The **R&A**

GOLFER'S HANDBOOK 2007

EDITOR RENTON LAIDLAW

The R&A is golf's world rules and development body and organiser of The Open Championship.
It operates with the consent of more than 125 national and international amateur and
professional organisations, from over 110 countries and on behalf of an estimated
28 million golfers in Europe, Africa, Asia Pacific and The Americas (outside the
USA and Mexico). The United States Golf Association (USGA) is the
game's governing body in the United States and Mexico.

MACMILLAN

First published 1984 by Macmillan
This edition published 2007 by Macmillan
an imprint of Pan Macmillan Ltd
Pan Macmillan, 20 New Wharf Road, London N1 9RR
Basingstoke and Oxford
Associated companies throughout the world
www.panmacmillan.com

ISBN: 978-1-4050-4936-8 (Cloth)

ISBN: 978-1-4050-4935-1 (Paper laminate case)

Note
Whilst every care has been taken in compiling the information contained in
this book, the Publishers, Editor and Sponsors accept no responsibility for
any errors or omissions.

Correspondence
Letters on editorial matters should be addressed to:
The Editor, The R&A Golfer's Handbook, Pan Macmillan,
20 New Wharf Road, London N1 9RR

> The information on golf courses and clubs contained in
> this Handbook is available for purchase on disk as
> mailing labels. For further information please
> e-mail golfmailing@macmillan.co.uk

9 8 7 6 5 4 3 2 1

A CIP catalogue record for this book is available from the British Library

Designed and typeset by Penrose Typography, Maidstone, Kent

Printed and bound in Great Britain by Mackays of Chatham plc, Chatham, Kent

Contents

Part X Awards

Part XI Who's Who in Golf

Part XII Governance of the Game

Part XIII Golf History

Part XIV Directory of Golfing Organisations Worldwide

Part XV Clubs and Courses in the British Isles and Europe

Amateur Champion is R&A Captain

Former Amateur Champion and Walker Cup player Michael Lunt is the new Captain of the Royal and Ancient Golf Club of St Andrews, having driven himself in for his year in office on the final day of the four-day Autumn Medal meeting last September.

Michael Lunt won his Amateur title at St Andrews in 1963 when he beat John Blackwell 2 and 1. The following year he again reached the final but on this occasion lost to Gordon Clark at Ganton, but only at the third extra hole. In 1966, 32 years after his father had won the title, he took the English Championship with victory over Dudley Millensted at Royal Lytham and St Annes.

He played in four Walker Cup matches including the drawn match at Five Farms in Maryland in 1965 and was a member of the Great Britain and Ireland team that won the Eisenhower Trophy (the World Amateur Team Championship) at Rome in 1964. He represented England for ten years from 1956 and was non-playing captain for four years from 1972.

Educated at Uppingham School and commissioned in 1953 into the Royal Warwickshire Regiment for two years service in Egypt, he returned to become a director in the family wholesale textile business before taking up a post as European golf sales manager for Slazenger. Later he was secretary/manager of the Royal Mid-Surrey club at Richmond for 11 years before retiring. A 4-handicapper who plays most of his golf at Walton Heath, he is married to Vicki, has a son, a daughter and two grandchildren. He has been a member of the Club since 1963 and has served on the Championship and Rules of Golf Committees.

Familiar faces and some new ones hit the headlines

Renton Laidlaw chooses his best six for 2006

In a year when golf lost one of its greats with the death of Byron Nelson and another golfing icon Arnold Palmer announced his retirement from competitive golf, Tiger Woods won two more majors in exemplary fashion. That was no surprise but when he missed the half-way cut for the first time in a major as a professional in the US Open at Winged Foot in June it was. Yet there were mitigating circumstances. That Championship came just weeks after the death of his father and mentor and emotionally Tiger was not ready to return to top-line competitive action. Indeed, a month later the strain was still apparent when he broke down completely in the arms of his long-time caddie Steve Williams at the end of The Open Championship, successfully staged at Hoylake again after a gap of 39 years.

As it was The Open, played on a brown, fast running course, that reminded us what links golf is really all about – manufacturing shots to suit the conditions – was a triumph for Woods' course management. He used the driver once and quickly learned how to hit the greens with longer than usual second shots and make the ball stick. It was a timely reminder of what Jack Nicklaus always said, that nobody could call himself truly a world class player until he had played and won on a British seaside links. Woods again proved his world class that week.

It is easy to choose **Tiger Woods** every year as one of the top six. Winning two more majors and stretching his tally to 12 as he tries to catch and pass Nicklaus' record might not have been enough on this occasion but when he finished the year with a record six straight stroke-play victories, his selection was guaranteed. The only pity is he appeared so uncomfortable as a team member at The Ryder Cup

– an event steeped in history and tradition about which Tiger has so much respect. Every two years the Cup match produces a passionate, dramatic three-day competition in which the contestants thrill us all with brilliant shot-making. This is a fixture which really does mean something and recent results only emphasise the growing strength and confidence of European golf.

Had it not been for an unusual incident on the final green on the last day when Paul McGinley, as a result, generously and rightly conceded a half to JJ Henry, Europe might have won by a record margin instead of emulating the score-line success of the team captained by Bernhard Langer at Oakland Hills in 2004. This time it was Ian Woosnam in charge and although criticised in some quarters for his low-key (almost silent) pre-match *modus operandi,* he galvanised the side to produce a brilliant performance in a week in which Ireland's **Darren Clarke** played such a huge role. Only weeks after the death from cancer of his wife Heather, Clarke stepped up to play his emotional part winning three points out of three, two in partnership with close friend and on course strength Lee Westwood. The inspiration Clarke provided to the rest of his team mates was incalculable. American captain Tom Lehman did almost everything right and came away a loser, no doubt reflecting on the wisdom of an outdated US Cup points system that did not take into consideration the impact of overseas golfers on leader boards on the other side of the Atlantic these days.

There was nothing but praise for Aberdonian **Richie Ramsay's** historic victory in the US Amateur Championship, the third by an overseas player in the last four years, the first by a British golfer since 1911 and the first by a Scot since 1898. The Stirling University student, able to afford to take

Tiger Woods

Darren Clarke

Richie Ramsay

Padraig Harrington   *Geoff Ogilvy*   *Lorena Ochoa*

part in the event because of a change in the USGA rules regarding amateur expenses, insists he is just someone who enjoys playing golf but he proved his steeliness as a competitor when he survived two concentration-sapping rules incidents in his quarter-final and semi-final ties before landing the trophy that Tiger won a record three times in a row and on which is also engraved the names of Bobby Jones, Jack Nicklaus and Arnold Palmer.

If it was a magnificent year for Ramsay, it was an emotional one for Arnie who announced his retirement from mainline competition after 50 glorious years. The man who transformed the game and gave it worldwide popularity played his last competitive round in the company of John Mahaffey and Lee Trevino in a Champions Tour event. The King, to whom all of us should be grateful, will turn his passionate attentions to his design work. Palmer talked enthusiastically about a project in the Carolinas when visiting the K Club during the Ryder Cup giving no hint then of his pending retirement as a player. The 77-year-old had flown his own plane across the Atlantic to the Cup being played on a course he had designed and was present at the official pre-Ryder Cup match banquet. If he has one regret it is never having had the chance to build a course in Scotland. Maybe there is still a chance!

Another much younger star at the K Club was Paul Casey, who after his fine amateur record – he was twice English champion and played well in the Walker Cup – has wasted no time in making the grade in the paid ranks. Two weeks in September were particularly note-worthy. He landed the £1m prize in the HSBC World Match Play Championship, restored in 2006 to having a truly world class field including Tiger and Jim Furyk, and then played his part in the European success in Ireland. In a close battle with David Howell, **Padraig Harrington** and Robert Karlsson, however, he missed out on the No.1 spot in Europe which went to the Irishman. Harrington, after twice finishing second and twice third in the money race, deserved his success although Casey was below his best in the final week because of illness.

Casey is just one of the band of new young Europeans making a name for themselves on the world stage and who may play more in the United States in future, following tournament schedule changes made by the American commissioner Tim Finchem which did little to ease the scheduling problems of

European executive director George O'Grady, who still managed to announce a 50-tournament main tour programme. Casey might have made the top six had not Harrington finished No.1 to edge him out! Harrington is worthy of his place because he is a fine ambassador for European golf.

It seemed one Sunday afternoon in June as if Colin Montgomerie was at last going to win a major but his brave battle to do so at Winged Foot in the US Open came to nothing when he missed the green with a 7-iron at the last and took 6. Had he hit the green he would almost certainly have two-putted for a winning par but again it was not to be. Five times he has come close to winning a prized major and five times has come away disappointed. Time is running out for him and he may never get a better chance than he did last summer. I hope he does win one. He is a resilient fellow who has bounced back from disappointment and controversy in the past.

As Montgomerie stumbled along with Jim Furyk, Padraig Harrington and most spectacularly Phil Mickelson in the closing stages at Winged Foot, Australian **Geoff Ogilvy** finished in cast-iron style to give Australia a first major victory since Steve Elkington beat, ironically enough, Montgomerie in the 1995 US PGA Championship at Riviera. Ogilvy admitted he was surprised to have been the Australian to do so but those of us who have followed the career of the young man with strong Scottish connections were not surprised. There may be more major titles for him.

It would be remiss not to have a lady in the top six and there is an excellent candidate for diploma honours on this occasion in the talented young Mexican **Lorena Ochoa** who toppled Annika Sörenstam from the top money spot on the LPGA Tour. Annika did add to her major title tally and it was good to see Se Ri Pak back on the major winners list but although Ochoa did not take a major she was still the star winning regularly. No first major either for Michelle Wie. The talented teenager continues to make headlines, mostly by taking on the men unsuccessfully from time to time. In Europe, evergreen Laura Davies deserves to be congratulated for taking the No.1 spot for a seventh time. She has always been a superbly enthusiastic competitor.

Mickelson started well but Tiger took over in the end

David Davies reports on a dramatic year for the majors

The 2006 majors were essentially about two men. Phil Mickleson won The Masters and lost a golden opportunity to win the US Open while Tiger Woods, after missing his first cut in a major as a professional at the US Open, won The Open and US PGA Championships with a 36-under par record bringing his tally of major titles to 12.

It was impossible to keep Mickelson out of the headlines in the first half of the year. He dominated his rival from April to June but Tiger took over with a vengeance in the second half emphasising that on this form he is more than likely to beat Jack Nicklaus' record 18 professional majors – the principal goal of a golfing millionaire for whom prize-money has not been an incentive for some time.

Let's start chronologically with Mickelson picking up the story the week before The Masters at the TPC at Sugarloaf, just outside Atlanta. This is a difficult test – a course built on such an unlikely bit of land that it is necessary to ride a cart or take crampons and a rope! Yet in the BellSouth Classic Mickelson returned a score so far under par that it was positively subterranean. He ended up on 28-under beating a distant José María Olazábal and Zach Johnson by 13 shots. By any standards that is a fair bit of form leading up to the first major of the year and his confidence was given a further boost when he claimed Augusta had similar shot values and greens. It was the perfect preparation.

This was never more apparent than on Augusta's back nine on the final day – the stretch where traditionally players have their nerves shredded. Mickelson has often been referred cruelly as the best putter in the world for the first three rounds and in the years before he won his first major in 2004 it did seem sadly apt. The extremely talented Mickelson never doubted he could win majors through those first 12 drought years of his professional career but, after winning his first major at Augusta in 2004, he had told us that he would go on to win a bunch of them. He still has only a posy worth of majors but, he insists, winning the first had been the problem. In 2005 he took the US PGA and at Augusta last year he won again. This time he was at his very best.

While playing partner and former Masters winner Fred Couples was demonstrating five times how to miss from inside three feet on the final day,

Mickelson was indomitable. The best of his putts was at the long 15th where after hitting the hole with his chip and running eight feet past he confidently sank the return putt to move eight-under-par. It was a telling blow. Ahead Tiger Woods, whose putting on the final day had been distinctly cool, had been maintaining the pressure by birdieing the 15th, almost holing his tee shot at the short 16th and setting up a 12 foot birdie chance at the 17th where the World No.1 surprised us all by three-putting, missing latterly from four feet and raising his eyes to the heavens in disbelief that he was being denied. Did he not after all have a god-given right to hole those important putts?

The fact is that during the week Woods, worried about the health of his ill father, did not play well enough to win. In the earlier rounds only his magical short game had saved him. Not that the television commentary indicated there was anything wrong with Tiger's game. A year earlier noted

Phil Mickelson, going for a third successive major win, blew it at Winged Foot with a last-hole nightmare

teacher turned commentator Peter Kostis told viewers he thought he spotted a flaw in Tiger's swing. Tiger reacted by sending him to golfing Coventry! This time after Woods had missed three of five fairways and two of five greens Lanny Wadkins, when asked about Tiger's swing suggested he was "in the groove".

Make no mistake, the only man in the groove at Augusta in 2006 was Mickelson who won his third major in nine starts and his second in a row with a closing 69 for seven-under-par 281. "What I am proud of most is the fact that I never let anyone back in. I'll cherish that final round."

For a long time it looked as if Mickelson would win the US Open at the always testing Winged Foot golf club north of New York but it was snatched by Geoff Ogilvy, the affable Australian, getting the reward for some consistently great golf for almost two years. Hopefully he will get the credit due him in time but his win was lost in the rubble caused by the implosion of Mickelson and Colin Montgomerie in particular.

Ogvilvy, who had chipped in from 15 feet downhill for par at the 17th and got down in two for par from off the green at the last where he holed a tricky six-footer, finished five-over-par but probably felt he had not just done enough to win. After all both Mickelson and first Montgomerie standing on the 72nd tee needed a par 4 to win or 5 to tie. Both took 6. Ogilvy was left the last man standing the beneficiary of some unexpected charity. "I got a bit lucky," he said.

He did in a sense because having posted his score and established the mark he could hardly have expected that the two experienced golfers coming along behind would both double-bogey a difficult

Colin Montgomerie's club change cost him the chance of an elusive first major

but far from impossible 450 yards hole. Indeed Jim Furyk, another title contender who slipped up in the closing stages, said: "It's a good finish but what does the damage is not so much the hole but the pressure you are under attempting to win a major."

Nonetheless, Mickelson trying to win his third major in a row and Montgomerie attempting to take his first in 58 starts contrived to make so many mistakes at the last hole that the normally raucous New York crowds were stunned into sympathetic or embarrassed silence. It was the manner in which the players made their 6's that was the most shocking aspect of the Championship.

Montgomerie made the first mistake despite having hit a fine drive down the middle – arguably the difficult part. He had left himself with 172 yards to the pin cut on the right side of the left-to-right sloping elevated green. This was normally a 6-iron and indeed that was the club he took out of his bag to play the shot but playing partner Vijay Singh was in all sorts of trouble and, crucially, was delaying things. As he waited Colin changed his mind and opted instead for a 7-iron arguing that the adrenalin of the moment would kick-in and he would hit it further than usual. The shot called for a slight fade but he overdid it sending the ball into deep rough 30 yards short and right of the green – a position so difficult that par could only have been achieved by a fluke.

No fluke was on offer. Hitting the ball hard enough to get it out of the grass the ball ran to the back of the green. In making sure he got the ball down to the hole with his fourth he hit it eight feet past and missed the return. Had he made 5 he would have played-off. A golden chance to get that elusive major title had been lost.

Back on the tee, Mickelson must have realised that he had been given a life but he blew it too. His driving had been worse than erratic. He had hit only two of 13 fairways so discretion may have been called for here but, no, out came the driver again. This time he not only missed the fairway he missed the rough and hit a hospitality tent well off line. It was a dramatically crooked shot. The ball had bounced back behind an enormous stand of trees. What to do? Hack out and hope to get down from 7-iron range or try to fade a long iron round the trees to get up by the green if not on it.

Neither option was enticing but Mickelson chose the heroic one with damaging consequences. He hit the trees in front of him, then plugged his third in a greenside bunker with no chance of an up and down 5. "I'm such an idiot," he said. "I had it won."

In one of those finishes to a major you simply could not make up it is as well to remember, too, that Jim Furyk was in the mix and Ireland's Padraig Harrington also had a chance of winning only to drop shots at each of the last three holes. So many potential winners but the desperate deeds of others should not obscure the fact that Ogilvy kept his

© Getty Images

Ernie Els has a depressing record against Tiger Woods in majors

at Hoylake before The Open but to no avail. Almost from the off there was a sense of inevitability about the first Championship to be played over the links of the Royal Liverpool Club since 1967. The reason was that Tiger was back after having missed the half-way cut at Winged Foot, his first in a major since turning professional. When he teed up in the US Open he was returning after a nine week break following the death of his father and mentor Earl Woods. Now at Hoylake he was ready for the fray again and ready to win without using his driver. In fact he used it once in 72-holes but it was a strategy that worked well for him despite the fact that he was more often hitting longer shots into the greens than some of his rivals. Jack Nicklaus, people recalled, had not used his driver much when he won his first Open at Muirfield in 1966.

Woods did not lead from start to finish. The first day belonged to jaunty Northern Irishman Graeme McDowell with his 66, one better than Tiger, but in the end he would finish 20 shots behind the winner who took the lead dramatically enough on day two with a glorious eagle at the last for 67. Woods reining himself in as he never has before on the fiery sunburnt links won, if not comfortably, without being seriously pressed.

Admittedly there was a point in the final round when Ernie Els, who is building a depressing record when matched against Woods, drew level on 13-under-par but that was after the South African had birdied the par 5 fifth. Moments later Woods eagled the hole! Els dropped shots at the eighth and 10th and would go on to finish third.

Els has a wonderfully effortless swing producing great power and he never seems ruffled but there is a suspicion that he ceded the high ground in 2000

head when all around others were losing theirs. When he finished he thought that five-over might be good enough for a play-off, second or, at worst, third but in the end he took the title, the first Australian to pick up a major since Steve Elkington won the US PGA in 1995. He was a far from unworthy winner.

Determined to put right the wrongs of Winged Foot, Mickelson played at least ten practice rounds

Ten made the cut in all four men's majors

Three Australians – Geoff Ogilvy, Adam Scott and Robert Allenby; two Americans – Phil Mickelson and Jim Furyk; two Spaniards – José María Olazábal and Miguel Angel Jiménez along with Canada's Mike Weir, South African Ernie Els and Luke Donald from England were the only golfers to make the cut in all four majors in 2006.

None finished in the top 10 in more than two majors. Tiger Woods won two majors, was third in the Masters but missed the cut for the first time in a major when he bowed out at the half-way stage of the US Open at Winged Foot.

	Masters	US Open	The Open	US PGA
Robert Allenby (AUS)	tied 22nd	tied 16th	tied 16th	20th
Luke Donald (ENG)	tied 42nd	tied 12th	tied 35th	3rd
Ernie Els (RSA)	tied 27th	tied 26th	3rd	tied 16th
Jim Furyk (USA)	tied 22nd	tied 2nd	4th	tied 29th
Miguel Angel Jiménez (ESP)	tied 11th	tied 16th	tied 41st	tied 65th
Phil Mickelson (USA)	1st	tied 2nd	tied 22nd	tied 16th
Geoff Ogilvy (AUS)	16th	1st	tied 16th	9th
José María Olazábal (ESP)	tied 3rd	tied 21st	tied 56th	tied 55th
Adam Scott (AUS)	tied 27th	tied 21st	tied 8th	tied 3rd
Mike Weir (CAN)	tied 11th	tied 6th	tied 56th	tied 6th

when Woods won three majors, two by huge margins, and has never regained it. Els at least got as far as the 10th before his chance was lost. Sergio García three putted two (and nearly three) of the first three holes and his last day challenge was over. His putter had let him down again. At the time of The Open he was 179th out of 194 players on the putting statistics table on the PGA Tour and has been showing a worrying propensity for failing to score when the pressure is on. His last round average in the States is two shots higher than Els, Woods or Mickelson, who would play no significant part at Hoylake.

It was left to Chris DiMarco to threaten Woods on the last day. After Woods bogeyed the 12th, Ryder Cup golfer DiMarco rolled in a 20-footer for a birdie at the 13th to get to within a shot but the World No.1 had the perfect response − three birdies in a row from the 14th and that was the job done.

DiMarco talked later of Woods' ability to switch up a gear whenever he needed to but the winner countered by saying that the switch went on at the first tee and remained on throughout the round. "If things happen at the end it is because I've done it before and feel comfortable. The more you do it the stronger the feeling of calm as you come down the stretch."

The only controversial point of the Championship was Woods using his driver only once. The fact is Hoylake was not long enough for Woods to need to use the driver, co-incidentally the club that consistently lets him down. It was argued that using irons off the tee − a plan he stuck with throughout − enabled fans to see one of the greatest displays of approach iron play.

His winning total of 270 − 18-under-par and one short of the record he set at St Andrews in 2000 − was good enough for a two shot victory over DiMarco. Although the scoring was low it was reasonable given there was scarcely a breath of

wind all week. It demolished the rather bilious piece of writing in an American magazine that had predicted that records at The Open would fall like rotten apples unless the wind howled all week. The scoring also demonstrated how wrong the bookmakers can be. Before the start odds of 66-1 were being offered for a score below 60 and 12-1 on 61 being bettered. Nobody got near or even threatened those scores.

In the end Woods notched up his 11th major, successfully defending the title for the first time since Tom Watson in 1983. He left Hoylake knowing that he now needed just eight more majors to overtake Jack Nicklaus' previously thought impregnable total. At 30 he has plenty of time to achieve his goal. By the time Nicklaus was 40 he had won 17 majors and took his last at the age of 46. If Tiger were to play on as long as Jack he has 60 or so more chances to win the eight he needs for the record.

He reduced that number to seven just four weeks later when he passed Walter Hagen's all-time record and landed his 12th major title by taking the 88th US PGA Championship for the second time. Phil Mickelson had been right when, in the aftermath of the US Open where Tiger had missed the cut, he had predicted the World No. 1 would win in Britain. He failed to predict he would also play even finer golf and win at Medinah in Chicago.

On the week, Tiger dropped only three shots to equal his own under-par record in majors and again finish on 18-under-par 270 to win by five from another former winner Shaun Micheel with Luke Donald, Adam Scott and Sergio García a further shot back.

In Chicago, Woods was at his imperious best. In his ten years as a professional he has left golfers of exceptional calibre − Ben Hogan, Sam Snead, Tom Watson and Severiano Ballesteros for instance − in his wake. Only Jack Nicklaus remains as a roadblock to Tiger totally rewriting the record book but the World No. 1 is on track to do so. Woods has won two majors in each of the last two years and with the remainder of the world's best mesmerised by him it is not difficult to imagine his winning, at a conservative estimate one major a year for the next seven years.

That would take him past Nicklaus, the man whose pictures and records have adorned a wall in every house in which Woods has lived.

Only Chris DiMarco challenged Tiger Woods over the last nine at Hoylake

He is determined, some might say obsessed, to win more majors than Jack and must be odds-on to do so.

There are, however, considerations. Nicklaus remained fit enough to play in over 150 majors winning his last at the age of 46 and all that while raising five children. No mean feat and we shall have to wait and see what the future brings for Woods who believes he is a better player now than he was in 1999–2000 during which time he won four majors in a row including the US Open by 15

Major title contender Luke Donald learned much on the final day at Medinah

shots and The Open at St Andrews by eight. Yet he insists he has a better understanding of how to get more out of a round, of the mechanics of his swing, of his putting stroke and of how to handle his emotions better.

Certainly the statistics (perhaps not always the best guide) show that he is acquiring consistency to go with his amazing all-round ability. At Medinah averaging 318 yards off the tee he was second only to the monstrous driving of JB Holmes whose average was 331.5 yards. Incidentally the top 15 long drivers were all over 300 yards. Luke Donald, who tied with Tiger with a round to go only to slip away, had an average drive of only 285 yards.

With his distance as a solid foundation, Woods was jointly top of the "greens in regulation" category that means most to the professionals and he was third best at making birdies with a total of 21 on the week.

In the end it was a disappointing Championship for Donald who had opened with rounds of 68, 68 and 66 on a course he had played often enough in his days at the North-Western University. Just as Sergio García in Tiger's company on the last day at Hoylake had slipped out of contention early, so too did Donald at Chicago unlucky perhaps to come up against Tiger on one of those days when his putter worked brilliantly for him. Twice in the first nine holes Tiger holed from nearly 40 feet while Donald, perhaps a little tense, lipped out three times *en route* to a closing 74. Still in contention for the first time in a major, Donald was positive about his performance. "I know if I am in that position again I am not going to hit good solid shots and maybe next time the putts will drop for me." He did admit, however, that he had a chance on that final day to watch Tiger at his best.

Medinah no monster for the top professionals

They thought Medinah was going to be a monster, stretched as it was to 7,561 yards for the US PGA Championship. It was the longest course in major championship history but it did not bring the golfers to their knees. Even Tiger Woods said that it did not really feel like a major as there were so many birdies being scored. For them, Medinah was not the severe examination they expected.

The problem was that the greens were too soft, too ready to accept the not-too-well hit shot. Luke Donald explained, too, that at the par 5 16th, the hardest hole on the course, he hit a 2-iron second and stopped it 12 feet from the pin. Instead of the cut coming at four or five over par it came at level par. In the third round both Woods and Canadian Mike Weir, who once shot 81 round Medinah, both shot record 65s.

Maybe it was easy for the professionals but Teddy Greenstein, a 15 handicapper, who writes on golf for the *Chicago Tribune*, was determined to prove how difficult the course was for ordinary mortals. He managed one par and returned a card littered with 6s and adding up to 104 – 17 over his handicap. Two Medinah members who played with him finished 10 and eight over their handicaps. Medinah too easy? – It all depends whose talking!

Tiger Woods' career record on the PGA Tour

Year	Played	Wins	2nds	3rds	Top 10	Official prize-money
1996	11	2	0	2	5	0	$790,594
1997	21	4	1	1	9	1	$2,066,833
1998	20	1	2	2	13	0	$1,841,117
1999	21	8	1	2	16	0	$6,616,585
2000	20	9	4	1	17	0	$9,188,321
2001	19	5	-	1	9	0	$5,687,777
2002	18	5	2	2	13	0	$6,912,625
2003	18	5	2	0	12	0	$6,673,413
2004	19	1	3	3	14	0	$5,365,472
2005	21	6	4	2	13	2	$10,628,024
2006	15	8	1	1	11	1	$9,941,563
Total	203	54	20	17	132	4	$65,712,324

In his 11 year career Tiger has missed only four cuts.

Tiger Woods' six tournament winning run in 2006

Event	Score	Par	Prize-money
The Open Championship	67–65–71–67—270	–18	$1,338,480
Buick	66–66–66–66—264	–24	$864,000
US PGA Championship	69–68–65–68—270	–18	$1,224,000
WGC Bridgestone	67–64–71–68—270	–10	$1,300,000
Deutsche Bank	66–72–67–63—268	–16	$990,000
American Express	63–64–67–67—261	–23	$1,300,000

For his six wins, Tiger was collectively 109 under par for 432 holes

Tiger makes 50 in record time

With his win in The Open at Hoylake, Tiger Woods joined the exclusive PGA Tour 50-win club as the seventh member to reach the coveted total ... and broke the record in doing so.

At the age of 30, he stole the crown previously held by Jack Nicklaus, who reached the magic 50 in 1973 at the age of 33.

The Tour career wins list is:

Sam Snead	82	Tiger Woods	53
Jack Nicklaus	73	Byron Nelson	52
Ben Hogan	64	Billy Casper	51
Arnold Palmer	62		

Tigers' lowest scores on the PGA Tour

61 (-11) 2002 PGA Grand Slam
            2005 Buick Open
61 (-9)   1999 GTE Byron Nelson Classic
            2000 WGC NEC Invitational

62 (-10) 1999 Buick Invitational

62 (-8)   1999 WGC NEC Invitational

63 (-9)   1996 Las Vegas Invitational
            1996 Disneyworld/Oldsmobile
            1997 AT&T Pebble Beach
            1998 BellSouth Classic
            2000 Memorial Tournament
            2000 National Car Rental Classic

63 (-9) continued
            2001 Deutsche Bank – SAP Open
            2002 Buick Open
            2002 Disney Golf Classic
            2003 Western Open
            2005 Buick Invitational
            2005 Ford Championship

63 (-8)   1999 World Cup
            2006 Deutsche Bank Championship
            2006 WGC American Express

63 (-7)   2000 GTE Byron Nelson Classic
            2001 Verizon Byron Nelson Classic

Brilliant Europeans delight record Ryder Cup crowd

Andy Farrell relives the glory moments at the K Club

As with every Ryder Cup these days, the 2006 match at the K Club seemed to have everything. Just more so than usual.

There was drama and passion, emotion and excitement, thunderous roars, respectful silences, modest winners, gracious losers, champagne and, being Ireland, Guinness. Mostly Guinness, in fact! Yet one thing was missing. Ironically, it is the one thing that has made the Ryder Cup the marvellous global celebration of golf it is every two years. In these international team competitions, the fortunes of either side are meant to fluctuate, often wildly, like an out of control pendulum desperately trying to obey the law of conservation of momentum.

In the last two Ryder Cups, however, momentum has been something the Europeans have kept all to themselves. At the K Club, Ian Woosnam's inspired side became the first under the current format to win all five sessions. Of course there were little moments of crisis but that is all they were.

So many matches followed a similar pattern. The home team taking the lead early on, the Americans fighting back on the second nine, but the Europeans holding firm. They won each of the first four sessions by the margin of 2½–1½, maintaining the upper hand effectively as emphasised when Colin Montgomerie holed from six feet on the 18th late on the first night. As always, he played a leading role in maintaining the momentum.

Tom Lehman was an eloquent and gracious leader of the American side but neither he nor his men could figure out a way to get that pendulum swinging strongly back in their direction. Lehman worked hard all year to engender a resolute team spirit, including an advanced trip to the K Club two weeks before the match, but the home side were always more comfortable producing their best golf on a familiar venue thanks to years of staging the Smurfit European Open on the Arnold Palmer designed course.

This was a Ryder Cup won early. Six of the first eight holes were won more often by European players than Americans. Blue was on the board early and that was translated into points despite the closeness of the matches. Eight of the first nine matches went all the way to the 18th but the Americans won only one of them. Still it was a reflection, perhaps, that early on the match was closer than the final result indicated.

The one US point on the first day came in the first match of the first series of fourballs, and that despite the unexpected – Tiger Woods driving into the water off the first tee. Brilliantly, Jim Furyk, his partner, birdied the hole anyway and made up for the great man's struggles. Yet, while Woods and Furyk would win two of their four matches together, the only other American partnership to score a point was that of Zach Johnson and Scott Verplank in the Saturday fourballs. Lehman might have had an inexperienced tail to his team, but it was not the rookies who let him down. Johnson prospered, as did JJ Henry, who came of age at the highest level. He was involved in two cracking fourballs alongside Stewart Cink, each time claiming a dramatic half against Paul Casey and Robert Karlsson.

It was the more senior men who let Lehman down, not least the partnership of Phil Mickelson and Chris DiMarco, so strong in the Presidents Cup

Tom Lehman did everything right but in the end played the role of the gracious loser

Sergio García enjoyed every minute, winning four points

but gleaning only half a point in three attempts this time.

Although the early games were close, only four of the last 17 matches went the distance and by the Saturday afternoon foursomes, the Europeans were beginning to enjoy themselves. Casey and David Howell combined as a foursome for four birdies in the first five holes and Casey ended the match in style by holing in one at the 14th. He used a four-

iron for the fifth ace in Ryder Cup history and because the match was already dormie, Johnson and Cink could only turn round on the tee and shake hands with their opponents. The following day, at the same hole, Verplank became the first American to hole in one in the Ryder Cup.

Casey was again in terrific form as he defeated Furyk in the singles. Monty led off the order in his natural position, got ahead by a couple of holes early on and posted a point on the board, although David Toms, for the second match running, did not make it easy. Stewart Cink pulverised Sergio García, who had been electric alongside José María Olazábal in the fourballs and with Luke Donald in the foursomes preventing the Spaniard from winning five points out of a possible five. Woods edged past the resilient Karlsson but Woosnam had sent his team out to win the singles and there was never going to be a repeat of Brookline, when a similar four-point lead after two days was swept away by the Americans.

Howell romped to victory and then the end came quickly. Luke Donald holed the putt that made sure Europe retained the Cup. Then Henrik Stenson holed the one which actually won it. Then came the emotional climax of the week. It was probably asking too much for Darren Clarke to hole the winning putt and he was genuinely not bothered but after beating Johnson at the 16th, he could not hold back the tears. His wife, Heather, following a long and courageous fight, had died from breast cancer only six weeks before. Clarke made himself available for a wild card selection determined he could contribute to the team. The roar as he approached the first tee on Friday morning was possibly the loudest, most intense sound ever heard on a golf course. Somehow, he hit a driver 340 yards down the middle and made a birdie.

Europe leads USA 5–1 on Cup aces

No holes in one were scored in the Ryder Cup until 1973 when Peter Butler playing in a four-ball match with Brian Barnes against Jack Nicklaus and Tom Weiskopf on the second day aced the short 16th at the Muirfield course of the Honourable Company of Edinburgh Golfers. Despite the ace, the Americans won that game and subsequently the match 19–13.

Next man to ace in 1993 was 2008 European captain Nick Faldo, in his game against Paul Azinger, who will captain the American side at Valhalla next year. Faldo's hole-in-one came at the 14th hole at The Belfry but it did not help him win the point. The game was halved and Europe lost the match 15–13.

There were two holes-in-one at the Oak Hill match in 1995 and both were achieved by Europeans. Italy's Constantino Rocca, playing with Sam Torrance aced the sixth in their foursomes against Davis Love III and Jeff Maggert. The Europeans won the game 6 and 5. Later in the singles Howard Clark holed in one at the 11th while playing against and beating Peter Jacobsen one hole. On that occasion it was the Europeans who emerged victorious by a point.

The latest aces came at The K Club last year when in dramatic fashion Paul Casey finished off his game with David Howell against Stewart Cink and Zach Johnson by using a 4-iron at the 14th for a hole in one then conceded a half to the Americans! The next day in the singles Scott Verplank became the first American in the history of the competition to hole-in-one. Like Casey he achieved his ace at the 14th *en route* to beating Padraig Harrington.

Days of triumph, pride and raw emotion

As much as Darren Clarke insisted it was a team effort and that he was just one member of the European team, the fairy tale events at the K Club conspired to put the Northern Irishman firmly in the spotlight. He may not have holed the winning putt, but when his match against Zach Johnson ended at the 16th the celebrations began and the emotions overflowed.

"Darren being here was an inspiration in itself", said Tiger Woods, a close friend of Clarke's who had counselled him to play despite the passing of his late wife Heather. "His play was remarkable considering his loss and what his family are going through. I kept telling him he is a hell of a player and unfortunately for us he went out there and showed us."

The ovation that greeted Clarke on the first tee on Friday had his caddie, Billy Foster, and his partner, Lee Westwood, in tears. But not Clarke, who promptly birdied the hole. Partnering his friend Westwood was ideal for the first two days as they extended their record together with two more wins, and then he defeated Johnson 3 and 2 on Sunday.

"The crowd's support was fantastic. They were so supportive and very vocal for me", Clarke said. "They showed me they cared and I was very grateful. The support I've received this week from my team-mates, their wives, from the American team, their wives, the captains, vice-captains, everyone, has been fantastic. I am just delighted Woosie chose me and that I have managed to contribute to the team and put some points on the board. We have been an unbelievable team this week and it has been fantastic to be a part of it."

It was an emotional time for Darren Clarke and Westwood was a perfect partner for him again

Ian Woosnam dedicated Europe's victory to Heather. Paul McGinley told Clarke: "We miss Heather dearly. She would have been right in the middle of this if she had been here. Big D, you've been great this week, we're so proud of the way you have handled everything and the way you have played."

David Howell celebrates with Paul Casey after his 4-iron tee-shot at the 14th went into the hole

Alongside his friend and fellow wild card, Lee Westwood, the old firm were back in business. They won both their fourballs. On the Saturday Clarke chipped in to defeat Woods and Furyk at the 16th. Woods, who lost his father earlier in the year, had been supportive during Clarke's time of need and the pair embraced. The scenes the following afternoon were more intense. There were many hugs and tears. "It's destiny", Woosnam told Clarke. Lehman said: "You beat up on us pretty bad, but we're glad you're here."

Clarke finished with three points out of three, as did Olazábal, playing for the first time since 1999, and so too did Donald. Incredibly, Woosnam had left out Donald, Howell and Stenson, all ranked in the world's top 13, on the first morning such was the strength in depth he had available. "Woosie was fantastic", said Clarke. "He had some difficult decisions because he had 12 players playing well, but you can tell from the scoreline, he chose well." García and Westwood, for the second match running, were the top scorers with four points out of five.

Oakland Hills was meant to be a one-off. Europe started the week at the K Club as the favourites but

Ian Woosnam and his dedicated team celebrate another Cup triumph

no one expected another nine-point victory but it was nothing less than the players and the Irish fans who created such a wonderful atmosphere deserved.

"I'm so proud", said Paul McGinley. "It is so emotional but I am so proud of this team and of the Irish people. It has been a great show and we have highlighted Ireland in the right way. Everyone has behaved so well. Sinking the winning putt at the Belfry was great for me but this is even more special."

How right he was.

Results of the match since 1979

1979	The Greenbrier	Europe	11	–	**USA** 17
1981	Walton Heath	Europe	9½	–	**USA** 18½
1983	PGA National	Europe	13½	–	**USA** 14½
1985	De Vere Belfry	**Europe** 16½	–	USA	11½
1987	Muirfield Village	**Europe** 15	–	USA	13
1989	De Vere Belfry	**Europe** 14	–	**USA**	14
1991	Kiawah Island	Europe	13½	–	**USA** 14½
1993	De Vere Belfry	Europe	13	–	**USA** 15
1995	Oak Hill	**Europe** 14½	–	USA	13½
1997	Valderrama	**Europe** 14½	–	USA	13½
1999	Brookline	Europe	13½	–	**USA** 14½
2002	De Vere Belfry	**Europe** 15½	–	USA	12½
2004	Oakland Hills	**Europe** 18½	–	USA	9½
2006	The K Club	**Europe** 18½	–	USA	9½
Overall points		**Europe** 201	–	USA	191

Ramsay adds his name to the list of US Amateur winners

Mark Garrod on the Scot who made golfing history at Hazeltine

Richie Ramsay describes himself as "just a guy from Aberdeen who loves playing golf", but now, after a simply stunning achievement on the Hazeltine National course made famous by Tony Jacklin's 1970 United States Open victory, he delights in another description – first British winner of the US Amateur Championship since Harold Hilton in 1911 and first Scot to lift the title since Findlay Douglas in 1898.

The 23-year-old Stirling University student added his name to a list of champions which also includes Francis Ouimet, Bobby Jones, Arnold Palmer, Jack Nicklaus, Mark O'Meara, Phil Mickelson and, of course, Tiger Woods.

Ramsay was a member of the 2005 Great Britain and Ireland Walker Cup side which narrowly lost in Chicago, but having been left out of both series of singles that week there was no reason to pay particular attention to him as he began his bid on a layout measuring 7,473 yards, the longest ever used for the event.

He survived the qualifying rounds, then embarked on a run through the match play stages which was not without incident, but ended with a convincing 4 and 2 victory over American John Kelly in the 36-hole final.

"I'm quite speechless right now and close to tears," said Ramsay on receiving the famous trophy. "Everything went according to plan. I worked hard and it just shows what someone can do when they put their mind to something. Yet I can't believe it."

Well might he have needed to pinch himself. With the win comes entry into The Masters at Augusta – he will partner defending champion Mickelson there in the opening two rounds – the US Open at Oakmont and The Open Championship at Carnoustie, the course where Paul Lawrie triumphed in 1999.

Lawrie sent daily good luck text messages to his fellow Aberdonian in Minnesota once Ramsay and Walker Cup teammates Lloyd Saltman, Oliver Fisher and Rhys Davies had come through two days of stroke play during which Billy Horschel, a 19-year-old from Florida, made championship history by returning an 11 under par 60 on the Chaska Town course which was also used for the Championship.

Saltman and Davies were beaten in the opening round of match play, but Fisher, the 17-year-old from Essex who 12 months earlier had become the youngest-ever Walker Cup player, joined Ramsay in the quarter-finals before going out.

It was at that point that Ramsay might easily have exited too. After being three-up on Californian Ricky Fowler the Scot came under attack and found himself all square when his caddie touched the line of his putt with his finger on the 17th and lost him the hole. Minutes later he had to make a 12-footer to stay alive, but he did so and eventually went through with a birdie putt of 15 feet at the third extra hole.

Amazingly, Ramsay incurred another loss-of-hole penalty at the 16th hole of his semi-final, this time for grounding a club in a hazard, but he had been two-up when it happened and he survived that shock to win on the last. Much to his relief, another mishap was avoided in the final and by hitting 30 out of 34 greens in regulation his solid play was something which Kelly could not match.

© Getty Images

Richie Ramsay, just a "guy from Aberdeen who loves playing golf", gave Scottish golf a boost with his win in America

No Briton had even reached the final for 70 years, but with his victory Ramsay made it an astonishing three overseas winners of the title in four years following Australian Nick Flanagan in 2003 and Italian Edoardo Molinari – the first European champion since Hilton 94 years earlier – in 2005.

While the US Amateur trophy crossed the Atlantic the Amateur Championship went across the English Channel. No Frenchman had won since Phillippe Ploujoux in 1981, but Julien Guerrier ended their wait for a successor by beating England's Adam Gee 4 and 3 at Royal St George's.

The plus-four handicapper had already knocked out opponents from Italy, Sweden and Australia when he clashed with Gee. They were level after 24 of the 36 holes, but Guerrier eagled the next and won the following three holes as well. Gee, winner of the Lake Macquarie Invitational in Sydney earlier in the year, did pull two back, but that was as close as he was allowed to get.

Ramsay's memorable year continued when he helped both Britain and Ireland to retain the St Andrews Trophy against Continental Europe, and Scotland to keep the Home Internationals title for the first time in 24 years.

Nobody could deny that Ross McGowan deserved the English amateur crown after a season in which he had had five runners-up finishes. A sixth was a distinct possibility because it was St Andrews Links Trophy winner Fisher he faced in

Norwegian teenager Marius Thorp impressed Tom Watson at Hoylake when he took the Silver Medal as leading amateur

the final at Burnham and Berrow, but McGowan won 5 and 4.

Joining Ramsay in The Open at Carnoustie this year will be rising star Rory McIlroy, the 17-year-old who followed his successful defences of the West of Ireland and Irish Closed titles with victory at the European Men's Championship in Milan.

They will both be trying for the silver medal captured at Hoylake in 2006 by 18-year-old Norwegian Marius Thorp, who finished 48th and earned this tribute from final round playing partner Tom Watson: "He has the game to go far. He is fearless with the putter – I remember those days!"

The Scottish Amateur saw brothers Lloyd, Zack and Elliott Saltman all reach the last 16, but not one made it any further and the eventual winner was Kevin McAlpine by a thumping 8 and 7 over Paul O'Hara, while Llewellyn Matthews took the Welsh Amateur thanks to a last-green win over Rhys Davies.

Pride of place and therefore last word, though, goes to Ramsay. "Anything I can do to benefit Scottish golf is just repaying a debt that I owe them for all the help they have given me over the last four or five years," he said.

"If some kid sees me winning this and thinks 'I'll have a crack at golf' that's another person playing the game, another kid going out there and enjoying himself or herself. There's no reason why anybody else can't do this just like I did." Why not?

For English champion Ross McGowan victory at last. After five runner-up finishes earlier in the season a win at Burnham & Berrow

Curtis Cup at the Old Course will be played over three days

Lewine Mair on a decision not universally welcomed

Great Britain and Ireland collected only two and a half points out of a possible nine on the first day of the Curtis Cup at Bandon Dunes and, in the end did well to lose by nothing more than 11½–6½. Had the match taken place at home rather than a nine-hour time-change away in California it might have made for rather more of a talking point in the UK papers. Instead it received barely a mention at a time when Michelle Wie and her sister professionals were arriving in the UK for the Weetabix British Women's Open.

Ada O'Sullivan, who captained the GB&I side in America's Far West, had just the two difficult questions to field at her end-of-the-match press conference. The first concerned Kiran Matharu who was, in some eyes at any rate, held to be the strongest player on either side. Why, when Matharu had played top and won the leading single on the first day, was she never used thereafter?

The second question was about the overall state of the poll. Since the US had won 25 of the 34 matches and had not been beaten since 1996, did Sullivan not think the time had come when GB&I should metamorphose into a European team.

Regarding Matharu, O'Sullivan indicated that the player had not come across as the best of team members in the first foursome series in which she and Tricia Mangan played Paige Mackenzie and Amanda Blumenherst. "We needed people to rally one another", she said feelingly. When the three combinations she chose for the second day did gel well and emerged with two and a half points as opposed to the half point of the first day, O'Sullivan had felt duty bound to stay with that same sextet for the afternoon. "They were so upbeat that I decided to keep them out there".

Breanne Loucks was a particular success story. The only other player apart from Matharu to have picked up a full point on the first day, Loucks won morning and afternoon on Sunday to leave Bandon Dunes with a commendable three points out of four.

On the European question O'Sullivan, like Carol Semple Thompson, her US counterpart, was of the opinion that no change should be made to the Great Britain and Ireland status volunteering, somewhat obliquely, that she believed things would all work out for the better in 2008 when the match, scheduled to be played for the first time at St

Andrews, would become a three-day rather than a two-day fixture. "I'm sure", said O'Sullivan, "that you'll see a much closer game if not a GB&I triumph".

There was a feeling anyway that it was unfair on the players to expect them to reach their top form over two days. Yet it became apparent very quickly that O'Sullivan was in the minority in thinking that the extra day would be an improvement in any way. A host of past players, who were present at Bandon Dunes, disapproved wholeheartedly about the idea of introducing four-balls to the 73-year-old fixture and playing foursomes and four-balls on each of the first two days before rounding things off with eight singles.

"Why four-balls?" they chorused. One American Curtis Cup luminary pointed out that by agreeing to four balls, the Ladies' Golf Union "are playing into our hands because four-ball golf is a much more common format for women's friendly games in the United States than in Britain or Ireland".

In addition, there were concerns that the extra day would be added to the detriment of the immediacy and impact of the match – rather like the fears being expressed about proposals to extend the Ryder Cup from three days to four. Yet nobody could deny that certain aspects of the new plan for the Curtis Cup had their merits. The proposed eight singles, for example, was going to ensure that every player in the team would be involved, eliminating the situation in 1988 when supporters poured across the Irish Sea to watch Claire Hourihane in action only to be disappointed. Claire was not given a single game.

It is not too difficult, of course, to understand why the idea of stretching the contest appeals to the LGU, particularly when the next match is scheduled for the home of golf and could attract in excess of 20,000 spectators. As Susan Simpson, the LGU's Tournament Secretary, has explained, the time, effort and expense which go into setting up so prestigious a fixture cry out for something which has not come and gone within the space of 48 hours.

Although captain O'Sullivan's theory is that GB&I cannot be expected to hit top form in two days, that must surely apply equally to the Americans. Obviously there is a case for suggesting that

St Andrews could be a case apart. After all, it was at St Andrews, in 1938 and again in 1971, that Great Britain and Ireland's men recorded their only two wins in the first 50 years of the Walker Cup.

There have been years when a poor GB&I performance in the Curtis Cup was followed by some impressive performances in the World Cup but this was not one of them. The World Cup for the Espirito Santo Trophy was held in South Africa and won by the South Africans – the first time for years that a host nation has won. Curiously, the South Africans won on an unusual countback deci-

sion in which the two non-counting scores of the three returned daily were used.

Having been compared on the final day and found to be equal, the decision on which country won was taken on the third day's non-counting scores or they were non-counting originally! England finished 12 shots adrift and in a share of 11th place, Scotland finished 19th, Wales 20th and Ireland 23rd. Yet, for a quick glimpse at a brighter future, what of Scotland's Sally Watson? At a time when the World Cup players were still warming up, Watson was winning the Daily Telegraph Junior Championships in Dubai by a breathtaking ten-shot margin.

Michelle Wie happily doing it her way

For some people, the second half of Michelle Wie's season in 2006 was not so much a short hiccup as a period in her brief career which suggested that she should give up playing against the men and concentrate instead on the women's professional circuit. Wie, who turned 17 in October, was no better placed than 26th in the Weetabix British Women's Open at Lytham, while she had five less-than-memorable forays in the men's arena.

She had to withdraw from the John Deere Classic with heat exhaustion and finished bottom of the heap in the Omega European Masters on the European Tour and the Lumber Classic on the USPGA Tour.

Of course, it does not make it any easier for gifted teenager Wie that she is trying to juggle her golf with her schoolwork. She is a straight 'A' student in her Hawaiian high school and is intent on going to

college in California, with Stanford the most likely choice.

Wie, who was brought up playing with her father's friends in Hawaii, has never made any secret of her ambition to make her mark in the men's golfing world. The trouble is that from the moment she started to dip into the men's scene she was much more a centre of attention than when she played on the women's circuit. For instance, she had three top-5 finishes in the opening women's majors of 2006 but not too many saw these excellent performances for the success story it was. Rather, questions were asked why she

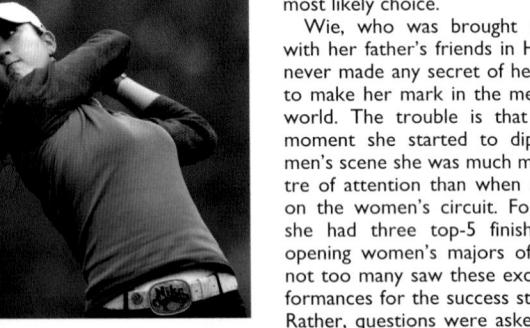

was not winning in that company. Again, whenever she turns up on the men's tour, she finds herself surrounded by photographers and the subject of controversial stories about whether or not she should be playing in men's events at all.

The Omega European Masters was typical. The pros and cons of her playing for a first time on the men's European Tour were discussed right up until the time she missed the cut with scores of 78 and 79. At that point, most of the column inches were devoted to her "failure".

Few mentioned the extent to which she had enhanced the tournament spectator figures, comfortably up on those for 2005. Nick Dougherty, who played with her, was quick to say, "Michelle has the same wow factor as a Tiger Woods".

There were plenty of other positives which were conveniently lost amid the criticisms. Aside from notching three top-five finishes in the women's majors, Wie made her first men's cut at the SK Telecom Open, an event in which Padraig Harrington also competed, on the secondary Korean circuit.

Through it all, the teenager stuck to her guns. "If I were to stay playing among the women, I would only get better at that discipline", she said. "If I am to succeed among the men, I have to keep playing with them".

Whatever the rights and wrongs of the situation, there is much to admire in someone who is so intent on doing things her way.

Scotland's Honest John has graced the game all the way

Jock MacVicar on the 70-year career of a gentleman golfer

There can never have been a more modest, gentle and, at the same time, successful man in sport than John Panton.

"Gentleman John", "Honest John". Those are names thoroughly merited, but because of his humility he never has quite received the credit his golf, and his life, deserve.

John's career in golf came in an era before spin elevated many people in sport well beyond their worth. John Panton received an MBE for his services to the game, was honorary professional to The R&A from 1988 to 2004, and during nearly 70 active years in the game met three Presidents of the United States.

It is perhaps not generally known that had Panton not become a professional golfer he would have been most probably a professional footballer. A few months after reaching the semi-final of the British Boys Championship at Moortown he had trials with Hearts and Dundee, and had it not been for the collapse of an Edinburgh clubmaker, a career with the Tynecastle club was more than a possibility.

John continued to play football for the 91st Field Artillery during the Second World War. Indeed, rumour has it that his army team once beat a Tom Finney touring select – which included Willie Redpath and Peter "Ma Ba" McKenna. Modesty prevents him from boasting about the scoreline that day but he believes his side won 9–2!

Some years after the war Panton was struck on the hand by a golf ball driven from another tee. The blow was so painful that he had to go to hospital to have it X-rayed. "I couldn't move my finger", he said.

It transpired that the reason for the extreme pain was that the ball had struck a war wound, and the doctor discovered pieces of shrapnel under the skin. He asked John if he wanted the bits taken out. "No, No", I told him. "They've served me well so far!"

Born in Pitlochry on October 9, 1916, Panton turned professional in 1935 and worked in the club shop under John Murray until the outbreak of war in 1939. He joined up in September and did not come out of the army until January 1946. By then he had been a professional for 11 years, but, apart from a few alliance meetings, he had been deprived of tournament play during some of the best years of his life.

© PGA

John Panton (far left back row) and Eric Brown (middle of back row) played together in Ryder Cup matches and were always a popular pairing in World Cups

However, Panton's talent for the game, and especially his mastery of the mid-irons, soon caught the attention of those who followed the game. He won his first Scottish Professional Championship in 1948, and from then until the mid-'70s he graced the fairways of the world, winning tournaments, making friends, and constantly pursuing the possibility of a cup of tea at the bar or a ginger beer and lime, later officially named "a John Panton". Few if any golfers can claim to have had a drink – albeit a soft one – named after them.

On those trips abroad he always took his cine-camera and today he has a wonderful archive chronicling golf in his era. He is particularly proud of the material featuring Ben Hogan who played in the World Cup (the old Canada Cup) at the same time as John.

Popular film shows

In the days before there was so much golf on television John was a regular performer at clubhouse evenings when he showed his films and, in the anonymity of the darkened room gave an entertaining, amusing and always insightful commentary.

In those 1950's and 1960's most professional golfers combined tournament play with their club job. "We thought nothing of playing two rounds on a Friday, driving back overnight and opening up at 8 o'clock in the morning," said John.

Panton moved from Pitlochry to Stenhousemuir after his appointment as Glenbervie club professional in September 1946 where he remained for 38 years, a remarkable record, made even more remarkable in that he also found time to compete all over Europe and in the United States as well.

Along with the redoubtable Eric Brown, Panton was a true ambassador for the game – and his country – wherever he went. As well as winning the Scottish Professional Championship eight times (on one occasion sharing the title with Brown), he won the Northern Open seven times, and was successful six times in PGA events, including the 1956 Match-Play Championship at Hoylake, where he and his fellow-finalist, Harry Weetman, played 13 rounds in five days.

"I remember Harry and I played in the Dunlop Masters at Prestwick the following week and we could hardly walk", John recalls. "We were absolutely exhausted."

He cites the Harry Vardon Trophy in 1951 as probably his best achievement, although he is proud to have won the Woodlawn Tournament at the US Air Force base at Ramstein three years in a row against some top Americans.

"Honest John" Panton played for Scotland in the World Cup 12 times, usually with Brown. They were a hugely popular double act very different in character. Brown was as extrovert as John was quiet but the partnership worked well although they never managed to bring the trophy home to Scotland. He played in three Ryder Cups, in 1951, 1953 and 1961.

In the early days of the Ryder Cup the Great Britain and Ireland golfers travelled to the United States on the Queen Elizabeth or the Queen Mary. The voyage took six days, and even when eventually they went by air the flight to New York took 16 hours, via Goose Bay and Gander. "So much has changed," says John. "In the old days even a trip down south from Scotland over Shap was not all that easy. There was no M74 and M6 then."

Panton has seen so many changes in the game, too, that it would take many pages to list them all. Suffice to say that when he began playing the game at Pitlochry it was with hickory-shafted clubs, although he later borrowed a few steel-shafted clubs from a couple of technologically advanced members.

He enjoys playing most at the Old Course at St Andrews – because of the "wee extra buzz" – although he has a great love of the courses in Berkshire not least Sunningdale, where he now lives close to his daughter, Cathy, herself a founder member of the European women's professional Tour, and her husband.

Over the years Panton met them all. He once caddied for Joyce Wethered just before she played Bobby Jones, and he saw the great Babe Zaharias, an Olympic athlete as well as one of the most powerful lady golfers in history whose career was cut short by cancer.

Hogan his hero

Not surprisingly Ben Hogan was the golfer he admired most. "I practiced alongside him at Panmure for the Carnoustie Open in 1953," he recalls. "His accuracy was incredible. There was a different sound off his shots. It was like the crack of a rifle. His biggest worry was that he would land in the sclaff mark left from his previous drive! I remember Tommy Bolt once saying that he never saw Hogan watching Nicklaus, but saw Nicklaus watching Hogan."

His post as honorary professional to the Royal and Ancient Golf Club of St Andrews has now gone to another talented Scottish player, Jim Farmer, but John still has a strong connection to The R&A. On his retirement he was made an honorary member of the Club – an honour reserved for only a very few professionals and most of them are former Open champions. It is a measure of the respect and esteem there is for him. John insists the game has been good to him. He played with the best, had a career unsurpassed by any other male Scottish golfer, and had the honour of being personally introduced to three Presidents, Eisenhower, Nixon and George Bush. Golf may have been good to him, but few have been better for the game than John Panton.

Darwin has earned his place in the World Golf Hall of Fame

John Hopkins on an outstanding literary master craftsman

There are many in golf to whom the name Darwin means only a little. It's a name lodged deep in the dark recesses of the mind, a half remembered name from school, rather like the number of Georgian Kings or the years the Stuart Kings reigned or how long Queen Victoria was on the throne

You can picture someone trying to think who Darwin is. "Come on now, I do know something about him. It's coming, it's coming. Ah yes, Darwin. Isn't he the fellow who defined where we all come from. He wrote a book about it, didn't he? What was it? Let me think. Um, er. *Origin of the Species?*"

Well, yes, Darwin IS the *Origin of the Species* fellow but that is Charles and the Darwin I am talking about here is Bernard, his grandson, who was born in Downe, in Kent, in 1876. Darwin became the best golf writer of all time. Listen to the late Herbert Warren Wind, the American who was himself a wonderful writer about sport and particularly golf: "There is little disagreement that the best golf writer of all time was an Englishman, Bernard Darwin," Herb wrote. "He was the finest talent ever to write about sport."

It took a long time before Darwin received his full weight of recognition around the world. It finally came on a warm evening in Florida in November in 2005 when Darwin was inducted into the World Golf Hall of Fame. If it was a bit late – after all, Darwin, *The Times'* golf correspondent, died in 1961 – then the pomp and ceremony more than made up for it. The World Golf Hall of Fame at St Augustine in Florida is only a few miles south of Jacksonville, the headquarters of the PGA Tour in the US.

Darwin made his name as the anonymous golf correspondent for *The Times* in the day when each story was described as having been written "By our correspondent." No vainglorious bylines with accompanying photographs of the author in those days. From 1907 until 1953 Darwin wrote essays and match reports in *The Times* and from 1907 until 1961 in *Country Life*. He also wrote an introduction to the *Oxford Book of Quotations*. He was an expert on Charles Dickens and could, and often would, recite passages from memory. You could tell a Darwin piece on any subject because more often than not there was a literary reference in it and more

often than not it was to a character in a Dickens novel. Darwin also wrote four volumes of autobiography, slim volumes about British clubs – men's clubs in London that is – and British public schools.

Darwin's style of writing was elegant, grammatically faultless and distinctive. He never inserted himself unnecessarily into his copy. He rarely used superlatives and, in complete contrast to today's practices, he never interviewed players. Darwin was so modest, in fact, that when he and Joyce Wethered won the Worplesdon mixed foursomes in 1933, he referred to himself as "the elderly gentleman whose name for the most part escapes me."

There is a saying in Britain that those who can, do, and those who can't, teach. Far from being unable to do any of these Darwin could have done them all with graceful ease. In his wide-ranging talents he was like Bobby Jones and it is sad and ironic that these two gifted men should end their lives crippled in such ways that one could not play golf and the other could not write about it.

Darwin could have taught. There is no doubt about that. Having attended Eton, he went on to study Classics at Cambridge which meant he was

Bernard Darwin, arguably the best golf writer of all time

© The Times

For visitors to the British Golf Museum at St Andrews there is a Bernard Darwin exhibit

@ The Times

comfortable with Latin and Greek. He had an acuity of mind that owed much to his forebears and his contemporaries. He trained as a lawyer and practised law for a few years until, in his early thirties, he sold his wig and gown and took up writing.

Most of all though, he could play golf. Twice a semi-finalist in The Amateur, he represented England on eight occasions. He reached the peak of his playing career in 1922 when he was 46 and was in the US to cover the Walker Cup. When the British and Irish captain fell ill, Darwin was drafted in to replace him as a player and captain and though he lost his foursomes he defeated WC Fownes Jr, the son of the founder of Oakmont Country Club, in the singles.

Darwin's career was as long as John Daly's backswing. He started writing at the time of The Great Triumvirate and though he had stopped writing for The Times, he continued wielding his pen for other publications until his death. Thus in the body of his work there is Darwin on Harry Vardon, James Braid, JH Taylor and Ted Ray and almost everyone else of significance up to the time when Jack Nicklaus was approaching the first tee. Writing about Gene Sarazen, Darwin said the American reminded him of the Cheshire Cat in *Alice in Wonderland* in the way that his grin remained with us long after Sarazen himself had disappeared.

If you want to know how to report live golf read Darwin on the 1913 US Open where Francis Ouimet, the amateur, sensationally tied with Vardon and Ray and then beat them in a playoff the next day. Darwin was the only British daily newspaperman to be present and it was he who marked Ouimet's card during the tumultuous playoff.

Darwin was present at Carnoustie when Hogan won The Open in 1953. We do not know what Hogan thought of Darwin but we can guess that Hogan liked the thoughtful and insightful approach of the writer. We do know what Darwin thought of Hogan. After Hogan had won The Open by four strokes, Darwin commented: "If he had needed a 64 on his last round, you were quite certain he could have played a 64. Hogan gave you the distinct impression he was capable of getting whatever score was needed to win."

Darwin saw a considerable amount of Bobby Jones and one suspects that he regarded Jones in much the same light as Herb Wind regarded him. Here is what Darwin wrote about the incomparable amateur. "I was in his company soon after he had finished his fourth round when he won the last of his three Open Championships here in 1930 and seeing him nearly past speech I thought the time had come for him to call a halt and that this game could not much longer be worth such an agonizing candle."

Darwin was always out on a golf course for he believed he had to see as much as he could in order to understand and report on it. Then in mid-afternoon he would retire to a corner of the clubhouse and quickly write his day's report in spidery handwriting. His writing was that of a master craftsman. He chipped away at paragraphs until they were as clear as a pane of glass and he chiselled away at sentences with the care of the craftsmen who built Chartres Cathedral.

In 1954, after the death of his wife, Darwin moved into the Dormy House Club just inside the Landgate in Rye, one of his favourite towns and near one of his favourite golf courses. "Just as the beautiful little old town, with its red roofs and huddled houses and cobbled streets, perching on top of a cliff, has a quality of its own, so has the golf course," Darwin wrote of Rye in 1925. "It can never be a championship course – and personally I thank goodness for that – because it lies on too narrow a strip of turf and is, therefore, no place for crowds, but it is a battlefield worthy of any champion. I know of no course on which it seems to blow so persistently across the player, never helping him or opposing him in a straightforward, open-hearted manner but harassing him by flanking attacks."

It was once noted that the quality of writing about sport gets better as the size of the ball used in that sport gets smaller. Thus the sports best served by literature are cricket and golf. Of these golf is the better and that is because of Darwin.

Salute the Carnoustie men who taught Americans the game

Keith Mackie on the pivotal role Scots played a century ago

The swing that won Bobby Jones enduring acclaim was copied in the leafy suburbs of Atlanta, Georgia, from the action of a stocky, taciturn Scot who had honed and polished his game more than 3,000 miles away on the mighty links of Carnoustie, venue of the 2007 Open Championship.

Stewart Maiden arrived in America to take over from his brother Jimmy as professional at East Lake, home club of the Jones family. He was just one of some 300 clubmakers, caddies and professionals to leave Carnoustie and its surrounding communities on Scotland's North Sea coast in the years on either side of the turn of the 19th and 20th centuries. All left in search of a better way of life.

Not all were great players, but as America woke up to the increasingly fashionable game, anyone with a Scottish accent, a reasonable game and the ability to whittle a hickory shaft, was accorded a level of respect unknown in Carnoustie. Many keen young golfers forced to work 12-hour shifts in the jute mills of nearby Dundee from the age of 13, were quick to pack their meagre belongings into cheap cardboard suitcases and set off across the Atlantic.

When Stewart Maiden arrived in Atlanta, Bobby Jones was a skinny and somewhat frail five-year-old who became instantly fascinated by the quietly spoken Scot. Maiden stood out from the local country club members, aloof from the endless social chatter, speaking only when he had something worth saying.

He paid little or no attention to the Jones boy, but whenever Maiden set foot outside the clubhouse to play or practise, the youngster would appear silently from the trees and follow his every move with intense concentration. At no time in those early years did the Scot give the young lad an ounce of encouragement, but he was eventually to become his coaching mentor and close friend.

Jones commented in later life: "Stewart had the finest and soundest style I had ever seen. Naturally I did not know this at the time, but I grew up swinging like him. I imitated his style, like a monkey I suppose."

When Jones won The Open at St Andrews in 1927 his father and Stewart Maiden were with him and they travelled on to Carnoustie, crossing the

River Tay by ferry, before Jones played an exhibition match and Maiden visited family and friends he had not seen for more than 20 years.

Jones went on, with Maiden's help and encouragement, to win The Open and Amateur Championships of Britain and America in a golden five-month period of 1930 and exhausted and made ill by his history-making exploits he immediately retired from competitive golf at the age of 28.

Carnoustie staged its first Open the following year, when, appropriately enough, it was won by another expatriate Scot, Tommy Armour, who gained a reputation as the Silver Scot because of his white hair.

While the Jones connection was influential in making the name of Carnoustie a byword in American golfing circles, his East Lake course was just one of some 250 throughout the USA where sons of

© Phil Sheldon Golf Picture Library

Tommy Armour, the Silver Scot, who triumphed at Carnoustie in 1931

In 1953, Ben Hogan arrived a week early to get to know Carnoustie, then stylishly won The Open

Carnoustie taught the game and its traditions to generations of golfers.

As new courses were opened in increasing numbers, professionals were actively recruited from all parts of Britain, but the group from Carnoustie enshrined the name of their birthplace into the roots of American golf.

The game first blossomed under the guidance of Carnoustie professionals at revered US Open courses like Medinah, Oakmont, Hazeltine and Pebble Beach. The club at Latrobe in Pennsylvania where Deacon Palmer told his son Arnold to learn to hit the ball hard, then learn to hit it straight, was also brought to life by another immigrant from the small Scottish town.

It was not just teaching and club professionals who made their mark. One Carnoustie family provided three brothers who played a dominant part in American tournament golf for 30 years.

Alex Smith won the US Open twice and was runner-up three times, losing once in a play-off. He was also third three times. He first played in the championship in 1898 and finished fifth at the age of 49 in 1921. Brother Willie, three years younger, won the title in 1899 by 11 shots and was second twice. They are still the only brothers to have won the title.

Alex Smith's victory in 1910 came after a three-way play-off, beating his own youngest brother, 20-year-old Macdonald Smith, and Johnny McDermott. Mac Smith was considered by many to be the finest player of the three brothers, but despite more than 40 tournament victories he was destined never to win one of golf's major championships.

He came close many times, but kept running into Bobby Jones at critical moments, finishing second to Jones in the Grand Slam year of 1930 in both The Open Championships of Britain and America. Among his many prestigious tournament titles were three victories in the Western Open. This brought about another unique family achievement – brothers Alex and Willie had also won. A wonderful collection of Macdonald Smith's medals is on display in Carnoustie Golf Club.

Scotland may have presented the world with the twin benefits of golf and whisky, but it also gave generously of its people, none more so than the small community in and around Carnoustie.

It is these people and the influence they exerted over the development of golf, particularly in the United States, that will be best remembered and celebrated when Carnoustie once again steps into the world spotlight as host to The Open Championship this year.

Carnoustie hosting The Open for the seventh time

The winners of the previous six Opens held at Carnoustie comprise three Americans (one originally from Scotland) an Englishman, a South African and a Scot.

Year	Winner	Score	Entry	Prize-fund	Winner
1931	T Armour (USA)	73-75-77-71—296	215	£500	£100
1937	H Cotton (ENG)	74-72-73-71—290	258	£500	£100
1953	B Hogan (USA)	73- 71-70-68—282	196	£2450	£500
1968	G Player (RSA)	74 71-71-73—289	309	£20,000	£3,000
1975	T Watson* (USA)	71-67-69-72—279	629	£75,000	£7,500
	*Watson beat Jack Newton 71-72 in 18-hole play-off				
1999	P Lawrie* (SCO)	73-74-76-67—290	2,222	£2,029,950	£350,000
	*Lawrie beat Justin Leonard and Jean Van de Velde in four-hole play-off				

How golf benefits from the largesse of The R&A

Mike Aitken finds out where The Open surpluses go

In his travels around the world, Duncan Weir, The R&A Director of Golf Development, is charged with the responsibility of re-investing some of the surpluses from The Open Championship at grassroots level in the conviction that golfers of international quality may one day emerge from countries where the game is still in its infancy.

"I think it is fantastic The Open has given The R&A enough financial clout to enable us to assist others," observed Weir. "Wouldn't it be great in ten or 15 years time to see a player from one of these countries where we're providing development support completing the circle by contending for the Claret Jug?"

In the past, most of the funds available for development projects have been distributed much closer to home but now the commitment is most certainly global.

If The R&A, apart from its work on the rules of the game, is best known for running the oldest major championship as well as other high profile events in Great Britain and Ireland as the Amateur Championship, the Boys Championship and the Walker Cup, Weir takes particular satisfaction from spreading the gospel of golf even further afield in Asia, Africa, the Caribbean, Eastern Europe, the Middle East and South America.

Where once The R&A offered mainly financial assistance to clubs and bodies at home, an operating profit of £9.1 million in 2005 enabled the organisation responsible for the governance of the international game to further extend its munificent reach around the world.

Pledged to invest more than £50 million in developing the game – the level of support annually approaches £4 million – The R&A now assists in staging international amateur team championships for men, women, boys and girls in many far flung corners of the globe. This helps provide a pathway for the development of aspiring golfers. It was in South America, for example, that Weir first caught sight of Colombia's Camilo Villegas, who went on to make such a flamboyant impact in his rookie season on the US PGA Tour during 2006.

"Camilo played in several events we supported," Weir recalled. "In the course of numerous trips to South America, we've encouraged the growth of Colombian golf in many ways. Camilo caught the eye right away and to see him go on to enjoy success is tremendously satisfying. We knew he was special, an aggressive player who is exciting to watch, and we are delighted for him."

As well as providing funds for the Copa los Andes, the long established team competitions for men and women in South America – the Peruvian Golf Federation received a grant of £28,000 last year. The R&A gave similar backing to the Queen Sirikit Cup, the Asia-Pacific Women's International Team Championship, and the Nomura Cup, the men's equivalent. The R&A also supported

Duncan Weir (left) and R&A Director Michael Tate (right) with the China team at the 2005 Nomura Cup played in Japan

© The R&A

the Pan-Arab Championships in Morocco to the tune of £20,000.

In Europe, the Young Masters, a tournament for boys and girls nominated by the national bodies of over 20 countries, received funding, as did the European Disabled Golf Association. The R&A has also worked diligently in Eastern Europe to support championships and other initiatives in places such as Bulgaria, Poland, Slovenia and Russia.

"We want to help others grow the game in any way we possibly can," enthused Weir. "Our aim is simple: to encourage more people in more places to play golf more often. Our role, however, is simply to offer support to others rather than to start projects on our own. Officials on the ground, who know the local scene, are in the best position to come to us with initiatives. If we can help in any way we will. Many of the awards we make come about as a result of approaches made by national governing bodies and other organisations. We are committed to consider every request for funding, no matter how small."

As well as supporting international team events, The R&A, in conjunction with affiliated national bodies in more than 110 countries, helps to deliver professional coaching resources as well as working on junior golf development. The organisation has distributed 1,000 TaylorMade starter sets for children. Among the first recipients were Guatemala, Peru, El Salvador, Bolivia and Argentina. The sets come in three different sizes and each comprises a wood, three irons and a putter in a golf bag.

In Brazil, The R&A contributed £130,000 towards the country's first public golf course in Japeri, some 50 miles from Rio de Janeiro, where Ronaldo, the celebrated footballer, is among those who have supported the project.

In Africa, where re-conditioned greenkeeping machinery is needed to improve the standard of playing surfaces, equipment sourced by Scottish Grass Machinery at Inverkeithing in Fife was sent to the Jinja Golf Club in Uganda. Fairways at the Toro Golf Club at nearby Fort Portal are now also cut with a set of trailed mowers while the Swaziland Golf Union was gifted mowers for greens and tees.

As far as assisting the growth of the game in China and Asia is concerned, Weir says The R&A is ready and willing to lend support when asked and will continue to fund the China-Scotland partnership at Elmwood College in Fife with a £400,000 grant over the next three years to promote the training of greenkeepers to cope with the boom of golf in China. In 1994 there were just a handful of courses in that country but as the interest in the game grows, the number will be closer to 500 in a very short time.

The R&A's Chief Executive, Peter Dawson, addressed a golf seminar in China last year aimed at encouraging and helping the expansion of golf – a game the Chinese claim they invented centuries before the Scots.

It was also significant The R&A chose Asia-Pacific, where a quarter of the world's golfers play the game, when the decision was taken to appoint Colin Phillips as their first Regional Director. "We'd made more than 100 visits to Asia-Pacific countries since 2000 and it made sense to have someone out there flying the flag," explained the Director of Development.

The game continues to spread and The R&A's willingness to help is clearly benefitting the sport the world over.

Youngsters enjoying golf at Japeri in Brazil

He enjoyed 50 glorious years but now "King Arnie" signs off

Renton Laidlaw on Arnold Palmer's decision to quit tournament golf

Golf has been Arnold Palmer's life so it was with real emotion that he pulled out of the Administaff Small Business Classic in Spring, Texas on Friday October 13 last year and announced his retirement from tournament play.

The end of his illustrious competitive career came quickly. As he battled with a bad back he hit two balls into the water at the par 4 440 yards fourth hole and told playing partners John Mahaffey and Lee Trevino that that was that. Naturally he would continue to play, he told them, but would not keep a score.

Suddenly and at the least likely location Arnie's gloriously loyal if ever ageing and dwindling army of fans – the army that marched initially at Augusta in 1956 when Palmer won The Masters – had had a last chance to see "The King" play tournament golf. He might play friendly matches or charity games but no more tournaments. His exciting and hugely significant 50 year career smashing drives charging putts and hitching up his trousers was over.

Palmer revolutionised and popularised the game for us all. He emerged at a time when television was looking for something different and for someone new to cover and golf and Palmer was it. Players on the US PGA Tour have often said that

Arnie's role was so important for the sport that if they handed him 25 cents of every prize-money dollar they earned it would not be enough.

Jim Murray the late much revered columnist for the *Los Angeles Times*, once wrote that only three people in America could be described as "The King" – film star Clark Gable, singer Elvis Presley and Palmer. He insisted that Palmer never tried to outsmart a course he just charged at it. He did not want to win on points, he wanted a knock-out. It meant his play was always aggressive, dramatic and so watchable.

In his heyday (and long after too) he was the boldest of putters. Murray recalls: "He never left a putt short. He treated 40 footers as tap-ins." Dave Marr, the former player and later commentator, always said that when Arnie got his ball to within 20 feet of the hole you felt like saying "That's good." The public have always loved Arnie. They still do. He is sporting royalty who often made bigger headlines not winning than the winner did taking the first prize cheque.

Arnie joined the US Tour in 1955, scored his first win at the Canadian Open and his last of 62 at the Bob Hope Desert Classic in 1973. Two years later he came to Europe and won the Spanish Open at La Manga and then the PGA Championship. He was as excited about those victories as he had been winning the Canadian title 20 years earlier. His enthusiasm was infectious. Later his participation ensured the success of the US Senior Tour, now the Champions Tour, where he scored a further ten victories. His involvement in the founding of The Golf Channel seen worldwide and with an audience of over 70 million homes in America alone was crucial at the start.

Arnold Palmer signs autographs for fans after his last tournament round

Arnie with his late caddie 'Tip' Anderson

Canada in 1955. His biggest winning margin was 12 shots at the Phoenix Open in 1962. More important than all his wins was the fact that he won over the hearts of the people watching him and that is still the case today. In his book *A Golfer's Life* he admits he never enjoyed being called "The King". "At times it makes me uncomfortable and even a bit irritated to be referred to in that way. There is no king in golf – never has and never will be. Golf is the most democratic of games, a pastime of the people that grants no special priviledges and pays no mind to whether a man is an hotel doorman or a corporate CEO. It punishes and exalts us all with splendid equal opportunity.

"I know I have said this before but it bears repeating: golf resembles life in so many ways and I also happen to believe that golf depends more than any other game on the simple timeless principles of courtesy and respect. I don't think that it is by accident that golf is the most polite, well-mannered game on earth. In a world where values are constantly shifting and, some believe, eroding, golf has not changed much."

In the same book he also has this to say to that loyal army of fans and to all who admired him and supported him throughout his career. "It's been a great life – rich with unexpected rewards and people at every turn in the road. Allow me to take my hat off to you all. Thank you for letting Arnold Palmer be Arnold Palmer. You will never know how deeply grateful I really am."

Arnie – no surname is ever required for you to know who that is – has left a wonderful legacy to golf – the legacy of always having played the game he loves in an exciting, passionate, entertaining and utterly sportsmanlike way. Everyone in golf is sad the tournaments are over but most assuredly wish golf's greatest ambassador a long and happy retirement. He has certainly earned it.

After announcing his retirement Palmer, one of the most warmly admired of golfers, said: "To stand out there on the course and not be able to make something happen is very traumatic. The people all want to see me hit a good shot and when I cannot give it to them you know that it's time. I am now going to concentrate on building courses. That will be my next great passion." At the end of his final round Trevino grabbed Arnie's ball and glove and asked him to sign them. "We didn't take his shoes!" quipped Trevino.

Curiously Arnold never scored better than 62 on the US PGA Tour and his lowest 72-hole score was the 265 he shot when winning that first event in

Arnie's Role in creating golf's modern Grand Slam

It has always been well-documented that the late Herbert Warren Wind, writing about the perils facing golfers at the 11th, 12th and 13th holes at Augusta, coined the always-to-be-remembered phrase "Amen Corner". We know too that it was the late Australian journalist Don Lawrence who first used the nickname "Golden Bear" to describe Jack Nicklaus. Less is known about the creating of the modern Grand Slam but Arnold Palmer was very much involved in it.

It was 1960 and Palmer had won The Masters and the US Open. Before getting to St Andrews for The Open, Palmer had a date with Sam Snead at Portmarnock playing for the United States in the Canada Cup, now the World Cup. Travelling with Palmer on that occasion was respected journalist Bob Drum and they got talking about Bobby Jones and his Grand Slam in 1930 when he won The Open and Amateur Championships of Britain and America in the same year. During the conversation, Drum said it was a pity that the the growth of the professional game had put an end to the old fashioned slam, to which Palmer suggested maybe they should produce a new Grand Slam to take its place.

Drum agreed that maybe it was not a bad idea to rope together The Masters and the US Open, already won by Palmer, with The Open and the US PGA and although Drum did not immediately write about it himself he planted the seed among the British journalists covering the World Cup. They wrote about it and the new Grand Slam had become reality.

Championship dates

	The Masters	US Open	The Open	US PGA Championship
2007	**April 5–8** Augusta National, Augusta, Georgia	**June 14–17** Oakmont CC, Pennsylvania	**July 19–22** Carnoustie	**August** Southern Hills, Tulsa, Oklahoma
2008	**April 10–13** Augusta National, Augusta, Georgia	**June 12–15** La Jolla Golf Club, Torrey Pines, California	**July 17–20** Royal Birkdale	**August** Oakland Hills, Bloomfield Hills CC, Michigan
2009	**April 9–12** Augusta National, Augusta, Georgia	**June 18–21** Bethpage State Park (Black Course), Farmingdale, New York	**July 16–19** Turnberry	**August** Hazeltine National GC, Chaska, Minnesota
2010	**April 8–11** Augusta National, Augusta, Georgia	**June 17–20** Pebble Beach Golf Links, California	**July 15–18** St Andrews	**August** Sahalee CC, Richmond, Washington
2011	**April 7–10** Augusta National, Augusta, Georgia	**June 16–19** Congressional (Md) CC (Blue Course), Bethesda, Maryland	TBA	**August** Atlanta AC, Deluth, Georgia

Ryder Cup

2008 at Valhalla Golf Club, Louisville, Kentucky
2010 at Celtic Manor Resort, Newport, Wales
2012 at Medinah Country Club, Illinois
2014 at Gleneagles Hotel, Perthshire, Scotland
2016 at Hazeltine National GC, Chaska, Minnesota
2018 to be decided
2020 at Whistling Straits, Kohler, Wisconsin

Presidents Cup

(USA v Rest of the World except Europe)
2007 Royal Montreal GC – September 24–27

Senior British Open

2007 Muirfield – July 26–29

R&A Contacts

Up-to-date news of The R&A and its activities can be found at
www.randa.org

Full details of The Open Championship can be found at
www.opengolf.com

R&A officials can be contacted on: Tel 01334 460000 Fax 01334 460001

Chief Executive: Peter Dawson

Director: Michael Tate

Director of Championships: David Hill

Director of Rules and Equipment Standards: David Rickman

Director of Golf Development: Duncan Weir

Commercial Director: Angus Farquhar

Financial Director: Mark Dobell

Golf Heritage Secretary: Peter Lewis

R&A dates, 2007–2009

	2007	2008	2009
The Amateur Championship	**June 18–23** Royal Lytham and St Annes Old Links	**June 16–21** Turnberry Ailsa & Kintyre	**June 15–20** Formby West Lancashire
The Open Championship Final Qualifying (local)	**July 9–10** Downfield Monifieth Montrose Panmure	**July 7–8** Formby Hillside Southport West Lancashire	**July 6–7** Glasgow Gailes Western Gailes Irvine Kilmarnock (Barassie)
The Junior Open Championship	—	**July 14–16** Hesketh	—
The Open Championship[1]	**July 19–22** Carnoustie	**July 17–20** Royal Birkdale	**July 16–19** Turnberry
The Senior Open Championship	**July 26–29** Muirfield	**July 24–27** TBA	**July 23–26** TBA
The Seniors' Open Amateur Championship	**August 8–10** Nairn and Nairn Dunbar	**August 6–8** Royal Cinque Ports and Prince's	**August 5–7** Prestwick Prestwick St Nicholas
The Boys' Home Internationals	**August 7–9** Ashburnham	**August 5–7** Royal County Down	**August 4–6** Sunningdale New
The Boys' Amateur Championship	**August 13–18** Royal Porthcawl	**August 11–16** Little Aston	**August 10–15** Royal St George's
The British Mid-Amateur Championship	**August 15–19** Allwoodley	**August 13–17** Royal St David's	**August 12–16** Blairgowrie (Rosemount)
The Jacques Léglise Trophy	**August 31–September 1** Notts GC, Hollinwell	**August 29–30** Kingsbarns	**September 4–5** Ganton
The St Andrews Trophy	—	**August 29–30** Kingsbarns	—
The Walker Cup	**September 8–9** Royal County Down, Northern Ireland	—	**September 12–13** Merion, USA
The Eisenhower Trophy	—	**October 30–Nov 2** Grange GC, Adelaide	—
Espirito Santo Trophy	—	**October 22–25** Grange GC, Adelaide	—

[1]The Open Championship returns to St Andrews from July 15–18 in 2010

Other fixtures and tour schedules can be found on pages 418–424

Abbreviations

ALB	Albania	IOM	Isle of Man	POR	Portugal
ARG	Argentina	IRL	Ireland	PUR	Puerto Rico
AUS	Australia	ISL	Iceland	RUS	Russia
AUT	Austria	ISR	Israel	LCA	Saint Lucia
BEL	Belgium	ITA	Italy	SIN	Singapore
BER	Bermuda	JAM	Jamaica	RSA	South Africa
BRA	Brazil	JPN	Japan	SCO	Scotland
BUL	Bulgaria	KOR	Korea (South)	SLO	Slovenia
CAN	Canada	MAS	Malaysia	SRI	Sri Lanka
CHN	China	MEX	Mexico	SWE	Sweden
CHI	Chile	MON	Monaco	SWZ	Swaziland
COL	Colombia	MYA	Myanmar	SUI	Switzerland
CZE	Czech Republic	NAM	Namibia	TPE	Taiwan
DEN	Denmark	NED	Netherlands		(Chinese Taipei)
EGY	Egypt	NCA	Nicaragua	THA	Thailand
ENG	England	NIR	Northern Ireland	TRI	Trinidad and
ESP	Spain	NOR	Norway		Tobago
FIJ	Fiji	NZL	New Zealand	TUN	Tunisia
FIN	Finland	PAK	Pakistan	TUR	Turkey
FRA	France	PAN	Panama	USA	United States
GER	Germany	PAR	Paraguay	VEN	Venezuela
GUA	Guatemala	PER	Peru	WAL	Wales
HUN	Hungary	PHI	Philippines	ZIM	Zimbabwe
IND	India	POL	Poland		

GBI   Great Britain and Ireland

(am)	Amateur	(M)	Match play	jr	Junior
(D)	Defending champion	(S)	Stroke play	sr	Senior

Where available, total course yardage and the par for a course are displayed in square brackets,
i.e. [6686–70]

* indicates winner after play-off

The Open benefits Scotland to the tune of £72m

Scotland benefitted to the tune of £72 million from the 2005 Open Championship at St Andrews according to a comprehensive report carried out for The R&A.

The value of The Open to Scotland was made up of £40 million worth of worldwide television exposure for the country and £32.3 million of new money for the economy in Fife from spending by spectators, media, players and The R&A, the Championship organisers.

In 2005 The Open attracted 223,000 spectators. A total of 47 broadcasters covering 194 territories worldwide carried coverage of The Open Championship in 2005.

The Masters gives $3.4 million to charity

Charity is a big winner each year at The Masters. In 2006, approximately $3.4 million was distributed to various charities. Over the last nine years, The Masters has made contributions in excess of $29 million.

The First Tee National Youth Development programme in the USA received $1 million in 2006, part of a $9 million total since 1998.

Among other charities to benefit from the success of The Masters is the Community Foundation for the CSRA – an Augusta-based foundation that evaluates and distibutes funds to worthwhile charities. It has received $11.2 million from The Masters,

Mickelson makes history with two drivers in his bag

It is rare that a golfer breaks free from convention and promptly wins a major but that is what Phil Mickelson did at the 2006 Masters. Having experimented successfully with the idea at the BellSouth event in Atlanta the week before, Mickelson decided to put two drivers in his bag – a driver with which to fade the ball and one with which to draw it.

There were mutterings at this manoeuvre, some saying this was taking an unfair advantage of new technology – an advantage that allowed him to use the same swing to produce two entirely different shots.

The fact is, of course, that there have always been clubs which help players hit a fade or a draw. All Mickelson did was recognise that fact. It worked brilliantly. He won a second Green Jacket.

Tiger never loses majors when ahead after 54 holes

Tiger Woods has a remarkable record in majors. He has never lost when leading or being tied for the lead going into the last day. He extended that run to 12 out of 12 with his victories last year in The Open at Royal Liverpool and the US PGA Championship at Medinah in Chicago. This is his record:

Year	Major	Venue	54 holes	Result	Total
1997	The Masters	Augusta	Led by 9	Won by 12 from T Kite	270
1999	US PGA	Medinah	Tied	Won by 1 from S García	277
2000	US Open	Pebble Beach	Led by 10	Won by 15 from E Els and M Jiménez	272
2000	The Open	St Andrews	Led by 6	Won by 8 from T Bjørn and E Els	269
2000	US PGA	Valhalla	Led by 1	Won 3-hole play-off with Bob May	270
2001	The Masters	Augusta	Led by 1	Won by 2 from D Duval	272
2002	The Masters	Augusta	Tied	Won by 3 from R Goosen	276
2002	US Open	Bethpage Park	Led by 4	Won by 3 from P Mickelson	277
2005	The Masters	Augusta	Led by 3	Won play-off with C DiMarco	276
2005	The Open	St Andrews	Led by 2	Won by 5 from C Montgomerie	274
2006	The Open	Hoylake	Led by 1	Won by 2 from C DiMarco	270
2006	US PGA	Medinah	Tied	Won by 5 from S Micheel	270

PART 1

The Major Championships

The Open Championship

Tiger Woods wins major title no. 11 as world golf welcomes Hoylake back to The Open rota

In winning his 11th major and becoming the first golfer to successfully defend The Open title since Tom Watson in 1983, Tiger Woods was always in control when the Championship returned for the first time in 39 years to the Hoylake course of the Royal Liverpool club.

His emotional victory following the death of his father earlier in the year, tied him for second in the all-time majors list with Walter Hagen. Woods led going into the second and third rounds but on the first day Ulsterman Graeme McDowell took pole position with a 66 – form that he was unable to maintain throughout the next three days. Woods second round 65 which was completed with a glorious early evening eagle gave him a one shot advantage over Ernie Els and his third round 71 saw him maintain that slender margin over the former winner from South Africa, American Chris DiMarco and Sergio García.

Occasionally Woods has not needed anything special in the last round to win but at Hoylake he closed with his best of the week – a 67. This enabled him to cope with García who stumbled quickly on the final day, Els who stayed with him until the 10th hole before falling back and DiMarco who was also grieving the loss of a parent – his mother had died two weeks earlier. He had a tougher job shaking off US Ryder Cup colleague DiMarco than the other two.

Playing with Tiger on the final day, García slipped out of contention as a result of poor putting. He missed from five feet for par at the second and third and from 10 feet at the eighth and ninth. His 39 out on the final day was ten shots worse than he had shot a day earlier. His problems on the last day were not surprising, however, as his fourth round scoring average on the PGA Tour is 74 – seventh worst out of 190 players on the list. Els drew level with Woods after making a birdie at the long fifth but when Tiger, coming behind, eagled the same hole to go two ahead the writing was on the wall for the South African who would go on to finish with a 71 for 13-under-par 275.

DiMarco became the main threat on the back nine, closing to within a shot thanks to birdies at the 10th and 13th and a brilliant par at the 14th where, after finding the rough, he chipped 60 feet past the hole only to sink the return. Threatened by his American colleague, Woods simply upped a gear. He birdied three in a row from the 14th where earlier in the Championship he had holed his second shot for an eagle and the Championship was won. At the end, in a rare show of emotion Tiger, remembering the role his late father Earl had played in his career, broke down and hugged his long-time caddie Steve Williams. Tiger's father had been with him when he had had his first taste of links golf in Britain as a 19-year-old amateur playing at Carnoustie in the Scottish Amateur Championship. "After the last putt I realised my dad was never going to see this again and I wished he could have seen this one last time". Victory in The Open more than made up for the missed cut at the US Open when making his return to competitive action after a nine-week break following his father's death.

Woods, who used his driver only once and frequently conceded yardage off the tee to his rivals, had produced some magnificent approach iron-play all week. His course management was superb.

In the end DiMarco, beaten in play-offs for the 2004 US PGA Championship and the 2005 Masters (by Woods) came second and Els finished third just ahead of Jim Furyk, the former US Open champion. García and Hideto Tanihara were tied fifth and Argentinian Angel Cabrera seventh. The silver medal for leading amateur went to Norwegian Marius Thorp who had his own last day battle with reigning US Amateur champion Eduardo Molinari.

First Round	Second Round	Third Round	Fourth Round
–6 McDowell	–12 Woods	–13 Woods	–18 Woods
–5 Owen	–11 Els	–12 García	–16 DiMarco
–5 Wall	–9 DiMarco	–12 DiMarco	–13 Els
–5 Jiménez	–8 Goosen	–12 Els	–12 Furyk
–5 Fukaboru	–7 Fukabori	–11 Furyk	–11 García
–5 Woods	–7 Ilonen	–11 Cabrera	–11 Tanihara
	–7 Jiménez	–10 Tanihara	–10 Cabrera

2006 Open Championship (135th) Royal Liverpool, Hoylake [7528–72]

Total Prize Money: £3,898,000. Entries: 2,434. 16 Regional Qualifying Courses: Ashridge, County Louth, Effingham, Little Aston, Minchinhampton, Musselburgh, Notts, Old Fold Manor, Orsett, Pannal, Pleasington, Prestbury, Rochester & Cobham Park, Royal Ashdown Forest, Silloth-on-Solway, Trentham.

International Final Qualifying:

Africa (Royal Johannesburg & Kensington)

Warren Abery (RSA)	66-70—136
Ross Wellington (RSA)	69-68—137
Bruce Vaughan (USA)	69-69—138
Thomas Aiken (RSA)	71-67—138

Australasia (Kingston Heath, Melbourne)

Michael Wright (AUS)	69-66—135
Ben Bunny (AUS)	69-69—138
Bradley Hughes (AUS)	69-69—138
Adam Bland (AUS)	73-66—139

America (Congressional, Maryland [cancelled; qualifiers from money list])

Tom Pernice (USA)	
Brett Wetterich (USA)	
Vaughn Taylor (USA)	
Lee Westwood (ENG)	
Greg Owen (ENG)	
Bo Van Pelt (USA)	
J B Holmes (USA)	
Jerry Kelly (USA)	
Ted Purdy (USA)	
Steve Elkington (AUS)	
Jeff Maggert (USA)	
Aaron Baddeley (AUS)	

Europe (Sunningdale, Old & New, England)

Louis Oosthuizen (RSA)	66-66—132
Marco Ruiz (PAR)	67-65—132
Richard Green (AUS)	69-66—135
Sam Little (ENG)	69-66—135
Mark Pilkington (WAL)	69-66—135
Barry Lane (ENG)	68-68—136
Carlos Rodiles (ESP)	68-68—136
Simon Wakefield (ENG)	67-69—136
Søren Kjeldsen (DEN)	68-68—136
Jamie Donaldson (WAL)	67-70—137
Peter Hedblom (SWE)	70-67—137
Lee Slattery (ENG)	70-67—137
Brett Rumford (AUS)	66-71—137
Phillip Price (WAL)	70-67—137
Richard Sterne (RSA)	71-67—138
Graeme McDowell (NIR)	69-69—138
Simon Dyson (ENG)	71-67—138
Robert Rock (ENG)	68-70—138

Asia (Sentosa, Singapore)

Jarrod Lyle (AUS)	67-71—138
Unho Park (AUS)	68-70—138
Shiv Kapur (IND)	69-70—139

Local Final Qualifying:

Conwy

Jon Bevan (ENG)	73-66—139
Warren Bladon (ENG)	70-72—142
Mikko Ilonen (FIN)	69-73—142

Wallasey

Gary Day (ENG)	67-72—139
Danny Denison (ENG) (am)	70-69—139
Markus Brier (AUT)	74-67—141

Formby

Jim Payne (ENG)	67-71—138
Andrew Marshall (ENG)	69-70—139
Darren Parris (ENG)	69-70—139

West Lancashire

Nick Ludwell (ENG)	72-68—140
Gary Lockerbie (ENG)	73-68—141
Adam Frayne (ENG)	69-73—142

Top shots at The Open

When Tiger Woods sunk a 211-yard four-iron shot at the 14th hole on the first day of the 2006 Open it was the latest in a series of remarkable shots in the classic tournament. In 1977 at Turnberry, Jack Nicklaus holed a long putt from the edge of the green at the last hole of the tournament ... but still lost to Tom Watson.

In 1979, Seve Ballesteros appeared to have lost his way when he drove into the car park at the 16th at Royal Lytham & St Annes. He recovered with a brilliant chip shot onto the green for a birdie ... and went on to take the title. Mark Calcavecchia holed a remarkable pitch at the 12th in 1989 at Royal Troon on his way to forcing a play-off and subsequently lifting the title.

At St Andrews in 1990, Nick Faldo holed from 60 feet at the 18th on his way to victory.

135th Open Championship continued

The final field of 156 players included 4 amateurs. 71 players (including 2 amateurs) qualified for the last two rounds with scores of 143 and better.

1	Tiger Woods (USA)	67-65-71-67—270	£720000	€1045965
2	Chris DiMarco (USA)	70-65-69-68—272	430000	624673
3	Ernie Els (RSA)	68-65-71-71—275	275000	399500
4	Jim Furyk (USA)	68-71-66-71—276	210000	305073
5	Sergio García (ESP)	68-71-65-73—277	159500	231710
	Hideto Tanihara (JPN)	72-68-66-71—277	159500	231710
7	Angel Cabrera (ARG)	71-68-66-73—278	128000	185949
8	Carl Pettersson (SWE)	68-72-70-69—279	95333	138493
	Andres Romero (ARG)	70-70-68-71—279	95333	138493
	Adam Scott (AUS)	68-69-70-72—279	95333	138493
11	Ben Crane (USA)	68-71-71-70—280	69333	100722
	S K Ho (KOR)	68-73-69-70—280	69333	100722
	Anthony Wall (ENG)	67-73-71-69—280	69333	100722
14	Retief Goosen (RSA)	70-66-72-73—281	56500	82079
	Sean O'Hair (USA)	69-73-72-67—281	56500	82079
16	Robert Allenby (AUS)	69-70-69-74—282	45000	65372
	Mikko Ilonen (FIN)	68-69-73-72—282	45000	65372
	Peter Lonard (AUS)	71-69-68-74—282	45000	65372
	Geoff Ogilvy (AUS)	71-69-70-72—282	45000	65372
	Robert Rock (ENG)	69-69-73-71—282	45000	65372
	Brett Rumford (AUS)	68-71-72-71—282	45000	65372
22	Mark Hensby (AUS)	68-72-74-69—283	35375	51390
	Phil Mickelson (USA)	69-71-73-70—283	35375	51390
	Greg Owen (ENG)	67-73-68-75—283	35375	51390
	Charl Schwartzel (RSA)	74-66-72-71—283	35375	51390
26	Paul Broadhurst (ENG)	71-71-73-69—284	29100	42274
	Jerry Kelly (USA)	72-67-69-76—284	29100	42274
	Hunter Mahan (USA)	73-70-68-73—284	29100	42274
	Rory Sabbatini (RSA)	69-70-73-72—284	29100	42274
	Lee Slattery (ENG)	69-72-71-72—284	29100	42274
31	Simon Khan (ENG)	70-72-68-75—285	24500	35591
	Scott Verplank (USA)	70-73-67-75—285	24500	35591
	Lee Westwood (ENG)	69-72-75-69—285	24500	35591
	Thaworn Wiratchant (THA)	71-68-74-72—285	24500	35591
35	Michael Campbell (NZL)	70-71-75-70—286	19625	28509
	Luke Donald (ENG)	74-68-73-71—286	19625	28509
	Marcus Fraser (AUS)	68-71-72-75—286	19625	28509
	Robert Karlsson (SWE)	70-71-71-74—286	19625	28509
	Rod Pampling (AUS)	69-71-74-72—286	19625	28509
	John Senden (AUS)	70-73-73-70—286	19625	28509
41	Stephen Ames (CAN)	70-71-72-74—287	14857	21583
	Thomas Bjørn (DEN)	72-71-73-71—287	14857	21583
	Mark Calcavecchia (USA)	71-68-68-80—287	14857	21583
	Miguel Angel Jiménez (ESP)	67-70-76-74—287	14857	21583
	Brandt Jobe (USA)	69-71-75-72—287	14857	21583
	Søren Kjeldsen (DEN)	71-71-71-74—287	14857	21583
	Jeff Sluman (USA)	71-72-68-76—287	14857	21583
48	John Bickerton (ENG)	72-70-70-76—288	11607	16862
	Simon Dyson (ENG)	74-69-70-75—288	11607	16862
	Gonzalo Fernandez Castano (ESP)	70-69-73-76—288	11607	16862
	Andrew Marshall (ENG)	72-71-68-77—288	11607	16862
	Henrik Stenson (SWE)	72-71-74-71—288	11607	16862
	Marius Thorp (NOR) (am)	71-71-75-71—288		
	Tom Watson (USA)	72-70-75-71—288	11607	16862
	Simon Wakefield (ENG)	72-71-70-75—288	11607	16862
56	Tim Clark (RSA)	72-69-69-79—289	10300	14963
	David Duval (USA)	70-70-78-71—289	10300	14963

56T	Keiichiro Fukabori (JPN)	67-73-70-79—289	10300	14963
	José-María Olazábal (ESP)	73-68-76-72—289	10300	14963
	Mike Weir (CAN)	68-72-73-76—289	10300	14963
61	Andrew Buckle (AUS)	72-69-72-77—290	9950	14454
	Graeme McDowell (NIR)	66-73-72-79—290	9950	14454
63	Mark O'Meara (USA)	71-70-77-73—291	9750	14164
	Marco Ruiz (PAR)	71-70-80-70—291	9750	14164
65	Chad Campbell (USA)	70-73-74-75—292	9600	13946
66	Fred Funk (USA)	69-74-75-76—294	9450	13728
	Vaughn Taylor (USA)	72-71-77-74—294	9450	13728
68	Todd Hamilton (USA)	72-71-74-78—295	9300	13510
	Edoardo Molinari (ITA) (am)	73-70-77-75—295		
70	Bart Bryant (USA)	69-74-77-76—296	9200	13365
71	Paul Casey (ENG)	72-70-79-77—298	9100	13219

The following players missed the cut:

72	Rich Beem (USA)	71-73—144	£3000	€4358
	Markus Brier (AUT)	71-73—144	3000	4358
	Bradley Dredge (WAL)	70-74—144	3000	4358
	Scott Drummond (SCO)	73-71—144	3000	4358
	Niclas Fasth (SWE)	69-75—144	3000	4358
	Mathew Goggin (AUS)	75-69—144	3000	4358
	Jarrod Lyle (AUS)	74-70—144	3000	4358
	Jeff Maggert (USA)	75-69—144	3000	4358
	Paul McGinley (IRL)	71-73—144	3000	4358
	Tom Pernice (USA)	71-73—144	3000	4358
	Mark Pilkington (WAL)	76-68—144	3000	4358
	Phillip Price (WAL)	74-70—144	3000	4358
84	John Daly (USA)	72-73—145	2500	3631
	Steve Elkington (AUS)	71-74—145	2500	3631
	Lucas Glover (USA)	72-73—145	2500	3631
	Shiv Kapur (IND)	72-73—145	2500	3631
	Tom Lehman (USA)	68-77—145	2500	3631
	Nick O'Hern (AUS)	70-75—145	2500	3631
	Ted Purdy (USA)	74-71—145	2500	3631
91	Thomas Aiken (RSA)	72-74—146	2500	3631
	Stuart Appleby (AUS)	74-72—146	2500	3631
	Aaron Baddeley (AUS)	70-76—146	2500	3631
	K J Choi (KOR)	72-74—146	2500	3631
	Fred Couples (USA)	70-76—146	2500	3631
	Ben Curtis (USA)	73-73—146	2500	3631
	Stephen Dodd (WAL)	73-73—146	2500	3631
	Richard Green (AUS)	71-75—146	2500	3631
	J J Henry (USA)	73-73—146	2500	3631
	Zach Johnson (USA)	73-73—146	2500	3631
	Sandy Lyle (SCO)	73-73—146	2500	3631
	Vijay Singh (FIJ)	70-76—146	2500	3631
	David Smail (NZL)	76-70—146	2500	3631
	Bo Van Pelt (USA)	74-72—146	2500	3631
	Brett Wetterich (USA)	74-72—146	2500	3631
106	Billy Andrade (USA)	72-75—147	2250	3268
	Adam Bland (AUS)	73-74—147	2250	3268

106T	Nick Dougherty (ENG)	74-73—147	2250	3268
	Julien Guerrier (FRA) (am)	72-75—147		
	Bradley Hughes (AUS)	72-75—147	2250	3268
	Davis Love III (USA)	72-75—147	2250	3268
	Shaun Micheel (USA)	72-75—147	2250	3268
	Louis Oosthuizen (RSA)	78-69—147	2250	3268
	Darren Parris (ENG)	75-72—147	2250	3268
	Kenny Perry (USA)	73-74—147	2250	3268
	Michael Wright (AUS)	72-75—147	2250	3268
117	Nick Faldo (ENG)	77-71—148	2250	3268
	Shingo Katayama (JPN)	74-74—148	2250	3268
	Bernhard Langer (GER)	74-74—148	2250	3268
	Colin Montgomerie (SCO)	73-75—148	2250	3268
	Arron Oberholser (USA)	73-75—148	2250	3268
	Ross Wellington (RSA)	75-73—148	2250	3268
123	Stewart Cink (USA)	72-77—149	2250	3268
	Johan Edfors (SWE)	75-74—149	2250	3268
	Padraig Harrington (IRL)	75-74—149	2250	3268
	Tim Herron (USA)	76-73—149	2250	3268
	J B Holmes (USA)	74-75—149	2250	3268
	Toshimori Muto (JPN)	75-74—149	2250	3268
	Jim Payne (ENG)	73-76—149	2250	3268
	Richard Sterne (RSA)	76-73—149	2250	3268
131	Peter Hedblom (SWE)	73-77—150	2000	2905
	David Howell (ENG)	74-76—150	2000	2905
	Barry Lane (ENG)	75-75—150	2000	2905
	Paul Lawrie (SCO)	76-74—150	2000	2905
	Brett Quigley (USA)	79-71—150	2000	2905
136	Severiano Ballesteros (ESP)	74-77—151	2000	2905
	Darren Clarke (NIR)	69-82—151	2000	2905

135th Open Championship continued

136T	Jamie Donaldson (WAL)	75-76—151	2000	2905		147T	Gary Lockerbie (ENG)	78-76—154	2000	2905
	Yasuharu Imano (JPN)	73-78—151	2000	2905		149	Wayne Perske (AUS)	76-79—155	2000	2905
	Mick Ludwell (ENG)	75-76—151	2000	2905		150	Unho Park (AUS)	82-74—156	2000	2905
	Ian Poulter (ENG)	75-76—151	2000	2905		151	Ben Bunny (AUS)	74-83—157	2000	2905
142	Warren Bladon (ENG)	76-76—152	2000	2905			Sam Little (ENG)	83-74—157	2000	2905
	Adam Frayne (ENG)	71-81—152	2000	2905			Carlos Rodiles (ESP)	81-76—157	2000	2905
	Tatsuhiko Ichihara (JPN)	78-74—152	2000	2905		154	Gary Day (ENG)	82-76—158	2000	2905
	Bruce Vaughn (USA)	75-77—152	2000	2905		155	Jon Bevan (ENG)	82-81—163	2000	2905
146	Warren Abery (RSA)	76-77—153	2000	2905			Kenneth Ferrie (ENG)	76 W/D		
147	Danny Denison (ENG) (am)	78-76—154								

2005 Open Championship St Andrews (Old Course) June 14–17   [7279–72]

Total Prize Money: £3,854,900. Entries: 2,499 (record). 16 Regional Qualifying Courses: Alwoodley, Ashridge, Hadley Wood, Hindhead, The Island, Little Aston, Minchinhampton, Notts, Orsett, Pleasington, Prestbury, Renfrew, Rochester & Cobham Park, Royal Ashdown Forest, Silloth-on-Solway, Trentham. Final Field: 156 (7 amateurs), of whom 80 (4 amateurs) made the half-way cut on 145 or less.

1	Tiger Woods (USA)	66-67-71-70—274	£720000		15T	Nick O'Hern (AUS)	73-69-71-70—283	46286
2	Colin Montgomerie (SCO)	71-66-70-72—279	430000			Lloyd Saltman (SCO) (am)	73-71-68-71—283	
3	Fred Couples (USA)	68-71-73-68—280	242500		23	Bart Bryant (USA)	69-70-71-74—284	32500
	José-María Olazábal (ESP)	68-70-68-74—280	242500			Tim Clark (RSA)	71-69-70-74—284	32500
5	Michael Campbell (NZL)	69-72-68-72—281	122167			Scott Drummond (SCO)	74-71-69-70—284	32500
	Sergio García (ESP)	70-69-69-73—281	122167			Brad Faxon (USA)	72-66-70-76—284	32500
	Retief Goosen (RSA)	68-73-66-74—281	122167			Nicholas Flanagan (AUS)	73-71-69-71—284	32500
	Bernhard Langer (GER)	71-69-70-71—281	122167			Tom Lehman (USA)	75-69-70-70—284	32500
	Geoff Ogilvy (AUS)	71-74-67-69—281	122167			Eric Ramsay (SCO) (am)	68-74-74-68—284	
	Vijay Singh (FIJ)	69-69-71-72—281	122167			Tadahiro Takayama (JPN)	72-72-70-70—284	32500
11	Nick Faldo (ENG)	74-69-70-69—282	66750			Scott Verplank (USA)	68-70-72-74—284	32500
	Graeme McDowell (NIR)	69-72-74-67—282	66750		32	Richard Green (AUS)	72-68-72-73—285	26500
	Kenny Perry (USA)	71-71-68-72—282	66750			Sandy Lyle (SCO)	74-67-69-75—285	26500
	Ian Poulter (ENG)	70-72-71-69—282	66750		34	Simon Dyson (ENG)	70-71-72-73—286	22000
15	Darren Clarke (NIR)	73-70-67-73—283	46286			Ernie Els (RSA)	74-67-75-70—286	22000
	John Daly (USA)	71-69-70-73—283	46286			Peter Hanson (SWE)	72-72-71-71—286	22000
	David Frost (RSA)	77-65-72-69—283	46286			Thomas Levet (FRA)	69-71-75-71—286	22000
	Mark Hensby (AUS)	67-77-69-70—283	46286			Joe Ogilvie (USA)	74-70-73-69—286	22000
	Trevor Immelman (RSA)	68-70-73-72—283	46286			Adam Scott (AUS)	70-71-70-75—286	22000
	Sean O'Hair (USA)	73-67-70-73—283	46286			Henrik Stenson (SWE)	74-67-73-72—286	22000

Other players who made the cut: Stuart Appleby (AUS), Choi Kyoung-Ju (KOR), Hiroyuki Fujita (JPN), Søren Hansen (DEN), Tim Herron (USA), Simon Khan (ENG), Maarten Lafeber (NED), Paul McGinley (IRL), Bob Tway (USA), Tom Watson (USA), Steve Webster (ENG), 287; Robert Allenby (AUS), Luke Donald (ENG), Fredrik Jacobson (SWE), Thongchai Jaidee (THA), Miguel Angel Jiménez (ESP), Paul Lawrie (SCO), Justin Leonard (USA), Bo Van Pelt (USA), 288; John Bickerton (ENG), Mark Calcavecchia (USA), Phil Mickelson (USA), Eduardo Molinari (ITA) (am), Greg Norman (AUS), Tino Schuster (GER), 289; Peter Lonard (USA), 290; Chris DiMarco (USA), Pat Perez (USA), Chris Riley (USA), Robert Rock (ENG), David Smail (NZL), Duffy Waldorf (USA), 291; Patrik Sjöland (SWE), 292; Scott Gutschewski (USA), S K Ho (KOR), Ted Purdy (USA), 293; Steve Flesch (USA), 294; Rodney Pampling (AUS), Graeme Storm (ENG), 296; Matthew Richardson (ENG) (am), 297

2004 Open Championship *Royal Troon* July 15–18 [7175–71]

Total Prize Money: £4,064,000. Entries: 2221 Regional Qualifying Courses: Alwoodley, Ashridge, Co.Louth, Hadley Wood, Hindhead, Little Aston, Minchinhampton, Notts, Orsett, Pleasington, Prestbury, Renfrew, Rochester & Cobham Park, Royal Ashdown Forest, Silloth-on-Solway, Trentham. Final qualifying courses: Glasgow (Gailes), Irvine, Turnberry Kintyre, Western Gailes. Final Field: 156 (5 amateurs), of whom 73 (1 amateur) made the half-way cut on 145 or less.

1	Todd Hamilton (USA)*	71-67-67-69—274	£720000	
2	Ernie Els (RSA)	69-69-68-68—274	430000	
Play-off: Hamilton 4-4-3-4–15; Els 4-4-4-4–16				
3	Phil Mickelson (USA)	73-66-68-68—275	275000	
4	Lee Westwood (ENG)	72-71-68-67—278	210000	
5	Thomas Levet (FRA)	66-70-71-72—279	159500	
	Davis Love III (USA)	72-69-71-67—279	159500	
7	Retief Goosen (RSA)	69-70-68-73—280	117500	
	Scott Verplank (USA)	69-70-70-71—280	117500	
9	Mike Weir (CAN)	71-68-71-71—281	89500	
	Tiger Woods (USA)	70-71-68-72—281	89500	
11	Mark Calcavecchia (USA)	72-73-69-68—282	69333	
	Darren Clarke (NIR)	69-72-73-68—282	69333	
	Skip Kendall (USA)	69-66-75-72—282	69333	
14	Stewart Fink (USA)	72-71-71-69—283	56500	
	Barry Lane (ENG)	69-68-71-75—283	56500	
16	Choi Kyung-Ju (KOR)	68-69-74-73—284	47000	
	Joakim Haeggman (SWE)	69-73-72-70—284	47000	
	Justin Leonard (USA)	70-72-71-71—284	47000	
	Kenny Perry (USA)	69-70-73-72—284	47000	
20	Michael Campbell (NZL)	67-71-74-73—285	38100	
20T	Paul Casey (ENG)	66-77-70-72—285	38100	
	Bob Estes (USA)	73-72-69-71—285	38100	
	Gary Evans (ENG)	68-73-73-71—285	38100	
	Vijay Singh (FIJ)	68-70-76-71—285	38100	
25	Colin Montgomerie (SCO)	69-69-72-76—286	32250	
	Ian Poulter (ENG)	71-72-71-72—286	32250	
27	Takashi Kamiyama (JPN)	70-73-71-73—287	29000	
	Rodney Pampling (AUS)	72-68-74-73—287	29000	
	Jyoti Randhawa (IND)	73-72-70-72—287	29000	
30	Kelichiro Fukabori (JPN)	73-71-70-74—288	24500	
	Shigeki Maruyama (JPN)	71-72-74-71—288	24500	
	Mark O'Meara (USA)	71-74-68-75—288	24500	
	Nick Price (ZIM)	71-71-69-77—288	24500	
	David Toms (USA)	71-71-74-72—288	24500	
	Bo Van Pelt (USA)	72-71-71-74—288	24500	
36	Stuart Appleby (AUS)	71-70-73-75—289	18750	
	Kim Felton (AUS)	73-67-72-77—289	18750	
	Tetsuji Hiratsuka (JPN)	70-74-70-75—289	18750	
	Steve Lowery (USA)	69-73-75-72—289	18750	
	Hunter Mahan (USA)	74-69-71-75—289	18750	
	Tjaart Van Der Walt (RSA)	70-73-72-74—289	18750	

Other players who made the cut: Kenneth Ferrie (ENG), Charles Howell III (USA), Trevor Immelman (RSA), Andrew Oldcorn (SCO), Adam Scott (AUS) 290; Paul Bradshaw (ENG), Alastair Forsyth (SCO), Mathias Grönberg (SWE), Migel Angel Jiménez (ESP), Jerry Kelly (USA), Shaun Micheel (USA), Sean Whiffin (ENG) 291; Steve Flesch (USA), Ignaçio Garrido (ESP), Rafaël Jacquelin (FRA) 292; James Kingston (RSA), Paul McGinley (IRL), Carl Pettersson (SWE) 293; Paul Broadhurst (ENG), Gary Emerson (ENG), Brad Faxon (USA) 294; Chris DiMarco (USA), Mark Foster (ENG), Stuart Wilson (SCO) (am) 296; Mårten Olander (SWE), Rory Sabbatini (RSA) 297; Martin Erlandsson (SWE), Paul Wesselingh (ENG) 298; Bob Tway (USA) 299; Rich Beem (USA), Christian Cévaër (FRA) 300; Sandy Lyle (SCO) 303

Turnberry to host the 2009 Open

The 2009 Open Championship will be played at the Westin Turnberry Resort from 16–19 July. It is the fourth time that Turnberry has hosted The Open since it was added in 1977 to the list of Open venues.

It is unsurpassed for its dramatic seascape as a 'backdrop' to the world's oldest major and as a challenging championship layout and has produced three winners of the highest calibre.

The 1977 Open will be remembered for its 'Duel in the Sun' when Tom Watson won by just one shot after both he and Jack Nicklaus halved the 72nd hole in birdies. Greg Norman, was the champion in 1986 when he is remembered for his record second round of 63 after opening with a 74. Zimbabwe's Nick Price took the title in 1994, remembered not only for his lengthy putt on the penultimate hole, but for his titanic struggle against Jesper Parnevik who had to be content with second place.

Since Price's win in 1994, the demands of The Open have substantially increased and while Turnberry could adequately cater as far as the infrastructure was concerned, traffic management implications had to be resolved before a return to the Ayrshire links could be considered.

David Hill, Director of Championships for The R&A said: "There was never any doubt that The Open would return to Turnberry, one of our very best links courses, but before reaching that decision we had to be convinced that every aspect of our forward planning process was in place.

"One element of that planning process was the implementation of a traffic management scheme to ease congestion and since South Ayrshire Council have commenced construction of a road link, essential to the scheme, we now have in place the final piece of the jigsaw."

2003 Open Championship *Royal St George's* July 17–20   [7034–71]

Prize Money £3.9 million. Entries: 2152. Regional qualifying courses: Alwoodley, Ashridge, Blackmoor, Co.Louth, Hadley Wood, Hindhead, Little Aston, Minchinhampton, Notts, Ormskirk, Orsett, Renfrew, Silloth-on-Solway, Stockport, Trentham, Wildernesse. Final qualifying courses: Littlestone, North Foreland, Prince's, Royal Cinque Ports. Final Field: 156 (3 amateurs), of whom 75 (no amateurs) made the half-way cut on 150 or less.

1	Ben Curtis (USA)	72-72-70-69—283	£700000
2	Thomas Bjørn (DEN)	73-70-69-72—284	345000
	Vijay Singh (FIJ)	75-70-69-70—284	345000
4	Davis Love III (USA)	69-72-72-72—285	185000
	Tiger Woods (USA)	73-72-69-71—285	185000
6	Brian Davis (ENG)	77-73-68-68—286	134500
	Fredrik Jacobson (SWE)	70-76-70-70—286	134500
8	Nick Faldo (ENG)	76-74-67-70—287	97750
	Kenny Perry (USA)	74-70-70-73—287	97750
10	Gary Evans (ENG)	71-75-70-72—288	68000
	Sergio García (ESP)	73-71-70-74—288	68000
	Retief Goosen (RSA)	73-75-71-69—288	68000
	Hennie Otto (RSA)	68-76-75-69—288	68000
	Phillip Price (WAL)	74-72-69-73—288	68000
15	Stuart Appleby (AUS)	75-71-71-72—289	49333
	Chad Campbell (USA)	74-71-72-72—289	49333
	Pierre Fulke (SWE)	77-72-67-73—289	49333
18	Ernie Els (RSA)	78-68-72-72—290	42000
	Mathias Grönberg (SWE)	71-74-73-72—290	42000
	Greg Norman (AUS)	69-79-74-68—290	42000
	Tom Watson (USA)	71-77-73-69—290	42000
22	Angel Cabrera (ARG)	75-73-70-73—291	32917
	Choi Kyung-Ju (KOR)	77-72-72-70—291	32917
	Peter Fowler (AUS)	77-73-70-71—291	32917
	Padraig Harrington (IRL)	75-73-74-69—297	32917
	Thomas Levet (FRA)	71-73-74-73—291	32917
	JL Lewis (USA)	78-70-72-71—291	32917
28	Mark Foster (ENG)	73-73-72-74—292	26000
	SK Ho (KOR)	70-73-72-77—292	26000
28T	Paul McGinley (IRL)	77-73-69-73—292	26000
	Andrew Oldcorn (SCO)	72-74-73-73—292	26000
	Nick Price (ZIM)	74-72-72-74—292	26000
	Mike Weir (CAN)	74-76-71-71—292	26000
34	Stewart Cink (USA)	75-75-75-68—293	18778
	José Coceres (ARG)	77-70-72-74—293	18778
	Bob Estes (USA)	77-71-76-69—293	18778
	Shingo Katayama (JPN)	76-73-73-71—293	18778
	Scott McCarron (USA)	71-74-73-75—293	18778
	Adam Mednick (SWE)	76-72-76-69—293	18778
	Gary Murphy (IRL)	73-74-73-73—293	18778
	Marco Ruiz (PAR)	73-71-75-74—293	18778
	Duffy Waldorf (USA)	76-73-71-73—293	18778
43	Robert Allenby (AUS)	73-75-74-72—294	14250
	Rich Beem (USA)	76-74-75-69—294	14250
	Tom Byrum (USA)	77-72-71-74—294	14250
46	Markus Brier (AUT)	76-71-74-74—295	11864
	Fred Couples (USA)	71-75-71-78—295	11864
	Brad Faxon (USA)	77-73-70-75—295	11864
	Mathew Goggin (AUS)	76-72-70-77—295	11864
	Tom Lehman (USA)	77-73-72-73—295	11864
	Ian Poulter (ENG)	78-72-70-75—295	11864
	Anthony Wall (ENG)	75-74-71-75—295	11864
53	Michael Campbell (NZL)	78-72-74-72—296	10200
	Trevor Immelman (RSA)	77-73-72-74—296	10200
	Raphaèl Jacquelin (FRA)	77-71-72-76—296	10200
	David Lynn (ENG)	73-76-71-76—296	10200
	Mark McNulty (ZIM)	79-71-77-69—296	10200
	Rory Sabbatini (RSA)	79-71-75-71—296	10200

Other players who made the cut: Darren Clarke (NIR), Alastair Forsyth (SCO), Skip Kendall (USA), Peter Lonard (AUS), Phil Mickelson (USA), Craig Parry (AUS) 297; Charles Howell III (USA), Stephen Leaney (AUS), Len Mattiace (USA), Mark O'Meara (USA) 298; Katsuyoshi Tomori (JPN) 300; John Rollins (USA) 301; Chris Smith (USA) 302; John Daly (USA), Ian Woosnam (WAL) 303; Jesper Parnevik (SWE), Mark Roe (ENG) DQ

2002 Open Championship *Muirfield* July 18–21   [7034–71]

Prize Money £3.885 million. Entries: 2260. Regional qualifying courses: Alwoodley, Blackmoor, Co.Louth, Hadley Wood, Hindhead, Little Aston, Minchinhampton, Northamptonshire County, Notts, Ormskirk, Orsett, Renfrew, Silloth-on-Solway, Stockport, Trentham, Wildernesse. Final qualifying courses: Dunbar, Gullane No.1, Luffness New, North Berwick. Final Field: 156 (3 amateurs), of whom 83 (no amateurs) made the half-way cut on 144 or less.

1	Ernie Els (RSA)	70-66-72-70—278	£700000
2	Stuart Appleby (AUS)	73-70-70-65—278	286667
	Steve Elkington (AUS)	71-73-68-66—278	286667
	Thomas Levet (FRA)	72-66-74-66—278	286667

After a four-hole play-off, Appleby and Elkington were eliminated; Els won the sudden-death play-off with Levet at the first extra hole.

5	Gary Evans (ENG)	72-68-74-65—279	140000
	Padraig Harrington (IRL)	69-67-76-67—279	140000
	Shigeki Maruyama (JPN)	68-68-75-68—279	140000
8	Thomas Bjørn (DEN)	68-70-73-69—280	77500
	Sergio García (ESP)	71-69-71-69—280	77500
	Retief Goosen (RSA)	71-68-74-67—280	77500
	Søren Hansen (DEN)	68-69-73-70—280	77500
	Scott Hoch (USA)	74-69-71-66—280	77500
	Peter O'Malley (AUS)	72-68-75-65—280	77500
14	Justin Leonard (USA)	71-72-68-70—281	49750
14T	Peter Lonard (AUS)	72-72-68-69—281	49750
	Davis Love III (USA)	71-72-71-67—281	49750
	Nick Price (ZIM)	68-70-75-68—281	49750
18	Bob Estes (USA)	71-70-73-68—282	41000
	Scott McCarron (USA)	71-68-72-71—282	41000
	Greg Norman (AUS)	71-72-71-68—282	41000
	Duffy Waldorf (USA)	67-69-77-69—282	41000
22	David Duval (USA)	72-71-70-70—283	32000
	Toshimitsu Izawa (JPN)	76-68-72-67—283	32000
	Mark O'Meara (USA)	69-69-77-68—283	32000
	Corey Pavin (USA)	69-70-75-69—283	32000
	Chris Riley (USA)	70-71-76-66—283	32000
	Justin Rose (ENG)	68-75-68-72—283	32000
28	Bradley Dredge (WAL)	70-72-74-68—284	24000
	Niclas Fasth (SWE)	70-73-71-70—284	24000
	Pierre Fulke (SWE)	72-69-78-65—284	24000
	Jerry Kelly (USA)	73-71-70-70—284	24000
	Bernhard Langer (GER)	72-72-71-69—284	24000

28T	Jesper Parnevik (SWE)	72-72-70-70—284	24000	47	Paul Eales (ENG)	73-71-76-67—287	12000
	Loren Roberts (USA)	74-69-70-71—284	24000		Jeff Maggert (USA)	71-68-80-68—287	12000
	Des Smyth (IRL)	68-69-74-73—284	24000		Rocco Mediate (USA)	71-72-74-70—287	12000
	Tiger Woods (USA)	70-68-81-65—284	24000	50	Fredrik Andersson (SWE)	74-70-74-70—288	10267
37	Darren Clarke (NIR)	72-67-77-69—285	16917		Warren Bennett (ENG)	71-68-82-67—288	10267
	Andrew Coltart (SCO)	71-69-74-71—285	16917		Ian Garbutt (ENG)	69-70-74-75—288	10267
	Neal Lancaster (USA)	71-71-76-67—285	16917		Mikko Ilonen (FIN)	71-70-77-70—288	10267
	Stephen Leaney (AUS)	71-70-75-69—285	16917		Shingo Katayama (JPN)	72-68-74-74—288	10267
	Scott Verplank (USA)	72-68-74-71—285	16917		Barry Lane (ENG)	74-68-72-74—288	10267
	Ian Woosnam (WAL)	72-72-73-68—285	16917		Ian Poulter (ENG)	69-69-78-72—288	10267
43	Trevor Immelman (RSA)	72-72-71-71—286	13750		Bob Tway (USA)	70-66-78-74—288	10267
	Steve Jones (USA)	68-75-73-70—286	13750				
	Carl Pettersson (SWE)	67-70-76-73—286	13750				
	Esteban Toledo (MEX)	73-70-75-68—286	13750				

Other players who made the cut: Stewart Cink (USA), Joe Durant (USA), Nick Faldo (ENG), Richard Green (AUS), Kuboya Kenichi (JPN), Paul Lawrie (SCO), Steve Stricker (USA) 289; Chris DiMarco (USA), Phil Mickelson (USA), Jarrod Moseley (AUS) 290; Stephen Ames (TRI), Jim Carter (USA), Matthew Cort (ENG), Len Mattiace (USA), Toru Taniguchi (JPN), Mike Weir (CAN) 291; Sandy Lyle (SCO), Chris Smith (USA) 292; Anders Hansen (DEN), Roger Wessels (RSA) 293; David Park (WAL) 294; Mark Calcavecchia (USA), Lee Janzen (USA) 295; Colin Montgomerie (SCO) 297; David Toms (USA) 298.

2001 Open Championship *Royal Lytham & St Annes* July 19–22   [6905–71]

Prize Money £3,229,748. Entries 2255. Regional qualifying courses: Alwoodley, Blackmoor, Burnham & Berrow, Carlisle, County Louth, Copt Heath, Coxmoor, Hadley Wood, Hindhead, Little Aston, Northamptonshire County, Orsett, Renfrew, Stockport, Wildernesse, Wilmslow. Final qualifying courses: Fairhaven, Hillside, St Anne's Old Links, Southport & Ainsdale. Final field comprised 156 players, of whom 70 (including one amateur) made the half-way cut on 144 or better.

1	David Duval (USA)	69-73-65-67—274	£600000	21	Davis Love III (USA)	73-67-74-67—281	32500
2	Niclas Fasth (SWE)	69-69-72-67—277	360000		Nick Price (ZIM)	73-67-68-73—281	32500
3	Darren Clarke (NIR)	70-69-69-70—278	141667	23	Michael Campbell (NZL)	71-72-71-68—282	30500
	Ernie Els (RSA)	71-71-67-69—278	141667		Greg Owen (ENG)	69-68-72-73—282	30500
	Miguel Angel Jiménez (ESP)	69-72-67-70—278	141667	25	Bob Estes (USA)	74-70-73-66—283	27500
	Bernhard Langer (GER)	71-69-67-71—278	141667		Joe Ogilvie (USA)	69-68-71-75—283	27500
	Billy Mayfair (USA)	69-72-67-70—278	141667		Eduardo Romero (ARG)	70-68-72-73—283	27500
	Ian Woosnam (WAL)	72-68-67-71—278	141667		Tiger Woods (USA)	71-68-73-71—283	27500
9	Sergio García (ESP)	70-72-67-70—279	63750	29	Barry Lane (ENG)	70-72-72-70—284	25000
	Mikko Ilonen (FIN)	68-75-70-66—279	63750	30	Stewart Cink (USA)	71-72-72-70—285	21500
	Jesper Parnevik (SWE)	69-68-71-71—279	63750		David Dixon (ENG) (am)	70-71-70-74—285	
	Kevin Sutherland (USA)	75-69-68-67—279	63750		Phil Mickelson (USA)	70-72-72-71—285	21500
13	Billy Andrade (USA)	69-70-70-71—280	40036		Justin Rose (ENG)	69-72-74-70—285	21500
	Alex Cejka (GER)	69-69-69-73—280	40036		Phillip Price (WAL)	74-69-71-71—285	21500
	Retief Goosen (RSA)	74-68-67-71—280	40036		Nicolas Vanhootegem (BEL)	72-68-70-75—285	21500
	Raphaël Jacquelin (FRA)	71-68-69-72—280	40036		Scott Verplank (USA)	71-72-70-72—285	21500
	Colin Montgomerie (SCO)	65-70-73-72—280	40036	37	Andrew Coltart (SCO)	75-68-70-73—286	16300
	Loren Roberts (USA)	70-70-70-70—280	40036		Padraig Harrington (IRL)	75-66-74-71—286	16300
	Vijay Singh (FIJ)	70-70-71-69—280	40036		Dudley Hart (USA)	74-69-69-74—286	16300
	Des Smyth (IRL)	74-65-70-71—280	40036		Frank Lickliter (USA)	71-71-73-71—286	16300
					Toru Taniguchi (JPN)	72-69-72-73—286	16300

Other players who made the cut: Richard Green (AUS), JP Hayes (USA), Paul Lawrie (SCO), Mark O'Meara (USA), Steve Stricker (USA) 287; Robert Allenby (AUS), Chris DiMarco (USA), Brad Faxon (USA), Matt Gogel (USA), Peter Lonard (AUS), Adam Scott (AUS), Lee Westwood (ENG) 288; Mark Calcavecchia (USA), Paul Curry (ENG), Carlos Franco (PAR), Paul McGinley (IRL), José María Olazábal (ESP), Rory Sabbatini (RSA), Duffy Waldorf (USA) 289; Stuart Appleby (AUS) 290; Gordon Brand jr (SCO), Brandel Chamblee (USA), Pierre Fulke (SWE) 291; Neil Cheetham (ENG) 295; Alexandre Balicki (FRA), Thomas Levet (FRA) 296; David Smail (NZL) 298; Scott Henderson (SCO), Sandy Lyle (SCO) 301.

2000 Open Championship St Andrews Old Course. Fife July 20–23 [7115–72]

Prize Money £2,722,150. Entries 2477. Regional qualifying courses: Alwoodley, Beau Desert, Blackmoor, Burnham & Berrow, Camberley Heath, Carlisle, Copt Heath, County Louth, Coxmoor, Hadley Wood, Hindhead, Northamptonshire County, Ormskirk, Renfrew, Romford, Stockport, Wildernesse. Final qualifying courses: Ladybank, Leven, Lundin, Scotscraig. Final field comprised 156 players, of whom 74 (none amateur) made the half-way cut on 144 or better.

1	Tiger Woods (USA)	67-66-67-69—269	£500000	11T	Phil Mickelson (USA)	72-66-71-72—281	37111
2	Ernie Els (RSA)	66-72-70-69—277	245000		Bob May (USA)	72-72-66-71—281	37111
	Thomas Bjørn (DEN)	69-69-68-71—277	245000		Dennis Paulson (USA)	68-71-69-73—281	37111
4	Tom Lehman (USA)	68-70-70-70—278	130000	20	Steve Flesch (USA)	67-70-71-74—282	25500
	David Toms (USA)	69-67-71-71—278	130000		Padraig Harrington (IRL)	68-72-70-72—282	25500
6	Fred Couples (USA)	70-68-72-69—279	100000		Steve Pate (USA)	73-70-71-68—282	25500
7	Loren Roberts (USA)	69-68-70-73—280	66250		Bob Estes (USA)	72-69-70-71—282	25500
	Paul Azinger (USA)	69-72-72-67—280	66250		Paul McGinley (IRL)	69-72-71-70—282	25500
	Pierre Fulke (SWE)	69-72-70-69—280	66250		Notah Begay III (USA)	69-73-69-71—282	25500
	Darren Clarke (NIR)	70-69-68-73—280	66250	26	Mark O'Meara (USA)	70-73-69-71—283	20000
11	Bernhard Langer (GER)	74-70-66-71—281	37111		Colin Montgomerie	71-70-72-70—283	20000
	Mark McNulty (ZIM)	69-72-70-70—281	37111		(SCO)		
	David Duval (USA)	70-70-66-75—281	37111		Miguel Angel Jiménez	73-71-71-68—283	20000
	Stuart Appleby (AUS)	73-70-68-70—281	37111		(ESP)		
	Davis Love III (USA)	74-66-74-67—281	37111		Mark Calcavecchia (USA)	73-70-71-69—283	20000
	Vijay Singh (FIJ)	70-70-73-68—281	37111		Dean Robertson (SCO)	73-70-68-72—283	20000

Other players who made the cut: José Maria Olazábal (ESP), Jean Van de Velde (FRA), Steve Jones (USA), Jarmo Sandelin (SWE), 284; Eduardo Romero (ARG), Sergio García (ESP), Jesper Parnevik (SWE), Craig Parry (AUS), José Coceres (ARG), Robert Allenby (AUS) 286; Nick Faldo (ENG), Justin Leonard (USA), Stewart Cink (USA), Jim Furyk (USA), Nick O'Hern (AUS), Jarrod Moseley (AUS), Gary Orr (SCO), Jeff Maggert (USA), Retief Goosen (RSA), Lucas Parsons (AUS), Tsuyoshi Yoneyama (JPN) 287; Mike Weir (CAN), Ian Garbutt (ENG), Rocco Mediate (USA), 288; David Frost (RSA), Tom Watson (USA), Shigeki Maruyama (JPN), Greg Owen (ENG), Andrew Coltart (SCO) 289; Christy O'Connor jr (IRL), Jeff Sluman (USA), Steve Elkington (AUS), Kirk Triplett (USA) 290; Desvonde Botes (RSA), Ian Poulter (ENG), Per-Ulrik Johansson (SWE), Lee Westwood (ENG) 291; Gordon Brand jr (SCO), Ian Woosnam (WAL), 292; Tom Kite (USA), Kazuhiko Hosokawa (JPN) 294; Peter Senior (AUS), Lionel Alexandre (FRA) 295; Dudley Hart (USA) Retd.

1999 Open Championship Carnoustie, Angus July 15–18 [7361–71]

Prize Money £2,009,550. Entries 2222. Regional qualifying courses: Beau Desert, Blackmoor, Burnham & Berrow, Carlisle, Copt Heath, County Louth, Coxmoor, Glenbervie, Hankley Common, Moortown, Northamptonshire County, Ormskirk, Romford, South Herts, Stockport, Wildernesse. Final qualifying courses: Downfield, Monifieth Links, Montrose Links, Panmure. Final field comprised 156 players, of whom 73 (none amateurs) made the half-way cut on 154 or better.

1	P Lawrie* (SCO)	73-74-76-67—290	£350000	18	B Langer (GER)	72-77-73-75—297	20500
2	J Leonard (USA)	73-74-71-72—290	185000		A Coltart (SCO)	74-74-72-77—297	20500
	J Van de Velde (FRA)	75-68-70-77—290	185000		F Nobilo (NZL)	76-76-70-75—297	20500
*Lawrie won four-hole play-off (15th–18th): Lawrie 5-4-3-3—15;					P Sjöland (SWE)	74-72-77-74—297	20500
Leonard 5-4-4-5–18; Van de Velde 6-4-3-5–18					L Westwood (ENG)	76-75-74-72—297	20500
4	C Parry (AUS)	76-75-67-73—291	100000		C Rocca (ITA)	81-69-74-73—297	20500
	A Cabrera (ARG)	75-69-77-70—291	100000	24	P O'Malley (AUS)	76-75-74-73—298	15300
6	G Norman (AUS)	76-70-75-72—293	70000		E Els (RSA)	74-76-76-72—298	15300
7	D Frost (RSA)	80-69-71-74—294	50000		B Watts (USA)	74-73-77-74—298	15300
	D Love III (USA)	74-74-77-69—294	50000		I Woosnam (WAL)	76-74-74-74—298	15300
	T Woods (USA)	74-72-74-74—294	50000		MA Martin (ESP)	74-76-72-76—298	15300
10	J Parnevik (SWE)	74-71-78-72—295	34800	29	P Harrington (IRL)	77-74-74-74—299	13500
	S Dunlap (USA)	72-77-76-70—295	34800	30	J Maggert (USA)	75-77-75-73—300	11557
	R Goosen (RSA)	76-75-73-71—295	34800		D Clarke (NIR)	76-75-76-73—300	11557
	H Sutton (USA)	73-78-72-72—295	34800		P Stewart (USA)	79-73-74-74—300	11557
	J Furyk (USA)	78-71-76-70—295	34800		P Fulke (SWE)	75-75-77-73—300	11557
15	T Yoneyama (JPN)	77-74-73-72—296	26000		T Bjørn (DEN)	79-73-75-73—300	11557
	C Montgomerie (SCO)	74-76-72-74—296	26000		T Herron (USA)	81-70-74-75—300	11557
	S Verplank (USA)	80-74-73-69—296	26000		L Mattiace (USA)	73-74-75-78—300	11557

Other players who made the cut: M McNulty (ZIM), D Hart (USA), P Baker (ENG), N Price (ZIM), M Weir (CAN), P Affleck (WAL) 301; D Waldorf (USA), M James (ENG) 302; S Pate (USA), N Ozaki (JPN), J Sluman (USA), D Howell (ENG) 303; N Price (ENG), T Levet (FRA), K Tomori (JPN), Choi Kyung-Ju (KOR), B Hughes (AUS), D Robertson (SCO), B Estes (USA), S Allan (AUS), P Lonard (AUS) 304; D Paulson (USA), J Robinson (ENG), S Luna (ESP), P Price (WAL) 305; J Rystrom (SWE), D Duval (USA), M Brooks (USA) 306; J Sandelin (SWE) 307; S Strüver (GER) 308; L Thompson (ENG), B Davis (ENG), J Huston (USA) 310; L Janzen (USA) 311; K Shingo (JPN) 312; M Thompson (ENG), D Cooper (ENG) 313.

1998 Open Championship Royal Birkdale, Southport, Lancashire July 16–19 [7018–70]

Prize money: £1,750,000. Entries: 2336. Regional qualifying courses: Beau Desert, Blackmoor, Burnham & Berrow, Carlisle, Copt Heath, County Louth, Coxmoor, Glenbervie, Hankley Common, Moortown, Northamptonshire County, Ormskirk, Romford, South Herts, Stockport and Wildernesse. Final qualifying courses: Hesketh, Hillside, Southport & Ainsdale and West Lancashire. Final field comprised 151 players, of whom 78 (including 3 amateurs) made the half-way cut on 146 or better.

1	M O'Meara (USA)*	72-68-72-68—280	£300000	
	*O'Meara won four-hole play-off (15th–18th):			
	O'Meara 4-4-5-4–17;Watts 5-4-5-5–19			
2	B Watts (USA)	68-69-73-70—280	188000	
3	T Woods (USA)	65-73-77-66—281	135000	
4	J Furyk (USA)	70-70-72-70—282	76666	
	J Parnevik (SWE)	68-72-72-70—282	76666	
	R Russell (SCO)	68-73-75-66—282	76666	
	J Rose (ENG) (am)	72-66-75-69—282		
8	D Love III (USA)	67-73-77-68—285	49500	
9	T Bjørn (DEN)	68-71-76-71—286	40850	
	C Rocca (ITA)	72-74-70-70—286	40850	
11	J Huston (USA)	65-77-73-72—287	33333	
	B Faxon (USA)	67-74-74-72—287	33333	
	D Duval (USA)	70-71-75-71—287	33333	
14	G Brand jr (SCO)	71-70-76-71—288	29000	
15	P Baker (ENG)	69-72-77-71—289	23650	
	G Turner (NZL)	68-75-75-71—289	23650	
	JM Olazábal (ESP)	73-72-75-69—289	23650	
	D Smyth (IRL)	74-69-75-71—289	23650	
19	C Strange (USA)	73-73-74-70—290	17220	
	V Singh (FIJ)	67-74-78-71—290	17220	
	S Lyle (SCO)	71-72-75-72—290	17220	
	R Allenby (AUS)	67-76-78-69—290	17220	
	M James (ENG)	71-74-74-71—290	17220	
24	S Torrance (SCO)	69-77-75-70—291	12480	
	B Estes (USA)	72-70-76-73—291	12480	
	S Ames (TRI)	68-72-79-72—291	12480	
	P O'Malley (AUS)	71-71-78-71—291	12480	
	L Janzen (USA)	72-69-80-70—291	12480	
29	S Dunlap (USA)	72-69-80-71—292	10030	
	N Price (ZIM)	66-72-82-72—292	10030	
	S Maruyama (JPN)	70-73-75-74—292	10030	
	L Roberts (USA)	66-76-76-74—292	10030	
	E Els (RSA)	72-74-74-72—292	10030	
	S García (ESP) (am)	69-75-76-72—292		
35	M Calcavecchia (USA)	69-77-73-74—293	8900	
	S Luna (ESP)	70-72-80-71—293	8900	
	S Strüver (GER)	75-70-80-68—293	8900	

Other players who made the cut: P Sjöland (SWE), J Haeggman (SWE), P Walton (IRL), N Ozaki (JPN), T Kite (USA), S Tinning (DEN) 294; K Tomori (JPN), D Howell (ENG), D Frost (RSA), R Davis (AUS), D Carter (ENG), N Faldo (ENG), P Stewart (USA), A Coltart (SCO) 295; S Stricker (USA), B Mayfair (USA), B Jobe (USA), L Mize (USA), F Minoza (PHI) 296; T Dodds (NAM), E Romero (ARG), S Jones (USA), J Leonard (USA), I Garrido (ESP), I Woosnam (WAL), L Westwood (ENG), C Daniel Franco (PAR) 298; S Cink (USA), M Brooks (USA), M Campbell (NZL), F Couples (USA), M Long (NZL), D De Vooght (BEL) (am) 299; A Clapp (ENG) 300; G Evans (ENG) 301; B May (USA) 303; A McLardy (RSA) 304; F Jacobson (SWE) 305; K Hosokawa (JPN) 306; R Giles (IRL) 307; P Mickelson (USA) 308; A Oldcorn (SCO) 309; D Hart (USA) 310.

1997 Open Championship Royal Troon July 17–20 [7079–71]

Prize money: £1,586,300. Entries: 2133. Regional qualifying courses: Beau Desert, Burnham & Berrow, Carlisle, Copt Heath, Coxmoor, Glenbervie, Hankley Common, Moortown, North Hants, Romford, South Herts, Sundridge Park, Wilmslow. Final qualifying courses: Irvine Bogside, Glasgow Gailes, Kilmarnock Barassie, Western Gailes. 156 players took part, 70 (including 1 amateur) qualified for final 36 holes.

1	J Leonard (USA)	69-66-72-65—272	£250000	
2	D Clarke (NIR)	67-66-71-71—275	150000	
	J Parnevik (SWE)	70-66-66-73—275	150000	
4	J Furyk (USA)	67-72-70-70—279	90000	
5	S Ames (TRI)	74-69-66-71—280	62500	
	P Harrington (IRL)	75-69-69-67—280	62500	
7	F Couples (USA)	69-68-70-74—281	40666	
	E Romero (ARG)	74-68-67-72—281	40666	
	P O'Malley (AUS)	73-70-70-68—281	40666	
10	R Goosen (RSA)	75-69-70-68—282	24300	
	L Westwood (ENG)	73-70-67-72—282	24300	
	T Watson (USA)	71-70-70-71—282	24300	
	M Calcavecchia (USA)	74-67-72-69—282	24300	
	R Allenby (AUS)	76-68-66-72—282	24300	
	S Maruyama (JPN)	74-69-70-69—282	24300	
	T Kite (USA)	72-67-74-69—282	24300	
	D Love III (USA)	70-71-74-67—282	24300	
	E Els (RSA)	75-69-69-69—282	24300	
	F Nobilo (NZL)	74-72-68-68—282	24300	
20	JM Olazábal (ESP)	75-68-73-67—283	14500	
	M James (ENG)	76-67-70-70—283	14500	
	B Faxon (USA)	77-67-72-67—283	14500	
	S Appleby (AUS)	72-72-68-71—283	14500	
24	P Lonard (AUS)	72-70-69-73—284	10362	
	C Montgomerie (SCO)	76-69-69-70—284	10362	
	I Woosnam (WAL)	71-73-69-71—284	10362	
	D A Russell (ENG)	75-73-68-69—284	10362	
	T Woods (USA)	72-74-64-74—284	10362	
	T Lehman (USA)	74-72-72-66—284	10362	
	J Haas (USA)	71-70-73-70—284	10362	
	P Mickelson (USA)	76-68-69-71—284	10362	
32	M McNulty (ZIM)	78-67-72-68—285	8750	
33	J Lomas (ENG)	72-71-69-74—286	8283	
	D Clarke (USA)	73-69-73-71—286	8283	
	R Davis (USA)	73-73-70-70—286	8283	
36	A Magee (USA)	70-75-72-70—287	7950	
	G Norman (AUS)	69-73-70-75—287	7950	

Other players who made the cut: R Russell (SCO), M O'Meara (USA), J Kernohan (USA), M Bradley (USA), B Langer (GER), V Singh (FIJ) 288; J Coceres (ARG), D Tapping (ENG), C Strange (USA), J Kelly (USA) 289; S Jones (USA), J Payne (ENG), R Boxall (ENG) 290; A Cabrera (ARG), J Maggert (USA), W Riley (AUS), P Senior (AUS), C Pavin (USA), P Mitchell (ENG), G Turner (NZL) 291; P Stewart (USA) 292; J Nicklaus (USA), B Howard (SCO) (am) 293; T Purtzer (USA), J Spence (ENG), S Stricker (USA), P Teravainen (USA) 294; P McGinley (IRL), P-U Johansson (SWE), G Clark (ENG) 295; T Tolles (USA) 296; B Andrade (USA) 298.

Open Championship History

The Belt

Date		Winner	Score	Venue	Entrants	Prize-money £
1860	Oct 17	W Park, Musselburgh	174	Prestwick	8	—
1861	Sept 26	T Morris sr, Prestwick	163	Prestwick	12	—
1862	Sept 11	T Morris sr, Prestwick	163	Prestwick	6	—
1863	Sept 18	W Park, Musselburgh	168	Prestwick	14	10
1864	Sept 16	T Morris sr, Prestwick	167	Prestwick	6	15
1865	Sept 14	A Strath, St Andrews	162	Prestwick	10	20
1866	Sept 13	W Park, Musselburgh	169	Prestwick	12	11
1867	Sept 26	T Morris sr, St Andrews	170	Prestwick	10	16
1868	Sept 23	T Morris jr, St Andrews	154	Prestwick	12	12
1869	Sept 16	T Morris jr, St Andrews	157	Prestwick	14	12
1870	Sept 15	T Morris jr, St Andrews	149	Prestwick	17	12

Having won it three times in succession, the Belt became the property of Young Tom Morris and the Championship was held in abeyance for a year. In 1872 the Claret Jug was, and still is, offered for annual competition but it was not available to present at the time to Tom Morris jr in 1872.

The Claret Jug

Date		Winner	Score	Venue	Entrants	Prize-money £
1872	Sept 13	T Morris jr, St Andrews	166	Prestwick	8	20
1873	Oct 4	T Kidd, St Andrews	179	St Andrews	26	20
1874	April 10	M Park, Musselburgh	159	Musselburgh	32	29
1875	Sept 10	W Park, Musselburgh	166	Prestwick	18	20
1876	Sept 30	B Martin, St Andrews	176	St Andrews	34	27
(D Strath tied but refused to play off)						
1877	April 6	J Anderson, St Andrews	160	Musselburgh	24	20
1878	Oct 4	J Anderson, St Andrews	157	Prestwick	26	20
1879	Sept 27	J Anderson, St Andrews	169	St Andrews	46	45
1880	April 9	B Ferguson, Musselburgh	162	Musselburgh	30	†
1881	Oct 14	B Ferguson, Musselburgh	170	Prestwick	22	†
1882	Sept 30	B Ferguson, Musselburgh	171	St Andrews	40	45
1883	Nov 16	W Fernie*, Dumfries	158	Musselburgh	41	†
After a play-off with B Ferguson, Musselburgh: Fernie 158; Ferguson 159						
1884	Oct 3	J Simpson, Carnoustie	160	Prestwick	30	†
1885	Oct 3	B Martin, St Andrews	171	St Andrews	51	34
1886	Nov 5	D Brown, Musselburgh	157	Musselburgh	46	20
1887	Sept 16	W Park jr, Musselburgh	161	Prestwick	36	20
1888	Oct 6	J Burns, Warwick	171	St Andrews	53	24
1889		W Park Jr*, Musselburgh	155	Musselburgh	42	22
After a play-off with A Kirkaldy: Park Jr 158; Kirkaldy 163						
1890	Nov 8	J Ball, Royal Liverpool (am)	164	Prestwick	40	29.50
1891	Sept 11	H Kirkaldy, St Andrews	166	St Andrews	82	30.50

After 1891 the competition was extended to 72 holes and for the first time entry money was imposed

Date		Winner	Score	Venue	Entrants	Prize-money £
1892	Sept 22–23	H Hilton, Royal Liverpool (am)	305	Muirfield	66	100
1893	Aug 31–Sept 1	W Auchterlonie, St Andrews	322	Prestwick	72	100
1894	June 11–12	J Taylor, Winchester	326	Sandwich, R St George's	94	100
1895	June 12–13	J Taylor, Winchester	322	St Andrews	73	100
1896	June 10–11	H Vardon*, Ganton	316	Muirfield	64	100
After a 36-hole play-off with JH Taylor: Vardon 157; Taylor 161						
1897	May 19–20	H Hilton, Royal Liverpool (am)	314	Hoylake, R Liverpool	86	100
1898	June 8–9	H Vardon, Ganton	307	Prestwick	78	100
1899	June 7–8	H Vardon, Ganton	310	Sandwich, R St George's	98	100
1900	June 6–7	J Taylor, Mid-Surrey	309	St Andrews	81	125
1901	June 5–6	J Braid, Romford	309	Muirfield	101	125
1902	June 4–5	A Herd, Huddersfield	307	Hoylake, R Liverpool	112	125
1903	June 9–10	H Vardon, Totteridge	300	Prestwick	127	125

† prize-money not known

Date	Winner	Score	Venue	Entrants	Qualifiers	Prize-money £
1904 June 8–10	J White, Sunningdale	296	Sandwich, R St George's	144		125
1905 June 7–9	J Braid, Walton Heath	318	St Andrews	152		125
1906 June 13–15	J Braid, Walton Heath	300	Muirfield	183		125
1907 June 20–21	A Massy, La Boulie	312	Hoylake, R Liverpool	193		125
1908 June 18–19	J Braid, Walton Heath	291	Prestwick	180		125
1909 June 10–11	J Taylor, Mid-Surrey	295	Deal, R Cinque Ports	204		125
1910 June 22–24	J Braid, Walton Heath	299	St Andrews	210		135
1911 June 26–29	H Vardon*, Totteridge	303	Sandwich, R St George's	226		135

*After a play-off with A Massy. The play-off was over 36 holes, but Massy picked up at the 35th before holing out. He had taken 148 for 34 holes, and when Vardon holed out at the 35th hole his score was 143

Date	Winner	Score	Venue	Entrants	Qualifiers	Prize-money £
1912 June 24–25	E Ray, Oxhey	295	Muirfield	215		135
1913 June 23–24	J Taylor, Mid-Surrey	304	Hoylake, R Liverpool	269		135
1914 June 18–19	H Vardon, Totteridge	306	Prestwick	194		135
1915–19 No Championship						
1920 June 30–July 1	G Duncan, Hanger Hill	303	Deal, R Cinque Ports	190	81	225
1921 June 23–25	J Hutchison*, Glenview, Chicago	296	St Andrews	158	85	225

*After a play-off with R Wethered (am): Hutchison 150; Wethered 159

Date	Winner	Score	Venue	Entrants	Qualifiers	Prize-money £
1922 June 22–23	W Hagen, Detroit, USA	300	Sandwich, R St George's	225	80	225
1923 June 14–15	A Havers, Coombe Hill	295	Troon	222	88	225
1924 June 26–27	W Hagen, Detroit, USA	301	Hoylake, R Liverpool	277	86	225
1925 June 25–26	J Barnes, USA	300	Prestwick	200	83	225
1926 June 22–24	R Jones, USA (am)	291	R Lytham and St Annes	293	117	225
1927 July 13–15	R Jones, USA (am)	285	St Andrews	207	108	275
1928 May 9–11	W Hagen, USA	292	Sandwich, R St George's	271	113	275
1929 May 8–10	W Hagen, USA	292	Muirfield	242	109	275
1930 June 18–20	R Jones, USA (am)	291	Hoylake, R Liverpool	296	112	400
1931 June 3–5	T Armour, USA	296	Carnoustie	215	109	500
1932 June 8–10	G Sarazen, USA	283	Sandwich, Prince's	224	110	500
1933 July 5–7	D Shute*, USA	292	St Andrews	287	117	500

*After a play-off with C Wood, USA: Shute 149; Wood 154

Date	Winner	Score	Venue	Entrants	Qualifiers	Prize-money £
1934 June 27–29	T Cotton, Waterloo, Belgium	283	Sandwich, R St George's	312	101	500
1935 June 26–28	A Perry, Leatherhead	283	Muirfield	264	109	500
1936 June 24–26	A Padgham, Sundridge Park	287	Hoylake, R Liverpool	286	107	500
1937 July 7–9	T Cotton, Ashridge	290	Carnoustie	258	141	500
1938 July 6–8	R Whitcombe, Parkstone	295	Sandwich, R St George's	268	120	500
1939 July 5–7	R Burton, Sale	290	St Andrews	254	129	500
1940–45 No Championship						
1946 July 3–5	S Snead, USA	290	St Andrews	225	100	1,000
1947 July 2–4	F Daly, Balmoral	293	Hoylake, R Liverpool	263	100	1,000
1948 June 30–July 2	T Cotton, Royal Mid-Surrey	284	Muirfield	272	97	1,000
1949 July 6–8	A Locke*, RSA	283	Sandwich, R St George's	224	96	1,500

*After a play-off with H Bradshaw: Locke 135; Bradshaw 147

Date	Winner	Score	Venue	Entrants	Qualifiers	Prize-money £
1950 July 5–7	A Locke, RSA	279	Troon	262	93	1,500
1951 July 4–6	M Faulkner, England	285	R Portrush	180	98	1,700
1952 July 9–11	A Locke, RSA	287	R Lytham and St Annes	275	96	1,700
1953 July 8–10	B Hogan, USA	282	Carnoustie	196	91	2,500
1954 July 7–9	P Thomson, Australia	283	Birkdale	349	97	3,500
1955 July 6–8	P Thomson, Australia	281	St Andrews	301	94	3,750
1956 July 4–6	P Thomson, Australia	286	Hoylake, R Liverpool	360	96	3,750
1957 July 3–5	A Locke, RSA	279	St Andrews	282	96	3,750
1958 July 2–4	P Thomson*, Australia	278	R Lytham and St Annes	362	96	4,850

*After a play-off with D Thomas: Thomson 139; Thomas 143

Date	Winner	Score	Venue	Entrants	Qualifiers	Prize-money £
1959 July 1–3	G Player, RSA	284	Muirfield	285	90	5,000
1960 July 6–8	K Nagle, Australia	278	St Andrews	410	74	7,000
1961 July 12–14	A Palmer, USA	284	Birkdale	364	101	8,500
1962 July 11–13	A Palmer, USA	276	Troon	379	119	8,500
1963 July 10–12	R Charles*, New Zealand	277	R Lytham and St Annes	261	119	8,500

*After a play-off with P Rodgers, USA: Charles 140; Rodgers 148

Date	Winner	Score	Venue	Entrants	Qualifiers	Prize-money £
1964 July 8–10	T Lema, USA	279	St Andrews	327	119	8,500
1965 July 7–9	P Thomson, Australia	285	R Birkdale	372	130	10,000
1966 July 6–9	J Nicklaus, USA	282	Muirfield	310	130	15,000
1967 July 12–15	R De Vicenzo, Argentina	278	Hoylake, R Liverpool	326	130	15,000
1968 July 10–13	G Player, RSA	289	Carnoustie	309	130	20,000
1969 July 9–12	A Jacklin, England	280	R Lytham and St Annes	424	129	30,334
1970 July 8–11	J Nicklaus*, USA	283	St Andrews	468	134	40,000

*After a play-off with Doug Sanders, USA: Nicklaus 72; Sanders 73

Date	Winner	Score	Venue	Entrants	Qualifiers	Prize-money £
1971 July 7–10	L Trevino, USA	278	R Birkdale	528	150	45,000
1972 July 12–15	L Trevino, USA	278	Muirfield	570	150	50,000
1973 July 11–14	T Weiskopf, USA	276	Troon	569	150	50,000

Open Championship Claret Jug winners history *continued*

Date	Winner	Score	Venue	Entrants	Qualifiers	Prize-money £
1974 July 10–13	G Player, RSA	282	R Lytham and St Annes	679	150	50,000
1975 July 9–12	T Watson*, USA	279	Carnoustie	629	150	50,000
After a play-off with J Newton, Australia: Watson 71; Newton 72						
1976 July 7–10	J Miller, USA	279	R Birkdale	719	150	75,000
1977 July 6–9	T Watson, USA	268	Turnberry	730	150	100,000
1978 July 12–15	J Nicklaus, USA	281	St Andrews	788	150	125,000
1979 July 18–21	S Ballesteros, Spain	283	R Lytham and St Annes	885	150	155,000
1980 July 17–20	T Watson, USA	271	Muirfield	994	151	200,000
1981 July 16–19	B Rogers, USA	276	Sandwich, R St George's	971	153	200,000
1982 July 15–18	T Watson, USA	284	R Troon	1121	150	250,000
1983 July 14–17	T Watson, USA	275	R Birkdale	1107	151	310,000
1984 July 19–22	S Ballesteros, Spain	276	St Andrews	1413	156	445,000
1985 July 18–21	A Lyle, Scotland	282	Sandwich, R St George's	1361	149	530,000
1986 July 17–20	G Norman, Australia	280	Turnberry	1347	152	634,000
1987 July 16–19	N Faldo, England	279	Muirfield	1407	153	650,000
1988 July 14–18	S Ballesteros, Spain	273	R Lytham and St Annes	1393	153	700,000
1989 July 20–23	M Calcavecchia*, USA	275	R Troon	1481	156	750,000
After a four-hole play-off with W Grady, Australia, and G Norman, Australia (1st, 2nd, 17th, 18th): Calcavecchia 4-3-3; Grady 4-4-4; Norman 3-4-4-X						
1990 July 19–22	N Faldo, England	270	St Andrews	1707	152	825,000
1991 July 18–21	I Baker-Finch, Australia	272	R Birkdale	1496	156	900,000
1992 July 16–19	N Faldo, England	272	Muirfield	1666	156	950,000
1993 July 15–18	G Norman, Australia	267	Sandwich, R St George's	1827	156	1,000,000
1994 July 14–17	N Price, Zimbabwe	268	Turnberry	1701	156	1,100,000
1995 July 20–23	J Daly*, USA	282	St Andrews	1836	159	1,250,000
After a four-hole play-off with C Rocca, Italy (1st, 2nd, 17th, 18th): Daly 4-3-4-4–15; Rocca 5-4-7-3–19						
1996 July 18–21	T Lehman, USA	271	R Lytham and St Annes	1918	156	1,400,000
1997 July 17–20	J Leonard, USA	272	R Troon	2133	156	1,586,300
1998 July 16–19	M O'Meara*, USA	280	R Birkdale	2336	152	1,800,000
After a four-hole play-off with B Watts, USA (15th–18th): O'Meara 4-4-5-4–17; Watts 5-4-5-5–19						
1999 July 15–18	P Lawrie*, Scotland	290	Carnoustie	2222	156	2,000,000
After a four-hole play-off with J Leonard, USA, and J Van de Velde, France: Lawrie 5-4-3-3–15; Leonard 5-4-4-5–18; de Velde 6-4-3-5–18						
2000 July 20–23	T Woods, USA	269	St Andrews	2477	156	2,750,000
2001 July 19–22	David Duval, USA	274	R Lytham and St Annes	2255	156	3,300,000
2002 July 18–21	Ernie Els*, RSA	278	Muirfield	2260	156	3,800,000
After a four hole play-off with Steve Elkington, Stuart Appleby and Thomas Levet and sudden death with Levet: Els 4-3-5-4–16; Levet 4-2-5-5–16; Appleby 4-4-4-5–17; Elkington 5-3-4-5–17. Sudden death: Els 4, Levet 5						
2003 July 17–20	Ben Curtis, USA	283	Sandwich, R St George's	2152	156	3,898,000
After a four-hole play-off with E Els, RSA: Hamilton 4-4-3-4–15; Els 4-4-4-4–16						
2005 July 14–17	T Woods, USA	274	St Andrews	2499	156	4,000,000
2006 July 20–23	T Woods, USA	270	R Liverpool	2434	156	4,000,000

Mickelson's preparation to no avail

Nobody participating at the 135th Open Championship at Hoylake prepared more assiduously than Phil Mickelson. Taking as his *raison d'etre* that The Open had not been played at Hoylake since 1967 and therefore all the current players would be equal in their ignorance of it, Mickelson made up his mind he would be the one-eyed man in the kingdom of the blind.

He flew over to Liverpool three weeks before the Championship and worked on his game plan and then, instead of acclimatising at the Barclay's Scottish Open, he returned to Hoylake. By the time the Open began he had played at least 10 practice rounds plus innumerable hours analysing the contours on the greens and working out the lines to the expected pins.

He was about to discover, however, one of golf's immutable truths – that it is not possible to play well on purpose on any week in any year. You can prepare as much as you like but if, on the week, your game is off, that pre-Championship preparation counts for little. Sadly Mickelson did not play well. After rounds of 69, 71,73 and 70 he knew his planning had been for nothing. He finished tied 22nd, 13 shots behind the winner Tiger Woods.   *David Davies*

US Open Championship

Australian Geoff Ogilvy wins the US Open after Furyk, Montgomerie and Mickelson crash at the final hole

Geoff Ogilvy became the first Australian winner of a major since Steve Elkington's 1995 US PGA victory when he triumphed in a US Open at Winged Foot that produced a climax you could not believe. Ogilvy stood tall over the closing holes as some bigger names collapsed, notably the reigning Masters champion Phil Mickelson and Colin Montgomerie. Jim Furyk, a former winner of the title, Padraig Harrington and Kenneth Ferrie, tied for the lead at one point on the final day, were also in with a chance of winning but faltered at the end.

The big losers were Mickelson and Montgomerie, both of whom needed a par 4 at the last to win, or a 5 to be involved in a next day 18-hole play-off with Ogilvy – but both took 6.

"This hurts more than any other tournament because I had this one won," said a stunned Mickelson at the end while Montgomerie added that coping with the reality of what had happened was "as difficult as it gets." Montgomerie has still to win a major although he has lost two play-offs for major titles to Elkington in that 1995 US PGA Championship and to Ernie Els in the 1997 US Open Championship.

Winged Foot has always been a monster. When Hale Irwin won the title there in 1974 he shot seven over par! Ogilvy when winning was five over. "The Australian press kept asking when were we going to have another Aussie winner of a major. I knew it would come but I did not think it would be me," he said. "This is bizarre but it is pretty special."

In a finish any of the other title challengers would have hoped for, Ogilvy chipped in for par at the 17th and holed a downhill six-footer at the last for par to finish on 285 – a total he felt was not quite enough for victory. He was wrong!

One by one, those in contention fell away. Padraig Harrington, bogey-free for 15 holes on the final day, dropped shots at the last three to finish fifth on his own, Furyk bogeyed the last for six-over and Ferrie, joint third round leader, closed with 76 to lose his chance of glory. Then there were two.

Montgomerie, who had led Furyk, Mickelson, David Howell, Steve Stricker and Miguel Angel Jiménez by a shot with an opening day one-under-par 69 and was playing some of the best golf of his career, rolled in a difficult left-to-right 60 footer at the seventeenth to tie Mickelson for the lead on four-over. He drove perfectly down the last but, uncertain about the club to use for his approach, plumped for a 7-iron instead of a 6-iron, finished in nasty, penal rough and took four more to get down to finish with Furyk on six-over.

Mickelson, like Montgomerie, was one ahead playing the last but hit a wild push into the trees, tried an over ambitious second shot which hit the trees and rebounded back towards him. His next finished buried in a greenside trap from where he recovered through the green and took two more to get down for six-over. "I couldn't par the last hole," said a shocked Mickelson. In nine previous events when leading at the 54-hole stage Mickelson had won eight times!

In addition to his runner-up spot in the 2006 US Open, Mickelson lost to the late Payne Stewart in the 1999 US Open at Pinehurst, finished second to Tiger Woods at Bethpage Park in 2002 and came second to Retief Goosen at Shinnecock Hills in 2004.

The Championship was notable, too, for the failure of Tiger Woods to make the halfway cut in a major for the first time since turning professional. Returning to competitive action following the death of his father, Woods shot two rounds of 76.

Day One	Day Two	Day Three	Day Four
−1 Montgomerie	−1 Stricker	+2 Mickelson	+5 Ogilvy
☐ Furyk	☐ Montgomerie	+2 Ferrie	+6 Mickelson
☐ Mickelson	+1 Ogilvy	+3 Ogilvy	+6 Montgomerie
☐ Stricker	+1 Ferrie		+6 Furyk
☐ Jimenez			
☐ Howell			

2006 US Open Championship (106th)

Winged Foot, Mamaroneck, NY

[7264–70]

Prize Money: $6.25 million. Entries: 8,584.

Players are of American nationality unless stated

Final Qualifying   (*play-off for places on the indicated scores)

Walton Heath, England

Maarten Lafeber (NED)	64-66—130
Graeme McDowell (NIR)	70-68—138
Graeme Storm (ENG)	69-69—138
Jyoti Randhawa (IND)	71-67—138
Richard Green (AUS)	72-67—139
Jeev M Singh (IND)	70-69—139
Oliver Wilson (ENG)*	71-69—140
Phillip Archer (ENG)*	69-71—140

Sayama City, Japan

Toru Taniguchi (JPN)	70-66—136
Keiichiro Fukabori (JPN)	69-69—138
Tadahiro Katayama (JPN)*	67-72—139

Daly City, CA

Michael Derminio	70-68—138
Taylor Wood (am)	64-75—139
Alex Coe (am)*	69-71—140
Patrick Nagle (am)*	73-67—140

Littleton, CO

Dustin White	67-68—135

Koloa, HI

Tadd Fujikawa (am)	71-70—141

St Charles, IL

Steve C Stricker	65-64—129
Jason Allred	71-63—134

Rockville, MD

Tommy Armour III	68-67—135
Joey Sindelar	70-66—136
David Berganio jr*	70-67—137
Chad Collins*	69-68—137

Summit, NJ

Brett Quigley	68-63—131
Gregory Clark	67-67—134
Kent Jones	66-68—134
Kevin Stadler	66-68—134
Michael Harris	68-66—134
J J Henry	70-65—135
Mark Brooks	68-67—135
Rob Johnson	66-69—135
Andy Bare	70-66—136
John Mallinger	68-68—136
Nicholas Thompson	69-67—136
Tom Pernice jr	68-68—136
Andrew Svoboda	72-65—137
Chris Nallen	69-68—137
David Oh	67-70—137

Summit, NJ *continued*

Philip Tataurangi	71-66—137
Scott Hend	68-69—137
Brad Fritsch (CAN)*	72-66—138

Columbus, OH

Benjamin Hayes	67-64—131
Ian Poulter (ENG)	65-66—131
Woody Austin	66-69—135
Stephen Gangluff	65-70—135
Charley Hoffman	65-70—135
Bo Van Pelt	66-69—135
J B Holmes	70-66—136
Charl Schwartzel (RSA)	70-66—136
Jeff Sluman	65-71—136
Camilo Villegas (COL)	67-69—136
Mathew Goggin (AUS)	66-71—137
Skip Kendal	70-67—137
Steve Lowery	64-73—137
Craig Barlow	71-67—138
Nathan Green (AUS)	69-69—138
Dean Wilson	69-69—138
Jay Haas	69-70—139
Tag Ridings	70-69—139
John Rollins	72-37—139
D J Trahan	71-68—139
Duffy Waldorf*	68-72—140

Columbus #2, OH

Madalitso Muthiya (ZAM)	65-69—134
Stephen Woodard	70-68—138

Creswell, OR

Jonathan Moore*	70-67—137

Houston, TX

Ryan Baca (am)	67-69—136
Ryan Posey (am)	65-71—136

Tampa, FL

John Koskinen	71-69—140
Billy Horschel (am)	73-67—140
George McNeill*	70-71—141

Atlanta, GA

Jason Dufner	67-68—135
Matt Kuchar	68-67—135
Lee Williams	68-68—136
Andrew Morse	67-70—137

St Louis, MO

Travis Hurst	70-67—137
Jay Delfing	71-71—142

Final Field: 156 of whom 83 (including 2 amateurs) made the half-way cut on 148 or less.

1	Geoff Ogilvy (AUS)	71-70-72-72—285	$1225000
2	Jim Furyk	70-72-74-70—286	501249
	Phil Mickelson	70-73-69-74—286	501249
	Colin Montgomerie (SCO)	69-71-75-71—286	501249
5	Padraig Harrington (IRL)	73-69-74-71—287	255642
6	Kenneth Ferrie (ENG)	71-70-71-76—288	183255
	Nick O'Hern (AUS)	75-70-74-69—288	183255
	Vijay Singh (FIJ)	71-74-70-73—288	183255
	Jeff Sluman	74-73-72-69—288	183255
	Steve Stricker	70-69-76-73—288	183255
	Mike Weir (CAN)	71-74-71-72—288	183255
12	Luke Donald (ENG)	78-69-70-72—289	131670
	Ryuji Imada (JPN)	76-73-69-71—289	131670
	Ian Poulter (ENG)	74-71-70-74—289	131670
15	Paul Casey (ENG)	77-72-72-69—290	116735
16	Robert Allenby (AUS)	73-74-72-72—291	99417
	David Duval	77-68-75-71—291	99417
	David Howell (ENG)	70-78-74-69—291	99417
	Miguel Angel Jiménez (ESP)	70-75-74-72—291	99417
	Arron Oberholser	75-68-74-74—291	99417
21	Peter Hedblom (SWE)	72-74-71-75—292	74252
	Trevor Immelman (RSA)	76-71-70-75—292	74252
	José-María Olazábal (ESP)	75-73-73-71—292	74252
	Tom Pernice jr	79-70-72-71—292	74252
	Adam Scott (AUS)	72-76-70-74—292	74252
26	Craig Barlow	72-75-72-74—293	52314
	Angel Cabrera (ARG)	74-73-74-72—293	52314
	Ernie Els (RSA)	74-73-74-72—293	52314
	Sean O'Hair	76-72-74-71—293	52314
	Ted Purdy	78-71-71-73—293	52314
	Henrik Stenson (SWE)	75-71-73-74—293	52314
32	Woody Austin	72-76-72-74—294	41912
	Bart Bryant	72-72-73-77—294	41912
	Scott Hend (AUS)	72-72-75-75—294	41912
	Steve Jones	74-74-71-75—294	41912
	Rodney Pampling (AUS)	73-75-75-71—294	41912
37	Stewart Cink	75-71-77-72—295	36647
	Jay Haas	75-72-74-74—295	36647
	Charles Howell III	77-71-73-74—295	36647
40	Tommy Armour III	79-70-74-73—296	29459
	Chad Collins	76-71-72-77—296	29459
	John Cook	71-78-74-73—296	29459
	Jason Dufner	72-71-78-75—296	29459
	Fred Funk	71-75-73-77—296	29459
	Stephen Gangluff (CAN)	76-73-77-70—296	29459
	Bo Van Pelt	72-75-73-76—296	29459
	Lee Williams	75-73-73-75—296	29459
48	Phillip Archer (ENG)	72-72-75-78—297	20482
	Thomas Bjørn (DEN)	72-74-73-78—297	20482
	Fred Couples	73-74-71-79—297	20482
	Charley Hoffman	76-70-78-73—297	20482
	J B Holmes	74-73-75-75—297	20482
	Kent Jones	73-74-73-77—297	20482
	Graeme McDowell (NIR)	71-72-75-79—297	20482
	Charl Schwartzel (RSA)	74-72-76-75—297	20482
56	Darren Clarke (NIR)	73-72-79-74—298	18031
57	Ben Curtis	78-71-77-73—299	17614
58	Kenny Perry	77-71-79-74—301	17281
59	Skip Kendal	73-75-76-78—302	16676
	Jeev Milkha Singh (IND)	73-76-77-76—302	16676

106th US Open Championship *continued*

59T	Camilo Villegas (COL)	74-72-79-77—302	16676
62	Ben Crane	77-72-74-80—303	16126
63	Tim Herron	73-76-79-77—305	15836

The following players missed the half-way cut. All professionals received $2000 each:

64	Stephen Ames (CAN)	72-78—150	98	Rich Beem	74-79—153	128T	Brad Fritsch (CAN)	78-78—156
	Alex Coe (am)	77-73—150		Mark Brooks	78-75—153		Sergio García (ESP)	78-78—156
	Jay Delsing	78-72—150		Chad Campbell	76-77—153		Travis Hurst	78-78—156
	Allen Doyle	76-74—150		Nick Dougherty			Shingo Katayama	
	Zach Johnson	73-77—150		(ENG)	78-75—153		(JPN)	81-75—156
	Paul McGinley (IRL)	74-76—150		Ben Hayes	76-77—153		Patrick Nagle (am)	81-75—156
	Andrew Morse	74-76—150		John Koskinen	79-74—153		D J Trahan	75-81—156
	Rory Sabbatini (RSA)	74-76—150		Greg Kraft	76-77—153		Oliver Wilson (ENG)	80-76—156
	Andy Svoboda	75-75—150		Billy Mayfair	72-81—153		Stephen Woodard	79-77—156
73	Stuart Appleby (AUS)	72-79—151		Rocco Mediate	76-77—153	137	Michael Harris	76-81—157
	K J Choi (KOR)	76-75—151		Eduardo Molinari			Graeme Storm	
	Tim Clark (RSA)	77-74—151		(am) (ITA)	77-76—153		(ENG)	81-76—157
	Mark Hensby (AUS)	73-78—151		Chris Nallen	79-74—153		Toru Taniguchi (JPN)	75-82—157
	John Mallinger	77-74—151		Carl Pettersson		140	Tadd Fujikawa (am)	81-77—158
	Shaun Micheel	77-74—151		(SWE)	77-76—153	141	Mark Calcavecchia	80-79—159
	Corey Pavin	76-75—151		Brett Quigley	80-73—153		Mathew Goggin	
	Duffy Waldorf	75-76—151		Taggart Ridings	77-76—153		(AUS)	81-78—159
	Dean Wilson	76-75—151		Dustin White	78-75—153		Maarten Lafeber	
82	Olin Browne	80-72—152	113	Niclas Fasth (SWE)	78-76—154		(NED)	76-83—159
	Michael Campbell			Keiichiro Fukabori			George McNeill	77-82—159
	(NZL)	75-77—152		(JPN)	75-79—154		Nick Price (ZIM)	81-78—159
	Chris DiMarco	76-76—152		J J Henry	77-77—154		Philip Tataurangi	
	Bob Estes	80-72—152		Lee Janzen	82-72—154		(NZL)	86-73—159
	Lucas Glover	75-77—152		Matt Kuchar	78-76—154	147	Dillon Dougherty	
	Nathan Green (AUS)	77-75—152		Tom Lehman	78-76—154		(am)	85-75—160
	Billy Horschel (am)	75-77—152		Davis Love III	76-78—154		David Oh	83-77—160
	Peter Jacobsen	76-76—152		Steve Lowery	79-75—154	149	Ryan Baca (am)	78-83—161
	Brandt Jobe	76-76—152	121	David Berganio jr	77-78—155		Michael Derminio	81-80—161
	Justin Leonard	77-75—152		Retief Goosen (RSA)	77-78—155		Madalitso Muthiya	
	Jyoti Randhawa (IND)	77-75—152		Richard Green (AUS)	75-80—155		(ZAM)	81-80—161
	Kevin Stadler	71-81—152		Todd Hamilton	77-78—155	152	Andy Bare	84-78—162
	Tadahiro Takayama			Jonathan Moore			Ryan Posey (am)	84-78—162
	(JPN)	77-75—152		(am)	77-78—155	154	John Rollins	83-80—163
	Scott Verplank	76-76—152		Joey Sindelar	79-76—155	155	Rob Johnson	82-82—164
	Taylor Wood (am)	74-78—152		Nicholas Thompson	81-74—155	156	David Toms	79 WD
	Tiger Woods	76-76—152	128	Jason Allred	78-78—156			

Weekend off for Tiger and his wayward driver

On Saturday June 17, the *New York Daily News* devoted five pages to coverage of the US Open being played upstate at Winged Foot. Three of those pages plus pictures on both the front and back pages were devoted to a player who would not be competing over the weekend – Tiger Woods, the World No. 1.

For the first time in 38 majors as a professional, Tiger missed the cut. The 2006 US Open was the first return to action for Tiger after a nine-week break following the death of his father although he refused to make that his excuse. What happened was what he called "poor execution" – the missing of 21 of 28 fairways in his two rounds of 76.

His peers were much more sympathetic. His playing partner defending champion Michael Campbell, who also missed the cut, said: "Give him credit for turning up," and Phil Mickelson said: "He is still the best player in the world and will be back in top form at the Open." Phil was right. Tiger did win his third British title and his first in England.   *David Davies*

2005 US Open *Pinehurst No.2, NC* June 16–19 [7214–70]

Prize money: $6.25 million. Entries: 9,048

1	Michael Campbell (NZL)	71-69-71-69—280	$1170000	15T	Peter Jacobsen	72-73-69-75—289	88120
2	Tiger Woods	70-71-72-69—282	700000		David Toms	70-72-70-77—289	88120
3	Tim Clark (RSA)	76-69-70-70—285	320039	23	Olin Browne	67-71-72-80—290	59633
	Sergio García (ESP)	71-69-75-70—285	320039		Paul Claxton	72-72-72-74—290	59633
	Mark Hensby (AUS)	71-68-72-74—285	320039		Fred Funk	73-71-76-70—290	59633
6	Davis Love III	77-70-70-69—286	187813		Justin Leonard	76-71-70-73—290	59633
	Rocco Mediate	67-74-74-71—286	187813		Kenny Perry	75-70-71-74—290	59633
	Vijay Singh (FIJ)	70-70-74-72—286	187813	28	Stephen Allan (AUS)	72-69-73-77—291	44486
9	Arron Oberholser	76-67-71-73—287	150834		Matt Every (am)	75-73-73-70—291	44486
	Nick Price (ZIM)	72-71-72-72—287	150834		Jim Furyk	71-70-75-75—291	44486
11	Bob Estes	70-73-75-70—288	123857		Geoff Ogilvy (AUS)	72-74-71-74—291	44486
	Retief Goosen (RSA)	68-70-69-81—288	123857		Adam Scott (AUS)	70-71-74-76—291	44486
	Peter Hedblom (SWE)	77-66-70-75—288	123857	33	Angel Cabrera (ARG)	71-73-73-75—292	35759
	Corey Pavin	73-72-70-73—288	123857		Steve Elkington (AUS)	74-69-79-70—292	35759
15	Choi Kyoung-Ju (KOR)	69-70-74-76—289	88120		Tim Herron	74-73-70-75—292	35759
	Stewart Cink	73-74-73-69—289	88120		Brandt Jobe	68-73-79-72—292	35759
	John Cook	71-76-70-72—289	88120		Bernhard Langer (GER)	74-73-71-74—292	35759
	Fred Couples	71-74-74-70—289	88120		Shigeki Maruyama (JPN)	71-74-72-75—292	35759
	Ernie Els (RSA)	71-76-72-70—289	88120		Phil Mickelson	69-77-72-74—292	35759
	Ryuji Imada (JPN)	77-68-73-71—289	88120		Ted Purdy	73-71-73-75—292	35759
					Lee Westwood (ENG)	68-72-73-79—292	35759

Other players who made the cut: Chad Campbell, Peter Lonard (AUS), Paul McGinley (IRL), Colin Montgomerie (SCO), Tom Pernice, Rob Rashell, Mike Weir (CAN), 293; Jason Gore, J L Lewis, Nick O'Hern (AUS), 294; Thomas Bjørn (DEN), Nick Dougherty (ENG), Richard Green (AUS), Søren Kjeldsen (DEN), Thomas Levet (FRA), 295; Tommy Armour III, Luke Donald (ENG), Keiichiro Fukabori (JPN), J J Henry, Lee Janzen, Steve Jones, Frank Lickliter, Jonathan Lomas (ENG), Ryan Moore (am), Ian Poulter (ENG), 296; Michael Allen, Steve Flesch, Bill Glasson, John Mallinger, 297; Stephen Ames (TRI), D J Brigman, J Hayes, Rory Sabbatini (RSA), 298; John Daly, Charles Howell III, Omar Uresti, 299; Jeff Maggert, Bob Tway, 300; Graeme McDowell (NIR), Chris Nallen, 301; Craig Barlow. 303; Jerry Kelly, 305

2004 US Open *Shinnecock Hills, Southampton, NY* June 17–20 [6996–70]

Prize money: $6.25 million. Entries: 8726

1	Retief Goosen (RSA)	70-66-69-71—276	$1125000	20T	David Toms	73-72-70-76—291	80644
2	Phil Mickelson	68-66-73-71—278	675000		Kirk Triplett	71-70-73-77—291	80644
3	Jeff Maggert	68-67-74-72—281	424604	24	Daniel Chopra (SWE)	73-68-76-75—292	63328
4	Shigeki Maruyama (JPN)	66-68-74-76—284	267756		Lee Janzen	72-70-71-79—292	63328
	Mike Weir (CAN)	69-70-71-74—284	267756		Tim Petrovic	69-75-72-76—292	63328
6	Fred Funk	70-66-72-77—285	212444		Nick Price (ZIM)	73-70-72-77—292	63328
7	Robert Allenby (AUS)	70-72-74-70—286	183828	28	Shaun Micheel	71-72-70-80—293	51774
	Steve Flesch	68-74-70-74—286	183828		Vijay Singh (FIJ)	68-70-77-78—293	51774
9	Stephen Ames (TRI)	74-66-73-74—287	145282	30	Ben Curtis	68-75-72-79—294	46089
	Ernie Els (RSA)	70-67-70-80—287	145282	31	Choi Kyoung-Ju (KOR)	76-68-76-75—295	41759
	Chris DiMarco	71-71-70-75—287	145282		Padraig Harrington (IRL)	73-71-76-75—295	41759
	Jay Haas	66-74-76-71—287	145282		Peter Lonard (AUS)	71-73-77-74—295	41759
13	Tim Clark (RSA)	73-70-66-79—288	119770		David Roesch	68-73-74-80—295	41759
	Tim Herron	75-66-73-74—288	119770		Bo Van Pelt	69-73-73-80—295	41759
	Spencer Levin (am)	69-73-71-75—288		36	Charles Howell III	75-70-68-83—296	36813
16	Angel Cabrera (ARG)	66-71-77-75—289	109410		Hidemichi Tanaka (JPN)	70-74-73-79—296	36813
17	Skip Kendall	68-75-74-73—290	98477		Lee Westwood (ENG)	73-71-73-79—296	36813
	Corey Pavin	67-71-73-79—290	98477		Casey Wittenberg (am)	71-71-75-79—296	
	Tiger Woods	72-69-73-76—290	98477				
20	Mark Calcavecchia	71-71-74-75—291	80644				
	Sergio García (ESP)	72-68-71-80—291	80644				

Other players who made the cut: Bill Haas (am), Jerry Kelly, Stephen Leaney (AUS), Spike McRoy, Joe Ogilvie, Pat Perez, Geoffrey Sisk, Scott Verplank 297; Kristopher Cox, Jim Furyk, Zachary Johnson, Chris Riley, John Rollins 298; Dudley Hart, Scott Hoch 299; Tom Carter, Trevor Immelman (RSA) 300; Joakim Haeggman (SWE), Tom Kite, Phillip Price (WAL) 302; Alex Cejka (GER), Craig Parry (AUS) 303; Cliff Kresge, Chez Reavie (am) 304; J J Henry 306; Kevin Stadler 307; Billy Mayfair 310

2003 US Open Olympia Fields CC (North Course), IL June 12–15 [7190–70]

Prize money: $6 million. Entries: 7820

1	Jim Furyk	67-66-67-72—272	$1080000	20	Mark Calcavecchia	68-72-67-76—283	64170
2	Stephen Leaney (AUS)	67-68-68-72—275	650000		Robert Damron	69-68-73-73—283	64170
3	Kenny Perry	72-71-69-67—279	341367		Ian Leggatt (RSA)	68-70-68-77—283	64170
	Mike Weir (CAN)	73-67-68-71—279	341367		Justin Leonard	66-70-72-75—283	64170
5	Ernie Els (RSA)	69-70-69-72—280	185934		Peter Lonard (AUS)	72-69-74-68—283	64170
	Fredrik Jacobson (SWE)	69-67-73-71—280	185934		Vijay Singh (FIJ)	70-63-72-78—283	64170
	Nick Price (ZIM)	71-65-69-75—280	185934		Jay Williamson	72-69-69-73—283	64170
	Justin Rose (ENG)	70-71-70-69—280	185934		Tiger Woods	70-66-75-72—283	64170
	David Toms	72-67-70-71—280	185934	28	Stewart Cink	70-68-72-74—284	41254
10	Padraig Harrington (IRL)	69-72-72-68—281	124936		John Maginnes	72-70-72-70—284	41254
					Dicky Pride	71-69-66-78—284	41254
	Jonathan Kaye	70-70-72-69—281	124936		Brett Quigley	65-74-71-74—284	41254
	Cliff Kresge	69-70-72-70—281	124936		Kevin Sutherland	71-71-72-70—284	41254
	Billy Mayfair	69-71-67-74—281	124936		Kirk Triplett	71-68-73-72—284	41254
	Scott Verplank	76-67-68-70—281	124936		Tom Watson	65-72-75-72—284	41254
15	Jonathan Byrd	69-66-71-76—282	93359	35	Angel Cabrera (ARG)	72-68-73-72—285	32552
	Tom Byrum	69-69-71-73—282	93359		Chad Campbell	70-70-69-76—285	32552
	Tim Petrovic	69-70-70-73—282	93359		Chris DiMarco	72-71-71-71—285	32552
	Eduardo Romero (ARG)	70-66-70-76—282	93359		Fred Funk	70-73-71-71—285	32552
					Sergio García (ESP)	69-74-71-71—285	32552
	Higemichi Tamaka (JPN)	69-71-71-71—282	93359		Brandt Jobe	70-68-76-71—285	32552
					Mark O'Meara	72-68-67-78—285	32552

Other players who made the cut: Darren Clarke (NIR), Retief Goosen (RSA), Bernhard Langer (GER), Steve Lowery, Colin Montgomerie (SCO), Loren Roberts 286; Woody Austin, Marco Dawson, Niclas Fasth (SWE), Dan Forsman, Darron Stiles 287; Charles Howell III, John Rollins 288; Lee Janzen, Phil Mickelson 289; Trip Kuehne (am), Len Mattiace 290; Ricky Barnes (am), Olin Browne 291; Chris Anderson, Alexander Cejka (GER), Brian Davis (ENG) 292; Jay Don Blake, JP Hayes 293; Fred Couples, Brian Henninger 295; Ryan Dillon 301

2002 US Open Bethpage State Park, Black Course, Farmingdale, NY August 13–16 [7214–70]

Prize money: $5.5 million. Entries: 8468

1	Tiger Woods	67-68-70-72—277	$1000000	24	Jim Carter	77-73-70-71—291	47439
2	Phil Mickelson	70-73-67-70—280	585000		Darren Clarke (NIR)	74-74-72-71—291	47439
3	Jeff Maggert	69-73-68-72—282	362356		Chris DiMarco	74-74-72-71—291	47439
4	Sergio García (ESP)	68-74-67-74—283	252546		Ernie Els (RSA)	73-74-70-74—291	47439
5	Nick Faldo (ENG)	70-76-66-73—285	182882		Davis Love III	71-71-72-77—291	47439
	Scott Hoch	71-75-70-69—285	182882		Jeff Sluman	73-73-72-73—291	47439
	Billy Mayfair	69-74-68-74—285	182882	30	Jason Caron	75-72-72-73—292	35639
8	Tom Byrum	72-72-70-72—286	138669		Choi Kyung-ju (KOR)	69-73-73-77—292	35639
	Padraig Harrington (IRL)	70-68-73-75—286	138669		Paul Lawrie (SCO)	73-73-73-73—292	35639
	Nick Price (ZIM)	72-75-69-70—286	138669		Scott McCarron	72-72-70-78—292	35639
11	Peter Lonard (AUS)	73-74-73-67—287	119357		Vijay Singh (FIJ)	75-75-67-75—292	35639
12	Robert Allenby (AUS)	74-70-67-77—288	102338	35	Shingo Katayama (JPN)	74-72-74-73—293	31945
	Jay Haas	73-73-70-72—288	102338				
	Dudley Hart	69-76-70-73—288	102338		Bernhard Langer (GER)	72-76-70-75—293	31945
	Justin Leonard	73-71-68-76—288	102338				
16	Shigeki Maruyama (JPN)	76-67-73-73—289	86372	37	Stuart Appleby (AUS)	77-73-75-69—294	26783
					Thomas Bjørn (DEN)	71-79-73-71—294	26783
	Steve Stricker	72-77-69-71—289	86372		Niclas Fasth (SWE)	72-72-74-76—294	26783
18	Luke Donald (ENG)	76-72-70-72—290	68995		Donnie Hammond	73-77-71-73—294	26783
	Charles Howell III	71-74-70-75—290	68995		Franklin Langham	70-76-74-74—294	26783
	Steve Flesch	72-72-75-71—290	68995		Rocco Mediate	72-72-74-76—294	26783
	Thomas Levet (FRA)	71-77-70-72—290	68995		Kevin Sutherland	74-75-70-75—294	26783
	Mark O'Meara	76-70-69-75—290	68995		Hidemichi Tanaka (JPN)	73-73-72-76—294	26783
	Craig Stadler	74-72-70-74—290	68995				

Other players who made the cut: Tom Lehman, Frank Lickliter, Kenny Perry, David Toms, Jean Van de Velde (FRA) 295; Craig Bowden, Tim Herron, Robert Karlsson (SWE), José María Olazábal (ESP) 296; Harrison Frazar, Ian Leggatt (CAN), Jesper Parnevik (SWE), Corey Pavin 297; Brad Lardon 298; John Maginnes, Greg Norman (AUS), Bob Tway 299; Andy Miller, Jeev Milkha Singh (IND), Paul Stankowski 300; Spike McRoy 301; Angel Cabrera (ARG), Brad Faxon 302; Kent Jones, Len Mattiace 303; John Daly, Tom Gillis 304; Kevin Warrick (am) 307.

2001 US Open Southern Hills CC, Tulsa, OK June 14–18 [6973–70]

Prize money: $5,000,000. Entries: 8300

1	Retief Goosen* (RSA)	66-70-69-71—276	$900000
2	Mark Brooks	72-64-70-70—276	530000
Play-off: Goosen 70, Brooks 72			
3	Stewart Cink	69-69-67-72—277	325310
4	Rocco Mediate	71-68-67-72—278	226777
5	Tom Kite	73-72-72-64—281	172912
	Paul Azinger	74-67-69-71—281	172912
7	Davis Love III	72-69-71-70—282	125172
	Vijay Singh (FIJ)	74-70-74-64—282	125172
	Angel Cabrera (ARG)	70-71-72-69—282	125172
	Phil Mickelson	70-69-68-75—282	125172
	Kirk Triplett	72-69-71-70—282	125172
12	Tiger Woods	74-71-69-69—283	91734
	Sergio García (ESP)	70-68-68-77—283	91734
	Michael Allen	77-68-67-71—283	91734
	Matt Gogel	70-69-74-70—283	91734
16	David Duval	70-69-71-74—284	75337
	Scott Hoch	73-73-69-69—284	75337
	Chris DiMarco	69-73-70-72—284	75337
19	Corey Pavin	70-75-68-72—285	63426
	Chris Perry	72-71-73-69—285	63426
	Mike Weir (CAN)	67-76-68-74—285	63426

22T	Scott Verplank	71-71-73-71—286	54813
	Thomas Bjørn (DEN)	72-69-73-72—286	54813
24	Mark Calcavecchia	70-74-73-70—287	42523
	Hal Sutton	70-75-71-71—287	42523
	Tom Lehman	76-68-69-74—287	42523
	Olin Browne	71-74-71-71—287	42523
	Steve Lowery	71-73-72-71—287	42523
	Joe Durant	71-74-70-72—287	42523
30	Dean Wilson	71-74-72-71—288	30055
	Bob Estes	70-72-75-71—288	30055
	Steve Jones	73-73-72-70—288	30055
	Gabriel Hjertstedt (SWE)	72-74-70-72—288	30055
	Padraig Harrington (IRL)	73-70-71-74—288	30055
	Jesper Parnevik (SWE)	73-73-74-68—288	30055
	Darren Clarke (NIR)	74-71-71-72—288	30055
	Bob May	72-72-69-75—288	30055
	Bryce Molder (am)	75-71-68-74—288	
	JL Lewis	68-68-77-75—288	30055
40	Bernhard Langer (GER)	71-73-71-74—289	23933
	Tim Herron	71-74-73-71—289	23933
	Briny Baird	71-72-70-76—289	23933
	Shaun Micheel	73-70-75-71—289	23933

Other players who made the cut: Fred Funk, Toshimitsu Izawa (JPN), Brandel Chamblee, Jeff Maggert, Duffy Waldorf, Kevin Sutherland, Tom Byrum 290; Eduardo Romero (ARG) 291; Loren Roberts, Colin Montgomerie (SCO), Mark Wiebe, Bob Tway, Hale Irwin, José Coceres (ARG), Scott Dunlap, Brandt Jobe, Frank Lickliter, Jimmy Walker 292; Jim Furyk, Dudley Hart, Richard Zokol (CAN), Tim Petrovic 293; Ernie Els (RSA), Peter Lonard (AUS), Dan Forsman, David Toms, Harrison Frazer, David Peoples 294; Nick Faldo (ENG), Franklin Langham 295; Anthony Kang (KOR), Mathias Grönberg (SWE), Gary Orr (SCO), Thongchai Jaidee (THA) 296; Jim McGovern 297; Stephen Gangluff 301.

2000 US Open Pebble Beach, CA June 15–18 [6846–71]

Prize money: $4,500,000. Entries: 8457

1	Tiger Woods	65-69-71-67—272	$800000
2	Miguel Angel Jiménez (ESP)	66-74-76-71—287	391150
	Ernie Els (RSA)	74-73-68-72—287	391150
4	John Huston	67-75-76-70—288	212779
5	Padraig Harrington (IRL)	73-71-72-73—289	162526
	Lee Westwood (ENG)	71-71-76-71—289	162526
7	Nick Faldo (ENG)	69-74-76-71—290	137203
8	Loren Roberts	68-78-73-72—291	112766
	David Duval	75-71-74-71—291	112766
	Stewart Cink	77-72-72-70—291	112766
	Vijay Singh (FIJ)	70-73-80-68—291	112766
12	José María Olazábal (ESP)	70-71-76-75—292	86223
	Paul Azinger	71-73-79-69—292	86223
	Retief Goosen (RSA)	77-72-72-71—292	86223
	Michael Campbell (NZL)	71-77-71-73—292	86223
16	Justin Leonard	73-73-75-72—293	65214
	Mike Weir (CAN)	76-72-76-79—293	65214
	Fred Couples	70-75-75-73—293	65214
	Scott Hoch	73-76-75-69—293	65214
	Phil Mickelson	71-73-73-76—293	65214
	David Toms	73-76-72-72—293	65214

22	Notah Begay III	74-75-72-73—294	53105
23	Hal Sutton	69-73-83-70—295	45537
	Bob May	72-76-75-72—295	45537
	Tom Lehman	71-73-78-73—295	45537
	Mike Brisky	71-73-79-72—295	45537
27	Tom Watson	71-74-78-73—296	34066
	Nick Price (ZIM)	77-70-78-71—296	34066
	Steve Stricker	75-74-75-72—296	34066
	Steve Jones	75-73-75-73—296	34066
	Hale Irwin	68-78-81-69—296	34066
32	Tom Kite	72-77-77-71—297	28247
	Chris Perry	75-72-78-72—297	28247
	Richard Zokol (CAN)	74-74-80-69—297	28247
	Rocco Mediate	69-76-75-77—297	28247
	Lee Porter	74-70-83-70—297	28247
37	Woody Austin	77-70-78-73—298	22056
	Jerry Kelly	73-73-81-71—298	22056
	Larry Mize	73-72-76-77—298	22056
	Craig Parry (AUS)	73-74-76-75—298	22056
	Bobby Clampett	68-77-76-77—298	22056
	Angel Cabrera (ARG)	69-76-79-74—298	22056
	Lee Janzen	71-73-79-75—298	22056
	Ted Tryba	71-73-79-75—298	22056
	Charles Warren	75-74-75-74—298	22056

Other players who made the cut: Rick Hartmann, Sergio García (ESP), Colin Montgomerie (SCO), Scott Verplank, Thomas Bjørn (DEN) 299; Warren Schutte (SA), Mark O'Meara 300; Darren Clarke (NIR), Keith Clearwater, Jeff Coston 301; Kirk Triplett 302; Dave Eichelberger, Jimmy Green 303; Jeffrey Wilson (am) 304; Jim Furyk 305; Brandel Chamblee, Carlos Daniel Franco (PAR) 306; Robert Damron 313.

1999 US Open Pinehurst No. 2, NC June 17–20   [7175–70]

Prize money: $3,500,000. Entries: 7889

1	P Stewart	68-69-72-70—279	$625000	17T	S Verplank	72-73-72-74—291	46756
2	P Mickelson	67-70-73-70—280	370000	23	MA Jiménez (ESP)	73-70-72-77—292	33505
3	V Singh (FIJ)	69-70-73-69—281	196791		N Price (ZIM)	71-74-74-73—292	33505
	T Woods	68-71-72-70—281	196791		T Scherrer	72-72-74-74—292	33505
5	S Stricker	70-73-69-73—285	130655		B Watts	69-73-77-73—292	33505
6	T Herron	69-72-70-75—286	116935		DA Weibring	69-74-74-75—292	33505
7	D Duval	67-70-75-75—287	96260	28	D Berganio jr	68-77-76-72—293	26185
	J Maggert	71-69-74-73—287	96260		T Lehman	73-74-73-73—293	26185
	H Sutton	69-70-76-72—287	96260	30	B Estes	70-71-77-76—294	23804
10	D Clarke (NIR)	73-70-74-71—288	78862		G Sisk	71-72-76-75—294	23804
	B Mayfair	67-72-74-75—288	78862	32	S Cink	72-74-78-71—295	22448
12	P Azinger	72-72-75-70—289	67347		S Strüver (GER)	70-76-75-74—295	22448
	P Goydos	67-74-74-74—289	67347	34	B Fabel	69-75-78-74—296	19083
	D Love III	70-73-74-72—289	67347		C Franco (PAR)	69-77-73-77—296	19083
15	J Leonard	69-75-73-73—290	58214		G Hjertstedt (SWE)	75-72-79-70—296	19083
	C Montgomerie (SCO)	72-72-74-72—290	58214		R Mediate	69-72-76-79—296	19083
17	J Furyk	69-73-77-72—291	46756		C Parry (AUS)	69-73-79-75—296	19083
	J Haas	74-72-73-72—291	46756		S Pate	70-75-75-76—296	19083
	D Hart	73-73-76-69—291	46756		C Pavin	74-71-78-73—296	19083
	J Huston	71-69-75-76—291	46756		E Toledo (MEX)	70-72-76-78—296	19083
	J Parnevik (SWE)	71-71-76-73—291	46756				

Other players who made the cut: S Allan (AUS), G Hallberg, L Mattiace, C Perry 297; R Allenby (AUS), B Chamblee, L Janzen, D Lebeck, 298; S Elkington (AUS), C Tidland 299; G Kraft, S McRoy, P Price (WAL), J Tyska 300; J Kelly, T Watson, K Yokoo (JPN) 301; J Cook, T Kite 302; C Smith, B Tway 303; L Mize 304; H Kuehne (am) 306; B Burns, T Tryba 308; J Daly 309.

1998 US Open The Olympic Club, San Francisco, CA June 18–21   [6797–70]

Prize money: $3,000,000. Entries: 7117

1	L Janzen	73-66-73-68—280	$535000	18T	JM Olazábal (ESP)	68-77-71-74—290	41833
2	P Stewart	66-71-70-74—281	315000		T Woods	74-72-71-73—290	41833
3	B Tway	68-70-73-73—284	201730	23	C Martin	74-71-74-72—291	34043
4	N Price (ZIM)	73-68-71-73—285	140597		G Day	73-72-71-75—291	34043
5	S Stricker	73-71-69-73—286	107392	25	DA Weibring	72-72-75-73—292	25640
	T Lehman	68-75-68-75—286	107392		P-U Johansson (SWE)	71-75-73-73—292	25640
7	D Duval	75-68-75-69—287	83794		E Romero (ARG)	72-70-76-74—292	25640
	L Westwood (ENG)	72-74-70-71—287	83794		C Perry	74-71-72-75—292	25640
	J Maggert	69-69-75-74—287	83794		V Singh (FIJ)	73-72-73-74—292	25640
10	J Sluman	72-74-74-68—288	64490		T Bjørn (DEN)	72-75-70-75—292	25640
	P Mickelson	71-73-74-70—288	64490		M Carnevale	67-73-74-78—292	25640
	S Appleby (AUS)	73-74-70-71—288	64490	32	M O'Meara	70-76-78-69—293	18372
	S Cink	73-68-73-74—288	64490		P Harrington (IRL)	73-72-76-72—293	18372
14	P Azinger	75-72-77-65—289	52214		B Zabriski	74-71-74-74—293	18372
	J Parnevik (SWE)	69-74-76-70—289	52214		S Pate	72-75-73-73—293	18372
	M Kuchar (am)	70-69-76-74—289			J Huston	73-72-72-76—293	18372
	J Furyk	74-73-68-74—289	52214		J Durant	68-73-76-76—293	18372
18	C Montgomerie (SCO)	70-74-75-69—290	41833		C DiMarco	71-71-74-77—293	18372
	L Roberts	71-76-71-72—290	41833		L Porter	72-67-76-78—293	18372
	F Lickliter II	73-71-72-74—290	41833				

Other players who made the cut: J Leonard, S McCarron, F Nobilo (NZL) 294; D Clarke (NIR), J Sindelar, T Kite, J Acosta jr, O Browne, J Nicklaus 295; E Els (RSA), M Reid, B Faxon, S Verplank 296; F Couples, T Herron, J Johnston, J Daly 297; M Brooks 298; S Simpson 300; R Walcher 303; T Sipula 305.

1997 US Open *Congressional CC, Bethesda, MD* June 12–15 [7213–70]

Prize money: $2,600,000. Entries: 7013

1	E Els (SA)	71-67-69-69—276	$465000	19T	P Stankowski	75-70-68-73—286	31915
2	C Montgomerie (SCO)	65-76-67-69—277	275000		H Sutton	66-73-73-74—286	31915
3	T Lehman	67-70-68-73—278	172828	24	L Mattiace	71-75-73-68—287	24173
4	J Maggert	73-66-68-74—281	120454		E Fryatt	72-73-73-69—287	24173
5	B Tway	71-71-70-70—282	79875		S Dunlap	75-66-75-71—287	24173
	O Browne	71-71-69-71—282	79875		S Elkington (AUS)	75-68-72-72—287	24173
	J Furyk	74-68-69-71—282	79875	28	P Goydos	73-72-74-69—288	17443
	J Haas	73-69-68-72—282	79875		P Azinger	72-72-74-70—288	17443
	T Tolles	74-67-69-72—282	79875		P Stewart	71-73-73-71—288	17443
10	S McCarron	73-71-69-70—283	56949		M McNulty (ZIM)	67-73-75-73—288	17443
	S Hoch	71-68-72-72—283	56949		H Kase	68-73-73-74—288	17443
	D Ogrin	70-69-71-73—283	56949		F Zoeller	72-73-69-74—288	17443
13	L Roberts	72-69-72-71—284	47348		K Gibson	72-69-72-75—288	17443
	S Cink	71-67-74-72—284	47348	28	J Sluman	69-72-72-75—288	17443
	B Andrade	75-67-69-73—284	47348	36	J Leonard	69-72-78-70—289	13483
16	B Hughes (AUS)	75-70-71-69—285	40086		G Waite (NZL)	72-74-72-71—289	13483
	JM Olazábal (ESP)	71-71-72-71—285	40086		S Stricker	66-76-75-72—289	13483
	D Love III	75-70-69-71—285	40086		M O'Meara	73-73-71-72—289	13483
19	N Price (ZIM)	71-74-71-70—286	31915		S Appleby (AUS)	71-75-70-73—289	13483
	L Westwood (ENG)	71-71-73-71—286	31915		F Nobilo (NZL)	71-74-70-74—289	13483
	T Woods	74-67-73-72—286	31915		J Cook	72-71-71-75—289	13483

Other players who made the cut: D Clarke (NIR), P Mickelson, F Funk, C Perry, C Parry (AUS) 290; J Parnevik (SWE), D Duval, N Faldo (ENG) 291; D White 292; L Janzen, J Nicklaus, H Irwin, F Couples, P Teravainen, P Broadhurst (ENG) 293; L Mize, C Rose 294; C Smith, D Waldorf, R Butcher, S Jones 295; T Watson 296; D Schreyer, B Crenshaw, B Faxon 297; T Kite, M Hulbert, G Kraft, J Morse, S Ames (TRI), T Björn (DEN) 298; J Green 299; R Wylie, A Coltart (SCO) 300; D Mast, G Towne, V Singh (FIJ), P Parker, D Hammond 301; J Ferenz 303; M Dawson 304; S Adams 306.

US Open Championship History

Year	Winner	Runner-up	Venue	Score
1894	W Dunn	W Campbell	St Andrews, NY	2 holes

After 1894 decided by stroke-play. From 1895–1897. 36-holes From 1898 72-holes

Year	Winner	Venue	Score
1895	HJ Rawlins	Newport	173
1896	J Foulis	Southampton	152
1897	J Lloyd	Wheaton, IL	162
1898	F Herd	South Hamilton, MA	328
1899	W Smith	Baltimore	315
1900	H Vardon (ENG)	Wheaton, IL	313
1901	W Anderson*	Myopia, MA	315

After a play-off with A Smith: Anderson 85, Smith 86

Year	Winner	Venue	Score
1902	L Auchterlonie	Garden City	305
1903	W Anderson*	Baltusrol	307

After a play-off with D Brown: Anderson 82, Brown 84

1904	W Anderson	Glenview	304
1905	W Anderson	Myopia, MA	335
1906	A Smith	Onwentsia	291
1907	A Ross	Chestnut Hill, PA	302
1908	F McLeod*	Myopia, MA	322

After a play-off with W Smith: McLeod 77, Smith 83

1909	G Sargent	Englewood, NJ	290
1910	A Smith*	Philadelphia	289

After a play-off with J McDermott and M Smith: A Smith 71, McDermott 75, M Smith 77

1911	J McDermott*	Wheaton, IL	307

After a play-off with M Brady and G Simpson: McDermott 80, Brady 82, Simpson 85

Year	Winner	Venue	Score
1912	J McDermott	Buffalo, NY	294
1913	F Ouimet* (am)	Brookline, MA	304

After a play-off with Harry Vardon and Ted Ray: Ouimet 72, Vardon 77, Ray 78)

1914	W Hagen	Midlothian	297
1915	J Travers (am)	Baltusrol	290
1916	C Evans (am)	Minneapolis	286
1917-18	No Championship		
1919	W Hagen*	Braeburn	301

After a play-off with M Brady: Hagen 77, Brady 78

1920	E Ray (ENG)	Inverness	295
1921	J Barnes	Washington	289
1922	G Sarazen	Glencoe	288
1923	R Jones jr* (am)	Inwood, LI	295

After a play-off with R Cruikshank: Jones 76, Cruikshank 78

1924	C Walker	Oakland Hills	297
1925	W MacFarlane*	Worcester	291

After a play-off with R Jones jr: MacFarlane 147, Jones 148

1926	R Jones jr (am)	Scioto	293
1927	T Armour*	Oakmont	301

After a play-off with H Cooper: Armour 76, Cooper 79

1928	J Farrell*	Olympia Fields	294

After a play-off with R Jones jr (am): Farrell 143, Jones 144

US Open Championship History *continued*

Year	Winner	Venue	Score
1929	R Jones jr* (am)	Winged Foot, NY	294
After a play-off with A Espinosa: Jones 141, Espinosa 164			
1930	R Jones jr (am)	Interlachen	287
1931	B Burke*	Inverness	292
After a play-off with G von Elm: Burke 149-148, von Elm 149-149			
1932	G Sarazen	Fresh Meadow	286
1933	J Goodman (am)	North Shore	287
1934	O Dutra	Merion	293
1935	S Parks	Oakmont	299
1936	T Manero	Springfield	282
1937	R Guldahl	Oakland Hills	281
1938	R Guldahl	Cherry Hills	284
1939	B Nelson*	Philadelphia	284
After a play-off with C Wood and D Shute: Nelson 138, Wood 141, Shute 76			
1940	W Lawson Little*	Canterbury, OH	287
After a play-off with G Sarazen: Little 70, Sarazen 73			
1941	C Wood	Fort Worth, TX	284
1942–45	No Championship		
1946	L Mangrum*	Canterbury	284
After a play-off with Byron Nelson and Vic Ghezzi: Mangrum 144, Nelson 145, Ghezzi 145			
1947	L Worsham*	St Louis	282
After a play-off with S Snead: Worsham 69, Snead 70			
1948	B Hogan	Los Angeles	276
1949	Dr C Middlecoff	Medinah, IL	286
1950	B Hogan*	Merion, PA	287
After a play-off with L Mangrum and G Fazio: Hogan 69, Mangrum 73, Fazio 75			
1951	B Hogan	Oakland Hills, MI	287
1952	J Boros	Dallas, TX	281
1953	B Hogan	Oakmont	283
1954	E Furgol	Baltusrol	284
1955	J Fleck*	San Francisco	287
After a play-off with B Hogan: Fleck 69, Hogan 72			
1956	Dr C Middlecoff	Rochester, NY	281
1957	D Mayer*	Inverness	282
After a play-off with Dr C Middlecoff: Mayer 72, Middlecoff 79			
1958	T Bolt	Tulsa, OK	283
1959	W Casper	Winged Foot, NY	282
1960	A Palmer	Denver, CO	280
1961	G Littler	Birmingham, MI	281
1962	J Nicklaus*	Oakmont	283
After a play-off with A Palmer: Nicklaus 71, Palmer 74			
1963	J Boros	Brookline, MA	293
(After a play-off with J Boros and J Cupit: J Boros 70, J Cupit 73, A Palmer 76			
1964	K Venturi	Washington	278
1965	G Player* (RSA)	St Louis, MO	282
After a play-off with K Nagle: Player 71, Nagle 74			
1966	W Casper*	San Francisco	278
After a play-off with A Palmer: Casper 69, Palmer 73			

Year	Winner	Venue	Score
1967	J Nicklaus	Baltusrol	275
1968	L Trevino	Rochester, NY	275
1969	O Moody	Houston, TX	281
1970	A Jacklin (ENG)	Hazeltine, MN	281
1971	L Trevino*	Merion, PA	280
After a play-off with J Nicklaus: Trevino 68, Nicklaus 71			
1972	J Nicklaus	Pebble Beach	290
1973	J Miller	Oakmont, PA	279
1974	H Irwin	Winged Foot, NY	287
1975	L Graham*	Medinah, IL	287
After a play-off with J Mahaffey: Graham 71, Mahaffey 73			
1976	J Pate	Atlanta, GA	277
1977	H Green	Southern Hills, Tulsa	278
1978	A North	Cherry Hills	285
1979	H Irwin	Inverness, OH	284
1980	J Nicklaus	Baltusrol	272
1981	D Graham (AUS)	Merion, PA	273
1982	T Watson	Pebble Beach	282
1983	L Nelson	Oakmont, PA	280
1984	F Zoeller*	Winged Foot	276
After a play-off with G Norman: Zoeller 67, Norman 75			
1985	A North	Oakland Hills, MI	279
1986	R Floyd	Shinnecock Hills, NY	279
1987	S Simpson	Olympic, San Francisco	277
1988	C Strange*	Brookline, MA	278
After a play-off with N Faldo: Strange 71, Faldo 75			
1989	C Strange	Rochester, NY	278
1990	H Irwin*	Medinah	280
After a play-off with M Donald: Irwin 74, Donald 74; Irwin won sudden death play-off with 3 to 4 at first extra hole			
1991	P Stewart*	Hazeltine, MN	282
After a play-off with S Simpson: Stewart 75, Simpson 77			
1992	T Kite	Pebble Beach, FL	285
1993	L Janzen	Baltusrol	272
1994	E Els* (RSA)	Oakmont, PA	279
After a play-off with L Roberts and C Montgomerie: Els 74, Roberts 74, Montgomerie 78. Els won sudden death playoff: Els 4,4, Roberts 4,5			
1995	C Pavin	Shinnecock Hills, NY	280
1996	S Jones	Oakland Hills, MI	278
1997	E Els (RSA)	Congressional, Bethesda	276
1998	L Janzen	Olympic, San Francisco	280
1999	P Stewart	Pinehurst No. 2, NC	279
2000	T Woods	Pebble Beach, CA	272
2001	R Goosen* (RSA)	Southern Hills CC, OK	276
After a play-off with M Brooks: Goosen 70, Brooks 72			
2002	T Woods	Farmingdale, NY	277
2003	J Furyk	Olympia Fields, IL	272
2004	R Goosen (RSA)	Shinnecock Hills, NY	276
2005	M Campbell (NZL)	Pinehurst No.2, NC	280
2006	G Ogilvy (AUS)	Winged Foot, NY	285

The Masters

Controlled Mickelson outscores the rest of the 'Big Five' to deservedly pick up a second Green Jacket at Augusta

Just a week after blitzing the field for a 13 shot victory at the BellSouth Classic, Phil Mickelson won the year's first major with a seven-under-par 281 total which earned him a $1.26 million first prize and moved him into second place in the money list behind Tiger Woods.

It was the first time since Sandy Lyle in 1988 that the winner of The Masters had won the previous week as well. One shot clear of evergreen Fred Couples and Chad Campbell at the 54-hole stage, Mickelson closed with a near perfectly compiled 69. His only dropped shot came at the last by which time victory was assured. He knew he could win if he two-putted after missing the green with his approach and used both putts to beat second-placed Tim Clark from South Africa by two.

With the rest of the Big Five in behind him, Mickelson explained his delight at being able to win the event for a second time. "When I won this title three years ago, I felt a great sense of relief that I could win a major. This time what I feel is great satisfaction at beating such a great field". Mickelson, who had won the US PGA Championship title at the end of 2005, knew he would be going on to Winged Foot later in the year to try to win a third major in a row.

The Masters course at Augusta was stretched to 7,445 yards, making it the second longest for a major in history and it suited Mickelson who was in his element as he scored his 29th victory on Tour. On the final day, the longest putts which mattered were a five-footer he holed after coming out of the bunker at the 10th and an eight-footer at the 15th.

After the first round Mickelson trailed Vijay Singh, another former Masters winner, by three and was four behind Chad Campbell at half-way in fifth place on two under par. Just behind Campbell and ahead of Mickelson at that point came Rocco Mediate, Singh and Couples. A two-under-par round of 70 on Sunday morning when the rain-delayed third round was completed, was good enough to give Mickelson the lead by one from Couples and Campbell with a round to go. Mickelson's four-under-par aggregate of 212 was the highest 54-hole score to lead since 1989. It was tight at the top of the leaderboard, always shown in relation to par on the huge green scoreboard beside the eighteenth green. The Masters officials were the first to relate players' scores to par rather than display their actual score at the holes – a practice now followed universally. Ten players were within three shots of the lead including Tiger Woods and Singh. Ten more were just five behind.

Early on the final day, Mickelson had been caught by 46-year-old Couples, Campbell, Mediate and Miguel Angel Jiménez, but the eventual winner took the lead again at the eighth as the others slipped away. Couples' putter went cold, Campbell three-putted the 11th and Mediate ran up a 10 at the par 5 12th. As others faltered, Tim Clark from South Africa – with two late birdies including a holed bunker shot at the last for a closing 69 – eased himself into second place just one ahead of two-time Masters winner José María Olazábal, who finished with a tournament best of the week 66 that jumped him up from 22nd, two-time US Open champion Retief Goosen, Woods, Couples and Campbell. Mickelson's win meant that for the 16th consecutive time the eventual winner came from the final pairing. Double Masters champion Olazábal's performance went a long way to ensuring he earned his place later in the year in Europe's Ryder Cup team.

Day One	Day Two	Day Three	Day Four
−5 Singh	−6 C Campbell	−4 Mickelson	−7 Mickelson
−4 Mediate	−3 Mediate	−3 Couples	−5 T Clark
−3 Oberholser	−3 Singh	−3 Campbell	−4 Olazábal
−2 Mickelson	−3 Couples		−4 Goosen
	−2 Mickelson		−4 Woods
			−4 Couples
			−4 Campbell

2006 Masters (70th) *Augusta National GC, GA* April 6–9   [7445–72]

Prize money: $7 million. Final field of 90 players (5 amateurs) of whom 47 (including no amateurs) made the final half-way cut on 148 or less.

Players are of American nationality unless stated.

1	Phil Mickelson	70-72-70-69—281	$1260000
2	Tim Clark (RSA)	70-72-72-69—283	758000
3	Chad Campbell	71-67-75-71—284	315700
	Fred Couples	71-70-72-71—284	315700
	Retief Goosen (RSA)	70-73-72-69—284	315700
	José-María Olazábal (ESP)	76-71-71-66—284	315700
	Tiger Woods	72-71-71-70—284	315700
8	Angel Cabrera (ARG)	73-74-70-68—285	210000
	Vijay Singh (FIJ)	67-74-73-71—285	210000
10	Stewart Cink	72-73-71-70—286	189000
11	Stephen Ames (CAN)	74-70-70-73—287	161000
	Miguel Angel Jiménez (ESP)	72-74-69-72—287	161000
	Mike Weir (CAN)	71-73-73-70—287	161000
14	Billy Mayfair	71-72-73-72—288	129500
	Arron Oberholser	69-75-73-71—288	129500
16	Geoff Ogilvy (AUS)	70-75-73-71—289	112000
	Rod Pampling (AUS)	72-73-72-72—289	112000
	Scott Verplank	74-70-74-71—289	112000
19	Stuart Appleby (AUS)	71-75-73-71—290	91000
	David Howell (ENG)	71-71-76-72—290	91000
	Nick O'Hern (AUS)	71-72-76-71—290	91000
22	Robert Allenby (AUS)	73-73-74-71—291	67200
	Darren Clarke (NIR)	72-70-72-77—291	67200
	Jim Furyk	73-75-68-75—291	67200
	Mark Hensby (AUS)	80-67-70-74—291	67200
	Davis Love III	74-71-74-72—291	67200
27	Ernie Els (RSA)	71-71-74-76—292	49700
	Padraig Harrington (IRL)	73-70-75-74—292	49700
	Shingo Katayama (JPN)	75-70-73-74—292	49700
	Carl Pettersson (SWE)	72-74-73-73—292	49700
	Adam Scott (AUS)	72-74-75-71—292	49700
32	Thomas Bjørn (DEN)	73-75-76-69—293	40512
	Brandt Jobe	72-76-77-68—293	40512
	Zach Johnson	74-72-77-70—293	40512
	Ted Purdy	72-76-74-71—293	40512
36	Tim Herron	76-71-71-76—294	34416
	Rocco Mediate	68-73-73-80—294	34416
	Rory Sabbatini (RSA)	76-70-74-74—294	34416
39	Jason Bohn	73-71-77-74—295	30100
	Ben Curtis	71-74-77-73—295	30100
	Justin Leonard	75-70-79-71—295	30100
42	Rich Beem	71-73-73-79—296	25900
	Luke Donald (ENG)	74-72-76-74—296	25900
	Larry Mize	75-72-77-72—296	25900
45	Olin Browne	74-69-80-74—297	23100
46	Sergio García (ESP)	72-74-79-73—298	21700
47	Ben Crenshaw	71-72-78-79—300	20300

The following players missed the half-way cut. Each professional player received $5000:

Pos	Player	Score
48	Bart Bryant	76-73—149
	Michael Campbell (NZL)	75-74—149
	Ben Crane	74-75—149
	Thomas Levet (FRA)	78-71—149
	Colin Montgomerie (SCO)	74-75—149
	Vaughn Taylor	75-74—149
	Ian Woosnam (WAL)	77-72—149
55	Chris DiMarco	76-74—150
	Todd Hamilton	74-76—150
	Peter Lonard (AUS)	76-74—150
	David Toms	72-78—150
	Lee Westwood (ENG)	75-75—150
60	Lucas Glover	73-78—151
	Trevor Immelman (RSA)	75-76—151
60T	Tom Lehman	76-75—151
	Joe Ogilvie	74-77—151
	Henrik Stenson (SWE)	77-74—151
65	K J Choi (KOR)	76-76—152
	Raymond Floyd	79-73—152
	Shaun Micheel	82-70—152
	Sean O'Hair	76-76—152
69	John Daly	74-79—153
	Nick Faldo (ENG)	79-74—153
	Thongchai Jaidee (THA)	78-75—153
	Bernhard Langer (GER)	79-74—153
73	Shigeki Maruyama (JPN)	79-75—154
	Mark O'Meara	82-72—154
	Tom Watson	79-75—154
76	Brian McElhinney (IRL) (am)	80-75—155
	Paul McGinley (IRL)	78-77—155
	Craig Stadler	77-78—155
79	Mark Calcavecchia	80-76—156
80	Fred Funk	76-81—157
	Edoardo Molinari (ITA) (am)	80-77—157
82	David Duval	84-75—159
	Clay Ogden (am)	83-76—159
	Fuzzy Zoeller	78-81—159
85	Dillon Dougherty (am)	82-78—160
	Kevin Marsh (am)	79-81—160
	Gary Player (RSA)	79-81—160
88	Sandy Lyle (SCO)	80-81—161
89	Charles Coody	89-74—163
90	Charles Howell III	80-84—164

2005 Masters April 7–10

[7290–72]

Prize money: $7 million. Final field of 93 players, of whom 50 (including 2 amateurs) made the half-way cut.

Pos	Player	Score	Prize
1	Tiger Woods*	74-66-65-71—276	$1260000
2	Chris DiMarco	67-67-74-68—276	756000
	Play-off: Woods 3, DiMarco 4		
3	Luke Donald (ENG)	68-77-69-69—283	406000
	Retief Goosen (RSA)	71-75-70-67—283	406000
5	Mark Hensby (AUS)	69-73-70-72—284	237300
	Trevor Immelman (RSA)	73-73-65-73—284	237300
	Rodney Pampling (AUS)	73-71-70-70—284	237300
	Vijay Singh (FIJ)	68-73-71-72—284	237300
	Mike Weir (CAN)	74-71-68-71—284	237300
10	Phil Mickelson	70-72-69-74—285	189000
11	Tim Herron	76-68-70-72—286	168000
	David Howell (ENG)	72-69-76-69—286	168000
13	Tom Lehman	74-74-70-69—287	135333
	Justin Leonard	75-71-70-71—287	135333
	Thomas Levet (FRA)	71-75-68-73—287	135333
	Ryan Moore (am)	71-71-75-70—287	
17	Chad Campbell	73-73-67-75—288	112000
	Darren Clarke (NIR)	72-76-69-71—288	112000
	Kirk Triplett	75-68-72-73—288	112000
20	Stewart Cink	72-72-74-71—289	84840
	Jerry Kelly	75-70-73-71—289	84840
	Bernhard Langer (GER)	74-74-70-71—289	84840
	Jeff Maggert	74-74-72-69—289	84840
	Scott Verplank	72-75-69-73—289	84840
25	Thomas Bjørn (DEN)	71-67-71-81—290	61600
25T	Joe Ogilvie	74-73-73-70—290	61600
	Craig Parry (AUS)	72-75-69-74—290	61600
28	Jim Furyk	76-67-74-74—291	53900
29	Steve Flesch	76-70-70-76—292	50750
	Kenny Perry	76-68-71-77—292	50750
31	Miguel Angel Jiménez (ESP)	74-74-73-72—293	46550
	Mark O'Meara	72-74-72-75—293	46550
33	Choi Kyoung-Ju (KOR)	73-72-76-73—294	39620
	Shingo Katayama (JPN)	72-74-73-75—294	39620
	Luke List (am)	77-69-78-70—294	
	Ian Poulter (ENG)	72-74-72-76—294	39620
	Adam Scott (AUS)	71-76-72-75—294	39620
	Casey Wittenberg	72-72-74-76—294	39620
39	Tim Clark (RSA)	74-74-72-75—295	32200
	Fred Couples	75-71-77-72—295	32200
	Todd Hamilton	77-70-71-77—295	32200
	Ryan Palmer	70-74-74-77—295	32200
43	Stuart Appleby (AUS)	69-76-72-79—296	28000
	Jonathan Kaye	72-74-76-74—296	28000
45	Stephen Ames (CAN)	73-74-75-75—297	25200
	Nick O'Hern (AUS)	72-72-76-77—297	25200
47	Ernie Els (RSA)	75-73-78-72—298	23100
48	Jay Haas	76-71-76-78—301	21700
49	Chris Riley	71-77-78-78—304	20300
50	Craig Stadler	75-73-79-79—306	19180

Billy Payne takes over the running of The Masters

William Porter (Billy) Payne has taken over the Chairmanship of Augusta National Golf Club and The Masters tournament following the retirement of Hootie Johnson, who assumes the title of Chairman Emeritus. Johnson (75) oversaw significant changes to the course, initiated 18-hole television coverage and announced over $25 million in charitable contributions made by the tournament. Billy Payne (58), a native of Georgia, spearheaded the successful attempt to bring the Centennial Olympic Games to Atlanta.

Payne will be the Club and Masters sixth Chairman. Those who previously held the post are Clifford Roberts (1933–77), Bill Lane (1977–80), Hord Hardin (1980–81), Jack Stephens (1991–98) and Hootie Johnson (1998–2006).

2004 Masters April 8–11 [7290–72]

Prize money: $6,000,000. Entries: 93, of whom 44 (including two amateurs) made the half-way cut.

1	Phil Mickelson		72-69-69-69—279	$1170000	22T	Shaun Micheel	72-76-72-70—290	70200
2	Ernie Els (RSA)		70-72-71-67—280	702000		Justin Rose (ENG)	67-71-81-71—290	70200
3	Choi Kyung-Ju (KOR)		71-70-72-69—282	442000		Tiger Woods	75-69-75-71—290	70200
4	Sergio García (ESP)		72-72-75-66—285	286000	26	Alex Cejka (GER)	70-70-78-73—291	57200
	Bernhard Langer (GER)		71-73-69-72—285	286000	27	Mark O'Meara	73-70-75-74—292	51025
6	Paul Casey (ENG)		75-69-68-74—286	189893		Bob Tway	75-71-74-72—292	51025
	Fred Couples		73-69-74-70—286	189893	29	Scott Verplank	74-71-76-72—293	48100
	Chris DiMarco		69-73-68-76—286	189893	30	José María Olazábal	71-69-79-75—294	46150
	Davis Love III		75-67-74-70—286	189893		(ESP)		
	Nick Price (ZIM)		72-73-71-70—286	189893	31	Bob Estes	76-72-73-74—295	41275
	Vijay Singh (FIJ)		75-73-69-69—286	189893		Brad Faxon	72-76-76-71—295	41275
	Kirk Triplett		71-74-69-72—286	189893		Jerry Kelly	74-72-73-76—295	41275
13	Retief Goosen (RSA)		75-73-70-70—288	125667		Ian Poulter (ENG)	75-73-74-73—295	41275
	Padraig Harrington		74-74-68-72—288	125667	35	Justin Leonard	76-72-72-76—296	35913
	(IRL)					Phillip Price (WAL)	71-76-73-76—296	35913
	Charles Howell III		71-71-76-70—288	125667	37	Paul Lawrie (SCO)	77-70-73-77—297	32663
	Casey Wittenberg (am)		76-72-71-69—288			Sandy Lyle (SCO)	72-74-75-76—297	32663
17	Stewart Cink		74-73-69-73—289	97500	39	Eduardo Romero (ARG)	74-73-74-77—298	30550
	Steve Flesch		76-67-77-69—289	97500	40	Todd Hamilton	77-71-76-75—299	29250
	Jay Haas		69-75-72-73—289	97500	41	Tim Petrovic	72-75-75-78—300	27950
	Fredrik Jacobson (SWE)		74-74-67-74—289	97500		Brandt Snedeker (am)	73-75-75-77—300	
	Stephen Leaney (AUS)		76-71-73-69—289	97500	43	Jeff Sluman	73-70-82-77—302	26650
22	Stuart Appleby (AUS)		73-74-73-70—290	70200	44	Chris Riley	70-78-78-78—304	25350

2003 Masters April 10–13 [7290–72]

Prize money: $6,000,000. Entries: 93, of whom 49 (including three amateurs) made the half-way cut.

1	Mike Weir (CAN)*	70-68-75-68—281	$1080000	23T	Nick Price (ZIM)	70-75-72-76—293	57600
2	Len Mattiace	73-74-69-65—281	648000		Chris Riley	76-72-70-75—293	57600
*Play-off: Weir 4, Mattiace 6					Adam Scott (AUS)	77-72-74-70—293	57600
3	Phil Mickelson	73-70-72-68—283	408000	28	Darren Clarke (NIR)	66-76-78-74—294	43500
4	Jim Furyk	73-72-71-68—284	288000		Fred Couples	73-75-69-77—294	43500
5	Jeff Maggert	72-73-66-75—286	240000		Sergio García (ESP)	69-78-74-73—294	43500
6	Ernie Els (RSA)	79-66-72-70—287	208500		Charles Howell III	73-72-76-73—294	43500
	Vijay Singh (FIJ)	73-71-70-73—287	208500		Hunter Mahan (am)	73-72-73-76—294	
8	Jonathan Byrd	74-71-71-72—288	162000	33	Nick Faldo (ENG)	74-73-75-73—295	36375
	José María Olazábal	73-71-71-73—288	162000		Rocco Mediate	73-74-73-75—295	36375
	(ESP)				Loren Roberts	74-72-76-73—295	36375
	Mark O'Meara	76-71-70-71—288	162000		Kevin Sutherland	77-72-76-70—295	36375
	David Toms	71-73-70-74—288	162000	37	Shingo Katayama (JPN)	74-72-76-74—296	31650
	Scott Verplank	76-73-70-69—288	162000		Billy Mayfair	75-70-77-74—296	31650
13	Tim Clark (RSA)	72-75-71-71—289	120000	39	Robert Allenby (AUS)	76-73-74-74—297	27000
	Retief Goosen (RSA)	73-74-72-70—289	120000		Craig Parry (AUS)	74-73-75-75—297	27000
15	Rich Beem	74-72-71-73—290	93000		Kenny Perry	76-72-78-71—297	27000
	Angel Cabrera (ARG)	76-71-71-72—290	93000		Justin Rose (ENG)	73-76-71-77—297	27000
	Choi Kyoung-Ju (KOR)	76-69-72-73—290	93000		Phillip Tataurangi (NZL)	73-70-74-78—297	27000
	Paul Lawrie (SCO)	72-72-73-73—290	93000	44	Jeff Sluman	75-72-76-75—298	23400
	Davis Love III	77-71-71-71—290	93000	45	Ryan Moore (am)	73-74-75-79—301	
	Tiger Woods	76-73-66-75—290	93000		Pat Perez	74-73-79-75—301	22200
21	Ricky Barnes (am)	69-74-75-73—291		47	John Rollins	74-71-80-77—302	21000
22	Bob Estes	76-71-74-71—292	72000	48	Jerry Kelly	72-76-77-79—304	19800
23	Brad Faxon	73-71-79-70—293	57600	49	Craig Stadler	76-73-79-77—305	18600
	Scott McCarron	77-71-72-73—293	57600				

2002 Masters April 10–13   [7270–72]

Prize money: $5,600,000. Entries: 89, of whom two withdrew and 45 (with no amateurs) made the half-way cut.

1	Tiger Woods	70-69-66-71—276	$1008000	20T	Justin Leonard	70-75-74-70—289	65240
2	Retief Goosen (RSA)	69-67-69-74—279	604800		Nick Price (ZIM)	70-76-70-73—289	65240
3	Phil Mickelson	69-72-68-71—280	380800	24	Mark Brooks	74-72-71-73—290	46480
4	José María Olazábal	70-69-71-71—281	268800		Stewart Cink	74-70-72-74—290	46480
	(ESP)				Tom Pernice	74-72-71-73—290	46480
5	Ernie Els (RSA)	70-67-72-73—282	212800		Jeff Sluman	73-72-71-74—290	46480
	Padraig Harrington (IRL)	69-70-72-71—282	212800		Mike Weir (CAN)	72-71-71-76—290	46480
7	Vijay Singh (FIJ)	70-65-72-76—283	187600	29	Robert Allenby (AUS)	73-70-76-72—291	38080
8	Sergio García (ESP)	68-71-70-75—284	173600		Charles Howell III	74-73-71-73—291	38080
9	Angel Cabrera (ARG)	68-71-73-73—285	151200		Jesper Parnevik (SWE)	70-72-77-72—291	38080
	Miguel Angel Jiménez	70-71-74-70—285	151200	32	John Daly	74-73-70-75—292	32410
	(ESP)				Bernhard Langer (GER)	73-72-73-74—292	32410
	Adam Scott (AUS)	71-72-72-70—285	151200		Billy Mayfair	74-71-72-75—292	32410
12	Chris DiMarco	70-71-72-73—286	123200		Craig Stadler	73-72-76-71—292	32410
	Brad Faxon	71-75-69-71—286	123200	36	Fred Couples	73-73-76-72—294	26950
14	Nick Faldo (ENG)	75-67-73-72—287	98000		Rocco Mediate	75-68-77-74—294	26950
	Davis Love III	67-75-74-71—287	98000		Greg Norman (AUS)	71-76-72-75—294	26950
	Shigeki Maruyama	75-72-73-67—287	98000		David Toms	73-74-76-71—294	26950
	(JPN)			40	Steve Lowery	75-71-76-73—295	22960
	Colin Montgomerie	75-71-70-71—287	98000		Kirk Triplett	74-70-74-77—295	22960
	(SCO)				Tom Watson	71-76-76-72—295	22960
18	Thomas Bjørn (DEN)	74-67-70-77—288	81200	43	Scott Verplank	70-75-76-75—296	20720
	Paul McGinley (IRL)	72-74-71-71—288	81200	44	Lee Westwood (ENG)	75-72-74-76—297	19600
20	Darren Clarke (NIR)	70-74-73-72—289	65240	45	Bob Estes	73-72-75-78—298	18480
	Jerry Kelly	72-74-71-72—289	65240				

2001 Masters April 11–14   [6985–72]

Prize money: $5,574,920. Entries: 93, of whom 47 (with no amateurs) made the half-way cut.

1	Tiger Woods	70-66-68-68—272	$1008000	20T	Jeff Maggert	72-70-70-71—283	65240
2	David Duval	71-66-70-67—274	604800	24	Darren Clarke (NIR)	72-67-72-73—284	53760
3	Phil Mickelson	67-69-69-70—275	380800	25	Tom Scherrer	71-71-70-73—285	49280
4	Toshimitsu Izawa	71-66-74-67—278	246400	26	Fred Couples	74-71-73-68—286	44800
	(JPN)			27	Padraig Harrington	75-69-72-71—287	40600
	Mark Calcavecchia	72-66-68-72—278	246400		(IRL)		
6	Bernhard Langer	73-69-68-69—279	181300		Justin Leonard	73-71-72-71—287	40600
	(GER)				Mike Weir (CAN)	74-69-72-72—287	40600
	Jim Furyk	69-71-70-69—279	181300		Steve Jones	74-70-72-71—287	40600
	Ernie Els (RSA)	71-68-68-72—279	181300	31	Stuart Appleby	72-70-70-76—288	33208
	Kirk Triplett	68-70-70-71—279	181300		(AUS)		
10	Brad Faxon	73-68-68-71—280	128800		Mark Brooks	70-71-77-70—288	33208
	Steve Stricker	66-71-72-71—280	128800		Duffy Waldorf	72-70-71-75—288	33208
	Miguel Angel	68-72-71-69—280	128800		Lee Janzen	67-70-72-79—288	33208
	Jiménez (ESP)				David Toms	72-72-71-73—288	33208
	Angel Cabrera	66-71-70-73—280	128800	36	Hal Sutton	74-69-71-75—289	28840
	(ARG)			37	Loren Roberts	71-74-73-72—290	26320
	Chris DiMarco	65-69-72-74—280	128800		Chris Perry	68-74-74-74—290	26320
15	José María	70-68-71-72—281	95200		Scott Hoch	74-70-72-74—290	26320
	Olazábal (ESP)			40	Steve Lowery	72-72-78-70—292	22960
	Paul Azinger	70-71-71-69—281	95200		Shingo Katayama	75-70-73-74—292	22960
	Rocco Mediate	72-70-66-73—281	95200		(JPN)		
18	Vijay Singh (FIJ)	69-71-73-69—282	81200		Franklin Langham	72-73-75-72—292	22960
	Tom Lehman	75-68-71-68—282	81200	43	Dudley Hart	74-70-78-71—293	19600
20	Mark O'Meara	69-74-72-68—283	65240		Bob May	71-74-73-75—293	19600
	Jesper Parnevik	71-71-72-69—283	65240		Jonathan Kaye	74-71-74-74—293	19600
	(SWE)			46	Carlos Franco (PAR)	71-71-77-75—294	17360
	John Huston	67-75-72-69—283	65240	47	Robert Allenby (AUS)	71-74-75-75—295	16240

2000 Masters April 5–8 [6985–72]

Prize money: $4,617,000. Entries: 95, of whom 57 (with no amateurs) made the half-way cut.

1	Vijay Singh (FIJ)	72-67-70-69—278	$828000
2	Ernie Els (RSA)	72-67-74-68—281	496800
3	Loren Roberts	73-69-71-69—282	266800
	David Duval	73-65-74-70—282	266800
5	Tiger Woods	75-72-68-69—284	184000
6	Tom Lehman	69-72-75-69—285	165600
7	Davis Love III	75-72-68-71—286	143367
	Carlos Franco (PAR)	79-68-70-69—286	143367
	Phil Mickelson	71-68-76-71—286	143367
10	Hal Sutton	72-75-71-69—287	124200
11	Greg Norman (AUS)	80-68-70-70—288	105800
	Nick Price (ZIM)	74-69-73-72—288	105800
	Fred Couples	76-72-70-70—288	105800
14	Chris Perry	73-75-72-69—289	80500
	Jim Furyk	73-74-71-71—289	80500
	John Huston	77-69-72-71—289	80500
	Dennis Paulson	68-76-73-72—289	80500
18	Jeff Sluman	73-69-77-71—290	69000
19	Padraig Harrington (IRL)	76-69-75-71—291	53820
	Steve Stricker	70-73-75-73—291	53820
	Jean Van de Velde (FRA)	76-70-75-70—291	53820
	Colin Montgomerie (SCO)	76-69-77-69—291	53820
	Bob Estes	72-71-77-71—291	53820
	Glen Day	79-67-74-71—291	53820
25	Larry Mize	78-67-73-74—292	37567
	Craig Parry (AUS)	75-71-72-74—292	37567
	Steve Jones	71-70-76-75—292	37567
28	Nick Faldo (ENG)	72-72-74-75—293	28673
	Bernhard Langer (GER)	71-71-75-76—293	28673
28T	Justin Leonard	72-71-77-73—293	28673
	Stewart Cink	75-72-72-74—293	28673
	Mike Weir (CAN)	75-70-70-78—293	28673
	Dudley Hart	75-71-72-75—293	28673
	Paul Azinger	72-72-77-72—293	28673
	Masashi Ozaki (JPN)	72-72-74-75—293	28673
	Thomas Bjørn (DEN)	71-77-73-72—293	28673
37	Fred Funk	75-68-78-73—294	21620
	Jay Haas	75-71-75-73—294	21620
	Notah Begay III	74-74-73-73—294	21620
40	Ian Woosnam (WAL)	74-70-76-75—295	17480
	Sergio García (ESP)	70-72-75-78—295	17480
	Jesper Parnevik (SWE)	77-71-70-77—295	17480
	Darren Clarke (NIR)	72-71-78-74—295	17480
	Mark Brooks	72-76-73-74—295	17480
	Retief Goosen (RSA)	73-69-79-74—295	17480
46	Shigeki Maruyama (JPN)	76-71-74-75—296	13800
	Scott Gump	75-70-78-73—296	13800
48	Brandt Jobe	73-74-76-74—297	12604
49	Miguel Angel Jiménez (ESP)	76-71-79-72—298	11623
	Steve Pate	78-69-77-74—298	11623
	David Toms	74-72-73-79—298	11623
52	Steve Elkington (AUS)	74-74-78-73—299	10948
	Rocco Mediate	71-74-75-79—299	10948
54	Jack Nicklaus	74-70-81-78—303	10672
	David Gossett (am)	75-71-79-78—303	10672
56	Skip Kendall	76-72-77-83—308	10580
57	Tommy Aaron	72-74-86-81—313	10488

1999 Masters April 8–11 [6985–72]

Prize money: $3,200,000. Entries: 96, of whom 56 (including 4 amateurs) made the half-way cut.

1	JM Olazábal (ESP)	70-66-73-71—280	$720000
2	D Love III	69-72-70-71—282	432000
3	G Norman (AUS)	71-68-71-73—283	272000
4	B Estes	71-72-69-72—284	176000
	S Pate	71-75-65-73—284	176000
6	D Duval	71-74-70-70—285	125200
	C Franco (PAR)	72-72-68-73—285	125200
	P Mickelson	74-69-71-71—285	125200
	N Price (ZIM)	69-72-72-72—285	125200
	L Westwood (ENG)	75-71-68-71—285	125200
11	S Elkington (AUS)	72-70-71-74—287	92000
	B Langer (GER)	76-66-72-73—287	92000
	C Montgomerie (SCO)	70-72-71-74—287	92000
14	J Furyk	72-73-70-73—288	70000
	L Janzen	70-69-73-76—288	70000
	B Jobe	72-71-74-71—288	70000
	I Woosnam (WAL)	71-74-71-72—288	70000
18	B Chamblee	69-73-75-72—289	52160
	B Glasson	72-70-73-74—289	52160
	J Leonard	70-72-73-74—289	52160
	S McCarron	69-68-76-76—289	52160
	T Woods	72-72-70-75—289	52160
23	L Mize	76-70-72-72—290	41600
24	B Faxon	74-73-68-76—291	35200
	P-U Johansson (SWE)	75-72-71-73—291	35200
	V Singh (FIJ)	72-76-71-72—291	35200
27	S Cink	74-70-71-77—292	29000
	F Couples	74-71-76-71—292	29000
27T	E Els (RSA)	71-72-69-80—292	29000
	R Mediate	73-74-69-76—292	29000
31	T Lehman	73-72-73-75—293	23720
	S Maruyama (JPN)	78-70-71-74—293	23720
	M O'Meara	70-76-69-78—293	23720
	J Sluman	70-75-70-78—293	23720
	B Watts	73-73-70-77—293	23720
36	J Huston	74-72-71-77—294	20100
	A Magee	70-77-72-75—294	20100
38	B Andrade	76-72-72-75—295	18800
	M Brooks	76-72-75-72—295	18800
	R Floyd	74-73-72-76—295	18800
	C Stadler	72-76-70-77—295	18800
	S Stricker	75-72-69-79—295	18800
	S García (ESP) (am)	72-75-75-73—295	
44	J Haas	74-69-79-75—297	14000
	T Herron	75-69-74-79—297	14000
	S Hoch	75-73-70-79—297	14000
	T McKnight (am)	73-74-73-77—297	
48	S Lyle (SCO)	71-77-70-80—298	12000
	C Parry (AUS)	75-73-73-77—298	12000
50	C Perry	73-72-74-80—299	10960
	M Kuchar (am)	77-71-73-78—299	
52	O Browne	74-74-72-80—300	9980
	J Daly	72-76-71-81—300	9980
	P Stewart	73-75-77-75—300	9980
	B Tway	75-73-78-74—300	9980
56	T Immelman (RSA) (am)	72-76-78-79—305	

1998 Masters April 9–12 [6925–72]

Prize money: $3,200,000. Entries: 88, of whom 46 (incluing 2 amateurs) made the half-way cut.

Pos	Player	Scores	Money		Pos	Player	Scores	Money
1	M O'Meara	74-70-68-67—279	$576000		23T	J Huston	77-71-70-71—289	33280
2	D Duval	71-68-74-67—280	281600			J Maggert	72-73-72-72—289	33280
	F Couples	69-70-71-70—280	281600		26	D Frost (RSA)	72-73-74-71—290	26133
4	J Furyk	76-70-67-68—281	153600			S Jones	75-70-75-70—290	26133
5	P Azinger	71-72-69-70—282	128000			B Faxon	73-74-71-72—290	26133
6	J Nicklaus	73-72-70-68—283	111200		29	M Bradley	73-74-72-72—291	23680
	D Toms	75-72-72-64—283	111200		30	S Elkington (AUS)	75-75-71-71—292	22720
8	D Clarke (NIR)	76-73-67-69—285	89600		31	A Magee	74-72-74-73—293	21280
	J Leonard	74-73-69-69—285	89600			J Parnevik (SWE)	75-73-73-72—293	21280
	C Montgomerie (SCO)	71-75-69-70—285	89600		33	L Janzen	76-74-72-72—294	18112
	T Woods	71-72-72-70—285	89600			F Zoeller	71-74-75-74—294	18112
12	J Haas	72-71-71-72—286	64800			P Blackmar	71-78-75-70—294	18112
	P-U Johansson (SWE)	74-75-67-70—286	64800			J Daly	77-71-71-75—294	18112
	P Mickelson	74-69-69-74—286	64800			D Love III	74-75-67-78—294	18112
	JM Olazábal (ESP)	70-73-71-72—286	64800		38	T Kite	73-74-74-74—295	15680
16	M Calcavecchia	74-74-69-70—287	48000		39	B Langer (GER)	75-73-74-74—296	14720
	E Els (RSA)	75-70-70-72—287	48000			P Stankowski	70-80-72-74—296	14720
	S Hoch	70-71-73-73—287	48000		41	C Pavin	73-77-72-75—297	13440
	I Woosnam (WAL)	74-71-72-70—287	48000			C Stadler	79-68-73-77—297	13440
	S McCarron	73-71-72-71—287	48000		43	J Cook	75-73-74-76—298	12480
21	W Wood	74-74-70-70—288	38400		44	L Westwood (ENG)	74-76-72-78—300	11840
	M Kuchar (am)	72-76-68-72—288				J Kribel (am)	74-76-76-75—301	
23	S Cink	74-76-69-70—289	33280		46	G Player (RSA)	77-72-78-75—302	11200

1997 Masters April 10–13 [6925–72]

Prize money: $2,500,000. Entries: 86, of whom 46 (with no amateurs) made the half-way cut.

Pos	Player	Scores	Money		Pos	Player	Scores	Money
1	T Woods	70-66-65-69—270	$486000		24	N Price (ZIM)	71-71-75-74—291	24840
2	T Kite	77-69-66-70—282	291600			L Westwood (ENG)	77-71-73-70—291	24840
3	T Tolles	72-72-72-67—283	183600		26	L Janzen	72-73-74-73—292	21195
4	T Watson	75-68-69-72—284	129600			C Stadler	77-72-71-72—292	21195
5	C Rocca (ITA)	71-69-70-75—285	102600		28	P Azinger	69-73-77-74—293	19575
	P Stankowski	68-74-69-74—285	102600			J Furyk	74-75-72-72—293	19575
7	F Couples	72-69-73-72—286	78570		30	S McCarron	77-71-72-74—294	17145
	B Langer (GER)	72-72-74-68—286	78570			L Mize	79-69-74-72—294	17145
	J Leonard	76-69-71-70—286	78570			C Montgomerie (SCO)	72-67-74-81—294	17145
	D Love III	72-71-72-71—286	78570			M O'Meara	75-74-70-75—294	17145
	J Sluman	74-67-72-73—286	78570		34	A Lyle (SCO)	73-73-74-75—295	14918
12	S Elkington (AUS)	76-72-72-67—287	52920			F Zoeller	75-73-69-78—295	14918
	P-U Johansson (SWE)	72-73-73-69—287	52920		36	D Waldorf	74-75-72-75—296	13905
	T Lehman	73-76-69-69—287	52920		37	D Frost (SA)	74-71-73-79—297	13230
	JM Olazábal (ESP)	71-70-74-72—287	52920		38	S Hoch	79-68-73-78—298	12690
	W Wood	72-76-71-68—287	52920		39	J Nicklaus	77-70-74-78—299	11610
17	M Calcavecchia	74-73-72-69—288	39150			S Torrance (SCO)	75-73-73-78—299	11610
	E Els (RSA)	73-70-71-74—288	39150			I Woosnam (WAL)	77-68-75-79—299	11610
	F Funk	73-74-69-72—288	39150		42	M Ozaki (JPN)	74-74-74-78—300	10530
	V Singh (FIJ)	75-74-69-70—288	39150		43	C Pavin	75-74-78-74—301	9720
21	S Appleby (AUS)	72-76-70-71—289	30240			C Rose	73-75-79-74—301	9720
	J Huston	67-77-75-70—289	30240		45	B Crenshaw	75-73-74-80—302	8910
	J Parnevik (SWE)	73-72-71-73—289	30240		46	F Nobilo (NZL)	76-72-74-81—303	8370

The Masters History (players are of American nationality unless stated)

Date	Winner	Score
1934 Mar 22–25	H Smith	284
1935 Apr 4–8	G Sarazen*	282
After a play-off with Craig Wood: Sarazen 144, Wood 149		
1936 Apr 2–6	H Smith	285
1937 Apr 1–4	B Nelson	283
1938 Apr 1–4	H Picard	285
1939 Mar 30–Apr 2	R Guldahl	279
1940 Apr 4–7	J Demaret	280
1941 Apr 3–6	C Wood	280
1942 Apr 9–12	B Nelson*	280
After a play-off with Ben Hogan: Nelson 69, Hogan 70		
1946 Apr 4–7	H Keiser	282
1947 Apr 3–6	J Demaret	281
1948 Apr 8–11	C Harmon	279
1949 Apr 7–10	S Snead	283
1950 Apr 6–9	J Demaret	282
1951 Apr 5–8	B Hogan	280
1952 Apr 3–6	S Snead	286
1953 Apr 9–12	B Hogan	274
1954 Apr 8–12	S Snead*	289
After a play-off with Ben Hogan: Snead 69, Hogan 70		
1955 Apr 7–10	C Middlecoff	279
1956 Apr 5–8	J Burke	289
1957 Apr 4–7	D Ford	283
1958 Apr 3–6	A Palmer	284
1959 Apr 2–5	A Wall	284
1960 Apr 7–10	A Palmer	282
1961 Apr 6–10	G Player (RSA)	280
1962 Apr 5–9	A Palmer*	280
After a play-off with Gary Player and Dow Finsterwald: Palmer 68, Player 71, Finsterwald 77		
1963 Apr 4–10	J Nicklaus	286
1964 Apr 9–12	A Palmer	276
1965 Apr 8–11	J Nicklaus	271
1966 Apr 7–11	J Nicklaus*	288
After a play-off with Tommy Jacobs and Gay Brewer jr.: Nicklaus 70, Jacobs 72, Brewer jr. 78		
1967 Apr 6–9	G Brewer	280
1968 Apr 11–14	R Goalby	277
1969 Apr 10–13	G Archer	281
1970 Apr 9–13	W Casper*	279
After a play-off with Gene Littler: Casper 69, Littler 74		
1971 Apr 8–11	C Coody	279
1972 Apr 6–9	J Nicklaus	286

Date	Winner	Score
1973 Apr 5–9	T Aaron	283
1974 Apr 11–14	G Player (RSA)	278
1975 Apr 10–13	J Nicklaus	276
1976 Apr 8–11	R Floyd	271
1977 Apr 7–10	T Watson	276
1978 Apr 6–9	G Player (RSA)	277
1979 Apr 12–15	F Zoeller*	280
After a play-off with Ed Sneed and Tom Watson: Zoeller 4,3; Watson 4,4; Sneed 4,4		
1980 Apr 10–13	S Ballesteros (ESP)	275
1981 Apr 9–12	T Watson	280
1982 Apr 8–11	C Stadler*	284
After a play-off with Dan Pohl: Stadler 4, Pohl 5		
1983 Apr 7–11	S Ballesteros (ESP)	280
1984 Apr 12–15	B Crenshaw	277
1985 Apr 11–14	B Langer (GER)	282
1986 Apr 10–13	J Nicklaus	279
1987 Apr 9–12	L Mize*	285
After a play-off with Severiano Ballesteros and Greg Norman: Mize 4, 3; Norman 4, 4; Ballesteros 5		
1988 Apr 7–10	A Lyle (SCO)	281
1989 Apr 6–9	N Faldo (ENG)*	283
After a play-off with Scott: Faldo 5,3; Hoch 5, 4		
1990 Apr 5–8	N Faldo (ENG)*	278
After a play-off with Raymond Floyd: Faldo 4, 4; Floyd 4, 5		
1991 Apr 11–14	I Woosnam (WAL)	277
1992 Apr 9–12	F Couples	275
1993 Apr 8–11	B Langer (GER)	277
1994 Apr 7–10	JM Olazábal (ESP)	279
1995 Apr 6–9	B Crenshaw	274
1996 Apr 11–14	N Faldo (ENG)	276
1997 Apr 10–13	T Woods	270
1998 Apr 9–12	M O'Meara	279
1999 Apr 8–11	JM Olazábal (ESP)	280
2000 Apr 6–9	V Singh (FIJ)	278
2001 Apr 5–8	T Woods	272
2002 Apr 11–14	T Woods	276
2003 Apr 10–13	M Weir (CAN)*	281
After a play-off with Len Mattiace: Weir 4, Mattiace 6		
2004 Apr 8–11	P Mickelson	279
2005 Apr 7–10	T Woods*	276
After a play-off with Chris DiMarco: Woods 3, DiMarco 4		
2006 Apr 6–9	P Mickelson	281

US PGA Championship

World no.1 Woods closes in on Nicklaus' record with an almost flawless performance at Medinah

Thirty-year-old Tiger Woods continued his relentless march towards breaking Jack Nicklaus' 18 major professional titles record when he won his 12th at Medinah by taking his second US PGA Championship by a comfortable five shots. Woods finished with a four-under-par 68 for an 18-under-par 270 total which matched his winning score at Hoylake in The Open a few weeks earlier. Shaun Micheel, himself a former winner, finished second after British golfer Luke Donald, playing with Tiger on the last day, shot 74 and ended up tied third with Adam Scott of Australia and Sergio García of Spain.

With his win Tiger became the first player to win the PGA Championship twice at the same venue – he had won at Medinah in 1999 – and he edged ahead of Walter Hagen in the all-time majors titles league table. In addition, he joined Hagen and Nicklaus (who both won five US PGA's) and Gene Sarazen and Sam Snead as a three-time US PGA winner. Woods' other success had been at Valhalla in 2000.

Woods has now won his 12 majors when leading at the 54-hole stage each time. This was his third consecutive win on the PGA Tour (he would go on to win six in a row), his second straight major and his 51st career victory.

Woods, who opened with a four-under-par 68, moved on to the leader board on day two. He was tied with US Open champion Ogilvy and Davis Love III on seven-under-par but one ahead of that group were Tim Herron, Billy Andrade, Henrik Stenson and 28-year-old Donald who knew the course by having attended the North–Western University in Chicago.

With a round to go, Woods and Donald had grabbed the lead on 14-under-par, two clear of Canadian Mike Weir, a former Masters champion, with Ogilvy, Sergio García, Micheel and K J Choi in close attendance.

Woods blew away the opposition, however, with a dramatic start to the final round. He holed a 12 footer at the first to take over the lead on his own, made back-to-back birdies at the fifth and sixth and rolled in a 30 footer at the eighth to take a four shot lead over his new nearest challenger Weir. When he came out of deep rough at the 11th and holed from 12 feet he had moved to 19-under and had dropped only two shots to par all week. When he bogeyed the 17th, however, his chance of bettering his 19-under-par winning total at The Open at St Andrews in 2000 had gone. In 2000 he had dropped only three shots to par and he matched that at Medinah.

A delighted Micheel finished second but this was Tiger's week. "It took Jack over 20 years to get his 18 majors and I've just got to keep plugging along to keep trying to win these things," he said. "They are the most fun events to play in. I thoroughly enjoy coming down the stretch on the back nine with a chance to win. That, to me, is the ultimate rush in golf. That is why I practice as hard as I do and what I live for. I've still got a long way to go. Eighteen is a big number."

Maybe but he is ahead of Nicklaus in getting to 12 majors in both age and speed of collecting them and he has potentially another 40 plus majors to play in order to achieve his dream. In the end, Donald produced his best finish in a major taking third place, six behind Woods, on 12 under par tied with Adam Scott and García, who had chased Woods home in the same event at Medinah in 1999.

First Round	Second Round	Third Round	Fourth Round
–6 Glover	–8 Herron	–14 Donald	–18 Woods
–6 Riley	–8 Donald	–14 Woods	–13 Micheel
–5 Andrade	–8 Andrade	–12 Weir	–12 Donald
–4 Donald	–8 Stenson	–11 Ogilvy	–12 Scott
–4 Stenson	–7 Ogilvy	–10 García	–12 García
–4 Allenby	–7 Woods	–10 Micheel	–11 Weir
–4 Love III	–7 Love III	–9 Choi	–10 Stricker
–4 JJ Henry			–10 Choi
–4 Cink			

2006 US PGA Championship (88th) *Medinah, Illinois* August 16–20   [7561–72]

Prize money: $6.5 million. Entries: Final field of 156 players, of whom 70 made the half-way cut on 144 or less.

Players are of American nationality unless stated

1	Tiger Woods	69-68-65-68—270	$1224000
2	Shaun Micheel	69-70-67-69—275	734400
3	Luke Donald (ENG)	68-68-66-74—276	353600
	Sergio García (ESP)	69-70-67-70—276	353600
	Adam Scott (AUS)	71-69-69-67—276	353600
6	Mike Weir (CAN)	72-67-65-73—277	244800
7	K J Choi (KOR)	73-67-67-71—278	207787
	Steve Stricker	72-67-70-69—278	207787
9	Ryan Moore	71-72-67-69—279	165000
	Geoff Ogilvy (AUS)	69-68-68-74—279	165000
	Ian Poulter (ENG)	70-70-68-71—279	165000
12	Chris DiMarco	71-70-67-72—280	134500
	Sean O'Hair	72-70-70-68—280	134500
14	Tim Herron	69-67-72-73—281	115000
	Henrik Stenson (SWE)	68-68-73-72—281	115000
16	Woody Austin	71-69-69-73—282	94000
	Ernie Els (RSA)	71-70-72-69—282	94000
	Phil Mickelson	69-71-68-74—282	94000
	David Toms	71-67-71-73—282	94000
20	Robert Allenby (AUS)	68-74-71-70—283	71250
	Jonathan Byrd	69-72-74-68—283	71250
	Harrison Fraser	69-72-69-73—283	71250
	Fred Funk	69-69-74-71—283	71250
24	Chad Campbell	71-72-75-66—284	53100
	Stewart Cink	68-74-73-69—284	53100
	Tim Clark (RSA)	70-69-75-70—284	53100
	Steve Flesch	72-71-69-72—284	53100
	Anders Hansen (DEN)	72-71-70-71—284	53100
29	Jim Furyk	70-72-69-74—285	41100
	Robert Karlsson (SWE)	71-73-69-72—285	41100
	Heath Slocum	73-70-72-70—285	41100
	Lee Westwood (ENG)	69-72-71-73—285	41100
	Dean Wilson	74-70-74-67—285	41100
34	Retief Goosen (RSA)	70-73-68-75—286	34500
	Trevor Immelman (RSA)	73-71-70-72—286	34500
	Davis Love III	68-69-73-76—286	34500
37	Richard Green (AUS)	73-69-73-72—287	29250
	J B Holmes	71-70-68-78—287	29250
	Graeme McDowell (NIR)	75-68-72-72—287	29250
	Billy Mayfair	69-69-73-76—287	29250
41	Billy Andrade	67-69-78-74—288	23080
	Daniel Chopra (SWE)	72-67-76-73—288	23080
	J J Henry	68-73-73-74—288	23080
	Chris Riley	66-72-73-77—288	23080
	Justin Rose (ENG)	73-70-70-75—288	23080
46	Olin Browne	75-66-73-75—289	19025
	Lucas Glover	66-74-77-72—289	19025
48	Jerry Kelly	70-74-74-72—290	17300
49	Rich Beem	75-69-72-75—291	15533
	Nathan Green (AUS)	71-71-74-75—291	15533
	Ryan Palmer	70-73-72-76—291	15533
	Corey Pavin	72-71-72-76—291	15533
	Kenny Perry	72-71-71-77—291	15533
	Joey Sindelar	74-70-73-74—291	15533
55	Stephen Ames (CAN)	74-69-74-75—292	14320
	Stuart Appleby (AUS)	70-73-79-70—292	14320

55T	Aaron Baddeley (AUS)	70-74-75-73—292	14320
	José-María Olazábal (ESP)	72-68-75-77—292	14320
	Hideto Tanihara (JPN)	73-71-78-70—292	14320
60	Ben Curtis	72-72-73-76—293	13750
	Steve Lowery	70-72-76-75—293	13750
62	Jason Gore	70-73-75-77—295	13425
	Jeff Maggert	75-68-78-74—295	13425
	Charles Warren	73-70-77-75—295	13425
65	Miguel Angel Jiménez (ESP)	70-73-75-78—296	13175
	Bob Tway	72-71-75-78—296	13175
67	David Howell (ENG)	71-71-73-82—297	13025
68	Jay Haas	75-68-74-83—300	12875
	Don Yrene	71-72-77-80—300	12875
70	Jim Kane	71-71-80-79—301	12725

The following players missed the half-way cut. Each player received $2000:

71	Angel Cabrera (ARG)	74-71—145
	Chris Couch	74-71—145
	David Duval	73-72—145
	Charles Howell III	70-75—145
	Zach Johnson	71-74—145
	Arron Oberholser	75-70—145
	Greg Owen (ENG)	74-71—145
	Brett Quigley	76-69—145
	Rory Sabbatini (RSA)	72-73—145
	Charles Schwartzel (RSA)	72-73—145
	Vijay Singh (FIJ)	73-72—145
	Mike Small	72-73—145
	Anthony Wall (ENG)	73-72—145
84	Bart Bryant	72-74—146
	Andrew Buckle (AUS)	73-73—146
	Michael Campbell (NZL)	70-76—146
	John Daly	71-75—146
	Bob Estes	74-72—146
	Brad Faxon	70-76—146
	Robert Gamez	70-76—146
	Brandt Jobe	76-70—146
	Justin Leonard	75-71—146
	Shigeki Maruyama (JPN)	76-70—146
	Jesper Parnevik (SWE)	71-75—146
	Pat Perez	73-73—146
	John Rollins	73-73—146
	Wes Short jr	72-74—146
	Craig Thomas	76-70—146
	Camilo Villegas (COL)	75-71—146

100	Paul Azinger	74-73—147
	John Bickerton (ENG)	73-74—147
	Paul Casey (ENG)	74-73—147
	Fred Couples	71-76—147
	Nick O'Hern (AUS)	74-73—147
	Rod Pampling (AUS)	71-76—147
	Lee Rinker	72-75—147
	John Senden (AUS)	75-72—147
	Jeff Sluman	74-73—147
109	Craig Barlow	70-78—148
	Gregory Bisconti	70-78—148
	Mark Brooks	73-75—148
	Stephen Dodd (WAL)	73-75—148
	Bradley Dredge (WAL)	75-73—148
	Niclas Fasth (SWE)	74-74—148
	Kenneth Ferrie (ENG)	70-78—148
	Tom Lehman	77-71—148
	Peter Lonard (AUS)	70-78—148
	Colin Montgomerie (SCO)	77-71—148
	Carl Pettersson (SWE)	72-76—148
	Nick Price (ZIM)	75-73—148
	Ted Purdy	73-75—148
	Andres Romero (ARG)	71-77—148
	Scott Verplank	72-76—148
124	Ben Crane	72-77—149
	Johan Edfors (SWE)	76-73—149
	Padraig Harrington (IRL)	75-74—149
	Vaughn Taylor	71-78—149

124T	Chris Wiemers	73-76—149
129	Thomas Bjørn (DEN)	80-70—150
	Jason Bohn	77-73—150
	Paul Broadhurst (ENG)	74-76—150
	Gonzalo Fernandez-Castaño (ESP)	75-75—150
	Kelly Mitchum	71-79—150
134	John Aber	78-73—151
	Simon Khan (ENG)	74-77—151
	Bernhard Langer (GER)	76-75—151
	Steve Schneiter (CAN)	72-79—151
	Chip Sullivan	79-72—151
	Tim Weinhart	77-74—151
140	Jeff Crabford	77-75—152
	Nick Dougherty (ENG)	80-72—152
	Larry Nelson	80-72—152
	Alan Schulte	75-77—152
144	Jerry Haas	74-79—153
	Todd Hamilton	77-76—153
	S K Ho (KOR)	74-79—153
	Tom Pernice jr	77-76—153
	Kirk Triplett	75-78—153
	Brett Wetterich	76-77—153
150	Richard S Johnson (SWE)	79-76—155
	Ron Philo jr	82-73—155
152	Mark Brown	80-77—157
153	Barry Evans	81-79—160
154	Sam Arnold	78-84—162
	Mark Calcavecchia	77 WD
	Dudley Hart	78 WD

Europeans among those who set course records in America

60 (-11)	Justin Rose (ENG)	Palm Course, Walt Disney World	1st rd, Funai Classic
61 (-10)	Vijay Singh (FIJ)	TPC of Boston	3rd rd, Deutsche Bank C/ship
61 (-9)	David Toms	Waialae CC	3rd rd, Sony Open
62 (-10)	Jesper Parnevik (SWE)	Classic Club	4th rd, Bob Hope Chrysler
63 (-9)	Michael Allen	Atunyote GC	2nd rd, BC Open
63 (-8)	Tiger Woods	The Grove	1st rd, WGC – AmEx C/ship
65 (-7)	Chris Dimarco	Hoylake	2nd rd, The Open
63 (-7)	Jim Furyk	Hamilton G & CC	1st rd, Canadian Open
65 (-7)	Greg Owen (ENG)	Redstone GC	Shell Houston Open

Phil Mickelson set a new tournament record at the BellSouth Classic with a 28-under-par 260

2005 US PGA Championship Baltusrol, NJ August 11–15   [7392–70]

Prize money: $6,250,000. Entries: Final field of 156, of whom 79 made the half-way cut.

1	Phil Mickelson	67-65-72-72—276	$1170000
2	Thomas Bjørn (DEN)	71-71-63-72—277	572000
	Steve Elkington (AUS)	68-70-68-71—277	572000
4	Davis Love III	68-68-68-74—278	286000
	Tiger Woods	75-69-66-68—278	286000
6	Michael Campbell (NZL)	73-68-69-69—279	201500
	Retief Goosen (RSA)	68-70-69-72—279	201500
	Geoff Ogilvy (AUS)	69-69-72-69—279	201500
	Pat Perez	68-71-67-73—279	201500
10	Steve Flesch	70-71-69-70—280	131800
	Dudley Hart	70-73-66-71—280	131800
	Ted Purdy	69-75-70-66—280	131800
	Vijay Singh (FIJ)	70-67-69-74—280	131800
	David Toms	71-72-69-68—280	131800
15	Stuart Appleby (AUS)	67-70-69-75—281	102500
	Charles Howell III	70-71-68-72—281	102500
17	Tim Clark (RSA)	71-73-70-68—282	82500
	Trevor Immelman (RSA)	67-72-72-71—282	82500
	Jack Johnson	70-70-73-69—282	82500
	Joe Ogilvie	74-68-69-71—282	82500
	Bo Van Pelt	70-70-68-74—282	82500
	Lee Westwood (ENG)	68-68-71-75—282	82500
23	Sergio García (ESP)	72-70-71-70—283	56400
23T	Shingo Katayama (JPN)	71-66-74-72—283	56400
	Paul McGinley (IRL)	72-70-72-69—283	56400
	Tom Pernice jr	69-73-69-72—283	56400
	Kenny Perry	69-70-70-74—283	56400
28	Chad Campbell	71-71-70-72—284	41500
	Stewart Cink	71-72-66-75—284	41500
	Bob Estes	71-72-73-68—284	41500
	Arron Oberholser	74-68-69-73—284	41500
	Jesper Parnevik (SWE)	68-69-72-75—284	41500
	Vaughn Taylor	75-69-71-69—284	41500
34	Jason Bohn	71-68-68-78—285	31917
	Ben Curtis	67-73-67-78—285	31917
	Jim Furyk	72-71-69-73—285	31917
	Fredrik Jacobson (SWE)	72-69-73-71—285	31917
	Jerry Kelly	70-65-74-76—285	31917
	Scott Verplank	71-72-71-71—285	31917
40	K J Choi (KOR)	71-70-73-72—286	22300
	Ben Crane	68-76-72-70—286	22300
	Miguel Angel Jiménez (ESP)	72-72-69-73—286	22300
	John Rollins	68-71-73-74—286	22300
	Steve Schneiter (CAN)	72-72-72-70—286	22300
	Adam Scott (AUS)	74-69-72-71—286	22300
	Patrick Sheehan	73-71-71-71—286	22300

Other players who made the cut: Fred Funk, Todd Hamilton, Bernhard Langer (GER), JL Lewis, José María Olazábal (ESP), Greg Owen (ENG), Ryan Palmer, Ian Poulter (ENG), Heath Slocum, Henrik Stenson (SWE), Mike Wier (CAN), Yong-Eun Yang (KOR) 287; Paul Casey (ENG), Carlos Franco (PAR), Peter Hanson (SWE), Mark Hensby (AUS), Scott McCarron, Sean O'Hair, Steve Webster (ENG) 288; Woody Austin, Luke Donald (ENG), Ron Philo jr, Chris Riley 289; Mark Calcavecchia, Fred Couples 290; Stephen Ames (CAN), Joe Durant 291; John Daly, Rory Sabbatini (RSA) 292; Mike Small 295; Kevin Sutherland 296; Darrell Kestner 299; Hal Sutton 300.

2004 US PGA Championship Whistling Straits, Kohler, WI August 12–15   [7514–72]

Prize money: $6,250,000. Entries: Final field of 155, of whom 73 made the half-way cut.

1	Vijay Singh (FIJ)*	67-68-69-76—280	$1125000
2	Justin Leonard	66-69-70-75—280	550000
	Chris DiMarco	68-70-71-71—280	550000
*Three hole play-off: Singh 3-3-4; Leonard 4-3-4; DiMarco 4-3-4			
4	Ernie Els (RSA)	66-70-72-73—281	267500
	Chris Riley	69-70-69-73—281	267500
6	Choi Kyoung-Ju (KOR)	68-71-73-70—282	196000
	Paul McGinley (IRL)	69-74-70-69—282	196000
	Phil Mickelson	69-72-67-74—282	196000
9	Robert Allenby (AUS)	71-70-72-70—283	152000
	Stephen Ames (CAN)	68-71-69-75—283	152000
	Ben Crane	70-74-69-70—283	152000
	Adam Scott (AUS)	71-71-69-72—283	152000
13	Darren Clarke (NIR)	65-71-72-76—284	110250
	Brian Davis (ENG)	70-71-69-74—284	110250
	Brad Faxon	71-71-70-72—284	110250
	Arron Oberholser	73-71-70-70—284	110250
17	Stuart Appleby (AUS)	68-75-72-70—285	76857
	Stewart Cink	73-70-70-72—285	76857
	Matt Gogel	71-71-69-74—285	76857
	Fredrik Jacobson (SWE)	72-70-70-73—285	76857
	Jean-François Remesy (FRA)	72-71-70-72—285	76857
	Loren Roberts	68-72-70-75—285	76857
17T	David Toms	72-72-69-72—285	76857
24	Tom Byrum	72-73-71-70—286	46714
	Chad Campbell	73-70-71-72—286	46714
	Luke Donald (ENG)	67-73-71-75—286	46714
	JL Lewis	73-69-72-72—286	46714
	Shaun Micheel	77-68-70-71—286	46714
	Geoff Ogilvy (AUS)	68-73-71-74—286	46714
	Tiger Woods	75-69-69-73—286	46714
31	Carlos Daniel Franco (PAR)	69-75-72-71—287	34250
	Charles Howell III	70-71-72-74—287	34250
	Miguel Angel Jiménez (ESP)	76-65-75-71—287	34250
	Nick O'Hern (AUS)	73-71-68-75—287	34250
	Chip Sullivan	72-71-73-71—287	34250
	Bo Van Pelt	74-71-70-72—287	34250
37	Briny Baird	67-69-75-77—288	24687
	Steve Flesch	73-72-67-76—288	24687
	Jay Haas	68-72-71-77—288	24687
	Todd Hamilton	72-73-75-68—288	24687
	Trevor Immelman (RSA)	75-70-69-72—288	24687
	Zach Johnson	75-70-69-74—288	24687
	Ian Poulter (ENG)	73-72-70-73—288	24687
	Brett Quigley	74-69-73-72—288	24687

Other players who made the cut: Tommy Armour III, Niclas Fasth (SWE), Padraig Harrington (IRL), David Howell (ENG) 289; Michael Campbell (NZL), Nick Faldo (ENG), Joe Ogilvie, Patrick Sheehan, Duffy Waldorf 290; Carl Pettersson (SWE) 291; Paul Azinger, S K Ho (KOR), Rod Pampling (AUS), Craig Parry (AUS), Eduardo Romero (ARG), Hidemichi Tanaka (JPN), Bob Tway 292; Woody Austin, Shingo Katayama (JPN), Jeff Sluman, Scott Verplank 293; Scott Drummond (SCO), Bernhard Langer (GER) 294; Robert Gamez, Mark Hensby (AUS) 296; Colin Montgomerie (SCO) 297; Roy Biancalana 299; Jeff Coston 301; Skip Kendall 304.

2003 US PGA Championship Oak Hill CC, Rochester, NY August 14–17 [7134–70]

Prize money: $6,000,000. Entries: Final field of 156, of whom 70 made the half-way cut.

1	Shaun Micheel	69-68-69-70—276	$1080000	23T	Luke Donald (ENG)	73-72-71-72—288	52000
2	Chad Campbell	69-72-65-72—278	648000		Phil Mickelson	66-75-72-75—288	52000
3	Tim Clark (RSA)	72-70-68-69—279	408000		Adam Scott (AUS)	72-69-72-75—288	52000
4	Alex Cejka (GER)	74-69-68-69—280	288000	27	Woody Austin	72-73-69-75—289	43000
5	Ernie Els (RSA)	71-70-70-71—282	214000		Geoff Ogilvy (AUS)	71-71-77-70—289	43000
	Jay Haas	70-74-69-69—282	214000	29	Todd Hamilton	70-74-73-73—290	36600
7	Fred Funk	69-73-70-72—284	175667		Padraig Harrington		
	Loren Roberts	70-73-70-71—284	175667		(IRL)	72-76-69-73—290	36600
	Mike Weir (CAN)	68-71-70-75—284	175667		Frank Lickliter II	71-72-71-76—290	36600
10	Billy Andrade	67-72-72-74—285	135500		Peter Lonard (AUS)	74-74-69-73—290	36600
	Niclas Fasth (SWE)	76-70-71-68—285	135500		David Toms	75-72-71-72—290	36600
	Charles Howell III	70-72-70-73—285	135500	34	Fred Couples	74-71-72-74—291	29000
	Kenny Perry	75-72-70-68—285	135500		Lee Janzen	68-74-72-77—291	29000
14	Robert Gamez	70-73-70-73—286	98250		JL Lewis	71-75-71-74—291	29000
	Tim Herron	69-72-74-71—286	98250		Jesper Parnevik (SWE)	73-72-72-74—291	29000
	Scott McCarron	74-70-71-71—286	98250		Vijay Singh (FIJ)	69-73-70-79—291	29000
	Rod Pampling (AUS)	66-74-73-73—286	98250	39	Robert Allenby (AUS)	70-77-73-72—292	22000
18	Carlos Franco (PAR)	73-73-69-72—287	73000		Briny Baird	73-71-67-81—292	22000
	Jim Furyk	72-74-69-72—287	73000		Mark Calcavecchia	73-71-76-72—292	22000
	Toshimitsu Izawa (JPN)	71-72-71-73—287	73000		Joe Durant	71-76-75-70—292	22000
	Rocco Mediate	72-74-71-70—287	73000		Hal Sutton	75-71-67-79—292	22000
	Kevin Sutherland	69-74-71-73—287	73000		Tiger Woods	74-72-73-73—292	22000
23	Stuart Appleby (AUS)	74-73-71-70—288	52000				

Other players who made the cut: Angel Cabrera (ARG), Tom Pernice jr, Duffy Waldorf 293; Ben Crane, Trevor Immelman (RSA), Shigeki Maruyama (JPN) 294; José Coceres (ARG), Gary Evans (ENG), Brian Gay, Len Mattiace, José María Olazábal (ESP), 295; Chris DiMarco 296; Aaron Baddeley (AUS), Bob Estes, Scott Hoch, Bernhard Langer (GER) 297; Jonathan Kaye, Billy Mayfair, Ian Poulter (ENG), Eduardo Romero (ARG), Philip Tataurangi (NZL) 298; Paul Casey (ENG) 299; Bob Burns 300; Rory Sabbatini (RSA) 302; Michael Campbell (NZL), Choi Kyoung-Ju (KOR) 304.

2002 US PGA Championship Hazeltine National, Chaska, MN August 15–18 [7360–72]

Prize money: $5,500,000. Entries: Final field of 156 (one amateur), of whom 72 made the half-way cut.

1	Rich Beem	72-66-72-68—278	$990000	22	Heath Slocum	73-74-75-69—291	57000
2	Tiger Woods	71-69-72-67—279	594000	23	Michael Campbell (NZL)	73-70-77-72—292	44250
3	Chris Riley	71-70-72-70—283	374000		Retief Goosen (RSA)	69-69-79-75—292	44250
4	Fred Funk	68-70-73-73—284	235000		Bernhard Langer (GER)	70-72-77-73—292	44250
	Justin Leonard	72-66-69-77—284	235000		Justin Rose (ENG)	69-73-76-74—292	44250
6	Rocco Mediate	72-73-70-70—285	185000		Adam Scott (AUS)	71-71-76-74—292	44250
7	Mark Calcavecchia	70-68-74-74—286	172000		Jeff Sluman	70-75-74-73—292	44250
8	Vijay Singh (FIJ)	71-74-74-68—287	159000	29	Brad Faxon	74-72-75-72—293	33500
9	Jim Furyk	68-73-76-71—288	149000		Tom Lehman	71-72-77-73—293	33500
10	Robert Allenby (AUS)	76-66-77-70—289	110714		Craig Perks (NZL)	72-76-74-71—293	33500
	Stewart Cink	74-74-72-69—289	110714		Kenny Perry	73-68-78-74—293	33500
	José Coceres (ARG)	72-71-72-74—289	110714		Kirk Triplett	75-69-79-70—293	33500
	Pierre Fulke (SWE)	72-68-78-71—289	110714	34	David Duval	71-77-76-70—294	26300
	Sergio García (ESP)	75-73-73-68—289	110714		Ernie Els (RSA)	72-71-75-76—294	26300
	Ricardo Gonzalez (ARG)	74-73-71-71—289	110714		Neal Lancaster	72-73-75-74—294	26300
	Steve Lowery	71-71-73-74—289	110714		Phil Mickelson	76-71-78-68—294	26300
17	Stuart Appleby (AUS)	73-74-74-69—290	72000		Mike Weir (CAN)	73-74-77-70—294	26300
	Steve Flesch	72-74-73-71—290	72000	39	Chris DiMarco	76-69-77-73—295	21500
	Padraig Harrington (IRL)	71-73-74-72—290	72000		Joel Edwards	73-74-77-71—295	21500
	Charles Howell III	72-69-80-69—290	72000		John Huston	74-74-75-72—295	21500
	Peter Lonard (AUS)	69-73-75-73—290	72000		Scott McCarron	73-71-79-72—295	21500

Other players who made the cut: Briny Baird, Søren Hansen (DEN), Shigeki Maruyama (JPN), Loren Roberts, Kevin Sutherland 296; Angel Cabrera (ARG), Steve Elkington (AUS), Davis Love III, Len Mattiace, Tom Watson 297; Cameron Beckman, Tim Clark (RSA), Brian Gay, Toshimitsu Izawa (JPN), Lee Janzen, Greg Norman (AUS), Chris Smith 298; Joe Durant, Nick Faldo (ENG), Hal Sutton 299; JJ Henry 301; Don Berry, Matt Gogel, JP Hayes, Joey Sindelar 302; Dave Tentis 304; José María Olazábal (ESP) 305; Pat Perez 309; Thomas Levet (FRA) 310; Stephen Ames (TRI) W/D

2001 US PGA Championship Atlanta Athletic Club, Duluth, GA August 16–19   [7213–70]

Prize money: $5,205,049. Entries: Final field of 150, of whom 76 made the half-way cut.

1	David Toms	66-65-65-69—265	$936000	16T	Chris DiMarco	68-67-71-71—277	70666
2	Phil Mickelson	66-66-66-68—266	562000	22	Mark O'Meara	72-63-70-73—278	44285
3	Steve Lowery	67-67-66-68—268	354000		Shigeki Maruyama	68-72-71-67—278	44285
4	Mark Calcavecchia	71-68-66-65—270	222500		(JPN)		
	Shingo Katayama (JPN)	67-64-69-70—270	222500		Paul Azinger	68-67-69-74—278	44285
6	Billy Andrade	68-70-68-66—272	175000		Paul McGinley (IRL)	68-72-71-67—278	44285
7	Jim Furyk	70-64-71-69—274	152333		Briny Baird	70-69-72-67—278	44285
	Scott Verplank	69-68-70-67—274	152333		J Brian Gay	70-68-69-71—278	44285
	Scott Hoch	68-70-69-67—274	152333		Charles Howell III	71-67-69-71—278	44285
10	David Duval	66-68-67-74—275	122000	29	Greg Norman (AUS)	70-68-71-70—279	29437
	Justin Leonard	70-69-67-69—275	122000		Tiger Woods	73-67-69-70—279	29437
	Kirk Triplett	68-70-71-66—275	122000		Nick Price (ZIM)	71-67-71-70—279	29437
13	Steve Flesch	73-67-70-66—276	94666		Choi Kyung-ju (KOR)	66-68-72-73—279	29437
	Jesper Parnevik (SWE)	70-68-70-68—276	94666		Bob Tway	69-69-71-70—279	29437
	Ernie Els (RSA)	67-67-70-72—276	94666		Carlos Franco (PAR)	67-72-71-69—279	29437
16	Stuart Appleby (AUS)	66-70-68-73—277	70666		Niclas Fasth (SWE)	66-69-72-72—279	29437
	Mike Weir (CAN)	69-72-66-70—277	70666		Christopher Smith	69-71-68-71—279	29437
	Dudley Hart	66-68-73-70—277	70666		José María Olazábal	70-70-68-71—279	29437
	José Coceres (ARG)	69-68-73-67—277	70666		(ESP)		
	Robert Allenby (AUS)	69-67-73-68—277	70666				

Other players who made the cut: Fred Couples, Davis Love III, Bob Estes, Angel Cabrera (ARG), Andrew Coltart (SCO), Retief Goosen (RSA) 280; Andrew Oldcorn (SCO), Greg Chalmers (AUS), Jerry Kelly, Hal Sutton, Kenny Perry, Lee Westwood (ENG), Rick Schuller 281; Nick Faldo (ENG), Ian Woosnam (WAL), Joe Durant, Vijay Singh (FIJ), Scott Dunlap, Tom Pernice, Chris Riley, Frank Lickliter 282; Brad Faxon, Stewart Cink, Phillip Price (WAL), Grant Waite (NZL) 283; Skip Kendall, Thomas Bjørn (DEN), Jonathan Kaye, Rocco Mediate 284; Tom Watson, Steve Stricker, Robert Damron 285; Fred Funk, Scott McCarron 286; John Huston 287; Bob May 291; Paul Stankowski 293; Steve Pate 294; Colin Montgomerie (SCO) DQ

2000 US PGA Championship Valhalla GC, Louisville, KY August 17–20   [7167–72]

Prize money: $5,000,000. Entries: Final field of 150, of whom 80 made the half-way cut.

1	Tiger Woods*	66-67-70-67—270	$900000	19T	JP Hayes	69-68-68-86—281	56200
2	Bob May	72-66-66-66—270	540000		Angel Cabrera (ARG)	72-71-71-67—281	56200
*After a three hole play-off: Woods 3-4-5-12; May 4-4-5-13					Robert Allenby (AUS)	73-71-68-69—281	56200
3	Thomas Bjørn (DEN)	72-68-67-68—275	340000		Lee Janzen	76-70-70-65—281	56200
4	Greg Chalmers (AUS)	71-69-66-70—276	198667	24	Paul Azinger	72-71-66-73—282	41000
	José María Olazábal				Steve Jones	72-71-70-69—282	41000
	(ESP)	76-68-63-69—276	198667		Jarmo Sandelin (SWE)	74-72-68-68—282	41000
	Stuart Appleby (AUS)	70-69-68-69—276	198667	27	Brad Faxon	71-74-70-68—283	34167
7	Franklin Langham	72-71-65-69—277	157000		Skip Kendall	72-72-69-70—283	34167
8	Notah Begay III	72-66-70-70—278	145000		Tom Pernice	74-69-70-70—283	34167
9	Tom Watson	76-70-65-68—279	112500	30	Mike Weir (CAN)	76-69-68-71—284	28875
	Fred Funk	69-68-74-68—279	112500		Jean Van de Velde	70-74-69-71—284	28875
	Davis Love III	68-69-72-70—279	112500		(FRA)		
	Darren Clarke (NIR)	68-72-72-67—279	112500		Stephen Ames (TRI)	69-71-71-73—284	28875
	Scott Dunlap	66-68-70-75—279	112500		Kenny Perry	78-68-70-68—284	28875
	Phil Mickelson	70-70-69-70—279	112500	34	Sergio García (ESP)	74-69-73-69—285	24000
15	Stewart Cink	72-71-70-67—280	77500		Chris Perry	72-74-70-69—285	24000
	Lee Westwood (ENG)	72-72-69-67—280	77500		Mark Calcavecchia	73-74-71-67—285	24000
	Chris DiMarco	73-70-69-68—280	77500		Ernie Els (RSA)	74-68-72-71—285	24000
	Michael Clark II	73-70-67-70—280	77500		Blaine McCallister	73-71-70-71—285	24000
19	Tom Kite	70-72-69-70—281	56200				

Other players who made the cut: Toshimitsu Izawa (JPN), Colin Montgomerie (SCO) 286; Jeff Sluman, Justin Leonard, Paul Stankowski, Steve Pate, David Toms 287; Bernhard Langer (GER), Mark O'Meara, Shigeki Maruyama (JPN), Duffy Waldorf, Brian Henninger 288; Nick Faldo (ENG), Jesper Parnevik (SWE), Steve Lowery, Brian Watts, Glen Day, Andrew Coltart (SCO), Jonathan Kaye 289; Padraig Harrington (IRL), Loren Roberts, Curtis Strange, Carlos Franco (PAR), Dennis Paulson, Joe Ogilvie 290; Wayne Grady (AUS), Craig Stadler, Bill Glasson, Miguel Angel Jiménez (ESP), Jay Haas 291; Greg Kraft, Kirk Triplett 292; John Huston 293; Jim Furyk, Paul Lawrie (SCO) 294; Robert Damron, Billy Mayfair, Scott Hoch 297; Masashi Ozaki (JPN), Rory Sabbatini 299; Hidemichi Tanaka (JPN) 301; Frank Dobbs 313

1999 US PGA Championship *Medinah, IL* August 12–15   [7401–72]
Prize money: $3,000,000. Entries: Final field of 149, of whom 74 made the half-way cut.

1	T Woods	70-67-68-72—277	$630000	21	D Frost (RSA)	75-68-74-71—288	33200
2	S García (ESP)	66-73-68-71—278	378000		S Hoch	71-71-75-71—288	33200
3	S Cink	69-70-68-73—280	203000		S Kendall	74-65-71-78—288	33200
	J Haas	68-67-75-70—280	203000		JL Lewis	73-70-74-71—288	33200
5	N Price (ZIM)	70-71-69-71—281	129000		K Wentworth	72-70-72-74—288	33200
6	B Estes	71-70-72-69—282	112000	26	F Couples	73-69-75-72—289	24000
	C Montgomerie (SCO)	72-70-70-70—282	112000		C Franco (PAR)	72-71-71-75—289	24000
8	J Furyk	71-70-69-74—284	96500		J Kelly	69-74-71-75—289	24000
	S Pate	72-70-73-69—284	96500		H Sutton	72-73-73-71—289	24000
10	D Duval	70-71-72-72—285	72166		J Van de Velde (FRA)	74-70-75-70—289	24000
	MA Jiménez (ESP)	70-70-75-70—285	72166	31	P Goydos	73-70-71-76—290	20000
	J Parnevik (SWE)	72-70-73-70—285	72166		M James (ENG)	70-74-79-67—290	20000
	C Pavin	69-74-71-71—285	72166		T Tryba	70-72-76-72—290	20000
	C Perry	70-73-71-71—285	72166	34	S Flesch	73-71-72-75—291	15428
	M Weir (CAN)	68-68-69-80—285	72166		P Lawrie (SCO)	73-72-72-74—291	15428
16	M Brooks	70-73-70-74—287	48600		T Lehman	70-74-76-71—291	15428
	G Hjertstedt (SWE)	72-70-73-72—287	48600		B Mayfair	75-69-75-72—291	15428
	B Jobe	69-74-69-75—287	48600		K Perry	74-69-72-76—291	15428
	G Turner (NZL)	73-69-70-75—287	48600		S Verplank	73-72-73-73—291	15428
	L Westwood (ENG)	70-68-74-75—287	48600		L Wadkins	72-69-74-76—291	15428

Other players who made the cut: P Azinger, Angel Cabrera (ARG), C DiMarco, N Faldo (ENG), H Irwin, R Karlsson (SWE), D Waldorf, B Watts 292; O Browne, D Love III, R Mediate, V Singh (FIJ), K Triplett 293; JP Hayes, A Magee, J Sluman 294; P Mickelson, M O'Meara, P Stewart, B Tway 295; M Calcavecchia, B Faxon, G Kraft, B Langer (GER) 296; A Cejka (GER), A Coltart (SCO), M Reid 297; S Dunlap, B Zabriski 298; R Beem, T Bjørn (DEN), N Ozaki (JPN) 299; F Funk 300

1998 US PGA Championship *Sahalee, Redmond, WA* August 13–16   [6906–70]
Prize money: $3,000,000. Entries: Final field of 150, of whom 75 made the half-way cut.

1	V Singh (FIJ)	70-66-67-68—271	$540000	21	E Els (RSA)	72-72-71-66—281	32000
2	S Stricker	69-68-66-70—273	324000		A Magee	70-68-72-71—281	32000
3	S Elkington (AUS)	69-69-69-67—274	204000	23	P-U Johansson (SWE)	69-74-71-68—282	26000
4	F Lickliter	68-71-69-68—276	118000		F Funk	70-71-71-70—282	26000
	M O'Meara	69-70-69-68—276	118000		S Gump	68-69-72-73—282	26000
	N Price (ZIM)	70-73-68-65—276	118000		G Kraft	71-73-65-73—282	26000
7	B Mayfair	73-67-67-70—277	89500	27	J Sluman	71-73-70-69—283	20500
	D Love III	70-68-67-72—277	89500		H Sutton	72-68-72-71—283	20500
9	J Cook	71-68-70-69—278	80000	29	G Day	68-71-75-70—284	17100
10	K Perry	69-72-70-68—279	69000		T Lehman	71-71-70-72—284	17100
	T Woods	66-72-70-71—279	69000		I Woosnam (WAL)	70-75-67-72—284	17100
	S Kendall	72-68-68-71—279	69000		L Rinker	70-70-71-73—284	17100
13	B Faxon	70-68-74-68—280	46000		S Hoch	72-69-70-73—284	17100
	F Couples	74-71-67-68—280	46000	34	P Mickelson	70-70-78-67—285	14250
	B Tway	69-76-67-68—280	46000		B Estes	68-76-69-72—285	14250
	P Azinger	68-73-70-69—280	46000		P Goydos	70-70-72-73—285	14250
	B Glasson	68-74-69-69—280	46000		R Cochran	69-71-70-75—285	14250
	S Flesch	75-69-67-69—280	46000	38	C Stadler	69-74-71-72—286	12750
	J Huston	70-71-68-71—280	46000		D Waldorf	74-70-70-72—286	12750
	R Allenby (AUS)	72-68-69-71—280	46000				

Other players who made the cut: J Sindelar, J Haas, J Durant, C Franco (PAR) 287; J Ozaki (JPN), J Maggert, S Lowery, D Ogrin, K Sutherland, C Montgomerie (SCO), PH Horgan III, M Calcavecchia, D Hart, B Andrade 288; N Faldo (ENG), S Verplank 289; T Tryba, M Brooks, B Watts, J Carter, D Frost (RSA), JD Blake 290; T Dodds (NAM), T Byrum, O Browne 291; R Karlsson (SWE), S Maruyama (JPN), L Roberts 292; S Leaney (AUS) 293; A Coltart (SCO) 294; D Sutherland 295; B Geiberger, C Parry (AUS), B Fabel 296; C Perry 297; T Herron 298

1997 US PGA Championship Winged Foot CC, NY August 14–17 [6987–70]

Prize money: $2,600,000. Entries: Final field of 150, of whom 77 made the half-way cut.

1	D Love III	66-71-66-66—269	$470000	13T	B Tway	68-75-72-69—284	35100
2	J Leonard	68-70-65-71—274	280000		M O'Meara	69-73-75-67—284	35100
3	J Maggert	69-69-73-65—276	175000	23	M Calcavecchia	71-74-73-67—285	22500
4	L Janzen	69-67-74-69—279	125000		B Langer (GER)	73-71-72-69—285	22500
5	T Kite	68-71-71-70—280	105000		D Martin	69-75-74-67—285	22500
6	P Blackmar	70-68-74-69—281	85000		S Maruyama (JPN)	68-70-74-73—285	22500
	J Furyk	69-72-72-68—281	85000		K Perry	73-68-73-71—285	22500
	S Hoch	71-72-68-70—281	85000		J Cook	71-71-74-69—285	22500
9	T Byrum	69-73-70-70—282	70000	29	P Azinger	68-73-71-74—286	13625
10	T Lehman	69-72-72-70—283	60000		R Black	76-69-71-70—286	13625
	S McCarron	74-71-67-71—283	60000		F Couples	71-67-73-75—286	13625
	J Sindelar	72-71-71-69—283	60000		J Daly	66-73-77-70—286	13625
13	D Duval	70-70-71-73—284	35100		P Goydos	70-72-71-73—286	13625
	T Herron	72-73-68-71—284	35100		H Irwin	73-70-71-72—286	13625
	C Montgomerie (SCO)	74-71-67-72—284	35100		P Mickelson	69-69-73-75—286	13625
	G Norman (AUS)	68-71-74-71—284	35100		F Nobilo (NZL)	72-73-67-74—286	13625
	N Price (ZIM)	72-70-72-70—284	35100		D Pooley	72-74-70-70—286	13625
	V Singh (FIJ)	73-66-76-69—284	35100		P Stewart	70-70-72-74—286	13625
	T Tolles	75-70-73-66—284	35100		L Westwood (ENG)	74-68-71-73—286	13625
	K Triplett	73-70-71-70—284	35100		T Woods	70-70-71-75—286	13625

Other players who made the cut: I Garrido (ESP), S Jones, D Ogrin, E Romero (ARG) 287; T Bjørn (DEN), S Elkington (AUS), J Parnevik (SWE), S Torrance (SCO) 288; R Allenby (AUS), B Henninger, C Perry, L Roberts 289; O Browne, E Els (RSA), B Mayfair, T Smith, C Stadler 290; S Lowery, L Mize, L Wadkins 291; S Appleby (AUS), J Haas, R Cochran, F Funk, R Goosen (RSA), L Rinker 292; P Jacobsen, P-U Johansson (SWE), P Stankowski 293; C Franco (PAR) 294; M Bradley, Y Kaneko (JPN), L Nelson, C Rocca (ITA) 295; A Magee 296; P Jordan, K Sutherland 297.

US PGA Championship History

Date	Winner	Runner-up	Venue	By
1916 Oct 8–14	J Barnes	J Hutchison	Siwanoy, NY	1 hole
1919 Sept 15–20	J Barnes	F McLeod	Engineers' Club, NY	6 and 5
1920 Aug 17–21	J Hutchison	D Edgar	Flossmoor, IL	1 hole
1921 Sept 26–Oct 1	W Hagen	J Barnes	Inwood Club, NY	3 and 2
1922 Aug 12–18	G Sarazen	E French	Oakmont, PA	4 and 3
1923 Sept 23–29	G Sarazen	W Hagen	Pelham, NY	38th hole
1924 Sept 15–20	W Hagen	J Barnes	French Lick, IN	2 holes
1925 Sept 21–26	W Hagen	W Mehlhorn	Olympic Fields, IL	6 and 4
1926 Sept 20–25	W Hagen	L Diegel	Salisbury, NY	4 and 3
1927 Oct 31–Nov 5	W Hagen	J Turnesa	Dallas, TX	1 hole
1928 Oct 1–6	L Diegel	A Espinosa	Five Farms, MD	6 and 5
1929 Dec 2–7	L Diegel	J Farrell	Hill Crest, CA	6 and 4
1930 Sept 8–13	T Armour	G Sarazen	Fresh Meadows, NY	1 hole
1931 Sept 7–14	T Creavy	D Shute	Wannamoisett, RI	2 and 1
1932 Aug 31–Sept 4	O Dutra	F Walsh	St Paul, MN	4 and 3
1933 Aug 8–13	G Sarazen	W Goggin	Milwaukee, WI	5 and 4
1934 July 24–29	P Runyan	C Wood	Buffalo, NY	38th hole
1935 Oct 18–23	J Revolta	T Armour	Oklahoma, OK	5 and 4
1936 Nov 17–22	D Shute	J Thomson	Pinehurst, NC	3 and 2
1937 May 26–30	D Shute	H McSpaden	Pittsburgh, PA	37th hole
1938 July 10–16	P Runyan	S Snead	Shawnee, PA	8 and 7
1939 July 9–15	H Picard	B Nelson	Pomonok, NY	37th hole
1940 Aug 26–Sept 2	B Nelson	S Snead	Hershey, PA	1 hole
1941 July 7–13	V Ghezzie	B Nelson	Denver, CO	38th hole
1942 May 23–31	S Snead	J Turnesa	Atlantic City, NJ	2 and 1
1943 No Championship				
1944 Aug 14–20	B Hamilton	B Nelson	Spokane, WA	1 hole
1945 July 9–15	B Nelson	S Byrd	Dayton, OH	4 and 3
1946 Aug 19–25	B Hogan	E Oliver	Portland, OR	6 and 4
1947 June 18–24	J Ferrier	C Harbert	Detroit, MI	2 and 1
1948 May 19–25	B Hogan	M Turnesa	Norwood Hills, MO	7 and 6
1949 May 25–31	S Snead	J Palmer	Richmond, VA	3 and 2
1950 June 21–27	C Harper	H Williams	Scioto, OH	4 and 3

Date	Winner	Runner-up	Venue	By
1951 June 27–July 3	S Snead	W Burkemo	Oakmont, PA	7 and 6
1952 June 18–25	J Turnesa	C Harbert	Louisville, KY	I hole
1953 July 1–7	W Burkemo	F Lorza	Birmingham, MI	2 and I
1954 July 21–27	C Harbert	W Burkemo	St Paul, MN	4 and 3
1955 July 20–26	D Ford	C Middlecoff	Meadowbrook, MI	4 and 3
1956 July 20–24	J Burke	T Kroll	Canton, MA	3 and 2
1957 July 17–21	L Hebert	D Finsterwald	Dayton, OH	3 and I

Changed to stroke play in 1958

Date	Winner	Venue	Score
1958 July 17–20	D Finsterwald	Llanerch, PA	276
1959 July 30– Aug 2	B Rosburg	Minneapolis, MN	277
1960 July 21–24	J Hebert	Firestone, Akron, OH	281
1961 July 27–31	J Barber*	Olympia Fields, IL	277

After a play-off with Don January: Barber 67, January 68

Date	Winner	Venue	Score
1962 July 19–22	G Player (RSA)	Aronimink, PA	278
1963 July 18–21	J Nicklaus	Dallas, TX	279
1964 July 16–19	B Nichols	Columbus, OH	271
1965 Aug 12–15	D Marr	Laurel Valley, PA	280
1966 July 21–24	A Geiberger	Firestone, Akron, OH	280
1967 July 20–24	D January*	Columbine, CO	281

After a play-off with Don Massengale: January 69, Massengale 71

Date	Winner	Venue	Score
1968 July 18–21	J Boros	Pecan Valley, TX	281
1969 Aug 14–17	R Floyd	Dayton, OH	276
1970 Aug 13–16	D Stockton	Southern Hills, OK	279
1971 Feb 25–28	J Nicklaus	PGA national, FL	281
1972 Aug 3–6	G Player (RSA)	Oakland Hills, MI	281
1973 Aug 9–12	J Nicklaus	Canterbury, OH	277
1974 Aug 8–11	L Trevino	Tanglewood, NC	276
1975 Aug 7–10	J Nicklaus	Firestone, Akron, OH	276
1976 Aug 12–16	D Stockton	Congressional, MD	281
1977 Aug 11–14	L Wadkins*	Pebble Beach, CA	287

After a sudden death play-off with Gene Littler: Wadkins 4,4,3; Littler 4,4,4

1978 Aug 3–6	J Mahaffey*	Oakmont, PA	276

After a sudden death play-off with Jerry Pate and Tom Watson: Mahaffey 4,3; Pate 4,4; Watson 4,4

1979 Aug 2–5	D Graham (AUS)*	Oakland Hills, MI	272

After a sudden death play-off with Ben Crenshaw: Graham 4,4,2; Crenshaw 4,4,4

1980 Aug 7–10	J Nicklaus	Oak Hill, NY	274
1981 Aug 6–9	L Nelson	Atlanta, GA	273
1982 Aug 5–8	R Floyd	Southern Hills, OK	272
1983 Aug 4–7	H Sutton	Pacific Palisades, CA	274
1984 Aug 16–19	L Trevino	Shoal Creek, AL	273

Date	Winner	Venue	Score
1985 Aug 8–11	H Green	Cherry Hills, Denver, CO	278
1986 Aug 7–10	R Tway	Inverness, Toledo, OH	276
1987 Aug 6–9	L Nelson*	PGA National, FL	287

After a sudden death play-off with Lanny Wadkins: Nelson 4, Wadkins 5

1988 Aug 11–14	J Sluman	Oaktree, OK	272
1989 Aug 10–13	P Stewart	Kemper Lakes, IL	276
1990 Aug 9–12	W Grady (AUS)	Shoal Creek, AL	282
1991 Aug 8–11	J Daly	Crooked Stick, IN	276
1992 Aug 13–16	N Price (ZIM)	Bellerive, MS	278
1993 Aug 12–15	P Azinger*	Inverness, Toledo, OH	272

After a sudden death play-off with Greg Norman: Azinger 4,4, Norman 4,5

1994 Aug 11–14	N Price (ZIM)	Southern Hills, OK	269
1995 Aug 10–13	S Elkington (AUS)*	Riviera, LA	267

After a sudden death play-off against Colin Montgomerie: Elkington 3, Montgomerie 4

1996 Aug 8–11	M Brooks*	Valhalla, Kentucky	277

After a play-off against Kenny Perry: Brooks 4, Perry 5

1997 Aug 14–17	D Love III	Winged Foot, NY	269
1998 Aug 13–16	V Singh (FIJ)	Sahalee, Seattle, WA	271
1999 Aug 12–15	T Woods	Medinah, IL	277
2000 Aug 17–20	T Woods*	Valhalla, Louisville KY	270

After a three-hole play-off with Bob May: Woods 3-4-5–12, May 4-4-5–13

2001 Aug 16–19	D Toms	Atlanta Athletic Club, GA	265
2002 Aug 15–18	R Beem	Hazeltine National, MN	278
2003 Aug 14–17	S Micheel	Oak Hill, NY	276
2004 Aug 12–15	V Singh (FIJ)*	Whistling Straits, WI	280

After a three hole play-off with Chris DiMarco and Justin Leonard.: Singh 3-3-4–10, DiMarco 4-3-4–11, Leonard 4-3-4–11

2005 Aug 11–15	P Mickelson	Baltusrol, NJ	276
2006 Aug 16–20	T Woods	Medinah, IL	270

Growth of USPGA purses

1916	$2,580	1988	$1,000,.000
1926	$11,100	1990	$1,350,000
1936	$9,200	1992	$1,608,000
1946	$17,700	1994	$1,702,750
1956	$40,000	1996	$2,412,675
1966	$149,360	1998	$3,000,000
1976	$250,950	2000	$5,031,100
1980	$376,400	2002	$5,500,000
1982	$451,800	2004	$6,250,000
1984	$700,300	2006	$6,800,000
1986	$801,100		

International winners by country

Australia:			Scotland:	
Jim Ferrier	1947		Jock Hutchison	1920
D Graham	1979		Tommy Armour	1930
W Grady	1990		South Africa:	
S Elkington	1995		Gary Player	1962
Fiji:			Gary Player	1972
Vijay Singh	1998		Zimbabwe:	
Vijay Singh	2004		Nick Price	1992
			Nick Price	1994

Men's Grand Slam Titles

Jack Nicklaus   Tiger Woods   Walter Hagen

The modern Grand Slam comprises four events – the British and US Open Championships, the US PGA Championship and The Masters at Augusta.

	Open	US Open	Masters	US PGA	Total Titles
Jack Nicklaus (USA)	3	4	6	5	18
Tiger Woods (USA)	3	2	4	3	12
Walter Hagen (USA)	4	2	0	5	11
Ben Hogan (USA)	1	4	2	2	9
Gary Player (RSA)	3	1	3	2	9
Tom Watson (USA)	5	1	2	0	8
Arnold Palmer (USA)	2	1	4	0	7
Gene Sarazen (USA)	1	2	1	3	7
Sam Snead (USA)	1	0	3	3	7
Lee Trevino (USA)	2	2	0	2	6
Nick Faldo (ENG)	3	0	3	0	6

The original Grand Slam comprised the British and US Open Championships and the British and US Amateur Championships.

	Open	US Open	Amateur	US Amateur	Total Titles
Bobby Jones (USA)	3	4	1	5	13
John Ball (ENG)	1	0	8	0	9
Harold Hilton (ENG)	2	0	4	1	7
Harry Vardon (ENG)	6	1	0	0	7

Note: Tiger Woods won three consecutive US Amateur Championships in 1994, 1995 and 1996. Only Bobby Jones has won all four recognised Grand Slam events in the same year – 1930.

Weetabix Women's British Open Championship

American Sherri Steinhauer produces her best at Lytham to win the Open again – and now it's a major

History repeated itself when Sherri Steinhauer won the Weetabix Women's British Open at Royal Lytham and St Annes by four strokes over Sophie Gustafson and Cristie Kerr. In 1998 Steinhauer had won the title at t he Lancashire course and then, as on this occasion, Gustafson finished tied second.

"I feel like I'm living a dream," said Steinhauer whose seven-under-par winning total of 271 earned her a first prize cheque of $305,440 (£160,000). It was her third success in the event. She had also won the 1999 Women's British Open at Sunningdale. In 1998, her opening round of 81 was one of the highest opening rounds of a winner but in 2006 her highest score was 73. It was her first major victory in Britain. The Women's British Open was not declared a major until 2001.

Steinhauer's victory was built on her ability to avoid trouble and a brilliant six-hole stretch in the third round when she covered holes 11 to 16 in five-under-par. After a bogey at the fifth hole on the second day she played the next 48 holes without dropping a shot. In the final round she had 16 pars, a birdie and a tap-in bogey at the last. Kerr got to seven-under-par after 15 on Sunday but dropped three shots in the last three holes to finish second with Gustafson, the 2000 champion, who was second in 1998, 2005 and 2006. Lorena Ochoa and Julie Inkster finished in a tie for fourth on three-under-par.

At the age of 43 years, 7 months and 10 days, Steinhauer became the second oldest player to win a major. Fay Crocker was 45 years, 7 months and 11 days when she won the 1960 Titleholders' Championship – an event which is no longer included on the LPGA Calendar. Veteran Julie Inkster, who led after the first and second rounds, had been trying to win her first British title and join Karrie Webb as a super career Grand Slam winner – someone with victories in the British and US Opens, the McDonald's LPGA, the Kraft Nabisco and the now defunct due Maurier event. Her chance was lost when she shot 74-73 over the weekend to winner Steinhaur's 66-72.

Lee Ann Walker-Cooper aced the 156 yards ninth in the second round with an 8-iron and Lori Kane aced the 160 yards 12th hole with a 4-iron on the final day. Seventeen-year-old Amy Wang, who won the ANZ Australian Masters earlier in the year, won the Smyth Salver which goes to the leading amateur. The former New Zealand Amateur champion shot 301.

Michelle Wie finished on 294 after rounds of 74, 74, 72 and 74 but was positive about her performance. "This week I learned how to play the game. Playing links golf forces you to play and remain patient. When things go bad you have to play through it and make putts when you have to".

Annika Sörenstam, who closed with a round of 79, finished on seven over par.

First Round	Second Round	Third Round	Fourth Round
–6 Inkster	–6 Inkster	–7 Steinhauer	–7 Steinhauer
–3 Cavalieri	–3 Cavalieri	–4 Inkster	–4 Kerr
–3 Hjorth	–2 Stupples	–4 Gustafson	–4 Gustafson
–2 Reis	–2 Kane	–4 Ochoa	–3 Ochoa
–2 Nocera	–2 King	–3 Kerr	–3 Inkster
–2 Hanna	–2 Wright		

2006 Weetabix Women's British Open Championship
Royal Lytham & St Annes   [6308–72]

Prize money: £1.05 million (€1.5 million). Final field of 150 (4 amateurs), of whom 72 (2 amateurs) made the half-way cut on 151 or under.

Final Qualifying at St Annes Old Links:

Sofie Andersson (SWE)	Lynn Kenny (SCO)	Joanne Oliver (ENG)
Suzanne Dickens (ENG)	Erin Kerr (USA)	Clare Queen (SCO)
Stephanie Evans (WAL)	Jenni Kuosa (FIN)	Margherita Rigon (ITA)
Lora Fairclough (ENG)	Pernella Lindberg (SWE)	Marie-J Rouleau (CAN)
Kirsty J Fisher (ENG)	Clare Lipscombe (ENG)	Anna Temple (USA)
Louise Friberg (SWE)	Danielle Montgomery (ENG)	Laura Terebey (USA)
Melanie Holmes-Smith (AUS)	Susan Moon (USA)	Sophie Walker (ENG)
Katy Jarochowicz (AUS)	Nienke Mijenhuis (NED)	Emma Weeks (ENG)
Felicity Johnson (ENG)	Therese Nilsson (SWE)	

1	Sherri Steinhauer (USA)	73-70-66-72—281	£160000
2	Sophie Gustafson (SWE)	76-67-69-72—284	85000
	Cristie Kerr (USA)	71-76-66-71—284	85000
4	Juli Inkster (USA)	66-72-74-73—285	50000
	Lorena Ochoa (MEX)	74-73-65-73—285	50000
6	Beth Daniel (USA)	73-70-71-72—286	37000
	Lorie Kane (CAN)	73-69-74-70—286	37000
8	Julieta Granada (PAR)	71-73-70-73—287	32000
9	Ai Miyazato (JPN)	71-75-75-67—288	29000
10	Hee Won Han (KOR)	80-71-69-70—290	21250
	Karine Icher (FRA)	72-73-71-74—290	21250
	Joo Mi Kim (KOR)	73-73-73-71—290	21250
	Candie Kung (TPE)	72-70-71-77—290	21250
	Nina Reis (SWE)	70-76-69-75—290	21250
	Karen Stupples (ENG)	73-69-70-78—290	21250
16	Il-Mi Chung (KOR)	72-71-75-73—291	14041
	Laura Davies (ENG)	72-72-73-74—291	14041
	Natalie Gulbis (USA)	72-74-67-78—291	14041
	Gwladys Nocera (FRA)	70-73-71-77—291	14041
	Sukura Yokomine (JPN)	72-73-75-71—291	14041
	Heather Young (USA)	72-74-70-75—291	14041
22	Kyeong Bae (KOR)	73-73-75-71—292	11500
	Paula Creamer (USA)	72-71-73-76—292	11500
	Jee Young Lee (KOR)	72-77-69-74—292	11500
25	Shi Hyun Ahn (KOR)	75-73-69-76—293	10600
26	Jackie Gallagher-Smith (USA)	77-74-71-72—294	9460
	Tracy Hanson (USA)	74-77-70-73—294	9460
	Jeong Jang (KOR)	78-73-68-75—294	9460
	Michelle Wie (USA)	74-74-72-74—294	9460
	Young-A Yang (KOR)	72-75-68-79—294	9460
31	Nicole Castrale (USA)	73-75-71-76—295	7810
	Anja Monke (GER)	75-76-70-74—295	7810
	Liselotte Neumann (SWE)	76-72-70-77—295	7810
	Annika Sörenstam (SWE)	72-71-73-79—295	7810
	Lindsey Wright (USA)	71-71-74-79—295	7810
36	Becky Brewerton (WAL)	76-73-73-74—296	6375
	Vicki Goetze-Ackerman (USA)	75-72-71-78—296	6375
	Young Jo (KOR)	80-70-74-72—296	6375
	Angela Stanford (USA)	76-69-80-71—296	6375
	Sun Young Yoo (KOR)	76-74-71-75—296	6375
	Veronica Zorzi (ITA)	74-76-78-68—296	6375
42	Yuri Fudoh (JPN)	74-75-69-79—297	5250
	Nikki Garrett (AUS)	76-71-76-74—297	5250
	Patricia Meunier-Lebouc (FRA)	75-75-72-75—297	5250
45	Chieko Amanuma (JPN)	71-80-72-75—298	4310

45T	Silvia Cavalleri (ITA)	69-72-77-80—298	4310
	Maria Hjörth (SWE)	69-76-75-78—298	4310
	Christina Kim (USA)	71-73-71-83—298	4310
	Sarah Lee (KOR)	72-77-72-77—298	4310
50	Marisa Baena (COL)	75-75-76-73—299	3200
	Rita Hakkarainen (FIN)	76-75-74-74—299	3200
	Allison Hanna (USA)	70-76-78-75—299	3200
	Teresa Lu (TPE)	73-77-74-75—299	3200
	Joanne Morley (ENG)	73-77-73-76—299	3200
	Lee Ann Walker-Cooper (USA)	76-74-73-76—299	3200
56	Brittany Lincicome (USA)	74-76-75-75—300	2325
	Becky Morgan (WAL)	77-73-72-78—300	2325
	Morgan Pressel (USA)	75-75-72-78—300	2325
	Kris Tamulis (USA)	72-76-79-73—300	2325
60	Amy Yang (KOR) (am)	76-74-75-76—301	
61	Lynnette Brooky (NZL)	73-78-70-81—302	1850
	Seon Hwa Lee (KOR)	74-77-72-79—302	1850
	Elisa Serramia (ESP)	73-78-74-77—302	1850
	Ursula Wikstrom (FIN)	75-75-75-77—302	1850
65	Laura Diaz (USA)	75-73-72-83—303	1600
66	Marta Prieto (ESP)	75-70-76-83—304	1550
67	Helena Alterby (SWE)	74-74-77-80—305	1000
	Wendy Ward (USA)	71-74-75-85—305	1000
69	Rachel Hetherington (AUS)	71-79-83-73—306	1000
70	Belen Mozo (ESP) (am)	73-74-79-81—307	
71	Iben Tinning (DEN)	75-76-76-84—311	1000

The following players missed the cut. Each professional player received £300:

72	Helen Alfredsson (SWE)	76-76—152
	Beth Bader (USA)	73-79—152
	Sophie Giquel (FRA)	75-77—152
	Lisa Hall (ENG)	75-77—152
	Anna Highgate (WAL)	77-75—152
	Birdie Kim (KOR)	77-75—152
	Brittany Lang (USA)	76-76—152
	Stacy Prammanasudh (USA)	77-75—152
	Ashleigh Simon (RSA) (am)	77-75—152
	Louise Stahle (SWE)	76-76—152
	Shani Waugh (AUS)	76-76—152
83	Johanna Head (ENG)	80-73—153
	Pat Hurst (USA)	78-75—153
	Mi Hyun Kim (KOR)	78-75—153
	Isabella Maconi (ITA)	72-81—153
	Miriam Nagl (GER)	75-78—153
	Reilley Rankin (USA)	80-73—153
	Michele Redman (USA)	76-77—153
90	Minea Blomqvist (FIN)	76-78—154
	Tania Elosegui Mayor (ESP)	75-79—154
	Asa Gottmo (SWE)	78-76—154
	Candy Hannemann (BRA)	75-79—154
	Young Kim (KOR)	81-73—154
	Meena Lee (KOR)	77-77—154
	Stephanie Louden (USA)	75-79—154
	Catriona Matthew (SCO)	75-79—154
	Amanda Moltke-Leth (DEN)	75-79—154
	Soo-Young Moon (KOR)	83-71—154
	Mikaela Parmlid (SWE)	82-72—154
	Midori Yoneyama (JPN)	77-77—154
102	Diana D'Alessio (USA)	76-79—155
	Virada Nirapathpongporn (THA)	76-79—155
	Joanne Mills (AUS)	77-78—155
	Suzann Pettersen (NOR)	77-78—155
	Ana B Sanchez (ESP)	80-75—155
	Jade Schaeffer (FRA) (am)	79-76—155
	Frederique Seeholzer (SUI)	78-77—155
	Karin Sjodin (SWE)	82-73—155
	Linda Wessberg (SWE)	76-79—155
111	Nora Angehern (SUI)	71-85—156

111T	Stephanie Arricau (FRA)	78-78—156
	Tina Barrett (USA)	77-79—156
	Karen Margrethe Juul (DEN)	75-81—156
	Carin Koch (SWE)	78-78—156
	Laurette Maritz (RSA)	77-79—156
	Gloria Park (KOR)	76-80—156
	Jessica Reese (USA)	79-77—156
119	Nikki Campbell (AUS)	75-82—157
	Rebecca Coakley (IRL)	81-76—157
	Cecilia Ekelundh (SWE)	77-80—157
	Nicole Perrot (CHI)	75-82—157
	Marie-Josee Rouleau (CAN)	77-80—157
	Sophie Sandolo (ITA)	82-75—157
	Guilia Sergas (ITA)	77-80—157
	Aree Song (KOR)	77-80—157
	Rebecca Stevenson (AUS)	79-78—157
	Kirsty S Taylor (ENG)	78-79—157
129	Virginie Auffret (FRA)	76-82—158
	Marcy Hart (USA)	80-78—158
	Akane Iijima (JPN)	72-86—158
	Jill McGill (USA)	79-79—158
	Karrie Webb (AUS)	76-82—158
134	Laura Cabanillas (ESP)	80-79—159
	Rebecca Hudson (ENG)	82-77—159
	Hilary Lunke (USA)	74-85—159
	Meg Mallon (USA)	77-82—159
138	Sarah Kemp (AUS)	75-85—160
	Eleanor Pilgrim (WAL)	82-78—160
	Kirsty Taylor (ENG)	79-81—160
	Lotta Waylin (SWE)	80-80—160
142	Antonella Cvitan (SWE)	80-82—162
	Heather Macrae (SCO) (am)	82-80—162
144	Ludivine Kreutz (FRA)	81-82—163
145	Dorothy Delasin (PHI)	82-82—164
	Amy Hung (TPE)	81-83—164
	Mhairi McKay (SCO)	82-82—164
148	Anna Knutsson (SWE)	78-87—165
	Se Ri Pak (KOR)	78 Rtd
	Karen Weiss (USA)	89 DQ

2005 Weetabix Women's British Open   Royal Birkdale, Southport, Lancashire   [6463–72]

Prize money: £1.05 million

1	Jeong Jang (KOR)	68-66-69-69—272	£160000	21	Catriona Matthew (SCO)	73-72-72-67—284	13500
2	Sophie Gustafson (SWE)	69-73-67-67—276	100000	22	Brandie Burton (USA)	74-75-71-65—285	11767
3	Young Kim (KOR)	74-68-67-69—278	70000		Cecilia Ekelundh (SWE)	77-69-71-68—285	11767
	Michelle Wie (USA) (am)	75-67-67-69—278			Candie Kung (TAI)	76-71-67-71—285	11767
5	Cristie Kerr (USA)	73-66-69-71—279	46333		Nicole Perrot (CHI)	70-72-69-74—285	11767
	Liselotte Neumann (SWE)	71-70-68-70—279	46333		Sophie Sandolo (ITA)	71-73-73-68—285	11767
	Annika Sörenstam (SWE)	73-69-66-71—279	46333		Linda Wessberg (SWE)	72-71-73-69—285	11767
8	Natalie Gulbis (USA)	76-70-68-66—280	33500	28	Shi Hyun Ahn (KOR)	78-68-67-73—286	9283
	Grace Park (KOR)	77-68-67-68—280	33500		Becky Brewerton (WAL)	75-71-65-75—286	9283
	Louise Stahle (SWE) (am)	73-65-73-69—280			Laura Davies (ENG)	76-70-66-74—286	9283
11	Ai Miyazato (JPN)	72-73-69-67—281	25250		Christina Kim (USA)	79-70-71-66—286	9283
	Michele Redman (USA)	75-71-67-68—281	25250		Anja Monke (GER)	73-73-70-70—286	9283
	Karen Stupples (ENG)	74-71-65-71—281	25250		Miriam Nagl (GER)	74-75-69-68—286	9283
	Karrie Webb (AUS)	75-66-69-71—281	25250	34	Heather Bowie (USA)	74-69-72-72—287	7530
15	Paula Creamer (USA)	75-69-65-73—282	17300		Marty Hart (USA)	79-70-71-67—287	7530
	Yuri Fudoh (JPN)	75-69-68-70—282	17300		Rebecca Hudson (ENG)	78-70-71-68—287	7530
	Juli Inkster (USA)	74-68-68-72—282	17300		Emilee Klein (USA)	71-73-70-73—287	7530
	Carin Koch (SWE)	76-68-66-72—282	17300		Jill McGill (USA)	76-70-72-69—287	7530
	Becky Morgan (WAL)	79-66-67-70—282	17300	39	Minea Blomquist (SWE)	78-68-72-70—288	6500
20	Pat Hurst (USA)	75-65-70-73—283	14250		Wendy Doolan (AUS)	77-72-67-72—288	6500
					Sherri Steinhauer (USA)	74-73-70-71—288	6500

Other players who made the cut: Helen Alfredsson (SWE), Michelle Ellis (AUS), Riikka Hakkarainen (FIN), Rachel Hetherington (AUS), Riko Higashio (JPN), Amanda Moltke-Leth (DEN), Gwladys Nocera (FRA), Iben Tinning (DEN), Kris Tschetter (USA), 289; Carlota Ciganda (ESP) (am), Moira Dunn (USA), Kris Lindstrom (USA), Kimberley Williams (USA), 290; Catherine Cartwright (USA), Beth Daniel (USA), 291; Young Jo (KOR), Lorie Kane (CAN), Aree Song (KOR), Bo Bae Song (KOR). 292; Judith Van Hagen (NED), Shani Waugh (AUS), 293; Laura Diaz (USA), Sung Ah Yim (KOR), 294; Amy Hung (TAI), Paula Marti (ESP), 295; Siew-Ai Lim (MAS), Yu Ping Lin (TAI), 296; Karen Lunn (AUS), 301.

2004 Weetabix Women's British Open   Sunningdale (Old Course)   [6392–72]

Prize money: £1.05 million

1	Karen Stupples (ENG)	65-70-70-64—269	£160000	21T	Se Ri Pak (KOR)	73-70-69-69—281	12250
2	Rachel Teske (AUS)	70-69-65-70—274	100000	23	Jeong Jang (KOR)	70-68-73-71—282	11250
3	Heather Bowie (USA)	70-69-65-71—275	70000		Aree Song (KOR)	72-70-70-70—282	11250
4	Lorena Ochoa (MEX)	69-71-66-70—276	55000	25	Juli Inkster (USA)	71-75-69-68—283	10200
5	Beth Daniel (USA)	69-69-71-68—277	39667		Seol-An Jeon (KOR)	69-69-70-75—283	10200
	Michele Redman (USA)	70-71-70-66—277	39667		Toshimi Kimura (JPN)	70-75-68-70—283	10200
	Guilia Sergas (ITA)	72-71-67-67—277	39667	28	Alison Nicholas (ENG)	75-71-70-69—285	9450
8	Minea Blomqvist (FIN)	68-78-62-70—278	29000	29	Candie Kung (TPE)	73-69-71-73—286	8925
	Laura Davies (ENG)	70-69-69-70—278	29000		Catriona Matthew (SCO)	68-74-68-76—286	8925
	Jung Yeon Lee (KOR)	67-72-70-69—278	29000	31	Wendy Doolan (AUS)	71-72-74-70—287	7950
11	Pat Hurst (USA)	72-72-66-69—279	23000		Natascha Fink (AUT)	74-70-70-73—287	7950
	Cristie Kerr (USA)	69-73-63-74—279	23000		Gloria Park (KOR)	72-73-75-67—287	7950
13	Laura Diaz (USA)	70-69-70-71—280	15906		Kirsty Taylor (ENG)	72-74-72-69—287	7950
	Natalie Gulbis (USA)	68-71-70-71—280	15906	35	Soo-Yun Kang (KOR)	71-74-74-69—288	7000
	Hee Won Han (KOR)	72-68-70-70—280	15906		Becky Morgan (WAL)	74-72-69-73—288	7000
	Christina Kim (USA)	73-68-68-71—280	15906		Jennifer Rosales (PHI)	75-70-70-73—288	7000
	Carin Koch (SWE)	70-70-70-70—280	15906	38	Denise Killeen (USA)	72-72-70-75—289	6125
	Paula Marti (ESP)	73-66-68-73—280	15906		Jill McGill (USA)	71-72-71-75—289	6125
	Grace Park (KOR)	71-70-69-70—280	15906		Patricia Meunier-Lebouc (FRA)	70-75-71-73—289	6125
	Annika Sörenstam (SWE)	68-71-70-71—280	15906		Nadina Taylor (AUS)	69-74-72-74—289	6125
21	Michelle Estill (USA)	70-72-68-71—281	12250				

Other players who made the cut: Hiromi Mogi (JPN), Shiho Ohyama (JPN), Ana B Sanchez (ESP), Louise Stahle (SWE) (am), Sherri Steinhauer (USA) 290; Bettina Hauert (GER), Angela Jerman (USA), Pamela Kerrigan 291; Ashli Bunch (USA), Audra Burks (USA), Johanna Head (ENG), Katherine Hull (AUS), Kelli Kuehne (USA), Gwladys Nocera (FRA) 292; Lynnette Brooky (NZL), A J Eathorne (CAN), Wendy Ward (USA) 293; Emilee Klein (USA) 294; Helen Alfredsson (SWE), Hsiao Chuan Lu (CHN), Betsy King (USA), Janice Moodie (SCO) 295; Raquel Carriedo (ESP), Ana Larraneta (ESP) 296; Vicki Goetze-Ackerman (USA), Laurette Maritz (RSA) 297; Samantha Head (ENG) 298; Maria Hjörth (SWE) 305.

2003 Weetabix Women's British Open   Royal Lytham and St Annes, Lancashire   [6308-72]

Prize money: £1.05 million

1	Annika Sörenstam (SWE)	68-72-68-70—278	£160000
2	Se Ri Pak (KOR)	69-69-69-72—279	100000
3	Grace Park (KOR)	74-65-71-70—280	62500
	Karrie Webb (AUS)	67-72-70-71—280	62500
5	Patricia Meunier-Lebouc (FRA)	70-69-67-76—282	45000
6	Vicki Goetze-Ackerman (USA)	73-71-68-71—283	37000
	Wendy Ward (USA)	67-71-69-76—283	37000
8	Sophie Gustafson (SWE)	73-69-71-71—284	32000
9	Young Kim (KOR)	73-70-72-70—285	29000
10	Candie Kung (TPE)	73-71-69-73—286	25000
	Gloria Park (KOR)	70-75-69-72—286	25000
12	Paula Marti (ESP)	71-70-70-76—287	21000
	Karen Stupples (ENG)	69-74-70-74—287	21000
14	Lynnette Brooky (NZL)	70-74-75-69—288	16150
	Beth Daniel (USA)	74-71-67-76—288	16150
	Laura Diaz (USA)	73-74-71-70—288	16150
	Jeong Jang (KOR)	76-69-72-71—288	16150
	Cristie Kerr (USA)	74-71-71-72—288	16150
19	Heather Bowie (USA)	70-66-74-79—289	12500
19T	Laura Davies (ENG)	75-70-70-74—289	12500
	Hee Won Han (KOR)	75-71-70-73—289	12500
	Lorie Kane (CAN)	69-75-70-75—289	12500
	Becky Morgan (WAL)	72-70-71-76—289	12500
24	Brandie Burton (USA)	76-69-69-76—290	8996
	Moira Dunn (USA)	70-74-74-72—290	8996
	Michiko Hattori (JPN)	78-69-71-72—290	8996
	Pat Hurst (USA)	73-71-74-72—290	8996
	Soo-Yun Kang (KOR)	70-75-72-73—290	8996
	Emilee Klein (USA)	72-70-74-74—290	8996
	Lorena Ochoa (MEX)	74-65-77-74—290	8996
	Dottie Pepper (USA)	71-75-71-73—290	8996
	Jennifer Rosales (PHI)	69-72-76-73—290	8996
	Iben Tinning (DEN)	71-73-73-73—290	8996
	Hiroko Yamaguchi (JPN)	72-71-75-72—290	8996
	Young-A Yang (KOR)	71-75-71-73—290	8996
36	Georgina Simpson (ENG)	69-73-74-75—291	7000
37	Christine Kuld (DEN)	69-76-75-72—292	6375
	Meg Mallon (USA)	71-72-71-78—292	6375
	Michele Redman (USA)	71-69-76-76—292	6375
	Nadina Taylor (AUS)	71-74-72-75—292	6375

Other players who made the cut: Elisabeth Esterl (GER), Akiko Fukushima (JPN), Johanna Head (ENG), Juli Inkster (USA), Catrin Nilsmark (SWE) 293; Kelli Kuehne (USA), Elisa Serramia (ESP) (am), Rachel Teske (AUS), Karen Weiss (USA), 294; Kasumi Fujii (JPN), Angela Jerman (USA), Carin Koch (SWE), Kelly Robbins (USA) 295; Cherie Byrnes (AUS), Michelle Ellis (AUS), Woo-Soon Ko (KOR), Shani Waugh (AUS) 296; Heather Daly-Donofrio (USA), Susan Parry (USA), Kirsty Taylor (ENG) 297; Helen Alfredsson (SWE), Alison Nicholas (ENG) 298; Beth Bauer (USA) 299; Silvia Cavalleri (ITA), Sophie Sandolo (ITA), Angela Stanford (USA) 300; Suzanne Strudwick (ENG) 303; Marnie McGuire (NZL) 308.

2002 Weetabix Women's British Open   Turnberry, Ayrshire   [6407-72]

Prize money: £1,000,000

1	Karrie Webb (AUS)	66-71-70-66—273	£154982
2	Michelle Ellis (AUS)	69-70-68-68—275	84990
	Paula Marti (ESP)	69-68-69-69—275	84990
4	Jeong Jang (KOR)	73-69-66-69—277	42308
	Candie Kung (TPE)	65-71-71-70—277	42308
	Catrin Nilsmark (SWE)	70-69-69-69—277	42308
	Jennifer Rosales (PHI)	69-70-65-73—277	42308
8	Beth Bauer (USA)	70-67-70-71—278	25164
	Carin Koch (SWE)	68-68-68-74—278	25164
	Meg Mallon (USA)	69-71-68-70—278	25164
11	Sophie Gustafson (SWE)	69-73-69-68—279	19748
	Se Ri Pak (KOR)	67-72-69-71—279	19748
13	Natalie Gulbis (USA)	69-70-67-74—280	16581
	Pat Hurst (USA)	69-70-69-72—280	16581
	Angela Stanford (USA)	69-70-69-72—280	16581
16	Tina Barrett (USA)	67-70-70-76—283	14348
	Beth Daniel (USA)	73-68-68-74—283	14348
18	Jean Bartholomew (USA)	71-72-72-69—284	12099
	Wendy Doolan (AUS)	70-69-71-74—284	12099
	Jane Geddes (USA)	71-69-70-74—284	12099
	Marine Monnet (FRA)	71-70-70-73—284	12099
	Fiona Pike (AUS)	72-73-67-72—284	12099
	Rachel Teske (AUS)	67-74-68-75—284	12099
24	Patricia Meunier-Lebouc (FRA)	69-71-69-76—285	10249
	Suzann Pettersen (NOR)	72-71-72-70—285	10249
26	Dorothy Delasin (PHI)	70-71-70-75—286	9366
	Elisabeth Esterl (GER)	67-71-72-76—286	9366
	Emilee Klein (USA)	68-71-72-75—286	9366
29	Brandie Burton (USA)	71-70-71-75—287	7949
	Cristie Kerr (USA)	72-71-69-75—287	7949
	Kelli Kuehne (USA)	75-67-71-74—287	7949
	Yu Ping Lin (TPE)	73-69-74-71—287	7949
	Iben Tinning (DEN)	71-69-71-76—287	7949
34	Toshimi Kimura (JPN)	74-70-70-74—288	7249
35	Kathryn Marshall (SCO)	70-71-76-72—289	6499
	Catriona Matthew (SCO)	73-71-70-75—289	6499
	Liselotte Neumann (SWE)	70-71-71-77—289	6499
	Kelly Robbins (USA)	70-75-68-76—289	6499
	Shani Waugh (AUS)	70-73-74-72—289	6499
40	Helen Alfredsson (SWE)	70-75-71-74—290	5249
	Lora Fairclough (ENG)	71-69-73-77—290	5249
	Becky Iverson (USA)	69-76-72-73—290	5249
	Karen Lunn (AUS)	73-71-72-74—290	5249
	Sophie Sandolo (ITA)	71-74-68-77—290	5249

Other players who made the cut: Asa Gottmo (SWE), Mhairi McKay (SCO) 291; Heather Daly-Donofrio (USA), Federica Dassu (ITA), Tracy Hanson (USA), Johanna Head (ENG), Becky Morgan (WAL), Giulia Sergas (ITA) 292; Heather Bowie (USA), Grace Park (KOR), Suzanne Strudwick (ENG) 293; Raquel Carriedo (ESP), Karen Stupples (ENG), Wendy Ward (USA) 294; Betsy King (USA) 295; Vicki Goetze-Ackerman (USA) 296; Mi Hyun Kim (KOR), Charlotta Sörenstam (SWE) 297; Tonya Gill (USA) 298; Riikka Hakkarainen (FIN) 299; Marina Arruti (ESP) 301; Ana Larraneta (ESP) 302.

2001 Weetabix Women's British Open Sunningdale, Berkshire   [6245–72]

Prize money: £730,000

1	Se Ri Pak (KOR)	71-70-70-66—277	£155000	21T	Emilee Klein (USA)	71-70-71-73—285	11125
2	Mi Hyun Kim (KOR)	72-65-71-71—279	100000		Lora Fairclough (ENG)	71-70-67-77—285	11125
3	Laura Diaz (USA)	74-70-69-67—280	51813	25	Danielle Ammaccapane	75-68-74-69—286	9071
	Iben Tinning (DEN)	71-69-72-68—280	51813		(USA)		
	Janice Moodie (SCO)	67-70-71-72—280	51813		Dina Ammaccapane	72-71-74-69—286	9071
	Catriona Matthew (SCO)	70-65-72-73—280	51813		(USA)		
7	Kristal Parker (USA)	72-71-71-67—281	25600		Silvia Cavalleri (ITA)	71-73-72-70—286	9071
	Marina Arruti (ESP)	71-73-70-67—281	25600		Maria Hjörth (SWE)	72-73-71-70—286	9071
	Kathryn Marshall (SCO)	75-71-68-67—281	25600		Gloria Park (KOR)	71-73-71-71—286	9071
	Kelli Kuehne (USA)	71-70-71-69—281	25600		Lee Ji Hee (KOR)	75-71-69-71—286	9071
	Kasumi Fujii (JPN)	71-71-69-70—281	25600		Laura Davies (ENG)	68-73-69-76—286	9071
12	Raquel Carriedo (ESP)	73-70-70-69—282	17750	32	Annika Sörenstam (SWE)	70-74-74-69—287	6767
	Tracy Hanson (USA)	72-69-70-71—282	17750		Marisa Baena (COL)	72-74-72-69—287	6767
	Rosie Jones (USA)	70-69-71-72—282	17750		Suzann Pettersen (NOR)	78-64-74-71—287	6767
15	Brandie Burton (USA)	72-71-73-67—283	14400		Wendy Doolan (AUS)	72-68-75-72—287	6767
	Pearl Sinn (USA)	74-70-72-67—283	14400		Grace Park (KOR)	70-71-74-72—287	6767
	Jill McGill (USA)	70-70-72-71—283	14400		Kelly Robbins (USA)	69-72-73-73—287	6767
	Karrie Webb (AUS)	74-67-68-74—283	14400		Mhairi McKay (SCO)	70-72-72-73—287	6767
19	Becky Morgan (WAL)	73-68-71-72—284	12575		Hee Won Han (KOR)	72-73-69-73—287	6767
	Trish Johnson (ENG)	70-67-72-75—284	12575		Hiromi Kobayashi (JPN)	72-70-71-74—287	6767
21	Johanna Head (ENG)	68-70-75-72—285	11125		Rebecca Hudson (ENG)	71-70-70-76—287	
	Marlene Hedblom (SWE)	70-74-69-72—285	11125		(am)		

Other players who made the cut: Sophie Gustafson (SWE), Kellee Booth (USA), Joanne Morley (ENG), Vicki Goetze-Ackerman (USA) 288; Lorie Kane (CAN), Suzanne Strudwick (ENG), Tina Barrett (USA), Cindy Schreyer (USA), Elisabeth Esterl (GER), Riikka Hakkarainen (FIN) 289; Joanne Mills (AUS) 290; Becky Iverson (USA), Yu Ping Lin (TPE) 291; Liselotte Neumann (SWE) 292; Carin Koch (SWE), Jenny Lidback (PER), Marine Monnet (FRA), Diane Barnard (ENG) 293; Kaori Harada (JPN), Laurette Maritz (RSA), Karin Icher (FRA), Lisa Hed (SWE) 294; Nicola Moult (ENG), Helen Alfredsson (SWE), Patricia Meunier-Lebouc (FRA) 295; Kirsty Taylor (ENG) 296; Judith Van Hagen (NED), Claire Duffy (ENG) 297; Dorothy Delasin (PHI) 298.

2000 Women's British Open Championship Royal Birkdale   [6285–73]

Prize money: £730,000

1	Sophie Gustafson (SWE)	70-66-71-75—282	£120000	20	Kelly Robbins (USA)	73-74-73-70—290	8475
2	Kirsty Taylor (ENG)	71-74-72-67—284	50713		Karen Weiss (USA)	73-70-75-72—290	8475
	Becky Iverson (USA)	70-70-75-69—284	50713		Rachel Hetherington	71-74-73-72—290	8475
	Liselotte Neumann (SWE)	71-73-71-69—284	50713		(AUS)		
	Meg Mallon (USA)	74-69-71-70—284	50713		Brandie Burton (USA)	72-74-71-73—290	8475
6	Laura Philo (USA)	72-73-72-68—285	27500	24	Michele Redman (USA)	74-73-73-71—291	7275
7	Karrie Webb (AUS)	68-75-72-71—286	23250		Alicia Dibos (PER)	72-73-74-72—291	7275
8	Janice Moody (SCO)	73-74-73-67—287	19500		Marine Monnet (FRA)	72-73-74-72—291	7275
	Vicki Goetze-Ackerman	77-69-73-68—287	19500		Raquel Carriedo (ESP)	76-71-72-72—291	7275
	(USA)			28	Riko Higashio (JPN)	74-72-76-70—292	6313
10	Maggie Will (USA)	74-72-76-66—288	13250		Susan Redman (USA)	70-78-71-73—292	6313
	Michelle McGann (USA)	72-76-69-71—288	13250		Jill McGill (USA)	71-71-76-74—292	6313
	Juli Inkster (USA)	70-69-77-72—288	13250		Mhairi McKay (SCO)	74-71-71-76—292	6313
	Jenny Lidback (PER)	71-71-73-73—288	13250	32	Shani Waugh (AUS)	73-74-76-70—293	5400
	Trish Johnson (ENG)	71-72-72-73—288	13250		Michelle Estill (USA)	72-75-75-71—293	5400
	Kellee Booth (USA)	73-71-71-73—288	13250		Sofia Grönberg	80-69-73-71—293	5400
	Kathryn Marshall (SCO)	72-69-73-74—288	13250		Whitmore (SWE)		
17	Pat Bradley (USA)	74-71-74-70—289	9850		Gail Graham (CAN)	79-71-71-72—293	5400
	Rosie Jones (USA)	72-72-73-72—289	9850		Betsy King (USA)	74-73-73-73—293	5400
	Annika Sörenstam (SWE)	70-76-71-72—289	9850				

Other players who made the cut: Giulia Sergas (ITA), Maria Hjörth (SWE), Tina Barrett (USA), Leigh Ann Mills (USA), Julie Forbes (SCO), Wendy Daden (ENG), Pernilla Sterner (SWE), Laura Davies (ENG) 294; Anna Berg (SWE), Yu Ping Lin (TPE), Aki Takamura (JPN), Karen Pearce (AUS) 295; Silvia Cavalleri (ITA), Stephanie Arricau (FRA), Sara Eklund (SWE), Karen Stupples (ENG), Sandrine Mendiburu (FRA), Jenifer Feldott (USA), Helen Alfredsson (SWE), Anne-Marie Knight (AUS) 296; Federica Dassu (ITA) 297; Kristal Parker-Gregory (USA), Elizabeth Esterl (GER) 298; Catrin Nilsmark (SWE), Smriti Mehra (IND), Johanna Head (ENG) 299; Mardi Lunn (AUS), Mandy Adamson (RSA), Dale Reid (SCO) 300; Hiromi Kobayashi (JPN), Lisa De Paulo (USA) 301; Hsui Feng Tseng (CHN), Nina Karlsson (SWE), Judith Van Hagen (NED) 303; Emilee Klein (USA), Gina Marie Scott (NZL), Laurette Maritz (RSA) 304; Lora Fairclough (ENG) 306.

1999 Weetabix Women's British Open Woburn G&CC, Bedfordshire [6463–73]

Prize money: £575,000

1	S Steinhauer (USA)	71-71-68-73—283	£100000	17T	C Figg-Currier (USA)	69-76-72-73—290	6614
2	A Sörenstam (SWE)	69-71-72-72—284	60000		V Van	72-75-70-73—290	6614
3	H Dobson (ENG)	71-72-72-70—285	31666		Ryckeghem (BEL)		
	C Flom (USA)	71-74-69-71—285	31666		K Taylor (ENG)	73-71-72-74—290	6614
	F Pike (AUS)	70-70-71-74—285	31666	24	G Sergas (ITA) (am)	71-73-74-73—291	
6	E Klein (USA)	72-70-73-71—286	16000		J Morley (ENG)	70-75-73-73—291	5300
	S Gustafson (SWE)	73-69-72-72—286	16000		A Nicholas (ENG)	73-71-73-74—291	5300
	M Lunn (AUS)	71-72-70-73—286	16000		M Hjörth (SWE)	71-68-77-75—291	5300
	I Tinning (DEN)	68-69-75-74—286	16000		S Lowe (ENG)	72-74-70-75—291	5300
	C McCurdy (USA)	73-70-68-75—286	16000		P Meunier-	73-70-72-76—291	5300
11	S Mehra (IND)	70-70-76-71—287	11000		Lebouc (FRA)		
12	C Koch (SWE)	74-72-72-70—288	9625		M Yoneyama (JPN)	73-70-72-76—291	5300
	S Strudwick (ENG)	71-70-76-71—288	9625	31	C Nilsmark (SWE)	72-71-76-73—292	4150
14	R Jones (USA)	73-71-73-72—289	8033		M Hirase (JPN)	73-72-74-73—292	4150
	L Philo (USA)	69-71-75-74—289	8033		D Barnard (ENG)	73-72-74-73—292	4150
	L Neumann (SWE)	72-70-72-75—289	8033		K Marshall (SCO)	72-75-72-73—292	4150
17	D Richard (USA)	72-73-73-72—290	6614		S Cavalleri (ITA)	73-72-73-74—292	4150
	L Navarro (ESP)	70-70-77-73—290	6614		Yu Chen Huang (TPE)	71-75-72-74—292	4150
	M McNamara (AUS)	72-70-75-73—290	6614		R Hudson (ENG) (am)	72-69-75-76—292	
	T Kimura (JPN)	69-74-74-73—290	6614				

Other players who made the cut: L Davies (ENG), T Barrett (USA), M McKay (SCO), C Dibnah (AUS), K Webb (AUS) J Head (ENG), R Higashio (JPN) 293; C Sörenstam (SWE), J Moodie (SCO), L Hackney (ENG), J Forbes (SCO), J McGill (USA), K Orum (DEN), F Dassu (ITA), A Belen Sanchez (ESP) 294; N Scranton (USA), M Baena (COL), H Kobayashi (JPN), L Lambert (AUS), T Johnson (ENG), A Takamura (JPN), E Poburski (GER), M Dunn (USA), B Pestana (RSA) 297; J Mills (AUS), M Sutton (ENG), B Morgan (WAL) (am), C Schmitt (FRA) 299; P Wright (SCO), S Croce (ITA) 300; N Nijenhuis (NED) (am), C Matthew (SCO) 301; M Hageman (NED) 302; Le Kreutz (FRA), V Stensrud (NOR) 303.

1998 Weetabix Women's British Open Royal Lytham & St Annes, Lancashire [6355–72]

Prize money: £575,000

1	S Steinhauer (USA)	81-72-70-69—292	£100000	20T	J Gallacher-Smith	76-74-74-79—303	6300
2	S Gustafson (SWE)	78-71-74-70—293	50000		K Marshall (SCO)	79-74-71-79—303	6300
	B Burton (USA)	71-74-77-71—293	50000	24	D Andrews (USA)	81-72-76-75—304	5600
4	J Moodie (SCO)	75-72-72-75—294	30000		J Morley (ENG)	79-74-74-77—304	5600
5	K Webb (AUS)	76-76-71-73—296	25000		P Hurst (USA)	76-77-70-81—304	5600
6	L Spalding	76-70-75-76—297	17000	27	C Johnstone-Forbes	78-76-79-72—305	5100
	W Ward (USA)	76-71-74-76—297	17000		S Strudwick	75-72-75-83—305	5100
	S Mehra (IND)	73-77-71-76—297	17000	29	C Koch (SWE)	79-74-76-77—306	4700
	B King (USA)	71-77-72-77—297	17000		K Saiki (JPN)	80-76-73-77—306	4700
10	C Nilsmark (SWE)	77-77-69-75—298	12000	31	C McCurdy	80-77-75-75—307	4216
11	T Johnson (ENG)	72-77-77-73—299	9687		F Dassu (ITA)	82-72-77-76—307	4216
	J Inkster (USA)	75-75-76-73—299	9687		A Nicholas (ENG)	79-72-76-80—307	4216
	A Sörenstam (SWE)	75-73-77-74—299	9687	34	L Fairclough (ENG)	77-77-78-76—308	3300
	ML de Lorenzi (FRA)	79-70-76-74—299	9687		SR Pak (KOR)	78-74-79-77—308	3300
15	M McKay (SCO)	75-74-75-76—300	8000		W Doolan (AUS)	83-72-76-77—308	3300
16	M Murray (SCO)	81-76-69-75—301	7300		L Baugh (USA)	77-80-74-77—308	3300
	D Reid (SCO)	73-79-73-76—301	7300		C Dibnah (AUS)	77-80-74-77—308	3300
	H Wadsworth	79-74-72-76—301	7300		H Dobson (ENG)	80-71-79-78—308	3300
19	H Kobayashi (JPN)	77-74-75-76—302	6800		C McMillan	76-78-76-78—308	3300
20	M Hjörth (SWE)	82-73-76-72—303	6300		C Figg-Currier (USA)	78-78-74-78—308	3300
	K Tschetter	79-75-73-76—303	6300		V Odegard	82-73-74-79—308	3300

Other players who made the cut: E Klein, C Sörenstam, R Carriedo, S Lowe 309; S Dallongeville, L Philo 310; A Munt, C Hall, T Fischer 311; K Pearce, L Kane, B Whitehead, J Forbes, D Barnard 312; I Tinning, L Neumann 313; L Maritz, T Barrett, H Stacy 314; R Hakkarainen, A Berg 316; M Hirase 317; C Johnson 318; M Spencer-Devlin 319; E Knuth 321.

1997 Weetabix Women's British Open Sunningdale   [6255–72]

Prize money: £525,000

1	K Webb (AUS)	65-70-63-71—269	£82500	19T	C Dibnah (AUS)	72-71-70-73—286	5837
2	R Jones (USA)	70-70-66-71—277	52000		A Dibos (PER)	71-72-70-73—286	5837
3	A Sörenstam (SWE)	72-70-69-67—278	36750	23	L Davies (ENG)	74-73-69-71—287	5300
4	B Burton (USA)	73-69-71-67—280	27000		R Hetherington (AUS)	75-70-71-71—287	5300
5	L Hackney (ENG)	74-69-67-71—281	20000		K Tschetter	73-70-72-72—287	5300
	C Matthew (SCO)	70-70-70-71—281	20000	26	E Klein (USA)	69-74-70-75—288	5000
7	W Doolan (AUS)	74-70-68-70—282	14000	27	S Farron	72-75-75-67—289	4475
	T Barrett (USA)	70-72-70-70—282	14000		B Whitehead	71-74-77-67—289	4475
9	C Johnson (USA)	71-71-73-68—283	11500		J Morley (ENG)	75-69-76-69—289	4475
10	C Sörenstam (SWE)	71-70-72-71—284	10100		L Brooky (NED)	72-73-72-72—289	4475
	B King (USA)	71-72-68-73—284	10100		H Alfredsson (SWE)	69-76-72-72—289	4475
12	J Lidback (PER)	71-74-70-70—285	7414		J Moodie (SCO)	74-71-71-73—289	4475
	M Hirase (JPN)	76-65-74-70—285	7414	33	K Lunn (AUS)	74-71-75-70—290	3875
	L Neumann (SWE)	68-75-71-71—285	7414		P Hurst (USA)	76-72-70-72—290	3875
	J Inkster (USA)	69-71-73-72—285	7414		S Cavalleri (ITA) (am)	70-73-73-74—290	
	B Mucha (USA)	72-67-73-73—285	7414	36	S Maynor	72-74-74-71—291	3650
	H Dobson (ENG)	73-69-69-74—285	7414	37	S Strudwick (ENG)	72-74-74-72—292	3350
	K Marshall (SCO)	70-68-73-74—285	7414		D Richard	71-72-75-74—292	3350
19	C Koch (SWE)	76-71-71-68—286	5837		G Graham	73-73-71-75—292	3350
	L Lambert (AUS)	70-73-73-70—286	5837				

Other players who made the cut: M Estill, S Steinhauer, K Parker-Gregory 293; P Meunier Lebouc, A Gottmo, S Prosser, A Fruhwirth, S Waugh 294; M Spencer-Devlin, H Kobayashi, F Dassu 295; T Green, A Yamaoka, T Johnson, E Esterl (am) 296; S Croce, C Pierce, J Lee, W Dicks 297; M Koch, K Taylor, H Wadsworth, L Fairclough, L Kane, M Murray 298; C Figg-Currier 299; N Moult, D Barnard, S Gustafson 301; S Dallongeville 302.

Women's British Open History

Year	Winner	Country	Venue	Score
1976	J Lee Smith	England	Fulford	299
1977	V Saunders	England	Lindrick	306
1978	J Melville	England	Foxhills	310
1979	A Sheard	South Africa	Southport and Ainsdale	301
1980	D Massey	USA	Wentworth (East)	294
1981	D Massey	USA	Northumberland	295
1982	M Figueras-Dotti	Spain	Royal Birkdale	296
1983	Not played			
1984	A Okamoto	Japan	Woburn	289
1985	B King	USA	Moor Park	300
1986	L Davies	England	Royal Birkdale	283
1987	A Nicholas	England	St Mellion	296
1988	C Dibnah*	Australia	Lindrick	296
*Won play-off after a tie with S Little				
1989	J Geddes	USA	Ferndown	274
1990	H Alfredsson*	Sweden	Woburn	288
*Won play-off at fourth extra hole after a tie with J Hill				
1991	P Grice-Whittaker	England	Woburn	284
1992	P Sheehan	USA	Woburn	207
Reduced to 54 holes by rain				
1993	K Lunn	Australia	Woburn	275
1994	L Neumann	Sweden	Woburn	280
1995	K Webb	Australia	Woburn	278
1996	E Klein	USA	Woburn	277
1997	K Webb	Australia	Sunningdale	269
1998	S Steinhauer	USA	Royal Lytham & St Annes	292
1999	S Steinhauer	USA	Woburn	283
2000	S Gustafson	Sweden	Royal Birkdale	282
2001	SR Pak	Korea	Sunningdale	277
2002	K Webb	Australia	Turnberry	273

Year	Winner	Country	Venue	Score
2003	A Sörenstam	Sweden	Royal Lytham & St Annes	278
2004	Karen Stupples	England	Sunningdale (Old Course)	269
2005	Jeong Jang	Korea	Royal Birkdale	272
2006	Sherri Steinhauer	USA	Royal Lytham & St Annes	281

Nineteen LPGA players made all 19 cuts in 2006

Nineteen players made the cut in women's four majors but only five had top 5 positions in three of them – Shi Hyun Ahn, Juli Inkster, Lorena Ochoa, Annika Sörenstam and Michelle Wie.

	Kraft Nabisco	McDonald's LPGA	US Open	Weetabix British Open
Shi Hyun Ahn	tied 8	tied 5	tied 8	25
Paula Creamer	tied 24	tied 49	tied 16	tied 22
Yuri Fudoh	tied 15	tied 20	tied 46	tied 42
Natalie Gulbis	tied 3	tied 20	tied 16	tied 16
Rachel Hetherington	tied 42	tied 34	tied 8	69
Juli Inkster	5	tied 34	6	tied 4
Jeong Jang	tied 19	tied 58	tied 28	tied 26
Cristie Kerr	tied 35	tied 5	tied 28	tied 2
Candie Kung	tied 24	tied 44	tied 28	tied 10
Jee Young Lee	tied 56	tied 14	tied 10	tied 22
Seon Hwa Lee	tied 19	tied 16	tied 49	tied 61
Ai Miyazato	tied 29	tied 3	tied 28	9
Lorena Ochoa	2	tied 9	tied 20	tied 4
Morgan Pressel	tied 13	tied 69	tied 28	tied 56
Annika Sörenstam	tied 6	tied 9	1	tied 31
Sherri Steinhauer	tied 35	tied 16	tied 24	1
Karen Stupples	tied 17	tied 69	tied 20	tied 10
Wendy Ward	tied 35	tied 16	tied 41	tied 67
Michelle Wie	tied 3	tied 5	tied 3	tied 26

US Women's Open Championship

Another major for Sörenstam but this time she needs extra time to edge out Pat Hurst by four shots

It took 90 holes of gritty golf but 35-year-old Annika Sörenstam prevailed for her third US Women's Open title beating Pat Hurst in their 18-hole play-off. Both had tied on level par 284 at Newport Country Club, Rhode Island. In the end, Sörenstam won her tenth major by four shots with a play-off round of 70 and earned another $560,000. The tenth play-off in the US Women's Open history was the most lop-sided affair since Kathy Whitworth beat amateur Barbara McIntire by seven in 1956.

Thirty-seven-year-old Hurst, who was attempting to become the second woman golfer in history to win the US Girls' Junior, US Women's Amateur and US Women's Open, quickly found herself behind in the play-off when she missed the green at the par 5 first hole, dropped a shot and never recovered.

Sörenstam and Hurst had shared the lead at the end of the first and second rounds. Sörenstam edged ahead in their personal battle in the third round but Hurst caught the Swede again with a better final round – 69 to 71.

This was the third major of the year to be decided by a play-off. Karrie Webb beat Lorena Ochoa in a play-off for the Kraft Nabisco Championship and Se Ri Pak beat Webb in the McDonald's LPGA Championship, but both these were by sudden death.

This was Sörenstam's 20th career play-off and she has an impressive 15–5 record. Four amateurs were among the 68 players who made the half-way cut in the Championship with Amanda Blumenherst and Jane Park, who had shared the lead on day one, finishing joint 10th. Se Ri Pak's hopes of becoming the eighth player to win the McDonald's LPGA and US Women's Open in the same year failed by two shots and 46-year-old Juli Inkster lost her chance to become the oldest winner of a major by three after a closing round of 73. She finished sixth.

Michelle Wie, who finished tied third with Pak and Stacy Prammanasudh, was completing her fourth consecutive top-five finish in a major and her second top 10 finish in the 11 majors the 16-year-old had played up to that point.

First Round	Second Round	Third Round	Fourth Round
−2 Sörenstam	−2 Sörenstam	☐ Sörenstam	☐ Sörenstam
−2 Hurst	−2 Hurst	☐ Wie	☐ Hurst
−2 Pak	☐ Wie	+1 Prammanasudh	+2 Pak
−2 J Park (am)	☐ J Park (am)	+1 Inkster	+2 Prammanasudh
	☐ S H Ahn	+2 Hurst	+2 Wie

2006 US Women's Open Championship (61st)
Newport CC, Newport, RI   [6564–71]

Prize Money: $3.1 million. Entries 1,098. Final Field: 156 (29 amateurs), of whom 68 (including 4 amateurs) made the cut on 150 or less.

Players are of American nationality unless stated

1	Annika Sörenstam (SWE)*	69-71-73-71—284	$560000
2	Pat Hurst	69-71-75-69—284	335000

*Play off: 18 holes: Sörenstam 70, Hurst 74

3	Se Ri Pak (KOR)	69-74-74-69—286	156038
	Stacy Prammanasudh	72-71-71-72—286	156038
	Michelle Wie	70-72-71-73—286	156038
6	Juli Inkster	73-70-71-73—287	103575
7	Brittany Lincicome	72-72-69-78—291	93026

10	Amanda Blumenherst (am)	70-77-73-73—293	
	Sophie Gustafson (SWE)	72-72-71-78—293	66174
	Young Kim (KOR)	75-69-75-74—293	66174
	Jee Young Lee (KOR)	71-75-70-77—293	66174
	Patricia Meunier-Lebouc (FRA)	72-73-73-75—293	66174
	Jane Park (am)	69-73-75-76—293	
16	Paula Creamer	71-72-76-75—294	53577
	Natalie Gulbis	76-71-74-73—294	53577
	Sherri Turner	72-74-76-72—294	53577
19	Catriona Matthew (SCO)	74-76-72-73—295	48007
20	Lorena Ochoa (MEX)	71-73-77-75—296	41654
	Gloria Park (KOR)	70-78-76-72—296	41654
	Karen Stupples (ENG)	78-72-70-76—296	41654
	Kristina Tucker (SWE)	72-74-74-76—296	41654
24	Amy Hung (TPE)	76-72-77-72—297	32873
	Lorie Kane (CAN)	73-72-75-77—297	32873
	Sherri Steinhauer	72-75-72-78—297	32873
	Shani Waugh (AUS)	77-72-73-75—297	32873
28	Tracy Hanson	75-71-78-74—298	22529
	Jeong Jang (KOR)	72-71-75-80—298	22529
	Cristie Kerr	73-74-75-76—298	22529
	Carin Koch (SWE)	74-73-73-78—298	22529
	Candie Kung (TPE)	74-70-77-77—298	22529
	Ai Miyazato (JPN)	74-75-70-79—298	22529
	Becky Morgan (WAL)	70-74-77-77—298	22529
	Suzann Pettersen (NOR)	73-74-75-76—298	22529
	Morgan Pressel	76-74-75-73—298	22529
37	Dawn Coe-Jones (CAN)	74-75-73-77—299	17647
	Karrie Webb (AUS)	73-76-74-76—299	17647
	Lindsey Wright (AUS)	74-73-76-76—299	17647
	Heather Young	76-71-77-75—299	17647
41	Maria Hjörth (SWE)	74-75-73-78—300	14954
	Mi Hyun Kim (KOR)	75-72-75-78—300	14954
	Yu Ping Lin (TPE)	76-74-75-75—300	14954
	Aree Song (KOR)	77-72-79-72—300	14954
	Wendy Ward	77-73-77-73—300	14954
46	Yuri Fudoh (JPN)	73-76-75-77—301	12566
	Julieta Granada (PAR)	76-73-79-73—301	12566
	Nancy Scranton	75-71-77-78—301	12566
49	Dana Dormann	74-74-78-76—302	10052
	Seon Hwa Lee (KOR)	75-73-80-74—302	10052
	Siew-Ai Lin (MAS)	74-74-78-76—302	10052
	Alena Sharp (CAN)	77-72-77-76—302	10052
	Karin Sjodin (SWE)	78-72-76-76—302	10052
	Angela Stanford	72-76-77-77—302	10052
55	Moira Dunn	75-74-76-78—303	8749
	Karine Icher (FRA)	73-77-79-74—303	8749
57	Nicole Castrale	74-71-80-79—304	8154
	Silvia Cavalleri (ITA)	71-77-81-75—304	8154
	Rosie Jones	72-75-80-77—304	8154
	Ashley Knoll (am)	77-72-76-79—304	
	Diana Luna (MON)	77-73-77-77—304	8154
62	Beth Bader	75-73-77-80—305	7746
63	Dana Ammaccapane	76-74-79-77—306	7620
64	Denise Munzlinger	75-74-79-79—307	7432
	Sung Ah Yin (KOR)	70-79-75-83—307	7432
66	Kimberly Kim (am)	77-71-78-83—309	
	Kim Saiki	71-78-81-79—309	7243
68	Lynnette Brooky (NZL)	75-75-76-85—311	7107

US Women's Open Championship continued

The following players missed the half-way cut. :

69	Marisa Baena (COL)	80-71—151	94T	Kristen Samp	80-73—153	130T	Hee-Won Han (KOR)	77-80—157
	Minea Blomqvist (FIN)	73-78—151		Kim Welch	73-80—153		Nadina Light (AUS)	76-81—157
	Brandie Burton	71-80—151		Carri Wood	77-76—153		Kelly Robbins	81-76—157
	Vicki Goetze-Ackerman	76-75—151		May Wood	79-74—153	134	Colleen Cashman-McSween	77-81—158
	Candy Hannemann (BRA)	77-74—151	103	Amie Cochran	79-75—154		Dasol Chung (KOR) (am)	82-76—158
	Jamie Hullett	78-73—151		Laura Diaz	79-75—154		Lauren Espinosa (am)	79-79—158
	Soo-Yun Kang (KOR)	75-76—151		Cindy Figg-Currier	78-76—154			
	Sarah Jane Kenyon (AUS)	77-74—151		Allison Hanna	76-78—154		Brandi Jackson (am)	75-83—158
	Brittany Lang	76-75—151		Elizabeth Janangelo	78-76—154		Ayaka Kaneko (JPN) (am)	80-78—158
	Michelle Murphy	76-75—151		Birdie Kim (KOR)	79-75—154		Kristal Parker-Manzo (am)	76-82—158
	Kris Tschetter	80-71—151		In Kyung Kim (KOR) (am)	79-75—154	140	Vicky Hurst (am)	78-82—160
	Veronica Zorzi (ITA)	73-78—151		Taylor Leon (am)	76-78—154		Taylore Karle (am)	78-82—160
81	Helen Alfredsson (SWE)	79-73—152		Teresa Lu (TPE)	80-74—154		Stephanie Kono (am)	82-78—160
	Tina Barrett	79-73—152		Meg Mallon	75-79—154		Mhairi McKay (SCO)	80-80—160
	Randi Gauthier	80-72—152		Maru Martinez (VEN) (am)	77-77—154	144	Stacey Kim (am)	83-78—161
	Jen Hanna	75-77—152		Nicole Perrot (CHI)	76-78—154		Amanda McCurdy (am)	81-80—161
	Young Jo (KOR)	76-76—152		Iben Tinning (DEN)	74-80—154		Wendy Modic	81-80—161
	Christina Kim	78-74—152	116	Il Mi Chung (KOR)	76-79—155	147	Cristina Baena (COL)	84-79—163
	Jennie Lee (am)	76-76—152		Laura Davies (ENG)	78-77—155		Charlotte Campbell	79-84—163
	Sarah Lee (KOR)	76-76—152		Sarah Huarte	75-80—155	149	Beth Bauer	79-85—164
	Charlotte Mayortas	77-75—152		Hilary Lunke	72-83—155		Laree Sugg	82-82—164
	Virada Nirapathpongporn (THA)	74-78—152		Marianne Morris	75-80—155	151	Joanne Lee (am)	83-82—165
	Michele Redman	79-73—152		Jane Rah (am)	78-77—155	152	Sydnee Michaels (am)	81-85—166
	Ya-Ni Tseng (am)	73-79—152		Sophia Sheridan (MEX)	76-79—155	153	Michelle Jarman (am)	83-84—167
	Maria Jose Uribe (am)	76-76—152		Celeste Troche (PAR)	77-78—155		Nicole Hage (am)	89-78—167
94	Keyong Bae (KOR)	76-77—153	124	Beth Allen	79-77—156	155	Megan Grehan (am)	85-83—168
	Becky Iverson	79-74—153		Aimee Cho (KOR)	78-78—156	156	Jennifer Rosales (PHI)	78 WD
	Angela Jerman	80-73—153		Esther Choe (am)	79-77—156			
	Jill McGill	75-78—153		Sandra Gal (GER) (am)	78-78—156			
	Liselotte Neumann (SWE)	76-77—153		Hana Kim	78-78—156			
				Paige MacKenzie (am)	74-82—156			
			130	Jennie Arseneault (am)	77-80—157			

Golf pioneer Patty Berg passes away at 88

Patty Berg, who won an LPGA Tour record of 15 major titles and was on of the 13 founding members of the tour in 1950, died in 2006 aged 88.

She was the LPGA Tour's first president from 1950–52 and the Tour's money leader in 1954, 1955 and 1957. She scored 60 victories and was a member of the LPGA Tour and World Golf Halls of Fame.

Berg won the 1938 US Women's Amateur and swept the 1937–39 Titleholders as an amateur for her first three major victories. After turning pro, she won the 1946 US Women's Open, four more Titleholders and was a seven-times winner of the Women's Western Open.

"As a founder, Patty took the LPGA to new heights and it was the work, passion and dedication that she and her fellow co-founders exhibited that has allowed the association to grow and prosper for so many years", said Tour Commissioner Carolyn Bivens. "I, along with the entire LPGA family, mourn Patty's passing, but we will forever celebrate her legacy".

Patty and the other LPGA founders were honoured in 2000 with the Commissioner's Award and in 2002 she was the honorary chair for the 2002 Solheim Cup at her home course, Interlachen Country Club in Edina, Minnesota.

2005 US Women's Open Championship Cherry Hill, CO [6749–71]

Prize money: $1.5 million

1	Birdie Kim (KOR)	74-72-69-72—287	$560000		23T	Sarah Huarte	74-76-73-73—296	34556
2	Brittany Lang (am)	69-77-72-71—289				Gloria Park (KOR)	74-75-74-73—296	34556
	Morgan Pressel (am)	71-73-70-75—289				Nicole Perrot (CHI)	70-70-78-78—296	34556
4	Natalie Gulbis	70-75-74-71—290	272723			Jennifer Rosales (PHI)	72-76-73-75—296	34556
	Lorie Kane (CAN)	74-71-76-69—290	272723			Annika Sörenstam		
6	Karine Icher (FRA)	69-75-75-72—291	116310			(SWE)	71-75-73-77—296	34556
	Young Jo (KOR)	74-71-70-76—291	116310			Michelle Wie (am)	69-73-72-82—296	
	Candie Kung (TPE)	73-73-71-74—291	116310		31	Rachel Hetherington		
	Lorena Ochoa (MEX)	74-68-77-72—291	116310			(AUS)	74-69-76-78—297	23479
10	Cristie Kerr	74-71-72-75—292	80523			Mi Hyun Kim (KOR)	72-73-76-76—297	23479
	Angela Stanford	69-74-73-76—292	80523			Brittany Lincicome	74-74-78-71—297	23479
	Karen Stupples (ENG)	75-70-69-78—292	80523			Catriona Matthew		
13	Tina Barrett	73-74-71-75—293	61402			(SCO)	73-72-75-77—297	23479
	Heather Bowie	77-73-69-74—293	61402			Karrie Webb (AUS)	76-73-73-75—297	23479
	Jamie Hullett	75-72-70-76—293	61402		36	Kim Saiki	74-73-74-77—298	20386
	Soo Yun Kang (KOR)	74-74-74-71—293	61402			Wendy Ward	74-74-75-75—298	20386
	Paige MacKenzie (am)	75-75-69-74—293			38	Il Mi Chung (KOR)	75-71-76-77—299	17939
	Meg Mallon	71-74-75-73—293	61402			Johanna Head (ENG)	74-73-75-77—299	17939
19	Paula Creamer	74-69-72-79—294	47480			Juli Inkster	77-71-75-76—299	17939
	Rosie Jones	73-72-74-75—294	47480			Young Kim (KOR)	73-73-70-83—299	17939
	Leta Lindley	73-76-73-72—294	47480			Sarah Lee (KOR)	79-70-75-75—299	17939
	Liselotte Neumann	70-75-73-76—294	47480			Amanda McCurdy		
	(SWE)					(am)	75-75-71-78—299	17939
23	Helen Alfredsson (SWE)	72-73-74-77—296	34556			Aree Song (KOR)	77-70-72-80—299	17939
	Laura Diaz	75-73-72-76—296	34556					

Other players who made the cut: Se Ri Pak (KOR), Nancy Scranton, 300; Beth Bader, Dorothy Delasin (PHI), Hee Won Han (KOR), 301; Arnie Cochran (am), Jeong Janh (KOR), 302; Katie Allison, Eva Dahllof (SWE), Stephanie Louden, Grace Park (KOR), Suzann Pettersen (NOR), Kris Tschetter, 303; Katie Futcher, Sophie Gustafson (SWE), Kaori Higo (JPN), Carri Wood, 304; Candy Hannemann (BRA), 307; Jean Bartholomew, 309.

2004 US Women's Open Championship The Orchards, South Hadley, MA [6473–71]

Prize money: $3.1 million

1	Meg Mallon	73-69-67-65—274	$560000		20T	Kate Golden	74-71-72-71—288	38660
2	Annika Sörenstam	71-68-70-67—276	335000			Johanna Head (ENG)	76-69-70-73—288	38660
	(SWE)					Rosie Jones	74-72-72-70—288	38660
3	Kelly Robbins	74-67-68-69—278	208863			Young Kim (KOR)	71-73-76-68—288	38660
4	Jennifer Rosales (PHI)	70-67-69-75—281	145547			Kim Saiki	70-68-74-76—288	38660
5	Candie Kung (TPE)	70-68-74-70—282	111173			Liselotte Neumann	72-72-72-72—288	38660
	Michele Redman	70-72-73-67—282	111173			• (SWE)		
7	Moira Dunn	73-67-72-71—283	86744		27	Beth Daniel	69-74-71-75—289	29195
	Pat Hurst	70-71-71-71—283	86744			Cristie Kerr	73-71-74-71—289	29195
	Jeong Jang (KOR)	72-74-71-66—283	86744		29	Shi Hyun Ahn (KOR)	73-71-72-74—290	24533
10	Michelle Ellis (Aus)	70-69-72-73—284	68813			Lorie Kane (CAN)	75-70-72-73—290	24533
	Carin Koch (SWE)	72-67-75-70—284	68813			Deb Richard	71-73-72-74—290	24533
	Rachel Teske (AUS)	71-69-70-74—284	68813		32	Allison Hanna	71-75-74-71—291	20539
13	Paula Creamer (am)	72-69-72-72—285				Becky Morgan (WAL)	71-74-73-73—291	20539
	Patricia Meunier–					Se Ri Pak (KOR)	70-76-71-74—291	20539
	Labouc (FRA)	67-75-74-69—285	60602			Sherri Steinhauer	74-71-73-73—291	20539
	Michelle Wie (am)	71-70-71-73—285				Karen Stupples (ENG)	71-72-77-71—291	20539
16	Mi Hyun Kim (KOR)	76-68-71-71—286	54052		37	Jenna Daniels	76-71-72-73—292	16897
	Suzann Pettersen	74-72-71-69—286	54052			AJ Eathorne (CAN)	73-72-75-72—292	16897
	(NOR)					Natalie Gulbis	73-71-75-73—292	16897
	Karrie Webb (AUS)	72-71-71-72—286	54052			Jamie Hullett	72-74-74-72—292	16897
19	Catriona Matthew	73-71-72-71—287	48432			Christina Kim	74-71-76-71—292	16897
	(SCO)					Jill McGill	71-75-71-75—292	16897
20	Dawn Coe-Jones (CAN)	71-73-72-72—288	38660			Gloria Park (KOR)	76-71-73-72—292	16897

Other players who made the cut: Donna Andrews, Laura Diaz, Jennifer Greggain, Ji-Hee Lee, Mhairi McKay (SCO), Lorena Ochoa (MEX) 293; Jennie Lee (am) 294; Katherine Hull 295; Tina Barrett, Catherine Cartwright, Hee-Won Han (KOR) 296; Brittany Lincicome (am) 297; Loraine Lambert, Aree Song (KOR) 298; Liz Earley, Allison Finney, Juli Inkster 299; Mee Lee (KOR), Seol-An Jeon (KOR), Courtney Swaim 300; Hilary Lunke, Grace Park (KOR) 301; Li Ying Ye 304.

2003 US Women's Open Championship Pumpkin Ridge GC, North Plains, OR   [6509–71]

Prize money: $3.1 million

1	Hilary Lunke*	71-69-68-75—283	$560000	20	Beth Daniel	73-69-77-74—293	43491
2	Kelly Robbins	74-69-71-69—283	272004		Yuri Fudoh (JPN)	74-72-75-72—293	43491
	Angela Stanford	70-70-69-74—283	272004	22	Lorie Kane (CAN)	73-75-73-73—294	36575
Play-off rounds: Hilary Lunke 70, Angela Stanford 71,					Christina Kim	74-74-72-74—294	36575
Kelly Robbins 73					Leta Lindley	73-69-77-75—294	36575
4	Annika Sörenstam	72-72-67-73—284	150994		Catriona Matthew	74-70-76-74—294	36575
	(SWE)				(SCO)		
5	Aree Song (am)	70-73-68-74—285		26	Danielle Ammaccapane	74-74-73-74—295	28354
6	Jeong Jang (KOR)	73-69-69-75—286	115333		Dorothy Delasin (PHI)	79-70-76-70—295	28354
	Mhairi McKay (SCO)	66-70-75-75—286	115333		Kelli Kuehne	72-74-75-74—295	28354
8	Juli Inkster	69-71-74-73—287	97363		Paula Marti (ESP)	71-76-76-72—295	28354
9	Rosie Jones	70-72-73-73—288	90241	30	Ashli Bunch	71-73-77-75—296	22678
10	Grace Park (KOR)	72-76-73-68—289	79243		Annette DeLuca	71-73-78-74—296	22678
	Suzann Pettersen (NOR)	76-69-69-75—289	79243		Elizabeth Janangelo	75-73-73-75—296	
12	Donna Andrews	69-72-72-77—290	71362		(am)		
13	Laura Diaz	71-71-74-76—292	56500		Mi-Hyun Kim (KOR)	73-73-73-77—296	22678
	Natalie Gulbis	73-69-72-78—292	56500		Jane Park (am)	76-73-74-73—296	
	Cristie Kerr	72-73-73-74—292	56500	35	Candy Hannemann	75-69-73-80—297	20360
	Patricia Meunier-	73-69-74-76—292	56500		(BRA)		
	Lebouc (FRA)				Stephanie Louden	71-74-77-75—297	20360
	Lorena Ochoa (MEX)	71-75-72-74—292	56500		Guilia Sergas (ITA)	70-74-79-74—297	20360
	Jennifer Rosales (PHI)	74-69-76-73—292	56500		Kirsty Taylor (ENG)	71-75-73-78—297	20360
	Rachel Teske (AUS)	71-73-72-76—292	56500	39	Michele Redman	71-74-74-79—298	18783

Other players who made the cut: Heather Bowie, Karen Stupples (ENG) 299; Beth Bauer, Hee-Won Han (KOR), Jamie Hullett, Emilee Klein, Becky Morgan (WAL), Karen Weiss 300; Sherri Turner 301; Se Ri Pak (KOR) 302; Leigh Ann Hardin (am) 303; Morgan Pressel (am) 304; Alison Nicholas (ENG), Suzanne Strudwick (ENG), Michelle Vinieratos 305; Yu Ping Lin (TPE) 306; Mollie Fankhauser (am) 307; Irene Cho (am) 308; Mardi Lunn (AUS) 309

2002 US Women's Open Championship Prairie Dunes, Hutchinson, KS   [6253–70]

Prize money: $3,000,000

1	Juli Inkster	67-72-71-66—276	$535000	22T	Susan Ginter-Brooker	74-72-70-74—290	26894
2	Annika Sörenstam	70-69-69-70—278	315000		Jeong Jang (KOR)	73-73-74-70—290	26894
	(SWE)				Rosie Jones	71-77-69-73—290	26894
3	Shani Waugh (AUS)	67-73-71-72—283	202568		Mi Hyun Kim (KOR)	74-72-70-74—290	26894
4	Raquel Carriedo (ESP)	75-71-72-66—284	141219		Meg Mallon	73-75-73-69—290	26894
5	Se Ri Pak (KOR)	74-75-68-68—285	114370		Catriona Matthew		
6	Mhairi McKay (SCO)	70-75-71-70—286	101421		(SCO)	69-80-72-69—290	26894
7	Beth Daniel	71-76-71-69—287	78016		Stacy Prammanasudh	75-74-72-69—290	26894
	Laura Diaz	67-72-77-71—287	78016		Michele Redman	71-69-73-77—290	26894
	Kelli Kuehne	70-76-72-69—287	78016	32	Brandie Burton	70-74-76-71—291	18730
	Janice Moodie (SCO)	71-72-71-73—287	78016		Laura Davies (ENG)	75-73-68-75—291	18730
	Jennifer Rosales (PHI)	73-72-74-68—287	78016		Hee-Won Han (KOR)	72-77-70-72—291	18730
12	Lynnette Brooky (NZL)	73-73-69-73—288	54201		Cristie Kerr	74-71-72-74—291	18730
	Stephanie Keever	72-71-73-72—288	54201		Charlotta Sörenstam	73-70-77-71—291	18730
	Jill McGill	71-70-69-78—288	54201		(SWE)		
	Joanne Morley (ENG)	78-68-73-69—288	54201	37	Jenna Daniels	72-70-77-73—292	15209
	Kelly Robbins	71-74-74-69—288	54201		Wendy Doolan (AUS)	73-76-75-68—292	15209
	Rachel Teske (AUS)	75-71-72-70—288	54201		Jackie Gallagher-Smith	70-76-73-73—292	15209
18	Donna Andrews	74-74-70-71—289	40738		Carin Koch (SWE)	73-72-70-77—292	15209
	Beth Bauer	74-72-71-72—289	40738		Liselotte Neumann	72-74-70-76—292	15209
	Lorie Kane (CAN)	69-77-69-74—289	40738		(SWE)		
	Grace Park (KOR)	71-77-71-70—289	40738		Karen Stupples (ENG)	80-68-72-72—292	15209
22	Danielle Ammaccapane	74-71-73-72—290	26894		Kris Tschetter	72-77-72-71—292	15209
	Michelle Ellis (AUS)	71-71-75-73—290	26894				

Other players who made the cut: Jean Bartholomew, Audra Burke, Mitzi Edge, Jung Yeon Lee (KOR), Gloria Park (KOR), Cindy Schreyer, Leslie Spalding 293; Alicia Dibos (PER), Vicki Goetze-Ackerman, Angela Jerman (am), Ara Koh (KOR), Sherri Steinhauer, Karen Weiss, Aree Song Wongluekiet (THA) 294; Amy Fruhwirth, Kim Saiki; Sherri Turner 295; Heather Bowie, Soo Young Moon (KOR) 296; Patricia Meunier-Lebouc (FRA) 297; Dawn Coe-Jones (CAN), Dorothy Delasin (PHI), Pearl Sin (KOR) 298; Allison Finney 299; Tracy Hanson 300; Michele Vinieratos 301.

2001 US Women's Open Championship Southern Pines, NC [6256–70]

Prize money: $2,700,000

1	Karrie Webb (AUS)	70-65-69-69—273	$520000	19T	Dorothy Delasin (PHI)	75-70-70-73—288	37327
2	Se Ri Pak (KOR)	69-70-70-72—281	310000	24	Beth Daniel	73-70-71-75—289	30091
3	Dottie Pepper	74-69-70-69—282	202580		Audra Burks	70-72-72-75—289	30091
4	Cristie Kerr	69-73-71-70—283	118697	26	Brandie Burton	73-70-77-70—290	24649
	Sherri Turner	72-70-71-70—283	118697		Helen Alfredsson (SWE)	71-73 74-72—290	24649
	Catriona Matthew (SCO)	72-68-70-73—283	118697		Mi Hyun Kim (KOR)	68-76-72-74—290	24649
7	Lorie Kane (CAN)	75-68-72-69—284	80726		Janice Moodie (SCO)	71-70-73-76—290	24649
	Kristi Albers	71-69-74-70—284	80726	30	Kris Tschetter	72-74-77-68—291	20472
	Kelli Kuehne	70-71-72-71—284	80726		Michelle Ellis	75-69-75-72—291	20472
	Wendy Doolan	71-70-70-73—284	80726		Candy Hannemann	73-73-72-73—291	
11	Sophie Gustafson (SWE)	74-66-74-71—285	66581		(BRA) (am)		
12	Kelly Robbins	72-68-76-70—286	57088		Meg Mallon	72-70-76-73—291	20472
	AJ Eathorne (CAN)	67-71-75-73—286	57088	34	Pat Hurst	73-71-76-72—292	18408
	Juli Inkster	68-72-71-75—286	57088		Natalie Gulbis (am)	73-71-75-73—292	
	Yuri Fudoh (JPN)	73-68-70-75—286	57088		Catrin Nilsmark (SWE)	70-76-72-74—292	18408
16	Emilee Klein	72-69-75-71—287	46885		Dina Ammaccapane	69-73-75-75—292	18408
	Michele Redman	70-72-73-72—287	46885		Karen Weiss	74-71-71-76—292	18408
	Annika Sörenstam (SWE)	70-72-73-72—287	46885	39	Marcy Newton	74-72-74-73—293	16061
19	Maria Hjörth (SWE)	70-71-77-70—288	37327		Liselotte Neumann	70-73-76-74—293	16064
	Marisa Baena (COL)	71-72-75-70—288	37327		(SWE)		
	Jill McGill	68-76-72-72—288	37327		Rosie Jones	73-68-75-77—293	16061
	Wendy Ward	70-71-74-73—288	37327		Grace Park (KOR)	76-70-69-78—293	16061

Other players who made the cut: Leta Lindley, Paula Marti (ESP), Amy Fruhwirth, Aki Nakano, Cindy Figg-Currier, Alison Nicholas (ENG) 294; Pearl Sinn (KOR) 295; Stephanie Keever (am), Christina Kim (am), Sherri Steinhauer 296; Smriti Mehra (IND), Jean Bartholamew, Raquel Carriedo (ESP) 297; Terry-Jo Myers; Yu Ping Lin (TPE), Jamie Hullett 299, Lynnette Brooky, Lisa Strom 299.

2000 US Women's Open Championship Merit Club, Libertyville, IL [6540–72]

Prize money: $2,700,000

1	Karrie Webb (AUS)	69-72-68-73—282	$500000	21	Jackie Gallagher Smith	71-77-73-74—295	34113
2	Cristie Kerr	72-71-74-70—287	240228		Wendy Doolan (AUS)	77-69-74-75—295	34113
	Meg Mallon	68-72-73-74—287	240228	23	Donna Andrews	73-75-79-70—297	28404
4	Rosie Jones	73-71-72-72—288	120119		Kristi Albers	71-77-73-76—297	28404
	Mi Hyun Kim (KOR)	74-72-70-72—288	120119		Michele Redman	74-74-73-76—297	28404
6	Grace Park (KOR)	74-72-73-70—289	90458		Juli Inkster	70-74-73-80—297	28404
	Kelli Kuehne	71-74-73-71—289	90458	27	Charlotta Sörenstam	75-74-76-73—298	21740
8	Beth Daniel	71-74-72-73—290	79345		(SWE)		
9	Annika Sörenstam	73-75-73-70—291	67369		AJ Eathorne (CAN)	73-77-73-75—298	21740
	(SWE)				Silvia Cavalleri (ITA)	72-73-75-78—298	21740
	Kelly Robbins	74-73-71-73—291	67369		Joanne Morley (ENG)	73-72-74-79—298	21740
	Laura Davies (ENG)	73-71-72-75—291	67369	31	Tina Barrett	72-78-75-74—299	17067
12	Jennifer Rosales (PHI)	75-75-69-73—292	55355		Danielle Ammaccapane	72-73-79-75—299	17067
	Pat Hurst	73-72-72-75—292	55355		Emilee Klein	77-72-75-75—299	17067
	Dorothy Delasin (PHI)	76-68-72-76—292	55355		Fiona Pike (AUS)	72-74-77-76—299	17067
15	Se Ri Pak (KOR)	74-75-75-69—293	47846		Kate Golden	75-72-76-76—299	17067
	Kellee Booth	70-78-75-70—293	47846		Jenny Lidback (PER)	73-74-76-76—299	17067
17	Janice Moodie (SCO)	73-77-75-69—294	40586		Carin Koch (SWE)	75-73-73-78—299	17067
	Kathryn Marshall (SCO)	72-72-77-73—294	40586		Sophie Gustafson	72-78-71-78—299	17067
	Shani Waugh (AUS)	69-75-73-77—294	40586		(SWE)		
	Lorie Kane (CAN)	71-74-72-77—294	40586		Hiromi Kobayashi (JPN)	77-72-70-80—299	17067

Other players who made the cut: Michelle Ellis (AUS), Valerie Skinner, Mary Beth Zimmerman, Naree Wongluekiet (am) 300; Catriona Matthew (SCO), Jill McGill 301; Leta Lindley, Nancy Scranton, Nancy Lopez, Jan Stephenson (AUS), Jae Jean Ro (am), Betsy King, Sara Sanders 302; Jean Zedlitz 304; Marisa Baena (COL), Anna Macosko 305; Hilary Homeyer (am) 306; Carri Wood 307; Barb Mucha 308; Pearl Sinn (KOR) 310; Michelle McGann 311

1999 US Women's Open Championship Old Waverley, West Point, MS   [6421–72]

Prize money: $1,750,000

1	J Inkster	65-69-67-71—272	$315000	20T	L Lindley	72-72-73-70—287	21832
2	S Turner	69-69-68-71—277	185000		S Gustafson (SWE)	72-72-70-73—287	21832
3	K Kuehne	64-71-70-74—279	118227		D Andrews	69-71-72-75—287	21832
4	L Kane (CAN)	70-64-71-75—280	82399		H Fukushima (JPN)	69-70-71-77—287	21832
5	C Koch (SWE)	72-69-68-72—281	62938	25	K Saiki	70-71-73-74—288	16006
	M Mallon	70-70-69-72—281	62938		S Croce (ITA)	71-71-71-75—288	16006
7	K Webb (AUS)	70-70-68-74—282	53132		R Jones	71-70-72-75—288	16006
8	H Dobson (ENG)	71-70-73-69—283	45244		L Kiggens	71-67-73-77—288	16006
	M Hjörth (SWE)	73-69-70-71—283	45244		S Steinhauer	68-69-73-78—288	16006
	C Matthew (SCO)	69-68-74-72—283	45244	30	M Lunn (AUS)	72-71-74-72—289	11652
	G Park (KOR) (am)	70-67-73-73—283			J Zedlitz	75-67-75-72—289	11652
12	H Alfredsson (SWE)	72-68-70-74—284	37666		M McKay (SCO)	73-68-76-72—289	11652
	B Iverson	72-64-73-75—284	37666		N Scranton	69-72-75-73—289	11652
14	M Redman	72-71-75-67—285	32389		D Coe Jones	73-71-71-74—289	11652
	Se Ri Pak (KOR)	68-70-74-73—285	32389		A Acker Macosko	73-71-71-74—289	11652
	D Pepper	68-69-72-76—285	32389		K Robbins	70-70-74-75—289	11652
17	L Neumann (SWE)	73-71-69-73—286	27422	37	H Kobayashi (JPN)	74-70-76-70—290	10078
	AJ Eathorne (CAN)	69-71-71-75—286	27422		D Dormann	74-70-73-73—290	10078
	C Nilsmark (SWE)	69-71-70-76—286	27422		K Booth (am)	71-73-70-76—290	
20	C McCurdy	72-72-74-69—287	21832				

Other players who made the cut: M Estill, M Berteotti, K Tschetter, W Ward, M Dunn 291; P Kerrigan, S Strudwick (ENG) 292; B King, B Daniel, B Mucha, A Munt, W Doolan, V Odegard 293; M Will, R Hetherington (AUS) 294; J Lidback, L Hackney, C Figg-Currier, A Nicholas (ENG) 295; P Rizzo 296; J Feldott, P Hammel 297; K Millies 298; T Green 299

1998 US Women's Open Championship Blackwolf Run, Wisconsin, WI   [6412–71]

Prize money: $1,500,000

1	Se Ri Pak* (KOR)	69-70-75-76—290	$267500	19T	J Lidback (PER)	71-73-79-75—298	18998
2	J Chuasiriporn (am)	72-71-75-72—290			A Fukushima (JPN)	72-71-79-76—298	18998
*Se Ri Pak won at second extra hole after both had shot 73					R Jones	74-74-74-76—298	18998
in the play-off					W Ward	76-69-75-78—298	18998
3	L Neumann (SWE)	70-70-75-76—291	157500		D Andrews	70-75-75-78—298	18998
4	Dani Ammaccapane	76-71-74-71—292	77351		L Walters (CAN)	76-70-74-78—298	18998
	P Hurst	69-75-75-73—292	77351	26	D Dormann	72-76-79-72—299	12972
	C Johnson	72-70-76-74—292	77351		N Scranton	76-72-78-73—299	12972
7	S Croce (ITA)	74-71-76-72—293	46737		M Estill	75-74-76-74—299	12972
	T Green	73-71-76-73—293	46737		H Dobson (ENG)	71-75-77-76—299	12972
	M McKay (SCO)	72-70-73-78—293	46737		L Rinker Graham	75-71-77-76—299	12972
10	T Johnson (ENG)	73-71-77-73—294	39015	31	K Williams	68-81-79-72—300	10093
11	L Davies (ENG)	68-75-78-74—295	34929		P Hammel	71-79-77-73—300	10093
	D Pepper	71-71-78-75—295	34929		B Daniel	77-69-78-76—300	10093
13	C Koch (SWE)	72-74-77-73—296	30684		D Eggeling	71-72-79-78—300	10093
	H Alfredsson (SWE)	75-75-73-73—296	30684		K Webb (AUS)	76-73-73-78—300	10093
15	H Stacy	76-68-82-71—297	25871	36	D Coe Jones	71-74-83-73—301	8897
	A Acker Macosko	74-74-76-73—297	25871		I Blais (am)	74-73-78-76—301	
	Dina Ammaccapane	75-70-78-74—297	25871		K Tschetter	75-72-77-77—301	8897
	B Burton	74-72-77-74—297	25871		B Corrie Kuehn (am)	70-72-80-79—301	
19	L Kane (CAN)	74-72-82-70—298	18998		L Spalding	69-74-78-80—301	8897

Other players who made the cut: H Wadsworth, E Klein, N Bowen, A Sörenstam, B Mucha 302; P Bradley, P Rizzo, P Sinn 304; K Albers, M Redman, M Lovander, K Booth (am), A De Luca 305; H Kobayashi 306; ML de Lorenz 307; S Lowe 308; J Stephenson, TJ Myers 309; JJ Robertson (am) 310; C Kerr 311; K Parker 314; K Baue 316.

1997 US Women's Open Championship Pumpkin Ridge GC, Cornelius, OR [6365–71]

Prize money: $1,300,000

1	A Nicholas (ENG)	70-66-67-71—274	$232500	21	K Kuehne	72-73-74-67—286	13800
2	N Lopez	69-68-69-69—275	137500		K Weiss	74-72-72-68—286	13800
3	K Robbins	68-69-74-66—277	86708		Se Ri Pak (KOR)	68-74-75-69—286	13800
4	K Webb (AUS)	73-72-65-68—278	60432		P Hurst	72-74-70-70—286	13800
5	S Croce (ITA)	72-69-71-67—279	46159		L Bemvenuti	73-71-72-70—286	13800
	L Hackney (ENG)	71-70-67-71—279	46159		C Pierce	71-71-73-71—286	13800
7	T Green	74-70-71-65—280	37542	27	C Matthew (SCO)	76-69-70-72—287	10961
	M Redman	74-67-70-69—280	37542	28	S Smyers	71-71-75-71—288	9188
9	P Sheehan	72-71-71-68—282	28769		P Bradley	72-71-73-72—288	9188
	C Johnson	72-68-73-69—282	28769		K Marshall (SCO)	72-71-73-72—288	9188
	D Coe-Jones	72-67-73-70—282	28769		B King	74-72-69-73—288	9188
	D Andrews	74-71-66-71—282	28769		J Pitcock	71-69-75-73—288	9188
	A Fukushima (JPN)	71-71-69-71—282	28769	33	D Eggeling	71-74-76-70—291	7392
14	B Burton	73-72-69-70—284	21287		E Makings	72-73-75-71—291	7392
	D Pepper	72-70-72-70—284	21287		V Fergon	72-75-71-73—291	7392
	J Inkster	72-66-76-70—284	21287		M Morris	75-69-74-73—291	7392
	L Neumann (SWE)	67-70-76-71—284	21287		R Jones	70-74-73-74—291	7392
	D Richard	68-70-73-73—284	21287		P Sinn	70-73-74-74—291	7392
19	T Johnson (ENG)	69-74-71-71—285	17407		M McGann	73-70-73-75—291	7392
	K Williams	71-71-67-76—285	17407		C Nilsmark (SWE)	76-70-69-76—291	7392

Other players who made the cut: A Dibos, J McGill 292; N Bowen, M McGeorge, M Mallon, J Lidback, E Wicoff 293; J Stephenson, H Alfredsson, L Kane 294; B Iverson, B Mucha 295; E Klein, J Gallagher-Smith, M Spencer-Devlin 296; T Hanson, S Redman, J Chuasiriporn (am) 297; D Dormann, N Harvey 298; M Edge, R Walton 299; B Corrie Kuehn (am) 302; P Dunlap 303.

US Women's Open History

Year	Winner	Runner-up		Venue	Score
1946	P Berg	B Jamieson		Spokane	5 and 4

Changed to strokeplay

Year	Winner		Venue	Score
1947	B Jamieson		Greensboro	300
1948	B Zaharias		Atlantic City	300
1949	L Suggs		Maryland	291
1950	B Zaharias		Wichita	291
1951	B Rawls		Atlanta	294
1952	L Suggs		Bala, PA	284
1953	B Rawls*		Rochester, NY	302

*Won play-off after a tie with J Pung 71-77

1954	B Zaharias		Peabody, MA	291
1955	F Crocker		Wichita	299
1956	K Cornelius*		Duluth	302

*Won play-off after a tie with B McIntire (am) 75-82

1957	B Rawls		Mamaroneck	299
1958	M Wright		Bloomfield Hills, MI	290
1959	M Wright		Pittsburgh, PA	287
1960	B Rawls		Worchester, MA	292
1961	M Wright		Springfield, NJ	293
1962	M Lindstrom		Myrtle Beach	301
1963	M Mills		Kenwood	289
1964	M Wright*		San Diego	290

*Won play-off after a tie with R Jessen, Seattle 70-72

1965	C Mann		Northfield, NJ	290
1966	S Spuzich		Hazeltine National, MN	297
1967	C Lacoste (FRA) (am)		Hot Springs, VA	294

US Women's Open History *continued*

Year	Winner	Venue	Score
1968	S Berning	Moselem Springs, PA	289
1969	D Caponi	Scenic-Hills	294
1970	D Caponi	Muskogee, OK	287
1971	J Gunderson-Carner	Erie, PA	288
1972	S Berning	Mamaroneck, NY	299
1973	S Berning	Rochester, NY	290
1974	S Haynie	La Grange, IL	295
1975	S Palmer	Northfield, NJ	295
1976	J Carner*	Springfield, PA	292

Won play-off after a tie with S Palmer. Play-off scores: Carner 76, Palmer 78

1977	H Stacy	Hazeltine, MN	292
1978	H Stacy	Indianapolis	299
1979	J Britz	Brooklawn, CN	284
1980	A Alcott	Richland, TN	280
1981	P Bradley	La Grange, IL	279
1982	J Alex	Del Paso, Sacramento, CA	283
1983	J Stephenson (AUS)	Broken Arrow, OK	290
1984	H Stacy	Salem, MA	290
1985	K Baker	Baltusrol, NJ	280
1986	J Geddes*	NCR	287

Won play-off after a tie with J Carner and A Okamoto. Play-off scores: Davies 71, Okamoto 73, Carner 74

1987	L Davies (ENG)*	Plainfield	285

Won play-off after a tie with J Carner and A Okamoto. Play-off scores: Davies 71, Okamoto 73, Carner 74

1988	L Neumann (SWE)	Baltimore	277
1989	B King	Indianwood, MI	278
1990	B King	Atlanta Athletic Club, GA	284
1991	M Mallon	Colonial, TX	283
1992	P Sheehan*	Oakmont, PA	280

Won play-off after a tie with J Inkster. Play-off scores: Sheehan 72, Inkster 74

1993	L Merton	Crooked Stick	280
1994	P Sheehan	Indianwood, MI	277
1995	A Sörenstam (SWE)	The Broadmore, CO	278
1996	A Sörenstam (SWE)	Pine Needles Lodge, NC	272
1997	A Nicholas (ENG)	Pumpkin Ridge, OR	274
1998	SR Pak (KOR)*	Blackwolf Run, WI	290

Won play-off after a tie with J Chausiriporn (am). Play-off: Both shot 73 then in sudden death Pak 5,3; Chausiriporn 5,4

1999	J Inkster	Old Waverley, West Point, MS	272
2000	K Webb (AUS)	Merit Club, Libertyville, IL	282
2001	K Webb (AUS)	Pine Needles Lodge & GC, NC	273
2002	J Inkster	Prairie Dunes, KS	276
2003	H Lunke*	Pumpkin Ridge GC, OR	283

Won play-off after a tie with Kelly Robins and Angela Stanford. Play-off scores: Lunke 70, Stanford 71, Robins 73

2004	M Mallon	The Orchards, S Hadley, MA	274
2005	B Kim (KOR)	Cherry Hills CC, CO	287
2006	A Sörenstam (SWE)*	Newport CC, RI	284

Play off: 18 holes: Sörenstam 70, Pat Hurst 74

McDonald's LPGA Championship

Back to her best, Se Ri Pak returns to pick up her fifth major in a play-off with Webb

A tap-in birdie at the first extra hole at the Bulle Rock course at Havre de Grace in Maryland earned Se Ri Pak victory over Karrie Webb in the McDonald's LPGA Championship. Twenty-eight-year-old Pak had finished tied with the Australian on eight-under-par 280, missing a chance to win in regulation time by three-putting the final green. Second time around at the 385 yards 18th – the first hole of sudden death, she miss-hit her drive but then produced a glorious 4-iron second which flew all of 200 yards and finished inches from the cup to record her 23rd career victory and collect her fifth major.

It was Pak's first win since May 2004 and she was back to her very best after a lean period during which she had injuries to her neck, shoulder, lower back and finger. "My game right now has more consistency than before," said Pak who had finished 102nd in the money list the previous year after teeing up only 12 times.

Webb, winner of the Kraft Nabisco Championship, the first major of the year, in a play-off with Lorena Ochoa, had felt she had the upper hand but admitted "Se Ri hit an unbelievable shot." Webb missed a 12-footer to keep the play-off alive.

Mi Hyun Kim and Japanese golfer Ai Miyazato finished one shot back on seven-under-par 281 while Cristie Kerr, Michelle Wie, Shi Hyun Ahn and Pat Hurst all tied for fifth on six-under 282. Three-time defending champion Annika Sörenstam did not relinquish her crown without a final round surge. A day after her third round 75, she rebounded and put her self back into contention with four consecutive birdies in the mid-round but she ended three back tied ninth after making a bogey at the last in her closing 68, jointly best of the day with Webb, Cristie Kerr and Reilly Rankin.

With her runner-up spot, Webb passed the $1 million mark in season earnings for the fifth time. Nicole Castrale led after the first round by two from Pat Hurst thanks to a bogey-free 64, her best career round by three shots, but Hurst had taken over after half way from Castrale and Wie, who trailed by two. Pak was three behind after 36 holes.

Ai Miyazato joined Hurst in the lead by one from Michelle Wie and Mi Hyun Kim after three rounds with Pak two back but in the end it was welcome back to the winner's circle on the final day to a golfer who will be inducted in 2007 into the LPGA Tour and World Golf Hall of Fame.

First Round	Second Round	Third Round	Fourth Round
–8 Castrale	–7 Hurst	–7 Miyazato	–8 Pak
–6 Hurst	–5 Castrale	–7 Hurst	–8 Webb
–6 Kerr	–5 Wie	–6 Wie	–7 M H Kim
–5 S-H Lee	–5 S H Ahn	–6 M H Kim	–7 Miyazato
–5 C Kim	–5 M H Kim		

2006 McDonald's LPGA Championship

Bulle Rock, Havre de Grace, MD [6596–72]

Prize Money: $1.8 million. Field of 150 players, of whom 76 made the half-way cut on 146 or less.

Players are of American nationality unless stated

1	Se Ri Pak (KOR)*	71-69-71-69—280	$270000
2	Karrie Webb (AUS)	70-70-72-68—280	163998
Play-off: 1st extra hole: Pak 3, Webb 4			
3	Mi Hyun Kim (KOR)	68-71-71-71—281	105501
	Ai Miyazato (JPN)	68-72-69-72—281	105501
5	Shi Hyun Ahn (KOR)	69-70-71-72—282	57464

2006 McDonald's LPGA Championship *continued*

9	Young Kim (KOR)	69-72-73-69—283	34174
	Lorena Ochoa (MEX)	68-72-71-72—283	34174
	Reilley Rankin	68-73-74-68—283	34174
	Annika Sörenstam (SWE)	71-69-75-68—283	34174
	Sung Ah Yim (KOR)	72-68-74-69—283	34174
14	Jee Young Lee (KOR)	70-71-70-73—284	26847
	Meena Lee (KOR)	71-72-69-72—284	26847
16	Silvia Cavalleri (ITA)	69-71-72-73—285	22896
	Seon Hwa Lee (KOR)	67-74-75-69—285	22896
	Sherri Steinhauer	70-71-71-73—285	22896
	Wendy Ward	69-74-70-72—285	22896
20	Yuri Fudoh (JPN)	69-74-71-72—286	19215
	Natalie Gulbis	72-73-72-69—286	19215
	Young Jo (KOR)	72-72-70-72—286	19215
	Suzann Pettersen (NOR)	70-72-74-70—286	19215
	Lindsey Wright (AUS)	72-73-68-73—286	19215
25	Minea Blomqvist (FIN)	71-71-70-75—287	16207
	Laura Diaz	71-74-72-70—287	16207
	Hee-Won Han (KOR)	68-73-75-71—287	16207
	Heather Young	71-75-70-71—287	16207
29	Il-Ne Chung (KOR)	71-72-75-70—288	13558
	Liselotte Neumann (SWE)	69-74-75-70—288	13558
	Nancy Scranton	73-73-73-69—288	13558
	Angela Stanford	70-76-72-70—288	13558
	Kris Tamulis	73-71-75-69—288	13558
34	Marisa Baena (COL)	72-72-74-71—289	11044
	Nicole Castrale	64-75-74-76—289	11044
	Rachel Hetherington (AUS)	70-72-74-73—289	11044
	Juli Inkster	70-74-73-72—289	11044
	Nina Reis (SWE)	70-73-73-73—289	11044
39	Beth Daniel	71-71-73-75—290	8979
	Allison Hanna	74-69-78-69—290	8979
	Maria Hjörth (SWE)	68-77-73-72—290	8979
	Nicole Perrot (CHI)	70-71-76-73—290	8979
	Michele Redman	73-72-73-72—290	8979
44	Julieta Grenada (PAR)	71-73-71-76—291	7363
	Sophie Gustafson (SWE)	72-72-75-72—291	7363
	Candie Kung (TPE)	68-78-71-74—291	7363
	Yu Ping Lin (TPE)	74-72-72-73—291	7363
	Jessica Reese-Quayle	73-73-72-73—291	7363
49	Paula Creamer	71-75-75-71—292	6124
	Rosie Jones	71-75-72-74—292	6124
	Carin Koch (SWE)	72-74-75-71—292	6124
	Brittany Lincicome	72-70-73-77—292	6124
	Kim Saiki	71-73-74-74—292	6124
54	Michelle Ellis (AUS)	71-72-75-75—293	5298
54T	Jill McGill	75-71-74-73—293	5298
	Miriam Nagl (GER)	70-76-75-72—293	5298
	Mikaela Parmlid (SWE)	69-75-73-76—293	5298
58	Jackie Gallagher-Smith	70-74-78-72—294	4669
	Jeong Jang (KOR)	73-73-76-72—294	4669
	Teresa Lu (TPE)	75-69-77-73—294	4669
61	Christina Kim	67-71-75-82—295	4265
	Siew-Ai Lim (MAS)	71-72-76-76—295	4265
	Gloria Park (KOR)	70-76-73-76—295	4265
	Karin Sjodin (SWE)	74-72-78-71—295	4265
65	Laura Davies (ENG)	72-73-76-75—296	3906
	Wendy Doolan (AUS)	68-72-78-78—296	3906
	Birdie Kim (KOR)	70-75-75-76—296	3906
	Sarah Lee (KOR)	68-73-77-78—296	3906

69	Ashli Bunch	74-71-77-75—297	3581
	Dorothy Delasin	67-71-81-78—297	3581
	Morgan Pressel	73-67-79-78—297	3581
	Karen Stupples (ENG)	70-76-77-74—297	3581
73	Kristi Albers	71-73-76-79—299	3457
74	Moira Dunn	71-71-79-79—300	3412
75	Jamie Fischer	72-73-80-77—302	3346
	Becky Iverson	74-72-76-80—302	3346

The following players missed the half-way cut:

77	Beth Bader	74-73—147
	Michelle Estill	73-74—147
	Karine Icher (FRA)	73-74—147
	Marcy Hart	71-76—147
	Patricia Meunier-Lebouc (FRA)	73-74—147
	Stacy Prammanasudh	71-76—147
	Giulia Sergas (ITA)	69-78—147
	Lee Ann Walker-Cooper	74-73—147
85	Kyeong Bae (KOR)	71-77—148
	Diana D'Alessio	75-73—148
	Karen Davies	73-75—148
	Tracy Hanson	73-75—148
	Hilary Lunke	72-76—148
	Sun Young Yoo (KOR)	77-71—148
91	Helen Alfredsson (SWE)	72-77—149
	Brandie Burton	76-73—149
	Catherine Cartwright	72-77—149
	Amy Hung (TPE)	76-73—149
	Lorie Kane (CAN)	70-79—149
	Soo-Yun Kang (KOR)	74-75—149
	Ji Yeon Lee (KOR)	72-77—149
	Shinobu Moromizato (JPN)	72-77—149
	Grace Park (KOR)	76-73—149
	Laurie Rinker	74-75—149
	Kris Tschetter	75-74—149

102	Emily Bastel	78-72—150
	Candy Hannemann (BRA)	75-75—150
	Joo Mi Kim (KOR)	76-74—150
	Stephanie Louden	73-77—150
	Kelly Robbins	76-74—150
	Aree Song (KOR)	73-77—150
108	Tina Barrett	78-73—151
	Patricia Baxter-Johnson	75-76—151
	Dawn Coe-Jones (CAN)	74-77—151
	Jamie Hullett	70-81—151
	Michelle McGann	75-76—151
	Mhairi McKay (SCO)	77-74—151
	Joanne Morley (ENG)	74-77—151
	Brooke Tull	73-78—151
116	Audra Burks	76-76—152
	Alicia Dibos (PER)	76-76—152
	Dana Dormann	73-79—152
	Meredith Duncan	75-77—152
	Vicki Goetze-Ackerman	73-79—152
	Katherine Hull (AUS)	75-77—152
	Catriona Matthew (SCO)	72-80—152
	Virada Nirapathpongporn (THA)	75-77—152
124	Tina Fischer (GER)	75-78—153

124T	Louise Stahle (SWE)	75-78—153
	Young-A Yang (KOR)	74-79—153
127	Beth Bauer	81-73—154
	Kate Golden	72-82—154
	Johanna Head (ENG)	76-78—154
	Soo Young Moon (KOR)	75-79—154
	Alena Sharp (CAN)	73-81—154
132	Christa Johnson	78-77—155
	Cindy Rarick	76-79—155
	Sherri Turner	75-80—155
135	Jean Bartholomew	80-76—156
136	Katie Futcher	78-79—157
137	Tiffany Faucette	80-78—158
138	Sherry Smith	79-80—159
139	Angie Rizzo	79-81—160
140	Libby Smith	80-81—161
141	Amy Alcott	78 WD
	Danielle Ammaccapane	75 WD
	Eva Dahllof (SWE)	79 WD
	Jimin Kang (KOR)	69 WD
	Nadina Light (AUS)	77 WD
	Becky Morgan (WAL)	75 WD
	Diana Ramage	79 WD
	Jennifer Rosales (PHI)	77 WD
	Kim Williams	77 WD
	Jan Stephenson (AUS)	78 DQ

Month by month in 2006

If it's January it must be the Mercedes Championship. And if it's the Mercedes it must be Stuart Appleby. The Australian takes the PGA Tour season-opener in Hawaii for the third year running. Chris DiMarco knows whom to thank after ending four years without a win in Abu Dhabi – his wife Amy caddied for him. Tiger Woods starts his year by beating José María Olazábal and Nathan Green in a play-off at the Buick Invitational.

2005 McDonald's LPGA Championship Bulle Rock, Havre de Grace, MD

Prize money: $1.8 million

1	Annika Sörenstam (SWE)	68-67-69-73—277	$270000	20T	Laura Diaz	67-72-76-73—288	19797
2	Michelle Wie (am)	69-71-71-69—280			Meena Lee (KOR)	70-71-72-75—288	19797
3	Paula Creamer	68-73-74-67—282	140517		Karrie Webb (AUS)	74-75-72-67—288	19797
	Laura Davies (ENG)	67-70-74-71—282	140517	25	Shi Hyun Ahn (KOR)	78-71-72-68—289	16096
5	Natalie Gulbis	67-71-73-73—284	82486		Kirsti Albers	70-72-73-74—289	16096
	Lorena Ochoa (MEX)	72-72-68-72—284	82486		Il Mi Chung (KOR)	71-68-79-71—289	16096
7	Moira Dunn	71-68-72-74—285	43993		Hee-Won Han (KOR)	73-74-72-70—289	16096
	Pat Hurst	72-73-71-69—285	43993		Leta Lindley	72-72-75-70—289	16096
	Mi Hyun Kim (KOR)	69-75-74-67—285	43993		Karen Stupples (ENG)	72-71-71-75—289	16096
	Young Kim (KOR)	73-68-68-76—285	43993	31	Rosie Jones	72-69-74-75—290	13733
	Carin Koch (SWE)	74-70-69-72—285	43993		Liselotte Neumann		
	Gloria Park (KOR)	71-71-72-71—285	43993		(SWE)	70-71-74-75—290	13733
13	Juli Inkster	75-71-71-69—286	29309	33	Jamie Hullett	70-75-71-75—291	11225
	Jeong Jang (KOR)	71-71-69-75—286	29309		Jimin Kang (KOR)	73-74-72-72—291	11225
	Candie Kung (TAI)	72-73-73-68—286	29309		Cristie Kerr	74-72-67-78—291	11225
16	Marisa Baena (COL)	70-69-73-75—287	23899		Christina Kim	73-72-78-68—291	11225
	Jennifer Rosales (PHI)	71-73-69-74—287	23899		Brittany Lincicome	72-72-75-72—291	11225
	Angela Stanford	69-73-73-72—287	23899		Meg Mallon	74-69-76-72—291	11225
	Lindsey Wright (AUS)	71-72-72-72—287	23899		Janice Moodie (SCO)	73-72-74-72—291	11225
20	Beth Bader	72-72-72-72—288	19797		Stacy Prammanasudh	72-76-72-71—291	11225
	Heather Bowie	72-71-71-74—288	19797				

Other players who made the cut: Birdie Kim (KOR), 292, Rachel Hetherington (AUS), Hilary Lunke, Paula Marti (ESP), Joanne Morley (ENG), 293; Johanna Head (ENG), Lorie Kane (CAN), Aree Song (KOR), 294; Heather Daly-Donofrio, Catriona Matthew (SCO), Suzann Pettersen (NOR), Michele Redman, Kim Saiki, 295; Dawn Coe-Jones (CAN), Beth Daniel, Wendy Doolan (AUS), Yu Ping Lin (TAI), Stephanie Louden, Jill McGill, Nicole Perrot (CHI), Nancy Scranton, Sung Ah Yim (KOR), 296; Tina Barrett, Patricia Baxter-Johnson, Tina Fischer (GER), Laurel Kean, Emilee Klein, Bernadette Luse, Sae-Hee Son (KOR), Kris Tschetter, 297; Maria Hjörth (SWE), 298; Katie Allison, Catherine Cartwright, A J Eathorne (CAN), Katherine Hull (AUS), Reilley Rankin, 299; Laurie Rinker, Nadina Taylor (AUS), 300; Candy Hannemann (BRA), 302; Barb Mucha, 305.

2004 McDonald's LPGA Championship Du Pont CC, DE

Prize money: $1.6 million

1	Annika Sörenstam	68-67-64-72—271	$240000	17T	Betsy King	76-70-70-68—284	18654
	(SWE)				Se Ri Pak (KOR)	69-73-70-72—284	18654
2	Shi Hyun Ahn (KOR)	69-70-69-66—274	144780	23	Tina Barrett	75-71-68-71—285	14596
3	Grace Park (KOR)	68-70-70-68—276	105028		Jeong Jang (KOR)	71-71-71-72—285	14596
4	Gloria Park (KOR)	67-72-68-71—278	73322		Siew-Ai Lim (MAS)	72-70-71-72—285	14596
	Angela Stanford	69-71-67-71—278	73322		Stacy Prammanasudh	73-71-69-72—285	14596
6	Juli Inkster	70-66-70-73—279	49145		Kim Saiki	69-72-72-72—285	14596
	Christina Kim	74-69-64-72—279	49145		Sherri Steinhauer	69-72-74-70—285	14596
8	Wendy Doolan (AUS)	73-70-65-72—280	35538		Chiharu Yamaguchi	67-73-70-75—285	14596
	Soo-Yun Kang	69-68-71-72—280	35538		(JPN)		14596
	Lorena Ochoa (MEX)	71-67-67-75—280	35538	30	Moira Dunn	68-74-72-72—286	10631
11	Carin Koch (SWE)	69-71-68-73—281	28734		Mi-Hyun Kim (KOR)	72-70-74-70—286	10631
	Reilley Rankin	70-67-71-73—281	28734		Young Kim (KOR)	70-73-74-69—286	10631
13	Pat Hurst	69-69-75-69—282	24466		Patricia Meunier-	71-70-76-69—286	
	Mhairi McKay (SCO)	72-69-69-72—282	24466		Labouc (FRA)		
	Jennifer Rosales (PHI)	66-70-74-72—282	24466		Janice Moodie (SCO)	72-71-73-70—286	10631
16	Meg Mallon	69-73-70-71—283	21718		Aree Song (KOR)	71-72-69-74—286	10631
17	Kristi Albers	70-74-69-71—284	18654		Charlotta Sörenstam	74-70-70-72—286	
	Dawn Coe-Jones (CAN)	72-72-70-70—284	18654		(SWE)		10631
	Michelle Ellis (AUS)	72-70-69-73—284	18654		Karen Stupples (ENG)	67-73-73-73—286	10631
	Cristie Kerr	69-73-71-71—284	18654		Wendy Ward	72-72-71-71—286	10631

Other players who made the cut: Beth Daniel, Stephanie Louden (AUS), Karrie Webb (AUS) 287; Jean Bartholomew, Ashli Bunch, Laura Davies (ENG), Becky Iverson, Becky Morgan (WAL), Deb Richard, Karen Pearce (AUS) 289; Heather Daly-Donofrio, Hee-Won Han (KOR), Lorie Kane (CAN), Yu Ping Lin (TPE), Kelly Robbins, Giulia Sergas (ITA), Rachel Teske (AUS) 290; Pat Bradley, Diana D'Alessio, Kate Golden, Jamie Hullett, Emilee Klein 291; Helen Alfredsson (SWE), Natalie Gulbis, Catriona Matthew (SCO) 292; Amy Fruhwirth, Tammy Green, Seol-An Jeon (KOR), Angela Jerman, Candie Kung (TPE), Soo Young Moon (KOR) 293; Isabelle Beisiegel (CAN), Vicki Goetz-Ackerman, Jill McGill, Dotty Pepper 294; Jenna Daniels, Sophie Gustafson (SWE), Kim Williams 295; Candy Hannemann (BRA) 296; Jackie Gallagher-Smith 297; Heather Bowie 299.

2003 McDonald's LPGA Championship Du Pont CC, DE

Prize money: $1.6 million

1	Annika Sörenstam (SWE)*	70-64-72-72—278	$240000	20	Donna Andrews	73-70-70-74—287	16719
*Sörenstam winner at first extra hole of play-off with Grace Park					Tina Barrett	76-69-71-71—287	16719
2	Grace Park (KOR)	69-72-70-67—278	147934		Michelle Ellis (AUS)	73-70-71-73—287	16719
3	Beth Daniel	71-71-70-72—284	85718		Natalie Gulbis	71-69-78-69—287	16719
	Rosie Jones	73-68-72-71—284	85718		Kelli Kuehne	73-73-65-76—287	16719
	Rachel Teske (AUS)	69-70-74-71—284	85718		Lorena Ochoa (MEX)	72-72-71-72—287	16719
6	Kate Golden	72-70-68-75—285	41873		Karen Stupples (ENG)	73-73-71-70—287	16719
	Young Kim (KOR)	70-73-72-70—285	41873	27	Danielle Ammaccapane	74-72-74-68—288	13769
	JoAnne Mills (AUS)	68-73-75-69—285	41873		Meg Mallon	74-69-70-75—288	13769
	Becky Morgan (WAL)	73-70-70-72—285	41873		Angela Stanford	72-73-71-72—288	13769
	Young-A Yang (KOR)	73-74-69-69—285	41873	30	Laura Diaz	73-70-75-71—289	11987
11	Akiko Fukushima (JPN)	72-68-74-72—286	24037		Tracy Hanson	71-77-70-71—289	11987
	Hee-Wan Han (KOR)	67-69-74-76—286	24037		Mi-Hyun Kim (KOR)	72-72-71-74—289	11987
	Jeong Jang (KOR)	72-73-69-72—286	24037		Deb Richard	75-71-74-69—289	11987
	Angela Jerman	73-72-69-72—286	24037	34	Moira Dunn	78-70-72-70—290	10367
	Patricia Meunier-Lebouc (FRA)	75-69-72-70—286	24037		Lorie Kane (CAN)	72-75-70-73—290	10367
	Suzann Pettersen (NOR)	70-71-75-70—286	24037		Cristie Kerr	74-69-75-72—290	10367
	Michele Redman	74-70-69-73—286	24037	37	Juli Inkster	71-72-71-77—291	8970
	Jennifer Rosales (PHI)	74-68-74-70—286	24037		Hilary Lunke	72-70-75-74—291	8970
	Wendy Ward	68-69-75-74—286	24037		Catriona Matthew (SCO)	72-73-75-71—291	8970
					Jan Stephenson (AUS)	74-72-69-76—291	8970

Other players who made the cut: Jill McGill, Terry-Jo Myers 292; Vicki Goetze-Ackerman, Pat Hurst, Giulia Sergas (ITA) 293; Marisa Baena (COL), Brandie Burton, Jung Yeon Lee (KOR), Se Ri Pak (KOR), Leslie Spalding 294; Yu Ping Lin (TPE), Kathryn Marshall (SCO), Joanne Morley (ENG) 295; Dorothy Delasin (PHI), Kim Saiki 296; Dawn Coe-Jones (CAN), Jane Crafter (AUS), Wendy Doolan (AUS), Jackie Gallagher-Smith, Karrie Webb (AUS) 297; Fiona Pike (AUS) 298; Heather Bowie 299; Marnie McGuire (NZL) 300; Mitzi Edge, Marcy Hart, Michelle McGann 301; Marilyn Lovander, Liselotte Neumann (SWE), Dottie Pepper 304; Kim Williams 306.

2002 McDonald's LPGA Championship Du Pont CC, DE

Prize money: $1,400,000

1	Se Ri Pak (KOR)	71-70-68-70—279	$225000	20T	Barb Mucha	70-73-75-75—293	16950
2	Beth Daniel	67-70-68-77—282	136987	22	Silvia Cavalieri (ITA)	72-73-73-76—294	15450
3	Annika Sörenstam (SWE)	70-76-73-65—284	99375		Maria Hjörth (SWE)	78-70-75-71—294	15450
					Kelly Robbins	70-75-74-75—294	15450
4	Juli Inkster	69-75-70-71—285	69375	25	Danielle Ammaccapane	73-76-73-73—295	12543
	Karrie Webb (AUS)	68-71-72-74—285	69375		Brandie Burton	74-76-74-71—295	12543
6	Carin Koch (SWE)	68-73-73-72—286	46500		Vicki Goetze-Ackerman	72-72-74-77—295	12543
	Michele Redman	74-69-70-73—286	46500		Tammie Green	70-78-73-74—295	12543
8	Catriona Matthew (SCO)	70-73-75-70—288	37125		Leta Lindley	72-77-71-75—295	12543
					Kathryn Marshall (SCO)	73-73-72-77—295	12543
9	Kristi Albers	74-73-73-70—290	30625		Gloria Park (KOR)	75-72-73-75—295	12543
	Michelle McGann	71-72-72-75—290	30625		Kris Tschetter	74-75-75-71—295	12543
	Karen Stupples (ENG)	75-70-70-75—290	30625	33	Eva Dahllof (SWE)	75-73-75-73—296	9056
12	Meg Mallon	73-72-76-70—291	24650		Dorothy Delasin (PHI)	79-68-73-76—296	9056
	Kim Saiki	71-71-69-80—291	24650		Moira Dunn	74-75-75-72—296	9056
	Karen Weiss	70-74-75-72—291	24650		Michelle Ellis (AUS)	72-77-74-73—296	9056
15	Akiki Fukushima (JPN)	71-71-76-74—292	19650		Lorie Kane (CAN)	70-74-76-76—296	9056
	Natalie Gulbis	72-72-75-73—292	19650		Mi Hyun Kim (KOR)	77-71-72-76—296	9056
	Kelli Kuehne	71-75-74-72—292	19650		Charlotta Sörenstam (SWE)	75-73-74-74—296	9056
	Grace Park (KOR)	72-73-73-74—292	19650		Sherri Turner	74-73-76-73—296	9056
	Rachel Teske (AUS)	72-71-77-72—292	19650				
20	Laura Diaz	73-71-71-78—293	16950				

Other players who made the cut: Jane Crafter (AUS), Heather Daly-Donofrio, Tracy Hanson, Pat Hurst, Cristie Kerr, Mhairi McKay (SCO) 297; Angela Buzminski, Jackie Gallagher-Smith, Betsy King, Joanne Morley (ENG), Jennifer Rosales (PHI) 298; Beth Bauer, Jenna Daniels, Michelle Estill, Liselotte Neumann (SWE), Susie Parry 299; Hee-Won Han (KOR), Jeong Jang (KOR) 300; Stephanie Keever, Angela Stanford 301; Denise Killeen, Marnie McGuire (NZL), Patricia Meunier-Lebouc 302; Emilee Klein 303; Becky Iverson, Val Skinner 304; Chris Johnson 305; A J Eathorne (CAN) 307; Karen Pearce 308; Alicia Dibos (PER), Shiho Katano (JPN) 309.

2001 McDonald's LPGA Championship Du Pont CC, DE

Prize money: $1,500,000

1	Karrie Webb (AUS)	67-64-70-69—270	$225000	17T	Dottie Pepper	71-72-71-68—282	16819
2	Laura Diaz	67-71-66-68—272	139639		Kelly Robbins	69-74-71-68—282	16819
3	Maria Hjörth (SWE)	71-67-66-70—274	90577		Rachel Teske (AUS)	68-72-70-72—282	16819
	Wendy Ward	65-69-71-69—274	90577	26	Heather Daly-Donofrio	75-68-71-69—283	13162
5	Annika Sörenstam (SWE)	68-69-71-67—275	64157		Beth Daniel	71-71-70-71—283	13162
6	Laura Davies (ENG)	67-68-70-71—276	48684		Akiko Fukushima (JPN)	66-72-73-72—283	13162
	Becky Iverson	66-73-67-70—276	48684		Nancy Scranton	73-68-70-72—283	13162
8	Mi Hyun Kim (KOR)	70-70-68-69—277	39250	30	Dawn Coe-Jones	72-69-71-72—284	11603
9	Helen Alfredsson (SWE)	68-66-74-70—278	35476		Catriona Matthew (SCO)	71-72-72-69—284	1 603
10	Michele Redman	69-66-73-71—279	30245		Grace Park (KOR)	71 72-71-70—284	11633
	Maggie Will	68-74-67-70—279	30245	33	Danielle Ammaccapane	69-71-71-74—285	10257
12	Rosie Jones	71-69-71-69—280	25013		Jane Crafter (AUS)	71-71-69-74—285	10257
	Lorie Kane (CAN)	69-71-71-69—280	25013		Patricia Meunier-Lebouc	70-73-71-71—285	10257
	Liselotte Neumann (SWE)	69-72-68-71—280	25013		(FRA)		
15	Wendy Doolan (AUS)	70-71-72-68—281	21239		Sherri Turner	71-72-72-70—285	10257
	Juli Inkster	71-71-69-70—281	21239	37	Brandie Burton	69-74-68-75—286	9125
17	Pat Hurst	72-68-72-70—282	16819		Hee Won Han (KOR)	70-75-72-69—286	9125
	Carin Koch (SWE)	69-73-71-69—282	16819	39	Kathryn Marshall (SCO)	71-73-71-72—287	8011
	Leta Lindley	71-71-70-70—282	16819		Se Ri Pak (KOR)	71-73-69-74—287	8011
	Meg Mallon	71-74-67-70—282	16819		Deb Richard	72-71-73-71—287	8011
	Mhairi McKay (SCO)	68-72-70-72—282	16819		Kris Tschetter	71-74-69-73—287	8011
	Terry-Jo Myers	70-71-69-72—282	16819				

Other players who made the cut: Alicia Dibos, Vicki Goetze-Ackerman, Gloria Park (KOR), Kristal Parker 288; Suzy Green, Jenny Lidback (PER), Marnie McGuire 289; Mitzi Edge, Jackie Gallagher-Smith, Emilee Klein, Sara Sanders 290; Amy Alcott, Donna Andrews, Marisa Baena (COL), Susan Ginter, Betsy King, Charlotta Sörenstam (SWE), Leslie Spalding 291; Dorothy Delasin (PHI), Alison Nicholas (ENG) 292; Jean Bartholomew, Gail Graham (CAN), Joanne Morley (ENG) 293; Janice Moodie (SCO), Barb Mucha, Joan Pitcock 294; Annette DeLuca 296; Michelle McGann 299.

2000 McDonald's LPGA Championship Du Pont CC, DE

Prize money: $1,400,000

1	Juli Inkster*	72-69-65-75—281	$210000	23	Pat Bradley	68-76-67-76—287	13304
Inkster winner at second hole of play-off with Croce					Betsy King	68-78-67-74—287	13304
2	Stefania Croce (ITA)	72-67-74-68—281	130330		Janice Moodie (SCO)	72-73-71-71—287	13304
3	Se Ri Pak (KOR)	73-69-69-71—282	76319		Alison Nicholas (ENG)	72-72-71-72—287	13304
	Nancy Scranton	72-70-67-73—282	76319		Dottie Pepper	71-73-69-74—287	13304
	Wendy Ward	69-69-68-76—282	76319	28	Rosie Jones	70-74-74-70—288	11191
6	Heather Bowie	74-70-70-69—283	42503		Jenny Lidback (PER)	75-71-71-71—288	11191
	Jane Crafter (AUS)	72-69-69-73—283	42503		Gloria Park (KOR)	68-75-75-70—288	11191
	Laura Davies (ENG)	70-66-75-72—283	42503		Karen Weiss	73-71-70-74—288	11191
9	Akiko Fukushima (JPN)	71-72-71-70—284	29839		Barb Whitehead	73-72-70-73—288	11191
	Jan Stephenson (AUS)	70-69-69-76—284	29839	33	Beth Daniel	72-72-70-75—289	9698
	Karrie Webb (AUS)	72-70-69-73—284	29839		Emilee Klein	74-71-71-73—289	9698
12	Amy Fruhwirth	74-71-70-70—285	21885		Kim Saiki	77-69-71-72—289	9698
	Mi Hyun Kim (KOR)	70-73-70-72—285	21885	36	Jean Bartholomew	71-71-74-74—290	8464
	Leta Lindley	71-73-71-70—285	21885		Alicia Dibos (PER)	72-74-74-70—290	8464
	Kelly Robbins	72-72-73-68—285	21885		Cindy McCurdy	73-74-71-72—290	8464
	Annika Sörenstam (SWE)	70-73-70-72—285	21885		Maggie Will	74-72-67-77—290	8464
17	Dawn Coe-Jones	71-73-72-70—286	16602	40	Sophie Gustafson (SWE)	76-70-69-76—291	6820
	Wendy Doolan (AUS)	69-71-71-75—286	16602		Carin Koch (SWE)	74-70-73-74—291	6820
	Jane Geddes	66-74-73-73—286	16602		Barb Mucha	72-72-70-77—291	6820
	Pat Hurst	71-70-71-74—286	16602		Laura Philo	72-74-73-72—291	6820
	Meg Mallon	72-73-69-72—286	16602		Jennifer Rosales (PHI)	71-73-74-73—291	6820
	Michele Redman	70-70-70-76—286	16602		Sherri Steinhauer	70-75-68-78—291	6820

Other players who made the cut: Cindy Flom, Kathryn Marshall (SCO), Leigh Ann Mills, Patty Sheehan, Kris Tschetter, Mary Beth Zimmerman 292; Cindy Figg-Currier, Yu Ping Lin (TPE), 293; Jill McGill, Joanne Morley (ENG) 293; Marisa Baena (COL), AJ Eathorne (CAN), Vicki Goetze-Ackerman, Kate Golden, Tracy Hanson, Catrin Nilsmark (SWE) 294; Ashli Bunch, Val Skinner, Leslie Spalding 295; Pamela Kerrigan, Nancy Lopez, Shani Waugh (AUS) 296; Danielle Ammaccapane, Debbi Koyama (JPN) 298; Moira Dunn 299; Carmen Hajjar 300; Julie Piers 301; Dina Ammaccapane 305

1999 McDonald's LPGA Championship Du Pont CC, DE

Prize money: $1,400,000

1	J Inkster	68-66-69-65—268	$210000	22	L Kiggens	68-74-69-68—279	14063
2	L Neumann (SWE)	67-67-70-68—272	130330		A Fukushima (JPN)	70-70-69-70—279	14063
3	M Lunn (AUS)	68-74-65-66—273	84538		V Odegard	69-70-70-70—279	14063
	N Scranton	69-68-66-70—273	84538		A Finney	67-69-71-72—279	14063
5	R Jones	64-72-68-70—274	54596	26	P Sinn	71-71-70-68—280	11087
	C Kerr	70-64-69-71—274	54596		Mi Hyun Kim (KOR)	70-70-71-69—280	11087
7	E Klein	72-68-67-68—275	35224		V Fergon	67-73-70-70—280	11087
	J McGill	70-69-68-68—275	35224		J Crafter	70-69-71-70—280	11087
	L Davies (ENG)	65-71-71-68—275	35224		L Lindley	70-72-67-71—280	11087
	Se Ri Pak (KOR)	68-69-67-71—275	35224		B Mucha	70-70-69-71—280	11087
11	M Hirase	70-73-68-65—276	23487		K Kuehne	68-67-72-73—280	11087
	S Sanders	70-68-68-70—276	23487		A Nicholas (ENG)	67-73-66-74—280	11087
	T Green	68-70-68-70—276	23487		T Johnson (ENG)	67-70-69-74—280	11087
	J Lidback	67-67-72-70—276	23487		L Kane	70-66-70-74—280	11087
	M Mallon	70-71-63-72—276	23487	36	T Tombs	71-71-69-70—281	8164
16	A Sörenstam (SWE)	73-68-68-68—277	18415		H Stacy	73-68-70-70—281	8164
	S Redman	70-68-70-69—277	18415		C Koch	68-73-70-70—281	8164
	J Stephenson	69-69-69-70—277	18415		N Bowen	70-72-68-71—281	8164
19	D Pepper	71-72-68-67—278	16301		S Waugh	70-69-71-71—281	8164
	S Steinhauer	74-69-65-70—278	16301		C Figg-Currier	71-70-67-73—281	8164
	H Kobayashi (JPN)	70-67-71-70—278	16301				

Other players who made the cut: Dana Dormann, W Doolan, J Moodie (SCO), R Hetherington (AUS), M Spencer-Devlin 282; C Flom, M Nause, B Iverson, M McGann, D Eggeling, S Croce (ITA), T Barrett 283; K Coats, K Tschetter, P Hammel, C Nilsmark (SWE), K Saiki, D Richard, S Little, C Johnson, S Gustafson (SWE) 284; M Hjörth (SWE), M Will 285; P Bradley 286; K Robbins 287; D Barnard 288; M McGeorge 289; B King, D Killeen 290; K Lunn (AUS) 299

1998 McDonald's LPGA Championship Du Pont CC, DE

Prize money: $1,300,000

1	Se Ri Pak (KOR)	65-68-72-68—273	$195000	21T	H Dobson (ENG)	76-70-70-68—284	13558
2	D Andrews	71-67-69-69—276	104666		P Hurst	71-73-68-72—284	13558
	L Hackney (ENG)	70-66-69-71—276	104666		J Lidback	70-73-68-73—284	13558
4	K Webb (AUS)	71-73-67-66—277	62145	25	D Dormann	71-74-74-66—285	11579
	W Ward	71-67-69-70—277	62145		M McGann	68-74-73-70—285	11579
6	M Mallon	71-69-68-70—278	39467		N Scranton	73-73-67-72—285	11579
	C Johnson	69-71-67-71—278	39467		S Redman	68-76-69-72—285	11579
	E Klein	72-67-68-71—278	39467		D Eggeling	68-69-74-74—285	11579
9	C Nilsmark (SWE)	69-73-70-67—279	29110	30	W Doolan	73-72-71-70—286	9365
	K Robbins	69-71-68-71—279	29110		V Odegard	69-74-73-70—286	9365
11	J Pitcock	69-75-70-66—280	23180		A Sörenstam (SWE)	73-71-71-71—286	9365
	A DeLuca	70-70-71-69—280	23180		R Hetherington	71-71-72-72—286	9365
	J Geddes	69-69-70-72—280	23180		L Kane (CAN)	72-73-68-73—286	9365
14	T Green	72-68-70-71—281	19691		K Tschetter	71-71-71-73—286	9365
	L Walters	66-69-73-73—281	19691		J Morley	73-69-69-75—286	9365
16	M Hjörth (SWE)	71-70-73-68—282	17402	37	S Steinhauer	73-73-71-70—287	7093
	J Inkster	70-71-69-72—282	17402		B King	71-73-72-71—287	7093
18	M Redman	70-71-74-68—283	15767		M Spencer-Devlin	74-71-70-72—287	7093
	C Koch (SWE)	71-73-69-70—283	15767		L Neumann (SWE)	73-69-73-72—287	7093
	C Johnston-Forbes	71-70-70-72—283	15767		M Halpin	73-73-68-73—287	7093
21	J Moodie (SCO)	75-69-73-67—284	13558		M Estill	72-70-72-73—287	7093

Other players who made the cut: D Coe-Jones, S Little, N Lopez, L Davies, C McCurdy, M Figueras-Dotti, P Bradley 288; C Figg-Currier, K Saiki, B Mucha, D Barnard, H Alfredsson 289; E Dahllof, C Sörenstam 290; C McMillan, K Albers, K Monaghan, B Daniel, M Berteotti 291; H Stacy, M Dobek, P Hammel 292; G Graham, T Hanson 293; M McGeorge, B Burton 295; J Gallagher-Smith, M Morris 297; H Daly-Donofrio 298.

1997 McDonald's LPGA Championship Du Pont CC, DE

Prize money: $1,200,000

1	C Johnson*	68-73-69-71—281	$180000	16T	K Saiki (JPN)	68-75-69-77—289	15397
*Johnson won at second hole of play-off with Lindley				20	A Fruhwirth	72-75-73-70—290	13586
2	L Lindley	72-69-69-71—281	111711		J Wyatt	73-75-71-71—290	13586
3	A Sörenstam (SWE)	70-73-72-67—282	81519	22	M Lunn (AUS)	72-77-75-67—291	12176
4	L Davies (ENG)	67-75-74-68—284	57365		M Mallon	72-76-73-70—291	12176
	S Steinhauer	68-71-73-72—284	57365		T Barrett	69-77-75-70—291	12176
6	G Graham	69-79-71-66—285	38947	25	D Reid (SCO)	74-75-73-70—292	10446
	D Coe-Jones	70-75-71-69—285	38947		W Ward	72-78-71-71—292	10446
8	T Johnson (ENG)	70-73-72-71—286	31400		C Matthew (SCO)	71-75-75-71—292	10446
9	K Webb (AUS)	71-79-70-67—287	26871		M McGeorge	73-74-73-72—292	10446
	B Mucha	68-73-72-74—287	26871		A Dibos	71-76-73-72—292	10446
11	K Robbins	73-74-74-67—288	20047		C Figg-Currier	71-76-72-73—292	10446
	P Bradley	70-75-76-67—288	20047	31	S Strudwick (ENG)	72-74-77-70—293	8423
	B Burton	71-73-76-68—288	20047		M McGann	74-76-71-72—293	8423
	D Dormann	70-73-75-70—288	20047		H Dobson (ENG)	78-72-69-74—293	8423
	J Dickinson	75-72-68-73—288	20047		K Weiss	73-75-71-74—293	8423
16	W Doolan	74-72-74-69—289	15397		C Walker	72-74-73-74—293	8423
	L Kane (CAN)	73-74-71-71—289	15397		N Bowen	73-72-73-75—293	8423
	D Andrews	73-71-73-72—289	15397				

Other players who made the cut: N Lopez, K Monaghan, D Richard, N Ramsbottom, D Pepper, M Edge, M Estill, K Parker-Gregory, B Whitehead 294; A Miller, K Albers, A Finney, K Marshall, J Lidback, M Morris, J Pitcock 295; B King, H Stacy, C H Koch, M Berteotti, S Redman, J Inkster 296; M B Zimmerman 297; J McGill, V Goetze-Ackerman, H Kobayashi, J Crafter, R Hetherington, K Peterson-Parker, N Scranton 298; C Mockett, H Alfredsson, Danielle Ammaccapane, J Geddes, D Killeen, A Alcott, J Gallagher-Smith, E Klein 299; M Hirase, M Spencer-Devlin, C Johnston-Forbes, A-M Palli, P Hurst 300; L Walters, V Skinner 301; Vickie Odegard 302.

LPGA Championship History

The Championship was known simply as the LPGA Championship from its inauguration in 1955 until 1987. It was sponsored by Mazda from 1988 until 1993 when the sponsorship was taken over by McDonald's.

Year	Winner	Venue	Score
1955	B Hanson	Orchard Ridge	4 and 3
1956	M Hagge*	Forest Lake	291
*After a play-off with Patty Berg			
1957	L Suggs	Churchill Valley	285
1958	M Wright	Churchill CC	288
1959	B Rawls	Churchill CC	288
1960	M Wright	French Lick	292
1961	M Wright	Stardust	287
1962	J Kimball	Stardust	282
1963	M Wright	Stardust	294
1964	M Mills	Stardust	278
1965	S Haynie	Stardust	279
1966	G Ehret	Stardust	282
1967	K Whitworth	Pleasant Valley	284
1968	S Post*	Pleasant Valley	294
*After a play-off with K Whitworth			
1969	B Rawls	Concord	293
1970	S Englehorn*	Pleasant Valley	285
*After a play-off with K Whitworth			
1971	K Whitworth	Pleasant Valley	288
1972	K Ahern	Pleasant Valley	293
1973	M Mills	Pleasant Valley	288
1974	S Haynie	Pleasant Valley	288
1975	K Whitworth	Pine Ridge	288

Year	Winner	Venue	Score
1976	B Burfeindt	Pine Ridge	287
1977	C Higuchi (JPN)	Bay Tree	279
1978	N Lopez	Kings Island	275
1979	D Caponi	Kings Island	279
1980	S Little (SA)	Kings Island	285
1981	D Caponi	Kings Island	280
1982	J Stephenson (AUS)	Kings Island	279
1983	P Sheehan	Kings Island	279
1984	P Sheehan	Kings Island	272
1985	N Lopez	Kings Island	273
1986	P Bradley	Kings Island	277
1987	J Geddes	Kings Island	275
1988	S Turner	Kings Island	281
1989	N Lopez	King's Island	274
1990	B Daniel	Bethesda	280
1991	M Mallon	Bethesda	274
1992	B King	Bethesda	267
1993	P Sheehan	Bethesda	275
1994	L Davies (ENG)	Wilmington, Delaware	275
1995	K Robbins	Wilmington, Delaware	274
1996	L Davies (ENG)	Wilmington, Delaware	213

Reduced to 54 holes – bad weather

1997	C Johnson	Wilmington, Delaware	281
1998	Se Ri Pak (KOR)	Wilmington, Delaware	273
1999	J Inkster	Wilmington, Delaware	268
2000	J Inkster*	Wilmington, Delaware	281

After a tie with Stefania Croce (ITA)

2001	K Webb (AUS)	Wilmington, Delaware	270
2002	Se Ri Pak (KOR)	Wilmington, Delaware	279
2003	A Sörenstam (SWE)*	Wilmington, Delaware	271

After a play-off with Grace Park

2004	A Sörenstam (SWE)	Wilmington, Delaware	271
2005	A Sörenstam (SWE)	Bulle Rock, MD	277
2006	Se Ri Pak (KOR)*	Bulle Rock, MD	280

Pak beat Karrie Webb (AUS) at first extra hole

Month by month in 2006

Woods switches from California to the Middle East and this time it's Ernie Els he defeats in a play-off for the Dubai Desert Classic. American success on the European Tour continues with Craig Stadler's son Kevin eagling the last to lift the Johnnie Walker Classic in Perth, but back in the States Australian Geoff Ogilvy lives a charmed life to win the Accenture World Match Play.

Kraft Nabisco Championship

formerly known as the Nabisco Dinah Shore

Karrie eagles the last to catch Lorena Ochoa then caps her comeback with a play-off win

Australian Karie Webb holed a 116 yards shot for a closing eagle at Mission Hills to set up a play-off with Lorena Ochoa for the Kraft Nabisco Championship. Then she birdied the hole second time around from seven feet after Ochoa had missed from 12 feet to pick up the $270,000 first prize, her second Kraft Nabisco title and her ninth career major. She had started the day seven shots off the lead but fired a closing bogey-free 65 to tie Ochoa whose opening 62 tied the record for a low round in a major.

Webb, whose last win had been in 2004 at the Kellogg-Keebler Classic, said at the prize-giving ceremony "I feel so lucky to be here. A lot of hard work has paid off and I am enjoying the moment." It was her best come-from-behind of her career on the final day by two shots and the best comeback in a major since Patty Sheehan came from seven back to win the 1983 LPGA Championship.

The final round saw multiple lead changes with Webb, Michelle Wie and Natalie Gulbis all making moves on Ochoa whose chance of victory came unstuck on the back nine with some wayward driving. Wie, chasing her first major win at age 16, led by one with five to play and had a short birdie putt at the 16th to move to eight-under par. At that moment, Webb was holing from the fairway at the last for nine under.

Natalie Gulbis birdied the 17th to join Wie and Ochoa on eight under par, one off the lead. All three had the chance to catch Webb at the last. Ochoa and Wie were putting for an eagle and Gulbis for a birdie but only Ochoa was successful in making the play-off, holing from eight feet.

Gulbis and Wie finished tied for third with Juli Inkster continuing her solid play with a fifth place on 284.

It was only the seventh play-off in the 35-year history of the Championship and the fourth since it was designated a major in 1983. Winner Webb improved her play-off record to 4–4 but Ochoa has now lost all three play-offs in which she has been involved.

First Round	Second Round	Third Round	Fourth Round
–10 Ochoa	–11 Ochoa	–9 Ochoa	–9 Webb
–6 Wie	–7 Wi	–6 Wie	–9 Ochoa
–5 Prammanasudh	–6 Webb	–4 Gulbis	–8 Gulbis
–4 A Park	–6 S-H Lee	–4 S H Ahn	–8 Wie

2006 Kraft Nabisco Championship [6569–72]

Mission Hills CC, (Dinah Shore Tournament Course), Rancho Mirage, CA

Prize money: $1.8 million. Final field of 98 players, of whom 70 (including 4 amateurs) made the final halfway cut on 150 or less.

Players are of American nationality unless stated.

1	Karrie Webb* (AUS)	70-68-76-65—279	$270000
2	Lorena Ochoa (MEX)	62-71-74-72—279	168226
Webb won sudden death play-off:: Webb 5, Ochoa 6			
3	Natalie Gulbis	73-71-68-68—280	108222
	Michelle Wie	66-71-73-70—280	108222
5	Juli Inkster	69-73-74-68—284	75985
6	Hee-Won Han (KOR)	75-72-68-71—286	57104
	Annika Sörenstam (SWE)	71-72-73-70—286	57104
8	Shi Hyun Ahn (KOR)	70-71-71-75—287	41293
	Helen Alfredsson (SWE)	70-72-72-73—287	41293
	Brittany Lang	70-74-72-71—287	41293
11	Stacy Prammanasudh	67-73-76-72—288	33388

11T	Michele Redman	72-72-72-72—288	33388
13	Beth Daniel	72-72-72-73—289	29289
	Morgan Pressel	69-76-70-74—289	29289
15	Yuri Fudoh (JPN)	75-73-69-73—290	26710
	Angela Park (am)	68-73-75-74—290	
17	Pat Hurst	73-73-73-72—291	24592
	Karen Stupples (ENG)	69-74-72-76—291	24592
19	Tina Barrett	72-75-74-71—292	21221
	Jeong Jang (KOR)	71-75-76-70—292	21221
	Young Kim (KOR)	74-73-70-75—292	21221
	Seon Hwa Lee (KOR)	69-69-74-80—292	21221
	Veronica Zorzi (ITA)	74-72-75-71—292	21221
24	Paula Creamer	69-71-79-74—293	17610
	Dorothy Delasin	72-72-74-75—293	17610
	Karine Icher (FRA)	73-73-77-70—293	17610
	Carin Koch (SWE)	70-72-76-75—293	17610
	Candie King (TAI)	72-75-72-74—293	17610
29	Young Jo (KOR)	72-73-75-74—294	14199
	Meena Lee (KOR)	72-76-72-74—294	14199
	Patricia Meunier-Lebouc (FRA)	77-67-77-73—294	14199
	Ai Miyazato (JPN)	70-77-72-75—294	14199
	Becky Morgan (WAL)	76-70-75-73—294	14199
	Jennifer Rosales (PHI)	72-76-73-73—294	14199
35	Il Mi Chung (KOR)	72-77-73-73—295	11329
	Cristie Kerr	71-76-75-73—295	11329
	Grace Park (KOR)	74-72-78-71—295	11329
	Sherri Steinhauer	72-77-75-71—295	11329
	Wendy Ward	71-75-76-73—295	11329
40	Suzann Pettersen (NOR)	75-72-75-74—296	9763
	Aree Song (KOR)	74-76-72-74—296	9763
42	Marisa Baena (COL)	75-72-71-79—297	8842
	Mi Hyun Kim (KOR)	75-74-75-73—297	8842
	Rachel Hetherington (AUS)	74-75-76-72—297	8842
45	Kyeong Bae (KOR)	71-79-74-74—298	7276
	Jimin Kang (KOR)	73-73-77-75—298	7276
	Birdie Kim (KOR)	75-73-76-74—298	7276
	Sarah Lee (KOR)	75-74-72-77—298	7276
	Janice Moodie (SCO)	71-76-73-78—298	7276
	Liselotte Neumann (SWE)	72-75-77-74—298	7276
	Se Ri Pak (KOR)	74-74-76-74—298	7276
52	Johanna Head (ENG)	70-77-76-76—299	5987
	Christine Kim	74-73-78-74—299	5987
	Gwladys Nocera (FRA)	73-76-73-77—299	5987
	Kim Saiki	74-74-80-71—299	5987
56	Jee Young Lee (KOR)	73-76-77-74—300	5434
	Sung Ah Yim (KOR)	78-72-77-73—300	5434
58	Lorie Kane (CAN)	74-72-77-78—301	4974
	Soo Young Moon (KOR)	76-74-73-78—301	4974
	Reilley Rankin	71-74-81-75—301	4974
61	Brandie Burton	74-76-76-76—302	4605
62	Maru Martinez (am)	74-73-77-80—304	
	In-Bee Park (am)	72-78-77-77—304	
64	Joo Mi Kim (KOR)	80-70-78-77—305	4513
65	Nicole Perrot (CHI)	74-76-77-79—306	4421
66	Katherine Hull (AUS)	75-73-82-77—307	4283
	Meg Mallon	74-76-78-79—307	4283
68	Kate Golden	73-75-83-77—308	4145
	Sydnee Michaels (am)	77-73-80-78—308	
70	A J Eathorne (CAN)	78-68-83-85—314	4053

Kraft Nabisco Championship *continued*

The following players missed the cut:

Amy Alcott	75-76—151	Lindsey Wright (AUS)	75-78—153
Beth Bader	79-72—151	Cecilia Ekelundh (SWE)	77-77—154
Silvia Cavalleri (ITA)	74-77—151	Paige Mackenzie (am)	76-78—154
Trish Johnson (ENG)	73-78—151	Hee Jung Park (KOR)	80-74—154
Kelly Robbins	76-75—151	Jill McGill	81-74—155
Heather Young	73-78—151	Laura Diaz	77-79—156
Candy Hannemann (BRA)	75-77—152	Tina Fischer (GER)	78-78—156
Hilary Lunke	78-74—152	Anna Grzebien (am)	80-76—156
Angela Stanford	79-73—152	Ludivine Kreutz (FRA)	77-79—156
Sophie Gustafson (SWE)	77-76—153	Catriona Matthew (SCO)	79-77—156
Maria Hjörth (SWE)	80-73—153	Moira Dunn	79-78—157
Jamie Hullett	77-76—153	Laura Davies (ENG)	75-84—159
Rosie Jones	74-79—153	Ashli Bunch	75-85—160
Patty Sheehan	75-78—153	Soo-Yun Kang (KOR)	75-85—160

2005 Kraft Nabisco Championship

Prize money: $1.8 million

1	Annika Sörenstam (SWE)	70-69-66-68—273	$270000	
2	Rosie Jones	69-70-71-71—281	166003	
3	Laura Diaz	75-69-71-68—283	106791	
	Cristie Kerr	72-70-70-71—283	106791	
5	Mi Hyun Kim (KOR)	69-71-72-72—284	68165	
	Grace Park (KOR)	73-68-76-67—284	68165	
7	Juli Inkster	70-74-72-69—285	51350	
8	Lorie Kane (CAN)	71-76-69-70—286	44988	
9	Beth Daniel	74-72-69-72—287	34591	
	Dorothy Delasin (PHI)	71-72-73-71—287	34591	
	Wendy Doolan (AUS)	74-69-73-71—287	34591	
	Candie Kung (TPE)	72-73-71-71—287	34591	
	Reilley Rankin	73-68-74-72—287	34591	
14	Brandie Burton	72-71-72-73—288	27175	
	Kim Saiki	74-71-70-73—288	27175	
	Michelle Wie (am)	70-74-73-71—288		
17	Natalie Gulbis	73-71-72-73—289	24267	
	Hee-Won Han (KOR)	76-71-69-73—289	24267	
19	Shi Hyun Ahn (KOR)	77-76-71-66—290	21692	
	Paula Creamer	74-72-72-72—290	21692	
	Young Kim (KOR)	76-70-70-74—290	21692	
	Morgan Pressel (am)	70-73-72-75—290		

23	Laura Davies (ENG)	73-71-71-77—292	19086	
	Pat Hurst	71-74-74-73—292	19086	
	Sherri Steinhauer	71-72-75-74—292	19086	
	Karen Stupples (ENG)	69-80-70-73—292	19086	
27	Dawn Coe-Jones (CAN)	74-73-74-72—293	16723	
	Jeong Jang (KOR)	77-74-71-71—293	16723	
	Se Ri Pak (KOR)	77-70-70-76—293	16723	
30	Michelle Estill	71-79-71-73—294	14565	
	Julieta Granada (PAR) (am)	75-71-70-78—294		
	Carin Koch (SWE)	70-73-75-76—294	14565	
	Jill McGill	73-72-77-72—294	14565	
	Stacy Prammanasudh	75-74-74-71—294	14565	
35	Helen Alfredsson (SWE)	76-72-74-73—295	12383	
	Leta Lindley	74-77-73-71—295	12383	
	Lorena Ochoa (MEX)	76-75-73-71—295	12383	
	Jennifer Rosales (PHI)	71-79-74-71—295	12383	
39	Tina Barrett	73-77-71-75—296	10288	
	Yuri Fudoh (JPN)	75-75-75-71—296	10288	
	Rachel Hetherington (AUS)	77-73-72-74—296	10288	
	Christina Kim	76-71-73-76—296	10288	
	Janice Moodie (SCO)	74-77-74-71—296	10288	

Other players who made the cut: Joo Mi Kim (KOR), Catriona Matthew (SCO), Ai Miyazato (JPN), Gloria Park (KOR), Charlotta Sörenstam (SWE), Karrie Webb (AUS), 297; Heather Bowie, Tina Fischer (GER), Meg Mallon, Jane Park (am), Wendy Ward, 298; Liselotte Neumann (SWE), Giulia Sergas (ITA), Bo Bae Song (KOR), 299; Katherine Hull (AUS), Kelli Kuehne, Michele Redman, Angela Stanford, 300; Donna Andrews, Betsy King, 301; Trish Johnson (ENG), Aree Song (KOR), 302; Sophie Gustafson (SWE), Emilee Klein, 303; Stephanie Arricau (FRA), Hilary Lunke, 304; Heather Daly-Donofrio, Candy Hannemann (BRA), 305; Nancy Scranton, 306; Catrin Nilsmark (SWE), 310; Jamie Hullett, 311; Laurel Kean, 316.

2004 Nabisco Dinah Shore

Prize money: $1.6 million

Pos	Player	Score	Money
1	Grace Park (KOR)	72-69-67-69—277	$240000
2	Aree Song (KOR)	66-73-69-70—278	146826
3	Karrie Webb (AUS)	68-71-71-69—279	106512
4	Michelle Wie (am)	69-72-69-71—281	
5	Cristie Kerr	71-71-71-69—282	74358
	Catriona Matthew (SCO)	67-75-70-70—282	74358
7	Mi-Hyun Kim (KOR)	71-70-71-71—283	54261
8	Rosie Jones	67-73-71-73—284	36737
	Christina Kim	72-72-70-70—284	36737
	Candie Kung (TPE)	69-75-71-69—284	36737
	Jung Yeon Lee (KOR)	69-69-71-75—284	36737
	Lorena Ochoa (MEX)	67-76-74-67—284	36737
13	Hee-Won Han (KOR)	72-71-71-71—285	26420
	Stacy Prammanasudh	71-71-69-74—285	26420
	Annika Sörenstam (SWE)	71-76-69-69—285	26420
16	Laura Davies (ENG)	71-77-70-68—286	20633
	Wendy Doolan (AUS)	70-69-72-75—286	20633
	Young Kim (KOR)	74-72-67-73—286	20633
	Carin Koch (SWE)	70-72-71-73—286	20633
	Se Ri Pak (KOR)	72-73-72-69—286	20633
	Karen Stupples (ENG)	70-76-68-72—286	20633
22	Michele Redman	73-73-70-71—287	17846
23	Jeong Jang (KOR)	76-71-70-72—289	17203
24	Brandie Burton	70-76-71-73—290	15944
	Tammie Green	71-78-71-70—290	15944
	Jane Park (am)	71-74-73-72—290	
	Dottie Pepper	68-70-74-78—290	15944
28	Danielle Ammaccapane	75-77-73-66—291	13682
	Donna Andrews	70-74-73-74—291	13682
	Tina Barrett	75-70-73-73—291	13682
	Juli Inkster	74-74-73-70—291	13682
	Wendy Ward	72-74-70-75—291	13682
33	Vicki Goetze-Ackerman	73-79-71-69—292	11897
	Kelly Robbins	69-74-78-71—292	11897
35	Dorothy Delasin (PHI)	76-71-71-75—293	10306
	Pat Hurst	72-76-69-76—293	10306
	Lorie Kane (CAN)	72-74-76-71—293	10306
	Rachel Teske (AUS)	75-71-71-76—293	10306
	Iben Tinning (DEN)	70-75-77-71—293	10306
40	Helen Alfredsson (SWE)	75-72-71-76—294	8541
	Beth Daniel	72-74-74-74—294	8541
	Kate Golden	73-78-74-69—294	8541
	Elizabeth Janangelo (am)	71-78-70-75—294	
	Emilee Klein	71-73-76-74—294	8541

Other players who made the cut: Beth Bauer, Paula Creamer (am), Jill McGill 295; Sophie Gustafson (SWE), Stephanie Louden, Meg Mallon, Sherri Steinhauer 296; Michelle Ellis (AUS), Laurel Kean, Becky Morgan (WAL) 297; Jackie Gallagher-Smith, Ji-Hee Lee (KOR), Charlotta Sörenstam (SWE) 298; Moira Dunn, Natalie Gulbis, Betsy King, Jennifer Rosales (PHI) 300; Marisa Baena (COL), Heather Bowie, Heather Daly-Donofrio, Soo-Yun Kang (KOR), Miho Koga (JPN), Yu Ping Lin (TPE), Janice Moodie (SCO) 301; Hilary Lunke 302; JoAnne Carner, Dawn Coe-Jones, Joanne Mills (AUS) 303; Mhairi McKay (SCO), Shani Waugh (AUS) 304; Mardi Lunn (AUS) 305; Kelli Kuehne 306; Amy Alcott 308; Nancy Lopez WD

2003 Nabisco Dinah Shore

Prize money: $1.6 million

Pos	Player	Score	Money
1	Patricia Meunier Lebouc (FRA)	70-68-70-73—281	$240000
2	Annika Sörenstam (SWE)	68-72-71-71—282	146120
3	Lorena Ochoa (MEX)	71-70-74-68—283	106000
4	Laura Davies (ENG)	70-75-69-70—284	82000
5	Beth Daniel	75-74-68-70—287	51200
	Laura Diaz	76-71-69-71—287	51200
	Maria Hjörth (SWE)	72-72-73-70—287	51200
	Catriona Matthew (SCO)	71-74-72-70—287	51200
9	Jennifer Rosales (PHI)	74-70-72-72—288	35600
	Michelle Wie (am)	72-74-66-76—288	
11	Juli Inkster	75-74-66-75—290	29160
	Cristie Kerr	74-71-74-71—290	29160
	Woo-Soon Ko (KOR)	74-73-70-73—290	29160
	Rosie Jones	71-75-72-72—290	29160
15	Dawn Coe-Jones (CAN)	72-74-72-73—291	22080
	Dorothy Delasin (PHI)	71-71-76-73—291	22080
	Catrin Nilsmark (SWE)	71-78-73-69—291	22080
	Se Ri Pak (KOR)	71-72-71-77—291	22080
	Karen Stupples (ENG)	71-71-76-73—291	22080
20	Hee-Won Han (KOR)	73-74-75-70—292	19040
21	Danielle Ammaccapane	75-68-78-72—293	17440
21T	Jeong Jang (KOR)	75-73-76-69—293	17440
	Virada Nirapathpongporn (am)	76-72-72-73—293	
	Michele Redman	70-72-76-75—293	17440
	Aree Song (am)	72-77-73-71—293	
	Karrie Webb (AUS)	70-79-71-73—293	17440
27	Leta Lindley	76-70-75-73—294	15840
28	Tammie Green	77-71-73-74—295	14160
	Christina Kim	72-76-71-76—295	14160
	Betsy King	75-74-70-76—295	14160
	Candie Kung (TPE)	74-75-74-72—295	14160
	Charlotta Sörenstam (SWE)	73-74-71-77—295	14160
33	Heather Bowie	72-78-72-74—296	11373
	Heather Daly-Donofrio	74-77-72-73—296	11373
	Moira Dunn	74-80-73-69—296	11373
	Amy Fruhwirth	73-75-75-73—296	11373
	Vicki Goetze-Ackerman	75-74-74-73—296	11373
	Meg Mallon	72-76-73-75—296	11373
39	Beth Bauer	74-76-70-77—297	9440
	Jackie Gallagher-Smith	75-74-74-74—297	9440
	Lorie Kane (CAN)	72-72-78-75—297	9440

Other players who made the cut: Brandie Burton, Raquel Carriedo (ESP), Michelle Ellis (AUS), Liselotte Neumann (SWE), Gloria Park (KOR), Kelly Robbins 298; Natalie Gulbis, Rachel Teske (AUS), Wendy Ward 299; Sophie Gustafson (SWE), Pat Hurst, Kelli Kuehne, Barb Mucha, Dottie Pepper, Angela Stanford 300; Nanci Bowen, Akiko Fukushima (JPN), Laurel Kean, Mi-Hyun Kim (KOR), Joanne Morley (ENG), Kim Saiki, Lindsey Wright (AUS) (am) 301; Helen Alfredsson (SWE), Donna Andrews, Emilee Klein, Stephanie Louden, Janice Moodie (SCO), Shani Waugh (AUS) 302; Mhairi McKay (SCO), Patty Sheehan 303; Suzanne Strudwick (ENG) 304; Tina Fischer (GER) 305; Tracy Hanson 306; Kasumi Fujii (JPN), Yu Ping Lin (TPE) 307; Pat Bradley 308; Dale Eggeling 310; Mardi Lunn (AUS) 311

2002 Nabisco Dinah Shore

Prize money: $1,500,000

1	Annika Sörenstam (SWE)	70-71-71-68—280	$225000	21T	Janice Moodie (SCO)	73-73-73-70—289	16350
2	Liselotte Neuman (SWE)	69-70-73-69—281	136987	25	Sophie Gustafson (SWE)	77-69-71-73—290	13800
3	Rosie Jones	72-69-72-69—282	88125		Hee-Won Han (KOR)	74-74-73-69—290	13800
	Cristie Kerr	74-70-70-68—282	88125		Laurel Kean	79-74-71-66—290	13800
5	Akiko Fukushima (JPN)	73-76-68-66—283	56250		Suzann Pettersen (NOR)	74-71-73-72—290	13800
	Carin Koch (SWE)	73-73-71-66—283	56250		Michele Redman	75-70-72-73—290	13800
7	Karrie Webb (AUS)	75-70-67-72—284	42375	30	Laura Diaz	74-73-73-71—291	12225
8	Lorena Ochoa (am)	75-69-71-70—285			Aree Song Wongluekiet	71-74-73-73—291	
9	Becky Iverson	71-74-68-73—286	31050		(am)		
	Lorie Kane (CAN)	73-72-70-71—286	31050	32	Heather Daly-Donofrio	74-73-72-73—292	11100
	Leta Lindley	72-72-72-70—286	31050		Kathryn Marshall (SCO)	75-72-73-72—292	11100
	Se Ri Pak (KOR)	74-71-71-70—286	31050		Alison Nicholas (ENG)	76-71-70-75—292	11100
	Grace Park (KOR)	75-73-70-68—286	31050		Gloria Park (KOR)	70-76-75-71—292	11100
14	Vicki Goetze-Ackerman	74-73-68-72—287	21900	36	Marisa Baena (COL)	79-74-68-72—293	8524
	Heather Bowie	75-71-72-69—287	21900		Maria Hjörth (SWE)	76-73-69-75—293	8524
	Beth Daniel	71-70-75-71—287	21900		Pat Hurst	78-72-71-72—293	8524
	Dorothy Delasin (PHI)	72-73-69-73—287	21900		Chris Johnson	75-71-76-71—293	8524
	Kris Tschetter	74-69-73-71—287	21900		Betsy King	71-75-73-74—293	8524
19	Juli Inkster	73-76-71-68—288	18225		Kelli Kuehne	74-73-73-73—293	8524
	Mhairi McKay (SCO)	73-72-73-70—288	18225		Meg Mallon	75-73-74-71—293	8524
21	Laura Davies (ENG)	75-75-69-70—289	16350		Sherri Steinhauer	73-78-70-72—293	8524
	Wendy Doolan (AUS)	78-70-72-69—289	16350		Wendy Ward	77-74-73-69—293	8524
	Mi Hyun Kim (KOR)	74-75-69-71—289	16350				

Other players who made the cut: Helen Alfredsson (SWE), Yuri Fudoh (JPN), Jeong Jang (KOR), Yu Ping Lin (TPE) 294; Donna Andrews, Barb Mucha 295; Penny Hammel, Karin Icher (FRA), Catriona Matthew (SCO), Deb Richard 296; Tina Barrett, Amy Fruhwirth, Jill McGill 298; Moira Dunn, Kelly Robbins, Pearl Sinn (KOR), Naree Song Wongluekiet (am) 299; Brandie Burton, Charlotta Sörenstam (SWE), Sherri Turner 300; Dina Ammaccapane, Rachel Teske (AUS), Karen Weiss 301; Amy Alcott, Kate Golden 302; Emilee Klein 303; Patty Sheehan 305; Tammie Green 306; Meredith Duncan (am) 307; Hiromi Kobayashi (JPN) 312

2001 Nabisco Dinah Shore

Prize money: $1,250,000

1	Annika Sörenstam (SWE)	72-70-70-69—281	$225000	21T	Loreno Ochoa (MEX) (am)	72 71-74-73—290	
2	Karrie Webb (AUS)	73-72-70-69—284	87557	23	Becky Iverson	75-70-72-74—291	15955
	Janice Moodie (SCO)	72-72-70-70—284	87557	24	Maria Hjörth	73-72-75-72—292	14540
	Dottie Pepper	71-71-71-71—284	87557		Tammie Green	72-73-75-72—292	14540
	Akiko Fukushima (JPN)	74-68-70-72—284	87557		Kelly Robbins	75-72-72-73—292	14540
	Rachel Teske (AUS)	72-73-66-73—284	87557		Penny Hammel	70-75-72-75—292	14540
7	Sophie Gustafson (SWE)	72-74-70-69—285	41891	28	Meg Mallon	74-71-78-70—293	12063
	Brandie Burton	74-69-72-70—285	41891		Grace Park (KOR)	75-75-72-71—293	12063
9	Laura Diaz	71-74-69-72—286	33589		Dina Ammaccapane	74-74-73-72—293	12063
	Pat Hurst	70-68-74-74—286	33589		Rosie Jones	73-73-75-72—293	12063
11	Laura Davies (ENG)	71-73-75-68—287	25957		Alison Nicholas (ENG)	71-75-75-72—293	12063
	Dorothy Delasin (PHI)	73-70-74-70—287	25957		Stefania Croce (ITA)	74-72-73-74—293	12063
	Se Ri Pak (KOR)	73-69-73-72—287	25957		Emilee Klein	72-74-72-75—293	12063
	Tina Barrett	71-73-70-73—287	25957	35	Kelli Kuehne	75-70-75-74—294	10446
15	Mi Hyun Kim (KOR)	74-71-70-73—288	20736	36	Jan Crafter (AUS)	78-73-74-70—295	9124
	Carin Koch (SWE)	70-69-75-74—288	20736		Heather Bowie	77-73-74-71—295	9124
	Juli Inkster	70-75-68-75—288	20736		Charlotte Sörenstam	78-71-75-71—295	9124
18	Liselotte Neumann (SWE)	70-74-74-71—289	18220		(SWE)		
	Jeong Jang (KOR)	74-71-71-73—289	18220		Nancy Scranton	72-75-75-73—295	9124
	Michele Redman	71-72-71-75—289	18220		Moira Dunn	78-73-70-74—295	9124
21	Jill McGill	75-71-70-74—290	16711		Wendy Ward	76-73-70-76—295	9124

Other players who made the cut: Amy Fruhwirth, Joanne Morley (ENG), Danielle Ammaccapane, Lorie Kane (CAN) 296; Helen Alfredsson (SWE), Aree Wongluekiet (am) 297; Jenny Lidback (PER), Cindy Figg Currier, Nanci Bowen, Leta Lindley, Chris Johnson, Cathy Johnston Forbes, Donna Andrews 298; Beth Daniel, Laurie Kean, Pearl Sinn (KOR) 299; Jackie Gallagher-Smith, Vickie Goetze Ackerman, Caroline McMillan, Vicki Fergon, Naree Wongluekiet (am) 300; Wendy Doolan (AUS), Nancy Lopez, Hiromi Kobayashi (JPN) 301; Cristie Kerr, Susie Redman 302; Joan Pitcock, Catrin Nilsmark (SWE), Kellee Booth 303; Ok Hee Ku (JPN) 305; Dawn Coe-Jones, Marine Monnet (FRA) 306; Betsy King 309

2000 Nabisco Dinah Shore

Prize money: $1,250,000

1	Karrie Webb (AUS)	67-70-67-70—274	$187500	17T	Kaori Higo (JPN)	76-72-73-71—292	14321
2	Dottie Pepper	68-72-72-72—284	116366		Sherri Steinhauer	73-71-77-71—292	14321
3	Meg Mallon	75-70-73-67—285	84916		Charlotta Sörenstam	75-75-70-72—292	14321
4	Cathy Johnston-Forbes	74-71-71-70—286	59755		(SWE)		
					Juli Inkster	76-71-73-72—292	14321
5	Michele Redman	73-73-69-71—286	59755		Nancy Bowen	75-72-73-72—292	14321
6	Helen Dobson (ENG)	73-74-72-68—287	40750		Carin Koch (SWE)	79-70-70-73—292	14321
	Chris Johnson	73-68-73-73—287	40750		Nancy Scranton	78-70-71-73—292	14321
8	Rosie Jones	74-71-74-69—288	31135		Barb Mucha	77-71-70-74—292	14321
	Kim Saiki	72-77-68-71—288	31135	27	Jane Geddes	74-72-78-69—293	10969
10	Jenny Lidback (PER)	75-72-74-68—289	24170		Leta Lindley	73-76-73-71—293	10969
	Wendy Doolan (AUS)	73-73-69-74—289	24170		Catriona Matthew	72-77-73-71—293	10969
	Pat Hurst	72-72-70-75—289	24170		(SCO)		
	Aree Song Wongluekiet (am)	75-71-68-75—289			Alison Nicholas (ENG)	71-74-74-74—293	10969
				31	Susie Redman	73-75-74-72—294	9507
14	Kristi Albers	77-71-72-70—290	20845		Caroline McMillan	73-74-74-73—294	9507
	Se Ri Pak (KOR)	73-71-77-70—291	18957		(ENG)		
	Janice Moodie (SCO)	74-72-70-75—291	18957		Gail Graham (CAN)	71-75-75-73—294	9507
17	Kelly Robbins	79-69-73-71—292	14321		Brandie Burton	74-75-71-74—294	9507
	Annika Sörenstam (SWE)	76-72-73-71—292	14321				

Other players who made the cut: Akiko Fukushima (JPN), Tina Barrett, Dawn Coe Jones, Laura Davies (ENG), Cristie Kerr, Fumiko Muraguchi (JPN), Lorie Kane (CAN), Beth Bauer (am) 295; Pearl Sinn (KOR), Nancy Lopez, Wendy Ward, Barb Whitehead 296; Cindy McCurdy, Becky Iverson, Mi Hyun Kim (KOR), Jill McGill, Patty Sheehan, Beth Daniel 297; Kris Tschetter, Donna Andrews, Mary Beth Zimmerman, Jan Stephenson (AUS) 298; Helen Alfredsson (SWE), Eva Dahlloff (SWE), Jackie Gallagher-Smith, Catrin Nilsmark (SWE), Amy Fruhwirth 299; Mayumi Hirase (JPN), Penny Hammel, Tammie Green, Sherri Turner, Rachel Hetherington (AUS) 300; Maggie Will, Ayako Okamoto (JPN), Julie Piers, Kathryn Marshall (SCO) 301; Marnie McGuire (NZL) 302; Liselotte Neumann (SWE) 306; Dale Eggeling 309

1999 Nabisco Dinah Shore

Prize money: $1,000,000

1	D Pepper	70-66-67-66—269	$150000	13T	K Tschetter	68-70-73-75—286	13712
2	M Mallon	66-69-71-69—275	93093	21	M Spencer-Devlin	72-69-77-69—287	9692
3	K Webb (AUS)	73-71-70-66—280	67933		H Stacy	74-74-69-70—287	9692
4	K Robbins	69-73-67-72—281	52837		M Estill	70-76-71-70—287	9692
5	C Sörenstam (SWE)	72-68-76-66—282	42772		R Hetherington (AUS)	70-74-71-72—287	9692
6	J Inkster	72-66-71-74—283	35224		N Lopez	72-73-69-73—287	9692
7	C Matthew (SCO)	72-73-69-70—284	26502		D Eggeling	73-70-70-74—287	9692
	A Sörenstam (SWE)	70-73-71-70—284	26502		H Kobayashi (JPN)	70-69-74-74—287	9692
	J Moodie (SCO)	69-68-75-72—284	26502		D Andrews	70-69-74-74—287	9692
10	S Steinhauer	70-72-72-71—285	19289	29	H Dobson (ENG)	74-72-74-68—288	7812
	M Hjörth (SWE)	77-68-68-72—285	19289		D Dormann	74-73-71-70—288	7812
	H Alfredsson (SWE)	69-71-73-72—285	19289		L Kane (CAN)	73-74-71-70—288	7812
13	R Jones	73-70-73-70—286	13712		J Pitcock	77-68-73-70—288	7812
	M Will	72-71-73-70—286	13712	33	W Ward	74-73-72-70—289	6516
	M Redman	71-74-69-72—286	13712		A Alcott	74-71-71-73—289	6516
	P Bradley	73-69-72-72—286	13712		J Geddes	73-72-71-73—289	6516
	C McCurdy	70-74-69-73—286	13712		T Green	70-75-71-73—289	6516
	Se Ri Pak (KOR)	73-69-69-75—286	13712		B Mucha	73-75-67-74—289	6516
	M Hirase	70-72-69-75—286	13712		J Crafter (AUS)	70-74-71-74—289	6516

Other players who made the cut: K Saiki, T Tombs, N Bowen, G Park (am) 290; K Marshall (SCO), E Klein, M Nause, P Hurst, B Daniel 291; G Graham, T Johnson, C Figg-Currier 292; T Barrett, C Johnson, M McGeorge, D Coe-Jones, K Albers, S Turner, A Nicholas (ENG) 293; L Neumann (SWE), M McGann, T Hanson, M Hattori 294; C Johnston-Forbes, P Sinn, L Kiggens 295; V Fergon, Dina Ammaccapane 296; D Richard, J Piers, J Chuasiriporn (am) 297; E Crosby, C Flom, L Davies (ENG) 298; P Sheehan, TJ Myers, Dani Ammaccapane, K Harada 299; B King 300; B Iverson 301; V Skinner, S Gustafson 302

1998 Nabisco Dinah Shore

Prize money: $1,000,000

1	P Hurst	68-72-70-71—281	$150000	18T	M Spencer-Devlin	72-70-76-73—291	12147
2	H Dobson (ENG)	70-74-71-67—282	93093		L Hackney (ENG)	71-71-73-76—291	12147
3	L Davies (ENG)	75-70-70-68—283	60385	23	G Park (KOR) (am)	77-73-71-71—292	
	H Alfredsson (SWE)	70-73-70-70—283	60385	24	E Klein	76-74-73-70—293	9256
5	D Andrews	71-72-71-70—284	38998		J Inkster	74-75-74-70—293	9256
	L Neumann (SWE)	69-71-71-73—284	38998		C Figg-Currier	74-72-77-70—293	9256
7	A Sörenstam (SWE)	76-71-69-70—286	27928		B Iverson	74-72-77-70—293	9256
	K Webb (AUS)	71-72-70-73—286	27928		B Mucha	72-75-74-72—293	9256
9	D Pepper	73-72-74-68—287	22393		T Green	72-72-76-73—293	9256
	S Steinhauer	69-76-71-71—287	22393		Dani Ammaccapane	75-73-71-74—293	9256
11	A Fruhwirth	73-71-73-71—288	18438		M McGann	74-71-72-76—293	9256
	D Coe-Jones	70-72-74-72—288	18438		M Hirase	73-69-73-78—293	9256
13	C Matthew (SCO)	75-74-70-70—289	15670	33	H Kobayashi (JPN)	77-71-77-69—294	6964
	P Hammel	73-72-71-73—289	15670		T Barrett	76-73-74-71—294	6964
	N Lopez	71-71-73-74—289	15670		M Halpin	72-77-74-71—294	6964
16	M Mallon	75-69-76-70—290	13658		G Graham	71-75-74-74—294	6964
	B Bauer (am)	76-70-72-72—290			A Nicholas (ENG)	75-70-75-74—294	6964
18	L Kane (CAN)	76-71-74-70—291	12147		J Geddes	73-75-71-75—294	6964
	R Jones	75-66-78-72—291	12147		D Dormann	73-74-72-75—294	6964
	J Carner	73-72-73-73—291	12147				

Other players who made the cut: A Alcott, J Stephenson 295; C McCurdy, K Saiki, J Crafter, P Sheehan, M Redman, J Pitcock, P Bradley, K Robbins 296; V Fergon, D Richard, D Eggeling, J Piers, B Burton 297; J Lidback, MB Zimmerman, K Marshall, L Walters 298; T Tombs, R Hetherington 299; C Rarick, B King, K Weiss 300; V Skinner 301; S Redman, P Rizzo, N Bowen 302; S Hamlin, T Johnson 303; M Morris 304; L Kiggens 305; B Daniel 306

1997 Nabisco Dinah Shore

Prize money: $900,000

1	B King	71-67-67-71—276	$135000	16T	L Davies (ENG)	70-70-74-72—286	10898
2	K Tschetter	66-76-66-70—278	83783		K Marshall (SCO)	66-73-73-74—286	10898
3	A Fruhwirth	69-70-68-72—279	54346	23	C Schreyer	72-74-73-68—287	8690
	K Robbins	70-67-68-74—279	54346		M Baena (am)	74-71-73-69—287	
5	N Bowen	70-74-70-68—282	35097		P Hammel	76-72-67-72—287	8690
	L Hackney (ENG)	70-72-72-68—282	35097		T Johnson (ENG)	70-72-73-72—287	8690
7	T Barrett	70-71-70-72—283	26720		N Lopez	70-74-69-74—287	8690
8	MB Zimmerman	75-74-72-63—284	21285	28	B Mucha	71-72-73-72—288	8000
	H Kobayashi (JPN)	72-69-71-72—284	21285	29	K Webb (AUS)	69-74-71-75—289	7728
	A Sörenstam (SWE)	70-72-68-74—284	21285	30	M Hirase	70-77-72-71—290	6940
11	M Morris	71-75-72-67—285	15065		M Estill	72-73-73-72—290	6940
	D Andrews	73-71-72-69—285	15065		D Coe-Jones	73-72-72-73—290	6940
	J Geddes	68-75-72-70—285	15065		D Richard	68-75-74-73—290	6940
	J Crafter (AUS)	70-71-72-72—285	15065		D Eggeling	68-72-75-75—290	6940
	D Pepper	69-70-71-75—285	15065	35	J Briles-Hinton	72-76-74-69—291	5668
16	T Green	72-73-71-70—286	10898		C Johnson	75-72-72-72—291	5668
	J Inkster	72-74-69-71—286	10898		E Klein	73-74-71-73—291	5668
	M McGann	74-70-71-71—286	10898		A-M Palli (FRA)	73-74-70-74—291	5668
	L Neumann (SWE)	74-71-69-72—286	10898		H Stacy	72-73-72-74—291	5668
	P Hurst	74-69-71-72—286	10898		P Bradley	69-72-73-77—291	5668

Other players who made the cut: A Nicholas, C Walker 292; V Skinner, J Lidback, C Rarick, B Iverson, L Walters 293; S Turner, B Burton, S Steinhauer, K Harada, J Pitcock, V Goetze-Ackerman 294; J Piers, R Hood, H Alfredsson 295; T Hanson, A Finney, A Alcott, K Monaghan 296; N Ramsbottom, R Walton 298; P Sheehan 299; A Okamoto 300; M Spencer-Devlin 301; A Ritzman, TJ Myers 302; B Bunkowsky-Scherbak, A Fukushima, L Kiggens 303; V Fergon, B Whitehead 304; T Kerdyk, A Benz 305

Nabisco Dinah Shore History

This event was inaugurated in 1972 as the Colgate Dinah Shore and continued to be sponsored by Colgate until 1981. Nabisco took over the sponsorship in 1982; and the Nabisco Dinah Shore was designated a Major Championship in 1983. Mission Hills CC, Rancho Mirage, California, is the event's permanent venue.

Year	Winner	Score
1972	J Blalock	213
1973	M Wright	284
1974	J Prentice*	289
*After a play-off with Jane Blalock and Sandra Haynie		
1975	S Palmer	283
1976	J Rankin	285
1977	K Whitworth	289
1978	S Post*	283
*After a play-off with Penny Pulz		
1979	S Post*	276
*After a play-off with Nancy Lopez		
1980	D Caponi	275
1981	N Lopez	277
1982	S Little	278
1983	A Alcott	282
1984	J Inkster*	280
*After a play-off with P Bradley		
1985	A Miller	278
1986	P Bradley	280
1987	B King*	283
*After a play-off with P Sheehan		
1988	A Alcott	274

Year	Winner	Score
1989	J Inkster	279
1990	B King	283
1991	A Alcott	273
1992	D Mochrie*	279
*After a play-off with J Inkster		
1993	H Alfredsson (SWE)	284
1994	D Andrews	276
1995	N Bowen	285
1996	P Sheehan	281
1997	B King	276
1998	P Hurst	281
1999	D Pepper	269
2000	K Webb (AUS)	274
2001	A Sörenstam (SWE)	281
2002	A Sörenstam (SWE)	280
2003	P Meunier-Lebouc (FRA)	281
2004	G Park (KOR)	277
2005	A Sörenstam (SWE)	273
2006	K Webb (AUS)*	279
*After a play-off with L Ochoa		

du Maurier Classic History

The du Maurier Classic was inaugurated in 1973 and designated a Major Championship in 1979.
It was discontinued after 2000 and was replaced as a major on the US LPGA schedule by the Weetabix Women's British Open.

Players are of American nationality unless stated

Year	Winner	Venue	Score
1973	J Bourassa*	Montreal GC, Montreal	214
After a play-off with S Haynie and J Rankin			
1974	CJ Callison	Candiac GC, Montreal	208
1975	J Carner*	St George's CC, Toronto	214
After a play-off with C Mann			
1976	D Caponi*	Cedar Brae G&CC, Toronto	212
After a play-off with J Rankin			
1977	J Rankin	Lachute G&CC, Montreal	214
1978	J Carner	St George's CC, Toronto	278
1979	A Alcott	Richelieu Valley CC, Montreal	285
1980	P Bradley	St George's CC, Toronto	277
1981	J Stephenson (AUS)	Summerlea CC, Dorian, Quebec	278
1982	S Haynie	St George's CC, Toronto	280
1983	H Stacy	Beaconsfield CC, Montreal	277
1984	J Inkster	St George's CC, Toronto	279
1985	P Bradley	Beaconsfield CC, Montreal	278
1986	P Bradley*	Board of Trade CC, Toronto	276
After a play-off with A Okamoto			
1987	J Rosenthal	Islesmere GC, Laval, Quebec	272
1988	S Little (RSA)	Vancouver GC, Coquitlam, BC	279
1989	T Green	Beaconsfield GC, Montreal	279
1990	C Johnston	Westmount G&CC, Kitchener, Ontario	276
1991	N Scranton	Vancouver GC, Coquitlam, BC	279
1992	S Steinhauer	St Charles CC, Winnipeg, Manitoba	277
1993	B Burton*	London H&CC, Ontario	277
After a play-off with B King			
1994	M Nause	Ottawa Hunt Club, Ontario	279
1995	J Lidback	Beaconsfield CC, Montreal	280
1996	L Davies (ENG)	Edmonton CC, Edmonton, Alberta	277
1997	C Walker	Glen Abbey GC, Toronto	278
1998	B Burton	Essex G&CC, Ontario	270
1999	K Webb (AUS)	Priddis Greens G&CC, Calgary, Alberta	277
2000	M Mallon	Royal Ottawa GC, Aylmer, Quebec	282

Women's Grand Slam Titles

Patty Berg

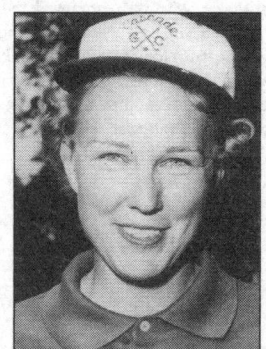

Mickey Wright

Louise Suggs

Photographs © Phil Sheldon and Empics

	British Open[1]	US Open[2]	McDonald's LPGA[3]	Kraft Nabisco[4]	du Maurier[5]	Title-holders[6]	Western[7]	Total Titles
Patty Berg (USA)	0	1	0	—	—	7	7	15
Mickey Wright (USA)	0	4	4	—	—	2	3	13
Louise Suggs (USA)	0	2	1	—	—	4	4	11
Annika Sörenstam (SWE)	1	3	3	3	0	—	—	10
'Babe' Zaharias (USA)	0	3	—	—	—	3	4	10
Karrie Webb (AUS)	3	2	1	2	1	—	—	9
Betsy Rawls (USA)	0	4	2	—	—	0	2	8
Juli Inkster (USA)	0	2	2	2	1	—	—	7

[1] The Weetabix Women's British Open was designated a major on the LPGA Tour in 2001
[2] The US Open became an LPGA major in 1950
[3] The McDonald's LPGA Championship was designated a major in 1955
[4] The Kraft Nabisco event was designated a major in 1983
[5] The du Maurier event was designated a major in 1979 but discontinued in 2001
[6] The Titleholders Championship was a major from 1937–1966 and in 1972
[7] The Western event was a major from 1937 to 1967

Super Career Grand Slam: Only Karrie Webb has won five of the qualifying majors – the Weetabix Women's British Open, the US Open, the LPGA Championship, the Kraft Nabisco and du Maurier. She completed her Super Grand Slam in 2002.

Career Grand Slam: Only Louise Suggs (1957), Mickey Wright (1962), Pat Bradley (1986), Julie Inkster (1999), Karrie Webb (2001) and Annika Sörenstam (2003) have won all the designated majors in their playing careers.

Grand Slam: Only Babe Zaharias in 1950 (three majors) and Sandra Haynie (USA) in 1964 (two majors) have won all the majors available that season.

Note: Glenna Collett Vare (USA) won six US Amateurs between 1922 and 1935 including three in a row in 1928, 1929 and 1930. Jo Anne Carner (USA) won five US Amateurs between 1957 and 1968. Julie Inkster won three US Amateurs in 1980, 1981 and 1982.

Ballesteros takes his trophy event to Ireland again

The five star Heritage Golf and Spa resort at Killenard in County Laois has been chosen as the venue for the Seve Trophy this year and again in 2009. The event is staged in alternate years to the Ryder Cup.

Nick Faldo, Europe's 2008 Ryder Cup captain, takes over this year as captain of the Great Britain and Ireland side from Colin Montgomerie, who has captained the team in four previous competitions at Sunningdale, El Saler, Druid's Glen and The Wynyard in north-east England. Seve will again captain the Continental team taking over from José María Olazábal, who captained the team in 2004.

The par-72 course which Seve helped design measures 7,319 yards. The Seve Trophy teams up 10 players for series of four-balls, greensomes, foursomes and singles and mirrors the Presidents Cup in which an American team takes on an International selection with no European involvement.

Justin Rose just misses out on a magical 59

European Tour player Justin Rose had a 14-foot putt on the final green of the Palm Course at Walt Disney World for 59 in the 2006 Funai Classic but pulled it slightly and the ball failed to drop, preventing his becoming only the fourth player on the US PGA Tour to shoot a sub-60 score.

Al Geiberger shot 59 in the Memphis Classic in 1977, Chip Beck did it in the 1991 Las Vegas Invitational and David Duval also shot a 13-under-par score in the Bob Hope Chrysler Classic in 1999.

Rose, who had ten birdies in his first 12 holes, needed three birdies over the closing holes for 59 and had chances after nearly hitting the stick with approaches to the last four. At the last his second shot landed six inches from the hole but the ball ran to the fringe of the green.

Chinese venue chosen for 2007 and 2008 World Cup

Mission Hills in China will stage the 2007 and 2008 World Cup competitions. This year's event, being held from November 9–25, will be over the José María Olazábal-designed course, one of ten at the club which is just 30 minutes from the Hong Kong border.

Mr Lui Peng, China's Minister of Sport, welcoming the decision to play the World Cup in China again – it was first played at Mission Hills in 1995 before it was part of the World Golf Championship schedule – said: "The World Golf Championship events present a significant cultural opportunity to take China to another level internationally. This event will help China to integrate on a global level."

Since the World Cup was started in 1953 as the Canada Cup, the USA has been the most regular winner. The dates for the 2008 event have been finalised as November 17–23. Dates, field and format for a World Golf Championship stroke-play event which is also to be played at Mission Hills will be decided later.

"Golf in China has only 20 years of history", said Mr Zhang Xiao Ling, Executive President and Secretary General of the China Golf Association, "Despite this the game has enormous potential for growth. Staging this prestigious event will help China and Asian Pacific region to compete at the highest level. The process of golf development will be accelerated."

In addition to the Olazábal course the complex, opened in 1994, also includes courses designed by Jack Nicklaus, Annika Sörenstam, Vijay Singh, Nick Faldo, Ernie Els, Greg Norman, David Duval, Jumbo Ozaki and David Leadbetter, who has an academy there. The residential community also includes a five-star hotel.

PART II

Men's Professional Tournaments

World Golf Rankings

Seventeen European golfers are in the top 50 on the world rankings at the end of 2006 with Padraig Harrington leading the way in eighth spot just ahead of Luke Donald who finished the year in ninth. Although Tiger Woods, Jim Furyk and Phil Mickelson filled the top three spots at the end of the year, there are only ten more Americans in the top 50. There are six Americans in the top 20 compared to eight Europeans.

Ranking		Name	Country	Points Average	Total Points	No. of Events	2004/2005 Pts Lost	2006 Pts Gained
1	(1)	Tiger Woods	USA	20.41	857.41	42	−644.06	+746.28
2	(7)	Jim Furyk	USA	8.88	479.58	54	−235.88	+477.66
3	(3)	Phil Mickelson	USA	7.17	293.99	41	−364.08	+291.82
4	(9)	Adam Scott	AUS	7.03	358.27	51	−241.21	+365.29
5	(5)	Ernie Els	RSA	6.05	290.24	48	−359.71	+272.52
6	(4)	Retief Goosen	RSA	5.61	336.53	60	−361.48	+268.67
7	(2)	Vijay Singh	FIJ	5.58	340.28	61	−554.44	+278.79
8	(17)	Padraig Harrington	IRL	5.46	300.15	55	−201.94	+294.03
9	(13)	Luke Donald	ENG	5.25	267.74	51	−226.83	+260.65
10	(50)	Geoff Ogilvy	AUS	5.21	260.51	50	−169.78	+302.56
11	(6)	Sergio Garcia	ESP	5.12	250.50	49	−269.34	+187.63
12	(32)	Henrik Stenson	SWE	4.62	240.00	52	−152.58	+245.54
13	(62)	Trevor Immelman	RSA	4.58	247.45	54	−125.37	+263.67
14	(11)	David Howell	ENG	3.80	208.92	55	−197.54	+172.93
15	(52)	Paul Casey	ENG	3.75	198.93	53	−119.19	+202.89
16	(19)	Davis Love III	USA	3.69	173.30	47	−163.29	+150.07
17	(8)	Colin Montgomerie	SCO	3.64	211.22	58	−190.69	+134.47
18	(26)	José María Olazábal	ESP	3.54	183.87	52	−159.68	+164.63
19	(15)	David Toms	USA	3.46	162.79	47	−214.34	+166.33
20	(10)	Chris DiMarco	USA	3.46	183.14	53	−209.60	+158.93
21	(24)	Nick O'Hern	AUS	3.33	166.53	50	−156.52	+137.22
22	(30)	Stuart Appleby	AUS	3.33	183.05	55	−169.80	+186.02
23	(20)	Tim Clark	RSA	3.24	181.61	56	−181.14	+148.93
24	(39)	Shingo Katayama	JPN	3.18	168.38	53	−111.17	+141.46
25	(16)	Michael Campbell	NZL	3.17	164.66	52	−159.04	+101.72
26	(27)	Stewart Cink	USA	3.12	162.10	52	−179.23	+166.05
27	(38)	Chad Campbell	USA	3.10	161.07	52	−152.51	+167.23
28	(12)	Angel Cabrera	ARG	3.08	154.15	50	−153.16	+120.68
29	(31)	Choi Kyung-Ju	KOR	3.01	183.35	61	−146.90	+154.34
30	(47)	Rod Pampling	AUS	2.93	160.91	55	−144.38	+170.47
31	(216)	Robert Karlsson	SWE	2.92	166.60	57	−54.60	+182.33
32	(112)	Joe Durant	USA	2.87	152.29	53	−61.67	+147.92
33	(106)	Yang Yong-Eun	KOR	2.86	134.57	47	−64.01	+124.74
34	(59)	Ian Poulter	ENG	2.82	174.67	62	−128.86	+180.20
35	(18)	Darren Clarke	NIR	2.81	118.07	42	−174.34	+90.77
36	(53)	Carl Pettersson	SWE	2.71	176.02	65	−127.99	+167.30
37	(376)	Jeev Milkha Singh	IND	2.63	192.07	73	−38.09	+207.14
38	(65)	Lucas Glover	USA	2.61	153.74	59	−101.58	+144.58
39	(71)	Rory Sabbatini	RSA	2.58	129.00	50	−129.28	+169.24
40	(294)	Brett Wetterich	USA	2.56	140.74	55	−51.57	+163.22
41	(34)	Ben Crane	USA	2.55	119.93	47	−99.88	+85.35
42	(60)	Niclas Fasth	SWE	2.54	127.20	50	−88.33	+106.73
43	(51)	Stephen Ames	CAN	2.52	113.55	45	−139.70	+139.13
44	(99)	Arron Oberholser	USA	2.51	110.34	44	−90.32	+137.64
45	(48)	Mike Weir	CAN	2.50	120.10	48	−124.73	+136.82
46	(22)	Thomas Bjørn	DEN	2.48	128.77	52	−148.68	+100.31
47	(35)	Robert Allenby	AUS	2.47	153.01	62	−147.30	+117.38
48	(410)	Johan Edfors	SWE	2.46	120.71	49	−39.31	+144.69
49	(41)	Lee Westwood	ENG	2.39	128.89	54	−128.15	+120.69
50	(83)	Bradley Dredge	WAL	2.37	106.68	45	−66.13	+88.45

Ranking in brackets indicates position at 31st December 2005

European Tour 2006

Final Order of Merit (Top 118 keep their cards for the 2007 season)

1	Padraig Harrington (IRL)	€2,489,337		61	Paul Lawrie (SCO)	394,034
2	Paul Casey (ENG)	2,454,084		62	Carl Pettersson (SWE)	392,585
3	David Howell (ENG)	2,321,166		63	José-Filipe Lima (POR)	381,222
4	Robert Karlsson (SWE)	2,044,936		64	Stephen Gallacher (SCO)	376,571
5	Ernie Els (RSA)	1,716,208		65	Marcus Fraser (AUS)	375,626
6	Henrik Stenson (SWE)	1,709,359		66	Ross Fisher (ENG)	370,275
7	Luke Donald (ENG)	1,658,060		67	Peter Lawrie (IRL)	360,889
8	Ian Poulter (ENG)	1,589,074		68	Jyoti Randhawa (IND)	351,468
9	Colin Montgomerie (SCO)	1,534,748		69	Darren Fichardt (RSA)	343,412
10	Johan Edfors (SWE)	1,505,583		70	Maarten Lafeber (NED)	340,705
11	Sergio García (ESP)	1,456,752		71	Oliver Wilson (ENG)	331,706
12	Retief Goosen (RSA)	1,367,399		72	Richard Bland (ENG)	319,391
13	Anthony Wall (ENG)	1,303,231		73	Andrew Marshall (ENG)	318,002
14	Thomas Bjørn (DEN)	1,188,504		74	Gary Houston (WAL)	315,751
15	Niclas Fasth (SWE)	1,180,140		75	Mattias Eliasson (SWE)	314,018
16	Jeev Milkha Singh (IND)	1,173,177		76	Gary Emerson (ENG)	312,330
17	Angel Cabrera (ARG)	1,166,918		77	Jean Van De Velde (FRA)	308,782
18	Charl Schwartzel (RSA)	1,148,275		78	Richard Sterne (RSA)	306,473
19	Paul Broadhurst (ENG)	1,141,431		79	Mark Foster (ENG)	302,660
20	John Bickerton (ENG)	1,140,281		80	Thaworn Wiratchant (THA)	296,693
21	Simon Dyson (ENG)	1,092,156		81	Steve Webster (ENG)	286,273
22	Bradley Dredge (WAL)	1,075,591		82	Alastair Forsyth (SCO)	285,494
23	Miguel Angel Jiménez (ESP)	985,389		83	Andrew Coltart (SCO)	285,309
24	Lee Westwood (ENG)	960,304		84	Jean-François Lucquin (FRA)	285,045
25	Simon Khan (ENG)	960,122		85	Stephen Ames (CAN)	282,708
26	Nick O'Hern (AUS)	919,332		86	Robert-Jan Derksen (NED)	278,977
27	Richard Green (AUS)	865,669		87	Ignacio Garrido (ESP)	277,058
28	José María Olazábal (ESP)	840,006		88	Jean-François Remesy (FRA)	274,818
29	Stephen Dodd (WAL)	795,146		89	Peter Hedblom (SWE)	270,495
30	José Manuel Lara (ESP)	784,987		90	Christian Cévaër (FRA)	261,545
31	Michael Campbell (NZL)	784,915		91	Lee Slattery (ENG)	260,549
32	Vijay Singh (FIJ)	752,403		92	Gregory Havret (FRA)	258,836
33	Anders Hansen (DEN)	731,041		93	Louis Oosthuizen (RSA)	256,466
34	Søren Hansen (DEN)	712,649		94	Martin Erlandsson (SWE)	254,661
35	Andres Romero (ARG)	694,363		95	Tom Whitehouse (ENG)	250,952
36	Søren Kjeldsen (DEN)	692,036		96	Andrew McLardy (RSA)	245,719
37	Thongchai Jaidee (THA)	669,226		97	Benn Barham (ENG)	245,310
38	Francesco Molinari (ITA)	657,143		98	Miles Tunnicliff (ENG)	241,538
39	Nick Dougherty (ENG)	653,080		99	David Park (WAL)	235,094
40	Gonzalo Fernandez-Castaño (ESP)	649,354		100	Peter Gustafsson (SWE)	230,761
41	Phillip Archer (ENG)	636,491		101	Christian L Nilsson (SWE)	226,789
42	Marc Warren (SCO)	610,885		102	Gregory Bourdy (FRA)	224,685
43	Darren Clarke (NIR)	583,348		103	Steven Jeppesen (SWE)	223,796
44	Jarmo Sandelin (SWE)	568,046		104	Gary Murphy (IRL)	220,782
45	Raphaël Jacquelin (FRA)	551,745		105	Barry Lane (ENG)	220,351
46	David Lynn (ENG)	543,467		106	James Kingston (RSA)	217,646
47	Peter O'Malley (AUS)	530,327		107	David Griffiths (ENG)	217,166
48	Gary Orr (SCO)	524,372		108	Joakim Bäckström (SWE)	217,070
49	Markus Brier (AUT)	506,359		109	Alejandro Canizares (ESP)	216,794
50	Marcel Siem (GER)	493,956		110	Alessandro Tadini (ITA)	215,571
51	Brett Rumford (AUS)	491,907		111	Steven O'Hara (SCO)	210,128
52	Paul McGinley (IRL)	478,244		112	Mikko Ilonen (FIN)	209,316
53	Graeme Storm (ENG)	474,651		113	Richard Finch (ENG)	208,815
54	Kenneth Ferrie (ENG)	471,775		114	Robert Rock (ENG)	208,637
55	Ricardo Gonzalez (ARG)	451,204		115	Matthew Millar (AUS)	207,386
56	Damien McGrane (IRL)	447,415		116	Shiv Kapur (IND)	207,042
57	Peter Hanson (SWE)	440,564		117	David Carter (ENG)	204,366
58	Graeme McDowell (NIR)	437,802		118	Ian Garbutt (ENG)	201,581
59	Emanuele Canonica (ITA)	437,672		119	David Drysdale (SCO)	200,392
60	Simon Wakefield (ENG)	430,786		120	Jonathan Lomas (ENG)	197,033

Career Money List (at end of 2006 season)

Colin Montgomerie still out in front

Scotland's Colin Montgomerie continues to lead the all-time career money list on the European Tour having won €21,338,938 since he joined in 1988. On five occasions since then he has topped €2 million in prize-money. Eight times European No.1, Montgomerie currently leads from two South African players Ernie Els and Retief Goosen, both of whom have been No.1 twice.

1	Colin Montgomerie (SCO)	€21,338,983	51	Jean Van De Velde (FRA)	3,905,856
2	Ernie Els (RSA)	18,627,884	52	Peter Baker (ENG)	3,813,351
3	Retief Goosen (RSA)	15,862,172	53	Søren Hansen (DEN)	3,795,893
4	Darren Clarke (NIR)	15,372,334	54	Jamie Spence (ENG)	3,772,727
5	Padraig Harrington (IRL)	14,492,702	55	David Gilford (ENG)	3,756,909
6	Lee Westwood (ENG)	12,601,924	56	Ricardo Gonzalez (ARG)	3,753,297
7	Bernhard Langer (GER)	12,231,109	57	Jarmo Sandelin (SWE)	3,739,498
8	Thomas Bjørn (DEN)	11,571,991	58	Sandy Lyle (SCO)	3,723,199
9	José María Olazábal (ESP)	11,272,476	59	David Lynn (ENG)	3,686,134
10	Vijay Singh (FIJ)	11,031,506	60	Jean-François Remesy (FRA)	3,630,235
11	Miguel Angel Jiménez (ESP)	11,029,176	61	Søren Kjeldsen (DEN)	3,552,522
12	Michael Campbell (NZL)	10,364,292	62	Anthony Wall (ENG)	3,490,604
13	Ian Woosnam (WAL)	9,584,347	63	Mark Roe (ENG)	3,454,502
14	Angel Cabrera (ARG)	9,378,782	64	Gary Evans (ENG)	3,433,122
15	Sergio García (ESP)	9,239,022	65	Steve Webster (ENG)	3,420,132
16	David Howell (ENG)	9,119,740	66	Stephen Gallacher (SCO)	3,405,378
17	Paul McGinley (IRL)	8,878,921	67	Roger Chapman (ENG)	3,394,673
18	Nick Faldo (ENG)	7,988,365	68	Miguel Angel Martin (ESP)	3,342,442
19	Ian Poulter (ENG)	7,619,190	69	Patrik Sjöland (SWE)	3,222,878
20	Eduardo Romero (ARG)	7,467,752	70	Ronan Rafferty (NIR)	3,165,250
21	Robert Karlsson (SWE)	7,235,701	71	Alastair Forsyth (SCO)	3,104,472
22	Paul Casey (ENG)	6,838,293	72	Anders Forsbrand (SWE)	3,086,484
23	Niclas Fasth (SWE)	6,602,613	73	Maarten Lafeber (NED)	3,078,567
24	Paul Lawrie (SCO)	6,459,835	74	Jonathan Lomas (ENG)	2,954,554
25	Adam Scott (AUS)	6,260,597	75	Peter Fowler (AUS)	2,952,288
26	Barry Lane (ENG)	6,246,231	76	Nick Dougherty (ENG)	2,942,347
27	Phillip Price (WAL)	6,075,084	77	Santiago Luna (ESP)	2,925,660
28	Peter O'Malley (AUS)	5,761,197	78	Stephen Dodd (WAL)	2,923,934
29	Paul Broadhurst (ENG)	5,584,111	79	Emanuele Canonica (ITA)	2,878,256
30	Sam Torrance (SCO)	5,491,084	80	Tony Johnstone (ZIM)	2,818,574
31	Mark McNulty (IRL)	5,366,794	81	Andrew Oldcorn (SCO)	2,767,260
32	Seve Ballesteros (ESP)	5,331,121	82	Sven Strüver (GER)	2,701,619
33	Andrew Coltart (SCO)	5,179,789	83	Greg Norman (AUS)	2,677,884
34	Nick O'Hern (AUS)	5,136,187	84	Graeme McDowell (NIR)	2,675,339
35	Henrik Stenson (SWE)	4,840,660	85	Peter Hedblom (SWE)	2,621,738
36	Thomas Levet (FRA)	4,785,900	86	David Carter (ENG)	2,617,641
37	Trevor Immelman (RSA)	4,606,841	87	Raymond Russell (SCO)	2,588,342
38	Gary Orr (SCO)	4,515,914	88	Tim Clark (RSA)	2,588,128
39	Anders Hansen (DEN)	4,448,610	89	Simon Dyson (ENG)	2,587,231
40	Richard Green (AUS)	4,410,840	90	Des Smyth (IRL)	2,539,099
41	Bradley Dredge (WAL)	4,402,881	91	Peter Senior (AUS)	2,459,759
42	Costantino Rocca (ITA)	4,368,165	92	Russell Claydon (ENG)	2,389,907
43	Luke Donald (ENG)	4,335,658	93	Simon Khan (ENG)	2,270,298
44	Pierre Fulke (SWE)	4,310,837	94	José Manuel Lara (ESP)	2,266,097
45	Brian Davis (ENG)	4,206,544	95	Jarrod Moseley (AUS)	2,258,380
46	Joakim Haeggman (SWE)	4,191,793	96	Carlos Rodiles (ESP)	2,236,042
47	John Bickerton (ENG)	4,179,958	97	Brett Rumford (AUS)	2,222,665
48	Raphaël Jacquelin (FRA)	4,109,682	98	Malcolm Mackenzie (ENG)	2,175,447
49	Gordon Brand Jr (SCO)	4,094,239	99	Kenneth Ferrie (ENG)	2,163,611
50	Ignacio Garrido (ESP)	4,008,370	100	Miles Tunnicliffe (ENG)	2,095,180

Tour Statistics (Reuters Performance Data)

Stroke average

Pos	Name	Total Rounds	Stroke Avg,
1	Ernie Els (RSA)	52	70.02
2	Sergio García (ESP)	46	70.04
3	Luke Donald (ENG)	44	70.09
4	Mikko Ilonen (FIN)	34	70.29
5	Robert Karlsson (SWE)	106	70.48
	Padraig Harrington (IRE)	69	70.48
7	Paul Casey (ENG)	86	70.50

Driving accuracy

Pos	Name	Rounds	%
1	Oliver Whiteley (ENG)	44	77.7
2	Peter O'Malley (AUS)	70	75.6
3	Felipe Aguilar (CHI)	48	72.6
4	Alexandre Rocha (BRA)	68	71.3
5	Raymond Russell (SCO)	41	71.8
6	John Bickerton (ENG)	72	70.2
7	Richard Green (AUS)	54	70.1

Driving distance

Pos	Name	Rounds	Avg.
1	Christian L Nilsson (SWE)	62	314.1
2	Titch Moore (RSA)	36	312.2
3	Tuomas Tuovinen (FIN)	26	306.8
4	Angel Cabrera (ARG)	36	305.1
5	Johan Edfors (SWE)	67	304.5
6	Joackim Backstrom SWE)	76	304.3
7	Emanuele Canonica (ITA)	73	303.2

Greens in regulation

Pos	Name	Rounds	%
1	Titch Moore (RSA)	36	75.6
2	Angel Cabrera (ARG)	36	75.2
3	Peter O'Malley (AUS)	70	74.6
	Paul Casey (ENG)	86	74.6
5	Steven O'Hara (SCO)	83	74.1
6	Peter Hanson (SWE)	77	73.8
7	Retief Goosen (RSA)	30	73.7

Putts per greens in regulation

Pos	Name	Rounds	Putts per GIR
1	Thaworn Wirachant (THA)	46	1.718
2	David Howell (ENG)	42	1.724
3	Darren Clarke (IRE)	30	1.727
4	Robert Karlsson (SWE)	86	1.736
	David Higgins (IRL)	79	1.736
6	Paul Broadhurst (ENG)	70	1.737
	Toni Karjalainen (FIN)	32	1.737

South African Ernie Els edged out Spaniard Sergio García in the stroke averages table

Average putts per round

Pos	Name	Rounds	Putts per round
1	Thaworn Wirachant (THA)	46	28.0
2	Paul Broadhurst (ENG)	70	28.2
	Matthew Millar (AUS)	78	28.2
4	Christian Cevear (FRA)	79	28.3
	David Howell (ENG)	42	28.3
6	Peter Baker (ENG)	25	28.4
	Padraig Harrington (IRL)	45	28.4

Sand saves

Pos	Name	Rounds	%
1	Emanuele Canonica (ITA)	73	75.9
2	David Howell (ENG)	42	71.1
3	Mark Roe (ENG)	54	70.9
4	Gordon Brand Jr (SCO)	26	69.0
5	Titch Moore (RSA)	36	68.9
6	Paul Lawrie (SCO)	57	68.4
	David Carter (ENG)	73	68.4
	Benoit Teilleria (FRA)	42	67.3
	Christian Cévaër (FRA)	79	65.8
	Andrews Romero (ARG)	52	64.7

Scrambles[1]

Pos	Name	Rounds	%
1	Sergio García (ESP)	24	66.1
2	Simon Dyson (ENG)	94	65.3
3	David Howell (ENG)	42	64.6
4	Thongchai Jaidee (THA)	71	64.1
5	Richard Green (AUS)	54	63.7
6	Padraig Harrington (IRL)	45	63.4
7	Soren Kjeldsen (DEN)	95	63.3

[1] Where player makes par after missing green in regulation

PGA European Tour statistics 2006

Sixteen course records

Chawalit Plaphol	65 (-7)	Volvo China Open
Simon Yates	61 (-9)	UBS Hong Kong Open
Patrick O'Brien	67 (-6)	SAA Open
Henrik Stenson	62 (-10)	Abu Dhabi Golf Championship
Lian Wen-Chong	62 (-10)	TCL Classic
Paul Broadhurst	64 (-8)	Algarve Open de Portugal
Jeev Milkha Singh	67 (-5)	Volvo China Open
Robert Karlsson	63 (-9)	Andalucia Open de España
	63 (-9)	Entercard Scandinavian Masters
Phillip Archer	60 (-9)	The Celtic Manor Wales Open
Gregory Havret	63 (-8)	BA-CA Golf Open
Tiger Woods	65 (-7)	The Open Championship
	63 (-8)	WGC–American Express
Lee Westwood	63 (-9)	Deutsche Bank PC of Europe
Richard Green	62 (-9)	KLM Dutch Open
Bradley Dredge	64 (-8)	Alfred Dunhill Links

Six albatrosses

Marcel Siem	8th hole, Leopard Creek – dunhill championship
Danny Chia	1st hole, Emeralda GC – Enjoy Jakarta HSBC Indonesian Open
Kieran Staunton	13th hole, Yalong Bay GC – TCL Classic
Max Kramer (am)	9th hole, Fontana GC – BA/CA Golf Open
Felipe Aguilar	9th hole, Gleneagles – Johnnie Walker Championship
Joey Sindelar	5th hole, Medinah GC – US PGA Championship

Largest winning margin

8 shots Bradley Dredge, Omega European Masters

8 shots Tiger Woods, WGC–American Express

Biggest catch-up in last round by a winner

6 shots Johan Edfors, Barclays Scottish Open

Ten multiple winners

Tiger Woods (5) – Dubai Desert Classic; The Open Championship; US PGA Championship; WGC–Bridgestone Invitational; WGC–American Express Championship

Johann Edfors (3) – TCL Classic; The Quinn Direct British Masters; The Barclays Scottish Open

Paul Casey (3) – Volvo China Open; Johnnie Walker Championship; HSBC World Match Play Championship

Robert Karlsson (2) – The Celtic Manor Wales Open; The Deutsche Bank Tournament Players Championship of Europe

David Howell (2) – HSBC Champions; BMW Championship

Geoff Ogilvy (2) – WGC–Accenture Match Play Championship; US Open

Simon Dyson (2) – Enjoy Jakarta HSBC Indonesian Open; The KLM Dutch Open

Henrik Stenson (2) – The Commercialbank Qatar Masters; BMW International Open

Niclas Fasth (2) – Andalucia Open de España Valle Romano; Mallorca Classic

Jeev Milkha Singh (2) – Volvo China Open; Volvo Masters

Thirteen first time winners on the European Tour

Golfers of 12 different nationalities were first time winners in 12 different countries on the 2006 European Tour:

Chris DiMarco (USA)	Abu Dhabi Championship	Abu Dhabi
Kevin Stadler (USA)	Johnnie Walker Classic	The Vines, Australia
Charlie Wi (KOR)	Maybank Malaysian Open	Kuala Lumpur
Geoff Ogilvy (AUS)	WGC Accenture Match Play	La Costa CA
Simon Dyson (ENG)	Enjoy Jakarta Indonesian Open	Emaralda
Mardan Mamat (SIN)	OSIM Singapore Masters	Laguna National
Johan Edfors (SWE)	TCL Classic	Yalong Bay
Jeev Milkha Singh (IND)	Volvo China Open	Honghu, Beijing
Francesco Molinari (ITA)	Telecom Italia Open	Castello di Tolcinasco
Markus Brier (AUT)	BA-CA Open	Fontana
Cesar Monasterio (ARG)	Aa St Omer Open	Aa St Omer, France
Marc Warren (SCO)	Entercard Scandinavian	Barsebäck, Sweden
Alejandro Canizares (ESP)	Imperial Collection Russian Open	Le Meridien, Russia

European Tour Top Earners 2006 (majors in bold type)

1   **PADRAIG HARRINGTON**[†] (IRL)   €2,489,337
Top Tens   1st Alfred Dunhill Links Championship. 2nd Open de France; BMW International; Volvo Masters. 4th Open de Madrid Golf Masters. 5th WGC – Accenture Match Play; **US Open Championship**. 6th BMW PGA Championship
Played 20: Wins 1; Top 5's 7; Top 10's 8; Missed cut 3

2   **PAUL CASEY** (ENG)   €2,454,084
Top Tens   1st Volvo China Open; Johnnie Walker Championship; HSBC World Match Play Championship. 2nd Nissan Irish Open. 4th WGC – Bridgestone Invitational; Volvo China Open. 5th BMW Asian Open; Quinn Direct British Masters. 6th Alfred Dunhill Links Championship. 7th HSBC Championship
Played 2: Wins 3; Top 5's 8; Top 10's 10; Missed cut 3

3   **DAVID HOWELL**[†] (ENG)   €2,321,116
Top Tens   1st HSBC Championship; BMW PGA Championship. 4th BMW International. 5th WGC – Accenture Match Play. 7th TCL Classic. 9th HSBC World Match Play Championship
Played 21: Wins 2; Top 5's 4; Top 10's 6; Missed cut 5

4   **ROBERT KARLSSON** (SWE)   €2,044,936
Top Tens   1st The Celtic Manor Wales Open; Deutsche Bank Players Championship of Europe. 2nd Entercard Scandinavian Masters. 3rd HSBC World Match Play Championship. 5th Nissan Irish Open. 8th Mallorca Classic. 9th Johnnie Walker Championship. 10th Andalusia Open de Espana Valle Romano
Played 30: Wins 2; Top 5's 5; Top 10's 8; Missed cut 3

5   **ERNIE ELS**[†] (RSA)   €1,716,208
Top Tens   1st dunhill championship. 2nd SAA Open Championship; Dubai Desert Classic. 3rd **The Open Championship**. 5th WGC – American Express Championship; Alfred Dunhill Links Championship. 9th Barclays Scottish Open; HSBC World Match Play Championship
Played 15: Wins 1; Top 5's 6; Top 10's 8; Missed cut 0

6   **HENRIK STENSON** (SWE)   €1,709,359
Top Tens   1st The Commercial Bank Qatar Masters; BMW International. 2nd The Abu Dhabi Golf Championship; BMW Asian Open. 7th Dubai Desert Classic. 8th Alfred Dunhill Links Championship. 9th Volvo Masters
Played 23: Wins 2; Top 5's 4; Top 10's 7; Missed cut 3

7   **LUKE DONALD**[†] (ENG)   €1,658,060
Top Tens   2nd Barclays Scottish Open; Volvo Masters. 3rd **US PGA Championship**. 5th HSBC World Match Play Championship. 6th BMW International Open; WGC – American Express Championship. 8th WGC – Bridgestone Invitational. 9th WGC – Accenture Match Play Championship
Played 13: Wins 0; Top 5's 4; Top 10's 9; Missed cut 0

8   **IAN POULTER**[†] (ENG)   €1,589,074
Top Tens   1st Open de Madrid Golf Masters. 2nd WGC – American Express Championship. 3rd Quinn Direct British Masters. 6th Johnnie Walker Classic. 9th **US PGA Championship**; Volvo Masters. 10th The Abu Dhabi Golf Championship
Played 22: Wins 1; Top 5's 3; Top 10's 7; Missed cut 2

9   **COLIN MONTGOMERIE** (SCO)   €1,534,748
Top Tens   1st UBS Hong Kong Open. 2nd **US Open Championship**. 3rd BMW Asian Open; HSBC World Match Play Championship. 4th Celtic Manor Wales Open; Johnnie Walker Championship. 6th The Abu Dhabi Golf Championship; BMW International. 9th Smurfit Kappa European Open
Played 26: Wins 1; Top 5's 6; Top 10's 9; Missed cut 8

10   **JOHAN EDFORS** (SWE)   €1,505,583
Top Tens   1st TCL Classic; Quinn Direct British Masters; Barclays Scottish Open. 8th Alfred Dunhill Links Championship
Played 25: Wins 3; Top 5's 3; Top 10's 4; Missed cut 6

[†] Also played on the PGA Tour

PGA European Tour top 20

MC Missed cut   —   Did not play   * Involved in play-off

Columns span **2005** (HSBC Champions Tourn., Volvo China Open) and **2006** (all remaining tournaments).

	HSBC Champions Tourn.	Volvo China Open	UBS Hong Kong Open	dunhill championship	South African Airways	Abu Dhabi Championship	Quatar Masters	Dubai Desert Classic	Johnnie Walker Classic	Malaysian Open	WGC-Accenture Match	Indonesian open	Singapore Masters	TCL Classic	Madeira Island Open	Open de Portugal	The Masters	Volvo China Open	BMW Asian Open	Open de España
1 Padraig Harrington (IRL)	15T	—	—	—	—	—	—	13T	5T	—	—	—	—	—	—	—	27T	—	—	—
2 Paul Casey (ENG)	7	1*	MC	—	—	45T	—	16T	15T	—	33T	—	10T	—	—	—	—	4T	5T	—
3 David Howell (ENG)	1	—	—	—	MC	24T	28T	—	—	—	5T	—	7T	—	—	19T	—	—	—	—
4 Robert Karlsson (SWE)	—	37T	MC	—	—	30T	15T	28T	47T	—	—	40T	37T	—	MC	32T	—	—	—	10
5 Ernie Els (RSA)	—	—	—	1	2	—	13T	2*	—	—	33T	—	—	—	—	—	27T	—	—	—
6 Henrik Stenson (SWE)	32T	—	—	—	—	2	1	7T	—	—	17T	—	—	—	—	—	MC	20T	2*	—
7 Luke Donald (ENG)	—	—	—	—	—	—	—	—	—	—	9T	—	—	—	—	—	—	42T	—	—
8 Ian Poulter (ENG)	19T	—	—	—	10T	43T	47T	6T	—	—	33T	—	—	—	—	—	—	—	—	—
9 Colin Montgomerie (SCO)	40T	—	1	—	—	6T	—	MC	MC	—	17T	—	—	—	—	—	—	MC	3T	28T
10 Johan Edfors (SWE)	—	—	15T	18T	—	—	13T	—	37T	—	—	—	—	1	—	MC	—	49T	56T	45T
11 Sergio García (ESP)	—	—	—	—	3	—	—	—	—	—	—	—	—	—	—	46	—	—	—	—
12 Retief Goosen (RSA)	—	—	—	—	1	—	—	6	MC	—	5T	—	—	—	—	—	—	3T	—	—
13 Anthony Wall (ENG)	—	19T	MC	—	—	45T	15T	MC	60T	—	—	RT	—	—	—	2	—	—	—	—
14 Thomas Bjørn (DEN)	5T	—	22T	—	—	24T	9T	47T	—	—	—	—	—	—	—	—	—	32T	26T	3T
15 Niclas Fasth (SWE)	25T	—	—	—	—	MC	4T	11T	—	—	33T	—	MC	—	17T	10T	—	—	—	1*
16 Jeev Milkha Singh (IND)	—	—	18T	—	—	24T	—	MC	MC	—	40T	MC	7T	—	—	—	—	1	26T	—
17 Angel Cabrera (ARG)	—	—	—	—	—	—	—	30T	—	—	17T	—	—	—	—	—	—	8T	—	—
18 Charl Schwartzel (RSA)	32T	—	—	2T	12T	8T	24T	—	—	—	—	40T	13T	—	—	4T	—	—	—	14T
19 Paul Broadhurst (ENG)	19T	—	—	—	—	17T	2	22T	—	—	33T	—	MC	MC	—	1	—	—	—	—
20 John Bickerton (ENG)	19T	—	—	MC	MC	24T	52T	72T	52T	4T	—	—	—	—	36T	60T	—	—	—	2*

2006 performances at a glance

RT Retired   WD Withdrew

Telecom Italia Open	British Masters	Nissan Irish Open	BMW Championship	Celtic Manor Wales Open	BA-CA Open	US Open	Aa St Omer Open	Johnnie Walker Champ.	Open de France	Smurfit European Open	Barclays Scottish Open	135th Open Championship	Deutsche Bank – SAP	Scandinavian Masters	KLM Open	US PGA Championship	Cadillac Russian Open	WGC–Bridgestone Inv.	BMW International Open	Omega European Masters	HSBC World Match Play	Madrid Golf Classic	WGC – Amex Champ.	dunhill linkschampionship	Mallorca Classic	Volvo Masters
—	14T	11	6T	—	5	—	—	2	20T	—	MC	28T	—	—	MC	—	27T	2T*	—	—	4T		17T	1	MC	2T
—	5T	2	11T	—	15	—	1	—	20T	—	71	MC	—	—	MC	—	4T	13T	—	1	—		56T	6T	—	21T
—	11T	—	1	—	—	16T	—	MC	—	35T	MC	MC	—	—	67	—	59T	4T	—	9T	—		13T	MC	—	5T
MC	27T	5T	14T	1	—	FQ	—	9T	17T	13T	—	35T	1	2*	—	29T	—	62T	—	—	3T	—	21	15T	8T	21T
—	—	—	19T	—	—	26T	—	—	—	—	9T	3	—	—	—	16T	—	31T	—	—	9T	—	5	5	—	—
—	MC	37T	19T	—	—	26T	—	—	29T	31T	—	48T	22T	MC	—	14T	—	31T	1*	—	—		13T	8T	—	9T
—	—	—	25T	—	—	12T	—	—	—	—	2T	35T	15T	—	—	3T	—	8T	6T	—	5T	—	6T	—	—	2T
—	14T	60T	MC	—	—	12T	—	—	3T	52T	14T	MC	22T	—	—	9T	—	13T	MC	—	—	1	2T	22T	—	9T
—	MC	MC	53T	4	13T	2T	—	4T	—	9T	24T	MC	—	—	14T	MC	—	—	6T	—	3T	—	41T	MC	—	28T
—	1	60T	MC	—	—	FQ	—	—	MC	—	1	MC	45T	MC	—	MC	—	62T	68T	12T	—	—	22T	8T	—	21T
—	—	—	—	—	—	MC	—	—	—	—	9T	5T	9T	—	—	3T	—	22T	—	4T	—	—	32T	—	2	2T
—	—	—	19T	—	—	MC	—	—	—	—	35T	14T	14T	4T	—	34T	—	48T	2T*	—	9T	—	45T	—	—	—
40T	33T	5T	6T	14T	—	FQ	—	42T	40T	2T	MC	11T	18T	—	—	MC	—	—	18T	17T	—	—	50T	2T	MC	35T
—	63T	1	MC	—	26T	48T	—	4T	MC	—	5T	41T	RT	—	—	MC	—	18T	13T	—	—	31T	41T	27T	54T	38T
—	60T	19T	29T	49T	—	MC	—	—	54T	35T	—	MC	11T	15T	—	MC	—	—	42T	—	—	23T	—	32T	1	5T
—	—	—	MC	21T	—	59T	—	—	—	4T	MC	FQ	—	—	—	—	—	—	—	—	—	—	—	—	13T	1
MC	MC	37T	29T	—	—	26T	—	—	12T	17T	14T	7	15T	—	—	MC	—	4T	—	—	5T	—	26T	38T	—	28T
—	27T	MC	MC	—	—	48T	—	—	40T	46T	2T	22T	2T	—	—	MC	—	36T	—	—	—	—	41T	22T	—	41T
MC	7	MC	47T	2	—	FQ	—	MC	12T	MC	47T	26T	MC	—	MC	MC	—	—	59T	33T	—	—	50T	8T	MC	28T
16T	MC	RT	MC	—	69T	—	—	MC	1	MC	MC	48T	—	—	—	MC	—	66T	MC	—	—	56T	45T	MC	—	21T

2006 European Tour and Past Results
(in chronological order)

HSBC Champions Tournament *Sheshan International, China*   [7143-72]

1	David Howell (ENG)	65-67-68-68—268	$474547	€704516
2	Tiger Woods (USA)	65-69-67-70—271	316802	469692
3	Nick Dougherty (ENG)	64-68-73-69—274	160308	237995
	Nick O'Hern (AUS)	67-67-67-73—274	160308	237995

Volvo China Open *Shenzhen GC*   [7127-72]

1995	Raul Fretes (PAR)	1999	Kyi Hla Han (MYA)	2003	Zhang Lian-Wei (CHI)
1996	Prayed Marksaeng (THA)	2000	Simon Dyson (ENG)	2004	Stephen Dodd (WAL)
1997	Cheng Jun (CHI)	2001	Charlie Wi (KOR)		
1998	Ed Fryatt (ENG)	2002	David Gleeson (AUS)		

1	Paul Casey (ENG)*	71-69-70-65—275	£126354	€184533
2	Oliver Wilson (ENG)	68-67-71-69—275	84236	123022
3	Barry Lane (ENG)	67-74-67-68—276	47460	69313

Casey won play-off at first extra hole

UBS Hong Kong Open *Hong Kong GC*   [6703-70]

1959	Lu Liang-Huan (TPE)	1975	Hsieh Yung-yo (TPE)	1990	Bernhard Langer (GER)
1960	Peter Thomson (AUS)	1976	Ho Ming-Chung (TPE)	1990	Tom Watson (USA)
1961	Kel Nagle (AUS)	1977	Hsieh Min-Nan (TPE)	1990	Brian Watts (USA)
1962	Len Woodward (AUS)	1978	Hsieh Yung-yo (TPE)	1990	David Frost (USA)
1963	Hsieh Yung-yo (TPE)	1979	Greg Norman (AUS)	1990	Gary Webb (USA)
1964	Hsieh Yung-yo (TPE)	1980	Kuo Chie-hsiung (TPE)	1990	Rodrigo Cuello (PHI)
1965	Peter Thomson (AUS)	1981	Chen Tse-Ming (TPE)	1990	Frank Nobilo (NZL)
1966	Frank Phillips (AUS)	1982	Kurt Cox (AUS)	1990	Kang Wook-soon (KOR)
1967	Peter Thomson (AUS)	1983	Greg Norman (AUS)	1990	Patrick Sjoland (SWE)
1968	Randall Vines (AUS)	1984	Bill Brask (USA)	2000	Simon Dyson (ENG)
1969	Teruo Suguhara (JPN)	1985	Mark Aebi (USA)	2001	Jose Maria Olazabal (ESP)
1970	Isao Katsumatu (JPN)	1986	Seichi Kanai (JPN)	2002	Frederik Jacobson (SWE)
1971	Orville Moody (USA)	1987	Ian Woosnam (WAL)	2003	Padraig Harrington (IRE)
1972	Walter Godfrey (NZL)	1988	Hsieh Chin-sheng (TPE)	2004	Miguel Angel Jiménez (ESP)
1973	Frank Phillips (AUS)	1989	Brian Claar (USA)		
1974	Lu Liang-huan (TPE)	1990	Ken Green (USA)		

1	Colin Montgomerie (SCO)	69-66-66-70—271	£116584	€170590
2	K J Choi (KOR)	67-72-64-69—272	42125	61639
	James Kingston (RSA)	68-69-64-71—272	42125	61639
	Jeng-Chi Lin (TAI)	68-69-66-69—272	42125	61639
	Edward Loar (USA)	68-64-71-69—272	42125	61639
	Thammanoon Srirot (THA)	71-67-66-68—272	42125	61639

dunhill championship *Leopard Creek, Mpumalanga, RSA*   [7350-72]
(1959–99 combined with South African PGA Championship)

1995	E Els	Wanderers Club	271	2002	J Rose	Houghton GC	268
1996	S Strüver	Houghton GC	202 (54)	2003	M Foster*	Houghton GC	273
1997	N Price*	Houghton GC	269				

Price beat D Frost at first extra hole   * Foster beat Paul Lawrie, T Immelman, B Vaughan,

1998	T Johnstone	Houghton GC	271	2004	M Siem*	Houghton GC	266
1999	E Els	Houghton GC	273				
2000	A Wall	Houghton GC	204	2005	C Schwartzel*	Leoard Creek	281
2001	A Scott	Houghton GC	267				

A Hansen and D McGuigan at second extra hole

Siem beat G Havret and R Jacquelin at third extra hole

Schwartzel beat N Cheetham at first extra hole

1	Ernie Els (RSA)	71-67-68-68—274	£107213	€158579
2	Louis Oosthuizen (RSA)	69-67-71-70—277	62264	92096
	Charl Schwartzel (RSA)	70-67-70-70—277	62264	92096

South African Airways Open *Fancourt, George, Western Cape* [7435–73]

1903	LB Waters	1931	SF Brews	1960	G Player	1983	C Bolling
1904	LB Waters	1932	C McIlvenny	1961	R Waltman	1984	T Johnstone (ZIM)
1905	AG Gray	1933	SF Brews	1962	HR Henning	1985	G Levenson
1906	AG Gray	1934	SF Brews	1963	R Waltman	1986	D Frost
1907	LB Waters	1935	AD Locke (am)	1964	A Henning	1987	M McNulty
1908	G Fotheringham	1936	CE Olander	1965	G Player	1988	W Westner
1909	J Fotheringham	1937	AD Locke (am)	1966	G Player	1989	S Wadsworth
1910	G Fotheringham	1938	AD Locke	1967	G Player	1990	T Dodds
1911	G Fotheringham	1939	AD Locke	1968	G Player	1991	W Westner
1912	G Fotheringham	1940	AD Locke	1969	G Player	1992	E Els
1913	JAW Prentice (am)	1946	AD Locke	1970	T Horton (ENG)	1993	C Whitelaw
1914	G Fotheringham	1947	RW Glennie (am)	1971	S Hobday	1994	T Johnstone (ZIM)
1919	WH Horne	1948	JM Janks (am)*	1972	G Player	1995	R Goosen
1920	LB Waters	1949	SF Brews	1973	RJ Charles (NZL)	1996	E Els
1921	J Brews	1950	AD Locke	1974	R Cole	1997	V Singh (Fij)
1922	F Jangle	1951	AD Locke	1975	G Player	1998	E Els
1923	J Brews	1952	SF Brews	1976	D Hayes	1999	D Frost
1924	BH Elkin	1953	JR Boyd (am)	1976	G Player	2000	M Grönberg (SWE)
1925	SF Brews	1954	RC Taylor (am)	1977	G Player	2001	M McNulty (ZIM)
1926	J Brews	1955	AD Locke	1978	H Baiocchi	2002	T Clark
1927	SF Brews	1956	G Player	1979	G Player	2003	T Immelman*
1928	J Brews	1957	HR Henning*	1980	R Cole		*Immelman beat T Clark at
1929	A Tosh	1958	AA Stewart (am)	1981	G Player		first extra hole
1930	SF Brews	1959	D Hutchinson (am)	1982	*Not played*	2004	T Immelman

1	Retief Goosen (RSA)	73-70-69-70—282	£106815	€158579
2	Ernie Els (RSA)	76-70-69-68—283	77500	115057
3	Gregory Bourdy (FRA)	75-75-70-70—290	39828	59219
	Darren Fichardt (RSA)	78-69-69-74—290	39828	59219

The Royal Trophy *Amata Spring, Bangkok, Thailand* [7381–72]

Europe beat Asia 9–7

Full details of this event can be found on page 202

Abu Dhabi Championship *Abu Dhabi, UAE* [7348–72]

1	Chris DiMarco (USA)	71-67-63-67—268	£188162	€275411
2	Henrik Stenson (SWE)	69-69-62-69—269	125441	183607
3	Sergio García (ESP)	70-69-65-66—270	70674	103445

Qatar Masters *Doha, Qatar* [7744–72]

1998	A Coltart	270		2003	D Fichardt*	275
1999	P. Lawrie	268			*Fichardt beat J Kingston at first extra hole*	
2000	R Muntz	280		2004	J Haeggman	272
2001	T Johnstone	274		2005	E Els	276
2002	A Scott	269				

1	Henrik Stenson (SWE)	66-68-71-68—273	£188716	€275456
2	Paul Broadhurst (ENG)	72-67-67-70—276	125811	183637
3	Darren Fichardt (RSA)	67-72-70-68—277	70882	103462

Dubai Desert Classic *Emirates GC, Dubai* [7264–72]

1989	M James*	Emirates	277
James beat P O'Malley at first extra hole			
1990	E Darcy	Emirates	276
1991	Not played		
1992	S Ballesteros*	Emirates	272
Ballesteros beat R Rafferty at second extra hole			
1993	W Westner	Emirates	274
1994	E Els	Emirates	268
1995	F Couples	Emirates	268
1996	C Montgomerie	Emirates	270

1997	R Green*	Emirates	272
Green beat I Woosnam & G Norman at first extra hole			
1998	JM Olazábal	Emirates	269
1999	D Howell	Dubai Creek	275
2000	J Coceres	Dubai Creek	274
2001	T Bjørn	Emirates	266
2002	E Els	Emirates	272
2003	R-J Derksen	Emirates	271
2004	M O'Meara	Emirates	271
2005	E Els	Emirates	269

1	Tiger Woods (USA)*	67-66-67-69—269	£225568	€329760
2	Ernie Els (RSA)	68-66-68-67—269	150375	219834
3	Richard Green (USA)	64-69-69-68—270	84723	123857

Woods won at first extra hole

Johnnie Walker Classic *The Vines, Perth, Australia* [7104–72]

1992	I Palmer	Bangkok, Thailand	268
1993	N Faldo	Singapore Island	269
1994	G Norman	Blue Canyon, Phuket	277
1995	F Couples	Orchard GC, Manila	277
1996	I Woosnam*	Tanah Merah, Singapore	272
Woosnam beat A Coltart at third extra hole			
1997	E Els	Hope Island, Queensland	278
1998	T Woods*	Blue Canyon CC, Phuket	279
Woods beat E Els at second extra hole			

1999	Not played		
2000	M Campbell	Ta Shee, Taiwan	276
2001	T Woods	Bangkok, Thailand	263
2002	R Goosen	Perth, Australia	274
2003	E Els	Perth, Australia	259
2004	MA Jiménez	Bangkok, Thailand	271
2005	A Scott	Beijing	270

1	Kevin Stadler (USA)	64-69-66-69—268	£208330	€305468
2	Nick O'Hern (AUS)	67-71-64-68—270	138880	203635
3	Robert Allenby (AUS)	69-68-69-66—272	70375	103188
	Richard Green (AUS)	66-69-66-71—272	70375	103188

Malaysian Open *Kuala Lumpur, Malaysia* [6936–72]

1992	V Singh (FIJ)	1998	E Fryatt
1993	G Norquist (USA)	1999	G Norquist (USA)
1994	J Haegmann (SWE)	2000	Y Wei Tze (TPE)
1995	C Devers (USA)	2001	V Singh (FIJ)*
1996	S Fiesch (USA)		*Singh beat Harrington at third extra
1997	L Westwood (ENG)		hole

2002   A Forsyth (SCO)*
*Forsyth beat S Leaney at second extra
hole of play-off*
2003   A Atwal (IND)
2004   T Jaidee (THA)
2005   T Jaidee (THA)

1	Charlie Wi (KOR)	66-68-63—197	£119359	€174773
2	Thongchai Jaidee (THA)	69-63-66—198	79569	116509
3	Raphaël Jacquelin (FRA)	72-65-62—199	44832	65645

Reduced to 54 holes due to extreme weather

WGC – Accenture Match Play Championship *La Costa, Carlsbad, CA, USA*

Final: Geoff Ogilvy (AUS) beat Davis Love III (USA) 3 and 2

Full details of this event can be found on pages 178 and 179

Enjoy Jakarta Indonesian Open *Emeralda, Jakarta* [7082–72]

2005 T Wiratchant (THA)   255

1	Simon Dyson (ENG)	66-68-67-67—268	£95517	€140261
2	Andrew Buckle (AUS)	67-69-65-69—270	63680	93510
3	Thongchai Jaidee (THA)	66-68-72-68—274	32267	47382
	Ter-Chang Wang (TPE)	66-68-70-70—274	32267	47382

OSIM Singapore Masters   *Laguna GCC, Singapore*   [7207–72]

2001	V Singh (FIJ)	263	2004	C Montgomerie (SCO)	272
2002	A Atwal (IND)	274	2005	N Dougherty (ENG)	270
2003	L-w Zhang (CHN)	278			

1	Mardan Mamat (SIN)	65-70-70-71—276	£95065	€138560
2	Nick Dougherty (ENG)	69-70-67-71—277	63379	92376
3	Ross Fisher (ENG)	71-68-68-71—278	32114	46807
	Charlie Wi (KOR)	69-73-65-71—278	32114	46807

TCL Classic   *Yalong Bay, Sana, Hainan Island, China*   [7172–72]

2005	P Casey (ENG)	266

1	Johan Edfors (SWE)	66-66-63-68—263	£96580	€140215
2	Andrew Buckle (AUS)	63-66-65-70—264	64389	93479
3	Prayad Marksaeng (THA)	66-66-68-65—265	36277	52666

Madeira Island Open   *Santo da Serra, Madeira*   [6826–72]

1993	M James	Campo de Golf da Madeira	281	2000	N Fasth	Santo da Serra GC	279
1994	M Lanner	Campo de Golf da Madeira	206 (54)	2001	D Smyth	Santo da Serra GC	270
1995	S Luna	Campo de Golf da Madeira	272	2002	D Borrego	Santo da Serra GC	281
1996	J Sandelin	Campo de Golf da Madeira	279	2003	B Dredge	Santo da Serra GC	272
1997	P Mitchell	Santo de Serra GC	204 (54)	2004	C Hanell	Santo da Serra GC	284
1998	M Lanner	Santo de Serra GC	277	2005	R-J Derksen	Santo da Serra GC	275
1999	P Linhart	Santo da Serra GC	276				

1	Jean Van de Velde (FRA)	69-65-71-68—273	£80998	€116660
2	Lee Slattery (ENG)	74-68-66-66—274	53996	77770
3	Pedro Linhart (ESP)	71-67-69-68—275	30424	43820

Algarve Open de Portugal Caixa Geral de Depositos   *Le Meridien Penina*

[6798–72]

1953	EC Brown	Estoril	260		1983	S Torrance	Troia	286
1954	A Miguel	Estoril	263		1984	A Johnstone	Quinta do Lago	274
1955	F van Donck	Estoril	267		1985	W Humphreys	Quinta do Lago	279
1956	A Miguel	Estoril	268		1986	M McNulty	Quinta do Lago	270
1958	P Alliss	Estoril	264		1987	R Lee	Estoril	195 (54)
1959	S Miguel	Estoril	265		1988	M Harwood	Quinta do Lago	280
1960	K Bousfield	Estoril	268		1989	C Montgomerie	Quinta do Lago	264
1961	K Bousfield	Estoril	263		1990	M McLean	Quinta do Lago	274
1962	A Angelini	Estoril	269		1991	S Richardson	Estela	283
1963	R Sota	Estoril	204 (54)		1992	R Rafferty	Vila Sol	273
1964	A Miguel	Estoril	279		1993	D Gilford*	Vila Sol	275
1966	A Angelini	Estoril	273		*Gilford beat J Berendt at first extra hole			
1967	A Gallardo	Estoril	214 (54)		1994	P Price	Penha Longa	278
1968	M Faulkner	Estoril	273		1995	A Hunter*	Penha Longa	277
1969	R Sota	Estoril	270		*Hunter beat D Clarke at first extra hole			
1970	R Sota	Estoril	274		1996	W Riley	Aroeira	271
1971	L Platts	Estoril	277		1997	M Jonzon	Aroeira	269
1972	G Garrido	Estoril	196 (54)		1998	P Mitchell	Algarve	274
1973	J Benito*	Penina	294		1999	V Phillips*	Penina	276
*Benito beat B Gallacher at first extra hole					*Phillips beat J Bicherton at first extra hole			
1974	BGC Huggett	Estoril	272		2000	G Orr	Penina	275
1975	H Underwood	Penina	292		2001	P Price	Algarve	273
1976	S Balbuena	Quinta do Lago	283		2002	C Pettersson*	Vale do Lobo	142 (36)
1977	M Ramos	Penina	287		*Pettersson beat D Gilford at first extra hole			
1978	H Clark	Penina	291		2003	F Jacobson	Vale do Lobo	283
1979	B Barnes	Vilamoura	287		2004	MG Jiménez	Vale do Lobo	272
1982	S Torrance	Penina	207 (54)		2005	P Broadhurst	Quinta de Marinha	271

Algarve Open de Portugal Caixa Geral de Depositos *continued*

1	Paul Broadhurst (ENG)	64-69-71-67—271	£143859	€208330
2	Anthony Wall (ENG)	71-67-67-67—272	95901	138880
3	Andres Romero (ARG)	69-70-68-66—273	54034	78250

The MASTERS   *Augusta National, GA, USA*   [7445–72]

1	Phil Mickelson (USA)	70-72-70-69—281	£724429	€1037977
2	Tim Clark (RSA)	70-72-72-69—283	434658	622786
3	Chad Campbell (USA)	71-67-75-71—284	181510	260071
	Fred Couples (USA)	71-70-72-71—284	181510	260071
	Retief Goosen (RSA)	70-73-72-69—284	181510	260071
	José-María Olazábal (ESP)	76-71-71-66—284	181510	260071
	Tiger Woods (USA)	72-71-71-70—284	181510	260071

Fuller details of this event are included in Part I The Majors page 61

Volvo China Open   *Honghua International, Beijing*   [7203-72]

1995	Raul Fretes (PAR)		1999	Kyi Hla Han (MYA)	2003	Zhang Lian-Wei (CHI)
1996	Prayed Marksaeng (THA)		2000	Simon Dyson (ENG)	2004	Stephen Dodd (WAL)
1997	Cheng Jun (CHI)		2001	Charlie Wi (KOR)	2005	Paul Casey (ENG)
1998	Ed Fryatt (ENG)		2002	David Gleeson (AUS)		

1	Jeev Milkha Singh (IND)	72-69-67-70—278	£172344	€247748
2	Gonzalo Fernandez-Castaño (ESP)	67-74-68-70—279	114896	165165
3	David Lynn (ENG)	68-67-72-73—280	64732	93054

BMW Asian Open   *Tomson, Shanghai Pudong, China*   [7300–72]

2002	J Sandelin (SWE)	278		2004	MA Jiménez (ESP)	274
2003	P Harrington (IRL)	273		2005	E Els (RSA)	262

1	Gonzalo Fernandez-Castaño (ESP)*	71-71-69-70—281	£171330	€247810
2	Henrik Stenson (SWE)	67-72-71-71—281	114220	165207
3	José-Filipe Lima (POR)	71-70-73-68—282	57875	83710
	Colin Montgomerie (SCO)	69-74-71-68—282	57875	83710

Fernandez-Castaño won at first extra hole

Andalucia Open de España Valle Romano   *San Roque, Cadiz*   [7105–72]

1912	A Massy (FRA)	Polo, Madrid	1941	M Provencio	Puerta de Hierro
1916	A de la Torre	Puerta de Hierro	1942	G Gonzalez	Sant Cugat
1917	A de la Torre	Puerta de Hierro	1943	M Provencio	Puerta de Hierro
1919	A de la Torre	Puerta de Hierro	1944	N Sagardia	Pedrena
1921	E Lafitte	Puerta de Hierro	1945	C Celles	Puerta de Hierro
1923	A de la Torre	Puerta de Hierro	1946	M Morcillo	Pedrena
1925	A de la Torre	Puerta de Hierro	1947	M Gonzalez (am)	Puerta de Hierro
1926	J Bernardino	Puerta de Hierro	1948	M Morcillo	Negun
1927	A Massy (FRA)	Puerta de Hierro	1949	M Morcillo	Puerta de Hierro
1928	A Massy (FRA)	Puerta de Hierro	1950	A Cerda	Cedana
1929	E Lafitte	Puerta de Hierro	1951	M Provencio	Puerta de Hierro
1930	J Bernardino	Puerta de Hierro	1952	M Faulkner (ENG)	Puerta de Hierro
1932	G Gonzalez	Puerta de Hierro	1953	M Faulkner (ENG)	Puerta de Hierro
1933	G Gonzalez	Puerta de Hierro	1954	S Miguel	Puerta de Hierro
1934	J Bernardino	Puerta de Hierro	1955	H de Lamaze (FRA) (am)	Puerta de Hierro
1935	A de la Torre	Puerta de Hierro	1956	P Alliss (ENG)	El Prat

1957	M Faulkner (ENG)	Club de Campo		1985	S Ballesteros	Vallromanos
1958	P Alliss (ENG)	Puerta de Hierro		1986	H Clark (ENG)	La Moraleja
1959	PW Thomson (AUS)	El Prat		1987	N Faldo (ENG)	La Brisas
1960	S Miguel	Club de Campo		1988	M James (ENG)	Pedrena
1961	A Miguel	Puerta de Hierro		1989	B Langer (GER)	El Saler
1963	R Sota	El Prat		1990	R Davis (AUS)	Club de Campo
1964	A Miguel	Tenerife		1991	E Romero* (ARG)	Club de Campo
1966	R de Vicenzo (ARG)	Sotogrande		*Romero beat S Ballesteros at seventh extra hole		
1967	S Miguel	Sant Cugat		1992	A Sherborne (ENG)	RACE, Madrid
1968	R Shaw	La Galea		1993	J Haeggman (SWE)	RACE, Madrid
1969	J Garaialde	RACE, Madrid		1994	C Montgomerie (SCO)	Club de Campo
1970	A Gallardo	Nueva Andalucia		1995	S Ballesteros	Club de Campo
1971	D Hayes (RSA)	El Prat		1996	P Harrington (IRL)	Club de Campo
1972	A Garrido*	Pals		1997	M James* (ENG)	La Moraleja II
*Garrido beat V Barrias at third extra hole				*James beat G Norman at third extra hole		
1973	NC Coles (ENG)	La Manga		1998	T Bjørn (SWE)	El Prat
1974	J Heard	La Manga		1999	J Sandelin (SWE)	El Prat
1975	A Palmer (USA)	La Manga		2000	B Davis	PGA Golf de
1976	E Polland (NIR)	La Manga				Catalunya
1977	B Gallacher (SCO)	La Manga				
1978	B Barnes (SCO)	El Prat		2001	R Karlsson (SWE)	El Saler
1979	D Hayes (RSA)	Torrequebrada		2002	S García (ESP)	El Cortij
1980	E Polland (NIR)	Escorpion		2003	K Ferrie (ENG)*	Golf Costa Adeje
1981	S Ballesteros	El Prat		*Ferrie bear P Hedblom and P Lawrie at second extra hole		
1982	S Torrance (SCO)	Club de Campo		2004	C Cévaër (FRA)	Golf Costa Adeje
1983	E Darcy (IRL)	Las Brisas		2005	P Hanson (SWE)*	San Roque, Cadiz
1984	B Langer (GER)	El Saler		*Hanson beat P Gustafsson (SWE) at first extra hole		

1	Niclas Fasth (SWE)*	67-68-66-69—270	£190464		€275000
2	John Bickerton (ENG)	68-65-74-63—270	126973		183330
3	Phillip Archer (ENG)	67-69-68-67—271	46663		67375
	Thomas Bjørn (DEN)	70-64-68-69—271	46663		67375
	Mattias Eliasson (SWE)	68-68-68-67—271	46663		67375
	David Griffiths (ENG)	68-65-66-72—271	46663		67375
	José Manuel Lara (ESP)	68-66-69-68—271	46663		67375
	Gary Orr (SCO)	72-64-68-67—271	46663		67375

Fasth won at fourth extra hole

63rd Telecom Italia Open Castello di Tolcinasco, Milan   [7225–72]

1925	F Pasquali	Stresa	154		1962–1971	Not played	
1926	A Boyer	Stresa	147		1972	N Wood	Villa d'Este	271
1927	P Alliss	Stresa	145		1973	A Jacklin	Rome	284
1928	A Boyer	Villa d'Este	145		1974	P Oosterhuis	Venice	249 (63)
1929	R Golias	Villa d'Este	143		1975	W Casper	Monticello	286
1930	A Boyer	Villa d'Este	140		1976	B Dassu	Is Molas	280
1931	A Boyer	Villa d'Este	141		1977	A Gallardo*	Monticello	286
1932	A Boomer	Villa d'Este	143		*Gallardo beat B Barnes at fourth extra hole		
1934	N Nutley	San Remo	132		1978	D Hayes	Pevero	293
1935	P Alliss	San Remo	262		1979	B Barnes*	Monticello	281
1936	H Cotton	Sestriere	268		*Barnes beat D Hayes at fourth extra hole		
1937	M Dallemagne	San Remo	276		1980	M Mannelli	Rome	276
1938	F van Donck	Villa d'Este	276		1981	J M Canizares*	Milan	280
1947	F van Donck	San Remo	263		*Canizares beat B Clampett at first extra hole		
1948	A Casera	San Remo	267		1982	M James	Is Molas	280
1949	H Hassanein	Villa d'Este	263		1983	B Langer*	Ugolino	271
1950	U Grappasonni	Rome	281		*Langer beat S Ballesteros and K Brown at second extra hole		
1951	J Adams	Milan	289		1984	A Lyle	Milan	277
1952	E Brown	Milan	273		1985	M Piñero	Molinetto	267
1953	F van Donck	Villa d'Este	267		1986	D Feherty*	Albarella, Venice	270
1954	U Grappasonni	Villa d'Este	272		*Feherty beat R Rafferty at second extra hole		
1955	F van Donck	Venice	287		1987	S Torrance*	Monticello	271
1956	A Cerda	Milan	284		*Torrance beat J Rivero at sixth extra hole		
1957	H Henning	Villa d'Este	273		1988	G Norman	Monticello	270
1958	P Alliss	Varese	282		1989	R Rafferty	Monticello	273
1959	P Thomson	Villa d'Este	269		1990	R Boxall	Milan	267
1960	B Wilkes	Venice	285		1991	C Parry	Castelconturbia	279
1961	R Sota	Garlenda	282		1992	A Lyle	Monticello	270

63rd Telecom Italia Open *continued*

1993	G Turner	Modena	267		2000	I Poulter	Is Molas	267
1994	E Romero	Marco Simone	272		2001	G Havret	Is Molas	268
1995	S Torrance	Le Rovedine	269		2002	I Poulter	Olgiata GC	197 (54)
1996	J Payne	Bergamo GC	275		2003	M Grönberg	Gardagolf, Brescia	271
1997	B Langer	Gardagolf	273		2004	G McDowell*	Castello di Tolcinasco	197 (54)
1998	JM Olazábal	Castelconturbia	195 (54)		*McDowell beat T Levet at fourth extra hole			
1999	D Robertson	Circolo GC, Torino	271		2005	S Webster	Castello di Tolcinasco	270

1	Francesco Molinari (ITA)	68-65-67-65—265	£161666		€233330
2	Anders Hansen (DEN)	70-67-66-66—269	84249		121595
	Jarmo Sandelin (SWE)	69-68-67-65—269	84249		121595

Quinn Direct British Masters *The Belfry* [7163–72]

1946T	AD Locke	Stoneham	286		1977	G Hunt*	Lindrick	291
	J Adams				*Hunt beat B Barnes at third extra hole		
1947	A Lees	Little Aston	283		1978	T Horton	St Pierre	279
1948	N Von Nida	Sunningdale	272		1979	G Marsh	Woburn	283
1949	C Ward	St Andrews	290		1980	B Langer	St Pierre	270
1950	D Rees	Hoylake	281		1981	G Norman	Woburn	273
1951	M Faulkner	Wentworth Club	281		1982	G Norman	St Pierre	267
1952	H Weetman	Mere	281		1983	L Woosnam	St Pierre	269
1953	H Bradshaw	Sunningdale	272		1985	L Trevino	Woburn	278
1954	AD Locke	Prince's	291		1986	S Ballesteros	Woburn	275
1955	H Bradshaw	Little Aston	277		1987	M McNulty	Woburn	274
1956	C O'Connor	Prestwick	277		1988	A Lyle	Woburn	273
1957	E Brown	Hollinwell	275		1989	N Faldo	Woburn	267
1958	H Weetman	Little Aston	276		1990	M James	Woburn	270
1959	C O'Connor	Portmarnock	276		1991	S Ballesteros	Woburn	275
1960	J Hitchcock	Sunningdale	275		1992	C O'Connor jr*	Woburn	270
1961	P Thomson	Porthcawl	284		*O'Connor beat P Johnstone at first extra hole		
1962	D Rees	Wentworth Club	278		1993	P Baker	Woburn	266
1963	B Hunt	Little Aston	282		1994	I Woosnam	Woburn	271
1964	C Legrange	Royal Birkdale	288		1995	S Torrance	Collingtree Park	270
1965	B Hunt	Portmarnock	283		1996	R Allenby*	Collingtree Park	284
1966	N Coles	Lindrick	278		*Allenby beat MA Martin at first extra hole		
1967	A Jacklin	R St George's	274		1997	G Turner	Forest of Arden	275
1968	P Thomson	Sunningdale	274		1998	C Montgomerie	Forest of Arden	281
1969	C Legrange	Little Aston	281		1999	B May	Woburn	269
1970	B Huggett	R Lytham & St Annes	293		2000	G Orr	Woburn	267
1971	M Bembridge	St Pierre	273		2001	T Levet*	Woburn	274
1972	RJ Charles	Northumberland	277		*Levet beat M Gronberg, D Howell and R Karlsson at third extra
1973	A Jacklin	St Pierre	272		hole			
1974	B Gallacher*	St Pierre	282		2002	J Rose	Woburn	269
*Gallacher beat G Player at first extra hole					2003	G Owen	Forest of Arden	274
1975	B Gallacher	Ganton	289		2004	B Lane	Forest of Arden	272
1976	B Dassu	St Pierre	271		2005	T Bjørn	Forest of Arden	282

1	Johan Edfors (SWE)	68-69-70-70—277	£300000		€437949
2	Gary Emerson (ENG)	68-70-73-67—278	134226		195948
	Stephen Gallacher (SCO)	71-66-70-71—278	134226		195948
	Jarmo Sandelin (SWE)	67-71-70-70—278	134226		195948

Nissan Irish Open *Carton House, Maynooth, Co. Kildare* [7301–72]

1927	G Duncan	Portmarnock	312		1936	R Whitcombe	Royal Dublin	281
1928	E Whitcombe	Newcastle	288		1937	B Gadd	Portrush	284
1929	A Mitchell	Portmarnock	309		1938	A Locke	Portmarnock	292
1930	C Whitcombe	Portrush	289		1939	A Lees	Newcastle	287
1931	E Kenyon	Royal Dublin	291		1946	F Daly	Portmarnock	288
1932	A Padgham	Cork	283		1947	H Bradshaw	Portrush	290
1933	E Kenyon	Malone	286		1948	D Rees	Portmarnock	295
1934	S Easterbrook	Portmarnock	284		1949	H Bradshaw	Belvoir Park	286
1935	E Whitcombe	Newcastle	292		1950	H Pickworth	Royal Dublin	287

1953	E Brown	Belvoir Park	272
1975	C O'Connor Jr	Woodbrook	275
1976	B Crenshaw	Portmarnock	284
1977	H Green	Portmarnock	283
1978	K Brown	Portmarnock	281
1979	M James	Portmarnock	282
1980	M James	Portmarnock	284
1981	S Torrance	Portmarnock	276
1982	J O'Leary	Portmarnock	287
1983	S Ballesteros	Royal Dublin	271
1984	B Langer	Royal Dublin	267
1985	S Ballesteros*	Royal Dublin	278

*Ballesteros beat B Langer at second extra hole

1986	S Ballesteros	Portmarnock	285
1987	B Langer	Portmarnock	269
1988	I Woosnam	Portmarnock	278
1989	I Woosnam*	Portmarnock	278

*Woosnam beat P Walton at first extra hole

1990	JM Olazábal	Portmarnock	282
1991	N Faldo	Killarney	283
1992	N Faldo*	Killarney	274

*Faldo beat W Westner at fourth extra hole

1993	N Faldo*	Mount Juliet	276

*Faldo beat JM Olazábal at first extra hole

1994	B Langer	Mount Juliet	275
1995	S Torrance*	Mount Juliet	277

*Torrance beat S Cage and H Clonk at second extra hole

1996	C Montgomerie	Druid's Glen	279
1997	C Montgomerie	Druid's Glen	269
1998	D Carter*	Druid's Glen	278

*Carter beat C Montgomerie at first extra hole

1999	S García	Druid's Glen	268
2000	P Sjöland	Ballybunion	270
2001	C Montgomerie	Fota Island	266
2002	S Hansen*	Fota Island	270

*Hansen beat N Fasth, D Fichardt and R Bland at fourth extra hole

2003	M Campbell*	Portmarnock	277

*Campbell beat T Bjørn and P Hedblom at first extra hole

2004	B Rumford	Portmarnock	274
2005	S Dodd	Maynooth	279

1	Thomas Bjørn (DEN)	78-66-67-72—283	£249882	€366660
2	Paul Casey (ENG)	73-70-68-73—284	166588	244440
3	Darren Clarke (NIR)	75-70-67-73—285	93857	137720

BMW Championship Wentworth Club, Surrey, England [7308–72]

1955	K Bousfield	Pannal	277
1956	CH Ward	Maesdu	282
1957	P Alliss	Maesdu	286
1958	H Bradshaw	Llandudno	287
1959	DJ Rees	Ashburnham	283
1960	AF Stickley	Coventry	247 (63)
1961	BJ Bamford	R Mid-Surrey	266
1962	P Alliss	Little Aston	287
1963	PJ Butler	R Birkdale	306
1964	AG Grubb	Western Gailes	287
1965	P Alliss	Prince's	286
1966	GB Wolstenholme	Saunton	278
1967	BGC Huggett	Thorndon Park	271
1967	ME Gregson	Hunstanton	275
1968	PM Townsend	R Mid-Surrey	275
1968	D Talbot	Dunbar	276
1969	B Gallacher	Ashburnham	293
1972	A Jacklin	Wentworth Club	279
1973	P Oosterhuis	Wentworth Club	280
1974	M Bembridge	Wentworth Club	278
1975	A Palmer	R St George's	285
1976	NC Coles*	R St George's	280

*Coles beat E Darcy and G Player at third extra hole

1977	M Piñero	R St George's	283
1978	N Faldo	R Birkdale	278
1979	V Fernandez	St Andrews	288
1980	N Faldo	R St George's	283
1981	N Faldo	Ganton	274
1982	A Jacklin*	Hillside	284

*Jacklin beat B Langer at first extra hole

1983	S Ballesteros	R St George's	278
1984	H Clark	Wentworth Club	204 (54)
1985	P Way*	Wentworth Club	282

*Way beat AWB Lyle at third extra hole

1986	R Davis*	Wentworth Club	281

*Davis beat D Smyth at third extra hole

1987	B Langer	Wentworth Club	270
1988	I Woosnam	Wentworth Club	274
1989	N Faldo	Wentworth Club	272
1990	M Harwood	Wentworth Club	271
1991	S Ballesteros*	Wentworth Club	271

*Ballesteros beat C Montgomerie at first extra hole

1992	T Johnstone	Wentworth Club	272
1993	B Langer	Wentworth Club	274
1994	JM Olazábal	Wentworth Club	271
1995	B Langer	Wentworth Club	279
1996	C Rocca	Wentworth Club	274
1997	I Woosnam	Wentworth Club	275
1998	C Montgomerie	Wentworth Club	274
1999	C Montgomerie	Wentworth Club	270
2000	C Montgomerie	Wentworth Club	271
2001	A Oldcorn	Wentworth Club	272
2002	A Hansen	Wentworth Club	269
2003	I Garrido*	Wentworth Club	270

*Garrido beat T Immelman at extra hole of play-off

2004	S Drummond	Wentworth Club	269
2005	A Cabrera	Wentworth Club	273

1	David Howell (ENG)	68-65-69-69—271	£481536	€708330
2	Simon Khan (ENG)	70-68-70-68—276	321024	472220
3	Miguel Angel Jiménez (ESP)	71-69-65-72—277	180865	266050
4	Brett Rumford (AUS)	72-73-69-65—279	144461	212500
5	Richard Bland (ENG)	73-68-71-68—280	122503	180200
6	Andrew Coltart (SCO)	71-72-69-69—281	76506	112540
	Padraig Harrington (IRL)	72-70-68-71—281	76506	112540
	Trevor Immelman (RSA)	70-73-73-65—281	76506	112540
	Gary Orr (SCO)	71-70-73-67—281	76506	112540

BMW Championship continued

6T	Anthony Wall (ENG)	71-71-73-66—281	76506	112540
11	Paul Casey (ENG)	67-72-69-74—282	49791	73241
	Søren Hansen (DEN)	70-72-69-71—282	49791	73241
	Garry Houston (WAL)	69-72-71-70—282	49791	73241
14	Richard Green (AUS)	70-71-72-70—283	40738	59925
	Robert Karlsson (SWE)	69-68-74-72—283	40738	59925
	Maarten Lafeber (NED)	71-71-71-70—283	40738	59925
	Jean-François Lucquin (FRA)	76-70-67-70—283	40738	59925
	José-María Olazábal (ESP)	69-74-72-68—283	40738	59925
19	Emanuele Canonica (ITA)	72-71-72-69—284	33226	48875
	Ernie Els (RSA)	69-74-69-72—284	33226	48875
	Retief Goosen (RSA)	70-71-73-70—284	33226	48875
	Raphaël Jacquelin (FRA)	68-72-75-69—284	33226	48875
	Henrik Stenson (SWE)	73-73-68-70—284	33226	48875
	Steve Webster (ENG)	71-70-74-69—284	33226	48875
25	Luke Donald (ENG)	67-72-74-72—285	28747	42287
	Kenneth Ferrie (ENG)	69-73-73-70—285	28747	42287
	Peter Lawrie (IRL)	68-72-74-71—285	28747	42287
	Nick O'Hern (AUS)	72-72-68-73—285	28747	42287
29	Angel Cabrera (ARG)	68-69-75-74—286	24414	35912
	François Delamontaigne (FRA)	69-70-71-76—286	24414	35912
	Niclas Fasth (SWE)	70-70-71-75—286	24414	35912
	Andrew McLardy (RSA)	67-74-75-70—286	24414	35912
	David Park (WAL)	76-69-70-71—286	24414	35912
	Miles Tunnicliffe (ENG)	72-73-70-71—286	24414	35912
35	Nicolas Colsaerts (BEL)	70-72-70-75—287	21380	31450
	Thaworn Wiratchant (THA)	71-71-75-70—287	21380	31450
37	Michael Campbell (NZL)	72-73-73-70—288	19646	28900
	Nick Dougherty (ENG)	67-69-74-78—288	19646	28900
	Simon Dyson (ENG)	73-73-70-72—288	19646	28900
	Paul Lawrie (SCO)	69-73-73-73—288	19646	28900
41	David Carter (ENG)	73-71-73-72—289	16757	24650
	Bradley Dredge (WAL)	75-71-72-71—289	16757	24650
	Ross Fisher (ENG)	71-72-75-71—289	16757	24650
	Mark Foster (ENG)	71-71-74-73—289	16757	24650
	Jean Van de Velde (FRA)	75-69-66-79—289	16757	24650
	Ian Woosnam (WAL)	71-74-74-70—289	16757	24650
47	Paul Broadhurst (ENG)	71-71-73-75—290	13290	19550
	Alastair Forsyth (SCO)	71-72-72-75—290	13290	19550
	Ian Garbutt (ENG)	73-71-74-72—290	13290	19550
	Ignacio Garrido (ESP)	76-70-70-74—290	13290	19550
	Graeme McDowell (NIR)	71-70-73-76—290	13290	19550
	Wade Ormsby (AUS)	74-69-69-78—290	13290	19550
53	Markus Brier (AUT)	70-76-72-73—291	10112	14875
	Colin Montgomerie (SCO)	73-72-74-72—291	10112	14875
	Phillip Price (WAL)	69-77-72-73—291	10112	14875
	Jarmo Sandelin (SWE)	77-69-75-70—291	10112	14875
	Alessandro Tadini (ITA)	77-68-69-77—291	10112	14875
58	Phillip Archer (ENG)	72-73-79-68—292	8234	12112
	Peter Gustafsson (SWE)	72-70-75-75—292	8234	12112
	Steven Jeppesen (SWE)	71-74-74-73—292	8234	12112
	Jyoti Randhawa (IND)	71-72-76-73—292	8234	12112
62	Simon Edwards (WAL)	71-75-74-73—293	7512	11050
63	Graeme Storm (ENG)	71-75-76-72—294	7223	10625
64	Søren Kjeldsen (DEN)	70-75-72-79—296	6934	10200
65	Darren Prosser (ENG)	72-71-78-77—298	6645	9775
66	John Wells (ENG)	69-77-82-72—300	6356	9350

The Celtic Manor Wales Open Celtic Manor Resort, Newport, Wales [6165–69]

2000	S Tinning	Newport	223	2003	I Poulter	Newport	270
2001	P McGinley*	Newport	138	2004	S Khan*	Newport	267
*McGinley beat D Lee and P Lawrie at fifth extra hole				*Khan beat P Casey at second extra hole			
2002	P Lawrie	Newport	272	2005	MA Jiménez	Newport	262

1	Robert Karlsson (SWE)	61-63-65-71—260	£250000	€364352
2	Paul Broadhurst (ENG)	64-64-67-68—263	166660	242891
3	José-Filipe Lima (POR)	69-61-70-64—264	93900	136850

BA-CA Telecom Austria Open Fontana, Vienna [7059–71]

1	Markus Brier (AUT)	65-67-66-68—266	£148669	€216660
2	Søren Hansen (DEN)	68-67-69-65—269	99112	144440
3	Simon Dyson (ENG)	66-66-67-71—270	55841	81380

US OPEN CHAMPIONSHIP Winged Foot, NY, USA [7264–70]

1	Geoff Ogilvy (AUS)	71-70-72-72—285	£664821	€969455
2	Jim Furyk (USA)	70-72-74-70—286	272033	396684
	Phil Mickelson (USA)	70-73-69-74—286	272033	396684
	Colin Montgomerie (SCO)	69-71-75-71—286	272033	396684

Fuller details of this event are included in Part 1 The Majors page 51

Aa St Omer Open St Omer, Lumbres, France [6845–71]

2000	P Edmond	274	2002	N Vanhootagem	277	2004	P Lima	279
2001	S Delagrange	272	2003	B Rumford	269	2005	J Bäckström	280

1	Cesar Monasterio (ARG)	68-68-71-67—274	£45713	€66660
2	Martin Maritz (RSA)	71-67-66-71—275	23823	34740
	Henrik Nystrom (SWE)	69-65-68-73—275	23823	34740

Johnnie Walker Championship Centenary Course, Gleneagles, Scotland [7260–73]

1999	W Bennett	282	2002	A Scott	262	2005	E Canonica	281
2000	P Fulke	271	2003	S Kjeldsen	279			
2001	P Casey	274	2004	M Tunnicliffe	275			

1	Paul Casey (ENG)	67-71-66-72—276	£233330	€341667
2	Søren Hansen (DEN)	69-70-68-70—277	121595	178052
	Andrew Marshall (ENG)	72-67-69-69—277	121595	178052

Open de France ALSTOM Le Golf National, Paris, France [7225–71]

1906	A Massy	La Boulie	292	1924	CJH Tolley (am)	La Boulie	290
1907	A Massy	La Boulie	294	1925	A Massy	Chantilly	291
1908	JH Taylor	La Boulie	300	1926	A Boomer	St Cloud	280
1909	JH Taylor	La Boulie	290	1927	G Duncan	St Germain	290
1910	J Braid	La Boulie	298	1928	CJH Tolley (am)	La Boulie	283
1911	A Massy	La Boulie	284	1929	A Boomer	Fourqueux	283
1912	J Gassiat	La Boulie	284	1930	ER Whitcombe	Dieppe	282
1913	G Duncan	Chantilly	304	1931	A Boomer	Deauville	291
1914	JD Edgar	Le Touquet	284	1932	AJ Lacey	St Cloud	296
1920	W Hagen	La Boulie	298	1933	B Gadd	Chantilly	283
1921	A Boomer	Le Touquet	284	1934	SF Brews	Dieppe	284
1922	A Boomer	La Boulie	284	1935	SF Brews	Le Touquet	292
1923	J Ockenden	Dieppe	284	1936	M Dallemagne	St Germain	277

Open de France ALSTOM *continued*

1937	M Dallemagne	St Cloud	278	1977	S Ballesteros	Le Touquet	282
1938	M Dallemagne	Fourqueux	282	1978	D Hayes	La Baule	269
1939	M Pose	Le Touquet	285	1979	B Gallacher	Lyons	284
1946	TH Cotton	St Cloud	269	1980	G Norman	St Cloud	268
1947	TH Cotton	Chantilly	285	1981	A Lyle	St Germain	270
1948	F Cavalo	St Cloud	287	1982	S Ballesteros	St Nom-la-Bretêche	278
1949	U Grappasonni	St Germain	275	1983	N Faldo*	La Boulie	277
1950	R De Vicenzo	Chantilly	279	*Faldo beat DJ Russell and JM Canizares at third extra hole			
1951	H Hassanein	St Cloud	278	1984	B Langer	St Cloud	270
1952	AD Locke	St Germain	268	1985	S Ballesteros	St Germain	263
1953	AD Locke	La Boulie	276	1986	S Ballesteros	La Boulie	269
1954	F van Donck	St Cloud	275	1987	J Rivero	St Cloud	269
1955	B Nelson	La Boulie	271	1988	N Faldo	Chantilly	274
1956	A Miguel	Deauville	277	1989	N Faldo	Chantilly	273
1957	F van Donck	St Cloud	266	1990	P Walton*	Chantilly	275
1958	F van Donck	St Germain	276	*Walton beat B Langer at second extra hole			
1959	DC Thomas	La Boulie	276	1991	E Romero	National GC	281
1960	R De Vicenzo	St Cloud	275	1992	MA Martin	National GC	276
1961	KDG Nagle	La Boulie	271	1993	C Rocca*	National GC	273
1962	A Murray	St Germain	274	*Rocca beat P McGinley at first extra hole			
1963	B Devlin	St Cloud	273	1994	M Roe	National GC	274
1964	R de Vicenzo	Chantilly	272	1995	P Broadhurst	National GC	274
1965	R Sota	St Nom-la-Bretêche	268	1996	R Allenby*	National GC	272
1966	DJ Hutchinson	La Boulie	274	*Allenby beat B Langer at first extra hole			
1967	BJ Hunt	St Germain	271	1997	R Goosen	National GC	271
1968	PJ Butler	St Cloud	272	1998	S Torrance	National GC	276
1969	J Garaialde	St Nom-la-Bretêche	277	1999	R Goosen*	Golf du Médoc	272
1970	D Graham	Chantaco	268	*Goosen beat G Turner at second extra hole of play-off			
1971	Lu Liang Huan	Biarritz	262	2000	C Montgomerie	Le Golf National	272
1972	B Jaeckel*	Biarritz & La Nivelle	265	2001	JM Olazábal	Lyon GC	268
*Jaeckel beat C Clarke at first extra hole				2002	M Mackenzie	Le Golf National	279
1973	P Oosterhuis	La Boulie	280	2003	P Golding	Le Golf National	273
1974	P Oosterhuis	Chantilly	284	2004	J-F Remesy	Le Golf National	272
1975	B Barnes	La Boulie	281	2005	J-F Remesy*	Le Golf National	273
1976	V Tshabalaia	Le Touquet	272	*Remesy beat J Van de Velde at first extra hole			

1	John Bickerton (ENG)	63-70-71-69—273	£458576		€666660
2	Padraig Harrington (IRL)	69-70-69-66—274	305717		444440
3	Michael Campbell (NZL)	65-70-68-73—276	142160		206666
	Marcus Fraser (AUS)	70-68-69-69—276	142160		206666
	Ian Poulte (ENG)	68-70-69-69—276	142160		206666

Smurfit Kappa European Open   The K Club, Co. Kildare, Ireland   [7313–72]

1978	B Wadkins*	Walton Heath	283	1992	N Faldo	Sunningdale	262
*Wadkins beat B Gallacher and G Morgan at first extra hole				1993	G Brand Jr	E. Sussex National	275
1979	A Lyle	Turnberry	275	1994	D Gilford	E. Sussex National	275
1980	T Kite	Walton Heath	284	1995	B Langer*	The K Club	280
1981	G Marsh	Royal Liverpool	275	*Langer beat B Lane at second extra hole			
1982	M Piñero	Sunningdale	266	1996	P-U Johansson	The K Club	277
1983	L Aoki	Sunningdale	274	1997	P-U Johansson	The K Club	267
1984	G Brand Jr	Sunningdale	270	1998	M Grönberg	The K Club	275
1985	B Langer	Sunningdale	269	1999	L Westwood	The K Club	271
1986	G Norman*	Sunningdale	269	2000	L Westwood	The K Club	276
*Norman beat K Brown at first extra hole				2001	D Clarke	The K Club	273
1987	P Way	Walton Heath	279	2002	M Campbell	The K Club	282
1988	I Woosnam	Sunningdale	260	2003	P Price	The K Club	272
1989	A Murray	Walton Heath	277	2004	R Goosen	The K Club	275
1990	P Senior	Sunningdale	267	2005	K Ferrie	The K Club	285
1991	M Harwood	Walton Heath	277				

1	Stephen Dodd (WAL)	67-69-73-70—279	£400000		€578792
2	José Manuel Lara (ESP)	72-68-67-74—281	208450		301622
	Anthony Wall (ENG)	70-68-70-73—281	208450		301622

The Barclay's Scottish Open Loch Lomond, Glasgow, Scotland [7139–71]

1986	D Feherty*	Haggs Castle	270	1996	I Woosnam	Carnoustie	289
*Feherty beat C O'Connor Jr and I Baker-Finch at second extra				1996	T Bjørn	Loch Lomond	277
hole				1997	T Lehman	Loch Lomond	265
1987	I Woosnam	Gleneagles	264	1998	L Westwood	Loch Lomond	276
1988	B Lane	Gleneagles	271	1999	C Montgomerie	Loch Lomond	268
1989	M Allen	Gleneagles	272	2000	E Els	Loch Lomond	273
1990	I Woosnam	Gleneagles	269	2001	R Goosen	Loch Lomond	268
1991	C Parry	Gleneagles	268	2002	E Romero*	Loch Lomond	273
1992	P O'Malley	Gleneagles	262	*Romero beat F Jacobsen at first extra hole of play-off			
1993	J Parnevik	Gleneagles	271	2003	E Els	Loch Lomond	267
1994	C Mason	Gleneagles	265	2004	T Levet	Loch Lomond	269
1995	W Riley	Carnoustie	276	2005	T Clark	Loch Lomond	265

I	Johan Edfors (SWE)	65-69-74-63—271	£400000	€577540	
2	Luke Donald (ENG)	68-69-70-66—273	178966	258401	
	Anders Romero (ARG)	72-64-68-69—273	178966	258401	
	Charl Schwartzel (RSA)	68-66-72-67—273	178966	258401	

The 135th OPEN CHAMPIONSHIP Hoylake [7258–72]

I	Tiger Woods (USA)	67-65-71-67—270	£720000	€1045965
2	Chris DiMarco (USA)	70-65-69-68—272	430000	624673
3	Ernie Els (RSA)	68-65-71-71—275	275000	319500

Past results and fuller details in Part I The Majors page 38

The Deutsche Bank Players' Championship of Europe

Gut Kaden, Hamburg, Germany [7290–72]

1977	N Coles	Foxhills	288	1992	not played		
1978	B Waites	Foxhills	286	1993	not played		
1979	M King	Moor Park	281	1994	not played		
1980	B Gallacher	Moortown	268	1995	B Langer	Gut Kaden	270
1981	B Barnes*	Dalmahoy	276	1996	F Nobilo	Gut Kaden	270
*Barnes beat B Waites at fourth extra hole				1997	R McFarlane	Gut Kaden	282
1982	N Faldo	Notts	270	1998	L Westwood	Gut Kaden	265
1983	B Langer	St Mellion	269	1999	T Woods	St Leon-Rot	273
1984	J Gonzalez*	St Mellion	265	2000	L Westwood	Gut Kaden, Hamburg	273
*Gonzalez beat M James at second extra hole				2001	T Woods	St Leon-Rot	266
1985	Not played			2002	T Woods*	St Leon-Rot	268
1986	I Woosnam	The Belfry	277	*Woods beat C Montgomerie at third extra hole of play-off			
1987	Not played			2003	P Harrington*	Gut Kaden	269
1988	Not played			*Harrington beat T Bjørn at first extra hole			
1989	C Montgomerie	Quinta do Lago	264	2004	T Immelman	Gut Kaden	271
1990	M McLean	Quinta do Lago	274	2005	N Fasth*	Gut Kaden	274
1991	not played			*Fasth won at third extra hole			

I	Robert Karlsson (SWE)	64-66-66-67—263	£409469	€600000
2	Charl Schwartzel (RSA)	68-64-68-67—267	213388	312680
	Lee Westwood (ENG)	63-68-67-69—267	213388	312680

EnterCard Scandinavian Masters Barsebäck, Malmo, Sweden [7365–72]

1991	C Montgomerie	Drottningholm	270	1998	J Parnevik	Kungsängen	273
1992	N Faldo	Barsebäck	277	1999	C Montgomerie	Barsebäck	268
1993	P Baker*	Forsgårdens	278	2000	L Westwood	Kungsängen	270
*Baker beat A Forsbrand at second extra hole				2001	C Montgomerie	Kungsängen	274
1994	V Singh	Drottningholm	268	2002	G McDowell (NIR)	Kungsängen	270
1995	J Parnevik	Barsebäck	270	2003	A Scott	Kungsängen	277
1996	L Westwood*	Forsgårdens	281	2004	L Donald	Kungsängen	272
*Westwood beat P Broadhurst & R Claydon at 2nd extra hole				2005	M Hensby*	Kungsängen	262
1997	J Haeggman	Barsebäck	270	*Hensby beat H Stenson at second extra hole			

EnterCard Scandinavian Masters *continued*

1	Marc Warren (SCO)*	67-69-73-69—278	£182321	€266660
2	Robert Karlsson (SWE)	75-69-63-71—278	121545	177770
3	Richard Sterne (RSA)	70-68-72-69—279	68481	100160

Warren won at second extra hole

The KLM Open   Kennemer, Zandvoort, Netherlands   [6862–71]

Year	Winner	Venue	Score	Year	Winner	Venue	Score
1919	D Oosterveer	The Hague	158	1967	P Townsend	The Hague	282
1920	H Burrows	Kennemer	155	1968	J Cockin	Hilversumsche	292
1921	H Burrows	Domburg	151	1969	G Wolstenholme	Utrecht	277
1922	G Pannell	Noordwijk	160	1970	V Fernandez	Eindhoven	279
1923	H Burrows	Hilversumsche	153	1971	R Sota	Kennemer	277
1924	A Boomer	The Hague	138	1972	J Newton	The Hague	277
1925	A Boomer	The Hague	144	1973	D McClelland	The Hague	279
1926	A Boomer	The Hague	151	1974	B Barnes	Hilversumsche	211 (54)
1927	P Boomer	The Hague	147	1975	H Baiocchi	Hilversumsche	279
1928	ER Whitcombe	The Hague	141	1976	S Ballesteros	Kennemer	275
1929	JJ Taylor	Hilversumsche	153	1977	R Byman	Kennemer	278
1930	J Oosterveer	The Hague	152	1978	R Byman	Noordwijkse	211 (54)
1931	F Dyer	Kennemer	145	1979	G Marsh	Noordwijkse	285
1932	A Boyer	The Hague	137	1980	S Ballesteros	Hilversumsche	280
1933	M Dallemagne	Kennemer	143	1981	H Henning	The Hague	280
1934	SF Brews	Utrecht	286	1982	P Way	Utrecht	276
1935	SF Brews	Kennemer	275	1983	K Brown	Kennemer	274
1936	F van Donck	Hilversumsche	285	1984	B Langer	Rosendaelsche	275
1937	F van Donck	Utrecht	286	1985	G Marsh	Noordwijkse	282
1938	AH Padgham	The Hague	281	1986	S Ballesteros	Noordwijkse	271 (70)
1939	AD Locke	Kennemer	281	1987	G Brand Jr	Hilversumsche	272
1946	F van Donck	Hilversumsche	290	1988	M Mouland	Hilversumsche	274
1947	G Ruhl	Eindhoven	290	1989	JM Olazábal*	Kennemer	277
1948	C Denny	Hilversumsche	290	*Olazábal beat R Chapman and R Rafferty at ninth extra hole
1949	J Adams	The Hague	294	1990	S McAllister	Kennemer	274
1950	R De Vicenzo	Breda	269	1991	P Stewart	Noordwijkse	267
1951	F van Donck	Kennemer	281	1992	B Langer*	Noordwijkse	277
1952	C Denny	Hilversumsche	284	*Langer beat G Brand Jr at second extra hole
1953	F van Donck	Eindhoven	286	1993	C Montgomerie	Noordwijkse	281
1954	U Grappasonni	The Hague	295	1994	MA Jiménez	Hilversumsche	270
1955	A Angelini	Kennemer	280	1995	S Hoch	Hilversumsche	269
1956	A Cerda	Eindhoven	277	1996	M McNulty	Hilversumsche	266
1957	J Jacobs	Hilversumsche	284	1997	S Strüver	Hilversumsche	266
1958	D Thomas	Kennemer	277	1998	S Leaney	Hilversumsche	266
1959	S Sewgolum	The Hague	283	1999	L Westwood	Hilversumsche	269
1960	S Sewgolum	Eindhoven	280	2000	S Leaney	Nordwijkse	269
1961	BBS Wilkes	Kennemer	279	2001	B Langer*	Nordwijkse	269
1962	BGC Huggett	Hilversumsche	274	*Langer beat W Bennett at first extra hole
1963	R Waltman	Wassenaar	279	2002	T Dier	Hilversum	263
1964	S Sewgolum	Eindhoven	275	2003	M Lafeber	Hilversum	267
1965	A Miguel	Breda	278	2004	D Lynn	Hilversum	264
1966	R Sota	Kennemer	276	2005	G F Castano	Hilversum	269

1	Simon Dyson (ENG)*	67-71-66-66—270	£180034	€266660
2	Richard Green (AUS)	73-70-62-65—270	120021	177770
3	Damien McGrane (IRL)	69-68-64-70—271	67623	100160

Dyson won at first extra hole

US PGA CHAMPIONSHIP   Medina IL   [7561–72]

1	Tiger Woods (USA)	69-68-65-68—270	£645843	€959469
2	Shaun Micheel (USA)	69-70-67-69—275	387505	575681
3	Luke Donald (ENG)	68-68-66-74—276	186576	277180
	Sergio García (ESP)	69-70-67-70—276	186576	277180
	Adam Scott (AUS)	71-69-69-67—276	186576	277180

Past results and fuller details in Part I The Majors page 69

Imperial Collection Russian Open Le Meridien, Moscow, Russia [7154–72]

1996	C Watts	203	2001	J Donaldson	270	2004	G Emerson	272
1997	M Reale	280	2002	I Pyman	269	2005	M Lundberg*	273
1998	W Bennett	270	2003	M Fraser*	269	*Lundberg won at 4th extra hole		
1999	I Pyman	273	*Fraser beat M Wiegele at 2nd extra					
2000	M Bernardini	269	hole					

1	Alejandro Cañizares (ESP)	66-67-67-66—266	£87937	€130641
2	David Drysdale (SCO)	62-70-69-69—270	58627	87096
3	Mikael Lundberg (SWE)	68-67-70-66—271	29706	44132
	Gary Murphy (IRL)	67-68-68-68—271	29706	44132

WGC – Bridgestone Invitational Firestone CC, Akron, OH, USA [7366–70]

1	Tiger Woods (USA)*	67-64-71-68—270	£691195	€1014833
2	Stewart Cink (USA)	70-67-64-69—270	398766	585480
3	Jim Furyk (USA)	69-65-69-68—271	239259	351288

*Woods won at fourth extra hole

Fuller details of this event are included in World Championship Events on pages 179 and 180

BMW International Open Golfclub München Nord-Eichenried, Munich [6963–72]

1989	D Feherty	Golfplatz, Munich	269	1996	M Farry	St Eurach L&GC	132 (36)
1990	P Azinger*	Golfplatz, Munich	277	1997	R Karlsson	GC München	264
*Azinger beat D Feherty at first extra hole				1998	R Claydon	GC München	270
1991	A Lyle	Golfplatz, Munich	268	1999	C Montgomerie	GC München	268
1992	P Azinger*	Golfplatz, Munich	266	2000	T Bjørn	GC München	368
*Azinger beat G Day, B Langer, A Forsbrand and M James at				2001	J Daly	GC München	261
first extra hole				2002	T Bjørn	GC München	264
1993	P Fowler	Golfplatz, Munich	267	2003	L Westwood	GC München	269
1994	M McNulty	St Eurach L&GC	274	2004	M A Jiménez	GC München	267
1995	F Nobilo	St Eurach L&GC	272	2005	D Howell	GC München	265

1	Henrik Stenson (SWE)*	71-68-66-68—273	£225356	€333330
2	Retief Goosen (RSA)	73-66-67-67—273	117441	173710
	Padraig Harrington (IRL)	70-70-64-69—273	117441	173710

*Stenson won at first extra hole

Omega European Masters Crans-sur-Sierre, Switzerland (since 1939) [6857–72]

1923	A Ross	Engen	149	1958	K Bousfield		272
1924	P Boomer	Engen	150	1959	DJ Rees		274
1925	A Ross	Engen	148	1960	H Henning		270
1926	A Ross	Lucerne	145	1961	KDG Nagle		268
1929	A Wilson	Lucerne	142	1962	RJ Charles*		272
1930	A Boyer	Samedan	150	1963	DJ Rees*		278
1931	M Dallemagne	Lucerne	145	1964	HR Henning		276
1934	A Boyer	Lausanne	133	1965	HR Henning		208 (54)
1935	A Boyer	Lausanne	137	1966	A Angelini		271
1936	F Francis (am)	Lausanne	134	1967	R Vines		272
1937	M Dallemagne	Samedan	138	1968	R Bernardini		272
1938	J Saubaber	Zumikon	139	1969	R Bernardini		277
1939	F Cavalo	Crans-sur-Sierre	273	1970	G Marsh		274
1948	U Grappasonni		285	1971	PM Townsend		270
1949	M Dallemagne		270	1972	G Marsh		270
1950	A Casera		276	1973	H Baiocchi		278
1951	EC Brown		267	1974	RJ Charles		275
1952	U Grappasonni		267	1975	D Hayes		273
1953	F van Donck		267	1976	M Piñero		274
1954	AD Locke		276	1977	S Ballesteros		273
1955	F van Donck		277	1978	S Ballesteros		272
1956	DJ Rees		278	1979	H Baiocchi		275
1957	A Angelini		270	1980	N Price		267

Omega European Masters continued

1981	M Piñero*	277	1993	B Lane		270
*Piñero beat T Johnstone and A Garrido at first extra hole			1994	E Romero		266
1982	I Woosnam*	272	1995	M Grönberg		270
*Woosnam beat W Longmuir at third extra hole			1996	C Montgomerie		260
1983	N Faldo*	268	1997	C Rocca		266
1984	J Anderson	261	1998	S Strüver*		263
1985	C Stadler	267	*Strüver beat P Sjoland at first extra hole			
1986	JM Olazábal	262	1999	L Westwood		270
1987	A Forsbrand	263	2000	E Romero		261
1988	C Moody	268	2001	R Gonzalez		268
1989	S Ballesteros	266	2002	R Karlsson		270
1990	R Rafferty	267	2003	E Els		267
1991	J Hawkes	268	2004	L Donald		265
1992	J Spence*	271	2005	S García		270
*Spence beat A Forsbrand at second extra hole						

1	Bradley Dredge (WAL)	68-67-65-67—267	£224546	€333330
2	Francesco Molinari (ITA)	68-68-70-69—275	117018	173710
	Marcel Siem (GER)	68-67-67-73—275	117018	173710

HSBC World Match Play Championship Wentworth West Course, Surrey, England

1964	A Palmer beat N Coles 2 and 1		1985	S Ballesteros beat B Langer 6 and 5
1965	G Player beat P Thomson 3 and 2		1986	G Norman beat A Lyle 2 and 1
1966	G Player beat J Nicklaus 6 and 4		1987	I Woosnam beat A Lyle 1 hole
1967	A Palmer beat P Thomson 1 hole		1988	A Lyle beat N Faldo 2 and 1
1968	G Player beat R Charles 1 hole		1989	N Faldo beat I Woosnam 1 hole
1969	R Charles beat G Littler 37th hole		1990	I Woosnam beat M McNulty 4 and 2
1970	J Nicklaus beat L Trevino 2 and 1		1991	S Ballesteros beat N Price 3 and 2
1971	G Player beat J Nicklaus 5 and 4		1992	N Faldo beat J Sluman 8 and 7
1972	T Weiskopf beat L Trevino 4 and 3		1993	C Pavin beat N Faldo 1 hole
1973	G Player beat G Marsh 40th hole		1994	E Els beat C Montgomerie 4 and 2
1974	H Irwin beat G Player 3 and 1		1995	E Els beat S Elkington 2 and 1
1975	H Irwin beat A Geiberger 4 and 2		1996	E Els beat V Singh 3 and 2
1976	D Graham beat H Irwin 38th hole		1997	V Singh beat E Els 1 hole
1977	G Marsh beat R Floyd 5 and 3		1998	M O'Meara beat T Woods 1 hole
1978	I Aoki beat S Owen 3 and 2		1999	C Montgomerie beat M O'Meara 3 and 2
1979	W Rogers beat I Aoki 1 hole		2000	L Westwood beat C Montgomerie 38th hole
1980	G Norman beat A Lyle 1 hole		2001	I Woosnam beat P Harrington 2 and 1
1981	S Ballesteros beat B Crenshaw 1 hole		2002	E Els beat S García 2 and 1
1982	S Ballesteros beat A Lyle 37th hole		2003	E Els beat T Bjørn 4 and 3
1983	G Norman beat N Faldo 3 and 2		2004	E Els beat L Westwood 2 and 1
1984	S Ballesteros beat B Langer 2 and 1		2005	M Campbell beat P McGinley 2 and 1

First Round:
Michael Campbell (NZL) beat Simon Khan (ENG) 3 and 1
Colin Montgomerie (SCO) beat David Howell (ENG) 1 hole
Paul Casey (ENG) beat Retief Goosen (RSA) 6 and 4
Mike Weir (CAN) beat Adam Scott (AUS) 3 and 2
Robert Karlsson (SWE) beat Jim Furyk (USA) 4 and 3
Angel Cabrera (ARG) beat Ernie Els (RSA) 2 and 1
Luke Donald (ENG) beat Tim Clark (RSA) 2 holes
Shaun Micheel (USA) beat Tiger Woods (USA) 4 and 3

Quarter Finals:
Montgomerie beat Campbell 1 hole
Casey beat Weir 5 and 3
Karlsson beat Cabrera 4 and 3
Micheel beat Donald 4 and 2

Semi-Finals:
Casey beat Montgomerie 6 and 5
Micheel beat Karlsson 2 holes

Final:
Paul Casey beat Shaun Micheel 10 and 8

Winner:	£1,000,000	€1,470,230
Runner-up:	£400,000	€588,092
Semi-finalists:	£120,000	€176,427

XXXII Banco Madrid Valle Romano Open de Madrid Masters

La Moraleja 2, Madrid   [7018–72]

1968	G Garrido	1974	M Pineto	1980	S Ballesteros	*Piñero beat JM Canizares at	
1969	R Soto	1975	K Shearer	1981	M Piñero	fourth extra hole	
1970	M Cabrera	1976	F Abreu	1982	S Ballesteros	1986	H Clark
1971	V Barrios	1977	A Garrido	1983	A Lyle	1987	I Woosnam
1972	J Kinsetta	1978	H Clark	1984	H Clark	1988	D Cooper
1973	G Garrido	1979	S Hobday	1985	M Piñero*	1989	S Ballesteros

1990	B Langer	1995	A Cejka	2000	P Harrington	2003	R Gonzales
1991	A Sherborne	1996	D Borrego	2001	R Goosen*	2004	R Sterne
1992	D Feherty	1997	JM Olazábal		*Goosen beat S Webster at	2005	R Jacquelin
1993	D Smyth	1998	MA Jiménez		third extra hole		
1994	C Mason	1999	MA Jiménez	2002	S Tinning		

1	Ian Poulter (ENG)	67-66-64-69—266	£113356	€166660
2	Ignacio Garrido (ESP)	68-66-71-66—271	75573	111110
3	Phillip Price (WAL)	70-67-68-67—272	42578	62600

Ryder Cup K Club, Straffan, Ireland

Result: Europe 18½ USA 9½

Fuller details of this event can be found in International Team Events on page 186

WGC – American Express Championship The Grove, Chandlers' Cross, Herts [7125–71]

1	Tiger Woods (USA)	63-64-67-67—261	£683778	€1015944
2	Ian Poulter (ENG)	64-71-68-66—269	320849	476712
	Adam Scott (AUS)	67-68-65-69—269	320849	476712

Fuller details of this event can be found in World Championship Events on page 181

Alfred Dunhill Links Championship St Andrews Old [72], Carnoustie [71], Kingsbarns [72]

2001	P Lawrie	270	2003	L Westwood	267	2005	C Montgomerie	279
2002	P Harrington*	269	2004	S Gallacher*	269			

*Harrington beat E Romero at second extra hole of play-off

*Gallacher beat G McDowell at first extra hole

1	Padraig Harrington (IRL)	66-69-68-68—271	£427441	€630566
2	Bradley Dredge (WAL)	64-67-71-74—276	191246	282128
	Edward Loar (USA)	70-66-70-70—276	191246	282128
	Anthony Wall (ENG)	70-70-69-67—276	191246	282128

Mallorca Classic Pula GC, Majorca, Spain [6850–70]

2003	MA Jiménez	204	2004	S García	268	2005	J-M Olazábal	270

1	Niclas Fasth (SWE)	66-71-70-68—275	£195107	€291660
2	Sergio García (ESP)	70-70-70-68—278	130071	194440
3	José Manuel Lara (ESP)	69-72-71-67—279	73283	98525
	Marc Warren (SCO)	70-68-71-70—279	73283	98525

Volvo Masters Valderrama, Sotogrande, Spain [6952–71]

1988	N Faldo	Valderrama	284	1999	MA Jiménez	Montecastillo	269
1989	R Rafferty	Valderrama	282	2000	P Fulke	Montecastillo	272
1990	M Harwood	Valderrama	286	2001	P Harrington	Montecastillo	204 (54)
1991	R Davis	Valderrama	280	2002	B Langer*	Valderrama	281
1992	A Lyle*	Valderrama	287		C Montgomerie*		281

*Lyle beat C Montgomerie at first extra hole

*declared a tie after bad light stopped play after two holes of their sudden-death play-off

1993	C Montgomerie	Valderrama	274	2003	F Jacobsen	Valderrama	276
1994	B Langer	Valderrama	276	2004	I Poulter*	Valderrama	277
1995	A Lyle	Valderrama	282				

*Poulter beat S García at first extra hole of play-off

1996	M McNulty	Valderrama	276	2005	P McGinley	Valderrama	274
1997	L Westwood	Montecastillo	200 (54)				
1998	D Clarke	Montecastillo	271				

Volvo Masters *continued*

1	Jeev Milkha Singh (IND)	71-71-68-72—282	£446598	€666660
2	Luke Donald (ENG)	69-71-74-69—283	199819	298280
	Padraig Harrington (IRL)	73-69-72-69—283	199819	298280
	Sergio García (ESP)	71-70-70-72—283	199819	298280

2007

HSBC Champions Tournament   *Sheshan GC, Shanghai*   [7143-72]

1	Yang Yong-eun (KOR)	66-72-67-69—274	£435826	€647928
2	Tiger Woods (USA)	72-64-73-67—276	290559	431965
3	Michael Campbell (NZL)	66-70-77-64—277	147140	218749
	Retief Goosen (RSA)	68-67-69-73—277	147140	218749

UBS Hong Kong Open   *Hong Kong GC, Fanling*   [6703-70]

1	Jose Manuel Lara (ESP)	64-66-66-69—265	£175081	€259178
2	Juvin Pagunson (PHI)	67-65-66-68—266	116720	172785
3	Jeev Milkha Singh (IND)	66-67-69-66—268	54724	80345
	Jyoti Randhawa (IND)	64-69-69-66—268	54724	80345
	Thongchai Jaidee (THA)	68-66-67-67—268	54724	80345

Mastercard Masters   (formerly Australian Masters)   *Huntingdale, Melbourne*   [6980-72]

1	Justin Rose (ENG)	69-66-68-73—276	£115370	€170353
2	Greg Chalmers (AUS)	70-67-68-73—278	54320	80208
	Richard Green (AUS)	70-71-68-69—278	54320	80208

Blue Chip New Zealand Open   *Gulf Harbour CC, Auckland*   [6951-71]

1	Nathan Green (AUS)	71-67-76-65—279	£98104	€145831
2	Nick Docherty (ENG)	69-66-79-67—281	29567	43951
	Brett Rumford (AUS)	71-70-69-71—281	29567	43951
	Marcus Fraser (AUS)	69-69-70-73—281	29567	43951
	Michael Campbell (NZL)	71-65-73-72—281	29567	43951
	Jarrod Moseley (AUS)	68-70-73-70—281	29567	43951
	Wade Ormsby (AUS)	72-63-76-70—281	29567	43951

dunhill championship   *Leopard Creek, Mpumalanga, RSA*   [7249-72]

1	Alvaro Quiros (ESP)	74-66-68-67—275	£107193	€158,500
2	Charl Schwartzel (RSA)	68-68-68-72—276	77774	115,000
3	Lee Westwood (ENG)	73-66-67-73—279	46732	69,100

South African Airways Open   *Humewood GC, Port Elizabeth*   [6963-72]

1	Ernie Els (RSA)	67-66-66-65—264	£105896	€158000
2	Trevor Immelman (RSA)	67-66-63-71—267	77076	115000
3	Patrick Sjoland (SWE)	68-64-69-67—268	46319	69100

World Cup of Golf   *The Sandy Lane Resort , Barbados*   [7069-71]

1	Germany (Bernhard Langer and Marcel Siem)	268	£716039 shared	€1508761 shared
2	Scotland (Colin Montgomerie and Marc Warren)	268	358019	529380
3	Sweden (Henrik Stenson and Carl Petterssen)	269	102291	151251

Fuller details can be found in World Championship Events, page 184

European Senior Tour 2006
www.europeantour.com

Final Ranking (Top 30 earn full Tour card for 2007)

1	Sam Torrance (SCO)	€347,525	41	Angel Fernandez (CHI)	40,527
2	Carl Mason (ENG)	268,453	42	Bob Larratt (ENG)	40,150
3	José Rivero (ESP)	233,374	43	Alan Tapie (USA)	38,325
4	Gordon J Brand (ENG)	196,002	44	Tony Allen (ENG)	32,067
5	Stewart Ginn (AUS)	178,260	45	Emilio Rodriguez (ESP)	31,991
6	Juan Quiros (ESP)	159,071	46	Seiji Ebihara (JPN)	31,655
7	Horacio Carbonetti (ARG)	147,655	47	Manuel Piñero (ESP)	31,170
8	David J Russell (ENG)	140,784	48	John Mashego (RSA)	30,361
9	Giuseppe Cali (ITA)	138,242	49	Ian Mosey (ENG)	26,640
10	Luis Carbonetti (ARG)	136,375	50	Rex Caldwell (USA)	26,426
11	Guillermo Encina (CHI)	126,616	51	Peter Teravainen (USA)	26,033
12	Nick Job (ENG)	120,017	52	Bob Lendzion (USA)	25,826
13	Tony Johnstone (ZIM)	115,929	53	Martin Foster (ENG)	24,120
14	Eamonn Darcy (IRL)	112,503	54	Jean Pierre Sallat (FRA)	23,576
15	Gery Watine (FRA)	104,676	55	Noel Ratcliffe (AUS)	23,550
16	Bertus Smit (RSA)	101,748	56	Mike Ferguson (AUS)	22,861
17	Simon Owen (NZL)	95,402	57	Tony Charnley (ENG)	22,318
18	Bobby Lincoln (RSA)	86,869	58	Bill Hardwick (CAN)	20,948
19	Bill Longmuir (SCO)	83,040	59	John Benda (USA)	20,553
20	Bob Cameron (ENG)	80,840	60	Maurice Bembridge (ENG)	20,469
21	Delroy Cambridge (JAM)	75,949	61	Ray Carrasco (USA)	16,723
22	Adan Sowa (ARG)	74,427	62	Hank Woodrome (USA)	15,961
23	Bruce Heuchan (CAN)	70,862	63	Jeff Hawkes (USA)	15,711
24	Martin Poxon (ENG)	67,537	64	David Creamer (ENG)	15,625
25	Martin Gray (SCO)	66,467	65	Malcolm Gregson (ENG)	15,199
26	Jim Rhodes (ENG)	64,238	66	Denis Durnian (ENG)	15,122
27	Terry Gale (AUS)	60,298	67	Gordon Townhill (ENG)	14,181
28	John Bland (RSA)	60,151	68	Alan Mew (TRI)	13,558
29	Kevin Spurgeon (ENG)	58,834	69	Craig Maltman (SCO)	12,756
30	Jerry Bruner (USA)	57,886	70	Eddie Polland (NIR)	10,387
			71	Robin Mann (ENG)	9,025
31	John Chillas (SCO)	57,852	72	Victor Garcia (ESP)	8,931
32	Gavan Levenson (RSA)	57,093	73	Antonio Garrido (ESP)	8,354
33	Pete Oakley (USA)	53,308	74	Neil Coles (ENG)	7,635
34	Jimmy Heggarty (NIR)	53,145	75	Liam Higgins (IRL)	7,600
35	Des Smyth (IRL)	50,261	76	Bill Malley (USA)	7,385
36	Glenn Ralph (ENG)	49,898	77	Craig Defoy (WAL)	7,061
37	Doug Johnson (CAN)	44,460	78	Stephen Chadwick (ENG)	5,351
38	Denis O'Sullivan (IRL)	43,520	79	Paul Leonard (NIR)	4,854
39	Mike Miller (SCO)	42,003	80	Philippe Dugeny (FRA)	4,038
40	David Good (AUS)	41,397			

Mackenzie completes 26 years and 600 tournaments

Malcolm Mackenzie reached the 600 mark in European Tour events when he played in the BMW International at Nord-Eichenried in 2006. Having turned professional in 1980 and played his first event in 1981 at the Cold Shield Greater Manchester Open, Mackenzie, at 44 and 335 days, is the youngest of the four players who have passed the 600 mark on Tour.

Sam Torrance has played 700, Roger Chapman 616 and Eamonn Darcy 610. The player with the most appearances on the US PGA Tour is Jay Haas with 796. He made his start on the US Tour as an amateur in 1973.

Career Money List

1	Tommy Horton (ENG)	€1,478,499	51	Gary Player (RSA)	380,736
2	Carl Mason (ENG)	1,230,584	52	David Jones (NIR)	374,369
3	Noel Ratcliffe (AUS)	1,201,150	53	John Fourie (RSA)	370,647
4	Jim Rhodes (ENG)	996,494	54	Ian Mosey (ENG)	364,054
5	Terry Gale (AUS)	959,184	55	Pete Oakley (USA)	361,520
6	Seiji Ebihara (JPN)	947,080	56	John Bland (RSA)	355,117
7	Denis O'Sullivan (IRL)	946,079	57	Des Smyth (IRL)	337,202
8	Neil Coles (ENG)	919,868	58	Craig Defoy (WAL)	323,213
9	Nick Job (ENG)	901,250	59	Renato Campagnoli (ITA)	317,192
10	Denis Durnian (ENG)	872,309	60	Gery Watine (FRA)	315,738
11	Jerry Bruner (USA)	845,493	61	Keith MacDonald (ENG)	297,834
12	Malcolm Gregson (ENG)	827,226	62	Loren Roberts (USA)	289,664
13	David Good (AUS)	794,169	63	Barry Vivian (NZL)	287,062
14	John Chillas (SCO)	789,695	64	Gordon J Brand (ENG)	277,807
15	Delroy Cambridge (JAM)	763,683	65	Jeff Van Wagenen (USA)	273,722
16	Sam Torrance (SCO)	742,819	66	Ross Metherell (AUS)	255,539
17	Maurice Bembridge (ENG)	716,379	67	John Irwin (CAN)	250,934
18	Bill Longmuir (SCO)	684,338	68	Steve Stull (USA)	249,583
19	David Creamer (ENG)	646,986	69	Bruce Heuchan (CAN)	246,839
20	Brian Huggett (WAL)	638,783	70	Brian Jones (AUS)	245,918
21	Eddie Polland (NIR)	617,228	71	Gavan Levenson (RSA)	239,135
22	Bob Charles (NZL)	614,375	72	Brian Barnes (SCO)	234,975
23	Ian Stanley (AUS)	607,584	73	Peter Townsend (ENG)	230,974
24	Antonio Garrido (ESP)	571,059	74	John McTear (SCO)	226,794
25	Giuseppe Cali (ITA)	568,300	75	Peter Dawson (ENG)	225,109
26	Alan Tapie (USA)	551,406	76	Stewart Ginn (AUS)	222,843
27	John Grace (USA)	539,694	77	Bill Brask (USA)	221,902
28	Simon Owen (NZL)	539,120	78	Jay Horton (USA)	219,067
29	Luis Carbonetti (ARG)	514,923	79	Tom Kite (USA)	217,407
30	David Huish (SCO)	512,325	80	Hank Woodrome (USA)	206,038
31	Guillermo Encina (CHI)	505,840	81	Manuel Piñero (ESP)	201,922
32	Bob Cameron (ENG)	503,749	82	John Mashego (RSA)	197,432
33	Bobby Verwey (RSA)	496,778	83	Joe McDermott (IRL)	189,114
34	Tom Watson (USA)	492,806	84	Russell Weir (SCO)	183,193
35	Brian Waites (ENG)	482,280	85	Norman Wood (SCO)	183,066
36	Ray Carrasco (USA)	479,658	86	Dragon Taki (JPN)	165,074
37	Alberto Croce (ITA)	463,545	87	Noboru Sugai (JPN)	163,016
38	Horacio Carbonetti (ARG)	461,400	88	Juan Quiros (ESP)	159,071
39	Liam Higgins (IRL)	459,108	89	Kevin Spurgeon (ENG)	156,421
40	Bob Shearer (AUS)	458,621	90	Peter Butler (ENG)	155,985
41	Bob Lendzion (USA)	445,160	91	Craig Stadler (USA)	155,053
42	Christy O'Connor Jr (IRL)	421,266	92	Steve Wild (ENG)	153,739
43	Eduardo Romero (ARG)	421,139	93	Hugh Inggs (RSA)	153,048
44	Paul Leonard (NIR)	410,777	94	Mike Ferguson (AUS)	152,816
45	Bill Hardwick (CAN)	399,703	95	Martin Foster (ENG)	152,213
46	David J Russell (ENG)	397,812	96	Bobby Lincoln (RSA)	151,555
47	Bernard Gallacher (SCO)	390,573	97	Jay Dolan III (USA)	148,141
48	Priscillo Diniz (BRA)	388,580	98	John Garner (ENG)	142,686
49	Mike Miller (SCO)	386,816	99	Gary Wintz (USA)	142,362
50	Martin Gray (SCO)	382,279	100	Chick Evans (USA)	141,712

Tour Results

DGM Barbados Open	Royal Westmoreland, Barbados	José Rivera (ESP)	207 (-9)
Sharp Italian Seniors Open	GC Venezia, Italy	Sam Torrance (SCO)	205 (-11)
US Senior PGA Championship	Oak Tree GC, Edmund, OK		
1 Jay Haas* (USA)	68-70-73-68—279		
2 Brad Bryant (USA)	69-67-72-71—279		
3 Gil Morgan (USA)	66-70-71-74—281		
Haas won at third extra hole			
AIB Irish Seniors Open	Fota Island	Sam Torrance (SCO)*	207 (-6)
Torrance beat Jerry Bruner, Guillermo Encina and Stewart Ginn at second extra hole			
Irvine Whitlock Seniors Classic	La Moye, Jersey	Guillermo Encina (CHI)	209 (-7)
Firstplus Wales Seniors Open	The Vale, Wales	José Rivera (ESP)	212 (-4)
Bendinat London Seniors Masters	London GC, Kent	Giuseppe Cali (ITA)*	210 (-6)
Cali beat Delroy Cambridge (JAM) at the fifth extra hole			
US Senior Open	Prairie Dunes, Hutchison, KS		
1 Allen Doyle (USA)	69-68-67-68—272		
2 Tom Watson (USA)	70-66-66-72—274		
3 Peter Jacobsen (USA)	72-66-68-69—275		
Bruce Lietzke (USA)	69-70-70-66—275		
Senior British Open	Turnberry		
1 Loren Roberts (USA)*	65-65-69-75—274		
2 Eduardo Romero (ARG)	67-63-73-71—274		
3 Dick Mast (USA)	71-67-70-67—275		
Roberts won at first extra hole			
Wentworth Senior Masters	Wentworth, England	Eduardo Romero (ARG)	207 (-9)
Bad Ragaz PGA Seniors Open	Bad Ragaz, Switzerland	Juan Quiros (ESP)	196 (-14)
Scandinavian Senior Open	Helsingør, Denmark	Katsuyoshi Tomori (JPN)	199 (-14)
PGA Seniors Championship	Stoke by Nayland	Sam Torrance (SCO)	268 (-20)
Charles Church Scottish Seniors Open	Dalmahoy	Sam Torrance (Sco)	213 (-3)
European Senior Masters	Woburn, England	Carl Mason (ENG)	209 (-7)
Midas Group English Seniors Open	St Mellion	Carl Mason (ENG)	212 (-4)
OKI Castellon Open de España	Club de Camp Mediterraneo	Gordon J Brand (ENG)	203 (-13)
Estoril Senior of Portugal	Quint a da Marinha Oitavos	Carl Mason (ENG)	204 (-9)
Arcapita Seniors Tour Championship	Riffa Views, Bahrain	Gordon J Brand*	211 (-5)
Brand beat Adan Sowa (ARG) at third extra hole			

Five seniors in Europe hit the 200 starts mark

England's Jim Rhodes became the fifth player to hit the 200 mark in starts on the European Seniors Tour when he played in the Estoril Senior Open of Portugal at Quinta da Marinha Oitavos in 2006.

The 60-year-old Midlander, a three-time winner on the Senior Tour, is still an enthusiastic competitor, practising a lot as he continues to try, as he puts it "to master the game". He has been ten years on Tour and joined Tommy Horton, David Creamer, Malcolm Gregson and Maurice Bembridge as a member of the "200 Club".

Creamer hit 200 when he played in the DGM Barbados Open, Gregson made the mark at the Bad Ragaz PGA Seniors Open and Bembridge registered his 200th event at the PGA Seniors Championship.

Senior Tour Records 1992–2006

Low 18 holes

61 (-8)	Bob Cameron	Sanremo Masters	Sanremo GC	2004
62 (-10)	Tommy Horton	Scottish Seniors Open	Newmachar	1997
62 (-10)	Noel Ratcliffe	De Vere PGA Seniors Championship	De Vere Carden Park	2004
62 (-10)	Sam Torrance	Travis Perkins Senior Masters	Wentworth Club	2004
62 (-8)	David Huish	Bad Ragaz PGA Seniors Open	Bad Ragaz GC	2000
62 (-8)	John Irwin	Bad Ragaz PGA Seniors Open	Bad Ragaz GC	2001
62 (-8)	Jim Colbert	Senior British Open, presented by MasterCard	Westin Turnberry Resort	2003
62 (-8)	Priscillo Diniz	Bad Ragaz PGA Seniors Open	Bad Ragaz GC	2003
62 (-8)	Denis Durnian	Bad Ragaz PGA Seniors Open	Bad Ragaz GC	2004
62 (-8)	Jerry Bruner	Bad Ragaz PGA Seniors Open	Bad Ragaz GC	2005
62 (-8)	Loren Roberts	US Senior Open	Prairie Dunes CC	2006
62 (-7)	Terry Gale	GIN Monte Carlo Invitational	Monte Carlo GC	2002

Low first 18 holes

62 (-10)	Noel Ratcliffe	De Vere PGA Seniors Championship	De Vere Carden Park	2004
62 (-8)	Denis Durnian	Bad Ragaz PGA Seniors Open	Bad Ragaz GC	2004
62 (-8)	Jerry Bruner	Bad Ragaz PGA Seniors Open	Bad Ragaz GC	2005
62 (-7)	Terry Gale	GIN Monte Carlo Invitational	Monte Carlo GC	2002

Low first 18 to par

62 (-10)	Noel Ratcliffe	De Vere PGA Seniors Championship	De Vere Carden Park	2004
63 (-9)	Luis Carbonetti	Digicel Jamaica Classic in association with Sony Ericsson	Half Moon Resort	2004
63 (-9)	David J Russell	Jolie Ville Sharm El Sheikh Seniors Open	Jolie Ville Golf Hotel	2005
62 (-8)	Denis Durnian	Bad Ragaz PGA Seniors Open	Bad Ragaz GC	2004
62 (-8)	Jerry Bruner	Bad Ragaz PGA Seniors Open	Bad Ragaz GC	2005
64 (-8)	José Maria Roca	La Bresse Seniors	Le Bresse	1992
64 (-8)	Seiji Ebihara	Coca-Cola Kaiser Karl European Trophy	Haus Kambach GC	2000
64 (-8)	Priscillo Diniz	The Royal Westmoreland Barbados Open	Royal Westmoreland GC	2001
64 (-8)	Bill Longmuir	Irvine Whitlock Jersey Seniors Classic	La Moye GC	2003
64 (-8)	Sam Torrance	Bendinat London Seniors Masters	The London Club	2005
64 (-8)	John Chillas	PGA Seniors Championship	The Stoke by Nayland GC	2006

Low first 36 holes

128 (-12)	Horacio Carbonetti	Bad Ragaz PGA Seniors Open	Bad Ragaz GC	2003
129 (-15)	David J Russell	Jolie Ville Sharm El Sheikh Seniors Open	Jolie Ville Golf Hotel	2005
129 (-9)	Terry Gale	GIN Monte Carlo Invitational	Monte Carlo GC	2002
129 (-9)	Keith MacDonald	GIN Monte Carlo Invitational	Monte Carlo GC	2002
129 (-9)	David Good	Sanremo Masters	Sanremo GC	2004
129 (-9)	Guillermo Encina	Sanremo Masters	Sanremo GC	2004

Low first 36 holes to par

129 (-15)	David J Russell	Jolie Ville Sharm El Sheikh Seniors Open	Jolie Ville Golf Hotel	2005
131 (-13)	Priscillo Diniz	The Royal Westmoreland Barbados Open	Royal Westmoreland GC	2001
131 (-13)	Sam Torrance	Bendinat London Seniors Masters	The London Club	2005
131 (-13)	Sam Torrance	PGA Seniors Championship	The Stoke by Nayland GC	2006
131 (-13)	Gordon J Brand	Oki Castellón Open de España Senior	Club de Campo del Mediterraneo	2006
128 (-12)	Horacio Carbonetti	Bad Ragaz PGA Seniors Open	Bad Ragaz GC	2003
132 (-12)	Tommy Horton	Scottish Seniors Open	Newmachar GC	1997
132 (-12)	Bob Lendzion	Jolie Ville Sharm El Sheikh Seniors Open	Jolie Ville Golf Hotel	2005

European Challenge Tour 2006

www.europeantour.com

Final Order of Merit (top 20 earn card for PGA European Tour)

#	Name	Earnings		#	Name	Earnings
1	Mark Pilkington (WAL)	€119,152		51	Carlos del Moral (ESP)	27,343
2	Johan Axgren (SWE)	105,699		52	Francisco Cea (ESP)	26,463
3	Alexander Noren (SWE)	99,631		53	Jamie Little (ENG)	26,372
4	Martin Kaymer (GER)	93,321		54	Mickael Dieu (FRA)	26,091
5	James Hepworth (ENG)	84,236		55	Gareth Paddison (NZL)	26,042
6	Kyron Sullivan (WAL)	83,364		56	Rodolfo Gonzalez (ARG)	26,039
7	Rafael Echenique (ARG)	82,737		57	Stuart Manley (WAL)	25,676
8	Juan Parron (ESP)	71,089		58	Peter Kaensche (NOR)	25,598
9	Sam Walker (ENG)	69,853		59	Toni Karjalainen (FIN)	25,460
10	Marcus Higley (ENG)	67,851		60	Kariem Baraka (GER)	24,781
11	Shaun P Webster (ENG)	65,536		61	John Wade (AUS)	24,033
12	Gary Lockerbie (ENG)	64,073		62	Chris Doak (SCO)	23,521
13	Rafael Cabrera Bello (ESP)	62,849		63	Luis Claverie (ESP)	21,708
14	James Heath (ENG)	60,346		64	Ben Mason (ENG)	21,075
15	Gareth Davies (ENG)	60,189		65	Klas Eriksson (SWE)	20,892
16	Lee S James (ENG)	59,704		66	Alessio Bruschi (ITA)	20,404
17	Jean-Baptiste Gonnet (FRA)	59,343		67	Pedro Linhart (ESP)	19,680
18	Alvaro Quiros (ESP)	57,278		68	Julien van Hauwe (FRA)	19,581
19	Mads Vibe-Hastrup (DEN)	52,485		69	Niki Zitny (AUT)	19,325
20	Adrien Mörk (FRA)	52,136		70	Stuart Davis (ENG)	19,136
				71	Peter Whiteford (SCO)	18,652
21	Hernan Rey (ARG)	50,570		72	Julio Zapata (ARG)	18,401
22	Nicolas Vanhootegem (BEL)	48,983		73	Mikko Korhonen (FIN)	17,769
23	Anthony Snobeck (FRA)	48,066		74	Cédric Menut (FRA)	17,633
24	Martin Maritz (RSA)	47,841		75	Olivier David (FRA)	17,530
25	Antonio Maldonado (MEX)	45,971		76	Edward Rush (ENG)	16,895
26	Jean Hugo (RSA)	45,778		77	Magnus Persson (SWE)	16,889
27	Andrew McArthur (SCO)	45,732		78	Neil Cheetham (ENG)	16,806
28	Alvaro Salto (ESP)	44,929		79	Fredrik Andersson Hed (SWE)	16,751
29	Jan-Are Larsen (NOR)	44,021				
30	Jesus Maria Arruti (ESP)	43,988		80	Inder van Weerelt (NED)	16,577
31	Sebastian Fernandez (ARG)	43,658		81	Carlos de Corral (ESP)	16,400
32	Chris Gane (ENG)	43,422		82	Matthew King (ENG)	16,310
33	Oskar Bergman (SWE)	43,332		83	Miguel Rodriguez (ARG)	16,222
34	Tim Milford (ENG)	42,634		84	Jerome Theunis (BEL)	16,217
35	Ivó Giner (ESP)	42,367		85	Jorge Benedetti (COL)	15,865
36	Sion E Bebb (WAL)	39,496		86	Gustavo Acosta (ARG)	15,714
37	Felipe Aguilar (CHI)	39,441		87	Mikko Ilonen (FIN)	15,308
38	Denny Lucas (ENG)	37,666		88	Birgir Hafthorsson (ISL)	15,253
39	Anders Schmidt Hansen (DEN)	36,878		89	José Manuel Carriles (ESP)	15,052
40	Gareth Wright (WAL)	36,745		90	Thomas Norret (DEN)	14,764
41	David Drysdale (SCO)	35,966		91	Michael McGeady (IRL)	14,678
42	Rafael Gomez (ARG)	35,056		92	Michiel Bothma (RSA)	14,356
43	Johan Sköld (SWE)	33,567		93	Michael Lorenzo-Vera (FRA)	14,305
44	Gustavo Rojas (ARG)	33,309		94	Wilhelm Schauman (SWE)	14,289
45	Julien Foret (FRA)	32,622		95	Zane Scotland (ENG)	13,954
46	Miguel Carballo (ARG)	30,614		96	Ben Willman (ENG)	13,877
47	Alvaro Velasco (ESP)	29,067		97	Gabriel Canizares (ESP)	13,791
48	Kalle Brink (SWE)	29,061		98	Peter Jespersen (DEN)	13,493
49	Roope Kakko (FIN)	27,854		99	Alfredo Garcia-Heredia (ESP)	13,435
50	Magnus A Carlsson (SWE)	27,580		100	Van Phillips (ENG)	13,176

Results

48th Abierto Mexicano	GC de Hacienda, Mexico City	Antonio Maldonado (MEX)	275 (-9)
Abierto Visa de la Republica	Buenos Aires	Kevin Stadler (USA)	274 (-6)
Abierto Movistar Guatemala	Hacienda Nueva, Guatemala City	Miguel Carnballo (Arg)*	273 (-15)

Carnballo beat G Rojas (ARG) at the first extra hole

Kai Fieberg Costa Rica Open	Cariari, San José	Johan Axgren (SWE)*	277 (-7)

Axgren beat A Noren (SWE) at the third extra hole

Estoril Challenge	Penha Longa	Kyron Sullivan (WAL)	284 (-4)
Tusker Kenya Open	Karen GC, Nairobi	Johan Axgren (SWE)	270 (-10)
Peugeot Challenge	El Prat, Barcelona	David Drysdale (SCO)	278 (-10)
Tessali-Metaponto Open di Puglia e Basilicata	Riva del Tessali & Metaponto, Italy	Anthony Snobeck (FRA)*	272 (-14)

Snobeck beat Kyron Sullivan at the first extra hole

Parco di Monza Challenge	Milano GC, Monza	Alvaro Salto (ESP)	271 (-13)
Telenet Trophy	Limburg, Belgium	Toni Karjalainen (FIN)	274 (-14)
Riu Tikida Moroccan Classic	Golf du Soleil, Agadir, Morocco	Adrien Mörk (FRA)	265 (-19)
Morson International Pro-Am Challenge	Worsley, Greater Manchester, England	Alvaro Quiros (ESP)	267 (-13)
Thomas Bjørn Open	Horsens, Denmark	Marcus Higley (ENG)	277 (-11)
Lexus Open	Larvik, Norway	Kalle Brink (SWE)	275 (-13)
Aa St Omer Open	St Omer, Lumbres	Cesar Monasterio (ARG)	274 (-10)
Credit Suisse Challenge	Wylihof, Luterbach	Francisco Cea (ESP)	276 (-16)
Open Mahou de Madrid	La Herreria, Madrid	Juan Parron (ESP)	271 (-13)
Scottish Challenge	Murcar	Sam Walker (ENG)	266 (-18)
Texbond Open	Gardagolf, Brescia, Italy	Carlos Del Moral (ESP)*	270 (-18)

Del Moral beat LS James at the third extra hole

MAN NO Open	Adanstal, Ramsal, Austria	Rafael Cabrera Bello (ESP)	264 (-16)
Ryder Cup Wales Challenge	Nefyn, Wales	Sion Bebb (WAL)	274 (-10)
Irish Ryder Cup Challenge	Killarney, Ireland	John Wade (AUS)	261 (-19)
Vodafone Challenge	Elfrather Mühle, Krefeld, Germany	Martin Kaymer (GER)	270 (-18)
Rolex Trophy	Geneva, Switzerland	Alexander Noren (SWE)	266 (-22)
ECCO Tour Championship	Odense	James Heath (ENG)	261 (-19)
Telia Challenge Waxholm	Waxholm, Sweden	Rafael Echenique (ARG)	270 (-22)
Open des Volcans	Golf des Volcans, France	Martin Kaymer (GER)	271 (-13)
OKI Mahou Challenge de España	Centro National, Madrid	Adrien Mörk (FRA)	271 (-17)
Kazakhstan Open	Nurtau, Almaty	Mark Pilkington (WAL)	272 (-16)
Open International de Toulouse	Golf de Toulouse-Seilh	Julien Foret (FRA)	274 (-14)
Apulia San Domenico Grand Final	San Domenico GC	James Hepworth (ENG)	271 (-13)

2007

101 Campeonato Abierto Visa de la Republica[1]	Pilar GC, Buenos Aries, Argentina	Rafael Echinque (ARG)	277 (-7)
Abierto Mexicano Corona[1]	Club de Golf de la Hacienda, Mexico City, Mexico	Fabrizio Zanotti (PAR)	275 (-9)

[1]Joint venture with Tour de Las Americas

Month by month in 2006

Woods wins again at the Ford Championship before Luke Donald takes the Honda Classic and Greg Owen is poised to make it back-to-back British victories until he three-putts from three feet on the 71st and bogeys the last at Bay Hill. Seven years after his Open nightmare Jean Van de Velde finally wins, but only after a closing double bogey in Madeira. Later the same day Stephen Ames captures the Players Championship at Sawgrass.

US PGA Tour 2006

www.pgatour.com

Players are of US nationality unless stated

Final Ranking

The top 125 on the money list retained their cards for the 2007 season. The top 40 earned a spot at The Masters.

1	Tiger Woods	$9,941,563	44	Frank Lickliter II	1,655,678	87	Billy Andrade	1,057,927
2	Jim Furyk	7,213,316	45	John Senden	1,650,674	88	Brian Gay	1,037,600
3	Adam Scott	4,978,858	46	Shaun Micheel	1,632,842	89	DJ Trahan	1,035,242
4	Vijay Singh (FIJ)	4,602,416	47	Justin Rose (ENG)	1,629,288	90	Bubba Watson	1,019,264
5	Geoff Ogilvy (AUS)	4,354,969	48	Fred Funk	1,579,837	91	Charles Warren	1,018,841
6	Phil Mickelson	4,256,505	49	Sergio García (ESP)	1,560,733	92	Ryuji Imada (JPN)	1,018,140
7	Stuart Appleby (AUS)	3,470,457	50	Richard Johnson	1,555,376	93	Craig Barlow	1,006,538
8	Trevor Immelman		51	Ian Poulter (ENG)	1,553,906	94	Nick O'Hern (AUS)	995,235
	(RSA)	3,884,189	52	Charles Howell III	1,553,105	95	Daisuke Maruyama	956,874
9	Luke Donald (ENG)	3,177,408	53	Chris DiMarco	1,537,926		(JPN)	
10	Brett Wetterich	3,023,185	54	Daniel Chopra	1,530,455	96	David Howell (ENG)	912,437
11	David Toms	2,911,187	55	Aaron Baddeley	1,516,513	97	Paul Goydos	890,392
12	Rory Sabbatini (RSA)	2,861,751	56	Robert Allenby	1,503,581	98	Harrison Frazar	889,022
13	Joe Durant	2,811,139		(AUS)		99	Bill Haas	887,024
14	Chad Campbell	2,811,067	57	John Rollins	1,498,828	100	Will MacKenzie	879,965
15	Stewart Cink	2,755,911	58	Ben Crane	1,489,093	101	Kent Jones	860,766
16	Davis Love III	2,747,206	59	JB Holmes	1,487,604	102	Briny Baird	844,547
17	Rod Pampling	2,664,673	60	Jeff Maggert	1,430,376	103	Peter Lonard	837,017
18	Carl Pettersson	2,647,982	61	Steve Flesch	1,417,615	104	Kenny Perry	818,698
	(SWE)		62	Sean O'Hair	1,411,387	105	Joey Sindelar	802,507
19	Retief Goosen (RSA)	2,617,453	63	Jonathan Byrd	1,408,418	106	Brandt Jobe	802,432
20	Brett Quigley	2,617,419	64	Bo Van Pelt	1,389,927	107	Jeff Gove	793,477
21	Lucas Glover	2,587,982	65	Billy Mayfair	1,367,998	108	Fredrik Jacobson	788,764
22	Dean Wilson	2,509,857	66	Chris Couch	1,356,731		(SWE)	
23	Arron Oberholser	2,467,772	67	Bob Estes	1,340,244	109	Justin Leonard	781,756
24	Zach Johnson	2,452,250	68	Padraig Harrington	1,339,675	110	Fred Couples	780,361
25	Tom Pernice Jr	2,396,548		(IRL)		111	Kirk Triplett	766,593
26	Stephen Ames (CAN)	2,395,155	69	Greg Owen	1,316,685	112	Dudley Hart	762,736
27	KJ Choi (KOR)	2,376,548	70	Bart Bryant	1,316,131	113	Brian Davis	762,281
28	Ernie Els (RSA)	2,326,220	71	Jesper Parnevik	1,308,310	114	Olin Browne	754,061
29	JJ Henry	2,301,480		(SWE)		115	Kevin Sutherland	751,626
30	Ben Curtis	2,256,326	72	Corey Pavin	1,308,084	116	Stephen Leaney	746,747
31	José María Olazábal	2,120,422	73	Eric Axley	1,274,580	117	Pat Perez	719,507
	(ESP)		74	Jeff Sluman	1,252,025	118	Jason Gore	717,005
32	Tim Clark (RSA)	1,974,931	75	Nick Watney	1,243,816	119	David Branshaw	706,346
33	Mike Weir (CAN)	1,883,724	76	Ted Purdy	1,216,428	120	Mark Calcavecchia	705,315
34	Steve Stricker	1,811,811	77	Heath Slocum	1,180,681	121	Paul Azinger	702,090
35	Vaughn Taylor	1,783,945	78	Woody Austin	1,179,321	122	JP Hayes	701,433
36	Troy Matteson	1,778,597	79	Shigeki Maruyama	1,154,115	123	Shane Bertsch	697,059
37	Tim Herron	1,776,142		(JPN)		124	Mathias Gronberg	674,002
38	Camilo Villegas	1,742,112	80	Steve Lowery	1,124,950	125	Darren Clarke (NIR)	660,898
	(COL)		81	Ryan Moore	1,122,118			
39	Jerry Kelly	1,737,800	82	Charley Hoffman	1,115,193	126	Rich Beem	658,225
40	Scott Verplank	1,729,319	83	Hunter Mahan	1,107,457	127	Bubba Dickerson	650,314
41	Nathan Green	1,700,803	84	Ryan Palmer	1,092,853			
42	Tom Lehman	1,692,081	85	Mathew Goggin	1,076,142			
43	Jason Bohn	1,676,893	86	Joe Ogilvie	1,073,111			

Career Money List (at end of 2006 season)

1	Tiger Woods	$65,712,324	51	Rocco Mediate	12,203,971
2	Vijay Singh (FIJ)	49,379,841	52	Steve Elkington (RSA)	11,927,717
3	Phil Mickelson	39,514,038	53	Payne Stewart	11,737,008
4	Davis Love III	34,613,823	54	Billy Andrade	11,618,464
5	Jim Furyk	31,200,066	55	KJ Choi (KOR)	11,530,338
6	Ernie Els (RSA)	28,420,395	56	Rory Sabbatini (RSA)	11,506,946
7	David Toms	25,816,115	57	Duffy Waldorf	11,271,906
8	Justin Leonard	21,086,669	58	Stephen Ames (TRI)	11,201,944
9	Nick Price (RSA)	20,551,208	59	Tom Kite	11,041,042
10	Kenny Perry	20,335,031	60	José María Olazábal (ESP)	10,963,145
11	Fred Funk	19,429,189	61	Joey Sindelar	10,851,395
12	Mark Calcavecchia	19,303,087	62	Tom Pernice Jr	10,602,694
13	Fred Couples	19,129,114	63	Geoff Ogilvy (AUS)	10,483,323
14	Stuart Appleby (AUS)	18,906,470	64	Joe Durant	10,428,026
15	Mike Weir (CAN)	18,853,935	65	Jonathan Kaye	10,166,329
16	Tom Lehman	18,821,038	66	Frank Lickliter II	10,146,618
17	Chris DiMarco	18,709,850	67	Steve Stricker	10,042,503
18	Stewart Cink	18,593,548	68	Craig Stadler	10,003,337
19	Scott Hoch	18,487,114	69	Tom Watson	9,939,949
20	Scott Verplank	17,956,383	70	Dudley Hart	9,890,031
21	Jeff Sluman	17,841,673	71	Scott McCarron	9,600,092
22	Brad Faxon	17,571,909	72	Luke Donald (ENG)	9,178,310
23	Retief Goosen (RSA)	17,231,017	73	David Frost	9,155,221
24	David Duval	16,682,256	74	Kevin Sutherland	9,151,954
25	Sergio García (ESP)	15,819,592	75	Mark Brooks	8,868,883
26	Bob Estes	15,518,055	76	Bernhard Langer (GER)	8,811,068
27	Hal Sutton	15,267,685	77	John Daly	8,804,750
28	Loren Roberts	15,090,850	78	Carlos Franco (PAR)	8,761,085
29	Bob Tway	14,489,049	79	Andrew Magee	8,500,515
30	Jeff Maggert	14,455,224	80	Chris Riley	8,494,630
31	Jay Haas	14,440,317	81	Craig Parry	8,395,145
32	Jerry Kelly	14,417,685	82	Dan Forsman	8,333,355
33	Paul Azinger	14,230,551	83	Woody Austin	8,315,510
34	John Huston	14,094,975	84	Padraig Harrington (IRL)	8,315,040
35	Billy Mayfair	14,088,197	85	Olin Browne	8,026,941
36	Mark O'Meara	14,082,183	86	Steve Pate	8,018,208
37	Greg Norman (AUS)	13,963,611	87	Rod Pampling	7,875,566
38	Tim Herron	13,569,182	88	Peter Jacobsen	7,799,810
39	Robert Allenby (AUS)	13,455,147	89	Curtis Strange	7,599,951
40	Jesper Parnevik (SWE)	13,438,150	90	Robert Gamez	7,580,573
41	Kirk Triplett	13,215,254	91	Larry Mize	7,528,673
42	Corey Pavin	13,183,622	92	Skip Kendall	7,508,316
43	Lee Janzen	13,048,403	93	Glen Day	7,504,674
44	Adam Scott (AUS)	12,977,216	94	Brett Quigley	7,454,046
45	Steve Flesch	12,773,344	95	JL Lewis	7,407,520
46	Steve Lowery	12,616,606	96	Ben Crane	7,323,526
47	Chad Campbell	12,479,591	97	Tim Clark (RSA)	7,301,208
48	Charles Howell III	12,386,786	98	Harrison Frazar	7,236,634
49	John Cook	12,313,843	99	Ben Crenshaw	7,123,226
50	Shigeki Maruyama (JPN)	12,241,561	100	Brent Geiberger	7,117,032

Tour Statistics

Driving accuracy
(Percentage of fairways hit in regulation)

Pos	Name	Rds	%
1	Joe Durant	101	78.43
2	Fred Funk	106	78.01
3	Scott Verplank	88	75.23
4	Heath Slocum	96	74.67
5	Larry Mize	53	74.33
6	Omar Uresti	61	74.30
7	Steve Elkington (AUS)	52	73.91
8	Jim Furyk	89	73.85
9	Olin Browne	108	73.56
10	Paul Goydos	72	72.90

Driving distance (Average yards per drive)

Pos	Name	Rds	Yds
1	Bubba Watson	83	319.6
2	JB Holmes	81	318.8
3	Robert Garrigus	85	309.8
4	Brett Wetterich	82	307.8
5	John Daly	51	307.1
6	Tiger Woods	55	306.4
7	Ryan Hietala	61	305.9
8	Tag Ridings	103	305.3
9	Harrison Frazar	95	304.6
10	Charley Hoffman	100	304.4

Sand saves

Pos	Name	Rds	%	Pos	Name	Rds	%
1	Luke Donald (ENG)	66	63.64	6	Doug Barron	74	60.50
2	Dudley Hart	83	62.20	7	David Toms	76	59.43
3	Steve Stricker	64	62.03	8	Rod Pampling (AUS)	89	59.15
4	Chris Riley	86	61.90	9	Michael Allen	84	59.09
5	Brian Gay	107	61.59	10	Duffy Waldorf	96	58.90

Greens in regulation

Pos	Name	Rds	%
1	Tiger Woods	55	74.15
2	Jeff Gove	91	72.03
3	John Senden (AUS)	96	71.15
4	Jim Furyk	89	70.71
5	Briny Baird	81	70.20
6	Joe Durant	101	69.75
7	David Branshaw	98	69.67
8	Jonathan Byrd	66	69.61
	Steve Elkington (AUS)	52	69.61
10	Chris Smith	67	69.32

Putting averages (Average per hole)

Pos	Name	Rds	Avg
1	Daniel Chopra (SWE)	110	1.712
2	Vaughn Taylor	88	1.725
3	Brian Gay	107	1.727
4	David Howell (ENG)	52	1.730
5	Phil Mickelson	74	1.731
6	Steve Stricker	64	1.734
7	Ben Crane	85	1.736
8	Jim Furyk	89	1.742
9	Stuart Appleby (AUS)	83	1.743
10	Todd Fischer	101	1.744

Scoring averages

Pos	Name	Rds	Avg	Pos	Name	Rds	Avg
1	Tiger Woods	55	68.11	11	Arron Oberholser	82	69.86
2	Jim Furyk	89	68.86	12	Robert Allenby (AUS)	79	69.99
3	Adam Scott (AUS)	70	68.95	13	Brett Quigley	109	70.02
4	Luke Donald (ENG)	66	69.17	14	David Toms	76	70.09
5	Steve Stricker	64	69.37	15	José María Olazábal (ESP)	62	70.18
6	Phil Mickelson	74	69.50	16	Jonathan Byrd	66	70.19
7	Trevor Immelman (RSA)	86	69.51	17	KJ Choi (KOR)	93	70.21
8	Vijay Singh (FIJ)	103	69.62	17	Ian Poulter (ENG)	53	70.21
9	Stewart Cink	93	69.66	19	Stuart Appleby (AUS)	83	70.25
10	Ernie Els (RSA)	69	69.76	20	Lucas Glover	105	70.26

US PGA Tour top 20

MC Missed cut   — Did not play

Players are of US nationality unless stated otherwise

	Mercedes Championships	Sony Open	Bob Hope Chrysler Classic	Buick Invitational	FBR Open	AT&T Pebble Beach	Nissan Open	WGC–Accenture MatchPlay	Chrysler Classic of Tucson	Ford Championship	Honda Classic	Bay Hill Invitational	Player's Championship	BellSouth Classic	The Masters	Verizon Heritage	Shell Houston Open	Zurich Classic	Wachovia Cup
1 Tiger Woods	—	—	—	1*	—	—	WD	9	—	1	—	20	22	—	3	—	—	—	—
2 Jim Furyk	3	7	—	—	27	12	33	—	MC	—	20	3	—	22	2	—	—	—	1*
3 Adam Scott (AUS)	—	18	—	—	—	—	2	17	—	—	MC	53	—	27	—	—	—	—	3
4 Vijay Singh (FIJ)	2	6	—	—	20	7	—	9	—	15	—	7	8	—	8	—	36	—	38
5 Geoff Ogilvy (AUS)	13	—	—	MC	20	—	19	1	—	—	2	26	MC	—	16	11	—	—	10
6 Phil Mickelson	—	—	5	8	7	38	—	9	—	12	—	—	14	1	1	—	—	15	35
7 Trevor Immelman (RSA)	—	—	—	MC	20	—	7	—	41	64	MC	MC	—	—	—	MC	11	—	2
8 Stuart Appleby (AUS)	1*	7	—	24	—	—	51	33	—	—	54	MC	—	19	—	—	1	4	52
9 Luke Donald (ENG)	—	—	—	24	—	7	12	9	—	—	1	—	MC	10	42	—	—	—	WD
10 Brett Wetterich	—	—	—	MC	—	64	—	—	24	—	MC	—	—	42	—	—	6	4	MC
11 David Toms	13	1	—	—	19	—	—	2	—	—	3	—	MC	15	MC	—	MC	47	—
12 Rory Sabbatini (RSA)	—	2	10	16	20	2	1	33	—	—	—	—	MC	MC	36	—	—	—	52
13 Joe Durant	—	53	44	MC	—	—	73	—	—	MC	65	—	36	66	—	36	MC	4	38
14 Chad Campbell	—	2	1	28	70	—	36	5	—	35	—	17	70	—	3	36	—	—	MC
15 Stewart Cink	—	10	—	28	15	—	45	33	—	—	MC	MC	24	10	27	—	—	—	26
16 Davis Love III	—	—	MC	24	MC	33	—	2	—	12	55	—	MC	57	22	47	—	—	14
17 Rod Pampling	—	—	MC	10	49	—	45	33	—	—	1	MC	—	16	40	—	—	—	56
18 Carl Pettersson (SWE)	21	10	35	43	—	—	7	17	—	—	55	15	8	—	27	68	—	—	38
19 Retief Goosen (RSA)	—	—	—	—	—	—	5	—	15	—	48	2	4	3	—	—	—	25	10
20 Brett Quigley	—	MC	—	16	53	68	MC	—	—	26	MC	—	MC	MC	—	5	21	—	14

2006 performances at a glance

* Involved in play-off   WD Withdrew

EDS Byron Nelson	Bank of America Colonial	FedEx St Jude Classic	Memorial Tournament	Barclays Classic	US Open Championship	Booz Allen Classic	Buick Championship	Cialis Western Open	John Deere Classic	The Open Championship	BC Open	US Bank Championship	Buick Open	The International	PGA Championship	Reno-Tahoe Open	WGC-Bridgestone Inv.	Deutsche Bank	Canadian Open	84 Lumber Classic	Valero Texas Open	WGC-AmEx Championship	Southern Farm Bureau	Chrysler Classic of G/boro	Frys.com	FUNAI Classic	Chrysler Championship	Tour Championship
—	—	—	—	MC	—	2	—	1	—	—	1	—	1	—	1*	1	—	—	—	1	—	—	—	—	—	—	—	—
MC	17	—	18	—	2	—	—	4	—	4	—	—	2	—	29	—	3	—	1	—	—	4	—	—	16	—	—	2
3	—	—	4	2	21	—	—	21	—	8	—	—	—	—	3	—	10	50	68	—	—	—	2	—	—	—	MC	1
48	—	—	38	1	6	—	—	4	—	MC	—	—	11	—	MC	—	45	2	35	27	—	56	—	—	—	5	19	8
MC	—	—	31	18	1	—	—	—	—	16	—	—	60	—	9	—	36	—	—	—	—	—	—	—	—	—	—	19
—	—	—	4	18	2	—	—	65	—	22	—	—	—	MC	16	—	54	—	—	—	—	—	—	—	—	—	—	—
2	—	—	7	13	21	—	16	1	—	—	—	—	—	—	34	—	13	—	5	—	—	9	—	—	—	14	44	5
—	—	—	28	18	MC	—	—	12	—	MC	—	—	—	19	55	—	71	—	—	—	—	6	—	—	—	30	31	10
6	—	—	—	5	12	—	—	21	—	35	—	—	—	—	3	—	8	—	—	—	—	6	—	—	—	—	—	5
1	MC	—	2	MC	—	53	MC	58	—	MC	—	24	MC	—	MC	—	36	—	—	75	—	6	—	—	43	2	—	22
—	30	10	—	15	WD	—	MC	—	—	—	—	—	19	16	—	8	—	—	51	—	53	—	—	—	—	—	—	14
61	64	—	18	MC	MC	—	—	—	—	26	—	—	—	—	MC	—	36	—	5	20	—	41	—	—	—	—	62	22
—	MC	—	46	70	—	MC	68	58	—	—	—	62	3	—	—	46	—	—	MC	72	—	—	2	6	—	1	4	3
5	30	—	—	MC	MC	—	—	MC	—	65	—	—	—	—	24	—	50	—	—	MC	—	32	—	—	16	—	19	24
—	4	MC	12	—	37	—	5	4	—	MC	—	24	—	—	—	—	2	—	11	—	—	13	—	—	—	—	19	25
—	17	—	29	—	MC	—	—	42	—	MC	—	—	—	40	34	—	4	—	—	—	—	—	—	1	—	5	—	27
8	3	—	18	36	32	—	—	30	—	35	—	—	70	10	MC	—	45	—	—	—	—	38	—	—	—	—	6	14
21	MC	—	1	MC	MC	—	31	4	—	8	—	—	—	—	MC	—	27	MC	—	—	—	17	—	MC	—	MC	MC	18
—	—	—	62	29	MC	—	—	—	14	—	—	—	36	34	—	48	—	—	—	—	45	—	—	—	—	—	MC	4
26	4	10	57	3	MC	6	—	MC	—	MC	—	31	7	10	MC	—	—	MC	4	3	—	9	—	19	—	36	MC	12

US PGA Tour Top Earners 2006 (majors in bold type)

1   **TIGER WOODS** $9,941,563
Top Tens   1st Buick Invitational; Ford Championship at Doral; **The Open Championship**; Buick
Open; **USPGA Championship**; WGC – Bridgestone Invitational; Deutsche Bank
Championship; WGC – American Express Championship. 2nd Cialis Western Open. 3rd
The Masters. 9th WGC – Accenture Match Play Championship
Played 15: Wins 8; Top 5's 10; Top 10's 11; Missed cut 1; Withdrew 1

2   **JIM FURYK** $7,213,316
Top Tens   1st Wachovia Championship; Canadian Open. 2nd Verizon Heritage Classic; **US Open
Championship**; Buick Open; The Tour Championship. 3rd Mercedes Championship; The
Players' Championship; WGC – Bridgestone Invitational. 4th Cialis Western Open; **The
Open Championship**; WGC – American Express Championship. 7th Sony Open in Hawaii
Played 24: Wins 2; Top 5's 12; Top 10's 13; Missed cut 2

3   **ADAM SCOTT** (AUS) $4,978,858
Top Tens   1st The Tour Championship. 2nd Nissan Open; Barclays Classic; WGC – American Express
Championship. 3rd Wachovia Championship; EDS Byron Nelson Championship; **USPGA
Championship**. 4th Memorial Tournament. 8th **The Open Championship**. 10th
WGC – Bridgestone Invitational
Played 19: Wins 1; Top 5's 8; Top 10's 9; Missed cut 2

4   **VIJAY SINGH** (FIJ) $4,602,416
Top Tens   1st Barclays Classic. 2nd Mercedes Championship; Deutsche Bank Open. 4th Cialis Western
Open. 5th Funai Classic at Walt Disney World. 6th Sony Open in Hawaii; **US Open
Championship**. 7th AT&T Pebble Beach National Pro-am; Bay Hill Invitational. 8th The
Players' Championship; **The Masters**; The Tour Championship. 9th WGC – Accenture
Match Play Championship
Played 27: Wins 1; Top 5's 3; Top 10's 13; Missed cut 4

5   **GEOFF OGILVY** (AUS) $4,354,969
Top Tens   1st WGC–Accenture Match Play Championship; **US Open Championship**. 2nd The
Honda Classic. 9th **USPGA Championship**. 10th Wachovia Championship
Played 20: Wins 2; Top 5's 3; Top 10's 4; Missed cut 3

6   **PHIL MICKELSON** $4,256,505
Top Tens   1st BellSouth Classic; **The Masters**. 2nd **US Open Championship**. 4th Memorial
Tournament; Bob Hope Chrysler Classic. 7th FBR Open. 8th Buick Invitational;
WGC – Accenture Match Play Championship
Played 19: Wins 2; Top 5's 5; Top 10's 8; Missed cut 1

7   **TREVOR IMMELMAN** (RSA) $3,844,189
Top Tens   1st Cialis Western Open. 2nd Wachovia Championship; EDS Byron Nelson Championship.
5th Canadian Open; The Tour Championship. 7th Nissan Open; Memorial Tournament. 9th
WGC – American Express Championship.
Played 24: Wins 1; Top 5's 5; Top 10's 8; Missed cut 5

8   **STUART APPLEBY** (AUS) $3,470,475
Top Tens   1st Mercedes Championship; Shell Houston Open. 4th Zurich Classic of New Orleans. 6th
WGC – American Express Championship. 7th Sony Open in Hawaii. 10th The Tour
Championship
Played 23: Wins 2; Top 5's 3; Top 10's 6; Missed cut 3

9   **LUKE DONALD**[†] (ENG) $3,177,408
Top Tens   1st The Honda Classic. 3rd **USPGA Championship**. 5th Barclays Classic; The Tour
Championship. 6th EDS Byron Nelson Championship; WGC – American Express
Championship; AT&T Pebble Beach National Pro-am. 8th WGC – Bridgestone Invitational.
9th WGC – Accenture Match Play Championship. 10th BellSouth Classic
Played 18: Wins 1; Top 5's 4; Top 10's 10; Missed cut 2; Withdrew 1

10   **BRETT WETTERICH** $ 3,023,185
Top Tens   1st EDS Byron Nelson Championship. 2nd Memorial Tournament; Chrysler Championship.
4th Zurich Classic of New Orleans. 6th Shell Houston Open; WGC – American Express
Championship
Played 25: Wins 1; Top 5's 4; Top 10's 6; Missed cut 9

† Also played on the European Tour

Tour Results 2006 (in chronological order)

Players are of American nationality unless stated

Mercedes Championships Plantation Course, Lahaina. Maui, HI [7411–73]

1	Stuart Appleby (AUS)*	71-72-70-71—284	$1080000
2	Vijay Singh (FIJ)	70-74-74-66—284	630000
3	Jim Furyk	72-72-72-72—288	420000

Appleby won at first extra hole

Sony Open Waialae CC, Honolulu, HI [7060–70]

1	David Toms	66-69-61-65—261	$918000
2	Chad Campbell	67-67-62-70—266	448800
	Rory Sabbatini (RSA)	65-72-67-62—266	448800

Bob Hope Chrysler Classic The Classic Club, La Quinta [7305–72]

1	Chad Campbell	63-66-68-67-71—335	$900000
2	Jesper Parnevik (SWE)	69-69-71-62-67—338	440000
	Scott Verplank	68-68-65-64-73—338	440000

Buick Invitational Torrey Pines (South), San Diego, CA [7208–72]

1	Tiger Woods*	71-68-67-72—278	$918000
2	José-María Olazábal (ESP)	74-64-71-69—278	448800
	Nathan Green	67-70-69-72—278	448800

Woods won at second extra hole

FBR Open TPC Scottsdale, AZ [7216–71]

1	JB Holmes	68-64-65-66—263	$936000
2	JJ Henry	67-61-70-72—270	312000
	Steve Lowery	65-68-70-67—270	312000
	Ryan Palmer	68-66-64-72—270	312000
	Scott Verplank	69-66-67-68—270	312000
	Camilo Villegas (COL)	68-67-66-69—270	312000

AT&T Pebble Beach National Pro-Am Pebble Beach [6816–72]

1	Arron Oberholser	65-68-66-72—271	$972000
2	Rory Sabbatibi (RSA)	69-69-68-70—276	583200
3	Jonathan Byrd	69-65-74-69—277	313200
	Mike Weir (CAN)	63-67-69-78—277	313200

Nissan Open Riviera CC, Pacific Palisades, CA [7078–71]

1	Rory Sabbatini (RSA)	67-65-67-72—271	$918000
2	Adam Scott (AUS)	68-71-69-64—272	550800
3	Craig Barlow	67-69-67-70—273	346800

WGC – Accenture Match Play Championship
La Costa, Carlsbad, CA

Final: Geoff Ogilvy (AUS) beat Davis Love III 3 and 2

Full details of this event can be found on pages 178 and 179

Chrysler Classic of Tucson *Tucson, AZ*   [7109–72]

1	Kirk Triplett	68-71-64-63—266	$540000
2	Jerry Kelly	66-68-68-65—267	324000
3	Heath Slocum	67-69-65-68—269	156000
	Duffy Waldorf	66-66-65-72—269	156000
	Bubba Watson	67-67-65-70—269	156000

Ford Championship *Doral, Miami, FL*   [7266–72]

1	Tiger Woods	64-67-68-69—268	$990000
2	David Toms	66-66-70-67—269	484000
	Camilo Villegas (COL)	65-66-71-67—269	484000

Honda Classic *Mirasol, Palm Beach Gardens, FL*   [7157-72]

1	Luke Donald (ENG)	72-67-68-69—276	$990000
2	Geoff Ogilvy (AUS)	67-71-71-69—278	594000
3	Billy Mayfair	68-67-72-72—279	319000
	David Toms	67-67-76-69—279	319000

Bay Hill Invitational *Orlando, FL*   [7207–72]

1	Rod Pampling (AUS)	70-65-67-72—274	$990000
2	Greg Owen (ENG)	70-69-67-69—275	594000
3	Darren Clarke (NIR)	73-70-63-70—276	374000

The Players Championship *TPC, Sawgrass, Ponte Vedra Beach, FL*
[7093-72]

1	Stephen Ames (CAN)	71-66-70-67—274	$1440000
2	Retief Goosen (RSA)	69-71-71-69—280	864000
3	Jim Furyk	65-71-75-72—283	384000
	Pat Perez	71-72-69-71—283	384000
	Henrik Stensons (SWE)	69-71-70-73—283	384000
	Camilo Villegas (COL)	74-70-68-71—283	384000

BellSouth Classic *TPC Sugarloaf, Duluth, GA*   [7259–72]

1	Phil Mickelson	63-65-67-65—260	$954000
2	Zach Johnson	69-70-64-70—273	466400
	José-María Olazábal (ESP)	71-64-69-69—273	466400

THE MASTERS *Augusta National, GA* [7445–72]

1	Phil Mickelson	70-72-70-69—281	$1260000
2	Tim Clark (RSA)	70-72-72-69—283	758000
3	Chad Campbell	71-67-75-71—284	315700
	Fred Couples	71-70-72-71—284	315700
	Retief Goosen (RSA)	70-73-72-69—284	315700
	José-María Olazábal (ESP)	76-71-71-66—284	315700
	Tiger Woods	72-71-71-70—284	315700

Fuller details of this event are to be found in Part I The Majors page 61

Verizon Heritage *Harbour Town, Hilton Head Island, SC* [6973–71]

1	Aaron Baddeley (AUS)	66-67-66-70—269	$954000
2	Jim Furyk	64-67-68-71—270	572000
3	Billy Mayfair	65-69-68-69—271	307400
	Vaughn Taylor	63-70-72-66—271	307400

Shell Houston Open *Redstone, Humble, TX* [7457–72]

1	Stuart Appleby (AUS)	66-67-69-67—269	$990000
2	Bob Estes	71-69-66-69—275	594000
3	Steve Stricker	72-70-68-66—276	374000

Zurich Classic of New Orleans *TPC Avondale, New Orleans, LA*
[7082–72]

1	Chris Couch	70-70-64-65—269	$1080000
2	Fred Funk	70-69-69-62—270	528000
	Charles Howell III	70-69-66-65—270	528000

Wachovia Championship *Quail Hollow, Charlotte, NC* [7438–72]

1	Jim Furyk*	68-69-68-71—276	$1134000
2	Trevor Immelman (RSA)	68-72-66-70—276	680400
3	Adam Scott (AUS)	71-72-66-71—280	428400

*Furyk won at first extra hole

EDS Byron Nelson Championship *TPC Four Seasons, Irving, TX*
[7022–70]

1	Brett Wetterich	66-64-70-68—268	$1116000
2	Trevor Immelman (RSA)	68-67-64-70—269	669600
3	Adam Scott (AUS)	65-65-69-71—270	359600
	Omar Uresti	67-66-69-68—270	359600

Bank of America Colonial Championship
Colonial CC, Fort Worth, TX [7054–70]

1	Tim Herron*	67-65-68-68—268	$1080000
2	Richard Johnson (SWE)	68-65-68-67—268	648000
3	Rod Pampling (AUS)	67-63-70-70—270	408000

*Herron won at second extra hole

FedEx St Jude Classic *TPC Southwind, Memphis, TN*   [7244–70]

1	Jeff Maggert	72-66-68-65—271	$936000
2	Tom Pernice Jr	67-68-68-71—274	561600
3	John Cook	69-69-67-71—276	301600
	Kris Cox	74-67-63-72—276	301600

Memorial Tournament *Muirfield Village, Dublin, OH*   [7300–72]

1	Carl Pettersson (SWE)	69-67-69-71—276	$1035000
2	Zach Johnson	70-68-70-70—278	506000
	Brett Wetterich	69-69-73-67—278	506000

Barclays Classic *Westchester CC, Harrison, NY*   [6839–71]

1	Vijay Singh (FIJ)	70-64-72-68—274	$1035000
2	Adam Scott (AUS)	65-72-69-70—276	621000
3	Billy Andrade	66-70-69-72—277	333500
	Brett Quigley	71-66-70-70—277	333500

US OPEN Championship *Winged Foot, NY*   [7264–70]

1	Geoff Ogilvy (AUS)	71-70-72-72—285	$1225000
2	Jim Furyk	70-72-74-70—286	501249
	Phil Mickelson	70-73-69-74—286	501249
	Colin Montgomerie (SCO)	69-71-75-71—286	501249

Fuller details of this event are to be found in Part I The Majors page 51

Booz Allen Classic *TPC Avenal, Potomac, MD*   [7005–71]

1	Ben Curtis	62-65-67-70—264	$900000
2	Billy Andrade	69-68-68-64—269	330000
	Padraig Harrington (IRL)	70-65-68-66—269	330000
	Nick O'Hern (AUS)	74-64-64-67—269	330000
	Steve Stricker	68-67-66-68—269	330000

Buick Championship *TPC River Highlands, Cromwell, CT*   [6820–70]

1	J J Henry	68-68-63-67—266	$792000
2	Hunter Mahan	69-67-68-65—269	387200
	Ryan Moore	69-66-67-67—269	387200

Cialis Western Open *Cog Hill, Lemont, IL*   [7326–72]

1	Trevor Immelman (RSA)	69-66-69-67—271	$900000
2	Matthew Goggin (AUS)	69-69-66-69—273	440000
	Tiger Woods	72-67-66-68—273	440000

John Deere Classic *Deere Run, Silvis, IL*   [6762-71]

1	John Senden (AUS)	64-69-64-68—265	$720000
2	J P Hayes	64-71-66-65—266	432000
3	Alex Cejka (GER)	69-68-64-67—268	232000
	Heath Slocum	69-65-66-68—268	232000

135th OPEN CHAMPIONSHIP R Liverpool, Hoylake   [7258–72]

1	Tiger Woods	67-65-71-67—270	$1338480
2	Chris DiMarco	70-65-69-68—272	719370
3	Ernie Els (RSA)	68-65-71-71—275	511225

Fuller details of this event are to be found in Part 1 The Majors page 38

BC Open Atunyote, Vernon, NY   [7315–72]

1	John Rollins	67-70-68-64—269	$540000
2	Bob May	73-66-67-64—270	324000
3	Shigeki Maruyama (JPN)	68-71-67-65—271	204000

US Bank Championship Brown Deer Park, Milwaukee, WI   [6759–70]

1	Corey Pavin	61-64-68-67—260	$720000
2	Jerry Kelly	64-67-64-67—262	432000
3	Jeff Sluman	66-65-68-64—263	272000

Buick Open Warwick Hills, Grand Blanc, MI   [7127–72]

1	Tiger Woods	66-66-66-66—264	$864000
2	Jim Furyk	66-68-69-64—267	518400
3	Joe Durant	65-69-67-67—268	326400

The International Castle Pines, Castle Rock, CO   [7619–72]

Modified Stableford

1	Dean Wilson*	2-11-9-12—34 points	$990000
2	Tom Lehman	5-11-8-10—34	594000
3	Steve Flesch	8-5-13-6—32	319000
	Daisuke Maruyama (JPN)	2-10-7-13—32	319000

Wilson won at second extra hole

US PGA CHAMPIONSHIP Baltusrol, Springfield, NJ   [7561–72]

1	Tiger Woods	69-68-65-68—270	$1224000
2	Shaun Micheel	69-70-67-69—275	734400
3	Luke Donald (ENG)	68-68-66-74—276	353600
	Sergio García (ESP)	69-70-67-70—276	353600
	Adam Scott (AUS)	71-69-69-67—276	353600

Fuller details of this event are included in Part 1 The Majors page 69

WGC – Bridgestone Invitational Firestone CC, Akron, OH   [7283–70]

1	Tiger Woods*	67-64-71-68—270	$1300000
2	Stewart Cink	70-67-64-69—270	750000
3	Jim Furyk	69-65-69-68—271	450000

Woods won at fourth extra hole

Fuller details of this event are to be found on page 179

Reno-Tahoe Open *Montreux GCC, Reno, NV*   [7472–72]

1	Will MacKenzie	63-67-67-71—268	$540000
2	Bob Estes	64-65-68-72—269	324000
3	Joe Ogilvie	71-68-69-62—270	204000

Deutsche Bank US Championship *TPC Boston, Norton, MA* [7415–71]

1	Tiger Woods	66-72-67-63—268	$990000
2	Vijay Singh (FIJ)	70-71-61-68—270	594000
3	Brian Bateman	69-71-70-66—276	374000

Canadian Open *Hamilton GCC, BC*   [6946–70]

1	Jim Furyk	63-71-67-65—266	$900000
2	Bart Bryant	69-67-64-67—267	540000
3	Sean O'Hair	65-69-66-68—268	340000

84 Lumber Classic of Pennsylvania *Mystic Rock, Farmington, PA*
[7516-72]

1	Ben Curtis	66-69-69-70—274	$828000
2	Charles Howell III	67-69-68-72—276	496800
3	Brett Quigley	69-70-68-70—277	312800

Ryder Cup *K Club, Straffan, Ireland*
Result: Europe 18½. USA 9½.
Fuller details of this event can be found in International Team Events on page 186

Valero Texas Open *LaCantera, San Antonio, TX*   [6881-70]

1	Eric Axley	68-63-63-71—265	$720000
2	Anthony Kim	69-68-66-65—268	298666
	Justin Rose (ENG)	64-71-65-68—268	298666
	Dean Wilson	66-67-66-69—268	298666

WGC – American Express Championship
The Grove, Chandlers Cross, England   [7125–71]

1	Tiger Woods	63-64-67-67—261	$1300000
2	Ian Poulter (ENG)	64-71-68-66—269	610000
	Adam Scott (AUS)	67-68-65-69—269	610000

Fuller details can be found in World Championship Events on page 178

Southern Farm Bureau Classic *Annandale GC, Madison, MA* [7199–72]

1	D J Trahan*	65-68-71-71—275	$540000
2	Joe Durant	70-65-74-66—275	324000
3	Lee Janzen	70-69-67-70—276	204000

Trahan won at second extra hole

Chrysler Classic of Greensboro Forest Oaks, Greensboro, NC

[7311–72]

1	Davis Love III	69-69-68-66—272	$900000
2	Jason Bohn	69-69-70-66—274	540000
3	Eric Axley	68-69-71-67—275	290000
	Steve Flesch	69-69-69-68—275	290000

Frys.com TPC at Summerlin

[7243–72]

1	Troy Matteson	67-65-64-69—265	$720000
2	Daniel Chopra	69-67-64-66—266	352000
	Ben Crane	66-71-64-65—266	352000

FUNAI Classic at Walt Disney World
Magnolia and Palm Courses, Lake, Buena Vista, FL

[7516–72, 6957–72]

1	Joe Durant	69-65-64-65—263	$828000
2	Frank Lickliter II	68-70-67-62—267	404800
	Troy Matteson	67-65-65-70—267	404800

Chrysler Championship
Westin Innisbrook Golf Resort (Copperhead course), Tampa Bay, FL

[7295–72]

1	KJ Choi (KOR)	68-66-70-67—271	$954,000
2	Brett Wetterich	72-70-67-66—275	466,400
	Paul Goydos	68-68-69-70—275	466,400

Tour Championship East Lake GC, Atlanta, GA

[7154–70]

1	Adam Scott (AUS)	69-67-67-66—269	$1170000
2	Jim Furyk	69-71-67-65—272	715000
3	Joe Durant	68-68-70-67—273	461500

Merrill Lynch Shoot-out Tiburon GC, Naples, FL

[7288–72]

1	R Pampling (AUS) and J Kelly* (USA)	64-62-59—185	$337500 each
2	S Verplank and J Leonard (USA)	63-63-59—185	$215000 each
3	J Huston and K Perry (USA)	68-61-59—188	$104166 each
	T Immelman R Sabatini (RSA)	66-63-59—188	$104166 each
	C Campbell (USA) and N Price (ZIM)	67-63-58—188	$104166 each

* Won play-off at first extra hole

Wendy's 3-Tour Challenge Recreation Resort GC, Lake Las Vegas, Nevada

1	PGA Tour (Zach Johnson, Scott Verplank, Stewart Cink)	202
2	Champions Tour (Craig Stadler, Tom Kite, Jay Haas)	207
3	LPGA Tour (Juli Inkster, Natalie Gulbis, Cristie Kerr)	209

Del-Webb Fathers-Sons Challenge   *Champions Gate Golf Resort, Orlando, Florida*

1	Bernard and Stefan Langer (GER)	59-61—120
2	Bob and Kevin Tway (USA)	61-60—121
	Vijay and Qass Singh (FIJ)	60-61—121

Target World Challenge Challenge   *Sherwood Oaks, California*   [7097–72]

1	Tiger Woods	68-68-70-66—272	$1,350,000
2	Geoff Ogilvy (AUS)	68-70-67-71—276	840,000
3	Chris DiMarco	70-68-68-71—277	570,000

WGC World Cup   *The Sandy Lane Resort , Barbados*   [7069–71]

1	Germany (Bernhard Langer and Marcel Siem)	268	$1400000 shared
2	Scotland (Colin Montgomerie and Marc Warren)	268	700000
3	Sweden (Henrik Stenson and Carl Petterssen)	269	200,000

Fuller details can be found in World Championship Events, page 184

Luke Donald makes top ten in Europe and America

European Ryder Cup golfer Luke Donald made the top ten money-earners' list on both sides of the Atlantic in 2006. He would have been joined by Tiger Woods but the World No.1 did not play in enough European Tour events to be included on that money list.

Donald played 13 events on the European schedule and although he did not win he finished with nine top 10 placings. He ended the season in seventh place having won £1,658,059 in prize-money.

He did win on the US PGA Tour taking the Honda Classic and had ten top 10 finishes on that circuit completing the season in 9th spot with $3,177,408.

Four of the events in which he finished in the top ten were included on both the European and US Tour schedules. He finished third behind Tiger Woods in the USPGA Championship, and in three of the World Golf Championship events – in the Accenture Match Play Championship he came ninth, in the Bridgestone Invitational he finished eighth and in the American Express Championship he was sixth.

First time winners on the US PGA Tour

JB Holmes (USA)	FBR Open	TPC of Scotsdale
Aaron Oberholser (USA)	AT&T	Pebble Beach
Aaron Baddeley (AUS)	Verizon Heritage	Harbour Town
Chris Couch (USA)	Zurich Classic	English Turn
Brett Wetterich (USA)	EDS Byron Nelson	Cottonwood Valley
JJ Henry (USA)	Buick Classic	River Highlands
Trevor Immelman (RSA)	Cialis Western Open	Cog Hill
John Senden (AUS)	John Deere Classic	TPC Deere Run
Dean Wilson (USA)	The International	Castle Pines
Will MacKenzie (USA)	Reno-Tahoe Open	Montreux
Eric Axley	Valero Texas Open	
DJ Trahan	Southern Farm Bureau Classic	Madison
Troy Matteson	Frys.com Open	TPC Summerlin and The Canyons, Las Vegas

PGA's Doug Smith honoured

Doug Smith, a past chairman and captain of the PGA and a founder of modern PGA training, has been honoured with life membership reflecting his outstanding contribution to the game over a 50 year association with the PGA.

Doug will be best remembered for his chairmanship during the mid-1970s when he helped to steer the association through a period of upheaval during which the tournament division split from the PGA leading to the creation of the European Tour in 1974.

The PGA has gone on to produce highly qualified club professionals and coaches and Smith played a crucial part in PGA education and training.

"I'm proud to have worked with the four founding fathers of the training programme – Eddie Whitcombe, Eddie Mustey, Reg Cox and Sid Collins – and of developing that programme subsequently with Keith Hockey and others", said Smith.

The current list of PGA Life Members features Keith Hockey, Geoff Cotton, Tony Jacklin, Bernard Hunt, John Panton, Peter Alliss, John Stirling, John Jacobs, Derek Nash and Dave Thomas.

St Andrews degree for Charlie Sifford

The University of St Andrews gave an Honorary Degree in 2006 to Charlie Sifford, the father of African–American golf and the man whose career began the dismantling of racial barriers in the sport. Mr Sifford (84) travelled to the home of golf last June where Scotland's oldest University conferred upon him a Degree of Doctor of Laws.

Dr Brian Lang, Principal and Vice-Chancellor of the University of St Andrews, said: "Charlie Sifford is a pioneer of the Civil Rights era whose career exemplifies courage, determination and the will to succeed in the face of substantial prejudice and adversity. He changed the landscape of sport and his story is one which should challenge and inspire us all."

Sifford, whom Tiger Woods describes as his "honorary grandfather", challenged the PGA's Caucasian-only clause to become its first black member in 1960 at a time when the only blacks on tour were caddies. During his career he endured death threats, heard racial slurs shouted from the galleries, was refused entry to clubhouses and in the 1952 Phoenix Open found human faeces in the cup when he and partner Joe Louis got to the first green.

He won the Hartford Open in 1967 and two years later took the Los Angeles Open. He played 422 events on the PGA tour and made 399 cuts. Despite being the top black player on tour in the 60s, he was never invited to play in The Masters. In his autobiography *Just Let Me Play* he recalls meeting Jackie Robinson at the time Robinson was trying to break the colour barrier in major league baseball and Sifford was taking his first steps as a pro. "He asked me if I was a quitter," Sifford said. "I told him no. He said, 'If you're not a quitter, there's going to be a lot of obstacles you're going to have to go through to be successful in what you're trying to do.' I made up my mind I was going to do it. I just did it. Everything worked out perfect I think."

Golf went some way to repaying its debt to Charlie Sifford when he was inducted into the World Golf Hall of Fame in 2004, the first black player to be honoured.

Sifford travelled to Scotland with a group of young American golfers, courtesy of the Young Golfers of America Association which promotes education and reaches out to disadvantaged children, mostly minorities, through golf. The University of St Andrews has a history of honouring sports personalities, particularly golfers, whose lives have been inspirational to others. It has previously conferred Honorary Degrees on Gary Player, Seve Ballesteros, Colin Montgomerie, Peter Thomson, Nick Faldo, Jack Nicklaus and Peter Alliss.

US Champions Tour 2006

Final Ranking *Players are of American nationality unless stated*

1	Jay Haas	$2,420,227	26	Bruce Lietzke		724,874
2	Loren Roberts	2,365,395	27	Lonnie Nielsen		694,212
3	Brad Bryant	1,692,417	28	Peter Jacobsen		685,844
4	Tom Kite	1,643,348	29	John Harris		651,016
5	Gil Morgan	1,525,050	30	Mark McNulty (IRL)		646,459
6	Scott Simpson	1,340,676	31	Mark James (ENG)		593,100
7	Jim Thorpe	1,296,784	32	Jerry Pate		571,358
8	Tom Jenkins	1,287,666	33	Mark Johnson		562,962
9	Bobby Wadkins	1,193,173	34	Larry Nelson		519,931
10	David Edwards	1,191,086	35	Chip Beck		505,467
11	Allen Doyle	1,072,840	36	Wayne Levi		495,808
12	Andy Bean	1,020,678	37	Massy Kuramoto (JPN)		491,104
13	Bob Gilder	994,842	38	Bruce Summerhays		459,267
14	Tom Watson	961,741	39	Mike Reid		444,813
15	Craig Stadler	936,601	40	Bruce Fleisher		434,533
16	Don Pooley	924,614	41	Fuzzy Zoeller		423,918
17	Eduardo Romero (ARG)	909,229	42	David Eger		423,347
18	Morris Hatalsky	902,677	43	Danny Edwards		416,623
19	Keith Fergus	898,531	44	Dick Mast		408,900
20	Tom Purtzer	888,216	45	Joe Ozaki (JPN)		398,187
21	Dana Quigley	833,234	46	Tim Simpson		359,073
22	Hale Irwin	808,144	47	Tom McKnight		358,686
23	Des Smyth (IRL)	791,192	48	Fred Funk		344,122
24	DA Weibring	783,896	49	Ben Crenshaw		343,492
25	RW Eaks	751,923	50	Hajime Meshiai (JPN)		339,652

Career Money List

1	Hale Irwin	$29,350,736	26	Bob Charles (NZL)		9,556,184
2	Gil Morgan	22,467,636	27	JC Snead		9,526,788
3	Tom Kite	21,183,011	28	Jim Dent		9,453,272
4	Fred Funk	19,773,311	29	DA Weibring		9,248,277
5	Tom Watson	18,626,067	30	Wayne Levi		9,205,602
6	Scott Hoch	18,556,224	31	Graham Marsh (AUS)		9,115,307
7	Loren Roberts	18,416,126	32	Jack Nicklaus		9,108,352
8	Jay Haas	18,401,117	33	Jay Sigel		9,077,554
9	Larry Nelson	16,721,136	34	Tom Purtzer		9,026,551
10	Craig Stadler	15,713,000	35	Fuzzy Zoeller		8,989,316
11	Bruce Fleisher	14,959,206	36	Mike Hill		8,940,339
12	Raymond Floyd	14,637,668	37	Bob Murphy		8,799,264
13	Greg Norman (AUS)	14,188,469	38	Bruce Summerhays		8,618,435
14	Jim Thorpe	13,375,425	39	Ben Crenshaw		8,222,895
15	Lee Trevino	13,308,697	40	Curtis Strange		8,221,408
16	Dana Quigley	13,259,023	41	Scott Simpson		8,194,130
17	Jim Colbert	13,128,297	42	John Jacobs		8,164,044
18	Bruce Lietzke	12,984,028	43	Bobby Wadkins		8,040,778
19	Allen Doyle	12,374,770	44	Hubert Green		8,026,634
20	Dave Stockton	12,143,512	45	Vicente Fernandez (ARG)		7,965,942
21	Bob Gilder	11,178,877	46	Gary Player (RSA)		7,807,649
22	Tom Jenkins	11,094,426	47	Don Pooley		7,728,071
23	Doug Tewell	10,436,296	48	Mike McCullough		7,694,204
24	Isao Aoki (JPN)	10,197,639	49	Chi Chi Rodriguez (PUR)		7,679,140
25	Peter Jacobsen	10,167,627	50	Lanny Wadkins		7,608,600

Tour Statistics

Scoring average

Pos	Name	Rounds	Avg
1	Loren Roberts	67	69.01
2	Jay Haas	67	69.07
3	Tom Watson	45	69.67
4	Brad Bryant	63	69.71
5	David Edwards	64	69.94
6	Gil Morgan	85	69.99
7	Tom Kite	79	70.29
8	Tom Jenkins	82	70.38
9	Bob Gilder	86	70.42
10	Keith Fergus	74	70.50

Driving accuracy

Pos	Name	Rounds	%
1	David Edwards	64	83.79
2	John Bland	46	81.56
3	Doug Tewell	61	81.10
4	Allen Doyle	75	79.31
5	Graham Marsh (AUS)	64	78.26
6	Tom McKnight	78	78.07
7	Ed Dougherty	65	78.00
8	Jim Albus	63	77.75
9	Wayne Levi	75	77.50
10	Mark McNulty (IRL)	82	77.27

Driving distance

(Average yards per drive)

Pos	Name	Rounds	Yds
1	Dan Pohl	63	293.0
2	Tom Purtzer	73	291.2
3	RW Eaks	68	291.1
4	Hajime Meshiai (JPN)	46	288.8
5	Keith Fergus	74	287.4
6	Gil Morgan	85	284.8
7	Andy Bean	82	282.8
8	John Harris	78	280.4
9	Craig Stadler	70	279.8
10	Mark Johnson	78	279.5

Putting leaders

(Average putts per hole)

Pos	Name	Rounds	Avg
1	Loren Roberts	67	1.726
2	Jay Haas	67	1.741
3	Bob Gilder	86	1.743
4	Gil Morgan	85	1.748
5	Scott Simpson	85	1.758
6	Allen Doyle	75	1.759
7	Ben Crenshaw	46	1.760
8	Brad Bryant	63	1.761
9	Gary McCord	44	1.762
	Tom Watson	45	1.762

Sand saves

Pos	Name	Rounds	%
1	Jerry Pate	43	62.07
2	Morris Hatalsky	80	61.90
3	Tom Watson	45	61.36
4	Tim Simpson	50	60.00
5	Bob Gilder	86	54.39
6	Dana Quigley	82	53.85
7	Massy Kuramoto (JPN)	74	53.54
8	Scott Simpson	85	53.49
9	Vicente Fernandez (ARG)	71	53.09
10	Ben Crenshaw	46	52.60

Greens in regulation

Pos	Name	Rounds	%
1	Tom Watson	45	76.42
2	Loren Roberts	67	75.75
3	Brad Bryant	63	74.43
4	Jay Haas	67	74.16
5	David Edwards	64	73.89
6	Keith Fergus	74	73.27
7	Tom Jenkins	82	73.04
8	Danny Edwards	68	72.74
	Tom Kite	79	72.44
10	Hale Irwin	70	72.39

Haas is double winner in race to the wire with Roberts

Jay Haas won the money title on the US Champions Tour and the Charles Schwab Cup competition after a close battle with Loren Roberts all season. Haas finished the year ahead of his rival and the battle for the Schwab Cup was even closer coming down to the last putt on the final green of the last event. Had Roberts, the Tour's best putter often referred to as "King of the Moss" holed from four and a half feet he would have won the Cup but he missed by half an inch. Haas won the Gold Cup and the $1 million annuity that goes with it. Roberts took the second place prize of a $500,000 annuity. Both had matched each other's performances throughout the season. In majors Haas won the Senior PGA Championship and Roberts took the Senior British Open. In normal tournament play Roberts won three of the first four events – the Mastercard Championship at Hualalai, the Turtle Bay Championship and the Ace Group Classic – while Haas was winner of the Liberty Mutual Legends of Golf, the FedEx Kinko's Classic and the Administaff Small Business Classic.

Tour Results

MasterCard Championship	Hualalai, Ka'upulehu-Kona, HI	Loren Roberts	191 (-25)
Turtle Bay Championship	Kahuku, HI	Loren Roberts	204 (-12)
Wendy's Champions Skins Game	Wallea, Maui, HI	Raymond Floyd & Dana Quigley	10
The ACE Group Classic	Twin Eagles, Naples, FL	Loren Roberts	202 (-14)
Outback Steakhouse Pro-Am	TPC Tampa Bay, Lutz, FL	Jerry Pate	202 (-11)
AT&T Classic	Valencia, CA	Tom Kite	204 (-12)
Toshiba Senior Classic	Newport Beach, CA	Brad Bryant	204 (-9)
Puerta Vallarta Classic	Puerta Vallarta, Mexico	Morris Hatalsky	207 (-9)
Liberty Mutual Legends of Golf	Savannah Harbor, GA	Jay Haas	201 (-15)
FedEx Kinko's Classic	The Hills, Austin, TX	Jay Haas	205 (-11)
Regions Charity Classic	RT Jones Trail, Birmingham, AL	Brad Bryant	199 (-17)
Boeing Championship	Raven GC, Sandestin, FL	Bobby Wadkins	203 (-10)

Senior PGA Championship — Oak Tree GC, Edmund, OK

1	Jay Haas*	68-70-73-68—279
2	Brad Bryant	69-67-72-71—279
3	Gil Morgan	66-70-71-74—281

Haas won at third extra hole

Allianz Championship	Glen Oaks, West Des Moines, IA	Gil Morgan	197 (-16)
Bank of America Championship	Nashawtuc, Concord, MA	*Cancelled (weather)*	
Commerce Bank Championship	Eisenhower Park, East Meadow, NY	John Harris*	202 (-11)

Harris beat Tom Jenkins at first extra hole

Greater Kansas City Classic	Lions Gate, Overland Park, KS	Dana Quigley	198 (-18)

US Senior Open — Prairie Dunes, Hutchison, KS

1	Allen Doyle	69-68-67-68—272 (-8)
2	Tom Watson	70-66-66-72—274
3	Peter Jacobsen	72-66-68-69—275
	Bruce Lietzke	69-70-70-66—275

Ford Senior Players Championship — TPC Dearborn, MI

1	Bobby Wadkins	69-72-65-68—274
2	Jim Thorpe	67-70-69-69—275
3	Jay Haas	68-70-70-68—276
	Gil Morgan	70-66-71-69—276
	Des Smyth (IRL)	71-67-68-70—276
	Loren Roberts	71-67-64-74—276

Senior British Open — Turnberry

1	Loren Roberts (USA)*	65-65-69-75—274 (-6)
2	Eduardo Romero (ARG)	67-63-73-71—274
3	Dick Mast (USA)	71-67-70-67—275

Roberts won at first extra hole

3M Chp	TPC Twin Cities, Blaine, MN	David Edwards	204 (-12)
Boeing Greater Seattle Classic	TPC Snoqualmie, WA	Tom Kite*	201 (-15)

Kite beat Keith Fergus at first extra hole

JELD-WEN Tradition	Reserve Vineyards, Aloha, OR	Eduardo Romero (ARG)	275 (-13)
Wal-Mart First Tee Open	Pebble Beach	Scott Simpson	204 (-12)
Georgia-Pacific Grand Champions	Hawks Ridge, Ball Ground, GA	Jay Sigel	134 (-10)
Constellation Energy Classic	Hayfields, Hunt Valley, MD	Bob Gilder	202 (-14)
Greater Hickory Classic	Rock Barn, Conover, NC	Andy Bean	201 (-15)
SAS Championship	Prestonwood CC, Cary, NC	Tom Jenkins	134 (-10)
Administaff Small Business Classic	Augusta Pines, Spring, TX	Jay Haas	128 (-16)

(Thirty-six holes only. Rain cause cancellation of final round)

AT&T Championship	Oak Hills, San Antonio, TX	Fred Funk	201 (-12)
Schwab Cup Championship	Sonoma GC, Sonoma, CA	Jim Thorpe	271 (-17)

US Nationwide Tour 2006

www.pgatour.com

Players are of American nationality unless stated

Final Ranking (Top 20 earned US Tour Card)

Pos	Name	Events	Prize $	Pos	Name	Events	Prize $
1	Ken Duke	27	$382,443	51	Chris Baryla	18	120,229
2	Johnson Wagner	28	372,069	52	Aron Price	11	117,858
3	Cliff Kresge	26	339,763	53	Kyle Thompson	26	117,046
4	Craig Bowden	28	334,671	54	Kevin Johnson	25	116,823
5	Tripp Isenhour	26	321,996	55	Roland Thatcher	29	116,641
6	Jeff Quinney	27	317,802	56	Scott Dunlap	26	112,559
7	Boo Weekley	24	312,843	57	David Hearn	26	111,163
8	Jason Dufner	24	310,666	58	Gary Christian	24	110,875
9	Brandt Snedeker	26	300,918	59	Richard Johnson (SWE)	21	107,833
10	Matt Kuchar	21	300,867	60	Michael Long (NZL)	29	107,355
11	Craig Kanada	27	297,744	61	Scott Gardiner (AUS)	20	105,011
12	Kevin Stadler	15	294,657	62	Cameron Beckman	8	102,977
13	Andrew Buckle (AUS)	18	277,976	63	Chez Reavie	22	93,713
14	Jim Rutledge (CAN)	25	257,979	64	Jason Caron	22	92,922
15	Doug LaBelle II	28	240,174	65	Kevin Na	1	90,000
16	Gavin Coles (AUS)	23	239,141	66	Deane Pappas (RSA)	24	87,414
17	Michael Putnam	26	230,049	67	Fran Quinn	28	86,336
18	Jarrod Lyle (AUS)	21	227,909	68	Matt Hendrix	28	86,164
19	Michael Sim	17	220,432	69	Matt Weibring	28	84,560
20	Paul Sheehan (AUS)	9	216,407	70	Tom Scherrer	24	82,714
21	John Merrick	29	208,506	71	Brad Adamonis	28	81,599
22	Bryce Molder	24	205,413	72	Erik Compton	21	76,885
23	Ricky Barnes	26	199,276	73	Tim Wilkinson	25	75,676
24	Brenden Pappas (AUS)	25	193,745	74	Grant Waite (NZL)	17	72,839
25	Jess Daley	22	193,589	75	Mario Tiziani	25	72,292
26	Paul Gow	26	187,093	76	Kevin Gessino-Kraft	29	72,027
27	Craig Lile	24	186,840	77	Tom Johnson	26	71,947
28	Chad Collins	26	180,167	78	John Mallinger	15	69,515
29	Parker McLachlin	28	176,882	79	Scott Petersen	27	68,663
30	Hunter Haas	29	175,189	80	Jim McGovern	22	67,767
31	Ryan Armour	27	174,267	81	Kim Felton (AUS)	23	65,170
32	Nick Flanagan (AUS)	24	169,812	82	Rick Price	28	65,107
33	Darron Stiles	15	167,457	83	Jamie Broce	19	64,587
34	Justin Bolli	26	163,981	84	Zoran Zorkic	27	64,217
35	Glen Day	19	156,055	85	Steve Wheatcroft	21	62,542
36	Tim O'Neal	26	150,205	86	Steven Alker (AUS)	25	62,070
37	Brendon de Jonge	27	149,288	87	Tommy Tolles	25	61,838
38	Jason Allred	23	147,540	88	Scott Weatherly	30	60,267
39	Bradley Hughes (AUS)	24	137,408	89	Jeremy Anderson	23	59,591
40	Charlie Wi (KOR)	17	137,238	90	Joe Daley	28	59,086
41	Franklin Langham	26	136,246	91	Josh Broadaway	29	57,112
42	Stephen Marino	20	134,038	92	Andrew Pratt	18	56,615
43	Bob Heintz	29	127,432	93	Dan Olsen	27	56,333
44	Kyle Reifers	15	127,424	94	Brett Rumford	2	55,122
45	Paul Claxton	30	125,668	95	Glen Hnatiuk	20	54,675
46	Steve Allan (AUS)	25	125,203	96	Chris Stroud	9	53,919
47	Peter Tomasulo	29	124,293	97	Scott Parel	21	53,521
48	Jason Enloe	25	124,129	98	Joel Kribel	19	53,279
49	Matthew Jones	24	123,066	99	David Mathis	27	51,303
50	Chris Tidland	27	122,033	100	Jeff Klauk	23	50,553

Tour Results

Moviestar Panama Championship	Panama City	Tripp Isenhour	269 (-11)
Jacob's Creek Open	R Adelaide, S Australia	Paul Sheehan (AUS)	281 (-7)
NZ PGA Championship	Clearwater, Christchurch, NZ	Jim Rutledge (CAN)	279 (-9)
Chitimacha Louisiana Open	Broussard, LA	Johnson Wagner	272 (-12)
Livermore Valley Wine Country Championship	Livermore CA	Tripp Isenhour	279 (-9)
Athens Foundation Classic	Jenings Mill, Athens GA	Paul Gow	267 (-21)
BMW Charity Pro-Am	The Cliffs, Greenville, SC	Ken Duke	273 (-15)
Virginia Beach Open	Virginia Beach VA	Andrew Buckle (AUS)	268 (-20)
Rheem Classic	Hardscrabble, Fort Smith, AR	Darron Stiles*	267 (-13
*Stiles won at first extra hole			
Henrico County Open	Dominion Club, Richmond, VA	Matt Kuchar	279 (-9)
Rex Hospital Open	Wakefield Plantation, Raleigh NC	Brenden Pappas (RSA)	268 (-16)
LaSalle Bank Open	Glen Club, Glenview, IL	Jason Dufner	279 (-5)
Knoxville Open	Fox Den, Knoxville, TN	Hunter Haas	269 (-19)
Chattanooga Classic	Black Creek, Chattanooga, TN	Kyle Reifers*	262 (-26)
*Reifers beat Brandt Snedeker at first extra hole			
Peek'n Peak Classic	Peek'n Peak, Findley Lake, NY	John Merrick*	277 (-11)
*Merick beat Gavin Coles at third extra hole			
Scholarship America Showdown	Troy Burne, Hudson, WI	Brandt Snedeker*	272 (-16)
*Snedeker beat Jeff Quinney at second extra hole			
Price Cutter Charity Championship	Highland Springs, Springfield, MO	Doug LaBelle	261 (-17)
Preferred Health Systems Wichita Open	Crestview, Wichita, KS	Kevin Johnson	266 (-18)
Cox Classic	Champions Run, Omaha, NV	Johnson Wagner	263 (-21)
Xerox Classic	Jirondequiot, Rochester, NY	Kevin Stadler	271 (-9)
Northeast Pennsylvania Classic	Glenmaura, Scranton,, PA	Craig Bowden*	268 (-16)
*Bowden beat Jess Daley at first extra hole			
National Mining Association Pete Dye Classic	Bridgeport, WV	Jason Enloe*	274 (-14)
*Enloe beat Boo Weekley at first extra hole			
Legend Group Classic	Stone Water, Highland Heights, OH	Gavin Coles	274 (-10)
Utah Energy Solutions	Willow Creek, Sandy, UT	Craig Kanada	272 (-16)
Albertsons Boise Open	Hillcrest, Boise, ID	Kevin Stadler	264 (-20)
Oregon Classic	Shadow Hills, Junction City, OR	Cliff Kresge*	271 (-17)
*Kresge beat Ricky Barnes at third extra hole			
Mark Christopher Charity Classic	Empire Lakes, Rancho Cucamonga, CA	Kevin Na	268 (-16)
Permian Basin Charity Classic	Midland, TX	Brandt Snedeker*	272 (-16)
*Snedeker beat Aron Price at first extra hole			
Palmetto Pride Classic	Daniel Island Club, Charleston, SC	Michael Sim* (AUS)	276 (-12)
*Sim beat Ken Duke at first extra hole			
Miccosukee Championship	Miccosukee GC, Miami, FL	Bryce Molder	270 (-16)
Nationwide Tour Championship	The Houstonian	Craig Kanada	275 (-13)

US Nationwide Tour statistics leaders

Driving distance – Scott Hend (AUS) (9 rounds), 315 yards average.
Driving accuracy (fairways hit) – Jeff Hart, 79.21%
Greens in regulation – Boo Weekley, 74.31%
Putts per round – Parker McLachlin (77 rounds), 28.36 average
Sand saves – Jason Caron (64 rounds), 64.37%
Scrambling – Jarrod Lyle (AUS) (76 rounds), 65.93%
Scoring average– Boo Weekley, 69.59
Top Ten finishes – Ken Duke (9), Boo Weekley (9)

Japan PGA Tour

Players are of Japanese nationality unless stated

Results

2005

Okinawa Open	Naha, Okinawa	Tadahiro Takayama * 276 (-8)

Takayama beat Kiyoshi Miyazato at first extra hole

Final ranking 2005

1	Shingo Katayama	¥120,483,266	11	Hidemasa Hoshino	60,153,666
2	Yasuharu Imano	111,696,913	12	Ryoken Kawagishi	59,572,772
3	Keiichiro Fukabori	92,016,703	13	Tadahiro Takayama	58,011,360
4	S K Ho (KOR)	86,206,541	14	Shinichi Yokota	57,919,014
5	David Smail (NZL)	77,025,388	15	Kaname Yokoo	55,936,085
6	Daisuke Maruyama	74,160,817	16	Naomichi Joe Ozaki	54,909,332
7	Toru Taniguchi	64,907,775	17	Taichi Teshima	54,163,490
8	Dinesh Chand (FIJ)	63,409,935	18	Hiroyuki Fujita	53,042,900
9	Toshimitsu Izawa	62,832,150	19	Kazuhiko Hosokawa	52,887,044
10	Y E Yang (KOR)	61,752,125	20	Paul Sheehan (AUS)	51,740,935

2006

Token Homemate Cup	Token Shuga, Gifu	Wayne Perske (AUS)	267 (-21)
Tsuruya Open	Yamanohara, Hyogo	Brendan Jones (AUS)	273 (-11)
THE CROWNS	Nagoya, Aichi	Shingo Katayama	262 (-18)
JPGA Championship	Tanigumi, Gifu	Tomohiro Kondo*	278 (-10)
Kondo beat Katsuyashi Tomori at first extra hole			
Munsingwear Open KSB Cup	Tojigaoka Marine Hills, Okayama	Toshinori Muto	274 (-8)
Mitsubishi Diamond Cup	Sayama, Saitama	Kaname Yokoo	275 (-5)
JCB Classic Sendai	Omotezao Kokusai, Miyagi	Hideto Tanihara	266 (-18)
Mandom Lucido Yomiuri Open	Yomiuri, Hyogo	Nobuhiro Masuda	274 (-14)
Mizuno OPEN	Setonaikai, Okayama	S K Ho (KOR)	274 (-14)
Japan Golf Tour Championship	Shishido Hills, Ibaraki	Tatsuhiko Takahashi	273 (-7)
Woodone Open	Hiroshima	Tetsuji Hiratsuka	265 (-19)
Sega Sammy Cup	North Country CC, Hokkaido	Wei-Tze Yeh (TPE)	276 (-12)
Omaezaki Tournament	Hamaoka, Shizuoka	Toru Taniguchi*	273 (-11)
Taniguchi beat S K Ho and Tomohiro Kondo at third extra hole			
Sun-Chorella Classic	Otaru, Hokkaido	Hideto Tanihara	283 (-5)
KBC Augusta	Keya, Fukuoka	Taichi Teshima	268 (16)
FUJISANKEI CLASSIC	Fujizakura, Yamanashi	Shingo Katayama	274 (-10)
Suntory Open	Sobu, Chiba	Yang Yong-eun (KOR)	266 (-14)
ANA Open	Sapporo, Hokkaido	Tomohiro Kondo	274 (-10)
Acom International	Ishioka, Ibaraki	Mamo Osanai*	270 (-14)
Osani beat Taichi Teshima at first extra hole			
Coca-Cola Tokai Classic	Miyoshi, Aichi	Hidemasa Hoshimo	282 (-2)
Japan Open	Kasumigaseki, Saitama	Paul Sheehan (Aus)	277 (-7)
Bridgestone Open	Sodegaura CC, Chiba	Taichi Teshima	266 (-22)
Japan ABC Championship	ABC GC	Shingo Katayama*	271 (-17)
Katayama beat Yang Yong-eun (KOR) at second extra hole			
Asahiryokuken Yomiuri Memorial	Asoiizuka, Fukuoka	Tatsuhiko Ichihara	277 (-18)
Mitsui Sumitomo VISA Taiheiyo Masters	Taiheiyo Club Gotemba Course, Shizuoka	Tommy Nakajima	275 (-13)

Dunlop Phoenix Open	Phoenix GC, Miyazato	Padraig Harrington* (IRL) 271 (-17)

*Harrington beat Tiger Woods at second extra hole

Casio World Open	Kochi Kuroshio CC, Kochi	Jeev Milkha Singh (IND) 272 (-16)
Golf Nippon Series JT Cup	Tokyo Yomiuri Country Club	Jeev Milkha Singh (IND) 269 (-11)

Final ranking 2006 (Japanese events only; does not include major or WGC event money)

1	Shingo Katayama	¥157,881,928	11	Paul Sheehan (AUS)	63,735,333
2	Jeev Milkha Singh (IND)	111,579,411	12	Kaname Yokoo	62,490,386
3	Toru Taniguchi	109,298,615	13	Nobuhiro Masuda	61,932,103
4	Taichi Teshima	96,488,270	14	Hiroyuki Fujita	59,463,650
5	Tetsuji Hiratsuka	90,566,642	15	Mamo Osanai	58,864,050
6	Hideto Tanihara	85,250,600	16	Katsumasa Miyamoto	58,294,663
7	Hidemasa Hoshino	85,236,370	17	Toshinori Muto	57,672,877
8	S K Ho (KOR)	81,254,966	18	Azuma Yano	57,197,766
9	Y E Yang (KOR)	75,710,084	19	David Smail (NZL)	53,442,964
10	Tomohiro Kondo	75,490,851	20	Keiichiro Fukabori	52,349,330

Singh sweeps top honours at Asian Tour's UBS Awards gala

UBS Order of Merit winner: Jeev Milkha Singh (IND)
Players' Player of the Year: Jeev Milkha Singh (IND)
UBS Special Achievement Awards: Jeev Milkha Singh (IND)
Rookie of the Year: Juvic Pagunsan (PHI)

First time winners on the Asian Tour

Johan Edfors (SWE)	TCL Classic, China
Tadahiro Takayama (JPN)	Asia Japan Okinawa Open
Chris Rogers (ENG)	Pakistan Open
Henrik Stenson (SWE)	Commercialbank Qatar Masters
Kevin Stadler (USA)	Johnnie Walker Classic, Australia
Gonzalo Fernandez-Castano (ESP)	BMW Asian Open
Suk Jong-ryul (KOR)	GS Caltex Maekyung Open
Prom Meesawatt (THA)	SK Telecom Open
Hendrik Buhrmann (RSA)	Aamby Valley Asian Masters
Kane Webber (AUS)	Macau Open
Anton Haig (RSA)	Pulai Springs Malaysian Masters
Yang Yong-eun (KOR)	Kolon-Hana Bank Korea Open
Lin Wen-tang (TPE)	Taiwan Open

Sparkling finish from Jeev Milkha Singh

Indian golfer Jeev Milkha Singh, who topped the Asian Order of Merit in 2006, came second in the Japanese money list and made the top 20 on the European money table, hit his best form late in the year to move into the top 50 in the world for the first time.

Although the 34-year-old won the Volvo China Open, a joint venture between the Asian and European Tours, in April he left the best to last winning the Volvo Masters at Valderrama in Spain and the Casio World and Golf Nippon Series JT Cup tournaments in Japan in the space of five weeks. His Volvo Masters win was the first by an Indian golfer in Europe and was helped by a classic 6-iron second shot to the dreaded par 5 17th hole at Valderrama on the final day – a shot worthy of a champion

Singh's top place finish on the Asia Tour and his top 50 spot in the world earned him entry to all four majors in 2007.

Asian Tour

Results

Asia Japan Okinawa Open	Naha, Okinawa	Tadahiro Takayama (JPN)*	276 (-8)
*Takayama beat Kiyoshi Miyazato at first extra hole			
The Royal Trophy	Amata Spring CC, Bangkok	Asia 7, Europe 9	
Pakistan Open	Karachi	Chris Rodgers* (ENG)	273 (-15)
*Chris Rodgers beat Ross Bain (SCO) at first extra hole			
The Commercial Bank Qatar Masters	Doha, Qatar	Henrik Stenson (SWE)	273 (-15)
Johnnie Walker Classic	The Vines, Perth	Kevin Stadler (USA)	268 (-20)
Maybank Malaysian Open	Kuala Lumpur	Charlie Wi (KOR)	197 (-19)
Enjoy Jacarta HSBC Indonesian Open	Emeralda GCC	Simon Dyson (ENG)	268 (-20)
OSIM Singapore Masters	Laguna	Mardan Mamat (SIN)	276 (-12)
TCL Classic	Yalong Bay, Sanya, Hainan Is, China	Johan Edfors (SWE)	263 (-25)
Volvo China Open	Honghua International, Beijing	Jeev Milkha Singh (IND)	278 (-10)
BMW Asian Open	Tomson, Shanghai Pudong	Gonzalo Fernandez-Castano* (ESP)	281 (-7)
*Fernandez-Castano beat H Stenson at the first extra hole			
GS Caltex Maekyung Open	Lakeside CC, Seoul, Korea	Suk Jong-ryul (KOR)	271 (-17)
SK Telecom Open	Il Dong Lakes, Seoul	Prom Meesawat (THA)	201 (-15)
Aamby Valley Masters	Sahara Lake City, Mumbai, India	Hendrik Buhrmann (RSA)	277 (-11)
Macau Open	Macau	Kane Webber (AUS)	275 (-9)
90th Philippine Open	Cagayan De Oro, Manila	Scott Strange (AUS)	280 (-8)
Bangkok Airways Open	Santiburi Samui CC, Koh Samui, Thailand	Chawalit Plaphol (THA)*	281 (-3)
*Plaphol beat Rick Gibson (CAN) at first extra hole			
Crowne Plaza Open	Tycoon GC, Beijing	Chinarat Phadungsil (THA)*	272 (-16)
*Chinarat Phadungsil beat Prom Meesawat and Lin Wen-tang at second extra hole			
Brunei Open	Bandar Seri Begawan, Brunei	Wang Ter-chang (TPE)*	268 (-16)
*Wang Ter-Chang beat David Gleeson (AUS) at second extra hole			
Pulai Springs Malaysian Masters	Pulai Springs, Johor Bahru, Malaysia	Anton Haig (RSA)	266 (-22)
Barclays Singapore Open	Sentosa, Singapore	Adam Scott (AUS)*	205 (-8)
*Scott beat Ernie Els (RSA) in three-hole play-off – event reduced to 54 holes because of rain			
49th KOLON-Hana Bank Korean Open	Woo Jeong Hills, Korea	Yang Yong-eun (KOR)	270 (-14)
Mercuries Taiwan Masters	Taiwan G and CC, Taipei	Gaurau Ghei (IND)	278 (-10)
Taiwan Open	Sunrise G and CC, Taipei	Lin Wen-tang (TPE)	275 (-13)
Volkswagen Masters–China	Yalong Bay GC, Sanya, China	Retief Goosen (RSA)	267 (-21)
Hero Honda Indian Open,	Delhi GC	Jyoti Randhawa* (IND)	270 (-18)
*Randhawa beat V Kumar and SSP Chowrasia at second extra hole			
HSBC Champions Tournament	Sheshan GC, Shanghai	Yang Yong-eun (KOR)	274 (-14)
UBS Hong Kong Open	Hong Kong GC, Fanling	José Manuel Lara (ESP)	265 (-15)
Volvo Masters of Asia	Thai CC, Bangkok	Thongchai Jaidee (THA)	277 (-11)

Final 2006 Order of Merit

1 Jeev Milkha Singh (IND)	US$591,884	6 Jyoti Randhawa (IND)	301,728
2 Thongchai Jaidee (THA)	444,736	7 Juvic Pagunsan (PHI)	291,847
3 Prom Meesawat (THA)	392,671	8 Shiv Kapur (IND)	271,343
4 Charlie Wi (KOR)	369,880	9 Thaworn Wirichant (THA)	263,287
5 Andrew Buckle (AUS)	348.295	10 Brad Kennedy (AUS)	263,218

Von Nida Tour

www.pga.org.au

Results 2006   *Players are of Australian nationality unless stated*

National Bank Victorian PGA Championship	Sanctuary Lakes Resort	Steven Jeffress	272 (-16)
Victorian Open Championship	Woodlands Golf Club	David Diaz	202 (-14)
Bega Cheese NSW PGA Championship	Tura Beach & Pambula-Merimbula Golf Club	Paul Marantz	267 (-25)
Toyota Southern Classic	Woolooware Golf Club	Marc Leishman	190 (-20)
South Australian PGA Championship	Tanunda Pines Golf Club	David Diaz	279 (-9)
Western Australian PGA Championship	Western Australian Golf Club	Andrew Pitt	268 (-12)
North Queensland X-Ray Services Cairns Classic	Paradise Palms Golf Club	Marc Leishman	283 (-5)
Minniecon & Burke Queensland Masters	The Willows Golf Club	Cameron Percy*	272 (-16)
*Percy beat Marc Leishman at first extra hole			
Roadcon Queensland Open Championship	Ipswich Golf Club	Ricky Schmidt	274 (-14)
Greater Building Society Queensland PGA Championship	Emerald Lakes Golf Club	Cameron Percy	264 (-20)
Proton NSW Championship	Moore Park GC	Rick Kulacz* (am)	270 (-10)
*Kulacz beat Tony McFadyean at first extra hole			

Final Order of Merit (top ten earn cards for the Australasian Tour)

1	M Leishman	Aus$54,679	6	M Brennan	23,281
2	C Percy	45,612	7	D Alaban	22,921
3	D Diaz	35,809	8	A Townsend	22,782
4	T McFadyean	23,749	9	AJ Painter	20,855
5	R Schmidt	23,453	10	P Marantz	18,697

Omega China Tour

www.worldsportgroup.com

Players are of Chinese nationality unless stated

Hainan Leg	Kangle Garden Spa and GC	Liang Wenchong	273 (-15)
Zhuhai Leg	Golden Gulf Golf Club	Zhang Lianwei	296 (+8)
Shandong Leg	Tiger Beach Golf Club	Li Chao	291(+3)
Shanghai Leg	Grand Shanghai G and HR	Zhang Lianwei	282 (-6)
Kunming Leg	Kunming C and GC	Li Chao	277 (-11)
Omega Championship	Tianin GC, Beijing	Liang Wenchong	273 (-15)

Final Order of Merit

1	Zhang Lianwei	RMB540,000	6	Zheng Wengen	142,800
2	Li Chao	498,000	7	Jimmy Qi Zengfa	135,850
3	Liang Wenchong	300,000	8	Wu Weihuang	114,325
4	Huang Mingjie	244,450	9	Liao Guiming	110,350
5	Yuan Hao	175,000	10	Xiao Zhijin	95,050

Australasian Tour

www.pgatour.com.au

Players are of Australian nationality unless stated

Johnnie Walker Classic[2]	The Vines, Perth, WA	Kevin Stadler (USA)	268 (-20)
Jacobs Creek Open[1]	Royal Adelaide GC	Paul Sheehan*	281 (-7)
Sheehan beat Michael Sim at second extra hole			
ING New Zealand PGA Championship[1]	Clearwater Resort	Jim Rutledge (CAN)	279 (-9)
HSBC Champions Tournament	Sheshan International, Shanghai	Yang Yong-eun (KOR)	274 (-14)
MFS Australian Open	Royal Sydney GC	John Senden	280 (-8)
Mastercard Masters	Huntingdale	Justin Rose (ENG)	276 (-12)
Blue Chip New Zealand Open[3]	Gulf Harbour Country Club	Nathan Green	279 (-5)
Cadbury-Schweppes Australian PGA Championship	Hyatt Coolum Resort	Nick O'Hern*	266 (-11)
O'Hern beat P Lonard at fourth extra hole			

Final Order of Merit

1	Nick O'Hern	AU$583,820	6	Wade Ormsby		210,606
2	Kevin Stadler (USA)	523,098	7	Brett Rumford (USA)		204,828
3	Nathan Green	346,108	8	Robert Allenby		196,642
4	Richard Green	343,048	9	Jarrod Lyle		188,429
5	Paul Sheehan	215,964	10	Peter Lonard		183,150

Fixtures 2007 (early season)

Jacobs Creek Open[1]	Royal Adelaide GC	Paul Sheehan (D)
Johnnie Walker Classic[2]	The Vines, Perth, WA	Kevin Stadler (USA) (D)
Sheehan beat Michael Sim in the play-off		
HSBC New Zealand PGA Championship[1]	Clearwater Resort	Jim Rutledge (CAN) (D)

[1]Joint sanction with US PGA Tour
[2]Joint sanction with European Tour and Asian Tour
[3]Joint sanction with European Tour

Stellar year for Australians around the world

Australian golfers produced sterling performances around the world in 2006 without recording a win in Europe. They did well elsewhere scoring successes on the US, Asian and Japanese Tours.

Their 2006 roll of honour makes impressive reading and is testament to the Australian coaching techniques and the quality of the courses they play when back in their own country.

American Tour

Stuart Appleby	Mercedes Championship	Geoff Ogilvy	WGC – Accenture Match Play
	Shell Houston Open		US Open Championship
Rod Pampling	Bay Hill Invitational	Aaron Baddeley	Verizon Heritage
John Senden	John Deere Classic	Adam Scott	The Tour Championship

Asian Tour

Scott Strange	Philippine Open	Adam Scott	Barclays Singapore Open
Kane Webber	Macau Open		

Japanese Tour

Wayne Peske	Token Homemate Cup	Brendan Jones	Tsuruya Open
Paul Sheehan	Japan Open Championship		

South African Sunshine Tour
www.sunshinetour.com

Players are of South African nationality unless stated

2005–2006

Dimension Data Pro-Am	Gary Player CC/Lost City CC	Alan McLean (SCO)*	285 [-3]
after tie with Tyrone van Aswegen and Anton Haig			
Nashua Masters	Wild Coast Sun CC	Warren Abery	265 [-15]
Telkom PGA Championship	Country Club, Johannesburg	Gregory Bourdy (FRA)	267 [-21]
Vodacom Tour Championship	Pretoria CC	Charl Schwartzel	270 [-14]

Final Order of Merit 2005–2006

1	Charl Schwartzel	SAR 1207459	11	Doug McGuigan (SCO)	395635
2	Gregory Bourdy (FRA)	936394	12	Bradford Vaughan	333073
3	Louis Oosthuizen	842091	13	Titch Moore	323640
4	Thomas Aiken	779565	14	Ross Wellington	314181
5	Darren Fichardt	763324	15	Alan Michell	304971
6	Ulrich van den Berg	500454	16	Hennie Otto	280182
7	Warren Abery	458136	17	Mark Murless	275377
8	Keith Horne	454700	18	Michiel Bothma	273925
9	Bobby Lincoln	438784	19	Tyrone van Aswegen	272475
10	Jaco Van Zyl	400838	20	Desvonde Botes	259484

2006–2007

Stanbic Zambia Open	Nchanga GC, Chingola	Steve Basson	207 (-9)
Vodacom Western Cape	Arabella CE, Hermanus	Jean Hugo	208 (-8)
SA Airways Pro-am Invitational	Cape Town	Jean Hugo	200 (-16)
Samsung Royal Swazi Sun Open	Royal Swazi, Mbabane	Thomas Aiken	59 pts
Suncoast Classic	Durban CC	Alex Haindl	207 (-9)
SAAirways Pro-am Invitationa	Kempton Park, Johannesburg	Toongoona Charamba (ZIM)	199 (-17)
Vodacom Pretoria	Pretoria CC	Vaughn Groenewald	205 (-11)
Vodacom Kwazulu Natal	Selborne CC	Rossouw Loubser	205 (-8)
Vodacom Blomfontein	Blomfontein CC	Rossouw Loubser	205 (-11)
Telkom PGA Pro-am	Centurion CC, Pretoria	Doug McGuigan	205 (-11)
Eskom Power Cup	Wanderers GC Johannesburg	Trevor Fisher	202 (-11)
Vodacom Eastern Cape	Pezula	Kevin Stone	207 (-9)
Seekers Travel Pro-am	Dainfern CC Johannesburg	Desvonde Botes	196 (-20)
Vodacom Final	Fancourt	Darren Fichardt	212 (-4)
Bearingham Highveld Classic	Witbank GC	Darren Fichardt*	204 (-12)
Fitchardt beat Alex Haindl at the second extra hole			
MTC Namibia PGA Championship	Windhoek CC	Anton Haig	196 (-20)
Platinum Classic	Mooi Nooi GC Rustenburg	Vaughn Groenewald	202 (-14)
†HSBC Champions Tournament	Sheshan International GC, Shanghai	Yang Yong-eun (KOR)	274 (-14)
Limpopo Classic	Polokwane GC	Bradford Vaughan*	266 (-18)
Vaughan beat Warren Abery at first extra hole			

†Not included in Order of Merit

Nelson Mandela Invitational	Arabella GC, Hermanas	Bobby Lincoln and Retief Goosen*	128 (-16)

*Lincoln and Goosen beat John Bland and Alan Michell at second extra hole

Nedbank Challenge‡	Gary Player CC, Sun City	Jim Furyk (USA)	276 (-12)
dunhill championship	Leopard Creek	Alvaro Quiros (ESP)	275 (-13)
South African Airways Open	Humewood GC, Port Elizabeth	Ernie Els	264 (-24)
Johannesburg Classic	Royal Johannesburg GC and Kensington GC	new event	
Dimension Data Pro-am	Gary Player CC/ Lost City CC	Alan McLean (D)	
Nashua Masters	Wild Coast Sun Country Club	Warren Abery (D)	
Telcom PGA Championship	Country Club, Johannesburg	Gregory Bourdy (D)	
Vodacom Tour Championship	Pretoria CC, Pretoria	Charl Schwartzel (D)	

‡ Approved event but prize-money unofficial

Current Season 2006–2007 Top Ten

1	Ernie Els	SAR1,700,913	6	Lee Westwood (ENG)	866,313
2	Alvaro Quiros (ESP)	1,497,033	7	Hennie Otto	518,171
3	Charl Schwartzel	1,249,021	8	Bradford Vaughan	389,395
4	Trevor Immelman	1,087,222	9	Adilson da Silva (BRA)	357,398
5	Darren Fichardt	1,038,141	10	Louis Oosthuizen	347,479

Gary Player is Payne Stewart Award winner

South African Gary Player was the recipient of the 2006 Payne Stewart Award, named in honour of Stewart, an 11-times winner on the PGA Tour, including three major championships, who died in the week of The Tour Championship in 1999.

"Gary Player represents everything this award stands for", said PGA Tour Commissioner Tim Finchem. "The PGA Tour's core values of honesty, integrity, sportsmanship, respect for the game, growing the game, making a positive contribution to charity and helping each other achieve our highest potential, are all values that could certainly be used to describe Gary Player.

"As one of the most travelled athletes in all of sport, Gary's love of the game and thirst for life spread to everyone around him".

Player has won more than 163 titles worldwide and was a member of the inaugural class into the World Golf Hall of Fame in 1974. He won nine major championships and was the third player in the game's history to win the career Grand Slam.

While his accomplishments on the course are more than impressive, his accomplishments off the course are equally notable. Perhaps one of the most significant is the Gary Player Foundation which helped to build the Blair Atholl Schools in Johannesburg, South Africa, which have educational facilities for more than 500 students while also supporting other educational projects worldwide.

Canadian Tour 2006

www.cantour.com

Players are of Canadian nationality unless stated

Yes Golf BCR Classic	Barton Creek Resort, Austin, TX	Rob Oppenheim (USA)*	271 (-15)
Oppenheim beat Omar Uresti and Jim Rutledge at first extra hole			
Yes Golf BCR Challenge	Barton Creek Resort, Austin, TX	Brian Guetz (USA)*	279 (-9)
Guetz beat John Mallinger at first extra hole			
Northern California Classic	Brookside CC Stockton, CA	Matt Hansen (USA)*	269 (-19)
Hansen beat Jeff Quinney and John Mallinger at first extra hole			
Diablo Grande California Classic	The Legends West Course, Diablo Grande, Patterson, CA	Lee Williamson (USA)	272 (-16)
Corona Mazatlan Classic	El Cid Resort, Mazatlan, Mexico	Rob Oppenheim (USA)*	273(-15)
Oppenheim beat Stephen Gangluff at first extra hole			
Greater Vancouver Charity Classic	Hazlemere GC, South Surrey, BC	Lee Williamson (USA)	280 (-8)
Times Colonist Open	Royal Colwood GC, Victoria, BC	Mike Grob (USA)	269 (-11)
Telus Edmonton Open	Gendale G and CC, Edmonton, AB	Stephen Gangluff (USA)	272 (-16)
MTS Classic	Pine Ridge GC, Winnipeg, MB	Josh Habig (USA)	271 (-17)
Casino de Montreal Open Players Championship	Quatre Domaines GC, Montreal, QC	Wes Heffernan*	270 (-18)
Heffernan beat Brock Mackenzie at first extra hole			
Fallsview Casinio Resort Pro-Am Classic	Grand Niagara/Thundering Waters, Niagara Falls, ON	Stephen Gangluff (USA)	274 (-14)
Bell Canadian Open	Hamilton, Ancaster ON	Jim Furyk	266 [-14]
Canadian Tour Championship	Highlands GC, Horseshoe Resort, Barrie, ON	Stuart Anderson	273 (-11)

Final Order of Merit

1	Stephen Gangluff (USA)	$67,336	11	Stuart Anderson		28,685
2	Rob Oppenheim (USA)	62,973	12	Wil Collins (USA)		26,780
3	Wes Heffernan	55,633	13	Brendan Steele (USA)		25,699
4	Lee Williamson (USA)	46,551	14	John Mallinger (USA)		25,067
5	Darren Griff	42,470	15	Matt McQuillan		24,890
6	Brian Guetz (USA)	42,388	16	Steve Friesen (USA)		23,607
7	Brock Mackenzie (AUS)	38,197	17	Lee Curry		23,055
8	Josh Habig (USA)	33,353	18	Jason Hartwick (USA)		21,146
9	Mike Grob (USA)	31,188	19	Eugene Smith (USA)		21,086
10	Anthony Rodriguez (USA)	30,099	20	Brad Fritsch		20,834

Month by month in 2006

People wonder if Phil Mickelson has peaked too soon when he wins the BellSouth Classic by an incredible 13 strokes, but a week later he proves them wrong by claiming a second Masters title - and second successive major. Karrie Webb wins the first of the women's majors after a thrilling finish to the Kraft Nabisco. The US Tour returns to New Orleans eight months after the devastation caused by Hurricane Katrina.

Tour de las Americas
www.tourdelasamericas.com

Results

2005

47th Abierto Mexicano	GC de Hacienda, Mexico City	Antonio Maldonado (MEX)	275 (-9)
Abierto Visa de la Republica	Buenos Aires	Kevin Stadler (USA)	274 (-6)

2006

Abierto del Sur Personal	Mar del Plata	Luciano Giometti (ARG)	278 (-2)
Abierto Movistar Guatemala	Hacienda Nueva, Guatemala City	Miguel Carballo (ARG)*	273 (-15)
*Carballo beat G Rojas (ARG) at first extra hole			
Kai Fieberg Costa Rica Open	Cariari, San Jose	Johan Axgren (SWE)*	277 (-7)
*Axgren beat A Noren (SWE) at third extra hole			
Abierto Visa Del Centro de la Republica	Cordoba, Villa Allende, Argentina	Angel Cabrera (ARG)	275 (-9)
Copa Mitsubishi 3 Diamantes†	Barquisimeto, Venezuela	Otto Solis (VEN)	274 (-10)
TLA Players Championship	Acapulco, Mexico	Julio Zapata (ARG)	197 (-13)
Abierto de Venezuela	Valle Arriba, Caracas	Fabian Gomez (ARG)	265 (-15)
Abierto de Colombia	Campestre de Cali, Cali, Colombia	Manuel Merizalde (COL)	280 (-4)
Copa de Naciones	Tierra del Sol Aruba	Mexico (Toledo, Gonzalez)	276 (-8)
Torneo de Maestros Personal	Olivos, Buenos Aries	Andres Romero (ARG)	204 (-9)
Event reduced to 54 holes because of electrical storms			
Samsung Brazil Classic	San Fernando	Paulo Pinto (ARG)	274 (-10)
Abierto de San Luis	Villa Mercedes	Raphael Gomez (ARG)	195 (-18)
101 Campeonato Abierto Viusa de la Republica¹	Pilar GC, Buenos Arie	Rafael Echenique (ARG)	277 (-7)
Abierto Mexicano Corona¹	Club de Golf de la Hacienda, Mexico City	Fabrizio Zanotti (PAR)	275 (-9)

Fixtures 2007

Colombia Masters	Bogota GC		
Guatemala Open¹	Hacienda Nueva CC	Rafael Gomez (ARG)	D
Kei Feiberg Costa Rica Open¹	Cariari GC, San José	Johan Axgren (SWE)	D

†Not included in official money list
¹Joint venture with European Challenge Tour

Final Order of Merit 2005–2006

1	Fabrizio Zanotti (PAR)	US$68789	11	Mark Tullo (CHI)		22783
2	Rafael Echenique (ARG)	44747	12	Pablo de Grosso (ARG)		20537
3	Julio Zapata (ARG)	37883	13	Gustavo Acosta (ARG)		20122
4	Hernan Rey (ARG)	30419	14	Jesus Amaya (COL)		20005
5	Rafael Gomez (ARG)	29336	15	Miguel Guznman (ARG)		17400
6	Gustavo Rojas (ARG)	27321	16	Mauricio Molina (ARG)		16676
7	Rodolfo Gonzalez (ARG)	26237	17	Alejandro Villavicencio (GUA)		16116
8	Paulo Pinto (ARG)	24995	18	Augustin Jauretche (ARG)		15992
9	Fabian Gomez (ARG)	24708	19	Luciano Giometti (ARG)		15677
10	Carlos Cardera (ARG)	23732	20	Juan Abbate (ARG)		13728

World Championship Events

WGC – Accenture Match Play Championship
(formerly Anderson Consulting Match Play Championship)

2000   Darren Clarke (NIR) beat Tiger Woods (USA) 4 and 3 at La Costa, Carlsbad, CA, USA
2001   Steve Stricker (USA) beat Pierre Fulke (SWE) 4 and 3 at Metropolitan GC, Melbourne, Australia
2002   Kevin Sutherland (USA) beat Scott McCarron (USA) 1 hole at La Costa, Carlsbad, CA, USA
2003   Tiger Woods (USA) beat David Toms (USA) 2 and 1 at La Costa, Carlsbad, CA, USA
2004   Tiger Woods (USA) beat Davis Love III (USA) 3 and 2 at La Costa, Carlsbad, CA, USA
2005   David Toms (USA) beat Chris DiMarco (USA) 6 and 5 at La Costa, Carlsbad, CA, USA

2006 *at La Costa, Carlsbad, CA, USA*   [7247–72]

First Round
Tiger Woods (USA) beat Stephen Ames (TRI) 9 and 8
Robert Allenby (AUS) beat K J Choi (KOR) 3 and 2
Henrik Stenson (SWE) beat Paul Casey (ENG) 1 hole
Chad Campbell (USA) beat Tim Herron (USA) 4 and 2
David Toms (USA) beat Ian Poulter (ENG) at 19th
José-María Olazábal (ESP) beat Brandt Jobe (USA) 3 and 2
Adam Scott (AUS) beat Lucas Glover (USA) 2 and 1
Tom Lehman (USA) beat Stuart Appleby (AUS) 3 and 2

Bernhard Langer (GER) beat Ernie Els (RSA) 1 hole
Mike Weir (CAN) beat Stewart Cink (USA) 4 and 3
Geoff Ogilvy (AUS) beat Michael Campbell (NZL) at 19th
Nick O'Hern (AUS) beat Fred Funk (USA) 4 and 3
Phil Mickelson (USA) beat Charles Howell III (USA) 2 holes
John Daly (USA) beat Bart Bryant (USA) 4 and 2
David Howell (ENG) beat Steve Elkington (AUS) at 22nd
Scott Verplank (USA) beat Lee Westwood (ENG) at 26th

Vijay Singh (FIJ) beat Graeme McDowell (NIR) 5 and 4
Miguel Angel Jiménez (ESP) beat Rory Sabbatini (RSA) 2 and 1
Angel Cabrera (COL) beat Peter Lonard (AUS) 1 hole
Padraig Harrington (IRL) beat Rod Pampling (AUS) 4 and 2
Chris DiMarco (USA) beat Mark Calcavecchia (USA) 2 and 1
Arron Oberholser (USA) beat Tim Clark (RSA) at 21st
Carl Pettersson (SWE) beat Kenny Perry (USA) 1 hole
Davis Love III (USA) beat Mark Hensby (AUS) 2 and 1

Retief Goosen (RSA) beat Paul Broadhurst (ENG) 5 and 4
Ben Crane (USA) beat Justin Leonard (USA) 4 and 3
Luke Donald (ENG) beat Richard Green (AUS) 2 and 1
Shigeki Maruyama (JPN) beat Darren Clarke (NIR) 4 and 3
Zach Johnson (USA) beat Jim Furyk (USA) 1 hole
Sean O'Hair (USA) beat Fred Couples (USA) at 19th
Colin Montgomerie (SCO) beat Niclas Fasth (SWE) at 23rd
Shingo Katayama (JPN) beat Paul McGinley (IRL) 2 and 1

Second Round

Woods beat Allenby 1 hole
Campbell beat Stenson 1 hole
Toms beat Olazábal 2 and 1
Lehman beat Scott 1 hole
Weir beat Langer at 20th
Ogilvy beat O'Hern at 21st
Mickelson beat Daly 2 and 1
Howell beat Verplank 3 and 2
Singh beat Jiménez 2 and 1
Harrington beat Cabrera at 19th
DiMarco beat Oberholser 6 and 5
Love beat Pettersson 1 hole
Goosen beat Crane 2 and 1
Donald beat Maruyama 4 and 3
Johnson beat O'Hair 1 hole
Katayama beat Montgomerie 3 and 2

Third Round

Campbell beat Woods 1 hole
Lehman beat Toms 4 and 3
Ogilvy beat Weir at 21st
Howell beat Mickelson 3 and 1
Harrington beat Singh at 19th
Love beat DiMarco 3 and 2
Goosen beat Donald 1 hole
Johnson beat Katayama 4 and 3

Quarter-finals

Lehman beat Campbell at 21st
Ogilvy beat Howell at 19th
Love beat Harrington 1 hole
Johnson beat Goosen 3 and 2

Semi-finals

Ogilvy beat Lehman 4 and 3
Love beat Johnson 4 and 2

Final

Geoff Ogilvy (AUS) beat Davis Love III (USA)
3 and 2

Consolation Match

Zach Johnson beat Tom Lehman 1 hole

Winner	$1300000
Runner-up	750000
Third Place	560000
Fourth Place	450000
Quarter Finals	240000
Third Round	125000
Second Round	85000
First Round	35000

WGC – Bridgestone Invitational *Firestone CC, Akron, OH* [7283–70]

1999	T Woods (USA)	66-71-62-71—270	at Firestone CC, Akron, OH
2000	T Woods (USA)	64-61-67-67—259	at Firestone CC, Akron, OH
2001	T Woods (USA)	66-67-66-69—268	at Firestone CC, Akron, OH
2002	C Parry (AUS)	72-65-66-65—268	at Sahalee, Redmond, WA
2003	D Clarke (NIR)	65-70-66-67—268	at Firestone CC, Akron, OH
2004	S Cink (USA)	63-68-68-70—269	at Firestone CC, Akron, OH
2005	T Woods (USA)	66-70-67-71—274	at Firestone CC, Akron, OH

1	Tiger Woods (USA)*	67-64-71-68—270	$1300000
2	Stewart Cink (USA)	70-67-64-69—270	750000

Woods won at fourth extra hole

3	Jim Furyk (USA)	69-65-69-68—271	450000
4	Angel Cabrera (ARG)	70-68-70-65—273	246250
	Paul Casey (ENG)	69-69-64-71—273	246250
	Lucas Glover (USA)	66-69-69-69—273	246250
	Davis Love III (USA)	67-65-70-71—273	246250
8	Luke Donald (ENG)	67-69-70-68—274	152500
	David Toms (USA)	67-74-65-68—274	152500
10	J J Henry (USA)	70-68-68-69—275	120000
	Arron Oberholser (USA)	70-71-69-65—275	120000
	Adam Scott (AUS)	63-71-71-70—275	120000
13	Trevor Immelman (RSA)	69-70-68-70—277	95000
	Ian Poulter (ENG)	71-71-67-68—277	95000
	Kevin Stadler (USA)	68-67-70-72—277	95000
16	Ben Crane (USA)	73-67-70-68—278	85000
17	Michael Campbell (NZL)	67-71-70-71—279	81327
18	Stephen Ames (CAN)	69-70-71-70—280	77000
	Thomas Bjørn (DEN)	72-67-67-74—280	77000
	Robert Gamez (USA)	70-67-72-71—280	77000
	Vaughn Taylor (USA)	71-67-71-71—280	77000
22	Robert Allenby (AUS)	71-71-68-71—281	68000
	K J Choi (KOR)	75-70-67-69—281	68000
	Sergio García (ESP)	69-73-68-71—281	68000

WEC – Bridgestone Invitational   *continued*

22T	José-María Olazábal (ESP)	68-70-74-69—281	68000
	Mike Weir (CAN)	69-71-69-72—281	68000
27	Chris DiMarco (USA)	68-72-71-71—282	60500
	Padraig Harrington (IRL)	73-71-70-68—282	60500
	Kenny Perry (USA)	73-70-66-73—282	60500
	Carl Pettersson (SWE)	70-72-68-72—282	60500
31	Ernie Els (RSA)	68-67-70-78—283	56000
	Brad Faxon (USA)	69-69-75-70—283	56000
	Justin Leonard (USA)	70-69-72-72—283	56000
	Nick O'Hern (AUS)	72-69-71-71—283	56000
	Henrik Stenson (SWE)	75-73-67-68—283	56000
36	Jason Gore (USA)	65-76-73-70—284	50500
	Zach Johnson (USA)	71-68-72-73—284	50500
	Geoff Ogilvie (AUS)	69-76-70-69—284	50500
	Rory Sabbatini (RSA)	75-71-68-70—284	50500
	Charl Schwartzel (RSA)	72-69-70-73—284	50500
	Brett Wetterich (USA)	72-73-71-68—284	50500
42	Ben Curtis (USA)	71-72-72-70—285	46167
	Fred Funk (USA)	72-70-72-71—285	46167
	Tom Lehman (USA)	72-69-73-71—285	46167
45	Rod Pampling (AUS)	75-71-71-69—286	44500
	Vijay Singh (FIJ)	70-74-73-69—286	44500
	Dean Wilson (USA)	75-70-68-73—286	44500
48	Retief Goosen (RSA)	71-73-74-69—287	43250
	Corey Pavin (USA)	74-73-68-72—287	43250
50	Olin Browne (USA)	68-75-70-75—288	41750
	Chad Campbell (USA)	68-76-72-72—288	41750
	Stephen Dodd (WAL)	74-73-69-72—288	41750
	J B Holmes (USA)	71-72-68-77—288	41750
54	Aaron Baddeley (AUS)	73-74-69-73—289	39500
	Mark Hensby (AUS)	74-76-68-71—289	39500
	Miguel Angel Jiménez (ESP)	70-72-77-70—289	39500
	Thomas Levet (FRA)	77-69-69-74—289	39500
	Phil Mickelson (USA)	74-74-68-73—289	39500
59	David Howell (ENG)	67-79-71-74—291	37500
	Jeff Maggert (USA)	75-70-75-71—291	37500
	Scott Verplank (USA)	71-75-70-75—291	37500
62	Bart Bryant (USA)	72-83-69-68—292	36000
	Johan Edfors (SWE)	75-76-71-70—292	36000
	Robert Karlsson (SWE)	75-70-73-74—292	36000
65	Shiv Kapur (IND)	72-75-72-74—293	34712
66	John Bickerton (ENG)	74-75-70-75—294	33968
	Paul McGinley (IRL)	77-75-70-72—294	33968
68	Mark Calcavecchia (USA)	75-72-77-71—295	33000
	Chris Couch (USA)	72-74-72-77—295	33000
	Tim Herron (USA)	76-74-73-72—295	33000
71	Stuart Appleby (AUS)	76-75-76-69—296	31750
	Peter Lonard (USA)	74-73-77-72—296	31750
	Wes Short jr (USA)	76-71-73-76—296	31750
74	Tim Clark (RSA)	68-75-80-77—300	31250
75	Gonzalo Fernandez-Castaño (ESP)	74-76-81-70—301	30744
76	Tatsuhiko Takahashi (JPN)	81-73-75-75—304	30497
77	Fred Couples (USA)	73-71-71 WD	
	Lee Westwood (ENG)	79-67-74 WD	

WGC – American Express Championship The Grove, Chandlers Cross, Herts [7125–71]

1999	Tiger Woods* (USA)	71-69-70-68—278	at Valderrama GC, Cadiz, Spain

*Woods beat Miguel Angel Jiménez (ESP) at first extra hole

2000	Mike Weir (CAN)	68-75-65-69—277	at Valderrama GC, Cadiz, Spain
2001	Cancelled		
2002	Tiger Woods (USA)	65-65-67-66—263	at Mount Juliet, Kilkenny, Ireland
2003	Tiger Woods (USA)	67-66-69-72—274	at Capital City, Atlanta, GA
2004	Ernie Els (RSA)	69-64-68-69—270	at Mount Juliet, Kilkenny, Ireland
2005	Tiger Woods* (USA)	67-68-68-67—270	at Harding Park, San Francisco, CA

*Woods beat John Daly at second extra hole

1	Tiger Woods (USA)	63-64-67-67—261	$1300000
2	Ian Poulter (ENG)	64-71-68-66—269	610000
	Adam Scott (AUS)	67-68-65-69—269	610000
4	Jim Furyk (USA)	67-65-69-69—270	345000
5	Ernie Els (RSA)	65-70-69-67—271	290000
6	Stuart Appleby (AUS)	71-66-70-66—273	216666
	Luke Donald (ENG)	68-70-67-68—273	216666
	Brett Wetterich (USA)	70-66-69-68—273	216666
9	Trevor Immelman (RSA)	68-68-68-70—274	150000
	Thongchai Jaidee (THA)	71-67-71-65—274	150000
	Brett Quigley (USA)	70-64-67-73—274	150000
12	Arron Oberholser (USA)	69-72-66-68—275	120000
13	Stewart Cink (USA)	65-67-70-74—276	98375
	Lucas Glover (USA)	69-68-68-71—276	98375
	David Howell (ENG)	66-66-71-73—276	98375
	Henrik Stenson (SWE)	68-67-68-73—276	98375
17	Padraig Harrington (IRL)	64-69-71-73—277	85000
	José-María Olazábal (ESP)	70-67-71-69—277	85000
	Carl Pettersson (SWE)	69-70-67-71—277	85000
	Jyoti Randhawa (IND)	66-71-71-69—277	85000
21	Robert Karlsson (SWE)	67-76-72-64—279	80500
22	Michael Campbell (NZL)	69-71-69-71—280	75000
	Chris DiMarco (USA)	69-70-70-71—280	75000
	Johan Edfors (SWE)	70-68-71-71—280	75000
	Dean Wilson (USA)	71-70-70-69—280	75000
26	Robert Allenby (AUS)	69-73-69-70—281	66666
	Bart Bryant (USA)	70-74-67-70—281	66666
	Angel Cabrera (ARG)	71-70-67-73—281	66666
	Tim Clark (RSA)	68-70-73-70—281	66666
	Darren Clarke (NIR)	68-71-72-70—281	66666
	Nick O'Hern (AUS)	67-69-75-70—281	66666
32	Chad Campbell (USA)	67-70-73-72—282	61000
	K J Choi (KOR)	72-66-73-71—282	61000
	Sergio García (ESP)	69-73-71-69—282	61000
	Louis Oosthuizen (RSA)	71-70-72-69—282	61000
	Lee Westwood (ENG)	71-66-73-72—282	61000
37	J J Henry (USA)	70-70-70-73—283	58000
38	Simon Dyson (ENG)	67-69-75-73—284	56000
	Rodney Pampling (AUS)	70-69-72-73—284	56000
	Scott Verplank (USA)	70-68-73-73—284	56000
41	Thomas Bjørn (DEN)	70-71-73-71—285	52500
	Colin Montgomerie (SCO)	72-67-69-77—285	52500
	Rory Sabbatini (RSA)	73-67-73-72—285	52500
	Charl Schwartzel (RSA)	73-69-70-73—285	52500
45	John Bickerton (ENG)	72-73-75-67—287	49000
	Retief Goosen (RSA)	71-70-75-71—287	49000
	Zach Johnson (USA)	70-71-73-73—287	49000
48	Tim Herron (USA)	73-69-71-75—288	46500
	Tom Pernice jr (USA)	69-70-71-78—288	46500
50	Paul Broadhurst (ENG)	74-72-70-73—289	44000
	Tetsuji Hiratsuka (JPN)	73-69-71-76—289	44000
	Anthony Wall (ENG)	71-76-68-74—289	44000
53	David Toms (USA)	73-75-69-73—290	42500
54	Sean O'Hair (USA)	70-75-71-75—291	40500

WGC – American Express Championship *continued*

54T	Thaworn Wiratchant (THA)	71-71-75-74—291	40500
56	Paul Casey (ENG)	74-75-72-71—292	38500
	Vijay Singh (FIJ)	73-75-72-72—292	38500
58	Craig Parry (AUS)	74-74-70-75—293	37500
59	Gregory Bourdy (FRA)	74-77-71-75—297	35500
	Toru Taniguchi (JPN)	73-73-76-75—297	35500
61	Stephen Ames (CAN)	73 WD	
	Ben Crane (USA)	74 WD	
63	Tom Lehman (USA)	WD	

WGC – World Cup of Golf (formerly known as the Canada Cup)

Year	Winner	Runners-up	Venue	Score
1953	Argentina	Canada	Montreal	287
	(A Cerda and R de Vicenzo)	(S Leonard and B Kerr)		
	(Individual: A Cerda, Argentina, 140)			
1954	Australia	Argentina	Laval-Sur-Lac	556
	(P Thomson and K Nagle)	(A Cerda and R de Vicenzo)		
	(Individual: S Leonard, Canada, 275)			
1955	United States	Australia	Washington	560
	(C Harbert and E Furgol)	(P Thomson and K Nagle)		
	(Individual: E Furgol, USA, after a play-off with P Thomson and F van Donck, 279)			
1956	United States	South Africa	Wentworth	567
	(B Hogan and S Snead)	(A Locke and G Player)		
	(Individual: B Hogan, USA, 277)			
1957	Japan	United States	Tokyo	557
	(T Nakamura and K Ono)	(S Snead and J Demaret)		
	(Individual: T Nakamura, Japan, 274)			
1958	Ireland	Spain	Mexico City	579
	(H Bradshaw and C O'Connor)	(A Miguel and S Miguel)		
	(Individual: A Miguel, Spain, after a play-off with H Bradshaw, 286)			
1959	Australia	United States	Melbourne	563
	(P Thomson and K Nagle)	(S Snead and C Middlecoff)		
	(Individual: S Leonard, Canada, 275, after a tie with P Thomson, Australia)			
1960	United States	England	Portmarnock	565
	(S Snead and A Palmer)	(H Weetman and B Hunt)		
	(Individual: F van Donck, Belgium, 279)			
1961	United States	Australia	Puerto Rico	560
	(S Snead and J Demaret)	(P Thomson and K Nagle)		
	(Individual: S Snead, USA, 272)			
1962	United States	Argentina	Buenos Aires	557
	(S Snead and A Palmer)	(F de Luca and R De Vicenzo)		
	(Individual: R De Vicenzo, Argentina, 276)			
1963	United States	Spain	St Nom-La-Breteche	482
	(A Palmer and J Nicklaus)	(S Miguel and R Sota)		
	(Individual: J Nicklaus, USA, 237 – tournament reduced to 36 holes because of fog)			
1964	United States	Argentina	Maui, Hawaii	554
	(A Palmer and J Nicklaus)	(R De Vicenzo and L Ruiz)		
	(Individual: J Nicklaus, USA, 276)			
1965	South Africa	Spain	Madrid	571
	(G Player and H Henning)	(A Miguel and R Sota)		
	(Individual: G Player, South Africa, 281)			
1966	United States	South Africa	Tokyo	548
	(J Nicklaus and A Palmer)	(G Player and H Henning)		
	(Individual: G Knudson* Canada, 272 (*after a play-off with H Sugimoto, Japan)			
1967	United States	New Zealand	Mexico City	557
	(J Nicklaus and A Palmer)	(R Charles and W Godfrey)		
	(Individual: A Palmer, USA, 276)			
1968	Canada	United States	Olgiata, Rome	569
	(A Balding and G Knudson)	(J Boros and L Trevino)		
	(Individual: A Balding, Canada, 274)			
1969	United States	Japan	Singapore	552
	(O Moody and L Trevino)	(T Kono and H Yasuda)		
	(Individual: L Trevino, USA, 275)			
1970	Australia	Argentina	Buenos Aires	545
	(B Devlin and D Graham)	(R De Vicenzo and V Fernandez)		
	(Individual: R De Vicenzo, Argentina, 269)			
1971	United States	South Africa	Palm Beach, Florida	555
	(J Nicklaus and L Trevino)	(H Henning and G Player)		
	(Individual: J Nicklaus, USA, 271)			

Year	Winner	Runners-up	Venue	Score
1972	Taiwan	Japan	Melbourne	438
	(H Min-Nan and LL Huan)	(T Kono and T Murakami)		
	(Three rounds only – Individual: H Min-Nan, Taiwan, 217)			
1973	United States	South Africa	Marbella, Spain	558
	(J Nicklaus and J Miller)	(G Player and H Baiocchi)		
	(Individual: J Miller, USA, 277)			
1974	South Africa	Japan	Caracas	554
	(R Cole and D Hayes)	(I Aoki and M Ozaki)		
	(Individual: R Cole, South Africa, 271)			
1975	United States	Taiwan	Bangkok	554
	(J Miller and L Graham)	(H Min-Nan and KC Hsiung)		
	(Individual: J Miller, USA, 275)			
1976	Spain	United States	Palm Springs	574
	(S Ballesteros and M Pinero)	(J Pate and D Stockton)		
	(Individual: EP Acosta, Mexico, 282)			
1977	Spain	Philippines	Manilla, Philippines	591
	(S Ballesteros and A Garrido)	(R Lavares and B Arda)		
	(Individual: G Player, South Africa, 289)			
1978	United States	Australia	Hawaii	564
	(J Mahaffey and A North)	(G Norman and W Grady)		
	(Individual: J Mahaffey, USA, 281)			
1979	United States	Scotland	Glyfada, Greece	575
	(J Mahaffey and H Irwin)	(A Lyle and K Brown)		
	(Individual: H Irwin, USA, 285)			
1980	Canada	Scotland	Bogota	572
	(D Halldorson and J Nelford)	(A Lyle and S Martin)		
	(Individual: A Lyle, Scotland, 282)			
1981	Not played			
1982	Spain	United States	Acapulco	563
	(M Pinero and JM Canizares)	(B Gilder and B Clampett)		
	(Individual: M Pinero, Spain, 281)			
1983	United States	Canada	Pondok Inah, Jakarta	565
	(R Caldwell and J Cook)	(D Barr and J Anderson)		
	(Individual: D Barr, Canada, 276)			
1984	Spain	Scotland	Olgiata, Rome	414
	(JM Canizares and J Rivero)	(S Torrance and G Brand Jr)		
	(Played over 54 holes because of storms – Individual: JM Canizares, Spain, 205)			
1985	Canada	England	La Quinta, Calif.	559
	(D Halidorson and D Barr)	(H Clark and P Way)		
	(Individual: H Clark, England, 272)			
1986	Not played			
1987	Wales (won play-off)	Scotland	Kapalua, Hawaii	574
	(I Woosnam and D Llewelyn)	(S Torrance and A Lyle)		
	(Individual: I Woosnam, Wales, 274)			
1988	United States	Japan	Royal Melbourne,	560
	(B Crenshaw and M McCumber)	(T Ozaki and M Ozaki)	Australia	
	(Individual: B Crenshaw, USA, 275)			
1989	Australia	Spain	Las Brisas, Spain	278
	(P Fowler and W Grady)	(JM Olazábal and JM Canizares)		
	(Played over 36 holes because of storms – Individual: P Fowler)			
1990	Germany	T England (M James and R Boxall)	Grand Cypress Resort,	
	(B Langer and T Giedeon)	Ireland (R Rafferty and D Feherty)	Orlando, Florida	556
	(Individual: P Stewart, USA, 271)			
1991	Sweden	Wales	La Querce, Rome	563
	(A Forsbrand and P-U Johansson)	(I Woosnam and P Price)		
	(Individual: I Woosnam, Wales, 273)			
1992	USA	Sweden	La Moraleja II,	548
	(F Couples and D Love III)	(A Forsbrand and P-U Johansson)	Madrid, Spain	
	(Individual: B Ogle*, Australia, 270 (after a tie with Ian Woosnam, Wales)			
1993	USA	Zimbabwe	Lake Nona, Orlando, FL	556
	(F Couples and D Love III)	(N Price and M McNulty)		
	(Individual: B Langer, Germany, 272)			
1994	USA	Zimbabwe	Dorado Beach,	536
	(F Couples and D Love III)	(M McNulty and T Johnstone)	Puerto Rico	
	(Individual: F Couples, USA, 265)			
1995	USA	Australia	Mission Hills, Shenzhen,	543
	(F Couples and D Love III)	(B Ogle and R Allenby)	China	
	(Individual: D Love III, USA, 267)			
1996	South Africa	USA	Erinvale, Cape Town	547
	(E Els and W Westner)	(T Lehman and S Jones)	South Africa	
	(Individual: E Els, S. Africa, 272)			
1997	Ireland	Scotland	Kiawah Island, SC	545
	(P Harrington and P McGinley)	(C Montgomerie and R Russell)		
	(Individual: C Montgomerie, Scotland, 266)			

WGC – World Cup of Golf continued

Year	Winner	Runners-up	Venue	Score
1998	England	Italy	Gulf Harbour, Auckland	568
	(N Faldo and D Carter)	(C Rocca and M Florioli)	New Zealand	
	(Individual: Scott Verplank, USA, 279)			
1999	USA	Spain	The Mines Resort, KL	545
	(T Woods and M O'Meara)	(S Luna and MA Martin)	Malaysia	
	(Individual: Tiger Woods, USA, 263)			
2000	USA	Argentina	Buenos Aires GC	254
	(T Woods and D Duval)	(A Cabrera & E Romero)	Argentina	
2001	South Africa*	New Zealand	The Taiheiyo Club,	254
	(E Els and R Goosen)	(M Campbell and D Smail)	Japan	
		USA		
		(D Duval and T Woods)		
		Denmark		
		(T Bjørn and S Hansen)		
*South Africa won at second extra hole				
2002	Japan	USA	Puerto Vallarta, Mexico	252
	(S Maruyama and T Izawa)	(P Mickelson and D Toms)		
2003	South Africa	England	Kiawah Island, SC	275
	(T Immelman and R Sabbatini)	(J Rose and P Casey)		
2004	England	Spain	Real Club de Sevilla, Spain	257
	(L Donald and P Casey)	(MA Jiménez and S García)		
Reduced to 54 holes because of rain				
2005	Wales	Sweden	Vilamoura, Portugal	189
	(B Dredge and S Dodd)	(N Fasth and H Stenson)		
Reduced to 54 holes because of bad weather				

2006 The Sandy Lane Resort, Barbados   [7069–71]

				$ per team
1	Germany*	Bernhard Langer and Marcel Siem	65-69-66-68—268	1400000

Germany beat Scotland at first extra hole

2	Scotland	Colin Montgomerie and Marc Warren	67-67-65-69—268	700000
3	Sweden	Carl Petterssen and Henrik Stenson	64-70-63-72—269	400000
4	South Africa	Rory Sabbatini and Trevor Immelman	64-71-67-68—270	200000
5	Spain	Gonzalo Fernandez-Castano and Miguel Angel Jiménez	69-66-67-69—271	126666
	United States	Stewart Cink and JJ Henry	66-73-63-69—271	126666
	Argentina	Andres Romero and Angel Cabrera	64-67-67-73—271	126666
8	Australia	John Senden and Mark Hensby	68-72-64-69—273	77500
	Mexico	Octavio Gonzalez and Esteban Toledo	69-68-65-71—273	77500
	Wales	Stephen Dodd and Bradley Dredge	65-75-62-71—273	77500
	Italy	Emanuele Canonica and Francisco Molinari	68-70-64-71—273	77500
12	Ireland	Padraig Harrington and Paul McGinlay	67-73-66-69—275	57500
	Switzerland	Nicolas Sulzer and Martin Rominger	73-70-64-68—275	57500
14	Colombia	Camilo Villegas and Manuel Merizalde	67-74-66-70—277	50000
15	Canada	Mike Weir and Jim Rutledge	69-72-66-71—278	48500
	England	Luke Donald and David Howell	66-70-70-72—278	48500
17	Singapore	Mardan Mamat and Chih-Bing Lam	71-72-68-69—280	47000
18	Denmark	Thomas Bjørn and Soren Hansen	70-70-71-70—281	46000
19	South Korea	SK Ho and Charlie Wi	66-72-70-75—283	45000
20	France	Raphael Jacquelin and Jean Van De Velde	68-75-65-77—285	44000
21	Barbados	Roger Beale jr and James Johnson	69-76-71-72—288	42500
	Trinidad and Tobago	Stephen Ames and Robert Ames	70-73-67-78—288	42500
23	Japan	Hideto Tanihara and Testsuji Hiratsuka	67-74-74-74—289	41000
24	Jamaica	Peter Horrobin and Delroy Cambridge	72-76-67-80—295	40000

WGC – World Cup Qualifiers

Asian Competition qualifiers   Singapore and Italy
Latin American qualifiers   Mexico and Jamaica

For fuller results see Nations Cup in International Team Events, page 202

Other International Events

Hassan II Trophy   *Dar-es-Salaam, Rabat, Morocco*

1971	O Moody (USA)	1983	R Streck (USA)	1999	D Toms (USA)*
1972	R Cerrudo (USA)	1984	R Maltbie (USA)	2000	R Chapman (ENG)
1973	W Casper (USA)	1985	K Green (USA)	2001	J Haegmann (SWE)
1974	L Ziegler (USA)	1986–90	Not played	2002	S Luna (ESP)
1975	W Casper (USA)	1991	V Singh (FIJ)	2003	S Luna (ESP)
1976	S Balbuena (USA)	1992	P Stewart (USA)	2004	S Luna (ESP)
1977	L Trevino (USA)	1993	P Stewart (USA)	2005	E Compton (USA)
1978	P Townsend (ENG)	1994	M Gates (ENG)	2006	S Torrance (SCO)*
1979	M Brannan (USA)	1995	N Price (ZIM)	*Torrance beat Raphael Jacquelin (FRA)
1980	E Sneed (USA)	1996	I Garrido (ESP)	at first extra hole
1981	B Eastwood (USA)	1997	C Montgomerie (SCO)	
1982	F Connor (USA)	1998	S Luna (ESP)	

Nedbank Golf Challenge   *Sun City, Bophutatswana, South Africa*   [7597–72]

1982 (Jan)	J Miller (USA)	277	1992	D Frost (RSA)	276	2001	S García* (ESP)	268
1982 (Dec)	R Floyd* (USA)	280	1993	N Price (ZIM)	264	*García beat E Els (RSA) in play-off

*Floyd beat Craig Stadler (USA) in play-off

1983	S Ballesteros (ESP)	274	1994	N Faldo (ENG)	272	2002	E Els (ESP)	267
1984	S Ballesteros (ESP)	279	1995	C Pavin (USA)	276	2003	S García* (ESP)	274
1985	B Langer (GER)	278	1996	C Montgomerie* (SCO)	274	*García beat R Goosen (RSA) in play-off
1986	M McNulty (ZIM)	282	*Montgomerie beat E Els (RSA) in play-off	2004	R Goosen (RSA)	281
1987	I Woosnam (WAL)	274	1997	N Price (ZIM)	275	2005	J Furyk* (USA)	282
1988	F Allem (RSA)	278	1998	N Price* (ZIM)	273	*Furyk beat D Clarke (NIR), R Goosen
1989	D Frost (RSA)	276	*Price beat T Woods (USA) in play-off	(RSA) and A Scott (AUS) at second extra
1990	D Frost (RSA)	284	1999	E Els (RSA)	263	hole
1991	B Langer (GER)	272	2000	E Els* (RSA)	268	2006	J Furyk (USA)	276

*Els beat L Westwood (ENG) in play-off

Mauritius Open   *Belle Mare Plage, Mauritius*

1994	Michael McLean (ENG)	2000	Michael McLean (ENG)	2006	Van Philips (men)
1995	Marcello Santi (ITA)	2001	Sebastian Delagrange (FRA)		Lara Fairclough (women)
1996	Philip Golding (ENG)	2002	Mark Mouland (WAL)	(From 2006 men and women
1997	Gordon Sherry (SCO)	2003	Mark Mouland (WAL)	professionals were involved in
1998	Roger Davis (AUS)	2004	Miles Tunnicliffe (ENG)	separate competitions)
1999	Jonathan Lomas (ENG)	2005	Miles Tunnicliffe (ENG)	

Target World Challenge   *Sherwood Thousand Oaks, California*

1999	Tom Lehman (USA)	2002	Padraig Harrington (IRE)	2005	Luke Donald (ENG)
2000	Davis Love III (USA)	2003	Davis Love III (USA)	2006	Tiger Woods (USA)
2001	Tiger Woods (USA)	2004	Tiger Woods (USA)	

Nelson Mandela Invitational   *Arabella CC, Hermanas, South Africa*

2002	Hugh Baiocchi and Deane Pappas (RSA)	2006	Bobby Lincoln and Retief Goosen* (RSA)
2003	Lee Westwood (ENG) and Simon Hobday (RSA)		*Lincoln and Goosen beat John Bland and Alan Michell (RSA)
2004	Ernie Els and Vincent Tshabalala (RSA)		at second extra hole
2005	Tim Clark and Vincent Tshabalala (RSA)	

International Team Events

35th Ryder Cup   *K Club, Straffan, Ireland*   September 22–24

Non-playing captains: Ian Woosnam (Europe), Tom Lehman (USA)

Europe		USA	
First Day, Morning – Fourballs			
Harrington & Montgomerie	0	Woods & Furyk (1 hole)	1
Casey & Karlsson (halved)	½	Cink & Henry (halved)	½
García & Olazábal (3 and 2)	1	Toms & Wetterich	0
Clarke & Westwood (1 hole)	1	Mickelson & DiMarco	0
	2½		1½
Afternoon – Foursomes			
Harrington & McGinley (halved)	½	Campbell & Johnson (halved)	½
Howell & Stenson (halved)	½	Cink & Toms (halved)	½
Westwood & Montgomerie (halved)	½	Mickelson & DiMarco (halved)	½
Donald & García (2 holes)	1	Woods & Furyk	0
	2½		1½

First day match position: Europe 5, USA 3

Europe		USA	
Second Day, Morning – Fourballs			
Casey & Karlsson (halved)	½	Cink & Henry (halved)	½
García & Olazábal (3 and 2)	1	Mickelson & DiMarco	0
Clarke & Westwood (3 and 2)	1	Woods & Furyk	0
Stenson & Harrington	0	Verplank & Johnson (2 and 1)	1
	2½		1½
Afternoon – Foursomes			
García & Donald (2 and 1)	1	Mickelson & Toms	0
Montgomerie & Westwood (halved)	½	Campbell & Taylor (halved)	½
Casey & Howell (5 and 4)	1	Cink & Johnson	0
Harrington & McGinley	0	Woods & Furyk (3 and 2)	1
	2½		1½

Second day match position: Europe 10, USA 6

Europe		USA	
Third Day – Singles			
Colin Montgomerie (SCO) (1 hole)	1	David Toms	0
Sergio García (ESP)	0	Stewart Cink (4 and 3)	1
Paul Casey (ENG) (2 and 1)	1	Jim Furyk	0
Robert Karlsson (SWE)	0	Tiger Woods (3 and 2	1
Luke Donald (ENG) (2 and 1)	1	Chad Campbell	0
Paul McGinley (IRL) (halved)	½	JJ Henry (halved)	½
Darren Clarke (NIR) (3 and 2)	1	Zach Johnson	0
Henrik Stenson (SWE) (4 and 3)	1	Vaughn Taylor	0
David Howell (ENG) (5 and 4)	1	Brett Wetterich	0
José María Olazábal (ESP) (2 and 1)	1	Phil Mickelson	0
Lee Westwood (ENG) (2 holes)	1	Chris DiMarco	0
Padraig Harrington (IRL)	0	Scott Verplank (4 and 3)	1
	8½		3½

Result: Europe 18½, USA 9½,

Unoffical Ryder Cups

Great Britain v USA

1921 *King's Course, Gleneagles Hotel, Perthshire, Scotland* June 6
Result: GB 9 USA 3 (no half points were awarded)

Singles
George Duncan beat Jock Hutchison 2 and 1
Abe Mitchell halved with Walter Hagen
Ted Ray lost to Emmet French 2 and 1
JH Taylor lost to Fred McLeod 1 hole
Harry Vardon beat Tom Kerrigan 3 and 1
James Braid beat Charles Hoffner 5 and 4
AG Havers lost to WE Reid 2 and 1
J Ockenden beat G McLean 5 and 4
J Sherlock beat Clarence Hackney 3 and 2
Joshua Taylor beat Bill Melhorn 3&2

Foursomes
George Duncan & Abe Mitchell halved with Jock Hutchison & Walter Hagen
Ted Ray & Harry Vardon beat Emmet French & Tom Kerrigan 5 and 4
James Braid & JH Taylor halved with Charles Hoffner & Fred McLeod
AG Havers & J Ockenden beat WE Reid & G McLean 6 and 5
J Sherlock & Joshua Taylor beat Clarence Hackney & W Melhorn 1 hole

Three matches were halved

1926 *West Course, Wentworth GC, Surrey, England* June 4–5
Result: GB 13½, USA 1½

Singles
Abe Mitchell beat Jim Barnes 8 and 7
George Duncan beat Walter Hagen 6 and 5
Aubrey Boomer beat Tommy Armour 2 and 1
Archie Compston lost to Bill Mehlhorn 1 hole
George Gadd beat Joe Kirkwood 8 and 7
Ted Ray beat Al Watrous 6 and 5
Fred Robson beat Cyril Walker 5 and 4
Arthur Havers beat Fred McLeod 10 and 9
Ernest Whitcombe halved with Emmett French
Herbert Jolly beat Joe Stein 3 and 2

Foursomes
Mitchell & Duncan beat Barnes & Hagen 9 and 8
Boomer & Compston beat Armour & Kirkwood 3 and 2
Gadd & Havers beat Mehlhorn & Watrous 3 and 2
Ray & Robson beat Walker & McLeod 3 and 2
Whitcombe & Jolly beat French & Stein 3 and 2

Ryder Cup – Inaugurated 1927

1927 *Worcester Country Club, Worcester, MA, USA* June 3–4
Result: USA 9½, GB 2½
Captains: W Hagen (USA), E Ray (GB)

Foursomes
Hagen & Golden beat Ray & Robson 2 and 1
Farrell & Turnesa beat Duncan & Compston 8 and 6
Sarazen & Watrous beat Havers & Jolly 3 and 2
Diegel & Mehlhorn lost to Boomer & Whitcombe 7 and 5

Singles
Bill Mehlhorn beat Archie Compston 1 hole
Johnny Farrell beat Aubrey Boomer 5 and 4

Johnny Golden beat Herbert Jolly 8 and 7
Leo Diegel beat Ted Ray 7 and 5
Gene Sarazen halved with Charles Whitcombe
Walter Hagen beat Arthur Havers 2 and 1
Al Watrous beat Fred Robson 3 and 2
Joe Turnesa lost to George Duncan 1 hole

1929 *Moortown Golf Club, Leeds, Yorkshire, England* May 26–27
Result: GB 7, USA 5
Captains: George Duncan (GB), Walter Hagen (USA)

Foursomes
C Whitcombe & Compston halved with Farrell & Turnesa
Boomer & Duncan lost to Diegel & Espinosa 7 and 5
Mitchell & Robson beat Sarazen & Dudley 2 and 1
E Whitcombe & Cotton lost to Golden & Hagen 2 holes

Singles
Charles Whitcombe beat Johnny Farrell 8 and 6
George Duncan beat Walter Hagen 10 and 8
Abe Mitchell lost to Leo Diegel 9 and 8
Archie Compston beat Gene Sarazen 6 and 4
Aubrey Boomer beat Joe Turnesa 4 and 3
Fred Robson lost to Horton Smith 4 and 2
Henry Cotton beat Al Watrous 4 and 3
Ernest Whitcombe halved with Al Espinosa

1931 *Scioto Country Club, Columbus, OH, USA* June 26–27
Result: USA 9, GB 3
Captains: Walter Hagen (USA), Charles Whitcombe (GB)

Foursomes
Sarazen & Farrell beat Compston & Davies 8 and 7
Hagen & Shute beat Duncan & Havers 10 and 9
Diegel & Espinosa lost to Mitchell & Robson 3 and 1
Burke & Cox beat Easterbrook & E Whitcombe 3 and 2

Singles
Billy Burke beat Archie Compston 7 and 6
Gene Sarazen beat Fred Robson 7 and 6
Johnny Farrell lost to William H Davies 4 and 3
Wilfred Cox beat Abe Mitchell 3 and 1
Walter Hagen beat Charles Whitcombe 4 and 3
Densmore Shute beat Bert Hodson 8 and 6
Al Espinosa beat Ernest Whitcombe 2 and 1
Craig Wood lost to Arthur Havers 4 and 3

1933 *Southport & Ainsdale GC, Southport, Lancs, England* June 26–27
Result: GB 6½, USA 5½
Captains: JH Taylor (GB), Walter Hagen (USA)

Foursomes
Alliss & Whitcombe halved with Sarazen & Hagen
Mitchell & Havers beat Dutra & Shute 3 and 2
Davies & Easterbrook beat Wood & Runyan 1 hole
Padgham & Perry lost to Dudley & Burke 1 hole

Singles
Alf Padgham lost to Gene Sarazen 6 and 4
Abe Mitchell beat Olin Dutra 9 and 8
Arthur Lacey lost to Walter Hagen 2 and 1
William H Davies lost to Craig Wood 4 and 3
Percy Alliss beat Paul Runyan 2 and 1
Arthur Havers beat Leo Diegel 4 and 3
Syd Easterbrook beat Densmore Shute 1 hole
Charles Whitcombe lost to Horton Smith 2 and 1

1935 *Ridgewood Country Club, Paramus, NJ, USA*
      Sept 28–29
Result: USA 9, GB 3
Captains: Walter Hagen (USA),
      Charles Whitcombe (GB)

Foursomes
Sarazen & Hagen beat Perry & Busson 7 and 6
Picard & Revolta beat Padgham & Alliss 6 and 5
Runyan & Smith beat Cox & Jarman 9 and 8
Dutra & Laffoon lost to C Whitcombe & E Whitcombe
      1 hole

Singles
Gene Sarazen beat Jack Busson 3 and 2
Paul Runyon beat Dick Burton 5 and 3
Johnny Revolta beat Charles Whitcombe 2 and 1
Olin Dutra beat Alf Padgham 4 and 2
Craig Wood lost to Percy Alliss 1 hole
Horton Smith halved with Bill Cox
Henry Picard beat Ernest Whitcombe 3 and 2
Sam Parks halved with Alf Perry

1937 *Southport & Ainsdale GC, Southport, Lancs,*
      England June 29–30
Result: USA 8, GB 4
Captains: Charles Whitcombe (GB),
      Walter Hagen (USA)

Foursomes
Padgham & Cotton lost to Dudley & Nelson 4 and 2
Lacey & Bill Cox lost to Guldahl & Manero 2 and 1
Whitcombe & Rees halved with Sarazen & Shute
Alliss & Burton beat Picard & Johnny Revolta 2 and 1

Singles
Alf Padgham lost to Ralph Guldahl 8 and 7
Sam King halved with Densmore Shute
Dai Rees beat Byron Nelson 3 and 1
Henry Cotton beat Tony Manero 5 and 3
Percy Alliss lost to Gene Sarazen 1 hole
Dick Burton lost to Sam Snead 5 and 4
Alf Perry lost to Ed Dudley 2 and 1
Arthur Lacey lost to Henry Picard 2 and 1

1947 *Portland Golf Club, Portland, OR, USA* Nov 1–2
Result: USA 11, GB 1
Captains: Ben Hogan (USA), Henry Cotton (GB)

Foursomes
Oliver & Worsham beat Cotton & Lees 10 and 9
Snead & Mangrum beat Daly & Ward 6 and 5
Hogan & Demaret beat Adams & Faulkner 2 holes
Nelson & Herman Barron beat Rees & King 2 and 1

Singles
Dutch Harrison beat Fred Daly 5 and 4
Lew Worsham beat Jimmy Adams 3 and 2
Lloyd Mangrum beat Max Faulkner 6 and 5
Ed Oliver beat Charlie Ward 4 and 3
Byron Nelson beat Arthur Lees 2 and 1
Sam Snead beat Henry Cotton 5 and 4
Jimmy Demaret beat Dai Rees 3 and 2
Herman Keiser lost to Sam King 4 and 3

1949 *Ganton Golf Club, Scarborough, Yorks, England*
      Sept 16–17
Result: USA 7, GB 5
Captains: Charles Whitcombe (GB),
      Ben Hogan (USA)

Foursomes
Faulkner & Adams beat Harrison & Palmer 2 and 1
Daly & Ken Bousfield beat Hamilton & Alexander
      4 and 2
Ward & King lost to Demaret & Heafner 4 and 3
Burton & Lees beat Snead & Mangrum 1 hole

Singles
Max Faulkner lost to Dutch Harrison 8 and 7
Jimmy Adams beat Johnny Palmer 2 and 1
Charlie Ward lost to Sam Snead 6 and 5
Dai Rees beat Bob Hamilton 6 and 4
Dick Burton lost to Clayton Heafner 3 and 2
Sam King lost to Chick Harbert 4 and 3
Arthur Lees lost to Jimmy Demaret 7 and 6
Fred Daly lost to Lloyd Mangrum 1 hole

1951 *Pinehurst No.2, Pinehurst, NC, USA* Nov 2–4
Result: USA 9½, GB 2½
Captains: Sam Snead (USA), Arthur Lacey (GB)

Foursomes
Heafner & Burke beat Faulkner & Rees 5 and 3
Oliver & Henry Ransom lost to Ward & Lees
      2 and 1
Mangrum & Snead beat Adams & Panton 5 and 4
Hogan & Demaret beat Daly & Bousfield 5 and 4

Singles
Jack Burke beat Jimmy Adams 4 and 3
Jimmy Demaret beat Dai Rees 2 holes
Clayton Heafner halved with Fred Daly
Lloyd Mangrum beat Harry Weetman 6 and 5
Ed Oliver lost to Arthur Lees 2 and 1
Ben Hogan beat Charlie Ward 3 and 2
Skip Alexander beat John Panton 8 and 7
Sam Snead beat Max Faulkner 4 and 3

1953 *West Course, Wentworth GC, Surrey,*
      England Oct 2–3
Result: USA 6½, GB 5½
Captains: Henry Cotton (GB), Lloyd Mangrum (USA)

Foursomes
Weetman & Alliss lost to Douglas & Oliver 2 and 1
Brown & Panton lost to Mangrum & Snead 8 and 7
Adams & Hunt lost to Kroll & Burke 7 and 5
Daly & Bradshaw beat Burkemo & Middlecoff 1 hole

Singles
Dai Rees lost to Jack Burke 2 and 1
Fred Daly beat Ted Kroll 9 and 7
Eric Brown beat Lloyd Mangrum 2 holes
Harry Weetman beat Sam Snead 1 hole
Max Faulkner lost to Cary Middlecoff 3 and 1
Peter Alliss lost to Jim Turnesa 1 hole
Bernard Hunt halved with Dave Douglas
Harry Bradshaw beat Fred Haas jr 3 and 2

Although no matches were played between 1939 and 1945, Great Britain selected a side in 1939 and
the Americans chose sides in 1939 to 1943. No alternative fixture was played in 1939 but the
Americans played matches amongst themselves in the other four years. They resulted in:

      1940 Cup Team 7, Gene Sarazen's Challengers 5   1942 Cup Team 10, Walter Hagen's Challengers 5
      1941 Cup Team 6½, Bobby Jones' Challengers 8½   1943 Cup Team 8½, Walter Hagen's Challengers 3½

1955 *Thunderbird G and C Club, Palm Springs, CA, USA* Nov 5–6
Result: USA 8, GBI 4
Captains: Chick Harbert (USA), Dai Rees (GBI)
Foursomes
Harper & Barber lost to Fallon & Jacobs 1 hole
Ford & Kroll beat Brown & Scott 5 and 4
Burke & Bolt beat Lees & Weetman 1 hole
Snead & Middlecoff beat Rees & Bradshaw 3 and 2
Singles
Tommy Bolt beat Christy O'Connor 4 and 2
Chick Harbert beat Syd Scott 3 and 2
Cary Middlecoff lost to John Jacobs 1 hole
Sam Snead beat Dai Rees 3 and 1
Marty Furgol lost to Arthur Lees 3 and 1
Jerry Barber lost to Eric Brown 3 and 2
Jack Burke beat Harry Bradshaw 3 and 2
Doug Ford beat Harry Weetman 3 and 2

1957 *Lindrick Golf Club, Sheffield, Yorks, England* Oct 4–5
Result: GBI 7½, USA 4½
Captains: Dai Rees (GBI), Jack Burke (USA)
Foursomes
Alliss & Hunt lost to Ford & Finsterwald 2 and 1
Bousfield & Rees beat Art Wall jr & Hawkins 3 and 2
Faulkner & Weetman lost to Kroll & Burke 4 and 3
O'Connor & Brown lost to Mayer & Bolt 7 and 5
Singles
Eric Brown beat Tommy Bolt 4 and 3
Peter Mills beat Jack Burke 5 and 3
Peter Alliss lost to Fred Hawkins 2 and 1
Ken Bousfield beat Lionel Hebert 4 and 3
Dai Rees beat Ed Furgol 7 and 6
Bernard Hunt beat Doug Ford 6 and 5
Christy O'Connor beat Dow Finsterwald 7 and 6
Harry Bradshaw halved with Dick Mayer

1959 *Eldorado Country Club, Palm Desert, CA, USA* Nov 6–7
Result: USA 8½, GBI 3½
Captains: Sam Snead (USA), Dai Rees (GBI)
Foursomes
Rosburg & Souchak beat Hunt & Brown 5 and 4
Ford & Wall lost to O'Connor & Alliss 3 and 2
Boros & Finsterwald beat Rees & Bousfield 2 holes
Snead & Middlecoff halved with Weetman & Thomas
Singles
Doug Ford halved with Norman Drew
Mike Souchak beat Ken Bousfield 3 and 2
Bob Rosburg beat Harry Weetman 6 and 5
Sam Snead beat Dave Thomas 6 and 5
Dow Finsterwald beat Dai Rees 1 hole
Jay Hebert halved with Peter Alliss
Art Wall jr beat Christy O'Connor 7 and 6
Cary Middlecoff lost to Eric Brown 4 and 3

1961 *Royal Lytham & St Annes GC, St Annes, Lancs, England* Oct 13–14
Result: USA 14½, GBI 9½
Captains: Jerry Barber (USA), Dai Rees (GBI)
First Day: Foursomes – Morning
O'Connor & Alliss beat Littler & Ford 4 and 3
Panton & Hunt lost to Wall & Hebert 4 and 3
Rees & Bousfield lost to Casper & Palmer 2 and 1
Haliburton & Coles lost to Souchak & Collins 1 hole

Foursomes – Afternoon
O'Connor & Alliss lost to Wall & Hebert 1 hole
Panton & Hunt lost to Casper & Palmer 5 and 4
Rees & Bousfield beat Souchak & Collins 4 and 2
Haliburton & Coles lost to Barber & Finsterwald 1 hole
Second Day: Singles – Morning
Harry Weetman lost to Doug Ford 1 hole
Ralph Moffitt lost to Mike Souchak 5 and 4
Peter Alliss halved with Arnold Palmer
Ken Bousfield lost to Billy Casper 5 and 3
Dai Rees beat Jay Hebert 2 and 1
Neil Coles halved with Gene Littler
Bernard Hunt beat Jerry Barber 5 and 4
Christy O'Connor lost to Dow Finsterwald 2 and 1
Singles – Afternoon
Weetman lost to Wall 1 hole
Alliss beat Bill Collins 3 and 2
Hunt lost to Souchak 2 and 1
Tom Haliburton lost to Palmer 2 and 1
Rees beat Ford 4 and 3
Bousfield beat Barber 1 hole
Coles beat Finsterwald 1 hole
O'Connor halved with Littler

1963 *East Lake CC, Atlanta, GA, USA* Oct 11–13
Result: USA 23, GBI 9
Captains: Arnold Palmer (USA), John Fallon (GBI)
First Day: Foursomes – Morning
Palmer & Pott lost to Huggett & Will 3 and 2
Casper & Ragan beat Alliss & O'Connor 1 hole
Boros & Lema halved with Coles & B Hunt
Littler & Finsterwald halved with Thomas & Weetman
Foursomes – Afternoon
Maxwell & Goalby beat Thomas & Weetman 4 and 3
Palmer & Casper beat Huggett & Will 5 and 4
Littler & Finsterwald beat Coles & G Hunt 2 and 1
Boros & Lema beat Haliburton & B Hunt 1 hole
Second Day: Fourball – Morning
Palmer & Finsterwald beat Huggett & Thomas 5 and 4
Littler & Boros halved with Alliss & B Hunt
Casper & Maxwell beat Weetman & Will 3 and 2
Goalby & Ragan lost to Coles & O'Connor 1 hole
Fourball – Afternoon
Palmer & Finsterwald beat Coles & O'Connor 3 and 2
Lema & Pott beat Alliss & B Hunt 1 hole
Casper & Maxwell beat Haliburton & G Hunt 2 and 1
Goalby & Ragan halved with Huggett & Thomas
Third Day: Singles – Morning
Tony Lema beat Geoffrey Hunt 5 and 3
Johnny Pott lost to Brian Huggett 3 and 1
Arnold Palmer lost to Peter Alliss 1 hole
Billy Casper halved with Neil Coles
Bob Goalby beat Dave Thomas 3 and 2
Gene Littler lost to Tom Haliburton 6 and 5
Julius Boros lost to Harry Weetman 1 hole
Dow Finsterwald lost to Bernard Hunt 2 holes
Singles – Afternoon
Arnold Palmer beat George Will 3 and 2
Dave Ragan beat Neil Coles 2 and 1
Tony Lema halved with Peter Alliss
Gene Littler beat Tom Haliburton 6 and 5
Julius Boros beat Harry Weetman 2 and 1
Billy Maxwell beat Christy O'Connor 2 and 1
Dow Finsterwald beat Dave Thomas 4 and 3
Bob Goalby beat Bernard Hunt 2 and 1

1965 *Royal Birkdale Golf Club, Southport, Lancs,*
England Oct 7–9
Result: GBI 12½, USA 19½
Captains: Harry Weetman (GBI),
Byron Nelson (USA)
First Day: Foursomes – Morning
Thomas & Will beat Marr & Palmer 6 and 5
O'Connor & Alliss beat Venturi & January 5 and 4
Platts & Butler lost to Boros & Lema 1 hole
Hunt & Coles lost to Casper & Littler 2 and 1
Foursomes – Afternoon
Thomas & Will lost to Marr & Palmer 6 and 5
Martin & Hitchcock lost to Boros & Lema 5 and 4
O'Connor & Alliss beat Casper & Littler 2 and 1
Hunt & Coles beat Venturi & January 3 and 2
Second Day: Fourball – Morning
Thomas & Will lost to January & Jacobs 1 hole
Platts & Butler halved with Casper & Littler
Alliss & O'Connor lost to Marr & Palmer 5 and 4
Coles & Hunt beat Boros & Lema 1 hole
Fourball – Afternoon
Alliss & O'Connor beat Marr & Palmer 1 hole
Thomas & Will lost to January & Jacobs 1 hole
Platts & Butler halved with Casper & Littler
Coles & Hunt lost to Lema & Venturi 1 hole
Third Day: Singles – Morning
Jimmy Hitchcock lost to Arnold Palmer 3 and 2
Lionel Platts lost to Julius Boros 4 and 2
Peter Butler lost to Tony Lema 1 hole
Neil Coles lost to Dave Marr 2 holes
Bernard Hunt beat Gene Littler 2 holes
Peter Alliss beat Billy Casper 1 hole
Dave Thomas lost to Tommy Jacobs 2 and 1
George Will halved with Don January
Singles – Afternoon
Butler lost to Palmer 2 holes
Hitchcock lost to Boros 2 and 1
Christy O'Connor lost to Lema 6 and 4
Alliss beat Ken Venturi 3 and 1
Hunt lost to Marr 1 hole
Coles beat Casper 3 and 2
Will lost to Littler 2 and 1
Platts beat Jacobs 1 hole

1967 *Champions Golf Club, Houston, TX, USA*
Oct 20–22
Result: USA 23½, GBI 8½
Captains: Ben Hogan (USA), Dai Rees (GBI)
First Day: Foursomes – Morning
Casper & Boros halved with Huggett & Will
Palmer & Dickinson beat Alliss & O'Connor 2 and 1
Sanders & Brewer lost to Jacklin & Thomas 4 and 3
Nichols & Pott beat Hunt & Coles 6 and 5
Foursomes – Afternoon
Boros & Casper beat Huggett & Will 1 hole
Dickinson & Palmer beat Gregson & Boyle 5 and 4
Littler & Geiberger lost to Jacklin & Thomas 3 and 2
Nichols & Pott beat Alliss & O'Connor 2 and 1
Second Day: Fourball – Morning
Casper & Brewer beat Alliss & O'Connor 3 and 2
Nichols & Pott beat Hunt & Coles 1 hole
Littler & Geiberger beat Jacklin & Thomas 1 hole
Dickinson & Sanders beat Huggett & Will 3 and 2
Fourball – Afternoon
Casper & Brewer beat Hunt & Coles 5 and 3
Dickinson & Sanders beat Alliss & Gregson 4 and 3
Palmer & Boros beat Will & Boyle 1 hole
Littler & Geiberger halved with Jacklin & Thomas

Third Day: Singles – Morning
Gay Brewer beat Hugh Boyle 4 and 3
Billy Casper beat Peter Alliss 2 and 1
Arnold Palmer beat Tony Jacklin 3 and 2
Julius Boros lost to Brian Huggett 1 hole
Doug Sanders lost to Neil Coles 2 and 1
Al Geiberger beat Malcolm Gregson 4 and 2
Gene Littler halved with Dave Thomas
Bobby Nichols halved with Bernard Hunt
Singles – Afternoon
Palmer beat Huggett 5 and 3
Brewer lost to Alliss 2 and 1
Gardner Dickinson beat Jacklin 3 and 2
Nichols beat Christy O'Connor 3 and 2
Johnny Pott beat George Will 3 and 1
Geiberger beat Gregson 2 and 1
Boros halved with Hunt
Sanders lost to Coles 2 and 1

1969 *Royal Birkdale Golf Club, Southport, Lancs,*
England Sept 18–20
Result: USA 16, GBI 16
Captains: Eric Brown (GBI), Sam Snead (USA)
First Day: Foursomes – Morning
Coles & Huggett beat Barber & Floyd 3 and 2
Gallacher & Bembridge beat Trevino & Still 2 and 1
Jacklin & Townsend beat Hill & Aaron 3 and 1
O'Connor & Alliss halved with Casper & Beard
Foursomes – Afternoon
Coles & Huggett lost to Hill & Aaron 1 hole
Gallacher & Bembridge lost to Trevino & Littler 2 holes
Jacklin & Townsend beat Casper & Beard 1 hole
Hunt & Butler lost to Nicklaus & Sikes
Second Day: Fourball – Morning
O'Connor & Townsend beat Hill & Douglass 1 hole
Huggett & Alex Caygill halved with Floyd & Barber
Barnes & Alliss lost to Trevino & Littler 1 hole
Jacklin & Coles beat Nicklaus & Sikes 1 hole
Fourball – Afternoon
Townsend & Butler lost to Casper & Beard 2 holes
Huggett & Gallacher lost to Hill & Still 2 and 1
Bembridge & Hunt halved with Aaron & Floyd
Jacklin & Coles halved with Trevino & Barber
Third Day: Singles – Morning
Peter Alliss lost to Lee Trevino 2 and 1
Peter Townsend lost to Dave Hill 5 and 4
Neil Coles beat Tommy Aaron 1 hole
Brian Barnes lost to Billy Casper 1 hole
Christy O'Connor beat Frank Beard 5 and 4
Maurice Bembridge beat Ken Still 1 hole
Peter Butler beat Ray Floyd 1 hole
Tony Jacklin beat Jack Nicklaus 4 and 3
Singles – Afternoon
Barnes lost to Hill 4 and 2
Bernard Gallacher beat Trevino 4 and 3
Bembridge lost to Miller Barber 7 and 6
Butler beat Dale Douglass 3 and 2
O'Connor lost to Gene Littler 2 and 1
Brian Huggett halved with Casper
Coles lost to Dan Sikes 4 and 3
Jacklin halved with Nicklaus

1971 *Old Warson Country Club, St Louis, MO, USA*
Sept 16–18
Result: USA 18½, GBI 13½
Captains: Jay Hebert (USA), Eric Brown (GBI)
First Day: Foursomes – Morning
Casper & Barber lost to Coles & O'Connor 2 and 1
Palmer & Dickinson beat Townsend & Oosterhuis 2 holes

Nicklaus & Stockton lost to Huggett & Jacklin 3 and 2
Coody & Beard lost to Bembridge & Butler 1 hole
Foursomes – Afternoon
Casper & Barber lost to Bannerman & Gallacher 2 and 1
Palmer & Dickinson beat Townsend & Oosterhuis 1 hole
Trevino & Rudolph halved with Huggett and Jacklin
Nicklaus & Snead beat Bembridge & Butler 5 and 3
Second Day: Fourball – Morning
Trevino & Rudolph beat O'Connor & Barnes 2 and 1
Beard & Snead beat Coles & John Garner 2 and 1
Palmer & Dickinson beat Oosterhuis & Gallacher 5 and 4
Nicklaus & Littler beat Townsend & Bannerman 2 and 1
Fourball – Afternoon
Trevino & Casper lost to Oosterhuis & Gallacher 1 hole
Littler & Snead beat Huggett & Jacklin 2 and 1
Palmer & Nicklaus beat Townsend & Bannerman 1 hole
Coody & Beard halved with Coles & O'Connor
Third Day: Singles – Morning
Lee Trevino beat Tony Jacklin 1 hole
Dave Stockton halved with Bernard Gallacher
Mason Rudolph lost to Brian Barnes 1 hole
Gene Littler lost to Peter Oosterhuis 4 and 3
Jack Nicklaus beat Peter Townsend 3 and 2
Gardner Dickinson beat Christy O'Connor 5 and 4
Arnold Palmer halved with Harry Bannerman
Frank Beard halved with Neil Coles
Singles – Afternoon
Trevino beat Brian Huggett 7 and 6
JC Snead beat Jacklin 1 hole
Miller Barber lost to Barnes 2 and 1
Stockton beat Townsend 1 hole
Charles Coody lost to Gallacher 2 and 1
Nicklaus beat Coles 5 and 3
Palmer lost to Oosterhuis 3 and 2
Dickinson lost to Bannerman 2 and 1

1973 Honourable Company of Edinburgh Golfers, Muirfield, Gullane, East Lothian, Scotland Sept 20–22

Result: USA 19, GBI 13
Captains: Bernard Hunt (GBI), Jack Burke (USA)
First Day: Foursomes – Morning
Barnes & Gallacher beat Trevino & Casper 1 hole
O'Connor & Coles beat Weiskopf & Snead 3 and 2
Jacklin & Oosterhuis halved with Rodriguez & Graham
Bembridge & Polland lost to Nicklaus & Palmer 6 and 5
Fourball – Afternoon
Barnes & Gallacher beat Aaron & Brewer 5 and 4
Bembridge & Huggett beat Nicklaus & Palmer 3 and 1
Jacklin & Oosterhuis beat Weiskopf & Casper 3 and 1
O'Connor & Coles lost to Trevino & Blancas 2 and 1
Second Day: Foursomes – Morning
Barnes & Butler lost to Nicklaus & Weiskopf 1 hole
Jacklin & Oosterhuis beat Palmer & Hill 2 holes
Bembridge & Huggett beat Rodriguez & Graham 5 and 4
O'Connor & Coles lost to Trevino & Casper 2 and 1
Fourball – Afternoon
Barnes & Butler lost to Snead & Palmer 2 holes
Jacklin & Oosterhuis lost to Brewer & Casper 3 and 2
Clark & Polland lost to Nicklaus & Weiskopf 3 and 2
Bembridge & Huggett halved with Trevino & Blancas
Third Day: Singles – Morning
Brian Barnes lost to Billy Casper 2 and 1
Bernard Gallacher lost to Tom Weiskopf 3 and 1
Peter Butler lost to Homero Blancas 5 and 4
Tony Jacklin beat Tommy Aaron 3 and 1
Neil Coles halved with Gay Brewer
Christy O'Connor lost to JC Snead 1 hole
Maurice Bembridge halved with Jack Nicklaus
Peter Oosterhuis halved with Lee Trevino

Singles – Afternoon
Brian Huggett beat Blancas 4 and 2
Barnes lost to Snead 3 and 1
Gallacher lost to Brewer 6 and 5
Jacklin lost to Casper 2 and 1
Coles lost to Trevino 6 and 5
O'Connor halved with Weiskopf
Bembridge lost to Nicklaus 2 holes
Oosterhuis beat Arnold Palmer 4 and 2

1975 Laurel Valley Golf Club, Ligonier, PA, USA Sept 19–21

Result: USA 21, GBI 11
Captains: Arnold Palmer (USA), Bernard Hunt (GBI)
First Day: Foursomes – Morning
Nicklaus & Weiskopf beat Barnes & Gallacher 5 and 4
Littler & Irwin beat Wood & Bembridge 4 and 3
Geiberger & Miller beat Jacklin & Oosterhuis 3 and 1
Trevino & Snead beat Horton & O'Leary 2 and 1
Fourball – Afternoon
Casper & Floyd lost to Jacklin & Oosterhuis 2 and 1
Weiskopf & Graham beat Darcy & Christy O'Connor jr 3 and 2
Nicklaus & Murphy halved with Barnes & Gallacher
Trevino & Irwin beat Horton & O'Leary 2 and 1
Second Day: Fourball – Morning
Casper & Miller halved with Jacklin & Oosterhuis
Nicklaus & Snead beat Horton & Wood 4 and 2
Littler & Graham beat Barnes & Gallacher 5 and 3
Geiberger & Floyd halved with Darcy & Hunt
Foursomes – Afternoon
Trevino & Murphy lost to Jacklin & Barnes 3 and 2
Weiskopf & Miller beat O'Connor & O'Leary 5 and 3
Irwin & Casper beat Oosterhuis & Bembridge 3 and 2
Geiberger & Graham beat Darcy & Hunt 3 and 2
Third Day: Singles – Morning
Bob Murphy beat Tony Jacklin 2 and 1
Johnny Miller lost to Peter Oosterhuis 2 holes
Lee Trevino halved with Bernard Gallacher
Hale Irwin halved with Tommy Horton
Gene Littler beat Brian Huggett 4 and 2
Billy Casper beat Eamonn Darcy 3 and 2
Tom Weiskopf beat Guy Hunt 5 and 3
Jack Nicklaus lost to Brian Barnes 4 and 2
Singles – Afternoon
Ray Floyd beat Jacklin 1 hole
JC Snead lost to Oosterhuis 3 and 2
Al Geiberger halved with Gallacher
Lou Graham lost to Horton 2 and 1
Irwin beat John O'Leary 2 and 1
Murphy beat Maurice Bembridge 2 and 1
Trevino lost to Norman Wood 2 and 1
Nicklaus lost to Barnes 2 and 1

1977 Royal Lytham & St Annes GC, St Annes, Lancs, England Sept 15–17

Result: USA 12½, GBI 7½
Captains: Brian Huggett (GBI), Dow Finsterwald (USA)
First Day: Foursomes
Gallacher & Barnes lost to Wadkins & Irwin 3 and 1
Coles & Dawson lost to Stockton & McGee 1 hole
Faldo & Oosterhuis beat Floyd & Graham 2 and 1
Darcy & Jacklin halved with Sneed & January
Horton & James lost to Nicklaus & Watson 5 and 4

1977 continued

Second Day: Fourball
Barnes & Horton lost to Watson & Green 5 and 4
Coles & Dawson lost to Sneed & Wadkins 5 and 3
Faldo & Oosterhuis beat Nicklaus & Floyd 3 and 1
Darcy & Jacklin lost to Hill & Stockton 5 and 3
James & Brown lost to Irwin & Graham 1 hole
Third Day: Singles
Howard Clark lost to Lanny Wadkins 4 and 3
Neil Coles lost to Lou Graham 5 and 3
Peter Dawson beat Don January 5 and 4
Brian Barnes beat Hale Irwin 1 hole
Tommy Horton lost to Dave Hill 5 and 4
Bernard Gallacher beat Jack Nicklaus 1 hole
Eamonn Darcy lost to Hubert Green 1 hole
Mark James lost to Ray Floyd 2 and 1
Nick Faldo beat Tom Watson 1 hole
Peter Oosterhuis beat Jerry McGee 2 holes

From 1979 GBI became a European team

1979 The Greenbrier, White Sulphur Springs, WV, USA Sept 14–16
Result: USA 17, Europe 11
Captains: Billy Casper (USA), John Jacobs (Eur)
First Day: Fourball – Morning
Wadkins & Nelson beat Garrido & Ballesteros 2 and 1
Trevino & Zoeller beat Brown & James 3 and 2
Bean & Elder beat Oosterhuis & Faldo 2 and 1
Irwin & Mahaffey lost to Gallacher & Barnes 2 and 1
Foursomes – Afternoon
Irwin & Kite beat Brown & Smyth 7 and 6
Zoeller & Green lost to Garrido & Ballesteros 3 and 2
Trevino & Morgan halved with Lyle & Jacklin
Wadkins & Nelson beat Gallacher & Barnes 4 and 3
Second Day: Foursomes – Morning
Elder & Mahaffey lost to Lyle & Jacklin 5 and 4
Bean & Kite lost to Oosterhuis & Faldo 6 and 5
Zoeller & Hayes halved with Gallacher & Barnes
Wadkins & Nelson beat Garrido & Ballesteros 3 and 2
Fourball – Afternoon
Wadkins & Nelson beat Garrido & Ballesteros 5 and 4
Irwin & Kite beat Lyle & Jacklin 1 hole
Trevino & Zoeller lost to Gallacher & Barnes 3 and 2
Elder & Hayes lost to Oosterhuis & Faldo 1 hole
Third Day: Singles
Lanny Wadkins lost to Bernard Gallacher 3 and 2
Larry Nelson beat Seve Ballesteros 3 and 2
Tom Kite beat Tony Jacklin 1 hole
Mark Hayes beat Antonio Garrido 1 hole
Andy Bean beat Michael King 4 and 3
John Mahaffey beat Brian Barnes 1 hole
Lee Elder lost to Nick Faldo 3 and 2
Hale Irwin beat Des Smyth 5 and 3
Hubert Green beat Peter Oosterhuis 2 holes
Fuzzy Zoeller lost to Ken Brown 1 hole
Lee Trevino beat Sandy Lyle 2 and 1
Gil Morgan, Mark James: injury; match a half

1981 Walton Heath GC, Tadworth, Surrey, England Sept 18–20
Result: USA 18½, Europe 9½
Captains: John Jacobs (Eur), Dave Marr (USA)
First Day: Foursomes – Morning
Langer & Pinero lost to Trevino & Nelson 1 hole
Lyle & James beat Rogers & Lietzke 2 and 1
Gallacher & Smyth beat Irwin & Floyd 3 and 2
Oosterhuis & Faldo lost to Watson & Nicklaus 4 and 3

Fourball – Afternoon
Torrance & Clark halved with Kite & Miller
Lyle & James beat Crenshaw & Pate 3 and 2
Smyth & Canizares beat Rogers & Lietzke 6 and 5
Gallacher & Darcy lost to Irwin & Floyd 2 and 1
Second Day: Fourball – Morning
Faldo & Torrance lost to Trevino & Pate 7 and 5
Lyle & James lost to Nelson & Kite 1 hole
Langer & Pinero beat Irwin & Floyd 2 and 1
Smyth & Canizares lost to Watson & Nicklaus 3 and 2
Foursomes – Afternoon
Oosterhuis & Torrance lost to Trevino & Pate 2 and 1
Langer & Pinero lost to Watson & Nicklaus 3 and 2
Lyle & James lost to Rogers & Floyd 3 and 2
Gallacher & Smyth lost to Nelson & Kite 3 and 2
Third Day: Singles
Sam Torrance lost to Lee Trevino 5 and 3
Sandy Lyle lost to Tom Kite 3 and 2
Bernard Gallacher halved with Bill Rogers
Mark James lost to Larry Nelson 2 holes
Des Smyth lost to Ben Crenshaw 6 and 4
Bernhard Langer halved with Bruce Lietzke
Manuel Pinero beat Jerry Pate 4 and 2
José Maria Canizares lost to Hale Irwin 1 hole
Nick Faldo beat Johnny Miller 2 and 1
Howard Clark beat Tom Watson 4 and 3
Peter Oosterhuis lost to Ray Floyd 2 holes
Eamonn Darcy lost to Jack Nicklaus 5 and 3

1983 PGA National Golf Club, Palm Beach Gardens, FL, USA Oct 14–16
Result: USA 14½, Europe 13½
Captains: Jack Nicklaus (USA), Tony Jacklin (Eur)
First Day: Foursomes – Morning
Watson & Crenshaw beat Gallacher & Lyle 5 and 4
Wadkins & Stadler lost to Faldo & Langer 4 and 2
Floyd & Gilder lost to Canizares & Torrance 4 and 3
Kite & Peete beat Ballesteros & Way 2 and 1
Fourball – Afternoon
Morgan & Zoeller lost to Waites & Brown 2 and 1
Watson & Haas beat Faldo & Langer 2 and 1
Floyd & Strange lost to Ballesteros & Way 1 hole
Crenshaw & Peete halved with Torrance & Woosnam
Second Day: Foursomes – Morning
Floyd & Kite lost to Faldo & Langer 3 and 2
Wadkins & Morgan beat Canizares & Torrance 7 and 5
Gilder & Watson lost to Ballesteros & Way 2 and 1
Haas & Strange beat Waites & Brown 3 and 2
Fourball – Afternoon
Wadkins & Stadler beat Waites & Brown 1 hole
Crenshaw & Peete lost to Faldo & Langer 2 and 1
Haas & Morgan halved with Ballesteros & Way
Gilder & Watson beat Torrance & Woosnam 5 and 4
Third Day: Singles
Fuzzy Zoeller halved with Seve Ballesteros
Jay Haas lost to Nick Faldo 2 and 1
Gil Morgan lost to Bernhard Langer 2 holes
Bob Gilder beat Gordon J Brand 2 holes
Ben Crenshaw beat Sandy Lyle 3 and 1
Calvin Peete beat Brian Waites 1 hole
Curtis Strange lost to Paul Way 2 and 1
Tom Kite halved with Sam Torrance
Craig Stadler beat Ian Woosnam 3 and 2
Lanny Wadkins halved with José Maria Canizares
Ray Floyd lost to Ken Brown 4 and 3
Tom Watson beat Bernard Gallacher 2 and 1

1985 *The Brabazon Course, The De Vere Belfry,*
Sutton Coldfield, West Midlands, England
Sept 13–15
Result: Europe 16½, USA 11½
Captains: Tony Jacklin (Eur), Lee Trevino (USA)
First Day: Foursomes – Morning
Ballesteros & Pinero beat Strange & O'Meara 2 and 1
Faldo & Langer lost to Kite & Peete 3 and 2
Brown & Lyle lost to Floyd & Wadkins 4 and 3
Clark & Torrance lost to Stadler & Sutton 3 and 2
Fourball – Afternoon
Way & Woosnam beat Green & Zoeller 1 hole
Ballesteros & Pinero beat Jacobsen & North 2 and 1
Canizares & Langer halved with Stadler & Sutton
Clark & Torrance lost to Floyd & Wadkins 1 hole
Second Day: Fourball – Morning
Clark & Torrance beat Kite & North 2 and 1
Way & Woosnam beat Green & Zoeller 4 and 3
Ballesteros & Pinero lost to O'Meara & Wadkins 3 and 2
Langer & Lyle halved with Stadler & Strange
Foursomes – Afternoon
Canizares & Rivero beat Kite & Peete 7 and 5
Ballesteros & Pinero beat Stadler & Sutton 5 and 4
Way & Woosnam lost to Jacobsen & Strange 4 and 3
Brown & Langer beat Floyd & Wadkins 3 and 2
Third Day: Singles
Manuel Pinero beat Lanny Wadkins 3 and 1
Ian Woosnam lost to Craig Stadler 2 and 1
Paul Way beat Ray Floyd 2 holes
Seve Ballesteros halved with Tom Kite
Sandy Lyle beat Peter Jacobsen 3 and 2
Bernhard Langer beat Hal Sutton 5 and 4
Sam Torrance beat Andy North 1 hole
Howard Clark beat Mark O'Meara 1 hole
Nick Faldo lost to Hubert Green 3 and 1
José Rivero lost to Calvin Peete 1 hole
José Maria Canizares beat Fuzzy Zoeller 2 holes
Ken Brown lost to Curtis Strange 4 and 2

1987 *Muirfield Village Golf Club, Dublin, OH, USA*
Sept 25–27
Result: Europe 15, USA 13
Captains: Jack Nicklaus (USA), Tony Jacklin (Eur)
First Day: Foursomes – Morning
Kite & Strange beat Clark & Torrance 4 and 2
Pohl & Sutton beat Brown & Langer 2 and 1
Mize & Wadkins lost to Faldo & Woosnam 2 holes
Nelson & Stewart lost to Ballesteros & Olazábal 1 hole
Fourball – Afternoon
Crenshaw & Simpson lost to Brand & Rivero 3 and 2
Bean & Calcavecchia lost to Langer & Lyle 1 hole
Pohl & Sutton lost to Faldo & Woosnam 2 and 1
Kite & Strange lost to Ballesteros & Olazábal 2 and 1
Second Day: Foursomes – Morning
Kite & Strange beat Brand & Rivero 3 and 1
Mize & Sutton halved with Faldo & Woosnam
Nelson & Wadkins lost to Langer & Lyle 2 and 1
Crenshaw & Stewart lost to Ballesteros & Olazábal 1 hole
Fourball – Afternoon
Kite & Strange lost to Faldo & Woosnam 5 and 4
Bean & Stewart beat Brand & Darcy 3 and 2
Mize & Sutton beat Ballesteros & Olazábal 2 and 1
Nelson & Wadkins lost to Langer & Lyle 1 hole
Third Day: Singles
Andy Bean beat Ian Woosnam 1 hole
Dan Pohl lost to Howard Clark 1 hole
Larry Mize halved with Sam Torrance

Mark Calcavecchia beat Nick Faldo 1 hole
Payne Stewart beat José Maria Olazábal 2 holes
Scott Simpson beat José Rivero 2 and 1
Tom Kite beat Sandy Lyle 3 and 2
Ben Crenshaw lost to Eamonn Darcy 1 hole
Larry Nelson halved with Bernhard Langer
Curtis Strange lost to Seve Ballesteros 2 and 1
Lanny Wadkins beat Ken Brown 3 and 2
Hal Sutton halved with Gordon Brand jr

1989 *The Brabazon Course, The De Vere Belfry,*
Sutton Coldfield, West Midlands, England
Sept 22–24
Result: Europe 14, USA 14
Captains: Tony Jacklin (Eur), Ray Floyd (USA)
First Day: Foursomes – Morning
Faldo & Woosnam halved with Kite & Strange
Clark & James lost to Stewart & Wadkins 1 hole
Ballesteros & Olazábal halved with Beck & Watson
Langer & Rafferty lost to Calcavecchia & Green 2 and 1
Fourball – Afternoon
Brand & Torrance beat Azinger & Strange 1 hole
Clark & James beat Couples & Wadkins 3 and 2
Faldo & Woosnam beat Calcavecchia & McCumber
  1 hole
Ballesteros & Olazábal beat O'Meara & Watson 6 and 5
Second Day: Foursomes – Morning
Faldo & Woosnam beat Stewart & Wadkins 3 and 2
Brand & Torrance lost to Azinger & Beck 4 and 3
O'Connor & Rafferty lost to Calcavecchia & Green
  3 and 2
Ballesteros & Olazábal beat Kite & Strange 1 hole
Fourball – Afternoon
Faldo & Woosnam lost to Azinger & Beck 2 and 1
Canizares & Langer lost to Kite & McCumber 2 and 1
Clark & James beat Stewart & Strange 1 hole
Ballesteros & Olazábal beat Calcavecchia & Green 4 and 2
Third Day: Singles
Seve Ballesteros lost to Paul Azinger 1 hole
Bernhard Langer lost to Chip Beck 3 and 1
José Maria Olazábal beat Payne Stewart 1 hole
Ronan Rafferty beat Mark Calvecchia 1 hole
Howard Clark lost to Tom Kite 8 and 7
Mark James beat Mark O'Meara 3 and 2
Christy O'Connor jr beat Fred Couples 1 hole
José Maria Canizares beat Ken Green 1 hole
Gordon Brand jr lost to Mark McCumber 1 hole
Sam Torrance lost to Tom Watson 3 and 1
Nick Faldo lost to Lanny Wadkins 1 hole
Ian Woosnam lost to Curtis Strange 1 hole

1991 *The Ocean Course, Kiawah Island, SC, USA*
Sept 26–29
Result: USA 14½, Europe 13½
Captains: Dave Stockton (USA),
Bernard Gallacher (Eur)
First Day: Morning – Foursomes
Ballesteros & Olazábal beat Azinger & Beck 2 and 1
Langer & James lost to Floyd & Couples 2 and 1
Gilford & Montgomerie lost to Wadkins & Irwin 4 and 2
Faldo & Woosnam lost to Stewart & Calcavecchia 1 hole
Afternoon – Fourball
Torrance & Feherty halved with Wadkins & O'Meara
Ballesteros & Olazábal beat Azinger & Beck 2 and 1
Richardson & James beat Pavin & Calcavecchia 5 and 4
Faldo & Woosnam lost to Floyd & Couples 5 and 3

1991 *continued*

Second Day: Morning – Foursomes
Torrance & Feherty lost to Irwin & Wadkins 4 and 2
James & Richardson lost to Calcavecchia & Stewart
 I hole
Faldo & Gilford lost to Azinger & O'Meara 7 and 6
Ballesteros & Olazábal beat Couples & Floyd 3 and 2

Afternoon – Fourball
Woosnam & Broadhurst beat Azinger & Irwin 2 and I
Langer & Montgomerie beat Pate & Pavin 2 and I
James & Richardson beat Wadkins & Levi 3 and I
Ballesteros & Olazábal halved with Couples & Stewart

Third Day – Singles
Nick Faldo beat Ray Floyd 2 holes
David Feherty beat Payne Stewart 2 and I
Colin Montgomerie halved with Mark Calcavecchia
José Maria Olazábal lost to Paul Azinger 2 holes
Steven Richardson lost to Corey Pavin 2 and I
Seve Ballesteros beat Wayne Levi 3 and 2
Ian Woosnam lost to Chip Beck 3 and I
Paul Broadhurst bat Mark O'Meara 3 and I
Sam Torrance lost to Fred Couples 3 and 2
Mark James lost to Lanny Wadkins 3 and 2
Bernhard Langer halved with Hale Irwin
David Gilford (withdrawn) halved with Steve Pate
 (withdrawn – injured)

1993 *The Brabazon Course, The De Vere Belfry,*
Sutton Coldfield, West Midlands, England
Sept 24–26
Result: Europe 13, USA 15
Captains: Bernard Gallacher (Eur)
 Tom Watson (USA)

First Day: Morning – Foursomes
Torrance & James lost to Wadkins & Pavin 4 and 3
Woosnam & Langer beat Azinger & Stewart 7 and 5
Ballesteros & Olazábal lost to Kite & Love 2 and I
Faldo & Montgomerie beat Floyd & Couples 4 and 3

Afternoon – Fourball
Woosnam & Baker beat Gallagher & Janzen I hole
Lane & Langer lost to Wadkins & Pavin 4 and 2
Faldo & Montgomerie halved with Azinger & Couples
Ballesteros & Olazábal beat Kite & Love 4 and 3

Second Day: Morning – Foursomes
Faldo & Montgomerie beat Wadkins & Pavin 3 and 2
Langer & Woosnam beat Couples & Azinger 2 and I
Baker & Lane lost to Floyd & Stewart 3 and 2
Ballesteros & Olazábal beat Kite & Love 2 and I

Afternoon – Fourball
Faldo & Montgomerie lost to Beck & Cook 2 holes
James & Rocca lost to Pavin & Gallagher 5 and 4
Woosnam & Baker beat Couples & Azinger 6 and 5
Olazábal & Haeggman lost to Floyd & Stewart 2 and I

Third Day – Singles
Ian Woosnam halved with Fred Couples
Barry Lane lost to Chip Beck I hole
Colin Montgomerie beat Lee Janzen I hole
Peter Baker beat Corey Pavin 2 holes
Joakim Haeggman beat J Cook I hole
Sam Torrance (withdrawn at start of day) halved with
 Lanny Wadkins (withdrawn at start of day)
Mark James lost to Payne Stewart 3 and 2
Constantino Rocca lost to Davis Love III I hole
Seve Ballesteros lost to Jim Gallagher jr 3 and 2
José Maria Olazábal lost to Ray Floyd 2 holes
Bernhard Langer lost to Tom Kite 5 and 3
Nick Faldo halved with Paul Azinger

1995 *Oak Hill Country Club, Rochester, NY, USA*
Sept 22–24
Result: USA 13½, Europe 14½
Captains: Lanny Wadkins (USA),
 Bernard Gallacher (Eur)

First Day: Morning – Foursomes
Faldo & Montgomerie lost to Pavin & Lehman I hole
Torrance & Rocca beat Haas & Couples 3 and 2
Clark & James lost to Love & Maggert 4 and 3
Langer & Johansson beat Crenshaw & Strange I hole

Afternoon – Fourball
Gilford & Ballesteros beat Faxon & Jacobsen 4 and 3
Torrance & Rocca lost to Maggert & Roberts 6 and 5
Faldo & Montgomerie lost to Couples & Love 3 and 2
Langer & Johansson lost to Pavin & Mickelson 6 and 4

Second Day: Morning – Foursomes
Faldo & Montgomerie beat Haas & Strange 4 and 2
Torrance & Rocca beat Love & Maggert 6 and 5
Woosnam & Walton lost to Roberts & Jacobsen I hole
Langer & Gilford beat Pavin & Lehman 4 and 3

Afternoon – Fourball
Torrance & Montgomerie lost to Faxon & Couples
 4 and 2
Woosnam & Rocca beat Love & Crenshaw 3 and 2
Ballesteros & Gilford lost to Haas & Mickelson 3 and 2
Faldo & Langer lost to Pavin & Roberts I hole

Third Day – Singles
Seve Ballesteros lost to Tom Lehman 4 and 3
Howard Clark beat Peter Jacobsen I hole
Mark James beat Jeff Maggert 4 and 3
Ian Woosnam halved with Fred Couples
Costantino Rocca lost to Davis Love III 3 and 2
David Gilford beat Brad Faxon I hole
Colin Montgomerie beat Ben Crenshaw 3 and I
Nick Faldo beat Curtis Strange I hole
Sam Torrance beat Loren Roberts 2 and I
Bernhard Langer lost to Corey Pavin 3 and 2
Philip Walton beat Jay Haas I hole
Per-Ulrik Johansson lost to Phil Mickelson 2 and I

1997 *at Valderrama Golf Club, Sotogrande, Cadiz,*
Spain Sept 26–28
Result: Europe 14½, USA 13½
Captains: Seve Ballesteros (Eur), Tom Kite (USA)

First Day: Morning – Fourball
Olazábal & Rocca beat Love & Mickelson I hole
Faldo & Westwood lost to Couples & Faxon I hole
Parnevik & Johansson beat Lehman & Furyk I hole
Montgomerie & Langer lost to Woods & O'Meara 3 and 2

Afternoon – Foursomes
Rocca & Olazábal lost to Hoch & Janzen I hole
Langer & Montgomerie beat O'Meara & Woods 5 and 3
Faldo & Westwood beat Leonard & Maggert 3 and 2
Parnevik & Garrido halved with Lehman & Mickelson

Second Day: Morning – Fourball
Montgomerie & Clarke beat Couples & Love I hole
Woosnam & Bjørn beat Leonard & Faxon 2 and I
Faldo & Westwood beat Woods & O'Meara 2 and I
Olazábal & Garrido halved with Mickelson & Lehman

Afternoon – Foursomes
Montgomerie & Langer beat Janzen & Furyk I hole
Faldo & Westwood lost to Hoch & Maggert 2 and I
Parnevik & Garrido halved with Leonard & Woods
Olazábal & Rocca beat Love & Couples 5 and 4

Third Day – Singles
Ian Woosnam lost to Fred Couples 8 and 7
Per-Ulrik Johansson beat Davis Love III 3 and 2

Costantino Rocca beat Tiger Woods 4 and 2
Thomas Bjørn halved with Justin Leonard
Darren Clarke lost to Phil Mickelson 2 and 1
Jesper Parnevik lost to Mark O'Meara 5 and 4
José Maria Olazábal lost to Lee Janzen 1 hole
Bernhard Langer beat Brad Faxon 2 and 1
Lee Westwood lost to Jeff Maggert 3 and 2
Colin Montgomerie halved with Scott Hoch
Nick Faldo lost to Jim Furyk 3 and 2
Ignacio Garrido lost to Tom Lehman 7 and 6

1999 The Country Club, Brookline, MA., USA Sept 24–26

Result: USA 14½, Europe 13½
Captains: Ben Crenshaw (USA), Mark James (Eur)
First Day: Morning – Foursomes
Montgomerie & Lawrie beat Duval & Mickelson 3 and 2
Parnevik & García beat Lehman & Woods 2 and 1
Jiménez & Harrington halved halved with Love & Stewart
Clarke & Westwood lost to Sutton & Maggert 3 and 2
Afternoon – Fourball
Montgomerie & Lawrie halved with Love & Leonard
Parnevik & García beat Mickelson & Furyk 1 hole
Jiménez & Olazábal beat Sutton & Maggert 2 and 1
Clarke & Westwood beat Duval & Woods 1 hole

Second Day: Morning – Foursomes
Montgomerie & Lawrie lost to Sutton & Maggert 1 hole
Clarke & Westwood beat Furyk & O'Meara 3 and 2
Jiménez & Harrington lost to Pate & Woods 1 hole
Parnevik & García beat Stewart & Leonard 3 and 2
Afternoon – Fourball
Clarke & Westwood lost to Mickelson & Lehman 2 and 1
Parnevik & García halved with Love & Duval
Jiménez & Olazábal halved with Leonard & Sutton
Montgomerie & Lawrie beat Pate & Woods 2 and 1

Third Day – Singles
Lee Westwood lost to Tom Lehman 3 and 2
Darren Clarke lost to Hal Sutton 4 and 2
Jarmo Sandelin lost to Phil Mickelson 4 and 3
Jean Van de Velde lost to Davis Love III 6 and 5
Andrew Coltart lost to Tiger Woods 3 and 2
Jesper Parnevik lost to David Duval 5 and 4
Padraig Harrington beat Mark O'Meara 1 hole
Miguel Angel Jiménez lost to Steve Pate 2 and 1
José Maria Olazábal halved with Justin Leonard
Colin Montgomerie beat Payne Stewart 1 hole
Sergio García lost to Jim Furyk 4 and 3
Paul Lawrie beat Jeff Maggert 4 and 3

2002 The Brabazon Course, The De Vere Belfry, Sutton Coldfield, West Midlands, England September

Result: Europe 13½, USA 12½
Captains: Sam Torrance (Eur), Curtis Strange (USA)
First Day, Morning – Fourball
Bjørn & Clarke beat Azinger & Woods 1 hole
García & Westwood beat Duval & Love 4 and 3
Langer & Montgomerie Beat Furyk & Hoch 4 and 3
Fasth & Harrington lost to Mickelson & Toms 1 hole

Afternoon – Foursomes
Bjørn & Clarke lost to Sutton & Verplank 2 and 1
García & Westwood beat Calcavecchia & Woods 2 and 1
Langer & Montgomerie halved with Mickelson & Toms
Harrington & McGinley lost to Cink & Furyk 3 and 2

Second Day, Morning – Foursomes
Fulke & Price lost to Mickelson & Toms 2 and 1
García & Westwood beat Cink & Furyk 2 and 1
Langer & Montgomerie beat Hoch & Verplank 1 hole
Bjørn & Clarke lost to Love & Woods 4 and 3

Afternoon – Fourball
Fasth & Parnevik lost to Calcavecchia & Duval 1 hole
García & Westwood lost to Love & Woods 1 hole
Harrington & Montgomerie beat Mickelson & Toms 2 and 1
Clarke & McGinley halved with Furyk & Hoch

Third Day – Singles
Colin Montgomerie (Sco) beat Scott Hoch 5 and 4
Sergio García (Esp) lost to David Toms 1 hole
Darren Clarke (NI) halved with David Duval
Bernhard Langer (Ger) beat Hal Sutton 4 and 3
Padraig Harrington (Irl) beat Mark Calcavecchia 5 and 4
Thomas Bjørn (Den) beat Stewart Cink 2 and 1
Lee Westwood (Eng) lost to Scott Verplank 2 and 1
Niclas Fasth (Swe) halved with Paul Azinger
Paul McGinley (Irl) halved with Jim Furyk
Pierre Fulke (Swe) halved with Davis Love III
Phillip Price (Wal) beat Phil Mickelson 3 and 2
Jesper Parnevik (Swe) halved with Tiger Woods

2004 Oakland Hills Country Club, Bloomfield, Detroit, MI, USA Sept 17–19

Result: USA 9½, Europe 18½
Captains: Hal Sutton (USA), Bernhard Langer (Eur)
First Day, Morning – Fourball
Woods & Mickelson lost to Montgomerie & Harrington 2 and 1
Love & Campbell lost to Clarke & Jiménez 5 and 4
Riley & Cink halved with McGinley & Donald
Toms & Furyk lost to García & Westwood 5 and 3

Afternoon – Foursomes
DiMarco & Haas beat Jiménez & Levet 3 and 2
Love & Funk lost to Montgomerie & Harrington 4 and 2
Mickelson & Woods lost to Clarke & Westwood 1 hole
Perry & Cink lost to García & Donald 2 and 1

Second Day, Morning – Fourball
Haas & DiMarco halved with García & Westwood
Woods & Riley beat Clarke & Poulter 4 and 3
Furyk & Campbell lost to Casey & Howell 1 hole
Cink & Love beat Montgomerie & Harrington 3 and 2

Afternoon – Foursomes
DiMarco & Haas lost to Clarke & Westwood 5 and 4
Mickelson & Toms beat Jiménez & Levet 4 and 3
Funk & Furyk lost to Donald & García 1 hole
Love & Woods lost to Harrington & McGinley 4 and 3

Third Day – Singles
Tiger Woods beat Paul Casey (Eng) 3 and 2
Phil Mickelson lost to Sergio García (Esp) 3 and 2
Davis Love III halved with Darren Clarke (NI)
Jim Furyk beat David Howell (Eng) 6 and 4
Kenny Perry lost to Lee Westwood (Eng) 1 hole
David Toms lost to Colin Montgomerie (Sco) 1 hole
Chad Campbell beat Luke Donald (Eng) 5 and 3
Chris DiMarco beat Miguel Angel Jiménez (Esp) 1 hole
Fred Funk lost to Thomas Levet (Fra) 1 hole
Chris Riley lost to Ian Poulter (Eng) 3 and 2
Jay Haas lost to Padraig Harrington (Irl) 1 hole
Stewart Cink lost to Paul McGinley (Irl) 3 and 2

INDIVIDUAL RECORDS

Matches were contested as Great Britain v USA from 1927 to 1953; as Great Britain & Ireland v USA from 1955 to 1977 and as Europe v USA from 1979. Non-playing captains are shown in brackets.

GB/GBI/Europe

Name	Year	Played	Won	Lost	Halved
Jimmy Adams	*1939-47-49-51-53	7	2	5	0
Percy Alliss	1929-33-35-37	6	3	2	1
Peter Alliss	1953-57-59-61-63-65-67-69	30	10	15	5
Laurie Ayton	1949	0	0	0	0
Peter Baker	1993	4	3	1	0
Severiano Ballesteros (ESP)	1979-83-85-87-89-91-93-95-(97)	37	20	12	5
Harry Bannerman	1971	5	2	2	1
Brian Barnes	1969-71-73-75-77-79	25	10	14	1
Maurice Bembridge	1969-71-73-75	16	5	8	3
Thomas Bjørn (DEN)	1997-2002	6	3	2	1
Aubrey Boomer	1927-29	4	2	2	0
Ken Bousfield	1949-51-55-57-59-61	10	5	5	0
Hugh Boyle	1967	3	0	3	0
Harry Bradshaw	1953-55-57	5	2	2	1
Gordon J Brand	1983	1	0	1	0
Gordon Brand jr	1987-89	7	2	4	1
Paul Broadhurst	1991	2	2	0	0
Eric Brown	1953-55-57-59-(69)-(71)	8	4	4	0
Ken Brown	1977-79-83-85-87	13	4	9	0
Stewart Burns	1929	0	0	0	0
Dick Burton	1935-37-*39-49	5	2	3	0
Jack Busson	1935	2	0	2	0
Peter Butler	1965-69-71-73	14	3	9	2
José Maria Canizares (ESP)	1981-83-85-89	11	5	4	2
Paul Casey	2004-06	6	3	1	2
Alex Caygill	1969	1	0	0	1
Clive Clark	1973	1	0	1	0
Howard Clark	1977-81-85-87-89-95	15	10	7	3
Darren Clarke	1997-99-2002-04-06	20	7	7	3
Neil Coles	1961-63-65-67-69-71-73-77	40	12	21	7
Andrew Coltart	1999	1	0	1	0
Archie Compston	1927-29-31	6	1	4	1
Henry Cotton	1929-37-*39-47-(53)	6	2	4	0
Bill Cox	1935-37	3	0	2	1
Allan Dailey	1933	0	0	0	0
Fred Daly	1947-49-51-53	8	3	4	1
Eamonn Darcy	1975-77-81-87	11	1	8	2
William Davies	1931-33	4	2	2	0
Peter Dawson	1977	3	1	2	0
Luke Donald	2004-06	7	5	1	1
Norman Drew	1959	1	0	0	1
George Duncan	1927-29-31	5	2	3	0
Syd Easterbrook	1931-33	3	2	1	0
Nick Faldo	1977-79-81-83-85-87-89-91-93-95-97	46	23	19	4
John Fallon	1955-(63)	1	1	0	0
Niclas Fasth (SWE)	2002	3	0	2	1
Max Faulkner	1947-49-51-53-57	8	1	7	0
David Feherty	1991	3	1	1	1
Pierre Fulke (SWE)	2002	2	0	1	1
George Gadd	1927	0	0	0	0
Bernard Gallacher	1969-71-73-75-77-79-81-83-(91)-(93)-(95)	31	13	13	5
Sergio García (ESP)	1999-2002-04-06	20	14	4	2
John Garner	1971-73	1	0	1	0
Antonio Garrido (ESP)	1979	5	0	4	1
Ignacio Garrido (ESP)	1997	4	0	1	3
David Gilford	1991-95	6	3	3	0
Eric Green	1947	0	0	0	0
Malcolm Gregson	1967	4	0	4	0
Joakim Haeggman (SWE)	1993	2	1	1	0
Tom Haliburton	1961-63	6	0	6	0
Jack Hargreaves	1951	0	0	0	0
Padraig Harrington	1999-2002-04-06	17	7	8	2
Arthur Havers	1927-31-33	6	3	3	0
Jimmy Hitchcock	1965	3	0	3	0
Bert Hodson	1931	1	0	1	0

In 1939 a GB team was named but the match was not played because of the Second World War

Name	Year	Played	Won	Lost	Halved
Reg Horne	1947	0	0	0	0
Tommy Horton	1975-77	8	1	6	1
David Howell	2004-06	5	3	1	1
Brian Huggett	1963-67-69-71-73-75-(77)	25	9	10	6
Bernard Hunt	1953-57-59-61-63-65-67-69-(73)-(75)	28	6	16	6
Geoffrey Hunt	1963	3	0	3	0
Guy Hunt	1975	3	0	2	1
Tony Jacklin	1967-69-71-73-75-77-79-(83)-(85)-(87)-(89)	35	13	14	8
John Jacobs	1955-(79)-(81)	2	2	0	0
Mark James	1977-79-81-89-91-93-95-(99)	24	8	15	1
Edward Jarman	1935	1	0	1	0
Miguel Angel Jiménez (ESP)	1999-2004	9	2	5	2
Per-Ulrik Johansson (SWE)	1995-97	5	3	2	0
Herbert Jolly	1927	2	0	2	0
Robert Karlsson (SWE)	2006	3	0	1	2
Michael King	1979	1	0	1	0
Sam King	1937-*39-47-49	5	1	3	1
Arthur Lacey	1933-37-(51)	3	0	3	0
Barry Lane	1993	3	0	3	0
Bernhard Langer (GER)	1981-83-85-87-89-91-93-95-97-2002-(04)	42	21	15	6
Paul Lawrie	1999	5	3	1	1
Arthur Lees	1947-49-51-55	8	4	4	0
Thomas Levet (FRA)	2004	3	1	2	0
Sandy Lyle	1979-81-83-85-87	18	7	9	2
Paul McGinley (IRL)	2002-04-06	9	2	2	5
Jimmy Martin	1965	1	0	1	0
Peter Mills	1957-59	1	1	0	0
Abe Mitchell	1929-31-33	6	4	2	0
Ralph Moffitt	1961	1	0	1	0
Colin Montgomerie	1991-93-95-97-99-2002-04-06	36	20	9	7
Christy O'Connor jr	1975-89	4	1	3	0
Christy O'Connor sr	1955-57-59-61-63-65-67-69-71-73	36	11	21	4
José María Olazábal (ESP)	1987-89-91-93-97-99-2006	31	18	8	5
John O'Leary	1975	4	0	4	0
Peter Oosterhuis	1971-73-75-77-79-81	28	14	11	3
Alf Padgham	1933-35-37-*39	6	0	6	0
John Panton	1951-53-61	5	0	5	0
Jesper Parnevik (SWE)	1997-99-2002	11	4	3	4
Alf Perry	1933-35-37	4	0	3	1
Manuel Pinero (ESP)	1981-85	9	6	3	0
Lionel Platts	1965	5	1	2	2
Eddie Polland	1973	2	0	2	0
Ian Poulter	2004	2	1	1	0
Phillip Price	2002	2	1	1	0
Ronan Rafferty	1989	3	1	2	0
Ted Ray	1927	2	0	2	0
Dai Rees	1937-*39-47-49-51-53-55-57-59-61-(67)	18	7	10	1
Steven Richardson	1991	4	2	2	0
José Rivero (ESP)	1985-87	5	2	3	0
Fred Robson	1927-29-31	6	2	4	0
Costantino Rocca (ITA)	1993-95-97	11	6	5	0
Jarmo Sandelin (SWE)	1999	1	0	1	0
Syd Scott	1955	2	0	2	0
Des Smyth	1979-81	7	2	5	0
Henrik Stenson (SWE)	2006	3	1	1	1
Dave Thomas	1959-63-65-67	18	3	10	5
Sam Torrance	1981-83-85-87-89-91-93-95-(2002)	27	7	15	5
Peter Townsend	1969-71	11	3	8	0
Jean Van de Velde (FRA)	1999	1	0	1	0
Brian Waites	1983	4	1	3	0
Philip Walton	1995	2	1	1	0
Charlie Ward	1947-49-51	6	1	5	0
Paul Way	1983-85	9	6	2	1
Harry Weetman	1951-53-55-57-59-61-63-(65)	15	2	11	2
Lee Westwood	1997-99-2002-04-06	20	12	5	3
Charles Whitcombe	1927-29-31-33-35-37-*39-(49)	9	3	2	4
Ernest Whitcombe	1929-31-35	6	1	4	1
Reg Whitcombe	1935-*39	1	0	1	0
George Will	1963-65-67	15	2	11	2
Norman Wood	1975	3	1	2	0
Ian Woosnam	1983-85-87-89-91-93-95-97-(2006)	31	14	12	5

In 1939 a GB team was named but the match was not played because of the Second World War

United States of America

Name	Year	Played	Won	Lost	Halved
Tommy Aaron	1969-73	6	1	4	1
Skip Alexander	1949-51	2	1	1	0
Paul Azinger	1989-91-93-2002	16	5	8	3
Jerry Barber	1955-61	5	1	4	0
Miller Barber	1969-71	7	1	4	2
Herman Barron	1947	1	1	0	0
Andy Bean	1979-87	6	4	2	0
Frank Beard	1969-71	8	2	3	3
Chip Beck	1989-91-93	9	6	2	1
Homero Blancas	1973	4	2	1	1
Tommy Bolt	1955-57	4	3	1	0
Julius Boros	1959-63-65-67	16	9	3	4
Gay Brewer	1967-73	9	5	3	1
Billy Burke	1931-33	3	3	0	0
Jack Burke	1951-53-55-57-59-(73)	8	7	1	0
Walter Burkemo	1953	1	0	1	0
Mark Calcavecchia	1987-89-91-2002	14	6	7	1
Chad Campbell	2004-06	6	1	3	2
Billy Casper	1961-63-65-67-69-71-73-75-(79)	37	20	10	7
Stewart Cink	2002-04-06	12	3	5	4
Bill Collins	1961	3	1	2	0
Charles Coody	1971	3	0	2	1
John Cook	1993	2	1	1	0
Fred Couples	1989-91-93-95-97	20	7	9	4
Wilfred Cox	1931	2	2	0	0
Ben Crenshaw	1981-83-87-95-(99)	12	3	8	1
Jimmy Demaret	*1941-47-49-51	6	6	0	0
Gardner Dickinson	1967-71	10	9	1	0
Leo Diegel	1927-29-31-33	6	3	3	0
Chris DiMarco	2004-06	8	2	4	2
Dale Douglass	1969	2	0	2	0
Dave Douglas	1953	2	1	0	1
Ed Dudley	1929-33-37	4	3	1	0
Olin Dutra	1933-35	4	1	3	0
David Duval	1999-2002	7	2	3	2
Lee Elder	1979	4	1	3	0
Al Espinosa	1927-29-31	4	2	1	1
Johnny Farrell	1927-29-31	6	3	2	1
Brad Faxon	1995-97	6	2	4	0
Dow Finsterwald	1957-59-61-63-(77)	13	9	3	1
Ray Floyd	1969-75-77-81-83-85-(89)-91-93	31	12	16	3
Doug Ford	1955-57-59-61	9	4	4	1
Fred Funk	2004	3	0	3	0
Ed Furgol	1957	1	0	1	0
Marty Furgol	1955	1	0	1	0
Jim Furyk	1997-99-2002-04-06	20	6	12	2
Jim Gallagher jr	1993	3	2	1	0
Al Geiberger	1967-75	9	5	1	3
Vic Ghezzi	*1939-*41	0	0	0	0
Bob Gilder	1983	4	2	2	0
Bob Goalby	1963	5	3	1	1
Johnny Golden	1927-29	3	3	0	0
Lou Graham	1973-75-77	9	5	3	1
Hubert Green	1977-79-85	7	4	3	0
Ken Green	1989	4	2	2	0
Ralph Guldahl	1937-*39	2	2	0	0
Fred Haas jr	1953	1	0	1	0
Jay Haas	1983-95-2004	12	4	6	2
Walter Hagen	1927-29-31-33-35-(37)	9	7	1	1
Bob Hamilton	1949	2	0	2	0
Chick Harbert	1949-55	2	2	0	0
Chandler Harper	1955	1	0	1	0
EJ (Dutch) Harrison	1947-49-51	3	2	1	0
Fred Hawkins	1957	2	1	1	0
Mark Hayes	1979	3	1	2	0
Clayton Heafner	1949-51	4	3	0	1
Jay Hebert	1959-61-(71)	4	2	1	1
Lionel Hebert	1957	1	0	1	0
J J Henry	2006	3	0	0	3
Dave Hill	1969-73-77	9	6	3	0
Jimmy Hines	*1939	0	0	0	0

* US teams were selected in 1939 and 1941, but did not play because of the Second World War

Name	Year	Played	Won	Lost	Halved
Scott Hoch	1997-2002	7	2	3	2
Ben Hogan	*1941-47-(49)-51-(67)	3	3	0	0
Hale Irwin	1975-77-79-81-91	20	13	5	2
Tommy Jacobs	1965	4	3	1	0
Peter Jacobsen	1985-95	6	2	4	0
Don January	1965-77	7	2	3	2
Lee Janzen	1993-97	5	2	3	0
Zach Johnson	2006	4	1	2	1
Herman Keiser	1947	1	0	1	0
Tom Kite	1979-81-83-85-87-89-93-(97)	28	15	9	4
Ted Kroll	1953-55-57	4	3	1	0
Ky Laffoon	1935	1	0	1	0
Tom Lehman	1995-97-99-(2006)	10	5	3	2
Tony Lema	1963-65	11	8	1	2
Justin Leonard	1997-99	8	0	3	5
Wayne Levi	1991	2	0	2	0
Bruce Lietzke	1981	3	0	2	1
Gene Littler	1961-63-65-67-69-71-75	27	14	5	8
Davis Love III	1993-95-97-99-2002-04	26	9	12	5
Jeff Maggert	1995-97-99	11	6	5	0
John Mahaffey	1979	3	1	2	0
Mark McCumber	1989	3	2	1	0
Jerry McGee	1977	2	1	1	0
Harold McSpaden	*1939-*41	0	0	0	0
Tony Manero	1937	2	1	1	0
Lloyd Mangrum	*1941-47-49-51-53	8	6	2	0
Dave Marr	1965-(81)	6	4	2	0
Billy Maxwell	1963	4	4	0	0
Dick Mayer	1957	2	1	0	1
Bill Mehlhorn	1927	2	1	1	0
Dick Metz	*1939	0	0	0	0
Phil Mickelson	1995-97-99-2002-04-06	29	9	12	4
Cary Middlecoff	1953-55-59	6	2	3	1
Johnny Miller	1975-81	6	2	2	2
Larry Mize	1987	4	1	1	2
Gil Morgan	1979-83	6	1	2	3
Bob Murphy	1975	4	2	1	1
Byron Nelson	1937-*39-*41-47-(65)	4	3	1	0
Larry Nelson	1979-81-87	13	9	3	1
Bobby Nichols	1967	5	4	0	1
Jack Nicklaus	1969-71-73-75-77-81-(83)-(87)	28	17	8	3
Andy North	1985	3	0	3	0
Ed Oliver	1947-51-53	5	3	2	0
Mark O'Meara	1985-89-91-97-99	14	4	9	1
Arnold Palmer	1961-63-65-67-71-73-(75)	32	22	8	2
Johnny Palmer	1949	2	0	2	0
Sam Parks	1935	1	0	0	1
Jerry Pate	1981	4	2	2	0
Steve Pate	1991-99	4	2	2	0
Corey Pavin	1991-93-95	8	5	3	0
Calvin Peete	1983-85	7	4	2	1
Kenny Perry	2004	2	0	2	0
Henry Picard	1935-37-*39	4	3	1	0
Dan Pohl	1987	3	1	2	0
Johnny Pott	1963-65-67	7	5	2	0
Dave Ragan	1963	4	2	1	1
Henry Ransom	1951	1	0	1	0
Johnny Revolta	1935-37	3	2	1	0
Chris Riley	2004	3	1	1	1
Loren Roberts	1995	4	3	1	0
Chi Chi Rodriguez	1973	2	0	1	1
Bill Rogers	1981	4	1	2	1
Bob Rosburg	1959	2	2	0	0
Mason Rudolph	1971	3	1	1	1
Paul Runyan	1933-35-*39	4	2	2	0
Doug Sanders	1967	5	2	3	0
Gene Sarazen	1927-29-31-33-35-37-*41	12	7	2	3
Densmore Shute	1931-33-37	6	2	2	2
Dan Sikes	1969	3	2	1	0
Scott Simpson	1987	2	1	1	0
Horton Smith	1929-31-33-35-37-*39-*41	4	3	0	1
JC Snead	1971-73-75	11	9	2	0
Sam Snead	1937-*39-*41-47-49-51-53-55-59-(69)	13	10	2	1

US teams were selected in 1939 and 1941, but did not play because of the Second World War

Ryder Cup American Individual Records *continued*

Name	Year	Played	Won	Lost	Halved
Ed Sneed	1977	2	1	0	1
Mike Souchak	1959-61	6	5	1	0
Craig Stadler	1983-85	8	4	2	2
Payne Stewart	1987-89-91-93-99	19	7	10	2
Ken Still	1969	3	1	2	0
Dave Stockton	1971-77-(91)	5	3	1	1
Curtis Strange	1983-85-87-89-95-2002	20	6	12	2
Hal Sutton	1985-87-99-2002-(04)	16	7	5	4
Vaughn Taylor	2006	2	0	1	1
David Toms	2002-04-06	12	4	6	2
Lee Trevino	1969-71-73-75-79-81-(85)	30	17	7	6
Jim Turnesa	1953	1	1	0	0
Joe Turnesa	1927-29	4	1	2	1
Ken Venturi	1965	4	1	3	0
Scott Verplank	2002-06	5	4	1	0
Lanny Wadkins	1977-79-83-85-87-89-91-93-(95)	33	20	11	2
Art Wall jr	1957-59-61	6	4	2	0
Al Watrous	1927-29	3	2	1	0
Tom Watson	1977-81-83-89-(93)	15	10	4	1
Tom Weiskopf	1973-75	10	7	2	1
Brett Wetterich	2006	2	0	2	0
Craig Wood	1931-33-35-*41	4	1	3	0
Tiger Woods	1997-99-2002-04-06	25	10	13	2
Lew Worsham	1947	2	2	0	0
Fuzzy Zoeller	1979-83-85	10	1	8	1

Paul Azinger to lead Americans in 2008 Ryder Cup

The announcement that Paul Azinger, the former USPGA champion, would captain the American team in the next Ryder Cup at Valhalla in Louisville, Kentucky, was no surprise. He had been widely tipped to land the role opposite Nick Faldo who will captain the European side in their bid to win the trophy for a fourth time in a row.

© Getty Images

Azinger, who played in the 1989, 1991, 1993 and 2002 Ryder Cup matches, described his appointment as "The proudest honour you can bestow on a professional golfer". Winner of 12 events on the USPGA Tour, Azinger won his major in a play-off against Greg Norman just a few months before being diagnosed with lymphoma cancer from which he has made a full recovery.

Azinger and Faldo will be seeing a lot of each other in the next two years. Both commentate in the box for CBS Television in America.

Nick Faldo and Paul Azinger

As expected, the Americans have made changes to their points selection system for the 2008 match from which eight players will be chosen, leaving the captain with four instead of two picks. Points will only be awarded in 2007 for the majors and in 2008 all events will carry Cup points with the majors offering the most.

PGA Cup (Instituted 1973)

Great Britain and Ireland Club Professionals v United States Club Professionals

1973	USA	Pinehurst, NC	13–3	1986	USA	Knollwood, Lake Fore, IL	16–9
1974	USA	Pinehurst, NC	11½–4½	1988	USA	The Belfry, England	15½–10½
1975	USA	Hillside, Southport, England	9½–6½	1990	USA	Turtle Point, Kiawah Island, SC	19–7
1976	USA	Moortown, Leeds, England	9½–6½	1992	USA	K Club, Ireland	15–11
1977	Halved	Mission Hills, Palm Springs	8½–8½	1994	USA	Palm Beach, Florida	15–11
1978	GB&I	St Mellion, Cornwall	10½–6½	1996	Halved	Gleneagles, Scotland	13–13
1979	GB&I	Castletown, Isle of Man	12½–4½	1998	USA	The Broadmoor, Colorado	
1980	USA	Oak Tree, Edmond, OK	15–6			Springs, CO	11½–4½
1981	Halved	Turnberry Isle, Miami, FL	10½–10½	2000	USA	Celtic Manor, Newport, Wales	13½–12½
1982	USA	Holston Hills, Knoxville, TN	13–7	2002	Cancelled		
1983	GB&I	Muirfield, Scotland	14½–6½	2003	USA	Port St Lucie, FL	19–7
1984	GB&I	Turnberry, Scotland	12½–8½	2005	GBI	K Club, Dublin, R.o.I.	15–11

Played alternate years from 1984

This event is being played this year at the Reynolds Plantation, Georgia, USA

The Seve Trophy (Instituted 2000)

2000	Sunningdale, England	GBI 12½, Europe 13½	2002	Druid's Glen, Ireland	Europe 12½, GBI 14½
2003	El Saler, Spain	Europe 13, GBI 15	2005	The Wynard, England	GBI 16½, Europe, 11½

This event is being played this year at The Heritage, Killenard, from September 27–30

Presidents Cup (Instituted 1994)

1994	USA	Lake Manassas, Virginia	20–12
1996	USA	Lake Manassas, Virginia	16½–15½
1998	International	Royal Melbourne, Australia	20½–11½
2000	USA	Robert Trent Jones GC, VA	20½–11½
2003	Tied	Fancourt Hotel and CC, S. Africa	17–17

Play-off: Els and Woods halved three sudden-death holes when darkness forced a stoppage. It was agreed that both teams should share the cup for the next two years.

2005	USA	Robert Trent Jones GC, VA	18½–15½

This event is being played this year at Royal Montreal GC from September 24–27

Alfred Dunhill Cup *Old Course, St Andrews*

Year	Winner	Runner-up	Score
1985	Australia (G Norman, G Marsh, D Graham)	USA (M O'Meara, R Floyd, C Strange)	3–0
1986	Australia (R Davis, D Graham, G Norman)	Japan (T Ozaki, N Ozaki, T Nakajima)	3–0
1987	England (N Faldo, G Brand, H Clark)	Scotland (S Lyle, S Torrance, G Brand jr)	2–1
1988	Ireland (D Smyth, R Rafferty, E Darcy)	Australia (R Davis, D Graham, G Norman)	2–1
1989	USA (M Calcavecchia, T Kite, C Strange)	Japan (H Meshiai, N Ozaki, K Suzuki)	3½–2½
1990	Ireland (P Walton, R Rafferty, D Feherty)	England (M James, R Boxall, H Clark)	3½–2½
1991	Sweden (A Forsbrand, P-U Johansson,	South Africa (J Bland, D Frost, G Player)	2–1
	M Lanner)		
1992	England (S Richardson, J Spence, D Gilford)	Scotland (G Brand Jr, C Montgomerie, S Lyle)	2–0
1993	USA (P Stewart, F Couples, J Daly)	England (M James, N Faldo, P Baker)	2–1
1994	Canada (D Barr, R Gibson, R Stewart)	USA (T Kite, C Strange, F Couples)	2–1
1995	Scotland (A Coltart, C Montgomerie,	Zimbabwe (T Johnstone, M McNulty, N Price)	
	S Torrance)		2–1
1996	USA (M O'Meara, P Mickelson, S Stricker)	New Zealand (F Nobilo, G Turner, G Waite)	2–1
1997	South Africa (R Goosen, D Frost, E Els)	Sweden (J Parnevik, P-U Johansson, J Haeggman)	2–1
1998	South Africa (R Goosen, D Frost, E Els)	Spain (MA Jiménez, S Luna, JM Olazábal)	2–1
1999	Spain (S García, JM Olazábal, MA Jiménez)	Australia (C Parry, PO'Malley, S Leaney)	2–1
2000	Spain (MA Martin, MA Jiménez, JM Olazábal)	South Africa (D Frost, R Goosen, E Els)	2–1

Discontinued

UBS Warburg Cup USA v Rest of World (Instituted 2001)

2001	USA	2002	USA	2003	Rest of World	2004	Rest of World

Discontinued

Nations Cup (World Cup Qualifiers)

Asian Qualifier Seri Selangor Golf Club,Kuala Lumpur

2000	Korea	2002	Switzerland	2004	Korea
2001	China	2003	Myanmar	2005	Singapore

1	Singapore	Mardan Mamat and Lam Chih Bing	65-73-63-70--271
2	Italy	Emanuele Canonica and Francesco Molinari	68-75-64-71--278

Other scores: 3 Switzerland, India 280; 5 Hong Kong, Malaysia 281;7 Philippines, Finland 282; 9 Chinese Taipei 286; 10 Myanmar 287; 11 Holland 290; 12 Pakistan 294;13 Ghana 296; 14 Mauritius 316

Latin American Qualifier Holiday Inn,Tierra de Sol GC,Aruba

2003	Chile	2004	Mexico	2005	Venezuela

1	Mexico	Esteban Toledo and Octavio Gonzalez	64-75-67-70—276
2	Jamaica*	Peter Horrobin and Delroy Cambridge	70-71-70-67—278
	Venezuela	Carlos Larrain and Miguel Martinez	64-77-65-72—278

* Jamaica won second qualifying spot after two hole play-off with Venezuela

Other scores: 4 Paraguay 280; 5 Bermuda 283; 6 Peru 284; 7 Bahamas, Chile 285; 9 Austria 288; 10 Puerto Rico 294; 11 Brazil 295; Aruba 306

The Royal Trophy (Asia/Japan v Europe)

2005 Amata Spring, Bangkok,Thailand

Captains: Asia: Masahiro Kuramoto (JPN); Europe: Seve Ballesteros (ESP)

First Day, Morning – Foursomes
S K Ho & Fukabori lost to Howell & Ferrie 2 holes
Atwal & Randhawa lost to McGinley & McDowell 4 and 3
Imano & Zhang lost to Bjørn & Stenson 1 hole
Wiratchant & Jaidee beat Faldo & Woosnam 6 and 5

Afternoon – Fourball
Atwal & Randhawa beat Howell & Ferrie 1 hole
S K Ho & Zhang lost to McGinley & McDowell 2 and 1
Wiratchant & Jaidee lost to Bjørn & Woosnam 3 and 2
Fukabori & Imano lost to Faldo & Stenson 1 hole

First day match position: Asia/Japan 2 Europe 6

Second Day – Singles
Yasuharo Imano (JPN) beat David Howell (ENG) 2 holes
Zhang Lian-wei (CHN) lost to Paul McGinley (IRL) 2 and 1
Jyoti Randhawa (IND) lost to Graeme McDowell (NIR) 3 and 2
Arjun Atwal (IND) beat Nick Faldo (ENG) 3 and 2
Thaworn Wiratchant (THA) beat Ian Woosnam (WAL) 2 and 1
S K Ho (KOR) beat Kenneth Ferrie (ENG) 2 and 1
Keiichiro Fukibori (JPN) beat Thomas Bjørn (DEN) 4 and 3
Thongchai Jaidee (THA) lost to Henrik Stenson (SWE) 5 and 4

Singles: Asia/Japan 5, Europe 3

Final result: Asia/Japan 7, Europe 9

Visa Dynasty Cup (Instituted 2003)

2003	Asia	16½, Japan 7½	2005	Asia	14½, Japan 9½

National and Regional Championships

National Championships

PGA Seniors' Championship *Stoke by Nayland*

1970	M Faulkner	Longniddry	288		1989	N Coles	West Hill	277	
1971	K Nagle	Elie	269		1990	B Waites	Brough	269	
1972	K Bousfield	Longniddry	291		1991	B Waites	Wollaton Park	277	
1973	K Nagle	Elie	270		1992	T Horton	R Dublin	290	
1974	E Lester	Lundin	282		1993	B Huggett	Sunningdale	204	(54)
1975	K Nagle	Longniddry	268		1994	J Morgan	Sunningdale	203	
1976	C O'Connor	Cambridgeshire Hotel	284		1995	J Morgan	Sunningdale	204	
1977	C O'Connor	Cambridgeshire Hotel	288		1996	T Gale	The Belfry	284	
1978	P Skerritt	Cambridgeshire Hotel	288		1997	W Hall	The Belfry	277	
1979	C O'Connor	Cambridgeshire Hotel	280		1998	T Horton	The Belfry	277	
1980	P Skerritt	Gleneagles Hotel	286		1999	R Metherall	The Belfry	276	
1981	C O'Connor	North Berwick	287		2000	J Grace	The Belfry	282	
1982	C O'Connor	Longniddry	285		2001	I Stanley	Carden Park	278	
1983	C O'Connor	Burnham and Berrow	277		2002	S Ebihara	Carden Park	267	
1984	E Jones	Stratford-upon-Avon	280		2003	W Longmuir	Carden Park	271	
1985	N Coles	Pannal, Harrogate	284		2004	C Mason*	Carden Park	275	
1986	N Coles	Mere, Cheshire	276		*Mason beat Jim Rhodes and Seiji Ebihara after two extra holes				
1987	N Coles	Turnberry	279		2005	S Torrance	Carden Park	271	
1988	P Thomson	North Berwick	287						

1	Sam Torrance (De Vere Belfry)	66-65-71-66—268
2	Luis Carbonetti (ARG)	68-69-65-69—271
3	Giuseppe Cali (ITA)	67-66-66-74—273

Glenmuir Club Professionals' Championship *Princes*

1973	DN Sewell	Calcot Park	276		1991	W McGill	King's Lynn	285
1974	WB Murray	Calcot Park	275		1992	J Hoskison	St Pierre	275
1975	DN Sewell	Calcot Park	276		1993	C Hall	Coventry	274
1976	WJ Ferguson	Moortown	283		1994	D Jones	North Berwick	278
1977	D Huish	Notts	284		1995	P Carman	West Hill	269
1978	D Jones	Pannal	281		1996	B Longmuir	Co Louth	280
1979	D Jones	Pannal	278		1997	B Rimmer	Northop	268
1980	D Jagger	Turnberry	286		1998	M Jones	Royal St David's	280
1981	M Steadman	Woburn	289		1999	S Bebb*	Kings Lynn	283
1982	D Durnian	Hill Valley	285		*Bebb beat Chris Hall and Paul Wesselingh at first extra hole			
1983	J Farmer	Heaton Park	270		2000	R Cameron*	St Andrews	295
1984	D Durnian	Bolton Old Links	278		*Cameron beat Russell Weir at second extra hole			
1985	R Mann	The Belfry	291		2001	S Edwards	County Louth	275
1986	D Huish	R Birkdale	278		2002	B Cameron	Saunton	280
1987	R Weir	Sandiway	273		2003	G Law	St Andrews Bay	280
1988	R Weir	Harlech	269		2004	T Nash	Southport & Ainsdale	270
1989	B Barnes	Sandwich, Prince's	280		2005	M Ellis*	Woodhall Spa	285
1990	A Webster	Carnoustie	292					

1	Paul Wesselingh (Kedleston Park)*	69-73-69-68—279
2	Duncan Muscroft (Montecchia)	73-74-67-65—279
3	John Wells (Beverley & East Riding)	69-73-69-69—280

*Wesselingh won at first extra hole

Irish Club Professionals' Championship Rathsallagh

1993	D Mooney	Royal Tara	208
1994	K O'Donnell	Knockanally	216
1995	D Jones	Fota Island	145
1996	B McGovern	Headfort	140
1997	N Manchip	Mount Wolseley	141
1998	L Robinson	Nuremore	140
1999	N Manchip	Nuremore	139
2000	L Walker	Nuremore	134
2001	M Allen*	Nuremore	142

*Allen won at second extra hole

2002	N Manchip	Nuremore	135
2003	D Mooney*	Tulfarris	142

*Mooney wn at first extra hole

2004	C Mallon*	Enniscrone	144

*Mallon won at second extra hole

2005	S Thornton*	Lisburn	138

*Thornton won at fourth extra hole

1	Peter O'Hagan (K Club)	70-68—138
2	Eamonn Brady (Clontarf)	70-70—140
	Ian Kerr (Carlow GR)	69-71—140
	Simon Thornton (Royal County Down)	68-72—140

PGA Senior Club Professionals Championship King's Lynn

1	Stewart Graham (Golf de Bondues)	70-73-70—213
2	Graham Burroughs (Boyce Hill)	74-72-69—215
	David Jagger (Hull)	70-73-72—215

PGA Assistants Championship The London Club, Kent

1984	G Weir	Coombe Hill	286
1985	G Coles	Coombe Hill	284
1986	J Brennand	Sand Moor	280
1987	J Hawksworth	Coombe Hill	282
1988	J Oates	Coventry	284
1989	C Brooks	Hillside	291
1990	A Ashton	Hillside	213 (54)
1991	S Wood	Wentworth	288
1992	P Mayo	E Sussex National	285
1993	C Everett	Oaklands	280
1994	M Plummer	Burnham & Berrow	278
1995	I Sparkes	The Warwickshire	285

1996	S Purves	Moor Allerton	281
1997	P Sefton	De Vere, Blackpool	273
1998	A Raitt	Bearwood Lakes	280
1999	I Harrison	Bearwood Lakes	274
2000	T Anderson	St Annes Old Links	273
2001	C Goodfellow	St Annes Old Links	207
2002	D Orr	St Annes Old Links	271
2003	M Tottey*	St Annes Old Links	204

*Tottey beat Neil Ridewood at first extra hole

2004	M Ford	Coventry	208
2005	M Tottey	The London Club	211

1	Brett Taylor (Chelmsford)	69-69-68—206
2	Ryan Fenwick (Ifield)	64-78-69—211
3	Matthew March (unattached)	71-71-71—213

PGA Irish Championship Druids Heath

1944	H Bradshaw	Hermitage	291
1945	J McKenna	Newlands	283
1946	F Daly	Clandeboye	285
1947	H Bradshaw	County Louth	291
1948	J McKenna	Galway	285
1949	C Kane	Portrush	301
1950	H Bradshaw	Grange	277
1951	H Bradshaw	Balmoral	280
1952	F Daly	Mullingar	284
1953	H Bradshaw	Dundalk	272
1954	H Bradshaw	Newcastle	300
1955	E Jones	Castleroy	276
1956	C Greene	Clandeboye	281
1957	H Bradshaw	Ballybunion	286
1958	C O'Connor	Royal Belfast	279
1959	NV Drew	Mullingar	282
1960	C O'Connor	Warrenpoint	271
1961	C O'Connor	Lahinch	280
1962	C O'Connor	Bangor	264
1963	C O'Connor	Little Island	271
1964	E Jones	Knock	279
1965	C O'Connor	Mullingar	283
1966	C O'Connor	Warrenpoint	269

1967	H Boyle	Tullamore	214 (54)
1968	C Greene	Knock	282
1969	J Martin	Dundalk	268
1970	H Jackson	Massareene	283
1971	C O'Connor	Galway	278
1972	J Kinsella	Bundoran	289
1973	J Kinsella	Limerick	284
1974	E Polland	Portstewart	277
1975	C O'Connor	Carlow	275
1976	P McGuirk	Waterville	291
1977	P Skerritt	Woodbrook	281
1978	C O'Connor	Dollymount	286
1979	D Smyth	Dollymount	215 (54)
1980	D Feherty	Dollymount	283
1981	D Jones	Woodbrook	283
1982	D Feherty	Woodbrook	287
1983	L Higgins	Woodbrook	275
1984	M Sludds	Skerries	277
1985	D Smyth	Co Louth	204 (54)
1986	D Smyth	Waterville	282
1987	P Walton	Co Louth	144 (36)
1988	E Darcy	Castle, Dublin	269
1989	P Walton	Castle, Dublin	266

1990	D Smyth	Woodbrook	271
1991	P Walton	Woodbrook	277
1992	E Darcy	K Club	285
1993	M Sludds	K Club	285
1994	D Clarke	Galway Bay	285
1995	P Walton	Belvoir Park	273
1996	D Smyth	Slieve Russell GC	281
1997	P McGinley	Fota Island	285
1998	P Harrington*	Powerscourt	216 (54)

*Harrington won at first extra hole

1999	N Manchip	The Island	271
2000	P McGinley	Co Louth	270
2001	D Smyth	Castle Rock	273
2002	P McGinley	Westport	213
2003	P McGinley	Adare Manor	280
2004	P Harrington	St Margaret's	287
2005	P Harrington*	Palmerston House	285

*Harrington won at first extra hole

1	David Mortimer (Newlands)	68-72-76-70—286
2	John Dwyer (Ashbourne)	75-72-69-71—287
	Robert Giles (Greenore)	69-73-71-74—287

Scottish PGA Championship *Gleneagles*

1907	J Hunter	1933	M Seymour	1961	RT Walker	1983	BJ Gallacher
1908	R Thomson	1934	M Seymour	1962	EC Brown	1984	I Young
1909	TR Fernie	1935	M McDowall	1963	WM Miller	1985	S Torrance
1910	TR Fernie	1936	J Forrester	1964	RT Walker	1986	R Drummond
1911	E Sinclair	1937	WM Hastings	1965	EC Brown	1987	R Drummond
1912	WM Watt	1938	JH Ballingall	1966	EC Brown	1988	S Stephen
1913	A Marling	1939	W Davis		J Panton	1989	R Drummond
1914	DP Watt	1940–1945 Not played		1967	H Bannerman	1990	R Drummond
1915–1918 Not played		1946	W Anderson	1968	EC Brown	1991	S Torrance
1919	TR Fernie	1947	J McCondichie	1969	G Cunningham	1992	P Lawrie
1920	TR Fernie	1948	J Panton	1970	RDBM Shade	1993	S Torrance
1921	P Robertson	1949	J Panton	1971	BJ Gallacher	1994	A Coltart
1922	GE Smith	1950	J Panton	1972	H Bannerman	1995	C Gillies
1923	AW Butchart	1951	J Panton	1973	BJ Gallacher	1996	B Marchbank
1924	P Robertson	1952	J Campbell	1974	BJ Gallacher	1997	G Law
1925	S Burns	1953	H Thomson	1975	D Huish	1998	C Gillies
1926	T Wilson	1954	J Panton	1976	John Chillas	1999	G Hutcheon
1927	S Burns	1955	J Panton	1977	BJ Gallacher	2000	A Forsyth
1928	S Burns	1956	EC Brown	1978	S Torrance	2001	J Chillas
1929	D McCulloch	1957	EC Brown	1979	AWB Lyle	2002	F Mann
1930	D McCulloch	1958	EC Brown	1980	S Torrance	2003	C Kelly
1931	M Seymour	1959	J Panton	1981	B Barnes	2004	C Ronald*
1932	R Dornan	1960	EC Brown	1982	B Barnes	2005	P Lawrie

1	Dean Robertson (Czech Design)*	69-70-63-73—275
2	Craig Lee (All Golf Swing Centre)	67-69-68-71—275

Young Professionals Scottish Championship *Forres*
(formerly Macallan Spey Scottish Assistant's Championship)

1958	J Carter			
1959	W Mcondichie			
1960	RT Walker			
1961	RT Walker			
1962	RT Walker			
1963	RT Walker			
1964	L Taylor			
1965	D Huish			
1966	J Steven			
1967	H McCorquodale			
1968	N Wood			
1969	D Ross			
1970	WR Lockie			
1971	J Hamilton			
1972	TC Maltman			
1973	R Fyfe			
1974	J Noon			
1975	TC Maltman			
1976	TC Maltman			
1977	Not played			
1978	J McCallum			
1979	S Kelly			
1980	N Cameron			
1980	F Mann	Dunbar	294
played twice in 1980			
1981	M Brown	West Kilbride	290
1982	R Collinson	West Kilbride	294
1983	A Webster	Stirling	285
1984	C Elliott	Stirling	285
1985	C Elliott	Falkirk Tryst	284
1986	P Helsby	Erskine	295
1987	C Innes	Hilton Park	284
1988	G Collinson	Turnberry	289
1989	C Brooks	Windyhill	282
1990	P Lawrie	Cruden Bay	279
1991	G Hume	Kilmarnock Barassie	299
1992	E McIntosh	Turnberry Hotel	266
1993	J Wither	Alloa	280
1994	S Henderson	Newmacher	283
1995	A Tait	Newmacher	276

Young Professionals Scottish Championship *continued*

1996	S Thompson	Newmacher	278	2001	C Kelly	Spey Bay	275
1997	M Hastie	Balbirnie Park	275	2002	C Kelly	Spey Bay	277
1998	D Orr	Balbirnie Park	272	2003	G Dingwall	Balbirnie Park	281
1999	A Forsyth	Balbirnie Park	269	2004	G Duncan	Forres	269
2000	C Lee	Balbirnie Park	275	2005	A Lockhart	Forres	275

1	Callum Nicoll (Prestwick)	68-67-66-65—266
2	Mark Loftus (Cowglen)	70-64-70-65—269
3	Graeme Lornie (Aspire)	70-70-64-72—276

Welsh Open PGA Championship *St Pierre*

1	Liam Bond (St Pierre)	67-68-74—209
2	Sion Bebb (Vale of Glamorgan)	71-69-71—211
	Simon Edwards (Clays)	70-68-73—211
	Michael Watson (Weymouth)	74-65-72—211
	Ian Walley (Mickleover)	69-72-70—211

Welsh National Championship *Tenby*

1960	RH Kemp jr	Llandudno	288	1983	S Cox	Cardiff	136
1961	S Mouland	Southerndown	286	1984	K Jones	Cardiff	135
1962	S Mouland	Porthcawl	302	1985	D Llewellyn	Whitchurch	132
1963	H Gould	Wrexham	291	1986	P Parkin	Whitchurch	142
1964	B Bielby	Tenby	297	1987	A Dodman	Cardiff	132
1965	S Mouland	Penarth	281	1988	I Woosnam	Cardiff	137
1966	S Mouland	Conway	281	1989	K Jones	Royal Porthcawl	140
1967	S Mouland	Pyle and Kenfig	219 (54)	1990	P Mayo	Fairwood Park	136
1968	RJ Davies	Southerndown	292	1991	P Mayo	Fairwood Park	138
1969	S Mouland	Llandudno	277	1992	C Evans	Asburnham	142
1970	W Evans	Tredegar Park	289	1993	P Price	Caerphilly	138
1971	J Buckley	St Pierre	291	1994	M Plummer	Northop	133
1972	J Buckley	Porthcawl	298	1995	S Dodd	Northop	139
1973	A Griffiths	Newport	289	1996	M Stanford	Northop	137
1974	M Hughes	Cardiff	284	1997	M Ellis	Vale of Glamorgan	139
1975	C DeFoy	Whitchurch	285	1998	L Bond	Vale of Glamorgan	69 (18)
1976	S Cox	Radyr	284	1999	R Dinsdale	Vale of Glamorgan	134
1977	C DeFoy	Glamorganshire	135	2000	M Plummer	Newport	136
1978	BCC Huggett	Whitchurch	145	2001	S Dodd	Ashburnham	214
1979	*Cancelled*			2002	S Edwards	Pyle & Kenfig	210
1980	A Griffiths	Cardiff	139	2003	S Edwards	Porthmadog	196
1981	C DeFoy	Cardiff	139	2004	M Plummer	Vale of Llangollen	203
1982	C DeFoy	Cardiff	137	2005	S Bebb	Vale of Glamorgan	199

1	Sion Bebb (Vale of Glamorgan)	68-65-70—203
2	Mark Litton (The Bedford)	69-70-65—204
3	Simon Edwards (Clays)	62-73-71—206

Grampian International Freight Northern Open *(formerly the Northern Open)*
Carnegie Links, Skibo

1931	J McDowell	1950	EC Brown	1962	J Panton	1975	WTG Milne
1931	JT Henderson	1951	J Panton	1963	G Will	1976	D Chillas
1932	Jack McLean	1952	J Panton	1964	LR Taylor	1977	JE Murray
1933	James Forrester	1953	EC Brown	1965	JT Brown	1978	B Barnes
1934	RS Walker	1954	EC Brown	1966	R Liddle	1979	JC Farmer
1935	RS Walker	1955	EC Brown	1967	H Bannerman	1980	D Huish
1936	Jack McLean	1956	J Panton	1968	DK Webster	1981	AP Thomson
1937	TB Haliburton	1957	EC Brown	1969	H Bannerman	1982	AR Marshall
1938	Jack McLean	1958	G Will	1970	AK Pirie	1983	DA Cooper (ENG)
1939–1946	*Not played*	1959	J Panton	1971	F Rennie	1984	D Huish
1947	JH Ballingall	1960	J Panton	1972	H Bannerman	1985	B Barnes
1948	J Panton	1961	H Weetman	1973	D Huish	1986	RD Weir
1949	JH Ballingall		(ENG)	1974	WTG Milne	1987	AJ Hunter

1988	D Huish	1993	K Stables	1998	L James	2003	G Law
1989	C Brooks	1994	K Stables	1999	A Forsyth	2004	J McCreadie
1990	C Brooks	1995	J Higgins	2000	J Payne (ENG)	2005	C Doak
1991	C Cassells	1996	S Henderson	2001	G Rankin		
1992	P Smith	1997	D Thomson	2002	F Mann		

1	Jason McCready (Buchanan Castle)*	71-65-75-65—276
2	Chris Doak (unattached)	72-68-72-64—276

*McCready won at the first extra hole

3	Greig Hutcheon (Peterculter)	73-68-70-66—277

Southern Open Drift

1	Gary Marks (World of Golf)	69-68-72-70—279
2	Glenn Ralph (Camberley Heath)	72-72-66-70—280
3	Mark Belsham (Stonelees)	71-68-70-73—282

PGAs of Europe International Team Championship

Roda Golf and Beach Club, Murcia, Spain   (best two scores of three counting daily)

1990	Scotland	1994	Not played	1998	Ireland	2002	Spain
1991	Netherlands	1995	Spain	1999	England	2003	Spain
1992	Scotland	1996	Scotland	2000	Wales	2004	England
1993	Scotland	1997	Scotland	2001	Spain	2005	France

1	Scotland	134-136-138-139—547 (C Lee, J McKinnon, S Cairns)
2	Ireland	139-137-136-138—550 (J Dwyer, L Walker, R Giles)
3	Wales	136-140-141-136—553 (A Evans, S Edwards, M Litton)
	Norway	142-135-139-137—553 (J Elgborn, J Uppard, N Diethelm)
5	England	139-142-138-136—555 (P Simpson, P Wesselingh, D Muscroft)

Other scores: 565 Austria, Italy; 567 Finland; 568 South Africa; 573 Czech Republic, Germany; 574 France, Sweden; 576 Switzerland; 583 Belgium; 587 Poland, United Arab Emirates; 588 Slovenia; 592 Holland; 593 Bulgaria, Portugal; 597 Croatia; 601 Luxembourg; 606 Spain; 612 Russia

PGAs of Europe Championship

1983	Cees Renders (NED)	1988	Russell Weir (SCO)	1997	Claud Grenier (AUT)	2002	Paul Wesselingh (ENG)
1984	Donald Armour (NED)	1989	Russell Weir (SCO)	1998	Simon Brown (ENG)	2003	Not played
		1990	John Woof (NED)	1999	Richard Dinsdale (WAL)	2004	Andrew George (ENG)
1985	John Woof (NED)	1991	Paul Carman (ENG)	2000	Sion Bebb (WAL)	2005	Not played
1986	Stuart Brown (ENG)	1992	Tim Giles (ENG)	2001	Andrew George (ENG)		
1987	Jim Rhodes (ENG)	1993	Russell Weir (SCO)				
		1994–96	Not played				

2006 not played

PGAs of Europe Fourball Championship Atalaya Park, Spain

2002	S Edwards & J Lee (Wales)	2004	S Edwards & D Shacklady (Wales and England)
2003	R Davis & S McDonagh (England)	2005	Not played

2006 Not played

Regional Championships

Bedford & Cambridge PGA

1997	M Roberts	2003	M Litton
1998	A George	2004	D Armor (M)
1999	P Simpson		D Charlton (S)
2000	F Kiddie	2005	D Charlton
2001	P Abbott	2006	D Charlton
2002	P Abbott		

Berks, Bucks & Oxon

Professionals		Players	
2001	B Newman	2001	P Simpson
2002	P Simpson	2002	P Robshaw
2003	S Wells	2003	P Robshaw
2004	R Campbell	2004	4 way tie
2005	N Rowlands	2005	P Simpson
2006	G Laird	2006	J Hoskinson

Cheshire & North Wales

1997	N Dunroe	2002	P Archer
1998	N Price	2003	S Edwards
1999	P Archer	2004	S Edwards
2000	M Boothroyd	2005	C Hodges
2001	P Archer	2006	I Keenan

Derbyshire Professionals

1997	A Carnall	2002	M Poxon
1998	J Mellor	2003	P Wesselingh
1999	D Russell	2004	P Wesselingh
2000	M Smith	2005	P Wesselingh
2001	M Smith	2006	D Bartlett

Devon Open

1997	J Langmead	2002	B Austin
1998	D Sheppard	2003	R Knott (am)
1999	J Langmead	2004	J Langmead
2000	B Austin	2005	B Austin
2001	B Austin	2006	B Austin

East Anglian Open

1997	I Poulter	2002	I Ellis
1998	P Curry	2003	I Ellis
1999	P Curry	2004	D Parker
2000	J Bevan	2005	I Ellis
2001	D Parker	2006	D Charlton

East Region PGA

1997	R Mann	2002	D Parker
1998	T Charnley	2003	P Cherry
1999	S Khan	2004	F Madden
2000	I Ellis	2005	S Standing
2001	P Barham	2006	J Bevitt

Essex Open

1997	V Cox	2002	D Parker
1998	J Robson	2003	S Cipa/M Stokes
1999	P Joiner	2004	J Fryatt
2000	S Khan	2005	M Davis
2001	R Coles	2006	S Khan

Essex PGA

1997	M Stokes	2002	R Green
1998	G Carter	2003	M Stokes
1999	P Curry	2004	D Wood
2000	W McColl	2005	S Cipa
2001	J Fryatt	2006	D Turner

Hampshire PGA

1997	J Lovell	2002	K Saunders
1998	G Hughes	2003	J Barnes
1999	J Barnes	2004	E Rawlings
2000	K Saunders	2005	R Edwards
2001	S Cowle	2006	D Porter

Hampshire Match Play

1997	D Harris	2002	J Barnes
1998	D Harris	2003	R Tate
1999	J Lovell	2004	J Barnes
2000	M Robbins	2005	D Porter
2001	P Bryden	2006	A Mew

Hampshire, Isle of Wight and Channel Islands Open

1997	M Blackey	2002	R Tate
1998	R Bland	2003	M Treleaven
1999	R Bland	2004	D Porter
2000	R Bland	2005	N Smith
2001	S Cowle	2006	M Blackey

Herts Professionals

1997	P Winston	2003	J Pinsent (M)
1998T	R Mitchell		D Tapping (S)
	I Parker	2004	R Hurd (M)
1999	L Jones		S Harris (S)
2000	R Mitchell	2005	A Clapp
2001	A Bailey	2006	M Bird
2002	D Field		

Kent Open

1997	S Page	2002	M Day
1998	D Parris	2003	M McLean
1999	R Cameron	2004	T Milford
2000	M McLean	2005	M Belsham
2001	J Marshall	2006	R McGuirk

Kent PGA

1997	P Lyons	2002	S Stevens
1998	T Milford	2003	S Green
1999	R Cameron	2004	S Green
2000	B Coomber	2005	Not played
2001	S Wood	2006	A Tarchetti

Lancashire Open

1997	G Furey	2002	S Astin
1998	J Cheetham	2003	D Shacklady
1999	C Corrigan	2004	D Shacklady
2000	G Furey	2005	D Shacklady
2001	M Hollingsworth	2006	S Walsh

Leeds Cup (Stroke Play)

1997	P Scott	2002	G Bell
1998	N Price	2003	J Cheetham
1999	M Bradley	2004	J Godbold
2000	P Archer	2005	S Edwards (WAL)
2001	R Giles	2006	N Price*

Leicestershire & Rutland Open

1997	N Bland	2003	G Shaw
1998	J Caylis (am)	2004	I Bailey, I Lyner,
1999	I Ball		D Mee
2000	M Cort	2005	J Palmer (am)
2001	I Ball	2006	J Herbert
2002	G Shaw		

Lincolnshire Open

1997	M King (am)	2002	S Emery
1998	M King (am)	2003	D Greenwood
1999	M King (am)	2004	B Greenwood
2000	M King (am)	2005	P Streeter
2001	S Emery	2006	P Streeter

Lincolnshire Professionals

1997	S Bennett (M and S)	2002	D Greenwood (M and S)
1998	S Brown (M) P Streeter (S)	2003	P Streeter (M and S)
1999	C Elliott (M) D Greenwood (S)	2004	P Streeter (M) S Bennett (S)
2000	P Spence (M) J Dowland (S)	2005	D Drake (M) M Evans* (S)
2001	S Austwick (M) I Fulton (S)	2006	S Bennett (M) N Evans (S)

Manchester Open (Stroke Play)

2002	G Houston	2005	R Bean
2003	J Cheetham	2006	R Wragg*
2004	D Clark		

Middlesex PGA (Stroke Play)

1997	L Jones	2002	P Winston
1998	L Jones	2003	S Whiffin
1999	N Wichelow	2004	Cancelled
2000	S Whiffin	2005	N Wichelow
2001	N Wichelow	2006	L Clarke

Midland Professionals

1997	J Higgins (M and S)	2001	J Robinson (M) T Rouse (S)
1998	J Robinson (M) S Webster (S)	2002	I Lyner (M) R Rock (S)
1999	I Ball (M) C Hall (S)	2003	P Edwards (S)
2000	R Rock (M) DJ Russell (S)	2004	P Streeter (S)
		2005	A Carey
		2006	P Streeter

Midland Open

1997–2002	Not played	2005	D Prosser
2003	D Prosser	2006	P Streeter (S)
2004	P Edwards		

Norfolk Open

1997	N Lythgoe	2002	T Varney
1998	R Wilson	2003	T Varney
1999	P Little (am)	2004	T Varney
2000	M Jubb	2005	N Lythgoe
2001	D Henderson (am)	2006	S Ballingale (am)

North East Masters (Stroke Play)

2001	M Nesbit	2004	M Nesbit
2002	N Cheetham	2005	K Ferrie
2003	M Bradley	2006	A Wainwright

Northern Region PGA

1997	G Furey	2002	P Archer
1998	P Carman	2003	J Cheetham
1999	R Wragg	2004	P Eales
2000	C Hislop	2005	C Corrigan
2001	B Sharrock	2006	M Bradley

Northumberland & Durham Open

2002	B Rumney	2005	G Bell
2003	S McKenna	2006	T Henderson
2004	G Lockerbie (am)		

Notts Championship

2004	P Edwards	2006	K Crossland (M) P Edwards (S)
2005	M Foulkes		

Shropshire & Hereford Open

1997	AR Minshall	2002	D Richards (am)
1998	P Hinton	2003	L Rooke
1999	D James	2004	P Hinton
2000	J Griffiths	2005	B Ruddick
2001	P Wesselingh	2006	D Harris (am)

Shropshire & Hereford PGA

2005	S Russell	2006	S Russell

South West PGA

1997	M Stanford	2002	B Austin
1998	S Little	2003	Not played
1999	G Ryall	2004	Not played
2000	K Spurgeon	2005	Not played
2001	M Wiggett	2006	Not played

Southern Assistants

1997	B Hodkin (M)	2002	G Lingard (M)
	A Lovelace (S)		P Schunter (S)
1998	B Hodkin (M)	2003	R Campbell (M)
	D Parris (S)		N Reilly (S)
1999	M Nichols (M)	2004	B Willman (M)
	C Fromant (S)		C Gordon (S)
2000	S Wells (M)	2005	G Willman (M)
	N Reilly (S)		J Ablett (S)
2001	S Crooks (M)	2006	N Clark (M)
	C Roake (S)		M Freeland (S)

Southern Professionals

1997	P Sherman	2002	A Lovelace
1998	P Simpson	2003	M Hazelden
1999	S Wood	2004	A Tarchetti
2000	P Robshaw	2005	P Sherman
2001	K Saunders	2006	G Shoesmith

Staffordshire Open

1997	A Roger	2002	I Proverbs
1998	R Peace	2003	I Benson
1999	G Beddow	2004	S Lynn
2000	J Cookson (am)	2005	B Rimmer
2001	R Maxfield (am)	2006	B Rimmer

Staffordshire PGA

2005	B Rimmer	2006	B Rimmer

Suffolk Open

1997	P Wilby	2002	A Lucas
1998	J Wright (am)	2003	S Keely
1999	S MacPherson	2004	A Lucas
2000	J Keeley	2005	J Abbott (am)
2001	J Moul (am)	2006	S Dainty

Suffolk Professionals

1997	A Cotton (M)	2002	A Cottom (M)
	A Lucas (S)		R Mann (S)
	C Jenkins (S)	2003	N Grundtvig (M)
1998	K Golding (M)		S Keely (S)
	S MacPherson (S)	2004	A Cotton (M)
1999	R Mann (M)		R Mann (S)
	S MacPherson (S)	2005	S Harrison (M)
2000	R Hitchcock (M)		R Mann (S)
	J Bevan (S)	2006	P Bate (M)
2001	P Kent (M)		R Mann (S)
	A Cotton (S)		

Surrey Open

1997	M Nichols	2002	M Nichols
1998	P Sefton	2003	R Humphrey
1999	H Stott	2004	G Marks
2000	C Gane	2005	I Golding
2001	N Reilly	2006	L Atkinson

Sussex Open

1997	K Macdonald	2002	T Spence
1998	J Doherty (am)	2003	J Harris
1999	P Lyons	2004	S Graham (am)
2000	P Lyons	2005	P Jones
2001	G Murray	2006	R Fenwick

Ulster Professionals

1997	D Mooney	2002	L Walker
1998	D Mooney	2003	L Walker
1999	D Mooney	2004	D Higgins
2000	P Collins	2005	S Thornton
2001	J Dwyer	2006	D Mooney

Warwickshire Open

1997	D Barton	2002	M Morris
1998	SJ Walker	2003	A Carey
1999	D Clayton	2004	C Phillips
2000	T Whitehouse (am)	2005	A Carey
2001	A Carey	2006	A Sullivan (am)

Warwickshire Professionals

1997	L Bashford (M)	2002	M Morris
	C Phillips (S)		(M and S)
1998	C Phillips (M)	2003	A Bownes (M)
	J Corns* (S)		A Carey (S)
1999	D Clayton (M)	2004	R Smith (S)
	A Bownes (S)	2005	A Bownes (S)
2000	A Carey (M)	2006	C Clark*
	A Stokes (S)		*After 6-hole play-off
2001	A Stokes (M)		
	A Bownes (S)		

West Region PGA

1997	M Thompson	2002	M Thompson
1998	J Taylor	2003	B Austin
1999	S Little	2004	G Ryall
2000	M Higley	2005	M Plummer
2001	I Ferrie	2006	G Brand Jr

Hills Wiltshire Professionals

1997	M Smith	2002	D Hutton
1998	R Blake	2003	D Hutton
1999	S McDonald	2004	G Laing
2000	A Beal	2005	M Griffin
2001	S Robertson	2006	M Butler

Worcestershire Open

1997	I Clark	2002	M Toombes
1998	D Eddiford	2003	M Quigley
1999	F Clark	2004	R Wassell
2000	J Jones	2005	J Jones
2001	N Turley	2006	M Butler

Worcestershire PGA

1997	P Scarrett	2002	R Wassell
1998	D Eddiford*	2003	M Butler
1999	S Edwards	2004	M Butler
2000	N Turley	2005	M Sandry
2001	N Turley	2006	D Hutton

Yorkshire Open

2003	A Gray	2005	J Wells
2004	JP Samuel	2006	Not played

Yorkshire Professionals

1997	S Robinson	2002	A Ambler
1998	G Brown	2003	A Wainwright
1999	G Brown	2004	A Ambler
2000	G Walker	2005	G Brand
2001	A Ambler	2006	J Wells

Scotland's nine-year drought ends

It took nine years of frustrating effort, but when Scotland finally ended their drought in the Glenmuir PGAsE International Team Championship they did so as front-runners all the way. Their victory at Roda Golf & Beach Resort in Murcia, Spain, was their first since their record-setting run of five wins in seven years from 1990 when the competition started.

Scotland's current Tartan Tour heroes are Craig Lee, Jim McKinnon and Sam Cairns, who led from start to finish with a best-two-from-three total of 29-under-par 547 to share the €6,000 first prize. Lee was the inspiration of the Scotland team, and the competition's individual lowest scorer overall, with a four-round total of 21-under-par 267.

"I couldn't have asked for a better retirement present," said Peter Lloyd, secretary of the Scottish PGA, who retired at the end of the year after more than 20 years' service.

Ireland's Robert Giles, John Dwyer and Leslie Walker made a bold attempt to outscore Scotland to record their second victory but settled for runners-up place on 26-under-par 550 after pulling to within two shots of the Scots with one hole to play. Giles, who was a member of the last Ireland team to win the tournament in 1998, was second lowest individual scorer with an 18-under-par total of 270 to help his team to finish three shots clear of Norway and Wales, with pre-tournament favourites England taking fifth place.

Month by month in 2006

Brett Wetterich and Johan Edfors, survivors of their respective qualifying schools at the end of 2005, win on the US and European Tours on the same day. Thomas Bjorn takes the Irish Open, then David Howell stretches his Order of Merit lead with runaway victory at BMW Championship. Michelle Wie wins local qualifying competition for US Open, but later fails in her bid to become the first woman to play in a major.

Overseas National Championships

(Excluding European Tour or Affiliated Events)

Australian Open (Australian unless stated)

1904	Hon Michael Scott (am)	1961	Frank Phillips
1905	Dan Soutar	1962	Gary Player (RSA)
1906	Carnegie Clark (am)	1963	Gary Player (RSA)
1907	Hon Michael Scott (am)	1964	Jack Nicklaus (USA)
1908	Clyde Pearce (am)	1965	Gary Player (RSA)
1909	C Felstead (am)	1966	Arnold Palmer (USA)
1910	Carnegie Clark (am)	1967	Peter Thomson
1911	Carnegie Clark (am)	1968	Jack Nicklaus (USA)
1912	Ivo Whitton (am)	1969	Gary Player (RSA)
1913	Ivo Whitton (am)	1970	Gary Player (RSA)
1914–1919	not played	1971	Jack Nicklaus (USA)
1920	Joe Kirkwood	1972	Peter Thomson
1921	A Le Fevre	1973	J C Snead (USA)
1922	C Campbell	1974	Gary Player (RSA)
1923	T Howard	1975	Jack Nicklaus (USA)
1924	A Russell (am)	1976	Jack Nicklaus (USA)
1925	Fred Popplewell	1977	David Graham
1926	Ivo Whitton (am)	1978	Jack Nicklaus (USA)
1927	R Stewart	1979	Jack Newton
1928	Fred Popplewell	1980	Greg Norman
1929	Ivo Whitton (am)	1981	Bill Rogers (USA)
1930	F Eyre	1982	Bob Shearer
1931	Ivo Whitton (am)	1983	Peter Fowler
1932	Mick Ryan (am)	1984	Tom Watson (USA)
1933	M Kelly	1985	Greg Norman
1934	Bill Bolger	1986	Rodger Davis
1935	F McMahon	1987	Greg Norman
1936	Gene Sarazen (USA)	1988	Mark Calcavecchia
1937	George Naismith		(USA)
1938	Jim Ferrier (am)	1989	Peter Senior
1939	Jim Ferrier (am)	1990	John Morse (USA)
1940–1945	not played	1991	Wayne Riley
1946	Ossie Pickworth	1992	Steve Elkington
1947	Ossie Pickworth	1993	Brad Faxon (USA)
1948	Ossie Pickworth	1994	Robert Allenby
1949	Eric Cremin	1995	Greg Norman
1950	Norman Von Nida	1996	Greg Norman
1951	Peter Thomson	1997	Lee Westwood (ENG)
1952	Norman Von Nida	1998	Greg Chalmers
1953	Norman Von Nida	1999	Aaron Baddeley (am)
1954	Ossie Pickworth	2000	Aaron Baddeley
1955	Bobby Locke (RSA)	2001	Stuart Appleby
1956	Bruce Crampton	2002	Steve Allan
1957	Frank Phillips	2003	Peter Lonard
1958	Gary Player (RSA)	2004	Peter Lonard
1959	Kel Nagle	2005	Robert Allenby
1960	Bruce Devlin (am)	2006	John Senden

Canadian Open (Canadian unless stated)

1904	J H Oke	1958	W Ellis jr (USA)
1905	G Cumming	1959	D Ford (USA)
1906	C Murray	1960	A Wall jr (USA)
1907	P Barrett	1961	J Cupit (USA)
1908	A Murray	1962	T Kroll (USA)
1909	K Keffer	1963	D Ford (USA)
1910	D Kenny	1964	KDG Nagle (AUS)
1911	C Murray	1965	G Littler (USA)
1912	G Sargent	1966	D Massengale (USA)
1913	A Murray	1967	W Casper (USA)
1914	K Kesser	1968	RJ Charles (NZL)
1915–1918	not played	1969	T Aaron (USA)
1919	J D Edgar	1970	D Zarley (USA)
1920	J D Edgar	1971	L Trevino (USA)
1921	W H Trovinger	1972	G Brewer jr (USA)
1922	A Watrous	1973	T Weiskopf (USA)
1923	C W Hackney	1974	B Nichols (USA)
1924	L Diegel	1975	T Weiskopf (USA)
1925	L Diegel	1976	J Pate (USA)
1926	M Smith	1977	L Trevino (USA)
1927	T Armour	1978	B Lietzke (USA)
1928	L Diegel	1979	L Trevino (USA)
1929	L Diegel	1980	B Gilder (USA)
1930	T Armour	1981	P Oosterhuis (ENG)
1931	W Hagen	1982	B Lietzke (USA)
1932	H Cooper	1983	J Cook (USA)
1933	J Kirkwood	1984	G Norman (AUS)
1934	T Armour	1985	C Strange (USA)
1935	G Kunes	1986	B Murphy (USA)
1936	L Little	1987	C Strange (USA)
1937	H Cooper	1988	K Green (USA)
1938	S Snead (USA)	1989	S Jones (USA)
1939	H McSpaden (USA)	1990	W Levi (USA)
1940	S Snead (USA)	1991	N Price (ZIM)
1941	S Snead (USA)	1992	G Norman (AUS)
1942	C Wood (USA)	1993	D Frost (RSA)
1943–1944	not played	1994	N Price (ZIM)
1945	B Nelson (USA)	1995	M O'Meara (USA)
1946	G Fazio (USA)	1996	D Hart (USA)
1947	AD Locke (RSA)	1997	S Jones (USA)
1948	CW Congdon	1998	B Andrade (USA)
1949	E J Harrison	1999	H Sutton (USA)
1950	J Ferrier	2000	T Woods (USA)
1951	J Ferrier	2001	S Verplank (USA)
1952	J Palmer (USA)	2002	J Rollins (USA)
1953	D Douglas (USA)	2003	R Tway (USA)
1954	P Fletcher	2004	V Singh (FIJ)
1955	A Palmer (USA)	2005	Mark Calcavecchia
1956	D Sanders (am) (USA)		(USA)
1957	G Bayer (USA)	2006	Jim Furyk (USA)

Austrian Open (Austrian unless stated)

1995	A Cejka (GER)	2001	C Gane (ENG)
1996	P McGinley (IRL)	2002	M Brier
1997	E Simsek (GER)	2003	M Brier
1998	K Carissimi (GER)	2004	M Brier
1999	J Ciola	2005	Michael Hoey (NIR)
2000	Not played	2006	Marcus Brier

Hong Kong Open

1995	G Webb	2002	F Jacobson (SWE)
1996	Rodrigo Cuello (PHI)	2003	P Harrington (IRL)
1997	F Nobilo (NZL)	2004	MA Jiménez (ESP)
1998	WS Kang	2005	C Montgomerie
1999	P Sjöland (SWE)		(SCO)
2000	S Dyson (ENG)	2006	JM Lara (ESP)
2001	JM Olazábal (ESP)		

Indian Open

1995	J Rutledge (CAN)	2001	T Jaidee (THA)
1996	H Shirakata (IND)	2002	V Kumar (IND)
1997	E Fryatt (ENG)	2003	M Cunning (USA)
1998	A Firoz	2004	M Mamat (SIN)
1999	A Atwal (IND)	2005	T Wiratchant (THA)
2000	J Randhawa (IND)	2006	J Randhawa (IND)

Japanese Open

1995	T Izwa (JPN)	2001	T Teshima (JPN)
1996	P Teravainen (USA)	2002	D Smail (NZL)
1997	C Parry (AUS)	2003	K Fukabori (JPN)
1998	H Tanaka (JPN)	2004	T Taniguchi (JPN)
1999	N Ozaki (JPN)	2005	S Katayama (JPN)
2000	N Ozaki (JPN)	2006	P Sheehan (AUS)

Kenya Open

1995	J Lee	2001	A Roestoff (RSA)
1996	M Miller (SCO)	2002	I James (ENG)
1997	J Berendt (USA)	2003	Not played
1998	R Gonzalez (ARG)	2004	M Cayeux (ZIM)
1999	M Lafeber (NED)	2005	D Vancsik (ARG)
2000	T Immelman (RSA)	2006	J Axgren (SWE)

Korean Open

1995	B Jobe (USA)	2001	DS Kim (am)
1996	K-JChoi	2002	S García (ESP)
1997	K Jong-Duck	2003	J Daly (USA)
1998	DS Kim (am)	2004	E Loar (USA)
1999	K-JChoi	2005	Not played
2000	T Jaidee (THA)	2006	Yang Yong-Eun

New Zealand Open

1995	L Parsons (AUS)	2001	C Parry (AUS)
1996	M Long	2002	C Parry (AUS)
1997	G Turner	2003	M Pearce
1998	G Turner	2004	G Coles (ENG)
1999	M Lane (AUS)	2005	N Fasth (SWE)
2000	M Campbell	2006	N Green (AUS)

Singapore Open

1995	S Conran (AUS)	2002	Not played
1996	J Kernohan	2003	Not played
1997	Z Moe	2004	Not played
1998	S Micheel (USA)	2005	A Scott (AUS)
1999	J Milkha Singh (IND)	2006	A Scott* (AUS)
2000	J Randhawa (IND)		*Scott beat E Els in three-hole
2001	T Warachant (THA)		play-off

Zambian Open

1995	Not played	2001	M Foster (ENG)
1996	D Botes (RSA)	2002	M Cayeux (ZIM)
1997	Not played	2003	J Edfors (SWE)
1998	M Cayeux (ZIM)	2004	M Kirk
1999	Not played	2005	Not played
2000	J Loughnane (RSA)	2006	S Basson (RSA)

Other 2006 Overseas National Championships

Argentine Open	Kevin Stadler (USA)
China Open	Jeev Milkha Singh (IND)
Colombian Open	Manuel Marizalde
Costa Rican Open	Johan Axgren (SWE)
Dutch Open	Simon Dyson (ENG)
Finnish Open	Jaako Mäkitalo
French Open	John Bickerton (ENG)
Guatemala Open	Miguel Carballo (ARG)
Indonesian Open	Simon Dyson (ENG)
Italian Open	Francesco Molinari
Kazakhstan Open	Mark Pilkington (WAL)
Malaysian Open	Charlie Wi (KOR)

Mexican Open	Antonio Maldonado
	(Dec 2005)
Pakistan Open	Chris Rodgers (ENG)
Philippines Open	Scott Strange (AUS)
Portuguese Open	Paul Broadhurst (ENG)
Russian Open	Alejandro Cañizares (ESP)
Singapore Open	Adam Scott (ASU)
South African Open	Retief Goosen (RSA)
Spanish Open	Niclas Fasth (SWE)
Taiwan Open	Lin Wen-tang (TPE)
Venezuela Open	Fabian Gomez (ARG)

European Ryder Cup team wins top honour as Golf Writers reward K Club triumph

Members of the Association of Golf Writers, who vote annually for the person or persons who did most for European golf in 2006, sprung no surprise when they chose the European Ryder Cup team captained by Ian Woosnam.

The Cup team won by a record equalling winning margin at the K Club over the Americans led by Tom Lehman. It was the sixth time in the past 20 years that a Ryder Cup team has been successful.

When they ended a 28-year drought and won in 1985 they received the award and with Tony Jacklin still captain in 1987 they took it again when scoring their first victory on American soil.

As a result of Bernard Gallacher leading his side to victory at Oak Hill they won the Golf Writers' Trophy again in 1995 and took it for a fourth time in 2002 under the captaincy of Sam Torrance at The Belfry. The outstanding performance of the team in 2004 at Oakland Hills when Bernhard Langer was in charge earned them the trophy and their third-in-a-row victory last September in Ireland meant the name of the team went on the cup for the sixth time.

After the Ryder Cup team surprisingly missed out at a BBC sports awards ceremony last week, Woosnam was particularly pleased to win the Golf Writers' Trophy.

"I am very honoured, both for myself and on behalf of the players," he added. "It was an unbelievable performance. To get 18½ points, to equal the record, and also to win all five series of play for the first time ever, is the stuff of dreams.

"It was a very special week. It was the best week of my life without question, very hard but the best. I can't say enough about my wonderful players and the way they played."

Darren Clarke, whose courageous performance just weeks after losing his wife, Heather, to cancer was the highlight of an emotional week in Ireland, was the runner-up in the annual poll. Richie Ramsay, the first Scot to win the US Amateur Championship since 1898, finished a close third.

Clarke won three matches out of three at the K Club despite having played only one tournament in the previous two months. "I am very grateful for all the recognition I have received and I would especially like to thank the golf writers for their support, not just this year, but throughout my career," said the Northern Irishman.

"For the Ryder Cup team to win this trophy, however, is absolutely the right result. To win as we did was a stunning performance and Woosie was fantastic as our captain. We had 12 players all playing to their best and I was just proud to play my part."

Ramsay described himself as "just a guy from Aberdeen who loves playing golf," after he defeated John Kelly 4 and 2 in the final of the US Amateur at Hazeltine. He became the first Scot to win the title since Finlay Douglas in 1898 and the first Briton since Harold Hilton in 1911. He will play in three major championships in 2007, including The Open at Carnoustie.

Ramsay finished ahead of Ryder Cup players Paul Casey and Padraig Harrington. Laura Davies, No.1 on the Ladies European Tour money list for the seventh time also featured in the voting.

Woosnam will receive the trophy during The Open Championship at Carnoustie in July. The award dates back to 1951.

Severiano Ballesteros honoured by the PGA

Five-time Major champion Seve Ballesteros has collected the PGA Recognition Award for his outstanding contribution to golf.

The 49-year-old Spaniard, who has announced his return to competitive golf in 2007, captured three Open Championship and two Masters titles and played a huge part in revitalising The Ryder Cup both as a player and captain.

Renowned for his shot-making around the greens, Seve's charisma and flair made him into golf's biggest attraction for over 20 years.

In presenting the award, PGA Chief Executive Sandy Jones said: "The PGA is delighted to honour Seve with this award which recognises his outstanding contribution to golf since he first burst onto the scene at Royal Birkdale in 1976.

"We always recognise greatness but in life we get very few occasions to recognise genius and Seve is simply that – a golfing genius. Throughout his career he lit up world golf with his charisma, skill and flair, winning millions of fans in the process and playing a significant part in making The European Tour what it is today. He has also left a lasting impact on The Ryder Cup and richly deserves the acclaim and recognition he is receiving from the Association."

PART III

Women's Professional Tournaments

Rolex Women's World Golf Rankings

Rank	Name	Country	Events	Total	Average
1	Annika Sörenstam	SWE	43	716.66	16.67
2	Lorena Ochoa	MEX	50	623.89	12.48
3	Karrie Webb	AUS	46	523.86	11.39
4	Cristie Kerr	USA	49	406.19	8.29
5	Juli Inkster	USA	41	308.84	7.53
6	Ai Miyazato	JPN	53	371.37	7.01
7	Paula Creamer	USA	57	376.47	6.60
8	Jeong Jang	KOR	58	382.88	6.60
9	Shiho Ohyama	JPN	67	410.56	6.13
10	Se-Ri Pak	KOR	36	198.38	5.51
11	Michelle Wie	USA	16	192.39	5.50
12	Pat Hurst	USA	48	259.71	5.41
13	Yuri Fudoh	JPN	50	266.49	5.33
14	Hee-Won Han	KOR	56	296.45	5.29
15	Mi Hyun Kim	KOR	59	307.29	5.21
16	Julieta Granada	PAR	42	181.38	4.32
17	Seon-Hwa Lee	KOR	53	224.98	4.24
18	Natalie Gulbis	USA	54	227.41	4.21
19	Akiko Fukushima	JPN	51	212.88	4.17
20	Sakura Yokomine	JPN	66	274.62	4.16
21	Morgan Pressel	USA	31	139.05	3.97
22	Ji-Hee Lee	KOR	57	222.57	3.90
23	Sherri Steinhauer	USA	51	197.73	3.88
24	Jee Young Lee	KOR	39	150.01	3.85
25	Sophie Gustafson	SWE	53	202.94	3.83
26	Brittany Lang	USA	34	130.35	3.72
27	Hyun-Ju Shin	KOR	63	233.93	3.71
28	Mi-Jeong Jeon	KOR	63	232.88	3.70
29	Stacy Prammanasudh	USA	51	164.51	3.23
30	Brittany Lincicome	USA	44	138.23	3.14
31	Miho Koga	JPN	64	198.22	3.10
32	Meena Lee	KOR	59	176.36	2.99
33	Shi-Hyun Ahn	KOR	44	125.40	2.85
34	Ji-yai Shin	KOR	17	96.63	2.76
35	Shinobu Moromizato	JPN	44	116.11	2.64
36	Laura Davies	ENG	58	152.65	2.63
37	Gloria Hee Jung Park	KOR	55	142.22	2.59
38	Wendy Ward	USA	49	124.89	2.55
39	Young Kim	KOR	50	125.89	2.52
40	Candie Kung	TPE	52	129.89	2.50
41	Yun-Jye Wei	TPE	65	161.30	2.48
42	Momoko Ueda	JPN	36	89.10	2.47
43	Catriona Matthew	SCO	47	115.10	2.45
44	Michele Redman	USA	43	105.21	2.45
45	Joo Mi Kim	KOR	52	125.57	2.41
46	Karine Icher	FRA	53	126.63	2.39
47	Gwladys Nocera	FRA	40	94.65	2.37
48	Liselotte Neumann	SWE	44	101.35	2.30
49	Kasumi Fujii	JPN	51	114.94	2.25
50	Mie Nakata	JPN	59	132.74	2.25

Ladies' European Tour, 2006

www.ladieseuropeantour.com

Final Order of Merit (The top 90 players retain a full card)

1	Laura Davies (ENG)	€471,727	52	Carmen Alonso (ESP)	32,052
2	Gwladys Nocera (FRA)	415,020	53	Stefania Croce (ITA)	31,330
3	Annika Sörenstam (SWE)	225,822	54	Nina Reis (SWE)	31,195
4	Sophie Gustafson (SWE)	193,773	55	Joanne Mills (AUS)	30,884
5	Veronica Zorzi (ITA)	143,881	56	Ursula Wikstrom (FIN)	30,809
6	Linda Wessberg (SWE)	142,414	57	Eleanor Pilgrim (WAL)	30,626
7	Stephanie Arricau (FRA)	140,376	58	Laura Cabanillas (ESP)	30,560
8	Rebecca Hudson (ENG)	123,835	59	Anna Highgate (WAL)	28,646
9	Riikka Hakkarainen (FIN)	112,361	60	Ellen Smets (BEL)	27,692
10	Karen Margrethe Juul (DEN)	107,531	61	Lisa Holm Sorensen (DEN)	27,256
11	Cecilia Ekelundh (SWE)	102,379	62	Carlie Butler (AUS)	27,188
12	Nikki Garrett (AUS)	99,445	63	Kris Lindstrom (USA)	27,024
13	Sophie Giquel (FRA)	98,851	64	Anne-Marie Knight (AUS)	26,710
14	Anja Monke (GER)	97,540	65	Sofia Renell (SWE)	26,213
15	Becky Brewerton (WAL)	96,700	66	Leah Hart (AUS)	25,786
16	Helen Alfredsson (SWE)	96,407	67	Elin Ohlsson (SWE)	25,605
17	Lynn Brooky (NZL)	87,336	68	Nathalie David-Mila (FRA)	25,516
18	Ludivine Kreutz (FRA)	85,477	69	Isabella Maconi (ITA)	25,508
19	Virginie Lagoutte (FRA)	83,760	70	Ana Larraneta (ESP)	25,444
20	Iben Tinning (DEN)	82,413	71	Catriona Matthew (SCO)	25,060
21	Maria Hjorth (SWE)	80,173	72	Liselotte Neumann (SWE)	25,007
22	Ana B Sanchez (ESP)	76,256	73	Beatriz Recari Eransus (ESP)	24,990
23	Tania Elosegui Mayor (ESP)	74,893	74	Anna Rawson (AUS)	24,981
24	Trish Johnson (ENG)	72,288	75	Lara Tadiotto (BEL)	24,604
25	Amanda Moltke-Leth (DEN)	70,753	76	Amy Yang (KOR)	24,100
26	Karine Icher (FRA)	67,892	77	Tullia Calzavara (ITA)	23,863
27	Asa Gottmo (SWE)	65,585	78	Federica Piovano (ITA)	23,722
28	Sarah Kemp (AUS)	65,567	79	Georgina Simpson (ENG)	23,208
29	Karen Stupples (ENG)	60,123	80	Sara Beautell (ESP)	22,953
30	Sophie Sandolo (ITA)	59,433	81	Marina Arruti (ESP)	22,575
31	Marta Prieto (ESP)	58,384	82	Catrin Nilsmark (SWE)	22,008
32	Elisa Serramia (ESP)	57,494	83	Denise Simon (GER)	21,871
33	Lisa Hall (ENG)	55,140	84	Anna Tybring (SWE)	19,809
34	Suzann Pettersen (NOR)	52,903	85	Karen Lunn (AUS)	19,622
35	Virginie Auffret (FRA)	52,585	86	Fame More (ENG)	18,839
36	Rebecca Coakley (IRL)	52,417	87	Carin Koch (SWE)	18,769
37	Kirsty Taylor (ENG)	51,549	88	Eva Steinberger (AUT)	18,155
38	Rebecca Stevenson (AUS)	50,251	89	Lisa Jean (AUS)	17,957
39	Lotta Wahlin (SWE)	48,394	90	Patricia Meunier Lebouc (FRA)	17,702
40	Kirsty S Taylor (ENG)	46,442			
41	Nora Angehrn (SUI)	44,463	91	Mianne Bagger (DEN)	17,385
42	Lora Fairclough (ENG)	43,233	92	Alison Munt (AUS)	17,264
43	Bettina Hauert (GER)	42,579	93	Maria Boden (SWE)	16,813
44	Cherie Byrnes (AUS)	41,998	94	Liza Walters (ENG)	16,738
45	Laurette Maritz (RSA)	41,970	95	Kathryn Imrie (SCO)	16,425
46	Shani Waugh (AUS)	40,984	96	Nienke Nijenhuis (NED)	16,082
47	Martina Eberl (GER)	40,798	97	Margherita Rigon (ITA)	14,893
48	Danielle Masters (ENG)	39,676	98	Diana Luna (ITA)	14,872
49	Louise Friberg (SWE)	39,303	99	Clare Queen (SCO)	14,679
50	Anna Knutsson (SWE)	36,561	100	Sarah Heath (ENG)	14,559
51	Helena Alterby (SWE)	32,140			

Ladies European Tour 2006 Money List

1	Laura Davies (ENG)	€471,727	51	Nina Reis (SWE)	31,195
2	Gwladys Nocera (FRA)	407,570	52	Eleanor Pilgrim (WAL)	30,626
3	Sophie Gustafson (SWE)	193,773	53	Laura Cabanillas (ESP)	30,560
4	Annika Sörenstam (SWE)	150,822	54	Carmen Alonso (ESP)	30,427
5	Linda Wessberg (SWE)	142,414	55	Martina Eberl (GER)	28,948
6	Stephanie Arricau (FRA)	137,576	56	Anna Highgate (WAL)	28,646
7	Rebecca Hudson (ENG)	123,835	57	Ellen Smets (BEL)	27,692
8	Veronica Zorzi (ITA)	119,781	58	Lisa Holm Sorensen (DEN)	27,256
9	Riikka Hakkarainen (FIN)	112,361	59	Anne-Marie Knight (AUS)	26,710
10	Cecilia Ekelundh (SWE)	98,713	60	Joanne Mills (AUS)	26,159
11	Karen Margrethe Juul (DEN)	95,681	61	Leah Hart (AUS)	25,786
12	Anja Monke (GER)	92,815	62	Kris Lindstrom (USA)	25,774
13	Sophie Giquel (FRA)	91,851	63	Elin Ohlsson (SWE)	25,605
14	Nikki Garrett (AUS)	90,482	64	Isabella Maconi (ITA)	25,508
15	Becky Brewerton (WAL)	87,737	65	Catriona Matthew (SCO)	25,060
16	Lynn Brooky (NZL)	85,536	66	Liselotte Neumann (SWE)	25,007
17	Ludivine Kreutz (FRA)	85,477	67	Anna Rawson (AUS)	24,981
18	Virginie Lagoutte (FRA)	83,760	68	Carlie Butler (AUS)	24,938
19	Maria Hjorth (SWE)	80,173	69	Ursula Wikstrom (FIN)	24,884
20	Ana B Sanchez (ESP)	70,331	70	Nathalie David-Mila (FRA)	24,191
21	Tania Elosegui Mayor (ESP)	68,443	71	Federica Piovano (ITA)	23,722
22	Karine Icher (FRA)	67,892	72	Georgina Simpson (ENG)	23,208
23	Iben Tinning (DEN)	67,413	73	Sara Beautell (ESP)	22,953
24	Amanda Moltke-Leth (DEN)	67,086	74	Marina Arruti (ESP)	22,575
25	Trish Johnson (ENG)	63,325	75	Tullia Calzavara (ITA)	22,063
26	Asa Gottmo (SWE)	61,919	76	Catrin Nilsmark (SWE)	22,008
27	Karen Stupples (ENG)	60,123	77	Denise Simon (GER)	21,871
28	Elisa Serramia (ESP)	57,494	78	Louise Friberg (SWE)	21,803
29	Sarah Kemp (AUS)	56,605	79	Ana Larraneta (ESP)	21,778
30	Marta Prieto (ESP)	56,584	80	Beatriz Recari Eransus (ESP)	21,323
31	Lisa Hall (ENG)	55,140	81	Sofia Renell (SWE)	19,763
32	Suzann Pettersen (NOR)	52,903	82	Fame More (ENG)	18,839
33	Rebecca Coakley (IRL)	52,417	83	Carin Koch (SWE)	18,769
34	Sophie Sandolo (ITA)	51,983	84	Lara Tadiotto (BEL)	18,679
35	Rebecca Stevenson (AUS)	50,251	85	Eva Steinberger (AUT)	18,155
36	Virginie Auffret (FRA)	47,860	86	Patricia Meunier Lebouc (FRA)	17,702
37	Helen Alfredsson (SWE)	45,657	87	Mianne Bagger (DEN)	17,385
38	Kirsty S Taylor (ENG)	44,917	88	Anna Tybring (SWE)	17,009
39	Kirsty Taylor (ENG)	44,749	89	Maria Boden (SWE)	16,813
40	Lora Fairclough (ENG)	43,233	90	Liza Walters (ENG)	16,738
41	Lotta Wahlin (SWE)	42,919	91	Kathryn Imrie (SCO)	16,425
42	Nora Angehrn (SUI)	39,738	92	Alison Munt (AUS)	15,939
43	Bettina Hauert (GER)	38,912	93	Lisa Jean (AUS)	15,707
44	Laurette Maritz (RSA)	37,245	94	Diana Luna (ITA)	14,872
45	Danielle Masters (ENG)	36,876	95	Clare Queen (SCO)	14,679
46	Anna Knutsson (SWE)	36,561	96	Karen Lunn (AUS)	14,147
47	Shani Waugh (AUS)	36,259	97	Bo Bae Song (KOR)	13,501
48	Cherie Byrnes (AUS)	36,073	98	Nienke Nijenhuis (NED)	13,282
49	Helena Alterby (SWE)	32,140	99	Carina Vagner (DEN)	13,212
50	Stefania Croce (ITA)	31,330	100	Jehanne Jail (FRA)	13,152

Tour Results (in chronological order)

Women's World Cup Gary Player GC, Sun City, RSA [6384–72]

1	Sweden	65-69-147 (Annika Sörenstam 70, Liselotte Neumann 77)—281
2	Scotland	70-73-141 (Catriona Matthew 69, Janice Moodie 72)—284
3	Wales	70-70-148 (Becky Brewerton 73, Becky Morgan 75)—288

Other scores: 290 South Korea; 291 Colombia; 292 South Africa, Finland; 294 Australia, Germany; 295 Italy; 296 Japan; 298 France; 299 Brazil, Taiwan; 301 England; 302 Canada, Spain; 305 Philippines; 306 New Zealand

For full results see page 236

ANZ Ladies' Masters Royal Pines, Gold Coast, Queensland, Australia [6397–72]

1998	K Webb	2002	A Sörenstam
1999	K Webb	2003	L Davies
2000	K Webb	2004	A Sörenstam
2001	K Webb	2005	K Webb

1	Amy Yang (KOR) (am)*	69-66-70-70—275	
2	Catherine Cartwright (USA)	70-67-70-68—275	€83374
3	Tiffany Joh (USA) (am)	72-66-69-69—276	
	Louise Stahle (SWE)	72-68-68-68—276	55027
	Ya-Ni Tseng (TAI) (am)	73-69-70-64—276	

*Yang won at first extra hole

Tenerife Ladies Open Abama [6095–72]

1	Rikka Hakkarainen (FIN)	73-70-74-71—288	€37500
2	Tania Elosegui Mayor (ESP)	71-72-76-71—290	25375
3	Virginie Auffret (FRA)	73-76-75-67—291	11570
	Rebecca Coakley (IRL)	74-73-73-71—291	11570
	Rebecca Hudson (ENG)	78-76-69-68—291	11570
	Kirsty S Taylor (ENG)	72-69-73-77—291	11570
	Shani Waugh (AUS)	73-73-74-71—291	11570

Open de España Femenino Panorámica, Castellón [6252–72]

1982	R Jones	Sotogrande	1988	M-L de Taya	La Manga
1983	not played		1989–2002	not played	
1984	M Burton	La Manga	2003	K Icher	Salamanca
1985	A Sheard	La Manga	2004	F Dassu	Salamanca
1986	L Davies	La Manga	2005	I Tinning	Panorámica
1987	C Dibnah	La Manga			

1	Lynnette Brooky (NZL)	66-74-65-70—275	€41250
2	Gwladys Nocera (FRA)	67-68-73-70—278	27912
3	Nora Angehrn (SUI)	71-72-66-71—280	19250

Deutsche Bank Swiss Open Gerre Losone

1	Gwladys Nocera (FRA)	69-70-63-71—273	€75000
2	Laura Davies (ENG)	66-71-69-70—276	50750
3	Lisa Hall (ENG)	68-67-66-76—277	35000

Vediorbis Open de France *Le Golf d'Arras, Anzin, France* [6195–72]

1987	L Neumann	Fourqueux	1998	not played	
1988	M-L de Taya	Fourqueux	1999	T Johnson	Paris International
1989	S Strudwick	Fourqueux	2000	P Meunier Lebouc	Le Golf d'Arras
1990–1993 not played			2001	S Pettersen	Le Golf d'Arras
1994	J Forbes	Saint-Endreol	2002	L Brooky	Le Golf d'Arras
1995	M-L de Lorenzi	Saint-Endreol	2003	L Brooky	Le Golf d'Arras
1996	T Johnson	Le Golf d'Arras	2004	S Arricau	Le Golf d'Arras
1997	K Lunn	Paris International	2005	V Zorzi	Le Golf d'Arras

1	Veronica Zorzi (ITA)	71-69-69-72—281	€48750
2	Laura Davies (ENG)	72-73-68-69—282	32987
3	Stephanie Arricau (FRA)	73-70-70-72—285	22750

KLM Ladies Open *Eindhovensche Valkenswaard, Netherlands* [6195–72]

1	Stephanie Arricau (FRA)	67-67-70—204	€24750
2	Anja Monke (GER)	69-67-69—205	16747
3	Leah Hart (AUS)	65-71-70—206	11550

BMW Ladies Italian Open *Parco de' Medici, Rome* [6145–72]

1987	L Davies	Croara	1997	V van Ryckeghem	Il Picciolo GC
1988	L Davies	Ca'Della Nave	1998	not played	
1989	X Wunsch-Ruiz	Carimate	1999	S Head	Poggio dei Medici
1990	F Descampe	Lake Garda	2000	S Gustafson	Poggio dei Medici
1991	C Dibnah	Albarella	2001	P Marti	Poggio dei Medici
1992	L Davies	Frasanelle	2002	I Tinning	Poggio dei Medici
1993	A Arruti	GC Lignano	2003	L Kreutz	Poggio dei Medici
1994	C Dibnah	GC Lignano	2004	AB Sanchez	Parco di Roma GC
1995	D Booker	Il Picciolo GC	2005	I Tinning	Parco de' Medici
1996	L Davies	Il Picciolo GC			

1	Gwladys Nocera (FRA)	71-66-65-72—274	€60000
2	Sophie Giquel (FRA)	70-69-66-71—276	40600
3	Laura Cabanillas (ESP)	71-71-68-70—280	15931
	Rebecca Hudson (ENG)	72-71-66-71—280	15931
	Ana B Sanchez (ESP)	72-74-65-69—280	15931
	Elisa Serramia (ESP)	68-70-73-69—280	15931
	Iben Tinning (DEN)	72-69-67-72—280	15931
	Linda Wessberg (SWE)	67-72-69-72—280	15931
	Veronica Zorzi (ITA)	71-72-68-69—280	15931

Estoril Open of Portugal *Quinta da Marinha Oitavos, Portugal* [6199–72]

1	Stephanie Arricau (FRA)	71-71-65—207	€45000
2	Gwladys Nocera (FRA)	69-73-70—212	30450
3	Sarah Kemp (AUS)	69-72-72—213	21000

OTP Bank Ladies Central European Open *Old Lake GC, Tata, Hungary* [6037–71]

1	Rebecca Hudson (ENG)	66-65-70—201	€24750
2	Anja Monke (GER)	64-66-73—203	16747
3	Lora Fairclough (ENG)	67-69-68—204	10230
	Riikka Hakkarainen (FIN)	69-64-71—204	10230

Catalonia Masters GC D'Aro, Costa Brava, Spain [6153-72]

1	Gwladys Nocera (FRA)	69-69-69—207	€55000
2	Sarah Kemp (AUS)	70-74-68—212	22800
3	Maria Hjörth (SWE)	73-73-67—213	11400
	Ludivine Kreutz (FRA)	75-72-66—213	11400

Evian Masters Evian Les Bains, France [6283-72]

1998	H Alfredsson	Royal GC Evian	2002	A Sörenstam	Evian Masters GC
1999	C Nilsmark	Evian Masters GC	2003	J Inkster	Evian Masters GC
2000	A Sörenstam	Royal GC Evian	2004	W Doolan	Evian Masters GC
2001	R Teske	Evian Masters GC	2005	P Creamer	Evian Masters GC

1	Karrie Webb (AUS)	67-68-69-68—272	€380268
2	Laura Davies (ENG)	68-71-67-67—273	215766
	Michelle Wie (USA)	69-66-70-68—273	215766

WEETABIX WOMEN'S BRITISH OPEN Royal Lytham & St Annes, England [7308-72]

1	Sherri Steinhauer (USA)	73-70-66-72—281	€160000
2	Sophie Gustafson (SWE)	76-67-69-72—284	85000
	Cristie Kerr (USA)	71-76-66-71—284	85000

Fuller details of this event and former winners are included in Part I The Majors page 79

Scandinavian TPC Bro-Balsta GC, Stockholm [6530-73]

1	Annika Sörenstam (SWE)	66-71-69-65—271	€75000
2	Lorena Ochoa (MEX)	72-65-69-66—272	50750
3	Suzann Pettersen (NOR)	71-69-68-68—276	35000

Wales Championship of Europe Machynys Peninsula, Llanelli, Wales [6126-72]

1	Linda Wessberg (SWE)	67-67-69-71—274	€77070
2	Laura Davies (ENG)	66-69-73-67—275	52150
3	Nikki Garrett (AUS)	69-67-69-71—276	31855
	Gwladys Nocera (FRA)	70-72-68-66—276	31855

SAS Masters Oslo, Norway [6172-72]

1	Laura Davies (ENG)	69-68-68—205	€30000
2	Ellen Smets (BEL)	72-69-70—211	20300
3	Nikki Garrett (AUS)	69-73-70—212	12400
	Virginie Lagoutte (FRA)	67-74-71—212	12400

Finnair Masters Helsinki GC, Finland [5916-71]

1	Virginie Lagoutte (FRA)	68-68-67—203	€30000
2	Elin Ohlsson (SWE)	67-70-68—205	20300
3	Kris Lindstrom (USA)	68-69-71—208	12400
	Gwladys Nocera (FRA)	68-72-68—208	12400

Nykredit Masters Odense Eventyr Golf Klub, Copenhagen [6372-72]

1	Karen Margrethe Juul (DEN)	72-67-66-68—273	€30000
2	Laura Davies (ENG)	70-69-72-66—277	17150
	Trish Johnson (ENG)	72-71-66-68—277	17150

Siemens Austrian Ladies Open   *Föhrenwald, Wiener Neustadt, Austria*   [6194-72]

1	Sophie Gustafson (SWE)	71-64-65-71—271	€37500
2	Laura Davies (ENG)	70-70-66-67—273	25375
3	Ana Belen Sanchez (ESP)	75-66-67-69—277	17500

BBC Radio Kent English Open   *Chart Hills, Kent, England*   [6250-72]

1	Cecilia Ekelundh (SWE)	71-69-70—210	€24750
2	Martina Ebert (GER)	70-71-70—211	16747
3	Danielle Masters (ENG)	69-73-70—212	11550

Dubai Ladies Masters   *Emirates GC Dubai UAE*

1	Annika Sörenstam (SWE)	65-68-68-69—270	€58315
2	Helen Alfredsson (SWE)	70-71-68-67—276	39460
3	Karen Webb (AUS)	70-68-70-70—278	27214

Six first time winners on Ladies European Tour

There were six first-time winners on the Ladies European Tour in 2006 and all were from different countries. Korean Amy Yang, who won in Australia as an amateur, has since turned professional and joined the Tour. Another of the first-timers, Gwladys Nocera from France, won three events during the year. After her break-through success in the Deutsche Bank Ladies Swiss Open, she also won the BMW Ladies Open and the Catalonia Ladies Masters. The golfers who scored their first wins were:

Amy Yang (KOR)	ANZ Ladies Masters
Rikka Hakkarainen (FIN)	Tenerife Ladies Open
Gwyladys Nocera (FRA)	Deutsche Bank Ladies Swiss Open
	BMW Ladies Italian Open
	Catalonia Ladies Masters
Rebecca Hudson (ENG)	OTP Bank Central European Open, Hungary
Linda Wessberg (SWE)	Welsh Ladies Championship of Europe
Karen Margrethe Juul (DEN)	Nykredit Masters, Denmark

Five first time winners on the US LPGA Tour

Julieta Granada (PAR)	ADT Championship
Brittany Lincicome (USA)	HSBC Women's World Match Play Championship
Seon-Hua Lee (KOR)	ShopRite LPGA Classic
Sung-Ah Yim (KOR)	Florida's Natural Charity Championship
Joo-Mi Kim (KOR)	SBS Open at Turtle Bay

LPGA Tour 2006

www.lpga.com

Players are of American nationality unless stated

Money List

1	Lorena Ochoa (MEX)	$2,592,872
2	Karrie Webb (AUS)	2,090,113
3	Annika Sörenstam (SWE)	1,971,741
4	Julieta Granada (PAR)	1,633,586
5	Cristie Kerr	1,578,362
6	Mi Hyun Kim (KOR)	1,332,274
7	Juli Inkster	1,326,442
8	Jeong Jang (KOR)	1,151,070
9	Hee-Won Han (KOR)	1,147,651
10	Pat Hurst	1,128,662
11	Paula Creamer	1,076,163
12	Seon Hwa Lee (KOR)	915,590
13	Se Ri Pak (KOR)	884,961
14	Brittany Lincicome	853,013
15	Sherri Steinhauer	707,932
16	Natalie Gulbis	693,968
17	Sophie Gustafson (SWE)	655,548
18	Stacy Prammanasudh	653,613
19	Meena Lee (KOR)	645,350
20	Jee Young Lee (KOR)	575,125
21	Brittany Lang	538,552
22	Ai Miyazato (JPN)	532,053
23	Angela Stanford	473,218
24	Morgan Pressel	465,685
25	Gloria Park (KOR)	443,163
26	Shi Hyun Ahn (KOR)	438,154
27	Joo Mi Kim (KOR)	408,699
28	Young Kim (KOR)	398,784
29	Candie Kung (KOR)	397,235
30	Karine Icher (FRA)	392,847
31	Sung Ah Yim (KOR)	385,224
32	Wendy Ward	383,441
33	Nicole Castrale	375,106
34	Laura Davies (ENG)	364,531
35	Christina Kim	355,656
36	Laura Diaz	342,432
37	Il Mi Chung (KOR)	339,914
38	Diana D'Alessio	328,396
39	Heather Young	323,871
40	Rachel Hetherington (AUS)	319,288
41	Michele Redman	307,948
42	Lorie Kane	307,301
43	Patricia Meunier-Lebouc (FRA)	303,747
44	Maria Hjorth (SWE)	299,634
45	Lindsey Wright (AUS)	295,398
46	Suzann Pettersen (NOR)	292,621
47	Aree Song (KOR)	289,240
48	Kyeong Bae (KOR)	286,931
49	Karen Stupples (ENG)	276,188
50	Nancy Scranton	274,304

Tour Results (in chronological order)

Women's World Cup *Gary Player GC, Sun City, RSA*   [6384–72]

1	Sweden	65-69-147 (Annika Sörenstam 70, Liselotte Neumann 77)—281
2	Scotland	70-73-141 (Catriona Matthew 69, Janice Moodie 72)—284
3	Wales	70-70-148 (Becky Brewerton 73, Becky Morgan 75)—288

Other scores: 290 South Korea; 291 Colombia; 292 South Africa, Finland; 294 Australia, Germany; 295 Italy; 296 Japan; 298 France; 299 Brazil, Taiwan; 301 England; 302 Canada, Spain; 305 Philippines; 306 New Zealand

For full results see page 236

SBS Open *Turtle Bay (Palmer Course), Oahu, HI*   [6520–72]

1	Joo Mi Kim (KOR)*	70-65-71—206	$150000

*Joo Mi Kim won at the second extra hole

2	Lorena Ochoa (MEX)	74-65-67—206	77722
	Soo Young Moon (KOR)	70-67-69—206	77722

Fields Open *Kolina, Hawaii*   [6519–72]

1	Meena Lee (KOR)*	69-68-65—202	$165000

*Meena Lee beat Seon Hwa Lee at third extra hole

2	Seon Hwa Lee (KOR)	65-66-71—202	100942
3	Michelle Wie	67-70-66—203	73227

MasterCard Classic *Bosque Real, Mexico City*   [6932–72]

1	Annika Sörenstam (SWE)	67-71-70—208	$180000
2	Helen Alfredsson (SWE)	72-70-67—209	95966
	Seon Hwa Lee (KOR)	70-69-70—209	95966

Safeway International

Prospector Course, Superstition Mountain, AZ   [6629–72]

1	Juli Inkster	68-68-70-67—273	$210000
2	Sarah Lee (KOR)	65-67-70-73—275	128161
3	Aree Song (KOR)	64-69-70-73—276	92972

KRAFT NABISCO CHAMPIONSHIP

Mission Hills, Rancho Mirage, CA   [6569–72]

1	Karrie Webb (AUS)*	70-68-76-65—279	$270000
2	Lorena Ochoa (MEX)	62-71-74-72—279	168226
3	Natalie Gulbis	73-71-68-68—280	108222
	Michelle Wie	66-71-73-70—280	108222

*Play-off: Webb 5, Ochoa 6 at first extra hole

Fuller details of this event are included in Part I The Majors page 106

LPGA Takefuji Classic Las Vegas CC, NV   [6550–72]

1	Lorena Ochoa (MEX)	63-68-66—197	$165000
2	Sean Hwa Lee (KOR)	67-67-66—200	99316
3	Brittany Lincicome	68-65-69—202	72046

Florida's Natural Charity Championship
Eagle's Landing, Stockbridge, GA   [6401–72]

1	Sung Ah Yin (KOR)	68-64-68-72—272	$210000
2	Cristie Kerr	65-75-65-69—274	96775
	Annika Sörenstam (SWE)	66-69-64-75—274	96775
	Karrie Webb (AUS)	67-67-70-70—274	96775

Ginn Clubs & Resorts Open Reunion, Orlando, FL   [6531–72]

1	Mi Hyun Kim (KOR)	70-66-69-71—276	$375000
2	Lorena Ochoa (MEX)	67-70-75-66—278	193477
	Karrie Webb (AUS)	75-67-69-67—278	193477

Franklin American Mortgage Championship
Vanderbilt Legends, Franklin, TN   [6458–72]

1	Cristie Kerr	67-69-66-67—269	$165000
2	Pat Hurst	70-67-66-68—271	77322
	Lorena Ochoa (MEX)	67-71-67-66—271	77322
	Angela Stanford	65-67-66-73—271	77322

Michelob ULTRA Open Kingsmill, Williamsburg, VA   [6306–71]

1	Karrie Webb (AUS)	66-68-66-70—270	$330000
2	Hee-Won Han (KOR)	71-67-69-70—277	175038
	Lorena Ochoa (MEX)	73-67-65-72—277	175038

Sybase Classic Wykagyl, New Rochelle, NY   [6223–71]

1	Lorena Ochoa (MEX)	71-71-66—208	$195000
2	Kyeong Bae (KOR)	71-73-66—210	103431
	Hee-Won Han (KOR)	68-73-69—210	103431

LPGA Corning Classic Corning CC, NY   [6132–72]

1	Hee-Won Han (KOR)*	66-70-69-68—273	$180000
2	Meena Lee (KOR)	65-72-70-66—273	110392
3	Brandie Burton	66-68-70-70—274	80081

*Hee-Won Han won after 4 hole sudden death play-off

ShopRite LPGA Classic

Bay Course, Marriott Seaview, Galloway Township, NJ   [6071–71]

1	Seon Hwa Lee (KOR)	65-69-63—197	$225000
2	Jeong Jang (KOR)	67-69-64—200	104167
	Annika Sörenstam (SWE)	64-69-67—200	104167
	Sherri Steinhauer	68-66-66—200	104167

McDONALD'S LPGA CHAMPIONSHIP

Bulle Rock, Havre de Grace, MD   [6486–72]

1	Se Ri Pak (KOR)*	71-69-71-69—280	$270000
2	Karrie Webb (AUS)	70-70-72-68—280	163998
3	Mi Hyun Kim (KOR)	68-71-71-71—281	105501
	Ai Miyazato (JPN)	68-72-69-72—281	105501

Play-off: 1st extra hole: Pak 3, Webb 4

Fuller details of this event are included in Part 1 The Majors page 97

Wegman's LPGA *Locust Hill, Pittsford, NY*   [6221–72]

1	Jeong Jang (KOR)	69-70-66-70—275	$270000
2	Julieta Grenada (PAR)	72-70-67-67—276	166003
3	Marcy Hart	70-72-66-69—277	106791
	Brittany Lang	66-71-69-71—277	106791

US WOMEN'S OPEN CHAMPIONSHIP

Newport, RI   [6564–71]

1	Annika Sörenstam (SWE)*	69-71-73-71—284	$560000
2	Pat Hurst	69-71-75-69—284	335000
3	Se Ri Pak (KOR)	69-74-74-69—286	156038
	Stacy Prammanasudh	72-71-71-72—286	156038
	Michelle Wie	70-72-71-73—286	156038

Play off, 18 holes: Sörenstam 70, Hurst 74

Fuller details of this event are included in Part 1 The Majors page 88

HSBC World MatchPlay Championship

Hamilton Farm, Gladstone, NJ   [6598–72]

First Round

Annika Sörenstam (SWE) beat Vira Nira Pathpongporn (THA) 3 and 2
Heather Young beat Sung Ah Yim (KOR) at 19th
Seon Hwa Lee (KOR) beat Aree Song (KOR) 3 and 2
Brittany Lang beat Patricia Meunier-Lebouc (FRA) 3 and 2
Juli Inkster beat Tina Barrett 2 and 1
Catriona Matthew (SCO) beat Beth Daniel at 21st
Marcy Hart beat Jeong Jang (KOR) 2 holes
Liselotte Neumann (SWE) beat Karren Stupples (ENG) 3 and 1
Karrie Webb (AUS) beat Nancy Scranton 4 and 2
Gloria Park (KOR) beat Rachel Hetherington (AUS) 1 hole
Pat Hurst beat Reilley Rankin at 21st
Helen Alfredsson (SWE) beat Julieta Granada (PAR) 3 and 2
Paula Creamer beat Miriam Nagl (GER) 2 and 1
Marisa Baena (COL) beat Wendy Ward at 21st
Morgan Pressel beat Sarah Lee (KOR) at 20th

First Round *continued*
Meena Lee beat Sherri Steinhauer 2 and 1
Michelle Wie beat Candy Hannemann (BRA) 5 and 3
Christina Kim beat Joo Mi Kim 2 and 1
Se Ri Pak (KOR) beat Angela Stanford 5 and 4
Lorie Kane (CAN) beat Natalie Gulbis 3 and 2
Brandie Burton beat Yuri Fudoh (JPN) 4 and 3
Brittany Lincicome beat Michele Redman at 20th
Kyeong Bae (KOR) beat Ai Miyazoto (JPN) 2 holes
Suzann Pettersen (NOR) beat Young Kim 2 and 1
Lorena Ochoa (MEX) beat Il-Me Chung (KOR) 3 and 1
Karine Icher (FRA) beat Stacy Prammanasudh 4 and 3
Mi Hyun Kim (KOR) beat Nicole Castrale 4 and 2
Laura Davies (ENG) beat Jee Young Lee (KOR) 2 and 1
Cristie Kerr beat Young Jo 1 hole
Sophie Gustafson (SWE) beat Gwladys Nocera (FRA) 3 and 2
Lindsey Wright (AUS) beat Hee-Won Han (KOR) 5 and 4
Laura Diaz w/o Shi Hyun Hahn (KOR)

Second Round
Sörenstam beat Young 3 and 2
Lang beat Lee 3 and 2
Inkster beat Matthew 4 and 3
Hart beat Neumann 4 and 3
Webb beat Park 5 and 4
Hurst beat Alfredsson 4 and 2
Creamer beat Baena 5 and 3
Pressel beat Lee 2 and 1
Wie beat C Kim 3 and 2
Pak beat Kane 1 hole
Lincicome beat Burton 2 and 1
Bae beat Pettersen 1 hole
Ochoa beat Icher 1 hole
M H Kim beat Davies 5 and 4
Gustafson beat Kerr 4 and 2
Diaz beat Wright 2 holes

Third Round
Sörenstam beat Lang 6 and 5
Inkster beat Hart 3 and 2
Webb beat Hurst 3 and 2
Creamer beat Pressel 3 and 1
Wie beat Pak 2 and 1
Lincicome beat Bae 3 and 2
Ochoa beat Kim 3 and 2
Gustafson beat Diaz 2 and 1

Quarter Finals
Inkster beat Sörenstam 1 hole
Creamer beat Webb 3 and 2
Lincicome beat Wie 4 and 3
Ochoa beat Gustafson 3 and 2

Semi-Finals
Inkster beat Creamer 5 and 4
Lincicome beat Ochoa at 19th

ThirdPlace: Lorena Ochoa beat Paula Creamer
  3 and 2

1	$500000
2	$300000
3	$200000
4	$150000

Final
Brittany Lincicome beat Juli Inkster 3 and 2

Jamie Farr Owens Corning Classic
Highland Meadows, Sylvania, OH   [6408–71]

1	Mi Hyun Kim (KOR)*	68-66-67-65—266	$180000
2	Natalie Gulbis	67-66-68-65—266	106155
3	Paula Creamer	67-67-68-65—267	77007

*Mi Hyun Kim won at the third extra hole

Evian Masters *Evian-les-Bains, France* [6283–72]

1	Karrie Webb (AUS)	67-68-69-68—272	$450000
2	Laura Davies (ENG)	68-71-67-67—273	255333
	Michelle Wie	69-66-70-68—273	255333

WEETABIX WOMEN'S BRITISH OPEN
Royal Lytham & St Annes, England [7308–72]

1	Sherri Steinhauer	73-70-66-72—281	$305440
2	Sophie Gustafson (SWE)	76-67-69-72—284	162265
	Cristie Kerr	71-76-66-71—284	162265

Fuller details of this event are included in Part 1 The Majors page 79

CN Canadian Women's Open *London Hunt Club, ON* [6611–72]

1	Cristie Kerr	67-70-74-65—276	$255000
2	Angela Stanford	64-70-69-74—277	152823
3	Pat Hurst	69-71-70-68—278	110863

Safeway Classic *Columbia Edgewater, Portland, OR* [6377–72]

1	Pat Hurst	69-69-68—206	$210000
2	Jeong Jang (KOR)	69-68-70—207	109291
	Kim Saiki	68-72-67—207	109291

Wendy's Championship for Children
Tartan Fields, Dublin, OH [6509–72]

1	Lorena Ochoa (MEX)	67-68-64-65—264	$165000
2	Jee Young Lee (KOR)	66-67-68-66—267	87085
	Stacy Prammanasudh	66-70-67-64—267	87085

State Farm Classic *Rail GC, Springfield, IL* [6666–72]

1	Annika Sörenstam (SWE)	70-68-69-62—269	$195000
2	Cristie Kerr	68-64-72-67—271	120827
3	Il Mi Chung (KOR)	67-66-70-69—272	70011
	Maria Hjörth (SWE)	65-67-70-70—272	70011
	Seon-Hwa Lee (KOR)	67-67-69-69—272	70011

John Q Hammons Hotel Classic *Cedar Ridge, Tulsa, OK* [6602–71]

1	Cristie Kerr	70-61-68—199	$150000
2	Annika Sörenstam (SWE)	64-68-69—201	91766
3	Lorena Ochoa (MEX)	69-69-65—203	66570

Longs Drugs Challenge Blackhawk CC, Danville, CA [6212–72]

1	Karrie Webb (AUS)	67-70-66-70—273	$165000
2	Annika Sörenstam (SWE)	70-70-69-65—274	101192
3	Morgan Pressel	71-68-69-68—276	73408

Corona Morelia Championship Tres Marias, Morelia, Mexico
[6600–73]

1	Lorena Ochoa (MEX)	71-64-68-69—272	$150000
2	Julieta Granada (PAR)	70-70-66-71—277	92698
3	Paula Creamer	76-66-71-65—278	67246

Samsung World Championship Bighorn GC, Palm Desert, CA
[6644–72]

1	Lorena Ochoa (MEX)	67-73-67-65—272	$218750
2	Annika Sörenstam (SWE)	67-71-66-70—274	136718
3	Sophie Gustafson (SWE)	68-70-70-69—277	92968

Honda LPGA Thailand Amata Spring CC, Chonburi [6392–72]

1	Hee Won Han (KOR)	67-68-67—202	$195000
2	Diana D'Alessio	68-69-70—207	125042
3	Gloria Park (KOR)	69-68-71—208	72454
	Nicole Castrale	65-68-75—208	72454
	Candie Kung (THA)	72-67-69—208	72454

Kolon-Hana Bank Championship
Mauna Ocean GR, Yangnam, South Korea [6381–72]

1	Jin Joo Hong (KOR)	68-67-70—205	$202500
2	Jeong Jang (KOR)	68-72-68—208	125817
3	Se Ri Pak (KOR)	74-69-67—210	91272

Mizuno Classic Kashikojama GC, Shima, Japan [6506–72]

1	Karrie Webb (AUS)	69-67-66—202	$180000
2	Kaori Higo (JPN)	73-68-65—206	109333
3	Brittany Lang	68-69-70—207	57615
	Jeong Eun Lee (KOR)	72-65-70—207	57615
	Annika Sörenstam (SWE)	71-66-70—207	57615
	Aree Song (KOR)	69-68-70—207	57615

Mitchell Company LPGA Tournament of Champions
Magnolia Grove, Mobile, AL [6253–72]

1	Lorena Ochoa (MEX)	66-73-63-65—267	$150,000
2	Julie Inkster	67-69-73-68—277	92,177
	Paula Creamer	64-74-69-70—277	92,177

ADT Championship *Trump International, West Palm Beach, FL*   [6514–72]

Field of 32, cut to 16 after two rounds and eight after three but then all previous scores eliminated.
Eight played one round for the $1 million jackpot Figure in brackets is their opening three round score.

1	Julieta Granada (PAR)	(208)	68	$1,000,000
2	Lorena Ochoa (MEX)	(212)	70	100,000
3	Karrie Webb (AUS)	(210)	71	20,500
4	Il Mi Chung (KOR)	(207)	72	18,125
5	Natalie Gulbis	(212)	72	18,125
6	Mi Hyun Kim (KOR)	(208)	72	18,125
7	Ai Miyazato (JPN)	(209)	72	18,125
8	Paula Creamer	(212)	75	6,250

The following failed to make the third round cut: Jeong Jang (KOR), 213; Diana D'Alessio, Juli Inkster, Cristie Kerr, 215; Hee-Won Han (KOR), Se Ri Pak (KOR), 217; Morgan Pressel, 220; Wendy Ward, 224

The following missed the half-way cut: Pat Hurst, Brittany Lang, Jee Young Lee (KOR), 145; Annika Sörenstam (SWE), 146; Lorie Kane, Angela Stanford, 147; Brittany Lincicome, 148; Sophie Gustafson (SWE), Stacy Prammanaasudh, 149; Maria Hjörth (SWE), 150; Sun Young Yoo (KOR), 151; Candie Kung (THA), Seon-Hwa Lee (KOR), Sung Ah Yim (KOR), 153; Sherri Steinhauer 160

Wendy's 3-Tour Challenge *Recreation Resort GC, Lake Las Vegas, Nevada*

1	PGA Tour (Zach Johnson, Scott Verplank, Stewart Cink)	202
2	Champions Tour (Craig Stadler, Tom Kite, Jay Haas)	207
3	LPGA Tour (Juli Inkster, Natalie Gulbis, Cristie Kerr)	209

How the LPGA Big Three compared in 2006

	Lorena Ochoa (Mexico)	Karrie Webb (Australia)	Annika Sörenstam (Sweden)
On the US LPGA Tour:			
Played	25	20	19
Wins	6	5	5
Majors	0	1	1
2nds	6	4	5
Top 5s	16	10	11
Top 10s	20	13	16
Missed cut	0	1	2
Rounds	89	73	67
Rounds under par	62	56	48
In 60s	46	31	30
Average score	69.24	70.10	69.82
Average drive	269 yards	259.7 yards	261.3 yards
Birdies	395	297	281
Eagles	15	8	6
In the 2006 majors:			
Kraft Nabisco	2	1	6
McDonald's LPGA	9	2	9
US Open	20	37	1
British Open	4	MC	31
Other comparisons:			
Age	25	31	36
Years on Tour	4 years	11 years	13 years
Major wins	0	7	9
Career wins	9	35	69
Earnings 2006	$2,592,872 (1)	$2.090,113 (2)	$1,971,741 (3)
Career earnings	$6,069,222 (14)	$12,826,995 (2)	$20,304,562 (1)

The Legends Tour 2006
Formerly the Women's Senior Golf Tour   www.thelegendstour.com

Players are of American nationality unless stated

Women's Senior Ladies Open *Gotemba, Japan*

2005	Ai-Yu-Tu (TPE)	134	
1	Patty Sheehan	70-72–142	$50000
2	Alicia Dibos	75-72–147	35000
3	Cindy Rarik	75-73–148	26000

Hy-Vee Classic *Hyperion Field Club, Johnston, IA*

2001	C Walker	142	2003	M Lovander	139	2005	K Young-Robyn	140
2002	L West	140	2004	E Crosby	135			

1	Martha Nause	65-72—137	$100000
2	Alicia Dibos	70-69—139	57000
3	Jan Stephenson	68-72—140	22333
	Val Skinner	70-70—140	22333
	JoAnne Carner	71-69—140	22333

BJ's Charity Championship *Granite Links Club, Quincy, MA*

2005	Pat Bradley & Patty Sheehan		
	Cindy Rarick & Jan Stephenson (tie)	129	

1	Nancy Scranton and Christa Johnson	63-58—121	$100000
2	Cindy Figg-Currier and Sherri Turner	63-59—122	70000
3	Barb Scherbak and Cathy Gerring	66-62—128	30000
	Colleen Walker and Barb Mucha	67-61—128	30000
	Pat Bradley and Patty Sheehan	68-60—128	30000

Handa Cup (USA v Rest of World) *World Golf Village, St. Augustine, FL*
Captains: Kathy Whitworth (USA), Hisako Higuchi (JPN) (Rest of World)

First day – Foursomes:
Pat Bradley & Patty Sheehan beat Alicia Dibo (PER) & Jan Stephenson (AUS) 1 up
Martha Nause & Marylin Lovander lost to Dawn Coe-Jones (CAN) & Nayoko Yoshikawa (JPN) 1 up
Amy Alcott & Rosie Jones beat Anne-Marie Palli (FRA) & Cathy Panton-Lewis (SCO) 2 and 1
JoAnne Carner & Christa Johnson halved with Barb Scherbak (CAN) & Maria Gonzales (BRA)
Jane Geddes & Sandra Haynie beat Mieko Nomura (JPN) & Angie Tsai (TPE) 2 up

First day – Fourballs:
Nause & Lovander beat Coe-Jones & Yoshikawa 3 and 2
Bradley & Sheehan beat Dibos & Michiko Okada (JPN) 2 up
Jones & Cindy Rarik lost to Nomura & Gonzales 1 up

Second day – Singles:

Nause halved with Coe-Jones	Bradley beat Tsai 3 and 1
Geddes beat Palli 3 and 2	Johnson beat Gonzales 7 and 6
Lovander beat Scherbak 4 and 3	Alcott lost to Nomura 1 up
Rarik beat Okada 2 and 1	Jones beat Yoshikawa 3 and 1
Sheehan halved with Stephenson	Haynie beat Panton-Lewis 1 up
Carner lost to Dibos 2 and 1	

Result: USA 13½, Rest of World 5½

International Team Events

Solheim Cup

1990 *Lake Nona, FL*　Nov 16–18
Result: USA 11½, Europe 4½
Captains: Kathy Whitworth (USA),
　Mickey Walker (Europe)

First Day – Foursomes
Bradley & Lopez lost to Davies & Nicholas　2 and 1
Gerring & Mochrie beat Wright & Neumann　6 and 5
Sheehan & Jones beat Reid & Alfredsson　6 and 5
Daniel & King beat Johnson & de Lorenzi　5 and 4

Second Day – Fourball
Sheehan & Jones beat　Johnson & de Lorenzi　2 and 1
Bradley & Lopez beat　Reid & Alfredsson　2 and 1
King & Daniel beat Davies & Nicholas　4 and 3
Gerring & Mochrie lost to Neumann & Wright
　4 and 2

Third Day – Singles
Cathy Gerring beat Helen Alfredsson　4 and 3
Rosie Jones lost to Laura Davies　3 and 2
Nancy Lopez beat Alison Nicholas　6 and 4
Betsy King halved with Pam Wright
Beth Daniel beat Liselotte Neumann　7 and 6
Patty Sheehan lost to Dale Reid　2 and 1
Dottie Mochrie beat Marie Laure de Lorenzi
　4 and 2
Pat Bradley beat Trish Johnson　8 and 7

1992 *Dalmahoy, Edinburgh*　Oct 2–4
Result: Europe 11½, USA 6½
Captains: Mickey Walker (Europe),
　Kathy Whitworth (USA)

First Day – Foursomes
Davies & Nicholas beat King & Daniel　1 hole
Neumann & Alfredsson beat　Bradley & Mochrie
　2 and 1
Descampe & Johnson lost to Ammaccapane & Mallon
　1 hole
Reid & Wright halved with Sheehan & Inkster

Second Day – Fourball
Davies & Nicholas beat Sheehan & Inkster　1 hole
Johnson & Descampe halved with Burton & Richard
Wright & Reid lost to Mallon & King　1 hole
Alfredsson & Neumann halved with Bradley & Mochrie

Third Day – Singles
Laura Davies beat Brandie Burton　4 and 2
Helen Alfredsson beat Danielle Ammaccapane
　4 and 3
Trish Johnson beat Patty Sheehan　2 and 1
Alison Nicholas lost to Juli Inkster　3 and 2
Florence Descampe lost to Beth Daniel　2 and 1
Pam Wright beat Pat Bradley　4 and 3
Catrin Nilsmark beat Meg Mallon　3 and 2
Kitrina Douglas lost to Deb Richard　7 and 6
Liselotte Neumann beat Betsy King　2 and 1
Dale Reid beat Dottie Pepper Mochrie　3 and 2

1994 *The Greenbrier, WA*　Oct 21–23
Result: USA 13, Europe 7
Captains: JoAnne Carner (USA),
　Mickey Walker (Europe)

First Day – Foursomes
Burton & Mochrie beat Alfredsson & Neuman　3 and 2
Daniel & Mallon lost to Nilsmark & Sörenstam　1 hole
Green & Robbins lost to Fairclough & Reid　2 and 1
Andrews & King lost to Davies & Nicholas　2 holes
Sheehan & Steinhauer　beat Johnson & Wright　2 holes

Second Day – Fourball
Burton & Mochrie beat Davies & Nicholas　2 and 1
Daniel & Mallon beat Nilsmark & Sörenstam　6 and 5
Green & Robbins lost to Fairclough & Reid　4 and 3
Andrews & King beat Johnson & Wright　3 and 2
Sheehan & Steinhauer lost to Alfredsson & Neumann
　1 hole

Third Day – Singles
Betsy King lost to Helen Alfredsson　2 and 1
Dottie Pepper Mochrie beat Catrin Nilsmark　6 and 5
Beth Daniel beat Trish Johnson　1 hole
Kelly Robbins beat Lora Fairclough　4 and 2
Meg Mallon beat Pam Wright　1 hole
Patty Sheehan lost to Alison Nicholas　3 and 2
Brandie Burton beat Laura Davies　1 hole
Tammie Green beat Annika Sörenstam　3 and 2
Sherri Steinhauer beat Dale Reid　2 holes
Donna Andrews beat Liselotte Neumann　3 and 2

1996 *St Pierre, Chepstow*　Sept 20–22
Result: USA 17, Europe 11
Captains: Judy Rankin (USA),
　Mickey Walker (Europe)

First Day – Foursomes
Sörenstam & Nilsmark halved with Robbins & McGann
Davies & Nicholas lost to Sheehan & Jones　1 hole
de Lorenzi & Reid lost to Daniel & Skinner 1 hole
Alfredsson & Neumann lost to Pepper & Burton
　2 and 1

Fourball
Davies & Johnson beat Robbins & Bradley　6 and 5
Sörenstam & Marshall beat Skinner & Geddes　1 hole
Neumann & Nilsmark lost to Pepper & King　1 hole
Alfredsson & Nicholas halved with Mallon & Daniel

Second Day – Foursomes
Davies & Johnson beat Daniel & Skinner　4 and 3
Sörenstam & Nilsmark beat Pepper & Burton　1 hole
Neumann & Marshall halved with Mallon & Geddes
de Lorenzi & Alfredsson beat Robbins & McGann
　4 and 3

Fourball
Davies & Hackney beat Daniel & Skinner　6 and 5
Sörenstam & Johnson halved with McGann & Mallon
de Lorenzi & Morley lost to Robbins & King　2 and 1
Nilsmark & Neumann beat Sheehan & Geddes　2 and 1

Third Day – Singles
Annika Sörenstam beat Pat Bradley 2 and 1
Kathryn Marshall lost to Val Skinner 2 and 1
Laura Davies lost to Michelle McGann 3 and 2
Liselotte Neumann halved with Beth Daniel
Lisa Hackney lost to Brandie Burton 1 hole
Trish Johnson lost to Dottie Pepper 3 and 2
Alison Nicholas halved with Kelly Robbins
Marie Laure de Lorenzi lost to Betsy King 6 and 4
Joanne Morley lost to Rosie Jones 5 and 4
Dale Reid lost to Jane Geddes 2 holes
Catrin Nilsmark lost to Patty Sheehan 2 and 1
Helen Alfredsson lost to Meg Mallon 4 and 2

1998 *Muirfield Village, Dublin, OH* Sept 18–20
Result: USA 16, Europe 12
Captains: Judy Rankin (USA),
Pia Nilsson (Europe)

First Day – Foursomes
Pepper & Inkster beat Davies & Johnson 3 and 1
Mallon & Burton beat Alfredsson & Nicholas 3 and 1
Robbins & Hurst beat Hackney & Neumann 1 hole
A Sörenstam & Matthew lost to Andrews & Green
3 and 2
Fourball
King & Johnson halved with Davies & C Sörenstam
Hurst & Jones beat Hackney & Gustafson 7 and 5
Robbins & Steinhauer lost to Alfredsson & de Lorenzi
2 and 1
Pepper & Burton beat A Sörenstam & Nilsmark
2 holes
Second Day – Foursomes
Andrews & Steinhauer beat A Sörenstam & Matthew
3 and 2
Mallon & Burton lost to Davies & C Sörenstam 3 and 2
Pepper & Inkster beat Alfredsson & de Lorenzi 1 hole
Robbins & Hurst beat Neumann & Nilsmark 1 hole
Fourball
King & Jones lost to A Sörenstam & Nilsmark 5 and 3
Johnson & Green lost to Davies & Hackney 2 holes
Andrews & Steinhauer beat Alfredsson & de Lorenzi
4 and 3
Mallon & Inkster beat Neumann & C Sörenstam
2 and 1
Third Day – Singles
Pat Hurst lost to Laura Davies 1 hole
Juli Inkster lost to Helen Alfredsson 2 and 1
Donna Andrews lost to Annika Sörenstam 2 and 1
Brandie Burton lost to Liselotte Neumann 1 hole
Dottie Pepper beat Trish Johnson 3 and 2
Kelly Robbins beat Charlotta Sörenstam 2 and 1
Chris Johnson lost to Marie Laure de Lorenzi 1 hole
Rosie Jones beat Catrin Nilsmark 6 and 4
Tammie Green beat Alison Nicholas 1 hole
Sherri Steinhauer beat Catriona Matthew 3 and 2
Betsy King lost to Lisa Hackney 6 and 5
Meg Mallon halved with Sophie Gustafson

2000 *Loch Lomond* Oct 6–8
Result: Europe 14½, USA 11½
Captains: Dale Reid (Europe),
Pat Bradley (USA)

First Day – Foursomes
Davies & Nicholas beat Pepper & Inkster 4 and 3
Johnson & Gustafson beat Robbins & Hurst 3 and 2
Nilsmark & Koch beat Burton & Iverson 2 and 1
Sörenstam & Moodie beat Mallon & Daniel 1 hole

First Day – Foursomes
Davies & Nicholas lost to Iverson & Jones 6 and 5
Johnson & Gustafson halved with Inkster & Steinhauer
Neumann & Alfredsson lost to Robbins & Hurst
2 holes
Moodie & Sörenstam beat Mallon & Daniel 1 hole
Second Day – Fourball
Nilsmark & Koch beat Scranton & Redman 2 and 1
Neumann & Meunier Labouc halved with Pepper &
Burton
Davies & Carriedo halved with Mallon & Daniel
Sörenstam & Moodie lost to Hurst & Robbins 2 and 1
Johnson & Gustafson beat Jones & Iverson 3 and 2
Nicholas & Alfredsson beat Inkster & Steinhauer
3 and 2
Third Day – Singles
Annika Sörenstam lost to Juli Inkster 5 and 4
Sophie Gustafson lost to Brandie Burton 4 and 3
Helen Alfredsson beat Beth Daniel 4 and 3
Trish Johnson lost to Dottie Pepper 2 and 1
Laura Davies lost to Kelly Robbins 3 and 2
Liselotte Neumann halved with Pat Hurst
Alison Nicholas halved with Sherri Steinhauer
Patricia Meunier Labouc lost to Meg Mallon 1 hole
Catrin Nilsmark beat Rosie Jones 1 hole
Raquel Carriedo lost to Becky Iverson 3 and 2
Carin Koch beat Michele Redman 2 and 1
Janice Moodie beat Nancy Scranton 1 hole

2002 *Interlachen CC, Madina, MN* Sept 20–22
Result: USA 15½, Europe 12½
Captains: Patty Sheehan (USA),
Dale Reid (Europe)

First Day – Foursomes
Inkster & Diaz lost to Davies & Marti 2 holes
Daniel & Ward beat Carriedo & Tinning 1 hole
Hurst & Robbins lost to Alfredsson & Pettersen
4 and 2
Kuehne & Mallon lost to Koch & Sörenstam 3 and 2
Fourball
Jones & Kerr beat Davies & Marti 1 hole
Diaz & Klein beat Gustafson & Icher 4 and 3
Mallon & Redman beat Hjörth & Sörenstam 3 and 1
Inkster & Kuehne lost to Koch & McKay 3 and 2
Second Day – Foursomes
Kerr & Redman lost to Koch & Sörenstam 4 and 3
Klein & Ward beat McKay & Tinning 3 and 2
Inkster & Mallon beat Davies & Marti 2 and 1
Diaz & Robbins beat Alfredsson & Pettersen 3 and 1
Fourball
Daniel & Ward lost to Koch & Sörenstam 4 and 3
Hurst & Kuehne lost to Hjörth & Tinning 1 hole
Jones & Kerr lost to Carriedo & Icher 1 hole
Klein & Robbins lost to Davies & Gustafson 1 hole
Third Day – Singles
Juli Inkster beat Raquel Carriedo (ESP) 4 and 3
Laura Diaz beat Paula Marti (ESP) 5 and 3
Emilee Klein beat Helen Alfredsson (SWE) 2 and 1
Kelli Kuehne lost to Iben Tinning (DEN) 3 and 2
Michele Redman halved with Suzann Pettersen (NOR)
Wendy Ward halved with Annika Sörenstam (SWE)
Kelly Robbins beat Maria Hjörth (SWE) 5 and 3
Cristie Kerr lost to Sophie Gustafson (SWE) 3 and 2
Meg Mallon beat Laura Davies (ENG) 3 and 2
Pat Hurst beat Mhairi McKay (SCO) 4 and 2
Beth Daniel halved with Carin Koch (SWE)
Rosie Jones beat Karine Icher (FRA) 3 and 2

2003 *Barsebäck, Sweden* Sept 12–14
Result: Europe 17½, USA 10½
Captains: Catrin Nilsmark (Europe),
Patty Sheehan (USA)

First Day – Foursomes
Koch & Davies halved with Daniel & Robbins
Moodie & Matthew beat Inkster & Ward 5 and 3
Sörenstam & Pettersen beat Diaz & Bowie 4 and 3
Gustafson & Esterl beat Mallon & Jones 3 and 2

Fourball
Davies & Matthew lost to Kuehne & Kerr 2 and 1
Sörenstam & Koch lost to Inkster & Daniel 1 hole
Pettersen & Meunier-Labouc beat Stanford & Mallon
3 and 2
Tinning & Gustafson lost to Redman & Jones 2 holes

Second Day – Foursomes
Gustafson & Pettersen beat Kuehne & Kerr 3 and 1
Esterl & Tinning halved with Stanford & Redman
Sörenstam & Koch beat Ward and Bowie 3 and 4
Moodie & Matthew halved with Mallon & Robbins

Fourball
Sanchez & McKay lost to Daniel & Inkster 5 and 4
Gustafson & Davies lost to Kerr & Kuehne 2 and 1
Matthew & Moodie beat Ward & Jones 4 and 3
Sörenstam & Pettersen beat Robbins & Diaz 1 hole

Third Day – Singles
Janice Moodie (SCO) beat Kelli Kuehne 3 and 2
Carin Koch (SWE) lost to Juli Inkster 5 and 4
Sophie Gustafson (SWE) beat Heather Bowie 5 and 4
Iben Tinning (DEN) beat Wendy Ward 2 and 1
Ana Belen Sanchez (ESP) lost to Michele Redman 3 and 1
Catriona Matthew (SCO) beat Rosie Jones 2 and 1
Annika Sörenstam (SWE) beat Angela Stanford 3 and 2
Suzann Pettersen (NOR) lost to Cristie Kerr conceded
Laura Davies (ENG) beat Meg Mallon conceded
Elisabeth Esterl (GER) lost to Laura Diaz 5 and 4
Mhairi McKay (SCO) beat Beth Daniel conceded
Patricia Meunier-Labouc (FRA) beat Kelly Robbins
conceded

2005 *Crooked Stick GC, Carmel, IN, USA* Sept 9–11
Result: USA 15½, Europe 12½
Captains: Nancy Lopez (USA),
Catrin Nilsmark (Europe)

First Day – Foursomes
Daniel & Creamer halved with Koch & Matthew
Kerr & Gulbis lost to Davies & Hjörth 2 and 1
Kim & Hurst halved with Gustafson & Johnson
Redman & Diaz lost to Sörenstam & Pettersen 1 hole

Fourballs
Jones & Mallon beat Hjörth & Tinning 3 and 2
Hurst & Ward beat Sörenstam & Matthew 2 and 1
Kerr & Gulbis lost to Gustafson & Stupples 2 and 1
Creamer & Inkster lost to Davies & Pettersen 4 and 3

Second Day – Foursomes
Kim & Gulbis beat Nocera & Kreutz 4 and 2
Creamer & Inkster beat Davies & Hjörth 3 and 2
Diaz & Ward lost to Gustafson & Koch 5 and 3
Redman & Hurst beat Sörenstam & Matthew 2 holes

Fourballs
Hurst & Kim lost to Davies & Sörenstam 4 and 2
Daniel & Inkster halved with Tinning & Johnson
Kerr & Creamer beat Koch & Matthew 1 hole
Jones & Mallon halved with Gustafson & Pettersen

Third Day – Singles
Juli Inkster beat Sophie Gustafson (SWE) 2 and 1
Paula Creamer beat Laura Davies (ENG) 7 and 5
Pat Hurst beat Trish Johnson (ENG) 2 and 1
Laura Diaz beat Iben Tinning (DEN) 6 and 5
Christina Kim beat Ludivine Kreutz (FRA) 5 and 4
Beth Daniel lost to Annika Sörenstam (SWE) 4 and 3
Natalie Gulbis beat Maria Hjörth (SWE) 2 and 1
Wendy Ward lost to Catriona Matthew (SCO)
3 and 2
Michele Redman lost to Carin Koch (SWE) 2 and 1
Cristie Kerr lost to Gwladys Nocera (FRA) 2 and 1
Meg Mallon beat Karen Stupples (ENG) 3 and 1
Rosie Jones halved with Suzann Pettersen (NOR)

Solheim Cup – Individual Records

Brackets indicate non-playing captain

Europe

Name		Year	Played	Won	Lost	Halved
Helen Alfredsson	SWE	1990-92-94-96-98-2000-02	24	10	12	2
Raquel Carriedo	ESP	2000-02	5	1	3	1
Laura Davies	ENG	1990-92-94-96-98-2000-02-03-05	37	19	15	3
Florence Descampe	BEL	1992	3	0	2	1
Kitrina Douglas	ENG	1992	1	0	1	0
Elisabeth Esterl	GER	2003	3	1	1	1
Lora Fairclough	ENG	1994	3	2	1	0
Sophie Gustafson	SWE	1998-2000-02-03-05	19	9	6	4
Lisa Hackney	ENG	1996-98	6	3	3	0
Maria Hjörth	SWE	2000-04-05	7	0	5	0
Karine Icher	FRA	2002	3	1	2	0
Trish Johnson	ENG	1990-92-94-96-98-2000-05	22	5	12	5
Carin Koch	SWE	2000-02-03-05	16	10	3	3
Ludivine Kreutz	FRA	2005	2	0	2	0
Laure de Lorenzi	FRA	1990-96-98	11	3	8	0
Mhairi McKay	SCO	2002-03	5	2	3	0
Kathryn Marshall	SCO	1996	3	1	1	1
Paula Marti	ESP	2002	4	1	3	0

Name		Year	Played	Won	Lost	Halved
Catriona Matthew	SCO	1998-03-05	13	5	6	2
Patricia Meunier Labouc	FRA	2000-03	4	2	I	I
Janice Moodie	SCO	2000-03	8	6	I	I
Joanne Morley	ENG	1996	2	0	2	0
Liselotte Neumann	SWE	1990-92-94-96-98-2000	21	6	10	5
Alison Nicholas	ENG	1990-92-94-96-98-2000	18	7	8	3
Catrin Nilsmark	SWE	1992-94-96-98-2000-(03)-(05)	16	8	7	I
Pia Nilsson	SWE	(1998)	0	0	0	0
Gwladys Nocera	FRA	2005	2	I	I	0
Suzann Pettersen	NOR	2002-03-05	12	7	2	3
Dale Reid	SCO	1990-92-94-96-(2000-02)	11	4	6	I
Ana Belen Sanchez	ESP	2003	2	0	2	0
Annika Sörenstam	SWE	1994-96-98-2000-02-03-05	32	19	10	3
Charlotta Sörenstam	SWE	1998	4	I	2	I
Karen Stupples	ENG	2005	2	I	I	0
Iben Tinning	DEN	2002-03-05	10	3	5	2
Mickey Walker	ENG	(1990)-(92)-(94)-(96)	0	0	0	0
Pam Wright	SCO	1990-92-94	6	I	4	I

United States

Name	Year	Played	Won	Lost	Halved
Danielle Ammaccapane	1992	2	I	I	0
Donna Andrews	1994-98	7	4	3	0
Heathert Bowie	2003	3	0	3	0
Pat Bradley	1990-92-96-(2000)	8	2	5	I
Brandie Burton	1992-94-96-98-2000	14	8	4	2
Jo Anne Carner	(1994)	0	0	0	0
Paula Creamer	2005	5	3	I	I
Beth Daniel	1990-92-94-96-2000-02-03-05	29	10	9	7
Laura Diaz	2002-03-05	10	5	5	0
Jane Geddes	1996	4	I	2	I
Cathy Gerring	1990	3	2	I	0
Tammie Green	1994-98	6	2	4	0
Natalie Gulbis	2005	4	2	2	0
Pat Hurst	1998-2000-02-05	16	9	5	2
Juli Inkster	1992-98-2000-02-03-05	23	12	8	3
Becky Iverson	2000	4	2	2	0
Chris Johnson	1998	3	0	2	I
Rosie Jones	1990-96-98-2000-02-03-05	22	11	9	2
Cristie Kerr	2002-03-05	12	5	7	0
Christina Kim	2005	4	2	I	I
Betsy King	1990-92-94-96-98	15	7	6	2
Emilee Klein	2002	4	3	I	0
Kelli Kuehne	2002-03	8	2	6	0
Nancy Lopez	1990-(2005)	3	2	I	0
Michelle McGann	1996	4	I	I	2
Meg Mallon	1992-94-96-98-2000-02-03-05	29	13	9	7
Alice Miller	(1992)*	0	0	0	0
Dottie Pepper	1990-92-94-96-98-2000	20	13	5	2
Judy Rankin	(1996)-(98)	0	0	0	0
Michele Redman	2000-02-03-05	11	4	5	2
Deb Richard	1992	2	I	0	I
Kelly Robbins	1994-96-98-2000-02-03	24	10	10	4
Nancy Scranton	2000	2	0	2	0
Patty Sheehan	1990-92-94-96-(2002)-(03)	13	5	7	I
Val Skinner	1996	4	2	2	0
Angela Stanford	2003	3	0	2	I
Sherri Steinhauer	1994-98-2000	10	5	I	2
Wendy Ward	2002-03-05	11	3	7	I
Kathy Whitworth	(1990)-(92)*	0	0	0	0

Women's World Cup *Gary Player CC, Sun City, RSA*   [6384–72]

2005   Japan (Ai Miyazato and Rui Kitada)

1	Sweden	65-69-147 (Annika Sörenstam 70, Liselotte Neumann 77)—281
2	Scotland	70-73-141 (Catriona Matthew 69, Janice Moodie 72)—284
3	Wales	70-70-148 (Becky Brewerton 73, Becky Morgan 75)—288
4	United States	68-75-146 (Paula Creamer 73, Natalie Gulbis 73)—289
5	Korea	65-72-153 (Meena Lee 77, Bo Bae Song 76)—290
6	Colombia	69-69-153 (Marissa Baena 73, Cristina Baena 80)—291
7	South Africa	69-77-146 (Laurette Maritz 74, Ashleigh Simon (am) 72)—292
8	Finland	69-69-154 (Minea Blomqvist 78, Rikka Hakkarainnen 76)—292
9	Australia	72-77-145 (Rachel Hetherington 71, Shani Waugh 74)—294
	Germany	70-72-152 (Anja Monke 79, Miriam Nagl 73)—294
11	Italy	73-74-148 (Veronica Sorzi 75, Silvia Cavalleri 73)—295
12	Japan	73-74-149 (Ai Miyazato 76, Sakura Yokomine 73)—296
13	France	73-74-149 (Gwladys Nocera 75, Karine Icher 77)—296
14	Brazil	72-77-150 (Candy Hannemann 76, Luciana Benvenuti 74)—299
	Taiwan	67-77-155 (Amy Hung 74, Yu Ping Lin 81)—299
16	England	71-78-152 (Kirsty Taylor 79, Laura Davies 73)—301
17	Canada	70-75-157 (Lori Kane 77, A J Eathorne 80)—302
	Spain	69-74-159 (Marta Prieto 80, Paula Marti 79)—302
19	Philippines	71-82-152 (Dorothy Delasin 73, Ria Quiazon 79)—305
20	New Zealand	69-82-155 (Lynnette Brooky 70, Gina Scott 80)—306

Lexus Cup (Team Asia v Team International) *Tanah Merah GC, Singapore*   [7022–72]
(inaugurated 2005)

2005 Asia 8, International 16   Tanah Merah GC, Singapore

Captains: Grace Park (Team Asia), Annika Sörenstam (Team International)

First Day – Foursomes
Young Kim and Seon Hwa Lee beat Brittany Lincicome and Laura Davies 6 and 5
Jee Young Lee and Meena Lee beat Natalie Gulbis and Paula Creamer 2 holes
Grace Park and Shi Hyun Ahn halved with Stacy Prammanasudh and Angela Stanford
Hee Wan Han and Se Ri Pak lost to Morgan Pressel and Julieta Granada 4 and 3
Joo Mi Kim and Sakura Yokomine lost to Carin Koch and Annika Sörenstam 3 and 2
Candie Kung and Jennifer Rosales halved with Sherri Steinhauer and Nikki Campbell

Match position: Team Asia 3, Team International 3

Second Day – Fourballs
M Lee and JY Lee lost to N Gulbis and A Sörenstam 2 holes
HW Han and G Park beat J Granada and M Pressel 1 hole
SH Ahn and JM Kim lost to P Creanmer and S Prammanasudh 3 and 2
C Kung and J Rosales beat B Lincicome and N Campbell 3 and 1
Y Kim and S Yokomine beat L Davies and C Koch 2 holes
SH Lee and SR Pak beat S Steinhauer and A Stanford 4 and 2

Match position: Team Asia 4, Team International 2

Third Day – Singles
Grace Park (KOR) lost to Annika Sörenstam (SWE) 4 and 3
Candie Kung (TPE) lost to Paula Creamer (USA) 1 hole
Meen Lee (KOR) halved with Angela Stanford (USA)
Jee Young Lee (KOR) beat Morgan Pressel (USA) 5 and 4
Shi Hyun Ahn (KOR) lost to Stacy Prammanasudh (THA) 4 and 3
Young Kim (KOR) beat Carin Koch (SWE) 3 and 2
Hee Won Han (KOR) beat Nikki Campbell (AUS) 3 and 2
Jennifer Rosales (PHII) lost to Sherri Steinhauer (USA) 4 and 3
Sakura Yokomine JPN) beat Laura Davies (ENG) 4 and 3
Joo Mi Kim (KOR) lost to Natalie Gulbis (USA) 5 and 4

Third Day – Singles (continued)
Seon Hwa Lee (KOR) beat Julieta Granada (PAR) 2 and 1
Se Ri Pak (KOR) lost to Brittany Lincicome (USA) 4 and 2

Result: Team Asia 12½, Team International 13½

Louise Suggs is Bobby Jones Award winner

Two times US Open champion and founding member of the LPGA Louise Suggs has been honoured with the prestigious Bobby Jones Award for 2007.

Presented since 1955, the United States Golf Association's highest honour is awarded in recognition of distinguished sportsmanship in golf. The award recognises a person who emulates Jones' spirit, personal qualities and his attitude to the game and its players.

Louise, now 83 and iving in St Augustine, Florida, was introduced to the game by her father and as a native of Atlanta had the opportunity to play with Jones on several occasions. "It is an incredible honour to win this award. I admired and respected Bobby Jones immensely and even patterned my own game after him. This is the ultimate accolade I could receive."

Louise Suggs, who played in the 1948 Curtis Cup, had won the 1947 US Amateur Championship and completed the transatlantic double with a one hole victory over Jean Donald in the 1948 British Amateur at Royal Lytham and St Annes before turning professional.

She won her first US Open in 1949 beating Babe Zaharias by 14 shots – still a record winning margin – and took the 1952 Championship by seven shots. She had 14 top-5 finishes and 19 top 10's in that event. Eleven of her 58 victories on the LPGA Tour were majors. She was inducted as a player into the LPGA Hall of Fame in 1952, the World Golf Hall of Fame in 1979 and to the LPGA Hall of Fame again in 2000 as a teacher and club professional based at Sea Island GC. In 2000 she also won the Patty Berg award for her contribution to the LPGA Tour. The Louise Suggs award is presented annually to the Rookie of the Year.

Month by month in 2006

Colin Montgomerie, seeking his first major, and Mickelson, seeking his third in a row, both double bogey the final hole of the US Open at Winged Foot to hand title to Ogilvy. Woods misses the cut – for the first time in a major as a professional – on his return from the death of his father Earl six weeks earlier. Webb ties another major, but this time loses play-off to Se Ri Pak at the McDonalds LPGA.

FUTURES Tour

www.duramedfuturestour.com

Players American unless stated

Results

Lakeland FUTURES Golf Classic	Cleveland Heights, Lakeland, FL	Meaghan Francella	209 (-7)
Greater Tampa FGC	Summerfield Crossings, River View, FL	Ashley Prange	203 (-10)
Louisiana FC	The Wetlands, Lafayette, LA	Song-Hee Kim (KOR)	213 (-3)
Power of the Green FGC	The Trails at Frisco, TX	Hye Jung Choi (KOR)	206 (-7)
Jalapeno FGC	Palm View Municipal, McAllen, TX	Kristy McPherson	205 (-11)
IOS FGC	El Paso, TX	Song-Hee Kim (KOR)*	208 (-8)

* Song-Hee Kim beat Sarah Huarte in the play-off

Tucson FGC	Dell Urich, Tucson, AZ	Charlotte Mayorkas*	199 (-11)

*Mayorkas beat Karen Dennison in the play-off

Aurora FC	Geneva National, WI	Song-Hee Kim (KOR)	214 (-2)
Team WLF.org Classic	Kankakee Elks GC, Saint Anne, IL	Mollie Fankhauser*	212 (-4)

*Fankhauser beat Brandi Jackson at second extra hole

Michelob ULTRA F Players Chp	Hickory Point, Forsyth, IL	Salimah Mussani	272 (-16)
Lima Memorial Hospital FC	Lost Creek, Lima, OH	Ji Min Jeong (KOR)	203 (-13)
Horseshoe Casino FGC	Lost Marsh, Hammond, IN	Ashley Prange	214 (-2)
CIGNA Chip In For A Cure FGC	Gilette Ridge, Bloomfield, CT	Song-Hee Kim (KOR)	216 (E)
Alliance Bank FGC	Elie Village, Syracuse, NY	Ha-Ma Chae (Kor)	204 (-9)
Laconia Savings Bank FGC	Beaver Meadow, Concord, NH	Charlotte Mayorkas	207 (-9)
Betty Puskar FGC	The Pines, Morgantown, WV	Kristy McPherson	207 (-9)
Hunters Oak FGC	Queenstown, MD	Ashley Hoagland	206 (-10)
The Gettysburg Championship	Gettysburg, PA	Song-Hee Kim (KOR)*	206 (-10)

* Song-Hee Kim beat Jin Young Pak (KOR) in the play-off

ILOVENY Championship	Capital Hills, Albany, NY	Ji Min Jeong (KOR)	206 (-7)

Final Money List

1	Song-Hee Kim (KOR)	$76287	6	Allison Fouch	36826
2	Charlotte Mayorkas	66351	7	Ashley Prange	36107
3	In-Bee Park	49079	8	Angela Park	34861
4	Kristy McPherson	40558	9	Hye Jung Choi (KOR)	33366
5	Meaghan Francella	39416	10	Mollie Fankhauser	30612

Japan LPGA Tour www.lpga.or.jp (Japanese only)

Players are of Japanese nationality unless stated

Results 2006

Daikin Orchid Ladies Golf Tournament	Ryukyu GC, Okinawa	Mikiyo Nishizuka	208 (-8)
Accordia Golf Ladies	Aoshima GC, Miyazaki	Yuri Fudoh	211 (-5)
Kinmirai Tsuushin Queens Open Ladies Golf Tournament	Kagoshima Takamaki CC, Kagoshima	Akane Iijima	211 (-5)
Studio Alice Ladies Open	Hanayashiki GC, Hyogo	Ji-Hee Lee (KOR)	218 (+2)
Life Card Ladies Golf Tournament	Kumamoto Kuko CC, Kumamoto	Yuri Fudoh	208 (-8)
Fujisankei Ladies Classic	Kawana Hotel GC, Shizuoka	Shiho Oyama	215 (-1)
Katokichi Queens Golf Tournament	Yashima CC, Kagawa	Mie Nakata	206 (-10)
Salonpas World Ladies Golf Tournament	Tokyo Yomiuri CC, Tokyo	Shiho Oyama	281 (-7)
Vernal Ladies	Fukuoka Century GC, Fukuoka	Ji-Hee Lee (KOR)	204 (-12)
Chukyo TV Bridgestone Ladies Open	Chukyo GC, Aichi	Ji-Hee Lee (KOR)	211 (-5)
Kosaido Ladies Golf Cup	Chiba Kosaido GC, Chiba	Chieko Amanuma	209 (-7)
Resort Trust Ladies	Grandie Nasu Shirakawa GC, Fukushima	Mie Nakata	207 (-9)
We Love KOBE Suntory Ladies Open Golf Tournament	Rokko Kokusai GC, Hyogo	Nikki Campbell (CAN)	277 (-11)
Nichirei Ladies	Miho GC, Ibaraki	Sakura Yokomine	210 (-6)
Promise Ladies Golf Tournament	Water Hills GC, Hyogo	Saiki Fujita	206 (-10)
Belluna Ladies Cup Golf Tournament	Obatago GC, Gunma	Sakura Yokomine	201 (-15)
Meiji Chocolate Cup	Sapporo Kokusai CC, Hokkaido	Mi-Jung Jeon (KOR)	208 (-8)
Stanley Ladies Golf Tournament	Tomei CC, Shizuoka	Miho Koga	206 (-10)
Philanthrophy LPGA Players Championship	Itako CC, Ibaraki	Mi-Jeong Jeon (KOR)	277 (-11)
Crystal Gayser Ladies Golf Tournament	Keiyo CC, Chiba	Shiho Oyama	205 (-11)
NEC Karuizawa 72 Golf Tournament	Karuizawa 72 G, Nagano	Shiho Oyama	170 (-10)
New Caterpillar Mitsubishi Ladies	Daihakone CC, Kanagawa	Mikiyo Nishizuka	210 (-9)
Yonex Ladies Golf Tournament	Yonex CC, Niigata	Shiho Oyama	208 (-8)
Golf 5 Ladies	Alpen GC, Hokkaido	Yun-Jye Wei (KOR)	209 (-7)
LPGA Championship Konica Minolta Cup	Nidom Classic Course, Hokkaido	Ai Miyazato	282 (-6)
Munsingwear Ladies Tokai Classic	Ryosen GC, Mie	Akiko Fukushima	202 (-14)
Miyagi TV Cup Dunlop Ladies Open Golf Tournament	Rifu GC, Miyagi	Ai Miyazato	214 (-2)
Japan Women's Open	Ibaraki GC, Oosaka	Jeong Jang (KOR)	279 (-9)
SANKYO Ladies Open	Akagi CC, Gunma	Shinobu Moromizato	143 (-1)

Japan LPGA Tour Results *continued*

Fujitsu Ladies	Tokyu 700 C, Chiba	Mi-Jeong Jeon (KOR)	210 (-6)
Masters GC Ladies	Masters GC, Hyogo	Miho Koga	207 (-9)
Higuchi Hisako IDC Otsuka Kagu Ladies	Musashigaoka GC, Saitama	Akiko Fukushima	207 (-9)
Mizuno Classic	Kashikojima CC, Mie	Karrie Webb (AUS)	214 (-2)
Ito-En Ladies Golf Tournament	Great Island C, Chiba	Hyun-Ju Shin (KOR)	207 (-9)
Daiohseishi Elleair Ladies Open	Elleair GC, Ehime	Yun-Jye Wei (KOR)	207 (-9)
LPGA Tour Championship (Ricoh Cup)	Miyazaki CC, Miyazaki	Sakura Yokomine	277 (-11)

Final ranking 2006

1	Shiho Ohyama	¥166,290,957	11	Akane Iijima	54,285,626
2	Jeon Mi Jung (KOR)	102,614,030	12	Nikki Campbell (CAN)	48,294,394
3	Sakura Yokomine	96,387,662	13	Momoko Ueda	46,751,163
4	Ji-Hee Lee (KOR)	92,545,091	14	Shinobu Moromizato	46,394,001
5	Hyun-Ju Shin (KOR)	91,450,224	15	Yuri Fudoh	46,010,000
6	Miho Koga	86,323,105	16	Jeong-Eun Lee (KOR)	43,430,855
7	Akiko Fukushima	81,360,557	17	Hiromi Mogi	43,023,346
8	Yun-Jye Wei (KOR)	62,199,000	18	Mikiyo Nishizuka	38,724,470
9	Mie Nakata	59,963,803	19	Kaori Higo	37,100,506
10	Ai Miyazato	58,604,501	20	Michiko Hattori	36,171,695

Nedbank Women's Tour

www.wpga.co.za

Players are of South African nationality unless stated

Pam Golding International	Dainfern GC, Johannesburg	Nora Anghern (SWI)	210
Acer SA Open	Durban CC, Durban	Rebecca Hudson (ENG)	217
Telknom Classic	Zwartkop CC, Pretoria	Laurette Maritz	207
Nedbank Masters	Killarney GC, Johannesburg	Ashleigh Simon (am)	209

Final Order of Merit 2006

1	Rebecca Hudson (ENG)	327.50 pts	6	Bettina Hauert (GER)	160.00
2	Ashleigh Simon (am)	307.50	7	Mandy Adamson (ENG)	140.00
3	Laurette Maritz	218.50	8	Kirsty Fisher (ENG)	130.00
4	Cecilie Lundgren (NOR)	170.00	9	Nora Anghern (SWI)	108.66
5	Helena Alterby (SWE)	168.00	10	Salima Mussani (CAN)	107.50

Ladies Asian Golf Tour

www.lagt.org

Orient Golf Zhuhai Open	Zhuhai, China	Kim Hae-jung (KOR)	209
Malaysian Open	Eastwood Valley G and CC, Miri, Sarawak	Ji Eun-hee (KOR)	214
Thailand Open	Pattana Sports Club, Bangkok	Park Hee-young (KOR)	209
Hong Kong Masters	Kau Sai Chau (North Course)	Pornanong Phatlum (THA) (am)	216
Macau Championship	Macau Grand CC	Ji-Eun-hee* (KOR)	143

*Ji Eun-hee beat Porani Chutichai (THA) at the third extra hole
(Reduced to 36-holes. Second round abandoned because of heavy rain and thick fog)

Final Order of Merit 2006

1	Ji Eun-hee (KOR)	$28,845	6	Zhong Xiao Long (CHN)	14,645
2	Kim Hae-jung (KOR)	24,220	7	Lee Jeong-yun (KOR)	10,309
3	Russamee Gulyanamitta (THA)	22,060	8	Walailak Satarak (THA)	10,168
4	Park Hee-young (KOR)	19,200	9	Eleanor Pilgrim (WAL)	8,685
5	Porani Chutachai (THA)	18,812	10	Nontaya Srisawang (THA)	8,321

Ladies Australian Golf Tour

www.alpgtour.com

Players are of Australian nationality unless stated

2005

Bermagui Country Club Pro-Am	Bermagui Country Club	Vicky Uwland	143 (-3)
Eden Country Club Pro-Am	Eden Country Club	Katherine Hull	66 (-6)
Sapphire Coast Ladies Classic	Tura Beach Country Club	Katherine Hull	137 (-9)
Mollymook Womens Classic	Mollymook Hilltop Golf Club	Belinda Kerr	145 (+1)
Catalina Country Club Pro-Am	Catalina Country Club	Helen Beatty	139 (-5)
St Georges Basin Country Club Pro-Am	St Georges Basin Country Club	Tamara Johns	139 (-5)
Moss Vale Golf Club Pro-Am	Moss Vale Golf Club	Karen Pearce	69 (-2)
Peugeot Kangaroo Valley Resort Pro-Am	Kangaroo Valley Resort	Shani Waugh	71 (-1)
Bing Lee LG Oatlands Trophy	Oatlands Golf Club, Sydney	Jane Leary	67 (-5)
Titanium Golf Ladies Classic	Club Pelican	Sarah Kemp	67 (-5)
Jack Newton Celebrity Classic	Peregian Springs Resort	Sarah Kemp	139 (-5)

2006

Womensport Queensland ALPG Pro-Am	Royal Pines Resort	Cancelled	
Optus World Coraki Golf Club Pro-Am	Coraki Golf Club	Sarah Kemp	67 (-6)
Titanium Enterprises ALPG Players Championship	Club Pelican	Rebecca Stevenson	212 (-4)
ANZ Ladies Masters	Royal Pines Resort	Amy Yang* (KOR)	275 (-13)

*Yang beat Catherine Cartwright (USA) at first extra hole of play-off

2007 fixtures:

Feb 1–4	MFS Women's Australian Open, Royal Sydney
Feb 8–11	ANZ Ladies Masters, Royal Pines Resort
TBC	Titanium Enterprises ALPG Players Championship, Club Pelican

Professional Women's Overseas Championships

ANZ Ladies Masters

1998	K Webb	2003	L Davies (ENG)
1999	K Webb	2004	A Sörenstam (SWE)
2000	K Webb	2005	K Webb
2001	K Webb	2006	Amy Yung (KOR)
2002	A Sörenstam (SWE)		

AAMI Australian Women's Open

1995	L Neumann (SWE)	2001	S Gustafson (SWE)
1996	C Matthew (SCO)	2002	K Webb
1997	J Crafter	2003	M McKay (SCO)
1998	M McGuire	2004	L Davies (ENG)
1999	Not played	2005	Not played
2000	K Webb	2006	Not played

French Ladies Open

1992	Not played	2000	P Meunier-Lebouc
1993	Not played	2001	S Pettersen (NOR)
1994	J Forbes (ENG)	2002	L Brooky (NZL)
1995	L Kreutz (GER)	2003	L Brooky (NZL)
1996	L Rolner	2004	S Arricau
1997	K Lunn (AUS)	2005	V Zorzi (ITA)
1998	Not played	2006	V Zorzi (ITA)
1999	T Johnson (ENG)		

Italian Ladies Open

1992	L Davies (ENG)	2000	S Gustafson (SWE)
1993	A Arruti	2001	P Marti (ESP)
1994	C Dibnah (AUS)	2002	I Tinning (DEN)
1995	D Booker	2003	L Kreutz (GER)
1996	L Davies (ENG)	2004	AB Sanchez (ESP)
1997	V Van Ryckegham	2005	I Tinning (DEN)
1998	Not played	2006	G Nocera (FRA)
1999	S Head (ENG)		

Other 2006 Overseas Championships

Austrian	Sophie Gustafson (SWE)
Canadian Open	Paula Creamer (USA)
Finnish Masters	Virginie Lagoutte (FRA)
Hungarian Open	Rebecca Hudson (ENG)
Japanese Open	Jeong Jang (KOR)
Netherlands	Stephanie Arricau (FRA)
Portuguese Masters	Stephanie Arricau (FRA)
South African Ladies Masters	Rebecca Hudson (ENG)
South African Ladies Open	Ashleigh Simon (am)
Spanish Open	Lynne Brooky (NZL)
Thailand Open	Park Hee-young (KOR)

PART IV

Men's Amateur Tournaments

Men's Amateur Ranking

After an 18-month trial run, the WAGR – the World Amateur Golf Ranking – proposed by The R&A, started this year. From January and on a weekly basis amateurs will be ranked according to where and in what events they choose to play their golf. The qualifying list of tournaments currently tops the 280 mark with, currently, the following representation: South Africa (17 events), Asia/Pacific (40), Continental Europe (33), Great Britain and Ireland (55) Latin America and the Caribbean (15) and North America (125). The list also includes the four majors plus entries from a number of other Tours including the Canadian, Challenge, Korean, Nationwide, Scandic League and the Tour de las Americas. Below is a list of some of the qualifying events this year and the top 10 as it would have looked last year had it been official. Heading the table is the US Amateur champion Richie Ramsay from Aberdeen.

New Zealand Under-23 – Danny Lee (NZL)
Lake Macquarie – Adam Gee* (ENG)
KwaZulu-Natal Open – Michael van de Venter (RSA)
Ping Arizona Inter-Collegiate – Henry Liaw* (USA)
Gauteng North Open – Jan Carel Nel* (RSA)
NSW Amateur* – Won Joon Lee* (AUS)
Mercedes-Benz Collegiate Championship – Oscar Floren (SWE)
All India Amateur – Himmat Rai (IND)
Portuguese Amateur – Adrien Bernadet* (FRA)
Tasmanian Open – Ben Parker* (ENG)
Jones Cup – Not played in 2006
Free State and Northern Cape Open – JBE Kruger (RSA)
Puerto Rico Classic – Chris Kirk (USA)
Ashworth Invitational – Anthony Kim (USA)
Spanish Amateur – Sam Hutsby* (ENG)
South African Amateur – Nigel Edwards* (WAL)
Southern Highlands Collegiate – Matt Kinsinger (USA)
Riversdale Cup – Stephen Dartnall* (AUS)
General Hackler Invitational – Alex Coe (USA)
South Island Amateur – Leighton James (NZL)
Hall of Fame Invitational – Anthony Kim (USA)
Schenkel E-Z-GO Inv.– Matt Harmon (USA)
Mexican Amateur – Sebastian Saavedra (ARG)
Australian Amateur – Tim Stewart* (AUS)
North West Open – Kyle Scott (RSA)
São Paulo City Open – Roberto Gomez (BRA)
Azalea Invitational – Not played in 2006
Hootie at Bulls Bay – Jamie Miller (USA)
National Invitational Tourn. – Jay Choi (USA)
Philippines Nat. Am. – Marvin Dumandan (PHI)
Copa del Jerez – Nigel Edwards* (WAL)
Scottish Champion of Champions – George Murray (SCO)
Administaff ASU Inv. – Scott Brown (USA)
Northern Open – George Coetzee* (RSA)
New Zealand Am.– Andrew Green* (NZL)
Morris Williams Intercollegiate – Oscar Alvarez (COL)
US Collegiate C/ship – Stephen Poole (USA)
South American Junior Team – Andres Echavarria (COL)
North Island Amateur – Josh Geary (NZL)
US Collegiate by The Maple Fund – Rob Grube (USA)
Mandurah Easter Amateur – Ben Pisani* (AUS)
The Aggie Invitational – Oscar Floren (SWE)
Craigmillar Park Open – Scott Jamieson (SCO)
Duncan Putter – Neil Chaudhuri (ENG)
West of Ireland – Rory McIlroy (IRL)
SAGA Invitational – Andrew Martin (AUS)
Lima International – Sebastian Saavedra (ARG)
SEC Championship – Brett Stegmaier (USA)
ACC Men's C/ship – Cameron Tringale (USA)
Brasilia City Open – Eduardi Pesenti (BRA)

Hampshire Salver – James Crampton (ENG)
Big 12 C/ship – Matthew Rosenfeld (USA)
Pac-10 Championship – Daniel Im (USA)
Mountain West Men's Conf. – Jay Choi (USA)
Big Ten's Mens C/ship – Chris Wilson (USA)
West of England – David Horsey (ENG)
South of Brazil Open – Felipe Lessa (BRA)
Boland Open – Brandon Grace* (RSA)
Trubshaw Cup – Rhys Enoch (WAL)
Western Province Am. – Charl Coetzee* (RSA)
Lytham Trophy – Jamie Moul* (ENG)
Keperra Bowl – Andrew Tampion* (AUS)
Irish Open Amateur – Antti Ahokas* – (FIN)
West of Scotland – Callum Macaulay (SCO)
Clwyd Trophy – Stuart Runcie (WAL)
NCAA Division II Men's Championship – Jamie Amoretti (USA)
Gambro Open – Johan Carlsson (SWE)
NCAA Central Final – Jonathan Moore (USA)
NCAA East Final – Kevin Chappell (USA)
NCAA West Final – Billy Horschel (USA)
Malaysian Amateur – Andrew Dodt (AUS)
English Open Am. – Robert Dinwiddie (ENG)
HLA Saujana Amateur Open – Stephen Dartnell (AUS)
Lagonda Trophy – Mark Thistleton (ENG)
Kinnaborg Open – Johan Carlsson (SWE)
Welsh Open Stroke Play – Cancelled – inclement weather
Thunderbird Int. Junior – Philip Francis (USA)
Parana State Open – Eduardo Pesenti (BRA)
NCAA Divisional Championship – Jonathan Moore (USA)
Scottish Stroke Play – Scott Henry (SCO)
Austrian Am.– Sigmundur Einar Masson (ISL)
East of Ireland – Brendan McCarroll (IRL)
Taiwan Amateur – Kim Do-Hoon (TPE)
Telia Masters – Bjorn Akesson (SWE)
Sunnehanna Amateur – Webb Simpson (USA)
St Andrews Links – Oliver Fisher (ENG)
French Open Amateur – Sean Einhaus (GER)
Aberconwy Cup – Craig Evans (WAL)
Irish Amateur Closed – Rory McIlroy (IRL)
Southwestern Amateur – Ben Fox (USA)
Footjoy Boys Invitational – Andrew Yun (USA)
Monroe Invitational – Phillip Mollica (USA)
Southeastern Amateur – Seth Brandon (USA)
Husqvarna Open – Tobias Rosendahl (SWE)
Rio State Open – Felipe Lessa (BRA)
The Amateur – Julien Guerrier (FRA)
California State Am. – Jordan Nasser (USA)
Copa de Las Americas – Not played in 2006
Northeast Amateur – Carlton Forrester (USA)
The Berkshire – David Hewan (RSA)
The Tennant Cup – John Gallagher (SCO)
Dogwood Inv. – Hudson Swafford (USA)
Russian Open Amateur – Seve Benson (ENG)
Midland Amateur – Edward Richardson (ENG)
East of Scotland – Keir McNicoll (SCO)

Danish Amateur – Morten Findsen Schou (DEN)
North and South Am.– Brady Schnell (USA)
Japan Amateur Golf Championship – Kyung-Tae Kim (KOR)
Rice Planters Amateur – Tanner Erwin (USA)
Sahalee Players C/ship – Kyle Stanley (USA)
Rolex Tournament of Champions – Philip Francis (USA)
Skane Open – Alexander Jacobsson (SWE)
Cameron Corbett Vase – Glenn Campbell (SCO)
Tucker Trophy – Nigel Edwards (WAL)
US Public Links – Casey Watabu (USA)
North of Ireland – Darren Crowe (IRL)
European Youths Team (Individual) – European Boys Team (Individual) (SWE)
Ontario Amateur C/ship – Andrew Parr (CAN)
Players Amateur – Jonathan Moore (USA)
Luxembourg Amateur – Steven Rojas – (SUI)
Chiberta Grand Prix – Duncan Stewart (SCO)
Salem Open – Henrik Norlander (SWE)
Eastern Amateur – Mark Ogren (USA)
Sutherland Chalice – George Murray (SCO)
Tillman Trophy – Robert Dinwiddie (ENG)
US Junior Amateur – Philip Francis (USA)
BC Amateur C/ship – Bryan Toth (CAN)
Southern Amateur – Kyle Stanley (USA)
Brazil Am. C/ship – Eduardo Pesenti (BRA)
Saskatchewan Amateur Men – Graham DeLaet (CAN)
St David's Gold Cross – Rya (KOR)
The Porter Cup – Steve Han (KOR)
South of England – Gary Wolstenholme (ENG)
Alberta Men's Amateur Championship – Kris Wasylowich (CAN)
German Amateur – Christian Schunck (GER)
Baltic Open – Iiro Sutinen (FIN)
Limpopo Province Open – Matthew Carvell (RSA)
South of Ireland – Simon Ward (IRL)
English Amateur – Ross McGowan (ENG)
Scottish Amateur – Kevin McAlpine (SCO)
Western Amateur – Bronson LaCassie (AUS)
Welsh Amateur – Llewellyn Matthews (WAL)
Pacific Coast – Patrick Nagle (USA)
Finnish Amateur – Jukka-Pekka Savolampi (FIN)
Swiss Amateur – Marc Dobias* (SUI)
Mullingar Scratch Trophy – Rory McIlroy* (IRL)
South American Match Play – Sebastian Saavedra (ARG)
St Mellion International Amateur – Gary Wolstenholme (ENG)
Czech Amateur – Nuno Henriques (POR)
Vasteras Open – Johan Carlsson (SWE)
Cardinal Amateur – Not played in 2006
Amateur Gold Medal – George Murray (SCO)
Canadian Amateur – Richard Scott (CAN)
The Boys Am. C/ship – Matthew Nixon (ENG)

Scratch Players C/ship – Rhys Davies (WAL)
British Mid-Am. C/ship – Simon Young (ENG)
Japan Junior Championship – Dan Maeda (JPN)
PGA Landman Open – Johan Carlsson (SWE)
Southern Cape Open – Justin Harding (RSA)
North East Open Am. – Mark Halliday (SCO)
US Amateur – Richie Ramsay (SCO)
Singapore Open Am. – Chiragh Kumar (IND)
Japan Collegiate Golf C/ship – Yuta Ikeda (JPN)
Sime Darby KL Amateur Open – S Sivachandran (MAS)
European International Individual – Rory McIlroy (IRL)
North of Scotland – Kevin McAlpine (SCO)
Lee Westwood Trophy – David Horsey (ENG)
2nd International Collegiate – Gordon Yates (SCO)
Labor Day Invitational – Garrett Osborn (USA)
State Fair Amateur – Bob Niger* (USA)
Golf University World C/ship – Yuta Ikeda (JPN)
Turkish Amateur – Peter Baunsoe (DEN)
Mpumalanga Open – David Hewan (RSA)
Newlands Trophy – James Byrne (SCO)
Rich Harvest Farms – Derek Fathauer (USA)
Scenic City Inv. – Garrett Osborn (USA)
Inverness Intercollegiate – Jon McLean (USA)
European Tour School Stage 1A – Heikki Mantyla (leading amateur) (FTQ) (FIN)
European Tour School Stage 1A – Adam Gee (leading amateur qualifier) (ENG)
European Tour School Stage 1A – Steven Uzzell (leading amateur qualifier) (ENG)
Duke of York Young Champions Trophy – Sam Hutsby (ENG)
Wairakei Open – Danny Lee (NZL)
US Mid-Amateur – Dave Womack (USA)
Italian International Am. – Jason Palmer (ENG)
Carpet Capital Collegiate – Chris Kirk (USA)
South East District Open – Glenn Campbell* (SCO)
Gopher Invitational – Colt Knost (USA)
Canadian Fall Qualifying – James Love (leading qualifier – amateur) (CAN)
Acer International Amateur – Chiang Chen-Chih (TPE)
Purple & Red Inv. – Dave Lewinski (USA)
Raines Development Group – Duncan Stewart (SCO)
Kansas Invitational – Gary Woodland (USA)
William H Tucker Intercollegiate – Charlie Beljan (USA)
Fighting Illini Inv. – Niklas Lemke (SWE)
VCU/Mattaponi Springs Shootout – Dan Woltman (USA)
Opus NW Husky Inv. – John Wise (USA)
Shoal Creek Intercollegiate – Jonas Blixt (SWE)
Moe O'Brien Intercollegiate – Sigmundur Einar Masson (ISL)
Vandal Fall Classic – Nick Travers (USA)
Adams Cup of Newport – Joel Myrick (USA)
European Tour School Stage 1B – Joost Luiten – leading amateur qualifier (NED)

European Tour School Stage 1B – James Morrison – leading amateur qualifier (ENG)
European Tour School Stage 1B – Oliver Fisher – leading amateur qualifier (ENG)
Federal Amateur – Rick Kulacz (AUS)
Cornell Invitational – Tyler Brewington (USA)
Murray State Invitational – Scott Stallings (USA)
Northwest Collegiate Classic – Matt Ma (USA)
Joe Agee Invitational – Jordan Utley (USA)
Wolf Pack Classic – Dustin Pimm (USA)
Ping/Golfweek Preview – Billy Horschel (USA)
Xavier Invitational – Jason Kokrak (USA)
Memphis Intercollegiate – Franklin Corpening (USA)
Faldo Series Final – Ben Evans (ENG)
Chile Open – Alan Wagner (ARG)
Wolf Run Intercollegiate – Derek Fathauer (USA)
MacDonald Cup – Robert Lindstrom (USA)
Mission Inn Collegiate Classic – Daniel Willett (ENG)
Coca-Cola Duke Golf Classic – Dustin Johnson (USA)
Ekurhuleni Open – Adrian Schwartzel (RSA)
Bulgarian Amateur – Michael Kanev (BUL)
Windon Memorial – Colt Knost (USA)
SFA Bill Hill Crown Classic – Bill Alcorn (USA)
Rex Chaney Eagle Classic – Matt Gann (USA)
Fighting Irish Gridiron Classic – Justin Harding (RSA)
2006 Earl Yestingsmeier Invite – Jeff Lanier (USA)
Jerry Pate National Intercollegiate – Joseph Sykora (USA)
District 7 Shootout – Aaron Goldberg (USA)
Stocker Cup – Bob Niger (USA)
Cape Province Open – JBE Kruger (RSA)
Alister MacKenzie Invitational – Michael Wilson (USA)
Bank of Tennessee at The Ridges – Rhys Davie (WAL)
Oklahoma Intercollegiate – Sam Korbe (USA)
NSU Fall Classic – Federico Damus (ARG)
The Prestige at PGA WEST – Zack Miller (USA)
TLA Tour School A – Sebastian Saavedra - leading amateur (ARG)
St Augustine Amateur – Peter Uihlein* (USA)
Mason Rudolph Intercollegiate – Kyle Peterman (USA)
Isleworth-UCF Collegiate Invitational – Brian Harman (USA)
Barona Collegiate Cup – Taylor Coffman (USA)
F&M Bank APSU Intercollegiate – Grant Leaver (USA)
49er Classic/SleepInn&Suites – Ray Sheedy (USA)
Big Ten/Pac-10 Challenge – Jamie Lovemark (USA)
The Club Glove Intercollegiate – Charlie Beljan (USA)
SCU Invitational – Brandon Crick (USA)
ORU Invitational – Alex Hogben (ENG)

Poplar Hill Intercollegiate – Kris Shepherd (USA)
The Eisenhower Trophy (Individual) – Will Besseling (NED)
Landfall Tradition – Mitch Cohlmia/Nicolas Geyger (USA/CHI)
Rollins College Invitational – Greg Koch (USA)
Herb Wimberly Intercollegiate – Brady Schnell (USA)
Sam Hall Invitational – Justin Fetcho (USA)
Buffalo Rock/Southern Showdown – Andy Rauscher (USA)
Bill Cullum Intercollegiate – Brian Locke (USA)
European Tour School Stage 2 – Oliver Fisher (leading amateur qualifier) (ENG)
European Tour School Stage 2 – James Morrison (leading amateur qualifier) (ENG)
European Tour School Stage 2 – Antti Ahokas (leading amateur qualifier) (FIN)
European Tour School Stage 2 – John Parry - leading amateur (ENG)
European Club Cup (Individual) – Sean Einhaus (GER)
Big East/MAC Challenge – Ben Sieg (USA)
Eastern Province Open – JBE Kruger (RSA)
CordeValle Collegiate – Rob Grube/Zach Miller (USA)
Stetson/CFCS Invitational – Daniel Laughlin (USA)
Food4Less Pacific Invitational – Clay Ogden (USA)
U of Hawaii Fall Intercollegiate – Brian Locke (USA)
Sri Lanka Amateur – Mithun Perera (SRI)
Putra Cup – Choo Tze Huang (SIN)
European Tour, Final Qualifying – Oliver Fisher (leading amateur qualifier) (ENG)
Selangor Amateur Open – Alex Tiong Wei Zen (MAS)
Central Gauteng Open – Neil Schietekat (RSA)
Western Refining Classic – Chris Kirk (USA)
Aloha Purdue Collegiate – Kyle Stanley (USA)
Pakistan Open Amateur – Tariq Mahmoud (PAK)
National Teams Championship (Individual) – Christiaan Basson (RSA)
Asia-Pacific Open Amateur – Gary Boyd (ENG)
The Dunes Medal – Rick Kulacz (AUS)
Copa Juan Carlos Tailhade (Individual) – Luciano Dodda (ARG)
Asian Games Golf – Kyung Tae Kim (KOR)
Asian Tour Qualifying – Final Stage – †
Australasian Tour Qualifying – Final Stage – †
Philippine Amateur – †
Junior Orange Bowl International – †
Dixie Amateur – †

† Not played at time of going to press

		Points				Points
1	Richie Ramsay (SCO)	1181.08	6	Oliver Fisher (ENG)		1120.37
2	Jamie Moul (ENG)	1162.79	7	Won Joon Lee (AUS)		1104.44
3	Ross McGowan (ENG)	1151.92	8	Adam Gee (ENG)		1093.02
4	Pablo Martin (ESP)	1151.11	9	Nigel Edwards (WAL)		1044.74
5	Rory McIlroy (IRL)	1138.30	10	Webb Simpson (USA)		1035.56

National and International Championships

Amateur Championship (inaugurated 1885)   (British or Irish unless stated)

Year	Winner	Runner-up	Venue	By	Ent
1885	A MacFie	H Hutchinson	Hoylake, Royal Liverpool	7 and 6	44
1886	H Hutchinson	H Lamb	St Andrews	7 and 6	42
1887	H Hutchinson	J Ball	Hoylake, Royal Liverpool	1 hole	33
1888	J Ball	J Laidlay	Prestwick	5 and 4	38
1889	J Laidlay	L Melville	St Andrews	2 and 1	40
1890	J Ball	J Laidlay	Hoylake, Royal Liverpool	4 and 3	44
1891	J Laidlay	H Hilton	St Andrews	20th hole	50
1892	J Ball	H Hilton	Sandwich, Royal St George's	3 and 1	45
1893	P Anderson	J Laidlay	Prestwick	1 hole	44
1894	J Ball	S Fergusson	Hoylake, Royal Liverpool	1 hole	64
1895	L Melville	J Ball	St Andrews	19th hole	68

From 1896 final played over 36 holes

Year	Winner	Runner-up	Venue	By	Ent
1896	F Tait	H Hilton	Sandwich, Royal St George's	8 and 7	64
1897	A Allan	J Robb	Muirfield	4 and 2	74
1898	F Tait	S Fergusson	Hoylake, Royal Liverpool	7 and 5	77
1899	J Ball	F Tait	Prestwick	37th hole	101
1900	H Hilton	J Robb	Sandwich, Royal St George's	8 and 7	68
1901	H Hilton	J Low	St Andrews	1 hole	116
1902	C Hutchings	S Fry	Hoylake, Royal Liverpool	1 hole	114
1903	R Maxwell	H Hutchinson	Muirfield	7 and 5	142
1904	W Travis (USA)	E Blackwell	Sandwich, Royal St George's	4 and 3	104
1905	A Barry	Hon O Scott	Prestwick	3 and 2	148
1906	J Robb	C Lingen	Hoylake, Royal Liverpool	4 and 3	166
1907	J Ball	C Palmer	St Andrews	6 and 4	200
1908	E Lassen	H Taylor	Sandwich, Royal St George's	7 and 6	197
1909	R Maxwell	Capt C Hutchison	Muirfield	1 hole	170
1910	J Ball	C Aylmer	Hoylake, Royal Liverpool	10 and 9	160
1911	H Hilton	E Lassen	Prestwick	4 and 3	146
1912	J Ball	A Mitchell	Westward Ho!, Royal North Devon	38th hole	134
1913	H Hilton	R Harris	St Andrews	6 and 5	198
1914	J Jenkins	C Hezlet	Sandwich, Royal St George's	3 and 2	232
1915–19	*Not played*				
1920	C Tolley	R Gardner (USA)	Muirfield	37th hole	165
1921	W Hunter	A Graham	Hoylake, Royal Liverpool	12 and 11	223
1922	E Holderness	J Caven	Prestwick	1 hole	252
1923	R Wethered	R Harris	Deal, Royal Cinque Ports	7 and 6	209
1924	E Holderness	E Storey	St Andrews	3 and 2	201
1925	R Harris	K Fradgley	Westward Ho!, Royal North Devon	13 and 12	151
1926	J Sweetser (USA)	A Simpson	Muirfield	6 and 5	216
1927	Dr W Tweddell	D Landale	Hoylake, Royal Liverpool	7 and 6	197
1928	T Perkins	R Wethered	Prestwick	6 and 4	220
1929	C Tolley	J Smith	Sandwich, Royal St George's	4 and 3	253
1930	R Jones (USA)	R Wethered	St Andrews	7 and 6	271
1931	E Smith	J De Forest	Westward Ho!, Royal North Devon	1 hole	171
1932	J De Forest	E Fiddian	Muirfield	3 and 1	235
1933	Hon M Scott	T Bourn	Hoylake, Royal Liverpool	4 and 3	269
1934	W Lawson Little (USA)	J Wallace	Prestwick	14 and 13	225
1935	W Lawson Little (USA)	Dr W Tweddell	R Lytham and St Annes	1 hole	232
1936	H Thomson	J Ferrier (AUS)	St Andrews	2 holes	283
1937	R Sweeney jr (USA)	L Munn	Sandwich, Royal St George's	3 and 2	223
1938	C Yates (USA)	R Ewing	Troon	3 and 2	241
1939	A Kyle	A Duncan	Hoylake, Royal Liverpool	2 and 1	167
1940–45	*Not played*				
1946	J Bruen	R Sweeny (USA)	Birkdale	4 and 3	263
1947	W Turnesa (USA)	R Chapman (USA)	Carnoustie	3 and 2	200
1948	F Stranahan (USA)	C Stowe	Sandwich, Royal St George's	5 and 4	168
1949	S McCready	W Turnesa (USA)	Portmarnock	2 and 1	204

Year	Winner	Runner-up	Venue	By	Ent
1950	F Stranahan (USA)	R Chapman (USA)	St Andrews	8 and 6	324
1951	R Chapman (USA)	C Coe (USA)	Royal Porthcawl	5 and 4	192
1952	E Ward (USA)	F Stranahan (USA)	Prestwick	6 and 5	286
1953	J Carr	E Harvie Ward (USA)	Hoylake, Royal Liverpool	2 holes	279
1954	D Bachli (AUS)	W Campbell (USA)	Muirfield	2 and 1	286
1955	J Conrad (USA)	A Slater	Royal Lytham and St Annes	3 and 2	240
1956	J Beharrell	L Taylor	Troon	5 and 4	200
1957	R Reid Jack	H Ridgley (USA)	Formby	2 and 1	200
In 1956 and 1957 the Quarter Finals, Semi-Finals and Final were played over 36 holes					
1958	J Carr	A Thirlwell	St Andrews	3 and 2	488
In 1958, Semi-Finals and Final only were played over 36 holes					
1959	D Beman (USA)	W Hyndman (USA)	Sandwich, Royal St George's	3 and 2	362
1960	J Carr	R Cochran (USA)	Royal Portrush	8 and 7	183
1961	MF Bonallack	J Walker	Turnberry	6 and 4	250
1962	R Davies (USA)	J Povall	Hoylake, Royal Liverpool	1 hole	256
1963	M Lunt	J Blackwell	St Andrews	2 and 1	256
1964	G Clark	M Lunt	Ganton	39th hole	220
1965	MF Bonallack	C Clark	Royal Porthcawl	2 and 1	176
1966	R Cole (RSA)	R Shade	Carnoustie (18 holes)	3 and 2	206
Final played over 18 holes because of sea mist					
1967	R Dickson (USA)	R Cerrudo (USA)	Formby	2 and 1	
1968	MF Bonallack	J Carr	Royal Troon	7 and 6	249
1969	MF Bonallack	W Hyndman (USA)	Hoylake, Royal Liverpool	3 and 2	245
1970	MF Bonallack	W Hyndman (USA)	Newcastle, Royal Co Down	8 and 7	256
1971	S Melnyk (USA)	J Simons (USA)	Carnoustie	3 and 2	256
1972	T Homer	A Thirlwell	Sandwich, Royal St George's	4 and 3	253
1973	R Siderowf (USA)	P Moody	Royal Porthcawl	5 and 3	222
1974	T Homer	J Gabrielsen (USA)	Muirfield	2 holes	330
1975	M Giles (USA)	M James	Hoylake, Royal Liverpool	8 and 7	206
1976	R Siderowf (USA)	J Davies	St Andrews	37th hole	289
1977	P McEvoy	H Campbell	Ganton	5 and 4	235
1978	P McEvoy	P McKellar	Royal Troon	4 and 3	353
1979	J Sigel (USA)	S Hoch (USA)	Hillside	3 and 2	285
1980	D Evans	D Suddards (RSA)	Royal Porthcawl	4 and 3	265
1981	P Ploujoux (FRA)	J Hirsch (USA)	St Andrews	4 and 2	256
1982	M Thompson	A Stubbs	Deal, Royal Cinque Ports	4 and 3	245
Qualifying round introduced					
1983	P Parkin	J Holtgrieve (USA)	Turnberry	5 and 4	288
1984	JM Olazábal (ESP)	C Montgomerie	Formby	5 and 4	291
1985	G McGimpsey	G Homewood	Royal Dornoch	8 and 7	457
1986	D Curry	G Birtwell	Royal Lytham and St Annes	11 and 9	427
1987	P Mayo	P McEvoy	Prestwick	3 and 1	373
1988	C Hardin (SWE)	B Fouchee (RSA)	Royal Porthcawl	1 hole	391
1989	S Dodd	C Cassells	Royal Birkdale	5 and 3	378
1990	R Muntz (NED)	A Macara	Muirfield	7 and 6	510
1991	G Wolstenholme	B May (USA)	Ganton	8 and 6	345
1992	S Dundas	B Dredge	Carnoustie	7 and 6	364
1993	I Pyman	P Page	Royal Portrush	37th hole	279
1994	L James	G Sherry	Nairn	2 and 1	288
1995	G Sherry	M Reynard	Hoylake, Royal Liverpool	7 and 6	288
1996	W Bladon	R Beames	Turnberry	1 hole	288
1997	C Watson	T Immelman (RSA)	Royal St Georges, Royal Cinque Ports	3 and 2	369
1998	S García (ESP)	C Williams	Muirfield	7 and 6	537
1999	G Storm	A Wainwright	Royal County Down, Kilkeel	7 and 6	433
2000	M Ilonen (FIN)	C Reimbold	Royal Liverpool and Wallasey	2 and 1	376
2001	M Hoey	I Campbell	Prestwick & Kilmarnock	1 hole	288
2002	A Larrazábal (ESP)	M Sell	Royal Porthcawl and Pyle & Kenfig	1 hole	286
2003	G Wolstenholme	R De Sousa (SUI)	Royal Troon and Irvine	6 and 5	289
2004	S Wilson	L Corfield	St Andrews, Old and Jubilee Courses	4 and 3	288
2005	B McElhinney	J Gallagher	Royal Birkdale and Southport & Ainsdale	5 and 4	406

111th Amateur Championship 2006 *Royal St George's and Prince's*

284 entries from 26 countries played in the 36-hole qualifying competition, 76 of whom qualified on 152 or better for the match play stage.

Leading Qualifier: Llewellyn Matthews (Southerndown) 74-68—142

First Round

Alex Prugh (USA) beat Jacques Blaauw (RSA) at 21st

Jamie Moul (Stoke by Nayland) beat John Parry (Harrogate) 4 and 3

Duncan Stewart (Grantown-on-Spey) beat Ben Westgate (Perranporth) 2 and 1

Alejandro Canizares (ESP) beat James Taverner (Enfield) 2 and 1

Amateur Championship *continued*

Oscar Floren (SWE) beat Ben Montgomery
(Frinton) 1 hole
Dustin Pimm (USA) beat Wallace Booth (Comrie)
6 and 5
Lorenzo Gagli (ITA) beat Craig Watson
(East Renfrewshire) 2 and 1
Stuart Moore (USA) beat Cian McNamara
(Limerick) 3 and 2
Niklas Lemke (SWE) beat Morgan Hoffmann
(USA) 6 and 4
Bryan Fotheringham (Forres) beat Martin Young
(Brokenhurst Manor) 2 and 1
Scott Jamieson (Cathkin Braes) beat Paul Waring
(Bromborough) 3 and 2
Heikki Mantyla (FIN) beat James Ruth (Tavistock)
3 and 2

Second Round
Llewellyn Matthews (Southerndown) beat
Richard Ramsay (Royal Aberdeen) 1 hole
Chandler Cocco (USA) beat Daniel Denison
(Howley Hall) 2 and 1
Ryan Harrison (Wentworth) beat
Arnond Vongvanij (USA) 2 holes
Matteo Del Podio (ITA) beat Ben Rickett
(Surbiton) 5 and 4
Luke Collins (Mendip Spring) beat Lloyd Campbell
(Rochester & Cobham Park) 3 and 2
Julien Guerrier (FRA) beat Simon Cedergren
(SWE) 5 and 3
Andrew Parr (CAN) beat William Bowe
(Workington) 6 and 4
James Morrison (St George's Hill) beat
Graham Delaet (CAN) 1 hole
Oliver Fisher (West Essex) beat Remi Dupuis
(FRA) 1 hole
Stephen Lewton (Woburn) beat John Kemp
(John O'Gaunt) 1 hole
Rhys Davies (Royal Porthcawl) beat Jonathan King
(Glasgow) at 22nd
Mitchell Brown (AUS) beat James Smith
(Sundridge Park) 3 and 1
Florian Fritsch (GER) beat Kevin Chappell (USA)
7 and 6
Dale Whitnell (Forrester Park) beat
Mark Haastrup (DEN) 2 and 1
Gary Wolstenholme (Kilworth Springs) beat
Andrew Martin (AUS) 2 and 1
Ben Evans (Rye) beat Jean-Jacques Wolff (FRA)
4 and 3
Gary Boyd (Cherwell Edge) beat Joost Luiten
(NED) 4 and 3
Pablo Martin (ESP) beat Michael Bush
(Rochester & Cobham Park) 1 hole
Jason Palmer (Kirby Muxloe) beat Stephen Gross
(GER) 4 and 2
Stephen Dartnell (AUS) beat José Luis Adarraga
(ESP) 4 and 3
Alex Prugh beat James Crampton (Spalding)
5 and 4

Jamie Moul beat Nigel Edwards (Whitchurch)
1 hole
Duncan Stewart beat John Gallagher (Swanston)
3 and 2
Ross McGowan (Banstead Downs) beat
Alejandro Canizares 6 and 4
James Mason (Rotherham) beat Oscar Floren
3 and 2
Yuki Ito (JPN) beat Dustin Pimm 3 and 2
Adam Gee (Leatherhead) beat Lorenzo Gagli
5 and 4
Stuart Moore beat Kevin Kean
(Ashton-on-Mersey) 3 and 2
Niklas Lemke beat Daniel Brooks (Mill Hill)
4 and 3
Bryan Fotheringham beat Tino Weiss (SUI)
2 and 1
Scott Jamieson beat Nicklas Glans (SWE) 3 and 2
Jamie Arnold (AUS) beat Heikki Mantyla 3 and 2

Third Round
Matthews beat Cocco 2 and 1
Del Podio beat Harrison at 20th
Guerrier beat Collins 2 and 1
Morrison beat Parr 1 hole
Lewton beat Fisher 1 hole
Brown beat Davies 1 hole
Whitnell beat Fritsch at 21st
Wolstenholme beat Evans 3 and 2
Martin beat Boyd at 20th
Palmer beat Dartnell 1 hole
Moul beat Prugh 4 and 3
McGowan beat Stewart 5 and 4
Ito beat Mason 2 and 1
Gee beat Moore 7 and 6
Fotheringham beat Lemke 1 hole
Jamieson beat Arnold 3 and 2

Fourth Round
Del Podio beat Matthews 1 hole
Guerrier beat Morrison 2 and 1
Brown beat Lewton 1 hole
Wolstenholme beat Whitnell 1 hole
Palmer beat Martin 1 hole
Moul beat McGowan 4 and 3
Gee beat Ito 3 and 2
Jamieson beat Fotheringham 5 and 4

Quarter Finals
Guerrier beat Del Podio at 19th
Brown beat Wolstenholme 4 and 3
Moul beat Palmer 4 and 3
Gee beat Jamieson 1 hole

Semi-Finals
Guerrier beat Brown 3 and 2
Gee beat Moul 5 and 4

Final (36 holes)
Julien Guerrier beat Adam Gee 4 and 3

British Seniors' Open Amateur Championship (inaugurated 1969) 2006 Saunton

1969	R Pattinson	Formby	154		1988	CW Green	Royal Burgess	221
1970	K Bamber	Prestwick	150		1989	CW Green	Moortown, Alwoodley	226
1971	GH Pickard	Royal Cinque Ports;			1990	CW Green	The Berkshire	207
		Royal St George's	150		1991	CW Green	Prestwick	219
1972	TC Hartley	St Andrews	147		1992	C Hartland	Purdis Heath	221
1973	JT Jones	Longniddry	142		1993	CW Green	Royal Aberdeen	150
1974	MA Ivor-Jones	Moortown	149		1994	CW Green	Formby, Southport &	
1975	HJ Roberts	Turnberry	138				Ainsdale	223
1976	WM Crichton	Berkshire	149		1995	G Steel	Hankley Common	218
1977	Dr TE Donaldson	Panmure	228		1996	J Hirsch	Blairgowrie	210
1978	RJ White	Formby	225		1997	G Bradley (USA)	Sherwood Forest	216
1979	RJ White	Harlech, R St David's	226		1998	D Lane	Western Gailes/	
1980	JM Cannon	Prestwick St Nicholas	218				Glasgow Gailes	221
1981	T Branton	Hoylake, R Liverpool	227		1999	W Shean (USA)	Frilford Heath	219
1982	RL Glading	Blairgowrie	218		2000	J Hirsch (USA)	Gullane	218
1983	AJ Swann (USA)	Walton Heath	222		2001	K Richardson (USA)	Royal Portrush	217
1984	JC Owens (USA)	Western Gailes	222		2002	J Baldwin (USA)	Woodhall Spa	216
1985	D Morey (USA)	Hesketh	223		2003	R Smethurst	Blairgowrie	215
1986	AN Sturrock	Panmure	229		2004	K Richardson (USA)	The Berkshire	213
1987	B Soyars (USA)	Royal Cinque Ports	226		2005	A Foster (USA)	Woburn	222

1	Paul Simson (USA)	74-73-76—223
2	Rick Woulfe (USA)	74-80-74—228
3	John Baldwin (USA)	80-73-75—228

British Mid-Amateur Championship (inaugurated 1995) 2006 Southport & Ainsdale

1995	GP Wolstenholme	S Vale	Sunningdale
1996	GP Wolstenholme	G Steel	Hillside, Lancs
1997	S Philipson	G Thomson	Prestwick
1998	GP Wolstenholme	S Twynholm	Ganton
1999	J Kemp	S East	Walton Heath
2000	A Farmer	J Kemp	Royal Troon
2001	S East	J McGroarty	Seaton Carew
2002	J Kemp	J Williams	Formby
2003	J Kemp	R Roper	St Andrews
2004	D Perrett	M Hunt	Royal Liverpool
2005	D Perrett	S Sansome	Muirfield

Leading Qualifier: George Cowan (Bellingham) 70-65—135

Quarter Finals
François Illouz (FRA) beat George Cowan 3 and 1
John Carroll (Huyton & Prescot) beat Brian Harris (USA)
5 and 4
Simon Young (Workington) beat Sandy Twynholm (Morpeth)
1 hole
John Kemp (John O'Gaunt) beat Stephen Brennan (Wheatley)
at 21st

Semi-Finals
Carroll beat Illouz 5 and 4
Young beat Kemp 5 and 3

Final
Simon Young beat John Carroll
at 19th

English Amateur Championship (inaugurated 1925) 2006 Burnham & Berrow

1925	TF Ellison	S Robinson	Royal Liverpool	1 hole
1926	TF Ellison	Sq Ldr CH Hayward	Walton Heath	6 and 4
1927	TP Perkins	JB Beddard	Little Aston	2 and 1
1928	JA Stout	TP Perkins	R Lytham and St Annes	3 and 2
1929	W Sutton	EB Tipping	Northumberland	3 and 2
1930	TA Bourn	CE Hardman	Burnham & Berrow	3 and 2
1931	LG Crawley	W Sutton	Hunstanton	1 hole
1932	EW Fiddian	AS Bradshaw	Royal St George's	1 hole
1933	J Woollam	TA Bourn	Ganton	4 and 3
1934	S Lunt	LG Crawley	Formby	37th hole
1935	J Woollam	EW Fiddian	Hollinwell	2 and 1
1936	HG Bentley	JDA Langley	Royal Cinque Ports	5 and 4
1937	JJ Pennink	LG Crawley	Saunton	6 and 5
1938	JJ Pennink	SE Banks	Moortown	2 and 1
1939	AL Bentley	W Sutton	Royal Birkdale	5 and 4
1946	IR Patey	K Thom	Mid-Surrey	5 and 4

English Amateur Championship continued

1947	GH Micklem	C Stow	Ganton	1 hole
1948	AGB Helm	HJR Roberts	Little Aston	2 and 1
1949	RJ White	C Stowe	Formby	5 and 4
1950	JDA Langley	IR Patey	Royal Cinque Ports	1 hole
1951	GP Roberts	H Bennett	Hunstanton	39th hole
1952	E Millward	TJ Shorrock	Burnham and Berrow	2 holes
1953	GH Micklem	RJ White	Royal Birkdale	2 and 1
1954	A Thirlwell	HG Bentley	Royal St George's	2 and 1
1955	A Thirlwell	M Burgess	Ganton	7 and 6
1956	GB Wolstenholme	H Bennett	R Lytham and St Annes	1 hole
1957	A Walker	G Whitehead	Royal Liverpool	4 and 3
1958	DN Sewell	DA Procter	Walton Heath	8 and 7
1959	GB Wolstenholme	MF Bonallack	Formby	1 hole
1960	DN Sewell	MJ Christmas	Hunstanton	41st hole
1961	I Caldwell	GJ Clark	Wentworth	37th hole
1962	MF Bonallack	MSR Lunt	Moortown	2 and 1
1963	MF Bonallack	A Thirlwell	Burnham and Berrow	4 and 3
1964	Dr D Marsh	R Foster	Hollinwell	1 hole
1965	MF Bonallack	CA Clark	The Berkshire	3 and 2
1966	MSR Lunt	DJ Millensted	R Lytham and St Annes	3 and 2
1967	MF Bonallack	GE Hyde	Woodhall Spa	4 and 2
1968	MF Bonallack	PD Kelley	Ganton	12 and 11
1969	JH Cook	P Dawson	Royal St George's	6 and 4
1970	Dr D Marsh	SG Birtwell	R Birkdale	6 and 4
1971	W Humphreys	JC Davies	Burnham and Berrow	9 and 8
1972	H Ashby	R Revell	Northumberland	5 and 4
1973	H Ashby	SC Mason	Formby	5 and 4
1974	M James	JA Watts	Woodhall Spa	6 and 5
1975	N Faldo	D Eccleston	Royal Lytham and St Annes	6 and 4
1976	P Deeble	JC Davies	Ganton	3 and 1
1977	TR Shingler	J Mayell	Walton Heath	4 and 3
1978	P Downes	P Hoad	Royal Birkdale	1 hole
1979	R Chapman	A Carman	Royal St George's	6 and 5
1980	P Deeble	P McEvoy	Moortown	4 and 3
1981	D Blakeman	A Stubbs	Burnham & Berrow	3 and 1
1982	A Oldcorn	I Bradshaw	Royal Liverpool	4 and 3
1983	G Laurence	A Brewer	Wentworth	7 and 6
1984	D Gilford	M Gerrard	Woodhall Spa	4 and 3
1985	R Winchester	P Robinson	Little Aston	1 hole
1986	J Langmead	B White	Hillside	2 and 1
1987	K Weeks	R Eggo	Frilford Heath	37th hole
1988	R Claydon	D Curry	R Birkdale	38th hole
1989	S Richardson	R Eggo	Royal St George's	2 and 1
1990	I Garbutt	G Evans	Woodhall Spa	8 and 7
1991	R Willison	M Pullan	Formby	10 and 8
1992	S Cage	R Hutt	Royal Cinque Ports	3 and 2
1993	D Fisher	R Bland	Saunton	3 and 1
1994	M Foster	A Johnson	Moortown	8 and 7
1995	M Foster	S Jarman	Hunstanton	6 and 5
1996	S Webster	D Lucas	Hollinwell	6 and 4
1997	A Wainwright	P Rowe	Royal Liverpool	2 and 1
1998	M Sanders	S Gorry	Woodhall Spa	6 and 5
1999	P Casey	S Dyson	St Mellion	2 and 1
2000	P Casey	G Wolstenholme	Royal Lytham and St Annes	4 and 2
2001	S Godfrey	S Robinson	Saunton	4 and 3
2002	R Finch	G Legg	Walton Heath	6 and 5
2003	G Lockerbie	M Skelton	Alwoodley	6 and 5
2004	J Heath	D Horsey	Notts (Hollinwell)	3 and 2
2005	P Waring	S Capper	Bromborough	3 and 2

Quarter Finals

Ross McGowan (Banstead Downs) beat Gary Boyd (Cherwell Edge) 1 hole

Jamie Moul (Stoke-by-Nayland) beat Ben Parker (Royal Birkdale) 3 and 2

Matthew Cryer (Coventry) beat Kevin Kean (Ashton-on-Mersey) 3 and 2

Oliver Fisher (West Essex) beat Adam Gee (Leatherhead) 7 and 5

Semi-Finals

McGowan beat Moul at 20th

Fisher beat Cryer at 19th

Final

Ross McGowan beat Oliver Fisher 5 and 4

English Open Amateur Stroke Play Championship (Brabazon Trophy)
(inaugurated 1957) 2006 *Ganton*

1957	D Sewell	Moortown	287	1982	P Downes	Woburn	299
1958	AH Perowne	Birkdale	289	1983	C Banks	Hollinwell	294
1959	D Sewell	Hollinwell	300	1984	M Davis	Deal, R Cinque Ports	286
1960	GB Wolstenholme	Ganton	286	1985T	R Roper	Seaton Carew	296
1961	RDBM Shade	Hoylake, R Liverpool	284		P Baker		
1962	A Slater	Woodhall Spa	209	1986	R Kaplan	Sunningdale	286
1963	RDBM Shade	R Birkdale	306	1987	JG Robinson	Ganton	287
1964	MF Bonallack	Deal, R Cinque Ports	290	1988	R Eggo	Saunton	289
1965T	CA Clark	Formby	289	1989T	C Rivett	Hoylake, R Liverpool	293
	DJ Millensted				RN Roderick		
	MJ Burgess			1990T	O Edmond	Burnham and Berrow	287
1966	PM Townsend	Hunstanton	282		G Evans		
1967	RDBM Shade	Saunton	299	1991T	G Evans	Hunstanton	284
1968	MF Bonallack	Walton Heath	210		M Pullan		
1969T	R Foster	Moortown	290	1992	I Garrido	Notts	280
	MF Bonallack			1993	D Fisher	Stoneham	277
1970	R Foster	Little Aston	287	1994	G Harris	Little Aston	280
1971	MF Bonallack	Hillside	294	1995T	M Foster	Hillside	283
1972	PH Moody	Hoylake, R Liverpool	296		CS Edwards		
1973	R Revell	Hunstanton	294	1996	P Fenton	R St Georges	297
1974	N Sundelson	Moortown	291	1997	D Park	Saunton	271
1975	A Lyle	Hollinwell	298	1998	P Hanson	Formby	287
1976	P Hedges	Saunton	294	1999	M Side	Moortown	279
1977	A Lyle	Royal Liverpool	293	2000	J Lupprien (GER)	Woodhall Spa	284
1978	G Brand Jr	Woodhall Spa	289	2001	R Walker	Royal Birkdale	280
1979	D Long	Little Aston	291	2002	C Schwartzel (RSA)	Royal Cinque Ports	282
1980T	R Rafferty	Hunstanton	293	2003	J Lupton	Hunstanton	287
	P McEvoy			2004	M Richardson	West Lancashire	279
1981	P Way	Hillside	292	2005	L Saltman (SCO)	The Oxfordshire	278

1	Robert Dinwiddie (Barnard Castle)	70-73-70-69—282
2	Ross McGowan (Banstead Downs)	71-68-73-73—285
3	Knut Bersheim (NOR)	75-75-69-72—291
	Jamie Moul (Stoke-by-Nayland)	66-81-73-71—291
	Jean-Jacques Wolff (FRA)	75-76-69-71—291

English Seniors' Amateur Championship (inaugurated 1981) 2006 *Yelverton*

1981	CR Spalding	Copt Heath	152	1995	H Hopkinson	Copt Heath	226
1982	JL Whitworth	Lindrick	152	1996T	G Edwards		224
1983	B Cawthray	Ross-on-Wye	154		B Berney	West Lancs	
1984	RL Glading	Thetford	150	1997	D Lane	West Hill	215
1985	JR Marriott	Bristol and Clifton	153	1998	J Marks	Saunton	217
1986	R Hiatt	Northants County	153	1999	D Lane	Shifnal	73 (18)
1987	I Caldwell	North Hants	72 (18)	2000	R Smethurst	Moor Park	212
1988	G Edwards	Bromborough	222	2001	R Smethurst	Sherwood Forest	220
1989	G Clark	West Sussex	212	2002	D Arnold	Heswall & Bromborough	224
1990	N Paul	Enville, Bridgnorth	217	2003	D Arnold	Frilford Heath	218
1991	W Williams	Gerrards7 Cross	217	2004	R Smethurst	John O'Gaunt	215
1992	B Cawthray	Fulford	223	2005	R Smethurst	Prestbury & Lymm	223
1993	G Edwards	John O'Gaunt	221				
1994T	G Steel	Parkstone,					
	F Jones	Broadstone	72 (18)				

1	Douglas Arnold (Copthorne)	71-71-79—221
2	Bob Knott (Churston)	72-75-78—225
	Alan Squires (Oldham)	75-69-81—225

English Open Mid-Amateur Championship (Logan Trophy)   2006 Delamere Forest
(inaugurated 1988)

1988	P McEvoy	Little Aston	284	1998	S East	Broadstone	216
1989	A Mew	Moortown	290	1999	S East	Little Aston	217
1990	A Mew	Wentworth	214	2000	B Downing	Ponteland	208
1991	I Richardson	West Lancashire	223	2001	S East	Lindrick	206
1992	A Mew	King's Lynn	222	2002T	F Illouz	Prince's, Sandwich	217
1993	R Godley	Southport & Ainsdale	210		S Crosby		
1994T	I Richardson	Trentham	217	2003	J Longcake	Royal Birkdale	213
	A McLure			2004	S Sansome	Fairhaven	211
1995	C Banks	Seacroft	222	2005	N Chesters	Delamere Forest	212
1997	C Banks	Stockport	211				

1	Martin Young (Brokenhurst Manor)	66-71-71—208
2	Barry Downing (Hallamshire)	71-73-69—213
	Craig Townsend (Teignmouth)	71-73-69—213

English County Champions' Tournament (formerly President's Bowl)   2006 Woodhall Spa
(inaugurated 1962)

1962T	G Edwards, Cheshire	1985	P Robinson, Herts
	A Thirwell, Northumberland	1986	A Gelsthorpe, Yorks
1963T	M Burgess, Sussex/R Foster, Yorks	1987T	F George, Berks, Bucks & Oxon
1964	M Attenborough, Kent		D Fay, Surrey
1965	M Lees, Lincs	1988	R Claydon, Cambridge
1966	R Stephenson, Middx	1989	R Willison, Middlesex
1967	P Benka, Surrey	1990T	P Streeter, Lincs/R Sloman, Kent
1968	G Hyde, Sussex	1991	T Allen, Warwickshire
1969	A Holmes, Herts	1992	L Westwood, Notts
1970	M King, Berks, Bucks and Oxon	1993	R Walker, Durham
1971	M Lee, Yorks	1994	GP Wolstenholme, Glos
1972	P Berry, Glos	1995	S Webster, Warwickshire
1973	A Chandler, Lancs	1996T	J Herbert, Leics/G Wolstenholme, Glos
1974T	G Hyde, Sussex/A Lyle, Shrops & Hereford	1997	J Herbert, Leicestershire & Rutland
1975	N Faldo, Herts	1998	GP Wolstenholme, Leics
1976	R Brown, Devon	1999	D Griffiths, Herts
1977	M Walls, Cumbria	2000	P Bradshaw, Lincolnshire
1978	I Simpson, Notts	2001	G Wolstenholme, Leicestershire & Rutland
1979	N Burch, Essex	2002	G Evans, Middlesex
1980	D Lane, Berks, Bucks and Oxon	2003	J Crampton, Lincolnshire
1981	M Kelly, Yorks	2004	J Phelps, Middlesex
1982	P Deeble, Northumberland	2005	D Horsey, Cheshire
1983	N Chesses, Warwickshire		(David Horsey's second round 64 is a record)
1984T	N Briggs, Herts/P McEvoy, Warwickshire		

1	Gareth Evans (Yorkshire)	72-69—141
2	George Cowan (Northumberland)	73-69—142
3	Tom Lawson (Berks, Bucks, & Oxon)	71-71—142

Irish Amateur Open Championship (inaugurated 1892)   2006 Portmarnock

1892	A Stuart	JH Andrew	Royal Portrush	1 hole
1893	John Ball	LS Anderson	Newcastle	8 and 7
1894	John Ball	DL Low	Dollymount	9 and 7
1895	WB Taylor	JM Williamson	Royal Portrush	13 and 11
1896	WB Taylor	D Anderson	Newcastle	9 and 8
1897	HH Hilton	LS Anderson	Dollymount	5 and 4
1898	WB Taylor	ROJ Dallmyer	Royal Portrush	at 37th
1899	John Ball	JM Williamson	Portmarnock	13 and 11
1900	HH Hilton	SH Fry	Newcastle	11 and 9
1901	HH Hilton	P Dowie	Dollymount	6 and 5
1902	HH Hilton	WH Hamilton	Royal Portrush	5 and 4
1903	G Wilkie	HA Boyd	Portmarnock	1 hole
1904	JS Worthington	JF Mitchell	Newcastle	6 and 4
1905	HA Boyd	JF Mitchell	Dollymount	3 and 2
1906	HH Barker	JS Worthington	Royal Portrush	5 and 4
1907	JD Brown	SH Fry	Portmarnock	2 and 1

1908	JF Mitchell	HM Cairnes	Newcastle	3 and 2
1909	LO Munn	R Garson	Dollymount	2 holes
1910	LO Munn	G Lockhart	Royal Portrush	9 and 7
1911	LO Munn	Hon. Michael Scott	Portmarnock	7 and 6
1912	G Lockhart	P Jenkins	Newcastle	11 and 9
1913	CA Palmer	LA Phillips	Dollymount	4 and 3
1914–1918	*Not played*			
1919	C Bretherton	TD Armour	Royal Portrush	5 and 3
1920	GNC Martin	CW Robertson	Portmarnock	6 and 5
1921	D Smyth	J Gorry	Newcastle	2 holes
1922	A Lowe	J Henderson	Royal Portrush	6 and 4
1923	GNC Martin	CO Hezlet	Newcastle	1 hole
1924	EF Spiller	JDA McCormack	Dollymount	3 and 1
1925	TA Torrance	CO Hezlet	Royal Portrush	4 and 3
1926	CO Hezlet	RM McConnell	Portmarnock	7 and 6
1927	RM McConnell	DEB Soulby	Newcastle	5 and 3
1928	GS Moon	EF Spiller	Dollymount	1 hole
1929	CO Hezlet	JA Lang	Royal Portrush	1 hole
1930	W Sutton	DA Fiddian	Portmarnock	4 and 2
1931	EA McRuvie	DEB Soulby	Newcastle	7 and 5
1932	J McLean	JC Brown	Dollymount	9 and 8
1933	J McLean	E Fiddian	Newcastle	3 and 2
1934	H Thomson	HG Bentley	Portmarnock	3 and 2
1935	H Thomson	J McLean	Royal Portrush	5 and 4
1936	JC Brown	WM O'Sullivan	Portmarnock	at 39th
1937	J Fitzsimmons	RA McKinna	Dollymount	4 and 3
1938	J Bruen jr	JR Mahon	Newcastle	9 and 8
1939–1945	*Not played*			
1946	JB Carr	AT Kyle	Royal Portrush	3 and 1
1947	J Burke	JB Carr	Dollymount	1 hole
1948	RC Ewing	JB Carr	Newcastle	1 hole
1949	WM O'Sullivan	BJ Scannell	Killarney	2 holes
1950	JB Carr	RC Ewing	Rosses Point	at 40th
1951	RC Ewing	JB Carr	Portmarnock	2 and 1
1952	NV Drew	CH Beamish	Royal Portrush	5 and 4
1953	NV Drew	WM O'Sullivan	Killarney	3 and 2
1954	JB Carr	RC Ewing	Dollymount	6 and 4
1955	JF Fitzgibbon	JW Hulme	Royal County Down	1 hole
1956	JB Carr	JR Mahon	Portmarnock	1 hole
1957	JL Bamford	W Meharg	Royal Portrush	at 37th

From 1958 decided by Stroke Play

1958	T Craddock	Dollymount	484
1959	J Duncan	Newcastle	313

From 1960–1994 not played

1995	P Harrington	Fota Island	283
1996	K Nolan	Fota Island	286
1997	K Nolan	Fota Island	279
1998	M Hoey	Royal Dublin	286
1999	G Cullen	Royal Dublin	282
2000	N Fox	Royal Dublin	284
2001	R McEvoy*	Royal Dublin	277
2002	L Oosthuizen (RSA)	Royal Dublin	283
2003	N Fox	Royal Dublin	282
2004	C Smith	Carton House	289
2005	R Ramsay	Carton House	283

2006 *Portmarnock*

1	Antti Ahokas (FIN)*	71-71-76-73—291
2	Rory McIlroy (Holywood)	73-71-74-73—291
3	Tim Dykes (Wrexham)	72-75-74-71—292

Play-off: Ahokas 4,4,3; McIlroy 4,4,4

Irish Amateur Close Championship (inaugurated 1893)

1893	T Dickson	G Combe	Royal Portrush	2 holes
1894	R Magill jr	T Dickson	Newcastle	3 and 1
1895	WH Webb	J Stevenson	Dollymount	10 and 9
1896	J Stewart-Moore jr	HAS Upton	Royal Portrush	8 and 7
1897	HE Reade	WH Webb	Newcastle	2 and 1
1898	WH Webb	J Stewart-Moore jr	Dollymount	9 and 8
1899	HE Reade	JP Todd	Royal Portrush	3 and 2
1900	RGN Henry	J McAvoy	Portmarnock	4 and 3
1901	WH Boyd	HE Reade	Newcastle	7 and 5
1902	FB Newett	R Shaw	Dollymount	1 hole
1903	HE Reade	DRA Campbell	Royal Portrush	5 and 4
1904	HA Boyd	JP Todd	Portmarnock	4 and 2
1905	FB Newett	B O'Brien	Newcastle	6 and 5
1906	HA Boyd	HM Cairnes	Dollymount	at 38th
1907	HM Cairnes	HA Boyd	Royal Portrush	7 and 6
1908	LO Munn	A Babbington	Portmarnock	10 and 9
1909	AH Patterson	EF Spiller	Newcastle	at 37th
1910	JF Jameson	LO Munn	Dollymount	2 and 1
1911	LO Munn	HA Boyd	Royal Portrush	7 and 6
1912	AH Craig	P Halligan	Castlerock	13 and 11
1913	LO Munn	HA Boyd	Portmarnock	6 and 5
1914	LO Munn	Earl Annesley	Hermitage	10 and 8
1915–1918	*Not played*			
1919	E Carter	WG McConnell	Portmarnock	9 and 7
1920	CO Hezlet	CL Crawford	Castlerock	12 and 11
1921	E Carter	G Moore	Portmarnock	9 and 8
1922	EM Munn	WK Tillie	Royal Portrush	3 and 1
1923	JD McCormack	LE Werner	Milltown	2 and 1
1924	JD McCormack	DEB Soulby	Newcastle	4 and 2
1925	CW Robertson	HM Cairnes	Portmarnock	4 and 3
1926	AC Allison	OW Madden	Royal Portrush	7 and 6
1927	JD McCormack	HM Cairnes	Cork	at 37th
1928	DEB Soulby	JO Wisdom	Castlerock	7 and 5
1929	DEB Soulby	FP McConnell	Dollymount	4 and 3
1930	J Burke	FP McConnell	Lahinch	6 and 5
1931	J Burke	FP McConnell	Rosses Point	6 and 4
1932	J Burke	M Crowley	Royal Portrush	6 and 5
1933	J Burke	GT McMullan	Cork	3 and 2
1934	JC Brown	RM McConnell	Rosslare	6 and 5
1935	RM McConnell	J Burke	Galway	2 and 1
1936	J Burke	RM McConnell	Castlerock	7 and 6
1937	J Bruen jr	J Burke	Ballybunion	3 and 2
1938	J Bruen jr	R Simcox	Rathfarnham Castle	3 and 2
1939	GH Owens	RM McConnell	Rosses Point	6 and 5
1940	J Burke	WM O'Sullivan	Dollymount	4 and 3
1941–1945	*Not played*			
1946	J Burke	RC Ewing	Dollymount	2 and 1
1947	J Burke	J Fitzsimmons	Lahinch	2 holes
1948	RC Ewing	BJ Scannell	Royal Portrush	3 and 2
1949	J Carroll	P Murphy	Galway	4 and 3
1950	B Herlihy	BC McManus	Baltray	4 and 3
1951	M Power	JB Carr	Cork	3 and 2
1952	TW Egan	JC Brown	Royal Belfast at 41st	
1953	J Malone	M Power	Rosses Point	2 and 1
1954	JB Carr	I Forsythe	Carlow	4 and 3
1955	JR Mahon	G Crosbie	Lahinch	3 and 2
1956	AGH Love	G Crosbie	Malone	at 37th
1957	JB Carr	G Crosbie	Galway	2 holes
1958	RC Ewing	GA Young	Ballybunion	5 and 3
1959	T Craddock	JB Carr	Portmarnock	at 38th
1960	M Edwards	N Fogarty	Portstewart	6 and 5
1961	D Sheahan	J Brown	Rosses Point	5 and 4
1962	M Edwards	J Harrington	Baltray	42nd hole
1963	JB Carr	EC O'Brien	Killarney	2 and 1
1964	JB Carr	A McDade	Co Down	6 and 5
1965	JB Carr	T Craddock	Rosses Point	3 and 2
1966	D Sheahan	J Faith	Dollymount	3 and 2
1967	JB Carr	PD Flaherty	Lahinch	1 hole
1968	M O'Brien	F McCarroll	Royal Portrush	2 and 1
1969	V Nevin	J O'Leary	Co Sligo	1 hole
1970	D Sheahan	M Bloom	Grange	2 holes
1971	P Kane	M O'Brien	Ballybunion	3 and 2

1972	K Stevenson	B Hoey	Co Down	2 and 1
1973	RKM Pollin	RM Staunton	Rosses Point	1 hole
1974	R Kane	M Gannon	Portmarnock	5 and 4
1975	MD O'Brien	JA Bryan	Cork	5 and 4
1976	D Brannigan	D O'Sullivan	Royal Portrush	2 holes
1977	M Gannon	A Hayes	Westport	19th hole
1978	M Morris	T Cleary	Carlow	1 hole
1979	J Harrington	MA Gannon	Ballybunion	2 and 1
1980	R Rafferty	MJ Bannon	Co Down	8 and 7
1981	D Brannigan	E McMenamin	Co Sligo	19th hole
1982	P Walton	B Smyth	Woodbrook	7 and 6
1983	T Corridan	E Power	Killarney	2 holes
1984	CB Hoey	L McNamara	Malone	20th hole
1985	D O'Sullivan	D Branigan	Westport	1 hole
1986	J McHenry	P Rayfus	Dublin	4 and 3
1987	E Power	JP Fitzgerald	Tranmore	2 holes
1988	G McGimpsey	D Mulholland	Royal Portrush	2 and 1
1989	P McGinley	N Goulding	Rosses Point	3 and 2
1990	D Clarke	P Harrington	Baltray	3 and 2
1991	G McNeill	N Goulding	Ballybunion	3 and 1
1992	G Murphy	JP Fitzgerald	Portstewart	2 and 1
1993	E Power	D Higgins	Enniscrone	3 and 2
1994	D Higgins	P Harrington	Portmarnock	20th hole
1995	P Harrington	D Coughlan	Lahinch	3 and 2
1996	P Lawrie	G McGimpsey	Royal Co Down	3 and 2
1997	K Kearney	P Lawrie	Fota Island	5 and 4
1998	E Power	B Omelia	The Island	1 hole
1999	C McMonagle	M Sinclair	Killarney	2 and 1
2000	G McDowell	A McCormick	Royal Portrush	7 and 6
2001	G McNeill	S Browne	Co Sligo	20th hole
2002	J McGinn	K Kearney	Carlow	3 and 1
2003	M O'Sullivan	D Carroll	Tramore	1 hole
2004	B McElhinney	M McGeady	Donegal	1 hole
2005	R McIlroy	E McCormack	Westport	3 and 2

2006 *The European Club*

Leading Qualifiers: 150 – Rory McIlroy (Holywood) 70-80; Andrew Pitcher (The Island) 75-75

Quarter Finals

Connor Doran (Banbridge) beat Jonathan Caldwell (Clandeboye) 2 and 1

Rory McIlroy (Holywood) beat Darren Crowe (Dunmurry) 1 hole

Simon Ward (Co. Louth) beat David Finn (Mallow) 6 and 5

Paul O'Kane (Moyola Park) beat Fergal Rafferty (Dungannon) at 19th

Semi-Finals

McIlroy beat Doran 2 and 1

Ward beat O'Kane 2 and 1

Final

Rory McIlroy beat Simon Ward 3 and 2

Irish Seniors' Open Amateur Championship (inaugurated 1970) 2006 *Limerick*

1970	RC Ewing	Lahinch	153	1988	WB Buckley	Westport	154
1971	J O'Sullivan	Rosslare	159	1989	B McCrea	Royal Belfast	150
1972	BJ Scannell	Co. Sligo	152	1990	C Hartland	Cork	149
1973	JW Hulme	Warrenpoint	147	1991	C Hartland	Mullingar	147
1974	P Walsh	Cork	155	1992	C Hartland	Athlone	145
1975	SA O'Connor	Woodbrook	152	1993	P Breen	Bangor	147
1976	BJ Scannell	Athlone	150	1994	B Buckley	Tramore	151
1977	DB Somers	Warrenpoint	150	1995	B Hoey	Dundalk	151
1978	DP Herlihy	Limerick	150	1996	E Condren	Oughterard	148
1979	P Kelly	Royal Tara	153	1997	B Wilson	The Knock	152
1980	GN Fogarty	Galway	144	1998	J Harrington	Thurles	149
1981	GN Fogarty	Bundoran	149	1999	A Lee	Thurles	150
1982	J Murray	Douglas	141	2000	D Jackson	Westport	151
1983	F Sharpe	Courtown	153	2001	D Jackson	Clandeboye	153
1984	J Boston	Connemara	147	2002	T Fox	Limerick	146
1985	J Boston	Newcastle	155	2003	P Jones	Mullingar	150
1986	J Coey	Waterford	141	2004	MF Morris*	Roscommon	145
1987	J Murray	Castleroy	150	2005	J Baldwin	Royal County Down	149

(continued over)

Irish Senior's Open Amateur Championship – 2006 *Limerick – continued*

1	John Baldwin (USA)	72-70-72—214
2	Arthur Pierse (Tipperary)	72-74-69—215
3	Peter Cowley (Cork)	73-74-72—219 (winner, over 60s)
2	Maurice Kelly (Killeen)	75-72-72—219

Scottish Amateur Championship (inaugurated 1922)

1922	J Wilson	E Blackwell	St Andrews	19th hole
1923	TM Burrell	Dr A McCallum	Troon	1 hole
1924	WW Mackenzie	W Tulloch	Aberdeen	3 and 2
1925	JT Dobson	W Mackenzie	Muirfield	3 and 2
1926	WJ Guild	SO Shepherd	Leven	2 and 1
1927	A Jamieson jr	Rev D Rutherford	Gailes	22nd hole
1928	WW Mackenzie	W Dodds	Muirfield	5 and 3
1929	JT Bookless	J Dawson	Aberdeen	5 and 4
1930	K Greig	T Wallace	Carnoustie	9 and 8
1931	J Wilson	A Jamieson Jr	Prestwick	2 and 1
1932	J McLean	K Greig	Dunbar	5 and 4
1933	J McLean	KC Forbes	Aberdeen	6 and 4
1934	J McLean	W Campbell	Western Gailes	3 and 1
1935	H Thomson	J McLean	St Andrews	2 and 1
1936	ED Hamilton	R Neill	Carnoustie	1 hole
1937	H McInally	K Patrick	Barassie	6 and 5
1938	ED Hamilton	R Rutherford	Muirfield	4 and 2
1939	H McInally	H Thomson	Prestwick	6 and 5
1946	EC Brown	R Rutherford	Carnoustie	3 and 2
1947	H McInally	J Pressley	Glasgow Gailes	10 and 8
1948	AS Flockhart	G Taylor	Royal Aberdeen	7 and 6
1949	R Wright	H McInally	Muirfield	1 hole
1950	WC Gibson	D Blair	Prestwick	2 and 1
1951	JM Dykes	J Wilson	St Andrews	4 and 2
1952	FG Dewar	J Wilson	Carnoustie	4 and 3
1953	DA Blair	J McKay	Western Gailes	3 and 1
1954	JW Draper	W Gray	Nairn	4 and 3
1955	RR Jack	AC Miller	Muirfield	2 and 1
1956	Dr FWG Deighton	A MacGregor	Troon	8 and 7
1957	JS Montgomerie	J Burnside	Balgownie	2 and 1
1958	WD Smith	I Harris	Prestwick	6 and 5
1959	Dr FWG Deighton	R Murray	St Andrews	6 and 5
1960	JR Young	S Saddler	Carnoustie	5 and 3
1961	J Walker	ST Murray	Western Gailes	4 and 3
1962	SWT Murray	RDBM Shade	Muirfield	2 and 1
1963	RDBM Shade	N Henderson	Troon	4 and 3
1964	RDBM Shade	J McBeath	Nairn	8 and 7
1965	RDBM Shade	G Cosh	St Andrews	4 and 2
1966	RDBM Shade	C Strachan	Western Gailes	9 and 8
1967	RDBM Shade	A Murphy	Carnoustie	5 and 4
1968	GB Cosh	R Renfrew	Muirfield	4 and 3
1969	JM Cannon	A Hall	Troon	6 and 4
1970	CW Green	H Stuart	Royal Aberdeen	1 hole
1971	S Stephen	C Green	St Andrews	3 and 2
1972	HB Stuart	A Pirie	Prestwick	3 and 1
1973	IC Hutcheon	A Brodie	Carnoustie	3 and 2
1974	GH Murray	A Pirie	Western Gailes	2 and 1
1975	D Greig	G Murray	Montrose	7 and 6
1976	GH Murray	H Stuart	St Andrews	6 and 5
1977	A Brodie	P McKellar	Troon	1 hole
1978	IA Carslaw	J Cuddihy	Downfield	7 and 6
1979	K Macintosh	P McKellar	Prestwick	5 and 4
1980	D Jamieson	C Green	Royal Aberdeen	2 and 1 (18)
1981	C Dalgleish	A Thomson	Western Gailes	7 and 6
1982	CW Green	G Macgregor	Carnoustie	1 hole
1983	CW Green	J Huggan	Gullane	1 hole
1984	A Moir	K Buchan	Renfrew	3 and 3
1985	D Carrick	D James	Southerness	4 and 2
1986	C Brooks	A Thomson	Monifieth	3 and 2
1987	C Montgomerie	A Watt	Nairn	9 and 8
1988	J Milligan	A Coltart	Kilmarnock (Barassie)	1 hole
1989	A Thomson	A Tait	Moray	1 hole
1990	C Everett	M Thomson	Gullane	7 and 5

1991	G Lowson	L Salariya	Downfield	4 and 3
1992	S Gallacher	D Kirkpatrick	Glasgow Gailes	37th hole
1993	D Robertson	R Russell	Royal Dornoch	2 holes
1994	H McKibben	A Reid	Renfrew	39th hole
1995	S Mackenzie	H McKibben	Southerness	8 and 7
1996	M Brooks	A Turnbull	Dunbar	7 and 6
1997	C Hislop	S Cairns	Carnoustie	5 and 3
1998	G Rankin	M Donaldson	Prestwick	6 and 5
1999	C Heap	M Loftus	Cruden Bay	7 and 5
2000	S O'Hara	C Heap	Royal Dornoch	I hole
2001	B Hume	C Watson	Downfield	4 and 3
2002	A McArthur	S Jamieson	Western Gailes	2 and I
2003	G Gordon	S Wilson	St Andrews	4 and 3
2004	G Murray	P O'Hara	Gullane No.I	I hole
2005	G Campbell	B Shamash	Southerness	at 37th

2006 *Nairn*

Quarter Finals

Paul O'Hara (Colville Park) beat Scott Jamieson (Cathkin Braes) 3 and 2

Jonathan King (Glasgow) beat Callum Macaulay (Tulliallan) 4 and 3

Bobby Rushford (Grangemouth) beat Gordon Stevenson (Whitecraigs) 2 and I

Kevin McAlpine (Alyth) beat Terry Mathieson (Murcar) 4 and 3

Semi-Finals

O'Hara beat King I hole

McAlpine beat Rushford 4 and 3

Final

Kevin McAlpine beat Paul O'Hara 8 and 7

Scottish Open Amateur Stroke Play Championship (inaugurated 1967) 2006 *Craigielaw*

1967	BJ Gallacher	Muirfield and Gullane	291
1968	RDBM Shade	Prestwick and Prestwick St Nicholas	282
1969	JS Macdonald	Carnoustie and Monifieth	288
1970	D Hayes	Glasgow Gailes and Barassie	275
1971	IC Hutcheon	Leven and Lundin	277
1972	BN Nicholas	Dalmahoy and Ratho Park	290
1973T	DM Robertson/GJ Clark	Dunbar and North Berwick	284
1974	IC Hutcheon	Blairgowrie and Alyth	283
1975	CW Green	Nairn and Nairn Dunbar	295
1976	S Martin	Monifieth and Carnoustie	299
1977	PJ McKellar	Muirfield and Gullane	299
1978	AR Taylor	Cawder	281
1979	IC Hutcheon	Blairgowrie	286
1980	G Brand jr	Musselburgh and R Musselburgh	207 (54 holes)
1981	F Walton	Erskine and Renfrew	287
1982	C Macgregor	Downfield and Camperdown	287
1983	C Murray	Irvine and Irvine Ravenspark	291
1984	CW Green	Blairgowrie	287
1985	C Montgomerie	Dunbar and North Berwick	274
1986	KH Walker	Carnoustie	289
1987	D Carrick	Lundin and Ladybank	282
1988	S Easingwood	Cathkin Braes and East Kilbride	277
1989	F Illouz	Blairgowrie	281
1990	G Hay	Royal Aberdeen and Murcar	133 (36 holes)
1991	A Coltart	Royal Troon and Troon Portland	291
1992	D Robertson	Mortonhall and Bruntsfield Links	281
1993	A Reid	St Andrews Jubilee and New	289
1994	D Downie	Letham Grange	288
1995	S Gallacher	Paisley and Renfrew	284
1996	A Forsyth	Cardross and Helensburgh	279
1997	DB Howard	Monifieth and Panmure	271
1998	L Kelly	Moray and Elgin	275
1999	G Rankin	St Andrews Old and Jubilee	286
2000	S McKenzie*	Letham Grange	278
2001	J Sutherland*	Nairn and Nairn Dunbar	279
2002	B Hume	Southerness	277
2003	G Wolstenholme	Turnberry Kintyre	273
2004	R Ramsay	Lundin	269
2005	R Dinwiddie	Royal Aberdeen	281

(continued over)

Scottish Open Amateur Stroke Play Championship – 2006 *Craigielaw* – *continued*

1	Scott Henry (Cardross)	71-69-68-69—277
2	Ross McGowan (Banstead Downs)	68-68-68-74—278
3	Matthew Baldwin (Royal Birkdale)	74-66-67-72—279
	Ross Kellett (Colville Park)	74-65-69-71—279
	Ben Parker (GER)	71-72-71-65—279

Scottish Senior Championship (inaugurated 1978) 2006 *Ranfurly Castle*

1978T	JM Cannon	Glasgow	149	1990	C Hartland	Royal Burgess	146
	GR Carmichael			1991	CW Green	Glasgow	140
1979	A Sinclair	Glasgow	143	1992	G Clark	Royal Burgess	148
1980	JM Cannon	Royal Burgess	149	1993	J Maclean	Glasgow	141
1981T	IR Harris	Glasgow	146	1994	DM Lawrie	Ladybank	149
	Dr J Hastings			1995	CW Green	Glasgow	141
	AN Sturrock			1996	CW Green	Western Gailes	146
1982T	JM Cannon	Royal Burgess	143	1997	CW Green	Glasgow	137
	J Niven			1998	CW Green	Ladybank	146
1983	WD Smith	Glasgow	145	1999	G Steel*	Glasgow	145
1984	A Sinclair	Royal Burgess	148	2000	N Grant	Falkirk Tryst	142
1985	AN Sturrock	Glasgow	143	2001	D Lane	Glasgow	140
1986	RL Glading	Royal Burgess	153	2002	D Lane	Scotscraig	142
1987	I Hornsby	Glasgow	145	2003	I Hutcheon	Glasgow	221
1988	J Hayes	Royal Burgess	143	2004	I Hutcheon	Alyth	140 (36)
1989	AS Mayer	Glasgow	139	2005	G MacDonald	Stranraer	215

1	Stephen Ellis (Cowal)	75-74-75—224
2	John Baldwin (USA)	77-79-69—225
3	Brian Grieve (King James VI)	72-81-72—225
	David Lane (Goring & Streatley)	73-76-76—225
	Glen MacBryde (Newcastle-under-Lyme)	74-80-71—225
	Gordon MacDonald (Callander)	73-77-75—225

Scottish Champion of Champions (inaugurated 1970) *always at Leven*

1970	A Horne	1982	G Macgregor	1994	G Sherry
1971	D Black	1983	D Carrick	1995	S Gallacher
1972	R Strachan	1984	S Stephen	1996	M Brooks
1973	*Not held*	1985	I Brotherston	1997	G Rankin
1974	M Niven	1986	I Hutcheon	1998	G Rankin
1975	A Brodie	1987	G Shaw	1999	D Patrick
1976	A Brodie	1988	I Hutcheon	2000	G Fox
1977	V Reid	1989	J Milligan	2001	M Loftus
1978	D Greig	1990	J Milligan	2002	S Carmichael
1979	B Marchbank	1991	G Hay	2003	S Wilson
1980	I Hutcheon	1992	D Robertson	2004	A McArthur
1981	I Hutcheon	1993	R Russell	2005	C Watson

1	George Murray (Earlsferry Thistle)	71-69-68-65—273
2	Iain Colquhoun (Ranfurly Castle)	72-75-64-65—276
	Barry Scott (Dumfries & Galloway)	70-69-68-69—276

Scottish Mid-Amateur Championship (inaugurated 1994) 2006 *Dullatur*

1994	C Watson	1998	G Campbell	2002	C Elliot
1995	M Thomson	1999	G Crawford	2003	C Gordon
1996	B Smith	2000	J Cameron	2004	R Roper
1997	H McDonald	2001	M Thomson	2005	A Dick

Leading Qualifier: 135 – Stuart Smith (Duddingston) 135

(continued over)

Quarter Finals

Allyn Dick (Shotts) beat Thomas McInally (Loudoun Gowf)
1 hole
Kenneth Ralston (Shotts) beat Tony Fraser (Annanhill)
1 hole
Terry Mathieson (Murcar) beat John Fowler (Hayston)
2 holes
Craig Elliot (Carrickvale) beat Clark Riddick (Dumfries &
Galloway) 5 and 4

Semi-Finals

Dick beat Ralston 3 and 2
Mathieson beat Elliot 4 and 3

Final

Allyn Dick beat Terry Mathieson
at 19th

Welsh Amateur Championship (inaugurated 1895) 2006 Pyle & Kenfig

Year	Winner	Runner-up	Venue	Score
1895	J Hunter	TM Barlow	Aberdovey	2 holes
1896	J Hunter	P Plunkett	Rhyl	1 hole
1897	FE Woodhead	J Hunter	Penarth	4 and 3
1898	FE Woodhead	Dr E Reid	Aberdovey	5 and 4
1899	FE Woodhead	TD Cummins	Conway	6 and 5
1900	TM Barlow	H Ludlow	Royal Porthcawl	2 and 1
1901	Major Green	P Plunkett	Aberdovey	8 and 7
1902	J Hunter	H Ludlow	Penarth	5 and 4
1903	J Hunter	TM Barlow	Rhos-on-Sea	2 holes
1904	H Ludlow	RM Brown	Ashburnham	13 and 11
1905	J Duncan jr	AP Cary Thomas	Conway	6 and 5
1906	G Renwick	WT Davies	Radyr	9 and 7
1907	LA Phillips	LH Gottwaltz	Royal Porthcawl	3 and 1
1908	G Renwick	LA Phillips	Southerndown	7 and 5
1909	J Duncan jr	EJ Byrne	Rhyl	9 and 8
1910	G Renwick	RM Brown	Swansea	2 holes
1911	HM Lloyd	TC Mellor	Conway	4 and 2
1912	LA Phillips	CH Turnbull	Royal Porthcawl	4 and 3
1913	HN Atkinson	CJ Hamilton	Chester	at 38th
1914–1919 Not played				
1920	HR Howell	J Duncan jr	Southerndown	2 holes
1921	CEL Fairchild	E Rowe	Aberdovey	1 hole
1922	HR Howell	EDSN Carne	Tenby	12 and 11
1923	HR Howell	CEL Fairchild	Rhyl	3 and 1
1924	HR Howell	CH Turnbull	Radyr	2 and 1
1925	CEL Fairchild	GS Emery	Rhyl	10 and 8
1926	DR Lewis	K Stoker	Royal Porthcawl	1 hole
1927	DR Lewis	JL Jones	Tenby	4 and 3
1928	CC Marston	DR Lewis	Royal St David's	at 37th
1929	HR Howell	R Chapman	Southerndown	4 and 3
1930	HR Howell	DR Lewis	Tenby	2 and 1
1931	HR Howell	WG Morgan	Aberdovey	7 and 6
1932	HR Howell	HE Davies	Ashburnham	7 and 6
1933	JL Black	AA Duncan	Royal Porthcawl	2 and 1
1934	SB Roberts	GS Noon	Prestatyn	4 and 3
1935	R Chapman	GS Noon	Tenby	1 hole
1936	RM de Lloyd	G Wallis	Aberdovey	1 hole
1937	DH Lewis	R Glossop	Porthcawl	2 holes
1938	AA Duncan	SB Roberts	Rhyl	2 and 1
1939–1945 Not played				
1946	JV Moody	A Marshman	Porthcawl	9 and 8
1947	SB Roberts	G Breen Turner	Royal St David's	8 and 7
1948	AA Duncan	SB Roberts	Porthcawl	2 and 1
1949	AD Evans	MA Jones	Aberdovey	2 and 1
1950	JL Morgan	DJ Bonnell	Southerndown	9 and 7
1951	JL Morgan	WI Tucker	Royal St David's	3 and 2
1952	AA Duncan	JL Morgan	Ashburnham	4 and 3
1953	SB Roberts	D Pearson	Prestatyn	5 and 3
1954	AA Duncan	K Thomas	Tenby	6 and 5
1955	TJ Davies	P Dunn	Royal St David's	38th hole
1956	A Lockley	WI Tucker	Southerndown	2 and 1
1957	ES Mills	H Griffiths	Royal St David's	2 and 1
1958	HC Squirrell	AD Lake	Conway	4 and 3
1959	HC Squirrell	N Rees	Porthcawl	8 and 7
1960	HC Squirrell	P Richards	Aberdovey	2 and 1
1961	AD Evans	J Toye	Ashburnham	3 and 2
1962	J Povall	HC Squirrell	Royal St David's	3 and 2

Welsh Amateur Championship *continued*

1963	WI Tucker	J Povall	Southerndown	4 and 3
1964	HC Squirrell	WI Tucker	Royal St David's	1 hole
1965	HC Squirrell	G Clay	Porthcawl	6 and 4
1966	WI Tucker	EN Davies	Aberdovey	6 and 5
1967	JK Povall	WI Tucker	Asburnham	3 and 2
1968	J Buckley	J Povall	Conway	8 and 7
1969	JL Toye	EN Davies	Porthcawl	1 hole
1970	EN Davies	J Povall	Royal St David's	1 hole
1971	CT Brown	HC Squirrell	Southerndown	6 and 5
1972	EN Davies	JL Toye	Prestatyn	40th hole
1973	D McLean	T Holder	Ashburnham	6 and 4
1974	S Cox	EN Davies	Caernarvonshire	3 and 2
1975	JL Toye	WI Tucker	Porthcawl	5 and 4
1976	MPD Adams	WI Tucker	Royal St David's	6 and 5
1977	D Stevens	JKD Povall	Southerndown	3 and 2
1978	D McLean	A Ingram	Caernarvonshire	11 and 10
1979	TJ Melia	MS Roper	Ashburnham	5 and 4
1980	DL Stevens	G Clement	Prestatyn	10 and 9
1981	S Jones	C Davies	Porthcawl	5 and 3
1982	D Wood	C Davies	Royal St David's	8 and 7
1983	JR Jones	AP Parkin	Southerndown	2 holes
1984	JR Jones	A Llyr	Prestatyn	1 hole
1985	ED Jones	MA Macara	Ashburnham	2 and 1
1986	C Rees	B Knight	Conwy	1 hole
1987	PM Mayo	DK Wood	Porthcawl	2 holes
1988	K Jones	RN Roderick	Royal St David's	40th hole
1989	S Dodd	K Jones	Tenby	2 and 1
1990	A Barnett	A Jones	Prestatyn	1 hole
1991	S Pardoe	S Jones	Ashburnham	7 and 5
1992	H Roberts	R Johnson	Pyle & Kenfig	3 and 2
1993	B Dredge	M Ellis	Southerndown	3 and 1
1994	C Evans	M Smith	Royal Porthcawl	5 and 4
1995	G Houston	C Evans	Royal St David's	3 and 2
1996	Y Taylor	DH Park	Ashburnham	3 and 2
1997	JR Donaldson	M Pilkington	Pyle & Kenfig	5 and 4
1998	M Pilkington	K Sullivan	Prestatyn	2 and 1
1999	M Griffiths	R Brookman	Tenby	7 and 6
2000	JG Jermine	R Brookman	Royal St David's	1 hole
2001	C Williams	L Harpin	Royal Porthcawl	1 hole
2002	D Price	L Harpin	Conwy	20th hole
2003	S Manley	R Davies	Southerndown	8 and 7
2004	R Thomas	J Williams	Ashburnham	at 41st
2005	C Wakeley	C Mills	Prestatyn	7 and 6

2006

Quarter Finals

Rhys Davies (Royal Porthcawl) beat Lee Lewis (Gower) 4 and 3

Chris Cousins (Aberdare) beat Craig Evans (West Monmouthshire) 6 and 5

Jason Shufflebotham (Prestatyn) beat Keiron Thomas (Hinckley) 2 and 1

Llewellyn Matthews (Southerndown) beat Rhys Enoch (Truro) 5 and 4

Semi-Finals

Davies beat Cousins 1 hole

Matthews beat Shufflebotham 2 and 1

Final

Llewellyn Matthews beat Rhys Davies 1 hole

Welsh Open Amateur Stroke Play Championship (inaugurated 1967)

1967	EN Davies	Harlech	295	1977	JA Buckley	Prestatyn	302
1968	JA Buckley	Harlech	294	1978	HJ Evans	Pyle & Kenfig	300
1969	DL Stevens	Tenby	288	1979	D McLean	Holyhead	289
1970	JK Povall	Newport	292	1980	TJ Melia	Tenby	291
1971T	EN Davies	Harlech	296	1981	D Evans	Wrexham	270
	JL Toye			1982	JR Jones	Cradoc	287
1972	JR Jones	Pyle & Kenfig	299	1983	G Davies	Aberdovey	287
1973	JR Jones	Llandudno (Maesdu)	300	1984	RN Roderick	Newport	292
1974	JL Toye	Tenby	307	1985	MA Macara	Harlech	291
1975	D McLean	Wrexham	288	1986	M Calvert	Pyle & Kenfig	299
1976	WI Tucker	Newport	282	1987	MA Macara	Llandudno (Maesdu)	290

1988	RN Roderick	Tenby	283	1997	G Wolstenholme	Conwy	286
1989	SC Dodd	Conwy	304	1998	DAJ Patrick	Southerndown	279
Open event since 1990				1999	C Williams	Northop	288
1990	G Houston	Pyle & Kenfig	288	2000	J Donaldson	Ashburnham	283
1991	A Jones	Royal Porthcawl	290	2001	J Lupton	Maesdu	266
1992	AJ Barnett	Royal St David's	278	2002	J Doherty	Pyle & Kenfig	282
1993	M Macara	Maesdu	280	2003	M Skelton	Prestatyn	278
1994	N Van Hootegem	St Pierre	290	2004	H Bragason (ISL)	Royal Porthcawl	286
1995	M Peet	Prestatyn	282	2005	R Dinwiddie*	Royal St David's	268
1996	M Blackey	Tenby	276				

First round not completed due to bad weather; further play impossible.
2006 – event cancelled *Southerndown*

Welsh Seniors' Amateur Championship (inaugurated 1975) 2006 *Aberdovey*

1975	A Marshman	77 (18)	1991	RO Ward	155
1976	AD Evans	156	1992	I Hughes	150
1977	AE Lockley	154	1993	G Perks	149
1978	AE Lockley	75 (18)	1994T	G Perks/I Hughes/	
1979	CR Morgan	158		A Prytherch	157
1980	ES Mills	152	1995	I Hughes	147
1981	T Branton	153	1996	G Isaac	152
1982	WI Tucker	147	1997	I Hughes	148
1983	WS Gronow	153	1998	D Reidford	158
1984	WI Tucker	150	1999	G Isaac	150
1985	NA Lycett	149	2000	JR Jones*	145
1986	E Mills	154	2001	W Stowe	222
1987	WS Gronow	146	2002	B Cramb	221
1988	NA Lycett	150	2003	P Jones	213
1989	WI Tucker	150	2004	P Jones	220
1990	I Hughes	159	2005	P Jones*	218

1	K Stimpson (Wenvoe Castle)	65-72-72—209
2	J Jones (Bromborough)	73-74-70—217
3	B Griffiths (Llanymynech)	72-73-74—219

Welsh Tournament of Champions (inaugurated 1979) *always at Cradoc*

1979	J L Toye (Radyr)	1988	S C Dodd (Brynhill)	1997	M Pilkington (Nefyn)
1980	J M Morrow (Porthmadog)	1989	P Sykes (Pontypridd)	1998	M Gwyther (Morlais Castle)
1981	A P Vicary (St Pierre)	1990	G Houston (Flint)	1999	R Williams (Conwy)
1982	P M Mayo (Newport)	1991	G Houston (Flint)	2000	J Davidson (Llanwern)
1983	P M Mayo (Newport)	1992	B Dredge (Bryn Meadows)	2001	N Oakley (St Mellons)
1984	M Bearcroft (St Pierre)	1993	B Dredge (Bryn Meadows)	2002	T Hayward (Pontnewydd)
1985	S C Dodd (Brynhill)	1994	B Dredge (Bryn Meadows)	2003	L James (Brynhill)
1986	S C Dodd (Brynhill)	1995	G Houston (Flint)	2004	P Grimley (Chirk)
1987	J R Jones (Langland Bay)	1996	M H Peat (Pyle & Kenfig)	2005	I Flower (Mountain Ash)

1	James Zanotti (Llanwern)	71-71—142
2	Lee Thomas Lewis (Gower)	75-68—143
3	M S Davies (Llandrindod)	71-72—143

European Amateur Championship (inaugurated 1986) 2006 *Bella, Italy*

1986	A Haglund (SWE)	Eindhoven, Netherlands	1998	P Gribben (IRL)	Golf du Medoc, France
1988	D Ecob (AUS)	Falkenstein, Germany	1999	G Havret (FRA)	Ascona, Switzerland
1990	K Erikson (SWE)	Aalborg, Denmark	2000	C Pettersson (SWE)	Murhof, Austria
1991	J Payne (ENG)	Hillside, England	2001	S Browne (IRL)	Odense, Denmark
1992	M Scarpa (ITA)	Le Querce, Italy	2002	R Pellicioli (FRA)	Tróia, Portugal
1993	M Backhausen (DEN)	Dalmahoy, Scotland	2003	B McElhinney (IRL)	Nairn, Scotland
1994	S Gallacher (SCO)	Aura, Finland	2004	M Richardson (ENG)	Skövde, Sweden
1995	S García (ESP)	El Prat, Spain	2005	M Thorp (NOR)	Rinkven, Belgium
1996	D Olsson (SEW)	Karlstad, Sweden			
1997	D de Vooght (BEL)	Domaine Imperial, Switzerland			

(continued over)

European Amateur Championship – 2006 *Bella, Italy – continued*

1	Rory McIlroy (IRL)	65-69-72-68—274
2	Stephen Lewton (ENG)	69-72-68-68—277
3	Jamie Moul (ENG)	71-70-71-66—278

European Seniors' Championship (inaugurated 1999)   2006 *Ribagolfe, Portugal*

1999	H-J Ecklebe (GER)	Switzerland	216	2003	DJ Smith (SCO)	France	216
2000	HH Giesen (GER)	Spain	217	2004	D Smith (SCO)*	France	213
2001	G Steel (ENG)	Spain	216	*Smith won at fifth extra hole			
2002	A Morrison (ENG)	Spain	212	2005	R Smethurst (ENG)	France	218

1	Miguel Preysler de la Riva (ESP)	72-73—145
2	Ghirardi Francesco (ITA)	73-75—148
3	Hugh Smyth (IRL)	74-76—150

One round cancelled due to bad weather

European Mid-Amateur Championship (inaugurated 1999)   2006 *Grand-Ducal, Luxembourg*

1999	H-G Reiter (GER)	Luxembourg	215	2003	H-G Reiter (GER)	Sweden	216
2000	F Illouz (FRA)	England	221	2004	F Clerici (ITA)	Italy	210
2001	B Downing (ENG)	Turkey	216	2005	JM Zamora (ESP)	Slovenia	216
2002	H-G Reiter (GER)	Austria	210				

1	Gary Wolstenholme (ENG)*	73-70-67—210
2	Jakob Thomsen (DEN)	68-74-68—210
3	Roger Roper (ENG)	73-68-72—213

Wolstenholme beat Thomsen at first extra hole

New course at Machrihanish in Argyll

There are not too many areas of linksland where it would be possible to build a new golf course but a site has been located at Machrihanish on the Argyll peninsula.

Australian entrepreneur Brian Keating leads the development team for the new project with David McLay Kidd having been asked to design the new course through the dunes.

"There are only 200 true links in the world," says the developer, "and it is our intention to develop Machrihanish Dunes in the spirit of past golf pioneers by building a course that reminds us of the way golf began".

The project has the full support of the Scottish Natural Heritage and has been given the go-ahead despite being an area of Special Scientific Interest. Poor quality grazing and lack of appropriate management to preserve the dunes and its associated vegetation and wildlife persuaded Scottish Natural Heritage to approve it.

National Orders of Merit

English champion Ross McGowan (Banstead Downs) topped the English National Order of Merit and European Amateur champion Rory McIlroy (Holywood) was Ireland's No. 1 in 2006. Scott Jamieson (Cathkin Braes) topped Scotland's Order of Merit but Richie Ramsay, the American champion from Aberdeen) was No. 1 in the Scottish Rankings. Llewellyn Matthews was top amateur of the year in Wales.

England – PING/EGU Order of Merit 2006

1	Ross McGowan (Banstead Downs)	1746	6	Oliver Fisher (West Essex)	800
2	Jamie Moul (Stoke-by-Nayland)	1497	7	Jason Palmer (Kirby Muxloe)	736
3	Gary Wolstenholme (Kilworth Springs)	1210	8	David Horsey (Styal)	602
4	Robert Dinwiddie (Barnard Castle)	881	9	Stephen Lewton (Woburn)	575
5	Adam Gee (Leatherhead)	811	10	Matthew Cryer (Coventry)	554

Ireland – Willie Gill Award 2006

1	Rory McIlroy (Holywood)	180	7	Desmond Morgan (Mullingar)	80
2	Darren Crowe (Dunmurry)	155	8	Paul O'Hanlon (The Curragh)	65
3	Simon Ward (Co. Louth)	120	9	Joe Lyons (Galway)	55
	Jonathan Caldwell (Clandeboye)	120		Greg Bowden (Hermitage)	55
	Connor Doran (Banbridge)	120		Rory Leonard (Banbridge)	55
6	Pat Murray (Limerick)	95			

Scotland – Order of Merit 2006

1	Scott Jamieson (Cathkin Braes)	615	6	Elliot Saltman (Craigielaw)	478
2	Glenn Campbell (Blairgowrie)	564	7	Kevin McAlpine (Alyth)	470
3	George Murray (Earlsferry Thistle)	525	8	Callum Macaulay (Tulliallan)	452
4	John Gallagher (Swanston)	512	9	Steven McEwan (Kilmarnock [Barassie])	426
5	Keir McNicoll (Carnoustie)	485	10	Paul O'Hara (Colville Park)	390

Scottish Golf Ranking 2006

1	Richie Ramsay (Royal Aberdeen)	1191	6	Callum Macaulay (Tulliallan)	821
2	Scott Jamieson (Cathkin Braes)	968	7	John Gallagher (Swanston)	779
3	George Murray (Earlsferry Thistle)	925	8	Jonathan King (Glasgow)	742
4	Lloyd Saltman (Craigielaw)	857	9	Scott Henry (Cardross)	740
5	Paul O'Hara (Colville Park)	840	10	Keir McNicoll (Carnoustie)	734

Wales – Konica Minolta Order of Merit 2006

1	Llewellyn Matthews (Southerndown)	404	6	Tim Dykes (Wrexham)	273
2	Nigel Edwards (Whitchurch)	370	7	Ryan Thomas (Aberdare)	209
3	Rhys Enoch (Truro)	343	8	Cennydd Mills (Vale of Glamorgan)	205
4	Craig Evans (West Monmouthshire)	318	9	Rhys Davies (Royal Porthcawl)	190
5	Chris Cousins (Aberdare)	281	10	Jason Shufflebotham (Prestatyn)	185

Team Events

Walker Cup (Instituted 1922)
Great Britain & Ireland v USA (home team names first)

Unofficial match
1921 *Hoylake* 21 May
Result: USA 9, GBI 3
Foursomes
Simpson & Jenkins lost to Evans & Jones 5 and 3
Tolley & Holderness lost to Ouimet & Guilford 3 and 2
de Montmorency & Wethered lost to Hunter & Platt
　1 hole
Aylmer & Armour lost to Wright & Fownes 4 and 2
Singles
CJH Tolley beat C Evans jr 4 and 3
JLC Jenkins lost to FD Ouimet 6 and 5
RH de Montmorency lost to RT Jones jr 4 and 3
JG Simpson lost to JP Guilford 2 and 1
CC Aylmer beat P Hunter 2 and 1
TD Armour beat JW Platt 2 and 1
EWE Holderness lost to F Wright 2 holes
RH Wethered lost to WC Fownes jr 3 and 1

Walker Cup
1922 *National Golf Links, New York* Aug 28–29
Result: USA 8, GBI 4
Captains: WC Fownes (USA), R Harris (GBI)
Foursomes
Guilford & Ouimet beat Tolley & Darwin 8 and 7
Evans & Gardner lost to Wethered & Aylmer 5 and 4
Jones & Sweetser beat Torrance & Hooman 3 and 2
Marston & Fownes beat Caven & Mackenzie 2 and 1
Singles
JP Guilford beat CJH Tolley 2 and 1
RT Jones jr beat RH Wethered 3 and 2
C Evans jr beat J Caven 5 and 4
FD Ouimet beat CC Aylmer 8 and 7
RA Gardner beat WB Torrance 7 and 5
MR Marston lost to WW Mackenzie 6 and 5
WC Fownes jr lost to B Darwin 3 and 1
JW Sweetser lost to CVL Hooman at 37th

1923 *Old Course, St Andrews* May 18–19
Result: USA 6½, GBI 5½
Captains: R Harris (GBI), RA Gardner (USA)
Foursomes
Tolley & Wethered beat Ouimet & Sweetser 6 and 5
Harris & Hooman lost to Gardner & Marston
　7 and 6
Holderness & Hope beat Rotan & Herron 1 hole
Wilson & Murray beat Johnston & Neville
　4 and 3
Singles
RH Wethered halved with FD Ouimet
CJH Tolley beat JW Sweetser 4 and 3
R Harris lost to RA Gardner 1 hole
WW Mackenzie lost to GV Rotan 4 and 4
WL Hope lost to MR Marston 6 and 5
EWE Holderness lost to FJ Wright jr 1 hole
J Wilson beat SD Herron 1 hole
WA Murray lost to OF Willing 2 and 1

1924 *Garden City, New York* Sept 12–13
Result: USA 9, GBI 3
Captains: RA Gardner (USA), CJH Tolley (GBI)
Foursomes
Marston & Gardner beat Storey & Murray 3 and 1
Guilford & Ouimet beat Tolley & Hezlet 2 and 1
Jones & Fownes jr lost to Scott & Scott jr 1 hole
Sweetser & Johnston beat Torrance & Bristowe 4 and 3
Singles
MR Marston lost to CJH Tolley 1 hole
RT Jones jr beat CO Hezlet 4 and 3
C Evans jr beat WA Murray 2 and 1
FD Ouimet beat EF Storey 1 hole
JW Sweetser lost to Hon M Scott 7 and 6
RA Gardner beat WL Hope 3 and 2
JP Guilford beat TA Torrance 2 and 1
OF Willing beat DH Kyle 3 and 2

1926 *Old Course, St Andrews* June 2–3
Result: USA 6½, GBI 5½
Captains: R Harris (GBI), RA Gardner (USA)
Foursomes
Wethered & Holderness beat Ouimet &
　Guilford 5 and 4
Tolley & Jamieson lost to Jones & Gunn 4 and 3
Harris & Hezlet lost to Von Elm & Sweetser 8 and 7
Storey & Brownlow lost to Gardner & MacKenzie
　1 hole
Singles
CJH Tolley lost to RT Jones jr 12 and 11
EWE Holderness lost to JW Sweetser 4 and 3
RH Wethered beat FD Ouimet 5 and 4
CO Hezlet halved with G Von Elm
R Harris beat JP Guilford 2 and 1
Hon WGE Brownlow lost to W Gunn 9 and 8
EF Storey beat RR MacKenzie 2 and 1
A Jamieson jr beat RA Gardner 5 and 4

1928 *Wheaton, Chicago, IL* Aug 30–31
Result: USA 11, GBI 1
Captains: RT Jones jr (USA),
　W Tweddell (GBI)
Foursomes
Sweetser & Von Elm beat Perkins & Tweddell
　7 and 6
Jones & Evans beat Hezlet & Hope 5 and 3
Ouimet & Johnston beat Torrance & Storey
　4 and 2
Gunn & MacKenzie beat Beck & Martin 7 and 5
Singles
RT Jones jr beat TP Perkins 13 and 12
G Von Elm beat W Tweddell 3 and 2
FD Ouimet beat CO Hezlet 8 and 7
JW Sweetser beat WL Hope 5 and 4
HR Johnston beat EF Storey 4 and 2
C Evans jr lost to TA Torrance 1 hole
W Gunn beat RH Hardman 11 and 10
RR MacKenzie beat GNC Martin 2 and 1

1930 St George's, Sandwich May 15–16
Result: USA 10, GBI 2
Captains: RH Wethered (GBI),
RT Jones jr (USA)

Foursomes
Tolley & Wethered beat Von Elm & Voigt 2 holes
Hartley & Torrance lost to Jones & Willing 8 and 7
Holderness & Stout lost to MacKenzie & Moe 2 and 1
Campbell & Smith lost to Johnston & Ouimet 2 and 1

Singles
CJH Tolley lost to HR Johnston 5 and 4
RH Wethered lost to RT Jones jr 9 and 8
RW Hartley lost to G Von Elm 3 and 2
EWE Holderness lost to GJ Voigt 10 and 8
JN Smith lost to OF Willing 2 and 1
TA Torrance beat FD Ouimet 7 and 6
JA Stout lost to DK Moe 1 hole
W Campbell lost to RR MacKenzie 6 and 5

1932 Brookline, MA Sept 1–2
Result: USA 9½, GBI 2½
Captains: FD Ouimet (USA), TA Torrance (GBI)

Foursomes
Sweetser & Voigt beat Hartley & Hartley 7 and 6
Seaver & Moreland beat Torrance & de Forest
6 and 5
Ouimet & Dunlap beat Stout & Burke 7 and 6
Moe & Howell beat Fiddian & McRuvie 5 and 4

Singles
FD Ouimet halved with TA Torrance
JW Sweetser halved with JA Stout
GT Moreland beat RW Hartley 2 and 1
J Westland halved with J Burke
GJ Voigt lost to LG Crawley 1 hole
MJ McCarthy jr beat WL Hartley 3 and 2
CH Seaver beat EW Fiddian 7 and 6
GT Dunlap jr beat EA McRuvie 10 and 9

1934 Old Course, St Andrews May 11–12
Result: USA 9½, GBI 2½
Captains: Hon M Scott (GBI), FD Ouimet (USA)

Foursomes
Wethered & Tolley lost to Goodman & Little 8 and 6
Bentley & Fiddian lost to Moreland & Westland 6 and 5
Scott & McKinlay lost to Egan & Marston 3 and 2
McRuvie & McLean beat Ouimet & Dunlap 4 and 2

Singles
Hon M Scott lost to JG Goodman 7 and 6
CJH Tolley lost to WL Little jr 6 and 5
LG Crawley lost to FD Ouimet 5 and 4
J McLean lost to GT Dunlap jr 4 and 3
EW Fiddian lost to JW Fischer 5 and 4
SL McKinlay lost to GT Moreland 3 and 1
EA McRuvie halved with J Westland
TA Torrance beat MR Marston 4 and 3

1936 Pine Valley, NJ Sept 2–3
Result: USA 10½, GBI 1½
Captains: FD Ouimet (USA),
W Tweddell (GBI)

Foursomes
Goodman & Campbell beat Thomson & Bentley
7 and 5
Smith & White beat McLean & Langley 8 and 7
Yates & Emery halved with Peters & Dykes
Givan & Voigt halved with Hill & Ewing

Singles
JG Goodman beat H Thomson 3 and 2
AE Campbell beat J McLean 5 and 4
JW Fischer beat RC Ewing 8 and 7
R Smith beat GA Hill 11 and 9
W Emery beat GB Peters 1 hole
CR Yates beat JM Dykes 8 and 7
GT Dunlap jr halved with HG Bentley
E White beat JDA Langley 6 and 5

1938 St Andrews June 3–4
Result: GBI 7½, USA 4½
Captains: JB Beck (GBI),
FD Ouimet (USA)

Foursomes
Bentley & Bruen halved with Fischer & Kocsis
Peters & Thomson beat Goodman & Ward 4 and 2
Kyle & Stowe lost to Yates & Billows 3 and 2
Pennink & Crawley beat Smith & Haas 3 and 1

Singles
J Bruen jr lost to CR Yates 2 and 1
H Thomson beat JG Goodman 6 and 4
LG Crawley lost to JW Fischer 3 and 2
C Stowe beat CR Kocsis 2 and 1
JJF Pennink lost to MH Ward 12 and 11
RC Ewing beat RE Billows 1 hole
GB Peters beat R Smith 9 and 8
AT Kyle beat F Haas jr 5 and 4

1947 Old Course, St Andrews May 16–17
Result: USA 8, GBI 4
Captains: JB Beck (GBI),
FD Ouimet (USA)

Foursomes
Carr & Ewing lost to Bishop & Riegel 3 and 2
Crawley & Lucas beat Ward & Quick 5 and 4
Kyle & Wilson lost to Turnesa & Kammer 5 and 4
White & Stowe beat Stranahan & Chapman 4 and 3

Singles
LG Crawley lost to MH Ward 5 and 3
JB Carr beat SE Bishop 5 and 3
GH Micklem lost to RH Riegel 6 and 5
RC Ewing lost to WP Turnesa 6 and 5
C Stowe lost to FR Stranahan 2 and 1
RJ White beat AF Kammer jr 4 and 3
JC Wilson lost to SL Quick 8 and 6
PB Lucas lost to RD Chapman 4 and 3

1949 Winged Foot, New York Aug 19–20
Result: USA 10, GBI 2
Captains: FD Ouimet (USA), PB Lucas (GBI)

Foursomes
Billows & Turnesa lost to Carr & White 3 and 2
Kocsis & Stranahan beat Bruen & McCready 2 and 1
Bishop & Riegel beat Ewing & Micklem 9 and 7
Dawson & McCormick beat Thom & Perowne
8 and 7

Singles
WP Turnesa lost to RJ White 4 and 3
FR Stranahan beat SM McCready 6 and 5
RH Riegel beat J Bruen jr 5 and 4
JW Dawson beat JB Carr 5 and 3
CR Coe beat RC Ewing 1 hole
RE Billows beat KG Thom 2 and 1
CR Kocsis beat AH Perowne 4 and 2
JB McHale jr beat GH Micklem 5 and 4

1951 *Royal Birkdale, Southport* May 11–12
Result: USA 7½, GBI 4½
Captains: RH Oppenheimer (GBI),
WP Turnesa (USA)

Foursomes
White & Carr halved with Stranahan & Campbell
Ewing & Langley halved with Coe & McHale
Kyle & Caldwell lost to Chapman & Knowles jr 1 hole
Bruen jr & Morgan lost to Turnesa & Urzetta 5 and 4

Singles
SM McCready lost to S Urzetta 4 and 3
JB Carr beat FR Stranahan 2 and 1
RJ White beat CR Coe 2 and 1
JDA Langley lost to JB McHale jr 2 holes
RC Ewing lost to WC Campbell 5 and 4
AT Kyle beat WP Turnesa 2 holes
I Caldwell halved with HD Paddock jr
JL Morgan lost to RD Chapman 7 and 6

1953 *Kittansett, MA* Sept 4–5
Result: USA 9, GBI 3
Captains: CR Yates (USA), AA Duncan (GBI)

Foursomes
Urzetta & Venturi beat Carr & White 6 and 4
Ward & Westland beat Langley & AH Perowne
　9 and 8
Jackson & Littler beat Wilson & MacGregor 3 and 2
Campbell & Coe lost to Micklem & Morgan 4 and 3

Singles
EH Ward jr beat JB Carr 4 and 3
RD Chapman lost to RJ White 1 hole
GA Littler beat GH Micklem 5 and 3
J Westland beat RC MacGregor 7 and 5
DR Cherry beat NV Drew 9 and 7
K Venturi beat JC Wilson 9 and 8
CR Coe lost to JL Morgan 3 and 2
S Urzetta beat JDA Langley 3 and 2

1955 *Old Course, St Andrews* May 20–21
Result: USA 10, GBI 2
Captains: GA Hill (GBI), WC Campbell (USA)

Foursomes
Carr & White lost to Ward & Cherry 1 hole
Micklem & Morgan lost to Patton & Yost 2 and 1
Caldwell & Millward lost to Conrad & Morey 3 and 2
Blair & Cater lost to Cudd & Jackson 5 and 4

Singles
RJ White lost to EH Ward jr 6 and 5
PF Scrutton lost to WJ Patton 2 and 1
I Caldwell beat D Morey 1 hole
JB Carr lost to DR Cherry 5 and 4
DA Blair beat JW Conrad 1 hole
EB Millward lost to BH Cudd 2 holes
RC Ewing lost to JG Jackson 6 and 4
JL Morgan lost to RL Yost 8 and 7

1957 *Minikahda, MN* Aug 30–31
Result: USA 8½, GBI 3½
Captains: CR Coe (USA), GH Micklem (GBI)

Foursomes
Baxter & Patton beat Carr & Deighton 2 and 1
Campbell & Taylor beat Bussell & Scrutton 4 and 3
Blum & Kocsis lost to Jack & Sewell 1 hole
Robbins & Rudolph halved with Shepperson &
　Wolstenholme

Singles
WJ Patton beat RR Jack 1 hole
WC Campbell beat JB Carr 3 and 2
R Baxter jr beat A Thirlwell 4 and 3
W Hyndman III beat FWG Deighton 7 and 6
JE Campbell lost to AF Bussell 2 and 1
FM Taylor jr beat D Sewell 1 hole
EM Rudolph beat PF Scrutton 3 and 2
H Robbins jr lost to GB Wolstenholme 2 and 1

1959 *Muirfield, Gullane* May 15–16
Result: USA 9, GBI 3
Captains: GH Micklem (GBI), CR Coe (USA)

Foursomes
Jack & Sewell lost to Ward & Taylor 1 hole
Carr & Wolstenholme lost to Hyndman & Aaron 1 hole
Bonallack & Perowne lost to Patton & Coe 9 and 8
Lunt & Shepperson lost to Wettlander & Nicklaus 2 and 1

Singles
JB Carr beat CR Coe 3 and 1
GB Wolstenholme lost to EH Ward jr 9 and 8
RR Jack beat WJ Patton 5 and 3
DN Sewell lost to W Hyndman III 4 and 3
AE Shepperson beat TD Aaron 2 and 1
MF Bonallack lost to DR Beman 2 holes
MSR Lunt lost to HW Wettlander 6 and 5
WD Smith lost to JW Nicklaus 5 and 4

1961 *Seattle, WA* Sept 1–2
Result: USA 11, GBI 1
Captains: J Westland (USA), CD Lawrie (GBI)

Foursomes
Beman & Nicklaus beat Walker & Chapman 6 and 5
Coe & Cherry beat Blair & Christmas 1 hole
Hyndman & Gardner beat Carr & G Huddy 4 and 3
Cochran & Andrews beat Bonallack & Shade 4 and 3

Singles
DR Beman beat MF Bonallack 3 and 2
CR Coe beat MSR Lunt 5 and 4
FM Taylor jr beat J Walker 3 and 2
W Hyndman III beat DW Frame 7 and 6
JW Nicklaus beat JB Carr 6 and 4
CB Smith lost to MJ Christmas 3 and 2
RW Gardner beat RDBM Shade 1 hole
DR Cherry beat DA Blair 5 and 4

1963 *Ailsa Course, Turnberry* May 24–25
Result: USA 14, GBI 10
Captains: CD Lawrie (GBI), RS Tufts (USA)

First Day – Foursomes
Bonallack & Murray beat Patton & Sikes
　4 and 3
Carr & Green lost to Gray & Harris 2 holes
Lunt & Sheahan lost to Beman & Coe 5 and 3
Madeley & Shade halved with Gardner &
　Updegraff

Singles
SWT Murray beat DR Beman 3 and 1
MJ Christmas lost to WJ Patton 3 and 2
JB Carr beat RH Sikes 7 and 5
DB Sheahan beat LE Harris 1 hole
MF Bonallack beat RD Davies 1 hole
AC Saddler halved with CR Coe
RDBM Shade beat AD Gray jr 4 and 3
MSR Lunt halved with CB Smith

Second Day – Foursomes
Bonallack & Murray lost to Patton & Sikes 1 hole
Lunt & Sheahan lost to Gray & Harris 3 and 2
Green & Saddler lost to Gardner & Updegraff 3 and 1
Madeley & Shade lost to Beman & Coe 3 and 2

Singles
Murray lost to Patton 3 and 2
Sheahan beat Davies 1 hole
Carr lost to Updegraff 4 and 3
Bonallack lost to Harris 3 and 2
Lunt lost to Gardner 3 and 2
Saddler halved with Beman
Shade beat Gray 2 and 1
Green lost to Coe 4 and 3

1965 *Five Farms, MD* Sept 3–4
Result: USA 11, GBI 11[†]
Captains: JW Fischer (USA), JB Carr (GBI)
First Day – Foursomes
Campbell & Gray lost to Lunt & Cosh 1 hole
Beman & Allen halved with Bonallack & Clark
Patton & Tutwiler beat Foster & Clark 5 and 4
Hopkins & Eichelberger lost to Townsend & Shade 2 and 1

Singles
WC Campbell beat MF Bonallack 6 and 5
DR Beman beat R Foster 2 holes
AD Gray jr lost to RDBM Shade 3 and 1
JM Hopkins lost to CA Clark 5 and 3
WJ Patton lost to P Townsend 3 and 2
D Morey lost to AC Saddler 2 and 1
DC Allen lost to GB Cosh 2 holes
ER Updegraff lost to MSR Lunt 2 and 1

Second Day – Foursomes
Campbell & Gray beat Saddler & Foster 4 and 3
Beman & Eichelberger lost to Townsend & Shade 2 and 1
Tutwiler & Patton beat Cosh & Lunt 2 and 1
Allen & Morey lost to CA Clark & Bonallack 2 and 1

Singles
Campbell beat Foster 3 and 2
Beman beat Saddler 1 hole
Tutwiler beat Shade 5 and 3
Allen lost to Cosh 4 and 3
Gray beat Townsend 1 hole
Hopkins halved with CA Clark
Eichelberger beat Bonallack 5 and 3
Patton beat Lunt 4 and 2

1967 *Royal St George's, Sandwich* May 19–20
Result: USA 13, GBI 7[†]
Captains: JB Carr (GBI), JW Sweetser (USA)
First Day – Foursomes
Shade & Oosterhuis halved with Murphy & Cerrudo
Foster & Saddler lost to Campbell & Lewis 1 hole
Bonallack & Attenborough lost to Gray & Tutwiler 4 and 2
Carr & Craddock lost to Dickson & Grant 3 and 1

Singles
RDBM Shade lost to WC Campbell 2 and 1
R Foster lost to RJ Murphy jr 2 and 1
MF Bonallack halved with AD Gray jr
MF Attenborough lost to RJ Cerrudo 4 and 3
P Oosterhuis lost to RB Dickson 6 and 4
T Craddock lost to JW Lewis jr 2 and 1
AK Pirie halved with DC Allen
AC Saddler beat MA Fleckman 3 and 2

Second Day – Foursomes
Bonallack & Craddock beat Murphy & Cerrudo 2 holes
Saddler & Pirie lost to Campbell & Lewis 1 hole
Shade & Oosterhuis beat Gray & Tutwiler 3 and 1
Foster & Millensted beat Allen & Fleckman 2 and 1

Singles
Shade lost to Campbell 3 and 2
Bonallack beat Murphy 4 and 2
Saddler beat Gray 3 and 2
Foster halved with Cerrudo
Pirie lost to Dickson 4 and 3
Craddock beat Lewis 5 and 4
Oosterhuis lost to Grant 1 hole
Millensted lost to Tutwiler 3 and 1

1969 *Milwaukee, WI* Aug 22–23
Result: USA 10, GBI 8[†]
Captains: WJ Patton (USA), MF Bonallack (GBI)
First Day – Foursomes
Giles & Melnyk beat Bonallack & Craddock 3 and 2
Fleisher & Miller halved with Benka & Critchley
Wadkins & Siderowf lost to Green & A Brooks
W Hyndman III & Inman jr beat Foster & Marks 2 and 1

Singles
B Fleisher halved with MF Bonallack
M Giles III beat CW Green 1 hole
AL Miller III beat B Critchley 1 hole
RL Siderowf beat LP Tupling 6 and 5
S Melnyk lost to PJ Benka 3 and 1
L Wadkins lost to GC Marks 1 hole
J Bohmann beat MG King 2 and 1
ER Updegraff beat R Foster 6 and 5

Second Day – Foursomes
Giles & Melnyk halved with Green & Brooks
Fleisher & Miller lost to Benka & Critchley 2 and 1
Siderowf & Wadkins beat Foster & King 6 and 5
Updegraff & Bohmann lost to Bonallack & Tupling 4 and 3

Singles
Fleisher lost to Bonallack 5 and 4
Siderowf halved with Critchley
Miller beat King 1 hole
Giles halved with Craddock
Inman beat Benka 2 and 1
Bohmann lost to Brooks 4 and 3
Hyndman halved with Green
Updegraff lost to Marks 3 and 2

1971 *Old Course, St Andrews* May 26–27
Result: GBI 13, USA 11
Captains: MF Bonallack (GBI), JM Winters jr (USA)
First Day – Foursomes
Bonallack & Humphreys beat Wadkins & Simons 1 hole
Green & Carr beat Melnyk & Giles 1 hole
Marsh & Macgregor beat Miller & Farquhar 2 and 1
Macdonald & Foster beat Campbell & Kite 2 and 1

Singles
CW Green lost to L Wadkins 1 hole
MF Bonallack lost to M Giles III 1 hole
GC Marks lost to AL Miller III 1 hole
JS Macdonald lost to S Melnyk 3 and 2
RJ Carr halved with W Hyndman III
W Humphreys lost to JR Gabrielsen 1 hole
HB Stuart beat J Farquhar 3 and 2
R Foster lost to T Kite 3 and 2

---

† *Some matches were halved but no half points were awarded*

1971 *continued*

Second Day – Foursomes
Marks & Green lost to Melnyk & Giles 1 hole
Stuart & Carr beat Wadkins & Gabrielsen 1 hole
Marsh & Bonallack lost to Miller & Farquhar 5 and 4
Macdonald & Foster halved with Campbell & Kite

Singles
Bonallack lost to Wadkins 3 and 1
Stuart beat Giles 2 and 1
Humphreys beat Melnyk 2 and 1
Green beat Miller 1 hole
Carr beat Simons 2 holes
Macgregor beat Gabrielsen 1 hole
Marsh beat Hyndman 1 hole
Marks lost to Kite 3 and 2

1973 *Brookline, MA* Aug 24–25
Result: USA 14, GBI 10
Captains: JW Sweetser (USA), DM Marsh (GBI)

First Day – Foursomes
Giles & Koch halved with King & Hedges
Siderowf & Pfeil beat Stuart & Davies 5 and 4
Edwards & Ellis beat Green & Milne 2 and 1
West & Ballenger beat Foster & Homer 2 and 1

Singles
M Giles III beat HB Stuart 5 and 4
RL Siderowf beat MF Bonallack 4 and 2
G Koch lost to JC Davies 1 hole
M West lost to HK Clark 2 and 1
D Edwards beat R Foster 2 holes
M Killian lost to MG King 1 hole
W Rodgers lost to CW Green 1 hole
M Pfeil lost to WT Milne 4 and 3

Second Day – Foursomes
Giles & Koch & Homer & Foster 7 and 5
Siderowf & Pfeil halved with Clark & Davies
Edwards & Ellis beat Hedges & King 2 and 1
Rodgers & Killian beat Stuart & Milne 1 hole

Singles
Ellis lost to Stuart 5 and 4
Siderowf lost to Davies 3 and 2
Edwards beat Homer 2 and 1
Giles halved with Green
West beat King 1 hole
Killian lost to Milne 2 and 1
Koch halved with Hedges
Pfeil beat Clark 1 hole

1975 *Old Course, St Andrews* May 28–29
Result: USA 15½, GBI 8½
Captains: DM Marsh (GBI), ER Updegraff (USA)

First Day – Foursomes
James & Eyles beat Pate & Siderowf 1 hole
Davies & Poxon lost to Burns & Stadler 5 and 4
Green & Stuart lost to Haas & Strange 2 and 1
Macgregor & Hutcheon lost to Giles & Koch 5 and 4

Singles
M James beat J Pate 2 and 1
JC Davies halved with C Strange
P Mulcare beat RL Siderowf 1 hole
HB Stuart lost to G Koch 3 and 1
MA Poxon lost to J Grace 3 and 1
IC Hutcheon halved with WC Campbell
GRD Eyles lost to J Haas 2 and 1
G Macgregor lost to M Giles III 5 and 4

Second Day – Foursomes
Mulcare & Hutcheon beat Pate & Siderowf 1 hole
Green & Stuart lost to Burns & Stadler 1 hole
James & Eyles beat Campbell & Grace 5 and 3
Hedges & Davies lost to Haas & Strange 3 and 2

Singles
Hutcheon beat Pate 3 and 2
Mulcare lost to Strange 4 and 3
James lost to Koch 5 and 4
Davies beat Burns 2 and 1
Green lost to Grace 2 and 1
Macgregor lost to Stadler 3 and 2
Eyles lost to Campbell 2 and 1
Hedges halved with Giles

1977 *Shinnecock Hills, NY* Aug 26–27
Result: USA 16, GBI 8
Captains: LW Oehmig(USA), AC Saddler (GBI)

First Day – Foursomes
Fought & Heafner beat Lyle & McEvoy 4 and 3
Simpson & Miller beat Davies & Kelley 5 and 4
Siderowf & Hallberg lost to Hutcheon & Deeble 1 hole
Sigel & Brannan beat Brodie & Martin 1 hole

Singles
L Miller beat P McEvoy 2 holes
J Fought beat IC Hutcheon 4 and 3
S Simpson beat GH Murray 7 and 6
V Heafner beat JC Davies 4 and 3
B Sander lost to A Brodie 4 and 3
G Hallberg lost to S Martin 3 and 2
F Ridley beat AWB Lyle 2 holes
J Sigel beat P McKellar 5 and 3

Second Day – Foursomes
Fought & Heafner beat Hutcheon & Deeble 4 and 3
Miller & Simpson beat McEvoy & Davies 2 holes
Siderowf & Sander lost to Brodie & Martin 6 and 4
Ridley & Brannan lost to Murray & Kelley 4 and 3

Singles
Miller beat Martin 1 hole
Fought beat Davies 2 and 1
Sander lost to Brodie 2 and 1
Hallberg beat McEvoy 4 and 3
Siderowf lost to Kelley 2 and 1
Brannan lost to Hutcheon 2 holes
Ridley beat Lyle 5 and 3
Sigel beat Deeble 1 hole

1979 *Muirfield, Gullane* May 30–31
Result: USA 15½, GBI 8½
Captains: R Foster (GBI), RL Siderowf (USA)

First Day – Foursomes
McEvoy & Marchbank lost to Hoch & Sigel 1 hole
Godwin & Hutcheon beat West & Sutton 2 holes
Brand jr & Kelley lost to Fischesser & Holtgrieve 1 hole
Brodie & Carslaw beat Moody & Gove 2 and 1

Singles
P McEvoy halved with J Sigel
JC Davies lost to D Clarke 8 and 7
J Buckley lost to S Hoch 9 and 7
IC Hutcheon lost to J Holtgrieve 6 and 4
B Marchbank beat M Peck 1 hole
G Godwin beat G Moody 3 and 2
MJ Kelley beat D Fischesser 3 and 2
A Brodie lost to M Gove 3 and 2

Second Day – Foursomes
Godwin & Brand lost to Hoch & Sigel 4 and 3
McEvoy & Marchbank beat Fischesser & Holtgrieve
2 and 1
Kelley & Hutcheon halved with West & Sutton
Carslaw & Brodie halved with Clarke & Peck
Singles
McEvoy lost to Hoch 3 and 1
Brand lost to Clarke 2 and 1
Godwin lost to Gove 3 and 2
Hutcheon lost to Peck 2 and 1
Brodie beat West 3 and 2
Kelley lost to Moody 3 and 2
Marchbank lost to Sutton 3 and 1
Carslaw lost to Sigel 2 and 1

1981 *Cypress Point, CA* Aug 28–29
Result: USA 15, GBI 9
Captains: J Gabrielsen (USA), R Foster (GBI)
First Day – Foursomes
Sutton & Sigel lost to Walton & Rafferty 4 and 2
Holtgrieve & Fuhrer beat Chapman & McEvoy 1 hole
Lewis & von Tacky beat Deeble & Hutcheon 2 and 1
Commans & Pavin beat Evans & Way 5 and 4
Singles
H Sutton beat R Rafferty 3 and 1
J Rassett beat CR Dalgleish 1 hole
R Commans lost to P Walton 1 hole
B Lewis lost to R Chapman 2 and 1
J Mudd beat G Godwin 1 hole
C Pavin beat IC Hutcheon 4 and 3
D von Tacky lost to P Way 3 and 1
J Sigel beat P McEvoy 4 and 2
Second Day – Foursomes
Sutton & Sigel lost to Chapman & Way 1 hole
Holtgrieve & Fuhrer lost to Walton & Rafferty
6 and 4
Lewis & von Tacky lost to Evans & Dalgleish
3 and 2
Rassett & Mudd beat Hutcheon & Godwin 5 and 4
Singles
Sutton lost to Chapman 1 hole
Holtgrieve beat Rafferty 2 and 1
Fuhrer beat Walton 4 and 3
Sigel beat Way 6 and 5
Mudd beat Dalgleish 7 and 5
Commans halved with Godwin
Rassett beat Deeble 4 and 3
Pavin halved with Evans

1983 *Royal Liverpool, Hoylake* May 25–26
Result: USA 13½, GBI 10½
Captains: CW Green (GBI), J Sigel (USA)
First Day – Foursomes
Macgregor & Walton beat Sigel & Fehr 3 and 2
Keppler & Pierse lost to Wood & Faxon 3 and 1
Lewis & Thompson lost to Lewis & Holtgrieve
7 and 6
Mann & Oldcorn beat Hoffer & Tentis 5 and 4
Singles
P Walton beat J Sigel 1 hole
SD Keppler lost to R Fehr 1 hole
G Macgregor halved with W Wood
DG Carrick lost to B Faxon 3 and 1
A Oldcorn beat B Tuten 4 and 3
P Parkin beat N Crosby 5 and 4
AD Pierse lost to B Lewis jr 3 and 1
LS Mann lost to J Holtgrieve 6 and 5

Second Day – Foursomes
Macgregor & Walton lost to Crosby & Hoffer 2 holes
Parkin & Thompson beat Faxon & Wood 1 hole
Mann & Oldcorn beat Lewis & Holtgrieve 1 hole
Keppler & Pierse halved with Sigel & Fehr
Singles
Walton beat Wood 2 and 1
Parkin lost to Faxon 3 and 2
Macgregor lost to Fehr 2 and 1
Thompson lost to Tuten 3 and 2
Mann halved with Tentis
Keppler lost to Lewis 6 and 5
Oldcorn beat Holtgrieve 3 and 2
Carrick lost to Sigel 3 and 2

1985 *Pine Valley, NJ* Aug 21–22
Result: USA 13, GBI 11
Captains: J Sigel (USA), CW Green (GBI)
First Day – Foursomes
Verplank & Sigel beat Montgomerie & Macgregor
1 hole
Waldorf & Randolph lost to Hawksworth & McGimpsey
4 and 3
Sonnier & Haas lost to Baker & McEvoy 6 and 5
Podolak & Love halved with Bloice & Stephen
Singles
S Verplank beat G McGimpsey 2 and 1
S Randolph beat P Mayo 5 and 4
R Sonnier halved with J Hawksworth
J Sigel beat CS Montgomerie 5 and 4
B Lewis lost to P McEvoy 2 and 1
C Burroughs lost to G Macgregor 2 holes
D Waldorf beat D Gilford 4 and 2
J Haas lost to AR Stephen 2 and 1
Second Day – Foursomes
Verplank & Sigel halved with Mayo & Montgomerie
Randolph & Haas beat Hawksworth & McGimpsey
3 and 2
Lewis & Burroughs beat Baker & McEvoy 2 and 1
Podolak & Love beat Bloice & Stephen 3 and 2
Singles
Randolph halved with McGimpsey
Verplank beat Montgomerie 1 hole
Sigel lost to Hawksworth 4 and 3
Love beat McEvoy 5 and 3
Sonnier beat Baker 5 and 4
Burroughs lost to Macgregor 3 and 2
Lewis beat Bloice 4 and 3
Waldorf lost to Stephen 2 and 1

1987 *Sunningdale Old* May 27–28
Result: USA 16½, GBI 7½
Captains: GC Marks (GBI), F Ridley (USA)
First Day – Foursomes
Montgomerie & Shaw lost to Alexander & Mayfair
5 and 4
Currey & Mayo lost to Kite & Mattice 2 and 1
Macgregor & Robinson lost to Lewis & Loeffler 2 and 1
McHenry & Girvan lost to Sigel & Andrade 3 and 2
Singles
D Currey beat B Alexander 2 holes
J Robinson lost to B Andrade 7 and 5
CS Montgomerie beat J Sorenson 3 and 2
R Eggo lost to J Sigel 3 and 2
J McHenry lost to B Montgomery 1 hole
P Girvan lost to B Lewis 3 and 2
DG Carrick lost to B Mayfair 2 holes
G Shaw beat C Kite 1 hole

1987 *continued*

Second Day – Foursomes
Currey & Carrick lost to Lewis & Loeffler 4 and 3
Montgomerie & Shaw lost to Kite & Mattice 5 and 3
Mayo & Macgregor lost to Sorenson & Montgomery 4 and 3
McHenry & Robinson beat Sigel & Andrade 4 and 2

Singles
Currey lost to Alexander 5 and 4
Montgomerie beat Andrade 4 and 2
McHenry beat Loeffler 3 and 2
Shaw halved with Sorenson
Robinson beat Mattice 1 hole
Carrick lost to Lewis 3 and 2
Eggo lost to Mayfair 1 hole
Girvan lost to Sigel 6 and 5

1989 *Peachtree, GA* Aug 16–17
Result: GBI 12½, USA 11½
Captains: F Ridley (USA), GC Marks (GBI)

First Day – Foursomes
Gamez & Martin beat Claydon & Prosser 3 and 2
Yates & Mickelson halved with Dodd & McGimpsey
Lesher & Sigel lost to McEvoy & O'Connell 6 and 5
Eger & Johnson lost to Milligan & Hare 2 and 1

Singles
R Gamez beat JW Milligan 7 and 6
D Martin lost to R Claydon 5 and 4
E Meeks halved with SC Dodd
R Howe lost to E O'Connell 5 and 4
D Yates lost to P McEvoy 2 and 1
P Mickelson beat G McGimpsey 4 and 2
G Lesher lost to C Cassells 1 hole
J Sigel halved with RN Roderick

Second Day – Foursomes
Gamez & Martin halved with McEvoy & O'Connell
Sigel & Lesher lost to Claydon & Cassells 3 and 2
Eger & Johnson lost to Milligan & Hare 2 and 1
Mickelson & Yates lost to McGimpsey & Dodd 2 and 1

Singles
Gamez beat Dodd 1 hole
Martin halved with Hare
Lesher beat Claydon 3 and 2
Yates beat McEvoy 4 and 3
Mickelson halved with O'Connell
Eger beat Roderick 4 and 2
Johnson beat Cassells 4 and 2
Sigel halved with Milligan

1991 *Portmarnock, Dublin, Ireland* Sept 5–6
Result: USA 14, GBI 10
Captains: G Macgregor (GBI),
*   JR Gabrielsen (USA)*

First Day – Foursomes
Milligan & Hay lost to Mickelson & May 5 and 3
Payne & Evans lost to Duval & Sposa 1 hole
McGimpsey & Willison lost to Voges & Eger 1 hole
McGinley & Harrington lost to Sigel & Doyle 2 and 1

Singles
A Coltart lost to P Mickelson 4 and 3
J Payne beat F Langham 2 and 1
G Evans beat D Duval 2 and 1
R Willison lost to B May 2 and 1
G McGimpsey beat M Sposa 1 hole
P McGinley lost to A Doyle 6 and 4
G Hay beat T Scherrer 1 hole
L White lost to J Sigel 4 and 3

Second Day – Foursomes
Milligan & McGimpsey beat Voges & Eger 2 and 1
Payne & Willison lost to Duval & Sposa 1 hole
Evans & Coltart beat Langham & Scherrer 4 and 3
White & McGinley beat Mickelson & May 1 hole

Singles
Milligan lost to Mickelson 1 hole
Payne beat Doyle 3 and 1
Evans lost to Langham 4 and 2
Coltart beat Sigel 1 hole
Willison beat Scherrer 3 and 2
Harrington lost to Eger 3 and 2
McGimpsey lost to May 4 and 3
Hay lost to Voges 3 and 1

1993 *Interlachen, Edina, MN* Aug 18–19
Result: USA 19, GBI 5
Captains: M Giles III (USA), G Macgregor (GBI)

First Day – Foursomes
Abandoned – rain & flooding

Singles
A Doyle beat I Pyman 1 hole
D Berganio lost to M Stanford 3 and 2
J Sigel lost to D Robertson 3 and 2
K Mitchum halved with S Cage
T Herron beat P Harrington 1 hole
D Yates beat P Page 2 and 1
T Demsey beat R Russell 2 and 1
J Leonard beat R Burns 4 and 3
B Gay lost to V Phillips 2 and 1
J Harris beat B Dredge 4 and 3

Second Day – Foursomes
Doyle & Leonard beat Pyman & Cage 4 and 3
Berganio & Demsey beat Stanford & Harrington 3 and 2
Sigel & Mitchum beat Dredge & Phillips 3 and 2
Harris & Herron beat Russell & Robertson 1 hole

Singles
Doyle beat Robertson 4 and 3
Harris beat Pyman 3 and 2
Yates beat Cage 2 and 1
Gay halved with Harrington
Sigel beat Page 5 and 4
Herron beat Phillips 3 and 2
Mitchum beat Russell 4 and 2
Berganio lost to Burns 1 hole
Demsey beat Dredge 3 and 2
Leonard beat Stanford 5 and 4

1995 *Royal Porthcawl, Wales* Sept 9–10
Result: GBI 14, USA 10
Captains: C Brown (GBI),
*   AD Gray jr (USA)*

First Day – Foursomes
Sherry & Gallacher lost to Harris & Woods 4 and 3
Foster & Howell halved with Bratton & Riley
Rankin & Howard lost to Begay & Jackson 4 and 3
Harrington & Fanagan beat Cox & Kuehne 5 and 3

Singles
G Sherry beat N Begay 3 and 2
L James lost to K Cox 1 hole
M Foster beat B Marucci 4 and 3
S Gallacher beat T Jackson 4 and 3
P Harrington beat J Courville jr 2 holes
B Howard halved with A Bratton
G Rankin lost to J Harris 1 hole
GP Wolstenholme beat T Woods 1 hole

Second Day – Foursomes
Sherry & Gallacher lost to Bratton & Riley 4 and 2
Howell & Foster beat Cox & Kuehne 3 and 2
Wolstenholme & James lost to Marucci & Courville
6 and 5
Harrington & Fanagan beat Harris & Woods 2 and 1

Singles
Sherry beat Riley 2 holes
Howell beat Begay 2 and 1
Gallacher beat Kuehne 3 and 2
Fanagan beat Courville 3 and 2
Howard halved with Jackson
Foster halved with Marucci
Harrington lost to Harris 3 and 2
Wolstenholme lost to Woods 4 and 3

1997 *Quaker Ridge, NY* Aug 9–10
Result: USA 18, GBI 6
Captains: AD Gray jr (USA), C Brown (GBI)
First Day – Foursomes
Howard & Young lost to Elder & Kribel 4 and 3
Rose & Brooks lost to Courville & Marucci 5 and 4
Wolstenholme & Nolan lost to Gore & Harris 6 and 4
Coughlan & Park lost to Leen & Wollman 1 hole

Singles
S Young beat D Delcher 5 and 4
C Watson beat S Scott 1 hole
B Howard lost to B Elder 5 and 4
J Rose beat J Kribel 1 hole
K Nolan lost to R Leen 3 and 2
G Rankin lost to J Gore 3 and 2
R Coughlan halved with C Wollman
GP Wolstenholme lost to J Harris 1 hole

Second Day – Foursomes
Young & Watson lost to Harris & Elder 3 and 2
Howard & Rankin lost to Courville & Marucci 5 and 4
Coughlan & Park lost to Delcher & Scott 1 hole
Wolstenholme & Rose beat Leen & Wollman 2 and 1

Singles
Young beat Kribel 2 and 1
Watson halved with Gore
Rose lost to Courville 3 and 2
Nolan lost to Elder 2 and 1
Brooks lost to Harris 6 and 5
Park lost to Marucci 4 and 3
Wolstenholme lost to Delcher 2 and 1
Coughlan lost to Scott 2 and 1

1999 *Nairn, Scotland* Sept 11–12
Result: GBI 15, USA 9
Captains: P McEvoy (GBI), D Yates jr (USA)
First Day – Foursomes
Rankin & Storm lost to Haas & Miller 1 hole
Casey & Donald beat Byrd & Scott 5 and 3
Gribben & Kelly lost to Gossett & Jackson 3 and 1
Rowe & Wolstenholme beat Kuchar & Molder 1 hole

Singles
G Rankin lost to E Loar 4 and 3
L Donald beat T McKnight 4 and 3
G Storm lost to H Haas 5 and 3
P Casey beat S Scott 4 and 3
D Patrick lost to J Byrd 6 and 5
S Dyson halved with D Gossett
P Gribben halved with B Molder
L Kelly lost to T Jackson 3 and 1

Second Day – Foursomes
Rankin & Storm beat Loar & McKnight 4 and 3
Dyson & Gribben lost to Haas & Miller 1 hole
Casey & Donald beat Gossett & Jackson 1 hole
Rowe & Wolstenholme beat Kuchar & Molder 4 and 3

Singles
Rankin beat Scott 1 hole
Dyson lost to Loar 5 and 4
Casey beat Miller 3 and 2
Storm beat Byrd 1 hole
Donald beat Molder 3 and 2
Rowe beat Kuchar 1 hole
Gribben beat Haas 3 and 2
Wolstenholme beat Gossett 1 hole

2001 *Ocean Forest, Sea Island, GA* Aug 11–12
Result: GBI 15, USA 9
Captains: D Yates jr (USA), P McEvoy (GBI)
First Day – Foursomes
D Green & DJ Trahan lost to S O'Hara &
GP Wolstenholme 5 and 3
N Cassini & L Glover beat L Donald & N Dougherty
4 and 3
D Eger & B Molder halved with J Elson & R McEvoy
J Driscoll & J Quinney lost to G McDowell & M Hoey
3 and 1

Singles
E Compton beat G Wolstenholme 3 and 2
DJ Trahan beat S O'Hara 2 and 1
J Driscoll lost to N Dougherty 2 and 1
N Cassini beat N Edwards 5 and 4
J Harris lost to M Warren 5 and 4
J Quinney lost to L Donald 3 and 2
B Molder beat G McDowell 2 and 1
L Glover beat M Hoey 1 hole

Second Day – Foursomes
E Compton & J Harris lost to L Donald & N Dougherty
3 and 2
N Cassini & L Glover lost to G McDowell & M Hoey
2 and 1
D Eger & B Molder beat S O'Hara & M Warren 7 and 6
D Green & DJ Trahan lost to J Elson & R McEvoy
1 hole

Singles
L Glover lost to L Donald 3 and 2
J Harris lost to S O'Hara 4 and 3
DJ Trahan lost to N Dougherty 1 hole
J Driscoll lost to M Warren 2 and 1
B Molder beat G McDowell 1 hole
D Green lost to M Hoey 1 hole
E Compton halved with J Elson
N Cassini lost to GP Wolstenholme 4 and 3

2003 *Ganton, Yorkshire* Sept 6–7
Result: GBI 12½, USA 11½
Captains: Garth McGimpsey (GBI),
Bob Lewis (USA)
First Day – Foursomes
GP Wolstenholme & M Skelton lost to W Haas
& T Kuehne 2 and 1
S Wilson & D Inglis beat L Williams & G Zahringer
2 holes
NB Edwards & S Manley beat C Nallen & R Moore
3 and 2
N Fox & C Moriarty beat A Rubinson & C Wittenberg
4 and 2

2003 *continued*

Singles
GP Wolstenholme lost to W Haas 1 hole
O Wilson halved with T Kuehne
D Inglis lost to B Mackenzie 3 and 2
S Wilson halved with M Hendrix
NB Edwards beat G Zahringer 3 and 2
C Moriarty lost to C Nallen 1 hole
N Fox lost to A Rubinson 3 and 2
G Gordon lost to C Wittenberg 5 and 4

Second Day – Foursomes
GP Wolstenholme & O Wilson beat W Haas & T Kuehne
 5 and 4
N Fox & C Moriarty lost to B Mackenzie & M Hendrix
 6 and 5
S Wilson & D Inglis halved with C Wittenberg &
 A Rubinson
NB Edwards & S Manley halved with L Williams &
 G Zahringer

Singles
O Wilson beat W Haas 1 hole
GP Wolstenholme beat C Wittenberg 3 and 2
M Skelton beat A Rubinson 3 and 2
C Moriarty lost to B Mackenzie 3 and 1
S Wilson lost to M Hendrix 5 and 4
D Inglis beat R Moore 4 and 3
NB Edwards halved with L Williams
S Manley beat T Kuehne 3 and 2

2005 *Chicago GC, Wheaton, IL* Aug 13–14

Result: USA 12½, GBI 11½
Captains: Bob Lewis (USA), Garth McGimpsey (GBI)

First Day – Foursomes
A Kim & B Harman halved with NB Edwards & R Davies
L Williams & M Every beat G Lockerbie & R Dinwiddie
 1 hole
J Overton & M Putnam beat O Fisher & M Richardson
 2 and 1
K Reifers & B Hurley lost to R Ramsay & L Saltman
 4 and 3

Singles
M Every lost to R Davies 4 and 3
A Kim beat G Lockerbie 6 and 5
L Overton beat NB Edwards 5 and 4
M Putnam lost to O Fisher 2 holes
N Thompson lost to M Richardson 5 and 4
B Hurley lost to L Saltman 1 hole
J Holmes beat G Wolstenholme 1 hole
L Williams beat B McElhinney 2 and 1

Second Day – Foursomes
Kim & Harman beat Ramsay & Saltman 4 and 2
Every & Williams lost to Davies & Edwards 2 and 1
Thompson & Holmes beat Fisher & Richardson 2 and 1
Putnam & Overton lost to Lockerbie & Dinwiddie 5 and 3

Singles
Kim lost to Wolstenholme 1 hole
Harman beat Davies 6 and 5
Putnam halved with Fisher
Every halved with Dinwiddie
Holmes lost to Richardson 5 and 4
Reifers lost to Saltman 1 hole
Overton beat Edwards 1 hole
Williams beat Lockerbie 4 and 3

Walker Cup – INDIVIDUAL RECORDS

Notes: Bold type indicates captain; in brackets, did not play
 † indicates players who have also played in the Ryder Cup

Great Britain and Ireland

Name		Year	Played	Won	Lost	Halved
MF Attenborough	ENG	1967	2	0	2	0
CC Aylmer	ENG	1922	2	1	1	0
†P Baker	ENG	1985	3	2	1	0
JB Beck	ENG	1928-(38)-(47)	1	0	1	0
PJ Benka	ENG	1969	4	2	1	1
HG Bentley	ENG	1934-36-38	4	0	2	2
DA Blair	SCO	1955-61	4	1	3	0
C Bloice	SCO	1985	3	0	2	1
MF Bonallack	ENG	1957-59-61-63-65-67-**69-71-73**	25	8	14	3
†G Brand jr	SCO	1979	3	0	3	0
OC Bristowe	ENG	(1923)-24	1	0	1	0
A Brodie	SCO	1977-79	8	5	2	1
A Brooks	SCO	1969	3	2	0	1
M Brooks	SCO	1997	2	0	2	0
C Brown	WAL	**1995-(97)**	0	0	0	0
Hon WGE Brownlow	ENG	1926	2	0	2	0
J Bruen	IRL	1938-49-51	5	0	4	1
JA Buckley	WAL	1979	1	0	1	0
J Burke	IRL	1932	2	0	1	1
R Burns	IRL	1993	2	1	1	0
AF Bussell	SCO	1957	2	1	1	0
S Cage	ENG	1993	3	0	2	1
I Caldwell	ENG	1951-55	4	1	2	1

Name		Year	Played	Won	Lost	Halved
W Campbell	SCO	1930	2	0	2	0
JB Carr	IRL	1947-49-51-53-55-57-59-61-63-**(65)-67**	20	5	14	1
RJ Carr	IRL	1971	4	3	0	1
DG Carrick	SCO	1983-87	5	0	5	0
IA Carslaw	SCO	1979	3	1	1	1
P Casey	ENG	1999	4	4	0	0
C Cassells	ENG	1989	3	2	1	0
JR Cater	SCO	1955	1	0	1	0
J Caven	SCO	1922	2	0	2	0
BHG Chapman	ENG	1961	1	0	1	0
R Chapman	ENG	1981	4	3	1	0
MJ Christmas	ENG	1961-63	3	1	2	0
†CA Clark	ENG	1965	4	2	0	2
GJ Clark	ENG	1965	1	0	1	0
†HK Clark	ENG	1973	3	1	1	1
R Claydon	ENG	1989	4	2	2	0
†A Coltart	SCO	1991	3	2	1	0
GB Cosh	SCO	1965	4	3	1	0
R Coughlan	IRL	1997	4	0	3	1
T Craddock	IRL	1967-69	6	2	3	1
LG Crawley	ENG	1932-34-38-47	6	3	3	0
B Critchley	ENG	1969	4	1	1	2
D Curry	ENG	1987	4	1	3	0
CR Dalgleish	SCO	1981	3	1	2	0
B Darwin	ENG	1922	2	1	1	0
JC Davies	ENG	1973-75-77-79	13	3	8	2
R Davies	WAL	2005	4	2	1	1
P Deeble	ENG	1977-81	5	1	4	0
FWG Deighton	SCO	(1951)-57	2	0	2	0
R Dinwiddie	ENG	2005	2	1	1	0
SC Dodd	WAL	1989	4	1	1	2
L Donald	ENG	1999-01	8	7	1	0
N Dougherty	ENG	2001	4	3	1	0
B Dredge	WAL	1993	3	0	3	0
†NV Drew	IRL	1953	1	0	1	0
AA Duncan	WAL	**(1953)**	0	0	0	0
JM Dykes	SCO	1936	2	0	1	1
S Dyson	ENG	1999	3	0	2	1
NB Edwards	WAL	2001-03-05	9	3	3	3
R Eggo	ENG	1987	2	0	2	0
J Elson	ENG	2001	3	1	0	2
D Evans	WAL	1981	3	1	1	1
G Evans	ENG	1991	4	2	2	0
RC Ewing	IRL	1936-38-47-49-51-55	10	1	7	2
GRD Eyles	ENG	1975	4	2	2	0
J Fanagan	IRL	1995	3	3	0	0
EW Fiddian	ENG	1932-34	4	0	4	0
O Fisher	ENG	2005	4	2	2	1
J de Forest	ENG	1932	1	0	1	0
M Foster	ENG	1995	4	2	0	2
R Foster	ENG	1965-67-69-71-73-**(79)-(81)**	17	2	13	2
N Fox	IRL	2003	3	1	2	0
DW Frame	ENG	1961	1	0	1	0
S Gallacher	SCO	1995	4	2	2	0
†D Gilford	ENG	1985	1	0	1	0
P Girvan	SCO	1987	3	0	3	0
G Godwin	ENG	1979-81	7	2	4	1
G Gordon	SCO	2003	1	0	1	0
CW Green	SCO	1963-69-71-73-75-**(83)-(85)**	17	4	10	3
P Gribben	IRL	1999	4	1	2	1
RH Hardman	ENG	1928	1	0	1	0
A Hare	ENG	1989	3	2	2	0
†P Harrington	IRL	1991-93-95	9	3	5	1
R Harris	SCO	**(1922)-23-26**	4	1	3	0
RW Hartley	ENG	1930-32	4	0	4	0
WL Hartley	ENG	1932	2	0	2	0
J Hawksworth	ENG	1985	4	2	2	0
G Hay	SCO	1991	3	1	2	0
P Hedges	ENG	1973-75	5	0	2	3
CO Hezlet	IRL	1924-26-28	6	0	5	1

Walker Cup Individual Records *continued*

Name		Year	Played	Won	Lost	Halved
GA Hill	ENG	1936-(55)	2	0	1	1
M Hoey	IRL	2001	4	3	1	0
Sir EWE Holderness	ENG	1923-26-30	6	2	4	0
TWB Homer	ENG	1973	3	0	3	0
‡CVL Hooman	ENG	1922-23	3	†1	2	†0
WL Hope	SCO	1923-24-28	5	1	4	0
DB Howard	SCO	1995-97	6	0	4	2
D Howell	ENG	1995	3	2	0	1
G Huddy	ENG	1961	1	0	1	0
W Humphreys	ENG	1971	3	2	1	0
IC Hutcheon	SCO	1975-77-79-81	15	5	8	2
D Inglis	SCO	2003	4	2	1	1
RR Jack	SCO	1957-59	4	2	2	0
L James	ENG	1995	2	0	2	0
†M James	ENG	1975	4	3	1	0
A Jamieson jr	SCO	1926	2	1	1	0
MJ Kelley	ENG	1977-79	7	3	3	1
L Kelly	SCO	1999	2	0	2	0
SD Keppler	ENG	1983	4	0	3	1
†MG King	ENG	1969-73	7	1	5	1
AT Kyle	SCO	1938-47-51	5	2	3	0
DH Kyle	SCO	1924	1	0	1	0
JA Lang	SCO	(1930)	0	0	0	0
JDA Langley	ENG	1936-51-53	6	0	5	1
CD Lawrie	SCO	(1961)-(63)	0	0	0	0
ME Lewis	ENG	1983	1	0	1	0
G Lockerbie	ENG	2005	4	1	3	0
PB Lucas	ENG	(1936)-47-(49)	2	1	1	0
MSR Lunt	ENG	1959-61-63-65	11	2	8	1
†AWB Lyle	SCO	1977	3	0	3	0
AR McCallum	SCO	1928	1	0	1	0
SM McCready	IRL	1949-51	3	0	3	0
JS Macdonald	SCO	1971	3	1	1	1
G McDowell	IRL	2001	4	2	2	0
B McElhinney	IRL	2005	1	0	1	0
P McEvoy	ENG	1977-79-81-85-89-(99)-(01)	18	5	11	2
R McEvoy	ENG	2001	2	1	0	1
G McGimpsey	IRL	1985-89-91-(03)-(05)	11	4	5	2
P McGinley	IRL	1991	3	1	2	0
G Macgregor	SCO	1971-75-83-85-87-(91)-(93)	14	5	8	1
RC MacGregor	SCO	1953	2	0	2	0
J McHenry	IRL	1987	4	2	2	0
P McKellar	SCO	1977	1	0	1	0
WW Mackenzie	SCO	1922-23	3	1	2	0
SL McKinlay	SCO	1934	2	0	2	0
J McLean	SCO	1934-36	4	1	3	0
EA McRuvie	SCO	1932-34	4	1	2	1
JFD Madeley	IRL	1963	2	0	1	1
S Manley	WAL	2003	3	2	0	1
LS Mann	SCO	1983	4	2	1	1
B Marchbank	SCO	1979	4	2	2	0
GC Marks	ENG	1969-71-(87)-(89)	6	2	4	0
DM Marsh	ENG	71-(73)-(75)	3	2	1	0
GNC Martin	IRL	1928	1	0	1	0
S Martin	SCO	1977	4	2	2	0
P Mayo	WAL	1985-87	4	0	3	1
GH Micklem	ENG	1947-49-53-55-(57)-(59)	6	1	5	0
DJ Millensted	ENG	1967	2	1	1	0
JW Milligan	SCO	1989-91	7	3	3	1
EB Millward	ENG	(1949)-55	2	0	2	0
WTG Milne	SCO	1973	4	2	2	0
†CS Montgomerie	SCO	1985-87	8	2	5	1
JL Morgan	WAL	1951-53-55	6	2	4	0
C Moriarty	IRL	2003	4	1	3	0
P Mulcare	IRL	1975	3	2	1	0
GH Murray	SCO	1977	2	1	1	0
SWT Murray	SCO	1963	4	2	2	0
WA Murray	SCO	1923-24-(26)	4	1	3	0

‡In 1922 Hooman beat Sweetser at the 37th – on all other occasions halved matches have counted as such.

Name		Year	Played	Won	Lost	Halved
K Nolan	IRL	1997	3	0	3	0
E O'Connell	IRL	1989	4	2	0	2
S O'Hara	SCO	2001	4	2	2	0
A Oldcorn	ENG	1983	4	4	0	0
†PA Oosterhuis	ENG	1967	4	1	2	1
R Oppenheimer	ENG	(1951)	0	0	0	0
P Page	ENG	1993	2	0	2	0
D Park	WAL	1997	3	0	3	0
P Parkin	WAL	1983	3	2	1	0
D Patrick	SCO	1999	1	0	1	0
J Payne	ENG	1991	4	2	2	0
JJF Pennink	ENG	1938	2	1	1	0
TP Perkins	ENG	1928	2	0	2	0
GB Peters	SCO	1936-38	4	2	1	1
V Phillips	ENG	1993	3	1	2	0
AD Pierse	IRL	1983	3	0	2	1
AH Perowne	ENG	1949-53-59	4	0	4	0
AK Pirie	SCO	1967	3	0	2	1
MA Poxon	ENG	1975	2	0	2	0
D Prosser	ENG	1989	1	0	1	2
I Pyman	ENG	1993	3	0	3	0
†R Rafferty	IRL	1981	4	2	2	0
R Ramsay	SCO	2005	2	1	1	0
G Rankin	SCO	1995-97-99	8	2	6	0
M Richardson	ENG	2005	4	2	2	0
D Robertson	SCO	1993	3	1	2	0
J Robinson	ENG	1987	4	2	2	0
RN Roderick	WAL	1989	2	0	1	1
J Rose	ENG	1997	4	2	2	0
P Rowe	ENG	1999	3	3	0	0
R Russell	SCO	1993	3	0	3	0
AC Saddler	SCO	1963-65-67-(**77**)	10	3	5	2
L Saltman	SCO	2005	4	3	1	0
Hon M Scott	ENG	1924-**34**	4	2	2	0
R Scott, jr	SCO	1924	1	1	0	0
PF Scrutton	ENG	1955-57	3	0	3	0
DN Sewell	ENG	1957-59	4	1	3	0
RDBM Shade	SCO	1961-63-65-67	14	6	6	2
G Shaw	SCO	1987	4	1	2	1
DB Sheahan	IRL	1963	4	2	2	0
AE Shepperson	ENG	1957-59	3	1	1	1
G Sherry	SCO	1995	4	2	2	0
AF Simpson	SCO	(1926)	0	0	0	0
M Skelton	ENG	2003	2	1	1	0
JN Smith	SCO	1930	2	0	2	0
WD Smith	SCO	1959	1	0	1	0
M Stanford	ENG	1993	3	1	2	0
AR Stephen	SCO	1985	4	2	1	1
EF Storey	ENG	1924-26-28	6	1	5	0
G Storm	ENG	1999	4	2	2	0
JA Stout	ENG	1930-32	4	0	3	1
C Stowe	ENG	1938-47	4	2	2	0
HB Stuart	SCO	1971-73-75	10	4	6	0
A Thirlwell	ENG	1957	1	0	1	0
KG Thom	ENG	1949	2	0	2	0
MS Thompson	ENG	1983	3	1	2	0
H Thomson	SCO	1936-38	4	2	2	0
CJH Tolley	ENG	1922-23-**24**-26-30-34	12	4	8	0
TA Torrance	SCO	1924-28-30-**32**-34	9	3	5	1
WB Torrance	SCO	1922	2	0	2	0
†PM Townsend	ENG	1965	4	3	1	0
LP Tupling	ENG	1969	2	1	1	0
W Tweddell	ENG	**1928**-(36)	2	0	2	0
J Walker	SCO	1961	2	0	2	0
†P Walton	IRL	1981-83	8	6	2	0
M Warren	SCO	2001	3	2	1	0
C Watson	SCO	1997	3	1	1	1
†P Way	ENG	1981	4	2	2	0
RH Wethered	ENG	1922-23-26-**30**-34	9	5	3	1
L White	ENG	1991	2	1	1	0

Walker Cup Individual Records *continued*

Name		Year	Played	Won	Lost	Halved
RJ White	ENG	1947-49-51-53-55	10	6	3	1
R Willison	ENG	1991	4	1	3	0
J Wilson	SCO	1923	2	2	0	0
JC Wilson	SCO	1947-53	4	0	4	0
O Wilson	ENG	2003	3	2	0	1
S Wilson	SCO	2003	4	1	1	2
GB Wolstenholme	ENG	1957-59	4	1	2	1
GP Wolstenholme	ENG	1995-97-99-01-03-05	19	10	9	0
S Young	SCO	1997	4	2	2	0

United States of America

Name	Year	Played	Won	Lost	Halved
†TD Aaron	1959	2	1	1	0
B Alexander	1987	3	2	1	0
DC Allen	1965-67	6	0	4	2
B Andrade	1987	4	2	2	0
ES Andrews	1961	1	1	0	0
D Ballenger	1973	1	1	0	0
R Baxter, jr	1957	2	2	0	0
N Begay III	1995	3	1	2	0
DR Beman	1959-61-63-65	11	7	2	2
D Berganio	1993	3	1	2	0
RE Billows	1938-49	4	2	2	0
SE Bishop	1947-49	3	2	1	0
AS Blum	1957	1	0	1	0
J Bohmann	1969	3	1	2	0
M Brannan	1977	3	1	2	0
A Bratton	1995	3	1	0	2
GF Burns	1975	3	2	1	0
C Burroughs	1985	3	1	2	0
J Byrd	1999	3	1	2	0
AE Campbell	1936	2	2	0	0
JE Campbell	1957	1	0	1	0
WC Campbell	1951-53-(**55**)-57-65-67-71-75	18	11	4	3
N Cassini	2001	4	2	2	0
RJ Cerrudo	1967	4	1	1	2
RD Chapman	1947-51-53	5	3	2	0
D Cherry	1953-55-61	5	5	0	0
D Clarke	1979	3	2	0	1
RE Cochran	1961	1	1	0	0
CR Coe	1949-51-53-(**57**)-**59**-61-63	13	7	4	2
R Commans	1981	3	1	1	1
E Compton	2001	3	1	1	1
JW Conrad	1955	2	1	1	0
J Courville jr	1995-97	6	4	2	0
K Cox	1995	3	1	2	0
N Crosby	1983	2	1	1	0
BH Cudd	1955	2	2	0	0
RD Davies	1963	2	0	2	0
JW Dawson	1949	2	2	0	0
D Delcher	1997	3	2	1	0
T Demsey	1993	3	3	0	0
RB Dickson	1967	3	3	0	0
A Doyle	1991-93	6	5	1	0
J Driscoll	2001	3	0	3	0
GT Dunlap jr	1932-34-36	5	3	1	1
†D Duval	1991	3	2	1	0
D Edwards	1973	4	4	0	0
HC Egan	1934	1	1	0	0
D Eger	1991-01	5	3	1	1
HC Eger	1989	3	1	2	0
D Eichelberger	1965	3	1	2	0
B Elder	1997	4	4	0	0
J Ellis	1973	3	2	1	0

Name	Year	Played	Won	Lost	Halved
W Emery	1936	2	1	0	1
C Evans jr	1922-24-28	5	3	2	0
M Every	2005	4	1	2	1
J Farquhar	1971	3	1	2	0
†B Faxon	1983	4	3	1	0
R Fehr	1983	4	2	1	1
JW Fischer	1934-36-38-(65)	4	3	0	1
D Fischesser	1979	3	1	2	0
MA Fleckman	1967	2	0	2	0
B Fleisher	1969	4	0	2	2
J Fought	1977	4	4	0	0
WC Fownes jr	**1922-24**	3	1	2	0
F Fuhrer	1981	3	2	1	0
JR Gabrielsen	1977-(81)-(91)	3	1	2	0
R Gamez	1989	4	3	0	1
RA Gardner	1922-**23-24-26**	8	6	2	0
RW Gardner	1961-63	5	4	0	1
B Gay	1993	2	0	1	1
M Giles	1969-71-73-75	15	8	2	5
HL Givan	1936	1	0	0	1
L Glover	2001	4	2	2	0
JG Goodman	1934-36-38	6	4	2	0
J Gore	1997	3	2	0	1
D Gossett	1999	4	1	2	1
M Gove	1979	3	2	1	0
J Grace	1975	3	2	1	0
JA Grant	1967	2	2	0	0
AD Gray jr	1963-65-67-(95)-(97)	12	5	6	1
D Green	2001	3	0	3	0
JP Guilford	1922-24-26	6	4	2	0
W Gunn	1926-28	4	4	0	0
†F Haas jr	1938	2	0	2	0
H Haas	1999	4	3	1	0
†J Haas	1975	3	3	0	0
J Haas	1985	3	1	2	0
W Haas	2003	4	2	2	0
G Hallberg	1977	3	1	2	0
GS Hamer jr	(1947)	0	0	0	0
B Harman	2005	3	2	0	1
J Harris	1993-95-97-01	14	10	4	0
LE Harris jr	1963	4	3	1	0
V Heafner	1977	3	3	0	0
M Hendrix	2003	3	2	0	1
SD Herron	1923	2	0	2	0
T Herron	1993	3	3	0	0
†S Hoch	1979	4	4	0	0
W Hoffer	1983	2	1	1	0
J Holmes	2005	3	2	1	0
J Holtgrieve	1979-81-83	10	6	4	0
JM Hopkins	1965	3	0	2	1
R Howe	1989	1	0	1	0
W Howell	1932	1	1	0	0
B Hurley	2005	2	0	2	0
W Hyndman	1957-59-61-69-71	9	6	1	2
J Inman	1969	2	2	0	0
JG Jackson	1953-55	3	3	0	0
T Jackson	1995-99	6	3	2	1
K Johnson	1989	3	1	2	0
HR Johnston	1923-24-28-30	6	5	1	0
RT Jones jr	1922-24-26-**28-30**	10	9	1	0
AF Kammer	1947	2	1	1	0
M Killian	1973	3	1	2	0
A Kim	2005	4	2	1	1
C Kite	1987	3	2	1	0
†TO Kite	1971	4	2	1	1
RE Knepper	(1922)	0	0	0	0
RW Knowles	1951	1	1	0	0
G Koch	1973-75	7	4	1	2
CR Kocsis	1938-49-57	5	2	2	1
J Kribel	1997	3	1	2	0

Walker Cup Individual Records *continued*

Name	Year	Played	Won	Lost	Halved
M Kuchar	1999	3	0	3	0
T Kuehne	1995-03	7	I	5	I
F Langham	1991	3	I	2	0
R Leen	1997	3	2	I	0
†J Leonard	1993	3	3	0	0
G Lesher	1989	4	I	3	0
B Lewis jr	1981-83-85-87-(03)-(05)	14	10	4	0
JW Lewis	1967	4	3	I	0
WL Little jr	1934	2	2	0	0
†GA Littler	1953	2	2	0	0
E Loar	1999	3	2	I	0
B Loeffler	1987	3	2	I	0
†D Love III	1985	3	2	0	I
B Mackenzie	2003	3	3	0	0
RR Mackenzie	1926-28-30	6	5	I	0
MJ McCarthy jr	(1928)-32	I	I	0	0
BN McCormick	1949	I	I	0	0
T McKnight	1999	2	0	2	0
JB McHale	1949-51	3	2	0	I
MR Marston	1922-23-24-34	8	5	3	0
D Martin	1989	4	I	I	2
B Marucci	1995-97	6	4	I	I
L Mattiace	1987	3	2	I	0
R May	1991	4	3	I	0
B Mayfair	1987	3	3	0	0
E Meeks	1989	I	0	0	I
SN Melnyk	1969-71	7	3	3	I
†P Mickelson	1989-91	8	4	2	2
AL Miller	1969-71	8	4	3	I
J Miller	1999	3	2	I	0
L Miller	1977	4	4	0	0
K Mitchum	1993	3	2	0	I
DK Moe	1930-32	3	3	0	0
B Molder	1999-01	8	3	3	2
B Montgomery	1987	2	2	0	0
G Moody	1979	3	I	2	0
R Moore	2003	2	0	2	0
GT Moreland	1932-34	4	4	0	0
D Morey	1955-65	4	I	3	0
J Mudd	1981	3	3	0	0
†RJ Murphy	1967	4	I	2	I
C Nallen	2003	2	I	I	0
JF Neville	1923	I	0	I	0
†JW Nicklaus	1959-61	4	4	0	0
LW Oehmig	(1977)	0	0	0	0
FD Ouimet	1922-23-24-26-30-**32-34**-(36)-(38)-(47)-(49)	16	9	5	2
J Overton	2005	4	3	I	0
HD Paddock jr	1951	I	0	0	I
†J Pate	1975	4	0	4	0
WJ Patton	1955-57-59-63-65-(69)	14	11	3	0
†C Pavin	1981	3	2	0	I
M Peck	1979	3	I	I	I
M Pfeil	1973	4	2	I	I
M Podolak	1985	2	I	0	I
M Putnam	2005	4	I	2	I
SL Quick	1947	2	I	I	0
J Quinney	2001	2	0	2	0
S Randolph	1985	4	2	I	I
J Rassett	1981	3	3	0	0
K Reifers	2005	2	0	2	0
F Ridley	1977-(**87**)-(**89**)	3	2	I	0
RH Riegel	1947-49	4	4	0	0
C Riley	1995	3	I	I	I
H Robbins jr	1957	2	0	I	I
†W Rogers	1973	2	I	I	0
GV Rotan	1923	2	I	I	0
A Rubinson	2003	4	I	3	0
†EM Rudolph	1957	2	I	0	I

Name	Year	Played	Won	Lost	Halved
B Sander	1977	3	0	3	0
T Scherrer	1991	3	0	3	0
S Scott	1997-99	6	2	4	0
CH Seaver	1932	2	2	0	0
RL Siderowf	1969-73-75-77-(79)	14	4	8	2
J Sigel	1977-79-81-83-85-87-89-91-93	33	18	10	5
RH Sikes	1963	3	1	2	0
JB Simons	1971	2	0	2	0
†S Simpson	1977	3	3	0	0
CB Smith	1961-63	2	0	1	1
R Smith	1936-38	4	2	2	0
R Sonnier	1985	3	0	2	1
J Sorensen	1987	3	1	1	1
M Sposa	1991	3	2	1	0
†C Stadler	1975	3	3	0	0
FR Stranahan	1947-49-51	6	3	2	1
†C Strange	1975	4	3	0	1
†H Sutton	1979-81	7	2	4	1
‡JW Sweetser	1922-23-24-26-28-32-(67)-(73)	12	7	†4	*1
FM Taylor	1957-59-61	4	4	0	0
D Tentis	1983	2	0	1	1
N Thompson	2005	2	1	1	0
DJ Trahan	2001	4	1	3	0
RS Tufts	(1963)	0	0	0	0
WP Turnesa	1947-49-51	6	3	3	0
B Tuten	1983	2	1	1	0
EM Tutweiler	1965-67	6	5	1	0
ER Updegraff	1963-65-69-(75)	7	3	3	1
S Urzetta	1951-53	4	4	0	0
K Venturi	1953	2	2	0	0
S Verplank	1985	4	3	0	1
M Voges	1991	3	2	1	0
GJ Voigt	1930-32-36	5	2	2	1
G Von Elm	1926-28-30	6	4	1	1
D von Tacky	1981	3	1	2	0
†JL Wadkins	1969-71	7	3	4	0
D Waldorf	1985	3	1	2	0
EH Ward	1953-55-59	6	6	0	0
MH Ward	1938-47	4	2	2	0
M West	1973-79	6	2	3	1
J Westland	1932-34-53-(61)	5	3	0	2
HW Wettlaufer	1959	2	2	0	0
E White	1936	2	2	0	0
L Williams	2003-05	7	3	2	2
OF Willing	1923-24-30	4	4	0	0
JM Winters jr	(1971)	0	0	0	0
C Wittenberg	2003	4	1	3	0
C Wollman	1997	3	1	1	1
W Wood	1983	4	1	2	1
†T Woods	1995	4	2	2	0
FJ Wright	1923	1	1	0	0
CR Yates	1936-38-(53)	4	3	0	1
D Yates jr	1989-93-(99)-01	6	3	2	1
RL Yost	1955	2	2	0	0
G Zahringer	2003	3	0	2	1

‡In 1922 Hooman beat Sweetser at the 37th – on all other occasions halved matches have counted as such.

European Seniors Nations Cup   2006 *Ruuhikoskigolf, Finland*

1 Scotland; 2 Ireland; 3 England; 4 Germany; 5 Italy; 6 Spain; 7 Wales; 8 Switzerland; 9 Finland; 10 France; 11 Sweden; 12 Belgium; 13 Netherlands; 14 Norway; 15 Czech Republic; 16 Austria

In the match-play section of the event Scotland were in the first flight with England, Ireland and Germany. The results of this section were: Scotland beat Germany 3½–1½; Scotland beat Ireland 3½–1½; England beat Germany 4½–½; Ireland beat England 4½–½

Winning team: Gordon MacDonald, Alan Ferguson, Stephen Ellis, Ian Hutcheon, Donald McCart, Brian Grieve

Individual: 1 D Lane (ENG) 70-74–144; 2 I Hutcheon (SCO) 74-71–145; 3 H-G Reiter (GER) 76-70

World Amateur Team Championship (Eisenhower Trophy)

2006 *Stellenbosch GC and De Zalza GC, Stellenbosch, South Africa*   [6966–72; 6835–72]

Year	Winners	Runners-up	Venue	Score
1958	Australia	United States	St Andrews	918
(After a tie, Australia won the play-off by two strokes: Australia 222, United States 224)				
1960	United States	Australia	Ardmore, USA	834
1962	United States	Canada	Kawana, Japan	854
1964	Great Britain & Ireland	Canada	Olgiata, Rome	895
1966	Australia	United States	Mexico City	877
1968	United States	Great Britain & Ireland	Melbourne	868
1970	United States	New Zealand	Madrid	857
1972	United States	Australia	Buenos Aires	865
1974	United States	Japan	Dominican Rep.	888
1976	Great Britain & Ireland	Japan	Penina, Portugal	892
1978	United States	Canada	Fiji	873
1980	United States	South Africa	Pinehurst, USA	848
1982	United States	Sweden	Lausanne	859
1984	Japan	United States	Hong Kong	870
1986	Canada	United States	Caracas, Venezuela	860
1988	Great Britain & Ireland	United States	Ullva, Sweden	882
1990	Sweden	New Zealand	Christchurch, New Zealand	879
1992	New Zealand	United States	Capilano, Canada	823
1994	United States	Great Britain & Ireland	Paris, France	838
1996	Australia	Sweden	Manila, Philippines	838
1998	Great Britain and Ireland	Australia	Los Leones/La Dehesa, Chile	852
2000	United States	Great Britain & Ireland	Sporting Club, Berlin	841
2002	United States	France	Saujana, Malaysia	568
2004	United States	Spain	Rio Grande, Puerto Rico	407 (54)

Only two scores to count each day

1   NETHERLANDS   141-140-136-137—554
    (Wil Besseling 69-70-66-70—275, Joost Luiten 74-71-70-67—282, Tim Sluiter 72-70-75-72—289)

2   CANADA   139-139-141-137—556
    (Richard Scott 69-68-71-68—276, James Love 73-75-70-69—287, Andrew Parr 70-71-77-71—289)

3   UNITED STATES OF AMERICA   143-136-140-138—557
    (Chris Kirk 71-66-70-69—276, Trip Keuhne 78-70-70-69—287, Jonathan Moore 72-72-72-74—290)

4   WALES   144-143-132-140—559
    (Nigel Edwards 75-70-68-69—282, Rhys Davies 73-76-64-71—284, Llewellyn Matthews 71-73-73-72—289)

Wales come fourth as the Dutch take the World Amateur title

Wales led the home countries with a 17-under-par four-round total of 559 to take fourth place in the World Amateur Team Championship in South Africa as the Netherlands swept to victory over Canada and the United States.

Joost Luiten of the Netherlands played his last five holes in six-under-par and finished with a 67 as the Dutch captured the Eisenhower Trophy. The 20-year-old Luiten began his run with a birdie on the par-five 14th hole at De Zalze Golf Club, then holed a sand wedge from 93 yards on the par-four 15th for an eagle and closed with three further birdies.

With Luiten's 67 and a two-under-par 70 from individual low scorer Wil Besseling, the Netherlands won by two strokes over Canada and by three from the USA with a 22-under-par total of 554, the lowest since the two counting scores format was instituted in 2002.

In a field of 60 national teams, Nigel Edwards, Rhys Davies and Llewellyn Matthews took Wales into fourth place, two shots ahead of Korea, with England, Scotland and Argentina sharing sixth place on 563 and Ireland tied for ninth with France on 564.

"We didn't lose it," said Canada's captain Doug Roxburgh. "The Netherlands won it. They made the birdies coming home."

The previous best finish for the Netherlands was a tie for eighth place in 1992 and 1994. Host country South Africa finished tied for 22nd. Although there is no official recognition, Wil Besseling of the Netherlands returned the lowest four-round individual score at 13-under-par 275.

The biennial event will next be be played in 2008 in Adelaide, Australia.

Other scores: 561 South Korea; 563 Scotland (George Murray 72-70-70-70—282; Richie Ramsay 72-73-67-70—282; Scott Jamieson 78-72-74-70—294), England (Oliver Fisher 74-66-70-67—277, Ross McGowan 75-72-70-69—286, Jamie Moul 75-74-74-70—293), Argentina; 564 Ireland (Rory McIlroy 73-69-72-67—281, Gareth Shaw 73-69-73-73—288, Simon Ward 76-72-68-76—292), France; 565 Spain; 569 Australia, Sweden, Germany, Mexico; 570 Japan, Switzerland; 571 Malaysia; 572 New Zealand, Denmark; 573 Portugal; 574 Belgium, South Africa, Colombia, Norway; 575 Chinese Taipei, Finland; 576 Chile; 577 Italy; 578 Austria; 584 Brazil; 585 India, Czech Republic; 590 Iceland; 593 Trinidad and Tobago; 594 Puerto Rico; 596 Bolivia; 599 Philippines; 603 Bermuda, Hong Kong, China; 605 Russian Federation; 606 Pakistan; 607 Zimbabwe; 611 Turkey; 613 Peru, Ecuador, El Salvador; 614 Guatemala; 616 Namibia; 618 Tunisia; 620 Venezuela; 622 Fiji; 626 Uruguay; 628 Latvia; 630 Estonia; 634 Slovakia; 635 Greece; 638 Egypt; 647 Honduras; 648 US Virgin Islands, Botswana; 655 Cote d'Ivoire; 657 United Arab Emirates; 659 Saudi Arabia; 673 Croatia; 699 Gabon; 702 Bulgaria; 704 Bosnia and Herzegovina; 725 Nigeria; 774 Mauritius

Individual:

I	Wil Besseling (NED)	69-70-66-70—275
2	Julien Grillon (FRA)	72-68-69-67—276
	Chris Kirk (USA)	71-66-70-69—276
	Richard Scott (CAN)	69-68-71-68—276
5	Oliver Fisher (ENG)	74-66-70-67—277

Europe v Asia–Pacific (Sir Michael Bonallack Trophy)

2006 Auckland GC, Auckland, New Zealand

2000	Europe	Puerta de Hierro, Spain	2004	Asia–Pacific	Circolo Golf Roma, Italy
2002	Asia–Pacific	Hirono GC, Japan			

Captains: Asia–Pacific – Roger Brennand (NZL); Europe – Gonzaga Escauriaza (ESP)

Asia–Pacific		Europe	
First Day: **Morning – Fourball**			
Hu & Sandu	0	Edwards & Gould (6 and 5)	I
Ikeda & Ito	0	McIlroy & Thorp (I hole)	I
Purser & Geary	0	Ahokas & Oriol (2 and I)	I
Kim & Kang (halved)	½	Luiten & Guerrier (halved)	½
Lee & Dodt	0	Wolstenholme & Fisher (3 and 2)	I
	½		4½
Afternoon – Foursomes			
Leong & Hirunratanakorn (I hole)	I	Edwards & Gould	0
Ikeda & Ito	0	McIlroy & Ramsay (5 and 3)	I
Purser & Geary (4 and 3)	I	Luiten & Thorp	0
Lee & Dodt	0	Wolstenholme & Fisher (I hole)	I
Kim & Kang (5 and 4)	I	Oriol & Guerrier	0
	3		2

Match positions: Asia-Pacific 3½, Europe 6½

Asia–Pacific		Europe	
Second Day: **Morning – Fourball**			
Ikeda & Ito (I hole)	I	Edwards & Gould	0
Leong & Hirunratanakorn	0	Ahokas & Oriol (I hole)	I
Lee & Dodt	0	McIlroy & Ramsay (I hole)	I
Purser & Geary (2 holes)	I	Wolstenholme & Fisher	0
Kim & Kang (halved)	½	Thorp & Luiten (halved)	½
	2½		2½
Afternoon – Foursomes			
Ikeda & Ito (I hole)	I	Edwards & Gould	0
Leong & Hirunratanakorn (4 and 3)	I	Ahokas & Guerrier	0
Lee & Dodt (I hole)	I	McIlroy & Ramsay	0
Purser & Geary (halved)	½	Wolstenholme & Fisher (halved)	½
Kim & Kang (2 holes)	I	Thorp & Oriol	0
	4½		½

Match position: Asia–Pacific 10½, Europe 9½

(continued over)

Europe v Asia–Pacific (Bonallack Trophy) – 2006 – *continued*

Third Day: **Singles**

Anujit Hirunratanakorn (THA) (3 and 1)	1	Zac Gould (WAL)	0
Ajeetesh Sandu (IND)	0	Joost Luiten (NED) (3 and 1)	1
Nu Hu (CHN)	0	Rory McIlroy (IRL) (3 and 2)	1
Yuta Ikeda (JPN)	0	Marius Thorp (NOR) (1 hole)	1
Yuki Ito (JPN) (5 and 3)	1	Nigel Edwards (WAL)	0
Ben Leong (MAS)	0	Pedro Oriol (ESP) (3 and 2)	1
Andrew Dodt (AUS)	0	Richard Ramsay (SCO) (4 and 3)	1
Josh Geary (NZL) (1 hole)	1	Damian Ulrich (SUI)	0
Mark Purser (NZL)	0	Julien Guerrier (FRA) (1 hole)	1
Kyung Tae Kim (KOR)	0	Gary Wolstenholme (ENG) (3 and 2)	1
Sung Hoon Kang (KOR)	0	Antti Ahokas (FIN) (1 hole)	1
Won Joon Lee (AUS) (halved)	½	Oliver Fisher (ENG) (halved)	½
	3½		**8½**

Result: Europe 18, Asia–Pacific 14

European Amateur Team Championship

Year	Winner	Runner-up	Venue	Year	Winner	Runner-up	Venue
1959	Sweden	France	Barcelona, Spain	1985	Scotland	Sweden	Halmstad, Sweden
1961	Sweden	England	Brussels, Belgium	1987	Ireland	England	Murhof, Austria
1963	England	Sweden	Falsterbo, Sweden	1989	England	Scotland	Royal Porthcawl, Wales
1965	Ireland	Scotland	St George's, England	1991	England	Italy	Puerta de Hierro, Spain
1967	Ireland	France	Turin, Italy	1993	Wales	England	Marianske Lasne, Czech
1969	England	Germany	Hamburg, Germany				Republic
1971	England	Scotland	Lausanne, Switzerland	1995	Scotland	England	Royal Antwerp, Belgium
1973	England	Scotland	Penina, Portugal	1997	Spain	Scotland	Portmarnock, Ireland
1975	Scotland	Italy	Killarney, Ireland	1999	Italy	Germany	Monticello, Italy
1977	Scotland	Sweden	The Haagsche,	2001	Scotland	Ireland	Ljunghusens, Sweden
			Netherlands	2003	Spain	Sweden	Royal Hague,
1979	England	Wales	Esbjerg, Denmark				Netherlands
1981	England	Scotland	St Andrews, Scotland	2005	England	Germany	Hillside, England
1983	Ireland	Spain	Chantilly, France				

Sherry Cup (Copa de Jerez) 2006 *Sotogrande, Spain*

1 Spain 848; 2 Wales 857; 3 England 860   19 teams took part

Winning team: José Luis Adarraga Gomez, Bosco de Checa Mato, Pedro Oriol Sanchez-Blanco, Jordi García del Moral

For individual scores see page 294

EGA Challenge Trophy 2006 *Ptuj, Slovenia*

1 Belgium 1090; 2 Turkey 1120; 3 Czech Republic 1122; 4 Slovenia 1129; 5 Estonia 1188; 6 Hungary 1192; 7 Slovakia 1209; 8 Greece 1241; 9 Croatia 1244; 10 Poland 1295

Winning team: Pierre Belecom, Xavier Feyaerts, Patrick Hanaeuer, Hugues Joannes, Alban Lammens, Guillauime Watremez

Individual: 1 Hugues Joannes (BEL) 74-70-71—215; 2 Matjaz Gojcic (SLO) 69-75-72—216; 3 Hamza Sayin (TUR) 75-71-72—218

European Club Cup (Albacom Trophy) 2006 Corfu

1975	Club de Campo, Spain	Club de Campo	1992	Hillerod, Denmark		La Quinta
1976	Växjö Golfklub, Sweden	El Prat	1993	Lahden, Finland		La Quinta
1977	Chantilly, France	RC Belgique	1994	Kilmarnock (Barassie),		
1978	Hamburger, Germany	Deauville		Scotland		Vilamoura
1979	Hamburger, Germany	Santa Ponsa	1995	Racing C de France, France		Vilamoura
1980	Limerick, Ireland	Santa Ponsa	1996	Racing C de France, France		Vilamoura
1981	El Prat, Spain	Aloha	1997	Racing C de France, France		Parco de Medici
1982	El Prat, Spain	Aloha	1998	Aalborg, Denmark		Parco de Medici
1983	Rapallo, Italy	Aloha	1999	Aalborg, Denmark		Parco de Medici
1984	Hamburger, Germany	Aloha	2000	Shandon Park,		
1985	El Prat, Spain	Aloha		Northern Ireland		Parco de Medici
1986	Hamburger, Germany	Aloha	2001	Shandon Park		La Boulie
1987	Puerto de Hierro, Spain	Aloha	2002	Bordelais, France		Parco de Medici
1988	Brokenhurst Manor, England	Aloha	2003	Deauville, France		Antalyn
1989	Ealing, England	Aloha	2004	De Houtrak		Glyfada
1990	Ealing, England	Aloha	2005	Klassis		Klassis
1991	Club de Golf Terramar, Spain	La Quinta				

1	St Leon-Rot (GER)	426	(Sean Einhaus, Christian Schunk, Allen John)
2	Kilworth Springs (ENG)	430	
3	Aura Golf (FIN)	437	

Best Individuals: 212 Sean Einhaus (GER), Gary Wolstenholme (ENG)   *24 countries competed*

St Andrews Trophy (Great Britain & Ireland v Continent of Europe)

Match instituted 1956, trophy presented 1964

1956	Great Britain & Ireland	Wentworth	12½–2½
1958	Great Britain & Ireland	St Cloud, France	10–5
1960	Great Britain & Ireland	Walton Heath	13–5
1962	Great Britain & Ireland	Halmstead, Sweden	18–12
1964	Great Britain & Ireland	Muirfield	23–7
1966	Great Britain & Ireland	Bilbao, Spain	19½–10½
1968	Great Britain & Ireland	Portmarnock	20–10
1970	Great Britain & Ireland	La Zoute, Belgium	17½–12½
1972	Great Britain & Ireland	Berkshire	19½–10½
1974	Continent of Europe	Punta Ala, Italy	16–14
1976	Great Britain & Ireland	St Andrews	18½–11½
1978	Great Britain & Ireland	Bremen, Germany	20½–9½
1980	Great Britain & Ireland	Sandwich, Royal St George's	19½–10½
1982	Continent of Europe	Rosendaelsche, Netherlands	14–10
1984	Great Britain & Ireland	Saunton, Devon	13–11
1986	Great Britain & Ireland	Halmstead, Sweden	14½–9½
1988	Great Britain & Ireland	St Andrews	15½–8½
1990	Great Britain & Ireland	El Saler, Spain	13–11
1992	Great Britain & Ireland	Royal Cinque Ports	14–10
1994	Great Britain & Ireland	Chantilly, France	14–10
1996	Great Britain & Ireland	Woodhall Spa	16–8
1998	Continent of Europe	Villa d'Este, Italy	14–10
2000	Great Britain & Ireland	The Ailsa Course, Turnberry	13–11
2002	Great Britain & Ireland	Lausanne, Switzerland	14–10
2004	Great Britain & Ireland	Nairn, Ireland	17–7

2006 Marianske Lazne, Czech Republic

Non-playing Captains: Eur: Wolfgang Wiegand (GER); GB&I: Colin Dalgleish (SCO)

Continent of Europe		**GB&I**	
First Day – **Foursomes**			
A Ahokas & W Besseling	0	R Ramsay & L Saltman (1 hole)	1
J García del Moral & J L Adarraga	0	R McIlroy & O Fisher (2 and 1)	1
M Delpodio & L Gagli	0	R McGowan & J Moul (4 and 3)	1
J Guerrier & J Grillon	0	N Edwards & R Davies (3 and 1)	1
	—		—
	0		4

St Andrews Trophy *continued*

Singles

Antti Ahokas (FIN) (4 and 3)	I	Richard Ramsay (SCO)	0
Damian Ulrich (SUI) (halved)	½	Rory McIlroy (IRL) (halved)	½
Jordi García del Moral (ESP)	0	Oliver Fisher (ENG) (5 and 4)	I
José Luis Adarraga (ESP)	0	Lloyd Saltman (SCO) (2 and I)	I
Julien Grillon (FRA)	0	Robert Dinwiddie (ENG) (3 and I)	I
Matteo Delpodio (ITA)	0	Rhys Davies (WAL) (I hole)	I
Lorenzo Gagli (ITA) (2 and I)	I	Ross McGowan (ENG)	0
Julien Guerrier (FRA)	0	Nigel Edwards (WAL) (3 and 2)	I
	—		—
	2½		5½

Match position: Continent of Europe 2½, GB&I 9½

Second Day – **Foursomes**

J Guerrier & J Grillon	0	R McIlroy & O Fisher (I hole)	I
A Ahokas & W Besseling	0	N Edwards & R Davies (2 and I)	I
M Delpodio & L Gagli (5 and 3)	I	L Saltman & R Dinwiddie	0
J García del Moral & J L Adarraga (2 and I)	I	R McGowan & J Moul	0
	—		—
	2		2

Singles

J Guerrier (halved)	½	R McIlroy (halved)	½
A Ahokas	0	R Ramsay (3 and 2)	I
M Delpodio lost	0	O Fisher (4 and 3)	I
L Gagli (I hole)	I	N Edwards	0
D Ulrich (2 and I)	I	R Dinwiddie	0
J García del Moral (3 and 2)	I	Jamie Moul (ENG)	0
J Grillon	0	R Davies (4 and 3)	I
Will Besseling (NED) (6 and 5)	I	L Saltman	0
	—		—
	4½		3½

Match Result: Continent of Europe 9, GB&I 15

Home Internationals (Raymond Trophy)

1932	Scotland	1960	England	1981	Scotland		
1933	Scotland	1961	Scotland	1982	Scotland		
1934	Scotland	1962T	England/Ireland/Scotland	1983	Ireland		
1935T	England/Ireland/Scotland	1963T	England/Ireland/Scotland	1984	England		
1936	Scotland	1964	England	1985	England		
1937	Scotland	1965	England	1986	Scotland		
1938	England	1966	England	1987	Ireland		
1939–46	No Internationals held	1967	Scotland	1988	England		
1947	England	1968	England	1989	England		
1948	England	1969	England	1990	Ireland		
1949	England	1970	Scotland	1991	Ireland		
1950	Ireland	1971	Scotland	1992T	England and Ireland		
1951T	Ireland and Scotland	1972T	Scotland/England	1993	England		
1952	Scotland	1973	England	1994	England		
1953	Scotland	1974	England	1995	England		
1954	England	1975	Scotland	1996	England		
1955	Ireland	1976	Scotland	1997	England		
1956	Scotland	1977	England	1998	England		
1957	England	1978	England	1999	England		
1958	England	1979	*No Internationals held*				
1959T	England/Ireland/Scotland	1980	England				

2000 Carnoustie

England halved with Wales	7½ matches to 7½
Ireland halved with Scotland	7½ matches to 7½
England halved with Scotland	7½ matches to 7½
Wales beat Ireland	8 matches to 7
Scotland beat Wales	8½ matches to 6½
Ireland beat England	9½ matches to 5½

Winners: Scotland

2001 Woodhall Spa

England beat Scotland	9 matches to 6
Ireland beat Wales	10½ matches to 4½
England halved with Wales	7½ matches to 7½
Scotland beat Ireland	8½ matches to 6½
Scotland beat Wales	10½ matches to 4½
England beat Ireland	11½ matches to 3½

Winners: England

2002 Royal St David's

Wales beat England	8 matches to 7
Ireland halved with Scotland	7½ matches to 7½
Wales beat Ireland	8½ matches to 6½
Scotland beat England	10 matches to 5
England beat Ireland	10 matches to 5
Wales beat Scotland	9 matches to 6

Winners: Wales

2003 Ballybunion

Ireland beat Wales	8 matches to 7
Scotland halved with England	7½ matches to 7½
Ireland beat England	8 matches to 7
Scotland beat Wales	9½ matches to 5½
Wales beat England	11 matches to 4
Ireland halved with Scotland	7½ matches to 7½

Winners: Ireland

2004 Prestwick

England beat Ireland	8½ matches to 6½
Wales beat Scotland	9½ matches to 5½
Scotland beat England	8 matches to 7
Ireland beat Wales	9 matches to 6
Scotland beat Ireland	1 matches to 4
England beat Wales	0 matches to 5

Winners: England

2005 Royal St George's

England beat Ireland	8½ matches to 6½
Wales beat Scotland	0 matches to 5
Scotland beat England	1½ matches to 3½
Ireland beat Wales	9 matches to 6
England beat Wales	9½ matches to 5½
Scotland beat Ireland	0 matches to 5

Winners: Scotland

2006 Pyle & Kenfig

Scotland beat Ireland	8 matches to 7
England beat Wales	8½ matches to 6½
Scotland beat Wales	9 matches to 6
England beat Ireland	9 matches to 6
Wales beat Ireland	8 matches to 7
Scotland beat England	10 matches to 5

Winners: Scotland

Winning team: George Crawford (Williamwood) (non-playing captain); Glenn Campbell (Blairgowrie), John Gallagher (Swanston), Scott Henry (Cardross), Scott Jamieson (Cathkin Braes), Jonathan King (Glasgow), Kevin McAlpine (Alyth), Keir McNicoll (Carnoustie), George Murray (Earlsferry Thistle), Paul O'Hara (Colville Park), Richie Ramsay (Royal Aberdeen), Lloyd Saltman (Craigielaw)

Senior Home Internationals 2006 Dunbar

2002	England	Nairn Dunbar	2004	England	Aberdovey
2003	Ireland & Wales	Seaton Carew	2005	Ireland	Lahinch

Ireland tied with England	4½ matches to 4½
Scotland beat Wales	7 matches to 2
Ireland beat Wales	7 matches to 2
England beat Scotland	6 matches to 3
Wales beat England	5½ matches to 3½
Scotland beat Ireland	5½ matches to 3½

Result: 1 Scotland 2 (15½); 2 Ireland 1½ (15); 3 England 1½ (14); 4 Wales 1 (9½)

Winning team: Stephen Ellis, Alan Ferguson, Brian Grieve, Ian Hutcheon, John Johnston, Donald McCart, Gordon MacDonald

English County Championship

1928	Warwickshire	1937	Lancashire	1953	Yorkshire
1929	Lancashire	1938	Staffordshire	1954	Cheshire
1930	Lancashire	1939	Worcestershire	1955	Yorkshire
1931	Yorkshire	1947	Staffordshire	1956	Staffordshire
1932	Surrey	1948	Staffordshire	1957	Surrey
1933	Yorkshire	1949	Lancashire	1958	Surrey
1934	Worcestershire	1950	Not played	1959	Northumberland
1935	Worcestershire	1951	Lancashire	1961	Lancashire
1936	Surrey	1952	Yorkshire	1962	Northumberland

English County Championship *continued*

1963	Yorkshire	1978	Kent	1993	Yorkshire
1964	Northumberland	1979	Gloucestershire	1994	Middlesex
1965	Northumberland	1980	Surrey	1995	Lancashire
1966	Surrey	1981	Surrey	1996	Hampshire
1967	Lancashire	1982	Yorkshire	1997	Yorkshire
1968	Surrey	1983	Berks, Bucks, Oxon	1998	Yorkshire
1969	Berks, Bucks, Oxon	1984	Yorkshire	1999	Yorkshire
1970	Gloucestershire	1985T	Devon/Hertfordshire	2000	Surrey
1971	Staffordshire	1986	Hertfordshire	2001	Yorkshire
1972	Berks, Bucks, Oxon	1987	Yorkshire	2002	Yorkshire
1973	Yorkshire	1988	Warwickshire	2003	Devon
1974	Lincolnshire	1989	Middlesex	2004	Surrey
1975	Staffordshire	1990	Warwickshire	2005	Yorkshire
1976	Warwickshire	1991	Middlesex		
1977	Warwickshire	1992	Dorset		

2006 *Prince's*

Yorkshire beat Warwickshire	7 matches to 2
Surrey beat Gloucestershire	5½ matches to 3½
Yorkshire beat Gloucestershire	6½ matches to 2½
Warwickshire beat Surrey	5 matches to 4
Gloucestershire beat Warwickshire	6½ matches to 2½
Yorkshire beat Surrey	6½ matches to 2½

Result: 1 Yorkshire 3 (20); 2 Gloucestershire 1 (12½); 3 Surrey 1 (12); 4 Warwickshire 1 (9½)

Winning team: David Appleyard, Simon Bell, Gareth Evans, Nicholas McCarthy, James Mason, John Parry, Stephen Uzzell

English Club Championship 2006 *Stoke Park*

1989	Ealing	Southport and Ainsdale	1998	Moor Park	Northumberland
1990	Ealing	Goring and Streatley	1999	Royal Mid-Surrey	Moor Park
1991	Trentham	Porters Park	2000	Coxmoor	Berkhampstead
1992	Bristol & Clifton	South Staffs	2001	St Mellion	Minchinhampton
1993	Worksop	Rotherham	2002	Woodcote Park	Northamptonshire County
1994	Sandmoor	Coxmoor	2003	Southern Valley	King's Lynn
1995	Sandmoor	Ipswich	2004	Tavistock	Sandwell Park
1996	Hartlepool	Frilford Heath	2005	Rotherham	Brancepeth Castle
1997	Royal Mid-Surrey	Sandiway			

1	Kilworth Springs*	428	(Sam Mayfield, Dion Stevens, Gary Wolstenholme)
2	Stoke Park	428	
3	John O'Gaunt	431	

Kilworth Springs won by having lower total for last 18 holes

Scottish Club Championship 2006 *Cowglen*

1985	Cochrane Castle	Helensburgh	1993	Troon Wellbeck	Helensburgh
1986	Thornhill	Dunblane New	1994	Kilmarnock Barassie	North Berwick
1987	Alloa	Cruden Bay	1995	Kelso	Cochrane Castle
1988	Cowglen	Tulliallan	1996	Cochrane Castle	Alloa
1989	Cowglen	Crieff	1997	Blairgowrie	Burnstone Castle
1990	Haggs Castle	Haggs Cstle	1998	Turvill	Boat of Garven
1991	Cochrane Castle	Ranfurley Castle	1999	Tulliallan	Kilmarnock Barassie
1992	Kilmarnock Barassie	Scotscraig	2000	Cowglen	Crow Wood

1	Cruden Bay	135
	(Laurie Phillips, Ross Cooper, Michael Buchan)	
2	Glenbervie	137
3	Tulliallan	139

Bad weather reduced event to one round

Scottish Club Handicap Championship 2006 *Cardrona*

2001	Dunbar	2003	Galashields	2005	Downfield
2002	Newmachar	2004	Braehead		

1	Balmore	63	(Gordon Campbell, Scott Chisholm)
2	Burntisland	65	
3	Duns	67	
	Bruntsfield Links	67	

Scottish Area Team Championship 2006 *Glasgow Gailes*

1990	North East	1996	Renfrewshire	2002	Perth and Kinross
1991	Glasgow	1997	Lothians	2003	Lothians
1992	North East	1998	Lanarkshire	2004	Lothians
1993	Lothians	1999	Lothians	2005	Renfrewshire
1994	Lothians	2000	North		
1995	North	2001	Perth and Kinross		

Semi-finals

Lothians beat Renfrewshire	6 matches to 3
Angus beat Perth & Kinross	5½ matches to 3½

Final

Lothians beat Angus	5½ matches to 3½

Winning team: Steven Armstrong, Alexander Culverwell, John Gallagher, Mark Kerr, Shaun McAllister, Keith Reilly, Keith Young

Scottish Foursomes Tournament – *Glasgow Evening Times* Trophy

1923 Gullane Comrades	1949 Troon Portland	1968 Troon St Meddans	1985 East Renfrewshire
1924 St Andrews New	1950 '36 Club	1969 Irvine	1986 Hamilton
1925 St Andrews New	1951 Troon Portland	1970 Cardross	1987 Drumpellier
1926 Pollok	1952 Western Gailes	1971 Airdrie	1988 Irvine Ravenspark
1927 Erskine	1953 Irvine	1972 Scottish Building	1989 Cochrane Castle
1928 Earlsferry Thistle	1954 Glasgow University	Contractors	1990 Pitreavie
1929 Pollok	1955 Haggs Castle	1973 Glasgow Insurance	1991 Irvine Ravenspark
1930 Mortonhall	1956 Prestonfield	1974 Baberton	1992 Cochrane Castle
1931 Royal Burgess	1957 Falkirk Tryst	1975 Prestwick St	1993 Baberton
1932 Hayston	1958 Troon St Meddans	Cuthbert	1994 Standard Life
1933 Lothianburn	1959 Cambuslang	1976 Wishaw	1995 Ratho Park
1934 Ayr Academy FP	1960 Irvine	1977 Stirlingshire Jun.&	1996 Cardross
1935 Ayr Academy FP	1961 Falkirk Tryst	Youth Society	1997 Cardross
1936 Ayr Academy FP	1962 Irvine	1978 Helensburgh	1998 Haggs Castle
1937 Ayr Academy FP	1963 Clydebank & Dist	1979 Helensburgh	1999 Scottish Life
1938 Western Gailes	1964 Scottish Building	1980 Helensburgh	2000 Colville Park
1939–45 *Not played*	Contractors	1981 Duddingston	2001 Hamilton
1946 St Andrews New	1965 Falkirk Tryst	1982 Haggs Castle	2002 Wishaw
1947 Western Gailes	1966 Bathgate	1983 Haggs Castle	2003 Whitecraigs
1948 Melville College FP	1967 Prestonfield	1984 Royal Musselburgh	

The event was discontinued after 2003

Welsh Inter-Counties Championship 2006 *Borth & Ynyslas*

2003	Gwent		2004	Caernarvon	2005	Glamorgan

1	Glamorgan	711
2	Flint	714
3	Caernarvonshire	736

Winning Team: R Hooper, M Jones, L Lewis, L Matthews, C O'Neill, L Thomas

Welsh Team Championship 2006 *Maesdu*

2003   Pontnewydd   2004   Monmouthshire   2005   Whitchurch

Semi-Finals:
Llandudno (Maesdu) beat Newport   3 matches to 2
Pontypridd beat Whitchurch   3½ matches to 1½

Final
Llandudno (Maesdu) beat Pontypridd   3 matches to 2

Winning team: Mark Hanson (non-playing captain); James Gresty, Antony Hanson, Gary Marfell, Howard Williams, Mark Yates

107th *Edinburgh Evening News Dispatch* Trophy (inaugurated 1890)   2006 *The Braids*

1980	Scottish Universities	1987	Whitehill	1994	Lochend	2001	Barnton Hotel
1981	Royal Bank	1988	Edinburgh Thistle	1995	Harrison	2002	Westermont
1982	Royal Bank	1989	Westermont	1996	Observers	2003	Rhodes
1983	Torphin 20	1990	Edinburgh Thistle	1997	Crags	2004	Carrick Knowe
1984	Silverknowes	1991	Scottish Life	1998	Silverknowes	2005	Riccarton
1985	Bank of Scotland	1992	Harrison	1999	Carrick Knowe		
1986	Bank of Scotland	1993	Crags	2000	Harrison		

Semi-Finals:
Silverknowes beat MCBA, Mortonhall   12 and 11
Harrison beat Barnton Hotel   3 and 2

Final
Silverknowes beat Harrison   2 and 1

Winning team: Tom Caldwell, Graham Robertson, Keith Reilly, Ian Doig

Copa Los Andes   (inaugurated 1974)   2006 *Caracas CC, Venezuela*

Men:
1   Argentina   15 points (individual match wins 74)
2   Chile   14 (63)
3   Colombia   12 (69)
4 Peru; 5 Brazil; 6 Bolivia; 7 Ecuador; 8 Uruguay; 9 Venezuela

Ladies:
1   Colombia   14 (68)
2   Argentina   13 (74)
3   Peru   12 (66)
4 Brazil; 5 Chile; 6 Paraguay; 7 Uruguay; 8 Ecuador; 9 Bolivia

Spirit International

2001 Mexico   525   2003 USA   523   2005 England   533

This event will next be held at Whispering Pines, Houston, TX in October

Nomura Cup – Asia-Pacific Amateur Team Championship

1963	Japan	1544	Wack Wack GCC, Manilla	1987	Japan	877	Royal Hua Hin GC, Thailand
1965	Japan	876	Nikko Country Club, Japan	1989	Japan	887	Taiwan GC, Chinese Taipei
1967	Chinese Taipei	861	Taiwan GC, Chinese Taipei	1991	Australia	883	Wack Wack GCC, Manilla
1969	Chinese Taipei	891	Seoul Country Club, Korea	1993	Australia	852	Royal Selangor GC, Malaysia
1971	Japan	894	Wack Wack GCC, Manilla				
1973	India	876	Jakarta GCC, Indonesia	1995	New Zealand	889	Russley GC, New Zealand
1975	Japan	850	Tokyo GC, Japan	1997	Chinese Taipei	829	Hong Kong GC, China
1977	Chinese Taipei	865	Royal Selangor GC, Malaysia	1999	Australia	845	Lahore Gymkhana GC, Pakistan
1979	Japan	850	Singapore Island CC	2001	Australia	814	Wu Fi Fountain Palm GC, China
1981	Japan	879	Royal Calcutta GC, India				
1983	Chinese Taipei	869	Nam Seoul CC, Korea	2003	Australia	852	Links GC, Australia
1985	Australia	874	Royal Adelaide GC, Australia	2005	Australia	814	Narita GC, Japan

Principal 72 hole Tournaments

Including the National District Championships

Aberconwy Trophy (inaugurated 1976) *always at Conwy and Llandudno (Maesdu), Gwynedd*

1976	JR Jones	1986	JR Berry	1996	R Williams
1977	EN Davies	1987	M Sheppard	1997	I Campbell
1978	MG Mouland	1988	MG Hughes	1998	J Donaldson
1979	JM Morrow	1989	JN Lee	1999	J Donaldson
1980	JM Morrow	1990	S Wilkinson	2000	J Donaldson
1981	D Evans	1991	S Wilkinson	2001	L Harpin*
1982	G Tuttle	1992	MJ Ellis	2002	R Scott
1983	GH Brown	1993	S Wilkinson	2003	R Scott
1984	D McLean	1994	G Marsden	2004	B Briscoe
1985	MA Macara	1995	S Andrew	2005	T Dykes

1	Craig Evans (West Monmouthshire)	73-80-74-72—299
2	Luke Thomas (Pontypridd)	78-78-73-73—302
3	Jason Shufflebotham (Prestatyn)	79-79-74-73—305

Berkshire Trophy (inaugurated 1946) *always at The Berkshire*

1946	R Sweeney	148	1966	P Oosterhuis	287	1987	J Robinson	275
1947	PB Lucas	298	1967	DJ Millensted	283	1988	R Claydon	276
1948	LG Crawley	301	1968	MF Bonallack	273	1989	J Metcalfe	272
1949	PB Lucas	300	1969	JC Davies	278	1990	J O'Shea	271
1950	PF Scrutton	296	1970	MF Bonallack	274	1991	J Bickerton	280
1951	PF Scrutton	301	1971T	MF Bonallack	277	1992	V Phillips	274
1952	PF Scrutton	286		J Davies		1993	V Phillips	271
1953	JL Morgan	289	1972	DP Davidson	280	1994T	J Knight	274
1954T	Ft Lt K Hall	303	1973	PJ Hedges	278		A Marshall	
	E Bromley-Davenport		1974	J Downie	280	1995	G Harris	275
1955	GH Micklem	282	1975	N Faldo	281	1996	GP Wolstenholme	274
1956	GB Wolstenholme	285	1976	PJ Hedges	284	1997	GP Wolstenholme	275
1957	MF Bonallack	291	1977	A Lyle	279	1998	M Hilton	284
1958T	GB Wolstenholme	284	1978	PJ Hedges	281	1999	D Henley	275
	AH Perowne		1979	D Williams	274	2000	C Edwards	281
1959	JB Carr	279	1980	P Downes	280	2001	G Evans	283
1960	GB Wolstenholme	276	1981	D Blakeman	280	2002	G Wolstenholme	267
1961	MF Bonallack	275	1982	SD Keppler	278	2003	R Fisher	275
1962	SC Saddler	279	1983	S Hamer	288	2004	S Osborne	267
1963	DW Frame	289	1984	JL Plaxton	276	2005	A Gee	275
1964	R Foster	281	1985	P McEvoy	279			
1965	MF Bonallack	278	1986	R Muscroft	280			

1	David Shewan (RSA)	68-67-70-68—273
2	James Kruger (RSA)	70-67-68-69—274
3	Ross McGowan (Banstead Downs)	68-70-70-67—275

Cameron Corbett Vase (inaugurated 1897) *always at Haggs Castle, Glasgow*

1897	AF Duncan	1935	H Thomson	1972	HB Stuart		
1898	AF Duncan	1936	J Gray	1973	MJ Miller		
1899	W Laidlaw	1937	TI Craig jr	1974	M Rae		
1900	GH Hutcheson	1938	JS Logan	1975	D Barclay Howard		
1901	G Fox jr	1939	A Steel	1976	GH Murray		
1902	AF Duncan	1940–41	*No competition*	1977	MJ Miller		
1903	G Fox jr	1942	AC Taylor	1978	GH Murray		
1904	R Bone	1943–45	*No competition*	1979	KW Macintosh		
1905	R Bone	1946	JS Montgomerie	1980	IA Carslaw		
1906	W Gemmill	1947	W Maclaren	1981	GH Murray		
1907	G Wilkie	1948	J Pressley	1982	GH Murray		
1908	AF Duncan	1949	GB Peters	1983	AS Oldcorn		
1909	EB Tipping	1950	J Gray	1984	D Barclay Howard		
1910	JH Irons	1951	GB Peters	1985	J McDonald		
1911	G Morris	1952	J Stewart Thomson	1986	JW Milligan		
1912	R Scott jr	1953	J Orr	1987	J Semple		
1913	R Scott jr	1954	JR Cater	1988	C Everett		
1914	D Martin	1955	RC Macgregor	1989	AG Tait		
1915–18	*No competition*	1956	RC Macgregor	1990	D Robertson	290	
1919	HR Orr	1957	I Rennie	1991	K Gallacher	281	
1920	DJ Murray Campbell	1958	DH Reid	1992	D Kirkpatrick	284	
1921	HM Dickson	1959	AS Kerr	1993	R Russell	278	
1922	WS Macfarlane	1960	J Mackenzie	1994	J Hodson	280	
1923	JO Stevenson	1961	GB Cosh	1995	D Barclay Howard	268	
1924	JO Stevenson	1962	JH Richmond	1996	C Watson	282	
1925	A Jamieson jr	1963	JA Davidson	1997	C Watson	268	
1926	G Chapple	1964	IA MacCaskill	1998	E Wilson	140	(36)
1927	RS Rodger	1965	H Frazer	1999	W Bryson	278	
1928	SL McKinlay	1966	D Black	2000	P McKechnie	277	
1929	D McBride	1967	JRW Walkinshaw	2001	P Gault	291	
1930	HM Dickson	1968	CW Green	2002	B Hume*	275	
1931	HM Dickson	1969	A Brooks	2003	J McLeary	276	
1932	W Stringer	1970T	J McTear	2004	J McGhee	275	
1933	W Tulloch		D Hayes	2005	G Campbell	280	
1934	JM Dykes	1971	G Macgregor				

1	Glenn Campbell (Blairgowrie)		68-69-69-68—274
2	Kevin McAlpine (Alyth)		73-64-68-70—275
3	Wallace Booth (Comrie)		70-70-71-65—276
	Mark Kerr (Dalmahoy)		67-72-72-65—276

Clwyd Open (inaugurated 1991) *always at Prestatyn and Wrexham*

1991	G Houston	1996	M Ellis	2001	A Campbell
1992	C O'Carrol	1997	D Park	2002	G Wright
1993	M Ellis	1998	R Donovan	2003	T Dykes
1994	G Houston	1999	L Harpin	2004	B Westgate
1995	M Ellis	2000	K Sullivan	2005	M Trow

1	Stuart Runcie (Abergele)	76-68-71-68—283
2	Jonathan Holmes (Southerndown)	72-69-74-70—285
3	Richard Merchant (Monmouthshire)	71-72-75-70—288

Craigmillar Park Open (inaugurated 1961) *always at Craigmillar Park, Edinburgh*

1961	RDBM Shade	1972	CW Green	1983	G Macgregor
1962	A Sinclair	1973	DF Campbell	1984	G Macgregor
1963	HM Campbell	1974	GH Murray	1985	C Bloice
1964	RDBM Shade	1975	IC Hutcheon	1986	SR Easingwood
1965	GB Cosh	1976	NA Faldo	1987	RM Roper
1966	RDBM Shade	1977	CW Green	1988	B Shields
1967	RDBM Shade	1978	DM McCart	1989	RM Roper
1968	RDBM Shade	1979	IC Hutcheon	1990	SJ Bannerman
1969	GB Cosh	1980	JB Dunlop	1991	N Walton
1970	PJ Smith	1981	GK MacDonald	1992	SJ Knowles
1971	CW Green	1982	AS Oldcorn	1993	R Russell

1994	BW Collier	1998	G Rankin	2002	M Warren
1995	C Watson	1999	S Mackenzie	2003	G Gordon
1996	GW Tough	2000	M Warren	2004	J McLeary
1997	CD Hislop	2001	S O'Hara	2005	J Gallagher

1	Scott Jamieson (Cathkin Braes)	66-66-68-70—270
2	Scott Henry (Cardross)	68-69-65-69—271
3	George Murray (Earlsferry Thistle)	72-65-67-70—274
	Paul O'Hara (Colville Park)	66-69-69-70—274

Duncan Putter (inaugurated 1959) always at Southerndown, Bridgend, Glamorgan

1959	G Huddy	301	1975	JG Jermine	295	1990	R Willison	311
1960	WI Tucker	289	1976T	WI Tucker	286	1991	R Willison	267
1961T	G Huddy	295		H Stott		1992	R Dinsdale	213
	WI Tucker		1977	H Stott	295	1993	M Thomson	289
1962	EN Davies	297	1978	P McEvoy	295	1994	GP Wolstenholme	226
1963	WI Tucker	296	1979	HJ Evans	292	1995	B Dredge	293
1964	JL Toye	293	1980	P McEvoy	296	1996	GP Wolstenholme	291
1965	P Townsend	305	1981T	R Chapman	294	1997	M Pilkington	283
1966	MF Attenborough	291		PG Way		1998	M King	291
1967	D Millensted	297	1982	D McLean	283	1999	GP Wolstenholme	216 (54)
1968	JL Morgan	299	1983	JG Jermine	297	2000	J Donaldson	285
1969	WI Tucker	304	1984	JP Price	284	2001	N Edwards	140 (36)
1970	JL Toye	305	1985	P McEvoy	299	2002T	S Manley	286
1971	W Humphreys	295	1986	D Wood	300		N Oakley	
1972	P Berry (3 rounds)	230	1987	P McEvoy	278	2003	S Manley	290
1973	JKD Povall	299	1988	S Dodd	290	2004	N Edwards	276
1974	S Cox	302	1989	RN Roderick	280	2005	G Wright	288

1	Neil Chaudhuri (The Leicestershire)	63-67-71-73—274	tied
	Bjørn Akesson (DEN)	67-65-69-73—274	
3	Danny Belch (Hillside)	68-70-70-68—276	
	James Ruth (Tavistock)	69-65-69-73—276	

Hampshire Salver (inaugurated 1979) always at North Hants/Blackmoor

1979	P McEvoy	280	1988	NE Holman	279	1997	JP Rose	275
1980	J Morrow	282	1989	P Dougan	286	1998	SJ Dyson	275
1981	AP Sherbourne	211 (54)	1990	J Metcalfe	272	1999	B Mason	273
1982	I Gray	293	1991	G Evans	281	2000	M Young	207 (54)
1983	DG Lane	281	1992	SR Cage	276	2001	G Wolstenholme	271
1984	DH Currie	283	1993	DJ Hamilton	281	2002	J Moul	277
1985	AJ Clapp	285	1994	W Bennett	279	2003	M Sell	278
1986	D Gilford	287	1995	M Treleaven	275	2004	R Fisher	206
1987	A Rogers	286	1996	J Knight	272	2005	R Henley	272

1	James Crampton (Spalding)	68-69-67-63—267
2	Jamie Moul (Stoke-by-Nayland)	67-69-65-67—268
3	Lawrence Dodd (Thetford)	67-69-66-67—269

Lagonda Trophy 1975 at Camberley and from 1990 at Gog Magog

1975	WJ Reid	143	1986	D Gilford	282	1997	L Donald	279
1976	JC Davies	142	1987	DG Lane	290	1998	K Ferrie	284
1977	WS Gronow	145	1988	R Claydon	275	1999	Z Scotland	284
1978	JC Davies	135	1989	T Spence	280	2000	M Young	279
1979	JG Bennett	142	1990	L Parsons	273	2001	D Skinns	271
1980	P McEvoy	139	1991	J Cook	277	2002	G Wolstenholme	275
1981	N Mitchell	138	1992	L Westwood	279	2003	S Tiley	269
1982	A Sherborne	290	1993	L James	279	2004	O Fisher	268
1983	I Sparkes	216 (54)	1994	S Webster	276	2005	L Allen	275
1984	MS Davis	289	1995	P Nelson	274			
1985	J Robinson	283	1996	S Collingwood	283			

(continued over)

Lagonda Trophy – 2006 *Gog Magog – continued*

1	Mark Thistleton (Hayling)	66-67-68-68—269
2	Simon Bell (Baildon)	70-63-71-67—271
	James Smith (Sundridge Park)	69-67-69-66—271

Standard Life Leven Gold Medal (inaugurated 1870) *always at Leven Links, Fife*

1870	J Elder	85
1871	R Wallace	91
1872	P Anderson	91
1873	R Armit	95
1874	D Campbell	93
1875	AM Ross	90
1876	AM Ross	88
1877	J Wilkie	88
1878	R Wallace	90
1879	C Anderson	89
1880	C Anderson	89
1881	J Foggo	91
1882	J Wilkie	89
1883	J Foggo	86
1884	C Anderson	89
1885	R Adam	84
1886	R Adam	87
1887	J Foggo	81
1888	DA Leitch	86
1889	R Adam	81
1890	W Marshall	80
1891	DM Jackson	80
1892	Col DW Mackinnon	85
1893	HS Colt	79
1894	J Bell jr	82
1895	C Wilkie jr	80
1896	J Bell jr	78
1897	J Bell jr	79
1898	G Wilkie jr	82
1899	G Wilkie jr	78
1900	W Henderson	78
1901	R Simpson	76
1902	J Bell	76
1903	W Henderson	76
1904	W Henderson	77
1905	G Wilkie	76
1906	G Wilkie	78
1907	M Goodwillie	73
1908	W Henderson	77
1909	W Henderson	77
1910	W Whyte	76
1911	G Wilkie	73
1912	G Wilkie	73
1913	W Whyte	73

1914	GB Rattray	76
1915–18	No competition	
1919	G Wilkie	77
1920	JJ Smith	76
1921	GV Donaldson	77
1922	SO Shepperd	72
1923	GV Donaldson	73
1924	JN Smith	76
1925	A Robertson	73
1926	T Ainslie	75
1927	EA McRuvie	72
1928	EA McRuvie	70
1929	EA McRuvie	72
1930	EA McRuvie	68
1931	A Dunsire	71
1932	J Ballingall	72
1933	CA Danks	73
1934	EA McRuvie	67
1935	EG Stoddart	71
1936	GA Buist	73
1937	JY Strachan	75
1938	S Macdonald	71
1939	D Jamieson	72
1940–45	No competition	
1946	EA McRuvie	77
1947	JE Young	74
1948	J Imrie	77
1949	WM Ogg	76
1950	E McRuvie	77
1951	J Imrie	72
1952	HVS Thomson	69
1953	O Rolland	70
1954	JW Draper	73
1955	JW Draper	72
1956	R Dishart	72
1957	I Pearson	72
1958	W McIntyre	71
1959	W Moyes	71
1960	T Taylor	69
1963	W Moyes	68
1961	A Cunningham	69
1962	W Moyes	71
1964	A Cunningham	68
1965	PG Buchanan	71

Two rounds played from 1966

1966	GM Rutherford	144
1967	AO Maxwell	140
1968	A Cunningham	140

Four rounds played from 1969

1969	P Smith	284
1970	JC Farmer	277
1971	J Scott Macdonald	207
1972	J Rankine	282
1973	S Stephen	288
1974	P Smith	282
1975	HB Stuart	286
1976	IC Hutcheon	266
1977	IC Hutcheon	289
1978	R Wallace	287
1979	B Marchbank	274
1980	J Huggan	279
1981	IC Hutcheon	282
1982	IC Hutcheon	272
1983	J Huggan	274
1984	S Stephen	278
1985	AD Turnbull	281
1986	P-U Johansson	275
1987	G Macgregor	271
1988	CE Everett	280
1989	AJ Coltart	280
1990	CE Everett	280
1991	GA Lowson	284
1992	D Robertson	279
1993	L Westwood	276
1994	B Howard	265
1995	S Mackenzie	273
1996	M Eliasson	267
1997	S Carmichael	278
1998	G Rankin	268
1999	J Mathers	291
2000	G Gordon	269
2001	P Whiteford*	271
2002	J Doherty	263
2003	J White	262
2004	J King	265
2005	G Murray	275

1	George Murray (Earlsferry Thistle)	72-69-76-67—284
2	Callum Macaulay (Tulliallan)	72-69-71-75—287
3	Philip McLean (Peterhead)	72-73-67-76—288

Lytham Trophy (inaugurated 1965) *always at Royal Lytham & St Annes and Fairhaven*

1965T	MF Bonallack	295
	CA Clark	
1966	PM Townsend	290
1967	R Foster	296
1968	R Foster	286
1969T	T Craddock	290
	SG Birtwell	

1970T	JC Farmer	296
	CW Green	
	GC Marks	
1971	W Humphreys	292
1972	MF Bonallack	281
1973T	MG King	292
	SG Birtwell	292
1974	CW Green	291

1975	G Macgregor	299
1976	MJ Kelley	292
1977	P Deeble	296
1978	B Marchbank	288
1979	P McEvoy	279
1980	IC Hutcheon	293
1981	R Chapman	221
1982	MF Sludds	306

1983	S McAllister	299	1991	G Evans	284	1999	T Schuster	283
1984	J Hawksworth	289	1992	S Cage	294	2000	D Dixon	285
1985	MPD Walls	291	1993	T McLure	292	2001	R McEvoy	276
1986	S McKenna	297	1994	W Bennett	285	2002	L Corfield	283
1987	D Wood	293	1995	S Gallacher	281	2003	S Wilson	283
1988	P Broadhurst	296	1996	M Carver	284	2004	J Heath	266
1989	N Williamson	286	1997	G Rankin	279	2005	G Lockerbie	276
1990	G Evans	291	1998	L Kelly	288			

1	Jamie Moul (Stoke-by-Nayland)*	68-72-69-70—279
2	George Murray (Earlsferry Thistle	73066-73-69—279
3	Lawrence Dodd (Thetford)	71-71-67-71—280
	Rory McIlroy (Holywood)	71-71-67-71—280
	Lloyd Saltman (Craigielaw)	71-72-68-69—280

*3-hole play-off (Moul 3-4-4, Murray 3-6-5)

Newlands Trophy 2006 Lanark

1	James Byrne (Banchory)	68-66-71-66—271
2	Chris Orr (Lanark)	71-67-73-64—275
3	Scott Borrowman (Dollar)	70-70-71-69—280
	David McMillan (Lanark)	71-68-69-72—280

St Andrews Links Trophy (inaugurated 1989) always at St Andrews

1989	R Claydon	284	1995	G Rankin	276	2001	S O'Hara	281
1990	S Bouvier (Aus)	280	1996	DB Howard	282	2002	S Mackenzie	289
1991	R Willison	289	1997	J Rose	284	2003	R Finch	276
1992	C Watson	281	1998	C Watson	276	2004	J McLeary	284
1993	G Hay	280	1999	D Patrick	152 (36)	2005	L Saltman	275
1994	DB Howard	294	2000	M King	140			

1	Oliver Fisher (West Essex)	66-70-71-73—280
2	Stephen Dartnall (AUS)	69-73-68-72—282
3	Keir McNicoll (Carnoustie)	68-71-72-73—284

St David's Gold Cross (inaugurated 1930) always at Royal St David's, Gwynedd

1930	GC Stokoe	1959	MSR Lunt	1983	RD James
1931	EW Fiddian	1960	LJ Ranells	1984	RJ Green
1932	Dr W Tweddell	1961	MSR Lunt	1985	KH Williams
1933	IS Thomas	1962	PD Kelley	1986	RN Roderick
1934	SB Roberts	1963	JKD Povall	1987	SR Andrew
1935	IS Thomas	1964	MSR Lunt	1988	MW Calvert
1936	RMW Pritchard	1965	MSR Lunt	1989	AJ Barnett
1937	IS Thomas	1966	MSR Lunt	1990	MA Macara
1938	SB Roberts	1967	MSR Lunt	1991	RJ Dinsdale
1939	IS Thomas	1968	AW Holmes	1992	B Dredge
1940–45	No competition	1969	AJ Thomson	1993	B Dredge
1946	SB Roberts	1970	AJ Thomson	1994	C Evans
1947	G Mills	1971	A Smith	1995	M Skinner
1948	CH Eaves	1972	EN Davies	1996	L Harpin
1949	SB Roberts	1973	RD James	1997	M Pilkington
1950	DMG Sutherland	1974	GC Marks	1998	L Harpin
1951	JL Morgan	1975	CP Hodgkinson	1999	D Jones
1952	SB Roberts	1976	JR Jones	2000	D Price
1953	S Lunt	1977	JA Fagan	2001	C Williams
1954	GB Turner	1978	S Wild	2002	A Smith
1955	JL Morgan	1979	MA Smith	2003	S Manley
1956	W Cdr CH Beamish	1980	CP Hodgkinson	2004	Z Gould
1957	CD Lawrie	1981	G Broadbent	2005	T Dykes
1958	GB Turner	1982	MW Calvert		

1	Ryan Thomas (Aberdare)	68-66-74-69—277
2	Nigel Edwards (Whitchurch)	69-68-66-77—280
3	Craig Evans (West Monmouthshire)	68-69-73-71—281

Sherry Cup(Copa de Jerez) 2006 *Sotogrande, Spain*

1990	Alvaro Prat	1996	Alvaro Salto	2002	L Harpin
1991	Padraig Harrington	1997	Sergio García	2003	G Wolstenholme
1992	Frederic Cupillard	1998	Sergio García	2004	F Molinari
1993	Francisco Valera	1999	Marcel Siem	2005	G Wolstenholme
1994	Francisco Cea	2000	G Wolstenholme		
1995	José Maria Zamora	2001	G Wolstenholme*		

1	Nigel Edwards (WAL)*	71-69-71-71—282
2	José Luis Adarraga (ESP)	74-67-71-70—282
3	Marius Thorp (NOR)	69-72-72-71—284

Edwards won at second extra hole

For team results see page 281

Sutherland Chalice (inaugurated 2000) 2006 *Dumfries & Galloway*

2000	G Gordon	275	2002	G Gordon	264	2004	J King	268
2001	S Carmichael	274	2003	D Sutton	275	2005	B Scott	277

1	George Murray (Earlsferry Thistle)	70-64-63-64—261
2	Glenn Campbell (Blairgowrie)	67-69-67-71—274
3	Mark Lamb (Haddington)	70-70-68-68—276

Tennant Cup (inaugurated 1880) *always at Glasgow GC*

1880	AW Smith	1923	FW Baldie	1967	BJ Gallacher
1881	AW Smith	1924	J Barrie Cooper	1968	CW Green
1882	AM Ross	1925	R Scott jr	1969	J Scott Cochran
1883	J Kirk	1926	W Tulloch	1970	CW Green
1884	W Doleman	1927	W Tulloch	1971	Andrew Brodie
1885	TR Lamb	1928	A Jamieson jr	1972	Allan Brodie
1886	D Bone	1929	R Scott jr	1973	PJ Smith
1887	JR Motion	1930	JE Dawson	1974	D McCart
1888	D Bone	1931	GNS Tweedale	1975	CW Green
1889	W Milne	1932	SL McInlay	1976	IC Hutcheon
1890	W Marshall	1933	H Thomson	1977	S Martin
1891	D Bone	1934	K Lindsay jr	1978	IA Carslaw
1892	D Bone	1935	JM Dykes jr	1979	G Hay
1893	W Doleman	1936	JNW Dall	1980	Allan Brodie
1894	W Doleman	1937	WS McCleod	1981	G MacDonald
1895	JA Shaw	1938	A Jamieson jr	1982	LS Mann
1896	J Thomson	1939	GB Peters	1983	C Dalgleish
1897	D Bone	1940–45	No competition	1984	E Wilson
1898	R Bone	1946	JB Stevenson	1985	CJ Brooks
1899	W Hunter	1947	JC Wilson	1986	PG Girvan
1900	JG Macfarlane	1948	J Wallace	1987	J Rasmussen
1901	R Bone	1949	W Irvine	1988	C Dalgleish
1902	CB Macfarlane	1950	JW Mill	1989	DG Carrick
1903	CB Macfarlane	1951	WS McCleod	1990	C Everett
1904	WS Colville	1952	GT Black	1991	C Everett
1905	TW Robb	1953	AD Gray	1992	D Robertson
1906	JG Macfarlane	1954	H McInally	1993	D Robertson
1907	R Andrew	1955	LG Taylor	1994	G Rankin
1908	R Carson	1956	JM Dykes	1995	S Gallacher
1909	WS Colville	1957	LG Taylor	1996	G Rankin
1910	R Andrew	1958	Dr FWG Deighton	1997	C Hislop
1911	WS Colville	1959	JF Milligan	1998	G Rankin
1912	R Scott jr	1960	Dr FWG Deighton	1999	G Fox
1913	SO Shepherd	1961	R Reid Jack	2000	G Fox
1914	John Caven	1962	WS Jack	2001	C Watson
1915–19	No competition	1963	SWT Murray	2002	B Hume
1920	G Lockhart	1964	Dr FWG Deighton	2003	G Gordon
1921	R Scott jr	1965	J Scott Cochran	2004	M Leishman
1922	WD Macleod	1966	AH Hall	2005	A Hall (AUS)

(continued over)

1	John Gallagher (Swanston)	69-72-68-69—278
2	Gavin Dear (Murrayshall)	72-72-65-70—279
	Scott Jamieson (Cathkin Braes)	76-64-68-71—279
	Craig Watson (East Renfrewshire)	68-67-75-69—279

Tillman Trophy (inaugurated 1989) 2006 *Alwoodley*

1989	J Cook	1995	P Stuart	2001	R Fisher
1990	M Wiggett	1996	S Wakefield	2002	A Gee
1991	A Tillman	1997	M Searle	2003	J Smith
1992	D Probert	1998	R Blaxhill	2004	D Belch
1993	C Nowicki	1999	J Conteh	2005	J Mason
1994	*Not played*	2000	B Welch		

1	Robert Dinwiddie (Barnard Castle)*	71-67-72-72—282
2	Luke Cornford (East Sussex National)	70-69-68-75—282
3	Gary Wolstenholme (Kilworth Springs)	72-67-70-74—283

Dinwiddie won at the first extra hole

Trubshaw Cup (inaugurated 1989) *always at Ashburnham and Tenby*

1989	MA Macara	1994	C Evans	2001	N Edwards
1990	TSM Wilkinson	1995	B Dredge	2002	J Doherty
1991	S Pardoe	1997	M Pilkington	2003	N Edwards
1992	B Dredge	1998	M Pilkington	2004	J Williams
1993	B Dredge	1999	N Matthews	2005	C Smith
1996	M Ellis	2000	N Edwards		

1	Rhys Enoch (Truro)	73-71-68-74—286
2	Richard Merchant (Monmouthshire)	76-69-66-77—288
3	Ben Westgate (Perranporth)	71-71-75-72—289

Tucker Trophy (inaugurated 1991) 2006 *Whitchurch and Newport*

1991	C Evans (W. Monmouthshire)	1996	M Searle (High Post)	2001	NB Edwards (Whitchurch)
1992	R Dinsdale (Newport)	1997	J Donaldson (Macclesfield)	2002	NB Edwards (Whitchurch)
1993	B Dredge (Bryn Meadows)	1998	NB Edwards (Whitchurch)	2003	NB Edwards (Whitchurch)
1994	D Park (Burghill)	1999	J Donaldson (Macclesfield)	2004	NB Edwards (Whitchurch)
1995	M Ellis (Wrexham)	2000	I Campbell (Marlborough)	2005	J Williams (Pontypridd)

1	Nigel Edwards (Whitchurch)	69-69-70-70—278
2	Cennydd Mills (Vale of Glamorgan)	74-68-75-64—281
3	Tim Dykes (Wrexham)	74-69-74-69—286

Lake Macquarie Tournament (inaugurated 1958) *Belmont GC, NSW, Australia*
(Australian unless stated)

1958	B Devlin	1975	C Kaye	1992	S Leaney
1959	P Billings	1976	C Kaye	1993	S Collins
1960	P Billings	1977	D Sharpe	1994	M Wheelhouse (NZL)
1961	P Billings	1978	R Carlin	1995	L Peterson
1962	K Johnstone	1979	C Kaye	1996	S Allan
1963	K Donohue	1980	G Power	1997	G Ogilvy
1964	P Billings	1981	R Chapman (ENG)	1998	B Rumford*
1965	P Billings	1982	C Byrum (USA)		*beat G Wolstenholme in play-off*
1966	P Billings	1983	C Dalgleish (SCO)	1999	J Sutherland
1967	T Jones	1984	J Crowe (USA)	2000	S Strange
1968	J Bennett	1985	R Picker	2001	N Docherty (ENG)*
1969	J Newton	1986	P O'Malley		*beat L Hickmott in play-off*
1970	D Sharpe	1987	S Robinson	2002	C Campbell
1971	D Sharpe	1988	D Ecob	2003	J Lyle
1972	B Boyle	1989	R Claydon (ENG)	2004	J Lyle
1973	R Davis	1990	R Willison (ENG)	2005	M Leishman
1974	P Billings	1991	S Tait		

(continued over

Lake Macquarie Tournament *continued*

2006

1	Adam Gee (Leatherhead (ENG))*	69-69-66-69—273
2	Jason Day (AUS)	68-72-70-63—273
3	Won Joon Lee (AUS)	66-71-73-64—274

Chiberta Grand Prix Europe 2006 *Biarritz, France*

2005   J Campillo (ESP)

1	Duncan Stewart (SCO)	69-66-65-73—273
2	Jamie Abbott (ENG)	70-68-66-70—274
3	Rudy Thuillier (FRA)	67-73-69-68—277

Callaway Handicapping

It frequently occurs in social competitions such as office or business association outings that many of the competitors do not have official handicaps. In such cases the best solution is to use the Callaway handicapping system, so called after the name of its inventor, as it is simple to use yet has proved equitable.

Competitors complete their round marking in their gross figures at every hole and their handicaps are awarded and deducted at the end of the 18 holes using the following table:

Competitor's Gross Score	*Handicap Deduction*
par or less	none
one over par – 75	½ worst hole
76–80	worst hole
81–85	worst hole plus ½ next worse
86–90	two worst holes
91–95	two worst holes plus ½ next
96–100	three worst holes
101–105	three worst holes plus ½ next
106–110	four worst holes
111–115	four worst holes plus ½ next
116–120	five worst holes
121–125	five worst holes plus ½ next
126–130	six worst holes

Note 1: Worst hole equals highest score at any hole regardless of the par of the hole except that the maximum score allowed for any one hole is twice the par of the hole.

Note 2: The 17th and 18th holes are not allowed to be deducted.

Example: Competitor scores 104. From the table he should deduct as his handicap the total of his three worst (i.e. highest) individual hole scores plus half of his fourth worst hole. If he scored one 9, one 8 and several 7's he would therefore deduct a total of 27½ from his gross score of 104 to give a net score of 76½.

National District Championships

Midland Open (inaugurated 1976) 2006 *Newcastle-under-Lyme and Trentham Park*

1976	P Downes	1984	K Valentine	1992	M McGuire	2000	D Dixon
1977	P Downes	1985	MC Hassall	1993	N Williamson	2001	M Lock
1978	P McEvoy	1986	G Wolstenholme	1994	D Howell	2002	G Wolstenholme
1979	M Tomlinson	1987	C Suneson	1995	G Harris	2003	J Kemp
1980	P Downes	1988	R Winchester	1996	M Carver	2004	R Steele
1981	P Baxter	1989	J Cook	1997	P Streeter	2005	M Cryer
1982	NJ Chesses	1990	J Bickerton	1998	L Donald		
1983	CA Banks	1991	P Sefton	1999	G Davies		

1	Ed Richardson (Southern Valley)	66-71-70-71—278
2	James Morrison (St George's Hill)	76-65-70-70—281
3	Charles Ford (Kirkby Muxloe)	71-71-68-73—283

South of England Open Amateur 2006 *Walton Heath*

1	Gary Wolstenholme* (Kilworth Springs)	71-68-65-72—276
2	Ross McGowan (Banstead Downs)	66-71-70-69—276
3	Ben Evans (Rye)	72-69-70-70—281
	Joost Luiten (NED)	67-71-69-74—281

Wolstenholme won at second extra hole

West of England Open Match Play (inaugurated 1912) *always at Burnham & Berrow*

1912	RA Riddell	1937	O Austreng	1964	DC Allen	1986	J Bennett
1913	Hon M Scott	1938	HJ Roberts	1965	DE Jones	1987	D Rosier
1914–18	No competition	1939–45	No competition	1966	A Forrester	1988	N Holman
1919	Hon M Scott	1946	JH Neal	1967	A Forrester	1989	N Holman
1920	Hon D Scott	1947	WF Wise	1968	SR Warrin	1990	I West
1921	CVL Hooman	1948	WF Wise	1969	SR Warrin	1991	S Amor
1922	Hon M Scott	1949	J Payne	1970	C Ball	1992	K Baker
1923	D Grant	1950	EB Millward	1971	G Irlam	1993	D Haines
1924	D Grant	1951	J Payne	1972	JA Bloxham	1994	A Emery
1925	D Grant	1952	EB Millward	1973	SC Mason	1995	A March
1926	K Whetstone	1953	F Griffin	1974	CS Mitchell	1996	M Carver
1927	GC Brooks	1954	EB Millward	1975	MR Lovett	1997	SJ Martin
1928	JA Pierson	1955	SJ Fox	1976	No competition	1998	D Dixon
1929	DE Landale	1956	SJ Fox	1977	AR Dunlop	1999	D Dixon
1930	RH de	1957	D Gardner	1978	R Broad	2000	J Morgan
	Montmorency	1958	AJN Young	1979	N Burch	2001	L Corfield
1931	DR Howard	1959	DM Woolmer	1980	JM Durbin	2002	J Donaldson
1932	R Straker	1960	AW Holmes	1981	M Mouland	2003	E Butler
1933	DM Anderson	1961	JM Leach	1982	M Higgins	2004	T Burley
1934	Hon M Scott	1962	Sq Ldr WE	1983	C Peacock	2005	M Mackman
1935	JJF Pennink		McCrea	1984	GB Hickman		
1936	PH White	1963	KT Warren	1985	AC Nash		

Quarter-Finals
Edward Butler (Lansdown) beat Richard Scarrott (Wrag Barn) 2 holes
Mark Searle (High Post) beat Max Burrow (Exeter) 3 and 2
Peter Godfrey (Wentworth) beat Kristian Branum-Burns (Bearwood Lakes) 4 and 3
Ross Jones (Orchardleigh) beat Warren Harmston (Wentworth) 6 and 5

Semi-Finals
Searle beat Butler 6 and 5
Godfrey beat Jones 6 and 4

Final
Peter Godfrey beat Mark Searle 3 and 2

West of England Open Stroke Play (inaugurated 1968) 2006 *Royal North Devon*

1968	PJ Yeo	Saunton	297	1987	G Wolstenholme	Saunton	296
1969	A Forrester	Saunton	304	1988	MC Evans	R North Devon	291
1970	PJ Yeo	R North Devon	312	1989	AD Hare	Saunton	289
1971	P Berry	Saunton	303	1990	J Payne	Saunton	290
1972	P Berry	R North Devon	310	1991	D Lee	Saunton	286
1973	SC Mason	Saunton	287	1992	M Stanford	R North Devon	291
1974	R Abbott	R North Devon	301	1993	PR Trew	Saunton	279
1975	BG Steer	Saunton	290	1994	CP Nowicki	R North Devon	294
1976	R Abbott	R North Devon	304	1995	G Clark	Saunton	141 (36)
1977	PE McEvoy	Saunton	298	1996	R Wiggins	Saunton	288
1978	JG Bennett*	R North Devon	291	1997	M Reynard	R North Devon	280
After play-off with PE McEvoy				1998	C Edwards	R North Devon	287
1979	R Kane	Saunton	296	1999	D Griffiths	Saunton	286
1980	PE McEvoy	R North Devon	288	2000	S Grewal	R North Devon	279
1981	N Taee	Saunton	245 (54)	2001	R Finch	Saunton	279
1982	MP Higgins	R North Devon	286	2002	D Barnes	Royal North Devon	219
1983	PE McEvoy	Saunton	298	2003	E Butler	Royal North Devon	282
1984	A Sherborne	R North Devon	288	2004	L Corfield	Royal North Devon	279
1985	PE McEvoy	Saunton	307	2005	E Richardson	Saunton	280
1986	P Baker*	R North Devon	282				

Won at second extra hole after play-off with PE McEvoy

1	David Horsey (Styal)	74-68-72-69—283	
2	Adam Gee (Leatherhead)	72-72-69-73—286	
	Ross McGowan (Banstead Downs)	77-73-66-70—286	
	Paul Waring (Bromborough)	69-74-72-71—286	

East of Ireland Open 2006 *Co. Louth*

1989	D Clarke	1994	G McGimpsey	1999	K Kearney	2002	N Fox
1990	D O'Sullivan	1995	D Brannigan	2000	N Fox*	2003	M Sinclair
1991	P Hogan	1996	N Fox		*Fox beat M Murphy (better	2004	M Campbell
1992	R Burns	1997	S Quinlivan		last round)*	2005	J Carvill
1993	R Burns	1998	G McGimpsey	2001	K Kearney		

1	Brendan McCarroll (Ballyliffin)	73-71-68-71—283
2	Jonathan Caldwell (Clandeboye)	69-68-74-74—285
3	Shane Lowry (Esker Hills)	71-73-73-72—289

North of Ireland Open 2006 *Cork*

1989	N Anderson	1994	N Ludwell	1999	P Gribben	2004	T Coulter
1990	D Clarke	1995	F Nolan	2000	M Hoey	2005	G Shaw
1991	G McGimpsey	1996	M McGinley	2001	S Paul		
1992	G McGimpsey	1997	M Sinclair	2002	G Maybin		
1993	G McGimpsey	1998	P Gribben	2003	B McElhinney		

Leading Qualifier: Connor Doran (Banbridge)   68-68—136

Quarter-Finals

Rory Leonard (Banbridge) beat Andrew McCormick (Scrabo) 3 and 2

Darren Crowe (Dunmurry) beat Michael Lavelle (Belmullet) 5 and 4

Connor Doran (Banbridge) beat Robert McCarthy (The Island) 3 and 2

Andrew Pitcher (The Island) beat Nick Scholey (Henbury) 3 and 2

Semi-Finals

Crowe beat Leonard 1 hole
Doran beat Pitcher 5 and 3

Final: Darren Crowe beat Connor Doran 2 holes

South of Ireland Open 2006 *Lahinch*

1989	S Keenan	1994	D Higgins	1999	M Campbell	2004	C McNamara
1990	D Clarke	1995	J Fanagan	2000	G McDowell	2005	J Carvill
1991	P McGinley	1996	A Morrow	2001	J Kehoe		
1992	L MacNamara	1997	P Collier	2002	C Moriarty		
1993	P Sheehan	1998	J Foster	2003	M Owens		

Quarter-Finals

Darren Crowe (Dunmurry) beat Mark Campbell
(Stackstown) 2 and 1
Michael O'Kelly (Limerick) beat Robert McCarthy
(The Island) 5 and 4
Simon Ward (Co.Louth) beat Jonathan Caldwell (Clandeboye)
5 and 3
Pat Murray (Limerick) beat Gary O'Flaherty (Cork) 5 and 4

Semi-Finals

Crowe beat O'Kelly 2 and 1
Ward beat Murray 2 and 1

Final: Simon Ward beat Darren
Crowe 2 and 1

West of Ireland Open 2006 *Co Sligo*

1989	P McInerney	1994	P Harrington	1999	M Ilonen (FIN)	2004	P McDonald
1990	N Goulding	1995	E Brady	2000	E Brady	2005	R McIlroy
1991	N Goulding	1996	G McGimpsey	2001	M McDermott		
1992	K Kearney	1997	J Fanagan	2002	S Paul		
1993	G McGimpsey	1998	N Fox	2003	M Ryan		

Leading Qualifiers: 140 – Paul O'Hanlon (Curragh) 71-69; David Horsey (Styal) 67-73

Quarter-Finals

David Horsey beat Randal Evans (Moyola Park) 5 and 4
Rory McIlroy (Holywood) beat Connor Doran
(Banbridge) 5 and 4
Andrew McCormick (Scrabo) beat Seamus Power
(West Waterford) 2 and 1
Paul O'Hanlon beat Darren Crowe (Dunmurry) 2 and 1

Semi-Finals

McIlroy beat Horsey at 21st
O'Hanlon beat McCormick 1 hole

Final

Rory McIlroy beat Paul O'Hanlon
3 and 1

East of Scotland Open Stroke Play 2006 *Lundin GC*

1989	K Hird	1994	A Reid	1999	R Beames	2004	R Ramsay
1990	G Lawrie	1995	G Davidson	2000	C Watson	2005	W Booth
1991	R Clark	1996	C Hislop	2001	J King		
1992	ST Knowles	1997	S Meiklejohn	2002	D Inglis		
1993	S Meiklejohn	1998	B Lamb (Aus)	2003	J King		

1	Keir McNicoll (Carnoustie)	72-64-67-65—268
2	John Gallagher (Swanston)	66-64-69-72—269
	Lloyd Saltman (Craigielaw)	69-66-67-67—269

North of Scotland Open Stroke Play 2006 *Nairn Dunbar*

1989	G Hickman	1994	E Forbes	1999	N Steven*	2004	B Fotheringham
1990	S McIntosh	1995	R Beames	2000	C Watson	2005	E Saltman
1991	S Henderson	1996	C Dunan	2001	G Thomson		
1992	K Buchan	1997	G Crawford	2002	W Booth		
1993	D Downie	1998	C Taylor	2003	G Murray		

1	Kevin McAlpine (Alyth)	71-69-68-74—282
2	Arthur Culverwell (Dunbar)	70-69-75-70—284
3	Philip McLean (Peterhead)	67-75-72-71—285

North-East Scotland District Championship 2006 Fraserburgh

1999	BA Innes	2001	G Gordon	2003	J McLeary	2005	M Kerr* (at 4th extra hole)
2000	E Forbes	2002	B Innes	2004	G Campbell*		

1	Mark Halliday (Royal Aberdeen)	68-68-67—203
2	Steven McEwan (Kilmarnock [Barassie])	68-66-70—204
3	James Byrne (Banchory)	69-66-70—205

South-East Scotland District Championship 2006 Longniddry

1999	S Carmichael	2001	J Doherty	2003	S Wilson	2005	S Smith
2000	J King	2002	S Armstrong	2004	E Ramsay		

1	Glenn Campbell (Blairgowrie)*	65-66-63-69—263
2	Shaun McAllister (Craigielaw)	66-66-68-63—263
	Rob McKnight (Kilmarnock Barassie)	64-66-65-68—263

*Campbell won at the 4th extra hole

West of Scotland Open 2006 Cawder

1989	A Elliot	1994	J Hodgson	1999	L Kelly	2004	Not played
1990	S Knowles	1995	G Rankin	2000	S O'Hara	2005	A Dick
1991	A Coltart	1996	C Hislop	2001	B Fitzsimmons		
1992	S Henderson	1997	C Hislop	2002	G Gordon		
1993	B Howard	1998	L Kelly	2003	G Gordon		

1	Callum McAulay (Tulliallan)	66-66-68-68—268
2	Graeme Gorrie (Glasgow)	68-67-67-68—270
3	Glenn Campbell (Blairgowrie)	70-68-67-67—272
	Matthew Clark (Kilmacolm)	71-67-65-69—272
	Ross Kellett (Colville Park)	68-68-65-71—272

David Pepper lands top role with IGF

David Pepper, chairman of the General Committee of the Royal and Ancient Golf Cub of St Andrews, has taken over from David Harrison as joint chairman of the International Golf Federation, the organisation founded in 1958 as the World Amateur Golf Council to encourage the international development of the game and as vehicle to foster friendship and sportsmanship.

Recognized by the International Olympic Committee as the official federation for golf, the IGF comprises the national governing bodies of golf in more than 100 countries and also conducts the bi-ennial World Amateur Team Championships for the Eisenhower Trophy and Espirito Santo Trophy.

Married with four children, 66-year-old Pepper has been a member of the R and A since 1967 and during that time has served on and chaired the Rules of Golf Committee. He has also served on the Implements and Ball Committee, the Commercial Committee and the 250th Anniversary Committee. He was on the Championship Committee from 1988 to 1992 and again from 2000 to 2004 when he was chairman with responsibility for running the Open Championship.

Mr Pepper will work closely with Vicky Whyte, the women's chairman and the joint secretaries Peter Dawson, secretary of the Royal and Ancient Golf Club of St Andrews, and David Fay, Executive Director of the USGA. A long-time member of Little Aston where, having served as treasurer and captain, he is now president he is also past treasurer and captain of the Midland Junior Golf Society and is currently a committee member of The Senior Golfers' Society.

Other Men's Amateur Tournaments

Berkhamsted Trophy (inaugurated 1960) *always at Berkhamsted*

Year	Name	Score	Year	Name	Score	Year	Name	Score
1960	HC Squirrell	150	1976	JC Davies	144	1992	P Page	141
1961	DW Frame	147	1977	AWB Lyle	144	1993	S Burnell	143
1962	DG Neech	149	1978	JC Davies	146	1994	M Treleaven	140
1963	HC Squirrell	149	1979	JC Davies	147	1995	J Crampton	142
1964	PD Flaherty	149	1980	R Knott	143	1996	L Donald	139
1965	LF Millar	153	1981	P Dennett	146	1997	P Streeter	143
1966	P Townsend	150	1982	DG Lane	148	1998	G Storm	69 (18)
1967	DJ Millensted	150	1983	J Hawksworth	146	1999	GP Wolstenholme*	140
1968	PD Flaherty	144	1984	R Willison	139	2000	J Wormald*	141
1969	MM Niven	149	1985	F George	144	2001	S Godfrey	140
1970	R Hunter	145	1986	P McEvoy	144	2002	G Wolstenholme	140
1971	A Millar	144	1987	F George	141	2003	J Knight	140
1972	C Cieslewicz	148	1988	J Cowgill	146	2004	J Ruth	140
1973	SC Mason	141	1989	J Payne	142	2005	I Parnaby	135
1974	P Fisher	144	1990	J Barnes	144			
1975	PG Deeble	147	1991	G Homewood	141			

1	Adam Norman (Moseley)	68-69—137
2	Ross McGowan (Banstead Downs)	69-74—143
3	George Woolgar (Chesterfield)	71-73—144

John Cross Bowl (inaugurated 1957) *always at Worplesdon, Surrey*

Year	Name	Year	Name	Year	Name
1957	DW Frame	1974	RPF Brown	1991	P Sefton
1958	G Evans	1975	BJ Winteridge	1992	R Watts
1959	G Evans	1976	DW Frame	1993	J Collier
1960	DW Frame	1977	DW Frame	1994	P Benka
1961	DW Frame	1978	RPF Brown	1995	M Galway
1962	DW Frame	1979	JG Bennett	1996	B Barham
1963	PO Green	1980	JG Bennett	1997	C Banks
1964	RL Glading	1981	ME Johnson	1998	J Wormald
1965	P Townsend	1982	R Boxall	1999	M Galway
1966	P Townsend	1983	DG Lane	2000	R Mann*
1967	MJ Burgess	1984	I Gray	2001	J Bint
1968	PJ Benka	1985	M Devetta	2002	D Holmes
1969	DW Frame	1986	C Rotheroe	2003	D Curtis
1970	P Dawson	1987	B White	2004	J Brown*
1971	PBQ Drayson	1988	B White	2005	M Galway
1972	AR Kerr	1989	KG Jones		
1973	DW Frame	1990	D Lee		

1	A Shields (Worplesdon)	69-69—138
2	M Galway (Brighton & Hove)	71-68—139
3	N Taee (Queenwood)	69-70—139

Frame Trophy (inaugurated 1986 for players aged 50+) *always at Worplesdon, Surrey*

Year	Name	Score	Year	Name	Score	Year	Name	Score
1988	DW Frame	229	1994	DG Lane	222	2000	DW Frame	213
1989	JRW Walkinshaw	219	1995	M Christmas	223	2001	DW Frame	217
1990	WJ Williams	224	1996	DG Lane	217	2002	BK Turner	209
1991	DB Sheahan	223	1997	B Turner	226	2003	BK Turner	219
1992	DW Frame	223	1998	DG Lane	211	2004	DG Lane*	221
1993	DW Frame	216	1999	NH Barnes	220	2005	ND Coleman	220

(continued over)

Frame Trophy *continued*

1	N H Barnes (Brokenhurst Manor)	74-69-77—220
2	M L Kirby (Hayling)	75-73-75—223
3	M J Wigley (Hankley Common)	74-78-72—224

Golf Illustrated Gold Vase (inaugurated 1909)

1909	CK Hutchison	1950	AW Whyte	1977	J Davies
1910	Abe Mitchell	1951	JB Carr	1978	P Thomas
1911	R Harris	1952	JDA Langley	1979	KJ Miller
1912	R Harris	1953	JDA Langley	1980	G Brand Jr
1913	Abe Mitchell	1954	H Ridgeley	1981	P Garner
1914	H Hilton	1955	Major DA Blair	1982	I Carslaw
1919	D Darwin	1956	Major DA Blair	1983	S Keppler
1920	DS Crowther	1957	GB Wolstenholme	1984	JV Marks
1921	M Seymour	1958	M Lunt	1985	M Davis
1922	WA Murray	1959	A Bussell	1986	R Eggo
1923	CJH Tolley	1960	D Sewell	1987	D Lane
1924	CC Aylmer	1961T	DJ Harrison/MF Bonallack	1988	M Turner
1925	JB Beck	1962	BHG Chapman	1989	GP Wolstenholme
1926T	CJH Tolley/TA Torrance	1963	RH Mummery	1990	A Rogers
1927	RH Wethered	1964	D Moffat	1991	R Scott
1928	CJH Tolley	1965	C Clark	1992	P Page
1929	D Grant	1966	PM Townsend	1993T	C Challen/V Phillips
1930	RT Jones (US)	1967T	MF Bonallack/	1994	S Burnell
1931	WA Murray		RA Durrant	1995	A Wall
1932	RW Hartley	1968	MF Bonallack	1996	*Not played*
1933	RW Hartley	1969T	MF Bonallack/J Hayes	1997	M James
1934	WL Hartley	1970	D Harrison	1998	R Rea*
1935	J Thomas	1971	MF Bonallack	1999	M Side
1936	J Ferrier	1972T	H Ashby/DP Davidson/	2000	J Kemp
1937	R Sweeney		R Hunter	2001	J Heath
1938	CJ Anderson	1973	J Davies	2002	A Inglis
1939	SB Robert	1974	P Hedges	2003	R Roper
1948	RD Chapman	1975	MF Bonallack		
1949	RJ White	1976	A Brodie		

Discontinued

Hampshire Hog (inaugurated 1957) *always at North Hants*

1957	MF Bonallack	1974	TJ Giles	1991	M Welch
1958	PF Scrutton	1975	HAN Stott	1992	S Graham
1959	Col AA Duncan	1976	MC Hughesdon	1993	D Hamilton
1960	MF Attenborough	1977	AWB Lyle	1994	B Ingleby
1961	HC Squirrell	1978	GF Godwin	1995	J Rose
1962	FD Physick	1979	MF Bonallack	1996	R Tate
1963	Sqn Ldr WE McCrea	1980	RA Durrant	1997	GP Wolstenholme
1964	DF Wilkie	1981	G Brand jr	1998	P Rowe
1965	T Koch de Gooreynd	1982	A Sherborne	1999	C Rodgers
1966	Major DA Blair	1983	I Gray	2000	M Booker
1967	Major DA Blair	1984	J Hawksworth	2001	J Lupton
1968	MJ Burgess	1985	A Clapp	2002	G Wolstenholme
1969	B Critchley	1986	R Eggo	2003	M Sell
1970	Major DA Blair	1987	A Rogers	2004	L Kennedy
1971	DW Frame	1988	S Richardson	2005	L Dodd
1972	R Revell	1989	P McEvoy		
1973	SC Mason	1990	J Metcalfe		

1	James Crampton (Spalding)	67-63—130
2	Jamie Moul (Stoke-by-Nayland)	65-67—132
3	Lawrence Dodd (Thetford)	66-67—133

King George V Coronation Cup *always at Porters Park, Herts*

1990	C Boal	141	1996	N Swaffield	134	2002	G Evans	141
1991	S Hoffman	142	1997	J Knight	136	2003	L Gauthier	137
1992	R Watts	141	1998	M King	65 (18)	2004	J Ruebotham	144
1993	D Hamilton	134	1999	J Field*	141	2005	A Bravant	137
1994	S Webster	146	2000	R Chattaway	142			
1995	S Jarvis	140	2001	M Payne*	143			

1	Alan Glynn (Porters Park)	69-65—134
2	Laurence Allen (Brookmans Park)	70-68—138
3	Daniel Brooks (Mill Hill)	69-72—141

Prince of Wales Challenge Cup (inaugurated 1928) *always at Royal Cinque Ports*

1928	D Grant	142	1960	CG Moore	162	1984	F Wood	146
1929	NR Reeves	153	1961	RH Bazell	151		DH Niven	146
1930	R Harris	156	1962	Dr J Pittar	154	1985	RJ Tickner	141
1931	RW Hartley	149	1963	Sq Ldr WE McCrea	155	1986	JM Baldwin	149
1932	EN Layton	151	1964	NA Paul	153	1987	S Finch	148
1933	JB Nash	148	1965	NA Paul	150	1988	MP Palmer	144
1934	R Sweeney	304		VE Barton	150	1989	T Lloyd	146
1935	HG Bentley	301	1966	P Townsend	150		NA Farrell	146
1936	LOM Munn	301	1967	MF Bonallack	141	1990	G Homewood	145
1937	DHR Martin	291	1968	NA Paul	144		BS Ingleby	145
1938	EA Head	291		GC Marks	144	1991	S Pardoe	152
1939–46	No competition		1969	MF Attenborough	152	1992	L Westwood	160
1947	PB Lucas	154	1970	J Butterworth	153	1993	ML Welch	143
1948	Capt DA Blair	151	1971	VE Barton	147	1994	I Hardy	149
1949	C Stowe	142	1972	PJ Hedges	162	1995	L Ferris	152
1950	I Caldwell	151	1973	PJ Hedges	138	1996	J Maddock	142
1951	I Caldwell	151	1974	PJ Hedges	146	1997	J Carter	154
1952	I Caldwell	150	1975	JC Davies	150	1998	G Woodman	144
1953	JG Blackwell	159	1976	MJ Inglis	162	1999	A Webster (AUS)	147
1954	DLW Woon	143	1977	PJ Hedges	154	2000	JM Bint	145
1955	C Taylor	153	1978	ER Dexter	145	2001	A Webster	140
	GT Duncan	153	1979	GF Godwin	148	2002	G Homewood	151
1956	PF Scrutton	151	1980	GM Dunsire	149	2003	S Tiley	142
1957	No competition			B Nicholson	149	2004	A Tampion (AUS)	143
1958	KR Mackenzie	158	1981	JM Baldwin	146	2005	D Pike*	146
	BAF Belmore	158	1982	SG Homewood	145	*Pike beat D Harris at 1st extra hole		
1959	D Johnstone	149	1983	M Davis	141			

1	Jason Barnes (Ashford)	69-67—136
2	Daniel Brooks (Mill Hill)	70-69—139
3	Steven Tiley (Royal Cinque Ports)	73-67—140

Rosebery Challenge Cup (inaugurated 1933) *always at Ashridge*

1962	PR Johnston	1977	J Ambridge	1992	R Harris
1963	CA Murray	1978	RJ Bevan	1993	M Hooper
1964	A Millar	1979	JB Berney	1994	P Wilkins
1965	EJ Wiggs	1980	JA Watts	1995	P Wilkins
1966	A Holmes	1981	RY Mitchell	1996	J Kemp
1967	A Holmes	1982	DG Lane	1997	L Watcham
1968	A Holmes	1983	N Briggs	1998	S Vinnicombe
1969	A Holmes	1984	DG Lane	1999	J Kemp
1970	PW Bent	1985	P Wharton	2000	J Kemp
1971	AW Holmes	1986	JE Ambridge	2001	J Ruebotham
1972	AW Holmes	1987	HA Wilkerson	2002	R Leonard
1973	AJ Mason	1988	N Leconte	2003	D Stockwell
1974	G Stradling	1989	C Slattery	2004	K Freeman
1975	JA Watts	1990	C Tingey	2005	J York
1976	G Stradling	1991	M Thompson		

(continued over)

Rosebery Challenge Cup *continued*

1	Gregory Schmidt (Welwyn Garden City)	67-69—136
2	Luke Goddard (Hendon)	67-70—137
3	Nick Pateman (Porters Park)	73-66—139
	Robert Watkins (Bush Hill Park)	68-71—139

St George's Grand Challenge Cup *always at Royal St George's, Sandwich, Kent*

(inaugurated 1888)

Year	Winner	Score	Year	Winner	Score	Year	Winner	Score
1888	J Ball	180	1928	D Grant	146	1970	PJ Hedges	150
1889	J Ball	169	1929	TA Torrance	148	1971	EJS Garrett	143
1890	J Ball	175	1930	RW Hartley	148	1972	JC Davies	149
1891	J Ball	174	1931	WL Hartley	149	1973	JC Davies	141
1892	FA Fairlie	167	1932	HG Bentley	151	1974	JC Davies	140
1893	HH Hilton	165	1933	JB Beck	151	1975	JC Davies	147
1894	HH Hilton	167	1934	AGS Penman	153	1976	JC Davies	158
1895	E Blackwell	176	1935	Maj WHH Aitken	158	1977	JC Davies	154
1896	FG Tait	165	1936	DHR Martin	150	1978	C Phillips	145
1897	CE Hambro	162	1937	DHR Martin	144	1979	CF Godwin	146
1898	FG Tait	163	1938	JJF Pennink	142	1980	J Simmance	150
1899	FG Tait	155	1939	AA McNair	153	1981	MF Bonallack	151
1900	R Maxwell	155	1940–46	No competition		1982	SJ Wood	145
1901	SH Fry	165	1947	PB Lucas	147	1983	R Willison	155
1902	H Castle	162	1948	M Gonzalez	144	1984	SJ Wood	142
1903	CK Hutchison	158	1949	PF Scrutton	143	1985	SJ Wood	144
1904	J Graham jr	154	1950	E Bromley-Davenport	148	1986	RC Claydon	143
1905	R Harris	154	1951	PF Scrutton	142	1987	MR Coodwin	147
1906	S Mure Fergusson	155	1952	GH Micklem	148	1988	T Ryan	143
1907	CE Dick	161	1953	Major DA Blair	148	1989	S Green	149
1908	AC Lincoln	157	1954	H Berwick (Aus)	141	1990	P Sullivan	144
1909	SH Fry	153	1955	PF Scrutton	150	1991	D Fisher	141
1910	Capt CK Hutchison	157	1956	DAC Marr	148	1992	L Westwood	146
1911	E Martin Smith	148	1957	PF Scrutton	148	1993	P Sefton	137
1912	Hon Michael Scott	146	1958	PF Scrutton	144	1994	M Welch	142
1913	HD Gillies	153	1959	J Nicklaus (USA)	149	1995	J Harris	142
1914	J Graham jr	146	1960	JG Blackwell	152	1996	M Brooks	137
1915–19	No competition		1961	Sq Ldr WE McCrea	143	1997	Abandoned due to rain	
1920	R Harris	162	1962	Sq Ldr WE McCrea	145	1998	C Gold*	145
1921	WB Torrance	154	1963	Sq Ldr WE McCrea	150	1999	M Williamson (Aus)	149
1922	WI Hunter	156	1964	Major DA Blair	153	2000	P Appleyard	151
1923	F Ouimet (USA)	153	1965	MF Bonallack	144	2001	A Gee	140
1924	RH Wethered	149	1966	P Townsend	148	2002	B St John	145
1925	D Grant	149	1967	Major DA Blair	154	2003	N Olsen	141
1926	Maj CO Hezlet	158	1968	MF Bonallack	142	2004	D Crompton	145
1927	WL Hartley	153	1969	PJ Benka	150	2005	W Hayter	149

1	Jamie Moul (Stoke-by-Nayland)	73-72—145
2	Stephen Tiley (Royal Cinque Ports)	76-69—145
3	John Macklen (Sundridge Park)	71-75—146

Selborne Salver *(inaugurated 1976)* *always at Blackmoor*

Year	Winner	Year	Winner	Year	Winner
1976	A Miller	1986	TE Clarke	1996	J Knight
1977	CS Mitchell	1987	A Clapp	1997	R Binney
1978	GM Brand	1988	NE Holman	1998	M Side
1979	P McEvoy	1989	M Stamford	1999	B Mason
1980	P McEvoy	1990	J Metcalfe	2000	J Franks
1981	A Sherborne	1991	J Payne	2001	G Wolstenholme
1982	IA Cray	1992	M Treleaven	2002	G Clark
1983	DG Lane	1993	M Welch	2003	Z Scotland
1984	D Curry	1994	W Bennett	2004	R Fisher
1985	SM Bottomley	1995	S Drummond	2005	R Henley

(continued over)

1	Jamie Moul (Stoke-by-Nayland)*	67-69—136
2	Lawrence Dodd (Thetford)	67-69—136
3	Mike Bush (Rochester & Cobham)	72-65—137
	James Crampton (Spalding)	68-69—137

Moul beat Dodd at first extra hole

Month by month in 2006

Woods hits his driver just once in 72 holes, but is far too good for the rest on The Open's return to Hoylake after 39 years. At 18 under par he is just one off the record he set himself at St Andrews in 2000. It gives him 11 majors, while Annika Sörenstam moves on to 10 when she beats Pat Hurst in US Women's Open play-off at Newport, Rhode Island. Corey Pavin ends 10 years without a win.

Foursomes Events

The Antlers (inaugurated 1933) *always at Royal Mid-Surrey*

1933	TFB Law and PWL Risdon	147	1971	I Mosey and I Gradwell	144
1934	GA Hill and HS Malik	153	1972	MJ Kelley and W Smith	144
1935	EF Storey and Sir WS Worthington Evans	152	1973	DOJ Albutt and P Flaherty	148
1936	HG Bentley and F Francis	144	1974	BF Critchley and MC Hughesdon	140
1937	LG Crawley and C Stowe	145	1975	JC Davies and PJ Davies	140
1938	RW Hartley and PWL Risdon	149	1976	JK Tate and P Deeble	144
1939	LG Crawley and H Thomson	148	1977	JC Davies and PJ Davies	141
1940–47	*Not played*		1978	R Chapman and R Fish	148
1948	RC Quilter and E Bromley-Davenport	151	1979	N Roche and D Williams	143
1949	LG Crawley and JC Wilson	143	1980	G Coles and M Johnson	148
1950	L Gracey and I Caldwell	151	1981	R Boxall and R Chapman	143
1951	LG Crawley and JC Wilson	147	1982	IA Carslaw and J Huggan	139
1952T	Major DA Blair and GH Micklem	145	1983	N Fox and G Lashford	147
	LG Crawley and JC Wilson		1984	M Palmer and M Belsham	147
1953	D Wilson and G Simmons	148	1985	S Blight and R Wilkins	143
1954	JR Thornhill and PF Scrutton	147	1986	M Gerrard and B White	146
1955	G Evans and D Sewell	147	1987	IA Carslaw and J Huggan	141
1956	GH Micklem and AF Bussell	141	1988	A Raitt and P Thornley	143
1957	Major DA Blair and CD Lawrie	138	1989	A Howard and R Hunter	146
1958	D Sewell and G Evans	143	1990	AC Livesey and RG Payne	143
1959	HC Squirrell and P Dunn	146	1991	WM Hopkinson and MR Cook	143
1960	MSR Lunt and JC Beharrell	139	1992	J C Davies and P J Davies	148
1961	HC Squirrell and P Dunn	145	1993	M Benka and S Seman	138
1962	AW Holmes and JM Leach	142	1994	D Cowap and J Brant	142
1963	RC Pickering and MJ Cooper	146	1995	R Neill and G Evans	141
1964	MF Bonallack and Dr DM Marsh	145	1996	I Tottingham and R Harris	144
1965	MSR Lunt and DE Rodway	146	1997	S Kay and R Peacock	143
1966	PD Kelley and Dr DM Marsh	144	1998	G Willman and B Willman	142
1967	*Play abandoned*		1999	D Lomas and K Staunton*	104
1968	H Broadbent and G Birtwell	144	2000	MA Booker and RET Rea	143
1969T	SR Warrin and JH Cook		2001	MA Booker and RET Rea	142
	J Povall and K Dabson		2002	MA Booker and RET Rea	138
	JC Davies and W Humphreys		2003	*Not played*	
	RD Watson-Jones and LOM Smith	146	2004	MA Booker and RET Rea	138
1970	JB Carr and R Carr	142	2005	C and W Harmston	144

2006   John Poulton (Hindhead) & Michael Lowe (Wentworth)   71-71—142

Burhill Family Foursomes (inaugurated 1937) *always at Burhill, Surrey*

1937	Captain JR Stroyan and Miss S Stroyan			Miss 'Pooh' Rowan Robinson
1938	W Price and Miss E Price		1964	Mrs P Todhunter and T Todhunter
1939–1946	*Not played – Second World War*		1965	Mrs WT Warrin and SR Warrin
1947	Mrs GH Brooks and PJ Brooks		1966	Mrs WT Warrin and SR Warrin
1948	W Price and Miss E Price		1967	Mrs WT Warrin and SR Warrin
1949	Mrs EC Pepper and W Pepper		1968	Mrs CHP Trollope and Nigel Trollope
1950	A Forbes Ilsley and Miss J Ilsley		1969	Mrs EPP D'A Walton and JF Walton
1951	Major E Loxley Land and Miss J Land		1970	JF Young and Miss EJ Young
1952	CHV Elliot and Miss S Elliott		1971	PHA Brownrigg and Miss D Brownrigg
1953	JC Hubbard and Miss A Hubbard		1972	Mrs S Grant and NJ Grant
1954	JC Hubbard and Miss A Hubbard		1973	MV Blake and Miss B Blake
1955	Mrs HP Thornhill and JR Thornhill		1974	Mrs NR Bailhache and WJ Bailhache
1956	Mrs HP Thornhill and JR Thornhill		1975	Mrs PR Williams and PM Williams
1957	CH Young and Mrs PBK Gracey		1976	Mrs D Gotla and C Gotla
1958	Mrs HM Winckley and JB Winckley		1977	Mrs J Maudsley and C Maudsley
1959	Jack and Anna van Zwanenberg		1978	Mrs H Calderwood and WR Calderwood
1960	Mrs M Kippax and JM Kippax		1979	Dr AG Wells and Miss E Wells
1961	Mrs R Sutherland Pilch and J Sutherland Pilch		1980	JL Hall and Miss Cynthia Hall
1962	JC Hubbard and Miss Trudi Hubbard		1981	Mrs J Fox and N Fox
1963T	GA Rowan-Robinson and		1982	Mrs J Fox and N Fox

(continued over)

1983	Mrs J Rowe and D Rowe		1995	Mrs G Warner and R Warner
1984	Mrs JS Gilbert and AS Gilbert		1996	Mrs AP Croft and MC Croft
1985	Mrs MM Pollitt and R Pollitt		1997	Mrs J Clink and T Clink
1986	Mrs J Maudesley and C Maudesley		1998	MJ Toole and Miss SJ Toole
1987	Mrs A Croft and M Croft		1999	MJ Toole and Miss SJ Toole
1988	Mrs V Hargreaves and R Hargreaves		2000	Mrs V Marchbanks and R Marchbanks
1989	Mrs J Lawson and P Lawson		2001	Mrs C Warren and R Warren
1990	Mrs M Maisey and S Maisey		2002	GR and TG Clark
1991	Mrs M Pollitt and R Pollitt		2003	M & R-L Hall
1992	R Stocks and Miss Joanna Stocks		2004	J & S Burrage
1993	Mrs M Bartlett and Jerome Bartlett		2005	S and A Russell
1994	MJ Toole and Miss SJ Toole			

Semi-Finals:
M & S Hiscocks (Banstead Downs) beat D & J Richards (Burhill) 5 and 4
A & A Gems (Malden) beat J & S Burrage (Walton Heath) 3 and 2
Final:
A & A Gems beat M & S Hiscocks 7 and 6

Fathers and Sons Foursomes *always at West Hill, Surrey*

1991	DM and WK Laing	1996	MJ and J Hickey	2001	J and D Niven
1992	JA and R Piggott	1997	DR and M Baxter	2002	GR and TG Clark
1993	B and R Groce	1998	SF and P Brown	2003	R and T Stocks
1994	RJ and P Hill	1999	R and K Boxall	2004	CEG & JC Kemp
1995	J and D Niven	2000	G and M Steele	2005	CEG & JC Kemp

2006 RA & SA Briars (North Hants) beat C & J Stapleton (Gerrard's Cross) at 19th

Sunningdale Foursomes (inaugurated 1934) *always at Sunningdale*

1934	Miss D Fishwick and EN Layton	1974	PJ Butler and CA Clark
1935	Miss J Wethered and JSF Morrison	1975	*Cancelled due to snow*
1936	Miss J Wethered and JSF Morrison	1976	CA Clark and M Hughesdon
1937	AS Anderson and Dai Rees	1977	GN Hunt and D Matthew
1938	Miss P Barton and Alf Padgham	1978	GA Caygill and Miss J Greenhalgh
1939	C Rissik and EWH Kenyon	1979	G Will and R Chapman
1940-47 *Not played*		1980	NC Coles and D McClelland
1948	Miss Wanda Morgan and Sam King	1981	A Lyddon and G Brand jr
1949	RG French and SS Field	1982	Miss MA McKenna and Miss M Madill
1950	M Faulkner and J Knipe	1983	J Davies and M Devetta
1951	Miss J Donald and TB Haliburton	1984	Miss M McKenna and Miss M Madill
1952	PF Scrutton and Alan Waters	1985	J O'Leary and S Torrance
1953	Miss J Donald and TB Haliburton	1986	R Rafferty and R Chapman
1954	PF Scrutton and Alan Waters	1987	I Mosey and W Humphreys
1955	W Sharp and SS Scott	1988	SC Mason and A Chandler
1956	G Knipe and DC Smalldon	1989	AD Hare and R Claydon
1957	BGC Huggett and R Whitehead	1990	Miss D Reid and Miss C Dibnah
1958	Miss J Donald and Peter Alliss	1991	J Robinson and W Henry
1959	MF Bonallack and D Sewell	1992	R Boxall and D Cooper
1960	Miss B McCorkindale and MJ Moir	1993	A Beal and L James
1961	Mrs J Anderson and Peter Alliss	1994	S Webster and A Wall
1962	ER Whitehead and NC Coles	1995	D Cooper and R Boxall
1963	L Platts and D Snell	1996	L Donald and M O'Connor
1964	B Critchley and R Hunter	1997	Mrs J Hall and Miss H Wadsworth
1965	Mrs AD Spearman and T Fisher	1998	D Fisher and W Bennett
1966	RRW Davenport and A Walker	1999	Miss L Walters and R McEvoy
1967	NC Coles and K Warren	2000	Mrs C Caldwell and R Caldwell
1968	JC Davies and W Humphreys	2001	Miss C Lipscombe and S Little
1969	P Oosterhuis and PJ Benka	2002	J Kemp and M Wharton
1970	R Barrell and Miss A Willard	2003	R Fisher & S Griffiths
1971	A Bird and H Flatman	2004	R Fisher & S Griffiths
1972	JC Davies and MG King	2005	G Lockerbie & P Jenkinson
1973	J Putt and Miss M Everard		

(continued over)

Sunningdale Foursomes *continued*

Semi-Finals:
Danielle Masters (Chart Hill) & Ben Evans (Rye) beat Sophie Walker (Kenwick Park) & Oliver Fisher (West Essex) 2 and 1
James Morrison (St George's Hill) & Colin Roope (Farnham) beat D Thomas & J Pease (Braintree) 2 and 1

Final:
Danielle Masters & Ben Evans beat James Morrison & Colin Roope 2 and 1

Worplesdon Mixed Foursomes (inaugurated 1921) *always at Worplesdon, Surrey*

1921	Miss Helme and TA Torrance	1967	JF Gancedo and Mlle C Lacoste
1922	Miss Joyce Wethered and R Wethered	1968	JD van Heel and Miss Dinah Oxley
1923	Miss Joyce Wethered and CJ Tolley	1969	Mrs R Ferguson and Alistair Wilson
1924	Miss SR Fowler and EN Layton	1970	Miss R Roberts and RL Glading
1925	Miss Cecil Leitch and E Esmond	1971	Mrs D Frearson and A Smith
1926	Mlle de la Chaume and R Wethered	1972	Miss B Le Garreres and CA Strang
1927	Miss Joyce Wethered and CJH Tolley	1973	Miss T Perkins and RJ Evans
1928	Miss Joyce Wethered and JSF Morrison	1974	Mrs S Birley and RL Glading
1929	Miss M Gourlay and Maj CO Hezlet	1975	Mr and Mrs JR Thornhill
1930	Miss M Gourlay and Maj CO Hezlet	1976	Mrs B Lewis and J Caplan
1931	Miss J Wethered and Hon M Scott	1977	Mrs D Henson and J Caplan
1932	Miss J Wethered and RH Oppenheimer	1978	Miss T Perkins and R Thomas
1933	Miss J Wethered and B Darwin beat	1979	Miss J Melville and A Melville
1934	Miss M Gourlay and TA Torrance	1980	Mrs L Bayman and I Boyd
1935,	Miss G and J Craddock-Hartopp	1981	Mrs J Nicholsen and MN Stern
1936	Miss J Wethered and Hon T Coke	1982	Miss B New and K Dobson
1937	Mrs Heppel and LG Crawley	1983	Miss B New and K Dobson
1938	Mrs MR Garon and EF Storey	1984	Mrs L Bayman and MC Hughesdon
1939–45	*Not played*	1985	Mrs H Kaye and D Longmuir
1946	Miss J Gordon and AA Duncan	1986	Miss P Johnson and RN Roderick
1947	Miss J Gordon and AA Duncan	1987	Miss J Nicholson and B White
1948	Miss W Morgan and EF Storey	1988	Mme A Larrezac and JJ Caplan
1949	Miss F Stephens and LG Crawley	1989	Miss J Kershaw and M Kershaw
1950	Miss F Stephens and LG Crawley	1990	Miss S Keogh and A Rodgers
1951	Mrs AC Barclay and G Evans	1991	J Rhodes and C Banks
1952	Mrs RT Peel and GW Mackie	1992	D Henson and B Turner
1953	Miss J Gordon and G Knipe	1993	A Macdonald and S Skeldon
1954	Miss F Stephens and WA Slark	1994	Mr and Mrs K Quinn
1955	Miss P Garvey and PF Scrutton	1995	Mrs C Caldwell and P Carr
1956	Mrs L Abrahams and Maj WD Henderson	1996	Miss L Walters and M Naylor
1957	Mrs B Singleton and WD Smith	1997	Miss K Burton and G Wolstenholme
1958	Mr and Mrs M Bonallack	1998	Miss K Burton and J Smith
1959	Miss J Robertson and I Wright	1999	Miss AM Boatman and RG Hodgkinson
1960	Miss B Jackson and MJ Burgess	2000	Mr and Mrs Galway
1961	Mrs R Smith and B Critchley	2001	Miss K Fisher and J Harper
1962	Viscomtesse de Saint Sauveur and DW Frame	2002	C Court and J Donaldson
1963	Mrs G Valentine and JE Behrend	2003	A Downer and L Boxall
1964	Mrs G Valentine and JE Behrend	2004	Miss L Webb and G O'Connor
1965	Mrs G Valentine and JE Behrend	2005	Miss A Coffey and A Shields
1966	Mrs C Barclay and DJ Miller		

Semi-Finals:
A Coffey & A Shields (Worplesdon) beat Mr & Mrs T Greenfield (Pycombe) 3 and 1
S Lovell (Stock Brook Manor) & M Stam (Worplesdon) beat Mr & Mrs G Legg (Ferndown, Broadstone) 1 hole

Final:
Alison Coffey & Anthony Shields beat Samantha Lovell & Marcus Stam 4 and 3

University and School Events

Halford-Hewitt Cup (inaugurated 1924) *always at Royal Cinque Ports, Deal, and Royal. St George's*

1924	Eton	1956	Eton	1982	Charterhouse
1925	Eton	1957	George Watson's	1983	Charterhouse
1926	Eton	1958	Harrow	1984	Charterhouse
1927	Harrow	1959	Wellington	1985	Harrow
1928	Eton	1960	Rossall	1986	Repton
1929	Harrow	1961	Rossall	1987	Merchiston
1930	Charterhouse	1962	Oundle	1988	Stowe
1931	Harrow	1963	Repton	1989	Eton
1932	Charterhouse	1964	Fettes	1990	Tonbridge
1933	Rugby	1965	Rugby	1991	Shrewsbury
1934	Charterhouse	1966	Charterhouse	1992	Tonbridge
1935	Charterhouse	1967	Eton	1993	Shrewsbury
1936	Charterhouse	1968	Eton	1994	Tonbridge
1937	Charterhouse	1969	Eton	1995	Harrow
1938	Marlborough	1970	Merchiston	1996	Radley
1939	Charterhouse	1971	Charterhouse	1997	Oundle
1940–46	No competition	1972	Marlborough	1998	Charterhouse
1947	Harrow	1973	Rossall	1999	George Watson's
1948	Winchester	1974	Charterhouse	2000	Epsom
1949	Charterhouse	1975	Harrow	2001	Tonbridge
1950	Rugby	1976	Merchiston	2002	Charterhouse
1951	Rugby	1977	George Watson's	2003	Edinburgh Academy
1952	Harrow	1978	Harrow	2004	Tonbridge
1953	Harrow	1979	Stowe	2005	Tonbridge
1954	Rugby	1980	Shrewsbury		
1955	Eton	1981	George Watson's		

Semi-Finals:
Sherborne beat Tonbridge 3–2
Malvern beat George Watson's 3–2

Final:
Malvern beat Sherborne 3–2

Winning team: Jeremy Lowe, Adrian Coleman, Richard Thompson, Sebastien Blanchet, Adrian Barrett-Greene, Tim Duerr, Ian Timberlake, William Beeson, Henry Aldridge, Edward James

Senior Halford-Hewitt Competitions (inaugurated 2000)

Bernard Darwin Trophy (Original 16) *always at Woking GC*

2000	Wellington	2003	Tonbridge	2006	Tonbridge
2001	Malvern	2004	Charterhouse		
2002	Wellington	2005	Rugby		

GL Mellin Salver (Second 16) *always at West Hill GC*

2000	Lancing	2003	Haileybury	2006	Cranleigh
2001	Cheltenham	2004	Shrewsbury		
2002	Shrewsbury	2005	Shrewsbury		

Cyril Gray Trophy (Remaining 32) *always at Worplesdon*

2000	Stoneyhurst	2003	Stowe	2006	Canford
2001	Canford	2004	Edinburgh Academy		
2002	George Watson's	2005	Fettes		

Senior Halford-Hewitt Trophy (Play-off between winners of Darwin, Mellin and Gray Trophies)

2000	Wellington	2003	Haileybury	2006	Cranleigh
2001	Canford	2004	Charterhouse		
2002	George Watson's	2005	Shrewsbury		

Grafton Morrish Trophy (inaugurated 1963) *always at Hunstanton and Royal West Norfolk*

1963	Tonbridge	1978	Charterhouse	1993	Malvern
1964	Tonbridge	1979	Harrow	1994	George Heriot's
1965	Charterhouse	1980	Charterhouse	1995	Repton
1966	Charterhouse	1981	Charterhouse	1996	Coventry
1967	Charterhouse	1982	Marlborough	1997	George Heriot's
1968	Wellington	1983	Wellington	1998	Solihull
1969	Sedbergh	1984	Sedbergh	1999	George Heriot's
1970	Sedbergh	1985	Warwick	2000	Lancing
1971	Dulwich	1986	Tonbridge	2001	King's College School
1972	Sedbergh	1987	Harrow	2002	George Heriot's
1973	Pangbourne	1988	Robert Gordon's	2003	Glasgow Academy
1974	Millfield	1989	Tonbridge	2004	KCS, Wimbledon
1975	Oundle	1990	Clifton	2005	Malvern
1976	Charterhouse	1991	Repton		
1977	Haileybury	1992	Charterhouse		

Semi-Finals
Dollar beat Birkenhead 2–1
Malvern beat Berkhamsted 2½–½
Final
Malvern beat Dollar 2–1

Winning team: Jeremy Lowe, Henry Aldridge, William Beeson, Sebastien Blanchet, Adrian Coleman, Tim Duerr

---

117th Oxford v Cambridge Varsity Match (inaugurated 1878)　2006 *Muirfield*

1878	Oxford	Wimbledon	1925	Oxford	Hunstanton
1879	Cambridge	Wimbledon	1926	Cambridge	Burnham and Berrow
1880	Oxford	Wimbledon	1927	Cambridge	Hoylake
1881	*Not played*		1928	Cambridge	Prince's, Sandwich
1882	Cambridge	Wimbledon	1929	Cambridge	Rye
1883	Oxford	Wimbledon	1930	Oxford	Hoylake
1884	Oxford	Wimbledon	1931	Oxford	Prince's, Sandwich
1885	Oxford	Wimbledon	1932	Oxford	Lytham St Annes
1886	Oxford	Wimbledon	1933	Cambridge	Prince's, Sandwich
1887	Cambridge	Wimbledon	1934	Oxford	Formby
1888	Cambridge	Wimbledon	1935	Cambridge	Burnham and Berrow
1889	Oxford	Wimbledon	1936	Cambridge	Hoylake
1890	Cambridge	Wimbledon	1937	Cambridge	Prince's, Sandwich
1891	Cambridge	Wimbledon	1938	Cambridge	Westward Ho!
1892	Cambridge	Wrlmbledon	1939	Cambridge	Royal St George's
1893	Cambridge	Wimbledon	1940–45	*Not played*	
1894	Oxford	Sandwich	1946	Cambridge	Royal Lytham & St Annes
1895	Cambridge	Sandwich	1947	Oxford	Rye
1896	Halved	Wimbledon	1948	Oxford	Royal St George's
1897	Cambridge	Sandwich	1949	Cambridge	Hoylake
1898	Cambridge	Sandwich	1950	Oxford	Royal Lytham & St Annes
1899	Oxford	Sandwich	1951	Cambridge	Rye
1900	Oxford	Sandwich	1952	Cambridge	Rye
1901	Oxford	Sandwich	1953	Cambridge	Rye
1902	Oxford	Sandwich	1954	Cambridge	Rye
1903	Oxford	Sandwich	1955	Cambridge	Rye
1904	Oxford	Woking	1956	Oxford	Formby
1905	Cambridge	Sunningdale	1957	Oxford	Royal St George's
1906	Cambridge	Hoylake	1958	Cambridge	Rye
1907	Cambridge	Hoylake	1959	Cambridge	Burnham & Berrow
			1960	Cambridge	Royal Lytham & St Annes

After 1907 the result was arrived at by matches won

			1961	Oxford	Royal St George's
1908	Cambridge	Sunningdale	1962	Halved	Hunstanton
1909	Oxford	Royal St George's	1963	Cambridge	Royal Birkdale
1910	Cambridge	Hoylake	1964	Oxford	Rye
1911	Oxford	Rye	1965	Cambridge	Royal St George's
1912	Halved	Prince's, Sanswich	1966	Cambridge	Hunstanton
1913	Halved	Hoylake	1967	Cambridge	Rye
1914	Oxford	Rye	1968	Cambridge	Porthcawl
1915–19	*Not played*		1969	Cambridge	Formby
1920	Cambridge	Sunningdale	1970	Halved	Royal St George's
1921	Oxford	Hoylake	1971	Oxford	Rye
1922	Oxford	Prince's, Sandwich	1972	Cambridge	Formby
1923	Oxford	Rye	1973	Oxford	Saunton
1924	Cambridge	Hoylake	1974	Cambridge	Ganton

1975	Cambridge	Hoylake	1991	Cambridge	Royal St George's
1976	Cambridge	Woodhall Spa	1992	Oxford	Royal Cinque Ports
1977	Cambridge	Porthcawl	1993	Oxford	Royal Liverpool
1978	Oxford	Rye	1994	Oxford	Rye
1979	Oxford	Harlech	1995	Oxford	Royal Lytham & St Annes
1980	Oxford	Hoylake	1996	Oxford	Royal West Norfolk
1981	Cambridge	Formby	1997	Oxford	Royal St George's
1982	Cambridge	Hunstanton	1998	Cambridge	Rye
1983	Cambridge	Royal St George's	1999	Oxford	Royal Cinque Ports
1984	Cambridge	Sunningdale	2000	Cambridge	Porthcawl
1985	Oxford	Rye	2001	Oxford	Formby
1986	Oxford	Ganton	2002	Cambridge	Royal St George's
1987	Cambridge	Formby	2003	Oxford	Walton Heath
1988	Cambridge	Royal Porthcawl	2004	Tie	Ganton
1989	Cambridge	Rye	2005	Oxford	Ganton
1990	Cambridge	Muirfield			

Captains: Oxford: Michael Gray (Somerville); Cambridge: Duncan Reid (Fitzwilliam)

Foursomes (Oxford names first):
P Bickerton & G Jones lost to J Nierinck & R Stewart 4 and 3
M McFadden & D Stewart lost to T Clougherty & T Woolsey 2 and 1
M Canty & M Grower lost to C Bellingham & D Reid 2 and 1
S Baird & R Balmer lost to A Habibi & E Zaaymann 8 and 7
M Gray & T Smith beat G Powell & J Smit 3 and 2

Singles:
Michael Gray (Somerville) beat Duncan Reid (Fitzwilliam) 3 and 2
Michael Canty (Worcester) beat Edward Zaaymann (Magdalene) 1 hole
Gareth Jones (Hertford) beat Thomas Clougherty (Churchill) 2 and 1
Mason Grower (Oriel) lost to Ruaraidh Stewart (Peterhouse) 2 and 1
Thomas Smith (Worcester) lost to Amir Habibi (Queens') 9 and 8
Philip Bickerton (Lady Margaret Hall) beat James Nierinck (Sidney Sussex) 1 hole
David Stewart (Magdalen) beat Chris Bellingham (Christ's) 4 and 3
Michael McFadden (Worcester) lost to Thomas Woolsey (Queens') 3 and 2
Ritchie Balmer (Keble) halved with Johannes Smit (Darwin)
Stuart Baird (Wadham) beat Gerald Powell (Churchill) 2 and 1

Result: Oxford 7½, Cambridge 7½

Oxford and Cambridge Golfing Society for the President's Putter

(inaugurated 1920)   2006 *Littlestone and Rye*

1920	EWE Holderness	1951	LG Crawley	1977	AWJ Holmes
1921	EWE Holderness	1952	LG Crawley	1978	MJ Reece
1922	EWE Holderness	1953	GH Micklem	1979	*Cancelled – snow*
1923	EWE Holderness	1954	G Huddy	1980	S Melville
1924	B Darwin	1955	G Huddy	1981	AWJ Holmes
1925	HD Gillies	1956	GT Duncan	1982	DMA Steel
1926T	EF Storey	1957	AE Shepperson	1983	ER Dexter
	RH Wethered	1958	Lt-Col AA Duncan	1984	A Edmond
1927	RH Wethered	1959	ID Wheater	1985	ER Dexter
1928	RH Wethered	1960	JME Anderson	1986	J Caplan
1929	Sir EWE Holderness	1961	ID Wheater	1987	CD Meacher
1930	TA Bourn	1962	MF Attenborough	1988	G Woollett
1931	AG Pearson	1963	JG Blackwell	1989	M Froggatt
1932	LG Crawley	1964	DMA Steel	1990	G Woollett
1933	AJ Peech	1965	WJ Uzielli	1991	B Ingleby
1934	DHR Martin	1966	MF Attenborough	1992	M Cox
1935	RH Wethered	1967	JR Midgley	1993	C Weight
1936	RH Wethered	1968	AWJ Holmes	1994	S Seman
1937	JB Beck	1969	P Moody	1995	A Woolnough
1938	CJH Tolley	1970	DMA Steel	1996	C Rotheroe
1939	JOH Greenly	1971	GT Duncan	1997	C Rotheroe
1940–46	*Not played*	1972	P Moody	1998	N Pabari
1947	LG Crawley	1973	AD Swanston	1999	C Dale
1948	Major AA Duncan	1974	R Biggs	2000	C Dale
1949	PB Lucas	1975	CJ Weight	2001	B Streather
1950	DHR Martin	1976	MJ Reece	2002	T Etridge

Oxford and Cambridge Golfing Society for the President's Putter *continued*

| 2003 | D Hayes | 2004 | I Henderson | 2005 | O Lindsay |

Quarter-Finals

Mark Williamson (Fitzwilliam, Cambridge) beat
  Richard Bisson (Christ Church, Oxford) 2 holes
David Hayes (Corpus Christi, Oxford) beat
  Tom Etridge (St Catherine's, Oxford) 3 and 2
Harry Westall (Balliol, Oxford) beat Bill Barclay
  (St John's, Cambridge) 5 and 4
Alan Holmes (St John's, Cambridge) beat
  John Hargreaves (Magdalen, Oxford) at 19th

Semi-Finals

Hayes beat Williamson 2 and 1
Westall beat Holmes 2 and 1

Final

David Hayes beat Harry Westall 4 and 2

Palmer Cup (USA university students v Europe university students) 2006 *Prestwick*

1997	USA	19–5	Bay Hill, Orlando, Florida	2002	USA	15½–8½	Doonbeg, Ireland
1998	USA	12–12	St Andrews, Scotland	2003	Europe	14–10	Kiawah Island, SC
1999	USA	17½–6½	Honors, Tennessee	2004	Europe	14½–9½	Ballybunion, Ireland
2000	GB&I	12½–11½	Royal Liverpool	2005	USA	14–10	Whistling Straits, WI
2001	USA	14–2	Springfield, NJ	2006	Europe	19½–4½	Prestwick

First Day – Fourball:

A Cañizares & P Martin beat B Harman & C Kirk
  5 and 3
M Haastrup & J Luiten beat L List & C Ogden 4 and 3
R Davies & R Ramsay beat R Baca & R Blaum 6 and 4
O Floren & S Lewton beat R Castro & K Larsen
  2 and 1

Singles:

Pablo Martin (ESP) beat Brian Harman 6 and 5
Alejandro Cañizares (ESP) beat Clay Ogden 2 and 1
Mark Haastrup (DEN) lost to Ryan Baca 3 and 2
Joost Luiten (NED) beat Luke List 1 hole
Richard Ramsay (SCO) lost to Roberto Castro
  1 hole
Oscar Floren (SWE) beat Kevin Larsen 5 and 4
Stephen Lewton (ENG) beat Chris Kirk 1 hole
Rhys Davies (WAL) beat Ryan Blaum 4 and 3

Result: Europe 19½, USA 4½

Second Day – Foursomes:

A Cañizares & P Martin beat R Blaum &
  R Castro 6 and 5
O Floren & M Haastrup beat R Baca &
  C Ogden 1 hole
J Luiten & R Ramsay beat B Harman & L List
  3 and 2
R Davis beat S Lewton beat C Kirk &
  K Larsen 4 and 3

Singles:

P Martin beat R Castro 3 and 2
O Floren lost to R Blaum 4 and 2
M Haastrup beat B Harman 5 and 3
A Cañizares beat R Baca 1 hole
J Luiten beat K Larsen 2 holes
S Lewton halved with C Ogden
R Davis beat L List 3 and 2
R Ramsay lost to C Kirk 1 hole

Boyd Quaich (University Championship) *always at St Andrews*

1946	AS Mayer	Glasgow	161	1968	JW Johnston	Aberdeen	291
1947T	H Brews	Johannesburg	148	1969	PH Moody	Cambride	286
	FWG Deighton	Glasgow	148	1970	JT Moffat	Strathclyde	297
1948	JL Lindsay	St Andrews	203	1971	JW Johnston	Aberdeen	289
1949	FD Tatum	Oxford	217	1972	D Greig	Aberdeen	288
1950	GP Roberts	Liverpool	294	1973	J Rube	Sweden	285
1951	H Dooley	Nottingham	299	1974	G Cairns	Edinburgh	297
1952	G Parker	Glasgow	297	1975	S Dunlop	Trinity, Dublin	291
1953	JL Bamford	Trinity, Dublin	290	1976	R Watson	Dundee	297
1954	I Caldwell	London	287	1977	R Watson	Dundee	297
1955	HC Squirrll	Birmingham	292	1978	R Watson	Dundee	298
1956	JL Bamford	Trinity, Dublin	295	1979	D McLeary	St Andrews	302
1957	DM Marsh	Liverpool	293	1980	ME Lewis	Bath	290
1958	R Mummery	London	299	1981	P Gallagher	Heriot-Watt	302
1959-61	*Not played*			1982	ME Lewis	Bath	297
1962	DB Sheahan	Univ. Coll., Dublin	217	1983	R Risan	Lund, Sweden	296
1963	S MacDonald	Edinburgh	295	1984	J Huggan	Stirling	297
1964	AJ Low	St Andrews	299	1985	S Elgie	W. Ontario, Canada	299
1965	S MacDonald	Edinburgh	295	1986	A Roberts	Hull	291
1966	FE McCarroll	Queen's, Belfast	291	1987	M Pask	St Andrews	293
1967	B Nicholson	Aberdeen	294	1988	A Mathers	Stirling	289

1989	A Mathers	Stirling	300		1998	D Simpson	Edinburgh	283
1990	A Mathers	Stirling	297		1999	O Lindsay	St Andrews	290
1991	C Somner	Friberg, Switzerland	302		2000	G Greer	Glasgow	288
1992	L Walker	Trinity, Dublin	286		2001	P Botha*	Pretoria	292
1993	G Sherry	Stirling	298		2002	G Duncan	Heriot-Watt	283
1994	C Sanderson	Stellenbosch, SA	283		2003	R Hooper	St Andrews	287
1995	C Sanderson	Stellenbosch, SA	290		2004	G Blainey	St Andrews	289
1996	B Templeton	Heriot-Watt	294		2005	B Westgate	St Andrews	288
1997	G Maly	St Andrews	289					

1	Niall O'Connor (UCD)	75-70-73-71—289
2	Justin Fluit (Waterloo, ON) (CAN)	73-71-73-72—289 (count back)
3	Gordon Yates (Stirling)	75-72-75-71—293

54th Queen Elizabeth Coronation Schools Trophy *always at Royal Burgess, Barnton*

(inaugurated 1953)

1953	Watsonians	1980	George Heriot's FP
1954	Daniel Stewart's FP	1981	Ayr Academicals
1955	Watsonians	1982	George Heriot's FP
1956	Watsonians	1983	Perth Academy FP
1957	Hillhead High School FP	1984	Glasgow High School FP
1958	Watsonians	1985	Glasgow High School FP
1959	Glasgow High School FP	1986	Watsonians
1960	Glasgow High School FP	1987	Daniel Stewart's/Melville FP
1961	Watsonians	1988	Watsonians
1962	Glasgow High School FP	1989	Kelvinside Academicals
1963	Glasgow High School FP	1990	Hutchesons' Grammar School FP
1964	Dollar Academicals	1991	Glasgow High School FP
1965	Old Lorettonians	1992	Daniel Stewart's/Melville FP
1966	Merchistonians	1993	Merchistonians
1967	Merchistonians	1994	Perth Academy FP
1968	Hillhead High School FP	1995	Glasgow High School FP
1969	Kelvinside Academicals	1996	Glasgow High School FP
1970	Dollar Academicals	1997	Old Uppinghamians
1971	Merchistonians	1998	Watsonians
1972	Merchistonians	1999	Morrisonians
1973	Merchistonians	2000	Breadalbane Academicals
1974	Old Carthusians	2001	Old Carthusians
1975	Old Lorettonians	2002	Old Campbellians
1976	Watsonians	2003	Breadalbane Academicals
1977	Glasgow High School FP	2004	Glasgow Academicals
1978	Old Lorettonians	2005	Watsonians
1979	Gordonians		

Semi-Finals:
Fettesians beat Lenzie Academicals 2 – 1
Old Carthusians beat Merchistonians 2 – 1

Final:
Fettesians beat Old Carthusians 2½ – ½

Winning team: Richard Philip (captain); Gordon Archibald, Francis Clark, Gavin Lawrie, Chris Mather, Douglas Philip, Andrew Soulsby, Ramsay Wilson.

County and Other Regional Championships

England

Bedfordshire

1997	K Kemp	2002	M Wharton
1998	M Wharton	2003	G Benson
1999	J Kemp	2004	M Wharton
2000	S Vinnecombe	2005	M Round
2001	J Kemp	2006	J Kemp

Berks, Bucks & Oxon

1997	L Donald	2002	A Walton
1998	L Donald	2003	L Gauthier
1999	L Rusher	2004	T Lawson
2000	K Freeman	2005	T Lawson
2001	C Bowler	2006	T Lawson

Cambridgeshire

1997	O Cousins	2002	K Arthur
1998	L Yearn	2003	L Tearn
1999	O Cousins	2004	J Greenall
2000	LG Yearn	2005	S Jarvis
2001	LG Yearn	2006	J Mynott

Channel Islands

1997	R Williamson	2002	R Ramskill
1998	D Rowlandson	2003	M Jones
1999	N Vaudin	2004	P Le Chevalier
2000	B Eggo	2005	G O'Neill
2001	P Le Chevalier	2006	M Parkman

Cheshire

1997	N Pabari	2004	J Murphy (M)
1998	J Donaldson		D Peel (S)
1999	SS Grewal	2005	M Jones (M)
2000	FA Bibby		D Horsey (S)
2001	GJ Bradley	2006	D Horsey
2002	D Wardrop		
2003	S Dixon (M)		
	M Pilling (S)		

Cornwall

1997	P Darlington	2002	IT Veale
1998	I Atkinson	2003	IC Veale
1999	I Veale	2004	M Reynard
2000	S Chapman	2005	I Veale
2001	C Llewellyn	2006	M Reynard

Cumbria

1997	G Watson	2002	N Bell
1998	P Jack	2003	W Bowe
1999	J Longcake	2004	W Bowe
2000	J Carr	2005	C Morrow
2001	S Young	2006	W Bowe

Derbyshire

1997	AS Humpston	2002	P Gration
1998	L Walley	2003	E Vernon
1999	JP Feeney	2004	D Clarke
2000	N Vowles	2005	G Woolgar
2001	P Gration	2006	G Woolgar

Devon

1997	G Ruth	2002	K Harper
1998	S Pike	2003	C Townsend
1999	G Ruth	2004	P Newcombe
2000	S Davey	2005	K Harper
2001	G Ruth	2006	D Gee

Dorset

1997	J Baldwin	2002	T Peacock
1998	J Pounder	2003	T Peacock
1999	C Jessup	2004	D Cook
2000	M Davies	2005	B Churchill
2001	A Lawrence	2006	R Morris

Durham

1997	J Dryden	2002	J Harper
1998	C Hamilton	2003	R Aisbitt
1999	A McLure	2004	H Hamilton
2000	AJ McLure	2005	M Curry
2001	M Ridley	2006	M Curry

Essex

1997	B Taylor	2002	P Ring
1998	B Taylor	2003	L Kennedy
1999	R Blaxhill	2004	O Fisher
2000	S Middleton	2005	L Kennedy
2001	R Blaxill	2006	D Whitnell

Gloucestershire

1997	M Unwin	2002	P Reed
1998	TP Smith	2003	M Unwin
1999	D Young	2004	A Rudge
2000	C Newman	2005	D Lake
2001	M Unwin	2006	C Wood

Hampshire, Isle of Wight and Channel Islands

1997	S Stanley	2002	R Elmes
1998	C Hudson	2003	D Porter
1999	D Henley	2004	M Thistleton
2000	C McLaughlin	2005	R Henley
2001	D Henley	2006	S Archibald

Hertfordshire

1997	C Duke	2002	B Connelly
1998	R Conway-Lye	2003	B Connelly
1999	D Griffiths	2004	R Leonard
2000	I Farrant	2005	T Shadbolt
2001	M Payne	2006	N Pateman

Isle of Man

1997	P McMullan	2002	M Sutton
1998	P McMullan	2003	D Jones
1999	G Wilson	2004	K Moore
2000	S Ellis	2005	P Lowey
2001	G Wilson	2006	P Lowey

Kent

1997	D Ottoway	2002	L Campbell
1998	D Ottoway	2003	M Ford
1999	J Carter	2004	E Richardson
2000	D Curtis	2005	J Smith
2001	L Godwin	2006	M Bush

Lancashire

1997	D Johnson	2002	R Walker
1998	P Wiliams	2003	R Bardsley
1999	A Jackson	2004	M Baldwin
2000	M Cox	2005	R Bardsley
2001	R Bardsley	2006	J Carroll

Leicestershire and Rutland

1997	J Herbert	2002	C Shave
1998	G Wolstenholme	2003	D Gibson
1999	D Gibson	2004	N Chaudhuri
2000	N Knighton	2005	S Sansome
2001	G Wolstenholme	2006	R Wells

Lincolnshire

1997	P Streeter	2002	P Bradshaw
1998	A White	2003	J Crampton
1999	D Skinns	2004	D Skinns*
2000	P Bradshaw	2005	R Harris
2001	LJ Toyne	2006	D Rowland

Middlesex

1997	C Austin	2002	G Evans
1998	R Vaney	2003	M Richardson
1999	G Evans	2004	J Phelps
2000	S Samphire	2005	L Cameron
2001	S Samphire	2006	J Taverner

Norfolk

1997	G Price	2002	D Henderson
1998	CJ Lamb	2003	A Brydon
1999	CJ Lamb	2004	C Waugh
2000	NJ Williamson	2005	D Henderson
2001	D Henderson	2006	D Henderson

Northamptonshire

1997	P Langrish-Smith	2002	M Peacock
1998	G Keates	2003	G Keates
1999	N Soto	2004	S Ashwood
2000	A Print	2005	D Wood
2001	N Soto	2006	G Boyd

Northumberland

1997	D Clark	2004	S Twynholm (M and S)
1998	J McCallum		
1999	SE Philipson	2005	P Fiddes (M) S Twynholm (S)
2000	AR Paisley		
2001	C McDonnell	2006	G Cowan
2002	SE Phillipson		
2003	A Minnikin (M) C McDonnell (S)		

Nottinghamshire

1997	O Wilson	2002	T Payne
1998	AJ Liddle	2003	M Betteridge
1999	AJ Liddle	2004	M Foulkes
2000	M Allen	2005	M Foulkes
2001	D McJannet	2006	D Brooks

Shropshire and Herefordshire

1997	K Preece	2003	B Ruddick
1998	O Pughe	2004	M Jones
1999	K Baker	2005	N Chesters (M) A Stephenson (S)
2000	R Brown		
2001	D McDonnell	2006	K Williams
2002	K Williams		

Somerset

1997	R Swords	2002	B Porter
1998	J Morgan	2003	C Edwards
1999	G Legg	2004	J Baker-Odlin
2000	D Dixon	2005	G Morgan
2001	C Edwards	2006	R Jones

Staffordshire

1997	SD Wakefield	2002	A Cheese
1998	KD Hale	2003	JJ Kendall
1999	R Chattaway	2004	J Bandurak
2000	C Russell	2005	N Johnson
2001	MA Payne	2006	K Bridgen

Suffolk

1997	J Maddock	2003	K Day
1998	J Wright	2004	S Crosby
1999	P Barnard	2005	J Abbott (M)
2000	L Dodd		J Moul (S)
2001	L Dodd	2006	A Holmes
2002	J Wright		

Surrey

1997	T Paterson	2002	D Lomas
1998	C Rodgers	2003	J Heath
1999	N Pimm	2004	R Rea
2000	J Franks	2005	F Keenan
2001	Z Scotland	2006	C Roope

Sussex

1997	M Harris	2002	C Newman
1998	M Harris	2003	J Budgen
1999	M Galway	2004	W Hawes
2000	J Doherty	2005	O Turnhill
2001	S Nightingale	2006	S Nightingale

Warwickshire

1997	T Whitehouse	2002	J Hemphill
1998	T Whitehouse	2003	R Steele
1999	T Whitehouse	2004	M Cryer
2000	T Whitehouse	2005	P Randle
2001	T Whitehouse	2006	B Stafford

Wiltshire

1997	P Bicknell	2002	J Huffam
1998	P Bicknell	2003	M Searle
1999	P Bicknell	2004	M White
2000	S Surry	2005	B Newman
2001	I Campbell	2006	M Searle

Worcestershire

1997	S Braithwaite	2002	S Braithwaite
1998	D Glover	2003	A Norman
1999	P Scarrett	2004	J Toman
2000	R Wassell	2005	J Ferguson
2001	M Reynard	2006	P Garey

Yorkshire

1997	R Jones (M)	2001	R Finch (M & S)
	A Wright (S)	2002	DJ Berry (M)
1998	S Tarplett (M)	2003	G Clark (M)
	M Bugg /	2004	D Appleyard
	R Hodgkinson (S)		(M & S)
	(tied)	2005	J Parry (M & S)
1999	GA Clark (M)	2006	G Evans
	SJ Dyson (S)		
2000	JB Godbold (M)		
	GA Clark (S)		
	RM Hollins (S)		

Scotland

Angus

1997	P Cunningham	2003	G Bell (M)
1998	E Ramsay		G Brown (S)
1999	J Flynn	2004	R Coull (M)
2000	S Wilson		G Bell (S)
2001	M Lindsay (M)	2005	A Serrells (M)
	A Johnston (S)		J Watt (S)
2002	GW Tough (M)	2006	R Coull (M)
	JA Watt (S)		G Bell (S)

Argyll and Bute

1998	J Sharp	2003	I McLennan (M)
1999	G Bolton		G Bolton (S)
2000	G McMillan	2004	S Campbell (M)
2001	G Bolton (M)		G Reynolds (S)
	G Reynolds (S)	2005	G Bolton (M & S)
2002	G Bolton (M)	2006	R Currie (M)
	G Tyre (S)		C Timms (S)

Ayrshire

1997	G Fox (M)	2003	B Crawford (M)
	B Aitken (S)		T McInally (S)
1998	I Robertson (M)	2004	D McLure (M)
	D Glass (S)		A Gourlay and
1999	G Holland		R Duncan (S)
	(M and S)	2005	D Addison (M)
2000	L Bagnall (M)		D McLure (S)
	A Gourlay (S)	2006	S McEwan (M)
2001	A Gourlay (M)		T McInally (S)
	G Bryden (S)		
2002	A Gourlay (M)		
	R Duncan (S)		

Borders Golfers' Association

1997	W Simpson	2004	C Fraser (M)
1998	D Ballantyne		K Fortune (S)
1999	J Paterson	2005	M Thomson (M)
2000	M Thomson		S Lamb (S)
2001	M Thomson	2006	D Gillie (M & S)
2002	RD Ballantyne		
2003	M Thomson		

Clackmannanshire

1997	G Bowie	2004	B Paterson (M)
1998	B Stewart		C O'Connor (S)
1999	M Crichton	2005	M Rust (M)
2000	AC Fairbrother		A Hyem (S)
2001	I Macaulay (M & S)	2006	N Scaife M)
2002	M Crichton (S)		C O'Connor (S)
	C Macaulay (M)		
2003	N Scaife (S)		
	I Ross (M)		

Dunbartonshire

1997	S Carmichael (M)	2002	P Gault jr (M)
	S McLeitch (S)		K Smyth (S)
1998	S Carmichael (M)	2003	C Peddie (M)
	G Murphy (S)		J Hamilton (S)
1999	G Greer (M)	2004	C Harper (M)
	J Hughes (S)		K Smyth (S)
2000	J Devonney (M)	2005	M Ferguson (M)
	SR McIntosh (S)		C Harper (S)
2001	F Bone (M)	2006	C Checkley (M)
	P Gault (S)		J Meechan (S)

Fife

1997	S Meiklejohn	2003	K McGowan (M)
1998	J Bunch		S Mackie (S)
1999	J McLeary	2004	B Erskine (M)
2000	R Bremner		K Weir (S)
2001	J McLeary (M)	2005	G McNab (M)
	S Meiklejohn (S)		J White (S)
2002	R Dickson (M)	2006	G Sharp (M & S)
	JT Bunch (S)		

Glasgow

1997	J Finnegan (M)	2002	A Syme (M and S)
	DA Lamond (S)	2003	J Laurie (M)
1998	M Loftus (M)		C Kerr (S)
	I Mackie (S)	2004	C Robertson (M)
1999	A Doherty (M)		AP Craig (S)
	M Loftus (S)	2005	S Robertson (M)
2000	M Loftus (M)		N McBride (S)
	S Jamieson (S)	2006	G Corrie (M)
2001	E Wood (M)		M Bookless (S)
	N MacRae (S)		

Lanarkshire

1997	W Bryson (M)	2002	G Rodger (M)
	E Moir (S)		S Douglas (S)
1998	R Hinshelwood (M)	2003	R Hinshelwood (M)
	M Warren (S)		G Rodger (S)
1999	W Bryson	2004	R McKenzie (M)
	(M and S)		G Robertson (S)
	W Bryson (S)	2005	W Bryson (M)
2000	I Duff (M)		C Gibson (S)
	C Heap (S)	2006	M Moir (M)
2001	C Gibson (M)		E Moir (S)
	W Bryson (S)		

Lothians

1997	K Nicholson	2003	J Gallagher (M)
1998	K Nicholson		K Nicholson (S)
1999	C Swanston	2004	S Armstrong (M)
2000	M Timmins		R Moffat (S)
2001	K Nicholson (M)	2005	D Warner (M)
	D Thomson (S)		C Neilson (S)
2002	B Smith (M)	2006	A Culverwell (M)
	G Corrigan (S)		S Armstrong (S)

North-East (Scotland)

2003	B Edmond (M)	2006	G Taylor (M)
	E McIntosh (S)		M Halliday (S)
2004	L Phillips (M & S)		
2005	M Halliday (M)		
	A Reith (S)		

Perth and Kinross

1997	N Macdonald	2003	G Campbell (M & S)
1998	K Grant	2004	G Stubbs (M)
1999	N Macdonald		K McAlpine (S)
2000	G Campbell	2005	S Graham (M)
2001	G Campbell (M & S)		N Barr (S)
2002	S Carruthers (M)	2006	S Hume (M)
	G Campbell (S)		K McAlpine (S)

Renfrewshire

1997	D Owens	2003	M Clark (M)
1998	A McKay		R Clark (S)
1999	A McKay	2004	D McFarlane (M)
2000	S Robertson		M Clark (S)
2001	A Craig (M)	2005	L Jenkins (M)
	G Murphy (S)		C Watson (S)
2002	C Rossi (M)	2006	A Farmer (M & S)
	GW Urquhart (S)		

SE Scotland Championship

1997	I Brotherston	2003	B Scott (M & S)
1998	D Sutton	2004	I Brotherston (M)
1999	I Thomson		B Scott (S)
2000	BJ Scott	2005	I Thomson (M)
2001	I Brotherston (M)		D Brodie (S)
	C Haddow (S)	2006	N Hamilton (M)
2002	BJ Scott (S)		M Grunwell (S)
	J Power (M)		

Stirlingshire

1997	A Ellison	2003	S McLachlan (M)
1998	JR Johnson		G Barrie (S)
1999	K McArthur	2004	D Wallace (M)
2000	H Anderson		M Hislop (S)
2001	H Anderson (M)	2005	R Rushford (M)
	D Todd (S)		A Ellison (S)
2002	H Anderson (M)	2006	A Lynch (M & S)
	D Buchanan (S)		

Wales

Anglesey

1997	M Perdue	2002	M Perdue
1998	EO Jones	2003	L Baynes
1999	A Williams	2004	E Jones
2000	H Hughes	2005	B Thompson
2001	H Hughes	2006	S Thomas

Brecon & Radnor

2003	M Maddock	2005	GD Jones
2004	C Trott	2006	M Davies

Caernarfon and District

1997	Not played	2002	A Williams
1998	A Clishem	2003	A Thomas
1999	R Williams	2004	G Marfell
2000	H Hughes	2005	A Clishem
2001	M Tottey	2006	E Angel

Caernarfonshire Cup

1997	Not played	2002	A Thomas
1998	M Pilkington	2003	E Williams
1999	E Angel	2004	N Lloyd
2000	M Wyn Jones	2005	M Wyn Jones
2001	A Thomas	2006	M Ellison

Denbigh

2004	P Grimley	2006	A Runcie
2005	T Dykes		

Dyfed

2003	R Scott	2005	R Stone
2004	R Lindquist	2006	R Scott

Flintshire

2003	R Caldecott	2005	M Davies
2004	J Snead	2006	J Shufflebotham

Glamorgan

1997	Y Taylor	2002	L James
1998	C Williams	2003	J Holmes
1999	S Roberts	2004	R Hooper
2000	N Edwards	2005	J Holmes
2001	N Edwards	2006	C Rowe

Gwent (Formerly Monmouthshire Amateur)

1997	R Price	2003	A Mason
1998	N Povall	2004	C Evans
1999	A Williams	2005	N Povall
2000	CJ Dinsdale	2006	R Collett (M)
2001	S Westley		C Evans (S)
2002	J Davidson		

Month by month in 2006

Sherri Steinhauer claims third Weetabix Women's British Open title in nine years, but the month belongs to Woods. He wins the Buick Open by three, the PGA Championship by five and then the WGC – Bridgestone Invitational after a play-off with Stewart Cink, who a week earlier was given a Ryder Cup wild card along with Scott Verplank. Darren Clarke loses his wife Heather to cancer at the age of 39.

Overseas Amateur Championships

Australian (inaugurated 1894) (Australian unless stated)

1894	LA Whyte	1925	H Sinclair	1956	H Berwick	1983	WJ Smith
1895	RAA Balfour	1926	Len Nettlefold	1957	BH Warren	1984	BP King
	Melville	1927	WS Nankivell	1958	K Hartley	1985	B Ruangkit (THA)
1896	HA Howden	1928	Len Nettlefold	1959	BW Devlin	1986	DJ Ecob
1897	HA Howden	1929	MJ Ryan	1960	Ted Ball	1987	B Johns
1898	HA Howden	1930	HW Hattersley	1961	T Crow	1988	S Bouvier
1899	CES Gillies	1931	HL William	1962	D Bachli	1989	SJ Conran
1900	LA Whyte	1932	Dr RH Bettington	1963	J Hayes (RSA)	1990	CD Gray
1901	HA Howden	1933	WL Hope	1964	B Baker	1991	LKJ Parsons
1902	H Macneil	1934	TS McKay	1965	K Donohoe	1992	MS Campbell (NZL)
1903	DG Soutar	1935	J Ferrier	1966	W Britten	1993	GJ Chalmers
1904	JD Howden	1936	J Ferrier	1967	J Muller	1994	W Bennett (ENG)
1905	Hon. Michael Scott	1937	HL Williams	1968	R Stott	1995	MC Goggin
1906	EA Gill	1938	J Ferrier	1969	RA Shearer	1996	DC Gleeson
1907	Hon. Michael Scott	1939	J Ferrier	1970	PA Bennett	1997	K Felton
1908	Clyde Pearce	1940–45	Not played	1971	GR Hicks	1998	B Rumford
1909	Hon. Michael Scott	1946	AN Waterson	1972	CR Kaye	1999	BM Jones
1910	Hon. Michael Scott	1947	HW Hattersley	1973	RJ Jenner	2000	BP Lamb
1911	JD Howden	1948	D Bachli	1974	TR Gale	2001	S Bowditch
1912	Hector Morrison	1949	WD Ackland-	1975	C Bonython	2002	K Barnes
1913	AR Lempriere		Horman	1976	P Sweeney	2003	J Doherty (SCO)
1914–19	Not played	1950	H Berwick	1977	AY Gresham	2004	A Martin
1920	EL Apperley	1951	Peter Heard	1978	MA Clayton	2005	E Ramsay (SCO)
1921	CL Winser	1952	R Stevens	1979	J Kelly	2006	T Stewart
1922	Ivo Witton	1953	Peter Heard	1980	R Mackay		
1923	Ivo Witton	1954	P Toogood	1981	O Moore		
1924	H Sinclair	1955	J Rayner	1982	EM Couper		

Canadian (inaugurated 1895) (Canadian unless stated)

1895	TH Harley	1925	DD Carrick	1956	M Norman	1982	D Roxburgh
1896	JS Gillespie	1926	CR Somerville	1957	N Weslock	1983	D Milovic
1897	WAH Kerr	1927	DD Carrick	1958	B Castator	1984	W Swartz
1898	GS Lyon	1928	CR Somerville	1959	J Johnston	1985	B Franklin
1899	Vere C Brown	1929	E Held	1960	RK Alexander	1986	B Franklin
1900	GS Lyon	1930	CR Somerville	1961	G Cowan	1987	B Franklin
1901	WAH Kerr	1931	CR Somerville	1962	R Taylor	1988	D Roxburgh
1902	FR Martin	1932	GB Taylor	1963	N Weslock	1989	P Major
1903	GS Lyon	1933	A Campbell	1964	N Weslock	1990	W Sye
1904	J Percy Taylor	1934	A Campbell	1965	G Henry	1991	J Kraemer
1905	GS Lyon	1935	CR Somerville	1966	N Weslock	1992	D Ritchie
1906	GS Lyon	1936	F Haas jr	1967	S Jones	1993	G Simpson
1907	GS Lyon	1937	CR Somerville	1968	J Doyle	1994	W Sye
1908	Alex Wilson	1938	T Adams	1969	Wayne McDonald	1995	G Willis (USA)
1909	E Legge	1939	K Black	1970	A Miller	1996	R McMillan
1910	F Martin	1940–44	Not played	1971	R Siderowf	1997	D Goehring
1911	GH Hutton	1946	H Martell	1972	D Roxburgh	1998	C Matthew
1912	George S Lyon	1947	FR Stranahan	1973	G Burns	1999	Han Lee (USA)
1913	GH Turpin	1948	FR Stranahan	1974	D Roxburgh	2000	Han Lee (USA)
1914	George S Lyon	1949	RD Chapman	1975	J Nelford	2001	G Paddison (NZL)
1915–19	Not played	1950	W Mawhinney	1976	J Nelford	2002	D Pruitt (USA)
1920	CB Grier	1951	W McElroy	1977	R Spittle	2003	R Scott
1921	F Thompson	1952	L Bouchey	1978	R Spittle	2004	D Wallace
1922	CC Fraser	1953	D Cherry	1979	R Alarcon (MEX)	2005	R Scott
1923	WJ Thompson	1954	E Harvie Ward	1980	G Olson	2006	R Scott
1924	F Thompson	1955	M Norman	1981	R Zokol		

New Zealand (inaugurated 1893)   (New Zealand unless stated)

1893	JA Somerville	1923	J Goss jr	1955	SG Jones	1982	J Peters
1894	H Macneil	1924	L Quin	1956	PA Toogood	1983	C Taylor
1895	G Gosset	1925	TH Horton	1957	EJ McDougall	1984	J Wagner
1896	MS Todd	1926	ADS Duncan	1958	WJ Godfrey	1985	G Power
1897	D Pryde	1927	S Morpeth	1959	SG Jones	1986	P O'Malley
1898	W Pryde	1928	TH Horton	1960	R Newdick	1987	O. Kendall
1899	ADS Duncan	1929	S Morpeth	1961	SG Jones	1988	B Hughes
1900	ADS Duncan	1930	HA Black	1962	SG Jones	1989	L Peterson
1901	ADS Duncan	1931	R Wagg	1963	J Durry	1990	M Long
1902	SH Gollan	1932	R Wagg	1964	SG Jones	1991	L Parsons
1903	K Tareha	1933	BV Wright	1965	J Durry	1992	R Lee
1904	AH Fisher	1934	BM Silk	1966	SG Jones	1993	P Tatamaugi
1905	ADS Duncan	1935	JP Hornabrook	1967	J Durry	1994	P Fitzgibbon
1906	SH Gollan	1936	JP Hornabrook	1968	BA Stevens	1995	S Bittle
1907	ADS Duncan	1937	BM Silk	1969	G Stevenson	1996	D Somerville
1908	HC Smith	1938	PGF Smith	1970	EJ McDougall	1997	C Johns
1909	ADS Duncan	1939	JP Hornabrook	1971	SG Jones	1998	B MacDonald
1910	HB Lusk	1940–45	Not played	1972	RC Murray	1999	A Duffin
1911	ADS Duncan	1946	WG Horne	1973	MN Nicholson	2000	E Burgess
1912	BB Wood	1947	BM Silk	1974	RM Barltrop	2001	B Gallie
1913	BB Wood	1948	A Gibbs	1975	SF Reese	2002	M Fraser
1914	ADS Duncan	1949	J Holden	1976	TR Pulman	2003	J Nitties (AUS)
1915–18	Not played	1950	DL Woon	1977	TR Pulman	2004	G Flint (AUS)
1919	H Crosse	1951	DL Woon	1978	F Nobilo	2005	MI Brown (AUS)
1920	S Morpeth	1952	H Berwick	1979	J Durry	2006	A Green
1921	AG Syme	1953	DL Woon	1980	PE Hartstone		
1922	ADS Duncan	1954	DL Woon	1981	T Cochrane		

South African (inaugurated 1892)   (South African unless stated)

1892	D Walker	1923	WCE Stent	1954	A Jackson	1981	D Suddards
1893	DG Proudfoot	1924	AL Forster	1955	B Keyter	1982	N James
1894	DG Proudfoot	1925	TG McLelland	1956	RC Taylor	1983	C-C Yuan (CHN)
1895	DG Proudfoot	1926	WS Bryant	1957	A Stewart	1984	M Wiltshire
1896	DG Proudfoot	1927	GJ Chantler	1958	JR Boyd	1985	N Clarke
1897	DG Proudfoot	1928	B Wynne	1959	A Walker	1986	E Els
1898	DG Proudfoot	1929	C Hunter	1960	WM Grinrod	1987	B Fouche
1899	DG Proudfoot	1930	B Wynne	1961	JG Le Roux	1988	N Clarke
1900–01	Not played	1931	C Coetzer	1962	J Hayes	1989	C Rivett
1902	DG Proudfoot	1932	CE Olander	1963	D Symons	1990	R Goosen
1903	R Law	1933	B Wynne	1964	JR Langridge	1991	D Botes
1904	JR Southey	1934	CE Olander	1965	P Vorster	1992	B Davidson
1905	HCV Nicholson	1935	AD Locke	1966	Comrie du Toit	1993	L Chitengwa (ZIM)
1906	Lt. HM Ballinghall	1936	CE Olander	1967	Derek Kemp	1994	B Vaughan
1907	Lt. HM Ballinghall	1937	AD Locke	1968	R Williams	1995	W Abery
1908	JAW Prentice	1938	B Wynne	1969	D Thornton	1996	T Moore
1909	JAW Prentice	1939	O Hayes	1970	H Baiocchi	1997	T Immelman
1910	Dr EL Steyn	1940	HEP Watermeyer	1971	C Dreyer	1998	J Hugo
1911	JAW Prentice	1941–45	Not played	1972	N Dundelson	1999	R Sterne
1912	HG Stewart	1946	JR Boyd	1973	A. Oosthuizen	2000	J Van Zyl
1913	JAW Prentice	1947	C de G Watermeyer	1974	T Lagerwey	2001	D Dixon (ENG)
1914	SM McPherson	1948	RR Ryan	1975	P Vorster	2002	R Loubser
1915–18	Not played	1949	RW Glennie	1976	R Kotzen	2003	A Haig
1919	HG Stewart	1950	EA Dalton	1977	EA Webber (ZIM)	2004	H Rootman
1920	HG Stewart	1951	ES Irwin	1978	EA Webber (ZIM)	2005	G Coetzee
1921	AL Forster	1952	M Janks	1979	L Norval	2006	N Edwards (WAL)
1922	WCE Stent	1953	R Brews	1980	E Grienewald		

South African Stroke Play (inaugurated 1969) (South African unless stated)

1969 D van der Walt	1979 D Suddards	1989 E Els	1999 J Hugo
1970 D Hayes	1980 E Groenewald	1990 P Pascoe	2000 C McMonagle (IRL)
1971 K Suddards	1981 C-C Yuan (CHN)	1991 N Henning	2001 R Sterne
1972 P Dunne	1982 Li Wen-sheng	1992 J Nelson	2002 G Wolstenholme
1973 G Harvey (ZIM)	1983 Peter van der Riet	1993 D Kinnear	(ENG)
1974 N Sundelson	1984 D James	1994 N Homann	2003 A Kruger
1975 G Levenson	1985 D van Steden	1995 M Murless	2004 H Rootman
1976 G Harvey (ZIM)	1986 C-S Hsieh	1996 T Moore	2005 J Cunliffe
1977 M McNulty	1987 B Fouchee	1997 U van den Berg	2006 B Grace
1978 D Suddards	1988 N Clarke	1998 T Immelman	

106th United States Amateur Championship 2006 *Hazeltine, Cheska, MN*

Year	Winner	Runner-up	Venue	By
1895	CB Macdonald	C Sands	Newport, RI	12 and 11
1896	HJ Whigham	JG Thorp	Shinnecock Hills, NY	8 and 7
1897	HJ Whigham	WR Betts	Wheaton, IL	8 and 6
1898	FS Douglas	WB Smith	Morris County, NJ	5 and 3
1899	HM Harriman	FS Douglas	Onwentsia, IL	3 and 2
1900	WJ Travis	FS Douglas	Garden City, NY	2 holes
1901	WJ Travis	WE Egan	Atlantic City, NJ	5 and 4
1902	LN James	EM Byers	Glenview, IL	4 and 3
1903	WJ Travis	EM Byers	Nassau, NY	5 and 4
1904	HC Egan	F Herreshof	Baltusrol, NJ	8 and 6
1905	HC Egan	DE Sawyer	Wheaton, IL	6 and 5
1906	EM Byers	GS Lyon	Englewood, NJ	2 holes
1907	JD Travers	A Graham	Cleveland, OH	6 and 5
1908	JD Travers	MH Behr	Garden City, NY	8 and 7
1909	RA Gardner	HC Egan	Wheaton, IL	4 and 3
1910	WC Fownes jr	WK Wood	Brookline, MA	4 and 3
1911	HH Hilton (ENG)	F Herreshof	Apawamis, NY	37th
1912	JD Travers	C Evans jr	Wheaton, IL	7 and 6
1913	JD Travers	JG Anderson	Garden City, NY	5 and 4
1914	F Ouimet	JD Travers	Ekwanok, VT	6 and 5
1915	RA Gardner	JG Anderson	Detroit, MI	5 and 4
1916	C Evans jr	RA Gardner	Merion, PA	4 and 3
1917–18 Not played				
1919	SD Herron	RT Jones jr	Oakmont, PA	5 and 4
1920	C Evans jr	F Ouimet	Roslyn, NY	7 and 6
1921	JP Guildford	RA Gardner	Clayton, MO	7 and 6
1922	JW Sweetser	C Evans jr	Brookline, MA	3 and 2
1923	MR Marston	JW Sweetser	Flossmoor, IL	38th
1924	RT Jones jr	G Von Elm	Merion, PA	9 and 8
1925	RT Jones jr	W Gunn	Oakmont, PA	8 and 7
1926	G Von Elm	RT Jones jr	Baltusrol, NJ	2 and 1
1927	RT Jones jr	C Evans jr	Minikahda, MN	8 and 7
1928	RT Jones jr	TP Perkins	Brae Burn, MA	10 and 9
1929	HR Johnston	OF Willing	Pebble Beach, CA	4 and 3
1930	RT Jones jr	EV Homans	Merion, PA	8 and 7
1931	F Ouimet	J Westland	Beverley, IL	6 and 5
1932	CR Somerville	J Goodman	Baltimore, MD	2 and 1
1933	GT Dunlap jr	MR Marston	Kenwood, OH	6 and 5
1934	W Lawson Little jr	D Goldman	Brookline, MA	8 and 7
1935	W Lawson Little jr	W Emery	Cleveland, OH	4 and 2
1936	JW Fischer	J McLean	Garden City, NY	37th
1937	J Goodman	RE Billows	Portland, OR	2 holes
1938	WP Turnesa	BP Abbott	Oakmont, PA	8 and 7
1939	MH Ward	RE Billows	Glenview, IL	7 and 5
1940	RD Chapman	WB McCullough	Winged Foot, NY	11 and 9
1941	MH Ward	BP Abbott	Omaha, NE	4 and 3
1942–45 Not played				
1946	SE Bishop	S Quick	Baltusrol, NJ	37th
1947	RH Riegel	JW Dawson	Pebble Beach, CA	2 and 1
1948	WP Turnesa	RE Billows	Memphis, TN	2 and 1
1949	CR Coe	R King	Rochester, NY	11 and 10
1950	S Urzetta	FR Stranahan	Minneapolis, MN	39th
1951	WJ Maxwell	J Gagliardi	Saucon Valley, PA	4 and 3
1952	J Westland	A Mengert	Seattle, WA	3 and 2

106th United States Amateur Championship *continued*

Year	Winner	Runner-up	Venue	By
1953	G Littler	D Morey	Oklahoma City, OK	I hole
1954	A Palmer	R Sweeney	Detroit, MI	I hole
1955	E Harvie Ward	W Hyndman	Richmond, VA	9 and 8
1956	E Harvie Ward	C Kocsis	Lake Forest, IL	5 and 4
1957	H Robbins	FM Taylor	Brookline, MA	5 and 4
1958	CR Coe	TD Aaron	San Francisco, CA	5 and 4
1959	JW Nicklaus	CR Coe	Broadmoor, CO	I hole
1960	DR Beman	RW Gardner	St Louis, MO	6 and 4
1961	JW Nicklaus	HD Wysong	Pebble Beach, CA	8 and 6
1962	LE Harris jr	D Gray	Pinehurst, NC	I hole
1963	DR Beman	RH Sikes	Des Moines, IA	2 and I
1964	WC Campbell	EM Tutweiler	Canterbury, OH	I hole

Changed to stroke play

Year	Winner	Venue	Score
1965	RJ Murphy	Tulsa, OK	291
1966	G Cowan (CAN)	Merion, PA	285
1967	RB Dickson	Broadmoor, CO	285
1968	B Fleisher	Columbus, OH	284
1969	S Melnyk	Oakmont, PA	286
1970	L Wadkins	Portland, OR	280
1971	G Cowan (CAN)	Wilmington, DE	280
1972	M Giles	Charlotte, NC	285

Reverted to match play

Year	Winner	Runner-up	Venue	By
1973	C Stadler	D Strawn	Inverness, OH	6 and 5
1974	J Pate	J Grace	Ridgewood, NJ	2 and I
1975	F Ridley	K Fergus	Richmond, VA	2 holes
1976	B Sander	CP Moore	Bel-Air, CA	8 and 6
1977	J Fought	D Fischesser	Aronimink, PA	9 and 8
1978	J Cook	S Hoch	Plainfield, NJ	5 and 4
1979	M O'Meara	J Cook	Cleveland, OH	8 and 7
1980	H Sutton	B Lewis	Pinehurst, NC	9 and 8
1981	N Crosby	B Lindley	San Francisco, CA	37th
1982	J Sigel	D Tolley	Brookline, MA	8 and 7
1983	J Sigel	C Perry	Glenview, IL	8 and 7
1984	S Verplank	S Randolph	Oak Tree, OK	4 and 3
1985	S Randolph	P Persons	Montclair, NJ	I hole
1986	S Alexander	C Kite	Shoal Creek, AL	5 and 3
1987	W Mayfair	E Rebmann	Jupiter Hills, FL	4 and 3
1988	E Meeks	D Yates	Hot Springs, VA	7 and 6
1989	C Patton	D Green	Merion, PA	3 and I
1990	P Mickelson	M Zerman	Cherry Hills, CO	5 and 4
1991	M Voges	M Zerman	Chattanooga, TN	7 and 6
1992	J Leonard	T Scherrer	Muirfield Village, OH	8 and 7
1993	J Harris	D Ellis	Houston, TX	5 and 3
1994	T Woods	T Kuehne	Sawgrass, FL	2 holes
1995	T Woods	G Marucci	Newport, RI	2 holes
1996	T Woods	S Scott	Pumpkin Ridge, OR	38th
1997	M Kuchar	J Kribel	Cog Hill, Lemont, IL	2 and I
1998	H Kuehne	T McKnight	Oak Hill, Rochester, NY	2 and I
1999	D Gossett	Sung Yoon Kim	Pebble Beach, CA	9 and 8
2000	J Quinney	J Driscoll	Springfield, NJ	39th hole
2001	B Dickerson	R Hamilton	East Lake, Atlanta, GA	I hole
2002	R Barnes	H Mahon	Oakland Hills, MI	2 and I
2003	N Flanagan (AUS)	C Wittenberg	Okmont, PA	37th
2004	R Moore	L List	Mamaroneck, NY	2 holes
2005	E Molinari (ITA)	D Dougherty	Merion, PA	4 and 3

2006 *Hazeltine*

Leading Qualifier: Billy Horshel 60-78—138

Quarter Finals:

Ryan Yip (CAN) beat Oliver Fisher (ENG) 4 and 3
John Kelly (Saint Louis, MO) beat Trip Kuehne (Dallas, TX) 3 and 2
Webb Simpson (Raleigh, NC) beat Alex Prugh (Spokane, WA)
Richie Ramsay (SCO) beat Rickie Fowler (Murrieta, CA) at 21st

Semi-Finals:
Kelly beat Yip 2 and 1
Ramsay beat Simpson 1 hole
Final: Richie Ramsay beat John Kelly 4 and 2

Boyd triumphs in China

Young England international Gary Boyd came from five shots back to win the inaugural Asia–Pacific Open Amateur Championship at Mission Hills in China. A closing round of 71 for a level par aggregate of 288 left the 20-year-old from Northamptonshire tied with Japan's Ryutaro Nagano but Boyd took the title at the first playoff hole.

The pair finished a stroke ahead of T Choo from Singapore and third round leader Anthony Fernando from the Philippines while veteran Walker Cup man Gary Wolstenholme finished down the field on 312.

Boyd, who lost only one of five matches when making his full England début in September's Home Internationals in Wales, trailed Fernando by five shots going into the final round over the 7,323 yard Mission Hills course in Shenzhen. But while Fernando was posting a closing 77, Boyd was making up ground fast. He was out in 35, one under par, with birdies at the sixth and seventh holes, while an eagle-three at the long 11th proved the key despite his dropping shots at the short 15th and par four 18th.

In the playoff on the par four tenth hole, both Boyd and Nagano had putts from around six feet but while the Japanese missed, Boyd holed out for his first major international title.

2006 National Amateur Championship winners

American	Richie Ramsay (SCO)	Japanese	Kyung-Tae Kim (KOR)
Australian	Tim Stewart	Luxembourg	Steven Rojas (SUI)
Austrian	Sigmundur Einar Masson (ISL)	Malaysian	Andrew Dodt (AUS)
Baltic	Liro Sutinen (FIN)	Mexican	Sebastian Saavedra (ARG)
Brazilian	Eduardo Pesenti	New Zealand	Andrew Green
Bulgarian	Michael Kanev	Pakistan	Tariq Mahmoud
Canadian	Richard Scott	Philippines	Marvin Dumandan
Czech	Nuno Henriques (POR)	Polish	Thomas Ortner (AUT)
Danish	Morten Findsen Schou	Portuguese	Adrien Bernadet (FRA)
English	Ross McGowan	Russian	Seve Benson (ENG)
Estonian	Paul Pohi	Scottish	Kevin McAlpine
Finnish	Jukka-Pekka Savolampi	Singapore	Chiragh Kumar (IND)
French	Sean Einhaus (GER)	Slovenian	Matjaí Gojčič
German	Christian Schunck	Spanish	Sam Hutsby (ENG)
Hellenic	Gencer Oxcan (TUR)	Sri Lanka	Mithun Perera
Hungarian	Ifj. János Tóth	Swiss	Marc Dobias
Indian	Himmat Rai	Taiwan	Kim Do-Hoon
Irish	Antti Ahokas (FIN)	Turkish	Peter Baunsoe (DEN)
Italian	Jason Palmer (ENG)	Welsh	Llewellyn Matthews

Month by month in 2006

Just three weeks after the death of his wife, Darren Clarke makes himself available for the Ryder Cup and is picked along with Lee Westwood. Europe not only achieve an unprecedented third successive victory, but repeat their record 18½–9½ win in 2004. Clarke's three wins out of three make him the focal point of the celebrations. Paul Casey and Verplank both hole-in-one at 14th. Casey to finish his game just a week after winning the £1 million HSBC Match Play title.

PART V

Women's Amateur Tournaments

National and International Tournaments

Ladies British Amateur Championship (inaugurated 1893)   2006 *Royal County Down*

1893	M Scott	I Pearson	St Annes	7 and 5
1894	M Scott	I Pearson	Littlestone	3 and 2
1895	M Scott	E Lythgoe	Portrush	5 and 4
1896	Miss Pascoe	L Thomson	Hoylake, Royal Liverpool	3 and 2
1897	EC Orr	Miss Orr	Gullane	4 and 2
1898	L Thomson	EC Neville	Yarmouth	7 and 5
1899	M Hezlet	Magill	Newcastle Co Down	2 and 1
1900	Adair	Neville	Westward Ho!, R North Devon	6 and 5
1901	Graham	Adair	Aberdovey	3 and 1
1902	M Hezlet	E Neville	Deal	19th hole
1903	Adair	F Walker-Leigh	Portrush	4 and 3
1904	L Dod	M Hezlet	Troon	I hole
1905	B Thompson	ME Stuart	Cromer	3 and 2
1906	Kennon	B Thompson	Burnham	4 and 3
1907	M Hezlet	F Hezlet	Newcastle Co Down	2 and 1
1908	M Titterton	D Campbell	St Andrews	19th hole
1909	D Campbell	F Hezlet	Birkdale	4 and 3
1910	Miss Grant Suttie	L Moore	Westward Ho!, R North Devon	6 and 4
1911	D Campbell	V Hezlet	Portrush	3 and 2
1912	G Ravenscroft	S Temple	Turnberry	3 and 2

(Final played over 36 holes after 1912)

1913	M Dodd	Chubb	St Annes	8 and 6
1914	C Leitch	G Ravenscroft	Hunstanton	2 and 1
1915–18	*Not played*			
1919	*Should have been played at Burnham in October, but abandoned because of railway strike*			
1920	C Leitch	M Griffiths	Newcastle Co Down	7 and 6
1921	C Leitch	J Wethered	Turnberry	4 and 3
1922	J Wethered	C Leitch	Prince's, Sandwich, Royal St George's	9 and 7
1923	D Chambers	A Macbeth	Burnham, Somerset	2 holes
1924	J Wethered	Mrs Cautley	Portrush	7 and 6
1925	J Wethered	C Leitch	Troon	37th hole
1926	C Leitch	Mrs Garon	Harlech	8 and 7
1927	T de la Chaume (FRA)	Miss Pearson	Newcastle Co Down	5 and 4
1928	N Le Blan (FRA)	S Marshall	Hunstanton	3 and 2
1929	J Wethered	G Collett (USA)	St Andrews	3 and 1
1930	D Fishwick	G Collett (USA)	Formby	4 and 3
1931	E Wilson	W Morgan	Portmarnock	7 and 6
1932	E Wilson	CPR Montgomery	Saunton	7 and 6
1933	E Wilson	D Plumpton	Gleneagles	5 and 4
1934	AM Holm	P Barton	Porthcawl	6 and 5
1935	W Morgan	P Barton	Newcastle Co Down	3 and 2
1936	P Barton	B Newell	Southport and Ainsdale	5 and 3
1937	J Anderson	D Park	Turnberry	6 and 4
1938	AM Holm	E Corlett	Burnham	4 and 3
1939	P Barton	T Marks	Portrush	2 and 1
1940–45	*Not played*			
1946	GW Hetherington	P Garvey	Hunstanton	I hole
1947	B Zaharias (USA)	J Gordon	Gullane	5 and 4
1948	L Suggs (USA)	J Donald	Lytham St Annes	I hole
1949	F Stephens	V Reddan	Harlech	5 and 4
1950	Vicomtesse de St Sauveur (FRA)	J Valentine	Newcastle Co Down	3 and 2
1951	PJ MacCann	F Stephens	Broadstone	4 and 3
1952	M Paterson	F Stephens	Troon	39th hole
1953	M Stewart (CAN)	P Garvey	Porthcawl	7 and 6
1954	F Stephens	E Price	Ganton	4 and 3
1955	J Valentine	B Romack (USA)	Portrush	7 and 6

1956	M Smith (USA)	M Janssen (USA)	Sunningdale	8 and 7
1957	P Garvey	J Valentine	Gleneagles	4 and 3
1958	J Valentine	E Price	Hunstanton	I hole
1959	E Price	B McCorkindale	Ascot	37th hole
1960	B McIntyre (USA)	P Garvey	Harlech	4 and 2
1961	M Spearman	DJ Robb	Carnoustie	7 and 6
1962	M Spearman	A Bonallack	Royal Birkdale	I hole
1963	B Varangot (FRA)	P Garvey	Newcastle Co Down	3 and I
1964	C Sorenson (USA)	BAB Jackson	Sandwich, Prince's,	
			Royal St George's	37th hole
1965	B Varangot (FRA)	IC Robertson	St Andrews	4 and 3
1966	E Chadwick	V Saunders	Ganton	3 and 2
1967	E Chadwick	M Everard	Harlech	I hole
1968	B Varangot (FRA)	C Rubin (FRA)	Walton Heath	20th hole
1969	C Lacoste (FRA)	A Irvin	Portrush	I hole
1970	D Oxley	IC Robertson	Gullane	I hole
1971	M Walker	B Huke	Alwoodley	3 and I
1972	M Walker	C Rubin (FRA)	Hunstanton	2 holes
1973	A Irvin	M Walker	Carnoustie	3 and 2
1974	C Semple (USA)	A Bonallack	Porthcawl	2 and I
1975	N Syms (USA)	S Cadden	St Andrews	3 and 2
1976	C Panton	A Sheard	Silloth	I hole
1977	A Uzielli	V Marvin	Hillside	6 and 5
1978	E Kennedy (AUS)	J Greenhalgh	Notts	I hole
1979	M Madill	J Lock (AUS)	Nairn	2 and I
1980	A Quast (USA)	L Wollin (SWE)	Woodhall Spa	3 and I
1981	IC Robertson	W Aitken	Conway	20th hole
1982	K Douglas	G Stewart	Walton Heath	4 and 2
1983	J Thornhill	R Lautens (SUI)	Silloth	4 and 2
1984	J Rosenthal (USA)	J Brown	Royal Troon	4 and 3
1985	L Beman (IRL)	C Waite	Ganton	I hole
1986	M McGuire (NZL)	L Briars (AUS)	West Sussex	2 and I
1987	J Collingham	S Shapcott	Harlech	19th hole
1988	J Furby	J Wade	Deal	4 and 3
1989	H Dobson	E Farquharson	Royal Liverpool	6 and 5
1990	J Hall	H Wadsworth	Dunbar	3 and 2
1991	V Michaud (FRA)	W Doolan (AUS)	Pannal	3 and 2
1992	P Pedersen (DEN)	J Morley	Saunton	I hole
1993	C Lambert	K Speak	Royal Lytham	3 and 2
1994	E Duggleby	C Mourgue d'Algue	Newport	3 and I
1995	J Hall	K Mourgue d'Algue	Royal Portrush	3 and 2
1996	K Kuehne (USA)	B Morgan	Royal Liverpool	5 and 3
1997	A Rose	M McKay	Cruden Bay	4 and 3
1998	K Rostron	G Nocera (FRA)	Little Aston	3 and 2
1999	M Monnet (FRA)	R Hudson	Royal Birkdale	I hole
2000	R Hudson	E Duggleby	Walton Heath	5 and 4
2001	M Prieto (ESP)	E Duggleby	Ladybank	4 and 3
2002	R Hudson	L Wright	Ashburnham	5 and 4
2003	E Serramia (ESP)	P Odefey (GER)	Lindrick	2 holes
2004	L Stahle (SWE)	A Highgate	Gullane	4 and 2
2005	L Stahle (SWE)	C Coughlan	Littlestone	3 and 2

2006 Royal County Down

Leading Qualifier: 142 – Azahara Muñoz (ESP) 69-73

First Round

Stacy Bregman (RSA) beat Azahara Muñoz (ESP) 2 and I
Malene Jorgensen (DEN) beat Charlotte Ellis (Minchinhampton) 3 and 2
Sophie Walker (Kenwick Park) beat Stephanie Evans (Vale of Llangollen) 4 and 3
Dewi Claire Schreefel (NED) beat Kiran Matharu (Cookridge Hall) 2 and I
Martina Gillen (Beaverstown) beat Gemma Webster (Hilton Park) 2 and I
Maura Morrin (The Curragh) beat Devan Anderson (MEX) 4 and 3
Maria Hernandez (ESP) beat Roseanne Niven (Crieff) 2 and I
Breanne Loucks (Wrexham) beat Lene Krog (NOR) 2 holes
Maude-Aimee Leblanc (CAN) beat Mikaela Backstedt (SWE) 4 and 3
Krystle Caithness (St Regulus) beat Melissa Reid (Chevin) at 19th
Myrte Eikenaar (NED) beat Christel Boeljon (NED) at 19th
Anna Nordqvist (SWE) beat Stephanie Doering (GER) 6 and 4
Florentyna Parker (Gut Waldhof) beat Kira Meixner (CAN) 8 and 7
Jade Schaeffer (FRA) beat Rachel Jennings (Izaak Walton) 4 and 3

2006 Ladies British Amateur Championship *continued*

First Round *continued*

Joanna Klatten (FRA) beat Deirdre Smith (Co. Louth) 2 holes
Sandra Gal (GER) beat Lisa Ball (Matfen Hall) 3 and 1
Belen Mozo (ESP) beat Meaghan Leblanc (CAN) 6 and 5
Thea Hoffmeister (GER) beat Danielle McVeigh (Royal County Down) 4 and 3
Py Bengtsson (SWE) beat Emilie Geury (BEL) 4 and 3
Marjet van der Graaff (NED) beat Charlotte Lorentzen (DEN) 2 and 1
Lucie Gendronneau (FRA) beat Felicity Johnson (Harborne) at 20th
Laura Matthews (CAN) beat Carlota Ciganda (ESP) 2 and 1
Jody Fleming (AUS) beat Kerry Smith (Waterlooville) 1 hole
Katharina Schallenberg (GER) beat Karen Delaney (Carlow) 6 and 4
Tricia Mangan (Ennis) beat Caroline Westrup (SWE) 1 hole
Louise Kenney (Pitreavie) beat Mary-Ann Lapointe (CAN) at 19th
Emma Bennett (AUS) beat Emily Ogilvy (Auchterarder) 3 and 2
Tara Delaney (Carlow) beat Sofie Andersson (SWE) 3 and 2
Mariana Macias (ESP) beat Anne-Lise Caudal (FRA) 4 and 2
Kate Combes (AUS) beat Heather Macrae (Dunblane New) 4 and 3
Naomi Edwards (Ganton) beat Sinead Keane (The Curragh) 5 and 4
Claire Coughlan (Cork) beat Morgane Bazin de Jessey (FRA) 4 and 3

Second Round
Bregman beat Jorgensen 4 and 2
Walker beat Schreefel 3 and 2
Morrin beat Gillen 4 and 3
Hernandez beat Loucks 6 and 4
Caithness beat Leblanc 4 and 3
Nordqvist beat Eikenaar 1 hole
Parker beat Schaeffer 1 hole
Gal beat Klatten 4 and 3
Mozo beat Hoffmeister 2 and 1
Bengtsson beat van der Graaff 4 and 2
Matthews beat Gendronneau 5 and 4
Schallenberg beat Fleming 2 and 1
Mangan beat Kenney 5 and 4
Bennett beat Delaney 5 and 4
Macias beat Combes 1 hole
Edwards beat Coughlan 3 and 2

Third Round
Walker beat Bregman 3 and 2
Hernandez beat Morrin 2 and 1

Third Round *continued*
Nordqvist beat Caithness 4 and 3
Parker beat Gal 1 hole
Mozo beat Bengtsson 1 hole
Schallenberg beat Matthews at 19th
Mangan beat Bennett at 20th
Edwards beat Macias 5 and 3

Quarter Finals
Hernandez beat Walker 7 and 6
Nordqvist beat Parker 1 hole
Mozo beat Schallenberg 1 hole
Edwards beat Mangan 2 holes

Semi-Finals
Nordqvist beat Hernandez 2 and 1
Mozo beat Edwards 7 and 6

Final
Belen Mozo (ESP) beat Anna Nordqvist (SWE)
  3 and 1

Ladies British Open Amateur Stroke Play Championship 2006 *Prince's*

(inaugurated 1969)

1969	A Irvin	Gosforth Park	295	1984	C Waite	Caernarvonshire	295
1970	M Everard	Birkdale	313	1985	IC Robertson	Formby	300
1971	IC Robertson	Ayr Belleisle	302	1986	C Hourihane	Blairgowrie	291
1972	IC Robertson	Silloth	296	1987	L Bayman	Ipswich	297
1973	A Stant	Purdis Heath	298	1988	K Mitchell	Porthcawl	317
1974	J Greenhalgh	Seaton Carew	302	1989	H Dobson	Southerness	298
1975	J Greenhalgh	Gosforth Park	298	1990	V Thomas	Strathaven	287
1976	J Lee Smith	Fulford	299	1991	J Morley	Long Ashton	297
1977	M Everard	Lindrick	306	1992	J Hockley	Frilford Heath	287
1978	J Melville	Foxhills	310	1993	J Hall	Gullane	290
1979	M McKenna	Moseley	305	1994	K Speak	Woodhall Spa	297
1980	M Mahill	Brancepeth Castle	304	1995	MJ Pons (ESP)	Princes	289
1981	J Soulsby	Norwich	300	1996	C Kuld (DEN)	Conwy (Caernarvonshire)	289
1982	J Connachan	Downfield	294	1997	KM Juul (DEN)	Silloth-on-Solway	293
1983	A Nicholas	Moortown	292	1998	N Nijenhuis	Stirling	297

1999	B Brewerton	Huddersfield	294	2003	S McKevitt	Royal Portrush	306
2000	R Hudson	Newcastle, NI	294	2004	C Queen*	Alwoodley	294
2001	R Hudson	Kilmarnock	300	2005	H Macrae*	Nairn	288
2002	B Brewerton	Hunstanton	291				

2006 *Prince's*

I	Anna Rossi (ITA)	74-76-70-70—290
2	Rachel Bell (Ganton)	74-73-73-71—291
3	Sahra Hassan (Vale of Glamorgan)	76-76-68-72—292

Ladies British Open Mid-Amateur Championship (inaugurated 2002) 2006 *Nairn*

| 2002 | A Laing | The Berkshire | 214 | 2004 | J Nicolson | Hunstanton | 239 |
| 2003 | S Walton | Royal Liverpool | 229 | 2005 | L McGowan | Walton Heath | 224 |

I	Martine Pow (Selkirk)	72-75-73—220
2	Jo Nicolson (Wrexham)	74-79-75—228
3	Fiona Lockhart (St Regulus)	76-79-76—231

Senior Ladies British Open Amateur Championship 2006 *Dumfries & County*

1981	BM King	Formby	159	1994	D Williams	Nottingham	154
1982	P Riddiford	Ilkley	161	1995	A Uzielli	Blairgowrie	152
1983	M Birtwistle	Troon Portland	167	1996	V Hassett	Pyle & Kenfig	236
1984	O Semelaigne	Woodbridge	152	1997	T Wiesner (USA)	Frilford Heath	231
1985	Dr G Costello	Prestatyn	158	1998	A Uzielli	Powfoot	227
1986	P Riddiford	Longniddry	154	1999	A Uzielli	Malone	229
1987	O Semelaigne	Copt Heath	152	2000	B Mogensen (DEN)	West Kilbride	242
1988	C Bailey	Littlestone	156	2001	M McKenna	Aberdovy	230
1989	C Bailey	Wrexham	149	2002	R Page	Longniddry	229
1990	A Uzielli	Harrogate	153	2003	C Burke (SWE)	South Staffordshire	226
1991	A Uzielli	Ladybank	154	2004	E Ansgarius (SWE)	Portstewart	246
1992	A Uzielli	Stratford-upon-Avon	148	2005	E Ansgarius (SWE)	Newport	226
1993	J Thornhill	Ashburnham	151				

I	Christine Quinn (Hockley)	71-75-78—224
2	Viveca Hoff (SWE)	73-79-78—230
3	Rozalyn Adams (Addington Court)	77-76-78—231

English Ladies Close Amateur Championship (inaugurated 1912)

1912	M Gardner	Mrs Cautley	Sandwich	at 20th
1913	FW Brown	Mrs McNair	Hollinwell	I hole
1914	Cecil Leitch	Miss Bastin	Walton Heath	2 and I
1915–1918	*Not played*			
1919	Cecil Leitch	Mrs Temple Dobell	St Annes Old	10 and 8
1920	Joyce Wethered	Cecil Leitch	Sheringham	2 and I
1921	Joyce Wethered	Mrs Mudford	Lytham St Annes	12 and II
1922	Joyce Wethered	J Stocker	Hunstanton	7 and 6
1923	Joyce Wethered	Mrs TA Lodge	Ganton	8 and 7
1924	Joyce Wethered	DR Fowler	Cooden Beach	8 and 7
1925	DR Fowler	J Winn	Westward Ho!	9 and 7
1926	Molly Gourlay	Elsie Corlett	Woodhall Spa	6 and 4
1927	Mrs H Guedalla	Enid Wilson	Pannal	I hole
1928	Enid Wilson	Dorothy Pearson	Walton Heath	9 and 8
1929	Molly Gourlay	Diana Fishwick	Broadstone	6 and 5
1930	Enid Wilson	Mrs RO Porter	Aldeburgh	12 and II
1931	Wanda Morgan	Molly Gourlay	Ganton	3 and I
1932	Diana Fishwick	Miss B Brown	Royal Ashdown Forest	5 and 4
1933	Dorothy Pearson	M Johnson	Westward Ho!	5 and 3
1934	P Wade	M Johnson	Seacroft	4 and 3
1935	Mrs M Garon	Elsie Corlett	Birkdale	at 38th
1936	Wanda Morgan	P Wade	Hayling Island	2 and I
1937	Wanda Morgan	M Fyshe	St Enodoc	4 and 2
1938	Elsie Corlett	J Winn	Aldeburgh	2 and I
1939–1946	*Not played*			

English Ladies Close Amateur Championship *continued*

1947	M Wallis	Elizabeth Price	Ganton	3 and 1
1948	Frances Stephens	Zara Bolton	Hayling Island	1 hole
1949	Diana Critchley	Lady Katharine Cairns	Burnham & Berrow	3 and 2
1950	Hon Mrs A Gee	Pamela Davies	Sheringham	8 and 6
1951	Jeanne Bisgood	A Keiller	St Annes Old	2 and 1
1952	Pamela Davies	Jacqueline Gordon	Westwood Ho!	6 and 5
1953	Jeanne Bisgood	J McIntyre	Sandwich	6 and 5
1954	Frances Stephens	Elizabeth Price	Woodhall Spa	at 37th
1955	Frances Smith	Elizabeth Price	Moortown	4 and 3
1956	Bridget Jackson	Ruth Ferguson	Hunstanton	2 and 1
1957	Jeanne Bisgood	Margaret Nichol	Bournemouth	10 and 8
1958	Angela Bonallack	Bridget Jackson	Formby	3 and 2
1959	Ruth Porter	Frances Smith	Aldeburgh	5 and 4
1960	Margaret Nichol	Angela Bonallack	Burnham & Berrow	3 and 1
1961	Ruth Porter	Peggy Reece	Littlestone	2 holes
1962	Jean Roberts	Angela Bonallack	Woodhall Spa	3 and 1
1963	Angela Bonallack	Elizabeth Chadwick	Liphook	7 and 6
1964	Marley Spearman	Mary Everard	Lytham St Annes	6 and 5
1965	Ruth Porter	G Cheetham	Whittington Barracks	6 and 5
1966	Julia Greenhalgh	Jean Holmes	Hayling Island	3 and 1
1967	Ann Irvin	Margaret Pickard	Alwoodley	3 and 2
1968	Sally Barber	Dinah Oxley	Hunstanton	5 and 4
1969	Barbara Dixon	M Wenyon	Burnham & Berrow	6 and 4
1970	Dinah Oxley	Sally Barber	Rye	3 and 2
1971	Dinah Oxley	Sally Barber	Hoylake	5 and 4
1972	Mary Everard	Angela Bonallack	Woodhall Spa	2 and 1
1973	Mickey Walker	Carol Le Feuvre	Broadstone	6 and 5
1974	Ann Irvin	Jill Thornhill	Sunningdale	1 hole
1975	Beverly Huke	Lynne Harrold	Birkdale	2 and 1
1976	Lynne Harrold	Angela Uzielli	Hollinwell	3 and 2
1977	Vanessa Marvin	Mary Everard	Burnham & Berrow	1 hole
1978	Vanessa Marvin	Ruth Porter	West Sussex	2 and 1
1979	Julia Greenhalgh	Susan Hedges	Hoylake	2 and 1
1980	Beverley New	Julie Walker	Aldeburgh	3 and 2
1981	Diane Christison	S Cohen	Cotswold Hills	2 holes
1982	Julie Walker	C Nelson	Brancepeth Castle	4 and 3
1983	Linda Bayman	C Macintosh	Hayling Island	4 and 3
1984	Claire Waite	Linda Bayman	Hunstanton	3 and 2
1985	Patricia Johnson	Linda Bayman	Ferndown	1 hole
1986	Jill Thornhill	Susan Shapcott	Sandwich	3 and 1
1987	Joanne Furby	Maria King	Alwoodley	4 and 3
1988	Julie Wade	Susan Shapcott	Little Aston	at 19t
1989	Helen Dobson	Simone Morgan	Burnham & Berrow	4 and 3
1990	Angela Uzielli	Linzi Fletcher	Rye	2 and 1
1991	Nicola Buxton	Karen Stupples	Sheringham	2 holes
1992	Caroline Hall	Joanne Hockley	St Annes Old	1 hole
1993	Nicola Buxton	Sarah Burnell	St Enodoc	2 and 1
1994	Julie Wade	S Sharpe	The Berkshire	1 hole
1995	Julie Wade	Elaine Ratcliffe	Ipswich	2 and 1
1996	Joanne Hockley	Lisa Educate	Silloth-on-Solway	4 and 3
1997	Kim Rostron	K Burton	Saunton	4 and 2
1998	Elaine Ratcliffe	Lisa Walters	Walton Heath	at 19th
1999	Fiona Brown	Kerry Smith	Ganton	2 and 1
2000	Emma Duggleby	Rebecca Hudson	Hunstanton	4 and 3
2001	Rebecca Hudson	Emma Duggleby	West Sussex	at 20th
2002	Kerry Knowles	C Court	Littlestone	6 and 5
2003	Emma Duggleby	N Edwards	Aldburgh	2 and 1
2004	Kerry Smith	S McKevitt	Northants County	4 and 3
2005	Felicity Johnson	S Walker	Burnham & Berrow	at 20th

2006 *West Lancashire*

Leading Qualifiers: 153: Kerry Smith (Waterlooville) 77-76; Sophie Walker (Kenwick Park) 74-79

Quarter Finals
Felicity Johnson (Harborne) beat Emma Duggleby (Malton & Norton) 2 holes
Kiran Matharu (Cookridge Hall) beat Clara Leathers (Ellesborough) 3 and 1
Danielle Montgomery (Lambourne) beat Corisande Lee (West Lancashire) 2 and 1
Naomi Edwards (Ganton) beat Rachel Bell (Ganton) 3 and 1

Semi-Finals
Matharu beat Johnson 5 and 4
Edwards beat Montgomery 4 and 2

Final
Kiran Matharu beat Naomi Edwards 5 and 4

English Ladies Close Amateur Stroke Play Championship 2006 *Little Aston*
(inaugurated 1984)

1984	P Grice	Moor Park	300	1995	L Walton	Hallamshire	289
1985	P Johnson	Northants County	301	1996	S Gallagher	Little Aston	290
1986	S Shapcott	Broadstone	301	1997	L Tupholme	Hankley Common	293
1987	J Wade	Northumberland	296	1998	E Duggleby	Broadstone	306
1988	S Prosser	Wentworth	297	1999	C Lipscombe	Gog Magog	300
1989	S Robinson	Notts	302	2000	R Hudson	Silloth-on-Solway	290
1990	K Tebbet	Saunton	299	2001	C Marron*	Stoneham	291
1991	J Morley	Ganton	301	2002	S Garbutt	Whittington Heath	294
1992	J Morley	Littlestone	289	2003	S Walker*	Saunton	303
1993	J Hall	King's Norton	298	2004	S Reddick	Woodhall Spa	285
1994	F Brown	Ferndown	289	2005	L Eastwood	St Annes Old Links	287

1	Elizabeth Bennett (Brokenhurst Manor)	75-72-70-73—290
2	Sophie Walker (Kenwick Park)	71-72-78-71—292
3	Kerry Smith (Waterlooville)	77-71-76-73—297

English Ladies Under-23 Championship
Elizabeth Bennett (Brokenhurst Manor)

English Senior Ladies Stroke Play Championship (inaugurated 1986) 2006 *Hillside*

1988	A Thompson	Wentworth	158	1997	A Thompson	Formby Ladies	152
1989	C Bailey	Notts Ladies	163	1998	E Boatman	Royal Liverpool	154
1990	A Thompson	Fairhaven	162	1999	S Westall	Northants County	151
1991	C Bailey	Burnham and Berrow	155	2000	E McCombe	Formby	162
1992	A Thompson	Pleasington	154	2001	R Page	Woodhall Spa	159
1993	A Uzielli	Hunstanton	150	2002	C Caldwell	Saunton	158
1994	S Bassindale	Littlestone	163	2003	C Caldwell*	Rye	154
1995	V Morgan	Tandridge	151	2004	V Saunders	Sandiway	154
1996	A Uzielli	Royal North Devon	153	2005	C Stirling	Little Aston	156

1	Geraldine Bray (Littlestone)	79-77—156
2	Susan Dye (Delamere Forest)	78-80—158
3	Susan Pickles (Lee-on-the-Solent)	83-81—164
	Fiona Anderson (Formby Ladies)	77-87—164

English Senior Ladies Match Play Championship (inaugurated 1994) 2006 *Sunningdale*

1994	E Annison	S Bassindale	Whitting Heath
1995	A Thompson	G Palmer	R Ashdown Forest
1996	R Farrow	V Morgan	Lindrick
1997	G Palmer	C Means	S Winchester
1998	E McCombe	J Thornhill	West Sussex
1999	E McCombe	V Morgan	Lindrick
2000	E McCombe	M Griffiths	Burnham & Berrow
2001	A Vine	V Morgan	Beau Desert
2002	C Stirling	C Caldwell	Ganton
2003	C Watson	R Page	The Berkshire
2004	C Stirling	R Lindley	Notts GC & Notts Ladies GC
2005	G Bray	C Kirk	Hayling Island

(continued over)

English Senior Ladies Match Play Championship – 2006 *Sunningdale – continued*

Semi-Finals
Christine Watson (Beaconsfield)) beat Carole Caldwell (Sunningdale) 3 and 2
Chris Quinn (Hockley) beat Susan Pickles (Lee-on-the-Solent) 2 holes

Final
Christine Watson beat Chris Quinn at 20th

English Ladies Open Mid-Amateur Championship 2006 *Cotswold Hills*
(inaugurated 1982)

1982	J Rhodes	Headingley	19th hole	1994	J Oliver	Beaconsfield	2 up
1983	L Davies	Worksop	2 and 1	1995	K Smith	Clitheroe	5 and 4
1984	P Grice	Whittington Barracks	3 and 2	1996	R Bailey	Sandiway	3 and 2
1985	S Lowe	Caldy	2 and 1	1997	K Smith	Abbotsley	2 and 1
1986	S Moorcroft	Hexham	6 and 5	1998	J Lamb	Hornsea	1 hole
1987	J Wade	Sheringham	2 and 1	1999	K Fisher	Woodbury Park	1 hole
1988	S Morgan	Enville, Staffs	20th hole	2000	K Keogh	Woodbury Park	1 hole
1989	L Fairclough	Warrington	4 and 3	2001	A Keighley	Pleasington	22nd hole
1990	L Fletcher	Whitley Bay	7 and 6	2002	Not played		
1991	J Morley	West Lancashire	6 and 5	2003	N Timmins	Notts Ladies	2 and 1
1992	K Speak	South Staffs	3 and 1	2004	F More	Moor Park	2 and 1
1993	K Speak	Seascale	2 and 1	2005	N Edwards	Huddersfield	at 22nd

Leading Qualifier: 147 – Claire Aitken (Mid-Kent) 74-73

Quarter-Finals
Charlotte Ellis (Minchinhampton) beat Claire Aitken
2 holes
Rachel Lomas (Hallowes) beat Fiona Lockhart (St Regulus)
1 hole
Elizabeth Bennett (Brokenhurst Manor) beat Kerry Smith
(Waterlooville) 2 and 1
Corisande Lee (West Lancashire) beat Lisa Ball (Matfen Hall)
at 19th

Semi-Finals
Ellis beat Lomas 4 and 3
Bennett beat Lee 3 and 2

Final
Charlotte Ellis beat Elizabeth Bennett
3 and 2

Irish Ladies Close Amateur Championship (inaugurated 1894) 2006 *The European*

Year	Winner	Runner-up	Venue	Score
1894	Miss Mulligan	N Graham	Carnalea	3 and 2
1895	Miss Cox	Miss MacLaine	Portrush	3 and 2
1896	N Graham	N Brownrigg	Newcastle	4 and 3
1897	N Graham	Miss Magill	Dollymount	4 and 3
1898	Miss Magill	M Hezlet	Malone	1 hole
1899*	M Hezlet	Miss Adair	Newcastle	5 and 4
1900*	Miss Adair	V Hezlet	Portrush	9 and 7
1901	Miss Adair	F Walker-Leigh	Portmarnock	4 and 2
1902	Miss Adair	ME Stuart	Newcastle	9 and 7
1903	Miss Adair	V Hezlet	Portrush	7 and 5
1904	M Hezlet	F Walker-Leigh	Lahinch	3 and 2
1905	M Hezlet	F Hezlet	Portsalon	2 and 1
1906	M Hezlet	F Hezlet	Newcastle	2 and 1
1907	F Walker-Leigh	Mrs Fitzgibbon	Dollymount	4 and 3
1908	M Hezlet	F Hezlet	Portrush	5 and 4
1909	Miss Ormsby	V Hezlet	Lahinch	4 and 2
1910	M Harrison	Miss Magill	Newcastle	5 and 4
1911	M Harrison	F Walker-Leigh	Malahide	6 and 4
1912	M Harrison	Mrs Cramsie	Portsalon	5 and 3
1913	J Jackson	M Harrison	Lahinch	4 and 3
1914	J Jackson	Miss Meldon	Castlerock	3 and 2
1915–1918	Not played			
1919	J Jackson	M Alexander	Portmarnock	5 and 4
1920	J Jackson	Mrs Cramsie	Portrush	5 and 4
1921	Miss Stuart French	M Fitzgibbon	Hermitage	4 and 3
1922	Mrs Claude Gotto	MR Hirsch	Newcastle	2 holes

* Final played over 36 holes

Year	Winner	Runner-up	Venue	Score
1923	J Jackson	Mrs Babington	Portmarnock	5 and 4
1924	CG Thornton	Miss Hewitt	Castlerock	4 and 3
1925	J Jackson	JF Jameson	Lahinch	2 and 1
1926	P Jameson	CH Murland	Newcastle	5 and 3
1927	Miss McLoughlin	F Blake	Dollymount	2 holes
1928	Mrs Dwyer	H Clarke	Cork	3 and 2
1929	MA Hall	I Taylor	Rosapenna	1 hole
1930	JB Walker	JF Jameson	Portmarnock	2 and 1
1931	Miss Pentony	JH Todd	Rosses Point	2 and 1
1932	B. Latchford	D Ferguson	Ballybunion	7 and 5
1933	Miss Pentony	F Blacke	Newcastle	3 and 2
1934	P Sherlock Fletcher	JB Walker	Portmarnock	3 and 2
1935	D Ferguson	Miss Ellis	Rospenna	2 and 1
1936	C Tiernan	S Moore	Ballybunion	7 and 6
1937	HV Glendinning	EL Kidd	Portrush	37th hole
1938	J Beck	B Jackson	Portmarnock	5 and 4
1939	C MacGeagh	E Gikdea	Bundoran	1 hole
1940–1945	*Not played*			
1946	P Garvey	V Reddan	Lahinch	39th hole
1947	P Garvey	C Syme	Portrush	5 and 4
1948	P Garvey	V Reddan	Rosslare	9 and 7
1949	C Syme	J Beck	Baltray	9 and 7
1950	P Garvey	T Marks	Rosses Point	6 and 4
1951	P Garvey	D Forster	Ballybunion	12 and 10
1952	DM Forster	PG McCann	Newcastle	3 and 2
1953	P Garvey	Mrs Hegarty	Rosslare	8 and 7
1954	P Garvey	HV Glendinning	Portmarnock	13 and 12
1955	P Garvey	A O'Donohoe	Rosses Point	10 and 9
1956	P O'Sullivan	JF Hegarty	Killarney	14 and 12
1957	P Garvey	K McCann	Portrush	3 and 2
1958	P Garvey	Z Fallon	Carlow	7 and 6
1959	P Garvey	H Colhoun	Lahinch	12 and 10
1960	P Garvey	PG McCann	Cork	5 and 3
1961	K McCann	A Sweeney	Newcastle	5 and 3
1962	P Garvey	M Earner	Baltray	7 and 6
1963	P Garvey	E Barnett	Killarney	9 and 7
1964	Z Fallon	P O'Sullivan	Portrush	37th hole
1965	E Purcell	P O'Sullivan	Mullingar	3 and 2
1966	E Bradshaw	P O'Sullivan	Rosslare	3 and 2
1967	G Brandom	P O'Sullivan	Castlerock	3 and 2
1968	E Bradshaw	M McKenna	Lahinch	3 and 2
1969	M McKenna	C Hickey	Ballybunion	3 and 2
1970	P Garvey	M Earner	Portrush	2 and 1
1971	E Bradshaw	M Mooney	Baltray	3 and 1
1972	M McKenna	I Butler	Killarney	5 and 4
1973	M Mooney	M McKenna	Bundoran	2 and 1
1974	M McKenna	V Singleton	Lahinch	3 and 2
1975	M Gorry	E Bradshaw	Tramore	1 hole
1976	C Nesbitt	M McKenna	Rosses Point	20th hole
1977	M McKenna	R Hegarty	Ballybunion	2 holes
1978	M Gorry	I Butler	Grange	4 and 3
1979	M McKenna	C Nesbitt	Donegal	6 and 5
1980	C Nesbitt	C Hourihane	Lahinch	1 hole
1981	M McKenna	M Kenny	Laytown & Bettystown	1 hole
1982	M McKenna	M Madill	Portrush	2 and 1
1983	C Hourihane	V Hassett	Cork	6 and 4
1984	C Hourihane	M Madill	Rosses Point	19th hole
1985	C Hourihane	M McKenna	Waterville	4 and 3
1986	T O'Reilly	E Higgins	Castlerock	4 and 3
1987	C Hourihane	C Hickey	Lahinch	5 and 4
1988	L Bolton	E Higgins	Tramore	2 and 1
1989	M McKenna	C Wickham	West Port	19th hole
1990	ER McDaid	L Callan	The Island	2 and 1
1991	C Hourihane	E McDaid	Ballybunion	1 hole
1992	ER Power	C Hourihane	Co. Louth	1 hole
1993	E Higgins	A Rogers	R Belfast	2 and 1
1994	L Webb	H Kavanagh	Rosses Point	20th hole
1995	ER Power	S O'Brien-Kenney	Cork	1 hole
1996	B Hackett	L Behan	Tullamore	3 and 2
1997	S Fanagan	ER Power	Enniscrone	4 and 3
1998	L Behan	O Purfield	Clandeboye	19th hole

Irish Ladies Close Amateur Championship – 2006 *The European – continued*

Year	Winner	Runner-up	Venue	Score
1999	C Coughlan	ER Power	Carlow	4 and 3
2000	A Coffey	C Coughlan	Co Louth	3 and 2
2001	A Coffey	C Coughlan	The European Club	4 and 3
2002	R Coakley	A Coffey	Cork	4 and 3
2003	M Gillen	M Dunne	Donegal	2 holes
2004	D Smith	T Delaney	The Island	20th hole
2005	T Mangan	C Tucker	Portsalon	3 and 2

Leading Qualifiers: 153: Mary Dowling (New Ross) 80-73; Martina Gillen 73-80; Tricia Mangan 80-73

Quarter Finals
Tricia Mangan (Ennis) beat Jennifer Gannon
　(Co.Louth) 2 and 1
Deirdre Smith (Co.Louth) beat Darragh McGowan
　(Ballybofey & Stranorlar) 2 and 1
Martina Gillen (Beaverstown) beat Maria Dunne
　(Skerries) 2 holes
Danielle McVeigh (RCDL) beat Victoria Bradshaw
　(Bangor) 8 and 6

Semi-Finals
Mangan beat Smith 1 hole
Gillen beat McVeigh 3 and 2

Final
Tricia Mangan beat Martina Gillen 2 and 1

Irish Ladies Open Amateur Stroke Play Championship
(inaugurated 1993)

1993	T Eakin	Milltown	293
1994	H Kavanagh	Milltown	286
1995	N Quigg	Grange	300
1996	ER Power	Grange	218
1997	Y Cassidy	Waterford Castle	217
1998	S O'Brien	Waterford Castle	141
1999	H Kavanagh	Waterford Castle	217
2000	R Cookley	Birr	205
2001	A Laing	Birr	214
2002	R Coakley	Dundalk	214
2003	C Coughlan	Rathsallagh	215
2004	T Delaney*	Cork	220

*Delaney won at eighth extra hole

2005	T Delaney	Hermitage	219

2006 *Rosses Point, Co. Sligo*

1	Martina Gillen (Beaverstown)	75-80-69—224
2	Deirdre Smith (Co.Louth)	75-76-76—227
3	Tara Delaney (Carlow)	77-74-77—228

Irish Senior Ladies Amateur Championship (inaugurated 1988)

1988	M Magan		1994	G Costello	80	2000	S Kearney	80
1989	Dr G Costello		1995	A Gaynor	81	2001	M McKenna*	162
1990	A Hesketh		1996	M Stuart	81	2002	P Williamson	157
1991	C Hickey	77	1997	M O'Donnell	85	2003	P Williamson	153
1992	C Hickey	79	1998	M Moran	78	2004	A Murdoch (CAN)	152
1993	G Costello	81	1999	R Fanagan	80	2005	A Murdoch (CAN)	156

2006 *Thurles*

1	Therese O'Reilly (Grange)	79-77—156
2	Sheena O'Brien-Kenney (Grange)	78-80—158
3	Valerie Hassett (Ennis)	82-80—162

Scottish Ladies Close Amateur Championship (inaugurated 1903)

Year	Winner	Runner-up	Venue	Score
1903	AM Glover	MA Graham	St Andrews	1 hole
1904	MA Graham	M Bishop	Prestwick St Nicholas	6 and 5
1905	D Campbell	MA Graham	North Berwick	at 19th
1906	D Campbell	AM Glover	Cruden Bay	3 and 1
1907	FS Teacher	D Campbell	Troon	at 21st
1908	D Campbell	MA Cairns	Gullane	7 and 6
1909	EL Kyle	D Campbell	Machrihanish	3 and 1
1910	EL Kyle	AM Glover	Nairn	4 and 3
1911	E Grant-Suttie	EL Kyle	St Andrews	1 hole
1912	DM Jenkins	M Neil Fraser	Lossiemouth	4 and 2
1913	JW McCulloch	R Mackintosh	Machrihanish	4 and 3
1914	ER Anderson	FS Teacher	Muirfield	at 20th
1915–1919	*Not played*			
1920	Mrs JB Watson	L Scroggie	Cruden Bay	5 and 3
1921	Mrs JB Watson	Mrs M Martin	Machrihanish	1 hole
1922	Mrs JB Watson	A Kyle	St Andrews	2 and 1
1923	Mrs WH Nicholson	Mrs JB Watson	Lossiemouth	2 and 1
1924	CPR Montgomery	H Cameron	Turnberry	5 and 4
1925	J Percy	E Grant-Suttie	Gullane	2 and 1
1926	MJ Wood	Mrs J Cochrane	Cruden Bay	2 and 1
1927	B Inglis	H Cameron	Machrihanish	1 hole
1928	JW McCulloch	P Ramsay	St Andrews	3 and 1
1929	Mrs JB Watson	Doris Park	Nairn	3 and 1
1930	Helen Holm	Doris Park	Turnberry	1 hole
1931	JW McCulloch	Doris Park	Gullane	at 19th
1932	Helen Holm	Mrs G Coates	Cruden Bay	at 23rd
1933	MJ Couper	Helen Holm	Turnberry	at 22nd
1934	Nan Baird	J Anderson	North Berwick	1 hole
1935	M Robertson-Durham	Nan Baird	Lossiemouth	at 20th
1936	Doris Park	CPR Montgomery	Turnberry	at 19th
1937	Helen Holm	Mrs I Bowhill	Gleneagles	3 and 2
1938	Jessie Anderson	Helen Holm	Nairn	2 holes
1939	Jessie Anderson	Catherine Park	Turnberry	at 19th
1939–1946	*Not played*			
1947	Jean Donald	J Kerr	Elie	5 and 3
1948	Helen Holm	Vivien Falconer	Gleneagles	5 and 4
1949	Jean Donald	Helen Holm	Troon	6 and 4
1950	Helen Holm	Charlotte Beddows (Mrs JB Watson)	St Andrews	6 and 5
1951	Mrs G Valentine	Moira Paterson	Nairn	3 and 2
1952	Jean Donald	Mrs RT Peel	Gullane	13 and 11
1953	Mrs G Valentine	Jean Donald	Carnoustie	8 and 7
1954	Mrs RT Peel	Mrs G Valentine	Turnberry	7 and 6
1955	Mrs G Valentine	Millicent Couper	North Berwick	8 and 6
1956	Mrs G Valentine	Helen Holm	Dornoch	8 and 7
1957	Marigold Speir	Helen Holm	Troon	7 and 5
1958	Dorothea Sommerville	Janette Robertson	Elie	1 hole
1959	Janette Robertson	Belle McCorkindale	Nairn	6 and 5
1960	Janette Robertson	Dorothea Sommerville	Turnberry	2 and 1
1961	JS Wright (née Robertson)	AM Lurie	St Andrews	1 hole
1962	JB Lawrence	C Draper	R Dornoch	5 and 4
1963	JB Lawrence	IC Robertson	Troon	2 and 1
1964	JB Lawrence	SM Reid	Gullane	5 and 3
1965	IC Robertson	JB Lawrence	Nairn	5 and 4
1966	IC Robertson	M Fowler	Machrihanish	2 and 1
1967	J Hastings	A Laing	North Berwick	5 and 3
1968	Joan Smith	J Rennie	Carnoustie	10 and 9
1969	JH Anderson	K Lackie	West Kilbride	5 and 4
1970	A Laing	IC Robertson	Dunbar	1 hole
1971	IC Robertson	A Ferguson	R Dornoch	3 and 2
1972	IC Robertson	CJ Lugton	Machrihanish	5 and 3
1973	I Wright	Dr AJ Wilson	St Andrews	2 holes
1974	Dr AJ Wilson	K Lackie	Nairn	22nd hole
1975	LA Hope	JW Smith	Elie	1 hole
1976	S Needham	T Walker	Machrihanish	3 and 2
1977	CJ Lugton	M Thomson	R Dornoch	1 hole
1978	IC Robertson	JW Smith	Prestwick	2 holes
1979	G Stewart	LA Hope	Gullane	2 and 1

(continued over)

Scottish Ladies Close Amateur Championship *continued*

Year	Winner	Runner-up	Venue	Score
1980	IC Robertson	F Anderson	Carnoustie	I hole
1981	A Gemmill	W Aitken	Stranraer	2 and I
1982	J Connachan	P Wright	R Troon	19th hole
1983	G Stewart	F Anderson	North Berwick	3 and I
1984	G Stewart	A Gemmill	R Dornoch	3 and 2
1985	A Gemmill	D Thomson	Barassie	2 and I
1986	IC Robertson	L Hope	St Andrews	3 and 2
1987	F Anderson	C Middleton	Nairn	4 and 3
1988	S Lawson	F Anderson	Southerness	3 and I
1989	J Huggon	L Anderson	Lossiemouth	5 and 4
1990	E Farquharson	S Huggan	Machrihanish	3 and 2
1991	C Lambert	F Anderson	Carnoustie	3 and 2
1992	J Moody	E Farquharson	R Aberdeen	2 and I
1993	C Lambert	M McKay	Prestwick St Nicholas	5 and 4
1994	C Matthew	V Melvin	Gullane	I hole
1995	H Monaghan	S McMaster	Portpatrick	21st hole
1996	A Laing	A Rose	R Dornoch	I hole
1997	A Rose	H Monaghan	W Kilbride	3 and 2
1998	E Moffat	C Agnew	North Berwick	4 and 3
1999	J Smith	A Laing	Nairn Dunbar	2 and I
2000	L Kenny	H Stirling	Machrihanish	I hole
2001	L Morton	L Mackay	Carnoustie	6 and 4
2002	H Stirling	A Laing	Stranraer	3 and I
2003	A Laing	C Hargan	Old Course, St Andrews	4 and 2
2004	A Laing	C Queen	Prestwick	2 holes
2005	F Lockhart	A Laing	Cruden Bay	3 and 2

2006 *Dunbar*

Leading Qualifiers: 138: Louise Kenney 65-73; Heather MacRae 68-70

Quarter Finals

Heather MacRae (Dunblane New) beat Lesley
Hendry (Routenburn) 5 and 3

Martine Pow (Selkirk) beat Emily Ogilvie
(Auchterarder) 2 and I

Anne Laing (Vale of Leven) beat Fiona Lockhart
(St Regulus) 5 and 4

Louise Kenney (Pitreavie) beat Hilary Laughland
(Mortonhall) at 20th

Semi-Finals

Pow beat MacRae I hole

Laing beat Kenney I hole

Final

Martine Pow beat Anne Laing 2 and I

Scottish Ladies Open Stroke Play Championship (Helen Holm Trophy)

(inaugurated 1973)

1973 Belle Robertson	1982 Wilma Aitken	1991 Julie Wade (ENG)	1999 L Nicholson
1974 Sandra Needham	1983 Jane Connachan	1992 Mhairi McKay	2000 Rebecca Hudson
1975 Muriel Thomson	1984 Gillian Stewart	1993 Julie Wade (ENG)	2001 Fiona Brown
1976 Muriel Thomson	1985 Pamela Wright	1994 K Tebbet	2002 Heather Stirling
1977 Beverly Huke (ENG)	1986 Belle Robertson	1995 Maria Hjörth (SWE)	2003 Nathalie David
1978 Wilma Aitken	1987 Elaine Farquharson	1996 J Hockley	2004 Emma Duggleby
1979 Belle Robertson	1988 Elaine Farquharson	1997 Kim Rostron	(ENG)
1980 Wilma Aitken	1989 Sara Robinson	1998 K-M Juul Esbjerg	2005 Martina Gillen (IRL)
1981 Gillian Stewart	1990 Catriona Lambert	(SWE)	

2006 *Royal Troon and Troon Portland*

I	Melissa Reid (Chevin)	71-69-72—212
2	Emma Duggleby (Malton & Norton)	71-68-74—213
3	Rachel Bell (Ganton)	74-72-71—217

Scottish Senior Ladies (Close) Amateur Championship 2006 *Machrihanish*

(inaugurated 1997)

1997	A Wilson		2000	P Hutton		2003	K Ballantyne
1998	I McIntosh		2001	F Liddle		2004	K Sutherland
1999	P Williamson		2002	P Williamson		2005	P Williamson

Stroke Play

1	Ruth Brown (Lothianburn)	81-74—155
2	Lorna Bennett (Ladybank)	77-79—156
3	Lynne Terry (Cruden Bay)	81-76—157

Match Play

Quarter Finals
E Campbell (Torwoodlee) beat S McGregor (Edzell) 3 and 1
F De Vries (St Rule) beat M Thomson (North Berwick) 2 and 1
H Faulds (Douglas Park) beat J Mack (Haggs Castle) 2 and 1
P Williamson (Baberton) beat K Ballantyne (Craigmillar Park) 6 and 5

Semi-Finals
De Vries beat Campbell 4 and 3
Faulds beat Williamson 1 hole

Final
F De Vries beat H Faulds 4 and 3

Scottish Veteran Ladies Championship 2006 *Blairgowrie*

Semi-Finals
N Fenton (Merchants of Edinburgh) beat L Campbell (Torwoodlee) 5 and 3
K Sutherland (Royal Montrose) beat H Faulds (Douglas Park) 2 and 1

Final
Kathleen Sutherland beat Noreen Fenton 4 and 3

Welsh Ladies Close Amateur Championship (inaugurated 1905) 2006 *Conwy*

1905	E Young	B Duncan	Penarth	2 and 1
1906	B Duncan	Mrs Storry	Radyr	5 and 4
1907	B Duncan	Mrs Wenham	Royal Porthcawl	5 and 4
1908	B Duncan	Miss Lloyd Williams	Conwy	4 and 2
1909	B Duncan	Mrs Ellis Griffiths	Southerndown	4 and 3
1910	Miss Lloyd Roberts	Miss Leaver	Rhyl	4 and 3
1911	Miss Clay	Miss Allington-Hughes	Royal Porthcawl	2 and 1
1912	B Duncan	P Williams	Llandrindod Wells	4 and 2
1913	Miss Brooke	Miss Shaw	Rhos-on-Sea	at 19th
1914	Mrs Vivian Phillips	Miss Morgan	Tenby	4 and 3
1915–1919	*Not played*			
1920	Mrs Rupert Phillips	M Marley	Royal Porthcawl	8 and 6
1921	M Marley	I Rieben	Aberdovey	7 and 5
1922	J Duncan	H Franklyn Thomas	Llandrindod Wells	9 and 8
1923	MR Cox	M Marley	Southerndown	at 39th
1924	MR Cox	B Pyman	Rhyl	11 and 10
1925	MR Cox	J Rhys	Tenby	9 and 7
1926	MC Justice	A Smalley	Aberdovey	4 and 3
1927	J Duncan	Mrs Blake	Porthcawl	1 hole
1928	J Duncan	I Rieben	Harlech	2 and 1
1929	I Rieben	B Pyman	Tenby	2 and 1
1930	MJ Jeffreys	I Rieben	Llandudno	2 holes
1931	MJ Jeffreys	B Pyman	Southerndown	4 and 3
1932	I Rieben	MJ Jeffreys	Aberdovey	2 and 1
1933	MJ Jeffreys	Mrs Bridge	Porthcawl	2 and 1
1934	I Rieben	MJ Jeffreys	Harlech	3 and 2
1935	*Abandoned*			
1936	I Rieben	M Thompson	Prestatyn	2 and 1
1937	GS Emery	Dr P Whitaker	Porthcawl	10 and 9
1938	B Pyman	GS Emery	Llandudno	1 hole
1939	B Burrell	H Reynolds	Swansea	2 and 1
1940–1946	*Not played*			
1947	M Barron	E Jones	Prestatyn	1 hole

(continued over)

Welsh Ladies Close Amateur Championship – 2006 Conwy – continued

1948	N Seely	M Barron	Prestatyn	12 and 11
1949	S Bryan Smith	E Brown	Newport	3 and 2
1950	Dr Garfield Evans	Nancy Cook	Porthcawl	2 and 1
1951	E Bromley-Davenport	Nancy Cook	Harlech	1 hole
1952	Elsie Lever	Pat Roberts	Southerndown	6 and 5
1953	Nancy Cook	Elsie Lever	Llandudno	3 and 2
1954	Nancy Cook	ED Brown	Tenby	1 hole
1955	Nancy Cook	Pat Roberts	Holyhead	2 holes
1956	Pat Roberts	M Barron	Royal Porthcawl	2 and 1
1957	M Barron	Pat Roberts	Royal St David's	6 and 4
1958	Nancy Cook Wright	Pat Roberts	Newport	1 hole
1959	Pat Roberts	A Gwyther	Conwy	6 and 4
1960	M Barron	E Brown	Tenby	8 and 6
1961	M Oliver	N Sneddon	Aberdovey	5 and 4
1962	M Oliver	P Roberts	Radyr	4 and 2
1963	P Roberts	N Sneddon	Royal St David's	7 and 5
1964	M Oliver	M Wright	Southerndown	1 hole
1965	M Wright	E Brown	Prestatyn	3 and 2
1966	A Hughes	P Roberts	Ashburnham	5 and 4
1967	M Wright	C Phipps	Royal St David's	21st hole
1968	S Hales	M Wright	Royal Porthcawl	3 and 2
1969	P Roberts	A Hughes	Caernarvonshire	3 and 2
1970	A Briggs	J Morris	Newport	19th hole
1971	A Briggs	EN Davies	Royal St David's	2 and 1
1972	A Hughes	J Rogers	Tenby	3 and 2
1973	A Briggs	J John	Holyhead	3 and 2
1974	A Briggs	Dr H Lyall	Ashburnham	3 and 2
1975	A Johnson (née Hughes)	K Rawlings	Prestatyn	1 hole
1976	T Perkins	A Johnson	Royal Porthcawl	4 and 2
1977	T Perkins	P Whitley	Aberdovey	5 and 4
1978	P Light	A Briggs	Newport	2 and 1
1979	V Rawlings	A Briggs	Caernarvonshire	2 holes
1980	M Rawlings	A Briggs	Tenby	2 and 1
1981	M Rawlings	A Briggs	Royal St David's	5 and 3
1982	V Thomas (née Rawlings)	M Rawlings	Ashburnham	7 and 6
1983	V Thomas	T Thomas (née Perkins)	Llandudno	1 hole
1984	S Roberts	K Davies	Newport	5 and 4
1985	V Thomas	S Jump	Prestatyn	1 hole
1986	V Thomas	L Isherwood	Royal Porthcawl	7 and 6
1987	V Thomas	S Roberts	Aberdovey	3 and 1
1988	S Roberts	F Connor	Tenby	4 and 2
1989	H Lawson	V Thomas	Conwy	2 and 1
1990	S Roberts	H Wadsworth	Ashburnham	3 and 2
1991	V Thomas	H Lawson	Royal St David's	4 and 3
1992	J Foster	S Boyes	Newport	4 and 3
1993	A Donne	V Thomas	Abergele & Pensarn	19th hole
1994	V Thomas	L Dermott	Royal Porthcawl	19th hole
1995	L Dermott	K Stark	Aberdovey	19th hole
1996	L Dermott	V Thomas	Tenby	4 and 3
1997	E Pilgrim	L Davis	Northop	4 and 2
1998	L Davis	R Morgan	Ashburnham	1 hole
1999	R Brewerton	R Morgan	Conwy	19th hole
2000	K Evans	K Phillips	Pyle & Kenfig	19th hole
2001	B Brewerton	S Jones	Royal St David's	2 and 1
2002	E Pilgrim	A Highgate	Newport	1 hole
2003	K Phillips	K Walls	Aberdovey	2 and 1
2004	S Jones	A Highgate	Royal Porthcawl	1 hole
2005	S Jones	S Evans	Conwy	5 and 4

Leading Qualifier: Stephanie Evans 77 (reduced to one round – weather)

Quarter Finals
Stephanie Evans (Vale of Llangollen) beat
  Kelly Miller (Penrhos) 7 and 6
Tara Davies (Holyhead) beat Sahra Hassan
  (Vale of Glamorgan) 5 and 3
Becky Harries (Haverfordwest) beat Jo Nicolson
  (Wrexham) 3 and 2
Rhian Wyn Thomas (Vale of Glamorgan) beat
  Breanne Loucks (Wrexham) 4 and 3

Semi-Finals
Evans beat Davies 3 and 2
Harries beat Wyn Thomas 3 and 1

Final
Stephanie Evans beat Becky Harries 3 and 2

Welsh Senior Ladies Match Play Championship 2006 Tenby

1990	E Higgs	Vale of Llangollen	171	1998	C Thomas	Padeswood	163
1991	H Lyall	Pyle and Kenfig	160	1999	V Mackenzie	St Mellons	153
1992	P Morgan	Cardigan	83	2000	F Shehan	Carmarthen	159
1993	P Morgan	Pwllheli	157	2001	F Shehan	Porthmadog	159
1994	C Thomas	Llandudno	163	2002	C Thomas	Creigiau	154
1995	C Thomas	Tredegar Park	157	2003	C Thomas	Cardigan	165
1996	C Thomas	Vale of Llangollen	157	2004	C Thomas	Haverfordwest	156
1997	C Thomas	Fairwood Park	160	2005	V Thomas	Nefyn	161

Semi-Finals
Janet Doleman (Ruchcliffe) beat Trudy Carradice (Pyle & Kenfig) 2 and 1
Vicki Thomas (Carmarthen) beat Helen Joyce (Long Ashton) 1 hole

Final
Vicki Thomas beat Janet Doleman 6 and 5

Welsh Ladies Open Amateur Strokeplay Championship 2006 Whitchurch
(inaugurated 1976)

1976	P Light	Aberdovey	227	1991	M Sutton	R Porthcawl	224
1977	J Greenhalgh	Aberdovey	239	1992	C Lambert	R Porthcawl	218
1978	S Hedges	Aberdovey	49 holes	1993	J Hall	Newport	221
1979	S Crowcroft	Aberdovey	228	1994	A Rose	Newport	217
1980	T Thomas	Aberdovey	233	1995	F Brown	Newport	221
1981	V Thomas	Aberdovey	224	1996	E Duggleby	Whitchurch	223
1982	V Thomas	Aberdovey	225	1997	K Edwards	Whitchurch	216
1983	J Thornhill	Aberdovey	239	1998	G Simpson	Rolls of Monmouth	154
1984	L Davies	Aberdovey	230	1999	A Walker	Celtic Manor	230
1985	C Swallow	Aberdovey	219	2000	R Prout	Ashburnham	228
1986	H Wadsworth	Aberdovey	223	2001	V Laing	Royal Porthcawl	229
1987	S Shapcott	Newport	225	2002	V Laing	Northop Country Park	218
1988	S Shapcott	Newport	218	2003	V Laing	Southerndown	213
1989	V Thomas	Newport	220	2004	D Masters	Ashburnham	216
1990	L Hackney	Newport	218	2005	H Brockway*	Pyle & Kenfig	218

1	Naomi Edwards (Ganton)	73-74-74—221
2	Felicity Johnson (Harborne)	71-72-79—222
3	Henni Brockway (Yeovil)	76-74-73—223

Welsh Senior Ladies Championship (inaugurated 1990) 2006 Cardiff

1	Vicki Thomas (Carmarthen)	78-72—150
2	Helen Joyce (Long Ashton)	76-82—158
3	Jean O'Connor (Newport)	82-79—161

International European Ladies Amateur Championship 2006 Falkenstein, Hamburg
(inaugurated 1986)

1986	M Koch (GER)	Morfontaine, France	286
1988	F Descampe (BEL)	Pedrena, Spain	289
1990	M Koch (GER)	Zumicon, Switzerland	295
1991	D Bourson (FRA)	Schönborn, Austria	294
1992	J Morley (ENG)	Estoril, Portugal	284
1993	V Steinsrud (NOR)	Torino, Italy	277
1994	M Fischer (GER)	Bastad, Sweden	288
1995	M Hjörth (SWE)	Berlin, Germany	284
1996	S Cavalleri (ITA)	Furesoe, Denmark	288
1997	S Cavalleri (ITA)	Formby, England	297
1998	G Sergas (ITA)	Noordwijk, Netherlands	295
1999	S Sandolo (ITA)	Karlovy Vary, Czech Republic	284
2000	E Duggleby (ENG)	Amber Baltic GC, Poland	283
2001	M Eberl (GER)	Biella, Italy	217
2002	B Brewerton (WAL)	Kristianstad, Sweden	288
2003	V Beauchet (FRA)	Shannon, Ireland	293
2004	C Ciganda (ESP)	Ulzama, Navarra, Spain	282
2005	J Schaeffer (FRA)	Santo da Serra, Madeira, Portugal	286

International European Ladies Amateur Championship – 2006 *Falkenstein, Hamburg – continued*

1	Belen Mozo (ESP)	69-72-68-69—278
2	Kerry Smith (ENG)	71-72-72-65—280
3	Thea Hoffmeister (GER)	70-69-69-74—282
	Stephanie Kirchmayr (GER)	73-69-69-71—282

European Senior Ladies Championship (inaugurated 2000) 2006 *Ribagolfe, Portugal*

2000	C Mourgue d'Algue (FRA)	La Manga	226
2001	C Mourgue d'Algue (FRA)	Torremirona	219
2002	C Mourgue d'Algue (FRA)	La Manga	220
2003	C Cros Chatrier (FRA)	Chantaco	221
2004	M-B Heden (SWE)	La Baule	220
2005	C Mourgue D'Algue (FRA)	Chantilly	222

1	Gunilla Ekman (SWE)	77-69—146
2	Karin Gumpert (GER)	78-71—149
3	Viveka Hoff (SWE)	76-76—152

(event reduced to 36 holes because of bad weather)

National Orders of Merit 2006

English Order of Merit

1	Naomi Edwards (Ganton)	1040
2	Kerry Smith (Waterlooville)	939
3	Rachel Bell (Ganton)	904
4	Melissa Reid (Chevin)	745
5	Kiran Matharu (Cookridge Park)	745
6	Sophie Walker (Kenwick Park)	741
7	Emma Duggleby (Malton & Norton)	687
8	Elizabeth Bennett (Brokenhurst Manor)	641
9	Felicity Johnson (Harborne)	608
10	Florentyna Parker (Royal Birkdale)	594

Paull & Williamson Scottish Ranking

1	Jenna Wilson (Strathaven)	–3.60
2	Louise Kenney (Pitreavie)	–1.10
3	Heather MacRae (Dunblane New)	–0.60
4	Anne Laing (Vale of Leven)	–0.50
5	Fiona Lockhart (St Regulus)	–0.10
6	Sara Bishop (Windyhill)	0.00
7	Cara Gruber (Royal Dornoch)	0.20
8	Jocelyn Carthew (Ladybank)	0.30
	Claire Hargan (Mortonhall)	0.30
10	Emily Ogilvy (Auchterarder)	0.60

ILGU Irish Order of Merit

1	Martina Gillen (Beaverstown)	1584
2	Tricia Mangan (Ennis)	1310
3	Deirdre Smith (Co.Louth)	895
4	Maura Morrin (The Curragh)	831
5	Claire Coughlan (Cork)	648
6	Tara Delaney (Carlow)	500
7	Marian Riordan (Tipperary)	491
8	Danielle McVeigh (RCDL)	490
9	Sinead Keane (The Curragh)	386
10	Niamh Kitching (Claremorris)	380

Welsh Order of Merit

Not declared for 2006

British Golf Museum

Award winning museum at the heart of the Home of Golf

The British Golf Museum sits at the heart of the Home of Golf, directly opposite The Royal and Ancient Golf Clubhouse and a mere 67½ yards from the 1st tee of the Old Course.

The British Golf Museum opened in 1990 and won seven major awards. It is currently one of four museums to have been awarded five stars by the Scottish Tourist Board, the highest rating under its quality assurance programme.

Inside the Museum, the history of golf is brought to life through many wondrous exhibits, which are enhanced by stunning interactive displays. Early treasures include a set of golf clubs dating to the late 17th and early 18th centuries, which were discovered in a concealed cupboard in 1898. Each gallery reflects the style and tastes of the time, none more so than the Victorian Gallery, where objects compete for attention around the centrepiece, a replica of the Claret Jug.

From club and ball development to the growth of the amateur and professional game, each display case is brimming with items from the game's rich past. Visual highlights include rare footage of Braid, Taylor and Vardon, captured on Kinora film, which has been digitised, giving visitors the chance to view three of the greatest players ever in action.

The Museum strives to continue improving displays and setting high standards of interpretation. *Open Championships since 1946* is a new exhibition, which focuses on each of The Open venues around the UK. This is accompanied by three other new exhibition spaces – *International Team Events*, *The R&A Room* and the *Cabinet of Curiosities*, a special display that brings together some of the more unusual items to delight the golf enthusiast, from radio-controlled golf games, to a ball removed from the jaws of a lioness.

Interactive displays provide alternative ways of enjoying and learning about the history of the game. In *Pages of History*, early documents from The Royal and Ancient Golf Club can be viewed digitally and in *Highlights of The Open Championship*, the victories of past champions can be followed from 1923 to 2006.

The opportunity to practice putting using replica clubs and balls from the last 175 years provides a grand finale to the museum experience.

Another recent addition is the online shop, offering an extensive range of golfing literature, stylish gifts and St Andrews souvenirs. Visit the Museum online at www.britishgolfmuseum.co.uk and shop online at www.britishgolfmuseumshop.co.uk

A visit to the British Golf Museum is the perfect break from playing golf.

Team Events

Curtis Cup (Instituted 1932)
Great Britain & Ireland v USA (home team names first)

2006 Bandon Dunes, OR July 29–30   [6221–71]
Captains: Carol Semple Thompson (USA); Ada O'Sullivan (Monkstown) (GBI)

USA		Great Britain and Ireland	
Saturday Foursomes			
Morning			
P Mackenzie & A Blumenherst (5 and 4)	1	T Mangan & K Matharu	0
D Grimes & A McCurdy (2 holes)	1	M Gillen & N Edwards	0
J Park & T Leon (1 hole)	1	C Coughlan & M Reid	0
	3		0
Afternoon			
Jenny Suh	0	Kiran Matharu (Cookridge Park) (2 and 1)	1
Jennie Lee (4 and 3)	1	Martina Gillen (Beaverstown)	0
Amanda Blumenherst	0	Breanne Loucks (Wrexham) (5 and 4)	1
Paige Mackenzie (5 and 4)	1	Melissa Reid (Chevin)	0
Jane Park (3 and 2)	1	Tara Delaney (Carlow)	0
Taylor Leon (5 and 4)	1	Claire Coughlan (Cork)	0
	7		2
Sunday Foursomes			
Morning			
J Park & T Leon	½	T Mangan & T Delaney	½
J Lee & J Suh	0	M Reid & B Loucks (7 and 5)	1
P.Mackenzie & A Blumenherst	0	M Gillen & N Edwards (1 hole)	1
	½		2½
Afternoon			
Virginia Grimes	0	M Gillen (3 and 2)	1
Amanda McCurdy	0	B Loucks (3 and 2)	1
P Mackenzie (1 hole)	1	Tricia Mangan (Ennis)	0
T Leon (5 and 4)	1	Naomi Edwards (Ganton)	0
J Lee (3 and 2)	1	M Reid	0
J Park (3 and 2)	1	T Delaney	0
	4		2

Result: United States of America 11½, Great Britain & Ireland 6½

1932 *Wentworth* May 21
Result: USA 5½, GBI 3½
Captains: J Wethered (GBI), M Hollins (USA)
Foursomes
Wethered & Morgan lost to Vare & Hill 1 hole
Wilson & JB Watson lost to Van Wie & Hicks 2 and 1
Gourlay & Doris Park lost to Orcutt & Cheney 1 hole
Singles
Joyce Wethered beat Glenna Collett Vare 6 and 4
Enid Wilson beat Helen Hicks 2 and 1
Wanda Morgan lost to Virginia Van Wie 2 and 1
Diana Fishwick beat Maureen Orcutt 4 and 3
Molly Gourlay halved with Opal Hill
Elsie Corlett lost to Leona Pressley Cheney 4 and 3

1934 *Chevy Chase, MD* Sept 27–28
Result: USA 6½, GBI 2½
*Captains: Glenna Collett Vare (USA),
    Doris Chambers (GBI)*

Foursomes
Van Wie & Glutting halved with Gourlay & Barton
Orcutt & Cheney beat Fishwick & Morgan 2 holes
Hill & Lucille Robinson lost to Plumpton & Walker 2 and 1
Singles
Virginia Van Wie beat Diana Fishwick 2 and 1
Maureen Orcutt beat Molly Gourlay 4 and 2
Leona Pressley Cheney beat Pamela Barton 7 and 5
Charlotte Glutting beat Wanda Morgan
Opal Hill beat Diana Plumpton 3 and 2
Aniela Goldthwaite lost to Charlotte Walker 3 and 2

1936 *Gleneagles* May 6
Result: USA 4½, GBI 4½
*Captains: Doris Chambers (GBI),
    Glenna Collett Vare (USA)*
Foursomes
Morgan & Garon halved with Vare & Berg
Barton & Walker lost to Orcutt & Cheney 2 and 1
Anderson & Holm beat Hill & Glutting 3 and 2

Singles
Wanda Morgan lost to Glenna Collett Vare 3 and 2
Helen Holm beat Patty Berg 4 and 3
Pamela Barton lost to Charlotte Glutting 1 hole
Charlotte Walker lost to Maureen Orcutt 1 hole
Jessie Anderson beat Leona Pressley Cheney 1 hole
Marjorie Garon beat Opal Hill 7 and 5

1938 *Essex, MA* Sept 7–8
Result: USA 5½, GBI 3½
Captains: Frances Stebbins (USA),
Mrs RH Wallace-Williamson (GBI)
Foursomes
Page & Orcutt lost to Holm & Tiernan 2 holes
Vare & Berg lost to Anderson & Corlett 1 hole
Miley & Kathryn Hemphill halved with Walker &
Phyllis Wade
Singles
Estelle Lawson Page beat Helen Holm 6 and 5
Patty Berg beat Jessie Anderson 1 hole
Marion Miley beat Elsie Corlett 2 and 1
Glenna Collett Vare beat Charlotte Walker 2 and 1
Maureen Orcutt lost to Clarrie Tiernan 2 and 1
Charlotte Glutting beat Nan Baird 1 hole

1948 *Birkdale* May 21–22
Result: USA 6½, GBI 2½
Captains: Doris Chambers (GBI),
Glenna Collett Vare (USA)
Foursomes
Donald & Gordon beat Suggs & Lenczyk 3 and 2
Garvey & Bolton lost to Kirby & Vare 4 and 3
Ruttle & Val Reddan lost to Page & Kielty 5 and 4
Singles
Philomena Garvey halved with Louise Suggs
Jean Donald beat Dorothy Kirby 1 hole
Jacqueline Gordon lost to Grace Lenczyk 5 and 3
Helen Holm lost to Estelle Lawson Page 3 and 2
Maureen Ruttle lost to Polly Riley 3 and 2
Zara Bolton lost to Dorothy Kielty 2 and 1

1950 *Buffalo, NY* Sept 4–5
Result: USA 7½, GBI 1½
Captains: Glenna Collett Vare (USA),
Diana Fishwick Critchley (GBI)
Foursomes
Hanson & Porter beat Valentine & Donald 3 and 2
Helen Sigel & Kirk lost to Stephens & Price 1 hole
Dorothy Kirby & Kielty beat Garvey & Bisgood 6 and 5
Singles
Dorothy Porter halved with Frances Stephens
Polly Riley beat Jessie Anderson Valentine 7 and 6
Beverly Hanson beat Jean Donald 4 holes
Dorothy Kielty beat Philomena Garvey 2 and 1
Peggy Kirk beat Jeanne Bisgood 1 hole
Grace Lenczyk beat Elizabeth Price 5 and 4

1952 *Muirfield* June 6–7
Result: GBI 5, USA 4
Captains: Lady Katherine Cairns (GBI),
Aniela Goldthwaite (USA)
Foursomes
Donald & Price beat Kirby & DeMoss 3 and 2
Stephens & JA Valentine lost to Doran & Lindsay 6 and 4
Paterson & Garvey beat Riley & Patricia O'Sullivan 2 and 1

Singles
Jean Donald lost to Dorothy Kirby 1 hole
Frances Stephens beat Marjorie Lindsay 2 and 1
Moira Paterson lost to Polly Riley 6 and 4
Jeanne Bisgood beat Mae Murray 6 and 5
Philomena Garvey lost to Claire Doran 3 and 2
Elizabeth Price beat Grace DeMoss 3 and 2

1954 *Merion, PA* Sept 2–3
Result: USA 6, GBI 3
Captains: Edith Flippin (USA), Mrs JB Beck (GBI)
Foursomes
Faulk & Riley beat Stephens & Price 6 and 4
Doran & Patricia Lesser beat Garvey & Valentine 6 and 5
Kirby & Barbara Romack beat Marjorie Peel &
Robertson 6 and 5
Singles
Mary Lena Faulk lost to Frances Stephens 1 hole
Claire Doran beat Jeanne Bisgood 4 and 3
Polly Riley beat Elizabeth Price 9 and 8
Dorothy Kirby lost to Philomena Garvey 3 and 1
Grace DeMoss Smith beat Jessie Anderson Valentine
4 and 3
Joyce Ziske lost to Janette Robertson 3 and 1

1956 *Prince's, Sandwich* June 8–9
Result: GBI 5, USA 4
Captains: Zara Davis Bolton (GBI), Edith Flippin (USA)
Foursomes
Valentine & Garvey lost to Lesser & Smith 2 and 1
Smith & Price beat Riley & Romack 5 and 3
Robertson & Veronica Anstey lost to Downey &
Carolyn Cudone 6 and 4
Singles
Jessie Anderson Valentine beat Patricia Lesser 6 and 4
Philomena Garvey lost to Margaret Smith 9 and 8
Frances Stephens Smith beat Polly Riley 1 hole
Janette Robertson lost to Barbara Romack 6 and 4
Angela Ward beat Mary Ann Downey 6 and 4
Elizabeth Price beat Jane Nelson 7 and 6

1958 *Brae Burn, MA* Aug 8–9
Result: GBI 4½, USA 4½
Captains: Virginia Dennehy (USA),
Daisy Ferguson (GBI)
Foursomes
Riley & Romack lost to Bonallack & Price 2 and 1
Gunderson & Quast lost to Robertson & Smith 3 and 2
Johnstone & McIntire beat Jackson & Valentine 6 and 5
Singles
JoAnne Gunderson beat Jessie Anderson Valentine 2 holes
Barbara McIntire halved with Angela Ward Bonallack
Anne Quast beat Elizabeth Price 4 and 2
Anna Johnstone lost to Janette Robertson 3 and 2
Barbara Romack beat Bridget Jackson 3 and 2
Polly Riley lost to Frances Stephens Smith 2 holes

1960 *Lindrick* May 20–21
Result: USA 6½, GBI 2½
Captains: Maureen Garrett (GBI),
Mildred Prunaret (USA)
Foursomes
Price & Bonallack beat Gunderson & McIntyre 1 hole
Robertson & McCorkindale lost to Eller & Quast 4 and 2
Frances Smith & Porter lost to Goodwin & Anna
Johnstone 3 and 2

1960 continued

Singles
Elizabeth Price halved with Barbara McIntyre
Angela Ward Bonallack lost to JoAnne Gunderson 2 and 1
Janette Robertson lost to Anne Quast 2 holes
Philomena Garvey lost to Judy Eller 4 and 3
Belle McCorkindale lost to Judy Bell 8 and 7
Ruth Porter beat Joanne Goodwin 1 hole

1962 Broadmoor, CO Aug 17–18

Result: USA 8, GBI 1
Captains: Polly Riley (USA),
Frances Stephens Smith (GBI)

Foursomes
Decker & McIntyre beat Spearman & Bonallack 7 and 5
Jean Ashley & Anna Johnstone beat Ruth Porter &
  Frearson 8 and 7
Creed & Gunderson beat Vaughan & Ann Irvin 4 and 3

Singles
Judy Bell lost to Diane Frearson 8 and 7
JoAnne Gunderson beat Angela Ward Bonallack 2 and 1
Clifford Ann Creed beat Sally Bonallack 6 and 5
Anne Quast Decker beat Marley Spearman 7 and 5
Phyllis Preuss beat Jean Roberts 1 hole
Barbara McIntyre beat Sheila Vaughan 5 and 4

1964 Porthcawl Sept 11–12

Result: USA 10½, GBI 1½
Captains: Elsie Corlett (GBI), Helen Hawes (USA)

First Day: Foursomes
Spearman & Bonallack beat McIntyre & Preuss 2 and 1
Sheila Vaughan & Porter beat Gunderson & Roth 3 and 2
Jackson & Susan Armitage lost to Sorenson & White
  8 and 6

Singles
Angela Ward Bonallack lost to JoAnne Gunderson 6 and 5
Marley Spearman halved with Barbara McIntyre
Julia Greenhalgh lost to Barbara White 3 and 2
Bridget Jackson beat Carol Sorenson 4 and 3
Joan Lawrence lost to Peggy Conley 1 hole
Ruth Porter beat Nancy Roth 1 hole

Second Day: Foursomes
Spearman & Bonallack beat McIntyre & Preuss 6 and 5
Armitage & Jackson lost to Gunderson & Roth 2 holes
Porter & Vaughan halved with Sorenson & White

Singles
Spearman halved with Gunderson
Lawrence lost to McIntyre 4 and 2
Greenhalgh beat Phyllis Preuss 5 and 3
Bonallack lost to White 3 and 2
Porter lost to Sorenson 3 and 2
Jackson lost to Conley 1 hole

1966 Hot Springs, VA July 29–30

Result: USA 13, GBI 5
Captains: Dorothy Germain Porter (USA),
Zara Bolton (GBI)

First Day: Foursomes
Ashley & Preuss beat Armitage & Bonallack 1 hole
Barbara McIntire & Welts halved with Joan Hastings &
  Robertson
Boddie & Flenniken beat Chadwick & Tredinnick
  1 hole

Singles
Jean Ashley beat Belle McCorkindale Robertson 1 hole
Anne Quast Welts halved with Susan Armitage
Barbara White Boddie beat Angela Ward Bonallack
  3 and 2
Nancy Roth Syms beat Elizabeth Chadwick 2 holes
Helen Wilson lost to Ita Burke 3 and 1
Carol Sorenson Flenniken beat Marjory Fowler 3 and 1

Second Day: Foursomes
Ashley & Preuss beat Armitage & Bonallack 2 and 1
McIntire & Welts lost to Burke & Chadwick 1 hole
Boddie & Flenniken beat Hastings & Robertson 2 and 1

Singles
Ashley lost to Bonallack 2 and 1
Welts halved with Robertson
Boddie beat Armitage 3 and 2
Syms halved with Pam Tredinnick
Phyllis Preuss beat Chadwick 3 and 2
Flenniken beat Burke 2 and 1

1968 Newcastle, Co Down June 14–15

Result: USA 10½, GBI 7½
Captains: Zara Bolton (GBI),
Evelyn Monsted (USA)

First Day: Foursomes
Irvin & Robertson beat Hamlin & Welts 6 and 5
Pickard & Saunders beat Conley & Dill 3 and 2
Howard & Pam Tredinnick lost to Ashley & Preuss 1 hole

Singles
Ann Irvin beat Anne Quast Welts 3 and 2
Vivien Saunders lost to Shelley Hamlin 1 hole
Belle McCorkindale Robertson lost to Roberta Albers
  1 hole
Bridget Jackson halved with Peggy Conley
Dinah Oxley halved with Phyllis Preuss
Margaret Pickard beat Jean Ashley 2 holes

Second Day: Foursomes
Oxley & Tredinnick lost to Ashley & Preuss 5 and 4
Irvin & Robertson halved with Conley & Dill
Pickard & Saunders lost to Hamlin & Welts 2 and 1

Singles
Irvin beat Hamlin 3 and 2
Robertson halved with Welts
Saunders halved with Albers
Ann Howard lost to Mary Lou Dill 4 and 2
Pickard lost to Conley 1 hole
Jackson lost to Preuss 2 and 1

1970 Brae Burn, MA Aug 7–8

Result: USA 11½, GBI 6½
Captains: Carolyn Cudone (USA),
Jeanne Bisgood (GBI)

First Day: Foursomes
Bastanchury & Hamlin lost to McKenna & Oxley
  4 and 3
Preuss & Wilkinson beat Irvin & Robertson 4 and 3
Jane Fassinger & Hill lost to Everard & Greenhalgh
  5 and 3

Singles
Jane Bastanchury beat Dinah Oxley 5 and 3
Martha Wilkinson beat Ann Irvin 1 hole
Shelley Hamlin halved with Belle McCorkindale
  Robertson
Phyllis Preuss lost to Mary McKenna 4 and 2
Nancy Hager beat Margaret Pickard 5 and 4
Alice Dye beat Julia Greenhalgh 1 hole

Second Day: Foursomes
Preuss & Wilkinson beat McKenna & Oxley 6 and 4
Dye & Hill halved with Everard & Greenhalgh
Bastanchury & Hamlin beat Irvin & Robertson 1 hole
Singles
Bastanchury beat Irvin 4 and 3
Hamlin halved with Oxley
Preuss beat Robertson 1 hole
Wilkinson lost to Greenhalgh 6 and 4
Hager lost to Mary Everard 4 and 3
Cindy Hill beat McKenna 2 and 1

1972 *Western Gailes* June 9–10
Result: USA 10, GBI 8
Captains: Frances Stephens Smith (GBI),
Jean Ashley Crawford (USA)
First Day: Foursomes
Everard & Beverly Huke lost to Baugh & Kirouac   2 and 1
Frearson & Robertson beat Booth & McIntyre 2 and 1
McKenna & Walker beat Barry & Hollis Stacy 1 hole
Singles
Mickey Walker halved with Laura Baugh
Belle McCorkindale Robertson lost to Jane Bastanchury
  Booth 3 and 1
Mary Everard lost to Martha Wilkinson Kirouac 4 and 3
Dinah Oxley lost to Barbara McIntire 4 and 3
Kathryn Phillips beat Lancy Smith 2 holes
Mary McKenna lost to Beth Barry 2 and 1
Second Day: Foursomes
McKenna & Walker beat Baugh & Kirouac 3 and 2
Everard & Huke lost to Booth & McIntyre 5 and 4
Frearson & Robertson halved with Barry & Stacy
Singles
Robertson lost to Baugh 6 and 5
Everard beat McIntyre 6 and 5
Walker beat Booth 1 hole
McKenna beat Kirouac 3 and 1
Diane Frearson lost to Smith 3 and 1
Phillips lost to Barry 3 and 1

1974 *San Francisco, CA* Aug 2–3
Result: USA 13, GBI 5
Captains: Sis Choate (USA),
  Belle McCorkindale Robertson (GBI)
First Day: Foursomes
Hill & Semple halved with Greenhalgh & McKenna
Booth & Sander beat Lee-Smith & LeFeuvre 6 and 5
Budke & Lauer lost to Everard & Walker 5 and 4
Singles
Carol Semple lost to Mickey Walker 2 and 1
Jane Bastanchury Booth beat Mary McKenna 5 and 3
Debbie Massey beat Mary Everard 1 hole
Bonnie Lauer beat Jennie Lee-Smith 6 and 5
Beth Barry beat Julia Greenhalgh 1 hole
Cindy Hill halved with Tegwen Perkins
Second Day: Foursomes
Booth & Sander beat McKenna & Walker 5 and 4
Budke & Lauer beat Everard & LeFeuvre 5 and 3
Hill & Semple lost to Greenhalgh & Perkins 3 and 2
Singles
Anne Quast Sander beat Everard 4 and 3
Booth beat Greenhalgh 7 and 5
Massey beat Carol LeFeuvre 6 and 5
Semple beat Walker 2 and 1
Mary Budke beat Perkins 5 and 4
Lauer lost to McKenna 2 and 1

1976 *Royal Lytham & St Annes* June 11–12
Result: USA 11½, GBI 6½
Captains: Belle McCorkindale Robertson (GBI),
  Barbara McIntyre (USA)
First Day: Foursomes
Greenhalgh & McKenna lost to Daniel & Hill
  3 and 2
Cadden & Henson lost to Horton & Massey 6 and 5
Irvin & Perkins beat Semple & Syms 3 and 2
Singles
Ann Irvin lost to Beth Daniel 4 and 3
Dinah Oxley Henson beat Cindy Hill 1 hole
Suzanne Cadden lost to Nancy Lopez 3 and 1
Mary McKenna lost to Nancy Roth Syms 1 hole
Tegwen Perkins lost to Debbie Massey 1 hole
Julia Greenhalgh halved with Barbara Barrow
Second Day: Foursomes
Cadden & Irvin lost to Daniel & Hill 4 and 3
Henson & Perkins beat Semple & Syms 2 and 1
McKenna & Anne Stant lost to Barrow & Lopez
  4 and 3
Singles
Henson lost to Daniel 3 and 2
Greenhalgh beat Syms 2 and 1
Cadden lost to Donna Horton 6 and 5
Jennie Lee-Smith lost to Massey 3 and 2
Perkins beat Hill 1 hole
McKenna beat Carol Semple 1 hole

1978 *Apawamis, NY* Aug 4–5
Result: USA 12, GBI 6
Captains: Helen Wilson (USA),
  Carol Comboy (GBI)
First Day: Foursomes
Daniel & Brenda Goldsmith lost to Greenhalgh &
  Marvin 3 and 2
Cindy Hill & Smith lost to Everard & Thomson 2 and 1
Cornett & Carolyn Hill halved with McKenna &
  Perkins
Singles
Beth Daniel beat Vanessa Marvin 5 and 4
Noreen Uihlein lost to Mary Everard 7 and 6
Lancy Smith beat Angela Uzielli 4 and 3
Cindy Hill beat Julia Greenhalgh 2 and 1
Carolyn Hill halved with Carole Caldwell
Judy Oliver beat Tegwen Perkins 2 and 1
Second Day: Foursomes
Cindy Hill & Smith beat Everard & Thomson 1 hole
Daniel & Goldsmith beat McKenna & Perkins 1 hole
Oliver & Uihlein beat Greenhalgh & Marvin 4 and 3
Singles
Daniel beat Mary McKenna 2 and 1
Patricia Cornett beat Caldwell 3 and 2
Cindy Hill lost to Muriel Thomson 2 and 1
Lancy Smith beat Perkins 2 holes
Oliver halved with Greenhalgh
Uihlein halved with Everard

1980 *St Pierre, Chepstow* June 6–7
Result: USA 13, GBI 5
Captains: Carol Comboy (GBI), Nancy Roth
  Syms (USA)
First Day: Foursomes
McKenna & Nesbitt halved with Terri Moody & Smith
Stewart & Thomas lost to Castillo & Sheehan 5 and 3
Caldwell & Madill halved with Oliver & Semple

1980 continued

Singles

Mary McKenna lost to Patty Sheehan 3 and 2
Claire Nesbitt halved with Lancy Smith
Jane Connachan lost to Brenda Goldsmith 2 holes
Maureen Madill lost to Carol Semple 4 and 3
Linda Moore halved with Mary Hafeman
Carole Caldwell lost to Judy Oliver 1 hole

Second Day: Foursomes

Caldwell & Madill lost to Castillo & Sheehan 3 and 2
McKenna & Nesbitt lost to Moody & Smith 6 and 5
Moore & Thomas lost to Oliver & Semple 1 hole

Singles

Madill lost to Sheehan 5 and 4
McKenna beat Lori Castillo 5 and 4
Connachan lost to Hafeman 6 and 5
Gillian Stewart beat Smith 5 and 4
Moore beat Goldsmith 1 hole
Tegwen Perkins Thomas lost to Semple 4 and 3

1982 Denver, CO Aug 5–6

Result: USA 14½, GBI 3½

Captains: Betty Probasco (USA),
Maire O'Donnell (GBI)

First Day: Foursomes

Inkster & Semple beat McKenna & Robertson 5 and 4
Baker & Smith halved with Douglas & Soulsby
Benz & Hanlon beat Connachan & Stewart 2 and 1

Singles

Amy Benz beat Mary McKenna 2 and 1
Cathy Hanlon beat Jane Connachan 5 and 4
Mari McDougall beat Wilma Aitken 2 holes
Kathy Baker beat Belle McCorkindale Robertson 7 and 6
Judy Oliver lost to Janet Soulsby 2 holes
Juli Inkster beat Kitrina Douglas 7 and 6

Second Day: Foursomes

Inkster & Semple beat Aitken & Connachan 3 and 2
Baker & Smith beat Douglas & Soulsby 1 hole
Benz & Hanlon lost to McKenna & Robertson 1 hole

Singles

Inkster beat Douglas 7 and 6
Baker beat Gillian Stewart 4 and 3
Oliver beat Vicki Thomas 5 and 4
McDougall beat Soulsby 2 and 1
Carol Semple beat McKenna 1 hole
Lancy Smith lost to Robertson 5 and 4

1984 Muirfield June 8–9

Result: USA 9½, GBI 8½

Captains: Diane Robb Bailey (GBI),
Phyllis Preuss (USA)

First Day: Foursomes

New & Waite beat Pacillo & Sander 2 holes
Grice & Thornhill halved with Rosenthal & Smith
Davies & McKenna lost to Farr & Widman 1 hole

Singles

Jill Thornhill halved with Joanne Pacillo
Claire Waite lost to Penny Hammel 4 and 2
Claire Hourihane lost to Jody Rosenthal 3 and 1
Vicki Thomas beat Dana Howe 2 and 1
Penny Grice beat Anne Quast Sander 2 holes
Beverley New lost to Mary Anne Widman 4 and 3

Second Day: Foursomes

New & Waite lost to Rosenthal & Smith 3 and 1
Grice & Thornhill beat Farr & Widman 2 and 1
Hourihane & Thomas halved with Hammel & Howe

Singles

Thornhill lost to Pacillo 3 and 2
Laura Davies beat Sander 1 hole
Waite beat Lancy Smith 5 and 4
Grice lost to Howe 2 holes
New lost to Heather Farr 6 and 5
Hourihane beat Hammel 2 and 1

1986 Prairie Dunes, KS Aug 1–2

Result: GBI 13, USA 5

Captains: Judy Bell (USA), Diane Robb Bailey (GBI)

First Day: Foursomes

Kessler & Schreyer lost to Behan & Thornhill 7 and 6
Ammaccapane & Mochrie lost to Davies & Johnson 2 and 1
Gardner & Scrivner lost to McKenna & Robertson 1 hole

Singles

Leslie Shannon lost to Patricia (Trish) Johnson 1 hole
Kim Williams lost to Jill Thornhill 4 and 3
Danielle Ammaccapane lost to Lillian Behan 4 and 3
Kandi Kessler beat Vicki Thomas 3 and 2
Dottie Pepper Mochrie halved with Karen Davies
Cindy Schreyer beat Claire Hourihane 2 and 1

Second Day: Foursomes

Ammaccapane & Mochrie lost to Davies & Johnson 1 hole
Shannon & Williams lost to Behan & Thornhill 5 and 3
Gardner & Scrivner halved with McKenna & Belle McCorkindale Robertson

Singles

Shannon halved with Thornhill
Kathleen McCarthy Scrivner lost to Trish Johnson 5 and 3
Kim Gardner beat Behan 1 hole
Williams lost to Thomas 4 and 3
Kessler halved with Davies
Schreyer lost to Hourihane 5 and 4

1988 Royal St George's June 10–11

Result: GBI 11, USA 7

Captains: Diane Robb Bailey (GBI),
Judy Bell (USA)

First Day: Foursomes

Bayman & Wade beat Kerdyk & Scrivner 2 and 1
Davies & Shapcott beat Scholefield & Thompson 5 and 4
Thomas & Thornhill halved with Keggi & Shannon

Singles

Linda Bayman halved with Tracy Kerdyk
Julie Wade beat Cindy Scholefield 2 holes
Susan Shapcott lost to Carol Semple Thompson 1 hole
Karen Davies lost to Pearl Sinn 4 and 3
Shirley Lawson beat Pat Cornett-Iker 1 hole
Jill Thornhill beat Leslie Shannon 3 and 2

Second Day: Foursomes

Bayman & Wade lost to Kerdyk & Scrivner 1 hole
Davies & Shapcott beat Keggi & Shannon 2 holes
Thomas & Thornhill beat Scholefield & Thompson 6 and 5

Singles

Wade lost to Kerdyk 2 and 1
Shapcott beat Caroline Keggi 3 and 2
Lawson lost to Kathleen McCarthy Scrivner 4 and 3
Vicki Thomas beat Cornett-Iker 5 and 3
Bayman beat Sinn 1 hole
Thornhill lost to Thompson 3 and 2

1990 *Somerset Hills, NJ* July 28–29
Result: USA 14, GBI 4
Captains: Leslie Shannon (USA), Jill Thornhill (GBI)
First Day: Foursomes
Goetze & Anne Quast Sander beat Dobson & Lambert
4 and 3
Noble & Margaret Platt lost to Wade & Imrie 2 and 1
Thompson & Weiss beat Farquharson & Helen
Wadsworth 3 and 1
Singles
Vicki Goetze lost to Julie Wade 2 and 1
Katie Peterson beat Kathryn Imrie 3 and 2
Brandie Burton beat Linzi Fletcher 3 and 1
Robin Weiss beat Elaine Farquharson 4 and 3
Karen Noble beat Catriona Lambert 1 hole
Carol Semple Thompson lost to Vicki Thomas 1 hole
Second Day: Foursomes
Goetze & Sander beat Wade & Imrie 3 and 1
Noble & Platt lost to Dobson & Lambert 1 hole
Burton & Peterson beat Farquharson & Wadsworth
5 and 4
Singles
Goetze beat Helen Dobson 4 and 3
Burton beat Lambert 4 and 3
Peterson beat Imrie 1 hole
Noble beat Wade 2 holes
Weiss beat Farquharson 2 and 1
Thompson beat Thomas 3 and 1

1992 *Hoylake* June 5–6
Result: GBI 10, USA 8
Captains: Elizabeth Boatman (GBI),
Judy Oliver (USA)
First Day: Foursomes
Hall & Wade halved with Fruhwirth & Goetze
Lambert & Thomas beat Ingram & Shannon 2 and 1
Hourihane & Morley beat Hanson & Thompson 2 and 1
Singles
Joanne Morley halved with Amy Fruhwirth
Julie Wade lost to Vicki Goetze 3 and 2
Elaine Farquharson beat Robin Weiss 2 and 1
Nicola Buxton lost to Martha Lang 2 holes
Catriona Lambert beat Carol Semple Thompson 3 and 2
Caroline Hall beat Leslie Shannon 6 and 5
Second Day: Foursomes
Hall & Wade halved with Fruhwirth & Goetze
Hourihane & Morley halved with Lang & Weiss
Lambert & Thomas lost to Hanson & Thompson
3 and 2
Singles
Morley beat Fruhwirth 2 and 1
Lambert beat Tracy Hanson 6 and 5
Farquharson lost to Sarah LeBrun Ingram 2 and 1
Vicki Thomas lost to Shannon 2 and 1
Claire Hourihane lost to Lang 2 and 1
Hall beat Goetze 1 hole

1994 *Chattanooga, TN* July 30–31
Result: GBI 9, USA 9
Captains: Lancy Smith (USA),
Elizabeth Boatman (GBI)
First Day: Foursomes
Sarah LeBrun Ingram & McGill halved with Matthew
& Moodie
Klein & Thompson beat McKay & Kirsty Speak 7 and 5
Kaupp & Port lost to Wade & Walton 6 and 5

Singles
Jill McGill halved with Julie Wade
Emilee Klein beat Janice Moodie 3 and 2
Wendy Ward lost to Lisa Walton 1 hole
Carol Semple Thompson beat Myra McKinlay 2 and 1
Ellen Port beat Mhairi McKay 2 and 1
Stephanie Sparks lost to Catriona Lambert Matthew
1 hole
Second Day: Foursomes
Ingram & McGill lost to Wade & Walton 2 and 1
Klein & Thompson beat McKinlay & Eileen Rose
Power 4 and 2
Sparks & Ward lost to Matthew & Moodie 3 and 2
Singles
McGill beat Wade 4 and 3
Klein lost to Matthew 2 and 1
Port beat McKay 7 and 5
Wendy Kaupp lost to McKinlay 3 and 2
Ward beat Walton 4 and 3
Thompson lost to Moodie 2 holes

1996 *Killarney* June 21–22
Result: GBI 11½, USA 6½
Captains: Ita Burke Butler (GBI),
Martha Lang (USA)
First Day: Foursomes
Lisa Walton Educate & Wade lost to K Kuehne & Port
2 and 1
Lisa Dermott & Rose beat B Corrie Kuehn & Jemsek
3 and 1
McKay & Moodie halved with Kerr & Thompson
Singles
Julie Wade lost to Sarah LeBrun Ingram 4 and 2
Karen Stupples beat Kellee Booth 3 and 2
Alison Rose beat Brenda Corrie Kuehn 5 and 4
Elaine Ratcliffe halved with Marla Jemsek
Mhairi McKay beat Cristie Kerr 1 hole
Janice Moodie beat Carol Semple Thompson 3 and 1
Second Day: Foursomes
McKay & Moodie beat Booth & Ingram 3 and 2
Dermott & Rose beat B Corrie Kuehn & Jemsek 2 and 1
Educate & Wade lost to K Kuehne & Port 1 hole
Singles
Wade lost to Kerr 1 hole
Ratcliffe beat Ingram 3 and 1
Stupples lost to Booth 3 and 2
Rose beat Ellen Port 6 and 5
McKay halved with Thompson
Moodie beat Kelli Kuehne 2 and 1

1998 *Minikahda, Minneapolis, MN* Aug 1–2
Result: USA 10, GBI 8
Captains: Barbara McIntire (USA),
Ita Burke Butler (GBI)
First Day: Foursomes
Bauer & Chuasiriporn lost to Ratcliffe & Rostron
1 hole
Booth & Corrie Kuehn beat Brown & Stupples 2 and 1
Burke & Derby Grimes beat Morgan & Rose 3 and 2
Singles
Kellee Booth beat Kim Rostron 2 and 1
Brenda Corrie Kuehn beat Alison Rose 3 and 2
Jenny Chuasiriporn halved with Rebecca Hudson
Beth Bauer beat Hilary Monaghan 5 and 3
Jo Jo Robertson lost to Becky Morgan 2 and 1
Carol Semple Thompson lost to Elaine Ratcliffe
3 and 2

1998 *continued*

Second Day: Foursomes
Booth & Corrie Kuehn beat Morgan & Rose 6 and 5
Bauer & Chuasiriporn lost to Brown & Hudson 2 holes
Burke & Derby Grimes beat Ratcliffe & Rostron 2 and 1

Singles
Booth beat Rostron 2 and 1
Corrie Kuehn beat Morgan 2 and 1
Thompson lost to Karen Stupples 1 hole
Robin Burke lost to Hudson 2 and 1
Robertson lost to Fiona Brown 1 hole
Virginia Derby Grimes halved with Ratcliffe

2000 *Ganton* June 24–25
Result: USA 10, GBI 8
Captains: Claire Hourihane Dowling (GBI),
*   Jane Bastanchury Booth (USA)*

First Day: Foursomes
Andrew & Morgan lost to Bauer & Carol Semple
   Thompson 1 hole
Brewerton & Hudson lost to Keever & Stanford 1 hole
Duggleby & O'Brien halved with Derby Grimes &
   Homeyer

Singles
Kim Rostron Andrew lost to Beth Bauer 3 and 2
Fiona Brown lost to Robin Weiss 1 hole
Rebecca Hudson lost to Stephanie Keever 4 and 2
Lesley Nicholson halved with Angela Stanford
Suzanne O'Brien beat Leland Beckel 3 and 1
Emma Duggleby lost to Hilary Homeyer 1 hole

Second Day: Foursomes
Brewerton & Hudson beat Bauer & Thompson 2 and 1
Duggleby & O'Brien beat Keever & Stanford 7 and 6
Andrew & Morgan lost to Derby Grimes & Homeyer 3 and 1

Singles
Hudson lost to Bauer 1 hole
O'Brien beat Weiss 3 and 2
Duggleby beat Keever 4 and 2
Becky Brewerton lost to Homeyer 3 and 2
Becky Morgan beat Stanford 5 and 4
Andrew beat Virginia Derby Grimes 6 and 5

2002 *Fox Chapel, PA* Aug 3–4
Result: USA 11, GBI 7
Captains: Mary Budke (USA), Pam Benka (GBI)
First Day: Foursomes
Duncan & Jerman beat Duggleby & Hudson 4 and 3
Fankhauser & Semple Thompson beat Laing & Stirling 1 hole
Myerscough & Swaim beat Coffey & Smith 3 and 2

Singles
Emily Bastel lost to Rebecca Hudson 2 holes
Leigh Anne Hardin beat Emma Duggleby 2 and 1
Meredith Duncan beat Fame More 5 and 4
Angela Jerman beat Sarah Jones 6 and 5
Courtney Swaim beat Heather Stirling 4 and 2
Mollie Fankhauser lost to Vikki Laing 1 hole

Second Day: Foursomes
Hardin & Bastel lost to Laing & Stirling 3 and 1
Myerscough & Swaim beat Hudson & Smith 4 and 2
Duncan & Jerman lost to Coffey & Dugglesby 4 and 2

Singles
Mollie Fankhauser beat Rebecca Hudson 3 and 1
Carol Semple Thompson Beat Vikki Laing 1 hole
Leigh Anne Hardin lost to Emma Duggleby 4 and 3
Laura Myerscough beat Heather Stirling 2 holes
Meredith Duncan beat Akison Coffey 3 and 1
Courtney Swaim lost to Sarah Jones 5 and 3

2004 *Formby* June 12–13
Result: GBI 8, USA 10
Captains: Ada O'Sullivan (Monkstown) (GBI);
*   Martha Kironac (USA)*
First Day: Foursomes
S McKevitt & E Duggleby beat P Creamer & J Park 3 and 2
N Timmins & D Masters beat S Huarte & A Thurman
   1 hole
A Laing & C Coughlan beat B Lang & M Wie 1 hole

Singles
Emma Duggleby beat Elizabeth Janangelo 3 and 2
Danielle Masters lost to Erica Blasberg 1 hole
Fame More lost to Paula Creamer 5 and 3
Anna Highgate lost to Michelle Wie 5 and 4
Shelley McKevitt lost to Jane Park 4 and 3
Anne Laing lost to Anne Thurman 4 and 3

Second Day: Foursomes
E Duggleby & S McKevitt beat E Blasberg & Sarah Huarte
   2 and 1
A Laing & C Coughlan beat E Janangelo & M Wie 3 and 2
N Timmins & D Masters lost to B Lang & A Thurman
   5 and 4

Singles
E Duggleby lost to P Creamer 3 and 2
A Laing beat J Park 3 and 1
S McKevitt lost to E Janangelo 1 hole
Nicola Timmins lost to M Wie 6 and 5
Claire Coughlan beat Brittany Lang 2 holes
D Masters lost to A Thurman 1 hole

Curtis Cup INDIVIDUAL RECORDS

Bold print: captain; bold print in brackets: non-playing captain
Maiden name in parentheses, former surname in square brackets

Great Britain and Ireland

Name		Year	Played	Won	Lost	Halved
Jean Anderson (Donald)	SCO	1948	6	3	3	0
Kim Andrew (Rostron)	ENG	1998-2000	8	2	6	0
Diane Bailey [Frearson] (Robb)	ENG	1962-72-(84)-(86)-(88)	5	2	2	1
Sally Barber (Bonallack)	ENG	1962	1	0	1	0
Pam Barton	ENG	1934-36	4	0	3	1
Linda Bayman	ENG	1988	4	2	1	1
Baba Beck (Pym)	IRL	(1954)	0	0	0	0
Charlotte Beddows [Watson] (Stevenson)	SCO	1932	1	0	1	0

Name		Year	Played	Won	Lost	Halved
Lilian Behan	IRL	1986	4	3	1	0
Veronica Beharrell (Anstey)	ENG	1956	1	0	1	0
Pam Benka (Tredinnick)	ENG	1966-68 (2002)	4	0	3	1
Jeanne Bisgood	ENG	1950-52-54-(70)	4	1	3	0
Elizabeth Boatman (Collis)	ENG	(1992)-(94)	0	0	0	0
Zara Bolton (Davis)	ENG	1948-(56)-(66)-(68)	2	0	2	0
Angela Bonallack (Ward)	ENG	1956-58-60-62-64-66	15	6	8	1
Becky Brewerton	WAL	2000	3	1	2	0
Fiona Brown	ENG	1998-2000	4	2	2	0
Ita Butler (Burke)	IRL	1966-(96)	3	2	1	0
Lady Katherine Cairns	ENG	(1952)	0	0	0	0
Carole Caldwell (Redford)	ENG	1978-80	5	0	3	2
Doris Chambers	ENG	(1934)-(36)-(48)	0	0	0	0
Alison Coffey	IRL	2002	3	1	2	0
Carol Comboy (Grott)	ENG	(1978)-(80)	0	0	0	0
Jane Connachan	SCO	1980-82	5	0	5	0
Elsie Corlett	ENG	1932-38-(64)	3	1	2	0
Claire Coughlan	IRL	2004-06	5	3	2	0
Diana Critchley (Fishwick)	ENG	1932-34-(50)	3	1	2	0
Alison Davidson (Rose)	SCO	1996-98	7	4	3	0
Karen Davies	WAL	1986-88	7	4	1	2
Laura Davies	ENG	1984	2	1	1	0
Tara Delanbey	ENG	2006	3	0	2	1
Lisa Dermott	WAL	1996	2	2	0	0
Helen Dobson	ENG	1990	3	1	2	0
Kitrina Douglas	ENG	1982	4	0	3	1
Claire Dowling (Hourihane)	IRL	1984-86-88-90-92-(2000)	8	3	3	2
Marjorie Draper [Peel] (Thomas)	SCO	1954	1	0	1	0
Emma Duggleby	ENG	2000-04	8	5	2	1
Lisa Educate (Walton)	ENG	1994-96	6	3	3	0
Naomi Edwards	ENG	2006	3	1	2	0
Mary Everard	ENG	1970-72-74-78	15	6	7	2
Elaine Farquharson	SCO	1990-92	6	1	5	0
Daisy Ferguson	IRL	(1958)	0	0	0	0
Marjory Ferguson (Fowler)	SCO	1966	1	0	1	0
Elizabeth Price Fisher (Price)	ENG	1950-52-54-56-58-60	12	7	4	1
Linzi Fletcher	ENG	1990	1	0	1	0
Maureen Garner (Madill)	IRL	1980	4	0	3	1
Marjorie Ross Garon	ENG	1936	2	1	0	1
Maureen Garrett (Ruttle)	ENG	1948-(60)	2	0	2	0
Philomena Garvey	IRL	1948-50-52-54-56-60	11	2	8	1
Carol Gibbs (Le Feuvre)	ENG	1974	3	0	3	0
Martine Gillen	IRL	2006	4	2	2	0
Jacqueline Gordon	ENG	1948	2	1	1	0
Molly Gourlay	ENG	1932-34	4	0	2	2
Julia Greenhalgh	ENG	1964-70-74-76-78	17	6	7	4
Penny Grice-Whittaker (Grice)	ENG	1984	4	2	1	1
Caroline Hall	ENG	1992	4	2	0	2
Marley Harris [Spearman] (Baker)	ENG	1960-62-64	6	2	2	2
Dorothea Hastings (Sommerville)	SCO	1958	0	0	0	0
Lady Heathcoat-Amory (Joyce Wethered)	ENG	1932	2	1	1	0
Dinah Henson (Oxley)	ENG	1968-70-72-76	11	3	6	2
Anna Highgate	WAL	2004	1	0	1	0
Helen Holm (Gray)	SCO	1936-38-48	5	3	2	0
Ann Howard (Phillips)	ENG	1956-68	2	0	2	0
Rebecca Hudson	ENG	1998-2000-02	11	5	5	1
Shirley Huggan (Lawson)	SCO	1988	2	1	1	0
Beverley Huke	ENG	1972	2	0	2	0
Ann Irvin	ENG	1962-68-70-76	12	4	7	1
Bridget Jackson	ENG	1958-64-68	8	1	6	1
Patricia Johnson	ENG	1986	4	4	0	0
Sarah Jones	WAL	2002	2	1	1	0
Anne Laing	SCO	2004	4	3	1	0
Vikki Laing	SCO	2002	4	2	2	0
Susan Langridge (Armitage)	ENG	1964-66	6	0	5	1
Joan Lawrence	SCO	1964	2	0	2	0
Wilma Leburn (Aitken)	SCO	1982	2	0	2	0
Jenny Lee Smith	ENG	1974-76	3	0	3	0
Breanne Loucks	WAL	2006	3	3	0	0
Kathryn Lumb (Phillips)	ENG	1970-72	2	1	1	0

Curtis Cup Individual Records *continued*

Name		Year	Played	Won	Lost	Halved
Mhairi McKay	SCO	1994-96	7	2	3	2
Mary McKenna	IRL	1970-72-74-76-78-80-82-84-86	30	10	16	4
Shelley McKevitt	ENG	2004	4	2	2	0
Myra McKinlay	SCO	1994	3	1	2	0
Suzanne McMahon (Cadden)	SCO	1976	4	0	4	0
Sheila Maher (Vaughan)	ENG	1962-64	4	1	2	1
Tricia Mangan	IRL	2006	3	0	2	1
Kathryn Marshall (Imrie)	SCO	1990	4	1	3	0
Vanessa Marvin	ENG	1978	4	1	3	0
Danielle Masters	ENG	2004	3	1	2	0
Kiran Matharu	ENG	2006	2	1	1	0
Catriona Matthew (Lambert)	SCO	1990-92-94	12	7	4	1
Tegwen Matthews [Thomas] (Perkins)	WAL	1974-76-78-80	14	4	8	2
Moira Milton (Paterson)	SCO	1952	2	1	1	0
Hilary Monaghan	SCO	1998	1	0	1	0
Janice Moodie	SCO	1994-96	8	5	1	2
Fame More	ENG	2002-04	2	0	2	0
Becky Morgan	WAL	1998-2000	7	2	5	0
Wanda Morgan	ENG	1932-34-36	6	0	5	1
Joanne Morley	ENG	1992	4	2	0	2
Nicola Murray (Buxton)	ENG	1992	1	0	1	0
Beverley New	ENG	1984	4	1	3	0
Lesley Nicholson	SCO	2000	1	0	0	1
Suzanne O'Brien	IRL	2000	4	3	0	1
Maire O'Donnell	IRL	**(1982)**	0	0	0	0
Ada O'Sullivan	IRL	**(2004-06)**	0	0	0	0
Margaret Pickard (Nichol)	ENG	1968-70	5	2	3	0
Diana Plumpton	ENG	1934	2	1	1	0
Elizabeth Pook (Chadwick)	ENG	1966	4	1	3	0
Doris Porter (Park)	SCO	1932	1	0	1	0
Eileen Rose Power (McDaid)	IRL	1994	1	0	1	0
Elaine Ratcliffe	ENG	1996-98	6	3	1	2
Clarrie Reddan (Tiernan)	IRL	1938-48	3	2	1	0
Joan Rennie (Hastings)	SCO	1966	2	1	1	0
Melissa Reid	ENG	2006	4	1	3	0
Maureen Richmond (Walker)	SCO	1974	1	0	1	0
Jean Roberts	ENG	1962	4	2	2	0
Belle Robertson (McCorkindale)	SCO	1960-66-68-70-72-**(74)**-**(76)**-82-86	24	5	12	7
Claire Robinson (Nesbitt)	IRL	1980	3	0	1	2
Vivien Saunders	ENG	1968	4	1	1	1
Susan Shapcott	ENG	1988	4	3	1	0
Linda Simpson (Moore)	ENG	1980	3	1	1	1
Ruth Slark (Porter)	ENG	1960-62-64	7	3	3	1
Anne Smith [Stant] (Willard)	ENG	1976	1	0	1	0
Frances Smith (Stephens)	ENG	1950-52-54-56-58-60-**(62)**-**(72)**	11	7	3	1
Kerry Smith	ENG	2002	2	0	2	0
Janet Soulsby	ENG	1982	4	1	2	1
Kirsty Speak	ENG	1994	1	0	1	0
Gillian Stewart	SCO	1980-82	4	1	3	0
Heather Stirling	SCO	2002	4	1	3	0
Karen Stupples	ENG	1996-98	4	2	2	0
Vicki Thomas (Rawlings)	WAL	1982-84-86-88-90-92	13	6	5	2
Muriel Thomson	SCO	1978	3	2	1	0
Jill Thornhill	ENG	1984-86-88	12	6	2	4
Nicola Timmins	ENG	2004	3	1	2	0
Angela Uzielli (Carrick)	ENG	1978	1	0	1	0
Jessie Valentine (Anderson)	SCO	1936-38-50-52-54-56-58	13	4	9	0
Julie Wade	ENG	1988-90-92-94-96	19	6	10	3
Helen Wadsworth	WAL	1990	2	0	2	0
Claire Waite	ENG	1984	4	2	2	0
Mickey Walker	ENG	1972-74	4	3	0	1
Pat Walker	IRL	1934-36-38	6	2	3	1
Verona Wallace-Williamson	SCO	**(1938)**	0	0	0	0
Nan Wardlaw (Baird)	SCO	1938	1	0	1	0
Enid Wilson	ENG	1932	2	1	1	0
Janette Wright (Robertson)	SCO	1954-56-58-60	8	3	5	0
Phyllis Wylie (Wade)	ENG	1938	1	0	0	1

United States of America

Name	Year	Played	Won	Lost	Halved
Roberta Albers	1968	2	1	0	1
Danielle Ammaccapane	1986	3	0	3	0
Kathy Baker	1982	4	3	0	1
Barbara Barrow	1976	2	1	0	1
Beth Barry	1972-74	5	3	1	1
Emily Bastel	2002	2	0	2	0
Beth Bauer	1998-2000	7	4	3	0
Laura Baugh	1972	4	2	1	1
Leland Beckel	2000	1	0	1	0
Judy Bell	1960-62-(**86**)-(**88**)	2	1	1	0
Peggy Kirk Bell (Kirk)	1950	2	1	1	0
Amy Benz	1982	3	2	1	0
Patty Berg	1936-38	4	1	2	1
Erica Blasberg	2004	2	1	2	1
Amanda Blumenherst	2006	3	1	2	0
Barbara Fay Boddie (White)	1964-66	8	7	0	1
Jane Booth (Bastanchury)	1970-72-74-(**2000**)	12	9	3	0
Kellee Booth	1996-98	7	5	2	0
Mary Budke	1974-(**2002**)	3	2	1	0
Robin Burke	1998	3	2	1	0
Brandie Burton	1990	3	3	0	0
Jo Anne Carner (Gunderson)	1958-60-62-64	10	6	3	1
Lori Castillo	1980	3	2	1	0
Leona Cheney (Pressler)	1932-34-36	6	5	1	0
Sis Choate	(**1974**)	0	0	0	0
Jenny Chuasiriporn	1998	3	0	2	1
Peggy Conley	1964-68	6	3	1	2
Mary Ann Cook (Downey)	1956	2	1	1	0
Patricia Cornett	1978-88	4	1	2	1
Brenda Corrie Kuehn	1996-98	7	4	3	0
Jean Crawford (Ashley)	1962-66-68-(**72**)	8	6	2	0
Paula Creamer	2004	3	2	1	0
Clifford Ann Creed	1962	2	2	0	0
Grace Cronin (Lenczyk)	1948-50	3	2	1	0
Carolyn Cudone	1956-(**70**)	1	1	0	0
Beth Daniel	1976-78	8	7	1	0
Virginia Dennehy	(**1958**)	0	0	0	0
Virginia Derby Grimes	1998-2000	6	3	1	2
Mary Lou Dill	1968	3	1	1	1
Meredith Duncan	2002	4	3	1	0
Alice Dye	1970	2	1	0	1
Mollie Fankhauser	2002	3	1	2	0
Heather Farr	1984	3	2	1	0
Jane Fassinger	1970	1	0	1	0
Mary Lena Faulk	1954	2	1	1	0
Carol Sorensen Flenniken (Sorensen)	1964-66	8	6	1	1
Edith Flippin (Quier)	(**1954**)-(**56**)	0	0	0	0
Amy Fruhwirth	1992	4	0	1	3
Kim Gardner	1986	3	1	1	1
Charlotte Glutting	1934-36-38	5	3	1	1
Vicki Goetze	1990-92	8	4	2	2
Brenda Goldsmith	1978-80	4	2	2	0
Aniela Goldthwaite	1934-(**52**)	1	0	1	0
Joanne Goodwin	1960	2	1	1	0
Virginia Grimes	2006	2	1	1	0
Mary Hafeman	1980	2	1	0	1
Shelley Hamkin	1968-70	8	3	3	2
Penny Hammel	1984	3	1	1	1
Nancy Hammer (Hager)	1970	2	1	1	0
Cathy Hanlon	1982	3	2	1	0
Beverley Hanson	1950	2	2	0	0
Tracy Hanson	1992	3	1	2	0
Patricia Harbottle (Lesser)	1954-56	3	2	1	0
Leigh Anne Hardin	2002	3	1	2	0
Helen Hawes	(**1964**)	0	0	0	0
Kathryn Hemphill	1938	1	0	0	1
Helen Hicks	1932	2	1	1	0
Carolyn Hill	1978	2	0	0	2
Cindy Hill	1970-74-76-78	14	5	6	3

Curtis Cup Individual Records *continued*

Name	Year	Played	Won	Lost	Halved
Opel Hill	1932-34-36	6	2	3	1
Marion Hollins	(1932)	0	0	0	0
Hilary Homeyer	2000	4	3	0	1
Dana Howe	1984	3	1	1	1
Sarah Huarte	2004	2	0	2	0
Juli Inkster	1982	4	4	0	0
Elizabeth Janangelo	2004	3	1	2	0
Maria Jemsek	1996	3	0	2	1
Angela Jerman	2002	3	2	1	0
Ann Casey Johnstone	1958-60-62	4	3	1	0
Mae Murray Jones (Murray)	1952	1	0	1	0
Wendy Kaupp	1994	2	0	2	0
Stephanie Keever	2000	4	2	2	0
Caroline Keggi	1988	3	0	2	1
Tracy Kerdyk	1988	4	2	1	1
Cristie Kerr	1996	3	1	1	1
Kandi Kessler	1986	3	1	1	1
Dorothy Kielty	1948-50	4	4	0	0
Dorothy Kirby	1948-50-52-54	7	4	3	0
Martha Kirouac (Wilkinson)	1970-72-(2004)	8	5	3	0
Emilee Klein	1994	4	3	1	0
Nancy Knight (Lopez)	1976	2	2	0	0
Kelli Kuehne	1996	3	2	1	0
Brittany Lang	2004	3	1	2	0
Martha Lang	1992-(96)	3	2	0	1
Bonnie Lauer	1974	4	2	2	0
Sarah Le Brun Ingram	1992-94-96	7	2	4	1
Jennie Lee	2006	3	2	1	0
Taylor Leon	2006	4	3	0	1
Marjorie Lindsay	1952	2	1	1	0
Patricia Lucey (O'Sullivan)	1952	1	0	1	0
Paige Mackenzie	2006	4	3	1	0
Amanda McCurdy	2006	2	1	1	0
Mari McDougall	1982	2	2	0	0
Jill McGill	1994	4	1	1	2
Barbara McIntire	1958-60-62-64-66-72-(76)	16	6	6	4
Lucile Mann (Robinson)	1934	1	0	1	0
Debbie Massey	1974-76	5	5	0	0
Marion Miley	1938	2	1	0	1
Dottie Mochrie (Pepper)	1986	3	0	2	1
Evelyn Monsted	(1968)	0	0	0	0
Terri Moody	1980	2	1	0	1
Laura Myerscough	2002	3	3	0	0
Karen Noble	1990	4	2	2	0
Judith Oliver	1978-80-82-(92)	8	5	1	2
Maureen Orcutt	1932-34-36-38	8	5	3	0
Joanne Pacillo	1984	3	1	1	1
Estelle Page (Lawson)	1938-48	4	3	1	0
Jane Park	2004-06	7	4	2	1
Katie Peterson	1990	3	3	0	0
Margaret Platt	1990	2	0	2	0
Frances Pond (Stebbins)	(1938)	0	0	0	0
Ellen Port	1994-96	6	4	2	0
Dorothy Germain Porter	1950-(66)	2	1	0	1
Phyllis Preuss	1962-64-66-68-70-(84)	15	10	4	1
Betty Probasco	(1982)	0	0	0	0
Mildred Prunaret	(1960)	0	0	0	0
Polly Riley	1948-50-52-54-56-58-(62)	10	5	5	0
Jo Jo Robertson	1998	2	0	2	0
Barbara Romack	1954-56-58	5	3	2	0
Jody Rosenthal	1984	3	2	0	1
Anne Sander [Welts] [Decker] (Quast)	1958-60-62-66-68-74-84-90	22	11	7	4
Cindy Scholefield	1988	3	0	3	0
Cindy Schreyer	1986	3	1	2	0
Kathleen McCarthy Scrivner (McCarthy)	1986-88	6	2	3	1
Carol Semple Thompson	1974-76-80-82-90-92-94-96-98-2000-02-06	33	16	13	4
Leslie Shannon	1986-88-90-92	9	1	6	2
Patty Sheehan	1980	4	4	0	0

Name	Year	Played	Won	Lost	Halved
Pearl Sinn	1988	2	1	1	0
Grace De Moss Smith (De Moss)	1952-54	3	1	2	0
Lancy Smith	1972-78-80-82-84-(94)	16	7	5	4
Margaret Smith	1956	2	2	0	0
Stephanie Sparks	1994	2	0	2	0
Hollis Stacy	1972	2	0	1	1
Claire Stancik (Doran)	1952-54	4	4	0	0
Angela Stanford	2000	4	1	2	1
Judy Street (Eller)	1960	2	2	0	0
Louise Suggs	1948	2	0	1	1
Jenny Suh	2006	2	0	2	0
Courtney Swaim	2002	4	3	1	0
Nancy Roth Syms (Roth)	1964-66-76-(80)	9	3	5	1
Anne Thurman	2004	4	3	1	0
Noreen Uihlein	1978	3	1	1	1
Virginia Van Wie	1932-34	4	3	0	1
Glenna Collett Vare (Collett)	1932-(34)-36-38-48-(50)	7	4	2	1
Wendy Ward	1994	3	1	2	0
Jane Weiss (Nelson)	1956	1	0	1	0
Robin Weiss	1990-92-2000	7	4	2	1
Donna White (Horton)	1976	2	2	0	0
Mary Anne Widman	1984	3	2	1	0
Michelle Wie	2004	4	2	2	0
Kimberley Williams	1986	3	0	3	0
Helen Sigel Wilson (Sigel)	1950-66-(78)	2	0	2	0
Joyce Ziske	1954	1	0	1	0

Commonwealth Tournament (Instituted 1959)

1959	Great Britain	St Andrews	1983	Australia	Glendale, Edmonton, Canada
1963	Great Britain	Royal Melbourne, Australia	1987	Canada	Christchurch, New Zealand
1967	Great Britain	Ancaster, Ontario, Canada	1991	Great Britain	Northumberland, England
1971	Great Britain	Hamilton, New Zealand	1995	Australia	Royal Sydney, Australia
1975	Great Britain	Ganton, England	1999	Australia	Marine Drive, Vancouver, Canada
1979	Canada	Lake Karrinup, Perth, Australia	2003	Australia	Remeura, New Zealand

Women's European Amateur Team Championship

1967	England	France	Penina, Portugal	1987	Sweden	Wales	Turnberry, Scotland
1969	France	England	Tylosand, Sweden	1989	France	England	Pals, Spain
1971	England	France	Ganton, England	1991	England	Sweden	Wentworth, England
1973	England	France	Brussels, Belgium	1993	England	Spain	Royal Haagshe
1975	France	Spain	Paris, France	1995	Spain	Scotland	Milan, Italy
1977	England	Spain	Sotogrande, Spain	1997	Sweden	Scotland	Nordcenter, Finland
1979	Ireland	Germany	Hermitage, Ireland	1999	France	England	St Germain, France
1981	Sweden	France	Troia, Portugal	2001	Sweden	Spain	Pontevedra, Spain
1983	Ireland	England	Waterloo, Belgium	2003	Spain	Sweden	Wittelsbacher, Germany
1985	England	Italy	Stavanger, Norway	2005	Spain	England	Karstad, Sweden

Vagliano Trophy – Great Britain & Ireland v Continent of Europe

1959	GBI	12–3	Wentworth	1983	GBI	14–10	Woodhall Spa
1961	GBI	8–7	Villa d'Este	1985	GBI	14–10	Hamburg
1963	GBI	20–10	Muirfield	1987	GBI	15–9	The Berkshire
1965	Europe	17–13	Cologne	1989	GBI	14½–9½	Venice
1967	Europe	15½–14½	Lytham	1991	GBI	13½–10½	Nairn
1969	Europe	16–14	Chantilly	1993	GBI	13½–10½	Morfontaine
1971	GBI	17½–12½	Worplesdon	1995	Europe	14–10	Ganton
1973	GBI	20–10	Eindhoven	1997	Europe	14–10	Halmstad
1975	GBI	13½–10½	Muirfield	1999	Europe	13–11	North Berwick
1977	GBI	15½–8½	Malmo	2001	Europe	7–5	Venice
1979	Halved	12–12	R Porthcawl	2003	GBI	12½–11½	Co Louth
1981	Europe	14–10	P de Hierro	2005	GBI	13–11	Chantilly

Women's World Amateur Team Championship for the Espirito Santo Trophy

2006 Stellenbosch GC and De Zalza GC, South Africa

Year				Score
1964	France	United States	St Germain	588
1966	United States	Canada	Mexico	580
1968	United States	Australia	Melbourne	616
1970	United States	France	Madrid	598
1972	United States	France	Buenos Aires	583
1974	United States	GBI, South Africa	Dominican Republic	620
1976	United States	France	Vilamoura, Portugal	605
1978	Australia	Canada	Fiji	596
1980	United States	Australia	Pinehurst, USA	588
1982	United States	New Zealand	Geneva, Switzerland	579
1984	United States	France	Hong Kong	585
1986	Spain	France	Caracas, Venezuela	580
1988	United States	Sweden	Drottningholm, Sweden	587
1990	United States	New Zealand	Christchurch, New Zealand	585
1992	Spain	GBI	Vancouver, Canada	588
1994	United States	Korea	Paris, France	569
1996	Korea	Italy	Manila, Philippines	438
1998	United States	Italy	Santiago, Chile	558
2000	France	Korea	Sporting Club, Berlin	580
2002	Australia	Thailand	Saujana, Kuala Lumpur	578
2004	Sweden	Canada	Rio Grande, Puerti Rico	567

1   South Africa* (Ashleigh Simon, Kelli Shean, Stacy Bregman)   139-138-141-148—566
*South Africa won on a countback
2   Sweden (Anna Nordqvist, Caroline Westrup, Sofie Andersson)   139-145-138-144—566
3   Colombia (Eileen Vargas, Maria José Uribe, Caroline Llano)   147-141-143-146—577

Other scores: 568 France; 569 Germany, Japan; 570 New Zealand; 572 Spain; 574 USA; 576 Chinese Taipei; 578 England (Kerri Smith 73-69-72-74—288; Sophie Walker 72-70-73-75—290; Mellisa Reid 75-74-76-77—302), South Korea, Netherlands; 581 Australia; 583 Canada; 585 Italy; 585 Russian Federation; 590 Mexico; 591 Scotland (Heather MacRae 76-72-76-71—295; Jenna Wilson 77-69-76-78—300; Krystle Caithness 77-78-74-76—305); 592 Wales (Breanne Loucks 77-75-75-68—295; Tara Davies 78-73-78-74—303; Sahra Hassan 73-78-78-74—303), Czech Republic; 593 Belgium; 594 Ireland (Claire Coughlan 81-74-72-72—299; Martina Gillen 75- 75-74- 75—299; Tricia Mangan 77-79-83-83—322), Austria; 597 Chile; 602 Brazil; 603 Finland; 605 Argentina; 608 Norway; 610 Venezuela, Philippines; 623 Bermuda; 624 Iceland; 625 Switzerland; 636 Puerto Rico; 638 Guatemala; 643 Egypt; 657 Trinidad and Tobago; 670 Slovakia; 694 Zambia; 705 Croatia; 760 Gabon

---

Hosts beat defenders for the World Amateur Championship

Host nation South Africa withstood a late challenge from defending champions Sweden to win the 2006 Women's World Amateur Team Championship at Stellenbosch but only after a tie-break when both teams finished with a 10-under-par four-round team aggregate of 566. Sweden made up a four-stroke deficit during the final round, taking the lead for a short time, but were unable to stop South Africa from becoming the first victorious host nation since 1980 and claiming the Espirito Santo Trophy.

The two leading scores from each team of three count towards the team total each day and the tie-break was decided by the lowest non-counting score in the final round. These were equal and the result was determined by South Africa's lower non-counting score in the third round.

For South Africa, Ashleigh Simon and Kelli Shean each scored 74 on their final day, with Stacy Bregman on 75. Sweden's counting scores were a three-under-par 69 from Caroline Westrup and 75s by Anna Nordqvist and Sofie Andersson. Their final round total was 144. Sweden had hoped to become the first team to win consecutive championships since the USA in 1988 and 1990. The Swedes are the only country to finish in the top 10 in all 22 championships.

Colombia moved from tied for 11th into third place thanks to a six-under-par 66 from Carolina Llano, the lowest round of the day, and a 70 from Eileen Vargas. Their 136 total was the lowest final round team score in championship history. France finished fourth at 568; Germany and Japan tied for fifth at 569; New Zealand seventh at 570; Spain eighth at 572; the USA ninth at 574; and Chinese Taipei 10th at 576.

England tied for 11th place with Korea and Australia; Scotland finished in 19th place; Wales tied for 20th with the Czech Republic and Belgium; and Ireland tied for 23rd place with Austria. Although there is no official recognition, Sweden's Caroline Westrup recorded the lowest individual total of the championship at eight-under-par 2.

Individual:

1	C Westrup (SWE)	72-73-66-69—280
2	R Morita (JPN)	65-72-70-75—282
3	P-L Yu (THA)	66-73-71-73—283
	A Munoz (ESP)	74-72-68-69—283

European Seniors Ladies Team Championship 2006 *Royal Waterloo, Belgium*

1 France, 2 England, 3 Spain, 4 Italy, 5 Germany, 6 Sweden, 7 Switzerland, 8 Belgium, 9 Netherlands, 10 Ireland 11 Finland

Match-play First Flight results: France beat Italy 3–2; France beat England 3–2; England beat Spain 3–2; Spain beat Italy 3–2

Winning Team: Claudine Chartrier, Françoise Freiss, Cécilia Morgue D'Algue, Laurence Neuhaus, Anyta Remoleur, Marie-Christine Ubald-Bocquet

Individual: 1 Christine Quinn (ENG) 77-76; Ana Vilella (ESP) 77-76—153

European Club Cup 2006 *Royal GC du Hainaut, Belgium (2001–2003 La Boulie, France)*

2001	Spain (Jarama Race GC)
2002	Germany (Bergisch-Land GC)
2003	Germany (Bergisch-Land GC)

2004	Germany (St Leon Rot GC)
2005	RCF La Boulie (FRA)

2006

1	Italy (Asolo GC)	441 (Anna Rossi 69-71-72; Ilaria Cinel 77-79-73; Guilia Abram 90-90-87)
2	Germany (GC Berlin Wannsee)	445
3	Belgium (Royal Waterloo)	449

Other scores: 453 GC De Pan; 452 GC San Cugat; 457 GC Hilleroed; 460 GV Geneve; 464 RGC Marianske Lazne; 471 Estoril GC; 474 GC Keiler; 475 Arboretum GC; 507 GC Wien; Disqualified – Racing GC de France (disqualified because a member of the team used a mobile phone on the course)

Best individual score: Anna Rossi (BEL) 69-71-72—212 (won by 11 shots)

Women's Home Internationals

1948	England	R Lytham and St Annes	1974T	England/Scotland/	
1949	Scotland	Harlech		Ireland	Sandwich, Princes
1950	Scotland	Newcastle Co Down	1975	England	Newport
1951	Scotland	Broadstone	1976	England	Troon
1952	Scotland	Troon	1977	England	Cork
1953	England	Porthcawl	1978	England	Moortown
1954T	England/Scotland	Ganton, Scotland	1979T	Scotland/Ireland	Harlech
1955	England	Western Gailes	1980	Ireland	Cruden Bay
1956	Scotland	Sunningdale	1981	Scotland	Portmarnock
1957	Scotland	Troon	1982	England	Burnham and Barrow
1958	England	Hunstanton	1983	*Matches abandoned due to weather*	
1959	England	Hoylake	1984	England	Gullane
1960	England	Gullane	1985	England	Waterville
1961	Scotland	Portmarnock	1986	Ireland	Whittington Barracks
1962	Scotland	Porthcawl	1987	England	Ashburnham
1963	England	Formby	1988	Scotland	Kilmarnock (Barassie)
1964	England	Troon	1989	England	Westport
1965	England	Portrush	1990	Scotland	Hunstanton
1966	England	Woodhall Spa	1991	Scotland	Aberdovey
1967	England	Sunningdale	1992	England	Hamilton
1968	England	Porthcawl	1993	England	Dublin
1969T	England/Scotland	Western Gailes	1994	England	Huddersfield
1970	England	Killarney	1995	England	Wrexham
1971	England	Longniddry	1996	England	Longniddry
1972	England	R Lytham and St Annes	1997	England	L:ahinch
1973	England	Harlech	1998	England	Burnham & Berrow
			1999	Wales	Royal Dornoch

Women's Home Internationals *continued*

2000 *Royal St David's*

Ireland halved with Wales	4½ matches to 4½
England beat Scotland	6 matches to 3
Wales beat Scotland	8 matches to 1
England beat Ireland	8 matches to 1
Ireland beat Scotland	5 matches to 4
England beat Wales	5 matches to 4

Result: England 3; Wales 1½; Ireland 1½; Scotland 0

2001 *Carlow*

Ireland beat Wales	6 matches to 3
England beat Scotland	5½ matches to 3½
Wales halved with Scotland	4½ matches to 4½
England beat Ireland	5½ matches to 3½
England beat Wales	5 matches to 4
Ireland beat Scotland	5½ matches to 3½

Result: England 3; Ireland 2; Scotland & Wales ½

2002 *The Berkshire*

Ireland beat England	5 matches to 4
Scotland beat Wales	5 matches to 4
England beat Scotland	5½ matches to 3½
Wales beat England	5 matches to 4
England beat Wales	6½ matches to 2½
Scotland beat Ireland	6 matches to 3

Result: England 2; Scotland 2; Ireland 1; Wales 1

2003 *Cruden Bay*

Scotland halved with Ireland	4½ matches to 4½
England halved with Wales	4½ matches to 4½
Ireland beat Wales	5 matches to 4
England halved with Scotland	4½ matches to 4½
Ireland beat England	5 matches to 4
Scotland beat Wales	5½ matches to 3½

Result: Ireland 2½; Scotland 2; England 1; Wales ½

2004 *Royal Porthcawl*

England beat Wales	6½ matches to 2½
Ireland beat England	5½ matches to 3½
Engand beat Scotland	5 matches to 4
Wales beat Ireland	7 matches to 2
Ireland beat Scotland	7 matches to 1
Scotland halved with Wales	4 matches to 4

Result: Ireland 2; Wales 1½; England 1½; Scotland 1

2005 *Dundalk*

England beat Wales	6½ matches to 2½
Scotland beat Ireland	6½ matches to 2½
Wales beat Ireland	5½ matches to 3½
England beat Scotland	5 matches to 4
England beat Ireland	5½ matches to 3½
Scotland beat Wales	6 matches to 3

Result: England 3; Scotland 2; Wales 1; Ireland 0

2006 *Frilford Heath*

Ireland 3½, England 5½
Wales 5, Scotland 4
Scotland 6, England 3
Wales 4½, Ireland 4½
England 6, Wales 3
Ireland 6, Scotland 3

Result: 1 England 2 (14½); 2 Ireland 1½ (14); 3 Wales 1½ (13); 4 Scotland 1 (12½)

Winning Team: Rachel Bell (Ganton), Elizabeth Bennett (Brokenhurst Manor), Naomi Edwards (Ganton), Felicity Johnson (Harborne), Florentyna Parker (Royal Birkdale), Melissa Reid (Chevin), Kerry Smith (Waterlooville), Sophie Walker (Kenwick Park)

Senior Home Internationals 2006 *Hamilton*

2003	England; Ireland; Wales; Scotland	Whittington Heath
2004	England; Scotland; Wales; Ireland	Kilkeel
2005	England; Scotland, Wales, Ireland	Radyr

England beat Ireland	6 matches to 1	Wales beat Ireland	6 matches to 1
Scotland beat Wales	4½ matches to 2½	England beat Wales	4½ matches to 2½
England beat Scotland	5 matches to 2	Scotland beat Ireland	4½ matches to 2½

Result: 1 England 3 (15½); 2 Scotland 2 (11); 3 Wales 1 (11); 4 Ireland 0 (4½)

Winning team: Geraldine Bray (Littlestone), Carole Caldwell (Sunningdale), Susan Pickles (Lee-on-the-Solent), Christine Quinn (Hockley) Christine Stirling (Meon Valley), Christine Watson (Beaconsfield), Pat Wrightson (Huddersfield)

All-Africa Challenge (inaugurated 1992) 2006 *Lusaka*

1	Egypt	484 (Donia Scarello jr, Naela El Attar, Sophie Sallab)
2	South Africa	485 (count back) (Millie Zim, Tsebo Mokoena, Meriton Sandys jr)
3	Zambia	485 (Tara Allin, Hilda Edwards, Melissa Nawa jr)

Best Individual: 1 Naela Al Attar (EGY) 234; 2 Betty Mokoena (RSA) 240; 3 Melissa Nawa (ZAM) 242

Junior Winner: Melissa Nawa (ZAM)

Other scores: 4 Kenya 516; 5 Namibia 525; 6 Zimbabwe 529; 7 Swaziland 534; 8 Tanzania 541; 9 Botswana 556; 10 Ghana, Uganda, Côte d'Ivoire 561; 13 Gabon 578; 14 Malawi 589; 15 Togo 622; 16 Senegal 665; 17 Rwanda 895

England and Wales Ladies County Championship 2006 *Brancepeth Castle*

1908	Lancashire	1935	Essex	1964	Lancashire	1985	Surrey
1909	Surrey	1936	Surrey	1965	Staffordshire	1986	Glamorgan
1910	Cheshire	1937	Surrey	1966	Lancashire	1987	Lancashire
1911	Cheshire	1938	Lancashire	1967	Lancashire	1988	Surrey
1912	Cheshire	1947	Surrey	1968	Surrey	1989	Cheshire
1913	Surrey	1948	Yorkshire	1969	Lancashire	1990	Cheshire
1920	Middlesex	1949	Surrey	1970	Yorkshire	1991	Glamorgan
1921	Surrey	1950	Yorkshire	1971	Kent	1992	Hampshire
1922	Surrey	1951	Lancashire	1972	Kent	1993	Lancashire
1923	Surrey	1952	Lancashire	1973	Northumberland	1994	Staffordshire
1924	Surrey	1953	Surrey	1974	Surrey	1995	Hampshire
1925	Surrey	1954	Warwickshire	1975	Glamorgan	1996	Cheshire
1926	Surrey	1955	Surrey	1976	Staffordshire	1997	Surrey
1927	Yorkshire	1956	Kent	1977	Essex	1998	Yorkshire
1928	Cheshire	1957	Middlesex	1978	Glamorgan	1999	Yorkshire
1929	Yorkshire	1958	Lancashire	1979	Essex	2000	Yorkshire
1930	Surrey	1959	Middlesex	1980	Lancashire	2001	Yorkshire
1931	Middlesex	1960	Lancashire	1981	Glamorgan	2002	Lancashire
1932	Cheshire	1961	Middlesex	1982	Surrey	2003	Kent
1933	Yorkshire	1962	Staffordshire	1983	Surrey	2004	Yorkshire
1934	Surrey	1963	Warwickshire	1984	Surrey/Yorkshire	2005	Yorkshire

Yorkshire beat Cambs & Hunts	6½ matches to 2½
Gloucestershire beat Hertfordshire	8½ matches to ½
Cambs & Hunts tied with Hertfordshire	4½ matches to 4½
Gloucestershire tied with Yorkshire	4½ matches to 4½
Gloucestershire beat Cambs & Hunts	6 matches to 3
Yorkshire beat Hertfordshire	9 matches to 0

Result: I Yorkshire 2½ (20); 2 Gloucestershire 2½ (19); 3 Cambs & Hunts ½ (10); 4 Hertfordshire ½ (5)

Winning team: Rachel Bell (Ganton), Emma Duggleby (Malton & Norton), Nicola Dunn, Naomi Edwards (Ganton), Sara Garbutt (Ganton), Laura Harvey (Richmond), Laura Holmes (Hessle), Rachael Lomas (Hallowes)

Scottish Ladies County Championship 2006 *The Hirsel*

1992	Dunbartonshire & Argyll	1998	East Lothian	2002	Stirlingshire & Clackmannanshire
1993	East Lothian	1999	East Lothian		
1994	East Lothian	2000	Northern Counties	2003	Northern Counties
1995	Fife	2001	Stirlingshire & Clackmannanshire	2004	Northern Counties
1996	East Lothian			2005	Midlothian
1997	Dunbartonshire & Argyll				

Fife beat Renfrewshire	6½ matches to 2½	Renfrewshire beat Galloway	5½ matches to 3½
Perth & Kinross beat Galloway	6 matches to 3	Renfrewshire beat Perth & Kinross	5 matches to 4
Fife beat Perth & Kinross	6 matches to 3	Fife beat Galloway	7 matches to 2

Result: I Fife 3 (19½); 2 Renfrewshire 2 (13); 3 Perth & Kinross 1 (13); 4 Galloway 0 (8½)

Winning team: Lorna Bennett, Krystle Cathness, Jocelyn Carthew, Becky Copland, Louise Kenney, Fiona Lockhart, Katrina Milne, Elaine Moffat

Scottish Ladies Foursomes

1992	Haggs Castle	1997	Stirling	2002	Ladies Panmure, Barry
1993	North Berwick	1998	Prestonfield	2003	Drumpellier
1994	Turnberry	1999	Dunblane New	2004	Dunblane New
1995	Gullane	2000	Windyhill	2005	Stirling
1996	Hilton Park	2001	Stirling		

2006 *Cowglen*

I	Fiona Lockhart and Elaine Moffat (St Regulus)	77-73—150
2	Karen Marshall and Fiona Hunter (Baberton)	71-80—151

Welsh Ladies Team Championship

1992	Whitchurch	1997	St Pierre	2002	Abergele
1993	Pennard	1998	Wrexham	2003	Pennard
1994	St Pierre	1999	Pennard	2004	Rhuddlan
1995	R. St Davids	2000	Pennard	2005	St Pierre
1996	R. St Davids	2001	Whitchurch		

2006 *Wrexham*

Semi-Finals:
Whitchurch beat Cradoc
Llandudno (Maesdu) beat Rhuddlan

Final:
Llandudno (Maesdu) beat Whitchurch

Winning team: Janet Barrington, Amy Boulden, Hayley Boulden, Kim Boulden, Nia Carrington-Jones, Jane Hallows

---

Asia-Pacific Women's Team Championship: Queen Sirikit Cup 2006 *Royal Adelaide*
(inaugurated 1979)

1	449	Chinese Taipei* (Su-Peng Yao (captain), Ya-Ni Tseng, Yu-Ling Hsieh, Pei-Lin Yu)
2	449	New Zealand (Gaylene Eyre (captain), Sharon Ahn, Natasha Krishna, Sarah Nicholson)
3	455	Korea (Mi Jung Hur, He Yong Choi, So Yeon Ryu)

Chinese Taipei won at the first extra hole

Other scores: 4 Australia 462; 5 Thailand 467; 6 Japan 470; 7 China 473; 8 Malaysia 479; 9 India 486; 10 Philippines, Singapore 497; 12 HK–China 504; 13 Sri Lanka 506

Women's Foursomes Events

London Ladies Foursomes

1992	Chelmsford	1997	The Berkshire	2002	Porter's Park
1993	Knebworth	1998	The Berkshire	2003	Chelmsford
1994	Knebworth	1999	The Berkshire	2004	Worplesdon
1995	The Berkshire	2000	Worplesdon	2005	Chelmsford
1996	The Berkshire	2001	Porter's Park		

2006 *Grim's Dyke*

Final: Cowdray Park (Hannah Ralph & Debbie Cheasley) beat Brocket Hall (Helen Hayward & Charlie Douglas) 5 and 4

Mothers and Daughters Foursomes

1992	Mrs P Carrick and Mrs A Uzielli	1998	Mrs H Joyce and Miss C Joyce
1993	Mrs P Carrick and Mrs A Uzielli	1999	Mrs E Boatman and Miss A Boatman
1994	Mrs P Carrick and Mrs A Uzielli	2000	Lady Bonallack and Mrs G Beasley
1995T	Mrs P Carrick and Mrs A Uzielli	2001	Mrs and Miss Gay
	Mrs P Huntley and Miss J Huntley	2002	Mrs J Thornhill and Mrs C Weeks
1996T	Mrs A Uzielli and Miss C Uzielli	2003	A Laughland and R Jenner
	Mrs E Boatman and Miss A Boatman	2004	E Proven and S Saggers tied with W and K Laud
	Mrs S Lines and Miss K Lines	2005	L and A Boatman
1997	Mrs S Lines and Miss K Lines		

2006 *Royal Mid-Surrey*

1	Liz Boatman (Royal Worlington) & Alex Howe (Royal County Down)	74-39—113
2	Ann & Alexandra Peters (Notts Ladies)	78-38—116
3	Elsie Provan & Sarah Saggers (East Herts)	74-43—117

Other Women's Amateur Tournaments

Lady Astor Salver (inaugurated 1951) *always at The Berkshire*

1951	Jeanne Bisgood	1965	Marley Spearman	1979	Julia Greenhalgh	1993	S Lambert
1952	Jeanne Bisgood	1966	Angela Bonallack	1980	Jane Lock	1994	S Lambert
1953	Jeanne Bisgood	1967	Mary Everard	1981	Angela Uzielli	1995	J Oliver
1954	Jean Donald	1968	Mary Everard	1982	*Abandoned*	1996	S Gallagher
1955	Elizabeth Price	1969	Julia Greenhalgh	1983	Linda Denison-	1997	J Lamb
1956T	J Barton,	1970	B Whitehead		Pender Bayman	1998	R Morgan
	Elizabeth Price	1971	Angela Uzielli	1984	Linda Bayman	1999	*Not played*
1957	Angela Ward	1972	Jill Thornhill	1985	Helen Wadsworth	2000T	C Court,
1958	Angela Bonallack	1973T	Linda Denison-	1986	Caroline Pierce		K Taylor
	nee Ward		Pender, Angela	1987	Vicki Thomas	2001	E Pilgrim
1959	Elizabeth Price		Uzielli	1988	Jill Thornhill	2002	*Abandoned – rain*
1960	Angela Bonallack	1974	Cathy Barclay	1989	Sarah Sutton	2003	K Smith
1961	Angela Bonallack	1975	Jill Thornhill	1990T	Joanne Morley,	2004	F Johnston
1962	Ruth Porter	1976	Heather Clifford		Julie Wade	2005	C Court
1963	Ruth Porter	1977	Angela Uzielli	1991	EJ Smith		
1964	Marley Spearman	1978	Mary Everard	1992	Lisa Walton		

1	Emma Duggleby (Malton & Norton)	71-72—143
2	Tracey Boyes (Meon Valley)	76-70—146
	Kate Combes (AUS)	73-73—146
	Lucy Gould (Bargoed)	71-75—146
	Kerry Smith (Waterlooville)	74-72—146

Bridget Jackson Bowl (inaugurated 1982) *always at Handsworth*

1982	Julie Brown (Leek)	1991	Fiona Edmund (Frinton-on-	1998	Claire Dowling (Copt Heath)
1983	Julie Brown (Leek)		Sea)	1999	Shelley McKevitt (Reading)
1984	Trish Johnson (Pyle & Kenfig)	1992	Fiona Brown (Heswall)	2000	Rebecca Hudson (Wheatley)
1985	Trish Johnson (Pyle & Kenfig)	1993	Simone Morgan (Hearsall)	2001	Laura Wright (Stanton-on-the-
1986	Julia Hill (Hazel Grove)	1994	Kirsty Speak (Clitheroe)		Wolds)
1987	Vicki Thomas (Pennard)	1995	Karen Stupples (Royal Cinque	2002	Claire Dowling (Copt Heath)
1988	Vicki Thomas (Pennard)		Ports)	2003	Shelley McKevitt (Reading)
1989	Helen Dobson (Seacroft)	1996	Rebecca Hudson (Wheatley)	2004	Felicity Johnston (Harborne)
1990	Susan Elliott (Henbury)	1997	Kate MacIntosh (AUS)	2005	Anna Scott (Consett)

1	Sophie Stubbs (Shifnal)	70-72—142
2	Joanne Hodge (Knowle)	75-68—143
	Emma Lyons (West Surrey)	72-71—143

Critchley Salver (inaugurated 1982) *always at Sunningdale*

1982	H Reid	1989	L Fletcher	1995	K Tebbet	2001	E Duggleby
1983	K Douglas	1990	S Hourihane	1996	S Gallagher	2002	E Pilgrim
1984	L Bayman	1991	NL Buxton	1997	L Waters	2003	A Highgate
1985	L Bayman	1992	C Caldwell	1998	L Waters	2004	N Cruse
1986	W Wooldridge	1993	CG Watson	1999	LC Tupholme	2005	K Smith
1987	S Moorcraft	1994	S Lambert	2000	C Court		
1988	L Bayman		K Speak				
	J Wade						

1	Felicity Johnson (Harborne)	73-71—144
2	Elizabeth Bennett (Brokenhurst Manor)	71-75—146
	Emma Duggleby (Malton & Norton)	76-70—146
	Kerry Smith (Waterlooville)	72-74—146

Hampshire Rose (inaugurated 1973) *always at North Hants*

1973	Carole Redford	1980	Beverley New	1989	Alison MacDonald	1998	C Court
1974	Pru Riddiford	1981	Jillian Nicolson	1990	S Keogh	1999	C Court
1975	Vanessa Marvin	1982	Jill Thornhill	1991	K Egford	2000	K Fisher
1976T	Heather Clifford,	1983	J Pool	1992	Angela Uzielli	2001	K Smith
	Wendy Pithers	1984	Carole Redford	1993	C Hourihane	2002	K Smith
1977	Julia Greenhalgh		Caldwell	1994T	K Shepherd,	2003	F More
1978T	Heather Clifford	1985	Angela Uzielli		K Egford	2004	E Sheffield
	Glyn-Jones,	1986	Claire Hourihane	1995	J Oliver	2005	H Burke
	Vanessa Marvin	1987	Jill Thornhill	1996	K Stupples		
1979	Carol Larkin	1988	Jill Thornhill	1997	S Sanderson		

1	Claire Aitken (Mid-Kent)	65-70—135
2	Hannah Barwood (Knowle)	72-75—147
	Charlie Douglass (Brocket Hall)	77-70—147
	Danielle Montgomery (Lambourne)	75-72—147

Liphook Scratch Cup (inaugurated 1992) *always at Liphook*

1992T	T Kernan,	1995	K Shepherd	1999	R Prout	2003	S McKEvitt
	K Shepherd	1996	K Shepherd	2000	K Smith	2004	M Allen
1993	K Egford	1997	E Weeks	2001	N Timmins	2005	E Bennett/F Smith
1994	S Sharpe	1998	K Knowles	2002	F More		

1	Henrietta Brockway (Yeovil)	72-65—137[†]
2	Kerry Smith (Waterlooville)	70-71—141
3	Elizabeth Bennett (Brokenhurst Manor)	74-68—142

[†]Henrietta Brockway's second round 65 is a record

Roehampton Gold Cup (inaugurated 1926) *always at Roehampton*

(This event has included women professionals since 1982 and has been an Open event since 1987)

1926	Mrs WM McNair	1954	Isabella Bromley	1974	Lyn Harrold	1989T	Catriona Lambert,
1927	Molly Gourlay		Davenport	1975T	Wendy Pithers,		Cathy Panton
1928	Cecil Leitch	1955	Louisa Abrahams		Carole Redford	1990	Kathryn Imrie
1929	I Doxford	1956	Shirley Allom	1976T	Ann Irvin,	1991	K Hurley
1930	Enid Wilson	1957	Mary Roberts		Vanessa Marvin	1992	Kathryn Marshall
1931	V Lamb	1958	Patricia Moore	1977	Angela Uzielli	1993	Beverley New
1932	Mrs A Gold	1959	Mavis G lidewell	1978T	Carole Redford	1994	C Hall
1933	A Ramsden	1960	Elizabeth Price		Caldwell,	1995	S Gallagher
1934	J Hamilton	1961	Louisa Abrahams		Belle Robertson	1996T	Joanne Morley,
1935	Pam Barton	1962	Louisa Abrahams	1979	Belle Robertson		J Soulsby
1936	B Newell	1963	Ruth Porter	1980	Angela Bonallack	1997T	J Forbes, J Oliver
1937	Pam Barton	1964	RC Archer	1981	Belle Robertson	1998T	K Lunn, J Head
1938	Pam Barton	1965	Marley Spearman	1982	Belle Robertson	1999	K Taylor
1939	Pam Barton	1966	Gwen Brandon	1983T	Beverley New,	2000	S Forster
1940–47	Not played	1967	Ann Irvin		Vicki Thomas	2001	T Loveys
1948	Maureen Ruttle	1968	Ann Irvin	1984	Beverley New	2002	F More
1949	Frances Stephens	1969	Ann Irvin	1985	Vicki Thomas	2003	T Loveys
1950	Maureen Ruttle	1970	Mary Everard	1986T	Katherine	2004	A Coffey
	Garrett	1971	Beverly Huke		Harridge,	2005	S Heath
1951	Jeanne Bisgood	1972	Ann Irvin		Patricia Johnson		
1952	Jeanne Bisgood	1973T	Ann Irvin,	1987	Diane Barnard		
1953	Jeanne Bisgood		Carole Redford	1988	Alison Johns		

1	Joanne Oliver (Quindell)	77-70—147 } tied
	Tracy Loveys (Broadstone)	74-73—147 }
3	Marie Allen (Brookman's Park)	78-70—148
	Vanessa Bell (Ipswich)	75-73—148
	Emma Duggleby (Malton & Norton)	73-75—148 (leading amateur)

St Rule Trophy (inaugurated 1984) *always at St Andrews*

1984	P Hammel (USA)	149	1992	M Wright	222	2000	V Laing*	153 (36)
1985	K Imrie	151	1993	C Lambert	215	2001	A Coffey	221
1986	T Hammond	153	1994	C Matthew	217	2002	H Stirling	218
1987	J Morley	153	1995	M Hjörth	220	2003	K Borjeskog	217
1988	C Middleton	152	1996	A Laing	227	2004	L Stahle (SWE)	141
1989	C Middleton	232	1997	K Rostron	217	2005	N Edwards	225
1990	A Sörenstam	228	1998	N Clau†	154 (36)			
1991	A Rose	237	1999	L Nicholson	227			

† At 16 years, the youngest ever winner

1	Krystle Caithness (St Regulus)	71-72-73—216
2	Katherina Schallenberg (GER)	71-74-72—217
3	Tricia Mangan (Ennis)	72-74-74—220

Sherry Cup (Copa de Jerez) *always at Sotogrande, Cadiz, Spain*

1991	Caterina Quintarelli	1996	Maria Hjörth	2001	Carmen Alonso Fuentes
1992	Estafania Knuth	1997	Marieke Zelsman	2002	Kathryn Evans
1993	Ana F Johansson	1998	Nicole Stillia	2003	Bettina Hauert
1994	Ada O'Sullivan	1999	Martina Eberl	2004	Tania Elosegui Mayor
1995	Maria Hjörth	2000	Martina Eberl	2005	S Endstrasser

1	Katharina Schallenberg (GER)*	72-74-71-72—289
2	Sophie Walker (ENG)	69-71-73-76—289
3	Breanne Loucks (WAL)	73-72-75-74—294

Schallenberg beat Walker at second extra hole

Team event: 1 Germany (Stephanie Doering, Carolin Loehr, Katharina Schallenberg) 589; 2 England 594; 3 Italy 597

11 countries took part.

The Leveret *always at Formby*

1	Corisande Lee (West Lancashire)*	70-72—142
2	Hannah Barwood (Knowle)	68-74—142
3	Holly Aitchison (The Bedfordshire)	73-72—145
	Rachel Connor (Manchester)	73-72—145

Cori Lee tied with Hannah Barwood. Lee won on a count back

Tenby Ladies *always at Tenby*

1	Sian James (Bristol & Clifton)	71-73—144
2	Sahra Hassan (Vale of Glamorgan)	72-75—147
3	Tara Davies (Holyhead)	80-69—149

Pleasington Putter *always at Pleasington*

1	Kate Combes (AUS)	70-71—141 (record)
2	Laura Eastwood (Yelverton)	76-73—149
3	Stephanie Evans (Vale of Llangollen)	76-75—151
	Sarah-Jane Eaves (Cosby)	76-75—151
	Rachel Lomas (Hallowes)	75-76—151

Royal Birkdale Scratch Trophy *always at Royal Birkdale*

1	Jenna Wilson (Strathaven)	74-72—146
2	Corisande Lee (West Lancashire)	73-74—147
3	Sophie Walker (Kenwick Park)	75-73—148

Wentworth Scratch Trophy *always at Wentworth*
Cancelled

Munross Trophy (inaugurated 1986) *always at Montrose*

1986	Elaine Farquharson (Deeside)	144	1992	Catriona Lambert (Stirling U)	137	1999	Anne Laing (Edinburgh U)	144
1987	Shirley Lawson (Stirling U)	145	1993	Janice Moodie (Windyhill)	142	2000	Lynn Kenny (Stirling U)*	150
1988	Catriona Lambert (Stirling U)	141	1994	Lesley Nicholson (Haddington)	149	2001	Alison Davidson (Stirling)	142
1989	Catriona Lambert (Stirling U)	146	1995	Lesley Nicholson (Haddington)	145	2002	Heather MacRae (Dunblane New)	147
1990	Catriona Lambert (North Berwick)	141	1996	Susan Simpson (Kirriemuir)	148	2003	Anne Laing (Vale of Leven)	138
1991	Morag Wright (Dumfries & County)*	141	1997	Vikki Laing (Musselburgh)	146	2004	Lisa Jean (AUS)	140
			1998	Elaine Farquharson-Black (Deeside)	161	2005	Jenna Wilson (Strathaven)	141

2006

1	Jenna Wilson (Strathaven)	69-69—138
2	Jocelyn Carthew (Ladybank)	75-68—143
	Jane Turner (Mortonhall)	73-70—143
	Roseanne Niven (Crieff)	72-71—143
	Claire MacDonald (Gullane Ladies)	72-71—143

Mackie Bowl *always at Gullane No 1*

1	Jenna Wilson (Strathaven)	71-71—142
2	Jocelyn Carthew (Ladybank)	74-71—145
3	Jane Turner (Mortonhall)	70-75—145

Riccarton Rose Bowl *always at Hamilton*

1	Jenna Wilson (Strathaven)	68-68—136
2	Claire Hargan (Mortonhall)	70-71—141
3	Louise Kenny (Pitreavie)	71-71—142
	Fiona Norris (Hamilton)	68-74—142

Mary McCallay Trophy *always at Dumfries & Galloway*

1	Emily Ogilvie (Auchterarder)	72-69—141
2	Jenna Wilson (Strathaven)	69-73—142
3	Jocelyn Carthew (Ladybank)	72-72—144

Ness Open *always at Inverness*

1	Laura Murray (Alford)	72-77—149
2	Jane Turner (Mortonhall)	73-80—153
3	Laura Walker (Nairn Dunbar)	80-77—157

Women's Regional Amateur Championships

England

Bedfordshire Ladies

1997	J Faris	2002	B Quinn
1998	S Cormack	2003	H Carr
1999	E Bruce	2004	H Aitchison
2000	C Hoskin	2005	L Collin
2001	P Gale	2006	F Dalton

Berkshire Ladies

1997	L Meredith	2002	L Webb
1998	S Sanderson	2003	L Webb
1999	L Webb	2004	L Webb
2000	L Webb	2005	L Webb
2001	E Cooper	2006	J Florey

Buckinghamshire Ladies

1997	C Watson	2002	C Watson
1998	C Watson	2003	K Platt
1999	C Watson	2004	C Watson
2000	C Watson	2005	L King
2001	S Mace	2006	C Leathers

Cambridgeshire and Huntingdonshire Ladies

1997	J Walter	2002	J Walter
1998	J Walter	2003	S Attwood
1999	R Farrow	2004	J Gregg
2000	J Walter	2005	J Gregg
2001	P Parker	2006	H Fitzgerald

Cheshire Ladies

1997	E Ratcliffe	2002	S Beardsall
1998	E Ratcliffe	2003	S Beardsall
1999	R Adby	2004	N Podmore
2000	O Briggs	2005	N Podmore
2001	R Adby	2006	N Podmore

Cornwall Ladies

1997	L Simpson	2002	S Sanderson
1998	G Dowling	2003	J Teague
1999	G Dowling	2004	L Bird
2000	G Dowling	2005	J Teague
2001	S Sanderson	2006	R Phillips

Cumbria Ladies

1997	J Blaydes	2002	E Woodhouse
1998	A Wood	2003	J Blaydes
1999	J Blaydes	2004	A Wood
2000	J Viles	2005	C Brown
2001	J Blades	2006	R Edwards

Derbyshire Ladies

1997	L Walters	2002	R Wood
1998	L Shaw	2003	M Reid
1999	L Walters	2004	E Griggs
2000	R Wood	2005	M Reid
2001	L Shaw	2006	C Russell

Devon Ladies

1997	J Roberts	2002	E Frayn
1998	C Copping	2003	L Eastwood
1999	K Clarke	2004	L Eastwood
2000	K Clarke	2005	E Frain
2001	K Clarke	2006	G Whitehead

Dorset Ladies

1997	A Monk	2002	C Jones
1998	A Monk	2003	H Brockway
1999	S Phillips	2004	K-A Haskell
2000	J Topp	2005	J Terry
2001	C Jones	2006	N Stone

Durham Ladies

1997	K Lee	2002	D Roseberry
1998	P Dobson	2003	F Sanderson
1999	L Keers	2004	P Simpson
2000	P Simpson	2005	F Sanderson
2001	A Dobson	2006	L Richardson

Essex Ladies

1997	S Barber	2002	J Dartford
1998	M Williams	2003	F Smith
1999	E Gibson	2004	C Rogers
2000	S Smith	2005	H Moul
2001	J Dartford	2006	T Wilson

Gloucestershire Ladies

1997	C Lipscombe	2002	Z Lennox
1998	C Lipscombe	2003	R Rowntree
1999	N Lumb	2004	J Hodge
2000	L Occleshaw	2005	L Carruthers
2001	C Lipscombe	2006	J Hodge

Hampshire Ladies

1997	H Wheeler	2002	K Smith
1998	E Weekes	2003	K Smith
1999	K Taylor	2004	S White
2000	K Taylor	2005	E Bennett
2001	N Booth	2006	K Smith

Hertfordshire Ladies

1997	K Evans	2002	K Hutcherson
1998	M Allen	2003	M Allen
1999	H Skinner	2004	A Waller
2000	K Evans	2005	T Jeary
2001	S Matthews	2006	L Williams

Kent Ladies

1997	S Butchers	2002	D Masters
1998	K Stupples	2003	N Timmins
1999	N Timmins	2004	H Batt
2000	D Masters	2005	A Wheble
2001	N Timmins	2006	C Aitken

Lancashire Ladies

1997	G Nutter	2002	K Fisher
1998	A Murray	2003	A Peacock
1999	K Fisher	2004	N Evans
2000	C Blackshaw	2005	C Lee
2001	K Fisher	2006	F Parker

Leicestershire and Rutland Ladies

1997	J Morris	2002	R Rowlands
1998	C Gay	2003	J Morris
1999	J Morris	2004	S-J Eaves
2000	H Lowe	2005	C Gay
2001	C Gay	2006	C Gay

Lincolnshire Ladies

1997	A Thompson	2002	S Walker
1998	M Willerton	2003	S Walker
1999	S Hunter	2004	E Taylor
2000	S Walker	2005	P West
2001	N Chantry	2006	E Taylor

Middlesex Ladies

1997	J Barnett	2002	P Ranchard
1998	J Sadler	2003	T Watters
1999	P Costello	2004	L Housman
2000	D McCormack	2005	B McCormack
2001	C Irons	2006	L Tarn

Midland Division (England)

1997	R Bailey	2002	S Walker
1998	N Lawrenson	2003	M Reid
1999	S Pidgeon	2004	S Hinton
2000	S Walker	2005	K Holford
2001	K Hanwell	2006	S Birks

Norfolk Ladies

1997	T Williamson	2002	J Wilkerson
1998	T Williamson	2003	T Williamson
1999	R Shubrook	2004	J Ashmore
2000	J Wilkerson	2005	K Young
2001	J Wilkerson	2006	K Young

Northamptonshire Ladies

1997	S Carter	2002	K Hanwell
1998	C Gibbs	2003	K Jennings
1999	S Turbayne	2004	C Gibbs
2000	C Gibbs	2005	R Youngman
2001	S Carter	2006	K Hanwell

Northern Division (England)

1997	G Nutter	2002	N Edwards
1998	R Lomas	2003	C Lee
1999	C Ritson	2004	J Ross
2000	L Mackay	2005	C Roberts
2001	N Evans	2006	J Ewart

Northumberland Ladies

1997	C Hall	2002	C Hall
1998	C Hall	2003	K McKenna
1999	J Ross	2004	J Ross
2000	J Ross	2005	J Ross
2001	J Ross	2006	A Storey

Nottinghamshire Ladies

1997	J Collingham	2002	L Slack
1998	J Collingham	2003	J Doleman
1999	L Wright	2004	J Collingham
2000	L Wright	2005	A Peters
2001	*Event cancelled*	2006	E Sheffield

Oxfordshire Ladies

1997	L King	2002	J de Vere Hunt
1998	N Woolford	2003	J Corkish
1999	K Humphris	2004	J Corkish
2000	N Woolford	2005	G Porter
2001	N Woolford	2006	S Round

Shropshire Ladies

1997	S Heath	2002	S Heath
1998	L Archer	2003	S Hinton
1999	S Heath	2004	J Frooms
2000	L Archer	2005	L Warrilow
2001	S Heath	2006	B Smith

Somerset Ladies

1997	L Wixon	2002	K Walls
1998	G Pritchard	2003	K Walls
1999	V McFarlane	2004	R Dowell
2000	A Pitt	2005	B New
2001	B New	2006	K Walls

South-Eastern Division (England)

1997	L Evans	2002	R Prout
1998	A Waller	2003	N Booth
1999	K Knowles	2004	K Smith
2000	A Waller	2005	E Lyons
2001	K Smith	2006	S Tyson

South-Western Division (England)

1997	E Pilgrim	2002	K Walls
1998	C Lipscombe	2003	L Eastwood
1999	J Clingan	2004	H Barwood
2000	E Pilgrim	2005	E Taylor
2001	C Lipsombe	2006	C Ellis

Staffordshire Ladies

1997	K Edwards	2002	S Spenser
1998	K Edwards	2003	D Warren
1999	C Champion	2004	K Holford
2000	J Peacock	2005	K Holford
2001	R Bolas	2006	J Rhodes

Suffolk Ladies

1997	L Wright	2002	A Boatman
1998	J Hockley	2003	H Rees
1999	A Boatman	2004	H Rees
2000	L Steadman	2005	H Rees
2001	A Boatman	2006	S Luckman

Surrey Ladies

1997	J Thornhill	2002	R Prout
1998	K Burton	2003	M Bruck
1999	R Prout	2004	L McGowan
2000	K Knowles	2005	A Coffey
2001	L McGowan	2006	A Coffey

Sussex Ladies

1997	C Court	2002	A Greenfield
1998	J Galway	2003	K Sykes
1999	P Carver	2004	J Summer
2000	C Court	2005	H Ralph
2001	C Court	2006	S Rodger

Warwickshire Ladies

1997	C Dowling	2002	F Johnson
1998	C Dowling	2003	H Coles
1999	C Dowling	2004	C Dowling
2000	T Atkin	2005	T Atkin
2001	C Dowling	2006	F Johnson

Wiltshire Ladies

1997	J Lamb	2002	G Loughrey
1998	W Martin	2003	P Abbott
1999	J Wheaton	2004	E Brown
2000	J Wheaton	2005	C Boulton
2001	G Loughrey	2006	J Long

Worcestershire Ladies

1997	N Lawrenson	2002	L Day
1998	N Lawrenson	2003	W Bill
1999	S Haslam	2004	S Cranton
2000	S Nicklin	2005	K Greenfield
2001	K Greenfield	2006	S Cranton

Yorkshire Ladies

1997	R Hudson	2002	E Duggleby
1998	R Hudson	2003	A Keighley
1999	R Hudson	2004	N Edwards
2000	E Duggleby	2005	R Bell
2001	A Keighley	2006	R Bell

Ireland

Munster Ladies

2003	T Mangan	2005	H Nolan
2004	S O'Sullivan	2006	M Riordan

Ulster Open Ladies

2003	H Jones	2005	G Hegarty
2004	H Jones	2006	N Quigg

Connacht Ladies

2003	D Judge	2005	C Tucker
2004	C Tucker	2006	S Meadow

Leinster Ladies

2003	M Morrin	2005	M Dunne
2004	M Morrin	2006	M Dunne

Midland Ladies

2003	K Delaney	2005	K Delaney
2004	R Cassidy	2006	S Meadow

Scotland

Aberdeenshire Ladies

1997	K Moggach	2002	S Wood
1998	L Urquhart	2003	J Henderson
1999	L Urquhart	2004	SD Wilson
2000	S Wood	2005	J Henderson
2001	S Wood	2006	K Thomson

Angus Ladies

1997	S Raitt	2002	D Dewar
1998	L Fenton	2003	D Carcary
1999	L Fenton	2004	L Fotheringham
2000	A Ramsay	2005	M Summers
2001	K Sutherland	2006	J Tough

Ayrshire Ladies

1997	A Gemmill	2002	S Lambie
1998	S Lambie	2003	L Moffat
1999	S Lambie	2004	A Glennie
2000	R Kennedy	2005	L Hendry
2001	L Keohone	2006	L Hendry

Border Counties Ladies

1997	J Anderson	2002	J Anderson
1998	A Hunter	2003	M Pow
1999	J Anderson	2004	E Fairnie
2000	M Pow	2005	E Fairnie
2001	M Pow	2006	J Anderson

Dumfriesshire Ladies

1997	L Wells	2002	F Macgregor
1998	D MacDonald	2003	D MacDonald
1999	L Wells	2004	F MacGregor
2000	L Wells	2005	D McDonald
2001	K Wells	2006	F McGregor

Dunbartonshire and Argyll Ladies

1997	K Burns	2002	C McNeil
1998	A Laing	2003	S Bishop
1999	V Melvin	2004	S Bishop
2000	V Melvin	2005	S Bishop
2001	A Laing	2006	K Walker

East Lothian Ladies

1997	S McMaster	2002	S McMaster
1998	S McEwan	2003	J Smith
1999	L Nicholson	2004	M Thomson
2000	L Nicholson	2005	K Brotherton
2001	J Smith	2006	F Prior

Eastern Division Ladies (Scotland)

1997	S Grant	2002	H Stirling
1998	F Lockhart	2003	J Carthew
1999	L Kenny	2004	E Moffat
2000	H Stirling	2005	F Lockhart
2001	H Stirling	2006	C Hargan

Fife County Ladies

1997	J Hall	2002	S Millar
1998	K Milne	2003	L Bennett
1999	L Fury	2004	K Milne
2000	E Moffat	2005	F Lockhart
2001	L Kenney	2006	E Moffat

Galloway Ladies

1997	S McMurtrie	2002	S McMurtrie
1998	S McMurtrie	2003	S McMurtrie
1999	S Booth	2004	P McGill
2000	S McMurtrie	2005	S McMurtrie
2001	S McMurtrie	2006	A Shamash

Lanarkshire Ladies County

1997	L Lloyd	2002	C Queen
1998	F Prior	2003	M Hughes
1999	F Prior	2004	M Hughes
2000	A Bell	2005	J Wilson
2001	C Queen	2006	J Wilson

Midlothian Ladies

1997	P Silver	2002	B Murphy
1998	V Laing	2003	C Hargan
1999	C Williamson	2004	C Hargan
2000	B Murphy	2005	C Hargan
2001	F Hunter	2006	C Hargan

Northern Counties (Scotland) Ladies

1997	E Vass	2002	L McKinnon
1998	L Vass	2003	M Smith
1999	L Mackay	2004	L McKinnon
2000	L Mackay	2005	K MacDonald
2001	C Gruber	2006	K MacDonald

Northern Division Ladies (Scotland)

1997	C Hunter	2002	L Devenish
1998	J Tough	2003	A Scott
1999	L McLardy	2004	A Bushby
2000	J Yellowlees	2005	M Thomson
2001	S Wood	2006	M Thomson

Perth and Kinross Ladies

1997	N Harding	2002	D Butchart
1998	J Yellowlees	2003	N Harding
1999	A Murray	2004	R Niven
2000	C Meir	2005	C Booth
2001	J Yellowlees	2006	J Milne

Renfrewshire County Ladies

1997	L Robertson	2002	S Harman
1998	K Fitzgerald	2003	C-M Carlton
1999	D Jackson	2004	K Fitzgerald
2000	D Jackson	2005	D Jackson
2001	D Jackson	2006	M Briggs

Southern Division Ladies (Scotland)

1997	J Anderson	2002	L Fleming
1998	D MacDonald	2003	L Wells
1999	J Anderson	2004	A Shamash
2000	M Pow	2005	S McMurtrie
2001	A Shamash	2006	I Craigie

Stirling and Clackmannan County Ladies

1997	S Grant	2002	H Stirling
1998	L Kenny	2003	L Kenny
1999	H Stirling	2004	L Kenny
2000	H Stirling	2005	A Davidson
2001	L Kenny	2006	L Robertson

Western Division Ladies (Scotland)

1997	C Malcolm	2002	A Laing
1998	A Laing	2003	A Laing
1999	A Laing	2004	C Queen
2000	A Laing	2005	C Queen
2001	C Hargan	2006	C-M Carlton

Wales

Caernarfonshire and Anglesey Ladies

1997	F Vaughan-Thomas	2002	K Evans
1998	F Vaughan-Thomas	2003	F Vaughan-Thomas
1999	K Evans	2004	F Vaughan-Thomas
2000	L Davies	2005	T Davies
2001	L Davies	2006	T Davies

Denbighshire and Flintshire Ladies

1997	R Brewerton	2002	Cancelled
1998	B Jones	2003	S Mountford
1999	R Brewerton	2004	J Nicols
2000	S Mountford	2005	J Nicolson
2001	J Nicolson	2006	J Nicolson

Glamorgan County Ladies

1997	V Thomas	2002	A Highgate
1998	P Chugg	2003	A Highgate
1999	K Phillips	2004	L Hall
2000	V Thomas	2005	L Weatherill
2001	A Highgate	2006	B Harries

Mid-Wales Ladies

1997	K Humphries	2003	G Badham
1998	A Hubbard	2004	Sherrie Gore
1999	S Hughes		[Hughes]
2000	J Dyer	2005	R Vaughan-Jones
2001	J Dyer	2006	A Hubbard
2002	D Tuffnell		

Monmouthshire Ladies

1997	S O'Sullivan	2002	E Pilgrim
1998	S O'Sullivan	2003	L Diggle
1999	R Morgan	2004	L Diggle
2000	J Pritchard	2005	L Diggle
2001	L Diggle	2006	C Cole

Overseas Amateur Championships

106th United States Women's Amateur Championship (inaugurated 1895)

Year	Winner	Runner-up	Venue	Margin
1895	CS Brown	N Sargent	Meadowbrook, NY	132
Changed to match play				
1896	B Hoyt	A Tunure	Morristown, NJ	2 and 1
1897	B Hoyt	N Sargent	Essex County, MA	5 and 4
1898	B Hoyt	M Wetmore	Ardsley, NY	5 and 3
1899	R Underhill	M Fox	Philadelphia, PA	2 and 1
1900	FC Griscom	M Curtis	Shinnecock Hills, NY	6 and 5
1901	G Hecker	L Herron	Baltusrol, NJ	5 and 3
1902	G Hecker	LA Wells	Brookline, MA	4 and 3
1903	B Anthony	JA Carpenter	Wheaton, IL	7 and 6
1904	GM Bishop	EF Sanford	Merion, PA	5 and 3
1905	P Mackay	M Curtis	Morris County, NJ	1 hole
1906	HS Curtis	MB Adams	West Newton, MA	2 and 1
1907	M Curtis	HS Curtis	Blue Island, IL	7 and 6
1908	KC Harley	TH Polhemus	Chevy Chase, MD	6 and 5
1909	D Campbell	N Barlow	Merion, PA	3 and 2
1910	D Campbell	GM Martin	Homewood, IL	2 and 1
1911	M Curtis	LB Hyde	Baltusrol, NJ	5 and 4
1912	M Curtis	N Barlow	Essex County, MA	3 and 2
1913	G Ravenscroft	M Hollins	Wilmington, DE	2 holes
1914	KC Harley	EV Rosenthal	Nassau, NY	1 hole
1915	F Vanderbeck	M Gavin (ENG)	Onwentsia, IL	3 and 2
1916	A Stirling	M Caverly	Belmont Springs, MA	2 and 1
1917–1918 *Not played*				
1919	A Stirling	M Gavin (ENG)	Shawnee, PA	6 and 5
1920	A Stirling	D Campbell Hurd	Cleveland, OH	5 and 4
1921	M Hollins	A Stirling	Deal, NJ	5 and 4
1922	G Collett	M Gavin (ENG)	Greenbrier, WV	5 and 4
1923	E Cummings	A Stirling	Westchester, NY	3 and 2
1924	D Campbell Hurd	MK Browne	Nyatt, RI	7 and 6
1925	G Collett	A Stirling Fraser	Clayton, MO	9 and 8
1926	H Stetson	E Goss	Merion, PA	2 and 1
1927	MB Horn	M Orcutt	Garden City, NY	5 and 4
1928	G Collett	V Van Wie	Hot Springs, VA	13 and 12
1929	G Collett	L Pressler	Oakland Hills, MI	4 and 3
1930	G Collett	V Van Wie	Beverly Hills, CA	6 and 5
1931	H Hicks	G Collett Vare	Williamsville, NY	2 and 1
1932	V Van Wie	G Collett Vare	Peabody, MA	10 and 8
1933	V Van Wie	H Hicks	Highland Park, IL	4 and 3
1934	V Van Wie	D Traung	Whitemarsh Valley, PA	2 and 1
1935	G Collett Vare	P Berg	Interlachen, MN	3 and 2
1936	P Barton (ENG)	M Orcutt	Canoe Brook, NJ	4 and 3
1937	EL Page	P Berg	Memphis, TN	7 and 6
1938	P Berg	EL Page	Westmoreland, IL	6 and 5
1939	B Jameson	D Kirby	Wee Burn, CT	3 and 2
1940	B Jameson	J Cochran	Pebble Beach, CA	6 and 5
1941	E Hicks Newell	H Sigel	Brookline, MA	5 and 3
1942–1945 *Not played*				
1946	B Zaharias	C Sherman	Tulsa, OK	11 and 9
1947	L Suggs	D Kirby	Franklin, MI	2 holes
1948	G Lenczyk	H Sigel	Pebble Beach, CA	4 and 3
1949	D Porter	D Kielty	Merion, PA	3 and 2

Year	Winner	Runner-up	Venue	By
1950	B Hanson	M Murray	Atlanta, GA	6 and 4
1951	D Kirby	C Doran	St Paul, MN	2 and 1
1952	J Pung	S McFedters	Portland, OR	2 and 1
1953	ML Faulk	P Riley	West Barrington, RI	3 and 2
1954	B Romack	M Wright	Sewickley, PA	4 and 2
1955	P Lesser	J Nelson	Charlotte, NC	7 and 6
1956	M Stewart	J Gunderson	Indianapolis, IN	2 and 1
1957	J Gunderson	AC Johnstone	Del Paso, CA	8 and 6
1958	A Quast	B Romack	Wee Burn, CT	3 and 2
1959	B McIntyre	J Goodwin	Washington, DC	4 and 3
1960	J Gunderson	J Ashley	Tulsa, OK	6 and 5
1961	A Quast	P Preuss	Tacomac, WA	14 and 13
1962	J Gunderson	A Baker	Rochester, NY	9 and 8
1963	A Quast	P Conley	Williamstown, MA	2 and 1
1964	B McIntyre	J Gunderson	Prairie Dunes, KA	3 and 2
1965	J Ashley	A Quast	Denver, CO	5 and 4
1966	J Gunderson Carner	JD Stewart Streit	Sewickley, PA	41st hole
1967	ML Dill	J Ashley	Pasadena, CA	5 and 4
1968	J Gunderson Carner	A Quast	Birmingham, MI	5 and 4
1969	C Lacoste (FRA)	S Hamlin	Las Colinas, TX	3 and 2
1970	M Wilkinson	C Hill	Wee Burn, CT	3 and 2
1971	L Baugh	B Barry	Atlanta, GA	1 hole
1972	M Budke	C Hill	St Louis, MO	5 and 4
1973	C Semple	A Quast	Montclair, NJ	1 hole
1974	C Hill	C Semple	Seattle, WA	5 and 4
1975	B Daniel	D Horton	Brae Burn, MA	3 and 2
1976	D Horton	M Bretton	Del Paso, CA	2 and 1
1977	B Daniel	C Sherk	Cincinnati, OH	3 and 1
1978	C Sherk	J Oliver	Sunnybrook, PA	4 and 3
1979	C Hill	P Sheehan	Memphis, TN	7 and 6
1980	J Inkster	P Rizzo	Prairie Dunes, KA	2 holes
1981	J Inkster	L Goggin (AUS)	Portland, OR	1 hole
1982	J Inkster	C Hanlon	Colorado Springs, CO	4 and 3
1983	J Pacillo	S Quinlan	Canoe Brook, NJ	2 and 1
1984	D Richard	K Williams	Seattle, WA	37th hole
1985	M Hattori (JPN)	C Stacy	Pittsburgh, PA	5 and 4
1986	K Cockerill	K McCarthy	Pasatiempo, CA	9 and 7
1987	K Cockerill	T Kerdyk	Barrington, RI	3 and 2
1988	P Sinn	K Noble	Minikahda, MN	6 and 5
1989	V Goetze	B Burton	Pinehurst, NC	4 and 3
1990	P Hurst	S Davis	Canoe Brook, NJ	37th hole
1991	A Fruhwirth	H Voorhees	Prairie Dunes, KA	5 and 4
1992	V Goetze	A Sörenstam (SWE)	Kemper Lakes, IL	1 hole
1993	J McGill	S Ingram	San Diego, CA	1 hole
1994	W Ward	J McGill	Hot Springs, VA	2 and 1
1995	K Kuehne	A-M Knight	Brookline, MA	4 and 2
1996	K Kuehne	M Baena	Lincoln, NE	2 and 1
1997	S Cavalleri (ITA)	R Burke	Brae Burn, MA	5 and 4
1998	G Park (KOR)	J Chuasiriporn	Blackwolf Run, WI	7 and 6
1999	D Delasin	J Kang	Biltmore Forest, NC	4 and 3
2000	N Newton	L Myerscough	Biltmore Forest, NC	8 and 7
2001	M Duncan	N Perrot	Flint Hills, KS	37th hole
2002	B Lucidi	B Jackson	Sleepy Hollow, NY	3 and 2
2003	V Nirapathpongporn	J Park	Philadelphia CC, PA	2 and 1
2004	J Park	A McCurdy	Kahkwa GC, Erie, PA	2 holes
2005	M Pressel	M Martinez	Roswell, GA	9 and 8

(continued over)

106th United States Women's Amateur Championship *continued*

2006 *Witch Hollow, Pumpkin Ridge OR*

Leading Qualifier: Paige Mackenzie   69-70-139

Quarter Finals:
Katharina Schallenberg (GER) beat Jennie Lee (Huntington Beach, CA)   1 hole
Stacy Lewis (The Woodlands, TX) beat Ayaka Kaneko (Honolulu, HI)   6 and 4
Lindy Duncan (Plantation, FL) beat Jennie Arseneault (Grinnell, IA)   at 19th
Kimberley Kim (Hilo, HI) beat Eileen Vargas (COL)   3 and 1

Semi-Finals:
Schallenberg beat Lewis   at 19th
Kim beat Duncan   1 hole

Final:
Kimberley Kim beat Katharina Schallenberg

Other 2006 Overseas Amateur Championships

South Africa's Ashleigh Simon not only helped her country win the World Amateur Team Championship (Espirito Santo Trophy) at Stellenbosch and De Salza Golf Clubs in the Cape in 2006, she also completed the South African National title double winning the 100th Match Play Championship and the Stroke Play event as well. Playing as an amateur on the women's professional circuit in South Africa, she won the Nedbank Masters and finished second in the professional tour's final order of merit. Among other results were:

Australian	Helen Oh	Italian	Marjet Van Der Graaf (NED)
Australian SP	Sarah Nicholson (NZL)	Japanese	Sakurako Mori
Austrian	Maria Verchenova (RUS)	Luxembourg	Anne Harles
Bulgarian	Iliana Dimitrova	New Zealand	Larissa Eruera
Canadan	Jessica Potter	Polish	Krisztina Fodor (HUN)
Cypriot	Myrna Raad	Portuguese	Marta Silva (ESP)
Czech	Stefanie Endstrasser (AUT)	Russian	Maria Verchenova
Danish	Sara Monberg	Slovenian	Fanny Wolte (AUT)
Estonian	Galina Rothmistrova	South African MP	Ashleigh Simon
Finnish	Hanna-Lenna Salonen	South African SP	Ashleigh Simon
French SP	Isabelle Boineau	Spanish	Carlota Ciganda
German	Katharina Schallenberg	Swiss	Diana Terol
Hungarian	Donia Carolina Scarello	Thai	Lorelia Roberto (PHI)

Month by month in 2006

Woods, on the losing side for the fourth time in five Ryder Cup matches, strolls to an eight-shot win at WGC–American Express Championship – his sixth successive stroke play victory and 13th World Championship in 24 starts. Padraig Harrington pips Casey for European Order of Merit with Alfred Dunhill Links Championship win and then joint second place behind Jeev Milkha Singh at the Volvo Masters. Sergio García's closing bogey makes all the difference. The Netherlands and South Africa win men's and women's world amateur team titles.

PART VI

Junior Tournaments and Events

Boys' and Youths' Tournaments

Boys Amateur Championship 2006 *Royal Aberdeen*

Year	Winner	Runner-up	Venue	By
1921	ADD Mathieson	GH Lintott	Ascot	37th hole
1922	HS Mitchell	W Greenfield	Ascot	4 and 2
1923	ADD Mathieson	HS Mitchell	Dunbar	3 and 2
1924	RW Peattie	P Manuevrier (FRA)	Coombe Hill	2 holes
1925	RW Peattie	A McNair	Barnton	4 and 3
1926	EA McRuvie	CW Timmis	Coombe Hill	1 hole
1927	EW Fiddian	K Forbes	Royal Burgess	4 and 2
1928	S Scheftel	A Dobbie	Formby	6 and 5
1929	J Lindsay	J Scott-Riddell	Royal Burgess	6 and 4
1930	J Lindsay	J Todd	Fulwell	9 and 8
1931	H Thomson	F McGloin	Glasgow (Killermont)	5 and 4
1932	IS MacDonald	LA Hardie	Royal Lytham and St Annes	2 and 1
1933	PB Lucas	W McLachlan	Carnoustie	3 and 2
1934	RS Burles	FB Allpass	Moortown	12 and 10
1935	JDA Langley	R Norris	Royal Aberdeen	6 and 5
1936	J Bruen	W Innes	Birkdale	11 and 9
1937	IM Roberts	J Stewart	Bruntsfield	8 and 7
1938	W Smeaton	T Snowball	Moor Park	3 and 2
1939	SB Williamson	KG Thom	Carnoustie	4 and 2
1940–45	*Not played*			
1946	AFD MacGregor	DF Dunstan	Bruntsfield	7 and 5
1947	J Armour	I Caldwell	Hoylake	5 and 4
1948	JD Pritchett	DH Reid	Kilmarnock (Barasssie)	37th hole
1949	H MacAnespie	NV Drew	St Andrews	3 and 2
1950	J Glover	I Young	Royal Lytham and St Annes	2 and 1
1951	N Dunn	MSR Lunt	Prestwick	6 and 5
1952	M Bonallack	AE Shepperson	Formby	37th hole
1953	AE Shepperson	AT Booth	Dunbar	6 and 4
1954	AF Bussell	K Warren	Hoylake	38th hole
1955	SC Wilson	BJK Aitken	Kilmarnock (Barassie)	39th hole
1956	JF Ferguson	CW Cole	Sunningdale	2 and 1
1957	D Ball	J Wilson	Carnoustie	2 and 1
1958	R Braddon	IM Stungo	Moortown	4 and 3
1959	AR Murphy	EM Shamash	Pollok	3 and 1
1960	P Cros (FRA)	PO Green	Olton	5 and 3
1961	FS Morris	C Clark	Dalmahoy	3 and 2
1962	PM Townsend	DC Penman	Royal Mid-Surrey	1 hole
1963	AHC Soutar	DI Rigby	Prestwick	2 and 1
1964	PM Townsend	RD Gray	Formby	9 and 8
1965	GR Milne	DK Midgley	Gullane	4 and 2
1966	A Phillips	A Muller	Moortown	12 and 11
1967	LP Tupling	SC Evans	Western Gailes	4 and 2
1968	SC Evans	K Dabson	St Annes Old Links	3 and 2
1969	M Foster	M Gray	Dunbar	37th hole
1970	ID Gradwell	JE Murray	Hillside	1 hole
1971	H Clark	G Harvey	Kilmarnock (Barassie)	6 and 5
1972	G Harvey	R Newsome	Moortown	7 and 5
1973	DM Robertson	S Betti (ITA)	Blairgowrie	5 and 3
1974	TR Shannon	A Lyle	Hoylake	10 and 9
1975	B Marchbank	A Lyle	Bruntsfield	1 hole
1976	M Mouland	G Hargreaves	Sunningdale	6 and 5
1977	I Ford	CR Dalgleish	Downfield	1 hole
1978	S Keppler	M Stokes	Seaton Carew	3 and 2
1979	R Rafferty	D Ray	Kilmarnock (Barassie)	6 and 5
1980	D Muscroft	A Llyr	Formby	7 and 6
1981	J Lopez (ESP)	R Weedon	Gullane	4 and 3
1982	M Grieve	G Hickman	Burnham and Barrow	37th hole
1983	JM Olazábal (ESP)	M Pendaries (FRA)	Glenbervie	6 and 5
1984	L Vannet	A Mednick (SWE)	Royal Porthcawl	2 and 1
1985	J Cook	W Henry	Royal Burgess	5 and 4
1986	L Walker	G King	Seaton Carew	5 and 4

Year	Winner	Runner-up	Venue	By
1987	C O'Carrol	P Olsson (SWE)	Barassie	3 and 1
1988	S Pardoe	D Haines	Formby	3 and 2
1989	C Watts	C Fraser	Nairn	5 and 3
1990	M Welch	M Ellis	Hunstanton	3 and 1
1991	F Valera (ESP)	R Walton	Montrose	4 and 3
1992	L Westerberg (SWE)	F Jacobson (SWE)	Royal Mid-Surrey	3 and 2
1993	D Howell	V Gustavsson (SWE)	Glenbervie	3 and 1
1994	C Smith	C Rodgers	Little Aston	2 and 1
1995	S Young	S Walker	Dunbar	7 and 6
1996	K Ferrie	M Pilkington	Littlestone	2 and 1
1997	S García (ESP)	R Jones	Saunton	6 and 5
1998	S O'Hara	S Reale (ITA)	Ladybank	1 hole
1999	A Gutierrez (ESP)	M Skelton	Royal St David's	1 hole
2000	D Inglis	D Skinns	Hillside	1 hole
2001	P Martin (ESP)	R Cabrera (ESP)	Ganton	3 and 2
2002	M Pilling	R Davies	Carnoustie	at 37th
2003	R Davies	P Martin (ESP)	Royal Liverpool	1 hole
2004	J Findlay	T Sherreard	Conwy	2 and 1
2005	B Neumann (GER)	J Findlay	Hunstanton	3 and 2

Quarter Finals

Matthew Nixon (Ashton-under-Lyne) beat Billy Fowles (Wentworth) 3 and 1

Andrew Johnston (North Middlesex) beat Marius Junker (GER) 3 and 1

Björn Akesson (SWE) beat Thibaud Fourest (FRA) 2 and 1

Sam Stuart (Chorley) beat Michael Stewart (Troon Welbeck) 6 and 5

Semi-Finals

Nixon beat Johnston 2 holes

Akesson beat Stuart 2 and 1

Final

Matthew Nixon beat Björn Akesson at 38th

British Youths Open Amateur Championship

This championship bridged the gap between the Boys and the Men's tournaments from 1954 until 1994, when it was discontinued because it was no longer needed. The date on the schedule was used to introduce the Mid-Amateur (over 25s).

Year	Winner	Club	Venue	Score
1954	JS More	Swanston	Erskine	287
1955	B Stockdale	Royal Lytham & St Annes	Pannal	287
1956	AF Bussell	Coxmoor	Royal Burgess	287
1957	G Will	St Andrews	Pannal	290
1958	RH Kemp	Glamorganshire	Dumfries & County	281
1959	RA Jowle	Moseley	Pannal	286
1960	GA Caygill	Sunningdale	Pannal	279
1961	JS Martin	Kilbirnie Place	Bruntsfield	284
1962	GA Caygill	Sunningdale	Pannal	287
1963	AJ Low	St Andrews U	Pollok	283
1964	BW Barnes	Burnham & Berrow	Pannal	290
1965	PM Townsend	Porters Park	Gosforth Park	281
1966	PA Easterhouse	Dulwich & Sydenham Hill	Dalmahoy	219 (54 holes)
1967	PJ Benka	Addington	Copt Heath	278
1968	PJ Benka	Addington	Ayr Belleisle	281
1969	JH Cook	Calcot Park	Lindrick	289
1970	B Dassu	Italy	Royal Burgess	276
1971	P Elson	Coventry	Northamptonshire County	277
1972	AH Chandler	Regent Park (Bolton)	Glasgow Gailes	281
1973	SC Mason	Goring & Streatley	Southport & Ainsdale	284
1974	DM Robertson	Dunbar	Downfield	284
1975	N Faldo	Welwyn Garden City	Pannal	278
1976	ME Lewis	Henbury	Gullane	277
1977	AWB Lyle	Hawkstone Park	Moor Park	285
1978	B Marchbank	Auchterarder	East Renfrewshire	278
1979	G Brand jr	Knowle	Woodhall Spa	291
1980	G Hay	Hilton Park	Royal Troon	303
1981	T Antevik	Sweden	West Lancashire	290
1982	AP Parkin	Newtown	St Andrews New	280
1983	P Mayo	Newport	Sunningdale	290
1984	R Morris	Padeswick & Buckley	Blairgowrie	281
1985	JM Olazábal	Spain	Ganton	281

British Youths Open Amateur Championship *continued*

Year	Winner	Club	Venue	Score
1986	D Gilford	Trentham Park	Carnoustie	283
1987	J Cook*	Leamington & County	Hollinwell	283
1988	C Cevaer*	France	Royal Aberdeen	275
1989	M Smith*	Brokenhurst Manor	Ashburnham	285
1990	M Gronberg	Sweden	Southerness	275
1991	J Payne	Sandilands	Woodhall Spa	287
1992	W Bennett	Ruislip	Northumberland	283
1993	L Westwood	Worksop	Glasgow Gailes	278
1994	F Jacobson	Sweden	Royal St Davids	277

English Boys Stroke Play Championship (formerly Carris Trophy)   2006 *Sherwood Forest*

1935	R Upex	75 (18)	1963	EJ Threlfall	147	1985	P Baker	286
1936	JDA Langley	152	1964	PM Townsend	148	1986	G Evans	292
1937	RJ White	149	1965	G McKay	145	1987	D Bathgate	289
1938	IP Garrow	147	1966	A Black	151	1988	P Page	284
1939	CW Warren	149	1967	RF Brown	147	1989	I Garbutt	285
1946	AH Perowne	158	1968	P Dawson	149	1990	M Welch	276
1947	I Caldwell	159	1969	ID Gradwell	150	1991	I Pyman	284
1948	I Caldwell	152	1970	MF Foster	146	1992	M Foster	286
1949	PB Hine	148	1971	RJ Evans	146	1993	J Harris	285
1950	J Glover	144	1972	L Donovan	143	1994	R Duck	280
1951	I Young	154	1973	S Hadfield	148	1995	J Rose	266
1952	N Thygesen	150	1974	KJ Brown	304	1996	G Storm	281
1953	N Johnson	148	1975	A Lyle	270	1997	D Griffiths	283
1954	K Warren	149	1976	H Stott	285	1998	S Godfrey	286
1955	ID Wheater	151	1977	R Mugglestone	293	1999	D Porter	275
1956	G Maisey	141	1978	J Plaxton	144	2000	G Lockerbie	279
1957	G Maisey	145	1979	P Hammond	288	2001	M Richardson*	138
1958	J Hamilton	149	1980	MP McLean	290	2002	C Del Moral	282
1959	RT Walker	152	1981	D Gilford	290	2003	D Denison	286
1960	PM Baxter	150	1982	M Jarvis	298	2004	P Martin (ESP)	276
1961	DJ Miller	143	1983	P Baker	288	2005	T Haylock	283
1962	FS Morris	145	1984	J Coe	283			

1	Darren Wright (Rowlands Castle)	71-74-64-67—276
2	Hugues Joannes (BEL)	69-65-72-73—279
3	Dale Whitnell (Forrester Park)	68-72-72-68—280

English Boys Under-16 Championship (McGregor Trophy) 2006 *Worthing*

1994	G Storm	291	1998	MY Ali	280	2002	M Baldwin	289
1995	J Rose	287	1999	J Heath	280	2003	W De Vries	281
1996	E Molinari	291	2000	M Skelton	289	2004	O Fisher	290
1997	R Paolillo	285	2001	P Waring	212	2005	A Myers	286

1	Oscar Sharpe (Minchinhampton)	70-72-72-73—287
2	Eddie Repperell (Frilford Heath)	74-72-71-71—288
3	Stiggy Hodfson (Sunningdale)	74-71-70-74—289

Nissan Irish Boys Championship (formerly IMSL Irish Boys Championship)   2006 *Kinsale*
(inaugurated 1983)

Year	Winner		Venue	Score
1983	J Carvill	J Farrell	Curragh	144
1984	E O'Connell	J Farrell	Mullingar	142
1985	K Kearney	D Clarke	Athlone	145
1986	D Errity	G McNeill	Royal Tara	147
1987	G McNeill	P McCartan	Warrenpoint	143
1988	D McGrane	P Harrington	Birr	219
1989	D Higgins	JWH Clark	Mullingar	221
1990	R Burns	G Murphy	Kilkenny	213
1991	R Coughlan	R Burns	Thurles	207

(continued over)

1992	J O'Sullivan	D Dunne	Athlone	210
1993	H Armstrong	C McMonagle/P Byrne	Warrenpoint	222
1994	P Byrne	R Leonard/A Thomas	Nenagh	209
1995	L Dalton	M McGreedy	Mullingar	222
1996	M Campbell	L Dalton	Galway	213
1997	M Hoey	D Jones	Galway	217
1998	D Jones	D O'Connor	Youghal	214
1999	M McTernan	M O'Sullivan	Kilkenny	210
2000	D McNamara	C Doran	Strandhill	268
2001	M McHugh*	K Fahey	Donaghadee	280
2002	M McNamara	G Shaw	Thurles	279
2003	B McCarroll	K Gilbert	Hermitage	291
2004	R McIlroy*	A O'Callaghan	Castlebar	283
2005	N Kearney	S Ward	Kilkeel	288

1	Stephen Healy (Claremorris)	73-70-71-74—288	
2	Simon Doherty (Malone)	71-75-72-72—290	
3	Garth Boyd (Donaghadee)	77-72-71-72—292	[winner of Under-16]
	Simon Gallivan (Killarney)	73-69-71-79—292	

Irish Youths Open Amateur Championship (inaugurated 1969) 2006 *Royal Tara*

1969	D Branigan	Delgany	142	1988	P McGinley	Malone	283
1970	LA Owens	Tullamore	286	1989	A Mathers	Athlone	280
1971	MA Gannon	Athlone	277	1990	D Errity	Dundalk	293
1972	MA Gannon	Mullingar	291	1991	R Coughlan	Lahinch	288
1973	J Purcell	Tullamore	289	1992	K Nolan	Clandeboye	275
1974	S Dunlop	Athlone	293	1993	CD Hislop	Co Sligo	279
1975	P McNally	Mullingar	287	1994	B O'Melia	Tullamore	272
1976	R McCormack	Tullamore	294	1995	S Young	Ballybunion	286
1977	B McDaid	Athlone	290	1996	S Young	Royal Portrush	291
1978	T Corridan	Thurles	279	1997	N Howley	Galway	284
1979	R Rafferty	Tullamore	293	1998	A Murray	Headfort	281
1980	J McHenry	Clandeboye	296	1999	G McDowall	Cork	284
1981	J McHenry	Westport	303	2000	G McDowall	Malone	276
1982	K O'Donnell	Mullingar	286	2001	M Ryan	Enniscrone	298
1983	P Murphy	Cork	287	2002	G Wright	Seapoint	288
1984	JC Morris	Bangor	292	2003	C Mills	Cork	294
1985	J McHenry	Co Sligo	287	2004	R McIlroy	Clandeboye	289
1986	JC Morris	Carlow	280	2005	S Power	Portumna	284
1987	C Everett	Killarney	300				

1	Gareth Shaw (Lurgan)	66-67-73-73—279
2	Paul Cutler (Portstewart)	71-70-73-70—284
	Rhys Enoch (WAL)	69-75-69-71—284
	Seamus Power (West Waterford)	71-73-69-71—284

Scottish Boys Championship

1960	L Carver	S Wilson	North Berwick	6 and 5
1961	K Thomson	G Wilson	North Berwick	10 and 8
1962	HF Urquhart	S MacDonald	North Berwick	3 and 2
1963	FS Morris	I Clark	North Berwick	9 and 8
1964	WR Lockie	MD Cleghorn	North Berwick	1 hole
1965	RL Penman	J Wood	North Berwick	9 and 8
1966	J McTear	DG Greig	North Berwick	4 and 3
1967	DG Greig	I Cannon	North Berwick	2 and 1
1968	RD Weir	M Grubb	North Berwick	6 and 4
1969	RP Fyfe	IP Doig	North Berwick	4 and 2
1970	S Stephen	M Henry	North Berwick	38th hole
1971	JE Murray	AA Mackay	North Berwick	4 and 3
1972	DM Robertson	G Cairns	North Berwick	9 and 8
1973	R Watson	H Alexander	North Berwick	8 and 7
1974	DM Robertson	J Cuddihy	North Berwick	6 and 5
1975	A Brown	J Cuddihy	North Berwick	6 and 4
1976	B Marchbank	J Cuddihy	Dunbar	2 and 1
1977	JS Taylor	GJ Webster	Dunbar	3 and 2
1978	J Huggan	KW Stables	Dunbar	2 and 1
1979	DR Weir	S Morrison	West Kilbride	5 and 3

Scottish Boys Championship *continued*

1980	R Gregan	AJ Currie	Dunbar	2 and 1
1981	C Stewart	G Mellon	Dunbar	3 and 2
1982	A Smith	J White	Dunbar	39th hole
1983	C Gillies	C Innes	Dunbar	38th hole
1984	K Buchan	L Vannet	Dunbar	2 and 1
1985	AD McQueen	FJ McCulloch	Dunbar	1 hole
1986	AG Tait	EA McIntosh	Dunbar	6 and 5
1987	AJ Coltart	SJ Bannerman	Dunbar	37th hole
1988	CA Fraser	F Clark	Dunbar	9 and 8
1989	M King	D Brolls	Dunbar	8 and 7
1990	B Collier	D Keeney	West Kilbride	2 and 1
1991	C Hislop	R Thorton	West Kilbride	11 and 9
1992	A Reid	A Forsyth	West Kilbride	2 and 1
1993	S Young	A Campbell	West Kilbride	4 and 2
1994	S Young	E Little	Dunbar	2 and 1
1995	S Young	M Donaldson	Royal Aberdeen	7 and 6
1996	S Whiteford	I McLaughlin	West Kilbride	3 and 2
1997	M Donaldson	L Rhind	Dunbar	1 hole
1998	S O'Hara	D Sutton	Murcar	2 holes
1999	L Harper	M Syme	West Kilbride	6 and 5
2000	S Buckley	M Risbridger	Dunbar	7 and 6
2001	S Brown	R Gill	Royal Aberdeen	6 and 4
2002	J Hempstock	R Taylor	West Kilbride	4 and 2
From 2003, final played over 36 holes				
2003	P Doherty	G Wood	Dunbar	7 and 5
2004	S Henry	D Yeats	Southerness	12 and 11
2005	S Henry	E Polson	Murcar	6 and 5

2006 *West Kilbride*

Quarter Finals

Michael Main (Thornton) beat Daniel Torrance
(Wentworth) at 20th

James Byrne (Banchory) beat Cameron Gray
(West Kilbride) 1 hole

Jamie Neilson (Dunbar) beat John Shanks
(Ardeer) 4 and 3

James White (Lundin) beat Jack Meechan
(Dullatur) 6 and 5

Semi-Finals

Main beat Byrne 2 and 1
White beat Neilson at 20th

Final

James White beat Michael Main 4 and 3

Scottish Boys Stroke Play Championship (Inaugurated 1970)

1970	D Chillas	Carnoustie	298		1988	M Urquhart	Dumfries and County	280
1971	JE Murray	Lanark	274		1989	C Fraser	Stirling	282
1972	S Martin	Montrose	280		1990	N Archibald	Monifieth	292
1973	S Martin	Royal Burgess	284		1991	S Gallacher	Crieff	280
1974	PW Gallacher	Lundin Links	290		1992	S Gallacher	Monifieth	288
1975	A Webster	Kilmarnock (Barassie)	286		1993	J Bunch	Powfoot	292
1976	A Webster	Forfar	292		1994	S Young	Drumpellier	288
1977T	J Huggan	Renfrew	303		1995	C Lee	Arbroath	284
	L Mann				1996	M Brown	Dullatur	286
1978	R Fraser	Arbroath	283		1997	L Rhind	Downfield	287
1979	L Mann	Stirling	289		1998	G Holland	Burntisland	281
1980	ASK Glen	Forfar	288		1999	B Hume	Nairn Dunbar	281
1981	J Gullen	Bellshill	296		2000	C Ries (RSA)	Cawder	275
1982	D Purdie	Monifieth	296		2001	S Jamieson	Lanark	275
1983	L Vannet	Kilmarnock (Barassie)	286		2002	M Lamb	Peterhead	275
1984	K Walker	Carnoustie	280		2003	L Saltman	Prestwick	286
1985	G Matthew	Baberton	297		2004	S Henry	Macrihanish	286
1986	G Cassells	Edzell	294		2005	S McEwan	Monifieth	283
1987	C Ronald	Lanark	287					

2006 *Alloa*

1	Shaun McAllister (Craigielaw)	64-67-68-77—276	
2	Zack Saltman (Craigielaw)	69-64-70-74—277	
3	Tom Hayes (West Byfleet)	68-70-74-69—281	

Scottish Boys Under-16 Stroke Play Championship (Inaugurated 1990) 2006 Deeside

1990	G Davidson	W Linton	148	1998	D Inglis	Braehead	139
1991	D Patrick	R Musselburgh	152	1999	G Murray	Lundin	141
1992	*Not played*			2000	W Booth	The Hirsel	138
1993	S Lamond	Old Ranfurly	150	2001	C Johnston	Edzell	143
1994	S Fraser	Crieff	142	2002	S Borrowman	Ratho Park	142
1995	C Campbell	Shotts	73 (18)	2003	D Addison	Helensburgh	128
1996	P Whiteford	Bothwell	143	2004	G Stevenson*	Ralston	142
1997	D Inglis	Glenbervie	139	2005	D Renwick	Longniddry	207

1	Sam McLaren (King James VI)	71-74-72—217
2	Oliver Young (Hollins Hall)	76-73-70—219
3	Sam Binning (Old Ranfurly)	77-75-68—220
	Gavin Stirling (Caldwell)	72-77-71—220

Scottish Youths Stroke Play Championship (Inaugurated 1979) 2006 Mortonhall

1979	A Oldcorn	Dalmahoy	217	1993	CD Hislop	West Kilbride	284
1980	G Brand jr	Monifieth & Ashludie	281	1994	S Gallacher	Crieff	275
1981	S Campbell	Cawder and Keir	279	1995	E Little	Irvine, Ayr	280
1982	LS Mann	Leven and Scoonie	270	1996	E Little	Stranraer & Portpatrick	280
1983	A Moir	Mortonhall	284	1997	S Young	Cawder	269
1984	B Shields	Eastwood, Renfrew	280	1998	T Rice*	Bruntsfield/R. Burgess	287
1985	H Kemp	East Kilbride	282	1999	J Hendry*	Crieff & Aucterarder	142 (36)
1986	A Mednick	Cawder	282	2000	J Hendry	Newmachar	285
1987	K Walker	Bogside	291	2001	J McLeary	Crail	287
1988	P McGinley	Ladybank & Glenrothes	281	2002	G Bourdy	Murrayshall	276
1989	J Mackenzie	Longniddry	281	2003	M Laird	Letham Grange (Old)	297
1990	S Bannerman	Portpatrick & Stranraer	213	2004	W Booth	Brunston Castle	275
1991	D Robertson	Hilton Park	273	2005	P McLachlan	Glenbervie	270
1992	R Russell	Nairn	296				

1	Francisco Pintor (ESP)	69-73-68-74—284
2	Ross Kellett (Colville Park)	74-69-72-71—286
	James White (Lundin)	75-69-75-67—286

Welsh Boys Championship (inaugurated 1954) 2006 Pennard

1954	JWH Mitchell	DA Rees	Llandrindod Wells	8 and 6
1955	EW Griffith	DA Rees	Llandrindod Wells	3 and 2
1956	DA Rees	JP Hales	Llandrindod Wells	2 and 1
1957	P Waddilove	JG Jones	Llandrindod Wells	2 and 1
1958	P Waddilove	J Williams	Llandrindod Wells	1 hole
1959	C Gilford	JG Jones	Llandrindod Wells	6 and 4
1960	C Gilford	JL Toye	Llandrindod Wells	5 and 4
1961	AR Porter	JL Toye	Llandrindod Wells	3 and 2
1962	RC Waddilove	W Wadrup	Harlech	20th hole
1963	G Matthews	R Witchell	Penarth	6 and 5
1964	D Lloyd	M Walters	Conway	2 and 1
1965	G Matthews	DG Lloyd	Wenvoe Castle	7 and 6
1966	J Buckley	DP Owen	Holyhead	4 and 2
1967	J Buckley	DL Stevens	Glamorganshire	2 and 1
1968	J Buckley	C Brown	Maesdu	1 hole
1969	K Dabson	P Light	Glamorganshire	5 and 3
1970	P Tadman	A Morgan	Conway	2 and 1
1971	R Jenkins	TJ Melia	Ashburnham	3 and 2
1972	MG Chugg	RM Jones	Wrexham	3 and 2
1973	R Tate	N Duncan	Penarth	2 and 1
1974	D Williams	S Lewis	Llandudno	5 and 4
1975	G Davies	PG Garrett	Glamorganshire	20th hole
1976	JM Morrow	MG Mouland	Caernarvonshire	1 hole
1977	JM Morrow	MG Mouland	Glamorganshire	2 and 1
1978	JM Morrow	A Laking	Harlech	2 and 1
1979	P Mayo	M Hayward	Penarth	24th hole
1980	A Llyr	DK Wood	Llandudno (Maesdu)	2 and 1
1981	M Evans	P Webborn	Pontypool	5 and 4
1982	CM Rees	KH Williams	Prestatyn	2 holes

Welsh Boys Championship *continued*

Year	Winner	Runner-up	Venue	Margin
1983	MA Macara	RN Roderick	Radyr	I hole
1984	GA Macara	D Bagg	Llandudno	I hole
1985	B Macfarlane	R Herbert	Cardiff	I hole
1986	C O'Carroll	A Salmon	Rhuddlan	I hole
1987	SJ Edwards	A Herbert	Abergavenny	19th hole
1988	C Platt	P Murphy	Holyhead	2 and I
1989	R Johnson	RL Evans	Southerndown	2 holes
1990	M Ellis	C Sheppard	Llandudno (Maesdu)	3 and 2
1991	B Dredge	A Cooper	Tenby	2 and I
1992	Y Taylor	J Pugh	Wrexham	I hole
1993	R Davies	S Raybould	Pyle and Kenfig	3 and 2
1994	R Peet	K Sullivan	Abergele & Pensarn	7 and 6
1995	M Palmer	O Pughe	Newport	4 and 3
1996	A Smith	M Griffiths	Borth & Ynyslas	19th hole
1997	A Lee	I Campbell	Glamorganshire	4 and 3
1998	M Setterfield	D Price	Llandudno	3 and 2
1999	C Mills	D Price	Neath	3 and 2
2000	R Narduzzo	G Dobson-Jones	Pwllheli	I hole
2001	J Morgan	B Briscoe	St Mellons	3 and 2
2002	C Cole	J Morgan	Radyr	4 and 3
2003	T Light	R Young	Porthmadog	7 and 6
2004	M Jones	L Lewis	Carmarthen	3 and 2
2005	A Runcie	R Merchant	Abergele	2 and I

Quarter Finals

Richard Merchant (Monmouthshire) beat Lloyd Evans
(Wenvoe Castle) 2 and I

Richard Bentham (Celtic Manor) beat Jamie Howie
(Royal St David's) 4 and 2

Jonathan Williams (Vale of Glamorgan) beat Rhys Enoch
(Truro) 4 and 3

Zac Gould (Vale of Glamorgan) beat Christopher O'Neill
(Radyr) 7 and 5

Semi-Finals

Merchant beat Bentham　2 and I

Gould beat Williams　I hole

Final

Richard Merchant beat Zac Gould　3 and I

Welsh Boys Stroke Play Championship　(inaugurated 1995)　2006 *Pennard*

1995　M Pillington (Nefyn & Dist.)	1999　G Bennett (Cirencester)	2003　C Wakely (Whitchurch)
1996　A Lee (St Mellons)	2000　C Mills (Vale of Glamorgan)	2004　L Jones (Conwy)
1997　GM James (Wrexham)	2001　J Morgan (Alice Springs)	2005　J Frazer (Morriston)
1998　G Bennett (Cirencester)	2002　C Cole (Monmouthshire)	

I	Richard Merchant (Monmouthshire)	68-72—140
2	Zac Gould (Vale of Glamorgan)	70-75—142
3	Rhys Enoch (Truro)	66-79—145

Welsh Boys Under-15 Championship　(inaugurated 1985)　2006 *Holywell*

1985　A Wesson (Tredegar Park)	1992　MC Gordon (Pyle & Kenfig)	1999　L James (Brynhill)
1986　A Wesson (Tredegar Park)	1993　G Jones (Builth Wells)	2000　M Jones (Pontypridd)
1987　J Grundy (Radyr)	1994　AGL Smith (Rhondda)	2001　P Smith (Dewston)
1988　S Rees (Carmarthen)	1995　C Thomas (Oxley Park)	2002　Z Gould (Vale of Glamorgan)
1989　Y Taylor (Brynhill)	1996　J Lloyd (Southerndown)	2003　T Smith (Pontypridd)
1990　R Morgan (Morlais Castle)	1997　RW Johnson (Cardiff)	2004　*Cancelled (bad weather)*
1991　M Lucas (Brynhill)	1998　BM Briscoe (Old Colwyn)	2005　B Enoch (Truro)

I	Rhodri Harston (Felixstowe Ferry)	76-63—139
2	Luke Parry (Moss Valley)	71-71—142
3	Ross McLister (Cardiff)	73-70—143

Welsh Open Youths Championship (inaugurated 1993) 2006 *Monmouthshire*

1993	A McKenna	Langland Bay	310	2000	B Welch	Cottrell Park	276
1994	D Quinney	Vale of Llangollen	290	2001	T Dykes	Wrexham	281
1995	R Warner	Glamorganshire	289	2002	J Ruth	Cardiff	283
1996	D Harris	Porthmadog	295	2003	M Laskey	Northop Country Park	280
1997	N Matthews	Cradoc	294	2004	G Slater	Rolls of Monmouth	286
1998	M Hearne	Carmarthen	294	2005	D Lake	Langland Bay	291
1999	D Price	Rhuddlan	281				

1	Joe Favata (Cuddington)	66-71-71-69—277
2	Joe Vickery (Newport)	70-73-64-75—282
3	Miles Mackman (Broome Manor)	68-73-70-74—285

Peter McEvoy Trophy (Inaugurated 1988) *always at Copt Heath*

1988	P Sefton	1994	J Harris	2000	Z Scotland
1989	D Bathgate	1995	C Duke	2001	B Harvey
1990	P Sherman	1996	M Pilkington	2002	M Richardson
1991	L Westwood	1997	P Rowe	2003	T Hunter
1992	B Davis	1998	J Rose	2004	J Parry
1993	S Webster	1999	D Porter	2005	T Sherreard

1	Luke Goddard (Hendon)	68-67-73-70—278
2	Tom Hesketh (Oakdale)	71-68-71-72—282
	Sam Hutsby (Lee-on-the-Solent)	74-71-70-67—282
	James Watts (East Herts)	69-69-76-68—282
	Dale Whitnell (Forrester Park)	72-71-67-72—282

Midland Boys Amateur Championship 2006 *Maxstoke Park*

1989	M Wilson	1995	C Richardson	2000	J Prince
1990	ML Welch	1996T	S Walker	2001	O West
1991	S Drummond		K Cliffe	2002	B Stafford
1992	S Drummond	1997	K Hale	2003	C Evans
1993	S Webster	1998	E Vernon	2004	R Harris
1994	R Duck	1999	C Stevenson	2005	A Chesters

1	Daniel Rowland (Boston West)	74-68—142 (better last round)
2	Adam Keogh (Boston West)	71-71—142
3	Andrew Smedley (Notts)	71-72—143
	Ross Love (Enville)	69-74—143

Team Events

European Youths Team Championship 2006 San Roque, Spain

1990	Italy	Sweden	Turin, Italy
1992	Sweden	England	Helsinki, Finland
1994	Ireland	Sweden	Esbjerg, Denmark
1996	Scotland	Spain	Madeira
1998	Wales	Sweden	Royal Waterloo, Belgium
2000	England	Scotland	Kilmarnock (Barassie), Scotland
2002	Sweden	England	Gdansk, Poland
2004	Scotland	England	The Island, Dublin, Ireland

Final ranking: 1 Spain; 2 Italy; 3 England; 4 Scotland; 5 Netherlands; 6 Ireland; 7 France; 8 Wales; 9 Germany; 10 Sweden; 11 Austria; 12 Finland; 13 Turkey; 14 Belgium; 15 Denmark

Winning Team: Jorge Campillo, Ignacio Elvira, Ion García Avis, Jordi García del Moral, Pedro Oriol, Marc Perez

European Boys Team Championship 2006 Bokskogens, Malmö, Sweden

1980	Spain	El Prat, Barcelona	1993	Sweden	Ascona, Switzerland
1981	England	Olgiata, Rome	1994	England	Vilamoura, Portugal
1982	Italy	Frankfurt, Germany	1995	England	Woodhall Spa
1983	Sweden	Helsinki, Finland	1996	Spain	Gut Murstatten, Austria
1984	Scotland	Royal St George's, England	1997	Spain	Bled, Slovenia
1985	England	Troia, Portugal	1998	Ireland	Gullane, Scotland
1986	England	Turin, Italy	1999	England	Uppsala, Sweden
1987	Scotland	Chantilly, France	2000	Scotland	Noord Nederlandse
1988	France	Renfrew, Scotland	2001	Sweden	Amber Baltic, Poland
1989	England	Lyckoma, Sweden	2002	Spain	Reykjavik, Iceland
1990	Spain	Reykjavik, Iceland	2003	Italy	Karlovy Vary, Czech Republic
1991	Sweden	Oslo, Norway	2004	England	Kymen GC, Finland
1992	Scotland	Conwy, Wales	2005	Netherlands	Monticello, Italy

Final Ranking: 1 Norway; 2 Scotland; 3 Sweden; 4 Spain; 5 Netherlands; 6 France; 7 Belgium; 8 Wales; 9 Ireland; 10 Germany; 11 Denmark; 12 Italy; 13 Portugal; 14 England; 15 Switzerland; 16 Finland; 17 Austria, Czech Republic, Iceland, Poland

Winning Team: Are Friestad, Daniel Böe Jacobsen, Fredrik Kollevold, Anders Kristiansen, Joakim Nikkelsen, Marius Thorp

Great Britain & Ireland v Continent of Europe (Jacques Léglise Trophy)

1958	GBI	11½–½	Moortown	1987	GBI	7½–4½	Kilmarnock (Barassie)
1959	GBI	7–2	Pollok	1988	GBI	5½–2½	Formby
1960	GBI	8–7	Olton	1989	GBI	7½–4½	Nairn
1961	GBI	11–4	Dalmahoy	1990	GBI	10–2	Hunstanton
1962	GBI	11–4	Royal Mid-Surrey	1991	GBI	6½–5½	Montrose
1963	GBI	12–3	Prestwick	1992	GBI	8–7	Royal Mid-Surrey
1964	GBI	12–1	Formby	1993	GBI	8–7	Glenbervie
1965	GBI	12–1	Gullane	1994	GBI	12½–2½	Little Aston
1966	GBI	10–2	Moortown	1995	GBI	9–6	Dunbar
1967–76	Not played			1996	Europe	13–11	Woodhall Spa
1977	Europe	7–6	Downfield	1997	Europe	12½–11½	Aberdeen
1978	Europe	7–6	Seaton Carew	1998	GBI	14–10	Villa d'Este, Italy
1979	GBI	9½–2½	Kilmarnock (Barassie)	1999	GBI	15–9	Burnham & Berrow
1980	GBI	7–5	Formby	2000	GBI	16–8	Turnberry
1981	GBI	8–4	Gullane	2001	Europe	16–8	Chantilly
1982	GBI	11–1	Burnham & Berrow	2002	Europe	14–10	Lausanne, Switzerland
1983	GBI	6½–5½	Glenbervie	2003	GBI	16½–7½	Lahinch, Ireland
1984	GBI	6½–5½	Royal Porthcawl	2004	GBI	14½–9½	Nairn
1985	GBI	7½–4½	Royal Burgess	2005	Europe	14–10	Royal Porthcawl
1986	Europe	8½–3½	Seaton Carew	2006	Europe	19½–4½	Marianske Lazne

2006 *Marianske Lazne, Czech Republic*

Non-playing Captains: Europe: Andreas Pallauf; GBI: Niall Kearney

European names first:

First Day – **Foursomes**

T Sluiter & L García del Moral beat S Hutsby & L Goddard 2 and 1

J Kennegard & B Akesson beat R Enoch & A Runcie 1 hole

M Thorp & A Kristiansen beat P Cutler & N Kearney 3 and 1

V Dubuisson & A Pavan beat J Byrne & L Kirton 2 and 1

Singles

Pedro Figuieredo (POR) beat Luke Goddard (ENG) 1 hole

Tim Sluiter (NED) beat Rhys Enoch (WAL) 1 hole

Björn Akesson (SWE) beat Paul Cutler (IRL) 4 and 2

Jesper Kennegard (SWE) beat Lewis Kirton (SCO) 5 and 4

Lluis García del Moral (ESP) lost to Adam Runcie (WAL) 2 and 1

Victor Dubuisson (FRA) beat Sam Hutsby (ENG) 2 and 1

Anders Kristiansen (NOR) beat James Byrne (SCO) 2 and 1

Marius Thorp (NOR) beat Niall Kearney (IRL) 1 hole

Second Day – **Foursomes**

V Dubuisson & A Pavan lost to R Enoch & A Runcie 1 hole

T Sluiter & L García del Moral beat J Byrne & M Nixon 5 and 4

J Kennegard & B Akesson lost to P Cutler & N Kearney 1 hole

M Thorp & A Kristiansen beat S Hutsby & L Goddard 2 and 1

Singles

M Thorp beat N Kearney 2 and 1

B Akesson beat S Hutsby 2 and 1

J Kennegard beat L Kirton 1 hole

P Figuieredo beat J Byrne 1 hole

T Sluiter beat L Goddard 2 and 1

L García del Moral lost to Matthew Nixon (ENG) 1 hole

A Kristiansen beat A Runcie 3 and 2

Andrea Pavan halved with R Enoch

Match result: Europe 19½, GBI 4½

EGA Challenge Trophy 2006 *Tale, Slovakia*

1	Austria	1121 (L Nemecz 223; E Fuernwenger 223; P Feenat 224; L Piessi 228; D Angkawidjaja withdrew)
2	Slovenia	1136
3	Hungary	1151

Other scores: 1183 Estonia; 1228 Slovakia; 1236 Greece.

Individual winner: Benjamin Palanszki (HUN) 72-72-71—215

Boys' Home Internationals (R&A Trophy) (inaugurated 1985)

1985T	England/Ireland	Royal Burgess	1996	England	Littlestone
1986	Ireland	Seaton Carew	1997	Ireland	Royal North Devon
1987	Scotland	Barassie	1998	England	St Andrews
1988	England	Formby	1999	England	Conwy
1989	England	Nairn	2000	England	Portmanock
1990	Scotland	Hunstanton	2001	England	Moortown
1991	England	Montrose	2002	England	Lansdowne
1992T	Wales/Scotland	Royal Mid-Surrey	2003	England	Royal St David's
1993	England	Glenbervie	2004	England	Royal Dublin
1994	England	Little Aston	2005	England	Woodhall Spa
1995	Scotland	Dunbar	2006	Scotland	Moray

(continued over)

Boys' Home Internationals *continued*

2006 *Moray*

England 7, Ireland 8	**Winning Team:** Barrie Douglas (non-playing
Scotland 10½, Wales 4½	captain); James Byrne (Banchory), Jordan
Wales 4½, Ireland 10½	Findlay (Fraserburgh), Cameron Gray (West
England 7½, Scotland 7½	Kilbride), Ross Kellett (Colville Park), Lewis
England 9, Wales 6	Kirton (Newmachar), Shaun McAllister
Scotland 8, Ireland 7	(Craigielaw), Chris Robinson (Wigton &

Bladnoch), Zack Saltman (Craigielaw), Gordon
Result: 1 Scotland 2½ pts (26); 2 Ireland 2 (25½);   Stevenson (Whitecraigs), Michael Stewart
3 England 1½ (23½);   4 Wales 0 (15)   (Troon Welbeck), James White (Lundin)

English Boys County Finals 2006 *Little Aston*

2000 Surrey	2002 Yorkshire	2004 Essex and Yorkshire (tied)
2001 Lancashire	2003 Yorkshire	2005 Yorkshire

Results – Day One: Gloucestershire beat Shropshire and Herefordshire 5½–3½; Surrey beat Lancashire 5½–3½. **Day Two**: Lancashire beat Gloucestershire 6½–2½; Shropshire and Herefordshire beat Surrey 6½–½. **Day Three:** Surrey beat Gloucestershire 6½–2½; Lancashire beat Shropshire and Herefordshire 5–4

1 Lancashire 15 pts; 2 Surrey 14½; 3 Shropshire and Herefordshire 14; 4 Gloucestershire 10½

Winning team: Martin Edge, Tommy Fleetwood, Steven McGlynn, James Robinson, Jack Senior, Sam Stuart, Michael Williams

Scottish Boys Area Team Championship 2006 *Paisley*

2000 Lothians	355	2002 Lothians	370	2004 Dunbartonshire	360
2001 Dunbartonshire	347	2003 Lothians	350	2005 Lothians	377

1 Fife 355; 2 North East 371; 3 Angus 379; 4 South 379; 5 Renfrewshire 380; 6 Perth and Kinross 382; 7 Lothians, Stirlingshire 384; 9 Dunbartonshire, Ayrshire 387; 11 Borders 388; 12 North 389; 13 Lanarkshire 395; 14 Glasgow 400; 15 Argyll and Bute 411; 16 Clackmannanshire 421

Winning Team: Scott Crichton, Michael Main, Alex Moir, James White

Month by month in 2006

Korean Yang Yong-eun holds off Woods to become the surprise winner of the HSBC Champions event in Shanghai and there is another shock a week later when Woods, two ahead with three holes to play and the sport's greatest-ever front-runner, loses the Dunlop Phoenix title to Harrington after a play-off in Japan. The world number one does claim his seventh PGA Grand Slam crown, however, while Jeev Milkha Singh follows up his Volvo Masters success with victory in Japan's Casio World Open – after Michelle Wie crashes against the men again with rounds of 81 and 80.

Girls' and Junior Ladies' Tournaments

Girls British Open Championship _ 2006 *Portstewart*

Year	Winner	Runner-up	Venue	By
1960	S Clarke	AL Irvin	Kilmarnock (Barassie)	2 and 1
1961	D Robb	J Roberts	Beaconsfield	3 and 2
1962	S McLaren-Smith	A Murphy	Foxton Hall	2 and 1
1963	D Oxley	B Whitehead	Gullane	2 and 1
1964	P Tredinnick	K Cumming	Camberley Heath	2 and 1
1965	A Willard	A Ward	Formby	3 and 2
1966	J Hutton	D Oxley	Troon Portland	20th hole
1967	P Burrows	J Hutton	Liphook	2 and 1
1968	C Wallace	C Reybroeck	Leven	4 and 3
1969	J de Witt Puyt	C Reybroeck	Ilkley	2 and 1
1970	C Le Feuvre	Michelle Walker	North Wales	2 and 1
1971	J Mark	Maureen Walker	North Berwick	4 and 3
1972	Maureen Walker	S Cadden	Norwich	2 and 1
1973	AM Palli	N Jeanson	Northamptonshire	2 and 1
1974	R Barry	T Perkins	Dunbar	1 hole
1975	S Cadden	L Isherwood	Henbury	4 and 3
1976	G Stewart	S Rowlands	Pyle and Kenfig	5 and 4
1977	W Aitken	S Bamford	Formby Ladies	2 and 1
1978	M L de Lorenzi	D Glenn	Largs	2 and 1
1979	S Lapaire	P Smilie	Edgbaston	19th hole
1980	J Connachan	L Bolton	Wrexham	2 holes
1981	J Connachan	P Grice	Woodbridge	20th hole
1982	C Waite	M Mackie	Edzell	6 and 5
1983	E Orley	A Walters	Leeds	7 and 6
1984	C Swallow	E Farquharson	Maesdu	1 hole
1985	S Shapcott	E Farquharson	Hesketh	3 and 1
1986	S Croce	S Bennett	West Kilbride	5 and 4
1987	H Dobson	S Croce	Barnham Broom	19th hole
1988	A Macdonald	J Posener	Pyle and Kenfig	3 and 2
1989	M McKinlay	S Eriksson	Carlisle	19th hole
1990	S Cavalleri (ITA)	E Valera	Penrith	5 and 4
1991	M Hjorth (SWE)	J Moodie	Whitchurch	3 and 2
1992	M McKay	L Navarro	Northamptonshire	2 holes
1993	M McKay	A Vincent	Helensburgh	4 and 3
1994	A Vincent	R Hudson	Gog Magog	1 up
1995	A Lemoine	J Krantz	Northop Park	3 and 2
1996	M Monnet	C Laurens	Formby	4 and 3
1997	C Laurens	M Nagl (GER)	West Kilbride	2 and 1
1998	M Beautell (ESP)	M Nagl (GER)	Holyhead	4 and 3
1999	S Pettersen (NOR)	M Nagl (GER)	High Post	3 and 1
2000	T Calzavara (ITA)	R Bell	Blairgowrie	1 hole
2001	C Queen	C Alonso (ESP)	Brough	1 hole
2002	*Rain washed out this tournament in its later stages. Awards were made to the top qualifiers:*			
	E Cabrera (ESP)	L Stable (SWE)	Sandiway	
2003	M Skarpnord (NOR)	R Eransus (ESP)	Newport, Gwent	2 and 1
2004	A Muñoz (ESP)	V Derrey (FRA)	Lanark	4 and 2
2005	A Nordquist (SWE)	A Muñoz (ESP)	West Hill	2 and 1

Leading Qualifier: 141 Belen Mozo (ESP) 68-73

Girls British Open Championship *continued*

Quarter-Finals

Belen Mozo (ESP) beat Gabi Zuber (GER) 4 and 3

Valerie Sternebeck (GER) beat Marion Bernard (FRA) 4 and 3

Sally Watson (David Leadbetter Golf Academy) beat Ane Urchegui (ESP) 2 and 1

Junthima Gulyanamitta (THA) beat Sian James (Bristol & Clifton) 4 and 3

Semi-Finals

Mozo beat Sternebeck 4 and 3

Watson beat Gulyanamitta 4 and 3

Final

Belen Mozo beat Sally Watson 1 hole

English Girls Close Championship

Year	Winner	Runner–up	Venue	By
1964	S Ward	P Tredinnick	Wollaton Park	2 and 1
1965	D Oxley	A Payne	Edgbaston	2 holes
1966	B Whitehead	D Oxley	Woodbridge	1 hole
1967	A Willard	G Holloway	Burhill	1 hole
1968	K Phillips	C le Feuvre	Harrogate	6 and 5
1969	C le Feuvre	K Phillips	Hawkstone Park	2 and 1
1970	C le Feuvre	M Walker	High Post	2 and 1
1971	C Eckersley	J Stevens	Liphook	4 and 3
1972	C Barker	R Kelly	Trentham	4 and 3
1973	S Parker	S Thurston	Lincoln	19th hole
1974	C Langford	L Harrold	Knowle	2 and 1
1975	M Burton	R Barry	Formby	6 and 5
1976	H Latham	D Park	Moseley	3 and 2
1977	S Bamford	S Jolly	Chelmsford	21st hole
1978	P Smillie	J Smith	Willesley Park	3 and 2
1979	L Moore	P Barry	Cirencester	1 hole
1980	P Smillie	J Soulsby	Kedleston Park	3 and 2
1981	J Soulsby	C Waite	Worksop	7 and 5
1982	C Waite	P Grice	Wilmslow	3 and 2
1983	P Grice	K Mitchell	West Surrey	2 and 1
1984	C Swallow	S Duhig	Bath	3 and 1
1985	L Fairclough	K Mitchell	Coventry	6 and 5
1986	S Shapcott	N Way	Huddersfield	7 and 6
1987	S Shapcott	S Morgan	Sandy Lodge	1 hole
1988	H Dobson	S Shapcott	Long Ashton	1 hole
1989	H Dobson	A MacDonald	Edgbaston	3 and 1
1990	C Hall	J Hockley	Bolton Old Links	20th hole
1991	N Buxton	C Hall	Knole Park	2 and 1
1992	F Brown	L Nicholson	Finham Park	2 and 1
1993	G Simpson	L Wixon	Cotswold Hills	7 and 5
1994	K Hamilton	S Forster	Whitley Bay	3 and 2
1995	R Hudson	G Nutter	Porters Park	2 and 1
1996	R Hudson	D Rushworth	Bedford	8 and 6
1997	S McKevitt	C Ritson	Kingsdown	3 and 2
1998	L Walters	K Lawton	Harrogate	5 and 4
1999	S Heath	A Cook	Chigwell	6 and 4
2000	S Walker	R Wood	Sheringham	1 hole
2001	A Marshall	S Walker	Long Ashton	3 and 2
2002	L Eastwood	N Haywood	Fairhaven	1 hole
2003	K-A Haskell	J Hodge	Porters Park	4 and 3
2004	M Reid	K Matharu	Gainsborough	3 and 2
2005	M Reid	J Hodge	Liphook	3 and 2

2006 *Liphook*

Leading Qualifier: 142 Henrietta Brockway (Yeovil) 73-69

Quarter Finals

Henrietta Brockway (Yeovil) beat Jodi Ewart (Catterick) 4 and 3

Rachel Jennings (Izaak Walton) beat Hannah Moul (Chelmsford) 6 and 4

Charlie Douglass (Brocket Hall) beat Ellie Givens (Blackwell Grange) 1 hole

Sian James (Bristol & Clifton) beat Florentyna Parker (Royal Birkdale) 2 and 1

Semi-Finals

Jennings beat Brockway 2 and 1

Douglass beat James 2 and 1

Final

Rachel Jennings beat Charlie Douglass 1 hole

Irish Girls Championship (Blake Cup) (inaugurated 1951)

Year	Winner	Runner–up	Venue	By
1951	J Davies	I Hurst	Milltown	3 and 2
1952	J Redgate	A Phillips	Grange	at 22nd
1953	J Redgate	I Hurst	Grange	4 and 3
1954–60	Suspended			
1961	M Coburn	C McAuley	Portrush	6 and 5
1962	P Boyd	P Atkinson	Elm Park	4 and 3
1963	P Atkinson	C Scarlett	Donaghadee	8 and 7
1964	C Scarlett	A Maher	Milltown	6 and 5
1965	V Singleton	P McKenzie	Ballycastle	7 and 6
1966	M McConnell	D Hulme	Dun Laoghaire	3 and 2
1967	M McConnell	C Wallace	Portrush	6 and 5
1968	C Wallace	A McCoy	Louth	3 and 1
1969	EA McGregor	M Sheenan	Knock	6 and 5
1970	EA McGregor	J Mark	Greystones	3 and 2
1971	J Mark	C Nesbitt	Belfast	3 and 2
1972	P Smyth	M Governey	Elm Park	1 hole
1973	M Governey	R Hegarty	Mullingar	3 and 1
1974	R Hegarty	M Irvine	Castletroy	2 holes
1975	M Irvine	P Wickham	Carlow	2 and 1
1976	P Wickham	R Hegarty	Castle	5 and 3
1977	A Ferguson	R Walsh	Birr	3 and 2
1978	C Wickham	B Gleeson	Killarney	1 hole
1979	L Bolton	B Gleeson	Milltown	3 and 2
1980	B Gleeson	L Bolton	Kilkenny	5 and 3
1981	B Gleeson	E Lynn	Donegal	1 hole
1982	D Langan	S Lynn	Headfort	5 and 4
1983	E McDaid	S Lynn	Ennis	20th hole
1984	S Sheehan	L Tormey	Thurles	6 and 4
1985	S Sheehan	D Hanna	Laytown/Bettystown	5 and 4
1986	D Mahon	T Eakin	Mallow	4 and 3
1987	V Greevy	B Ryan	Galway	8 and 7
1988	L McCool	P Gorman	Courtown	3 and 2
1989	A Rogers	R MacGuigan	Athlone	2 and 1
1990	G Doran	L McCool	Royal Portrush	3 and 1
1991	A Rogers	D Powell	Mallow	2 and 1
1992	M McGreevy	N Gorman	Kilkenny	2 and 1
1993	M McGreevy	E Dowdall	Strandhill	2 and 1
1994	A O'Leary	D Doyle	Mullingar	23rd hole
1995	P Murphy	G Hegarty	Douglas	5 and 4
1996	P Murphy	C Smyth	Warren Point	2 holes
1997	J Gannon	C Coughlan	Lay/Bettystown	3 and 2
1998	P Murphy	C Coughlan	Galway	5 and 4
1999	P Murphy	M Gillen	Tullamore	20th hole
2000	M Gillen	N Mullooly	Limerick	6 and 5
2001	DM Conaty	H Nolan	Belvoir Park	3 and 2
2002	K Delaney	H Nolan	Athenry	4 and 3
2003	K Delaney	T Delaney	Ardee	4 and 3
2004	T Delaney	S Meadow	Portarlington	8 and 6
2005	D McVeigh	L Toomey	Charleville	4 and 3

2006 *Malone*

Quarter Finals

Louise Coffey (Warrenpoint) beat Charlene Reid
(Gracehill) 7 and 6

Stephanie Meadow (Royal Portrush) beat Sarah Faller
(Galway) 3 and 2

Victoria Bradshaw (Bangor) beat Sarah Cunningham
(Ennis) 3 and 2

Louise Mernagh (Woodenbridge) beat Kate Gallagher
(Claremorris) at 19th

Semi-Finals

Meadow beat Coffey 5 and 4
Bradshaw beat Mernagh 2 and 1

Final

Stephanie Meadow beat Victoria Bradshaw
5 and 4

Scottish Ladies Junior Open Stroke Play Championship 2006 *Stirling*
(inaugurated 1955)

1955	M Fowler	Erskine		1981	K Douglas	Downfield
1956	B McCorkindale	Erskine		1982	J Rhodes	Dumfries & Galloway
1957	M Fowler	Kilmacolm		1983	S Lawson	Largs
1958	R Porter	Ranfurly Castle		1984	S Lawson	Dunbar
1959	D Robb	Helensburgh		1985	K Imrie	Ballater
1960	J Greenhalgh	Ranfurly Castle		1986	K Imrie	Dumfries and County
1961	D Robb	Whitecraigs		1987	K Imrie	Douglas Park
1962	S Armitage	Dalmahoy		1988	C Lambert	Baberton
1963	A Irvin	Dumfries		1989	C Lambert	Dunblane New
1964	M Nuttall	Dalmahoy		1990	J Moodie	Royal Troon
1965	I Wylie	Carnoustie		1991	C Macdonald	Alyth
1966	J Smith	Douglas Park		1992	L McCool	North Berwick
1967	J Bourassa	Dunbar		1993	J Moodie	Dumfries and County
1968	K Phillips	Dumfries		1994	C Agnew	Dumfries and County
1969	K Phillips	Prestonfield		1995	R Hakkarainen (Fin)	Lanark
1970	B Huke	Leven		1996	L Moffat	Auchterarder
1971	B Huke	Dalmahoy		1997	L Nicholson	Stranraer
1972	L Hope	Troon, Portland		1998	V Laing	Duff House Royal
1973	G Cadden	Edzell		1999	L Kenny	Alyth
1974	S Lambie	Stranraer		2000	L Morton	Cardross
1975	S Cadden	Lanark		2001	L Kenny	Southerness
1976	S Cadden	Prestonfield		2002	K Brotherton	Baberton
1977	S Cadden	Edzell		2003	J Wilson*	Kilmalcolm
1978	J Connachan	Peebles		2004	C Queen	Kircaldy
1979	A Gemmill	Royal Troon, Portland		2005	L Fleming	West Kilbride
1980	J Connachan	Kirkcaldy				

1	Krystle Caithness (St Regulus)	64-69-69—202
2	Katy McNicoll (Carnoustie Ladies)	71-72-70—213
3	Kelsey MacDonald (Nairn Dunbar)	70-73-72—215

Scottish Girls Close Championship (inaugurated 1960) 2006 *Peebles*

Year	Winner	Runner–up	Venue	By
1960	J Hastings	A Lurie	Kilmacolm	6 and 4
1961	I Wylie	W Clark	Murrayfield	3 and 1
1962	I Wylie	U Burnet	West Kilbride	3 and 1
1963	M Norval	S MacDonald	Carnoustie	6 and 4
1964	JW Smith	C Workman	West Kilbride	2 and 1
1965	JW Smith	I Walker	Leven	7 and 5
1966	J Hutton	F Jamieson	Arbroath	2 holes
1967	J Hutton	K Lackie	West Kilbride	4 and 2
1968	M Dewar	J Crawford	Dalmahoy	2 holes
1969	C Panton	A Coutts	Edzell	23rd hole
1970	M Walker	L Bennett	Largs	3 and 2
1971	M Walker	S Kennedy	Edzell	1 hole
1972	G Cadden	C Panton	Stirling	3 and 2
1973	M Walker	M Thomson	Cowal, Dunoon	1 hole
1974	S Cadden	D Reid	Arbroath	3 and 1
1975	W Aitken	S Cadden	Leven	1 hole
1976	S Cadden	D Mitchell	Dumfries and County	4 and 2
1977	W Aitken	G Wilson	West Kilbride	2 holes
1978	J Connachan	D Mitchell	Stirling	7 and 5
1979	J Connachan	G Wilson	Dunbar	3 and 1
1980	J Connachan	P Wright	Dumfries and County	21st hole
1981	D Thomson	P Wright	Kilmarnock (Barassie)	2 and 1
1982	S Lawson	D Thomson	Montrose	1 hole
1983	K Imrie	D Martin	Leven	2 and 1
1984	T Craik	D Jackson	Peebles	3 and 2
1985	E Farquharson	E Moffat	West Kilbride	2 holes
1986	C Lambert	F McKay	Nairn	4 and 3
1987	S Little	L Moretti	Stirling	3 and 2
1988	J Jenkins	F McKay	Dumfries and County	4 and 3
1989	J Moodie	V Melvin	Kilmacolm	19th hole
1990	M McKay	J Moodie	Duff House Royal	3 and 2
1991	J Moodie	M McKay	Leven Links	5 and 4

Year	Winner	Runner–up	Venue	By
1992	M McKay	L Nicholson	Powfoot	2 and 1
1993	C Agnew	H Stirling	Baberton	19th hole
1994	C Nicholson	L Moffat	Deeside	3 and 1
1995	L Moffat	F Lockhart	Paisley	2 and 1
1996	V Laing	C Hunter	Peebles	5 and 4
1997	V Laing	A Walker	Dunfermline	5 and 4
1998	V Laing	L Moffat	Kilmarnock Barassie	at 21st hole
1999	V Laing	L Wells	Edzell	3 and 2
2000	L Kenney	F Gilbert	Dunblane New	3 and 2
2001	H MacRea	L Kenney	Glenbervie	1 hole
2002	L Walker	G Webster	Powfoot	2 and 1
2003	K Brotherton	K Caithness	Newmachar	3 and 2
2004	K Caithness	K Brotherton	Pumpherston	2 holes
2005	S Watson	C Booth	Tain	2 and 1

Leading Qualifier: 143 Kelsey MacDonald (Nairn Dunbar) 69-74

Quarter Finals

Rachael Livingstone (Musselburgh Old) beat Kelsey
MacDonald 3 and 1

Edwina Lowrey-Gold (Eaton) beat Krystle Caithness
(St Regulus) 4 and 3

Katy McNicoll (Carnoustie Ladies) beat Gillian Monteith
(Portpatrick Dunskey) at 19th

Roseanne Niven (Crieff) 1 hole beat Michele Thomson
(McDonald) 1 hole

Semi-Finals

Livingstone beat Lowrey-Gold 5 and 3
Niven beat McNicoll 4 and 3

Final

Roseanne Niven beat Rachael Livingstone
3 and 2

SLGA St Leonards' Under-16 Stroke Play Championship

2006 *St Andrews (Strathtyrum)*

1	Carly Booth (Comrie)	76-73—149
2	Rachel Connor (Manchester)	72-78—150
3	Kelsey MacDonald (Nairn Dunbar)	77-74—151

Welsh Girls Championship (inaugurated 1957)

Year	Winner	Runner–up	Venue	By
1957	A Coulman	S Wynne-Jones	Newport	1 hole
1958	S Wynne-Jones	A Coulman	Conwy	3 and 1
1959	C Mason	T Williams	Glamorgan	3 and 2
1960	A Hughes	D Wilson	Llandrindod Wells	6 and 4
1961	J Morris	S Kelly	North Wales	3 and 2
1962	J Morris	P Morgan	Southerndown	4 and 3
1963	A Hughes	A Brown	Conway	8 and 7
1964	A Hughes	M Leigh	Holyhead	5 and 3
1965	A Hughes	A Reardon-Hughes	Swansea Bay	19th hole
1966	S Hales	J Rogers	Prestatyn	1 hole
1967	E Wilkie	L Humphreys	Pyle and Kenfig	1 hole
1968	L Morris	J Rogers	Portmadoc	1 hole
1969	L Morris	L Humphreys	Wenvoe Castle	5 and 3
1970	T Perkins	P Light	Rhuddlan	2 and 1
1971	P Light	P Whitley	Glamorganshire	4 and 3
1972	P Whitley	P Light	Llandudno (Maesdu)	2 and 1
1973	V Rawlings	T Perkins	Whitchurch	19th hole
1974	L Isherwood	S Rowlands	Wrexham	4 and 3
1975	L Isherwood	S Rowlands	Swansea Bay	1 hole
1976	K Rawlings	C Parry	Rhuddlan	5 and 4
1977	S Rowlands	D Taylor	Clyne	7 and 5
1978	S Rowlands	G Rees	Abergele	3 and 2
1979	M Rawlings	J Richards	St Mellons	19th hole
1980	K Davies	M Rawlings	Vale of Llangollen	19th hole
1981	M Rawlings	F Connor	Radyr	4 and 3
1982	K Davies	K Beckett	Wrexham	6 and 5
1983	N Wesley	J Foster	Whitchurch	4 and 2
1984	J Foster	J Evans	Pwllheli	6 and 5
1985	J Foster	S Caley	Langland Bay	6 and 5
1986	J Foster	L Dermott	Holyhead	3 and 2

Welsh Girls Championship *continued*

Year	Winner	Runner–up	Venue	By
1987	J Lloyd	S Bibbs	Cardiff	2 and 1
1988	L Dermott	A Perriam	Builth Wells	2 holes
1989	L Dermott	N Stroud	Carmarthen	4 and 2
1990	L Dermott	N Stroud	Padeswood and Buckley	6 and 4
1991	S Boyes	R Morgan	Clyne	3 and 1
1992	B Jones	S Musto	Rhuddlan	2 and 1
1993	K Stark	S Tudor-Jones	Radyr	3 and 2
1994	K Stark	J Evans	Wrexham	4 and 3
1995	E Pilgrim	L Davis	Borth and Ynyslas	2 holes
1996	K Stark	S Bourne	Monmouth	4 and 3
1997	R Brewerton	K Stark	Perhos	19th hole
1998	B Brewerton	L Archer	Old Padeswood	3 and 1
1999	K Phillips	R Last	Pontardawe	6 and 5
2000	K Phillips	J Pritchard	Northop Country Park	1 hole
2001	S Jones	J Dyer	Carmarthen	3 and 2
2002	L Gould	R Vaughan-Jones	North Wales GC	4 and 3
2003	L Gould	B Loucks	North Wales GC	4 and 2
2004	T Davies	B Loucks	Padeswood & Buckley	2 and 1
2005	S Hassan	L Hall	Ashburnham	1 hole

Ashburnham

Quarter Finals

Katherine O'Connor (Tadmarton Heath) beat Bethan Jones (Llantrisant & Pontyclun) 3 and 1

Amy Rees (Southerndown) beat Rachael Lewis (Pontypool) 3 and 1

Hayley Boulden (Maesdu) beat Natasha Gobey (Rhondda) 2 holes

Tara Davies (Holyhead) beat Beth Davies (Mold) at 21st

Semi-Finals

O'Connor beat Rees 3 and 2
Davies beat Boulden 5 and 4

Final

Tara Davies beat Katherine O'Connor 7 and 6

Month by month in 2006

The rise and rise of Jeev Milkha Singh continues with another win in Japan, this time at the Golf Nippon Series JT Cup, and he makes the world's top 50 as a result. Jim Furyk successfully defends the Nedbank Challenge in South Africa, while Colin Montgomerie goes straight from last place there to the World Cup in Barbados and with European Tour Rookie of the Year Marc Warren battles his way into a play-off. A bogey on the first extra hole, though, means the title goes to Germans Bernhard Langer and Marcel Siem. Spaniard Alvaro Quiros wins in South Africa less than a month after surviving the qualifying school.

Team Events

European Lady Juniors Team Championship 2006 GC de Pan, Netherlands

Year	Winner	Second	Venue
1990	Sweden	England	Shannon, Ireland
1992	Spain	Sweden	St Nom–La–Bretêche, France
1994	Sweden	France	Gutenhof, Vienna, Austria
1996	Spain	France	Nairn, Scotland
1998	Spain	Italy	Oslo, Norway
2000	Italy	England	Castelconturbia, Italy
2002	Spain	Germany	Moscow, Russia
2004	Spain	Wales	Royal Cinque Ports

Qualifying scores for knock-out order (5 out of 6 scores count): I Spain 716; 2 England 742; 3 Sweden 742; 4 France 744; 5 Netherlands 744; 6 Germany 748; 7 Belgium 754; 8 Wales 756; also: Austria, Ireland, Denmark, Scotland, Italy, Finland

Final Ranking: I Sweden; 2 Spain; 3 England; 4 France; 5 Germany; 6 Netherlands; 7 Belgium; 8 Wales; 9 Italy; 10 Denmark; 11 Ireland; 12 Austria; 13 Finland; 14 Scotland

Winning team: Mikaela Backstedt, Py Bengtsson, Karin Kinnerud, Pernilla Lindberg, Anna Nordqvist, Caroline Westrup

European Girls Team Championship 2006 Esbjerg, Denmark

Year	Winner	Venue	Year	Winner	Venue	Year	Winner	Venue
1995	Sweden	Luxembourg	2001	Spain	Portugal	2005	England	Lucerne
1997	Spain	Germany	2003	Spain	Esjberg, Denmark			
1999	Germany	Finland	2004	Sweden	Golf National, France			

Qualifying scores for knock-out order (3 out of 4 scores count): I Spain 427; 2 Sweden 432; 3 Germany 440; 4 Denmark 444; 5 Scotland 445; 6 Belgium 449; 7 France 452; 8 Netherlands 452

Final Ranking: I Germany; 2 Spain; 3 Denmark; 4 France; 5 Sweden; 6 Scotland; 7 Belgium; 8 Netherlands; 9 Italy; 10 Norway; 11 England; 12 Switzerland; 13 Czech Republic; 14 Wales; 15 Finland; 16 Ireland; 17 Iceland; 18 Latvia

Winning team: Pia Halbig, Caroline Masson, Nicola Rössler, Valerie Sternebeck

Girls Home Internationals (Stroyan Cup) 2006 Portstewart

1966	Scotland	Troon (Portland)	1979	England	Edgbaston	1992	Scotland	Moseley
1967	England	Liphook	1980	England	Wrexham	1993	Scotland	Helensburgh
1968	England	Leven	1981	England	Woodbridge	1994	Scotland	Gog Magog
1969	England	Ilkley	1982	England	Edzell	1995	England	Northop
1970	England	North Wales	1983	England	Alwoodley	1996	England	Formby
1971	England	North Berwick	1984	Scotland	Llandudno	1997	England	Forfar
1972	Scotland	Royal Norwich			(Maesdu)	1998	England	Mullingar
1973	Scotland	N'hamptonshire	1985	England	Hesketh GC	1999	Wales	High Post
		County	1986	England	West Kilbride	2000	England	Downfield
1974	England	Dunbar	1987	England	Barnham Broom	2001	England	Brough
1975	England	Henbury	1988	England	Pyle and Kenfig	2002	England	The Hermitage
1976	Scotland	Pyle and Kenfig	1989	England	Carlisle	2003	England	Pyle & Kenfig
1977	England	Formby Ladies	1990	England	Penrith	2004	England	Strathaven
1978	England	Largs	1991	England	Whitchurch	2005	England	Worplesdon

Wales 2, Scotland 7   Wales 3, Ireland 6   **Winning team:** Jenny Jenkins (Captain); Carly Booth
Ireland 2½, England 6½   Ireland 0, Scotland 9   (Comrie), Megan Briggs (Kilmacolm), Krystle Caithness (St
Scotland 7½, England 1½   England 6, Wales 3   Regulus), Rachael Livingstone (Musselburgh Old), Kelsey
                                                                             MacDonald (Nairn Dunbar), Roseanne Niven (Crieff), Michele
                                                                             Thomson (McDonald), Sally Watson (Elie & Earlsferry)

Result: I Scotland 3 [23½]; 2 England 2 [14]; 3 Ireland I [8½]; 4 Wales 0 [8]

Junior Solheim Cup

2002	USA 17	Europe 7	Oak Ridge CC, Hopkins MN
2003	Europe 12½	USA 11½	Bokskogen GC Bara, Sweden
2005	USA 16	Europe 8	The Bridgewater Club, Westfield, IN

Golf Foundation Events

Weetabix Age Group Championships 2006 Forest of Arden

Boys

Year	Under 16	Under 15	Under 14
1990	C Lane (Kingsthorpe)	G Harris (Broome Manor)	P Collier (Limerick)
1991	G Harris (Broome Manor)	C Richardson (Burghley Park)	J Bajcer (Church Stretton)
1992	C Leach (Gillingham)	S Walker (Walmley)	D Kirton (Worksop)
1993	K Godfrey (St Enodoc)	S Young (Seascale)	J Rose (North Hants)
1994	A Smith (Rhondda)	T Hilton (Lewes)	A Smith (Enville)
1995	G Legg (Enmore Park)	S Robinson (Seaton Carew)	D Inglis (Glencorse)
1996	S Fromant (Orsett)	D Skinns (Canwick Park)	C Smith (Cotgrave Place)
1997	M Stam (Royal Liverpool)	G Lockerbie (Keswick)	S Robinson (Thames Ditton)
1998	D Rix (Malton and Norton)	M Skelton (Hunley Hall)	L Shepherd (Cleckheaton & District)
1999	W Schucksmith (Sand Moor)	J Moul (Stoke by Nayland)	T Robinson (Middlesbrough)
2000	M Jones (Upton-by-Chester)	S Taylor (Blundells Hill)	S Hufton (Copt Heath)
2001	J Cundy (Kings Lynn)	M Baldwin (Hesketh)	T Chambers (Coxmoor)
2002	J Parry (Harrogate)	L Lewis (Fairwood Park)	M Swales (Bowood)
2003T	L Lewis (Gower)	L Edmunds (West Cornwall)	H Smart (Banstead)
	A Bates (Stressholme)		
2004	L Joy (Canford Magna)	A Chesters (Hawkstone Park)	S Hodgson (Sunningdale)
2005	O Pearl (Stoke-by-Nayland)	G Edwards (Llanymynech)	T Lewis (Mid Herts)

Year	Under 13
1990	S Walker (Boldmere)
1991	N Rossin (John O'Gaunt)
1992	D Main (Moray)
1993	S Godfrey (St Enodoc)
1994	D Tarbotton (Hull)
1995	D Porter (Wellow)
1996	J Maxwell (Muckhart)
1997	J Turner (Newmarket Links)
1998	C Paisley (Stocksfield)
1999	J Haugh (Salisbury and S Wilts)
2000	J Stevenson (Torrington)
2001	Z Gould (Vale of Glamorgan)
2002	N Eardley (Burslem)
2003	C Lloyd (Kendelshire)
2004	T Fleetwood (Salton Juniors, The Park)
2005	A Carson (Long Ashton)

Under 15

1	Reece Cranfield (Haigh Hall)	67-69—136
2	Tom Blennerhassett (Marriott Dalmahoy)	73-67—140
3	Tom Boys (Royal Liverpool)	78-66—144
	Hugo Dobson (Woodbridge)	75-69—144

Under 14

1	Luke Johnson (King's Lynn)*	75-73—148
2	Nigel Colbeck (Cleckheaton)	74-74—148
3	Jack Scott (Deeside)	72-77—149

Under 13

1	Rhys Pugh (Pontypridd)	73-73—146
2	Sam Williams (Castle Royle)	75-73—148
3	Joseph Holmes (Minchinhampton)	80-70—150

(continued over)

Girls

Year	Under 17	Under 16	Under 15
1990		T Poulton (Boyce Hill)	V Hanks (Broome Manor)
1991		G Simpson (Cleckheaton & District)	D Doyle (Lahinch)
1992		H Stirling (Bridge of Allan)	G Nutter (Prestwich)
1993		K Wrigglesworth (Hornsea)	R Hudson (Wheatley)
1994		L Meredith (Wentworth)	L Moffat (W. Kilbride)
1995	R Hudson (Wheatley)	L Moffat (W. Kilbride)	V Laing (Musselburgh)
1996	K Fisher (Leyland)	F More (Lindrick)	L Archer (Lilleshall Hall)
1997	V Laing (Musselburgh)	R Bell (Northcliff)	L Kenney (Pitreavie)
1998	J Pritchard (Tredegar Park)	L Archer (Lilleshall Hall)	A Marshall (Burghley Park)
1999	P Willett (Enfield)	H MacRae (Callander)	A Marshall (Burghley Park)
2000	C Queen (Drumpelier)	L Eastwood (Yelverton)	N Haywood (Rotherham)
2001	L Eastwood (Yelverton)	N Haywood (Rotherham)	F Johnson (Harborne)
2002	J Phipps (Gog Magog)	A Scott (Consett & District)	M Reid (Chevin)

Year	Under 16	Under 15	Under 14
2003	M Reid (Chevin)	J Ewart (Catterick)	K Matharu (Sand Moor)
2004	J Ewart (Catterick)	K Matharu (Sand Moor)	V Bradshaw (Bangor)
2005	E Taylor (Gainsborough)	G Lewis (Oswestry)	N Gobey (Rhondda

Under 15
1. Jenna Birch (Fleetwood) 75-74—149
2. Nikki Foster (Accrington & District) 74-76—150
3. Gemma Bradbury (Cottrell Park) 77-76—153

Under 14
1. Melissa McMahon (Yeovil) 80-75—155
2. Megan Illingworth (Stoke Rochford) 76-82—158
3. Victoria Homer (West Sussex) 85-82—167

Under 13
1. Alexandra Peters (Beeston Fields) 73-72—145
2. Bronte Law (Bramhall) 77-72—149
3. Poppy Lockwood (Cleveland) 79-77—156

Duke of York Trophy Winners (For best 36-hole aggregate)

Year	Boys	Girls
1991	Gary Harris (Broome Manor)	Georgina Simpson (Cleckheaton)
1992	Christopher Leach (Gillingham)	Heather Stirling (Bridge of Allan)
1993	Kristian Godfrey (St Enodoc)	Katy Wrigglesworth (Hornsea)
1994	Alex Smith (Rhondda)	Lisa Meredith (Wentworth)
1995	Gavin Legg (Enmore Park)	Rebecca Hudson (Wheatley)
1996	Stuart Fromant (Orsett)	Fame More (Lindrick)
1997	Marcus Stam (Royal Liverpool)	Louise Kenney (Pitreavie)
1998	Darren Rix (Malton & Norton)	Laura Archer (Lilleshall Hall)
1999	William Shucksmith (Sand Moor)	Alexandra Marshall (Burghley Park) and Polly Willett (Enfield)
2000	Sam Hufton (Copt Heath)	Natalie Haywood (Rotherham)
2001	James Cundy (King's Lynn)	Natalie Haywood (Rotherham)
2002	John Parry (Harrogate)	Melissa Reid (Chevin)
2003	Henry Smart (Banstead)	Melissa Reid (Chevin)
2004	Luke Joy (Canford Magna)	Jodi Ewart (Catterick)
2005	Owen Pearl (Stoke-by-Nayland)	Emilee Taylor (Gainsborough)
2006	Reece Cranfield (Haigh Hall)	Alexandra Peters (Beeston Fields)

Golf Foundation Schools Team Championship (for the R&A Trophy)

Year	Winner	Country	Venue
1990	Lycée Bellevue	France	St Andrews
1991	Lycée Bellevue	France	Sunningdale
1992	Lycée Bellevue	France	St Andrews
1993	Lycée Bellevue	France	Gleneagles
1994	Lycée Bellevue	France	St Andrews
1995	Kelvin Grove High School	Australia	Sunningdale
1996	Welkom Gymnasium	South Africa	Blairgowrie
1997	Lycée Bellevue	France	Loch Lomond

Golf Foundation Schools Team Championship continued

Year	Winner	Country	Venue
1998	Damelin College, Randburg	South Africa	Sunningdale
1999	Kooralbyn International School	Australia	St Andrews
2000	Rotorua Boys' High School	New Zealand	Royal County Down
2001	Rotorua Boys' High School	New Zealand	The Berkshire

Discontinued

Golf Foundation Award Winners

Year	Winner		Club	Year	Winner		Club
1982		Lindsey Anderson	Tain	1994	*Boys:*	Denny Lucas	Worksop
1983		Nigel Osborne Clarke	Shirehampton		*Girls:*	Rebecca Hudson	Wheatley
1984		Wayne Henry	Redbourn	1995	*Boys:*	Justin Rose	North Hants
1985		David Grantham	Hull		*Girls:*	Rebecca Hudson	Wheatley
1986		Matthew Stanford	Saltford	1996	*Boys:*	Mark Pilkington	Nefyn & District
1987		Jane Marchant	Whittington				GC and Pwllheli
			Barracks		*Girls:*	Fame More	Chesterfield GC
1988	*Boys:*	Ian Garbutt	Wheatley				and Lindrick GC
	Girls:	Lisa Dermott	St Melyd	1997	*Boys:*	Nicholas Dougherty	Shaw Hill, Lancs
1989	*Boys:*	Lee Westwood	Worksop		*Girls:*	Rebecca Brewerton	Abergele &
	Girls:	Lynn McCool	Strabane				Pensarn
1990	*Boys:*	Keith Law	Forfar	1998	*Boys:*	Steven O'Hara	Colville Park
	Girls:	Mhairi McKay	Turnberry		*Girls:*	Vikki Laing	Musselburgh
1991	*Boys:*	Gary Harris	Broome Manor	1999	*Boys:*	Barry Hume	Haggs Castle
	Girls:	Nicola Buxton	Woodsome Hall		*Girls:*	Rebecca Brewerton	Abergele
1992	*Boys:*	Shaun Devenney	Strabane	2000	*Boys:*	David Inglis	Glencorse
	Girls:	Mhairi McKay	Turnberry		*Girls:*	Sophie Walker	Kenwick Park
1993	*Boys:*	Craig Williams	Greigiau				
	Girls:	Georgina Simpson	Cleckheaton &				
			District				

Discontinued

Records tumble on the European international schedule

Spectacular scoring on the European Tour meant many records were set in 2006. Tiger Woods at The Open and US PGA Championships and Robert Karlsson at the Andalucia Open de España Valle Romano and the Entercard Scandinavian Masters were double record breakers. Records were broken in Wales, Hong Kong, Abu Dhabi, Holland, China, Portugal, Austria, Sweden, Germany, Portugal, England and America.

60 (–9)	Phillip Archer	Celtic Manor Wales Open	63 (–9)	Lee Westwood	Deutsche Bank Players Championship
61 (–9)	Simon Dyson	UBS Hong Kong Open	64 (–8)	Paul Broadhurst	Algarve Open de Portugal
62 (–10)	Henrik Stenson	Abu Dhabi Golf Championship	65 (–7)	Chawalit Plaphol	Volvo China Open
62 (–9)	Richard Green	KLM Dutch Open	65 (–7)	Tiger Woods	The Open
62 (–10)	Lian Wen-Chong	TCL Classic			Championship
63 (–9)	Robert Karlsson	Andalucia Open de España Valle Romano	65 (–7)	Tiger Woods	US PGA Championship
63 (–8)	Gregory Havret	BA-CA Telekom Austria Open	67 (–6)	Patrick O'Brien	South Africa Airways Open
63 (–9)	Robert Karlsson	Entercard Scandinavian Masters	67 (–5)	Jeev Milkha Singh	Volvo China Open

Mixed Boys' and Girls' Events

R&A Junior Open Championhips 2006 *Heswall*

Gold	Patrick Reed (USA)	73-70-74—217
Silver	Amanjyot Singh (IND)	77-75—152
Bronze	Saber Sahli (TUN)	85-78—163
Young Lady Golfer	Jungeun Han (KOR)	72-72—144
Under 14	Bertine Strauss (RSA)	71-76—147

Regional Trophies: African: Nobuhle Dlamini (SWZ) 145; Asia-Pacific: Michelle Koh (MAS) 39; Central European: Ben Enoch (WAL) 141; Eastern European: Petr Strycek (CZE) 147; Nordic: Patrick Winther (DEN) 154; Southern European: Koray Varli (TUR) 145; North American: Nicole Vandermade (CAN) 148; South American: Carina Cuculiza (NCA) 149; Special Invitation Category: Ignacio Rodriguez (ESP) 149

61 countries were represented

Next event: 2008 at Hesketh, Southport

European Young Masters 2006 *Styrian, Murhof, Austria*

European Young Masters Nations Cup

1 Germany 624 (Saskia Hausladen, Nicola Rössler; Sean Einhaus, Maximilian Kiefer); 2 France 645; 3 Spain 646   12 teams took part

Overall Individual Winner: Saskia Hausladen (GER)   72-71-64—207

Boys Individual

1	Victor Dubuisson (FRA)*	69-71-67—207
2	Maximilian Kiefer (GER)	70-68-69—207
3	Anders Kristiansen (NOR)	68-71-69—208

play-off: Kiefer 4, Dubuisson 5

14 countries were represented

Girls Individual

1	Saskia Hausladen (GER)	72-71-64—207
2	Carlota Ciganda (ESP)	72-71-68—211
3	Carly Booth (SCO)	70-73-71—214

Toyota World Junior Team Championship 2006 *Chukyo, Japan*

1995	USA	643	1999	England	863	2003	Korea	868
1996	Japan	625	2000	USA	859	2004	USA	839
1997	USA	864	2001	South Africa	856	2005	USA	824
1998	England	874	2002	Not played				

1	Norway	832 (Are Friesbad, Anders Kristiansen, Espen Kofstad, Marius Thorp)
2	Sweden	833 (Björn Akesson, Jesper Kennegard, Pontus Widegren, Robin Wingardh)
3	Japan	839 (Yusaku Matsuoka, Ryutaro Nagano, Naoto Nakanishi, Synnsuke Sonoda)

15 teams took part

Individual:

1	Marius Thorp (NOR)	68-71-65-67—271 (-17)
2	Björn Akesson (SWE)	69-67-70-70—276 (-12)
	Naoto Nakanishi (JPN)	72-69-65-70—276 (-12)

Faldo Series 2006 *Celtic Manor*

Boys

1997	N Dougherty			2002	J Heath	Burhill	138
1998	G Hyde	Loch Lomond	138	2003	M Pilling	Brocket Hall	134
1999	N Dougherty	The Belfry	109 (27 holes)	2004	O Fisher	Burhill	133
2000	N Dougherty	Royal Liverpool	140	2005	J Parry	Celtic Manor	137
2001	G Bondarenko*	Saunton	152				

Under 21: Ben Evans (Rye)   211

Under 18: Simon Doherty (Malone)   221

Under 17: Rory McIlroy (Holywood)   214

Under 16: Darren Renwick (Worthing)   219

Under 15: Eddie Pepperell (Frilford Heath)   220

Girls

1998	K Philips	Loch Lomond	154	2002	F Parker	Burhill	152
1999	A Highgate	The Belfry	114 (27 holes)	2003	T Delaney	Brocket Hall	145
2000	A Highgate	Royal Liverpool	146	2004	K Matharu	Burhill	142
2001	O Rotmistrova	Saunton	155				

Under 18: Stephanie Meadow (Royal Portrush) 241

Faldo Series International Trophy 2006 *Hong Kong*

1	Tsai Pei-ying (TPE)	77-74—151
2	Kiran Matharu (ENG)	76-76—152
	Tiffany Avern Taplin (RSA)	73-79—152

Junior Masters 2006 *Gleneagles (Queen's Course)*

Boys

2003	L Pirie	Gleneagles (Queen's Course)	42 pts	2005	L Pirie	Gleneagles (Queen's Course)	42 pts
2004	R MacNab	Gleneagles (Queen's Course)	42 pts				

1	John Gibson (Carnwath)	40 pts
2	Lewis Meston (Ayr Belleisle)	38
3	Ryan Boyle (Bathgate)	37
	Murray Winton (Mortonhall)	37

Girls

2003	M Thomson	Gleneagles (Queen's Course)	37 pts	2005	M Thomson	Gleneagles (Queen's Course)	37 pts
2004	R Livingstone	Gleneagles (Queen's Course)	40 pts				

1	Jennifer Sinclair (Elie & Earlsferry)	36 pts
2	Karen Mackay (Durness)	35
3	Ashley Alston (Royal Montrose)	34

The Junior Ryder Cup 2006 *Celtic Manor, Wales*

1995	Rochester, USA	Exhibition Match won by Europe
1997	San Roque & Alcaidesa, Spain	United States won 7–5
1999	Cape Cod, USA	Europe won 10½–1½
2002	K Club, Dublin, Ireland	Europe won 9½–2½
2004	Cleveland, OH, USA	Europe won 8½–3½

Captains: Europe: Andy Ingram; USA: Jack Connelly

First Day – Fourball
Anders Kristiansen (NOR) & Are Friestad (NOR) lost to Philip Francis & Drew Kittleson 3 and 1
Carlota Ciganda (ESP) & M Silva (ESP) lost to Vicky Hurst & Isabelle Lendl 1 hole
Pedro Figueiredo (POR) & V Dubuisson (FRA) beat Tony Mapu Finau & Joe Monte 2 and 1
Carly Booth (SCO) & G Molinaro (ITA) lost to Esther Choe & Kristen Schelling 1 hole
Sean Einhaus (GER) & Maximilian Kieffer (GER) beat Bud Cauley & Andrew Yun 4 and 2
Laura Gonzales-Escallon (BEL) & Saskia Hausladen (GER) beat Brittany Altomare & Cassandra Blaney
  2 and 1

Second Day – Mixed Fourball
C Ciganda & A Kristiansen beat E Choe & P Francis 2 and 1
S Hausladen & S Einhaus lost to I Landl & D Kittleson 3 and 1
C Booth & A Friestad beat K Schelling & A Yun 3 and 2
M Silva & P Figueiredo lost to V Hurst & B Cauley 3 and 2
L Gonzales-Escallon & M Kieffer lost to C Blaney & T Mapu Finau 1 hole
G Molinaro & V Dubuisson beat B Altomare & J Monte 4 and 3

Match result: Europe 6; USA 6 (Europe retain the trophy)

New 12-hole course in Edinburgh caters for juniors, beginners and the disabled

As sport's only international governing body based in Scotland, The R&A is committed to looking "outward rather than inward", according to chief executive Peter Dawson.

When it comes to the development of the game, however, the home of golf hasn't been omitted from The R&A's philanthropic vision. The organisation has made a three year commitment to the Paul Lawrie Junior Programme in Aberdeen as well as providing financial assistance for the public golf course at Ruchill in Glasgow and the Hermitage course in Edinburgh.

The R&A teamed up with Sportscotland to back the 12 hole facility at the Braid Hills which caters specifically for juniors, beginners and the disabled. The Hermitage is the first facility of its type in the UK and the charity which runs the course has paid special tribute to The R&A's support in completing the project. *Mike Aitken*

PART VII

Tournaments for the Disabled

Tournaments for the Disabled

British Blind Open *Ratho Park, Edinburgh*
1	Des Chandler (ENG)	62-67—129
2	Brad Eaton (USA)	67-67—134
3	Jan Dinsdale (NI)	67-72—139

World Invitation Trophy (for blind golfers) *Ratho Park, Edinburgh*
1	Paul Hennessey (SCO)	60-60—120
2	Cameron McDiarmid (SCO)	62-66—128
3	Gordon Dickson (SCO)	60-75—135

British Blind Masters *Patshull Park, Shropshire*
1	Steve Cook	66-69-71-59—265
2	Duncan Bickerton	63-71-59-74—267
3	Andrew Sellars	70-69-66-71—276

English MatchPlay Championships (for blind golfers) *Guadet Luce GC, Worcestershire*

Quarter Finals:
A Sellars beat D Bickerton 2 and 1
T Shearman beat R Tomlinson 2 and 1
D Field beat P Appleyard 7 and 6
M Elrick beat J Madsen 7 and 6

Semi-Finals:
A Sellars beat T Shearman 9 and 7
M Elrick beat D Field 1 up

Final:
A Sellars beat M Elrick 1 up

English StrokePlay Championships (for blind golfers) *Wharton Park, Worcestershire*
1	Sandy Burne	62-77—139
2	Simon Cookson	73-68—141
	Andy Sellars	71-70—141

Scottish MatchPlay Championships (for blind golfers)
Cawder GC, Dunblane GC, Strathmore GC

Semi finals:
John Imrie (Aberdeen) beat Gordon Dickson (Edinburgh) 2 and 1
Jim Eadie (Bellshill) beat Stuart Wilkie (Auchterarder) 4 and 3
Final:
John Imrie beat Jim Eadie 2 and 1

Scottish StrokePlay Championships (for blind golfers) *The Glen GC, North Berwick*
1	Myles Clark	63-65—128
2	Cameron McDiarmid	74-70—144
3	John Imrie	76-70—146

Scotland v England Blind Golf Competition for the Auld Enemies Cup

Meon Valley GC, Southampton (home team names first)

Day I – Foursomes:
Mike Loten & Duncan Bickerton lost to Peter Philip & Mike Mayo 2 & I
Ron Tomlinson & Peter Hodgkinson lost to Ally Reid & Myles Clark 7 & 6
Simon Cookson & Neil Baxter lost to John Miller & Sam Sloan 3 & 2
Steve Beevers & Derek Field beat John Imrie & Darren Healey 3 & I
Jay Cookson & Malcolm Elrick beat Gerry Kelly & Stuart Wilkie 4 & 3
Steve Cook & Andy Sellars beat Iain Prime & Cameron McDiarmid 7 & 6

Day 2 – Four balls:
Mike Loten & Paul Appleyard lost to Iain Prime & Stuart Wilkie 4 & 3
Steve Beevers & Derek Field lost to John Miller & Mike Mayo I up
Jay Cookson & Malcolm Elrick beat Ally Reid & Peter Philip I up
Simon Cookson & Ron Tomlinson beat Cameron McDiarmid & Jim Eadie I up
Andy Sellars & Steve Cook lost to Sam Sloan & Myles Clark 3 & 2
Peter Hodgkinson & Duncan Bickerton halved with John Imrie & Gerry Kelly

Day 3 – Singles:

Mike Loten halved with Iain Prime	Derek Field beat Mike Mayo I up
Andy Sellars halved with Cameron McDiarmid	Steve Cook lost to Stuart Wilkie 2 up
Simon Cookson lost to Jim Eadie 2 up	Paul Appleyard halved with Sam Sloan
Steve Beevers beat Ally Reid I up	Duncan Bickerton beat John Miller I up
Jay Cookson halved with Myles Clark	Neil Baxter lost to John Imrie 4 & 3
Malcolm Elrick halved with Darren Healey	Ron Tomlinson lost to Gerry Kelly 4 & 3

Match result: Scotland I3, England II

69th One Arm Golf Society World Championships *Tynemouth*

Quarter Finals
Nicholas Champness (ENG) beat Gary Marshal (USA)
  6 and 5
Tony Hamley (AUS) beat Keith Dewhurst (ENG)
  3 and 2
Michael O'Grady (IRL) beat Chris Court (ENG)
  6 and 4
Marcus Malo (SWE) beat David Waterhouse (ENG)
  6 and 5

Semi-Finals
Nicholas Champness beat Tony Hamley
  5 and 4
Michael O'Grady beat Marcus Malo 3 and 2

Final
Nicholas Champness beat Michael O'Grady
  I up

Society of One-Armed Golfers Stableford Competitions

Scottish *Eden, St Andrews* (I8 holes)
  Hugh Ross (Cawder)   4I points
Irish *Mullingar* (I8 holes)
  Michael O'Grady (Mullingar)   35 points
England and Wales *Staverton Park* (27 holes)
  Darren Masters (Feltwell)   62 points

I8th British Amputee Open Championship *Patshull Park, Shropshire*

AK	Bill Savage	172 gross/I36 net	BK	Bill West	173 gross/I45 net
AK	Roger Hurcombe	190 gross/I46 net	BK	Glen Burrage	165 gross/I47 net
AK	Nick Rawcliffe	190 gross/I46 net	BK	Mike Lincoln	169 gross/I49 net
Armie	George Carter	193 gross/I5I net	MUL	Paul O'Kelly	212 gross/I64 net
Armie	David Bailey	184 gross/I50 net	MUL	Dave Walker	219 gross/I7I net
Armie	Dave Mooney	202 gross/I62 net			

Net Champion Bill Savage
Senior Champion Robin Anderson (AK) 173 gross/I5I net
Overall Champion Glen Burrage

Amputee golf categories: Armie (above or below elbow); AK=above knee; BK=below knee; MUL=multiple

Bader Pipe Open *Bognor Regis GC, West Sussex*

1	John Byrne	39 pts
2	Robin Anderson	37 pts
3	Richard Coates	34 pts

Handigolf

National Championship winner	Mark Gibson (Belfast)	Southern Open	Ray Lee (Kent)
		Bolton Metro Unity	Alan Campbell (Lancashire)
North Lincs Open	Ray Lee (Kent)	Southport Links Open	Andy Gore (Lancashire)
Handigolf MK Masters	Keith Robinson (Kent)	Most Improved Player	Andy Gore (Lancashire)

8th Robinson Cup *Onion Creek GC, Austin, Texas*

Captains: Kenny Green (USA), Dallas Smith (International)

USA		International	
Morning – fourball:			
Green & Rowland	1	Smith & Stevens	0
Valentine-Andrews & Harding	1	Davies & Hewitt	0
Bemis & Hubbard	0	Cherry & McNaughton	1
Cox & Hudson	0	Isogai & Asano	1
Buck & Vincent	1	Ziegler & Friske	0
Novak & Ithal	½	Warrington & O'Grady	½
Valentine & Monroe	1	McClelland & Williams	0
Hodess & Larkin	1	Hart & Koyamada	0

Afternoon – singles:

Kenny Green	1	Dan Hewitt (CAN)	0	Bob Buck	0	Josh Williams (CAN)	1
Dan Cox	1	Dallas Smith (CAN)	0	Kevin Valentine	1	Masato Koyamada	0
John Novak	0	Danny Stevens (USA)	1			(JPN)	
Dennis Ithal	0	Ralph Warrington	1	Rick Monroe	1	Gwen Davies (CAN)	0
		(CAN)		Kellie Valentine-	1	Camilla Ziegler (ITA)	0
Brian Bemis	0	Shunro Isogai (JPN)	1	Andrews			
Matt Hubbard	1	Yoshio Asano (JPN)	0	Bob Larkin	1	Gary Hart (AUS)	0
Mike Hudson	0	John McNaughton	1	Dan Hodess	0	Vic McClelland (CAN)	1
		(CAN)		Tim Vincent	½	Michael O'Grady (IRL)	½
Bill Harding	½	Corbin Cherry (USA)	½	Brandon Roland	1	Reinhard Friske (GER)	0

Result: USA 14½, International 9½

Another win for the USA in the Robinson Cup

Photo courtesy of College Park Industries

Bob Buck of Pennsylvania, USA, and Reinhard Friske of Germany who competed in the morning fourballs

For the second year running, the USA team won the Robinson Cup, sponsored by College Park Industries of Fraser, MI, manufacturers of prosthetic feet. Led by captain Kenny Green, the USA team beat captain Dallas Smith and the International team, 14½ to 9½. The International team holds the overall record of 5–3.

Players on the International team represented Australia, Canada, Ireland, Germany, Italy and Japan but found themselves two players short. This deficit was rectified when two US golfers – Danny Stevens and Corbin Cherry – joined the International team to make up the 16 players required.

7th European Disabled Golf Championship *Koski-Golf, Finland*

Category 1 – Scratch:

1	Johan Kammerstad (SWE)	220
2	Manuel de los Santos (FRA)	248
3	Pierfederi Rocchetti (ITA)	252

Category 2 – Handicap:

1	Joakim Bjorkman (SWE)	225 net
2	John Andreas (GER)	229
3	Wolfgang Zum Berge (GER)	230

Category 3 – Stableford:

1	Richard Saunders (ENG)	94 points
2	Michael Sorensen (DEN)	90 points
3	Jeroen Coumou (NED)	89 points

Category 4 – Stableford:

1	Jussi Nuorti (FIN)	96 points
2	Heins Barnbeck (GER)	93 points
3	Antonio Vicari (ITA)	85 points

Ladies Championship Scratch:

1	Tineke Loogman (NED)	280
2	Cynthia van der Zwet (NED)	281
3	Marie Broholmer (SWE)	306

BALASA Federation Games *Broome Manor, Swindon*

Reduced to 27 holes due to bad weather

Category 1 – Scratch:

1	Duncan Hamilton-Martin (ENG)	109
2	Mark Smith (ENG)	121
3	Richard Willis (WAL)	123

Category 2 – Handicap:

1	William West (ENG)	101 net
2	Michael Clements (GER)	102
3	Michael Wright (ENG)	106

Category 3 – Stableford:

1	Graham Cox (AUS)	57
2	Jeroen Coumou (NED)	51
3	George Carter (ENG)	51

Other events

United Kingdom

Blind

Cowdrey Shield	Andrew Sellars
Northern Cup	Duncan Bickerton
Chairman's Cup	Steven Beavers
Fife Classic	Cameron McDiarmid
Tayside Classic	Myles Clark
Greater Glasgow Classic	Cameron McDiarmid
Grampian Classic	Jim Eadie
The Bendall Trophy	Darren Healey
Tuppy Trophy	George Derby
East Classic	Mike Mayo

Overseas

Physically Disabled

Canadian Amputee National Open	Men: Dan Cox
	Women: Gwen Davies
	Senior: John Getchell
17th National Seniors Invitational Ch. (USA)	Cory Crowell
5th National Amputee Championships (USA)	Men: Kenny Green
1st BurgGolf Dutch Disabled Open	Women: Kim Moore
	Hans van Elven

Blind

Canadian Blind Open	Bob Andrews (B1)
	Bruce Hope (B2)
	Ron Plath (B3)

Golf organisations for the disabled

International Blind Golf Association	www.blindgolf.com
English Blind Golf Association	www.blindgolf.co.uk
Scottish Blind Golf Association	www.scottishblindgolf.com
British Amputee & les Autres Sports Association (BALASA)	01206 298610
British Amputee Golf Association	www.baga.org.uk
The Society of One Armed Golfers	01360 622476
Handigolf	www.handigolf.org
European Disabled Golf Asociation	www.edgagolf.com
Physically Challenged Golf Association	www.townusa.com/pcga
Special Olympics Great Britain	www.specialolympicsgb.org
Deaf Golf Association	www.deafgolf.com
Sportability	www.sportability.org

Donations to special needs groups

Since 2002, The R&A have made donations to several special needs groups:

English Blind Golf Association
2002   £2,000
2003   £3,000
2004   £1,000
2005   £2,000
2006   £2,500
2007   £5,000

Scottish Blind Golf Society
2002   £2,000
2003   £2,000
2004   £2,500
2005   £3,000 + £1,000 for International match
2006   £2,500 + £5,000 for International match

British Amputee & Les Autres Sports Association (BALASA)
2002   £2,500
2003   £3,000
2004   £3,000
2005   £3,000

Disability Sport England
2003   £1,000

The Handigolf Foundation
2002   £500
2004   £1,000
2005   £1,000

Irish Deaf Golf Union
2002   £1,000

English Deaf Golf Association
2005   £1,000

Wales Deaf Golf Association
2006   £500

One Armed Golfers
2002   £1,250
2003   £1,500
2004   £1,000
2005   £1,000
2006   £1,000

Special Olympics Europe
2003   £2,000

Special Olympics Great Britain
2002   £2,000
2003 – 2007 incl. £5,000 per annum

Special Olympics Cardiff
2001   £1,750

Special Olympics Wales
2000   £1,250

European Disabled Golf Association
2005 – 2007 incl. £5,000 per annum

Murray Foundation
2006   £1,000

PART VIII

Record Scoring

Record Scoring

In the Major Championships nobody has shot lower than 63. There have been seven 63s in the Open, four 63s in the US Open, two 63s in The Masters and nine 63s in the USPGA Championship. The lowest first 36 holes is 130 by Nick Faldo in the 1992 Open at Muirfield and the lowest 72 hole total is 265 by David Toms in the 2001 USPGA Championship at the Atlanta Athletic Club.

The Open Championship

Most times champions
6 Harry Vardon, 1896–98–99–1903–11–14
5 James Braid, 1901–05–06–08–10; JH Taylor, 1894–95–1900–09–13; Peter Thomson, 1954–55–56–58–65; Tom Watson, 1975–77–80–82–83

Most times runner-up
7 Jack Nicklaus, 1964–67–68–72–76–77–79
6 JH Taylor, 1896–1904–05–06–07–14

Oldest winner
Old Tom Morris, 46 years 99 days, 1867
Roberto De Vicenzo, 44 years 93 days, 1967

Youngest winner
Young Tom Morris, 17 years 5 months 8 days, 1868
Willie Auchterlonie, 21 years 24 days, 1893
Severiano Ballesteros, 22 years 3 months 12 days, 1979

Youngest and oldest competitor
Young Tom Morris, 15 years, 4 months, 29 days, 1866
Gene Sarazen, 71 years 4 months 13 days, 1973

Widest margin of victory
13 strokes Old Tom Morris, 1862
12 strokes Young Tom Morris, 1870
8 strokes JH Taylor, 1900 and 1913; James Braid, 1908; Tiger Woods, 2000
6 strokes Harry Vardon, 1903; JH Taylor, 1909; Bobby Jones, 1927; Walter Hagen, 1929; Arnold Palmer, 1962; Johnny Miller, 1976

Lowest winning aggregates
267 Greg Norman, 66-68-69-64, Sandwich, 1993
268 Tom Watson, 68-70-65-65, Turnberry, 1977; Nick Price, 69-66-67-66, Turnberry, 1994
269 Tiger Woods, 67-66-67-69, St Andrews, 2000
270 Nick Faldo, 67-65-67-71, St Andrews, 1990; Tiger Woods 67-65-71-67, Hoylake, 2006

Lowest in relation to par
19 under Tiger Woods, St Andrews, 2000
18 under Nick Faldo, St Andrews, 1990; Tiger Woods, Hoylake, 2006

Lowest aggregate by runner-up
269 (68-70-65-66) Jack Nicklaus, Turnberry, 1977; (69-63-70-67) Nick Faldo, Sandwich, 1993; (68-66-68-67) Jesper Parnevik, Turnberry, 1994

Lowest aggregate by an amateur
281 (68-72-70-71), Iain Pyman, Sandwich, 1993; (75-66-70-70), Tiger Woods, Royal Lytham, 1996

Lowest round
63 Mark Hayes, second round, Turnberry, 1977; Isao Aoki, third round, Muirfield, 1980; Greg Norman, second round, Turnberry, 1986; Paul Broadhurst, third round, St Andrews, 1990; Jodie Mudd, fourth round, Royal Birkdale, 1991; Nick Faldo, second round, Payne Stewart, fourth round, Sandwich, 1993

Lowest round by an amateur
66 Frank Stranahan, fourth round, Troon, 1950; Tiger Woods, second round, Royal Lytham, 1996; Justin Rose, second round, Royal Birkdale, 1998

Lowest first round
64 Craig Stadler, Royal Birkdale, 1983; Christy O'Connor Jr, Royal St George's, 1985; Rodger Davis, Muirfield, 1987; Steve Pate, Ray Floyd, Muirfield, 1992

Lowest second round
63 Mark Hayes, Turnberry, 1977; Greg Norman, Turnberry, 1986; Nick Faldo, Sandwich, 1993

Lowest third round
63 Isao Aoki, Muirfield, 1980; Paul Broadhurst, St Andrews, 1990

Lowest fourth round
63 Jodie Mudd, Royal Birkdale, 1991; Payne Stewart, Sandwich, 1993

Lowest first 36 holes
130 (66-64), Nick Faldo, Muirfield, 1992
132 (67-65), Henry Cotton, Sandwich, 1934; Nick Faldo (67-65) and Greg Norman (66-66), St Andrews, 1990; Nick Faldo (69-63), Sandwich, 1993; Tiger Woods (67-65), Hoylake, 2006

Lowest second 36 holes
130 (65-65), Tom Watson, Turnberry, 1977; (64-66) Ian Baker-Finch, Royal Birkdale, 1991; (66-64) Anders Forsbrand, Turnberry, 1994

Lowest first 54 holes
198 (67-67-64) Tom Lehman, Royal Lytham, 1996
199 (67-65-67), Nick Faldo, St Andrews, 1990; (66-64-69) Nick Faldo, Muirfield, 1992

Lowest final 54 holes
199 (66-67-66) Nick Price, Turnberry, 1994
200 (70-65-65), Tom Watson, Turnberry, 1977; (63-70-67), Nick Faldo, Sandwich, 1993; (66-64-70), Fuzzy Zoeller, Turnberry, 1994; (66-70-64), Nick Faldo, Turnberry 1994

Lowest 9 holes
28 Denis Durnian, first 9, Royal Birkdale, 1983

Champions in three decades
Harry Vardon, 1896, 1903, 1911; JH Taylor, 1894, 1900, 1913; Gary Player, 1959, 1968, 1974

Biggest span between first and last victories
19 years, J.H. Taylor, 1894–1913

18 years, Harry Vardon, 1896–1914
15 years, Willie Park, 1860–75
15 years, Gary Player, 1959–74
14 years, Henry Cotton, 1934–48

Successive victories
4 Young Tom Morris, 1868–72 (no championship 1871)
3 Jamie Anderson, 1877–79; Bob Ferguson, 1880–82,
Peter Thomson, 1954–56
2 Old Tom Morris, 1861–62; JH Taylor, 1894–95;
Harry Vardon, 1898–99; James Braid, 1905–06; Bobby
Jones, 1926–27; Walter Hagen, 1928–29; Bobby Locke,
1949–50; Arnold Palmer, 1961–62; Lee Trevino,
1971–72; Tom Watson, 1982–83

Amateur champions
John Ball, 1890, Prestwick; Harold Hilton, 1892,
Muirfield; 1897, Royal Liverpool; Bobby Jones, 1926,
Royal Lytham; 1927, St Andrews; 1930 Royal
Liverpool

Highest number of top five finishes
16 JH Taylor and Jack Nicklaus
15 Harry Vardon and James Braid

Players with four rounds under 70
Ernie Els (68-69-69-68), Sandwich, 1993; Greg
Norman (66-68-69-64), Sandwich, 1993; Jesper
Parnevik (68-66-68-67), Turnberry, 1994; Nick Price
(69-66-67-66), Turnberry, 1994; Tiger Woods
(67-66-67-69), St Andrews, 2000; Ernie Els
(69-69-68-68), Royal Troon, 2004

Highest number of rounds under 70
37	Nick Faldo	26	Greg Norman
33	Jack Nicklaus	25	Nick Price
28	Tom Watson	22	Bernhard Langer
27	Ernie Els		

Outright leader after every round (since Championship became 72 holes in 1892)
James Braid, 1908; Ted Ray, 1912; Bobby Jones, 1927;
Gene Sarazen, 1932; Henry Cotton, 1934; Tom
Weiskopf, 1973

Record leads (since 1892)
After 18 holes: 4 strokes, Bobby Jones, 1927; Henry
Cotton, 1934; Christy O'Connor jr, 1985
After 36 holes: 9 strokes, Henry Cotton, 1934
After 54 holes: 10 strokes, Henry Cotton, 1934;
7 strokes, Tony Lema, 1964; 6 strokes, James Braid,
1908; Tom Lehman, 1996; Tiger Woods, 2000

Champions with each round lower than previous one
Jack White, 1904, Sandwich, 80-75-72-69; James Braid,
1906, Muirfield, 77-76-74-73; Ben Hogan, 1953,
Carnoustie, 73-71-70-68; Gary Player, 1959, Muirfield,
75-71-70-68

Champion with four rounds the same
Densmore Shute, 1933, St Andrews, 73-73-73-73
(excluding the play-off)

Biggest variation between rounds of a champion
14 strokes, Henry Cotton, 1934, second round 65,
fourth round 79; 11 strokes, Jack White, 1904, first
round 80, fourth round 69; Greg Norman, 1986, first
round 74, second round 63, third round 74

Biggest variation between two rounds
20 strokes: R.G. French, 1938, second round 71, third
round 91; Colin Montgomerie, 2002, second round 64,

third round 84; 18 strokes: A Tingey Jr, 1923, first
round 94, second 76; 17 strokes, Jack Nicklaus, 1981,
first round 83, second round 66; Ian Baker-Finch, 1986,
first round 86, second round 69

Best comeback by champions
After 18 holes: Harry Vardon, 1896, 11 strokes behind
the leader
After 36 holes: George Duncan, 1920, 13 strokes behind
leader
After 54 holes: Paul Lawrie, 1999, 10 strokes behind the
leader (won four-hole play-off)

Best comeback by non-champions
Of non-champions, Greg Norman, 1989, seven strokes
behind the leader and lost in a play-off

Best finishing round by a champion
64 Greg Norman, Sandwich, 1993
65 Tom Watson, Turnberry, 1977; Severiano
Ballesteros, Royal Lytham, 1988; Justin Leonard, Royal
Troon, 1997

Worst finishing round by a champion since 1920
79 Henry Cotton, Sandwich, 1934
78 Reg Whitcombe, Sandwich, 1938
77 Walter Hagen, Hoylake, 1924

Best opening round by a champion
66 Peter Thomson, Royal Lytham, 1958; NickFaldo,
Muirfield, 1992; Greg Norman, Sandwich, 1993
67 Henry Cotton, Sandwich, 1934; Tom Watson,
Royal Birkdale, 1983; Severiano Ballesteros, Royal
Lytham, 1988; Nick Faldo, St Andrews, 1990; John
Daly, St Andrews, 1995; Tom Lehman, Royal Lytham,
1996; Tiger Woods, St Andrews, 2000; Tiger Woods,
St Andrews, 2005; Tiger Woods, Hoylake, 2006

Worst opening round by a champion since 1919
80 George Duncan, Deal, 1920 (he also had a second
round of 80)
77 Walter Hagen, Hoylake, 1924

Biggest recovery in 18 holes by a champion
George Duncan, Deal, 1920, was 13 strokes behind the
leader, Abe Mitchell, after 36 holes and level after 54

Most consecutive appearances
47 Gary Player, 1955–2001

Championship since 1946 with the fewest rounds under 70
St Andrews, 1946; Hoylake, 1947; Portrush, 1951;
Hoylake, 1956; Carnoustie, 1968. All had only two
rounds under 70

Longest course
Carnoustie, 1999, 7361 yds

Largest entries
2,499 in 2005, St Andrews

Courses most often used
St Andrews, 27; Prestwick, 24 (but not since 1925);
Muirfield, 15; Sandwich, 12; Hoylake, 11; Royal Lytham
and St Annes, 10; Royal Birkdale, 8; Royal Troon 8;
Musselburgh, 6; Carnoustie, 6; Turnberry, 3; Deal, 2;
Royal Portrush and Prince's, 1

Albatrosses
Both Jeff Maggert (6th hole, 2nd round) and Greg
Owen (11th hole, 3rd round) made albatrosses during

Prize Money

Year	Total	First Prize £	Year	Total	First Prize £	Year	Total	First Prize £
1860	nil	nil	1960	7000	1,250	1987	650,000	75,000
1863	10	nil	1961	8500	1,400	19 88	700,000	80,000
1864	16	6	1963	8500	1,500	1989	750,000	80,000
1876	20	20	1965	10,000	1,750	1990	815,000	85,000
1889	22	8	1966	15,000	2,100	1991	900,000	90,000
1891	28.50	10	1968	20,000	3,000	1992	950,000	95,000
1892	110	(am)	1969	30,000	4,250	1993	1,000,000	100,000
1893	100	30	1970	40,000	5,250	1994	1,100,000	110,000
1910	125	50	1971	45,000	5,500	1995	1,250,000	125,000
1920	225	75	1972	50,000	5,500	1996	1,400,000	200,000
1927	275	100	1975	75,000	7,500	1997	1,586,300	250,000
1930	400	100	1977	100,000	10,000	1998	1,774,150	300,000
1931	500	100	1978	125,000	12,500	1999	2,029,950	350,000
1946	1000	150	1979	155,000	15,500	2000	2,722,150	500,000
1949	1700	300	1980	200,000	25,000	2001	3,229,748	600,000
1953	2450	500	1982	250,000	32,000	2002	3,880,998	700,000
1954	3500	750	1983	300,000	40,000	2003	3,931,000	700,000
1955	3750	1,000	1984	451,000	55,000	2004	4,006,950	720,000
1958	4850	1,000	1985	530,000	65,000	2005	3,854,900	720,000
1959	5000	1,000	1986	600,000	70,000	2006	3,990,916	720,000

the 2001 Open Championship at Royal Lytham and St Annes. No complete record of albatrosses in the history of the event is available but since 1979 there have been only four others – by Johnny Miller (Muirfield 5th hole) in 1980, Bill Rogers (Royal Birkdale 17th hole) 1983, Manny Zerman (St Andrews) 2000 and Gary Evans (Royal Troon 4th hole) 2004.

US Open

Most times champion
4 Willie Anderson, 1901–03–04–05; Bobby Jones, 1923–26–29–30; Ben Hogan, 1948–50–51–53; Jack Nicklaus, 1962–67–72–80

Most times runner-up
4 Bobby Jones, 1922–24–25–28; Sam Snead, 1937–47–49–53; Arnold Palmer, 1962–63–66–67; Jack Nicklaus, 1960 (am)–68–71–82

Oldest winner
Hale Irwin, 45 years, 15 days, Medinah, 1990

Youngest winner
Johnny McDermott, 19 years, 10 months, 12 days, Chicago, 1911

Biggest winning margin
15 strokes Tiger Woods, Pebble Beach, 2000

Lowest winning aggregate
272 Jack Nicklaus, Baltusrol, 1980; Lee Janzen, Baltusrol, 1993; Tiger Woods, Pebble Beach, 2000

Lowest in relation to par
12 under Tiger Woods, Pebble Beach, 2000

Lowest round
63 Johnny Miller, fourth round, Oakmont, 1973; Jack Nicklaus, first round, Baltusrol, 1980; Tom Weiskopf, first round, Baltusrol, 1980; Vijay Singh, second round, Olympia Fields, 2003

Lowest 9 holes
29 Neal Lancaster, Shinnecock Hills, 1995, and Oakland Hills, 1996

Lowest first 36 holes
133 Jim Furyk, Vijay Singh, Olympia Fields, 2003

Lowest final 36 holes
132 Larry Nelson, Oakmont, 1983

Lowest first 54 holes
200 Jim Furyk, Olympia Fields, 2003

Open attendances

Year	Attendance	Year	Attendance	Year	Attendance	Year	Attendance
1962	37,098	1974	92,796	1986	134,261	1998	180,000
1963	24,585	1975	85,258	1987	139,189	1999	158,000
1964	35,954	1976	92,021	1988	191,334	2000	230,000
1965	32,927	1977	87,615	1989	160,639	2001	178,000
1966	40,182	1978	125,271	1990	207,000	2002	161,000
1967	29,880	1979	134,501	1991	192,154	2003	182,585
1968	51,819	1980	131,610	1992	150,100	2004	176,000
1969	46,001	1981	111,987	1993	140,100	2005	223,000
1970	82,593	1982	133,299	1994	128,000	2006	230,000
1971	70,076	1983	142,892	1995	180,000		
1972	84,746	1984	193,126	1996	170,000		
1973	78,810	1985	141,619	1997	176,797		

Lowest final 54 holes
204 Jack Nicklaus, Baltusrol, 1967; Raymond Floyd, Shinnecock Hills, 1986; Steve Jones, Oaklands Hills, 1996

Most consecutive appearances
44 Jack Nicklaus 1957 to 2000

Successive victories
3 Willie Anderson, 1903–04–05

Players with four rounds under 70
Lee Trevino, 69-68-69-69, Oak Hill, 1968; Lee Janzen, 67-67-69-69, Baltusrol, 1993

Outright leader after every round
Walter Hagen, Midlothian, 1914; Jim Barnes, Columbia, 1921; Ben Hogan, Oakmont, 1953; Tony Jacklin, Hazeltine, 1970; Tiger Woods, Pebble Beach, 2000; Tiger Woods, Bethpage, 2002

Best opening round by a champion
63 Jack Nicklaus, Baltusrol, 1980

Worst opening round by a champion
91 Horace Rawlins, Newport, RI, 1895
Since World War II: 76 Ben Hogan, Oakland Hills, 1951; Jack Fleck, Olympic, 1955

Amateur champions
Francis Ouimet, Brookline, 1913; Jerome Travers, Baltusrol, 1915; Chick Evans, Minikahda, 1916; Bobby Jones, Inwood, 1923; Scioto, 1926, Winged Foot, 1929, Interlachen, 1930; Johnny Goodman, North Shore, 1933

The Masters

Most times champion
6 Jack Nicklaus, 1963–65–66–72–75–86
4 Arnold Palmer, 1958–60–62–64
4 Tiger Woods, 1997–2001–02–05

Most times runner-up
4 Ben Hogan, 1942–46–54–55; Jack Nicklaus, 1964–71–77–81

Oldest winner
Jack Nicklaus, 46 years, 2 months, 23 days, 1986

Youngest winner
Tiger Woods, 21 years, 3 months, 15 days, 1997

Biggest winning margin
12 strokes Tiger Woods, 1997

Lowest winning aggregate
270 Tiger Woods, 1997

Lowest in relation to par
18 under Tiger Woods, Augusta, 1997

Lowest aggregate by an amateur
281 Charles Coe, 1961 (joint second)

Lowest round
63 Nick Price, 1986; Greg Norman, 1996

Lowest 9 holes
29 Mark Calcavecchia, 1992; David Toms, 1998

Lowest first 36 holes
131 Raymond Floyd, 1976

Lowest final 36 holes
131 Johnny Miller, 1975

Lowest first 54 holes
201 Raymond Floyd, 1976; Tiger Woods, 1997

Lowest final 54 holes
200 Tiger Woods, 1997

Most appearances
50 Arnold Palmer 1955–2004
49 Doug Ford 1952 to 2001; Gary Player 1957 to 2006

Successive victories
2 Jack Nicklaus, 1965–66; Nick Faldo, 1989–90; Tiger Woods, 2001–02

Players with four rounds under 70
None

Outright leader after every round
Craig Wood, 1941; Arnold Palmer, 1960; Jack Nicklaus, 1972; Raymond Floyd, 1976

Best opening round by a champion
65 Raymond Floyd, 1976

Worst opening round by a champion
75 Craig Stadler, 1982

Albatrosses
There have been three albatross twos in the Masters at Augusta National: by Gene Sarazen at the 15th, 1935; by Bruce Devlin at the eighth, 1967; and by Jeff Maggert at the 13th, 1994.

USPGA Championship

Most times champion
5 Walter Hagen, 1921–24–25–26–27; Jack Nicklaus 1963–71–73–75–80

Most times runner-up
4 Jack Nicklaus, 1964–65–74–83

Oldest winner
Julius Boros, 48 years 4 months 18 days, Pecan Valley, 1968

Youngest winner
Gene Sarazen, 20 years 5 months 22 days, Oakmont, 1922

Biggest winning margin
7 strokes Jack Nicklaus, Oak Hill, 1980

Lowest winning aggregate
265 (–15) David Toms, Atlanta Athletic Club, 2001
267 Steve Elkington and Colin Montgomerie, Riviera, 1995 – Montgomerie lost sudden death play-off

Lowest aggregate by runner-up
266 (–14) Phil Michelson, Atlanta Athletic Club, 2001

Lowest in relation to par
18 under Tiger Woods and Bob May, Valhalla, 2000 (May lost three-hole play-off); Tiger Woods, Medinah, 2006

Lowest round
63 Bruce Crampton, Firestone, 1975; Raymond Floyd, Southern Hills, 1982; Gary Player, Shoal Creek, 1984;

Vijay Singh, Inverness, 1993; Michael Bradley and Brad Faxon, Riviera, 1995; José Maria Olazábal, Valhalla, 2000; Mark O'Meara, Atlanta Athletic Club, 2001; Thomas Bjørn, Baltusrol, 2005

Most successive victories
4　Walter Hagen, 1924–25–26–27

Lowest 9 holes
28　Brad Faxon, Riviera, 1995

Lowest first 36 holes
131　Hal Sutton, Riviera, 1983; Vijay Singh, Inverness, 1993; Ernie Els and Mark O'Meara, Riviera, 1995; Shingo Katayama and David Toms, Atlanta Athletic Club, 2001

Lowest final 36 holes
131　Mark Calcavecchia, Atlanta Athletic Club, 2001
132　Miller Barber, Dayton, 1969; Steve Elkington and Colin Montgomerie, Riviera, 1995

Lowest first 54 holes
196　David Toms, Atlanta Athletic Club, 2001

Lowest final 54 holes
199　Steve Elkington, Colin Montgomerie, Riviera, 1995; Mark Calcavecchia, David Toms, Atlanta Athletic Club, 2001

Most appearances
37　Arnold Palmer; Jack Nicklaus

Outright leader after every round
Bobby Nichols, Columbus, 1964; Jack Nicklaus, PGA National, 1971; Raymond Floyd, Southern Hills, 1982; Hal Sutton, Riviera, 1983

Best opening round by a champion
63　Raymond Floyd, Southern Hills, 1982

Worst opening round by a champion
75　John Mahaffey, Oakmont, 1978

Worst closing round by a champion
76　Vijay Singh, Whistling Straits, 2004 (worst in any major since Reg Whitcombe's 78 in 1938 Open)

Albatrosses
Joey Sindelar had an albatross at the fifth hole at Medinah Country Club during the third round of the 2006 PGA Championship

PGA European Tour

Lowest 72-hole aggregate
258　(–14)　David Llewellyn (WAL), AGF Biarritz Open, 1988; (18 under par) Ian Woosnam (WAL), Monte Carlo Open, 1990.
259　(–29) Ernie Els (RSA), Johnnie Walker Classic, Lake Karrinyup, 2003; (25 under par) Mark McNulty (ZIM), German Open, Frankfurt, 1987; (21 under par) Tiger Woods (USA), NEC Invitational, 2000

Lowest 9 holes
27　(9 under par) José María Canizares (ESP), Swiss Open at Crans-sur-Sierre, 1978; (7 under par) Robert Lee (ENG), Johnnie Walker Monte Carlo Open at Mont Agel, 1985; (6 under par) Robert Lee, Portuguese Open at Estoril, 1987; (9 under par) Joakim Haeggman (SWE), Alfred Dunhill Cup at St Andrews, 1997; (9 under par) Simon Khan, Wales Open at Celtic Manor, 2004

Lowest 18 holes
60　(–12) Jamie Spence, Canon European Masters at Crans-sur-Sierre, 1992; Bernhard Langer (GER), Linde German Masters at Motzener See, 1997; Darren Clarke, Smurfit European Open at K Club, 1999; Fredrik Jacobson, Linde German Masters, Gut Larchenhof, 2003; Ernie Els, Heineken Classic, Royal Melbourne, 2004; (–11) Baldovino Dassu (ITA), Swiss Open at Crans-sur-Sierre, 1971; David Llewellyn (WAL), AGF Biarritz Open, 1988; (–10) Paul Curry, Bell's Scottish Open at Gleneagles, 1992; Tobias Dier, TNT Open, Hilversum, 2002; (–9) Ian Woosnam (WAL), Torras Monte Carlo Open at Mont Agel, 1990; (–9) both Darren Clarke and Johan Rystrom, Monte Carlo Open at Mont Agel, 1992; Phillip Archer (ENG), Celtic Manor Wales Open, Celtic Manor, 2006

Lowest 36 holes
124　(–18) Colin Montgomerie (SCO), Canon European Masters at Crans-sur-Sierre, 1996 (3rd and 4th rounds); (–14) Robert Karlsson (SWE), Celtic Manor Wales Open at Celtic Manor, 2006 (1st and 2nd rounds)

Lowest 54 holes
189　(–18) Robert Karlsson (SWE), Celtic Manor Wales Open, Celtic Manor, 2006 (rounds 1-2-3)
192　(–24) Anders Forsbrand (SWE), Ebel European Masters Swiss Open, Crans-sur-Sierre, 1987 (rounds 2-3-4)
192　(–18) Tiger Woods, NEC Invitational, Firestone, Akron, Ohio, 2000 (first 3 rounds)

Lowest first 36 holes
125　(–17) Frankie Minoza, Caltex Singapore Masters, Singapore Island, 2001
125　(–15) Tiger Woods, NEC Invitational World Championship, Firestone, Akron, Ohio, 2000

Largest winning margin
15 strokes　Tiger Woods, United States Open, Pebble Beach, 2000 (Note: Bernhard Langer's 17-stroke victory in 1979 at Cacharel Under-25's Championship in Nîmes is not considered a full European Tour event)

Highest winning score
306　Peter Butler (ENG), Schweppes PGA Close Championship at Royal Birkdale, 1963

Youngest winner
Dale Hayes, 18 years 290 days, Spanish Open, 1971

Youngest to make cut
Sergio García, 15 years 46 days, Turespana Open Mediterrania, 1985

Oldest winner
Des Smyth (IRL), 48 years 34 days, Madeira Island Open, 2001

Most wins in one season
7　Norman von Nida (AUS), 1947

US PGA Tour

Lowest 72-hole aggregate
254　(–26) Tommy Armour III, Valero Texas Open, 2003 (Note: Ernie Els' 261 at the 2003 Mercedes Championship was a record 31 under par)

Lowest 54 holes
189 (−24) Chandler Harper, Texas Open (last three rounds), 1954; John Cook, St Jude Classic (first three rounds), 1996; Mark Calcavecchia, Phoenix Open (first three rounds), 2001; (−21) Tommy Armour III, Valero Texas Open (first three rounds), 2003 (Note: Tim Herron's 190 at the 2003 Bob Hope Chrysler Classic (rounds 2-4) was a record 26 under par)

Lowest 36 holes
124 (−18) Mark Calcavecchia (USA), Phoenix Open, 2001 (2nd and 3rd rounds) (Note: Gay Brewer's 125 at the 1967 Pensacola Open (2nd and 3rd rounds), John Cook's 125 at the 1997 Bob Hope Chrysler Classic (last two rounds), Tom Lehman's 125 at the 2001 Invensys Classic (1st and 2nd rounds) and Tim Herron's 125 at the 2003 Bob Hope Chrysler Classic (2nd and 3rd rounds) were a record 19 under par)

Lowest 18 holes
59 Sam Snead, 3rd round, Greenbrier Open (Sam Snead Festival), White Sulphur Springs, West Virginia, 1959; Al Geiberger, 2nd round, Danny Thomas Memphis Classic, Colonial CC, 1977 (when preferred lies were in operation); (−13) Chip Beck on the 6,914-yards Sunrise GC course, Las Vegas, 3rd round, Las Vegas Invitational, 1991 (finished third but won a bonus prize of $500,000 and another $500,000 for charities; David Duval on 6,940-yd PGA West Arnold Palmer course, CA, final round, Bob Hope Chrysler Classic, 1999 (won tournament with last hole eagle)

Lowest 9 holes
26 (−8) Corey Pavin, US Bank Championship, 2006
27 (−9) Billy Mayfair, Buick Open, 2001; Robert Gamez, Bob Hope Chrysler Classic, 2004; (−8) Mike Souchak, Texas Open, 1955; (−7) Andy North, BC Open, 1975

Lowest first 36 holes
125 (−19) Tom Lehman (USA), Invensys Classic 2001; (−17) Mark Calcavecchia (USA), Phoenix Open, 2001; (−15) Tiger Woods, NEC Invitational World Championship, Firestone, Akron, Ohio, 2000; Corey Pavin, US Bank Championship, 2006

Largest winning margin
16 strokes J. Douglas Edgar, Canadian Open Championship, 1919; Joe Kirkwood, Corpus Christi Open 1924; Bobby Locke, Chicago Victory National Championship, 1948

Youngest winner
Johnny McDermott, 19 years 10 months, US Open, 1911

Youngest to make cut
Bob Panasik, 15 years 8 months 20 days, Canadian Open, 1957

Oldest winner
Sam Snead, 52 years 10 months, Greater Greensboro Open, 1965

Most wins in one season
18 Byron Nelson, 1945

National opens – excluding Europe and USA

Lowest 72-hole aggregate
255 Peter Tupling, Nigerian Open, Lagos, 1981

Lowest 36-hole aggregate
124 (18 under par) Sandy Lyle, Nigerian Open, Ikoyi GC, Lagos, 1978 (his first year as a professional)

Lowest 18 holes
59 Gary Player, second round, Brazilian Open, Gavea GC (6,185 yards), Rio de Janeiro, 1974.

Professional events – excluding Europe and USA

Lowest 72-hole aggregate
260 Bob Charles, Spalding Masters at Tauranga, New Zealand, 1969; Jason Bohn, Bayer Classic, Huron Oaks, Canada, 2001; Brian Kontak, Alberta Open, Canada, 1998.

Lowest 18-hole aggregate
58 (13 under par) Jason Bohn (USA), Bayer Classic, Huron Oaks, Canada, 2001 (Note: Miguel Angel Martin had round of 59 at South Argentine Open, 1987)

Lowest 9-hole aggregate
27 Bill Brask (USA) at Tauranga in the New Zealand PGA in 1976

Amateur winners
Charles Evans, 1910 Western Open, Beverly, Illinois; John Dawson, 1942 Bing Crosby, Rancho Santa Fe, California; Gene Littler, 1954 San Diego Open, Rancho Santa Fe, California; Doug Sanders, 1956 Canadian Open, Beaconsfield, Quebec; Scott Verplank 1985 Western Open, Butler National, Illinois; Phil Mickelson 1991 Northern Telecom Open, Tucson, Arizona; Brett Rumford, 1999 ANZ Players Championship, Royal Queensland; Aaron Baddeley, 1999 Australian Open, Royal Sydney

Asian PGA Tour

Lowest 72 holes
259 (−29) Ernie Els, 2003 Johnnie Walker Classic
262 (−26) Jeev Milkha Singh, 1996 Philip Morris Asia Cup (Limited Field); (−26) Ernie Els, 2005 BMW Asian Open
263 (−25) Tiger Woods, 2000 Johnnie Walker Classic (Note: Thaworn Wiratchant achieved a 25 under par total of 255 in the 2005 Enjoy Jakarta Standard Chartered Indonesian Open, but preferred lies were in use)

Only players to shoot 20-under par or better more than once
Tiger Woods, 2000 Johnnie Walker Classic; 1997 Asian Honda Classic; Ernie Els, 2003 Johnnie Walker Classic and 2005 BMW Asian Open

Highest winning score
293   (+5) Boonchu Tuangkit, 1996 Myanmar Open

Lowest 54 holes
193   (–23) Ernie Els, 2003 Johnnie Walker Classic;
David Howell, 2006 TCL Classic (Note: Thaworn
Wiratchant achieved an 18 under par total of 192 in
the 2005 Enjoy Jakarta Standard Chartered Indonesia
Open, but preferred lies were in use)

Lowest 36 holes
125   (–17) Frankie Minoza, 2001 Caltex Singapore
Masters

Lowest 18 holes
61   (–11) Chung Chun-hsing, 2001 Maekyung LG
Fashion Open; Chanin Puntawong (am), 2003 Thailand
Open; (–10) Frankie Minoza, 2001 Caltex Singapore
Masters; Henrik Bjornstad, 2001 Omega Hong Kong
Open; Lu Wei-chih, 2004 Tianjin TEDA Open
(Note: Kim Felton and Colin Montgomerie had rounds
of 60 in the 2000 Omega Hong Kong Open and 2005
Enjoy Jakarta Standard Chartered Indonesian Open
respectively, but preferred lies were in operation.
Felton's round was 11 under par, Montgomerie's 10
under) (Note: David Howell's 127 in the 2006 TCL
Classic was also 17 under par)

Lowest 9 holes
28   (–8) Chung Chun-hsing, 2001 Maekyung LG
Fashion Open; (–7) Henrik Bjornstad, 2001 Omega
Hong Kong Open; (–6) Darren Griff, 2005 Standard
Chartered Indonesian Open; Maarten Lafeber, 2005
UBS Hong Kong Open

Biggest margin of victory
13 strokes Ernie Els, 2005 BMW Asian Open
12 strokes   Bradley Hughes, 1996 Players
Championship

Youngest winners
Kim Dae-sub (am), 17 years 83 days, 1998 Korean
Open; Eddie Lee (am) 18 years and 170 days, 2002
Maekyung LG Fashion Open; Chinarat Phadungsil (am),
17 years 5 days, 2005 Double A International Open

Youngest to play in an Asian event
Ye Jian-fe, 13 years and 20 days, 2004 Sanya Open

Oldest winner
Choi Sang-ho, 50 years and 145 days, 2005 Maekyung
Open; Boonchu Ruangkit, 47 years and 258 days, 2004
Thailand Open

Most wins in a season
4 Thaworn Wiratchant, 2005
3 Lin Keng-chi 1995 (Tournament Players
Championship, Singapore PGA Championship,
Samsung Masters); Simon Dyson 2000 (Omega Hong
Kong Open, Macau Open, Volvo China Open)

Most wins on Tour
8 Thaworn Wiratchant
7 Kang Wook-soon; Thongchai Jaidee, Thaworn
Wiratchant

Youngest player to make the cut
Lo Shih-kai, 14 years and 275 days, 2003 Acer Taiwan
Open

Oldest player to make the cut
Gary Player, 66 years and 323 days, 2002 Acer Taiwan
Open

Holes in one at same hole
Chen Chung-cheng, 2004 Thailand Open, fourth hole,
days 1 and 3

Japan Golf Tour

Lowest 72 holes
260   (–20) Masashi 'Jumbo' Ozaki, 1995 Chunichi
Crowns, Nagoya Wago
262   (–26) Masashi Ozaki, 1996 Japan Series, Tokyo
Yomiuri
266   (–26) Brandt Jobe, 1995 Mitsubishi Gallant, Aso
Prince Hotel

Lowest 54 holes
193   (–23) Masahiro Kuramoto, 1987 Maruman
Open, Higashi Matsuyama; (–17) Masashi Ozaki, 1995
Chunichi Crowns, Nagoya Wago

Lowest 36 holes
126   (–18) Masahiro Kuramoto, 1987 Maruman
Open, Higashi Matsuyama

Lowest 18 holes
59   (–12) Masahiro Kuramoto, 2003 Acom
International

Lowest 9 holes
28   (–8) Isao Aoki, 1972 Kanto Pro, Isogo; Takashi
Murakami, 1972 Kanto Pro, Isogo; Yoshinori Kaneko,
1994 Nikkei Cup, Mitsui-kanko Tomakomai; Masayuki
Kawamura, 1995 Gene Sarazen Jun Classic; Tsuyoshi
Yoneyama, 1998 Sapporo Tokyu, Sapporo Kokusai;
Toshimitsu Izawa, 2000 TPC Iiyama Cup, Horai

Largest winning margin
15 Masashi Ozaki, 1994 Daiwa International
Hatoyama (pre-1973 tour formation: 19 Akira Muraki,
1930 Japan PGA Championship, Takarazuka)

Youngest winner
Seve Ballesteros, 20 years 5 months, 1977 Japan Open,
Narashino (pre-1973 tour formation: Toichiro Toda,
18 years 6 months, 1933 Kansai Open)

Oldest winner
Masashi Ozaki, 55 years 8 months, 2002 ANA Open,
Sapporo Wattsu

Most wins in a season
9 Tsuneyuki 'Tommy' Nakajima, 1983; Masashi
'Jumbo' Ozaki, 1972

South African Sunshine Tour

Lowest 9-hole score
28 Simon Hobday, 2nd round of the 1987 Royal Swazi
Sun Pro Am at Royal Swazi Sun Country Club; Mark
McNulty (IRL), 2nd round of 1996 Zimbabwe Open at
Chapman Golf Club; David Frost, 2nd round of the
1997 Alfred Dunhill PGA Championship at Houghton
Golf Club; Tertius Claassens, 1st round of the 1982
SAB Masters at Milnerton; Brenden Pappas, 2nd round
of the 1996 Dimension Data Pro-Am at Gary Player
Country Club; Murray Urquhart, 2nd round of the
2001 Royal Swazi Sun Open at Royal Swazi Sun
Country Club

Lowest 18-hole score
60 Shane Pringle (ZIM) 30-30, 2002 Botswana Open, Gabarone Golf Club

Lowest first 36 holes
127 Barry Painting (ZIM) 62-65, 2004 FNB Botswana Open, Gabarone Golf Club

Lowest last 36 holes
126 Mark McNulty (IRL) 64-62, 1987 Royal Swazi Sun Pro-Am, Royal Swazi Sun Country Club

Lowest 54 holes
195 Nick Price (ZIM) 61-69-65, 1994 ICL International; Barry Painting (ZIM) 62-65-68, 2004 FNB Botswana Open, Gaberone GC

Lowest 72-hole score
259 Mark McNulty (IRL) 68-65-64-62, 1987 Royal Swazi Sun Pro-Am, Royal Swazi Sun Country Club; David Frost 64-67-65-63, 1994 Lexington PGA, Wanderers Golf Club

Largest winning margin
12 strokes Nick Price (ZIM), 1993 Nedbank Million Dollar, Sun City (non-order of merit event)
11 strokes Nico van Rensburg, 2000 Vodacom Series Gauteng, Silver Lakes

Most wins in a season
Seven wins in 11 tournaments by Mark McNulty (IRL), 1986-87 season – Southern Suns SA Open, AECI Charity Classic, Royal Swazi Sun Pro-Am, Trust Bank Tournament of Champions, Germiston Centenary Golf Tournament, Safmarine Masters, Helix Wild Coast Sun Classic

Most wins in succession
Four Gary Player, 1979-80 – Lexington PGA, Krönenbrau SA Masters, B.A. / Yellow Pages SA Open, Sun City Classic; Mark McNulty (IRL), 1986-87 – Southern SA Open, AECI Charity Classic, Royal Swazi Sun Pro-Am, Trust Bank Tournament of Champions

Most birdies in one round
11 Allan Henning, 1st round of the 1975 Rolux Toro Classic, Glendower Golf Club; John Bland, 1st round of the 1993 SA Open Championship, Durban Country Club; Mark McNulty (IRL), 2nd round of the 1996 Zimbabwe Open, Royal Harare Golf Club; Alan McLean, 3rd round of the 2005 Telkom PGA Championship at Woodhill Country Club (Note: Shane Pringle had 10 birdies and an eagle in the 2nd round of the 2002 FNB Botswana Open at Gaborone Golf Club; Marc Cayeux had nine birdies and an eagle in the final round of the 2004 Vodacom Players Championship at Country Club Johannesburg)

Most birdies in a row
9 Alan McLean, from the seventh to the 15th in the 3rd round of the 2005 Telkom PGA Championship at Woodhill Country Club
8 Bobby Lincoln, from the eighth to the 15th in the final round of the AECI Classic, Randpark Golf Club; Mark McNulty (IRL), from the ninth to the 16th in the 2nd round of the 1996 Zimbabwe Open, Royal Harare Golf Club

Lowest finish by a winner
62 Gavan Levenson, last round of the 1983 Vaal Reefs Open, Orkney Golf Club; Mark McNulty (IRL), 1987

Royal Swazi Sun Pro-Am, Royal Swazi Sun Country Club

Most Order of Merit victories
Eight Mark McNulty (IRL), 1981, 82, 85, 86, 87, 93, 98

Youngest winners
Anton Haig, 19 years 4 months, 2005 Seekers Travel Pro-Am, Dainfern; Dale Hayes, 19 years 5 months, Bert Hagerman Invitational, Zwartkops, Dec 1971; Charl Schwartzel, 20 years 3 months, 2004 dunhill championship at Leopard Creek (Note: Dale Hayes was 18 years 6 months when he won the unofficial Newcastle Open at Newcastle Golf Club in 1971); Mark Murless, 20 years 5 months, 1996 Platinum Classic, Mooinooi Golf Club; Adam Scott (AUS), 20 years 6 months, 2001 Alfred Dunhill Championship, Houghton Golf Club; Marc Cayeux (ZIM), 20 years 9 months, 1998 Zambia Open, Lusaka Golf Club; Trevor Immelman, 20 years 11 months, Vodacom Players Championship, Royal Cape Golf Club

Oldest winner
Mark McNulty (IRL), 49 years 44 days, 2003 Vodacom Players Championship, Royal Cape Golf Club

Australasian Tour

Most wins
31 Greg Norman

Youngest winner
A Baddeley (19 years), 1999 Australian Open

Oldest winner
Kel Nagle (54 years), 1975 Clearwater Classic (now the New Zealand PGA Championship

Lowest round
60 (–12) Paul Gow, 2001 Canon Challenge, Castle Hill; (–12) Ernie Els, 2004 Heineken Classic, Royal Melbourne

Canadian Tour

Lowest 72 holes
260 (–24) Jason Bohn, 2001 Bayer Championship; (–20) Brian Kontak, 1998 Alberta Open (Note: Tim Clark's 261 at 1998 Royal Oaks New Brunswick Open was a record 27 under par)

Lowest 54 holes
194 Brian Kontak, 1999 Telus Henry Singer Alberta Open

Lowest 36 holes
126 Matt Cole, 1988 Windsor Charity Classic (first two rounds)

Lowest 18 holes
58 (–13) Jason Bohn, 2001 Bayer Championship

Lowest 9 holes
26 (–9) Jason Bohn, 2001 Bayer Championship

Largest winning margin
11 Arron Oberholser, 1999 Ontario Open Heritage Classic

Most wins in one season
4   Moe Norman, 1966 (Manitoba Open, CPGA Championship, Quebec Open, Alberta Open); Trevor Dodds, 1996 (Henry Singer Alberta Open, ED TEL Planet Open, Infiniti Championship, Canadian Masters)

Tour de las Americas

Youngest winner
Andres Romero, 21 years, 2003 Cable and Wireless Masters, Panama City, Panama

Oldest winner
Vicente Fernandez, 54 years, Argentina Open, Jockey Club, Buenos Aires, 2002

Lowest winning aggregate
260 (–20) Rafael Ponce, Acapulco Fest, Fairmont Princess, Acapulco, Mexico, 2004

Biggest comeback to win
9 strokes Venezuela, Copa de Naciones, El Tigre, Nueva Vallarta, Mexico 2004; Rafael Ponce, Acapulco Fest, Fairmont Princess, Acapulco, Mexico, 2004 LPGA Tour

LPGA TOUR

Lowest 72 holes
258 (–22 Karen Stupples, Welch's/Fry's Championship, Dell Urich, Arizona, 2004 (Note: Annika Sörenstam's 261 at 2001 Standard Register Ping, Moon Valley, Arizona, was a record 27 under par)

Lowest 54 holes
192   (–24) Annika Sörenstam, Mizuno Classic, Shiga, Japan, 2003

Lowest 36 holes
124   (–20) Annika Sörenstam, Standard Register Ping, Moon Valley, Arizona, 2001; (–16 Meg Mallon, Welch's/Fry Championship, Dell Urich, Arizona, 2003

Lowest 18 holes
59   (–13) Annika Sörenstam, Standard Register Ping, Moon Valley, Arizona, 2001

Lowest 9 holes
27   (–8) Jimin Kang, ShopRite Classic, Seaview, New Jersey, 2005 (Note: the 28s by Mary Beth Zimmerman, Rail Charity Classic, Springfield, Illinois, 1984, and by Annika Sörenstam, Standard Register Ping, Moon Valley, Arizona, 2001, were also 8 under par)

Largest winning margin
14 strokes   Cindy Mackey, MasterCard International Pro-am, Knollwood, New York, 1986

Youngest winner
Marlene Hagge, 18 years 14 days, Sarasota Open, 1952

Oldest winner
Beth Daniel, 46 years 8 months 29 days, Canadian Open, 2003

Most wins in a season
13   Mickey Wright, 1963

Ladies European Tour

Lowest 72 holes
267   Laura Davies, 1988 Biarritz Ladies Open, Biarritz; Laura Davies, 1995 Guardian Irish Holidays Open, St Margaret's; Juli Inkster, 2003 Evian Masters, Evian

Lowest 54 holes
190 Karine Icher, 2004 Catalonia Masters, Sant Cugat

Lowest 36 holes
129   (–17) Sophie Gustafson, 2003 Ladies Irish Open, Killarney; (–15) Kirsty Taylor, 2005 Wales Ladies Championship, Machynys Peninsula

Lowest 18 holes
61 (–11) Kirsty Taylor, 2005 Wales Ladies Championship, Machynys Peninsula. (Note: Trish Johnson's 62 in the 1996 Ladies French Open was also 11 under par)

Lowest 9 holes
29 Kitrina Douglas, 1988 Italian Ladies Open, Cá Della Nave; Regine Lautens, 1988 Godiva European Masters, Royal Antwerp; Laura Davies, 1987 First Open de France, Feminin, Fourqueux; Anne Jones, 1990 Trophée International Coconut Skol, Fourqueux; Trish Johnson, 1999 Cantor Fitzgerald, Laura Davies Invitational, Brocket Hall; Trish Johnson, 1999 Marrakech Palmeraie Open, Palmeraie Golf Palace; Rachel Hetherington, 2000 AAMI Women's Australian Open, Yarra Yarra; Federica Dassu, 2000 Chrysler Open, Halmstad; Susan Redman, 2000 Evian Masters, Evian; Minea Blomqvist, 2004 OTP Bank Central European Masters, Old Lake, Hungary; Karine Icher, 2004 Catalonia Masters, Sant Cugat; Paula Marti, 2004 Catalonia Masters, Sant Cugat; Veronica Zorzi, 2005 Arras Open de France Dames, Le Golf d'Arras; Nina Karlsson, 2005 OTP Bank Ladies Central European Open, Old Lake; Sophie Gustafson, 2006 Siemens Austrian Ladies Open presented by Uniqa, Golfclub Fohrenwald-Wiener; Stephanie Arricau, 2006 Ladies Open of Portugal, Quinta da Marinha Oitavos; Ludivine Kreutz, 2006 ANZ Ladies Masters, Royal Pines

Largest winning margin
16 strokes   Laura Davies, 1995 Guardian Irish Holidays Open, St Margaret's

Youngest winner
Amy Yang (amateur), 16 years 191 days, 2006 ANZ Ladies Masters, Royal Pines

Oldest winner
Federica Dassu, 46 years 105 days, 2003 Open de España Femenino, Campo De Golf De Salamanca

Most wins in a year
7   Marie-Laure de Lorenzi, 1988 (French Open, Volmac Open, Hennessy Cup, Gothenburg Open, Laing Charity Classic, Woolmark Matchplay, Qualitair Spanish Open)

Miscellaneous British

72-hole aggregate
Andrew Brooks recorded a 72-hole aggregate of 259 in winning the Skol (Scotland) tournament at Williamwood in 1974.

Lowest rounds
Playing on the ladies' course (4,020 yards) at Sunningdale on 26th September, 1961, Arthur Lees, the professional there, went round in 52, 10 under par. He went out in 26 (2, 3, 3, 4, 3, 3, 3, 3, 2) and came back in 26 (2, 3, 3, 3, 2, 3, 4, 3, 3).

On 1st January, 1936, A.E. Smith, Woolacombe Bay professional, recorded a score of 55 in a game there with a club member. The course measured 4,248 yards. Smith went out in 29 and came back in 26 finishing with a hole-in-one at the 18th.

Other low scores recorded in Britain are by CC Aylmer, an English International who went round Ranelagh in 56; George Duncan, Axenfels in 56; Harry Bannerman, Banchory in 56 in 1971; Ian Connelly, Welwyn Garden City in 56 in 1972; James Braid, Hedderwick near Dunbar in 57; H. Hardman, Wirral in 58; Norman Quigley, Windermere in 58 in 1937; Robert Webster, Eaglescliffe in 58, in 1970. Harry Weetman scored 58 in a round at the 6171 yards Croham Hurst on 30th January, 1956.

D. Sewell had a round of 60 in an Alliance Meeting at Ferndown, Bournemouth, a full-size course. He scored 30 for each half and had a total of 26 putts. In September 1986, Jeffrey Burn, handicap 1, of Shrewsbury GC, scored 60 in a club competition, made up of 8 birdies, an eagle and 9 pars. He was 30 out and 30 home and no. 5 on his card. Andrew Sherborne, as a 20-year-old amateur, went round Cirencester in 60 strokes. Dennis Gray completed a round at Broome Manor, Swindon (6906 yards, SSS 73) in the summer of 1976 in 60 (28 out, 32 in).

Playing over Aberdour on 13th June, 1936, Hector Thomson, British Amateur champion, 1936, and Jack McLean, former Scottish Amateur champion, each did 61 in the second round of an exhibition. McLean in his first round had a 63, which gave him an aggregate 124 for 36 holes.

Steve Tredinnick in a friendly match against business tycoon Joe Hyman scored a 61 over West Sussex (6211 yards) in 1970. It included a hole-in-one at the 12th (198 yards) and a 2 at the 17th (445 yards).

Another round of 61 on a full-size course was achieved by 18-year-old Michael Jones on his home course, Worthing GC (6274 yards), in the first round of the President's Cup in May, 1974.

In the Second City Pro-Am tournament in 1970, at Handsworth, Simon Fogarty did the second 9 holes in 27 against the par of 36.

Miscellaneous USA

Lowest rounds
The lowest known scores recorded for 18 holes in America are 55 by E.F. Staugaard in 1935 over the 6419 yards Montebello Park, California, and 55 by Homero Blancas in 1962 over the 5002 yards Premier course in Longview, Texas. Staugaard in his round had 2 eagles, 13 birdies and 3 pars.

Equally outstanding is a round of 58 (13 under par) achieved by a 13-year-old boy, Douglas Beecher, on 6th July, 1976, at Pitman CC, New Jersey. The course measured 6180 yards from the back tees, and the middle tees, off which Douglas played, were estimated by the club professional to reduce the yardage by under 180 yards.

In 1941 at a 6100 yards course in Portsmouth, Virginia, Chandler Harper scored 58.

Jack Nicklaus in an exhibition match at Breakers Club, Palm Beach, California, in 1973 scored 59 over the 6200-yard course.

The lowest 9-hole score in America is 25, held jointly by Bill Burke over the second half of the 6384 yards Normandie CC, St Louis in May, 1970 at the age of 29; by Daniel Cavin, who had seven 3s and two 2s on the par 36 Bill Brewer Course, Texas, in September, 1959; and by Douglas Beecher over the second half of Pitman CC, New Jersey, on 6th July, 1976, at the amazingly young age of 13. The back 9 holes of the Pitman course measured 3150 yards (par 35) from the back tees, but even though Douglas played off the middle tees, the yardage was still over 3000 yards for the 9 holes. He scored 8 birdies and 1 eagle.

Horton Smith scored 119 for two consecutive rounds in winning the Catalina Open in California in December, 1928. The course, however, measured only 4700 yards.

Miscellaneous – excluding GB and USA

Tony Jacklin won the 1973 Los Lagartos Open with an aggregate of 261, 27 under par.

Henry Cotton in 1950 had a round of 56 at Monte Carlo (29 out, 27 in).

In a Pro-Am tournament prior to the 1973 Nigerian Open, British professional David Jagger went round in 59.

Max Banbury recorded a 9-hole score of 26 at Woodstock, Ontario, playing in a competition in 1952.

Women
The lowest score recorded on a full-size course by a woman is 59 by Sweden's Annika Sörenstam on the 6459 yards, par 72 Moon Valley course in Phoenix, Arizona. It broke by two the previous record of 61 by South Korean Se Ri Pak. Sörenstam had begun the tournament with a 65 and by adding rounds of 69 and 68 she equalled the LPGA record of 261 set by Pak (71-61-63-66) at Highland Meadows in Ohio in 1998. Sörenstam's score represents 27 under par, Pak's 23 under.

The lowest 9-hole score on the US Ladies' PGA circuit is 28, first achieved by Mary Beth Zimmerman in the 1984 Rail Charity Classic and since equalled by Pat Bradley, Muffin Spencer-Devlin, Peggy Kirsch, Renee Heiken, Anika Sörenstam and Danielle Ammaccapane.

The Lowest 36-hole score is the 124 (20 under par) by Sörenstam at Moon Valley and the lowest 54-hole score 193 (23 under par) by Karrie Webb at Walnut Hills, Michigan, in the 2000 Oldsmobile Classic and equalled by Sörenstam at Moon Valley.

Patty Berg holds the record for the most number of women's majors with 15; Kathy Whitworth achieved a record number of tournament wins with 88; Mickey Wright's 13 wins in 1963 was the most in one season and the youngest and oldest winners of LPGA events were Marlene Hagge, 18 years and 14 days when she won the 1952 Sarasota Open and JoAnne Carner, 46 years 5 months 11 days when she won the 1985 Safeco Classic.

The lowest round on the European LPGA is 62 (11 under par) by Trish Johnson in the 1996 French Open. A 62 was also achieved by New Zealand's Janice Arnold at Coventry in 1990 during a Women's Professional Golfers' Association tournament.

The lowest 9-hole score on the European LPGA circuit is 29 by Kitrina Douglas, Regine Lautens, Laura Davies, Anne Jones and Trish Johnson.

In the Women's World Team Championship in Mexico in 1966, Mrs Belle Robertson, playing for the British team, was the only player to break 70. She scored 69 in the third round.

At Westgate-on-Sea GC (measuring 5002 yards), Wanda Morgan scored 60 in an open tournament in 1929.

Since scores cannot properly be taken in matchplay no stroke records can be made in matchplay events. Nevertheless we record here two outstanding examples of low scoring in the finals of national championships. Mrs Catherine Lacoste de Prado is credited with a score of 62 in the first round of the 36-hole final of the 1972 French Ladies' Open Championship at Morfontaine. She went out in 29 and came back in 33 on a course measuring 5933 yards. In the final of the English Ladies' Championship at Woodhall Spa in 1954, Frances Stephens (later Mrs Smith) did the first nine holes against Elizabeth Price (later Mrs Fisher) in 30. It included a hole-in-one at the 5th. The nine holes measured 3280 yards.

Amateurs

National championships

The following examples of low scoring cannot be regarded as genuine stroke play records since they took place in match play. Nevertheless they are recorded here as being worthy of note.

Michael Bonallack in beating David Kelley in the final of the English championship in 1968 at Ganton did the first 18 holes in 61 with only one putt under two feet conceded. He was out in 32 and home in 29. The par of the course was 71.

Charles McFarlane, playing in the fourth round of the Amateur Championship at Sandwich in 1914 against Charles Evans did the first nine holes in 31, winning by 6 and 5.

This score of 31 at Sandwich was equalled on several occasions in later years there. Then, in 1948, Richard Chapman of America went out in 29 in the fourth round eventually beating Hamilton McInally, Scottish Champion in 1937, 1939 and 1947, by 9 and 7.

Francis Ouimet in the first round of the American Amateur Championship in 1932 against George Voigt did the first nine holes in 30. Ouimet won by 6 and 5.

Open competitions

The 1970 South African Dunlop Masters Tournament was won by an amateur, John Fourie, with a score of 266, 14 under par. He led from start to finish with rounds of 65, 68, 65, 68, finally winning by six shots from Gary Player.

Jim Ferrier, Manly, won the New South Wales championship at Sydney in 1935 with 266. His rounds were: 67, 65, 70, 64, giving an aggregate 16 strokes better than that of the runner-up. At the time he did this amazing score Ferrier was 20 years old and an amateur.

Aaron Baddeley became the first amateur to win the Australian Open since Bruce Devlin in 1960 when he took the title at Royal Sydney in 1999. After turning pro he successfully defended the title the following year at Kingston Heath.

Holes below par

Most holes below par

E.F. Staugaard in a round of 55 over the 6419 yards Montbello Park, California, in 1935, had two eagles, 13 birdies and three pars.

American Jim Clouette scored 14 birdies in a round at Longhills GC, Arkansas, in 1974. The course measured 6257 yards.

Jimmy Martin in his round of 63 in the Swallow-Penfold at Stoneham in 1961 had one eagle and 11 birdies.

In the Ricarton Rose Bowl at Hamilton, Scotland, in August, 1981, Wilma Aitken, a women's amateur internationalist, had 11 birdies in a round of 64, including nine consecutive birdies from the 3rd to the 11th.

Mrs Donna Young scored nine birdies and one eagle in one round in the 1975 Colgate European Women's Open.

Jason Bohn had two eagles and 10 birdies in his closing 58 at the 2001 Bayer Classic on the Canadian Tour at the par 71 Huron Oaks.

Consecutive holes below par

Lionel Platts had ten consecutive birdies from the 8th to 17th holes at Blairgowrie GC during a practice round for the 1973 Sumrie Better-Ball tournament.

Roberto De Vicenzo in the Argentine Centre of the Republic Championship in April, 1974 at the Cordoba GC, Villa Allende, broke par at each of the first nine holes. (By starting his round at the 10th hole they were in fact the second nine holes played by Vicenzo.) He had one eagle (at the 7th hole) and eight birdies. The par for the 3,602 yards half was 37, completed by Vicenzo in 27.

Nine consecutive holes under par have been recorded by Claude Harmon in a friendly match over Winged Foot GC, Mamaroneck, NY, in 1931; by Les Hardie at Eastern GC, Melbourne, in April, 1934; by Jimmy Smith at McCabe GC, Nashville, Tenn, in 1969; by 13-year-old Douglas Beecher, in 1976, at Pitman CC, New Jersey; by Rick Sigda at Greenfield CC, Mass, in 1979; and by Ian Jelley at Brookman Park in 1994.

TW Egan in winning the East of Ireland Championship in 1962 at Baltray had eight consecutive birdies (2nd to 9th) in the third round.

On the United States PGA tour, eight consecutive holes below par have been achieved by six players – Bob Goalby (1961 St Petersburg Open), Fuzzy Zoeller (1976 Quad Cities Open), Dewey Arnette (1987 Buick Open), Edward Fryatt (2000 Doral-Ryder Open), JP Hayes (2002 Bob Hope Chrysler Classic) and Jerry Kelly (2003 Las Vegas Invitational).

Fred Couples set a PGA European Tour record with 12 birdies in a round of 61 during the 1991 Scandinavian

Masters on the 72-par Drottningholm course. This has since been equalled by Ernie Els (1994 Dubai Desert Classic), Russell Claydon (1995 German Masters) and Darren Clarke (1999 European Open). Ian Woosnam, Tony Johnstone, Severiano Ballesteros, John Bickerton, Mark O'Meara, Raymond Russell, Darren Clarke, Marcello Santi, Mårten Olander and Craig Spence share another record with eight successive birdies.

The United States Ladies' PGA record is seven consecutive holes below par achieved by Carol Mann in the Borden Classic at Columbus, Ohio in 1975.

Miss Wilma Aitken recorded nine successive birdies (from the 3rd to the 11th) in the 1981 Ricarton Rose Bowl.

This has since been equalled by Ernie Els (1994 Dubai Desert Classic), Russell Claydon and Fredrik Lindgren (1995 Mercedes German Masters) and Darreb Clarke (1999 Smurfit European Open). Ian Woosnam, Tony Johnstone, Severiano Ballesteros, John Bickerton, Mark O'Meara, Raymond Russell, Darren Clarke and Marcello Santi and Marten Olander share another record with eight successive birdies.

Low scoring rarities

At Standerton GC, South Africa, in May 1937, F.F. Bennett, playing for Standerton against Witwatersrand University, did the 2nd hole, 110 yards, in three 2s and a 1. Standerton is a 9-hole course, and in the match Bennett had to play four rounds.

In 1957 a fourball comprising HJ Marr, E Stevenson, C Bennett and WS May completed the 2nd hole (160 yards) in the grand total of six strokes. Marr and Stevenson both holed in one while Bennett and May both made 2.

The old Meadow Brook Club of Long Island, USA, had five par 3 holes and George Low in a round there in the 1950s scored two at each of them.

In a friendly match on a course near Chicago in 1971, assistant professional Tom Doty (23 years) had a remarkable low run over four consecutive holes: 4th (500 yards) 2; 5th (360 yards, dogleg) 1; 6th (175 yards) 1; 7th (375 yards) 2.

RW Bishop, playing in the Oxley Park, July medal competition in 1966, scored three consecutive 2s. They occurred at the 12th, 13th and 14th holes which measured 151, 500 and 136 yards respectively.

In the 1959 PGA Close Championship at Ashburnham, Bob Boobyer scored five 2s in one of the rounds. American Art Wall scored three consecutive 2s in the first round of the US Masters in 1974. They were at the 4th, 5th and 6th holes, the par of which was 3, 4 and 3.

Nine consecutive 3s have been recorded by RH Corbett in 1916 in the semi-final of the Tangye Cup; by Dr James Stothers of Ralston GC over the 2056 yards 9-hole course at Carradale, Argyll, during the summer of 1971; by Irish internationalist Brian

Kissock in the Homebright Open at Carnalea GC, Bangor, in June, 1975; and by American club professional Ben Toski.

The most consecutive 3s in a British PGA event is seven by Eric Brown in the Dunlop at Gleneagles (Queen's Course) in 1960.

Hubert Green scored eight consecutive 3s in a round in the 1980 US Open.

The greatest number of 3s in one round in a British PGA event is 11 by Brian Barnes in the 1977 Skol Lager tournament at Gleneagles.

Fewest putts

The lowest known number of putts in one round is 14, achieved by Colin Collen-Smith in a round at Betchworth Park, Dorking, in June, 1947. He single-putted 14 greens and chipped into the hole on four occasions.

Professional Richard Stanwood in a round at Riverside GC, Pocatello, Idaho on 17th May, 1976 took 15 putts, chipping into the hole on five occasions. Several instances of 16 putts in one round have been recorded in friendly games.

For 9 holes, the fewest putts is five by Ron Stutesman for the first 9 holes at Orchard Hills G&CC, Washington, USA in 1978.

Walter Hagen in nine consecutive holes on one occasion took only seven putts. He holed long putts on seven greens and chips at the other two holes.

In competitive stroke rounds in Britain and Ireland, the lowest known number of putts in one round is 18, in a medal round at Portpatrick Dunskey GC, Wilmslow GC professional Fred Taggart is reported to have taken 20 putts in one round of the 1934 Open Championship. Padraigh Hogan (Elm Park), when competing in the Junior Scratch Cup at Carlow in 1976, took only 20 putts in a round of 67.

The fewest putts in a British PGA event is believed to be 22 by Bill Large in a qualifying round over Moor Park High Course for the 1972 Benson and Hedges Match Play.

Overseas, outside the United States of America, the fewest putts is 19 achieved by Robert Wynn (ENG) in a round in the 1973 Nigerian Open and by Mary Bohen (USA) in the final round of the 1977 South Australian Open at Adelaide.

The USPGA record for fewest putts in one round is 18, achieved by Andy North (1990); Kenny Knox (1989); Mike McGee (1987) and Sam Trehan (1979). For 9 holes the record is eight putts by Kenny Knox (1989), Jim Colbert (1987) and Sam Trehan (1979).

The fewest putts recorded for a 72-hole US PGA Tour event is 93 by Kenny Knox in the 1989 Heritage Classic at Harbour Town Golf Links.

The fewest putts recorded by a woman is 17, by Joan Joyce in the Lady Michelob tournament, Georgia, in May, 1982.

Men's Amateur Championship Schedule 2007

Mar 21–24	Sherry Cup, Sotogrande, Spain	Jul 12–14	EGA Challenge Trophy–Boys, Binowo, Poland
Apr 6–10	West of Ireland Open, Co Sligo		
May 4–6	Lytham Trophy, R. Lytham & St Annes	Jul 19–22	**136th Open Championship, Carnoustie**
May 11–13	Irish Open Stroke Play, Royal Dublin		
May 12–13	West of Scotland Open, Cawder	Jul 26–28	European Young Masters, Golf de Bondues, France
May 18–20	English Open Stroke Play (Brabazon), Forest of Arden	Jul 28–Aug 1	South of Ireland Open, Lahinch
May 22–24	Scottish Seniors Open Stroke Play, Drumpellier	Jul 30–Aug 4	English Am. Close, Royal St George's
		Jul 30–Aug 4	Scottish Am. Close, Prestwick
May 25–27	Welsh Open Stroke Play, Machynys	Jul 31–Aug 4	Welsh Am. Close, Royal St David's
May 30–Jun 1	Irish Senior Open, Hermitage	Aug 8–10	British Seniors Open, Nairn Dunbar
June 1–3	Scottish Open Stroke Play, R. Dornoch	Aug 8–10	Boys Home Internationals, Machynys
Jun 2–4	East of Ireland Open, Co Louth	Aug 13–18	British Boys C/ship, Royal Porthcawl
Jun 6–8	English Seniors, Enville	Aug 15–18	European Men's Senior Team C/ship, Bled, Slovenia
Jun 7–9	European Mid-Am., Domaine Impérial, Switzerland	Aug 15–19	British Mid-Am. C/ship, Alwoodley
Jun 8–10	St Andrews Links Trophy, St Andrews (Old & Jubilee)	Aug 17–19	Welsh Team C/ship, Carmarthen
		Aug 20–26	United States Am., Olympic, CA
Jun 9–13	Irish Close Amateur, Cork	Aug 22–25	European Am. C/ship, Sporting Club, Berlin
Jun 12–14	Welsh Seniors Close, Aberdovey		
Jun 14–16	European Seniors, Vilamoura, Portugal	Aug 24–26	English Open Mid-Am. (Logan), Minchinhampton
Jun 16–18	Scottish Mid-Am., Duddingston		
Jun 18–23	**Amateur C/ship, R. Lytham & St Annes**	Aug 31–Sep 1	Jacques Léglise, Notts
		Sep 8–9	**Walker Cup, Royal County Down**
Jun 26–28	Welsh Sen. Open, Llandudno (Maesdu)		
Jun 30–Jul 1	East of Scotland Open, Lundin	Sep 19–21	Home Internationals, Co Louth
Jul 3–7	European Team C/ship, Western Gailes	Sep 28–30	English County Finals, Cleveland
Jul 5–7	EGA Challenge Trophy, Tallinn, Estonia	Oct 2–4	Seniors Home Internationals, Caldy
Jul 9–13	North of Ireland Open, Royal Portrush	Oct 6–7	Scottish Area Team Finals, Powfoot
Jul 10–14	European Boys Team C/ship, Rold Skov, Denmark	Nov 1–3	European Club Trophy (Albacom), Porto-Carras, Greece

Women's Amateur Championship Schedule 2007

Mar 28–31	Sherry Cup, Sotogrande	Jul 24–27	European Ladies Seniors Team C/ship, R. Drottningholm, Sweden
Apr 23–27	English Senior Ladies Match Play, Delamere Forest	Jul 27–28	**Vagliano Trophy, Fairmount St Andrews**
Apr 27–29	Scottish Ladies Open Am. [Helen Holm], Royal Troon & Troon Portland	Aug 8–10	Girls Home Internationals, Southerndown
May 5–6	Welsh Ladies Open Am. SP, Newport		
May 7–11	**Commonwealth Tournament, Johannesburg, RSA**	Aug 13–17	Girls British Open Am., Southerndown
		Aug 14–17	English Ladies Open Mid-Am., Sherwood Forest
May 15–19	Scottish Ladies Close Am., Kilmarnock (Barassie)	Aug 22–24	Ladies British Open Am. SP, Conwy
May 19–22	Welsh Ladies Close Am., R. St David's	Aug 29–Sep 1	European Ladies C/ship [Individual], Golf National, France
May 19–22	Welsh Senior Ladies MP, R. St David's		
May 19–22	Irish Ladies Close Am., Lahinch	Aug 31–Sep 2	Scottish County Finals, Tulliallan
May 22–26	English Ladies Close Am., Littlestone	Sep 5–6	Welsh Senior Ladies C/ship, Pwllheli
Jun 2–3	St Rule Trophy, St Andrews	Sep 6–9	Scottish Senior Ladies Close, Glenbervie
Jun 12–16	Ladies British Am., Alwoodley		
Jun 18–20	English Senior Ladies SP, Northumberland	Sep 10–11	Irish Senior Ladies Open, Ennis
		Sep 12–14	Home Internationals, Dunbar
Jun 19–20	Irish Senior Ladies Close, Portumna	Sep 19–21	Senior Ladies British Open, Copt Heath
Jun 30–Jul 1	Irish Ladies Open Am. SP, Clandeboye		
Jul 6–8	Ladies British Open Mid-Am., Frilford Heath	Sep 19–21	English & Welsh County Finals, Brokenhurst Manor
Jul 10–14	European Ladies Team C/ship, Castelconturdia, Italy	Sep 23–25	Scottish Veteran Ladies, Blairgowrie
		Sep 27–29	European Club Trophy, Wuppertal, Germany
Jul 10–14	European Girls Team C/ship, Oslo, Norway	Oct 2–4	Senior Ladies Home Internationals, Royal Tara
Jul 24–26	English Close Am. SP, Silloth-on-Solway		

PART IX

Fixtures 2007

European Tour international schedule

Early results 2007 season

HSBC Champions Tour	Shenshan International GC, Shanghai	Yang Yong-eun (KOR)	274
UBS Hong Kong Open	Fanling GC, Hong Kong	Jose Manuel Lara (ESP)	265
MasterCard Masters	Huntingdale GC, Melbourne	Justin Rose (ENG)	276
Blue Chip New Zealand Open	Gulf Harbour GC, Auckland	Nathan Green (AUS)	279
dunhill championship	Leopard Creek GC, RSA	Alvaro Quiros (ESP)	275
South African Airways Open	Humewood GC, Port Elizabeth	Ernie Els (RSA)	264

Jan 11–14	Johannesburg Open	Royal Johannesburg and kensington GC
Jan 18–21	The Abu Dhabi Golf Championship	Abu Dhabi Golf Club, United Arab Emirates
Jan 25–28	The Commercial Bank Qatar Master	Doha GC, Qatar
Feb 1–4	Dubai Desert Classic	Emirates GC, Dubai, United Arab Emirates
Feb 8–11	Maybank Malaysian Open	Saujana G & CC, Malaysia
Feb 15–18	Indonesian Open	Damai Indah G&CC, Indonesia
Feb 22–25	**WGC – Accenture Match Play** USA	The Gallery at Dove Mountain, Tucson, Arizona,
Mar 1–4	Johnnie Walker Classic	TBC
Mar 8–11	Singapore Masters	Laguna National G&CC, Singapore
Mar 15–18	TCL Classic	TBC
Mar 22–25	Madeira Island Open	Santo da Serra, Madeira
Mar 22–25	**WGC – CA Championship**	Doral Golf Resort & Spa, Doral, Florida, USA
Mar 29–Apr 1	Open de Portugal	Oitavos, Portugal
Apr 5–8	**MASTERS TOURNAMENT**	Augusta National, Georgia, USA
Apr 12–15	Volvo China Open	Shanghai Silport GC, China
Apr 19–22	BMW Asian Open	Tomson Shanghai Pudong GC, Shanghai, China
Apr 26–29	Open de España	Centro National de Golf, Madrid, Spain
May 3–6	Telecom Italia Open	Castello di Tolcinasco G & CC, Milan, Italy
May 10–13	TBC	TBC
May 17–20	Irish Open	Adare Manor Hotel & Golf Resort, Limerick, Ireland
May 24–27	BMW Championship	Wentworth Club, Surrey
May 31–Jun 3	The Celtic Manor Wales Open	The Celtic Manor Resort, Newport, Wales
Jun 7–10	BA-CA Golf Open Presented by Telekom Austria	Fontana GC, Vienna, Austria
Jun 14–17	Aa St Omer Open	Aa Saint Omer GC, St Omer, Lumbres, France
Jun 14–17	**US OPEN CHAMPIONSHIP**	Oakmont CC, Pittsburgh, PA, USA
Jun 21–24	BMW International Open	Golfclub München-Nord Eichereid, Germany
Jun 28–Jul 1	Open de France ALSTOM	Le Golf National, Paris, France
Jul 5–8	Smurfit Kappa European Open	The K Club, Straffan, Co Kildare, Ireland
Jul 12–15	The Barclays Scottish Open	Loch Lomond, Glasgow, Scotland
Jul 19–23	**136th OPEN CHAMPIONSHIP**	Championship Course, Carnoustie, Scotland
Jul 26–29	The Deutsche Bank Players' Championship of Europe	Gut Kaden, Hamburg, Germany
Aug 2–5	**WGC – Bridgestone Invitational**	Firestone CC, Akron, Ohio, USA
Aug 2–5	Russian Open	Le Meridien Moscow CC, Moscow, Russia
Aug 9–12	**US PGA CHAMPIONSHIP**	Southern Hills CC, Tulsa, Oklahoma, USA
Aug 16–19	Scandinavian Masters	Arlandastad Golf, Rosersberg, Sweden
Aug 23–26	The KLM Open	TBC
Aug 30–Sep 2	Johnnie Walker Championship at Gleneagles	The Gleneagles Hotel, Auchterarder, Scotland
Sep 6–9	Omega European Masters	Crans-sur-Sierre, Crans Montana, Switzerland
Sep 13–16	Mercedes-Benz Championship	TBC
Sep 20–23	The Quinn Direct British Masters	The De Vere Belfry, Warwickshire
Sep 27–30	Seve Trophy[†]	The Heritage at Killenard, Co Laois, Ireland
Oct 4–7	Alfred Dunhill Links Championship	St Andrews, Carnoustie & Kingsbarns, Scotland
Oct 11–14	HSBC World Match Play Championship	Wentworth Club, Surrey, England
Oct 11–14	Open de Madrid	TBC

Oct 18–21	Portugal Masters	Victoria Clube de Golfe, Vilamoura, Portugal
Oct 25–28	Mallorca Classic	Pula GC, Majorca, Spain
Nov 1–4	Volvo Masters	Club de Golf Valderrama, Sotorande, Spain
Nov 22–25	**WGC – World Cup**	Mission Hills GC, Hong Kong, China

† Denotes Approved Special Event

US PGA Tour schedule

Jan 1–7	Mercedes-Benz Championship, Plantation Course at Kapalua, Kapalua, HI
Jan 8–14	Sony Open in Hawaii, Waialae Country Club, Honolulu, HI
Jan 15–21	Bob Hope Chrysler Classic, The Classic Club, LaQuinta, Palm Desert, CA
Jan 22–28	Buick Invitational, Torrey Pines GC, San Diego, CA
Jan 29–Feb 4	FBR Open, TPC Scottsdale, Scottsdale, AZ
Feb 5–11	AT&T Pebble Beach National Pro-Am, Pebble Beach Golf Links, Pebble Beach, CA
Feb 12–18	Nissan Open, Riviera Country Club, Pacific Palisades, CA
Feb 19–25	**WGC – Accenture Match Play Championship**, The Gallery at Dove Mountain, Tucson, AZ
Feb 19–25	Mayakoba Classic at Riviera Maya, El Camaleon, Mayakoba Resort, Riviera Maya, MX
Feb 26–Mar 4	The Honda Classic, PGA National, Palm Beach Gardens, FL
Mar 5–11	Tampa Bay Championship, Westin Innisbrook Resort, Tampa Bay, FL
Mar 12–18	Arnold Palmer Invitational Presented by MasterCard, Bay Hill Golf Club and Lodge, Orlando, FL
Mar 19–25	**WGC – CA Championship**, Doral Golf Resort and Spa, Doral, FL
Mar 26–Apr 1	Shell Houston Open, Redstone Golf Club, Houston, TX
Apr 2–8	**THE MASTERS**, Augusta National Golf Club, Augusta, GA
Apr 9–15	Verizon Heritage, Harbour Town Golf Links, Hilton Head Island, SC
Apr 16–22	Zurich Classic of New Orleans, TPC Louisiana, New Orleans, LA
Apr 23–29	EDS Byron Nelson Championship, TPC Four Seasons Resort, Irving, TX
Apr 30–May 6	Wachovia Championship, Quail Hollow Club, Charlotte, NC
May 7–13	THE PLAYERS Championship, TPC Sawgrass, Ponte Vedra Beach, FL
May 14–20	BellSouth Classic, TPC Sugarloaf, Duluth, GA
May 21–27	Crowne Plaza Invitational at Colonial, Colonial Country Club, Fort Worth, TX
May 28–Jun 3	The Memorial Tournament Presented by Morgan Stanley, Muirfield Village Golf Club, Dublin, OH
Jun 4–10	Stanford St. Jude Championship, TPC Southwind, Memphis, TN
Jun 11–17	**US OPEN**, Oakmont Country Club, Oakmont, PA
Jun 18–24	Travelers Championship, TPC River Highlands, Cromwell, CT
Jun 25–Jul 1	Buick Open, Warwick Hills Golf and Country Club, Grand Blanc, MI
Jul 2–8	The INTERNATIONAL, Castle Pines Golf Club, Castle Rock, CO
Jul 9–15	John Deere Classic, TPC Deere Run, Silvis, IL
Jul 16–22	**BRITISH OPEN**, Carnoustie Golf Links, Angus, Scotland
Jul 16–22	US Bank Championship in Milwaukee, Brown Deer Park Golf Course, Milwaukee, WI
Jul 23–29	Bell Canadian Open, Angus Glen Golf Course (North), Ontario, CA
Jul 30–Aug 5	**WGC – Bridgestone Invitational**, Firestone Country Club, Akron, OH
Jul 30–Aug 5	Reno Tahoe Open, Montreux Golf and Country Club, Reno, NV
Aug 6–12	PGA Championship, Southern Hills Country Club, Tulsa, OK
Aug 13–19	Wyndham Championship, Forest Oaks Country Club, Greensboro, NC
Aug 20–26	**Barclays Classic**, Westchester Country Club, Harrison, NY
Aug 27–Sep 3	**Deutsche Bank Championship**, TPC Boston, Norton, MA
Sep 3–9	**BMW Championship,** Cog Hill Golf and Country Club, Lemont, IL
Sep 10–16	**THE TOUR Championship** presented by Coca-Cola, East Lake Golf Club, Atlanta, GA

European Golf Association Championships

Feb 7–11	Portuguese International Ladies Amateur Championship, Quinta de Cima GC (Algarve)
	Portuguese International Amateur Championship, Quinta de Cima GC (Algarve)
Feb 28–Mar 3	Spanish International Ladies Amateur Championship, Sherry Golf
	Spanish International Amateur Championship, Desert Springs
Apr 5–9	French Lady Juniors Championship (Esmond Trophy), Saint-Cloud Golf Club
	French Boys Championship (Michel Carlhian Trophy), Toulouse Seilh Golf Club
Apr 27–29	Scottish Ladies Open Stroke Play Championship, Troon
Apr 27–29	Cyprus Mens Amateur Open, TBA
May 4–6	Lytham Trophy, Royal Lytham & St Annes
May 5–6	Welsh Ladies Amateur Open Stroke Play Championship, Newport GC
May 6–8	Israel Juniors Boys and Girls Championship, Caesarea GC
May 7–10	Israel Amateur Open Championship, Caesarea GC
May 8–10	Israel Ladies Amateur Open Championship, Caesarea GC
May 9–13	Spanish International Lady Junior Championship, La Cala Golf
May 11–13	Irish Amateur Open Stroke Play Championship, Royal Dublin
May 18–20	English Mens Open Stroke Play Championship (Brabazon Trophy), Forest of Arden
May 19–20	Cyprus Ladies Amateur Open, TBA
May 24–27	German International Ladies Amateur Championship, Düsseldorfer GC
May 24–27	Austrian Ladies Amateur Championship, TBA
	Austrian Amateur Championship, TBA
May 25–27	Welsh Open Amateur Stroke Play Championship, Machynys GC
May 25–27	Skandia Lady Junior Open (Youth), Bastad GC
	Skandia Junior Open (Youth), TBA
Jun 1–3	Scottish Open Amateur Stroke Play Championship, Royal Dornoch GC
Jun 1–3	French Ladies Amateur Stroke Play Championship (Cécile de Rothschild Trophy), TBA
Jun 2–3	Welsh Open Youths Championship, Whitchurch, Cardiff
Jun 8–10	German Girls Open, GC St. Leon-Rot, Heidelberg
	German Boys Open, GC St. Leon-Rot, Heidelberg
Jun 8–10	French Men Amateur Stroke Play Championship (Coupe Murat), Chantilly GC
Jun 12–16	Ladies British Open Amateur Championship, Alwoodley
Jun 14–16	Slovenian Ladies Amateur Championship, TBA
	Slovenian Amateur Championship, TBA
Jun 18–23	The Amateur Championship, Royal Lytham & St Annes
Jun 22–24	Scottish Youths Open Amateur Stroke Play Championship, TBC
Jun 25–29	Russian Ladies Amateur Open Championship, Le Meridien Moscow CC
	Russian Amateur Open Championship, Le Meridien Moscow CC
Jun 28–29	Scottish Ladies Junior Open Stroke Play Championship, Auchterarder GC
Jun 28–29	Irish Youth Open Stroke Play Championship, West Waterford
Jun 30–Jul 1	Irish Ladies Open Stroke Play Championship, Clandeboye GC
Jul 6–8	Ladies British Open Mid Amateur Championship, TBA
Jul 11–13	Slovak Ladies Amateur Championship, Lomnicky GC
	Slovak Amateur Championship, Lomnicky GC
Jul 12–14	Luxembourg Ladies Amateur Championship, Golf de Clervaux
	Luxembourg Amateur Championship, Golf de Clervaux
Jul 13–15	Polish Open Amateur Championship, TBA
Jul 18–21	Dutch Lady Junior International, Toxandria GC
	Dutch Junior International, Toxandria GC
Jul 23–25	Danish International Lady Junior Championship, Smörum
	Danish International Youth Championship, Smörum
Jul 24–26	English Boys (under 18) Open Amateur Stroke Play Championship (Carris Trophy), Saunton
Jul 26–28	Czech International Lady Junior Championship, GC Karlstejn
	Czech International Junior Championship, GC Karlstejn
Jul 27–29	Estonian Open Ladies Amateur Championship, TBA
	Estonian Open Amateur Championship, TBA
Jul 28–29	Danish International Ladies Amateur Championship, Silkeborg
	Danish International Amateur Championship, Silkeborg

Aug 3–5	Swiss Ladies Amateur Championship, Basel GC
	Swiss Amateur Championship, Basel GC
Aug 4–5	Polish Ladies Open Amateur Championship, TBA
Aug 8–10	British Senior Championship, Nairn Dunbar
Aug 8–11	Czech International Ladies Amateur Championship, Cihelny GC
	Czech International Amateur Championship, Cihelny GC
Aug 9–11	Finnish Ladies Amateur Championship, Helsinki GC
	Finnish Amateur Championship, Helsinki GC
Aug 9–12	German International Amateur Championship, G&LC Seddiner See, Berlin
Aug 10–12	Latvian Ladies Amateur Open Championship, OZO GC (Riga)
	Latvian Amateur Open Championship, OZO GC (Riga)
Aug 13–17	Girls British Open Amateur Championship, Southerndown
Aug 13–18	British Boys Championship, Royal Porthcawl
Aug 14–17	English Ladies Open Mid Amateur Championship, Sherwood Forest GC
Aug 15–19	British Mid-Amateur Championship, Alwoodley
Aug 22–24	Ladies British Open Amateur Stroke Play Championship, Conwy
Aug 22–25	Belgian International Lady Junior Championship, Royal GC of Belgium in Ravenstein
	Belgian International Junior Championship, Royal GC of Belgium in Ravenstein
Aug 25–26	Hungarian Junior Amateur Open Championship, TBA
Sept 3–9	Spanish International Junior Championship, PGA de Cataluña
Sept 4–5	Irish Senior Ladies Open Amateur Stroke Play Championship, Ennis GC
Sept 6–8	Hungarian Open Ladies Amateur Championship, TBA
	Hungarian Open Amateur Championship, TBA
Sept 6–9	Turkish Open Amateur Championship (Men), Antalya GC
Sept 12–16	Italian International Ladies Amateur Championship, Parco di Roma GC
Sept 19–21	Senior Ladies British Open Amateur Championship, Copt Heath
Sept 19–23	Italian International Amateur Championship, Villa d'Este GC
Sept 20–23	Hellenic Ladies Amateur Championship, Glyfada GC
	Hellenic Amateur Championship, Glyfada GC
Oct 6–7	Bulgarian Amateur Championship, TBA

European Team Championships

Jul 3–7	Amateur, Western Gailes GC, Scotland
Jul 5–7	Challenge Trophy – Men, TBA
Jul 10–14	Ladies, Castelconturbia, Italy
Jul 10–14	Girls, Oslo Golf Club, Norway
Jul 10–14	Boys, Rold Skov GC, Denmark
Jul 12–14	Challenge Trophy – Boys, TBA
Jul 24–27	Lady Seniors, Royal Dottingholm, Sweden
Aug 15–18	Men Seniors, Bled GC, Slovenia

International European Championships

Jun 7–9	Mid-Amateur, Domaine Impérial, Switzerland
Jun 14–16	Seniors, Portugal
Jul 26–28	European Young Masters, Golf de Bondues, France
Aug 22–25	Amateur, Sporting Club, Berlin, Germany
Aug 29–Sept 1	Ladies, Golf National, France
Sept 27–29	European Club Cup Trophy – Ladies, GC Bergisch Land, Düsseldorf, Germany
Nov 2–4	European Club Cup Trophy – Men, Porto-Carras, Thessaloniki, Greece

International Matches

Jul 28–29	Vagliano Trophy, St Andrews Bay Golf Resort and Spa, Scotland
Aug 31–Sept 1	Jacques Léglise Trophy, Notts GC, England

United States Golf Association Championships

Jun 14–17	**US Open**	Oakmont CC, Oakmont, PA
Jun 19–24	US Women's Amateur Public Links	Kearney Hill Golf Links, Lexington, KY
Jul 5–8	US Senior Open	Whistling Straits CC, Kohler, WI
Jun 28–Jul 1	**US Women's Open**	Pine Needles L & GC, Southern Pines, NC
Jul 9–14	US Amateur Public Links	Cantigny GC, Wheaton, IL
Jul 23–28	US Junior Amateur	Boone Valley Golf Club, Augusta, MO
Jul 23–28	US Girls' Junior	Tacoma C & GC, Lakewood, WA
Aug 6–12	US Women's Amateur	Crooked Stick GC, Carmel, IN
Aug 20–26	US Amateur	The Olympic Club, San Francisco, CA
Sep 8–9	**Walker Cup**	Royal County Down GC, Newcastle, County Down, Northern Ireland
Sep 1–6	USGA Senior Women's Amateur	Sunriver Resort, Sunriver, OR
Sep 29–Oct 4	US Women's Mid-Amateur	Desert Forest GC, Carefree, AZ
Sep 29–Oct 4	US Mid-Amateur	Bandon Dunes Golf Resort, Bandon, OR
Sep 1–6	USGA Senior Amateur	Flint Hills National GC, Andover, KS
Sept 18–20	USGA Men's State Team Championship	The Club at Carlton Woods, The Woodlands, TX
Sept 18–20	USGA Women's State Team Championship	The Club at Carlton Woods, The Woodlands, TX

Japan LPGA Tour

Jun 2	Resort Trust Ladies, Grande Nasu Shirakawa GC
Jun 8	We Love KOBE Suntory Ladies Open Golf Tournament, Rokko Kokusai GC
Jun 16	Nichirei Ladies, Miho GC
Jun 23	Promise Ladies Golf Tournament, Water Hills GC
Jun 30	Belluna Ladies Cup Golf Tournament, Obatago GC
Jul 7	Meiji Chocolate Cup, Sapporo Kokusai CC
Jul 14	Stanley Ladies Golf Tournament, Tomei CC
Aug 4	CrystalGayser Ladies Golf Tournament, Keiyo CC
Aug 11	Karuizawa 72 Golf Tournament, Karuizawa 72 GC
Aug 18	New Caterpillar Mitsubishi Ladies, Daihakone CC
Aug 25	Yonex Ladies Golf Tournament, Yonex CC
Sept 1	Golf 5 Ladies, Alpen GC
Sept 7	LPGA Championship KONICA MINOLTA Cup, Nidom Classic Course
Sept 15	Munsingwear Ladies Tokai Classic, Ryosen GC
Sept 22	Miyagi TV Cup Dunlop Ladies Open Golf Tournament, Rifu GC
Sept 22	Japan Women's Open, Ibaraki GC
Oct 6	Ladies Open, Akagi CC
Oct 13	Fujitsu Ladies, Tokyo 700 CC
Oct 13	Masters GC Ladies, Masters GC
Oct 27	Higuchi Hisako IDC Otsuka Kagu Ladies, Musashigaoka GC
Nov 3	Mizuno Classic, Kashikojima CC
Nov 11	Itoen Ladies Golf Tournament, Great Island CC
Nov 17	Daiohseishi Elleair Ladies Open, Chukyo
Nov 17	Bridgestone Ladies Open Philanthrophy LPGA Players Championship, Tokyo
Mar 3,	Daikin Orchid Ladies Golf Tournament, Ryukyu GC, Okinawa
Mar 10	Accordia Golf Ladies, Aoshima GC
Mar 17	KINMIRAI TSUUSHIN Queens Open Ladies Golf Tournament, Kagoshima Takamaki CC, Kagoshima
Apr 7	Studio Alice Ladies Open, Hanayashiki GC
Apr 14	Life Card Ladies Golf Tournament, Kumamoto Kuko CC, Kumamoto
Apr 21	Fujisankei Ladies Classic, Kawana Hotel GC
Apr 28	Katokichi Queens Golf Tournament, Yashima CC
May 4	Salonpas World Ladies Golf Tournament, Tokyo Yomiuri CC
May 12	Vernal Ladies, Fukuoka Century GC
May 26	Kosaido Ladies Golf Cup, TBA

Asian Tour

Jan 11-14	Philippine Open, Wack Wack GCC, Manila
Jan 18-21	Pakistan Open, Karachi GC, Karachi
Jan 25-28	Commercialbank Qatar Masters[1], Doha GC, Doha
Feb 8-11	Maybank Malaysian Open[1], Saujana GCC, Kuala Lumpur
Feb 15-18	Indonesia Open[1], Damai Indah GCC, Jakarta
Mar 1-4	Johnnie Walker Classic[3], venue TBC
Mar 8-11	Singapore Masters[1], Laguna National Golf and CC
Mar 15-18	TCL Classic[1], venue TBC
Mar 22-25	Motorola International Bintan, Ria Bintan GC, Bintan
Mar 27-28	British Open Qualifier, Sentosa GC, Singapore
Apr 12-15	Volvo China Open[1], Shanghai Silport GC, Shanghai
Apr 19-22	BMW Asian Open[1], venue TBC
May 3-6	Maekyung Open, venue TBC, Seoul
May 17-20	Macau Open, Macau GCC, Macau
May 24-27	SK Telecom Open, venue TBC, Seoul
May 31-Jun 3	Jakarta Masters, venue TBC
Jun 14-17	Bangkok Airways Open, Santiburi Samui CC, Samui
Jun 28-Jul 1	Crowne Plaza Open, venue TBC, Malaysia
Jul 5-8	Johor Classic, Royal Johor GC, Johor, Malaysia
Jul 12-15	Brunei Open, Empire Hotel and CC, Bandar Seri Begawan
Aug 16-19	Visa Dynasty Cup[2], venue TBC
Aug 23-26	Indonesian International Championship, venue TBC, Jakarta
Sept 13-16	Pulai Springs Malaysian Masters, Pulai Springs Resort, Johor Bahru
Sept 20-23	Taiwan Open, Sunrise GCC, Taipei
Sept 27-30	Mercuries Taiwan Masters, Taiwan GCC, Taipei
Oct 4-7	Kolon-Hana Bank Korea Open, Woo Jeong Hills CC, Seoul
Oct 11-14	Hero Honda Indian Open, Delhi GC, New Delhi
Oct 25-28	TBA
Nov 1-4	Barclays Singapore Open, Sentosa GC, Singapore
Nov 8-11	HSBC Champions[4], Sheshan International Golf Club, Shanghai
Nov 15-18	UBS Hong Kong Open[1], Hong Kong GC, Hong Kong
Nov 22-25	WGC-World Cup, Mission Hills GC, Shenzhen, China
Dec 6-9	Cambodian Open, Phokeethra CC, Siem Reap
Dec 13-16	Volvo Masters of Asia, Thai Country Club, Bangkok

[1] Co-sanctioned with European Tour
[2] Co-sanctioned with Japan Golf Tour Organisation
[3] Tri-sanctioned with European Tour and Australasian Tour
[4] Special Event.

Ladies European Tour

Jan 19-21	Women's World Cup of Golf, Gary Player Country Club, Sun City, Johannesburg
Feb 1-4	MFS Women's Australian Open[1], Royal Sydney Golf Club, Sydney, Australia
Feb 8-11	ANZ Ladies Masters[1], Royal Pines Resort, Gold Coast, Queensland, Australia
May 3-6	Tenerife Ladies Open, venue TBC
May 10-13	Open De España Femenino–Castellón, CC Mediterráneo, Castellón, Spain
May 17-20	Deutsche Bank Ladies Swiss Open, Golf Gerre Losone, Ticino, Switzerland
TBC	BMW Ladies Italian Open, venue TBC
May 31-Jun 3	Northern Ireland Ladies Open, Hilton Templepatrick Hotel and CC, Belfast, N. Ireland
Jun 8-10	KLM Ladies Open, Eindhovensche Golf, Valkenswaard, Holland
Jun 14-17	Ladies European Masters, The Oxfordshire Golf Club, Thame, Oxfordshire, England
Jun 21-24	Vediorbis Open de France, Le Golf d'Arras, Anzin St Aubin, France
Jul 6-8	Ladies English Open, Chart Hills Golf Club, Biddenden, Kent, England
Jul 13-15	OTP Bank Ladies Central European Open – Hungary, Old Lake Golf Club, Tata, Hungary
TBC	Catalonia Ladies Masters, venue TBC
Jul 25-28	**Evian Masters**[1], Evian Masters GC, Evian Les Bains, France

Ladies European Tour *continued*

Aug 2–5	**Weetabix Women's British Open**[1], The Old Course, St Andrews, Scotland
Aug 9–12	Scandinavian TPC hosted by Annika, Barsebäck G&CC, Malmo, Sweden
Aug 16–19	Wales Ladies Championship of Europe, Machynys Peninsula GC, Llanelli, Wales
Aug 24–26	SAS Masters, Losby Golf Club, Oslo, Norway
Aug 31–Sep 2	Finnair Masters, Helsinki Golf Club, Tali, Finland
Sep 6–9	Nykredit Masters, Helsingør Golf Club, Denmark
Sep 14–16	**The Solheim Cup**, Halmstad Golf Club, Halmstad, Sweden
Sep 21–23	De Vere Ladies Scottish Open, De Vere Cameron House, The Carrick on Loch Lomond, Scotland
Sep 27–30	Siemens Austrian Ladies Open, Golfclub Fohrenwald-Wiener, Neustadt, Austria
Oct 5–7	TBA
Dec 6–9	Dubai Ladies Masters, Emirates Golf Club (Majlis Course), Dubai, UAE

[1]Joint sanction event

LPGA Tour

Jan 19–21	Women's World Cup of Golf, Gary Player CC, Sun City, RSA
Feb 15–17	SBS Open at Turtle Bay, Turtle Bay Resort, Oahu, HI
Feb 22–24	Fields Open in Hawaii, Ko Olina Resort, Honolulu, HI
Mar 9–11	MasterCard Classic Bosque Real CC, Huixquilucan, Mexico
Mar 22–25	Safeway International, Superstition Mountain G&CC, Superstition Mountain, AZ
Mar 29–Apr 1	**Kraft Nabisco Championship**, Mission Hills CC, Rancho Mirage, CA
Apr 12–15	Ginn Open, Reunion Resort & Club, Reunion, FL
Apr 19–22	Franklin American Mortgage Championship, Vanderbilt Legends Club, Franklin, TN
Apr 26–29	Corona Morelia Championship, Tres Marias Residential CC, Michoacan, Mexico
May 4–6	SemGroup Championship, Cedar Ridge CC, Broken Arrow, OK
May 10–13	Michelob ULTRA Open at Kingsmill, Kingsmill Resort & Spa, Williamsburg, VA
May 17–20	TBA
May 24–27	LPGA Corning Classic, Corning CC, Corning, NY
May 31–Jun 3	Ginn Tribute, RiverTowne CC, Mount Pleasant, SC
Jun 7–10	**McDonald's LPGA Championship**, Bulle Rock GC, Havre de Grace, MD
Jun 21–24	Wegmans LPGA, Locust Hill Country Club, Pittsford, NY
Jun 28–Jul 1	**US Women's Open**, Pine Needles Lodge & GC, Southern Pines, NC
Jul 12–15	Jamie Farr Owens Corning Classic, Highland Meadows GC, Sylvania, OH
Jul 19–22	HSBC Women's World Match Play Championship, Wykagyl CC, New Rochelle, NY
Jul 25–28	Evian Masters, Evian Masters GC, Evian-les-Bains, France
Aug 2–5	**Weetabix Women's British Open**, Old Course at St Andrews, Scotland
Aug 16–19	CN Canadian Women's Open, Royal Mayfair G&CC, Edmonton, Alberta, Canada
Aug 24–26	Safeway Classic, Columbia Edgewater CC, Portland, OR
Aug 30–2	LPGA State Farm Classic, Panther Creek CC, Springfield, IL
Sep 7–9	NW Arkansas LPGA Classic, Pinnacle CC, Rogers, AR
Sep 14–16	The Solheim Cup, Halmstad GC, Halmstad, Sweden
Sept 27–30	Navistar LPGA Classic, RTJ Golf Trail, Prattville, AL
Oct 4–7	Longs Drugs Challenge, Blackhawk CC, Danville, CA
Oct 11–14	Samsung World Championship, Bighorn GC, Palm Desert, CA
TBA	Honda LPGA Thailand, Amata Spring CC, Chonburi, Thailand
TBA	Korea Championship, South Korea
TBA	Mizuno Classic, Japan
Nov 8–11	The Mitchell Company LPGA Tournament of Champions, RTJ Golf Trail, Mobile, AL
Nov 15–18	ADT Championship, TBA
TBA	Lexus Cup, TBA
Dec 21–23	Wendy's 3-Tour Challenge, TBA

Men's and Women's Amateur Championship schedules for 2007
can be found on page 416

PART X

Awards

Awards

Association of Golf Writers' Trophy   (Awarded to the man or woman who, in the opinion of golf writers, has done most for European golf during the year)

1951	Max Faulkner
1952	Miss Elizabeth Price
1953	Joe Carr
1954	Mrs Roy Smith (Miss Frances Stephens)
1955	Ladies' Golf Union's Touring Team
1956	John Beharrell
1957	Dai Rees
1958	Harry Bradshaw
1959	Eric Brown
1960	Sir Stuart Goodwin (sponsor of international golf)
1961	Commdr Charles Roe (ex-hon secretary, PGA)
1962	Mrs Marley Spearman, British Ladies' Champion 1961–1962
1963	Michael Lunt, Amateur Champion, 1963
1964	GBI Eisenhower Trophy Team
1965	Gerald Micklem, golf administrator, President, English Golf Union
1966	Ronnie Shade
1967	John Panton
1968	Michael Bonallack
1969	Tony Jacklin
1970	Tony Jacklin
1971	Great Britain & Ireland Walker Cup Team
1972	Miss Michelle Walker
1973	Peter Oosterhuis
1974	Peter Oosterhuis
1975	Golf Foundation
1976	Great Britain & Ireland Eisenhower Trophy Team
1977	Christy O'Connor

1978	Peter McEvoy
1979	Severiano Ballesteros
1980	Sandy Lyle
1981	Bernhard Langer
1982	Gordon Brand Jr
1983	Nick Faldo
1984	Severiano Ballesteros
1985	European Ryder Cup Team
1986	GBI Curtis Cup Team
1987	European Ryder Cup Team
1988	Sandy Lyle
1989	Great Britain & Ireland Walker Cup Team
1990	Nick Faldo
1991	Severiano Ballesteros
1992	European Solheim Cup Team
1993	Bernhard Langer
1994	Laura Davies
1995	European Ryder Cup Team
1996	Colin Montgomerie
1997	Alison Nicholas
1998	Lee Westwood
1999	Sergio García
2000	Lee Westwood
2001	Great Britain & Ireland Walker Cup Team
2002	Ernie Els (RSA)
2003	Annika Sörenstam
2004	European Ryder Cup team (Bernhard Langer capt.)
2005	Annika Sörenstam
2006	European Ryder Cup team (Ian Woosnam capt.)

Daily Telegraph Woman Golfer of the Year

1982	Jane Connachan
1983	Jill Thornhill
1984	Gillian Stewart and Claire Waite
1985	Belle Robertson
1986	GBI Curtis Cup Team
1987	Linda Bayman
1988	GBI Curtis Cup Team
1989	Helen Dobson
1990	Angela Uzielli
1991	Joanne Morley
1992	GBI Curtis Cup Team, Captain Liz Boatman
1993	Catriona Lambert and Julie Hall
1994	GBI Curtis Cup Team, Captain Liz Boatman
1995	Julie Hall
1996	GBI Curtis Cup Team
1997	Alison Rose
1998	Kim Andrew
1999	Welsh International Team
2000	Rebecca Hudson
2001	Rebecca Hudson
2002	Becky Brewerton
2003	Becky Brewerton
2004	Emma Duggleby
2005	Felicity Johnson
2006	Not awarded

Joyce Wethered Trophy

(Awarded to the outstanding amateur under 25)

1994	Janice Moodie	2001	Clare Queen
1995	Rebecca Hudson	2002	Sarah Jones
1996	Mhairi McKay	2003	Sophie Walker
1997	Rebecca Hudson	2004	Melissa Reid
1998	Liza Walters	2005	Becky Harries
1999	Becky Brewerton	2006	Not awarded
2000	Sophie Walker		

LET Players' Player of the Year

1995	Annika Sörenstam (SWE)
1996	Laura Davies (ENG)
1997	Alison Nicholas (ENG)
1998	Sophie Gustafson (SWE)
1999	Laura Davies (ENG)
2000	Sophie Gustafson (SWE)
2001	Raquel Carriedo (ESP)
2002	Annika Sörenstam (SWE)
2003	Sophie Gustafson (SWE)
2004	Stephanie Arricau (FRA)
2005	Iben Tinning (DEN)
2006	Gwladys Nocera (FRA)

Robe Di Kappa LET Order of Merit

1979	Catherine Panton-Lewis (SCO)	1993	Karen Lunn (AUS)
1980	Muriel Thomson (SCO)	1994	Liselotte Neumann (SWE)
1981	Jenny Lee-Smith (ENG)	1995	Annika Sörenstam (SWE)
1982	Jenny Lee-Smith (ENG)	1996	Laura Davies (ENG)
1983	Muriel Thomson (SCO)	1997	Alison Nicholas (ENG)
1984	Dale Reid (SCO)	1998	Helen Alfredsson (SWE)
1985	Laura Davies (ENG)	1999	Laura Davies (ENG)
1986	Laura Davies (ENG)	2000	Sophie Gustafson (SWE)
1987	Dale Reid (SCO)	2001	Raquel Carriedo (ESP)
1988	Marie-Laure Taud (FRA)	2002	Paula Marti (ESP)
1989	Marie-Laure de Laurenzi (FRA)	2003	Sophie Gustafson (SWE)
1990	Trish Johnson (ENG)	2004	Laura Davies (ENG)
1991	Corinne Dibnah (AUS)	2005	Iben Tinning (DEN)
1992	Laura Davies (ENG)	2006	Laura Davies (ENG)

Ryder Cup Wales Rookie of the Year

(formerly Bill Johnson Trophy)

Awarded to the Rookie of the Year on the Robe Di Kappa Tour

1984	Katrina Douglas (ENG)
1985	Laura Davies (ENG)
1986	Patricia Gonzales (COL)
1987	Trish Johnson (ENG)
1988	Laurette Maritz (USA)
1989	Helen Alfredsson (SWE)
1990	Pearl Sinn (KOR)
1991	Helen Wadsworth (WAL)
1992	Sandrine Mendiburu (FRA)
1993	Annika Sörenstam (SWE)
1994	Tracy Hansen (USA)
1995	Karrie Webb (AUS)
1996	Anne-Marie Knight (AUS)
1997	Anna Berg (SWE)
1998	Laura Philo (USA)
1999	Elaine Ratcliffe (ENG)
2000	Guila Sergas (ITA)
2001	Suzann Pettersen (NOR)
2002	Kirsty S Taylor (ENG)
2003	Rebecca Stevenson (AUS)
2004	Minea Blomqvist (FIN)
2005	Elisa Serramia (ESP)
2006	Nikki Garrett (AUS)

US LPGA Rolex Player of the Year

1966	Kathy Whitworth	1987	Ayako Okamoto
1967	Kathy Whitworth	1988	Nancy Lopez
1968	Kathy Whitworth	1989	Betsy King
1969	Kathy Whitworth	1990	Beth Daniel
1970	Sandra Haynie	1991	Pat Bradley
1971	Kathy Whitworth	1992	Dottie Mochrie
1972	Kathy Whitworth	1993	Betsy King
1973	Kathy Whitworth	1994	Beth Daniel
1974	JoAnne Carner	1995	Annika Sörenstam
1975	Sandra Palmer	1996	Laura Davies
1976	Judy Rankin	1997	Annika Sörenstam
1977	Judy Rankin	1998	Annika Sörenstam
1978	Nancy Lopez	1999	Karrie Webb
1979	Nancy Lopez	2000	Karrie Webb
1980	Beth Daniel	2001	Annika Sörenstam
1981	Jo Anne Carner	2002	Annika Sörenstam
1982	Jo Anne Carner	2003	Annika Sörenstam
1983	Patty Sheehan	2004	Annika Sörenstam
1984	Betsy King	2005	Annika Sörenstam
1985	Nancy Lopez	2006	Lorena Ochoa
1986	Pat Bradley		

Vivien Saunders Trophy

Low average score | **Scoring average**

1991	Alison Nicholas (ENG)	71.71
1992	Laura Davies (ENG)	70.35
1993	Laura Davies (ENG)	71.63
1994	Liselotte Neumann (SWE)	69.56
1995	Annika Sörenstam (SWE)	69.75
1996	Marie Laure de Lorenzi (FRA)	71.39
1997	Marie Laure de Lorenzi (FRA)	72.20
1998	Laura Davies (ENG)	71.96
1999	Elaine Ratcliffe	73.76
2000	Laura Davies (ENG)	70.50
2001	Catriona Mathew (SCO)	70.08
2002	Sophie Gustafson (SWE)	70.59
2003	Sophie Gustafson (SWE)	69.93
2004	Annika Sörenstam (SWE)	67.92
2005	Laura Davies (ENG)	70.35
2006	*Not awarded*	

US LPGA Louise Suggs

Rookie of the Year (American unless stated)

1962	Mary Mills	1988	Liselotte Neumann (SWE)
1963	Clifford Ann Creed		
1964	Susie Berning	1989	Pamela Wright (SCO)
1965	Margie Masters	1990	Hiromi Kobayashi (JPN)
1966	Jan Ferraris		
1967	Sharron Moran	1991	Brandie Burton
1968	Sandra Post	1992	Helen Alfredsson (SWE)
1969	Jane Blalock		
1970	JoAnne Carner	1993	Suzanne Strudwick (ENG)
1971	Sally Little (RSA)		
1972	Jocelyne Bourassa	1994	Annika Sörenstam (SWE)
1973	Laura Baugh		
1974	Jan Stephenson	1995	Pat Hurst
1975	Amy Alcott	1996	Karrie Webb (AUS)
1976	Bonnie Lauer	1997	Lisa Hackney (ENG)
1977	Debbie Massey	1998	Se Ri Pak (KOR)
1978	Nancy Lopez	1999	Mi Hyun Kim (KOR)
1979	Beth Daniel	2000	Dorothy Delasin (PHI)
1980	Myra Van Hoose	2001	Hee Won Han (KOR)
1981	Patty Sheehan	2002	Beth Bauer
1982	Patti Rizzo	2003	Lorena Ochoa (MEX)
1983	Stephanie Farwig	2004	Shi Hyun Ahn (KOR)
1984	Juli Inkster	2005	Paula Creamer
1985	Penny Hammel	2006	Seon-Hua Lee (KOR)
1986	Jody Rosenthal		
1987	Tammi Green		

LPGA Vare Trophy

		Scoring average			Scoring average
1953	Patty Berg	75.00	1980	Amy Alcott	71.51
1954	Babe Zaharias	75.48	1981	Jo Anne Carner	71.75
1955	Patty Berg	74.47	1982	Jo Anne Carner	71.49
1956	Patty Berg	74.57	1983	Jo Anne Carner	71.41
1957	Louise Suggs	74.64	1984	Patty Sheehan	71.40
1958	Beverly Hanson	74.92	1985	Nancy Lopez	70.73
1959	Betsy Rawls	74.03	1986	Pat Bradley	71.10
1960	Mickey Wright	73.25	1987	Betsy King	71.14
1961	Mickey Wright	73.55	1988	Colleen Walker	71.26
1962	Mickey Wright	73.67	1989	Beth Daniel	70.38
1963	Mickey Wright	72.81	1990	Beth Daniel	70.54
1964	Mickey Wright	72.46	1991	Pat Bradley	70.66
1965	Kathy Whitworth	72.61	1992	Dottie Mochrie	70.80
1966	Kathy Whitworth	72.60	1993	Nancy Lopez	70.83
1967	Kathy Whitworth	72.74	1994	Beth Daniel	70.90
1968	Carol Mann	72.04	1995	Annika Sörenstam (SWE)	71.00
1969	Kathy Whitworth	72.38	1996	Annika Sörenstam (SWE)	70.47
1970	Kathy Whitworth	72.26	1997	Karrie Webb (AUS)	70.01
1971	Kathy Whitworth	72.88	1998	Annika Sörenstam (SWE)	69.99
1972	Kathy Whitworth	72.38	1999	Karrie Webb (AUS)	69.43
1973	Judy Rankin	73.08	2000	Karrie Webb (AUS)	70.05
1974	JoAnne Carner	72.87	2001	Annika Sörenstam (SWE)	69.42
1975	JoAnne Carner	72.40	2002	Annika Sörenstam (SWE)	68.70
1976	Judy Rankin	72.25	2003	Se Ri Pak (KOR)	70.03
1977	Judy Rankin	72.16	2004	Grace Park (KOR)	69.99
1978	Nancy Lopez	71.76	2005	Annika Sörenstam (SWE)	69.25
1979	Nancy Lopez	71.20	2006	Lorena Ochoa (MEX)	69.23

Arnold Palmer Award

(Awarded to the US Tour's leading money winner)

1981	Tom Kite	1994	Nick Price (ZIM)
1982	Craig Stadler	1995	Greg Norman (AUS)
1983	Hal Sutton	1996	Tom Lehman
1984	Tom Watson	1997	Tiger Woods
1985	Curtis Strange	1998	David Duval
1986	Greg Norman (AUS)	1999	Tiger Woods
1987	Paul Azinger	2000	Tiger Woods
1988	Curtis Strange	2001	Tiger Woods
1989	Tom Kite	2002	Tiger Woods
1990	Greg Norman (AUS)	2003	Tiger Woods
1991	Corey Pavin	2004	Vijay Singh (FIJ)
1992	Fred Couples	2005	Tiger Woods
1993	Nick Price (ZIM)	2006	Tiger Woods

Payne Stewart Award

(presented to the player who respects and upholds the traditions of the game)

2000	Byron Nelson, Jack Nicklaus, Arnold Palmer
2001	Ben Crenshaw
2002	Nick Price (ZIM)
2003	Tom Watson
2004	Jay Haas
2005	Brad Faxon
2006	Gary Player (RSA)

Jack Nicklaus Award

(US Tour Player of the Year – decided by player ballot)

1990	Wayne Levi	1999	Tiger Woods
1991	Fred Couples	2000	Tiger Woods
1992	Fred Couples	2001	Tiger Woods
1993	Nick Price (ZIM)	2002	Tiger Woods
1994	Nick Price (ZIM)	2003	Tiger Woods
1995	Greg Norman (AUS)	2004	Vijay Singh (FIJ)
1996	Tom Lehman	2005	Tiger Woods
1997	Tiger Woods	2006	Tiger Woods
1998	Mark O'Meara		

First Lady of Golf Award

(PGA of America award for women who have made a significant contribution to the game)

1998	Barbara Nicklaus
1999	Judy Rankin
2000	No award given
2001	Judy Bell
2002	Nancy Lopez
2003	Renee Powell
2004	Alice Dye
2005	Carole Semple-Thompson
2006	Kathy Whitworth

PGA of America Vardon Trophy (The award is made by the PGA of America to the member of the US Tour who completes 60 rounds or more, with the lowest scoring average over the calendar year)

1937	Harry Cooper		1963	Billy Casper	70.58	1985	Don Pooley	70.36
1938	Sam Snead		1964	Arnold Palmer	70.01	1986	Scott Hoch	70.08
1939	Byron Nelson		1965	Billy Casper	70.85	1987	Dan Pohl	70.25
1940	Ben Hogan		1966	Billy Casper	70.27	1988	Chip Beck	69.46
1941	Ben Hogan		1967	Arnold Palmer	70.18	1989	Greg Norman (AUS)	69.49
1942–46	No Awards – World War II		1968	Billy Casper	69.82	1990	Greg Norman (AUS)	69.10
1947	Jimmy Demarel	69.90	1969	Dave Hill	70.34	1991	Fred Couples	69.59
1948	Ben Hogan	69.30	1970	Lee Trevino	70.64	1992	Fred Couples	69.38
1949	Sam Snead	69.37	1971	Lee Trevino	70.27	1993	Nick Price (ZIM)	69.11
1950	Sam Snead	69.23	1972	Lee Trevino	70.89	1994	Greg Norman (AUS)	69.81
1951	Lloyd Mangrum	70.05	1973	Bruce Crampton (AUS)	70.57	1995	Steve Elkington (AUS)	69.82
1952	Jack Burke	70.54	1974	Lee Trevino	70.53	1996	Tom Lehman	69.32
1953	Lloyd Mangrum	70.22	1975	Bruce Crampton (AUS)	70.51	1997	Nick Price (ZIM)	68.98
1954	Ed Harrison	70.41	1976	Don January	70.56	1998	David Duval	69.13
1955	Sam Snead	69.86	1977	Tom Watson	70.32	1999	Tiger Woods	68.43
1956	Cary Middlecoff	70.35	1978	Tom Watson	70.16	2000	Tiger Woods	67.79
1957	Dow Finsterwald	70.30	1979	Tom Watson	70.27	2001	Tiger Woods	68.81
1958	Bob Rosburg	70.11	1980	Lee Trevino	69.73	2002	Tiger Woods	68.56
1959	Art Wall	70.35	1981	Tom Kite	69.80	2003	Tiger Woods	68.41
1960	Billy Casper	69.95	1982	Tom Kite	70.21	2004	Vijay Singh (FIJ)	68.84
1961	Arnold Palmer	69.85	1983	Ray Floyd	70.61	2005	Tiger Woods	68.66
1962	Arnold Palmer	70.27	1984	Calvin Peete	70.56	2006	Jim Furyk	68.66

US Tour Player of the Year
(Decided on merit points)

1948	Ben Hogan	1978	Tom Watson
1949	Sam Snead	1979	Tom Watson
1950	Ben Hogan	1980	Tom Watson
1951	Ben Hogan	1981	Bill Rogers
1952	Julius Boros	1982	Tom Watson
1953	Ben Hogan	1983	Hal Sutton
1954	Ed Furgol	1984	Tom Watson
1955	Doug Ford	1985	Lanny Wadkins
1956	Jack Burke	1986	Bob Tway
1957	Dick Mayer	1987	Paul Azinger
1958	Dow Finsterwald	1988	Curtis Strange
1959	Art Wall	1989	Tom Kite
1960	Arnold Palmer	1990	Nick Faldo (ENG)
1961	Jerry Barner	1991	Corey Pavin
1962	Arnold Palmer	1992	Fred Couples
1963	Julius Boros	1993	Nick Price (ZIM)
1964	Ken Venturi	1994	Nick Price (ZIM)
1965	Dave Marr	1995	Greg Norman (AUS)
1966	Billy Casper	1996	Tom Lehman
1967	Jack Nicklaus	1997	Tiger Woods
1968	not awarded	1998	Mark O'Meara
1969	Orville Moody	1999	Tiger Woods
1970	Billy Casper	2000	Tiger Woods
1971	Lee Trevino	2001	Tiger Woods
1972	Jack Nicklaus	2002	Tiger Woods
1973	Jack Nicklaus	2003	Tiger Woods
1974	Johnny Miller	2004	Vijay Singh (FIJ)
1975	Jack Nicklaus	2005	Tiger Woods
1976	Jack Nicklaus	2006	Tiger Woods
1977	Tom Watson		

European Tour Player of the Year

1995	C Montgomerie (SCO)	2001	R Goosen (RSA)
1996	C Montgomerie (SCO)	2002	E Els (RSA)
1997	C Montgomerie (SCO)	2003	E Els (RSA)
1998	L Westwood (ENG)	2004	V Singh (FIJ)
1999	C Montgomerie (SCO)	2005	M Campbell (NZL)
2000	L Westwood (ENG)	2006	Paul Casey (ENG)

US Tour Rookie of the Year
(Decided by PGA Tour members ballot)

1990	Robert Gamez	1999	Carlos Franco (PAR)
1991	John Daly	2000	Michael Clark II
1992	Mark Carnevale	2001	Charles Howell III
1993	Vijay Singh (FIJ)	2002	Jonathan Byrd
1994	Ernie Els (RSA)	2003	Ben Curtis
1995	Woody Austin	2004	Todd Hamilton
1996	Tiger Woods	2005	Sean O'Hair
1997	Stewart Cink	2006	Trevor Immelman (RSA)
1998	Steve Flesch		

Sir Henry Cotton European Rookie of the Year

1960	Tommy Goodwin	1985	Paul Thomas
1961	Alex Caygill	1986	José Maria Olazàbal
1962	No Award	1987	Peter Baker
1963	Tony Jacklin	1988	Colin Montgomerie
1964	No Award	1989	Paul Broadhurst
1966	Robin Liddle	1990	Russell Claydon
1967	No Award	1991	Per-Ulrik Johansson
1968	Bernard Gallacher	1992	Jim Payne
1969	Peter Oosterhuis	1993	Gary Orr
1970	Stuart Brown	1994	Jonathan Lomas
1971	David Llewellyn	1995	Jarmo Sandelin
1972	Sam Torrance	1996	Thomas Bjørn
1973	Philip Elson	1997	Scott Henderson
1974	Carl Mason	1998	Olivier Edmond
1975	No Award	1999	Sergio García
1976	Mark James	2000	Ian Poulter
1977	Nick Faldo	2001	Paul Casey
1978	Sandy Lyle	2002	Nick Dougherty
1979	Mike Miller	2003	Peter Lawrie
1980	Paul Hoad	2004	Scott Drummond
1981	Jeremy Bennett	2005	Gonzalo Fernandez-Castano
1982	Gordon Brand Jr		
1983	Grant Turner	2006	Marc Warren
1984	Philip Parkin		

Harry Vardon Trophy (Awarded to the PGA member heading the Order of Merit at the end of the season)

1937	Charles Whitcombe	1964	Peter Alliss	1986	Severiano Ballesteros
1938	Henry Cotton	1965	Bernard Hunt	1987	Ian Woosnam
1939	Roger Whitcombe	1966	Peter Alliss	1988	Severiano Ballesteros
1940–45	In abeyance	1967	Malcolm Gregson	1989	Ronan Rafferty
1946	Bobby Locke	1968	Brian Huggett	1990	Ian Woosnam
1947	Norman Von Nida	1969	Bernard Gallacher	1991	Severiano Ballesteros
1948	Charlie Ward	1970	Neil Coles	1992	Nick Faldo
1949	Charlie Ward	1971	Peter Oosterhuis	1993	Colin Montgomerie
1950	Bobby Locke	1972	Peter Oosterhuis	1994	Colin Montgomerie
1951	John Panton	1973	Peter Oosterhuis	1995	Colin Montgomerie
1952	Harry Weetman	1974	Peter Oosterhuis	1996	Colin Montgomerie
1953	Flory van Donck	1975	Dale Hayes	1997	Colin Montgomerie
1954	Bobby Locke	1976	Severiano Ballesteros	1998	Colin Montgomerie
1955	Dai Rees	1977	Severiano Ballesteros	1999	Colin Montgomerie
1956	Harry Weetman	1978	Severiano Ballesteros	2000	Lee Westwood
1957	Eric Brown	1979	Sandy Lyle	2001	Retief Goosen
1958	Bernard Hunt	1980	Sandy Lyle	2002	Retief Goosen
1959	Dai Rees	1981	Bernhard Langer	2003	Ernie Els
1960	Bernard Hunt	1982	Greg Norman	2004	Ernie Els
1961	Christy O'Connor	1983	Nick Faldo	2005	Colin Montgomerie
1962	Christy O'Connor	1984	Bernhard Langer	2006	Padraig Harrington
1963	Neil Coles	1985	Sandy Lyle		

Bob Jones Award

(Awarded by USGA for distinguished sportsmanship in golf)

1955	Francis Ouimet	1973	Gene Littler	1991	Ben Crenshaw
1956	Bill Campbell	1974	Byron Nelson	1992	Gene Sarazen
1957	Babe Zaharias	1975	Jack Nicklaus	1993	PJ Boatwright Jr
1958	Margaret Curtis	1976	Ben Hogan	1994	Lewis Oehmig
1959	Findlay Douglas	1977	Joseph C Dey	1995	Herbert Warren Wind
1960	Charles Evans Jr	1978	Bob Hope and Bing Crosby	1996	Betsy Rawls
1961	Joe Carr	1979	Tom Kite	1997	Fred Brand
1962	Horton-Smith	1980	Charles Yates	1998	Nancy Lopez
1963	Patty Berg	1981	JoAnne Carner	1999	Ed Updegraff
1964	Charles Coe	1982	Billy Joe Patton	2000	Barbara McIntyre
1965	Mrs Edwin Vare	1983	Maureen Garrett	2001	Thomas Cousins
1966	Gary Player	1984	Jay Sigel	2002	Judy Rankin
1967	Richard Tufts	1985	Fuzzy Zoeller	2003	Carol Semple Thompson
1968	Robert Dickson	1986	Jess W Sweetser	2004	Jackie Burke
1969	Gerald Micklem	1987	Tom Watson	2005	Nick Price
1970	Roberto De Vicenzo	1988	Isaac B Grainger	2006	Louise Suggs
1971	Arnold Palmer	1989	Chi-Chi Rodriquez		
1972	Michael Bonallack	1990	Peggy Kirk Bell		

PGA of America Distinguished Service Award

1988	Herb Graffis	1993	Byron Nelson	1998	Paul Runyan	2003	Vince Gill
1989	Bob Hope	1994	Arnold Palmer	1999	Bill Dickey	2004	Pete Dye
1990	No award	1995	Patty Berg	2000	Jack Nicklaus	2005	Wally Uihlein
1991	Gerald Ford	1996	Frank Chirkinian	2001	Mark McCormack	2006	Jay Haas
1992	Gene Sarazen	1997	George Bush	2002	Tim Finchem		

Gustafson named Life Member of the Ladies European Tour

With her victory in the Siemens Austrian Ladies Open in September 2006, Sophie Gustafson earned Life Membership of the Ladies European Tour. Her victory earned her the minimum 20 points required to be eligible. Having joined the LET in 1994, she also met the second requirement with more than 10 years as a member of the Tour. She received lifetime eligibility for all LET standard ranking full-field events from December 1, 2006, and will no longer be required to pay annual subscription fees. She won the Tour Order of Merit in 2000 and 2003, having won three times in Europe in each of those years.

PART XI

Who's Who in Golf

European Golfers – Men

Great Britain and Ireland

Alliss, P.	Darcy, E.	Green, C,	McDowell, G.	Price, P.
Baker, P.	Dodd, S.	Harrington, P.	McEvoy, P.	Rafferty, R.
Barnes, B.	Donald, K.	Horton, T.	McGimpsey, G.	Ramsay, R.
Beharrell, J.C.	Dougherty, N.	Howell, D.	McGinley, P.	Rose, J.
Benka, P.	Dredge, B.	Howard, B.	Macgregor, G.	Saltman, L.
Bennett, W.	Drew, N.	Huggett, B.	McNulty, M.	Smyth, D.
Bickerton, J.	Drummond, S.	Hunt, B.	Marks, G.	Thomas, D.
Bonallack, M.	Dyson, S.	Jacklin, T.	Marsh, D.	Torrance, S.
Brown, K.	Edwards, N.	Jacobs, J.	Milligan, J.	Walton, P.
Casey, P.	Emerson, G.	James, M.	Montgomerie, C.	Warren, M.
Chapman, R.	Faldo, N.	Khan, S.	O'Connor, C., Sr	Webster, S.
Clark, C.	Feherty, D.	Lane, B.	O'Connor, C., Jr	Westwood, L.
Clark, H.	Fiddian, E.W.	Lawrie, P.	O'Leary, J.	White, R.
Clarke, D.	Fisher, O.	Lunt, M.	Oosterhuis, P.	Wolstenholme, G.
Coles, N.	Foster, R.	Lyle, S.	Panton, J.	Woosnam, I.
Coltart, A.	Gallacher, B.	Lynn, D.	Poulter, I.	

Alliss, Peter (ENG)
Born Berlin, 28 February 1931
Turned professional 1946
Following a distinguished career as a tournament golfer in which he won 18 titles between 1954 and 1966 and played eight times in the Ryder Cup between 1953 and 1969, he turned to golf commentating. In Britain he works for the BBC and in America for the ABC network. Twice captain of the PGA in 1962 and 1987 he won the Spanish, Italian and Portuguese Opens in 1958. Author or co-author of several golf books and a novel with a golfing background, he has also designed several courses including the Brabazon course at The Belfry in association with Dave Thomas. In 2003 he was awarded Life Membership of the PGA in honour of his lifelong contribution and commitment to the game. In 2005 he received an honorary degree from St Andrews University.

Baker, Peter (ENG)
Born Shifnal, Shropshire, 7 October 1967
Rookie of the year in 1987, Peter was hailed as the best young newcomer by Nick Faldo when he beat Faldo in a play-off for the Benson and Hedges International in 1988. Several times a winner since then he played in the 1993 Ryder Cup scoring three points out of four. In the singles he beat Corey Pavin. He was a vice-captain to Ian Woosnam in the 2006 Ryder Cup.

Barnes, Brian (SCO)
Born Addington, Surrey, 3 June 1945
Turned professional 1964
Extrovert Scottish professional whose father-in-law was the late former Open champion Max Faulkner. He was a ten times winner on the European Tour between 1972 and 1981 and was twice British Seniors champion successfully defending the title in 1996. He played in six Ryder Cup matches most notably at Laurel Valley in 1975 when, having beaten Jack Nicklaus in the morning, he beat him again in the afternoon. Now prevented from continuing to play on the US Senior Tour because of rheumatoid arthritis he is expanding his career as a commentator for Sky Television.

Beharrell, John Charles (ENG)
Born Birmingham, 14 January 1935
Youngest winner of the Amateur Championship when he took the title at Troon (now Royal Troon) in 1956. Held the post of captain of the Royal and Ancient Golf Club of St Andrews in 1998/99. Married Veronica Anstey, former Curtis Cup player, Australian and New Zealand Ladies champion.

Benka, Peter (ENG)
Born London, 18 September 1946
Former Walker Cup player who won the British Youths Championship in 1967 and 1968. Now chairman of the R&A Selection Committee.

Bennett, Warren (ENG)
Born Ruislip, 20 August 1971
Turned professional 1994
Leading amateur in the 1994 Open Championship and winner of the Australian Centennial Amateur Championship the same year. A former British Youths champion, Bennett won the 1999 Scottish PGA Championship but his career has been dogged by injury.

Bickerton, John (ENG)
Born Redditch, 23 December 1969
Turned professional 1991
Five seconds was his frustrating record on Tour until he came through to win the Abama Canaries Open in 2005. His break through success, which guaranteed him his card for 2006, came as he teed up for the 287th event.

He proved the exception to the rule when he was hit twice by lightening while playing as an amateur. Fortunately he was not injured. He won for the second time on the European Tour when he landed the French Open at Golf National.

Bonallack KT, OBE, Sir Michael (ENG)
Born Chigwell, Essex, 31 December 1934
One of only three golfing knights (the others are the late Sir Henry Cotton and Sir Bob Charles) he won the Amateur Championship five times between 1961 and 1970 and was five times English champion between 1962 and 1968. He also won the English stroke play title four times and was twice leading amateur in the Open in 1968 and 1971. In his hugely impressive career he played in nine Walker Cup matches captaining the side on two occasions. He participated in five Eisenhower Trophy matches and five Commonwealth team competitions. He scored his first national title win in the 1952 British Boys' Championship and took his Essex County title 11 times between 1954 and 1972. After serving as secretary of the R&A from 1983 to 1999 he was captain in 1999/2000. Twice winner of the Association of Golf Writers' award in 1968 and 1999, he also received the Bobby Jones award in 1972, the Donald Ross and Gerald Micklem awards in 1991 and the Ambassador of Golf award in 1995. In 2000 he was inducted into the World Hall Golf of Fame. A former chairman of the R&A selection committee, he served as chairman of the PGA from 1976 to 1981 and is now a non-executive director of the PGA European Tour. He was chairman of the Golf Foundation in 1977 and president of the English Golf Union in 1982. His wife Lady Angela is the former English champion Angela Ward.

Brown, Ken (SCO)
Born Harpenden, Hertfordshire, 9 January 1957
Turned professional 1974
Renowned as a great short game exponent, especially with his hickory-shafted putter, he won four times in Europe between 1978 and 85, and took the Southern Open on the US tour in 1987. He played in two winning Ryder Cup sides in 1985 and 1987 having previously played in the 1977, 1979 and 1983 matches. Latterly he has carved out a new career for himself as a television commentator working closely with Peter Alliss on the BBC team and providing the insight for Setanta Television in the satellite company's coverage of the PGA Tour in America. He also works for The Golf Channel.

Casey, Paul (ENG)
Born Cheltenham, 21 July 1977
Turned professional 2001
Winner of the English Amateur Championship in 1999 and 2000, he attended Arizona State University where he was a three time All American in NCAA Golf. While at college he broke records set by Phil Mickelson and Tiger Woods. In the 1999 Walker Cup match, which the Great Britain and Ireland side won at Nairn, he won all of his four games. After turning professional he earned his European Tour card after just five events helped by a second-equal finish in the Great North Open 2001 and twelfth place finishes in the Compass English Open and Benson and Hedges International. He became a winner in his 11th event when taking the Gleneagles Scottish PGA title over the PGA Centenary course. His coach is

Sir Michael Bonallack

Peter Kostis. In 2002 he shot a course record 62 at Gut Lärchenhof in the Linde German Masters won by Stephen Leaney. In the early part of the 2003 European season he won the ANZ Championship in Sydney and the last Benson and Hedges International at The Belfry and played with distinction in the 2004 Ryder Cup at Oakland Hills, Detroit, teaming up with David Howell for a vital foursomes point on the second morning. After mis-reported remarks he made about how he geared himself up for the Ryder Cup which some Americans found upsetting he had a quieter 2005 but did win the TCL Classic in China. His place in the England World Cup side, however, was taken by David Howell. He again played with distinction in the Ryder Cup at the K Club in 2006. He won three more events on the European Tour – the Volvo China Open (played in 2005 but on the 2006 fixture list), the Johnnie Walker Championship at Gleneagles and landed the £1m first prize by beating Shaun Micheel in the final of the HSBC World Match Play Championship at Wentworth. Leading the 2006 money list with only the Volvo Masters to come, he was pipped for the No.1 spot by Ireland's Padraig Harrington in a nail-biting finish to the season. Casey lost out when Sergio García bogeyed the last to let Harrington finish joint second with two others which was just enough to edge out Casey by €35,252

Chapman, Roger (ENG)
Born Nakuru, Kenya, 1 May 1959
Turned professional 1981
After playing on the European Tour for eighteen years without success, he lost his card and had to return to the qualifying school in 1999. Regaining his playing privileges with a twelfth place finish in the six round competition, he made his break-through win by beating Padraig

Harrington at the second hole of a play-off in the Brazil Rio de Janeiro Five Hundred Years Open. Later that year he won the Hassan II Trophy at Dar-Es-Salaam in Morocco. A former English Amateur Champion in 1981 he played in the Walker Cup the same year beating Hal Sutton twice in a day at Cypress Point.

Clark, Clive (ENG)
Born Winchester, 27 June 1945
Turned professional 1965
In the 1965 Walker Cup at Five Farms East in Maryland, he holed a 35-foot putt to earn a half point against Mark Hopkins and ensure a drawn match against the Americans. After turning professional he played in the 1973 Ryder Cup and was a four time winner of titles between 1966 and 1974. Following a career as commentator with the BBC he continued his golf course architecture work in America, and has received awards for his innovative designs.

Clark, Howard (ENG)
Born Leeds, 26 August 1954   Turned professional 1973
A scratch player by the age of 16 he turned professional after playing in the 1973 Walker Cup. An eleven-time winner on the European tour he played in six Ryder Cups and was in the winning team three times – in 1985 at The Belfry, 1987 at Muirfield Village, when the Europeans won for the first time on American soil, and in 1995 when he gained a vital point helped by a hole in one in the last day singles against Peter Jacobsen. In the 1985 World Cup played at La Quinta in Palm Springs he was the individual champion. He played 494 tournaments before giving up full-time competition to concentrate on his job as a golf analyst on the Sky TV commentary team.

Clarke, Darren (NIR)
Born Dungannon, Northern Ireland, 14 August 1968
Turned professional 1990
He became the first European Tour player to shoot 60 twice when he returned that record low score at the European Open at the K Club in 1999. Seven years earlier he had shot a nine under par 60 at Mont Agel in the European Monte Carlo Open, but his 60 in Dublin was 12 under par. With his second 60 he also equalled two other records. With twelve birdies on the card he matched the best birdie total in a round and he also scored a record-equalling eight birdies in a row. Tied second in the 1997 Open behind Justin Leonard and third equal in 2001 at Lytham, cigar-smoking Clarke played particularly well in the 2000 Andersen Consulting Match Play Championship at La Costa in California beating Paul Azinger, Mark O'Meara, Thomas Bjørn, Hal Sutton and David Duval to reach the final against Tiger Woods. He became the first European to win a World Golf Championship event when he beat Woods 4 and 3 and picked up the million dollar first prize. He took a second World Championship event in 2003 when he was an impressive winner of the NEC Invitational at Firestone. He played in the 1997, 1999, 2002 and 2004 Ryder Cup matches making a vital half point on the final day with David Duval in the 2002 match and halving with Davis Love III in 2004 at Detroit. Clarke's 2005 season was much reduced because of the illness of his wife while but he still managed a second place finish in the Barclays Scottish Open, a third place in the Open de Madrid and a fourth in the Smurfit European Open. Before the end of

the year he won the Visa Taiheiyo Masters in Japan. In 2006, is wife lost her battle with cancer but Clarke still managed to win a wild card in the Ryder Cup, winning twice in partnership with good friend Lee Westwood and taking his singles against Zach Johnson.

Coles MBE, Neil (ENG)
Born 26 September 1934   Turned professional 1950
Remarkably he has won golf tournaments in six decades and who is to say he will not win in seven decades. He turns 70 in September. In 2003 he did not win but in the Travis Perkins event at Wentworth's Edinburgh Course which he helped design he shot a 64 – great golf for a man who has been a prof for 54 years. In 1956 he won the Gor-Ray tournament and made golfing history when he took the Microlease Jersey Seniors Open at La Moye in 2000. From 1973 to 1979 he played in 68 events on the main European Tour without missing a half-way cut and became the then oldest winner when he won the Sanyo Open in Barcelona in 1982 at the age of 48 years and 14 days. (Des Smyth has since become an even older winner.) Coles remains, however, the oldest winner on the European Senior tour scoring his Jersey win when aged 65 years and 10 months and the following year won the Lawrence Batley Seniors Open at Huddersfield. A member of eight Ryder Cup teams, he has represented his country nineteen times since turning professional at the age of sixteen with a handicap of 14. He has been chairman of the PGA European Tour's Board of Directors since its inception in 1971 and in 2000 was inducted into the World Golf Hall of Fame. Internationally respected he might well have won more in America but for an aversion to flying caused by a bad experience on an internal flight from Edinburgh to London.

Coltart, Andrew (SCO)
Born Dumfries, 12 May 1970   Turned professional 1991
Twice Australian PGA champion in 1994 and 1997 he was the Australasian circuit's top money earner for the 1997/98 season. He made his Ryder Cup début at Brookline in 1999 as a captain's pick and on the final day found himself up against Tiger Woods. He played well but still lost. A former Walker Cup and Eisenhower Trophy player he was a member of the only Scottish team to win the Alfred Dunhill Cup at St Andrews in 1995. His European Tour successes include the 1998 Qatar Masters and 2001 Great North Open. His sister Laurae is married to fellow professional Lee Westwood.

Darcy, Eamonn (IRL)
Born Dalgeny, 7 August 1952   Turned professional 1969
One of Ireland's best known players who has played more than 600 tournament appearances on the European Tour despite suffering for many years with back trouble. First played when he was 10 years old and is renowned for his very distinctive swing incorporating a flying right elbow. He played in four Ryder Cups including the memorable one at Muirfield Village in 1987 when Europe won for the first time in America. He scored a vital point in the last day singles holing a tricky left to right downhill seven footer for a valuable point against Ben Crenshaw. In 2002 he joined the European Senior Tour. A year later he earned his card for the US Senior Tour – the Champions Tour.

Dodd, Stephen (WAL)
Born Cardiff, 15 July 1966   Turned professional 1990
Winner of the Amateur Championship at Royal Birkdale in 1989 when he also was a member of the winning Walker Cup team at Peachtree, he turned professional the following year but had to wait until the 2005 season for his first victory in Shanghai in the Volvo China Open. Later he added the Nissan Irish Open winning that in a play-off at Carton House against Australian Brett Rumford. With Bradley Dredge gave Wales their second win in the World Cup of Golf over 54 holes at Vilamoura in Portugal. Rainy weather caused cancellation of the last round.

Donald, Luke (ENG)
Born Hemel Hempstead, Herts., 7 December 1977
Turned professional 2001
Member of the winning Great Britain and Ireland team against the Americans in the 1999 Walker Cup at Nairn and again in 2001 before turning professional. In 1999 he won the NCAA Championship and was named NCAA Player of the Year. Has played most of his golf in America and he scored his first win on the US Tour when he took the rain-shortened Southern Farms Bureau title, becoming the 18th first-time winner of the season. He has continued to make steady progress and in 2004 lost a play-off to John Daly in the Buick Invitational on the US Tour and won the Scandinavian Masters and Omega European Masters of Europe. He was one of five rookies in the winning European Ryder Cup team in Detroit having been a captain's pick. Donald continued to play well in 2005 without managing to win any more titles on either side of the Atlantic. In the end he finished 12th on the European Money list and easily kept his US Tour card. In Europe he topped the "Putts per greens in regulation" stats with 1.684 average. He made the 2006 Ryder Cup by right and won his last day singles against Chad Campbell. Donald played on both sides of the Atlantic in 2006 and finished seventh on the European money list with €1,658,059 and ninth on the US PGA Tour with $3,177,408.

Dougherty, Nick (ENG)
Born Liverpool, 24 May 1982
Turned professional 2001
He was playing off plus 4 and had won the Australian Amateur Championship in 2001 when he turned professional. Started golfing at age 4 and won his first event at six years old. Sir Henry Cotton Rookie of the Year in 2002, Dougherty's career was hindered by a bout of glandular fever in 2003 but he made his break through win when holding off Colin Montgomerie to win the Caltex Masters, a joint venture between the Asian and European Tours in Singapore in 2005. In 2006, he nearly won in Singapore but had a miserable run when he lost form, failing to make 10 cuts in a row.

Dredge, Bradley (WAL)
Born Tredegar, Wales, 6 July 1973
Turned professional 1996
Winner of the Madeira Island Open in 2003, he had his biggest win when sharing the $1,400,000 first prize with Stephen Dodd in the 2005 World Cup of Golf played over 54 holes because of storms at Vilamoura in Portugal. The Welsh pair shot 61 twice in better-ball play and 67 in foursomes for a winning 27-under-par total.

Drew, Norman (NIR)
Born Belfast, 25 May 1932   Turned professional 1958
Twice Irish Open Amateur champion in 1952 and 1953 he played in the 1953 Walker Cup and six years later represented Great Britain and Ireland in the Ryder Cup.

Drummond, Scott (SCO)
Born Shrewsbury, 29 May 1974
Turned professional 1996
Like Sandy Lyle he is Scottish although born in Shropshire. Graduated from the Challenge Tour in 2004 and spectacularly won the Volvo PGA Championship at Wentworth from a star-studded field.

Dyson, Simon (ENG)
Born York, 21 December 1977
Turned professional 1999
Although a three-time winner on the Asian Tour where he was top earner in 2000, he scored his first European Tour success in the joint Asian–European venture in Indonesia in 2006 and later in the season he beat Australian Richard Green in a play-off for the KLM Open at Zandvoort. He finished the year in 21st spot on the money list.

Edwards, Nigel (WAL)
Born Caerphilly, 9 August 1968
Top scoring member of the winning Walker Cup sides in 2001 and in 2003 at Ganton when he teamed up with fellow countryman Nigel Manley to score 1½ points in the Fourballs, beat George Zahringer in the first day singles and halved with Lee Williams on day two holing from 30 yards with the putter at the 17th to ensure overall victory. He was again involved in a dramatic finish to the 2005 Walker Cup but one down with one to play needing to win the last against Jeff Overton his putt narrowly missed.

Emerson, Gary (ENG)
Born Salisbury, 26 September 1963
Turned professional 1982
Lost his card after finishing 128th in the 2003 Volvo Order of Merit but then gained a two year extension after winning the BMW Russian Open – a joint venture between the main Tour and the Challenge Tour.

Faldo MBE, Nick (ENG)
Born Welwyn Garden City, 18 July 1957
Turned professional 1976
Decided to turn professional after watching the US Masters on television and being impressed by Jack Nicklaus's performance. Europe's most successful major title winner having won three Open Champion-ships in 1987, 1990 at St Andrews and 1992 and three Masters titles in 1989, 1990 and 1996. Of current day players only Tom Watson with eight wins has won more majors. When he successfully defended the Masters in 1990 he became only the second man (after Nicklaus) to win in successive years. Staged a dramatic last day revival to win the 1996 Masters having started the last round six behind Greg Norman. When he realised his swing was not good enough to win majors he completely revamped it with the help of coach David Leadbetter. His 31 European Tour victories include a record three Irish Open victories in a row. In 1992 became the first player to win over £1

million in prize-money during a season. He played with distinction in 11 Ryder Cup matches including the winning teams in 1985, 1987, 1995 and 1997. He holds the record for most games played in the Cup – 46 – and most points won – 25. In 1995 at Oak Hill came from behind to score a vital last day point against Curtis Strange, the American who had beaten him in a play-off for the US Open title in 1988 at The Country Club in Boston. He became the first international player to be named USPGA Player of the Year in 1990 and led the official World Golf Rankings for 81 weeks in 1993–1994. After having teamed up with Swedish caddie Fanny Sunesson for ten years they split only to be reunited as one of golf's best-known partnerships in 2001. His hopes of one day captaining the European Ryder Cup side have been realized. He will be in charge for the match in 2008. His Faldo Junior Series, designed to encourage the best young players to improve, continues to expand. In 2006, he continued with his commentating career with the BBC, Sky, the Golf Channel and CBS with whom he signed an $8m eight-year contract

Feherty, David (NIR)
Born Bangor, Northern Ireland, 13 August 1958
Turned professional 1976
Quick-witted Ulsterman who gave up his competitive golfing career to become a hugely successful commentator for CBS in America where his one-liners are legendary. Had five European title wins and three victories on the South African circuit before switching his golf clubs for a more lucrative career with a microphone.

Fiddian, Eric Westwood (ENG)
Born Stourbridge, Worcestershire, 28 March 1910
Best remembered for having had two holes in one during the final of the 1933 Irish Open Amateur Championship but still lost by 3 and 2 to J McLean.

Fisher, Oliver (ENG)
Born Chingford, Essex, 19 August 1988
Became the youngest ever Walker Cup player when he made the 2005 Great Britain and Ireland side. He won the 2006 St Andrews Links Trophy, was runner-up in the 2006 English Amateur and reached the quarter-finals of the US Amateur Championship at Hazeltine.

Foster, Rodney (ENG)
Born Shipley, Yorkshire, 13 October 1941
Played in the Walker Cup five times between 1965 and 1973 and captained the side in 1979. He also captained the Eisenhower Trophy team in 1980.

Gallacher CBE, Bernard (SCO)
Born Bathgate, Scotland, 9 February 1949
Turned professional 1967
For many years combined tournament golf with the club professional's post at Wentworth where he was honoured in 2000 by being appointed captain. He took up golf at the age of 11 and nine years later was European No.1. He has scored 30 victories worldwide. Gallacher was the youngest Ryder Cup player when he made his début in the 1969 match in which he beat Lee Trevino in the singles. He played in eight Cup matches and captained the side three times losing narrowly in 1991 at Kiawah Island and 1993 at

The Belfry before leading the team to success at Oak Hill in 1995. A former member of the European Tour's Board of Directors, he now plays on the European Senior Tour making his break-through win in 2002 when he took first prize in the Mobile Cup at Stoke Park. In 2003 he was granted honorary membership of the European Tour but missed much of the Senior season through injury.

Green OBE, Charlie (SCO)
Born Dumbarton, 2 August 1932
One of Scotland's most successful amateur golfers who was leading amateur in the 1962 Open Championship. A prolific winner he took the Scottish Amateur title three times in 1970, 1982 and 1983. He played in five and was non-playing captain in two more Walker Cups and was awarded the Frank Moran Trophy for his services to Scottish sport in 1974.

Harrington, Padraig (IRL)
Born Dublin, Ireland, 31 August 1971
Turned professional 1995
A qualified accountant, he was Irish Open and Close Amateur champion (1995) and played three times in the Walker Cup player before turning professional. Played in the 1999 Ryder Cup at Brookline and beat Mark O'Meara in the singles. He was a member of the victorious European team for the 2002 match beating Mark Calcavecchia in the final day singles and was a key member of the winning Ryder Cup side at Oakland Hills in 2004 when he teamed up well with Colin Montgomerie and beat Jay Haas in the singles. In 2006, he was one of three Irishmen in Ian Woosnam's team that beat the Americans 18½–9½ at the K Club. Remembered in 2000 for being disqualified on the final day of the Benson and Hedges International at The Belfry after having moved into a five shot lead at the 54-hole stage. It was only then discovered that one of his playing partners had signed Harrington's card on the first day and not Harrington himself. The manner in which he accepted this dis-appointment greatly impressed observers. In the autumn of 2002 he won the US$800,000 first pize in the Dunhill Links Championship beating Eduardo Romero at the 2nd play-off hole at St Andrews. Won the BMW Asian Open in Taiwan and the Deutsche Bank SAP Open TPC of Europe in the early part of the 2003 European season. Continued to play well in 2004 and in 2005 won two events on the US Tour. Late in 2006, he took the dunhill links championship for the second time at St Andrews which helped him clinch the No.1 spot on the European money list for the first time. Harrington, who finished €35,252 ahead of Paul Casey, had twice come second and twice third in previous years races for the No.1 spot. Harrington's European winnings amounted to €2,489,336. He finished 68th on the US PGA Tour money list.

Horton MBE, Tommy (ENG)
Born St Helens, Lancashire, 16 June 1941
Turned professional 1957
A former Ryder Cup player who was no.1 earner on the European Seniors Tour in 1993 and for four successive seasons between 1996 and 1999. Awarded an MBE by Her Majesty the Queen for his services to golf, Tommy is a member of the European Tour Board and is chairman of the European Seniors Tour committee. A distinguished coach, broadcaster, author and golf course

architect, Tommy retired as club professional at Royal Jersey in 1999 after 25 years in the post. He continues to play on the Senior Tour.

Howell, David (ENG)
Born Swindon, 23 June 1975
Turned professional 1995
Winner of the 1999 Dubai Desert Classic, he made his Ryder Cup début in 2004 at Oakland Hills where he teamed up with Paul Casey to gain a valuable foursomes point on the second day. He continued to play well in 2005 adding a second victory to his European Tour CV when winning the BMW International in Munich. Finished seventh in the 2005 European Tour money list making over £1.2 million and in 2006, when his schedule was curtailed by injury, he made over £1.5 million in Europe and finished third in the list.

Howard, Barclay (SCO)
Born Johnstone, Scotland, 27 January 1953
Leading amateur in the Open Championship at Royal Troon in 1997, he has successfully battled cancer which affected his golfing career after he had played in both the 1995 and 1997 Walker Cup matches. When Dean Robertson won the Italian Open at Turin in 1999 he dedicated his victory to him as a tribute to his courage in adversity.

Huggett MBE, Brian (WAL)
Born Porthcawl, Wales, 18 November 1936
Turned professional 1951
Brian won the first of his 16 European Tour titles in Holland in 1962 and was still winning in 2000 when he landed the Beko Seniors Classic in Turkey after a play-off. A dogged competitor he played in six Ryder Cup matches before being given the honour of captaining the side in 1977 – the last year the Americans took on players from only Great Britain and Ireland. A respected golf course designer, Huggett was awarded the MBE for his services to golf and in particular Welsh golf.

Hunt MBE, Bernard (ENG)
Born Atherstone, Warwickshire, 2 February 1930
Turned professional 1946
One of Britain's most accomplished professionals he won 22 times between 1953 and 1973. He was third in the 1960 Open at the Old Course behind Kel Nagle and fourth in 1964 when Tony Lema took the title at St Andrews. Among his other victories were successes in Egypt and Brazil. Having made eight appearances in the Ryder Cup he captained the side in 1973 and again in 1975. He was PGA captain in 1966 and won the Harry Vardon Trophy as leading player in the Order of Merit on three occasions.

Jacklin CBE, Tony (ENG)
Born Scunthorpe, 7 July 1944
Turned professional 1962
Played an important and often under-rated role in the growth of the PGA European Tour after it became a self-supporting organisation in 1971. Although playing most of his golf in America he was encouraged by John Jacobs, the then executive director of the European Tour, to return to Europe to help build up the circuit. In 1969 he won the Open Championship at Royal Lytham and St Annes – the first British winner of the title since Max Faulkner in 1951. A year later he led from start to finish to win the US

Open at Hazeltine – the first British player to win that event since Ted Ray had been successful in 1920 and the only one to have done so to date. He was the first player since Harry Vardon to hold the British and American Open titles simultaneously. He might well have won further Opens but a thunderstorm halted his bid for the title at St Andrews in 1970, he came third in 1971 and in 1972 Lee Trevino chipped in at the 17th at Muirfield and went on to win a title the British player had seemed set to win. He is now one of just 13 honorary members of the Royal and Ancient Golf Club of St Andrews having been elected in 2003 along with Lee Trevino. Played in his last Open in 2005. He has built in Florida with Jack Nicklaus a course known as The Concession, so named because of the putt Jack conceded him in the 1969 Ryder Cup to ensure the overall match was halved.

Jacobs OBE, John (ENG)
Born Lindrick, Yorkshire, 14 March 1925
The first Executive Director of the independently run PGA European Tour, John Jacobs was awarded the OBE in 2000 for his services to golf as a player, administrator and coach. Known as 'Dr Golf' Jacobs has built up an awesome reputation as a teacher around the world and is held in high esteem by the golfing world. Top American coach Butch Harmon summed up Jacobs' contribution in this field of golf when he said: 'There is not one teacher who does not owe something to John. He wrote the book on coaching.' With 75 per cent of the votes he was inducted into the World Golf Teachers Hall of Fame and was described at that ceremony as 'the English genius'. Last year he was also, quite correctly, welcomed into the World Golf Hall of Fame in America. Having played in the 1955 Ryder Cup match he captained the side in 1979 when Continental players were included for the first time and again in 1981. Ken Schofield who succeeded him as European Tour supremo believes that Jacobs changed the face of golf sponsorship allowing, as he points out, far more than 10 players a season to earn a living. In 2002 he received the Association of Golf Writers award for outstanding services to golf.

James, Mark (ENG)
Born Manchester, 28 October 1953
Turned professional 1976
Veteran of over 500 European tournaments who is now chairman of the European Tour's Tournament committee. A seven-time Ryder Cup player including the 1995 match at Oak Hill when he scored a vital early last day point against Jeff Maggert, he captained the side in 1999 at Brookline. Four times a top five finisher in the Open Championship Mark has been involved in his fair share of controversy especially in the early days. He has won 18 European Tour events and four elsewhere but these days having successfully battled cancer, he is just as happy working in his Yorkshire garden. Caused some raised eyebrows with some of his comments in his book reviewing the 1999 Ryder Cup entitled 'Into the Bear Pit', then followed that up with a less controversial sequel. Affec-tionately known as Jesse to his friends. He qualified for the US Champions Tour in 2004 and won one of that Tour's five majors – the Ford Senior Players Championship. Through 2005 continued to play on the US Champions Tour with only infrequent visits back to play in European Senior events.

Khan, Simon (ENG)
Born Epping, 16 June 1972   Turned professional 1991
Inspired by friend Scott Drummond's victory a week earlier in the Volvo PGA Championship, Simon took first prize by overhauling Paul Casey in the final round of the 2004 Celtic Manor Resort Wales Open.

Lane, Barry (ENG)
Born Hayes, Middlesex, 21 June 1960
Turned professional 1976
After winning his way into the 1993 Ryder Cup he hit the headlines when he won the first prize of $1 million in beating David Frost in the final at Greyhawk in Arizona. He has played over 400 European events, winning five times between 1988 and 2004. In 2004 he won the *Daily Telegraph* Damovo British Masters at Marriott Forest of Arden.

Lawrie MBE, Paul (SCO)
Born Aberdeen, 1 January 1969
Turned professional 1986
Made golfing history when he came from 10 shots back on the final day to win the 1999 Open Championship at Carnoustie after a play-off against former winner Justin Leonard and Frenchman Jean Van de Velde. With his win he became the first home-based Scot since Willie Auchterlonie in 1893 to take the title. Still based in Aberdeen he hit the opening tee shot in the 1999 Ryder Cup and played well in partnership with Colin Montgomerie in foursomes and four balls and in the singles earned a point against Jeff Maggert. Originally an assistant at Banchory Golf Club on Royal Deeside Lawrie has had a hole named after him at the club. Coached by former Tour player Adam Hunter and Scottish Rugby Union psychologist Dr Richard Cox, Lawrie has been awarded an MBE for his achievements in golf.

Lunt, Michael (ENG)
Born Birmingham, 20 May 1935
From a well-known golfing family, Michael won the Amateur Championship in 1963 beating John Blackwell in the final then reached the final again the following year. He was English Amateur champion in 1966 and played four times in the Walker Cup. He drove himself into office as captain of the Royal and Ancient Golf Club of St Andrews in September 2006.

Lyle MBE, Sandy (SCO)
Born Shrewsbury, 9 February 1958
Turned professional in 1977
With his win in the 1985 Open Championship at Royal St George's he became the first British player to take the title since Tony Jacklin in 1969. He was also the first British player to win a Green Jacket in the Masters at Augusta in 1988 helped by a majestic 7-iron second shot out of sand at the last for a rare winning birdie 3. Although he represented England as an amateur at boys', youths' and senior level he became Scottish when he turned professional, something he was entitled to do at the time because his late father, the professional at Hawkstone Park, was a Scot. This is no longer allowed. He made his international début at age 14 and, two years later, qualified for and played 54 holes in the 1974 Open at Royal Lytham and St Annes. A tremendously talented natural golfer he fell a victim later in his career to

becoming over-technical. Now lives in Perthshire and is competing less and less frequently in the US and Europe. He was part of captain Ian Woosnam's team for the 2006 Ryder Cup at the K Club in 2006.

Lynn, David (ENG)
Born Billinge 20 October 1973
Turned professional 1995
Made his European Tour winning breakthrough when he won the 2004 KLM Dutch Open at Hilversum by three shots from Richard Green and Paul McGinley with a winning total of 264.

McDowell, Graeme (NIR)
Born Ballymoney, Northern Ireland, 30 July 1979
Turned professional 2002
A member of the winning Great Britain and Ireland Walker Cup team in 2001, he earned his European Tour card in just his fourth event as a professional. McDowell, who had been signed up to represent the Kungsangen Golf Club in Sweden just two weeks earlier, received a last minute sponsor's invitation to play there in the Volvo Scandinavian Masters ... and not only won the event but also broke the course record with an opening round of 64. He beat Trevor Immelman into second place with former USPGA champion Jeff Sluman third. McDowell's winning score of 270 – 14-under-par – earned him a first prize of over £200,000 and a place in the World Golf Championship NEC event at Sahalee in Washington. He was the European Tour's 12th first time winner of the season and at 23 the youngest winner of the title. In his amateur days he attended the University of Alabama where he was rated No. 1 Collegiate golfer winning six of 12 starts with a stroke average of 69.6. In 2004, scored his second European success when he won the Telecom Italia Open. He found it difficult to compete on both sides of the Atlantic in 2006.

McEvoy OBE, Peter (ENG)
Born London, 22 March 1953
The most capped player for England who has had further success as a captain of Great Britain and Ireland's Eisenhower Trophy and Walker Cup sides. The Eisenhower win came in 1998 and the Walker Cup triumphs at Nairn in 1999 and at Ocean Forest, Sea Island, Georgia in 2001. On both occasions his team won 15-9. A regular winner of amateur events McEvoy was amateur champion in 1977 and 1978 and won the English stroke play title in 1980. He reached the final of the English Amateur the same year. In 1978 he played all four rounds in the Masters at Augusta and that year received the Association of Golf Writers' Trophy for his contribution to European golf. He was leading amateur in two Open Championships – 1978 and 1979. In 2003 he was awarded the OBE by Her Majesty the Queen for his services to golf.

McGimpsey, Garth (IRL)
Born Bangor, 17 July 1955
A long hitter who was Irish long-driving champion in 1977 and UK long-driving title holder two years later. He was amateur champion in 1985 and Irish champion the same year and again in 1988. He played in three Walker Cup matches and competed in the home internationals for Ireland in 1978 and from 1980 to 1998. He captained the winning Great Britain and Ireland Walker Cup side that beat American 12½–11½ at

Ganton in 2003 and again two years later in Chicago when the Americans won by a point.

McGinley, Paul (IRL)
Born Dublin, 16 December 1966
Turned professional 1991
Popular Irish golfer who turned to the game after breaking his left kneecap playing Gaelic football. With Padraig Harrington won the 1977 World Cup at Kiawah and made his Ryder Cup début when the postponed 2001 match was played in 2002. In a tense finish to his match with Jim Furyk he holed from 9 feet to get the half point the Europeans needed for victory. He made the side again in 2004 and was unbeaten as Europe beat the USA 18½–9½ and was one of three Irishmen who helped Europe win by the same margin in 2006. Europe might have won 19–9 had he not conceded a half to JJ Henry at the last when a streaker ran over the line of the American's 20 foot downhill putt. In 2005 he finished third behind Colin Montgomerie and Michael Campbell in the European Tour Order of Merit making over £1.5 million. During the year he finished third behind Tiger Woods in the WGC–NEC Invitational at Firestone, lost the HSBC World MatchPlay at Wentworth to Michael Campbell but ended the season on a high note with victory in the Volvo Masters of Andalucia. He remains one of the most popular players on Tour.

Macgregor, George (SCO)
Born Edinburgh, 19 August 1944
After playing in five Walker Cup matches he captained the side in 1991 and later served as chairman of the R&A Selection committee. He won the Scottish Stroke Play title in 1982 after having been runner up three times.

McNulty, Mark (IRL)
Born Zimbabwe, 25 October 1953
Turned professional 1977
Recognised as one of the best putters in golf he was runner-up to Nick Faldo in the 1990 Open at St Andrews. Although hampered throughout his career by a series of injuries and illness he has scored 16 wins on the European Tour and 33 around the world including 23 on the South African Sunshine circuit. He won the South African Open in 1987 and again in 2001 holing an 18-foot putt on the last at East London to beat Justin Rose. Qualified in 2004 to join the US Champions Tour and quickly won the Outback Steakhouse event. He had another successful year on the US Champions Tour in 2005. He now plays out of Ireland.

Marks, Geoffrey (ENG)
Born Hanley, Stoke-on-Trent, November 1938
President of the English Golf Union in 1995 he captained the Walker Cup side in 1987 after having played on two previous occasions. He made eight appearances for England in the home internationals before captaining the team in a non-playing capacity at the start of the 1980s. He is a former England selector and was chairman of the R&A selection committee for four years from 1989.

Marsh, Dr David (ENG)
Born Southport, Lancashire, 29 April 1934
Twice winner of the English Amateur Championship in 1964 and 1970, he was captain of the R&A in 1990/1991. He played in the 1971 Walker Cup match at St Andrews and helped the home side win by scoring a vital one hole victory in the singles against Bill Hyndman. He captained the team in 1973 and 1975 and had a distinguished career as a player and then captain for England between 1956 and 1972. He was chairman of the R&A selection committee from 1979 to 1983 and in 1987 was president of the English Golf Union.

Milligan, Jim (SCO)
Born Irvine, Ayrshire, 15 June 1963
The 1988 Scottish Amateur champion had his moment of international glory in the 1989 Walker Cup which was won by the Great Britain and Ireland side for only the third time in the history of the event and for the first time on American soil. With GB&I leading by a point at Peachtree in Atlanta only Milligan and his experienced opponent Jay Sigel were left on the course. The American looked favourite to gain the final point and force a draw. The American was two up with three to play but Milligan hit his approach from 100 yards to a few inches to win the 16th with a birdie then chipped in after both had fluffed chips to square at the 17th. The last was halved leaving the Great Britain and Ireland side historic winners by a point.

Montgomerie OBE, Colin (SCO)
Born Glasgow, 23 June 1963   Turned professional 1987
Europe's most consistent golfer who topped the Volvo Order of Merit an unprecedented seven years in a row between 1993 and 1999. Although he has yet to win a major he has come close losing a play-off for the US Open to Ernie Els in 1994 and again being pipped by Els in the 1997 Championship. He was third behind Tom Kite in the 1992 US Open. In 1995 he was beaten in a play-off for the USPGA Championship by Australian Steve Elkington. He has had over 30 victories around the world and has played with distinction in seven Ryder Cups. At Brookline in 1999, at The Belfry in 2002, Oakland Hills in 2004 and at the K Club in 2006 he was a pillar of strength for the team in difficult on-course conditions. He has twice won the Association of Golf Writers' Golfer of the Year award and has been three times Johnnie Walker Golfer of the Year in Europe. His low round in Europe is 61 achieved at

Colin Montgomerie

Crans-sur-Sierre in the Canon European Masters in 1996. He has been honoured by Her Majesty the Queen for his record-breaking golfing exploits but is troubled these days by a persistent back injury and midway through 2003 had not added to his total of victories. He did, however, take first prize toward the end of the year at the Macau Open. In 2004 he won in Singapore after being chosen as a captain's pick by Bernhard Langer for the European Ryder Cup side and played inspired golf, holing the winning putt. It was a remarkable perform-ance considering a year of trauma off the course which culminated in divorce from wife Eimear. After a hesitant start to 2005, by which time he had slipped to 83rd in the world rankings, he staged a remarkable comeback in the latter half of the year. He produced his best ever finish in the Open when finishing second behind Tiger Woods at St Andrews, won the dunhill links championship – his first win since Singapore 2004 – and went on to finish European No.1 for a remarkable eighth time. In Europe he earned almost £1.9 million and before the end of the year had clawed his way back into the top 15 in the world. In the 2006 European season, he won the Hong Kong Open. Had his MBE upgraded to OBE for services to golf.

O'Connor Sr, Christy (IRL)
Born Galway, 21 December 1924
Turned professional 1946
Never managed to win the Open but came close on three occasions finishing runner-up to Peter Thomson in 1965 and being third on two other occasions. Played in ten Ryder Cup matches between 1955 and 1973 and scored 24 wins in tournament play between 1955 and 1972. Known affectionately as 'Himself' by Irish golfing fans who have long admired his talent with his clubs. He is a brilliant shot maker. He is now an Honorary Member of the PGA European Tour. In 2006, a special dinner was staged in his honour in Dublin by the Irish Food Board on the eve of the Ryder Cup.

O'Connor Jr, Christy (IRL)
Born Galway, 19 August 1948
Turned professional 1965
Nephew of Christy Sr, he finished third in the 1985 Open Championship. A winner on the European and Safari circuits he won the 1999 and 2000 Senior British Open – only the second man to successfully defend. Played in two Ryder Cup matches hitting a career best 2-iron to the last green at The Belfry in 1989 to beat Fred Couples and ensure a drawn match enabling Europe to keep the trophy. His US Senior Tour career was interrupted when he broke a leg in a motorcycle accident.

O'Leary, John (IRL)
Born Dublin, 19 August 1949   Turned professional 1979
After a successful career as a player including victory in the Carrolls Irish Open in 1982 he retired because of injury and now is director of golf at the Buckinghamshire Club. He is a member of the PGA European Tour Board of Directors.

Oosterhuis, Peter (ENG)
Born London, 3 May 1948   Turned professional 1968
Twice runner up in the Open Championship in 1974 and 1982, he was also the leading British player in 1975 and 1978. He finished third in the US Masters in 1973, had multiple wins on the European tour and in Africa and

won the Canadian Open on the US tour in 1981. He played in six Ryder Cups partnering Nick Faldo at Royal Lytham and St Annes in 1977 when Faldo made his début. He was top earner in Europe four years in a row from 1971. Following his retirement from top-line golf he moved to Arizona and after a spell working for the Golf Channel in Europe he is now a respected member of the CBS commentary team and makes guest appearances on the Golf Channel and Sky.

Panton MBE, John (SCO)
Born Pitlochry, Perthshire, 9 October 1916
Turned professional 1935
Recently retired honorary professional at the Royal and Ancient Golf Club of St Andrews – a post he had held since 1988. One of Scotland's best known, admired and loved professionals. He was leading British player in the 1956 Open and beat Sam Snead for the World Senior's title in 1967. He played in three Ryder Cup matches and was twelve times a contestant in the World Cup with the late Eric Brown as his regular partner. He won the Association of Golf Writer's Trophy for his contribution to the game in 1967 and has been honoured with an MBE.

Poulter, Ian (ENG)
Born Hitchen, England, 10 January 1976
Turned professional 1994
Having failed narrowly to make the 2002 European Ryder Cup side, he made the 2004 team and beat Chris Riley in the singles at Oakland Hills and later that year beat Sergio García in a play-off for the Volvo Masters Andalucia at Valderrama. He had won twice in 2003 at Celtic Manor and Copenhagen but had no victories in 2005. A real character with no shortage of talent, he insists he wants to be noticed for the quality of his golf rather than his hair-styles and colourful clothing. Missed out on the 2006 Ryder Cup but returned to winning ways when he won a European Tour event in Madrid in September. This victory moved him into the top 50 in the world. He also kept his card in America. Before the end of the season, he finished joint second to Tiger Woods in the American Express Championship at The Grove.

Price, Phillip (WAL)
Born Pontypridd, 21 October 1966
Turned professional 1989
Winner of the 1994 Portuguese Open he abandoned plans to play the US Tour in 2002. He made his Ryder Cup début in 2002 and produced a sterling last day per-formance when he beat the world no.2 Phil Mickelson 3 and 2 for a vital point. He was named Asprey Golfer of the Month of July after winning the Smurfit European Open at the K-Club and finishing in the top 10 at the Barclays Scottish Open and the Open at Royal St George's. Played in the United States through 2005 with limited success and, back in Europe in 2006, found it difficult to re-discover the old magic.

Ramsay, Richie (SCO)
Born Aberdeen, 15 June 1983
A student at Stirling University he became the first Scot since 1898 and the first British golfer since 1911 to win the US Amateur Championship when he beat John Kelly from St Louis 4 and 2 in the final at Hazeltine. His victory earned him automatic entry into

the 2007 US Open and The Open and he will receive an invitation to play at The Masters at Augusta. A member of the 2005 Great Britain and Ireland Walker Cup team, he has played in the Palmer Cup and was the winner of the 2004 Scottish Open Stroke-play title and the 2005 Irish Open Stroke-play. He has shot a 62 at Murcur in Aberdeenshire.

Rafferty, Ronan (NIR)
Born Newry, Northern Ireland, 13 January 1964
Turned professional 1981
Won the Irish Amateur Championship as a 16 year old in 1980 when he also won the English Amateur Open Stroke Play title, competed in the Eisenhower Trophy and played against Europe in the home internationals. Winner of the British Boys, Irish Youths' and Ulster Youths' titles in 1979, he also played in the senior Irish side against Wales that year. A regular winner on the European tour between 1988 and 1993 he was also victorious in tournaments played in South America, Australia and New Zealand. A wrist injury has curtailed his career but he is active on the corporate golf front and often commentates for Sky TV. He has an impressive wine collection.

Rose, Justin (ENG)
Born Johannesburg, South Africa, 30 July 1980
Turned professional 1998
Walker Cup player who shot to attention in the 1998 Open Championship when he finished top amateur and third behind winner Mark O'Meara after holing his third shot at the last on the final day for a closing birdie. Immediately after that Open he turned professional and missed his first 21 half-way cuts before finding his feet. In 2002 was a multiple winner in Europe and also won in Japan and South Africa. Delighted his father who watched him win the Victor Chandler British Masters just a few weeks before he died of leukemia. He has found winning more difficult in the last four years when he played most of his golf in the United States from his base in Lake Nona but in a strong finish to the 2006 season he shot a 60 in the Funai Classic at Walt Disney World. Overall he finished 47th on the American money list with over $1.6 million. He will continue to play in America but plans to rejoin the European Tour in 2007 in the hope of making the 2008 Ryder Cup side. He jumped from 69th to 51st in the world rankings when he scored his first win in four years when taking the 2006 Mastercard Masters title in Melbourne.

Saltman, Lloyd (SCO)
Born Edinburgh, 10 September 1985
Had a wonderful 2005 season winning the Brabazon Trophy, the St Andrews Links Championship, taking the silver medal in the Open at St Andrews, being top scorer for Great Britain and Ireland in the Walker Cup in Chicago and helping Scotland win the Home Internationals series for the first time since 2000. Elected to stay amateur throughout 2006 but turned professional at the end of the year and will again play amateur golf in 2007 having failed to earn his card for the European Tour at the annual school.

Smyth, Des (IRL)
Born Drogheda, Ireland, 12 February 1954
Turned professional 1973
Became the oldest winner on the PGA European Tour when he won the Madeira Island Open in 2001. Smyth was 48 years and 34 days – 20 days older than Neil Coles had been when he won the Sanyo Open in Barcelona in 1982. One of the Tour's most consistent performers – he played 592 events before switching to the European Seniors Tour and qualifying for the US Champions Tour where he has been a winner. Five times Irish National champion he was a member of the winning Irish side in the 1988 Alfred Dunhill Cup. Won twice on US Champions Tour in 2005 and in Abu Dhabi on the European Senior Tour. He was vice-captain for the European team in the 2006 Ryder Cup.

Thomas, Dave (WAL)
Born Newcastle-upon-Tyne, 16 August 1934
Twice runner-up in the Open Championship, Welshman Thomas lost a play-off to Peter Thomson in 1958. He played 11 times in the World Cup for Wales and four times in the Ryder Cup. In all he won 10 tournaments between 1961 and 1969 before retiring to concentrate on golf course design. Along with Peter Alliss designed the Ryder Cup course at The Belfry. He was captain of the Professional Golfers' Association for 2001 – their Centenary year – and for 2002.

Torrance OBE, Sam (SCO)
Born Largs, Ayrshire, 24 August 1953
Turned professional 1970
Between 1976 and 1998 he won 21 times on the European Tour in which he has played over 700 events. Captain of the 2002 European Ryder Cup side having previously played in eight matches notably holing the winning putt in 1985 to end a 28-year run of American domination. He was an inspired captain when the 2001 match was played in September 2002. Tied 8 points each, Torrance's men won the singles for only the third time since 1979 to win 15½–12½. His father Bob, who has been his only coach, looks after the swings these days of several others on the European Tour including Paul McGinley who holed the nine foot putt that brought the Ryder Cup back to Europe. He was awarded the MBE in 1996. European Tour officials worked out that in his first 28 years Torrance walked an estimated 14,000 miles and played 15,000 shots earning at the rate of £22 per stroke. In 2003 he retired from full-time competition on the European Tour and made his début in the Charles Church Scottish Seniors at The Roxburghe in late August. In 2004 he qualified for the US Champions Tour but returned to Europe to win the Travis Perkins Senior Masters with a brilliant final round of 61 over the Wentworth Edinburgh course. He played throughout 2005 and 2006 on the European Senior Tour and finished top earner both years. He hit the 700 mark on the main Tour at the Barclays Scottish Open at Loch Lomond. Is now a full-time member of the BBC commentary team working with Peter Alliss and Ken Brown.

Walton, Philip (IRL)
Born Dublin, 28 March 1962
Turned professional 1983
Twice a Walker Cup player he is best remembered for two-putting the last to beat Jay Haas by one hole and clinch victory in the 1995 Ryder Cup at Oak Hill. He played in five Alfred Dunhill Cup competitions at St Andrews and was in the winning side in 1990.

Warren, Mark (SCO)
Born Rutherglen, near Glasgow, 1 April 1981
Turned professional 2002
Mark, who holed the winning putt in Great Britain and Ireland's Walker Cup victory over America in 2001, had two play-off victories on the European Challenge Tour in 2005 – in the Ireland Ryder Cup Challenge and the Rolex Trophy. His joint second place finish behind Carl Sunesson in the end of season Apulia San Domenica Grand Final saw him finish leader of the Challenge Tour. In 2006 Warren, who is coached by Bob Torrance, scored his first victory on the main Tour when he beat Robert Karlsson in a play-off for the Eurocard Masters at Barsebäck. At the start of the 2007 season he finished fifth behind winner Yang Yong-eun, Tiger Woods, Michael Campbell and Retief Goosen in the HSBC Champions event.

Webster, Steve (ENG)
Born Nuneaton, England, 17 January 1975
Turned professional 1995
After five second place finishes on Tour twice in Spain, twice in South Africa and in Germany he finally hit the jackpot in Italy in 2005 when he won the Telecom Italia Open at Castello di Tolcinaco in Milan. Ten years earlier Steve won the silver medal as leading amateur in the Open at St Andrews.

Westwood, Lee (ENG)
Born Worksop, Nottinghamshire, 24 April 1973
Turned professional 1993
A former British Youths champion who missed out on Walker Cup honours, he quickly made the grade in the professional ranks. In 2000 he ended the seven-year reign of Colin Montgomerie by taking the top spot in the Volvo Order of Merit. He was six-time winner that year in Europe taking five order of merit titles and beating Montgomerie at the second extra hole of the Cisco World Match Play final at Wentworth. Among his overseas victories are three successful Taiheiyo Masters titles in Japan, the Australian Open in 1997 when he beat Greg Norman in a play-off and the Freeport McDermott Classic at New Orleans on the US Tour. He has already won titles on every major circuit. He is married to Laurae Coltart, sister of fellow professional Andrew Coltart. He has been a member of the last five Ryder Cup teams and in the 2002 match won 3 points out of 4. In 2004 he again produced some of his best golf, picking up points as Europe swept to a record win at Oakland Hills and more than justified being chosen as a captain's pick for the 2006 match in which he teamed up successfully with close friend Darren Clarke and won his singles against Chris DiMarco. Although he admits he had thoughts of giving up tournament play he persevered and won again for the first time in three years when he was successful in the BMW International at Nord Eichenried, Munich. A month later he picked up first prize in the Dunhill Links Championship bringing his earnings in five weeks to over $1 million. He credits David Lead-better for sorting out his game. He had five top 10 finishes in 2005 in Europe and finished 27th on the money list. In 2006 he finished 24th in Europe.

White, Ronnie (ENG)
Born Wallasey, Cheshire, 9 April 1921
A five times Walker Cup team member between 1947 and 1953 he was one of the most impressive players in post-war amateur golf. He won six and halved one of the 10 Walker Cup matches he played and won the English Amateur in 1949 and the English Open stroke play title the following two years.

Wolstenholme, Gary (ENG)
Born Egham, Surrey, 21 August 1960
The 1991 Amateur champion he has been one of the most regular title winners in the past 11 years and regained the Amateur title in 2003 when beating Raphael De Sousa, the first Swiss to reach the final, by 6 and 5. At 42 he was the oldest player in the field and not one of the longest hitters on a course measuring 7126 yards. In 1991 he had beaten Bob May 8 and 6 in the final. A week after his triumph at Troon when he won the Scottish StrokePlay title. Son of former professional the late Guy Wolstenholme he won the 1995 and 1996 British Mid-Amateur Championship, the Chinese Amateur title in 1993, the Emirates Amateur in 1995 and the Finnish Amateur in 1996. He also won the 2002 Australian Amateur Championship title and the 2002 and 2003 South African strokeplay title. He was England County champion of champions in 1994 and 1996 and he highlighted his appearances in Walker Cup golf by beating Tiger Woods by one hole in the first day singles of the 1995 match at Royal Porthcawl. Great Britain and Ireland won that year but Woods gained his revenge on Wolstenholme by beating him on the second day. He was named 2003 Ping English Golfer of the Year. He made his sixth appearance in the Walker Cup in Chicago in 2005 and became Great Britain and Ireland's record points scorer with 10 from 19 ties when he won his singles match.

Woosnam MBE, Ian (WAL)
Born Oswestry, Shropshire, 2 March 1958
Turned professional 1976
Highlight of his career was winning the Green Jacket at the Masters in 1991 after a last day battle with Spaniard José Maria Olazábal who went on to win in 1994 and again in 1999. Teamed up very successfully with Nick Faldo in Ryder Cup golf and was in four winning teams in 1985, 1987, 1995 and 1997. Was vice-captain in 2001 to Sam Torrance. He has scored 28 European Tour victories and twice won the World Match Play Championship in 1987 when he beat Sandy Lyle, with whom he used to play boys' golf in Shropshire, in 1990 when his opponent was Zimbabwean Mark McNulty and in 2001 when he beat Retief Goosen, then US Open Champion, Colin Montgomerie, Lee Westwood and then Padraig Harrington in the final. In 1989 he lost a low-scoring final to Nick Faldo on the last green. His lowest round was a 60 he returned in the 1990 Monte Carlo Open at Mont Agel. Partnered by David Llewellyn he won the World Cup of Golf in 1987 beating Scotland's Sam Torrance and Sandy Lyle in a play-off. Honoured with an MBE from Her Majesty the Queen he now lives with his family in Jersey. Finished joint third in the 2001 Open at Lytham after having been penalised two shots for discovering on the second tee he had 15 clubs (one over the limit) in his bag. He lost out the captaincy of the Ryder Cup in 2004 to Bernhard Langer but captained the side to victory in the 2006 match at the K Club just outside Dublin.

Continent of Europe

Bäckström, J.	Edfors, J.	Hanson, P.	Levet, T.	Rivero, J.
Ballesteros, S.	Fasth, N.	Ilonen, M.	Lima, J.-F.	Rocca, C.
Bjørn, T.	Fernandez	Jacobsen, F.	Lundberg, M.	Sandelin, J.
Brier, M.	Castano, G.	Jacquelin, R.	Molinari, E.	Siem, M.
Canizares, A.	Fulke, P.	Jiménez, M.A.	Molinari, F.	Stenson, H.
Canizares, J.M.	García, S.	Johansson, P.-U.	Olazábal, J.M.	Van de Velde, J.
Canonica, E.	Garrido, I.	Karlsson, R.	Parnevik, J.	
Céveär, C.	Haeggeman, J.	Langer, B.	Remsey, J.-F.	

Bäckström, Johan (SWE)
Born Umea, 16 March 1978
Turned professional 1998
Despite having a problem with his back, he played boys, youths and senior golf for Sweden as an amateur. Inspired by his golfing hero Fred Couples he won his first title when taking the 2005 Aa St Omer Championship – a joint venture between the Challenge and main European Tour.

Ballesteros, Severiano (ESP)
Born Pedrena, 9 April 1957
Turned professional 1974
Charismatic Spaniard who won 52 titles between 1976 and 1999 including three Opens (1979, 1984 at St Andrews and 1988) and The Masters at Augusta in 1980 and again in 1983. One of four brothers all of whom play golf. He was introduced to the game by big brother Manuel and first hit the headlines when he and Jack Nicklaus finished second to Johnny Miller at Royal Birkdale in 1976. He played in eight Ryder Cups and captained the side to victory at Valderrama in 2000. Never one of golf's straightest hitters his powers of recovery from seemingly impossible positions have been legendary throughout his career. He was the driving force in getting a match started between the British and Irish golfers and the Continentals in 2000. Although not the player he once was, he made a welcome return to competitive action in 2005 at the Open de Madrid. He planned to play throughout 2006 but his appearances were few and far between. He did play in The Open when his son caddied for him. He missed the cut. Although only a shadow of his former self on the course, he remains popular with the public who remember with great affection his charismatic performances which drew similarities with Arnold Palmer before him.

Bjørn, Thomas (DEN)
Born Silkeborg, 18 February 1971
Turned professional 1993
A former Danish Amateur champion in 1990 and 1991, he became the first Dane to play in the Ryder Cup when he made the team in 1997. Four down after four holes against Justin Leonard in the last day singles at Valderrama he fought back to halve the match and gain a valuable half-point in the European victory. He missed out on the 1999 match because of injury but was in the 2002 side and beat Stewart Cink in the singles. He made the side again in 2004 but narrowly missed out in 2006 despite having won the Nissan Irish Open. Won four times in the Challenge Tour before gaining his full European card. He came joint second to Tiger Woods in the 2000 Open at St Andrews just a few weeks after finishing third behind Woods in the US Open at Pebble Beach. In Japan in 1999 he beat Sergio García at the fourth hole of a play-off for the Dunlop Phoenix title. In 2001 he beat Tiger Woods in the Dubai Desert Classic. He looked set to win the 2003 Open at Royal St George's when three shots clear with four to play but took 3 to get out of a bunker at the short sixteenth and lost to Ben Curtis, the American playing in his first Open. A week later Bjørn lost a play-off to Michael Campbell in the Nissan Irish Open at Portmarnock. He remains one of Europe's most talented golfers and came close again to winning a major in 2005 when he finished third behind Phil Mickelson in the US PGA Championship at Baltusrol. In the third round he equalled the low round in a major when he shot a 63. A viral infection caused him to miss several events towards the end of the year. During 2005 he had eight top 10 finishes winning the *Daily Telegraph* Dunlop Masters in a play-off at Forest of Arden. He was ninth top earner in Europe in 2005 with just over £1 million in prize-money.

Brier, Markus (AUT)
Born Vienna, Austria, 5 July 1968
Turned professional 1995
Scored his first European Tour win "at home" when he won the BA/CA Austrian Open in 2006.

Canizares, Alejandro (ESP)
Born Manilva, Malaga, 9 January 1983
Turned professional 2006
A four-time All American golfer when studying at Arizona State University, he is the son of José Maria Canizares the European and US Champions Tour golfer. He turned professional in July and won his third event – the Imperial Collection Russian Open.

Canizares, José Maria (ESP)
Born Madrid, 18 February 1947
Turned professional 1967
A seven-time winner on the European Tour between 1972 and 1992 the popular Spaniard now plays full time on the US Senior Tour. A former caddie, he played in four Ryder Cup matches in the 80s winning five and halving two of his 11 games.

Canonica, Emanuele (ITA)
Born Turin, 7 January 1971
Turned professional 1991
He had been a professional for 14 years before he struck gold and won his first European title – the 2005 Johnnie Walker Championship at Gleneagles Hotel. Despite being only 5ft 2in tall he is a prodigous hitter of the golf

ball. With his win he became only the fifth Italian to win on Tour – the others being Baldovino Dassu, Massimo Mannelli, Massimo Scarpa and Costantino Rocca.

Céveär, Christian (FRA)
Born New Caledonia, 10 April 1970
Turned professional 1993
A former world junior champion and Stanford graduate, Christian scored his first victory on the European Tour in 2005 when taking top spot in the Canarias Open de España. He had previously been second in the 1995 Madeira Island Open and 2003 *Daily Telegraph* Damovo British Masters.

Edfors, Johan (SWE)
Born Varberg, Sweden, 10 October 1975
The number one player on the 2003 Challenge Tour but lost his card in 2004. Won back his card at the 2005 school and had a brilliant year, winning three events – the TCL Classic in China, the Quinn Direct British Masters and the Barclays Scottish Open at Loch Lomond.

Fasth, Niclas (SWE)
Born Gothenburg, Sweden, 29 April 1972
Turned professional 1989
The studious-looking Swede tried to play both US and European tours in 1998 but found it too difficult. He made the headlines in 2001 when finishing second to David Duval in the Open. In the 2002 Ryder Cup side he made a half point against Paul Azinger on the final day. He was a double winner in 2005 taking the New Zealand Open and the prestigious Deutsche Bank Tournament Players' Championship of Europe.

Fernandez-Castano, Gonzalo (ESP)
Born Madrid, 13 October 1980
Turned professional 2004
Began playing golf as a five-year-old and turned professional in 2004 when he was playing off plus 4. He represented Spain in the 2002 Eisenhower Trophy and played for the Continent of Europe against Great Britain and Ireland in 2004. He played twice in the Palmer Cup leading the European students to success against the Americans at Ballybunion in 2004. He picked up the fifth card in the European qualifying School later that year and won for the first time in Holland when he took the 2005 KLM Dutch Open title at Hilversum and was named Sir Henry Cotton Rookie of the Year. In 2006, he came second in the Volvo China Open in Beijing and the following week won the BMWAsian Open in a play-off with Henrik Stenson. As an amateur, he won the Spanish Amateur and was in two winning Palmer Cup teams.

Fulke, Pierre (SWE)
Born Nyköping, Sweden, 21 February 1971
Turned professional 1993
Son of a Swedish swimming champion he finished runner-up to Steve Stricker in the 2001 Accenture Matchplay Championship a few weeks after winning the Volvo Masters. Played on the 2002 winning Ryder Cup side. He still plays tournament golf but now commentates with Gorazv Zachrisson on Swedish television and designs courses.

García, Sergio (ESP)
Born Castellon, 9 January 1980
Turned professional 1999
The extrovert Spaniard having won the French and Amateur Championships in 1997 took the British title in 1998 and in both years was European Amateur Masters champion. Son of a greenkeeper/professional who now plays on the European Senior Tour, Sergio's future was always going to be in professional golf but he waited until after the 1999 Masters in which he was leading amateur before joining the paid ranks at the Spanish Open. Although only just starting to collect Ryder Cup points he easily made the 1999 team and formed an invaluable partnership with Jesper Parnevik at Brookline scoring three and a half points out of four on the first two days. Victories in the Murphy's Irish Open and Linde German Masters helped him to the 1999 Rookie of the Year title in Europe but arguably an even better performance was finishing runner-up to Tiger Woods in the US PGA Championship at Medinah outside Chicago. Although he did not win in 2000 he won the Mastercard Colonial and Buick Classic on the US Tour in 2001 and the Mercedes Championship, the Canaries Open de España and the Kolon Cup in Korea. He was in the 2002 Ryder Cup team and formed a useful partnership with Lee Westwood winning 3 out of 4 points on the first two days. They teamed up again in the winning 2004 side at Oakland Hills. He himself was unbeaten, winning 4½ out of five points including victory over Phil Mickelson in the singles. In the 2006 Ryder Cup at the K Club he again played well with José María Olazábal in the fourballs and Luke Donald in the foursomes. He scored four out of five points losing only his single to Stewart Cink. He continues to play on both sides of the Atlantic and in 2004 won the EDS Byron Nelson event and the Buick Classic through September. Later in the year he won the Mallorcan Open and lost a play-off to Ian Poulter in the Volvo Masters Andalusia at Valderrama. In 2005, García finished sixth on the European Tour money list and 10th on the US Order of Merit, winning on both sides of the Atlantic. In Europe he won the Omega European Masters and in America was successful in the Booz Allen Classic.

Garrido, Ignacio (ESP)
Born Madrid, 27 March 1972
Turned professional 1993
Eldest son of Antonio Garrido who played in the 1979 Ryder Cup, Ignacio emulated his father when he made the team at the 1997 match at Valderrama having earlier that year won the Volvo German Open. In 2003 he had his most impressive win when beating Trevor Immelman in a play-off for the Volvo PGA Championship at Wentworth. Before turning professional with a handicap of 4 he won the English Amateur Stroke Play title (the Brabazon Trophy) in 1992. In the 80s used to caddie for his father who has since caddied for him on occasion.

Haeggman, Joakim (SWE)
Born Kalmar, 28 August 1969
Turned professional 1989
Became the first Swedish player to play in the Ryder Cup when he made the side which lost to the Americans at The Belfry in 1993. He received one of

team captain Bernard Gallacher's 'wild cards' and beat John Cook in his last day singles. Gave up ice hockey after dislocating his shoulder and breaking ribs in 1994. Realised then that ice hockey and golf do not mix but has become an enthusiastic angler when not on the links. Equalled the world record of 27 for the first nine holes in the Alfred Dunhill Cup over the Old course at St Andrews in 1997. Occasionally acts as commentator for Swedish TV and was a member of Sam Torrance's Ryder Cup back-room team at The Belfry in 2002 and Bernhard Langer's vice-captain at Oakland Hills in 2004. Returned to the winner's circle in 2004 at Qatar. It was only his second win on the European Tour and his first since 1993.

Hanson, Peter (SWE)
Born Svedala, 4 October 1977
Turned professional 1998
Former winner of the English Strokeplay Championship (the Brabazon Trophy) in 1998 when he also represented Sweden in the Eisenhower Trophy and was in the winning Swedish Eisenhower Trophy team. He won his first European professional title when he won the 2005 Jazztel Open de España.

Ilonen, Mikko (FIN)
Born Lahti, 18 December 1979
Turned professional 2001
Became the first Finnish golfer to win the Amateur Championship when he beat Christian Reimbold from Germany 2 and 1 in the final at Royal Liverpool. He has won both the Finnish match play and stroke play titles. Represented Finland in the 1998 and 2000 Eisenhower Trophy events. Now plays professionally on the European Tour and in 2001 finished ninth behind David Duval in the Open at Royal Lytham.

Jacobsen, Frederik (SWE)
Born Moindal, Sweden, 26 September 1974
He made his European Tour winning breakthrough when he took the 2003 Omega Hong Kong Open and then followed that up with victory in the Algarve Open de Portugal. He finished fifth in the US Open, sixth in the Open and became the latest playeer to shoot 60 when he did so in the first round of the Linde German Masters. He won his third title of the European season when he beat Carlos Rodiles in the end-of-season Volvo Masters at Andalucia. With that win at Valderrama, Jacobsen became the first Swede to win three titles in a season and by doing so moved into the top 20 of the world rankings for the first time. He finished the European season fourth in the Volvo Order of Merit. Played almost exclusively in 2005 and 2006 in America but is still chasing his first win there.

Jacquelin, Rafaël (FRA)
Born Lyon, 8 May 1974
Turned professional 1995
Ten years after turning professional Rafaël Jacquelin became the latest French golfer to win on Tour when he won the 2005 Madrid Open at Club de Campo. The Frenchman with a most graceful swing had had four second place finishes previously. His success came in his 238th event. As an amateur he won the French title. Originally wanted to be a soccer player but a knee injury

Bernhard Langer

thwarted his plans and he turned instead to tennis and later to golf.

Jiménez, Miguel Angel (ESP)
Born Malaga, 4 January 1964
Turned professional 1982
Talented Spaniard who was runner-up to Tiger Woods in the 2000 US Open. This was a year after making his successful début in the Ryder Cup. One of seven brothers he did not take up golf until his mid-teens. He loves cars, drives a Ferrari and has been nicknamed 'The Mechanic' by his friends. His best-remembered shot was the 3-wood he hit into the hole for an albatross 2 at the infamous 17th hole at Valderrama in the Volvo Masters but he was credited with having played the Canon Shot of the Year when he chipped in at the last to win 1998 Trophée Lancôme. In 2000 lost in a play-off at Valderrama in a World Championship to Tiger Woods. He played in the 2002 and 2004 European Ryder Cup sides and won four times, taking the Johnnie Walker Classic title in Bangkok, the Algarve Portu-guese Open at Penina, the BMW Asian Open in Shanghai and the BMW German Open in Munich. He had a quieter 2005 but finished 14th in the money list helped by victories in the Omega Hong Kong Open and the Celtic Manor Resort Wales Open and four other top 10 finishes.

Johansson, Per-Ulrik (SWE)
Born Uppsala, 6 December 1966
Turned professional 1990
A former amateur international at both junior and senior level he became the first Swede to play in two Ryder Cups when he made the 1995 and 1997 teams. In 1997 he played Phil Mickelson with whom he had studied at Arizona State University. In 1991 he was winner of the Sir Henry Cotton Rookie of the Year award in Europe but now plays most of his golf in America although he played a few events in Europe last summer after recovering from injury.

Langer, Bernhard (GER)
Born Anhausen, 27 August 1957
Turned professional 1972
One of the game's most respected figures and consistent performers he is best known for having conquered the putting yips on more than one occasion. Twice winner of the US Masters in 1985 and 1993 he has never managed to win the Open despite coming second twice and third on three occasions. Deeply religious he was for many years Germany's only top player. He has been an inspiration to many taking his own National title on 12 occasions and winning 37 titles in Europe between 1980 and 2000. In 1979 he won the Cacherel Under 25s Championship by 17 shots. He played nine times in the Ryder Cup between 1981 and 1997 proving a mainstay in foursomes and fourballs with 11 different partners. He regained his place for the 2002 match after having been overlooked for a captain's pick in 1999 and made 3½ points – 2½ of them partnering Colin Montgomerie. He then captained with considerable success the winning 2004 team at Oakland Hills. Now plays both the US and European Tours. Has won 11 times in Germany including five German Opens.

Levet, Thomas (FRA)
Born Paris, 9 September 1968
Turned professional 1988
Although he was the first Frenchman to play full time on the US Tour, he lost his card and only regained his European Tour card when he was invited because of his French ranking to play in the 1998 Cannes Open – and won it. He won the 2001 British Masters and by late September 2004 had won the Barclays Scottish Open and finished 6th in the Open at Royal Troon. Lost in a play-off to Ernie Els in the 2002 Open at Muirfield. Thomas made his Ryder Cup début at Oakland Hills in 2004, winning his singles game against Fred Funk. He is a gifted linguist speaking six languages and learning a seventh – Japanese.

Lima, José-Filipe (POR)
Born Versailles, 26 November 1981
Turned professional 2002
Although he played all his early golf in France and represented that country on the European Tour when he won the AA St Omer event in 2004, he has since changed nationalities. His mother is Portuguese and he represented that country in the 2005 WGC–World Cup of Golf.

Lundberg, Mikael (SWE)
Born Helsingborg, 13 August 1973
Turned professional 1997
The former Challenge Tour player won his first main Tour event when he picked up the first prize in the Caddilac Russian Open at Le Meridien Moscow Country Club in 2005. He represented Sweden as an amateur in the Eisenhower Trophy.

Molinari, Eduardo (ITA)
Born Turin, 1981
Became the first Italian to win the US Amateur Championship when he beat Dillon Dougherty 4 and 3 in the 2005 final at Merion, Pennsylvania. The 24-year-old, who has earned an engineering degree in his home country. Turned professional and joined his brother on the European Tour in 2006.

Molinari, Francesco (ITA)
Born Turin, 8 Novemner 1982
Turned professional 2004
Brother of Eduardo Molinari, winner of the US Amateur in 2005, he won his first European Tour title when he took the Italian Open at Castello di Tolcinasco in 2006.

Olazábal, José María (ESP)
Born Fuenterrabia, 5 February 1966
Turned professional 1985
Twice a winner of the Masters, his second triumph was particularly emotional. He had won in 1994 but had to withdraw from the 1995 Ryder Cup with a foot problem eventually diagnosed as rheumatoid polyarthritis in three joints of the right foot and two of the left. He was out of golf for eighteen months but treatment from Munich doctor Hans-Wilhelm Muller-Wohlfahrt helped him back to full fitness after a period when he was house bound and unable to walk. At that point it seemed as if his career was over, but he came back in 1999 to beat Davis Love III by two shots at Augusta. With over twenty victories in Europe and a further seven abroad, the son of a Real Sebastian greenkeeper who took up the game at the age of four has been one of the most popular players in the game. He competed in six Ryder Cups between 1987 and 1999 frequently partnering Severiano Ballesteros. He is a former British Boys Youths and Amateur champion. His best performances in the Open have been third behind Nick Faldo in the 1992 Championship at Muirfield and behind Tiger Woods in the 2005 event at St Andrews. Olazábal, who played on both sides of the Atlantic in 2005, finished 10th on the European Money list finishing strongly with a 2nd place finish in the Linde German Masters, victory in the Open de Mallorca and a third place behind Paul McGinley in the Volvo Masters of Andalucia. In 2006 he regained his place in the Ryder Cup team and played well with Sergio García in the fourballs, winning twice. He beat Phil Mickelson in the singles.

Parnevik, Jesper (SWE)
Born Danderyd, Stockholm, 7 March 1965
Turned professional 1986
Son of a well-known Swedish entertainer he is one of the most extrovert of golfers best known for his habit of wearing a baseball cap with the brim turned up and brightly coloured drain-pipe style trousers. Winner of events on both sides of the Atlantic he plays most of his golf these days in America where he has won five times since 1998 but made history in 1995 when he became the first Swede to win in Sweden when he took the Scandinavian Masters at Barseback in Malmo. Has twice finished runner-up in the Open at Turnberry in 1994 when he was two ahead but made a bogey at the last and was passed by Nick Price who finished with an eagle and a birdie in the last three holes. He led by two with a round to go in 1998 but shot 73 and finished tied second with Darren Clarke behind Justin Leonard. Played in the 1997 and 1999 Ryder Cup teaming up successfully with Sergio García to win three and a half points in 1999.

Was also in the 2002 team and halved with Tiger Woods in the singles. Has had health problems suffering injuries and illness and has resorted at times to unusual remedies including, at one stage, eating volcanic dust to cleanse the system.

Remesy, Jean-Francois (FRA)
Born Nimes, 5 June 1964   Turned professional 1987
Became the first Frenchman since Jean Garaialde in 1969 to win the Open de France in 2004 then successfully defended the title at Golf National, Versailles when beating Jean Van de Velde in a play-off. Now lives in the Seychelles.

Rivero, José (ESP)
Born Madrid, 20 September 1955
Turned professional 1973
One of only eight Spaniards who have played in the Ryder Cup he competed in the winning 1985 and 1987 sides. Worked as a caddie but received a grant from the Spanish Federation to pursue his golf career. With José Maria Canizares won the World Cup in 1984 at Olgiata in Italy.

Rocca, Costantino (ITA)
Born Bergamo, 4 December 1956
Turned professional 1981
The first and to date only Italian to play in the Ryder Cup. In the 1999 match at Valderrama he beat Tiger Woods 4 and 2 in a vital singles. Left his job in a polystyrene box making factory to become a club professional and graduated to the tournament scene through Europe's Challenge Tour. In 1995 he fluffed a chip at the final hole in the Open at St Andrews only to hole from 60 feet out of the Valley of Sin to force a play-off against John Daly which he then lost. In recent years he has met with limited success in European Tour events.

Sandelin, Jarmo (SWE)
Born Imatra, Finland, 10 May 1967
Turned professional 1987
Extrovert Swede who made his début in the Ryder Cup at Brookline in 1999 although he did not play until the singles. Has always been a snazzy dresser on course where he is one of the game's longest hitters often in the early days with a 54-inch shafted driver. Five time winner on Tour he met his partner Linda when she asked to caddie for him at a Stockholm pro-am.

Siem, Marcel (GER)
Born Mettmann, 15 July 1980
Turned Professional 2000
Became the latest German to win on the European Tour when he beat Frenchmen Gregory Havret and Raphaël

Jaquelin in a play-off at Houghton to win the Dunhill Championship. Represented Germany in the 2000 Eisenhower Trophy.

Stenson, Henrik (SWE)
Born Gothenburg, 5 April 1976
Turned professional 1998
Ended a run without success following his initial Tour win in 2001 at the old Benson and Hedges Festival at The Belfry by winning the inaugural Heritage event at Woburn. In 2005 he failed to add to his success but had nine top 10 finishes including three second place finishes and four thirds. He ended the season eighth on the European money list making just over a £1 million in prize-money. He played for Sweden in the 1998 Eisenhower Trophy and made the 2006 Ryder Cup side helping Europe beat America 18½–9½ at the K Club. In the singles he beat Vaughn Taylor. Stenson finished the 2006 season with seventh place with €1.7 million earned in prize-money. He planned to play the first part of 2007 in America.

Van de Velde, Jean (FRA)
Born Mont de Marsan, 29 May 1966
Turned professional 1987
Who ever remembers who came second? Everybody will remember Jean Van de Velde, however, for finishing runner-up after a play-off with eventual winner Paul Lawrie and American Justin Leonard when the Open returned to a somewhat tricked-up Carnoustie in 1999. Playing the last hole he led by three but refused to play safe and paid a severe penalty. He ran up a triple bogey 7 after seeing his approach ricochet off a stand into the rough and his next into the Barry Burn. He appeared to contemplate playing the half-submerged ball when taking off his shoes and socks and wading in but that was never a possibility. Took up the game as a youngster when holidaying with his parents in Biarritz. Has scored only one win in Europe (the Roma Masters in 1993) and has returned to the European Tour after a spell in America. Made his Ryder Cup début at Brookline in 1999. Injury prevented him competing regularly in 2003 and 2004 during which time he was part of the BBC Golf Commentary team with, among others, Peter Alliss, Sam Torrance, Mark James and Ken Brown. Came close to winning his national title but lost out in a play-off to fellow Frenchman Jean-Francois Remesy at Golf National. Created headlines later in the year when he said that if it was to be made easier for women to play in the British Open he thought it only fair that he should be allowed to enter the Weetabix British Women's Open.

Severiano Ballesteros looks to the Champions Tour

Arthritis and back pain may have reduced Severiano Ballesteros' competitive appearances to just three in the last three years but he is not yet ready to quit playing the game he dominated for so long.

Expected to announce his retirement at the end of 2006, the charismatic Spaniard announced instead that he would be gearing himself up for a crack at the lucrative American Champions Tour, the former Seniors Tour for players 50 and over. Seve turns 50 in April this year.

He plans to play 14 events on the US Champions Tour and will warm up with some earlier appearances on the main Tour and at The Masters where he has not played since returning an 85 in 2003.

Overseas Golfers – Men

American

Aaron, T.	DiMarco, C.	Irwin, H.	Mize, L.	Stockton, D.
Azinger, P.	Dickson, B.	January, D.	Nelson, L.	Stranahan, F.R.
Beem, R.	Duval, D.	Janzen, L.	Nicklaus, J.	Strange, C.
Brooks, M.	Faxon, B.	Jones, S.	North, A.	Stricker, S.
Bryant, B.	Finsterwald, D.	Kite, T.	Oberholser, A.	Sutton, H.
Calcavecchia, M.	Floyd, R.	Kuchar, M.	O'Meara, M.	Taylor, V.
Campbell, C.	Ford, D.	Lehman, T.	Palmer, A.	Toms, D.
Campbell, W.C.	Funk, F.	Leonard, J.	Pate, J.	Trahan, D.J.
Casper, B.	Furyk, J.	Littler, G.	Pavin, C.	Trevino, L.
Cink, S.	Graham, L.	Love III, D.	Perry, K.	Verplank, S.
Coe, C.	Green, H.	MacKenzie, W.	Quigley, D.	Wadkins, L.
Cook, J.	Hamilton, T.	Maggert, J.	Rogers, B.	Ward, H.
Couch, C.	Harper, C.	Matteson, T.	Siderowf, D.	Watson, T.
Couples, F.	Haas, J.	Melnyk, S.	Sigel, J.	Weiskopf, T.
Crenshaw, B.	Henry, J.J.	Michael, S.	Simpson, S.	Wetterich, B.
Curtis, B.	Hoch, S.	Mickelson, P.	Stadler, C.	Woods, E.
Daly, J.	Holmes, J.B.	Miller, J.	Stadler, K.	Zoeller, F.

Aaron, Tommy
Born Gainesville, Georgia, 22 February 1937
Turned professional 1961
After finishing runner-up in the 1972 US PGA Championship he won the 1973 Masters. He was a member of the 1969 and 1973 Ryder Cup teams. Inadvertently marked down a 4 on Roberto de Vicenzo's card for the 17th hole in the 1968 Masters when the Argentinian took 3. De Vicenzo signed for the 4 and lost out by one shot on a play-off for the Green Jacket.

Azinger, Paul
Born Holyoke, Massachusetts, 6 January 1960
Turned professional 1981
Helped by a second hole play-off victory against Greg Norman in the 1993 US PGA Championship at Inverness he made almost $1.5 million to finish second on the US money list to Nick Price. The following year he played only four events after having been diagnosed with lymphoma in his right shoulder blade. Happily he made a good recovery and scored his 12th US Tour victory in 2000 and his first since his 1993 US PGA win when he opened with a 63 and led from start to finish in the Sony Open in Hawaii. He played in three Ryder Cup matches in 1989, 1991 and 1993 and was on the 2001 team making headlines by holing a bunker shot at the last to halve with Niclas Fasth. In 1987 he was joint runner-up with Rodger Davis in the Open at Muirfield won by Nick Faldo. Injury prevented his enjoying much success in the 2003 and 2004 seasons in the States. It was announced in 2006 that he would captain the US Ryder Cup side in 2010.

Beem, Rich
Born Phoenix Arizona 24 August 1974
Turned professional 1994.
Playing in only his fourth major championship he hit the headlines in 2002 when he held off the spirited challenge of Tiger Woods to win the US PGA Championship at Hazeltine. The 31-year-old from Phoenix who now lives in Texas admitted he was 'flabbergasted to have won' having arrived with no expectations, although a winner of two US Tour titles – the 1999 Kemper Open and the 2002 International event at Castle Pines just a few weeks before the US PGA title. Just a year after turning professional Beem had given up the game to sell car stereos and mobile phones before becoming an assistant club professional before returning once again to tournament play in 1999. On the final day at Hazeltine, Beem hit two great shots – a fairway wood to to seven feet for an eagle at the at the 587 yards 11th and a 40 foot putt for a birdie at the 16th which helped him hold off Woods who finished with four birdies in a row. Beem prevented Woods from winning three majors in a year for the second time. From 73rd in the World Rankings Beem jumped to 26th.

Brooks, Mark
Born Fort Worth, Texas, 25 March 1961
Turned professional 1983
A seven-time winner on the US Tour between 1988 and 1996 he took the US PGA Championship title in 1996 after a play-off with Kenny Perry at Valhalla. On that occasion he birdied the 72nd hole and the first extra hole to win but he was beaten by South African Retief Goosen in the 18-hole play-off for the 2000 US Open at Southern Hills in Tulsa. Goosen shot 70, Brooks 72.

Bryant, Bart
Born Gatesville, Texas, 18 November 1962
Turned professional 1986
Won The Memorial Tournament and the Tour Championship in 2005 to finish ninth in the US money list.

Calcavecchia, Mark
Born Laurel, Nebraska, 12 June 1960
Turned professional 1981
Winner of the 1989 Open Championship at Royal Troon after the first ever four-hole play-off against Australians Greg Norman and Wayne Grady. He was runner-up in the 1987 Masters at Augusta to Sandy Lyle and came second to Jodie Mudd in the 1990 Players' Championship. He played in the 1987, 1989, 1991 and 2002 Ryder Cup sides.

Campbell, Chad
Born Andrews, Texas, 31 May 1974
Turned professional 1996
Winner of the Tour Championship in 2003 he was beaten into second place in the 2003 USPGA Championship by Shaun Micheel who hit a wonder approach shot at the last hole at Oak Hill. His seven iron from 175 yards out finished inches from the cup. In 2004, Campbell made his Ryder Cup début and made the team again in 2006.

Campbell, William Cammack
Born West Virginia, 5 May 1923
One of America's most distinguished players and administrators. He won the US Amateur Championship in 1964 ten years after finishing runner-up in the Amateur Championship in Britain to Australian Doug Bachli at Muirfield. One of a select group who have been both President of the United States Golf Association (in 1983) and captain of the Royal and Ancient Golf Club of St Andrews (in 1987/88). He played in eight Ryder Cup matches between 1951 and 1975 as was captain in 1955.

Casper, Billy
Born San Diego, California, 24 June 1931
Turned professional 1954
A three-time major title winner he took the US Open in 1959 and 1966 and the US Masters in 1970. In 1966 came back from seven strokes behind Arnold Palmer with nine to play to force a play-off which he then won. Between 1956 and 1975 he picked up 51 first prize cheques on the US Tour. His European victories were the 1974 Trophée Lancôme and Lancia D'Oro and the 1975 Italian Open. As a senior golf he won nine times between 1982 and 1989 including the US Senior Open in 1983. Played in eight Ryder Cups and captained the American side in 1979 at Greenbrier. He and wife Shirley have 11 children several of them adopted. He was named Father of the Year in 1966. Started playing golf aged 5 and rates Ben Hogan, Byron Nelson and Sam Snead as his heroes. Five times Vardon Trophy winner (for low season stroke-average) and twice top money earner he was US PGA Player of the Year in 1966 and 1970. He was inducted into the World Golf Hall of Fame in 1978 and the US PGA Hall of Fame in 1982. Encouraged by his family to play in The Masters for one last time in 2005 he shot 106 but was disqualified for not handing in his card.

Cink, Stewart
Born Huntsville, Alabama, 21 May 1973
Turned professional 1995
The Rookie of the Year on the US Tour in 1997 when he won the Canon Greater Hartford Classic. The year before he had been top rookie on the Buy.com tour. Although he made the 2002 Ryder Cup side he missed a two foot putt on the last and, as a result, a play-off for the US Open with Mark Brooks and winner Retief

Goosen. He received a captain's pick from Hal Sutton for the 2004 Ryder Cup and immediately led from start to finish to win the World Championship NEC Invitational. In 2006, he was again a captain's pick for the Ryder Cup but on this occasion finished second to Woods in the Bridgestone Invitational. In the Cup match at the K Club, he beat Sergio García in the singles to prevent the Spaniard winning five points out of five.

Coe, Charles
Born Oklahoma City, 26 October 1923
Another fine American amateur golfer who finished runner-up with Arnold Palmer to Gary Player in the 1961 Masters at Augusta. Twice US Amateur champion in 1949 and 1958, he played in six Walker Cup matches and was non-playing captain in 1959. He won seven and halved two of the 13 games he played. Winner of the Bobby Jones award in 1964.

Cook, John
Born Toledo, Ohio, 2 October 1957
Turned professional 1979
A regular winner on the US Tour he gave Nick Faldo a fright in the 1992 Open at Muirfield. Three strokes behind with eight to play Cook had moved out in front after 16 holes on the final day but finished 5,5 to Faldo's 4,4. He was also tied second that year in the US PGA Championship. Given much help in his early years by Jack Nicklaus and Tom Weiskopf. Jointly with Mark Calcavecchia holds the low first-54 holes record of 189 at the St Jude Classic in 1996.

Couch, Chris
Born Fort Lauderdale, Florida, 1 May 1973
Turned professional 1995
Scored his first win on the US Tour when he took first prize in the Zurich Classic of New Orleans.

Couples, Fred
Born Seattle, Washington, 3 October 1959
Turned professional 1980
Troubled continually with a back problem he has managed to win only one major – the 1992 US Masters but is one of the most popular of all American players. Although he has been known to say he enjoys watching television lying on the sofa, he is no stay-at-home in a golfing sense. He has always been willing to travel and his overseas victories include two Johnnie Walker World Championships, the Johnnie Walker Classic, the Dubai Desert Classic and the Tournoi Perrier de Paris. On the US Tour he won 14 times between 1983 and 1998. He played in five Ryder Cup matches and has teed up four times for the US in the Presidents Cup. After an absence of years he returned to the winner's circle when he won the Shell Houston Open. In 2005 finished second behind Brad Bryant in The Memorial Tournament and beat Vijay Singh on the final day of the Presidents Cup. In 2006, he challenged for The Masters title at Augusta but lost out to Phil Mickelson.

Crenshaw, Ben
Born Austin, Texas, 11 January 1952
Turned professional 1973
One of golf's great putters who followed up his victory in the 1984 US Masters with an emotional repeat success in 1995 just a short time after the death of his long-time coach and mentor Harvey Pennick. He played

in four Ryder Cup matches between 1981 and 1995 before captaining the side in 1999 when the Americans came from four points back to win with a scintillating last day performance. Winner of the Byron Nelson award in 1976 he was also named Bobby Jones award winner in 1991. Now combines playing with an equally successful career as a golf course designer and is an acknowledged authority on every aspect of the history of the game. In 2002 he was named the Payne Stewart Award winner – an award that recognises a player's respect of and upholding of the traditions of the game.

Curtis, Ben
Born Columbus, Ohio, 26 May 1977
Turned professional 2000
Shock 750-1 outsider who played superbly at Royal St George's to get his name engraved with all the other golfing greats on the famous Claret Jug. His victory while well deserved was one of golf's biggest shocks in years. It was his first major appearance. He only qualified for the Open with a 14th place finish in the Western Open in Chicago – a designated qualifying event. He had never played in Britain nor had he any experience of links golf but he outplayed Tiger Woods, Thomas Bjørn, David Love III and Vijay Singh to take the title with a score of 283. He learned the game in Ohio at the golf course his grandfather built at Ostrander, Ohio. He was a double winner on the US Tour in 2006 taking the Booz Allen Classic and the 84 Lumber Classic titles.

Daly, John
Born Sacramento, California, 28 April 1966
Turned professional 1987
Winner of two majors – the 1991 US PGA Championship and the 1995 Open Championship at St Andrews after a play-off with Costantino Rocca, his career has not been without its ups and downs. He admits he has battled alcoholism and, on occasions, has been his own worst enemy when having run-ins with officialdom but he remains one of the most popular and likeable if sometimes unorthodox players on Tour because of his long hitting. His average drive is over 300 yards. When he won the US PGA Championship at Crooked Stick he got in as ninth alternate, drove through the night to tee it up without a practice round and shot 69, 67, 69, 71 to beat Bruce Lietzke by three. Given invaluable help at times by Fuzzy Zoeller he writes his own songs and is a mean performer on the guitar. In 2001 took the BMW International Open title at Munich. In 2002 was a member of both the US and European Tours. Curiously, despite winning two majors, he has never played in the Ryder Cup. In 2003 he won the Korean Open and in 2004 beat Luke Donald in a play-off at San Diego to take the Buick Invitational.

DiMarco, Chris
Born Huntingdon, New York, 23 August 1968
Turned professional 1990
He made his début in the Presidents Cup in 2003 and the Ryder Cup in 2004 when he also lost a play off to Vijay Singh in the US PGA Championship at Whistling Straits. In 2005 he was beaten at the first extra hole by Tiger Woods in The Masters at Augusta and later in the year holed the winning putt when making his second appearance in the Presidents Cup. In 2006 he won the Abu Dhabi event on the European Tour. Finished runner-up to Tiger Woods in The Open at Hoylake and

again made the Ryder Cup. Commentates with the Golf Channel in Orlando.

Dickson, Bob
Born McAlester, Oklahoma, 25 January 1944
Turned professional 1968
Best remembered for being one of only four players to complete a Transatlantic amateur double. In 1967 he won the US Amateur Championship at Broadmoor with a total of 285 (the Championship was played over 72 holes from 1965 to 1972) and the British Amateur title with a 2 and 1 win over fellow American Ron Cerrudo at Formby. After turning professional scored two wins on the US Tour.

Duval, David
Born Jacksonville, Florida, 19 November 1971
Turned professional 1993
A regular winner on the US Tour who wears dark glasses because of an eye stigmatism which is sensitive to light, he won his first major at Royal Lytham and St Annes last year when he became only the second American professional to win the Open over that course. He was the first player in US Tour history to win titles by play-off in consecutive weeks. Played 86 events and had seven second-place finishes and four thirds before making his break-through win in the Michelob Championship then won the following week as well. His father Bob plays the US Senior Tour. He was a winner of the US Tour Championship in 1997 and the Players' Championship in 1999. In the 1998 and 2001 Masters he came second and was third in that event in 2000. He played in 1991 Walker Cup and was a member of the winning Ryder Cup side on his début in 1999 and was also a member of the 2002 Cup side halving his match with Darren Clarke in the singles. Injury and illness meant he has not enjoyed a successful 2003, 2004 or 2005 season.

Faxon, Brad
Born Oceanport, New Jersey, 1 August 1961
Turned professional 1983
A former Walker Cup player who competed in the 1983 match he has played twice in the Ryder Cup (1995 and 1997). A seven-time winner on the US Tour he also putted superbly to win the Australian Open at Metropolitan in 1993. In 2005 was named recipient of the Payne Stewart award for respecting and upholding the traditions of the game.

Finsterwald, Dow
Born Athens, Ohio, 6 September 1929
Turned professional 1951
Winner of the 1958 US PGA Championship he won 11 other competitions between 1955 and 1963. He played in four Ryder Cup matches in a row from 1957 and captained the side in 1977. He was US PGA Player of the Year in 1958.

Floyd, Raymond
Born Fort Bragg, North Carolina, 4 September 1942
Turned professional 1961
A four time major winner whose failure to win an Open Championship title prevented his completing a Slam of Majors. He won the US Open in 1986, the Masters in 1976 when he matched the then 72-hole record set by Jack Nicklaus to win by eight strokes and took the US PGA title in 1969 and 1982. In addition to coming second and third in the Open he was also runner-up

three times in the Masters and in the US PGA once. After scoring 22 victories on the main US Tour he has continued to win as a senior. Inducted into the World Golf Hall of Fame in 1989 he is an avid Chicago Cubs baseball fan. Played in eight Ryder Cup matches between 1969 and 1993 making history with his last appearance by being the oldest player to take part in the match. He was 49. He was non-playing captain in 1989 when the match was drawn at The Belfry.

Ford, Doug
Born West Haven, Connecticut, 6 August 1922
Turned professional 1949
His 25 wins on the US Tour between 1955 and 1963 included the 1975 US Masters. US PGA Player of the Year in 1955, he competed in four Ryder Cup matches in succession from 1955.

Funk, Fred
Born Tacoma Park, Missouri, 14 June 1956
Turned professional 1981
One of five rookies in the 2004 US Ryder Cup side, he scored his sisth US Tour success a few weeks later when he won the Southern Farm Bureau Classic. In 2005 he won the Tournament Players' Championship at Sawgrass.

Furyk, Jim
Born West Chester, Pennsylvania, 12 May 1970
Turned professional 1992
Considered one of the best players not to have won a major, Furyk put that right when he won the US Open at Olympia Fields, Chicago. He was one of four first-time major winners in 2003. He clearly enjoys playing in Las Vegas where he has won three Invitational events in 1995, 1999 and 1998. Has teed it up in two Presidents Cups and two Ryder Cups beating Nick Faldo in the singles at Valderrama in 1997. He was also in the 2002 side. Has one of the most easily recognisable if idiosyncratic swings in top line golf. His father Mike has been his only coach. He played in the last four Ryder Cup matches and four Presidents Cups. In 2005 he finished fourth top money earner in the United States and was winner of the Cialis Western Open. In 2006 he came second to Tiger Woods in the US Tour money list earning $7,213,316. He won the Harry Vardon Trophy for the best scoring average of 68.66 for golfers who played 60m rounds or more on Tour. Furyk has made over $31 million in prize-money on the US Tour by the end of 2006.

Graham, Lou
Born Nashville, Tennessee, 7 January 1938
Turned professional 1962
Won the US Open at Medinah in 1975 after a play-off against John Mahaffey.

Green, Hubert
Born Birmingham, Alabama, 18 December 1946
Turned professional 1970
Beat Lou Graham for the 1977 US Open at Southern Hills despite being told with four holes to play that he had received a death threat. Three times a Ryder Cup player he also won the 1985 US PGA Championship. His only European Tour victory was the 1977 Irish Open. Best known for his unorthodox swing and distinctive crouching putting style. He is successfully beating throat cancer – an illness that has meant he has been unable to compete in the US Senior Tour.

Hamilton, Todd
Born Galesburg, Illinois, 18 October 1965
Turned professional 1997
Winner of the 2004 Open Chmpionship at Royal Troon beating Ernie Els in a four-hole play-off after both had tied on ten-under-par 274. Having learned his craft on the Asian Tour and Japanese circuit where he won four times in 2003, he earned his US Tour card in 2004 and won the Honda Classic. His performance in the Open was flawless as he kept his nerve to win against Els, Phil Mickelson and world No.1 Tiger Woods among others. He was Rookie of the Year in 2004.

Harper, Chandler
Born Portsmouth, Virginia, 10 March 1914
Turned professional 1934
Winner of the 1950 US PGA Championship he won over ten tournaments and was elected to the US PGA Hall of Fame in 1969. Once shot 58 (29-29) round a 6100 yards course in Portsmouth.

Haas, Jay
Born St Louis, Missouri, 2 December 1953
Turned professional 1976
Winner of nine events on the USPGA Tour, he played in his third Ryder Cup as an invitee of the US captain Hal Sutton. He had played in 1983 and 1995. He has played in three Presidents Cups and was a Walker Cup player in 1975. His uncle is former Masters champion Bob Goalby. In 2004 he was named recipient of the Payne Stewart award for respecting and upholding the traditions of the game and received the Bob Jones award for outstanding sportsmanship in 2005. In 2006 he edged out Loren Roberts for the No.1 spot on the US Champions Tour winning five times in the season.

Henry, J.J.
Born Fairfield, Connecticut, 2 April 1975
Turned professional 1998
Earned his place in the 2006 Ryder Cup and during the year won the Buick Classic at River Highlands.

Hoch, Scott
Born Raleigh, North Carolina, 24 November 1955
Turned professional 1979
Ryder Cup, Presidents Cup, Walker Cup and Eisenhower Trophy player who is a regular winner on the US Tour. Has scored 10 wins on the US Tour between 1980 and 2001 and has had six more victories worldwide. In 1989 he donated $100,000 of his Las Vegas Invitational winnings to the Arnold Palmer Children's Hospital in Orlando where his son Cameron had been successfully treated for a rare bone infection in his right knee. More unfortunately remembered for missing a short putt at the first extra hole of a play-off that would have won him a Masters Green Jacket.

Holmes, John B.
Born Campbellsville, Kentucky, 26 April 1982
Turned professional 2005
Big hitter who scored his first win on the US Tour when he won the FBR Open at the TPC at Scottsdale in impressive fashion.

Irwin, Hale
Born Joplin, Montana, 3 June 1945
Turned professional 1968
A three time winner of the US Open (1974, 1979 and 1990) he has been a prolific winner on the main US Tour and, since turning 50, on the US Senior Tour. He had 20 wins on the main Tour including the 1990 US Open triumph where he holed a 45-foot putt on the final green at Medinah to force a play-off with Mike Donald then after both were still tied following a further 18 holes became the oldest winner of the Championship at 45 when he sank a 10-foot birdie putt at the first extra hole of sudden death. Joint runner-up to Tom Watson in the 1983 Open at Royal Birkdale where he stubbed the ground and missed a tap-in putt on the final day – a slip that cost him the chance of a play-off. Three times top earner on the Senior Tour where, prior to the start of the 2001 season, he had averaged $90,573 per start in 130 events coming in the top three in 63 of those events and finishing over par in only nine of them.

January, Don
Born Plainview, Texas, 20 November 1929
Turned professional 1955
Winner of the US Open in 1967 he followed up his successful main Tour career in which he had 11 wins between 1956 and 1976 with double that success as a Senior winning 22 times. Much admired for his easy rhythmical style.

Janzen, Lee
Born Austin, Minnesota, 28 August 1964
Turned professional 1986
Twice a winner of the US Open in 1993 and again in 1998 when he staged the best final round comeback since Johnny Miller rallied from six back to win the title 25 years earlier. Five strokes behind the late Payne Stewart after 54 holes at Baltusrol he closed with a 67 to beat Stewart with whom he had also battled for the title in 1993.

Johnson, Zach
Born Iowa City, 24 February 1976
Turned professional 1998
The winner of the 2004 BellSouth Classic, he made his début in the Ryder Cup at the K Club in 2006.

Jones, Steve
Born Artesia, New Mexico, 27 December 1958
Turned professional 1981
First player since Jerry Pate in 1976 to win the US Open after having had to qualify. His 1996 victory was the result of inspiration he received from reading a Ben Hogan book given to him the week before the Championship at Oakland Hills. Uses a reverse overlapping grip as a result of injury. Indeed his career was put on hold for three years after injury to his left index finger following a dirt-bike accident. He dominated the 1997 Phoenix Open shooting 62, 64, 65 and 67 for an 11 shot victory over Jesper Parnevik That week his 258 winning total was just one outside the low US Tour record set by Mike Souchak in 1955.

Kite, Tom
Born Austin, Texas, 9 December 1949
Turned professional 1972
He won the US Open at Pebble Beach in 1992 in difficult conditions when aged 42 to lose the 'best player around

never to have won a Major' tag. With 19 wins on the main Tour he was the first to top $6million, $7 million, $8 million and $9 million dollars in prize money. Has been playing since he was 11 and after a lifetime wearing glasses had laser surgery to correct acute near-sightedness. The Ryder Cup captain in 1997 he now plays the US Senior Tour. He was inducted into the World Golf Hall of Fame in 2004.

Kuchar, Matt
Born Lake Mary, Florida, 21 June 1978
Turned professional 2002
Winner of the US Amateur in 1997 he was leading amateur in the 1998 Masters and US Open Championship. Scored his first win as a professional when he landed the 2002 Honda Classic.

Lehman, Tom
Born Austin, Minnesota, 7 March 1959
Turned professional 1982
Winner of the Open Championship at Royal Lytham and St Annes in 1996 he was runner-up in the US Open in 1996 and third in 1997. He was runner-up in the 1994 US Masters having come third the previous year. Has played in four Ryder Cup matches. He was appointed to lead the US team in the 2006 Ryder Cup side at the K Club when the Americans lost 18½–9½ to the Europeans led by Ian Woosnam.

Leonard, Justin
Born Dallas, Texas, 15 June 1972
Turned professional 1994
Winner of the 1997 Open at Royal Troon when he beat Jesper Parnevik and Darren Clarke into second place with a closing 65 and nearly won the title again in 1999 when he lost a four-hole play-off with Jean Van de Velde and Paul Lawrie to the Scotsman at Carnoustie. In 1998 came from five back to beat Lee Janzen in the Players Championship and is remembered for his fight back against José Maria Olazábal on the final day of the 1999 Ryder Cup at Brookline. Four down after 11 holes he managed to share a half-point with the Spaniard to help America win the Cup. He was a double winner in 2005 taking the Bob Hope Chrysler Classic at Palm Springs and the Fedex St Jude Classic.

Littler, Gene
Born San Diego, California, 21 July 1930
Turned professional 1954
Winner of the 1953 US Amateur Championship he had a distinguished professional career scoring 26 victories on the US Tour between 1955 and 1977. He scored his only major triumph at Pebble Beach in 1961 when he beat Bob Goalby and Doug Sanders at Oakland Hills. He had been runner-up in the US Open in 1954 and was runner-up in the 1977 US PGA Championship and the 1970 US Masters. A seven-time Ryder Cup player between 1961 and 1977 he is a former winner of the Ben Hogan, Bobby Jones and Byron Nelson awards. He won the Hogan award after successfully beating cancer. .

Love III, Davis
Born Charlotte, North Carolina, 13 April 1964
Turned professional 1985
Son of one of America's most highly rated teachers who died in a plane crash in 1988, Love has won only one major – the 1997 US PGA Championship at Winged

Foot where he beat Justin Leonard by five shots. He has been runner-up in the US Open (1996) and the US Masters (1999). In the World Cup of Golf won the title in partnership with Fred Couples four years in a row (1992–1995). He has played in five Ryder Cups and enjoyed a superb 2003 winning four times between February and August. His victories were the AT&T Pebble Beach National Pro-Am, the Players Championship, The Heritage and The International. Just failed to make the 2006 Ryder Cup side but two weeks later he returned to the winner's circle when he won the Chrysler Greensboro event.

MacKenzie, Will
Born Greenville, North Carolina, 28 September 1974
Turned professional 2000
He won his first event on the US Tour when he took the Reno-Tahoe Open.

Maggert, Jeff
Born Columbia, Missouri, 20 February 1964
Turned professional 1986
A three times Ryder Cup player who competed in the 1995, 1997 and 1999 matches he won the World Golf Championship Match Play event in 1999 to land a million. A quiet achiever he has come third in the US PGA Championship twice in 1995 and 1997.

Matteson, Troy
Born Rockledge, Florida, 8 November 1979
Turned professional 2003
He was a first-time winner on the 2006 PGA Tour when he won the Frys.com event in Las Vegas.

Melnyk, Steve
Born Brunswick, Georgia, 26 February 1947
Turned professional 1971
US Amateur champion in 1969 and British champion in 1971. His professional career was cut short because of an ankle injury. Today he commentates for CBS, one of the US networks.

Micheel, Shaun
Born Orlando, Florida, 5 January 1969
Turned professional 1962
Surprise winner of the USPGA Championship at Oak Hill in 2003. He fired rounds of 69, 68, 69 and 70 for a winning total of 276. He completed his victory with one of the most brilliant approach irons from the rough to just one foot of the hole at the last. Micheel was one of four first time winners in 2003. Three years later, at Medinah, he finished second to Tiger Woods in the US PGA Championship. Later he beat Woods en route to the final of the HSBC World Match Play at Wentworth but lost in the final to Paul Casey.

Mickelson, Phil
Born San Diego, California, 16 June 1970
Turned professional 1992
Plays all sports right-handed except golf and claims to have started hitting golf balls at 18 months. Although he won the 2000 Tour Championship is still without a major victory. His best finishes in Majors are second in the 2001 US PGA Championship and the 1999 US Open and third in the 1994 US PGA Championship. His 19 victories on the US Tour include a win as an amateur in the 1995 Tucson Open. His 65 at the Masters in 1996 is lowest score by a left-hander at that event. One of only three players to win the NCAA Championship and US Amateur in the same year. The others – Jack Nicklaus and Tiger Woods. He has played in two Walker Cups, four times in Presidents Cup and in six Ryder Cup matches. Like Colin Montgomerie, Mickelson finally won his first major when he took the Green Jacket in the 2004 Masters at Augusta by a shot from Ernie Els. Mickelson birdied five of the last seven holes. He was pipped by Retief Goosen for the US Open at Shinnecock Hills and was third in the Open at Troon. In 2005 he won four times on the US Tour including a second major – the USPGA Championship at Baltusrol. He started the 2006 season by winning The Masters for a second time and had the chance to win a third major in a row at the US Open at Winged Foot in June but double-bogeyed the last hole and finished with Jim Furyk and Colin Montgomerie.

Miller, Johnny
Born San Francisco, California, 29 April 1947
Turned professional 1969
Dreamed of winning the Open after Tony Lema, another member of the Olympic Club in San Francisco, did so in 1964. Realised his dream when he beat Jack Nicklaus and Seve Ballesteros into second place in the 1976 Open at Royal Birkdale. His US Open win in 1973 came with the help of a brilliant last round 63 which set the record, since equalled for the lowest round in the Championship. Was involved with Tom Weiskopf and Jack Nicklaus in one of the greatest finishes to a US Masters in 1975 which Nicklaus won. He scored 24 wins between 1971 and 1984 and in 1975 shot 49 under par when winning the Phoenix and Tucson Opens in successive weeks. Now commentates for NBC.

Mize, Larry
Born Augusta, Georgia, 23 September 1958
Turned professional 1980
Only local player ever to win the Masters and he did it in dramatic style holing a 140-foot pitch and run at the second extra hole to edge out Greg Norman and Seve Ballesteros. He had made the play-off by holing a 10-foot birdie on the final green. In 1993 he beat an international field to take the Johnnie Walker World Championship title at Tryall in Jamaica. His middle name is Hogan.

Nelson, Larry
Born Fort Payne, Alabama, 10 September 1947
Turned professional 1971
Often underrated he learned to play by reading Ben Hogan's The Five Fundamentals of Golf and broke 100 first time out and 70 after just nine months. Active as well these days on course design he has won the Jack Nicklaus award. He has been successful in the US Open (1983 at Oakmont) and two US PGA Championships (in 1981 at the Atlanta Athletic Club and in 1987 after a play-off with Lanny Wadkins at PGA National). Three times a Ryder Cup player he has competed equally successfully as a Senior having won 15 titles (at end of July 2001). He did not play as a youngster but visited a driving range after completing his military service and was hooked. He was named Senior PGA Tour Player of the Year for finishing top earner and winning six times in 2000. At the end of his third full season on the Senior Tour and after 87 events he had won just short of $10 million.

Nicklaus, Jack

Born Columbus, Ohio, 21 January 1940
Turned professional 1961

The greatest golfer of the 20th century and possibly of all time depending on what Tiger Woods manages to achieve. After winning two US Amateurs he went on to win 18 professional major titles. His record is phenomenal. He won the Open in 1966, 1970 and 1978, the last two at St Andrews and was runner-up seven times and third on two further occasions. He won the US Open in 1962, 1967, 1972 and 1980 and came second four times. He won five US PGA titles in 1963, 1971, 1973, 1975 and 1980 and was runner-up four times and third on two further occasions and he won six Masters in 1963, 1965, 1966, 1972, 1975 and 1986 when at the age of 46 he became the oldest winner of a Green Jacket. In addition he was runner-up four times and third twice. In 1966 he became the first player to successfully defend the Masters (a feat later matched by Nick Faldo in 1990). He won six Australian Opens (1964, 1968, 1971, 1975, 1976 and 1978) and played in six Ryder Cups, captaining two more in 1983 at Palm Beach Gardens when America won and in 1987 at Muirfield Village where his side were losers for the first time on home soil. Credited with saving the Cup match after suggesting that Continental golfers should be included in the side from 1979. Ten years earlier he conceded the 18-inch putt that Jacklin had for a half at the last when the result of the match depended on the result of that game. The match was drawn. After winning 71 times between 1962 and 1984 on the main Tour he won a further ten times on the Senior US Tour. He has won almost every honour you can win in golf including the Byron Nelson, Ben Hogan and Walter Hagen awards. He was the US top money earner in seasons 1964, 1965, 1967, 1971, 1972, 1973, 1975 and 1976 and is a honorary member of the Royal and Ancient Golf Club of St Andrews. Bobby Jones once said of Nicklaus that 'he played a game with which I am not familiar'. With the constant support of his wife Barbara, Nicklaus has been the personification of all that is good about the game. He has designed over 200 courses worldwide. He played in The Open Championship for the last time in 2005. It was his 44th appearance.

North, Andy

Born Thorp, Wisconsin, 9 March 1950
Turned professional 1972

Although this tall American found it difficult to win Tour events he did pick up two US Open titles. His first Championship success came at Cherry Hills in Denver in 1986 when he edged out Dave Stockton and J.C. Snead and the second at Oakland Hills in 1985 when finished just a shot ahead of Dave Barr, T.C. Chen and Denis Watson who had been penalised a shot during the Championship for waiting longer than the regulation 10 seconds at one hole to see if his ball would drop into the cup. North is now a very successful golf commentator whose analytical comments are much admired.

Oberholser, Aaron

Born San Luis Obispo, California, 2 February 1975
Turned professional 1998

Made his break-through win on the US Tour when he won the AT&T event at Pebble Beach.

O'Meara, Mark

Born Goldsboro, North Carolina, 13 January 1957
Turned professional 1980

A former US Amateur Champion in 1979 Mark was 41 when he won his first Major – the US Masters at Augusta. That week in 1998 he did not three putt once on Augusta's glassy greens. Three months later he won the Open at Royal Birkdale battling with, among others, Tiger Woods with whom he has had a particular friendship. They both live at Isleworth in Florida. He is the oldest player to win two Majors in the same year and was chosen as PGA Player of the Year that season. When he closed birdie, birdie to win the Masters he joined Arnold Palmer and Art Wall as the only players to do that and became only the fifth player in Masters history to win without leading in the first three rounds. He won his Open championship title in a four hole play-off against Brian Watts. O'Meara played in five Ryder Cups between 1985 and 1999.

Palmer, Arnold

Born Latrobe, Pennsylvania, 10 September 1929
Turned professional 1954

Winner of 61 titles on the US Tour between 1956 and 1980, he is one of the most charismatic players in golf who has been credited with starting the golfing boom in the latter part of the 20th century. A former US Amateur champion in 1954, his performances were always exciting to watch and for years he was followed around by his own ever-loyal army of fans ... indeed still is when he tees up on the US Senior Tour. He won eight Major titles – the 1960 US Open and the 1961 and 1962 Opens at Royal Birkdale in very stormy weather and at Royal Troon where he beat Kel Nagle by six shots and the rest of the field by 13. He won the US Masters in 1958, 1960, 1962 and 1964 but never managed to win the US PGA although he finished second three times. The first player to pass the $1 million mark in earnings he helped Keith

Arnold Palmer

Mackenzie the then secretary of the Royal and Ancient Golf Club of St Andrews revive the Open and is now a distinguished honorary member of the club. In 1960 having won The Masters and US Open he came to St Andrews for the Centenary Open hoping to match three majors in a season – a record held at the time by Ben Hogan but he was beaten by Australian Kel Nagle. Son of the greenkeeper at Ligonier in the Pennsylvanian mountains – he later bought the club – he has remained a respected golfing idol noted for his remarkable strength and his attacking golf. With Jack Nicklaus and Gary Player he became a member of the modern Big Three – a concept developed by his manager – the late Mark McCormack whose first client he was. Palmer, who had already played his last Open, US Open and USPGA Championhips, bowed out of The Masters in 2004. He helped to launch the now hugely successful Golf Channel in the United States and presented the Palmer Cup for annual competition between the best young college golfers in America and Europe. Retired from competitive golf in October 2006 after hitting two balls into the water at the fourth on the first day of the Adminstaff Bureau Classic. He will only play in charity events and among friends from now on and will concentrate on his new passion – building golf courses.

Pate, Jerry
Born Macon, Georgia, 16 September 1953
Turned professional 1975
Winner of the 1976 US Open when he hit a 5-iron across water to three feet at the 72nd hole at the Atlanta Athletic Club. He was a member of what is regarded as the strongest ever Ryder Cup side that beat the Europeans at Walton Heath in 1981. Has now retired from golf and commentates occasionally on American television.

Pavin, Corey
Born Oxnard, California, 26 May 1961
Turned professional 1983
Although not one of golf's longer hitters he battled with powerful Greg Norman to take the 1995 US Open title at Shinnecock Hills. A runner-up in the 1994 US PGA Championship and third in the 1992 US Masters he won 14 times between 1984 and 2006. His only victory in Europe came when he took the German Open title in 1983 while on honeymoon. In 2006, he ended a ten-year winning drought by taking the US Bank Championship in Milwaukee and was one of Tom Lehman's vice-captains at the Ryder Cup at the K Club.

Perry, Kenny
Born Elizabethtown, Kentucky, 10 August 1960
Turned professional 1982
After winning for times between 1991 and 2001, he had a marvellous 2003 winning the Bank of America Colonial, the Memorial Tournament and the Greater Milwaukee Open between May 25 and July 13. He made his Ryder Cup début at Detroit in 2004 having played in the 1996, 2003 and 2005 Presidents Cups. He was a double winner on the US Tour in 2005 taking the Bay Hill Invitational and Bank of America Colonial titles.

Quigley, Dana
Born Lynnfield Centre Massachussetts, 14 April 1947
Turned professional 1971
Iron man of the US Champions Tour who played in 278 consecutive events for which he was qualified before missing the Senior British Open at Royal Aberdeen. In 2005 he had passed the million dollars mark in prize-money by early June. He had two victories in the Mastercard Championship and the Bayer Advantage Classic. With official money of $2,170,258 he topped the Champions Tour money list.

Rogers, Bill
Born Waco, Texas, 10 September 1951
Turned professional 1974
US PGA Player of the Year in 1981 when he won the Open at Royal St George's and was runner-up in the US Open. That year he also won the Australian Open but retired from top line competitive golf not long after because he did not enjoy all the travelling. A former Walker Cup player in 1973 he only entered the Open in 1981 at the insistence of Ben Crenshaw. Now a successful club professional and sometime television commentator, he is also competing on the US Champions Tour – the US Seniors Tour.

Siderowf, Dick
Twice a winner of the British Amateur title in 1973 when he beat Peter Moody at Royal Porthcawl and again in 1976 when he had to go to the 37th hole to beat John Davies. He was leading amateur in the 1968 US Open and played in four Walker Cups (1969, 1973, 1975 and 1977) before captaining the winning side in 1979.

Sigel, Jay
Born Narbeth, Pennsylvania, 13 November 1943
Turned professional 1993
Winner of the Amateur Championship in 1979 when he beat Scott Hoch 3 and 2 at Hillside, he also won the US Amateur in successive years 1982 and 1983. He was leading amateur in the US Open in 1984 and leading amateur in the US Masters in 1981, 1982 and 1988. He played in nine Walker Cup matches between 1977 and 1993 and has a record 18 points to his credit. Turned professional in order to join the US Senior Tour where he has had several successes.

Simpson, Scott
Born San Diego, California, 17 September 1955
Turned professional 1977
Winner of the US Open in 1987 at San Francisco's Olympic Club, he was beaten in a play-off for the title four years later at Hazeltine when the late Payne Stewart won the 18-hole play-off.

Stadler, Craig
Born San Diego, California, 2 June 1953
Turned professional 1975
Nicknamed 'The Walrus' because of his moustache and stocky build, he was the winner of the 1982 Masters at Augusta. Winner of 12 titles on the US Tour between 1980 and 1996 he played in two Ryder Cups (1983 and 1985). As an amateur he played in the 1975 Walker Cup two years after winning the US Amateur. He won his first senior major title when he took the Ford Senior Players' Championship just a few weeks after turning 50 then went back to the main tour the following week and won the BC Open against many players half his age. Had a successful 2004 season. In 2004 he was top earner on the US Champions Tour with over $2 million.

Stadler, Kevin
Born Reno, Nevada, 5 February 1980
Turned professional 2002
Son of Craig Stadler, the former Masters champion, Kevin won the Abierto Visa de la Republica in Argentina on the European Challenge Tour in 2005 before making his breakthrough on the main tour when taking the first prize in the Johnnie Walker Classic at The Vines in Perth in 2006.

Stockton, Dave
Born San Bernardino, California, 2 November 1941
Turned professional 1964
Winner of two US PGA Championships in 1970 and 1976, he has won more Senior Tour titles (14 as of end July 2001) than he did on the main Tour (11). Captained the American Ryder Cup team controversially in the infamous 'War on the Shore' match at Kiawah Island in 1991.

Stranahan, Frank R
Born Toledo, Ohio, 5 August 1922
Turned professional 1954
One of America's most successful amateurs he won the Amateur championship at Royal St George's in 1948 and 1950. He also won the US Amateur in 1950, the Mexican Amateur in 1946, 1948 and 1951 and the Canadian title in 1947 and 1948. He was also leading amateur in the Open in 1947, 1949, 1950, 1951 and 1953 behind Ben Hogan. He played in three Walker Cups in 1947, 1949 and 1951.

Strange, Curtis
Born Norfolk, Virginia, 20 January 1955
Turned professional 1976
Winner of successive US Opens in 1988 and again in 1989 when he beat Nick Faldo in an 18-hole play-off at The Country Club Brookline after getting up and down from a bunker at the last to tie on 278. Winner of 17 US Tour titles he won at least one event for seven successive years from 1983. Having played in five Ryder Cup matches he captained the US side when the 2001 match was played at The Belfry in 2002. Now commentates for the ABC Network.

Stricker, Steve
Born Egerton, Wisconsin, 23 February 1967
Turned professional 1990
Started 2001 by winning the $1 million first prize in the Accenture Match Play Championship, one of the World Golf Championship series. In the final he beat Pierre Fulke. Was a member of the winning American Alfred Dunhill Cup side in 1996.

Sutton, Hal
Born Shreveport, Louisiana, 28 April 1958
Turned professional 1981
Winner of the 1983 US PGA Championship at the Riviera CC in Los Angeles beating Jack Nicklaus into second place. Played in the 1985 and 1987 Ryder Cup matches and returned to the side in 1999 at Brookline when he beat Darren Clarke 4 and 2 in the singles. He made the 2002 side as well and captained the American team which lost to the Europeans at Oakland Hills in 2004.

Taylor, Vaughn
Born Roanoke, Virginia, 9 March 1976
Turned professional 1999
Made his Ryder Cup début in the 2006 match at the K Club. Twice won the Reno-Tahoe Open in 2004 and 2005

Toms, David
Born Monroe, LA, 4 January 1967
Turned professional 1989
Most important of his six wins on the US Tour was his first Major success by beating Phil Mickelson into second place in the 2001 USPGA Championship. Toms shot 66, 65, 65 and 69 for a 265 record winning aggregate at the Atlanta Athletic Club. This is the lowest aggregate in any Major. The previous year he had come joint fourth to Tiger Woods in the Open. Made his Ryder Cup début in 2002 and was the American side's top points scorer with 3½ points. In 2003 he had won twice in the Wachovia Championship and the Fedex St Jude Classic by the end of August. In an injury-hit 2004 he still made the US Ryder Cup side at Oakland Hills and again at the K Club in 2006. In 2005 Toms won the WGC Accenture Match-play title beating Chris DiMarco 6 and 5 in the final. He finished fifth in the money list in 2005.

Trahan, DJ
Born Atlanta, Georgia, 18 December 1980
Turned professional 2003
He was a first-time winner in 2006 when he beat Joe Durant in a play-off for the Southern Farm Bureau Classic.

Trevino, Lee
Born Dallas, Texas, 1 December 1939
Turned professional 1961
Twenty times a winner on the US Tour between 1968 and 1981 'Supermex', as he was nicknamed by his peers, hit the headlines in 1971 when he won the US Open beating Jack Nicklaus in a play-off at Merion, the Canadian Open at Montreal and the Open at Royal Birkdale in succession. One of the most extrovert of golfers who followed up his 27 victories on the main Tour with 29 on the US Senior Tour was entirely self-taught. He won six Majors – the Open in 1971 and 1972 when he chipped in at the 71st hole to end Tony Jacklin's hopes of winning, the US Open in 1968 and 1971 and the US PGA Championship in 1974 and 1984 but he never finished better than tenth twice in the Masters at Augusta – a course with so many right to left dog-legs that he felt it did not suit his game. In 1975 he was hit by lightning while playing in the Western Open in Chicago and had to undergo back surgery in order to keep competing. He was involved in one of the low scoring matches in the World Match Play Championship with Tony Jacklin in 1972 when he again came out on top. In 2003 he was made an honorary member of the Royal & Ancient Golf Club of St Andrews.

Verplank, Scott
Born Dallas, Texas, 9 July 1964
When he won the Western Open as an amateur in 1985 he was the first to do so since Doug Sanders took the 1956 Canadian Open. Missed most of the 1991 and 1992 seasons because of an elbow injury and the injury also

affected his 1996 season. He has diabetes and wears an insulin pump while playing to regulate his medication. Curtis Strange chose him as one of his two picks for the 2002 US Ryder Cup side. In the singles on the final day he beat Lee Westwood 2 and 1. He was again a captain's pick in Tom Lehman's side in 2006 and again won his singles, this time against Padraig Harrington.

Wadkins, Lanny

Born Richmond, Virginia, 5 December 1949
Turned professional 1971
His 21 victories on the US Tour between 1972 and 1992 include the 1977 US PGA Championship, his only Major. He won that after a play-off with Gene Littler at Pebble Beach but lost a play-off for the same title in 1987 to Larry Nelson at Palm Beach Gardens. He was second on two other occasions to Ray Floyd in 1982 and to Lee Trevino in 1984. In other Majors his best finish was third three times in the US Masters (1990, 1991 and 1993), tied second in the US Open (1986) and tied fourth in the 1984 Open at St Andrews. One of the fiercest of competitors he played eight Ryder Cups between 1977 and 1993 winning 20 of his 33 games, but was a losing captain at Oak Hill in 1995.

Ward, Harvie

Born Tarboro, North Carolina 1926
Turned professional 1973
Winner of the Amateur Championship in 1952 when he beat Frank Stranahan 6 and 5 at Prestwick, he went on to win the US title in 1955 and 1956 and the Canadian Amateur in 1964. He played in the 1953, 1955 and 1959 Walker Cup matches and won all of his six games.

Watson, Tom

Born Kansas City, Missouri, 4 September 1949
Turned professional 1971
Winner of 34 career titles, he won at least three a year on the main US Tour in a six-year spell between 1977 and 1982. He is best known for having won five Open championships in eight years between 1975 and 1983 to match the feat of J.H. Taylor, James Braid and Peter Thomson. When he had a chance to win a sixth Open and tie Harry Vardon's record at St Andrews in 1984 he hit his second close to the wall through the green at the 17th and lost out to Seve Ballesteros. Watson's wins came at Carnoustie in 1975 after a play-off with Jack Newton; a memorable 1977 triumph in which he edged out Jack Nicklaus at Turnberry shooting 65, 65 over the weekend to Nicklaus' 65, 66; 1980 at Muirfield where he beat Lee Trevino; 1982 at Royal Troon where Peter Oosterhuis and Nick Price came second and 1983 when Andy Bean and Hale Irwin were runners-up. Watson also won the 1982 US Open chipping in from the rough at the 17th on the final day to go on and beat Nicklaus and two US Masters in 1977 and 1981 but he never did better than tied second in the 1978 US PGA Championship to miss out joining Gene Sarazen, Ben Hogan, Gary Player, Jack Nicklaus and Tiger Woods as a winner of all four Majors. Became the oldest winner on the US Tour when he won the Mastercard Colonial in 1998 nearly 24 years after scoring his first win in the Western Open. He was 48, two years older than the previous oldest Ben Hogan, when he won the same event for the fifth time in 1959. Six times

Player of the Year he played in four Ryder Cups and captained the side to victory in 1993 at The Belfry. Inducted into the World Golf Hall of Fame in 1988, he is an honorary member of the Royal and Ancient Golf Club of St Andrews. Now plays on the US Senior Tour and returned in triumph to Turnberry in 2003 to win the Senior British Open 26 years after his memorable shoot-out for the Open over the same course. Although Nicklaus was again in the field, Watson's main rival this time was rookie European Senior Tour player Carl Mason who let a two shot lead playing the last slip then lost the play-off to the American at the second extra hole. He retained the British title in 2005 at Royal Aberdeen and finished second behind Dana Quigley on the US Champions Tour money list .

Weiskopf, Tom

Born Massillon, Ohio, 9 November 1942
Turned professional 1964
Winner of only one Major – the 1973 Open Championship at Royal Troon, he lived in the shadow of Jack Nicklaus throughout his competitive career. He was runner-up in the 1976 US Open to Jerry Pate and was twice third in 1973 and 1977. His best finish in the US PGA Championship was third in 1975 – the year he had to be content for the fourth time with second place at the US Masters. He had been runner-up for a Green Jacket in 1969, 1972 and 1974 previously but played perhaps his best golf ever in 1975 only to be pipped at the post by Nicklaus. With 22 wins to his name he now plays the US Senior Tour with a curtailed schedule because of his course design work for which he and his original partner Jay Morrish have received much praise. One of their designs is Loch Lomond, venue of the revived Scottish Open. Played in just two Ryder Cup matches giving up a place in the team one year in order to go Bighorn sheep hunting in Alaska.

Wetterich, Brett

Born Cincinnati, Ohio, 9 August 1973
Turned professional 1994
Was one of the four rookies in Tom Lehman's side which lost 18½–9½ to the Europeans at the K Club in 2006. During the year, he had won the EDS Byron Nelson Classic at Cottonwood Valley.

Wilson, Dean

Born Kaneohe, Hawaii, 17 December 1969
Turned professional 1992
Scored his first victory on the US Tour when he won The International at Castle Pines in Colorado.

Woods, Eldrick 'Tiger'

Born Cypress, California, 30 December 1975
Turned professional 1996
First golfer in history to hold all four Majors simultaneously. He won the 2000 US Open, The Open at St Andrews and the US PGA Championship after a play-off with Bob May then scored his second victory at Augusta when he won the 2001 US Masters. He is rewriting the record books. As an amateur he successfully made two defences of the US Championship to win the event a record three years in a row but the meteoric start to his professional career gives rise to the view that he might beat Jack Nicklaus' 18 major title wins record. In

2000 he was 53-under-par for the four Majors with Ernie Els next best at 17-under. His nine Tour victories in a season was the most by anyone since Ben Hogan won 11 in 1950. When he won the AT and T at Pebble Beach in 2000 he became the first player since Ben Hogan in 1948 to win on six successive starts on the US Tour. At Pebble Beach in the US Open he shot 65, 69, 71, 67 to tie the US Open record of 272 but his 12-under-par score was a new sub-par record. Having won the US Masters for the first time with a record 270 total which gave him a 12 shot victory in 1997 and taken the US PGA title in 1999 he needed only to win the Open in Britain to become the youngest and only the fifth player in history (the others were Gene Sarazen, Ben Hogan, Gary Player and Jack Nicklaus) to have won all four Majors. At the Old Course at St Andrews he romped home by eight shots with a new British Open and major Championship record total of 269 – 19-under-par. He needed extra holes to beat Bob May at Valhalla to successfully defend the US PGA title a few weeks later. With that victory he joined Ben Hogan (1953) as a winner of three Majors in a season but beat that record when he took the US Masters Green Jacket for a second time in 2001. His current Majors tally is six. His chance of winning all four Majors in one season was lost when he did not successfully defend his US Open title later in the year. During the 2000 season he set or tied 27 records and his average score on the US Tour of 68.1 beat Sam Snead's record of 69.23 set in 1945. Named Tiger after a Vietnamese soldier who was a friend of his father's he was born to play golf, hitting shots on the Bob Hope Show when aged two and shooting 48 for nine holes at age three. He is the youngest player to have won 20 events on the US Tour. He is so far ahead in the World rankings that he is unlikely to be deposed for some considerable time. He played in the 1997 and 1999 Ryder Cup matches and was a member of the 2002 side. Woods won the Masters title again in 2002 beating Retief Goosen into second place at Augusta on a final day when both Ernie Els and Vijay Singh challenged strongly before the South African ran up a 7 and the Fijian a 9 on the back nine. When he also won the US Open again at Bethpage Park in New York State he was in line to win all four majors in the same year but just like Jack Nicklaus 30 years earlier he lost out at Muirfield where Ernie Els was the winner of the Open. Caught in severe weather on the third day Woods fired a career high professional score of 81 but hit back with a closing 65 to finish joint 28th. In the US PGA Championship at Hazeltine he closed with four birdies but lost his chance of a ninth major in six years when Rich Beem took the title. Although a regular winner in 2003 he did not win any of the four majors stretching his losing run to six. He created headlines when he decided to leave the Nike driver out of his bag in favour of his old Titleist club. He is contracted to Nike but was able to swich to the older club under the terms of his sponsorship. Woods still described telling Nike what he planned to do was one of the most difficult things he had had to do in his career. In the 2003 Open at Royal St George's he lost a ball off his opening drive when it plunged into the thick rough. At the beginning of October, Woods scored his 52nd victory in the seven years since turning pro and his fifth of the season when

he won the American Express Championship, part of the WGC circuit, at the Capital City Club in Atlanta. Woods was winning his eighth GC event in 15 starts – bringing his earnings in these competitions to over $10 million. His win moved him into top spot on the US money list as he attempted to finish No. 1 for the fifth consecutive year. His victory also marked the 100th. victory of his caddie Steve Williams. Woods other victories on the US Tour up to that point had comprised the Buick Invitational, the WGC Accenture Match-play Championship, the Bay Hill Invitational and the 100th Western Open. He has played in five Ryder Cups and with David Duval won the World Cup of Golf in 2001. His bid to finish No.1 on the PGA Tour in 2004 came to the very last event of the season when he needed to win the Tour Championship to have a chance of overhauling Vijay Singh who had moved over $700,000 ahead on the money list. Although Woods was again the low average scorer for the fifth successive year, he failed to catch Singh for the No.1 spot. He finished No.1 again, however, in 2005 after a season in which he won six times including adding another two majors to his tally. He beat Chris DiMarco at the first hole of a play-off at Augusta to win his fourth Masters Green Jacket and won his second Open at St Andrews when finishing ahead of Colin Montgomerie and José María Olazábal. His majors tally is now 10. He finished second behind Michael Campbell in the US Open and fourth behind Phil Mickelson in the US PGA Championship in 2005. He led the stroke averages again in 2005 and his official earnings came up just short of $11m for the season. In 2006, he won The Open at Royal Liverpool and the USPGA Championship at Winged Foot to move to second place in the major titles table. He has won 11. His USPGA victory was the first time any golfer had won that title at the same venue. He had previously won there in 1999. During the year, his father and mentor Earl Woods died and a few weeks later he missed the cut in a major for the first time at the US Open at Winged Foot. After his win at Hoylake he completed a run of six successive stroke-play victories on the US PGA Tour. In 2006 he again finished No.1 on the money list in the United States with a total of $9,941,563 earned. He won eight times in all and had a scoring average for 55 rounds of 68.11 – best on Tour but it did not qualify him for the Harry Vardon trophy because he needed to have played 60 rounds. Jim Furyk with an average of 68.66 won that. By the end of 2006 Woods had won 54 events on the US Tour and his victory in the Dubai Desert Classic brought his international victories total to ten. His total prize-money earnings on the US Tour now top $65.7 million.

Zoeller, Fuzzy

Born New Albany, Indiana, 11 November 1951
Turned professional 1973

Winner of the US Masters in 1979 after a play-off with Ed Sneed (who had dropped shots at the last three holes in regulation play) and Tom Watson and the US Open in 1984 at Winged Foot after an 18-hole play-off with Greg Norman. A regular winner on the US Tour between 1979 and 1986, he played in three Ryder Cups (1979, 1983 and 1985).

International

Allenby, R.	Fernandez, V.	Monasterio, C.	Player, G.	Thomson, P.
Aoki, I.	Franci, C.	Marsh, G.	Price, N.	De Vicenzo, R.
Atwal, A.	Frost, D.	Monasterio, C.	Randhawa, J.	Weir, M.
Baddeley, A.	Goosen, R.	Nagle, K.	Romero, E.	Wi, C.
Baiocchi, H.	Grady, W.	Newton, J.	Schwartzel, C.	Wirachant, T.
Baker-Finch, I.	Graham, D.	Nobilo, F.	Scott, A.	Yang, Y-e
Charles, B.	Hayes, D.	Norman, G.	Senden, J.	Yeh, W.-t.
Choi, K.-J.	Henning, H.	Ogilvy, G.	Senior, P.	Zhang, L.-W.
Cole, B.	Hensby, M.	Ozaki, M.	Sheehan, P.	
Davis, R.	Immelman, T.	Pampling, R.	Singh, J.M.	
Elkington, S.	Jaidee, T.	Parry, C.	Singh, V.	
Els, E.	Mamat, M.	Phadungsil, C.	Sterne, R.	

Allenby, Robert (AUS)
Born Melbourne, 12 July 1971
Turned professional 1992
Pipped by a shot from winning the Australian Open as an amateur in 1991 by Wayne Riley's birdie, birdie, birdie finish at Royal Melbourne, he won the title three years later as a professional. After competing on the European Tour and winning four times, he now plays on the US Tour. He has played in four Presidents Cup matches in 1996, 2000, 2003 and 2005. In 2005 returned to Australia to win the Australian Open for a second time. He had won it in 1994.

Aoki, Isao (JPN)
Born Abiko, Chiba, 31 August 1942
Turned professional 1964
Successful international performer whose only victory on the main US Tour came dramatically in Hawaii in 1983 when he holed a 128 yards pitch for an eagle 3 at the last at Waialae to beat Jack Renner. Only Japanese golfer to win on the main European Tour taking the European Open in 1983. He also won the World Match Play in 1978 beating Simon Owen and was runner up the following year. He holed in one at Wentworth in that event to win a condominium at Gleneagles. He was top earner five times in his own country and is the Japanese golfer who has come closest to winning a major title finishing runner-up two shots behind Jack Nicklaus in the 1980 US Open at Baltusrol. Inducted into the World Golf Hall of Fame in 2004.

Atwal, Arjun (IND)
Born Asansol, India, 20 March 1973
Turned professional 1995
Learned the game at Royal Calcutta and became the first Indian to win on the European Tour when he won the Caltex Singapore Masters in 2002. He won again in 2003 when he won the Carlsberg Malaysian Open. Only the second Indian to earn a card – the first was Jeev Milka Singh. He was top putter on the US Tour in 2005 but is still chasing his first win there.

Baddeley, Aaron (AUS)
Born New Hampshire, USA, 17 March 1981
Turned professional 2000
Became the first amateur to win the Australian Open since Bruce Devlin in 1969 and the youngest when he took the title at Royal Sydney in 2000. Then, having turned professional he successfully defended it at Kingston Heath. He had shown considerable promise when at age 15, he qualified for the Victorian Open. Represented Australia in the Eisenhower Trophy and holds both Australian and American passports. Played a limited schedule in 2002 despite having a European Tour card. Continues to play on the US Tour and scored his first victory in 2006 when he took the Verizon Heritage at Harbour Town.

Baiocchi, Hugh (RSA)
Born Johannesburg, 17 August 1946
Turned professional 1971
A scratch golfer when he was 15, Hugh Baiocchi joined the Senior PGA Tour after playing with distinction for 23 years on the European Tour. He has played in 31 different countries around the world winning in many of them. He gained an extra special delight at winning the 1978 South African Open emulating his long-time golfing hero Gary Player who is a multiple winner of that title.

Baker-Finch, Ian (AUS)
Born Namour, Queensland, 24 October 1960
Turned professional 1979
Impressive winner of the Open Championship in 1991 he emerged as a tremendous ambassador for golf. Sadly in attempting to hit the ball further off the tee he lost his game completely when teeing up in Tour events and was forced, after an agonising spell, to retire prematurely. After having been given the chance by Channel Seven producer Graeme Rowland to commentate in Australia, he took up the opportunity to do a similar job for the American ABC network until they ceased covering golf.

Charles, Sir Bob (NZL)
Born Auckland, 14 March 1936
Turned professional 1960
Three years after turning professional he became the first and still the only New Zealander to win the Open Championship. He defeated Phil Rodgers in the last 36-hole play-off for the title at Royal Lytham and St Annes then was runner-up in 1968 to Gary Player at Carnoustie and in 1969 to Tony Jacklin again at Lytham. Earlier in 1954 he had won the first of his four New Zealand Opens as an amateur. Between 1954 and 1960 worked in a bank before embarking on a golf career which has seen him win extensively around the world on golf's main Tours and the US Senior Tour. He won seven times on the US Tour, nine times in Europe, 24

times in New Zealand and has also won in Canada, Japan and South Africa. He does everything right-handed except games requiring two hands. In 1972 received the OBE from Her Majesty the Queen, the CBE in 1992 and was knighted in 1999 for his services to golf. He had for many years been the only left-hander to win a major but that changed when Canadian Mike Weir won the Masters in a play-off at Augusta in 2003. He has announced his retirement but continues to play a very limited schedule on the European Senior Tour and US Champions Tour.

Choi, Kyoung-Ju (KOR)

Born Wando, South Korea, 19 May 1970
When his high school teacher suggested he take up golf, he studied all Jack Nicklaus' videos. Son of a rice farmer he was the first Korean to earn a US Tour card and won twice in 2002. In 2003 he became the first Korean to win on the Euopean Tour when he won the Linde German Masters. Better known as KJ Choi, he won the Chrysler Championship in America in 2006.

Cole, Bobby (RSA)

Born Springs, 11 May 1948
Turned professional 1966
Winner of the Amateur Championship in 1966 when he beat R.D.B.M. Shade in the final which because of haar (fog) was reduced to 18 holes. Among his victories when he turned professional were two South African Opens in 1974 and 1980.

Davis, Rodger (AUS)

Born Sydney, 18 May 1951
Turned professional 1974
Experienced Australian competitor who came joint second in the 1987 Open Championship behind Nick Faldo at Muirfield. A regular on the European Tour he

Sir Bob Charles

© Phil Sheldon Golf Picture Library

hopes to extend his playing career on the US Senior circuit. Winner of 27 titles, 19 of them on the Australasian circuit where, in 1988, he picked up an Aus$1 million first prize in the Bicentennial event at Royal Melbourne. Gave up golf for a while but lost all his money in a hotel venture that went wrong and took up tournament play again. Usually plays in trademark 'plus twos'. Now a regular on the US Champions Tour.

Elkington, Steve (AUS)

Born Inverell, 8 December 1962
Turned professional 1985
A former Australian (1990 and 1991) and New Zealand (1990) champion he is a regular winner these days on the US Tour despite an allergy to grass. At Riviera CC in Los Angeles in 1995 he beat Colin Montgomerie in a play-off for the US PGA Championship, the only major he has won to date. Winner of the 1992 Australian Open he has one of the finest swings in golf. He is also an accomplished artist in his spare time. He has played four times since 1994 in the Presidents Cup. In 2002 after prequalifying for the event at Dunbar he played off for the Open title at Muirfield with Thomas Levet, Stuart Appleby and eventual winner Ernie Els. He nearly won the US PGA Championship in 2005 finishing second tied with Thomas Bjørn behind Phil Mickelson at Baltusrol.

Els, Ernie (RSA)

Born Johannesburg, 17 October 1969
Turned professional 1989
Teenage winner of the South African Amateur Championship in 1996 he is renowned as one of the game's big hitters. His short game can be deadly too and when on song he is one of the most impressive international performers. He has won two US Opens – in 1994 at Oakmont after a play-off against Loren Roberts and Colin Montgomerie and at Congressional where he beat Montgomerie into second place. Although proficient at Rugby Union and cricket he decided to concentrate on golf when he played off scratch at age 14. He has matched Gary Player's record of winning three successive South African Opens and has collected the South African PGA and Masters titles as well. In 1994 equalled the European Tour record of 12 birdies in the 61 he fired en route to victory in the Dubai Desert Classic. He was made an honorary member of the PGA European Tour in recognition of his two US Open wins and his three successive World Match Play title successes round the famous West Course. Going for a fourth successive win in 1997 he lost on the last green to Vijay Singh. In 2002 Els won the Heineken Classic at Royal Melbourne, the Dubai Desert Classic and the Genuity Championship on the US Tour before realising his life-long dream by winning the Open Championship at Muirfield 43 years after Gary Player had won at the same venue. He beat Frenchman Thomas Levet in a sudden-death play-off at the first extra hole after tieing with him in a four hole play-off which also involved Australians Stuart Appleby and Steve Elkington. All had finished on six-under-par 268. Els played a brilliant recovery from an awkward lie in a greenside trap at the 18th to make the par that earned him his third major title victory. By winning he ended Tiger Woods' hopes of winning all four majors in the same year. Woods had won the Masters and US Open earlier.

He made a whirlwind start of 2003 winning twice in America at the Mercedes Championship where he won with a record 31 under total and the Sony Open in Hawaii and twice on the European Tour taking the Heineken Classic at Royal Melbourne and the Johnnie Walker Classic for the second time. At the Johnnie Walker at Lake Karinyup he was at his blistering best, powering 315 yards plus drives and shooting a remarkable 29-under-par. By the start of September he had added the Barclay's Scottish Open and the Omega European Masters and the HSBC World Match Play Championship and ended up top money earner on the European Tour. At the start of 2004 he shot a record 60 in the first round of the Heineken Classic at Royal Melbourne, eventually winning that event for a third successive year. It proved to be a frustrating year for him in the majors. He lost The Masters by a shot to Phil Mickelson, was beaten in a play-off for the Open at Royal Troon by Todd Hamilton and missed the play-off for the USPGA Championship by a shot. His wins included the American Express Championship at Mount Juliet. He won the HSBC World Matchplay title for a record sixth time and for the second year running was European No 1 becoming the first player to earn more than 4 million euro in a season. During his 2004 European season he was out of the top ten just once in 15 starts. He made a fast start to 2005 winning the Dubai Desert Classic and Qatar Masters in successive weeks and later the BMW Asian Open by 13 shots in Shanghai. He played poorly at The Masters finishing 47th, was 15th in the US Open and 34th at St Andrews in the Open – his last event for six months following a cruciate ligament injury sustained while on holiday. He only returned to action at Sun City late in the year then won the dunhill at Leopard Creek and came second to Retief Goosen in the SAA Open at Fancourt. In 2006, he took time to get back to his best but was still one of ten golfers who played four rounds in all four majors. In 2006 he finished 5th on the European money list and 28th in America.

Fernandez, Vicente (ARG)
Born Corrientes, 5 May 1946
Turned professional 1964
After playing on the European Tour where he won five times between 1975 and 1992 he joined the US Senior Tour competing with considerable success. In this respect he was following in the footsteps of fellow Argentinian Roberto de Vicenzo. Born with one leg shorter than the other which is why he limps, he is remembered in Europe for the 87 foot putt he holed up three tiers on the final green at The Belfry in 1992 to win the Murphy's English Open. His nickname is 'Chino'.

Franco, Carlos (PAR)
Born Asunción, 24 May 1965
Turned professional 1986
Emerged on to the international stage from humble beginnings. He was one of a family of nine who shared a one-room home at the course where his father was greens superintendent and caddie. All five of his brothers play golf and he was appointed Paraguayan Minister of Sport in 1999. Won twice in his rookie year on the US Tour and became the first player to make more than $1 million in his first two seasons. Has scored

three wins on the US circuit, five times in Japan where he had 11 top 10 finishes in 1997, once in the Philippines and 19 times in South America. First made headlines at St Andrews when he beat Sam Torrance in the Alfred Dunhill Cup.

Frost, David (RSA)
Born Cape Town, 11 September 1959
Turned professional 1981
Although now based permanently in the United States has won as many titles overseas as on the US Tour. The 1993 season was his best in America when he made over $1 million in prize money and finished fifth on the money list. He has established a vineyard in South Africa growing 100 acres of vines on the 300-acre estate. He has very quickly earned a reputation for producing quality wines.

Goosen, Retief (RSA)
Born Pietersburg, 3 February 1969
Turned professional 1990
Introduced to golf at the age of 11 he scored his first major success when leading from start to finish at the 2001 US Open at Tulsa and then beating Mark Brooks in the 18-hole play-off by two shots. Although he suffered health problems after being hit by lightning as a teenager he has enjoyed a friendly rivalry with South Africa's other talented young player Ernie Els. Winner of the 1990 South African Amateur title, he scored his first professional victory in the Iscor Newcastle Classic a year later. In Europe where he has been helped by Belgian psychologist Jos Vanstiphout, golf's quiet achiever enjoys playing in France where he has won two French Championships (1997 and 1999) and the Trophée Lancôme in 2000. Just weeks after his US Open win in 2001 he led again from start to finish to win the Scottish Open at Loch Lomond. In 2002 he was a runaway eight shot winner in the Johnnie Walker Classic at Lake Karynup in Perth, Australia. In 2004 he again won the US Open, this time at Shinnecock Hills GC on Long Island producing in the process not only superb control from tee to green but incredibly controlled putting on lightning fast greens on the first day to prevent Phil Mickelson winning his second major of the year. Goosen single-putted 11 of the first 17 holes of his final round of 71. A week later he returned to Europe to win the Smurfit European Open at the K Club. In 2005 after finishing tied third at The Masters, he was leading going into the last round of the US Open but shot a closing 81 to miss out on a successful defence of his title. He finished 11th behind Michael Campbell but was fifth at The Open and 6th at the US PGA Championship. He played again in the Presidents Cup and beat Tiger Woods in the singles at Lake Mannassas. Playing on both sides of the Atlantic he finished fourth on the European money list and eighth on the US list in 2005. Late in the year he beat Ernie Els for the SAA Open at Fancourt. He continued to play steadily throughout 2006. In 2006 he finished 19th on the US money list and was 12th in Europe.

Grady, Wayne (AUS)
Born Brisbane, 26 July 1957
Turned professional 1973 and again in 1978
One of Australia's most popular players he won the US PGA Championship at Shoal Creek by three shots over

Fred Couples. A year earlier he had tied with Greg Norman and eventual winner Mark Calcavecchia for the Open Championship losing out in the first ever four-hole play-off for the title. Took over in 2001 as chairman of the Australasian Tour from Jack Newton and was the architect of a tie up between the Australasian Tour and the US Nationwide Tour for two joint events a year. With a reduced playing schedule he now commentates regularly for the BBC golf team with Peter Alliss.

Graham, David (AUS)
Born Windsor, Tasmania, 23 May 1946
Turned professional 1962
Played superbly for a closing 67 round Merion to win the 1981 US Open Championship from George Burns and Bill Rogers. That day he hit every green in regulation. Two years earlier he had beaten Ben Crenshaw at the third extra hole at Oakland Hills to win the US PGA Championship. When he took up the game at age 14 he played with left-handed clubs before making the switch to a right-handed set. Awarded the Order of Australia for his services to golf he is a member of the Cup and Tee committee that sets up Augusta each year for the Masters. A regular winner around the world in the 70s and 80s he won eight times on the US Tour between 1972 and 1983. Now plays on the US Senior Tour but also has gained a considerable reputation as a course designer.

Hayes, Dale (RSA)
Born Pretoria, 1 July 1952
Turned professional 1970
Former South African amateur stroke play champion who was a regular winner in South Africa and Europe after turning professional. He was Europe's top money earner in 1975 but retired from competitive golf to move into business. He is now a successful television commentator in South Africa with a weekly programme of his own often working as a double act with veteran Denis Hutchinson.

Hensby, Mark (AUS)
Born Melbourne, 29 June 1972
Turned professional 1995
Played well in three of the four majors in 2005 finishing fifth in The Masters, third in the US Open and just outside the top 10 in the Open. On a rare visit to Europe he landed first prize in the Scandinavian Masters at Kungsangen but only after a play-off with Henrik Stenson. Earned a place for the first time in the Rest of the World President's Cup side.

Immelman, Trevor (RSA)
Born Cape Town, South Africa, 16 December 1979
Turned professional 1999
Son of Johan Immelman, executive director of the South African Sunshine Tour, Trevor, who had played his early professional golf in Europe before moving to the United States, won his first PGA title when he held off a strong field at the Cialis Western Open at Cog Hill.

Jaidee, Thongchai (THA)
Born Lop Buri, Thailand, 8 November 1969
Turned professional 1999
The first Thai golfer to win a title on the European Tour when he won the Carlsberg Malaysian Open in 2004. Learned his golf using a bamboo pole with an old 5-iron head and did not play his first nine holes until he was 16. An ex-paratrooper, Jaidee qualified and played all four rounds in the 2001 US Open. An impressive regular on the Asian Tour.

Mamat, Mardan (SIN)
Born Singapore, 31 October 1967
Turned professional 1994
Became the first Singaporean to win an Asian/European joint venture in his home country when he took the Osim Singapore Masters in 2006.

Marsh, Graham (AUS)
Born Kalgoorlie, Western Australia, 14 January 1944
Turned professional 1968
A notable Australian who followed up his international playing career by gaining a reputation for designing fine courses. Although he played in Europe, America and Australasia he spent most of his time on the Japanese circuit where he had 17 wins between 1971 and 1982 but won 11 times in Europe and scored victories also in the United States, India, Thailand and Malaysia. He now plays on the US Senior Tour.

Monasterio, Cesar (ARG)
Born Buenos Aires, 28 November 1963
Turned professional 1990
Became the latest Argentinian to win on the European Tour when he triumphed at the Aa St Omer Open.

Nagle, Kel (AUS)
Born North Sydney, 21 December 1920
Turned professional 1946
In the dramatic Centenary Open at St Andrews in 1960 he edged out Arnold Palmer, winner already that year of the Masters and US Open, to become champion. It was the finest moment in the illustrious career of a golfer who has been a wonderful ambassador for his country. Along with Peter Thomson he competed nine times in the World Cup winning the event in 1954. He is an honorary member of the Royal and Ancient Golf Club of St Andrews.

Newton, Jack (AUS)
Born Sydney, 30 January 1950
Turned professional 1969
Runner-up to Tom Watson after a play-off in the 1975 Open at Carnoustie and runner-up to Seve Ballesteros in the 1980 Masters at Augusta, he was a popular personality on both sides of the Atlantic and in his native Australia only to have his playing career ended prematurely when he walked into the whirling propeller of a plane at Sydney airport. He lost an eye, an arm and had considerable internal injuries but the quick action of a surgeon who happened to be around

probably saved his life. Learned to play one-handed and still competes in pro-ams successfully. Until his retirement in 2000 he was chairman of the Australasian Tour and remains Australia's most respected golf commentator.

Nobilo, Frank (NZL)
Born Auckland, 14 May 1960
Turned professional 1979
Injury has affected his career in recent years but he remains one of his country's most popular players with an excellent swing. After winning regularly in Europe he moved to America where in 1997 he won the Greater Greensboro Classic. He has represented New Zealand in nine World Cup matches between 1982 and 1999, played in 11 Alfred Dunhill Cups and three Presidents Cup sides. Now a successful and much respected television analyst for the Golf Channel.

Norman, Greg (AUS)
Born Mount Isa, Queensland, 10 February 1955
Turned professional 1976
Australia's most prolific winner in recent years credited with 77 victories worldwide (as of July 2001) but has slowed down because of injury and trimmed his schedule in recent times. He won the Open in tough conditions at Turnberry in 1986 and again in glorious weather at Royal St George's in 1993 when he fired the lowest winning aggregate of 267 (66, 68, 69, 64). Decided to take up golf after caddying for his mother and abandoned plans to join the Australian Air Force. One of the few golfers to have topped the official money lists on both sides of the Atlantic he received his first winner's cheque in the Westlake Classic on the Australian Tour in 1976. Has the unhappy reputation of having lost Majors in three different types of play-off – the 1987 Masters to Larry Mize and the 1993 US PGA to Paul Azinger in sudden death, the Open to Mark Calcavecchia at Royal Troon in a four-hole play-off in 1989 and the US Open over 18 holes to Fuzzy Zoeller at Winged Foot in 1984. In 1986 he led going into the final round of all four Majors that year and won only the Open. During his career he has set all kinds of money records on the US Tour but is jinxed at the US Masters where he has finished second three times. He has also been runner-up on five other occasions in Majors. Today spends more time in the boardroom looking after his business interests than playing.

Ogilvy, Geoff (AUS)
Born Adelaide, South Australia
Turned professional 1998
He became the first Australian to win a major since Steve Elkington's success in the USPGA Championship in 1992 when he won the US Open at Winged Foot beating Colin Montgomerie, Jim Furyk and Phil Mickelson into second place.

Ozaki, 'Jumbo' Masashi (JPN)
Born Kaiman Town, Tokushima, 24 January 1947
Turned professional 1980
Along with Isao Aoki is Japan's best known player, but unlike Aoki has maintained his base in Japan where he

Greg Norman

has scored over 80 victories. His only overseas win was the New Zealand Open early in his career. He is a golfing icon in his native country. His two brothers Joe (Naomichi) and Jet also play professionally. In 2005 declared bankrupt.

Pampling, Rod (AUS)
Born Redcliffe, Queensland, 23 September 1969
Turned professional 1994
Made his breakthrough as a winner on the US Tour when he took The International in 2004. His wife Angela is a clinical psychologist. In 2006 he won the Bay Hill Invitational and later in the year partnered Jerry Kelly to success in the Merrill Lynch Shoot Out.

Parry Craig (AUS)
Born Sunshine, Victoria, Australia 12 January 1966.
Turned professional 1985.
Australian Parry, winner of 18 titles internationally but never a winner on the US Tour, put that right in 2002 when he landed the World Golf Championship NEC Invitational at Sahalee in Washington to pick up his largest career cheque – $1 million. After 15 years of trying to win in America the chances of him being successful at Salahee seemed slim having missed the four previous cuts. However, the 300-1 long-shot played and putted beautifully covering the last 48 holes without making a bogey to win by four from another Australian Robert Allenby and American Fred Funk. Tiger Woods, trying to win the event for a record fourth-successive year was fourth. Only Gene Sarazen and Walter Hagen have ever won the same four titles in successive years. It was Parry's 236th tournament in the United States and moved him from 118th in the world to 45th. In 2004 he eagled the hardest hole on the US Tour in a play-off with Scott Verplank to win the Ford Championship in Florida.

Phadungsil, Chinarat (THA)
Born Bangkok, Thailand   Turned professional 2005
He became the youngest winner on the Asian Tour when he beat Shiv Kapur at the second hole of their

play-off for the Double A International title at the St Andrews Hill (2000) GC in Rayong, Thailand. The reigning World Junior champion, he was only 17 years and 5 days when he won and immediately turned professional.

Player, Gary (RSA)
Born Johannesburg, 1 November 1935
Turned professional 1953
One of the modern Big Three with Arnold Palmer and Jack Nicklaus, he has won 167 titles worldwide including nine Majors between 1959 and 1978 and nine senior Majors between 1986 and 1997. His Major wins include three Open Championships in 1959 at Muirfield, 1968 at Carnoustie and 1974 at Royal Lytham and St Annes, three US Masters in 1961, 1974 and 1978, the US Open in 1965 when he completed a Grand Slam of major titles and the US PGA Championship in 1962 and 1972. A life-long fitness fanatic who has won titles in five decades he is one of only five players to have won all four Major titles. Gene Sarazen, Ben Hogan, Jack Nicklaus and Tiger Woods are the others. He considers the greatest thrill of his life was becoming the third man in history to do so. Having never based himself full-time in the US he has travelled more miles than any other golfer during his career – an estimated 12 million by the end of 2000. He entered his first Open in 1955 and failed to qualify but finished fourth in 1956 and played for the last time at Royal Lytham and St Annes in 2001 when 66. One of his most dramatic major performances came when he went into the last round seven shots behind Hubert Green at the 1974 US Masters, came home in 30 and equalled the then record 64 to win. He scored a record seven wins in the Australian Open, took the South African Open a record 13 times and won the World Match Play title a record-equalling five times coming from seven down after 19 holes in one tie in 1965 to beat Tony Lema at the 37th. Credited as being one of the game's greatest bunker players he remains as enthusiastic about competing today as he did when he first took up the game. In 2006, he received the Payne Stewart award for his services to golf and to charity work, especially in Africa.

Price, Nick (ZIM)
Born Durban, South Africa, 28 January 1957
Turned professional 1977
One of the game's most popular players his greatest season was 1990 when he took six titles including the Open at Turnberry when he beat Jesper Parnevik and the US PGA at Southern Hills when Corey Pavin was second. He had scored his first Major triumph two years earlier when he edged out John Cook, Nick Faldo, Jim Gallagher Jr and Gene Sauers at the US PGA at Bellerive, St Louis. Along with Tiger Woods his record of 15 wins in the 90s was the most by any player. One of only seven players to win consecutive Majors, the others being Ben Hogan, Jack Nicklaus, Arnold Palmer, Lee Trevino, Tom Watson and Tiger Woods. Four times a Presidents Cup player he jointly holds the Augusta National record of 63 with Greg Norman. One of only two players in the 90s to win two Majors in a year, the others being Nick Faldo in 1990 and Mark O'Meara in 1998. Born of English parents but brought up in Zimbabwe he played his early

golf with Mark McNulty and Tony Johnstone. Winner of 41 titles by end of August 2003. In 2002 he was named recipient of the Payne Stewart Award which goes to the player who respects the traditions of the game and works to uphold them. In 2003, ten years after being named PGA Tour Player of the Year, he was inducted into the World Golf Hall of Fame.

Randhawa, Jyoti (IND)
Born New Delhi, 4 May 1972
First Indian winner on the Japanese Tour when he triumphed in the 2003 Suntory Open. Son of an Indian general, he was top earner on the Asian PGA Tour in 2002 despite missing several events after breaking his collarbone in a motorcycle accident.

Romero, Eduardo (ARG)
Born Cordoba, Argentina, 12 July 1954
Turned professional 1982
Son of the Cordoba club professional he learned much from former Open champion Roberto de Vicenzo and has inherited his grace and elegance as a competitor. A wonderful ambassador for Argentina he briefly held a US Tour card in 1994 but prefers to play his golf these days on the European Tour where he has won seven times including impressively at the 1999 Canon European Masters where he improved his concentration after studying Indian yoga techniques. Used his own money to sponsor Angel Cabrera with whom he finished second in the 2000 World Cup in Buenos Aries behind Tiger Woods and David Duval. Beat Frederick Andersson in a play-off in 2002 to win the Barclays Scottish Open at Loch Lomond but lost to Padraig Harrington in a play-off for the US$800,000 first prize in the Dunhill Links Championship at St Andrews. Continued playing well in 2003 and insists practising yoga helps. Joined the Senior ranks in July 2004.

Schwartzel, Charl (RSA)
Born Johannesburg, 31 August 1984
Turned professional 2002
He was playing off plus 4 when he turned professional after an amateur career that had seen him represent South Africa in the Eisenhower Trophy. In only his third event as a professional he finished joint third in the South African Airways Open and became a winner in his 56th event when he won the dunhill championship in a play-off at Leopard Creek. He was South African No.1 in season 2004–5 and was again No.1 in the 2005–6 season.

Scott, Adam (AUS)
Born Adelaide, 16 July 1980
Turned professional 2000
Highly regarded young Australian who was ranked World No. 2 amateur when he turned professional in 2000. Coached in the early days by his father Phil, himself a golf professional, Scott now uses Butch Harmon whom he met while attending the University of Las Vegas. Swings very much like another Harmon client Tiger Woods. He made headlines as an amateur when he fired a 10-under-par 63 at the Lakes in the Greg Norman Holden International in 2000 but has shot 62 in the US Junior Championship at Los Coyotes CC. Made his European Tour card in just eight starts

and secured his first Tour win when beating Justin Rose in the 2001 Alfred Dunhill Championship at Houghton in Johannesburg. In 2002 he won at Qatar and at Gleneagles Hotel when he won the Diageo Scottish PGA Championship by ten shots with a 26 under par total. He was 22 under par that week for the par 5 holes. In 2003 he was an impressive winner of the Scandinavian Masters at Barsebäck in Sweden and the Deutsche Bank Championship on the US Tour. In 2005 when he again played in the Presidents Cup, his victories included the Johnnie Walker Classic on the European and Asian Tours, the Singapore Open on the Asian Tour and the Nissan Open on the US Tour. In 2006, he won the Players Championship and Tour Championship in America moving to third in the World rankings in mid November. He also won the Singapore Open again.

Senden, John (AUS)
Born Brisbane, Queensland, 20 April 1971
Turned professional 1992
After finishing in the top 10 of Australia's three main events in 2005 he played in America in 2006 and was one of seven Australian winners. His success came in the John Deere Classic. He made over $1 million and finished inside the top 50 on the money list.

Senior, Peter (AUS)
Born Singapore, 31 July 1959
Turned professional 1978
One of Australia's most likeable and underrated performers who has been a regular winner over the years on the Australian, Japanese and European circuits. Converted to the broomstick putter by Sam Torrance – a move that saved his playing career. A former winner of the Australian Open, Australian PGA and Australian Masters titles he had considerable success off the course when he bought a share in a pawn-broking business. Senior now plays irregularly outside Australia.

Sheehan, Paul (AUS)
Born Woolagong, NSW, 26 January 1977
Turned professional 1999
A former Australian junior tennis champion who turned to golf and played the Australasian, Asian and Japanese circuits. In 2006 he won the Japanese Open.

Singh, Jeev Milkha (IND)
Born Chandigarh, India, 15 December 1971
Turned professional 1993
Stylish swinger, he won his first European event when he took the Volvo China Open in Beijing in 2006 but he scored an even greater triumph when he picked up the first prize at the Volvo Masters at Valderrama later in the year. He is the son of the former Olympian Milkha Singh who won a medal in the 1980 games.

Singh, Vijay (FIJ)
Born Lautoka, 22 February 1963
Turned professional 1982
An international player who began his career in Australasia, he became the first Fijian to win a major when he won the 1998 US PGA Championship at Sahalee but may well be remembered more for his victory in the 2000 US Masters which effectively prevented Tiger Woods winning all four Majors in a year. Tiger went on to win the US Open, Open and US PGA Championship that year and won the Masters the following year to hold all four Major titles at the one time. Introduced to golf by his father, an aeroplane technician, Vijay modelled his swing on that of Tom Weiskopf. Before making the grade on the European Tour where he won the 1992 Volvo German Open by 11 shots he was a club professional in Borneo. He has won tournaments in South Africa, Malaysia, the Ivory Coast, Nigeria, France, Zimbabwe, Morocco, Spain, England, Germany, Sweden, Taiwan and the United States. He ended Ernie Els' run of victories in the World Match Play Championship when he beat him in the final by one hole in 1997 when the South African was going for a fourth successive title. One of the game's most dedicated practisers. In 2003 he won the Phoenix Open, the EDS Byron Nelson Championship, the John Deere Classic and the Funai Classic. With 10 top ten finishes in his last 11 starts, Singh ended Woods' run as top money earner when he finished with a grand total of $7,753,907 – the second largest total in Tour history but was not named Player of the Year. Woods was again the players' choice. In 2004 he had his best ever season and by mid-October was approaching $10 million in year-long winnings on the US Tour, having won eight times, matching Johnnie Miller's eight wins in 1974. Finally edged out Woods for the No.1 spot and earned his third major and second USPGA Championship title with a play-off victory at Whistling Straits. He won four times in 2005 – the Sony Open, the Shell Houston Open, the Buick Open, and the Wachovia Championship – played 30 events on the US Tour but had to be content with second place in the money list to Tiger Woods.

Sterne, Richard (RSA)
Born Pretoria 27 August 1981
Turned professional 2001
Former world junior champion he made history as an amateur in Siouth Africa when becoming the first player to win the junior and senior stroke and matchplay titles. He scored his first European Tour success when he won the Open de Madrid in 2004.

Thomson CBE, Peter (AUS)
Born Melbourne, 23 August 1929
Turned professional 1949
He is one of only four players who have won five Open Championships. At the start of the 20th century J.H. Taylor and James Braid won five, and Tom Watson won five in eight years from 1975 while Thomson completed his five victories between 1954 and 1965. In one seven-year spell from 1952 Thomson never finished worse than second in the Championship. His run of finishes from 1952 was 2, 2, 1, 1, 1, 2, 1. His fifth victory, arguably his most impressive, came at Royal Birkdale in 1965 when more Americans were in the field. He played only three times in the US Open finishing fourth in 1956. He played in five US Masters with fifth his best finish in 1957. He won three Australian Opens and in Europe had 24 victories between 1954 and 1972. With one of the most fluent and reliable swings he made golf look easy. Instrumental in developing the game throughout Asia, Africa and the Middle East he was ready to retire from

golf and pursue a career in Australian politics but he was not elected and turned instead to the US Senior Tour with great success. In 1985 he won nine Senior Tour titles. Has captained three Rest of the World Presidents Cup sides, was elected to the World Golf Hall of Fame in 1988 and is an honorary member of the Royal and Ancient Golf Club of St Andrews. After his retirement from top-line golf he concentrated on his hugely successful golf course designing business based in Melbourne completing projects in many countries around the world.

De Vicenzo, Roberto (ARG)
Born Buenos Aires, 14 April 1923
Turned professional 1938
Although he won the Open in 1967 at Royal Liverpool this impressive South American is perhaps best known for the Major title he might have won. In 1968 he finished tied with Bob Goalby at Augusta or he thought he had. He had finished birdie, bogey to do so but sadly signed for the par 4 that had been inadvertently and carelessly put down for the 17th by Tommy Aaron who was marking his card. Although everyone watching on television and at the course saw the Argentinian make 3 the fact that he signed for 4 was indisputable and he had to accept that there would be no play-off. It remains one of the saddest incidents in golf with the emotion heightened by the fact that that Sunday was de Vicenzo's 45th birthday. The gracious manner in which he accepted the disappointments was remarkable. What a contrast to the scenes at Hoylake nine months earlier when, after years of trying, he finally won the Open beating Jack Nicklaus and Clive Clark in the process thanks to a pressure-packed brilliant last round 70. In fact he was runner-up in the event in 1950 and came third six times. The father of South American golf he was a magnificent driver and is credited with having won over 200 titles in his extraordinary career including nine Argentinian Opens between 1944 and 1974 plus the 1957 Jamaican, 1950 Belgian, 1950 Dutch, 1950, 1960 and 1964 French, 1964 German Open and 1966 Spanish Open titles. He played 15 times for Argentina in the World Cup and four times for Mexico. Inducted into the World Golf Hall of Fame in 1989 he is an honorary member of the Royal and Ancient Golf Club of St Andrews. Planned to return to Britain for the 2006 Open Championship at Hoylake were he had won in 1967 but could not make it.

Weir, Mike (CAN)
Born Sarnia, Ontario, 12 May 1970
Turned professional 1992
A left-hander, he was the first Canadian to play in the Presidents Cup when he made the side in 2000 and the first from his country to win a World Golf Championship event when he took the American Express Championship at Valderrama in 2000. Wrote to Jack Nicklaus as a 13-year-old to enquire whether or not he should switch from playing golf left-handed to right-handed and was told not to switch. In 1997 he led the scoring averages on the Canadian Tour with a score of 69.29 but his greatest triumph came when he became

only the second left-hander to win a major when he played beautifully and putted outstandingly to beat Len Mattiace for a Masters Green Jacket. Weir had to hole from 15 feet at the last to take the tournament into extra holes but won his first major title when Mattiace failed to par the tenth – the first extra hole. He has now assumed hero status in Canada.

Wi, Charlie (KOR)
Born 3 January 1972
Turned professional 1995
The popular Korean-American won his first European Tour title when he won the jointly-promoted Asian/European event at Kuala Lumpur in 2006. His success in the Maybank Malaysian Open was well deserved.

Wirachant, Thawarn (THA)
Born Bangkok, Thailand, 28 December 1966
Turned professional 1987
He earned a full year's exemption on the European Tour when he won the Enjoy Jakarta Standard Chartered Indonesian Open – a joint venture between the Asian and European Tours. It was his sixth win on the Asian Tour which he joined 10 years earlier. Wirachant is best known for his unorthodox swing which works effectively for him. He is a former Thai Amateur champion.

Yang, Yong-eun (KOR)
Born Seoul, Korea, 15 January 1972
Turned professional 1996
Winner of four events on the Japanese Tour between 2004 and 2006 and with wins on the Korean circuit and Asian Tour on which he played from 1998 to 2003, he shot to prominence when he beat World No. 1 Tiger Woods into second place in the $5m dollar HSBC Champions tournament at Sheshan in Shanghai in 2006. Yang, who won a first prize cheque of $833,300, by far his largest, not only beat Woods but had former US Open champions Michael Campbell (NZL) and Retief Goosen (RSA) behind him in joint third spot. The HSBC event is the richest in Asia.

Yeh, Wei-tze (TPE)
Born Taiwan, 20 February 1973
Turned professional 1994
Fisherman's son who became the third Asia golfer after "Mr Lu" and Isao Aoki to win on the European Tour when he won the 2000 Benson and Hedges Malaysian Open. In 2003 he won the ANA Open on the Japanese Tour.

Zhang, Lian-Wei (CHN)
Born Shenzhen, 2 May1965
Turned professional 1994
Leading Chinese player whose victory in the 2003 Caltex Singapore Open when he edged out Ernie Els was the first by a Chinese golfer on Tour. Initially he trained as a javelin thrower before turning to golf. Self-taught he was also the first Asian golfer to win on the Canadian Tour but remains a stalwart on the Asian circuit.

European Golfers – Women

Great Britain and Ireland

Andrew, K.	Davies, L.	Irvin, A.	McKenna, M.	Reid, D.
Bailey, D.	Dowling, C.	Jackson, B.	Matthew, C.	Robertson, B.
Bisgood, J.	Duggleby, E.	Johnson, T.	Moodie, J.	Saunders, V.
Bonallack, A.	Gerrett, M.	Laing, A.	Nicholas, A.	Stupples, K.
Butler, I.	Garvey, P.	Lawrence, J.	Otto, J.	Thomas, V.
Coughlan, C.	Harris, M.	Lee-Smith, J.	Panton-Lewis, C.	Walker, M.
Davidson, A.	Hudson, R.	McKay, M.	Price Fisher, E.	Wright, J.

Andrew, Kim (née Rostron) (ENG)
Born 12 February 1974
After taking the English and Scottish Ladies stroke play titles in 1997 she won the Ladies British Open Amateur a year later. She played in the 1998 and 2000 Curtis Cup matches.

Bailey MBE, Mrs Diane (Frearson née Robb) (ENG)
Born Wolverhampton, 31 August 1943
After playing in the 1962 and 1972 Curtis Cup matches she captained the side in 1984, 1986 and 1988. In 1984 at Muirfield the Great Britain and Ireland side lost narrowly to the Americans but she led the side to a first ever victory on American soil at Prairie Dunes in Kansas two years later. The result was a convincing 13-5. She was in charge again when the GB & I side held on to the Cup two years later this time by 11-7 at Royal St George's.

Bisgood CBE, Jeanne (ENG)
Born Richmond, Surrey, 11 August 1923
Three times English Ladies champion in 1951, 1953 and 1957. Having played in three Curtis Cups she captained the side in 1970. Between 1952 and 1955 she won the Swedish, Italian, German, Portuguese and Norwegian Ladies titles.

Bonallack, Lady Angela (née Ward) (ENG)
Born Birchington, Kent, 7 April 1937
Wife of Sir Michael Bonallack OBE she played in six Curtis Cup matches. She was leading amateur in the 1975 and 1976 Colgate European Opens, won two English Ladies titles and had victories, too, in the Swedish, German, Scandinavian and Portuguese Championships.

Butler, Ita (née Burke) (IRL)
Born Nenagh, County Tipperary
Having played in the Curtis Cup in 1966, she captained the side that beat the Americans by 5 points at Killarney thirty years later.

Coughlan, Claire (IRL)
Born Cork, 11 March 1980
Made her début in the 2004 Curtis Cup and won three points.

Davidson, Alison (née Rose) (SCO)
Born Stirling, Scotland, 18 June 1968
Twice a Curtis Cup player in 1996 and 1998. She won the Ladies British Open Amateur in 1997.

Davies CBE, Laura (ENG)
Born 10 October 1963
Turned professional 1985
Record-breaking performer who has won over 60 events worldwide including the US and British Women's Opens. For six days in 1987 she held both titles having won the American event before joining the US Tour. Was a founder member of the Women's Tour in Europe where she has won a record 33 times. Still holds the record for the number of birdies in a round – 11 which she scored in the 1987 Open de France Feminin. Her 16-shot victory, by a margin of five shots, in the 1995 Guardian Irish Holidays Open at St Margaret's remains the biggest in European Tour history. Her 267 totals in the 1988 Biarritz Ladies Open and the 1995 Guardian Irish Holidays Open are the lowest on Tour and have been matched only by Julie Inkster in the 2002 Evian Masters. Other major victories include the LPGA Championship twice and the du Maurier Championship. In 1999 she became the first European Tour player to pass through the £1 million in prize-money earnings and finished European No. 1 that year for a record fifth time. She was No.1 again in 2004. The 1996 Rolex Player of the Year in America, she has won almost $5.5 million in US prize-money. Originally honoured with an MBE by Her Majesty the Queen in 1988, she became a CBE in 2000. Enjoys all sports including soccer (she supports Liverpool FC). Among other awards she has received during her career have been the Association of Golf Writers' Trophy for her contribution to European golf in 1994 and the American version in 1994 and 1996 for her performances on the US Tour. In 1994 she became the first golfer to score victories on five different

Laura Davies

Tours – European, American, Australasian, Japanese and Asian in one calendar year. As an amateur she played for Surrey and was a Curtis Cup player in 1984. She has competed in all nine Solheim Cup matches. In 2000 was recognised by the LPGA in their top 50 players and teachers honours list. Laura proved how strong a competitor she still is when she took the No.1 spot on the women's tour in Europe for a seventh time in 2006. Although she only won once she had six second-place finishes and ended the year with a total of €471,727 from the 11 events she played. By the end of 2006 she had stretched her winning record to 67 titles.

Dowling, Clare (née Hourihane) (IRL)
Born 18 February 1958
Won three Irish Ladies Championships in a row – 1983, 1984 and 1985 and won the title again in 1987 and 1991. She won the 1986 British Ladies Stroke play amateur title. Two years earlier she had made the first of five playing appearances in the Curtis Cup before acting as non-playing captain in 2000.

Duggelby, Emma (ENG)
Born Fulford, York, 5 October 1971
Talented English golfer who won the British Ladies Open Amateur Championship in 1994 and the English Ladies in 2000 when she made her Curtis Cup début. She also played in the 2002 and 2004 matches winning three points out of four in 2004.

Garrett, Maureen (née Ruttle) (ENG)
Born 22 August 1922
President of the Ladies' Golf Union from 1982 to 1985, she captained the Curtis Cup (1960) and Vagliano Trophy (1961) teams. In 1983 won the Bobby Jones award presented annually by the United States Golf Association to a person who emulates Jones' spirit, personal qualities and attitude to the game and its players.

Garvey, Philomena (IRL)
Born Drogheda, Co Louth, 27 April 1927
Turned professional 1964 but later reinstated
Winner of the Irish Ladies title 15 times between 1946 and 1970 and six times a Curtis Cup player between 1948 and 1960 she remains one of Ireland's most successful players. In 1957 she won the British Ladies Open Amateur title.

Harris, Marley (née Spearman) (ENG)
Born January 11 1988
Superb ambassador for golf in the 1950s and 1960s whose exuberance and joie de vivre is legendary. Three times a Curtis Cup player she won the British Ladies in 1961 and again in 1962. She was English champion in 1964. In 1962 was awarded the Association of Golf Writers' Trophy for her services to golf.

Hudson, Rebecca (ENG)
Born Doncaster, Yorkshire, 13 June 1979
Turned professional 2002
A member of the 1998, 2000 and 2002 Curtis Cup teams Rebecca is one of the most gifted of younger players. In 2000 she won both the British Match Play and Stroke Play titles, the Scottish and English Stroke play Championships and the Spanish Women's Open. In addition she made the birdie that ensured Great Britain and Ireland won a medal in the World Team Championship for the Espirito Santo Trophy in Berlin in 2000.

Irvin, Ann (ENG)
Born 11 April 1943
Winner of the British Ladies' title in 1973, she played in four Curtis Cup matches between 1962 and 1976. She was Daks Woman Golfer of the Year in 1968 and 1969 and has been active in administration at junior and county level.

Jackson, Bridget (ENG)
Born Birmingham, 10 July 1936
A former President of the Ladies Golf Union she played in three Curtis Cup matches and captained the Vagliano Trophy side twice after having played four times. Although the best she managed in the British Championship was runner-up in 1964 she did win the English, German and Canadian titles.

Johnson, Trish (ENG)
Born Bristol, 17 January 1966
Turned professional 1987
Another stalwart of the Women's Tour in Europe who learned the game at windy Westward Ho. Regular winner on Tour both in Europe and America, she

scored two and a half points out of four in Europe's dramatic Solheim Cup win over the Americans at Loch Lomond in 2000. She has played in seven Solheim Cup matches. She was European no.1 earner in 1990. A loyal supporter of Arsenal FC she regularly attends games at Highbury.

Laing, Anne (SCO)
Born Alexandria, Dunbartonshire, 14 March 1975
Winner of three Scottish Championships in 1996, 2003 and 2004. She made her début in the Curtis Cup in 2004 having played in the Vagliano Trophy in 2003.

Lawrence, Joan (SCO)
Born Kinghorn, Fife, 20 April 1930
After a competitive career in which she three times won the Scottish championship and played in the 1964 Curtis Cup, she has played her part in golf administration. She had two four-year spells as an LGU selector, is treasurer of the Scottish Ladies Golf Association and has also served on the LGU executive.

Lee-Smith, Jennifer (ENG)
Born Newcastle-upon-Tyne, 2 December 1948
Turned professional 1977
After winning the Ladies British Open as an amateur in 1976 was named Daks Woman Golfer of the Year. She played twice in the Curtis Cup before turning professional and winning nine times in a six year run from 1979. For a time she ran her own driving range in southern England and is back living in Kent again after having lived for a time in Florida.

McKay, Mhairi (SCO)
Born Glasgow 18 April 1975
Turned professional 1997
Former British Girls Champion (1992 and 1993) she has played in the Vagliano Trophy and Curtis Cup. She was an All-American when studying at Stanford University and made her first appearance in the Solheim Cup at Barsebäck, Sweden, in 2003.

McKenna, Mary (IRL)
Born Dublin, 29 April 1949
Winner of the British Ladies Amateur Stroke play title in 1979 and eight times Irish champion between 1969 and 1989. One of Ireland's most successful golfers she played in nine Curtis Cup matches and nine Vagliano Trophy matches between 1969 and 1987. She captained the Vagliano team in 1995. Three times a member of the Great Britain and Ireland Espirito Santo Trophy side she went on to captain the team in 1986. She was Daks Woman Golfer of the Year in 1979.

Matthew, Catriona (SCO)
Born Edinburgh, 25 August 1969
Turned professional 1995
Former Scottish Girls Under-21 and Amateur champion, Catriona also won the British Amateur in 1993. She played in the 1990, 1992 and 1994 Curtis Cup matches and made her début in the Solheim Cup at Barsebäck in 2003 and had the honour of holing the winning putt. She performed impressively throughout showing considerable coolness under pressure. She was also a member of the 2005 European team. Now

plays on both sides of the Atlantic. With Janice Moodie came second to Sweden's Annika Sörenstam and Liselotte Neumann in the 2006 Women's World Cup of Golf.

Moodie, Janice (SCO)
Born Glasgow, 31 May 1973
Turned professional 1997
The 1992 Scottish Women's Stroke play champion played in two winning Curtis Cup teams and earned All American honours at San José State University where she graduated with a degree in psychology. She plays both the European and American Tours and in 2000 finished 17th in America and ninth in Europe. Started playing at age 11 and has been helped considerably by Cawder professional Ken Stevely. In the 2000 Solheim Cup she won three out of four points but was controversially left out of the 2002 team despite having won the Asahi Ryokuken International on the LPGA tour. She was reinstated by captain Catrin Nilsmark for the 2003 match at Barsebäck in Sweden. She teamed up well with Catriona Matthew and also won her singles. She played well in the USA in 2004 without managing to win. With Catriona Matthew, came second to Sweden's Annika Sörenstam and Liselotte Neumann in the 2006 Women's World Cup of Golf at Sun City in South Africa.

Nicholas MBE, Alison (ENG)
Born Gibraltar, 6 February 1978
In Solheim Cup golf had a successful partnership with Laura Davies. In addition they have both won the British and US Open Championship. Alison's first win on the European Tour came in the 1987 Weetabix British Open and she added the US Open ten years later after battling with Nancy Lopez who was trying to win her national title for the first time. Alison is a former winner of the Association of Golf Writers' Golfer of the Year award and has been honoured with an MBE. She announced her retirement from top-line competition in 2004.

Otto, Julie (née Wade) (ENG)
Born Ipswich, Suffolk, 10 March 1967
Secretary of the Ladies Golf Union from 1996 to 2000 she was one of the most successful competitors in both individual and team golf. Among the many titles she won were the English Stroke Play in 1987 and 1993, the British Ladies Stroke Play in 1993 and the Scottish Stroke Play in 1991 and 1993. She shared Britain's Golfer of the Year award in 1993 and won it again in 1995 on her own. She played in five Curtis Cups matches including the victories at Royal Liverpool in 1992 and Killarney in 1996 and the drawn match in 1994 at Chattanooga. Now works with the R&A.

Panton-Lewis, Cathy (SCO)
Born Bridge of Allan, Stirlingshire, 14 June 1955
Turned professional 1978
A former Ladies British Open Amateur Champion in 1976 when she was named Scottish Sportswoman of the year. She notched up thirteen victories as a professional on the European tour between 1979 and 1988. Daughter of John Panton, MBE.

Price Fisher, Elizabeth (ENG)
Born London, 17 January 1923
Turned professional 1968 but reinstated as an amateur three years later
Between 1950 and 1960 she played in six Curtis Cup matches and, in addition to her 1959 victory in the British Ladies Championship, also won national titles in Denmark and Portugal. For many years worked for the *Daily Telegraph*.

Reid MBE, Dale (SCO)
Born Ladybank, Fife, 20 March 1959
Turned professional 1979
Scored twenty-one wins in her professional career between 1980 and 1991 and was so successful in leading Europe's Solheim Cup side to victory against the Americans at Loch Lomond in 2000 that she was again captain in 2002 when the Americans won. Following the team's success in the 2000 Solheim Cup she received an MBE.

Robertson MBE, Belle (SCO)
Born Southend, Argyll, 11 April 1936
One of Scotland's most talented amateur golfers who was Scottish Sportswoman of the Year in 1968, 1971, 1978 and 1981. She was Woman Golfer of the Year in 1971, 1981 and 1985. A former Ladies British Open Amateur Champion and six times Scottish Ladies Champion, she competed in nine Curtis Cups acting as non-playing captain in 1974 and 1976.

Saunders, Vivien (ENG)
Born Sutton, Surrey, 24 November 1946
Turned professional 1969
Founder of the Women's Professional Golfers' Association (European Tour) in 1978 and chairman for the first two years. In 1969 she was the first European golfer to qualify for the LPGA Tour in America. No longer playing top-line professional golf, she is keen to be reinstated as an amateur but not finding that easy.

Stupples, Karen (ENG)
Born Dover, England, 24 June 1973
English professional who lives in Orlando but hit the headlines at Sunningdale in the summer of 2004 when she won the Weetabix British Women's Open with a 19 under par total of 269. In the final round she began by making an eagle at the first and holing her second shot for an eagle 2 at the second. She finally clinched victory with the help of three birdies in a row on the back nine. Earlier in the year she had won on the LPGA Tour which she had joined in 1999. She has played golf

since she was 11. She made her début in the Solheim Cup in 2005.

Thomas, Vicki (née Rawlings) (WAL)
Born Northampton, 27 October 1954
One of Wales' most accomplished players who took part in six Curtis Cup matches between 1982 and 1992. She won the Welsh Championship eight times between 1979 and 1994 as well as the British Ladies Stroke Play in 1990.

Walker OBE, Mickey (ENG)
Born Alwoodley, Yorkshire, 17 December 1952
Turned professional 1973
Always a popular and modest competitor she followed up an excellent amateur career by doing well as a professional. Twice a Curtis Cup player she won the Ladies British Open Amateur in 1971 and 1972, the English Ladies in 1973 and had victories, too, in Portugal, Spain and America where she won the 1972 Trans-Mississippi title. She won six times as a professional but is perhaps best known for her stirring captaincy of the first four European Solheim Cup sides leading them to a five point success at Dalmahoy. In 1992 she galvanised her side by playing them tapes of the men's Ryder Cup triumphs. Now a club professional she also works regularly as a television commentator.

Wright, Janette (née Robertson) (SCO)
Born Glasgow, 7 January 1935
Another of Scotland's most accomplished amateur players she competed four times in the Curtis Cup and was four times Scottish champion between 1959 and 1973. Formerly married to the late golf professional Innes Wright her daughter Pamela plays professionally on the LPGA Tour in America.

Wright, Pamela (SCO)
Born Aboyne, Scotland, 26 June 1964
Turned professional 1988
Daughter of former Scottish champion and Curtis Cup golfer Janette Wright and the late Aboyne professional Innes Wright. She played in the first three Solheim Cup matches being a member of the winning team at Dalmahoy in 1992 and was vice-captain in 2000. She was an All-American in 1987 and again in 1988 when she also won Collegiate Golfer of the Year honours. She was LPGA Tour rookie of the year in 1989.

Continent of Europe

Alfredsson, H.	Hjörth, M.	Neumann, L.	Sanchez, A.B.	Varangot, B.
Cavalleri, S.	Koch, K.	Nilsmark, C.	Segard, P.	
Goldschmid, I.	De Lorenzi, M.-L.	Petterson, S.	Sörenstam, A.	
Gustafson, S.	Meunier-Lebouc, P.	Prado, C.	Tinning, I.	

Alfredsson, Helen (SWE)
Born Gothenburg, 9 April 1965
Turned professional 1989
After earning Rookie of the Year on the 1989 European Tour she won the 1992 Ladies' British Open. Two years later she was Gatorade Rookie of the Year on the American LPGA Tour. She has competed in seven Solheim Cup matches and has won titles in Europe, America, Japan and Australia. She has been chosen to captain the Solheim Cup side this year.

Cavalleri, Silvia (ITA)
Born Milan, 10 October 1972
Turned professional 1997
Became the first Italian to win the US Amateur when she beat Robin Burke 5 and 4 at Brae Burn in the final. She was five times Italian National Junior champion and won the British Girls title in 1990 with a 5 and 4 success over E. Valera at Penrith. As a professional her best finish to date is tied second in the 2000 Ladies' Italian Open.

Goldschmid Isa (*née Bevione*) (ITA)
Born Italy, 15 October 1925
One of Italy's greatest amateurs she won her national title 21 times between 1947 and 1974 and was ten times Italian Open champion between 1952 and 1969. Among her other triumphs were victories in the 1952 Spanish Ladies and the 1973 French Ladies.

Gustafson, Sophie (SWE)
Born Saro, 27 December 1973
Turned professional 1992
Winner of the 2000 Weetabix Women's British Open she had studied marketing, economics and law before turning to professional golf. Credits Seve Ballesteros and Laura Davies as the two players most influencing her career. Her first European victory was the 1996 Swiss Open and her first on the USLPGA Tour was the Chick-fil-A Charity Cup in 2000. Played in the 1998, 2000, 2002, 2003 and 2005 Solheim Cup matches.

Hjörth, Maria (SWE)
Born Falun, 10 October 1973
Turned professional 1996
After an excellent amateur career when she won titles in Finland, Norway and Spain (where she won the prestigious Sherry Cup), she attended Stirling University in Scotland on a golf bursary and graduated with a BA honours degree in English before turning professional. In 2002, 2003 and 2005 she played in the Solheim Cup.

Koch, Carin (SWE)
Born Kungalv, Sweden, 2 February 1971
She has been playing golf since she was nine and in the 2000 and 2002 Solheim Cup matches was unbeaten. In 2000 she won three points of three and in 2002 she won 2½ points out of three. She also played in the 2003 and 2005 matches.

De Lorenzi, Marie-Laure (FRA)
Born Biarritz, 21 January 1961
Turned professional 1986
The stylish French golfer won 20 titles in Europe between 1987 and 1997 setting a record in 1988 when she won eight times but for family reasons never spent time on the US Tour. Jointly holds the record for 54 holes on the European Tour with her 201 total in the 1995 Dutch Open.

Meunier-Lebouc, Patricia (FRA)
Born Dijon, 16 November 1972
Turned professional 1993
French amateur champion in 1992, she has been a regular winner on Europe's Evian Tour. She played in the 2000 Solheim Cup and again last year at Barsebäck. In 2003 she won the Kraft-Nabisco Championship on the US Tour.

Neumann, Liselotte (SWE)
Born Finspang, 20 May 1966
Turned professional 1985
Having won the US Women's Open in 1988 she won the Weetabix British Women's title in 1990 to become one of six players to complete the Transatlantic double. The others are Laura Davies, Alison Nicholas, Jane Geddes, Betsy King and Patty Sheehan. The 1988 Rookie of the Year on the LPGA Tour she played in the first six Solheim Cup matches but was a surprising omission from the team in 2005 when she had one of her best years on the US Tour. With Annika Sörenstam won the 2006 World Cup of Golf in South Africa.

Nilsmark, Catrin (SWE)
Born Gothenburg, Sweden, 28 Aug 1967
Turned professional 1987
Holed the winning putt in Europe's Solheim Cup victory in 1992. Her early career was affected by whiplash injury after a car crash. Used to hold a private pilot's licence but now rides Harley Davidson motorcycles. She captained the European team to victory in the 2003 Solheim Cup matches at Barsebäck in Sweden and captained the team again at Crooked Stick when America regained the trophy.

Petterson, Suzann (NOR)
Born Oslo, April 7 1981
Turned professional 2000
Five times Norwegian Amateur champion, Suzann was World Amateur champion in 2000. She won the French Open in 2001 and made her Solheim Cup début in the 2003 match at Barsebäck. One of the best

Catherine Prado

performers on the week and was unbeaten going into the singles. She also played in the 2005 Cup match at Crooked Stick.

Prado, Catherine (née Lacoste) (FRA)
Born Paris 27 June 1945
The only amateur golfer ever to win the US Women's Open she won the title at Hot Springs, Virginia in 1967. She was also the first non-American to take the title and the youngest. Two years later she won both the US and British Amateur titles. She was a four times winner of her own French Championship in 1967, 1969, 1970 and 1972 and won the Spanish title in 1969, 1972 and 1976. She comes from a well-known French sporting family.

Sanchez, Ana Belen (ESP)
Born Malaga, 16 February 1976
Turned professional 1997
As an amateur she was a member of the winning Spanish side in the 1995 European Team Championship. Now plays on the Evian Tour and made her Solheim Cup début at Barsebäck in 2003.

Segard, Mme Patrick (de St Saveur, née Lally Vagliano) (FRA)
Former chairperson of the Women's Committee of the World Amateur Golf Council holding the post

from 1964 to 1972. A four times French champion (1948, 50, 51 and 52) she also won the British (1950), Swiss (1949 and 1965), Luxembourg (1949), Italian (1949 and 1951) and Spanish (1951) amateur titles. She represented France from 1937 to 1939, from 1947 to 1965 and again in 1970.

Sörenstam, Annika (SWE)
Born Stockholm, 9 October 1970
Turned professional 1992
Winner of the US Open in 1995 and 1996 she and Karrie Webb of Australia have battled for the headlines on the USLPGA Tour over the past few years. A prolific winner of titles in America. She won four in a row in early summer 2000 as she and Webb battled again for the No. 1 spot in 2001. Sörenstam was the No. 1 earner in 1995, 1997 and 1998, Webb in 1996, 1999 and 2000. At the Standard Register Ping event she became the first golfer to shoot 59 on the LPGA Tour. Her second round score 59 included 13 birdies, 11 of them in her first 12 holes. Her 36-hole total of 124 beat the previous record set by Webb the previous season by three. Her 54-hole score of 193 matched the record set by Karrie Webb and her 72-hole total of 261 which gave her victory by three shots from Se Ri Pak matched the low total on Tour set by Se Ri Pak in 1998. Sörenstam's 27-under-par winning score was a new record for the Tour beating the 26-under-par score Webb returned in the Australian Ladies' Masters in 1999. Her sister Charlotta also plays on the LPGA and Evian Tours. Before turning professional she finished runner-up in the 1992 US Women's Championship. Sörenstam continued on her winning way in 2002 when her victories included another major – the Kraft Nabisco Championship. By the end of August she had won six times in the US and once more in Europe. By the beginning of October she had won nine times on the 2002 LPGA Tour and collected her 40th LPGA title. Only four players have won more than 9 events in one LPGA season. By October she had won $2.5 million world wide. In 2003 she was awarded the Golf Writers award in Britain for the golfer who had done most for European golf. In 2004 she quickly passed through the 50 mark in titles won in America. Before the middle of October her tally was 54 she had passed the $2 million mark in American Tour earnings for the year. In 2004 she added another major to her list of achievements winning the McDonald's LPGA Championship. She remains the dominant force in women's professional golf. When Annika won the Mizuno Classic in Japan she became the first player for 34 years to win 10 titles in a season. In 2003 she took up the challenge of playing on the US Men's Tour teeing up in a blaze of publicity in the Colonial event in Texas but missed the half-way cut. She won her fifth Major when she took the McDonald's LPGA Championship in June and when she won the Weetabix British Women's Open at Royal Lytham and St Annes she completed a Grand Slam of major titles. Her tally is now six Majors. Her win at Lytham was her sixth major success. By the end of August 2003 she had won 46 LPGA tournaments and was inducted into the World Golf Hall of Fame. When she won the Mizuno Classic for the third successive year she was winning her 46th LPGA title and had wrapped up the Player of the Year

and top money earner award. In 2004 she quickly passed through the 50 mark in titles won and before the middle of October had passed the £2 million mark in US PGA Tour earnings for a fourth successive year. She added another major to her personal tally when she won the McDonald's LPGA Championship. 2005 was another stellar year for Annika who took her career wins on the LPGA Tour to 66 with 10 more victories from her 20 starts. She easily topped the money list with over $2 million and moved her career earnings on the US Tour to $18,332,764. During the year she also won her own event in Sweden. Her majors total at the end of 2005 after further Grand Slam victories in the Kraft Nabisco Championship and McDonald's LPGA Championship moved to nine. Although she did not win Player of the Year honours in 2006 – that went to Mexico's Lorena Ochoa – Annika again had an excellent season, winning three times and coming second on a further five occasions. She has now won 69 times and her earnings in America have gone through $20 million. She added a further major win to her list of Grand Slam successes and with Liselotte Neumann won the World Cup of

Golf in South Africa early in the year. She also hosted and then won her own event in Sweden and beat Helen Alfredsson and Karrie Webb to the first prize at the Dubai Ladies Masters in November.

Tinning, Iben (DEN)
Born Copenhagen, 4 February 1974
Turned professional 1995
Cousin of the European Tour player Steen Tinning she is Denmark's leading lady professional and made her Solheim Cup début in 2003 at Barsebäck. She was also in the Cup line-up in 2005 when she finished No.1 money earner in Europe.

Varangot, Brigitte (FRA)
Born Biarritz, 1 May 1940
Winner of the French Amateur title five times in six years from 1961 and again in 1973. Her run in the French Championship was impressive from 1960 when her finishes were 2, 1, 1, 2, 1, 1, 1, 2. She was also a triple winner of the British Championship in 1963, 1965 and 1968. One of France's most successful players she also won the Italian title in 1970.

Solheim Cup goes to Ireland in 2011

The Solheim Cup – the women's equivalent of the Ryder Cup – will be played for the first time in Ireland in 2011.

The 12th biennial match between Europe and the United States will be staged north-west of Dublin at Killeen Castle, the Jack Nicklaus-designed course which only opens for play this year. The dates for the 2011 match have not been decided.

"We have chosen Ireland and Killeen Castle," explained LET executive director Alexandra Armas, "firstly because of the superb way the whole nation supported the Ryder Cup at The K Club in 2006. Secondly we believe that modern Ireland is a young vibrant society compatible with the image we wish to promote for ladies golf."

The Americans defend the Cup when the 10th Solheim Cup is played from September 14–16 this year in Halmstad, Sweden. It has already been announced that the 2009 tournament will be held at Sugar Grove, Illinois.

Overseas Golfers – Women

American

Bradley, P.	Haynie, S.	Lopez, N.	Pepper, D.	Steinhauser, S.
Caponi, D.	Hurst, P.	McIntire, B.	Rawls, B.	Suggs, L.
Carner, J.A.	Inkster, J.	Mallon, M.	Sander, A.	Whitworth, K.
Creamer, P.	King, B.	Mann, C.	Semple	Wie, M.
Daniel. B.	Klein, E.	Massey, D.	Thompson, C.	Wright, M.
Geddes, J.	Kuehne, K.	Park, G.	Sheehan, P.	

Bradley, Pat
Born Westford, Massachusetts, 24 March 1951
Turned professional 1974
Winner of four US LPGA majors – the Nabisco Championship, the US Women's Open, the LPGA Championship and the du Maurier Classic, she won 31 times on the American circuit. An outstanding skier and ski instructor as well, she started playing golf when she was 11. Every time she won her mother would ring a bell on the porch of the family home whatever the time of day. The bell is now in the World Golf Hall of Fame. She played in four Solheim Cup sides and captained the team in 2000 at Loch Lomond. Inducted into the LPGA Hall of Fame in 1991 she was Rolex Player of the Year in 1986 and 1991.

Caponi, Donna
Born Detroit, Michigan, 29 January 1945
Turned professional 1965
Twice winner of the US Women's Open in 1969 and 1970 she collected 24 titles between 1969 and 1981 on the LPGA Tour. Winner of the 1975 Colgate European Open at Sunningdale, she is now a respected commentator/analyst.

Carner, Jo Anne (*née* Gunderson)
Born Kirkland, Washington, 4 April 1939
Turned professional 1970
Had five victories in the US Ladies' Amateur Championship (1957, 1960, 1962, 1966 and 1968) before turning professional and winning the 1971 and 1976 US Women's Open. She remains the last amateur to win on the LPGA Tour after having taken the 1969 Burdine's Invitational. Between 1970 and 1985 scored 42 victories on the LPGA Tour and was Rolex Player of the Year in 1974, 1981 and 1982. She was inducted into the LPGA Hall of Fame in 1982 and the World Golf Hall of Fame in 1985. She won the Bobby Jones award in 1981 and the Mickey Wright award in 1974 and 1982.

Creamer, Paula
Born Pleasanton, California, 5 August 1986
Turned professional 2005
The youngest and first amateur to win the LPGA qualifying school in 2004. As an amateur she was top ranked American junior in 2003 and 2004 winning 19 national titles. She became a winner on the LPGA Tour in her ninth start after turning professional when she won the Sybase Classic. Later in 2005 she won the Evian Masters and played in the winning Solheim Cup side. She began playing golf at the age of 10. In 2006 she had 13 top 10 finishes in 26 starts but did not win.

Daniel, Beth
Born Charleston, South Carolina, 14 October 1956
Turned professional 1978
A member of the LPGA Hall of Fame she won 32 times between 1979 and 1995 including the 1990 US LPGA Championship. She was Rolex Player of the Year in 1980, 1990 and 1994. Before turning professional she won the US Women's Amateur title in 1975 and 1977 and played in the 1976 and 1978 Curtis Cup teams. She has played in five Solheim Cup competitions since it began in 1990, missing only the 1998 match.

Geddes, Jane
Born Huntingdon, New York, 5 February 1960
Turned professional 1983
In 1986 she was the 13th player on the LPGA Tour to score her first victory at the US Women's Open. A year later she won the US LPGA title and took the British Women's title in 1989. She won 11 times on the US Tour between 1986 and 1994.

Haynie, Sandra
Born Fort Worth, Texas, 4 June 1943
Turned professional 1961
Twice a winner of the US Open (1965 and 1974) she won 42 times between 1962 and 1982 on the US LPGA Tour. She was elected to the LPGA Hall of Fame in 1977.

Hurst, Pat
Born San Leandro, California, 23 May 1969
Turned professional 1995
Had eight top 10 finishes in 2006 and nearly won the US Women's Open. An 18-hole play-off was required and she lost out to Annika Sörenstam.

Inkster, Juli
Born Santa Cruz, California, 24 June 1960
Turned professional 1983

Winner of two majors in 1984 (the Nabisco Championship and the du Maurier) she also had a double Major year in 1999 when she won the US Women's Open and the LPGA Championship which she won for a second time in 2000. In 2002 she won the US Women's Open for a second time. In all she has won seven major titles. In her amateur career she became the first player since 1934 to win the US Women's amateur title three years in a row (1980, 81, 82). Only four other women and one man (Tiger Woods) have successfully defended their national titles twice in a row. Coached for a time by the late London-based Leslie King at Harrods Store. She is a regular in the Solheim Cup competition. The 46 year old won again (the Safeway Classic) in 2006 and had 12 top 10 finishes in 20 starts on the LPGA Tour. Her career earnings have now gone through $11 million.

King, Betsy
Born Reading, Pennsylvania, 13 August 1955
Turned professional 1977

Another stalwart of the LPGA Tour in America she has won 34 times between 1984 and 2001. Winner of the British Open in 1985 she has also won the US Open in 1989 and 1990, the Nabisco Championship three times in 1987, 1990 and 1997 and the LPGA Championship in 1990. She never managed to win the du Maurier event although finishing in the top six on nine occasions. Three times Rolex Player of the Year in 1984, 1989 and 1993 she was elected to the LPGA Hall of Fame in 1995.

Klein, Emilee
Born Santa Monica, California, 11 June 1974
Turned professional 1994

The former Curtis Cup player who played in the 1994 match scored her biggest triumph as a professional when winning the Weetabix British Women's Open at Woburn in 1996.

Kuehne, Kelli
Born Dallas, Texas, 11 May 1977
Turned professional 1998

Having won the US Women's Amateur Championship in 1995 she successfully defended the title the following year when she also won the British Women's title – the first player to win both in the same year. She was also the first player to follow up her win in the US Junior Girls Championship in 1994 with victory in the US Women's event the following year. Her brother Hank is also a professional.

Lopez, Nancy (née Knight)
Born Torrance, California, 6 January 1957
Turned professional 1977

One of the game's bubbliest personalities and impressive performers who took her first title – the New Mexico Women's Amateur title at age 12. Between 1978 and 1995 she won 48 times on the LPGA Tour and was Rolex Player of the Year on four occasions (1978, 79, 85 and 88). In 1978, her rookie

Nancy Lopez

© Phil Sheldon Golf Picture Library

year, she won nine titles including a record five in a row. That year she also lost two play-offs and remains the only player to have won the Rookie of the Year, Player of the Year and Vare Trophy (scoring average) in the same season. A year later she won eight tournaments. Three times a winner of the LPGA Championship in 1978, 1985 and 1989 she has never managed to win the US Open although she was runner-up in 1975 as an amateur, in 1977, 1989 and most recently 1997 when she lost out to Britain's Alison Nicholas. She has now retired from competitive golf and in 2002 was awarded the PGA's First Lady in Golf award for the contribution she has made to the game. In 2005 she captained the winning American Solheim Cup side at Crooked Stick.

McIntire, Barbara
Born Toledo, Ohio, 1935

One of America's best amateurs who finished runner-up in the 1956 US Women's Open to Kathy Cornelius at Northland Duluth. Winner of the US Women's Amateur title in 1959 and 1964 she also won the British Amateur title in 1960. She played in six Curtis Cups between 1958 and 1962.

Mallon, Meg
Born Natwick, Maryland, 14 April 1963
Turned professional 1986

Winner of the 1991 US Women's Open, 1991 Mazda LPGA Championship, the 2000 du Maurier Classic and 11 other events between 1991 and 2002. In 2004 she won the US Women's Open for the second time. She holed the winning putt in the 2005 Solheim Cup.

Mann, Carole
Born Buffalo, New York, 3 February 1940
Turned professional 1960
Winner of 38 events on the LPGA Tour in her 22 years on Tour. A former president of the LPGA she was a key figure in the founding of the Tour and received the prestigious Babe Zaharias award. In 1964 she won the Western Open, then a Major, and in 1965 the US Women's Open but in 1968 she had a then record 23 rounds in the 60s, won 11 times and won the scoring averages prize with a score of 72.04. Enjoys a hugely successful corporate career within golf.

Massey, Debbie
Born Grosse Pointe, Michigan, 5 November 1950
Turned professional 1977
Best known for winning the British Women's Open in 1980 and 1981.

Park, Grace
Born Seoul, Korea, 6 March 1979
Turned professional 1999
After having lost a sudden-death play-off to Annika Sörenstam at the McDonald's LPGA Championship in 2003 she did win her first major in 2004 when she was successful in the Nabisco Dinah Shore at Mission Hills in Palm Springs. She was a graduate of the Futures Tour where in 1999 she won five of the ten events . Before turning professional she attended Arizona State University and in 1998 became the first player since Patty Berg in 1931 to win the US Amateur, Western Amateur and Trans-Amateur titles in the same year. She won 55 national junior, college and amateur titles and tied eighth as an amateur in the 1999 US Women's Open.

Pepper (Mochrie, Scarinzi), Dottie
Born Saratoga Springs, Florida, 17 August 1965
Turned professional 1987
Winner of 17 events (through to July 2001) on the US LPGA Tour including two majors. A fierce competitor she took the Nabisco Dinah Shore title in 1992 and again in 1999. She played in all Solheim Cup matches to 2000. In 2004 she announced her retirement from the US LPGA Tour.

Rawls, Betsy
Born Spartanburg, South Carolina, 4 May 1928
Turned professional 1951
Winner of the 1951, 1953, 1957 and 1960 US Women's Open and the US LPGA Championship in 1959 and 1969 as well as two Western Opens when the Western Open was a Major, she scored 55 victories on the LPGA Tour between 1951 and 1972. One of the best shot makers in women's golf who was noted for her game around and on the greens.

Sander, Anne (Welts, Decker, née Quast)
Born Marysville, 1938
A three times winner of the US Ladies title in 1958, 1961 and 1963, she also won the British Ladies title in

1980. She made eight appearances in the Curtis Cup stretching from 1958 to 1990. Only Carole Semple Thompson has played more often having played ten times.

Semple Thompson, Carol
Born 1950
Winner of six USLPGA titles including the US Ladies title in 1973 and the British Ladies in 1974. She has played in 12 Curtis Cups between 1974 and 2002 and holed the 27-foot winning putt in the 2002 match. At 53 she is the oldest US Curtis Cup Player. In 2003 she was named winner of the Bob Jones award for sportsmanship and in 2005 received the PGA of America Lady of the Year trophy.

Sheehan, Patty
Born Middlebury, Vermont, 27 October 1956
Turned professional 1980
Scored 35 victories between 1981 and 1996 including six Majors – the LPGA Championship in 1983, 1984 and 1994, the US Women's Open in 1993 and 1994 and the Nabisco Championship in 1996. As an amateur she won all her four games in the 1980 Curtis Cup. She is a member of the LPGA Hall of Fame. Captained the 2003 US Solheim Cup side.

Steinhauer, Sherri
Born Madison, Wisconsin, 27 December 1962
Turned professional 1985
Winner of the Weetabix Women's British Open at Woburn in 1999 and at Royal Lytham and St Annes in 1998 and again there in 2006. Her third victory was her first major success because the British Women's Open was only recently awarded major status. She has also played in three Solheim Cup matches.

Suggs, Louise
Born Atlanta, Georgia, 7 September 1923
Turned professional 1948
Winner of 58 titles on the LPGA Tour after a brilliant amateur career which included victories in the 1947 US Amateur and the 1948 British Amateur Championships. She won 11 Majors including the US Open in 1949 and 1952 and the LPGA Championship in 1957. A founder member of the US Tour she was an inaugural honoree when the LPGA Hall of Fame was instituted in 1967. In 2006 she was awarded the Bob Jones award for outstanding sportsmanship and for being a perfect ambassador for the game. She comes from Atlanta and knew Bobby Jones when she was younger.

Whitworth, Kathy
Born Monahans, Texas, 27 September 1939
Turned professional 1958
Won 88 titles on the LPGA Tour between 1959 and 1991 – more than any one else male or female. Her golden period was in the 1960s when she won eight events in 1965, nine in 1966, eight in 1967 and 10 in 1968. When she finished third in the 1981 US Women's Open she became the first player to top $1 million in prize money on the LPGA Tour. She was

the seventh member of the LPGA Tour Hall of Fame when inducted in 1975. Began playing golf at the age of 15 and made golfing history when she teamed up with Mickey Wright to play in the previously all male Legends of Golf event. Winner of six Majors – including three LPGA Championship wins in 1967, 1971 and 1975. In addition she won two Titleholders Championships (1966 and 1967) and the 1967 Western Open when they were Majors. Enjoyed a winning streak of 17 successive years on the LPGA Tour.

Wie, Michelle
Born Hawaii, 11 October 1989
Turned professional 2005
As an amateur she finished third in the Weetabix British Women's Open in July 2005 and turned professional in October as a 16-year-old with multi-million contract guarantees. In her first event as a professional in the Samsung Championship she finished fourth behind Annika Sörenstam but then was disqualified for a dropped ball infringement incurred in the third round – and spotted by an American journalist who did not report it until the following day. In 2006 she continued to play in a few men's events

including the Omega European Masters at Crans-sur-Sierre but failed to make the cut in any. She did make the cut in all four majors in 2006. She combines her professional career with her school work in Hawaii and it is reported she hopes to go eventually to Stanford University.

Wright, Mickey
Born San Diego, California, 14 February 1935
Turned professional 1954
Her 82 victories on the LPGA Tour between 1956 and 1973 was bettered only by Kathy Whitworth who has 88 official victories. One of the greatest golfers in the history of the Tour she had a winning streak of 14 successive seasons. Winner of 13 Major titles she is the only player to date to have won three in one season. In 1961 she took the US Women's Open, the LPGA Championship and the Titleholders Championship. That year she became only the second player to win both the US Women's Open and LPGA Championship in the same year having done so previously in 1958. Scored 79 of her victories between 1956 and 1969 when averaging almost eight wins a season. During this time she enjoyed a tremendous rivalry with Miss Whitworth. Truly a golfing legend.

Casey earns top European Tour honour

Twenty-nine-year-old Paul Casey became the 11th golfer since 1985 to be chosen as European Tour Golfer of the Year by a panel comprising members of the Association of Golf Writers along with television and radio representatives.

During the year, Casey won three times, including the HSBC World Match-play Championship in which he scored a record 10 and 8 success in the final against Shaun Micheel at Wentworth and beat former US Open champion Retief Goosen, former Masters champion Mike Weir and Colin Montgomerie en route to it.

Although Padraig Harrington finished No.1 on the money list for the first time after two second place finishes and two thirds, second placed Casey's challenge in the last event of the year was affected by a virus which prevented his playing at his best for at least the first two days.

"I am disappointed not to have taken the top spot on the European money list and won the Vardon Trophy but the battle with Padraig, David Howell and Robert Karlsson was truly exceptional," said Casey, who highlighted an outstanding performance in the Ryder Cup by holing a 4-iron at the 14th on the Saturday to give Howell and himself victory over Stewart Cink and Zach Johnson.

Casey, who had slumped to 39th in the European money list and was outside the top 50 in the world rankings, made such a wonderful comeback after sorting out the game that he finished 14th in the world.

George O'Grady, Chief Executive of the European Tour, commenting when the decision was announced at the Tour's end-of-season dinner: "Paul is an outstanding role model in our sport and deserving of having won the Golfer of the Year accolade."

Others who have won the award since 1985 comprise Bernhard Langer, Seve Ballesteros, Nick Faldo, Ian Woosnam, Colin Montgomerie, Lee Westwood, Ernie Els, Retief Goosen, Vijay Singh and Michael Campbell.

International

Dibnah, C.	Jang, J.	Miyazato, A	Pak, S.R.	Webb, K.
Fudoh, Y.	Kim, B.	Ochoa, L.	Stephenson, J.	
Higuchi, H.	Lunn, K.	Olamoto, A.	Streit, M.S.	

Dibnah, Corinne (AUS)
Born Brisbane, 29 July 1962
Turned professional 1984
A former Australian and New Zealand amateur champion, she joined the European Tour after turning professional and won 13 times between 1986 and 1994. A pupil of Greg Norman's first coach Charlie Earp, she was Europe's top earner in 1991.

Fudoh, Yuri (JPN)
Born Kumamoto, 14 October 1976
Turned professional 1996
A multiple winner on the Japanese Tour who won her first Japanese event in 2003 when she won the Japan LPGA Championship. She has won 20 events on the Japanese Tour and her winnings in 2000 of ¥120,443,924 was a record.

Higuchi, Hisako "Chako" (JPN)
Born Saitama Prefecture, Japan, 13 October 1945
Turned professional 1967
A charter member and star of the Japan LPGA Tour she won 72 victories worldwide during her career. In 2003 she was elected to the World Golf Hall of Fame.

Hisako Higuchi

Jang, Jeong (KOR)
Born Daejeon, Korea, 11 June 1980
Turned professional 1999
She scored her breakthrough win on the LPGA Tour when winning the Weetabix Women's British Open at Royal Birkdale – a joint venture with the Ladies European Tour. She led from start to finish. As an amateur she won the Korean Women's Open in 1997 and the following year was Korean Women's Amateur champion. Just 5ft tall, she started playing golf at age 13 and has been influenced throughout her career by her father. She has made over 2.75 million dollars in prize money since 2000.

Kim, Birdie (KOR)
Born Ik-San, Korea, 26 August 1981
Turned professional 2000
She became the 14th player in the history of the LPGA Tour to score her first win at the US Women's Open and she did it dramatically holing a bunker shot at the last to beat amateurs Brittany Lang and Morgan Pressel by two shots at Cherry Hills, Colorado. A silver medallist at the 1998 Asian Games she won 19 events as an amateur before joining the US Futures Tour in 2001.

Lunn, Karen (AUS)
Born Sydney, 21 March 1966
Turned professional 1985
A former top amateur she won the British Women's Open in 1993 at Woburn following the success in the European Ladies Open earlier in the year by her younger sister Mardi. She is the chairperson of the Ladies European Tour.

Miyazato, Ai (JPN)
Born Okinawa, Japan, 1985
Turned professional 2005
A multiple winner on the Japanese women's circuit in her rookie year as a pro, she is being talked off as Japanese women's golf's Tiger Woods. Among her victories last year – the Japan Open, the Elleair Ladies, the Vernal Ladies and the Hisako Higuchi IDC Otsukakagu Ladies.

Ochoa, Lorena (MEX)
Born Guadalajara, 15 November 1981
Turned professional 2003
Became the fastest player to reach $3million in prize-money on the LPGA Tour in 2006. She did not win a major, losing the Kraft Nabisco to Karrie Webb in a play-off at Palm Springs, but she topped the money list for the first time and was Player of the Year. In 2006 she had six victories, five second place finishes, two thirds, two fourths and a fifth earning more than $2million.

Okamoto, Ayako (JPN)
Born Hiroshima, 12 April 1951
Turned professional 1976

Although she won the British Women's Open in 1984 she managed only a runner-up spot in the US Women's Open and US LPGA Championships despite finishing in the top 20 28 times and missing the cut only four times. In the LPGA Championships she finished second or third five times in six years from 1986. She scored 17 victories in the USA between 1982 and 1992, won the 1990 German Open and was Japanese Women's champion in 1993 and 1997. The LPGA Tour's Player of the Year in 1987, she was inducted into the World Golf Hall of Fame in 2005.

Pak, Se Ri (KOR)
Born Daejeon, 28 September 1977
Turned professional 1996

In 1998 she was awarded the Order of Merit by the South Korean government – the highest honour given to an athlete – for having won two Majors in her rookie year on the US Tour. She won the McDonald LPGA Championship matching Liselotte Neumann in making a major her first tour success. When she won the US Women's Open later that year after an 18-hole play-off followed by two extra holes of sudden death against amateur Jenny Chuasiriporn, she became the youngest golfer to take that title. By the middle of 2001 she had won 12 events on the US tour including the Weetabix Women's British Open at Sunningdale – an event included on the US Tour as well as the European Circuit for the first time. In 2002 she was again a multiple winner on the US Tour adding to her majors by winning the McDonald's LPGA Championship. As an amateur in Korea she won 30 titles and became the first lady professional to make the cut in a men's professional event for 58 years when she played four rounds in a Korean Tour event. In 2006 she returned to the major's winner's circle when she beat Karrie Webb in a play off for the McDonald's LPGA Championship. It was her fifth major victory but her first since 2002.

Stephenson, Jan (AUS)
Born Sydney, 22 December 1951
Turned professional 1973

She won three majors on the LPGA Tour – the 1981 du Maurier Classic, the 1982 LPGA Championship and the 1983 US Women's Open. She was twice Australian Ladies champion in 1973 and 1977.

Streit, Marlene Stewart (CAN)
Born Cereal, Alberta, 9 March 1934

One of Canada's most successful amateurs she won her national title ten times between 1951 and 1973. She won the 1953 British Amateur, the US Amateur in 1956 and the Australian Ladies in 1963. She was Canadian Woman Athlete of the Year in 1951, 1953, 1956, 1960 and 1963.

Webb, Karrie (AUS)
Born Ayr, Queensland, 21 December 1974
Turned professional 1994

Blonde Australian who is rewriting the record books with her performances on the LPGA Tour. Peter Thomson, the five times Open champion considers she is the best golfer male or female there is and Greg Norman, who was her inspiration as a teenager, believes she can play at times better than Tiger Woods although Webb herself hates comparisons. She scored her first Major win in 1995 when she took the Weetabix Women's British Open – a title she won again in 1997. When she joined the LPGA Tour she won the 1999 du Maurier Classic, the 2000 Nabisco Championship and the 2000 and 2001 US Women's Open – five Majors out of eight (by the end of July 2001) – the most impressive run since Mickey Wright won five out of six in the early 1960s. In 2002 she became the first player to complete a career Grand Slam when she won her third Weetabix British Open which had become an official major on the US LPGA Tour. It was her sixth major title in four years. Her winning total at Turnberry was 15 under par 273. Enjoys a close rivalry with Annika Sörenstam. In 2005 she was inducted into the World Golf Hall of Fame. She added to her majors tally in 2006 when she beat Lorena Ochoa in a play-off for the Kraft Nabisco Championship. Later she lost a play-off to Se Ri Pak for another major – the McDonald's LPGA Championship. She is the only player to have victories in the current four majors and the du Maurier event, now discarded as a major.

Famous Personalities of the Past

In making the difficult choice of the names to be included, effort has been made to acknowledge the outstanding players and personalities of each successive era from the early pioneers to the stars of recent times.

Alliss, Percy   (1897–1975)

Finished in the top six in the Open Championship seven times, including joint third at Carnoustie in 1931, two strokes behind Tommy Armour. Twice winner of the Match Play Championship, five times German Open champion and twice winner of the Italian Open. Ryder Cup player in 1933–35–37, an international honour also gained by his son Peter. Spent much of his career as professional at the Wansee Club in Berlin.

Anderson, Jamie   (1842–1912)

Winner of three consecutive Open Championships – 1877–78–79. A native St Andrean, he once claimed to have played 90 consecutive holes on the Old Course without a bad or unintended shot. He was noted for his straight hitting and accurate putting.

Anderson, Willie   (1878–1910)

Took his typically Scottish flat swing to America where he won the US Open four times in a five year period from 1901. Only Bobby Jones, Ben Hogan and Jack Nicklaus have also won the US Open four times.

Archer, George   (1940–2005)

The 6ft 5in tall former cowboy won The Masters in 1969 – one of four golfers who won their first major that year. A superb putter Archer was dogged throughout his career by injury but he won 12 times on the PGA Tour and a further 19 times on the US Senior Tour now the Champions Tour. Elizabeth, one of his two daughters, made headlines when she caddied for her father and became the first woman to do so at Augusta.

Armour, Tommy D.   (1896–1968)

Born in Edinburgh, he played for Britain against America as an amateur and, after emigrating, for America against Britain as a professional in the forerunners of the Walker and Ryder Cup matches. Won the US Open in 1927, the USPGA in 1930 and the 1931 Open at Carnoustie. Became an outstanding coach and wrote several bestselling instruction books. Known as 'The Silver Scot'.

Auchterlonie, William   (1872–1963)

Won the Open at Prestwick in 1893 at the age of 21 with a set of seven clubs he had made himself. Founded the famous family club-making business in St Andrews. He believed that golfers should master half, three-quarter and full shots with each club. Appointed Honorary Professional to the R&A in 1935.

Balding, Al   (1924–2006)

A lovely swinger of the club, he was the first Canadian to win on the US Tour when he took the Mayfair Inn Open in Florida in 1955. In 1968, in partnership with Stan Leonard, he won the World Cup in Rome and was himself low individual scorer that year.

Ball, John   (1861–1940)

Finished fourth in the Open of 1878 at the age of 16 and became the first amateur to win the title in 1890. He won the Amateur Championship eight times and shares with Bobby Jones the distinction of being the winner of the Open and Amateur in the same year. He grew up on the edge of the links area which became the Royal Liverpool Golf Club and the birthplace of the Amateur. He was a master at keeping the ball low in the wind, but with the same straight-faced club could cut the ball up for accurate approach shots. His

Pam Barton   Popperfoto

run of success could have been greater but for military service in the South African campaign and the First World War.

Barton, Pamela   (1917–1943)

At the age of 19 she held both the British and American Ladies Championships in 1936. She was French champion at 17, runner-up in the British in both 1934 and '35 and won the title again in 1939. A Curtis Cup team member in 1934 and '36 she was a Flight Officer in the WAAF when she was killed in a plane crash at an RAF airfield in Kent.

Berg, Patty   (1915–2006)

The golf pioneer who won an LPGA Tour record 15 major titles and was one of the 13 founding members of the tour in 1950. She was the LPGA Tour's first president from 1950–52 and was the tour's money leader in 1954, '55 and '57 ending her career with 60 victories. She was a member of the LPGA Tour and World Golf Halls of Fame. She was described as a pioneer, an athlete, a mentor, a friend and an entertainer and had a great sense of humour.

Boros, Julius   (1920–1994)

Became the oldest winner of a major championship when he won the USPGA in 1968 at the age of 48. He twice won the US Open, in 1952 and again 11 years later at Brookline when he was 43. In a play-off he beat Jackie Cupit by three shots and Arnold Palmer by six. He played in four Ryder Cup matches between 1959–67, winning nine of his 16 matches and losing only three.

Bousfield, Ken   (1919–2000)

Although a short hitter even by the standards of his era, he won five out of 10 matches in six Ryder Cup appearances from 1949–61. He captured the PGA Match Play Championship in 1955, one of eight tournament victories in Britain, and also won six European Opens. He represented England in the World Cup at Wentworth in 1956 and Tokyo in 1957.

Bradshaw, Harry (1913–1950)

One of Ireland's most loved golfers whose swing Bernard Darwin described as "rustic and rugged". With Christy O'Connor he won the Canadian Cup (World Cup) for Ireland in Mexico in 1958 but he is also remembered for losing the 1949 Open to Bobby Locke after having hit one shot out of a bottle at the fifth on the second day. That bit of bad luck, it was later considered, cost him £10,000.

Braid, James   (1870–1950)

Together with Harry Vardon and J.H. Taylor he formed the Great Triumvirate and dominated the game for 20 years before the 1914–18 war. In a 10-year period from 1901 he became the first player in the history of the event to win the Open five times – and also finished second on three occasions. In that same period he won the Match Play Championship

four times and the French Open. He was a tall, powerful player who hit the ball hard but always retained an appearance of outward calm. He was one of the founder members of the Professional Golfers' Association and did much to elevate the status of the professional golfer. He was responsible for the design of many golf courses and served as professional at Walton Heath for 45 years. He was an honorary member of that club for 25 years and became one of its directors. He was also an honorary member of the R&A.

Brown, Eric   (1925–1986)

Twice captained the Ryder Cup side and for many years partnered John Panton for Scotland in the World Cup. A larger-than-life personality, he was one of two Cup captains who came from the Bathgate club. The other was Bernard Gallacher, who played in the 1969 match which Brown captained.

Bruen, Jimmy   (1920–1972)

Won the Irish Amateur at the age of 17 and defended the title successfully the following year. At 18 he became the youngest ever Walker Cup player at that time and in practice for the match at St Andrews in 1938 equalled the then amateur course record of 68 set by Bobby Jones.

Campbell, Dorothy Iona   (1883–1946)

One of only two golfers to win the British, American and Canadian Ladies titles. In total she won these three major championships seven times.

Carr, Joe   (1922–2004)

The first Irishman to captain the Royal and Ancient Golf Club of St Andrews, he was winner of three British Amateur Championship titles in 1953, 1958 and 1960. He played or captained Walker Cup sides from 1947 to 1963 making a record 11 appearances. He was the first Irishman to play in The Masters at Augusta, made 23 consecutive appearances for Ireland in the Home Internationals and was a regular winner of the West of Ireland and East of Ireland Championships. At one point in an illustrious career he held 18 different course records. An ebullient, fast-talking personality with a somewhat eccentric swing, he was one of Ireland's best known and best loved golfers.

Compston, Archie   (1893–1962)

Beat Walter Hagen 18 and 17 in a 72-hole challenge match at Moor Park in 1928 and tied for second place in the 1925 Open. Played in the Ryder Cup in 1927–29–31.

Cotton, Sir Henry   (1907–1987)

The first player to be knighted for services to golf, he died a few days before the announcement of the award was made. He won the Open Championship three times, which included a round of 65 at Royal St George's in 1934 after which the famous Dunlop golf ball was named. His final 71 at Carnoustie to win the 1937 Championship in torrential rain gave him great satisfaction and he set another record with a 66 at Muirfield on the way to his third triumph in 1948. He won the Match Play Championship three times and was runner-up on three occasions. He also won 11 Open titles in Europe, played three times in the Ryder Cup and was non-playing captain in 1953. Sir Henry worked hard to promote the status of professional golf and also championed the cause of young golfers, becoming a founder member of the Golf Foundation. He was a highly successful teacher, author and architect, spending much time at Penina, a course he created in southern Portugal. He was an honorary member of the R&A.

Crawley, Leonard   (1903–1981)

Played four times in the Walker Cup in 1932–34–38–47 and won the English Amateur in 1931. He also played first-class cricket for Worcestershire and Essex and toured the West Indies with the MCC in 1936. After the Second World War he was golf correspondent for the *Daily Telegraph* for 30 years.

The Curtis sisters, Harriet   (1878–1944)
Margaret   (1880–1965)

Donors of the Curtis Cup still contested biennially between the USA and GB&I. Harriet won the US Women's Amateur in 1906 and lost in the following year's final to her sister Margaret, who went on to win the championship three times.

Daly, Fred   (1911–1990)

Daly won the Open at Royal Liverpool in 1947 and in four of the next five years was never out of the top four in the Championship. At Portrush, where he was born, he finished fourth to Max Faulkner in 1951, the only time the Open has been played in Northern Ireland. He was Ulster champion 11 times and three times captured the prestigious PGA Match Play Championship. He was a member of the Ryder Cup team four times, finishing on a high note at Wentworth in 1953 when he won his foursomes match in partnership with Harry Bradshaw and then beat Ted Kroll 9 and 7 in the singles.

Darwin, Bernard   (1876–1961)

One of the most gifted and authoritative writers on golf, he was also an accomplished England international player for more than 20 years. While in America to report the 1922 Walker Cup match for *The Times*, he was called in to play and captain the side when Robert Harris became ill. A grandson of Charles Darwin, he was captain of the R&A in 1934–35. In 1937 he was awarded the CBE for services to literature. He was inducted into the World Golf Hall of Fame in 2005.

Demaret, Jimmy   (1910–1983)

Three times Masters champion, coming from five strokes behind over the final six holes to beat Jim Ferrier by two in 1950, he also won six consecutive tournaments in 1940 while still performing as a night club singer. He won all six Ryder Cup matches he played in the encounters of 1947–49–51.

Duncan, George   (1884–1964)

Won the Open in 1920 by making up 13 shots on the leader over the last two rounds and came close to catching Walter Hagen for the title two years later. Renowned as one of the fastest players, his book was entitled *Golf at the Gallop*.

Faulkner, Max   (1916–2005)

One of the game's most extrovert and colourful personalities, who won the 1951 Open Championship at Royal Portrush, the only time the event was played in Northern Ireland. He played in five Ryder Cups and was deservedly if belatedly recognised for his contribution to the game with an honour in 2001 when he was awarded the OBE. His son-in-law is Brian Barnes, another golfing extrovert.

Ferguson, Bob   (1848–1915)

The Open Championship winner three times in succession between 1880–82. He then lost a 36-hole play-off for the title by one stroke to Willie Fernie in 1883. At 18 he had won the Leith Tournament against the game's leading professionals.

Fernie, Willie   (1851–1924)

In 1882 he was second to Bob Ferguson in the Open over his home course at St Andrews. The following year he beat the same player in a 36-hole play-off for the championship over Ferguson's home links at Musselburgh.

Hagen, Walter   (1892–1969)

A flamboyant character who used a hired Rolls Royce as a changing room because professionals were not allowed in many clubhouses, he once gave his £50 cheque for winning The Open to his caddie. He won four consecutive USPGA Championships from 1924 when it was still decided by matchplay. He was four times a winner of The Open, in 1922–24–28–29 and captured the US Open title in 1914 and 1919. He captained and played in five Ryder Cup encounters between 1927–35, winning seven of his nine matches and losing only once. He was non-playing captain in 1937.

Henning, Harold   (1934–2005)

One of three brothers from a well-known South African golf family he was a regular winner of golf events in his home country and Europe and had two wins on the US Tour. Played ten times for South Africa in the World Cup winning the event with Gary Player in Madrid in 1965.

Herd, Alexander 'Sandy'   (1868–1944)

When he first played in the Open at the age of 17 he possessed only four clubs. His only championship success came in the 1902 Open at Hoylake, the first on the Grand Slam, but his poor state of health after a near fatal car crash four years earlier would have made the matchplay format of 10 rounds in six days in the USPGA an impossibility. After his car collided with a Greyhound bus in fog, it was feared that Hogan might never walk again. He had won three majors before the accident and he returned to capture six more. His only appearance in the Open was in his tremendous season of 1953 and he recorded rounds of 73-71-70-68 to win by four strokes at Carnoustie. His dramatic life story was made into a Hollywood film entitled *Follow the Sun*.

Hutchinson, Horace (1859–1932)

Runner-up in the first Amateur Championship in 1885, he won the title in the next two years and reached the final again in 1903. Represented England from 1902–07. He was a prolific writer on golf and country life and became the first English captain of The R&A in 1908.

Jarman, Ted (1907–2003)

He competed in the 1935 Ryder Cup at Ridgewood, New Jersey, and until his death in 2003 he had been the oldest living Cup golfer. When he was 76 years old and before he had to stop playing because of arthritis he shot a 75.

Jones, Bobby (1902–1971)

Always remembered for his incredible and unrepeatable achievement in 1930 of winning the Open and Amateur Championships of Britain and America in one outstanding season – the original and unchallenged Grand Slam. At the end of that year he retired from competitive golf at the age of 28. His victories included four US Opens, five US Amateur titles, three Opens in Britain and one Amateur Championship. Although his swing was stylish and fluent, he suffered badly from nerves and was often sick and unable to eat during championships.

He was also an accomplished scholar, gaining first-class honours degrees in law, English literature and mechanical engineering at three different universities. He subsequently opened a law practice in Atlanta and developed the idea of creating the Augusta National course and staging an annual invitation event which was to become known as The Masters.

He was made an honorary member of the Royal and Ancient Golf Club in 1956 and two years later was given the freedom of the Burgh of St Andrews at an emotional ceremony. He died after many years of suffering from a crippling spinal disease. The tenth hole on the Old Course bears his name.

Bobby Jones   Popperfoto

player to capture the title using the new rubber-cored ball. He won the Match Play Championship at the age of 58 and took part in his last Open at St Andrews in 1939 at the age of 71.

Hilton, Harold (1869–1942)

Winner of the Amateur Championship four times between 1900 and 1913, he also became the first player and the only Briton to hold both the British and US Amateur titles in the same year 1911. He won the Open in 1892 at Muirfield, the first time the championship was extended to 72 holes. A small but powerful player he was the first editor of *Golf Monthly*.

Hogan, Ben (1912–1997)

One of only five players to have won all four major championships, his record of capturing three in the same season has been matched by Tiger Woods. He dominated the golfing scene in America after the Second World War and in 1953 won the Masters, US Open and the Open Championship. A clash of dates between the Open and USPGA prevented an attempt

King, Sam (1911–2003)

He played Ryder Cup golf immediately before and after World War II and came third in the 1939 Open behind Dick Burton at Royal St George's. In the 1947 Ryder Cup he prevented an American whitewash in the singles by beating Herman Kaiser. He was British Senior Champion in 1961 and 1962 and was often

Bobby Locke   Popperfoto

described as "the old master" – a golfer noted for his long, straight drives and superb putting.

Kirkaldy, Andrew   (1860–1934)

First honorary professional appointed by the R&A, he lost a play-off for the Open Championship of 1889 to Willie Park at Musselburgh. He was second in the championship three times, a further three times finished third and twice fourth. A powerful player, he was renowned for speaking his mind.

Laidlay, John Ernest   (1860–1940)

The man who first employed the overlapping grip which was later credited to Harry Vardon and universally known as the Vardon grip, Laidlay was a finalist in the Amateur Championship six times in seven years from 1888, winning the title twice at a time when John Ball, Horace Hutchinson and Harold Hilton were at their peak. He was runner-up in the Open to Willie Auchterlonie at Prestwick in 1893. Among the 130 medals he won, were the Gold Medal and Silver Cross in R&A competitions.

Leitch, 'Cecil'   (1891–1977)

Christened Charlotte Cecilia, but universally known as Cecil, her list of international victories would undoubtedly have been greater but for the blank golfing years of the first world war. She first won the British Ladies Championship in 1908 at the age of 17. In 1914 she took the English, French and British titles and successfully defended all three when competition was resumed after the war. In all she won the French Championship five times, the British four times, the English twice, the Canadian once. Her total of four victories in the British has never been beaten and has been equalled only by her great rival Joyce Wethered. The victory in Canada was by a margin of 17 and 15 in the 36-hole final.

Lema, Tony   (1934–1966)

His first visit to Britain, leaving time for only 27 holes of practice around the Old Course at St Andrews, culminated in Open Championship victory in 1964 by five shots over Jack Nicklaus. He had won three tournaments in four starts in America before arriving in Scotland and gave great credit for his Open success to local caddie Tip Anderson. He played in the Ryder Cup in 1963 and 1965 with an outstanding record. He lost only once in 11 matches, halved twice and won eight. Lema and his wife were killed when a private plane in which they were travelling to a tournament crashed in Illinois.

Little, Lawson   (1910–1968)

Won the Amateur Championships of Britain and America in 1934 and successfully defended both titles the following year. He then turned his amateur form into a successful professional career, starting in 1936 with victory in the Canadian Open. He won the US Open in 1940 after a play-off against Gene Sarazen.

Locke, Bobby   (1917–1987)

The son of Northern Irish emigrants to South Africa, Arthur D'Arcy Locke was playing off plus four by the age of 18 and won the South African Boys, Amateur and Open Championships. On his first visit to Britain in 1936 he was leading amateur in the Open Championship. Realising that his normal fade was leaving him well short of the leading players, he deliberately developed the hook shot to get more run on the ball. It was to become his trade-mark throughout a long career.

He was encouraged to try the American tour in 1947 and won five tournaments, one by the record margin of 16 shots. More successes followed and the USPGA framed a rule which banned him from playing in their events, an action described by Gene Sarazen as 'the most disgraceful action by any golf organisation'.

Disillusioned by the American attitude, Locke then played most of his golf in Europe, winning the Open four times. He shared a period of domination with Peter Thomson between 1949–1958 when they won the championship four times each, only Max Faulkner and Ben Hogan breaking the sequence. In his final Open victory at St Andrews in 1957 he failed to replace his ball in the correct spot on the 18th green after moving it from fellow competitor Bruce Crampton's line. The mistake, which could have led to disqualification, was only spotted on television replays. The R&A Championship Committee rightly decided that Locke, who had won by three strokes, had gained no advantage, and allowed the result to stand.

Following a career in which he won over 80 events around the world he was made an honorary member of the R&A in 1976.

Longhurst, Henry   (1909–1978)

Captain of Cambridge University golf team, runner-up in the French and Swiss Amateur Championships and winner of the German title in 1936, he became the most perceptive and readable golf correspondent of his time and a television commentator who never wasted a single word. His relaxed, chatty style was based on the premise that he was explaining the scene to a friend in his favourite golf club bar. For 25 years his *Sunday Times* column ran without a break and became compulsory reading for golfers and non-golfers alike. He had a brief spell as a member of parliament and was awarded the CBE for services to golf.

McCormack, Mark   (1931–2003)

The Cleveland lawyer who created a golf management empire after approaching Arnold Palmer to look after his affairs. A keen golfer himself, he became one of the most influential and powerful men in sport, managing many golfing legends including Tiger Woods. He was responsible for the development of the modern game commercially and started the World Match Play Championship at Wentworth in 1964.

Mackenzie, Alister   (1870–1934)

A family doctor and surgeon, he became involved with Harry S. Colt in the design of the Alwoodley course in Leeds, where he was a founder member and honorary secretary and eventually abandoned his medical career and worked full time at golf course architecture. There are many outstanding examples of his work in Britain, Australia, New Zealand and America. His most famous creation, in partnership with Bobby Jones, is the Augusta National course in Georgia, home of The Masters.

Massy, Arnaud   (1877–1958)

The first non-British player to win the Open Championship. Born in Biarritz, France, he defeated J.H. Taylor by two strokes at Hoylake in 1907. Four years later he tied for the title with Harry Vardon at Royal St George's, but in the play-off conceded at the 35th hole when he was five strokes behind. He won the French Open four times, the Spanish on three occasions and the Belgian title once.

Micklem, Gerald   (1911–1988)

A pre-war Oxford Blue, he won the English Amateur Championship in 1947 and 1953 and played in the Walker Cup team four times between 1947 and 1955. He was non-playing captain in 1957 and 1959. In 1976 he set a record of 36 consecutive appearances in the President's Putter, an event that he won in 1953. In addition to his playing success he was a tireless administrator, serving as chairman of the R&A Rules, Selection and Championship Committees. He was president of the English Golf Union and the European Golf Association and captain of the R&A. In 1969 he received the Bobby Jones award for distinguished sportsmanship and services to the game.

Middlecoff, Cary   (1921–1998)

Dentist turned golf professional, he became one of the most prolific winners on the US tour, with 37 victories that included two US Opens and a Masters victory. In the US Open of 1949 he beat Sam Snead and Clayton Heafner at Medinah, and seven years later recaptured the title by one shot ahead of Ben Hogan and Julius Boros at Oak Hill. His Masters success came in 1955 when he established a record seven-shot winning margin over Hogan.

Mitchell, Abe   (1897–1947)

Said by J.H. Taylor to be the finest player never to win an Open, he finished in the top six five times. He was more successful in the Match Play Championship, with victories in 1919, 1920 and 1929. He taught the game to St Albans seed merchant Samuel Ryder and is the figure depicted on top of the famous trophy.

Morgan, Wanda   (1910–1995)

Three-time English Amateur champion, in 1931–36–37, she also captured the British title in 1935 and played three times in the Curtis Cup from 1932–36.

Morris, Old Tom   (1821–1908)

Apprenticed as a feathery ball maker to Allan Robertson in St Andrews at the age of 18 he was one of the finest golfers of his day when he took up the position of Keeper of the Green at Prestwick, where he laid out the original 12-hole course. He was 39 when he finished second in the first Open in 1860, but subsequently won the title four times. His success rate might have been much greater if he had been a better putter. His son once said: 'He would be a much better player if the hole was a yard closer.'

A man of fierce conviction, he returned to St Andrews to take up the duties of looking after the Old Course at a salary of £50 per year, paid by the R&A. He came to regard the course as his own property and was once publicly reprimanded for closing it without authority because he considered it needed a rest. A testimonial in 1896 raised £1,240 pounds towards his old age from golfers around the world and when he retired in 1903 the R&A continued to pay his salary. He died after a fall on the stairs of the New Club in 1908, having outlived his wife, his daughter and his three sons.

Morris, Young Tom   (1851–1875)

Born in St Andrews, but brought up in Prestwick, where his father had moved to become Keeper of the Green, he won a tournament against leading professionals at the age of 13. He was only 17 when he succeeded his father as Open champion in 1868 and then defended the title successfully in the following two years to claim the winner's belt outright. There was no championship in 1871, but when the present silver trophy became the prize in 1872, Young Tom's was the first name engraved on its base.

His prodigious talent was best demonstrated in his third successive Open victory in 1870 when he played 36 holes at Prestwick in 149 strokes, 12 shots ahead of his nearest rival, superb scoring given the equipment and the condition of the course at that time.

He married in November 1874 and was playing with his father in a money match at North Berwick the following year when a telegram from St Andrews sent them hurrying back across the Firth of Forth in a private yacht. Young Tom's wife and baby had both died in childbirth. He played golf only twice after that, in matches that had been arranged long in advance, and fell into moods of deep depression. He died on Christmas morning of that same year from a burst artery in the lung. He was 24 years old. A public subscription paid for a memorial which still stands above his grave in the cathedral cemetery.

Nelson, Byron (1912–2006)

In the 1945 US season he won 18 times including 11 events in a row between March and August – a record unlikely ever to be broken. Between 1935 and 1946 he won 54 times but although he won the US Open in 1939, the US PGA Championship in 1940 and 1945 and the US Masters in 1937 and 1942 he never managed to complete the set of four majors. His only win in Europe was the 1955 French Open. He was a father figure in US golf and until he retired in 2001 was one of the Masters honorary starters along with the late Gene Sarazen and the late Sam Snead. With Ben Hogan and Sam Snead was one of golf's most revered figures.

Norman, Moe (1929–2004)

Eccentric Canadian golf star who was renowned for the accuracy of his unusual swing. Twice Canadian Amateur Champion and winner of 13 Canadian Tour titles, he was inducted into the Canadian Golf Hall of Fame in 1995. He played very quickly, seldom slowing to line up a putt. He never had a lesson. He was such a character that Wally Uihlein, president of Titleist and Footjoy, paid him $5,000 a month for the last 10 years of his life for just "being himself".

Ouimet, Francis (1893–1967)

Regarded as the player who started the American golf boom after beating Harry Vardon and Ted Ray in a play-off for the 1913 US Open as a young amateur. Twice a winner of the US Amateur, he was a member of every Walker Cup team from 1922 to 1934 and non-playing captain from then until 1949. In 1951 he became the first non-British individual to be elected captain of the R&A and was a committee member of the USPGA for many years.

Park, Willie (1834–1903)

Winner of the first Open Championship in 1860. He won the title three more times, in 1863, 1866 and 1875, and was runner-up on four occasions. For 20 years he issued a standing challenge to play any man in the world for £100 a side. His reputation was built largely around a successful putting stroke and he always stressed the importance of never leaving putts short.

Park, Mungo (1839–1904)

Younger brother to Willie Park, he spent much of his early life at sea, but won the Open Championship in 1874 at the age of 35, beating Young Tom Morris into second place by two shots on his home course at Musselburgh.

Park Jr, Willie (1864–1925)

Son of the man who won the first Open Championship, Willie Park jr captured the title twice – in 1887 and 1889 – and finished second to Harry Vardon in 1898. He was also an accomplished clubmaker who did much to popularise the bulger driver with its convex face and he patented the wry-neck putter in 1891. One of the first and most successful professionals to design golf courses, he was responsible for many layouts in Britain, Europe and America and also wrote two highly successful books on the game.

Philp, Hugh (1782–1856)

One of the master craftsmen in St Andrews in the early days of the 19th century, he was renowned for his skill in creating long-nosed putters. After his death his business was continued by Robert Forgan. Philp's clubs are much prized collector's items.

Picard, Henry (1907–1997)

Winner of The US Masters in 1938 and the 1939 USPGA Championship, where he birdied the final hole to tie with Byron Nelson and birdied the first extra hole for the title. Ill health cut short a career in which he won 27 tournaments.

Ray, Ted (1877–1943)

Born in Jersey, his early years in golf were in competition with Channel Islands compatriot Harry Vardon and his fellow members of the Great Triumvirate, J.H. Taylor and James Braid. His only victory in the Open came in 1912, but he was runner-up to Taylor the following year and second again, to Jim Barnes of America, in 1925 when he was 48 years of age He claimed the US Open title in 1920 and remains one of only three British players to win The Open and the US Open on both sides of the Atlantic. The others are Harry Vardon and Tony Jacklin.

Rees, Dai (1913–1983)

One of Britain's outstanding golfers for three decades, he played in nine Ryder Cup matches between 1937 and 1961 and was playing captain of the 1957 team which won the trophy for the first time since 1933. He was non-playing captain in 1967. He was runner-up in The Open three times and won the PGA Match Play title four times. He was made an honorary member of the Royal and Ancient Golf Club in 1976.

his way to Masters victory, holing a four-wood across the lake at the 15th for an albatross two. At the age of 71 he played in The Open at Troon and holed-in-one at the Postage Stamp eighth. The next day be holed from a bunker for a two at the same hole. He acted as an honorary starter at the Masters, hitting his final shot only a month before his death at the age of 97.

Sayers, Ben (1857–1924)

A twinkling, elphin figure, the diminutive Sayers played a leading part in the game for more than four decades. He represented Scotland against England from 1903 to 1913 and played in every Open from 1880 to 1923.

Shade, Ronnie DBM (1938–1984)

One of Scotland's greatest golfers whom many considered the world's top amateur in the mid 60s. After losing the 1962 Scottish Amateur Golf Championship final to Stuart Murray, he won that title five years in a row winning 43 consecutive ties before losing in the fourth round to tie Willie Smeaton at Muirfield in 1968. Taught by his father John, professional at the Duddingston club in Edinburgh, he was often referred to as "Right Down the Bloody Middle" because of his initials and consistent play. Shade won the Scottish and Irish Open Championships as a professional but was re-instated as an amateur shortly before his death from cancer at the age of 47.

Dai Rees Popperfoto

Robertson, Allan (1815–1858)

So fearsome was Robertson's reputation as a player that when the R&A staged an annual competition for local professionals, he was not allowed to take part so as to give the others a chance. A famous maker of feather golf balls, he strongly resisted the advance of the more robust gutta percha. Tom Morris senior was his apprentice and they were reputed never to have lost a foursomes match in which they were partners.

Ryder, Samuel (1858–1936)

The prosperous seed merchant was so impressed with the friendly rivalry between British and American professionals at an unofficial match at Wentworth in 1926 that he donated the famous gold trophy for the first Ryder Cup match the following year. The trophy is still presented today for the contest between America and Europe.

Sarazen, Gene (1902–1999)

Advised to find an outdoor job to improve his health, Sarazen became a caddie and then an assistant professional. At the age of 20 he became the first player to win the US Open and PGA titles in the same year. In claiming seven major titles he added The Open at Prince's in 1932 and when he won the second Masters tournament in 1935 he became the first of only five players to date who have won all four Grand Slam trophies during their careers. He played 'the shot heard around the world' on

Smith, Frances – née Bunty Stephens (1925–1978)

Dominated post-war women's golf, winning the British Ladies Championship in 1949 and 1954, was three times a winner of the English and once the victor in the French Championship. She represented Great Britain & Ireland in six consecutive encounters from 1950, losing only three of her 11 matches, and was non-playing captain of the team in 1962 and 1972. She was awarded the OBE for her services to golf.

Smith, Horton (1908–1963)

In his first winter on the US professional circuit as a 20-year-old in 1928–29 he won eight out of nine tournaments. He was promoted to that year's Ryder Cup team and played again in 1933 and 1935 and remained unbeaten He won the first Masters in 1934 and repeated that success two year's later. He received the Ben Hogan Award for overcoming illness or injury and the Bobby Jones Award for distinguished sportsmanship in golf.

Smith, Macdonald (1890–1949)

Born into a talented Carnoustie golfing family, he was destined to become one of the finest golfers never to win the Open. He was second in 1930 and 1932, was twice third and twice fourth. His best chance came at Prestwick in 1925 when he led the field by five strokes with one round to play, but the enthusiastic hordes of Scottish supporters destroyed his concentration and he finished with an 82 for fourth place.

Snead, Sam   (1912–2002)

Few would argue that 'Slammin' Sam Snead' possessed the sweetest swing in the history of the game. 'He just walked up to the ball and poured honey all over it', it was said. Raised during the Depression in Hot Springs, Virginia, he also died there on May 23 2002, four days short of his 90th birthday. His seven major titles comprised three Masters, three USPGA Championships and the 1946 Open at St Andrews, while he was runner-up four times in the US Open. But for the Second World War he would surely have added several more. He achieved a record 82 PGA Tour victories in America, the last of them at age 52, and was just as prolific round the world across six decades. He played in seven Ryder Cup matches, captained the 1969 United States team which tied at Royal Birkdale and after his retirement acted as honorary starter at The Masters until his death. Perhaps his greatest achievement came in the 1979 Quad Cities Open when he scored 67 and 66. He was 67 years of age at the time.

Solheim, Karsten   (1912–2000)

A golfing revolutionary who discovered the game at the age of 42 and, working in his garage, invented the Ping putter with its unique heel-toe weighting design, later adopted with his irons. A keen supporter of women's golf, he presented the Solheim Cup for a biennial competition between the American and European Ladies' Tours.

Stewart, Payne   (1957–1999)

Four months after winning his second US Open title Payne Stewart was killed in a plane crash. Only a month earlier he had been on the winning United States Ryder Cup team. His first major victory was in the 1989 USPGA Championship and he claimed his first US Open title two years later after a play-off against Scott Simpson. In 1999 he holed an 18-foot winning putt to beat Phil Mickleson for the US title he was never able to defend. In 1985 he finished a stroke behind Sandy Lyle in The Open at Royal St George's and five years later he shared second place as Nick Faldo won the Championship at St Andrews.

Tait, Freddie   (1870–1900)

In 1890 Tait set a new record of 77 for the Old Course, lowering that to 72 only four years later. He was three times the leading amateur in the Open Championship and twice won the Amateur Championship, in 1896 and 1898. The following year he lost at the 37th hole of an historic final to John Ball at Prestwick. He was killed while leading a charge of the Black Watch at Koodoosberg Drift in the Boer War.

Taylor, J.H.   (1871–1963)

Winner of the Open Championship five times between 1894 and 1913, Taylor was part of the Great Triumvirate with James Braid and Harry Vardon. He tied for the title with Vardon in 1896, but lost in the play-off and was runner-up another five times. He also won the French and German Opens and finished second in the US Open. A self-educated man, he was a thoughtful and compelling speaker and became the founding father of the Professional Golfers' Association. He was made an honorary member of the R&A in 1949.

Tolley, Cyril   (1896–1978)

Won the first of his two Amateur Championships in 1920 while still a student at Oxford and played in the unofficial match which preceded the Walker Cup a year later. He played in six Walker Cup encounters and was team captain in 1924. Tolley is the only amateur to have won the French Open, a title he captured in 1924 and 1928. After winning the Amateur for the second time in 1929 he was favourite to retain the title at St Andrews the following summer but was beaten by a stymie at the 19th hole in the fourth round by Bobby Jones in the American's Grand Slam year.

Travis, Walter   (1862–1925)

Born in Australia, he won the US Amateur Championship in 1900 at the age of 38, having taken up the game only four years earlier. He won again the following year and in 1903. He became the first overseas player to win the Amateur title in Britain in 1904, using a centre-shafted Schenectady putter he had just acquired. The club was banned a short time later. He was 52 years old when he last reached the semi-finals of the US Amateur in 1914.

Valentine, Jessie   (1915–2006)

A winner of titles before and after World War II, she was an impressive competitor and was one of the first ladies to make a career out of professional golf. She won the British Ladies as an amateur in 1937 and again in 1955 and 1958 and was Scottish champion in 1938 and 1939 and four times between 1951 and 1956. But for the war years it is certain she would have had more titles and victories. She played in seven Curtis Cups between 1936 and 1958 and represented Scotland in the Home Internationals on 17 occasions between 1934 and 1958.

Vardon, Harry   (1870–1937)

Still the only player to have won The Open Championship six times, Vardon, who was born in Jersey, won his first title in 1896, in a 36-hole play-off against J.H. Taylor and his last in 1914, this time beating Taylor by three shots. He won the US Open in 1900 and was beaten in a play-off by Francis Ouimet in 1913. He was one of the most popular of the players at the turn of the century and did much to popularise the game in America with his whistle-stop exhibition tours. He popularised the overlapping grip which still bears his name, although it was first used by Johnny Laidlay. He was also the originator of the modern upright swing, moving away from the flat sweeping action of previous eras. After his Open victory of 1903, during which he was so ill he thought he would not be able to finish, he was diagnosed with tuberculosis. His legendary accuracy and low scoring are commemorated with the award of two Vardon Trophies – in America for the player each year with the lowest scoring average and in Europe for the golfer who wins the money list.

Vare, Glenna – née Collett   (1903–1989)

Won the first of her six US Ladies Amateur titles at the age of 19 in 1922 and the last in 1935. A natural athlete, she attacked the ball with more power than was normal in the women's game. The British title eluded her, although at St Andrews in 1929 she was three-under par and five up on Joyce Wethered after 11 holes, but lost to a blistering counter-attack. She played in the first Curtis Cup match in 1932 and was a member of the team in 1936, 1938 and 1948 and was captain in 1934 and 1950.

Walker, George   (1874–1953)

The President of the United States Golf Association who donated the trophy for the first match in 1922, at Long Island, New York, and which is still presented to the winning team in the biennial matches beteeen the USA and Great Britain & Ireland. His grandson and great grandson, George Walker Bush and George Bush jr have both become Presidents of the United States.

Ward, Charles Harold   (1911–2001)

Charlie Ward played in three Ryder Cup matches from 1947–1951 and was twice third in the Open, behind Henry Cotton at Muirfield in 1948 and Max Faulkner at Royal Portrush in 1951.

Wethered, Joyce – Lady Heathcoat-Amory (1901–1997)

Entered her first English Ladies Championship in 1920 at the age of 18 and beat holder Cecil Leitch in the final. She remained unbeaten for four years, winning 33 successive matches. After they had played together at St Andrews, Bobby Jones remarked: 'I had never played golf with anyone, man or woman, amateur or professional, who made me feel so utterly outclassed.'

Wethered, Roger   (1899–1983)

Amateur champion in 1923 and runner-up in 1928 and 1930, he played five times in the Walker Cup, acting as playing captain at Royal St George's in 1930, and represented England against Scotland every year from 1922 to 1930. In the Open Championship at St Andrews in 1921 he tied with Jock Hutchison despite incurring a penalty for treading on his own ball. Due to play in a cricket match in England the following day, he was persuaded to stay in St Andrews for the play-off, but lost by 150–159 over 36 holes.

Whitcombe, Ernest   (1890–1971)
Charles   (1895–1978)
Reginald   (1898–1957)

The remarkable golfing brothers from Burnham, Somerset, were all selected for the Ryder Cup team of 1935.

Charlie and Eddie were paired togther and won the only point in the foursomes in a heavy 9-3 defeat by the American team. Reg won the gale-lashed Open at Royal St George's in 1938, with a final round of 78 as the exhibition tent was blown into the sea. Ernest finished second to Walter Hagen in 1924 and Charlie was third at Muirfield in 1935.

Wilson, Enid   (1910–1996)

Completed a hat-trick of victories in the Ladies British Amateur Championship from 1931–33. She was twice a semi-finalist in the American Championship, won the British Girls and English Ladies titles and played in the inaugural Curtis Cup match, beating Helen Hicks 2 and 1 in the singles. Retiring early from competitive golf, she was never afraid to express strongly held views on the game in her role as women's golf correspondent of the *Daily Telegraph*.

Wind, Herbert Warren   (1917–2005)

One of if not the most distinguished writers on golf in America, he authored 14 books on the game he loved with a passion. A long-time contributor to the *New Yorker* magazine, he is still the only writer to have received the United States Golf Association's Bobby Jones award for distinguished sportsmanship – an honour bestowed on him in 1995, the year the Association celebrated its centenary. The award was appropriate because he was a life-long admirer of Jones and was a regular at The Masters each year where he has been given the credit for naming, in 1958, the difficult stretch of holes from the 11th to the 13th as Amen Corner, arguing you said "Amen" if you negotiated them without dropping a shot.

Wood, Craig   (1901–1968)

Both Masters and US Open champion in 1941, Wood finally made up for a career of near misses, having lost play-offs for all four major championships between 1933 and 1939. He was three times a member of the American Ryder Cup team.

Yates, Charlie   (1913–2005)

Great friend of the late Bobby Jones he was top amateur in the US Masters in 1934, 1939 and 1940. In 1938 came to Royal Troon and won the British Amateur title beating R. Ewing 3 and 2. For many years acted as chairman of the press committee at The Masters and staged annual parties for visiting golf writers in the Augusta Clubhouse. He was a long-time Vice President of the Association of Golf Writers.

Zaharias, Mildred – née Didrickson (1915–1956)

As a 17-year-old, Babe, as she was universally known, broke three records in the 1932 Los Angeles Olympics – the javelin, 80 metres hurdles and high jump, but her high jump medal was denied her when judges decided her technique was illegal. Turning her attention to golf, she rapidly established herself as the most powerful woman golfer of the time and in 1945 played and made the cut in the LA Open on the men's PGA Tour. She won the final of the US Amateur by 11 and 9 in 1946, became the first American to win the British title the following year, then helped launch the women's profes-

sional tour. She won the US Women's Open in 1948, 1950 and 1954 and in 1950 won six of the nine events on the tour. In 1952 she had a major operation for cancer, but when she won her third and final Open two years later it was by the margin of 12 shots. She was voted Woman Athlete of the Year five times between 1932 and 1950 and Greatest Female Athlete of the Half-Century in 1949.

With the passing of Byron Nelson, golf loses an all-time great and an unbeaten record holder

With his death on September 26, 2006, John Byron Nelson, born in Fort Worth, Texas, on February 4 1912, left a legacy which many will aspire to emulate but which few will achieve. Nelson joined the professional ciruit in 1935 after a caddie shack apprenticeship which he shared with Ben Hogan and quickly established himself, winning the New Jersey Open in 1935 and going on to take The Masters title a mere two years later.

© Phil Sheldon Golf Picture Library

Between 1935 and 1946 he had 54 wins but although he won The Masters in 1937 and 1942, the US Open in 1939 and the US PGA Championship in 1940 and 1945 he didn't manage to pull off a Grand Slam having never won The Open Championship.

The 1939 US Open is probably best remembered as the tournament Sam Snead threw away, history tending to overlook the achievement of Byron Nelson, the man who eventually took the title. After a three-way play-off with Craig Wood and Densmore Shute, Nelson went on to win the decisive 18 holes by three shots from Wood.

America's entry into the second world war called a temporary halt to competitive golf for many. Nelson, denied the opportunity to serve his country due to a blood disorder, continued to play throughout 1943 and 1944, re-establishing his prominent position when full competition reassumed in 1945, winning 18 times including 11 events in a row between March and August – a record unlikely ever to be broken. He was twice a member of US Ryder Cup teams – in 1937 and 1947 and had been picked for the postponed matches in 1939 and 1941. He returned to that competition in 1965 when he captained the victorious US team. His only win in Europe was the 1955 French Open.

He was a father figure in US golf and until he retired in 2001 was one of The Masters honorary starters along with the late Gene Sarazen and Sam Snead. In company with Snead and his old sparring partner Ben Hogan, Byron Nelson was one of the sport's most revered figures and had a particularly close friendship with five times Open champion Tom Watson.

 The only shots you can be dead sure of are those you've had already. — *Byron Nelson*

British Isles International Players

Professional Men

Key

RC	Ryder Cup GBI till 1977; Europe thereafter.	DC	Dunhill Cup – by home country
		CC	Canada Cup
USA	1921, 1926: pre-Ryder Cup	WbC	Warburg Cup
RoW	Rest of World	(S)Eur	European Seniors v Ladies European Tour
FT	Four Tours World Championship, Players represented European Tour; also in Nissan Cup and Kirin Cup	*	indicates winning team
		'to' indicates inclusive dates: e.g.'1908 to 1911' means '1908-09-10-11'; otherwise individual years are shown.	
Eur	GBI v Continent of Europe (Seve Trophy)		
WC	World Cup – by home country; was Canada (Cup) till 1966	Captaincy is indicated by the year printed in bold type; non-playing captaincy in brackets	

ENGLAND

Alliss, Percy
RC 1929-31-33-35-37; Sco 1932 to 1937; Irl 1932-38; Wal 1938. GBI: Fra 1939

Alliss, Peter
RC 1953-57-59-61-63-65-67-69; CC 1954-55-57-58-59-61-62-64-66; WC 1967

Baker, Peter
RC 1993; DC 1993 (r/u)-98; WC 1999

Bamford, BJ
CC 1961

Barber, T
Irl 1932-33

Batley, JB
Sco 1912

Beck, AG
Wal, Irl 1938

Bembridge, Maurice
RC 1969-71-73-75; SA 1976; WC 1974-75; (S)Eur 1997

Bickerton, J
Eur 2000

Boomer, Aubrey
USA 1926; RC 1927-29

Bousfield, Ken
RC 1949-51-55-57-59-61; CC 1956-57

Boxall, R
WC 1990; DC 1990

Branch, WJ
Sco 1936

Brand, Gordon J
RC 1983; Nissan 1986; WC 1983; DC 1986-87*

Broadhurst, Paul
RC 1991; FT 1991-95; WC 1997; DC 1991

Burton, J
Irl 1933

Burton, R (Dick)
RC 1935-37-49; Sco 1935-36-37; Sco, Wal, Irl 1938

Busson, JH
Sco 1938

Busson, Jack J
RC 1935; Sco 1934-35-36-37

Butler, Peter J
RC 1965-69-71-73; Eur 1976; WC 1969-70-73

Carter, D
DC 1998; WC 1998*

Casey, Paul
RC 2004-06; WC 2004; Eur 2003-05

Cawsey, GH
Sco 1906-07

Caygill, G Alex
RC 1969

Chapman, R
DC 2000

Clark, Clive
RC 1973

Clark, Howard K
RC 1977-81-85-87-89-95; Aus 1988; Eur 1978-84; Nissan 1985; WC 1978-84-85-87; DC 1985-86-87*-89-90-94-95

Claydon, R
DC 1997

Coles, Neil C
RC 1961-63-65-67-69-71-73-77; Eur 1974-76-78-80; (S)Eur 1998-99; Can 1963; WC 1968

Collinge, T
Sco 1937

Collins, JF
Sco 1903-04

Compston, Archie
USA 1926; RC 1927-29-31; Fra 1929; Sco, Irl 1932; Sco 1935

Cotton, T Henry
RC 1929-37-47; Fra 1929

Cox, WJ (Bill)
RC 1935-37; Sco 1935-36-37

Curtis, D
Sco 1934; Sco, Wal, Irl 1938

Davis, Brian
DC 2000; Eur 2005

Davies, William H
RC 1931-33; Sco, Irl 1932-33

Dawson, Peter
RC 1977; WC 1977

Denny, Charles S
Sco 1936

Donald. Luke
RC 2004-06; **WC** 2004-06

Dougherty, Nick
Eur 2005

Durnian, Denis
WC 1989; DC 1989; WbC 2001-02

Easterbrook, Syd
RC 1931-33; Sco 1932 to 35; 38; Irl
1933

Faldo, Nick A
RC 1977-79-81-83-85-87-89-91-
93-95-97; Eur 1978-80-82-84;
RoW 1982; Nissan 1986; Kirin
1987; FT 1990; WC 1977-91-98*;
DC 1985-86-87*-88-91-93; WbC
2001-02

Faulkner, Max
RC 1947-49-51-53-57

Foster, M
Eur 1976; WC 1976

Gadd, B
Sco, Irl 1933; Sco 1935; Sco, Irl,
Wal 1938

Gadd, George
USA 1926; **RC** 1927

Garner, John R
RC 1971-71

Gaudin, PJ
Sco 1905-06-07-09-12-13

Gilford, David
RC 1991-95; WC 1992-93; DC
1992*

Gray, E
Sco 1904-05-07

Green, Eric
RC 1947

Green, T
Sco 1935; also Wal v Sco, Irl 1937
and Sco, Eng 1938

Gregson, Malcolm
RC 1967; WC 1967; (S) Eur 1997

Hargreaves, Jack
RC 1951

Havers, AG
USA 1921-26; **RC** 1927-31-33; Fra
1929; Sco, Irl 1932-33; Sco 1934

Hitchcock, Jimmy
RC 1965

Horne, Reg
RC 1947

Horton, Tommy
RC 1975-77; Eur 1974-76; WC
1976; (S) Eur 1997-(98)-(99)

Howell, David
RC 2004-06; Eur 2000-03-05; DC
1999; WC 2005

Hunt, Bernard J
RC 1953-57-59-61-63-65-67-69;
Can 1958-59-60-62-63-64; WC
1968

Hunt, Guy L
RC 1975; Eur 1974; WC 1972-75

Hunt, Geoffrey M
RC 1963

Jacklin, A (Tony)
RC 1967-69-71-73-75-77-79-
(83)-(85)-(87)-(89); Eur 1976-
82; RoW 1982; Can 1966; WC
1970-71-72

Jacobs, John RM
RC 1955

Jagger, D
Eur 1976

James, Mark H
RC 1977-79-81-89-91-93-95-(99);
Eur 1978-80-82; RoW 1982; Aus
1988; Kirin 1988; FT 1989-90; WC
1978-79-82-84-87-88-93-97-99; DC
1988-89-90-93-95-97-99

Jarman, Edward W
RC 1935; Sco 1935

Job, Nick
Eur 1980

Jolly, Herbert C
USA 1926; **RC** 1927; Fra 1929

Jones, D
(S)Eur 1998-99

Jones, R
Sco 1903 to 07; 09-10-12-13

Kenyon, EWH
Sco, Irl 1932

King, Michael
RC 1979; WC 1979

King, Sam L
RC 1937-47-49; Sco 1934-36-37;
Sco, Wal, Irl 1938

Lacey, Arthur J
RC 1933-37; Sco, Irl 1932-33; Sco
1934-36-37; Sco, Irl, Wal 1938

Lane, Barry
RC 1993; WC 1988-94; DC 1988-
94-95-96; WbC 2002

Lees, Arthur
RC 1947-49-51-55; Sco, Wal, Irl
1938

Mason, SC
Eur 1980; WC 1980

Mayo, CH
Sco 1907-09-10-12-13

Mills, R Peter
RC 1957-59

Mitchell, Abe
USA 1921-26; **RC** 1929-31-33; Sco
1932-33-34

Mitchell, P
WC 1996

Moffitt, Ralph
RC 1961

Morgan, J
(S)Eur 1997-99

Ockenden, J
USA 1921

Oke, WG
Sco 1932

Oosterhuis, Peter A
RC 1971-73-75-77-79-81; Eur
1974; WC 1971

O'Sullivan, DF
(S)Eur 1998

Padgham, Alf H
RC 1933-35-37; Sco, Irl 1932-33;
Sco 1934 to 37; Sco, Irl, Wal 1938

Payne, J
WC 1996

Perry, Alf
RC 1933-35-37; Irl 1932; Sco 1933-
36-38

Platts, Lionel
RC 1965

Poulter, Ian
RC 2004; Eur 2005

Price, Phillip
Eur 2003

Rainford, P
Sco 1903-07

Ray, E (Ted)
USA 1921-26; **RC** 1927; Sco 1903
to 07; 09-10-12-13

Reid, W
Sco 1906-07

Renouf, TG
Sco 1903-04-05-10-13

Rhodes, J
(S)Eur 1998

Richardson, Steven
RC 1991; FT 1991; WC 1992; DC
1991-92*

Robson, F
USA1926; **RC** 1927-29-31; Sco
1909-10

Roe, Mark
WC 1989-94-95; DC 1994

Rose, Justin
Eur 2003

Rowe, AJ
Sco 1903-06-07

Scott, Syd S
RC 1955

Seymour, M
SCO: Irl 1932. ENG: Sco, Irl 1932-33

Sherlock, JG
USA 1921; Sco 1903 to 07; 09-10-
12-13

Snell, D
Canada 1965

Spence, J
DC 1992*-2000

Sutton, M
Can 1955

Taylor, JH
USA 1921; Sco 1903 to 07; 09-10-12-13

Taylor, JJ
Sco 1937

Taylor, Josh
USA 1921; Sco 1913

Tingey, A
Sco 1903-05

Townsend, Peter
RC 1969-71; Eur 1974; WC 1969-74

Twine, WT
Irl 1932

Vardon, Harry
USA 1921

Waites, Brian J
RC 1983; Eur 1980-82-84; RoW 1982; WC 1980-82-83; (S)Eur 1997-98

Ward, Charlie H
RC 1947-49-51; Irl 1932

Way, Paul
RC 1983-85; WC 1985; DC 1985-99

Weetman, Harry
RC 1951-53-55-57*-59-61-63; Can 1954-56-60

Westwood, Lee
RC 1997-99-2002-04-06; Eur 2000-03; DC 1996-97-98-99

Whitcombe, Charles A
RC 1927-29-31-33-35-37; Fra 1929; Sco 1932 to 38; Irl 1933

Whitcombe, EE
Sco, Wal, Irl 1938

Whitcombe, Ernest R
USA 1926; RC 1929-31-35; Fra 1929; Sco 1932; Irl 1933

Whitcombe, Reg A
RC 1935; Sco 1933 to 38

Wilcock, P
WC 1973

Williamson, T
Sco 1904 to 07; 09-10-12-13

Wilson, RG
Sco 1913

Wolstenholme, Guy B
Can 1965

IRELAND

Boyle, Hugh F
RC 1967; WC 1967

Bradshaw, Harry
RC 1953-55-57; Can 1954 to 1959; Sco 1937-38; Wal 1937; Eng 1938

Carrol, LJ
Sco, Wal 1937; Sco, Eng 1938

Cassidy, D
Sco 1936; Sco, Wal 1937

Cassidy, J
Eng 1933; Sco 1934-35

Clarke, Darren
RC 1997-99-2002-04-06; Eur 2000; DC 1994 to 99; WC 1994-95-96

Daly, Fred
RC 1947-49-51-53; Sco 1936; Sco, Wal 1937; Sco, Eng 1938; Can 1954-55

Darcy, Eamonn
RC 1975-77-81-87; Eur 1976-84; SA 1976; WC 1976-77-83-84-85-87; DC 1987-88*-91

Drew, Norman V
RC 1959; Can 1960-61

Edgar, J
Sco 1938

Fairweather, S
Eng 1932; Sco 1933. Sco: Eng 1933-35-36; Irl, Wal 1938

Feherty, David
RC 1991; FT 1990-91; DC 1985-86-90*-91-93; WC 1990

Greene, C
Can 1965

Hamill, J
Eng 1932; Eng, Sco 33; Sco 34-35

Harrington, Padraig
RC 1999-2002-04-06; Eur 2000-03-05; DC 1996 to 99; WC 1996-97*-98-99-2000-04-05-06

Holley, W
Sco 1933-34-35-36-38; Eng 1932-33-38

Jackson, H
WC 1970-71

Jones, E
Can 1965

Kinsella, J
WC 1968-69-72-73

Kinsella, W
Sco 1937; Sco, Eng 1938

McCartney, J
Sco 1932 to 38; Eng 1932-33-38; Wal 1937

McDermott, M
Sco, Eng 1932

McDowell, Graeme
Eur 2005

McGinley, Paul
RC 2002-04-06; WC 1993-94-97*-98-99-2000-05-06; DC 1993-94-96-97-98-99-04; Eur 2005

McKenna, J
Sco 1936; Sco, Wal 1937; Sco, Wal, Eng 1938

McKenna, R
Sco, Eng 1933; Sco 1935

McNeill, H
Eng 1932

Mahon, PJ
Sco 1932 to 38; Eng 1932-33-38; Wal 1937-38

Martin, Jimmy
RC 1965; Can 1962-63-64-66; WC 1970

O'Brien, W
Sco 1934-36; Sco, Wal 1937

O'Connor, Christy
RC 1955-57-59-61-63-65-67-69-71-73; Can 1956 to 64; 66; WC 1967-68-69-71-73

O'Connor, Christy jr
RC 1975-89; Eur 1974-84; SA 1976; (S)Eur 1998; WC 1974-75-78-85-89-92; DC 1985-89-92

O'Connor, CJ
(S)Eur 1998

O'Connor, P
Sco, Eng 1932-33; Sco 1934-35-36

O'Leary, John E
RC 1975; Eur 1976-78-82; RoW 1982; WC 1972-80-82

O'Neill, J
Eng 1933

O'Neill, M
Sco, Eng 1933; Sco 1934

Patterson, E
Sco 1933 to 36; Eng 1933; Wal 1937

Polland, Eddie
RC 1973; Eur 1974-76-78-80; (S)Eur 1998-99; WC 1973-74-76-77-78-79

Pope, CW
Sco, Eng 1932

Rafferty, Ronan
RC 1989; Eur 1984; Kirin 1988; FT 1989-90-91; Aus 1988; WC 1983-84-87-88; 90 to 93; DC 1986-87-88*-89-90*-91-92-93-95

Smyth, Des
RC 1979-81; Eur 1980-82-84; RoW 1982; WC 1979-80-82-83-88-89; DC 1985-86-87-88*-2000; WbC 2001

Stevenson, P
Sco 1933 to 36; 38; Eng 1933-38

Wallace, L
Sco, Eng 1932

Walton, Philip
RC 1995; WC 1995; DC 1989-90*-92-94-95

SCOTLAND

Adams, J
RC 1947-49-51-53; Eng 1932 to 1938; Wal 1937-38; Irl 1937-38

Ainslie, T
Irl 1936

Anderson, Joe
Irl 1932

Anderson, W
Irl 1936; Eng, Wal 1937

Ayton, LB
Eng 1910-12-13-33-34

Ayton, Laurie B jr
RC 1949; Eng 1937

Ballantine, J
Eng 1932-36

Ballingall, J
Eng, Irl, Wal 1938

Bannerman, Harry
RC 1993; WC 1967-72

Barnes, Brian
RC 1969-71-73-75-77-79; Eur 1974-76-78-80; SA 1976; WC 1974-75-76-77

Braid, James
USA 1921; Eng 1903 to 07; 1910-12

Brand, Gordon jr
RC 1987-89; Aus 1988; Nissan 1985; Kirin 1988; FT 1989; WC 1984-85-88-89-90-92-94; DC 1985 to 89; 91 to 94; 97

Brown, Eric C
RC 1953-55-57-59; Can 1954 to 62; 65-66; WC 1967-68

Brown, Ken
RC 1977-79-83-85-87; Eur 1978; Kirin 1987; WC 1977-78-79-83

Burns, Stewart
RC 1929; Eng 1932

Callum, WS
Irl 1935

Campbell, J
Irl 1936

Coltart, Andrew
RC 1999; DC 1994-95*-96-98-2000; WC 1994-95-96-98

Coltart, F
Eng 1909

Dailey, Allan
RC 1933; Eng 1932 to 36; Eng, Irl, Wal 1938

Davis, W
Irl 1933 to 36; Irl, Eng, Wal 1937-38

Dobson, T
Eng, Irl 1932 to 1936; Eng, Irl, Wal 1937; Irl, Wal 1938

Don, W
Irl 1935-36

Donaldson, J
Eng 1932-35-38; Irl, Wal 1937

Dorman, R
Irl 1932

Drummond, Scott
WC 2005-06

Duncan, George
USA 1921-26; RC 1927-29-31; Eng 1906-07-09-10-12-13-32-34 to 37

Durward, JG
Irl 1934; Eng 1937

Fairweather, S
IRL: Eng 1932; Sco 1933. SCO: Eng 1933-35-36; Irl, Wal 1938

Fallon, John
RC 1955; Eng 1936; Eng, Irl, Wal 1937-38

Fenton, WB
Eng, Irl 1932; Irl 1933

Fernie, TR
Eng 1910-12-13-33

Gallacher, Bernard
RC 1969-71-73-75-77-79-81-83-(91)-(93)-(95); Eur 1974-78-82-84; SA 1976; RoW 1982; WC 1969-71-74-82-83

Gallacher, Stephen
WC 2005-06

Good, G
Eng 1934-36

Gow, A
Eng 1912

Grant, T
Eng 1913

Haliburton, Tom B
RC 1961-63; Can 1954; Irl 1935-36; Irl, Wal, Eng 1938

Hastings, W
Eng, Wal, Irl 1937-38

Hepburn, J
Eng 1903-05-06-07-09-10-12-13

Herd, A (Sandy)
Eng 1903-04-05-06-09-10-12-13-32

Houston, D
Irl 1934

Huish, D
WC 1973

Hunter, W
Eng 1906-07-09-10

Hutton, GC
Irl 1936; Irl, Eng, Wal 1937; Eng 1938

Ingram, D
WC 1973

Knight, G
Eng 1937

Laidlaw, W
Eng 1935-36-38; Irl, Wal 1937

Lawrie, Paul
RC 1999-06; WC 1996; DC 1999; Eur 2003

Lockhart, G
Irl 1934-35

Lyle, AWB (Sandy)
RC 1979-81-83-85-87; Eur 1980-82-84; RoW 1982; Aus 1988; Nissan 1985-86; Kirin 1987; WC 1979-80-87; DC 1985 to 90; 92

McCulloch, D
Eng, Irl 1932 to 35; Eng 1936-37

McDowall, J
Eng 1932; Eng, Irl 1933 to 36

McEwan, P
Eng 1907

McIntosh, G
Eng, Irl, Wal 1938

McMillan, J
Eng, Irl 1933-34; Eng 1935

McMinn, W
Eng 1932-33-34

Martin, S
WC 1980

Montgomerie, Colin
RC 1991-93-95-97-99-2002-04-06; Eur 2000-**03-05**; FT 1991; WC 1988-91-92-93-97 (individual winner)-98-99; DC 1988; 91 to 98 (winners 95); 2000

Orr, Gary
Eur 2000; DC 1998-99-2000

Panton, John
RC 1951-53-61; Can 1955 to 66; WC 1968

Park, J
Eng 1909

Ritchie, WL
Eng 1913

Robertson, F
Irl 1933; Eng 1938

Robertson, P
Eng, Irl 1932; Irl 1934

Russell, Raymond
WC 1997; DC 1996-97

Sayers, Ben jr
Eng 1906-07-09

Seymour, M
Irl 1932. ENG: Sco, Irl 1932-33

Shade, Ronnie DBM
WC 1970-71-72

Simpson, A
Eng 1904

Smith, CR
Eng 1903-04-07-09-13

Smith, GE
Irl 1932

Spark, W
Irl 1933; Irl, Eng 1935; Irl, Wal 1937

Thompson, R
Eng 1903 to 07; 09-10-12

Torrance, Sam
RC 1981-83-85-87-89-91-93-95-(2002); Eur 1976-78-80-82-84;

RoW 1982; Nissan 1985; FT 1991; WC 1976-78-82-84-85-87-89-90-93-95; DC 1985-86-87-89-90-91-93-95*; WbC 2001-02

Walker, RT
Can 1964

Watt, T
Eng 1907

Watt, W
Eng 1912-13

White, J
Eng 1903 to 07; 09; 12-13

Will, George
RC 1963-65-67; Can 1963; WC 1969-70

Wilson, T
Irl 1932; Irl, Eng 1933-34

Wood, Norman
RC 1975; WC 1975

WALES

Affleck, P
DC 1995-96

Cox, S
WC 1975

Davies, R
WC 1968

De Foy, Craig B
WC 1971; 73 to 78

Dobson, K
WC 1972

Dodd, Stephen
Eur 2005; WC 2005*-06

Dredge, Bradley
Eur 2005; WC 2005*-06

Gould, H
Can 1954-55

Grabham, C
Eng, Sco 1938

Healing, SF
Sco 1938

Hill, EF
Sco, Irl 1937; Sco, Eng 1938

Hodson, Bert
RC 1931; Sco, Irl 1937; Sco, Eng 1938; also Eng v Irl 1933

Huggett, Brian GC
RC 1963-67-69-71-73-75; Eur 1974-78; Can 1963-64-65; WC 1968-69-70-71-76-79; (S)Eur 1998

James, G
Sco, Irl 1937

Jones, DC
Sco, Irl 1937; Sco, Eng 1938

Jones, T
Sco 1936; Irl 1937; Eng 1938

Llewellyn, D
Eur 1984; WC 1974-85-87*-88; DC 1985-88

Lloyd, F
Sco, Irl 1937; Sco, Eng 1938

Mayo, Paul
DC 1993

Mouland, Mark
Kirin 1988; WC 1988-89-90-92-93-95-96; DC 1986-87-88-89-93-95-96

Mouland, S
Can 1965-66; WC 1967

Park, D
DC 2000

Parkin, P
Eur 1984; WC 1984-89; DC 1985-86-87-89-90-91

Pickett, C
Sco, Irl 1937; Sco, Eng 1938

Price, Phillip
RC 2002; Eur 2000; WC 1994-95-97-98-2000; DC 1991-96

Rees, Dai J
RC 1937-47-49-51-53-**(55)-(57)***-**(59)-(61)-(67)**

Smalldon, D
Can 1955-56

Thomas, Dave C
RC 1959-63-65-67; Can 1957 to 63; 66; WC 1967-69-70

Vaughan, DI
WC 1972-73-77-78-79-80

Williams, K
Sco, Irl 1937; Sco, Eng 1938

Williams, KL
WC 1982

Woosnam, Ian
RC 1983-85-87-89-91-93-95-97-**(2006)**; Eur 1982-84-2000; RoW 1982; Aus 1988; Nissan 1985-86; Kirin 1987; FT 1989-90; WC 1980; 82 to 85; 87*; 90 to 94; 96-97-98; DC 1985 to 91; 93-95-2000; WbC 2001-02

Sam Torrance hits the 700 mark at £21.42 a shot!

Former Ryder Cup captain Sam Torrance played in his 700th event on the main European Tour when he teed up in the 2006 Barclays Scottish Open at Loch Lomond.

Sam, son of club professional and top teacher Bob Torrance, turned professional in 1970 when he was 16, earned £35.10p when finished 39th in his first event – 1971 AGFA-Gevaert tournament at Stoke Poges (now Stoke Park) and scored the first of his 21 victories in his 77th tournament – the 1976 Piccadilly Medal at Finham Park for which he won £6,000.

He has played in 27 different countries on the European schedule – an indication of how international the Tour is – and has won first prize cheques in ten of them. It has been estimated that he has walked 16,330 miles playing on the European Tour, hit in the region of 178,000 shots (each worth £21.42p) for an average of 72.22.

Professional Women

Non-playing captaincy in brackets

ENGLAND

Davies, Laura
SOLHEIM CUP 1990-92-94-96-98-2000-2002-03-05; World Cup 2006

Douglas, Kitrina
SOLHEIM CUP 1992

Fairclough, Lora
SOLHEIM CUP 1994

Hackney, Lisa
SOLHEIM CUP 1996-98

Johnson, Trish
SOLHEIM CUP 1990-92-94-96-98-2000-05

Morley, Joanne
SOLHEIM CUP 1996

Nicholas, Alison
SOLHEIM CUP 1990-92-94-96-98-2000

Stupples, Karen
SOLHEIM CUP 2005

Taylor, Kirsty
World Cup 2006

Walker, Mickey
SOLHEIM CUP **(1990)-(92)-(94)-(96)**

SCOTLAND

McKay, Mhairi
SOLHEIM CUP 2002-03

Marshall, Kathryn
SOLHEIM CUP 1996

Matthew, Catriona
SOLHEIM CUP 1998-2003-05; World Cup 2006

Moodie, Janice
SOLHEIM CUP 2000-03; World Cup 2006

Reid, Dale
SOLHEIM CUP 1990-92-94-96-**(2000)-(2002)**

Wright, Pam
SOLHEIM CUP 1990-92-94

WALES

Brewerton, Becky
World Cup 2006

Morgan, Becky
World Cup 2006

Amateur Men

Key

WC	Walker Cup	NNC	Nixdorf Nations Cup
AP	Europe v Asia-Pacific (Bonallack Trophy)	Scan	Scandinavia
CT	Commonweath Tournament	*	indicates winning team
ET	Eisenhower Trophy		
ETC	played in European Team Championship for home country		
Eur	GBI v Cont of Europe (St Andrews Trophy)		
HI	played in Home International matches		

'to' indicates inclusive dates: e.g.'1908 to 1911' means '1908-09-10-11'; otherwise individual years are shown.

Captaincy is indicated by the year printed in bold type; non-playing captaincy in brackets

---

ENGLAND

Ashby, H
Dominican Int 1973; Eur 1974; HI 1972-73-74

Attenborough, MF
WC 1967; Eur 1966-68; HI 1964-66-67-68; ETC 1967

Aylmer, CC
USA 1921; WC 1922; Sco 1911-22-23-24

Baker, P
WC 1985; Eur 1986; HI 1985

Ball, J
Sco 1902 to 12

Banks, C
HI 1983

Banks, SE
HI 1934-38

Bardsley, R
HI 1987; Fra 1988

Barker, HH
Sco 1907

Barry, AG
Sco 1906-07

Bathgate, D
HI 1990

Bayliss, RP
Irl 1929; HI 1933-34

Beck, JB
WC 1928-(38)*-(47); Sco 1926-30; HI 1933

Beddard, JB
Wal/Irl 1925; Sco 1927-28; Sco, Irl 1929

Beharrell, JC
HI 1956

Bell, RK
HI 1947

Benka, PJ
WC 1969; Eur 1970; HI 1967-68-69-70; ETC 1969

Bennett, H
HI 1948-49-51

Bennett, S
Sco 1979

Bennett, W
ET 1994; Eur 1994; HI 1992-93-94; Fra 1994

Bentley, AL
HI 1936-37; Fra 1937-39

Bentley, HG
WC 1934-36-38; Sco, Irl 1931; HI 1932 to 38; 47; Fra 1934 to 37; 39; 54

Berry, P
Eur 1972; HI 1972

Birtwell, SG
HI 1968-70-73

Blackey, M
HI 1995-96-97; ETC 1997; Fra 1994-96; Esp 1995

Bladon,W
Eur 1996; HI 1996

Blakeman, D
HI 1981; Fra 1982

Bland, R
HI 1994-95; Esp 1995

Bloxham, JA
HI 1966

Bonallack, Sir Michael F
WC 1957 to 73; (69-71*); ET 1960 to 72; CT 1959-63-67-71; Eur 1958; 62 to 72; HI 1957 to 74; ETC 1969-71

Bottomley, S
HI 1986

Bourn, TA
Aus 1934; Irl 1928; Sco 1930; HI 1933-34; Fra 1934

Bowman, TH
HI 1932

Boyd, Gary
HI 2006

Boxall, R
HI 1980-81-82; Fra 1982

Bradshaw, AS
HI 1932

Bradshaw, EI
Sco 1979; ETC 1979

Bradshaw, Paul
HI 2003

Bramston, JAT
Sco 1902

Brand, GJ
Eur 1976; HI 1976

Bretherton, CF
Sco 1922 to 25; Wal/Irl 1925

Bristowe, OC
WC 1923-24

Broadhurst. P
Eur 1988; HI 1986-87; Fra 1988

Bromley-Davenport, E
HI 1938-51

Brough, S
Eur 1960; HI 1952-55-59-60; Fra 1952-60

Brownlow, Hon WGE
WC 1926

Burch, N
HI 1974

Burgess, MJ
HI 1963-64-67; ETC 1967

Butterworth, JR
Fra 1954

Cage, S
WC 1993; HI 1992

Caldwell, I
WC 1951-55; HI 1950 to 59; 61; Fra 1950

Cannon, JHS
Irl/Wal 1925

Carman, A
Sco 1979; HI 1980

Carr, FC
Sco 1911

Carrigill, PM
HI 1978

Carver, M
HI 1996; ETC 1997

Casey, P
WC 1999; ET 2000; Eur 2000; HI 1999

Cassells, C
HI 1989

Castle, H
Sco 1903-04

Chapman, BHG
WC 1961; Eur 1962; HI 1961-62

Chapman, R
WC 1981; Eur 1980; Sco 1979; HI 1980-81; ETC 1981

Christmas, MJ
WC 1961-63; Eur 1962-64; ET 1962; HI 1960 to 64

Clark, CA
WC 1965; Eur 1964; HI 1964

Clark, Graeme
HI 1995-2002-03; ETC 2001; Esp 2001-03 Fra 2002

Clark, GJ
WC 1965; Eur 1964-66

Clark, HK
WC 1973; HI 1973

Claydon, Russell
WC 1989; HI 1988; ETC 1989

Colt, HS
Sco 1908

Cook, J
HI 1989-90

Cook, JH
HI 1969

Corfield, Lee
Eur 2004; HI 2002-04; Esp 2005

Crampton, James
HI 2005

Crawley, Leonard G
WC 1932-34-38-47; Sco, Irl 1931; HI 1932-33-34-36-37-38-47-48-49-54-55; Fra 1936-37-38-49

Critchley, Bruce
WC 1969; Eur 1970; HI 1962-69-70; ETC 1969

Cryer, Matthew
HI 2005l Fra 2006

Curry, DH
WC 1987; ET 1986; Eur 1986-88; HI 1984-86-87; Fra 1988

Darwin, Bernard
WC 1922; Sco 1902-04-05-08-09-10-23-24

Davies, JC
WC 1973-75-77-79; ET 1974-76*; Eur 1972-74-76-78; HI 1969-71-72-73-74-78; ETC 1973-75-77

Davies, M
HI 1984-85

Davison, C
HI 1989

Dawson, P
HI 1969

De Bendern, Count J (John de Forest)
WC 1932; Sco, Irl 1931

Deeble, P
WC 1977-81; Eur 1978; Colombian Int 1978; HI 1975-76-77-78-80-81-83-84; Sco 1979; ETC 1979-81; Fra 1982

Dinwiddie, Robert
WC 2005; HI 2004-05-06; Eur 2006; Esp 2005; Fra 2006

Dixon, D
HI 2000; RSA Esp 2001

Dodd, Laurence
HI 2004

Donald, Luke
WC 1999-2001; ET 1998*-2000; Eur 2000; HI 1996-97-98; ETC 1999-2001; Fra 1996

Dougherty, Nick
WC 2001; Eur 2000; HI 2000; ETC 2001; Fra 2000; Esp 2001

Downes, P
Eur 1980; HI 1976-77-78-80-81-82; ETC 1977-79-81

Downie, JJ
HI 1974

Drummond, S
HI 1995

Duck, R
HI 1997

Dunn, NW
Irl 1928

Durrant, RA
HI 1967; ETC 1967

Dyson, S
WC 1999; HI 1998-99; ETC 1999; Esp 1999

Edwards, CS
AP 2002; HI 1991 to 95; 97-98; 2003; ETC 1995-99; Fra 1992-94-96-2000; Esp 1993-95-99-2001

Eggo, R
WC 1987; Eur 1988; HI 1986 to 90; Fra 1988

Ellis, HC
Sco 1902-12

Ellison, TF
Sco 1922-25-26-27

Elson, Jamie
WC 2001; HI 2000-01-02; Fra 2000-02; Esp 2001

Evans, G
HI 1961

Evans, G
WC 1991; ET 1990; HI 1990; ETC 1991

Eyles, GR
WC 1975; ET 1974; Eur 1974; HI 1974-75; ETC 1975

Fairbairn, KA
HI 1988

Faldo, N
CT 1975; HI 1975

Fenton, P
HI 1996

Ferrie, K
HI 1998

Fiddian, EW
WC 1932-34; Sco, Irl 1929-30-31; HI 1932 to 35; Fra 1934

Finch, Richard
HI 2000-02; ETC 2003; Fra 2000-02; Esp 2003

Fisher, D
Eur 1994; HI 1993-94; Fra 1994

Fisher, Oliver
WC 2005; ET 2006; ETC 2005; AP 2006; Eur 2006; HI 2005-06

Fisher, Ross
HI 2003; ETC 2003

Fogg, HN
HI 1933

Foster, M
WC 1995; HI 1994-95; ETC 1995; Esp 1995

Foster, MF
HI 1973

Foster, R
WC 1965-67-69-71-73-**(79)-(81)**; ET 1964-70-**80**; Eur 1964-66-68-70; CT 1967-71; HI 1963-64; 66 to 72; ETC 1967-69-71-73

Fowler, WH
Sco 1903-04-05

Fox, SJ
HI 1956-57-58

Frame, DW
WC 1961; HI 1958 to 63

Francis, F
HI 1936; Fra 1935-36

Frazier, K
HI 1938

Fry, SH
Sco 1902 to 09

Garbutt, I
Eur 1992; HI 1990-91-92; ETC 1991; Fra 1992

Garner, PF
HI 1977-78-80; Sco 1979

Garnet, LG
Aus 1934; Fra 1934

Gee, Adam
HI 2004-05-06; Esp 2005; Fra 2006

Gent, J
Irl 1930; HI 1938

Gilford, David
WC 1985; ET 1984; Eur 1986; HI 1983-84-85

Gillies, HD
Sco 1908-25-26-27

Godfrey, S
HI 2001

Godwin, G
WC 1979-81; HI 1976-77-78-80-81; Sco 1979; ETC 1979-81; Fra 1982

Gray, CD
HI 1932

Green, HB
Sco 1979

Green, PO
CT 1963; HI 1961-62-63

Griffiths, D
HI 1999-2000-01; Fra 2000; RSA, Esp 2001

Hambro, AV
Sco 1905-08-09-10-22

Hamer, S
HI 1983-84

Hardman, RH
WC 1928; Sco 1927-28

Hare, A
WC 1989; HI 1988; ETC 1989

Harris, G
HI 1994; ETC 1995; Esp 1995

Harris, M
Eur 2000; HI 1998-99

Hartley, RW
WC 1930-32; Sco 1926 to 31; Irl 1928 to 31; HI 1933-34-35

Hartley, WL
WC 1932; Irl/Wal 1925; Sco 1927-31; Irl 1928-31; HI 1932-33; Fra 1935

Hassall, JE
Sco 1923; Irl/Wal 1925

Hawksworth, J
WC 1985; HI 1984-85

Hayward, CH
Sco 1925; Irl 1928

Heath, James
ET 2004; Eur 2004; AP 2004; HI 2003-04

Hedges, PJ
WC 1973-75; ET 1976; Eur 1974-76; HI 1970; 73 to 78, 82-83; ETC 1973-75-77

Helm, AGB
HI 1948

Henriques, GLQ
Irl 1930

Henry, W
HI 1987; Fra 1988

Hill, GA
WC 1936-(1955); HI 1936-37

Hilton, HH
Sco 1902 to 07; 09 to 12

Hilton, M
Esp 1999

Hoad, PGJ
HI 1978; Sco 1979

Hodgson, C
Sco 1924

Hodgson, J
HI 1994

Holderness, Sir EWE
USA 1921; WC 1923-26-30; Sco 1922 to 26; 28

Holmes, AW
HI 1962

Homer, TWB
WC 1973; ET 1972; Eur 1972; HI 1972-73; ETC 1973

Homewood, G
HI 1985-91; ETC 1991

Hooman, CVL
WC 1922-23; Sco 1910-22

Horsey, David
Fra 2006

Howell, D
WC 1995; HI 1994-95; ETC 1995; Esp 1995

Huddy, G
WC 1961; HI 1960-61-62

Humphreys, W
WC 1971; Eur 1970; HI 1970-71; ETC 1971

Hutchings, C
Sco 1902

Hutchinson, HG
Sco 1902-03-04-06-07-09

Hutt, R
HI 1991-92-93

Hyde, GE
HI 1967-68

Illingworth, G
Sco 1929; Fra 1937

Inglis, MJ
HI 1977

James, L
WC 1995; ET 1994; Eur 1994; HI 1993-94-95; ETC 1995; Fra 1994; Esp 1995

James, M
WC 1975; HI 1974-75; ETC 1975

James, RD
HI 1974-75

Jobson, RH
Irl 1928

Jones, JW
HI 1948 to 52; 54-55

Kelley, MJ
WC 1977-79; ET 1976*; Eur 1976-78; Colombian Int 1978; HI 1974 to 78; 80-81-82-(88); ETC 1977-79; Fra 1982

Kelley, PD
HI 1965-66-68

Kemp, John
HI 2003

Keppler, SD
WC 1983; HI 1982-83; Fra 1982

King, M
WC 1969-73; Eur 1970-72; CT 1971; HI 1969 to 73; ETC 1971-73

Kitchin, JE
Fra 1949

Knight, J
Fra 1996

Langley, JDA
WC 1936-51-53; HI 1950 to 53; Fra 1950

Langmead, J
HI 1986

Lassen, EA
Sco 1909 to 12

Laurence, C
HI 1983-84-85

Layton, EN
Sco 1922-23-26; Irl/Wal 1925

Lee, M
HI 1950

Lee, MG
HI 1965

Lewis, ME
WC 1983; HI 1980-81-82-(99)-(2001); Fra 1982

Lewton, Stephen
HI 2006

Lincoln, AC
Sco 1907

Lockerbie, Gary
WC 2005, HI 2003-04; ETC 2005; Esp 2005

Logan, GW
HI 1973

Lucas, D
HI 1996

Lucas, PB
WC 1936-47-(49); HI 1936-48-49; Fra 1936

Ludwell, N
HI 1991; Fra 1992

Lunt, MSR
WC 1959-61-63-65; ET 1964; Eur 1964; CT 1963; HI 1956 to 60; 62-63-64-66

Lunt, S
HI 1932 to 35; Fra 1934-35-39

Lupton, Jonathan
HI 2001-02; ETC 2003; Fra 2002; Esp 2003

Lyle, AWB (Sandy)
WC 1977; Eur 1976; CT 1975; HI 1975-76-77; ETC 1977

Lynn, D
HI 1995

Lyon, JS
HI 1937-38

McCarthy, S
HI 1998

McEvoy, Peter
WC 1977-79-81-85-89-(1999)*-(2001)*; ET 1978-80-84-86-88*; Eur 1978-80-86-88; HI 1976-77-78; 80-81; 83 to 89; 91; (94) to (97);

Sco 1979; ETC 1977-79-81-89; Fra
1982-88-92-(02)

McEvoy, R
WC 2001; HI 2000-01; ETC 2001;
Fra 2000; Esp 2001

McGowan, Ross
ET 2006; Eur 2006; HI 2006

McGuire, M
HI 1992

Marks, GC
WC 1969-71-**(87)-(89)***; ET
1970; Eur 1968-70; CT 1975;
Colombian Int 1975; HI 1963; 67 to
71; 74-75-82; ETC 1967-69-71-75;
Fra **(1982)**

Marsh, David M
WC 1959-71-**(73)-(75)**; Eur 1958;
HI 1956 to 60; 64-66; 68 to 72;
ETC 1971

Martin, DHR
HI 1938; Fra 1934-49

Mason, B
HI 1998-99; Esp 1999

Mason, SC
HI 1973

Mellin, GL
Sco 1922

Metcalfe, J
Eur 1990; HI 1989

Micklem, Gerald H
WC 1947-49-53-55-**(57)-(59)**; ET
1958; HI 1947 to 55

Millensted, Dudley J
WC 1967; CT 1967; HI 1966; ETC
1967

Millward, EB
WC 1949-55; HI 1950; 52 to 55

Mitchell, Abe
Sco 1910-11-12

Mitchell, CS
HI 1975-76-78

Mitchell, FH
Sco 1906-07-08

Moffat, DM
HI 1961-63-67; Fra 1959-60

Montmorency, RH de
USA 1921; Sco 1908; Wal/Irl 1925;
SA 1927

Moody, PH
Eur 1972; HI 1971-72

Morgan, J
Fra 2000

Morrison, JSF
Irl 1930

Mosey, IJ
HI 1971

Moul, Jamie
ET 2006; ETC 2005; Eur 2006; HI
2005-06; Esp 2005; Fra 2006

Muscroft, R
HI 1986

Nash, A
HI 1988-89

Neech, DG
HI 1961

Nelson, P
Fra 1996

Newey, AS
HI 1932

Oldcorn, Andrew
WC 1983; ET 1982; HI 1982-83

Oosterhuis, Peter A
WC 1967; ET 1968; Eur 1968; HI
1966-67-68

Oppenheimer, RH
WC (1951); Irl 1928-29; Irl, Sco
1930

Osborne, Sam
Eur 2004

Page, P
WC 1993; HI 1993

Palmer, DJ
HI 1962-63

Parker, Ben
HI 2006

Parry, John
Fra 2006

Patey, IR
HI 1925; Fra 1948-49-50

Pattinson, R
HI 1949

Payne, J
HI 1950-51

Payne, J
WC 1991; Eur 1990; HI 1989-90;
ETC 1991

Pearson, AG
SA 1927

Pearson, MJ
HI 1951-52

Pease, JWB (Lord
Wardington) Sco 1903 to 06

Pennink, JJF
WC 1938; HI 1937-38-47; Fra
1937-38-39

Perkins, TP
WC 1928; Sco 1927-28-29

Perowne, AH
WC 1949-53-59; ET 1958; HI 1947
to 51; 53-54-55-57

Philipson, S
HI 1997

Phillips, V
WC 1993

Plaxton, J
HI 1983-84

Pollock, VA
Sco 1908

Powell, WA
Sco 1923-24; Wal/Irl 1925

Poxon, Martin A
WC 1975; HI 1975-76; ETC 1975

Prosser, D
ETC 1989

Pullan, M
HI 1991-92

Pyman, I
WC 1993; HI 1993

Rawlinson, D
HI 1949-50-52-53

Ray, D
HI 1982; Fra 1982

Revell, RP
HI 1972-73; ETC 1973

Reynard, M
HI 1996-97; Fra 1996

Richardson, Edward
HI 2005-06; Fra 2006

Richardson, Matthew
WC 2005; ET 2004; Eur 2004; HI
2004; Esp 2003; ETC 2005; Esp
2005

Richardson, S
HI 1986-87-88

Risdon, PWL
HI 1935-36

Roberts, GP
HI 1951-53; Fra 1949

Roberts, HJ
HI 1947-48-53

Robertson, A
HI 1986-87; Fra 1988

Robinson, J
Irl 1928

Robinson, J
WC 1987; HI 1986

Robinson, S
Sco 1925; Irl 1928-29-30

Rodgers, C
HI 1999; Esp 1999

Rogers, A
HI 1991; Fra 1992

Roper, HS
Sco, Irl 1931

Roper, R
HI 1984 to 87

Rose, Justin
WC 1997; HI 1997; ETC 1997

Rothwell, J
HI 1947-48

Rowe, Philip
WC 1999; AP 2000; HI 1997-98-
2000; ETC 1999; Esp 1999

Ruth, James
HI 2004-05; Esp 2005

Ryles, D
HI 2000

Sanders, M
HI 1998-99; Esp 1999

Sandywell, A
HI 1990; ETC 1991

Scotland, Zane
HI 2000-01-02; Fra 2000-02

Scott, KB
HI 1937-38; Fra 1938

Scott, Hon Michael
WC 1924-(34); Aus 1934; Sco 1911-12; 23 to 26

Scott, Hon O
Sco 1902-05-06

Scrutton, EWHB
Sco 1912

Scrutton, PF
WC 1955-57; HI 1950-55

Sell, Martin
Esp 2003

Sewell, D
WC 1957-59; ET 1960; CT 1959; HI 1956 to 60

Shepperson, AE
WC 1957-59; HI 1956 to 60; 62

Sherborne, A
HI 1982-83-84

Shingler, TR
HI 1977

Shorrock, TJ
Fra 1952

Side, M
HI 1999

Skelton, Michael
WC 2003*; HI 2003-04

Skinns, David
HI 2001-02-03; Fra 2002

Slark, WA
HI 1957

Slater, A
HI 1955-62

Smith, Eric M
Sco, Irl 1931

Smith, Everard
Sco 1908-09-10-12

Smith, GF
Sco 1902-03

Smith, JR
HI 1932

Smith, LOM
HI 1963

Smith, W
Eur 1972; HI 1972

Snowdon, J
HI 1934

Stanford, M
WC 1993; ET 1992; Eur 1992; HI 1991-92-93; Fra 1992

Steel, Donald MA
HI 1970

Stevens, LB
Sco 1912

Storey, EF
WC 1924-26-28; Sco 1924 to 28; 30; HI 1936; Fra 1936

Storm, G
WC 1999; HI 1999; ETC 1999

Stott, HAN
HI 1976-77

Stout, JA
WC 1930-32; Sco 1928 to 31; Irl 1929-31

Stowe, C
WC 1938-47; HI 1935 to 38; 47-49-54; Fra 1938-39-49

Straker, R
HI 1932

Streeter, P
HI 1992; Fra 1994-96

Stubbs, AK
HI 1982

Suneson, C
HI 1988; ETC 1989

Sutherland, DMG
HI 1947

Sutton, W
Sco 1929-31; Irl 1929-30-31

Tate, JK
HI 1954-55-56

Taylor, HE
Sco 1911

Thirlwell, A
WC 1957; Eur 1956-58-64; CT 1953-64; HI 1951-52; 54 to 58; 63-64

Thirsk, TJ
Irl 1929; HI 1933 to 38; Fra 1935 to 39

Thom, KG
WC 1949; HI 1947-48-49-53

Thomas, I
HI 1933

Thompson, ASG
HI 1935-37

Thompson, MS
WC 1983; HI 1982

Tiley, Steven
HI 2004-05; ETC 2005; Esp 2005

Timmis, CT
Irl 1930; HI 1936-37

Tipping, EB
Irl 1930

Tipple, ER
Irl 1928-29; HI 1932

Tolley, Cyril JH
USA 1921; WC 1922-23-24-26-30-34; SA 1927; Sco 1922 to 30; Irl/Wal 1925; HI 1936-37-38; Fra 1938

Townsend, Peter M
WC 1965; ET 1966; Eur 1966; HI 1965-66

Tredinnick, SV
HI 1950

Tupling, LP
WC 1969; HI 1969; ETC 1969

Turner A
HI 1952

Tweddell, W
WC 1928-(36); Sco 1928-29-30; HI 1935

Wainwright, A
HI 1997-99

Walker, MS
Irl/Wal 1925

Walker, Richard
ET 2002; HI 2001-02-03; ETC 2003; Fra 2002; Esp 2003

Wallbank, K
HI 1996-97; Fra 1996

Walls, MPD
HI 1980-81-85

Walters, Justin
Esp 2003

Walton, AR
HI 1934-35

Wardrop, Daniel
Esp 2003

Waring, Paul
HI 2005-06; Fra 2006

Warren, KT
HI 1962

Watts, C
HI 1991-92; Fra 1992

Way, Paul
WC 1981; HI 1981; ETC 1981

Webster, S
HI 1995-96; ETC 1997

Weeks, K
HI 1987-88; Fra 1988

Welch, M
HI 1993-94; Fra 1994

Wells, J
HI 1999

Westwood, Lee
HI 1993

Wethered, Roger H
USA 1921; WC 1922-23-26-30-34; Sco 1922 to 30

White, L
WC 1991; HI 1990; ETC 1991

White, RJ
WC 1947-49-51-53-55; HI 1947-48-49-53-54

Whitehouse, Tom
HI 2000

Wiggett, M
HI 1990

Wiggins, R
Eur 1996; HI 1996; ETC 1997

Williams, DF
Sco 1979

Willison, R
WC 1991; ET 1990; Eur 1990; HI 1988-89-90; ETC 1989-91

Wilson, Oliver
WC 2003*; HI 2002; ETC 2003, Fra 2002

Winchester, R
HI 1985-87-89

Winter, G
HI 1991

Wise, WS
HI 1947

Wolstenholme, Gary P
WC 1995-97-99*-2001*-03*-05;
ET 1996-98*-2002-**04**; Eur 1992-
94-2004; AP 2000-04-06; HI 1988
to 2006; ETC 1995-97-99-2001-03-
05; Fra 1988-92-94-2000-02-06;
Esp 1989-91-95-99-2001-03-05;
RSA 2001

Wolstenholme, Guy G
WC 1957-59; ET 1958-60; CT
1959; HI 1953; 55 to 60

Woollam, J
HI 1933-34-35; Fra 1935

Woolley, FA
Sco 1910-11-12

Worthington, JS
Sco 1905

Yasin Ali
HI 2002

Yeo, J
HI 1971

Zacharias, JP
HI 1935

Zoete, HW de
Sco 1903-04-06-07

IRELAND

Allison, A
Eng 1928; Sco 1929

Anderson, N
Eur 1988; HI 1985 to 90; 93; ETC
1989

Babington, A
Wal 1913

Baker, RN
HI 1975

Bamford, JL
HI 1954-56

Beamish, CH
HI 1950-51-53-56

Bell, HE
Wal 1930; HI 1932

Bowden, Greg
HI 2004

Bowen, J
HI 1961

Boyd, HA
Wal 1913-23

Brady, E
HI 1995-98; ETC 1999

Branigan, D
HI 1975-76-77-80-81-82-86; ETC
1977-81; WGer, Fra, Swe 1976

Briscoe, A
Eng 1928 to 31; Sco, Wal 1929-30-
31; HI 1932-33-38

Brown, JC
HI 1933 to 38; 48-52-53

Browne, S
HI 2001; ETC 2001

Bruen, J
WC 1938-49-51; HI 1937-38-49-50

Burke, J
WC 1932; Eng, Wal 1929; Eng,
Wal, Sco 1930-31; HI 1932 to 38;
47-48-49

Burns, M
HI 1973-75-83

Burns, R
WC 1993; ET 1992; Eur 1992; HI
1991-92

Cairnes, HM
Sco, Eng 1904; Wal 1913-25; Sco
1927

Caldwell, Jonathan
HI 2006

Campbell, MK
HI 1999-2003-04

Carr, Joe B
WC 1947 to 63; (65)-**(67)**; ET
1958-60; Eur 1954-56-64-66-68; HI
1947 to 69; ETC 1965-67-69

Carr, JJ
HI 1981-82-83

Carr, JR
Wal 1930; Wal, Eng 1931; HI 1933

Carr, R
WC 1971; HI 1970-71; ETC 1971

Carroll, CA
Wal 1924

Carroll, JP
HI 1948-49-50-51-62

Carroll, W
Wal 1913-23-24-25; Eng 1925; Sco
1929; HI 1932

Carvill, J
Eur 1990; HI 1989; ETC 1989

Carvill, Jim
ETC 2005

Cashell, BG
HI 1978; Fra, WGer, Swe 1978

Caul, P
HI 1968-69; 1971 to 75

Clarke, D
Eur 1990; HI 1987-89

Cleary, T
HI 1976-77-78; 82 to 86; Wal 1979;
Fra, WGer, Swe 1976

Corcoran, DK
HI 1972-73; ETC 1973

Corridan, T
HI 1983-84-91-92

Coughlan, R
WC 1997; HI 1991-94; ETC 1997

Crabbe, JL
Wal 1925; Sco 1927-28

Craddock, T
WC 1967-69; HI 1955 to 60; 67 to
70

Craigan, RM
HI 1963-64

Crosbie, GF
HI 1953-55-56-57-**(88)**

Crowe, Darren
ET 2004; HI 2002-03-04-05-06;
ETC 2005

Crowley, M
Eng 1928 to 31; Wal 1929-31; Sco
1929-30-31; HI 1932

Cullen, G
AP 2000; HI 1999; ETC 1999

Davies, FE
Wal 1923

Dickson, JR
HI 1980; ETC 1977

Donellan, B
HI 1952

Dooley, Padraig
HI 2002

Doran, Connor
HI 2005

Drew, Norman V
WC 1953; HI 1952-53

Duncan, J
HI 1959-60-61

Dunne, D
HI 1997

Dunne, E
HI 1973-74-76-77-**(2001)**; Wal
1979; ETC 1975

Edwards, B
HI 1961-62; 64 to 69; 73

Edwards, M
HI 1956-57-58-60-61-62

Egan, TW
HI 1952-53-59-60-62-67-68; ETC
1967-69

Elliot, IA
HI 1975-77-78; ETC 1975; Fra,
WGer, Swe 1978

Errity, D
HI 1990

Ewing, RC
WC 1936-38-47-49-51-55; HI 1934
to 38; 47 to 51; 53 to 58

Fanagan, J
WC 1995; Eur 1992-96; HI 1989 to
97; ETC 1995-97

Ferguson, M
HI 1952

Ferguson, WJ
HI 1952-54-55-58-59-61

French, WF
Sco 1929; HI 1932

Fitzgibbon, JF
HI 1955-56-57

Fitzsimmons, J
HI 1938-47-48

Flaherty, JA
HI 1934 to 37

Flaherty, PD
HI 1967; ETC 1967-69

Fleury, RA
HI 1974

Fogarty, GN
HI 1956-58-63-64-67

Foster, J
HI 1998-2000-01-03

Fox, Noel
WC 2003*; ET 2002; Eur 2000; AP 2004; HI 1996 to 99; 2001-02-03-04; ETC 1997-2001-03

Froggatt, P
HI 1957

Gannon, MA
Eur 1974-78; HI 1973-74-77-78-80-81-83-84; 87 to 90; ETC 1979-81-89-(2005); Fra, WGer, Swe 1978-80

Gill, WJ
Wal 1931; HI 1932 to 37

Glover, J
HI 1951-52-53-55-59-60-70

Goulding, N
HI 1988 to 92; ETC 1991

Graham, JSS
HI 1938-50-51

Greene, R
HI 1933

Gribben, P
WC 1999; ET 1998*; HI 1997-98-99

Guerin, M
HI 1961-62-63

Hanway, M
HI 1971-74

Harrington, J
HI 1960-61-74-75-76; Wal 1979; ETC 1975

Harrington, Padraig
WC 1991-93-95; Eur 1992-94; HI 1990 to 95; ETC 1991-95

Hayes, JA
HI 1977

Healy, TM
Sco, Eng 1931

Heather, D
HI 1976; Fra, WGer, Swe 1976

Hegarty, J
HI 1975

Hegarty, TD
HI 1957

Henderson, J
Wal 1923

Herlihy, B
HI 1950

Heverin, AJ
HI 1978; Fra, WGer, Swe 1978

Hezlet, CO
WC 1924-26-28; SA 1927; Wal 1923-25-27-29-31; Sco 1927 to 31; Eng 1929-30-31

Higgins, D
HI 1993-94

Higgins, L
HI 1968-70-71

Hoey, M
WC 2001; HI 1999-2000-01; ETC 1999-2001

Hoey, TBC
HI 1970 to 73; 77-84; ETC 1971-77

Hogan, P
HI 1985 to 88; ETC 1991

Hulme, WJ
HI 1955-56-57

Humphreys, AR
Eng 1957

Hutton, R
HI 1991

Jameson, JF
Wal 1913-24

Johnson, TWG
Eng 1929

Jones, D
HI 1998

Kane, RM
Eur 1974; HI 1967-68-71-72-74-78; Wal 1979; ETC 1971-79

Kearney, Ken
HI 1988-89-90-92-94-95-97-98-2002; ETC 1999

Kearney, Niall
HI 2006

Keenan, S
HI 1989

Kehoe, Justin
ET 2002; HI 2000-01-02-03; ETC 2003

Kelleher, WA
HI 1962

Kelly, NS
HI 1966

Kilduff, AJ
Sco 1928

Kilpatrick, Richard
HI 2003-04-05

Kissock, B
HI 1961-62-74-76; Fra, WGer, Swe 1978

Lawrie, P
HI 1996; ETC 1997

Lehane, N
HI 1976; Fra, WGer, Swe 1976

Leyden, PJ
HI 1953-55-56-57-59

Long, D
HI 1973-74; 80 to 84; Wal 1979; ETC 1979

Lowe, A
Wal 1924; Eng 1925-28; Sco 1927-28

Lowry, Shane
HI 2006

Lyons, P
HI 1986

McCarroll, F
HI 1968-69

McCarthy, L
HI 1953 to 56

McConnell, FP
Wal, Eng 1929; Wal, Eng, Sco 1930-31; HI 1934

McConnell, RM
Wal 1924-25-29-30-31; Eng 1925; 28 to 31; Sco 1927-28-29-31; HI 1934 to 37

McConnell, WG
Eng 1925

McCormack, JD
Wal 1913-24; Eng 1928; HI 1932 to 37

McCormick, Andrew
HI 1997 to 2002

McCrea, WE
HI 1965-66-67; ETC 1965

McCready, SM
WC 1949-51; HI 1947-49-50-52-54

McDaid, B
Wal 1979

McDermott, M
HI 2000-01; ETC 2001

McDowell, G
WC 2001; HI 2000; ETC 2001

McElhinney, Brian
WC 2005; ET 2004; AP 2004; HI 2003-04-05; ETC 2003-05

McGeady, Michael
HI 2003-04-05; ETC 2003-05

McGimpsey, G
WC 1985-89-91-(2003)*-(05); ET 1984-86-88*; Eur 1986-88-90-92-(2004); HI 1978; 80 to 99; Wal 1979; ETC 1981-89-91-95-97-99

McGinley, M
HI 1996

McGinley, P
WC 1991; HI 1989-90; ETC 1991

McGinn, John
HI 2002

McHenry, J
WC 1987; HI 1985-86

McIlroy, Rory
ET 2006; Eur 2006; AP 2006; HI 2005; ETC 2005

McInally, RH
HI 1949-51

Mackeown, HN
HI 1973; ETC 1973

McMenamin, E
HI 1981

McMonagle, C
HI 1999-2000; ETC 1999

McMullan, C
HI 1933-34-35

McNamara, Cian
HI 2004-05

MacNamara, L
HI 1977; 83 to 92; ETC 1977-91

McNeill, G
HI 1991-93-2001

McTernan, Sean
ET 2004; HI 2002-04-05; ETC 2005

Madeley, JFD
WC 1963; Eur 1962; HI 1959 to 64

Mahon, RJ
HI 1938-52-54-55

Malone, B
HI 1959-64-69-71-75; ETC 1971-75

Manley, N
Wal 1924; Sco 1927-28; Eng 1928

Marren, JM
Wal 1925

Martin, GNC
WC 1928; Wal 1923-29; Sco 1928-29-30; Eng 1929-30

Maybin, Gareth
HI 2002-04; ETC 2003

Meharg, W
HI 1957

Moore, GJ
Eng 1928; Wal 1929

Moriarty, Colm
WC 2003*; ET 2002; HI 2001-02; ETC 2003

Morris, JC
HI 1993 to 98; ETC 1995

Morris, MF
HI 1978-80-82-83-84; Wal 1979; ETC 1979; Fra, WGer, Swe 1980

Morrow, AJC
HI 1975-83-92-93-96-97-99-2000

Mulcare, P
WC 1975; Eur 1972; HI 1968 to 72; 74-78-80; ETC 1975-79; Fra, WGer, Swe 1978-80

Mulholland, D
HI 1988

Munn, E
Wal 1913-23-24; Sco 1927

Munn, L
Wal 1913-23-24; HI 1936-37

Murphy, G
HI 1992 to 95; ETC 1995

Murphy, M
HI 2000

Murphy, P
HI 1985-86

Murray, P
HI 1995-96

Murray, Pat
HI 1995-96-2005-06

Neill, JH
HI 1938-47-48-49

Nestor, JM
HI 1962-63-64

Nevin, V
HI 1960-63-65-67-69-72; ETC 1967-69-73

Nicholson, J
HI 1932

Nolan, K
WC 1997; ET 1996; Eur 1996; HI 1992 to 96; ETC 1995-97

O'Boyle, P
ETC 1977

O'Brien, MD
HI 1968 to 72; 75-76-77; ETC 1971; Fra, WGer, Swe 1976

O'Callaghan, Aaron
HI 2005-06

O'Connell, A
HI 1967-70-71

O'Connell, E
WC 1989; ET 1988*; Eur 1988; HI 1985; ETC 1989

O'Leary, JE
HI 1969-70; ETC 1969

O'Neill, JJ
HI 1968

O'Rourke, P
HI 1980-81-82-84-85

O'Sullivan, DF
HI 1976-85-86-87-91; ETC 1977

O'Sullivan, Mark
HI 2003

O'Sullivan, WM
HI 1934 to 38; 47 to 51; 53-54

Omelia, B
HI 1994 to 97

Owens, M
HI 2003

Ownes, GH
HI 1935-37-38-47

Patterson, AH
Wal 1913

Paul, Stuart
HI 2001-02

Pierse, AD
WC 1983; ET 1982; Eur 1980; HI 1976-77-78; 80 to 85; 87-88; Wal 1979; ETC 1981; Fra, WGer, Swe 1980

Pollin, RKM
HI 1971; ETC 1973

Power, E
HI 1987-88-93-94-95-97-98-99

Power, M
HI 1947 to 52; 54

Power, Seamus
HI 2006

Purcell, M
HI 1973

Rafferty, Ronan
WC 1981; ET 1980; Eur 1980; Wal 1979; HI 1980-81; ETC 1981; Fra, WGer, Swe 1980

Rainey, WHE
HI 1962

Rayfus, P
HI 1986-87-88

Reade, HE
Wal 1913

Reddan, B
HI 1987

Rice, JH
HI 1947-52

Rice, T
HI 2000-01; ETC 2001

Robertson, CT
Wal, Sco 1930

Scannel, BJ
HI 1947 to 51; 53-54

Shaw, Gareth
ET 2006; HI 2005-06

Sheals, HS
Wal 1929; Eng 1929-30-31; Sco 1930; HI 1932-33

Sheahan, D
WC 1963; Eur 1962-64-67; HI 1961 to 67; 70

Simcox, R
Wal, Sco 1930; Wal, Sco, Eng 1931; HI 1932 to 36; 38

Sinclair, Michael
HI 1999-04

Slattery, B
HI 1947-48

Sludds, MF
HI 1982

Smyth, D
HI 1972-73; ETC 1973

Smyth, DW
Wal 1923-30; Eng 1930; Sco 1931; HI 1933

Smyth, V
HI 1981-82

Soulby, DEB
Sco, Wal, Eng 1929-30

Spiller, EF
Wal 1924; Eng 1928; Sco 1928-29

Spring, G
HI 1996

Staunton, R
HI 1964-65-72; ETC 1973

Stevenson, JF
Wal 1923-24; Eng 1925

Stevenson, K
HI 1972

Taggart, J
HI 1953

Timbey, JC
Sco 1928-31; Wal 1931

Waddell, G
Wal 1925

Walton, P
WC 1981-83; ET 1982; Wal 1979; HI 1980-81; ETC 1981; Fra, WGer, Swe 1980

Ward, Simon
ET 2006; HI 2006

Webster, F
HI 1949

Welch, L
HI 1936

Werner, LE
Wal 1925

West, CH
Eng 1928; HI 1932

Young, D
HI 1969-70-77

SCOTLAND

Aitken, AR
Eng 1906-07-08

Alexander, DW
HI 1958; Scan 1958

Anderson, RB
HI 1962-63; Scan 1960-62

Andrew, R
Eng 1905 to 10

Armour, A
Eng 1922

Armour, TD
USA 1921

Bannerman, SJ
HI 1988; Swe 1990

Barrie, GC
HI 1981-83; Swe 1983

Beames, Roger
Eur 1996; HI 1995-96-99; Esp 1996;
Fra, Swe 1997

Beveridge, HW
Eng 1908

Birnie, J
Irl 1927

Black, D
HI 1966-67

Black, FC
Eur 1966; HI 1962-64-65-66-68;
ETC 1965-67; Scan 1962

Black, GT
HI 1952-53; SA 1954

Black, WC
HI 1964-65

Blackwell, EBH
Eng 1902, 1904 to 1907, 1909-10-
12, 1923-24-25

Blair, DA
WC 1955-61; CT 1954; HI 1948-
49-51-52-53-55-56-57; Scan 1956-
58-62

Bloice, C
WC 1985; HI 1985-86; ETC 1985;
Fra 1985; Ita, Swe 1986

Blyth, AD
Eng 1904

Bookless, JT
Eng, Irl 1930; Eng, Wal 1931

Booth, Wallace
Fra 2003

Braid, HM
Eng 1922-23

Brand, Gordon jr
WC 1979; ET 1978-80; Eur 1978-
80; HI 1978-80

Brock, J
Irl 1929; HI 1932

Brodie, Allan
WC 1977-79; ET 1978; Eur 1974-
76-78-80; HI 1970, 1972 to 1978,
1980; Eng 1979; ETC 1973-77; Bel,
Esp 1977; Fra 1978; Ita 1979

Brodie, Andrew
HI 1968-69; Esp 1974

Brooks, A
WC 1969; HI 1968-69; ETC 1969

Brooks, CJ
Eur 1986; HI 1984-85; Swe 1984;
Swe, Ita 1986

Brooks, M
WC 1997; ET 1996; Eur 1996; HI
1995-96; ETC 1997; Aut 1994; Esp
1996; Fra, Swe 1997

Brotherston, IR
HI 1984-85; ETC 1985; Fra 1985

Brown, Graeme
HI 2004

Bryson, WS
HI 1991-92-93; Swe, Ita 1992; Fra
1993; Esp 1994

Bucher, AMM
HI 1954-55-56; Scan 1956

Burnside, J
HI 1956-57

Burrell, TM
Eng 1924

Bussell, AF
WC 1957; Eur 1956-62; HI 1956-
57-58-61; Scan 1956-60

Cairns, S
HI 1997

Cameron, D
HI 1938-51

Campbell, C
HI 1999

Campbell, Glenn
HI 2003-04-05-06; Esp 06

Campbell, Sir Guy, Bt
Eng 1909-10-11

Campbell, HM
Eur 1964; HI 1962-64-68; ETC
1965-(79); Scan 1962; Aus 1964

Campbell, JGS
HI 1947-48

Campbell, W
WC 1930; Irl 1927; Irl, Eng 1928-
29-30; Irl, Eng, Wal 1931; HI 1933
to 36

Cannon, JM
HI 1969; Esp 1974

Carmichael, Steven
HI 1998-99-2001-02; Swe 1999;
Esp, Ita 2002; Fra 2003

Carrick, DG
WC 1983-87; Eur 1986; HI 1981 to
89; ETC 1987-(89)-(91); WGer
1987; Ita 1984-86-88; Fra 1987-89;
Swe 1983-84-86

Carslaw, IA
WC 1979; Eur 1978; HI 1976-77-
78-80-81; ETC 1977-79; Eng 1979;
Esp 1977; Fra 1978-83; Bel 1978; Ita
1979

Cater, JR
WC 1955; HI 1952 to 56; SA 1954;
Scan 1956

Caven, J
WC 1922; Eng 1926

Chillas, D
HI 1971

Cochran, JS
HI 1966

Collier, B
HI 1994; Aut 1994

Coltart, Andrew
WC 1991; ET 1990; Eur 1990; HI
1988-89-90; ETC 1989-91; NNC
1990; Ita, Swe 1990; Fra 1991

Cosh, GB
WC 1965; ET 1966-68; Eur 1966-
68; CT 1967; HI 1964 to 69; ETC
1965-(69)

Coutts, FJ
HI 1980-81-82; ETC 1981-83; Fra
1981-82-83

Crawford, DR
HI 1990-91; ETC 1991; Fra 1991

Crawford, G
Esp 2002; ETC (2005)

Cuddihy, J
HI 1977-78

Dalgleish, CR
WC 1981; Eur 1982; HI 81-82-83-
89-(95); ETC 1981-83-(93)-(95);
Fra 1982; NNC 1989

Dawson, JE
Irl 1927-29; Irl, Eng 1930; Irl, Eng,
Wal 1931; HI 1932-33-34-37

Dawson, M
HI 1963-65-66

Deboys, A
HI 1956-59-60; Scan 1960

Deighton, Frank WG
WC 1951-57; CT 1954-59; HI
1950-52-53-56-58-59-60; SA 1954;
NZ 1954; Scan 1956

Denholm, RB
Irl 1927-29; Irl, Wal, Eng 1931; HI
1932-33-34

Dewar, FG
HI 1952-53-55; SA 1954; ETC
(1971)-(73)

Dick, CE
Eng 1902-03-04-05-09-12

Dickson, HM
Irl 1929-31

Doherty, Jack
ET 2002; ETC 2003; HI 2001-02;
Swe 2001; Esp, Ita 2002

Dowie, Andrew
HI 1949

Downie, D
HI 1993-94; Esp, Ita 1994; Fra, Swe
1995

Draper, JW
HI 1954

Dundas, S
HI 1992-93

Dykes, J Morton
WC 1936; HI 1934-35-36-48-49-51

Easingwood, SR
HI 1986-87-88-90; ETC 1989; Fra
1987-89; Ita 1988-90

Elliot, A
HI 1989; ETC 1989; Fra 1989

Elliot, C
HI 1982; Fra 1983

Everett, C
HI 1988-89-90; ETC 1989-91; NNC
1989-90; Ita 1988-90; Fra 1988-89-
91; Swe 1990

Fairlie, WE
Eng 1912

Farmer, A
HI 1997; Swe 1999

Farmer, JC
HI 1970

Ferguson, S Mure
Eng 1902-03-04

Fleming, J
HI 1987

Flockhart, AS
HI 1948-49

Forbes, E
HI 1996-98-2000-01; Ita 1996-
2000; Fra 1997; Swe 1997-99; Esp
2002

Forsyth, A
HI 1996; ETC 1997; Ita 1996; Fra,
Swe 1997

Fotheringham, Bryan
HI 2005; Esp 2006

Fox, G
HI 1997-98-99; ETC 1999; Swe
1999

Gairdner, JR
Eng 1902

Gallacher, Bernard J
HI 1967

Gallacher, S
WC 1995; ET 1994; HI 1992 to 95;
ETC 1993-95; Ita, Esp 1994; Fra,
Swe 1995

Gallagher, John
HI 2005-06

Galloway, RF
HI 1957-58-59; Scan 1958

Garson, R
Irl 1927-28-29

Gibb, C
Eng 1927; Irl 1928

Gibson, WC
HI 1950-51

Girvan, P
WC 1987; HI 1986; ETC 1987;
WGer 1987

Gordon, Graham
WC 2003*; ET 2002; ETC 2003; HI
2000-02

Graham, AJ
Eng 1925

Graham, J
Eng 1902 to 11

Green, CT
WC 1963-69-71-73-75-**(83)**-**(85)**;
ET 1970-72-**(84)**-**(86)**;Eur 1962-
66-68-70-72-74-76; CT 1971; HI
1961 to 78; Eng 1979; ETC 1965 to
83; Scan 1962; Aus 1964; Bel 1973-
75-77-78; Esp 1977; Ita 1979

Greig, DG
CT 1975; HI 1972-73-75

Greig, K
HI 1933

Guild, WJ
Eng 1925; Eng, Irl 1927-28

Hall, AH
HI 1962-66-69

Hamilton, ED
HI 1936-37-38

Hare, WCD
HI 1953; NZ 1954

Harris, IR
HI 1955-56-58-59

Harris, R
WC 1922-23-26; Eng 1905-08-
10-11-12; 22 to 28

Hastings, JL
HI 1957-58; Scan 1958

Hay, G
WC 1991; Eur 1980; Eng 1979; HI
1980-88-90-91-92; ETC 1991-93; Bel
1980; Fra 1980-82-89-91-93; Ita
1988-92-94; Swe 1992; Esp 1994

Hay, J
HI 1972

Heap, Craig
HI 1999-2001; ETC 2001

Henderson, N
HI 1963-64

Henry, Scott
HI 2006

Hird, K
HI 1987-88-89; NNC 1989; Ita
1990

Hislop, Craig
HI 1994-96; Aut 1994; Ita 1996

Hope, WL
WC 1923-24-28; Eng 1923; 25 to
29

Horne, A
HI 1971

Horne, S
HI 1997-98

Hosie, JR
HI 1936

Howard, D Barclay
WC 1995-97; ET 1996; Eur 1980-
94-96; Eng 1979; HI 1980 to 83; 93
to 96; ETC 1981-95-97; Bel 1980;
Fra 1980-81-83-95-97; Ita 1984-94;
Esp 1994-96; Swe 1995-97

Huggan, J
HI 1981 to 84; ETC 1981; Fra 1982-
83; Swe 1983; Ita 1984

Hume, B
HI 1999-2000-01; ETC 2001; Ita
2000; Swe 2001

Hunter, NM
1903-12

Hunter, R
HI 1966

Hunter, WI
Eng 1922

Hutcheon, I
WC 1975-77-79-81; ET 1974-76*-
80; Eur 1974-76; CT 1975;
Dominican Int 1973; Colombian Int
1975; HI 1971 to 78; 80; ETC 1973-
75-77-79-81; Bel 1973-75-77-78-80;
Esp 1977; Fra 1978-80-81; Ita 1979;
Swe 1983

Hutchison, CK
Eng 1904 to 12

Inglis, David
WC 2003*; ETC 2003; HI 2001-
02

Innes, Brian
HI 2003

Jack, R Reid
WC 1957-59; ET 1958; Eur 1956;
CT 1959; HI 1950-51; 54 to 59; 61;
NZ 1954; Scan 1956-58

Jack, WS (Billy)
HI 1955

James, D
HI 1985

Jamieson, A jr
WC 1926; Eng 1927; Eng, Irl 1928;
Eng, Irl, Wal 1931; HI 1932-33-36-
37

Jamieson, D
HI 1980

Jamieson, Scott
ET 2006; HI 2002-04-05; Esp 06

Jenkins, JLC
USA 1921; Eng 1908-12-22-24-26-
28; Irl 1928

Johnston, JW
HI 1970-71

Kelly, L
WC 1999; ET 1998*; HI 1997-98;
ETC 1999; Swe 1999

Killey, GC
Irl 1928

King, Jonathan
HI 2001-02-03-04-05-06; Swe 2001;
Esp 2002-06; Fra 2003 ETC 2005

Kirkpatrick, D
HI 1992; ETC 1993; Fra 1993

Knowles, ST
HI 1990-91-92; Fra 1991

Kyle, AT
WC 1938-47-51; SA 1952; HI
1938-47; 49 to 53

Kyle, DH
WC 1924; Eng 1924-30

Kyle, EP
Eng 1925

Laidlay, JE
Eng 1902 to 11

Laird, Martin
HI 2003

Lang, JA
WC 1930; Irl, Eng 1929; Irl 1930;
Irl, Eng, Wal 1931

Lawrie, CD
WC (1961)-(1963); ET (1960)-
(1962); Eur (1960)-(1962); HI
1949-50; 55 to 58; Swe 1950; Scan
1956-58

Lee, IGF
HI 1958 to 62; Scan 1960

Lindsay, J
HI 1933 to 36

Little, E
Ita 1996

Lockhart, G
Eng 1911-12

Loftus, M
Eur 2000; HI 1999-2000; Ita 2000

Low, AJ
HI 1963-64; ETC 1965; Aus 1964

Low, JL
Eng 1904

Lowdon, CJ
Irl 1927

Lowson, AG
HI 1989-90-91-97; Swe 1990; Swe,
Ita 1992

Lygate, M
HI 1970-75-(88); ETC 1971-85-87

McAllister, SD
HI 1983; ETC 1983; Swe 1983

McAlpine, Kevin
HI 2006

McArthur, Andrew
Eur 2004; ETC 2003-05; HI 2002-
03-04-05

McArthur, W
HI 1952-54; SA 1954

McBeath, J
HI 1964

McBride, D
HI 1932

McCallum, AR
WC 1928; Eng 1929

McCart, DM
HI 1977-78; Bel, Fra 1978

MacDonald, GK
HI 1978-81-82; Eng 1979; Fra 1981-
82-83

McDonald, H
HI 1970

Macdonald, J Scott
WC 1971; Eur 1970; HI 1969 to
72; ETC 1971; Bel 1973

McEwan, Steven
Esp 2006

Macfarlane, CB
Eng 1912

Macgregor, A
Scan 1956

Macgregor, G
WC 1971-75-83-85-87-(91)-(93);
ET 1982; Eur 1970-74-84; CT 1971-
75; HI 1969 to 76; 80 to 87; (99);
Eng 1979; ETC 1971-73-75-81-83-
85-87; Bel 1973-75-80; Fra 1981-82-
85-87; Swe 1983-84-86; Ita 1984-86

MacGregor, RC
WC 1953; HI 1951 to 54; NZ 1954

McInally, H
HI 1937-47-48

McIntosh, EA
HI 1989

Macintosh, KW
Eur 1980; Eng 1979; HI 1980; Bel,
Fra 1980

McKay, G
HI 1969

McKay, JR
HI 1950-51-52-54; NZ 1954

McKechnie, P
HI 1998

McKellar, PJ
WC 1977; Eur 1978; HI 1976-77-
78; Eng 1979; Bel, Fra 1978

Mackenzie, F
Eng 1902-03

Mackenzie, S
ET 2002; HI 1990; 93 to 2001-03;
ETC 1999-2001; Esp 1994-96-02; Ita
1994-2000; Fra 1997; Swe 1997-99

Mackenzie, WW
WC 1922-23; Eng 1923-26-27-29;
Irl 1930

McKibbin, H
HI 1994-95; ETC 1995; Fra, Swe
1995; Esp 1996

Mackie, GW
HI 1948-50

McKinlay, SL
WC 1934; Eng 1929-30-31; Irl
1930; Wal 1931; HI 1932-33-35-37-
47

McKinna, RA
HI 1938

McKinnon, A
HI 1947-52

McLean, J
WC 1934-36; Aus 1934; HI 1932
to 36

McLeary, Jamie
Eur 2004; HI 2002-03-04-05; ET
2004

McLeod, AE
HI 1937-38

McLeod, WS
HI 1935-37-38; 47 to 51; Swe 1950

McNair, AA
Irl 1929

McNicol, Keir
HI 2006

MacRae, Neil
HI 2003; Ita 2002

McRuvie, Eric A
WC 1932-34; Eng 1929; Eng, Irl
1930; Eng, Irl, Wal 1931; HI 1932 to
36

McTear, J
HI 1971

Manford, GC
Eng 1922-23

Mann, LS
WC 1983; HI 1982-83; ETC 1983;
Swe 1983

Marchbank, Brian
WC 1979; ET 1978; Eur 1976-78;
HI 1978; ETC 1979; Ita 1979

Martin, S
WC 1977; ET 1976; Eur 1976; HI
1975-76-77; ETC 1977; Bel, Esp
1977

Maxwell, R
Eng 1902 to 07; 09-10

Melville, LM Balfour
Eng 1902-03

Melville, TE
HI 1974

Menzies, A
Eng 1925

Mill, JW
HI 1953-54

Miller, AC
HI 1954-55

Miller, MJ
HI 1974-75-77-78; Bel, Fra
1978

Milligan, JW
WC 1989-91; ET 1988*-90; Eur
1988-92; HI 1986 to 92; ETC 1987-
89-91; NNC 1989; Swe 1986-90-92;
WGer 1987; Fra 1987-89-91; Ita
1988-90-92

Milne, WTG
WC 1973; HI 1972-73; ETC 1973;
Bel 1973

Moir, A
Eur 1984; HI 1983-84; ETC 1985;
Swe, Ita 1984; Fra 1985

Montgomerie, Colin S
WC 1985-87; ET 1984-86; Eur
1986; HI 1984-85-86; ETC 1985-87;
Ita 1984; Swe 1984-86; Fra 1985;
WGer 1987

Montgomerie, JS
HI 1957; ETC 1965; Scan 1958

Morris, FS
HI 1963

Morrison, JH
Scan 1960

Munro, RAG
HI 1960

Murdoch, D
HI 1964

Murphy, AR
HI 1961-67

Murray, George
ET 2004; HI 2004-05-06; ETC 2005;
Esp 06

Murray, GH
WC 1977; Eur 1978; HI 1973 to
78; 83; ETC 1975-77; Esp 1974-77;
Bel 1975-77

Murray, SWT
WC 1963; Eur 1958-62; HI 1959 to
63; Scan 1960

Murray, WA
WC 1923-24; Eng 1923 to 27

Murray, WB
HI 1967-68-69; ETC 1969

Neill, R
HI 1936

Noon, J
HI 1987

O'Hara, Paul
ET 2006, Esp 06

O'Hara, Steven
WC 2001; ET 2000; Eur 2000; HI
1999-2000; ETC 2001; Ita 2000;
Swe 2001

Osgood, TH
Eng 1925

Paton, DA
HI 1991

Patrick, D
WC 1999; AP 2000; HI 1997-98-
99; ETC 1999; Swe 1999

Patrick, KG
HI 1937

Peters, GB
WC 1936-38; HI 1934 to 38

Pirie, AK
WC 1967; Eur 1970; HI 1966 to 75;
ETC 1967-69; Bel 1973-75; Esp 1974

Pressley, J
HI 1947-48-49

Raeside, A
Irl 1929

Ramsay, Eric
HI 2002-03-04-05; Ita 2002; ETC
2005

Ramsay, Richie
WC 2005; ET 2006; AP 2006; Eur
2006; HI 2004-06; ETC 2005

Rankin, G
WC 1995-97-99; HI 1994-95-97-
98; ETC 1995-97-99; Swe 1995-97-
99; Fra 1995-97; Esp 1996

Reid, A
HI 1993-94-95; ETC 1993-95; Esp,
Ita 1994; Fra 1995

Renfrew, RL
HI 1964

Robb, J jr
Eng 1902-03-05-06-07

Robb, WM
HI 1935

Roberts, AT
Irl 1931

Roberts, GW
HI 1937-38

Robertson, Dean
WC 1993; ET 1992; Eur 1992; HI
1991-92-93; ETC 1993; Swe, Ita
1992; Fra 1993

Robertson, DM
HI 1973-74; Esp 1974

Robertson-Durham, JA
Eng 1911

Russell, R
WC 1993; HI 1992-93; ETC 1993;
Fra 1993

Rutherford, DS
Irl 1929

Rutherford, R
HI 1938-47

Saddler, AC
WC 1963-65-67-**(77)**; ET 1962-
(76)*; Eur 1960-62-64-66; CT
1959-63-67; HI 1959 to 64; 66;
ETC 1965-67-**(75)-(77)**; Scan
1962

Saltman, Lloyd
WC 2005; Eur 2006; HI 2004-05-06;
ETC 2005; Esp 06

Scott, R jr
WC 1924; Eng 1924-28

Scott, WGF
Irl 1927

Scroggie, FH
Eng 1910

Shade, Ronnie DBM
WC 1961-63-65-67; ET 1962-64-
66-68; Eur 1960-62-64-66; CT
1963-67; Aus 1964; HI 1957; 60 to
68; ETC 1965-67; Scan 1960-62

Shaw, G
WC 1987; HI 1984-86-87-88-90;
ETC 1987; Swe 1984; Fra, WGer
1987

Sherry, Gordon
WC 1995; ET 1994; Eur 1994; HI
1993-94-95; ETC 1995; Fra 1993-
95; Esp 1994; Swe 1995

Shields, B
HI 1986

Simpson, AF
Eng 1927; Irl 1928

Simpson, JG
USA 1921; Eng 1907-08-09-11-12-
22-24-26

Sinclair, A
HI 1950; ETC **(1967)**

Smith, JN
WC 1930; Irl 1928; Irl, Eng 1930;
Irl, Eng, Wal 1931; HI 1932-33-
34

Smith, S
Aut 1994

Smith, WD
WC 1959; Eur 1958; HI 1957 to
60; 63; Scan 1958-60

Stephen, AR (Sandy)
WC 1985; Eur 1972; HI 1971 to
77; 84-85; ETC 1975-85; Esp 1974;
Bel 1975-77-78; Fra 1985

Stevenson, A
HI 1949

Stevenson, JB
Irl 1931; HI 1932-38-47-49-50-51

Strachan, CJL
HI 1965-66-67; ETC 1967

Stuart, HB
WC 1971-73-75; ET 1972; Eur
1968-72-74; CT 1971; HI 1967 to
74; 76; ETC 1969-71-73-75; Bel
1973-75

Stuart, JE
HI 1959

Tait, AG
HI 1987-88-89; NNC 1989

Taylor, GN
HI 1948

Taylor, JS
Eng 1979; HI 1980; Bel, Fra 1980

Taylor, LG
HI 1955-56

Thomson, AP
HI 1970; ETC 1971

Thomson, G
HI 1996

Thomson, Hector
WC 1936-38; HI 1934 to 38

Thomson, JA
HI 1981 to 89; 91-92; ETC 1983;
WGer 1987; Ita 1984-86-88-90;
Swe 1990

Thomson, Mike
HI 1998

Thorburn, K
Irl 1927; Eng 1928

Torrance, TA
WC 1924-28-30-**32**-34; Eng 1922-
23-25-26-28-29-30; HI 1933

Torrance, WB
WC 1922; Eng 1922-23-24-26-27-
28-30; Irl 1928-29-30

Tulloch, W
Eng 1927-29; Eng, Irl 1930; Eng, Irl, Wal 1931; HI 1932

Turnbull, A
HI 1995-96-97; Fra 1995; Esp 1996

Twynholm, S
HI 1990; NNC 1990

Urquhart, M
HI 1993; Ita 1996

Vannet, Lee
HI 1984

Walker, J
WC 1961; Eur 1958-60; HI 1954-55-57-58; 60 to 63; Scan 1958-62

Walker, KH
HI 1985-86

Walker, RS
HI 1935-36

Warren, Marc
WC 2001; HI 2000-01; ETC 2001; Ita 2000; Swe 2001

Watson, Craig R
WC 1997; HI 1991-92; 94 to 2000, **2001**, 2003; ETC 1997-99-2001-03; Swe 1992-97-2001; Ita 1992; Aut 1994; Esp 1996-2002; Fra 1997

Watt, AW
HI 1987

Webster, AJ
HI 1978

Wemyss, DS
HI 1937

Whyte, AW
HI 1934

Wight, R
Swe 1950

Wilkie, DF
HI 1962-63-65-67-68

Wilkie, G
Eng 1911

Williamson, SB
HI 1947-48-49-51-52

Wilson, E
HI 1985

Wilson, J
WC 1923; Eng 1922-23-24-26; Irl 1932

Wilson, JC
WC 1947-53; CT 1954; SA 1954; HI 1947-48-49-51-52-53; Swe 1950; NZ 1954

Wilson, P
HI 1976; Bel 1977

Wilson, Stuart
WC 2003*; ET 2004; Eur 2004; AP 2002-04; ETC 2003; HI 2000-02-03-04; Esp, Ita 2002; Fra 2003

Wright, I
HI 1958 to 61; Scan 1960-62

Young, ID
Eur 1982; HI 1981-82; Fra 1982

Young, JR
Eur 1960; HI 1960-61-65; Scan 1960

Young, S
WC 1997; HI 1996; ETC 1997; Ita 1996

WALES

Adams, MPD
HI 1969 to 72; 75-76-77

Atkinson, HN
Irl 1913

Barnett, A
HI 1989-90-91; ETC 1991

Bayne, PWGA
HI 1949

Bevan, RJ
HI 1964-65-66-67-73-74

Black, JL
HI 1932 to 1936

Bonnell, DJ
HI 1949-50-51

Broad, RD
Irl 1979; HI 1980-81-82-84; ETC 1981

Brookman, R
HI 1999-2000

Brown, CT
WC (1995)*-(97); Eur (1996); HI 1970 to 75; 77-78-80-(88); ETC 1973; Den 1977; Irl 1979; Den, Esp, Sui 1980

Brown, D
Irl 1923-30-31; Eng 1925; Sco 1931

Buckley, JA
WC 1979; HI 1967-68-69-76-77-78; ETC 1967-69; Den 1976-77

Calvert, M
HI 1983-84-86-87-89-91

Campbell, A
HI 1996-97-2000-01

Campbell, I
HI 1998-99-2001; ETC 1999-2001

Carr, JP
Irl 1913

Chapman, JA
Irl 1923-29-30-31; Eng 1925; Sco 1931

Chapman, R
Irl 1929; HI 1932-34-35-36

Charles, WB
Irl 1924

Clark, MD
Irl 1947

Clay, G
HI 1962

Clement, G
Irl 1979

Coulter, JG
HI 1951-52

Cousins, Chris
HI 2006

Cox, S
HI 1970 to 74; ETC 1971-73

Davies, EN
HI 1959 to 74; ETC 1969-71-73

Davies, G
HI 1981-82-83; Den 1977

Davies, HE
HI 1933-34-36

Davies, Rhys
WC 2005; ET 2006; Eur 2006; ET 2004; HI 2002-03-04-05-06; ETC 2005

Davies, TJ
HI 1954 to 60

Dinsdale, R
HI 1991-92-93

Disley, A
HI 1976-77-78-**(99)**; Irl 1979; Den 1977

Dodd, SC
WC 1989; HI 1985-87-88-89

Donaldson, J
ET 2000; Eur 2000; HI 1996 to 2000; ETC 1997-99

Dredge, Bradley
WC 1993; ET 1992; Eur 1994; HI 1992 to 95; ETC 1995

Duffy, I
HI 1975

Duncan, AA
WC (1953); HI 1933-34-36-38; 47 to 59

Duncan, GT
HI 1952 to 58

Duncan, J jr
Irl 1913

Dykes, Tim
HI 2001-02-03-04-05-06; Fin 2004; ETC 2005

Eaves, CH
HI 1935-36-38-47-48-49

Edwards, Nigel
WC 2001*-03*-05; ET 2002-04-06; Eur 2004-06; AP 2002-04-06; HI 1995 to 2002, 2004-05-06; ETC 1997-99-2001-03-05

Edwards, S
HI 1992

Edwards, TH
HI 1947

Ellis, M
Eur 1996; HI 1992 to 96

Emerson, T
HI 1932

Emery, G
Irl 1925; HI 1933-36-38

Enoch, Rhys
HI 2006

Evans, AD
Sco, Irl 1931; Sco 1935; HI 1932 to 35; 38; 47 to 56; 61

Evans, Craig
HI 2004-05-06

Evans, C
1990 to 95; ETC 1995

Evans, Craig
HI 2004-05

Evans, Duncan
WC 1981; Eur 1980; HI 1978-80-81; Irl 1979; ETC 1981

Evans, HJ
HI 1976-77-78-80-81-84-85-87-88; Irl 1979; ETC 1979-81; Fra 1976; Den 1977-80; Esp, Sui 1980

Evans, M Gear
Irl 1930; Sco, Irl 1931

Fairchild, CEL
Irl 1923; Eng 1925

Fairchild, IJ
Irl 1924

Gilford, CF
HI 1963 to 67

Glossop, R
HI 1935-37-38-47

Gould, Zach
AP 2006; HI 2005-06; ETC 2005

Griffiths, HGB
Irl 1923-24-25

Griffiths, HS
Eng 1958

Griffiths, JA
HI 1933

Griffiths, M
HI 1999-2000-01; ETC 2001

Hales, JP
Sco 1963

Hall, A
HI 1994

Hall, D
HI 1932-37

Hall, K
HI 1955-59

Hamilton, CJ
Irl 1913

Harpin, Lee
ET 2002; HI 1996; 1998 to 2003; ETC 1999-2001

Harrhy, A
HI 1988-89-95

Harris, D
HI 1997

Harrison, JW
HI 1937-50

Hendriksen, Paul
Fin 2004

Herne, KTC
Irl 1913

Houston, G
HI 1990 to 95; ETC 1991-95

Howell, HR
Irl 1923-24-25-29-30-31; Eng 1925; Sco 1931; HI 1932; 34 to 38; 47

Howell H Logan
Irl 1925

Hughes, I
HI 1954-55-56

Humphrey, JG
Irl 1925

Humphreys, DI
HI 1972

Isitt, GH
Irl 1923

Jacob, NE
HI 1932 to 36

Jermine, JG
HI 1972 to 76; 82; 2000; ETC 1975-77; Fra 1975

Johnson, R
Eur 1994; HI 1990-92-93-94; ETC 1991

Jones, A
HI 1989-90; ETC 1991

Jones, DK
HI 1973

Jones, EO
HI 1983-85-86

Jones, JG Parry
HI 1959-60

Jones, JL
HI 1933-34-36

Jones, JR
HI 1970-72-73-77-78; 80 to 85; Irl 1979; ETC 1973-79-81; Den 1976; Den, Sui, Esp 1980

Jones, KG
HI 1988

Jones, MA
HI 1947 to 51; 53-54-57

Jones, Malcolm F
HI 1933

Jones, SP
HI 1981 to 86; 88-89-91-93

Knight, B
HI 1986

Knipe, RG
HI 1953 to 56

Knowles, WR
Eng 1948

Lake, AD
HI 1958

Laskey, Mark
HI 2004

Last, CN
HI 1975

Lee, JN
HI 1988-89; ETC 1991

Lewis, DH
HI 1935 to 38

Lewis, DR
Irl 1925-29-30-31; Sco 1931; HI 1932-34

Lewis, R Cofe
Irl 1925

Lloyd, HM
Irl 1913

Lloyd, RM de
Sco, Irl 1931; HI 1932 to 38; 47-48

Llyr, A
HI 1984-85

Lockley, AE
HI 1956-57-58-62

Macara, MA
HI 1983-84-85; 87; 89 to 93

McLean, D
HI 1968 to 78; 80 to 83; 85-86-88-90; Irl 1979; ETC 1975-77-79-81; Fra 1975; Fra, Den 1976; Den, Sui, Esp 1980

Maliphant, FR
HI 1932

Manley, Stuart
WC 2003*; HI 2001-02; ETC 2003

Marsden, G
HI 1994

Marshman, A
HI 1952

Marston, CC
Irl 1929-30; Irl, Sco 1931

Mathias-Thomas, FEL
Irl 1924-25

Matthews, Llewellyn
ET 2006; HI 2003-05-06

Matthews, N
HI 1999; ETC 1999

Matthews, RL
HI 1935-37

Mayo, PM
WC 1985-87; HI 1982-88

Melia, TJ
HI 1976-77-78-80-81-82; Irl 1979; ETC 1977-79; Den 1976; Den, Sui, Esp 1980

Mills, Cennydd
HI 2003-05-06; Fin 2004

Mills, ES
HI 1957

Mitchell, JWH
HI 1964-65-66-67

Moody, JV
HI 1947-48-49-51-56; 58 to 61

Morgan, JL
WC 1951-53-55; HI 1948 to 62; 64-68

Morris, R
HI 1983-86-87

Morris, TS
Irl 1924-29-30

Morrow, JM
Irl 1979; HI 1980-81; ETC 1979-81; Den, Sui, Esp 1980

Moss, AV
HI 1965-66-68

Mouland, MG
HI 1978-81; Irl 1979; ETC 1979

Moxon, GA
Irl 1929-30

Newman, JE
HI 1932

Newton, H
Irl 1929

Noon, GS
HI 1935-36-37

Oakley, Neil
HI 2002

O'Carroll, C
HI 1989 to 93; ETC 1991

Owen, JB
HI 1971

Owens, GF
HI 1960-61

Palferman, H
HI 1950-53

Palmer, M
HI 1998

Pardoe, S
HI 1991

Parfitt, RWM
Irl 1924

Park, D
WC 1997; HI 1994 to 97; ETC 1995-97

Parkin, AP
WC 1983; HI 1980-81-82

Parry, JR
HI 1966-75-76-77; Fra 1976

Peet, M
HI 1995-96

Peters, JL
HI 1987-88-89

Phillips, LA
Irl 1913

Pilkington, M
HI 1997-98; ETC 1997

Pinch, AG
HI 1969

Povall, J
Eur 1962; HI 1960 to 63; 65 to 77; ETC 1967-69-71-73-75-77; Fra 1975; Fra, Den 1976

Pressdee, RNG
HI 1958 to 62

Price, David
ET 2002; HI 1999 to 2003; ETC 2003

Price, JP
HI 1986-87-88

Price, Rhodri
HI 1994-96-97

Pugh, RS
Irl 1923-24-29

Pughe, O
HI 1997-98

Rees, CN
HI 1986-88-89-91-92; 94 to 97

Rees, DA
HI 1961 to 64

Renwick, G jr
Irl 1923

Ricardo, W
Irl 1930; Irl, Sco 1931

Rice-Jones, L
Irl 1924

Richards, PM
HI 1960 to 63; 71

Roberts, H
HI 1992-93

Roberts, J
HI 1937

Roberts, S
HI 1998-99

Roberts, SB
HI 1932 to 35; 37-38; 47 to 54

Roberts, WJ
HI 1948 to 54

Roderick, RN
WC 1989; Eur 1988; HI 1983 to 88

Rolfe, B
HI 1963-65

Roobottom, EL
HI 1967

Roper, MS
Irl 1979

Scott, Richard
HI 2003; Fin 2004

Sheppard, M
HI 1990

Smith, Alex
HI 1998-2000-02-03-04; ETC 2003; Fin 2004

Smith, Craig
HI 2002-03-04-05; ETC 2003

Smith, M
HI 1993 to 97; ETC 1995-97

Smith, VH
Irl 1924-25

Squirrel, HC
HI 1955 to 71; 73-74-75; ETC 1967-69-71-75; Fra 1975

Stevens, DI
HI 1968-69-70; 74 to 78; 80-82; ETC 1969-77; Fra 1976; Den 1977

Stoker, K
Irl 1923-24

Stokoe, GC
Eng 1925; Irl 1929-30

Sullivan, Kyron
HI 1998 to 2001; ETC 2001

Symonds, A
Irl 1925

Taylor, TPD
HI 1963

Taylor, Y
HI 1995-96-97; ETC 1995-97

Thomas, KR
HI 1951-52

Thomas, Ryan
HI 2004-05-06

Tooth, EA
Irl 1913

Toye, JL
HI 1963 to 67; 69 to 74; 76-78-**(2006)**; ETC 1971-73-75-77-**(2005)**; Fra 1975

Tucker, WI
HI 1949 to 72; 74-75; ETC 1967-69-75; Fra 1975

Turnbull, CH
Irl 1913-25

Turner, GB
HI 1947 to 52; 55-56

Wakely, Carl
HI 2005

Wallis, G
HI 1934-36-37-38

Walters, EM
HI 1967-68-69; ETC 1969

Westgate, Ben
HI 2004-06

Wilkie, GT
HI 1938

Wilkinson, S
HI 1990-91

Willcox, FS
Sco, Irl 1931

Williams, Craig
AP 2000; HI 1998 to 2001; ETC 1999-2001

Williams, James
HI 2001-02-03-04-05; Fin 2004; ETC 2005

Williams, KH
HI 1983 to 87

Williams, PG
Irl 1925

Wills, M
HI 1990

Winfield, HB
Irl 1913

Wood, DK
HI 1982 to 87

Woosnam, Ian
Fra 1976

Wright, Garwth
HI 2002-03-04; ETC 2003-05; ET 2004

Amateur Women

Key

Entries for the Curtis Cup, Commonwealth Tournament, World Amateur Team Championship and Vagliano Trophy, indicate that the player is representing Great Britain and Ireland. Other entries are for the home

CC	Curtis Cup
CT	Commonwealth Tournament
ES	World Amateur Team Championship (Espirito Santo)
VT	Vagliano Trophy
ELTC	played in European Ladies Team Championship for home country
HI	played in Home International matches
*	indicates winning team

'to' indicates inclusive dates: e.g.'1908 to 1911' means '1908-09-10-11'; otherwise individual years are shown.

Captaincy is indicated by the year printed in bold type; non-playing captaincy in brackets

[1998] indicates Espirito Santo Team selection which was subsequently advised not to travel to Chile

Maiden names are shown in brackets; other surnames and titles in square brackets

ENGLAND

Allen, F
HI 1952

Andrew, Kim (Rostron)
CC 1998-2000; HI 1996-97-99-2001; ELTC 1997-2001; (GBI) VT 1997-99-2001; ES [1998]; CT 1999

Archer, A (Rampton)
HI (1968)

Bailey, D [Frearson] (Robb)
CC 1962-72-(84)-(86)*-(88)*;
VT 1961-(83)-(85); CT 1983; HI 1961-62-71; ELTC 1968-(93)

Ball, Lisa
HI 2004

Barber, S (Bonallack)
CC 1962; ES (1996); VT 1961-63-69; CT (1995); HI 1960-61-62-68-70-72-77-(78); ELTC 1969-71

Bargh Etherington, B (Whitehead)
HI 1974

Barry, L
HI 1911 to 14

Barry, P
HI 1982

Barton, Pam
CC 1934-36; HI 1935 to 39

Bastin, G
HI 1920 to 25

Bayman, Linda (Denison Pender)
CC 1988; ES 1988; VT 1971-85-87; HI 1971-72-73-83-84-85-87-88-(95)-(96); ELTC 1985-87-89-(97)-(2001)

Beharrell, Veronica (Anstey)
CC 1956; HI 1955-56-57-(61)

Bell, Rachel
HI 2006

Benka, Pam (Tredinnick)
CC 1966-68-(2002); CT (2003); VT 1967; HI 1967

Bennett, Elizabeth
HI 2006

Biggs, A (Whittaker)
VT 1959

Bisgood, Jeanne
CC 1950-52-54-(70); HI 1949 to 54; 56-58

Blaymire, J
HI 1971-88-(89)

Boatman, Elizabeth A (Collis) CC (1992)*-(94); CT (1987)-(91); HI 1974-80-(84)-(85)-(90)-(91); ELTC (1985)-(87)

Bolas, R
HI 1992

Bolton, Zara (Bonner Davis)
CC 1948-(56)-(66)-(68); CT 1967; HI 1939; 48 to 51; (55)-(56)

Bonallack, Angela (Ward) [Lady Bonallack]
CC 1956-58-60-62-64-66; VT 1959-61-63; HI 1956 to 66; 72

Bostock, M
HI (1954)

Bourn, Mrs
HI 1909-12

Brown, Fiona
CC 1998-2000; VT 1999-2001; CT 1999; HI 1994; 96 to 2001; ELTC 1997-99-2001

Brown, J
HI 1984

Burnell, S
HI 1993; ELTC 1993

Burton, M
ELTC 1997

Cairns, Lady Katherine
CC (1952)*; HI 1947-48; 50 to 54

Caldwell, Carole (Redford)
CC 1978-80; VT 1973; HI 1973-78-79-80

Cann, M (Nuttall)
HI 1966

Carrick, P (Bullard)
HI 1939-47

Cautley, B (Hawtrey)
HI 1912-13-14; 22 to 25; 27

Christison, D
HI 1981

Clark, G (Atkinson)
HI 1955

Clarke, Mrs ML
HI 1933-35

Clarke, Nickie
HI (2002)

Clarke, P
HI 1981

Clement, V
HI 1932-34-35

Close, M (Wenyon)
VT 1969; HI 1968-69; ELTC 1969

Collett, P
HI 1910

Collingham, J (Melville)
VT 1979-87; CT 1987; HI 1978-79-81-84-86-87-92; ELTC 1989

Comboy, Carol (Grott)
CC (1978)-(80); ES (1978); VT (1977)-(79); CT (1979); HI (1975)-(76)

Corlett, Elsie
CC 1932-38-(64); HI 1927; 29 to 33; 35 to 39

Cotton, S (German)
VT 1967; HI 1967-68; ELTC 1967

Like Jack Nicklaus, RBS sponsored Luke Donald knows that to be an effective performer takes more than just raw talent; success is determined by the ability to think on your feet and make adjustments mid game. This versatility is even more important when considering Luke's tough schedule, involving the totally different playing conditions of golf courses on both the European and US Tours.

At The Royal Bank of Scotland, we also believe that being responsive to market conditions is what sets us apart from our competition and enables us to consistently deliver results for our clients. It's one reason why we've grown to be one of the biggest banking groups in the world.

rbs.co.uk

Make it happen

LEXUS HYBRID DRIVE

EXHILARATION

WITH CONSIDERATION

GS 450h. The world's first performance hybrid sedan.

Our new petrol/electric sedan with its advanced Lexus Hybrid Drive technology is a true breakthrough. The driving experience is highly exhilarating, thanks to the combination of a 3.5L V6 petrol engine and a high-output electric motor. These two power sources work intelligently together to produce extraordinarily smooth, seamless acceleration, delivering a hybrid system output of over 345 DIN hp, performance that rivals that of a V8. However,

at the same time, it is an extremely considerate car because this hybrid technology also delivers category-beating CO_2 emission levels of 186g/km and economical fuel consumption of 7.9L/100km in the combined fuel cycle, whilst reducing engine noise to a mere whisper. Experience exhilaration and consideration in equal proportion, with the new Lexus GS 450h.

www.lexus.eu

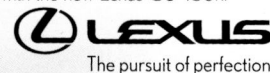

The pursuit of perfection

GS 450h fuel consumption figures: extra-urban 7.2 L/100 km (39.2 mpg), urban 9.2 L/100 km (30.7 mpg), combined 7.9 L/100 km (35.8 mpg). CO_2 emissions 186 g/km.

THE OPEN CHAMPIONSHIP

If you can't be there...
visit www.opengolf.com

Carnoustie, Angus 19th - 22nd July 2007

Please form an orderly queue.

Nikon

D80

The new 10.2 megapixel Nikon D80. RRP £699.99.   www.nikon.co.uk

D80 Nikon announce the D80, our 11th D-SLR, inheriting many features from our professional cameras, but at a price you wouldn't expect. It has a 10.2 megapixel CCD, 11 area wide autofocus, an advanced image processing engine, 0.94x viewfinder, a 2.5 inch LCD screen with a 170° viewing angle, a wide range of image enhancement options, start up in just 0.18 of a second and 3 fps continuous shooting. Body only - RRP £699.99. New AF-S DX 18-135 lens - RRP £299.99. New AF-S VR 70-300 lens - RRP £399.99. **Welcome to Nikon**

Whins – 13th hole, Carnoustie

A deceptively testing short hole often played down wind to a sloping green, surrounded by bunkers. Today's business environment can also be challenging and in times like these a little professional advice can be invaluable.

At Marsh & McLennan Companies, we offer advice and solutions in the fields of risk management, investment management and consulting. The more testing the terrain, the more we can help.

Use our resources to make the most of yours

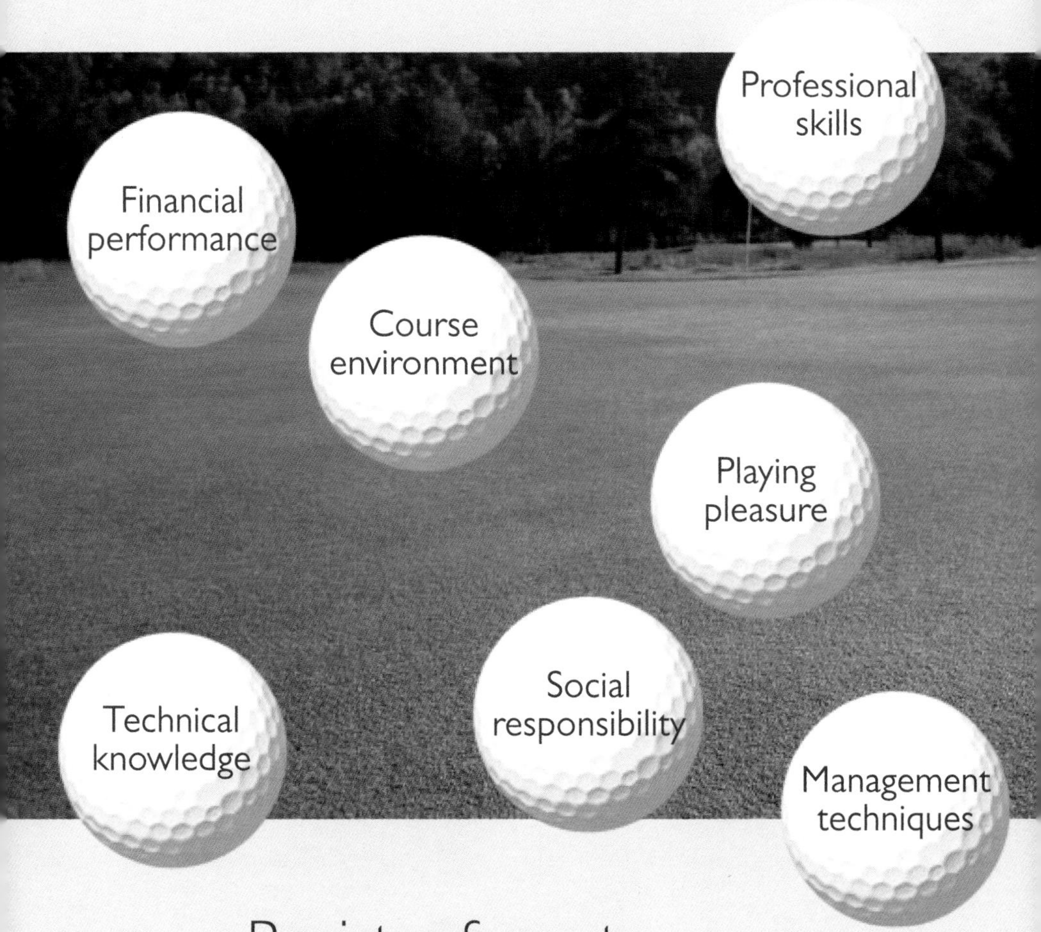

Professional skills

Financial performance

Course environment

Playing pleasure

Technical knowledge

Social responsibility

Management techniques

Register free at
www.bestcourseforgolf.org
today

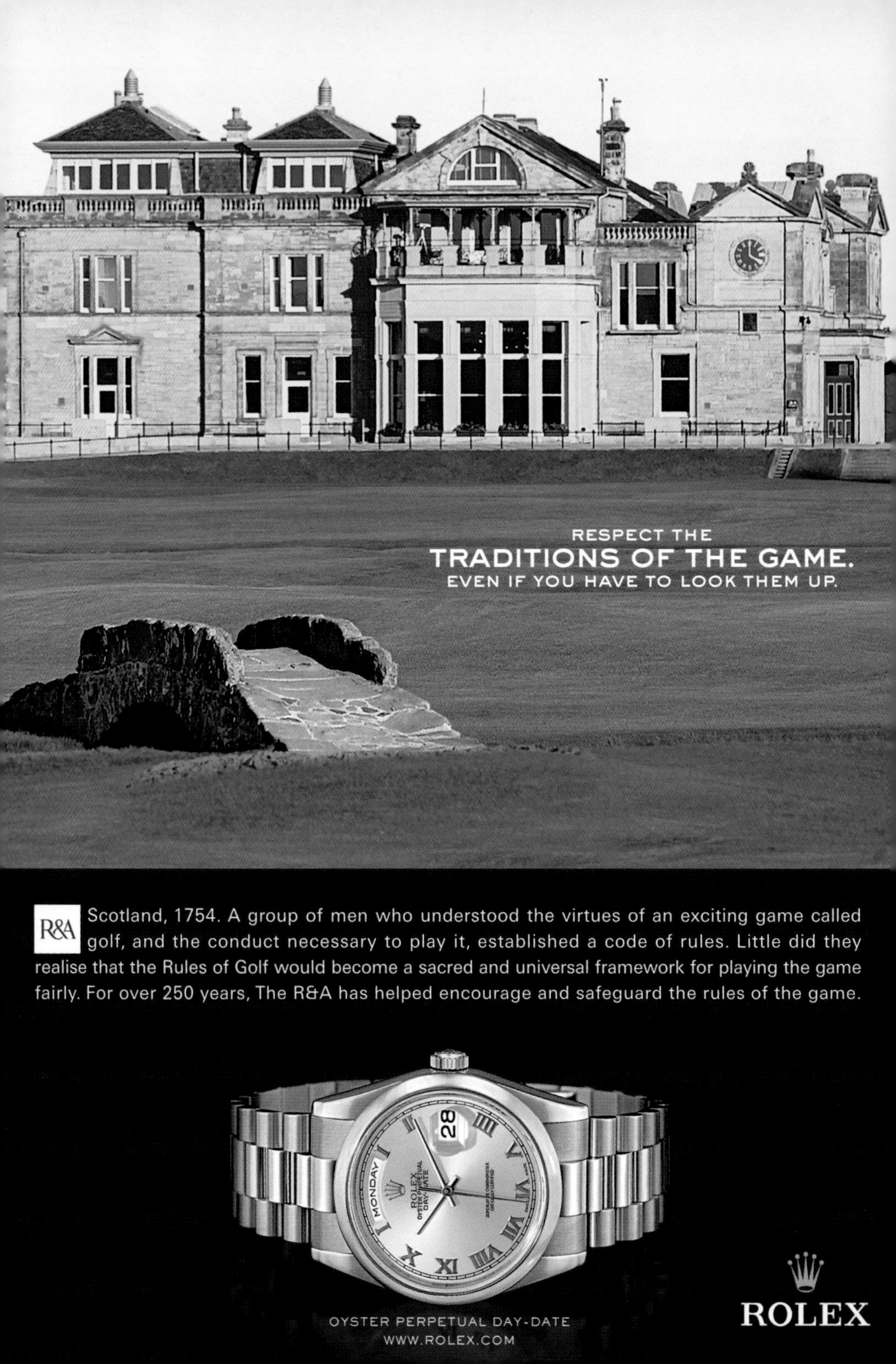

RESPECT THE
TRADITIONS OF THE GAME.
EVEN IF YOU HAVE TO LOOK THEM UP.

R&A Scotland, 1754. A group of men who understood the virtues of an exciting game called golf, and the conduct necessary to play it, established a code of rules. Little did they realise that the Rules of Golf would become a sacred and universal framework for playing the game fairly. For over 250 years, The R&A has helped encourage and safeguard the rules of the game.

OYSTER PERPETUAL DAY-DATE
WWW.ROLEX.COM

Court, C
HI 2000

Critchley, Diana (Fishwick)
CC 1932-34-(50); HI 1930 to 33;
35-36-(47)

Croft, A
HI 1927

Crummack, Miss
HI 1909

Davies, Laura
CC 1984; HI 1983-84

Dobson, Helen
CC 1990; VT 1989; HI 1987-88-89;
ELTC 1989

Dod, L
HI 1905

Douglas, K
CC 1982; VT 1983; HI 1981-82-83

Dowling, D
HI 1979

Duggleby, Emma
CC 2000-02-04; ES 2002-04; VT
1995-2001-03; HI 1994-95-96-99 to
2005; ELTC 1995-99-2001-03-05

Durrant, B [Green] (Lowe)
HI 1954

Eastwood, Laura
HI 2005

Edmond, F (Macdonald)
VT 1991; HI 1991; ELTC 1991

Educate, Lisa (Walton)
CC 1994-96; VT 1993-95; CT
1995; HI 1991-94-95; ELTC 1993-
95

Edwards, Naomi
CC 2006; HI 2004-05-06

Egford, K
HI 1992-94

Evans, H
HI 1908

Everard, Mary
CC 1970-72-74-78; ES 1968-72-78;
VT 1967-69-71-73; CT 1971; HI
1964-67-69-70-72-73-77-78; ELTC
1967-71-77

Ewart, Jodi
HI 2005

Fairclough, L
VT 1989; HI 1988-89-90; ELTC
1989

Ferguson, R (Ogden)
HI 1957

Fields, E
HI 1995-96

Fisher, Kirsty
VT 2001; HI 1998 to 2002; ELTC
1999-2001

Fletcher, Linzi
CC 1990; CT 1991; HI 1989-90;
ELTC 1991

Foster, C
HI 1905-06-09

Fowler, J
HI 1928

Furby, J
HI 1987-88; ELTC 1987

Fyshe, M
HI 1938

Garbutt, Sara
HI 2002-03

Garon, Marjorie Ross
CC 1936; HI 1927-28-32-33-34-36-
37-38

Garrett, Maureen (Ruttle)
CC 1948-(60); VT 1959; HI 1947-
48-50-53-(59)-(60)-(63)

Gee, Hon. J (Hives)
HI 1950-51-52

Gibb, M (Titterton)
HI 1906-07-08-10-12

Gibbs, Carol (Le Feuvre)
CC 1974; VT 1973; HI 1971 to 74

Gold, N
HI 1929-31-32

Gordon, Jacqueline
CC 1948; HI 1947-48-49-52-53

Gourlay, Molly
CC 1932-34; HI 1923-24; 27 to 30;
32-33-34-38-(57)

Green, B (Pockett)
HI 1939

Grice-Whitaker, Penny
(Grice) CC 1984; ES 1984; HI
1983-84

Griffiths, M
HI 1920-21

Guadella, E (Leitch)
HI 1908-10-20-21-22; 27 to 30;
33

Hackney, L
HI 1990

Hall, Caroline
CC 1992; VT 1991; HI 1991-92;
ELTC 1991

Hall, CM
HI 1985

Hambro, W (Martin Smith)
HI 1914

Hamilton, J
HI 1937-38-39

Hammond, T
HI 1985

Hampson, M
HI 1954

Harris, Marley [Spearman]
(Baker)
CC 1960-62-64; ES 1964; VT 1959-
61-65; HI 1955 to 65; ELTC 1965-
71

Harrold, L
HI 1974-75-76

Hartill, D
HI 1923

Hartley, E
HI (1964)

Hayter, J (Yuille)
HI 1956

Heath, Sarah (Gleeson)
HI 2001-02; ELTC 2001

Heathcoat-Amory, Lady
(Joyce Wethered)
CC 1932; HI 1921 to 25; 29

Hedges, S (Whitlock)
VT 1979; CT 1979; HI 1979

Helme, E
HI 1911-12-13-20

Heming Johnson, G
HI 1909-11-13

Henson, Dinah (Oxley)
CC 1968-70-72-76; ES 1970; VT
1967-69-71; CT 1967-71; HI 1967
to 70; 75 to 78; ELTC 1971-77

Hetherington, Mrs (Gittens)
HI 1909

Hill, J
HI 1986

Hockley, J
ES 1992; VT 1993; HI 1991-92-93-
96

Hodge, Susan (Shapcott)
CC 1988; ES 1988; VT 1987;
CT 1987; HI 1986-88; ELTC
1987

Hodgson, M
HI 1939

Holmes, A
HI 1931

Holmes [Hetherington]
(McClure)
HI 1956-66-(67)

Hooman, EM (Gavin)
HI 1910-11

Howard, Ann (Phillips)
CC 1956-58; HI 1953 to 58; (79)-
(80)

Hudson, Rebecca
CC 1998-2000-02; ES [1998]-2000;
VT 1997-2001; CT 1999; HI 1996-
2001-02; ELTC 1997-99-2001

Huke, Beverley
CC 1972; VT 1975; HI 1971-72-75-
76-77

Hunter, D (Tucker)
HI 1905

Irvin, Ann
CC 1962-68-70-76; ES (1982); VT
1961 to 75; CT 1967-75; HI 1962-
63-65; 67 to 73; 75; ELTC 1965-67-
69-71

Jackson, Bridget
CC 1958-64-68; ES 1964; VT 1959-63-65-67-**(73)-(75)**; CT 1959-67; HI 1955 to 59; 63 to 66; **(73)-(74)**

Johns, A
HI 1987-88-89

Johnson, Felicity
VT 2005; ELTC 2005; HI 2005-06

Johnson, M
HI 1934-35

Johnson, Patricia M
CC 1986; ES 1986; VT 1985; HI 1984-85-86; ELTC 1985

Kaye, H (Williamson)
HI **(1986)-(87)**

Keighley, Alex
HI 2002-03; ELTC 2003

Keiler, G (Style)
HI 1948-49-52

Kennedy, D (Fowler)
HI 1923-24-25-27-28-29

Kennion, Mrs (Kenyon Stow)
HI 1910

Kyle, B [Rhodes] (Norris)
HI 1937-38-39-48-49

Lamb, J
HI 1998-99

Lambert, S (Cohen)
VT 1979-95; HI 1979-80-93-94-95; ELTC 1995

Langridge, Susan (Armitage)
CC 1964-66; VT 1963-65; HI 1963 to 66; ELTC 1965

Large, P (Davies)
HI 1951-52-**(81)-(82)**

Latham Hall, E (Chubb)
HI 1928

Lee Smith, Jenny
CC 1974-76; ES 1976; CT 1975; HI 1973 to 76

Leitch, C
HI 1910 to 14; 20-21-22-24-25-27-28

Lipscombe, Clare
HI 1999

Lobbett, P
HI 1922-24-27-29-30

Luckin, B (Cooper)
HI 1980

Lumb, Kathryn (Phillips)
CC 1972; VT 1969-71; HI 1968 to 71; ELTC 1969

Lyons, T (Ross Steen)
VT 1959; HI 1959

Macbeth, M (Dodd)
HI 1913-14; 20 to 25

Macdonald, F
HI 1990

McIntosh, B (Dixon)
VT 1969; HI 1969-70; ELTC 1969

McIntyre, J
HI 1949-54

McKevitt, Shelley
CC 2004; CT 2003

McNair, W
HI 1921

Maher, Sheila (Vaughan)
CC 1962-64; VT 1961; CT 1963; HI 1960 to 64

Marshall, Alex
HI 2004

Marvin, Vanessa
CC 1978; VT 1977; HI 1977-78; ELTC 1977

Masters, Danielle
CC 2004; VT 2003; HI 2003; ELTC 2003

Matharu, Kiran
CC 2006; HI 2005

Merrill, Julia (Greenhalgh)
CC 1964-70-74-76-78; ES 1970-**74**-78; VT 1961-65-75-77; CT 1963; HI 1960-61-63-66-69-70-71; 75 to 78; ELTC 1971-77

Moorcroft, S
HI 1985-86; ELTC 1985-87

Morant, E
HI 1906-10

More, Fame
CC 2002-04; VT 2001-03; HI 2000-01-02-03; ELTC 2001-03

Morgan, S
HI 1989; ELTC 1989

Morgan, Wanda
CC 1932-34-36; HI 1931 to 37

Morley, Joanne
CC 1992; ES 1992; VT 1991-93; HI 1990 to 93; ELTC 1991-93

Morris, L (Moore)
HI 1912-13

Morrison, G (Cheetham)
VT 1965; HI 1965-**(69)**

Morrison, G (Cradock-Hartopp) HI 1936

Murray, Nicola (Buxton)
CC 1992; VT 1991-93; HI 1991-92-93; ELTC 1991-93

Murray, S (Jolly)
HI 1976

Nes, K (Garnham)
HI 1931-32-33; 36 to 39

Neville, E
HI 1905-06-08-10

New, Beverley
CC 1984; VT 1983; HI 1980 to 83

Newell, B
HI 1936

Newton, B (Brown)
HI 1930; 33 to 37

Oliver, J
HI 1995

Parker, Florentyne
HI 2006

Parker, S
HI 1973

Pearson, D
HI 1928 to 32; 34

Phillips, ME
HI 1905

Pickard, Margaret (Nichol)
CC 1968-70; VT 1959-61-67; HI 1958 to 61; 67-69; **(83)**

Pook, Elizabeth (Chadwick)
CC 1966; VT 1963-67; CT 1967; HI 1963-65-66-67

Porter, M (Lazenby)
HI 1931-32

Price, M (Greaves)
HI **(1956)**

Price Fisher, Elizabeth (Price) CC 1950-52-54-56-58-60; VT 1959; CT 1959; HI 1948; 51 to 60

Prout, Rebecca
HI 2000

Rabbidge, R
HI 1931

Ratcliffe, Elaine
CC 1998; ES 1996; VT 1997; HI 1995-96-97; ELTC 1995-97

Read, P
HI 1922

Reddick, Sian
ELTC 2005

Reece, P (Millington)
HI 1966

Reid, Melissa
CC 2006; ES 2006; HI 2006

Remer, H
HI 1909

Richardson, Mrs
HI 1907-09

Robinson, S
HI 1989

Roskrow, M
HI 1948-50

Ross, Julie
HI 2004

Rudgard, G
HI 1931-32-50-51-52

Sabine, Diana (Plumpton)
CC 1934; HI 1934-35

Sanderson, Fay
HI 2004; ELTC 2005

Saunders, Vivien
CC 1968; VT 1967; CT 1967; HI 1967-68; ELTC 1967

Sheppard, E (Pears)
HI 1947

Simpson, Linda (Moore)
CC 1980; HI 1979-80

Slark, Ruth (Porter)
CC 1960-62-64; ES 1964-66;
VT 1959-61-65; CT 1963; HI
1959 to 62; 64-65-66-68-78; ELTC
1965

Smillie, P
HI 1985-86

Smith, Anne [Stant]
(Willard)
CC 1976; VT 1975; CT **1959-63**;
HI 1974-75-76

Smith, E
HI 1991

Smith, Frances (Stephens)
CC 1950-52-54-56-58-60; **(62)-**
(72); VT 1959-71; CT 1959-63; HI
1947 to 55; 59; **(62)-(71)-(72)**

Smith, Kerry
CC 2002; ES 2006; VT 2001-05; HI
1997 to 2006; ELTC 1999-2003-05

Soulsby, Janet
CC 1982

Speak, Kirsty
CC 1994; ES 1994; VT 1993; HI
1993-94; ELTC 1993

Steel, E
HI 1905 to 08; 11

Stocker, J
HI 1922-23

Stuples, Karen
CC 1996-98; VT 1997; HI 1995 to
98; ELTC 1995-97

Sugden, J (Machin)
HI 1953-54-55

Sumpter, Mrs
HI 1907-08-12-14-24

Sutherland Pilch, R (Barton)
HI 1947-49-50-**(58)**

Swallow, C
HI 1985; ELTC 1985

Tamworth, Mrs
HI 1908

Tebbet, K
HI 1990-94

Temple, S
HI 1913-14

Temple Dobell, G
(Ravenscroft) HI 1911 to 14; 20-
21-25-30

Thompson, M (Wallis)
HI 1948-49

Thornhill, J (Woodside)
CC 1984-86-88; VT 1965-83-85-87-
(89); CT 1983-87; HI 1965-74; 82
to 88; ELTC 1965-85-87

Thomlinson, J [Evans]
(Roberts)
CC 1962; VT 1963; HI 1962-64

Timmins, Nicola
CC 2004; HI 2003; ELTC 2003

Turner, B
HI 1908

Uzielli, Angela (Carrick)
CC 1978; VT 1977; HI 1976-77-78-
90; **(92)-(93)**; ELTC 1977

Wade, Julie
CC 1988-90-92-94-96; ES 1988-90-
94; VT 1989-91-93-95; CT 1991-95;
HI 1987 to 95; ELTC 1987 to 95

Waite, Claire
CC 1984; ES 1984; VT 1983; CT
1983; HI 1981 to 84; ELTC 1985

Walker, B (Thompson)
HI 1905 to 09; 11

Walker, Mickey
CC 1972-74; VT 1971; CT 1971; HI
1970-72; ELTC 1971

Walker, Sophie
ES 2006; VT 2005; HI 2003-04-05-
06; ELTC 2005

Walker-Leigh, F
HI 1907-08-09; 11 to 14

Walter, J
HI 1974-79-80-82-86

Walters, L
HI 1998

Watson, C (Nelson)
HI 1982

Westall, S (Maudsley)
HI 1973

Williamson, C (Barker)
HI 1979-80-81

Willock-Pollen, G
HI 1907

Wilson, Enid
CC 1932; HI 1928-29-30

Winn, J
HI 1920-21-23-25

Wragg, M
HI 1929

Wylie, Phyllis (Wade)
CC 1938; HI 1934 to 38; 47

IRELAND

Alexander, M
HI 1920-21-22-30

Arbuthnot, M
HI 1921

Armstrong, M
HI 1906

Barlow, Mrs
HI 1921

Beck, Baba (Pim)
HI 1930 to 34; 36-37; 47 to 56; 58-
59-61

Beckett, J
HI 1962-66-67-68

Behan, L
CC 1986; VT 1985; HI 1984-85-86-
96-98

Birmingham, M
HI **(1967)**

Blake, Miss
HI 1931 to 36

Boyd, J
HI 1912-13-14

Bradshaw, E
VT 1969-71; HI 1964; 66 to 71; 74-
75-**(80)-(81)**; ELTC 1969-71-75

Brandom, G
VT 1967; HI 1965 to 68; ELTC
1967

Brennan, R (Hegarty)
HI 1974 to 79; 81

Brice, Mrs
HI 1948

Brinton, Mrs
HI 1922

Brooks, E
HI 1953-54-56

Brown, B
HI 1960

Brownlow, Miss
HI 1923

Butler, I (Burke)
CC 1966-**(96)***; ES 1964-66; VT
1965; 1962 to 66; 68; 70 to 73; 76
to 79; **(86)-(87)**; ELTC 1967

Byrne, A (Sweeney)
HI 1959 to 63; **(90)-(91)**

Callen, L
HI 1990

Casement, M (Harrison)
HI 1909 to 14

Cassidy, Yvonne
HI 1994-95-2000-01

Clarke, Mrs
HI 1922

Coffey, Alison
CC 2002; ES 2000; VT 1999-2001;
HI 1995 to 2002; ELTC 1997-99-
2001

Colquhoun, H
HI 1959-60-61-63

Coote, Miss
HI 1925-28-29

Costello, G
HI 1973-**(84)-(85)**

Coughlan, Claire
CC 2004-06; ES 2006; VT 2005; HI
1999-2000-01-03-04-05-06; ELTC
1999-2001-03-05

Cramsie, F (Hezlet)
HI 1905 to 10; 13-20-24

Cuming, Mrs
HI 1910

Cuthell, R (Adair)
HI 1908

Delaney, Tara
CC 2006; ELTC 2005; HI 2003-05

Dering, Mrs
HI 1923

Dickson, E
HI 1999-2000; ELTC 1999

Dickson, M
HI 1909

Dowdall, Elaine
HI 1997 to 2001

Dowling, Claire (Hourihane)
CC 1984-86-88-90-92-**(2000)**; ES 1986-90-[98]; VT 1981-83-85-87-89-91-**(99)**; HI 1979 to 92; ELTC 1981-83-85-87-89-**(97)**

Dunne, Maria
HI 2003-05-06; ELTC 2003

Durlacher, Mrs
HI 1905 to 10; 14

Dwyer, Mrs
HI 1928

Eakin, P (James)
HI 1967

Eakin, T
HI 1990 to 94; ELTC 1993

Earner, M
HI 1960 to 63; 70

Ellis, E
HI 1932-35-37-38

Ferguson, A
HI 1989

Ferguson, Daisy
CC **(1958)**; HI 1927 to 32; 34 to 38; **(61)**

Fitzgibbon, M
HI 1920-21; 29 to 33

Fitzpatrick, O (Heskin)
HI 1967

Fletcher, P (Sherlock)
HI 1932-34-35-36-38-39-54-55-**(66)**

Gardiner, A
HI 1927-29

Garvey, Philomena
CC 1948-50-52-54-56-60; VT 1959-63; HI 1947 to 53; 54-56-**57-58-59-60**-61-62-63-68-69

Gaynor, Z (Fallon)
ES 1964; HI 1952 to 65; 68-69-70; **(72)**

Gildea, Miss
HI 1936 to 39

Gillen, Martina
CC 2006; ES 2006; VT 2005; HI 1999-2001-02-04-05-06; ELTC 2001-03-05

Glendinning, D
HI 1937-54

Gorman, S
HI 1976; 79 to 82; **(92)-(93)**; ELTC **(1993)**

Gorry, Mary
VT 1977; HI 1971 to 80; 88-**(89)**; ELTC 1971-75

Gotto, Mrs C
HI 1923

Gotto, Mrs L
HI 1920

Graham, N
HI 1908-09-10-12

Gubbins, Miss
HI 1905

Hackett, B
HI 1993-94-96

Hall, Mrs
HI 1927-30

Hanna, D
HI 1987-88

Harrington, D
HI 1923

Hazlett, VP
HI **(1956)**

Healy, B
HI 1980-82

Hegarty, G
HI 1955-56-**(64)**

Heskin, A
HI 1968-69-70-72-75-77-**(82)-(83)**

Hewett, G
HI 1923-24

Hezlet, Mrs
HI 1910

Hickey, C
HI 1969-**(75)-(76)**

Higgins, E
HI 1981 to 88; 91 to 96; ELTC 1987-93-**(2001)**

Holland, I (Hurst)
HI 1958

Hulton, V (Hezlet)
HI 1905-07; 09 to 12; 20-21

Humphreys, D (Forster)
HI 1951-52-53-55-57

Hyland, B
HI 1964-65-66;

Jackson, B
HI 1937-38-39-50

Jackson, Mrs H
HI 1921

Jackson, J
HI 1912-13-14; 20 to 25; 27 to 30

Jackson, Mrs L
HI 1910-12-14-20-22-25

Jameson, S (Tobin)
HI 1913-14-20-24-25-27

Jones, Helen
HI 2003-04; ELTC 2003

Kavanagh, H
VT 1995; HI 1993-94-95-97-98-2001; ELTC 1997-2001

Keane, Sinead
HI 2000-02-03; ELTC 2001

Keenan, D
HI 1989

Kidd, Mrs
HI 1934-37

King, Mrs
HI 1923-25-27-29

Kirkwood, Mrs
HI 1955

Kitching, Niamh
HI 2006

Larkin, C (McAuley)
HI 1966 to 72; ELTC 1971

Latchford, B
HI 1931-33

Lauder, G
HI 1911

Lauder, R
HI 1911

Lowry, Mrs
HI 1947

MacCann, K
HI 1984-85-86

MacCann, K (Smye)
HI 1947 to 54; 56-57-58-60-61-62-64-**(65)**

McCarthy, A
HI 1951-52

McCarthy, D
HI 1988-90-91-95; ELTC 1993

McCool, L
HI 1993

McDaid, E (O'Grady)
HI 1959

MacGeach, C
HI 1938-39-48-49-50

McGowan, Darragh
HI 2002

McGreevy, V
HI 1987-90-92

McKenna, Mary
CC 1970 to 86; ES 1970-74-76-**(86)-(90)**; VT 1969 to 81; 85-87; **(95)**; HI 1968 to 91; 93; **(2002)**; ELTC 1969-71-75-87

McNeile, CL
HI 1906

McQuillan, Y
HI 1985-86

McVeigh, Danielle
HI 2006

Madeley, M (Coburn)
HI 1964-69; ELTC 1969

Madill, Maureen
CC 1980; ES 1980; VT 1979-81-85; CT 1979; HI 1978 to 85

Madill, Mrs
HI 1920-24-25-27-28-29-33

Magill, J
HI 1907-11-13

Mahon, D
HI 1989-90

Mallam, Mrs S
HI 1922-23

Mangan, Tricia
CC 2006; ES 2006; VT 2003-05; HI 1998-2000-02-03-04-05-06; ELTC 2003-05

Marks, Mrs T
HI 1950

Marks, Mrs
HI 1930-31-33-35

Menton, D
HI 1949

Millar, D
HI 1928

Milligan, J (Mark)
HI 1971-72-73

Mitchell, J
HI 1930

Mooney, M
VT 1973; HI 1972-73; ELTC 1971

Moore, S
HI 1937-38-39-47-48-49-(68)

Moran, V (Singleton)
HI 1970-71-73-74-75; ELTC 1971-75

Moriarty, M (Irvine)
HI 1979

Morrin, Maura
HI 2003-04-05-06; ELTC 2003

Morris, Mrs de B
HI 1933

Murray, Rachel
HI 1952

Nolan, Heather
HI 2002-03-04-05; ELTC 2005

Nutting, P (Jameson)
HI 1927-28

O'Brien, A
HI 1969

O'Brien, Suzanne (Fanagan)
CC 2000; ES 2000; VT 1999; HI 1995 to 2000; ELTC 1997-99

O'Brien Kenney, S
HI 1977-78; 83 to 86

O'Donnell, Maire
CC (1982); VT (1981); HI 1974-77-(78)-(79); ELTC (1980)

O'Donohue, A
HI 1948 to 51; 53; (73)-(74)

O'Hare, S
HI 1921-22

O'Reilly, T (Moran)
HI 1977-78-86-88; (95); ELTC 1987

O'Sullivan, Ada
CC (2006); HI 1982-83-84-92-94-95-96; ELTC 1993-97

O'Sullivan, P
HI 1950 to 60; 63 to 67; (69)-(70)-(71); ELTC (1971)

O'Sullivan, Sinead
HI 2004

Ormsby, Miss
HI 1909-10-11

Orr, P (Boyd)
HI 1971

Pim, Mrs
HI 1908

Power, Eileen Rose (McDaid)
CC 1994; VT 1995-97; HI 1987 to 97; 2001-02; ELTC 1987-93-97-99

Purcell, E
HI 1965-66-67-72-73

Purfield, O
HI 1998-99

Reddan, Clarrie (Tiernan)
CC 1938-48; HI 1935-36-38-39-47-48-49

Reddan, MV
HI 1955

Rice, J
HI 1924-27-29

Riordan, Marian
HI 2002

Roberts, E (Pentony)
HI 1932 to 36; 39

Roberts, E (Barnett)
HI 1961 to 65; ELTC 1964

Robinson, C (Nesbitt)
CC 1980; VT 1979; HI 1974 to 81

Robinson, R (Bayly)
HI 1947-56-57

Roche, Mrs
HI 1922

Rogers, A
HI 1992-93; ELTC 1993

Ross, M (Hezlet)
HI 1905 to 08; 11-12

Slade, Lady
HI 1906

Smith, Deirdre
HI 1999-2004-05-06; ELTC 2001-05

Smith, Mrs L
HI 1913-14-21-22-23-25

Smythe, M
HI 1947 to 56; 58-59; (62)

Starrett, L (Malone)
HI 1975 to 78; 80

Stuart, M
HI 1905-07-08

Stuart-French, Miss
HI 1922

Sweeney, L
HI 1991

Taylor, I
HI 1930

Thornhill, Miss
HI 1924-25

Thornton, Mrs
HI 1924

Todd, Mrs
HI 1931 to 36

Tynte, V
HI 1905-06-08-09; 11 to 14

Walker, Pat
CC 1934-36-38; HI 1928 to 39; 48

Walsh, R
HI 1987

Webb, L (Bolton)
HI 1981-82-88-89-91-92-94

Wickham, C
HI 1983-89

Wickham, P
HI 1976-83-87; ELTC 1987

Wilson, Mrs
HI 1931

SCOTLAND

Agnew, C
HI 1995

Aitken, E (Young)
HI 1954

Anderson, E
HI 1910-11-12-21-25

Anderson, F
VT 1987; HI 1977-79-80-81-83-84-87 to 92; ELTC 1979-83-87-91

Anderson, H
VT 1969; HI 1964-65-68-69-70-71; ELTC 1969

Anderson, Jean (Donald)
CC 1948-50-52; HI 1947 to 52

Anderson, L
HI 1986 to 89; ELTC 1987-89

Anderson, VH
HI 1907

Bald, J
HI 1968-69-71; ELTC 1969

Barclay, C (Brisbane)
HI 1953-61-68

Baynes, Mrs CE
HI 1921-22

Beddows, C [Watson] (Stevenson)
CC 1932; HI 1913-14-21-22-23-27; 29 to 37; 39; 47 to 51

Bennett, Lorna
HI 1977-80-81

Benton, MH
HI 1914

Bishop, Sara
HI 2006

Blair, N (Menzies)
HI 1955

Bowhill, M (Robertson-Durham) HI 1936-37-38

Broun, JG
HI 1905-06-07-21

Brown, Mrs FW (Gilroy)
HI 1905 to 11; 13-21

Brown, TWL
HI 1924-25

Burns, K
HI 1999

Burton, H (Mitchell)
VT 1961; HI 1931-55-56-(59)

Cadden, G
VT (1997); HI 1974-75-(95)-(96); ELTC (1997)

Caithness, Krystle
ES 2006; HI 2004-05-06

Campbell, J (Burnett)
HI 1960

Coats, Mrs G
HI 1931 to 34

Cochrane, K
HI 1924-25-28-29-30

Connachan, J
CC 1980-82; ES 1980-82; VT 1981-83; CT 1983; HI 1979 to 83

Copley, K (Lackie)
HI 1974-75

Couper, M
HI 1929; 34 to 37; 39-56

Craik, T
HI 1988

Crawford, I (Wylie)
HI 1970-71-72

Cresswell, K (Stuart)
HI 1909 to 12; 14

Cruickshank, DM (Jenkins)
HI 1910-11-12

Davidson, Alison (Rose)
CC 1996-98; VT 1995-97; CT 1995; HI 1990 to 98; 2000; ELTC 1991-93-95-97-99

Davidson, B (Inglis)
HI 1928

Draper, Marjorie [Peel] (Thomas)
CC 1954; VT (1963); HI 1929-34-38; 49 to 53; (54)-(55); 56-57-58; (61); 62

Duncan, MJ (Wood)
HI 1925-27-28-39

Falconer, V (Lamb)
HI 1932-36-37; 47 to 56

Farie-Anderson, J
HI 1924

Farquharson-Black, Elaine (Farquharson)
CC 1990-92; VT 1989-91; CT 1991; HI 1987 to 91; 97-98; (2002); ELTC 1989-91

Feggans, Pamela
HI 2002-03; ELTC 2005

Ferguson, Marjory (Fowler)
CC 1966; VT 1965; HI 1959; 62 to 67; 69-70-85; ELTC 1965-67-71

Forbes, J
HI 1985 to 89; ELTC 1987-89

Ford, J
HI 1993-94-95

Gallagher, S
HI 1983-84

Gemmill, A
HI 1981-82; 84 to 89; 91-(97)

Glennie, H
HI 1959

Glover, A
HI 1905-06-08-09-12

Gow, J
HI 1923-24-27-28

Graham, MA
HI 1905-06

Granger Harrison, Mrs
HI 1922

Grant-Suttie, E
HI 1908-10-11-14-22-23

Grant-Suttie, R
HI 1914

Greenlees, E
HI 1924

Greenlees, Y
HI 1928-30-31-33-34-35-38

Hamilton, S (McKinven)
HI 1965

Hargan, Claire
ELTC 2001-03; HI 1999-2000-01

Hastings, Dorothea (Sommerville)
CC 1958; VT 1963; HI 1955 to 63

Hay, J (Pelham Burn)
HI 1959

Holm, Helen (Gray)
CC 1936-38-48; HI 1932 to 38; 47-48-50-51-55-57

Hope, LA
HI 1975-76-80; 84 to 87; (88)-(89)-(90)

Huggan, Shirley (Lawson)
CC 1988; VT 1989; HI 1985 to 89; ELTC 1985-87-89

Hurd [Howe] (Campbell)
HI 1905-06-08-09-11-28-30

Jack, E (Philip)
HI 1962-63-64-(81)-(82)

Jackson, D
HI 1990

Kelway Bamber, Mrs
HI 1923-27-33

Kenny, Louise
HI 2003-06

Kenny, Lynn
VT 2003; CT 2003; ELTC 2003; HI 2000-01-03-04

Kerr, J
HI 1947-48-49-54

Kinloch, Miss
HI 1913-14

Knight, Mrs
HI 1922

Kyle, E
HI 1909-10

Laing, A
VT 1967; HI 1966-67-70-71-(73)-(74)

Laing, Anne
CC 2004; VT 1999-2003-05; CT 1999-2003; HI 1995 to 99; 2001 to 05; ELTC 1997-99-2001-03-05

Laing, Susannah
HI 2002

Laing, Vicki
CC 2002; VT 2003; HI 1997-98; ELTC 2001-03

Lambie, S
HI 1976

Lawrence, Joan B
CC 1964; ES 1964; VT 1963-65; CT 1971; HI 1959 to 70; (77); ELTC 1965-67-69-71

Leburn, Wilma (Aitken)
CC 1982; VT 1981-83; HI 1978 to 83; 85

Leete, Mrs IG
HI 1933

Little, S
HI 1993

Lockhart, Fiona
HI 2005; ELTC 2005

Lugton, C
HI 1968-72-73-**75**-**76**-77-78-80

MacAndrew, F
HI 1913-14

McCulloch, J
HI 1921 to 24; 27; 29 to 33; 35; (60)

Macdonald, K
HI 1928-29

MacIntosh, I
HI **(1991)-(92)-(93)**; ELTC **(1993)**

McKay, F
HI 1992-93-94; ELTC 1993

Mackay, Lesley
HI 1999 to 2003; ELTC 2001-03

McKay, Mhairi
CC 1994-96; ES 1996; VT 1993-95-97; CT 1995; HI 1991-93-94-96; ELTC 1993-95

Mackenzie, A
HI 1921

McKinlay, Myra
CC 1994; HI 1990-92-93; ELTC 1993

McLarty, E
HI **(1966)-(67)-(68)**

McMahon, Suzanne (Cadden)
CC 1976; VT 1975; HI 1974 to 77; 79

McMaster, S
HI 1994 to 97; ELTC 1995-97

McNeil, K
HI **(1969)-(70)**

MacRae, Heather
ES 2006; VT 2005; HI 2003-04-06; ELTC 2005

Main, M (Farquhar)
HI 1950-51

Maitland, M
HI 1905-06-08-12-13

Marr, H (Cameron)
HI 1927 to 31

Marshall, Kathryn (Imrie)
CC 1990; VT 1989; HI 1984-85-89; ELTC 1987-89

Mather, H
HI 1905-09-12-13-14

Matthew, Catriona (Lambert)
CC 1990-92-94; ES 1992; VT 1989-91-93; CT 1991; HI 1989 to 93; ELTC 1989-91-93

Mellis, Mrs
HI 1924-27

Melvin, V
HI 1994-96

Menzies, M
HI **(1962)**

Milton, Moira (Paterson)
CC 1952; HI 1948 to 52

Moffat, L
VT 1999; HI 1996-98-2001

Monaghan, Hilary
CC 1998; VT 1999; HI 1995 to 98; 2000; ELTC 1997-99

Moodie, Janice
CC 1994-96; ES 1996; VT 1993-95-97; CT 1995; HI 1990-91-92; ELTC 1991-93-95-97

Morton, Linzi
HI 2000-01-02; ELTC 2001

Myles, M
HI 1955-57-59-60-67

Neill-Fraser, M
HI 1905 to 14

Nicholson, J (Hutton)
CT 1971; HI 1969-70; ELTC 1971

Nicholson, Lesley
CC 2000; VT 1999; HI 1994 to 99; ELTC 1995-97-99

Nicholson, Mrs WH
HI 1910-13

Nimmo, H
HI 1936-38-39

Niven, Roseanne
HI 2006

Norris, J (Smith)
VT 1977; HI 1966 to 72; 75 to 79; **(83)-(84)**; ELTC 1971

Norwell, I (Watt)
HI 1954

Panton-Lewis, C (Panton)
ES 1976; VT 1977; HI 1972-73-76-77-78

Park, Mrs
HI 1952

Patey, Mrs
HI 1922-23

Percy, G (Mitchell)
HI 1927-28-30-31

Porter, Doris (Park)
CC 1932; HI 1922-25-27; 29 to 35; 37-38; 47-48

Pow, Martine
HI 2004-06

Provis, I (Kyle)
HI 1910-11

Purvis-Russell-Montgomery, C HI 1921-22-23-25; 28 to 39; 47 to 50; 52

Queen, Clare
VT 2003-05; ELTC 2003-05; HI 2002-03-04-05; ES 2004

Rawlinson, T (Walker)
VT 1973; HI 1970-71-73-76

Reid, A (Lurie)
VT 1961; HI 1960 to 64; 66

Reid, A (Kyle)
HI 1923-24-25

Reid, D
HI 1978-79

Rennie, J (Hastings)
CC 1966; VT 1961-67; 1961-65-66-67-71-72; ELTC 1967

Richmond, M (Walker)
CC 1974; VT 1975; HI 1972 to 75; 77-78

Rigby, F (Macbeth)
HI 1912-13

Ritchie, C (Park)
HI 1939-47-48-51-52-53-**(64)**

Roberts, M (Brown)
ES 1964; HI **(1965)**

Robertson, B (McCorkindale) CC 1960-66-68-70-72-**(74)-(76)**-82-86; ES 1964-66-**(68)**-72-80-82; VT 1959-63-69-71-81-85; CT 1971-**(75)**; HI 1958 to 66; 69-72-73-78-80-81-82-84-85-86; ELTC 1965-**67**-69-**71**

Robertson, D
HI 1907

Robertson, E
HI 1924

Robertson, G
HI 1907-08-09

Roxburgh, L
HI 1993-94-95

Roy, S (Needham)
VT 1973-75; HI 1969; 71 to 76; 83

Rusack, J
HI 1908

Singleton, B (Henderson)
HI 1939; 52 to 58; 60 to 65

Smith, J
HI 1999; ELTC 1999

Speir, Marigold
HI 1957-64-68-**(71)-(72)**

Stavert, M
HI 1979

Steel, Mrs DC
HI 1925

Stewart, Gillian
CC 1980-82; VT 1979-81-83; CT 1979-83; HI 1979 to 84; ELTC **1982-4**

Stewart, L (Scraggie)
HI 1921-22-23

Stirling, Heather
CC 2002; HI 1999-2000-01-02

Summers, M (Mackie)
HI 1986

Teacher, F
HI 1908-09-11-12-13

Thompson, M
HI 1949

Thomson, D
HI 1982-83-85-87

Thomson, M
HI 1907

Thomson, Muriel
CC 1978; VT 1977; HI 1974 to 78; ELTC 1978

Valentine, Jessie (Anderson)
CC 1938-48-50-52-54-56-58; CT
1959; HI 1934 to 39; 47; 49 to 55;
56; 57-58

Veitch, F
HI 1912

Walker, Kylie
HI 2004-05

Wallace-Williamson, Verona
CC **1938**; HI 1932

Walker, Kylie
HI 2004-05

Wardlaw, Nan (Baird)
CC 1938; HI 1932; 35 to 39; 47-
48

Watson, Sally
HI 2005-06

Webster, Gemma
HI 2005

Wells, Laura
HI 2003

Wilson, A
HI 1973-74-**(85)**

Wilson, Jenna
ES 2006; HI 2004-05-06; ELTC 2005

Wood, S
HI 1999-2000

Wooldridge, W (Shaw)
HI 1982

Wright, Janette (Robertson)
CC 1954-56-58-60; VT 1959-61-63;
CT 1959; HI 1952 to 61; 63-65-67-
73; **(78)-(79)-(80)-(86)**; ELTC
1965

Wright, M
HI 1990-91-92; ELTC 1991

Wright, P
VT 1981; HI 1981 to 84; ELTC
1987

WALES

Allington-Hughes, Miss
HI 1908-09-10-12-14-22-25

Archer, L
HI 1999

Ashcombe, Lady
HI 1950 to 54

Aubertin, Mrs
HI 1908-09-10

Baker, J
HI 1990

Barron, M
HI 1929-30-31; 34 to 39; 47 to 58;
60 to 63

Bayliss, Mrs
HI 1921

Bloodworth, D (Lewis)
HI 1954 to 57; 60

Boulden, Kimberley
HI 2005

Boyes, S
HI 1992

Bradley, K (Rawlings)
HI 1975 to 79; 82-83

Brearley, M
HI 1937-38

Brewerton, R (Becky)
CC 2000; ES 2002; VT 2001-03; HI
1997 to 2003; ELTC 1999-2001-
03

Bridges, Mrs
HI 1933-38-39

Briggs, A (Brown)
VT 1971-75; HI 1969 to 80; **81-
82-83**; 84; **93**; ELTC 1971-75

**Bromley-Davenport, I
(Rieben)** HI 1932 to 36; 48; 50 to
56

Brook, D
HI 1913

Brown, E (Jones)
HI 1947 to 50; 52-53; 57 to 66; 68-
69-70

Brown, J
HI 1960-61-62-64-65; ELTC 1965-
69

Brown, Mrs
HI 1924-25-27

Bryan-Smith, S
HI 1947 to 52; 56

Burrell, Mrs
HI 1939

Caryl, M
HI 1929

Chugg, Pam (Light)
HI 1973 to 78; 86-87-88; 96;
(2002); ELTC 1975-87-**(2001)**

Clarkson, H (Reynolds)
HI 1935-38-39

Clay, E
HI 1912

Cole, C
HI 1998

Cowley, Lady
HI 1907-09

Cox, Margaret
HI 1924-25

Cox, Nell
HI 1954

Cross, M
HI 1922

Cunninghame, S
HI 1922-25-29-31

Dampney, S
HI 1924-25; 27 to 30

David, Mrs
HI 1908

Davies, Karen
CC 1986-88; VT 1987; CT 1987; HI
1981-82-83; ELTC 1987

Davies, P (Griffiths)
HI 1965 to 68; 70-71-73; ELTC
1971

Davies, Tara
ES 2006; HI 2005-06

Davis, Louise
HI 1997-98-2000-01-02; ELTC
1997-99

Deacon, Mrs
HI 1912-14

Dermott, Lisa
CC 1996; HI 1987-88-89; 91 to 96;
ELTC 1991-93

Donne, A
HI 1993-94; ELTC 1993

Duncan, B
HI 1907 to 10; 12

Duncan, M
HI 1922-23-28-34

Edwards, E
HI 1949-50

Edwards, J
HI 1932-33-34-36-37

Edwards, J (Morris)
HI 1962-63; 66 to 70; **(77)-(78)-
(79)**; ELTC 1967-69-**(93)**

Ellis Griffiths, Mrs
HI 1907-08-09-12-13

Emery, MJ
HI 1928 to 38; 47

Evans, Kathryn
HI 1999-2000-01-02

Evans, N
HI 1908-09-10-13

Evans, Natalee
HI 1996 to 99; 2003-04; ELTC
1997-99-05

Evans, Stephanie
ES 2004; HI 2002-03-04-05-06;
ELTC 2003-05

Franklin Thomas, E
HI 1909

Freeguard, C
HI 1927

**Garfield Evans, PR
(Whittaker)** HI 1948 to 54;
(55)-(56)-(57)-(58)

Gear Evans, A
HI 1932-33-34

Gethin Griffith, S
HI 1914-22-23-24; 28 to 31; 35

Gibbs, S
HI 1933-34-39

Gould, Lucy
HI 2005

Griffith, W
HI 1981

Haig, J (Mathias Thomas)
HI 1938-39

Hall, Lydia
HI 2004-05; ELTC 2005

Harries, Rebecca Helen
HI 2006

Hartley, R
HI 1958-59-62

Hassan, Sahra
ES 2006; HI 2005-06

Hedley Hill, Miss
HI 1922

Highgate, Anna
CC 2004; CT 2003; HI 1999-2001-02-03-04; ELTC 2001-03

Hill, Mrs
HI 1924

Hort, K
HI 1929

Hughes, J
HI 1967-71-88-(89); ELTC 1971

Hughes, Miss
HI 1907

Humphreys, A (Coulman)
HI 1969-70-71

Hurst, Mrs
HI 1921-22-23-25-27-28

Inghram, E (Lever)
HI 1947 to 58; 64-65

Irvine, Miss
HI 1930

Isaac, Mrs
HI 1924

Isherwood, L
HI 1972-76-77-78-80-86; 88 to 91

Jenkin, B
HI 1959

Jenkins, J (Owen)
HI 1953-56

John, J
HI 1974

Johnson, A (Hughes)
HI 1964; 66 to 76; 78-79-85; (95); ELTC 1965-67-69-71

Johnson, J (Roberts)
HI 1955

Johnson, R
HI 1955

Jones, A (Gwyther)
HI 1959

Jones, B
HI 1994-95-96-98; ELTC 1993

Jones, K
HI (1959)-(60)-(61)

Jones, M (De Lloyd)
HI 1951

Jones, Sarah
CC 2002; HI 2000-01-02-03-04-05; ELTC 2001-03-05

Jones, Mrs
HI 1932-35

Justice, M
HI 1931-32

Laming Evans, Mrs
HI 1922-23

Langford, Mrs
HI 1937

Lawson, H
HI 1989 to 92; 97-98; ELTC 1991-93-97

Leaver, B
HI 1912-14-21

Llewellyn, Miss
HI 1912-13-14-21-22-23

Lloyd, J
HI 1988

Lloyd, P
HI 1935-36

Lloyd Davies, VH
HI 1913

Lloyd Roberts, V
HI 1907-08-10

Lloyd Williams, Miss
HI 1909-10-12-14

Loucks, Breanne
CC 2006; ES 2006; HI 2004-05-06; ELTC 2005

Lovatt, S
HI 1994-95

MacKean, Mrs
HI 1938-39-47

MacTier, Mrs
HI 1927

Magee, A-M
HI 1991 to 94

Marley, MV
HI 1921-22-23-30-37

Martin, P [Whitworth Jones] (Low)
HI 1948-50-56-59-60-61

Mason, Mrs
HI 1923

Matthews, Tegwen [Thomas] (Perkins)
CC 1974-76-78-80; ES 1974; VT 1973-75-77-79; CT 1975-79; HI 1972 to 84

Mills, I
HI 1935-36-37-39-47-48

Morgan, R [Becky]
CC 1998-2000; ES [1998]; VT 1997-99; CT 1999; HI 1996 to 99; ELTC 2001

Morgan, Miss
HI 1912-13-14

Mountford, Sara
HI 1989 to 92; ELTC 1991-2001

Musgrove, Mrs
HI 1923-24

Newman, L
HI 1927-31

Nicholls, M
HI (1962)

Nicolson, Jo
HI 2003-04-06; ELTC 2005

O'Connor, Katherine
HI 2006

Oliver, M (Jones)
ES 1964; HI 1955; 60 to 66

Orr, Mrs
HI 1924

Owen, E
HI 1947

Perriam, A
HI 1988-90-91-92

Phelips, M
HI 1913-14-21

Phillips, Kate
CT 2003; HI 1999 to 2004; ELTC 2001-03

Phillips, Mrs
HI 1921

Pilgrim, Eleanor
HI 1995-97-2000-01; ELTC 1997-99-2001

Powell, M
HI 1908-09-10-12

Pritchard, Jo
HI 2002-03; ELTC 2003

Proctor, Mrs
HI 1907

Pyman, B
HI 1921-22-23-25; 28 to 39; 47 to 50; 52

Rawlings, M
VT 1981; HI 1979-80-81; 83 to 87

Rees, G
HI 1981

Rees, MB
HI 1927-31

Rhys, J
HI 1979

Richards, D
HI 1994-95-96

Richards, J
HI 1980-82-83-85

Richards, S
HI 1967

Rieben, Mrs
HI 1927 to 33

Roberts, B
HI (1984)-(85)-(86)

Roberts, G
HI 1949-52-53-54

Roberts, P
ES 1964; HI 1950-51-53; 55 to 63; (64)-(65)-(66)-(67); 68-69-70; ELTC 1965-67-69

Roberts, S
HI 1983 to 90; ELTC 1983-87

Rogers, J
HI 1972

Scott Chard, Mrs
HI 1928-30

Seddon, N
HI 1962-63; **(74)-(75)-(76)**

Selkirk, H
HI 1925-28

Shaw, P
HI 1913

Sheldon, A
HI 1981

Slocombe, E (Davies)
HI 1974-75

Smalley, Mrs A
HI 1924-25; 31 to 34

Sowter, Mrs
HI 1923

Stark, K
HI 1995-96

Stockton, Mrs
HI 1949

Storry, Mrs
HI 1910-14

Stroud, N
HI 1989

Thomas, C (Phipps)
HI 1959; 63 to 73; 76-77-80

Thomas, I
HI 1910

Thomas, J (Foster)
HI 1984 to 87; 92-93-95; ELTC 1987-89-91-93

Thomas, O
HI 1921

Thomas, S (Rowlands)
HI 1977-82-84-85

Thomas, Vicki (Rawlings)
CC 1982-84-86-88-90; ES 1990; VT 1979-83-85-87-89-91; CT 1979-83-87-91; HI 1971 to 98; ELTC 1973 to 83; 87-91-97-99

Thompson, M
HI 1937-38-39

Treharne, A (Mills)
HI 1952-61

Turner, S (Jump)
HI 1982-84-85-86-91-93

Valentine, P (Whitley)
HI 1973-74-75; 77 to 80; **(90)**

Wadsworth, Helen
CC 1984; HI 1987 to 90; ELTC 1987-**90**

Wakelin, H
HI 1955

Webster, S (Hales)
HI 1968-69-72; **(91)**

Wesley, N
HI 1986

Weston, R
HI 1927

Whieldon, Miss
HI 1908

Williams, M
HI 1936

Wilson Jones, D
HI 1952

Wright, N (Cook)
ES 1964; HI 1938-47-48-49; 51 to 54; 57 to 60; 62-63-64-66-67-68; **(71)-(72)-(73)**; ELTC 1965; **(71)**

Woods wins the Nicklaus, Palmer and Nelson Awards

Tiger Woods' fellow competitors have voted him US PGA Tour Player of the Year. He will receive the Jack Nicklaus Trophy for the eighth time since 1997. Woods also won the Arnold Palmer Trophy as leading money winner – he earned $9.9 million in prize money – and the Tour's Byron Nelson Trophy for having the lowest stroke average at 68.11. Curiously, he did not play enough rounds to qualify for the PGA or America's Vardon Trophy which also goes to the player with the best stroke average over 60 rounds. Tiger only played 56.

"Tiger has shown a remarkable ability to raise his game to the highest level and sustain that excellence," said Tim Finchem, the Tour's commisioner. "Winning the Jack Nicklaus Trophy for the eighth time in 10 years is testimony to his greatness."

For Woods, the honour caps a season in which he won eight times. He won The Open at Hoylake and the US PGA Championship to raise his career major championship total to 12 and also won his 12th and 13th World Golf Championships events at the Bridgestone Invitational and the American Express Championship, his fifth victory in each.

He ended the season with a current streak of six consecutive victories, and raised his career victory total to 54, good for fifth on the all-time US winners list.

PART XII

Governance of the Game

RULES
OF GOLF

As Approved by
R&A Rules Limited
and the
United States Golf Association

30th EDITION
EFFECTIVE 1st JANUARY 2004

HOW TO USE THE RULE BOOK

Understand the words

The Rules book is written in a very precise and deliberate fashion. You should be aware of and understand the following differences in word use.

may	=	optional
should	=	recommendation
shall/must	=	instruction (and penalty if not carried out)
a ball	=	you may substitute another ball (e.g. Rules 26, 27 or 28)
the ball	=	you may not substitute another ball (e.g. Rules 24-2 or 25-1)

Know the definitions

There are over sixty defined terms and these form the foundation around which the Rules of play are written. A good knowledge of the defined terms (which are italicised throughout the book) is very important to the correct application of the Rules.

Which rule applies?

The Contents pages may help you find the relevant Rule, alternatively there is an Index at the back of the book.

What is the ruling

To answer any question on the Rules you must first establish the facts of the case. To do so, you should identify:

1. The form of play (e.g. match play or stroke play, single, foursome or four-ball?)
2. Who is involved (e.g. the player, his partner or caddie, an outside agency?)
3. Where the incident occurred (e.g. on the teeing ground, in a bunker or water hazard, on the putting green or elsewhere on the course).

In some cases it might also be necessary to establish:

4. The player's intentions (e.g. what was he doing and what does he want to do?)
5. Any subsequent events (e.g. the player has returned his score card or the competition has closed).

Refer to the book

It is recommended that you carry a Rule book in your golf bag and use it whenever a question arises. If in doubt, play the course as you find it and play the ball as it lies. Once back in the Clubhouse, reference to Decisions on the Rules of Golf should help resolve any outstanding queries.

CONTENTS

SECTION I —
ETIQUETTE; BEHAVIOUR ON THE COURSE

INTRODUCTION

This section provides guidelines on the manner in which the game of golf should be played. If they are followed, all players will gain maximum enjoyment from the game. The overriding principle is that consideration should be shown to others on the course at all times.

THE SPIRIT OF THE GAME

Unlike many sports, golf is played, for the most part, without the supervision of a referee or umpire. The game relies on the integrity of the individual to show consideration for other players and to abide by the Rules. All players should conduct themselves in a disciplined manner, demonstrating courtesy and sportsmanship at all times, irrespective of how competitive they may be. This is the spirit of the game of golf.

SAFETY

Players should ensure that no one is standing close by or in a position to be hit by the club, the ball or any stones, pebbles, twigs or the like when they make a stroke or practice swing.

Players should not play until the players in front are out of range.

Players should always alert greenstaff nearby or ahead when they are about to make a stroke that might endanger them.

If a player plays a ball in a direction where there is a danger of hitting someone, he should immediately shout a warning. The traditional word of warning in such situations is "fore".

CONSIDERATION FOR OTHER PLAYERS

No Disturbance or Distraction

Players should always show consideration for other players on the course and should not disturb their play by moving, talking or making unnecessary noise.

Players should ensure that any electronic device taken onto the course does not distract other players.

On the teeing ground, a player should not tee his ball until it is his turn to play.

Players should not stand close to or directly behind the ball, or directly behind the hole, when a player is about to play.

On the Putting Green

On the putting green, players should not stand on another player's line of putt or, when he is making a stroke, cast a shadow over his line of putt.

Players should remain on or close to the putting green until all other players in the group have holed out.

Scoring

In stroke play, a player who is acting as a marker should, if necessary, on the way to the next tee, check the score with the player concerned and record it.

PACE OF PLAY

Play at Good Pace and Keep Up

Players should play at a good pace. The Committee may establish pace of play guidelines that all players should follow.

It is a group's responsibility to keep up with the group in front. If it loses a clear hole and it is delaying the group behind, it should invite the group behind to play through, irrespective of the number of players in that group.

Be Ready to Play

Players should be ready to play as soon as it is their turn to play. When playing on or near the putting green, they should leave their bags or carts in such a position as will enable quick movement off the green and towards the next tee. When the play of a hole has been completed, players should immediately leave the putting green.

Lost Ball

If a player believes his ball may be lost outside a water hazard or is out of bounds, to save time, he should play a provisional ball.

Players searching for a ball should signal the players in the group behind them to play through as soon as it becomes apparent that the ball will not easily be found. They should not search for five minutes before doing so. Having allowed the group behind to play through, they should not continue play until that group has passed and is out of range.

Priority on the Course

Unless otherwise determined by the Committee, priority on the course is determined by a group's pace of play. Any group playing a whole round is entitled to pass a group playing a shorter round.

CARE OF THE COURSE

Bunkers

Before leaving a bunker, players should carefully fill up and smooth over all holes and footprints made by them and any nearby made by others. If a rake is within reasonable proximity of the bunker, the rake should be used for this purpose.

Repair of Divots, Ball-Marks and Damage by Shoes

Players should carefully repair any divot holes made by them and any damage to the putting green made by the impact of a ball (whether or not made by the player himself). On completion of the hole by all players in the group, damage to the putting green caused by golf shoes should be repaired.

Preventing Unnecessary Damage

Players should avoid causing damage to the course by removing divots when taking practice swings or by hitting the head of a club into the ground, whether in anger or for any other reason.

Players should ensure that no damage is done to the putting green when putting down bags or the flagstick.

In order to avoid damaging the hole, players and caddies should not stand too close to the hole and should take care during the handling of the flagstick and the removal of a ball from the hole. The head of a club should not be used to remove a ball from the hole.

Players should not lean on their clubs when on the putting green, particularly when removing the ball from the hole.

The flagstick should be properly replaced in the hole before the players leave the putting green.

Local notices regulating the movement of golf carts should be strictly observed.

CONCLUSION; PENALTIES FOR BREACH

If players follow the guidelines in this section, it will make the game more enjoyable for everyone.

If a player consistently disregards these guidelines during a round or over a period of time to the detriment of others, it is recommended that the Committee considers taking appropriate disciplinary action against the offending player. Such action may, for example, include prohibiting play for a limited time on the course or in a certain number of competitions. This is considered to be justifiable in terms of protecting the interest of the majority of golfers who wish to play in accordance with these guidelines.

In the case of a serious breach of etiquette, the Committee may disqualify a player under Rule 33-7.

SECTION II — DEFINITIONS

The Definitions are listed alphabetically and, in the *Rules* themselves, defined terms are in *italics*.

Abnormal Ground Conditions

An *"abnormal ground condition"* is any *casual water, ground under repair* or hole, cast or runway on the *course* made by a *burrowing animal*, a reptile or a bird.

Addressing the Ball

A player has *"addressed the ball"* when he has taken his *stance* and has also grounded his club, except that in a *hazard* a player has *addressed the ball* when he has taken his *stance*.

Advice

"Advice" is any counsel or suggestion that could influence a player in determining his play, the choice of a club or the method of making a *stroke*.

Information on the *Rules* or on matters of public information, such as the position of *hazards* or the *flagstick* on the *putting green*, is not *advice*.

Ball Deemed to Move

See *"Move or Moved"*.

Ball Holed

See *"Holed"*.

Ball Lost

See *"Lost Ball"*.

Ball in Play

A ball is *"in play"* as soon as the player has made a *stroke* on the *teeing ground*. It remains *in play* until it is *holed*, except when it is *lost, out of bounds* or lifted, or another ball has been *substituted* whether or not the substitution is permitted; a ball so *substituted* becomes the *ball in play*.

If a ball is played from outside the *teeing ground* when the player is starting play of a hole, or when attempting to correct this mistake, the ball is not *in play* and Rule 11-4 or 11-5 applies. Otherwise, *ball in play* includes a ball played from outside the *teeing ground* when the player elects or is required to play his next *stroke* from the *teeing ground*.

Exception in match play: *Ball in play* includes a ball played by the player from outside the *teeing ground* when starting play of a hole if the opponent does not require the *stroke* to be cancelled in accordance with Rule 11-4a.

Best-Ball

See *"Matches"*.

Bunker

A *"bunker"* is a *hazard* consisting of a prepared area of ground, often a hollow, from which turf or soil has been removed and replaced with sand or the like.

Grass-covered ground bordering or within a *bunker* including a stacked turf face (whether grass-covered or earthen), is not part of the *bunker*. A wall or lip of the *bunker* not covered with grass is part of the *bunker*.

The margin of a *bunker* extends vertically downwards, but not upwards. A ball is in a *bunker* when it lies in or any part of it touches the *bunker*.

Burrowing Animal

A *"burrowing animal"* is an animal that makes a hole for habitation or shelter, such as a rabbit, mole, groundhog, gopher or salamander.

Note: A hole made by a non-burrowing animal, such as a dog, is not an *abnormal ground condition* unless marked or declared as *ground under repair*.

Caddie

A *"caddie"* is one who assists the player in accordance with the *Rules*, which may include carrying or handling the player's clubs during play.

When one *caddie* is employed by more than one player, he is always deemed to be the *caddie* of the player whose ball is involved, and *equipment* carried by him is deemed to be that player's *equipment*, except when the *caddie* acts upon specific directions of another player, in which case he is considered to be that other player's *caddie*.

Casual Water

"Casual water" is any temporary accumulation of water on the *course* that is visible before or after the player takes his *stance* and is not in a *water hazard*. Snow and natural ice, other than frost, are either *casual water* or *loose impediments*, at the option of the player. Manufactured ice is an *obstruction*. Dew and frost are not *casual water*. A ball is in *casual water* when it lies in or any part of it touches the *casual water*.

Committee

The *"Committee"* is the committee in charge of the competition or, if the matter does not arise in a competition, the committee in charge of the *course*.

Competitor

A *"competitor"* is a player in a stroke play competition. A *"fellow-competitor"* is any person with whom the *competitor* plays. Neither is *partner* of the other.

In stroke play *foursome* and *four-ball* competitions, where the context so admits, the word *"competitor"* or *"fellow-competitor"* includes his *partner*.

Course

The *"course"* is the whole area within any boundaries established by the *Committee* (see Rule 33-2).

Equipment

"*Equipment*" is anything used, worn or carried by or for the player except any ball he has played at the hole being played and any small object, such as a coin or a tee, when used to mark the position of a ball or the extent of an area in which a ball is to be dropped. *Equipment* includes a golf cart, whether or not motorised. If such a cart is shared by two or more players, the cart and everything in it are deemed to be the *equipment* of the player whose ball is involved except that, when the cart is being moved by one of the players sharing it, the cart and everything in it are deemed to be that player's *equipment*.

Note: A ball played at the hole being played is *equipment* when it has been lifted and not put back into play.

Fellow-Competitor

See "*Competitor*".

Flagstick

The "*flagstick*" is a movable straight indicator, with or without bunting or other material attached, centered in the *hole* to show its position. It must be circular in cross-section. Padding or shock absorbent material that might unduly influence the movement of the ball is prohibited.

Forecaddie

A "*forecaddie*" is one who is employed by the *Committee* to indicate to players the position of balls during play. He is an *outside agency*.

Four-Ball

See "*Matches*".

Foursome

See "*Matches*".

Ground Under Repair

"*Ground under repair*" is any part of the *course* so marked by order of the *Committee* or so declared by its authorised representative. It includes material piled for removal and a hole made by a greenkeeper, even if not so marked.

All ground and any grass, bush, tree or other growing thing within the *ground under repair* is part of the *ground under repair*. The margin of *ground under repair* extends vertically downwards, but not upwards. Stakes and lines defining *ground under repair* are in such ground. Such stakes are *obstructions*. A ball is in *ground under repair* when it lies in or any part of it touches the *ground under repair*.

Note 1: Grass cuttings and other material left on the *course* that have been abandoned and are not intended to be removed are not *ground under repair* unless so marked.

Note 2: The *Committee* may make a Local Rule prohibiting play from *ground under repair* or an environmentally-sensitive area defined as *ground under repair*.

Hazards

A "*hazard*" is any *bunker* or *water hazard*.

Hole

The "*hole*" must be 4¼ inches (108 mm) in diameter and at least 4 inches (101.6 mm) deep. If a lining is used, it must be sunk at least 1 inch (25.4 mm) below the *putting green* surface unless the nature of the soil makes it impracticable to do so; its outer diameter must not exceed 4¼ inches (108 mm).

Holed

A ball is "*holed*" when it is at rest within the circumference of the *hole* and all of it is below the level of the lip of the *hole*.

Honour

The player who is to play first from the *teeing ground* is said to have the "*honour*".

Lateral Water Hazard

A "*lateral water hazard*" is a *water hazard* or that part of a *water hazard* so situated that it is not possible or is deemed by the *Committee* to be impracticable to drop a ball behind the *water hazard* in accordance with Rule 26-1b.

That part of a *water hazard* to be played as a *lateral water hazard* should be distinctively marked. A ball is in a *lateral water hazard* when it lies in or any part of it touches the *lateral water hazard*.

Note 1: Stakes or lines used to define a *lateral water hazard* must be red. When both stakes and lines are used to define *lateral water hazards*, the stakes identify the *hazard* and the lines define the *hazard* margin.

Note 2: The *Committee* may make a Local Rule prohibiting play from an environmentally-sensitive area defined as a *lateral water hazard*.

Note 3: The *Committee* may define a *lateral water hazard* as a *water hazard*.

Line of Play

The "*line of play*" is the direction that the player wishes his ball to take after a *stroke*, plus a reasonable distance on either side of the intended direction. The *line of play* extends vertically upwards from the ground, but does not extend beyond the *hole*.

Line of Putt

The "*line of putt*" is the line that the player wishes his ball to take after a *stroke* on the *putting green*. Except with respect to Rule 16-1e, the *line of putt* includes a reasonable distance on either side of the intended line. The *line of putt* does not extend beyond the *hole*.

Loose Impediments

"*Loose impediments*" are natural objects, including:
- stones, leaves, twigs, branches and the like,
- dung, and
- worms and insects and the casts and heaps made by them, provided they are not:
- fixed or growing,
- solidly embedded, or
- adhering to the ball.

Sand and loose soil are *loose impediments* on the *putting green*, but not elsewhere.

Snow and natural ice, other than frost, are either *casual water* or *loose impediments* at the option of the player.

Dew and frost are not *loose impediments*.

Lost Ball

A ball is deemed "*lost*" if:

a. It is not found or identified as his by the player within five minutes after the player's *side* or his or their *caddies* have begun to search for it; or

b. The player has made a *stroke* at a *substituted ball*; or

c. The player has made a *stroke* at a *provisional ball* from the place where the original ball is likely to be or from a point nearer the *hole* than that place.

Time spent in playing a *wrong ball* is not counted in the five-minute period allowed for search.

Marker

A "*marker*" is one who is appointed by the *Committee* to record a *competitor's* score in stroke play. He may be a *fellow-competitor*. He is not a *referee*.

Matches

Single: A match in which one plays against another.

Threesome: A match in which one plays against two, and each *side* plays one ball.

Foursome: A match in which two play against two, and each *side* plays one ball.

Three-Ball: A match play competition in which three play against one another, each playing his own ball. Each player is playing two distinct matches.

Best-Ball: A match in which one plays against the better ball of two or the best ball of three players.

Four-Ball: A match in which two play their better ball against the better ball of two other players.

Move or Moved
A ball is deemed to have "*moved*" if it leaves its position and comes to rest in any other place.

Nearest Point of Relief
The "*nearest point of relief*" is the reference point for taking relief without penalty from interference by an immovable *obstruction* (Rule 24-2), an *abnormal ground condition* (Rule 25-1) or a *wrong putting green* (Rule 25-3).

It is the point on the *course* nearest to where the ball lies:
(i) that is not nearer the *hole*, and
(ii) where, if the ball were so positioned, no interference by the condition from which relief is sought would exist for the *stroke* the player would have made from the original position if the condition were not there.

Note: In order to determine the *nearest point of relief* accurately, the player should use the club with which he would have made his next *stroke* if the condition were not there to simulate the *address* position, direction of play and swing for such a *stroke*.

Observer
An "*observer*" is one who is appointed by the *Committee* to assist a *referee* to decide questions of fact and to report to him any breach of a *Rule*. An *observer* should not attend the *flagstick*, stand at or mark the position of the *hole*, or lift the ball or mark its position.

Obstructions
An "*obstruction*" is anything artificial, including the artificial surfaces and sides of roads and paths and manufactured ice, except:
a. Objects defining *out of bounds*, such as walls, fences, stakes and railings;
b. Any part of an immovable artificial object that is *out of bounds*; and
c. Any construction declared by the *Committee* to be an integral part of the *course*.

An *obstruction* is a movable *obstruction* if it may be moved without unreasonable effort, without unduly delaying play and without causing damage. Otherwise it is an immovable *obstruction*.

Note: The *Committee* may make a Local Rule declaring a movable *obstruction* to be an immovable *obstruction*.

Out of Bounds
"*Out of bounds*" is beyond the boundaries of the *course* or any part of the *course* so marked by the *Committee*.

When *out of bounds* is defined by reference to stakes or a fence or as being beyond stakes or a fence, the *out of bounds* line is determined by the nearest inside points of the stakes or fence posts at ground level excluding angled supports.

Objects defining *out of bounds* such as walls, fences, stakes and railings, are not *obstructions* and are deemed to be fixed.

When *out of bounds* is defined by a line on the ground, the line itself is *out of bounds*.

The *out of bounds* line extends vertically upwards and downwards.

A ball is *out of bounds* when all of it lies *out of bounds*.

A player may stand *out of bounds* to play a ball lying within bounds.

Outside Agency
An "*outside agency*" is any agency not part of the match or, in stroke play, not part of the *competitor's side*, and includes a *referee*, a *marker*, an *observer* and a *forecaddie*. Neither wind nor water is an *outside agency*.

Partner
A "*partner*" is a player associated with another player on the same *side*.

In a *threesome*, *foursome*, *best-ball* or *four-ball* match, where the context so admits, the word "player" includes his *partner* or *partners*.

Penalty Stroke
A "*penalty stroke*" is one added to the score of a player or *side* under certain *Rules*. In a *threesome* or *foursome*, penalty *strokes* do not affect the order of play.

Provisional Ball
A "*provisional ball*" is a ball played under Rule 27-2 for a ball that may be *lost* outside a *water hazard* or may be *out of bounds*.

Putting Green
The "*putting green*" is all ground of the hole being played that is specially prepared for putting or otherwise defined as such by the *Committee*. A ball is on the *putting green* when any part of it touches the *putting green*.

R&A
The "*R&A*" means R&A Rules Limited.

Referee
A "*referee*" is one who is appointed by the *Committee* to accompany players to decide questions of fact and apply the *Rules*. He must act on any breach of a *Rule* that he observes or is reported to him.

A *referee* should not attend the *flagstick*, stand at or mark the position of the *hole*, or lift the ball or mark its position.

Rub of the Green
A "*rub of the green*" occurs when a ball in motion is accidentally deflected or stopped by any *outside agency* (see Rule 19-1).

Rule or Rules
The term "*Rule*" includes:
a. The Rules of Golf and their interpretations as contained in Decisions on the Rules of Golf;
b. Any Conditions of Competition established by the *Committee* under Rule 33-1 and Appendix I;
c. Any Local Rules established by the *Committee* under Rule 33-8a and Appendix I; and
d. The specifications on clubs and the ball in Appendices II and III.

Side
A "*side*" is a player, or two or more players who are *partners*.

Single
See "*Matches*".

Stance
Taking the "*stance*" consists in a player placing his feet in position for and preparatory to making a *stroke*.

Stipulated Round
The "*stipulated round*" consists of playing the holes of the *course* in their correct sequence unless otherwise authorised by the *Committee*. The number of holes in a *stipulated round* is 18 unless a smaller number is authorised by the *Committee*. As to extension of *stipulated round* in match play, see Rule 2-3.

Stroke
A "*stroke*" is the forward movement of the club made with the intention of striking at and moving the ball, but if a player checks his downswing voluntarily before the clubhead reaches the ball he has not made a *stroke*.

Substituted Ball
A "*substituted ball*" is a ball put into play for the original ball that was either *in play*, *lost*, *out of bounds* or lifted.

Tee

A "*tee*" is a device designed to raise the ball off the ground. It must not be longer than 4 inches (101.6 mm) and it must not be designed or manufactured in such a way that it could indicate the *line of play* or influence the movement of the ball.

Teeing Ground

The "*teeing ground*" is the starting place for the hole to be played. It is a rectangular area two club-lengths in depth, the front and the sides of which are defined by the outside limits of two tee-markers. A ball is outside the *teeing ground* when all of it lies outside the *teeing ground*.

Three-Ball

See "*Matches*".

Threesome

See "*Matches*".

Through the Green

"*Through the green*" is the whole area of the *course* except:

a. The *teeing ground* and *putting green* of the hole being played; and

b. All *hazards* on the *course*.

Water Hazard

A "*water hazard*" is any sea, lake, pond, river, ditch, surface drainage ditch or other open water course (whether or not containing water) and anything of a similar nature on the *course*.

All ground or water within the margin of a *water hazard* is part of the *water hazard*. The margin of a *water hazard* extends vertically upwards and downwards. Stakes and lines defining the margins of *water hazards* are in the *hazards*. Such stakes are *obstructions*. A ball is in a *water hazard* when it lies in or any part of it touches the *water hazard*.

Note 1: Stakes or lines used to define a *water hazard* must be yellow. When both stakes and lines are used to define *water hazards*, the stakes identify the *hazard* and the lines define the *hazard* margin.

Note 2: The *Committee* may make a Local Rule prohibiting play from an environmentally-sensitive area defined as a *water hazard*.

Wrong Ball

A "*wrong ball*" is any ball other than the player's:

- *ball in play*;
- *provisional ball*; or
- second ball played under Rule 3-3 or Rule 20-7c in stroke play;

and includes:

- another player's ball;
- an abandoned ball; and
- the player's original ball when it is no longer *in play*.

Note: *Ball in play* includes a ball *substituted* for the *ball in play*, whether or not the substitution is permitted.

Wrong Putting Green

A "*wrong putting green*" is any *putting green* other than that of the hole being played. Unless otherwise prescribed by the *Committee*, this term includes a practice *putting green* or pitching green on the *course*.

SECTION III — THE RULES OF PLAY

THE GAME

Rule 1 – The Game

Definitions

All defined terms are in *italics* and are listed alphabetically in the Definitions section – see pages 529–532.

1-1. General

The Game of Golf consists of playing a ball with a club from the *teeing ground* into the *hole* by a *stroke* or successive *strokes* in accordance with the *Rules*.

1-2. Exerting Influence on Ball

A player or *caddie* must not take any action to influence the position or the movement of a ball except in accordance with the *Rules*.

(Removal of movable obstruction – see Rule 24-1)

PENALTY FOR BREACH OF RULE 1-2:
Match play – Loss of hole; Stroke play –
Two strokes.

Note: In the case of a serious breach of Rule 1-2, the *Committee* may impose a penalty of disqualification.

1-3. Agreement to Waive Rules

Players must not agree to exclude the operation of any *Rule* or to waive any penalty incurred.

PENALTY FOR BREACH OF RULE 1-3:
Match play – Disqualification of both sides;
Stroke play – Disqualification of competitors concerned.

(Agreeing to play out of turn in stroke play – see Rule 10-2c)

1-4. Points Not Covered by Rules

If any point in dispute is not covered by the *Rules*, the decision should be made in accordance with equity.

Rule 2 – Match Play

Definitions

All defined terms are in *italics* and are listed alphabetically in the Definitions section – see pages 529–532.

2-1. General

A match consists of one *side* playing against another over a *stipulated round* unless otherwise decreed by the *Committee*.

In match play the game is played by holes.

Except as otherwise provided in the *Rules*, a hole is won by the *side* that *holes* its ball in the fewer *strokes*. In a handicap match the lower net score wins the hole.

The state of the match is expressed by the terms: so many "holes up" or "all square", and so many "to play".

A *side* is "dormie" when it is as many holes up as there are holes remaining to be played.

2-2. Halved Hole

A hole is halved if each *side holes* out in the same number of *strokes*.

When a player has *holed* out and his opponent has been left with a *stroke* for the half, if the player subsequently incurs a penalty, the hole is halved.

2-3. Winner of Match

A match is won when one *side* leads by a number of holes greater than the number remaining to be played.

If there is a tie, the *Committee* may extend the *stipulated round* by as many holes as are required for a match to be won.

2-4. Concession of Next Stroke, Hole or Match

A player may concede his opponent's next *stroke* at any time provided the opponent's ball is at rest. The opponent is considered to have *holed* out with his next *stroke* and the ball may be removed by either *side*.

A player may concede a hole at any time prior to the start or conclusion of that hole.

A player may concede a match at any time prior to the start or conclusion of that match.

A concession may not be declined or withdrawn.

(Ball overhanging hole – see Rule 16-2)

2-5. Doubt as to Procedure; Disputes and Claims

In match play, if a doubt or dispute arises between the players, a player may make a claim. If no duly authorised representative of the *Committee* is available within a reasonable time, the players must continue the match without delay. The *Committee* may consider a claim only if the player making the claim notifies his opponent (i) that he is making a claim, (ii) of the facts of the situation and (iii) that he wants a ruling. The claim must be made before any player in the match plays from the next *teeing ground* or, in the case of the last hole of the match, before all players in the match leave the *putting green*.

A later claim may not be considered by the *Committee* unless it is based on facts previously unknown to the player making the claim and he had been given wrong information (Rules 6-2a and 9) by an opponent.

Once the result of the match has been officially announced, a later claim may not be considered by the *Committee* unless it is satisfied that the opponent knew he was giving wrong information.

2-6. General Penalty

The penalty for a breach of a *Rule* in match play is loss of hole except when otherwise provided.

Rule 3 – Stroke Play

Definitions

All defined terms are in *italics* and are listed alphabetically in the Definitions section – see pages 529–532.

3-1. Winner

The *competitor* who plays the *stipulated round* or rounds in the fewest *strokes* is the winner.

In a handicap competition, the *competitor* with the lowest net score for the *stipulated round* or rounds is the winner.

3-2. Failure to Hole Out

If a *competitor* fails to hole out at any hole and does not correct his mistake before he makes a *stroke* on the next *teeing ground* or, in the case of the last hole of the round, before he leaves the *putting green*, he is disqualified.

3-3. Doubt as to Procedure
a. Procedure

In stroke play, if a *competitor* is doubtful of his rights or the correct procedure during play of a hole he may, without penalty, complete the hole with two balls.

After the doubtful situation has arisen and before taking further action, the *competitor* must announce to his *marker* or a *fellow-competitor* that he intends to play two balls and which ball he wishes to count if the *Rules* permit. If he fails to do so, the provisions of Rule 3-3b(ii) apply.

The *competitor* must report the facts of the situation to the *Committee* before returning his score card. If he fails to do so, he is disqualified.

b. Determination of Score for Hole

(i) If the ball that the *competitor* selected in advance to count has been played in accordance with the *Rules*, the score with that ball is the *competitor's* score for the hole. Otherwise, the score with the other ball counts if the *Rules* allow the procedure adopted for that ball.

(ii) If the *competitor* fails to announce in advance his decision to complete the hole with two balls, or which ball he wishes to count, the score with the original ball counts, provided it has been played in accordance with the *Rules*. If the original ball is not one of the balls being played, the first ball put into play counts, provided it has been played in accordance with the *Rules*. Otherwise, the score with the other ball counts if the *Rules* allow the procedure adopted for that ball.

Note 1: If a *competitor* plays a second ball under Rule 3-3, the *strokes* made after this Rule has been invoked with the ball ruled not to count and *penalty strokes* incurred solely by playing that ball are dis-regarded.

Note 2: A second ball played under Rule 3-3 is not a *provisional ball* under Rule 27-2.

3-4. Refusal to Comply with a Rule

If a *competitor* refuses to comply with a *Rule* affecting the rights of another *competitor*, he is disqualified.

3-5. General Penalty

The penalty for a breach of a *Rule* in stroke play is two strokes except when otherwise provided.

CLUBS AND THE BALL

The *R&A* reserves the right, at any time, to change the Rules relating to clubs and balls (see Appendices II and III) and make or change the interpretations relating to these Rules.

A player in doubt as to the conformity of a club should consult the *R&A*.

A manufacturer should submit to the *R&A* a sample of a club to be manufactured for a ruling as to whether the club conforms with the *Rules*. If a manufacturer fails to submit a sample or to await a ruling before manufacturing and/or marketing the club, the manufacturer assumes the risk of a ruling that the club does not conform with the *Rules*. Any sample submitted to the *R&A* becomes its property for reference purposes.

Rule 4 – Clubs

Definitions

All defined terms are in *italics* and are listed alphabetically in the Definitions section – see pages 529–532.

4-1. Form and Make of Clubs
a. General

The player's clubs must conform with this Rule and the provisions, specifications and interpretations set forth in Appendix II.

b. Wear and Alteration

A club that conforms with the *Rules* when new is deemed to conform after wear through normal use. Any part of a club that has been purposely altered is regarded as new and must, in its altered state, conform with the *Rules*.

4-2. Playing Characteristics Changed and Foreign Material

a. Playing Characteristics Changed

During a *stipulated round*, the playing characteristics of a club must not be purposely changed by adjustment or by any other means.

b. Foreign Material

Foreign material must not be applied to the club face for the purpose of influencing the movement of the ball.

PENALTY FOR BREACH OF RULE 4-1 or 4-2:
Disqualification.

4-3. Damaged Clubs: Repair and Replacement

a. Damage in Normal Course of Play

If, during a *stipulated round*, a player's club is damaged in the normal course of play, he may:

(i) use the club in its damaged state for the remainder of the *stipulated round*; or

(ii) without unduly delaying play, repair it or have it repaired; or

(iii) as an additional option available only if the club is unfit for play, replace the damaged club with any club. The replacement of a club must not unduly delay play and must not be made by borrowing any club selected for play by any other person playing on the *course*.

PENALTY FOR BREACH OF RULE 4-3a:
See Penalty Statement for Rule 4-4a or b, and c.

Note: A club is unfit for play if it is substantially damaged, e.g. the shaft is dented, significantly bent or breaks into pieces; the clubhead becomes loose, detached or significantly deformed; or the grip becomes loose. A club is not unfit for play solely because the club's lie or loft has been altered, or the clubhead is scratched.

b. Damage Other Than in Normal Course of Play

If, during a *stipulated round*, a player's club is damaged other than in the normal course of play rendering it non-conforming or changing its playing characteristics, the club must not subsequently be used or replaced during the round.

c. Damage Prior to Round

A player may use a club damaged prior to a round provided the club, in its damaged state, conforms with the *Rules*.

Damage to a club that occurred prior to a round may be repaired during the round, provided the playing characteristics are not changed and play is not unduly delayed.

PENALTY FOR BREACH OF RULE 4-3b or c:
Disqualification.

(Undue delay – see Rule 6-7)

4-4. Maximum of Fourteen Clubs

a. Selection and Addition of Clubs

The player must not start a *stipulated round* with more than fourteen clubs. He is limited to the clubs thus selected for that round except that, if he started with fewer than fourteen clubs, he may add any number provided his total number does not exceed fourteen.

The addition of a club or clubs must not unduly delay play (Rule 6-7) and the player must not add or borrow any club selected for play by any other person playing on the *course*.

b. Partners May Share Clubs

Partners may share clubs, provided that the total number of clubs carried by the *partners* so sharing does not exceed fourteen.

PENALTY FOR BREACH OF RULE 4-4a or b,
REGARDLESS OF NUMBER OF EXCESS
CLUBS CARRIED:
Match play – At the conclusion of the hole at which the breach is discovered, the state of the match is adjusted by deducting one hole for each hole at which a breach occurred. Maximum deduction per round:
Two holes.
Stroke play – Two strokes for each hole at which any breach occurred; maximum penalty per round: Four strokes.
Bogey and par competitions – Penalties as in match play.
Stableford competitions – See Note 1 to Rule 32-1b.

c. Excess Club Declared Out of Play

Any club or clubs carried or used in breach of Rule 4-3a(iii) or Rule 4-4 must be declared out of play by the player to his opponent in match play or his *marker* or a *fellow-competitor* in stroke play immediately upon discovery that a breach has occurred. The player must not use the club or clubs for the remainder of the *stipulated round*.

PENALTY FOR BREACH OF RULE 4-4c:
Disqualification.

Rule 5 – The Ball

Definitions

All defined terms are in *italics* and are listed alphabetically in the Definitions section – see pages 529–532.

5-1. General

The ball the player plays must conform to requirements specified in Appendix III.

Note: The *Committee* may require, in the conditions of a competition (Rule 33-1), that the ball the player plays must be named on the current List of Conforming Golf Balls issued by the *R&A*.

5-2. Foreign Material

Foreign material must not be applied to a ball for the purpose of changing its playing characteristics.

PENALTY FOR BREACH OF RULE 5-1 or 5-2:
Disqualification.

5-3. Ball Unfit for Play

A ball is unfit for play if it is visibly cut, cracked or out of shape. A ball is not unfit for play solely because mud or other materials adhere to it, its surface is scratched or scraped or its paint is damaged or discoloured.

If a player has reason to believe his ball has become unfit for play during play of the hole being played, he may lift the ball without penalty to determine whether it is unfit.

Before lifting the ball, the player must announce his intention to his opponent in match play or his *marker* or a *fellow-competitor* in stroke play and mark the position of the ball. He may then lift and examine it provided that he gives his opponent, *marker* or *fellow-competitor* an opportunity to examine the ball and observe the lifting and replacement. The ball must not be cleaned when lifted under Rule 5-3. If the player fails to comply with all or any part of this procedure, he incurs a penalty of one stroke.

If it is determined that the ball has become unfit for play during play of the hole being played, the player may *substitute* another ball, placing it on the spot where the original ball lay. Otherwise, the original ball must be replaced. If a player *substitutes* a ball when not permitted and he makes a *stroke* at the wrongly *substituted* ball, he incurs the general penalty for a breach of Rule 5-3, but there is no additional penalty under this Rule or Rule 15-1.

If a ball breaks into pieces as a result of a *stroke*, the *stroke* is cancelled and the player must play a ball without penalty as nearly as possible at the spot from which the original ball was played (see Rule 20-5).

*PENALTY FOR BREACH OF RULE 5-3:
Match play – Loss of hole; Stroke play – Two strokes.

*If a player incurs the general penalty for a breach of Rule 5-3, there is no additional penalty under this Rule.

Note: If the opponent, *marker* or *fellow-competitor* wishes to dispute a claim of unfitness, he must do so before the player plays another ball.

(Cleaning ball lifted from putting green or under any other Rule – see Rule 21)

PLAYER'S RESPONSIBILITIES

Rule 6 – The Player

Definitions

All defined terms are in *italics* and are listed alphabetically in the Definitions section – see pages 529–532.

6-1. Rules

The player and his *caddie* are responsible for knowing the *Rules*. During a *stipulated round*, for any breach of a *Rule* by his *caddie*, the player incurs the applicable penalty.

6-2. Handicap
a. Match Play

Before starting a match in a handicap competition, the players should determine from one another their respective handicaps. If a player begins a match having declared a handicap higher than that to which he is entitled and this affects the number of strokes given or received, he is disqualified; otherwise, the player must play off the declared handicap.

b. Stroke Play

In any round of a handicap competition, the *competitor* must ensure that his handicap is recorded on his score card before it is returned to the *Committee*. If no handicap is recorded on his score card before it is returned (Rule 6-6b), or if the recorded handicap is higher than that to which he is entitled and this affects the number of strokes received, he is disqualified from the handicap competition; otherwise, the score stands.

Note: It is the player's responsibility to know the holes at which handicap strokes are to be given or received.

6-3. Time of Starting and Groups
a. Time of Starting

The player must start at the time established by the *Committee*.

b. Groups

In stroke play, the *competitor* must remain throughout the round in the group arranged by the *Committee* unless the *Committee* authorises or ratifies a change.

PENALTY FOR BREACH OF RULE 6-3:
Disqualification.

(Best-ball and four-ball play – see Rules 30-3a and 31-2)

Note: The *Committee* may provide in the conditions of a competition (Rule 33-1) that, if the player arrives at his starting point, ready to play, within five minutes after his starting time, in the absence of circumstances that warrant waiving the penalty of disqualification as provided in Rule 33-7, the penalty for failure to start on time is loss of the first hole in match play or two strokes at the first hole in stroke play instead of disqualification.

6-4. Caddie

The player may be assisted by a *caddie*, but he is limited to only one *caddie* at any one time.

PENALTY FOR BREACH OF RULE 6-4:
Match play – At the conclusion of the hole at which the breach is discovered, the state of the match is adjusted by deducting one hole for each hole at which a breach occurred; maximum deduction per round – Two holes.
Stroke play – Two strokes for each hole at which any breach occurred; maximum penalty per round – Four strokes.
Match or stroke play – In the event of a breach between the play of two holes, the penalty applies to the next hole.

A player having more than one *caddie* in breach of this Rule must immediately upon discovery that a breach has occurred ensure that he has no more than one *caddie* at any one time during the remainder of the *stipulated round*. Otherwise, the player is disqualified.

Bogey and par competitions – Penalties as in match play.
Stableford competitions – See Note 2 to Rule 32-1b.

Note: The *Committee* may, in the conditions of a competition (Rule 33-1), prohibit the use of *caddies* or restrict a player in his choice of *caddie*.

6-5. Ball

The responsibility for playing the proper ball rests with the player. Each player should put an identification mark on his ball.

6-6. Scoring in Stroke Play
a. Recording Scores

After each hole the *marker* should check the score with the *competitor* and record it. On completion of the round the *marker* must sign the score card and hand it to the *competitor*. If more than one *marker* records the scores, each must sign for the part for which he is responsible.

b. Signing and Returning Score Card

After completion of the round, the *competitor* should check his score for each hole and settle any doubtful points with the *Committee*. He must ensure that the *marker* or *markers* have signed the score card, sign the score card himself and return it to the *Committee* as soon as possible.

PENALTY FOR BREACH OF RULE 6-6b:
Disqualification.

c. Alteration of Score Card

No alteration may be made on a score card after the *competitor* has returned it to the *Committee*.

d. Wrong Score for Hole

The *competitor* is responsible for the correctness of the score recorded for each hole on his score card. If he returns a score for any hole lower than actually taken, he is disqualified. If he returns a score for any hole higher than actually taken, the score as returned stands.

Note 1: The *Committee* is responsible for the addition of scores and application of the handicap recorded on the score card – see Rule 33-5.

Note 2: In *four-ball* stroke play, see also Rule 31-4 and -7a.

6-7. Undue Delay; Slow Play

The player must play without undue delay and in accordance with any pace of play guidelines that the *Committee* may establish. Between completion of a hole and playing from the next *teeing ground*, the player must not unduly delay play.

PENALTY FOR BREACH OF RULE 6-7:
Match play – Loss of hole; Stroke play – Two strokes.
Bogey and par competitions – See Note 3 to Rule 32-1a.
Stableford competitions – See Note 3 to Rule 32-1b.
For subsequent offence – Disqualification.

Note 1: If the player unduly delays play between holes, he is delaying the play of the next hole and, except for bogey, par and Stableford competitions (see Rule 32), the penalty applies to that hole.

Note 2: For the purpose of preventing slow play, the *Committee* may, in the conditions of a competition (Rule 33-1), establish pace of play guidelines including maximum periods of time allowed to complete a *stipulated round*, a hole or a *stroke*.

In stroke play only, the *Committee* may, in such a condition, modify the penalty for a breach of this Rule as follows:

First offence – One stroke;
Second offence – Two strokes.
For subsequent offence – Disqualification.

6-8. Discontinuance of Play; Resumption of Play

a. When Permitted

The player must not discontinue play unless:

(i) the *Committee* has suspended play;

(ii) he believes there is danger from lightning;

(iii) he is seeking a decision from the *Committee* on a doubtful or disputed point (see Rules 2-5 and 34-3); or

(iv) there is some other good reason such as sudden illness.

Bad weather is not of itself a good reason for discontinuing play.

If the player discontinues play without specific permission from the *Committee*, he must report to the *Committee* as soon as practicable. If he does so and the *Committee* considers his reason satisfactory, there is no penalty. Otherwise, the player is disqualified.

Exception in match play: Players discontinuing match play by agreement are not subject to disqualification unless by so doing the competition is delayed.

Note: Leaving the *course* does not of itself constitute discontinuance of play.

b. Procedure When Play Suspended by Committee

When play is suspended by the *Committee*, if the players in a match or group are between the play of two holes, they must not resume play until the *Committee* has ordered a resumption of play. If they have started play of a hole, they may discontinue play immediately or continue play of the hole, provided they do so without delay. If the players choose to continue play of the hole, they are permitted to discontinue play before completing it. In any case, play must be discontinued after the hole is completed.

The players must resume play when the *Committee* has ordered a resumption of play.

PENALTY FOR BREACH OF RULE 6-8b:
Disqualification.

Note: The *Committee* may provide in the conditions of a competition (Rule 33-1) that, in potentially dangerous situations, play must be discontinued immediately following a suspension of play by the *Committee*. If a player fails to discontinue play immediately, he is disqualified unless circumstances warrant waiving the penalty as provided in Rule 33-7.

c. Lifting Ball When Play Discontinued

When a player discontinues play of a hole under Rule 6-8a, he may lift his ball without penalty only if the *Committee* has suspended play or there is a good reason to lift it. Before lifting the ball the player must mark its position. If the player discontinues play and lifts his ball without specific permission from the *Committee*, he must, when reporting to the *Committee* (Rule 6-8a), report the lifting of the ball.

If the player lifts the ball without a good reason to do so, fails to mark the position of the ball before lifting it or fails to report the lifting of the ball, he incurs a penalty of one stroke.

d. Procedure When Play Resumed

Play must be resumed from where it was discontinued, even if resumption occurs on a subsequent day. The player must, either before or when play is resumed, proceed as follows:

(i) if the player has lifted the ball, he must, provided he was entitled to lift it under Rule 6-8c, place a ball on the spot from which the original ball was lifted. Otherwise, the original ball must be placed on the spot from which it was lifted;

(ii) if the player entitled to lift his ball under Rule 6-8c has not done so, he may lift, clean and replace the ball, or *substitute* a ball on the spot from which the original ball was lifted. Before lifting the ball he must mark its position; or

(iii) if the player's ball or ball-marker is moved (including by wind or water) while play is discontinued, a ball or ball-marker must be placed on the spot from which the original ball or ball-marker was moved.

Note: If the spot where the ball is to be placed is impossible to determine, it must be estimated and the ball placed on the estimated spot. The provisions of Rule 20-3c do not apply.

*PENALTY FOR BREACH OF RULE 6-8c or d:
Match play – Loss of hole; Stroke play –
Two strokes.
*If a player incurs the general penalty for a breach
of Rule
6-8d, there is no additional penalty under
Rule 6-8c.

Rule 7 – Practice

Definitions

All defined terms are in *italics* and are listed alphabetically in the Definitions section – see pages 529–532.

7-1. Before or Between Rounds

a. Match Play

On any day of a match play competition, a player may practise on the competition *course* before a round.

b. Stroke Play

Before a round or play-off on any day of a stroke play competition, a *competitor* must not practise on the competition *course* or test the surface of any *putting green* on the *course* by rolling a ball or roughening or scraping the surface.

When two or more rounds of a stroke play competition are to be played over consecutive days, a *competitor* must not practise between those rounds on any competition *course* remaining to be played, or test the surface of any *putting green* on such *course* by rolling a ball or roughening or scraping the surface.

Exception: Practice putting or chipping on or near the first *teeing ground* before starting a round or play-off is permitted.

PENALTY FOR BREACH OF RULE 7-1b:
Disqualification.

Note: The *Committee* may, in the conditions of a competition (Rule 33-1), prohibit practice on the competition *course* on any day of a match play competition or permit practice on the competition *course* or part of the *course* (Rule 33-2c) on any day of or between rounds of a stroke play competition.

7-2. During Round

A player must not make a practice *stroke* during play of a hole.

Between the play of two holes a player must not make a practice *stroke*, except that he may practise putting or chipping on or near:

(a) the *putting green* of the hole last played,

(b) any practice *putting green*, or

(c) the *teeing ground* of the next hole to be played in the round, provided a practice *stroke* is not made from a *hazard* and does not unduly delay play (Rule 6-7).

Strokes made in continuing the play of a hole, the result of which has been decided, are not practice *strokes*.

Exception: When play has been suspended by the *Committee*, a player may, prior to resumption of play, practise (a) as provided in this Rule, (b) anywhere other than on the competition *course* and (c) as otherwise permitted by the *Committee*.

PENALTY FOR BREACH OF RULE 7-2:

Match play – Loss of hole; Stroke play – Two strokes.

In the event of a breach between the play of two holes, the penalty applies to the next hole.

Note 1: A practice swing is not a practice *stroke* and may be taken at any place, provided the player does not breach the *Rules*.

Note 2: The *Committee* may, in the conditions of a competition (Rule 33-1), prohibit:

(a) practice on or near the *putting green* of the hole last played, and

(b) rolling a ball on the *putting green* of the hole last played.

Rule 8 – Advice: Indicating Line of Play

Definitions
All defined terms are in *italics* and are listed alphabetically in the Definitions section – see pages 529–532.

8-1. Advice
During a *stipulated round*, a player must not:

(a) give *advice* to anyone in the competition playing on the *course* other than his *partner*, or

(b) ask for *advice* from anyone other than his *partner* or either of their *caddies*.

8-2. Indicating Line of Play
a. Other Than on Putting Green
Except on the *putting green*, a player may have the *line of play* indicated to him by anyone, but no one may be positioned by the player on or close to the line or an extension of the line beyond the *hole* while the *stroke* is being made. Any mark placed by the player or with his knowledge to indicate the line must be removed before the *stroke* is made.

Exception: *Flagstick* attended or held up – see Rule 17-1.

b. On the Putting Green
When the player's ball is on the *putting green*, the player, his *partner* or either of their *caddies* may, before but not during the *stroke*, point out a line for putting, but in so doing the *putting green* must not be touched. A mark must not be placed anywhere to indicate a line for putting.

PENALTY FOR BREACH OF RULE:

Match play – Loss of hole; Stroke play – Two strokes.

Note: The *Committee* may, in the conditions of a team competition (Rule 33-1), permit each team to appoint one person who may give *advice* (including pointing out a line for putting) to members of that team. The *Committee* may establish conditions relating to the appointment and permitted conduct of that person, who must be identified to the *Committee* before giving *advice*.

Rule 9 – Information as to Strokes Taken

Definitions
All defined terms are in *italics* and are listed alphabetically in the Definitions section – see pages 529–532.

9-1. General
The number of *strokes* a player has taken includes any *penalty strokes* incurred.

9-2. Match Play
a. Information as to Strokes Taken
An opponent is entitled to ascertain from the player, during the play of a hole, the number of *strokes* he has taken and, after play of a hole, the number of *strokes* taken on the hole just completed.

b. Wrong Information
A player must not give wrong information to his opponent. If a player gives wrong information, he loses the hole.

A player is deemed to have given wrong information if he:

(i) fails to inform his opponent as soon as practicable that he has incurred a penalty, unless (a) he was obviously proceeding under a *Rule* involving a penalty and this was observed by his opponent, or (b) he corrects the mistake before his opponent makes his next *stroke*; or

(ii) gives incorrect information during play of a hole regarding the number of *strokes* taken and does not correct the mistake before his opponent makes his next *stroke*; or

(iii) gives incorrect information regarding the number of *strokes* taken to complete a hole and this affects the opponent's understanding of the result of the hole, unless he corrects the mistake before any player makes a *stroke* from the next *teeing ground* or, in the case of the last hole of the match, before all players leave the *putting green*.

A player has given wrong information even if it is due to the failure to include a penalty that he did not know he had incurred. It is the player's responsibility to know the *Rules*.

9-3. Stroke Play
A *competitor* who has incurred a penalty should inform his *marker* as soon as practicable.

ORDER OF PLAY

Rule 10 – Order of Play

Definitions
All defined terms are in *italics* and are listed alphabetically in the Definitions section – see pages 529–532.

10-1. Match Play
a. When Starting Play of Hole
The *side* that has the *honour* at the first *teeing ground* is determined by the order of the draw. In the absence of a draw, the *honour* should be decided by lot.

The *side* that wins a hole takes the *honour* at the next *teeing ground*. If a hole has been halved, the *side* that had the *honour* at the previous *teeing ground* retains it.

b. During Play of Hole
After both players have started play of the hole, the ball farther from the *hole* is played first. If the balls are equidistant from the *hole* or their positions relative to the *hole* are not determinable, the ball to be played first should be decided by lot.

Exception: Rule 30-3c (*best-ball* and *four-ball* match play).

Note: When the original ball is not to be played as it lies and the player is required to play a ball as nearly as possible at the spot from which the original ball was last played (see Rule 20-5), the order of play is determined by the spot from which the previous *stroke* was made. When a ball may be played from a spot other than where the previous *stroke* was made, the order of play is determined by the position where the original ball came to rest.

c. Playing Out of Turn

If a player plays when his opponent should have played, there is no penalty, but the opponent may immediately require the player to cancel the *stroke* so made and, in correct order, play a ball as nearly as possible at the spot from which the original ball was last played (see Rule 20-5).

10-2. Stroke Play

a. When Starting Play of Hole

The *competitor* who has the *honour* at the first *teeing ground* is determined by the order of the draw. In the absence of a draw, the *honour* should be decided by lot.

The *competitor* with the lowest score at a hole takes the *honour* at the next *teeing ground*. The *competitor* with the second lowest score plays next and so on. If two or more *competitors* have the same score at a hole, they play from the next *teeing ground* in the same order as at the previous *teeing ground*.

b. During Play of Hole

After the *competitors* have started play of the hole, the ball farthest from the *hole* is played first. If two or more balls are equidistant from the *hole* or their positions relative to the *hole* are not determinable, the ball to be played first should be decided by lot.

Exceptions: Rules 22 (ball assisting or interfering with play) and 31-5 (*four-ball* stroke play).

Note: When the original ball is not to be played as it lies and the player is required to play a ball as nearly as possible at the spot from which the original ball was last played (see Rule 20-5), the order of play is determined by the spot from which the previous *stroke* was made. When a ball may be played from a spot other than where the previous *stroke* was made, the order of play is determined by the position where the original ball came to rest.

c. Playing Out of Turn

If a *competitor* plays out of turn, there is no penalty and the ball is played as it lies. If, however, the *Committee* determines that *competitors* have agreed to play out of turn to give one of them an advantage, they are disqualified.

(Making stroke while another ball in motion after stroke from putting green – see Rule 16-1f)

(Incorrect order of play in threesomes and foursomes stroke play – see Rule 29-3)

10-3. Provisional Ball or Second Ball from Teeing Ground

If a player plays a *provisional ball* or a second ball from a *teeing ground*, he must do so after his opponent or *fellow-competitor* has played his first *stroke*. If a player plays a *provisional ball* or a second ball out of turn, Rule 10-1c or -2c applies.

Rule 11 – Teeing Ground

Definitions

All defined terms are in *italics* and are listed alphabetically in the Definitions section – see pages 529–532.

11-1. Teeing

When the player's ball is to be teed within the *teeing ground*, it must be placed on:

- the surface of the *teeing ground*, including an irregularity of surface (whether or not created by the player), or
- a *tee* placed in or on the surface of the *teeing ground*, or
- sand or other natural substance placed on the surface of the *teeing ground*.

A player may stand outside the *teeing ground* to play a ball within it.

In teeing, if a player uses a non-conforming *tee* or any other object to raise the ball off the ground, he is disqualified.

11-2. Tee-Markers

Before a player makes his first *stroke* with any ball on the *teeing ground* of the hole being played, the tee-markers are deemed to be fixed. In these circumstances, if the player moves or allows to be moved a tee-marker for the purpose of avoiding interference with his *stance*, the area of his intended swing or his *line of play*, he incurs the penalty for a breach of Rule 13-2.

11-3. Ball Falling off Tee

If a ball, when not *in play*, falls off a tee or is knocked off a tee by the player in *addressing* it, it may be re-teed without penalty. However, if a *stroke* is made at the ball in these circumstances, whether the ball is moving or not, the *stroke* counts but there is no penalty.

11-4. Playing from Outside Teeing Ground

a. Match Play

If a player, when starting a hole, plays a ball from outside the *teeing ground* there is no penalty, but the opponent may immediately require the player to cancel the *stroke* and play a ball from within the *teeing ground*.

b. Stroke Play

If a *competitor*, when starting a hole, plays a ball from outside the *teeing ground*, he incurs a penalty of two strokes and must then play a ball from within the *teeing ground*.

If the *competitor* plays a *stroke* from the next *teeing ground* without first correcting his mistake or, in the case of the last hole of the round, leaves the *putting green* without first declaring his intention to correct his mistake, he is disqualified.

The *stroke* from outside the *teeing ground* and any subsequent *strokes* by the *competitor* on the hole prior to his correction of the mistake do not count in his score.

11-5. Playing from Wrong Teeing Ground

The provisions of Rule 11-4 apply.

Rule 12 – Searching For and Identifying Ball

Definitions

All defined terms are in *italics* and are listed alphabetically in the Definitions section – see pages 529–532.

12-1. Searching for Ball; Seeing Ball

In searching for his ball anywhere on the *course*, the player may touch or bend long grass, rushes, bushes, whins, heather or the like, but only to the extent necessary to find and identify it, provided that this does not improve the lie of the ball, the area of his intended *stance* or swing or his *line of play*.

A player is not necessarily entitled to see his ball when making a *stroke*.

In a *hazard*, if a ball is believed to be covered by *loose impediments* or sand, the player may remove by probing or raking with a club or otherwise, as many *loose impediments* or as much sand as will enable him to see a part of the ball. If an excess is removed, there is no penalty and the ball must be re-covered so that only a part of it is visible. If the ball is *moved* during the removal, there is no penalty; the ball must be replaced and, if necessary, re-covered. As to removal of *loose impediments* outside a *hazard*, see Rule 23.

If a ball lying in an *abnormal ground condition* is accidentally *moved* during search, there is no penalty; the ball must be replaced, unless the player elects to proceed under Rule 25-1b. If the player replaces the ball, he may still proceed under Rule 25-1b if applicable.

If a ball is believed to be lying in water in a *water hazard*, the player may probe for it with a club or otherwise. If the ball is *moved* in probing, it must be replaced, unless the player elects to proceed under Rule 26-1. There is no penalty for causing the ball to *move* provided the movement of the ball was directly attributable to the specific act of probing. Otherwise, the player incurs a *penalty stroke* under Rule 18-2a.

PENALTY FOR BREACH OF RULE 12-1:
Match play – Loss of hole; Stroke play – Two strokes.

12-2. Identifying Ball

The responsibility for playing the proper ball rests with the player. Each player should put an identification mark on his ball.

Except in a *hazard*, if a player has reason to believe a ball is his, he may lift the ball without penalty to identify it.

Before lifting the ball, the player must announce his intention to his opponent in match play or his *marker* or a *fellow-competitor* in stroke play and mark the position of the ball. He may then lift the ball and identify it provided that he gives his opponent, *marker* or *fellow-competitor* an opportunity to observe the lifting and replacement. The ball must not be cleaned beyond the extent necessary for identification when lifted under Rule 12-2. If the player fails to comply with all or any part of this procedure, or if he lifts his ball for identification in a *hazard*, he incurs a penalty of one stroke.

If the lifted ball is the player's ball he must replace it. If he fails to do so, he incurs the general penalty for a breach of Rule 12-2, but there is no additional penalty under this Rule.

*PENALTY FOR BREACH OF RULE 12-2:
Match play – Loss of hole; Stroke play – Two strokes.
*If a player incurs the general penalty for a breach of Rule 12-2, there is no additional penalty under this Rule.

Rule 13 – Play Ball as it Lies

Definitions

All defined terms are in *italics* and are listed alphabetically in the Definitions section – see pages 529–532.

13-1. General

The ball must be played as it lies, except as otherwise provided in the *Rules*.
(Ball at rest moved – see Rule 18)

13-2. Improving Lie, Area of Intended Stance or Swing, or Line of Play

A player must not improve or allow to be improved:

- the position or lie of his ball,
- the area of his intended *stance* or swing,
- his *line of play* or a reasonable extension of that line beyond the *hole*, or
- the area in which he is to drop or place a ball,

by any of the following actions:

- moving, bending or breaking anything growing or fixed (including immovable *obstructions* and objects defining *out of bounds*),
- creating or eliminating irregularities of surface,
- removing or pressing down sand, loose soil, replaced divots or other cut turf placed in position, or
- removing dew, frost or water.

However, the player incurs no penalty if the action occurs:

- in fairly taking his *stance*,
- in making a *stroke* or the backward movement of his club for a *stroke* and the *stroke* is made,
- on the *teeing ground* in creating or eliminating irregularities of surface (Rule 11-1), or
- on the *putting green* in removing sand and loose soil or in repairing damage (Rule 16-1).

The club may be grounded only lightly and must not be pressed on the ground.

Exception: Ball in *hazard* – see Rule 13-4.

13-3. Building Stance

A player is entitled to place his feet firmly in taking his *stance*, but he must not build a *stance*.

13-4. Ball in Hazard; Prohibited Actions

Except as provided in the *Rules*, before making a *stroke* at a ball that is in a *hazard* (whether a *bunker* or a *water hazard*) or that, having been lifted from a *hazard*, may be dropped or placed in the *hazard*, the player must not:

a. Test the condition of the *hazard* or any similar *hazard*;

b. Touch the ground in the *hazard* or water in the *water hazard* with his hand or a club; or

c. Touch or move a *loose impediment* lying in or touching the *hazard*.

Exceptions:

1. Provided nothing is done that constitutes testing the condition of the *hazard* or improves the lie of the ball, there is no penalty if the player (a) touches the ground in any *hazard* or water in a *water hazard* as a result of or to prevent falling, in removing an *obstruction*, in measuring or in retrieving, lifting, placing or replacing a ball under any *Rule* or (b) places his clubs in a *hazard*.

2. After making the *stroke*, the player or his *caddie* may smooth sand or soil in the *hazard*, provided that, if the ball is still in the *hazard* or has been lifted from the *hazard* and may be dropped or placed in the *hazard*, nothing is done that improves the lie of the ball or assists the player in his subsequent play of the hole.

Note: At any time, including at *address* or in the backward movement for the *stroke*, the player may touch with a club or otherwise any construction declared by the *Committee* to be an integral part of the *course* or any grass, bush, tree or other growing thing.

PENALTY FOR BREACH OF RULE:
Match play – Loss of hole; Stroke play – Two strokes.
(Searching for ball – see Rule 12-1)
(Relief for ball in water hazard – see Rule 26)

Rule 14 – Striking the Ball

Definitions

All defined terms are in *italics* and are listed alphabetically in the Definitions section – see pages 529–532.

14-1. Ball to be Fairly Struck At

The ball must be fairly struck at with the head of the club and must not be pushed, scraped or spooned.

14-2. Assistance

In making a *stroke*, a player must not:

a. accept physical assistance or protection from the elements; or

b. allow his *caddie*, his *partner* or his *partner's caddie* to position himself on or close to an extension of the *line of play* or the *line of putt* behind the ball.

PENALTY FOR BREACH OF RULE 14-1 or
14-2:
Match play – Loss of hole; Stroke play –
Two strokes.

14-3. Artificial Devices and Unusual Equipment

The *R&A* reserves the right, at any time, to change the Rules relating to artificial devices and unusual equipment and make or change the interpretations relating to these Rules.

A player in doubt as to whether use of an item would constitute a breach of Rule 14-3 should consult the *R&A*.

A manufacturer may submit to the *R&A* a sample of an item to be manufactured for a ruling as to whether its use during a *stipulated round* would cause a player to be in breach of Rule 14-3. The sample becomes the property of the *R&A* for reference purposes. If a manufacturer fails to submit a sample before manufacturing and/or marketing the item, the manufacturer assumes the risk of a ruling that use of the item would be contrary to the *Rules*.

Except as provided in the *Rules*, during a *stipulated round* the player must not use any artificial device or unusual equipment:

a. That might assist him in making a *stroke* or in his play; or

b. For the purpose of gauging or measuring distance or conditions that might affect his play; or

c. That might assist him in gripping the club, except that:

   (i) plain gloves may be worn;

   (ii) resin, powder and drying or moisturising agents may be used; and

   (iii) a towel or handkerchief may be wrapped around the grip.

PENALTY FOR BREACH OF RULE 14-3:
Disqualification.

14-4. Striking the Ball More than Once

If a player's club strikes the ball more than once in the course of a *stroke*, the player must count the *stroke* and add a *penalty stroke*, making two *strokes* in all.

14-5. Playing Moving Ball

A player must not make a *stroke* at his ball while it is moving.

Exceptions:
- Ball falling off tee – Rule 11-3
- Striking the ball more than once – Rule 14-4
- Ball moving in water – Rule 14-6

When the ball begins to *move* only after the player has begun the *stroke* or the backward movement of his club for the *stroke*, he incurs no penalty under this Rule for playing a moving ball, but he is not exempt from any penalty under the following *Rules*:
- Ball at rest *moved* by player – Rule 18-2a
- Ball at rest moving after *address* – Rule 18-2b

(Ball purposely deflected or stopped by player, partner or caddie – see Rule 1-2)

14-6. Ball Moving in Water

When a ball is moving in water in a *water hazard*, the player may, without penalty, make a *stroke*, but he must not delay making his *stroke* in order to allow the wind or current to improve the position of the ball. A ball moving in water in a *water hazard* may be lifted if the player elects to invoke Rule 26.

PENALTY FOR BREACH OF RULE 14-5
or 14-6:
Match play – Loss of hole; Stroke play –
Two strokes.

Rule 15 – Substituted Ball; Wrong Ball

Definitions

All defined terms are in *italics* and are listed alphabetically in the Definitions section – see pages 529–532.

15-1. General

A player must hole out with the ball played from the *teeing ground* unless the ball is *lost*, *out of bounds* or the player *substitutes* another ball, whether or not substitution is permitted (see Rule 15-2). If a player plays a *wrong ball*, see Rule 15-3.

15-2. Substituted Ball

A player may *substitute* a ball when proceeding under a *Rule* that permits the player to play, drop or place another ball in completing the play of a hole. The *substituted ball* becomes the *ball in play*.

If a player *substitutes* a ball when not permitted to do so under the *Rules*, that *substituted ball* is not a *wrong ball*; it becomes the *ball in play*. If the mistake is not corrected as provided in Rule 20-6 and the player makes a *stroke* at a wrongly *substituted ball*, he incurs the penalty prescribed by the applicable Rule and, in stroke play, must play out the hole with the *substituted ball*.

(Playing from Wrong Place – see Rule 20-7)

15-3. Wrong Ball
a. Match Play

If a player makes a *stroke* at a *wrong ball* that is not in a *hazard*, he loses the hole.

There is no penalty if a player makes a *stroke* at a *wrong ball* in a *hazard*. Any *strokes* made at a *wrong ball* in a *hazard* do not count in the player's score.

If the *wrong ball* belongs to another player, its owner must place a ball on the spot from which the *wrong ball* was first played.

If the player and opponent exchange balls during the play of a hole, the first to make a *stroke* at a *wrong ball* that is not in a *hazard*, loses the hole; when this cannot be determined, the hole must be played out with the balls exchanged.

b. Stroke Play

If a *competitor* makes a *stroke* or *strokes* at a *wrong ball* that is not in a *hazard*, he incurs a penalty of two strokes.

There is no penalty if a *competitor* makes a *stroke* at a *wrong ball* in a *hazard*. Any *strokes* made at a *wrong ball* in a *hazard* do not count in the *competitor's* score.

The *competitor* must correct his mistake by playing the correct ball or by proceeding under the *Rules*. If he fails to correct his mistake before making a *stroke* on the next *teeing ground* or, in the case of the last hole of the round, fails to declare his intention to correct his mistake before leaving the *putting green*, he is disqualified.

Strokes made by a *competitor* with a *wrong ball* do not count in his score.

If the *wrong ball* belongs to another *competitor*, its owner must place a ball on the spot from which the *wrong ball* was first played.

(Lie of ball to be placed or replaced altered – see Rule 20-3b)

(Spot not determinable – see Rule 20-3c)

THE PUTTING GREEN

Rule 16 – The Putting Green

Definitions
All defined terms are in *italics* and are listed alphabetically in the Definitions section – see pages 529–532.

16-1. General
a. Touching Line of Putt
The *line of putt* must not be touched except:

(i) the player may remove *loose impediments*, provided he does not press anything down;

(ii) the player may place the club in front of the ball when *addressing* it, provided he does not press anything down;

(iii) in measuring – Rule 18-6;

(iv) in lifting the ball – Rule 16-1b;

(v) in pressing down a ball-marker;

(vi) in repairing old *hole* plugs or ball marks on the *putting green* – Rule 16-1c; and

(vii) in removing movable *obstructions* – Rule 24-1

(Indicating line for putting on putting green – see Rule 8-2b)

b. Lifting and Cleaning Ball
A ball on the *putting green* may be lifted and, if desired, cleaned. The position of the ball must be marked before it is lifted and the ball must be replaced (see Rule 20-1).

c. Repair of Hole Plugs, Ball Marks and Other Damage
The player may repair an old *hole* plug or damage to the *putting green* caused by the impact of a ball, whether or not the player's ball lies on the *putting green*. If a ball or ball-marker is accidentally *moved* in the process of the repair, the ball or ball-marker must be replaced. There is no penalty provided the movement of the ball is directly attributable to the specific act of repairing an old *hole* plug or damage to the *putting green* caused by the impact of a ball. Otherwise, the player incurs a *penalty stroke* under Rule 18-2a.

Any other damage to the *putting green* must not be repaired if it might assist the player in his subsequent play of the hole.

d. Testing Surface
During the play of a hole, a player must not test the surface of the *putting green* by rolling a ball or roughening or scraping the surface.

e. Standing Astride or on Line of Putt
The player must not make a *stroke* on the *putting green* from a *stance* astride, or with either foot touching, the *line of putt* or an extension of that line behind the ball.

f. Making Stroke While Another Ball in Motion
The player must not make a *stroke* while another ball is in motion after a *stroke* from the *putting green*, except that, if a player does so, there is no penalty if it was his turn to play.

(Lifting ball assisting or interfering with play while another ball in motion – see Rule 22)

PENALTY FOR BREACH OF RULE 16-1:
Match play – Loss of hole; Stroke play – Two strokes.

(Position of caddie or partner – see Rule 14-2)
(Wrong putting green – see Rule 25-3)

16-2. Ball Overhanging Hole
When any part of the ball overhangs the lip of the *hole*, the player is allowed enough time to reach the *hole* without unreasonable delay and an additional ten seconds to determine whether the ball is at rest. If by then the ball has not fallen into the *hole*, it is deemed to be at rest. If the ball subsequently falls into the *hole*, the player is deemed to have *holed* out with his last *stroke*, and must add a *penalty stroke* to his score for the hole; otherwise, there is no penalty under this Rule.

(Undue delay – see Rule 6-7)

Rule 17 – The Flagstick

Definitions
All defined terms are in *italics* and are listed alphabetically in the Definitions section – see pages 529–532.

17-1. Flagstick Attended, Removed or Held Up
Before making a *stroke* from anywhere on the *course*, the player may have the *flagstick* attended, removed or held up to indicate the position of the *hole*.

If the *flagstick* is not attended, removed or held up before the player makes a *stroke*, it must not be attended, removed or held up during the *stroke* or while the player's ball is in motion if doing so might influence the movement of the ball.

Note 1: If the *flagstick* is in the hole and anyone stands near it while a *stroke* is being made, he is deemed to be attending the *flagstick*.

Note 2: If, prior to the *stroke*, the *flagstick* is attended, removed or held up by anyone with the player's knowledge and he makes no objection, the player is deemed to have authorised it.

Note 3: If anyone attends or holds up the *flagstick* while a *stroke* is being made, he is deemed to be attending the *flagstick* until the ball comes to rest.

17-2. Unauthorised Attendance
If an opponent or his *caddie* in match play or a *fellow-competitor* or his *caddie* in stroke play, without the player's authority or prior knowledge, attends, removes or holds up the *flagstick* during the *stroke* or while the ball is in motion, and the act might influence the movement of the ball, the opponent or *fellow-competitor* incurs the applicable penalty.

*PENALTY FOR BREACH OF RULE 17-1 or 17-2:
Match play – Loss of hole; Stroke play – Two strokes.
*In stroke play, if a breach of Rule 17-2 occurs and the *competitor's* ball subsequently strikes the *flagstick*, the person attending or holding it or anything carried by him, the *competitor* incurs no penalty. The ball is played as it lies except that, if the *stroke* was made on the *putting green*, the *stroke* is cancelled and the ball must be replaced and replayed.

17-3. Ball Striking Flagstick or Attendant
The player's ball must not strike:

a. The *flagstick* when it is being attended, removed or held up;

b. The person attending or holding up the *flagstick*; or

c. The *flagstick* in the *hole*, unattended, when the *stroke* has been made on the *putting green*.

Exception: When the *flagstick* is attended, removed or held up without the player's authority – see Rule 17-2.

PENALTY FOR BREACH OF RULE 17-3:
Match play – Loss of hole; Stroke play – Two strokes and the ball must be played as it lies.

17-4. Ball Resting Against Flagstick
When the *flagstick* is in the *hole* and a player's ball when not *holed* rests against it, the player or another person authorised by him may move or remove the *flagstick* and if the ball falls into the *hole*, the player is deemed to have *holed* out with his last *stroke*; otherwise, the ball, if *moved*, must be placed on the lip of the *hole*, without penalty.

BALL MOVED, DEFLECTED OR STOPPED

Rule 18 – Ball at Rest Moved

Definitions

All defined terms are in *italics* and are listed alphabetically in the Definitions section – see pages 529–532.

18-1. By Outside Agency

If a ball at rest is *moved* by an *outside agency*, there is no penalty and the ball must be replaced.

(Player's ball at rest moved by another ball – see Rule 18-5)

18-2. By Player, Partner, Caddie or Equipment
a. General

When a player's ball is *in play*, if:

(i) the player, his *partner* or either of their *caddies* lifts or moves it, touches it purposely (except with a club in the act of *addressing* it) or causes it to *move* except as permitted by a *Rule*, or

(ii) *equipment* of the player or his *partner* causes the ball to *move*,

the player incurs a penalty of one stroke. If the ball is *moved*, it must be replaced unless the movement of the ball occurs after the player has begun the *stroke* or the backward movement of the club for the *stroke* and the *stroke* is made.

Under the *Rules* there is no penalty if a player accidentally causes his ball to *move* in the following circumstances:

- In searching for a ball in a *hazard* covered by *loose impediments* or sand, for a ball in an *abnormal ground condition* or for a ball believed to be in water in a *water hazard* – Rule 12-1
- In repairing a *hole* plug or ball mark – Rule 16-1c
- In measuring – Rule 18-6
- In lifting a ball under a *Rule* – Rule 20-1
- In placing or replacing a ball under a *Rule* – Rule 20-3a
- In removing a *loose impediment* on the *putting green* – Rule 23-1
- In removing movable *obstructions* – Rule 24-1

b. Ball Moving After Address

If a player's *ball in play* moves after he has *addressed* it (other than as a result of a *stroke*), the player is deemed to have *moved* the ball and incurs a penalty of one stroke. The ball must be replaced unless the movement of the ball occurs after the player has begun the *stroke* or the backward movement of the club for the *stroke* and the *stroke* is made.

18-3. By Opponent, Caddie or Equipment in Match Play
a. During Search

If, during search for a player's ball, an opponent, his *caddie* or his *equipment* moves the ball, touches it or causes it to *move*, there is no penalty. If the ball is *moved*, it must be replaced.

b. Other Than During Search

If, other than during search for a player's ball, an opponent, his *caddie* or his *equipment* moves the ball, touches it purposely or causes it to *move*, except as otherwise provided in the *Rules*, the opponent incurs a penalty of one stroke. If the ball is *moved*, it must be replaced.

(Playing a wrong ball – see Rule 15-3)
(Ball moved in measuring – see Rule 18-6)

18-4. By Fellow-Competitor, Caddie or Equipment in Stroke Play

If a *fellow-competitor*, his *caddie* or his *equipment* moves the player's ball, touches it or causes it to *move*, there is no penalty.

If the ball is *moved*, it must be replaced.
(Playing a wrong ball – see Rule 15-3)

18-5. By Another Ball

If a *ball in play* and at rest is *moved* by another ball in motion after a *stroke*, the *moved* ball must be replaced.

18-6. Ball Moved in Measuring

If a ball or ball-marker is *moved* in measuring while proceeding under or in determining the application of a *Rule*, the ball or ball-marker must be replaced. There is no penalty provided the movement of the ball or ball-marker is directly attributable to the specific act of measuring. Otherwise, the provisions of Rules 18-2a, 18-3b or 18-4 apply.

*PENALTY FOR BREACH OF RULE:

Match play – Loss of hole; Stroke play – Two strokes.

*If a player who is required to replace a ball fails to do so, he incurs the general penalty for breach of Rule 18. There is no additional penalty under Rule 18, except in the case of a wrongly *substituted* ball (Rule 15-2).

Note 1: If a ball to be replaced under this Rule is not immediately recoverable, another ball may be *substituted*.

Note 2: If the original lie of a ball to be placed or replaced has been altered, see Rule 20-3b.

Note 3: If it is impossible to determine the spot on which a ball is to be placed, see Rule 20-3c.

Rule 19 – Ball in Motion Deflected or Stopped

Definitions

All defined terms are in *italics* and are listed alphabetically in the Definitions section – see pages 529–532.

19-1. By Outside Agency

If a ball in motion is accidentally deflected or stopped by any *outside agency*, it is a *rub of the green*, there is no penalty and the ball must be played as it lies except:

a. If a ball in motion after a *stroke* other than on the *putting green* comes to rest in or on any moving or animate *outside agency*, the player must, *through the green* or in a *hazard*, drop the ball, or on the *putting green* place the ball, as near as possible to the spot where the *outside agency* was when the ball came to rest in or on it, and

b. If a ball in motion after a *stroke* on the *putting green* is deflected or stopped by, or comes to rest in or on, any moving or animate *outside agency* except a worm or an insect, the *stroke* is cancelled. The ball must be replaced and the *stroke* replayed.

If the ball is not immediately recoverable, another ball may be *substituted*.

(Player's ball deflected or stopped by another ball – see Rule 19-5)

Note: If the *referee* or the *Committee* determines that a player's ball has been purposely deflected or stopped by an *outside agency*, Rule 1-4 applies to the player. If the *outside agency* is a *fellow-competitor* or his *caddie*, Rule 1-2 applies to the *fellow-competitor*.

19-2. By Player, Partner, Caddie or Equipment
a. Match Play

If a player's ball is accidentally deflected or stopped by himself, his *partner* or either of their *caddies* or *equipment*, he loses the hole.

b. Stroke Play

If a *competitor's* ball is accidentally deflected or stopped by himself, his *partner* or either of their *caddies* or *equipment*, the *competitor* incurs a penalty of two strokes. The ball must be played as it lies, except when it comes to rest in or on the *competitor's*, his *partner's* or either of their *caddies'* clothes or *equipment*, in which case the *competitor* must *through the green* or in a *hazard* drop the ball, or on the *putting green* place the ball, as near as possible to where the article was when the ball came to rest in or on it.

Exception: Dropped ball – see Rule 20-2a.

(Ball purposely deflected or stopped by player, partner or caddie – see Rule 1-2)

19-3. By Opponent, Caddie or Equipment in Match Play

If a player's ball is accidentally deflected or stopped by an opponent, his *caddie* or his *equipment*, there is no penalty. The player may, before another *stroke* is made by either side, cancel the *stroke* and play a ball without penalty as nearly as possible at the spot from which the original ball was last played (see Rule 20-5) or he may play the ball as it lies. However, if the player elects not to cancel the *stroke* and the ball has come to rest in or on the opponent's or his *caddie's* clothes or *equipment*, the player must *through the green* or in a *hazard* drop the ball, or on the *putting green* place the ball, as near as possible to where the article was when the ball came to rest in or on it.

Exception: Ball striking person attending *flagstick* – see Rule 17-3b.

(Ball purposely deflected or stopped by opponent or caddie – see Rule 1-2)

19-4. By Fellow-Competitor, Caddie or Equipment in Stroke Play

See Rule 19-1 regarding ball deflected by *outside agency*.

19-5. By Another Ball
a. At Rest

If a player's ball in motion after a *stroke* is deflected or stopped by a *ball in play* and at rest, the player must play his ball as it lies. In match play, there is no penalty. In stroke play, there is no penalty unless both balls lay on the *putting green* prior to the *stroke*, in which case the player incurs a penalty of two strokes.

b. In Motion

If a player's ball in motion after a *stroke* is deflected or stopped by another ball in motion after a *stroke*, the player must play his ball as it lies. There is no penalty unless the player was in breach of Rule 16-1f, in which case he incurs the penalty for breach of that Rule.

Exception: If the player's ball is in motion after a *stroke* on the *putting green* and the other ball in motion is an *outside agency* – see Rule 19-1b.

PENALTY FOR BREACH OF RULE:
Match play – Loss of hole; Stroke play – Two strokes.

RELIEF SITUATIONS AND PROCEDURE

Rule 20 – Lifting, Dropping and Placing; Playing from Wrong Place

Definitions

All defined terms are in *italics* and are listed alphabetically in the Definitions section – see pages 529–532.

20-1. Lifting and Marking

A ball to be lifted under the *Rules* may be lifted by the player, his *partner* or another person authorised by the player. In any such case, the player is responsible for any breach of the *Rules*.

The position of the ball must be marked before it is lifted under a *Rule* that requires it to be replaced. If it is not marked, the player incurs a penalty of one stroke and the

ball must be replaced. If it is not replaced, the player incurs the general penalty for breach of this Rule but there is no additional penalty under Rule 20-1.

If a ball or ball-marker is accidentally *moved* in the process of lifting the ball under a *Rule* or marking its position, the ball or ball-marker must be replaced. There is no penalty provided the movement of the ball or ball-marker is directly attributable to the specific act of marking the position of or lifting the ball. Otherwise, the player incurs a penalty of one stroke under this Rule or Rule 18-2a.

Exception: If a player incurs a penalty for failing to act in accordance with Rule 5-3 or 12-2, there is no additional penalty under Rule 20-1.

Note: The position of a ball to be lifted should be marked by placing a ball-marker, a small coin or other similar object immediately behind the ball. If the ball-marker interferes with the play, *stance* or *stroke* of another player, it should be placed one or more clubhead-lengths to one side.

20-2. Dropping and Re-Dropping
a. By Whom and How

A ball to be dropped under the *Rules* must be dropped by the player himself. He must stand erect, hold the ball at shoulder height and arm's length and drop it. If a ball is dropped by any other person or in any other manner and the error is not corrected as provided in Rule 20-6, the player incurs a penalty of one stroke.

If the ball touches the player, his *partner*, either of their *caddies* or their *equipment* before or after it strikes a part of the *course*, the ball must be re-dropped, without penalty. There is no limit to the number of times a ball must be re-dropped in these circumstances.

(Taking action to influence position or movement of ball – see Rule 1-2)

b. Where to Drop

When a ball is to be dropped as near as possible to a specific spot, it must be dropped not nearer the *hole* than the specific spot which, if it is not precisely known to the player, must be estimated.

A ball when dropped must first strike a part of the *course* where the applicable *Rule* requires it to be dropped. If it is not so dropped, Rules 20-6 and -7 apply.

c. When to Re-Drop

A dropped ball must be re-dropped without penalty if it:

(i) rolls into and comes to rest in a *hazard*;
(ii) rolls out of and comes to rest outside a *hazard*;
(iii) rolls onto and comes to rest on a *putting green*;
(iv) rolls and comes to rest *out of bounds*;
(v) rolls to and comes to rest in a position where there is interference by the condition from which relief was taken under Rule 24-2b (immovable obstruction), Rule 25-1 (abnormal ground conditions), Rule 25-3 (wrong putting green) or a Local Rule (Rule 33-8a), or rolls back into the pitch-mark from which it was lifted under Rule 25-2 (embedded ball);
(vi) rolls and comes to rest more than two club-lengths from where it first struck a part of the *course*; or
(vii) rolls and comes to rest nearer the *hole* than:

   (a) its original position or estimated position (see Rule 20-2b) unless otherwise permitted by the *Rules*; or

   (b) the *nearest point of relief* or maximum available relief (Rule 24-2, 25-1 or 25-3); or

   (c) the point where the original ball last crossed the margin of the *water hazard* or *lateral water hazard* (Rule 26-1).

If the ball when re-dropped rolls into any position listed above, it must be placed as near as possible to the spot where it first struck a part of the *course* when re-dropped.

If a ball to be re-dropped or placed under this Rule is not immediately recoverable, another ball may be *substituted*.

Note: If a ball when dropped or re-dropped comes to rest and subsequently *moves*, the ball must be played as it lies, unless the provisions of any other *Rule* apply.

20-3. Placing and Replacing
a. By Whom and Where

A ball to be placed under the *Rules* must be placed by the player or his *partner*. If a ball is to be replaced, the player, his *partner* or the person who lifted or *moved* it must place it on the spot from which it was lifted or *moved*. In any such case, the player is responsible for any breach of the *Rules*.

If a ball or ball-marker is accidentally *moved* in the process of placing or replacing the ball, the ball or ball-marker must be replaced. There is no penalty provided the movement of the ball or ball-marker is directly attributable to the specific act of placing or replacing the ball or removing the ball-marker. Otherwise, the player incurs a *penalty stroke* under Rule 18-2a or 20-1.

b. Lie of Ball to be Placed or Replaced Altered

If the original lie of a ball to be placed or replaced has been altered:

(i) except in a *hazard*, the ball must be placed in the nearest lie most similar to the original lie that is not more than one club-length from the original lie, not nearer the *hole* and not in a *hazard*;

(ii) in a *water hazard*, the ball must be placed in accordance with Clause (i) above, except that the ball must be placed in the *water hazard*;

(iii) in a *bunker*, the original lie must be re-created as nearly as possible and the ball must be placed in that lie.

c. Spot Not Determinable

If it is impossible to determine the spot where the ball is to be placed or replaced:

(i) *through the green*, the ball must be dropped as near as possible to the place where it lay but not in a *hazard* or on a *putting green*;

(ii) in a *hazard*, the ball must be dropped in the *hazard* as near as possible to the place where it lay;

(iii) on the *putting green*, the ball must be placed as near as possible to the place where it lay but not in a *hazard*.

Exception: When resuming play (Rule 6-8d), if the spot where the ball is to be placed is impossible to determine, it must be estimated and the ball placed on the estimated spot.

d. Ball Fails to Come to Rest on Spot

If a ball when placed fails to come to rest on the spot on which it was placed, there is no penalty and the ball must be replaced. If it still fails to come to rest on that spot:

(i) except in a *hazard*, it must be placed at the nearest spot where it can be placed at rest that is not nearer the *hole* and not in a *hazard*;

(ii) in a *hazard*, it must be placed in the *hazard* at the nearest spot where it can be placed at rest that is not nearer the *hole*.

If a ball when placed comes to rest on the spot on which it is placed, and it subsequently *moves*, there is no penalty and the ball must be played as it lies, unless the provisions of any other *Rule* apply.

PENALTY FOR BREACH OF RULE 20-1,
20-2 or 20-3:
Match play – Loss of hole; Stroke play – Two strokes.

20-4. When Ball Dropped or Placed is in Play

If the player's *ball in play* has been lifted, it is again in play when dropped or placed.

A *substituted ball* becomes the *ball in play* when it has been dropped or placed.

(Ball incorrectly substituted – see Rule 15-2)
(Lifting ball incorrectly substituted, dropped or placed – see Rule 20-6)

20-5. Making Next Stroke from Where Previous Stroke Made

When a player elects or is required to make his next *stroke* from where a previous *stroke* was made, he must proceed as follows:

a. **On the Teeing Ground:** The ball to be played must be played from within the *teeing ground*. It may be played from anywhere within the *teeing ground* and may be teed.

b. **Through the Green and in a Hazard:** The ball to be played must be dropped.

c. **On the Putting Green:** The ball to be played must be placed.

PENALTY FOR BREACH OF RULE 20-5:
Match play – Loss of hole; Stroke play – Two strokes.

20-6. Lifting Ball Incorrectly Substituted, Dropped or Placed

A ball incorrectly *substituted*, dropped or placed in a wrong place or otherwise not in accordance with the *Rules* but not played may be lifted, without penalty, and the player must then proceed correctly.

20-7. Playing from Wrong Place
a. General

A player has played from a wrong place if he makes a *stroke* with his *ball in play*:

(i) on a part of the *course* where the *Rules* do not permit a *stroke* to be played or a ball to be dropped or placed; or

(ii) when the *Rules* require a dropped ball to be re-dropped or a *moved* ball to be replaced.

Note: For a ball played from outside the *teeing ground* or from a wrong *teeing ground* – see Rule 11-4.

b. Match Play

If a player makes a *stroke* from a wrong place, he loses the hole.

c. Stroke Play

If a *competitor* makes a *stroke* from a wrong place, he incurs a penalty of two strokes under the applicable *Rule*. He must play out the hole with the ball played from the wrong place, without correcting his error, provided he has not committed a serious breach (see Note 1).

If a *competitor* becomes aware that he has played from a wrong place and believes that he may have committed a serious breach, he must, before making a *stroke* on the next *teeing ground*, play out the hole with a second ball dropped or placed in accordance with the *Rules*. If the hole being played is the last hole of the round, he must declare, before leaving the *putting green*, that he will play out the hole with a second ball dropped or placed in accordance with the *Rules*.

The *competitor* must report the facts to the *Committee* before returning his score card; if he fails to do so, he is disqualified. The *Committee* must determine whether the *competitor* has committed a serious breach of the applicable *Rule*. If he has, the score with the second ball counts and the *competitor* must add two penalty strokes to his score with that ball. If the *competitor* has committed a serious breach and has failed to correct it as outlined above, he is disqualified.

Note 1: A *competitor* is deemed to have committed a serious breach of the applicable *Rule* if the *Committee* considers he has gained a significant advantage as a result of playing from a wrong place.

Note 2: If a *competitor* plays a second ball under Rule 20-7c and it is ruled not to count, *strokes* made with that ball and *penalty strokes* incurred solely by playing that ball are disregarded. If the second ball is ruled to count, the *stroke* made from the wrong place and any *strokes* subsequently taken with the original ball including *penalty strokes* incurred solely by playing that ball are disregarded.

Rule 21 – Cleaning Ball

Definitions
All defined terms are in *italics* and are listed alphabetically in the Definitions section – see pages 529–532.

A ball on the *putting green* may be cleaned when lifted under Rule 16-1b. Elsewhere, a ball may be cleaned when lifted except when it has been lifted:

a. To determine if it is unfit for play (Rule 5-3);

b. For identification (Rule 12-2), in which case it may be cleaned only to the extent necessary for identification; or

c. Because it is assisting or interfering with play (Rule 22).

If a player cleans his ball during play of a hole except as provided in this Rule, he incurs a penalty of one stroke and the ball, if lifted, must be replaced.

If a player who is required to replace a ball fails to do so, he incurs the penalty for breach of Rule 20-3a, but there is no additional penalty under Rule 21.

Exception: If a player incurs a penalty for failing to act in accordance with Rule 5-3, 12-2 or 22, there is no additional penalty under Rule 21.

Rule 22 – Ball Assisting or Interfering with Play

Definitions
All defined terms are in *italics* and are listed alphabetically in the Definitions section – see pages 529–532.

22-1. Ball Assisting Play
Except when a ball is in motion, if a player considers that a ball might assist any other player, he may:

a. lift the ball if it is his ball; or

b. have any other ball lifted.

A ball lifted under this Rule must be replaced (see Rule 20-3). The ball must not be cleaned unless it lies on the *putting green* (see Rule 21).

In stroke play, a player required to lift his ball may play first rather than lift the ball.

In stroke play, if the *Committee* determines that *competitors* have agreed not to lift a ball that might assist any other player, they are disqualified.

22-2. Ball Interfering with Play
Except when a ball is in motion, if a player considers that the ball of another player might interfere with his play, he may have it lifted.

A ball lifted under this Rule must be replaced (see Rule 20-3). The ball must not be cleaned unless it lies on the *putting green* (see Rule 21).

In stroke play, a player required to lift his ball may play first rather than lift the ball.

Note: Except on the *putting green*, a player may not lift his ball solely because he considers that it might interfere with the play of another player. If a player lifts his ball without being asked to do so, he incurs a penalty of one stroke for a breach of Rule 18-2a, but there is no additional penalty under Rule 22.

PENALTY FOR BREACH OF RULE:
Match play – Loss of hole; Stroke play –
Two strokes.

Rule 23 – Loose Impediments

Definitions
All defined terms are in *italics* and are listed alphabetically in the Definitions section – see pages 529–532.

23-1. Relief
Except when both the *loose impediment* and the ball lie in or touch the same *hazard*, any *loose impediment* may be removed without penalty.

If the ball lies anywhere other than on the *putting green* and the removal of a *loose impediment* by the player causes the ball to *move*, Rule 18-2a applies.

On the *putting green*, if the ball or ball-marker *moves* in the process of the player removing any *loose impediment*, the ball or ball-marker must be replaced. There is no penalty provided the movement of the ball or ball-marker is directly attributable to the removal of the *loose impediment*. Otherwise, if the player causes the ball to *move*, he incurs a penalty of one stroke under Rule 18-2a.

When a ball is in motion, a *loose impediment* that might influence the movement of the ball must not be removed.

Note: If the ball lies in a *hazard*, the player must not touch or move any *loose impediment* lying in or touching the same *hazard* – see Rule 13-4c.

PENALTY FOR BREACH OF RULE:
Match play – Loss of hole; Stroke play – Two strokes.

(Searching for ball in hazard – see Rule 12-1)
(Touching line of putt – see Rule 16-1a)

Rule 24 – Obstructions

Definitions
All defined terms are in *italics* and are listed alphabetically in the Definitions section – see pages 529–532.

24-1. Movable Obstruction
A player may take relief without penalty from a movable *obstruction* as follows:

a. If the ball does not lie in or on the *obstruction*, the *obstruction* may be removed. If the ball *moves*, it must be replaced, and there is no penalty provided that the movement of the ball is directly attributable to the removal of the *obstruction*. Otherwise, Rule 18-2a applies.

b. If the ball lies in or on the *obstruction*, the ball may be lifted and the *obstruction* removed. The ball must *through the green* or in a *hazard* be dropped, or on the *putting green* be placed, as near as possible to the spot directly under the place where the ball lay in or on the *obstruction*, but not nearer the *hole*.

The ball may be cleaned when lifted under this Rule.

When a ball is in motion, an *obstruction* that might influence the movement of the ball, other than an attended *flagstick* or *equipment* of the players, must not be removed.

(Exerting influence on ball – see Rule 1-2)

Note: If a ball to be dropped or placed under this Rule is not immediately recoverable, another ball may be *substituted*.

24-2. Immovable Obstruction
a. Interference
Interference by an immovable *obstruction* occurs when a ball lies in or on the *obstruction*, or when the *obstruction* interferes with the player's *stance* or the area of his intended swing. If the player's ball lies on the *putting green*,

interference also occurs if an immovable *obstruction* on the *putting green* intervenes on his *line of putt*. Otherwise, intervention on the *line of play* is not, of itself, interference under this Rule.

b. Relief

Except when the ball is in a *water hazard* or a *lateral water hazard*, a player may take relief from interference by an immovable *obstruction* as follows:

(i) Through the Green: If the ball lies *through the green*, the player must lift the ball and drop it without penalty within one club-length of and not nearer the *hole* than the *nearest point of relief*. The *nearest point of relief* must not be in a *hazard* or on a *putting green*. When the ball is dropped within one club-length of the *nearest point of relief*, the ball must first strike a part of the *course* at a spot that avoids interference by the immovable *obstruction* and is not in a *hazard* and not on a *putting green*.

(ii) In a Bunker: If the ball is in a *bunker*, the player must lift the ball and drop it either:

    (a) Without penalty, in accordance with Clause (i) above, except that the *nearest point of relief* must be in the *bunker* and the ball must be dropped in the *bunker*; or

    (b) Under penalty of one stroke, outside the *bunker* keeping the point where the ball lay directly between the *hole* and the spot on which the ball is dropped, with no limit to how far behind the *bunker* the ball may be dropped.

(iii) On the Putting Green: If the ball lies on the *putting green*, the player must lift the ball and place it without penalty at the *nearest point of relief* that is not in a *hazard*. The *nearest point of relief* may be off the *putting green*.

(iv) On the Teeing Ground: If the ball lies on the *teeing ground*, the player must lift the ball and drop it without penalty in accordance with Clause (i) above.

The ball may be cleaned when lifted under this Rule.

(Ball rolling to a position where there is interference by the condition from which relief was taken – see Rule 20-2c(v))

Exception: A player may not take relief under this Rule if (a) it is clearly unreasonable for him to make a *stroke* because of interference by anything other than an immovable *obstruction* or (b) interference by an immovable *obstruction* would occur only through use of an unnecessarily abnormal *stance*, swing or direction of play.

Note 1: If a ball is in a *water hazard* (including a *lateral water hazard*), the player may not take relief from interference by an immovable *obstruction*. The player must play the ball as it lies or proceed under Rule 26-1.

Note 2: If a ball to be dropped or placed under this Rule is not immediately recoverable, another ball may be *substituted*.

Note 3: The *Committee* may make a Local Rule stating that the player must determine the *nearest point of relief* without crossing over, through or under the *obstruction*.

24-3. Ball Lost in Obstruction

It is a question of fact whether a ball *lost* after having been struck toward an *obstruction* is *lost* in the *obstruction*. In order to treat the ball as *lost* in the *obstruction*, there must be reasonable evidence to that effect. In the absence of such evidence, the ball must be treated as a *lost ball* and Rule 27 applies.

a. Ball Lost in Movable Obstruction

If a ball is *lost* in a movable *obstruction*, a player may, without penalty, remove the *obstruction* and must *through the green*

or in a *hazard* drop a ball, or on the *putting green* place a ball, as near as possible to the spot directly under the place where the ball last crossed the outermost limits of the movable *obstruction*, but not nearer the *hole*.

b. Ball Lost in Immovable Obstruction

If a ball is *lost* in an immovable *obstruction*, the spot where the ball last crossed the outermost limits of the *obstruction* must be determined and, for the purpose of applying this Rule, the ball is deemed to lie at this spot and the player may take relief as follows:

(i) Through the Green: If the ball last crossed the outermost limits of the immovable *obstruction* at a spot *through the green*, the player may *substitute* another ball without penalty and take relief as prescribed in Rule 24-2b(i).

(ii) In a Bunker: If the ball last crossed the outermost limits of the immovable *obstruction* at a spot in a *bunker*, the player may *substitute* another ball without penalty and take relief as prescribed in Rule 24-2b(ii).

(iii) In a Water Hazard (including a Lateral Water Hazard): If the ball last crossed the outermost limits of the immovable *obstruction* at a spot in a *water hazard*, the player is not entitled to relief without penalty. The player must proceed under Rule 26-1.

(iv) On the Putting Green: If the ball last crossed the outermost limits of the immovable *obstruction* at a spot on the *putting green*, the player may *substitute* another ball without penalty and take relief as prescribed in Rule 24-2b(iii).

    PENALTY FOR BREACH OF RULE:
    Match play – Loss of hole; Stroke play – Two strokes.

Rule 25 – Abnormal Ground Conditions, Embedded Ball and Wrong Putting Green

Definitions

All defined terms are in *italics* and are listed alphabetically in the Definitions section – see pages 529–532.

25-1. Abnormal Ground Conditions
a. Interference

Interference by an *abnormal ground condition* occurs when a ball lies in or touches the condition or when the condition interferes with the player's *stance* or the area of his intended swing. If the player's ball lies on the *putting green*, interference also occurs if an *abnormal ground condition* on the *putting green* intervenes on his *line of putt*. Otherwise, intervention on the *line of play* is not, of itself, interference under this Rule.

    Note: The *Committee* may make a Local Rule denying the player relief from interference with his *stance* by an *abnormal ground condition*.

b. Relief

Except when the ball is in a *water hazard* or a *lateral water hazard*, a player may take relief from interference by an *abnormal ground condition* as follows:

(i) Through the Green: If the ball lies *through the green*, the player must lift the ball and drop it without penalty within one club-length of and not nearer the *hole* than the *nearest point of relief*. The *nearest point of relief* must not be in a *hazard* or on a *putting green*. When the ball is dropped within one club-length of the *nearest point of relief*, the ball must first strike a part of the *course* at a spot that avoids interference by the condition and is not in a *hazard* and not on a *putting green*.

(ii) In a Bunker: If the ball is in a *bunker*, the player must lift the ball and drop it either:

(a) Without penalty, in accordance with Clause (i) above, except that the *nearest point of relief* must be in the *bunker* and the ball must be dropped in the *bunker*, or if complete relief is impossible, as near as possible to the spot where the ball lay, but not nearer the *hole*, on a part of the *course* in the *bunker* that affords maximum available relief from the condition; or

(b) Under penalty of one stroke, outside the *bunker* keeping the point where the ball lay directly between the *hole* and the spot on which the ball is dropped, with no limit to how far behind the *bunker* the ball may be dropped.

(iii) On the Putting Green: If the ball lies on the *putting green*, the player must lift the ball and place it without penalty at the *nearest point of relief* that is not in a *hazard*, or if complete relief is impossible, at the nearest position to where it lay that affords maximum available relief from the condition, but not nearer the *hole* and not in a *hazard*. The *nearest point of relief* or maximum available relief may be off the *putting green*.

(iv) On the Teeing Ground: If the ball lies on the *teeing ground*, the player must lift the ball and drop it without penalty in accordance with Clause (i) above.

The ball may be cleaned when lifted under Rule 25-1b.

(Ball rolling to a position where there is interference by the condition from which relief was taken – see Rule 20-2c(v))

Exception: A player may not take relief under this Rule if (a) it is clearly unreasonable for him to make a *stroke* because of interference by anything other than an *abnormal ground condition* or (b) interference by an *abnormal ground condition* would occur only through use of an unnecessarily abnormal *stance*, swing or direction of play.

Note 1: If a ball is in a *water hazard* (including a *lateral water hazard*), the player is not entitled to relief without penalty from interference by an *abnormal ground condition*. The player must play the ball as it lies (unless prohibited by Local Rule) or proceed under Rule 26-1.

Note 2: If a ball to be dropped or placed under this Rule is not immediately recoverable, another ball may be substituted.

c. Ball Lost

It is a question of fact whether a ball *lost* after having been struck toward an *abnormal ground condition* is *lost* in such condition. In order to treat the ball as *lost* in the *abnormal ground condition*, there must be reasonable evidence to that effect. In the absence of such evidence, the ball must be treated as a *lost ball* and Rule 27 applies.

If a ball is *lost* in an *abnormal ground condition*, the spot where the ball last crossed the outermost limits of the condition must be determined and, for the purpose of applying this Rule, the ball is deemed to lie at this spot and the player may take relief as follows:

(i) Through the Green: If the ball last crossed the outermost limits of the *abnormal ground condition* at a spot *through the green*, the player may *substitute* another ball without penalty and take relief as prescribed in Rule 25-1b(i).

(ii) In a Bunker: If the ball last crossed the outermost limits of the *abnormal ground condition* at a spot in a *bunker*, the player may *substitute* another ball without penalty and take relief as prescribed in Rule 25-1b(ii).

(iii) In a Water Hazard (including a Lateral Water Hazard): If the ball last crossed the outermost limits of the *abnormal ground condition* at a spot in a *water hazard*, the player is not entitled to relief without penalty. The player must proceed under Rule 26-1.

(iv) On the Putting Green: If the ball last crossed the outermost limits of the *abnormal ground condition* at a spot on the *putting green*, the player may *substitute* another ball without penalty and take relief as prescribed in Rule 25-1b(iii).

25-2. Embedded Ball

A ball embedded in its own pitch-mark in the ground in any closely-mown area *through the green* may be lifted, cleaned and dropped, without penalty, as near as possible to the spot where it lay but not nearer the *hole*. The ball when dropped must first strike a part of the *course through the green*. "Closely-mown area" means any area of the *course*, including paths through the rough, cut to fairway height or less.

25-3. Wrong Putting Green

a. Interference

Interference by a *wrong putting green* occurs when a ball is on the *wrong putting green*.

Interference to a player's *stance* or the area of his intended swing is not, of itself, interference under this Rule.

b. Relief

If a player's ball lies on a *wrong putting green*, he must not play the ball as it lies. He must take relief, without penalty, as follows:

The player must lift the ball and drop it within one club-length of and not nearer the hole than the *nearest point of relief*. The *nearest point of relief* must not be in a *hazard* or on a *putting green*. When dropping the ball within one club-length of the *nearest point of relief*, the ball must first strike a part of the *course* at a spot that avoids interference by the *wrong putting green* and is not in a *hazard* and not on a *putting green*. The ball may be cleaned when lifted under this Rule.

PENALTY FOR BREACH OF RULE:
Match play – Loss of hole; Stroke play – Two strokes.

Rule 26 – Winter Hazards (Including Lateral Water Hazards)

Definitions

All defined terms are in *italics* and are listed alphabetically in the Definitions section – see pages 529–532.

26-1. Relief for Ball in Water Hazard

It is a question of fact whether a ball *lost* after having been struck toward a *water hazard* is *lost* inside or outside the *hazard*. In order to treat the ball as *lost* in the *hazard*, there must be reasonable evidence that the ball lodged in it. In the absence of such evidence, the ball must be treated as a *lost ball* and Rule 27 applies.

If a ball is in or is *lost* in a *water hazard* (whether the ball lies in water or not), the player may under penalty of one stroke:

a. Play a ball as nearly as possible at the spot from which the original ball was last played (see Rule 20-5); or

b. Drop a ball behind the *water hazard*, keeping the point at which the original ball last crossed the margin of the *water hazard* directly between the *hole* and the spot on which the ball is dropped, with no limit to how far behind the *water hazard* the ball may be dropped; or

c. As additional options available only if the ball last crossed the margin of a *lateral water hazard*, drop a ball outside the *water hazard* within two club-lengths of and not nearer the *hole* than (i) the point where the original ball last crossed the margin of the *water hazard* or (ii) a point on the opposite margin of the *water hazard* equidistant from the *hole*.

The ball may be lifted and cleaned when proceeding under this Rule.

(Prohibited actions when ball is in a hazard – see Rule 13-4)

(Ball moving in water in a water hazard – see Rule 14-6)

26-2. Ball Played Within Water Hazard
a. Ball Comes to Rest in Same or Another Water Hazard

If a ball played from within a *water hazard* comes to rest in the same or another *water hazard* after the *stroke*, the player may:

(i) proceed under Rule 26-1a. If, after dropping in the *hazard*, the player elects not to play the dropped ball, he may:

    (a) with reference to this *hazard*, proceed under Rule 26-1b, or if applicable Rule 26-1c, adding the additional penalty of one stroke prescribed by that Rule; or

    (b) add an additional penalty of one stroke and play a ball as nearly as possible at the spot from which the last *stroke* from outside a *water hazard* was made (see Rule 20-5); or

(ii) proceed under Rule 26-1b, or if applicable Rule 26-1c; or

(iii) under penalty of one stroke, play a ball as nearly as possible at the spot from which the last *stroke* from outside a *water hazard* was made (see Rule 20-5).

b. Ball Lost or Unplayable Outside Hazard or Out of Bounds

If a ball played from within a *water hazard* is *lost* or declared unplayable outside the *hazard* or is *out of bounds*, the player may, after taking a penalty of one stroke under Rule 27-1 or 28a:

(i) play a ball as nearly as possible at the spot in the *hazard* from which the original ball was last played (see Rule 20-5); or

(ii) proceed under Rule 26-1b, or if applicable Rule 26-1c, adding the additional penalty of one stroke prescribed by the Rule and using as the reference point the point where the original ball last crossed the margin of the *hazard* before it came to rest in the *hazard*; or

(iii) add an additional penalty of one stroke and play a ball as nearly as possible at the spot from which the last *stroke* from outside the *hazard* was made (see Rule 20-5).

Note 1: When proceeding under Rule 26-2b, the player is not required to drop a ball under Rule 27-1 or 28a. If he does not drop a ball, he is not required to play it. He may alternatively proceed under Rule 26-2b(ii) or (iii).

Note 2: If a ball played from within a *water hazard* is declared unplayable outside the *hazard*, nothing in Rule 26-2b precludes the player from proceeding under Rule 28b or c.

PENALTY FOR BREACH OF RULE:
Match play – Loss of hole; Stroke play – Two strokes.

Rule 27 – Lost Ball or Ball Out of Bounds; Provisional Ball

Definitions
All defined terms are in *italics* and are listed alphabetically in the Definitions section – see pages 529–532.

27-1. Ball Lost or Out of Bounds
If a ball is *lost* or is *out of bounds*, the player must play a ball, under penalty of one stroke, as nearly as possible at the spot from which the original ball was last played (see Rule 20-5).

Exceptions:
1. If there is reasonable evidence that the original ball is *lost* in a *water hazard*, the player must proceed in accordance with Rule 26-1.

2. If there is reasonable evidence that the original ball is *lost* in an *obstruction* (Rule 24-3) or an *abnormal ground condition* (Rule 25-1c) the player may proceed under the applicable Rule.

PENALTY FOR BREACH OF RULE 27-1:
Match play – Loss of hole; Stroke play – Two strokes.

27-2. Provisional Ball
a. Procedure

If a ball may be *lost* outside a *water hazard* or may be *out of bounds*, to save time the player may play another ball provisionally in accordance with Rule 27-1. The player must inform his opponent in match play or his *marker* or a *fellow-competitor* in stroke play that he intends to play a *provisional ball*, and he must play it before he or his *partner* goes forward to search for the original ball.

If he fails to do so and plays another ball, that ball is not a *provisional ball* and becomes the *ball in play* under penalty of stroke and distance (Rule 27-1); the original ball is *lost*.

(Order of play from teeing ground – see Rule 10-3)

Note: If a *provisional ball* played under Rule 27-2a might be *lost* outside a *water hazard* or *out of bounds*, the player may play another *provisional ball*. If another *provisional ball* is played, it bears the same relationship to the previous *provisional ball* as the first *provisional ball* bears to the original ball.

b. When Provisional Ball Becomes Ball in Play

The player may play a *provisional ball* until he reaches the place where the original ball is likely to be. If he makes a *stroke* with the *provisional ball* from the place where the original ball is likely to be or from a point nearer the *hole* than that place, the original ball is *lost* and the *provisional ball* becomes the *ball in play* under penalty of stroke and distance (Rule 27-1).

If the original ball is *lost* outside a *water hazard* or is *out of bounds*, the *provisional ball* becomes the *ball in play*, under penalty of stroke and distance (Rule 27-1).

If there is reasonable evidence that the original ball is *lost* in a *water hazard*, the player must proceed in accordance with Rule 26-1.

Exception: If there is reasonable evidence that the original ball is *lost* in an *obstruction* (Rule 24-3) or an *abnormal ground condition* (Rule 25-1c) the player may proceed under the applicable Rule.

c. When Provisional Ball to be Abandoned

If the original ball is neither *lost* nor *out of bounds*, the player must abandon the *provisional ball* and continue play with the original ball. If he makes any further *strokes* at the *provisional ball*, he is playing a *wrong ball* and the provisions of Rule 15 apply.

Note: If a player plays a *provisional ball* under Rule 27-2a, the *strokes* made after this Rule has been invoked with a *provisional ball* subsequently abandoned under Rule 27-2c and *penalty strokes* incurred solely by playing that ball are disregarded.

Rule 28 – Ball Unplayable

Definitions
All defined terms are in *italics* and are listed alphabetically in the Definitions section – see pages 529–532.

The player may deem his ball unplayable at any place on the *course* except when the ball is in a *water hazard*. The player is the sole judge as to whether his ball is unplayable.

If the player deems his ball to be unplayable, he must, under penalty of one stroke:

a. Play a ball as nearly as possible at the spot from which the original ball was last played (see Rule 20-5); or

b. Drop a ball behind the point where the ball lay, keeping that point directly between the *hole* and the spot on which the ball is dropped, with no limit to how far behind that point the ball may be dropped; or

c. Drop a ball within two club-lengths of the spot where the ball lay, but not nearer the *hole*.

If the unplayable ball is in a *bunker*, the player may proceed under Clause a, b or c. If he elects to proceed under Clause b or c, a ball must be dropped in the *bunker*.

The ball may be lifted and cleaned when proceeding under this Rule.

PENALTY FOR BREACH OF RULE:
Match play – Loss of hole; Stroke play –
Two strokes.

OTHER FORMS OF PLAY

Rule 29 – Threesomes and Foursomes

Definitions
All defined terms are in *italics* and are listed alphabetically in the Definitions section – see pages 529–532.

29-1. General
In a *threesome* or a *foursome*, during any *stipulated round* the *partners* must play alternately from the *teeing grounds* and alternately during the play of each hole. *Penalty strokes* do not affect the order of play.

29-2. Match Play
If a player plays when his *partner* should have played, his *side* loses the hole.

29-3. Stroke Play
If the *partners* make a *stroke* or *strokes* in incorrect order, such *stroke* or *strokes* are cancelled and the side incurs a penalty of two strokes. The *side* must correct the error by playing a ball in correct order as nearly as possible at the spot from which it first played in incorrect order (see Rule 20-5). If the *side* makes a *stroke* on the next *teeing ground* without first correcting the error or, in the case of the last hole of the round, leaves the *putting green* without declaring its intention to correct the error, the *side* is disqualified.

Rule 30 – Three-Ball, Best-Ball and Four-Ball Match Play

Definitions
All defined terms are in *italics* and are listed alphabetically in the Definitions section – see pages 529–532.

30-1. Rules of Golf Apply
The Rules of Golf, so far as they are not at variance with the following specific Rules, apply to *three-ball*, *best-ball* and *four-ball matches*.

30-2. Three-Ball Match Play
a. Ball at Rest Moved by an Opponent
Except as otherwise provided in the *Rules*, if the player's ball is touched or *moved* by an opponent, his *caddie* or *equipment* other than during search, Rule 18-3b applies. That opponent incurs a penalty of one stroke in his match with the player, but not in his match with the other opponent.

b. Ball Deflected or Stopped by an Opponent Accidentally
If a player's ball is accidentally deflected or stopped by an opponent, his *caddie* or *equipment*, there is no penalty. In his match with that opponent the player may play the ball as it lies or, before another *stroke* is played by either *side*, he may cancel the *stroke* and play a ball without penalty as nearly as possible at the spot from which the original ball was last played (see Rule 20-5). In his match with the other opponent, the ball must be played as it lies.

Exception: Ball striking person attending *flagstick* – see Rule 17-3b.

(Ball purposely deflected or stopped by opponent – see Rule 1-2)

30-3. Best-Ball and Four-Ball Match Play
a. Representation of Side
A *side* may be represented by one *partner* for all or any part of a match; all *partners* need not be present. An absent *partner* may join a match between holes, but not during play of a hole.

b. Maximum of Fourteen Clubs
The *side* is penalised for a breach of Rules 4-3a(iii) and 4-4 by any *partner*.

c. Order of Play
Balls belonging to the same *side* may be played in the order the *side* considers best.

d. Wrong Ball
If a player makes a *stroke* at a *wrong ball* that is not in a *hazard*, he is disqualified for that hole, but his *partner* incurs no penalty even if the *wrong ball* belongs to him. If the *wrong ball* belongs to another player, its owner must place a ball on the spot from which the *wrong ball* was first played.

e. Disqualification of Side
(i) A *side* is disqualified for a breach of any of the following by any *partner*:

Rule 1-3	Agreement to Waive Rules
Rule 4-1 or -2	Clubs
Rule 5-1 or -2	The Ball
Rule 6-2a	Handicap (playing off higher handicap)
Rule 6-4	Caddie (having more than one caddie; failure to correct breach immediately)
Rule 6-7	Undue Delay; Slow Play (repeated offence)
Rule 14-3	Artificial Devices and Unusual Equipment

(ii) A *side* is disqualified for a breach of any of the following by all *partners*:

Rule 6-3	Time of Starting and Groups
Rule 6-8	Discontinuance of Play

(iii) In all other cases where a breach of a *Rule* would result in disqualification, the player is disqualified for that hole only.

f. Effect of Other Penalties
If a player's breach of a *Rule* assists his *partner's* play or adversely affects an opponent's play, the *partner* incurs the applicable penalty in addition to any penalty incurred by the player.

In all other cases where a player incurs a penalty for breach of a *Rule*, the penalty does not apply to his *partner*. Where the penalty is stated to be loss of hole, the effect is to disqualify the player for that hole.

g. Another Form of Match Played Concurrently
In a *best-ball* or *four-ball* match when another form of match is played concurrently, the above specific Rules apply.

Rule 31 – Four-Ball Stroke Play

Definitions
All defined terms are in *italics* and are listed alphabetically in the Definitions section – see pages 529–532.

31-1. General
In *four-ball* stroke play two *competitors* play as *partners*, each playing his own ball. The lower score of the *partners* is the score for the hole. If one *partner* fails to complete the play of a hole, there is no penalty.

The Rules of Golf, so far as they are not at variance with the following specific Rules, apply to *four-ball* stroke play.

31-2. Representation of Side
A *side* may be represented by either *partner* for all or any part of a *stipulated round*; both *partners* need not be present. An absent *competitor* may join his *partner* between holes, but not during play of a hole.

31-3. Maximum of Fourteen Clubs
The *side* is penalised for a breach of Rules 4-3a (iii) and 4-4 by either *partner*.

31-4. Scoring
The *marker* is required to record for each hole only the gross score of whichever *partner's* score is to count. The gross scores to count must be individually identifiable; otherwise the *side* is disqualified. Only one of the *partners* need be responsible for complying with Rule 6-6b.

(Wrong score – see Rule 31-7a)

31-5. Order of Play
Balls belonging to the same *side* may be played in the order the *side* considers best.

31-6. Wrong Ball
If a *competitor* makes a *stroke* at a *wrong ball* that is not in a *hazard*, he incurs a penalty of two strokes and must correct his mistake by playing the correct ball or by proceeding under the *Rules*. His *partner* incurs no penalty even if the *wrong ball* belongs to him.

If the *wrong ball* belongs to another *competitor*, its owner must place a ball on the spot from which the *wrong ball* was first played.

31-7. Disqualification Penalties
a. Breach by One Partner
A *side* is disqualified from the competition for a breach of any of the following by either *partner*:

• Rule 1-3	Agreement to Waive Rules
• Rule 3-4	Refusal to Comply with Rule
• Rule 4-1 or -2	Clubs
• Rule 5-1 or -2	The Ball
• Rule 6-2b	Handicap (playing off higher handicap; failure to record handicap)
• Rule 6-4	Caddie (having more than one caddie; failure to correct breach immediately)
• Rule 6-6b	Signing and Returning Score Card
• Rule 6-6d	Wrong Score for Hole, i.e. when the recorded score of the *partner* whose score is to count is lower than actually taken. If the recorded score of the *partner* whose score is to count is higher than actually taken, it must stand as returned
• Rule 6-7	Undue Delay; Slow Play (repeated offence)
• Rule 7-1	Practice Before or Between Rounds
• Rule 14-3	Artificial Devices and Unusual Equipment
• Rule 31-4	Gross Scores to Count Not Individually Identifiable

b. Breach by Both Partners
A *side* is disqualified:

(i) for a breach by both of Rule 6-3 (Time of Starting and Groups) or Rule 6-8 (Discontinuance of Play), or

(ii) if, at the same hole, each *partner* is in breach of a *Rule* the penalty for which is disqualification from the competition or for a hole.

c. For the Hole Only
In all other cases where a breach of a *Rule* would result in disqualification, the *competitor* is disqualified only for the hole at which the breach occurred.

31-8. Effect of Other Penalties
If a *competitor's* breach of a *Rule* assists his *partner's* play, the *partner* incurs the applicable penalty in addition to any penalty incurred by the *competitor*.

In all other cases where a *competitor* incurs a penalty for breach of a *Rule*, the penalty does not apply to his *partner*.

Rule 32 – Bogey; Par and Stableford Competitions

Definitions
All defined terms are in *italics* and are listed alphabetically in the Definitions section – see pages 529–532.

32-1. Conditions
Bogey, par and Stableford competitions are forms of stroke play in which play is against a fixed score at each hole. The *Rules* for stroke play, so far as they are not at variance with the following specific Rules, apply.

a. Bogey and Par Competitions
The scoring for bogey and par competitions is made as in match play. Any hole for which a *competitor* makes no return is regarded as a loss. The winner is the *competitor* who is most successful in the aggregate of holes.

The *marker* is responsible for marking only the gross number of *strokes* for each hole where the *competitor* makes a net score equal to or less than the fixed score.

Note 1: Maximum of Fourteen Clubs – Penalties as in match play – see Rule 4-4.

Note 2: One Caddie at Any One Time – Penalties as in match play – see Rule 6-4.

Note 3: Undue Delay; Slow Play (Rule 6-7) – The *competitor's* score is adjusted by deducting one hole from the overall result.

b. Stableford Competitions
The scoring in Stableford competitions is made by points awarded in relation to a fixed score at each hole as follows:

Hole Played In	Points
More than one over fixed score or no score returned	0
One over fixed score	1
Fixed score	2
One under fixed score	3
Two under fixed score	4
Three under fixed score	5
Four under fixed score	6

The winner is the *competitor* who scores the highest number of points.

The *marker* is responsible for marking only the gross number of *strokes* at each hole where the *competitor's* net score earns one or more points.

Note 1: Maximum of Fourteen Clubs (Rule 4-4) – Penalties applied as follows: From total points scored for the round, deduction of two points for each hole at which any breach occurred; maximum deduction per round: four points.

Note 2: One Caddie at Any One Time (Rule 6-4) – Penalties applied as follows: From the points scored for the round, deduction of two points for each hole at which any breach occurred; maximum deduction per round: four points.

Note 3: Undue Delay; Slow Play (Rule 6-7) – The *competitor's* score is adjusted by deducting two points from the total points scored for the round.

32-2. Disqualification Penalties
a. From the Competition
A *competitor* is disqualified from the competition for a breach of any of the following:

• Rule 1-3	Agreement to Waive Rules
• Rule 3-4	Refusal to Comply with Rule
• Rule 4-1 or -2	Clubs
• Rule 5-1 or -2	The Ball
• Rule 6-2b	Handicap (playing off higher handicap; failure to record handicap)
• Rule 6-3	Time of Starting and Groups
• Rule 6-4	Caddie (having more than one caddie; failure to correct breach immediately)
• Rule 6-6b	Signing and Returning Score Card
• Rule 6-6d	Wrong Score for Hole, i.e. when the recorded score is lower than actually taken, except that no penalty is incurred when a breach of this Rule does not affect the result of the hole
• Rule 6-7	Undue Delay; Slow Play (repeated offence)
• Rule 6-8	Discontinuance of Play
• Rule 7-1	Practice Before or Between Rounds
• Rule 14-3	Artificial Devices and Unusual Equipment

b. For a Hole
In all other cases where a breach of a *Rule* would result in disqualification, the *competitor* is disqualified only for the hole at which the breach occurred.

ADMINISTRATION

Rule 33 – The Committee

Definitions
All defined terms are in *italics* and are listed alphabetically in the Definitions section – see pages 529–532.

33-1. Conditions; Waiving Rule
The *Committee* must establish the conditions under which a competition is to be played.

The *Committee* has no power to waive a Rule of Golf.

Certain specific *Rules* governing stroke play are so substantially different from those governing match play that combining the two forms of play is not practicable and is not permitted. The results of *matches* played and the scores returned in these circumstances must not be accepted.

In stroke play the *Committee* may limit a *referee's* duties.

33-2. The Course
a. Defining Bounds and Margins
The *Committee* must define accurately:

   (i) the *course* and *out of bounds*,
   (ii) the margins of *water hazards* and *lateral water hazards*,
   (iii) *ground under repair*, and
   (iv) *obstructions* and integral parts of the *course*.

b. New Holes
New *holes* should be made on the day on which a stroke play competition begins and at such other times as the *Committee* considers necessary, provided all *competitors* in a single round play with each *hole* cut in the same position.

Exception: When it is impossible for a damaged *hole* to be repaired so that it conforms with the Definition, the *Committee* may make a new *hole* in a nearby similar position.

Note: Where a single round is to be played on more than one day, the *Committee* may provide in the conditions of a competition that the *holes* and *teeing grounds* may be differently situated on each day of the competition, provided that, on any one day, all *competitors* play with each *hole* and each *teeing ground* in the same position.

c. Practice Ground
Where there is no practice ground available outside the area of a competition *course*, the *Committee* should establish the area on which players may practise on any day of a competition, if it is practicable to do so. On any day of a stroke play competition, the *Committee* should not normally permit practice on or to a *putting green* or from a *hazard* of the competition *course*.

d. Course Unplayable
If the *Committee* or its authorised representative considers that for any reason the *course* is not in a playable condition or that there are circumstances that render the proper playing of the game impossible, it may, in match play or stroke play, order a temporary suspension of play or, in stroke play, declare play null and void and cancel all scores for the round in question. When a round is cancelled, all penalties incurred in that round are cancelled.

(Procedure in discontinuing and resuming play – see Rule 6-8)

33-3. Times of Starting and Groups
The *Committee* must establish the times of starting and, in stroke play, arrange the groups in which *competitors* must play.

When a match play competition is played over an extended period, the *Committee* establishes the limit of time within which each round must be completed. When players are allowed to arrange the date of their match within these limits, the *Committee* should announce that the match must be played at a stated time on the last day of the period unless the players agree to a prior date.

33-4. Handicap Stroke Table
The *Committee* must publish a table indicating the order of holes at which handicap *strokes* are to be given or received.

33-5. Score Card
In stroke play, the *Committee* must provide each *competitor* with a score card containing the date and the *competitor's* name or, in *foursome* or *four-ball* stroke play, the *competitors'* names.

In stroke play, the *Committee* is responsible for the addition of scores and application of the handicap recorded on the score card.

In *four-ball* stroke play, the *Committee* is responsible for recording the better-ball score for each hole and in the process applying the handicaps recorded on the score card, and adding the better-ball scores.

In bogey, par and Stableford competitions, the *Committee* is responsible for applying the handicap recorded on the score card and determining the result of each hole and the overall result or points total.

Note: The *Committee* may request that each *competitor* records the date and his name on his score card.

33-6. Decision of Ties

The *Committee* must announce the manner, day and time for the decision of a halved match or of a tie, whether played on level terms or under handicap.

A halved match must not be decided by stroke play. A tie in stroke play must not be decided by a match.

33-7. Disqualification Penalty; Committee Discretion

A penalty of disqualification may in exceptional individual cases be waived, modified or imposed if the *Committee* considers such action warranted.

Any penalty less than disqualification must not be waived or modified.

If a *Committee* considers that a player is guilty of a serious breach of etiquette, it may impose a penalty of disqualification under this Rule.

33-8. Local Rules
a. Policy

The *Committee* may establish Local Rules for local abnormal conditions if they are consistent with the policy set forth in Appendix I.

b. Waiving or Modifying a Rule

A Rule of Golf must not be waived by a Local Rule. However, if a *Committee* considers that local abnormal conditions interfere with the proper playing of the game to the extent that it is necessary to make a Local Rule that modifies the Rules of Golf, the Local Rule must be authorised by the *R&A*.

Rule 34 – Disputes and Decisions

Definitions

All defined terms are in *italics* and are listed alphabetically in the Definitions section – see pages 529–532.

34-1. Claims and Penalties
a. Match Play

If a claim is lodged with the *Committee* under Rule 2-5, a decision should be given as soon as possible so that the state of the match may, if necessary, be adjusted. If a claim is not made in accordance with Rule 2-5, it must not be considered by the *Committee*.

There is no time limit on applying the disqualification penalty for a breach of Rule 1-3.

b. Stroke Play

In stroke play, a penalty must not be rescinded, modified or imposed after the competition has closed. A competition is closed when the result has been officially announced or, in stroke play qualifying followed by match play, when the player has teed off in his first match.

Exceptions: A penalty of disqualification must be imposed after the competition has closed if a *competitor*:

(i) was in breach of Rule 1-3 (Agreement to Waive Rules); or

(ii) returned a score card on which he had recorded a handicap that, before the competition closed, he knew was higher than that to which he was entitled, and this affected the number of strokes received (Rule 6-2b); or

(iii) returned a score for any hole lower than actually taken (Rule 6-6d) for any reason other than failure to include a penalty that, before the competition closed, he did not know he had incurred; or

(iv) knew, before the competition closed, that he had been in breach of any other *Rule* for which the penalty is disqualification.

34-2. Referee's Decision

If a *referee* has been appointed by the *Committee*, his decision is final.

34-3. Committee's Decision

In the absence of a *referee*, any dispute or doubtful point on the *Rules* must be referred to the *Committee*, whose decision is final.

If the *Committee* cannot come to a decision, it may refer the dispute or doubtful point to the Rules of Golf Committee of the *R&A*, whose decision is final.

If the dispute or doubtful point has not been referred to the Rules of Golf Committee, the player or players may request that an agreed statement be referred through a duly authorised representative of the *Committee* to the Rules of Golf Committee for an opinion as to the correctness of the decision given. The reply will be sent to this authorised representative.

If play is conducted other than in accordance with the Rules of Golf, the Rules of Golf Committee will not give a decision on any question.

APPENDIX I – CONTENTS

Part A – Local Rules

As provided in Rule 33-8a, the *Committee* may make and publish Local Rules for local abnormal conditions if they are consistent with the policy established in this Appendix. In addition, detailed information regarding acceptable and prohibited Local Rules is provided in "Decisions on the Rules of Golf" under Rule 33-8 and in "Guidance on Running a Competition".

If local abnormal conditions interfere with the proper playing of the game and the *Committee* considers it necessary to modify a Rule of Golf, authorisation from the *R&A* must be obtained.

1. Defining Bounds and Margins
Specifying means used to define *out of bounds*, *water hazards*, *lateral water hazards*, *ground under repair*, *obstructions* and integral parts of the *course* (Rule 33-2a).

2. Water Hazards
a. Lateral Water Hazards
Clarifying the status of *water hazards* that may be *lateral water hazards* (Rule 26).

b. Provisional Ball
Permitting play of a *provisional ball* under Rule 26-1 for a ball that may be in a *water hazard* of such character that if the original ball is not found, there is reasonable evidence that it is *lost* in the *water hazard* and it would be impracticable to determine whether the ball is in the *hazard* or to do so would unduly delay play. The ball is played provisionally under any of the available options under Rule 26-1 or any applicable Local Rule. In such a case, if a *provisional ball* is played and the original ball is in a *water hazard*, the player may play the original ball as it lies or continue with the *provisional ball* in play, but he may not proceed under Rule 26-1 with regard to the original ball.

3. Areas of the Course Requiring Preservation; Environmentally-Sensitive Areas
Assisting preservation of the *course* by defining areas, including turf nurseries, young plantations and other parts of the *course* under cultivation as "*ground under repair*" from which play is prohibited.

When the *Committee* is required to prohibit play from environmentally-sensitive areas that are on or adjoin the *course*, it should make a Local Rule clarifying the relief procedure.

4. Temporary Conditions – Mud, Extreme Wetness, Poor Conditions and Protection of Course
a. Lifting an Embedded Ball, Cleaning
Temporary conditions that might interfere with proper playing of the game, including mud and extreme wetness, warranting relief for an embedded ball anywhere *through the green* or permitting lifting, cleaning and replacing a ball anywhere *through the green* or on a closely-mown area *through the green*.

b. "Preferred Lies" and "Winter Rules"
Adverse conditions, including the poor condition of the *course* or the existence of mud, are sometimes so general, particularly during winter months, that the *Committee* may decide to grant relief by temporary Local Rule either to protect the *course* or to promote fair and pleasant play. The Local Rule must be withdrawn as soon as the conditions warrant.

5. Obstructions
a. General
Clarifying status of objects that may be *obstructions* (Rule 24).

Declaring any construction to be an integral part of the *course* and, accordingly, not an *obstruction*, e.g., built-up sides of *teeing grounds*, *putting greens* and *bunkers* (Rules 24 and 33-2a).

b. Stones in Bunkers
Allowing the removal of stones in *bunkers* by declaring them to be "movable *obstructions*" (Rule 24-1).

c. Roads and Paths
(i) Declaring artificial surfaces and sides of roads and paths to be integral parts of the *course*, or
(ii) Providing relief of the type afforded under Rule 24-2b from roads and paths not having artificial surfaces and sides if they could unfairly affect play.

d. Immovable Obstructions Close to Putting Green
Providing relief from intervention by immovable *obstructions* on or within two club-lengths of the *putting green* when the ball lies within two club-lengths of the *obstruction*.

e. Protection of Young Trees
Providing relief for the protection of young trees.

f. Temporary Obstructions
Providing relief from interference by temporary *obstructions* (e.g., grandstands, television cables and equipment, etc).

6. Dropping Zones (Ball Drops)
Establishing special areas on which balls may or must be dropped when it is not feasible or practicable to proceed exactly in conformity with Rule 24-2b or 24-3 (Immovable Obstruction), Rule 25-1b or 25-1c (Abnormal Ground Conditions), Rule 25-3 (Wrong Putting Green), Rule 26-1 (Water Hazards and Lateral Water Hazards) or Rule 28 (Ball Unplayable).

Part B – Specimen Local Rules

Within the policy established in Part A of this Appendix, the *Committee* may adopt a Specimen Local Rule by referring, on a score card or notice board, to the examples given below. However, Specimen Local Rules 3a, 3b, 3c, 6a and 6b should not be printed or referred to on a score card as they are all of limited duration.

1. Areas of the Course Requiring Preservation; Environmentally-Sensitive Areas
a. Ground Under Repair; Play Prohibited
If the *Committee* wishes to protect any area of the *course*, it should declare it to be *ground under repair* and prohibit

play from within that area. The following Local Rule is recommended:

"The _____(defined by ____) is *ground under repair* from which play is prohibited. If a player's ball lies in the area, or if it interferes with the player's *stance* or the area of his intended swing, the player must take relief under Rule 25-1.

PENALTY FOR BREACH OF LOCAL RULE:
Match play – Loss of hole; Stroke play – Two strokes."

b. Environmentally-Sensitive Areas
If an appropriate authority (i.e. a Government Agency or the like) prohibits entry into and/or play from an area on or adjoining the *course* for environmental reasons, the *Committee* should make a Local Rule clarifying the relief procedure.

The *Committee* has some discretion in terms of whether the area is defined as *ground under repair*, a *water hazard* or *out of bounds*. However, it may not simply define the area to be a *water hazard* if it does not meet the Definition of a "*Water Hazard*" and it should attempt to preserve the character of the hole.

The following Local Rule is recommended:

"**I. Definition**
An environmentally-sensitive area is an area so declared by an appropriate authority, entry into and/or play from which is prohibited for environmental reasons. These areas may be defined as *ground under repair*, a *water hazard*, a *lateral water hazard* or *out of bounds* at the discretion of the *Committee* provided that, in the case of an environmentally-sensitive area which has been defined as a *water hazard* or a *lateral water hazard*, the area is, by Definition, a *water hazard*.

Note: The *Committee* may not declare an area to be environmentally-sensitive.

**II. Ball in Environmentally-Sensitive Area
a. Ground Under Repair**
If a ball is in an environmentally-sensitive area that is defined as *ground under repair*, a ball must be dropped in accordance with Rule 25-1b.

If there is reasonable evidence that a ball is *lost* within an environmentally-sensitive area that is defined as *ground under repair*, the player may take relief without penalty as prescribed in Rule 25-1c.

b. Water Hazards and Lateral Water Hazards
If a ball is in or there is reasonable evidence that it is *lost* in an environmentally-sensitive area that is defined as a *water hazard* or *lateral water hazard*, the player must, under penalty of one stroke, proceed under Rule 26-1.

Note: If a ball, dropped in accordance with Rule 26 rolls into a position where the environmentally-sensitive area interferes with the player's *stance* or the area of his intended swing, the player must take relief as provided in Clause III of this Local Rule.

c. Out of Bounds
If a ball is in an environmentally-sensitive area that is defined as *out of bounds*, the player must play a ball, under penalty of one stroke, as nearly as possible at the spot from which the original ball was last played (see Rule 20-5).

III. Interference with Stance or Area of Intended Swing
Interference by an environmentally-sensitive area occurs when the condition interferes with the player's *stance* or the area of his intended swing. If interference exists, the player must take relief as follows:

(a) Through the Green: If the ball lies *through the green*, the point on the *course* nearest to where the ball lies must be determined that (a) is not nearer the *hole*, (b) avoids interference by the condition and (c) is not in

a *hazard* or on a *putting green*. The player must lift the ball and drop it without penalty within one club-length of the point so determined on a part of the *course* that fulfils (a), (b) and (c) above.

(b) In a Hazard: If the ball is in a *hazard*, the player must lift the ball and drop it either:

(i) Without penalty, in the *hazard*, as near as possible to the spot where the ball lay, but not nearer the *hole*, on a part of the *course* that provides complete relief from the condition; or

(ii) Under penalty of one stroke, outside the *hazard*, keeping the point where the ball lay directly between the *hole* and the spot on which the ball is dropped, with no limit to how far behind the *hazard* the ball may be dropped. Additionally, the player may proceed under Rule 26 or 28 if applicable.

(c) On the Putting Green: If the ball lies on the *putting green*, the player must lift the ball and place it without penalty in the nearest position to where it lay that affords complete relief from the condition, but not nearer the *hole* or in a *hazard*.

The ball may be cleaned when lifted under Clause III of this Local Rule.

Exception: A player may not obtain relief under Clause III of this Local Rule if (a) it is clearly unreasonable for him to make a *stroke* because of interference by anything other than a condition covered by this Local Rule or (b) interference by the condition would occur only through use of an unnecessarily abnormal *stance*, swing or direction of play.

PENALTY FOR BREACH OF LOCAL RULE:
Match play – Loss of hole; Stroke play – Two strokes.

Note: In the case of a serious breach of this Local Rule, the *Committee* may impose a penalty of disqualification."

2. Protection of Young Trees
When it is desired to prevent damage to young trees, the following Local Rule is recommended:

"Protection of young trees identified by _____. If such a tree interferes with a player's *stance* or the area of his intended swing, the ball must be lifted, without penalty, and dropped in accordance with the procedure prescribed in Rule 24-2b (Immovable Obstruction). If the ball lies in a *water hazard*, the player must lift and drop the ball in accordance with Rule 24-2b(i) except that the *nearest point of relief* must be in the *water hazard* and the ball must be dropped in the *water hazard* or the player may proceed under Rule 26. The ball may be cleaned when lifted under this Local Rule.

Exception: A player may not obtain relief under this Local Rule if (a) it is clearly unreasonable for him to make a *stroke* because of interference by anything other than the tree or (b) interference by the tree would occur only through use of an unnecessarily abnormal *stance*, swing or direction of play.

PENALTY FOR BREACH OF LOCAL RULE:
Match play – Loss of hole; Stroke play – Two strokes."

3. Temporary Conditions – Mud, Extreme Wetness, Poor Conditions and Protection of the Course
a. Relief for Embedded Ball; Cleaning Ball
Rule 25-2 provides relief without penalty for a ball embedded in its own pitch-mark in any closely-mown area *through the green*. On the *putting green*, a ball may be lifted and damage caused by the impact of a ball may be repaired (Rules 16-1b and c). When permission to take relief for an embedded ball anywhere *through the green* would be warranted, the following Local Rule is recommended:

"*Through the green*, a ball that is embedded in its own pitch-mark in the ground, other than sand, may be lifted without penalty, cleaned and dropped as near as possible to where it lay but not nearer the *hole*. The ball when dropped must first strike a part of the *course through the green*.

Exception: A player may not obtain relief under this Local Rule if it is clearly unreasonable for him to make a *stroke* because of interference by anything other than the condition covered by this Local Rule.

PENALTY FOR BREACH OF LOCAL RULE:
Match play – Loss of hole; Stroke play – Two strokes."

Alternatively, conditions may be such that permission to lift, clean and replace the ball will suffice. In these circumstances, the following Local Rule is recommended:

"(Specify area) a ball may be lifted, cleaned and replaced without penalty.

Note: The position of the ball must be marked before it is lifted under this Local Rule – see Rule 20-1.

PENALTY FOR BREACH OF LOCAL RULE:
Match play – Loss of hole; Stroke play – Two strokes."

b. "Preferred Lies" and "Winter Rules"

Ground under repair is provided for in Rule 25 and occasional local abnormal conditions that might interfere with fair play and are not widespread should be defined as *ground under repair*.

However, adverse conditions, such as heavy snows, spring thaws, prolonged rains or extreme heat can make fairways unsatisfactory and sometimes prevent use of heavy mowing equipment. When such conditions are so general throughout a *course* that the *Committee* believes "preferred lies" or "winter rules" would promote fair play or help protect the course, the following Local Rule is recommended:

"A ball lying on a closely-mown area *through the green* [or specify a more restricted area, e.g. at the 6th hole] may be lifted without penalty and cleaned. Before lifting the ball, the player must mark its position. Having lifted the ball, he must place it on a spot within [specify area, e.g. six inches, one club-length, etc.] of and not nearer the *hole* than where it originally lay, that is not in a *hazard* and not on a *putting green*.

A player may place his ball only once, and it is in play when it has been placed (Rule 20-4). If the ball fails to come to rest on the spot on which it is placed, Rule 20-3d applies. If the ball when placed comes to rest on the spot on which it is placed and it subsequently *moves*, there is no penalty and the ball must be played as it lies, unless the provisions of any other *Rule* apply.

If the player fails to mark the position of the ball before lifting it or *moves* the ball in any other manner, such as rolling it with a club, he incurs a penalty of one stroke.

*PENALTY FOR BREACH OF LOCAL RULE:
Match play – Loss of hole; Stroke play – Two strokes
*If a player incurs the general penalty for a breach of this Local Rule, no additional penalty under the Local Rule is applied."

c. Aeration Holes

When a *course* has been aerated, a Local Rule permitting relief, without penalty, from an aeration hole may be warranted. The following Local Rule is recommended:

"*Through the green*, a ball that comes to rest in or on an aeration hole may be lifted without penalty, cleaned and dropped, as near as possible to the spot where it lay but not nearer the *hole*. The ball when dropped must first strike a part of the *course through the green*.

On the *putting green*, a ball that comes to rest in or on an aeration hole may be placed at the nearest spot not nearer the *hole* that avoids the situation.

PENALTY FOR BREACH OF LOCAL RULE:
Match play – Loss of hole; Stroke play – Two strokes."

4. Stones in Bunkers

Stones are, by definition, *loose impediments* and, when a player's ball is in a *hazard*, a stone lying in or touching the *hazard* may not be touched or moved (Rule 13-4). However, stones in *bunkers* may represent a danger to players (a player could be injured by a stone struck by the player's club in an attempt to play the ball) and they may interfere with the proper playing of the game.

When permission to lift a stone in a *bunker* would be warranted, the following Local Rule is recommended:

"Stones in *bunkers* are movable *obstructions* (Rule 24-1 applies)."

5. Immovable Obstructions Close to Putting Green

Rule 24-2 provides relief without penalty from interference by an immovable *obstruction*, but it also provides that, except on the *putting green*, intervention on the *line of play* is not, of itself, interference under this Rule.

However, on some courses, the aprons of the *putting greens* are so closely mown that players may wish to putt from just off the green. In such conditions, immovable obstructions on the apron may interfere with the proper playing of the game and the introduction of the following Local Rule providing additional relief without penalty from intervention by an immovable *obstruction* would be warranted:

"Relief from interference by an immovable *obstruction* may be obtained under Rule 24-2. In addition, if a ball lies off the *putting green* but not in a *hazard* and an immovable *obstruction* on or within two club-lengths of the *putting green* and within two club-lengths of the ball intervenes on the *line of play* between the ball and the *hole*, the player may take relief as follows:

The ball must be lifted and dropped at the nearest point to where the ball lay that (a) is not nearer the *hole*, (b) avoids intervention and (c) is not in a *hazard* or on a *putting green*. The ball may be cleaned when lifted.

Relief under this Local Rule is also available if the player's ball lies on the *putting green* and an immovable *obstruction* within two club-lengths of the *putting green* intervenes on his *line of putt*. The player may take relief as follows:

The ball must be lifted and placed at the nearest point where the ball lay that (a) is not nearer the *hole*, (b) avoids intervention and (c) is not in a *hazard*. The ball may be cleaned when lifted.

PENALTY FOR BREACH OF LOCAL RULE:
Match play – Loss of hole; Stroke play – Two strokes."

6. Temporary Obstructions

When temporary *obstructions* are installed on or adjoining the *course*, the *Committee* should define the status of such *obstructions* as movable, immovable or temporary immovable *obstructions*.

a. Temporary Immovable Obstructions

If the *Committee* defines such *obstructions* as temporary immovable *obstructions*, the following Local Rule is recommended:

"I. Definition
A temporary immovable *obstruction* is a non-permanent artificial object that is often erected in conjunction with a competition and is fixed or not readily movable.

Examples of temporary immovable *obstructions* include, but are not limited to, tents, scoreboards, grandstands, television towers and lavatories.

Supporting guy wires are part of the temporary immovable *obstruction* unless the *Committee* declares that they are to be treated as elevated power lines or cables.

II. Interference
Interference by a temporary immovable *obstruction* occurs when (a) the ball lies in front of and so close to the

obstruction that the *obstruction* interferes with the player's stance or the area of his intended swing, or (b) the ball lies in, on, under or behind the *obstruction* so that any part of the *obstruction* intervenes directly between the player's ball and the *hole*; interference also exists if the ball lies within one club-length of a spot equidistant from the hole where such intervention would exist.

Note: A ball is under a temporary immovable *obstruction* when it is below the outer most edges of the *obstruction*, even if these edges do not extend downwards to the ground.

III. Relief

A player may obtain relief from interference by a temporary immovable *obstruction*, including a temporary immovable *obstruction* that is *out of bounds*, as follows:

(a) Through the Green: If the ball lies *through the green*, the point on the *course* nearest to where the ball lies must be determined that (a) is not nearer the *hole*, (b) avoids interference as defined in Clause II and (c) is not in a *hazard* or on a *putting green*. The player must lift the ball and drop it without penalty within one club-length of the point so determined on a part of the *course* that fulfils (a), (b) and (c) above.

(b) In a Hazard: If the ball is in a *hazard*, the player must lift and drop the ball either:

   (i) Without penalty, in accordance with Clause IIIa above, except that the nearest part of the *course* affording complete relief must be in the *hazard* and the ball must be dropped in the *hazard* or, if complete relief is impossible, on a part of the *course* within the *hazard* that affords maximum available relief; or

   (ii) Under penalty of one stroke, outside the *hazard* as follows: the point on the *course* nearest to where the ball lies must be determined that (a) is not nearer the *hole*, (b) avoids interference as defined in Clause II and (c) is not in a *hazard*. The player must drop the ball within one club-length of the point so determined on a part of the *course* that fulfils (a), (b) and (c) above.

The ball may be cleaned when lifted under Clause III.

Note 1: If the ball lies in a *hazard*, nothing in this Local Rule precludes the player from proceeding under Rule 26 or Rule 28, if applicable.

Note 2: If a ball to be dropped under this Local Rule is not immediately recoverable, another ball may be *substituted*.

Note 3: A *Committee* may make a Local Rule (a) permitting or requiring a player to use a dropping zone or ball drop when taking relief from a temporary immovable *obstruction* or (b) permitting a player, as an additional relief option, to drop the ball on the opposite side of the *obstruction* from the point established under Clause III, but otherwise in accordance with Clause III.

Exceptions: If a player's ball lies in front of or behind the temporary immovable *obstruction* (not in, on or under the *obstruction*) he may not obtain relief under Clause III if:

   1. It is clearly unreasonable for him to make a *stroke* or, in the case of intervention, to make a *stroke* such that the ball could finish on a direct line to the *hole*, because of interference by anything other than the temporary immovable *obstruction*;

   2. Interference by the temporary immovable *obstruction* would occur only through use of an unnecessarily abnormal stance, swing or direction of play; or

   3. In the case of intervention, it would be clearly unreasonable to expect the player to be able to strike the ball far enough towards the *hole* to reach the temporary immovable *obstruction*.

Note: A player not entitled to relief due to these exceptions may proceed under Rule 24-2, if applicable.

IV. Ball Lost

If there is reasonable evidence that the ball is *lost* in, on or under a temporary immovable *obstruction*, a ball may be dropped under the provisions of Clause III or Clause V, if applicable. For the purpose of applying Clauses III and V, the ball is deemed to lie at the spot where it last crossed the outermost limits of the *obstruction* (Rule 24-3).

V. Dropping Zones (Ball Drops)

If the player has interference from a temporary immovable *obstruction*, the *Committee* may permit or require the use of a dropping zone or ball drop. If the player uses a dropping zone in taking relief, he must drop the ball in the dropping zone nearest to where his ball originally lay or is deemed to lie under Clause IV (even though the nearest dropping zone may be nearer the *hole*).

Note 1: A *Committee* may make a Local Rule prohibiting the use of a dropping zone or ball drop that is nearer the *hole*.

Note 2: If the ball is dropped in a dropping zone, the ball must not be re-dropped if it comes to rest within two club-lengths of the spot where it first struck a part of the *course* even though it may come to rest nearer the *hole* or outside the boundaries of the dropping zone.

PENALTY FOR BREACH OF LOCAL RULE:
Match play – Loss of hole; Stroke play – Two strokes."

b. Temporary Power Lines and Cables

When temporary power lines, cables, or telephone lines are installed on the *course*, the following Local Rule is recommended:

"Temporary power lines, cables, telephone lines and mats covering or stanchions supporting them are *obstructions*:

   1. If they are readily movable, Rule 24-1 applies.

   2. If they are fixed or not readily movable, the player may, if the ball lies *through the green* or in a *bunker*, obtain relief as provided in Rule 24-2b. If the ball lies in a *water hazard*, the player may lift and drop the ball in accordance with Rule 24-2b(i) except that the *nearest point of relief* must be in the *water hazard* and the ball must be dropped in the *water hazard* or the player may proceed under Rule 26.

   3. If a ball strikes an elevated power line or cable, the *stroke* must be cancelled and replayed, without penalty (see Rule 20-5). If the ball is not immediately recoverable another ball may be *substituted*.

Note: Guy wires supporting a temporary immovable *obstruction* are part of the temporary immovable *obstruction* unless the *Committee*, by Local Rule, declares that they are to be treated as elevated power lines or cables.

Exception: Ball striking elevated junction section of cable rising from the ground must not be replayed.

   4. Grass-covered cable trenches are *ground under repair* even if not marked and Rule 25-1b applies."

Part C – Conditions of the Competition

Rule 33-1 provides, "The *Committee* must establish the conditions under which a competition is to be played." The conditions should include many matters such as method of entry, eligibility, number of rounds to be played, etc. which it is not appropriate to deal with in the Rules of Golf or this Appendix. Detailed information regarding these conditions is provided in "Decisions on the Rules of Golf" under Rule 33-1 and in "Guidance on Running a Competition".

However, there are a number of matters that might be covered in the Conditions of the Competition to which the *Committee's* attention is specifically drawn. These are:

1. Specification of the Ball (Note to Rule 5-1)

The following two conditions are recommended only for competitions involving expert players:

a. List of Conforming Golf Balls

The *R&A* periodically issues a List of Conforming Golf Balls which lists balls that have been tested and found to conform. If the *Committee* wishes to require players to play a brand of golf ball on the List, the List should be posted and the following condition of competition used:

"The ball the player plays must be named on the current List of Conforming Golf Balls issued by the *R&A*.

PENALTY FOR BREACH OF CONDITION:
Disqualification."

b. One Ball Condition

If it is desired to prohibit changing brands and types of golf balls during a *stipulated round*, the following condition is recommended:

"Limitation on Balls Used During Round: (Note to Rule 5-1)

(i) "One Ball" Condition

During a *stipulated round*, the balls a player plays must be of the same brand and type as detailed by a single entry on the current List of Conforming Golf Balls.

Note: If a ball of a different brand and/or type is dropped or placed it may be lifted, without penalty, and the player must then proceed by dropping or placing a proper ball (Rule 20-6).

PENALTY FOR BREACH OF CONDITION:

Match Play – At the conclusion of the hole at which the breach is discovered, the state of the match must be adjusted by deducting one hole for each hole at which a breach occurred; maximum deduction per round: Two holes.

Stroke Play – Two strokes for each hole at which any breach occurred; maximum penalty per round: Four strokes.

(ii) Procedure When Breach Discovered

When a player discovers that he has played a ball in breach of this condition, he must abandon that ball before playing from the next *teeing ground* and complete the round with a proper ball; otherwise, the player is disqualified. If discovery is made during play of a hole and the player elects to *substitute* a proper ball before completing that hole, the player must place a proper ball on the spot where the ball played in breach of the condition lay."

2. Time of Starting (Note to Rule 6-3a)

If the *Committee* wishes to act in accordance with the Note, the following wording is recommended:

"If the player arrives at his starting point, ready to play, within five minutes after his starting time, in the absence of circumstances that warrant waiving the penalty of disqualification as provided in Rule 33-7, the penalty for failure to start on time is loss of the first hole to be played in match play or two strokes in stroke play. Penalty for lateness beyond five minutes is disqualification."

3. Caddie (Note to Rule 6-4)

Rule 6-4 permits a player to use a *caddie* provided he has only one *caddie* at any one time. However, there may be circumstances where a *Committee* may wish to ban *caddies* or restrict a player in his choice of *caddie*, e.g. professional golfer, sibling, parent, another player in the competition, etc. In such cases, the following wording is recommended:

Use of Caddie Prohibited

"A player is prohibited from using a *caddie* during the *stipulated round*."

Restriction on Who May Serve as Caddie

"A player is prohibited from having _____ serve as his *caddie* during the *stipulated round*.

PENALTY FOR BREACH OF CONDITION:

Match play – At the conclusion of the hole at which the breach is discovered, the state of the match is adjusted by deducting one hole for each hole at which a breach occurred; maximum deduction per round – Two holes.

Stroke play – Two strokes for each hole at which any breach occurred; maximum penalty per round – Four strokes.

Match or stroke play – In the event of a breach between the play of two holes, the penalty applies to the next hole. A player having a *caddie* in breach of this condition must immediately upon discovery that a breach has occurred ensure that he conforms with this condition for the remainder of the *stipulated round*. Otherwise, the player is disqualified.

4. Pace of Play (Note 2 to Rule 6-7)

The *Committee* may establish pace of play guidelines to help prevent slow play, in accordance with Note 2 to Rule 6-7.

5. Suspension of Play Due to a Dangerous Situation (Note to Rule 6-8b)

As there have been many deaths and injuries from lightning on golf courses, all clubs and sponsors of golf competitions are urged to take precautions for the protection of persons against lightning. Attention is called to Rules 6-8 and 33-2d. If the *Committee* desires to adopt the condition in the Note under Rule 6-8b, the following wording is recommended:

"When play is suspended by the *Committee* for a dangerous situation, if the players in a match or group are between the play of two holes, they must not resume play until the *Committee* has ordered a resumption of play. If they are in the process of playing a hole, they must discontinue play immediately and not resume play until the *Committee* has ordered a resumption of play. If a player fails to discontinue play immediately, he is disqualified unless circumstances warrant waiving the penalty as provided in Rule 33-7.

The signal for suspending play due to a dangerous situation will be a prolonged note of the siren."

The following signals are generally used and it is recommended that all *Committees* do similarly:

Discontinue Play Immediately: One prolonged note of siren

Discontinue Play: Three consecutive notes of siren, repeated

Resume Play: Two short notes of siren, repeated

6. Practice
a. General

The *Committee* may make regulations governing practice in accordance with the Note to Rule 7-1, Exception (c) to Rule 7-2, Note 2 to Rule 7 and Rule 33-2c.

b. Practice Between Holes (Note 2 to Rule 7)

It is recommended that a condition of competition prohibiting practice putting or chipping on or near the *putting green* of the hole last played be introduced only in stroke play competitions. The following wording is recommended:

"A player must not play any practice *stroke* on or near the *putting green* of the hole last played. If a practice *stroke* is played on or near the *putting green* of the hole last played, the player incurs a penalty of two strokes at the next hole, except that in the case of the last hole of the round, he incurs the penalty at that hole."

7. Advice in Team Competitions (Note to Rule 8)

If the *Committee* wishes to act in accordance with the Note under Rule 8, the following wording is recommended:

"In accordance with the Note to Rule 8 of the Rules of Golf, each team may appoint one person (in addition to the persons from whom *advice* may be asked under that Rule) who may give *advice* to members of that team. Such person (if it is desired to insert any restriction on who may be nominated insert such restriction here) must be identified to the *Committee* before giving *advice*."

8. New Holes (Note to Rule 33-2b)
The *Committee* may provide, in accordance with the Note to Rule 33-2b, that the *holes* and *teeing grounds* for a single round competition, being held on more than one day, may be differently situated on each day.

9. Transportation
If it is desired to require players to walk in a competition, the following condition is recommended:
"Players must walk at all times during a *stipulated round*.

PENALTY FOR BREACH OF CONDITION:
Match play – At the conclusion of the hole at which the breach is discovered, the state of the match must be adjusted by deducting one hole for each hole at which a breach occurred. Maximum deduction per round:
Two holes.
Stroke play – Two strokes for each hole at which any breach occurred; maximum penalty per round: Four strokes. In the event of a breach between the play of two holes, the penalty applies to the next hole.
Match or stroke play – Use of any unauthorised form of transportation must be discontinued immediately upon discovery that a breach has occurred. Otherwise, the player is disqualified."

10. Anti-Doping
The *Committee* may require, in the Conditions of Competition, that players comply with an anti-doping policy.

11. How to Decide Ties
Rule 33-6 empowers the *Committee* to determine how and when a halved match or a stroke play tie is decided. The decision should be published in advance.
The *R&A* recommends:

Match Play
A match which ends all square should be played off hole by hole until one *side* wins a hole. The play-off should start on the hole where the match began. In a handicap match, handicap strokes should be allowed as in the prescribed round.

Stroke Play
(a) In the event of a tie in a scratch stroke play competition, a play-off is recommended. Such a play-off may be over 18 holes or a smaller number of holes as specified by the *Committee*. If that is not feasible or there is still a tie, a hole-by-hole play-off is recommended.

(b) In the event of a tie in a handicap stroke play competition, a play-off with handicaps is recommended. Such a play-off may be over 18 holes or a smaller number of holes as specified by the *Committee*. If the play-off is less than 18 holes the percentage of 18 holes to be played should be applied to the players' handicaps to determine their play-off handicaps. Handicap stroke fractions of one-half stroke or more should count as a full stroke and any lesser fraction should be disregarded.

(c) In either a scratch or handicap stroke play competition, if a play-off of any type is not feasible, matching score cards is recommended. The method of matching cards should be announced in advance. An acceptable method of matching cards is to determine the winner on the basis of the best score for the last nine holes. If the tying players have the same score for the last nine, determine the winner on the basis of the last six holes, last three holes and finally the 18th hole. If this method is used in a handicap stroke play competition, one-half, one-third, one-sixth, etc. of the handicaps should be deducted. Fractions should not be disregarded. If this method is used in a competition with a multiple tee start, it is recommended that the "last nine holes, last six holes, etc." is considered to be holes 10-18, 13-18, etc.

(d) If the conditions of the competition provide that ties are to be decided over the last nine, last six, last three and last hole, they should also provide what will happen if this procedure does not produce a winner.

12. Draw for Match Play
Although the draw for match play may be completely blind or certain players may be distributed through different quarters or eighths, the General Numerical Draw is recommended if matches are determined by a qualifying round.

General Numerical Draw
For purposes of determining places in the draw, ties in qualifying rounds other than those for the last qualifying place are decided by the order in which scores are returned, with the first score to be returned receiving the lowest available number, etc. If it is impossible to determine the order in which scores are returned, ties are determined by a blind draw.

UPPER HALF	LOWER HALF
64 QUALIFIERS	
1 vs. 64	2 vs. 63
32 vs. 33	31 vs. 34
16 vs. 49	15 vs. 50
17 vs. 48	18 vs. 47
8 vs. 57	7 vs. 58
25 vs. 40	26 vs. 39
9 vs. 56	10 vs. 55
24 vs. 41	23 vs. 42
4 vs. 61	3 vs. 62
29 vs. 36	30 vs. 35
13 vs. 52	14 vs. 51
20 vs. 45	19 vs. 46
5 vs. 60	6 vs. 59
28 vs. 37	27 vs. 38
12 vs. 53	11 vs. 54
21 vs. 44	22 vs. 43

UPPER HALF	LOWER HALF
32 QUALIFIERS	
1 vs. 32	2 vs. 31
16 vs. 17	15 vs. 18
8 vs. 25	7 vs. 26
9 vs. 24	10 vs. 23
4 vs. 29	3 vs. 30
13 vs. 20	14 vs. 19
5 vs. 28	6 vs. 27
12 vs. 21	11 vs. 22
16 QUALIFIERS	
1 vs. 16	2 vs.15
8 vs. 9	7 vs.10
4 vs. 13	3 vs.14
5 vs. 12	6 vs. 11
8 QUALIFIERS	
1 vs. 8	2 vs. 7
4 vs. 5	3 vs. 6

APPENDICES II AND III

Any design in a club or ball which is not covered by Rules 4 and 5 and Appendices II and III, or which might significantly change the nature of the game, will be ruled on by the R&A.

The dimensions contained in Appendices II and III are referenced in imperial measurements. A metric conversion is also referenced for information, calculated using a conversion rate of 1 inch = 25.4 mm. In the event of any dispute over the conformity of a club or ball, the imperial measurement takes precedence.

APPENDIX II – DESIGN OF CLUBS

A player in doubt as to the conformity of a club should consult the R&A.

A manufacturer should submit to the R&A a sample of a club, which is to be manufactured for a ruling as to whether the club conforms with the *Rules*. If a manufacturer fails to submit a sample or to await a ruling before manufacturing and/or marketing the club, the manufacturer assumes the risk of a ruling that the club does not conform with the *Rules*. Any sample submitted to the R&A becomes its property for reference purposes.

The following paragraphs prescribe general regulations for the design of clubs, together with specifications and interpretations. Further information relating to these regulations and their proper interpretation is provided in "A Guide to the Rules on Clubs and Balls".

Where a club, or part of a club, is required to have some specific property, this means that it must be designed and manufactured with the intention of having that property. The finished club or part must have that property within manufacturing tolerances appropriate to the material used.

1. Clubs
a. General

A club is an implement designed to be used for striking the ball and generally comes in three forms: woods, irons and putters distinguished by shape and intended use. A putter is a club with a loft not exceeding ten degrees designed primarily for use on the *putting green*.

The club must not be substantially different from the traditional and customary form and make. The club must be composed of a shaft and a head. All parts of the club must be fixed so that the club is one unit, and it must have no external attachments except as otherwise permitted by the *Rules*.

b. Adjustability

Woods and irons must not be designed to be adjustable except for weight. Putters may be designed to be adjustable for weight and some other forms of adjustability are also permitted. All methods of adjustment permitted by the *Rules* require that:

(i) the adjustment cannot be readily made;
(ii) all adjustable parts are firmly fixed and there is no reasonable likelihood of them working loose during a round; and
(iii) all configurations of adjustment conform with the *Rules*.

The disqualification penalty for purposely changing the playing characteristics of a club during a *stipulated round* (Rule 4-2a) applies to all clubs including a putter.

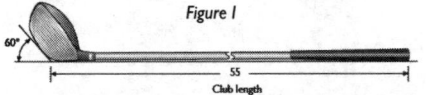

Figure I

c. Length

The overall length of the club must be at least 18 inches (457.2 mm) and, except for putters, must not exceed 48 inches (1,219.2 mm). For woods and irons, the measurement of length is taken when the club is lying on a horizontal plane and the sole is set against a 60 degree plane as shown in Fig. I. The length is defined as the distance from the point of the intersection between the two planes to the top of the grip. For putters, the measurement of length is taken from the top of the grip along the axis of the shaft or a straight line extension of it to the sole of the club.

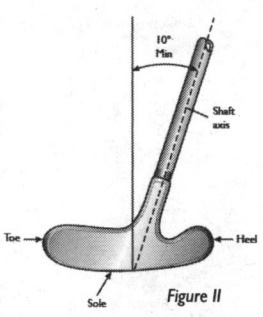

Figure II

Note: Clubs in breach of the maximum length limit as specified in Appendix II, 1c, which were in use or marketed prior to 1st January 2004 and which otherwise conform to the *Rules*, may be used until 31st December 2004.

d. Alignment

When the club is in its normal address position the shaft must be so aligned that:

(i) the projection of the straight part of the shaft on to the vertical plane through the toe and heel must diverge from the vertical by at least 10 degrees (see Fig. II);

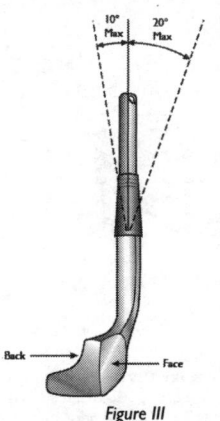

Figure III

(ii) the projection of the straight part of the shaft on to the vertical plane along the intended line of play must not diverge from the vertical by more than 20 degrees forwards or 10 degrees backwards (see Fig. III).

Except for putters, all of the heel portion of the club must lie within 0.625 inches (15.88 mm) of the plane containing the axis of the straight part of the shaft and the intended (horizontal) line of play (see Fig. IV).

2. Shaft
a. Straightness

The shaft must be straight from the

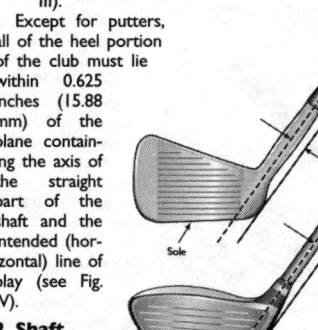

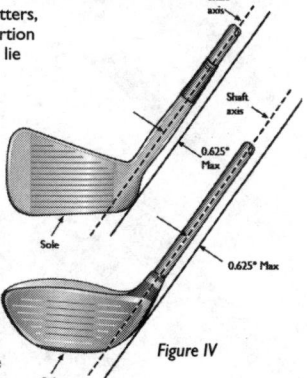

Figure IV

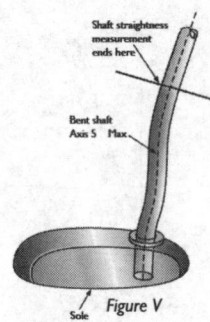

Figure V

top of the grip to a point not more than 5 inches (127 mm) above the sole, measured from the point where the shaft ceases to be straight along the axis of the bent part of the shaft and the neck and/or socket (see Fig. V).

b. Bending and Twisting Properties

At any point along its length, the shaft must:

(i) bend in such a way that the deflection is the same regardless of how the shaft is rotated about its longitudinal axis; and

(ii) twist the same amount in both directions.

c. Attachment to Clubhead

The shaft must be attached to the clubhead at the heel either directly or through a single plain neck and/or socket. The length from the top of the neck and/or socket to the sole of the club must not exceed 5 inches (127 mm), measured along the axis of, and following any bend in, the neck and/or socket (see Fig. VI).

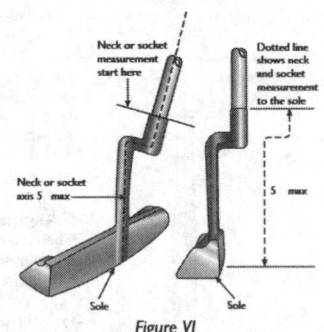

Figure VI

Exception for Putters: The shaft or neck or socket of a putter may be fixed at any point in the head.

3. Grip (see Fig. VII)

The grip consists of material added to the shaft to enable the player to obtain a firm hold. The grip must be straight and plain in form, must extend to the end of the shaft and must not be moulded for any part of the hands. If no material is added, that portion of the shaft designed to be held by the player must be considered the grip.

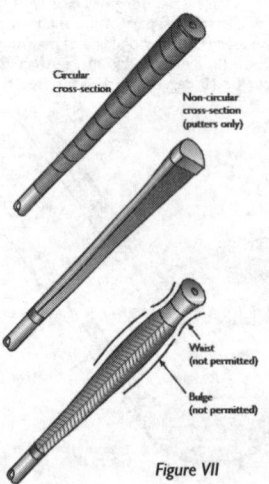

Figure VII

(i) For clubs other than putters the grip must be circular in cross-section, except that a continuous, straight, slightly raised rib may be incorporated along the full length of the grip, and a slightly indented spiral is permitted on a wrapped grip or a replica of one.

(ii) A putter grip may have a non-circular cross-section, provided the cross-section has no concavity, is symmetrical and remains generally similar through-out the length of the grip. (See Clause (v) overleaf).

(iii) The grip may be tapered but must not have any bulge or waist. Its cross-sectional dimensions measured in any direction must not exceed 1.75 inches (44.45 mm).

(iv) For clubs other than putters the axis of the grip must coincide with the axis of the shaft.

(v) A putter may have two grips provided each is circular in cross-section, the axis of each coincides with the axis of the shaft, and they are separated by at least 1.5 inches (38.1 mm).

4. Clubhead
a. Plain in Shape

The clubhead must be generally plain in shape. All parts must be rigid, structural in nature and functional. It is not practicable to define plain in shape precisely and comprehensively but features which are deemed to be in breach of this requirement and are therefore not permitted include:

(i) holes through the head,

(ii) transparent material added for other than decorative or structural purposes,

(iii) appendages to the main body of the head such as knobs, plates, rods or fins, for the purpose of meeting dimensional specifications, for aiming or for any other purpose. Exceptions may be made for putters.

Any furrows in or runners on the sole must not extend into the face.

b. Dimensions and Size
(i) Woods

When the club is in a 60 degree lie angle, the dimensions of the clubhead must be such that:

(a) the distance from the heel to the toe of the clubhead is greater than the distance from the face to the back;

(b) the distance from the heel to the toe of the clubhead is not greater than 5 inches (127 mm); and

(c) the distance from the sole to the crown of the clubhead is not greater than 2.8 inches (71.12 mm).

These dimensions are measured on horizontal lines between vertical projections of the outermost points of:

- the heel and the toe; and
- the face and the back (see Fig. VIII, dimension A);

and on vertical lines between the horizontal projections of the outermost points of the sole and the crown (see Fig. VIII, dimension B). If the outermost point of the heel is not clearly defined, it is deemed to be 0.875 inches (22.23 mm) above the horizontal plane on which the club is lying (see Fig. VIII, dimension C).

The size of the clubhead must not exceed 28.06 cubic

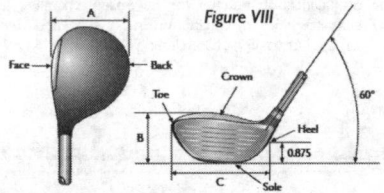

Figure VIII

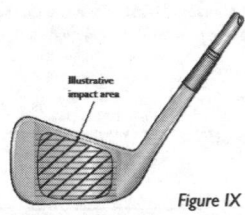

Illustrative
impact area

Figure IX

inches (460 cubic centimetres), plus a tolerance of 0.61 cubic inches (10 cubic centimetres).

Note: Clubs in breach of the maximum size limit as specified in Appendix II, 4b (i), which were in use or marketed prior to 1st January 2004 and which otherwise conform to the *Rules*, may be used until 31st December 2004.

(ii) Irons and Putters
When the clubhead is in its normal address position the dimensions of the head must be such that the distance from the heel to the toe is greater than the distance from the face to the back. For traditionally shaped heads, these dimensions will be measured on horizontal lines between vertical projections of the outermost points of:

- the heel and the toe; and
- the face and the back.

For unusually shaped heads, the toe to heel dimension may be made at the face.

c. Striking Faces
The clubhead must have only one striking face, except that a putter may have two such faces if their characteristics are the same, and they are opposite each other.

5. Club Face
a. General
The material and construction of, or any treatment to, the face or clubhead must not have the effect at impact of a spring (test on file), or impart significantly more or less spin to the ball than a standard steel face, or have any other effect which would unduly influence the movement of the ball.

The face of the club must be hard and rigid (some exceptions may be made for putters) and, except for such markings listed below, must be smooth and must not have any degree of concavity.

b. Impact Area Roughness and Material
Except for markings specified in the following paragraphs, the surface roughness within the area where impact is intended (the "impact area") must not exceed that of decorative sandblasting, or of fine milling (see Fig. IX).

The whole of the impact area must be of the same material. Exceptions may be made for wooden clubs.

c. Impact Area Markings
Markings in the impact area must not have sharp edges or raised lips as determined by a finger test. Grooves or punch marks in the impact area must meet the following specifications:

(i) Grooves. A series of straight grooves with diverging sides and a symmetrical cross-section may be used (see Fig. X).

- The width and cross-section must be consistent across the face of the club and along the length of the grooves.

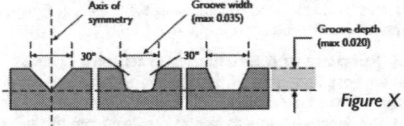

Axis of symmetry
Groove width (max 0.035)
Groove depth (max 0.020)
30° 30°

Figure X

- Any rounding of groove edges must be in the form of a radius which does not exceed 0.020 inches (0.508 mm).
- The width of the grooves must not exceed 0.035 inches (0.9 mm), using the 30 degree method of measurement on file with the R&A.
- The distance between edges of adjacent grooves must not be less than three times the width of a groove, and not less than 0.075 inches (1.905 mm).
- The depth of a groove must not exceed 0.020 inches (0.508 mm).

(ii) Punch Marks. Punch marks may be used.

- The area of any such mark must not exceed 0.0044 square inches (2.84 sq. mm).
- A mark must not be closer to an adjacent mark than 0.168 inches (4.27 mm) measured from centre to centre.
- The depth of a punch mark must not exceed 0.040 inches (1.02 mm).
- If punch marks are used in combination with grooves, a punch mark must not be closer to a groove than 0.168 inches (4.27 mm), measured from centre to centre.

d. Decorative Markings
The centre of the impact area may be indicated by a design within the boundary of a square whose sides are 0.375 inches (9.53 mm) in length. Such a design must not unduly influence the movement of the ball. Decorative markings are permitted outside the impact area.

e. Non-Metallic Club Face Markings
The above specifications apply to clubs on which the impact area of the face is of metal or a material of similar hardness. They do not apply to clubs with faces made of other materials and whose loft angle is 24 degrees or less, but markings which could unduly influence the movement of the ball are prohibited. Clubs with this type of face and a loft angle exceeding 24 degrees may have grooves of maximum width 0.040 inches (1.02 mm) and maximum depth 1½ times the groove width, but must otherwise conform to the markings specifications above.

f. Putter Face Markings
The specifications above with regard to roughness, material and markings in the impact area do not apply to putters.

APPENDIX III – THE BALL

1. Weight
The weight of the ball must not be greater than 1.620 ounces avoirdupois (45.93 gm).

2. Size
The diameter of the ball must not be less than 1.680 inches (42.67 mm). This specification will be satisfied if, under its own weight, a ball falls through a 1.680 inches diameter ring gauge in fewer than 25 out of 100 randomly selected positions, the test being carried out at a temperature of 23 +/- 1°C.

3. Spherical Symmetry
The ball must not be designed, manufactured or intentionally modified to have properties which differ from those of a spherically symmetrical ball.

4. Initial Velocity
The initial velocity of the ball must not exceed the limit specified (test on file) when measured on apparatus approved by the R&A.

5. Overall Distance Standard
The combined carry and roll of the ball, when tested on apparatus approved by the *R&A*, must not exceed the distance specified under the conditions set forth in the Overall Distance Standard for golf balls on file with the *R&A*.

HANDICAPS

The Rules of Golf do not legislate for the allocation and adjustment of handicaps. Such matters are within the jurisdiction of the National Union concerned and queries should be directed accordingly.

RULES OF AMATEUR STATUS

As approved by R&A Rules Limited
Effective from 1st January 2004

Preamble
The *R&A* reserves the right to change the *Rules* and to make and change the interpretations relating to Amateur Status at any time.
In the Rules of Amateur Status, the gender used in relation to any person is understood to include both genders.

DEFINITIONS

The Definitions are listed alphabetically and, in the *Rules* themselves, defined terms are in *italics*.

Amateur Golfer
An "Amateur Golfer" is one who plays the game as a non-remunerative and non-profit making sport and who does not receive remuneration for teaching golf or for other activities because of *golf skill or reputation*, except as provided in the *Rules*.

Committee
The "Committee" is the appropriate *Committee* of the *Governing Body*.

Golf Skill or Reputation
Generally, an *Amateur golfer* is only considered to have *golf skill* if he has gained representative honours at county or national level. *Golf reputation* can only be gained through *golf skill* and does not include prominence for service to the game of golf as an administrator. It is a matter for a *Governing Body* to decide whether a particular *Amateur golfer* has "golf skill or reputation".

Governing Body
The "Governing Body" for the Rules of Amateur Status in any country is the national union of that country.
    Note: In Great Britain and Ireland, the *R&A* is the *Governing Body*.

Instruction
"Instruction" covers teaching the physical aspects of playing golf i.e. the actual mechanics of swinging a golf club and hitting a golf ball.

Junior Golfer
A "junior golfer" is an *Amateur golfer* who has not reached his 18th birthday in the year prior to the event, unless a different age is decided by the *Governing Body*.

Prize Voucher
A "prize voucher" is a voucher issued by the *Committee* in charge of a competition for the purchase of goods from a Professional's shop or other retail source.

R&A
The "R&A" means R&A Rules Limited.

Retail Value
The "retail value" of a prize is the normal recommended selling price at which merchandise is available to anyone at a retail source.

Rule or Rules
The term "Rule" or "Rules" refers to the Rules of Amateur Status as determined by the *Governing Body*.

Symbolic Prize
A "symbolic prize" is a trophy made of gold, silver, ceramic, glass or the like which is permanently and distinctively engraved.

Testimonial Award
A "testimonial award" relates to notable performances or contributions to golf as distinguished from competition prizes. A *testimonial award* may not be a monetary award.

Rule 1 – Amateurism

Definitions
All defined terms are in *italics* and are listed alphabetically in the Definitions section – see pages 529–532.

1-1. General
An *Amateur golfer* must play the game and conduct himself in accordance with the *Rules*.

1-2. Amateur Status
Amateur Status is a universal condition of eligibility for playing in golf competitions as an *Amateur golfer*. A person who acts contrary to the *Rules* may forfeit his status as an *Amateur golfer* and as a result will be ineligible to play in Amateur competitions.

1-3. Purpose and Spirit of the Rules
The purpose and spirit of the *Rules* is to maintain the distinction between Amateur golf and Professional golf and keep the Amateur game as free as possible from the abuses

which may follow from uncontrolled sponsorship and financial incentive. It is considered necessary to safeguard Amateur golf, which is largely self-regulating with regard to the Rules of play and handicapping, so that it may be fully enjoyed by all *Amateur golfers*.

1-4. Doubt as to Rules

Any person who wishes to be an *Amateur golfer* and who is in doubt as to whether taking a proposed course of action is permitted under the *Rules* should consult the *Governing Body*.

Any organiser or sponsor of an Amateur golf competition or a competition involving *Amateur golfers*, who is in doubt as to whether a proposal is in accordance with the *Rules* should consult the *Governing Body*.

Rule 2 – Professionalism

Definitions

All defined terms are in italics and are listed alphabetically in the Definitions section – see pages 529–532.

2-1. General

An Amateur golfer must not take any action for the purpose of becoming a Professional golfer, including entering into an agreement, written or oral, with a sponsor or Professional agent.

Exception: Applying unsuccessfully for the position of an Assistant Professional.

Note: An Amateur golfer may enquire as to his likely prospects as a Professional and he may work in a Professional's shop and receive a salary, provided he does not infringe the Rules in any other way.

2-2. Professional Golfers' Associations

An Amateur golfer must not hold or retain membership of any Professional Golfers' Association.

2-3. Professional Tournament Players

An Amateur golfer must not hold or retain membership of a Professional Tour.

Note: If an Amateur golfer must compete in one or more qualifying competitions in order to be eligible for membership of a Professional Tour, he may enter and play in such qualifying competitions without forfeiting his Amateur Status, provided, in advance of play and in writing, he waives his right to any prize money in the competition.

Rule 3 – Prizes

Definitions

All defined terms are in *italics* and are listed alphabetically in the Definitions section – see pages 529–532.

3-1. Playing for Prize Money

An *Amateur golfer* must not play golf for prize money.

3-2. Prize Limits
a. General

An *Amateur golfer* must not accept a prize (other than a *symbolic prize*) or *prize voucher* of *retail value* in excess of £500 or the equivalent, or such a lesser figure as may be decided by the *Governing Body*. This limit applies to the total prizes or *prize vouchers* received by an *Amateur golfer* in any one competition or series of competitions, excluding any hole-in-one prize.

b. Hole-in-One Prizes

The limits prescribed in Rule 3-2a apply to a prize for a hole-in-one. However, such a prize may be accepted in addition to any other prize won in the same competition.

c. Exchanging Prizes

An *Amateur golfer* must not exchange a prize or *prize voucher* for cash.

Exception: An *Amateur golfer* may submit a *prize voucher* to a national or county union and thereafter be reimbursed from the value of that voucher for expenses incurred in participating in a golf competition, provided the reimbursement of such expenses is permitted under Rule 4-2.

Note 2: It is recommended that the total prize value of scratch prizes, or each division of handicap prizes, should not exceed twice the prescribed limit in an 18-hole competition, three times in a 36-hole competition, five times in a 54-hole competition and six times in a 72-hole competition.

3-3. Testimonial Awards
a. General

An *Amateur golfer* must not accept a *testimonial award* of *retail value* in excess of the limits prescribed in Rule 3-2a.

b. Multiple Awards

An *Amateur golfer* may accept more than one *testimonial award* from different donors, even though their total *retail value* exceeds the prescribed limit, provided they are not presented so as to evade the limit for a single award.

Rule 4 – Expenses

Definitions

All defined terms are in *italics* and are listed alphabetically in the Definitions section – see pages 529–532.

4-1. General

Except as provided in the *Rules*, an *Amateur golfer* must not accept expenses, in money or otherwise, from any source to play in a golf competition or exhibition.

4-2. Receipt of Expenses

An *Amateur golfer* may receive expenses, not exceeding the actual expenses incurred, to play in a golf competition or exhibition as follows:-

a. Family support

An *Amateur golfer* may receive expenses from a member of his family or a legal guardian.

b. Junior Golfers

A *junior golfer* may receive expenses when competing in a competition limited exclusively to *junior golfers*.

c. Team Events

(i) An *Amateur golfer*, who is representing his country, county or club (or similar body) in a team competition or at a training camp may receive expenses; and

(ii) An *Amateur golfer*, who is representing his country by taking part in a national championship abroad immediately before or after an international team competition may receive expenses.

The expenses must be paid by the body he represents or the body controlling golf in the country he is visiting.

d. Individual Events

An *Amateur golfer* may receive expenses when competing in individual events provided he complies with the following provisions:

(i) The player must be nominated to play in the competition by either his club, county or national union.

(ii) Where the competition is to take place in the player's own country and the nomination has been made by a club or county union, the approval of the national union, or the county union in the area in which the competition is to be staged, must first be obtained.

(iii) Where the competition is to take place in another country, the approval of the national union of the country in which the competition is to be staged and, if the nominating body is not the national union of the country from which the nomination is made, the approval of the national union must first be obtained by the nominating body.

(iv) The expenses must be paid only by the national union or county union responsible in the area from which the nomination is made or, subject to the approval of the nominating body, by the body controlling golf in the territory he is visiting.

(v) The expenses must be limited to a specific number of competitive days in any one calendar year as may be determined by the *Governing Body* in the country from which the nomination is made. The expenses are deemed to include reasonable travelling time and practice days in connection with the competitive days.

e. Celebrities, Business Associates, etc.
An *Amateur golfer* who is invited to take part in a competition for reasons unrelated to *golf skill* may receive expenses.

f. Exhibitions
An *Amateur golfer* who is participating in an exhibition in aid of a recognised charity may receive expenses, provided that the exhibition is not run in connection with another golfing event.

g. Sponsored Handicap Competitions
An *Amateur golfer* may receive expenses when competing in a sponsored handicap competition, provided the competition has been approved as follows:

(i) Where the competition is to take place in the player's own country, the annual approval of the *Governing Body* must first be obtained in advance by the sponsor; and

(ii) Where the competition is to take place in more than one country or involves golfers from another country, the approval of the two or more *Governing Bodies* must first be obtained in advance by the sponsor. The application for this approval should be sent to the *Governing Body* in the country where the competition commences.

Rule 5 – Instruction

Definitions
All defined terms are in *italics* and are listed alphabetically in the Definitions section – see pages 529–532.

5-1. General
Except as provided in the *Rules*, an *Amateur golfer* must not receive payment or compensation for giving *instruction* in playing golf.

5-2. Where Payment Permitted
a. Schools, Colleges, etc.
An *Amateur golfer*, who is an employee of an educational institution or system, may receive payment or compensation for golf *instruction* to students of the institution or system, provided that during a year the total time devoted to golf *instruction* comprises less than 50 percent of the time spent in the performance of all duties as such an employee.

b. Junior Golfers
An *Amateur golfer* may receive expenses, not exceeding the actual expenses incurred, for giving golf *instruction* to *junior golfers* as part of a programme which has been approved in advance by the *Governing Body*.

5-3. Instruction in Writing
An *Amateur golfer* may receive payment or compensation for *instruction* in writing, provided his ability or reputation as a golfer was not a major factor in his employment or in the commission or sale of his work.

Note: *Instruction* does not cover the many psychological aspects of the game or the Rules or Etiquette of Golf.

Rule 6 – Use of Golf Skill or Reputation

Definitions
All defined terms are in *italics* and are listed alphabetically in the Definitions section – see pages 529–532.

6-1. General
Except as provided in the *Rules*, an *Amateur golfer* of *golf skill or reputation* must not use that skill or reputation to promote, advertise or sell anything or for any financial gain.

6-2. Lending Name or Likeness
An *Amateur golfer* of *golf skill or reputation* must not use that skill or reputation to obtain payment, compensation, personal benefit or any financial gain for allowing his name or likeness to be used for the advertisement or sale of anything.

Note: An *Amateur golfer* may accept equipment from anyone dealing in such equipment provided no advertising is involved.

6-3. Personal Appearance
An *Amateur golfer* of *golf skill or reputation* must not use that skill or reputation to obtain payment, compensation, personal benefit or any financial gain for a personal appearance.

Exception: An *Amateur golfer* may receive actual expenses in connection with a personal appearance provided no golf competition or exhibition is involved.

6-4. Broadcasting and Writing
An *Amateur golfer* of *golf skill or reputation* must not use that skill or reputation to obtain payment, compensation, personal benefit or any financial gain for broadcasting concerning golf or writing golf articles or books.

Exception: An *Amateur golfer* may receive payment, compensation, personal benefit or any financial gain from broadcasting or writing provided:

(a) the player is actually the author of the commentary, article or books; and

(b) *instruction* in playing golf is not included.

6-5. Grants, Scholarships and Bursaries
An *Amateur golfer* of *golf skill or reputation* must not accept the benefits of a grant, scholarship or bursary, except one whose terms and conditions have been approved by the *Governing Body*.

6-6. Membership
An *Amateur golfer* of *golf skill or reputation* must not accept an offer of membership in a Golf Club without full payment for the class of membership if such an offer is made as an inducement to play for that Club.

Rule 7 – Other Conduct Incompatible with Amateurism

Definitions
All defined terms are in *italics* and are listed alphabetically in the Definitions section – see pages 529–532.

7-1. Conduct Detrimental to Amateurism
An *Amateur golfer* must not act in a manner which is considered detrimental to the best interests of the Amateur game.

7-2. Conduct Contrary to the Purpose and Spirit of the Rules
An *Amateur golfer* must not take any action, including actions relating to golf gambling, which is contrary to the purpose and spirit of the *Rules*.

Rule 8 – Procedure for Enforcement of the Rules

Definitions
All defined terms are in *italics* and are listed alphabetically in the Definitions section – see pages 529–532.

8-1. Decision on a Breach

If a possible breach of the *Rules* by a person claiming to be an *Amateur golfer* comes to the attention of the *Committee*, it is a matter for the *Committee* to decide whether a breach has occurred. Each case will be investigated to the extent deemed appropriate by the *Committee* and considered on its merits. The decision of the *Committee* shall be final, subject to an Appeal as provided in these *Rules*.

8-2. Enforcement

Upon a decision that a person has breached the *Rules*, the *Committee* may declare the Amateur Status of the person forfeited or require the person to refrain or desist from specified actions as a condition of retaining his Amateur Status.

The *Committee* must use its best endeavours to ensure that the person is notified and may notify any interested golf union of any action taken under Rule 8-2.

8-3. Appeals Procedure

Each *Governing Body* should put in place a procedure whereby any decision in respect of enforcement of these *Rules* may be appealed by the person affected by such decision.

Note: If a person, whose *Governing Body* is the R&A, is affected by a decision made by the Amateur Status Committee of the R&A in respect of the enforcement of these *Rules*, that person may raise an appeal of that decision with the Amateur Status Appeals Committee of the R&A.

Rule 9 – Reinstatement of Amateur Status

Definitions

All defined terms are in *italics* and are listed alphabetically in the Definitions section – see pages 529–532.

9-1. General

The *Committee* has sole power to reinstate a person to Amateur Status or to deny reinstatement, subject to an Appeal as provided in these *Rules*. Each application for reinstatement shall be considered on its merits.

9-2. Applications for Reinstatement

In considering an application for reinstatement, the *Committee* shall normally be guided by the following principles:

a. Awaiting Reinstatement

The Professional is considered to hold an advantage over the *Amateur golfer* by reason of having devoted himself to the game as his profession; other persons infringing the *Rules* also obtain advantages not available to the *Amateur golfer*. They do not necessarily lose such advantages merely by deciding to cease infringing the *Rules*. Therefore, an applicant for reinstatement to Amateur Status must undergo a period awaiting reinstatement as prescribed by the *Committee*.

The period awaiting reinstatement starts from the date of the person's last breach of the *Rules* unless the *Committee* decides that it starts from the date when the person's last breach became known to the *Committee*.

b. Period Awaiting Reinstatement

(i) Professionalism

The period awaiting reinstatement is normally related to the period the person was in breach. However, no applicant is normally eligible for reinstatement until he has conducted himself in accordance with the *Rules* for a period of at least one year.

It is recommended that the following guidelines on periods awaiting reinstatement are applied by the *Committee*:

Period of Breach:	Period Awaiting Reinstatement:
under 5 years	1 year
5 years or more	2 years

The *Committee* reserves the right to extend or to shorten such a period. Players of national prominence who have been in breach for more than five years are not normally eligible for reinstatement.

(ii) Other Breaches of the Rules

The period awaiting reinstatement is normally related to the seriousness of the breach i.e. the value of the excessive prize, the amount of unauthorised expenses received, etc. However, no applicant is normally eligible for reinstatement until he has conducted himself in accordance with the Rules for a period of at least one year. It is recommended that the *Committee* extends the period awaiting reinstatement as the seriousness of the breach increases, with a period of up to five years applied for the most serious cases.

The Committee reserves the right to extend or shorten such a period.

c. Number of Reinstatements

A person is not normally reinstated more than twice.

d. Status While Awaiting Reinstatement

During the period awaiting reinstatement an applicant for reinstatement must comply with these *Rules* as they apply to an *Amateur golfer*.

He is not eligible to enter competitions as an *Amateur golfer*. However, he may enter competitions and win a prize solely among members of a Club of which he is a member, subject to the approval of the Club; but he may not represent such Club against other Clubs.

9-3. Procedure for Applications

Each application for reinstatement must be submitted to the *Committee*, in accordance with such procedures as may be laid down and it must include such information as the *Committee* may require.

9-4. Appeals Procedure

Each *Governing Body* should put in place a procedure whereby any decision in respect of reinstatement of Amateur Status may be appealed by the person affected by such decision.

Note: If a person, whose *Governing Body* is the R&A, is affected by a decision made by the Amateur Status Committee of the R&A in respect of reinstatement of Amateur Status, that person may raise an appeal of that decision with the Amateur Status Appeals Committee of the R&A.

Rule 10 – Committee Decision

Definitions

All defined terms are in *italics* and are listed alphabetically in the Definitions section – see pages 529–532.

10-1. Committee's Decision

The *Committee's* decision is final, subject to an Appeal as provided in Rules 8-3 and 9-4.

10-2. Doubt as to Rules

If the *Committee* considers the case to be doubtful or not covered by the *Rules*, it may, prior to making its decision, consult with the Amateur Status Committee of the R&A.

INDEX

The Rules of Golf are here indexed according to the
pertinant rule number, definition or appendix that has gone before.

The R&A and the modern game

What is The R&A?

The R&A takes its name from The Royal and Ancient Golf Club of St Andrews, which traces its origins back 250 years. Although the golf club still exists to meet the needs of more than 2,000 international members, The R&A has grown apart to focus on its role as golf's world governance and development body and organiser of The Open Championship.

The R&A is the trust owned sports business behind The Open, golf's biggest major, and the international organisation that maintains the Rules of Golf. The R&A's activities are carried out with the consent of 127 national and international, amateur and professional organisations from 109 countries and on behalf of an estimated 26 million golfers in Europe, Africa, Asia, the Americas and Australasia.

The R&A and the United States Golf Association have jointly issued the Rules of Golf since 1952. The USGA is the governing body for the Rules of Golf in the United States and Mexico.

By making The Open Championship one of the world's great sporting events and an outstanding commercial success, The R&A is able to invest a substantial annual surplus for the development of the game through The R&A Foundation. The Foundation is the charitable body that channels money from The Open directly into grassroots development projects around the world.

Particular emphasis is placed on the encouragement of junior golf, on the development of the game in emerging golfing nations, on coaching and the provision of more accessible courses and improved practice facilities.

The R&A also provides best practice guidance on all aspects of golf course management, to help golf grow throughout the world in a commercially and environmentally sustainable way.

Useful links

www.randa.org
www.opengolf.com
www.bestcourseforgolf.org
www.theroyalandancientgolfclub.org
www.britishgolfmuseum.co.uk

The future of the game

The R&A is committed to promoting and developing golf both nationally and internationally. Two factors make this possible. One is the annual surplus from The Open Championship and the other is The R&A's

position of global influence. Combined, these give scope for the worldwide advancement of golf.

A major priority for The R&A is providing funding for training and the development of the game around the world. In recent years, a determined effort has been directed towards financing development in countries where golf is a relatively new sport. Major contributions are made to women's golf and the Golf Foundation receives substantial help to assist with its work of introducing young people to the game.

The R&A is highly conscious of the need and its obligation to serve the game worldwide. Since 1997 the R&A has provided financial support towards the African VI Tournament. The South American Men's and Women's Amateur Team Championship are also supported as are the equivalent events in the Asia-Pacific region.

The R&A Foundation supports University golf throughout Great Britain and Ireland with the aim of encouraging students to remain competitive while completing their formal education.

The R&A takes a lead in and offers advice on all aspects of golf course management worldwide, with developments in greenkeeping and environmental issues foremost among its concerns. Again, it is particularly concerned with offering assistance in countries where golf is still in its infancy.

Funding the future

Most of The R&A's funding comes from The Open Championship. Worldwide television rights are an important source of income, along with spectator ticket sales, catering, merchandising, corporate hospitality and sponsorship.

The Open Championship is broadcast throughout the world. In 2005 there were 1,661 global broadcast hours of the Open, an increase of 15 per cent over the previous year. The potential household reach was in the region of 404 million and covered 194 territories.

In recent years The R&A has been at the forefront of modern technology, extending its range of activities to New Media rights, whereby income is generated through the internet, and mobile communication devices. These, combined with merchandising, licensing and publishing, increase the ways in which The R&A is able to provide financial assistance for the development of golf throughout the world.

In 2004, Rolex began to sponsor the publication and distribution of the Rules of Golf book, ensuring that golfers worldwide can have a copy of the current

Rules of Golf free of charge. Over 4 million copies are distributed and the book is available in 21 different languages.

Marsh and McLennan, Nikon, Rolex, the Royal Bank of Scotland and Unisys are patrons of the Open Championship and they were joined in 2005 by luxury car-maker Lexus. Through their association with The Open, the Patrons provide additional income for the funding of golf development projects worldwide.

The rules of the game

In almost every country where the game is played, the rules followed are those set by The R&A. The exceptions are the USA and Mexico, where the code is set by the United States Golf Association, and Canada, which is self-governing but affiliated to The R&A. There are 127 associations and unions affiliated to The R&A.

The R&A is responsible for the Rules of Golf, the rules affecting equipment standards and the Rules of Amateur Status. The Rules of Golf Committee reviews the Rules of Golf and interprets and makes decisions on the playing Rules. The Equipment Standards Committee interprets and gives decisions on those rules that deal with the form and make of golf clubs and the specifications of the ball. The Amateur Status Committee reviews, interprets and amends the Rules of Amateur Status. All work closely with the equivalent committees of the USGA.

To meet the needs of golfers worldwide the Rules of Golf are published in over 20 languages and in audio CD format. Supplementing these are the biennial decisions on the Rules of Golf. Each volume contains over 1,100 decisions. Together, these help to ensure a consistent interpretation of the Rules throughout the world. The R&A also publish modifications of the Rules for golfers with disabilities.

The Rules Department answers thousands of queries from golf clubs, associations and professional tours on the playing Rules, the equipment Rules and on the Amateur Code.

Rules education is a priority for The R&A. Each year a Referees School is held in St Andrews, and overseas Rules Schools are held on a regular basis.

Since the beginning of 2001, countries visited include Argentina, Brazil, Ecuador, Venezuela, Germany, Luxembourg, Kenya, South Africa, United Arab Emirates, India, Thailand, the Dominican Republic and New Zealand. In 2005 schools were also held in China, South Korea and Singapore.

R&A Championships

The R&A promotes, organises and controls a number of championships and matches at both national and international level. Of these events, the biggest and most prestigious is The Open Championship.

In 1920, The Royal and Ancient Golf Club took over the running of the Amateur and Open Championships. The Boys Amateur Championship followed in 1948 and the British Youths Open Championship in 1963. The British Mid-Amateur Championship replaced the Youths event in 1995.

In 1969, the Club introduced the Seniors Open Amateur Championship for players aged 55 and over. In 1991, it became involved with and now organises the Senior British Open, in conjunction with the PGA European Seniors Tour. The Junior Open, first played in 1994, came under The R&A umbrella in 2000.

The Walker Cup, which is the largest of the international amateur matches, is played between teams from Great Britain & Ireland and the United States and is run jointly with the United States Golf Association.

The R&A also administers the St Andrews Trophy, inaugurated in 1956, and the Jacques Leglise Trophy, an event for boys. Both are played between teams from Great Britain & Ireland and the Continent of Europe. When these matches are played in Europe, they are organised by the European Golf Association.

The Great Britain and Ireland team selection for the Walker Cup and the St Andrews Trophy is undertaken by The R&A.

In 2004, The Royal and Ancient Golf Club transferred to The R&A the responsibilities and authority of the Club for all aspects of running championships and matches at national and international level.

Professional Governing Organisations

The Professional Golfers' Association (PGA)

The PGA was founded in 1901 and is the oldest PGA in the world. It has continued to develop steadily over the years; in the mid seventies major re-structuring of the Association took place with the development of two separate divisions. The administrative operation moved to The Belfry in 1977 to advance and develop the services available to club professionals, and shortly afterwards the Tournament Division established a new base at the Wentworth Club.

In 1984 it was decided that the interests of the members of each division would be best served by forming two separate organisations and on 1st January 1985 The Professional Golfers' Association and the European Tour became independent of each other.

The PGA's activities include training and further education of assistants and members and the organisation of tournaments at national level. National Headquarters is also the administrative base to accounts, marketing, media and the commercial activities of the Association.

There are seven regional headquarters located throughout Great Britain and Ireland and each region organises its own tournaments.

Classes of Membership

Class AA
Shall have passed the final examination of a PGA approved training programme, be actively engaged on a continuous basis in any field having a direct connection with or relevance to golf and has maintained the relevant requirements for the Professional Development Programme as defined by the Association.

Class A
Shall have passed the final examination of a PGA approved training programme and be actively engaged on a continuous basis in any field having a direct connection with or relevance to golf.

Class TP1
Must be a current full member of either the European Tour, Ladies' European Tour, European Seniors' Tour or any tour belonging to the International Federation of PGA Tours subject to the relevant categories as defined by the Association at the time.

Class TP2
Must be a current full member of either the European Tour, Ladies' European Tour or European Seniors' Tour subject to the relevant categories as defined by the Association at the time.

Class TP3
Must be a member of the PGA Europro Tour finishing 1–80 in the immediately preceding year's Order of Merit.

Life Member
Must be a member of the Association who has been recommended by the Board of Directors to Special General Meeting of the Association for appointment as a Life Member and whose recommendation has been approved.

Honorary Member
Must be a member who in the opinion of the Executive Committee through their past or continuing membership and contribution to the Association justifies retaining full privileges of membership as an Honorary Member.

Inactive Member
Shall have been a member for a continuous period of 10 years and no longer engaged in a direct or commercial capacity in the golf industry.

Retired Member
Shall be at least 60 years of age and been a member for a continuous period of 30 years.

Members may then proceed towards enhanced membership levels upon prior achievement and learning being recognised by the Association in the following categories:

Advanced Professional
Qualified members for a minimum of five years. Over a long period of time have demonstrated a strong desire to improve understanding and knowledge. Through attendance at courses, seminars and by taking qualifications related to golf, have shown commitment and willingness to develop self. Written articles and/or delivered seminars. Recognised by peers as having a high level of skill and knowledge, or qualified through the PGA Advanced Diploma programme.

Fellow Professional

Qualified members for a minimum of eight years. Consistently demonstrated an ability to work at a very high level with contribution to: development of players at different levels and/or a very strong reputation as an ethical business person who has established an extensive business that has benefited the golfing community and/or a strong reputation in equipment technology and/or repairs, which has enhanced the reputations of golf professionals and/or has written articles/books and presented at conferences, or has qualified through one of the PGA's Advanced Education programmes.

Advanced Fellow Professional

Qualified members for a minimum of ten years. Very strong national – possibly international reputation in one or more areas – coaching, course design, business, retail, equipment technology. Someone who has demonstrated strong leadership and has enhanced the world of golf and may have coached at the highest level or developed a programme method that has enabled ordinary players to play the game and/or designed a number of recognised golf courses and/or developed a strong golf business that has brought benefits to golf and golfers and/or innovative in the retail world with a strong sense of business ethics and/or designed/developed/improved some aspect of equipment (to include training aids or computer software) that has benefited a wide range of people in golf and/or a golf writer whose work has contributed strongly to the understanding and development of golf performance and/or a charity worker whose contribution has helped improve the lot of the disadvantaged through golf or in golf and/or written a number of books, articles and presented at prestigious conferences and seminars, or has qualified through one of the PGAís Advanced Education programmes.

Master Professional

Qualified member for a minimum of fifteen years. Held in high national or international esteem. Made a significant contribution to the development of golf as a player, coach, administrator or course designer. Someone who has left their mark at conferences and/or through books, articles or videos. Or an Advanced Fellow who has qualified as Master Professional through the submission of approved theses.

Tel 01675 470333   *Fax* 01675 477888

The Professional Golfers' Associations of Europe

The PGA of Europe was created in 1989 as an Association of national European PGAs to ensure uniformity of professional standards and objectives.

In its first ten years the PGAsE grew to a body comprising 33 member PGAs, five of them Associate Members from outside the continent of Europe. These 33 PGAs are made up of a total of 12,000 professionals comprising Directors of Golf, Club Professionals, Teaching Professionals, all of whom provide a comprehensive service to the entire golfing community.

The purpose of the PGAs of Europe is to:

(1) Unify and improve standards of education and qualification;

(2) Advise and assist golf professionals to achieve properly rewarded employment;

(3) Provide relevant playing opportunities;

(4) Be the central point of advice, information and support;

(5) Be a respected link with other golfing bodies throughout Europe and the rest of the world – all for the benefit of its members and the enhancement of the sport.

Tel 01675 477899

Fax 01675 4778980

European Tour

To be eligible to become a member of the European Tour a player must possess certain minimum standards which shall be determined by the Tournament Committee. In 1976 a Qualifying School for potential new members was introduced to be held annually. The leading players are awarded cards allowing them to compete in European Tour tournaments.

In 1985 the PGA European Tour became ALL EXEMPT with no more Monday pre-qualifying. Full details can be obtained from the Wentworth Headquarters.

Tel 01344 840400

Fax 01344 840444

Ladies' European Tour

The Evian Tour was founded in 1988 to further the development of women's professional golf throughout Europe and its membership is open to all nationalities. A qualifying school is held annually and an amateur wishing to participate must be 18 years of age and have a handicap of 1 or less. Full details can be obtained from the Tour Headquarters at Tytherington.

Tel 01625 611444

Fax 01625 610406

Amateur Governing Organisations

Home Unions

The English Golf Union

The English Golf Union was founded in 1924 and embraces 34 County Unions with 1895 affiliated clubs, 24 clubs overseas, and 500 Golfing Societies and Associations. Its objects are:

(1) To further the interests of Amateur Golf in England.

(2) To assist in maintaining a uniform system of handicapping.

(3) To arrange an English Championship; an English Strokeplay Championship; an English County Championship, International and other Matches and Competitions.

(4) To cooperate with The Royal and Ancient Golf Club of St Andrews and the Council of National Golf Unions.

(5) To cooperate with other National Golf Unions and Associations in such manner as may be decided.

Tel 01526 354500   *Fax* 01526 354020

The Scottish Golf Union

The Scottish Golf Union, the governing body for men's golf in Scotland, is dedicated to inspiring people to play golf and to developing and sustaining the game throughout the country. Its over-arching intention is to make golf available to everyone, in an environment that will actively encourage players to fulfil their potential.

Its aims are to:

* **Grow the game** – work with others to develop and grow golf in Scotland by increasing the number of people playing and enjoying golf

* **Develop talent** – ensure that the pathways to develop young talent are in place to produce excellent golfers at all levels

* **Support Clubs** – provide core services including handicapping, course rating, lobbying and training to improve the health and future success of member clubs.

The organisation is governed by a non executive board of directors who oversee the management of the organisation and an executive council, comprising representatives from 16 area associations, which provides the board with advice on policy matters.

Tel 01382 549500   *Fax* 01382 549510

Golfing Union of Ireland

The Golfing Union of Ireland, founded in 1891, embraces 398 Clubs. Its objects are:

(1) Securing the federation of the various Clubs.

(2) Arranging Amateur Championships, Inter-Provincial and Inter-Club Competitions, and International Matches.

(3) Securing a uniform standard of handicapping.

(4) Providing for advice and assistance, other than financial, to affiliated Clubs in all matters appertaining to Golf, and generally to promote the game in every way, in which this can be better done by the Union than by individual Clubs.

Its functions include the holding of the Close Championship for Amateur Golfers and Tournaments for Team Matches.

Its organisation consists of Provincial Councils in each of the four Provinces elected by the Clubs in the Province – each province electing a limited number of delegates to the Central Council which meets annually.

Tel 00 353 1 269411   *Fax* 00 353 1 693568

Welsh Golfing Union

The Welsh Golfing Union was founded in 1895 and is the second oldest of the four National Unions. Unlike the other Unions it is an association of Golf Clubs and Golfing Organisations. The present membership is 159. For the purpose of electing the Executive Council, Wales is divided into ten districts which between them return 22 members. The objects of the Union are:

(a) To take any steps which may be deemed necessary to further the interests of the amateur game in Wales.

(b) To hold a Championship Meeting or Meetings each year.

(c) To encourage, financially and/or otherwise, Inter-Club, Inter-County, and International Matches, and such other events as may be authorised by the Council.

(d) To assist in setting up and maintaining a uniform system of Handicapping.

(e) To assist in the establishment and maintenance of high standards of greenkeeping.

Note: The union recognises The Royal and Ancient Golf Club of St Andrews as the ruling authority.

Tel 01633 430830   *Fax* 01633 430843

The Council of National Golf Unions

At a meeting of Representatives of Golf Unions and Associations in Great Britain and Ireland, called at the special request of the Scottish Golf Union, and held in York, on 14th February, 1924, resolutions were adopted from which the Council of National Golf Unions was constituted.

The Council holds an Annual Meeting in March, and such other meetings as may be necessary. Two representatives are elected from each national Home Union – England, Scotland, Ireland and Wales and one from The Royal and Ancient Golf Club of St Andrews – and hold office until the next Annual meeting when they are eligible for re-election.

The principal function of the Council, as laid down by the York Conference, was to formulate a system of Standard Scratch Scores and Handicapping, and to co-operate with The Royal and Ancient Championship Committee in matters coming under their jurisdiction. The responsibilities undertaken by the Council at the instance of The Royal and Ancient Golf Club or the National Unions are as follows:

1   The Standard Scratch Score and Handicapping Scheme, formulated in March, 1926, approved by The Royal and Ancient, and last revised in 2001.
2   The nomination of one member on the Board of Management of The Sports Turf Research Institute, with an experimental station at St Ives, Bingley, Yorkshire.
3   The management of the Annual Amateur International Matches between the four countries – England, Scotland, Ireland and Wales.

Tel 00 353 416 861476

Government of the Amateur and Open Golf Championships

In December 1919, on the invitation of the clubs who had hitherto controlled the Amateur and Open Golf Championships, The Royal and Ancient Golf Club took over the government of those events. These two championships are now controlled by a committee appointed by The R&A.

Tel 01334 460000   *Fax* 01334 460001

European Golf Association
Association Européenne de Golf

Formed at a meeting held 20 November 1937 in Luxembourg, membership is restricted to European national amateur golf associations or unions. The Association concerns itself solely with matters of an international character. The association is presently composed of 30 member countries and is governed by the following committees:

- Executive Committee
- Championship Committee
- Professional Technical Committee
- EGA Handicapping & Course Rating Committee

Prime objectives are:

(a) To encourage international development of golf, to strengthen bonds of friendship existing between it members.
(b) To encourage the formation of new golf organisations representing the golf activities of European countries.
(c) To co-ordinate the dates of the Open and Amateur championships of its members and to arrange, in conjuction with host Federations, European championships and specific matches of international character.
(d) To ratify and publish the calendar dates of the major Amateur and Professional championships and international matches in Europe.
(e) To create and maintain international relationships in the field of golf and undertake any action useful to the cause of golf on an international level.

The headquarters are situated in Epalinges, Switzerland.

Ladies' Golf Union (LGU)

The Ladies' Golf Union was founded in 1893 with the following objectives:

(1) To promote the interests of the game of Golf.
(2) To obtain a uniformity of the rules of the game by establishing a representative legislative authority.
(3) To establish a uniform system of handicapping.
(4) To act as a tribunal and court of reference on points of uncertainty.
(5) To arrange the Annual Championship Competition and obtain the funds necessary for that purpose.

After 100 years, only the language has changed, the present Constitution defines the objectives as:

(1) To uphold the rules of golf, to advance and safeguard the interests of ladies' golf and to decide all doubtful and disputed points in connection therewith.
(2) To promote the CONGU Unified Handicapping System, the LGU Scratch Score System and the USGA Course Rating System. The National Organisations shall each retain responsibility to the LGU for the administration of the scratch score regulations as laid down by the LGU in their own country only.
(3) To employ the funds of the LGU in such manner as shall be deemed best for the interests of ladies' golf, with power to borrow or raise money for the same purpose.

Joan Neville, President of the Ladies' Golf Union

(4) To promote, maintain and regulate International Events, Championships and Competitions held under the LGU Regulations and to promote the interests of Great Britain and Ireland in ladies' international golf.
(5) To make, maintain, enforce and publish such regulations as may be considered necessary for the above purposes.

The constituents of the LGU are:

Home Countries. The English Ladies' Golf Association (founded 1952), the Irish Ladies' Golf Union (founded 1893), the Scottish Ladies' Golfing Association (founded 1904), the Welsh Ladies' Golf Union (founded 1904), ladies' golf clubs and ladies' sections of recognised golf clubs affiliated to these organisations.

Overseas. Affiliated overseas ladies' golf unions, ladies' golf clubs and ladies' sections of recognised golf clubs affiliated to their respective Overseas Union and affiliated Overseas Clubs.

Annual playing lady members of clubs within the above categories are regarded as members of the LGU.

The Rules of Golf and of Amateur Status, which the LGU is bound to uphold, are those published by R&A Rules Limited.

In endeavouring to fulfil its responsibilities towards advancing and safeguarding women's golf, the LGU maintains contact with other golfing organisations – The R&A, the Council of National Golf Unions, the United States Golf Association, the European Golf Association, the Ladies' Professional Golf Association, the Ladies' European Tour, the Golf Foundation, and the Central Council of Physical Recreation. This contact ensures that the LGU is informed of developments and projected developments and has an opportunity to comment upon and to influence the future of the game for women.

Either directly or through its constituent national organisations the LGU advises and is the ultimate authority on doubts or disputes which may arise in connection with the regulations governing competitions played under LGU conditions.

The funds of the LGU are administered by the Hon. Treasurer on the authority of the Executive Council, and the accounts are submitted annually for adoption in General Meeting.

The Women's British Open Championship, Ladies' British Open Amateur Championship, Ladies' British Open Amateur Stroke Play Championship, Girls' British Open Amateur Championship, Senior Ladies' British Open Amateur Championship, Ladies British Open Mid-Amateur Championship and the three Home International matches are organised annually by the LGU. International events involving a British or a combined British and Irish team are organised and controlled by the LGU when held in this country and the LGU acts as the coordinating body for the

Commonwealth Tournament in whichever of the five participating countries it is held, four-yearly, by rotation. The LGU selects and trains the teams, provides the uniforms and pays all the expenses of participation, whether held in this country or overseas. The LGU also maintains and regulates certain competitions played under handicap, such as Medal Competitions, Coronation Foursomes, Challenge Bowls, Australian Spoons and the LGU Pendant Competition.

The day-to-day administration of certain of the LGU responsibilities in the home countries is undertaken by the National Organisations, such as that concerned with Scratch Scores, and the organisation of LGU Medal Finals, Challenge Bowls and Australian Spoons Competitions.

Membership subscriptions to the LGU are assessed on a per capita basis of the club annual playing membership. To save unnecessary expense and duplication of administrative work in the home countries LGU subscriptions are collected by the National Organisations along with their own, and transmitted in bulk to the LGU.

Policy is determined and control over all the LGU's activities is exercised by an Executive Council of eight members – two each elected by the English, Irish, Scottish and Welsh national organisations. The Chairman is elected annually by the Councillors. During her chairmanship her place on the Council is taken by her Deputy and she has no vote other than a casting vote. The President and the Hon. Treasurer of the Union also attend and take part in Council meetings but with no vote. The Council meets five times a year.

The Annual General Meeting is held in January. The formal business includes presentation of the Report of the Executive Council for the previous year and of the Accounts for the last completed financial year, the election or re-election of President, Vice-Presidents, Hon. Treasurer and Auditors, and a report of the election of Councillors and their Deputies for the ensuing year. Voting is on the following basis: Executive Council, one each (8); members in the four home countries, one per national organisation (4) and in addition one per 100 affiliated clubs or part thereof; one per overseas Commonwealth Union with a membership of 50 or more clubs, and one per 100 individually affiliated clubs.

The Lady Golfer's Handbook is published annually by the LGU and is distributed free to all affiliated clubs and organisations. It is also available for sale to anyone interested. It contains the regulations for British Championships and international matches (with results for the past twenty years) and for LGU competitions, and sets out the Rules of the Union. It also lists every affiliated organisation, with names and addresses of officials, and every affiliated club, with Scratch Score, county of affiliation, number of members, and other useful information.

Tel 01334 475811   *Fax* 01334 472818

United States Golf Association

The USGA is the national governing body of golf in the United States, dedicated to promoting and conserving the best interests and true spirit of the game.

Founded on 22 December 1894 by representatives of five American golf clubs, the USGA was originally charged with conducting national championships, implementing a uniform code of rules, and maintaining a national system of handicapping.

Today, the principal functions of the association remain lagely unchanged. Each year, the USGA conducts thirteen national championships for amateur and professional golfers; biennial competitions include State Team Championships for men and women, the Walker Cup, Curtis Cup, and World Amateur Team Championships. In cooperation with the Royal & Ancient Golf Club of St. Andrews, Scotland, the USGA continues to write and interpret the Rules of Golf, and oversees the standards regulating the equipment used to play the game. The association also maintains a national handicapping system, providing handicap computation services to state and regional golf associations through the Golf Handicap and Information Network.

Additional responsibilities assumed by the association encompass turfgrass and environmental research conducted by the USGA Green Section; preservation and promotion of the game's rich history in the Museum and Archives; oversight of the Rules of Amateur Status; publication of *Golf Journal*, the USGA's official magazine; and direction of the USGA Members Program, with over 900,000 members globally. Since 1965, the USGA Foundation has functioned as the association's broad-based philanthropic arm, dedicated to maintaining and improving the opportunities for all individuals to participate fully in the game.

Tel 001 908 234 2300   *Fax* 001 908 234 9687

Championship and International Match Conditions

CHAMPIONSHIPS

Men

The Amateur Championship

The Championship, until 1982, was decided entirely by match play over 18 holes except for the final which was over 36 holes. Since 1983 the Championship has comprised two stroke play rounds of 18 holes each from which the leading 64 players and ties over the 36 holes qualify for the match play stages. Matches are over 18 holes except for the final which is over 36 holes. Full particulars can be obtained from the Championship Entries Department, R&A, St Andrews, Fife KY16 9JD. Tel: 01334 460000; Fax: 01334 460001.

The Seniors Open Amateur Championship

The Championship consists of 18 holes on each of two days, the leading 50 players and ties over the 36 holes then playing a further 18 holes the following day. Entrants must have attained the age of 55 years prior to the first day of the Championship. Full particulars can be obtained from the Championship Entries Department, R&A, St Andrews, Fife KY16 9JD. Tel: 01334 460000; Fax: 01334 460001.

National Championships

The English, Scottish, Irish and Welsh Amateur Championships are played by holes, each match consisting of one round of 18 holes except the final which is contested over 36 holes. Full particulars of conditions of entry and method of play can be obtained from the secretaries of the respective national Unions.

English Open Amateur Stroke Play Championship

The Championship consists of one round of 18 holes on each of two days after which the leading 40 and those tying for 40th place play a further two rounds. The remainder are eliminated.

Conditions for entry include: entrants must have a handicap not exceeding three; where the entries

exceed 130, an 18-hole qualifying round is held the day before the Championship. Certain players are exempt from qualifying.

Full particulars of conditions of entry and method of play can be obtained from the Secretary, English Golf Union, National Golf Centre, The Broadway, Woodhall Spa, Lincs LN10 6PU. Tel: 01526 354500; Fax: 01526 354020.

Scottish Open Amateur Stroke Play Championship

The Championship consists of one round of 18 holes on each of two days after which the leading 40 and those tying for 40th place play a further two rounds. The remainder are eliminated. Full particulars of conditions of entry and method of play can be obtained from the Scottish Golf Union, Scottish National Golf Centre, Drumoig, Leuchars, St Andrews, Fife KY16 0DW. Tel: 01382 549500   Fax: 01382 549510

British Mid-Amateur Championship

The Championship comprises two stroke play rounds of 18 holes from which the leading 64 players over the 36 holes qualify for the match play stages. All matches including the final are over 18 holes. Entrants must have attained the age of 25 years prior to the first day of the Championship. Full particulars can be obtained from the Championship Entries Department, R&A, St Andrews, Fife KY16 9JD. Tel: 01334 460000; Fax: 01334 460001.

Boys

Boys Amateur Championship

The Championship is played by match play, each match including the final consisting of one round of 18 holes. Entrants must be under 18 years of age at 00.00 hours on 1st January in the year of the Championship. Full particulars can be obtained from the Championship Entries Department, R&A, St Andrews, Fife KY16 9JD; Fax: 01334 460001.

Ladies

Ladies' British Open Amateur Championship

The Championship consists of one 18-hole qualifying round on each of two days. The players returning the 64 lowest scores over 36 holes shall qualify for match play. Ties for 64th place shall be decided by hole-by-hole play-off.

Ladies' British Open Amateur Stroke Play Championship

The Championship consists of 72 holes stroke play; 18 holes are played on each of two days after which the first 40 and all ties for 40th place qualify for a further 36 holes on the third day. Handicap limit is 6.4.

Ladies' British Open Championship

The Championship consists of 72 holes stroke play. 18 holes are played on each of four days, the field being reduced after the first 36 holes.

Entries accepted from lady amateurs with a handicap not exceeding scratch and from lady professionals. Full particulars for all three Championships can be obtained from the LGU, The Scores, St Andrews, Fife KY16 9AT. Tel: 01334 475811; Fax: 01334 472818.

National Championships

Conditions of entry and method of play for the English, Scottish, Welsh and Irish Ladies' Close Championships can be obtained from the Secretaries of the respective associations.

Other championships organised by the respective national associations, from whom full particulars can be obtained, include English Ladies', Intermediate, English Ladies' Stroke Play, Scottish Girls' Open Amateur Stroke Play (under 21) and Welsh Ladies' Open Amateur Stroke Play.

Girls

Girls' British Open Amateur Championship

The Championship consists of two 18-hole qualifying rounds, followed by match play in two flights, the first of 32 and the second of 16 players.

Conditions of entry include:

Entrants must be under 18 years of age on the 1st January in the year of the Championship.

Competitors are required to hold a certified LGU international handicap not exceeding 12.4.

Full particulars can be obtained from the Administrator, LGU, The Scores, St Andrews, Fife KY16 9AT. Tel: 01334 475811; Fax: 01334 472818.

National Championships

The English, Scottish, Irish and Welsh Girls' Close Championships are open to all girls of relevant nationality and appropriate age which may vary from country to country. A handicap limit may be set by some countries. Full particulars can be obtained via the secretaries of the respective associations.

International European Amateur Championships

Founded in 1986 by the European Golf Association, the International Amateur and Ladies Amateur Championships are held on an annual basis since 1990. These Championships consist of one round of 18 holes on each of three days after which the leading 70 and those tying for 70th place play one further round.

Full particulars of conditions of entry and method of play can be obtained from the European Golf Association.

Since 1991, the European Golf Association also holds an International Mid-Amateur Championship on an annual basis. The Championship consist of one round of 18 holes on each of two days after which the leading 90 and those tying for 90th place play one further round.

Full particulars of conditions of entry and method of play can be obtained from the European Golf Association.

Since 1996, the European Golf Association holds an International Seniors Championship for ladies and men on an annual basis.

The Championship consists of one round of 18 holes on each of two days after which there is a cut in both ladies and men categories. The competitors who pass the cut play one further round.

Additionally, a nation's cup is played within the tournament on the first two days. Teams are composed of three players. The two best gross scores out of three will count each day. The total aggregate of the four scores over two days will constitute the team's score.

Full particulars of conditions of entry and method of play can be obtained from the European Golf Association, Place de la Croix-Blanche 19, PO Box CH-1066 Epilanges, Switzerland. Tel: +41 21 784 32 32; Fax: +412 1 784 35 91.

TEAM CHAMPIONSHIPS

Men's Amateur

Walker Cup – Great Britain and Ireland v United States of America

Mr George Herbert Walker of the United States presented a Cup for international competition to be known as *The United States Golf Association International Challenge Trophy*, popularly described as *The Walker Cup*.

The Cup shall be played for by teams of amateur golfers selected from Clubs under the jurisdiction of the United States Golf Association on the one side and from England, Ireland, Scotland and Wales on the other.

The Walker Cup shall be held every two years in the United States of America and Great Britain and Ireland alternately.

The teams shall consist of not more than ten players and a captain.

The contest consists of four foursomes and eight singles matches over 18 holes on each of two days.

St Andrews Trophy – Great Britain and Ireland v Continent of Europe

First staged in 1956, the St Andrews Trophy is a biennial international match played between two selected teams of amateur golfers representing Great Britain and Ireland and the Continent of Europe. Each team consists of nine players and the match is played over two consecutive days with four morning foursomes followed each afternoon by eight singles. Selection of the Great Britain and Ireland team is carried out by the R&A Selection Committee. The European Golf Association select the Continent of Europe team.

Eisenhower Trophy – Men's World Team Championship

Founded in recognition of the need for an official world amateur team championship, the first event was played at St Andrews in 1958 and the Trophy has been played for every second year in different countries around the world.

Each country enters a team of four players who play strokeplay over 72 holes, the total of the three best individual scores to be counted for each round.

European Team Championship

Founded in 1959 by the European Golf Association for competition among member countries of the Association. The Championship is held biennially and played in rotation round the countries, which are grouped in four geographical zones.

Each team consists of six players who play two qualifying rounds of 18 holes, the five best scores of each round constituting the team aggregate. Flights for match play are then arranged according to qualifying rankings. The match play consists of two foursomes and five singles on each of three days.

A similar championship is held in alternate years for Youths teams, under 21 years of age and every year for Boys teams, under 18 years of age.

Raymond Trophy – Home Internationals

The first official International Match recorded was in 1902 at Hoylake between England and Scotland who won 32 to 25 on a holes up basis.

In 1932 International Week was inaugurated under the auspices of the British Golf Unions' Joint Advisory Council with the full approval of the four National Golf Unions. The Council of National Golf Unions is now responsible for running the matches. Teams of 11 players from England, Scotland, Ireland and Wales engage in matches consisting of five foursomes and ten singles over 18 holes, the foursomes being in the morning and the singles in the afternoon. Each team plays every other team.

The eligibility of players to play for their country shall be their eligibility to play in the Amateur Championship of their country.

Sir Michael Bonallack Trophy – Europe v Asia /Pacific

First staged in 1998, the Sir Michael Bonallack Trophy is a biennial international match played between two selected teams of amateur golfers representing Europe and Asia/Pacific. Each team consists of 12 players and the match is played over three days with five four balls in the morning and five foursomes in the afternoon of the first two days, followed by 12 singles on the last day. Selection of the European team is carried out by the European Golf Association. The Asia/Pacific Golf Confederation selects the Asia/Pacific team.

Men's Professional

Ryder Cup – Europe v United States of America

This Cup was presented by Mr Samuel Ryder, St Albans, England (who died 2nd January, 1936), for competition between a team of British professionals and a team of American professionals. The trophy was first competed for in 1927. In 1929 the original conditions were varied to confine the British team to British-born professionals resident in Great Britain, and the American team to American-born professionals resident in the United States, in the year of the match. In 1979 the British team was extended to include European players. The matches are played biennially, in alternate continents, in accordance with the conditions as agreed between the respective PGAs.

World Cup (formerly Canada Cup)

Founded in America by John Jay Hopkins in 1955 as a team event for professional golfers with the object of spreading international goodwill. Each country is represented by two players with the best team score over 72 holes producing the winners of the World Cup and the best individual score the winner of the International Trophy. Played for annually (but not in 1986) the event was run until 1999 by the International Gold Association but it is now organised as part of the new World Championship series of events by representatives of the leading professional golf tours.

Seve Ballesteros Trophy – Great Britain and Ireland v Continent of Europe

A match instituted in 2000 at Sunningdale and played along Ryder Cup lines in alternate years.

Llandudno Trophy (PGA Cup) – Great Britain and Ireland v United States of America

The Llandudno International Trophy was first awarded to England in 1939 after winning the first Home Tournament Series against Ireland, Scotland and Wales. With the outbreak of war the series was abolished and the Trophy formed part of Percy Alliss's personal collection. After Percy's death his son Peter donated the Llandudno Trophy to be awarded to the winner of the then annual PGA Cup Match. Now it is a biennial match played since 1973 in Ryder Cup format between Great Britain and Ireland and the United States of America involving top club professionals. No prize money is awarded to the competitors who compete solely for their country. Selection of the Great Britain and Ireland team is determined following completion of the Glenmuir PGA Club Professionals Championship.

Ladies Amateur

Curtis Cup – Great Britain and Ireland v United States

For a trophy presented by the late Misses Margaret and Harriot Curtis of Boston, USA, for biennial competition between amateur teams from the United States of America and Great Britain and Ireland. The match is sponsored jointly by the United States Golf Association and the Ladies' Golf Union who may select teams of not more than eight players.

The match consists of three foursomes and six singles of 18 holes on each of two days. The foursomes are played each morning.

Vagliano Trophy – Great Britain and Ireland v Continent of Europe

For a trophy presented to the Comité des Dames de la Fédération Française de Golf and the Ladies' Golf Union by Monsieur AA Vagliano, originally for annual competition between teams of women amateur golfers from France and Great Britain and Ireland but, since 1959, by mutual agreement, for competition between teams from the Continent of Europe and Great Britain and Ireland.

The match is played biennially, alternately in Great Britain and Ireland and on the Continent of Europe, with teams of not more than nine players plus a non-playing captain. The match consists of four foursomes and eight singles of 18 holes on each of two days. The foursomes are played each morning.

Espirito Santo Trophy – Women's World Team Championship

Presented by Mrs Ricardo Santo of Portugal for biennial competition between teams of not more than three women amateur golfers who represent a national association affiliated to the World Amateur Golf Council. First competed for in 1964. The Championship consists of 72 holes strokeplay, 18 holes on each of four days, the two best scores in each round constituting the team aggregate.

Lady Astor Trophy – Commonwealth Tournament

For a trophy presented by Nancy, Viscountess Astor CH, and the Ladies' Golf Union for competition once in every four years between teams of women amateur golfers from Commonwealth countries.

The inaugural Commonwealth Tournament was played at St Andrews in 1959 between teams from Australia, Canada, New Zealand, South Africa and Great Britain and was won by the British team. The tournament is played in rotation in the competing countries, for the present Great Britain, Australia, Canada, New Zealand and South Africa, each country being entitled to nominate six players including a playing or non-playing captain.

Each team plays every other team and each team match consists of two foursomes and four singles over 18 holes. The foursomes are played in the morning.

European Team Championships

Founded in 1959 by the European Golf Association for competition among member countries of the Association. The Championship is held biennially and played in rotation round the countries, which are grouped in four geographical zones.

Each team consists of six players who play two qualifying rounds of 18 holes, the five best scores of each round constituting the team aggregate. Flights for matchplay are then arranged according to qualifying rankings. The matchplay consists of two foursomes and five singles on each of three days.

A similar championship is held in alternate years for Lady Juniors teams, under 21 years of age and every year for Girls teams, under 18 years of age.

Home Internationals

Teams from England, Scotland, Ireland and Wales compete annually for a trophy presented to the LGU by the late Mr TH Miller. The qualifications for a player being eligible to play for her country are the same as those laid down by each country for its Close Championship.

Each team, consisting of not more than eight players, plays each other team, a draw taking place to decide the order of play between the teams. The matches consist of three foursomes and six singles, each of 18 holes.

Ladies Professional

Solheim Cup – Europe v United States

The Solheim Cup, named after Karsten Solheim who founded the sponsoring Ping company, is the women's equivalent of the Ryder Cup. In 1990 the inaugural competition between the top women professional golfers from Europe and America took place in Florida.

The matches are played biennially in alternate continents. The format is foursomes and fourball matches on the first two days, followed by singles on the third in accordance with the conditions as agreed between the Evian Tour and the United States LPGA Tour.

World Cup

Started in 2000 by the LPGA and the International Management Group, the event is held along similar lines to the men's World Cup with each country represented by two players. There is also an individual competiton incorporated in the regulations. It had been planned as an annual fixture but after the inaugural event held in Malaysia the 2001 Championship scheduled for Adelaide was cancelled. The event was restarted in South Africa in 2004.

Boys

R & A Trophy – Home Internationals

Teams comprising 11 players from England, Scotland, Ireland and Wales compete against one another over three days in a single round robin format. Each fixture comprises five morning foursomes followed by ten afternoon singles.

To be eligible for selection, players must be under the age of 18 at 00.00 hours on 1st January in the year of the matches and have eligibility to play in their national championships

Jacques Léglise Trophy – Great Britain and Ireland v Continent of Europe

The Jacques Léglise Trophy is an annual international match played between two selected teams of amateur boy golfers representing Great Britain and Ireland and the Continent of Europe. Each team consists of nine players and the match is played over two consecutive days with four morning foursomes followed each afternoon by eight singles. Selection of the Great Britain and Ireland team is carried out by the R&A Selection Committee. The European Golf Association selects the Continent of Europe team

To be eligible for selection, players must be under the age of 18 at 00.00 hours on 1st January in the year of the matches.

Junior Ryder Cup

First staged in 1995, the Junior Ryder Cup is a biennial international match played between two selected teams of amateur golfers representing Europe and the USA, prior to the Ryder Cup. Each team consists of four girls and four boys under 16 as well as two girls and two boys under 18. The match is played over two consecutive days with six four balls on the first day and six mixed four balls on the second day.

Selection of the European team is carried out by the European Golf Association. Players and captains are then invited to watch the Ryder Cup.

Girls

Home Internationals

Teams from England, Scotland, Ireland and Wales compete annually for the Stroyan Cup. The qualifications for a player for the Girls' International Matches shall be the same as those laid down by each country for its Girls' Close Championship except that a player shall be under 18 years on the 1st January in the year of the Tournament.

Each team, consisting of not more than eight players, plays each other team, a draw taking place to decide the order of play between the teams. The matches consist of three foursomes and six singles, each of 18 holes.

Websites

The R&A	www.randa.org
United States Golf Association	www.usga.org
English Golf Union	www.englishgolfunion.org
Golf Union of Ireland	www.gui.ie
Scottish Golf Union	www.scottishgolfunion.org
Welsh Golf Union	www.welshgolf.org
European Golf Association	www.ega-golf.ch
Ladies Golf Union (LGU)	www.lgu.org
English Ladies (ELGA)	www.englishladiesgolf.org
Irish Ladies (ILGU)	www.ilgu.ie
European Tour	www.europeantour.com
US PGA Tour	www.pgatour.com
Australasian Tour	www.pgatour.com.au
Asian Tour	www.asiantour.com
Japanese Tour	www.jgto.org
South African Sunshine Tour	www.sunshinetour.com
US LPGA Tour	www.lpga.com
Ladies European Tour (LET)	www.ladieseuropeantour.com
The Open	www.opengolf.com
US Open	www.usopen.com
The Masters	www.masters.org
US PGA Championship	www.pga.com/pgachampionship/2007
World Golf Championships	www.worldgolfchampionships.com
PGA (The Belfry)	www.pga.info
PGAs of Europe	www.pgae.com
PGA of America	www.pga.com

Websites

Severiano Ballesteros	www.seveballesteros.com
Michael Campbell	www.cambogolf.com
Paul Casey	www.paul-casey.com
Darren Clarke	www.darrenclarke.com
Ernie Els	www.ernieels.com
Nick Faldo	www.nickfaldo.com
Padraig Harrington	www.padraigharrington.com
David Howell	www.davidhowellgolf.com
Bernhard Langer	www.bernhardlanger.de
Paul McGinley	www.paulmcginley.net
Phil Mickelson	www.phil-mickelson.com
Colin Montgomerie	www.colinmontgomerie.com
Jack Nicklaus	www.nicklaus.com
Ian Poulter	www.ianpoulter.co.uk
Adam Scott	www.adamscott.com.au
Henrik Stenson	www.henrikstenson.com
Lee Westwood	www.westyuk.com
Tiger Woods	www.tigerwoods.com
Ian Woosnam	www.woosie.com

PART XIII

Golf History

R&A Championships and Team Events

In 2004, The Royal and Ancient Golf Club of St Andrews handed over responsibility for the running of The Open Championship and other key golfing events to The R&A. The following entries highlight the history of championship and team events that are organised by The R&A, or by The R&A in conjunction with other bodies.

Championships that come solely under the

administration of The R&A are:

The Open Championship
The Amateur Championship
The Seniors Open Amateur Championship
The British Mid-Amateur Championship
The Boys Amateur Championship
The Junior Open Championship

Team events organised by The R&A and other bodies are:

The Walker Cup (R&A/USGA)
The World Amateur Team Championships (R&A as part of the International Golf Federation)
The St Andrews Trophy (R&A/EGA)
The Jacques Léglise Trophy (R&A/EGA)

Team events run by The R&A are:

The Boys Home Internationals

The aim has been to focus on the origins and structural growth of each event, noting key changes in format and conditions. Current championship and international match conditions are defined elsewhere in the volume.

The Open Championship

The Open Championship began in 1860 at the Prestwick Golf Club and the original trophy was an ornate Challenge Belt, which was subscribed for and presented by the members of Prestwick Golf Club. What is now recognised as the first Open Championship was played on October 17, 1860 at the end of the club's autumn meeting. A total of eight players competed in three rounds of the 12 hole course. No prize money for The Open was awarded until 1863, the winner simply received the Belt for a year. In 1863 it was decided to give money prizes to those finishing second, third and fourth but the winner still only received the Belt. It was not until 1864 that the winner received £6. The average field in the 1860s was only 12 players.

The original rules of the competition stated that the Belt "becomes the property of the winner by being won three years in succession". In 1870 Tom Morris Junior won for the third year in a row and

took possession of the Belt. He won £6 for his efforts out of a total prize fund of £12. No Championship was held in 1871 whilst the Prestwick Club entered into discussions with The Royal and Ancient Golf Club and the Honourable Company of Edinburgh Golfers over the future of the event.

One of the key turning points in the history of The Open took place at the Spring Meeting of the Prestwick Club in April 1871. At that meeting it was proposed that "in contemplation of St Andrews, Musselburgh and other clubs joining in the purchase of a Belt to be played for over four or more greens, it is not expedient for the Club to provide a Belt to be played solely for at Prestwick". From that date onwards, The Open ceased to be under the sole control of the Prestwick Golf Club.

The Championship was played again under this new agreement in 1872. A new trophy, the now famous Claret Jug, was purchased for presentation to the winner. Until 1891, the host club remained responsible for all arrangements regarding the Championship, which continued to be played over 36 holes in one day.

In 1892, the Honourable Company of Edinburgh Golfers took four radical steps to transform The Open Championship. It extended play to 72 holes over two days, imposed an entrance charge for all competitors, changed the venue to a new course at Muirfield and increased the total prize fund from £28 10s to £100. These actions were all taken unilaterally by the club. The increased purse to counter a rival tournament held at Musselburgh.

A meeting was held between the three host clubs on June 9, 1893, for the purpose of "placing the competition for The Open Championship on a basis more commensurate with its importance than had hitherto existed". Three resolutions were agreed. Two English clubs, St George's, Sandwich and Royal Liverpool, would be invited to stage the Championship and join the rota, now of five clubs. Four rounds of 18 holes would be played over two days. Each of the five clubs would contribute £15 annually to the cost and the balance would come from an entry fee for all competitors. The prize money would total £100, with £30 for the winner. The date of each year's championship would be set by the host club, which would also bear any additional necessary expenses. The representatives of the five clubs became known as the Delegates of the Associated Clubs.

The increasing number of entrants caused a cut to be introduced after two rounds in 1898 and between 1904 and 1906 the Championship was played over three days. It then reverted to two days in 1907 with the introduction of qualifying rounds. The entire field had to qualify and there were no exemptions.

On January 24, 1920, the Delegates of the Associated Clubs asked The Royal and Ancient Golf Club to take over "the management of the Championship and the custody of the Challenge Cup". The new Championship Committee was responsible for running both The Open and Amateur Championships and in 1922 it was decided that The Open should only be played over links courses. The venues included in today's circuit are: Carnoustie, Muirfield, Royal Birkdale, Royal Liverpool, Royal Lytham & St Annes, Royal St George's, Royal Troon, the Old Course, St Andrews and Turnberry.

Prestwick, birth place of The Open, played host to the Championship 24 times, the last in 1925. Other courses that have been used in the past are: Musselburgh (1874, 1877, 1880, 1883, 1886, 1889); Royal Cinque Ports, Deal (1909, 1920); Princes, Sandwich (1932) and Royal Portrush (1951).

The Open was played regularly over three days starting in 1926, with a round on each of the first two days and two rounds on the final day, which from 1927 onwards was a Friday. The total prize money had reached £500 by 1939. The prize money was increased to £1000 in 1946 and reached £5000 in 1959.

As The Open went into its second century in the 1960s, it grew tremendously both as a Championship and a spectator event. In 1963, exemptions from pre-qualifying were introduced for the leading players. Play was extended to four days in 1966, with the Championship finishing with a single round on the Saturday. In 1968, a second cut after 54 holes was introduced to further reduce the field on the final day and this remained in effect until 1985. To cope with the increasing spectator numbers, facilities were much improved. Grandstands were first introduced at The Open in 1960 and they became a standard feature from 1963 onwards.

Regional qualifying had been tried as an experiment for one year in 1926, but did not become a regular feature until 1977. Some players were exempt but had to take part in final qualifying, while others were exempt from both regional and final qualifying.

Since 1980, the Championship has been scheduled to end on a Sunday instead of a Saturday. In the event of a tie for first place, play-offs took place over 36 holes up until 1963, when they were reduced to 18 holes. In 1985 a four-hole play-off, followed by sudden death, was introduced.

The Open Championship was first televised live in 1955 and was shown on the BBC. The first live broadcast to America in 1966 and was shown on ABC. In 1958, the television coverage lasted for a total of three hours, one and a half hours on each of the final two days. In 2003, The Open was broadcast for 1318 hours worldwide.

Admission charges to watch The Open were introduced in 1926. Paid admissions went over 50,000 for the first time in 1968 at Carnoustie and over 100,000 for the first time at St Andrews in 1978.

The 200,000 attendance figure was reached for the first time at St Andrews in 1990. A new record was set at the Home of Golf in 2000 when 238,787 watched the Millennium Open.

Growth of prize money

Year	Total Prize Money	First Prize
1860	£0	£0
1863	£10	£0
1866	£11	£6
1876	£27	£10
1886	£20	£8
1896	£90	£30
1906	£115	£50
1914	£125	£50
1926	£200	£75
1936	£500	£100
1946	£1,000	£150
1956	£3,750	£1,000
1966	£15,000	£2,100
1976	£75,000	£7,500
1986	£634,000	£70,000
1996	£1,400,000	£200,000
2006	£4,000,000	£720,000

Harry Vardon has scored most victories in The Open Championship. He won it six times between 1896 and 1914. JH Taylor, James Braid, Peter Thomson and Tom Watson have each won The Open five times. Between 1860 and 1889, all of The Open winners were Scottish. John Ball Jr became the first Englishman and the first amateur to claim the title in 1890. Arnaud Massy from France was the first Continental winner in 1907.

Four players have completed a hat trick of Open wins: Tom Morris Jr 1868–1870; Jamie Anderson 1877–1879; Bob Ferguson 1880–1882; Peter Thomson 1954–1956.

The Open Championship has been won by an amateur player six times – John Ball in 1890, Harold Hilton in 1892 and 1897 and Bobby Jones in 1926, 1927 and 1930. Walter Hagen was the first native born American to win The Open when he triumphed in 1922. Jock Hutchison, who had won the previous year, was resident in America at the time of his victory although he was born in St Andrews.

The Amateur Championship

What became recognised as the first Amateur Championship was held at Hoylake in 1885, although earlier national amateur competitions had been played at St Andrews in 1857, 1858 and 1859. The Royal and Ancient Golf Club had considered holding a national amateur tournament in 1876 but decided not to proceed with the idea.

In December 1884, Thomas Owen Potter, the Secretary of Royal Liverpool Golf Club, proposed holding a championship for amateur players. The event was to be open to members of recognised clubs and it was hoped that it would make the game more popular and lead to improved standards of play.

A total of 44 players from 12 clubs entered the first championship. The format was matchplay, with the ruling that if two players tied they would both advance to the following round and play one another again. There were three semi-finalists: John Ball, Horace Hutchinson and Allan Macfie. After a bye to the final, Macfie beat Hutchinson 7 and 6.

Following the success of the first tournament, it was agreed that a championship open to all amateurs should be played at St Andrews, Hoylake and Prestwick in rotation.

Twenty-four golf clubs subscribed for the trophy, which was acquired in 1886. They were:

Alnmouth	Royal Aberdeen
Bruntsfield	Royal Albert (Montrose)
Dalhousie	Royal and Ancient
Formby	Royal Blackheath
Gullane	Royal Burgess
Honourable Company	Royal Liverpool
Innerleven	Royal North Devon
Kilspindie	Royal St George's
King James VI	Royal Wimbledon
New North Berwick	Tantallon
Panmure	Troon
Prestwick	West Lancashire

Representatives, known as Delegates of the Associated Clubs, were elected from these clubs to run the Championship and in 1919 they approached The Royal and Ancient Golf Club to accept future management. The Club agreed and in 1920 the Championship Committee was formed. This committee became responsible for organising the Amateur and Open and for making decisions on the conditions of play. It was not until 1922, however, that the 1885 tournament was officially recognised as the first Amateur Championship and Allan Macfie the first winner.

The venue circuit gradually increased. Sandwich was added in 1892, Muirfield in 1897 and Westward Ho! in 1912. The Championship was first played in Ireland in 1949 (Portmarnock) and Wales in 1951 (Porthcawl).

Prior to 1930, only two non-British players won the Amateur Championship, Walter Travis, in 1904, and Jesse Sweetser, in 1926. Both hailed from the United States, the former via Australia.

The Americans began to make their presence felt more strongly in the 1930s, with four Americans winning five Amateur Championships. Bobby Jones took the title at St Andrews 1930, the year in which he achieved the Grand Slam. Lawson Little won in 1934 and 1935, Robert Sweeney in 1937 and Charles Yates in 1938.

Following a break during World War II, the Amateur Championship resumed in 1946 at Birkdale when the handicap limit was raised from one to two as an encouragement to those amateurs who had been on war service.

Attempts were made during the 1950s and 1960s to control large numbers of entries. In 1956 the field was limited to 200 so that the quarter-finals, semi-finals and the final could be played over 36 holes. This experiment lasted two years, when it was decided

that only the semi-finals and final should be played over two rounds.

Regional qualifying over 36 holes was introduced in 1958 when 14 courses throughout the UK were selected. Using this method, the original entry of 500 was reduced to 200. Any player with a handicap of 5 or better could enter.

In 1961 regional qualifying was scrapped and the quarter-finals and semi-finals were played over 18 holes. Then in 1983 at Turnberry, 36 holes of stroke-play qualifying were introduced during the first two days. This format continues, with the leading 64 players and ties qualifying for the matchplay stages.

The Seniors Open Amateur Championship

The Seniors Open Amateur Championship was the first tournament to be initiated by The Royal and Ancient Golf Club. Prestwick Golf Club had been responsible for starting the Open Championship, while Royal Liverpool Golf Club had introduced the Amateur Championship. Other events, such as the Boys Amateur Championship and Boys Home Internationals were introduced by private individuals and then handed over, by agreement, to The R&A.

The Seniors Open Amateur Championship made its début at Formby in 1969. It started as a means to help choose a Great Britain and Ireland team for the World Senior Amateur Team Championship which had begun in 1967 at Pinehurst, North Carolina, under the auspices of the World Amateur Golf Council.

Initially, the World Senior team event was to be played every two years, alternating with the competition for the Eisenhower Trophy, but it did not survive beyond 1969. The success of the Seniors Open Amateur Championship, however, was evident from the start and it became a popular event in its own right.

It began as a 36-hole strokeplay event, held over two days for players over the age of 55. The handicap limit was 5 and the field was restricted to 100. The winner was Reg Pattinson, who duly played his way onto the World Amateur Senior team in which he was partnered by Alan Cave, AL Bentley and AT Kyle. The short-lived World Senior event was played in 1969 over the Old Course at St Andrews and was won for the second time by the United States. Great Britain and Ireland finished third out of an entry of only 13 teams.

Before the present format was introduced, various alternatives were tried, in order to satisfy increasing entry demands. Two courses were used in 1971, allowing an entry of 250 with the handicap limit being increased to 9. In 1974, a limit of 130 was imposed. Subsidiary competitions were introduced according to age group: 55–59, 60–64 and 65 and over. A fourth age group was added in 1975 for the over 70s and the entry limit was increased to 140. The special categories changed in 1999, to one only for the 65 and over age group.

Today, the Seniors Open Amateur Championship attracts a wide international field, the initial entry of

252 playing two rounds and the leading 50 and ties completing a further 18 holes. Scotland's Charlie Green is a multiple winner, having claimed the title six times between 1988 and 1994.

The British Mid-Amateur Championship

Introduced as recently as 1995, the British Mid-Amateur Championship does, in fact, have a longer history. In 1954, Sam Bunton founded the British Youths Open Championship for amateurs and assistant professionals under the age of 22. The aim was to provide a category for those players who were too old to compete in the Boys Championship, which was aimed at players under the age of 18, and who were too young to compete in major tournaments.

By the end of the 1950s, the British Youths had become a well established, popular event, with entries exceeding 200. Its future came under discussion in 1962 when the Championship Committee of The Royal and Ancient Golf Club was notified that the sponsor was anxious to hand over the event to another authority.

The Club began its administration of the British Youths in 1963. While it continued as an event for youths aged between 18 and 22, it was decided that professional entries should be excluded. The Club also changed the title, renaming it the British Youths Open Amateur Championship.

The handicap limit, which was originally not more than six, was lowered in 1968 to four. At the same time, the minimum age requirement was abolished and this format continued until 1994 when the Championship Committee decided to replace it with a new fixture. The British Mid-Amateur Championship made its début at Sunningdale in 1995. Entries are accepted from competitors who have reached the age of 25 prior to the first day of the Championship.

The Boys Amateur Championship

The Boys Amateur Championship was introduced in 1921 for the under-16 age group. For the first two years it was played at Royal Ascot under the guidance of DM Mathieson and Colonel Thomas South. In 1948, Colonel South announced his intention to retire from his duties in connection with the event, declaring that "nothing would give him greater pleasure than that The Royal and Ancient Golf Club should take over the conduct of the Championship".

The venue for the first Boys Amateur Championship to be played under the administration of The Royal and Ancient Golf Club was the Old Course, St Andrews. A sub-committee ran the event until 1952 when it was finally handed over to the Championship Committee.

Since that year a prize has been presented to the best performing 16-year-old. This, the Peter Garner Bowl, commemorates the death of a competitor who was killed in a road accident while returning from the 1951 Championship.

Sir Michael Bonallack enjoyed early success in the Boys Amateur Championship. He won in 1952, and

went on to win the Amateur Championship in 1961, 1965, 1968, 1969 and 1970.

Professionals who won the title earlier in their careers include Ronan Rafferty (1979), José Maria Olazábal (1983) and more recently Sergio García (1997).

The Junior Open Championship

Inaugurated in 1994, the Junior Open Championship came under The R&A's administrative control in 2000. All national golf unions and federations are invited to send their leading boy and girl under the age of 16 to compete in the three-day event. In previous years, only one player from each union or federation could enter. The biennial event is run on a course close to the Open Championship and in the same week so that all participants can spend time watching the world's finest players in action.

To encourage entries worldwide, there are three categories of competition defined by varying handicap limits. Gold is for those with a handicap of 3 and under, silver 4–9 and bronze 10–21.

TEAM EVENTS

The Walker Cup

The United States Golf Association International Challenge Trophy was originally intended to be presented to the winners of a contest to which all golf playing nations would be invited to compete. However, as The R&A tactfully pointed out to their counterparts in the USGA in 1921, the only two countries capable of entering a team were Great Britain and America.

By this simple process of elimination the trophy presented by USGA President George Herbert Walker became the focal point of a biennial series between the finest amateur players of the two countries. The first unofficial match was played in 1921 on the eve of the Amateur Championship at Hoylake when 19-year-old Bobby Jones helped the American team to a 9–3 victory. For the next three years the event was played annually, but settled into its biennial pattern after 1924.

It was not until 1938 at St Andrews that Great Britain and Ireland recorded a first victory. In 1965 the score was 11–11. There were 2 halved matches.

Only after the first success in America, with a 12½–11½ victory at Peachtree in Georgia in 1989, did the GB&I team finally end American domination of the matches. In the years that followed there were home wins at Porthcawl in 1995 and Nairn in 1999. The GB&I run of victories continued at Ocean Forest in 2001 and Ganton in 2003.

The man after whom the trophy and the matches are named has another claim to a place in world history. His grandson, George Herbert Walker Bush and his great-grandson have both held office as President of the United States of America.

The Eisenhower Trophy

The United States Golf Association approached The Royal and Ancient Golf Club in 1958 with the proposal that the two bodies should sponsor a worldwide amateur golf event. The new competition would take place biennially in non-Walker Cup years, with the first being played at St Andrews in 1958. All golfing bodies that observed the Rules of Golf and Amateur Status as approved by The R&A and the USGA were invited to send one representative to a meeting in Washington at which President Dwight D Eisenhower presented a trophy to be awarded to the winning country. The committee of the event was to be known as the World Amateur Golf Council, which is now the International Golf Federation.

The key objective of the new council was "to foster friendship and sportsmanship among the peoples of the world through the conduct of an Amateur Team Championship for The Eisenhower Trophy". In a meeting with the President in the Rose Garden of the White House, Eisenhower offered his advice to the delegates: "I suggest, aside from the four hotshot golfers you bring, that you take along some high-handicap fellows and let them play at their full handicaps … This way golf doesn't become so important". This observation led to the creation of a "Delegates and Duffers Cup" for officials and non-playing captains.

The format decided for the Eisenhower Trophy was strokeplay. Each team consisted of four players who would play four rounds. The team score for each round was the three best individual scores. The first competition was held in St Andrews and attracted teams from 29 countries. After 72 holes of golf, the American and Australian teams were both tied on an aggregate score of 918. A play-off was held and the Australian team won by two strokes. So far this has been the only play-off in the history of the event.

Australia went on to win the trophy twice more, in 1966 and 1996. However, the USA have dominated the event, winning it 13 times in total. The Great Britain and Ireland team have won four times, in 1964, 1976, 1988 and 1998. In 2002 teams were reduced from four to three players with the best two scores counting in each round and for the first time England, Ireland, Scotland and Wales entered separate teams. A parallel event for women, playing for the Espirito Santo Trophy, is held at the same venue prior to the Eisenhower.

The St Andrews Trophy

In November 1955 the Championship Committee of The Royal and Ancient Golf Club put forward a recommendation that "the European Golf Association should be approached with a view to arranging an international match between a Great Britain and Ireland and European side".

The GB&I team, captained by Gerald Micklem, duly triumphed by a score of 12½ to 2½ in the first match played over the West Course at Wentworth in 1956.

A resounding success, the event immediately established as a biennial event in non-Walker Cup years and in 1964 the Club donated the St Andrews Trophy to be presented to the winning team.

Although Great Britain and Ireland have dominated the match, winning 23 of the 26 encounters, the Continent of Europe had a convincing victory at Villa d'Este in Italy in 1998 and suffered only a narrow 13–11 defeat at Turnberry in 2000. GB&I are the current holders of the trophy, winning in 2006 by a score of 15–9 at Marianske Lazne.

The Jacques Léglise Trophy

The annual boys international match involving GB&I against a team from the Continent of Europe was introduced in 1958. This event was dominated originally by the British and Irish side, which won every match through 1966 prompting the match to be discontinued because it was a one-sided affair.

The match was revived in 1977 when the Continental team won by 7 points to 6. A new trophy, donated by Jean-Louis Dupont on behalf of Golf de Chantilly in memory of Jacques Léglise, a leading French golf administrator, was presented for the first time in 1978 when the Continental team again won. Since then the Continental side has triumphed six times, most recently in 2006 at Marianske Lazne, where they won by a decisive 19½–4½. The match was played in conjunction with the Boys Amateur Championship and Home International events until 1995. Since 1996 it has been played concurrently with the St Andrews Trophy, although the Jacques Léglise Trophy remains an annual competition.

The Boys Home Internationals

Introduced at Dunbar in 1923, the Boys Home Internationals started off as a match played between England and Scotland. It was traditionally associated with the Boys Amateur Championship, being played the day before and acting as a prelude to the main event.

The Royal and Ancient Golf Club accepted responsibility for the Boys Amateur Championship in 1949 and with it the running of the England v Scotland match. The Championship Committee originally carried out team selection. Today, representatives from the four Home Unions select the teams.

In 1972, a team match between Ireland and Wales was added to the fixture and the current format was established in 1996. The four home countries compete against one another over three consecutive days in a round robin series. Each fixture comprises five morning foursomes, followed by ten afternoon singles.

In 1997, there was a significant break with the past when, for the first time, the venue chosen for the Boys Home Internationals differed to that for the Boys Amateur Championship. This practice has remained, helping to shape the individual identity of the inter-national matches. Since 1985, the R&A Trophy has been awarded to the winning team.

Important dates in the history of St Andrews, The Open Championship and The R&A

1123	King David I grants links to powerful bishops of St Andrews.
1413	Evidence of golf being a regular pastime on the links.
1457	Golf so popular King James II of Scotland bans it.
1552	Archbishop Hamilton grants citizens rights to play games including golf on the links.
1744	First set of 13 rules laid out by golfers at Leith.
1754	22 noblemen and gentlemen of Kingdom of Fife form Society of St Andrews golfers.
1764	Golfers at St Andrews play over 18 instead of 22 holes – and set the standard for a round of golf.
1834	King William IV confers his patronage and the Society of St Andrews Golfers becomes The Royal and Ancient Golf Club.
1854	Royal and Ancient Clubhouse completed and opened.
1860	First Open Championship held at Prestwick.
1870	Tom Morris jr wins Open Belt for third time and gets to keep it.
1872	The Royal and Ancient Golf Club, Prestwick and Honourable Company of Edinburgh Golfers take over running of The Open. Golfers play for Claret Jug.
1873	First Open at St Andrews.
1894	United States Golf Association responsible for rules in USA.
1897	Formation of Rules of Golf Committee. The R&A becomes accepted authority for golf.
1904	Lost ball search time reduced from 10 to five minutes.
1919	The R&A takes charge of Amateur Championship.
1920	The R&A takes charge of The Open Championship. First R&A–USGA rules conference.
1926	The Open Championship first played over three days.
1929	USGA legitimises larger ball (1.68in.). Smaller ball (1.62in.) still used elsewhere.
1929	Steel shafts legalised for the first time.
1951	The R&A and USGA meet to unify rules.
1952	The R&A and USGA standardise rules except for ball size. Stymie abolished.
1955	First live television coverage of The Open Championship.
1956	First four-yearly rules revision.
1960	First grandstands erected at The Open Championship.
1963	Last 36-hole play-off for The Open Championship.
1966	First live coverage of The Open Championship in America.
1966	Open played over four days for first time at Muirfield.
1974	Bigger American size ball (1.68in. compulsory in The Open Championship for first time).
1980	The Open Championship finished on a Sunday for the first time at Muirfield.
1985	The R&A change play-off arrangements for The Open Championship to four holes.
1984	New dropping procedure at arms length from the shoulder.
1990	The American size 1.68in. ball becomes the only legal ball.
2004	The Royal and Ancient Golf Club celebrates 250th anniversary.

Interesting Facts and Unusual Incidents

Royal golf clubs

● The right to the designation *Royal* is bestowed by the favour of the Sovereign or a member of the Royal House. In most cases the title is granted along with the bestowal of royal patronage on the club. The Perth Golfing Society was the first to receive the designation *Royal*. That was accorded in June 1833. King William IV bestowed the honour on The Royal and Ancient Club in 1834. The most recent Club to be so designated is Royal Mayfair Golf & Country Club in Edmonton, Canada. The club was granted Royal status in October 2005. The next most recent was Royal Marianske Lazne in the Czech Republic. In 2003, the club was given the Royal title as a result of its association in the early part of the 20th century with King Edward VII. A full list of Royal clubs can be found on pages 626–627.

Royal and Presidential golfers

● In the long history of the Royal and Ancient game no reigning British monarch has played in an open competition. In 1922 the Duke of Windsor, when Prince of Wales, competed in The Royal and Ancient Autumn Medal at St Andrews. He also took part in competitions at Mid-Surrey, Sunningdale, Royal St George's and in the Parliamentary Handicap. He occasionally competed in American events, sometimes partnered by a professional. On a private visit to London in 1952, he competed in the Autumn competition of Royal St George's at Sandwich, scoring 97. As Prince of Wales he played on courses all over the world and, after his abdication, as Duke of Windsor he continued to enjoy the game for many years.

● King George VI, when still Duke of York, in 1930, and the Duke of Kent, in 1937, also competed in the Autumn Meeting of The Royal and Ancient, when they had formally played themselves into the Captaincy of the Club and each returned his card in the medal round. So too did Prince Andrew, the Duke of York, when he became captain in 2003. He also played in the medal and won the mixed foursomes the following day playing with former British ladies champion Julie Otto who works at The R&A.

● King Leopold of Belgium played in the Belgian Amateur Championship at Le Zoute, the only reigning monarch ever to have played in a national championship. The Belgian King played in many competitions subsequent to his abdication. In 1949 he reached the quarter-finals of the French Amateur Championship at St Cloud, playing as Count de Rethy.

● King Baudouin of Belgium in 1958 played in the triangular match Belgium–France–Holland and won his match against a Dutch player. He also took part in the Gleneagles Hotel tournament (playing as Mr B. de Rethy), partnered by Dai Rees in 1959.

● United States President George Bush accepted an invitation in 1990 to become an Honorary Member of The Royal and Ancient Golf Club of St Andrews. The honour recognised his long connection and that of his family with golf and The R&A. Both President Bush's father, Prescott Bush Sr, and his grandfather, George Herbert Walker – who donated the Walker Cup – were presidents of the United States Golf Association. Other Honorary Members of the R&A include Kel Nagle, Jack Nicklaus, Arnold Palmer, Gene Sarazen, Peter Thomson, Roberto de Vicenzo, Gary Player and five-times Open Championship winner Tom Watson, who was made an honorary member in 1999 on his 50th birthday.

● In September 1992, The Royal and Ancient Golf Club of St Andrews announced that His Royal Highness The Duke of York had accepted the Club's invitation of Honorary Membership. The Duke of York is the sixth member of the Royal Family to accept membership along with Their Royal Highnesses The Duke of Edinburgh and The Duke of Kent. He has since become a single handicapper, and has appeared in a number of pro-ams, partnering The Open and Masters champion Mark O'Meara to victory in the Alfred Dunhill Cup pro-am at St Andrews in 1998. His Royal Highness was Captain for 2003–2004, the year in which the Club celebrated its 250th anniversary.

First lady golfer

● Mary Queen of Scots, who was beheaded on 8th February, 1587, was probably the first lady golfer so mentioned by name. As evidence of her indifference to the fate of Darnley, her husband who was murdered at Kirk o' Field, Edinburgh, she was charged at her trial with having played at golf in the fields beside Seton a few days after his death.

Record championship victories

● In the Amateur Championship at Muirfield, 1920, Captain Carter, an Irish golfer, defeated an American entrant by 10 and 8. This is the only known instance where a player has won every hole in an Amateur Championship tie.

● In the final of the Canadian Ladies' Championship at Rivermead, Ottawa, in 1921, Cecil Leitch defeated Mollie McBride by 17 and 15. Miss Leitch lost only 1 hole in the match, the ninth. She was 14 up at the end of the first round, making only 3 holes necessary in the second. She won 18 holes out of 21 played, lost 1, and halved 2.

● In the final of the French Ladies' Open Championship at Le Touquet in 1927, Mlle de la Chaume (St Cloud) defeated Mrs Alex Johnston (Moor Park) by 15 and 14, the largest victory in a European golf championship.

● At Prestwick in 1934, W. Lawson Little of Presidio, San Francisco, defeated James Wallace, Troon Portland, by 14 and 13 in the final of the Amateur Championship, the record victory in the Championship. Wallace failed to win a single hole.

Players who have won two or more majors in the same year

(The first Masters Tournament was played in 1934.)

1922 Gene Sarazen – USPGA, US Open
1924 Walter Hagen – USPGA, The Open
1926 Bobby Jones – US Open, The Open
1930 Bobby Jones – US Open, The Open (Bobby Jones also won the US Amateur and British Amateur in this year.)
1932 Gene Sarazen – US Open, The Open
1941 Craig Wood – Masters, US Open
1948 Ben Hogan – USPGA, US Open
1949 Sam Snead – USPGA, Masters
1951 Ben Hogan – Masters, US Open
1953 Ben Hogan – Masters, US Open, The Open
1956 Jack Burke – USPGA, Masters
1960 Arnold Palmer – Masters, US Open
1962 Arnold Palmer – Masters, The Open
1963 Jack Nicklaus – USPGA, Masters
1966 Jack Nicklaus – Masters, The Open
1971 Lee Trevino – US Open, The Open
1972 Jack Nicklaus – Masters, The Open
1974 Gary Player – Masters, The Open
1975 Jack Nicklaus – USPGA, Masters
1977 Tom Watson – Masters, The Open
1980 Jack Nicklaus – USPGA, US Open
1982 Tom Watson – US Open, The Open
1990 Nick Faldo – Masters, The Open
1994 Nick Price – The Open, US PGA
1998 Mark O'Meara – Masters, The Open
2000 *Tiger Woods – US Open, The Open, USPGA

*Woods also won the 2001 Masters to become the first player to hold all four Majors at the same time. He was 65-under-par for the four events.

Outstanding records in championships, international matches and on the professional circuit

● The record number of victories in The Open Championship is six, held by Harry Vardon who won in 1896-98-99-1903-11-14.

● Five-time winners of the Championship are J.H. Taylor in 1894-95-1900-09-13; James Braid in 1901-05-06-08-10; Peter Thomson in 1954-55-56-58-65 and Tom Watson in 1975-77-80-82-83. Thomson's 1965 win was achieved when the Championship had become a truly international event. In 1957 he finished second behind Bobby Locke. By winning again in 1958 Thomson was prevented only by Bobby Locke from winning five consecutive Open Championships.

● Four successive victories in The Open by *Young Tom Morris* is a record so far never equalled. He won in 1868-69-70-72. (The Championship was not played in 1871.) Other four-time winners are Bobby Locke in 1949-50-52-57, Walter Hagen in 1922-24-28-29, Willie Park 1860-63-66-75, and *Old Tom Morris* 1861-62-64-67.

● Since the Championship began in 1860, players who have won three times in succession are Jamie Anderson, Bob Ferguson, and Peter Thomson.

● Robert Tyre Jones won The Open three times in 1926-27-30; the Amateur in 1930; the American Open in 1923-26-29-30; and the American Amateur in 1924-25-27-28-30. In winning the four major golf titles of the world in one year (1930) he achieved a feat unlikely ever to be equalled. Jones retired from competitive golf after winning the 1930 American Open, the last of these Championships, at the age of 28.

● Jack Nicklaus has had the most wins (six) in the US Masters Tournament, followed by Arnold Palmer with four.

● In modern times there are four championships generally regarded as standing above all others – The Open, US Open, US Masters, and USPGA. Five players have held all these titles, Gene Sarazen, Ben Hogan, Gary Player, Jack Nicklaus and Tiger Woods in that order. In 1978 Nicklaus became the first player to have held each of them at least three times. His record in these events is: The Open 1966-70-78; US Open 1962-67-72-80; US Masters 1963-65-66-72-75-86; USPGA 1963-71-73-75-80. His total of major championships is now 18. In 1998 at the age of 58, Nicklaus finished joint sixth in the Masters. By not playing in The Open Championship that year, he ended a run of 154 successive major championships for which he was eligible (stretching back to 1957).

In 1953 Ben Hogan won the Masters, US Open and The Open, but did not compete in the USPGA because of a dates clash with The Open.

In 2000 Tiger Woods won the US Open by 15 strokes (a major championship record), The Open by eight strokes, and the USPGA in the play-off. In 2001 he then added the Masters winning by two shots to become the first player to hold all four major titles at the same time. He was 65-under-par for the four events.

● In the 1996 English Amateur Championship at Hollinwell, Ian Richardson (50) and his son, Carl, of Burghley Park, Lincolnshire, both reached the semi-finals. Both lost.

● The record number of victories in the US Open is four, held by Willie Anderson, Bobby Jones, Ben Hogan and Jack Nicklaus.

● Bobby Jones (amateur), Gene Sarazen, Ben Hogan, Lee Trevino, Tom Watson and Tiger Woods are the only players to have won The Open and US Open Championships in the same year. Tony Jacklin won The Open in 1969 and the US Open in 1970 and for a few weeks was the holder of both.

● In winning the Amateur Championship in 1970 Michael Bonallack became the first player to win in three consecutive years.

● The English Amateur record number of victories is held by Michael Bonallack, who won the title five times.

● John Ball holds the record number of victories in the Amateur Championship, which he won eight times. Next comes Michael Bonallack (who was internationally known as The Duke) with five wins.

● Cecil Leitch and Joyce Wethered each won the British Ladies' title four times.

● The Scottish Amateur record was held by Ronnie Shade, who won five titles in successive years, 1963 to 1967. His long reign as Champion ended when he was beaten in the fourth round of the 1968 Championship after winning 44 consecutive matches.

● Joyce Wethered established an unbeaten record by winning the English Ladies' in five successive years from 1920 to 1924 inclusive.

● In winning the Amateur Championships of Britain and America in 1934 and 1935 Lawson Little won 31 consecutive matches. Other dual winners of these championships in the same year are R.T. Jones (1930) and Bob Dickson (1967).

● Peter Thomson's victory in the 1971 New Zealand Open Championship was his ninth in that event.

● In a four-week spell in 1971, Lee Trevino won in succession the US Open, the Canadian Open and The Open Championships.

● Michael Bonallack and Bill Hyndman were the Amateur Championship finalists in both 1969 and 1970. This was the first time the same two players reached the final in successive years.

● On the US professional circuit the greatest number of consecutive victories is 11, achieved by Byron Nelson in 1945. Nelson also holds the record for most victories in one calendar year, again in 1945 when he won a total of 18 tournaments.

● Raymond Floyd, by winning the Doral Classic in March 1992, joined Sam Snead as the only winners of US Tour events in four different decades.

● Sam Snead won tournaments in six decades. His first win was the 1936 West Virginia PGA. In 1980 he won the Golf Digest Commemorative and in 1982 the Legends of Golf with Don January.

● Neil Coles has won official Tour events in six decades. His first victory was in 1958 and he was a winner on the European Senior Tour in June 2000 when he took the Microlease Jersey Senior Open. Coles still plays well enough to beat his age. Now 67, he shot a closing 64 in the final round of the 2003

Travis Perkins Senior Open over the Edinburgh course he helped design.

● Jack Nicklaus and the late Walter Hagen have had five wins each in the USPGA Championship. All Hagen's wins were at match play; all Nicklaus's at stroke play.

● In 1953 Flory van Donck of Belgium had seven major victories in Europe, including The Open Championships of Switzerland, Italy, Holland, Germany and Belgium.

● Mrs Anne Sander won four major amateur titles each under a different name. She won the US Ladies' in 1958 as Miss Quast, in 1961 as Mrs Decker, in 1963 as Mrs Welts and the British Ladies' in 1980 as Mrs Sander.

● The highest number of appearances in the Ryder Cup matches is held by Nick Faldo who made his eleventh appearance in 1997.

● The greatest number of appearances in the Walker Cup matches is held by Irishman Joe Carr who made his tenth appearance in 1967.

● In the Curtis Cup Mary McKenna made her ninth consecutive appearance in 1986.

● Players who have represented their country in both Walker and Ryder Cup matches are: for the United States, Fred Haas, Ken Venturi, Gene Littler, Jack Nicklaus, Tommy Aaron, Mason Rudolph, Bob Murphy, Lanny Wadkins, Scott Simpson, Tom Kite, Jerry Pate, Craig Stadler, Jay Haas, Bill Rodgers, Hal Sutton, Curtis Strange, Davis Love III, Brad Faxon, Scott Hoch, Phil Mickelson, Corey Pavin, Justin Leonard, Tiger Woods and David Duval; and for Great Britain & Ireland, Norman Drew, Peter Townsend, Clive Clark, Peter Oosterhuis, Howard Clark, Mark James, Michael King, Gordon Brand Jr, Paul Way, Ronan Rafferty, Sandy Lyle, Philip Walton, David Gilford, Colin Montgomerie, Peter Baker, Padraig Harrington and Andrew Coltart.

Remarkable recoveries in matchplay

● There have been two remarkable recoveries in the Walker Cup Matches. In 1930 at Sandwich, J.A. Stout, Great Britain, round in 68, was 4 up at the end of the first round against Donald Moe. Stout started in the second round, 3, 3, 3, and was 7 up. He was still 7 up with 13 to play. Moe, who went round in 67, won back the 7 holes to draw level at the 17th green. At the 18th or 36th of the match, Moe, after a long drive placed his iron shot within three feet of the hole and won the match by 1 hole.

● In 1936 at Pine Valley, George Voigt and Harry Girvan for America were 7 up with 11 to play against Alec Hill and Cecil Ewing. The British pair drew level at the 17th hole, or the 35th of the match, and the last hole was halved.

● In 1965 Piccadilly Match Play Championship Gary Player beat Tony Lema after being 7 down with 17 to play.

● Bobby Cruickshank, the old Edinburgh player, had an extraordinary recovery in a 36-hole match in a

USPGA Championship for he defeated Al Watrous after being 11 down with 12 to play.
● In a match at the Army GC, Aldershot, on 5th July, 1974, for the Gradoville Bowl, M.C. Smart was 8 down with 8 to play against Mike Cook. Smart succeeded in winning all the remaining holes and the 19th for victory.
● In the 1982 Suntory World Match Play Championship Sandy Lyle beat Nick Faldo after being 6 down with 18 to play.

Oldest champions

The Open Championship: Belt Tom Morris in 1867 – 46 years 99 days. *Cup* Roberto de Vicenzo, 44 years 93 days, in 1967; Harry Vardon, 44 years 42 days, in 1914; J.H. Taylor, 42 years 97 days, in 1913.
Amateur Championship Hon. Michael Scot, 54, at Hoylake in 1933.
British Ladies Amateur Mrs Jessie Valentine, 43, at Hunstanton in 1958.
Scottish Amateur J.M. Cannon, 53, at Troon in 1969.
English Amateur Terry Shingler, 41 years 11 months at Walton Heath 1977; Gerald Micklem, 41 years 8 months, at Royal Birkdale 1947.
Welsh Amateur John Jermine, 56, at St David's, in 2000
US Open Hale Irwin, 45, at Medinah, Illinois, in 1990.
US Amateur Jack Westland, 47, at Seattle in 1952 (He had been defeated in the 1931 final, 21 years previously, by Francis Ouimet).
US Masters Jack Nicklaus, 46, in 1986.
European Tour Des Smyth, 48 years, 14 days, Madeira Open 1982; Neil Coles, 48 years 14 days, Sanyo Open 1982
European Senior Tour Neil Coles, 65, in 2000
USPGA Julius Boros, 48, in 1968. Lee Trevino, 44, in 1984.
USPGA Tour Sam Snead, 52, at Greensborough Open in 1965. Sam Snead, 61, equal second in Glen Campbell Open 1974.

Youngest champions

The Open Championship: Belt Tom Morris, Jr, 17 years 5 months, in 1868. *Cup* Willie Auchterlonie, 21 years 24 days, in 1893; Tom Morris, Jr, 21 years 5 months, in 1872; Severiano Ballesteros, 22 years 103 days, in 1979.
Amateur Championship J.C. Beharrell, 18 years 1 month, at Troon in 1956; R. Cole (RSA) 18 years 1 month, at Carnoustie in 1966.
British Ladies Amateur May Hezlett, 17, at Newcastle, Co. Down, in 1899; Michelle Walker, 18, at Alwoodley in 1971.
English Amateur Nick Faldo, 18, at Lytham St Annes in 1975; Paul Downes, 18, at Birkdale in 1978; David Gilford, 18, at Woodhall Spa in 1984; Ian Garbutt, 18, at Woodhall Spa in 1990; Mark Foster, 18, at Moortown in 1994.
English Amateur Strokeplay Ronan Rafferty, 16, at Hunstanton in 1980.
British Ladies Open Strokeplay Helen Dobson, 18, at Southerness in 1989.

British Boys Championship Mark Mouland (WAL) 15 years 120 days at Sunningdale in 1976; Pablo Martin (ESP) 15 years 120 days at Ganton 2001.

More records can be found on pages 404–415

Disqualifications

Disqualifications are now numerous, usually for some irregularity over signing a scorecard or for late arrival at the first tee. We therefore show here only incidents in major events involving famous players or players who were in a winning position or incidents which were in themselves unusual.

● J.J. McDermott, the American Open Champion 1911–12, arrived for The Open Championship at Prestwick in 1914 to discover that he had made a mistake of a week in the date the championship began. The American could not play, as the qualifying rounds were completed on the day he arrived.
● In the Amateur Championship at Sandwich in 1937, Brigadier-General Critchley, arriving at Southampton from New York on the Queen Mary, which had been delayed by fog, flew by specially chartered aeroplane to Sandwich. He circled over the clubhouse, so the officials knew he was nearly there, but he arrived six minutes late, and his name had been struck out. At the same championship a player, entered from Burma, who had travelled across the Pacific and the American Continent, and was also on the Queen Mary, travelled from Southampton by motor car and arrived four hours after his starting time to find after journeying more than halfway round the world he was struck out.
● An unprecedented disqualification was that of A. Murray in the New Zealand Open Championship, 1937. Murray, who was New Zealand Champion in 1935, was playing with J.P. Hornabrook, New Zealand Amateur Champion, and at the 8th hole in the last round, while waiting for his partner to putt, Murray dropped a ball on the edge of the green and made a practice putt along the edge. Murray returned the lowest score in the championship, but he was disqualified for taking the practice putt.
● At The Open Championship at St Andrews in 1946, John Panton, Glenbervie, in the evening practised putting on a green on the New Course, which was one of the qualifying courses. He himself reported his inadvertence to The Royal and Ancient and he was disqualified.
● At The Open Championship, Sandwich, 1949, C. Rotar, an American, qualified by four strokes to compete in the championship but he was disqualified because he had used a putter which did not conform to the accepted form and make of a golf club, the socket being bent over the centre of the club head. This is the only case where a player has been disqualified in The Open Championship for using an illegal club.
● In the 1957 American Women's Open Championship, Mrs Jackie Pung had the lowest score, 298

over four rounds, but lost the championship. The card she signed for the final round read *five* at the 4th hole instead of the correct *six*. Her total of 72 was correct but the error, under rigid rules, resulted in her disqualification. Betty Jameson, who partnered Mrs Pung and also returned a wrong score, was also disqualified.

● Mark Roe and Jesper Parnevik were disqualified in bizarre circumstances in the 2003 Open at Royal St George's, Sandwich. Roe had shot 67 to move into contention but it was discovered after they left the recorder's hut that they had not exchanged cards. Roe's figures were returned on a card with Parnevik's name on it and vice versa. The R&A have since changed the rules to allow the official scorer to erase the wrong name and put the correct one on the card ensuring a Roe–Parnevik incident can never happen again.

● Teenager Michelle Wie will not be allowed to forget her début on the LPGA Tour as a professional in the Samsung World Championship. Although she completed four rounds and finished fourth behind Annika Sörenstam, she was disqualified for taking a drop nearer to the hole in the third round. A reporter, Michael Bamberger from *Sports Illustrated*, saw the incident but did not report it to officials until the next day after he had spoken with his editor. Officials only decided to disqualify the youngster after measuring out distances at the spot where she took the drop with a yard of string.

● Kevin Stadler, son of Ryder Cup and former Masters champion Craig Stadler, was disqualified in the 2005 Funai Classic in Orlando for disclosing he had a bent shaft in his wedge. Lying 163rd in the money list and needing a good finish to keep his card, he was lying joint fifth going into the final round. He discovered the shaft of his wedge was bent on the second hole on the final day and was disqualified for playing an illegal club – ironically, one that could never have helped him play a decent shot.

Longest match

● W.R. Chamberlain, a retired farmer, and George New, a postmaster at Chilton Foliat, on 1st August, 1922, met at Littlecote, the 9-hole course of Sir Ernest Wills, and agreed to play every Thursday afternoon over the course. This continued until New's sudden death on 13th January, 1938. An accurate record of the match was kept, giving details of each round including wind direction and playing conditions. In the elaborate system nearly two million facts were recorded. They played 814 rounds, and aggregated 86,397 strokes, of which Chamberlain took 44,008 and New 42,371. New, therefore, was 1,637 strokes up. The last round of all was halved, a suitable end to such an unusual contest.

Longest ties

● The longest known ties in 18-hole match play rounds in major events were in an early round of the News of the World Match Play Championship at Turnberry in 1960, when W.S. Collins beat W.J.

Branch at the 31st hole, and in the third round of the same tournament at Walton Heath in 1961 when Harold Henning beat Peter Alliss also at the 31st hole.

● In the 1970 Scottish Amateur Championship at Balgownie, Aberdeen, E. Hammond beat J. McIvor at the 29th hole in their second round tie.

● C.A. Palmer beat Lionel Munn at the 28th hole at Sandwich in 1908. This is the record tie of the British Amateur Championship. Munn has also been engaged in two other extended ties in the Amateur Championship. At Muirfield, in 1932, in the semi-final, he was defeated by John de Forest, the ultimate winner, at the 26th hole, and at St Andrews, in 1936, in the second round he was defeated by J.L. Mitchell, again at the 26th hole.

The following examples of long ties are in a different category for they occurred in competitions, either stroke play or match play, where the conditions stipulated that in the event of a tie, a further stated number of holes had to be played – in some cases 36 holes, but mostly 18. With this method a vast number of extra holes was sometimes necessary to settle ties.

● The longest known was between two American women in a tournament at Peterson (New Jersey) when 88 extra holes were required before Mrs Edwin Labaugh emerged as winner.

● In a match on the Queensland course, Australia, in October, 1933, H.B. Bonney and Col H.C.H. Robertson versus B.J. Canniffe and Dr Wallis Hoare required to play a further four 18-hole matches after being level at the end of the original 18 holes. In the fourth replay Hoare and Caniffe won by 3 and 2 which meant that 70 extra holes had been necessary to decide the tie.

● After finishing all square in the final of the Dudley GC's foursomes competition in 1950, F.W. Mannell and A.G. Walker played a further three 18-hole replays against T. Poole and E. Jones, each time finishing all square. A further 9 holes were arranged and Mannell and Walker won by 3 and 2 making a total of 61 extra holes to decide the tie.

● R.A. Whitcombe and Mark Seymour tied for first prize in the Penfold £750 Tournament at St Annes-on-Sea, in 1934. They had to play off over 36 holes and tied again. They were then required to play another 9 holes when Whitcombe won with 34 against 36. The tournament was over 72 holes. The first tie added 36 holes and the extra 9 holes made an aggregate of 117 holes to decide the winner. This is a record in first-class British golf but in no way compares with other long ties as it involved only two replays – one of 36 holes and one of 9.

● In the American Open Championship at Toledo, Ohio, in 1931, G. Von Elm and Billy Burke tied for the title. Each returned aggregates of 292. On the first replay both finished in 149 for 36 holes but on the second replay Burke won with a score of 148 against 149. This is a record tie in a national open championship.

● Cary Middlecoff and Lloyd Mangrum were declared co-winners of the 1949 Motor City Open on the USPGA Tour after halving 11 sudden death holes.

● Australian David Graham beat American Dave Stockton at the tenth extra hole in the 1998 Royal Caribbean Classic, a record on the US Senior Tour.

● Paul Downes was beaten by Robin Davenport at the 9th extra hole in the 4th round of the 1981 English Amateur Championship, a record marathon match for the Championship.

● Severiano Ballesteros was beaten by Johnny Miller at the 9th extra hole of a sudden-death play-off at the 1982 Million Dollar Sun City Challenge.

● José Maria Olazábal beat Ronan Rafferty at the 9th extra hole to win the 1989 Dutch Open on the Kennemer Golf and Country Club course. Roger Chapman had been eliminated at the first extra hole.

Long drives

It is impossible to state with any certainty what is the longest ever drive. Many long drives have never been measured and many others have most likely never been brought to our attention. Then there are several outside factors which can produce freakishly long drives, such as a strong following wind, downhill terrain or bonehard ground. Where all three of these favourable conditions prevail outstandingly long drives can be achieved. Another consideration is that a long drive made during a tournament is a different proposition from one made for length alone, either on the practice ground, a long driving competition or in a game of no consequence. All this should be borne in mind when considering the long drives shown here.

● When professional Carl Hooper hit a wayward drive on the 3rd hole (456 yards) at the Oak Hills Country Club, San Antonio, during the 1992 Texas Open, he wrote himself into the record books but out of the tournament. The ball kept bouncing and rolling on a tarmac cart path until it was stopped by a fence – 787 yards away. It took Hooper two recovery shots with a 4-iron and then an 8-iron to return to the fairway. He eventually holed out for a double bogey six and failed to survive the half-way qualifying cut.

● Tommie Campbell of Portmarnock hit a drive of 392 yards at Dun Laoghaire GC in July 1964.

● Playing in Australia, American George Bayer is reported to have driven to within chipping distance of a 589 yards hole. "It was certainly a drive of over 500 yards", said Bayer acknowledging the strong following wind, sharp downslope where his ball landed and the bone-hard ground.

● In September, 1934, over the East Devon course, T.H.V. Haydon, Wimbledon, drove to the edge of the 9th green which was a hole of 465 yards, giving a drive of not less than 450 yards.

● E.C. Bliss drove 445 yards at Herne Bay in August, 1913. The drive was measured by a government surveyor who also measured the drop in height from tee to resting place of the ball at 57 feet.

Long carries

● At Sitwell Park, Rotherham, in 1935 the home professional, W. Smithson, drove a ball which carried a dyke at 380 yards from the 2nd tee.

● George Bell, of Penrith GC, New South Wales, Australia, using a number 2 wood drove across the Nepean River, a certified carry of 309 yards in a driving contest in 1964.

● After the 1986 Irish Professional Championship at Waterville, Co. Kerry, four long-hitting professionals tried for the longest-carry record over water, across a lake in the Waterville Hotel grounds. Liam Higgins, the local professional, carried 310 yards and Paul Leonard 311, beating the previous record by 2 yards.

● In the 1972 Algarve Open at Penina, Henry Cotton vouched for a carry of 305 yards over a ditch at the 18th hole by long-hitting Spanish professional Francisco Abreu. There was virtually no wind assistance.

● At the Home International matches at Portmarnock in 1949 a driving competition was held in which all the players in all four teams competed. The actual carry was measured and the longest was 280 yards by Jimmy Bruen.

● On 6th April, 1976, Tony Jacklin hit a number of balls into Vancouver harbour, Canada, from the 495-foot high roof of a new building complex. The longest carry was measured at 389 yards.

Long hitting

There have been numerous long hits, not on golf courses, where an outside agency has assisted the length of the shot. Such an example was a "drive" by Liam Higgins in 1986, on the Airport runway at Baldonal, near Dublin, of 632 yards.

● How's this for a long shot? Odd Marthinussen was holidaying in Haparanda in Sweden when he holed in one at the 14th. So what! The curious thing about this ace is that while he teed up in Sweden the green is in Finland which is in a different time zone. Registered as an ace in both countries, the time it took for the ball to go from tee to cup was estimated at 1 hour and 4 seconds ... surely the longest hole ever reported by Simon Pia in his column in *The Scotsman* newspaper.

Longest albatrosses

● The longest-known albatrosses (three under par) recorded at par 5 holes are:

● 647 yards-2nd hole at Guam Navy Club by Chief Petty Officer Kevin Murray of Chicago on 3rd January, 1982.

● 609 yards-15th hole at Mahaka Inn West Course, Hawaii, by John Eakin of California on 12th November, 1972.

● 602 yards-16th hole at Whiting Field Golf Course, Milton, Florida, by 27-year-old Bill Graham with a drive and a 3-wood, aided by a 25 mph tail wind.

● The longest-known albatrosses in open championships are: 580 yards 14th hole at Crans-sur-Sierre, by American Billy Casper in the 1971 Swiss Open; 558 yards 5th hole at Muirfield by American Johnny Miller in the 1972 Open Championship.

● In the 1994 German Amateur Championship at Wittelsbacher GC, Rohrenfield, Graham Rankin, a member of the visiting Scottish national team, had a two at the 592 yard 18th.

Eagles (multiple and consecutive)

● Wilf Jones scored three consecutive eagles at the first three holes at Moor Hall GC when playing in a competition there on August Bank Holiday Monday 1968. He scored 3, 1, 2 at holes measuring 529 yards, 176 yards and 302 yards.

● In a round of the 1980 Jubilee Cup, a mixed four-somes match play event of Colchester GC, Mrs Nora Booth and her son Brendan scored three consecutive gross eagles of 1, 3, 2 at the eighth, ninth and tenth holes.

● Three players in a four-ball match at Kington GC, Herefordshire, on 22nd July, 1948, all had eagle 2s at the 18th hole (272 yards). They were R.N. Bird, R. Morgan and V. Timson.

● Four Americans from Wisconsin on holiday at Gleneagles in 1977 scored three eagles and a birdie at the 300-yard par-4 14th hole on the King's course. The birdie was by Dr Kim Lulloff and the eagles by Dr Gordon Meiklejohn, Richard Johnson and Jack Kubitz.

● In an open competition at Glen Innes GC, Australia on 13th November, 1977, three players in a four-ball scored eagle 3s at the 9th hole (442 metres). They were Terry Marshall, Roy McHarg and Jack Rohleder.

● David McCarthy, a member of Moortown Golf Club, Leeds, had three consecutive eagles (3, 3, 2) on the 4th, 5th and 6th holes during a Pro-Am competition at Lucerne, Switzerland, on 7th August, 1992.

Speed of golf ball and club head and effect of wind and temperature

● In The Search for the Perfect Swing, a scientific study of the golf swing, a first class golfer is said to have the club head travelling at 100 mph at impact. This will cause the ball to leave the club at 135 mph. An out-standingly long hitter might manage to have the club head travelling at 130 mph which would produce a ball send-off speed of 175 mph. The resultant shot would carry 280 yards.

● According to Thomas Hardman, Wilson's director of research and development, wind will reduce or increase the flight of a golf ball by approximately 1½ yards for every mile per hour of wind. Every two degrees of temperature will make a yard difference in a ball's flight.

Most northerly course

● Although the most northerly course used to be in Iceland, Björkliden Arctic Golf Club, Sweden, 250 km north of the Arctic Circle, has taken over that role. This may soon change, however, when a course opens in Narvic, Norway, which could be a few metres further north than Björkliden.

Most southerly course

● Golf's most southerly course is Scott Base Country Club, 13° north of the South Pole. The course is run by the New Zealand Antarctic Programme and players must be kitted in full survival gear. The most difficult aspect is finding the orange golf balls which tend to get buried in the snow. Other obstacles include penguins, seals and skuas. If the ball is stolen by a skua then a penalty of one shot is incurred; but if the ball hits a skua it counts as a birdie.

Highest golf courses

● The highest golf course in the world is thought to be the Tuctu GC in Peru which is 14,335 feet above sea-level. High courses are also found in Bolivia with the La Paz GC being about 13,500 feet. In the Himalayas, near the border with Tibet, a 9-hole course at 12,800 feet has been laid out by keen golfers in the Indian Army.

● The highest course in Europe is at Sestriere in the Italian Alps, 6,500 feet above sea-level.

● The highest courses in Great Britain are West Monmouthshire in Wales at 1,513 feet, Leadhills in Scotland at 1,500 feet and Church Stratton in England at 1,250 feet.

Longest courses

● The longest course in the world is Dub's Dread GC, Piper, Kansas, USA measuring 8,101 yards (par 78).

● The longest course for The Open Championship was 7,361 yards at Carnoustie in 1999.

Longest holes

● The longest hole in the world, as far as is known, is the 6th hole measuring 782 metres (860 yards) at Koolan Island GC, Western Australia. The par of the hole is 7. There are several holes over 700 yards throughout the world.

● The longest hole for The Open Championship is the 577 yards 6th hole at Royal Troon.

Longest tournaments

● The longest tournament held was over 144 holes in the World Open at Pinehurst, N Carolina, USA, first held in 1973. Play was over two weeks with a cut imposed at the halfway mark.

● An annual tournament, played in Germany on the longest day of the year, comprises 100 holes' medal play. Best return, in 1995, was 399 strokes.

Largest entries

● The Open – 2,477, St Andrews, 2000.
● The Amateur – 537, Muirfield, 1998.
● US Open – 8,457, Pebble Beach, 2000.
● The largest entry for a PGA European Tour event was 398 for the 1978 Colgate PGA Championship. Since 1985, when the all-exempt ruling was introduced, all PGA tournaments have had 144 competitors, slightly more or less.

● In 1952, Bobby Locke, The Open Champion, played a round at Wentworth against any golfer in Britain. Cards costing 2s. 6d. each (12½p) were taken out by 24,000 golfers. The challenge was to beat the local par by more than Locke could beat the par at Wentworth. 1,641 competitors, including women, succeeded in *beating* the Champion and each received a certificate signed by him. As a result of this challenge the British Golf Foundation benefited to the extent of £3,026, the proceeds from the sale of cards. A similar tournament was held in the US and Canada when 87,094 golfers participated; 14,667 players bettered Ben Hogan's score under handicap. The fund benefited by $80,024.

Largest prize money

● The Machrie Tournament of 1901 was the first tournament with a first prize of £100. It was won by J.H. Taylor, then The Open Champion, who beat James Braid in the final.

● The richest event in the world (at time of writing) will be the American Express Championship scheduled for Mount Juliet in 2004. Total prize money will be $7 million. The richest first prize in Europe is the $1.3 million which goes to the winner of the Nedbank Golf Challenge at Sun City in South Africa.

Holing-in-one – odds against

● At the Wanderers Club, Johannesburg in January, 1951, forty-nine amateurs and professionals each played three balls at a hole 146 yards long. Of the 147 balls hit, the nearest was by Koos de Beer, professional at Reading Country Club, which finished 10½ inches from the hole. Harry Bradshaw, the Irish professional who was touring with the British team in South Africa, touched the pin with his second shot, but the ball rolled on and stopped 3 feet 2 inches from the cup.

● A competition on similar lines was held in 1951 in New York when 1,409 players who had done a hole-in-one held a competition over several days at short holes on three New York courses. Each player was allowed a total of five shots, giving an aggregate of 7,045 shots. No player holed-in-one, and the nearest ball finished 3½ inches from the hole.

● A further illustration of the element of luck in holing-in-one is derived from an effort by Harry Gonder, an American professional, who in 1940 stood for 16 hours 25 minutes and hit 1,817 balls trying to do a 160 yard hole-in-one. He had two official witnesses and caddies to tee and retrieve the balls and count the strokes. His 1,756th shot struck the hole but stopped an inch from the hole. This was his nearest effort.

● From this and other similar information an estimate of the odds against holing-in-one at any particular hole within the range of one shot was made at somewhere between 1,500 and 2,000 to 1 by a proficient player. Subsequently, however, statistical analysis in America has come up with the following odds: a male professional or top amateur 3,708 to 1; a female professional or top amateur 4,648 to 1; an average golfer 42,952 to 1.

Hole-in-one first recorded

● The earliest recorded hole-in-one was in 1869 at The Open Championship when Tom Morris Jr completed the 145-yard 8th hole at Prestwick in one.

This was the first ace in competition for The Open Championship Challenge Belt.

● The first hole-in-one recorded with the 1.66 in ball was in 1972 by John G. Salvesen, a member of the R&A Championship Committee. At the time this size of ball was only experimental. Salvesen used a 7-iron for his historical feat at the 11th hole on the Old Course, St Andrews.

Holing-in-one in important events

Since the day of the first known hole-in-one by Tom Morris Jr, at the 8th hole (145 yards) at Prestwick in the 1869 Open Championship, holes-in-one, even in championships, have become too numerous for each to be recorded. Only where other unusual or interesting circumstances prevailed are the instances shown here.

● All hole-in-one achievements are remarkable. Many are extraordinary. Among the more amazing was that of 2-handicap Leicestershire golfer Bob Taylor, a member of the Scraptoft Club. During the final practice day for the 1974 Eastern Counties Foursomes Championship on the Hunstanton Links, he holed his tee shot with a one-iron at the 188-yard 16th. The next day, in the first round of the competition, he repeated the feat, the only difference being that because of a change of wind he used a six-iron. When he stepped on to the 16th tee the following day his partner jokingly offered him odds of 1,000,000 to one against holing-in-one for a third successive time. Taylor again used his six-iron – and holed in one!

● 1878 – Jamie Anderson, competing in The Open Championship at Prestwick, holed in one at the 11th. In these days The Open was played over three rounds of 12 holes so his ace, the first hole-in-one in competition for the Claret Jug – came at his penultimate hole in his third round. Although it seemed then that he was winning easily, it turned out afterwards that if he had not taken this hole in one stroke he would very likely have lost. Anderson was just about to make his tee shot when Andy Stuart (winner of the first Irish Open Championship in 1892), who was acting as marker to Anderson, remarked he was standing outside the teeing ground, and that if he played the stroke from there he would be disqualified. Anderson picked up his ball and teed it in a proper place. Then he holed-in-one. He won the Championship by one stroke.

● On a Friday the 13th in 1990, Richard Allen holed-in-one at the 13th at the Barwon Heads Golf Club, Victoria, Australia, and then lost the hole. He was giving a handicap stroke to his opponent, brother-in-law Jason Ennels, who also holed-in-one.

● 1906 – R. Johnston, North Berwick, competing in The Open Championship, did the 14th hole at Muirfield in one. Johnston played with only one club throughout – an adjustable head club.

● 1959 – The first hole-in-one in the US Women's Open Championship was recorded. It was by Patty Berg on the 7th hole (170 yards) at Churchill Valley CC, Pittsburgh.

● 1962 – On 6th April, playing in the second round of the Schweppes Close Championship at Little Aston, H. Middleton of Shandon Park, Belfast, holed his tee shot at the 159-yard 5th hole, winning a prize of £1,000. Ten minutes later, playing two matches ahead of Middleton, R.A. Jowle, son of the professional, Frank Jowle, holed his tee shot at the 179-yard 9th hole. As an amateur he was rewarded by the sponsors with a £30 voucher.

● 1963 – By holing out in one stroke at the 18th hole (156 yards) at Moor Park on the first day of the Esso Golden round-robin tournament, H.R. Henning, South Africa, won the £10,000 prize offered for this feat.

● 1967 – Tony Jacklin in winning the Masters tournament at St George's, Sandwich, did the 16th hole in one. His ace has an exceptional place in the records for it was seen by millions on TV, the ball was in view in its flight till it went into the hole in his final round of 64.

● 1971 – John Hudson, 25-year-old professional at Hendon, achieved a near miracle when he holed two consecutive holes-in-one in the Martini Tournament at Norwich. They were at the 11th and 12th holes (195 yards and 311 yards respectively) in the second round.

● 1971 – In The Open Championship at Birkdale, Lionel Platts holed-in-one at the 212-yard 4th hole in the second round. This was the first instance of an Open Championship hole-in-one being recorded by television. It was incidentally Platts' seventh ace of his career.

● There have been four holes-in-one in the Ryder Cup: by Peter Butler at Muirfield in 1973, Nick Faldo at the Belfry in 1993, and by Costantino Rocca and Howard Clark at Oak Hill in 1995. No American has holed in one in the Cup competition.

● 1973 – In the 1973 Open Championship at Troon, two holes-in-one were recorded, both at the 8th hole, known as the Postage Stamp, in the first round. They were achieved by Gene Sarazen and amateur David Russell, who were by coincidence respectively the oldest and youngest competitors.

● Mrs Argea Tissies, whose husband Hermann took 15 at Royal Troon's Postage Stamp 8th hole in the 1950 Open, scored a hole-in-one at the 2nd hole at Punta Ala in the second round of the Italian Ladies' Senior Open of 1978. Exactly five years later on the same date, at the same time of day, in the same round of the same tournament at the same hole, she did it again with the same club.

● In less than two hours play in the second round of the 1989 US Open at Oak Hill Country Club, Rochester, New York, four competitors – Doug Weaver, Mark Wiebe, Jerry Pate and Nick Price – each holed the 167-yard 6th hole in one. The odds against four professionals achieving such a record in a field of 156 are reckoned at 332,000 to 1.

● On 20th May, 1998, British golf journalist Derek Lawrenson, an eight-handicapper, won a Lamborghini Diablo car, valued at over £180,000, by holing his three-iron tee shot to the 175-yard 15th hole at Mill Ride, Berkshire. He was taking part in a charity

day and was partnering England football stars Paul Ince and Steve McManaman.

● David Toms took the lead in the 2001 USPGA Championship at Atlanta Athletic Club with a hole-in-one at the 15th hole in the third round and went on to win. Nick Faldo (4th hole) and Scott Hoch (17th hole) also had holes-in-one during the event.

● In the 2006 Ryder Cup at the K Club, Ireland, Paul Casey holed his 4-iron shot at the 14th to score the fifth ace in the history of the competition. The following day, at the same hole, Scott Verplank became the first American to score a Ryder Cup hole-in-one.

Holing-in-one – longest holes

● Bob Mitera, as a 21-year-old American student, standing 5 feet 6 inches and weighing under 12 stones, claimed the world record for the longest hole-in-one. Playing over the appropriately named Miracle Hill course at Omaha, on 7th October, 1965, Bob holed his drive at the 10th hole, 447 yards long. The ground sloped sharply downhill.

● Two longer holes-in-one have been achieved, but because they were at dog-leg holes they are not generally accepted as being the longest holes-in-one. They were 496 yards (17th hole, Teign Valley) by Shaun Lynch in July 1995 and 480 yards (5th hole, Hope CC, Arkansas) by L. Bruce on 15th November, 1962.

● In March, 1961, Lou Kretlow holed his tee shot at the 427-yard 16th hole at Lake Hefner course, Oklahoma City, USA.

● The longest known hole-in-one in Great Britain was the 393-yard 7th hole at West Lancashire GC, where in 1972 the assistant professional Peter Parkinson holed his tee shot.

● Paul Neilson, a 34-year-old golfer at South Winchester, holed in one at the club's par 4 fifth hole – 391 yards.

● Other long holes-in-one recorded in Great Britain have been 380 yards (5th hole at Tankersley Park) by David Hulley in 1961; 380 yards (12th hole at White Webbs) by Danny Dunne on 30th July, 1976; 370 yards (17th hole at Chilwell Manor, distance from the forward tee) by Ray Newton in 1977; 365 yards (10th hole at Harewood Downs) by K. Saunders in 1965; 365 yards (7th hole at Catterick Garrison GC) by Leslie Bruckner on 18th July, 1980.

● The longest-recorded hole-in-one by a woman was that accomplished in September, 1949 by Marie Robie – the 393-yard hole at Furnace Brook course, Wollaston, Mass, USA.

Holing-in-one – greatest number by one person

59–Amateur Norman Manley of Long Beach, California.

50–Mancil Davis, professional at the Trophy Club, Fort Worth, Texas.

31–British professional C.T. le Chevalier who died in 1973.

22–British amateur, Jim Hay of Kirkintilloch GC.

At One Hole

13–Joe Lucius at 15th hole of Mohawk, Ohio.

5–Left-hander, the late Fred Francis at 7th (now 16th) hole of Cardigan GC.

Holing-in-one – greatest frequency

● The greatest number of holes-in-one in a calendar year is 11, by J.O. Boydstone of California in 1962.

● John Putt of Frilford Heath GC had six holes-in-one in 1970, followed by three in 1971.

● Douglas Porteous, of Ruchill GC, Glasgow, achieved seven holes-in-one in the space of eight months. Four of them were scored in a five-day period from 26th to 30th September, 1974, in three consecutive rounds of golf. The first two were achieved at Ruchill GC in one round, the third there two days later, and the fourth at Clydebank and District GC after another two days. The following May, Porteous had three holes-in-one, the first at Linn Park GC incredibly followed by two more in the one round at Clober GC.

● Mrs Kathleen Hetherington of West Essex has holed-in-one five times, four being at the 15th hole at West Essex. Four of her five aces were within seven months in 1966.

● Mrs Dorothy Hill of Dumfries and Galloway GC holed-in-one three times in 11 days in 1977.

● James C. Reid of Brodick, aged 59 and 8 handicap in 1987, achieved 14 holes-in-one, all but one on Isle of Arran courses. His success was in spite of severe physical handicaps of a stiff left knee, a damaged right ankle, two discs removed from his back and a hip replacement.

● Jean Nield, a member at Chorlton-cum-Hardy and Bramall Park, has had eleven holes-in-one and her husband Brian, who plays at Bramall Park, has had five – a husband and wife total of 16.

● Peter Gibbins holed his tee shot at the 359 yards par 4 13th hole at Hazlemere on Novemeber 2 1984 using a 3-wood that was in his bag for the first time. That spectacular ace was his third but he has had nine more since then.

Holing successive holes-in-one

● Successive holes-in-one are rare; successive par 4 holes-in-one may be classed as near miracles. N.L. Manley performed the most incredible feat in September, 1964, at Del Valle Country Club, Saugus,

California, USA. The par 4 7th (330 yards) and 8th (290 yards) are both slightly downhill, dog-leg holes. Manley had *aces* at both, en route to a course record of 61 (par 71).

● The first recorded example in Britain of a player holing-in-one stroke at each of two successive holes was achieved on 6th February, 1964, at the Walmer and Kingsdown course, Kent. The young assistant professional at that club, Roger Game (aged 17) holed out with a 4-wood at the 244-yard 7th hole, and repeated the feat at the 256-yard 8th hole, using a 5-iron.

● The first occasion of holing-in-one at consecutive holes in a major professional event occurred when John Hudson, 25-year-old professional at Hendon, holed-in-one at the 11th and 12th holes at Norwich during the second round of the 1971 Martini tournament. Hudson used a 4-iron at the 195-yard 11th and a driver at the 311-yard downhill 12th hole.

● Assistant professional Tom Doty (23 years), playing in a friendly match on a course near Chicago in October, 1971, had a remarkable four-hole score which included two consecutive holes-in-one, sandwiched either side by an albatross and an eagle: 4th hole (500 yards)-2; 5th hole (360 yards dog-leg)-1; 6th hole (175 yards)-1; 7th hole (375 yards)-2. Thus he was 10 under par for four consecutive holes.

● At the Standard Life Loch Lomond tournament on the European Tour in July 2000 Jarmo Sandelin holed-in-one at the 17th with the final shot there in the third round and fellow Swede Mathias Gronberg holed-in-one with the first shot there in the last round. A prize of $100,000 was only on offer in the last round.

Holing-in-one twice (or more) in the same round by the same person

What might be thought to be a very rare feat indeed – that of holing-in-one twice in the same round – has in fact happened on many occasions as the following instances show. It is, nevertheless, compared to the number of golfers in the world, still something of an outstanding achievement. The first known occasion was in 1907 when J. Ireland playing in a three-ball match at Worlington holed the 5th and 18th holes in one stroke and two years later in 1909 H.C. Josecelyne holed the 3rd (175 yards) and the 14th (115 yards) at Acton on 24th November.

● The first mention of two holes-in-one in a round by a woman was followed later by a similar feat by

A pair of aces for Chris

In a remarkable feat given odds of 67 million to one, 25-year-old Chris Tugwell of Edinburgh sank two aces in the same round at Bruntsfield Links in June, 2006.

After acing the 157-yard seventh with a nine iron, Chris – who was representing his club, Lothianburn, in a club match – went on to hole-in-one again at the 168-yard 12th with a five-iron.

another lady at the same club. On 19th May, 1942, Mrs W. Driver, of Balgowlah Golf Club, New South Wales, holed out in one at the 3rd and 8th holes in the same round, while on 29th July, 1948, Mrs F. Burke at the same club holed out in one at the second and eighth holes.

● The Rev Harold Snider, aged 75, scored his first hole-in-one on 9th June, 1976 at the 8th hole of the Ironwood course, near Phoenix. By the end of his round he had scored three holes-in-one, the other two being at the 13th (110 yards) and 14th (135 yards). Ironwood is a par-3 course, giving more opportunity of scoring holes-in-one, but, nevertheless, three holes-in-one in one round on any type of course is an outstanding achievement.

● When the Hawarden course in North Wales comprised only nine holes, Frank Mills in 1994 had two holes-in-one at the same hole in the same round. Each time, he hit a seven iron to the 134-yard 3rd and 12th.

● The youngest player to achieve two holes-in-one in the same round is thought to be Christopher Anthony Jones on 14 September, 1994. At the age of 14 years and 11 months he holed-in-one at the Sand Moor, Leeds, 137-yard 10th and then at the 156-yard 17th.

● The youngest woman to have performed the feat was a 17-year-old, Marjorie Merchant, playing at the Lomas Athletic GC, Argentina, at the 4th (170 yards) and 8th (130 yards) holes.

● Tony Hannam, left-handed, handicap 16 and age 71, followed a hole-in-one at the 142 yards 4th of the Bude and North Cornwall Golf Club course with another at the 143-yard 10th on Friday, 18th September, 1992.

● Brothers Eric and John Wilkinson were playing together at the Ravensworth Golf Club on Tyneside in 2001 and both holed-in-one at the 148 yards eighth. Eric (46) played first and then John to the hidden green but there is no doubting this unusual double ace. The club's vice-captain Dave Johnstone saw both balls go in! Postman Eric plays off 9. John, a county planner, has a handicap of 20. Next time they played the hole both missed the green.

● Chris Valerro, a 22-handicapper from the Liberty Lake Golf Club, Spokane, Washington, aced the 143 yards 3rd hole at his home club with a 7-iron and then the 140 yards 11th hole with his 8-iron.

Holes-in-one on the same day

● In July 1987, at the Skerries Club, Co Dublin, Rank Xerox sponsored two tournaments, a men's 18-hole four-ball with 134 pairs competing and a 9-hole mixed foursomes with 33 pairs. During the day each of the four par-3 holes on the course were holed-in-one: the 2nd by Noel Bollard, the 5th by Bart Reynolds, the 12th by Jackie Carr and the 15th by Gerry Ellis.

● Wendy Russell holed-in-one at the consecutive par threes in the first round of the British Senior Ladies' at Wrexham in 1989.

● Clifford Briggs, aged 65, holed-in-one at the 14th at Parkstone GC on the same day as his wife Gwen, 60, aced the 16th.

● In the final round of the 2000 Victor Chandler British Masters at Woburn Alastair Forsyth holed-in-one at the second. Playing partner Roger Chapman then holed-in-one at the eighth.

Two holes-in-one at the same hole in the same game

● *First in World:* George Stewart and Fred Spellmeyer at the 18th hole, Forest Hills, New Jersey, USA in October 1919.

Two holes-in-one in the same round

Eugene O'Brien scored a unique hole-in-one double on one of Britain's most difficult courses when he aced the 13th and 16th holes at Carnoustie, where the Open Championship is being played this year and where Paul Lawrie won the title in 1999.

Three-handicapper O'Brien, who has been playing Carnoustie for 30 years, had had a previous hole-in one 20 years before but the 47-year-old made the double ace when he holed with a 5-iron at the 161 yards 13th and his driver at the 245 yards 16th. The chances of doing that in a round are reckoned to be 67 million to 1.

Yusuka Miyazato, a multiple winner on the Japanese circuit and playing in the Reno-Tahoe Open on a special foreign player exemption granted by Tour Commissioner Tim Finchem's office, had two holes in one in the same round on the second day at the Montreux Golf Club last year.

Miyazato, whose sister Ai plays on the LPGA Tour, aced the second most difficult hole on the course – the 231 yards 7th – with a 4-iron and then used a 7-iron to ace the 173 yards 12th hole. The balls he used have been sent for display at the World Golf Hall of Fame at St Augustine in Florida.

Helped by the two holes-in-one, Miyazato scored 66 in the second round but finished tied 21st on 279 – 11 shots behind the leader.

Milwaukee resident Sanjay Kuttemperoor scored two aces in 2006 at the Treetops Resort, Michigan, the first on the 150-yard fifth and the second on the 135-yard ninth.

● *First in Great Britain:* Miss G. Clutterbuck and Mrs H.M. Robinson at the 15th hole (120 yards), St Augustine GC, Ramsgate, on 8th May, 1925.

● *First in Denmark:* In a Club match in August 1987 at Himmerland, Steffan Jacobsen of Aalborg and Peter Forsberg of Himmerland halved the 15th hole in one shot, the first known occasion in Denmark.

● *First in Australia:* Dr & Mrs B. Rankine, playing in a mixed "Canadian foursome" event at the Osmond Club near Adelaide, South Australia in April 1987, holed-in-one in consecutive shots at the 2nd hole (162 metres), he from the men's tee with a 3-iron and his wife from the ladies' tee with a 1½ wood.

● Jack Ashton, aged 76, holed-in-one at the 8th hole of the West Kent Golf Club at Downe but only got a half. Opponent Ted Eagle, in receipt of shot, made a 2, net 1.

● Dr Martin Pucci and Trevor Ironside will never forget one round at the Macdonald Club in Ellon last year. Playing in an open competition the two golfers with Jamie Cowthorne making up the three-ball reached the tee at the 169yards short 11th. Dr Pucci, with the honour, hit a 5-iron, Mr Ironside a 6-iron at the hole where only the top of the flag is visible. Both hit good shots but when they reached the green they could spot only one ball and that was Mr Cowthorne's. Then they realised that something amazing might have happened. When they reached the putting surface they discovered that both Dr Pucci's and Mr Ironside's balls were wedged into the hole. Both had made aces. It was Dr Pucci's sixth and Mr Ironside's second.

● Eric and John Wilkinson went out for their usual weekly game at the Ravensworth Golf Club in Wrekenton on Tyneside in 2001 and both holed in one at the 148 yards eighth. Neither Eric, a 46-year-old 9-handicapper who has been playing golf since he was 14, nor John, who has been playing golf for ten years and has a handicap of 20, saw the balls go in because the green is over a hill but club vice-captain Dave Johnston did and described the incident as "amazing". Next time the brothers played the hole both missed the green!

● Richard Evans and Mark Evans may not be related but they have one thing in common – they both holed in one at the same hole when playing in a club competion. The double ace occurred in 2003 at Glynhir Golf Club's third hole which measures 189 yards. Thirty-seven-year-old surveyor Richard, who plays off 7, hit first and made his first hole-in-one in the 15 years he has played the game. His opponent, car worker Mark whose handicap is 12, then followed him in.

● Richard Hall, who plays off 12, and high handicapper Peter McEvoy had never had a hole-in-one until one Saturday night in 2003 at Shandon Park Golf Club in Belfast. Friends since their schooldays they play a lot of golf together so there was much excitement when Hall holed his 5-iron shot for an ace at the 180 yards eighth. Then he challenged McEvoy to match it. And he did!

Three holes-in-one at the same hole in the same game

● During the October monthly medal at Southport & Ainsdale Golf Club on Saturday October 18, 2003, three holes-in-one were achieved at the 153-yard 8th by Stuart Fawcett (5 handicap), Brian Verinder (17 handicap) and junior member Andrew Kent (12 handicap). The players were not playing in the same group.

Holing-in-one – youngest and oldest players

● In January 1985 Otto Bucher of Switzerland holed-in-one at the age of 99 on La Manga's 130-yard 12th hole.

● In 2005, Bim Smith, a member of Rochester & Cobham Park Golf Club, Kent, hit a hole-in-one – his fourth – three days before his 91st birthday.

● Bob Hope had a hole-in-one at Palm Springs, California, at the age of 90.

● 76-year-old lady golfer Mrs Felicity Sieghart achieved two holes-in-one when playing in a club Stableford competition at the Aldeburgh club in 2003. Mrs Sieghart aced the 134 yards eighth and the 130 yards 17th – but sadly did not win the competition.

● The youngest player ever to achieve a hole in one is now believed to be Matthew Draper, who was only five when he aced the 122-yard fourth hole at Cherwell Edge, Oxfordshire, in June 1997. He used a wood.

● Six-year-old Tommy Moore aced the 145-yard fourth hole at Woodbrier, West Virginia, in 1968. He had another at the same hole before his seventh birthday.

● Alex Evans, aged eight, holed-in-one with a 4-wood at the 136-yard 4th hole at Bromborough, Merseyside, in 1994.

● Nine-year-old Kate Langley from Scotter in Lincolnshire, is believed to have became the youngest girl to score an ace. It is reported that she holed in one at the 134 yards first hole at Forest Pines Beeches in Scunthorpe after having had a lesson from local professional David Edwards. Kate was nine years and 166 days when she hit the ace – 199 days younger than Australian Kathryn Webb who had held the record previously

Holing-in-one – miscellaneous incidents

● Chemistry student Jason Bohn, aged 19, of State College, Pennsylvania, supported a charity golf event at Tuscaloosa, Alabama, in 1992 when twelve competitors were invited to try to hole-in-one at the 135-yard second hole for a special prize covered by insurance. One attempt only was allowed. Bohn succeeded and was offered US$1m (paid at the rate of $5,000 a month for the next 20 years) at the cost of losing his amateur status. He took the money.

● The late Harry Vardon, who scored the greatest number of victories in The Open Championship, only once did a hole-in-one. That was in 1903 at Mundesley, Norfolk, where Vardon was convalescing from a long illness.

● In a guest day at Rochford Hundred, Essex, in 1994, there were holes-in-one at all the par threes. First Paul Cairns, of Langdon Hills, holed a 4-iron at the 205-yard 15th, next Paul Francis, a member of the home club, sank a 7-iron at the 156-yard seventh and finally Jim Crabb, of Three Rivers, holed a 9-iron at the 136-yard 11th.

● In April 1988, Mary Anderson, a bio-chemistry student at Trinity College, Dublin, holed-in-one at the 290-yard 6th hole at Island GC, Co Dublin.

● In April 1984 Joseph McCaffrey and his son, Gordon, each holed-in-one in the Spring Medal at the 164-yard 12th hole at Vale of Leven Club, Dunbartonshire.

● In 1977, 14-year-old Gillian Field after a series of lessons holed-in-one at the 10th hole at Moor Place GC in her first round of golf.

● When he holed-in-one at the second hole in a match against D. Graham in the 1979 Suntory World Match Play at Wentworth, Japanese professional Isao Aoki won himself a Bovis home at Gleneagles worth, inclusive of furnishings, £55,000. Brian Barnes has aced the short 10th and Thomas Bjørn won a car when he aced the short 14th in 2003.

● On the morning after being elected captain for 1973 of the Norwich GC, J.S. Murray hit his first shot as captain straight into the hole at the 169-yard 1st hole.

● At Nuneaton GC in 1999 the men's captain and the ladies' captain both holed-in-one during their captaincies.

● Using the same club and ball, 11-handicap left-hander Christopher Smyth holed-in-one at the 2nd hole (170 yards) in two consecutive medal competitions at Headfort GC, Co. Meath, in January, 1976.

● Playing over Rickmansworth course at Easter, 1960, Mrs A.E. (Paddy) Martin achieved a remarkable sequence of aces. On Good Friday she sank her tee shot at the 3rd hole (125 yards). The next day, using the same ball and the same 8-iron, at the same hole, she scored another one. And on the Monday (same ball, same club, same hole) she again holed out from the tee.

● At Barton-on-Sea in February 1989 Mrs Dorothy Huntley-Flindt, aged 91, holed-in-one at the par-3 13th. The following day Mr John Chape, a fellow member in his 80s, holed the par- 3 5th in one.

● In 1995 Roy Marsland of Ratho Park, Edinburgh, had three holes-in-one in nine days: at Prestonfield's 5th, at Ratho Park's 3rd and at Sandilands' 2nd.

● Michael Monk, age 82, a member of Tandridge Golf Club, Surrey, waited until 1992 to record his first hole-in-one. It continued a run of rare successes for his family. In the previous 12 months, Mr Monk's daughter, Elizabeth, 52, daughter-in-law, Celia, 48, and grandson, Jeremy, 16, had all holed-in-one on the same course.

● Lou Holloway, a left-hander, recorded his second hole-in-one at the Mount Derby course in New Zealand 13 years after acing the same hole while playing right-handed.

● Ryan Procop, an American schoolboy, holed-in-one at a 168-yard par 3 at Glen Eagles GC, Ohio, with a putter. He confessed that he was so disgusted with himself after a 12 on the previous hole that he just grabbed his putter and hit from the tee.

● Ernie and Shirley Marsden, of Warwick Golf Club, are believed in 1993 to have equalled the record for holes-in-one by a married couple. Each has had three, as have another English couple, Mr and Mrs B.E. Simmonds.

● Russell Pughe, a 12-handicapper from Nottinghamshire, holed-in-one twice in three days at the 274-yard par-4 18th hole at Sidmouth in Devon in 1998. The hole has a blind tee shot.

● Robert Looney aced the 170 yards 13th at the Thorny Lea Golf Club in Brockton, Massachussetts, 30 years after his father made a hole-in-one at the same hole.

● The odds on the chances of two players having a hole in one when playing together are long but it happened to former club captain Robert Smallwood, a 58-year-old retired IBM manager, and current captain Mike Wheeler, a 57-year-old retired financial consultant, when they went out for a round at Irvine GolfClub in Ayrshire in 2005. Playing in the rain, Mr Smallwood, using a driver, had his ace at the 289 yards fourth before Mr Wheeler holed in one at the 279 yards fifth.

● Texan blind golfer Charles Adams, sank his tee shot on the 102-yard 14th hole at Stone Creek Golf Club, Oregon City, Oregon, on October 4, 2006, during the US Blind Golf Association National Championship, the first hole-in-one in the 61-year history of the tournament.

Challenge matches

One of the first recorded professional challenge matches was in 1843 when Allan Robertson beat Willie Dunn in a 20-round match at St Andrews over 360 holes by 2 rounds and 1 to play. Thereafter until about 1905 many matches are recorded, some for up to £200 a side – a considerable sum for the time. The Morrises, the Dunns and the Parks were the main protagonists until Vardon, Braid and Taylor took over in the 1890s. Often matches were on a home-and-away basis over 72 holes or more, with many spectators; Vardon and Willie Park Jr attracted over 10,000 at North Berwick in 1899.

Between the wars Walter Hagen, Archie Compston, Henry Cotton and Bobby Locke all played several such matches. Compston surprisingly beat Hagen by 18 up and 17 to play at Moor Park in 1928; typically Hagen went on to win The Open the following week at Sandwich. Cotton played classic golf at Walton Heath in 1937 when he beat Densmore Shute for £500-a-side at Walton Heath by 6 and 5 over 72 holes.

Curious and large wagers

(See also bets recorded under Cross-Country Matches and in Challenge Matches)

● In The Royal and Ancient Golf Club minutes an entry on 3rd November, 1820 was made in the following terms:

> Sir David Moncrieffe, Bart, of Moncrieffe, backs his life against the life of John Whyte-Melville, Esq, of Strathkinnes, for a new silver club as a present to the St Andrews Golf Club, the price of the club to be paid by the survivor and the arms of the parties to be engraved on the club, and the present bet inscribed on it. No balls to be attached to it. In testimony of which this bet is subscribed by the parties thereto.

Thirteen years later, Mr Whyte-Melville, in a feeling and appropriate speech, expressed his deep regret at the lamented death of Sir David Moncrieffe, one of the most distinguished and zealous supporters of the club. Whyte-Melville, while lamenting the cause that led to it, had pleasure in fulfilling the duty imposed upon him by the bet, and accordingly delivered to the captain the silver putter. Whyte-Melville in 1883 was elected captain of the club a second time; he died in his eighty-sixth year in July, 1883, before he could take office and the captaincy remained vacant for a year. His portrait hangs in The Royal and Ancient clubhouse and is one of the finest and most distinguished pictures in the smoking room.

● In 1914 Francis Ouimet, who in the previous autumn had won the American Open Championship after a triangular tie with Harry Vardon and Ted Ray, came to Great Britain with Jerome D. Travers, the holder of the American amateur title, to compete in the British Amateur Championship at Sandwich. An American syndicate took a bet of £30,000 to £10,000 that one or other of the two United States champions would be the winner. It only took two rounds to decide the bet against the Americans. Ouimet was beaten by a then quite unknown player, H.S. Tubbs, while Travers was defeated by Charles Palmer, who was 56 years of age at the time.

● In 1907 John Ball for a wager undertook to go round Hoylake during a dense fog in under 90, in not more than two and a quarter hours and without losing a ball. Ball played with a black ball, went round in 81, and also beat the time.

● The late Ben Sayers, for a wager, played the 18 holes of the Burgess Society course scoring a four at every hole. Sayers was about to start against an American, when his opponent asked him what he could do the course in. Fours replied Sayers, meaning 72, or an average of 4s for the round. A bet was made, then the American added, Remember a three or a five is not a four. There were eight bogey 5s and two 3s on the Burgess course at the time Old Ben achieved his feat.

Feats of endurance

Although golf is not a game where endurance, in the ordinary sense in which the term is employed in sport, is required, there are several instances of feats on the links which demanded great physical exertion.

● Four British golfers, Simon Gard, Nick Harley, Patrick Maxwell and his brother Alastair Maxwell, completed 14 rounds in one day at Iceland's Akureyri Golf Club, the most northern 18-hole course in the world, during June 1991 when there was 24-hour daylight. It was claimed a record and £10,000 was raised for charity.

● In 1971 during a 24-hour period from 6 pm on 27th November until 5.15 pm on 28th November, Ian Colston completed 401 holes over the 6,061 yards Bendigo course, Victoria, Australia. Colston was a top marathon athlete but was not a golfer. However prior to his golfing marathon he took some lessons and became adept with a 6-iron, the only club he used throughout the 401 holes. The only assistance Colston had was a team of harriers to carry his 6-iron and look for his ball, and a band of motorcyclists who provided light during the night. This is, as far as is known, the greatest number of holes played in 24 hours on foot on a full-size course.

● In 1934 Col Bill Farnham played 376 holes in 24 hours 10 minutes at the Guildford Lake Course, Guildford, Connecticut, using only a mashie and a putter.

● To raise funds for extending the Skipton GC course from 12 to 18 holes, the club professional, 24-year-old Graham Webster, played 277 holes in the hours of daylight on Monday 20th June, 1977. Playing with nothing longer than a 5-iron he averaged 81 per 18-hole round. Included in his marathon was a hole-in-one.

● Michael Moore, a 7 handicap 26-year-old member of Okehampton GC, completed on foot 15 rounds 6 holes (276 holes) there on Sunday, 25th June, 1972, in the hours of daylight. He started at 4.15 am and stopped at 9.15 pm. The distance covered was estimated at 56 miles.

● On 21st June, 1976, 5-handicapper Sandy Small played 15 rounds (270 holes) over his home course Cosby GC, length 6,128 yards, to raise money for the Society of Physically Handicapped Children. Using only a 5-iron, 9-iron and putter, Small started at 4.10 am and completed his 270th hole at 10.39 pm with the aid of car headlights. His fastest round was his first (40 minutes) and slowest his last (82 minutes). His best round of 76 was achieved in the second round.

● During the weekend of 20th–21st June, 1970, Peter Chambers of Yorkshire completed over 14 rounds of golf over the Scarborough South Cliff course. In a non-stop marathon lasting just under 24 hours, Chambers played 257 holes in 1,168 strokes, an average of 84.4 strokes per round.

● Bruce Sutherland, on the Craiglockhart Links, Edinburgh, started at 8.15 pm on 21st June, 1927, and played almost continuously until 7.30 pm on 22nd June, 1927. During the night four caddies with acetylene lamps lit the way, and lost balls were reduced to a minimum. He completed fourteen rounds. Mr Sutherland, who was a physical culture teacher, never recovered from the physical strain and died a few years later.

● Sidney Gleave, motorcycle racer, and Ernest Smith, golf professional at Davyhulme Club, Manchester, on 12th June, 1939, played five rounds of golf in five different countries – Scotland, Ireland, Isle of Man, England and Wales. Smith had to play the five rounds under 80 in one day to win the £100 wager. They travelled by plane, and the following was their programme:

> Start 3.40a.m. at Prestwick St Nicholas (Scotland), finished 1 hour 35 minutes later on 70.
>
> 2nd Course – Bangor, Ireland. Started at 7.15 a.m. and took 1 hour 30 minutes to finish on 76.
>
> 3rd Course – Castletown, Isle of Man. Started 10.15 am, scored 76 in 1 hour 40 minutes.
>
> 4th Course – Blackpool, Stanley Park, England. Started at 1.30 pm and scored 72 in 1 hour 55 minutes.
>
> 5th Course – Hawarden, Wales, started at 6 pm and finished 2 hours 15 minutes later with a score of 72.

● On 19th June, 1995, Ian Botham, the former England cricketer, played four rounds of golf in Ireland, Wales, Scotland and England. His playing companions were Gary Price, the professional at Branston, and Tony Wright, owner of Craythorne, Burton-on-Trent, where the last 18 holes were completed. The other courses were St Margaret's, Anglesey and Dumfries & Galloway. The first round began at 4.30 am and the last was completed at 8.30 pm.

● On Wednesday, 3rd July, 1974, E.S. Wilson, Whitehead, Co. Antrim and Dr G.W. Donaldson, Newry, Co. Down, played a nine-hole match in each of seven countries in the one day. The first 9 holes was at La Moye (Channel Islands) followed by Hawarden (Wales), Chester (England), Turnberry (Scotland), Castletown (Isle of Man), Dundalk (Eire) and Warrenpoint (N Ireland). They started their first round at 4.25 am and their last round at 9.25 pm. Wilson piloted his own plane throughout.

● In June 1986 to raise money for the upkeep of his medieval church, the Rector of Mark with Allerton, Somerset, the Rev Michael Pavey, played a sponsored 18 holes on 18 different courses in the Bath & Wells Diocese. With his partner, the well-known broadcaster on music, Antony Hopkins, they played the 1st at Minehead at 5.55 am and finished playing the 18th at Burnham and Berrow at 6.05 pm. They covered 240 miles in the "round" including the distances to reach the correct tee for the "next" hole on each course. Par for the "round" was 70. Together the pair raised £10,500 for the church.

● To raise funds for the Marlborough Club's centenary year (1988), Laurence Ross, the Club professional, in June 1987, played eight rounds in 12 hours. Against a par of 72, he completed the 576 holes in 3 under par, playing from back tees and walking all the way.

● As part of the 1992 Centenary Celebrations of the Royal Cinque Ports Golf Club at Deal, Kent, and to support charity, a six-handicap member, John Brazell, played all 37 royal courses in Britain and Ireland in 17 days. He won 22 matches, halved three, lost 12; hit 2,834 shots for an average score of 76.6; lost 11 balls and made 62 birdies. The aim was to raise £30,000 for Leukaemia Research and the Spastics Society.

● To raise more than £500 for the Guide Dogs for the Blind charity in the summer of 1992, Mrs Cheryle Power, a member of the Langley Park Golf Club, Beckenham, Kent, played 100 holes in a day – starting at 5 am and finishing at 8.45 pm.

● David Steele, a former European Tour player, completed 17½ rounds, 315 holes, between 6 am and 9.45 pm in 1993 at the San Roque club near Gibraltar in a total of 1,291 shots. Steele was assisted by a caddie cart and raised £15,000 for charity.

● In 2005 Bernard Wood, a member of Rossendale Golf Club, played all the 18-hole courses in Scotland – 377 in all – to raise money for the Kirsty Appeal which supports the Frances House Children's Hospice in Manchester.

Fastest rounds

● Dick Kimbrough, 41, completed a round on foot on 8th August, 1972, at North Platte CC, Nebraska (6,068 yards) in 30 minutes 10 seconds. He carried only a 3-iron.

● At Mowbray Course, Cape Town, November 1931, Len Richardson, who had represented South Africa in the Olympic Games, played a round which measured 6,248 yards in 31 minutes 22 seconds.

● The women's all-time record for the fastest round played on a course of at least 5,600 yards is held by Sue Ledger, 20, who completed the East Berks course in 38 minutes 8 seconds, beating the previous record by 17 minutes.

● In April, 1934, after attending a wedding in Bournemouth, Hants, Captain Gerald Moxom hurried to his club, West Hill in Surrey, to play in the captain's prize competition. With daylight fading and still dressed in his morning suit, he went round in 65 minutes and won the competition with a net 71 into the bargain.

● On 14th June, 1922, Jock Hutchison and Joe Kirkwood (AUS) played round the Old Course at St Andrews in 1 hour 20 minutes. Hutchison, out in 37, led by three holes at the ninth and won by 4 and 3.

● Fastest rounds can also take another form – the time taken for a ball to be propelled round 18 holes. The fastest known round of this type is 8 minutes 53.8 seconds on 25th August, 1979 by 42 members at Ridgemount CC Rochester, New York, a course measuring 6,161 yards. The Rules of Golf were observed but a ball was available on each tee; to be driven off the instant the ball had been holed at the preceding hole.

● The fastest round with the same ball took place in January 1992 at the Paradise Golf Club, Arizona. It took only 11 minutes 24 seconds; 91 golfers being positioned around the course ready to hit the ball as soon as it came to rest and then throwing the ball from green to green.

● In 1992 John Daly and Mark Calcavecchia were both fined by the USPGA Tour for playing the final round of the Players' Championship in Florida in 123 minutes. Daly scored 80, Calcavecchia 81.

Curious scoring

● C.W. Allen of Leek Golf Club chipped-in four times in a round in which he was partnered by K. Brint against G. Davies and R. Hollins. The shortest chip was a yard, the longest 20 yards.

● Tony Blackwell, playing off a handicap of four, broke the course record at Bull Bay, Anglesey, by four strokes when he had a gross 60 (net 56) in winning the club's town trophy in 1996. The course measured 6,217 yards.

● In the third round of the 1994 Volvo PGA Championship at Wentworth, Des Smyth, of Ireland, made birdie twos at each of the four short holes, the 2nd, 5th, 10th and 14th. He also had a two at the second hole in the fourth round.

● Also at Wentworth, in the 1994 World Match Play Championship, Seve Ballesteros had seven successive twos at the short holes – and still lost his quarter-final against Ernie Els.

● R.H. Corbett, playing in the semi-final of the Tangye Cup at Mullion in 1916, did a score of 27. The remarkable part of Corbett's score was that it was made up of nine successive 3s, bogey being 5, 3, 4, 4, 5, 3, 4, 4, 3.

● At Little Chalfont in June 1985 Adrian Donkersley played six successive holes in 6, 5, 4, 3, 2, 1 from the 9th to the 14th holes against a par of 4, 4, 3, 4, 3, 3.

● On 2nd September, 1920, playing over Torphin, near Edinburgh, William Ingle did the first five holes in 1, 2, 3, 4, 5.

● In the summer of 1970, Keith McMillan, on holiday at Cullen, had a remarkable series of 1, 2, 3, 4, 5 at the 11th to 15th holes.

● Marc Osborne was only 14 years of age when he equalled the Betchworth Park amateur course record with a 66 in July, 1993. He was playing in the Mortimer Cup, a 36-hole medal competition, and had at the time a handicap of 6.8.

● Playing at Addington Palace, July, 1934, Ronald Jones, a member of Hendon Club, holed five consecutive holes in 5, 4, 3, 2, 1.

● Harry Dunderdale of Lincoln GC scored 5, 4, 3, 2, 1 in five consecutive holes during the first round of his club championship in 1978. The hole-in-one was the 7th, measuring 294 yards.

● At the Open Amateur Tournament of the Royal Ashdown Forest in 1936 Bobby Locke in his morning round had a score of 72, accomplishing every hole in 4.

● George Stewart of Cupar had a four at every hole over the Queen's course at Gleneagles despite forgetting to change into his golf shoes and therefore still wearing his street shoes.

● Henry Cotton told of one of the most extraordinary scoring feats ever. With some other professionals he was at Sestrieres in the 30s for the Italian Open Championship and Joe Ezar, a colourful character in those days on both sides of the Atlantic, accepted a wager from a club official – 1,000 lira for a 66 to break the course record; 2,000 for a 65; and 4,000 for a 64. *I'll do 64*, said Ezar, and proceeded to jot down the hole-by-hole score figures he would do next day for that total. With the exception of the ninth and tenth holes where his predicted score was 3, 4 and the actual score was 4, 3, he accomplished this amazing feat exactly as nominated.

● Nick Faldo scored par figures at all 18 holes in the final round of the 1987 Open Championship at Muirfield to win the title.

● During the Colts Championship at Knowle Golf Club, Bristol, Chris Newman (Cotswold Hills) scored eight consecutive 3s with birdies at four of the holes.

● At the Toft Hotel Golf Club captain's day event L. Heffernan had an ace, D. Patrick a 2, R. Barnett a 3 and D. Heffernan a 4 at the 240 yard par-4 ninth.

● In the European Club Championship played at the Parco de Medici Club in Rome in 1998, Belgian Dimitri van Hauwaert from Royal Antwerp had an albatross 2, Norwegian Marius Bjornstad from Oslo an eagle 3 and Scotsman Andrew Hogg from Turriff a birdie 4 at the 486 metre par-5 eighth hole.

● Earle F. Wilson from Brewerton, Alabama, has had an ace, an albatross and has fired eight birdies in a row.

High scores

● In the qualifying competition at Formby for the 1976 Open Championship, Maurice Flitcroft, a 46-year-old crane driver from Barrow-in-Furness, took 121 strokes for the first round and then withdrew saying, *I have no chance of qualifying*. Flitcroft entered as a professional but had never before played 18 holes. He had taken the game up 18 months previously but, as he was not a member of a club, had been limited to practising on a local beach. His round was made up thus: 7, 5, 6, 6, 6, 6, 12, 6, 7-61; 11, 5, 6, 8, 4, 9, 5, 7, 5-60, total 121. After his round Flitcroft said, "I've made a lot of progress in the last few months and I'm sorry I did not do better. I was trying too hard at the beginning but began to put things together at the end of the round". R&A officials, who were not amused by the bogus professional's efforts, refunded the £30 entry money to Flitcroft's two fellow-competitors. Flitcroft has since tried to qualify for The Open under assumed names: Gerard Hoppy from Switzerland and Beau Jolley (as in the wine)!

● Playing in the qualifying rounds of the 1965 Open Championship at Southport, an American self-styled professional entrant from Milwaukee, Walter Danecki, achieved the inglorious feat of scoring a total of 221 strokes for 36 holes, 81 over par. His first round over the Hillside course was 108, followed by a second round of 113. Walter, who afterwards admitted he felt *a little discouraged and sad*, declared that he entered because he was *after the money*.

● The highest individual scoring ever known in the rounds connected with The Open Championship occurred at Muirfield, 1935, when a Scottish professional started 7, 10, 5, 10, and took 65 to reach the 9th hole. Another 10 came at the 11th and the player decided to retire at the 12th hole. There was in a bunker, and after playing four shots he had not regained the fairway.

● In 1883 in The Open Championship at Musselburgh, Willie Fernie, the winner, had a 10, the only time double figures appeared on the card of The Open Champion of the year. Fernie won after a tie with Bob Ferguson, and his score for the last hole in the tie was 2. He holed from just off the green to win by one stroke.

● In the first Open Championship at Prestwick in 1860 a competitor took 21, the highest score for one hole ever recorded in this event. The record is preserved in the archives of the Prestwick Golf Club, where the championship was founded.

● In the first round of the 1980 US Masters, Tom Weiskopf hit his ball into the water hazard in front of the par-3 12th hole five times and scored 13 for the hole.

● In the French Open at St Cloud, in 1968, Brian Barnes took 15 for the short 8th hole in the second round. After missing putts at which he hurriedly snatched while the ball was moving he penalised himself further by standing astride the line of a putt. The amazing result was that he actually took 12 strokes from about three feet from the hole. The highest scores on the European Tour were also recorded in the French Open. Philippe Porquier had a 20 at La Baule in 1978 and Ian Woosnam a 16 at La Boulie in 1986.

● US professional Dave Hill 6-putted the fifth green at Oakmont in the 1962 US Open Championship.

● Many high scores have been made at the Road Hole at St Andrews. Davie Ayton, on one occasion, was coming in a certain winner of The Open Championship when he got on the road and took 11. In 1921, at The Open Championship, one professional took 13. In 1923, competing for the Autumn Medal of The Royal and Ancient, J.B. Anderson required a five and a four to win the second award, but he took 13 at the Road Hole. Anderson was close to the green in two, was twice in the bunkers in the face of the green, and once on the road. In 1935, R.H. Oppenheimer tied for the Royal Medal (the first award) in the Autumn Meeting of The Royal and Ancient. On the play-off he was one stroke behind Captain Aitken when they stood on the 17th tee. Oppenheimer drove three balls out of bounds and eventually took 11 to the Road Hole.

● British professional Mark James scored 111 in the second round of the 1978 Italian Open. He played the closing holes with only his right hand due to an injury to his left hand.

● In the 1927 Shawnee Open, Tommy Armour took 23 strokes to the 17th hole. Armour had won the American Open Championship a week earlier. In an effort to play the hole in a particular way, Armour hooked ball after ball out of bounds and finished with a 21 on the card. There was some doubt about the accuracy of this figure and on reaching the clubhouse Armour stated that it should be 23. This is the highest score by a professional in a tournament.

Freak matches

● In 1912, the late Harry Dearth, an eminent vocalist, attired in a complete suit of heavy armour, played a match at Bushey Hall. He was beaten 2 and 1.

● In 1914, at the start of the First World War, J.N. Farrar, a native of Hoylake, was stationed at Royston, Herts. A bet was made of 10-1 that he would not go round Royston under 100 strokes, equipped in full infantry marching order, water bottle, full field kit and haversack. Farrar went round in 94. At the camp were several golfers, including professionals, who tried the same feat but failed.

● Captain Pennington took part in a match *from the air* against A.J. Young, the professional at Sonning. Captain Pennington, with 80 golf balls in the locker of his machine, had to find the Sonning greens by dropping the balls as he circled over the course. The balls were covered in white cloth to ensure that they did not bounce once they struck the ground. The airman completed the course in 40 minutes, taking 29 *strokes*, while Young occupied two hours for his round of 68. Captain Pennington was eventually killed in an air crash in 1933.

● In April 1924, at Littlehampton, Harry Rowntree, an amateur golfer, played the better ball of Edward Ray and George Duncan, receiving an allowance of 150 yards to use as he required during the round. Rowntree won by 6 and 5 and had used only 50 yards 2 feet of his handicap. At one hole Duncan had a two – Rowntree, who was 25 yards from the hole, took this distance from his handicap and won the hole in one. Ray (died 1945) afterwards declared that, conceding a handicap of one yard per round, he could win every championship in the world. And he might, when reckoning is taken of the number of times a putt just stops an inch or two or how much difference to a shot three inches will make for the lie of the ball, either in a bunker or on the fairway. Many single matches on the same system have been played. An 18 handicap player opposed to a scratch player should make a close match with an allowance of 50 yards.

● The first known instance of a golf match by telephone occurred in 1957, when the Cotswold Hills Golf Club, Cheltenham, England, won a golf tournament against the Cheltenham Golf Club, Melbourne, Australia, by six strokes. A large crowd assembled at the English club to wait for the 12,000 miles telephone call from Australia. The match had been played at the suggestion of a former member of the Cotswold Hills Club, Harry Davies, and was open to every member of the two clubs. The result of the match was decided on the aggregate of the eight best scores on each side and the English club won by 564 strokes to 570.

Golf matches against other sports

● H.H. Hilton and Percy Ashworth, many times racket champion, contested a driving match, the former driving a golf ball with a driver, and the latter a racket ball with a racket. Best distances: Against breeze – Golfer 182 yards; Racket player 125 yards. Down wind – Golfer 230 yards; Racket player 140 yards. Afterwards Ashworth hit a golf ball with the racket and got a greater distance than with the racket ball, but was still a long way behind the ball driven by Hilton.

● In 1913, at Wellington, Shropshire, a match between a golfer and a fisherman casting a 2½ oz weight was played. The golfer, Rupert May, took 87; the fisherman J.J.D. Mackinlay, in difficulty because of his short casts, 102. His longest cast, 105 yards, was within 12 yards of the world record at the time, held by French angler, Decautelle. When within a rod's length of a hole he ran the weight to the rod end and dropped into the hole. Five times he broke his line, and was allowed another shot without penalty.

● In December, 1913, F.M.A. Webster, of the London Athletic Club, and Dora Roberts, with javelins, played a match with the late Harry Vardon and Mrs Gordon Robertson, who used the regulation clubs and golf balls. The golfers conceded two-thirds in the matter of distance, and they won by 5 up and 4 to play in a contest of 18 holes. The javelin throwers had a mark of two feet square in which to *hole out* while the golfers had to get their ball into the ordinary golf hole. Mr Webster's best throw was one of 160 feet.

● Several matches have taken place between a golfer on the one side and an archer on the other. The wielder of the bow and arrow has nearly always proved the victor. In 1953 at Kirkhill Golf Course, Lanarkshire, five archers beat six golfers by two games to one. There were two special rules for the match; when an archer's arrow landed six feet from the hole or the golfer's ball three feet from the hole, they were counted as holed. When the arrows landed in bunkers or in the rough, archers lifted their arrow and added a stroke. The sixth archer in this match called off and one archer shot two arrows from each of the 18 tees.

● In 1954, at the Southbroom Club, South Africa, a match over 9 holes was played between an archer and a fisherman against two golfers. The participants were all champions of their own sphere and consisted of Vernon Adams (archer), Dennis Burd (fisherman), Jeanette Wahl (champion of Southbroom and Port Shepstone), and Ron Burd (professional at Southbroom). The conditions were that the archer had holed out when his arrows struck a small leather bag placed on the green beside the hole and in the event of his placing his approach shot within a bow's length of the pin he was deemed to have 1-putted. The fisherman, to achieve a 1-putt, had to land his sinker within a rod's length of the pin. The two golfers were ahead for brief spells, but it was the opposition who led at the deciding 9th hole where *Robin Hood* played a perfect approach for a birdie.

● An *Across England* combined match was begun on 11th October, 1965, by four golfers and two archers from Crowborough Beacon Golf Club, Sussex, accompanied by *Penny*, a white Alsatian dog, whose duty it was to find lost balls. They teed off from Carlisle Castle via Hadrian's Wall, the Pennine Way, finally holing out in the 18th hole at Newcastle United GC in 612 teed shots. Casualties included 110 lost golf balls and 19 lost or broken arrows. The match

took 5½ days, and the distance travelled was about 60 miles. The golfers were Miss P. Ward, K. Meaney, K. Ashdown and C.A. Macey; the archers were W.H. Hulme and T. Scott. The first arrow was fired from the battlements of Carlisle Castle, a distance of nearly 300 yards, by Cumberland Champion R. Willis, who also fired the second arrow right across the River Eden. R. Clough, president of Newcastle United GC, holed the last two putts. The match was in aid of *Guide Dogs for the Blind* and *Friends of Crowborough Hospital.*

Cross-country matches

● Taking 1 year, 114 days, Floyd Rood golfed his way from coast to coast across the United States. He took 114,737 shots including 3,511 penalty shots for the 3,397 mile course.

● Two Californian teenagers, Bob Aube (17) and Phil Marrone (18) went on a golfing safari in 1974 from San Francisco to Los Angeles, a trip of over 500 miles lasting 16 days. The first six days they played alongside motorways. Over 1,000 balls were used.

● In 1830, the Gold Medal winner of The Royal and Ancient backed himself for 10 sovereigns to drive from the 1st hole at St Andrews to the toll bar at Cupar, distance nine miles, in 200 teed shots. He won easily.

● In 1848, two Edinburgh golfers played a match from Bruntsfield Links to the top of Arthur's Seat – an eminence overlooking the Scottish capital, 822 feet above sea level.

● On a winter's day in 1898, Freddie Tait backed himself to play a gutta ball in 40 teed shots from Royal St George's Clubhouse, Sandwich, to the Cinque Ports Club, Deal. He was to hole out by hitting any part of the Deal Clubhouse. The distance as the crow flies was three miles. The redoubtable Tait holed out with his 32nd shot, so effectively that the ball went through a window.

● In 1900 three members of the Hackensack (NJ) Club played a game of four-and-a-half hours over an extemporised course six miles long, which stretched from Hackensack to Paterson. Despite rain, cornfields, and wide streams, the three golfers – J.W. Hauleebeek, Dr E.R. Pfaare, and Eugene Crassons – completed the round, the first and the last named taking 305 strokes each, and Dr Pfaare 327 strokes. The players used only two clubs, the mashie and the cleek.

● On 3rd December, 1920, P. Rupert Phillips and W. Raymond Thomas teed up on the first tee of the Radyr Golf Club and played to the last hole at Southerndown. The distance as the crow flies was 15½ miles, but circumventing swamps, woods, and plough, they covered, approximately, 20 miles. The wager was that they would not do the hole in 1,000 strokes, but they holed out at their 608th stroke two days later. They carried large ordnance maps.

● On 12th March, 1921, A. Stanley Turner, Macclesfield, played from his house to the Cat and Fiddle Inn, five miles distance, in 64 strokes. The route was broken and hilly with a rise of nearly 1,000 feet. Turner was allowed to tee up within two club lengths after each shot and the wagering was 6-4 against his doing the distance in 170 strokes.

● In 1919, a golfer drove a ball from Piccadilly Circus and, proceeding via the Strand, Fleet Street and Ludgate Hill, *holed out* at the Royal Exchange, London. The player drove off at 8 am on a Sunday, a time when the usually thronged thoroughfares were deserted.

● On 23rd April, 1939, Richard Sutton, a London stockbroker, played from Tower Bridge, London, to White's Club, St James's Street, in 142 strokes. The bet was he would not do *the course* in under 200 shots. Sutton used a putter, crossed the Thames at Southwark Bridge, and hit the ball short distances to keep out of trouble.

● Golfers produced the most original event in Ireland's three-week national festival of An Tostal, in 1953 – a cross-country competition with an advertised £1,000,000 for the man who could hole out in one. The 150 golfers drove off from the first tee at Kildare Club to hole out eventually on the 18th green, five miles away, on the nearby Curragh course, a distance of 8,800 yards. The unusual hazards to be negotiated included the main Dublin-Cork railway line and highway, the Curragh Racecourse, hoofprints left by Irish thoroughbred racehorses out exercising on the plains from nearby stables, army tank tracks and about 150 telephone lines. The Golden Ball Trophy, which is played for annually – a standard size golf ball in gold, mounted on a black marble pillar beside the silver figure of a golfer on a green marble base, designed by Captain Maurice Cogan, Army GHQ, Dublin – was for the best gross. And it went to one of the longest hitters in international golf – Amateur Champion, Irish internationalist and British Walker Cup player Joe Carr, with the remarkable score of 52.

● In 1961, as a University Charities Week stunt, four Aberdeen University students set out to golf their way up Ben Nevis (4,406 feet). About half-way up, after losing 63 balls and expending 659 strokes, the quartet conceded victory to Britain's highest mountain.

● Among several cross-country golfing exploits, one of the most arduous was faced by Iain Williamson and Tony Kent, who teed off from Cained Point on the summit of Fairfield in the Lake District. With the hole cut in the lawn of the Bishop of Carlisle's home at Rydal Park, it measured 7,200 yards and passed through the summits of Great Rigg Mann, Heron Pike and Nab Scar, descending altogether 1,900 feet. Eight balls were lost and the two golfers holed out in a combined total of 303 strokes.

Long-lived golfers

● James Priddy, aged 80, played in the Seniors' Open at his home club, Weston-super-Mare, Avon, on 27th June, 1990, and scored a gross 70 to beat his age by ten shots.

● The oldest golfer who ever lived is believed to have been Arthur Thompson of British Columbia,

Canada. He equalled his age when 103 at Uplands GC, a course of over 6,000 yards. He died two years later.

● Nathaniel Vickers celebrated his 103rd birthday on Sunday, 9th October, 1949, and died the following day. He was the oldest member of the United States Senior Golf Association and until 1942 he competed regularly in their events and won many trophies in the various age divisions. When 100 years old, he apologised for being able to play only nine holes a day. Vickers predicted he would live until 103 and he died a few hours after he had celebrated his birthday.

● American George Miller, who died in 1979 aged 102, played regularly when 100 years old.

● In 1999 94-year-old Mr W. Seneviratne, a retired schoolmaster who lived and worked in Malaysia, was still practising every day and regularly competing in medal competitions at the Royal Colombo Golf Club which was founded in 1879.

● Bim Smith, a member of Rochester & Cobham Park Golf Club, Kent, achieved a hole-in-one three days before his 91st birthday.

● Phyllis Tidmarsh, aged 90, won a Stableford competition at Saltford Golf Club, near Bath, when she returned 42 points. Her handicap was cut from 28 to 27.

● George Swanwick, a member of Wallasey, celebrated his 90th birthday with a lunch at the club on 1st April, 1971. He played golf several times a week, carrying his own clubs, and had holed-in-one at the ages of 75 and 85. His ambition was to complete the sequence aged 95 ... but he died in 1973 aged 92.

● The 10th Earl of Wemyss played a round on his 92nd birthday, in 1910, at Craigielaw. At the age of 87 the Earl was partnered by Harry Vardon in a match at Kilspindie, the golf course on his East Lothian estate at Gosford. After playing his ball the venerable earl mounted a pony and rode to the next shot. He died on 30th June, 1914.

● F.L. Callender, aged 78, in September 1932, played nine consecutive rounds in the Jubilee Vase, St Andrews. He was defeated in the ninth, the final round, by 4 and 2. Callender's handicap was 12. This is the best known achievement of a septuagenarian in golf.

● George Evans shot a remarkable one over par 71 at Brockenhurst Manor – remarkable because Mr Evans was 87 at the time. Playing with him that day was Hampshire, Isle of Wight and Channel Islands President John Nettell and former Ferndown pro Doug Sewell. "It's good to shoot a score under your age, but when its 16 shots better that must be a record", said Mr Nettell. Mr Evans qualified for four opens while professional at West Hill, Surrey.

● Bernard Matthews, aged 82, of Banstead Downs Club, handicap 6, holed the course in 72 gross in August 1988. A week later he holed it in 70, twelve shots below his age. He came back in 31, finishing 4, 3, 3, 2, 3, against a par of 5, 4, 3, 3, 4. Mr Matthews's eclectic score at his Club is 37, or one over 2's.

Playing in the dark

On numerous occasions it has been necessary to hold lamps, lighted candles, or torches at holes in order that players might finish a competition. Large entries, slow play, early darkness and an eclipse of the sun have all been causes of playing in darkness.

● Since 1972, the Whitburn Golf Club at South Shields, Tyne and Wear, has held an annual Summer Solstice Competition. All competitors, who draw lots for starting tees, must begin before 4.24 and 13 seconds am, the time the sun rises over the first hole on the longest day of the year.

● At The Open Championship in Musselburgh in November 1889 many players finished when the light had so far gone that the adjacent street lamps were lit. The cards were checked by candlelight. Several players who had no chance of the championship were paid small sums to withdraw in order to permit others who had a chance to finish in daylight. This was the last championship at Musselburgh.

● At the Southern Section of the PGA tournament on 25th September, 1907, at Burnham Beeches, several players concluded the round by the aid of torch lights placed near the holes.

● In the Irish Open Championship at Portmarnock in September, 1907, a tie in the third round between W.C. Pickeman and A. Jeffcott was postponed owing to darkness, at the 22nd hole. The next morning Pickeman won at the 24th.

● The qualifying round of the American Amateur Championship in 1910 could not be finished in one day, and several competitors had to stop their round on account of darkness, and complete it early in the morning of the following day.

● On 10th January, 1926, in the final of the President's Putter, at Rye, E.F. Storey and R.H. Wethered were all square at the 24th hole. It was 5 pm and so dark that, although a fair crowd was present, the balls could not be followed. The tie was abandoned and the Putter held jointly for the year. Each winner of the Putter affixes the ball he played; for 1926 there are two balls, respectively engraved with the names of the finalists.

● In the 1932 Walker Cup contest at Brooklyn, a total eclipse of the sun occurred.

● At Perth, on 14th September, 1932, a competition was in progress under good clear evening light, and a full bright moon. The moon rose at 7.10 and an hour later came under eclipse to the earth's surface. The light then became so bad that on the last three greens competitors holed out by the aid of the light from matches.

● At Carnoustie, 1932, in the competition for the *Craw's Nest Tassie* the large entry necessitated competitors being sent off in 3-ball matches. The late players had to be assisted by electric torches flashed on the greens.

● In February, 1950, Max Faulkner and his partner, R. Dolman, in a Guildford Alliance event finished their round in complete darkness. A photographer's flash bulbs were used at the last hole to direct Faulkner's approach. Several of the other competitors also finished in darkness. At the last hole they had only the light from the clubhouse to aim at and one played his approach so boldly that he put his ball through the hall doorway and almost into the dressing room.

● On the second day of the 1969 Ryder Cup contest, the last 4-ball match ended in near total darkness on the 18th green at Royal Birkdale. With the help of the clubhouse lights the two American players, Lee Trevino and Miller Barber, along with Tony Jacklin for Britain each faced putts of around five feet to win their match. All missed and their game was halved.

The occasions mentioned above all occurred in competitions where it was not intended to play in the dark. There are, however, numerous instances where players set out to play in the dark either for bets or for novelty.

● On 29th November, 1878, R.W. Brown backed himself to go round the Hoylake links in 150 strokes, starting at 11 pm. The conditions of the match were that Mr Brown was only to be penalised *loss of distance* for a lost ball, and that no one was to help him to find it. He went round in 147 strokes, and won his bet by the narrow margin of three strokes.

● In 1876 David Strath backed himself to go round St Andrews under 100, in moonlight. He took 95, and did not lose a ball.

● In September 1928, at St Andrews, the first and last holes were illuminated by lanterns, and at 11 pm four members of The Royal and Ancient set out to play a foursome over the 2 holes. Electric lights, lanterns, and rockets were used to brighten the fairway, and the headlights of motor cars parked on Links Place formed a helpful battery. The 1st hole was won in four, and each side got a five at the 18th. About 1,000 spectators followed the freak match, which was played to celebrate the appointment of Angus Hambro to the captaincy of the club.

● In 1931, Rufus Stewart, professional, Kooyonga Club, South Australia, and former Australian Open Champion, played 18 holes of exhibition golf at night without losing a single ball over the Kooyonga course, and completed the round in 77.

● At Ashley Wood Golf Club, Blandford, Dorset, a night-time golf tournament was arranged annually with up to 180 golfers taking part over four nights. Over £6000 has been raised in four years for the Muscular Dystrophy Charity.

● At Pannal, 3rd July, 1937, R.H. Locke, playing in bright moonlight, holed his tee shot at the 15th hole, distance 220 yards, the only known case of holing-in-one under such conditions.

Fatal and other accidents on the links

The history of golf is, unfortunately, marred by a great number of fatal accidents on or near the course. In the vast majority of such cases they have been caused either by careless swinging of the club or by an uncontrolled shot when the ball has struck a spectator or bystander. In addi-

tion to the fatal accidents there is an even larger number on record which have resulted in serious injury or blindness. We do not propose to list these accidents except where they have some unusual feature. We would remind all golfers of the tragic consequences which have so often been caused by momentary carelessness. The fatal accidents which follow have an unusual cause and other accidents given may have their humorous aspect.

● English tournament professional Richard Boxall was three shots off the lead in the third round of the 1991 Open Championship when he fractured his left leg driving from the 9th tee at Royal Birkdale. He was taken from the course to hospital by ambulance and was listed in the official results as "retired" which entitled him to a consolation prize of £3000.

A month later, Russell Weir of Scotland, was competing in the European Teaching Professionals' Championship near Rotterdam when he also fractured his left leg driving from the 7th tee in the first round.

● In July, 1971, Rudolph Roy, aged 43, was killed at a Montreal course; in playing out of woods, the shaft of his club snapped, rebounded off a tree and the jagged edge plunged into his body.

● Harold Wallace, aged 75, playing at Lundin Links with two friends in 1950, was crossing the railway line which separates the fifth green and sixth tee, when a light engine knocked him down and he was killed instantly.

● In the summer of 1963, Harold Kalles, of Toronto, Canada, died six days after his throat had been cut by a golf club shaft, which broke against a tree as he was trying to play out of a bunker.

● At Jacksonville, Florida, on 18th March, 1952, two women golfers were instantly killed when hit simultaneously by the whirling propeller of a navy fighter plane. They were playing together when the plane with a dead engine coming in out of control, hit them from behind.

● In May, 1993, at Ponoka Community GC, Alberta, Canada, Richard McCulough hit a poor tee shot on the 13th hole and promptly smashed his driver angrily against a golf cart. The head of the driver and six inches of shaft flew through the air, piercing McCulough's throat and severing his carotid artery. He died in hospital.

● Britain's first national open event for competitors aged over 80, at Moortown, Leeds in September, 1992, was marred when 81-year-old Frank Hart collapsed on the fourth tee and died. Play continued and Charles Mitchell, aged 80, won the Stableford competition with a gross score of 81 for 39 points.

● Playing in the 1993 Carlesburg-Tetley Cornish Festival at Tehidy Park, Ian Cornwell was struck on the leg by a wayward shot from a player two groups behind. Later, as he was leaving the 16th green, he was hit again, this time below the ear, by the same player, knocking him unconscious. This may be the first time that a player has been hit twice in the same round by the same player.

Lightning on the links

There have been a considerable number of fatal and serious accidents through players and caddies having been struck by lightning on the course. The Royal and Ancient and the USGA have, since 1952, provided for discontinuance of play during lightning storms under the Rules of Golf (Rule 37, 6) and the United States Golf Association has given the following guide for personal safety during thunderstorms:

(a) Do not go out of doors or remain out during thunderstorms unless it is necessary. Stay inside of a building where it is dry, preferably away from fireplaces, stoves, and other metal objects.

(b) If there is any choice of shelter, choose in the following order:
   1. Large metal or metal-frame buildings.
   2. Dwellings or other buildings which are protected against lightning.
   3. Large unprotected buildings.
   4. Small unprotected buildings.

(c) If remaining out of doors is unavoidable, keep away from:
   1. Small sheds and shelters if in an exposed location.
   2. Isolated trees.
   3. Wire fences.
   4. Hilltops and wide open spaces.

(d) Seek shelter in:
   1. A cave.
   2. A depression in the ground.
   3. A deep valley or canyon.
   4. The foot of a steep or overhanging cliff.
   5. Dense woods.
   6. A grove of trees.

Note – Raising golf clubs or umbrellas above the head is dangerous.

● A serious incident with lightning involving well-known golfers was at the 1975 Western Open in Chicago when Lee Trevino, Jerry Heard and Bobby Nichols were all struck and had to be taken to hospital. At the same time Tony Jacklin had a club thrown 15 feet out of his hands.

● Two well-known competitors were struck by lightning in European events in 1977. They were Mark James of Britain in the Swiss Open and Severiano Ballesteros of Spain in the Scandinavian Open. Fortunately neither appeared to be badly injured.

● Two spectators were killed by lightning in 1991: one at the US Open and the other at US PGA Championship.

Spectators interfering with balls

● Deliberate interference by spectators with balls in play during important money matches was not unknown in the old days when there was intense rivalry between the schools of Musselburgh, St Andrews, and North Berwick, and disputes arose in stake matches caused by the action of spectators in kicking the ball into either a favourable or an unfavourable position.

● Tom Morris, in his last match with Willie Park at Musselburgh, refused to go on because of interference by the spectators, and in the match on the same course about 40 years later, in 1895, between Willie Park Jr and J.H. Taylor, the barracking of the crowd and interference with play was so bad that when the Park-Vardon match came to be arranged in 1899, Vardon refused to accept Musselburgh as a venue.

● Even in modern times spectators have been known to interfere deliberately with players' balls, though it is usually by children. In the 1972 Penfold Tournament at Queen's Park, Bournemouth, Christy O'Connor Jr had his ball stolen by a young boy, but not being told of this at the time had to take the penalty for a lost ball. O'Connor finished in a tie for first place, but lost the play-off.

● In 1912 in the last round of the final of the Amateur Championship at Westward Ho! between Abe Mitchell and John Ball, the drive of the former to the short 14th hit an open umbrella held by a lady protecting herself from the heavy rain, and instead of landing on the green the ball was diverted into a bunker. Mitchell, who was leading at the time by 2 holes, lost the hole and Ball won the Championship at the 38th hole.

● In the match between the professionals of Great Britain and America at Southport in 1937 a dense crowd collected round the 15th green waiting for the Sarazen-Alliss match. The American's ball landed in the lap of a woman, who picked it up and threw it so close to the hole that Sarazen got a two against Alliss' three.

● In a memorable tie between Bobby Jones and Cyril Tolley in the 1930 Amateur Championship at St Andrews, Jones' approach to the 17th green struck spectators massed at the left end of the green and led to controversy as to whether it would otherwise have gone on to the famous road. Jones himself had deliberately played for that part of the green and had requested stewards to get the crowd back. Had the ball gone on to the road, the historic Jones Quadrilateral of the year – The Open and Amateur Championships of Britain and the United States – might not have gone into the records.

● In the 1983 Suntory World Match Play Championship at Wentworth Nick Faldo hit his second shot over the green at the 16th hole into a group of spectators. To everyone's astonishment and discomfiture the ball reappeared on the green about 30ft from the hole, propelled there by a thoroughly misguided and anonymous spectator. The referee ruled that Faldo should play the ball where it lay on the green. Faldo's opponent, Graham Marsh, understandably upset by the incident, took three putts against Faldo's two, thus losing a hole he might well otherwise have won. Faldo won the match 2 and 1, but lost in the final to Marsh's fellow Australian Greg Norman by 3 and 2.

Golf balls killing animals and fish, and incidents with animals

● An astounding fatality to an animal through being hit by a golf ball occurred at St Margaret's-at-Cliffe Golf Club, Kent on 13th June, 1934, when W.J. Robinson, the professional, killed a cow with his tee shot to the 18th hole. The cow was standing in the fairway about 100 yards from the tee, and the ball struck her on the back of the head. She fell like a log, but staggered to her feet and walked about 50 yards before dropping again. When the players reached her she was dead.

● J.W. Perret, of Ystrad Mynach, playing with Chas R. Halliday, of Ralston, in the qualifying rounds of the Society of One Armed Golfers' Championship over the Darley course, Troon, on 27th August, 1935, killed two gulls at successive holes with his second shots. The deadly shots were at the 1st and 2nd holes.

● On the first day of grouse shooting of the 1975 season (12th August), 11-year-old schoolboy Willie Fraser, of Kingussie, beat all the guns when he killed a grouse with his tee shot on the local course.

● On 10th June, 1904, while playing in the Edinburgh High Constables' Competition at Kilspindie, Captain Ferguson sent a long ball into the rough at the Target hole, and on searching for it found that it had struck and killed a young hare.

● Playing in a mixed open tournament at the Waimairi Beach Golf Club in Christchurch, New Zealand, in the summer of 1961, Mrs R.T. Challis found her ball in fairly long spongy grass where a placing rule applied. She picked up, placed the ball and played her stroke. A young hare leaped into the air and fell dead at her feet. She had placed the ball on the leveret without seeing it and without disturbing it.

● In 1906 in the Border Championship at Hawick, a gull and a weasel were killed by balls during the afternoon's play.

● A golfer at Newark, in May, 1907, drove his ball into the river. The ball struck a trout 2lb in weight and killed it.

● On 24th April, 1975, at Scunthorpe GC, Jim Tollan's drive at the 14th hole, called The Mallard, struck and killed a female mallard duck in flight. The duck was stuffed and is displayed in the Scunthorpe Clubhouse.

● A. Samuel, Melbourne Club, at Sandringham, was driving with an iron club from the 17th tee, when a kitten, which had been playing in the long grass, sprang suddenly at the ball. Kitten and club arrived at the objective simultaneously, with the result that the kitten took an unexpected flight through the air, landing some 20 yards away.

● As Susan Rowlands was lining up a vital putt in the closing stages of the final of the 1978 Welsh Girls' Championship at Abergele, a tiny mouse scampered up her trouser leg. After holing the putt, the mouse ran down again. Susan, who won the final, admitted that she fortunately had not known it was there.

Interference by birds and animals

● Crows, ravens, hawks and seagulls frequently carry off golf balls, sometimes dropping the ball actually on the green, and it is a common incident for a cow to swallow a golf ball. A plague of crows on the Liverpool course at Hoylake are addicted to golf balls – they stole 26 in one day – selecting only new balls. It was suggested that members should carry shotguns as a 15th club!

● A match was approaching a hole in a rather low-lying course, when one of the players made a crisp chip from about 30 yards from the hole. The ball trickled slowly across the green and eventually disappeared into the hole. After a momentary pause, the ball was suddenly ejected on to the green, and out jumped a large frog.

● A large black crow named Jasper which frequented the Lithgow GC in New South Wales, Australia, stole 30 golf balls in the club's 1972 Easter Tournament.

● As Mrs Molly Whitaker was playing from a bunker at Beachwood course, Natal, South Africa, a large monkey leaped from a bush and clutched her round the neck. A caddie drove it off by clipping it with an iron club.

● In Massachusetts a goose, having been hit rather hard by a golf ball which then came to rest by the side of a water hazard, took revenge by waddling over to the ball and kicking it into the water.

● In the summer of 1963, S.C. King had a good drive to the 10th hole at the Guernsey Club. His partner, R.W. Clark, was in the rough, and King helped him to search. Returning to his ball, he found a cow eating it. Next day, at the same hole, the positions were reversed, and King was in the rough. Clark placed his woollen hat over his ball, remarking, *I'll make sure the cow doesn't eat mine.* On his return he found the cow thoroughly enjoying his hat; nothing was left but the pom-pom.

● On 5 August 2000 in the first round of the Royal Westmoreland Club Championship in Barbados, Kevin Edwards, a five-handicapper, hit a tee shot at the short 15th to a few feet of the hole. A monkey then ran onto the green, picked up the ball, threw it into the air a few times, then placed it in the hole before running off. Mr Edwards had to replace his ball, but was obliged afterwards to buy everyone a drink at the bar by virtue of a newly written rule.

Armless, one-armed, legless and ambidextrous players

● In September, 1933, at Burgess Golfing Society of Edinburgh, the first championship for one-armed golfers was held. There were 43 entries and 37 of the competitors had lost an arm in the 1914–18 war. Play was over two rounds and the championship was won by W.E. Thomson, Eastwood, Glasgow, with a score of 169 (82 and 87) for two rounds. The Burgess course was 6,300 yards long. Thomson drove the last green, 260 yards. The championship and an international match are played annually.

● In the Boys' Amateur Championship 1923, at Dunbar and 1949 at St Andrews, there were competitors each with one arm. The competitor in 1949, R.P. Reid, Cupar, Fife, who lost his arm working a machine in a butcher's shop, got through to the third round.

● There have been cases of persons with no arms playing golf. One, Thomas McAuliffe, who held the club between his right shoulder and cheek, once went round Buffalo CC, USA, in 108.

● Group Captain Bader, who lost both legs in a flying accident prior to the World War 1939–45, took part in golf competitions and reached a single-figure handicap in spite of his disability.

● In 1909, Scott of Silloth, and John Haskins of Hoylake, both one-armed golfers, played a home and away match for £20-a-side. Scott finished five up at Silloth. He was seven up and 14 to play at Hoylake but Haskins played so well that Scott eventually only won by 3 and 1. This was the first match between one-armed golfers. Haskins in 1919 was challenged by Mr Mycock, of Buxton, another one-armed player. The match was 36 holes, home and away. The first half was played over the Buxton and High Peak Links, and the latter half over the Liverpool Links, and resulted in a win for Haskins by 11 and 10. Later in the same year Haskins received another challenge to play against Alexander Smart of Aberdeen. The match was 18 holes over the Balgownie Course, and ended in favour of Haskins.

● In a match, November, 1926, between the Geduld and Sub Nigel Clubs – two golf clubs connected with the South African gold mines of the same names – each club had two players minus an arm. The natural consequence was that the quartet were matched. The players were – A.W.P. Charteris and E. Mitchell, Sub Nigel; and E.P. Coles and J. Kirby, Geduld. This is the first record of four one-armed players in a foursome.

● At Joliet Country Club, USA, a one-armed golfer named D.R. Anderson drove a ball 300 yards.

● Left-handedness, but playing golf right-handed, is prevalent and for a man to throw with his left hand and play golf right-handed is considered an advantage, for Bobby Jones, Jesse Sweetser, Walter Hagen, Jim Barnes, Joe Kirkwood and more recently Johnny Miller were eminent golfers who were left-handed and ambidextrous.

● In a practice round for The Open Championship in July, 1927, at St Andrews, Len Nettlefold and Joe Kirkwood changed sets of clubs at the 9th hole. Nettlefold was a left-handed golfer and Kirkwood right-handed. They played the last nine, Kirkwood with the left-handed clubs and Nettlefold with the right-handed clubs.

● The late Harry Vardon, when he was at Ganton, got tired of giving impossible odds to his members and beating them, so he collected a set of left-handed clubs, and rating himself at scratch, conceded the handicap odds to them. He won with the same monotonous regularity.

● Ernest Jones, who was professional at the Chislehurst Club, was badly wounded in the war in France in 1916 and his right leg had to be amputated below the knee. He persevered with the game, and before the end of the year he went round the Clacton course balanced on his one leg in 72. Jones later settled in the United States where he built fame and fortune as a golf teacher.

● Major Alexander McDonald Fraser of Edinburgh had the distinction of holding two handicaps simultaneously in the same club – one when he played left-handed and the other for his right-handed play. In medal competitions he had to state before teeing up which method he would use.

● Former England test cricketer Brian Close once held a handicap of 2 playing right-handed, but after retiring from cricket in 1977 decided to apply himself as a left-handed player. His left-handed handicap at the time of his retirement was 7. Close had the distinction of once beating Ted Dexter, another distinguished test cricketer and noted golfer twice in the one day, playing right-handed in the morning and left-handed in the afternoon.

Blind and blindfolded golf

● Major Towse, VC, whose eyes were shot out during the South African War, 1899, was probably the first blind man to play golf. His only stipulations when playing the game were that he should be allowed to touch the ball with his hands to ascertain its position, and that his caddie could ring a small bell to indicate the position of the hole. Major Towse, who played with considerable skill, was also an expert oarsman and bridge player. He died in 1945, aged 81.

● The United States Blind Golfers' Association in 1946 promoted an Invitational Golf Tournament for the blind at Inglewood, California, to be held annually. In 1953 there were 24 competitors, of which 11 completed the two rounds of 36 holes. The winner was Charley Boswell who lost his eyesight leading a tank unit in Germany in 1944.

● In July, 1954, at Lambton Golf and Country Club, Toronto, the first international championship for the blind was held. It resulted in a win for Joe Lazaro, of Waltham, Mass., with a score of 220 for the two rounds. He drove the 215-yard 16th hole and just missed an ace, his ball stopping 18 inches from the hole. Charley Boswell, who won the United States Blind Golfers' Association Tournament in 1953, was second. The same Charles Boswell, of Birmingham, Alabama holed the 141-yard 14th hole at the Vestavia CC in one in October, 1970.

● Another blind person to have holed-in-one was American Ben Thomas while on holiday in South Carolina in 1978.

● Rick Sorenson undertook a bet in which, playing 18 holes blindfolded at Meadowbrook Course, Minneapolis, on 25th May, 1973, he was to pay $10 for every hole over par and receive $100 for every hole in par or better. He went round in 86 losing $70 on the deal.

● Alfred Toogood played blindfolded in a match against Tindal Atkinson at Sunningdale in 1912.

Toogood was beaten 8 and 7. Previously, in 1908, I. Millar, Newcastle-upon-Tyne, played a match blindfolded against A.T. Broughton, Birkdale, at Newcastle, County Down.

● Wing-Commander *Laddie* Lucas, DSO, DFC, MP, played over Sandy Lodge golf course in Hertfordshire on 7th August, 1954, completely blindfolded and had a score of 87.

Trick shots

● Joe Kirkwood, Australia, specialised in public exhibitions of trick and fancy shots. He played all kinds of strokes after nominating them, and among his ordinary strokes nothing was more impressive than those hit for low flight. He played a full drive from the face of a wrist watch, and the toe of a spectator's shoe, full strokes at a suspended ball, and played for slice and pull at will, and exhibited his ambidexterity by playing left-handed strokes with right-handed clubs. Holing six balls, stymieing, a full shot at a ball catching it as it descended, and hitting 12 full shots in rapid succession, with his face turned away from the ball, were shots among his repertoire. In playing the last named Kirkwood placed the balls in a row, about six inches apart, and moved quickly along the line. Kirkwood, who was born in Australia lived for many years in America. He died in November, 1970 aged 73.

● On 2nd April, 1894, a 3-ball match was played over Musselburgh course between Messrs Grant, Bowden, and Waggot, the clubmaker, the latter teeing on the face of a watch at each tee. He finished the round in 41 the watch being undamaged in any way.

● In a match at Esher on 23rd November, 1931, George Ashdown, the professional, played his tee shot for each of the 18 holes from a rubber tee strapped to the forehead of Miss Ena Shaw.

● E.A. Forrest, a South African professional in a music hall turn of trick golf shots, played blindfolded shots, one being from the ball teed on the chin of his recumbent partner.

● The late Paul Hahn, an American trick specialist could hit four balls with two clubs. Holding a club in each hand he hit two balls, hooking one and slicing the other with the same swing. Hahn had a repertoire of 30 trick shots. In 1955 he flew round the world, exhibiting in 14 countries and on all five continents.

Balls colliding and touching

● Competing in the 1980 Corfu International Championship, Sharon Peachey drove from one tee and her ball collided in mid-air with one from a competitor playing another hole. Her ball ended in a pond.

● Playing in the Cornish team championship in 1973 at West Cornwall GC Tom Scott-Brown, of West Cornwall GC, and Paddy Bradley, of Tehidy GC, saw their drives from the fourth and eighth tees collide in mid-air.

● During a fourball match at Guernsey Club in June, 1966, near the 13th green from the tee, two of the

players, D.G. Hare and S. Machin, chipped up simultaneously; the balls collided in mid-air and Machin's ball
hit the green, then the flagstick, and dropped into the
hole for a birdie 2.

● In May, 1926, during the meeting of the Army
Golfing Society at St Andrews, Colonel Howard and
Lieutenant-Colonel Buchanan Dunlop, while playing
in the foursomes against J. Rodger and J. Mackie, hit
full iron shots for the seconds to the 16th green.
Each thought he had to play his ball first, and hidden
by a bunker the players struck their balls simultaneously. The balls, going towards the hole about 20
yards from the pin and five feet in the air, met with
great force and dropped either side of the hole five
yards apart.

● In 1972, before a luncheon celebrating the centenary year of the Ladies' Section of Royal Wimbledon
GC, a 12-hole competition was held during which
two competitors, Mrs L. Champion and Mrs A.
McKendrick, driving from the eighth and ninth tees
respectively, saw their balls collide in mid-air.

● In 1928, at Wentworth Falls, Australia, Dr Alcorn
and E.A. Avery, of Leura Club, were playing with professional E. Barnes. The tee shots of Avery and
Barnes at the 9th hole finished on opposite sides of
the fairway. Both players unknowingly hit their seconds (chip shots) at the same time. Dr Alcorn, standing at the pin, suddenly saw two balls approaching the
hole from different angles. They met in the air and
dropped into the hole.

● At Rugby, 1931, playing in a 4-ball match,
H. Fraser pulled his drive from the 10th tee in the
direction of the ninth tee. Simultaneously a club
member, driving from the ninth tee, pulled his drive.
The tees were about 350 yards apart. The two balls
collided in mid-air.

● Two golf balls, being played in opposite directions,
collided in flight over Longniddry Golf Course on
27th June, 1953. Immediately after Stewart Elder, of
Longniddry, had driven from the third tee, another
ball, which had been pulled off line from the second
fairway, which runs alongside the third, struck his
ball about 20 feet above the ground. S.J. Fleming, of
Tranent, who was playing with Elder, heard a loud
crack and thought Elder's ball had exploded. The balls
were found undamaged about 70 yards apart.

Three and two balls dislodged by one shot

● In 1934 on the short 3rd hole (now the 13th) of
Olton Course, Warwickshire, J.R. Horden, a scratch
golfer of the club, sent his tee shot into long wet
grass a few feet over the back of the green. When he
played an *explosion* shot three balls dropped on to the
putting green, his own and two others.

● A.M. Chevalier, playing at Hale, Cheshire, March,
1935, drove his ball into a grass bunker, and when he
reached it there was only part of it showing. He
played the shot with a niblick and to his amazement
not one but three balls shot into the air. They all
dropped back into the bunker and came to rest within a foot of each other. Then came another surprise.

One of the *finds* was of the same manufacture and
bore the same number as the ball he was playing
with.

● Playing to the 9th hole, at Osborne House Club,
Isle of Wight, George A. Sherman lost his ball which
had sunk out of sight on the sodden fairway. A few
weeks later, playing from the same tee, his ball again
was plugged, only the top showing. Under a local rule
he lifted his ball to place it, and exactly under it lay
the ball he had lost previously.

Balls in strange places

● Playing at the John O' Gaunt Club, Sutton, near
Biggleswade (Beds), a member drove a ball which did
not touch the ground until it reached London – over
40 miles away. The ball landed in a vegetable lorry
which was passing the golf course and later fell out of
a package of cabbages when they were unloaded at
Covent Garden, London.

● In the English Open Amateur Stroke Play at Moortown in 1974, Nigel Denham, a Yorkshire County
player, in the first round saw his overhit second shot
to the 18th green bounce up some steps into the
clubhouse. His ball went through an open door, rico-
cheted off a wall and came to rest in the men's bar,
20 feet from the windows. As the clubhouse was not
out of bounds Denham decided to play the shot back
to the green and opened a window 4 feet by 2 feet
through which he pitched his ball to 12 feet from the
flag. (Several weeks later the R&A declared that Denham should have been penalised two shots for opening the window. The clubhouse was an immovable
obstruction and no part of it should have been
moved.)

● In The Open Championship at Sandwich, 1949,
Harry Bradshaw, Kilcroney, Dublin, at the 5th hole in
his second round, drove into the rough and found his
ball inside a beer bottle with the neck and shoulder
broken off and four sharp points sticking up. Bradshaw, if he had treated the ball as in an unplayable lie
might have been involved in a disqualification, so he
decided to play it where it lay. With his blaster he
smashed the bottle and sent the ball about 30 yards.
The hole, a par 4, cost him 6.

● Kevin Sharman of Woodbridge GC hit a low, very
straight drive at the club's 8th hole in 1979. After
some minutes' searching, his ball was found embedded in a plastic sphere on top of the direction post.

● On the Dublin Course, 16th July, 1936, in the Irish
Open Championship, A.D. Locke, the South African,
played his tee shot at the 100-yard 12th hole, but the
ball could not be found on arrival on the green. The
marker removed the pin and it was discovered that
the ball had been entangled in the flag. It dropped
near the edge of the hole and Locke holed the short
putt for a birdie two.

● While playing a round on the Geelong Golf Club
Course, Australia, Easter, 1923, Captain Charteris
topped his tee shot to the short 2nd hole, which lies
over a creek with deep and steep clay banks. His ball
came to rest on the near slope of the creek bank. He

elected to play the ball as it lay, and took his niblick. After the shot, the ball was nowhere to be seen. It was found later embedded in a mass of gluey clay stuck fast to the face of the niblick. It could not be shaken off. Charteris did what was afterwards approved by the R&A, cleaned the ball and dropped it behind without penalty.

● In October, 1929, at Blackmoor Golf Club, Bordon, Hants, a player driving from the first tee holed out his ball in the chimney of a house some 120 yards distant and some 40 yards out of bounds on the right. The owner and his wife were sitting in front of the fire when they heard a rattle in the chimney and were astonished to see a golf ball drop into the fire.

● A similar incident occurred in an inter-club match between Musselburgh and Lothianburn at Prestongrange in 1938 when a member of the former team hooked his ball at the 2nd hole and gave it up for lost. To his amazement a woman emerged from one of the houses adjacent to this part of the course and handed back the ball which she said had come down the chimney and landed on a pot which was on the fire.

● In July, 1955, J. Lowrie, starter at the Eden Course, St Andrews, witnessed a freak shot. A visitor drove from the first tee just as a north-bound train was passing. He sliced the shot and the ball disappeared through an open window of a passenger compartment. Almost immediately the ball emerged again, having been thrown back on to the fairway by a man in the compartment, who waved a greeting which presumably indicated that no one was hurt.

● At Coombe Wood Golf Club, a player hit a ball towards the 16th green where it landed in the vertical exhaust of a tractor which was mowing the fairway. The greenkeeper was somewhat surprised to find a temporary loss of power in the tractor. When sufficient compression had built up in the exhaust system, the ball was forced out with tremendous velocity, hit the roof of a house nearby, bounced off and landed some three feet from the pin on the green.

● When carrying out an inspection of the air conditioning system at St John's Hospital, Chelmsford, in 1993, a golf ball was found in the ventilator immediately above the operating theatre. It was probably the result of a hooked drive from the first tee at Chelmsford Golf Club, which is close by, but the ball can only have entered the duct on a rebound through a three-inch gap under a ventilator hood and then descended through a series of sharp bends to its final resting place.

● There have been many occasions when misdirected shots have finished in strange places after an unusual line of flight and bounce. At Ashford, Middlesex, John Miller, aged 69, hit his tee shot out of bounds at the 12th hole (237 yards). It struck a parked car, passed through a copse, hit more cars, jumped a canopy, flew through the clubhouse kitchen window, finishing in a cooking stock-pot, without once touching the ground. Mr Miller had previously done the hole in one on four occasions.

Balls Hit To and From Great Heights

● In 1798 two Edinburgh golfers undertook to drive a ball over the spire of St Giles' Cathedral, Edinburgh, for a wager. Mr Sceales, of Leith, and Mr Smellie, a printer, were each allowed six shots and succeeded in sending the balls well over the weather-cock, a height of more than 160 feet from the ground.

● Some years later Donald McLean, an Edinburgh lawyer, won a substantial bet by driving a ball over the Melville Monument in St Andrew Square, Edinburgh – height, 154 feet.

● Tom Morris in 1860, at the famous bridge of Ballochmyle, stood in the quarry beneath and, from a stick elevated horizontally, attempted to send golf balls over the bridge. He could raise them only to the pathway, 400 feet high, which was in itself a great feat with the gutta ball.

● Captain Ernest Carter, on 28th September, 1922, drove a ball from the roadway at the 1st tee on Harlech Links against the wall of Harlech Castle. The embattlements are 200 feet over the level of the roadway, and the point where the ball struck the embattlements was 180 yards from the point where the ball was teed. Captain Carter, who was laid odds of £100 to £1, used a baffy.

● In 1896 Freddie Tait, then a subaltern in the Black Watch, drove a ball from the Rookery, the highest building on Edinburgh Castle, in a match against a brother officer to hole out in the fountain in Princes Street Gardens 350 feet below and about 300 yards distant.

● Prior to the 1977 Lancôme Tournament in Paris, Arnold Palmer hit three balls from the second stage of the Eiffel Tower, over 300 feet above ground. The longest was measured at 403 yards. One ball was hooked and hit a bus but no serious damage was done as all traffic had been stopped for safety reasons.

● Long drives have been made from mountain peaks, across the gorge at Victoria Falls, from the Pyramids, high buildings in New York, and from many other similar places. As an illustration of such freakish *drives* a member of the New York Rangers' Hockey Team from the top of Mount Edith Cavell, 11,033 feet high, drove a ball which struck the Ghost Glacier 5000 feet below and bounced off the rocky ledge another 1000 feet – a total drop of 2000 yards. Later, in June, 1968, from Pikes Peak, Colorado (14,110 feet), Arthur Lynskey hit a ball which travelled 200 yards horizontally but 2 miles vertically.

Remarkable Shots

● Remarkable shots are as numerous as the grains of sand; around every 19th hole, legends are recalled of astounding shots. One shot is commemorated by a memorial tablet at the 17th hole at the Lytham and St Annes Club. It was made by Bobby Jones in the final round of The Open Championship in 1926. He was partnered by Al Watrous, another American player. They had been running neck and neck and at the end of the third round, Watrous was just leading Jones with 215 against 217. At the 16th Jones drew level then on the 17th he drove into a sandy lie in broken ground. Watrous reached the green with his second. Jones took a mashie-iron (the equivalent to a 4-iron today) and hit a magnificent shot to the green to get his 4. This remarkable recovery unnerved Watrous, who 3-putted, and Jones, getting another 4 at the last hole against 5, won his first Open Championship with 291 against Watrous' 293. The tablet is near the spot where Jones played his second shot.

● Arnold Palmer (USA), playing in the second round of the Australian Wills Masters tournament at Melbourne, in October, 1964, hooked his second shot at the 9th hole high into the fork of a gum tree. Climbing 20 feet up the tree, Palmer, with the head of his 1-iron reversed, played a hammer stroke and knocked the ball some 30 yards forward, followed by a brilliant chip to the green and a putt.

● In the foursome during the Ryder Cup at Moortown in 1929, Joe Turnesa hooked the American side's second shot at the last hole behind the marquee adjoining the clubhouse, Johnny Farrel then pitched the ball over the marquee on to the green only feet away from the pin and Turnesa holed out for a 4.

Miscellaneous Incidents and Strange Golfing Facts

● Gary Player of South Africa was honoured by his country by having his portrait on new postage stamps which were issued on 12th December, 1976. It was the first time a specific golfer had ever been depicted on any country's postage stamps. In 1981 the US Postal Service introduced stamps featuring Bobby Jones and Babe Zaharias. They are the first golfers to be thus honoured by the United States.

● Gary Harris, aged 18, became the first player to make five consecutive appearances for England in the European Boys Team Championship at Vilamoura, Portugal, in 1994.

● In February, 1971, the first ever golf shots on the moon's surface were played by Captain Alan Shepard, commander of the Apollo 14 spacecraft. Captain Shepard hit two balls with an iron head attached to a makeshift shaft. With a one-handed swing he claimed he hit the first ball 200 yards aided by the reduced force of gravity on the moon. Subsequent findings put this distance in doubt. The second was a shank. Acknowledging the occasion the R&A sent Captain Shepard the following telegram: *Warmest congratulations to all of you on your great achievement and safe return. Please refer to Rules of Golf section on etiquette, paragraph 6, quote – before leaving a bunker a player should carefully fill up all holes made by him therein, unquote.* Shepard presented the club to the USGA Museum in 1974.

● Charles (Chick) Evans competed in every US Amateur Championship held between 1907 and 1962 by which time he was 72 years old. This amounted to 50 consecutive occasions discounting the six years of the two World Wars when the championship was not held.

●. In winning the 1977 US Open at Southern Hills CC, Tulsa, Oklahoma, Hubert Green had to contend with a death threat. Coming off the 14th green in the final round, he was advised by USGA officials that a phone call had been received saying that he would be killed. Green decided that play should continue and happily he went on to win, unharmed.

● It was discovered at the 1977 USPGA Championship that the clubs with which Tom Watson had won The Open Championship and the US Masters earlier in the year were illegal, having grooves which exceeded the permitted specifications. The set he used in winning the 1975 Open Championship were then flown out to him and they too were found to be illegal. No retrospective action was taken.

● Mrs Fred Daly, wife of the former Open champion, saved the clubhouse of Balmoral GC, Belfast, from destruction when three men entered the professional's shop on 5th August, 1976, and left a bag containing a bomb outside the shop beside the clubhouse when refused money. Mrs Daly carried the bag over to a hedge some distance away where the bomb exploded 15 minutes later. The only damage was broken windows. On the same day several hours afterwards, Dungannon GC in Co. Tyrone suffered extensive damage to the clubhouse from terrorist bombs. Co. Down GC, proposed venue of the 1979 home international matches suffered bomb damage in May that year and through fear for the safety of team members the 1979 matches were cancelled.

● The Army Golfing Society and St Andrews on 21st April, 1934, played a match 200-a-side, the largest golf match ever played. Play was by foursomes. The Army won 58, St Andrews 31 and 11 were halved.

● Jamie Ortiz-Patino, owner of the Valderrama Golf Club at Sotogrande, Spain, paid a record £84,000 (increased to £92,400 with ten per cent buyers premium) for a late seventeenth- or early eighteenth-century rake iron offered at auction in Musselburgh in July, 1992. The iron, which had been kept in a garden shed, was bought to be exhibited in a museum being created in Valderrama.

● In 1986 Alistair Risk and three colleagues on the 17th green at Brora, Sutherland, watched a cow giving birth to twin calves between the markers on the 18th tee, causing them to play their next tee shots from in front of the tee. Their application for a ruling from the R&A brought a Rules Committee reply that while technically a rule had been broken, their action was considered within the spirit of the game and there should be no penalty. The Secretary added that the Rules Committee hoped that mother and twins were doing well.

● In view of the increasing number of people crossing the road (known as Granny Clark's Wynd) which runs across the first and 18th fairways of the Old Course, St Andrews, as a right of way, the St Andrews Links committee decided in 1969 to control the flow by erecting traffic lights, with appropriate green for go, yellow for caution and red for stop. The lights are controlled from the starter's box on the first tee. Golfers on the first tee must wait until the lights turn to green before driving off and a notice has been erected at the Wynd warning pedestrians not to cross at yellow or stop.

● A traffic light for golfers was also installed in 1971 on one of Japan's most congested courses. After putting on the uphill 9th hole of the Fukuoka course in Southern Japan, players have to switch on a go-ahead signal for following golfers waiting to play their shots to the green.

● A 22-year-old professional at Brett Essex GC, Brentwood, David Moore, who was playing in the Mufulira Open in Zambia in 1976, was shot dead it is alleged by the man with whom he was staying for the duration of the tournament. It appeared his host then shot himself.

● Peggy Carrick and her daughter, Angela Uzielli, won the Mothers and Daughters Tournament at Royal Mid-Surrey in 1994 for the 21st time.

● Patricia Shepherd has won the ladies' club championship at Turriff GC Aberdeenshire 30 consecutive times from 1959 to 1988.

● Mrs Jackie Mercer won the South African Ladies' Championship in 1979, 31 years after her first victory in the event as Miss Jacqueline Smith.

● During The Royal and Ancient Golf Club of St Andrews' medal meeting on 25th September, 1907, a member of The Royal and Ancient drove a ball which struck the sharp point of a hatpin in the hat of a lady who was crossing the course. The ball was so firmly impaled that it remained in position. The lady was not hurt.

● John Cook, former English Amateur Champion, narrowly escaped death during an attempted coup against King Hassan of Morocco in July 1971. Cook had been playing in a tournament arranged by King Hassan, a keen golfer, and was at the King's birthday party in Rabat when rebels broke into the party demanding that the King give up his throne. Cook and many others present were taken hostage.

● When playing from the 9th tee at Lossiemouth golf course in June, 1971, Martin Robertson struck a Royal Navy jet aircraft which was coming in to land at the nearby airfield. The plane was not damaged.

● At a court in Inglewood, California, in 1978, Jim Brown was convicted of beating and choking an opponent during a dispute over where a ball should have been placed on the green.

● During the Northern Ireland troubles a home-made hand grenade was found in a bunker at Dungannon GC, Co. Tyrone, on Sunday, 12th September, 1976.

● Tiger Woods, 18, became both the youngest and the first black golfer to win the United States Amateur Championship at Sawgrass in 1994. He went on to win the title three years in a row and then won the first major championship he played as a professional, the 1997 Masters, by a record 12 strokes and with a record low aggregate of 270, 18 under par.

● To mark the centenary of the Jersey Golf Club in 1978, the Jersey Post Office issued a set of four special stamps featuring Jersey's most famous golfer, Harry Vardon. The background of the 13p stamp was a brief biography of Vardon's career reproduced from the Golfer's Handbook.

● Forty-one-year-old John Mosley went for a round of golf at Delaware Park GC, Buffalo, New York, in July, 1972. He stepped on to the first tee and was challenged over a green fee by an official guard. A scuffle developed, a shot was fired and Mosley, a bullet in his chest, died on the way to hospital. His wife was awarded $131,250 in an action against the City of Buffalo and the guard. The guard was sentenced to 7¹/₂ years for second-degree manslaughter.

● When three competitors in a 1968 Pennsylvania pro-am event were about to drive from the 16th tee, two bandits (one with pistol) suddenly emerged from the bushes, struck one of the players and robbed them of wristwatches and $300.

● In the 1932 Walker Cup match at Brooklyn, Leonard Crawley succeeded in denting the cup. An errant iron shot to the 18th green hit the cup, which was on display outside the clubhouse.

● In Johannesburg, South Africa, three golf officials appeared in court accused of violating a 75-year-old Sunday Observance Law by staging the final round of the South African PGA championship on Sunday, 28th February, 1971. The Championship should have been completed on the Saturday but heavy rain prevented any play.

● In The Open Championship of 1876, at St Andrews, Bob Martin and David Strath tied at 176. A protest was lodged against Strath alleging he played his approach to the 17th green and struck a spectator. The Royal and Ancient ordered the replay, but Strath refused to play off the tie until a decision had been given on the protest. No decision was given and Bob Martin was declared the Champion.

● At Rose Bay, New South Wales, on 11th July, 1931, D.J. Bayly MacArthur, on stepping into a bunker, began to sink. MacArthur, who weighed 14 stone, shouted for help. He was rescued when up to the armpits. He had stepped on a patch of quicksand, aggravated by excess of moisture.

● The late Bobby Cruickshank was the victim of his own jubilation in the 1934 US Open at Merion. In the 4th round while in with a chance of winning he half-topped his second shot at the 11th hole. The ball was heading for a pond in front of the green but instead of ending up in the water it hit a rock and bounced on to the green. In his delight Cruickshank threw his club into the air only to receive a resounding blow on the head as it returned to earth.

● A dog with an infallible nose for finding lost golf balls was, in 1971, given honorary membership of the Waihi GC, Hamilton, New Zealand. The dog, called Chico, was trained to search for lost balls, to be sold back to the members, the money being put into club funds.

● By 1980 Waddy, an 11-year-old beagle belonging to Bob Inglis, the secretary of Brokenhurst Manor GC, had found over 35,000 golf balls.

● Herbert M. Hepworth, Headingley, Leeds, Lord Mayor of Leeds in 1906, scored one thousand holes in 2, a feat which took him 30 years to accomplish. It was celebrated by a dinner in 1931 at the Leeds club. The first 2 of all was scored on 12th June, 1901, at Cobble Hall Course, Leeds, and the 1,000th in 1931 at Alwoodley, Leeds. Hepworth died in November, 1942.

● Fiona MacDonald was the first female to play in the Oxford and Cambridge University match at Ganton in 1986.

● Mrs Sara Gibbon won the Farnham (Surrey) Club's Grandmother's competition 48 hours after her first grand-child was born.

● At Carnoustie in the first qualifying round for the 1952 Scottish Amateur Championship a competitor drove three balls in succession out of bounds at the 1st hole and thereupon withdrew.

● In 1993, the Clark family from Hagley GC, Worcs, set a record for the county's three major professional events. The Worcestershire Stroke Play Championship was won by Finlay Clark, the eldest son, who beat his father Iain and younger brother Cameron, who tied second. In the Match Play Iain beat his son Finlay by 2 and 1 in the final; Cameron won the play-off for third place. Then in the Worcestershire Annual Pro-Am it was Cameron's turn to win, with his brother Finlay coming second and father Iain third. To add to the achievements of the family, Cameron also won the Midland Professional Match Play Championship.

● During a Captain–Pro foursomes challenge match at Chelmsford in 1993, Club Professional Dennis Bailey, put the ball into a hole only once in all 18 holes – when he holed-in-one at the fourth.

● In 1891, a new kind of matchplay – bogey – was introduced at Great Yarmouth Golf Club where the scratch score of the course was taken and each hole given a value known as the ground score. One of the club's members was described as a "regular bogeyman", a name suggested by a music hall song that was currently popular … and the name stuck.

Strange local rules

● The Duke of Windsor, who played on an extraordinary variety of the world's courses, once took advantage of a local rule at Jinja in Uganda and lifted his ball from a hippo's footprint without penalty.

● At the Glen Canyon course in Arizona a local rule provides that *If your ball lands within a club length of a rattlesnake you are allowed to move the ball.*

● Another local rule in Uganda read: *If a ball comes to rest in dangerous proximity to a crocodile, another ball may be dropped.*

● The 6th hole at Koolan Island GC, Western Australia, also serves as a local air strip and a local rule reads: *Aircraft and vehicular traffic have right of way at all times.*

● A local rule at the RAF Waddington GC reads: *When teeing off from the 2nd, right of way must be given to taxiing aircraft.*

Puerto Rican's chilly win

The first Chivas Snow Golf Championship to be staged in South America, held in Chile in 2006 against the backdrop of the Andes, was attended by golf professionals and amateurs as well as a number of well-known personalities. Among the professional players was Chilean Mark Tullo but victory went to the Puerto Rican amateur Cesar Serrano who won the Chivas Regal trophy and also gained automatic entry to the Chivas Snow Golf Championship at St Moritz later in the year.

The Chilean tournament was played on a nine-hole course with over 100 competitors from Canada, Argentina, Uruguay, Bolivia, Puerto Rico, Guatemala, Brazil, Peru and elsewhere taking part. The tournament was played on snow fairways and greens ("whites" might prove a better description) of smoothed and frozen snow.

Timeline for the Rules of Golf

The earliest known Rules of Golf were drawn up in 1744 by what was to become the Honourable Company of Edinburgh Golfers. For the next 100 years, each club could issue and revise its own code of Rules, and these were mainly based on the codes issued by The Royal and Ancient Golf Club, the Edinburgh Burgess Golfing Society or the Honourable Company. Some of the rules followed by individual clubs were identical to one of these codes, while others were worded with reference to the features of a particular course.

Starting in the second half of the 19th century, more and more clubs based their codes on those issued by The Royal and Ancient Golf Club. In 1897 its governance role was formalised with the creation of the Rules of Golf Committee.

1744 The Honourable company of Edinburgh Golfers produce a written code of rules. Known as the Thirteen Articles, Rule 1 states: "You must tee your ball within a club-length of the hole".

1754 Largely copying from the 1744 Rules, the Society of St Andrews Golfers (later to become The Royal and Ancient Golf Club) record their own Rules in the minutes.

1775 Methods of settling disputes first appear in the Honourable Company's Rules. "Any dispute arising between parties on the green shall be determined by the Captain for the time, if present, or by the latest Captain who may be on the ground".

1812 The R&A's 1754 code is revised and for the first time the Rules of Golf refer to bunkers and the putting green.

1842 The revised R&A code stipulates that "one round of the links, or 18 holes, is reckoned a match" for the first time.

1851 A revised R&A code is issued. In response to the advent of the gutta percha ball, a new rule allows that: "If a ball shall split into two or more pieces, a fresh ball shall be put down in playing for a medal".

1875 Attending the flagstick and dealing with balls resting against the flagstick appear in the Rules for the first time.

1882 The revised R&A code contains an index and a glossary of terms for the first time.

1882 The glossary of terms in the R&A code defines the size of the hole as being four inches in diameter and lined with iron.

1886 The Royal Isle of Wight Golf Club issues a version of the Rules of Golf, which defines the size of the hole as being four inches in diameter and six inches deep.

1888 Local Rules for Playing the Links at St Andrews are separated out from the main Rules of Golf for the first time by The R&A.

1891 The revised R&A code defines the hole as being four and a quarter inches in diameter and at least four inches deep. This remains the definition.

1897 The Royal and Ancient Golf Club is officially recognised as the game's governing body for the Rules of Golf.

1909 Limits on the form and make of clubs are applied for the first time.

1920 The R&A and the USGA agreed that from May 1st, 1921, "the weight of the ball should be no greater than 1.62 ounces and the size not less than 1.62 inches in diameter".

1929 Steel shafts are legalised.

1939 The maximum number of clubs that can be carried is 14.

1952 The R&A and the USGA establish a unified code of Rules.

1960 Distance measuring devices are banned.

1984 The ball is no longer dropped over the player's shoulder, but at arm's length and at shoulder height.

1988 First Joint Decisions on the Rules of Golf book published by The R&A and the USGA.

1990 The 1.68-inch ball becomes the only legal ball, marking the demise of the 1.62-inch British ball.

Royal Clubs

There are currently 61 clubs worldwide with a Royal title. In October 2005, the Mayfair Golf & Country Club in Edmonton, Canada, was granted Royal status by Her Majesty Queen Elizabeth II. In 2004, Wellington Golf Club received the title from HRH The Duke of York. Marianske Lazne Golf Club was honoured in 2003. The club had strong connections with British Royalty in the past; King Edward VII holidayed there, in what is now the Czech Republic. Apart from Marianske Lazne, the Royal Clubs are in the United Kingdom or the Commonwealth. The oldest club with Royal connections is The Royal and Ancient Golf Club of St Andrews, founded in 1745 and given Royal patronage by King William IV in 1834. Royal Perth Golf Club, which was founded in 1824, received the patronage of King William IV a year earlier, in 1833.

Club	Year Founded	Year of Royal Patronage	Royal Patron
Royal Ancient Golf Club, St Andrews	1745	1834	William IV
Royal Aberdeen	1780	1903	Edward VII (Leopold patron in 1872)
Royal Adelaide	1892	1923	George V
Royal Ascot	1887	1887	Victoria 1887; Elizabeth II 1977
Royal Ashdown Forest	1888	1893	Victoria
Royal Belfast	1881	1885	Edward, Prince of Wales
Royal Birkdale	1889	1951	George VI
Royal Blackheath	1766	1857	*Not known*
Royal Burgess	1773	1929	George V
Royal Calcutta	1829	1911	George V
Royal Canberra	1926	1933	George V
Royal Cape	1885	1910	George V
Royal Cinque Ports	1892	1910	George V
Royal Colombo	1879	1928	George V
Royal Colwood	1913	1931	George V
Royal County Down	1889	1908	Edward VII
Royal Cromer	1888	1887	Edward, Prince of Wales (later Edward VII)
Royal Dornoch	1877	1906	Edward VII
Royal Dublin	1885	1891	Victoria
Duff House Royal Golf Club	1909	1925	Princess Louise, Dowager Duchess of Fife
Royal Durban	1892	1932	George V
Royal Eastbourne	1887	1887	Prince Albert Victor, Duke of Clarence; Victoria
Royal Epping Forest	1888	1888	Prince Arthur, Duke of Connaught
Royal Fremantle	—	1930	George V

Club	Year Founded	Year of Royal Patronage	Royal Patron
Royal Guernsey	1890	1891	Victoria
Royal Harare	1898	1929	George V
Royal Hobart	—	1925	George V
Royal Jersey	1878	1879	Victoria
Royal Johannesburg	1890	1931	George V
Royal Liverpool	1869	1871	Prince Arthur, Duke of Connaught
Royal Lytham	1886	1926	George V
Royal Malta	1888	1888	Prince Alfred, Duke of Edinburgh
Royal Marianske Lazne	1905	2003	Elizabeth II
Royal Mayfair Golf & Country Club	1922	2005	Elizabeth II
Royal Melbourne	1891	1895	Victoria
Royal Mid Surrey	1892	1926	George V
Royal Montreal	1873	1884	Victoria
Royal Montrose	1810	1845	Prince Albert
Royal Musselburgh	1774	1876	Prince Arthur, Duke of Connaught
Royal Nairobi	1906	1935	George V
Royal North Devon	1864	1865	Edward, Prince of Wales
Royal Norwich	1893	1893	Duke of York (later George V)
Royal Ottawa	1891	1912	George V
Royal Perth	1824	1833	William IV
Royal Perth (Australia)	—	1937	George VI
Royal Port Alfred	—	1924	George V
Royal Porthcawl	1891	1909	Edward VII
Royal Portrush	1888	1892	Duke of York
Royal Quebec	1874	1934	George V
Royal Queensland	1920	1921	George V
Royal Regina	1899	1999	Elizabeth II
Royal Selangor	1893	1953	Elizabeth II
Royal St Davids	1894	1908	Edward VII
Royal St Georges	1887	1902	Edward VII
Royal Sydney	1893	1897	Victoria
Royal Tarlair	1925	1926	Princess Louise, Dowager Duchess of Fife
Royal Troon	1878	1978	Elizabeth II
Royal Wellington	1895	2004	Prince Andrew
Royal West Norfolk	1892	1892	Edward, Prince of Wales (later Edward VII)
Royal Wimbledon	1865	1882	Edward, Prince of Wales
Royal Winchester	1888	1913	Edward VII
Royal Worlington and Newmarket	1893	1895	Victoria

PART XIV

Directory of Golfing Organisations Worldwide

Directory of Golfing Organisations Worldwide

National Associations

The R&A
Ch Exec, Peter Dawson, St Andrews, Fife KY16 9JD
Tel (01334) 460000   Fax (01334) 460001
E-mail The Chief Executive@RandAgc.org
Website www.randa.org

Council of National Golf Unions
Sec, Kevin McIntyre, Dromin, Dunleer, Co. Louth,
Ireland
Tel +353 41 686 1476
E-mail golfinmcinere@hotmail.com
Website www.congu.com

Ladies European Tour Ltd
Exec Dir, A Armas,
The Old Hall, Macclesfield, Cheshire SK10 2LQ
Tel (01625) 611444   Fax (01625) 610406
E-mail mail@ladieseuropeantour.com
Website www.ladieseuropeantour.com

Ladies' Golf Union
Sec, Mrs Lesley Burn, The Scores, St Andrews, Fife
KY16 9AT
Tel (01334) 475811   Fax (01334) 472818
E-mail info@lgu.org   Website www.lgu.org

The Professional Golfers' Association
Ch Exec, Sandy Jones, Centenary House,
The Belfry, Sutton Coldfield B76 9PT
Tel (01675) 470333   Fax (01675) 477888
Website www.pga.info

East Region: Sec, J Smith, Bishop's Stortford GC,
Dunmow Road, Bishop's Stortford, Herts
CM23 5HP
Tel (01279) 652070   Fax (01279) 652732
E-mail john.smith@pga.org.uk

Midland Region: Sec, G Maly, Forest Hill GC,
Markfield Lane, Botcheston, Leicester LE9 9FS
Tel (01455) 824393   Fax (01455) 828751
E-mail graham.maly@pga.org.uk

North Region: Sec, J Croxton, No 2 Cottage,
Bolton GC, Lostock Park, Chorley New Road, Bolton,
Lancs BL6 4AJ
Tel (01204) 496137   Fax (01204) 847959
E-mail jim.croxton@pga.org.uk

South Region: Sec, J Sewell, Clandon Regis GC,
Epsom Road, West Clandon, Guildford, Surrey
GU4 7TT
Tel (01483) 224200   Fax (01483) 223224
E-mail jon.sewell@pga.org.uk

West Region: Sec, R Ellis, Exeter G&CC, Topsham
Road, Countess Wear, Exeter EX2 7AE
Tel (01392) 877657   Fax (01392) 876382
E-mail ray.ellis@pga.org.uk

Irish Region: Sec, M McCumiskey, Dundalk GC,
Blackrock, Dundalk, Co Louth, Eire
Tel (00 353) 42 932 1193   Fax (00 353) 42 932 1899
E-mail michael.mccumiskey@pga.org.uk

Scottish Region: Sec, G Dewar, King's Lodge,
Gleneagles, Auchterarder PH3 1NE
Tel (01764) 661840   Fax (01764) 661841
E-mail gordon.dewar@pga.org.uk

PGA European Tour
Exec Dir, G O'Grady, PGA European Tour,
Wentworth Drive, Virginia Water, Surrey GU25 4LX
Tel (01344) 840400   Fax (01344) 840500
E-mail info@europeantour.com
Website www.europeantour.com

PGAs of Europe
Sec, Centenary House, The Belfry, Sutton Coldfield,
B76 9PT
Tel (01675) 477899   Fax (01675) 477890
E-mail info@pgae.com   Website www.pgae.com

Artisan Golfers' Association
Hon Sec, K Stevens, 48 The Avenue, Lightwater,
Surrey GU18 5RG
Tel (01276) 475103
E-mail kevin@stevens85.freeserve.co.uk
Website www.agagolf.co.uk

Association of Golf Club Secretaries
Membership of the Association is over 2,300 consisting
of managers/secretaries and retired secretaries of
clubs and golfing associations situated in the UK and
Europe. The Association offers advice on all aspects of
managing a golf club and has an extensive information
library available to its members through its website.

National Sec, K Lloyd, 7a Beaconsfield Road,
Weston-super-Mare BS23 1YE
Tel (01934) 641166   Fax (01934) 644254
E-mail hq@agcs.org.uk   Website www.agcs.org.uk

Association of Golf Writers
A group of 30 newspapermen attending the Walker
Cup match at St Andrews in 1938 founded the Asso-
ciation to protect the interests of golf writers. The

principal objective is to maintain a close liaison with all the governing bodies and promoters to ensure good working conditions.

Sec, Andrew Farrell, I Pilgrims Bungalow, Mulberry Hill, Chilham, Kent CT4 8AH
Tel/Fax (01227) 732496
E-mail andyfarrell@compuserve.com

BAGCC – British Association of Golf Course Constructors

The BAGCC has a small but highly prestigious membership of constructors who have performed work to the highest standard from initial consultation to survey work and design through to the construction of a course and then its regular maintenance. Membership is granted only if the candidates satisfy the demanding criteria of experience, professionalism and workmanship set down by the Association.

Sec, D White, Fore! The Dormy House, Cooden Beach GC, Bexhill-on-Sea TN39 4TR
Tel (01424) 842380
Fax (01424) 843375
E-mail mightyspyder@onetel.net
Website www.bagcc.org.uk

BALASA – British Amputee & Les Autres Sports Association

Chair, R Saunders, 24 Notcutts, East Bergholt, Colchester CO7 6TS
Tel (01206) 298 610
E-mail richardsaunders@fingers32.freeserve.co.uk

British Golf Collectors' Society

Sec, A Thorpe, 22 Cherry Tree Close, Brinsley, Nottingham NG16 5BA
Tel/Fax (01773) 780420
E-mail anthonythorpe@ntlworld.com
Website www.britgolfcollectors.wyenet.co.uk

BGIA – British Golf Industry Association

Federation House, Stoneleigh Park, Warks CV8 2RF
Tel (024) 7641 7141   *Fax* (024) 7641 4990
E-mail bgia@sportsandplay.com
Website www.bgia.org.uk

British Golf Museum

Dir, PN Lewis, Bruce Embankment, St Andrews, Fife KY16 9AB
Tel (01334) 460046   *Fax* (01334) 460064
Website www.britishgolfmuseum.co.uk

BIGGA – British & International Golf Greenkeepers Association

BIGGA, which was formed in 1987, is an amalgamation of the British, English and Scottish Associations and promotes and advances all aspects of greenkeeping and assists and encourages the proficiency of the members. In addition to its annual conference the Association organizes the annual Turf Management Exhibition, Europe's largest indoor turf show. Currently the Association has over 7,300 members.

Ch Exec, J Pemberton, BIGGA House, Aldwark, Alne, York Y061 1UF
Tel (01347) 833800   *Fax* (01347) 833801
E-mail reception@bigga.co.uk
Website www.bigga.org.uk

BRTMA – British Rootzone & Topdressing Manufacturers Association

Federation House, Stoneleigh Park, Warks CV8 2RF
Tel (024) 7641 4999   *Fax* (024) 7641 4990
E-mail brtma@sportsandplay.com
Website www.brtma.com

British Turf & Landscape Irrigation Association

Sec, M Jones, 41 Pennine Way, Great Eccleston, Preston PR3 0YPO Box 709, Garstang PR3 1GT
Tel/Fax (01995) 670675
E-mail info@btlia.org.uk
Website www.btlia.org.uk

EDGA – European Disabled Golf Association

Sec/Treas, Pieter van Duyn, Wederikof 8, 2215 GJ Voorhout, The Netherlands
Tel +31 252 224161   *Fax* +31 653 161470
E-mail p.vanduyn@tiscali.ni
British contact: see BALASA

EGIA – European Golf Industry Association

Federation House, Stoneleigh Park, Warks CV8 2RF
Tel (024) 7641 4999   *Fax* (024) 7641 4990
E-mail egia@sportsandplay.com

EIGCA – European Institute of Golf Course Architects

The EIGCA represents the vast majority of qualified and experienced golf course architects throughout Europe. Its goals are to enhance the professional status of the profession and to provide educational courses to train future course architects.

Exec Off, Mrs Julia Green, Chiddingfold GC, Petworth Rd, Chiddingfold GU8 4SL
Tel/Fax (01428) 681528
E-mail info@eigca.org   *Website* www.eigca.org

Golf Club Stewards' Association

The Golf Club Stewards' Association was founded in 1912 to promote the interests of members and to serve as an employment agency for golf club stewards.

Sec, Peter Payne, 3 St George's Drive, Ickenham, Middx UB10 4HW
Tel (01895) 674325   *E-mail* golfclubstewards@aol.com
Website www.club_noticeboard.co.uk

Golf Consultants Association

Federation House, Stoneleigh Park, Warks CV8 2RF
Tel (024) 7641 4999   *Fax* (024) 7641 4990
E-mail gca@sportsandplay.com
Website www.golfconsultants.org.uk

Golf Foundation

Ch. Exec, Michael Round, Foundation House, The Spinney, Hoddesdon Rd, Stanstead Abbots SG12 8GF
Tel (01920) 876200   *Fax* (01920) 876211
E-mail info@golf-foundation.org
Website www.golf-foundation.org

Handigolf Foundation

Sec, Ray Lee, 404 Westthorne Ave, Eltham, London SE9 5TL
Tel (0208) 850 7407   *E-mail* rayndpam@hotmail.com
Website www.handigolf.org

National Association of Public Golf Courses
Affiliated to the English Golf Union, the Association was founded in 1927 by golf course architect FG Hawtree and five times Open champion JH Taylor to provide a relationship between private golf clubs, public golf clubs and local councils.

Hon Sec, E Mitchell, 12 Newton Close, Redditch B98 7YR
Tel (01527) 542106
Fax (01527) 455320
E-mail eddiemitchell@blueyonder.co.uk

National Golf Clubs' Advisory Association
Founded in 1922, the Association's aims are to protect the interests of golf clubs in general, give legal advice and direction, under the opinion of Counsel, on the administrative and legal responsibilities of golf clubs. Financial assistance may sometimes be given in cases taken to court which involve, in the opinion of the Asssociation's Executive Committee, principles affecting the general interests of affiliated clubs.

Sec, Michael Shaw LLM, Tranzart Business Centre, Owl Gate, Roberts End, Hanley Swan WR8 0DN
Tel (01684) 311353
Fax (01684) 311924
E-mail ngcaa@idealnet.co.uk
Website www.ngcaa.org.uk

One-Armed Golfers, Society of
Hon Sec, Jim Darragh, 29 Sunnybank Drive, Clarkston, Glasgow G76 7SS
Tel (0141) 571 7480
E-mail hail.hail@ntlworld.com

Public Schools Old Boys Golf Association
Hon Sec, P de Pinna, Bruins, Wythwood, Haywards Heath, West Sussex RH16 4RD
Tel/Fax (01444) 454883

Public Schools' Golfing Society
Hon Sec, N Owen,1 Bruce Grove, Orpington, Kent BR6 0HF
Tel 01689 810225　　*E-mail* nick.owen@ndowen.com

STRI – Sports Turf Research Institute
The STRI is recognised officially as the national centre for sports and amenity turf and provides agronomy advice to the Royal and Ancient Golf Club's Championship committee. The Institute's mission is to carry out research and promote innovation, to provide advisory and consultancy services and to provide education and publications for subscribing clubs, sports controlling bodies and the turfgrass industry.

Ch Exec, Dr IG McKillop; *Ext Affairs*, Anne Wilson, St Ives Estate, Bingley, West Yorks BD16 1AU
Tel (01274) 565131　　*Fax* (01274) 561891
E-mail info@stri.co.uk　　*Website* www.stri.co.uk

Home Unions and Regional Associations

England

English Golf Union
Ch Exec, PM Baxter, National Golf Centre, The Broadway, Woodhall Spa, Lincs LN10 6PU
Tel (01526) 354500
Fax (01526) 354020
E-mail info@englishgolfunion.org
Website www.englishgolfunion.org

Midland Group: *Sec*, TG Arnold, 5 Manor Drive, Corby, Northants NN18 0TN
Tel (01536) 743829
Fax (07005) 801 042
E-mail secretary@midlandgolfunion.co.uk
Website www.midlandgolfunion.co.uk

Northern Group: *Sec*, JE Allen, West Pines, 16 Macclesfield Rd, Presbury, Cheshire SK10 4BN
Tel/Fax (01625) 265373
E-mail john.allen87@ntlworld.com

South Eastern Group: *Sec*, JW Gilding, 10 Mansion Lane, Iver, Bucks SL0 9RH
Tel (01753) 819686
Fax (01753) 771809
E-mail secretary@southeastgolfunion.co.uk

South Western Group: *Sec*, DR King, 41 West Town Lane, Brislington, Bristol BS4 5DD
Tel/Fax (01179) 773330
E-mail davidswcga@btopenworld.com

English Men's County Unions

Bedfordshire CGU
Hon Sec, D Parrett, 49 Manor Road, Barton le Clay MK45 4NP
Tel (01582) 883089
E-mail secretary@bedsgolfunion.org
Website www.bedsgolfunion.org

Berks & Bucks & Oxon UGC
Sec, PMJ York, Bridge House, Station Approach, Great Missenden HP16 9AZ
Tel (01494) 867341　　*Fax* (01494) 867342
E-mail secretary@bbogolf.com
Website www.bbogolf.com

Cambridgeshire Area GU
Sec, RAC Blows, 73 Pheasant Rise, Bar Hill, Cambridge CB3 8SB
Tel (01954) 780887

Cheshire UGC
Sec, SJ Foster, 15 Barley Croft, Boughton, Chester CH3 5SP
Tel/Fax (01244) 346662
E-mail secretary@cheshiregolf.org.uk
Website www.cheshiregolf.org.uk

Cornwall GU
Hon Sec, P F Batty, 3 Clemens Close, Newquay, Cornwall TR7 2SG
Tel/Fax (01637) 873117
E-mail secretary@cornwallgolfunion.org.uk
Website www.cornwallgolfunion.org.uk

Cumbria UGC
Hon Sec, T F Stout, Kingston House, Moresby,
Whitehaven CA28 8UW
Tel/Fax (01946) 693 036
E-mail cumbriaugcsec@yahoo.co.uk
Website www.cumbrian-golf-union.org.uk

Derbyshire UGC
Hon Sec, CRJ Ibbotson, 4 The Spinney, Luke Lane,
Brailsford DE6 3BS
Tel (01335) 360889   *Fax* (01335) 361198
E-mail secretary@dugc.co.uk
Website www.dugc.co.uk

Devon CGU
Sec, John Hirst, 20 Plymouth Rd, Tavistock
PL19 8AY
Tel (01822) 610640   *Fax* (01822) 610540
E-mail info@devongolfunion.org.uk
Website www.devongolfunion.org.uk

Dorset CGU
Sec, Douglas Pratt, 5 Farm Close, Southill, Weymouth
DT4 0EG
Tel (01305) 786184   *Fax* (01305) 759134
E-mail douglas.pratt@virgin.net
Website www.dorsetgolfunion.com

Durham CGU
Sec, GP Hope, 7 Merrion Close, Moorside,
Sunderland SR3 2QP
Tel/Fax (0191) 522 8605
E-mail secretary@durhamcountygolfunion.co.uk
Website www.durhamcountygolfunion.co.uk

Essex GU
Sec, AT Lockwood, 2d Maldon Road, Witham, Essex
CM8 2AB
Tel (01376) 500998   *Fax* (01376) 500842
E-mail info@essexgolfunion.org
Website www.essexgolfunion.org

Gloucestershire GU
Sec, I Watkins, The Vyse, Olde Lane,
Toddington, Glos GL54 5DW
Tel/Fax (01242) 621476
E-mail secretary@gloucestershiregolfunion.co.uk
Website www.gloucestershiregolfunion.co.uk

Hampshire, Isle of Wight & Channel Islands GU
Sec, Barry Morgan, c/o Liphook GC, Wheatsheaf
Enclosure, Liphook, Hants GU30 7EH
Tel/Fax (01428) 725580
E-mail hgu@hampshiregolf.co.uk
Website www.hampshiregolf.org.uk

Hertfordshire GU
Hon Sec, J R Newton, 16 Ranworth Ave, Stevenage
SG2 8SL
Tel/Fax (01438) 244 858
E-mail secretary@hertsgolfunion.com
Website www.hertsgolfunion.com

Isle of Man GU
Hon Sec, Joe Boyd, Cheu-Ny-Hawiney,
Phildraw Rd, Ballasalla, Isle of Man IM9 3EG
Tel/Fax (01624) 823098
E-mail joeboyd@manx.net

Kent CGU
Sec, BL Sparkes, Littlestone GC, St Andrew's Road,
Littlestone, New Romney, Kent TN28 8RB
Tel (01797) 367725   *Fax* (01797) 367726
E-mail kcgu@kentgolf.co.uk
Website www.kentgolf.org.uk

Lancashire UGC
Sec, AV Moss, 5 Dicconson Terrace, Lytham
St Annes FY8 5JY
Tel (01253) 733323   *Fax* (01253) 795721
E-mail secretary@lancashiregolf.org
Website www.lancashiregolf.org

Leicestershire & Rutland GU
Hon Sec, C Chamberlain, 10 Shipton Close, The
Meadows, Wigston Magna, Leicester LE18 3WL
Tel/Fax (0116) 288 9862
E-mail secretary@lrgu.co.uk
Website www.lrgu.co.uk

Lincolnshire UGC
Hon Sec, H Harrison, 27 Orchard Close, Morton,
Gainsborough DN21 3BP
Tel (01427) 616904   *E-mail* secretary@lugc.co.uk

Middlesex CGU
Sec, JAL Williams, Northwick Park Golf Centre,
Watford Rd, Harrow HA1 3TZ
Tel (0208) 864 4744   *Fax* (0208) 864 4554
E-mail secretary@mcgu.co.uk
Website www.mcgu.co.uk

Norfolk CGU
Hon Sec, S Howlett, 49 Russell Ave, Sprowston,
Norfolk NR7 8XE
Tel (01603) 470047
E-mail steven.howlett@lycos.co.uk

Northamptonshire GU
Hon Sec, J Pearson, 150 Church Green Rd, Bletchley,
Milton Keynes MK3 6DD
Tel (01908) 648657
E-mail secretary@northantsgolfunion.co.uk

Northumberland UGC
Hon Sec, WE Procter, Eastfield House, Moor Road
South, Gosforth, Newcastle upon Tyne NE3 1NP
Tel/Fax (0191) 285 4981
E-mail secretary@nugc.org.uk
Website www.nugc.org.uk

Nottinghamshire UGC
Hon Sec, R Case, 68a Cropwell Rd, Radcliffe-on-Trent,
Nottingham NG12 2JG
Tel/Fax (0115) 933 4777
E-mail notts.jun.golf@bluecom.net
Website www.nottsgolf.com

Shropshire & Herefordshire UGC
Hon Sec, JR Davies, 23 Poplar Crescent, Bayston Hill,
Shrewsbury SY3 0QB
Tel/Fax (01743) 872655
E-mail bdavies@blueyonder.co.uk

Somerset GU
Hon Sec, GA Yates, Little Manor, Greinton,
Nr Bridgwater TA7 9BW
Tel/Fax (01458) 210179
E-mail gyates@greinton.freeserve.co.uk
Website www.somerset.golfunion.com

Staffordshire UGC
Sec, MA Payne, 20 Kingsbrook Drive, Hillfield, Solihull
B91 3UU

Tel (0121) 704 4779   *Fax* (0121) 711 2841
E-mail martin@mpayne99.freeserve.co.uk

Suffolk GU
Hon Sec, RA Kent, 77 Bennett Avenue, Bury St
Edmunds IP33 3JJ
Tel (01284) 705765   *Fax* (01284) 767607
E-mail golfsgu@aol.com

Surrey CGU
Sec, JA Davies, Sutton Green GC, New Lane,
Sutton Green GU4 7QF
Tel (01483) 755788
E-mail secretary@surreygolf.org
Website www.surreygolf.org

Sussex CGU
Sec, A Vasant, Eastbourne Down GC, East Dean Road,
Eastbourne, East Sussex BN20 8ES
Tel (01323) 746677   *Fax* (01323) 746777
E-mail info@sussexgolf.org
Website www.sussexgolf.org

Warwickshire UGC
Sec, G G Hayes, 114 Stonebury Ave, Eastern Green,
Coventry CV5 7NX
Tel/Fax (02476) 422793
E-mail grahamhayes@warksgolf.co.uk
Website www.warksgolf.co.uk

Wiltshire CGU
Sec, EK Hodges, 13 Elm Close, Bowerhill,
Melksham, Wilts SN12 6SD
E-mail secretary@wcgu.org.uk
Website www.wcgu.org.uk

Worcestershire UGC
Hon Sec, A Boyd, The Bear's Den, Upper Street,
Defford, Worcester WR8 9BG
Tel (01386) 750657
Fax (01386) 750472
E-mail aboydgolf@aol.com
Website www.wugc.co.uk

Yorkshire UGC
Hon Sec, KH Dowswell, 33 George Street,
Wakefield WF1 1LX
Tel (01924) 383869
Fax (01924) 383634
E-mail yorkshiregolf@lineone.net
Website www.yorkshireunionofgolf.co.uk

English Ladies' Golf Association
Sec, Mrs P Perla, Edgbaston GC,
Church Road, Birmingham B15 3TB
Tel (0121) 456 2088
Fax (0121) 454 5542
E-mail office@englishladiesgolf.org
Website www.englishladiesgolf.org

Midlands Division: *Hon Sec*, Mrs S Ramsay, 35
Kooreman Av, Wisbech PE13 3HY
Tel (01945) 467 732
E-mail susan.ramsay@btinternet.com

Northern Division: *Hon Sec*, Mrs D V Wilson,
27 Wilton Ave, Hartlepool TS26 9PT
Tel (01429) 261 473
E-mail diane.wilson@btinternet.com

South-Eastern Division: *Hon Sec*, Mrs A Green,
40a Woodside Avenue, Beaconsfield HP9 1JH
Tel (01494) 674791
E-mail agreen.beaconsfield@virgin.net

South-Western Division: *Hon Sec*, Lady
Beauchamp, The Coach House, 4 Balfour Mews,
Sidmouth EX10 8XL
Tel (01395) 513141
E-mail margot.beauchamp@btinternet.com

English Senior Ladies Golf Association
(contact ELGA)

English Ladies' County Associations

Bedfordshire LCGA
Hon Sec, Miss K Harris, 14 Tanqueray Ave, Clophill
MK45 4AW
Tel (01525) 862180
E-mail bkh.home@btinternet.com *Website* blcga.co.uk

Berkshire LCGA
Hon Sec, Mrs L Dyne, Tangle Wood, 122 Nine Mile
Ride, Finchampstead, Wokingham RG40 3JA
Tel (0118) 932 8791
E-mail lindyne@talktalk.net

Buckinghamshire CLGA
Hon Sec, Mrs H Mines, Sobalym, Manor Road, Princes
Risborough HP27 9DJ
Tel (01844) 274353
E-mail helen_mines@btinternet.com
Website bclga.org.uk

Cambs & Hunts LCGA
Hon Sec, Mrs C Ratcliffe, Roseberry House, 50
Witchford Rd, Ely CB6 3DP
Tel (01353) 664 136
E-mail christine.ratcliffe3@ntlworld.com
Website chlgca.co.uk

Cheshire CLGA
Hon Sec, Mrs L Lanceley, 41 Croft Drive East, Caldy,
Wirral CH48 1LX
Tel (0151) 6250183
E-mail libbylanceley@hotmail.com

Cornwall LCGA
Hon Sec, Mrs C Ryder, 7 Choughs Close, Camborne
TR14 7XH
Tel (01209) 717 564
E-mail clcga@btinternet.com
Website clga.co.uk

Cumbria LCGA
Hon Sec, Mrs S Cotter, Park Rigg Bungalow, Easton,
nr Longtown CA6 5RS
Tel (01228) 577 347
E-mail ue@cumbriakitchens.fsnet.co.uk

Derbyshire LCGA
Hon Sec, Mrs M Watson, 22 Seagrave Drive, Hasland,
Chesterfield S41 0YE
Tel (01246) 209426
E-mail mariewatson@tiscali.co.uk

Devon CLGA
Hon Sec, Mrs P Lyne, 8 The Broadway, Exmouth
EX8 2NW
Tel (01395) 275435
E-mail lyne.broadway@tinyworld.co.uk

Dorset LCGA
Hon Sec, Miss S Davidge, 88 Holyrood St, St Chard,
Somerset TA20 2AL
Tel (01460) 63504   E-mail suedavidge@aol.com

Durham CLGA
Hon Sec, Mrs E Whittle, 23 Kitswell Road,
Lanchester, Co Durham DH7 0JJ
Tel (01207) 520581
E-mail alenawhittle@supanet.com
Website durhamladiesgolf.org.uk

Essex LCGA
Hon Sec, Mrs D Castle, 8 Seven Ash Green,
Chelmsford, CM1 7SE
Tel (01245) 359 558
E-mail d.m.castle@talk21.com
Website essexladiesgolf.org

Gloucestershire LCGA
Hon Sec, Mrs C Williams, 7 The Tramshed, Beehive
Yard, Walcot St, Bath BA1 5BB
Tel (01225) 337 484
E-mail cmewilliams@hotmail.com

Hampshire LCGA
Hon Sec, Mrs L Brearley, Verderers Lodge, Moonhill
Lane, Beaulieu SO42 7YW
Tel (01590) 612 164
E-mail hlcgahonsec@freenet.co.uk
Website www.hampshireladiesgolf.co.uk

Hertfordshire CLGA
Hon Sec, Mrs M Oram, 80 Stansted Road, Bishop's
Stortford, Herts CM23 2DZ
Tel (01279) 659353
E-mail hclgamarcia@aol.com Website www.hclga.co.uk

Kent CLGA
Hon Sec, Mrs D Featherstone, 5 St Giles Close,
Farnborough BR6 7DT
Tel (01689) 858105
E-mail dorothyfeathers@aol.com
Website kentladiesgolf.org.uk

Lancashire LCGA
Hon Sec, Mrs J Smart, Romney, Pleasington Lane,
Pleasington, Blackburn BB2 5JH
Tel (01254) 208 935
E-mail janettesmart@btinternet.com

Leicestershire & Rutland LCGA
Hon Sec, Mrs D Jones, 73 Cunningham Drive,
Lutterworth LE17 4YR
Tel (01455) 554310
E-mail k.t-djones_73@tiscali.co.uk

Lincolnshire LCGA
Hon Sec, Mrs K Craigs, 11 Sylvan Avenue,
Woodhall Spa LN10 6SL
Tel (01526) 352293   E-mail kmcraigs@aol.com

Middlesex LCGA
Hon Sec, Mrs D Rowlands, 3 Meadowbank Close,
Bovingdon HP3 0FB
Tel (01442) 831 414   E-mail drowlands@helpplc.com

Norfolk LCGA
Hon Sec, Miss MA Fisher, 33 Brettingham Avenue,
Cringleford, Norwich NR4 6XQ
Tel (01603) 501181
E-mail fisher.m@btinternet.com

Northamptonshire LCGA
Hon Sec, Mrs SE Clark, Abid'or, Chapel le Dale,
Ingleton LA6 3JG
Tel (01524) 241636   E-mail sandraclark@aol.com

Northumberland LCGA
Hon Sec, Mrs S Gowens, 3 Lydbury Close,
Cramlington NE23 3XY
Tel (01670) 735 426   E-mail suegowens@aol.com
Website www.nlcga.co.uk

Nottinghamshire CLGA
Hon Sec, Mrs BA Patrick, 18 Delville Avenue,
Keyworth, Nottingham NG12 5JA
Tel (0115) 937 3237   E-mail bapatrick@beeb.net

Oxfordshire LCGA
Hon Sec, Mrs C Cowley, The Old Farmhouse, Upper
Brailes, nr Banbury OX15 5AX
Tel (01608) 685 763
E-mail ac.fmhse@btinternet.com
Website olcga.org.uk

Shropshire LCGA
Hon Sec, Mrs A Jarvis, 38 Harley Rd, Condover,
Shrewsbury SY5 7BB
Tel (01743) 872225
E-mail annecondover@aol.com

Somerset LCGA
Hon Sec, Mrs R Gait, 20 West Hill, Portishead,
N Somerset BS20 6LQ
Tel (01275) 848 500
E-mail bellavista@tesco.net

Staffordshire LCGA
Hon Sec, Mrs P Siviter, 69 Ward St, Coseley,
W Midlands WV14 9LQ
Tel/Fax (01902) 689940
E-mail pamsiviter@blueyonder.co.uk

Suffolk LCGA
Hon Sec, Mrs T Pearson, 12 Rydal Av, Felixstowe
IP11 9SE
Tel (01394) 270 319
E-mail mojo@rydal12.freeserve.co.uk
Website suffolkladiesgolf.org.uk

Surrey LCGA
Sec, Ms W Elliott, SLGCA, c/o Sutton Green GC,
Sutton Green, Guildford GU4 7QF
Tel (01483) 751 622
E-mail slcga@tiscali.co.uk Website slcga.org

Sussex CLGA
Hon Sec, Mrs S Holman, The Wattles, Piltdown, East
Sussex TN22 3XL
Tel (01825) 723 443
E-mail holman@wattles.force9.co.uk
Website sclga.com

Warwickshire LCGA
Hon Sec, Mrs D Beanland, Oak Grange, 106 Bridge
End, Warwick CV34 6PD
Tel (01926) 400416
E-mail dbean98879@aol.com Website warksgolf.co.uk

Wiltshire LCGA
Hon Sec, Mrs V Evans, 46 The Mall, Old Town,
Swindon SN1 4JG
Tel (01793) 340 045
E-mail vanessaievans@ntlworld.com

Worcestershire and Herefordshire CLGA
Hon Sec, Mrs S M Mullen, 28 Baveney Rd, Worcester
WR2 6DS
Tel (01905) 426 049
E-mail padbat1@hotmail.com

Yorkshire LCGA
Hon Sec, Mrs E Haw, Orchard Cross, Stonegate,
Whixley, York YO26 8AS
Tel (01423) 339 503
E-mail johliz@btopenworld.com
Website www.ylcga.org

English County PGAs

Bedfordshire & Cambridgeshire PGA
Sec, B Wake, 6 Gazelle Close, Eaton Socon,
St Neots PE19 3QF
Tel (01480) 219760
E-mail brian.wake@btopenworld.com

Berks, Bucks & Oxon PGA
Hon Sec, Mrs M Green, Wayside, Aylesbury Road,
Monks Risborough, Princes Risborough
HP27 0JS
Tel (01844) 343012

Cheshire and North Wales PGA
Sec, J Croxton, No 2 Cottage, Bolton GC, Lostock
Park, Chorley New Road, Bolton BL6 4AJ
Tel (01204) 496137   Fax (01204) 847959
E-mail jim.croxton@pga.org.uk

Cornwall PGA
Sec, C Willis, Bowood Park GC, Camelford
PL32 9RF
Tel (01840) 213017   Fax (01840) 212622

Derbyshire PGA
Sec, F McCabe, Hillside, Lower Hall Close,
Holbrook, Derby DE56 0TN
Tel (01332) 880411
E-mail flmccabe@hotmail.com

Devon PGA
Sec, Robin Goodey, 1 Brookside Cres., Exeter EX4 8NF
Tel (07967) 769485
E-mail robingoodey@blueyonder.co.uk

Dorset PGA
Sec/Treas, JM Nicholls, 230 St Michaels Avenue, Yeovil,
Somerset BA21 4LZ
Tel (01935) 472839
E-mail nicholls.john@lineone.net

Essex PGA
Sec, S Garland-Collins, 27 Willowdene Court,
Brentwood, Essex CM14 5ET
Tel/Fax (01277) 223510
E-mail entries@essexpga.co.uk
Website www.essexpga.co.uk

Gloucestershire & Somerset PGA
Sec, E Goodwin, Cotswold Hills GC,
Ullenwood, Cheltenham GL53 9QT
Tel (01242) 515263

Hampshire PGA
Sec, DL Wheeler, South Winchester GC, Pitt,
Winchester SO22 5QW
Tel/Fax (01962) 860928
E-mail hampshirepga@yahoo.co.uk
Website www.hampshirepga.co.uk

Hertfordshire PGA
Sec, Malcolm Plumbley, Stavonga Dell, Pasture Rd,
Letchworth SG6 3LP
Tel/Fax (01462) 485268
E-mail meplumbley@stavonga.co.uk
Website www.hertspga.org

Kent PGA
Contact South Region PGA

Lancashire PGA
Sec, J Croxton, No 2 Cottage, Bolton GC, Lostock
Park, Chorley New Road, Bolton BL6 4AJ
Tel (01204) 496137
Fax (01204) 847959
E-mail jim.croxton@pga.org.uk

Leicestershire PGA
Sec, J Ashton, 2 Rose Tree Avenue, Birstall,
Leicester LE4 4CR
Tel (0116) 267 1316

Lincolnshire PGA
Sec, D Drake, Gainsborough GC, Thonock,
Gainsborough DN21 1PZ
Tel (01522) 703331

Middlesex PGA
Sec, B Eady, 8 Woodbank Drive, Chalfont
St Giles HP8 4RP
Tel (01494) 874487
E-mail brianeady@ukonline.co.uk

Norfolk PGA
Sec, R Evans, 4 Melton Drive, Thorpe Marriott,
Norwich NR8 6TT
Tel (01603) 868404
E-mail golfevans@tiscali.co.uk
Website www.club-noticeboard.co.uk

North East & North West PGA
Hon Sec, T Flowers, 10 Rosedale Rd, Belmont,
Durham DH1 2AS
Tel/Fax (07958) 043 403
E-mail tom.flowers@fsmail.net

Northamptonshire PGA
Sec, R Lobb, 15 Manor Road, Pitsford, Northampton
NN6 9AR
Tel (01604) 887367
E-mail richardlobb@supanet.com

Nottinghamshire PGA
Sec, D Revill, 132 Nuncargate Road, Kirby-in-
Ashfield, Nottingham NG17 9EQ
Tel (01623) 477934
E-mail dave.revill@ntlworld.com
Website www.nottspga.co.uk

Shropshire & Hereford PGA
Sec, P Hinton, 1 Stanley Lane Cottages, Bridgnorth,
Shropshire
Tel (01746) 762045
E-mail paulhinton@enta.net
Website www.a1golf.biz

Staffordshire PGA
Sec, D Unwin, 56 Sycamore Rd, Great Barr,
Birmingham B43 7SS
Tel/Fax (0121) 358 1053
E-mail dave.unwin2@btopenworld.com

Suffolk PGA
Sec, AED Garnett, 9 Furness Close, Ipswich IP2 9YA
Tel (01473) 685529
E-mail garnett1@onetel.com

Surrey PGA
Contact South Region PGA

Sussex PGU
Sec, C Pluck, 96 Cranston Avenue, Bexhill,
East Sussex TN39 3NL
Tel/Fax (01424) 221298
E-mail cliff@spgu.freeserve.co.uk
Website www.spgu.freeserve.co.uk

Warwickshire PGA
Sec, J Tunnicliff, 80 Wychwood Ave, Knowle,
Solihull B93 9DQ
Tel (01564) 773168

Wiltshire PGA
Sec, M Walters, Erlestoke Sands GC, Erlestoke,
Devizes SN10 5UB
Tel (01380) 831027

Worcestershire PGA
Sec, K Ball, 136 Alvechurch Road, West Heath,
Birmingham B31 3PW
Tel (0121) 475 7400

Yorkshire PGA
Sec, J Pape, 1 Summerhill Gdns, Leeds, Yorks
LS8 2EL
Tel (0113) 266 4746

English Blind Golf Association
Sec, N Baxter, 11 Higham View, North Weald, Essex
CM16 6DD
Tel/Fax (01992) 525172
Website www.blindgolf.co.uk

Ireland

Golfing Union of Ireland
Gen Sec, S Smith, National Headquarters, Carton
Demesne, Maynooth, Co. Kildare
Tel +353 1 505 4000
Fax +353 1 505 4001
E-mail information@gui.ie   *Website* www.gui.ie

Irish Men's Branches

Connacht Branch: *Gen Sec*, E Lonergan,
2 Springfield Terrace, Castlebar, Mayo
Tel +353 94 90 28141   *Fax* +353 94 90 28143
E-mail guicb@eircom.net

Leinster Branch: *Hon Sec*, K McIntyre, Carton
Demesne, Maynooth, Co.Kildare
Tel +353 1 601 6842   *Fax* +353 1 601 685
E-mail info@leinster.gui.ie

Munster Branch: *Hon Sec*, J Moloughney,
6 Townview, Mallow, Co Cork
Tel +353 22 21026   *Fax* +353 22 42373
E-mail guimb@iol.ie

Ulster Branch: *Sec*, BG Edwards, MBE,
Unit 5, Forestgrove Business Park, Newtownbreda Rd,
Belfast BT8 6AW

Tel (028) 9049 1891   *Fax* (028) 9049 1615
E-mail ulster.gui@btconnect.com

Irish Ladies' Golf Union
Ch Exec, Ms S Heraty, 1 Clonskeagh Square,
Clonskeagh Road, Dublin 14
Tel +353 1 269 6244   *Fax* +353 1 283 8670
E-mail info@ilgu.ie   *Website* www.ilgu.ie

Irish Ladies' Districts

Eastern District: *Ch Exec*, Mrs T Morgan, Orchid
House, Station Road, Dunleer, Co.Louth
Tel +353 41 686 2857
E-mail easterndistrict@eircom.net

Midland District: *Hon Sec*, Ms R Tully, Kilmeany,
Carlow
Tel +353 59 913 7672   *E-mail* rosemary.tully@tully.ie

Northern District: *Hon Sec*, Mrs M Mawhinney,
7 Hillcrest Avenue, Newtownards, Co Down
BT23 7AW
Tel (028) 918 14497
E-mail maureen.mawhinney@gmail.com

Southern District: *Hon Sec*, Mrs M Power,
Garrai-Ard, St Anne's Rise, Golf Links Road, Youghal,
Co Cork
Tel +353 2425 867   *E-mail* poweress@eircom.net

Western District: *Hon Sec*, Mrs B Hughes,
Rampert Woods, Golf Cub Road, Westport, Co Mayo
Tel +353 98 25870
E-mail ilguwest@eircom.net

Scotland

Scottish Golf Union
Sec, H Grey, PO Box 29212, St Andrews KY16 0YG
Tel (01382) 549500   *Fax* (01382) 549510
E-mail sgu@scottishgolfunion.org
Website www.scottishgolfunion.org

Scottish Men's Area Golf Associations

Angus: *Sec*, D Speed, 7 Eastgate, Friockheim,
Arbroath DD11 4TG
Tel (01241) 828544   *Fax* (01241) 828455
E-mail david.speed2@btopenworld.com

Argyll & Bute: *Sec*, G Bolton, 20 Bridge Park,
Rothesay, Isle of Bute PA20 0HF
Tel (01700) 500189
E-mail bolton@argyllandbutegolfunion.com

Ayrshire: *Sec*, R L Crawford, 81 Connel Crescent,
Mauchline, Ayrshire KA5 5AU
Tel (01290) 551 434   *Fax* (01290) 551 078
E-mail secretary@ballochmylegolf.wanadoo.co.uk

Borders: *Sec*, RG Scott, 3 Whytbank Row,
Clovenfords, Nr Galashiels TD1 3NE
Tel/Fax (01896) 850570
E-mail rscott.bga@btinternet.com

Clackmannanshire: *Sec*, T Johnson, 75 Dewar
Avenue, Kincardine on Forth FK10 4RR
Tel 01259) 731 168   *Fax* (01259) 769 445
E-mail thjohn01@aol.com

Dunbartonshire: Sec, AW Jones, 107 Larkfield Road, Lenzie, Glasgow G66 3AS
Tel/Fax (0141) 776 4377
E-mail alanjones@larky14.fsnet.co.uk

Fife: Sec, J Scott, Lauriston, East Links, Leven KY8 4JL
Tel (01333) 423798   Fax (01333) 439910
E-mail jscottfga@blueyonder.co.uk

Glasgow: Sec, RJG Jamieson, 32 Eglinton Street, Beith KA15 1AH
Tel/Fax (01505) 503000
E-mail r.jamieson-accountant@fsmail.net

Lanarkshire: Sec, T Logan, 41 Woodlands Drive, Coatbridge ML5 1LB
Tel (01236) 428799   Fax (01236) 429358
E-mail tlogan.lga@hotmail.co.uk

Lothians: Sec, A Shaw, 34 Caroline Terrace, Edinburgh EH12 8QX
Tel 0131 334 7291   Fax 0131 334 9269
E-mail AllanGShaw@hotmail.com

North: Sec, D Black, 4 Drumduan Park, Forres, Moray ICV36 1FQ
Tel (01309) 673 102
E-mail secretary@sgunorthgolf.com

North-East: Sec, G McIntosh, 4 Polinar Place, Inverurie, Aberdeen AB51 3YZ
Tel (01467) 620330
E-mail kayashish@hotmail.com

Perth & Kinross: Sec, DY Rae, 18 Carlownie Place, Auchterarder PH3 1BT
Tel (01764) 662837   Fax (01764) 662886

Renfrewshire: Sec, IJ Walker, 12 Langcraigs Drive, Glenburn, Paisley PA2 8JW
Tel (0141) 560 3515   Fax (0141) 560 5649
E-mail walker.ian@ntlworld.com

South: Sec, J Burns, Glanavon, 14 Millfield Avenue, Stranraer DG9 0EG
Tel (01776) 704 778   Fax (01776) 706 087
E-mail jburns.sosga@tiscali.co.uk

Stirlingshire: Sec, J Elliott, 65 Rosebank Avenue, Falkirk FK1 5JR
Tel (01324) 634 118   Fax (01324) 639 573
E-mail johnelliott65@blueyonder.co.uk

Scottish Blind Golf Society
Co.Sec, Jim Gales, 38 Crawley Crescent, Springfield, Cupar KY15 5SF
Tel/Fax (01334) 650963
E-mail j.gales@btopenworld.com

Scottish Golfers' Alliance
Sec/Treas, Mrs MA Caldwell, 5 Deveron Avenue, Giffnock, Glasgow G46 6NH
Tel (0141) 638 2066

Scottish Ladies' Golfing Association
Sec, Dr S Hartley, The Den, 2 Dundee Road, Perth PH2 7DW
Tel (01738) 442357
Fax (01738) 442380
E-mail secretary@slga.co.uk
Website www.slga.scottishgolf.com

Scottish Ladies County Golf Associations

Aberdeen LCGA
Hon Sec, Miss K Stalker, 2 Braemar Court, Fraserburgh AB43 9XE
Tel (01346) 513308
E-mail karen@fairways.eclipse.co.uk
Website www.alcga.co.uk

Angus LCGA
Hon Sec, Mrs D Gordon, 11 Golf Avenue, Monifieth, DD5 4AS
Tel (01382) 532799   E-mail mgordon498@aol.com

Ayrshire LCGA
Hon Sec, Miss AD Cree, 19 Woodfield Road, Ayr KA8 8LZ
Tel (01292) 260702
E-mail dotcree@hotmail.com

Border Counties' LGA
Hon Sec, Mrs C J Michie, Peniel View, The Wynd, Denholm, nr Hawick TD9 8LY
Tel (01450) 870 714
E-mail cjmichie@penielview.freeserve.co.uk
Website www.borderladiesgolf.com

Dumfriesshire LCGA
Hon Sec, Mrs C Glen, 1a Annan Rd, Eastriggs, Annan DG12 6PZ
Tel (01461) 40266

Dunbartonshire & Argyll LCGA
Hon Sec, Mrs M Gibb, Auchinedean Farmhouse, Blanefield, Glasgow G63 9AX
Tel (01360) 771 026
E-mail gmgibb@compuserve.com
Website www.dalcga.ik.com

East Lothian LCGA
Hon Sec, Mrs R Thoresen, Westerlea, Abbotsford Rd, North Berwick EH39 5DB
Tel (01620) 892626

Fife CLGA
Hon Sec, Mrs S Campsie, 17 Albert Crescent, Newport-on-Tay DD6 8DT
Tel (01382) 542084

Galloway LCGA
Hon Sec, Mrs AM McClymont, 26 Kerrsland Rd, Stranraer DG9 7SF
Tel (01776) 704 935

Lanarkshire LCGA
Hon Sec, Mrs J Macintyre, 4 Midcroft Place, Strathaven ML10 6EX
Tel (01357) 520 648
E-mail secretary@llcga.wanadoo/co/uk
Website www.llcga.co.uk

Midlothian CLGA
Hon Sec, Mrs A Leslie, 18 Swanston Grove, Edinburgh EH10 7BW
Tel (0131) 445 2411   Website www.mclga.co.uk

Northern Counties' LGA
Hon Sec, Mrs M Hayden, Uisgi-Beatha, Tarlogie Rd, Tarlogie, Tain IV19 1QA
Tel (01862) 892 545   E-mail maryhayden1@aol.com

Perth & Kinross LCGA
Hon Sec, Mrs J Milne, 69 Newmiln Rd, Perth PH1 1QX
Tel (01738) 442 651

Renfrewshire LCGA
Hon Sec, Mrs E J Thomson, 21 Craignethan Rd,
Whitecraigs, Glasgow G46 6SH
Tel (0141) 639 3428
E-mail e.j.thomson@btinternet.com
Website rlgca.co.uk

Stirling & Clackmannan LGA
Hon Sec, Mrs A Hunter, 22 Muirhead Road,
Stenhousemuir, FK5 4JA
Tel (01324) 554515
E-mail annahunter@btinternet.com

Scottish Veteran Ladies' Golfing Association
Hon Sec, Mrs JC Lambert, Balcary, Barcloy Road,
Rockcliffe, Dalbeattie DG5 4QJ
Tel (01556) 630419   *E-mail* jeanc.lambert@tesco.net

Wales

Golf Union of Wales
Sec, Catsash, Newport, Gwent NP18 1JQ
Tel (01633) 430830/422911
Fax (01633) 430843/431106
E-mail wgu@welshgolf.org   info@wlgu.org.uk
Website www.welshgolf.org.uk   www.wlgu.org.uk

Welsh Men's Golf Unions

Anglesey GU
Hon Sec, GP Jones, 20 Gwelfor Estate, Cemaes Bay,
Anglesey LL67 0NL
Tel (01407) 710755   *E-mail* garethgwelfor@aol.com

Brecon & Radnor GU
Hon Sec, DJ Davies, Garden House, Howey,
Llandrindod Wells, Powys LD1 5PU
Tel (01597) 824316

Caernarfonshire & District GU
Hon Sec, RE Jones, 23 Bryn Rhos, Rhosbodrual,
Caernarfon, Gwynedd LL55 2BT
Tel (01286) 673486

Denbighshire GU
Hon Sec, EG Howells, 10 Lon Howell, Myddleton
Park, Dinbych, LL16 4AN, North Wales
Tel/Fax (01745) 813849

Dyfed GU
B Booth, Rhyd, Croes Y Llan, Llangoedmor, Cardigan
SA43 2LH
Tel (01239) 615 334

Union of Flintshire Golf Clubs
Hon Sec, Mrs G Snead, 1 Cornist Cottages, Flint
CH6 5RH
E-mail johnsnead@hotmail.co.uk

Glamorgan County GU
Hon Sec, P Austerberry, 10 Chestnut Tree Close,
Radyr, Cardiff CF4 8RY
Tel (02920) 419823

Gwent GU
Sec, G Harris, 4 Rolls Walk, Mount Pleasant,
Rogerstone, Gwent NP10 0AE
Tel (01633) 663750

North Wales PGA
See Cheshire & North Wales PGA, page 635

South Wales PGA
See West Region PGA, page 630

Welsh Ladies' Golf Union
See Golf Union of Wales

Welsh Ladies' County Golf Associations

Caernarvonshire & Anglesey LCGA
Hon Sec, Mrs GT Williams, Llais y Mor, Llanfaes,
Beaumaris, Anglesey LL58 8RH
Tel (01248) 490825
E-mail derek_williams@btinternet.co.uk

Denbighshire & Flintshire LCGA
Hon Sec, Mrs K Harcombe, 6 Birch Drive, Gresford,
Wrexham LL12 8YZ
Tel (01978) 855933

Glamorgan LCGA
Hon Sec, Miss J Brown, Trefelin, 2 Windmill Lane,
Cowbridge, Vale of Glamorgan CF71 7HX
Tel (01446) 773292
E-mail jane@glcga.freeserve.co.uk

Mid Wales LCGA
Hon Sec, Mrs L Price, Coygen, Lower Chapel, Brecon,
Powys LD3 9RE
Tel (01874) 690 258
E-mail coygen@btclick.com

Monmouthshire LCGA
Hon Sec, Mrs EL Davidson, Jon-Len, Goldcliff,
Newport NP10 8RF
Tel (01633) 274477
E-mail lena@mlcga.fsnet.co.uk

Overseas Associations

Europe

European Golf Association
Gen Sec, JC Storjohann, Place de la Croix Blanche 19, Case Postale CH-1066 Epalinges, Switzerland
Tel +41 21 784 35 32   Fax +41 21 784 35 91
E-mail info@ega-golf.ch   Website www.ega-golf.ch

Austrian Golf Association
Gen Sec, Mrs Y Yolbulur-Nissim, Haus des Sports, Prinz-Eugen-Strasse 12, A-1040 Wien
Tel +43 1 505 3245   Fax +43 1 505 4962
E-mail oegv@golf.at   Website www.golf.at

Royal Belgian Golf Federation
Pres, Philippe Relecom, Chausée de la Hulpe 110, B-1000 Brussels
Tel +32 2 672 2389   Fax +32 2 675 4619
E-mail info@golfbelgium.be
Website www.golfbelgium.be

Bulgarian Golf Association
Gen Sec, S Underwood, 19 Oborishte Street, 1504 Sofia
Tel +359 2943 0610   Fax +359 2946 3740
E-mail s.underwood@golfbg.com
Website www.golfbg.com

Croatian Golf Federation
Sec, D Kasapovic, Hotel Esplanade, Mihanoviceva 1, HR-10 000 Zagreb
Tel +385 1 456 6631   Fax +385 1 456 6050

Cyprus Golf Federation
Gen Sec, N Rossides, PO Box 62085, 8062 Pafos
Tel +357 2664 2978   Fax +357 2664 2776
E-mail cgf@cyprusgolffed.org
Website www.cgf.org.cy

Czech Golf Federation
Gen Sec, M Holub, Erpet Golf Centre, Strakonickà 2860, CZ-150 00 Prague 5-Smichov
Tel +420 2 5731 7865   Fax +420 2 5731 8618
E-mail cgf@cgf.cz   Website www.cgf.cz

Danish Golf Union
Gen Sec, K Thuen, Idrættens Hus, Brøndby Stadion 20, DK-2605 Brøndby
Tel +45 43 262 700   Fax +45 43 262 701
E-mail info@dgu.org   Website www.dgu.org

Estonian Golf Association
Sec Gen, C Marcus, Liivalaia, EE-10118 Tallinn
Tel +372 630 3080
E-mail christine@golf.ee

Finnish Golf Union
Gen Sec, M Rantanen, Radiokatu 20, FIN-00093 SLU
Tel +358 9 3481 2520
Fax +358 9 147 145
E-mail office@golf.fi   Website www.golf.fi

French Golf Federation
Exec Dir, C Muniesa, 68 rue Anatole France, F-92309 Levallois-Perret Cedex
Tel +33 1 41 497 700
Fax +33 1 41 497 701
E-mail ffg@ffgolf.org
Website www.ffgolf.org

German Golf Association
Man Dir, Jan Kadelke, Postfach 2106, D-65011 Wiesbaden
Tel +49 611 990 200   Fax +49 611 990 2040
E-mail info@dgv.golf.de   Website www.golf.de

Hellenic Golf Federation
Gen Sec, M Sideris, PO Box 70003,GR-166 10 Glyfada Athens
Tel +30 210 894 1933   Fax +30 210 894 5162
E-mail info@hgf.gr   Website www.hgf.gr

Hungarian Golf Federation
Gen Sec, Mrs T Fucskó, Istvanmezei út 1-3, H-1146 Budapest
Tel +36 61 460 6859   Fax +36 61 460 6860
E-mail hungolf@hungolf.hu
Website: www.hungolf.hu

Golf Union of Iceland
Gen Sec, H Thorsteinsson, Sport Center, Laugardal, IS-104 Reykjavik
Tel +354 514 4050   Fax +354 514 4051
E-mail gsi@golf.is   Website www.golf.is

Italian Golf Federation
Sec Gen, S Manca, Viale Tiziano 74, I-00196 Roma
Tel +39 06 323 1825   Fax +39 06 322 0250
E-mail fig@federgolf.it   Website www.federgolf.it

National Golf Federation of Republic of Kazakhstan
Gen Sec, K Mukhanov, c/o Mr K Lifanov, Nurtau GC, "Alatan" Sanatorium, Tausamaly Village, 483110 Almaty Oblast
Tel +7 3272 958 823   Fax +7 3272 958 830
E-mail golf_almaty@mail.ru
Website www.nurtau.kz

Latvia Golf Federation
Gen Sec, I Krodere-Imsa, Milgravja Iela 16, LV–1034 Riga
Tel/Fax +371 739 4034
E-mail info@golfaskola.lv   Website www.lgf.lv

Lithuanian Golf Federation
Gen Sec, A Keserauskas, D Lapiu km, Lapiu sen, Kuano Rajonas
Tel +370 687 81579   E-mail adas@mail.balt.net

Luxembourg Golf Federation
Sec, P Ronkar, Domaine de Belenhaff, L-6141 Junglinster
Tel +352 26 78 2383   Fax +352 26 78 2393
E-mail flgsecretariat@flgolf.lu
Website www.flgolf.lu

Malta Golf Federation
Hon Sec, Alexander Mangion, c/o Royal Malta GC, Marsa LQA 06, Malta
Tel +356 2122 7019   Fax +356 2122 7020
E-mail info@maltagolf.org
Website www.maltagolf.org

Netherlands Golf Federation
Gen Sec, HL Heyster, PO Box 221, NL-3454 ZL De Meern.
Tel +31 30 242 6370   Fax +31 30 242 6380
E-mail golf@ngf.nl   Website www.ngf.nl

Norwegian Golf Federation
Gen Sec, G-O Berg, N-0840 Oslo
Tel +47 21 029 150   Fax +47 21 029 151
E-mail post@golfforbundet.no
Website www.ngf golf.no

Polish Golf Union
Sec, J Gazecki, Lim Couter, Al.Jerozolimskie 65/79,
PL-00-697 Warszawa
65/79, PL-00-697 Warszawa
Tel +48 22 630 5560   Fax +48 22 630 5561
E-mail pzg@pzgolf.pl   Website www.pzgolf.pl

Portuguese Golf Federation
Gen Sec, P Vicente, Av das Tulipas Edifico
Miraflores17°, Miraflores, P-1495-161 Algés
Tel +351 214 123 780   Fax +351 214 107 972
E-mail fpg@fpg.pt   Website www.fpg.pt

Romanian Golf Federation
Pres, D Hintescu, 24 Carierei Str., Breaza, 105400
Prahova
Tel +40 244 343 525
E-mail president@lacdeverde.ro
Website romaniangolffederation.ro

Russian Golf Association
Pres, K Kozhevnikov, 12 Khamovnitchesky Val,
RU-119871 Moskow
Tel +7 095 242 7464   Fax +7 095 242 7467
E-mail info@rusgolf.ru   Website www.rusgolf.ru

San Marino Golf Federation
Sec Gen, Dr E Casali, Via Rancagalia 30, 47899
Serravalle, San Marino
Tel +378 (0549) 885 600   Fax +378 (0549) 885 651
E-mail dzanotti@omniway.sm

Serbia Golf Association
Pres, A Andjelkovic, Ada Ciganlija 5, YU-11000
Belgrade
Tel/Fax +381 11 551 559
E-mail office@golfclub.co.yu
Website www.golfclub.co.yu

Slovak Golf Association
Gen Sec, A Hauskrecht, Dom SOV, Kukucinova 26,
SK-831 02 Bratislava, Slovak Republic
Tel/Fax +421 2 4445 0727
E-mail skga@skga.sk   Website www.skga.sk

Slovenian Golf Association
Sec, G Kogoj, Dunajska 22, SLO-1511 Ljubljana
Tel +386 1 430 3200   Fax +386 1 430 3201
E-mail golfzveza@golfzveza-slovenije.si
Website www.golfzveza-slovenije.si

Royal Spanish Golf Federation
Sec, L Alvarez de Bohorques, c/o Gabriela Mistral s/n,
E-280 35 Madrid
Tel +34 91 555 2682   Fax +34 91 556 3290
E-mail rfeg@golfspain.com
Website www.golfspainfederacion.com

Swedish Golf Federation
Gen Sec, Mats Enquist, PO Box 84, Kevingestrand,
S-182 11 Danderyd
Tel +46 8 622 1500   Fax +46 8 755 8439
E-mail info@sgf.golf.se   Website www.sgf.golf.se

Swiss Golf Association
Sec, JC Storjohann, Place de la Croix Blanche 19, CH-
1066 Epalinges
Tel +41 21 784 3531   Fax +41 21 784 3536
E-mail info@asg.ch   Website www.asg.ch

Turkish Golf Federation
Co-ord, I Aktekin, GSGM Ulus Is Hani A Blok 2,
Kat 205 Ulus 06050, Ankara
Tel +90 312 309 3945   Fax +90 312 309 1840
E-mail info@tgf.org.tr   Website www.tgf.org.tr

Professional Associations

Austria PGA
Sec, R Hagan, Neuseiersbergerstr. 115/1, A-8055 Graz
Tel +43 316 890 503   Fax +43 316 890 50315
E-mail office@apga.info
Website www.apga.info

Belgian PGA
Sec, B De Bruyckere, Bergstraat 41, B-8790
Waregem
Tel +32 56 621 821   Fax +32 56 621 874
E-mail info@pga.be
Website www.pga.be

Bulgarian PGA
Sec, N Turley, Oborishte St, 1504 Sofia
E-mail n.turley@stsofiagolf.com

Croatia PGA
Sec, N Smoljenovic, Fancevljec Prilaz 16, HR-10010
Zagreb
Tel +385 1 211030   Fax +385 1 667 3308
E-mail golf-pga@zg.tel.hr

Czech Republic PGA
Sec, P Nitra, Villa Golfista, Amerika 782/1C,
CZ - 353 01 Marianske Lazne
Tel +420 354 623071   Fax +420 354 621357
E-mail villa.golfista@wo.cz
Website www.pgac.cz

Denmark PGA
Sec, J Ejlertsen, Centervej 1, Gatten 9640, Farsø
Tel +45 98 662 235   Fax +45 98 662 236
E-mail info@pga.dk   Website www.pga.dk

Finland PGA
Gen Sec, Teemu Laakso, Radiokatu 20, FIN-00093
SLU
Tel +358 9 3481 2377   Fax +358 9 3481 2378
E-mail pgafinland@pga.fi   Website www.pga.fi

French PGA
Sec, A Vannier, National Golf Club, 2 Avenue du Golf,
78 280 Guyancourt
Tel +33 1 34 52 0846   Fax +33 1 34 52 0548
E-mail contact@pgafrance.net
Website www.pgafrance.net

PGA of Germany
Exec Dir, Rainer Goldrian, Arnulfstrasse 295,
D-80639 München
Tel +49 8917 95880   Fax +49 8917 958829
E-mail info@pga.de   Website www.pga.de

Greece PGA
Gen Sec, A Sofronis, Ethnarhou Makariou 90,
GR-85103 Afandou, Rhodes

Tel +30 22410 52798   *E-mail* info@greekpga.com
Website www.greekpga.com

Iceland PGA
Sec, H Hilmarsson, Engiavegur 6, 104 Reykjavik
Tel +354 514 4050   *Fax* +354 514 4051
E-mail hinni@isisport.is

Italy PGA
Sec, L Rendina, Via Marangoni 3, I-20124 Milano
Tel +39 02 670 5670   *Fax* +39 02 669 3600
E-mail pgaitaly@tin.it   *Website* www.pga.it

Luxembourg PGA
Sec, L Cain, 1 Route de Tréves, L-2633 Senningerberg
Tel/Fax +352 348394
E-mail info@pga.lu   *Website* www.pga.lu

Malta PGA
Sec, The Royal Malta GC, Aldo Moro St, HMR-15 Marsa
Tel/Fax +356 239 320
E-mail info@maltagolf.org
Website www.maltagolf.org

Netherlands PGA
Sec, Mrs R Vonk Mundt, Burg van der Borchlaan 1, 3722 GZ Bilthoven
Tel +31 30 228 7018   *Fax* +31 30 225 0261
E-mail npga@wxs.nl
Website www.pgaholland.nl

Norway PGA
Sec, T Baardseng, PO Box 226, N-2402 Elverum
Tel +47 913 13912
E-mail pga@pga.no   *Website* www.pga.no

Poland PGA
Sec, M Podstolski, ul.Kwiatowa, PL-81638 Gdynia
Tel +48 5834 22312
Fax +48 5834 22313
E-mail m.podstolski@ndh.net
Website www.golf24.pl

Portugal PGA
Sec, David Silva, Apartado 1025, Vilamoura, 8125-914 Algarve
Tel +351 289 300 120
Fax +351 289 300 128
E-mail rosalia_oliveira@silvagolf.com
Website www.pgaportugal.com

Russia PGA
Sec, D Zherebko, Office 242A House 8, Luzhnetskaya nab, RU-119992 Moscow
Tel/Fax +7 095 977 7872
E-mail deniszherebko@hotmail.com
Website www.rusga.ru

Slovakia PGA
Sec, M Forro, Orenburska Str.66, SK-821 06 Bratislava
E-mail forro@pga.sk

Slovenia PGA
Sec, M Jamar, Kidriceva 10c, SL-4260 Bled
Tel +386 4 537 7716   *Fax* +386 4 537 7722
E-mail metka.jamar@golf.bled.si

Spain PGA
Sec, M Santamaría, c/o Capitán Haya 22-5C, E-28020 Madrid

Tel +34 91 555 1393
Fax +34 91 597 0170
E-mail apge@wanadoo.es
Website www.pgaspain.com.es

Swedish PGA
Exec Dir, A Strivall, Tylösand, S-302 73 Halmstad
Tel +46 35 320 30   *Fax* +46 35 320 25
E-mail pga@golf.se   *Website* www.pgasweden.se

Swiss PGA
Gen Sec, André Glauser, PO Box 107, CH-3177 Laupen
Tel +41 31 748 0312   *Fax* +41 31 748 0313
E-mail info@swisspga.ch
Website www.swisspga.ch

Turkey PGA
Sec, A Menabola, Doktorlar Sitesi B3 Blok Daire 14, Bosna Bulvari, Nato Yolu, Cengelkoy, Istanbul
Tel +90 533 773 3019
E-mail amc@igk.org.tr

North America: Canada and USA

Royal Canadian Golf Association
Exec Dir, Stephen Ross, Suite 1 1333 Dorval Drive, Oakville, Ontario L6M 4X7
Tel 001 905 849 9700   *Fax* 001 905 845 7040
Email sross@rcga.org
Website www.rcga.org

Canadian Ladies' Golf Association
See Royal Canadian Golf Association

National Golf Foundation
Chief Exec Off, Joseph Beditz, 1150 South US Highway One, Jupiter, Florida 33477
Tel +1 561 744 6006   *Website* www.ngf.org

United States Golf Association
Pres, Walter W Driver jr, Golf House, PO Box 708, Far Hills, NJ 07931-0708
Tel +1 908 234 2300   *Fax* +1 908 234 9687
E-mail usga@usga.org   *Website* www.usga.org

Professional Associations

Canadian PGA
Ch Exec, David J Colling, 13450 Dublin Line RR#1, Acton, Ontario L7J 2W7
Tel +1 519 853 5450   *Fax* +1 519 853 5449
E-mail cpga@canadianpga.org
Website www.cpga.com

Canadian Tour
Comm, Ian Mansfield, 212 King Street West, Suite 203, Toronto, Ontario M58 1K5
Tel +1 416 204 1564   *Fax* +1 416 204 1368
Website cantour.com

Ladies' Professional Golf Association
Pres, 100 International Golf Drive, Daytona Beach, Florida 32124-1092
Tel +1 386 274 6200   *Fax* +1 386 274 1099
Website www.lpga.com

PGA of America
Pres, Brian Whitcomb, Box 109601, 100 Avenue of the Champions, Palm Beach Gardens, Florida 33418

Tel +1 561 624 8400   *Fax* +1 561 624 8448
Website www.pgaonline.com

PGA Tour
Comm, Tim Finchem, PGA Tour, 112 PGA Tour
Boulevard, Ponte Vedra Beach, Florida 32082
Tel +1 904 285 3700   *Fax* +1 904 285 7913
Website www.pgatour.com

The Caribbean and Central America

Caribbean Golf Association
Sec, David G Bird, PO Box 31329 SMB, Grand
Cayman, Cayman Islands
Tel +345 947 1903   *Fax* +345 947 3439
E-mail bird@candw.ky   *Website* www.cgagolf.com

Bahamas Golf Federation
Pres, Agatha Delancey, PO Box F-41790, Freeport,
Grand Bahama
Tel +242 373 7295   *Fax* +242 373 7926
E-mail admin@bgfnet.com
Website www.bgfnet.com

Barbados Golf Association
Pres, Birchmore Griffith, PO Box 585, Bridgetown,
Barbados
Tel +246 430 0808   *Fax* +246 437 7792
E-mail carib@caribsurf.com
Website www.barbadosgolfassociation.org

Bermuda Golf Association
Sec, Richard Bartlett, PO Box HM 433, Hamilton
HM BX, Bermuda
Tel +1 441 295 9972   *Fax* +1 441 295 0304
Website www.bermudagolf.org

Cayman Islands Golf Association
Sec, David G Bird, PO Box 31329 SMB, Grand
Cayman
Tel +345 947 1903   *Fax* +345 947 3439
E-mail bird@candw.ky

Costa Rica Golf Federation
Sec, F T Deunas, PO Box 10969, San José 1000,
Costa Rica
Tel +506 296 5772   *Fax* +506 231 1914
E-mail info@anagolf.com   *Website* www.anagolf.com

Fedogolf (Dominican Republic)
Pres, Marcos Troncoso, Calle Macao No.7,
Urbanizacion Tennis Club, Arroyo Hondo, Santo
Domingo, Dominican Republic
Tel +809 338 1004   *Fax* +809 338 1008
E-mail fedogolf@verizon.net.do
Website www.golfdominicano.com

El Salvador Golf Federation
Pres, Jose Maria Duran Pacheco, VIP SAL 1256, PO
Box 2-5364, Miami FL 33102-5364
Tel +1 305 264 1583   *Fax* +1 305 298 3354
E-mail figueroa@telesal.net

National Golf Association of Guatemala
Pres, Gustavo Evertsz H., 23 Avenida 31-01 zona 5,
Edificio Espectrum oficina 210, Guatemala
Tel +502 2336 5079
E-mail asogolf@asogolfguatemala.org
Website www.asogolfguatemala.org

Hondurena Golf Association
Sec, LF Gutierrez Falla, Apartado Postal No.3175,
Tegucigalpa, Honduras
Tel +504 37 2084   *Fax* +504 38 0456

Jamaica Golf Association
Pres, Gordon Hutchinson, PO Box 743, Kingston 8
Tel 876 906 7636   *Fax* 876 906 7635
E-mail jamgolf@n5.com.jm
Website www.jamaicagolfassociation.com

Mexican Golf Federation
Exec Dir, Fernando Erana, Av.Insurgentes Sur 1605
10° Piso Torre Mural, Col. San Jose Insurgentes,
C.P. 03900 México, D.F.
Tel +525 1084 2176   *Fax* +525 1084 2179
E-mail direccionfmg@mexgolf.org
Website www.mexgolf.org

Nicaraguan Golf Federation
Exec Sec, J A Narvaez, Nejapa GCC, Managua
Tel +505 822 5522
E-mail procalsa1@hotmail.com

OECS Golf Association
Sec, Dessie Henry, c/o PO Box 895, Basseterre,
St Kitts
Tel +758 452 3486
Fax +758 453 1933
E-mail pearldes@thecable.net

Panama Golf Association
Pres, Roberto Duran Jr, PO Box 8613, Panama 5
Tel +507 266 7436   *Fax* +507 220 3994
E-mail master@pty.com

Puerto Rico Golf Association
Pres, Luiz Elvin Gonzalez, 58 Caribe St, San Juan,
Puerto Rico 00907-1909
Tel +787 721 7742   *Fax* +787 723 5760
E-mail golfpuertorico@prga.org
Website www.prga.org

Trinidad & Tobago Golf Association
Pres, Asraph Ali, c/o St Andrews GC, PO Box 3403,
Moka, Masaval, Trinidad
Tel +868 629 7127
Fax +868 629 0411
E-mail ttga@tstt.net.tt
Website www.trinidadandtobagogolfassociation.com

Turks & Caicos Golf Association
Pres, Thomas Waite, PO Box 319, Providenciales,
Turks & Caicos Islands
Tel +649 946 4417
Fax +649 946 4437
E-mail thomasw@tciway.tc

Virgin Islands Golf Federation
Pres, Greg Manigault, PO Box 5187, Kingshill, St Croix,
US Virgin Islands 00851
Tel +340 779 2315
Fax +340 714 5393
E-mail gregmanigault@hotmail.com

Professional Association

Jamaica PGA
Chairman, O Marshall, 9 Park Ave., Kingston 5
E-mail chairman@pgaj.com

South America

South American Golf Federation
Exec Sec, Rafael Enrique Otero D., Carrera 12
No 79-43 Of 704, Bogotá, Colombia
Tel +57 1 313 0624   *Fax* +57 1 313 0391
E-mail fedesud@etb.net.co
Website www.fedesudgolf.com

Argentine Golf Association
Exec Dir, Mark Lawrie, Av Corrientes 538-Pisos 11y12,
1043 CF, Buenos Aires
Tel +54 11 4325 1113   *Fax* +54 11 4325 8660
E-mail golf@aag.com.ar   *Website* www.aag.com.ar

Bolivian Golf Federation
Sec, Jaime Gonzalez, Ave. Mariscal Santa Cruz, Edif.
Camara de Comercio Of 604, Casilla Postal 10217,
La Paz
Tel/Fax +591 2 315853
E-mail fbgolf@ceibo.entelnet.bo
Website www.boliviagolf.com

Brasilian Golf Confederation
Exec Sec, M A Aguiar Giusti, Rua Paez de Araújo
29 cnj 42e43, CEP 04531 090 São Paulo
Tel/Fax +55 11 3168 4366
E-mail golfe@cbg.com.br   *Website* www.cbg.com.br

Chilean Golf Federation
Dir, Carlos Celis, Málaga 655, Las Condes, Santiago
Tel +56 2 208 7080   *Fax* +56 2 208 6566
E-mail secretaria@chilegolf.cl
Website www.chilegolf.cl

Colombian Golf Federation
Sec, Jaime Rodríguez Posada, Carrera 7#72-64 Int 26,
Bogotá DC
Tel +57 1 310 7664   *Fax* +57 1 235 5091
E-mail fedegolf@federacioncolombianadegolf.com
Website www.federacioncolombianadegolf.com

Ecuador Golf Federation
Sec, Carlos Javier Vallarino, Av Amazonas N.28-17 y
Alemania, Edif.Skorpios Piso 8 of.812, Quito
Tel +593 2 2922 128   *Fax* +593 2 2442 986
E-mail fedecuat@feg.org.ec   *Website* www.feg.org.ec

Guyana Golf Union
Sec, c/o Demerara Bauxite Co Ltd, Mackenzie, Guyana

Paraguay Golf Association
Sec, Roberto Berino, Manduriva 709, Casilla de
Correo No 76, Asunción
Tel +595 21 494 8011   *Fax* +595 21 447 923
E-mail secretaria@apg.org.py
Website www.apg.org.py

Peru Golf Federation
Exec Dir, Eduardo Ibarra, Calle Conde de la Monclova
315 Of 308, San Isidro, Lima 27
Tel +51 1 441 1500   *Fax* +51 1 441 1992
E-mail fepegolf@terra.com,pe
Website www.fpg.org.pe

Uruguay Golf Association
Sec, Nelson Silva, Bulevar Artigas 379, Montevideo
Tel +598 2 7101 721   *Fax* +598 2 7115285
E-mail augolf@adinet.com.uy
Website www.aug.com.uy

Venezuela Golf Federation
Exec Dir, Julio L Torres, Av. Juan B Arismendi Unidad
Comercial La Florida, Nivel Mezzanina, local 8,
La Florida, Caracas
Tel +582 12 731 7662   *Fax* +582 12 730 2731
E-mail fvg@fvg.org   *Website* www.fvg.org

Africa

Algerian Golf Federation
Sec, Ben Miloude Noureddine, rue Ahmed Ouaked,
Dely Ibrahim
Tel +213 213 75 362   *Fax* +213 213 75 790

Arab Golf Federation
Sec Gen, Dr Mohamed El Attar, 39 Abdel Moneim
Hafez St, Heliopolis, Cairo, Egypt
Tel +202 291 9101   *Fax* +202 291 9102
E-mail mohamedattar@eescoegypt.com
Website www.arabgolf.org

Botswana Golf Union
Exec Sec, Joseph Marudu, PO Box 1033, Gaborone
Tel +267 316 1116   *Fax* +267 391 2262
E-mail bgu@it.bw

Botswana Ladies Golf Union
Hon Sec, Mrs C de Villiers, PO Box 1362, Gaborone

Egyptian Golf Federation
Pres, Khaled Abu Taleb, Katameya GTR, District Ring
Road, New Cairo City
Tel +202 758 8433   *Fax* +202 757 5233
E-mail khaled.ataleb@katameya.com

Gabon Golf Federation
Sec, BP 15159 Libreville
Tel +241 760 378 *Fax* +241 729 079
E-mail golfclublibreville@inet.ga

Ghana Golf Association
Sec, J Wartemberg, PO Box 8, Achimota
Tel/Fax +233 21 400221
E-mail ghanagolf@yahoo.co.uk
Website www.achimotagolf.com

Ghana Ladies Golf Union
Hon Sec, Mrs M Amu, PO Box 70, Accra

Ivory Coast Golf Federation
Sec, I Keita, O8 BP 1297, Abidjan 08
Tel +225 213 874   *Fax* +225 227 112
E-mail tsr@aviso.ci

Kenya Golf Union
Chair, D S Bhavra, PO Box 43561, 00100 Nairobi
Tel +254 2 376 3898
Fax +254 2 376 5118
E-mail kgu@iconnect.co.ke
Website www.kgu.org.ke

Kenya Ladies' Golf Union
Hon Sec, Mrs S Royle, PO Box 7785, 00100 Nairobi
Tel +254 2 273 3794

KwaZulu-Natal Golf Union
Sec, RT Runge, PO Box 1939, Durban 4000
Tel +27 (0)31 202 7636   *Fax* +27 (0)31 202 1022
E-mail kzngu@kzngolf.co.za

Libyan Golf Federation
Gen Sec, Mustafa Ewkaiat, PO Box 3674, Tripoli
Tel +218 21 478 0510

Malawi Golf Union
Sec, S Langford, PO Box 1198, Blantyre 8
Tel +265 1 824 108   Fax +265 1 824 027
E-mail medlife@malawi.net

Malawi Ladies' Golf Union
Hon Sec, Mrs H Wallace, PO Box 30328, Lilongwe 3

Mauritius Golf Federation
Pres, Raj Ramlackhan, 42 Sir William Newton Street,
Port Louis
Tel +230 208 4224   Fax +230 483 5163
E-mail mgolffed@intnet.mu

The Royal Moroccan Golf Federation
Sec Gen, Abdelal Latif Benali, Route des Zaers, Rabat,
Dar El Salam
Tel +212 3775 5636   Fax +212 3775 1026
E-mail abdellatif.benali@manara.ma

Namibia Golf Federation
Treas, Hugh Mortimer, PO Box 2122, Windhoek,
Namibia
Tel +264 61 205 5223   Fax +264 61 205 5220
E-mail gm@wccgolf.com.na
Website www.wccgolf.com.na

Nigeria Golf Federation
Sec, Patrick Uwagbale, National Stadium Surulere,
PO Box 145, Lagos
Tel +234 1 545 6209   Fax +234 1 545 0530
E-mail nigeriagolffederation@yahoo.com

Nigerian Ladies Golf Union
Sec, Mrs OR Ogunleye, c/o Ikoyi GC, PO Box 239,
Ikoyi, Lagos

Sierra Leone Golf Federation
Pres, Freetown GC, PO Box 237, Lumley Beach,
Freetown
E-mail fadi@sierratel.sl

South African Golf Association
Exec Dir, BA Younge, PO Box 65303, Benmore 2010
RSA
Tel +27 11 442 3723   Fax +27 11 442 3753
E-mail sagolf@global.co.za
Website www.saga.co.za

Women's Golf South Africa
Hon Sec, Mrs V Horak, PO Box 209, Randfontein
1760, RSA
Tel/Fax +27 11 416 1263
E-mail salgu@global.co.za   Website www.salgu.co.za

Swaziland Golf Union
Sec, AP Dunn, PO Box 1739, Mbabane, H100
Swaziland
Tel +268 404 4735   Fax +268 404 5401
E-mail adunn2@fnb.co.za

Tanzania Golf Union
Hon Sec, Perfect A Lyimo, PO Box 15606, Arusha
Tel +255 22 250 4347
E-mail info@tgu.com
Website www.tgu.com

Tanzania Ladies Golf Union
Hon Sec, Mrs T Anthony, Gymkana Club, PO Box 286,
Dar es Salaam
E-mail magapye@netscape.net

Tunisian Golf Federation
Pres, Marwan Mabrouk, 4 Rue de la Ligue Arabe, 1002
Belvédère, Tunis
Tel +216 718 657 45   Fax +216 71 280 922
E-mail ftg@ftg.org.tn

Uganda Golf Union
Pres, N J Okwir, Kitante Road, PO Box 2574, Kampala
Tel +256 41 259 528   Fax +256 077 759 746
E-mail okwirn@hfcultd.co.ug

Uganda Ladies Golf Union
Hon Sec, Mrs R Tumusiime, PO Box 624, Kampala
E-mail ugagolf@africaonline.co.ug

Zaire Golf Federation
Pres, Tshilombo Mwin Tshitol, BP 1648, Lubumbashi

Zambia Golf Union
Hon Sec, A C Mwangata, 37A Twaliilubula Ave,
Parklands, PO Box 21602, Kitwe
Tel +260 96 780 095   Fax +260 2 226 884
E-mail anthony@coppernet.zm

Zambia Ladies Golf Union
Hon Sec, Mrs H Kapya, PO Box 22151, Kitwe

Zimbabwe Golf Association
Sec, John Nixon, PO Box 3327, Harare
Tel +263 4 746 141 Fax +263 4 746 228

Zimbabwe Ladies Golf Union
Hon Sec, Mrs JM Hall, PO Box HG 182, Highlands,
Harare

Professional Associations

South African PGA
Sec, Anne Du Toit, PO Box 949 Bedfordview 2008, RSA
Tel +27 11 485 1370   Fax +27 11 640 4372
E-mail admin@pgasa.com   Website www.pgasa.com

South African Women's PGA
Sec, Mrs V Harrington, PO Box 781547, Sandton 2146
Tel/Fax +27 11 477 8606

South Africa Sunshine Tour
Exec Dir, Louis Martin, 15 Postnet Suite #185,
Private Bag X15, Somerset West 7129
Tel +27 21 850 6500   Fax +27 21 852 8271

Middle East

Bahrain Golf Committee
Sec Gen, Muneer Ahmed, PO Box 38938, Riffa,
Kingdom of Bahrain
Tel +973 778 620   Fax +973 778 595
E-mail bgcom@batelco.com.bh

Islamic Republic of Iran Golf Federation
Pres, E Eshaghi, Enghelab Club, Val-e-Asr Ave, PO Box
15815, 1881-Tehran
Tel/Fax +98 21 883 6040
E-mail golf_ir@parsonline.net

Israel Golf Federation
Sec, Mrs Gili Peleg, PO Box 4858, Caesarea 38900
Tel +972 4 610 9600   *Fax* +972 4 636 1173
E-mail golf@caesarea.cc

Jordan Golf Federation
Pres, Amer El Salty, PO Box 888, Amman
Tel +962 6569 6206   *E-mail* rsalti@go.com.jo

Kuwait Golf Federation
Pres, Saud Al Hajeri, PO Box 1192, Fintas Z-code 51013
Tel +965 390 5287

Lebanese Golf Federation
Pres, Dr Faisal Alamuddin, c/o GC of Lebanon, PO Box 11-3099, Beirut
Tel +961 1 822 470   *Fax* +961 1 822 474
E-mail info@golfclub.org.lb

Qatar Golf Association
Pres, Fahad Nasser Al Noaimi, PO Box 13530, Doha
Tel +974 483 7815   *Fax* +974 483 2610
E-mail info@qgagolf.com
Website www.qatargolfassociation.com

Saudi Golf Committee
Sec Gen, PO Box 325422, Riyadh 11371, Saudi Arabia
Tel +966 1 464 1662   *Fax* +966 1 464 2608
E-mail info@ksagolf.com   *Website* www.ksagolf.com

United Arab Emirates Golf Association
Gen Man, A Flaherty, PO Box 31410, Dubai, UAE
Tel +971 4 380 1777   *Fax* +971 4 380 1818
E-mail uaegolf@emirates.net.ae
Website www.ugagolf.com

Professional Associations

Israel PGA
Sec, R Cordoba-Core, Sokolov 10, Block B Floor 12 Apartment 12, Hertzilia
Tel +972 4 6636 1172   *Fax* +972 4 6636 1173

United Arab Emirates PGA
Sec, C Reynolds, PO Box 32375, Abu Dhabi
Tel +971 2 575 5046   *Fax* +971 2 575 8041
E-mail niklaus@emirates.net.ae

Asia

Asia-Pacific Golf Confederation
Sec Gen, Colin Phillips, Golf Australia, Level 3-95 Coventry St, South Melbourne, VIC-3205
Tel +613 9626 5050   *Fax* +613 9626 5095
E-mail apgc@agu.org.au

Bangladesh Golf Federation
Sec Gen, Gp Capt M Aminul Haque (Retd), C/- Kurmitola GC, Dhaka Cantonment, Dhaka-1206
Tel/Fax +880 2 988 1615
E-mail kgcdhaka@hotmail.com

Bhutan Golf Confederation
Sec Gen, D K Chhetri, PO Box 939, Thimphu, Bhutan
Tel 975 2 322 138
Fax 975 2 323 937
E-mail bhusport@druknet.net.bt

Cambodian Golf Association
Sec, Pok Yuthea, No 202 Norodom Blvd, Senak Building, Chamcar Morn, Phnom Penh

China Golf Association
Sec Gen, Qiang Cui Zhi, 5 Tiyuguan Rd, Beijing, 100763 China
Tel +86 10 8582 5990   *Fax* +86 10 8582 5994
E-mail chinagolf@263.net   *Website* www.golf.org.cn

Chinese Taipei Golf Association
Dep Sec Gen, Bob Hsu, 12 F-1, 125 Nanking East Road, Section 2, Taipei, Taiwan 104, ROC
Tel +886 22 516 5611   *Fax* +886 22 516 3208
E-mail garoc.tw@msa.hinet.net
Website www.garoc.com.tw

Guam National Golf Federation
Pres, Samuel Teker, Suite 2A 130 Aspinall Ave, Agana, Guam 96910
Tel +1 671 447 9891   *Fax* +1 671 472 2601
E-mail st@tttguamlawyers.com

Hong Kong Golf Association Ltd
Ch Exec, F 1 Valentine, Rm 2003, Olympic House, 1 Stadium Path, So Kon Po, Causeway Bay, Hong Kong
Tel +852 2504 8659   *Fax* +852 2845 1553
E-mail hkgolf@hkga.com

Indian Golf Union
Sec-Gen, W/Cdr Satish Aparajit (Retd), Rm No.1138-B, Gate No 27 Jawaharlal Nehru Stadium, Lodhi Rd, New Delhi 110 003
Tel +91 11 436 7161   *Fax* +91 11 436 7162
E-mail tigu@vsnl.net

Indonesian Golf Association
Sec Gen, Kusnan Ismukanto, Gd Direksi Gelora Bung Karno 2nd Floor, Jl.Pintu I,, Senayan-Jakarta, Indonesia-10270
Tel +62 21 573 2811   *Fax* +62 21 573 1291
E-mail pgi@pgionline.org
Website www.pgionline.org

Japan Golf Association
Sec Gen, Ryo Shioda, Kyobashi YS Bldg 2nd Floor, 1-12-5 Kyobashi, Chuo-Ku, Tokyo 104-0031
Tel +81 3 3566 0003   *Fax* +81 3 3566 0101
E-mail info@jga.or.jp   *Website* www.jga.or.jp

Korean Golf Association
Exec Dir, Dong-Wook Kim, Rm 1318, Manhattan Bldg, 36-2 Yeo Eui Du-Dong, Yeong Deung Po-Ku, Seoul
Tel +82 2 783 4748   *Fax* +82 2 783 4747
E-mail kga@kgagolf.or.kr
Website www.kgagolf.or.kr

Golf Association of Macau
Sec, Michelle Leong, Rm 15, Estrada Vitoria S/N, Centro Desportivo, Vitoria, Macau
Tel +853 831 555   *Fax* +853 832 555

Malaysian Golf Association
Pres, Thomas M L Lee, No.14 Jalan 4/76C, Desa Pandan, 55100 Kuala Lumpur
Tel +60 3 9283 7300
Fax +60 3 9282 9300
E-mail mga@tm.net.my
Website www.mgaonline.com.my

Golf Federation of the Union of Myanmar
Gen Sec, U Aung Kyi, Nawaday Compound, Kaba Aye
Pagoda Rd, Mayangon Township, Yangon
Tel +95 1 663 930   *Fax* +95 1 579 911
E-mail mits@cybertech.net.mm

Nepal Golf Association
Sec, Prachanda Bdr Shrestha, GPO Box 1665 Naya,
Baneshwar, Kathmandu
Tel +977 1 449 4247   *Fax* +977 1 478 0141
E-mail pranec@mos.com.np

Pakistan Golf Federation
Pres, Lt Gen Ashfaq Kayani, Jhelum Road, PO Box
1295, Rawalpindi
Tel +92 51 556 8177   *Fax* +92 51 225 5440
E-mail pakgolffed@yahoo.com

**National Golf Association of the
Philippines**
Sec, S Facundo, 209 Admin Bldg, Philippine Sports
Commission, Rizal Memorial Sports Complex, Pablo
Ocampo Sr. St, Manila
Tel +63 2 525 6987   *Fax* +63 2 521 1587
E-mail ngapgolf@hotmail.com

Singapore Golf Association
Gen Manager, Tracey Tay, Tanglin Post Office,
PO Box 457, Singapore 912416
Tel +65 6 256 1318   *Fax* +65 6 256 1917
E-mail sga@pacific.net.sg

Sri Lanka Golf Union & Ladies Golf Union
Hon Sec, Mark Silva, PO Box 309, 223 Model Farm
Road, Colombo 8, Sri Lanka
Tel +94 1 695431   *Fax* +94 1 687592
E-mail golfsrilanka@lanka.com.lk

Thailand Golf Association
Sec Gen, Air Marshal Bureerat Ratanavanich, Rm
211/213, Rajmangala National Stadium, 2088
Ramkamhaeng Rd, Hua Mark, Bangkok 10240
Tel +66 2 369 3777   *Fax* +66 2 369 3776
E-mail info@tga.or.th
Website www.tga.or.th

Professional Associations

Asian PGA
Sec, Ramlan Dato harun, 415-417 Block A Kelana Busi-
ness Centre, 97 Jalan SS 7/2 Kelana Jaya,
Selangor, Malaysia
Tel +603 7492 0099   *Fax* +603 7492 0098
Website www.asianpgatour.com

Asia PGA Tour
Chief Exec Off, Justin Strachan, 15/F, One
Harbourfront, 18 Tak Fung Street, Hunghom,
Kowloon, Hong Kong
Tel +852 2330 8227
Fax +852 2801 5743
E-mail apgatour@asiaonline.net
Website www.asianpgatour.com

PGA Republic of China
2nd Floor 196 Cheng-Teh Road, Taipei, Taiwan
Tel +886 2 8220318   *Fax* +886 2 8229684
E-mail garoc.tw@msa.hinet.net
Website www.twgolf.org

Hong Kong PGA
Sec, Mr M Lai Wai Sing, Room 702 Landmark North,
Sheung Shui, NT Hong Kong
Tel +852 523 3171

Indian PGA
Sec, S P Mathur, 1136-A, 27th Gate Jawaharlal Nehru
Stadium, New Delhi – 110 003
Tel +91 11 2432 66331
Fax +91 11 243 65305
E-mail pgai@ndf.vsnl.net.in

Japan Ladies PGA
7-16-3 Ginza, Nitetsu Kobiki Bldg 8F, Chuo-ku, Tokyo
104-0061
Tel +81 3 3546 7801   *Fax* +81 3 3546 7805

Japan PGA
Int Com, Seien Kobayakawa, Top Hamamatsucho Bldg,
1-5-12 Shiba.Minato-Ku, 8FL, Tokyo 105-0014
Tel +81 3 5419 2614   *Fax* +81 3 5419 2622
E-mail bp@pga.or.jp

PGA of Malaysia
Sec, Brig-Gen Mahendran, 1B Jalan Mamanda 7,
Ampang Point, 6800 Selangor Darul Ehsan, Malaysia

Australasia and the Pacific

Golf Australia
Ch Exec Officer, Tony Hallam, Level 3-95 Coventry St,
South Melbourne, VIC-3205
Tel +613 9626 5050   *Fax* +613 9626 5095
E-mail info@golfaustralia.org.au
Website www.golfaustralia.org.au

Womens Golf Australia
See Golf Australia

Cook Islands Golf Association
Sec, Mrs Tereapii Urlich, Rarotonga GC, PO Box 151,
Rarotonga, Cook Islands
Tel +682 20621   *Fax* +682 20631
E-mail toots@oyster.net.ck

National Golf Association of Fiji
Pres, I Bainimara c/o Air Terminal Services (Fiji) Ltd,
PO Box 18140, Suva, Fiji Islands
Tel +679 338 5089   *Fax* +679 992 2601
E-mail ibainimara@hotmail.com

New Zealand Golf Incorporated
Ch Exec, Larry Graham, PO Box 11-842, Wellington,
New Zealand
Tel +64 4 471 0990
Fax +64 4 471 0991
E-mail nzgolf@nzgolf.org.nz
Website www.nzgolf.org.nz

Womens' Golf New Zealand Inc
See New Zealand Golf Incorporated

Papua New Guinea Golf Association
Pres, S Walker, PO Box 4632, Boroko, NCD
Tel +675 323 1120
Fax +675 323 1300
E-mail swalker@brianbell.com.pg

Papua New Guinea Ladies Golf Association
Hon Sec, Mrs L Illidge, PO Box 348, Lae MP 411

Vanuatu Golf Association
Chairman, Bernie Cain, PO Box 358, Port Vila,
Vanuatu, Pacific Ocean
Tel +678 22178   *Fax* +678 25037
E-mail vilare@vanuatu.com.vu

Professional Associations

Australian PGA
Ch Exec, Max Garske, PO Box 1314, Crows Nest,
New South Wales
Tel +61 2 9439 8111   *Fax* +61 2 9439 7888
E-mail maxgpga@oze-mail.com.au
Website www.pga.org.au

PGA Tour Australasia
Exec Dir, Andrew Georgiou, Suite 302, 77 Berry St,
North Sydney, NSW 2060
Tel +61 2 9956 0000
Fax +61 2 9956 0099
Website pgatour.com.au

New Zealand PGA
Exec Dir, PO Box 11-934, Wellington
Tel +64 4 4722 687
Fax +64 4 4722 925
E-mail postmaster@pga.org.nz
Website www.pga.org.nz

Tiger chooses Dubai for his first course

Tiger Woods is to develop his first golf course in Dubai, in the United Arab Emirate, that hosts two European Tour events and has seen a remarkable growth in golf following the opening of The Emirates, the first all-grass course in the Middle East.

The Tiger Woods Dubai will be a 7700-yard, par-72 with a large clubhouse, a golf academy, 320 exclusive villas and a boutique hotel with 80 suites built into the overall plan.

"I look at this project not only as an opportunity, but also as a great responsibility," Woods said. "Hopefully I will create a memorable and everlasting legacy."

Dubai already has eight golf courses, including The Emirates where Woods won the 2006 Desert Classic in a play-off with Ernie Els. Woods lost in Dubai five years ago when he made double bogey on the final hole to finish two shots behind Thomas Bjørn.

Els, Bjørn, Colin Montgomerie and Ian Baker-Finch are among those who have built or are building golf courses in Dubai. Until the idea of using water from the desalination plants along the Gulf to provide the millions of gallons needed every day to keep the courses green, golfers in Dubai played on the sandy country club courses with browns – a mixture of sand and oil – as the putting surfaces.

Woods' Dubai course is a joint venture with Tiger, who last month created Tiger Woods Design, and Tatweer, a member of the government-affiliated Dubai Holding. "I have been amazed by the progress of Dubai. From the time I first came to play here in 2000, I wanted to be a part of this amazing vision," he said in an exclusive interview with Associated Press.

He said he chose Dubai for his first golf course because he was excited about the "challenge of transforming a desert terrain into a world-class golf course." The development is scheduled to be finished in late 2009 at Dubailand, the region's largest tourism and leisure project.

Saeed al-Muntafiq, the CEO of Tatweer, said: "We never looked for anyone beyond Tiger for the project because we believe in only working with the very best."

PART XIII

Clubs and Courses in the British Isles and Europe

Compiled by Shirley Card

Club Centenaries

1907	1908	1909	1910
Abersoch	Alton	Arcot Hall	Abergele
Alderley Edge	Carlisle	Arkley	Bacup
Alnwick	Chester-le-Street	Bexleyheath	Ballina
The Alwoodley	Darlington	Brampton (Talkin Tarn)	Bandon
Andover	Delgany	Charleville	Blairbeth
Basingstoke	Dunscar	Cowes	Bishop's Stortford
Bishopbriggs	Eastbourne Downs	Craaigie Hill	Carrick-on-Shannon
Blackley	Elderslie	Denton	Castlebar
Borris	Frilford Heath	Douglas	Dartmouth
Burhill	Glencruitten	Filton	Delamere Forest
Burslem	Hollingbury Park	Glynhir	Denham
Caldy	Holme Hall	Greenway Hall	Dinsdale Spa
Carmarthen	Houghton-le-Spring	Grim's Dyke	Duff House Royal
Carnwath	Kemnay	Hickleton	Dunlaoghaire
Colchester	Kingsthorpe	Hopeman	Eaton
Copt Heath	Knebworth	Kidderminster	Edenberry
Daventry & District	Ladbrook Park	Laytown & Bettystown	Elland
Ennis	Leamington & County	Loudoun Gowf	Haggs Castle
Enniscorthy	Little Aston	Lydney	Heysham
Ghyll	Lochcarron	Merthyr Tydfil	Houldsworth
Halifax Bradley Hall	Meltham	Mold	Kirkhill
Harewood Downs	The Mendip	Moortown	Knott End
Headley	Mid Kent	Murcar	Langley Park
Henley	Middlesbrough	Northamptonshire County	Longley Park
Ilford	Mitchelstown	Parkstone	Malton & Norton
Irvine Ravenspark	Monkstown	Pike Fold	Milnathort
Kingsknowe	Muckhart	Pitlochry	North Shore
Lees Hall	Newcastle-under-Lyme	Radcliffe-on-Trent	Nottingham City
Lightcliffe	Penn	Ringway	Old Fold Manor
Lymm	Penwortham	Royal Town of Caernarfon	Omagh
Mapperley	Portarlington	Runcorn	Penmaenmawr
Merchants of Edinburgh	Prestwich	Rushcliffe	Reading
Milltown	Ripon City	Scarborough North Cliff	Rhondda
Mountain Ash	Seaham	Sheerness	Ryborn
Muskerry	Selsey	Strathtay	Sandy Lodge
Nefyn & District	Stoke Park	Swinley Forest	Tarbert
New Mills	Stoneham	Tarbat	West Hove
Newton Green	Strabane	Temple	West Surrey
North Oxford	Strathaven	Thurles	Western Park
North Worcestershire	Tarland	Torquay	Wetherby
Ogbourne Downs	Tidworth Garrison	Troon St Meddans	
Old Colwyn	Turton	Walmer & Kingsdown	
Scrabo	Vale of Llangollen	West Hill	
The Spa	Wareham	Withernsea	
Seaford Head	Werneth		
Selby	Westport		
Spalding	Weymouth		
St Augustines	Wimbledon Common		
Tankersley Park	Windyhill		
Thorpe Hall	Worlebury		
Vale of Leven	Worplesdon		
Walsall			
Waterlooville			
Welshpool			
Whiteleaf			
Yeovil			

Golf Clubs and Courses in the British Isles and Europe

How to use this section

Clubs in England, Ireland and Wales are listed in alphabetical order by country and county. Note that some clubs and courses are affiliated to a county different to that in which they are physically located. Clubs in Scotland are grouped under recognised administrative regions. The Great Britain and Ireland county index can be found on page 638.

European clubs are listed alphabetically by country and grouped under regional headings. The index for these can be found on page 829. In most European countries, only 18 hole courses are included.

All clubs and courses are listed in the the general index at the back of the book.

Contact details are shown for all clubs. Full course details are included where these have been made available.

Club details (see Key to Symbols below)

The date after the name of the club indicates the year it was founded. Courses are private unless otherwise stated. Many public courses play host to members' clubs. Information on these can be obtained from the course concerned.

The address is the postal address.

Telephone: club telephone number for general use.

Membership: total number of playing members. The number of lady members (L) and juniors (J) is sometimes shown separately.

Secretary/Professional: telephone numbers for secretaries and professionals are shown separately.

Holes: the length of the course refers in most cases to the yardage from the medal tees.

Visitors: indicates the playing opportunities and restrictions for unaccompanied visitors.

Fees: green fees, the most up-to-date supplied, are quoted for visitors playing without a member. The basic cost per round or per day (D) is shown first, with the weekend rate in brackets. The cost of a weekly (W) ticket is sometimes shown.

Location: general location of club/course.

Miscellaneous: other golf facilities.

Architect: course architect/designer.

Abbreviations

WD   Weekdays.
WE   Weekends.
BH   Bank Holidays.
H   Handicap certificate required.
M   With a member, i.e. casual visitors are not allowed: only visitors playing with a member are permitted on the days stated.
NA   No visitors allowed.
SOC   Recognised Golfing Societies welcome if previous arrangements made with secretary.
U   Unrestricted.
CR   Course Rating (Europe)
SR   Slope Rating (Europe)

We are indebted to club secretaries in the British Isles and continental Europe for the information supplied.

Key to Symbols		International Dialling Codes		
☎ Telephone	👥 Visitors	Austria +43	Iceland +354	Poland +48
🖵 Fax	££ Fees	Belgium +32	Repubic of	Portugal +351
✉ E-mail	🐾 Location	Czech Republic	Ireland +353	Slovenia +386
📖 Membership	⊕ Miscellaneous	+420	Italy +39	Spain +34
✍ Secretary	🏠 Architect	Denmark +45	Luxembourg	Sweden +46
✓ Professional	📄 Website	Finland +358	+352	Switzerland
⊳ Holes		France +33	Malta +356	+41
		Germany +49	Netherlands	Turkey +90
		Greece +30	+31	
		Hungary +36	Norway +47	

Great Britain and Ireland County Index

England

Bedfordshire

Aspley Guise & Woburn Sands (1914)
West Hill, Aspley Guise, Milton Keynes, MK17 8DX
- ☎ **(01908) 583596**
- 🖥 (01908) 583596
- 📖 590
- ✍ Richard Norris (01908) 583596
- ⚐ C Clingan (01908) 582974
- ⮞ 18 L 6079 yds Par 71 SSS 70
- 👥 WD–H WE/BH–MH SOC–Wed & Fri
- ££ £32 (£48)
- 🚗 2 miles W of M1 Junction 13
- ⌂ Herd/Sandow

Aylesbury Vale (1991)
Proprietary
Wing, Leighton Buzzard, LU7 0UJ
- ☎ **(01525) 240196**
- 🖥 (01525) 240848
- 📖 500
- ✍ C Wright (Sec/Mgr)
- ⚐ T Bunyan (01525) 240196
- ⮞ 18 L 6612 yds Par 72 SSS 72
- 👥 WD–U WE–U–phone first SOC–WD
- ££ £19 (£30)
- 🚗 3 miles W of Leighton Buzzard on Wing-Stewkley road
- ⊕ Driving range
- ⌂ Sq Ldr Don Wright
- 📧 www.avgc.co.uk

Beadlow Manor Hotel G&CC (1973)
Proprietary
Beadlow, Shefford, SG17 5PH
- ☎ **(01525) 860800**
- 🖥 (01525) 861345
- 📖 700
- ✍ Graham Wilson (Gen Mgr)
- ⚐ Paul Simpson (01525) 860666
- ⮞ 18 L 6238 yds SSS 71
  18 L 6042 yds SSS 70
- 👥 U SOC WD WE
- ££ Mon–Thur £17.50 (£20) Fri £20 WE+BH £25
- 🚗 2 miles W of Shefford on A507
- ⊕ Driving range
- 📧 www.beadlowmanor.co.uk

The Bedford (1999)
Proprietary
Carnoustie Drive, Great Denham Golf Village, Biddenham, MK40 4FF
- ☎ **(01234) 320022**
- 🖥 (01234) 320023
- 📧 thebedford@btopenworld.com
- 📖 500
- ✍ Simon Pepper (01234) 330559
- ⚐ Zac Thompson
- ⮞ 18 L 6560 yds Par 72
- 👥 WD–U WE–U SOC–WD

- ££ £30 (£40)
- 🚗 2 miles W of Bedford (A428)
- ⊕ Driving range; chipping green; putting green
- ⌂ David Pottage
- 📧 www.kolvengolf.com

Bedford & County (1912)
Green Lane, Clapham, Bedford, MK41 6ET
- ☎ **(01234) 352617**
- 🖥 (01234) 357195
- 📧 olga@bedfordandcountygolfclub.co.uk
- 📖 600
- ✍ RP Walker (Mgr), O Ebsworth (Asst Mgr)
- ⚐ R Tattersall (01234) 359189
- ⮞ 18 L 6420 yds SSS 70
- 👥 WD–U H SOC WE–M
- ££ £28 D–£35
- 🚗 2 miles NW of Bedford on the old A6 in the village of Clapham
- 📧 www.bedfordandcountygolfclub.co.uk

Bedfordshire (1891)
Spring Lane, Stagsden, Bedford, MK43 8SR
- ☎ **(01234) 822555**
- 📧 office@bedfordshiregolf.com

Chalgrave Manor (1994)
Dunstable Road, Chalgrave, Toddington, LU5 6JN
- ☎ **(01525) 876556**
- 🖥 (01525) 876556
- 📧 steve@chalgravegolf.co.uk
- 📖 450
- ✍ S Rumball
- ⚐ Geoff Swain
- ⮞ 18 L 6382 yds Par 72 SSS 70
- 👥 U SOC–WD WE–U after 1 pm
- ££ £20 (£30)
- 🚗 2 miles W of M1 Junction 12 on A5120
- ⊕ Practice range
- ⌂ Mike Palmer
- 📧 www.chalgravegolf.co.uk

Colmworth (1992)
Proprietary
New Road, Colmworth, MK44 2NU
- ☎ **(01234) 378181**
- 📧 julie@colmworthgc.fsnet.co.uk

Colworth (1985)
Colworth House, Sharnbrook, Bedford, MK44 1LQ
- ☎ **(01933) 353269 (Sec)**
- 📖 450
- ✍ E Thompson
- ⮞ 9 L 5208 yds Par 68 SSS 66
- 👥 M
- ££ D–£10
- 🚗 Sharnbrook, 10 miles N of Bedford, off A6

Dunstable Downs (1906)
Whipsnade Road, Dunstable, LU6 2NB
- ☎ **(01582) 604472**
- 🖥 (01582) 478700
- 📧 ddgc@btconnect.com
- 📖 640
- ✍ Alan Sigee
- ⚐ M Weldon (01582) 662806
- ⮞ 18 L 5903 yds SSS 69
- 👥 WD–H WE–M SOC–WD exc Wed
- ££ On request
- 🚗 2 miles SW of Dunstable on B4541. M1 Junction 11
- ⌂ James Braid
- 📧 www.dunstable-golf.co.uk

Griffin (1985)
Chaul End Road, Caddington, LU1 4AX
- ☎ **(01582) 415573**
- 🖥 (01582) 415314
- 📧 info@griffingolfclub.co.uk
- 📖 460
- ✍ D Isger
- ⚐ D Housden (07725) 648412
- ⮞ 18 L 6226 yds Par 71 SSS 70
- 👥 WD–U WE/BH–after 2pm
- ££ £18 (£25)
- 🚗 3 miles W of Luton off A505 between Dunstable and Caddington. M1 Junction 10/11
- 📧 www.griffingolfclub.co.uk

Henlow (1985)
RAF Henlow, Henlow, SG16 6DN
- ☎ **(01462) 851515 Ext 7083**
- 🖥 (01462) 816780
- 📖 250
- ✍ S Bowen (01462) 851515 (Ext 7501)
- ⮞ 9 L 5618 yds SSS 67
- 👥 M
- ££ D–£10
- 🚗 3 miles SE of Shefford on A600
- ⊕ Driving range
- 📧 www.henlowgolfclub.co.uk

John O'Gaunt (1948)
Sutton Park, Sandy, Biggleswade, SG19 2LY
- ☎ **(01767) 260360**
- 🖥 (01767) 262834
- 📧 admin@johnogauntgolfclub.co.uk
- 📖 1450
- ✍ SD Anthony
- ⚐ L Scarbrow (01767) 260094
- ⮞ John O'Gaunt 18 L 6513 yds Par 71 SSS 71
  Carthagena 18 L 5869 yds Par 69 SSS 69
- 👥 H–phone first SOC–WD
- ££ £35 D–£50 (£60)
- 🚗 3 miles NE of Biggleswade on B1040
- ⌂ Hawtree
- 📧 www.johnogauntgolfclub.co.uk

Leighton Buzzard (1925)
Plantation Road, Leighton Buzzard, LU7 3JF
☎ **(01525) 244800**
🖳 (01525) 244801
✉ secretary@leightonbuzzardgolf.net
📖 650
🏌 D Mutton (01525) 244800
🏌 M Campbell (01525) 244815
🏳 18 L 6101 yds SSS 70
👥 WD exc Tues–U H WE/BH–MH
££ £39 D–£42
⛳ Heath and Reach, I mile N of Leighton Buzzard. M1 Junction 12
🖥 www.leightonbuzzardgolf.net

The Millbrook (1980)
Ampthill, MK45 2JB
☎ **(01525) 840252**
🖳 (01525) 406249
✉ info@themillbrook.com
📖 500
🏌 DC Cooke (01525) 840252
🏌 G Dixon (01525) 402269
🏳 18 L 7021 yds SSS 73
👥 WD–U WE after 12.00pm SOC
££ £26 (£35)
⛳ 4 miles from M1 Junctions 12 or 13 on A507
⊕ Practice range; buggies–£20 per 18 holes
🏠 W Sutherland
🖥 www.themillbrook.com

Mount Pleasant (1992)
Proprietary
Station Road, Lower Stondon, Henlow, SG16 6JL
☎ **(01462) 850999**
🖳 (01462) 850257
✉ manager@mountpleasantgolfclub.co.uk
📖 300
🏌 D Simkins (Prop) (01462) 850999
🏌 Glen Kemble (01462) 850999
🏳 9 L 6185 yds Par 70 SSS 70
👥 U SOC–WD
££ 9: £9 (£11.50) 18: £16 (£20)
⛳ 4 miles N of Hitchin, off A600
⊕ Practice chipping green with bunker; 9 hole putting green; undercover nets
🏠 Derek Young
🖥 www.mountpleasantgolfclub.co.uk

Mowsbury (1975)
Public
Kimbolton Road, Bedford, MK41 8DQ
☎ **(01234) 216374/771041**

Pavenham Park (1994)
Pavenham, Bedford, MK43 7PE
☎ **(01234) 822202**
✉ kolvengolf@ukonline.co.uk

South Beds (1892)
Warden Hill Road, Luton, LU2 7AE
☎ **(01582) 591500**
🖳 (01582) 495381
✉ office@southbedsgolfclub.co.uk
📖 850
🏌 RJ Wright (01582) 591500

🏌 E Cogle (01582) 591209
🏳 Galley 18 L 6438 yds SSS 71
  Warden 9 L 4784 yds SSS 63
👥 Galley WD–H (Ladies Day–Tues)
  WE/BH–H exc comp days–NA
  Warden–U
££ Galley £23 D–£35 (£32 D–£45)
  Warden £10 (£13)
⛳ 3 miles N of Luton, E of A6
🖥 www.southbedsgolfclub.co.uk

Stockwood Park (1973)
Public
Stockwood Park, London Rd, Luton, LU1 4LX
☎ **(01582) 413704**
🖳 (01582) 481001
✉ spgc@hotmail.co.uk
📖 500
🏌 Brian E Clark (Club Admin Officer) (01582) 431788 (answerphone)
🏌 Matt Green, Mark Jones
🏳 18 L 6049 yds SSS 69
👥 U SOC by prior arrangement
££ £11.40 D–£17 (£14)
⛳ Adjacent exit 10/10a M1 exit for Luton Airport
⊕ Driving range; Par 3 9-hole mini course

Tilsworth (1972)
Pay and play
Dunstable Rd, Tilsworth, Dunstable, LU7 9PU
☎ **(01525) 210721/210722**
🖳 (01525) 210465
✉ enquiries@tilsworthgolf.co.uk
📖 370
🏌 G Brandon-White
🏌 N Webb (Mgr)
🏳 18 L 5306 yds Par 69 SSS 67
👥 U SOC
££ £17 (£19.50)
⛳ 2 miles N of Dunstable (A5)
⊕ Driving range
🖥 www.tilsworthgolf.co.uk

Wyboston Lakes (1978)
Public
Wyboston Lakes, Wyboston, MK44 3AL
☎ **(01480) 223004**
🖳 (01480) 407330
📖 300
🏌 DJ Little (Mgr)
🏌 P Ashwell (01480) 223004
🏳 18 L 5995 yds Par 70 SSS 69
👥 WD–U WE–booking SOC
££ Under revision
⛳ S of St Neots, off A1 and St Neots by-pass
⊕ Driving range
🏠 Neil Ockden
🖥 www.wybostonlakes.co.uk

Berkshire

Bearwood (1986)
Mole Road, Sindlesham, Wokingham, RG41 5DB
☎ **(0118) 976 0060**

Bearwood Lakes (1996)
Bearwood Road, Sindlesham, RG41 4SJ
☎ **(0118) 979 7900**
✉ info@bearwoodlakes.co.uk

The Berkshire (1928)
Swinley Road, Ascot, SL5 8AY
☎ **(01344) 621495**
🖳 (01344) 623328
📖 900
🏌 Lt Col JCF Hunt (01344) 621496
🏌 P Anderson (01344) 622351
🏳 Red 18 L 6452 yds Par 72 SSS 71
  Blue 18 L 6343 yds Par 71 SSS 71
👥 WD–I WE/BH–M
££ On application
⛳ 3 miles from Ascot on A332. M3 Junction 3
⊕ Practice range and short course academy
🏠 Herbert Fowler

Billingbear Park
Pay and play
The Straight Mile, Wokingham, RG40 5SJ
☎ **(01344) 869259**
🖳 (01344) 869259
✉ jrblainey@hotmail.com
📖 100
🏌 Mrs JR Blainey
🏌 MW Blainey
🏳 9 L 5700 yds Par 68
  9 hole Par 3 course
👥 U
££ £8 (£10)
⛳ 2 miles E of Wokingham via B3034. M4 Junction 10
🖥 www.billingbeargolf.co.uk

Bird Hills Golf Centre (1985)
Public
Drift Road, Hawthorn Hill, Maidenhead, SL6 3ST
☎ **(01628) 771030**
🖳 (01628) 631023
✉ info@birdhills.co.uk
📖 400
🏌 Eve Lane
🏌 N Slimming
🏳 18 L 6212 yds SSS 71
👥 U SOC–WD/WE
££ On application
⛳ 4 miles S of Maidenhead on A330
⊕ Floodlit driving range; putting green
🖥 www.birdhills.co.uk

Blue Mountain Golf Centre (1993)
Pay and play
Wood Lane, Binfield, RG42 4EX
☎ **(01344) 300220**
🖳 (01344) 360960
✉ bluemountain@crown-golf.co.uk
📖 350
🏌 Guy Riggott (Gen Mgr)
🏌 C Lilleystone (01344) 488858
🏳 18 L 6097 yds SSS 70
👥 U SOC
££ Mon–Thur £19, Fri £21 (£26)
⛳ I mile W of Bracknell on B3408. M4 Junction 10

For list of abbreviations and key to symbols see page 651

⊕ Driving range. Golf Academy
▤ www.crown-golf.co.uk

Calcot Park (1930)

Bath Road, Calcot, Reading, RG31 7RN
☎ **(0118) 942 7124**
▱ (0118) 945 3373
✉ info@calcotpark.com
▥ 550
♟ Kim Brake
✓ M Grieve (0118) 942 7797
▷ 18 L 6216 yds SSS 70
♟♟ WD–H WE/BH–M SOC–WD
££ £50. After 2pm–£30
⊷ 3 miles W of Reading on A4. 1¹/₂
   miles E of M4 Junction 12
⌂ HS Colt
▤ www.calcotpark.com

Castle Royle (1994)

Knowl Hill, Reading, RG10 9XA
☎ **(01628) 825442**

Caversham Heath (2000)

Chazey Heath, Mapledurham, Reading,
RG4 7UT
☎ **(0118) 947 8600**
▱ (0118) 947 8700
✉ info@cavershamgolf.co.uk
✓ Adam Harrison (0118) 947 9400
▷ 18 7151 yds Par 73 SSS 74
♟♟ U–restricted WD. WE–NA before
   3.00 pm SOC
££ £36 (£50)
⊷ 3 miles N of Reading
⌂ David Williams
▤ www.cavershamgolf.co.uk

Datchet (1890)

Buccleuch Road, Datchet, SL3 9BP
☎ **(01753) 543887 (Clubhouse)**
▱ (01753) 541872
✉ secretary@datchetgolfclub.co.uk
▥ 435 60(L) 30(J)
♟ KR Smith (01753) 541872
✓ I Godleman (01753) 545222
▷ 9 L 6087 yds SSS 69
♟♟ WD–U M SOC WE–M
££ £25 D–£35
⊷ Slough, Windsor 2 miles
⌂ JH Taylor
▤ www.datchetgolfclub.co.uk

Deanwood Park (1995)

Pay and play
Stockcross, Newbury, RG20 8JP
☎ **(01635) 48772**
▱ (01635) 48772
✉ golf@deanwoodpark.co.uk
▥ 400
♟ John Bowness
✓ Claire Waite
▷ 9 L 4230 yds Par 64 SSS 60
♟♟ U
££ 9: £8.50 (£10.50) 18: £14.50
   (£17.50)
⊷ 2 miles W of Newbury (B4000).
   M4 Junction 13, 2 miles
⊕ Driving range; putting green
▤ www.deanwoodpark.co.uk

Donnington Valley (1985)

Proprietary
Snelsmore House, Snelsmore Common,
Newbury, RG14 3BG
☎ **(01635) 568140**
▱ (01635) 568141
✉ golf@donningtonvalley.co.uk
▥ 550
♟ Peter Smith (01635) 568144
✓ M Balfour
▷ 18 L 6353 yds SSS 71
♟♟ U
££ £27 (£36)
⊷ N of Newbury, off Old Oxford
   road; 5 min M4 Jct 14
⊕ Putting green
⌂ Mike Smith
▤ www.donningtonvalleygolfclub.co.uk

Downshire (1973)

Public
Easthampstead Park, Wokingham,
RG40 3DH
☎ **(01344) 302030**
▱ (01344) 301020
✉ downshire@bracknell.forest.gov.uk
▥ 500
♟ P Stanwick (Golf
   Mgr) (01344) 422708
✓ W Owers
▷ 18 L 6416 yds Par 73 SSS 69
♟♟ U SOC WD WE
££ £19.45 (£25.95)
⊷ Off Nine Mile Ride
⊕ 30-bay floodlit driving range; 9-hole
   pitch & putt
▤ www.bracknell.forest.gov.uk/be

East Berkshire (1903)

Ravenswood Ave, Crowthorne, RG45 6BD
☎ **(01344) 772041**
▱ (01344) 777378
✉ thesecretary@eastberksgc.fsnet
   .co.uk
▥ 700
♟ C Day
✓ J Brant (01344) 774112
▷ 18 L 6345 yds SSS 70
♟♟ WD–H SOC (only Thur/Fri)
   WE/BH–M
££ £50
⊷ Nr Crowthorne Railway Station
⌂ P Paxton
▤ www.eastberkshiregolfclub.co.uk

Goring & Streatley (1895)

Rectory Road, Streatley-on-Thames,
RG8 9QA
☎ **(01491) 873229**
▱ (01491) 875224
✉ secretary@goringgc.org
▥ 740 115(L) 50(J)
♟ ABW James
✓ J Hadland (01491) 873715
▷ 18 L 6355 yds SSS 70
♟♟ WD–U WE/BH–M SOC–WD
££ £33 D–£44 (£44)
⊷ 10 miles NW of Reading on A417
⌂ Tom Dunne
▤ www.goringgc.org

Hennerton (1992)

Crazies Hill Road, Wargrave, RG10 8LT
☎ **(0118) 940 1000/4778**
▱ (0118) 940 1042
✉ info@hennertongolfclub.co.uk
▥ 450
♟ Zara Hearn (0118) 940 1000
✓ W Farrow (0118) 940 4778
▷ 18 L 4391 yds Par 65 SSS 62
♟♟ WD–U WE–pm only SOC WE
   only
££ 9: £14 (£18); 18: £20 (£30)
⊷ Between Maidenhead and Reading
   (A4/A321)
⊕ Driving range, floodlit, covered;
   practice putting green
⌂ Dion Beard; Gaunt & Marnoch
▤ www.hennertongolfclub.co.uk

Hurst (1979)

Public
Sandford Lane, Hurst, Wokingham,
RG10 0SQ
☎ **(01734) 344355**

Maidenhead (1896)

Shoppenhangers Road, Maidenhead,
SL6 2PZ
☎ **(01628) 624693**
▱ (01628) 780758
✉ manager@maidenheadgolf.co.uk
▥ 600
♟ NJ Randall
✓ S Geary (01628) 624067
▷ 18 L 6360 yds SSS 70
♟♟ WD–H Mon–Thur Fri M only H
   SOC Tue am/Wed–Thur WD only
££ D–£35 W–£50
⊷ Off A308, nr Maidenhead Station
⌂ A Simpson/JH Taylor
▤ www.maidenheadgolf.co.uk

Mapledurham (1992)

Mapledurham, Reading, RG4 7UD
☎ **(0118) 946 3353**
▱ (0118) 946 3363
✉ d.reeves@clubhaus.com
▥ 750
♟ R Davies
✓ T Gilpin
▷ 18 L 5635 yds SSS 67
♟♟ WE–NA before 11am
££ On application
⊷ 4 miles NW of Reading, off
   A4074
⌂ MRM Sandow

Mill Ride (1990)

Mill Ride, Ascot, SL5 8LT
☎ **(01344) 886777**
▱ (01344) 886820
▥ 300
♟ W Sheffield
✓ T Wild
▷ 18 L 6752 yds SSS 72
♟♟ H SOC WD, WE–NA before
   noon
££ On application
⊷ 2 miles W of Ascot
⌂ Donald Steel
▤ www.mill-ride.com

For list of abbreviations and key to symbols see page 651

Newbury & Crookham

(1873)

Bury's Bank Road, Greenham Common, Newbury, RG19 8BZ

☎ **(01635) 40035**
🖳 (01635) 40045
📧 steve.myers@newburygolf.co.uk
📖 620
🏌 S Myers MBE (01635) 40035
✓ DW Harris (01635) 31201
▷ 18 L 5961 yds SSS 69
👥 WD–U H WE–M (recognised club members)
££ £35 D–£40
⛳ 4 miles SE of Newbury. M4 Junction 13
🖥 www.newburygolf.co.uk

Newbury Racecourse

(1994)

The Racecourse, Newbury, RG14 7NZ

☎ **(01635) 551464**

Parasampia G&CC

Donnington Grove, Grove Road, Donnington, RG14 2LA

☎ **(01635) 581000**
📧 enquiries@parasampia.com

Reading

(1910)

17 Kidmore End Road, Emmer Green, Reading, RG4 8SG

☎ **(0118) 947 2909**
🖳 (0118) 946 4468
📧 secretary@readinggolfclub.com
📖 600
🏌 A Chaundy (0118) 947 2909
✓ S Fotheringham (0118) 947 6115
▷ 18 L 6251 yds SSS 70
👥 Mon–Thurs–UH Fri/WE/BH–M SOC–Tues–Thurs
££ £35 D–£50
⛳ 2 miles N of Reading, off Peppard Road (B481)
🏛 James Braid
🖥 www.readinggolfclub.com

Royal Ascot

(1887)

Winkfield Road, Ascot, SL5 7LJ

☎ **(01344) 625175**
🖳 (01344) 872330
📧 secretary@royalascotgolfclub.co.uk
📖 600
🏌 Mrs S Thompson (01344) 625175
✓ A White (01344) 624656
▷ 18 L 6294 yds Par 70 SSS 70
👥 M SOC
££ On application
⛳ Now on new course, formerly Ascot Farm, off A330; Windsor 4 miles; M3
🏛 STRI

The Royal Household

(1901)

Buckingham Palace, London SW1 1AA

☎ **(0207) 930 4832**
🖳 (0207) 024 5853
📧 rhgc@royal.gsx.gov.uk
📖 250

🏌 Peter Walter
▷ 9 (18 tees) L 4925 yds Par 66 SSS 64
👥 Strictly by invitation only
⛳ The Home Park, Windsor Castle; M25 Jct 13
🏛 Samuel Mure Fergusson

Sand Martins

(1993)

Proprietary

Finchampstead Road, Wokingham, RG40 3RQ

☎ **(0118) 979 2711**
🖳 (0118) 977 0282
📧 info@sandmartins.com
📖 750
🏌 J McDonald (0118) 902 9965
✓ AJ Hall (0118) 977 0265
▷ 18 L 6204 yds Par 70 SSS 70
👥 WD–U WE–NA before 1pm SOC
££ £35.50 (£42.50)
⛳ 1 mile S of Wokingham. M4 Jct 10
⊕ Driving range
🏛 ET Fox
🖥 www.sandmartins.com

Sonning

(1911)

Duffield Road, Sonning, Reading, RG4 6GJ

☎ **(0118) 969 3332**
🖳 (0118) 944 8409
📧 secretary@sonning-golf-club.co.uk
📖 750
🏌 AJ Tanner
✓ RT McDougall (0118) 969 2910
▷ 18 L 6366 yds Par 70 SSS 70
👥 WD–H WE–M
££ £40.50 before 10.30 £30.50 after 10.30 £18.50 with member
⛳ 1½ miles E of A329(M). S of A4, nr Sonning
🏛 JH Taylor (1911)
🖥 www.sonning-golf-club.co.uk

Swinley Forest

(1909)

Coronation Road, Ascot, SL5 9LE

☎ **(01344) 620197**
🖳 (01344) 874733
📧 swinleyfgc@aol.com
📖 350
🏌 IL Pearce (01344) 874979
✓ S Hill (01344) 874811
▷ 18 L 6062 yds Par 69 SSS 70
👥 M
££ £125
⛳ S of Ascot
🏛 HS Colt

Temple

(1909)

Henley Road, Hurley, Maidenhead, SL6 5LH

☎ **(01628) 824795**
🖳 (01628) 828119
📧 templegolfclub@btconnect.com
📖 566
🏌 KGM Adderley (01628) 824795
✓ J Whiteley (01628) 824254
▷ 18 L 6266 yds SSS 70
👥 H SOC
££ £44 D–£56 (£50 D–£60)
⛳ Between Maidenhead and Henley on A4130. M4 Junction 8/9. M40 Jct 4

🏛 Willie Park Jr
🖥 www.templegolfclub.co.uk

Theale

North Street, Theale, Reading, RG6 5EX

☎ **(01189) 305331**

West Berkshire

(1975)

Chaddleworth, Newbury, RG20 7DU

☎ **(01488) 638574**
🖳 (01488) 638781
📧 info@thewbgc.co.uk
📖 700
🏌 Mrs CM Clayton
✓ P Simpson (01488) 638851
▷ 18 L 7022 yds SSS 74
👥 WD–U WE–M SOC–WD
££ £28 D–£40 (£35)
⛳ Off A338 to Wantage. M4 Junction 14
🖥 www.thewbgc.co.uk

Winter Hill

(1976)

Grange Lane, Cookham, SL6 9RP

☎ **(01628) 527613**
📖 800
✓ R Frost (01628) 527610
▷ 18 L 6408 yds SSS 71
👥 WD–U WE–M SOC
££ D–£36 After 2pm–£24
⛳ Maidenhead 3 miles
🏛 Charles Lawrie

Wokefield Park

(1998)

Mortimer, Reading, RG7 3AE

☎ **(0118) 933 4013/4018/4017**
🖳 (0118) 933 4031
📧 wokefieldgolf@initialstyle.co.uk
✓ G Smith (0118) 933 4078
▷ 18 L 6961 yds Par 72 SSS 73
👥 WD–U WE–NA before 9.30am SOC
££ £30 (£45)
⛳ 8 miles SW of Reading, off A33. M4 Junction 11
⊕ Driving range
🏛 Jonathan Gaunt
🖥 www.golf-isc.co.uk

Buckinghamshire

Abbey Hill

(1975)

Monks Way, Two Mile Ash, Milton Keynes, MK8 8AA

☎ **(01908) 563845**

Aylesbury Golf Centre

(1992)

Public

Hulcott Lane, Bierton, HP22 5GA

☎ **(01296) 393644**
🏌 K Partington (Mgr)
✓ R Wooster
▷ 18 L 5965 yds SSS 69
👥 U
££ £12 (£17)
⛳ 1 mile N of Aylesbury on A418
⊕ Driving range
🏛 TS Benwell

Aylesbury Park (1996)

Andrews Way, off Coldharbour Way, Oxford Road, Aylesbury, HP17 8QQ
- ☎ (01296) 399196
- 🖳 (01296) 336830
- 📖 360
- ✍ J Scheu
- ✓ G Legouix
- ⊳ 18 L 6166 yds SSS 69
  9-hole Par 3 short course
- 👥 U
- ££ 9: £5; 18: £18 (£23)
- ⬥ SW of Aylesbury (A418). M40 Junction 8, 12 miles
- ⊕ Practice nets & putting green
- ⌂ Martin Hawtree
- 🖳 www.aylesburyparkgolf.com

Beaconsfield (1902)

Seer Green, Beaconsfield, HP9 2UR
- ☎ (01494) 676545
- 🖳 (01494) 681148
- ✉ secretary@beaconsfieldgolfclub .co.uk
- 📖 850
- ✍ KR Wilcox
- ✓ M Brothers (01494) 676616
- ⊳ 18 L 6508 yds Par 72 SSS 71
- 👥 WD–H WE–M SOC
- ££ £50 D–£60
- ⬥ 2 miles E of Beaconsfield. M40 Junction 2
- ⊕ Driving range
- ⌂ HS Colt
- 🖳 www.beaconsfieldgolfclub.co.uk

Buckingham (1914)

Tingewick Road, Buckingham, MK18 4AE
- ☎ (01280) 815566
- 🖳 (01280) 821812
- ✉ admin@buckinghamgolfclub.co.uk
- 📖 680
- ✍ GL Pearce (Sec/Mgr)
- ✓ G Hannah (01280) 815210
- ⊳ 18 L 6162 yds SSS 70
- 👥 WD–U WE–M SOC–Tues & Thurs
- ££ £30
- ⬥ 2 miles SW of Buckingham on A421
- ⌂ Peter Jones
- 🖳 www.buckinghamgolfclub.co.uk

Buckinghamshire (1992)

Denham Court Mansion, Denham Court Drive, Denham, UB9 5PG
- ☎ (01895) 835777
- 🖳 (01895) 835210
- ✉ enquiries@buckinghamshiregc.co.uk
- 📖 550
- ✍ D Barancek (01895) 836803 John O'Leary (Dir of Golf)
- ✓ Paul Schunter (01895) 836814
- ⊳ 18 L 6880 yds Par 72 SSS 73
- 👥 I or M SOC–WD exc Fri
- ££ £90 Mon–Thur (£100 Fri–Sun)
- ⬥ Off A40(M). M25 Junction 16b/M40 Junction 1
- ⊕ Driving range; chipping green; putting green
- ⌂ John Jacobs
- 🖳 www.buckinghamshiregc.com

Burnham Beeches (1891)

Green Lane, Burnham, Slough, SL1 8EG
- ☎ (01628) 661448
- 🖳 (01628) 668968
- ✉ enquiries@bbgc.co.uk
- 📖 670
- ✍ TP Jackson (Mgr) (01628) 661448
- ✓ R Bolton (01628) 661661
- ⊳ 18 L 6449 yds SSS 71
- 👥 WD–I WE/BH–M H
- ££ £40 D–£60
- ⬥ 4 miles W of Slough
- 🖳 www.bbgc.co.uk

Chartridge Park (1989)

Chartridge, Chesham, HP5 2TF
- ☎ (01494) 791772
- 🖳 (01494) 786462
- ✉ info@cpgc.co.uk
- 📖 700
- ✍ E Roca
- ✓ J Reilly
- ⊳ 18 L 5409 yds SSS 66
- 👥 U SOC
- ££ £20 (£30)
- ⬥ 2 miles NW of Chesham. 9 miles W of M25 Junction 18
- ⌂ John Jacobs
- 🖳 www.cpgc.co.uk

Chesham & Ley Hill (1900)

Ley Hill, Chesham, HP5 1UZ
- ☎ (01494) 784541
- 🖳 (01494) 785506
- ✉ secretary@cheshamgolf.co.uk
- 📖 322
- ✍ James Short
- ✓ James Short (07773) 367079
- ⊳ 9 L 5240 yds Par 67 SSS 65
- 👥 WD–U exc Tues–NA before 3pm WE/BH–M SOC–Thurs & Fri
- ££ £15
- ⬥ Chesham 2 miles
- ⊕ Course closed Sun after 2pm from 1st Apr–30th Sept
- 🖳 www.cheshamgolf.co.uk

Chiltern Forest

Aston Hill, Halton, Aylesbury, HP22 5NQ
- ☎ (01296) 631267
- 🖳 (01296) 632709
- ✉ secretary@chilternforest.co.uk
- 📖 650
- ✍ R Clift (01296) 631267
- ✓ A Lavers (01296) 631817
- ⊳ 18 L 5765 yds Par 70 SSS 69
- 👥 WD–U WE–M SOC
- ££ £34
- ⬥ 5 miles SE of Aylesbury, off A4011
- 🖳 www.chilternforest.co.uk

Denham (1910)

Tilehouse Lane, Denham, UB9 5DE
- ☎ (01895) 832022
- 🖳 (01895) 835340
- 📖 775
- ✍ JW Tucker
- ✓ S Campbell (01895) 832801
- ⊳ 18 L 6470 yds SSS 71
- 👥 Mon–Thurs–I H Fri–Sun/BH–M
- ££ £50–£75
- ⬥ 2 miles NW of Uxbridge
- ⌂ HS Colt

Ellesborough (1905)

Butlers Cross, Aylesbury, HP17 0TZ
- ☎ (01296) 622114
- 🖳 (01296) 622114
- ✉ admin@ellesboroughgolf.co.uk
- 📖 700
- ✍ PG Miles (Gen Mgr)
- ✓ M Squire (01296) 623126
- ⊳ 18 L 6384 yds SSS 71
- 👥 WE/BH–M WD–I or H SOC–on application
- ££ On application
- ⬥ 1 mile W of Wendover
- 🖳 www.ellesboroughgolf.co.uk

Farnham Park (1974)

Public
Park Road, Stoke Poges, Slough, SL2 4PJ
- ☎ (01753) 643332

Flackwell Heath (1904)

Treadaway Road, Flackwell Heath, High Wycombe, HP10 9PE
- ☎ (01628) 520929
- 🖳 (01628) 530040
- 📖 700
- ✍ SJ Chandler
- ✓ P Watson (01628) 523017
- ⊳ 18 L 6211 yds SSS 70
- 👥 WD–H WE–M SOC–Wed & Thurs
- ££ £30
- ⬥ Between High Wycombe and Beaconsfield, off A40. M40 Jct 3/4
- ⌂ J Turner
- 🖳 www.flackwellheathgolfclub.co.uk

Gerrards Cross (1921)

Chalfont Park, Gerrards Cross, SL9 0QA
- ☎ (01753) 883263
- 🖳 (01753) 883593
- ✉ secretary@gxgolf.co.uk
- 📖 640
- ✍ Simon Maynard
- ✓ M Barr (01753) 885300
- ⊳ 18 L 6212 yds SSS 70
- 👥 WD–H WE/H–M SOC
- ££ £45 D–£55
- ⬥ 1 mile from Station, off A413
- ⌂ B Pedlar

Harewood Downs (1907)

Cokes Lane, Chalfont St Giles, HP8 4TA
- ☎ (01494) 762184
- 🖳 (01494) 766869
- ✉ secretary@hdgc.co.uk
- 📖 500
- ✍ SJ Thornton (01494) 762184
- ✓ GC Morris (01494) 764102
- ⊳ 18 L 6028 yds SSS 69
- 👥 H
- ££ £40 (£45)
- ⬥ 2 miles E of Amersham, off A413
- ⌂ JH Taylor
- 🖳 www.hdgc.co.uk

Harleyford (1996)

Harleyford Estate, Henley Road, Marlow, SL7 2SP
- ☎ (01628) 816164
- 🖳 (01628) 816160
- ✉ info@harleyfordgolf.co.uk

☐ 750
🏌 Gary Ivory
⚬ D Brewer
▷ 18 L 6708 yds Par 72 SSS 72
👥 U SOC–WD after 10am SOC–WE after 1pm
££ £45 (£65)
⚙ 1 mile W of Marlow on A4155
⊕ Driving range
🏠 Donald Steel
▤ www.harleyfordgolf.co.uk

Hazlemere (1982)
Penn Road, Hazlemere, High Wycombe, HP15 7LR
☎ **(01494) 719300**
🖳 (01494) 713914
✉ enquiries@hazlemeregolfclub.co.uk
☐ 600
🏌 PS Dawson
⚬ G Cousins (01494) 719306
▷ 18 L 5828 yds SSS 69
👥 WD–U WE–booking req SOC–WD
££ £36 (£45)
⚙ 3 miles NE of High Wycombe on B474
🏠 Terry Murray
▤ www.hazlemeregolfclub.co.uk

Hedsor (2000)
Pay and play
Broad Lane, Wooburn Common, Bucks, HP10 0JW
☎ **(01628) 851285**
✉ info@hedsorgolfcourse.co.uk
☐ 150
🏌 S Morris (Gen Mgr) (01628) 851285
⚬ S Cannon (01628) 851285
▷ 9 L 5158 yds (18 holes) Par 68 SSS 64
👥 U
££ 9 holes £10 (£12); Seniors £6 WD
⚙ M40 Jct 2, take A355 to Slough and follow signs to Hedsor Golf Club
⊕ Practice area
🏠 Steve Morris
▤ www.hedsorgolfcourse.co.uk

Huntswood (1996)
Taplow Common Road, Burnham, SL1 8LS
☎ **(01628) 667144**
🖳 (01628) 663145
✉ chrislewis.huntswood @btopenworld.com
☐ 450
🏌 R Balm (01628) 810590
⚬ G Beynon (01628) 667144
▷ 18 L 5078 yds Par 68 SSS 64
👥 U SOC WD WE
££ £13 (£18)
⚙ M4 Junction 7
⊕ 6 buggies
▤ www.huntswoodgolf.com

Iver (1983)
Hollow Hill Lane, Iver, SL0 0JJ
☎ **(01753) 655615**
🖳 (01753) 654225
✉ ivergolf@fsmail.net
☐ 500

🏌 J Lynch (Golf Dir)
⚬ J Lynch
▷ 9 L 5146 yds SSS 66
9 hole short course 1407 yds
👥 U SOC Book time WE
££ 9: £8 (£9.50); 18: £14 (£17) Short: Adults 9: £4 (£4.50) 18: £7 (£8) reductions for juniors
⚙ M4 Slough East Langley
⊕ Driving range on site
▤ www.ivergolfcourse.co.uk

Ivinghoe (1967)
Wellcroft, Ivinghoe, Leighton Buzzard, LU7 9EF
☎ **(01296) 668696**
🖳 (01296) 662755
✉ ivinghoegolfclub@tesco.net
☐ 150
🏌 Mrs SE Garrad (01296) 662478
⚬ M Flitney (01296) 668696
▷ 9 L 4508 yds SSS 62
👥 WD–U WE–U after 8am SOC
££ 9: £6, 18: £10
⚙ 3 miles N of Tring. M1 Junction 11, 5 miles
🏠 R Garrad
▤ golfshopbuckinghamshire.co.uk

Kingfisher CC (1995)
Proprietary
Buckingham Road, Deanshanger, Milton Keynes, MK19 6JY
☎ **(01908) 560354**
🖳 (01908) 260857
✉ sales.kingfisher@btopenworld.com
☐ 80
🏌 Matthew Brand (01908) 562332
⚬ Brian Mudge (01604) 643555
▷ 9 L 5552 yds Par 70 SSS 67 (18 tees)
👥 U SOC
££ 9: £9.50 (£12.50) 18: £14 (£17)
⚙ 10 min W central Milton Keynes, Junction 15
⊕ Driving range - phone for availability
🏠 Donald Steele
▤ www.kingfisher-uk.com

The Lambourne Club (1992)
Dropmore Road, Burnham, SL1 8NF
☎ **(01628) 666755**
🖳 (01628) 663301
✉ info@lambourneclub.co.uk
☐ 670
🏌 D Hart (Gen Mgr)
⚬ D Hart/S Marshall (01628) 662936
▷ 18 L 6771 yds SSS 73
👥 H SOC–Thur only
££ £60 (£90)
⚙ 1 mile N of Burnham. M40 Junction 2. M4 Junction 7
⊕ Driving range
🏠 Donald Steel
▤ www.lambourneclub.co.uk

Little Chalfont (1981)
Lodge Lane, Little Chalfont, Amersham, HP8 4AJ
☎ **(01494) 764877**

Magnolia Park
Arncott Road, Boarstall, HP18 9XX
☎ **(01844) 239700**
🖳 (01844 238991
☐ 400
🏌 G Strong
⚬ I Godleman
▷ 18 holes Par 73 SSS 73
9 hole course
👥 U SOC–WD
££ D–£40
⚙ 10 miles NW of Thame (B4011)
⊕ Golf Academy
🏠 Johnathan Gaunt

Mentmore G&CC (1992)
Mentmore, Leighton Buzzard, LU7 0UA
☎ **(01296) 662020**
✉ s.clark@clubhaus.com

Oakland Park (1994)
Proprietary
Three Households, Chalfont St Giles, HP8 4LW
☎ **(01494) 871277**
🖳 (01494) 874692
✉ info@oaklandparkgolf.co.uk
☐ 600
🏌 I Donnelly (Gen Mgr)
⚬ A Thatcher (01494) 877333
▷ 18 L 5246 yds Par 67 SSS 66
👥 U SOC–WD–WE
££ £28.50 (£30.50)
⚙ 3 miles N of M40 Junction 2
⊕ Driving range
🏠 Jonathan Gaunt
▤ www.oaklandparkgolf.co.uk

Princes Risborough (1990)
Lee Road, Saunderton Lee, Princes Risborough, HP27 9NX
☎ **(01844) 346989 (Clubhouse)**
🖳 (01844) 274938
☐ 320
🏌 J Murray (Man Dir)
⚬ S Lowry (01844) 274567
▷ 9 L 5440 yds Par 68 SSS 67
👥 U SOC
££ 9: £12 (£14) 18: £17 (£22)
⚙ 7 miles NW of High Wycombe on A4010; M40 Jct 4 or 5
🏠 Guy Hunt
▤ www.princesrisboroughgc.uwclub.net

Richings Park (1996)
Proprietary
North Park, Iver, SL0 9DL
☎ **(01753) 655352**
🖳 (01753) 655409
☐ 550
🏌 R Mullane (01753) 655370
⚬ R Mullane (01753) 655352
▷ 18 L 6210 yds Par 70 SSS 70
👥 WD–U WE–NA
££ £24 (£30)
⚙ Nr M4 Junction 5
⊕ Driving range
🏠 Alan Higgins
▤ www.richingspark.co.uk

Silverstone (1992)
Proprietary
Silverstone Road, Stowe, Buckingham, MK18 5LH
☎ (01280) 850005
✉ proshop@silverstonegolfclub .co.uk

Stoke Park (1908)
Park Road, Stoke Poges, SL2 4PG
☎ (01753) 717171
🖷 (01753) 717181
✉ info@stokeparkclub.com
🛏 850
🏌 Miss Kelly Ford (01753) 717116
✓ S Collier
⊳ 18 L 6721 yds SSS 72
   9 L 3074 yds
👥 U H WE–NA unless playing with
   member
££ £125
⊶ 5 miles N of Windsor
⌂ HS Colt
▤ www.stokeparkclub.com

Thorney Park (1992)
Proprietary
Thorney Mill Lane, Iver, SL0 9AL
☎ (01895) 422095
🖷 (01895) 431307
✉ sales@thorneypark.co.uk
🛏 300
🏌 P Gray
✓ A Killing
⊳ 18 L 5731 yds Par 69 SSS 68
👥 U SOC WE U after 12 noon
££ £22 (£28)
⊶ 3 miles N of M4 Junction 5 (B470)
⊕ Practice facility; putting green
⌂ D Walker
▤ www.thorneypark.com

Three Locks (1992)
Great Brickhill, Milton Keynes, MK17 9BH
☎ (01525) 270050
🖷 (01525) 270470
✉ info@threelocksgolfclub.co.uk
🛏 300
🏌 P Critchley
⊳ 18 L 6025 yds Par 70 SSS 68
👥 U SOC exc Sun
££ £19 (£25)
⊶ N of Leighton Buzzard on A4146.
   M1 Junction 14
⌂ MRM Sandow
▤ www.threelocksgolfclub.co.uk

Wavendon Golf Centre
(1990)
Pay and play
Lower End Road, Wavendon, Milton Keynes, MK17 8DA
☎ (01908) 281811
🖷 (01908) 281257
🛏 250
🏌 G Iron
✓ G Iron
⊳ 18 L 5460 yds Par 67 SSS 66
   9 hole par 3 pitch & putt course
👥 U SOC
££ Mon–Thur £14.50, Fri £15 (£20)

⊶ 2 miles W of M1 Junction 13
⊕ Floodlit driving range

Weston Turville (1973)
New Road, Weston Turville, Aylesbury, HP22 5QT
☎ (01296) 424084
🖷 (01296) 395376
🛏 600
🏌 D Allen
✓ G George (01296) 425949
⊳ 18 L 6008 yds SSS 69
👥 U
££ £25 (£30)
⊶ 1½ miles SE of Aylesbury

Wexham Park (1977)
Pay and play
Wexham Street, Wexham, Slough, SL3 6ND
☎ (01753) 663271
🖷 (01753) 663318
✉ info@wexhamparkgolfcourse.co.uk
🛏 900
🏌 J Dunne
✓ J Kennedy (01753) 663425
⊳ 18 L 5251 yds SSS 66
   Green 9 L 2219 yds SSS 32
   Red 9 L 2727 yds SSS 34
👥 U SOC–WD/Sat pm
££ 9: £9 (£12) 18: £15 (£21)
⊶ 2 miles N of Slough. M4 Junction 4
⊕ Driving range (18 covered, 18
   open); practice area; putting green
⌂ David Morgan
▤ www.wexhamparkgolfcourse.co.uk

Whiteleaf (1907)
Whiteleaf, Princes Risborough, HP27 0LY
☎ (01844) 343097/274058
🖷 (01844) 275551
✉ whiteleafgc@tiscali.co.uk
🛏 300
🏌 D Hill (01844) 274058
   KS Ward (01844) 345472
⊳ 9 L 5391 yds SSS 66
👥 WD–U WE–M SOC
££ £17.50
⊶ Princes Risborough 2 miles
▤ www.whiteleafgolfclub.co.uk

Windmill Hill (1972)
Pay and play
Tattenhoe Lane, Bletchley, MK3 7RB
☎ (01908) 631113 (Bookings)
🖷 (01908) 630034
🛏 130
🏌 Diana Allen (01908) 647615
✓ C Clingan (01908) 378623
⊳ 18 L 6720 yds Par 73 SSS 72
👥 U SOC after 11am
££ £12.50 (£18)
⊶ W of Milton Keynes on A421. M1
   Junctions 13 & 14
⊕ Driving range
⌂ Sir Henry Cotton

Woburn (1976)
Little Brickhill, Milton Keynes, MK17 9LJ
☎ (01908) 370756
🖷 (01908) 378436
✉ enquiries@woburngolf.com

🛏 1400
🏌 E Bullock (Man Dir)
   Glenna Beasley (Sec)
✓ L Blacklock (01908) 626600
⊳ Duke's 18 L 6976 yds SSS 74
   Duchess 18 L 6651 yds SSS 72
   Marquess 18 L 7214 yds SSS 74
👥 WD–H (by arrangement) WE–M
££ By arrangement
⊶ ½ mile E of A5. 4 miles W of M1
   Junction 13
⌂ Charles Lawrie (Duke's/Duchess),
   Peter Alliss and Clive Clark,
   European Golf Design (Ross
   McMurray), Alex Hay (Marquess)
▤ www.discoverwoburn.co.uk

Wycombe Heights (1991)
Public
Rayners Avenue, Loudwater, High Wycombe, HP10 9SZ
☎ (01494) 816686
🖷 (01494) 816728
✉ info@wycombeheightsgc.co.uk
🛏 625
🏌 Rob Barker (Gen Mgr)
✓ Joe McKie (Head Pro)
⊳ 18 L 6300 yds Par 70 SSS 72
   18 hole Par 3 course
👥 U SOC
££ £17 (£25)
⊶ ½ mile from M40 Junction 3, on
   A40 to Wycombe
⊕ 24-bay driving range, heated; short
   game area; putting green
⌂ John Jacobs
▤ www.wycombeheightsgc.co.uk

Cambridgeshire

Abbotsley (1986)
Proprietary
Eynesbury Hardwicke, St Neots, PE19 6XN
☎ (01480) 474000
🖷 (01480) 403280
✉ abbotsley@crown-golf.co.uk
🛏 500
🏌 Nicky Briggs (01480) 474000
✓ S Connolly
⊳ 18 L 6311 yds SSS 72
👥 WD/BH–U WE–M before 1pm –U
   after 1pm SOC
££ £25 (£41.50)
⊶ 2 miles SE of St Neots on B1046.
   M11 Junction 13 (A428)
⌂ Vivien Saunders

Bourn (1991)
Proprietary
Toft Road, Bourn, Cambridge, CB3 7TT
☎ (01954) 718057
🖷 (01954) 718908
🛏 600
✓ C Watson (01954) 718958
⊳ 18 L 6528 yds SSS 71
👥 WD–U WE–U after 1pm
   SOC–WD
££ On application
⊶ 8 miles W of Cambridge, off
   B1046. M11 Junction 12
⊕ Par 3 course; driving range

Brampton Park (1991)

Buckden Road, Brampton, Huntingdon, PE28 4NF
- ☎ **(01480) 434700**
- 📠 (01480) 411145
- ✉ admin@bramptonparkgc.co.uk
- 📖 720
- ✍ RK Oakes (Gen Mgr)
- ⚲ A Currie (01480) 434705
- ⛳ 18 L 6300 yds SSS 71
- 👥 U SOC
- ££ £28 (D–£35)
- ⊕ 3 miles W of Huntingdon, off A1/A604
- ⊕ Driving range; buggies
- ⌂ Simon Gidman
- 🖥 www.bramptonparkgc.co.uk

Cambridge

Station Road, Longstanton, Cambridge, CB4 5DS
- ☎ **(01954) 789388**
- 📖 300
- ✍ K Green
- ⚲ G Huggett, Julie Knight
- ⛳ 18 L 6736 yds Par 72 SSS 74
- 👥 U SOC
- ££ 9: £10 (£12) 18: £14 (£18)
- ⊕ 5 miles NW of Cambridge, off A14 (B1050)
- ⊕ Floodlit driving range

Cambridge National (1944)

Proprietary
Comberton Road, Toft, Cambridge, CB3 7RY
- ☎ **(01223) 264700**
- 📠 (01223) 264701
- ✉ meridian@golfsocieties.com
- 📖 500
- ✍ Dale Brightman, Vivien Saunders
- ⛳ 18 L 6732 yds Par 73 SSS 72
- 👥 U SOC
- ££ £25 (£30)
- ⊕ 3 miles SW of Cambridge on B1046. M11 Junction 12
- ⌂ Alliss/Clark
- 🖥 www.golfsocieties.com

Cromwell (1986)

Proprietary
Eynesbury Hardwicke, St Neots, PE19 6XN
- ☎ **(01480) 215153**
- 📠 (01480) 406463
- ✉ abbotsley@crown-golf.co.uk
- 📖 300
- ✍ Nicky Briggs (01480) 474000
- ⚲ S Connolly
- ⛳ 18 L 6087 yds SSS 69
- 9 hole Par 3 course
- 👥 U SOC
- ££ £16 (£22)
- ⊕ 2 miles SE of St Neots on B1046. M11 Junction 13 (A428)
- ⊕ Floodlit driving range; 9 hole par 3
- ⌂ Vivien Saunders

Elton Furze (1993)

Proprietary
Bullock Road, Haddon, Peterborough, PE7 3TT
- ☎ **(01832) 280118 (bar)**
- 📠 (01832) 280299
- ✉ helen@efgc.co.uk
- 📖 540
- ✍ Helen Barron (01832) 280189
- ⚲ G Krause (01832) 280614
- ⛳ 18 L 6279 yds Par 70 SSS 71
- 👥 WD–phone in advance SOC
- ££ £33 (£37)
- ⊕ 4 miles W of Peterborough on old A605
- ⊕ Driving range
- ⌂ Roger Fitton
- 🖥 www.efgc.co.uk

Ely City (1961)

107 Cambridge Road, Ely, CB7 4HX
- ☎ **(01353) 662751**
- 📠 (01353) 668636
- ✉ elygolf@lineone.net
- 📖 775
- ✍ MS Hoare (Mgr) (01353) 662751
- ⚲ A George (01353) 663317
- ⛳ 18 L 6627 yds SSS 72
- 👥 WD–H WE–H SOC–Tues–Fri
- ££ £34 (£40)
- ⊕ 12 miles N of Cambridge
- ⌂ Henry Cotton
- 🖥 www.elygolf.co.uk

Girton (1936)

Dodford Lane, Girton, CB3 0QE
- ☎ **(01223) 276169**
- 📠 (01223) 277150
- ✉ secretary@girtongolfclub.co.uk
- 📖 800
- ✍ Miss VM Webb
- ⚲ S Thomson (01223) 276991
- ⛳ 18 L 6012 yds SSS 69
- 👥 WD–U WE/BH–M SOC–WD
- ££ £25
- ⊕ 3 miles N of Cambridge (A14)
- 🖥 www.club-noticeboard.co.uk /girton

The Gog Magog (1901)

Shelford Bottom, Cambridge, CB22 4AB
- ☎ **(01223) 247626**
- 📠 (01223) 414990
- ✉ secretary@gogmagog.co.uk
- 📖 1300
- ✍ Mrs C Davison
- ⚲ I Bamborough (01223) 246058
- ⛳ Old 18 L 6398 yds SSS 70
- Wandlebury 18 L 6735 yds SSS 72
- 👥 WD–I or H WE/BH–M SOC on application, not Wed/Sat/Sun
- ££ £40 D–£50 (£60) (fee reduction for winter)
- ⊕ 2 miles S of Cambridge on A1307 (A604)
- ⊕ Driving range
- ⌂ Hawtree
- 🖥 www.gogmagog.co.uk

Hemingford Abbots (1991)

Proprietary
New Farm Lodge, Cambridge Road, Hemingford Abbots, PE28 9HQ
- ☎ **(01480) 495000**

Heydon Grange G&CC (1994)

Heydon, Royston, SG8 7NS
- ☎ **(01763) 208988**
- 📠 (01763) 208926
- ✉ enquiries@heydongrange.co.uk
- 📖 200
- ✍ S Akhtar
- ⛳ 18 L 6512 yds SSS 72
- 9 L 3249 yds SSS 36
- 👥 U SOC
- ££ £17.50 (£23.00)
- ⊕ 4 miles E of Royston on A505. M11 Junction 10
- ⊕ Driving range
- ⌂ Cameron Sinclair
- 🖥 www.heydongrange.co.uk

Lakeside Lodge (1992)

Fen Road, Pidley, Huntingdon, PE28 3DF
- ☎ **(01487) 740540**
- 📠 (01487) 740852
- ✉ info@lakeside-lodge.co.uk
- 📖 1200
- ✍ Mrs J Hopkins
- ⚲ S Waterman (01487) 741541
- ⛳ 18 L 6865 yds SSS 73
- 9 L 2601 yds SSS 33
- 👥 U SOC
- ££ £16 (£25)
- ⊕ 4 miles N of St Ives on B1040
- ⊕ Driving range; 9 hole Manor course; 12 hole Church course; Par 3 course
- ⌂ A Headley
- 🖥 www.lakeside-lodge.co.uk

Malton (1993)

Pay and play
Malton Lane, Meldreth, Royston, SG8 6PE
- ☎ **(01763) 262200**
- 📠 (01763) 262209
- ✉ info@maltongolf.co.uk
- 📖 300
- ✍ P Bancroft
- ⚲ B Lyon
- ⛳ 18 L 6708 yds Par 72 SSS 72
- 👥 U SOC–exc WE
- ££ £10 (£16)
- ⊕ 8 miles SW of Cambridge, off A10. 5 miles SW of M11 Junction 11
- ⊕ Driving range
- ⌂ Bruce Critchley
- 🖥 www.maltongolf.co.uk

March (1922)

Frogs Abbey, Grange Rd, March, PE15 0YH
- ☎ **(01354) 652364**
- 📠 (01354) 658142
- ✉ secretary@marchgolfclub.co.uk
- 📖 360
- ✍ M Simpson
- ⚲ A Oldham (01354) 657255
- ⛳ 9 L 6204 yds SSS 70

♟ H SOC–WD
££ £21 (£25)
⊷ 18 miles E of Peterborough on A141
▤ www.marchgolfclub.co.uk

Menzies Cambridgeshire (1974)
Proprietary
Bar Hill, Cambridge, CB3 8EU
☎ (01954) 780098
⌨ (01954) 780010
✉ cambridge@menzies-hotels.co.uk
▯ 500
✍ Tom Turner (Golf Ops Mgr)
✓ Michael Clemons
⌁ 18 L 6775 yds Par 71 SSS 72
♟ U SOC–WD
££ £25 (£35)
⊷ 5 miles NW of Cambridge on A14
▤ www.cambridgeshiregolf.co.uk

Old Nene G&CC (1992)
Muchwood Lane, Bodsey, Ramsey, PE26 2XQ
☎ (01487) 815622
    (01487) 813610 (Golf Shop)
⌨ (01487) 813519
✉ george.stoneman@virgin.net
▯ 200
✍ GHD Stoneman
✓ GHD Stoneman
⌁ 9 L 5605 yds SSS 68
♟ U SOC
££ 9: £9 (£14) 18: £12 (£18)
⊷ 1 mile N of Ramsey, towards Ramsey Mereside; 10 miles A1(M)
⊕ Floodlit driving range

Orton Meadows (1987)
Public
Ham Lane, Peterborough, PE2 5UU
☎ (01733) 237478

Peterborough Milton (1937)
Milton Ferry, Peterborough, PE6 7AG
☎ (01733) 380489
⌨ (01733) 380380
✉ miltongolfclub@aol.com
▯ 730
✍ AB Izod (01733) 380489
✓ Jasen Barker (01733) 380793
⌁ 18 L 6505 yds SSS 72
♟ U SOC H WD
££ £31 D–£41 (£40 D–£50)
⊷ 4 miles W of Peterborough on A47
⊕ Practice ground
⌂ James Braid
▤ www.club-noticeboard.co.uk

Ramsey (1964)
4 Abbey Terrace, Ramsey, Huntingdon, PE26 1DD
☎ (01487) 812600
⌨ (01487) 815746
✉ admin@ramseyclub.co.uk
▯ 750
✍ Mr Kjenstad
✓ S Scott (01487) 813022

⌁ 18 L 6163 yds Par 71 SSS 70
♟ WD–H WE/BH–M SOC
££ £25
⊷ 12 miles SE of Peterborough
⌂ J Hamilton Stutt
▤ www.ramseyclub.co.uk

St Ives (1923)
Westwood Road, St Ives, PE27 6DH
☎ (01480) 468392 (Mgr)
⌨ (01480) 468392
✉ stivesgolfclub@zoom.co.uk
▯ 450
✍ BE Dunn (01480) 468392
✓ M Pond (01480) 466067
⌁ 9 L 6180 yds SSS 70
♟ WD–U H WE–M WD–SOC
££ D–£26
⊷ 5 miles E of Huntingdon
⊕ Practice ground

St Neots (1890)
Crosshall Road, St Neots, PE19 7GE
☎ (01480) 472363
⌨ (01480) 472363
✉ office@stneots-golfclub.co.uk
▯ 600
✓ P Toyer (01480) 476513
⌁ 18 L 6074 yds SSS 69
♟ WD–H WE–M
££ On application
⊷ By A1/B1048 junction
⌂ Harry Vardon

Stilton Oaks (1997)
Proprietary
High Street, Stilton, Peterborough, PE7 3RA
☎ (01733) 245233
▯ 200
✍ Mrs M Smith
✓ None
⌁ 18 hole course Par 71 SSS 67
♟ U SOC
££ £13 (£15)
⊷ 5 miles S of Peterborough. A1(M) Junction 16

Thorney Golf Centre (1991)
Public
English Drove, Thorney, Peterborough, PE6 0TJ
☎ (01733) 270570
⌨ (01733) 270842
▯ 400
✍ Jane Hind
✓ M Templeman
⌁ Fen 18 L 6104 yds SSS 69
    Lakes 18 L 6402 yds SSS 71
    9 hole Par 3 course
♟ Lakes WD–U SOC WE–M
££ Fen £9.25 (£11.25) Lakes £16 (£24)
⊷ 8 miles E of Peterborough, off A47
⊕ Floodlit driving range
⌂ A Dow
▤ www.thorneygolfcentre.com

Thorpe Wood (1975)
Pay and play
Nene Parkway, Peterborough, PE3 6SE
☎ (01733) 267701
⌨ (01733) 332774

✉ enquiries@thorpewoodgolfcourse .co.uk
✍ R Palmer
✓ R Fitton
⌁ 18 L 7086 yds SSS 74
♟ U–booking required SOC–WD
££ £13.80 (£18.50)
⊷ 3 miles W of Peterborough on A47 (Junction 15)
⌂ Alliss/Thomas
▤ www.thorpewoodgolfcourse.co.uk

Waterbeach (1968)
Waterbeach Barracks, Waterbeach, Cambridge, CB5 9PA
☎ (01223) 575260 (Sec)

Channel Islands

Alderney
Route des Carrieres, Alderney, GY9 3YD
☎ (01481) 822835

La Grande Mare (1994)
Proprietary
Vazon Bay, Castel, Guernsey, GY5 7LL
☎ (01481) 253544
⌨ (01481) 255194
✉ golf@lagrandemare.com
▯ 800
✍ N Graham (01481) 253544
✓ M Groves (01481) 253432
⌁ 18 L 4755 yds SSS 64
♟ U–booking necessary SOC
££ D–£33 (£37)
⊷ Vazon Bay, W coast of Guernsey
⊕ Driving range
⌂ Hawtree
▤ www.LGM.Guernsey.net

Les Mielles G&CC (1994)
St Ouens Bay, Jersey, JE3 7FQ
☎ (01534) 482787
⌨ (01534) 485414
✉ enquiries@lesmielles.co.je
▯ 1500
✍ J Le Brun (Golf Dir) (01534) 482787
✓ Ms L Cummins (01534) 483699
    W Osmand (01534) 483252
⌁ 18 L 5770 yds Par 70 SSS 68
♟ U
££ £26.50 (£30)
⊷ Five Mile Road, St Ouens Bay
⊕ Driving range; Breakers Miniature Golf
⌂ Le Brun/Whitehead
▤ www.lesmielles.com

La Moye (1902)
La Moye, St Brelade, Jersey, JE3 8GQ
☎ (01534) 743401
    (01534) 747166 (Bookings)
⌨ (01534) 747289
✉ secretary@lamoyegolfclub.co.uk
▯ 1350
✍ IN Prentice
✓ M Deeley (01534) 743130
⌁ 18 L 6664 yds SSS 73

🕎 U H SOC–9.30–11am and
   2.30–4pm WE–after 2.30pm
££ £55 D–£80 (£60)
🚗 2 miles from Jersey Airport
⊕ Driving range
🏌 James Braid
▤ www.lamoyegolfclub.co.uk

Les Ormes   (1996)
Pay and play
Mont à la Brune, St Brelade, Jersey, JE3 8FL
☎ **(01534) 497000**
🖳 (01534) 499122
🕮 1200
✍ M Graham (01534) 497002
✓ A Chamberlain (01534) 497000
🏳 9 L 5018 yds Par 66 SSS 65
🕎 U SOC
££ 9: Various 18: Various
🚗 Mont à la Brune, nr Airport
⊕ Driving range

Royal Guernsey   (1890)
L'Ancresse, Guernsey, GY3 5BY
☎ **(01481) 247022**
🖳 (01481) 243960
🖂 bob.rggc@cwgsy.net
🕮 1520
✍ R Bushby (01481) 246523
   R Eggo (Golf Mgr)
✓ N Wood (01481) 245070
🏳 18 L 6215 yds SSS 70
🕎 WD–H WE–M
££ £45
🚗 3 miles N of St Peter Port
⊕ Driving range
▤ www.royalguernseygolfclub.com

Royal Jersey   (1878)
Grouville, Jersey, JE3 9BD
☎ **(01534) 854416**
🖳 (01534) 854684
🖂 thesecretary@royaljersey.com
🕮 1300
✍ DJ Attwood
✓ D Morgan (01534) 852234
🏳 18 L 6116 yds SSS 70
🕎 WD 10–12 & 2–4 (H), WE/BH
   after 2.30pm
££ £50 (£50)
🚗 4 miles E of St Helier
▤ www.royaljersey.com

St Clements   (1925)
Public
St Clements, Jersey, JE2 6QN
☎ **(01534) 721938**

St Pierre Park
Rohais, St Peter Port, Guernsey, GY1 1FD
☎ **(01481) 727039**

Cheshire

Alder Root   (1993)
*Alder Root Lane, Winwick, Warrington,
WA2 8RZ*
☎ **(01925) 291919**
🖳 (01925) 291961

🖂 admin@alderroot.wanadoo.co.uk
🕮 450
✍ E Lander
✓ C McKevitt (01925) 291932
🏳 10 L 5820 yds Par 69 SSS 68
   WD–U SOC
££ £15 (£20)
🚗 4 miles N of Warrington (A49). M6
   Junction 22. M62 Junction 9
🏠 Millington/Lander
▤ www.alderroot.com

Alderley Edge   (1907)
Brook Lane, Alderley Edge, SK9 7RU
☎ **(01625) 586200**
🕮 225 65(L) 60(J)
✍ RC Harrison (01625) 583073
✓ P Bowring (01625) 584493
🏳 9 L 5823 yds SSS 68
🕎 SOC U H
££ £30 (£35); 2 for 1 scheme
🚗 12 miles S of Manchester
▤ www.aegc.co.uk

Aldersey Green   (1993)
Proprietary
Aldersey, Chester, CH3 9EH
☎ **(01829) 782157**
🖂 bradburygolf@aol.com
🕮 300
✍ S Bradbury
✓ S Bradbury (01829) 782157
🏳 18 L 6150 yds Par 70
🕎 U SOC
££ £15 (£20)
🚗 8 miles S of Chester, off A41
▤ alderseygreengolfclub.co.uk

Altrincham Municipal
   (1893)
Public
*Stockport Road, Timperley, Altrincham,
WA15 7LP*
☎ **(0161) 928 0761**
🕮 180
✍ BJ Cooper (0161) 905 2914
✓ S Partington
🏳 18 L 6385 yds Par 71 SSS 70
🕎 U SOC
££ £11 (£14)
🚗 1 mile W of Altrincham (A560)
⊕ Driving range
▤ www.altrinchamgolfclub.org

Alvaston Hall   (1992)
Proprietary
Middlewich Road, Nantwich, CW5 6PD
☎ **(01270) 628473**
🖳 (01270) 623395
🕮 120
✍ K Valentine (01270) 628473
✓ K Valentine
🏳 9 L 3708 yds Par 64 SSS 59
🕎 U
££ £10 (£10)
🚗 11 miles W of M6 Junction 16 on
   A530
⊕ Driving range
🏠 K Valentine

Antrobus   (1993)
Proprietary
Foggs Lane, Antrobus, Northwich, CW9 6JQ
☎ **(01925) 730890**
🖳 (01925) 730100
🕮 550
✍ Miss C Axford
✓ P Farrance (01925) 730900
🏳 18 L 6220 yds Par 71 SSS 72
🕎 H SOC
££ £25 (£28)
🚗 Nr M56 Junction 10, on A559 to
   Northwich
⊕ Driving range
🏠 Michael Slater
▤ www.antrobusgolfclub.co.uk

Ashton-on-Mersey   (1897)
Church Lane, Sale, M33 5QQ
☎ **(0161) 976 4390 (Clubhouse)**
🖳 (0161) 976 4390
🖂 golf@aomgc.fsnet.co.uk
🕮 190 65(L) 40(J)
✍ R Tomlinson (0161) 976 4390
✓ Kris Andrews (0161) 976 4390
🏳 9 L 3073 yds SSS 69
🕎 WD–U H exc Tues–NA before
   3pm WE–M
££ £25.50
🚗 5 miles W of Manchester. M60
   Junction 7, 1½ miles
▤ www.aomgc.co.uk

Astbury   (1922)
Peel Lane, Astbury, Congleton, CW12 4RE
☎ **(01260) 272772**
🕮 700
✍ FM Reed (01260) 272772
✓ N Dawson (01260) 272772
🏳 18 L 6296 yds SSS 70
🕎 WD–H or M WE–M SOC–Thurs
   only
££ £30 SOC–£27.50
🚗 1 mile S of Congleton, off A34
▤ www.astburygolfclub.com

Birchwood   (1979)
*Kelvin Close, Birchwood, Warrington,
WA3 7PB*
☎ **(01925) 818819**
🖳 (01925) 822403
🖂 birchwoodgolfclub.com@lineone
   .net
🕮 745
✍ M Cullen
✓ P McEwan (01925) 825216
🏳 18 L 6727 yds Par 71 SSS 72
🕎 U SOC–Mon/Wed/Thurs
££ £24 D–£29 (£39)
🚗 M62 Junction 11, 2 miles. Signs to
   'Science Park North'
🏠 TJA Macauley
▤ www.birchwoodgolfclub.org

Bramall Park   (1894)
*20 Manor Road, Bramhall, Stockport,
SK7 3LY*
☎ **(0161) 485 3119
   (Clubhouse)**
🖳 (0161) 485 7101
🖂 secretary@bramallparkgolfclub
   .co.uk

📖 400 160(L) 75(J)
🖊 CJ Shallcross (Hon) (0161) 485 7101
⛳ M Proffitt (0161) 485 2205
📋 18 L 6247 yds SSS 70
👥 SOC–WD (enquire of Sec)
££ £34 D–£38 (£40 D–£45)
🚗 8 miles S of Manchester (A5102)
🖥 www.bramallparkgolfclub.co.uk

Bramhall (1905)

Ladythorn Road, Bramhall, Stockport, SK7 2EY
☎ **(0161) 439 6092**
📠 (0161) 439 0264
📧 office@bramhallgolfclub.com
📖 700
🖊 B Hill (Hon) (0161) 439 6092
⛳ R Green (0161) 439 1171
📋 18 L 6340 yds SSS 70
👥 U H exc Thurs SOC–Wed, Fri
££ £40 (£55)
🚗 S of Stockport, off A5102
🖥 www.bramhallgolfclub.com

Carden Park

Chester, CH3 9DQ
☎ **(01829) 731600**
📠 (01829) 731629
📧 golf.carden@devere-hotels.com
📖 270
🖊 A Taylor (01829) 731000
⛳ P Hodgson (01829) 731500
📋 Cheshire 18 L 6824 yds SSS 72
   Nicklaus 18 L 7096 yds Par 72
   Azalea 9 hole Par 3 course
👥 SOC
££ Cheshire–£40 Nicklaus–£45
🚗 10 miles S of Chester on A534
⊕ Golf Academy. Driving range
🖥 www.devere.co.uk

Cheadle (1885)

Shiers Drive, Cheadle Road, Cheadle, SK8 1HW
☎ **(0161) 491 4452**
📧 cheadlegolfclub@msn.com
📖 350
🖊 CT Openshaw
⛳ D Cain (0161) 428 9878
📋 9 L 4993 yds SSS 65
👥 H or I exc Tues & Sat–NA SOC
££ £23 (£28)
🚗 1 mile S of Cheadle. M60 Jct 2
🏠 Mr Renouf
🖥 www.cheadlegolfclub.com

Chester (1901)

Curzon Park, Chester, CH4 8AR
☎ **(01244) 675130**
📠 (01244) 676667
📧 www@chestergolfclub.co.uk
📖 840
🖊 DR Kevan (01244) 677760
⛳ Scott Booth (01244) 671185
📋 18 L 6461 yds SSS 71
👥 U H SOC
££ £30 (£35)
🚗 Chester 1 mile
🖥 www.chestergolfclub.co.uk

Congleton (1898)

Biddulph Road, Congleton, CW12 3LZ
☎ **(01260) 273540**
📠 (01260) 290902
📧 congletongolfclub@hotmail.com
📖 440
🖊 D Lancake
⛳ A Preston
📋 12 L 5119 yds Par 68 SSS 65
👥 U H SOC
££ £24 (£34)
🚗 1½ miles E of Congleton on A527

Crewe (1911)

Fields Road, Haslington, Crewe, CW1 5TB
☎ **(01270) 584227 (Steward)**
📠 (01270) 256482
📧 secretary@crewegolfclub.co.uk
📖 628
🖊 J Stubbs (01270) 584099
⛳ D Wheeler (01270) 585032
📋 18 L 6404 yds SSS 71
👥 WD–U WE/BH–M SOC
££ £36 After 1pm–£28
🚗 Haslington, 2 miles NE of Crewe Station, off A534. 5 miles W of M6
🖥 www.crewegolfclub.co.uk

Davenport (1913)

Worth Hall, Middlewood Road, Poynton, SK12 1TS
☎ **(01625) 876951**
📠 (01625) 877489
📧 chris@davenportgolf.co.uk
📖 650
🖊 JC Souter (01625) 876951
⛳ T Stevens (01625) 877319
📋 18 L 6034 yds SSS 69
👥 U exc Wed & Sat–NA SOC–Tues & Thurs
££ £30 (£40)
🚗 5 miles S of Stockport. 7 miles N of Macclesfield
⊕ Practice ground and indoor custom fit and training facilities
🖥 www.davenportgolf.co.uk

Delamere Forest (1910)

Station Road, Delamere, Northwich, CW8 2JE
☎ **(01606) 883264**
📠 (01606) 889444
📧 delamere@btconnect.com
   info@delameregolf.com
📖 400
🖊 JJ Mulder (01606) 883800
⛳ EB Jones (01606) 883307
📋 18 L 6348 yds Par 72 SSS 71
👥 WD–U WE–SOC
££ £40 D–£60 (£55 D–£100)
🚗 10 miles E of Chester, off B5152
⊕ 9-bay warm-up area; practice bunker; nets
🏠 Herbert Fowler
🖥 www.delameregolf.co.uk

Disley (1889)

Stanley Hall Lane, Disley, Stockport, SK12 2JX
☎ **(01663) 764001**
📠 (01663) 762678
📧 secretary@disleygolfclub.co.uk

📖 500
🖊 P Smallwood
⛳ AG Esplin (01663) 764001
📋 18 L 5942 yds Par 70
👥 WD–U exc Thurs WE/BH–M
££ £30 (£40)
🚗 6 miles S of Stockport on A6
🏠 James Braid
🖥 www.disleygolfclub.co.uk

Dukinfield (1913)

Yew Tree Lane, Dukinfield, SK16 5DB
☎ **(0161) 338 2340**
📧 dgc@telinco.co.uk

Dunham Forest G&CC (1961)

Oldfield Lane, Altrincham, WA14 4TY
☎ **(0161) 928 2605**
📠 (0161) 929 8975
📧 email@dunhamforestgolfclub.com
📖 600
🖊 Mrs A Woolf
⛳ I Wrigley (0161) 928 2727
📋 18 L 6636 yds SSS 72
👥 WD–U WE/BH–M SOC exc 12–1pm
££ £46 (£60)
🚗 1 mile SW of Altrincham. M56 Junction 7
⊕ Driving range, indoor facility
🏠 John Bealey/Dave Thomas
🖥 www.dunhamforest.com

Eaton (1965)

Guy Lane, Waverton, Chester, CH3 7PH
☎ **(01244) 335885**
📠 (01244) 335782
📧 office@eatongolfclub.co.uk
📖 550
🖊 K Brown
⛳ W Tye (01244) 335826
📋 18 L 6580 yds SSS 72
👥 H SOC
££ On application
🚗 3 miles SE of Chester, off A41
⊕ Driving range; chipping area
🏠 Donald Steel
🖥 www.eatongolfclub.co.uk

Ellesmere Port (1971)

Public
Chester Road, Childer Thornton, South Wirral, CH66 1QF
☎ **(0151) 339 7689**
📖 350
🖊 C Craggs
⛳ Danny Youd
📋 18 L 6432 yds SSS 71
👥 WD–U WE–arrange with Pro SOC–WD
££ £9 (£10.50)
🚗 9 miles N of Chester on A41. M53 Junction 5

Frodsham (1990)

Simons Lane, Frodsham, WA6 6HE
☎ **(01928) 732159**
📧 office@frodshamgolf.co.uk

Gatley   (1911)
Waterfall Farm, Styal Road, Heald Green, Cheadle, SK8 3TW
☎ **(0161) 437 2091**

Hale   (1903)
Rappax Road, Hale, WA15 0NU
☎ **(0161) 980 4225**

Hazel Grove   (1913)
Buxton Road, Hazel Grove, Stockport, SK7 6LU
☎ **(0161) 483 3217 (Clubhouse)**
⌨ 550
🖎 DJ Billington (0161) 483 3978
✓ J Hopley (0161) 483 7272
↦ 18 L 6263 yds SSS 70
👥 U SOC–Mon, Thurs & Fri
££ £25.50 D–£30.50 (£30.50 D–£35.50)
🏌 3 miles S of Stockport (A6)

Heaton Moor   (1892)
Mauldeth Road, Heaton Mersey, Stockport, SK4 3NX
☎ **(0161) 432 2134**
🖳 (0161) 432 2134
🖎 heatonmoorgolfclub@yahoo.co.uk
⌨ 550
🖎 G Gell
✓ SJ Marsh (0161) 432 0846
↦ 18 L 5968 yds Par 70 SSS 69
👥 U SOC WD WE
££ £26 (£34)
🏌 2 miles from M60 J1, Stockport Town Centre
⊕ Practice nets; practice ground; putting green
▤ www.heatonmoorgolfclub.co.uk

Helsby   (1901)
Tower's Lane, Helsby, WA6 0JB
☎ **(01928) 722021**
🖳 (01928) 725384
🖎 secathgc@aol.com
⌨ 640
🖎 LJ Norbury
✓ M Jones (01928) 725457
↦ 18 L 6265 yds SSS 70
👥 H WE–NA SOC–Tues & Thurs
££ £27.50 (£37)
🏌 1 mile SE of M56 Junction 14, off Primrose Lane
⊕ Driving range
🏌 James Braid
▤ www.helsbygolfclub.org

Heyrose   (1989)
Proprietary
Budworth Road, Tabley, Knutsford, WA16 0HZ
☎ **(01565) 733664**
🖳 (01565) 734578
🖎 info@heyrosegolfclub.com
⌨ 600
🖎 Mrs H Marsh
✓ P Bills (01565) 734267
↦ 18 L 6499 yds SSS 71
👥 U SOC
££ £26 (£31)

🏌 3 miles W of Knutsford, off Pickmere Lane, Tabley. M6 Junction 19, 1 mile
⊕ Driving range; practice bunker; practice net; pitching practice area
🏌 CN Bridge, B.Sc Hons
▤ www.heyrosegolfclub.com

Houldsworth   (1910)
Houldsworth Park, Houldsworth Street, Reddish, Stockport, SK5 6BN
☎ **(0161) 442 1712**
🖳 (0161) 947 9678
🖎 secretary@houldsworthgolfclub.co.uk
⌨ 625
🖎 K Smith (0161) 442 1712
✓ S McLean (0161) 442 1714
↦ 18 L 6209 yds Par 70 SSS 70
👥 U SOC
££ £30 (£36)
🏌 4 miles S of Manchester, M60 Jct26
🏌 Redesigned 1992 by Dave Thomas
▤ www.houldsworthgolfclub.co.uk

Knights Grange   (1983)
Public
Grange Lane, Winsford, CW7 2PT
☎ **(01606) 552780**
🖎 p.littler@valeroyal.gov.uk
🖎 Mrs P Littler (Mgr)
↦ 18 L 6253 yds SSS 70
👥 U SOC
££ £9.80 (£12) Juniors playing with adult half price
🏌 Knights Grange Sports Complex. M6 Junctions 18 & 19

Knutsford   (1891)
Mereheath Lane, Knutsford, WA16 6HS
☎ **(01565) 633355**
⌨ 250
🖎 DM Burgess
↦ 9 L 6203 yds SSS 70
👥 H exc Wed–NA SOC
££ £28 (£35)
🏌 Knutsford ½ mile

Leigh   (1906)
Kenyon Hall, Broseley Lane, Culcheth, Warrington, WA3 4BG
☎ **(01925) 763130**
🖳 (01925) 765097
🖎 golf@leighgolf.fsnet.co.uk
⌨ 850
🖎 DA Taylor (01925) 762943
✓ A Baguley (01925) 762013
↦ 18 L 5892 yds SSS 69
👥 U H SOC
££ £32 (£40)
🏌 5 miles NE of Warrington
🏌 James Braid
▤ www.leighgolf.co.uk

Lymm   (1907)
Whitbarrow Road, Lymm, WA13 9AN
☎ **(01925) 755020**
🖳 (01925) 755020
🖎 lymmgolfclub@btconnect.com
⌨ 400 100(L) 75(J) 50(S)
🖎 TH Glover

✓ S McCarthy (01925) 755054
↦ 18 L 6341 yds SSS 70
👥 WD–H WE–M SOC–Wed
££ £32 (£36)
🏌 5 miles SE of Warrington. M6 Junction 20
▤ www.lymm-golf-club.co.uk

Macclesfield   (1889)
The Hollins, Macclesfield, SK11 7EA
☎ **(01625) 423227**
🖳 (01625) 260061
🖎 secretary@maccgolfclub.co.uk
⌨ 600
🖎 DJ English
✓ T Taylor
↦ 18 L 5714 yds SSS 68
👥 WD/BH–H WE–M SOC–WD
££ £30 (£40)
🏌 SE edge of Macclesfield, off A523
🏌 Hawtree
▤ www.maccgolfclub.co.uk

Malkins Bank Golf Course   (1980)
Public
Betchton Road, Malkins Bank, Sandbach, CW11 4XN
☎ **(01270) 765931**
🖳 (01270) 764730
🖎 phil.pleasance@congleton.gov.uk
🖎 P Pleasance (Mgr) (01270) 760233
✓ D Hackney
↦ 18 L 6005 yds SSS 69
👥 U SOC
££ £11 (£13)
🏌 2 miles S of Sandbach via A534/A533. M6 Junction 17
⊕ Practice area; net; putting green
🏌 Hawtree & Son
▤ www.congleton.gov.uk

Marple   (1892)
Barnsfold Road, Hawk Green, Marple, Stockport, SK6 7EL
☎ **(0161) 427 2311**
🖳 (0161) 427 2311
🖎 marple.golfclub@virgin.net
⌨ 415 84(L) 90(J)
🖎 R Hough (0161) 427 2311
✓ D Myers (0161) 427 1195
↦ 18 L 5554 yds SSS 67
👥 WD–U exc Thurs–NA WE/BH–M SOC
££ £30 (£40)
🏌 2 miles from High Lane North, off A6
▤ www.marplegolfclub.co.uk

Mellor & Towncliffe   (1894)
Tarden, Gibb Lane, Mellor, Stockport, SK6 5NA
☎ **(0161) 427 9700 (Clubhouse)**
🖳 (0161) 427 9700
⌨ 600
🖎 G Lee (0161) 427 2208
✓ G Broadley (0161) 427 5759
↦ 18 L 5925 yds SSS 69
👥 WD–U WE–M SOC
££ £24 (£32)

For list of abbreviations and key to symbols see page 651

⚐ 7 miles SE of Stockport, off A626
🖪 www.mellorgolf.co.uk

Mere G&CC (1934)
Chester Road, Mere, Knutsford,
WA16 6LJ
☎ (01565) 830155
🖵 (01565) 830713
✉ enquiries@meregolf.co.uk
📖 375 140(L) 40(J)
🏌 J Leeman
✓ P Eyre (01565) 830219
▷ 18 L 6817 yds SSS 73
👥 WE/BH–M Wed & Fri–M
   Mon/Tues/Thurs–H SOC
££ D–£70
⚐ 1 mile E of M6 Junction 19. 2 miles
   W of M56 Junction 7
⊕ Driving range-members and green
   fees only
🏠 James Braid
🖪 www.meregolf.co.uk

Mersey Valley (1995)
Proprietary
Warrington Road, Bold Heath, Widnes,
WA8 3XL
☎ (0151) 424 6060
🖵 (0151) 257 9097
✉ chrismgerrard@yahoo.co.uk
📖 550
🏌 RM Bush (Man Dir) Alan Robinson
   (Sec)
✓ Advanced PGA Pro
▷ 18 L 6511 yds SSS 71
👥 U
££ £20 (£25)
⚐ M62 Junction 7, 2 miles
🏠 RMR Bush
🖪 www.merseyvalleygolfclub.co.uk

Mobberley
Burleyhurst Lane, Mobberley, Knutsford,
WA16 7JZ
☎ (01505) 880188
🖵 (01505) 880178
🏌 N Donaghy
✓ D Whitaker
▷ 9 L 5542 yds Par 67
👥 U SOC
££ £14.50 (£18)
⚐ Mobberley. M56 Junction 6

Mollington Grange
(1999)
Townfield Lane, Mollington, Chester,
CH1 6NJ
☎ (01244) 851185

Mottram Hall Hotel
(1991)
Wilmslow Road, Mottram St Andrew,
Prestbury, SK10 4QT
☎ (01625) 820064
🖵 (01625) 829284
📖 200
🏌 M Turnock
✓ M Turnock/A Buckley/T Maxwell
▷ 18 L 7006 yds SSS 74
👥 U H SOC
££ £60

⚐ 4 miles SE of Wilmslow
⊕ Driving range; short game area; 2
   putting greens
🏠 Dave Thomas

Peover (1996)
Proprietary
Plumley Moor Road, Lower Peover,
WA16 9SE
☎ (01565) 723337
🖵 (01565) 723311
✉ mail@peovergolfclub.co.uk
📖 350
🏌 PA Naylor (Man Dir)
   J Baker (Sec)
✓ Mike Grantham (07976) 894357
▷ 18 L 6702 yds Par 72
👥 U SOC–WD
££ £25 (£30)
⚐ 3 miles SW of Knutsford, off
   A556. M6 Junction 19
🏠 Peter Naylor
🖪 www.peovergolfclub.co.uk

Portal G&CC (1992)
Cobblers Cross Lane, Tarporley, CW6 0DJ
☎ (01829) 733933
✉ enquiries@portalgolf.co.uk

Portal Premier (1990)
Forest Road, Tarporley, CW6 0JA
☎ (01829) 733884
✉ enquiries.premier@portalgolf
   .co.uk

Poulton Park (1978)
Dig Lane, Cinnamon Brow, Warrington,
WA2 0SH
☎ (01925) 812034/822802
🖵 (01925) 822802
✉ secretary@poultonparkgolfclub
   .co.uk
📖 360
🏌 Jeff Perkin (01925) 822802
✓ Ian Orrell (01925) 825220
▷ 9 L 5048 m Par 68 SSS 67
👥 WD–NA 5–6pm WE–NA before
   2pm
££ £20 (£22)
⚐ Off Crab Lane, Fearnhead (M6 Jct
   21)
🖪 www.poultonparkgolfclub.co.uk

Prestbury (1920)
Macclesfield Road, Prestbury, Macclesfield,
SK10 4BJ
☎ (01625) 828241
🖵 (01625) 828241
✉ office@prestburygolfclub.com
📖 650
🏌 N Young (01625) 828241
✓ N Summerfield (01625) 828242
▷ 18 L 6371 yds SSS 71
👥 WD–I WE–M SOC–Thurs
££ £45
⚐ 2 miles NW of Macclesfield
⊕ Practice ground inc. driving range
🏠 HS Colt
🖪 www.prestburygolfclub.com

Pryors Hayes (1993)
Proprietary
Willington Road, Oscroft, Tarvin, CH3 8NL
☎ (01829) 741250
🖵 (01829) 749077
✉ info@pryors-hayes.co.uk
📖 600
🏌 JM Quinn
✓ M Redrup (01829) 740140
▷ 18 L 6054 yds Par 69 SSS 69
👥 U SOC
££ £30 (£40)
⚐ Tarvin, 5 miles E of Chester
🏠 John Day
🖪 www.pryors-hayes.co.uk

Queens Park (1985)
Public
Queens Park Drive, Crewe, CW2 7SB
☎ (01270) 662378

Reaseheath (1987)
Reaseheath College, Reaseheath, Nantwich,
CW5 6DF
☎ (01270) 625131
🖵 (01270) 625665
✉ chrisb@reaseheath.ac.uk
📖 600
🏌 CK Bishop (Hon)
▷ 9 L 3726 yds SSS 58
👥 M SOC–WD/WE
££ Winter: D–£8 Summer: D–£10
⚐ 2 miles NW of Nantwich on
   College campus
🏠 D Mortram
🖪 www.reaseheath.ac.uk/golf

Reddish Vale (1912)
Southcliffe Road, Reddish, Stockport,
SK5 7EE
☎ (0161) 480 2359
🖵 (0161) 480 2359
✉ admin@reddishvalegolfclub.co.uk
📖 550
🏌 RG Dean
✓ RE Freeman (0161) 480 2359
▷ 18 L 6086 yds SSS 69
👥 WD–U exc 12.30-1.30pm–M
   WE–M SOC–WD
££ £28 (£40)
⚐ 1 mile NNE of Stockport
🏠 Dr A MacKenzie
🖪 www.reddishvalegolfclub.co.uk

Ringway (1909)
Hale Mount, Hale Barns, Altrincham,
WA15 8SW
☎ (0161) 980 2630
🖵 (0161) 980 4414
✉ andrew@ringwaygolfclub.co.uk
📖 360 175(L) 60(J)
🏌 A Scully
✓ N Ryan (0161) 980 2630
▷ 18 L 6482 yds SSS 71
👥 Tues–NA before 3pm, Fri–M,
   Sun–NA before 11am, SOC–Thurs
££ £40 (£50)
⚐ 8 miles S of Manchester, off M56
   Junction 6 (A538)
🏠 Harry Colt/James Braid
🖪 www.ringwaygolfclub.co.uk

Romiley   (1897)

Goosehouse Green, Romiley, Stockport, SK6 4LJ
- ☎ **(0161) 430 2392**
- 🖥 (0161) 430 7258
- 📧 office@romileygolfclub.org
- 📖 625
- ♙ DH Mason
- ✎ (0161) 430 7122
- ▷ 18 L 6412 yds Par 70 SSS 71
- ♚ U SOC
- ££ £30 (£40)
- ⚬ Station 3/4 mile (B6104)
- 🖳 www.romileygolfclub.org

Runcorn   (1909)

Clifton Road, Runcorn, WA7 4SU
- ☎ **(01928) 572093 (Members)**
- 🖥 (01928) 574214
- 📧 secretary@runcorngolfclub.co.uk
- 📖 375 80(L) 60(J)
- ♙ BR Griffiths (01928) 574214
- ✎ K Hartley (01928) 564791
- ▷ 18 L 6035 yds SSS 69
- ♚ WD–U H exc comp days WE–M SOC–Mon & Fri only
- ££ £26
- ⚬ Runcorn (A557). M56 Junction 12

Sale   (1913)

Sale Lodge, Golf Road, Sale, M33 2XU
- ☎ **(0161) 973 1638**
- 🖥 (0161) 962 4217
- 📧 mail@salegolfclub.com
- 📖 750
- ♙ CJ Boyles (Hon Sec)
- ✎ M Stewart (0161) 973 1730
- ▷ 18 L 6301 yds Par 70 SSS 70
- ♚ U SOC–WD
- ££ £32 (£35)
- ⚬ N of Sale. M60 Junction 6
- 🖳 www.salegolfclub.com

Sandbach   (1895)

Middlewich Road, Sandbach, CW11 1FH
- ☎ **(01270) 762117**

Sandiway   (1921)

Chester Road, Sandiway, CW8 2DJ
- ☎ **(01606) 883247**
- 🖥 (01606) 888548
- 📧 info@sandiwaygolf.fsnet.co.uk
- 📖 730
- ♙ RH Owens
- ✎ W Laird (01606) 883180
- ▷ 18 L 6435 yds SSS 72
- ♚ H SOC
- ££ £45 (£55)
- ⚬ 15 miles E of Chester on A556
- ♜ Ted Ray
- 🖳 www.sandiwaygolf.co.uk

Stamford   (1901)

Oakfield House, Huddersfield Road, Stalybridge, SK15 3PY
- ☎ **(01457) 832126**
- 🖥 (01457) 836550
- 📧 stamford.golfclub@totalise.co.uk
- 📖 600
- ♙ BD Matthews
- ✎ B Badger (01457) 834829

- ▷ 18 L 5701 yds SSS 68
- ♚ WD–U WE comp days–after 2.30pm SOC–WD
- ££ £20 (£25)
- ⚬ NE boundary of Stalybridge on B6175

Stockport   (1905)

Offerton Road, Offerton, Stockport, SK2 5HL
- ☎ **(0161) 427 8369**
- 🖥 (0161) 427 8369
- 📧 info@stockportgolf.co.uk
- 📖 510
- ♙ DRG Mitchell
- ✎ M Peel
- ▷ 18 L 6326 yds SSS 71
- ♚ SOC–WD
- ££ £40 (£50)
- ⚬ 4 miles SE of Stockport on A627
- ♜ Herd/Hawtree
- 🖳 www.stockportgolf.co.uk

Styal   (1994)

Proprietary
Station Road, Styal, SK9 4JN
- ☎ **(01625) 531359 (Bookings)**
- 🖥 (01625) 416373
- 📧 gtraynor@styalgolf.co.uk
- 📖 850
- ♙ G Traynor (01625) 530063 ext 214
- ✎ S Forrest (01625) 528910
- ▷ 18 L 6194 yds Par 70 SSS 70
  9 9 L 1203 yds Par 27
- ♚ U SOC
- ££ 18 hole course £22 (£27)
- ⚬ 2 miles from M56 Junction 5. Manchester Airport 5 mins
- ⊕ Floodlit driving range; tuition; buggies for hire
- ♜ T Holmes
- 🖳 www.styalgolf.co.uk

Sutton Hall

Aston Lane, Sutton Weaver, Runcorn, WA7 3ED
- ☎ **(01928) 790747**
- 🖥 (01928) 759174
- 📖 600 30(J)
- ♙ M Faulkner
- ✎ J Hope (01928) 714872
- ▷ 18 L 6608 yds Par 72
- ♚ U SOC–WD
- ££ £20 (£25)
- ⚬ 2 miles E of M56 Junction 12
- ♜ Steve Wunoke

The Tytherington Club   (1986)

Macclesfield, SK10 2JP
- ☎ **(01625) 506000**

Upton-by-Chester   (1934)

Upton Lane, Chester, CH2 1EE
- ☎ **(01244) 381183**
- 🖥 (01244) 376955
- 📧 secretary@uptongc.com
- 📖 750
- ♙ F Hopley (01244) 381183
- ✎ S Dewhurst (01244) 381183
- ▷ 18 L 5850 yds SSS 68

- ♚ U SOC–WD
- ££ £25 D–£35 (£25 D–£35)
- ⚬ Off Liverpool road, near 'Frog' PH

Vale Royal Abbey   (1998)

Whitegate, Northwich, CW8 2BA
- ☎ **(01606) 301291**
- 🖥 (01606) 301414
- 📧 golf@vra.co.uk
- 📖 400
- ♙ Alastair Griffiths
- ✎ D Ingman (01606) 301702
- ▷ 18 holes Par 72 SSS 71
- ⚬ 2 miles W of Hartford, off A556
- ♜ Simon Gidman
- 🖳 www.vra.co.uk

Vicars Cross   (1939)

Tarvin Road, Great Barrow, Chester, CH3 7HN
- ☎ **(01244) 335174**
- 🖥 (01244) 335686
- 📧 manager@vicarscrossgolf.co.uk
- 📖 800
- ♙ Mrs K Hunt
- ✎ JA Forsythe (01244) 335595
- ▷ 18 L 6446 yds SSS 71
- ♚ U SOC–Tue, Thur, Fri
- ££ £30 (£35)
- ⚬ 3 miles E of Chester on A51
- ⊕ Driving range
- ♜ E Parr
- 🖳 www.vicarscrossgolf.co.uk

Walton Hall   (1972)

Public
Warrington Road, Higher Walton, Warrington, WA4 5LU
- ☎ **(01925) 266775**
- 📧 theclub@waltonhallgolfclub.co.uk
- 📖 200
- ♙ Dave Johnson (01925) 266775
- ✎ J Jackson (01925) 263061
- ▷ 18 L 6647 yds Par 72 SSS 73
- ♚ U SOC
- ££ £13.50 (£17)
- ⚬ 2 miles S of Warrington. M56 J10/11
- ♜ Dave Thomas/Peter Alliss
- 🖳 www.waltonhallgolfclub.co.uk

Warrington   (1903)

Hill Warren, London Road, Appleton, WA4 5HR
- ☎ **(01925) 261775**
- 🖥 (01925) 265933
- 📧 secretary@warringtongolfclub.co.uk
- 📖 875
- ♙ S Dunlop (01925) 261775
- ✎ R Mackay (01925) 265431
- ▷ 18 L 6210 yds SSS 70
- ♚ U SOC–Wed
- ££ £30 (£35)
- ⚬ 3 miles S of Warrington on A49. M56 Junction 10
- ♜ James Braid/Creative Golf Design
- 🖳 www.warringtongolfclub.co.uk

Werneth Low   (1912)

Werneth Low Road, Gee Cross, Hyde, SK14 3AF
- ☎ **(0161) 368 2503**

Widnes (1924)
Highfield Road, Widnes, WA8 7DT
- ☎ **(0151) 424 2995**
- 📠 (0151) 495 2849
- ✉ office@widnesgolfclub.co.uk
- 📖 600
- ♙ Nicola Farrington
- ✎ J O'Brien (0151) 420 7467
- ⏰ 18 L 5729 yds SSS 68
- ♟ WD–H WE–H NA on comp days
- ££ D–£22 (£30)
- ⛳ Station ¹/₂ mile. M62 Junction 7

Wilmslow
Great Warford, Mobberley, Knutsford, WA16 7AY
- ☎ **(01565) 872148**
- 📠 (01565) 872172
- ✉ info@wilmslowgolfclub.co.uk
- 📖 855
- ♙ Mrs MI Padfield
- ✎ LJ Nowicki (01565) 873620
- ⏰ 18 L 6607 yds SSS 72
- ♟ U H exc Wed–NA before 3pm
- ££ £45 (£55)
- ⛳ 3 miles W of Alderley Edge
- 🖥 www.wilmslowgolfclub.co.uk

Woodside
Knutsford Road, Holmes Chapel, CW4 8HT
- ☎ **(01477) 532388**

Cornwall

Bowood Park (1992)
Valley Truckle, Lanteglos, Camelford, PL32 9RF
- ☎ **(01840) 213017**
- 📠 (01840) 212622
- ✉ info@bowoodpark.org
- 📖 300
- ♙ Tony Nash
- ✎ Tony Nash
- ⏰ 18 L 6692 yds SSS 72
- ♟ H (phone first) SOC WD WE
- ££ £30 (£33)
- ⛳ 2 miles SW of Camelford, off A39, on to B3266
- ⊕ Driving range; chipping green; 9 hole putting green
- 🏠 Bob Sandow
- 🖥 www.bowoodpark.org

Bude & North Cornwall
(1891)
Burn View, Bude, EX23 8DA
- ☎ **(01288) 352006**
- 📠 (01288) 356855
- ✉ secretary@budegolf.co.uk
- 📖 682 106(L) 38(J)
- ♙ Mrs PM Ralph
- ✎ J Yeo (01288) 353635
- ⏰ 18 L 6006 yds Par 71 SSS 70
- ♟ WD–U 9.30–12.30pm, 2–5pm and after 6.30pm WE–restricted
- ££ D–£27 (+BH £27)
- 🏠 Bude town centre
- 🏠 Tom Dunn
- 🖥 www.budegolf.co.uk

Budock Vean Hotel (1922)
Mawnan Smith, Falmouth, TR11 5LG
- ☎ **(01326) 252102**
- 📠 (01326) 250892
- ✉ relax@budockvean.co.uk
- 📖 150
- ♙ D McFarlane
- ✎ A Ramsden (Golf Mgr)
- ⏰ 9 L 5286 yds SSS 66
- ♟ H
- ££ D–£18 (D–£20)
- ⛳ Falmouth 5 miles
- 🏠 James Braid

Cape Cornwall G&CC
(1990)
St Just, Penzance, TR19 7NL
- ☎ **(01736) 788611**
- ✉ info@capecornwall.com

Carlyon Bay (1926)
Proprietary
Carlyon Bay, St Austell, PL25 3RD
- ☎ **(01726) 814250**
- 📠 (01726) 814250
- ✉ golf@carlyonbay.com
- 📖 500
- ♙ P Clemo
- ✎ M Rowe (01726) 814228
- ⏰ 18 L 6597 yds SSS 71
- ♟ U–book with Pro
- ££ £25–£42
- ⛳ 2 miles E of St Austell
- ⊕ Large practice ground; golf tuition holidays
- 🏠 J Hamilton Stutt
- 🖥 www.carlyonbay.com

China Fleet CC (1991)
Saltash, PL12 6LJ
- ☎ **(01752) 848668**
- 📠 (01752) 848456
- ✉ golf@china-fleet.co.uk
- 📖 600
- ♙ Mrs L Goddard
- ✎ P Kent
- ⏰ 18 L 6551 yds SSS 72
- ♟ H–by arrangement SOC
- ££ On application
- ⛳ 1 mile from Tamar Bridge, off A38
- ⊕ Floodlit driving range
- 🏠 Martin Hawtree
- 🖥 www.china-fleet.co.uk

Falmouth (1894)
Proprietary
Swanpool Road, Falmouth, TR11 5BQ
- ☎ **(01326) 311262/314296**
- 📠 (01326) 317783
- ✉ falmouth@onetel.com
- 📖 500
- ♙ (01326) 314296
- ✎ N Rogers
- ⏰ 18 L 6037 yds Par 71 SSS 70
- ♟ U SOC
- ££ On application
- ⛳ ¹/₄ mile W of Swanpool Beach
- ⊕ Driving range
- 🖥 www.falmouthgolfclub.com

Isles of Scilly (1904)
Carn Morval, St Mary's, Isles of Scilly, TR21 0NF
- ☎ **(01720) 422692**
- 📖 170
- ♙ Sam Ellis (Hon Sec)
- ⏰ 9 L 5898 yds Par 73 SSS 69
- ♟ U
- ££ £23.50
- ⛳ Hughtown 1¹/₂ miles
- 🏠 Horace Hutchinson

Killiow (1987)
Proprietary
Killiow, Kea, Truro, TR3 6AG
- ☎ **(01872) 270246**
- 📠 (01872) 240915
- ✉ killiowsec@yahoo.co.uk
- 📖 500
- ♙ J Crowson (01872) 266876
- ⏰ 18 L 6266 yds Par 72 SSS 71
- ♟ U
- ££ £15.50–£25 D–£30
- ⛳ 2¹/₂ miles S of Truro, off A39
- ⊕ Driving range

Lanhydrock Hotel & Golf Club (1991)
Lostwithiel Road, Bodmin, PL30 5AQ
- ☎ **(01208) 262570**
- 📠 (01208) 262579
- ✉ info@lanhydrockhotel.com
- 📖 350
- ♙ G Bond (Dir)
- ✎ P Brookes
- ⏰ 18 L 6100 yds Par 70 SSS 70
- ♟ U SOC H
- ££ On application (see web page)
- ⛳ A30 exit for Bodmin; follow tourist signs for Lanhydrock then hotel; 1 mile S of Bodmin on B3268
- ⊕ Driving range
- 🏠 J Hamilton Stutt
- 🖥 www.lanhydrockhotel.com

Launceston (1927)
St Stephen, Launceston, PL15 8HF
- ☎ **(01566) 773442**
- 📠 (01566) 777506
- ✉ secretary@tiscali.co.uk
- 📖 600
- ♙ PM Jones
- ✎ J Tozer
- ⏰ 18 L 6415 yds SSS 71
- ♟ WD–U H WE by prior arrangement
- ££ D–£30
- ⛳ 1 mile N of Launceston, off Bude road
- 🏠 J Hamilton Stutt
- 🖥 www.launcestongolfclub.com

Looe (1933)
Bin Down, Looe, PL13 1PX
- ☎ **(01503) 240239**
- 📠 (01503) 240864
- ✉ enquiries@looegolfclub.co.uk
- 📖 450
- ♙ T Day (Hon)
- ✎ J Bowen
- ⏰ 18 L 5940 yds Par 70 SSS 69

👫 U SOC
££ On application
⊶ 3 miles E of Looe
🏠 Harry Vardon
▤ www.looegolfclub.co.uk

Lostwithiel G&CC   (1990)
Lower Polscoe, Lostwithiel, PL22 0HQ
☎ **(01208) 873550**
📠 (01208) 873479
✉ reception@golf-hotel.co.uk
📖 350
🏌 D Higman
/ T Nash (01208) 873822
▷ 18 L 5984 yds Par 72
👫 U SOC
££ £30 (£34)
⊶ ¹/₂ mile E of Lostwithiel, off A390
⊕ Driving range
🏠 Stuart Wood
▤ www.golf-hotel.co.uk

Merlin   (1991)
Proprietary
Mawgan Porth, Newquay, TR8 4DN
☎ **(01841) 540222**
✉ rossoliver@merlingolfcourse.co.uk

Mullion   (1895)
Cury, Helston, TR12 7BP
☎ **(01326) 240685**
📠 (01326) 241527
✉ secretary@mulliongolfclub.plus
   .com
📖 700
🏌 G Fitter
/ I Harris (01326) 241176
▷ 18 L 6037 yds SSS 70
👫 H (restricted comp days and open
   days) SOC–WD
££ £25 D–£30 (+BH £30 D–£35)
⊶ 6 miles S of Helston
⊕ Golf academy
🏠 W Sich
▤ www.mulliongolfclub.co.uk

Newquay   (1890)
Tower Road, Newquay, TR7 1LT
☎ **(01637) 872091**
📠 (01637) 874066
✉ newquaygolf@btconnect.com
📖 600
🏌 G Binney (01637) 874354
/ M Bevan (01637) 874830
▷ 18 L 6151 yds SSS 69
👫 WD/Sat–H Sun–H SOC
££ £30 (£30) W–£90
⊶ Newquay town centre
🏠 HS Colt
▤ www.newquaygolfclub.co.uk

Perranporth   (1927)
Budnic Hill, Perranporth, TR6 0AB
☎ **(01872) 573701**
✉ secretary@perranporthgolfclub
   .co.uk
📖 600
🏌 DC Mugford
/ DC Michell (01872) 572317
▷ 18 L 6252 yds SSS 72
👫 WD–U WE–H SOC

££ £30 (£35)
⊶ ¹/₂ mile NW of Perranporth
⊕ Golf Academy
🏠 James Braid
▤ www.perranporthgolfclub.co.uk

Porthpean   (1992)
Proprietary
Porthpean, St Austell, PL26 6AY
☎ **(01726) 64613**
📠 (01726) 64613
✉ info@porthpeangolfclub.co.uk
📖 430
🏌 Roger French
▷ 18 L 5210 yds Par 67 SSS 66
👫 U SOC
££ £18
⊶ 2 miles SE of St Austell on coast
⊕ Driving range
▤ www.porthpeangolfclub.co.uk

Praa Sands   (1971)
Praa Sands, Penzance, TR20 9TQ
☎ **(01736) 763445**
✉ praasandsgolf@aol.com
📖 200
🏌 D & K Phillips (Props)
▷ 9 L 4122 yds Par 62 SSS 60 (men)
   Par 64 SSS 65 (ladies)
👫 U exc Sun am
££ £17 D–£24
⊶ 7 miles E of Penzance on A394
   Penzance-Helston road
⊕ Practice net; chipping green;
   putting green
🏠 RA Hamilton
▤ www.praasandsgolf.com

Roserrow   (1996)
Proprietary
St Minver, Wadebridge, PL27 6QT
☎ **(01208) 863000**
📠 (01208) 863002
✉ mail@roserrow.co.uk
📖 300
🏌 Simon Welch
▷ 18 L 6494 yds Par 72 SSS 72
👫 U SOC
££ Winter £20; summer £28
⊶ Polzeath, 15 min from A30
⊕ Driving range; practice facilities
🏠 David Feherty
▤ www.roserrow.co.uk

St Austell   (1911)
Tregongeeves, St Austell, PL26 7DS
☎ **(01726) 74756**
📠 (01726) 71978
✉ office@staustellgolf.co.uk
📖 780
🏌 K Trahair
/ T Pitts (01726) 68621
▷ 18 L 6091 yds SSS 69
👫 SOC exc comp days
££ On application
⊶ 1¹/₂ miles W of St Austell

St Enodoc   (1890)
Rock, Wadebridge, PL27 6LD
☎ **(01208) 863216**
✉ stenodocgolfclub@tiscali.co.uk

St Kew   (1993)
Proprietary
*St Kew Highway, Wadebridge, Bodmin,
PL30 3EF*
☎ **(01208) 841500**
📠 (01208) 841500
✉ stkewgolf@btconnect.com
📖 350
🏌 J Brown (Prop)
/ Mike Derry
▷ 9 L 4543 yds SSS 62
👫 U SOC WE booking after midday
££ 9: £11; 18: £15
⊶ 2¹/₂ miles N of Wadebridge on A39
⊕ Covered driving range
🏠 David Derry

St Mellion Hotel G&CC   (1976)
St Mellion, Saltash, PL12 6SD
☎ **(01579) 351351**

Tehidy Park   (1922)
Camborne, TR14 0HH
☎ **(01209) 842208**
📠 (01209) 842208
✉ secretary-manager
   @tehidyparkgolfclub.co.uk
📖 850
🏌 I J Veale (Sec/Mgr)
/ J Lamb (01209) 842914
▷ 18 L 6241 yds SSS 71
👫 H SOC
££ £25 (£30)
⊶ 3 miles N of Camborne
⊕ Practice ground; putting green
🏠 CK Cotton
▤ www.tehidyparkgolfclub.co.uk

Tregenna Castle Hotel   (1982)
St Ives, TR26 2DE
☎ **(01736) 795254**
📠 (01736) 796066
✉ hotel@tregenna-castle.co.uk
📖 297
🏌 S Davey
▷ 14 L 1846 yds Par 42
👫 U SOC
££ On application
⊶ St Ives 1 mile, off A3074
▤ www.tregenna-castle.co.uk

Treloy   (1991)
Treloy, Newquay, TR7 4JN
☎ **(01637) 878554**

Trethorne   (1991)
Kennards House, Launceston, PL15 8QE
☎ **(01566) 86903**
📠 (01566) 86929
✉ gen@trethornegolfclub.com
📖 450
🏌 M Boundy
/ M Boundy
▷ 18 L 6188 yds Par 71 SSS 71
👫 U
££ £28 (£35)
⊶ 2 miles SW of Launceston (A30)
⊕ Driving range; buggy hire

⌂ Frank Frayne
✉ www.trethornegolfclub.com

Trevose   (1924)
Constantine Bay, Padstow, PL28 8JB
☎ (01841) 520208
📠 (01841) 521057
✉ info@trevose-gc.co.uk
📖 1500
⚐ P Gammon (Prop),
  N Gammon (Sec/Mgr)
⚊ G Lenaghan (01841) 520261
↱ 18 L 6863 yds SSS 72
  9 L 3031 yds SSS 35
  9 L 1360 yds SSS 29
♟ H SOC
££ On application
⚲ 4 miles W of Padstow
⊕ 3 & 4 ball times restricted (phone
  first)
⌂ HS Colt
✉ www.trevose-gc.co.uk

Truro   (1937)
Treliske, Truro, TR1 3LG
☎ (01872) 272640/278684
📠 (01872) 225972
✉ trurogolfclub@tiscali.co.uk
📖 1000
⚐ HWD Leicester (Sec/Mgr)
  (01872) 278684
⚊ NK Bicknell (01872) 276595
↱ 18 L 5306 yds SSS 66
♟ U H SOC
££ £25 (£30)
⚲ 1 mile W of Truro on A390
⌂ Colt/Alison/Morrison
✉ www.trurogolf.co.uk

West Cornwall   (1889)
Lelant, St Ives, TR26 3DZ
☎ (01736) 753401
📠 (01736) 753401
✉ secretary@westcornwallgolfclub
  .co.uk
📖 825
⚐ GM Evans
⚊ J Broadway (01736) 753177
↱ 18 L 5884 yds SSS 69
♟ H SOC
££ £28 (£33)
⚲ 2 miles E of St Ives
⊕ Practice ground
⌂ Rev RF Tyack
✉ www.westcornwallgolfclub.co.uk

Whitsand Bay Hotel   (1906)
Portwrinkle, Torpoint, PL11 3BU
☎ (01503) 230276 (Clubhouse)
📠 (01503) 230329
📖 400
⚐ Paul Phillips
⚊ Steve Dougan (01503) 230778
↱ 18 L 5770 yds Par 70 SSS 68
♟ U SOC
££ £22 (£28)
⚲ 6 miles W of Plymouth
⌂ Willie Fernie
✉ www.whitsandbayhotel.co.uk

Cumbria

Alston Moor   (1906)
The Hermitage, Alston, CA9 3DB
☎ (01434) 381675
📠 (01434) 381675
📖 106
⚐ Paul Parkin (01434) 381704
↱ 10 L 5380 yds SSS 66
♟ U SOC
££ D–£13 (D–£15)
⚲ 2 miles S of Alston on B6277
✉ www.cybermoor.org.guest.golf

Appleby   (1903)
Brackenber Moor, Appleby, CA16 6LP
☎ (017683) 51432
📠 (017683) 52773
✉ appleby.gc@tiscali.co.uk
📖 740
⚐ JMF Doig (Hon)
⚊ J Taylor (017683) 52922
↱ 18 L 5901 yds SSS 68
♟ U H
££ £22 (£27)
⚲ 2 miles SE of Appleby. ½ mile N of
  A66
⌂ Willie Fernie
✉ www.applebygolfclub.co.uk

Barrow   (1922)
Rakesmoor Lane, Hawcoat, Barrow-in-
Furness, LA14 4QB
☎ (01229) 825444
✉ barrowgolf@supanet.com
📖 505 91(L) 67(J)
⚐ WR Edwards (Hon)
↱ 18 L 6184 yds Par 71 SSS 70
♟ U H Ladies Day–Fri SOC
££ D–£25 (£30 inc BH)
⚲ 2 miles E of Barrow, off A590
⌂ AM Duncan

Brampton (Talkin Tarn)
(1909)
Tarn Road, Brampton, CA8 1HN
☎ (016977) 2255
📠 (016977) 41487
✉ secretary@bramptongolfclub.com
📖 750
⚐ IJ Meldrum (01900) 827985
⚊ S Wilkinson (016977) 2000
↱ 18 L 6407 yds Par 72 SSS 71
♟ U
££ £20, D–£35 (+BH £35, D–£42)
⚲ B6413, 1 mile SE of Brampton
⊕ Driving range
⌂ James Braid
✉ www.bramptongolfclub.com

Brayton Park   (1986)
Pay and play
The Garth, Home Farm, Brayton, Aspatria,
CA7 3SX
☎ (01697) 323539
📖 60
⚐ D Warwick
⚊ Graham Batey (01697) 332072
↱ 9 L 2521 yds SSS 65
♟ U
££ 9: £6, 18: £10

⚲ 1 mile N of Aspatria. 10 miles N of
  Cockermouth
⌂ JB Ward

Carlisle   (1908)
Aglionby, Carlisle, CA4 8AG
☎ (01228) 513029
📠 (01228) 513303
✉ secretary@carlislegolfclub.org
📖 700
⚐ Roger Johnson
⚊ Graeme Lisle (01228) 513241
↱ 18 L 6263 yds SSS 70
♟ WD–U exc Tues–NA Sat–M
  Sun–restricted
  SOC–Mon/Wed/Thur/Fri
££ £35 D–£45 (£40 D–£45)
⚲ ½ mile E of M6 Junction 43, on
  A69
⌂ Mackenzie Ross
✉ www.carlislegolfclub.org

Carus Green   (1996)
Pay and play
Burneside Road, Kendal, LA9 6EB
☎ (01539) 721097

Casterton
Sedbergh Road, Casterton, Nr Kirkby
Lonsdale, LA6 2LA
☎ (015242) 71592
📠 (015242) 74387
✉ castertongc@hotmail.com
📖 300
⚐ J & E Makinson (Props)
⚊ R Williamson
↱ 9 L 2900 yds Par 35 SSS 67
♟ U SOC
££ £14 (£17)
⚲ 1 mile NE of Kirkby Lonsdale on
  A683. M6 Junction 36, 6 miles
⌂ Will Adamson
✉ www.castertongolf.co.uk

Cockermouth   (1896)
Embleton, Cockermouth, CA13 9SG
☎ (017687) 76223/76941
📠 (017687) 76941
✉ secretary@cockermouthgolf.co.uk
📖 539
⚐ RS Wimpress (01900) 825431
⚊ None
↱ 18 L 5496 yds Par 69 SSS 66
♟ WD–U before 3.30pm exc Wed
  (also 10–11am) and Thur (also
  9–10am) WE restricted – ring club
££ £20 (£25)
⚲ 3 m E of Cockermouth, 2 m W of
  Bassenthwaite Lake
⌂ James Braid
✉ www.cockermouthgolf.co.uk

Dalston Hall   (1990)
Dalston Hall, Dalston, Carlisle, CA5 7JX
☎ (01228) 710165
📠 (01228) 710165
✉ nigel@etmanco.fsnet.co.uk
📖 290
⚐ N Farthing
↱ 9 L 2700 yds SSS 67
♟ U
££ 9: £8 (£9) 18: £14 (£18)

⚶ 3 miles SW of Carlisle on B5299. 6 miles W of M6 Junction 42
🖥 www.dalstonhall.co.uk

The Dunnerholme   (1905)
Duddon Road, Askam-in-Furness, LA16 7AW
☎ (01229) 462675
🖴 (01229) 462675
✉ dunnerholmegolfclub@btinternet.com
📖 400
🖎 LA Haines (01229) 826198
🏴 10 L 6138 yds SSS 70
👥 U
££ £15 any day
⚶ 6 miles N of Barrow on A595

Eden   (1992)
Proprietary
Crosby-on-Eden, Carlisle, CA6 4RA
☎ (01228) 573003
🖴 (01228) 818435
📖 700
✓ S Harrison (01228) 573003
🏴 18 L 6368 yds SSS 72, additional 9 holes Par 36 – new for 2007
👥 U SOC
££ £28 (£32)
⚶ 5 miles NE of Carlisle, off A689. M6 Junction 44
⊕ Driving range; golf academy; extensive practice facilities
🏠 G Wannop & Son
🖥 www.edengolf.co.uk

Furness   (1872)
Central Drive, Walney Island, Barrow-in-Furness, LA14 3LN
☎ (01229) 475100
✉ furnessgolfclub@onetel.com
📖 625
🖎 WT French
✓ None
🏴 18 L 6363 yds SSS 70
👥 H SOC
££ £26
⚶ Walney Island. M6 Junction 36
🖥 www.furnessgolfclub.co.uk

Grange Fell   (1952)
Fell Road, Grange-over-Sands, LA11 6HB
☎ (015395) 32536
📖 300
🖎 JG Park (015395) 58513
🏴 9 L 4840 metres SSS 66
👥 U
££ £15 (£20)
⚶ W of Grange-over-Sands, towards Cartmel

Grange-over-Sands   (1919)
Meathop Road, Grange-over-Sands, LA11 6QX
☎ (015395) 33180
🖴 (015395) 33754
✉ dwright@ktdinternet.com
📖 490 140(L) 96(J)
🖎 SD Wright (015395) 33180

✓ N Lowe (015395) 35937
🏴 18 L 5938 yds SSS 69
👥 H SOC
££ £25 D–£30 (£30 D–£35)
⚶ E of Grange, off B5277
🏠 A Mackenzie
🖥 www.grangegolfclub.co.uk

Haltwhistle   (1967)
Wallend Farm, Greenhead, Carlisle, CA8 7HN
☎ (01697) 747367
📖 300
🖎 KL Dickinson (Hon)
✓ None
🏴 18 L 5532 yds Par 69 SSS 67
👥 U SOC
££ D–£16 (£20)
⚶ 3 miles W of Haltwhistle on A69
🏠 Andrew Mair

Kendal   (1891)
The Heights, Kendal, LA9 4PQ
☎ (01539) 723499 (Bookings)
🖴 (01539) 736466
✉ secretary@kendalgolfclub.co.uk
📖 475
🖎 I Clancy (01539) 733708
✓ P Scott (01539) 723499
🏴 18 L 5785 yds Par 70 SSS 68
👥 H SOC U–midweek WE–not Sat
££ £23 D–£30 (£30 D–£40)
⚶ 1 mile NW of Kendal
⊕ Buggy hire
🖥 www.kendalgolfclub.co.uk

Keswick   (1978)
Threlkeld Hall, Keswick, CA12 4SX
☎ (017687) 79324 (Bookings)

Kirkby Lonsdale   (1906)
Scaleber Lane, Barbon, Kirkby Lonsdale, LA6 2LJ
☎ (015242) 76365
🖴 (015242) 76503
✉ KLGolf@Dial.Pipex.com
📖 550 50(J)
🖎 G Hall (015242) 76365
✓ C Barrett (015242) 76366
🏴 18 L 6538 yds Par 72 SSS 71
👥 U SOC
££ D–£30 (D–£35)
⚶ 3 miles N of Kirkby Lonsdale, off A683
⊕ Practice facilities
🏠 W Squires
🖥 www.klgolf.dial.pipex.com

Maryport   (1905)
Bankend, Maryport, CA15 6PA
☎ (01900) 812605
🖴 (01900) 815626
✉ maryportgolfclub@tiscali.co.uk
📖 532
🖎 Mrs L Hayton (01900) 815626
🏴 18 L 5982 yds SSS 70
👥 U SOC
££ On application
⚶ 1 mile N of Maryport, off B5300

Penrith   (1890)
Salkeld Road, Penrith, CA11 8SG
☎ (01768) 891919/865429
📖 750
🖎 D Noble (01768) 891919
✓ G Key (01768) 891919
🏴 18 L 6026 yds SSS 69
👥 WD–H WE/BH–H 10.06–11.30am & after 3pm
££ £26 D–£31 (£31 D–£36)
⚶ ½ mile E of Penrith

Seascale   (1893)
Seascale, CA20 1QL
☎ (019467) 28202/28800
🖴 (019467) 28202
✉ seascalegolfclub@googlemail.com
📖 570
🖎 JDH Stobart (019467) 28202
🏴 18 L 6416 yds Par 71 SSS 71
👥 U SOC
££ £28 D–£33 (£33 D–£38)
⚶ 15 miles S of Whitehaven
🏠 Campbell/Lowe
🖥 www.seascalegolfclub.co.uk

Sedbergh   (1896)
Dent Road, Sedbergh, LA10 5SS
☎ (015396) 21551
🖴 (015396) 21827
✉ sedberghgolfclub@tiscali.co.uk
📖 170
🖎 Craig or Steve Gardner
🏴 9 L 5588 yds Par 70 SSS 67
👥 U–phone in advance SOC
££ £20 D–£26 WD+WE
⚶ 1 mile S of Sedbergh on Dent road. M6 Junction 37, 5 miles
🏠 WG Squires
🖥 www.sedberghgolfclub.co.uk

Silecroft   (1903)
Silecroft, Millom, LA18 4NX
☎ (01229) 774250
🖴 (01229) 774342
📖 240
🖎 DLA MacLardie (01229) 774342
✓ None
🏴 9 L 5877 yds Par 68 SSS 68
👥 WD–U WE/BH–restricted
££ D–£15 (£20)
⚶ 3 miles W of Millom

Silloth-on-Solway   (1892)
Silloth, Wigton, CA7 4BL
☎ (016973) 31304
🖴 (016973) 31782
✉ sillothgolfclub@lineone.net
📖 700
🖎 John Hill
✓ (016973) 32404
🏴 18 L 6600 yds SSS 71
Visitors normally play 6041 yds Par 72 SSS 69
👥 U H–booking advisable SOC
££ D–£37 (£50)
⚶ 22 miles W of Carlisle (B5302). M6 Junction 43
🏠 David Grant
🖥 www.sillothgolfclub.co.uk

Silverdale (1906)

Red Bridge Lane, Silverdale, Carnforth, LA5 0SP
- ☎ **(01524) 701300**
- 🖵 (01524) 702074
- ✉ silverdalegolfclub@ecosse.net
- 📖 500
- 🏌 KD Smith (01524) 702074
- 🏌 Ryan Grimsaw, PGA Pro
- ▷ 18 L 5535 yds Par 70 SSS 68
- 👥 U exc Sun (Summer)—M
- ££ £20 (£25)
- 🚗 3 miles NW of Carnforth, by Silverdale Station
- 📧 www.silverdalegolfclub.com

St Bees (1929)

Peckmill, Beach Road, St Bees, CA27 0EJ
- ☎ **(01946) 822515**
  (01946) 824300 (Clubhouse)

Stony Holme (1974)

Public
St Aidan's Road, Carlisle, CA1 1LS
- ☎ **(01228) 625511**
- 📖 375
- 🏌 WJ Hodgson (01228) 527112
- 🏌 S Ling (01228) 625511
- ▷ 18 L 5775 yds Par 69 SSS 68
- 👥 U SOC
- ££ £9.75 (£12.50)
- 🚗 1 mile E of Carlisle, off A69. M6 Junction 43
- 🏛 Frank Pennink

Ulverston (1895)

Bardsea Park, Ulverston, LA12 9QJ
- ☎ **(01229) 582824**
- 🖵 (01229) 588910
- ✉ enquiries@ulverstongolf.co.uk
- 📖 822
- 🏌 R Rushforth
- 🏌 PA Stoller (01229) 582806
- ▷ 18 L 6191 yds Par 71 SSS 70
- 👥 H or I SOC
- ££ £30 D—£35 (£35 D—£40) Summer £15 D—£20 (£20 D—£25) Winter
- 🚗 1½ miles SW of Ulverston on A5087
- ⊕ Driving range/ball dispenser
- 🏛 Herd/Colt
- 📧 www.ulverstongolf.co.uk

Windermere (1891)

Cleabarrow, Windermere, LA23 3NB
- ☎ **(015394) 43123**
- 🖵 (015394) 46370
- ✉ office@windermeregc.demon.co.uk
- 📖 700
- 🏌 RM Cox (Sec/Mgr)
- 🏌 WSM Rooke (015394) 43550
- ▷ 18 L 5143 yds SSS 65
- 👥 H SOC
- ££ £30 D—£43 (£37 D—£49)
- 🚗 1½ miles E of Bowness on B5264
- ⊕ Short game practice area
- 🏛 George Lowe
- 📧 www.windermeregolfclub.net

Workington (1893)

Branthwaite Road, Workington, CA14 4SS
- ☎ **(01900) 603460**
- ✉ workingtongolf@aol.com

Derbyshire

Alfreton (1892)

Oakerthorpe, Alfreton, DE55 7LH
- ☎ **(01773) 832070**
- 📖 350
- 🏌 S Bradley (07712) 136647
- 🏌 (01773) 831901
- ▷ 11 L 5393 yds SSS 66
- 👥 WD—U H before 4.30pm —M after 4.30pm WE—M SOC H
- ££ £20 (£28)
- 🚗 W of Alfreton (A38). M1 Junction 28
- 📧 www.alfretongolfclub.co.uk

Allestree Park (1949)

Public
Allestree Hall, Allestree, Derby, DE22 2EU
- ☎ **(01332) 550616**

Ashbourne (1886)

Wyaston Road, Ashbourne, DE6 1NB
- ☎ **(01335) 342078**
- 🖵 (01335) 347937
- ✉ sec@ashbournegc.fsnet.co.uk
- 📖 600
- 🏌 John Hammond
- 🏌 A Smith (01335) 347960
- ▷ 18 L 6365 yds SSS 71
- 👥 WD—U SOC
- ££ £27 D—£45 (£33)
- 🚗 1½ miles SW of Ashbourne, off A52
- ⊕ Telephone to confirm green fee and starting time. Practice area
- 🏛 David Hemstock
- 📧 www.ashbournegolfclub.co.uk

Bakewell (1899)

Station Road, Bakewell, DE4 1GB
- ☎ **(01629) 812307**
- 📖 305 67(L) 25(J)
- 🏌 Mrs P Moody
- 🏌 None
- ▷ 9 L 5244 yds SSS 65
- 👥 WD—U WE/BH—by arrangement SOC
- ££ D—£17 (D—£21)
- 🚗 ½ mile NE of Bakewell and A6
- 📧 www.bakewellgolfclub.co.uk

Birch Hall

Sheffield Road, Unstone, S18 5DH
- ☎ **(01246) 291979**
- 📖 290
- 🏌 E Gallagher (Hon Gen)
- 🏌 P Ball
- ▷ 18 L 6505 yds Par 73 SSS 71
- 👥 U
- ££ On application
- 🚗 Jct 29 on M1 then 2 miles N of Chesterfield (B6057)
- 🏛 David Tucker

Blue Circle (1985)

Cement Works, Hope, S33 2RP
- ☎ **(01433) 622315**

Bondhay (1991)

Bondhay Lane, Whitwell, Worksop, S80 3EH
- ☎ **(01909) 723608**
- 🖵 (01909) 720226
- ✉ enquiries@bondhay.com
- 📖 520
- 🏌 H Hardisty
- 🏌 M Ramsden
- ▷ 18 L 6807 yds Par 72
  9 hole course Par 3
- 👥 U SOC
- ££ £20 (£25)
- 🚗 2 miles E of M1 Junction 30, off A619
- ⊕ Driving range
- 🏛 Donald Steel
- 📧 www.bondhay.com

Brailsford (1994)

Proprietary
Pools Head Lane, Brailsford, Ashbourne, DE6 3BU
- ☎ **(01335) 360096**
- 🖵 (01335) 360077
- ✉ info@brailsfordgolfcourse.co.uk
- 📖 189
- 🏌 K Wilson (01332) 553703
- 🏌 D McCarthy (01335) 360096
- ▷ 12 L 5758 yds Par 68 SSS 68
- 👥 U SOC
- ££ 9: £12 (£14) 18: £17 (£22)
- 🚗 On A52 between Derby and Ashbourne
- ⊕ Driving range; PGA tuition
- 🏛 RW Baldwin (EGU)

Breadsall Priory Hotel G&CC (1976)

Moor Road, Morley, Derby, DE7 6DL
- ☎ **(01332) 836106**
- 🖵 (01332) 833438
- 📖 900
- 🏌 I Knox (Dir of Golf)
- 🏌 D Steels (01332) 836082
- ▷ 18 L 6201 yds SSS 70
  18 L 6028 yds SSS 69
- 👥 U
- ££ £25—£50
- 🚗 Morley, 5 miles N of Derby (A61). M1 Junction 25, 9 miles
- ⊕ Driving range

Broughton Heath

Proprietary
Bent Lane, Church Broughton, DE65 5BA
- ☎ **(01283) 521235**
- ✉ info@bhgcpar3.co.uk
- 📖 492
- 🏌 J Bentley (Mgr)
- 🏌 A Hyland
- ▷ 18 L 3125 yds Par 54 SSS 53
- 👥 WD—U WE—booking necessary SOC
- ££ £9 (£12)
- 🚗 Church Broughton, 1 mile off A516 at Hatton

⊕ Driving range
⌂ K Tunnicliffe
▤ www.bhgcpar3.co.uk

Burton-on-Trent   (1894)
43 Ashby Road East, Burton-on-Trent, DE15 0PS
☎ **(01283) 568708 (Clubhouse)**
⌨ (01283) 544551
✉ TheSecretary@BurtonGolfClub
.co.uk
▥ 700
♠ MJ Leggett (01283) 544551
✓ G Stafford (01283) 562240
▷ 18 L 6579 yds SSS 71
♙ H WD–NA before 9am or
12.30–14.00pm SOC WE–M
££ £38 D–£50 (£44 D–£57)
⊶ 3 miles E of Burton on A511
⌂ HS Colt
▤ www.burtongolfclub.co.uk

Buxton & High Peak   (1887)
Townend, Buxton, SK17 7EN
☎ **(01298) 26263**
⌨ (01298) 26333
✉ sec@bhpgc.co.uk
▥ 450
♠ J Harris
✓ J Lines (01298) 23112
▷ 18 L 5997 yds SSS 69
♙ U
££ £24 (£30)
⊶ NE boundary of Buxton (A6)
⊕ Driving range adj. to course
(separate business)
⌂ J Morris
▤ www.buxtonandhighpeakgolfclub
.co.uk

Cavendish   (1925)
Gadley Lane, Buxton, SK17 6XD
☎ **(01298) 79708**
⌨ (01298) 79708
✉ admin@cavendishgolfcourse.com
▥ 600
♠ PG Nicholls
✓ S Townend
▷ 18 L 5833 yds SSS 68
♙ U H SOC–by prior arrangement
with Sec
££ £30 (£33)
⊶ ³/₄ mile W of Buxton Station. St
John's Road (A53)
⊕ Practice area
⌂ Dr A Mackenzie
▤ www.cavendishgolfcourse.com

Chapel-en-le-Frith   (1905)
The Cockyard, Manchester Road, Chapel-en-le-Frith, SK23 9UH
☎ **(01298) 812118**
⌨ (01298) 814990
✉ info@chapelgolf.co.uk
▥ 640
♠ S Smith (01298) 813943
✓ DJ Cullen (01298) 812118
▷ 18 L 6434 yds SSS 71
♙ U
££ £28 (£38)
⊶ 13 miles SE of Stockport, off A6
(B5470)
▤ www.chapelgolf.co.uk

Chesterfield   (1897)
Walton, Chesterfield, S42 7LA
☎ **(01246) 279256**
⌨ (01246) 276622
✉ secretary@chesterfieldgolfclub
.co.uk
▥ 600
♠ T Marshall
✓ M McLean (01246) 276297
▷ 18 L 6281 yds Par 71 SSS 70
♙ WD–U before 4.00pm WE Sat (if
with member) Sun after 1.30pm (if
not with member) SOC–WD
££ £32–£40
⊶ 2 miles SW of Chesterfield on
A623 (Matlock Road)
⊕ Practice ground
▤ www.chesterfieldgolfclub.co.uk

Chevin   (1894)
Duffield, Derby, DE56 4EE
☎ **(01332) 841864**
✉ secretary@chevingolf.fsnet.co.uk

Derby   (1923)
Public
Wilmore Road, Sinfin, Derby, DE24 9HD
☎ **(01332) 766323**
♠ D Anderson
✓ D Delaney (01332) 766462
▷ 18 L 6185 yds SSS 70
♙ U SOC
££ On application
⊶ 1 mile S of Derby, off A52

Erewash Valley   (1905)
Stanton-by-Dale, DE7 4QR
☎ **(0115) 932 3258**
⌨ (0115) 944 0061
✉ secretary@erewashvalley.co.uk
▥ 675
♠ C Huckle (0115) 932 2984
✓ MJ Ronan (0115) 932 4667
▷ 18 L 6547 yds SSS 71
♙ WE/BH–NA before noon
SOC–WD
££ £30 D–£40 (£40)
⊶ 10 miles E of Derby, off A52. M1
Junction 25, 3 miles
⌂ Hawtree
▤ www.erewashvalley.co.uk

Glossop & District   (1894)
Sheffield Road, Glossop, SK13 7PU
☎ **(01457) 865247 (Clubhouse)**
▥ 300
♠ R Hargreaves
✓ D Marsh (01457) 853117
▷ 11 L 5800 yds SSS 68
♙ U SOC
££ £12.50 Mon £17.50 weekdays £20
⊶ 1 mile E of Glossop, off A57

Grassmoor Golf Centre
(1990)
Proprietary
North Wingfield Road, Grassmoor, Chesterfield, S42 5EA
☎ **(01246) 856044**
⌨ (01246) 853486
✉ enquiries@grassmoorgolf.co.uk

▥ 390
♠ H Hagues
✓ G Hagues
▷ 18 L 5721 yds Par 69
♙ U–advance booking required SOC
££ £12 (£15)
⊶ 2 miles S of Chesterfield on B6038.
M1 Junction 29, 3 miles
⊕ Floodlit driving range, 26 bay with
electric tee system
⌂ Hawtree
▤ www.grassmoorgolf.co.uk

Horsley Lodge   (1990)
Smalley Mill Road, Horsley, DE21 5BL
☎ **(01332) 780838**
⌨ (01332) 781118
✉ richard@horsleylodgegc.co.uk
▥ 650
♠ Dennis Wake
✓ Mark Whithorn (01332) 780838
▷ 18 L 6418 yds SSS 71
♙ WD–U H WE–NA before noon
££ On application
⊶ 4 miles NE of Derby. M1 Junction
28
⊕ Driving range
⌂ GM White/P McEvoy
▤ www.horsleylodgegc.co.uk

Kedleston Park   (1947)
Kedleston, Quarndon, Derby, DE22 5JD
☎ **(01332) 840035**
⌨ (01332) 840035
✉ secretary@kedleston-park-golf-club.co.uk
▥ 719
♠ GR Duckmanton
✓ P Wesselingh (01332) 841685
▷ 18 L 6731 yds SSS 72
♙ WD–H SOC
££ £45 (£45)
⊶ 3 miles NE of Derby. National
Trust signs to Kedleston Hall
⌂ James Braid
▤ www.kedlestonparkgolf.co.uk

Matlock   (1906)
Chesterfield Road, Matlock Moor, Matlock, DE4 5LZ
☎ **(01629) 582191**
⌨ (01629) 582135
✉ www.matlockgolfclub.co.uk
▥ 500 80(L) 65(J)
♠ J Odell (01629) 582191
✓ M Whithorn (01629) 584934
▷ 18 L 5804 yds SSS 68
♙ WD–U exc 12.30–1.30pm–NA
WE/BH–M SOC–WD
££ D–£25
⊶ 1½ miles NE of Matlock (A632)
⊕ Practice area
⌂ Tom Williamson

Maywood   (1990)
Rushy Lane, Risley, Derby, DE7 3ST
☎ **(0115) 939 2306**
✉ maywoodgolfclub@btinternet.com
▥ 350
♠ WJ Cockeram (0115) 932 6772
✓ S Jackson (0115) 949 0043
▷ 18 L 6424 yds Par 72 SSS 71

WD–U before 4pm WE–restricted SOC
££ £15 (£20)
⟷ Between Nottingham and Derby. M1 Junction 25
⌂ P Moon

Mickleover (1923)
Uttoxeter Road, Mickleover, DE3 9AD
☎ **(01332) 516011 (Clubhouse)**
🖳 (01332) 516011
✉ secretary@mickleovergolfclub.com
📖 800
🏌 GW Finney (01332) 516011
🏌 T Coxon (01332) 518662
🏳 18 L 5708 yds SSS 68
👥 U SOC–Tues & Thurs
££ £30 (D–£40)
⟷ 3 miles W of Derby on A516/B5020
🖳 www.mickleovergolfclub.com

New Mills (1907)
Shaw Marsh, New Mills, High Peak, SK22 4QE
☎ **(01663) 743485**
🖳 (01663) 746161
📖 420
🏌 P Jenkinson (01663) 744305
🏌 C Cross (01663) 746161
🏳 18 L 5604 yds SSS 67
👥 WD–U WE–U SOC
££ £20 (£25)
⟷ 8 miles SE of Stockport
⌂ David Williams

Ormonde Fields (1926)
Nottingham Road, Codnor, Ripley, DE5 9RG
☎ **(01773) 742987**
🖳 (01773) 744848
📖 660
🏌 K Constable
🏌 M Myford
🏳 18 L 6504 yds SSS 72
👥 U SOC
££ On application
⟷ A610 Ripley to Nottingham road. M1 Junction 26, 5 miles
⌂ John Fearn

Shirland (1977)
Proprietary
Lower Delves, Shirland, DE55 6AU
☎ **(01773) 834935**
✉ geofftowle@hotmail.com
📖 450
🏌 G Towle (01773) 874224
🏌 NB Hallam (01773) 834935
🏳 18 L 6072 yds SSS 70
👥 WD–U WE–U after 2pm SOC
££ £24 (£30)
⟷ 1 mile N of Alfreton, off A61 by Shirland Church

Sickleholme (1898)
Bamford, Sheffield, S33 0BH
☎ **(01433) 651306**

Stanedge (1934)
Walton Hay Farm, Chesterfield, S45 0LW
☎ **(01246) 566156**
📖 325

🏌 W Tyzack (01246) 276568 (home)
🏳 9 L 5786 yds SSS 68
👥 WD–U before 2pm –M after 2pm WE–M SOC
££ £15
⟷ 5 miles SW of Chesterfield, off B5057
🖳 www.stanedgegolfclub.co.uk

Devon

Ashbury (1991)
Higher Maddaford, Okehampton, EX20 4NL
☎ **(01837) 55453**
🖳 (01837) 55468
📖 100
🏌 I Gill
🏳 18 L 5460 yds SSS 67
18 L 5628 yds SSS 67
18 L 5400 yds SSS 66
18 L 2018 yds Par 3
18 L 6355 yds SSS 68 (open 04/07)
👥 Subject to availability
££ £25 (£30)
⟷ 4 miles W of Okehampton, off A3079
⊕ Driving range on site
⌂ DJ Fensom
🖳 www.ashburyhotel.co.uk

Axe Cliff (1894)
Proprietary
Squires Lane, Axmouth, Seaton, EX12 4AB
☎ **(01297) 21754**
🖳 (01297) 24371
✉ D.Quinn@axecliff.co.uk
📖 300
🏌 David Quinn
🏌 Mark Dack
🏳 18 L 5969 yds SSS 70
👥 U SOC WD WE
££ D–£17 (£22)
⟷ Nr Yacht Club at Axmouth Bridge off Sidmouth to Lyme Regis Road
⊕ Putting green; driving net
⌂ James Braid
🖳 www.axecliff.co.uk

Bigbury (1923)
Bigbury-on-Sea, South Devon, TQ7 4BB
☎ **(01548) 810055 (Clubhouse)**
🖳 (01548) 810207
✉ secretary@bigburygolfclub.co.uk
📖 750
🏌 MJ Lowry (01548) 810557
🏌 S Lloyd (01548) 810412
🏳 18 L 6061 yds Par 70 SSS 69
👥 H–preferred SOC–Tue & Thur
££ Dec–Feb: D–£15; Mar–Nov £30 (£35)
⟷ 15 miles SE of Plymouth on B3392
⌂ JH Taylor
🖳 www.bigburygolfclub.com

Bovey Castle (1929)
North Bovey, Devon TQ13 8RE
☎ **(01647) 445009**
🖳 (01647) 440961
✉ richard.lewis@boveycastle.com
📖 150

🏌 R Lewis
🏌 R Lewis
🏳 18 L 6303 yds Par 70 SSS 70
👥 U H SOC
££ £125
⟷ 15 miles SW of Exeter on B3212; M5 Junction 31
⌂ JF Abercromby
🖳 www.boveycastle.com

Chulmleigh (1976)
Pay and play
Leigh Road, Chulmleigh, EX18 7BL
☎ **(01769) 580519**
🖳 (01769) 580519
✉ chulmleighgolf@aol.com
📖 100
🏌 RW Dow
🏳 Summer 18 L 1450 yds SSS 54
Winter 9 L 2309 yds SSS 54
👥 U
££ £8.50 £7.50 before 10 am D–£15
⟷ 1 mile N of A377 at Chulmleigh
⌂ John Goodban
🖳 www.chulmleighgolf.co.uk

Churston (1890)
Churston, Brixham, TQ5 0LA
☎ **(01803) 842751**
🖳 (01803) 845738
✉ manager@churstongolf.com
📖 983
🏌 SR Bawden (01803) 842751
🏌 R Butterworth (01803) 843442
🏳 18 L 6208 yds SSS 70
👥 H exc Tues am–NA SOC–Mon/Thurs/Fri
££ £40 (£45)
⟷ 5 miles S of Torquay
⊕ Practice area
⌂ HS Colt
🖳 www.churstongolf.com

Dainton Park (1993)
Proprietary
Totnes Road, Ipplepen, Newton Abbot, TQ12 5TN
☎ **(01803) 815000**
✉ info@daintonparkgolf.co.uk
📖 600
🏌 Mrs M Selway
🏌 J Fullard
🏳 18 L 6400 yds SSS 71
👥 U SOC
££ £22 (£25)
⟷ 2 miles S of Newton Abbot on A381
⊕ Driving range
⌂ Adrian Stiff
🖳 www.daintonparkgolf.co.uk

Dartmouth G&CC (1992)
Blackawton, Nr Dartmouth, Devon TQ9 7DE
☎ **(01803) 712686**
✉ info@dgcc.co.uk

Dinnaton – McCaulays Health Club (1989)
Ivybridge, PL21 9HU
☎ **(01752) 892512**

☎ (01752) 698334
✉ info@mccaulays.com
📖 300
✓ P Hendriksen
✓ R Stephenson
⊳ 9 L 4089 yds Par 64
👥 U SOC WD–All WE–All
££ 9: £8 Mon–Thur (£9 Fri–Sun)
   18: £10 Mon–Thur (£11 Fri–Sun)
🚗 12 miles SE of Plymouth, off
   A38/B3213
🏠 Pink/Cotton
🖳 www.mccaulays.com

Downes Crediton   (1976)
Hookway, Crediton, EX17 3PT
☎ **(01363) 773025**
🖷 (01363) 775060
✉ secretary@downescreditongc.co.uk
📖 700
✓ PT Lee (01363) 773025
✓ B Austin (01363) 774464
⊳ 18 L 5962 yds Par 70 SSS 69
👥 H SOC
££ £28 (£32)
🚗 2 miles S of Crediton, off A377
🖳 www.downescreditongc.co.uk

East Devon   (1902)
Links Road, Budleigh Salterton, EX9 6DG
☎ **(01395) 443370**
🖷 (01395) 445547
✉ secretary@edgc.co.uk
📖 850
✓ J Reynolds (01395) 443370
✓ T Underwood (01395) 445195
⊳ 18 L 6231 yds SSS 70
👥 H SOC–Thurs only
££ £36 D–£48
🚗 12 miles SE of Exeter – M5 J30 –
   A376
🖳 www.edgc.co.uk

Elfordleigh Hotel G&CC
(1932)
Colebrook, Plympton, Plymouth, PL7 5EB
☎ **(01752) 348425**
🖷 (01752) 344581
✉ enquiries@elfordleigh.co.uk
📖 500
✓ Jeff Hobbs (01752) 218660
✓ Nick Cook (01752) 348425
⊳ 18 L 5527 yds SSS 67
👥 U H–phone first SOC
££ £25 (£30)
🚗 4 miles E of Plymouth, off Plympton
   road
🏠 JH Taylor

Exeter G&CC   (1895)
Countess Wear, Exeter, EX2 7AE
☎ **(01392) 874139**
🖷 (01392) 874139
✉ golf@exetergcc.co.uk
📖 850
✓ KJ Ham (Golf Sec)
✓ G Milne (01392) 875028
⊳ 18 L 5980 yds SSS 69
👥 WD–U H WE–I H SOC–Thurs
££ On application
🚗 4 miles SE of Exeter
🏠 James Braid

Fingle Glen   (1992)
Tedburn St Mary, Exeter, EX6 6AF
☎ **(01647) 61817**
🖷 (01647) 61135
✉ fingle.glen@btinternet.com
📖 700
✓ P Miliffe
✓ S Gould
⊳ 18 L 5878 yds Par 70 SSS 68
👥 U SOC
££ £20 (£22)
🚗 5 miles W of Exeter on A30
⊕ Driving range
🖳 www.fingleglen.com

Hartland Forest   (1980)
Hartland Forest Golf & Leisure Parc,
Woolsery, Bideford, EX39 5RA
☎ **(01237) 431442**
🖷 (01237) 431734
✉ hfgolf@googlemail.com
📖 150
✓ Kevin Murphy (01271) 343160
⊳ 18 L 6004 yds Par 71 SSS 70
👥 U SOC
££ £25
🚗 6 miles S of Clovelly, off A39
⊕ Buggies–£15/round
🏠 Alan Cartwright
🖳 www.hartlandforestgolf.com

Hele Park Golf Centre
(1993)
Proprietary
Ashburton Road, Newton Abbot, TQ12 6JN
☎ **(01626) 336060**
🖷 (01626) 332661
✉ info@heleparkgolf.co.uk
📖 400
✓ Wendy Stanbury
✓ Duncan Arnold (Dir of Golf)
⊳ 9 L 2584 yds SSS 65
👥 U SOC
££ £20 (£22)
🚗 W of Newton Abbot on A383
⊕ Driving range with Power Tees
🏠 M Craig
🖳 www.heleparkgolf.co.uk

Highbullen Hotel G&CC
(2002)
Proprietary
Chittlehamholt, Umberleigh, EX37 9HD
☎ **(01769) 540561**
✉ info@highbullen.co.uk

Holsworthy   (1937)
Kilatree, Holsworthy, EX22 6LP
☎ **(01409) 253177**
🖷 (01409) 253177
✉ hgcsecretary@aol.com
📖 450
✓ B Megson
✓ AR Johnston
⊳ 18 L 6059 yds SSS 69
👥 WD–U Sun–U after 2.30pm
££ £25
🚗 1 mile W of Holsworthy. 7 miles E
   of Bude (A3072)

Honiton   (1896)
Middlehills, Honiton, EX14 9TR
☎ **(01404) 44422**
🖷 (01404) 46383
✉ secretary@honitongolfclub.fsnet
   .co.uk
📖 750
✓ BM Young
✓ A Cave (01404) 42943
⊳ 18 L 5875 yds Par 69 SSS 68
👥 U (recognised club member) SOC
££ £26 (£30)
🚗 2 miles S of Honiton towards
   Farway off A35
🖳 www.honitongolf club.co.uk

Hurdwick   (1990)
Tavistock Hamlets, Tavistock, PL19 0LL
☎ **(01822) 612746**
📖 175
✓ Maj RW Cullen (Mgr) R Hurle
   (Golf Sec)
⊳ 18 L 5335 yds Par 67
👥 U SOC
££ £17
🚗 1 mile N of Tavistock, on Brentor
   Church road
🏠 Hawtree/Bartlett

Ilfracombe   (1892)
Hele Bay, Ilfracombe, EX34 9RT
☎ **(01271) 862176**
🖷 (01271) 867731
✉ ilfracombegolfclub@btinternet.com
📖 500
✓ A Williams
✓ M Davies (01271) 863328
⊳ 18 L 5795 yds Par 69 SSS 68
👥 WD–H SOC WE/BH–U after
   10am–NA 12–1pm
££ £25 D–£35 (£30 D–£40)
🚗 2 miles E of Ilfracombe, towards
   Combe Martin
⊕ Driving range
🏠 TK Weir
🖳 www.ilfracombegolfclub.com

Libbaton   (1988)
High Bickington, Umberleigh, EX37 9BS
☎ **(01769) 560269**
🖷 (01769) 560342
✉ gerald.herniman@tesco.net
📖 475
✓ Gerald Herniman
✓ Andrew Norman (01769) 560167
⊳ 18 L 6481 yds SSS 71
👥 U SOC
££ £22 (£26)
🚗 1 mile S of High Bickington on
   B3217. M5 Junction 27
⊕ Floodlit driving range
🖳 www.libbaton-golf-club.com

Mortehoe & Woolacombe
(1992)
Easewell, Mortehoe, Ilfracombe, EX34 7EH
☎ **(01271) 870566**
📖 225
✓ M Wilkinson (01271) 870745
⊳ 9 L 4729 yds Par 66 SSS 63
👥 U

££ 9: £10 18: £16 D–£20
⊕⊕ E of Mortehoe village
⌂ David Hoare

Okehampton (1913)

Okehampton, EX20 1EF
☎ **(01837) 52113**
⌨ (01837) 53541
✉ okehamptongc@btconnect.com
📖 550
✍ C Yeo
✓ A Moon (01837) 53541
▷ 18 L 5294 yds SSS 66 Par 68
♛ H SOC
££ £25 D–£30 (£30)
⊕⊕ S boundary of Okehampton
⌂ JH Taylor
▤ www.okehamptongc.co.uk

Padbrook Park (1992)

Pay and play
Cullompton, EX15 1RU
☎ **(01884) 836100**
⌨ (01884) 836101
✉ info@padbrookpark.co.uk
📖 250
✍ Cary Rawlings (Mgr)
✓ Richard Coffin
▷ 9 L 6108 yds SSS 70
♛ U SOC–WD
££ 9: £13 (£17); 18: £18 (£22)
⊕⊕ 10 miles E of Exeter. M5 Junction
28, 1 mile
⊕ Driving range (10 bays)
⌂ Bob Sandow

Portmore Golf Park (1993)

Proprietary
Landkey Road, Barnstaple, EX32 9LB
☎ **(01271) 378378**
✉ colin@portmoregolfpark.freeserve
.co.uk
📖 550
✍ C Webber
✓ S Gould, D Everett
▷ 27 holes
Barum: 18 L 6500 yds Par 71
SSS 70
Landkey: 9 hole Par 3
♛ U
££ Landkey: 9 holes £7.50, 18 holes
£12.50; Barum: 9 holes £12, 18
holes £20
⊕⊕ 1 mile E of Barnstaple, off A361
⊕ 24-bay floodlit driving range &
practice area
⌂ Hawtree

Royal North Devon (1864)

Golf Links Road, Westward Ho!, EX39 1HD
☎ **(01237) 473824 (Clubhouse)**
⌨ (01237) 423456
✉ info@royalnorthdevongolfclub
.co.uk
📖 1100
✍ R Fowler (01237) 473817
✓ I Parker (01237) 477598
▷ 18 L 6665 yds Par 72 SSS 72
9 hole short par 3 course
♛ U H
££ £38 D–£44 (£44 D–£50)
⊕⊕ 2 miles N of Bideford (A39)

⊕ Golf museum; indoor practice bays
⌂ Old Tom Morris
▤ www.royalnorthdevongolfclub
.co.uk

Saunton (1897)

Saunton, Braunton, EX33 1LG
☎ **(01271) 812436**
⌨ (01271) 814241
✉ info@sauntongolf.co.uk
📖 1450
✍ D Cliffe
✓ AT Mackenzie (01271) 812013
▷ East 18 L 6779 yds Par 71 SSS 72
West 18 L 6403 yds Par 71 SSS 71
♛ U H SOC
££ £60 D–£85 inc lunch
⊕⊕ 6 miles W of Barnstaple
⊕ Driving range
⌂ Fowler/Pennink
▤ www.sauntongolf.co.uk

Sidmouth (1889)

Cotmaton Road, Sidmouth, EX10 8SX
☎ **(01395) 513023**
⌨ (01395) 514661
✉ secretary@sidmouthgolfclub.co.uk
📖 580
✍ JP Lee (Mgr) (01395) 513451
✓ C Haigh (01395) 516407
▷ 18 L 5068 yds SSS 65
♛ U SOC
££ £28 (£28)
⊕⊕ 1/2 mile W of Sidmouth. 12 miles SE
of M5 Junction 30
⌂ JH Taylor
▤ www.sidmouthgolfclub.co.uk

Sparkwell (1993)

Pay and play
Sparkwell, Plymouth, PL7 5DF
☎ **(01752) 837219**
⌨ (01752) 837219
📖 108
✍ G Adamson
✓ None
▷ 9 L 5772 yds SSS 68
♛ U SOC
££ 9: £7 (£8) 18: £12 (£14)
⊕⊕ 8 miles NE of Plymouth. A38
Plympton Junction
⊕ 9 hole pitch & putt
⌂ J Gabb

Staddon Heights (1904)

Plymstock, Plymouth, PL9 9SP
☎ **(01752) 402475**
⌨ (01752) 401998
✉ roger.brown@btconnect.com
📖 740
✍ RW Brown
✓ (01752) 492630
▷ 18 L 6164 yds SSS 70
♛ WE–H SOC–WD
££ D–£25 (D–£30)
⊕⊕ SE Plymouth, via Plymstock
▤ www.staddon-heights.co.uk

Stover (1930)

Bovey Road, Newton Abbot, TQ12 6QQ
☎ **(01626) 352460**

⌨ (01626) 330210
✉ info@stovergolfclub.co.uk
📖 750
✍ W Hendry
✓ J Langmead (01626) 362078
▷ 18 L 5764 yds SSS 68
♛ U H SOC
££ £32 D–£40 (£40)
⊕⊕ 3 miles N of Newton Abbot on
A382. A38 Drumbridges Junction
⌂ James Braid
▤ www.stovergolfclub.co.uk

Tavistock (1890)

Down Road, Tavistock, PL19 9AQ
☎ **(01822) 612344**
⌨ (01822) 612344
✉ tavygolf@hotmail.com
📖 700
✍ J Coe
✓ D Rehaag (01822) 612316
▷ 18 L 6546 yds SSS 71
♛ H SOC–WD
££ £28 (£36)
⊕⊕ Whitchurch Down
▤ www.tavistockgolfclub.org

Teign Valley (1995)

Christow, Exeter, EX6 7PA
☎ **(01647) 253026**
⌨ (01647) 253026
✉ welcome@teignvalleygolf.co.uk
📖 480
✍ Ray Parker (01647) 253026
✓ S Amiet (01647) 253127
▷ 18 L 5958 yds Par 70 SSS 69
♛ U SOC
££ £20 (£28)
⊕⊕ SW of Exeter, via A38 (B3193)
⌂ Peter Nicholson
▤ www.teignvalleygolf.co.uk

Teignmouth (1924)

*Haldon Moor, Exeter Road, Teignmouth
TQ14 9NY*
☎ **(01626) 777070**
⌨ (01626) 777304
✉ tgc@btconnect.com
📖 900
✍ A Stubbs (01626) 777070
✓ R Selley (01626) 7728984
▷ 18 L 6073 yds SSS 69
♛ WD–H (recognised club member)
WE–by appointment SOC–Tues &
Thur only
££ £40
⊕⊕ 2 miles N of Teignmouth on B3192
⌂ Dr A Mackenzie
▤ www.teignmouthgolfclub.com

Thurlestone (1897)

Thurlestone, Kingsbridge, TQ7 3NZ
☎ **(01548) 560405**
⌨ (01548) 562149
✉ info@thurlestonegc.co.uk
📖 770
✍ TE Gibbons (01548) 560405
✓ P Laugher (01548) 560715
▷ 18 L 6340 yds Par 71 SSS 70
♛ I or H
££ £36
⊕⊕ 5 miles W of Kingsbridge, off A379

⌂ HS Colt
▤ www.thurlestonegc.co.uk

Tiverton   (1932)
Post Hill, Tiverton, EX16 4NE
☎ **(01884) 252114 (Clubhouse)**
▭ (01884) 251607
✉ tivertongolfclub@lineone.net
▥ 600 150(L) 100(J)
♤ R Jessop (Gen Mgr)
  (01884) 252187
✓ M Hawton (01884) 254836
▷ 18 L 6346 yds SSS 70
⚲ H
££ On application
⚙ 5 miles W of M5 Junction 27. 1½
  miles E of Tiverton on B3391
⌂ Braid/Cotton
▤ www.tivertongolfclub.co.uk

Torquay   (1909)
Petitor Road, St Marychurch, Torquay,
TQ1 4QF
☎ **(01803) 327471**
▭ (01803) 316116
✉ info@torquaygolfclub.org.uk
▥ 800
♤ TJ Fensom (01803) 314591
✓ M Ruth (01803) 329113
▷ 18 L 6164 yds Par 69 SSS 69
⚲ H SOC
££ £29 (£35)
⚙ 2 miles N of Torquay
▤ www.torquaygolfclub.org.uk

Torrington   (1895)
Weare Trees, Torrington, EX38 7EZ
☎ **(01805) 622229**
▭ (01805) 623878
✉ theoffice@tottingtongolf.fsnet
  .co.uk
▥ 400
♤ Mrs JM Cudmore
✓ None
▷ 9 L 4423 yds Par 64 SSS 62
⚲ U exc Sat/Sun am–NA
  SOC–Tues/Wed am
££ D–£15
⚙ 1 mile W of Torrington on Weare
  Giffard road
▤ www.greattorringtongolfclub.co.uk

Warren   (1892)
Dawlish Warren, EX7 0NF
☎ **(01626) 862255**
▭ (01626) 888005
✉ secretary@dwgc.co.uk
▥ 600
♤ T Aggett
✓ D Prowse (01626) 864002
▷ 18 L 5954 yds Par 69 SSS 69
⚲ U SOC–WD
££ £31 (£35)
⚙ 1½ miles E of Dawlish. M5 Jct 30
⌂ James Braid
▤ www.dwgc.co.uk

Waterbridge   (1992)
Pay and play
Down St Mary, Crediton, EX17 5LG
☎ **(01363) 85111**

Willingcott Valley   (1996)
Willingcott, Woolacombe, EX34 7HN
☎ **(01271) 870173**
▭ (01271) 870800
✉ secretary.willingcottgolfclub
  @virgin.net
▥ 239
♤ Jackie Kingsley (07939) 345434
✓ David Elliott (01271) 8837801
  Mobile: (07774) 211740
▷ 18 L 6422 SSS 71 Par 72 (White
  tees)
  18 L 5865 SSS 68 Par 72 (Yellow
  tees)
  18 L 5195 SSS 70 Par 72 (Red tees)
⚲ U SOC
££ £22 (£28)
⚙ Near Barnstaple, 45 min from M5
  J27
⊕ Practice facilities available
⌂ Hawtree (1st 9), Peter Lang (2nd 9)
▤ www.willingcott.co.uk

Woodbury Park   (1992)
Woodbury Castle, Woodbury, EX5 1JJ
☎ **(01395) 233500**

Wrangaton   (1895)
Golf Links Road, Wrangaton, South Brent,
TQ10 9HJ
☎ **(01364) 73229**
▭ (01364) 73229
✉ wrangatongolf@btconnect.com
▥ 660
♤ M Daniels (01364) 73229
✓ G Richards (01364) 72161
▷ 18 L 6065 yds Par 70 SSS 69
⚲ U SOC
££ £25 (£30)
⚙ Off A38 between South Brent and
  Ivybridge
⌂ Donald Steel
▤ www.wrangatongolfclub.co.uk

Yelverton   (1904)
Golf Links Road, Yelverton, PL20 6BN
☎ **(01822) 852824**
▭ (01822) 854869
✉ secretary@yelvertongc.co.uk
▥ 600
♤ SM Barnes (01822) 852824
✓ T McSherry (01822) 853593
▷ 18 L 6353 yds Par 71 SSS 71
⚲ H SOC
££ D–£34 (£40)
⚙ 6 miles N of Plymouth on A386
⊕ Practice ground; putting & chipping
  areas; Academy course
⌂ Herbert Fowler
▤ www.yelvertongc.co.uk

Dorset

The Ashley Wood   (1896)
Wimborne Road, Blandford Forum,
DT11 9HN
☎ **(01258) 452253**
▭ (01258) 450590
✉ generalmanager
  @ashleywoodgolfclub.com

▥ 600
♤ Y Brown
✓ J Shimmons (01258) 480379
▷ 18 L 6284 yds Par 70 SSS 70
⚲ WD after 10am WE–H after 1pm
  SOC–WD
££ Phone in advance
⚙ 1½ miles SE of Blandford on B3082
⊕ Practice area
⌂ Patrick Tallack
▤ www.ashleywoodgolfclub.com

Bridport & West Dorset
   (1891)
The Clubhouse, Burton Road, Bridport
DT6 4PS
☎ **(01308) 421095/422597
   (Clubhouse)**
▭ (01308) 421095
✉ secretary@bridportgolfclub.org.uk
▥ 600
♤ PJ Ridler (01308) 421095
✓ D Parsons (01308) 421491
▷ 18 L 5875 yds Par 70 SSS 68
⚲ WD/Sat–U after 9.30am Sun–U
  after 1pm SOC
££ £26. Afternoon £20
⚙ 1 mile E of A35 Bridport by-pass
  on B3157
⊕ Driving range. 9 hole pitch & putt
  course (Summer).
⌂ F Hawtree
▤ www.bridportgolfclub.org.uk

Broadstone (Dorset)
   (1898)
Wentworth Drive, Broadstone, BH18 8DQ
☎ **(01202) 692595**
▭ (01202) 642520
✉ admin@broadstonegolfclub.com
▥ 650
♤ C Robinson (01202) 642521
✓ M Wilson (01202) 692835
▷ 18 L 6349 yds SSS 70
⚲ WD–H from 9.30–11.30am and
  2–4pm WE/BH–restricted
  SOC–WD
££ £46 (£70 D–£60)
⚙ 4 miles N of Poole, off A349
⊕ Incorporates The Dorset Golf Club
⌂ Dunn (1898)/Colt (1920)/Sparks
  (2005)
▤ www.broadstonegolfclub.com

Bulbury Woods   (1989)
Bulbury Lane, Lytchett Minster, Poole,
BH16 6EP
☎ **(01929) 459574**
✉ enquiries@bulbury-woods.co.uk

Came Down   (1896)
Higher Came, Dorchester, DT2 8NR
☎ **(01305) 813494**
▭ (01305) 813494
✉ manager@camedowngolfclub.co.uk
▥ 700
♤ David Simpson (Mgr)
  (01305) 813494
✓ N Rodgers (01305) 812670
▷ 18 L 6255 yds Par 70 SSS 70
⚲ U Sun am–NA SOC H

££ £28 (£32)
⊷ 2 miles S of Dorchester on A354
⌂ Harry S Colt
▤ www.camedowngolfclub.co.uk

Canford Magna (1994)
Proprietary
Knighton Lane, Wimborne, BH21 3AS
☎ (01202) 592552
📠 (01202) 592550
✉ admin@canfordmagnagc.co.uk
▣ 1000
✍ S Hudson (Dir) (01202) 592505
✓ M Cummins (01202) 591212
▷ Parkland 18 L 6515 yds Par 71
    SSS 71
    Riverside 18 L 6213 yds Par 70
    SSS 69
    Knighton 9 L 1377 yds Par 27
👥 U
££ £7–£23 (£8–£26.50)
⊷ 2 miles E of Wimborne on A341
⊕ Driving range. Golf Academy. 6
    holes pitch & putt course
⌂ Swan/Smith
▤ www.canfordmagnagc.co.uk

Canford School (1987)
Canford School, Wimborne, BH21 3AD
☎ (01202) 841254
📠 (01202) 881009
✉ msb@canford.com
▣ 360
✍ M Burley (Mgr) (01202) 847522
▷ 9 L 5787 yds SSS 68
👥 M SOC
££ £12
⊷ 1 mile SE of Wimborne, off A341
⌂ P Boult
▤ www.canford.com

Charminster (1998)
Proprietary
Wolfedale Golf Course, Charminster,
Dorchester, DT2 7SG
☎ (01305) 260186
📠 (01305) 257074
▣ 140
✍ D Cox (Prop/Mgr) (01305) 260186
✓ T Lovegrove (01305) 260186
▷ 18 L 5467 yds Par 69 SSS 67
👥 U
££ £15.90 (£15.90)
⊷ 2 miles N of Dorchester
⊕ 6-hole beginners' course
⌂ D Cox

Chedington Court (1991)
South Perrott, Beaminster, DT8 3HU
☎ (01935) 891413
📠 (01935) 891217
✉ admincgc@tiscali.co.uk
▣ 450
✍ B Ritchie
✓ S Ritchie
▷ 18 L 6047 yds SSS 70
    9 hole par 3
👥 U SOC
££ £20 (£25)
⊷ 4 miles SE of Crewkerne on A356
⊕ 15 acre practice field; driving range
    planned

⌂ Chapman/Hemstock/Steel
▤ www.chedingtoncourtgolfclub.co.uk

Christchurch (1977)
Pay and play
Riverside Avenue, Bournemouth, BH7 7ES
☎ (01202) 436436 (Bookings)
📠 (01202) 436400
▣ 231
✍ ME Harvey (01202) 436412
✓ L Moxon (01202) 436436
▷ 18 L 6277 yds course
    9 hole short course
👥 U SOC
££ 9: £10 (£12) 18: £15 (£18.50)
⊷ Bournemouth/Christchurch
    boundary
⊕ Driving range

Crane Valley (1992)
The Clubhouse, Verwood, BH31 7LE
☎ (01202) 814088
📠 (01202) 813407
✉ general@crane-valley.co.uk
▣ 700
✍ A Blackwell (Gen Mgr)
✓ S Steele/G Hunt
▷ 18 L 6421 yds Par 72 SSS 71
    9 L 2060 yds Par 33 SSS 60
👥 U SOC (9 hole–U)
££ 9: £6.50 (£7.50) 18: £30 (£40)
⊷ Nr Ringwood, on B3081 Verwood-
    Cranborne road
⊕ Floodlit driving range
⌂ Donald Steel
▤ www.crane-valley.co.uk

The Dorset G&CC (1978)
Bere Regis, Wareham, BH20 7NT
☎ (01929) 472244
📠 (01929) 471294
✉ admin@dorsetgolfresort.com
▣ 850
✍ G Packer (Gen Mgr)
✓ S Porter
▷ Lakeland 18 L 7027 yds Par 72
    SSS 72
    Woodland 18 L 4887 yds Par 66
    SSS 64
    Parkland 18 L 5901 yds Par 69
    SSS 68
👥 U SOC
££ £38 (£42)
⊷ 5 miles S of Bere Regis, off Wool
    road
⊕ Driving range; hotel; luxury log
    homes for rent
⌂ Martin Hawtree
▤ www.dorsetgolfresort.com

Dudsbury (1992)
Proprietary
64 Christchurch Road, Ferndown,
BH22 8ST
☎ (01202) 593499
📠 (01202) 594555
✉ golf@dudsbury.demon.co.uk
✍ Micella Chamberlain (Mgr)
✓ Steve Pocknell (01202) 584488
    Head Pro & Sec
▷ 18 L 6904 yds Par 71 SSS 73
👥 U

££ £35 (£40)
⊷ 3 miles N of Bournemouth (B3073)
⊕ Driving range. Academy course
⌂ Donald Steel
▤ www.dudsburygolfclub.co.uk

Ferndown (1923)
119 Golf Links Road, Ferndown, BH22 8BU
☎ (01202) 874602
📠 (01202) 873926
✉ ferndowngc@lineone.net
▣ 700
✍ MC Davies (Mgr) (01202) 874602
✓ (01202) 873825
▷ 18 L 6509 yds Par 71 SSS 71
    9 L 5604 yds SSS 68
👥 WD–I H after 9.30am SOC–Tues
    & Fri
££ Old £60 (£70) President's £20
    (£25)
⊷ 6 miles N of Bournemouth
⌂ Harold Hilton
▤ www.ferndown-golf-club.co.uk

Ferndown Forest (1993)
Forest Links Road, Ferndown, BH22 9QE
☎ (01202) 876096
📠 (01202) 894095
▣ 300
✍ Chris Lawford
✓ G Howell (01202) 894990
▷ 18 L 5200 yds Par 68 SSS 65
👥 U SOC
££ £13 (£15)
⊷ 5 miles N of Bournemouth. N of
    Ferndown Bypass. Off A31
⊕ Floodlit driving range
⌂ Hunt/Grafham
▤ www.ferndownforestgolf.co.uk

Halstock (1988)
Pay and play
Common Lane, Halstock, BA22 9SF
☎ (01935) 891689

Highcliffe Castle (1913)
107 Lymington Road, Highcliffe-on-Sea,
Christchurch, BH23 4LA
☎ (01425) 272210/272953
📠 (01425) 272953
▣ 350 100(L) 50(J)
✍ G Fisher (01425) 272210
▷ 18 L 4776 yds Par 64 SSS 63
👥 H SOC
££ £26 (£36)
⊷ 8 miles E of Bournemouth

Isle of Purbeck (1892)
Studland, BH19 3AB
☎ (01929) 450361
📠 (01929) 450501
✉ enquiries@purbeckgolf.co.uk
▣ 400
✍ Mrs C Robinson
✓ I Brake (01929) 450354
▷ 18 L 6295 yds SSS 70
    9 L 2007 yds SSS 30
👥 U SOC
££ £38 D–£46 (£43 D–£49) (2006)
⊷ 3 miles N of Swanage on B3351.
    Ferry from Sandbanks to Studland

For list of abbreviations and key to symbols see page 651

☎ HS Colt
▤ www.purbeckgolf.co.uk

Knighton Heath　(1976)

Francis Avenue, West Howe, Bournemouth, BH11 8NX
- ☎ **(01202) 572633**
- 🖷 (01202) 590774
- ✉ khgc@btinternet.com
- 📖 700
- ♧ P Bodle
- ✎ P Brown (01202) 578275
- ⊳ 18 L 6065 yds SSS 69
- 👥 WD–H after 9.30am WE–M
- ££ On application
- ♣ 3 miles N of Poole, at junction of A348/A3049

Lyme Regis　(1893)

Timber Hill, Lyme Regis, DT7 3HQ
- ☎ **(01297) 442963**
- 🖷 (01297) 442963
- ✉ secretary@lymeregisgolfclub.co.uk
- 📖 750
- ♧ S Wright (01297) 442963
- ✎ D Driver (01297) 443822
- ⊳ 18 L 6283 yds SSS 70
- 👥 H WD–U after 9.30am (2.30pm Thurs) Sun–U after noon SOC
- ££ £30 D–£35 Last 3 hours £15 inc drink
- ♣ Between Lyme Regis and Charmouth, off A3502/A35
- ▤ www.lymeregisgolfclub.co.uk

Meyrick Park　(1890)

Pay and play
Central Drive, Meyrick Park, Bournemouth, BH2 6LH
- ☎ **(01202) 786000**
  (01202) 786040 (Bookings)
- ✉ m.gracehaus.com

Moors Valley　(1988)

Public
Horton Road, Ringwood, BH24 2ET
- ☎ **(01425) 479776**
- ✉ golf@eastdorset.gov.uk
- 📖 300
- ♧ Desmond Meharg (Mgr)
- ⊳ 18 L 6337 yds Par 72 SSS 70 4-hole short course
- 👥 U
- ££ £15.50 Mon–Thur, £21 Fri–Sun Twilight £11
- ♣ 4 miles SW of Ringwood, off A31
- ♠ Martin Hawtree
- ▤ www.moors-valley.co.uk/golf

Parkstone　(1909)

Links Road, Parkstone, Poole, BH14 9QS
- ☎ **(01202) 707138**
- 🖷 (01202) 706027
- ✉ admin@parkstonegolfclub.co.uk
- 📖 500 160(L) 75(J)
- ♧ Christine Radford (Gen Mgr) (01202) 707138
- ✎ M Thompson (01202) 708092
- ⊳ 18 L 6250 yds SSS 70
- 👥 H WD–NA before 9.30am and 12.30–2.10pm WE–NA before 9.45am and 12.30–2.30pm

££ £50 D–£75 (£60 D–£85)
♣ 3 miles W of Bournemouth, off A35
⊕ Practice range
♠ W Park Jr/Braid
▤ www.parkstonegolfclub.co.uk

Parley Court　(1992)

Proprietary
Parley Green Lane, Hurn, Christchurch, BH23 6BB
- ☎ **(01202) 591600**
- 🖷 (01202) 579043
- ✉ info@parleygolf.co.uk
- 📖 200
- ♧ Mrs SD Mitchell
- ✎ R Hill (07746) 850901/(01202) 591600
- ⊳ 9 L 2469 yds Par 68 SSS 64 18 tee positions
- 👥 U SOC
- ££ 9: £9 (£10.50) 18: £12 (£13)
- ♣ Opp Bournemouth Airport situated B3073
- ▤ www.parleygolf.co.uk

Queens Park (Bournemouth)　(1905)

Public
Queens Park West Drive, Queens Park, Bournemouth, BH8 9BY
- ☎ **(01202) 302611**
  (01202) 437807 (Bookings)
- 🖷 (01202) 302611
- ✉ queenspark@fsmail.net
- 📖 350
- ♧ R Polden (01202) 302611
- ⊳ 18 L 6132 yds SSS 70
- 👥 U SOC
- ££ £15 (£19.50)
- ♣ 2 miles NE of Bournemouth

Sherborne　(1894)

Higher Clatcombe, Sherborne, DT9 4RN
- ☎ **(01935) 812274**
- 🖷 (01935) 814218
- ✉ sherbornegc@btconnect.com
- 📖 700
- ✎ A Tresidder (01935) 812274
- ⊳ 18 L 6415 yds Par 72 SSS 71
- 👥 H
- ££ £25 (£36)
- ♣ 1 mile N of Sherborne, off B3145
- ♠ James Braid

Solent Meads Golf Centre　(1965)

Public
Rolls Drive, Southbourne, Bournemouth, BH6 4NA
- ☎ **(01202) 420795**
- ✉ solentmeads@yahoo.co.uk
- ♧ Matt Steward (01202) 420795
- ✎ Roddy Watkins (01202) 420795
- ⊳ 18 L 2159 yds Par 54
- 👥 U Groups welcome
- ££ £5.65–£7.50
- ♣ Hengistbury Head, S of Christchurch, E of Bournemouth
- ⊕ Driving range, 9 hole pitch and putt course
- ▤ www.solentmeads.com

Sturminster Marshall　(1992)

Moor Lane, Sturminster Marshall, BH21 4AH
- ☎ **(01258) 858444**
- 🖷 (01258) 858262
- ✉ info@sturminstermarshallgolfclub.co.uk
- 📖 160
- ♧ Mike Dodd
- ✎ Tracy Loveys, Mike Dodd
- ⊳ 9 L 3850 yds SSS 59
- 👥 U SOC
- ££ 9: £10; 18: £15
- ♣ 8 miles N of Poole on A350
- ⊕ Coaching range/short game area; children's golf academy; ladies golf academy
- ♠ John Sharkey
- ▤ www.sturminstermarshallgolfclub.co.uk

Wareham　(1908)

Sandford Road, Wareham, BH20 4DH
- ☎ **(01929) 554147/557995**
- 🖷 (01929) 557993
- ✉ warehamgolf@tiscali.co.uk
- 📖 550
- ♧ Richard Murgatroyd
- ⊳ 18 L 5753 yds SSS 68
- 👥 WD–after 9.30am WE–after 1pm SOC–WD
- ££ £22 D–£30 (£25)
- ♣ N of Wareham on A351
- ♠ C Whitcombe
- ▤ www.warehamgolfclub.com

Weymouth　(1909)

Links Road, Weymouth, DT4 0PF
- ☎ **(01305) 773981**
- 🖷 (01305) 788029
- ✉ weymouthgolfclub@aol.com
- 📖 700
- ♧ SB Elliott
- ✎ D Lochrie (01305) 773997
- ⊳ 18 L 5996 yds Par 70 SSS 69
- 👥 H SOC–WD
- ££ £30 (£36)
- ♣ 1 mile from town centre (A354), off Manor roundabout
- ⊕ Practice facility
- ♠ Braid/Hamilton Stutt
- ▤ www.weymouthgolfclub.co.uk

Durham

Barnard Castle　(1898)

Harmire Road, Barnard Castle, DL12 8QN
- ☎ **(01833) 638355**
- 🖷 (01833) 695551
- 📖 700
- ♧ J Kilgarriff
- ✎ D Pearce (01833) 631980
- ⊳ 18 L 6406 yds SSS 71
- 👥 U SOC
- ££ £20 D–£26 (£27 D–£32)
- ♣ N boundary of Barnard Castle on B6278
- ▤ www.barnardcastlegolfclub.org.uk

Beamish Park (1906)

Beamish, Stanley, DH9 0RH
☎ (0191) 370 1382

Billingham (1967)

Sandy Lane, Billingham, TS22 5NA
☎ (01642) 554494/533816
📠 (01642) 533816
✉ billingham@onetel.com
📖 850
🏌 Peter B Hodgson (Sec/Mgr) (01642) 533816
⛳ M Ure (01642) 557060
🚩 18 L 6346 yds Par 71 SSS 70
👥 WD–H after 9am WE/BH–H after 10am SOC
££ D–£28 Reduction for parties D–£40 weekends
⛰ W boundary of Billingham by A19, E of bypass
⊕ Practice ground
🏠 Frank Pennink
🖳 www.billinghamgolfclub.com

Bishop Auckland (1894)

High Plains, Durham Road, Bishop Auckland, DL14 8DL
☎ (01388) 661618
📠 (01388) 607005
✉ enquiries@bagc.co.uk
📖 788
🏌 MS Metcalf (01388) 661618
⛳ D Skiffington (01388) 661618
🚩 18 L 6420 yds SSS 70
👥 H (closed Good Friday and Christmas Day) SOC WD/WE
££ £25 D–£30 (£25 D–£30)
⛰ ½ mile NE of Bishop Auckland
🏠 James Kay
🖳 www.bagc.co.uk

Blackwell Grange (1930)

Briar Close, Blackwell, Darlington, DL3 8QX
☎ (01325) 464458
📠 (01325) 464458
✉ secretary@blackwellgrangegolf.com
📖 700
🏌 P Wraith (Hon) (01325) 464458
⛳ J Furby (01325) 462088
🚩 18 L 5621 yds Par 68 SSS 67
👥 U exc Wed 11am–2.30pm–NA Sat–booking req Sun–restricted SOC
££ £25 D–£35 (£35)
⛰ 1 mile S of Darlington on A66
🏠 Frank Pennink
🖳 www.blackwellgrangegolf.com

Brancepeth Castle (1924)

The Clubhouse, Brancepeth Village, Durham, DH7 8EA
☎ (0191) 378 0075
📠 (0191) 378 3835
✉ enquiries@brancepeth-castle-golf.co.uk
📖 768 68(L) 100(J)
🏌 S Haslam
⛳ D Howdon (0191) 378 0183
🚩 18 L 6400 yds SSS 70
👥 SOC–WD WE–by arrangement
££ £35 (£40) Society discounts
⛰ 4 miles W of Durham on A690

⊕ Practice area
🏠 HS Colt
🖳 www.brancepeth-castle-golf.co.uk

Castle Eden (1927)

Castle Eden, Hartlepool, TS27 4SS
☎ (01429) 836220
📖 650
🏌 D Livingston (01429) 836510
⛳ P Jackson (01429) 836689
🚩 18 L 6247 yds SSS 70
👥 U
££ £28 (£36)
⛰ 2 miles S of Peterlee
🏠 Henry Cotton
🖳 www.btinternet.com/ ~derek.livingston2

Chester-Le-Street (1908)

Lumley Park, Chester-Le-Street, DH3 4NS
☎ (0191) 388 3218
✉ clsgc@ukonline.co.uk
📖 510 75(L) 78(J)
🏌 Bill Routledge
⛳ D Fletcher (0191) 389 0157
🚩 18 L 6479 yds SSS 71
👥 WD–H after 9.30am –NA 12–1pm WE–NA before 10.30am or 12–2pm
££ £25 (£30)
⛰ E of Chester-Le-Street in grounds of Lumley Castle
⊕ Large practice area
🏠 JH Taylor
🖳 www.clsgc.co.uk

Consett & District (1911)

Elmfield Road, Consett, DH8 5NN
☎ (01207) 502186
📠 (01207) 505060
✉ consettgolfclub@btconnect.com
📖 650
🏌 W McMaster (01207) 507834
⛳ S Cowell (01207) 580210
🚩 18 L 6020 yds SSS 69
👥 WD–U SOC WE–limited to 20
££ £20 (£30)
⛰ 14 miles N of Durham on A691
🏠 Harry Vardon
🖳 www.consettgolfclub.com

Crook (1919)

Low Job's Hill, Crook, DL15 9AA
☎ (01388) 762429
📠 (01388) 762137
✉ secretary@crookgolfclub.com
📖 450
🏌 L Shaw
⛳ G Catrell (01388) 768145
🚩 18 L 6102 yds SSS 69
👥 U SOC
££ From £18
⛰ ½ mile E of Crook (A689)
🖳 www.crookgolfclub.com

Darlington (1908)

Haughton Grange, Darlington, DL1 3JD
☎ (01325) 355324
📠 (01325) 366086
✉ mdilley@darlington-gc.co.uk
📖 725

🏌 AR Ellis
⛳ C Dilley (01325) 484198
🚩 18 L 6181 yds Par 70 SSS 69
👥 WD–U WE–M
££ £27 D–£32
⛰ Off Salters Lane, NE of Darlington (A1150)
🏠 Dr Alistair Mackenzie
🖳 www.darlington-gc.co.uk

Dinsdale Spa (1910)

Middleton St George, Darlington, DL2 1DW
☎ (01325) 332297
📠 (01325) 332297
✉ dinsdalespagolf@btconnect.com
📖 875
🏌 EP Davison
⛳ M Stubbings (01325) 332515
🚩 18 L 6107 yds Par 71 SSS 69 Yellow
👥 WD–U exc Tues–NA WE–M
££ D–£25
⛰ 5 miles SE of Darlington
⊕ Large practice area; 2 bays undercover

Durham City (1887)

Littleburn, Langley Moor, Durham, DH7 8HL
☎ (0191) 378 0069
📠 (0191) 378 4265
📖 750
🏌 LTI Wilson (0191) 386 4434
⛳ S Corbally (0191) 378 0029
🚩 18 L 6326 yds SSS 70
👥 WD–U SOC
££ £24 (£30)
⛰ 1½ miles W of Durham, off A690
🏠 CC Stanton

Eaglescliffe (1914)

Yarm Road, Eaglescliffe, Stockton-on-Tees, TS16 0DQ
☎ (01642) 780098 (Clubhouse) (01642) 780238 (office)
📠 (01642) 780238
✉ eaglescliffegcsec@tiscali.co.uk
📖 835
🏌 Michael Sample (01642) 780238
⛳ Graeme Bell (01642) 790122
🚩 18 L 6275 yds SSS 70
👥 U SOC WD
££ £35 D–£45 (£45 D–£55)
⛰ 3 miles S of Stockton-on-Tees on A135
🏠 Braid/Cotton
🖳 www.eaglescliffegolfclub.co.uk

Hartlepool (1906)

Hart Warren, Hartlepool, TS24 9QF
☎ (01429) 274398
📠 (01429) 274129
✉ hartlepoolgolf@btconnect.com
📖 700
🏌 LG Gordon (01429) 261723
⛳ G Laidlaw (01429) 267473
🚩 18 L 6255 yds SSS 70
👥 WD–U SOC
££ £30 (£42)
⛰ N boundary of Hartlepool
🖳 www.hartlepoolgolfclub.co.uk

High Throston   (1997)

Hart Lane, Hartlepool, TS26 0UG
- ☎ **(01429) 275325**
- 📖 240
- ♟ Mrs J Sturrock
- ✓ None
- ▷ 18 L 6247 yds Par 71 SSS 70
- ♘ U SOC
- ££ £16 (£20)
- ⊕ 2 miles NW of Hartlepool (A179)
- ⌂ Jonathan Gaunt

Hobson   (1978)

Hobson, Burnopfield, Newcastle-upon-Tyne, NE16 6BZ
- ☎ **(01207) 271605**
- ♟ CP Taylor (01207) 270941
- ✓ J Ord (01207) 271605
- ▷ 18 L 6371 yds SSS 70
- ♘ U SOC
- ££ £19 (£22)
- ⊕ Between Gateshead and Consett on A692

Knotty Hill Golf Centre
(1992)
Pay and play
Sedgefield, Stockton-on-Tees, TS21 2BB
- ☎ **(01740) 620320**
- 🖷 (01740) 622227
- ✉ khgc21@btopenworld.com
- ♟ D Craggs (Mgr)
- ▷ Princes 18 L 6433 yds Par 72 SSS 71
- Bishops 18 L 5976 yds Par 70
- ♘ U SOC
- ££ £12 (£14)
- ⊕ 1 mile N of Sedgefield on A177. A1(M) Junction 60, 2 miles
- ⊕ Floodlit driving range
- ⌂ Chris Stanton

Mount Oswald   (1924)

South Road, Durham City, DH1 3TQ
- ☎ **(0191) 386 7527**
- 🖷 (0191) 386 0975
- ✉ info@mountoswald.co.uk
- 📖 200
- ♟ N Galvin
- ✓ C Calder (0191) 384 8941
- ▷ 18 L 6027 yds SSS 69
- ♘ U SOC
- ££ £14.50 D–£26 (£17.50 D–£28)
- ⊕ SW of Durham on A177
- ⊕ Driving range; putting green
- ▤ www.mountoswald.co.uk

Norton   (1989)

Pay and play
Junction Road, Norton, Stockton-on-Tees, TS20 1SU
- ☎ **(01642) 676385**
- 🖷 (01642) 608467
- ▷ 18 L 5870 yds SSS 71
- ♘ U SOC
- ££ £11.50 (£13.50)
- ⊕ 1 mile E of A177 on B1274
- ⌂ Tim Harper

Oakleaf Golf Complex
(1993)
Pay and play
School Aycliffe Lane, Newton Aycliffe, DL5 6QZ
- ☎ **(01325) 310820**
- 🖷 (01325) 300873
- ✉ info@great-aycliffe.gov.uk
- ♟ A Bailey (Mgr) (01325) 300700
- ✓ E Wilson
- ▷ 18 L 5568 yds SSS 67
- ♘ WD–U WE–booking necessary
- ££ £11.75 D–£15 (£14 D–£20)
- ⊕ 1 mile W of Aycliffe on A6072, from A68
- ⊕ Floodlit driving range; buggies for hire
- ▤ www.great-aycliffe.gov.uk

Ramside   (1995)

Ramside Hall Hotel, Carrville, Durham, DH1 1TD
- ☎ **(0191) 386 9514**
- 🖷 (0191) 386 9519
- ✉ golf@ramsidehallgolf.co.uk
- 📖 400
- ♟ MJ Davis
- ✓ K Jackson (0191) 386 9514
- ▷ 27 holes:
  6217-6851 yds SSS 70-73
- ♘ U SOC Soft spikes only
- ££ £37 (£45)
- ⊕ 2 miles NE of Durham on A690. A1(M) Junction 62
- ⊕ Driving range. Golf Academy
- ⌂ J Gaunt
- ▤ www.ramsidehallgolf.co.uk

Roseberry Grange   (1986)

Public
Grange Villa, Chester-Le-Street, DH2 3NF
- ☎ **(0191) 370 0660**
- 🖷 (0191) 370 2047
- ✉ chrisjones@chester-le-street.gov.uk
- 📖 500
- ♟ R McDermott (Hon)
- ✓ C Jones (0191) 370 0660
- ▷ 18 L 5892 yds SSS 68
- ♘ U SOC
- ££ £16 (£22)
- ⊕ 3 miles W of Chester-Le-Street on A693
- ⊕ Driving range

Seaham   (1908)

Shrewsbury Street, Dawdon, Seaham, SR7 7RD
- ☎ **(0191) 581 2354**
- ✉ seaham@onetel.com
- 📖 550
- ♟ T Johnson (0191) 581 1268
- ✓ A Blunt (0191) 513 0837
- ▷ 18 L 6009 yds SSS 69
- ♘ WE–NA before 3pm
- ££ On application
- ⊕ Dawdon, 2 miles NE of A19
- ▤ www.seahamgolfclub.co.uk

Seaton Carew   (1874)

Tees Road, Hartlepool, TS25 1DE
- ☎ **(01429) 266249/261040**

- 🖷 (01429) 267952
- ✉ info@seatoncarewgolf.co.uk
- 📖 700
- ♟ J Hall (01429) 296496
- ♟ M Rogers (01429) 890660
- ▷ Old 18 L 6613 yds SSS 72
  Brabazon 18 L 6855 yds SSS 73
- ♘ U SOC
- ££ On application
- ⊕ Hartlepool 2 m, A1(M) J60
- ⌂ Dr A Mackenzie
- ▤ www.seatoncarewgolf.co.uk

South Moor   (1923)

The Middles, Craghead, Stanley, DH9 6AG
- ☎ **(01207) 232848/283525**
- ✉ bryandavison@southmoorgc.freeserve.co.uk

Stressholme   (1976)

Public
Snipe Lane, Darlington, DL2 2SA
- ☎ **(01325) 461002**
- 🖷 (01325) 461002
- ✉ stressholme@btconnect.com
- ♟ R Givens
- ✓ R Givens
- ▷ 18 L 6511 yds SSS 71
- ♘ U
- ££ On application
- ⊕ 2 miles S of Darlington on A66
- ⊕ Floodlit driving range
- ▤ www.darlington.gov.uk/golf

Woodham G&CC   (1983)

Proprietary
Burnhill Way, Newton Aycliffe, DL5 4PN
- ☎ **(01325) 320574**
- 🖷 (01325) 315254
- 📖 610
- ♟ JD Jenkinson
- ✓ Peter Kelly (01325) 315257
- ▷ 18 L 6688 yds Par 73 SSS 72
- ♘ WD–SOC–U WD/WE U call for details
- ££ £20 D–£27 (£32 D–£40)
- ⊕ 1 mile N of Newton Aycliffe. 6 miles from A1 (A689)
- ⌂ J Hamilton Stutt

The Wynyard Club
(1996)
Proprietary
Wellington Drive, Wynyard Park, Billingham, TS22 5QJ
- ☎ **(01740) 644399**
- 🖷 (01740) 644599
- ✉ chris@wynardgolfclub.co.uk
- 📖 350
- ♟ C Mounter (Golf Dir)
- ✓ C Mounter
- ▷ 18 holes Par 72 SSS 73
- ♘ SOC–H WD WE
- ££ On application
- ⊕ 5 miles E of Sedgefield, between A1 and A19
- ⊕ Floodlit driving range. David Leadbetter Golf Academy
- ⌂ Hawtree
- ▤ www.wynardgolfclub.co.uk

Essex

Abridge G&CC (1964)
Epping Lane, Stapleford Tawney, RM4 1ST
- ☎ **(01708) 688396**
- 🖥 (01708) 688550
- 📧 info@abridgegolf.com
- 📖 500
- ✍ Manager (01708) 688932
- 🏌 S Layton (01708) 688333
- ⛳ 18 L 6704 yds SSS 72
- 👥 WD–H WE–NA before noon
- ££ £35 (£45)
- 🚗 Theydon Bois/Epping Stations 3 miles
- ⊕ Driving range & full practice facilities
- 🏠 Henry Cotton
- 🖥 www.abridgegolf.com

Ballards Gore G&CC (1980)
Proprietary
Gore Road, Canewdon, Rochford, SS4 2DA
- ☎ **(01702) 258917**
- 🖥 (01702) 258571
- 📧 iain@ballardsgore.com
- 📖 600
- ✍ Iain Evans
- 🏌 G McCarthy
- ⛳ 18 L 6874 yds SSS 73
- 👥 WD–U WE–M after 12.30pm (summer) 11.30am (winter) SOC
- ££ £35
- 🚗 1½ miles NE of Rochford
- ⊕ Practice hole; practice field 250 yards
- 🏠 Arthur Elvin
- 🖥 www.ballardsgore.com

Basildon (1967)
Public
Clayhill Lane, Kingswood, Basildon, SS16 5JP
- ☎ **(01268) 533297**
- 🖥 (01268) 284163
- 📧 basildongc@onetel.com
- 📖 300
- ✍ A Merrington
- 🏌 M Oliver (01268) 533532
- ⛳ 18 L 6236 yds Par 72 SSS 70
- 👥 U SOC
- ££ £14 (£18.40)
- 🚗 1 mile S of Basildon, off A176 at Kingswood roundabout
- ⊕ Practice area
- 🖥 www.basildongolfclub.org.uk

Belfairs (1926)
Public
Eastwood Road North, Leigh-on-Sea, SS9 4LR
- ☎ **(01702) 525345 (Starter)**

Belhus Park G&CC (1972)
Pay and play
Belhus Park, South Ockendon, RM15 4QR
- ☎ **(01708) 854260**

Bentley (1972)
Ongar Road, Brentwood, CM15 9SS
- ☎ **(01277) 373179**

- 🖥 (01277) 375097
- 📧 info@bentleygolfclub.com
- 📖 550
- ✍ Andy Hall
- 🏌 N Garrett (01277) 372933
- ⛳ 18 L 6709 yds SSS 72
- 👥 WD–UH WE–M after noon BH–after 11am SOC–WD
- ££ £27.50 D–£42
- 🚗 18 miles E of London. M25 Junction 28, 3 miles
- 🏠 Alec Swan
- 🖥 www.bentleygolfclub.com

Benton Hall (1993)
Proprietary
Wickham Hill, Witham, CM8 3LH
- ☎ **(01376) 502454**
- 🖥 (01376) 521050
- 📧 bentonhall.sales@theclubcompany .com
- ✍ James Gathercole
- 🏌 C Fairweather
- ⛳ 18 L 6570 yds SSS 72 9 hole Par 3 course
- 👥 U SOC–WD
- ££ £26 (£32)
- 🚗 Witham, 8 miles NE of Chelmsford, off A12
- 🏠 Walker/Cox
- 🖥 www.theclubcompany.com

Birch Grove (1970)
Layer Road, Colchester, CO2 0HS
- ☎ **(01206) 734276**
- 🖥 (01206) 734276
- 📖 280
- ✍ Mrs M Marston
- ⛳ 9 L 4532 yds SSS 63
- 👥 U exc Sun–U after 1pm SOC
- ££ D–£14 (£10 for nine holes)
- 🚗 3 miles S of Colchester on B1026
- 🖥 www.birchgrovegolfclub.co.uk

Boyce Hill (1921)
Vicarage Hill, Benfleet, SS7 1PD
- ☎ **(01268) 793625**
- 🖥 (01268) 750497
- 📧 secretary@boycehillgolfclub.co.uk
- 📖 700
- ✍ D Kelly
- 🏌 G Burroughs (01268) 752565
- ⛳ 18 L 6003 yds SSS 69
- 👥 WD–UH WE/BH–MH SOC–Thurs only
- ££ D–£35
- 🚗 4 miles W of Southend
- 🏠 James Braid
- 🖥 www.boycehillgolfclub.co.uk

Braintree (1891)
Kings Lane, Stisted, Braintree, CM77 8DD
- ☎ **(01376) 346079**
- 🖥 (01376) 348677
- 📧 manager@braintreegolfclub .freeserve.co.uk
- 📖 700
- ✍ Mrs N Wells
- 🏌 T Parcell (01376) 343465
- ⛳ 18 L 6228 yds SSS 70
- 👥 WD–U H SOC
- ££ £35 (£50)

- 🚗 1 mile E of Braintree, off A120 towards Stisted
- 🏠 Hawtree
- 🖥 www.braintreegolfclub.freeserve .co.uk

Braxted Park (1953)
Braxted Park, Witham, CM8 3EN
- ☎ **(01376) 572372**
- 🖥 (01376) 572372
- 📧 golf@braxtedpark.com
- 📖 100
- ✍ Mrs V Keeble
- ⛳ 9 L 5704 yds Par 70 SSS 68
- 👥 WD–U SOC–WD
- ££ 9: £10; 18: £17
- 🚗 1½ miles off A12, nr Kelvedon
- 🏠 Sir Allen Clark
- 🖥 www.braxtedpark.com

Bunsay Downs (1982)
Public
Little Baddow Road, Woodham Walter, Maldon, CM9 6RW
- ☎ **(01245) 412648/412369**

Burnham-on-Crouch (1923)
Ferry Road, Creeksea, Burnham-on-Crouch, CM0 8PQ
- ☎ **(01621) 782282/785508**
- 🖥 (01621) 784489
- 📧 burnhamgolf@hotmail.com
- 📖 600
- ✍ C Rumble
- 🏌 S Cardy (01621) 782282
- ⛳ 18 L 6056 yds SSS 69
- 👥 WD–H SOC WE–NA before 2pm
- ££ £36 (£42) 2–4–1 accepted
- 🚗 1½ miles W of Burnham
- ⊕ Putting green; practice area, buggies
- 🏠 D Swan
- 🖥 www.burnhamgolfclub.co.uk

The Burstead (1993)
Tye Common Road, Little Burstead, Billericay, CM12 9SS
- ☎ **(01277) 631171**
- 🖥 (01277) 632766
- 📖 800
- ✍ L Mence
- 🏌 K Bridges
- ⛳ 18 L 6275 yds SSS 70
- 👥 WD–U H WE–NA pm SOC
- ££ £26 (£32)
- 🚗 2 miles S of Billericay, off A176
- 🏠 Patrick Tallack

Canons Brook (1962)
Elizabeth Way, Harlow, CM19 5BE
- ☎ **(01279) 421482**
- 🖥 (01279) 626393
- 📧 manager@canonsbrook.com
- 📖 700
- ✍ Mrs SJ Langton
- 🏌 A McGinn (01279) 418357
- ⛳ 18 L 6763 yds SSS 73
- 👥 WD–U WE/BH–M
- ££ £30 D–£35
- 🚗 25 miles N of London

⛨ Henry Cotton
🖥 www.canonsbrook.com

Castle Point   (1988)
Public
Waterside Farm, Somnes Avenue, Canvey Island, SS8 9FG
☎ **(01268) 510830**

Channels   (1974)
Belsteads Farm Lane, Little Waltham, Chelmsford, CM3 3PT
☎ **(01245) 440005**
📠 (01245) 442032
📧 info@channelsgolf.co.uk
📖 650
🏌 Mrs SJ Larner
⛳ IB Sinclair (01245) 441056
🏳 Channels: 18 L 6413 yds Par 71 SSS 71
Belsteads: 18 L 4779 yds Par 67 SSS 63
👫 WD–U WE–M SOC
££ £40 D–£55
🚗 3 miles NE of Chelmsford on A130
⊕ Pitch & putt course. Driving range
🖥 www.channelsgolf.co.uk

Chelmsford   (1893)
Widford Road, Chelmsford, CM2 9AP
☎ **(01245) 256483**
📠 (01245) 256483
📧 office@chelmsfordgc.co.uk
📖 650
🏌 G Winckless (01245) 256483
⛳ M Welch (01245) 257079
🏳 18 L 5981 yds SSS 69
👫 WD–H WE/BH–M SOC
££ £40 D–£50
🚗 Off A414 at Widford roundabout
⛨ HS Colt
🖥 www.chelmsfordgc.co.uk

Chigwell   (1925)
High Road, Chigwell, IG7 5BH
☎ **(020) 8500 2059**
📠 (020) 8501 3410
📧 info@chigwellgolfclub.co.uk
📖 780
🏌 RH Danzey
⛳ J Fuller (020) 8500 2384
🏳 18 L 6279 yds SSS 70
👫 WD–H WE/BH–M
££ £35 D–£50
🚗 13 miles NE of London (A113)
⛨ Hawtree/Taylor
🖥 www.chigwellgolfclub.co.uk

Chingford   (1923)
158 Station Road, Chingford, London E4
☎ **(0208) 529 2107**
🏌 B Sinden
⛳ A Trainor (0208) 529 5708
🏳 18 L 6342 yds Par 71 SSS 70
👫 U
££ £14 (£18)

Clacton-on-Sea   (1892)
West Road, Clacton-on-Sea, CO15 1AJ
☎ **(01255) 421919**
📠 (01255) 424602
📧 secretary@clactongolfclub.com

📖 650
🏌 Miss HL Woodrow
⛳ SJ Levermore (01255) 426304
🏳 18 L 6448 yds SSS 71
👫 H WE/BH–H after 2pm SOC–WD
££ £30 (£35)
🚗 On Clacton sea front. 13 miles E of Colchester (A120)
⊕ Pactice field; driving nets
🖥 www.clactongolfclub.com

Colchester GC   (1907)
21 Braiswick, Colchester, CO4 5AU
☎ **(01206) 853396**
📠 (01206) 852698
📧 secretary@colchestergolfclub.co.uk
📖 790
🏌 JH Wiggam
⛳ M Angel (01206) 853920
🏳 18 L 6347 yds SSS 70
👫 WD/WE–H BH–NA SOC
££ £38 D–£40 (£40)
🚗 ¾ mile NW of Colchester North Station, towards West Berholt on B1508
⊕ Driving range; practice area
⛨ James Braid
🖥 www.colchestergolfclub.co.uk

Colne Valley   (1991)
Station Road, Earls Colne, CO6 2LT
☎ **(01787) 224343**
📠 (01787) 224126
📧 info@colnevalleygolfclub.co.uk
📖 500
🏌 T Smith (01787) 224343
⛳ P Garlick (01787) 220770
🏳 18 L 6286 yds SSS 71
👫 WD–U WE/BH–after 10 (11am SOC) BH–U
££ £25 (£30)
🚗 12 miles W of Colchester (A1124)
⛨ Howard Swann
🖥 www.colnevalleygolfclub.co.uk

Crondon Park   (1994)
Proprietary
Stock Road, Stock, CM4 9DP
☎ **(01277) 841115**

Elsenham Golf Centre   (1997)
Hall Road, Elsenham, Bishop's Stortford, CM22 6DH
☎ **(01279) 812865**
📠 (01279) 816970
📧 owen-mckenna@btconnect.com
🏌 O McKenna (Prop)
⛳ O McKenna/S Smith
🏳 9 L 5854 yds Par 70
👫 U
££ 9 holes–£12 (£14) 18 holes–£16 (£18)
🚗 Off M11, by Stansted Airport
⊕ Driving range; gym
🖥 www.egcltd.co.uk

Essex G&CC   (1990)
Earls Colne, Colchester, CO6 2NS
☎ **(01787) 224466**

📠 (01787) 224410
📧 essex.golfops@theclubcompany.com
📖 800
🏌 J Gathercole (Mgr)
⛳ L Cocker, P Grotier
🏳 18 L 7019 yds Par 73
9 L 2190 yds Par 34
👫 WD–U WE–U after 11.30am SOC
££ £26 (£31)
🚗 2 miles N of A120 at Coggeshall on B1024
⊕ Floodlit driving range
⛨ Reg Plumbridge
🖥 www.theclubcompany.com

Essex Golf Centres, Hainault Forest   (1912)
Public
Romford Road, Chigwell Row, IG7 4QW
☎ **(020) 8500 2131 (Proshop/Reception)**
📧 info@essexgolfcentre.com

Five Lakes Resort   (1995)
Colchester Road, Tolleshunt Knights, Maldon, CM9 8HX
☎ **(01621) 868888 (Hotel) (01621) 862307 (Bookings)**
📠 (01621) 869696
📧 office@fivelakes.co.uk
📖 550
🏌 AD Bermingham (Dir) (01621) 862326
⛳ G Carter (01621) 862326
🏳 Links 18 L 6250 yds SSS 70
Lakes 18 L 6765 yds SSS 72
👫 U BH–U after 1pm SOC
££ Links £25 (£32). Lakes £32 (£42)
🚗 8 miles S of Colchester, on B1026
⊕ Driving range; chipping & putting green
⛨ Neil Coles
🖥 www.fivelakes.co.uk

Forrester Park   (1975)
Beckingham Road, Great Totham, Maldon, CM9 8EA
☎ **(01621) 891406**
📠 (01621) 891406
📖 900
🏌 T Forrester-Muir
⛳ G Pike (01621) 893456
🏳 18 L 6073 yds SSS 69
👫 WD–U WE–NA before noon SOC–WD
££ £21 (£22)
🚗 3 miles NE of Maldon on B1022
⊕ Practice ground; par 3 loop
⛨ Everett/Forrester-Muir
🖥 www.forresterparkltd.com

Frinton   (1895)
1 The Esplanade, Frinton-on-Sea, CO13 9EP
☎ **(01255) 674618**
📠 (01255) 682450
📧 frintongolf@lineone.net
📖 850
🏌 PH Jones
⛳ P Taggart (01255) 671618

☞ 18 L 6265 yds SSS 70
9 L 3062 yds SSS 60
⚭ 18 hole: H WE/BH–NA before
11.30am SOC
££ 9: £10 18: D–£35 (£40)
🚗 18 miles E of Colchester
⌂ W Park Jr/HS Colt
🖥 www.frintongolfclub.com

Garon Park Golf Complex
(1993)
Pay and play
Garon Park, Eastern Avenue, Southend-on-Sea, SS2 4PT
☎ **(01702) 601701**
🖳 (01702) 601033
📖 700
🖎 Mrs J Jacom
⚲ G Jacom
☞ 27 L 6156 yds SSS 70
9 hole Par 3 course
⚭ U SOC
££ £18 (£25)
🚗 E side of Southend-on-Sea. M25 Junction 29
⊕ Floodlit driving range
⌂ Walker/Cox

Gosfield Lake   (1986)
The Manor House, Gosfield, Halstead, CO9 1SE
☎ **(01787) 474747**
🖳 (01787) 476044
🖎 gosfieldlakegc@btconnect.com
📖 800
🖎 JA O'Shea (Sec/Mgr)
(01787) 474747
⚲ R Wheeler (01787) 474488
☞ Lakes 18 L 6756 yds Par 72 SSS 72
Meadows 9 L 4990 yds Par 66
⚭ Lakes WD–H WE (pm)–H by arrangement SOC. Meadows–U
££ Lakes £30 D–£35. Meadows £15 D–£18
🚗 7 miles N of Braintree (A1017)
⌂ Sir H Cotton/Swann
🖥 www.gosfield-lake-golf-club.co.uk

Hanover G&CC   (1991)
Proprietary
Hullbridge Road, Rayleigh, SS6 9QS
☎ **(01702) 232377**
🖎 hanovergolf@aol.com

Hartswood   (1967)
Pay and play
King George's Playing Fields, Brentwood, CM14 5AE
☎ **(01277) 214830 (Bookings)**
📖 270
🖎 JR Gander (01227) 218850
⚲ S Cole (01277) 218714
☞ 18 L 6192 yds SSS 70
⚭ WD–U after 10am SOC
££ £13 (£18)
🚗 E of Brentwood on A128

Harwich & Dovercourt
(1906)
Station Road, Parkeston, Harwich, CO12 4NZ
☎ **(01255) 503616**

🖳 (01255) 503323
🖎 harwichgolfclub@btinternet.com
📖 400
🖎 AR Boddy (Hon)
⚲ None
☞ 9 L 2950 yds SSS 69
⚭ WD–H WE–U after 11 am SOC
££ £20
🚗 A120 to roundabout to Parkeston Village & Golf Club (first exit)

Ilford   (1907)
291 Wanstead Park Road, Ilford, IG1 3TR
☎ **(020) 8554 2930**
🖳 (020) 8554 0822
🖎 ilfordgolfclub@btconnect.com
📖 500
🖎 Scott Vass (Mgr)
⚲ S Jackson (020) 8554 0094
☞ 18 L 5299 yds SSS 66
⚭ WD–U WE–phone Pro SOC
££ £17 (£22)
🚗 S end of M11, off A406
🖥 www.ilfordgolfclub.com

Langdon Hills   (1991)
Proprietary
Lower Dunton Road, Bulphan, RM14 3TY
☎ **(01268) 548444/544300**
🖳 (01268) 490084
🖎 secretary@golflangdon.co.uk
📖 700
🖎 K Thompson
⚲ T Moncur (01268) 544300
☞ 27 holes:
Langdon 9 L 3128 yds Par 35
Bulphan 9 L 3395 yds Par 37
Horndon 9 L 3028 yds Par 36
⚭ U SOC WD WE–NA before noon
££ £20 (£30)
🚗 SW of Basildon between A127 and A13. M25 Junction 29, 8 miles
⊕ Floodlit driving range
⌂ MRM Sandow
🖥 www.langdonhillsgolfclub.co.uk

Lexden Wood   (1993)
Pay and play
Bakers Lane, Colchester, CO3 4AU
☎ **(01206) 843333**
🖳 (01206) 854775
🖎 enquiries@lexdenwood.co.uk
📖 850
🖎 L Cole
⚲ P Grice
☞ 18 L 5160 yds Par 67 SSS 65
⚭ U SOC
££ £20 (£25)
🚗 NW of Colchester, off A12
⊕ Driving range. Pitch & putt course
⌂ Jon Johnson
🖥 www.lexdenwood.co.uk

Loughton   (1981)
Pay and play
Clays Lane, Debden Green, Loughton, IG10 2RZ
☎ **(020) 8502 2923**
📖 60
🖎 A Day
☞ 9 L 4735 yds Par 66 SSS 63
⚭ U–booking required SOC

££ 9: £8.50 (£9.50) 18: £14 (£16)
🚗 M25 Junction 26

Maldon   (1891)
Beeleigh Langford, Maldon, CM9 6LL
☎ **(01621) 853212**
🖳 (01621) 855232
🖎 maldon.golf@virgin.net
📖 350
🖎 D Kelly
☞ 9 L 6253 yds Par 71 SSS 70
⚭ WD–U WE–M SOC
££ £18 D–£25
🚗 3 miles NW of Maldon on B1019

Maylands   (1936)
Colchester Road, Harold Park, Romford RM3 0AZ
☎ **(01708) 341777**

North Weald   (1996)
Rayley Lane, North Weald, Epping, CM16 6AR
☎ **(01992) 522118**
🖳 (01992) 522881
🖎 info@northwealdgolfclub.co.uk
📖 500
🖎 S Lloyd
☞ 18 L 6377 yds Par 71 SSS 71
⚭ U SOC–WD/WE
££ £20 (£30)
🚗 1½ miles E of M11 Junction 7 on A414
⊕ Chipping area; putting green
⌂ David Williams
🖥 www.northwealdgolfclub.co.uk

The Notleys   (1995)
The Green, White Notley, Witham, CM8 1RG
☎ **(01376) 329328**
🖳 (01376) 569051
🖎 michael@notleygolf.co.uk
📖 600
🖎 M Roughan
⚲ J Lowe
☞ 18 L 6022 yds Par 71
9 hole Par 3 course
⚭ U SOC
££ £15 (£20)
🚗 Black Notley, S of Braintree, off A120
⊕ Driving range; private function hire; gym
⌂ John Day
🖥 www.notleygolf.co.uk

Orsett   (1899)
Brentwood Road, Orsett, RM16 3DS
☎ **(01375) 891352**

Regiment Way Golf Centre
(1995)
Pay and play
Back Lane, Little Waltham, Chelmsford, CM3 3PR
☎ **(01245) 361100**
🖳 (01245) 442032
🖎 info@regimentway.co.uk
📖 210
🖎 R Pamphilon

√ D Marsh
⮞ 9 L 4887 yds Par 65 SSS 64
👥 U
££ 9: £11 (£12) 18: £15 (£17)
⮞ 3 miles NE of Chelmsford (A130)
⊕ Floodlit driving range
▤ www.channelgolf.co.uk

Risebridge   (1972)
Pay and play
Risebridge Chase, Lower Bedfords Road,
Romford, RM1 4DG
☎ (01708) 741429

Rivenhall Oaks   (1994)
Pay and play
Forest Road, Witham, Essex, CM8 2PS
☎ (01376) 510222
📠 (01376) 500316
✉ info@rivenhalloaksgolf.co.uk
📖 260
📇 B Chapman
√ B Chapman/J Hudson
⮞ 9 L 3128 yds Par 36
   9 hole Par 3 course
👥 U SOC
££ £9 (£13)
⮞ 4 miles E of Witham, off A12
⊕ Floodlit driving range
⌂ Alan Walker
▤ www.rivenhalloaksgolf.co.uk

Rochford Hundred   (1893)
Rochford Hall, Hall Road, Rochford,
SS4 1NW
☎ (01702) 544302
📠 (01702) 541343
✉ admin@rochfordhundredgolfclub
   .co.uk
📖 375 90(L) 60(J)
📇 MA Boon
√ GS Hill
⮞ 18 L 6256 yds SSS 70
👥 WD–U H WE–M
££ On application
⮞ 4 miles N of Southend-on-Sea
⌂ James Braid
▤ www.rochfordhundredgolfclub
   .co.uk

Romford   (1894)
Heath Drive, Gidea Park, Romford,
RM2 5QB
☎ (01708) 740007 (Members)
📠 (01708) 752157
✉ info@romfordgolfclub.co.uk
📖 680
📇 Mrs H Robinson (01708) 740986
√ C Goddard (01708) 749393
⮞ 18 L 6410 yds SSS 71
👥 WD–I WE–NA SOC
££ £30 D–£40
⮞ 1 mile E of Romford. 3 miles W of
   M25 Junction 29
⌂ HS Colt
▤ www.romfordgolfclub.com

Royal Epping Forest   (1888)
Forest Approach, Station Road, Chingford,
London E4 7AZ
☎ (020) 8529 2195
📠 (020) 8559 4664
✉ office@refgc.co.uk

📖 160 35(L) 35(J)
📇 R Bright-Thomas (0208) 529 2195
√ A Traynor (0181) 529 5708
⮞ 18 L 6281 yds Par 71 SSS 70
   U–booking necessary SOC
££ £15 (£19)
⮞ Nr Chingford station. M25 Jct 26
   Red coats or trousers compulsory
▤ www.refgc.co.uk

Saffron Walden   (1919)
Windmill Hill, Saffron Walden, CB10 1BX
☎ (01799) 522786
📠 (01799) 520313
✉ office@swgc.com
📖 950
📇 Chris Charlton
√ P Davis (01799) 527728
⮞ 18 L 6632 yds SSS 72 (men),
   SSS 74 (ladies)
👥 WD–U H SOC WE–M NA before
   1pm Sat
££ £40 D–£50
⮞ Saffron Walden, on B184 towards
   Cambridge
▤ www.swgc.com

South Essex G&CC
Herongate, Brentwood, CM13 3LW
☎ (01277) 811289
✉ southessex@americangolf.uk.com

St Cleres
St Cleres Hall, Stanford-le-Hope, SS17 0LX
☎ (01375) 361565
📠 (01375) 361565
📖 500
📇 D Wood (01375) 361565
√ D Wood (01375) 361565
⮞ 18 holes Par 72 SSS 71
👥 U H SOC
££ £17 (£23)
⮞ 5 miles E of M25 Junction 30/31
   (A13)
⊕ Driving range; 9 hole par 3 course
   £5
⌂ Adrian Stiff

Stapleford Abbotts   (1989)
Horseman's Side, Tysea Hill, Stapleford
Abbotts, RM4 1JU
☎ (01708) 381108
   (01708) 381278 (bookings)
📠 (01708) 386345
✉ staplefordabbotts@crown-
   golf.co.uk
📖 750
📇 M Gallop (Gen Mgr)
√ J Walpole
⮞ 18 L 6501 yds SSS 71
   9 hole Par 3 course
👥 WD–U WE–H SOC
££ £31–£36
⮞ 3 miles N of Romford. M25
   Junction 28
⌂ Howard Swann
▤ www.crown-golf.co.uk

Stock Brook Manor   (1992)
Queen's Park Avenue, Stock, Billericay,
CM12 0SP
☎ (01277) 658181

📠 (01277) 633063
✉ events@stockbrook.com
📖 850
📇 C Laurence (Golf Dir)
√ C Laurence
⮞ 18 L 6905 yds SSS 73
   9 L 2952 yds SSS 69
👥 After 12 noon WE+BH
££ £30 (£35 +BH))
⮞ 5 miles S of Chelmsford on B1007
⊕ Driving range; par 3 practice area
⌂ Martin Gillett
▤ www.stockbrook.com

Theydon Bois   (1897)
Theydon Road, Theydon Bois, Epping,
CM16 4EH
☎ (01992) 813054
📠 (01992) 815602
✉ theydonboisgolf@btconnect.com
📖 600
📇 MC Slatter (01992) 813054
√ RJ Hall (01992) 812460
⮞ 18 L 5480 yds SSS 68
👥 U exc Thurs am–restricted SOC
££ £30 (£20); £18 after 5pm
⮞ 1 mile S of Epping. M25 Junction 26
⌂ James Braid

Thorndon Park   (1920)
Ingrave, Brentwood, CM13 3RH
☎ (01277) 810345
📠 (01277) 810645
✉ office@thorndonpark.com
📖 415 140(L) 50(J)
📇 Lt Col RM Estcourt
√ BV White (01277) 810736
⮞ 18 L 6512 yds SSS 71
👥 WD–U WE/BH–M
££ £45 D–£60
⮞ 2 miles SE of Brentwood on A128
⌂ HS Colt
▤ www.thorndonparkgolfclub.com

Thorpe Hall   (1907)
Thorpe Hall Avenue, Thorpe Bay, SS1 3AT
☎ (01702) 582205
📠 (01702) 584498
✉ sec@thorpehallgc.co.uk
📖 1000
📇 GH Smith
√ WJ McColl (01702) 588195
⮞ 18 L 6290 yds SSS 70
👥 WD–H SOC–Fri only
££ On application
⮞ E of Southend-on-Sea

Three Rivers G&CC
   (1973)
Stow Road, Purleigh, Chelmsford, CM3 6RR
☎ (01621) 828631

Toot Hill   (1991)
School Road, Toot Hill, Ongar, CM5 9PU
☎ (01277) 365747
📠 (01277) 364509
📖 400
📇 Mrs Cameron
√ M Bishop
⮞ 18 L 6053 yds Par 70 SSS 69
👥 WE after 1pm SOC–WD

££ £25 (£30)
⊶ 2 miles W of Ongar
⊕ Practice range
⌂ Martin Gillett

Top Meadow (1986)
Fen Lane, North Ockendon, RM14 3PR
☎ **(01708) 852239 (Clubhouse)**
✉ info@topmeadow.co.uk

Unex Towerlands
(1985)
Panfield Road, Braintree, CM7 5BJ
☎ **(01376) 326802**
🖷 (01376) 552487
✉ info@unextowerlands.com
📖 250
🏌 Brian Clark
➢ 9 L 5559 yds Par 68
👥 WD–U exc Wed–NA after 4.30pm
    WE–NA before 1pm SOC
££ 9: £10; 18: £12 (£14)
⊶ 1 mile NW of Braintree (B1053)
▤ www.unextowerlands.com

Upminster (1928)
114 Hall Lane, Upminster, RM14 1AU
☎ **(01708) 222788**
🖷 (01708) 222484
✉ secretary@upminstergolfclub.co.uk
📖 936
🏌 RP Winmill
⁄ S Cipa (01708) 220000
➢ 18 L 6031 yds SSS 69
👥 WD–U H exc Tues am Ladies Day
    WE/BH–NA SOC
££ £26 D–£31
⊶ Station 3/4 mile
⊕ Practice school; practice nets
▤ www.upminstergolfclub.co.uk

Wanstead (1893)
*Overton Drive, Wanstead, London
E11 2LW*
☎ **(0208) 989 3938**
🖷 (020) 8532 9138
✉ wgclub@aol.com
📖 650
🏌 K Jones (020) 8989 3938
⁄ D Hawkins (020) 8989 9876
➢ 18 L 6015 yds SSS 69
👥 WD–H WE/BH–M
££ D–£40
⊶ Off A12, nr Wanstead station
⌂ James Braid
▤ www.wansteadgolf.org.uk

Warley Park (1975)
*Magpie Lane, Little Warley, Brentwood,
CM13 3DX*
☎ **(01277) 224891**
🖷 (01277) 200679
✉ enquiries@warleyparkgc.co.uk
📖 800
🏌 S Young
⁄ K Smith (01277) 200441
➢ 27 hole course
👥 WD–H
££ £50
⊶ 2 miles S of Brentwood. M25
    Junction 29

⊕ Practice ground
⌂ Reg Plumbridge
▤ www.warleyparkgc.co.uk

Warren (1932)
Woodham Walter, Maldon, CM9 6RW
☎ **(01245) 223258/223198**
🖷 (01245) 223989
✉ enquiries@warrengolfclub.co.uk
📖 800
🏌 MFL Durham (01245) 223258
⁄ D Brooks (01245) 224662
➢ 18 L 6263 yds SSS 70
👥 WD–H WE–M SOC
££ £30 D–£36
⊶ 7 miles E of Chelmsford, off A414
⊕ Golf Academy (01245) 224662;
    large practice area
▤ www.warrengolfclub.co.uk

Weald Park (1994)
*Coxtie Green Road, South Weald,
Brentwood, CM14 5RJ*
☎ **(01277) 375101**

West Essex (1900)
*Bury Road, Sewardstonebury, Chingford,
London E4 7QL*
☎ **(020) 8529 7558**
🖷 (020) 8524 7870
✉ sec@westessexgolfclub.co.uk
📖 720
🏌 Peter J Clarke
⁄ R Joyce (020) 8529 4367
➢ 18 L 6289 yds SSS 70
👥 WD–U H WE/BH–M H
    SOC–Mon/Wed/Fri
££ £45 D–£50
⊶ 2 miles N of Chingford BR station.
    M25 Junction 26
⊕ Driving range; short game area; dry
    bays; putting green; practice bunker
⌂ James Braid
▤ www.westessexgolfclub.co.uk

Woodford (1890)
*2, Sunset Avenue, Woodford Green,
IG8 0ST*
☎ **(020) 8504 0553
    (Clubhouse)**
🖷 (020) 8559 0504
✉ office@woodfordgolf.co.uk
📖 400
🏌 PS Willett (020) 8504 3330
⁄ J Robson (020) 8504 4254
➢ 9 L 5867 yds Par 70 SSS 69
👥 WD–U exc Tues am WE–NA Sat
    before 12.30pm U–Sun after
    9.45am SOC
££ £9–£16
⊶ 11 miles NE of London
⊕ Major item of red clothing to be
    worn on course
⌂ Tom Dunn
▤ www.woodfordgolf.co.uk

Woolston Manor
(1994)
*Woolston Manor, Abridge Road, Chigwell,
IG7 6BX*
☎ **(020) 8500 2549**

Brickhampton Court Golf Complex
Proprietary
*Cheltenham Road East, Churchdown,
Gloucestershire GL2 9QF*
☎ **(01452) 859444**
✉ info@brickhampton.co.uk

Bristol & Clifton (1891)
*Beggar Bush Lane, Failand, Clifton, Bristol
BS8 3TH*
☎ **(01275) 393474/393117**
🖷 (01275) 394611
📖 850
🏌 CR Vane Percy (01275) 393474
⁄ P Mitchell (01275) 393031
➢ 18 L 6387 yds SSS 71
👥 WD–UH WE/BH–UH after 11am
    SOC
££ On request
⊶ 2 miles W of suspension bridge. 4
    miles S of M5 Junction 19
⊕ Driving range; chipping green;
    practice bunkers
▤ www.bristolgolf.co.uk

Broadway (1895)
*Willersey Hill, Broadway, Worcs,
WR12 7LG*
☎ **(01386) 853683**
🖷 (01386) 858643
✉ secretary@broadwaygolfclub.co.uk
📖 515 165(L) 75(J)
🏌 Mr V Tofts (01386) 853683
⁄ M Freeman (01386) 853275
➢ 18 L 6228 yds Par 72 SSS 70
👥 H exc Sat–M SOC
££ £30 (£38)
⊶ 1½ miles E of Broadway (A44)
⊕ Driving/practice range
⌂ James Braid
▤ www.broadwaygolfclub.co.uk

Canons Court (1982)
*Bradley Green, Wotton-under-Edge,
GL12 7PN*
☎ **(01453) 843128**
📖 200
🏌 A Bennett
⁄ I Watts
➢ 9 L 5724 yds SSS 65
👥 U
££ £10 (£15)
⊶ 3 miles E of M5 Junction 14, off
    B4058
⊕ Driving range
▤ www.figolf.com

Chipping Sodbury (1905)
*Trinity Lane, Chipping Sodbury, Bristol
BS37 6PU*
☎ **(01454) 312024 (Members)**
🖷 (01454) 319042
✉ info@chippingsodburygolfclub.co.uk
📖 750
🏌 Bob Williams
⁄ M Watts (01454) 314087
➢ 18 L 6786 yds SSS 73

WD–U WE–pm only
££ £32 (£45)
⊕ 12 miles NE of Bristol. M4 Jct 18, 5 miles. M5 Jct 14, 9 miles.
⊕ Practice range
⌂ Fred Hawtree
▤ www.chippingsodburygolfclub.co.uk

Cirencester   (1893)

Cheltenham Road, Bagendon, Cirencester, GL7 7BH
☎ (01285) 652465
▢ (01285) 650665
✉ info@cirencestergolfclub.co.uk
▥ 800
⚲ R Caldecott (01285) 652465
⌖ E Goodwin (01285) 656124
▷ 18 L 6055 yds Par 70 SSS 69
▩ H SOC–WD
££ £32 (£38)
⊕ 1½ miles N of Cirencester on A435
⊕ Driving range; 6 hole par 3 academy
⌂ James Braid
▤ www.cirencestergolfclub.co.uk

Cleeve Hill   (1892)

Pay and play
Cleeve Hill, Cheltenham, GL52 3PW
☎ (01242) 672025
▢ (01242) 678444
✉ hugh.fitzsimons@btconnect.com
⚲ Hugh Fitzsimons (Mgr)
⌖ D Finch (01242) 672592
▷ 18 L 6448 yds Par 72 SSS 71
▩ U
££ £15 (£18+BH)
⊕ 3 miles N of Cheltenham on A46 to Winchcombe
⊕ Putting green
▤ www.clevehillgolfcourse.com

Cotswold Edge   (1980)

Upper Rushmire, Wotton-under-Edge, GL12 7PT
☎ (01453) 844167

Cotswold Hills   (1902)

Ullenwood, Cheltenham, GL53 9QT
☎ (01242) 515264
▢ (01242) 515317
✉ contact.us@cotswoldhills-golfclub.com
▥ 750
⚲ Mrs A Hale (Mgr)
⌖ J Latham (01242) 515263
▷ 18 L 6849 yds Par 72 SSS 72
▩ U–recognised club members SOC After 9.30 until 12.30 then after 2pm
££ £33 D–£36 (£38 D–£40)
⊕ 3 miles S of Cheltenham. M5 Junction 11A
⌂ MD Little
▤ www.cotswoldhills-golfclub.com

Dymock Grange   (1995)

The Old Grange, Leominster Road, Dymock, GL18 2AN
☎ (01531) 890840

Filton   (1909)

Golf Course Lane, Bristol, BS34 7QS
☎ (0117) 969 4169
▢ (0117) 931 4359
✉ thesecretary@filtongolfclub.co.uk
▥ 700
⚲ T Atkinson (0117) 969 6968
⌖ D Kelley (0117) 969 6968
▷ 18 L 6174 yds SSS 70
▩ WD–U WE/BH–M SOC–WD H
££ D–£28
⊕ 4 miles N of Bristol, M5 J16
⌂ Hawtree
▤ www.filtongolfclub.co.uk

Forest Hills   (1992)

Proprietary
Mile End Road, Coleford, GL16 7BY
☎ (01594) 810620
▢ (01594) 810823
▥ 550
⚲ D Bowen (01594) 837134
⌖ R Ballard (01594) 810620
▷ 18 L 6300 yds SSS 72
▩ U SOC
££ £17 (£22)
⊕ 1 mile E of Coleford (B4028)
⊕ Driving range
⌂ Adrian Stiff
▤ www.fweb.org.uk/forestgolf

Forest of Dean   (1973)

Lords Hill, Coleford, GL16 8BE
☎ (01594) 832583
▢ (01594) 832584
✉ enquiries@bellshotel.co.uk
▥ 500
⚲ R Sanzen-Baker (Hon Sec) E Ludlam (Man Dir)
⌖ Paul Davies (01594) 833689
▷ 18 L 5682 yds SSS 69
▩ U SOC
££ £18 (£25)
⊕ ½ mile SE of Coleford on Parkend road. M50, 10 miles
⌂ John Day
▤ www.bellshotel.co.uk

The Gloucestershire   (1976)

Tracy Park Estate, Bath Road, Wick, Bristol, BS30 5RN
☎ (0117) 937 2251
✉ golf@thegloucestershire.com

Gloucester Hotel   (1976)

Matson Lane, Gloucester, GL4 9EA
☎ (01452) 525653

Henbury   (1891)

Westbury-on-Trym, Bristol, BS10 7QB
☎ (0117) 950 0660

Hilton Puckrup Hall Hotel   (1992)

Puckrup, Tewkesbury, GL20 6EL
☎ (01684) 296200/271591
▢ (01684) 850788
▥ 400
⚲ J Stuart

⌖ M Fenning
▷ 18 L 6219 yds SSS 70
▩ WD SOC WE–residents
££ £30 (£35)
⊕ 2 miles N of Tewkesbury on A38. M50 Junction 1. M5 Junction 8
⌂ Simon Gidman
▤ www.puckrupgolf.co.uk

The Kendleshire

Proprietary
Henfield Road, Coalpit Heath, Bristol, BS36 2TG
☎ (0117) 956 7007
▢ (0117) 957 3433
✉ info@kendleshire.com
▥ 750
⚲ P Murphy
⌖ T Mealing (0117) 956 7000
▷ 27 L 6249-6544 yds Par 70-71
▩ U SOC
££ £32 (£35)
⊕ 1 mile NE of Bristol. M32 Jct 1
⊕ Driving range. Golf Academy
⌂ Adrian Stiff/Peter McEvoy
▤ www.kendleshire.com

Knowle   (1905)

Fairway, West Town Lane, Brislington, Bristol, BS4 5DF
☎ (0117) 977 0660
▢ (0117) 972 0615
▥ 600
⚲ MJ Harrington (0117) 977 0660
⌖ R Hayward (0117) 977 9193
▷ 18 L 6006 yds SSS 69
▩ WD exc Thurs–H WE/BH–H SOC–Thurs
££ £28 D–£35 (£33 D–£40)
⊕ Brislington Hill, 3 miles S of Bristol, off A4
⌂ JH Taylor
▤ www.knowlegolfclub.co.uk

Lilley Brook   (1922)

Cirencester Road, Charlton Kings, Cheltenham, GL53 8EG
☎ (01242) 526785
▢ (01242) 256880
✉ secretary@lilleybrook.co.uk
▥ 750
⚲ MF Jordan (Gen Mgr)
⌖ K Hayler (01242) 525201
▷ 18 L 6226 yds SSS 70
▩ WD–H or I (recognised club members) WE–M SOC–WD
££ £30 D–£35 (£35 pm only)
⊕ 3 miles SE of Cheltenham on A435. M5 Junction 11A
⌂ McKenzie
▤ www.lilleybrook.co.uk

Long Ashton   (1893)

Clarken Coombe, Long Ashton, Bristol, BS41 9DW
☎ (01275) 392229
▢ (01275) 394395
✉ secretary@longashtongolfclub.co.uk
▥ 750
⌖ M Hart (01275) 392229
▷ 18 L 6077 yds SSS 70

🏌 WD–U H WE/BH–I H SOC–Wed
& Fri
££ £30 (£35)
🚗 3 miles S of Bristol on B3128
🏠 JH Taylor
🖳 www.longashtongolfclub.co.uk

Lydney (1909)
*The Links, Off Lakeside Avenue, Lydney,
GL15 5QA*
☎ (01594) 842614

Minchinhampton (1889)
Minchinhampton, Stroud, GL6 9BE
☎ (01453) 832642 (Old)
(01453) 833840 (New)
📠 (01453) 837360
📧 secretary@mgcnew.co.uk
📖 1860
🏌 R East (01453) 833866
⛳ C Steele (01453) 837351
🏞 Old 18 L 6019 yds SSS 69
Avening 18 L 6263 yds SSS 70
Cherington 18 L 6430 yds SSS 71
🏌 H SOC
££ Old–£16 (£19). New–£40 (£50)
(2006 rates – subject to review)
🚗 Old-3 miles E of Stroud. New-5
miles E of Stroud
🏠 Old: R Wilson. Avening: F
Hawtree. Cherington: M Hawtree
🖳 www.mgcnew.co.uk

Naunton Downs (1993)
Proprietary
Naunton, Cheltenham, GL54 3AE
☎ (01451) 850090
📠 (01451) 850091
📧 admin@nauntondowns.co.uk
📖 750
🏌 Jane Ayers
⛳ N Ellis (01451) 850092
🏞 18 L 6135 yds Par 71 SSS 69
🏌 WD–U–by arrangement WE–NA
before 11am
££ £22 (£28)
🚗 5 miles SW of Stow-on-the-Wold,
on B4068
🏠 Jacob Pott
🖳 www.nauntondowns.co.uk

Newent (1994)
Pay and play
Coldharbour Lane, Newent, GL18 1DJ
☎ (01531) 820478

Painswick (1891)
*Golf Course Road, Painswick, Stroud,
GL6 6TL*
☎ (01452) 812180
📧 hello@painswickgolf.com
📖 300
🏌 Mrs Ann Smith
⛳ None
🏞 18 L 4780 yds SSS 63
🏌 WD/Sat–U Sun–M SOC
££ £17.50 (Sat £20). With member
£12.50 (Sat £15)
🚗 ½ mile N of Painswick on A46
⊕ Practice nets; putting green
🏠 David Brown
🖳 www.painswickgolf.com

Rodway Hill (1991)
Pay and play
Newent Road, Highnam, GL2 8DN
☎ (01452) 384222
📠 (01452) 313814
📖 400
🏌 A Price
🏞 18 L 6040 yds Par 70 SSS 69
🏌 U SOC
££ 18: £14 (£16). 9: £8 (£9)
🚗 2 miles W of Gloucester (B4215)
🏠 J Gabb

Sherdons Golf Centre (1993)
Pay and play
Tredington, Tewkesbury, GL20 7BP
☎ (01684) 274782
📠 (01684) 275358
📧 info@sherdons.co.uk
📖 300
🏌 R Chatham
⛳ P Clark, J Parker
🏞 9 L 2654 yds Par 34 SSS 65
🏌 U
££ 9: £9 (£10) 18: £15 (£17)
🚗 2 miles S of Tewkesbury, off A38
⊕ Driving range
🖳 www.sherdons.co.uk

Shirehampton Park (1904)
Park Hill, Shirehampton, Bristol, BS11 0UL
☎ (0117) 982 2083
📠 (0117) 982 5280
📧 info@shirehamptonparkgolfclub
.co.uk
📖 600
🏌 Karen Rix (0117) 982 2083
⛳ B Ellis (0117) 982 2488
🏞 18 L 5430 yds Par 67 SSS 66
🏌 WD–H WE–M SOC
££ £22 (£20)
🚗 2 miles E of M5 Junction 18, on
B4054
🖳 www.shirehamptonparkgolfclub
.co.uk

Stinchcombe Hill (1889)
Stinchcombe Hill, Dursley, GL11 6AQ
☎ (01453) 542015
📠 (01453) 549545
📧 secretary@stinchcombehill.plus
.com
📖 550
🏌 Ian Crowther
⛳ P Bushell (01453) 543878
🏞 18 L 5734 yds SSS 68
🏌 U–phone Pro SOC
££ £26 (£36)
🚗 1 mile W of Dursley. M5 J14
northbound, J13 southbound
🏠 A Hoare
🖳 www.stinchcombehillgolfclub.com

Tewkesbury Park Hotel (1976)
*Lincoln Green Lane, Tewkesbury,
GL20 7DN*
☎ (01684) 295405 (Hotel)
📠 (01684) 292386
📧 golfsec.tewkesburypark
@corushotels.com

📖 600
🏌 RH Love (01684) 272322
⛳ Marc Cottrell (01684) 272320
🏞 18 L 6533 yds Par 73 SSS 71
6 hole Par 3 course
🏌 WD–U H WE–restricted
SOC–WD
££ £25 (£35)
🚗 ½ mile S of Tewkesbury on A38.
M5 Junction 9, 2 miles
⊕ Driving range; putting green;
practice area
🖳 www.tewkesburyparkgolfclub.co.uk

Thornbury Golf Centre (1992)
Bristol Road, Thornbury, BS35 3XL
☎ (01454) 281144
📠 (01454) 281177
📧 info@thornburygc.co.uk
📖 500
🏌 K Pickett (Mgr)
⛳ M Smedley
🏞 18 L 6308 yds SSS 70 Par 71
18 L 2195 yds Par 54
🏌 U SOC–WD
££ £19 (£23)
🚗 10 miles N of Bristol, off A38
⊕ Driving range
🏠 Hawtree
🖳 www.thornburygc.co.uk

Woodlands G&CC (1989)
Pay and play
*Woodlands Lane, Almondsbury, Bristol,
BS32 4JZ*
☎ (01454) 619319
📠 (01454) 619397
📧 golf@woodlands-golf.com
🏌 D Knipe
⛳ L Riddiford
🏞 18 L 6100 yds SSS 70
🏌 U SOC
££ £14 (£16)
🚗 Nr M5 Junction 16
🖳 www.woodlands-golf.com

Woodspring G&CC (1994)
Yanley Lane, Long Ashton, Bristol, BS41 9LR
☎ (01275) 394378
📠 (01275) 394473
📧 info@woodspring-golf.com
🏌 D Knipe
⛳ K Pitts
🏞 27 holes:
6209-6587 yds Par 71 SSS 70-71
🏌 WD WE SOC
££ £30 (£34). Fairway rate £15 (£17)
🚗 2 miles S of Bristol on A38.
⊕ Floodlit driving range
🏠 Allis/Clark/Steel
🖳 www.woodspring-golf.com

Hampshire

Alresford (1890)
*Cheriton Road, Tichborne Down, Alresford,
SO24 0PN*
☎ (01962) 733746
📠 (01962) 736040

secretary@alresfordgolf.co.uk
625
D Maskery
M Scott (01962) 733998
18 L 5905 yds Par 69 SSS 69
U SOC–WD
£22–£28 (£30–£35)
1 m S of Alresford on B3046, 2 m N of A272
Practice ground, covered bays
Scott Webb Young
www.alresfordgolf.co.uk

Alton   (1908)
Old Odiham Road, Alton, GU34 4BU
(01420) 82042

Ampfield Par Three
(1963)
Winchester Road, Ampfield, Romsey, SO51 9BQ
(01794) 368480

Andover   (1907)
51 Winchester Road, Andover, SP10 2EF
(01264) 323980
(01264) 358040
secretary@andovergolfclub.co.uk
455 48(L) 80(J)
G Davis (01264) 358040
I Powell (01264) 324151
9 L 6096 yds SSS 69
U H SOC WD
£21 (£26)
1/2 mile S of Andover on A3057
JH Taylor
www.andovergolfclub.co.uk

Army   (1883)
Laffan's Road, Aldershot, GU11 2HF
(01252) 337272
(01252) 337562
secretary@armygolfclub.com
750
John Hiscock (01252) 337272
G Cowley (01252) 336722
18 L 6579 yds SSS 71
WD–H–contact Sec/Mgr SOC
Special rates for military per
Between Aldershot and Farnborough
www.armygolfclub.com

Barton-on-Sea   (1897)
Milford Road, New Milton, BH25 5PP
(01425) 615308
(01425) 621457
admin@barton-on-sea-golf.co.uk
800
G Prince
P Rodgers (01425) 611210
27 holes:
L 6289-6505 yds Par 72
H NA before 9am SOC–WD exc Tues
D–£42 (D–£50)
1 mile from New Milton, off B3058
J Hamilton Stutt/H Colt
www.barton-on-sea-golf.co.uk

Basingstoke   (1907)
Kempshott Park, Basingstoke, RG23 7LL
(01256) 465990
(01256) 331793
enquiries@basingstokegolfclub.co.uk
700
S Lawrence
G Shoesmith (01256) 351332
18 L 6350 yds SSS 70
WD–H WE–M SOC–Wed & Thurs
£40 D–£50
3 miles W of Basingstoke on A30. M3 Junction 7
Practice area
James Braid
www.basingstokegolfclub.co.uk

Bishopswood   (1978)
Proprietary
Bishopswood Lane, Tadley, Basingstoke, RG26 4AT
(0118) 981 2200/5213
(0118) 940 8606
420
Mrs J Jackson-Smith (0118) 982 0312
S Ward
9 L 6474 yds Par 72 SSS 71
WD–U WE–M SOC
9: £13; 18: £19
6 miles N of Basingstoke, off A340
12- bay floodlit driving range
Blake/Phillips
www.bishopswoodgolfcourse.co.uk

Blackmoor   (1913)
Whitehill, Bordon, GU35 9EH
(01420) 472775
(01420) 487666
admin@blackmoorgolf.co.uk
680 100(L) 70(J)
Mrs J Dean (Admin Mgr)
S Clay (01420) 472345
18 L 6164 yds SSS 70
WD–H SOC–WD
£40 D–£55
1/2 mile W of Whitehill on A325
HS Colt
www.blackmoorgolf.co.uk

Blacknest   (1993)
Blacknest, GU34 4QL
(01420) 22888
(01420) 22001
blacknestgc@btconnect.com
500
A Corbett
D Burgess
18 L 5938 yds SSS 69
6 hole Par 3 course
U SOC
£20 (£25)
7 miles SW of Farnham, off A325
Driving range

Blackwater Valley
Chandlers Lane, Yateley, Hampshire, GU46 7SZ
(01252) 874725

Botley Park Hotel G&CC
(1989)
Winchester Road, Boorley Green, Botley, SO3 2UA
(01489) 780888 Ext 451
(01489) 789242
golf.botley@mcdonald-hotels.co.uk
700
Dean Rossilli (Gen Mgr)
Mark Smith (01489) 789771
18 L 6389 yds SSS 70
SOC WD–U WE–NA before noon
£30 (£40) SOC on request
6 miles E of Southampton on B3354. M27 Junction 7. 8 miles SE of M3 Junction 11
Driving range; leisure club; swimming pool; squash courts; tennis courts
Potterton/Murray
www.mcdonald-hotels.co.uk

Bramshaw   (1880)
Brook, Lyndhurst, SO43 7HE
(023) 8081 3433
(023) 8081 3460
1075
Ian Baker
C Bonner (023) 8081 3434
Forest 18 L 5774 yds SSS 68
Manor 18 L 6527 yds SSS 71
WD–U WE–by arrangement H Soc–WD only
Forest: £28 D–£50 (£35) Manor: £37 D–£50 (£42)
10 miles SW of Southampton. M27 Junction 1, 1 mile
www.bramshaw.co.uk

Brokenhurst Manor   (1915)
Sway Road, Brockenhurst, SO42 7SG
(01590) 623332
(01590) 624140
secretary@brokenhurst-manor.org.uk
800
PE Clifford
B Parker (01590) 623092
18 L 6222 yds SSS 70
WD–H after 9.30am exc Tues–Ladies' Day SOC–Thurs only
£48 D–£58 (£58 D–£73)
1 mile SW of Brockenhurst on B3055
HS Colt
www.brokenhurst-manor.org.uk

Burley   (1905)
Cott Lane, Burley, Ringwood, BH24 4BB
(01425) 403737 (Clubhouse)
(01425) 404168
secretary@burleygolfclub.co.uk
520
DC Gough (01425) 402431
9 L 6149 yds Par 71 SSS 69
Bona fide club members only – H preferred
£16 (£20) W–£75
4 miles SE of Ringwood
www.burleygolfclub.co.uk

Cams Hall Estate

Cams Hall Estate, Fareham, PO16 8UP
☎ **(01329) 827222**

Chilworth   (1989)

*Main Road, Chilworth, Southampton,
SO16 7JP*
☎ **(023) 8074 0544**

Corhampton   (1891)

Corhampton, Southampton, SO32 3LP
☎ **(01489) 877279**
⌨ (01489) 877680
✉ secretary@corhamptongc.co.uk
📖 550
🏌 Margaret Middleton
⌁ I Roper (01489) 877638
🏴 18 L 6444 yds SSS 71
👫 WD–U H WE/BH–M SOC–Mons
& Thurs
££ £30 D–£40
⊷ 9 miles S of Winchester
🖥 www.corhamptongc.co.uk

Dibden Golf Centre   (1974)

Public
*Main Road, Dibden, Southampton,
SO45 5TB*
☎ **(023) 8020 7508 (Bookings)**

Dummer   (1993)

Dummer, Basingstoke, RG25 2AF
☎ **(01256) 397888**
⌨ (01256) 397889
✉ enquiries@dummergolfclub.com
📖 650
🏌 Steve Wright (Mgr)
⌁ A Fannon (01256) 397950
🏴 18 L 6500 yds SSS 71
👫 U SOC
££ £28 all week; twilight rates
available 25% off if played as 4–ball
Monthly Web offers
⊷ 4 miles SW of Basingstoke, by M3
Junction 7
⊕ 10 bay covered driving range, open
to public
🏠 Peter Alliss
🖥 www.dummergolfclub.com

Dunwood Manor   (1969)

Danes Road, Awbridge, Romsey, SO51 0GF
☎ **(01794) 340549**
⌨ (01794) 341215
✉ admin@dunwood-golf.co.uk
📖 480
🏌 Hazel Johnson
⌁ H Teschner (01794) 340663
🏴 18 L 5767 yds SSS 69
👫 WE/BH–restricted SOC–WD
££ £32 D–£45 (£45)
⊷ Romsey 4 miles, off A27
🖥 www.dunwood-golf.co.uk

Fleetlands   (1961)

Fareham Road, Gosport, PO13 0AW
☎ **(023) 9254 4492**

Four Marks   (1994)

*Headmore Lane, Four Marks, Alton,
GU34 3ES*
☎ **(01420) 587214**

⌨ (01420) 587324
📖 180
⌁ P Chapman (01420) 587214
🏴 9 L 2077 yds Par 62 SSS 61
👫 U SOC
££ 9: £7.50 (£8.50)
⊷ 4.4 miles SW of Alton, Hampshire
🏠 Wright/Falloon/Wrigglesworth

Furzeley   (1993)

Pay and play
Furzeley Road, Denmead, PO7 6TX
☎ **(023) 9223 1180**

Gosport & Stokes Bay

    (1885)
Fort Road, Haslar, Gosport, PO12 2AT
☎ **(023) 925 27941**
⌨ (023) 925 27941
✉ secretary@gosportandstokesbay
golfclub.co.uk
📖 500
🏌 Mark Chivers (023) 925 27941
🏴 9 L 5995 yds SSS 69
👫 U exc Sun am–NA
SOC–Mon/Tues/Wed/Fri/Sat
££ £17 (£22)
⊷ S boundary of Gosport
⊕ Putting green, chipping area, driving
nets
🖥 www.gosportandstokesbaygolfclub
.co.uk

The Hampshire   (1993)

*Winchester Road, Goodworth Clatford,
Andover, SP11 7TB*
☎ **(01264) 357555**
⌨ (01264) 356606
✉ enquiries@thehampshiregolfclub
.co.uk
📖 500
🏌 T Fiducia
⌁ I Powell
🏴 18 L 6382 yds Par 72
9 hole Par 3 course
👫 U SOC WD WE after midday
££ £20 (£27)
⊷ 1 mile SW of Andover (A3057)
⊕ Covered driving range
🏠 T Fiducia
🖥 www.thehampshiregolfclub.co.uk

Hartley Wintney   (1891)

*London Road, Hartley Wintney, Hook,
RG27 8PT*
☎ **(01252) 844211**
⌨ (01252) 844211
✉ office@hartleywintneygolfclub.com
📖 750
🏌 AH Jackson
⌁ M Smith
🏴 18 L 6240 yds Par 71 SSS 71
👫 Wed–Ladies Day
WE/BH–restricted SOC
££ £33 (£38)
⊷ A30 between Camberley and
Basingstoke
🖥 www.hartleywintneygolfclub.com

Hayling   (1883)

Links Lane, Hayling Island, PO11 0BX
☎ **(023) 9246 4446**

⌨ (023) 9246 1119
✉ generaloffice@haylinggolf.co.uk
📖 1020
🏌 Ian Walton (023) 9246 4446
⌁ R Gadd (023) 9246 4491
🏴 18 L 6531 yds SSS 71
👫 H WE/BH–after 10am SOC–Tues
& Wed
££ £45 (£60)
⊷ 5 miles S of Havant on A3023
🏠 Taylor (1905)/Simpson (1933)

Hockley   (1914)

Twyford, Winchester, SO21 1PL
☎ **(01962) 713165**
⌨ (01962) 713612
✉ secretary@hockleygolfclub.com
📖 750
🏌 Mrs L Dyer
⌁ G Stubbington
🏴 18 L 6336 yds SSS 70
👫 U H SOC
££ On application
⊷ 2 miles S of Winchester on B3335
🏠 James Braid
🖥 www.hockleygolfclub.com

Lee-on-the-Solent   (1905)

Brune Lane, Lee-on-the-Solent, PO13 9PB
☎ **(023) 925 51170**
⌨ (023) 925 54233
✉ enquiries@leeonthesolentgolfclub
.co.uk
📖 700
🏌 Rob Henderson (Mgr)
(023) 925 51170
⌁ R Edwards (023) 925 51181
🏴 18 L 5926 yds SSS 69
👫 WD–U H WE H SOC–U
££ D–£36 (£40)
⊷ 3 miles S of Fareham. M27 Jct 11
⊕ Practice area; putting, chipping and
practice bunkers
🏠 John D Dunn & John H Stutt
🖥 www.leegolf.co.uk

Liphook   (1922)

Liphook, GU30 7EH
☎ **(01428) 723271/723785**
⌨ (01428) 724853
✉ secretary@liphookgolfclub.com
📖 700
🏌 John Douglass
(01428) 723785/723271
⌁ I Mowbray
🏴 18 L 6167 yds SSS 69
👫 I H (max 24) Sun–NA before 1pm
SOC
££ £50 D–£63 (tbc)
⊷ 1 mile S of Liphook on B2070 (old
A3)
🏠 ACG Croome
🖥 www.liphookgolfclub.com

Meon Valley   (1979)

*Sandy Lane, Shedfield, Southampton,
SO32 2HQ*
☎ **(01329) 833455**
⌨ (01329) 834411
📖 730
🏌 GF McMenemy (Golf Dir)
⌁ R Cameron

☞ 18 L 6520 yds SSS 71
9 L 2885 yds SSS 68
🏌 H SOC
££ 9: £12 18: £44 (£52)
🚗 2 miles NW of Wickham. N off
A334
⊕ Driving range; full practice facilities
🏠 J Hamilton Stutt

New Forest (1888)
Southampton Road, Lyndhurst, SO43 7BU
☎ (023) 8028 2752
📧 tonyatnfgc@aol.com
📖 500
🏌 AJ Taylor (023) 8028 2484
⚐ K Nolan
☞ 18 L 5526 yds SSS 67
🏌 U exc Sun am SOC–WD
££ £17 D–£27 (£23 D–£32)
🚗 8 miles W of Southampton on A35
📧 www.newforestgolfclub.co.uk

North Hants (1904)
Minley Road, Fleet, GU51 1RF
☎ (01252) 616443
📠 (01252) 811627
📧 secretary@north-hants-fleetgc
.co.uk
📖 650
🏌 G Hogg
⚐ S Porter (01252) 616655
☞ 18 L 6472 yds Par 70 SSS 72
🏌 WD–H by prior arrangement
WE/BH–MH SOC–Tues & Wed
££ On application
🚗 3 miles W of Farnborough on
B3013. M3 Junction 4A
🏠 James Braid
📧 www.northhantsgolf..co.uk

Old Thorns (1982)
Pay and play
Longmoor Road, Griggs Green, Liphook,
GU30 7PE
☎ (01428) 724555

Otterbourne Golf Centre (1995)
Pay and play
Poles Lane, Otterbourne, Winchester,
SO21 2EL
☎ (01962) 775225
🏌 G Buck
☞ 9 L 1939 yds Par
🏌 U
££ £4 (£6.50)
🚗 On A31 between Otterbourne and
Hursley
⊕ Driving range

Park (1995)
Pay and play
Avington, Winchester, SO21 1DA
☎ (01962) 779945 (Clubhouse)
📠 (01962) 779530
📧 office@avingtongolf.co.uk
📖 350
🏌 R Stent (Prop) (01962) 779955
⚐ None
☞ 9 L 1907 yds Par 61 SSS 58
🏌 U SOC

££ 9: £9.80 (£12). 18: £14.70 (£18)
🚗 4 miles E of Winchester. M3
Junction 9
🏠 R Stent
📧 www.avingtongolf.co.uk

Paultons Golf Centre (1922)
Pay and play
Old Salisbury Road, Ower, Romsey,
SO51 6AN
☎ (023) 8081 3992
📠 (023) 8081 3993
🏌 M Rollinson
⚐ M Williamson
☞ 18 L 6238 yds SSS 71
9 hole Academy course Par 3
🏌 U SOC
££ 9: £7.50 (£8) 18: £20 (£26)
🚗 Nr M27 Junction 2, at Ower
⊕ Driving range; practice area
📧 www.crown-golf.co.uk

Petersfield (1892)
Tankerdale Lane, Liss, GU33 7QY
☎ (01730) 895165
📠 (01730) 894713
📧 manager@pgc1892.net
📖 730
🏌 PD Badger
⚐ G Hughes (01730) 895216
☞ 18 L 6450 yds Par 72 SSS 71
🏌 WD–U WE/BH–NA before noon
SOC–Mon/Wed/Fri
££ £28 (£33)
🚗 Off A3, at Liss exit (B3006)
🏠 Hawtree
📧 www.petersfieldgolfclub.co.uk

Petersfield Sussex Road
Pay and play
Sussex Road, Petersfield
☎ (01730) 267732

Portsmouth (1926)
Public
Crookhorn Lane, Widley, Waterlooville,
PO7 5QL
☎ (023) 9237 2210 ext 24
📖 650
🏌 S Richard (023) 9220 1827 ext 21
⚐ (023) 9237 2210 ext 24
☞ 18 L 6139 yds SSS 70
🏌 U SOC–arrange with Pro
££ £9–£16
🚗 1 mile N of Portsmouth, on B2177
⊕ Practice area, putting green,
practice nets
🏠 Hawtree
📧 www.portsmouthgc.com

Quindell (1997)
Skylark Meadows, Whiteley, Fareham,
PO15 6RS
☎ (01329) 844441
📠 (01329) 844442
📖 600
🏌 Rob Terry
⚐ Jason Bantine
☞ 18 L 5683 yds Par 70 SSS 67
🏌 WD–U WE–M SOC–WD

££ £28 (£35)
🚗 6 miles W of Fareham. M27
Junction 9

Romsey (1900)
Nursling, Southampton, SO16 0XW
☎ (023) 8073 4637
📠 (023) 8074 1036
📧 mike@romseygolf.co.uk
📖 655
🏌 J Pitcher
⚐ M Desmond (023) 8073 6673
☞ 18 L 5856 yds SSS 68
🏌 WD–H WE/BH–M H
££ £30 D–£36
🚗 2 miles SE of Romsey on A3057.
M27/M271 Junction 3
📧 www.romseygolfclub.com

Rowlands Castle (1902)
Links Lane, Rowlands Castle, PO9 6AE
☎ (023) 9241 2216
📠 (023) 9241 3649
📧 manager@rowlandscastlegolfclub
.co.uk
📖 800 150(L) 50(J)
🏌 KD Fisher (023) 9241 2784
⚐ P Klepacz (023) 9241 2785
☞ 18 L 6630 yds Par 72 SSS 72
🏌 WD–U H exc Wed am–restricted
WE–phone first Sat–M SOC–Tues
& Thurs
££ D–£36 (D–£40)
🚗 9 miles S of Petersfield, off A3(M).
3 miles N of Havant
🏠 HS Colt
📧 www.rowlandscastlegolfclub.co.uk

Royal Winchester (1888)
Sarum Road, Winchester, SO22 5QE
☎ (01962) 852462
📠 (01962) 865048
📧 manager@royalwinchestergolfclub
.com
📖 750
🏌 A Buck
⚐ S Hunter (01962) 862473
☞ 18 L 6216 yds SSS 70
🏌 WD–U H WE/BH–M
SOC–Mon/Tues/Wed
££ On application
🚗 W of Winchester. M3 Junction 11
🏠 JH Taylor
📧 www.royalwinchestergolfclub.com

Sandford Springs (1988)
Wolverton, Tadley, RG26 5RT
☎ (01635) 296800
📧 garye@leaderboardgolf.co.uk

Somerley Park (1995)
Somerley, Ringwood, BH24 3PL
☎ (01425) 461496
📖 169
🏌 C Trounce (01202) 820722
⚐ J Waring (01202) 821703
☞ 9 L 2155 yds Par 33 SSS 62
🏌 M SOC
££ £10 (£10)
🚗 5 miles W of Ringwood
🏠 John Jacobs OBE

South Winchester
Romsey Road, Pitt, Winchester, SO22 5QX
☎ **(01962) 877800**
✉ winchester-sales@crown-golf.co.uk

Southampton Municipal
(1935)
Public
1 Golf Course Road, Bassett, Southampton, SO16 7AY
☎ **(023) 8076 8407**
✉ mick.carter7@ntlworld.com
🖎 E Hemsley (02380) 476582
✓ Eddy Rawlings (02380) 760546
⊳ 18 L 6218 yds SSS 70
9 L 2391 yds SSS 33
🏌 U
££ On application
⊕ 2 miles N of Southampton
🏠 JH Taylor
🖥 www.southamptongolfclub.co.uk

Southsea
(1914)
Public
The Clubhouse, Burrfields Road, Portsmouth, PO3 5JJ
☎ **(023) 9266 8667**
📠 (023) 9266 8667
📖 350
🖎 R Collinson
✓ T Healy (02392) 664549
⊳ 18 L 5970 yds SSS 68
18 L 5620 Par 69 SSS 67
🏌 U SOC
££ £14 (£17)
⊕ 1 mile off M27 on A2030
⊕ Driving range

Southwick Park
(1977)
Pinsley Drive, Southwick, PO17 6EL
☎ **(023) 9238 0131**
📠 (023) 9221 0289
✉ southwickpark@btconnect.com
📖 650 80(L)
🖎 NW Price
✓ J Green (023) 9238 0442
⊳ 18 L 5884 yds Par 69 SSS 69
🏌 WD–U booking necessary WE–NA before 2pm SOC
££ Visitor £23 D–£32 (£26) Service personnel reduced rate
⊕ 5 miles N of Portsmouth, off B2177
🏠 Charles Lawrie

Southwood
(1977)
Public
Ively Road, Farnborough, GU14 0LJ
☎ **(01252) 548700**
📠 (01252) 549091
✉ mandybarter@dcleisure.co.uk
📖 350
🖎 DJ Main
✓ C Hudson
⊳ 18 L 5738 yds Par 69 SSS 68
🏌 U
££ £17.50 (£20)
⊕ 1 mile W of Farnborough, off A325; 2 miles from M3 J4A
🏠 M Hawtree
🖥 www.southwoodgolfclub.co.uk

Stoneham
(1908)
Monks Wood Close, Bassett, Southampton, SO16 3TT
☎ **(023) 8076 9272**
📠 (023) 8076 6320
✉ richard.penley-martin@stonehamgolfclub.org.uk
📖 600
🖎 R Penley-Martin (Mgr) (023) 8076 9272
✓ I Young (023) 8076 8397
⊳ 18 L 6392 yds Par 72 SSS 70
🏌 H SOC–Mon/Thurs/Fri
££ £40 D–£45 (£50 D–£60)
⊕ 2 miles N of Southampton on A27; 2 miles from M27 J5 or M3 J14
🏠 Willie Park jr
🖥 www.stonehamgolfclub.org.uk

Test Valley
(1992)
Micheldever Road, Overton, Basingstoke, RG25 3DS
☎ **(01256) 771737**
📠 (01256) 771285
✉ info@testvalleygolf.com
📖 550
🖎 A Briggs (Mgr) (01256) 771737
✓ A Briggs
⊳ 18 L 6897 yds SSS 71
🏌 U SOC WD–U WE–NA before noon SOC WD U WE NA before 2pm
££ £24 D–£36 (£30)
⊕ 2 miles S of Overton on Micheldever road. M3 Junction 8 (A303)
⊕ 10-bay driving range; short game practice area; putting green
🏠 Wright/Darcy
🖥 www.testvalleygolf.com

Tylney Park
(1973)
Proprietary
Rotherwick, Hook, RG27 9AY
☎ **(01256) 762079**
📠 (01256) 763079
✉ contact@tylneypark.co.uk
📖 700
🖎 MA Brain
✓ C de Bruin (Mgr)
⊳ 18 L 7017 yds Par 72 SSS 74
🏌 WD–U WE–H or U SOC
££ £43 (D–£60)
⊕ 2 miles NW of Hook. M3 J5, 8 miles S M4 J11
⊕ Driving range
🏠 Donald Steel/Tom MacKenzie
🖥 www.tylneypark.co.uk

Waterlooville
(1907)
Cherry Tree Ave, Cowplain, Waterlooville, PO8 8AP
☎ **(023) 9226 3388**
📠 (023) 9224 2980
✉ secretary@waterloovillegolfclub.co.uk
📖 800
🖎 D Nairne
✓ J Hay (023) 9225 6911
⊳ 18 L 6602 yds SSS 72
🏌 WD/WE–M H (Sun am–XL) SOC
££ £34 D–£44

⊕ 10 miles N of Portsmouth on A3
⊕ Practice area and putting green
🏠 Henry Cotton
🖥 www.waterloovillegolfclub.co.uk

Wellow
(1991)
Ryedown Lane, East Wellow, Romsey, SO51 6BD
☎ **(01794) 322872**
📠 (01794) 323832
📖 600
🖎 Mrs C Gurd
✓ N Bratley (01794) 323833
⊳ 27 L 6000 yds SSS 69
🏌 U SOC–WD
££ £20 (£25)
⊕ 2 miles W of Romsey. M27 Junction 2, via A36
🏠 W Wiltshire
🖥 www.wellowgolfclub.co.uk

Weybrook Park
(1971)
Rooksdown Lane, Basingstoke, RG24 9NT
☎ **(01256) 320347**
📠 (01256) 812973
✉ info@weybrookpark.co.uk
📖 600
🖎 A Dillon (Mgr)
✓ A Dillon (01256) 333232
⊳ 18 L 6468 yds SSS 71
🏌 WD–U WE–contact Mgr SOC
££ £24 (£28)
⊕ 1½ miles N of Basingstoke
🖥 www.weybrookpark.co.uk

Wickham Park
(1991)
Proprietary
Titchfield Lane, Wickham, Fareham, PO17 5PJ
☎ **(01329) 833342**
📠 (01329) 834798
✉ wickhampark@crown-golf.co.uk
🖎 Jonathon Tubb
✓ Dean Elder
⊳ 18 L 5868 yds Par 69 SSS 68
🏌 U SOC–WD
££ £15 (£20)
⊕ 2 miles N of Fareham. M27 Junction 10
⊕ Driving range
🏠 Jon Payn
🖥 www.crown-golf.co.uk

Worldham
(1993)
Proprietary
Cakers Lane, Worldham, Alton, GU34 3AG
☎ **(01420) 543151/544606**
📠 (01420) 544606
✉ manager@worldhamgolfclub.com
📖 350
🖎 Ian Yates (01420) 544606
✓ Anthony Cook (01420) 543151
⊳ 18 L 6196 yds SSS 70
🏌 WD–U WE–U SOC–WD/WE
££ £14 (£18)
⊕ ½ mile E of Alton on B3004 to Bordon
⊕ Driving range
🏠 Troth/Whidborne
🖥 www.worldhamgolfclub.com

Herefordshire

Belmont Lodge   (1983)
Ruckhall Lane, Belmont, Hereford, HR2 9SA
☎ **(01432) 352666**
📠 (01432) 358090
📧 info@belmont-hereford.co.uk
📖 500
🏌 B Macaskill (Mgr)
✎ M Welsh (01432) 352717
🏳 18 L 6511 yds SSS 71
👥 U SOC
££ On application
🚗 1½ miles S of Hereford on A465
🏠 B Sandow
🖳 www.belmont-hereford.co.uk

Burghill Valley   (1991)
*Tillington Road, Burghill, Hereford,
HR4 7RW*
☎ **(01432) 760456**
📠 (01432) 761654
📧 info@bvgc.co.uk
🏌 K Smith (Gen Mgr)
✎ K Preece (01432) 760808
🏳 18 L 6204 yds SSS 70
👥 U SOC
££ £26 (£31)
🚗 3 miles N of Hereford, off A4110
🖳 www.bvgc.co.uk

Cadmore Lodge   (1990)
Pay and play
*Berrington Green, Tenbury Wells,
Worcester, WR15 8TQ*
☎ **(01584) 810044**
📠 (01584) 810044
📖 150
🏌 RV Farr
✎ None
🏳 9 L 5129 yds Par 68 SSS 65
👥 U
££ D–£10 (D–£14)
🚗 2 miles S of Tenbury Wells on
A4112
🖳 www.cadmorelodge.demon.co.uk

Hereford Municipal
(1983)
Public
Holmer Road, Hereford, HR4 9UD
☎ **(01432) 344376**
📠 (01432) 266281
📖 200
🏌 G Morgan (Mgr)
✎ G Morgan (01432) 344376
🏳 9 L 3060 yds Par 70 SSS 68
👥 U SOC
££ 9: £5.50 18: £8
🚗 Hereford Leisure Centre, A49
Leominster road
⊕ Practice area and putting green;
leisure centre attached

Herefordshire   (1896)
*Raven's Causeway, Wormsley, Hereford,
HR4 8LY*
☎ **(01432) 830219**
📠 (01432) 830095
📧 herefordshire.golf@breathe.com

📖 770 150(L) 55(J)
🏌 T Horobin
✎ R Hemming (01432) 830465
🏳 18 L 6031 yds Par 70 SSS 69
👥 U–phone first SOC
££ £25 D–£30 (£35 D–£40)
🚗 6 miles NW of Hereford
🖳 www.herefordshiregolfclub.co.uk

Kington   (1926)
Bradnor Hill, Kington, HR5 3RE
☎ **(01544) 230340**
📠 (01544) 340270
📧 kington@ukonline.co.uk
📖 440
🏌 GR Wictome (01544) 340270
✎ A Gealy (01544) 231320
🏳 18 L 5840 yds SSS 68
👥 WE–NA before 10.15am
–restricted 1.30–2.45pm SOC
££ £20 D–£26 (£26 D–£32)
🚗 1 mile N of Kington
⊕ Practice area
🏠 CK Hutchison

Leominster   (1967)
Ford Bridge, Leominster, HR6 0LE
☎ **(01568) 612863 (Clubhouse)**
📠 (01568) 610055
📧 contact@leominstergolfclub.co.uk
📖 450
🏌 L Green (01568) 610055
✎ N Clarke (01568) 611402
🏳 18 L 6026 yds SSS 69
👥 U SOC
££ £16 D–£20 (£25 D–£30)
🚗 3 miles S of Leominster on A49
(Leominster Bypass)
🏠 R Sandow
🖳 leominstergolfclub.co.uk

Ross-on-Wye   (1903)
Two Park, Gorsley, Ross-on-Wye, HR9 7UT
☎ **(01989) 720267**
📠 (01989) 720212
📧 secretary@therossonwyegolfclub
.co.uk
📖 760
🏌 Sarah Creighton (Administrator)
✎ Paul Middleton (01989) 720439
🏳 18 L 6500 yds Par 72 SSS 71
👥 U SOC–Wed–Fri (min 16 players)
££ £40–£50 SOC–£34–£44 (subject
to review)
🚗 5 miles N of Ross-on-Wye, by M50
Junction 3
⊕ Parkland driving range
🏠 CK Cotton
🖳 www.rossonwyegolfclub.co.uk

Sapey   (1991)
Proprietary
Upper Sapey, Worcester, WR6 6XT
☎ **(01886) 853288**
📠 (01886) 853485
📧 anybody@sapeygolf.co.uk
📖 380
🏌 Miss L Stevenson
✎ C Knowles
🏳 18 L 5939 yds SSS 68
9 hole Par 3 course
👥 WD–U WE–NA before 11am SOC

££ £22 D–£26 (£27 D–£30)
🚗 6 miles N of Bromyard on B4203.
M5 Junction 5
🖳 www.sapeygolf.co.uk

South Herefordshire   (1992)
*Twin Lakes, Upton Bishop, Ross-on-Wye,
HR9 7UA*
☎ **(01989) 780535**
📠 (01989) 740611
📖 350
🏌 James Leaver
✎ Leo Tarrant
🏳 18 L 6672 yds Par 71 SSS 72
9 hole Par 3 course
👥 U SOC
££ £18 (£23)
🚗 3 miles NE of Ross-on-Wye. M50
Junction 4
⊕ Floodlit driving range
🏠 John Day

Hertfordshire

Aldenham G&CC   (1975)
*Church Lane, Aldenham, Watford,
WD25 8NN*
☎ **(01923) 853929**
📠 (01923) 858472
📧 info@aldenhamgolfclub.co.uk
📖 500
🏌 Mrs J Phillips
✎ T Dunstan (01923) 857889
🏳 18 L 6456 yds SSS 71
9 L 2350 yds
👥 WD–U WE–U after 12.30pm
££ 9: £12 (£15) 18: £30 (£40)
🚗 3 miles E of Watford, off B462. M1
Junction 5
🖳 www.aldenhamgolfclub.co.uk

Aldwickbury Park   (1995)
Proprietary
*Piggottshill Lane, Wheathampstead Road,
Harpenden, AL5 1AB*
☎ **(01582) 760112**
📠 (01582) 760113
📧 enquiries@aldwickburyparkgolfclub
.com
📖 700
🏌 T Hall (01582) 765112
✎ R Turley
🏳 18 L 6032 yds Par 71 SSS 69
9 hole Par 3 Academy course
👥 WD–U booking necessary WE–U
after 12.00 SOC–WD
££ £30 (£35)
🚗 E of Harpenden on
Wheathampstead road. M1
Junction 9. A1(M) Junction 4
🏠 Martin Gillett/Ken Brown
🖳 www.aldwickburyparkgolfclub.com

Arkley   (1909)
Rowley Green Road, Barnet, EN5 3HL
☎ **(020) 8449 0394**
📠 (020) 8440 5214
📧 secretary@arkleygolfclub.co.uk
📖 350
🏌 DDR Campbell

✓ A Hurley (020) 8440 8473
➢ 9 L 6046 yds SSS 69 - 18 tees
⚇ WD–U WE–M
SOC–Mon–Wed–Fri
££ £25 D–£32 (£20)
⊶ NW of Barnet, off A1(M)
⊕ Practice area
⌂ James Braid
▤ www.arkleygolfclub.co.uk

Ashridge   (1932)
Little Gaddesden, Berkhamsted, HP4 1LY
☎ (01442) 842244
⌨ (01442) 843770
✉ info@ashridgegolfclub.ltd.uk
⌘ 740
✍ MS Silver
✓ P Cherry (01442) 842307
➢ 18 L 6625 yds SSS 71
⚇ WD only–phone Sec
££ On application
⊶ 5 miles N of Berkhamsted on
B4506
⌂ Campbell/Hutchison/Hotchkin
▤ www.ashridgegolfclub.ltd.uk

Barkway Park   (1992)
Nuthampstead Road, Barkway, Royston,
SG8 8EN
☎ (01763) 849070

Batchwood Hall   (1935)
Pay and play
Batchwood Drive, St Albans, AL3 5XA
☎ (01727) 833349

Batchworth Park   (1996)
London Road, Rickmansworth, WD3 1JS
☎ (01923) 711400
⌨ (01923) 710200
✉ bpgc@crown-golf.co.uk
⌘ 750
✍ AD Lawrence
✓ S Proudfoot (01923) 714922
➢ 18 L 6723 yds Par 72 SSS 72
⚇ M
££ N/A
⊶ 1 mile SE of Rickmansworth on
A404. M25 Junction 18
⊕ Indoor Academy. Practice range
⌂ Dave Thomas
▤ www.crown-golf.co.uk

Berkhamsted   (1890)
The Common, Berkhamsted, HP4 2QB
☎ (01442) 865832
⌨ (01442) 863730
✉ barryh@berkhamstedgc.co.uk
⌘ 450 120(L) 50(J)
✍ BJ Hill
✓ J Clarke (01442) 865851
➢ 18 L 6605 yds Par 71 SSS 72
⚇ U H WD after 8.30am WE after
11.30am SOC Mon–Wed–Fri
££ On application
⊶ 1 mile N of Berkhamsted. M25
Junction 21 (A41). M1 Junction 8
⌂ HS Colt/James Braid
▤ www.berkhamstedgolfclub.co.uk

Bishop's Stortford   (1910)
Dunmow Road, Bishop's Stortford,
CM23 5HP
☎ (01279) 654715
⌨ (01279) 655215
✉ office@bsgc.co.uk
⌘ 900
✍ Judy Barker
✓ S Sheppard (01279) 651324
➢ 18 L 6404 yds SSS 71
⚇ WD–U H WE–M SOC–WD exc
Tues
££ £32 D–£40
⊶ E of Bishop's Stortford on A1250;
M11 J8
⌂ James Braid
▤ www.bsgc.co.uk

Boxmoor   (1890)
18 Box Lane, Hemel Hempstead, HP3 0DJ
☎ (01442) 242434 (Clubhouse)
⌘ 290
✍ B Swann
✓ None
➢ 9 L 4854 yds SSS 64
⚇ WE–Sun after 1pm WD–U
££ £10 (£10)
⊶ 1 mile W of Hemel Hempstead on
B4505 to Chesham
▤ www.boxmoorgolfclub.co.uk

Brickendon Grange   (1964)
Pembridge Lane, Brickendon, Hertford,
SG13 8PD
☎ (01992) 511258
⌨ (01992) 511411
✉ play@brickendongrangegc.co.uk
⌘ 700
✍ Martin Bennet
✓ G Tippett (01992) 511218
➢ 18 L 6458 yds SSS 71
⚇ WD–U H WE/BH–M SOC
££ £36 D–£45
⊶ Bayford, 3 miles S of Hertford
⌂ CK Cotton
▤ www.brickendongrangegc.co.uk

Briggens House Hotel
(1988)
Briggens Park, Stanstead Road, Stanstead
Abbotts, SG12 8LD
☎ (01279) 793742
⌨ (01279) 793685
✉ briggenshouse@corushotels.com
⌘ 280
✍ A Battle (Mgr)
➢ 9 L 5825 yds SSS 69
⚇ U SOC
££ 9 holes–£10 (£12)
⊶ 4 miles E of Hertford, off A414
▤ www.corushotels.co.uk
/briggenshouse

Brocket Hall   (1992)
Welwyn, AL8 7XG
☎ (01707) 368808
⌨ (01707) 390052
✉ paulden@brocket-hall.co.uk
⌘ 850
✍ P Densham (01707) 368808
✓ K Wood (01707) 390063

➢ Melbourne 18 L 6616 yds SSS 72
Palmerston 18 L 7096 yds SSS 73
⚇ M H Play & Stay
££ Play & Stay from £125 (B&B + 18
holes)
⊶ On B653 to Wheathampstead.
A1(M) Junction 4
⊕ Driving range. Faldo Golf Institute,
Melbourne Lodge
⌂ Melbourne-Alliss/Clark.
Palmerston-Steel
▤ www.brocket-hall.co.uk

Brookmans Park   (1930)
Brookmans Park, Hatfield, AL9 7AT
☎ (01707) 652487
⌨ (01707) 661851
✉ info@bpgc.co.uk
⌘ 800
✍ PA Gill
✓ I Jelley (01707) 652468
➢ 18 L 6473 yds SSS 71
⚇ WD–UH WE/BH–M SOC
££ £32
⊶ 3 miles S of Hatfield, off A1000
⌂ Hawtree/Taylor
▤ www.bpgc.co.uk

Bushey G&CC   (1980)
High Street, Bushey, WD23 1TT
☎ (020) 8950 2283
⌨ (020) 8386 1181
✉ info@busheycountryclub.com
⌘ 446
✍ B Worthington
✓ Martin Siggins (020) 8950 2215
➢ 9 L 3030 yds SSS 70
⚇ WD–U except Wed/Thur before 6
pm WE–NA before 2 pm SOC
££ 9: £13 (£15) 18: £21 (£26)
⊶ 2 miles S of Watford on A4008
⊕ Driving range
⌂ Donald Steel
▤ www.busheycountryclub.com

Bushey Hall   (1890)
Bushey Hall Drive, Bushey, WD23 2EP
☎ (01923) 222253
✉ gordon@golfclubuk.co.uk

Chadwell Springs   (1974)
Hertford Road, Ware, SG12 9LE
☎ (01920) 463647
⌨ (01920) 466596
⌘ 400
✍ D Robertson (01920) 461447
✓ S Smith (01920) 462075
➢ 9 L 3021 yds SSS 69
⚇ WD–U WE–M
££ £25 (£30)
⊶ Between Ware and Hertford on
A119

Chesfield Downs   (1991)
Pay and play
Jack's Hill, Graveley, Stevenage, SG4 7EQ
☎ (08707) 460020

Cheshunt   (1976)
Public
Park Lane, Cheshunt, EN7 6QD
☎ (01992) 29777

Chorleywood   (1890)

Common Road, Chorleywood, WD3 5LN
- ☎ **(01923) 282009**
- 🖥 (01923) 286739
- ✉ secretary@chorleywoodgolfclub
  .co.uk
- 🔲 320
- 🏌 RA Botham
- ✔ RM Mandeville
- ⓟ 9 L 2843 yds SSS 67
- 🚹 WD–U exc Tues am WE–U after
  11.30am SOC
- ££ £20 (£25)
- ⌘ 3 miles N of Rickmansworth, off
  A404. M25 Junction 18

Danesbury Park   (1991)

Codicote Road, Welwyn, AL6 9SD
- ☎ **(01438) 840100**
- ✉ d.s@snowdongolf.com

Dyrham Park CC   (1963)

Galley Lane, Barnet, EN5 4RA
- ☎ **(020) 8440 3361**
- 🖥 (020) 8441 9836
- 🔲 600
- 🏌 K Sutton
- ✔ W Large (020) 8440 3904
- ⓟ 18 L 6422 yds SSS 71
- 🚹 M SOC–Wed
- ⌘ 10 miles N of London. M25
  Junction 23
- ⌂ CK Cotton

East Herts   (1899)

Hamels Park, Buntingford, SG9 9NA
- ☎ **(01920) 821978**
- 🖥 (01920) 823700
- ✉ brian@ehgc.co.uk
- 🔲 700
- 🏌 B Palmer
- ✔ D Field (01920) 821922
- ⓟ 18 L 6456 yds SSS 71
- 🚹 WD–H exc Wed–NA before 1pm
  WE–M
- ££ £30 £32+8 holes D–£44
- ⌘ ¼ mile N of Puckeridge on A10
- 🖥 www.ehgc.co.uk

Elstree   (1984)

Watling Street, Elstree, WD6 3AA
- ☎ **(020) 8238 6947 (Clubhouse)**
  (020) 8953 6115 (General)
- 🖥 (020) 8207 6390
- ✉ admin@elstree-golf.co.uk
- 🔲 400
- 🏌 K Roberts (020) 8238 6942
- ✔ M Warwick (020) 8238 6941/9
- ⓟ 18 L 6556 yds Par 73 SSS 72
- 🚹 U SOC
- ££ Approx. £18.50 (£22.50)
- ⌘ A5183, 1 mile N of Elstree. M1
  Junction 4
- ⊕ Floodlit driving range
- ⌂ Donald Steel
- 🖥 www.elstree-golfclub.co.uk

Forest Hills   (1994)

Newgate Street, SG13 8EW
- ☎ **(01707) 876825**

Great Hadham   (1993)

Great Hadham Road, Bishop's Stortford,
SG10 6JE
- ☎ **(01279) 843558**
- 🖥 (01279) 842122
- ✉ ian@ghgcc.co.uk
- 🔲 700
- 🏌 I Bailey
- ✔ K Lunt (01279) 843888
- ⓟ 18 L 6854 yds Par 72 SSS 73
- 🚹 WD–U WE/BH–NA before 12
  noon SOC
- ££ £21 (£27)
- ⌘ 3 miles SW of Bishops Stortford
  (B1004). M11 Junction 8
- ⊕ Driving range
- 🖥 www.ghgcc.co.uk

The Grove   (2003)

Chandler`s Cross, Rickmansworth,
WD3 4TG
- ☎ **(01923) 807807**
- 🖥 (01923) 294268
- ✉ golf@thegrove.co.uk
- 🏌 Blyth Reid (Dir. of Golf)
- ✔ Spencer Schaub
- ⓟ 18 L 7152 yds
- 🚹 U
- ££ £75–£155 depending on time of
  year
- ⌘ 2 miles S of M25 (J20) on the A411
- ⊕ Range; short game area
- ⌂ Kyle Phillips
- 🖥 www.thegrove.co.uk

Hadley Wood   (1922)

Beech Hill, Hadley Wood, Barnet, EN4 0JJ
- ☎ **(020) 8449 4328**
- 🖥 (020) 8364 8633
- ✉ gm@hadleywoodgc.com
- 🔲 660
- 🏌 WM Beckett (Gen Mgr)
- ✔ P Jones (020) 8449 3285
- ⓟ 18 L 6514 yds SSS 71
- 🚹 WD–H WE/BH–M SOC
  Mon/Thur/Fri
- ££ On application
- ⌘ 10 miles N of London, off A111
  between Potters Bar and
  Cockfosters. 2 miles S of M25
  Junction 24
- ⊕ Practice range
- ⌂ Dr A Mackenzie
- 🖥 www.hadleywoodgc.com

Hanbury Manor G&CC
   (1990)

Ware, SG12 0SD
- ☎ **(01920) 487722**
- 🖥 (01920) 487692
- ✉ golf.hanbury@marriotthotels.co.uk
- 🔲 400
- 🏌 J O'Malley (Dir. of Golf)
- ✔ (01920) 885000
- ⓟ 18 L 7016 yds SSS 74
- 🚹 M H + Hotel guests SOC
- ££ £85
- ⌘ 8 miles N of M25 Junction 25 on
  A10 at Thundridge
- ⌂ Jack Nicklaus II
- 🖥 www.hanbury-manor.com

Harpenden   (1894)

Hammonds End, Harpenden, AL5 2AX
- ☎ **(01582) 712580**
- 🖥 (01582) 712725
- ✉ office@harpendengolfclub.co.uk
- 🔲 800
- 🏌 FLK Clapp (Gen Mgr)
- ✔ Peter Lane (01582) 767124
- ⓟ 18 L 6377 yds SSS 70
- 🚹 WD–U exc Thurs WE/BH–H
  SOC–WD exc Thurs
- ££ £35 D–£45 (£40)
- ⌘ 6 miles N of St Albans on B487
- ⌂ Hawtree/Taylor
- 🖥 www.harpendengolfclub.co.uk

Harpenden Common   (1931)

East Common, Harpenden, AL5 1BL
- ☎ **(01582) 711320**
- 🖥 (01582) 711321
- ✉ admin@hcgc.co.uk
- 🔲 740
- 🏌 CH Bailey (01582) 711320
- ✔ D Fitzsimmons (01582) 460655
- ⓟ 18 L 6214 yds SSS 70
- 🚹 WD–U H WE–M SOC
- ££ £40
- ⌘ 4 miles N of St Albans, on A1081
  M1, J9
- ⌂ K Brown (1995)
- 🖥 www.hcgc.co.uk

Hartsbourne G&CC   (1946)

Hartsbourne Avenue, Bushey Heath,
WD23 1JW
- ☎ **(020) 8421 7272**
- 🖥 (020) 8950 5357
- 🔲 750
- 🏌 I Thomas
- ✔ R Weedon (020) 8421 7266
- ⓟ 18 L 6385 yds SSS 70
  9 L 5773 yds SSS 68
- 🚹 NA SOC
- ⌘ 5 miles SE of Watford, off A4008
- ⌂ Hawtree/Taylor

Hatfield London CC   (1976)

Bedwell Park, Essendon, Hatfield, AL9 6HN
- ☎ **(01707) 260360**
- 🖥 (01707) 278475
- ✉ info@hatfieldlondon.co.uk
- 🔲 260
- 🏌 H Takeda
- ✔ Andrew Clapp (07711) 547391
- ⓟ 18 L 6808 yds SSS 72
  18 L 6938 yds SSS 73
  36 hole course
- 🚹 U SOC
- ££ £25 (£35)
- ⌘ 4 miles E of Hatfield on B158. M25
  Junction 24. A1(M) Junction 4
- ⊕ 9 hole pitch & putt course
- ⌂ Fred Hawtree
- 🖥 www.hatfieldlondon.co.uk

The Hertfordshire   (1995)

Proprietary
Broxbournebury Mansion, White Stubbs
Lane, Broxbourne, EN10 7PY
- ☎ **(01992) 466666**
- ✉ hertfordshire@americangolf.co.uk

Kingsway Golf Centre

(1991)

*Cambridge Road, Melbourn, Royston,
SG8 6EY*

- ☎ **(01763) 262727**
- 🖥 (01763) 263298
- 📖 150
- ✍ B Smith
- ✓ S Brown
- ⊳ 9 L 2500 yds Par 33
  9 hole Par 3 course
- 👥 U SOC
- ££ 9: £7.50 (£9). 18: £11 (£13)
- 🚗 N of Royston on A10
- ⊕ Driving range; Par 3 course; golf shop

Knebworth   (1908)

Deards End Lane, Knebworth, SG3 6NL

- ☎ **(01438) 812752
  (Clubhouse)**
- 🖥 (01438) 815216
- ✉ knebworth1@btconnect.com
- 📖 750
- ✍ AS Hobbs
- ✓ G Parker (01438) 812757
- ⊳ 18 L 6492 yds SSS 71
- 👥 WD–U H WE–M
  SOC–Mon/Tues/Thurs
- ££ £35
- 🚗 1 mile S of Stevenage on B197.
  A1(M) Junction 7
- 🏠 Willie Park
- 🖥 www.knebworthgolfclub.com

Lamerwood   (1996)

*Codicote Road, Wheathampstead,
AL4 8GB*

- ☎ **(01582) 833013**
- 🖥 (01582) 832604
- ✉ lamerwood.cc@virgin.net
- 📖 350
- ✍ R Darling (Gen Mgr)
- ✓ M Masters (01582) 833013
- ⊳ 18 L 6953 yds Par 72
- 👥 U
- ££ £27 (£40)
- 🚗 5 miles W of A1(M) Junction 4 on
  B653
- ⊕ Driving range; 9 hole par 3 course
- 🏠 Cameron Sinclair
- 🖥 www.lamerwood.humaxuk.com

Letchworth   (1905)

*Letchworth Lane, Letchworth Garden City,
SG6 3NQ*

- ☎ **(01462) 683203**
- 🖥 (01462) 484567
- ✉ secretary@letchworthgolfclub.com
- 📖 900
- ✍ Michael Jordan
- ✓ (01462) 682713
- ⊳ 18 L 6459 yds SSS 71
- 👥 WD–H WE–M SOC–Wed–Fri
- ££ £18 Mon Tue–Fri £32 D–£42 (£36)
- 🚗 S of Letchworth, off A505. A1(M)
  Junction 9
- ⊕ Driving range; 9 hole course
- 🏠 Harry Vardon
- 🖥 www.letchworthgolfclub.com

Little Hay Golf Complex

(1977)

Pay and play
*Box Lane, Bovingdon, Hemel Hempstead,
HP3 0DQ*

- ☎ **(01442) 833798**
- 🖥 (01442) 831399
- ✍ C Gordon (Golf Mgr)
- ✓ N Allen and M Perry
- ⊳ 18 L 6592 yds SSS 71
- 👥 U SOC
- ££ £14.50 (£19.50)
- 🚗 2 miles W of Hemel Hempstead,
  on B4505 to Chesham
- ⊕ Driving range; pitch & putt
- 🏠 Hawtree

Manor of Groves G&CC

(1991)

Proprietary
High Wych, Sawbridgeworth, CM21 0JU

- ☎ **(01279) 600777**
- 🖥 (01279) 600374
- ✉ golfsecretary@manorofgroves.com
- 📖 650
- ✍ R Walker (01279) 722247
- ✓ C Charlise
- ⊳ 18 L 6227 yds par 71 SSS 70
- 👥 WD–U WE–NA before 11am SOC
- ££ On application
- 🚗 1 mile N of Harlow (M11 J7)
- 🖥 www.manorgolf.net

Mid Herts   (1892)

Gustard Wood, Wheathampstead, AL4 8RS

- ☎ **(01582) 832242**
- 🖥 (01582) 834834
- ✉ secretary@mid-hertsgolfclub.co.uk
- 📖 500(M) 125(L)
- ✍ Miss A McDonald
- ✓ B Puttick (01582) 832788
- ⊳ 18 L 6060 yds SSS 69
- 👥 WD–UH exc Tues & Wed pm
  WE/BH–M SOC
- ££ £30
- 🚗 6 miles N of St Albans on B651
- 🏠 James Braid
- 🖥 www.mid-hertsgolfclub.co.uk

Mill Green   (1994)

*Gypsy Lane, Mill Green, Welwyn Garden
City, AL7 4TY*

- ☎ **(01707) 276900**
- 🖥 (01707) 276898
- ✉ millgreen@crown-golf.co.uk
- ✍ Tim Hudson
- ✓ I Parker (01707) 270542
- ⊳ 18 L 6615 yds Par 72 SSS 72
  Par 3 course
- 👥 SOC–WD Visitors–WD–U
  WE–NA before noon
- ££ £27.50 (£35)
- 🚗 S of Welwyn Garden City, off
  A414. A1 Junction 4
- ⊕ Driving range
- 🏠 Clark/Alliss
- 🖥 www.crown-golf.co.uk

Moor Park   (1923)

Rickmansworth, WD3 1QN

- ☎ **(01923) 773146**
- 🖥 (01923) 777109

- ✉ jon.moore@moorparkgc.co.uk
- 📖 1475
- ✍ JM Moore (01923) 773146
- ✓ L Farmer (01923) 774113
- ⊳ High 18 L 6722 yds SSS 72
  West 18 L 5851 yds SSS 68
- 👥 WD–H SOC WE/BH–NA before
  2pm
- ££ High £80 D–£110 (£120). West
  £50 (£80)
- 🚗 1 mile SE of Rickmansworth, off
  Batchworth roundabout (A4145).
  M25 Junction 18, 2 miles
- ⊕ Practice ground and nets; chipping
  green
- 🏠 HS Colt
- 🖥 www.moorparkgc.co.uk

Old Fold Manor   (1910)

*Old Fold Lane, Hadley Green, Barnet,
EN5 4QN*

- ☎ **(020) 8440 9185**
- 🖥 (020) 8441 4863
- ✉ manager@oldfoldmanor.co.uk
- 📖 450
- ✍ B Cullen (Mgr)
- ✓ P McEvoy (020) 8440 7488
- ⊳ 18 L 6466 yds SSS 71
- 👥 WD–H WE–M after 3pm
  SOC–Mon–Fri
- ££ £30 D–£38
- 🚗 1 mile N of Barnet on A1000
- 🖥 www.oldfoldmanor.co.uk

Oxhey Park

*Prestwick Road, South Oxhey, Watford,
WD19 7EX*

- ☎ **(01923) 248213/210118**

Panshanger Golf Complex

(1976)

Public
*Old Herns Lane, Welwyn Garden City,
AL7 2ED*

- ☎ **(01707) 333312/333350
  (Bookings)**
- 🖥 (01707) 390010
- ✉ panshanger.golfclub@virgin.net
- 📖 300
- ✍ Trish Skinner (01707) 332837
- ⊳ 18 L 6167 yds SSS 70
  9 hole Par 3 course
- 👥 U SOC
- ££ £15.50 (£19.60) Snr £8.30 (£19.60)
  Jnr £6.70 (£9)
- 🚗 2 miles off A1, via B1000 to
  Hertford
- 🖥 www.finesseleisure.co.uk

Porters Park   (1899)

Shenley Hill, Radlett, WD7 7AZ

- ☎ **(01923) 854127**
- 🖥 (01923) 855475
- 📖 850
- ✍ P Marshall
- ✓ D Gleeson (01923) 854366
- ⊳ 18 L 6313 yds SSS 70
- 👥 WD–H (phone first) WE/BH–M
  SOC–Wed & Thurs
- ££ £40–£55
- 🚗 E of Radlett on Shenley road. M25
  Junction 22

Potters Bar (1923)

Darkes Lane, Potters Bar, EN6 1DE
- ☎ **(01707) 652020**
- 🖥 (01707) 655051
- ✉ info@pottersbargolfclub.com
- 📖 600
- 🏌 PK Watson (Mgr)
- ✓ G A'ris, J Harding (01707) 652987
- ⛳ 18 L 6279 yds SSS 70
- 👥 WD–H WE/BH–M SOC–WD exc Wed
- ££ £26 D–£36
- 🚗 1 mile N of M25 Junction 24, off A1000
- 🏠 James Braid
- 🖳 www.pottersbargolfclub.com

Redbourn (1970)

Proprietary
Kinsbourne Green Lane, Redbourn, St Albans, AL3 7QA
- ☎ **(01582) 793493**
- 🖥 (01582) 794362
- ✉ enquiries@redbourngolfclub.com
- 📖 750
- 🏌 S Hatch (01582) 794888
- ✓ S Hunter (01592) 793493
- ⛳ 18 L 6506 yds SSS 71
  9 hole Par 3 course
- 👥 WD–U booking necessary WE/BH–H SOC–WD
- ££ 9: £7.25 (£8.25) 18: £30 (£35)
- 🚗 4 miles N of St Albans, off A5. 1 mile S of M1 Junction 9
- ⊕ Floodlit golf range
- 🖳 www.redbourngolfclub.com

Rickmansworth (1937)

Public
Moor Lane, Rickmansworth, WD3 1QL
- ☎ **(01923) 775278**

Royston (1892)

Baldock Road, Royston, SG8 5BG
- ☎ **(01763) 242696**
- 🖥 (01763) 246910
- ✉ roystongolf@btconnect.com
- 📖 500
- 🏌 S Clark (Mgr)
- ✓ S Clark (01763) 243476
- ⛳ 18 L 6042 yds SSS 70
- 👥 WD–U WE–M SOC–WD
- ££ £35 (£35)
- 🚗 SW of Royston on A505
- 🏠 H Vardon
- 🖳 www.roystongolfclub.co.uk

Sandy Lodge (1910)

Sandy Lodge Lane, Northwood, Middx, HA6 2JD
- ☎ **(01923) 825429**
- 🖥 (01923) 824319
- ✉ info@sandylodge.co.uk
- 📖 700
- 🏌 JC Coombes
- ✓ J Pinsent (01923) 825321
- ⛳ 18 L 6328 yds SSS 71
- 👥 H or M SOC
- ££ On application
- 🚗 Adjacent Moor Park Station
- 🏠 Harry Vardon
- 🖳 www.sandylodge.co.uk

Shendish Manor (1988)

Pay and play
Shendish Manor, London Road, Apsley, HP3 0AA
- ☎ **(01442) 251806**
- 🖥 (01442) 230683
- ✉ golf@shendish-manor.com
- 🏌 Seema Patel (Mgr) (01442) 251806
- ⛳ 18 L 5660 yds Par 70 SSS 68
- 👥 U SOC
- ££ £18 (£28)
- 🚗 S of Hemel Hempstead, off A41. M25 Junction 20
- 🏠 Cotton/Steel
- 🖳 www.shendish-manor.com

South Herts (1899)

Links Drive, Totteridge, London, N20 8QU
- ☎ **(020) 8445 0117**
- 🖥 (020) 8445 7569
- ✉ secretary@southhertsgolfclub.co.uk
- 📖 850
- 🏌 RJ Weeds (020) 8445 2035
- ✓ RY Mitchell (020) 8445 4633
- ⛳ 18 L 6470 yds SSS 71
  9 L 1581 yds
- 👥 WD–IH WE/BH–M
- ££ On application
- 🚗 Totteridge Lane
- 🏠 Harry Vardon
- 🖳 www.southhertsgolfclub.co.uk

Stevenage (1980)

Public
Aston Lane, Stevenage, SG2 7EL
- ☎ **(01438) 880424**
- 📖 250
- 🏌 Mrs S Elwin (01438) 880322
- ✓ P Winston (01438) 880424
- ⛳ 18 L 6451 yds SSS 71
  9 hole Par 3 course
- 👥 U
- ££ £16 (£21)
- 🚗 Off A602 to Hertford. A1(M) Junction 7
- ⊕ Driving range
- 🏠 John Jacobs

Verulam (1905)

226 London Road, St Albans, AL1 1JG
- ☎ **(01727) 853327**
- 🖥 (01727) 812201
- ✉ gm@verulamgolf.co.uk
- 📖 650
- 🏌 D Cliffe
- ✓ N Burch (01727) 861401
- ⛳ 18 L 6448 yds Par 72 SSS 71
- 👥 WD–H WE/BH–M SOC
- ££ £35 D–£50 Mon–£24 (£50)
- 🚗 1 mile SE of St Albans on A1081. M25 Junction 21A or 22. M1 Junction 6
- ⊕ Practice range
- 🏠 Braid/Steel
- 🖳 www.verulamgolf.co.uk

Welwyn Garden City (1922)

Mannicotts, High Oaks Road, Welwyn Garden City, AL8 7BP
- ☎ **(01707) 325243**
- 🖥 (01707) 393213
- ✉ secretary@welwyngardencitygolfclub.co.uk
- 📖 900
- 🏌 D Spring (Gen Mgr) (01707) 325243
- ✓ R May (01707) 325525
- ⛳ 18 L 6100 yds Par 70 SSS 69
- 👥 WD–H WE/BH–NA
- ££ On application
- 🚗 1 mile N of Hatfield. A1(M) Junction 4 – B197 to Valley Road
- 🏠 Hawtree
- 🖳 www.welwyngardencitygolfclub.co.uk

West Herts (1890)

Cassiobury Park, Watford, WD3 3GG
- ☎ **(01923) 236484**
- 🖥 (01923) 222300
- 📖 700
- 🏌 CC Dodman
- ✓ CS Gough (01923) 220352
- ⛳ 18 L 6602 yds SSS 72
- 👥 WD–U WE/BH–M SOC–Mon, Wed & Fri
- ££ £40 (£50)
- 🚗 Off A412, between Watford and Rickmansworth
- 🏠 Morris/Mackenzie

Wheathampstead (2001)

Pay and play
Harpenden Road, Wheathampstead, St Albans, AL4 8EZ
- ☎ **(01582) 833941**
- 🖥 (01582) 833941
- ✉ wheathampsteadgolfcourse@hotmail.co.uk
- 🏌 JD Edgar (mob - 07960 364212)
- ✓ JD Edgar
- ⛳ 9 L 2100 yds Par 31 SSS 31
- 👥 U SOC
- ££ £13 (£14). 9 holes–£9 Seniors: 9: £7, 18: £10 Children under 14– 9: £6, 18: £10
- 🚗 1 mile W of Wheathampstead (B653)
- ⊕ Driving range
- 🏠 JD Edgar

Whipsnade Park (1974)

Studham Lane, Dagnall, HP4 1RH
- ☎ **(01442) 842330**
- 🖥 (01442) 842090
- ✉ whipsnadeparkgolfc@btopenworld.com
- 📖 600
- 🏌 R Whalley
- ✓ M Day (01442) 842310
- ⛳ 18 L 6812 yds SSS 72
- 👥 WD–U WE–U after 1pm SOC–WD
- ££ £29 D–£40 (£35 D–£46)
- 🚗 8 miles N of Hemel Hempstead, off A4147
- ⊕ Driving range; grass practice ground; putting green
- 🖳 www.whipsnadeparkgolf.co.uk

Whitehill (1990)

Proprietary
Dane End, Ware, SG12 0JS
- ☎ **(01920) 438495**

□ (01920) 438891
✉ whitehillgolf@btconnect.com
☐ 550
🏌 Mr A Smith (Prop)
✓ M Belsham
📏 18 L 6802 yds SSS 72
👤 U
££ £23 (£30)
🚗 4 miles N of Ware (A10)
⊕ Floodlit driving range; practice putting green
🖥 www.whitehillgolf.co.uk

Isle of Man

Castletown Golf Links
(1892)
Fort Island, Derbyhaven, IM9 1UA
☎ **(01624) 822220**
□ (01624) 829661
✉ 1sttee@manx.net
☐ 500
📏 Mrs D Barron
✓ (01624) 822211
📏 18 L 6707 yds SSS 72
👤 U SOC
££ £39 (£45)
🚗 1 mile E of Castletown. 3 miles from Airport
🏠 Old Tom Morris
🖥 www.golfiom.com

Douglas (1891)
Public
Pulrose Park, Douglas, IM2 1AE
☎ **(01624) 675952 (Clubhouse)**
□ (01624) 616865
✉ douglasgolfclub@manx.net
☐ 280
📏 Mrs E Vincent (01624) 616865
✓ M Vipond/A Seddon (01624) 661558
📏 18 L 5922 yds Par 69 SSS 69
👤 U
££ £12.50 (£15) (2006)
🚗 Douglas Pier 2 miles
🏠 Dr A Mackenzie
🖥 www.douglasgolfclub.com

King Edward Bay (1893)
Groudle Road, Onchan, IM3 2JR
☎ **(01624) 620430/673821**

Mount Murray G&CC
(1994)
Santon, IM4 2HT
☎ **(01624) 661111**
□ (01624) 611116
✉ sales@mountmurray.com
☐ 360
📏 AD Dyson (Ext 3023)
✓ AD Dyson (Ext 3023)
📏 18 L 6361 yds SSS 71
👤 U H SOC
££ £25 (£32)
🚗 3 miles SW of Douglas
⊕ Driving range
🖥 www.mountmurray.com

Peel (1895)
Rheast Lane, Peel, IM5 1BG
☎ **(01624) 842227**
□ (01624) 843456
✉ peelgc@manx.net
☐ 600
📏 N Richmond (01624) 843456
✓ M Crowe
📏 18 L 5874 yds SSS 69
👤 WD–U WE/BH–NA before 10.30am SOC
££ £20 (£28)
🚗 10 miles W of Douglas via A1
🏠 James Braid

Port St Mary (1903)
Public
Kallow Road, Port St Mary, IM9 5EJ
☎ **(01624) 834932**
□ (01624) 837231
📏 T Boyle (Hon) (07624) 497387
📏 9 L 2711 yds SSS 68
👤 WD–U WE–NA before 10.30am SOC
££ On application
🚗 6 miles S of Castletown via A5
🏠 George Duncan

Ramsey (1891)
Brookfield, Ramsey, IM8 2AH
☎ **(01624) 813365/812244**
□ (01624) 815833
✉ ramseygolfclub@manx.net
☐ 700
📏 MND Robinson (01624) 812244
✓ A Dyson (01624) 814736
📏 18 L 5982 yds Par 71 SSS 70
👤 WD–U after 10am WE–M SOC
££ £28 (£38)
🚗 N of Douglas via A18. W boundary of Ramsey
🏠 James Braid
🖥 www.ramseygolfclub.com

Rowany (1895)
Rowany Drive, Port Erin, IM9 6LN
☎ **(01624) 834108**
□ (01624) 834072
✉ rowany@iommail.net
☐ 500
📏 CA Corrin (Mgr) (01624) 834072
📏 18 L 5774 yds SSS 69
👤 U SOC
££ £20 (£28)
🚗 6 miles W of Castletown via A5
🖥 www.rowanygolfclub.com

Isle of Wight

Cowes (1909)
Crossfield Avenue, Cowes, PO31 8HN
☎ **(01983) 280135 (Steward)**
☐ 300
📏 D Weaver (01983) 292303
Members (01983) 280135
📏 9 L 5878 yds SSS 68
👤 H Thurs–NA before 3pm (Ladies Day) Sun am–NA
££ £20 (£25)
🚗 Nr Cowes High School
🏠 J Hamilton Stutt

Freshwater Bay (1894)
Afton Down, Freshwater, PO40 9TZ
☎ **(01983) 752955**
□ (01983) 756704
✉ tr.fbgc@btopenworld.com
☐ 550
📏 T Riddett (01983) 752955
📏 18 L 5725 yds SSS 68
👤 NA before 9.30am SOC
££ £24 (£28)
🚗 400 yds off Military Road (A3055)
🖥 www.isle-of-wight.uk.com/golf

Newport (1896)
St George's Down, Shide, Newport, PO30 3BA
☎ **(01983) 525076**
✉ info@newportgolfclub.co.uk
☐ 350
📏 Dave Boon (01983) 525076
📏 9 L 5674 yds SSS 68
(18 holes from Aug 2007)
👤 WD–U exc Wed–NA 12–2.30pm Sat–NA before 3.30pm Sun–NA before noon SOC
££ £20 (£25)
🚗 1 mile SE of Newport
🏠 Guy Hunt
🖥 www.newportgolfclub.co.uk

Osborne (1904)
Osborne House Estate, East Cowes, PO32 6JX
□ (01983) 295421
✉ info@osbornegolfclub.wanadoo.co.uk
☐ 350
📏 AC Waite
📏 9 L 6358 yds SSS 70
👤 WD–U exc Ladies Day (Tues) 9am–12.30pm–NA WE–NA before noon SOC
££ £23 (£27) 5D–£70 (to April 1, 2007)
🚗 S of East Cowes in grounds of Osborne House
🖥 www.osbornegolfclub.co.uk

Ryde (1895)
Binstead Road, Ryde, PO33 3NF
☎ **(01983) 614809**
□ (01983) 567418
✉ ryde.golfclub@btinternet.com
☐ 450
📏 RA Dean
✓ None
📏 9 L 5772 yds Par 70 SSS 69
👤 WD–NA before 10am Wed–NA before 2pm (Ladies Day) WE–NA before 11am
££ £20 (£24) – 18 holes
🚗 On main Ryde/Newport road
🏠 J Hamilton Stutt
🖥 www.rydegolf.co.uk

Shanklin & Sandown
(1900)
The Fairway, Lake, Sandown, PO36 9PR
☎ **(01983) 403217**
□ (01983) 403007
✉ club@ssgolfclub.com

☐ 700
🖉 AC Creed
✔ P Hammond (01983) 404424
🏳 18 L 6062 yds SSS 69
👥 WD–U WE–NA before 12 noon
££ £32 (£37.50) 3WD–£75
🚗 I mile off A3055 in Lake
🏠 James Braid
🗐 www.ssgolfclub.com

Ventnor   (1892)

Steephill Down Road, Ventnor, PO38 IBP
☎ (01983) 853326/853388
🖳 (01983) 853326
🖂 secretary@ventnorgolfclub.co.uk
☐ 250
🖉 S Blackmore
🏳 12 L 5767 yds Par 70 SSS 68 (18 tees)
👥 WD–U Sun–NA before Ipm SOC
££ £15 (£20 + BH)
🚗 NW boundary of Ventnor
⊕ Nets; putting green
🗐 www.ventnorgolfclub.co.uk

Westridge   (1990)

Pay and play
Brading Road, Ryde, PO33 IQS
☎ (01983) 613131
🖳 (01983) 567017
🖂 westgc@aol.com
🖉 Simon Hayward
✔ Mark Wright
🏳 9 L 3768 yds Par 60
👥 U
££ D–£11 Week–£12
🚗 2 miles S of Ryde (A3054)
⊕ Driving range with power tees; practice bunker, green, chipping
🏠 Mark Wright
🗐 www.westridgegc.co.uk

Kent

Aquarius   (1912)

Marmora Rd, Honor Oak, London, SE22 0RY
☎ (020) 8693 1626
☐ 400
🖉 J Halliday
✔ F Private
🏳 9 L 5246 yds SSS 66
👥 M
🗐 aquariusgolfclub@btopenworld.com

Ashford   (1903)

Sandyhurst Lane, Ashford, TN25 4NT
☎ (01233) 620180

Austin Lodge   (1991)

Upper Auston Lodge Road, Eynsford, Swanley, DA4 0HU
☎ (01322) 863000

Barnehurst   (1903)

Public
Mayplace Road East, Bexley Heath, DA7 6JU
☎ (01322) 523746

Bearsted   (1895)

Ware Street, Bearsted, Maidstone, ME14 4PQ
☎ (01622) 738389
🖳 (01622) 735608
☐ 780
🖉 (01622) 738198
✔ T Simpson (01622) 738024
🏳 18 L 6253 yds SSS 70
👥 WD–I H WE–H M (recognised GC members) SOC
££ £32–£42 (£37)
🚗 2½ miles E of Maidstone; J7 off M20

Bexleyheath   (1909)

Mount Road, Bexleyheath, DA6 8JS
☎ (020) 8303 6951
🖂 bexleyheathgolf@aol.com
☐ 350
🖉 Mrs J Smith
🏳 9 L 5239 yds SSS 66
👥 WD–H before 4pm
££ £20
🚗 Station I mile

Birchwood Park   (1990)

Birchwood Road, Wilmington, Dartford, DA2 7HJ
☎ (01322) 662038

Boughton   (1993)

Pay and play
Brickfield Lane, Boughton, Faversham, ME13 9AJ
☎ (01227) 752277
🖳 (01227) 752361
🖂 greg@pentlandgolf.co.uk
☐ 300
🖉 G Haenen (Mgr)
✔ T Dungate, G Naenen
🏳 18 L 6452 yds SSS 71
9 hole par 3 course
👥 U SOC–WD/WE
££ £20 (£27.50)
🚗 NE of Boughton, nr M2/A2 interchange. 6 miles W of Canterbury
⊕ Driving range; putting green; short game area
🏠 Philip Sparks
🗐 www.pentlandgolf.co.uk

Broke Hill   (1993)

Sevenoaks Road, Halstead, TN14 7HR
☎ (01959) 533225
🖳 (01959) 532680
🖂 broke-sales@crows-golf.co.uk
🖉 Mark Clarke
✔ Iain Naylor (01959) 533810
🏳 18 L 6374 yds Par 72 SSS 71
👥 WD–U before 5pm WE–NA SOC–WD
££ £35
🚗 4 miles S of Bromley on A21. M25 Junction 4
⊕ Practice and chipping area
🏠 David Williams
🗐 www.brokehillgolf.co.uk

Bromley   (1948)

Public
Magpie Hall Lane, Bromley, BR2 8JF
☎ (020) 8462 7014
🖳 (020) 8462 6916
🖂 bromleygolfcourse@wanadoo.co.uk
☐ 200
🖉 Ian Smith
✔ A Hodgson
🏳 9 L 5590 yds SSS 67
👥 U
££ £8.50 (£11)
🚗 Off Bromley Common (A21)
⊕ Floodlit 20-bay driving range

Broome Park   (1981)

Broome Park Estate, Barham, Canterbury, CT4 6QX
☎ (01227) 830728
🖳 (01227) 832591
🖂 admin@broomepark.co.uk
☐ 600
🖉 G Robins
✔ T Britz (01227) 831126
🏳 18 L 6580 yds SSS 71
👥 H WE–NA before noon SOC–WD
££ £40 (£50)
🚗 M2/A2-A260 Folkestone road, 1½ miles on RH side
⊕ Driving range
🏠 Donald Steel
🗐 www.broomepark.co.uk

Canterbury   (1927)

Scotland Hills, Littlebourne Road, Canterbury, CT1 1TW
☎ (01227) 453532
🖳 (01227) 784277
🖂 cgc@freeola.com
☐ 705
🖉 John Morgan
✔ P Everard (01227) 462865
🏳 18 L 6272 yds Par 71 SSS 70
👥 WD–U H WE–NA before 11.30am SOC–Tues/Thurs/Fri
££ £45 (£50)
🚗 I mile E of Canterbury on A257
🏠 HS Colt
🗐 www.canterburygolfclub.org.uk

Chart Hills   (1993)

Weeks Lane, Biddenden, Ashford, TN27 8JX
☎ (01580) 292222
🖳 (01580) 292233
🖂 info@charthills.co.uk
☐ 495
🖉 Roed Park, PGA (Gen Mgr)
✔ James Cornish, PGA (Dir of Golf) (01580) 292148
🏳 18 L 7135 yds SSS 74
👥 Mon–Fri restricted times, Sat–sun+BH pm only, SOC
££ On application
🚗 12 miles W of Ashford (A262). M20 Jcts 8 or 9
⊕ Golf Academy
🏠 Nick Faldo
🗐 www.charthills.co.uk

Chelsfield Lakes Golf Centre   (1992)

Pay and play
Court Road, Orpington, BR6 9BX
- ☎ **(01689) 896266**
- 🖷 (01689) 824577
- 📖 650
- 🖉 Roger Tomey (Mgr)
- ✓ N Lee
- ⮞ 18 L 6077 yds Par 71 SSS 69
  9 hole Par 3 course
- 👥 SOC
- ££ £20 (£28)
- 🚗 1 mile from M25 Junction 4 (A224)
- ⊕ Target golf range
- 🏠 MRM Sandow
- 🖳 www.crown-golf.co.uk

Cherry Lodge   (1969)

Jail Lane, Biggin Hill, Westerham, TN16 3AX
- ☎ **(01959) 572250**
- 🖷 (01959) 540672
- 🖾 info@cherrylodgegc.co.uk
- 📖 650
- ✓ N Child (01959) 572989
- ⮞ 18 L 6593 yds SSS 73
- 👥 WD–U WE–M SOC–WD before 3pm
- ££ £40 D–£55
- 🚗 3 miles N of Westerham, off A233
- ⊕ Practice facilities
- 🏠 John Day
- 🖳 www.cherrylodgegc.co.uk

Chestfield   (1925)

103 Chestfield Road, Whitstable, CT5 3LU
- ☎ **(01227) 794411**
- 🖷 (01227) 794454
- 🖾 secretary@chestfield-golfclub.co.uk
- 📖 700
- 🖉 Nick Pout
- ✓ J Brotherton (01227) 793563
- ⮞ 18 L 6208 yds SSS 70
- 👥 WD–U WE–NA before noon SOC
- ££ £28 (£35)
- 🚗 ½ mile S of A2990 and Chestfield Station
- 🏠 Donald Steel
- 🖳 www.chestfield-golfclub.co.uk

Chislehurst   (1894)

Camden Place, Camden Park Road, Chislehurst, BR7 5HJ
- ☎ **(020) 8467 3055**
- 🖷 (020) 8295 0874
- 🖾 thesecretary@chislehurstgolfclub.co.uk
- 📖 740
- 🖉 P Foord (020) 8467 2782
- ✓ J Bird (020) 8467 6798
- ⮞ 18 L 5128 yds SSS 65
- 👥 WD–H WE–M SOC
- ££ £30
- 🚗 M25 Junction 3/A20/A222
- 🖳 www.chislehurstgolfclub.co.uk

Cobtree Manor Park   (1984)

Public
Chatham Road, Boxley, Maidstone, ME14 3AZ
- ☎ **(01622) 753276**

- 🖷 (01622) 620387
- 🖾 paul@medwaygolf.co.uk
- 📖 300
- 🖉 Steve Mattingly
- ✓ Paul Foston (01622) 753276
- ⮞ 18 L 5611 yds Par 69 SSS 69
- 👥 WD–U WE/BH–(book 1 wk in advance) SOC–WD
- ££ From £17.50 (£19)
- 🚗 3 miles N of Maidstone on A229
- 🏠 F Hawtree
- 🖳 www.medwaygolf.co.uk

Darenth Valley   (1973)

Pay and play
Station Road, Shoreham, Sevenoaks, TN14 7SA
- ☎ **(01959) 522944 (Clubhouse)**
  (01959) 522922 (Bookings)
- 🖷 (01959) 525089
- 🖾 enquiries@dvgc.co.uk
- 🖉 JR Cooper (Mgr)
- ✓ A Weller (01959) 522922
- ⮞ 18 L 6258 yds Par 72 SSS 71
- 👥 U–booking required SOC
- ££ £20 (£27)
- 🚗 3 miles N of Sevenoaks, off A225. M25 Junctions 3 or 5
- 🖳 www.dvgc.co.uk

Dartford   (1897)

The Clubhouse, Heath Lane (Upper), Dartford DA1 2TN
- ☎ **(01322) 223616**
- 🖾 dartfordgolf@hotmail.com
- 📖 750
- 🖉 Mrs Amanda Malas (01322) 226455
- ✓ J Gregory (01322) 226409
- ⮞ 18 L 5909 yds Par 69 SSS 69
- 👥 WD–I WE–M H
- ££ £23.50
- 🚗 Dartford 2 miles. Dartford Heath turn off A2
- 🏠 James Braid

Deangate Ridge   (1972)

Public
Duxcourt Road, Hoo, Rochester, ME3 8RZ
- ☎ **(01634) 254481 (Gen Mgr)**
  (01634) 254481 (Soc Bookings)
- 📖 560
- 🖉 Mrs CJ Williams (01634) 251950
- ✓ R Fox (01634) 251180
- ⮞ 18 L 6300 yds SSS 70
- 👥 U SOC
- ££ On application
- 🚗 7 miles NE of Rochester on A228. M2, 5 miles
- ⊕ 11 bay driving range; pitch & putt (18 holes)
- 🏠 Hawtree
- 🖳 www.medway.gov.uk/leisure

Eltham Warren   (1890)

Bexley Road, Eltham, London, SE9 2PE
- ☎ **(0208) 331 2831**
- 🖾 secretary@elthamwarren.tdps.co.uk
- 📖 430
- 🖉 DJ Clare (020) 8850 4477
- ✓ G Brett (020) 8859 7909
- ⮞ 9 L 5850 yds SSS 68

- 👥 WD–I WE/BH–M SOC–Thurs only
- ££ D–£28 (£14)
- 🚗 ½ mile from Eltham station on A210
- 🏠 James Braid
- 🖳 www.elthamwarrengolfclub.co.uk

Etchinghill   (1995)

Pay and play
Canterbury Road, Etchinghill, Folkestone, CT18 8FA
- ☎ **(01303) 863863**
- 🖷 (01303) 863210
- 📖 550
- 🖉 J Callister (01303) 862280
- ✓ C Hodgson (01303) 863966
- ⮞ Valley: 18 L 6101 Par 70 SSS 69
  Leas: 18 L 5824 Par 70 SSS 69
  9 hole Par 3 course
- 👥 WD–U WE–NA 7am–11am
- ££ Leas: £19.50 (£26) Valley: £14 (£21)
- 🚗 1 mile N of M20 Junction 12 on B2065
- ⊕ Driving range
- 🏠 John Sturdy

Faversham   (1902)

Belmont Park, Faversham, ME13 0HB
- ☎ **(01795) 890561**
- 🖷 (01795) 890760
- 🖾 themanager@favershamgolf.co.uk
- 📖 800
- 🖉 J Edgington
- ✓ S Rokes (01795) 890275
- ⮞ 18 L 5978 yds Par 70 SSS 69
- 👥 WD–I or H WE–M
- ££ £35 D–£45
- 🚗 Faversham and M2, 2 miles
- 🖳 www.favershamgolf.co.uk

Fawkham Valley   (1987)

Gay Dawn Farm, Fawkham, Dartford, DA3 8LZ
- ☎ **(01474) 707144**
- 🖷 (01474) 707911
- 🖾 info@fawkhamvalleygolf.co.uk
- 📖 300
- 🖉 J Marchant
- ✓ N Willis
- ⮞ 9 L 6547 yds Par 72 SSS 72
- 👥 U SOC
- ££ £25 (£35)
- 🚗 4 miles S of Dartford Tunnel. E of Brands Hatch along Fawkham Valley road
- ⊕ Practice ground, nets & putting green
- 🖳 www.fawkhamvalleygolf.co.uk

Gillingham   (1905)

Woodlands Road, Gillingham, ME7 2AP
- ☎ **(01634) 853017/850999**
- 🖷 (01634) 574749
- 🖾 golf@gillinghamgolf.idps.co.uk
- 📖 800
- 🖉 Miss K Snow (01634) 853017
- ✓ A Brooks (01634) 855862
- ⮞ 18 L 5260 yds SSS 66
- 👥 WD–I H WE/BH–M
- ££ £20 D–£28
- 🚗 A2/M2, 2 miles

For list of abbreviations and key to symbols see page 651

⌂ Braid/Steel
🖳 www.gillinghamgolfclub.co.uk

Hawkhurst (1968)
High Street, Hawkhurst, TN18 4JS
☎ (01580) 754074/752396
🖳 (01580) 754074
📠 hawkhurstgolfclub@tiscali.co.uk
📖 450
🔑 B Morrison (Gen Mgr)
✓ P Chandler (01580) 754396
ᐳ 9 L 5751 yds Par 70 SSS 68
🚶 WD–U WE–M SOC
££ 9: £13.50 (£16.50) 18: £22 (£26)
⛳ 14 miles S of Tunbridge Wells on A268
🖳 HawkhurstGolfClub.org.uk

Hemsted Forest (1969)
Golford Road, Cranbrook, TN17 4AL
☎ (01580) 712833
🖳 (01580) 714274
📠 golf@hemsteadforest.co.uk
🔑 K Stevenson
✓ C Weston
ᐳ 18 L 6305 yds SSS 70
🚶 WD–U WE/BH–restricted SOC
££ £30 (£40)
⛳ 15 miles S of Maidstone. M25 Junction 5–A21/A262
⌂ Cdr J Harris
🖳 www.hemsteadforest.co.uk

Herne Bay (1895)
Eddington, Herne Bay, CT6 7PG
☎ (01227) 374097
📠 sue.brown@hernebaygolfclub.co.uk
📖 500
🔑 SU Brown (01227) 373964
✓ D Ledingham (01227) 374727
ᐳ 18 L 5567 yds SSS 68
🚶 WD–U WE/BH–H after noon SOC–WD
££ £20 D–£27(£27)
⛳ A2299 Thanet road
🖳 www.hernebaygolfclub.co.uk

Hever Castle (1993)
Proprietary
Hever Road, Hever, TN8 7NP
☎ (01732) 700771
🖳 (01732) 700775
📠 mail@hevercastlegolfcub.co.uk
📖 500
🔑 Jon Wittenberg
✓ Peter Parks
ᐳ 18 L 7002 yds SSS 75
9 L 2784 yds
🚶 H SOC WD–U after 11am WE–U after 10.30am
££ £37 (£45)
⛳ 2 miles E of Edenbridge
⊕ Driving range; putting green; chipping area
⌂ Peter Nicholson
🖳 www.hevercastlegolflcub.co.uk

High Elms (1969)
Public
High Elms Road, Downe, Orpington, BR6 7SZ
☎ (01689) 858175

🖳 (01689) 856326
📠 hegc@pgr.org.uk
📖 423
🔑 Mrs P O'Keeffe (Hon)
✓ P Remy
ᐳ 18 L 6221 yds Par 71 SSS 70
🚶 U
££ On application
⛳ M25 J4, off A21 via Shire Lane
⌂ Hawtree
🖳 www.highelmsgolfclub.com

Hilden Golf Centre
Pay and play
Rings Hill, Hildenborough, Tonbridge, TN11 8LX
☎ (01732) 833607
🖳 (01732) 834484
📠 info@hildenpark.co.uk
🔑 Vicki Brett
✓ Rupert Hunter, Matt Jarvis, Nicky Way, Karl Steptoe
ᐳ 9 L 1554 yds Par 3 SSS 54 (men), SSS 60 (ladies)
🚶 U
££ 9: £7.50 (£10) 18: £11.50 (£15)
⛳ M25/A21
⊕ Driving range
🖳 www.hildenpark.co.uk

Hythe Imperial (1950)
Prince's Parade, Hythe, CT21 6AE
☎ (01303) 233745
🖳 (01303) 267554
📖 445
🔑 B Duncan (01303) 267554
✓ J Leaver (01303) 233745
ᐳ 9 L 5560 yds SSS 67
🚶 H SOC
££ £15 (£20)
⛳ On coast, 4 miles W of Folkestone

The Kent & Surrey G&CC (2006)
Proprietary
Crouch House Road, Edenbridge, TN8 5LQ
☎ (01732) 867381
🖳 (01732) 867029
📠 info@thekentandsurrey.com
📖 350
🔑 Simon Earl
✓ Nigel Burch (01732) 865202
ᐳ 18 L 6577 yds SSS 72
18 L 5605 yds SSS 67
9 hole course
🚶 WD/WE–booking necessary
££ £20 (£27.50)
⛳ 2 miles W of Edenbridge. M25 Junction 6
⊕ Floodlit driving range
⌂ David Williams
🖳 www.thekentandsurrey.com

Kent National G&CC (1993)
Watermans Lane, Brenchley, Tonbridge, TN12 6ND
☎ (01892) 724400
🖳 (01892) 723300
📠 info@kentnational.com

🔑 M Orwin (Dir of Ops)
✓ J Eldridge
ᐳ 18 L 7060 yds Par 72 SSS 74
🚶 WD/WE–U SOC–WD
££ £35 (£45); Twilight £20 (£25)
⛳ Between Matfield and Paddock Wood, off B2160
⊕ Driving range
⌂ T Saito
🖳 www.@kentnational.com

Kings Hill (1996)
Kings Hill, West Malling, ME19 4AF
☎ (01732) 875040/842121 (Bookings)

Knole Park (1924)
Seal Hollow Road, Sevenoaks, TN15 0HJ
☎ (01732) 452150
🖳 (01732) 463159
📠 secretary@knowleparkgolfclub .co.uk
📖 700
🔑 AP Mitchell (01732) 452150
✓ P Sykes (01732) 451740
ᐳ 18 L 6246 yds SSS 70
🚶 WD–restricted WE/BH–M H SOC
££ £36 D–£46
⛳ 1/2 mile from Sevenoaks centre
⌂ JF Abercromby
🖳 www.knoleparkgolfclub.co.uk

Lamberhurst (1890)
Church Road, Lamberhurst, TN3 8DT
☎ (01892) 890241
🖳 (01892) 891140
📠 secretary@lamberhurstgolfclub .com
📖 600
🔑 KJ Rawlins (01892) 890591
✓ BM Impett (01892) 890552
ᐳ 18 L 6409 yds SSS 71
🚶 WD–U H WE–NA before noon
££ £31 D–£41 Oct–Mar £33 D–£43 Apr–Sept
⛳ 5 miles SE of Tunbridge Wells, off A21
⊕ Small limited club practice area
🖳 www.lamberhurstgolfclub.com

Langley Park (1910)
Barnfield Wood Road, Beckenham, BR3 6SZ
☎ (020) 8658 6849
🖳 (020) 8658 6310
📠 manager@langleyparkgolf.co.uk
📖 750
🔑 R Pollard (Gen Mgr) (020) 8658 6849
✓ C Staff (020) 8650 1663
ᐳ 18 L 6453 yds SSS 71
🚶 WD–H WE–M SOC–WD
££ £40
⛳ Bromley South Station 1 mile. M25 Junction 4
⌂ JH Taylor
🖳 www.langleyparkgolf.co.uk

Leeds Castle (1928)

Pay and play
Leeds Castle, Hollingbourne, Maidstone, ME17 1PL
- ☎ **(01622) 880467/767828**
- 🖥 (01622) 735616
- ✉ stevepurves@leeds-castle.co.uk
- ✓ S Purves
- ⏸ 9 L 2451 yds Par 33
- 👥 U SOC–WD 6–day advance booking
- ££ 9: £11 (£13) 18: £18.50 (£26)
- 🚗 4 miles E of Maidstone (A20). M20 Junction 8, 1 mile
- ⊕ Practice ground and nets; free admission to Leeds Castle park, gardens and attractions
- 🏠 Neil Coles
- 📧 www.leeds-castle.com

Littlestone (1888)

St Andrews Road, Littlestone, New Romney, TN28 8RB
- ☎ **(01797) 362310**
- 🖥 (01797) 362740
- ✉ secretary@littlestonegolfclub.org.uk
- 📖 450
- 🏌 Col C Moorhouse (01797) 363355
- ✓ A Jones (01797) 362231
- ⏸ 18 L 6676 yds Par 71 SSS 73
- 👥 WD–H WE–by arrangement SOC
- ££ £45 (£65)
- 🚗 2 miles E of New Romney. 15 miles SE of Ashford. M20 Junction 10
- 🏠 W Laidlaw Purves/Dr A Mackenzie
- 📧 www.littlestonegolfclub.org.uk

London Beach (1998)

Pay and play
Ashford Road, St Michaels, Tenterden, TN30 6SP
- ☎ **(01580) 766279**
- ✉ enquiries@londonbeach.net

The London Golf Club (1993)

South Ash Manor Estate, Ash, Nr Brands Hatch, TN15 7EN
- ☎ **(01474) 879899**
- 🖥 (01474) 879912
- ✉ golf@londongolf.co.uk
- 📖 550
- 🏌 Scott Evans
- ✓ P Stuart, A Robertson
- ⏸ Heritage 18 L 7208 yds Par 72 SSS 74
  International 18 L 7005 yds Par 72 SSS 74
- 👥 M 1 SOC–WD Heritage–M International SOC WD
- ££ On application
- 🚗 Off A20, nr Brands Hatch
- ⊕ Driving range. Academy
- 🏠 Nicklaus/Kirby
- 📧 www.londongolf.co.uk

Lullingstone Park (1967)

Public
Parkgate Road, Chelsfield, Orpington, BR6 7PX
- ☎ **(01959) 533793**

- 🏌 CJ Pocock (0208) 303 9535
- ✓ M Watt
- ⏸ 18 L 6734 yds SSS 72
  9 L 2379 yds Par 33
- 👥 U SOC WD/WE
- ££ On application
- 🚗 Off Orpington Bypass (A224) towards Well Hill. M25 Junction 4
- ⊕ Driving range; 9 hole pitch & putt course

Lydd (1994)

Proprietary
Romney Road, Lydd, Romney Marsh, TN29 9LS
- ☎ **(01797) 320808**
- 🖥 (01797) 321482
- ✉ info@lyddgolfclub.co.uk
- 📖 400
- 🏌 Graham Barrett
- ✓ Richard Perkins (01797) 321201
- ⏸ 18 L 6529 yds Par 71 SSS 71
- 👥 U SOC
- ££ £21 (£30)
- 🚗 15 miles SE of Ashford, by Lydd Airport (B2075). M20 Junction 10
- ⊕ Driving range; Academy course
- 🏠 M Smith
- 📧 www.lyddgolfclub.co.uk

Mid Kent (1908)

Singlewell Road, Gravesend, DA11 7RB
- ☎ **(01474) 568035**
- 🖥 (01474) 564218
- ✉ secretary@mkgc.co.uk
- 📖 870
- 🏌 P Gleeson (01474) 568035
- ✓ M Foreman (01474) 332810
- ⏸ 18 L 6106 yds Par 70 SSS 69
- 👥 WD–H WE–M
- ££ £30/£35 weekdays only
- 🚗 SE of Gravesend, nr A2
- ⊕ Practice area - irons only
- 🏠 Frank Pennink
- 📧 www.mkgc.co.uk

Nizels (1992)

Nizels Lane, Hildenborough, Tonbridge, TN11 8NU
- ☎ **(01732) 833833**
- 🖥 (01732) 835492
- ✉ nizels@theclubcompany.com
- 📖 800
- 🏌 P Ferguson (Gen Mgr)
- ✓ D Vickerman
- ⏸ 18 L 6297 yds SSS 71
- 👥 WD–U SOC
- ££ £30 (£40)
- 🚗 4 miles from M25 on B245. A21 Tonbridge North Junction
- 🏠 Lennan/Purnell
- 📧 www.theclubcompany.com

North Foreland (1903)

Convent Road, Broadstairs, Kent, CT10 3PU
- ☎ **(01843) 862140**
- 🖥 (01843) 862663
- ✉ office@northforeland.co.uk
- 📖 1100
- 🏌 AJ Adams (01843) 862140
- ✓ D Parris (01843) 604471

- ⏸ 18 L 6430 yds SSS 71
  18 hole Par 3 course L 1752 yds
- 👥 WD–H WE–NA am –H pm
- ££ £39 D–£51 (£51)
- 🚗 B2052, 1½ miles N of Broadstairs
- ⊕ Practice ground and putting green
- 🏠 Fowler/Simpson
- 📧 www.northforeland.co.uk

Oastpark (1992)

Pay and play
Malling Road, Snodland, ME6 5LG
- ☎ **(01634) 242661**
- 🖥 (01634) 240744
- ✉ oastparkgolfclub@btconnect.com
- 📖 320
- 🏌 Lesley Murrock (01634) 242818
- ✓ D Porthouse (01634) 242661
- ⏸ 9 L 2850 yds Par 34 SSS 34
- 👥 U SOC
- ££ 9: £7 (£8) 18: £12 (£14)
- 🚗 1 mile E of M20 Junction 4
- ⊕ Driving range

Park Wood (1994)

Proprietary
Chestnut Avenue, Tatsfield, Westerham, TN16 2EG
- ☎ **(01959) 577744**
- 🖥 (01959) 572702
- ✉ mail@parkwoodgolf.co.uk
- 📖 450
- 🏌 Miss RLR Goldsmith (Man Dir)
- ✓ N Terry (01959) 577177
- ⏸ 18 L 6527 yds Par 72 SSS 72
- 👥 U SOC
- ££ On application
- 🚗 Tatsfield, nr Westerham. M25 J4/5
- ⊕ Large practice area with bunker and green; 18-hole putting green
- 📧 www.parkwoodgolf.co.uk

Pedham Place Golf Centre (1996)

Proprietary
London Road, Swanley, BR8 8PP
- ☎ **(01322) 867000**
- 🖥 (01322) 861646
- ✉ golf@ppgc.co.uk
- 📖 456
- 🏌 Beverley Smith
- ✓ Jon Woodroffe
- ⏸ 18 L 6444 yds Par 72 SSS 71
  9 hole Par 3 course
- 👥 WD–U WE–U SOC WD WE
- ££ £19.50 (£26.50)
- 🚗 Swanley 1 mile. M25 J3 300 m
- ⊕ Driving range; putting green
- 🏠 John Fortune
- 📧 www.ppgc.co.uk

Poult Wood (1974)

Public
Higham Lane, Tonbridge, TN11 9QR
- ☎ **(01732) 364039 (Bookings)**
  (01732) 366180 (Clubhouse)

Prince's (1906)

Proprietary
Sandwich Bay, Sandwich, CT13 9QB
- ☎ **(01304) 611118**

☐ (01304) 612000
✉ office@princesgolfclub.co.uk
☐ 300
✍ WM Howie (Dir) (01304) 626909
✓ R McGuirk (01304) 613797
▷ 27 hole course (3 x 9 holes):
   Dunes/Himalayas/Shore
   Length 6813-7204 yds
   Par 71-72 SSS 72-73
☗ U SOC
££ Winter: £40 (£50) Summer: £70
   D–£80 (£80 D–£90)
⊶ Sandwich Bay (A256)
⊕ Driving range; extensive practice
   areas inc. bunkers, chipping area,
   practice hole
☗ Morrison/Campbell
☷ www.princesgolfclub.co.uk

Redlibbets   (1996)
Proprietary
West Yoke, Ash, Nr Sevenoaks, TN15 7HT
☎ **(01474) 879190**
☐ (01474) 879290
✉ redlibbets@golfandsport.co.uk
☐ 500
✍ J Potter
✓ R Taylor (01474) 872278
▷ 18 L 6651 yds Par 72
☗ WD SOC
££ £40
⊶ Off A20 between Fawkham and
   Ash. M20 Jct 2. M25 Jct 3
⊕ Practice ground; indoor net room
☗ Jonathan Gaunt
☷ www.golfandsport.co.uk

The Ridge   (1993)
*Chartway Street, East Sutton, Maidstone,
ME17 3JB*
☎ **(01622) 844382**

Riverside   (1991)
Pay and play
*Fairway Drive, Thamesmead, London,
SE28 8PP*
☎ **(020) 8310 7975**

Rochester & Cobham Park
(1891)
Park Pale, by Rochester, ME2 3UL
☎ **(01474) 823411**
☐ (01474) 824446
✉ rcpgc@talk21.com
☐ 630
✍ DW Smith (Mgr)
✓ I Higgins (01474) 823658
▷ 18 L 6597 yds SSS 71
☗ WD–U H WE–M SOC–Tues &
   Thurs. Soft spikes only
££ £37.50
⊶ 3 miles E of Gravesend exit (A2)
⊕ Full practice facilities
☗ D Steel
☷ www.rochesterandcobhamgc.co.uk

Romney Warren   (1993)
Pay and play
*St Andrews Road, Littlestone, New Romney,
TN28 8RB*
☎ **(01797) 362231**

☐ (01797) 362740
✉ secretary@romneywarrengolfclub
   .org.uk
☐ 300
✍ J Purkiss (Hon Sec) (01797) 362768
   Col C Moorhouse (Mgr)
✓ A Jones
▷ 18 L 5126 yds SSS 65
☗ U SOC
££ £18 (£23)
⊶ 2 miles E of New Romney. 15 miles
   SE of Ashford
⊕ 9-bay driving range; video studio
☗ Evans/Lewis
☷ www.romneywarrengolfclub.org.uk

Royal Blackheath   (1608)
Court Road, Eltham, London, SE9 5AF
☎ **(020) 8850 1795**
☐ (020) 8859 0150
✉ info@rbgc.com
☐ 700
✍ MJ Miller
✓ R Harrison (020) 8850 1763
▷ 18 L 6219 yds SSS 70
☗ WD–I or H WE/BH–M SOC
££ £50 D–£70
⊶ 5 miles W of M25 Junction 3
⊕ Golf Museum
☗ James Braid
☷ www.rbgc.com

Royal Cinque Ports
(1892)
Golf Road, Deal, CT14 6RF
☎ **(01304) 374007 (Office)**
☐ (01304) 379530
✉ ian.symington@royalcinqueports
   .com
☐ 650
✍ Ian Symington (01304) 374007
✓ A Reynolds (01304) 374170
▷ 18 L 6899 yds SSS 73
☗ WD–H after 9.30am SOC
££ On application
⊶ A258, N of Deal
⊕ Full practice facilities
☗ H Hunter
☷ www.royalcinqueports.com

Royal St George's   (1887)
Sandwich, CT13 9PB
☎ **(01304) 613090**
☐ (01304) 611245
✉ secretary@royalstgeorges.com
☐ 775
✍ HCG Gabbey
✓ A Brooks (01304) 615236
▷ 18 L 7102 yds Par 70 SSS 74
☗ WD–I H WE–M SOC–WD
££ £120 D–£150
⊶ 1 mile E of Sandwich
☗ Dr Laidlaw Purves
☷ www.royalstgeorges.com

Sene Valley   (1888)
Sene, Folkestone, CT18 8BL
☎ **(01303) 268513**
☐ (01303) 237513
✉ senevalleygolf@btconnect.com
☐ 650
✍ Stuart More (Mgr)

✓ N Watson (01303) 268514
▷ 18 L 6271 yds SSS 70 Par 71
☗ WD SOC Tue pm & Thur all day;
   WE NA before noon; WD–U H
££ £30 (£35)
⊶ 2 miles N of Hythe on B2065; M20
   J12
☗ Henry Cotton
☷ www.senevalleygolfclub.co.uk

Sheerness   (1909)
Power Station Road, Sheerness, ME12 3AE
☎ **(01795) 662585**
☐ (01795) 668100
✉ thesecretary@sheernessgc
   .freeserve.co.uk
☐ 600
✍ AF Jones
✓ L Stanford (01795) 583060
▷ 18 L 6390 yds SSS 71
☗ WD–U SOC
££ £22
⊶ 9 miles N of Sittingbourne. M20,
   M2 or A2 to A249

Shooter's Hill   (1903)
Lowood, Eaglesfield Road, London, SE18 3DA
☎ **(020) 8854 6368**
☐ (020) 8854 0469
✉ secretary@shootershillgc.co.uk
☐ 600 60(L) 60(J)
✍ Mrs S Deadman (020) 8854 6368
✓ D Brotherton (020) 8854 0073
▷ 18 L 5721 yds SSS 68
☗ WD–H WE/BH–M SOC–Tues &
   Thurs only H
££ £28 D–£35
⊶ Off A207 nr Blackheath
☗ Willie Park
☷ www.shootershillgc.co.uk

Shortlands   (1894)
*Meadow Road, Shortlands, Bromley,
BR2 0DX*
☎ **(020) 8460 2471**
☐ (020) 8460 8828
☐ 525
✍ PS May (020) 8460 8828
✓ M Wood (020) 8464 6182
▷ 9 L 5222 yds SSS 65
☗ M
££ 9: £10, 18: £15
⊶ Ravensbourne Ave, Shortlands

Sidcup   (1891)
7 Hurst Road, Sidcup, DA15 9AE
☎ **(020) 8300 2864**
☐ (020) 8300 2150
✉ sidcupgolfclub@tiscali.co.uk
☐ 400
✍ J Aughterlony (020) 8300 2150
▷ 9 L 5571 yds Par 68 SSS 68
☗ WD–H WE/BH–M SOC–WD
££ £25
⊶ On A222. A2/A20, 2 miles

Sittingbourne & Milton
Regis   (1929)
*Wormdale, Newington, Sittingbourne,
ME9 7PX*
☎ **(01795) 842261**

☎ (01795) 844117
✉ sittingbournegc@btconnect.com
📖 725
✍ Charles Maxted
✓ John Hearn (01795) 842775
► 18 L 6291 yds SSS 70
♟ WD–U Sat–M Sun–M SOC–Tues & Thurs
££ £32 D–£40
🚗 N of M2 Junction 5, towards Danaway
▤ www.sittingbournegolfclub.com

Southern Valley   (1999)
Pay and play
Thong Lane, Shorne, Gravesend, DA12 4LF
☎ (01474) 740026,
(01474) 568568 (Bookings)
✉ info@southernvalley.co.uk

St Augustines   (1907)
Cottington Road, Cliffsend, Ramsgate, CT12 5JN
☎ (01843) 590333
🖷 (01843) 590444
✉ sagc@ic24.net
📖 650 55(J)
✍ RF Tranckle
✓ DB Scott (01843) 590222
► 18 L 5254 yds SS 66
♟ H SOC–WD
££ £22 (£28)
🚗 2 miles SW of Ramsgate from A253 or A256. Signs to St Augustines Cross
⌂ Tom Vardon

Staplehurst Golf Centre
Cradducks Lane, Staplehurst, TN12 0DR
☎ (01580) 893362
🖷 (01580) 893372
✍ C Jenkins
✓ C Jenkins/R Stilman/S Stevens
► 9 L 6114 yds Par 72 SSS 70
♟ U
££ £11 (£14)
🚗 8 miles S of Staplehurst on A229
⊕ Driving range
⌂ Sayner/Jenkins
▤ www.staplehurstgolfcentre.co.uk

Sundridge Park   (1901)
Garden Road, Bromley, BR1 3NE
☎ (020) 8460 0278
🖷 (020) 8289 3050
✉ gm@spgc.co.uk
📖 1200
✍ RJ Walden (020) 8460 0278
✓ S Dowsett (020) 8460 5540
► East 18 L 6538 yds SSS 71
West 18 L 6019 yds SSS 69
♟ H SOC–WD
££ D–£85 East £65, West £55
🚗 1 mile N of Bromley, by Sundridge Park Station. M25 Junctions 3/4
▤ www.spgc.co.uk

Sweetwoods Park   (1994)
Cowden, Edenbridge, TN8 7JN
☎ (01342) 850729

☎ (01342) 850866
✉ louisepalmer@sweetwoodspark.com
📖 750
✍ Louise Palmer
✓ P Lyons (01342) 850729
► 18 L 5299-6610 yds Par 72 SSS 69-73
♟ U SOC
££ £28 (£34)
🚗 5 miles E of E Grinstead on A264
⊕ Driving range; home to Sussex College of Golf
⌂ P Strand
▤ www.sweetwoodspark.com

Tenterden   (1905)
Woodchurch Road, Tenterden, TN30 7DR
☎ (01580) 763987
🖷 (01580) 763430
✉ enquiries@tenterdengolfclub.co.uk
📖 480
✍ N Taylor (Sec/Mgr)
✓ K Kelsall (01580) 762409
► 18 L 6001 yds Par 70 SSS 69
♟ WD–U WE/BH–M Sun–NA before noon SOC–WD
££ On application
🚗 1 mile E of Tenterden on B2067
▤ www.tenterdengolfclub.co.uk

Tudor Park   (1988)
Proprietary
Ashford Road, Bearsted, Maidstone, ME14 4NQ
☎ (01622) 734334
🖷 (01622) 735360
📖 750
✍ J Ladbrook (01622) 737119
✓ N McNally (01622) 739412
► 18 L 6085 yds SSS 69
♟ SOC WE–NA before 11am
££ £35 (£40)
🚗 3 miles E of Maidstone on A20. M20 Junction 8
⊕ Driving range (no woods allowed); putting and chipping area
⌂ Donald Steel

Tunbridge Wells   (1889)
Langton Road, Tunbridge Wells, TN4 8XH
☎ (01892) 523034

Upchurch River Valley   (1991)
Pay and play
Oak Lane, Upchurch, Sittingbourne, ME9 7AY
☎ (01634) 360626
🖷 (01634) 387784
📖 652
✍ D Candy (01634) 260594
✓ R Cornwell (01634) 379592
► 18 L 6237 yds SSS 70
9 hole course
♟ U SOC–WD
££ 18 hole: £12.95 (£16.45) 9 hole: £6.75 (£7.75)
🚗 3 miles NE of Rainham, off A2. M2 J4
⊕ Floodlit driving range
⌂ David Smart

Walmer & Kingsdown   (1909)
The Leas, Kingsdown, Deal, CT14 8EP
☎ (01304) 373256
🖷 (01304) 382336
✉ info@kingsdowngolf.co.uk
📖 627
✍ R Harrison
✓ J Read (01304) 363017
► 18 L 6471 yds Par 72 SSS 71
♟ WD–H WE–after noon SOC
££ D–£35 (£45)
🚗 2¹/₂ miles S of Deal on clifftop
⌂ James Braid
▤ www.kingsdowngolf.co.uk

Weald of Kent   (1992)
Proprietary
Maidstone Road, Headcorn, TN27 9PT
☎ (01622) 890866
🖷 (01622) 890070
✉ info@weald-of-kent.co.uk
📖 500
✍ K Brown (Golf Dir)
✓ R Goodway (01622) 890866
► 18 L 6289 yds SSS 70
♟ U–booking 7 days in advance SOC
££ £18 (£25) 4 balls £20 at WE
🚗 5 miles S of Maidstone on A274. M20 J8
⊕ Practice green (USPGA spec)
⌂ John Millen
▤ www.weald-of-kent.co.uk

West Kent   (1916)
Malking Lane, Downe, Orpington, BR6 7LD
☎ (01689) 851323
🖷 (01689) 858693
✉ golf@wkgc.co.uk
📖 700
✍ AP Barclay
✓ CW Forsyth (01689) 856863
► 18 L 6426 yds Par 71 SSS 71
♟ WD–H or I–phone to arrange
££ £40 Twilight £20 after 4pm WD
🚗 5 miles S of Orpington
⌂ DHS Colt
▤ www.wkgc.co.uk

West Malling   (1974)
Addington, Maidstone, ME19 5AR
☎ (01732) 844785
🖷 (01732) 844795
✉ mail@westmallinggolf.com
📖 900
✍ MR Ellis
✓ D Lambert
► Spitfire 18 L 6142 yds Par 70
Hurricane 18 L 6240 yds Par 70
♟ WD–U WE–U H after 1pm
££ £30 D–£50 (£30 after 1pm)
🚗 12 miles W of Maidstone (A20); M20 J4
⊕ Driving range
⌂ Max Faulkner
▤ www.westmallinggolf.com

Westerham   (1997)
Proprietary
Valence Park, Brasted Road, Westerham, TN16 1LJ
☎ (01959) 567100
🖷 (01959) 567101

✉ terri.willison@westerhamgc.co.uk
⌂ 600
⚐ R Sturgeon (Gen Mgr)
⚘ J Marshal
⚑ 18 L 6329 yds Par 72
♜ WD–U WE–after 12.00pm
££ £32 (£40)
⚶ E of Westerham (A25), off M25 Junction 5
⊕ Driving range; short game practice area
⌂ David Williams
✎ www.westerhamgc.co.uk

Westgate & Birchington
(1893)
176 Canterbury Road, Westgate-on-Sea, CT8 8LT
☎ (01843) 831115/833905
✉ wandbgc@btopenworld.com
⌂ 350
⚐ TJ Sharp
⚘ R Game
⚑ 18 L 4889 yds SSS 64
♜ WD–NA before 10am WE–NA before 11am SOC
££ £20 (£18)
⚶ 1 mile W of Birchington (A28)

Whitstable & Seasalter
(1911)
Collingwood Road, Whitstable, CT5 1EB
☎ (01227) 272020
⌨ (01227) 280822
⌂ 350
⚐ MD Moore
⚑ 9 L 5321 yds Par 66 SSS 65
♜ U
££ 18 holes–£15
⚶ 1 mile W of Whitstable

Wildernesse
(1890)
Seal, Sevenoaks, TN15 0JE
☎ (01732) 761199
⌨ (01732) 763809
✉ secretary@wildernesse.co.uk
⌂ 700
⚐ Maj (ret.) KP Loosemore
⚘ Craig Walker (01732) 761527
⚑ 18 L 6541 yds Par 72 SSS 71
♜ WD–U H SOC–Mon/Thurs/Fri
££ £50 D–£75
⚶ 2 miles E of Sevenoaks (A25). M25 Junction 5
⊕ Large practice ground and short game academy
✎ www.wildernesse.co.uk

Woodlands Manor
(1928)
Woodlands, Tinkerpot Lane, Sevenoaks, TN15 6AB
☎ (01959) 523806
⌨ (01959) 524398
✉ info@woodlandsmanorgolf.co.uk
⌂ 650
⚐ CG Robins (01959) 523806
⚘ P Womack (01959) 523806
⚑ 18 L 6100 yds SSS 69
♜ WD–U WE–H NA before noon SOC–WD
££ On application

⚶ 4 miles S of M25 Junction 3. Off A20 between West Kingsdown and Otford
⊕ Driving range
⌂ Coles/Lyons
✎ www.woodlandsmanorgolf.co.uk

Wrotham Heath
(1906)
Seven Mile Lane Comp, Sevenoaks, TN15 8QZ
☎ (01732) 884800
⌂ 424 75(L) 50(J)
⚐ M Lang
⚘ H Dearden (01732) 883854
⚑ 18 L 5954 yds SSS 69
♜ WD–H SOC–Fri only
££ £35 D–£45
⚶ 8 miles W of Maidstone on B2016. M26/A20 Junction, 1 mile
⌂ Donald Steel

Lancashire

Accrington & District
(1893)
West End, Oswaldtwistle, Accrington, BB5 4LS
☎ (01254) 381614
✉ info@accrington-golf-club.fsnet.co.uk

Ashton & Lea
(1913)
Tudor Ave, Off Blackpool Rd, Lea, Preston PR4 0XA
☎ (01772) 735282
⌨ (01772) 735762
✉ info@ashtonleagolfclub.co.uk
⌂ 655
⚐ I Hulley (01772) 735282
⚘ M Greenough (01772) 720374
⚑ 18 L 6334 yds SSS 71
♜ U SOC
££ £30 (£35) Members times: 8.30–9.15am WD 12.15–1.30pm WD
⚶ 3 miles W of Preston, off A5085. Nr M6, M55 and M65
⌂ J Steer
✎ www.ashtonleagolfclub.co.uk

Ashton-in-Makerfield
(1902)
Garswood Park, Liverpool Road, Ashton-in-Makerfield, WN4 0YT
☎ (01942) 727267
⌨ (01942) 719330
✉ secretary@ashton-in-makerfieldgolfclub.co.uk
⌂ 675
⚐ HG Williams (01942) 719330
⚘ P Allan (01942) 724229
⚑ 18 L 6205 yds SSS 70 Par 70
♜ WD–U exc Wed WE/BH–M SOC
££ £30
⚶ 1 mile W of Ashton-in-Makerfield on A58. M6 Junction 23/24
⌂ Fred Hawtree
✎ www.ashton-in-makerfieldgolfclub.co.uk

Ashton-under-Lyne
(1912)
Gorsey Way, Hurst, Ashton-under-Lyne, OL6 9HT
☎ (0161) 330 1537
⌨ (0161) 330 6673
✉ info@ashtongolfclub.co.uk
⌂ 600
⚐ A Jackson (0161) 330 1537
⚘ C Boyle (0161) 308 2095
⚑ 18 L 6209 yds SSS 70
♜ WD–U WE/BH–M SOC
££ £27.50 (£13.75 +BH)
⚶ 8 miles E of Manchester. M60 Junction 23
✎ www.ashtongolfclub.co.uk

Bacup
(1910)
Maden Road, Bankside Lane, Bacup, OL13 8HN
☎ (01706) 873170
✉ bacup@onetel.net.uk

Baxenden & District
(1913)
Top o' th' Meadow, Baxenden, Accrington, BB5 2EA
☎ (01254) 234555
✉ baxgolf@hotmail.com
⌂ 400
⚐ N Turner (01706) 225423
⚑ 9 L 5702 yds SSS 68
♜ WD–U WE/BH–M
££ £15
⚶ 2 miles SE of Accrington
⊕ Small practice area
✎ www.baxendengolf.co.uk

Beacon Park G&CC
(1982)
Public
Beacon Lane, Dalton, Up Holland, WN8 7RU
☎ (01695) 625551
⌨ (01695) 628362
✉ info@beaconparkgolf.com
⌂ 250
⚐ Mark Prosser
⚘ C Parkinson (01695) 622700
⚑ 18 L 6155 yds SSS 70
♜ U–book 6 days in advance SOC
££ £11 (£15)
⚶ Nr Ashurst Beacon and M58/M6 Junction 26
⊕ Driving range; practice area
⌂ Donald Steel
✎ www.beaconparkgolf.com

Blackburn
(1894)
Beardwood Brow, Blackburn, BB2 7AX
☎ (01254) 51122
⌨ (01254) 665578
⌂ 476 65(L) 104(J)
⚐ G Readett (01254) 51122
⚘ A Rodwell (01254) 55942
⚑ 18 L 6144 yds SSS 70
♜ U SOC–WD WE/BH–restricted
££ £26 (£30)
⚶ 1 mile NW of Blackburn (A677). M6 Junction 31

Blackpool North Shore
(1904)
Devonshire Road, Blackpool, FY2 0RD
☎ (01253) 352054

☎ (01253) 591240
✉ office@bnsgc.com
📖 750
🏌 JW Morris (01253) 352054 ext 1
⛳ B Ward (01253) 354640
▷ 18 L 6443 yds SSS 71
👥 WD–U WE–restricted SOC
££ £26 D–£33 (£33 D–£39)
🚗 ½ mile E of Queens Promenade (B5124)
🏠 HS Colt
🖥 www.bnsgc.com

Blackpool Park (1925)

Public
North Park Drive, Blackpool, FY3 8LS
☎ **(01253) 397916**
🖥 (01253) 397916
📖 600
🏌 D Stones (01253) 397916
⛳ B Purdie (01253) 391004
▷ 18 L 6048 yds SSS 69
👥 U–no telephone booking SOC (01253) 478478
££ £17 (£19.60 inc BH)
🚗 2 miles E of Blackpool, signposted off M55
⊕ Phone bookings for tee times – (01253) 478176 (up to 1 week in advance)
🏠 Dr A Mackenzie

Bolton (1891)

Lostock Park, Bolton, BL6 4AJ
☎ **(01204) 843278**
🖥 (01204) 843067
✉ boltongolf@lostockpark.fsbusiness .co.uk
📖 500
🏌 S Higham (01204) 843067
⛳ R Longworth (01204) 843073
▷ 18 L 6213 yds Par 70 SSS 70
👥 U SOC
££ Summer: £25, fourball £90 Winter: £20, fourball £75
🚗 3 miles W of Bolton. M61 Junction 6, 2 miles on A673

Bolton Old Links (1891)

Chorley Old Road, Montserrat, Bolton, BL1 5SU
☎ **(01204) 840050**
🖥 (01204) 842307
✉ mail@boltonoldlinksgolfclub .co.uk
📖 600
🏌 Mrs J Boardman (01204) 842307
⛳ P Horridge (01204) 843089
▷ 18 L 6469 yds SSS 71
👥 U H exc comp Sats SOC
££ £35 (£45)
🚗 3 miles NW of Bolton on B6226
🏠 Dr A Mackenzie
🖥 www.boltonoldlinksgolfclub.co.uk

Bolton Open Golf Course

Pay and play
Longsight Park, Longsight Lane, Harwood, BL2 4JX
☎ **(01204) 597659/309778**

Brackley Municipal (1977)

Public
Bullows Road, Little Hulton, Worsley, M38 9TR
☎ **(0161) 790 6076**

Breightmet (1911)

Red Bridge, Ainsworth, Bolton, BL2 5PA
☎ **(01204) 399275**
📖 400
🏌 ID Cooke
▷ 18 L 6405 yds Par 72 SSS 72
👥 WD–H WE–NA SOC–WD
££ £20
🚗 3 miles E of Bolton
🏠 David Griffiths

Brookdale (1896)

Medlock Road, Woodhouses, Failsworth, M35 9WQ
☎ **(0161) 681 4534**
🖥 (0161) 688 6872
📖 725
🏌 D Hegarty
⛳ T Cuppello (0161) 681 2655
▷ 18 L 5841 yds SSS 68
👥 WD–U SOC–WD
££ £26
🚗 5 miles NE of Manchester, M60 Jct 22
🖥 www.brookdalegolfclub.co.uk

Burnley (1905)

Glen View, Burnley, BB11 3RW
☎ **(01282) 451281**
✉ burnleygolfclub@onthegreen.co.uk

Bury (1890)

Unsworth Hall, Blackford Bridge, Bury, BL9 9TJ
☎ **(0161) 766 4897**
🖥 (0161) 796 3480
✉ secretary@burygolfclub.com
📖 650
🏌 R Adams
⛳ G Coope (0161) 766 2213
▷ 18 L 5927 yds Par 69 SSS 69
👥 SOC WD WE
££ £30 (£35)
🚗 A56, 5 miles N of Manchester. 3 miles N of M62 Junction 17
🏠 McKenzie
🖥 www.burygolfclub.com

Castle Hawk (1975)

Chadwick Lane, Castleton, Rochdale, OL11 3BY
☎ **(01706) 640841**
✉ teeoff@castlehawk.co.uk

Chorley (1897)

Hall o' th' Hill, Heath Charnock, Chorley, PR6 9HX
☎ **(01257) 480263**
🖥 (01257) 480722
✉ secretary@chorleygolfclub .freeserve.co.uk
📖 550
🏌 Mrs A Green (01257) 480263
⛳ M Bradley (01257) 481245

▷ 18 L 6240 yds SSS 70
👥 WD–I or H WE–NA SOC
££ On application
🚗 1 mile S of Chorley at junction A6/A673
🏠 JA Steer
🖥 www.chorleygolfclub.co.uk

Clitheroe (1891)

Whalley Road, Clitheroe, BB7 1PP
☎ **(01200) 422618 (Clubhouse)**
✉ secretary@clitheroegolfclub.com

Colne (1901)

Law Farm, Skipton Old Road, Colne, BB8 7EB
☎ **(01282) 863391**
🖥 (01282) 870547
📖 440
🏌 A Turpin (Hon)
⛳ None
▷ 9 L 6053 yds SSS 69
👥 U exc comp days SOC–WD
££ £20 (£25)
🚗 1½ miles N of Colne. From end of M65, signs to Keighley and then Lothersdale

Crompton & Royton (1914)

High Barn, Royton, Oldham, OL2 6RW
☎ **(0161) 624 2154**
🖥 (0161) 652 4711
✉ secretary@cromptonandroyton golfclub.co.uk
📖 620
🏌 R Smith (0161) 624 0986
⛳ DA Melling (0161) 624 2154
▷ 18 L 6186 yds SSS 70
👥 U SOC–WD
££ £25 (£35)
🚗 3 miles NW of Oldham
🖥 www.cromptonandroytongolfclub .co.uk

Darwen (1893)

Winter Hill, Duddon Avenue, Darwen, BB3 0LB
☎ **(01254) 701287**
✉ admin@darwengolfclub.com

Dean Wood (1922)

Lafford Lane, Up Holland, Skelmersdale, WN8 0QZ
☎ **(01695) 622219**
🖥 (01695) 622245
✉ john.ball@deanwoodgolfclub.co.uk
📖 750
🏌 JH Ball
⛳ S Danchin (01695) 627480
▷ 18 L 6148 yds SSS 70
👥 WD–U WE/BH–M SOC–Mon/Thur/Fri only
££ D–£30 (£35)
🚗 1 mile W of M6 J26
⊕ Small driving range; chipping facility; practice nets
🏠 James Braid
🖥 www.deanwoodgolfclub.co.uk

Deane (1906)

Broadford Road, Deane, Bolton, BL3 4NS
☎ **(01204) 61944**

📖 (01204) 652047
📖 490
🏌 P Parry (01204) 651808
✓ D Martindale
⛳ 18 L 5652 yds SSS 67
👥 WD–U WE–restricted
SOC–Tues/Thurs/Fri
££ £25 (£30)
🚗 2 miles W of Bolton. M61 Junction 5, I mile
🖥 www.deanegolfclub.co.uk

Dunscar   (1908)
Longworth Lane, Bromley Cross, Bolton, BL7 9QY
☎ (01204) 598228
📧 secretary@dunscargolfclub.fsnet.co.uk

Duxbury Park   (1975)
Public
Duxbury Hall Road, Duxbury Park, Chorley, PR7 4AS
☎ (01257) 265380
(01257) 241634 (Clubhouse)
📖 (01257) 241378
🏌 F Holding (01257) 262209
✓ Pro shop (01257) 265380
⛳ 18 L 6270 yds SSS 70
👥 U
££ £12 (£15)
🚗 1½ miles S of Chorley, off Wigan Lane

Fairhaven   (1895)
Oakwood Avenue, Ansdell, Lytham St Annes, FY8 4JU
☎ (01253) 736741
📖 (01253) 736741
📧 secretary@fairhavengolf.co.uk
📖 900
🏌 R Thompson
✓ B Plunkett (01253) 736976
⛳ 18 L 6883 yds SSS 73
👥 WD–U WE–NA before 9am SOC–WD
££ £45 (£50)
🚗 Lytham 2 miles. St Annes 2 miles. M55 Junction 4

Fishwick Hall   (1912)
Glenluce Drive, Farringdon Park, Preston, PR1 5TD
☎ (01772) 798300
📖 (01772) 704600
📧 fishwickhallgolfclub@supanet.com
📖 620
🏌 RE Stamp
✓ M Watson (01772) 795870
⛳ 18 L 6045 yds Par 70 SSS 69
👥 Apply to Sec SOC
££ £20 D–£28 (£32)
🚗 1 mile E of Preston, nr junction of A59 and M6 Junction 31
🖥 www.fishwickhallgolfclub.co.uk

Fleetwood   (1932)
Golf House, Princes Way, Fleetwood, FY7 8AF
☎ (01253) 773573 (Clubhouse)
📖 (01253) 773573
📧 fleetwoodgc@aol.com

📖 548
🏌 N Robinson (01253) 773573
✓ S McLaughlin (01253) 873661
⛳ L 18 L 6308 yds SSS 70
👥 U H exc Tues SOC
££ £30 (£40)
🚗 I mile W of Fleetwood centre
🏠 A Steer
🖥 www.fleetwoodgolfclub.org.uk

Gathurst   (1913)
Miles Lane, Shevington, Wigan, WN6 8EW
☎ (01257) 252861 (Clubhouse)
📖 (01257) 255953
📧 mail@gathurstgolfclub.ltd.uk
📖 675
🏌 Mrs I Fyffe (01257) 255235
✓ D Clarke (01257) 255882
⛳ 18 L 6089 yds Par 70 SSS 69
👥 WD–U before 5pm WE/BH/Wed–M SOC–WD
££ £30
🚗 4 miles W of Wigan. I mile S of M6 Junction 27
🏠 N Pearson-ADAS

Ghyll   (1907)
Ghyll Brow, Barnoldswick, Colne, BB18 6JH
☎ (01282) 842466
📧 secretary@ghyllgc.freeserve.com
📖 310
🏌 JL Gill (01524) 412958
⛳ 9 L 5708 yds SSS 68
👥 U exc Sun–NA; Tues NA before 3pm
££ D–£15 (D–£20)
🚗 7 miles N of Colne, off A56 (B6252)
🖥 www.ghyllgc.co.uk

Great Harwood   (1896)
Harwood Bar, Great Harwood, BB6 7TE
☎ (01254) 884391
📖 195 65(L) 45(J)
🏌 J Spibey (01254) 879494
⛳ 9 L 6404 yds SSS 71
👥 U SOC
££ £20 (£26)
🚗 5 miles NE of Blackburn. M65 Junction 7

Green Haworth   (1914)
Green Haworth, Accrington, BB5 3SL
☎ (01254) 237580
📖 (01254) 396176
📧 enquiries@greenhaworth.co.uk
📖 250
🏌 W Halstead
⛳ 9 L 5526 yds SSS 67
👥 WD–U exc Wed–Ladies only after 5pm WE/BH–M SOC
££ On application
🚗 Willows Lane
🖥 www.greenhaworthgolfclub.co.uk

Greenmount   (1920)
Greenmount, Bury, BL8 4LH
☎ (01204) 883712
📖 220
🏌 MD Barron (Hon)
⛳ 9 L 5874 yds SSS 69
👥 WD–U exc Tues WE–M

££ £20
🚗 3 miles N of Bury
⊕ Visiting Professional by arrangement
🏠 M Renouf (1936)

Haigh Hall   (1972)
Public
Haigh Hall Country Park, Haigh, Wigan, WN2 1PE
☎ (01942) 833337 (Clubhouse)
📖 (01942) 831417
📧 secretary@haighhall-golfclub.co.uk
📖 180
🏌 SG Eyres
✓ I Lee (01942) 832895
⛳ 9 L 1446 yds
18 L 6358 yds
👥 U WD/WE–NA SOC–WD/WE
££ 9: £4.20 (£5.30) 18: £13 (£16) Summer prices
🚗 2 miles NW of Wigan. M6 Junction 27. M61 Junction 6
🏠 Gaunt/Marnoch
🖥 www.haighhall-golfclub.co.uk

Hart Common   (1995)
Proprietary
Westhoughton Golf Centre, Wigan Road, Westhoughton, BL5 2BX
☎ (01942) 813195
📧 hartcommon@ukgolfer.org

Harwood   (1926)
Roading Brook Road, Bolton, BL2 4JD
☎ (01204) 522878
📖 (01204) 524233
📧 secretary@harwoodgolfclub.co.uk
📖 553
🏌 IW Lund (01204) 524233
✓ Colin Maroney (01204) 362834
⛳ 18 L 5813 yds Par 70 SSS 68
👥 WD WE–M SOC–WD
££ £20 (£12)
🚗 4 miles NE of Bolton off B6196
🏠 J Shuttleworth
🖥 www.harwoodgolfclub.co.uk

De Vere Herons Reach   (1993)
Pay and play
East Park Drive, Blackpool, FY3 8LL
☎ (01253) 766156

Heysham   (1910)
Trumacar Park, Middleton Road, Heysham, Morecambe, LA3 3JH
☎ (01524) 851011
📖 (01524) 853030
📧 secretary@heyshamgolf.freeserve.co.uk
📖 685
🏌 FA Bland (Sec/Mgr)
✓ R Dône (01524) 852000
⛳ 18 L 6258 yds SSS 70
👥 U H SOC
££ £30 (£40)
🚗 2 miles S of Morecambe. M6 Junction 34, 5 miles
⊕ Floodlit driving range; buggy hire
🏠 A Herd
🖥 www.heyshamgolfclub.co.uk

Hindley Hall (1905)

Hall Lane, Hindley, Wigan, WN2 2SQ
☎ **(01942) 255131**
🖥 (01942) 253871
✉ sechindley@aol.com
📖 430
♘ Louise Hedley (01942) 255131
⚲ D Clarke (01942) 255991
🏳 18 L 5913 yds SSS 68
👥 U SOC WD/WE after 3pm
££ £25 (£32)
🚗 2 miles E of Wigan. M61 Junction 6

Horwich (1895)

Victoria Road, Horwich, BL6 5PH
☎ **(01204) 696980**

Hurlston Hall (1994)

Proprietary
Hurlston Lane, Southport Road, Scarisbrick, L40 8HB
☎ **(01704) 840400**
🖥 (01704) 841404
✉ info@hurlstonhall.co.uk
📖 650
♘ M Atherton
⚲ (01704) 841120
🏳 18 L 6601 yds SSS 72
👥 SOC
££ £35 (£40)
🚗 2 miles NW of Ormskirk (A570). M58 Junction 3
⊕ Floodlit driving range with power tee
🏠 Donald Steel
🖥 www.hurlstonhall.co.uk

Ingol (1981)

Proprietary
Tanterton Hall Road, Ingol, Preston, PR2 7BY
☎ **(01772) 734556**
🖥 (01772) 729815
✉ ingol@golfers.net
📖 700
♘ M Ross
⚲ R Grimshaw (01772) 769646
🏳 18 L 6284 yds SSS 70
👥 U SOC–WD WE
££ £25 (£30)
🚗 1½ miles NW of Preston (A6). M6 Junction 32
⊕ Practice ground
🏠 Henry Cotton
🖥 www.ingolgolfclub.co.uk

Knott End (1910)

Wyreside, Knott End-on-Sea, Poulton-le-Fylde, FY6 0AA
☎ **(01253) 81576**
🖥 (01253) 813446
✉ louise@knottendgolfclub.com
📖 660
♘ Louise Freeman (01253) 810576
⚲ P Walker (01253) 811365
🏳 18 L 5849 yds SSS 68
👥 WD–U WE/BH–by arrangement SOC–WD
££ £30 (£38)
🚗 Over Wyre, 12 miles NE of Blackpool (A588). M55 J3 off M6
⊕ Practice ground; driving net; lessons; buggies

🏠 James Braid
🖥 www.knottendgolfclub.com

Lancaster (1932)

Ashton Hall, Ashton-with-Stodday, Lancaster, LA2 0AJ
☎ **(01524) 752090**
    (Clubhouse)
🖥 (01524) 752742
✉ office@lancastergc.co.uk
📖 530 170(L) 62(J)
♘ PJ Irvine (01524) 751247
⚲ DE Sutcliffe (01524) 751802
🏳 18 L 6500 yds SSS 71
££ £38 D–£45
🚗 2 miles S of Lancaster (A588)
⊕ Dormy House
🏠 James Braid
🖥 www.lancastergc.co.uk

Lansil (1947)

Caton Road, Lancaster, LA4 3PE
☎ **(01524) 39269**
📖 450
♘ D Burns (07751 089702)
🏳 9 L 5608 yds Par 70 SSS 67
👥 WD–U Sun–U after 1pm
££ £12 (£12)
🚗 A683, 2 miles E of Lancaster

Leyland (1924)

Wigan Road, Leyland, PR25 5UD
☎ **(01772) 436457**
🖥 (01772) 435605
✉ manager@leylandgolfclub.co.uk
📖 750
♘ S Drinkall
⚲ C Burgess (Dir of Golf) (01772) 423425
🏳 18 L 6298 yds SSS 70
👥 WD–U WE–M SOC–WD
££ £27
🚗 M6 Junction 28, ½mile
🖥 www.leylandgolfclub.co.uk

Lobden (1888)

Whitworth, Rochdale, OL12 8XJ
☎ **(01706) 343228**
🖥 (01706) 343228
✉ lobdengc@hotmail.com
📖 230
♘ B Harrison (01706) 852752
🏳 9 L 5697 yds Par 70 SSS 68
👥 U
££ £12 (£15)
🚗 4 miles N of Rochdale

Longridge (1877)

Fell Barn, Jeffrey Hill, Longridge, Preston, PR3 2TU
☎ **(01772) 783291**
🖥 (01772) 783022
✉ secretary@longridgegolfclub.fsnet .co.uk
📖 600
♘ D Simpson
⚲ S Taylor (01772) 783291
🏳 18 L 5969 yds SSS 69
👥 U
££ £20
🚗 8 miles NE of Preston, off B6243

⊕ Large practice area; 9 hole par 3 Academy course
🖥 www.longridgegolfclub.com

Lowes Park (1915)

Hilltop, Lowes Road, Bury, BL9 6SU
☎ **(0161) 764 1231**
🖥 (0161) 763 9503
✉ lowes@parkgc.fsnet.co.uk
📖 350
♘ J Entwistle
🏳 9 L 6006 yds Par 70 SSS 69
👥 WD–U exc Wed–NA WE/BH–by arrangement
££ Summer £10 (£15) Winter £5 (£10)
🚗 1 mile NE of Bury, off A56

Lytham Green Drive (1922)

Ballam Road, Lytham, FY8 4LE
☎ **(01253) 737390**
🖥 (01253) 731350
✉ secretary@lythamgreendrive.co.uk
📖 700
♘ I Stuart (01253) 737390
⚲ A Lancaster (01253) 737379
🏳 18 L 6363 yds SSS 70
👥 WD–U H WE–NA SOC–WD
££ £38 (£45) to be confirmed
🚗 Lytham St Annes. M55 Junction 4
🏠 JA Steer
🖥 www.lythamgreendrive.co.uk

Marland (1928)

Public
Springfield Park, Bolton Road, Rochdale, OL11 4RE
☎ **(01706) 649801**

Marsden Park (1969)

Public
Townhouse Road, Nelson, BB9 8DG
☎ **(01282) 661912**
🖥 (01282) 661384
✉ martin.robinson@pendleleisuretrust .co.uk
📖 300
♘ D Walton (01282) 697766
⚲ Martin Robinson (Mgr)
🏳 18 L 5909 yds Par 70 SSS 68
👥 U SOC
££ On application
🚗 M65 Junction 13, signposted Walton Lane
🖥 www.pendleleisuretrust.co.uk

Morecambe (1905)

Bare, Morecambe, LA4 6AJ
☎ **(01524) 418050**
🖥 (01524) 400088
✉ secretary@morecambegolfclub .com
📖 850
♘ Mrs J Atkinson (01524) 412841
⚲ S Fletcher (01524) 415596
🏳 18 L 5750 yds SSS 69
👥 U H SOC
££ On application
🚗 On coast road towards Carnforth (A5105)
🏠 Dr Alister Mackenzie
🖥 www.morecambegolfclub.com

Mossock Hall   (1996)
Liverpool Road, Bickerstaffe, L39 0EE
- ☎ **(01695) 421717**
- 🖳 (01695) 424961
- 🕮 600
- ♨ Jacqueline Fray
- ✓ B Millar (01695) 424969
- ⏵ 18 L 6375 yds Par 71 SSS 71
- ⅍ WD–U WE–after 12.30 SOC
- ££ £22 (£30)
- ⊛ 4 miles S of Ormskirk
- ⌂ Steve Marnoch

Mytton Fold Hotel & Golf Complex   (1994)
Proprietary
Whalley Road, Langho, BB6 8AB
- ☎ **(01254) 240662 (Hotel)**
- 🖂 golfshop@myttonfold.co.uk

Nelson   (1902)
Kings Causeway, Brierfield, Nelson, BB9 0EU
- ☎ **(01282) 614583**
- 🖳 (01282) 611834
- 🖂 secretary@nelsongolfclub.co.uk
- 🕮 550
- ♨ BR Thomason (01282) 611834
- ✓ N Reeves (01282) 617000
- ⏵ 18 L 6006 yds Par 70 SSS 69
- ⅍ WD–U H exc Thurs–NA WE–U exc Sat before 4pm SOC
- ££ £30 D–£35
- ⊛ 2 miles N of Burnley. M65 Junction 12
- ⊕ Large practice field
- ⌂ Dr A MacKenzie
- 🖺 www.nelsongolfclub.co.uk

Oldham   (1892)
Lees New Road, Oldham, OL4 5PN
- ☎ **(0161) 624 4986**
- 🕮 230 45(L) 20(J)
- ♨ J Brooks
- ✓ R Heginbotham (0161) 626 8346
- ⏵ 18 L 5045 yds SSS 65
- ⅍ U SOC
- ££ On application
- ⊛ Off Oldham-Stalybridge road

Ormskirk   (1899)
Cranes Lane, Lathom, Ormskirk, L40 5UJ
- ☎ **(01695) 572112**

Pennington
Pennington Country Park, Leigh, WN7 3PA
- ☎ **(01942) 741873**
- 🕮 122
- ♨ Mrs A Lythgoe
- ✓ (01942) 682852
- ⏵ 9 L 5521 yds Par 70 SSS 67
- ⅍ U SOC
- ££ £4 (£5)
- ⊛ ½ mile off A580, on Leigh By-Pass. Follow signs for Pennington Flash

Penwortham   (1908)
Blundell Lane, Penwortham, Preston, PR1 0AX
- ☎ **(01772) 744630**

- 🖳 (01772) 740172
- 🖂 admin@penworthamgc.co.uk
- 🕮 820
- ♨ N Annandale
- ✓ D Hopwood (01772) 742345
- ⏵ 18 L 5877 yds SSS 69
- ⅍ WD–U WE–no parties
- ££ £25 (£33)
- ⊛ 1½ miles W of Preston (A59)
- ⌂ Ken Moodie
- 🖺 www.penworthamgc.co.uk

Pleasington   (1891)
Pleasington, Blackburn, BB2 5JF
- ☎ **(01254) 202177**
- 🖳 (01254) 201028
- 🖂 secretary-manager@pleasington-golf.co.uk
- 🕮 545
- ♨ T Ashton
- ✓ GJ Furey (01254) 201630
- ⏵ 18 L 6402 yds SSS 71
- ⅍ H
- ££ £45 (£50)
- ⊛ 3 miles SW of Blackburn; M65 J3
- ⊕ Practice range available
- 🖺 www.pleasington-golf.co.uk

Poulton-le-Fylde   (1982)
Public
Myrtle Farm, Breck Road, Poulton-le-Fylde, FY6 7HJ
- ☎ **(01253) 892444**

Preston   (1892)
Fulwood Hall Lane, Fulwood, Preston, PR2 8DD
- ☎ **(01772) 700011**
- 🖳 (01772) 794234
- 🖂 secretary@prestongolfclub.com
- 🕮 800
- ♨ RM Lees
- ✓ A Greenbank (01772) 700022
- ⏵ 18 L 6312 yds SSS 71
- ⅍ WD–U H WE–M SOC–WD
- ££ D–£40
- ⊛ 1½ miles W of M6 Junction 32
- ⊕ Driving range. Golf academy
- ⌂ James Braid
- 🖺 www.prestongolfclub.com

Regent Park (Bolton)   (1931)
Public
Links Road, Chorley New Road, Bolton, BL6 4AF
- ☎ **(01204) 844170**

Rishton   (1927)
Eachill Links, Hawthorn Drive, Rishton, BB1 4HG
- ☎ **(01254) 884442**
- 🖂 rishtongc@onetel.net

Rochdale   (1888)
Edenfield Road, Bagslate, Rochdale, OL11 5YR
- ☎ **(01706) 643818 (Clubhouse)**
- 🖳 (01706) 861113
- 🕮 750
- ♨ P Kershaw (01706) 643818

- ✓ A Laverty (01706) 522104
- ⏵ 18 L 6031 yds SSS 69
- ⅍ U
- ££ £22 (£29)
- ⊛ 3 miles from M62 Junction 20 on A680
- ⌂ George Lowe

Rossendale   (1903)
Ewood Lane Head, Haslingden, Rossendale, BB4 6LH
- ☎ **(01706) 831339**
- 🖳 (01706) 228669
- 🖂 rgc@golfers.net
- 🕮 750
- ♨ K Wilson
- ✓ SJ Nicholls (01706) 213616
- ⏵ 18 L 6293 yds SSS 71
- ⅍ WD/Sun–U Sat–M
- ££ £30 (£35)
- ⊛ 7 miles N of Bury, nr end of M66
- 🖺 www.rossendalegolfclub.net

Royal Lytham & St Annes   (1886)
Links Gate, Lytham St Annes, FY8 3LQ
- ☎ **(01253) 724206**
- 🖳 (01253) 780946
- 🖂 bookings@royallytham.org
- 🕮 500
- ♨ RJG Cochrane
- ✓ E Birchenough (01253) 720094
- ⏵ 18 L 6685 yds SSS 73
- ⅍ WD–I H
- ££ £120 (£165) D–£180 (inc. £10 lunch)
- ⊛ St Annes 1 mile (A584)
- ⊕ Dormy House
- ⌂ George Lowe
- 🖺 www.royallytham.org

Saddleworth   (1904)
Mountain Ash, Uppermill, Oldham, OL3 6LT
- ☎ **(01457) 873653**
- 🖳 (01457) 820647
- 🖂 secretary@saddleworthgolfclub.org.uk
- 🕮 700
- ♨ Paul Green
- ✓ RI Johnson
- ⏵ 18 L 6196 yds SSS 69
- ⅍ U
- ££ £25 (£35)
- ⊛ Uppermill, 5 miles E of Oldham
- ⌂ Mackenzie/Leaver

Shaw Hill Hotel G&CC   (1925)
Preston Road, Whittle-le-Woods, Chorley, PR6 7PP
- ☎ **(01257) 269221**
- 🖂 info@shaw-hill.co.uk

St Annes Old Links   (1901)
Highbury Road East, Lytham St Annes, FY8 2LD
- ☎ **(01253) 723597**
- 🖳 (01253) 781506
- 🖂 secretary@stannesoldlinks.com
- 🕮 945
- ♨ Stephen Mainwaring

For list of abbreviations and key to symbols see page 651

✓ D Webster (01253) 722432
▷ 18 L 6684 yds SSS 72
♙ WD–NA before 9.30am and
12–1.30pm WE/BH–arrange with
Sec SOC
££ £55 am £40 pm (£50)
♣ Between St Annes and Blackpool,
off A584
🏠 Herd
▤ www.stannesoldlinks.com

Standish Court   (1995)
Pay and play
Rectory Lane, Standish, Wigan, WN6 0XD
☎ (01257) 425777
🖳 (01257) 425777
✉ info@standishgolf.co.uk
▥ 300
♙ S McGrath
✓ S McGrath
▷ 18 L 4860 yds Par 68 SSS 64
♙ U SOC
££ £10–£12 (£16)
♣ M6 Junction 27, 2 miles
🏠 Patrick Dawson
▤ www.standishgolf.co.uk

Stonyhurst Park   (1979)
Stonyhurst, Hurst Green, Clitheroe, BB7 9QB
☎ (01254) 826478 (not manned)
🖳 jandbaus@btinternet.com
▥ 436
♙ JR Austin (01200) 427720
▷ 9 L 5715 yds SSS 69
♙ WD–U WE–NA
££ £20
♣ 5 miles SW of Clitheroe (B6243)
⊕ Green fees payable at Bayley Arms
or Shireburn Arms, Hurst Green

Towneley   (1932)
Public
*Towneley Park, Todmorden Road, Burnley,
BB11 3ED*
☎ (01282) 451636

Tunshill   (1901)
Kiln Lane, Milnrow, Rochdale, OL16 3TS
☎ (01706) 342095
▥ 300
♙ P Lowthian (01706) 342095
▷ 9 L 5745 yds SSS 68
♙ WD–U WE–M SOC
££ £16
♣ 2 miles E of Rochdale. M62 Jct 21
▤ www.tunshillgolfclub.co.uk

Turton   (1908)
*Wood End Farm, Hospital Road, Bromley
Cross, Bolton, BL7 9QD*
☎ (01204) 852235
🖳 (01204) 856921
✉ info@turtongolfclub.com
▥ 300 56(L) 51(J)
♙ SP Kay (01204) 306971
✓ Mark Saunders (01204) 853576
▷ 18 L 6124 yds Par 70 SSS 69
♙ WD–U exc Wed–NA
10.00–2.30pm WE Sat–NA before
4 pm SOC
££ £26 D–£36 (£33 D–£45)
♣ 3¹/₂ miles N of Bolton, nr Last

Drop Village
▤ www.turtongolfclub.com

Walmersley   (1906)
Garrett's Close, Walmersley, Bury, BL9 6TE
☎ (0161) 764 1429
🖳 (0161) 764 7770
▥ 450
♙ DL Thomas (0161) 764 7770
✓ P Thorpe (0161) 763 9050
▷ 18 L 5341 yds SSS 67
♙ WD–U exc Tues–NA Sat–after
1pm SOC W–F Sun
££ D–£25 (£28)
♣ 2 miles N of Bury (A56). S of M66
Junction 1
🏠 SG Marnoch

Werneth   (1908)
*Green Lane, Garden Suburb, Oldham,
OL8 3AZ*
☎ (0161) 624 1190
✉ secretary@wernethgolfclub.co.uk
▥ 400
♙ JH Barlow
▷ 18 L 5363 yds SSS 66
♙ WD–U WE–M SOC
££ D–£16.50
♣ 2 miles S of Oldham centre
🏠 Sandy Herd
▤ www.wernethgolfclub.co.uk

Westhoughton   (1929)
*Long Island, Westhoughton, Bolton,
BL5 2BR*
☎ (01942) 811085
🖳 (01942) 811085
✉ honsec@westhoughtongc/fsnet
.co.uk
▥ 340
♙ Brian Axon
▷ 18 L 5918 yds SSS 69
♙ WD–U WE/BH–M
££ D–£20
♣ 4 miles SW of Bolton on A58

Whalley   (1912)
*Long Leese Barn, Clerkhill Road, Whalley,
BB7 9DR*
☎ (01254) 822236
🖳 (01254) 824766
▥ 350
♙ JS Dawson (01254) 886313
✓ J Hunt (01254) 824766
▷ 9 L 6258 yds Par 72 SSS 71
♙ U exc Sat (Apr–Oct) SOC–WD
££ £20 (£25)
♣ 7 miles NE of Blackburn off A59
▤ www.whalleygolfclub.co.uk

Whittaker   (1906)
Littleborough, OL15 0LH
☎ (01706) 378310
▥ 186
♙ S Noblett (01706) 842541
▷ 9 L 5666 yds SSS 67
♙ WD/Sat–U Sun–NA
££ £15 (£20)
♣ 1¹/₂ miles N of Littleborough, off
A58. M62 Junction 21
🏠 NP Stott

Wigan   (1898)
Arley Hall, Haigh, Wigan, WN1 2UH
☎ (01257) 421360
✉ info@wigangolfclub.co.uk
▥ 300
♙ E Walmsley
▷ 18 L 6008 yds SSS 70
♙ U exc Tues & Sat
££ £30 (£30)
♣ 4 miles N of Wigan, off
A5106/B5329. M6 Junction 27
🏠 Gaunt/Marnoch
▤ www.wigangolfclub.co.uk

Wilpshire   (1890)
*72 Whalley Road, Wilpshire, Blackburn,
BB1 9LF*
☎ (01254) 248260
🖳 (01254) 246745
✉ admin@wilpshiregolfclub.co.uk
▥ 650
♙ SH Tart
✓ W Slaven (01254) 249558
▷ 18 L 5843 yds SSS 69
♙ WD–U WE/BH–on request
££ £25 (£30)
♣ 3 miles NE of Blackburn, off A666
🏠 James Braid
▤ www.wilpshiregolfclub.co.uk

Leicestershire

Beedles Lake   (1993)
170 Broome Lane, East Goscote, LE7 3WQ
☎ (0116) 260 6759/7086
🖳 (0116) 260 4414
✉ ian@jelson.co.uk
▥ 480
♙ Ian Needham (Mgr) (0116) 260
4414
✓ S Byrne
▷ 18 L 6641 yds Par 72 SSS 72
♙ U SOC WD (WE restricted)
££ £14 (£20)
♣ 4 miles N of Leicester on B5328,
off A46. M1, 8 miles
⊕ Driving range
🏠 D Tucker
▤ www.beedleslake.co.uk

Birstall   (1900)
Station Road, Birstall, Leicester, LE4 3BB
☎ (0116) 267 4450
🖳 (0116) 267 4322
✉ sue@birstallgolfclub.co.uk
▥ 400 80(L) 50(J)
♙ Mrs SE Chilton (0116) 267 4322
✓ D Clark (0116) 267 5245
▷ 18 L 6213 yds SSS 70
♙ WD–I WE–M SOC
££ £30 (£40)
♣ 3 miles N of Leicester (A6)
▤ www.birstallgolfclub.co.uk

Breedon Priory   (1990)
Green Lane, Wilson, Derby, DE73 1LG
☎ (01332) 863081
✉ bpgc@barbox.net

Charnwood Forest (1890)

Breakback Road, Woodhouse Eaves,
Loughborough, LE12 8TA
- ☎ (01509) 890259
  (01509) 890925 (Steward)
- 📠 (01509) 890925
- ✉ secretary@charnwoodforestgc
  .co.uk
- 📖 360
- 🏌 PK Field
- ⚐ 9 L 5972 yds SSS 69
- 👥 UH SOC–Wed–Fri (not Tue)
- ££ £25 D–£30 (£30)
- 🚗 M1 Junction 22/23, 3 miles
- 🏠 James Braid
- 📠 www.charnwoodforestgc.co.uk

Cosby (1895)

Chapel Lane, Broughton Road, Cosby,
Leicester, LE9 1RG
- ☎ (0116) 286 4759
- ✉ secretary@cosby-golf-club.co.uk

Enderby (1986)

Public
Mill Lane, Enderby, Leicester, LE19 4LX
- ☎ (0116) 284 9388
- 📠 (0116) 284 9388
- ✓ C D'Araujo
- ⚐ 9 L 5800 yds Par 72 SSS 71
- 👥 U
- ££ 18 holes: £8.20 (£10.50)
- 🚗 Enderby 2 miles. M1 Junction 21

Forest Hill (1991)

Proprietary
Markfield Lane, Botcheston, LE9 9FJ
- ☎ (01455) 824800
- 📠 (01455) 828522
- ✉ gerry@hyde14.fsnet.co.uk
- 📖 650
- 🏌 GD Hyde
- ✓ G Quilter
- ⚐ 18 L 6450 yds Par 72 SSS 71
- 👥 WD–U WE–M
- ££ On application
- 🚗 6 miles W of Leicester. M1
  Junction 22, 4 miles
- ⊕ Driving range; putting green; 9 hole
  par 3
- 🏠 Redevelopment Gaunt & Marnock

Glen Gorse (1933)

Glen Road, Oadby, Leicester, LE2 4RF
- ☎ (0116) 271 4159
- 📠 (0116) 271 4159
- ✉ secretary@gggc.org
- 📖 440 115(L) 60(J)
- 🏌 Mrs J James (0116) 271 4159
- ✓ D Fitzpatrick (0116) 271 3748
- ⚐ 18 L 6648 yds SSS 72
- 👥 WD–U WE/BH–M SOC–WD
- ££ £30 D–£35
- 🚗 3 miles S of Leicester on A6
- 📠 www.gggc.org

Hinckley (1894)

Leicester Road, Hinckley, LE10 3DR
- ☎ (01455) 615124
- 📠 (01455) 890841
- ✉ proshop@hinckleygolfclub.com

- 📖 650
- 🏌 D Gray (Sec), Y Watts (Finance &
  Admin)
- ✓ R Jones (01455) 615014
- ⚐ 18 L 6527 yds SSS 71
- 👥 WD–U exc Tues before 2pm M
  after 11am SOC
- ££ £30 D–£40
- 🚗 NE of Hinckley on B4668, near
  M69
- 🏠 Southern Golf
- 📠 www.hinckleygolfclub.com

Humberstone Heights (1978)

Public
Gipsy Lane, Leicester, LE5 0TB
- ☎ (0116) 299 5570/1

Kibworth (1904)

Weir Road, Kibworth Beauchamp, Leicester,
LE8 0LP
- ☎ (0116) 279 2301
- 📠 (0116) 279 6434
- ✉ secretary@kibworthgolfclub
  .freeserve.co.uk
- 📖 700
- 🏌 J Noble
- ✓ M Herbert (0116) 279 2283
- ⚐ 18 L 6354 yds Par 71 SSS 71
- 👥 WD–U WE–M SOC–WD
- ££ £30 D–£40
- 🚗 9 miles SE of Leicester, off A6
- ⊕ Driving range & practice area

Kilworth Springs (1993)

South Kilworth Road, North Kilworth,
Lutterworth, LE17 6HJ
- ☎ (01858) 575082
  (01858) 575974 (Pro Shop)
- 📠 (01858) 575078
- ✉ kilworthsprings@ukonline.co.uk
- 📖 850
- 🏌 Ann Vicary (Sec)
  Jeremy Wilkinson (Mgr)
- ✓ A Mankert (01858) 575974
- ⚐ 18 L 6718 yds SSS 72
- 👥 U SOC
- ££ £24 (£27)
- 🚗 4 miles E of M1 Junction 20
- ⊕ Floodlit driving range; additional
  practice facilities; computerised
  teaching studio
- 🏠 Ray Baldwin
- 📠 www.kilworthsprings.co.uk

Kirby Muxloe (1893)

Station Road, Kirby Muxloe, Leicester,
LE9 2EP
- ☎ (0116) 239 3457
- 📠 (0116) 238 8891
- ✉ kirbymuxloegolf@btconnect.com
- 📖 630
- 🏌 GB Woodcock (0116) 239 3457
- ✓ B Whipham (0116) 239 2813
- ⚐ 18 L 6307 yds Par 71 SSS 70
- 👥 WD–U before 3.45pm exc
  Tues–NA WE–by arrangement
  SOC–H
- ££ £30 D–£35
- 🚗 3 miles W of Leicester. M1
  Junctions 21 or 21A

- ⊕ Driving range for members and
  green fees only
- 📠 www.kirbymuxloe-golf.co.uk

Leicestershire (1890)

Evington Lane, Leicester, LE5 6DJ
- ☎ (0116) 273 8825
- 📠 (0116) 249 8799
- ✉ secretary@leicestershiregolfclub
  .co.uk
- 📖 750
- 🏌 CR Chapman (0116) 273 8825
- ✓ DT Jones (0116) 273 8825
- ⚐ 18 L 6329 yds SSS 71
- 👥 U H SOC–arrange with Sec
- ££ £35 (£40)
- 🚗 2 miles E of Leicester
- ⊕ Practice area
- 📠 www.leicestershiregolfclub.co.uk

Lingdale (1967)

Joe Moore's Lane, Woodhouse Eaves,
Loughborough, LE12 8TF
- ☎ (01509) 890703
- 📠 (01509) 890703
- ✉ secretary@lingdale-golf-club.com
- 📖 718
- 🏌 T Stephens
- ✓ P Sellears
- ⚐ 18 L 6545 yds SSS 71
- 👥 SOC WD–U phone for availability
  WE–NA before 2pm
- ££ £28 D–£32 (£46 D–£33)
- 🚗 6 miles S of Loughborough. M1
  Junction 23, 4 miles
- ⊕ Practice ground
- 📠 www.lingdale-golf-club.com

Longcliffe (1906)

Snells Nook Lane, Nanpantan,
Loughborough, LE11 3YA
- ☎ (01509) 216321
- ✉ longcliffegolf@btconnect.com

Lutterworth (1904)

Rugby Road, Lutterworth, LE17 4HN
- ☎ (01455) 552532
- 📠 (01455) 553586
- ✉ sec@lutterworthgc.co.uk
- 📖 712
- 🏌 J Faulks (01455) 552532
- ✓ L Challinor (01455) 557199
- ⚐ 18 L 6226 yds SSS 70
- 👥 WD–U WE–M SOC–WD
- ££ £28 D–£36
- 🚗 By M1 Junction 20 and M6 Jct 1
- 📠 www.lutterworthgc.co.uk

Market Harborough (1898)

Great Oxendon Road, Market Harborough,
LE16 8NF
- ☎ (01858) 463684
- 📠 (01858) 432906
- ✉ mhgc@premier-opt.co.uk
- 📖 650
- 🏌 P Weston
- ✓ FJ Baxter (01858) 463684
- ⚐ 18 L 6022 yds Par 70 SSS 69
- 👥 WD–U WE–M SOC–WD
- ££ £30 D–£40

⚐ I mile S of Market Harborough on A508
⌂ Howard Swan
▤ www.mhgolf.co.uk

Melton Mowbray (1925)
Waltham Rd, Thorpe Arnold, Melton Mowbray, LE14 4SD
☎ (01664) 562118
⌨ (01664) 562118
✉ mmgc@le144sd.fsbusiness.co.uk
▥ 660
⚲ Sue Millward/Marilyn Connelly
⌕ N Curtis (01664) 569629
▷ 18 L 6222 yds SSS 70
👥 U Full green fee WD–U WE–U;
2–for–I WD–U WE–Sat after 2pm,
Sun after 120.30am SOC
££ £25 (£30)
⚐ 2 miles NE of Melton Mowbray on A607
⊕ Driving range; short game area
▤ www.mmgc.org

Oadby (1974)
Public
Leicester Road, Oadby, Leicester, LE2 4AJ
☎ (0116) 270 9052/270 0215
▥ 350
⚲ RA Primrose (0116) 270 3828
⌕ A Wells (0116) 270 9052
▷ 18 L 6311 yds Par 72 SSS 70
👥 WD–U WE/BH–book with Pro
SOC–WD
££ D–£12 (£15)
⚐ Leicester Racecourse, 2 miles SE of Leicester (A6)

Park Hill (1994)
Park Hill, Seagrave, LE12 7NG
☎ (01509) 815454
⌨ (01509) 816062
✉ mail@parkhillgolf.co.uk
▥ 500
⚲ JP Hutson
⌕ M Ulyett (01509) 815775
▷ 18 L 7219 yds Par 73 SSS 74
👥 U SOC
££ £25 D–£35 (£30 D–£45)
⚐ 6 miles N of Leicester on A46. 10 min from MI Junction 21A
⊕ Driving range (20 bay), grass tees; practice bunker; Par 3 academy course
▤ www.parkhillgolf.co.uk

Rothley Park (1911)
Westfield Lane, Rothley, Leicester, LE7 7LH
☎ (0116) 230 2019
⌨ (0116) 230 2809
✉ secretary@rothleypark.co.uk
▥ 600
⚲ SG Winterton (0116) 230 2809
⌕ D Spillane (0116) 230 3023
▷ 18 L 6487 yds SSS 71
👥 WD–H exc Tues–NA WE/BH–NA SOC
££ £30 D–£40
⚐ 6 miles N of Leicester, W of A6
▤ www.rothleypark.com

Scraptoft (1928)
Beeby Road, Scraptoft, Leicester, LE7 9SJ
☎ (0116) 241 9000
⌨ (0116) 241 9000
✉ secretary@scraptoft-golf.co.uk
▥ 600
⚲ Paul Henry (0116) 241 9000
⌕ Simon Wood (0116) 241 9138
▷ 18 L 6151 yds Par 70 SSS 70
👥 WD–U WE–M SOC–WD
££ £24 D–£29 (£29 after noon)
⚐ 3 miles E of Leicester
▤ www.scraptoft-golf.co.uk

Six Hills (1986)
Pay and play
Six Hills, Melton Mowbray, LE14 3PR
☎ (01509) 881225
⌨ (01509) 889090
▥ 120
⚲ Mrs J Showler
⌕ J Hawley
▷ 18 L 5758 yds Par 71 SSS 69
👥 U
££ £13 (£16)
⚐ 10 miles N of Leicester, off A46
⊕ Driving range

Stapleford Park (2000)
Stapleford park, Melton Mowbray, LE14 2EF
☎ (01572) 787044
⌨ (01572) 787001
✉ club@stapleford.co.uk
▥ 100
⚲ Richard Alderson
⌕ Richard Alderson
▷ 18 L 6944 yds Par 73 SSS 73
👥 H WD–U WE–NA before 11am
SOC–NA WE before 11am
SOC–WD–U
££ 9: £25; 18: £50 D–£75 Same rates apply at WE
⚐ 4 miles E of Melton Mowbray off B676
⊕ Driving range; putting green; pro shop
⌂ Donald Steel
▤ www.staplefordpark.com

Ullesthorpe Court Hotel (1976)
Frolesworth Road, Ullesthorpe, Lutterworth, LE17 5BZ
☎ (01455) 209023
⌨ (01455) 202537
▥ 600
⚲ AP Parr (ext 2446)
⌕ D Bowring (01455) 209150
▷ 18 L 6650 yds SSS 72
👥 U SOC–WD
££ £22 D–£30
⚐ 3 miles NW of Lutterworth, off B577. MI Junction 20, 5 miles
▤ www.ullesthorpecourt.co.uk

Western Park (1910)
Public
Scudamore Road, Leicester, LE3 1UQ
☎ (0116) 287 5211
▥ 300

⚲ Lee Preston
⌕ D Butler (0116) 299 5565
▷ 18 L 6532 yds SSS 71
👥 U
££ On application
⚐ 4 miles W of Leicester. MI Junction 21, 3 miles

Whetstone (1965)
Cambridge Road, Cosby, Leicester, LE9 5SH
☎ (0116) 286 1424
⌨ (0116) 286 1424
✉ daviddalbywgc@aol.com
▥ 550
⚲ D Dalby
⌕ D Raitt
▷ 18 L 6182 yds Par 70 SSS 70
👥 U SOC
££ £18 (£20)
⚐ S boundary of Leicester
⊕ Driving range
⌂ E Callaway
▤ www.whetstonegolf.co.uk

Willesley Park (1921)
Measham Road, Ashby-de-la-Zouch, LE65 2PF
☎ (01530) 414596
✉ info@willesleypark.com

Lincolnshire

Ashby Decoy (1936)
Ashby Decoy, Burringham Road, Scunthorpe, DN17 2AB
☎ (01724) 842913
⌨ (01724) 271708
✉ info@ashbydecoygolfclub.co.uk
▥ 640
⚲ Mrs J Harrison (01724) 866561
⌕ A Miller (01724) 868972
▷ 18 L 6281 yds SSS 71
👥 WD–Mon/Wed/Thur/Fri, Tue after 2pm WE–NA
££ £25 (£30)
⚐ 2 miles SW of Scunthorpe
▤ www.ashbydecoy.co.uk

Belton Park (1890)
Belton Lane, Londonthorpe Road, Grantham, NG31 9SH
☎ (01476) 567399
⌨ (01476) 592078
✉ greatgolf@beltonpark.co.uk
▥ 900
⚲ S Rowley (01476) 542900
⌕ S Williams (01476) 542903
▷ 27 holes:
Brownlow L 6427 yds SSS 71
Ancaster L 6227 yds SSS 70
Belmont L 6016 yds SSS 69
👥 U H SOC–WD exc Tues
££ £30 (£40)
⚐ 2 miles N of Grantham
⊕ Long & short game practice area
⌂ T Williamson
▤ www.beltonpark.co.uk

De Vere Belton Woods Hotel   (1991)

Belton, Grantham, NG32 2LN
- ☎ **(01476) 593200**
- 🖥 (01476) 574547
- ✉ belton.woods@devere-hotels
  .co.uk
- 🏛 350
- ✍ A Cameron (01476) 514364
- ✓ S Sayers (01476) 514634
- ▷ Lakes 18 L 6831 yds SSS 73
  Woodside 18 L 6623 yds SSS 72
  9 hole Par 3 course
- 👥 U SOC
- ££ £35 D–£45 (£45 D–£60)
- ⊶ 2 miles N of Grantham on A607
  towards Lincoln; 5 min from A1
- ⊕ Driving range
- 🏠 Cayford
- 🖥 www.devere.co.uk

Blankney   (1904)

Proprietary
Blankney, Lincoln, LN4 3AZ
- ☎ **(01526) 320263**
- 🖥 (01526) 322521
- ✉ grahambradley5@btconnect.com
- 🏛 664 138(L) 50(J)
- ✍ G Bradley (01526) 320202
- ✓ G Bradley (01526) 320202
- ▷ 18 L 6638 yds SSS 73
- 👥 U SOC WD WE U
- ££ £28 D–£36 (£34)
- ⊶ 10 miles SE of Lincoln on B1188
- ⊕ Good practice facilities
- 🏠 Cameron Sinclair
- 🖥 www.blankneygolf.co.uk

Boston   (1900)

Cowbridge, Horncastle Road, Boston,
PE22 7EL
- ☎ **(01205) 350589**
- 🖥 (01205) 367526
- ✉ steveshaw@bostongc.co.uk
- 🏛 650 115(L) 60(J)
- ✍ SP Shaw (01205) 350589
- ✓ N Hiom (01205) 362306
- ▷ 18 L 6415 yds Par 72 SSS 71
- 👥 WD–U WE/BH–U H
- ££ £30 anytime
- ⊶ 2 miles N of Boston on B1183
- ⊕ Driving range; putting green;
  practice ground
- 🖥 www.bostongc.co.uk

Boston West   (1995)

Hubbert's Bridge, Boston, PE20 3QX
- ☎ **(01205) 290670**
- 🖥 (01205) 290725
- ✉ info@bostonwestgolfclub.co.uk
- 🏛 650
- ✍ MJ Couture (01205) 290670
- ✓ S Collingwood (01205) 290540
- ▷ 18 L 6354 yds Par 72 SSS 70
  6 hole Par 3 course
- 👥 U SOC WD WE
- ££ £18 (£22)
- ⊶ 2 miles W of Boston on B1192
- ⊕ Floodlit driving range; 24-room
  hotel on site – golf packages
  available

- 🏠 Michael Zara
- 🖥 www.bostonwestgolfclub.co.uk

Burghley Park   (1890)

St Martin's, Stamford, PE9 3JX
- ☎ **(01780) 753789**
- 🖥 (01780) 753789
- ✉ burghley.golf@lineone.net
- 🏛 750 140(L) 100(J)
- ✍ S Last (Sec/Mgr)
- ✓ Glenn Davies (01780) 762100
- ▷ 18 L 6236 yds SSS 70
- 👥 WD–I or H WE/BH–M SOC–WD
- ££ D–£30
- ⊶ 1 mile S of Stamford, off A1 to
  B1081
- 🏠 Rev JD Day

Canwick Park   (1893)

Canwick Park, Washingborough Road,
Lincoln, LN4 1EF
- ☎ **(01522) 542912/522166**
- 🖥 (01522) 526997
- ✉ manager@canwickpark.org
- 🏛 650
- ✍ N Porteus (01522) 542912
- ✓ S Williamson (01522) 536870
- ▷ 18 L 6150 yds SSS 69
- 👥 WD–U WE–M before 2.30pm
  SOC–WD
- ££ £22 D–£30 (£25) 10am–noon &
  2–4pm £15
- ⊶ 1 mile SE of Lincoln
- 🏠 Hawtree
- 🖥 www.canwickpark.org

Carholme   (1906)

Carholme Road, Lincoln, LN1 1SE
- ☎ **(01522) 523725**
- 🖥 (01522) 533733
- ✉ info@carholme-golf-club.co.uk
- 🏛 600
- ✍ J Lammin
- ▷ 18 L 6215 yds Par 71 SSS 70
- 👥 WD–U WE–U after 2pm BH–SOC
- ££ £18 (£22)
- ⊶ Lincoln 1 mile (A57)
- 🏠 William Park jr
- 🖥 www.carholme-golf-club.co.uk

Cleethorpes   (1894)

Kings Road, Cleethorpes, DN35 0PN
- ☎ **(01472) 814060 (Pro)**
- 🖥 (01472) 814060
- ✉ secretary@cleethorpesgolfclub
  .co.uk
- 🏛 650
- ✍ AJ Thompson (01472) 816110
- ✓ P Davies (01472) 814060
- ▷ 18 L 6272 yds SSS 71
- 👥 WD–U exc Tues am Wed pm
  SOC–exc Tues/Wed/Sat
- ££ £25 D–£35 (£30 D–£40)
- ⊶ 1 mile S of Cleethorpes
- 🏠 Harry Vardon/Dr Alister
  Mackenzie
- 🖥 www.cleethorpesgolfclub.co.uk

Elsham   (1900)

Barton Road, Elsham, Brigg, DN20 0LS
- ☎ **(01652) 680291**
- 🖥 (01652) 680308

- ✉ manager@elshamgolfclub.co.uk
- 🏛 650
- ✍ T Hartley (Mgr) (01652) 680291
- ✓ S Brewer (01652) 680432
- ▷ 18 L 6426 yds SSS 71
- 👥 H SOC–WD
- ££ £27 D–£37
- ⊶ 3 miles N of Brigg. M180 Junction 5
- 🖥 www.elshamgolfclub.co.uk

Forest Pines G&CC Hotel   (1996)

Ermine Street, Brigg, DN20 0AQ
- ☎ **(01652) 650756**
- 🖥 (01652) 650495
- ✉ forestpines@qhotels.co.uk
- 🏛 400
- ✍ D Edwards (Golf Dir)
- ✓ D Edwards
- ▷ 27 holes: 6393-6859 yds
  Par 71-73 SSS 70-73
- 👥 U SOC
- ££ £40 D–£50
- ⊶ M180 Junction 4, on A15 to
  Scunthorpe
- ⊕ Golf range, hotel and leisure
  facilities
- 🏠 John Morgan
- 🖥 www.forestpines.co.uk

Gainsborough   (1894)

Thonock, Gainsborough, DN21 1PZ
- ☎ **(01427) 613088**
- 🖥 (01427) 810172
- ✉ emma@gainsboroughgc.co.uk
- 🏛 600
- ✍ D Bowers
- ✓ S Cooper
- ▷ 18 L 6266 yds Par 70 SSS 70
  18 L 6724 yds Par 72 SSS 72
- 👥 U
- ££ £30 D–£40
- ⊶ N of Gainsborough
- ⊕ Floodlit driving range
- 🏠 Neil Coles
- 🖥 www.gainsboroughgc.co.uk

Gedney Hill   (1991)

Public
West Drove, Gedney End Hill, PE12 0NT
- ☎ **(01406) 330922**
- 🖥 (01945) 581903
- 🏛 115
- ✍ R Newns (01945) 581903
- ▷ 18 L 5450 yds SSS 66
- 👥 U SOC–WD/WE
- ££ £9.50 (£13.50) D–£15 Seniors £7
  (£13.50)
- ⊶ 4 miles from A47 on B1166
- 🏠 C Britton

Grange Park   (1992)

Pay and play
Butterwick Road, Messingham, Scunthorpe,
DN17 3PP
- ☎ **(01724) 762945**
- ✉ info@grangepark.com
- ✍ I Cannon (Mgr)
- ✓ J Drury
- ▷ 18 L 6180 yds Par 70
  9 hole Par 3 course
- 👥 U SOC–WD/WE

££ £16 (£18)
🔺 5 miles from Scunthorpe. M180 Junction 3
⊕ Floodlit driving range
🏠 RW Price
▤ www.grangepark.com

Grimsby (1922)

Littlecoates Road, Grimsby, DN34 4LU
☎ **(01472) 342823 (Clubhouse)**
✉ secretary@grimsbygc.fsnet.co.uk
📖 650 150(L) 70(J)
🏌 D McCully (01472) 342630
🏌 R Smith (01472) 356981
🏁 18 L 6057 yds Par 70 SSS 69
🚶 WD–U Sat pm/Sun am–XL SOC–Mon & Fri H
££ £25 (£30)
🔺 1 mile W of Grimsby, off A46. 1 mile from M180
🏠 HS Colt
▤ www.grimsbygolfclub.com

Hirst Priory Park

Crowle, Scunthorpe, DN17 4BU
☎ **(07715) 420519**

Holme Hall (1908)

Holme Lane, Bottesford, Scunthorpe, DN16 3RF
☎ **(01724) 862078**
📠 (01724) 862081
✉ rogerbickley@hotmail.com
📖 470 90(L) 30(J)
🏌 Roger B. Bickley
🏌 R McKiernan (01724) 851816
🏁 18 L 6404 yds SSS 71
🚶 WD–U WE–M H SOC–WD
££ £25 D–£35
🔺 4 miles SE of Scunthorpe. M180 Junction 4

Horncastle (1990)

West Ashby, Horncastle, LN9 5PP
☎ **(01507) 526800**
📠 (01507) 517069
✉ info@twinlakescentre.com
📖 100
🏌 C Redfearn
🏌 A Johns
🏁 18 L 5717 yds SSS 70
🚶 U SOC
££ £15 (£18)
🔺 1 mile N of Horncastle, off A158
⊕ Golf Academy; driving range
🏠 EC Wright
▤ www.horncastlegolfclub.com

Humberston Park

Humberston Avenue, Humberston, DN36 4SJ
☎ **(01472) 210404**

Immingham (1975)

St Andrews Lane, Off Church Lane, Immingham, DN40 2EU
☎ **(01469) 575298**
📠 (01469) 577636
📖 650
🏌 D McCully (Mgr)
🏌 N Harding (01469) 575493

🏁 18 L 6215 yds SSS 70
🚶 WD–U WE–restricted (ring for details) SOC–WD
££ £18 (£23)
🔺 N of St Andrew's Church, Immingham
🏠 Hawtree/Pennink
▤ www.immgc.com

Kenwick Park (1992)

Kenwick, Louth, LN11 8NY
☎ **(01507) 605134**
📠 (01507) 606556
✉ golfatkenwick@nascr.net
📖 450
🏌 Mrs TL Baxter
🏌 E Sharp (01507) 607161
🏁 18 L 6782 yds Par 72 SSS 73
🚶 U SOC
££ £30 D–£40 (£40)
🔺 1 mile SE of Louth
⊕ Teaching Academy. Driving range
🏠 Patrick Tallack
▤ www.louthnet.co.uk

Kirton Holme (1992)

Proprietary
Holme Road, Kirton Holme, Boston, PE20 1SY
☎ **(01205) 290669**
📖 320
🏌 Mrs T Welberry
🏌 Alison Jones
🏁 9 L 2884 yds Par 70 SSS 68
🚶 U SOC
££ D–£10 (D–£11)
🔺 3 miles W of Boston, off A52
🏠 DW Welberry
▤ www.kirtonholmegolfcourse.co.uk

Lincoln (1891)

Torksey, Lincoln, LN1 2EG
☎ **(01427) 718721**
📠 (01427) 718721
✉ info@lincolngc.co.uk
📖 625
🏌 DB Linton
🏌 A Carter (01427) 718273
🏁 18 L 6438 yds SSS 71
🚶 WD–H SOC
££ £30 D–£38 (£35 D–£45)
🔺 12 miles NW of Lincoln, off A156
⊕ 3-hole pitch & putt practice course; large practice area; driving net
🏠 JH Taylor
▤ www.lincolngc.co.uk

Louth (1965)

Crowtree Lane, Louth, LN11 9LJ
☎ **(01507) 603681**
📠 (01507) 608501
✉ enquiries@louthgolfclub.com
📖 700
🏌 Simon Moody (Gen Mgr) T Moody (Golf Dev Mgr)
🏌 AJ Blundell (01507) 604648
🏁 18 L 6436 yds SSS 71
🚶 WD U SOC WE – not Sat/Sun after 11
££ £24 D–£30 (£30 D–£35)
🔺 W side of Louth
▤ www.louthgolfclub.com

Manor (Laceby) (1992)

Laceby Manor, Laceby, Grimsby, DN37 7EA
☎ **(01472) 873468**
📠 (01472) 871266
✉ judith@manorgolfclub.wanadoo.co.uk
📖 550
🏌 Mrs J Mackay, G Mackay (Mgr)
🏌 Neil Laybourne
🏁 18 L 6354 yds SSS 70
🚶 U SOC
££ D–£20 (£24)
🔺 5 miles W of Grimsby at Barton Street (A18)
🏠 Nicholson/Rushton

Market Rasen & District (1912)

Legsby Road, Market Rasen, LN8 3DZ
☎ **(01673) 842319**
📠 (01673) 849245
✉ marketrasengolf@onetel.net
📖 600
🏌 JP Smith
🏌 AM Chester (01673) 842416
🏁 18 L 6239 yds SSS 70
🚶 WD–I WE/BH–M SOC
££ £25 D–£35
🔺 1 mile E of Market Rasen
▤ www.marketrasengolfclub.co.uk

Market Rasen Racecourse (1990)

Legsby Road, Market Rasen, LN8 3EA
☎ **(01673) 843434**
📠 (01673) 844532
✉ marketrasen@rht.net
🏁 9 L 2350 yds Par
🚶 U
££ On application
🔺 Market Rasen Racecourse
▤ www.marketrasenraces.co.uk

Martin Moor

Martin Road, Blankney, LN4 3BE
☎ **(01526) 378243**

Millfield (1984)

Laughterton, Lincoln, LN1 2LB
☎ **(01427) 718473**
📠 (01427) 718473
📖 500
🏌 Paul Grey-Guthrie
🏌 Brian Cummings
🏁 18 L 6098 yds SSS 69
18 L 4585 yds
9 hole Par 3 course
🚶 U
££ £10
🔺 9 miles W of Lincoln, nr Torksey (B1133)
⊕ Driving range
🏠 C Watson

Normanby Hall (1978)

Public
Normanby Park, Scunthorpe, DN15 9HU
☎ **(01724) 280444 Ext 852 (Bookings)**

North Shore   (1910)
North Shore Road, Skegness, PE25 1DN
☎ **(01754) 763298**

Pottergate   (1992)
Owned privately
Moor Lane, Branston, Lincoln
☎ **(01522) 794867**

RAF Coningsby   (1972)
RAF Coningsby, Lincoln, LN4 4SY
☎ **(01526) 342581 Ext 6828**

Sandilands   (1901)
Proprietary
Sandilands, Sutton-on-Sea, LN12 2RJ
☎ **(01507) 441432**
🖳 (01507) 441617
✉ grangeandlinkshotel@btconnect
.com
📖 300
♠ P Ross (01507) 441432
✎ Andrew Myers
⛳ 18 L 6068 yds Par 70 SSS 69
👥 U SOC
££ £18 (£20)
⚲ 1 mile S of Sutton-on-Sea, off A52
🖥 www.grangeandlinkshotel.co.uk

Seacroft   (1895)
*Drummond Road, Seacroft, Skegness,
PE25 3AU*
☎ **(01754) 763020**
🖳 (01754) 763020
✉ enquiries@seacroft-golfclub.co.uk
📖 328 107(L) 87(J)
♠ R England (Sec/Mgr)
✎ R Lawie (01754) 769624
⛳ 18 L 6492 yds SSS 71
👥 U H SOC
££ £40 (£50)
⚲ S boundary of Skegness, nr Nature
Reserve
🏠 Willie Fernie/Tom Dunn
🖥 www.seacroft-golfclub.co.uk

Sleaford   (1905)
*Greylees, South Rauceby, Sleaford,
NG34 8PL*
☎ **(01529) 488273**
🖳 (01529) 488644
✉ sleafordgolfclub@btinternet.com
📖 630
♠ Ms EN Downey
✎ N Pearce (01529) 488644
⛳ 18 L 6503 yds SSS 71
👥 U H exc Sun–NA (Winter)
SOC–WD
££ £25 (£36)
⚲ 1 mile W of Sleaford on A153
🏠 Tom Williamson
🖥 www.sleafordgolfclub.co.uk

South Kyme   (1990)
*Skinners Lane, South Kyme, Lincoln,
LN4 4AT*
☎ **(01526) 861113**
🖳 (01526) 861080
✉ southkymegc@hotmail.com
♠ P Chamberlain (Golf Dir)

✎ P Chamberlain
⛳ 18 L 6482 yds Par 72 SSS 71
👥 U SOC
££ £20 (£24)
⚲ 2 miles from A17 on B1395
⊕ 6 hole practice course
🖥 www.skgc.co.uk

Spalding   (1907)
Surfleet, Spalding, PE11 4EA
☎ **(01775) 680386**
🖳 (01775) 680988
✉ secretary@spaldinggolfclub.co.uk
📖 825
♠ BW Walker (01775) 680386
✎ J Spencer (01775) 680474
⛳ 18 L 6483 yds SSS 71
👥 U H SOC–Tues after 2pm & Thurs
all day
££ £25 D–£30 (£40)
⚲ 4 miles N of Spalding, off A16
⊕ Driving range
🏠 Spencer/Ward/Price
🖥 www.spaldinggolfclub.co.uk

Stoke Rochford   (1924)
Great North Rd, Grantham, NG33 5EW
☎ **(01476) 530275**
🖳 (01476) 530237
📖 580
♠ J Martindale (01572) 756305
✎ A Dow (01476) 530218
⛳ 18 L 6252 yds SSS 70
👥 WD–U WE/BH–U after 10.30am
££ On application
⚲ 6 miles S of Grantham (A1)
🏠 Maj Hotchkin (1935)

Sudbrook Moor   (1991)
Public
*Charity Street, Carlton Scroop, Grantham,
NG32 3AT*
☎ **(01400) 250796 all enquiries**
♠ Judith Hutton
✎ Tim Hutton (01400) 250796
⛳ 9 L 4827 yds Par 66 SSS 64
👥 U–phone first
££ £9 (£12)
⚲ Carlton Scroop, 6 miles NE of
Grantham (A607)
⊕ Driving range on site; putting and
practice facilities
🏠 Tim Hutton
🖥 www.sudbrookmoor.co.uk

Sutton Bridge   (1914)
*New Road, Sutton Bridge, Spalding,
PE12 9RQ*
☎ **(01406) 350323 (Clubhouse)**
✉ suttonbridgegc@yahoo.co.uk
📖 320
♠ NE Davis (01945) 582447
✎ Antony Lowther (01406) 351422
⛳ 9 L 5820 yds SSS 68
👥 WD–H WE–M SOC
££ £20
⚲ 8 miles N of Wisbech (A17)
⊕ Driving range
🖥 www.club-noticeboard.co.uk
/suttonbridge

Tetney   (1993)
Station Road, Tetney, Grimsby, DN36 5HY
☎ **(01472) 211644**
🖳 (01472) 211644
📖 350
♠ J Abrams
✎ J Abrams
⛳ 18 L 6100 yds Par 71 SSS 69
👥 U SOC
££ £12
⚲ 5 miles S of Grimsby, off A16
⊕ Driving range

Toft Hotel   (1988)
Proprietary
Toft, Bourne, PE10 0JT
☎ **(01778) 590616**

Waltham Windmill   (1997)
Proprietary
Cheapside, Waltham, Grimsby, DN37 0HT
☎ **(01472) 824109**
🖳 (01472) 828391
📖 600
♠ S Bennett (01472) 821883
✎ N Burkitt (01472) 823963
⛳ 18 L 6400 yds Par 71 SSS 71
👥 WD–U SOC
££ £26 (£32)
⚲ 2 miles S of Grimsby, off A16
🏠 Fox/Payne
🖥 www.walthamgolf.co.uk

Welton Manor   (1995)
Proprietary
Hackthorn Road, Welton, LN2 3PD
☎ **(01673) 862827**
🖳 (01673) 860917
✉ golf@weltonmanorgolfcentre.co.uk
📖 650
♠ TM Coates MBE
✎ G Leslie (01673) 862827
⛳ 18 L 5703 yds SSS 67
👥 U SOC
££ £12 (£15)
⚲ Off A46 Lincoln to Grimsby road
⊕ Driving range
🖥 www.weltonmanorgolfcentre.co.uk

Woodhall Spa   (1891)
Proprietary
Woodhall Spa, LN10 6PU
☎ **(01526) 351835**
  (01526) 352511 (Bookings)
🖳 (01526) 352778
✉ secretary@woodhallgolfclub.co.uk
📖 600
♠ Mike Underwood
✎ Andrew Hare (01526) 830945
⛳ Hotchkin 18 L 7080 yds SSS 75
Bracken 18 L 6735 yds SSS 74
👥 Booking essential SOC
££ Hotchkin–£65 D–£100 (non–EGU
rate – 2006) Bracken–£50 D–£75
(non–EGU rate – 2006)
⚲ 19 miles SE of Lincoln (B1191)
⊕ Driving range. Teaching Academy
🏠 Hotchkin/Steel
🖥 www.woodhallspagolfclub.co.uk

Woodthorpe Hall   (1986)

Woodthorpe, Alford, LN13 0DD
☎ **(01507) 450000**
🖥 (01507) 450000
📧 secretary@woodthorpehallgolfclub
.fsnet.co.uk
📖 200
🏌 Joan Smith (01507) 450000
🏳 18 L 5140 yds Par 67 SSS 65
👥 U SOC
££ £12 (£15 inc. BH)
⛳ 3 miles N of Alford, off B1373. 8
miles SE of Louth
▤ www.woodthorpehall.co.uk

London Clubs

Aquarius *Kent*
Central London Golf Centre *Surrey*
Dulwich & Sydenham Hill *Surrey*
Eltham Warren *Kent*
Finchley *Middlesex*
Hampstead *Middlesex*
Hendon *Middlesex*
Highgate *Middlesex*
London Scottish *Surrey*
Mill Hill *Middlesex*
Muswell Hill *Middlesex*
North Middlesex *Middlesex*
Richmond Park *Surrey*
Roehampton Club *Surrey*
Royal Blackheath *Kent*
Royal Epping Forest *Essex*
Royal Wimbledon *Surrey*
Shooter's Hill *Kent*
South Herts *Hertfordshire*
Trent Park *Middlesex*
Wanstead *Essex*
West Essex *Essex*
Wimbledon Common *Surrey*
Wimbledon Park *Surrey*

Manchester

Blackley   (1907)

*Victoria Avenue East, Manchester,
M9 7HW*
☎ **(0161) 643 2980**
🖥 (0161) 653 8300
📧 office@blackleygolfclub.com
📖 800
🏌 B Beddoes (0161) 654 7770
☑ C Gould (0161) 643 3912
🏳 18 L 6235 yds SSS 70
👥 WD–U WE–M SOC–WD exc Thur
££ £24
⛳ North Manchester – M60 J20
🏠 Gaunt and Marnoch
▤ www.blackleygolfclub.com

Boysnope Park   (1998)

Proprietary
*Liverpool Road, Barton Moss, Eccles,
M30 7RF*
☎ **(0161) 707 6125**
🖥 (0161) 707 1888

🏌 Jean Stringer (0161) 707 6125
☑ S Currie (0161) 787 8687
🏳 18 L 3506 yds Par 72 SSS 71
👥 U SOC
££ £13 (£16)
⛳ SW of Manchester on A57. M60
Junction 11, 1 mile
⊕ Driving range
▤ www.boysnopegolfclub.co.uk

Chorlton-cum-Hardy   (1902)

*Barlow Hall, Barlow Hall Road, Manchester,
M21 7JJ*
☎ **(0161) 881 3139**
🖥 (0161) 881 4532
📧 chorltongolf@hotmail.com
📖 600
🏌 IR Booth (0161) 881 5830
☑ DR Valentine (0161) 881 9911
🏳 18 L 6039 yds SSS 69
👥 U H SOC–Thurs & Fri
££ £27 (£32)
⛳ 4 miles S of Manchester
(A5103/A5145)
▤ www.chorltoncumhardygolfclub
.sagenet.co.uk

Davyhulme Park   (1911)

*Gleneagles Road, Davyhulme, Manchester,
M41 8SA*
☎ **(0161) 748 2260**

Denton   (1909)

*Manchester Road, Denton, Manchester,
M34 2GG*
☎ **(0161) 336 3218**
🖥 (0161) 336 4751
📧 dentongolfclub@btinternet.com
📖 678
🏌 ID McIlvanney
☑ M Hollingworth (0161) 336 2070
🏳 18 L 6443 yds SSS 71
👥 WD–U WE/BH–NA before
3.30pm SOC
££ £28 (£35)
⛳ M60 Junction 24, A57 to
Manchester
▤ www.dentongolfclub.co.uk

Didsbury   (1891)

*Ford Lane, Northenden, Manchester,
M22 4NQ*
☎ **(0161) 998 9278**
🖥 (0161) 902 3060
📧 golf@didsburygolfclub.com
📖 760
🏌 AL Watson (Mgr)
☑ P Barber (0161) 998 2811
🏳 18 L 6210 yds SSS 70
👥 WD–U H exc 9–10am &
12–1.30pm–NA WE–U H
10.30–11.30am & after 4pm
££ £29 (£33) – includes insurance
⛳ 6 miles S of Manchester. M60
Junction 5
▤ www.didsburygolfclub.com

Ellesmere   (1913)

*Old Clough Lane, Worsley, Manchester,
M28 7HZ*
☎ **(0161) 790 2122**

🖥 (0161) 790 7322
📧 honsec@ellesmeregolf.fsnet.co.uk
📖 380 80(L) 75(J)
🏌 MJ Farrington (0161) 799 0554
☑ S Wakefield (0161) 790 8591
🏳 18 L 6238 yds SSS 70
👥 U exc comp days (check with Pro)
SOC–WD
££ £33
⛳ 6 miles W of Manchester, nr
junction of M60/A580
▤ www.ellesmeregolfclub.co.uk

Fairfield Golf & Sailing Club   (1892)

*Booth Road, Audenshaw, Manchester,
M34 5GA*
☎ **(0161) 301 4528**
🖥 (0161) 301 4524
📧 fairfieldgolf@btconnect.com
📖 550
🏌 M Jones (Sec/Mgr)
☑ SA Pownell (0161) 370 2292
🏳 18 L 5664 yds SSS 68
👥 WD–U WE–NA before noon
SOC–WD
££ £20 (£25)
⛳ 5 miles E of Manchester on A635

Flixton   (1893)

*Church Road, Flixton, Urmston, Manchester,
M41 6EP*
☎ **(0161) 748 2116**
🖥 (0161) 748 2116
📧 flixtongolfclub@mail.com
📖 400
🏌 F Baker
☑ A Bridgewood (0161) 746 7160
🏳 9 L 6410 yds SSS 71
👥 WD–U exc Wed SOC
££ £25 (£32)
⛳ 6 miles SW of Manchester on
B5213. M60 Junction 10
▤ www.flixtongolfclub.co.uk

Great Lever & Farnworth   (1901)

Plodder Lane, Farnworth, Bolton, BL4 0LQ
☎ **(01204) 656493**
🖥 (01204) 656137
📖 520
🏌 MJ Ivill (01204) 656137
☑ T Howarth (01204) 656650
🏳 18 L 6044 yds SSS 69
👥 H SOC–WD
££ £25 (£30)
⛳ 2 miles S of Bolton. M61 Junction 4

Heaton Park Golf Centre   (1912)

Pay and play
*Heaton Park, Middleton Road, Prestwich,
M25 2SW*
☎ **(0161) 654 9899**
🖥 (0161) 653 2003
🏌 Brian Dique (Gen Mgr)
☑ Gary Dermott
🏳 18 L 5755 yds Par 70 SSS 68
18 hole Par 3 course
👥 U SOC
££ £10.50 (£14) Concessions available

North Manchester, via M60
Junction 19 to Middleton Road
⊕ Pitch & putt course; teaching
academy
⌂ JH Taylor

Manchester   (1882)
Hopwood Cottage, Rochdale Road,
Middleton, Manchester M24 6QP
☎ **(0161) 643 3202**
🖳 (0161) 643 9174
📧 secretary@mangc.co.uk
📖 700
🎣 Stephen Armstead
✎ B Connor (0161) 643 2638
🏌 18 L 6450 yds SSS 72
🏃 WD–H WE–NA SOC
££ £25 D–£40
🏧 7 miles N of Manchester. M62
Junction 20
⊕ Driving range-members and green
fees only
⌂ HS Colt
🖥 www.mangc.co.uk

New North Manchester
(1923)
Rhodes House, Manchester Old Road,
Middleton, M24 4PE
☎ **(0161) 643 9033**
🖳 (0161) 643 7775
📧 tee@nmgc.co.uk
📖 650
🎣 D Parkinson
✎ J Peel (0161) 643 7094
🏌 18 L 6598 yds SSS 71
🏃 H WD
££ £30 (£35)
🏧 5 miles N of Manchester. M60
Junction 19
⌂ A Compston
🖥 www.northmanchestergolfclub
.co.uk

Northenden   (1913)
Palatine Road, Manchester, M22 4FR
☎ **(0161) 998 4738**
🖳 (0161) 945 5592
📧 manager@northendengolfclub.com
📖 700
🎣 P Powell (Sec/Mgr) (0161) 998
4738
✎ J Curtis (0161) 945 3386
🏌 18 L 6432 yds SSS 72
🏃 U SOC
££ £28 (£32)
🏧 5 miles S of Manchester. M56 Jct 2

Old Manchester   (1818)
Club
☎ **(0161) 766 4157**
🎣 PT Goodall
🏌 Club without a course

Pike Fold   (1909)
Hills Lane, Pole Lane, Unsworth, Bury
BL9 8QP
☎ **(0161) 766 3561**
📧 john@pikefold.co.uk

Prestwich   (1908)
Hilton Lane, Prestwich, M25 9XB
☎ **(0161) 772 0700**
🖳 (0161) 772 0700
📧 1908@prestwichgc.fsnet.co.uk
📖 500
🎣 R Mason
✎ S Wakefield (0161) 773 1404
🏌 18 L 5103 yds SSS 64
🏃 WD WE–NA before 2pm SOC
££ £20 (£20)
🏧 2½ miles N of Manchester, off
A56. M60 Junction 17
🖥 www.prestwichgolf.co.uk

Stand   (1904)
The Dales, Ashbourne Grove, Whitefield,
Manchester M45 7NL
☎ **(0161) 766 2388**
🖳 (0161) 796 3234
📖 600
🎣 TE Thacker (0161) 766 3197
✎ M Dance (0161) 766 2214
🏌 18 L 6411 yds SSS 71
🏃 U SOC–WD
££ £30 (£35)
🏧 5 miles N of Manchester. M60
Junction 17
⌂ Alex Herd

Swinton Park   (1906)
East Lancashire Road, Swinton, Manchester,
M27 5LX
☎ **(0161) 794 1785**
🖳 (0161) 281 0698
📧 info@spgolf.co.uk
📖 450 120(L) 50(J)
🎣 Barbara Wood (0161) 794 0861
✎ J Wilson (0161) 793 8077
🏌 18 L 6726 yds SSS 72
🏃 WD–U WE–M SOC–not
Thur/Sat/Bank Hols
££ On application + 2 for 1 vouchers
accepted
🏧 On A580, 5 miles NW of
Manchester
⊕ Corporate membership; 2 putting
greens; practice area
⌂ James Braid
🖥 www.spgolf.co.uk

Whitefield   (1932)
Higher Lane, Whitefield, Manchester,
M45 7EZ
☎ **(0161) 351 2700**
🖳 (0161) 351 2712
📧 enquiries@whitefieldgolfclub.com
📖 538
🎣 Mrs M Rothwell
✎ R Penney (0161) 351 2709
🏌 18 L 6047 yds SSS 69
18 L 5752 yds SSS 68
🏃 U SOC–WD
££ £25 (£35)
🏧 4 miles N of Manchester. M60
Junction 17
🖥 www.whitefieldgolfclub.co.uk

Withington   (1892)
243 Palatine Road, West Didsbury,
Manchester, M20 2UE
☎ **(0161) 445 9544**

🖳 (0161) 445 5210
📧 secretary@withingtongolfclub
.co.uk
📖 600
🎣 PJ Keane
✎ S Marr (0161) 445 4861
🏌 18 L 6410 yds SSS 70
🏃 WD–H exc Thurs SOC
££ On application
🏧 6 miles S of Manchester on B5166
🖥 www.withingtongolfclub.co.uk

Worsley   (1894)
Stableford Avenue, Monton Green, Eccles,
Manchester M30 8AP
☎ **(0161) 789 4202**
🖳 (0161) 789 3200
📖 625
🎣 M Heath (Hon)
✎ C Cousins
🏌 18 L 6217 yds SSS 70
🏃 H SOC
££ £30 (£35)
🏧 5 miles W of Manchester

Merseyside

Allerton Municipal   (1934)
Public
Allerton Road, Liverpool, L18 3JT
☎ **(0151) 428 1046**
✎ B Large
🏌 18 L 5494 yds SSS 65
9 hole course
🏃 U SOC
££ On application
🏧 5 miles S of Liverpool

Arrowe Park   (1931)
Public
Arrowe Park, Woodchurch, Birkenhead,
CH49 5LW
☎ **(0151) 677 1527**
🎣 P Hickey
✎ C Disbury
🏌 18 L 6396 yds SSS 70
🏃 U
££ £10
🏧 3 miles S of Birkenhead on A552.
M53 Junction 3, 1 mile
⊕ 9 hole pitch & putt

Bidston   (1913)
Bidston Link Road, Wallasey, Wirral,
CH44 2HR
☎ **(0151) 638 3412**
📖 550
🎣 K Povall (Hon)
✎ Alan Norwood (0151) 638 3412
🏌 18 L 6207 yds SSS 70
🏃 WD–U WE–U after 3pm SOC
££ £24.50 (£32.50)
🏧 Off Bidston Link Road. M53
Junction 1
🖥 www.bidstongolf.co.uk

Blundells Hill
Blundells Lane, Rainhill, L35 6NA
☎ **(0151) 430 0100**

Bootle (1934)
Pay and play
Dunnings Bridge Road, Litherland, L30 2PP
- ☎ **(0151) 949 1815**
- 🖥 (0151) 949 1815
- ✉ bootlegolfcourse@btconnect.com
- 📖 400
- ⚲ G Howarth
- ✓ A Bradshaw (0151) 928 1371
- ⊳ 18 L 6362 yds SSS 70
- 👥 U–book by phone SOC
- ££ £8.60 (£10.90)
- ⛳ 5 miles N of Liverpool (A565)
- ⌂ Fred Stevens

Bowring (1913)
Public
Bowring Park, Roby Road, Huyton,
L36 4HD
- ☎ **(0151) 489 1901**
- ✉ dgwalker36@tiscali.co.uk
- 📖 90
- ⚲ W Earps (0151) 480 6859
- ⊳ 18 L 6082 yds Par 70 SSS 69
- 👥 U
- ££ On application
- ⛳ 6 miles N of Liverpool. M62
  Junction 5

Brackenwood (1933)
Public
Bracken Lane, Bebington, Wirral, L63 2LY
- ☎ **(0151) 608 3093**
- ✉ secretary@brackenwoodgolfclub
  .co.uk
- 📖 220
- ⚲ GW Brogan (0151) 339 9817
- ✓ K Lamb
- ⊳ 18 L 6232 yds SSS 70
- 👥 U SOC
- ££ On application
- ⛳ Nr M53 Junction 4
- 🖥 www.brackenwoodgolfclub.co.uk

Bromborough (1903)
Raby Hall Road, Bromborough,
CH63 0NW
- ☎ **(0151) 334 2155**
- 🖥 (0151) 334 7300
- ✉ enquiries@bromboroughgolfclub
  .org.uk
- 📖 800
- ⚲ (0151) 334 2155
- ✓ G Berry (0151) 334 4499
- ⊳ 18 L 6585 yds SSS 72
- 👥 U–contact Pro in advance
- ££ £32 D–£50
- ⛳ Mid Wirral, M53 Junction 4
- ⌂ JE Hassall (redesign 1972
  Hawtree & Son)
- 🖥 www.bromboroughgolf-club
  .org.uk

Caldy (1907)
Links Hey Road, Caldy, Wirral, CH48 1NB
- ☎ **(0151) 625 5660**
- 🖥 (0151) 625 7394
- ✉ secretarycaldygc@btconnect.com
- 📖 900
- ⚲ Gail M Copple
- ✓ AG Gibbons (0151) 625 1818
- ⊳ 18 L 6693 yds Par 72 SSS 72

- 👥 WD–U exc before 9.30am and
  from 1–2pm (booking necessary)
  SOC
- ££ On application
- ⛳ 1½ miles S of West Kirby
- ⊕ Practice ground with ball collection
- ⌂ James Braid/Cameron Sinclair
- 🖥 www.caldygolfclub.co.uk

Childwall (1913)
Naylors Road, Gateacre, Liverpool, L27 2YB
- ☎ **(0151) 487 0654**
- 🖥 (0151) 487 0654
- ✉ office@childwallgolfclub.co.uk
- 📖 650
- ⚲ Peter Bowen
- ✓ N Parr (0151) 487 9871
- ⊳ 18 L 6470 yds SSS 71
- 👥 WD–Tues–restricted.
  WE/BH–restricted SOC
- ££ £35 (£45)
- ⛳ 7 miles E of Liverpool. M62
  Junction 6, 2 miles
- ⌂ James Braid
- 🖥 www.childwallgolfclub.co.uk

Eastham Lodge (1973)
117 Ferry Road, Eastham, Wirral,
CH62 0AP
- ☎ **(0151) 327 1483 (Clubhouse)**
- 🖥 (0151) 327 7574
- 📖 800
- ⚲ Mrs JL Lyon (0151) 327 3003
- ✓ N Sargent (0151) 327 3008
- ⊳ 18 L 5706 yds SSS 68
- 👥 WD–U WE/BH–M SOC
- ££ £24.50
- ⛳ 6 miles S of Birkenhead, off A41.
  M53 Junction 5. Signs to Eastham
  Country Park
- ⌂ Hawtree/Hemstock

Formby (1884)
Golf Road, Formby, Liverpool, L37 1LQ
- ☎ **(01704) 872164**
- 🖥 (01704) 833028
- ✉ info@formbygolfclub.co.uk
- 📖 690
- ⚲ CCH Barker (01704) 872164
- ✓ GH Butler (01704) 873090
- ⊳ 18 L 7024 yds SSS 74
- 👥 WD–I H SOC WE–NA before
  3.30pm WD–NA before 9.30am
- ££ £85 (£95)
- ⛳ By Freshfield Station, Formby. 8
  miles S of Southport
- ⌂ Willie Park
- 🖥 www.formbygolfclub.co.uk

Formby Hall
Southport Old Road, Formby, L37 0AB
- ☎ **(01704) 875699**
- 🖥 (01704) 832134
- ✉ proshop@formby-hall.co.uk
- ⚲ Joe Fleetwood (Dir of Golf)
- ✓ D Lloyd
- ⊳ 18 L 6875 yds Par 73
- 👥 WD–U SOC
- ££ On application
- ⛳ Off Formby by-pass
- ⊕ Floodlit driving range
- 🖥 www.formbyhallgolfclub.co.uk

Formby Ladies' (1896)
Golf Road, Formby, Liverpool, L37 1YH
- ☎ **(01704) 873493**
- 🖥 (01704) 834654
- ✉ secretary@formbyladiesgolfclub
  .co.uk
- ⚲ Mrs CA Bromley (01704) 873493
- ✓ G Butler (01704) 873090
- ⊳ 18 L 5374 yds SSS 71
- 👥 U–phone first SOC
- ££ £45 (£50)
- ⛳ Formby, off A565
- ⊕ Practice ground
- 🖥 www.formbyladiesgolfclub.co.uk

Grange Park (1891)
Prescot Road, St Helens, WA10 3AD
- ☎ **(01744) 22980 (Members)**
- 🖥 (01744) 26318
- ✉ secretary@grangeparkgolfclub.co.uk
- 📖 730
- ⚲ G Brown (01744) 26318
- ✓ P Roberts (01744) 28785
- ⊳ 18 L 6446 yds SSS 71
- 👥 I SOC–WD exc Tues
- ££ £30 (£35)
- ⛳ 1½ miles W of St Helens on A58
- ⊕ Practice ground
- 🖥 www.grangeparkgolfclub.co.uk

Haydock Park (1877)
Golborne Park, Newton Lane, Newton-le-
Willows, WA12 0HX
- ☎ **(01925) 228525**
- 🖥 (01925) 224984
- ✉ secretary@haydockparkgc.co.uk
- 📖 610 120(L)
- ⚲ Steve Dale
- ✓ PE Kenwright (01925) 226944
- ⊳ 18 L 6058 yds SSS 69
- 👥 H SOC–WD exc Tues
- ££ £30
- ⛳ 1 mile E of M6 Junction 23
- ⊕ Large practice area
- 🖥 www.haydockparkgc.co.uk

Hesketh (1885)
Cockle Dick's Lane, Cambridge Road,
Southport, PR9 9QQ
- ☎ **(01704) 536897**
- 🖥 (01704) 539250
- ✉ secretary@heskethgolfclub.co.uk
- 📖 650
- ⚲ MG Senior (01704) 536897
- ✓ S Astin (01704) 530050
- ⊳ 18 L 6655 yds SSS 72
- 👥 WD–U WE/BH–restricted SOC
- ££ £55 D–£70 (£70)
- ⛳ 1 mile N of Southport (A565)
- ⊕ Indoor golf academy
- ⌂ JOF Morris
- 🖥 www.heskethgolfclub.co.uk

Heswall (1902)
Cottage Lane, Gayton, Heswall, CH60 8PB
- ☎ **(0151) 342 1237**
- 🖥 (0151) 342 6140
- ✉ dawn@heswallgolfclub.com
- 📖 902
- ⚲ A Brooker
- ✓ AE Thompson (0151) 342 7431
- ⊳ 18 L 6492 yds SSS 72

🏌 U H BH–NA SOC–Wed & Fri
££ £50 (£60)
🚗 8 miles NW of Chester off A540.
  M53 Junction 4
🖥 www.heswallgolfclub.com

Hillside   (1911)
Hastings Road, Hillside, Southport, PR8 2LU
☎ **(01704) 567169**
📠 (01704) 563192
📧 secretary@hillside-golfclub.co.uk
📖 800
🏌 SH Newland (01704) 567169
✓ B Seddon (01704) 568360
🏴 18 L 6850 yds SSS 74
🏌 By arrangement with Sec
££ £70 D–£90
🚗 Southport
⊕ Buggies for hire
🏠 Hawtree
🖥 www.hillside-golfclub.co.uk

Houghwood   (1996)
Proprietary
*Billinge Hill, Crank Road, Crank, St Helens,
WA11 8RL*
☎ **(01744) 894754**
📠 (01744) 894754
📧 houghwoodgolf@btinternet.com
📖 600
🏌 P Turner (Man Dir)
✓ P Dickenson (01744) 894444
🏴 18 L 6268 yds SSS 70
🏌 WD–U SOC–WD
££ £30 (£40)
🚗 3 miles N of St Helens, off A580
  (B5201). M6 Junctions 23 or 26
🏠 N Pearson
🖥 www.houghwoodgolfclub.co.uk

Hoylake Municipal   (1933)
Public
Carr Lane, Hoylake, Wirral, L47 4BG
☎ **(0151) 632 2956/4883
  (Bookings)**
🏌 P Davies (0151) 632 0523
✓ S Hooton
🏴 18 L 6330 yds SSS 70
🏌 WD–U WE–phone booking 1
  week in advance SOC
££ £11
🚗 4 miles W of Birkenhead
🏠 James Braid
🖥 www.hoylakegolfclub.com

Huyton & Prescot   (1905)
Hurst Park, Huyton Lane, Huyton, L36 1UA
☎ **(0151) 489 1138**
📠 (0151) 489 0797
📖 700
🏌 D Hughes (0151) 489 3948
✓ J Fisher (0151) 489 2022
🏴 18 L 5839 yds SSS 68
🏌 WD–U WE–H SOC–WD
££ On application
🚗 7 miles E of Liverpool. 1 mile S of
  Prescot on B5199. M57 Junction 2
🏠 James Braid

Leasowe   (1891)
*Leasowe Road, Moreton, Wirral,
CH46 3RD*
☎ **(0151) 677 5852**

📠 (0151) 641 8519
📧 secretary@leasowegolfclub.co.uk
📖 610
🏌 L Jukes (0151) 677 5852
✓ AJ Ayre (0151) 678 5460
🏴 18 L 6151 yds SSS 70
🏌 U SOC–H
££ D–£30.50 (D–£35.50)
🚗 1 mile N of Queensway Tunnel.
  M53 Junction 1
🏠 John Ball Jr
🖥 www.leasowegolfclub.co.uk

Lee Park   (1954)
*Childwall Valley Road, Gateacre, Liverpool,
L27 3YA*
☎ **(0151) 487 3882 (Clubhouse)**
📠 (0151) 498 4666
📧 lee.park@virgin.net
📖 580
🏌 Steve Settle (0151) 487 3882
✓ Chris Crowder (07984) 253821
🏴 18 L 5959 yds Par 70 SSS 69
🏌 WD SOC (Mon/Thur/Fri)
££ £27 (£35)
🚗 7 miles SE of Liverpool (B5171); 10
  min from Liverpool Airport; M62
  J6
⊕ Practice nets; practice area;
  chipping area
🏠 CK Cotton
🖥 www.leepark.co.uk

Prenton   (1905)
*Golf Links Road, Prenton, Birkenhead,
CH42 8LW*
☎ **(0151) 609 3426**
📠 (0151) 609 3421
📖 470 100(L) 80(J)
🏌 N Brown
✓ R Thompson (0151) 608 1636
🏴 18 L 6429 yds SSS 71
🏌 U SOC–Mon/Wed/Fri
££ £35 (£40)
🚗 Outskirts of Birkenhead. M53
  Junction 3
🖥 www.prentongolfclub.co.uk

RLGC Village Play   (1895)
Club
*c/o 18 Waverley Road, Hoylake, Wirral,
CH47 3DD*
☎ **(07885) 507263**
📠 (0151) 632 5156
📧 pdwbritesparks@btinternet.com
📖 40
🏌 PD Williams (0151) 632 5156
🏴 Play over Royal Liverpool, Hoylake
🚗 M53 Jct 2

Royal Birkdale   (1889)
*Waterloo Road, Birkdale, Southport,
PR8 2LX*
☎ **(01704) 567920**
📠 (01704) 562327
📧 secretary@royalbirkdale.com
🏌 MC Gilyeat
✓ B Hodgkinson (01704) 568857
🏴 18 L 6703 yds Par 72 SSS 73
🏌 I H SOC
££ £150 (£175)
🚗 1½ miles S of Southport (A565)

🏠 George Lowe
🖥 www.royalbirkdale.com

Royal Liverpool   (1869)
Meols Drive, Hoylake, CH47 4AL
☎ **(0151) 632 3101/3102**
📠 (0151) 632 6737
📧 sec@royal-liverpool-golf.com
📖 810
🏌 Gp Capt CT Moore CBE
✓ J Heggarty (0151) 632 5868
🏴 18 L 7222 yds SSS 74
🏌 H SOC
££ On application
🚗 On A553 from M53 Junction 2
⊕ Golf bookings: bookings@royal-
  liverpool-golf.com
🏠 Robert Chambers & George
  Morris/Donald Steel
🖥 www.royal-liverpool-golf.com

Sherdley Park Municipal
   (1974)
Public
*Eltonhead Road, Sutton, St Helens,
Merseyside WA9 5DE*
☎ **(01744) 813149**
📠 (01744) 817967
📧 sherdleyparkgolfcourse@sthelens
  .gov.uk
🏌 J Barston (Mgr)
🏴 18 L 5974 yds SSS 69
🏌 U SOC
££ £12 (£14) £7 after 2pm Mon &
  Tues £7 every other day
🚗 2 miles E of St Helens (A570). M62
  Junction 7, 2 miles
⊕ Driving range
🖥 www.sthelens.gov.uk

Southport & Ainsdale
   (1906)
*Bradshaws Lane, Ainsdale, Southport,
PR8 3LG*
☎ **(01704) 578000**
📠 (01704) 570896
📧 secretary@sandagolfclub.co.uk
📖 452 94(L) 51(J)
🏌 CA Birrell
✓ J Payne (01704) 577316
🏴 18 L 6749 yds Par 72 SSS 73
🏌 WD–H WE–NA morning
££ £65 D–£90 (£90)
🚗 3 miles S of Southport on A565
🏠 James Braid
🖥 www.sandagolfclub.co.uk

Southport Golf Links
   (1912)
Public
Park Road West, Southport, PR9 0JS
☎ **(01704) 535286**

Southport Old Links
   (1926)
Moss Lane, Southport, PR9 7QS
☎ **(01704) 228207**
📠 (01704) 505353
📧 secretary@solgc.freeserve.co.uk
📖 450

🏌 BE Kenyon
✓ Gary Copeman (07802) 653909
▷ 9 L 6450 yds Par 72 SSS 71
👥 U exc Wed & Sun & B Hols NA/H
££ £25 (£30)
🚗 Churchtown, 3 miles NE of Southport

Wallasey   (1891)
Bayswater Road, Wallasey, CH45 8LA
☎ **(0151) 691 1024**
🖰 (0151) 638 8988
📧 wallaseygc@aol.com
📖 515 82(L) 61(J)
🏌 JT Barraclough (0151) 691 1024
✓ M Adams (0151) 638 3888
▷ 18 L 6572 yds SSS 72
👥 H SOC
££ £70 (£85)
🚗 M53-signs to New Brighton
🏠 Tom Morris
🖳 www.wallaseygolfclub.com

Warren   (1911)
Public
Grove Road, Wallasey, Wirral, CH45 0JA
☎ **(0151) 639 8323 (Clubhouse)**

West Derby   (1896)
Yew Tree Lane, Liverpool, L12 9HQ
☎ **(0151) 254 1034**
🖰 (0151) 259 0505
📧 pmilne@westderbygc.freeserve.co.uk
📖 550
🏌 AP Milne (0151) 254 1034
✓ A Witherup (0151) 254 1034
▷ 18 L 6275 yds SSS 70
👥 SOC–WD after 9.30am
££ £29.50 (£37)
🚗 2 miles E of Liverpool, off A580-West Derby Junction
🖳 www.wdgcliverpool.piczo.com

West Lancashire   (1873)
Hall Road West, Blundellsands, Liverpool, L23 8SZ
☎ **(0151) 924 1076**
🖰 (0151) 931 4448
📧 sec@westlancashiregolf.co.uk
📖 700
🏌 S King (0151) 924 1076
✓ G Edge (0151) 924 5662
▷ 18 L 6767 yds SSS 73
👥 H SOC–WD exc Tues
££ £60 D–£75 (£85)
🚗 Between Liverpool and Southport, off A565
🏠 CK Cotton
🖳 www.westlancashiregolf.co.uk

Wirral Ladies   (1894)
93 Bidston Road, Birkenhead, Wirral, CH43 6TS
☎ **(0151) 652 1255**
🖰 (0151) 651 3775
📧 sue.headford@virgin.co.uk
📖 480
🏌 Mrs SA Headford
✓ A Law (0151) 652 2468
▷ 18 L 4948 yds SSS 69 (Ladies)
   18 L 5185 yds SSS 65 (Men)

👥 U H SOC–WD
££ £30
🚗 Birkenhead ¹/₂ mile. M53, 2 miles

Woolton   (1900)
Doe Park, Speke Road, Woolton, Liverpool, L25 7TZ
☎ **(0151) 486 2298**
🖰 (0151) 486 1664
📧 golf@wooltongolf.co.uk
📖 500
🏌 K Hamilton (0151) 486 2298
✓ D Thompson (0151) 486 1298
▷ 18 L 5747 yds SSS 68
👥 U exc comp days
££ £30 (£40)
🚗 SE Liverpool. End of M62/M57. 2 miles Liverpool airport
🖳 www.thewooltongolfclub.com

Middlesex

Airlinks   (1984)
Public
Southall Lane, Hounslow, TW5 9PE
☎ **(020) 8561 1418**
🖰 (020) 8813 6284
📖 570
🏌 S Brewster
✓ T Martin
▷ 18 L 5813 yds SSS 68
👥 U
££ £18 (£25)
🚗 Just off M4 Junction 3
⊕ Floodlit driving range
🏠 Alliss/Taylor

Amida Golf   (1977)
Pay and play
Staines Road, Twickenham, TW2 5JD
☎ **(020) 8783 1698**

Ashford Manor   (1898)
Fordbridge Road, Ashford, TW15 3RT
☎ **(01784) 424644**
🖰 (01784) 424649
📧 secretary@amgc.co.uk
📖 700
🏌 Gina Rivett (Gen Mgr) (01784) 424644
✓ Ian Campbell (01784) 255940
▷ 18 L 6332 yds SSS 71
👥 WD–U WE–M H SOC–WD
££ £40 WD
🚗 A308 Ashford. M25 Junction 13
🏠 T Hogg
🖳 www.amgc.co.uk

Brent Valley   (1938)
Public
Church Road, Hanwell, London, W7 3BE
☎ **(020) 8567 4230 (Clubhouse)**
   (020) 8567 1287 (Bookings)

Bush Hill Park   (1895)
Bush Hill, Winchmore Hill, London, N21 2BU
☎ **(020) 8360 5738**
🖰 (020) 8360 5583

📧 info@bushhillparkgolfclub.co.uk
📖 630
🏌 Miss R Meade
✓ L Fickling (020) 8360 4103
▷ 18 L 5825 yds SSS 68
👥 WD–H WE–M SOC. Members only WE
££ £28.50
🚗 S of Enfield
🖳 www.bushhillparkgolfclub.co.uk

Crews Hill   (1920)
Cattlegate Road, Crews Hill, Enfield, EN2 8AZ
☎ **(020) 8363 6674**
🖰 (020) 8363 2343
📖 600
🏌 RC Williams
✓ N Wichelow (020) 8366 7422
▷ 18 L 6281 yds SSS 70
👥 WD–I H WE/BH–M SOC
££ On application
🚗 2¹/₂ miles N of Enfield. M25 Junction 24
🏠 HS Colt
🖳 www.crewshillgolfclub.co.uk

Ealing   (1898)
Perivale Lane, Greenford, UB6 8TS
☎ **(020) 8997 0937**
🖰 (020) 8998 0756
📖 600
✓ R Willison (020) 8997 3959
▷ 18 L 6191 yds SSS 70
👥 WD–U H WE/BH–M
££ £35 (£50)
🚗 Marble Arch 6 miles on A40-Perivale junction
🏠 HS Colt

Enfield   (1893)
Old Park Road South, Enfield, EN2 7DA
☎ **(020) 8363 3970**
🖰 (020) 8342 0381
📧 secretary@enfieldgolfclub.co.uk
📖 450
🏌 Peter Monument
✓ Martin Porter (020) 8366 4492
▷ 18 L 6154 yds SSS 70
👥 WD–H WE/BH–M SOC–WD
££ £28 D–£37 (£36)
🚗 1 mile NE of Enfield. M25 Junction 24-A1005
🏠 James Braid
🖳 www.enfieldgolfclub.co.uk

Finchley   (1929)
Nether Court, Frith Lane, London, NW7 1PU
☎ **(020) 8346 2436**
🖰 (020) 8343 4205
📧 secretary@finchleygolfclub.co.uk
📖 550
🏌 JM Seatter
✓ DM Brown (020) 8346 5086
▷ 18 L 6356 yds SSS 71
👥 WD–U WE–pm only SOC
££ On application
🚗 M1 Junction 2
🏠 James Braid
🖳 www.finchleygolfclub.co.uk

Fulwell   (1904)
Wellington Road, Hampton Hill, TW12 1JY
- ☎ **(020) 8977 2733**
- 🖴 (020) 8977 7732
- 📧 secretary@fulwellgolfclub.co.uk
- 📖 750
- ⛳ Mark Walden
- ✓ N Turner (020) 8977 3844
- ▷ 18 L 6529 yds SSS 71
- 👫 WD–U WE–NA before noon SOC
- ££ £40 (£55)
- 🌣 Opposite Fulwell Station, close to A316, M25, M3
- ⌂ John Morrison
- 🖥 www.fulwellgolfclub.co.uk

Grim's Dyke   (1909)
Oxhey Lane, Hatch End, Pinner, HA5 4AL
- ☎ **(020) 8428 4539**
- 🖴 (020) 8421 5494
- 📧 secretary@grimsdyke.co.uk
- 📖 600
- ⛳ K Loddy (020) 8428 4539
- ✓ L Curling (020) 8428 4539
- ▷ 18 L 5600 yds Par 69 SSS 67
- 👫 WD–U H WE–M SOC exc BH–NA
- ££ £30 D–£35 (£17 with member)
- 🌣 2 miles NW of Harrow (A4008). M1 Junctions 4/5
- ⌂ James Braid
- 🖥 www.club-noticeboard.co.uk /grimsdyke

Hampstead   (1893)
Winnington Road, London, N2 0TU
- ☎ **(020) 8455 0203**
- 🖴 (020) 8731 6194
- 📧 golf@hgc.uk.com
- 📖 450
- ⛳ Bob Blower
- ✓ PJ Brown (020) 8455 7089
- ▷ 9 L 5812 yds SSS 68
- 👫 H–phone Pro first
- ££ £30 (£35)
- 🌣 1 mile from Hampstead, nr Spaniards Inn
- ⌂ Tom Dunn

Harrow Hill Golf Course   (1982)
Public
Kenton Road, Harrow, Middx HA1 2BW
- ☎ **(0208) 8643754**
- 📧 harrowhillgolf@supanet.com
- ⛳ S Bishop
- ✓ S Bishop
- ▷ 9 holes Par 3
- ££ £4.50 (£5.50)
- 🌣 A4001
- 🖥 www.harrowhillgolfcourse.co.uk

Harrow School   (1978)
High Street, Harrow-on-the-Hill, HA1 3HW
- ☎ **(0208) 872 8000**
- 📖 440 100(L) 10(J)
- ⛳ CV Davies (020) 8872 8232
- ▷ 9 L 3690 yds SSS 57
- 👫 M H NA
- ££ £8 with member only
- 🌣 Harrow School, NW London

Haste Hill   (1930)
Public
The Drive, Northwood, HA6 1HN
- ☎ **(01923) 825224**

Heath Park   (1975)
Stockley Road, West Drayton
- ☎ **(01895) 444232**
- 📧 heathparkgolf@yahoo.co.uk

Hendon   (1903)
Ashley Walk, Devonshire Road, London, NW7 1DG
- ☎ **(020) 8346 6023**
- 🖴 (020) 8343 1974
- 📧 hendongolfclub@globalnet.co.uk
- 📖 560
- ⛳ CH Bailey
- ✓ M Deal (020) 8346 8990
- ▷ 18 L 6289 yds Par 70 SSS 70
- 👫 WD–U WE/BH–bookings SOC
- ££ £35 D–£45 (£45)
- 🌣 M1 Junction 2, on to Holders Hill Road
- ⊕ Practice ground; nets
- ⌂ HS Colt
- 🖥 www.hendongolfclub.co.uk

Highgate   (1904)
Denewood Road, Highgate, London, N6 4AH
- ☎ **(020) 8340 1906 (Clubhouse)**
- 🖴 (020) 8348 9152
- 📧 admin@highgategc.co.uk
- 📖 700
- ⛳ NA Challis (020) 8340 3745
- ✓ R Turner (020) 8340 5467
- ▷ 18 L 5964 yds SSS 69
- 👫 WD–U exc Wed–NA before noon WE/BH–M SOC
- ££ £35
- 🌣 Off Sheldon Avenue/Hampstead Lane
- ⌂ Cuthbert Butchart
- 🖥 www.highgategc.co.uk

Horsenden Hill   (1935)
Public
Woodland Rise, Greenford, UB6 0RD
- ☎ **(020) 8902 4555**
- 📖 84
- ⛳ AK Witte (020) 8458 5433
- ✓ J Quarshie
- ▷ 9 L 3264 yds SSS 56
- 👫 U
- ££ 9 holes–£4.80 (£7.50)
- 🌣 Greenford, near Sudbury Town tube station
- 🖥 www.horsendenhillgolfclub.co.uk

Hounslow Heath   (1979)
Public
Staines Road, Hounslow, TW4 5DS
- ☎ **(020) 8570 5271**
- 📖 120
- ⛳ R Mulford
- ▷ 18 L 5901 yds Par 69 SSS 68
- 👫 WD–U WE–booking essential

- ££ £9.85 (£14.30)
- 🌣 Opposite Green Lane, Staines Road (A315)
- ⌂ Fraser

Leaside GC   (1974)
Pay and play
Lee Valley Leisure, Picketts Lock Lane, Edmonton, London N9 0AS
- ☎ **(020) 8803 3611**

Mill Hill   (1925)
100 Barnet Way, Mill Hill, London, NW7 3AL
- ☎ **(020) 8959 2339**
- 🖴 (020) 8906 0731
- 📧 cluboffice@millhillgc.co.uk
- 📖 570
- ⛳ R Bauser
- ✓ D Beal (020) 8959 7261
- ▷ 18 L 6247 yds SSS 70
- 👫 WD–U SOC–WD. WE/BH: Prior booking in Pro Shop (WE pm only)
- ££ £30 (£37)
- 🌣 1/2 mile N of Apex Corner, nr A1/A41 junction
- ⊕ Driving range; chipping area; putting green
- ⌂ Abercrombie/Colt
- 🖥 www.millhillgc.co.uk

Muswell Hill   (1893)
Rhodes Avenue, London, N22 7UT
- ☎ **(020) 8888 2044 (members)**
- 🖴 (020) 8889 9380
- 📧 mlgcclubsecretary@btconnect.com
- 📖 600
- ⛳ V Benson (020) 8888 1764
- ✓ D Wilton (020) 8888 8046
- ▷ 18 L 6474 yds SSS 71
- 👫 WD–U WE–book with Pro SOC
- ££ £30 D–£40 (£40)
- 🌣 1 mile from Bounds Green Station. Central London 7 miles
- ⌂ Braid/Wilson
- 🖥 www.muswellhillgolfclub.co.uk

North Middlesex   (1905)
The Manor House, Friern Barnet Lane, Whetstone, London, N20 0NL
- ☎ **(020) 8445 1732**
- 🖴 (020) 8445 5023
- 📧 manager@northmiddlesexgc.co.uk
- 📖 500
- ⛳ Mrs J Underhill (Mgr) (020) 8445 1604
- ✓ (020) 8445 3060
- ▷ 18 L 5594 yds SSS 67
- 👫 WE/BH–restricted SOC–WD
- ££ £29 (£34)
- 🌣 5 miles S of M25 Junction 23, between Barnet and Finchley
- ⌂ Willie Park Jr
- 🖥 www.northmiddlesexgc.co.uk

Northwood   (1891)
Rickmansworth Road, Northwood, HA6 2QW
- ☎ **(01923) 821384**
- 🖴 (01923) 840150
- 📧 secretary@northwoodgolf.co.uk

☐ 560
🏌 T Collingwood (01923) 821384
✍ CJ Holdsworth (01923) 820112
🏳 18 L 6553 yds Par 71 SSS 71
👫 WD–H WE/BH–NA SOC
££ £36
⛳ 3 miles SE of Rickmansworth (A404)
🏠 James Braid
🖥 www.northwoodgolf.co.uk

Perivale Park   (1932)
Public
Stockdove Way, Argyle Road, Greenford, UB6 8EN
☎ (020) 8575 7116

Pinner Hill   (1927)
Southview Road, Pinner Hill, HA5 3YA
☎ (020) 8866 0963
☐ (020) 8868 4817
✉ phgc@pinnerhillgc.com
☐ 770
🏌 Michael Gottlieb (Gen Mgr)
✍ C Duck (020) 8866 2109
🏳 18 L 6393 yds Par 71 SSS 71
👫 WD–H exc Wed & Thurs–U Sun/BH–M SOC
££ £35 (£35) exc Wed & Thurs–£18.50
⛳ 1 mile W from Pinner Green
🏠 JH Taylor
🖥 www.pinnerhillgc.com

Ruislip   (1936)
Public
Ickenham Road, Ruislip, HA4 7DQ
☎ (01895) 638835

Stanmore   (1893)
29 Gordon Avenue, Stanmore, HA7 2RL
☎ (020) 8954 2599
☐ (020) 8954 2599
✉ secretary@stanmoregolfclub.co.uk
☐ 500
🏌 Allan Knott (020) 8954 2599
✍ J Reynolds (020) 8954 2599
🏳 18 L 5885 yds SSS 68
👫 WD–H WE/BH–M SOC
££ Mon & Fri £17, Tues, Wed, Thur £25, WE £35
⛳ Between Stanmore and Belmont, off Old Church Lane; 5 min from M1 Jct 4
🖥 www.stanmoregolfclub.co.uk

Stockley Park   (1993)
Pay and play
The Clubhouse, Stockley Park, Uxbridge, UB11 1AQ
☎ (020) 8813 5700/561 6339 (Bookings)
☐ (020) 8813 5655
✉ k.soper@stockleyparkgolf.com
🏌 K Soper
✍ S Birch
🏳 18 L 6548 yds SSS 71
👫 U SOC
££ £26 (£36)
⛳ Heathrow Airport, 1 mile. M4 Junction 4, 1 mile

🏠 Robert Trent Jones Sr
🖥 www.stockleyparkgolf.com

Strawberry Hill   (1900)
Wellesley Road, Strawberry Hill, Twickenham, TW2 5SD
☎ (020) 8894 0165

Sudbury   (1920)
Bridgewater Road, Wembley, HA0 1AL
☎ (020) 8902 3713 (office), (020) 8902 7910 (bookings)
☐ (020) 8902 3713
✉ enquiries@sudburygolfclubltd.co.uk
☐ 610
🏌 N Cropley (Gen Mgr)
✍ N Jordan (020) 8902 7910
🏳 18 L 6282 yds SSS 70
👫 WD–H WE–M SOC–Tues–Fri
££ On application
⛳ Junction of A4005/A4090
🏠 HS Colt
🖥 www.sudburygolfclubltd.co.uk

Sunbury   (1993)
Proprietary
Charlton Lane, Shepperton, TW17 8QA
☎ (01932) 771414
☐ (01932) 789300
✉ sunbury@crown-golf.co.uk
☐ 350
🏌 P Dawson (Gen Mgr)
✍ A McColgan
🏳 18 L 5103 yds Par 68 SSS 65
    9 L 2444 yds Par 33
👫 U–phone Pro SOC
££ £16.50 (£21)
⛳ SE of Queen Mary Reservoir, nr Chalton. M3 Junction 1, 2 miles
⊕ Floodlit driving range
🏠 Peter Alliss
🖥 www.crown-golf.co.uk

Trent Park   (1973)
Public
Bramley Road, Southgate, London, N14 4UW
☎ (020) 8367 4653

Uxbridge   (1947)
Public
The Drive, Harefield Place, Uxbridge, UB10 8AQ
☎ (01895) 231169
☐ (01895) 810262
✉ uxbridgegolf@btconnect.com
🏌 Mrs A James (01895) 272457
✍ Phil Howard (01895) 237287
🏳 18 L 5711 yds SSS 68
👫 U SOC
££ £16.50 (£24)
⛳ 2 miles N of Uxbridge. B467 off A40 towards Ruislip. M25 Jct 16
🖥 www.middlesexgolf.com

West Middlesex   (1891)
Greenford Road, Southall, UB1 3EE
☎ (020) 8574 3450
☐ (020) 8574 2383
✉ westmid.gc@virgin.net
☐ 407

🏌 Miss R Khanna
✍ T Talbot (020) 8574 1800
🏳 18 L 6119 yds SSS 69
👫 WD–U WE–NA before 2pm (phone Pro) SOC–Tues/Thurs/Fri
££ Mon–£16 Tues/Thurs/Fri–£18 Wed–£18 WE–£25
⛳ Junction of Uxbridge Road and Greenford Road
🏠 James Braid
🖥 www.westmiddxgolfclub.co.uk

Wyke Green   (1928)
Syon Lane, Isleworth, Osterley, TW7 5PT
☎ (020) 8560 8777
☐ (020) 8569 8392
✉ office@wykegreengolfclub.co.uk
☐ 550
🏌 D Pearson
✍ N Smith (020) 8847 0685
🏳 18 L 6282 yds SSS 70
👫 WD–U WE/BH–H after 4pm SOC
££ £30 D–£40, after 5pm–£20 (Mon/Tues only) WE £35 after 4pm
⛳ ½ mile from Gillette Corner (A4)
⊕ Practice range
🏠 Hawtree/Taylor
🖥 www.wykegreengolfclub.co.uk

Norfolk

Barnham Broom Hotel (1977)
Honingham Road, Barnham Broom, Norwich, NR9 4DD
☎ (01603) 759393 (Hotel) (01603) 757505 (Golf Shop)
☐ (01603) 758224
✉ alan@barnham-broom.co.uk
☐ 500
🏌 A Battle (01603) 757501
✍ I Rollett
🏳 Valley 18 L 6483 yds Par 72 SSS 71 Hill 18 L 6495 yds Par 71 SSS 71
👫 U SOC
££ £40 (£50)
⛳ 10 miles SW of Norwich, off A47. 5 miles NW of Wymondham, off A11
⊕ 3 Academy holes; driving range
🏠 Pennink/Steel
🖥 www.barnham-broom.co.uk

Bawburgh   (1978)
Glen Lodge, Marlingford Road, Bawburgh, Norwich NR9 3LU
☎ (01603) 740404
☐ (01603) 740403
✉ info@bawburgh.com
☐ 650
🏌 I Ladbrooke (Gen Mgr)
✍ C Potter (01603) 742323
🏳 18 L 6209 yds SSS 70
👫 U–phone first SOC
££ £27 (£30)
⛳ 2 miles W of Norwich, off A47 Norwich Southern Bypass
⊕ Floodlit driving range. Golf Academy

⌂ John Barnard
🖳 www.bawburgh.com

Caldecott Hall   (1993)
Caldecott Hall, Beccles Road, Fritton, Great Yarmouth, NR31 9EY
☎ **(01493) 488488**
🖷 (01493) 488561
▥ 600
🏌 P Oakes
✓ M Tungate
ᕦ 18 L 6685 yds Par 73 SSS 72
  18 L 2658 yds Par 3
👥 H SOC WD WE
££ £25 (£30)
⊶ 5 miles SW of Gt Yarmouth on A413
⊕ Floodlit driving range
🖳 www.caldecotthall.co.uk

Costessey Park   (1983)
Costessey Park, Costessey, Norwich, NR8 5AL
☎ **(01603) 746333**
🖷 (01603) 746185
✉ cpgc@ljgroup.com
▥ 600
🏌 GC Stangoe
✓ A Young (01603) 747085
ᕦ 18 L 5900 yds Par 71 SSS 69
👥 U SOC–WD
££ £20 D–£32 (£30)
⊶ 3 miles W of Norwich, off A47 at Round Well PH
🖳 www.costesseypark.com

Dereham   (1934)
Quebec Road, Dereham, NR19 2DS
☎ **(01362) 695900**
🖷 (01362) 695904
✉ derehamgolfclub@dgolfclub .freeserve.co.uk
▥ 400
🏌 D Mayers
✓ N Allsebrook (01362) 695631
ᕦ 9 L 6267 yds SSS 70
👥 H
££ £20 D–£30
⊶ Dereham ¹/₂ mile
🖳 www.club-noticeboard.co.uk

Dunham   (1979)
Proprietary
Little Dunham, Swaffham, PE32 2DF
☎ **(01328) 701906**
✉ info@dunhamgolfclub.com

De Vere Dunston Hall
   (1994)
Pay and play
Ipswich Road, Dunston, Norwich, NR14 8PQ
☎ **(01508) 470178**

Eagles   (1990)
39 School Road, Tilney All Saints, Kings Lynn, PE34 4RS
☎ **(01553) 827147**
🖷 (01553) 829777
▥ 200
🏌 RK Shipman

✓ N Pickerell
ᕦ 9 L 2142 yds SSS 61
  9 hole Par 3 course
👥 U
££ 9: £10.50 (+BH £11.50) 18: £14.50 (+BH £17.50)
⊶ 5 miles W of Kings Lynn on A47
⊕ Driving range
⌂ David Horn
🖳 www.eagles-golf-tennis.co.uk

Eaton   (1910)
Newmarket Road, Norwich, NR4 6SF
☎ **(01603) 451686**
🖷 (01603) 457539
✉ administrator@eatongc.co.uk
▥ 906 160(L) 62(J)
🏌 Mrs LA Bovill
✓ M Allen (01603) 251394
ᕦ 18 L 6118 yds SSS 70
👥 H WE–NA before noon SOC–WD
££ £35 D–£43 (£45)
⊶ S Norwich, off A11
⊕ Driving bays
⌂ Ernest Riseborough
🖳 www.eatongc.co.uk

Fakenham   (1973)
The Race Course, Fakenham, NR21 7NY
☎ **(01328) 862867**
✉ grahamc21@tiscali.com

Feltwell   (1976)
Thor Ave, Wilton Road, Feltwell, Thetford, IP26 4AY
☎ **(01842) 827644**
🖷 (01842) 827644
✉ sec.feltwellgc@virgin.net
▥ 400
🏌 David Rodwell
✓ Tom Ball (01842) 829089
ᕦ 9 L 6488 yds Par 72 SSS 71
👥 U SOC–WD
££ D–£16 (£25)
⊶ 1 mile S of Feltwell on B1112
⊕ Former Feltwell aerodrome
🖳 www.club-noticeboard.co.uk

Gorleston   (1906)
Warren Road, Gorleston, Gt Yarmouth, NR31 6JT
☎ **(01493) 661911**
🖷 (01493) 661911
✉ manager@gorlestongolfclub.co.uk
▥ 900
🏌 JE Woodhouse (01493) 661911
✓ N Brown (01493) 662103
ᕦ 18 L 6391 yds SSS 71
👥 U H SOC
££ £25 (£30) W–£85
⊶ S of Gorleston, off A12
⌂ JH Taylor

Great Yarmouth & Caister
   (1882)
Beach House, Caister-on-Sea, Gt Yarmouth, NR30 5TD
☎ **(01493) 728699**
🖷 (01493) 728831
✉ office@caistergolf.co.uk
▥ 700

🏌 RA Peck
✓ M Clarke (01493) 720421
ᕦ 18 L 6330 yds SSS 70
👥 WE–NA before noon WD SOC after 9 am
££ £35 (£45) WD £25 after noon
⊶ Caister-on-Sea
⊕ Practice field
⌂ HS Colt
🖳 www.caistergolf.co.uk

Hunstanton   (1891)
Golf Course Road, Old Hunstanton, PE36 6JQ
☎ **(01485) 532811**
🖷 (01485) 532319
✉ hunstanton.golf@eidosnet.co.uk
▥ 662 136(L) 83(J)
🏌 DP Thomson
✓ J Dodds (01485) 532751
ᕦ 18 L 6759 yds SSS 73
👥 WD–H after 9.30am WE–H after 10.30am SOC
££ D–£70 (£80)
⊶ 1¹/₂ miles NE of Hunstanton
⊕ 2 ball play (4 ball on Tues)
⌂ George Fernie
🖳 www.hunstantongolfclub.com

King's Lynn   (1923)
Castle Rising, King's Lynn, PE31 6BD
☎ **(01553) 631654**
🖷 (01553) 631036
✉ secretary@kingslynngc.co.uk
▥ 910
🏌 AH Mackenzie (01553) 633000
✓ J Reynolds (01553) 631655
ᕦ 18 L 6609 yds SSS 73
👥 U H SOC
££ £45 (£55)
⊶ 4 miles NE of King's Lynn, off A149
⊕ Practice ground
⌂ Alliss/Thomas
🖳 www.club-noticeboard.co.uk

Links Country Park Hotel & Golf Club   (1903)
West Runton, Cromer, NR27 9QH
☎ **(01263) 838383**
🖷 (01263) 838264
✉ sales@links-hotel.co.uk
▥ 300
🏌 CB Abbott
✓ N Catchpole (01263) 838215
ᕦ 9 L 4814 yds Par 66 SSS 64
👥 U
££ £18 D–£25
⊶ 3 miles W of Cromer (A149)
⌂ JH Taylor
🖳 www.links-hotel.co.uk

Marriott Sprowston Manor Hotel   (1980)
Wroxham Road, Sprowston, Norwich, NR7 8RP
☎ **(0870) 400 7229**
🖷 (0870) 400 7329
✉ ryan.oconnor@marriotthotels.com
▥ 620
🏌 A Moule (Golf Dir) (0870) 400 7229

✓ G Ireson (0870) 400 7229
▷ 18 L 6547 yds Par 71 SSS 71
👤 U SOC
££ £40/£50 Varying rates on
application
⛳ 4 miles NE of Norwich on A1151
⊕ Floodlit driving range
🏠 Ross McMurray
▤ www.marriott.co.uk/nwigs

Mattishall   (1990)

South Green, Mattishall, Dereham
☎ (01362) 850464
▦ 180
♣ B Hall
▷ 9 L 6170 yds Par 70 SSS 69
👤 WD–U WE–U before noon SOC
££ 9: £10 18: £14
⛳ 6 miles E of Dereham (B1063)
⊕ 9 hole pitch & putt
🏠 BC Todd

Middleton Hall   (1989)

Proprietary
Middleton, King's Lynn, PE32 1RH
☎ (01553) 841800
🖫 (01553) 841800
📧 middleton-hall@btclick.com
▦ 600
♣ J Holland
✓ S White (01553) 841801
▷ 18 L 5756 yds Par 71 SSS 68
👤 U SOC
££ £25 (£30)
⛳ 2 miles SE of King's Lynn on A47
⊕ Driving range
🏠 D Scott
▤ www.middletonhall.co.uk

Mundesley   (1901)

Links Road, Mundesley, NR11 8ES
☎ (01263) 720095
🖫 (01263) 722849
📧 manager@mundesleygolfclub.co.uk
▦ 500
♣ TE Duke (Gen Mgr)
(01263) 720095
✓ TG Symmons (01263) 720279
▷ 9 L 5377 yds SSS 66
👤 WD–U H exc Wed 10.00–2.30pm
WE–NA before 11.30am
££ £25 (£30)
⛳ 5 miles SE of Cromer
⊕ Driving range and practice area
🏠 Harry Vardon
▤ www.mundesleygolfclub.co.uk

The Norfolk G&CC
(1993)
Proprietary
Hingham Road, Reymerston, Norwich,
NR9 4QQ
☎ (01362) 850297
🖫 (01362) 850614
📧 norfolkgolfse@ukonline.co.uk
▦ 530
♣ M de Boltz
✓ T Varney (01362) 850297
▷ 18 L 6609 yds SSS 72
👤 WD–U before 4pm –M after 4pm
WE/BH–NA before noon SOC
££ £30 (£30)

⛳ 14 miles W of Norwich, off B1135
Dereham to Wymondham road
⊕ Driving range. 9 hole pitch & putt
course
▤ www.thenorfolk.co.uk

RAF Marham   (1974)

RAF Marham, Kings Lynn, PE33 9NP
☎ (01760) 337261 ext 7262
▦ 290
♣ PG Williams (ext 7387)
▷ 9 L 5976 yds Par 71 SSS 69
👤 SOC by prior arrangement
WD/WE subject to security
clearance and state
££ £10 non–member, £7 with
member,
⛳ 11 miles SE of King's Lynn, nr
Narborough
⊕ Course situated on MOD land, and
may be closed without prior notice
▤ www.marhamgolf.co.uk

Richmond Park   (1990)

Saham Road, Watton, IP25 6EA
☎ (01953) 881803
🖫 (01953) 881817
📧 info@richmondpark.co.uk
▦ 500
♣ A Hemsley
✓ A Hemsley
▷ 18 L 6300 yds SSS 71
👤 WD–U WE–H before noon SOC
££ £24 (£35)
⛳ ½ mile NW of Watton
⊕ Driving range
🏠 Scott/Jessup
▤ www.richmondpark.co.uk

Royal Cromer   (1888)

Overstrand Road, Cromer, NR27 0JH
☎ (01263) 512884
🖫 (01263) 512430
📧 general.manager@royal-cromer
.com
▦ 700
♣ Mrs G Richardson
✓ Lee D Patterson (01263) 512267
▷ 18 L 6508 yds SSS 72
👤 H SOC–WD after 9.30 pm; WE
after 10.30 pm
££ D–£45 (D–£55)
⛳ 1 mile E of Cromer on B1159
🏠 Morris/Taylor/Braid/Pennink
▤ www.royalcromergolfclub.com

Royal Norwich   (1893)

Drayton High Road, Hellesdon, Norwich,
NR6 5AH
☎ (01603) 425712
🖫 (01603) 417945
📧 mail@royalnorwichgolf.co.uk
▦ 650
♣ J Meggy (Mgr) (01603) 429928
✓ S Youd (01603) 408459
▷ 18 L 6506 yds Par 72 SSS 72
👤 WE/BH–restricted SOC
££ £25 D–£40 (£25 D–£40)
⛳ ½ mile W of Norwich ring road,
on Fakenham road (A1067)
🏠 James Braid
▤ www.royalnorwichgolf.co.uk

Royal West Norfolk   (1892)

Brancaster, King's Lynn, PE31 8AX
☎ (01485) 210223
🖫 (01485) 210087
📧 rwngc@btinternet.com
▦ 890
♣ Maj NA Carrington Smith
(01485) 210087
✓ S Rayner (01485) 210616
▷ 18 L 6457 yds SSS 71
👤 M mid July–mid Sept WE–NA
before 10am SOC No three or
four balls
££ £70 (£85)
⛳ 7 miles E of Hunstanton on A419
⊕ Practice ground
🏠 Holcombe Ingleby

Ryston Park   (1932)

Ely Road, Denver, Downham Market,
PE38 0HH
☎ (01366) 382133
📧 rystonparkgc.fsnet.co.uk

Sheringham   (1891)

Sheringham, NR26 8HG
☎ (01263) 822038
(Bar & Catering)
🖫 (01263) 826129
📧 info@sheringhamgolfclub.co.uk
▦ 800
♣ PJ Mounfield (01263) 823488
✓ MW Jubb (01263) 822980
▷ 18 L 6456 yds SSS 71
👤 WD & WE NA before 9–30am H
SOC
££ £47.50 (£60)
⛳ ½ mile W of Sheringham (A149)
🏠 Tom Dunn
▤ www.sheringhamgolfclub.co.uk

Swaffham   (1922)

Cley Road, Swaffham, PE37 8AE
☎ (01760) 721621
🖫 (01760) 721621
📧 swaffhamgc@supanet.co.uk
▦ 500
♣ MA Rust
✓ P Field (01760) 721611
▷ 18 L 6554 yds SSS 71
👤 WD–U WE–M exc Sun am–NA
SOC–WD
££ £40/day, £30/half day, £17 county
cards, £6 juniors.
⛳ 1½ miles SW of Swaffham
⊕ 4 acre practice area with bunkers
🏠 Gaunt & Marnoch Ltd
▤ www.club-noticeboard.co.uk

Thetford   (1912)

Brandon Road, Thetford, IP24 3NE
☎ (01842) 752258 (Clubhouse)
🖫 (01842) 766212
📧 thetfordgolfclub@btconnect.com
▦ 700
♣ Mrs Diane Hopkins
(01842) 752169
✓ G Kitley (01842) 752662
▷ 18 L 6879 yds SSS 73
👤 H SOC–Mon/Wed/Thur/Fri WE
after 1pm
££ £32 D–£43. Soc from £35

⊕ 2 miles W of Thetford (B1107), off
All By-pass
⊕ Long and short gtame practice
grounds
⌂ CH Mayo
▤ www.club-
noticeboard.com/thetford

Wensum Valley   (1990)
Beech Avenue, Taverham, Norwich,
NR8 6HP
☎ (01603) 261012
⌨ (01603) 261664
▦ 850
✍ Mrs B Hall
✓ P Whittle
▷ 18 L 6223 yds SSS 70
18 L 6942 yds SSS 73
⋔ U SOC
££ £20
⊕ 4 miles NW of Norwich on
A1067
⊕ Floodlit driving range
⌂ BC Todd
▤ www.wensumvalleyhotel.co.uk

Weston Park   (1993)
Weston Longville, Norwich, NR9 5JW
☎ (01603) 872363
⌨ (01603) 873040
✉ golf@weston-park.co.uk
▦ 550
✍ AN Payne (MD) (01603) 876300
✓ MR Few (01603) 872998
▷ 18 L 6603 yds SSS 72
⋔ WD–U H
££ £35 (£45)
⊕ 9 miles NW of Norwich, off A1067
⊕ Practice ground
⌂ John Glasgow
▤ www.weston-park.co.uk

Northamptonshire

Brampton Heath   (1995)
Sandy Lane, Church Brampton, NN6 8AX
☎ (01604) 843939
⌨ (01604) 843885
✉ slawrence@bhgc.co.uk
▦ 500
✍ K Brett
✓ A Wright
▷ 18 L 6533 yds Par 72 SSS 71
9 hole short course
⋔ U SOC
££ £18 (£23)
⊕ 4 miles N of Northampton
between A508 and A428
⊕ Driving range
▤ www.bhgc.co.uk

Cold Ashby   (1974)
Proprietary
Stanford Road, Cold Ashby, Northampton,
NN6 6EP
☎ (01604) 740548
⌨ (01604) 740548
✉ info@coldashbygolfclub.com
▦ 600 40(L) 40(J)
✍ DA Croxton (Prop) (01604) 740548

✓ S Rose (01604) 740099
▷ 27 L 6308 yds Par 72 SSS 71
⋔ U–WD/WE SOC–WD/WE
££ £18 D–£23 (£27)
⊕ 11 miles N of Northampton, nr
A5199/A14 Junction 1. 7 miles E of
M1 Junction 18
⊕ Driving range
⌂ David Croxton
▤ www.coldashbygolfclub.com

Collingtree Park   (1990)
Proprietary
Windingbrook Lane, Northampton,
NN4 0XN
☎ (01604) 700000
⌨ (01604) 702600
▦ 900
✍ Frank Prescott (Dir of Golf)
Les Pullan (Sec)
✓ G Pook, A Carter
▷ 18 L 6776 yds SSS 72
⋔ H SOC WD WE (after 12.30)
££ £50 (£60)
⊕ ½ mile E of M1 Junction 15
⊕ Floodlit driving range
⌂ Johnny Miller
▤ www.collingtreeparkgolf.com

Daventry & District
(1907)
Norton Road, Daventry, NN11 5LS
☎ (01327) 702829
✉ ms@teltec.com
▦ 350
✍ Mike Sheppard (07801) 860843
✓ None
▷ 9 L 5812 yds Par 69 SSS 68
⋔ WD–U Sun–NA before 11am
SOC–phone Sec
££ £10 (£10)
⊕ ½ mile E of Daventry
⊕ Practice area; putting green
▤ www.ddgc.co.uk

Delapre   (1976)
Pay and play
Eagle Drive, Nene Valley Way,
Northampton, NN4 7DU
☎ (01604) 764036
⌨ (01604) 706378
✉ delapre@jbgolf.co.uk
▦ 350
✍ J Howes (Mgr) (01604) 764036
✓ J Cuddihy, S Harlock
▷ Oaks 18 L 6299 yds SSS 70
Hardingstone 9 L 2109 yds SSS 32
2 x 9 holes Par 3 courses
⋔ U SOC
££ £13.50, £15 Fri (£17.50)
⊕ 3 miles from M1 Junction 15, on
A508/A45
⊕ Pitch & putt. Driving range
⌂ Jacobs/Corby
▤ www.jackbarker.com

Farthingstone Hotel   (1974)
Farthingstone, Towcester, NN12 8HA
☎ (01327) 361291
✉ interest@farthingstone.co.uk

Hellidon Lakes Hotel G&CC
(1991)
Hellidon, Daventry, NN11 6GG
☎ (01327) 262550
⌨ (01327) 262559
▦ 500
✍ MA Thomas
✓ J Kingston (01327) 262551
▷ 18 L 6700 yds SSS 72
9 L 5582 yds SSS 67
⋔ U H SOC
££ £20 (£30)
⊕ 7 miles SW of Daventry, via A361.
M40 Jct 11 and M1 Jct 16
⌂ David Snell
▤ www.hellidon.co.uk

Kettering   (1891)
Headlands, Kettering, NN15 6XA
☎ (01536) 511104
⌨ (01536) 511104
✉ secretary@kettering-golf.co.uk
▦ 700 100(L) 50(J)
✍ NA Sandell (01536) 511104
✓ K Theobald (01536) 481014
▷ 18 L 6057 yds SSS 69
⋔ WD–U WE/BH–M SOC
££ D–£36
⊕ Jct 8 of A14 – follow signs
⌂ Tom Morris
▤ www.kettering-golf.co.uk

Kingfisher Hotel   (1995)
Proprietary
Buckingham Road, Deanshanger, Milton
Keynes, MK19 6JY
☎ (01908) 560354/562332
⌨ (01908) 260857
✉ sales.kingfisher@btopenworld.com
▦ 98
✍ Roland Carlish
✓ B Mudge
▷ 9 L 5552 yds Par 70 SSS 67 (18
tees)
⋔ U SOC
££ 9: £9.50 (£12.50) 18: £14 (£17)
⊕ NW of Milton Keynes on A422 to
Buckingham. M1 Junction 15
⊕ Driving range
⌂ Donald Steel
▤ www.kingfisher-hotelandgolf.co.uk

Kingsthorpe   (1908)
Kingsley Road, Northampton, NN2 7BU
☎ (01604) 711173
⌨ (01604) 710610
✉ secretary@kingsthorpe-golf.co.uk
▦ 600
✍ JE Harris (01604) 710610
✓ P Armstrong (01604) 719602
▷ 18 L 5903 yds SSS 69
⋔ WD–U WE/BH–M H SOC–WD
££ £30 D–£40
⊕ 2 miles N of Northampton centre,
off A508
⊕ Putting green
⌂ Alison /Colt
▤ www.kingsthorpe-golf.co.uk

Northampton   (1893)
Harlestone, Northampton, NN7 4EF
☎ (01604) 845102 (Clubhouse)

⌨ (01604) 820262
✉ golf@northamptongolfclub.co.uk
📖 700
🏌 S Malherbe (01604) 845155
✓ B Randall (01604) 845167
▷ 18 L 6615 yds Par 72 SSS 72
🚶 H WD–U (except Weds) WE–M SOC–WD (except Weds)
££ D–£40
⛳ 4 miles NW of Northampton, on A428 beyond Harlestone
🏠 Donald Steel
📱 www.northamptongolfclub.co.uk

Northamptonshire County
(1909)

Church Brampton, Northampton, NN6 8AZ
☎ **(01604) 843025**
⌨ (01604) 843463
✉ secretary@countygolfclub.org.uk
📖 650
🏌 Peter Walsh (01604) 843025
✓ T Rouse (01604) 842226
▷ 18 L 6505 yds SSS 72 x 3
🚶 H SOC
££ Summer: 18 £40, 27 £50, 36 £60 Winter: £30 (£30)
⛳ 5 miles NW of Northampton, between A428 and A50
⊕ Driving range
🏠 HS Colt
📱 www.countygolfclub.org.uk

Oundle   (1893)

Benefield Road, Oundle, PE8 4EZ
☎ **(01832) 273267**
⌨ (01832) 273008
✉ office@oundlegolfclub.com
📖 630
🏌 D Foley (01832) 272267
✓ R Keys (01832) 272267
▷ 18 L 6265 yds Par 72 SSS 70
🚶 WD–U H WE–M before 10.30am –U H after 10.30am SOC
££ £26.50 D–£35.50 (£30)
⛳ 1½ miles W of Oundle on A427
📱 www.oundlegolfclub.com

Overstone Park   (1994)
Proprietary

Overstone Park Ltd, Billing Lane, Northampton, NN6 0A5
☎ **(01604) 647666**
⌨ (01604) 642635
✉ enquiries@overstonepark.com
📖 450
🏌 Allan McLundie (Gen Mgr)
✓ B Mudge (01604) 643555
▷ 18 L 6602 yds SSS 72
🚶 WD–U SOC
££ £30 (£40)
⛳ 4 miles E of Northampton, off A45. M1 Junction 15
⊕ Practice area
🏠 Donald Steel
📱 www.overstonepark.com

Priors Hall   (1965)
Public

Stamford Road, Weldon, Corby, NN17 3JH
☎ **(01536) 260756**
⌨ (01536) 260756

✉ p.ackroyd1@btinternet.com
📖 300
🏌 P Ackroyd
✓ G Bradbrook
▷ 18 L 6631 yds SSS 72
🚶 U SOC–WD+WE
££ On application
⛳ 4 miles E of Corby (A43)
⊕ Practice nets; buggies
🏠 Hawtree

Rushden   (1919)
Kimbolton Road, Chelveston, Wellingborough, Northamptonshire NN9 6AN
☎ **(01933) 418511**
⌨ (01933) 418511
✉ secretary@rushdengolfclub.org
📖 400
🏌 DL Waite
✓ Adrian Clifford (07710) 759265
▷ 10 L 6249 yds Par 71 SSS 70
🚶 WD–U exc Wed pm WE/BH–M SOC
££ £18
⛳ On B645, 2 miles E of Higham Ferrers
📱 www.rushdengolfclub.org

Staverton Park   (1977)
Staverton Park, Staverton, Daventry, NN11 6JT
☎ **(01327) 302000/302118**

Stoke Albany   (1995)
Proprietary
Ashley Road, Stoke Albany, Market Harborough, LE16 8PL
☎ **(01858) 535208**
⌨ (01858) 535505
✉ info@stokealbanygolfclub.co.uk
📖 450
🏌 R Want
✓ A Clifford
▷ 18 L 6175 yds Par 71 SSS 70
🚶 U SOC
££ D–£20 (£25 before 11, £23 after 11)
⛳ Between Market Harborough and Corby (A427)
⊕ Large practice area and putting green
🏠 Hawtree
📱 www.stokealbanygolfclub.com

Wellingborough   (1893)
Harrowden Hall, Great Harrowden, Wellingborough, NN9 5AD
☎ **(01933) 677234/673022**
⌨ (01933) 679379
✉ david.waite@wellingboroughgolfclub.com
📖 850
🏌 David Waite (01933) 677234
✓ D Clifford (01933) 678752
▷ 18 L 6651 yds SSS 72
🚶 WD–U H exc Tues WE–M SOC–WD exc Tues
££ D–£48
⛳ 2 miles N of Wellingborough on A509
⊕ No metal spikes May 1-Oct 31

🏠 Hawtree
📱 www.wellingboroughgolfclub.org

Whittlebury Park G&CC
(1992)

Whittlebury, Towcester, NN12 8WP
☎ **(01327) 850000**
⌨ (01327) 850001
✉ enquiries@whittlebury.com
📖 500
🏌 Penny Clarke
✓ Mark Booth (01327 858588)
▷ 36 holes: 5000-7000 yds SSS 68-72
🚶 U SOC
££ £25 (£35)
⛳ 4 miles S of Towcester on A413. M1 J15a. M40 J10
⊕ Driving range; indoor golf academy and club fitting centre
🏠 Cameron Sinclair
📱 www.whittlebury.com

Northumberland

Allendale   (1906)
High Studdon, Allenheads Road, Allendale, Hexham NE47 9DH
☎ **(0700) 580 8246**
📖 96
🏌 I Robinson (Hon)
▷ 9 L 4541 yds Par 66 SSS 64
🚶 U
££ D–£12 (D–£15)
⛳ 1½ miles S of Allendale on B6295
📱 www.allendale-golf.org

Alnmouth   (1869)
Foxton Hall, Alnmouth, NE66 3BE
☎ **(01665) 830231**
⌨ (01665) 830922
✉ secretary@alnmouthgolfclub.com
📖 750
🏌 H Sutherland
✓ Shop (01665) 830043
▷ 18 L 6484 yds SSS 71
🚶 Mon/Tues/Wed/Thurs/Sun–H SOC
££ £30 D–£40 (£35)
⛳ 5 miles SE of Alnwick
⊕ Dormy House
🏠 HS Colt
📱 www.alnmouthgolfclub.com

Alnmouth Village   (1869)
Marine Road, Alnmouth, NE66 2RZ
☎ **(01665) 830370**
✉ golf@alnmouth-village.fsnet.co.uk
📖 340
🏌 JE Clark (01665) 603797
▷ 9 L 6020 yds SSS 70
🚶 U
££ £16 (£20)
⛳ Alnmouth

Alnwick   (1907)
Swansfield Park, Alnwick, NE66 1AB
☎ **(01665) 602632**
✉ mail@alnwickgolfclub.co.uk
📖 450

🖉 LE Stewart (01665) 602499
⊵ 18 L 6250 yds SSS 70
♘ U
££ D–£20 (D–£25)
♨ Alnwick, off A1
♙ Rochester/Rae
▤ www.alnwickgolfclub.co.uk

Arcot Hall   (1909)

Dudley, Cramlington, NE23 7QP
☎ **(0191) 236 2794**
🖳 (0191) 217 0370
✉ arcothall@tiscali.co.uk
▥ 700
🖉 F Elliott (0191) 236 2794
⌇ J Metcalfe (0191) 236 2794
⊵ 18 L 6389 yds SSS 70
♘ WD–H WE/BH–M SOC
££ D–£28 (£32) After 3pm–£23
♨ 7 miles N of Newcastle, off A1
♙ James Braid
▤ www.arcothallgolfclub.com

Bamburgh Castle   (1904)

*The Club House, 40 The Wynding,
Bamburgh, NE69 7DE*
☎ **(01668) 214378**
🖳 (01668) 214607
✉ bamburghcastlegolfclub@hotmail
.com
▥ 730
🖉 RA Patterson (01668) 214321
⊵ 18 L 5621 yds Par 68 SSS 67
♘ WD–U H WE/BH–M SOC
££ £33 (£38)
♨ 5 miles E of A1, via B1341 or
B1342
♙ George Rochester
▤ www.bamburghcastlegolfclub.co.uk

Bedlingtonshire   (1972)

*Acorn Bank, Hartford Road, Bedlington,
NE22 6AA*
☎ **(01670) 822457**
🖳 (01670) 823048
✉ secretary@bedlingtongolfclub.com
▥ 820
🖉 J Laverick (01670) 822457
⌇ M Webb (01670) 822457
⊵ 18 L 6224 metres SSS 73
♘ U SOC
££ £24 (£30)
♨ 12 miles N of Newcastle (A1068)
♙ Frank Pennink
▤ www.bedlingtongolfclub.com

The Belford   (1993)

South Road, Belford, NE70 7DP
☎ **(01668) 213323**
🖳 (01668) 213282
▥ 250
🖉 HS Adair
⌇ A Brown
⊵ 9 L 6412 yds SSS 71 (18 tee boxes)
♘ U SOC
££ 9: £14 (£16) 18: £20 (£22)
♨ 15 miles N of Alnwick, off A1
⊕ Driving range
♙ Nigel Williams
▤ www.thebelford.com

Bellingham   (1893)

Boggle Hole, Bellingham, NE48 2DT
☎ **(01434) 220530/220152**
✉ admin@bellinghamgolfclub.com
▥ 400
🖉 Jaimie Self
⊵ 18 L 6093 yds Par 70 SSS 70
♘ U SOC
££ £25 (£30)
♨ 15 miles N of Hexham, off B6320
⊕ Driving range
♙ I Wilson
▤ www.bellinghamgolfclub.com

Berwick-upon-Tweed   (1890)

*Goswick, Berwick-upon-Tweed,
TD15 2RW*
☎ **(01289) 387256**
🖳 (01289) 387392
✉ goswickgc@btconnect.com
▥ 700
🖉 IAM Alsop
⌇ P Terras (01289) 387380
⊵ 18 L 6803 yds SSS 72
♘ WD–U 9.30–11.30am & after 2pm
WE–U 10–11.30am & after 2.30pm
SOC
££ £30 D–£37 (£37 D–£45)
♨ 5 miles S of Berwick, off A1
⊕ Driving range and large practice
area
♙ James Braid
▤ www.goswicklinksgc.co.uk

Blyth   (1905)

New Delaval, Blyth, NE24 4DB
☎ **(01670) 540110**
🖳 (01670) 540134
✉ clubmanager@blythgolf.co.uk
▥ 840
🖉 J Wright
⌇ A Brown (01670) 356514
⊵ 18 L 6424 yds SSS 71
♘ WD–U before 4pm WE/BH–U
after 2pm SOC
££ £25 D–£28 (£28)
♨ 10 miles NE of Newcastle. Close
to Northumberland Spine Road
A189
♙ J Hamilton Stutt
▤ www.blythgolf.co.uk

Burgham Park   (1994)

Felton, Morpeth, NE65 9QP
☎ **(01670) 787898**
🖳 (01670) 787164
✉ info@burghampark.co.uk
▥ 570
🖉 Terry Minett
⌇ D Mather (01670) 787898
⊵ 18 L 6751 yds SSS 72
♘ U SOC
££ £26 (£32)
♨ 7 miles N of Morpeth on A1
⊕ Pitch & putt course; driving range.
Home to the North Region PGA
Championship
♙ Andrew Mair
▤ www.burghampark.co.uk

Close House Country Club   (1968)

Proprietary
*Close House, Heddon-on-the-Wall,
Newcastle-upon-Tyne, NE15 0HT*
☎ **(01661) 852953**
🖳 (01661) 853322
✉ events@closehouse.co.uk
▥ 900
🖉 John Glendinning
⊵ 18 L 5671 yds SSS 67
♘ U–SOC
££ £15
♨ 9 miles W of Newcastle on A69
♙ Hawtree
▤ www.closehouse.co.uk

Dunstanburgh Castle   (1900)

Embleton, NE66 3XQ
☎ **(01665) 576562**
✉ enquiries@dunstanburgh.com
▥ 322
🖉 PFC Gilbert (Mgr)
⊵ 18 L 6298 yds SSS 70
♘ U
££ £22 (£26)
♨ 7 miles NE of Alnwick on B1339
♙ James Braid
▤ www.dunstanburgh.com

Hexham   (1892)

Spital Park, Hexham, NE46 3RZ
☎ **(01434) 603072**
🖳 (01434) 601865
✉ info@hexhamgolf.co.uk
▥ 750
🖉 Dawn Wylie (01434) 603072
⌇ Ben West
⊵ 18 L 6272 yds SSS 70
♘ U
££ £30 (£40)
♨ 21 miles W of Newcastle (A69)
♙ Vardon/Caird
▤ www.hexhamgolf.co.uk

Linden Hall   (1997)

Longhorsley, Morpeth, NE65 8XF
☎ **(01670) 500011**
✉ golf@lindenhall.co.uk

Longhirst Hall Golf Course   (1997)

Longhirst Hall, Longhirst, NE61 3LL
☎ **(01670) 791562 (Clubhouse)**
(01670) 858562 (Admin)
🖳 (01670) 791768
✉ enquiries@longhirstgolf.co.uk
▥ 1400
🖉 Ian Brodie
⌇ G Cant
⊵ The Lakes 18 L 6101 yds
White tees Par 70
Dawson 18 L 6713 yds
White tees Par 72
Old Course (Nov-Mar) 18
L 6572 yds
♘ U SOC
££ £30, £20, £15 (depending on tee
time) subject to review
♨ 4 miles NE of Morpeth, via
A197/B1337
⊕ Driving range

⌂ B Poole
▤ www.longhirstgolf.co.uk

Magdalene Fields   (1903)
Pay and play
Magdalene Fields, Berwick-upon-Tweed, TD15 1NE
☎ **(01289) 306130**
⌨ (01289) 306384
✉ mail@magdalene-fields.co.uk
▥ 330
♣ MJ Lynch
▷ 18 L 6407 yds SSS 71
♟ U SOC
££ £20 (£22)
🚗 Berwick-upon-Tweed 1 mile
⌂ Park/Jefferson/Thompson
▤ www.magdalene-fields.co.uk

Matfen Hall Hotel   (1994)
Matfen, Hexham, NE20 0RH
☎ **(01661) 886500 (Hotel)**
   (01661) 886400 (Bookings)
⌨ (01661) 886055
✉ golf@matfenhall.com
▥ 500
♣ D Burton
✓ J Harrison (01661) 886146
▷ 18 L 6700 yds Par 72
   9 hole Par 3 course
♟ WD–U WE–U after 11am
££ £35 (£40)
🚗 12 miles W of Newcastle, off B6318
⊕ Driving range; new 9 holes opening May 2007
⌂ Mair/James/Gaunt
▤ www.matfenhall.com

Morpeth   (1906)
The Clubhouse, Morpeth, NE61 2BT
☎ **(01670) 504942**
⌨ (01670) 504918
✉ morpethgolfclub@btconnect.com
▥ 800
♣ K Hunter (Mgr)
✓ MR Jackson (01670) 515675
▷ 18 L 5834 metres SSS 70
♟ H SOC
££ £25 (£30)
🚗 1 mile S of Morpeth on A197
⌂ Henry Vardon
▤ www.morpethgolf.co.uk

Newbiggin   (1884)
Newbiggin-by-the-Sea, NE64 6DW
☎ **(01670) 817344 (Clubhouse)**
✉ info@newbiggingolfclub.co.uk
▥ 500
♣ J Storey
✓ James Kerr
▷ 18 L 6516 yds SSS 71
♟ U after 10am exc comp days SOC by arrangement with Sec
££ D–£15 (D–£20)
🚗 Newbiggin, nr Church Point
⌂ Willie Park
▤ www.newbiggingolfclub.co.uk

Ponteland   (1927)
53 Bell Villas, Ponteland, Newcastle-upon-Tyne, NE20 9BD
☎ **(01661) 822689**

⌨ (01661) 860077
✉ secretary@thepontelandgolfclub.co.uk
▥ 480 170(L) 115(J)
♣ Mrs PM Spong
✓ A Robson-Crosby
▷ 18 L 6587 yds SSS 72
♟ WD–U SOC–Tues & Thurs
££ £30
🚗 6 miles NW of Newcastle on A696, nr Airport
▤ www.thepontelandgolfclub.co.uk

Prudhoe   (1930)
Eastwood Park, Prudhoe-on-Tyne, NE42 5DX
☎ **(01661) 832466 ext 20**
⌨ (01661) 830710
✉ secretary@prudhoegolfclub.co.uk
▥ 500
♣ ID Pauw
✓ J Crawford (01661) 832466 ext 23
▷ 18 L 5839 yds SSS 69
♟ WD–U WE–NA before 3pm SOC
££ £24 (£32)
🚗 12 miles W of Newcastle (A1/A695 junction)
▤ www.prudhoegolfclub.co.uk

Rothbury   (1891)
Whitton Road, Rothbury, Morpeth, NE65 7RX
☎ **(01669) 621271**
▥ 300
♣ LF Brown (0191) 215 0268
✓ None
▷ 18 L 6100 yds Par 70
♟ WD–U exc Tues after 4pm & Wed am WE–by arrangement
££ £18 D–£25 (£23)
🚗 15 miles N of Morpeth on A697. S side of Rothbury
⌂ JB Radcliffe
▤ www.rothburygolfclub.com

Seahouses   (1913)
Beadnell Road, Seahouses, NE68 7XT
☎ **(01665) 720794**
⌨ (01665) 721994
✉ secretary@seahousesgolf.co.uk
▥ 600
♣ John Rhind
▷ 18 L 5542 yds SSS 67
♟ U SOC
££ £20 (£27+Bank Hols) under review for 2007
🚗 14 miles N of Alnwick. 9 miles E of A1 on B1340
▤ www.seahousesgolf.co.uk

De Vere Slaley Hall   (1988)
Slaley, Hexham, NE47 0BX
☎ **(01434) 673154**
⌨ (01434) 673050
✉ slaley.hall@devere-hotels.com
▥ 350
♣ M Stancer (Golf Mgr)
✓ M Stancer (01434) 673154
▷ Hunting 18 L 7073 yds Par 72 SSS 71-74
   Priestman 18 L 6951 Par 72 SSS 71-74

♟ U SOC
££ Hunting: Low season £40, High season £80; Priestman: Low season £32, High season £45
🚗 20 miles W of Newcastle. 7 miles S of Corbridge, off A68
⊕ Driving range. Golf Academy
⌂ Hunting-Dave Thomas. Priestman-Neil Coles
▤ www.devere.co.uk

Stocksfield   (1913)
New Ridley, Stocksfield, NE43 7RE
☎ **(01661) 843041**
⌨ (01661) 843046
✉ info@sgcgolf.co.uk
▥ 570 70(L) 160(J)
♣ B Garrow
✓ S Harrison
▷ 18 L 5991 yds SSS 70
♟ U SOC–exc Wed am
££ £20 D–£25 (£28)
🚗 Off A695 at Branch End, 3 miles E of A68
⌂ F Pennink
▤ www.sgcgolf.co.uk

Swarland Hall   (1993)
Coast View, Swarland, Morpeth, NE65 9JG
☎ **(01670) 787940 (Clubhouse)**

Warkworth   (1891)
The Links, Warkworth, Morpeth, NE65 0SW
☎ **(01665) 711596**
▥ 400
♣ M Rowe
▷ 9 L 5986 yds Par 70 SSS 69
♟ U exc Tues & Sat SOC
££ D–£15 (D–£20)
🚗 9 miles SE of Alnwick (A1068)
⌂ Old Tom Morris

Wooler   (1975)
Dod Law, Doddington, Wooler, NE71 6AL
☎ **(01668) 282135**
▥ 250
♣ S Lowrey (01668) 281631
✓ None
▷ 9 L 6411 yds SSS 71
♟ U SOC
££ £15 (£20) £10 for 9 holes
🚗 3 miles N of Wooler on B6525
▤ www.woolergolf.co.uk

Nottinghamshire

Beeston Fields   (1923)
Beeston, Nottingham, NG9 3DD
☎ **(0115) 925 7062**
⌨ (0115) 925 4280
✉ beestonfields@btconnect.com
▥ 500 110(L) 60(J)
♣ J Lewis
✓ A Wardle (0115) 925 7062
▷ 18 L 6404 yds SSS 71
♟ U H SOC
££ £33 D–£43 (£39)
🚗 4 miles W of Nottingham. M1 J 25

♙ Tom Williamson
🖥 www.beestonfields.co.uk

Brierley Forest (1993)
Main Street, Huthwaite, Sutton-in-Ashfield, NG17 2LG
☎ **(01623) 550761**
🖳 (01623) 550761
🏛 130
🖊 D Crafts
✓ None
🏌 18 L 6008 yds Par 72 SSS 69
👥 WD–U bookings only WE–U before noon
££ £12 (£15)
🛦 W of Sutton-in-Ashfield. M1 Junction 28, 2 miles
♙ Dave Hibbert, Malc Walsh, P Roberts

Bulwell Forest (1902)
Hucknall Road, Bulwell, Nottingham, NG6 9LQ
☎ **(0115) 977 0576 (Clubhouse)**
🖳 (0115) 976 3172 (Pro)
🏛 350
🖊 D Nehra (07974) 754342
✓ B Hurt (0115) 976 3172
🏌 18 L 5746 yds Par 68 SSS 67
👥 U SOC
££ £13 (£16). 4 ball–£50 (£60)
🛦 4 miles N of Nottingham. M1 Junction 26, 3 miles

Chilwell Manor (1906)
Meadow Lane, Chilwell, Nottingham, NG9 5AE
☎ **(0115) 925 8958**
🖳 (0115) 922 0575
📧 chilwellmanorgolfclub@barbox .net
🏛 700
🖊 D Shakespeare
✓ P Wilson (0115) 925 8993
🏌 18 L 6028 yds Par 70 SSS 71
👥 U SOC
££ £30 D–£35 (£30)
🛦 4 miles W of Nottingham on A6005
♙ Tom Williamson
🖥 www.chilwellmanorgolfclub .co.uk

College Pines (1994)
Proprietary
Worksop College Drive, Sparken Hill, Worksop, S80 3AP
☎ **(01909) 501431**
🖳 (01909) 481227
🏛 550
🖊 C Snell (Golf Dir)
✓ C Snell (01909) 501431
🏌 18 L 6801 yds SSS 73
👥 U–phone first SOC
££ £14 D–£20 (£20 D–£30)
🛦 1 mile SE of Worksop on B6034, off Worksop Bypass
⊕ Driving range; buggies for hire
♙ David Snell
🖥 www.collegepinesgolfclub.co.uk

Cotgrave Place G&CC (1991)
Owned privately
Stragglethorpe, Nr Cotgrave Village, Cotgrave, NG12 3HB
☎ **(0115) 933 3344**
🖳 (0115) 933 4567
📧 cotgrave@crown-golf.co.uk
🏛 1100
🖊 M Evans
✓ R Smith
🏌 Open 18 L 6302 yds SSS 70 Masters 18 L 5933 yds SSS 69
👥 SOC WE after 12pm
££ Open £25 (£30.50). Masters £25 (£28.50)
🛦 4 miles SE of Nottingham, off A52
⊕ 9 bay driving range
♙ Small/Glasgow/Alliss
🖥 www.crown-golf.co.uk

Coxmoor (1913)
Coxmoor Road, Sutton-in-Ashfield, NG17 5LF
☎ **(01623) 557359**
🖳 (01623) 557435
📧 coxmoor@btconnect.com
🏛 650
🖊 P Snow
✓ D Ridley (01623) 559906
🏌 18 L 6577 yds SSS 72
👥 H exc Ladies Day–Tues WE–NA SOC
££ £40 D–£55
🛦 1½ miles S of Mansfield. 4 miles NE of M1 Junction 27 on A611
⊕ Practice nets/area
🖥 www.coxmoor.freeuk.com

Edwalton (1982)
Wellin Lane, Edwalton, Nottingham NG12 4AS
☎ **(0115) 923 4775**
🖳 (0115) 923 1647
📧 edwalton@glendale-services.co.uk
🏛 700
🖊 Mrs DJ Parkes (Hon) (0115) 914 8978
✓ L Rawlings
🏌 9 L 3336 yds SSS 36 9 hole Par 3 course
👥 U SOC
££ £7.95 (£8.95)
🛦 2 miles S of Nottingham (A606)
⊕ Driving range/practice facilities; putting green; buggy and club hire
🖥 www.glendale-golf.com

Kilton Forest (1978)
Public
Blyth Road, Worksop, S81 0TL
☎ **(01909) 486563**
🏛 300
🖊 JA Eyre (Hon)
✓ S Betteridge (01909) 486563
🏌 18 L 6424 yds Par 72 SSS 71
👥 WD–U WE–booking necessary SOC
££ £12 (£15)
🛦 1 mile NE of Worksop on B6045

Leen Valley Golf Centre (1994)
Pay and play
Wigwam Lane, Hucknall, NG15 7TA
☎ **(0115) 964 2037**
🖳 (0115) 964 2724
📧 leen@jbgolf.co.uk
🏛 350
🖊 R Hanson
🏌 18 L 6001 yds Par 71 SSS 70
👥 U SOC
££ Mon–Thur £12.50 Fri £13.50 WE+BH £16
🛦 ½ mile from Hucknall town centre
♙ Tom Hodgetts
🖥 www.jackbarker.com

Mapperley (1907)
Central Avenue, Plains Road, Mapperley, Nottingham, NG3 6RH
☎ **(0115) 955 6672**
🖳 (0115) 955 6670
📧 secretary@mapperleygolfclub.org
🏛 735
✓ A Newham (0115) 955 6672
🏌 18 L 6307 yds SSS 70
👥 U SOC
££ £25 (£30)
🛦 3 miles NE of Nottingham, off B684
♙ J Mason
🖥 www.mapperleygolfclub.org

Newark (1901)
Coddington, Newark, NG24 2QX
☎ **(01636) 626282**
🖳 (01636) 626497
📧 secretary@newark-golf-club.co.uk
🏛 650
🖊 DA Collingwood (01636) 626282
✓ PA Lockley (01636) 626492
🏌 18 L 6458 yds SSS 71
👥 H SOC
££ £28 (£34)
🛦 4 miles E of Newark on A17
⊕ Driving range on site
♙ Tom Williamson
🖥 www.newark-golf-club.co.uk

Norwood Park (1999)
Norwood Park, Southwell, NG25 0PF
☎ **(01636) 816626**
🖳 (01636) 815756
📧 mail@norwoodgolf.co.uk
🏛 600
🖊 H Starkey
✓ P Thornton (01636) 816626
🏌 18 L 6805 yds Par 72 SSS 72
👥 U SOC
££ £18 D–£26 (£25 D–£35)
🛦 ½ mile W of Southwell, off Kirklington road. Nearest road A617/612
⊕ Driving range
♙ Clyde Johnston
🖥 www.norwoodpark.org.uk

Nottingham City (1910)
Public
Norwich Gardens, Bulwell, Nottingham, NG6 8LF
☎ **(0115) 927 2767 (Pro Shop)**

460
GJ Chappell (0115) 927 2606
18 L 6218 yds SSS 70
WD–U WE–NA before noon SOC
££ £12.50 (£16)
5 miles N of Nottingham. M1
Junction 26

Notts (1887)
Hollinwell, Kirkby-in-Ashfield, NG17 7QR
☎ (01623) 753225
🖳 (01623) 753655
✉ office@nottsgolfclub.co.uk
🏛 330
♨ JB Noble
✒ M Bradley (01623) 753087
🏌 18 L 7153 yds Par 72 SSS 75
👫 WD–H WE/BH–M
££ £66 D–£99
🚗 4 miles S of Mansfield on A611. M1
Junction 27
⊕ Driving range–green fees only
🏠 Willie Park Jr
🖳 www.nottsgolfclub.co.uk

Oakmere Park (1974)
Oaks Lane, Oxton, NG25 0RH
☎ (0115) 965 3545
🖳 (0115) 965 5628
✉ enquiries@oakmerepark.co.uk
🏛 450
♨ D St-John Jones
✒ D St-John Jones (0115) 965 3545
🏌 18 L 6617 yds SSS 72
9 L 3495 yds SSS 37
👫 WD–U WE/BH–arrange times with
Mgr SOC
££ 9: £7 (£9) 18: £20 (£28)
🚗 8 miles NE of Nottingham on A614
⊕ Floodlit driving range
🏠 F Pennink
🖳 www.oakmerepark.co.uk

Radcliffe-on-Trent (1909)
Dewberry Lane, Cropwell Road, Radcliffe-
on-Trent, NG12 2JH
☎ (0115) 933 3000
🖳 (0115) 911 6991
✉ les.wake@radcliffeontrentgc.co.uk
🏛 700
♨ L Wake
✒ C George
🏌 18 L 6374 yds Par 70 SSS 71
👫 H SOC–Wed only
££ 18: £25 (£32); 18+: £35 (£40)
🚗 6 miles E of Nottingham, off A52
🏠 Tom Williamson
🖳 www.radcliffeontrentgc.co.uk

Ramsdale Park Golf Centre
(1992)
Pay and play
Oxton Road, Calverton, NG14 6NU
☎ (0115) 965 5600
🖳 (0115) 965 4105
✉ info@ramsdaleparkgc.co.uk
🏛 400
♨ N Birch (Mgr)
✒ R Macey
🏌 Seely: 18 L 6546 yds SSS 71
Lee: 18 hole Par 3 course
👫 U SOC–WD WE restricted

££ £20.50 D–£32 (£26)
🚗 5 miles NE of Nottingham on
B6386. M1 Junction 27
⊕ 26 bay floodlit driving range
🏠 Hawtree
🖳 www.ramsdaleparkgc.co.uk

Retford (1921)
Brecks Road, Ordsall, Retford, DN22 7UA
☎ (01777) 703733
✉ retfordgolfclub@lineone.net

Ruddington Grange (1988)
Wilford Road, Ruddington, Nottingham,
NG11 6NB
☎ (0115) 984 6141
🖳 (0115) 940 5165
✉ info@ruddingtongrange.co.uk
🏛 700
♨ P Deacon
✒ R Simpson (0115) 921 1951
🏌 18 L 6515 yds SSS 72
👫 WD–U SOC
££ D–£17.50 (£25)
🚗 3 miles S of Nottingham
🏠 J Small
🖳 www.ruddingtongrange.co.uk

Rufford Park G&CC
Rufford Lane, Rufford, Newark, NG22 9DG
☎ (01623) 825253
🖳 (01623) 825254
✉ enquiries@ruffordpark.co.uk
🏛 500
♨ Mrs K Whitehead (01623) 825253
✒ J Vaughan, J Thompson
🏌 18 L 6368 yds Par 70 SSS 70
👫 U–booking necessary
SOC–WD/WEpm
££ £22 (£28)
🚗 Nr Rufford Abbey on A614. 8 miles
S of A1/A614 junction
⊕ Floodlit driving range
🏠 Ken Moodie/Ken Brown
🖳 www.ruffordpark.co.uk

Rushcliffe (1909)
Stocking Lane, East Leake, Loughborough,
LE12 5RL
☎ (01509) 852959
✉ secretary.rushcliffegc
@btopenworld.com

Serlby Park (1906)
Serlby, Doncaster, DN10 6BA
☎ (01777) 818268
🏛 250
♨ KJ Crook (01302) 742280
🏌 9 L 5396 yds SSS 66
👫 M SOC–WD
££ £20
🚗 12 miles S of Doncaster, between
A614 and A638
🏠 Lord Galway

Sherwood Forest (1895)
Eakring Road, Mansfield, NG18 3EW
☎ (01623) 626689/627403
🖳 (01623) 420412
🏛 648
♨ Ms A Miles (01623) 626689

✒ K Hall (01623) 627403
🏌 18 L 6843 yds SSS 74
👫 H SOC–WD
££ 18: £50; 32: £70
🚗 2 miles E of Mansfield (A617)
🏠 HS Colt/James Braid

Southwell (1993)
Proprietary
Southwell Racecourse, Rolleston, Newark,
NG25 0TS
☎ (01636) 816501/816795
🖳 (01636) 812271
✉ info@southwellgolfclub.com
🏛 450
♨ M Harness (01636) 821651
✒ Chris White (01636) 813706
🏌 18 L 5767 yds Par 69 SSS 68
👫 U SOC
££ £15 (£18)
🚗 6 miles W of Newark on A617.
Course adjacent to racetrack
🏠 RA Muddle
🖳 www.southwellgolfclub.com

Springwater (1991)
Proprietary
Moor Lane, Calverton, Nottingham,
NG14 6FZ
☎ (0115) 965 4946
✉ springwater@rapidial.co.uk
🏛 450
♨ W Turner (0115) 965 2129
✒ P Drew (0115) 965 2129
🏌 18 L 6262 yds Par 71
👫 U SOC WD WE after 12.30pm
££ £20 (£25)
🚗 Off A6097 between Lowdham and
Oxton
⊕ Driving range
🏠 N Footit/P Wharmsby
🖳 www.springwatergolfclub.co.uk

Stanton-on-the-Wolds
(1906)
Golf Course Road, Stanton-on-the-Wolds,
Nottingham, NG12 5BH
☎ (0115) 937 4885
🖳 (0115) 937 4885
✉ swgc@zoom.co.uk
🏛 500 167(L) 100(J)
♨ MJ Price (0115) 937 4885
✒ N Hernon ((0115) 937 2390
🏌 18 L 6421 yds SSS 71
👫 WD–U SOC exc comp days
WE–M
££ On application
🚗 9 miles S of Nottingham
⊕ Practice field and putting green

Trent Lock Golf Centre
(1991)
Lock Lane, Sawley, Long Eaton,
NG10 2FY
☎ (0115) 946 4398
🖳 (0115) 946 1183
✉ emccausland@aol.com
🏛 550
♨ R Gregory
✒ M Taylor

℞ 18 L 5868 yds Par 69 SSS 68
9 L 2911 yds Par 36
♟ U SOC
££ 9: £6 (£7.50) 18: £17.50 (£22.50)
Summer rates
⛳ S of Long Eaton. M1 Junction 25
⊕ Driving range, 24 bays; power tees
(floodlit); custom fitting centre
⌂ E McCausland
▤ www.trenlock.co.uk

Wollaton Park   (1927)
Wollaton Park, Nottingham, NG8 1BT
☎ **(0115) 978 7574**
🖬 (0115) 970 0736
✉ wollatonparkgc@aol.com
📖 700
♟ Avril J Jamieson
✓ J Lower (0115) 978 4834
℞ 18 L 6445 yds SSS 71
♟ U SOC
££ £35 (£40) D–£48 (D–£55)
⛳ 2 miles SW of Nottingham. M1
Junction 25, 5 miles
⌂ T Williamson
▤ www.wollatonparkgolfclub.com

Worksop   (1911)
Windmill Lane, Worksop, S80 2SQ
☎ **(01909) 477731**
🖬 (01909) 530917
✉ thesecretary@worksopgolfclub
.com
📖 500
♟ DA Dufall (01909) 477731
✓ K Crossland
℞ 18 L 6628 yds Par 72 SSS 72
♟ WD–H (phone first) WE/BH–M
SOC
££ On application
⛳ 1 mile SE of Worksop, off A6034
via by-pass (A57). M1 Junction 30,
9 miles
▤ www.worksopgolfclub.com

Oxfordshire

Aspect Park   (1988)
*Remenham Hill, Henley-on-Thames,
RG9 3EH*
☎ **(01491) 578306**

Badgemore Park   (1972)
Proprietary
Henley-on-Thames, RG9 4NR
☎ **(01491) 637300**
🖬 (01491) 576899
✉ info@badgemorepark.com
📖 600
♟ J Connell (Mgr) (01491) 637300
✓ J Dunn (01491) 574175
℞ 18 L 6129 yds SSS 69
♟ WD–U exc Tues am–NA WE–U
after 12 noon SOC–Wed to Fri
££ £29 (£38)
⛳ 1 mile NW of Henley on
Rotherfield Greys road
⌂ B Sandow
▤ www.badgemorepark.com

Banbury Golf Centre
(1993)
*Aynho Road, Adderbury, Banbury,
OX17 3NT*
☎ **(01295) 810419**
🖬 (01295) 810056
✉ office@banburygolfcentre.co.uk
📖 350
♟ Mrs A Prestidge
✓ (01295) 812880
℞ 27 holes :
L 5766-6706 yds Par 72 SSS 72
♟ U SOC
££ £23 (£29)
⛳ 6 miles S of Banbury on B4100.
M40 Junction 10/11
⌂ Reed/Payn
▤ www.banburygolfcentre.co.uk

Bicester G&CC   (1973)
Chesterton, Bicester, OX26 1TE
☎ **(01869) 241204**
✉ bicestergolf@ukonline.co.uk

Brailes   (1992)
Proprietary
*Sutton Lane, Lower Brailes, Banbury,
OX15 5BB*
☎ **(01608) 685633**
🖬 (01608) 685205
✉ office@brailesgolfclub.co.uk
📖 580
♟ P Gibbs (Gen Mgr) (01608) 685336
✓ Mark McGeehan (07787) 937672
℞ 18 L 6304 yds Par 71 SSS 70
♟ U SOC–WD anytime WE after
noon
££ £25 (£35)
⛳ 4 miles E of Shipston-on-Stour on
B4035. M40 Junction 11, 10 miles
⊕ Golf Academy & driving range
⌂ R Baldwin
▤ www.brailesgolfclub.co.uk

Burford   (1936)
Burford, OX18 4JG
☎ **(01993) 822583**
🖬 (01993) 822801
✉ secretary@burfordgc.co.uk
📖 785
♟ RP Thompson
✓ M Ridge (01993) 822344
℞ 18 L 6401 yds SSS 71
♟ WD–H SOC
££ On application
⛳ 19 miles W of Oxford on A40
⌂ JH Turner
▤ www.burfordgolfclub.co.uk

Carswell CC   (1993)
Carswell, Faringdon, SN7 8PU
☎ **(01367) 870422**
🖬 (01367) 870592
✉ info@carswellgolfandcountryclub
.co.uk
📖 500
♟ G Lisi (Prop)
✓ Jamie Clutterbuck
℞ 18 L 6133 yds Par 72
♟ U SOC–WD
££ £20 (£28)

⛳ 12 miles W of Oxford on A420
⊕ Floodlit driving range
⌂ J & E Ely
▤ www.carswellgolfandcountryclub
.co.uk

Cherwell Edge   (1980)
Chacombe, Banbury, OX17 2EN
☎ **(01295) 711591**
🖬 (01295) 713674
✉ enquiries@cherwelledgegolfclub
.co.uk
📖 530
♟ RA Beare (Sec) David Newman
(Gen Mgr)
✓ Jason Roberts-Newman
℞ 18 L 6085 yds SSS 69
♟ U SOC–WD WE after 11am
££ From £20 (from £25)
⛳ 2 miles N M40 Jct 11 (see website)
⊕ Driving range
▤ www.cherwelledgegolfclub.co.uk

Chipping Norton   (1890)
Southcombe, Chipping Norton, OX7 5QH
☎ **(01608) 642383**
✉ chipping.nortongc@virgin.net

Drayton Park   (1992)
Pay and play
*Steventon Road, Drayton, Abingdon,
OX14 4la*
☎ **(01235) 550607/528989**
🖬 (01235) 525731
✉ draytonpark@btclick.com
📖 400
♟ IR Head (01235) 528989
✓ M Morbey (01235) 550607
℞ 18 L 6214 yds SSS 70
9 hole Par 3 course
♟ U SOC
££ £19 (£25)
⛳ 10 miles S of Oxford on A34. M4
J13
⊕ Floodlit driving range; chipping
green; putting green
⌂ Hawtree
▤ www.draytonparkgolfclubabingdon
.co.uk

Frilford Heath   (1908)
Frilford Heath, Abingdon, OX13 5NW
☎ **(01865) 390864**
🖬 (01865) 390823
✉ secretary@frilfordheath.co.uk
📖 1350 210(L)
♟ S Styles
✓ DC Craik (01865) 390887
℞ Red 18 L 6884 yds SSS 73
Green 18 L 6006 yds SSS 69
Blue 18 L 6728 yds SSS 72
♟ H SOC
££ £65 (£80)
⛳ 3 miles W of Abingdon on A338
⌂ Blue-Simon Gidman
▤ www.frilfordheath.co.uk

Hadden Hill   (1990)
Proprietary
Wallingford Road, Didcot, OX11 9BJ
☎ **(01235) 510410**

☎ (01235) 511260
✉ info@haddenhillgolf.co.uk
📖 420 52(L)
🏌 MV Morley
⚐ I Mitchell
🏴 18 L 6563 yds SSS 71
🏌 WD–U SOC–WD
££ £19 (£24)
🚗 E of Didcot on A4130
⊕ Floodlit driving range
🏠 MV Morley
🖥 www.haddenhillgolf.co.uk

Henley   (1907)
Harpsden, Henley-on-Thames, RG9 4HG
☎ **(01491) 575742**
🖥 (01491) 412179
✉ info@henleygc.com
📖 750
🏌 Gary Oatham (01491) 575781
⚐ Mark Howell (01491) 575710
🏴 18 L 6256 yds SSS 70
🏌 WD–H WE–M SOC
££ £45
🚗 I mile S of Henley (A4155)
🏠 James Braid
🖥 www.henleygc.com

Hinksey Heights   (1995)
Public
South Hinksey, Oxford, OX1 5AB
☎ **(01865) 327775**
🖥 (01865) 736930
✉ play@oxford-golf.co.uk
📖 575
🏌 K McCallum (01865) 327775 ext 2
⚐ D Davis (01865) 327775 ext 1
🏴 18 L 6936 yds Par 72 SSS 73
9 hole Par 3 course
9/18 L 5212 yds Par 70 SSS 65
🏌 U SOC
££ £21 (£27)
🚗 W of Oxford, off A34 at South
Hinksey, between Oxford and
Abingdon
⊕ Practice range. Golf academy
🏠 D Heads
🖥 www.oxford-golf.co.uk

Huntercombe   (1901)
Nuffield, Henley-on-Thames, RG9 5SL
☎ **(01491) 641207**
🖥 (01491) 642060
✉ office@huntercombegolfclub.co.uk
📖 650
🏌 KS McCrea
⚐ IM Roberts (01491) 641241
🏴 18 L 6271 yds SSS 70
🏌 H–by appointment only SOC–WD
££ £40 D–£60 (£60 D–£75)
🚗 6 miles W of Henley on A4130
⊕ Practice ground
🏠 Willie Park Jr
🖥 www.huntercombegolfclub.co.uk

Kirtlington   (1995)
Proprietary
Kirtlington, Oxon OX5 3JY
☎ **(01869) 351133**
🖥 (01869) 331143
✉ info@kirtlingtongolfclub.com
📖 450

🏌 P Smith (Sec/Mgr)
⚐ Andy Taylor (0800) 587 2489
🏴 18 holes Par 70 SSS 69
9 hole Par 30
🏌 U SOC
££ £22 (£27)
🚗 I mile from Kirtlington on A4095.
M40 Junction 9
⊕ Driving range; putting green; short
game practice area
🏠 G Webster
🖥 www.kirtlingtongolfclub.com

North Oxford   (1907)
Banbury Road, Oxford, OX2 8EZ
☎ **(01865) 554415**
🖥 (01865) 515921
✉ manager@nogc.co.uk
📖 701
🏌 C Page (01865) 554924
⚐ R Harris (01865) 553977
🏴 18 L 5741 yds SSS 67
🏌 WD–U SOC–WD exc Thurs
££ £25 D–£30 (£30 D–£38)
🚗 4 miles N of Oxford, off A4260 to
Kidlington
🖥 www.nogc.co.uk

The Oxfordshire   (1993)
Proprietary
Rycote Lane, Milton Common, Thame,
OX9 2PU
☎ **(01844) 278300**
🖥 (01844) 278003
✉ info@theoxfordshiregolfclub.com
📖 470
🏌 Mr M Harris
⚐ S Gibson (01844) 278505
🏴 18 L 7187 yds Par 72 SSS 75
🏌 I H before noon SOC WD
WE–NA before noon
££ On application
🚗 1½ miles W of Thame on A329.
M40 Junction 7, 1½ miles. M40
Junction 8, 4 miles
⊕ Driving range
🏠 Rees Jones
🖥 www.theoxfordshiregolfclub.com

RAF Benson   (1975)
Royal Air Force, Benson, Wallingford,
OX10 6AA
☎ **(01491) 837766 Ext 7322**

Rye Hill   (1992)
Proprietary
Milcombe, Banbury, OX15 4RU
☎ **(01295) 721818**
🖥 (01295) 720089
✉ info@ryehill.co.uk
🏌 Tony Pennock
⚐ T Pennock (01295) 721818
🏴 18 L 6919 yds Par 72
🏌 U–booking necessary SOC
££ £25 D–£40 (£32 D–£55) 5 holes
£10 (£12) 10 holes £19 (£21)
🚗 5 miles SW of Banbury, off A361.
M40 Junction 11
⊕ Golf Parc, purpose-built junior golf
facility inc. driving school
🖥 www.ryehill.co.uk

Southfield   (1875)
Hill Top Road, Oxford, OX4 1PF
☎ **(01865) 242158**
🖥 (01865) 250023
✉ sgcltd@btopenworld.com
📖 700
🏌 M Blight (01865) 242158
⚐ A Rees (01865) 244258
🏴 18 L 6230 yds SSS 70
🏌 WD–U WE/BH–M H SOC
££ £37
🚗 2 miles E of Oxford City Centre
🏠 HS Colt
🖥 www.southfieldgolf.com

The Springs Hotel & Golf Club   (1998)
Proprietary
Wallingford Road, North Stoke, Wallingford,
OX10 6BE
☎ **(01491) 827310**
🖥 (01491) 827312
✉ proshop@thespringshotel.com
📖 550
🏌 D Allen (01491) 827315
⚐ D Boyce (01491) 827310
🏴 18 L 6470 yds Par 72 SSS 71
18 L 5651 yds Par 72 SSS 72
(ladies)
🏌 By arrangement SOC; U of
handicap standard
££ D–£37 (£45)
🚗 2 miles SW of Wallingford on
B4009. M40 Junction 6
⊕ Short game practice area
🏠 Brian Huggett
🖥 www.thespringshotel.com

Studley Wood   (1996)
The Straight Mile, Horton-cum-Studley,
Oxford, OX33 1BF
☎ **(01865) 351144**
🖥 (01865) 351166
✉ admin@swgc.co.uk
📖 750
🏌 Annie Anderson (01865) 351144
⚐ T Williams (01865) 351122
🏴 18 L 6722 yds Par 73 SSS 72
🏌 WD–U WE–NA before noon SOC
££ £39 (£47)
🚗 4 miles NE of Oxford. M40 J8 from
London, J9 from Birmingham
⊕ Driving range. Golf academy
🏠 Simon Gidman
🖥 www.studleywoodgolf.co.uk

Tadmarton Heath   (1922)
Wigginton, Banbury, OX15 5HL
☎ **(01608) 737278**
🖥 (01608) 730548
✉ thgc@btinternet.com
📖 560
🏌 JR Cox (01608) 737278
⚐ T Jones (01608) 730047
🏴 18 L 5936 yds Par 69 SSS 69
🏌 WD–H by appointment WE–M
SOC–WD
££ £45 (£50). After 10am–£40 (12
noon £40)
🚗 5 miles SW of Banbury, off B4035
🏠 Maj CJ Hutchison
🖥 www.thgc.btinternet.co.uk

Waterstock   (1994)

Pay and play
*Thame Road, Waterstock, Oxford,
OX33 1HT*
☎ (01844) 338093
🖂 (01844) 338036
✉ wgc_oxford@btinternet.com
📖 500
🏌 AJ Wyatt
↗ P Bryant
↦ 18 L 6535 yds Par 72
👥 U SOC
££ £22 D–£36 (£27 D–£44); 9–hole,
day fees available and twilight fees
available
⛳ E of Oxford on A418. M40 Jct 8
⊕ 22-bay floodlit driving range;
practice putting green; grass
practice area
🏠 Donald Steel
🖥 www.waterstockgolf.co.uk

Witney Lakes   (1994)

Downs Road, Witney, OX29 0SY
☎ (01993) 893011
🖂 (01993) 778866
✉ golf@witney-lakes.co.uk
📖 450
🏌 G Brown
↗ A Souter
↦ 18 L 6460 yds SSS 71
👥 U SOC WD/WE
££ £20 (£28)
⛳ 2 miles W of Witney on B4047
⊕ Floodlit driving range
🏠 Simon Gidman
🖥 www.witney-lakes.co.uk

The Wychwood   (1992)

Proprietary
Lyneham, Chipping Norton, OX7 6QQ
☎ (01993) 831841
🖂 (01993) 831775
✉ golf@wychwoodgc.freeserve.co.uk
📖 750
🏌 CJT Howkins
↗ D Griffin
↦ 18 L 6844 yds SSS 72
👥 WD–U WE–U after 11am SOC
££ £25 (£30)
⛳ 4 miles W of Chipping Norton, off
A361
⊕ Driving range
🏠 D Carpenter
🖥 www.golf@lynehamgc.freeserve
.co.uk

Rutland

Greetham Valley   (1992)

Greetham, Oakham, LE15 7NP
☎ (01780) 460444
🖂 (01780) 460623
✉ info@gvgc.co.uk
📖 1000
🏌 FE Hinch
↗ Neil Evans (01780) 460666
↦ 18 holes SSS 71
18 holes SSS 68
9 hole Par 3 course

👥 U SOC–WD
££ £25 (£30)
⛳ 5 miles NE of Oakham (B668), nr
A1
⊕ Floodlit driving range; 35 room
hotel
🖥 www.greethamvalley.co.uk

Luffenham Heath   (1911)

Ketton, Stamford, PE9 3UU
☎ (01780) 720205
🖂 (01780) 722146
✉ jringleby@theluffenhamheathgc
.co.uk
📖 555
🏌 JR Ingleby
↗ I Burnett (01780) 720298
↦ 18 L 6563 yds Par 70 SSS 72
👥 U H SOC–WD
££ £40 D–£50 (£40 D–£50) (under
review)
⛳ 5 miles W of Stamford on A6121
🏠 James Braid
🖥 www.luffenhamheath.co.uk

RAF Cottesmore   (1982)

Oakham, Leicester, LE15 7BL
☎ (01572) 812241 Ext 6706
📖 150
🏌 I Westcott
↦ 9 L 5767 yds SSS 69
👥 By arrangement
££ £10
⛳ RAF Cottesmore

Rutland County   (1991)

Great Casterton, Stamford, PE9 4AQ
☎ (01780) 460239/460330
🖂 (01780) 460437
✉ info@rutlandcountygolf.co.uk
🏌 S Lowe (Golf Dir)
Ian Melville
↦ 18 L 6401 yds SSS 71
9 hole Par 3 course
👥 U H SOC
££ £25 (£30)
⛳ 3 miles N of Stamford on A1
⊕ Driving range
🏠 Cameron Sinclair
🖥 www.rutlandcountygolf.co.uk

Shropshire

Aqualate   (1995)

Pay and play
Stafford Road, Newport, TF10 9JT
☎ (01952) 811699
🖂 (01952) 825343
📖 160
🏌 HB Dawes (Mgr) (01952) 811699
↗ K Short (01952) 811699
↦ 18 L 5659 yds Par 69 SSS 67
👥 U (Pay & Play)
££ £12 (£15)
⛳ 1 mile E of Newport (A518/A41
junction)
⊕ Floodlit driving range
🖥 www.aqualategolf..co.uk

Arscott   (1992)

Arscott, Pontesbury, Shrewsbury, SY5 0XP
☎ (01743) 860114
🖂 (01743) 860114
✉ golf@arscott.dydirect.net
📖 650
🏌 Sian Cadwallader
↗ Glynn Sadd (01743) 860881
↦ 18 L 6112 yds SSS 69
👥 WD–U WE/BH–M before 2pm
SOC
££ £20 (£25)
⛳ 5 miles SW of Shrewsbury, off
A488
🏠 Martin Hamer
🖥 www.arscottgolfclub.co.uk

Bridgnorth   (1889)

Stanley Lane, Bridgnorth, WV16 4SF
☎ (01746) 763315
🖂 (01746) 763315
✉ bridgnorthgolfclub@tiscali.co.uk
📖 690
🏌 GC Kelsall
↗ P Hinton (01746) 762045
↦ 18 L 6582 yds Par 73 SSS 72
👥 H SOC WD
££ £25 (£31)
⛳ 1 mile N of Bridgnorth
🖥 www.bridgnorthgolfclub.co.uk

Brow

Proprietary
Welsh Frankton, Ellesmere, SY12 9HW
☎ (01691) 622628
✉ browgolf@btinternet.com
📖 130
🏌 David Davies
↗ Alan Strange
↦ 9 L 4220 yds Par 66
👥 U SOC WD WE
££ D–£11 (D–£12.50)
⛳ On A495 2 m from Ellesmere on
the Oswestry Road
⊕ Club and trolley hire
🖥 www.thebrowgolfclub.com

Chesterton Valley

*Chesterton, Worfield, Bridgnorth,
WV15 5NX*
☎ (01746) 783682
📖 450
🏌 P Hinton
↗ P Hinton
↦ 18 L 6000 yds Par 71 SSS 69
👥 U–phone first SOC
££ £15.50 (£18)
⛳ 10 miles W of Wolverhampton on
B4176
🏠 Mike Davis

Church Stretton   (1898)

Trevor Hill, Church Stretton, SY6 6JH
☎ (01694) 722281
✉ secretary@churchstrettongolfclub
.co.uk
📖 410
🏌 John Povall (01743) 860679
↗ J Townsend (01694) 722281
↦ 18 L 5020 yds SSS 65
👥 U WE–NA before 10.30am SOC
££ £20 (£25)

⛳ ½ mile W of Church Stretton, off A49 above Carding Mill Valley
🏠 Jack Morris, James Hepburn, Harry Vardon, James Braid
🖥 www.churchstrettongolfclub.co.uk

Cleobury Mortimer (1993)

Wyre Common, Cleobury Mortimer, DY14 8HQ
☎ (01299) 271112 (Clubhouse)
🖷 (01299) 271468
📧 enquiries@cleoburygolfclub.com
📖 704
♪ G Pain (Gen Mgr)
✓ J Jones, M Payne
🏌 27 holes:
L 6147-6438 yds SSS 69-71
👥 WD–U H WE–M H SOC
££ £20 (£30)
⛳ 10 miles SW of Kidderminster on A4117
⊕ Driving range and short game practice area
🏠 Ray Baldwin E.G.U.
🖥 www.cleoburygolfclub.com

Hawkstone Park (1920)

Weston-under-Redcastle, Shrewsbury, SY4 5UY
☎ (01939) 200611
🖷 (01939) 200311
📧 secretary@hawkstone.co.uk
📖 700
♪ T Harrop
✓ S Leech
🏌 Hawkstone 18 L 6491 yds SSS 72
Championship 18 L 6764 yds SSS 72
Academy 6 holes Par 3 course
👥 U SOC
££ £35 D–£50 (£45 D–£65)
⛳ 10 miles S of Whitchurch. 14 miles N of Shrewsbury on A49
⊕ Driving range
🏠 Braid/Huggett
🖥 www.hpgcgolf.com

Hill Valley G&CC (1975)

Proprietary
Terrick Road, Whitchurch, SY13 4JZ
☎ (01948) 667788
🖷 (01948) 665927
📧 general.hillvalley@mcdonald-hotels.co.uk
📖 350
♪ A De Barro (01948) 664039
✓ AJ Minshall (01948) 663032
🏌 Emerald 18 L 6628 yds Par 73
Sapphire 18 L 4801 yds Par 66
👥 U
££ Emerald £20 (£25) Sapphire £11 (£15)
⛳ 1 mile N of Whitchurch, off A41/A49 Bypass
🏠 Alliss/Thomas
🖥 www.hillvalleygolfclub.co.uk

Horsehay Village Golf Centre (1999)

Pay and play
Wellington Road, Horsehay, Telford, TF4 3BT
☎ (01952) 632070

📧 horsehayvillagegolfcentre@telford.gov.uk

Lilleshall Hall (1937)

Abbey Road, Lilleshall, Newport, TF10 9AS
☎ (01952) 604776
🖷 (01952) 604272
📧 honsec@lhgc.entdsl.com
📖 700
♪ A Marklew (01952) 604776
✓ R Bluck (01952) 604104
🏌 18 L 5813 yds SSS 68
👥 WD–U WE SOC
££ £30
⛳ 3 miles S of Newport between Lilleshall and Sheriffhales. M54 Junction 4
⊕ Indoor teaching academy
🏠 HS Colt
🖥 www.lilleshallhallgolfclub.co.uk

Llanymynech (1933)

Pant, Oswestry, SY10 8LB
☎ (01691) 830983
📧 secretary.llanygc@btinternet.com
📖 760
♪ Howard Jones
✓ A Griffiths (01691) 830879
🏌 18 L 6114 yds Par 70 SSS 69
👥 U between 9.30–4pm M after 4pm SOC–WD
££ £25 D–£35 (£30)
⛳ 5 miles S of Oswestry on A483
⊕ Practice area
🖥 www.llanymynechgolfclub.co.uk

Ludlow (1889)

Bromfield, Ludlow, SY8 2BT
☎ (01584) 856285
🖷 (01584) 856366
📧 secretary@ludlowgolfclub.com
📖 650
♪ E Wilks (01584) 856285
✓ R Price (01584) 856366
🏌 18 L 6277 yds SSS 70
👥 H SOC–WD
££ £28 D–£35 (£35)
⛳ 2 miles N of Ludlow (A49)
⊕ Buggies available
🖥 www.ludlowgolfclub.com

Market Drayton (1906)

Sutton, Market Drayton, TF9 2HX
☎ (01630) 652266
🖷 (01630) 656564
📧 marketdrayton@btinternet.com
📖 650
♪ DB Palmer
✓ R Clewes (01630) 656237
🏌 18 L 6290 yds SSS 71
👥 WD–U WE–M
££ £28
⛳ 1 mile S of Market Drayton off A41
🖥 www.marketdraytongolfclub.co.uk

Meole Brace (1976)

Public
Meole Brace, Shrewsbury SY2 6QQ
☎ (01743) 364050

Mile End (1992)

Proprietary
Mile End, Oswestry, SY11 4JF
☎ (01691) 671246
🖷 (01691) 670580
📧 info@mileendgolfclub.co.uk
♪ R Thompson
✓ S Carpenter (01691) 671246
🏌 18 L 6233 yds SSS 70
👥 U SOC
££ £16 D–£24 (£25 D–£37)
⛳ 1 mile SE of Oswestry, off A5/A483
⊕ Driving range, PGA tuition
🏠 Price/Gough
🖥 www.mileendgolfclub.co.uk

Oswestry (1903)

Aston Park, Queens Head, Oswestry, SY11 4JJ
☎ (01691) 610535
🖷 (01691) 610535
📧 secretary@oswestrygolfclub.co.uk
📖 880
♪ Peter Turner (01691) 610535
✓ David Skelton (01691) 610448
🏌 18 L 6038 yds Par 70 SSS 69
👥 M or H SOC–WD + some WE
££ £27 (£31 Sat)
⛳ 3 miles SE of Oswestry on A5
🏠 James Braid
🖥 www.oswestrygolfclub.co.uk

Patshull Park Hotel G&CC (1980)

Pattingham, WV6 7HR
☎ (01902) 700100
🖷 (01902) 700874
📖 395
♪ B Poole
✓ R Bissell (01902) 700342
🏌 18 L 6345 yds SSS 71
👥 U H SOC
££ £40
⛳ 7 miles W of Wolverhampton, off A41. M54 Junction 3, 5 miles
⊕ Practice facilities, putting green, on-site hotel
🏠 John Jacobs
🖥 www.patshull-park.co.uk

Severn Meadows (1990)

Pay and play
Highley, Bridgnorth, WV16 6HZ
☎ (01746) 862212
📖 150
♪ C Harrison
✓ None
🏌 18 L 6357 yds Par 72 SSS 70
👥 WD–U WE–booking required
££ £15 (£20)
⛳ 8 miles S of Bridgnorth on B4555

Shifnal (1929)

Decker Hill, Shifnal, TF11 8QL
☎ (01952) 460330
🖷 (01952) 460330
📧 secretary@shifnalgolfclub.co.uk
📖 700
♪ M Vanner (01952) 460330
✓ D Ashton (01952) 460330 ext 3
🏌 18 L 6422 yds SSS 71

WD–phone first WE/BH–M
££ £30
🚗 1 mile NE of Shifnal. M54 Junction 4, 2 miles
🏠 Pennink
🖥 www.shifnalgolfclub.co.uk

Shrewsbury (1891)
Condover, Shrewsbury, SY5 7BL
☎ (01743) 872977
🖶 (01743) 872977
📧 info@shrewsbury-golf-club.co.uk
📖 525 184(L) 70(J)
🏌 Mrs SM Kenny (01743) 872977
⛳ P Seal (01743) 872977
🏁 18 L 6178 yds Par 70 SSS 69
👥 H SOC
££ £28 (£34)
🚗 4 miles S of Shrewsbury
🖥 www.club-noticeboard.co.uk/shrewsbury

The Shropshire (1992)
Muxton, Telford, TF2 8PQ
☎ (01952) 677866/677800

Telford (1976)
Proprietary
Great Hay Drive, Sutton Heights, Telford, TF7 4DT
☎ (01952) 429977
🖶 (01952) 586602
📧 ibarklem@aol.com
📖 340
🏌 I Lucas (01952) 422960
⛳ George Boden (01952) 586052
🏁 18 L 6741 yds SSS 72
👥 H SOC
££ On application
🚗 4 miles SE of Telford, M54 J4, off A442
⊕ Driving range
🏠 John Harris
🖥 www.telford-golfclub.co.uk

Worfield (1991)
Worfield, Bridgnorth, WV15 5HE
☎ (01746) 716541
🖶 (01746) 716302
📧 enquiries@worfieldgolf.co.uk
📖 500
🏌 W Weaver (Gen Mgr) (01746) 716372
⛳ S Russell (01746) 716541
🏁 18 L 6660 yds SSS 72
👥 U SOC
££ £22 (£25)
🚗 7 miles W of Wolverhampton on A454
🏠 Williams
🖥 www.worfieldgolf.co.uk

Wrekin (1905)
Wellington, Telford, TF6 5BX
☎ (01952) 244032
🖶 (01952) 252906
📧 wrekingolfclub@lineone.net
📖 500 100(L) 90(J)
🏌 D Briscoe
⛳ K Housden (01952) 223101
🏁 18 L 5570 yds SSS 67

WD–U before 5pm –M after 5pm
SOC
££ £22 (£30)
🚗 Wellington, off B5061

Somerset

Bath (1880)
Sham Castle, North Road, Bath, BA2 6JG
☎ (01225) 463834
🖶 (01225) 331027
📧 enquiries@bathgolfclub.org.uk
📖 730
🏌 JM Galley (01225) 463834
⛳ P Hancox (01225) 466953
🏁 18 L 6442 yds Par 71 SSS 71
👥 H SOC WD–NA before 9.30 am WE
££ £38 (£42)
🚗 1½ miles SE of Bath, off A36. M4 J18 (A46)
⊕ Warm-up range
🏠 HS Colt
🖥 www.bathgolfclub.org.uk

Brean (1973)
Coast Road, Brean, Burnham-on-Sea, TA8 2QY
☎ (01278) 752111
📧 proshop@brean.com

Burnham & Berrow (1890)
St Christopher's Way, Burnham-on-Sea, TA8 2PE
☎ (01278) 785760
🖶 (01278) 795440
📧 secretary@burnhamandberrow.plus.com
📖 800
🏌 PE Ware (01278) 785760
⛳ M Crowther-Smith (01278) 785760
🏁 18 L 6616 yds Par 71 SSS 72
9 L 5819 yds Par 70 SSS 69
👥 I H SOC
££ 9: £15 (£18) 18: £48 (£60)
🚗 1 mile N of Burnham-on-Sea on B3140. M5 Junction 22
⊕ Dormy House
🏠 HS Colt
🖥 www.burnhamandberrowgolfclub.co.uk

Cannington (1993)
Pay and play
Cannington Centre for Land Based Studies, Bridgwater, TA5 2LS
☎ (01278) 655050
🖶 (01278) 655055
📖 280
🏌 R Macrow (Mgr)
⛳ R Macrow
🏁 9 L 6077 yds Par 68 SSS 70
👥 U exc Wed eve–restricted
££ 9: £9.50 (£12.50); 18: £14 (£18.50)
🚗 4 miles NW of Bridgwater on A39. M5 Junction 24
⊕ Driving range
🏠 Hawtree
🖥 www.bridgwater.ac.uk

Clevedon (1891)
Castle Road, Clevedon, BS21 7AA
☎ (01275) 874057
🖶 (01275) 341228
📧 secretary@clevedongolfclub.co.uk
📖 800
🏌 J Cunning (01275) 874057
⛳ R Scanlan (01275) 874704
🏁 18 L 6557 yds Par 72 SSS 72
👥 WD–U H exc Wed am WE/BH–U H (phone first) SOC–WD
££ £30 (£40)
🚗 Off Holly Lane, Walton, Clevedon. M5 Junction 20
🏠 JH Taylor
🖥 www.clevedongolfclub.co.uk

Enmore Park (1906)
Enmore, Bridgwater, TA5 2AN
☎ (01278) 672103 (Members)
🖶 (01278) 672101
📧 golfclub@enmore.fsnet.co.uk
📖 780
🏌 I Wallace (01278) 672100
⛳ N Wixon (01278) 672102
🏁 18 L 6411 yds SSS 71
👥 SOC–WD–H
££ £32 (£44)
🚗 3 miles W of Bridgwater, off Durleigh road. M5 Junctions 23/24
⊕ Full practice range 300 yds
🏠 Hawtree
🖥 www.enmore-park-gc.co.uk

Entry Hill (1985)
Public
Entry Hill, Bath, BA2 5NA
☎ (01225) 834248
🏌 J Sercombe
⛳ T Tapley
🏁 9 L 4206 yds SSS 61
👥 WD/WE–booking only
££ 9: £7.50; 18: £11.75
🚗 1 mile S of Bath city centre, off A367

Farrington (1992)
Proprietary
Marsh Lane, Farrington Gurney, Bristol, BS39 6TS
☎ (01761) 451596
📧 info@farringtongolfclub.net

Fosseway CC (1970)
Charlton Lane, Midsomer Norton, Radstock, BA3 4BD
☎ (01761) 412214

Frome (1994)
Proprietary
Critchill Manor, Frome, BA11 4LJ
☎ (01373) 453410
📧 fromegolfclub@yahoo.co.uk
📖 460
🏌 Mrs S Austin
⛳ Lawrence Wilkin
🏁 18 L 5527 yds Par 69 SSS 67
👥 U
££ £21 D–£25 (£24 D–£28)
🚗 1 mile from centre of Frome (easiest access from A361 Nunney

junction following signs back to
Frome)
⊕ Driving range; putting green;
practice bunker & pitching area.
Course can be played as 2 x 9 if
time limited
▤ www.fromegolfclub.fsnet.co.uk

Isle of Wedmore (1992)
*Lineage, Lascots Hill, Wedmore,
BS28 4QT*
☎ (01934) 712452
▭ (01934) 713696
✉ wedmoregolfclub@supanet.com
▥ 670
✍ AC Edwards (01934) 712222
◢ G Coombe (01934) 712452
➢ 18 L 6006 yds Par 70 SSS 69
⋈ U SOC–WD
££ £24 (£24)
⊷ ³/₄ mile N of Wedmore. M5
Junction 22
⌂ Terry Murray
▤ www.wedmoregolfclub.com

Kingweston (1983)
*12 Lowerside Road, Glastonbury, Somerset
BA6 9BH*
☎ (01458) 834086
▥ 200
✍ I Price
➢ 9 L 4809 yds SSS 65
⋈ M exc Wed & Sat 2–5pm–NA
££ NA
⊷ I mile SE of Butleigh. 2 miles SE of
Glastonbury

Lansdown (1894)
Lansdown, Bath, BA1 9BT
☎ (01225) 422138
▭ (01225) 339252
✉ admin@lansdowngolfclub.co.uk
▥ 750
✍ Mrs E Bacon
◢ T Mercer (01225) 420242
➢ 18 L 6428 yds SSS 70
⋈ H SOC
££ £24 (£30)
⊷ 2 miles NW of Bath, by
racecourse. M4 Junction 18, 6 miles
⌂ HS Colt
▤ www.lansdowngolfclub.co.uk

Long Sutton (1991)
Pay and play
Long Load, Langport, TA10 9JU
☎ (01458) 241017
▭ (01458) 241022
✉ reservations@longsuttongolf.com
▥ 700
✍ T Tulk
◢ A Hayes
➢ 18 L 6367 yds SSS 71
⋈ WD–U WE–booking required
SOC
££ £18 (£22)
⊷ 3 miles E of Langport
⊕ Floodlit driving range
⌂ Patrick Dawson
▤ www.longsuttongolf.com

The Mendip (1908)
Gurney Slade, Radstock, BA3 4UT
☎ (01749) 840570
▭ (01749) 841439
✉ secretary@mendipgolfclub.com
▥ 800
✍ J Scott
◢ A Marsh (01749) 840793
➢ 18 L 6383 yds SSS 71
⋈ WD–U WE–H SOC–WD
££ £27 (£38)
⊷ 3 miles N of Shepton Mallet (A37)
⌂ CK Cotton
▤ www.mendipgolfclub.com

Mendip Spring (1992)
Honeyhall Lane, Congresbury, BS49 5JT
☎ (01934) 853337/852322
▭ (01934) 853021
✉ info@mendipspringgolfclub.com
▥ 500
✍ A Melhuish
◢ J Blackburn, R Moss
➢ 18 L 6352 yds SSS 70
9 L 4784 yds SSS 66
⋈ U
££ 9: £9 (£9.50) 18: £26 (£35)
⊷ Congresbury. M5 Junction 21.
⊕ Driving range
⌂ Langholt
▤ www.mendipspring.co.uk

Minehead & West
Somerset (1882)
The Warren, Minehead, TA24 5SJ
☎ (01643) 702057
▭ (01643) 705095
✉ secretary.mwsgc@btconnect.com
▥ 604
✍ G Mason
◢ I Read (01643) 702057
➢ 18 L 6226 yds SSS 70
⋈ U after 9.30am SOC
££ £35 (£40) W–£130
⊷ E end of sea front
▤ www.minehead-golf-club.co.uk

Oake Manor (1993)
Oake, Taunton, TA4 1BA
☎ (01823) 461993

Orchardleigh (1996)
Frome, BA11 2PH
☎ (01373) 454200
▭ (01373) 454202
✉ info@orchardleighgolf.co.uk
▥ 500
✍ David Forrest (Gen Mgr)
◢ I Ridsdale
➢ 18 L 6824 yds Par 72 SSS 73
⋈ WD/BH–U WE–U after 11am SOC
££ £35 (£40)
⊷ 2 miles NW of Frome on A362. 12
miles S of Bath
⊕ Driving range and practice facilities
⌂ Brian Huggett
▤ www.orchardleighgolf.co.uk

Saltford (1904)
Golf Club Lane, Saltford, Bristol, BS31 3AA
☎ (01225) 873220

▭ (01225) 873525
▥ 650
✍ V Radnedge (01225) 873513
◢ D Millensted (01225) 872043
➢ 18 L 6225 yds SSS 70
⋈ WD–U SOC–Mon & Thurs
££ £26 (£33)
⊷ 7 miles SE of Bristol

Stockwood Vale (1991)
Public
*Stockwood Lane, Keynsham, Bristol,
BS31 2ER*
☎ (0117) 986 6505
✉ stockwoodvale@aol.com

Tall Pines (1990)
*Cooks Bridle Path, Downside, Backwell,
Bristol, BS48 3DJ*
☎ (01275) 472076
▭ (01275) 474869
▥ 500
✍ T Murray
◢ A Murray
➢ 18 L 6067 yds Par 70 SSS 70
⋈ U SOC
££ £20 (£20)
⊷ 8 miles SW of Bristol (A470/A38)
⌂ Terry Murray

Taunton & Pickeridge
(1892)
Corfe, Taunton, TA3 7BY
☎ (01823) 421876
▭ (01823) 421742
✉ admin@tauntongolf.co.uk
▥ 660
✍ MPD Walls (01823) 421537
◢ S Stevenson (01823) 421790
➢ 18 L 6056 yds Par 69 SSS 69
⋈ H SOC
££ £26 (£40)
⊷ 5 miles S of Taunton on B3170
⌂ Hawtree
▤ www.tauntongolf.co.uk

Taunton Vale (1991)
Proprietary
Creech Heathfield, Taunton, TA3 5EY
☎ (01823) 412220
▭ (01823) 413583
✉ tvgc@gotadsl.co.uk
▥ 700
✍ Mrs J Wyatt
◢ M Keitch (01823) 412880
➢ 18 L 6158 yds Par 70 SSS 70
9 L 2004 yds Par 64 SSS 60
⋈ U SOC
££ 9 hole: £10 (£12) 18 hole: £20
(£25).
⊷ 3 miles N of Taunton, off A361. M5
Junctions 24/25
⊕ Floodlit driving range; practice
chipping area & putting green
⌂ John Pyne
▤ www.tauntonvalegolf.co.uk

Tickenham (1994)
*Clevedon Road, Tickenham, Bristol,
BS21 6RY*
☎ (01275) 856626

✓　A Sutcliffe, S Jarrett, A Smith, F
Amey
▶　9 L 2000 yds Par 60 SSS 58
♙♙　U–phone first SOC
££　18 holes–£12 (£15)
⇔　2 miles E of M5 Junction 20 on
B3130, nr Nailsea
⊕　Floodlit driving range
♙　Andrew Sutcliffe
▤　www.tickenhamgolf.co.uk

Vivary　(1928)
Public
Vivary Park, Taunton, TA1 3JW
☎　**(01823) 289274**
(Clubhouse)

Wells　(1893)
East Horrington Road, Wells, BA5 3DS
☎　**(01749) 675005**
📠　(01749) 683170
✉　secretary@wellsgolfclub99
.freeserve.co.uk
📖　750
♙　Christine Searle (01749) 683171
✓　A Bishop (01749) 679059
▶　18 L 6053 yds SSS 69
♙♙　WD–U WE–H SOC–WD
££　£30 (£35)
⇔　1¹/₂ miles E of Wells, off Bath road
(B3139)
⊕　Floodlit driving range
▤　www.wellsgolfclub.co.uk

Weston-super-Mare
(1892)
*Uphill Road North, Weston-super-Mare,
BS23 4NQ*
☎　**(01934) 626968**
📠　(01934) 621360
✉　wsmgolfclub@eurotelbroadband
.com
📖　752
♙　Mrs K Drake (01934) 626968
✓　M La Band (01934) 633360
▶　18 L 6251 yds SSS 70
♙♙　H SOC
££　£36 D–£48
⇔　Weston-super-Mare, M5 J21
♙　T Dunn - redesigned A Mackenzie
▤　www.westonsupermaregolfclub
.com

Wheathill　(1993)
Wheathill, Somerton, TA11 7HG
☎　**(01963) 240667**
📠　(01963) 240230
✉　wheathill@wheathill.fsnet.co.uk
📖　600
♙　A England
✓　A England
▶　18 L 5362 yds SSS 66
8 hole Par 3 course
♙♙　U
££　£17 D–£25 (£22 D–£30)
⇔　3 miles W of Castle Cary on B3153
⊕　10 acre practice ground
♙　John Baine
▤　www.foremostonline.com/wheathill

Wincanton Golf Course
Proprietary
The Racecourse, Wincanton, BA9 8BJ
☎　**(01963) 34606**
📠　(01963) 34668
✉　wincanton@rht.net
📖　200
♙　Andrew England
✓　Andrew England
▶　9/18 L 6182 yds Par 70 SSS 69
♙♙　U SOC
££　9 holes £10 (£12)
⇔　A303 Wincanton
⊕　Practice ground
♙　Eagle Golf
▤　wincantonracecourse.co.uk

Windwhistle　(1932)
Cricket St Thomas, Chard, TA20 4DG
☎　**(01460) 30231**
✉　info@windwhistlegolf.co.uk

Worlebury　(1908)
*Monks Hill, Worlebury, Weston-super-
Mare, BS22 9SX*
☎　**(01934) 625789**
📠　(01934) 621935
✉　secretary@worleburygc.co.uk
📖　640
♙　MW Wake
✓　G Marks (01934) 418473
▶　18 L 5963 yds SSS 69
♙♙　H SOC–WD
££　£27.50 (£35)
⇔　2 miles NE of Weston, off A370
♙　H Vardon
▤　www.worleburygc.co.uk

Yeovil　(1907)
Sherborne Road, Yeovil, BA21 5BW
☎　**(01935) 422965**
📠　(01935) 411283
✉　office@yeovilgolfclub.com
📖　710 122(L) 101(J)
♙　M Betteridge (01935) 422965
✓　G Kite (01935) 473763
▶　18 L 6150 yds SSS 70
9 L 4905 yds SSS 65
♙♙　WD–U H WE/BH–H
(WD/WE–phone Pro) SOC
££　18: £25 (£30) Nov–Mar £35 (£45)
Apr–Oct 9: £20 (£20)
⇔　1 mile from Yeovil on A30 to
Sherborne
⊕　20-bay floodlit driving range open
7am-9pm WD, 7am-6pm WE
♙　Alison
▤　www.yeovilgolfclub.com

Staffordshire

Alsager G&CC　(1992)
*Audley Road, Alsager, Stoke-on-Trent,
ST7 2UR*
☎　**(01270) 875700**
📠　(01270) 882207
📖　660
♙　M Davenport
✓　R Brown
▶　18 L 6225 yds SSS 70

♙♙　WD–U before 5pm –M after 5pm
SOC
££　£12.50 (£15) with member
⇔　5 miles W of Crewe. M6 Junction
16
▤　www.alsagergolfclub.com

Aston Wood　(1994)
Blake Street, Sutton Coldfield, B74 4EU
☎　**(0121) 580 7803**
📠　(0121) 353 0354
✉　enquiries@astonwoodgolfclub
.co.uk
📖　850
♙　K Heathcote (0121) 580 7803
✓　S Smith (0121) 580 7801
▶　18 holes Par 71 SSS 71
♙♙　WD–SOC before 5pm WE–M
after 1pm
££　£22 (£33)
⇔　3 miles NE of Sutton Coldfield on
A4026. M6 Junc 7; M42 Junc 9
⊕　Driving range
♙　Alliss/Clarke
▤　www.astonwoodgolfclub.co.uk

Barlaston　(1987)
Meaford Road, Stone, ST15 8UX
☎　**(01782) 372867**
📠　(01782) 372867
✉　barlaston.gc@virgin.net
📖　650
♙　H Thompson (01782 372867)
✓　I Rogers (01782) 372795
▶　18 L 5800 yds SSS 68
♙♙　WD–U WE–NA before 10am
££　On application
⇔　¹/₂ mile S of Barlaston. M6 Junction
14/15
♙　P Aliss
▤　www.bgc.everplay.net

Beau Desert　(1921)
Hazel Slade, Cannock, WS12 0PJ
☎　**(01543) 422626/422773**
📠　(01543) 451137
✉　bdgc@btconnect.com
📖　650
♙　John Bradbury (01543) 422626
✓　Barrie Stevens (01543) 422492
▶　18 L 6310 yds Par 70 SSS 71
♙♙　WD–U WE–phone in advance
BH–NA SOC
££　£45 (£55)
⇔　4 miles NE of Cannock, off A460
⊕　Driving range
♙　WH Fowler
▤　www.bdgc.co.uk

Bloxwich　(1924)
136 Stafford Road, Bloxwich, WS3 3PQ
☎　**(01922) 476593**
📠　(01922) 493449
✉　secretary@bloxwichgolfclub.com
📖　700
♙　RJ Wormstone
✓　RJ Dance (01922) 476889
▶　18 L 6257 yds SSS 71
♙♙　WD–U WE–M SOC
££　£30 (£35)
⇔　N of Walsall on A34; 4m M6 J11
▤　www.bloxwichgolfclub.com

Branston G&CC (1975)
Burton Road, Branston, Burton-on-Trent, DE14 3DP
- ☎ **(01283) 528320**
- 🖳 (01283) 566984
- ✉ sales@branston-golf-club.co.uk
- 📖 800
- ✍ G Pyle (Golf Mgr)
- ✓ J Sture
- ⏵ 18 L 6697 yds Par 72 SSS 72
  9 L 1856 yds Par 30
- 👥 WD–U WE–M before noon SOC
- ££ £32 (£42)
- ♣ ¹/₂ mile S of Burton (A38)
- ⊕ Driving range
- ⌂ G Hamshall

Brocton Hall (1894)
Brocton, Stafford, ST17 0TH
- ☎ **(01785) 661901**
- 🖳 (01785) 661591
- ✉ secretary@broctonhall.com
- 📖 500
- ✍ JDS Duffy (01785) 661901
- ✓ N Bland (01785) 661485
- ⏵ 18 L 6095 yds SSS 69
- 👥 I H SOC
- ££ £38 (£45)
- ♣ 4 miles SE of Stafford, off A34
- ⌂ Harry Vardon
- 🖱 www.broctonhall.com

Burslem (1907)
Wood Farm, High Lane, Stoke-on-Trent, ST6 7JT
- ☎ **(01782) 837006**
- 📖 300
- ✍ A Porter (01782) 839645
- ⏵ 9 L 5274 yds SSS 66
- 👥 WD–U WE–NA
- ££ £10 D–£16
- ♣ Burslem 2 miles

Calderfields (1983)
Proprietary
Aldridge Road, Walsall, WS4 2JS
- ☎ **(01922) 646888 (Clubhouse)**
  (01922) 632243 (Bookings)
- 🖳 (01922) 640540
- ✉ calderfields@bigfoot.com
- 📖 750
- ✍ MR Andrews
- ✓ Cranfield Academy (01922) 613675
- ⏵ 18 L 6509 yds Par 73 SSS 71
- 👥 U SOC
- ££ £18 (£20) – under review
- ♣ 1 mile N of Walsall (A454). M6 J10
- ⊕ 27 bay floodlit driving range with Auto Tech golf tees; 18 hole putting green
- 🖱 www.calderfieldsgolf.com

Cannock Park (1993)
Public
Stafford Road, Cannock, WS11 2AL
- ☎ **(01543) 578850**
- 🖳 (01543) 578850
- ✉ seccpgc@yahoo.co.uk
- 📖 175
- ✍ CB Milne (01543) 571091
- ⏵ 18 L 5149 yds SSS 65
- 👥 U SOC–WD

- ££ £11.50 (£14.50)
- ♣ ¹/₂ mile N of Cannock on A34. M6 Junction 11, 2 miles
- ⌂ John Mainland
- 🖱 www.cpgc.freeserve.co.uk

The Chase (1999)
Pottal Pool Road, Penkridge, ST19 5RN
- ☎ **(01785) 712191**
- ✉ chase-sales@crowngolf.co.uk

The Craythorne (1972)
Craythorne Road, Rolleston on Dove, Burton upon Trent, DE13 0AZ
- ☎ **(01283) 564329**
- 🖳 (01283) 511908
- ✉ admin@craythorne.co.uk
- 📖 475
- ✍ AA Wright (Man Dir/Owner)
- ✓ S Hadfield (01283) 533745
- ⏵ 18 L 5602 yds Par 68 SSS 68
- 👥 WD–U SOC
- ££ £28 (£34)
- ♣ Stretton, 1¹/₂ miles N of Burton. A38/A5121 Junction
- ⊕ Floodlit driving range
- ⌂ A.A. Wright
- 🖱 www.craythorne.co.uk

Dartmouth (1910)
Vale Street, West Bromwich, B71 4DW
- ☎ **(0121) 588 2131**
- 🖳 (0121) 588 5746
- 📖 350
- ✍ CF Wade (0121) 532 4070
- ⏵ 9 L 6036 yds SSS 71
- 👥 WD–U WE–M after 12 SOC–Tues & Thurs
- ££ D–£25 (£17)
- ♣ 1 mile from W Bromwich, behind site of new estate. M5 J1, M6 J7
- 🖱 www.dartmouth-golf-club.co.uk

Denstone College (1991)
Denstone, Uttoxeter, ST14 5HN
- ☎ **(01889) 590484**
- 🖳 (01889) 590744
- ✉ moor.house.farm@farmline.com
- ✍ Ann Tweddle
- ✓ None
- ⏵ 9 L 4404 yds Par 64 SSS 62
- 👥 M SOC
- ££ £7
- ♣ Grounds of Denstone College. 6 miles N of Uttoxeter
- ⌂ MP Raisbeck
- 🖱 www.denstone.staffs.sch.uk

Drayton Park (1897)
Drayton Park, Tamworth, B78 3TN
- ☎ **(01827) 251139**
- 🖳 (01827) 284035
- ✉ admin@draytonparkgc.com
- 📖 650
- ✍ DO Winter
- ✓ MW Passmore (01827) 251478
- ⏵ 18 L 6473 yds SSS 71
- 👥 WD–H WE/BH–NA SOC–Tues & Thurs
- ££ £44 D–£44

- ♣ 2 miles S of Tamworth (A4091); M42 J9 or 10
- ⌂ James Braid
- 🖱 www.draytonparkgc.com

Druids Heath (1974)
Stonnall Road, Aldridge, WS9 8JZ
- ☎ **(01922) 455595**
- 🖳 (01922) 452887
- ✉ dhgcadmin@uku.co.uk
- 📖 539 80(L) 50(J)
- ✍ KI Taylor
- ✓ G Williams (01922) 459523
- ⏵ 18 L 6661 yds Par 72 SSS 73
- 👥 WD–U WE–NA before 2pm SOC–WD
- ££ £32 (£42)
- ♣ 6 miles NW of Sutton Coldfield, off A452
- 🖱 www.druidsheathgc.co.uk

Enville (1935)
Highgate Common, Enville, Stourbridge, DY7 5BN
- ☎ **(01384) 872074**
- 🖳 (01384) 873396
- ✉ secretary@envillegolfclub.com
- 📖 900
- ✍ JJ Bishop (Sec/Mgr) (01384) 872074
- ✓ S Power (01384) 872585
- ⏵ Highgate 18 L 6531 yds SSS 72
  Lodge 18 L 6290 yds SSS 70
- 👥 WD–U WE/BH–M H SOC
- ££ £35–£45
- ♣ 6 miles W of Stourbridge
- 🖱 www.envillegolfclub.com

Great Barr (1961)
Chapel Lane, Birmingham, B43 7BA
- ☎ **(0121) 358 4376**
- 🖳 (0121) 358 4376
- ✉ info@greatbarrgolfclub.co.uk
- 📖 600
- ✍ Mrs D Smith (0121) 358 4376
- ✓ R Spragg (0121) 357 5270
- ⏵ 18 L 6459 yds SSS 72
- 👥 WD–U WE–I (h'cap max 18) SOC
- ££ £32
- ♣ 6 miles NW of Birmingham. M6 Junction 7
- 🖱 www.greatbarrgolfclub.co.uk

Greenway Hall (1908)
Stockton Brook, Stoke-on-Trent, ST9 9LJ
- ☎ **(01782) 503158**
- 🖳 (01782) 504691
- ✉ jackbarker_greenwayhallgolfclub @hotmail.com
- 📖 250
- ✍ J Latham (Mgr)
- ⏵ 18 L 5676 yds SSS 67
- 👥 U SOC + Pay & Play
- ££ £10 (£15)
- ♣ 5 miles N of Stoke, off A53
- 🖱 www.jackbarker.com

Handsworth (1895)
11 Sunningdale Close, Handsworth Wood, Birmingham, B20 1NP
- ☎ **(0121) 554 3387**
- 🖳 (0121) 554 6144

For list of abbreviations and key to symbols see page 651

▪▪ info@handsworthgolfclub.net
□ 850
⚉ PS Hodnett (Hon)
/ L Bashford (0121) 523 3594
▶ 18 L 6267 yds SSS 70
⛹ WD–U WE/BH–M SOC
££ £35
∾ 3 miles NW of Birmingham. M5
Junction 1. M6 Junction 7

Himley Hall   (1980)
Pay and play
Himley Hall Park, Dudley, DY3 4DF
☏ **(01902) 895207**
□ (01902) 895207
▪▪ msgplt@aol.com
□ 63
⚉ B Sparrow (01902) 894973 Mobile:
(07702) 554229
/ Mark Sparrow (07951) 440777
▶ 9 L 3145 yds SSS 35
9 hole short course
⛹ WD–U WE/BH–restricted
££ 9: £8.50, 18: £12 all week
∾ Grounds of Himley Hall Park.
B4176, off A449
⊕ Practice area
☗ A & K Baker
≡ www.himleygolf.co.uk

Ingestre Park   (1977)
Ingestre, Stafford, ST18 0RE
☏ **(01889) 270061**
□ (01889) 271434
▪▪ manager@ingestregolf.co.uk
□ 740
⚉ D Warrilow (Mgr) (01889) 270845
/ D Scullion (01889) 270304
▶ 18 L 6352 yds SSS 71
⛹ WD–H before 3.30pm WE/BH–M
SOC–WD exc Wed
££ £30 D–£38
∾ 6 miles E of Stafford, off Tixall
Road. M6 Junctions 13/14
☗ Hawtree
≡ www.ingestregolf.com

Izaak Walton   (1993)
Cold Norton, Stone, ST15 0NS
☏ **(01785) 760900**
▪▪ secretary@izaakwaltongolfclub
.co.uk
□ 500
⚉ TT Tyler
/ CP Brunt (01785) 760808
▶ 18 L 6398 yds SSS 72
⛹ U SOC
££ £20 (£25 D–£30)
∾ 7 miles NW of Stafford on B5026.
M6 Junction 14
⊕ Driving range
≡ www.izaakwaltongolfclub.co.uk

Keele Golf Centre
(1973)
Pay and play
*Keele Road, Newcastle-under-Lyme,
ST5 5AB*
☏ **(01782) 627596**
□ (01782) 714555
⚉ GA Bytheway (01782) 619317
/ N Worrall (Mgr)

▶ 18 L 5822 metres SSS 70
⛹ U
££ £10 Mon–Thur, £12 Fri (£15)
∾ 2 miles W of Newcastle on A525,
opposite University. M6 Jct 15
⊕ Floodlit driving range; buggy hire
☗ Hawtree

Lakeside   (1969)
Rugeley Power Station, Rugeley, WS15 1PR
☏ **(01889) 575667**
□ (01889) 572146
□ 500
⚉ TA Yates
▶ 18 L 5686 yds Par 69 SSS 68
⛹ M SOC
∾ 2 miles SE of Rugeley on A513
≡ www.lakesidegolf.20m.com

Leek   (1892)
Birchall, Leek, ST13 5RE
☏ **(01538) 384779**
□ (01538) 384779
▪▪ enquiries@leekgolfclub.co.uk
□ 520 135(L) 65(J)
⚉ DT Brookhouse
/ Fred Fearn
▶ 18 L 6218 yds SSS 70
⛹ U H before 3pm –M after 3pm
SOC–Wed
££ £26 (£32)
∾ 1 mile S of Leek on A520
≡ www.leekgolfclub.co.uk

Little Aston   (1908)
*Roman Road, Streetly, Sutton Coldfield,
B74 3AN*
☏ **(0121) 353 2066**
□ (0121) 580 8387
▪▪ manager@littleastongolf.co.uk
□ 250
⚉ G Ridley (Mgr) (0121) 353 2942
/ Brian Rimmer (0121) 353 0330
▶ 18 L 6670 yds SSS 73
⛹ H WE–by prior arrangement
SOC–WD
££ £75 D–£95
∾ 4 miles NW of Sutton Coldfield, off
A454
⊕ Professional all-weather teaching
academy
☗ Harry Vardon
≡ www.littleastongolf.co.uk

Manor (Kingstone)
(1991)
Proprietary
Leese Hill, Kingstone, Uttoxeter, ST14 8QT
☏ **(01889) 563234**
□ (01889) 563234
▪▪ manorgc@btinternet.com
□ 300
⚉ A Foulds
/ Chris Miller
▶ 18 L 6019 yds Par 71 SSS 69
⛹ U–SOC (SOC WD)
££ £18 (£28)
∾ 4 miles W of Uttoxeter on A518
☗ A Foulds
≡ www.manorgolfclub.org.uk

Newcastle-under-Lyme
(1908)
*Whitmore Road, Newcastle-under-Lyme,
ST5 2QB*
☏ **(01782) 616583**
□ (01782) 617531
▪▪ info@newcastlegolfclub.co.uk
□ 575
⚉ Vicki Wiseman (Sec/Mgr)
(01782) 617006
/ A Salt (01782) 618526
▶ 18 L 6395 yds SSS 71
⛹ WD–U H WE/BH–M SOC
££ 18 holes £25; 36 holes £35
∾ 2 miles SW of Newcastle-under-
Lyme on A53
≡ www.newcastlegolfclub.co.uk

Onneley   (1968)
Onneley, Crewe, Cheshire, CW3 5QF
☏ **(01782) 750577**
▪▪ all@onneleygolf.co.uk
□ 410
⚉ P Ball (01782) 846759
/ Simon Arnold
▶ 18 L 5728 yds SSS 68
⛹ WD–U Sat/BH–M Sun–NA
SOC–by appointment
££ D–£20
∾ 8 miles W of Newcastle, off A525
☗ A Benson
≡ www.onneleygolf.co.uk

Oxley Park   (1913)
*Stafford Road, Bushbury, Wolverhampton,
WV10 6DE*
☏ **(01902) 425892**
▪▪ secretary@oxleyparkgolfclub.fsnet
.co.uk

Parkhall   (1989)
Public
*Hulme Road, Weston Coyney, Stoke-on-
Trent, ST3 5BH*
☏ **(01782) 599584**
□ (01782) 599584
⚉ M Robson
/ T Earl
▶ 18 L 2335 yds Par 54
⛹ WE–booking necessary SOC
££ On application
∾ 3 miles E of Stoke. Longton 1 mile

Penn   (1908)
*Penn Common, Wolverhampton,
WV4 5JN*
☏ **(01902) 341142**
□ (01902) 620504
▪▪ secretary@penn-golf.freeserve
.co.uk
□ 650
⚉ MH Jones
/ (01902) 330472
▶ 18 L 6492 yds SSS 72
⛹ WD–U WE–M SOC
££ £28. Nov–Feb £17
∾ 2 miles SW of Wolverhampton, off
A449

Perton Park   (1990)

Proprietary
Wrottesley Park Road, Perton,
Wolverhampton, WV6 7HL
☎ **(01902) 380103/380073**
🖥 (01902) 326219
📧 golf@swindonperton.fsbusiness
.co.uk
📖 300
🏌 Simon Edwin (Gen Mgr)
⟟ 18 L 6520 yds SSS 72
👥 U SOC
££ £16 D–£22 (£21 D–£27)
🚗 6 miles W of Wolverhampton, off
A454
⊕ Driving range
🖳 www.pertongolfclub.co.uk

Sandwell Park   (1895)

Birmingham Road, West Bromwich, B71 4JJ
☎ **(0121) 553 4637**
🖥 (0121) 525 1651
📧 secretary@sandwellparkgolfclub
.co.uk
📖 600
🏌 DA Paterson (0121) 553 4637
⟋ N Wylie (0121) 553 4384
⟟ 18 L 6468 yds Par 71 SSS 73
👥 WD–U WE–MH SOC–WD
££ £35 D–£50
🚗 West Bromwich/Birmingham
boundary. By M5 Junction 1
🏠 HS Colt
🖳 www.sandwellparkgolfclub.co.uk

Sedgley   (1992)

Pay and play
Sandyfields Road, Sedgley, Dudley,
DY3 3DL
☎ **(01902) 880503**
📧 info@sedgleygolf.co.uk
📖 150
🏌 JA Cox
⟋ G Mercer
⟟ 9 L 3150 yds SSS 71
👥 U
££ 9: £7.50 18: £10
🚗 ¹/₂ mile from Sedgley, off A463
between Dudley and
Wolverhampton
⊕ Driving range
🏠 WG Cox
🖳 www.sedgleygolf.co.uk

Seedy Mill   (1991)

Pay and play
Elmhurst, Lichfield, WS13 8HE
☎ **(01543) 417333**
📧 seedymill.sales@clubhaus.com

South Staffordshire   (1892)

Danescourt Road, Tettenhall,
Wolverhampton, WV6 9BQ
☎ **(01902) 751065**
🖥 (01902) 751159
📧 suelebeau@southstaffsgc.co.uk
📖 550
🏌 P Baker (Dir of Golf)
⟋ Shaun Ball
⟟ 18 L 6500 yds SSS 71
👥 WD–U WE/BH–M or by
arrangement SOC

££ £36
🚗 3 miles W of Wolverhampton, off
A41; 7 miles off M54 J3
⊕ Driving range (under construction)
🏠 Harry Vardon
🖳 www.southstaffordshiregolfclub
.co.uk

St Thomas's Priory   (1995)

Armitage Lane, Armitage, Rugeley,
WS15 1ED
☎ **(01543) 492096**
🖥 (01543) 492096
📧 rohanlonpro@acl.com
📖 450
🏌 RMR O'Hanlon
⟋ RMR O'Hanlon (01543) 492096
⟟ 18 L 5969 yds SSS 70
👥 SOC–WD/WE
££ £30 (£40) 2 for 1 except WE
🚗 1 mile SE of Rugeley on A513, opp
Ash Tree Inn
🏠 Paul Mulholland
🖳 www.st-thomass-golfclub.com

Stafford Castle   (1906)

Newport Road, Stafford, ST16 1BP
☎ **(01785) 223821**
🖥 (01785) 223821
📖 440
🏌 Mrs S Calvert
⟟ 9 L 6383 yds Par 71 SSS 70
👥 WD–U WE–after 1pm
££ £18 (£22)
🚗 ¹/₂ mile W of Stafford

Stone   (1896)

The Fillybrooks, Stone, ST15 0NB
☎ **(01785) 813103**
📧 stonegolfc@onetel.net
📖 314
🏌 PR Farley (01785) 284875
⟟ 9 L 6299 yds Par 71 SSS 70
👥 WD–U WE/BH–M SOC–WD
££ £20
🚗 ¹/₂ mile W of Stone on A34

Swindon   (1976)

Proprietary
Bridgnorth Road, Swindon, Dudley,
DY3 4PU
☎ **(01902) 897031**
🖥 (01902) 326219
📧 admin@swindongolfclub.co.uk
📖 500
🏌 Simon Edwin (Gen Mgr)
⟟ 18 L 6121 yds Par 71 SSS 70
👥 U SOC–WD/WE
££ £24+ D–£36+ (£32+ D–£48+)
🚗 5 miles SW of Wolverhampton on
B4176, Dudley to Bridgnorth road
⊕ Driving range
🖳 www.swindongolfclub.co.uk

Tamworth   (1976)

Public
Eagle Drive, Amington, Tamworth, B77 4EG
☎ **(01827) 709303**
🖥 (01827) 709304
📖 395
🏌 Trish Norton
⟋ W Alcock

⟟ 18 L 6488 yds SSS 72
👥 U SOC–WD WE
££ £14 (£15)
🚗 2¹/₂ miles E of Tamworth on
B5000. M42 J10, 3 miles
⊕ Practice range
🏠 Hawtree

Trentham   (1894)

14 Barlaston Old Road, Trentham, Stoke-
on-Trent, ST4 8HB
☎ **(01782) 658109**
🖥 (01782) 644024
📧 secretary@trenthamgolf.org
📖 420
🏌 RN Portas
⟋ S Wilson (01782) 657309
⟟ 18 L 6644 yds SSS 72
👥 WD–H WE/BH–M (or enquire
Sec) SOC–WD
££ £50 (£50)
🚗 3 miles S of Newcastle-under-Lyme
on A5305, off A34. M6 Junction 15
🖳 www.trenthamgolf.org

Trentham Park   (1936)

Trentham Park, Stoke-on-Trent, ST4 8AE
☎ **(01782) 642245**
📧 trevor.berrisford@barbox.net

Uttoxeter   (1970)

Wood Lane, Uttoxeter, ST14 8JR
☎ **(01889) 566552**
🖥 (01889) 566552
📧 admin@uttoxetergolfclub.com
📖 700
🏌 RW Harvey
⟋ AD McCandless (01889) 564884
⟟ 18 L 5801 yds Par 70 SSS 69
👥 WD–U WE–by arrangement SOC
££ D–£28 (£30)
🚗 Close to A50, 1/2 mile past
entrance to Uttoxeter racecourse
🖳 www.uttoxetergolfclub.com

Walsall   (1907)

Broadway, Walsall, WS1 3EY
☎ **(01922) 613512**
🖥 (01922) 616460
📧 secretary@walsallgolfclub.co.uk
📖 600
🏌 HJ Durkin (01922) 613512
⟋ R Lambert (01922) 626766
⟟ 18 L 6259 yds SSS 70
👥 WD–U WE–M SOC
££ £33
🚗 1 mile S of Walsall, off A34. M6
Junction 7
🏠 McKenzie
🖳 www.walsallgolfclub.co.uk

Wergs   (1990)

Pay and play
Keepers Lane, Tettenhall, WV6 8UA
☎ **(01902) 742225**
🖥 (01902) 844553
📧 wergs.golfclub@btinternet.com
📖 150
🏌 Mrs G Parsons
⟋ S Weir (07973) 899607
⟟ 18 L 6949 yds Par 72 SSS 73
👥 U

£€ D–£17 (£22)
🚗 3 miles W of Wolverhampton on A41
⊕ 20 acre practice area
🏠 CW Moseley
📧 www.wergs.com

Westwood   (1923)
Newcastle Road, Wallbridge, Leek, ST13 7AA
☎ **(01538) 398385**
📠 (01538) 382485
📧 carol@cpoveyo.wanadoo.co.uk
📖 800
🖊 Ms C Povey
✓ D Squire
🏳 18 L 6207 yds SSS 70
👥 U SOC–WD
£€ D–£30
🚗 W boundary of Leek on A53
📧 www.leekwestwoodgolfclub.co.uk

Whiston Hall   (1971)
Whiston, Cheadle, ST10 2HZ
☎ **(01538) 266260**
📠 (01538) 266820
📧 enq@whistonhall.com
📖 500
🖊 LC & RM Cliff (Mgr)
🏳 18 L 5742 yds SSS 69
👥 U SOC
£€ £10
🚗 8 miles NE of Stoke-on-Trent on A52, nr Alton Towers (3 miles away)
⊕ Hotel available for golfing breaks
🏠 T Cooper
📧 www.whistonhall.com

Whittington Heath (1886)
Tamworth Road, Lichfield, WS14 9PW
☎ **(01543) 432317 (Admin), (01543) 432212 (Steward)**
📠 (01543) 433962
📧 info@whittingtonheathgc.co.uk
📖 670
🖊 Mrs JA Burton
✓ AR Sadler (01543) 432261
🏳 18 L 6490 yds SSS 71
👥 WD–H or I WE/BH–M SOC–Wed & Thurs
£€ £40 D–£55
🚗 2½ miles E of Lichfield on Tamworth road (A51)
📧 www.whittingtonheathgc.co.uk

Wolstanton   (1904)
Dimsdale Old Hall, Hassam Parade, Wolstanton, Newcastle, ST5 9DR
☎ **(01782) 616995**
📠 (01782) 622413
📖 625
🖊 Mrs VJ Keenan (01782) 622413
✓ S Arnold (01782) 622718
🏳 18 L 5533 yds SSS 68
👥 WD–H WE–M SOC–WD
£€ £25
🚗 1½ miles NW of Newcastle (A34)

Suffolk

Aldeburgh   (1884)
Aldeburgh, IP15 5PE
☎ **(01728) 452890**
📠 (01728) 452937
📧 info@aldeburghgolfclub.co.uk
📖 879
🖊 GM Gadney
✓ K Preston (01728) 453309
🏳 18 L 6349 yds Par 68 SSS 71
9 L 2114 yds SSS 64
👥 H–2 ball play only SOC
£€ On application
🚗 6 miles E of A12 (A1094)
🏠 W Fernie/J Thompson
📧 www.aldeburghgolfclub.co.uk

Beccles   (1899)
The Common, Beccles, NR34 9BX
☎ **(01502) 712244**
📧 alan@ereira.wanadoo.co.uk
📖 145
🖊 A Ereira (01502) 715222 (07896) 08797
🏳 9 L 2696 yds SSS 68
👥 WD–U Sun–M SOC
£€ £5 (£10)
🚗 10 miles W of Lowestoft (A146)
📧 www.becclesgolfclub.co.uk

Brett Vale   (1992)
Proprietary
Noakes Road, Raydon, Ipswich, IP7 5LR
☎ **(01473) 310718**
📧 info@brettvalegolf.com
📖 500
🖊 JS Reid
✓ Paul Bate
🏳 18 L 5813 yds Par 70 SSS 67
👥 U–booking advisable. Soft spikes only. SOC–WD
£€ £22.50 (£28)
🚗 5 miles N of Colchester, off A12 (B1070), towards Hadleigh
⊕ Driving range. 3 x 3 Par 3 holes
🏠 Howard Swan
📧 www.brettvale.com

Bungay & Waveney Valley (1889)
Outney Common, Bungay, NR35 1DS
☎ **(01986) 892337**
📠 (01986) 892222
📖 673
🖊 JR Lunniss
✓ AR Collison
🏳 18 L 6050 yds Par 69 SSS 69
👥 WD–U WE–M SOC–WD
£€ £26 D–£32
🚗 N side of A143/A144 roundabout
⊕ Practice ground
🏠 James Braid

Bury St Edmunds   (1922)
Tut Hill, Bury St Edmunds, IP28 6LG
☎ **(01284) 755979**
📠 (01284) 763288
📧 info@burygolf.co.uk
📖 570(m) 180(L)

🖊 JF Taylor
✓ M Jillings (01284) 755978
🏳 18 L 6675 yds Par 72 SSS 72
9 L 2217 yds Par 31 SSS 31 (Pay & Play)
👥 18 WD–U SOC–WD 9 U
£€ 9: £13 (£16) 18: D–£35
🚗 2 miles W of Bury St Edmunds on B1106, off A14
🏠 Ted Ray
📧 www.club-noticeboard.co.uk /burystedmunds

Cretingham   (1984)
Grove Farm, Cretingham, Woodbridge, IP13 7BA
☎ **(01728) 685275**
📠 (01728) 685488
📖 400
🖊 Mrs K Jackson
✓ N Jackson
🏳 18 L 5278 yds
9 L 4969 yds Par 34
9 hole short course
👥 U SOC
£€ 18: £18 D–£24 (+BH £20 D–£26)
🚗 2 miles SE of Earl Soham. 11 miles N of Ipswich
⊕ Practice range; putting green
🏠 J Austin

Diss   (1903)
Stuston Common, Diss, IP21 4AA
☎ **(01379) 641025**
📠 (01379) 644586
📧 sec.dissgolf@virgin.net
📖 700
🖊 Chris Wellstead (01379) 641025
✓ Nigel Taylor (01379) 644399
🏳 18 L 6206 yds Par 70 SSS 70
👥 WD–U WE–phone first (SOC)
£€ £28 D–£36
🚗 1 mile SE of Diss, off A140, on B1077
⊕ Driving range 1 mile E of clubhouse on A143/A140 junction
🏠 Michael Pinner (extension to 18 holes)
📧 www.club-noticeboard.co.uk

Felixstowe Ferry   (1880)
Ferry Road, Felixstowe, ID11 9RY
☎ **(01394) 283060**
📠 (01394) 273679
📧 secretary@felixstowegolf.co.uk
📖 1000
🖊 R Tibbs (01394) 286834
✓ I Macpherson (01394) 283975
🏳 18 L 6308 yds SSS 70
9 L 2986 yds Par 35
👥 WD–H after 9am WE–H after 2.30pm SOC. 9 hole course–U
£€ 9: £10 D–£12.50 18: £25 D–£35 (£40)
🚗 2 miles NE of Felixstowe, towards Ferry
🏠 Henry Cotton (1947)
📧 www.felixstowegolf.co.uk

Flempton   (1895)
Bury St Edmunds, IP28 6EQ
☎ **(01284) 728291**

flemptongolfclub@freebie.net
260
MS Clark
C Aldred
9 L 6240 yds Par 70 SSS 70
WD–H WE/BH–H by prior arrangement
D–£30 (£30)
4 miles NW of Bury St Edmunds on A1101
JH Taylor

Fynn Valley (1991)
Proprietary
Witnesham, Ipswich, IP6 9JA
(01473) 785267
(01473) 785632
enquiries@fynn-valley.co.uk
650
AR Tyrrell (01473) 785267
P Wilby (01473) 785463
18 L 6371 yds Par 70 SSS 71
9 hole Par 3 course
U exc Sun am SOC
£26 (£32)
2 miles N of Ipswich on B1077
Driving range; restaurant; conference facilities
Antonio Primavera
www.fynn-valley.co.uk

Halesworth (1990)
Bramfield Road, Halesworth, IP19 9XA
(01986) 875567
(01986) 874565
info@halesworthgc.co.uk
400
D Cotton (Mgr)
S Harrison
18 L 6506 yds SSS 72
9 L 2280 yds SSS 33
U
9: £5 18: £18 D–£22 (£25)
1 mile S of Halesworth, off A144
Floodlit driving range
www.club-noticeboard.co.uk

Haverhill (1974)
Coupals Road, Haverhill, CB9 7UW
(01440) 761951
(01440) 761951
haverhillgolf@coupalsroad.fsnet.co.uk
700
Mrs L Farrant, D Renyard (Mgr)
N Duc (01440) 712628
18 L 5956 yds SSS 70
U–phone Pro SOC–WD
£25 (£35)
1 mile E of Haverhill, off A1107
Lawrie/Pilgrem
www.club-noticeboard.co.uk

Hintlesham (1991)
Hintlesham, Ipswich, IP8 3JG
(01473) 652761
(01473) 652750
office@hintleshamgolfclub.com
425
T Sunderland (Dir)
A Spink
18 L 6580 yds SSS 72

WD–U WE SOC
£36 (£46)
4 miles W of Ipswich on A1071
Hawtree
www.hintleshamgolfclub.com

Ipswich (Purdis Heath) (1895)
Purdis Heath, Bucklesham Road, Ipswich, IP3 8UQ
(01473) 727474 (F&B)
(01473) 715236
neill@ipswichgolfclub.com
740
NM Ellice (01473) 728941
SJ Whymark (01473) 724017
18 L 6439 yds Par 71 SSS 71
9 L 1930 yds Par 31
18 hole: H SOC 9 hole: U
9: D–£10 (£12.50) 18: £35 (£40) (D–£45 D–£50)
3 miles E of Ipswich
James Braid
www.ipswichgolfclub.com

Links (Newmarket) (1902)
Cambridge Road, Newmarket, CB8 0TG
(01638) 663000
(01638) 661476
secretary@linksgc.fsbusiness.co.uk
750
ML Hartley
J Sharkey (01638) 662395
18 L 6558 yds SSS 72
H exc Sun–M before 11.30am SOC
£26 D–£34 (£30 D–£38) (2006)
1 mile SW of Newmarket
www.club-noticeboard.co.uk/newmarket

Newton Green (1907)
Newton Green, Sudbury, CO10 0QN
(01787) 377217
(01787) 377549
info@newtongreengolfclub.co.uk
550
Mrs C List
T Cooper (01787) 313215
18 L 5893 yds SSS 69
WD WE SOC
£23 (£27)
4 miles S of Sudbury on A134
www.newtongolfclub.co.uk

Rookery Park (1891)
Beccles Road, Carlton Colville, Lowestoft, NR33 8HJ
(01502) 509190
(01502) 509191
office@rookeryparkgolfclub.co.uk
860
RF Jones
M Elsworthy (01502) 515103
18 L 6714 yds Par 72 SSS 72
9 hole Par 3 course
WD–U Sat/BH–after 11am Sun–NA SOC H
£29.50 D–£35 (£35 D–£41 – inc BH)
3 miles W of Lowestoft (A146)
Par 3 9-hole course; driving range with teaching facilities

CD Lawrie
www.club-noticeboard.co.uk

Royal Worlington & Newmarket (1893)
Golf Links Road, Worlington, Bury St Edmunds, IP28 8SD
(01638) 712216 (Clubhouse)
(01638) 717787
325
S Ballentine (01638) 717787
S Barker (01638) 715224
9 L 6246 yds SSS 70
I or H–phone first (2 ball or foursomes only) WE–NA
D–£55. After 2pm–£40
6 miles NE of Newmarket, off A11
Tom Dunn
www.royalworlington.co.uk

Rushmere (1927)
Rushmere Heath, Ipswich, IP4 5QQ
(01473) 725648
(01473) 273852
rushmeregolfclub@btconnect.com
770
RWG Tawell (01473) 725648
K Vince (01473) 728076
18 L 6262 yds SSS 70
WD–H WE/BH–H after 2.30pm
£38
3 miles E of Ipswich, off Woodbridge road (A1214)
David Williams (bunkers 1999)
www.club-noticeboard.co.uk/rushmere

Seckford (1991)
Seckford Hall Road, Great Bealings, Woodbridge, IP13 6NT
(01394) 388000
(01394) 382818
info@seckfordgolf.co.uk
400
G Cook
S Jay
18 L 4752 yds Par 66 SSS 63
U–booking necessary SOC WD WE after 12
Summer: £22 (£30) Winter: Please apply
SW of Woodbridge, off A12
Driving range, practice green, practice bunker
J Johnson
www.seckfordgolf.co.uk

Southwold (1884)
The Common, Southwold, IP18 6TB
(01502) 723234
380
PJ Obern (01502) 723248
B Allen (01502) 723790
9 L 6050 yds Par 70 SSS 69
U (subject to fixtures) SOC
£26 (£28) £15 after 2.30 summer/ 12.30 winter
35 miles NE of Ipswich
J Braid

Stoke-by-Nayland   (1972)
Keepers Lane, Leavenheath, Colchester, CO6 4PZ
- ☎ **(01206) 262836**
- 🖴 (01206) 263356
- 🖂 info@golf-club.co.uk
- 🎏 1400
- ✍ PG Barfield (01206) 265815
- ✓ K Lovelock (01206) 262769
- ⊳ Gainsborough 18 L 6498 yds SSS 71
     Constable 18 L 6544 yds SSS 71
- 👥 WD–U WE/BH–H after 12 noon SOC
- ££ £28.50 (£38.50)
- 🚗 Off A134 Colchester-Sudbury road on B1068
- ⊕ Driving range
- 🖳 www.stokebynaylandclub.co.uk

Stowmarket   (1962)
Lower Road, Onehouse, Stowmarket, IP14 3DA
- ☎ **(01449) 736473**

The Swallow Suffolk Hotel G&CC   (1974)
Fornham St Genevieve, Bury St Edmunds, IP28 6JQ
- ☎ **(01284) 706777**
- 🖴 (01284) 706721
- 🖂 swallow.suffolk@swallowhotels.com
- 🎏 652
- ✍ P Thorpe
- ✓ S Hall
- ⊳ 18 L 6376 yds SSS 71
- 👥 U SOC WD WE
- ££ £32 (£37)
- 🚗 2 miles NW of Bury St Edmunds (A14), off B1106
- 🖳 www.swallowhotels.com

Thorpeness Hotel & Golf Course   (1923)
Thorpeness, Leiston, IP16 4NH
- ☎ **(01728) 452176**
- 🖴 (01728) 453868
- 🖂 charlie@thorpeness.co.uk
- 🎏 700
- ✍ Charlie Damonsing (01728) 452176
- ✓ F Hill (01728) 454926
- ⊳ 18 L 6281 yds SSS 71
- 👥 H
- ££ £37 (£42)
- 🚗 2 miles N of Aldeburgh
- ⊕ Buggies available for hire
- 🏛 James Braid
- 🖳 www.thorpeness.co.uk

Ufford Park   (1992)
Yarmouth Road, Ufford, Woodbridge, IP12 1QW
- ☎ **(01394) 382836**
- 🖴 (01394) 383582
- 🖂 uffordparkhotelgolf@tiscali.co.uk
- 🎏 400
- ✍ Ray Baines
- ✓ S Robertson (01394) 383480
- ⊳ 18 L 6312 yds SSS 71
- 👥 U H SOC

- ££ £30 (£40)
- 🚗 2 miles N of Woodbridge, off A12
- ⊕ Golf Academy; 32 bay 2-storey driving range
- 🏛 P Pilgrim
- 🖳 www.uffordpark.co.uk

Waldringfield   (1983)
Newbourne Road, Waldringfield, Woodbridge, IP12 4PT
- ☎ **(01473) 736768**
- 🖴 (01473) 736793
- 🎏 520
- ✍ Pat Whitham
- ✓ T Huffer (01473) 736417
- ⊳ 18 L 6141 yds SSS 69
- 👥 WD–U WE/BH–M before noon SOC–WD
- ££ £24 (£28)
- 🚗 3 miles E of Ipswich, off A12
- 🏛 P Pilgrem

Woodbridge   (1893)
Bromeswell Heath, Woodbridge, IP12 2PF
- ☎ **(01394) 382038**
- 🖴 (01394) 382392
- 🖂 woodbridgegc@anglianet.co.uk
- 🎏 925
- ✍ A Theunissen
- ✓ C Elliott (01394) 383213
- ⊳ 18 L 6299 yds Par 70 SSS 71
     9 L 6382 yds SSS 70
- 👥 WD–H WE/BH–M SOC
- ££ 9: D–£18. 18: D–£42
- 🚗 2 miles E of Woodbridge on A1152 towards Orford
- 🏛 F Hawtree
- 🖳 www.woodbridgegolfclub.co.uk

Surrey

Abbey Moor   (1991)
Pay and play
Green Lane, Addlestone, KT15 2XU
- ☎ **(01932) 570741/570765**
- 🖴 (01932) 561313
- 🎏 300
- ✍ M Gyues (01932) 561313
- ✓ R Wiltshire (01932) 570741
- ⊳ 9 L 5142 yds Par 68 SSS 65
- 👥 U
- ££ £11 (£12.50)
- 🚗 Nr M25 Junction 11, off A318
- 🏛 D Walker

The Addington   (1913)
Proprietary
205 Shirley Church Road, Croydon, CR0 5AB
- ☎ **(020) 8777 1055**
- 🖴 (020) 8777 6661
- 🖂 secretary@addingtongolf.com
- 🎏 restricted
- ✍ Oliver Peel
- ⊳ 18 L 6338 yds SSS 71
- 👥 SOC–WD WE–after 10.30 am
- ££ £50 (£70+BH)
- 🚗 E Croydon 2½ miles
- ⊕ Practice hole, par 4
- 🏛 JF Abercromby
- 🖳 www.addingtongolf.com

Addington Court   (1931)
Pay and play
Featherbed Lane, Addington, Croydon, CR0 9AA
- ☎ **(020) 8657 0281 (Bookings)**
- 🖂 addington@americangolf.uk.com

Addington Palace   (1930)
Addington Park, Gravel Hill, Addington, CR0 5BB
- ☎ **(020) 8654 3061**
- 🖴 (020) 8655 3632
- 🖂 johnb@addingtonpalacegolf.co.uk
- 🎏 600
- ✍ JD Bowen
- ✓ R Williams (020) 8654 1786
- ⊳ 18 L 6373 yds Par 71 SSS 70
- 👥 WD–M WD–U SOC
- ££ £40 D–£45
- 🚗 2 miles E of Croydon Station
- 🏛 JH Taylor
- 🖳 www.addingtonpalacegolf.co.uk

Banstead Downs   (1890)
Burdon Lane, Belmont, Sutton, SM2 7DD
- ☎ **(020) 8642 2284**
- 🖴 (020) 8642 5252
- 🖂 secretary@bansteaddowns.com
- 🎏 700
- ✍ Mrs KS Cote
- ✓ I Golding (020) 8642 6884
- ⊳ 18 L 6192 yds SSS 69
- 👥 WD–H M,T,W,T/BH–M SOC–Thurs
- ££ £40 am, £30 pm
- 🚗 6 miles north of M25 J8
- 🏛 JH Braid
- 🖳 www.bansteaddowns.com

Barrow Hills   (1970)
Longcross, Chertsey, KT16 0DS
- ☎ **(01344) 635770**
- 🎏 300
- ✍ R Hammond (01483) 234807
- ⊳ 18 L 3090 yds SSS 53
- 👥 M
- ££ On application
- 🚗 4 miles W of Chertsey

Betchworth Park   (1911)
Reigate Road, Dorking, RH4 1NZ
- ☎ **(01306) 882052**
- 🖴 (01306) 877462
- 🖂 manager@betchworthparkgc.co.uk
- 🎏 560
- ✍ John Holton (Sec/Mgr)
- ✓ Andy Tocher (01306) 884334
- ⊳ 18 L 6325 yds Par 69 SSS 70
- 👥 WD exc Tues am WE–NA exc Sun pm SOC–Mon & Thurs
- ££ £40 (£50); £22 (£30) (after 4pm)
- 🚗 1 mile E of Dorking on A25; Jcts 8 & 9 M25
- ⊕ Large practice area
- 🏛 HS Colt
- 🖳 www.betchworthparkgc.co.uk

Bletchingley   (1993)
Proprietary
Church Lane, Bletchingley, RH1 4LP
- ☎ **(01883) 744666**

📞 (01883) 744284
📠 info@bletchingleygolf.co.uk
📖 500
🏌 R Borer (Mgr)
⛳ A Dyer (01883) 744848
⛳ 18 L 6513 yds Par 72 SSS 71
👥 WD–U WE after 12 noon
££ £32 (£45)
🚗 1 mile S of M25 Junction 6 on A25
💻 www.bletchingleygolf.co.uk

Bowenhurst Golf Centre
Mill Lane, Crondall, Farnham, GU10 5RP
📞 **(01252) 851695**
📠 (01252) 852225
🏌 GL Corbey (01252) 851695
⛳ Alastair Hardaway (01252) 851344
⛳ 9 L 2023/4046 yds Par 62 SSS 63
👥 U SOC WD
££ 9: £10 (£12) 18: £14 (£16.50). WD reduced fees for Snr/Jnr
🚗 2 miles SW of Farnham on A287. M3 Jct 5 (4 miles)
⊕ 20 bay floodlit driving range open 8-10pm
🏛 G Finn, N Finn

Bramley (1913)
Bramley, Guildford, GU5 0AL
📞 **(01483) 892696**
📠 (01483) 894673
📧 secretary@bramleygolfclub.co.uk
📖 775
🏌 Gary Peddie (Gen Mgr) (01483) 892696
⛳ G Peddie (01483) 893685
⛳ 18 L 5930 yds SSS 69
👥 WD–U WE–M SOC–WD
££ £44
🚗 3 miles S of Guildford on A281
⊕ Driving range - members and green fees only
🏛 Mayo/Braid
💻 www.bramleygolfclub.co.uk

Broadwater Park
Guildford Road, Farncombe, Godalming, GU7 3BU
📞 **(01483) 429955**
📖 126
🏌 MJ Winwright (Dir)
⛳ KD Milton
⛳ 9 L 1301 yds Par 27
👥 U
££ £5.25 (£6)
🚗 1 mile SE of Godalming (A3100)
⊕ 16-bay floodlit driving range
🏛 KD Milton

Burhill (1907)
Burwood Road, Walton-on-Thames, KT12 4BL
📞 **(01932) 227345**
📠 (01932) 267159
📧 info@burhillgolf-club.co.uk
📖 1100
🏌 D Cook (Gen Mgr)
⛳ I Partington (01932) 221729
⛳ Old 18 L 6479 yds SSS 71
New 18 L 6597 yds SSS 71
👥 WD–H WE/BH–M
££ On application

🚗 Between Walton-on-Thames and Cobham, off Burwood Road
⊕ Driving range
🏛 Willie Park/Gidman
💻 www.burhillgolf-club.co.uk

Camberley Heath (1912)
Golf Drive, Camberley, GU15 1JG
📞 **(01276) 23258**
📠 (01276) 692505
📧 info@camberleyheathgolfclub.co.uk
📖 765
🏌 C Kennedy
⛳ G Ralph (01276) 27905
⛳ 18 L 6351 yds SSS 71
👥 WD–H WE–M SOC H
££ £57 (£74)
🚗 1½ miles S of Camberley on A325
🏛 HS Colt
💻 www.camberleyheathgolfclub.co.uk

Central London Golf Centre (1992)
Public
Burntwood Lane, Wandsworth, London, SW17 0AT
📞 **(020) 8871 2468**
📠 (020) 8874 7447
📖 200
🏌 J Robson
⛳ J Robson
⛳ 9 L 4658 yds SSS 62
👥 U SOC
££ £9 (£11)
🚗 Off Burntwood Lane SW17
⊕ Driving range
🏛 Patrick Tallack
💻 www.clgc.co.uk

Chessington Golf Centre (1983)
Pay and play
Garrison Lane, Chessington, KT9 2LW
📞 **(020) 8391 0948**
📠 (020) 8397 2068
📧 info@chessingtongolf.co.uk
📖 85
🏌 M Bedford
⛳ M Janes
⛳ 9 L 1679 yds Par 60 SSS 55
👥 U
££ £9 (£11)
🚗 Off A243, opp Chessington South Station. M25 Junction 9
⊕ Driving range (floodlit)
🏛 Patrick Tullach
💻 www.chessingtongolf.co.uk

Chiddingfold (1994)
Petworth Road, Chiddingfold, GU8 4SL
📞 **(01428) 685888**

Chipstead (1906)
How Lane, Chipstead, Coulsdon, CR5 3LN
📞 **(01737) 555781**
📠 (01737) 555404
📧 office@chipsteadgolf.co.uk
📖 600
🏌 Mrs SA Wallace (Admin) (01737) 555781
⛳ G Torbett (Golf Dir) (01737) 554939

⛳ 18 L 5450 yds SSS 67
👥 WD–U WE/BH–M
££ £30. After 4pm–£20
🚗 M25 Junction 8 (A217)
💻 www.chipsteadgolf.co.uk

Chobham (1994)
Chobham Road, Knaphill, Woking, GU21 2TZ
📞 **(01276) 855584**
📠 (01276) 855663
📧 info@chobhamgolfclub.co.uk
📖 750
🏌 Pam Reade-Hill
⛳ T Coombes (01276) 855748
⛳ 18 L 5959 yds Par 69 SSS 69
👥 M H–restricted SOC
££ £44
🚗 3 miles E of M3 Junction 3 between Chobham and Knaphill
🏛 Alliss/Clark
💻 www.chobhamgolfclub.co.uk

Clandon Regis (1994)
Epsom Road, West Clandon, GU4 7TT
📞 **(01483) 224888**
📠 (01483) 211781
📧 office@clandonregis-golfclub.co.uk
📖 650
🏌 Paul Napier (Gen Mgr)
⛳ S Lloyd (01483) 223922
⛳ 18 L 6485 yds Par 72 SSS 71
👥 WD–U WE–NA before 10.30am SOC–WD
££ £34 (£44)
🚗 3 miles E of Guildford on A246
⊕ Practice area; chipping area; indoor nets
🏛 David Williams
💻 www.clandonregis-golfclub.co.uk

Coombe Hill (1911)
Golf Club Drive, Coombe Lane West, Kingston, KT2 7DF
📞 **(0208) 336 7600**
📠 (0208) 336 7601
📧 thesecretary@chgc.net
📖 527
🏌 DR Crombie
⛳ A Dunn (0208) 336 7615
⛳ 18 L 6293 yds SSS 71
👥 WD–I or H WE–NA SOC
££ £80 D–£100
🚗 1 mile W of New Malden on A238
🏛 JF Abercromby
💻 www.coombehillgolfclub.com

Coombe Wood (1904)
George Road, Kingston Hill, Kingston-upon-Thames, KT2 7NS
📞 **(020) 8942 0388 (Clubhouse)**
📠 (020) 8942 5665
📧 info@coombewoodgolf.com
📖 600
🏌 G McKay (020) 8942 0388
⛳ P Wright (020) 8942 6764
⛳ 18 L 5312 yds SSS 65
👥 WD–U WE–NA before 2.30pm SOC–WD
££ £30 (£35)
🚗 1 mile E of Kingston-upon-Thames, off A3 at Robin Hood roundabout or Coombe junction

🏠 Williamson
🖳 www.coombewoodgolf.com

Coulsdon Manor   (1937)
Pay and play
Coulsdon Court Road, Old Coulsdon,
Croydon, CR5 2LL
☎ (020) 8660 6083
🖳 (020) 8668 3118
📖 80
🏌 A Oxby (020) 8668 0414
⚬ Matt Asbury (020) 8660 6083
🏴 18 L 6037 yds SSS 70
👥 U
£€ £17 (£22)
🚗 5 miles S of Croydon on B2030.
   M25 Junction 7
🏠 HS Colt
🖳 www.swallowhotels.com

Cranfield Golf at Sandown
(1970)
Public
More Lane, Esher, KT10 8AN
☎ (01372) 468093
🖳 (01372) 469260
🏌 P Johnstone (Mgr)
⚬ J Skinner (01372) 461282
🏴 9 L 5658 yds SSS 67
   9 hole Par 3 course
👥 U–closed on race days
£€ £8 (£10)
🚗 Sandown Park Racecourse
⊕ 33 bay floodlit driving range
🏠 John Jacobs
🖳 www.sandown.co.uk

The Cranleigh   (1985)
Barhatch Lane, Cranleigh, GU6 7NG
☎ (01483) 268855
🖳 (01483) 267251
✉ clubshop@cranleighgolfandleisure
   .co.uk
📖 650
🏌 MG Kateley
⚬ T Longmuir (01483) 277188
🏴 18 L 5648 yds SSS 67
👥 WD–U WE/BH subject to
   availability SOC–WD and WE after
   11.30am
£€ £30 D–£38 (£33)
🚗 1 mile from Cranleigh, off A281
⊕ Driving range
🖳 www.cranleighgolfandleisure.co.uk

Croham Hurst   (1911)
Croham Road, South Croydon, CR2 7HJ
☎ (020) 8657 5581
🖳 (020) 8657 3229
✉ secretary@chgc.co.uk
📖 515 110(L) 50(J)
🏌 M Paget
⚬ M Paget (020) 8657 7705
🏴 18 L 6373 yds SSS 70
👥 WD–I WE/BH–M
£€ £50
🚗 1 mile from S Croydon. M25
   Junction 6-A22-B270-B269
🏠 Braid/Hawtree
🖳 www.chgc.co.uk

Cuddington   (1929)
Banstead Road, Banstead, SM7 1RD
☎ (020) 8393 0952
🖳 (020) 8786 7025
✉ ds@cuddingtongc.co/uk
📖 760
🏌 S Davis (020) 8393 0952
⚬ M Warner (020) 8393 5850
🏴 18 L 6614 yds SSS 71
👥 WD–I WE–M H
£€ £45 (£55)
🚗 Nr Banstead Station
🏠 HS Colt
🖳 www.cuddingtongc.co.uk

Dorking   (1897)
Deepdene Avenue, Chart Park, Dorking,
RH5 4BX
☎ (01306) 886917
🖳 (01306) 886917
✉ info@dorkinggolfclub.co.uk
📖 360
🏌 A Smeal (Mgr)
⚬ A Smeal
🏴 9 L 5163 yds SSS 65
👥 WD–U WE/BH–M SOC–WD
£€ £15 (£20)
🚗 1 mile S of Dorking on A24
🏠 James Braid
🖳 www.dorkinggolfclub.co.uk

Drift   (1975)
Proprietary
The Drift, East Horsley, KT24 5HD
☎ (01483) 284641
🖳 (01483) 284642
✉ info@driftgolfclub.com
📖 700
🏌 L Greasley (Sec/Mgr)
⚬ (01483) 284772
🏴 18 L 6425 yds SSS 72
👥 WD–U WE–U after 12.00 SOC
£€ £39 (£49)
🚗 2 miles off A3 (B2039). M25
   Junction 10
⊕ Grass driving range in season; Lee
   Johnson Golf Academy
🏠 Sir Henry Cotton & Robert
   Sandow
🖳 www.driftgolfclub.com

Dulwich & Sydenham Hill
(1894)
Grange Lane, College Road, London,
SE21 7LH
☎ (020) 869 33961
🖳 (020) 869 32481
✉ secretary@dulwichgolf.co.uk
📖 710
🏌 MP Hickson
⚬ D Baillie (020) 869 38491
🏴 18 L 6079 yds SSS 69
👥 WD–UH SOC by arrangement
   WE/BH–M before 2pm U after
   2pm
£€ £40
🚗 Half mile from Dulwich College off
   A205
🏠 HS Colt
🖳 www.dulwichgolf.co.uk

Effingham   (1927)
Guildford Road, Effingham, KT24 5PZ
☎ (01372) 452203
🖳 (01372) 459959
✉ secretary@effinghamgolfclub.com
📖 710
🏌 Robin Easton
⚬ Steve Hoatson (01372) 452606
🏴 18 L 6524 yds Par 72 SSS 71
👥 WD–H WE/BH–M
£€ On application
🚗 8 miles E of Guildford on A246.
   M25 J9 (clockwise) or J10 (anti-
   clockwise)
⊕ Practice facilities available
🏠 HS Colt
🖳 www.effinghamgolfclub.com

Epsom   (1889)
Longdown Lane South, Epsom Downs,
Epsom, KT17 4JR
☎ (01372) 721666
🖳 (01372) 817183
✉ secretary@epsomgolfclub.co.uk
📖 650
🏌 D Bowles
⚬ R Goudie (01372) 741867
🏴 18 L 5656 yds SSS 68
👥 WD–U exc Tues am WE/BH–NA
   before noon SOC
£€ £24 (£30)
🚗 ³/₄ mile NE of Epsom Racecourse
🏠 The Masters of Epsom College
🖳 www.epsomgolfclub.co.uk

Farnham   (1896)
The Sands, Farnham, GU10 1PX
☎ (01252) 783163
🖳 (01252) 781185
✉ info@farnhamgolfclub.tiscali.co.uk
📖 750
🏌 Judy Elliott (01252) 782109
⚬ G Cowlishaw (01252) 782198
🏴 18 L 6447 yds SSS 71
👥 WD–H WE–M
   SOC–Wed/Thurs/Fri
£€ £40 D–£45
🚗 1 mile E of Farnham, off A31
🖳 www.farnhamgolfclub.co.uk

Farnham Park Par Three
(1966)
Pay and play
Farnham Park, Farnham, GU9 0AU
☎ (01252) 715216
🖳 (01252) 718246
📖 75
🏌 R Hutton
⚬ R Hutton
🏴 9 L 1163 yds Par 54
👥 U
£€ £6 (£7)
🚗 By Farnham Castle
🏠 Henry Cotton

Foxhills   (1975)
Stonehill Road, Ottershaw, KT16 0EL
☎ (01932) 872050
🖳 (01932) 874762
✉ golf@foxhills.co.uk
📖 1200

R Hyder
R Summerscales (01932) 704465
18 L 6680 yds SSS 73
18 L 6547 yds SSS 72
9 hole course
WD–U WE–NA before noon
SOC–WD am
£€ £75 D–£95 (£95)
2 miles off M25 Jct 11
Driving range, conference centre, spa, 70 bedrooms, 3 restaurants
FW Hawtree
www.foxhills.co.uk

Gatton Manor Hotel G&CC
(1969)
Standon Lane, Ockley, Dorking, RH5 5PQ
☎ (01306) 627555
(01306) 627713
info@gattonmanor.co.uk
275
Patrick Kiely (owner)
Rob Humphrey (01306) 627557
18 L 6563 yds Par 72 SSS 72
U exc Sun before 12 noon
SOC–WD
£€ £28 D–£45 (£38)
1½ miles SW of Ockley, off A29. M25 Junction 9, S on A24
Driving range; chipping green; bookings via website
Cmdr John D Harris (Canadian)
www.gattonmanor.co.uk

Goal Farm Par Three
Proprietary
Gole Road, Pirbright, GU24 0PZ
☎ (01483) 473183
(01483) 473205
secretary@gfgc.co.uk
320
GJ Williams
Peter Fuller
9 hole Par 3 course
Sat/Thurs am–restricted SOC–WD
£€ £5.50 (£5.95)
7 miles NW of Guildford
www.gfgc.co.uk

Guildford (1886)
High Path Road, Merrow, Guildford, GU1 2HL
☎ (01483) 563941
(01483) 453228
admin@guildfordgolfclub.co.uk
600
BJ Green
PG Hollington (01483) 566765
18 L 6090 yds SSS 69
WD–U WE–M SOC–WD
£€ £42
2 miles E of Guildford on A246
Taylor/Hawtree
www.guildfordgolfclub.co.uk

Hampton Court Palace
(1895)
Hampton Wick, Kingston-upon-Thames, KT1 4AD
☎ (020) 8977 2423
(020) 8614 4747
hamptoncourtpalace@crown-golf.co.uk
650
Christopher Bamford
Edward Litchfield (020) 8977 2658
18 L 6513 yds SSS 71
WD–U WE–U after 2.30pm
£€ Mon–Thur £30 Fri £40 (£50)
1 mile W of Kingston
Willie Park

Hankley Common (1896)
Tilford, Farnham, GU10 2DD
☎ (01252) 792493
(01252) 795699
jhay@hankley-commongc.co.uk
700
JSW Scott
P Stow (01252) 793761
18 L 6702 yds SSS 72
WD–U WE–H at discretion of Sec SOC
£€ £65 D–£80 (£80)
3 miles SE of Farnham on Tilford road
James Braid/Harry Colt
www.hankley.co.uk

Hazelwood Golf Centre
(1992)
Pay and play
Croysdale Avenue, Green Street, Sunbury-on-Thames, TW16 6QU
☎ (01932) 770932
(01932) 770933
200
AP Oades
R Catley-Smith (01932) 770932
9 L 5660 yds Par 35 SSS 67
U SOC
£€ 9: £9.50 (£12.50) 18: £15 (£19)
M3 Junction 1, 1 mile
Driving range (36 bays, floodlit). Golf academy
Jonathan Gaunt

Hersham Village
Asher Road, Hersham, Walton-on-Thames, KT12 4RA
☎ (01932) 267666
(01932) 240975
R Hutton (Golf Dir)
R Hutton
18 hole Par 67
U
£€ £18.50
5 miles N of M25 Jct 10 (B365)
22 bay floodlit driving range; golf academy

The Hindhead (1904)
Churt Road, Hindhead, GU26 6HX
☎ (01428) 604614
(01428) 608508
secretary@the-hindhead-golf-club.co.uk
500 76(L) 81(J)
N Hallam Jones
I Benson (01428) 604458
18 L 6356 yds SSS 70
WD–U WE–by arrangement H SOC–Wed & Thurs

£€ £42 (£55)
1½ miles N of A3 on A287. M25 Junction 10, 25 miles
www.the-hindhead-golf-club.co.uk

Hoebridge Golf Centre
(1982)
Public
Old Woking Road, Old Woking, GU22 8JH
☎ (01483) 722611
(01483) 740369
700
M O'Connell (Mgr)
C Butfoy
18 L 6587 yds SSS 71
Inter 9 L 2294 yds Par 33
18 hole Par 3 course
U SOC–WD
£€ 18 hole: £21 (£27.50) Inter: £11. Par 3: £9
Between Old Woking and West Byfleet on B382
Floodlit driving range
Jacobs/Hawtree
www.hoebridgegc.co.uk

Horne Park
Croydon Barn Lane, Horne, South Godstone, RH9 8JP
☎ (01342) 844443
hornepark@pncl.co.uk

Horton Park G&CC (1987)
Pay and play
Hook Road, Epsom, KT19 8QG
☎ (020) 8393 8400 (Enquiries)
(020) 8394 2626 (Bookings)
hortonparkgc@aol.com

Hurtmore (1992)
Pay and play
Hurtmore Road, Hurtmore, Godalming, GU7 2RN
☎ (01483) 426492
(01483) 426121
general@hurtmore-golf.co.uk
200
Maxine Burton (01483) 426492
Maxine Burton (01483) 426440
18 L 5530 yds Par 70 SSS 67
U SOC
£€ £14 (£20)
6 miles S of Guildford on A3. M25 Junction 10
Practice nets and putting green
Alliss/Clark
www.hurtmore-golf.co.uk

Kingswood (1928)
Sandy Lane, Kingswood, Tadworth, KT20 6NE
☎ (01737) 832188
(01737) 833920
sales@kingswood-golf.co.uk
770
Elaine Labbett (Corporate Golf Admin) Jackie Dunne (Membership Admin)
T Sims (01737) 832334
18 L 6904 yds SSS 73
U SOC

££ £40 (£55 Sat, £45 Sun)
&& 5 miles S of Sutton on A217. M25
Junction 8, 2 miles
⊕ Driving range
⌂ James Braid
🖳 www.kingswood-golf.co.uk

Laleham   (1903)
Laleham Reach, Chertsey KT16 8RP
☎ (01932) 564211
🖶 (01932) 564448
📧 sec@laleham-golf.co.uk
📖 600
🄅 RM McCue
✔ H Stott (01932) 562877
🏴 18 L 6291 yds SSS 70
👥 WD–U 9.30–4.30pm WE–M
SOC–Mon–Wed
££ £30 – £36
&& 2 miles S of Staines, opp Thorpe Pk
🖳 www.laleham-golf.co.uk

Leatherhead   (1903)
Proprietary
Kingston Road, Leatherhead, KT22 0EE
☎ (01372) 843966
🖶 (01372) 842241
📧 secretary@lgc-golf.co.uk
📖 600
🄅 Timothy Lowe
✔ Timothy Lowe (01372) 849413
🏴 18 L 6203 yds Par 71 SSS 70
👥 WD–U WE–NA before 2pm SOC
££ £37.50
&& On A243 to Chessington. M25
Junction 9
⊕ Practice area (own balls); putting
green; practice nets
🖳 www.lgc-golf.co.uk

Limpsfield Chart   (1889)
Westerham Road, Limpsfield, RH8 0SL
☎ (01883) 723405/722106
📧 secretary@limpsfieldchartgolf.co.uk
📖 300
🄅 RJ Smitherman
✔ None
🏴 9 L 5718 yds SSS 68
👥 WD–U exc Thurs (Ladies Day)
WE–M or by appointment SOC
££ £20 (£22)
&& 1 mile E of Oxted on A25
🖳 www.limpsfieldchartgolf.co.uk

Lingfield Park   (1987)
Racecourse Road, Lingfield, RH7 6PQ
☎ (01342) 834602
📧 cmorley@lingfieldpark.co.uk

London Scottish   (1865)
Windmill Enclosure, Wimbledon Common,
London, SW19 5NQ
☎ (020) 8788 0135
🖶 (020) 8789 7517
📧 secretary.lsgc@virgin.net
📖 250
🄅 S Barr (020) 8789 7517
✔ S Barr (020) 8789 1207
🏴 18 L 5458 yds Par 68 SSS 66
👥 WD–U WE/BH–NA SOC
££ £20 Mon–£15
&& Wimbledon Common

⊕ Red upper garment must be worn
⌂ Willie Dunn/Tom Dunn
🖳 www.londonscottishgolfclub.co.uk

Malden   (1893)
Traps Lane, New Malden, KT3 4RS
☎ (020) 8942 0654
🖶 (020) 8336 2219
📧 manager@maldengolfclub.com
📖 750
🄅 Mrs A Besant (Mgr)
✔ R Hunter
(professional@maldengolfclub.com)
(020) 8942 6009
🏴 18 L 6295 yds SSS 70
👥 WD–U WE–restricted
SOC–Wed–Fri
££ On application
&& Off A3, between Wimbledon and
Kingston
🖳 www.maldengolfclub.com

Merrist Wood   (1997)
Coombe Lane, Worplesdon, Guildford,
GU3 3PE
☎ (01483) 238890

Milford
Proprietary
Station Lane, Milford, GU8 5HS
☎ (01483) 419200
🖶 (01483) 419199
📧 milford@crown-golf.co.uk
📖 750
🄅 R Brewer
✔ P Creamer (01483) 416291
🏴 18 L 5960 yds Par 69 SSS 68
👥 WD–U WE–after 12 noon SOC
££ £25 £42
&& 3 miles SW of Guildford, off A3
⊕ Practice range
⌂ Alliss/Clark

Mitcham   (1924)
Carshalton Road, Mitcham Junction,
CR4 4HN
☎ (020) 8648 1508
(020) 8640 4280 (Bookings)

Moore Place   (1926)
Public
Portsmouth Road, Esher, KT10 9LN
☎ (01372) 463533
🖶 (01372) 463533
📖 80
🄅 R Egan (020) 8715 8851
✔ N Gadd
🏴 9 L 2078 yds SSS 61
👥 U
££ £10 (£12.50)
&& Centre of Esher
⌂ D Allen
🖳 www.moore-place.co.uk

New Zealand   (1895)
Woodham Lane, Addlestone, KT15 3QD
☎ (01932) 345049
🖶 (01932) 342891
📧 roger.marrett@nzgc.org
📖 300
🄅 RA Marrett (01932) 342891

✔ VR Elvidge (01932) 349619
🏴 18 L 6075 yds SSS 69
👥 By request
££ On application
&& Woking 3 miles. West Byfleet 1
mile. Weybridge 5 miles
⌂ Simpson/Fergusson

North Downs   (1899)
Northdown Road, Woldingham, Caterham,
CR3 7AA
☎ (01883) 652057
🖶 (01883) 652832
📧 info@northdownsgolfclub.co.uk
📖 550
🄅 DM Sinden (Sec/Mgr)
(01883) 652057
✔ MJ Homewood (01883) 653004
🏴 18 L 5857 yds Par 69 SSS 68
👥 WD–U WE–NA before 3pm
(summer), 12 noon (winter)
SOC–WD
££ £30 (£30)
&& 3 miles E of Caterham. M25 Jct 6
⊕ Practice ground; putting green
⌂ JF Pennink
🖳 www.northdownsgolfclub.co.uk

Oak Park   (1984)
Heath Lane, Crondall, Farnham, GU10 5PB
☎ (01252) 850850
🖶 (01252) 850851
📧 oakpark@crown-golf.co.uk
📖 550
🄅 R Brewer (Mgr)
✔ (01252) 850066
🏴 Woodland 18 L 6352 yds Par 70
SSS 70
Village 9 L 3279 yds Par 36
👥 WE pm only
££ Woodland Mon–Thur £25.50, Fri
(£28.50 pm only) Village £13
Mon–Thur, £14 Fri
&& Off A287 Farnham-Odiham road.
M3 Junction 5, 4 miles
⊕ Driving range; Teaching Academy
⌂ Patrick Dawson
🖳 www.crown-golf.co.uk /oakpark

Oaks Sports Centre
(1973)
Public
Woodmansterne Road, Carshalton,
SM5 4AN
☎ (020) 8643 8363
📧 golf@oaks.sagehost.co.uk

Pachesham Park Golf
Centre   (1990)
Pay and play
Oaklawn Road, Leatherhead, KT22 0BT
☎ (01372) 843453
📧 enquiries@pacheshamgolf.co.uk
📖 150
🄅 P Taylor
✔ P Taylor
🏴 9 L 2804 yds Par 35
👥 U SOC
££ 9: £10 (£14)
&& NW of Leatherhead, off A244. M25
Junction 9

⊕ Driving range
⌂ P Taylor
▤ www.pacheshamgolf.co.uk

Pine Ridge (1992)
Pay and play
Old Bisley Road, Frimley, Camberley, GU16 9NX
☎ **(01276) 20770**
✉ enquiry@pineridgegolf.co.uk

Purley Downs (1894)
106 Purley Downs Road, South Croydon, CR2 0RB
☎ **(020) 8657 8347**
🖷 (020) 8651 5044
✉ info@purleydowns.co.uk
▥ 660
🖉 Mrs SJ Burr
✓ S Iliffe (020) 8651 0819
🏳 18 L 6308 yds SSS 70
👫 WD–I WE–M SOC–WD exc Tues am
££ On application
⚑ 3 miles S of Croydon (A235)
▤ www.purleydowns.co.uk

Puttenham (1894)
Puttenham, Guildford, GU3 1AL
☎ **(01483) 810498**
🖷 (01483) 810988
✉ enquiries@puttenhamgolfclub.co.uk
▥ 600
🖉 G Simmons
✓ D Lintott (01483) 810277
🏳 18 L 6220 yds SSS 70
👫 WD–by prior appointment WE/BH–M SOC–Wed, Thurs & Fri
££ On application
⚑ Between Guildford and Farnham on B3000, just off Hog's Back
⊕ Driving range for green fee/society visitors & members
▤ www.puttenhamgolfclub.co.uk

Pyrford (1993)
Warren Lane, Pyrford, GU22 8XR
☎ **(01483) 723555**
✉ pyrford@americangolf.uk.com

Redhill (1993)
Pay and play
Canada Avenue, Redhill, RH1 5BF
☎ **(01737) 770204**
🖷 (01737) 760046
✉ info@redhillgolfcentre.co.uk
▥ 90
🖉 S Furlonger
✓ M Lovegrove
🏳 9 L 1903 yds Par 31 SSS 59
👫 U SOC
££ £6 (£6.50)
⚑ 1½ miles S of Redhill on A23, off Three Arch Road
⊕ Floodlit driving range
▤ www.redhillgolfcentre.co.uk

Redhill & Reigate (1887)
Clarence Lodge, Pendleton Road, Redhill, RH1 6LB
☎ **(01737) 244626/244433**

🖷 (01737) 242117
✉ mail@rrgc.net
▥ 500
🖉 D Simpson (01737) 240777
✓ W Pike (01737) 244433
🏳 18 L 5272 yds SSS 68
👫 WD–U WE–phone first SOC
££ £21
⚑ 1 mile S of Redhill on A23
▤ www.rrgc.net

Reigate Heath (1895)
The Club House, Reigate Heath, RH2 8QR
☎ **(01737) 242610**
🖷 (01737) 249226
✉ reigateheath@surreygolf.co.uk
▥ 330 80(L) 60(J)
🖉 RJ Perkins (01737) 226793
✓ B Davies
🏳 9 L 5658 yds SSS 68
👫 WD–U Sun/BH–M SOC–Thurs
££ On application
⚑ W boundary of Reigate Heath on Flanchford Road
▤ www.reigateheathgolfclub.co.uk

Reigate Hill
Gatton Bottom, Reigate, RH2 0TU
☎ **(01737) 645577**

The Richmond (1891)
Sudbrook Park, Richmond, TW10 7AS
☎ **(020) 8940 4351**
🖷 (020) 8332 7914
✉ gm@therichmondgolfclub.co.uk
▥ 600
🖉 J Maguire (020) 8940 4351
✓ S Burridge (020) 8940 7792
🏳 18 L 6100 yds SSS 70
👫 WD–H
££ £40 (£45)
⚑ Between Richmond and Kingston-upon-Thames
⊕ Driving range
⌂ T Dunn
▤ www.therichmondgolfclub.co.uk

Richmond Park (1923)
Public
Roehampton Gate, Richmond Park, London, SW15 5JR
☎ **(020) 8876 3205/1795**
🖷 (020) 8878 1354
✉ richmondpark@glendale-services.co.uk
🖉 AJ Gourvish
✓ D Bown, A Ocana, Stuart Hill, J Gillespie
🏳 Dukes 18 L 6036 yds SSS 68
Princes 18 L 5868 yds SSS 67
👫 WD–U WE–booking necessary SOC–WD
££ On application
⚑ In Richmond Park
⊕ Driving range
⌂ Hawtree
▤ www.richmondparkgolf.co.uk

Roehampton Club (1901)
Roehampton Lane, London, SW15 5LR
☎ **(020) 8480 4200**

🖷 (020) 8480 4265
✉ alistair.cook@roehamptonclub.co.uk
▥ 400
🖉 M Bouaird (Chief Exec) (020) 8480 4200 A Cook (Sports Mgr) (020) 8480 4200
✓ AL Scott (020) 8876 3858
🏳 18 L 6065 yds Par 71
👫 WD/WE–Introduced by member
££ On application
⚑ 1 mile W of Putney, off South Circular
▤ www.roehamptonclub.co.uk

Roker Park (1993)
Pay and play
Holly Lane, Aldershot Road, Guildford, GU3 3PB
☎ **(01483) 236677**
▥ 200
🖉 C Tegg
✓ A Carter (01483) 236677
🏳 9 L 3037 yds SSS 72
👫 U SOC
££ £9.50 D–£12.50 (£12.50)
⚑ 2 miles W of Guildford on A323
⊕ Driving range
⌂ Alan Helling

Royal Automobile Club (1913)
Woodcote Park, Epsom, KT18 7EW
☎ **(01372) 276311**
🖷 (01372) 276117
🖉 D Adams (01372) 273091
✓ I Howieson (01372) 279514
🏳 Old 18 L 6709 yds SSS 72
Coronation 18 L 6223 yds SSS 70
👫 M SOC
⚑ Epsom Station 2 miles
⌂ Fowler/Myddleton

Royal Mid-Surrey (1892)
Old Deer Park, Richmond, TW9 2SB
☎ **(020) 8940 1894**
🖷 (020) 8939 0150
✉ secretary@rmsgc.co.uk
▥ 1420
🖉 Marc Newey
✓ (020) 8939 0148
🏳 Outer 18 L 6402 yds Par 69 SSS 71
Inner 18 L 5544 yds Par 68 SSS 67
👫 WD–H or M WE/BH–M SOC
££ Outer £75 D–£90 WD only Inner £60 D–£90 WD only
⚑ Nr Richmond roundabout, off A316
⊕ Practice ground; short game practice area; indoor nets
⌂ Outer: JH Taylor
Inner: JH Taylor/Hawtree
▤ www.rmsgc.co.uk

Royal Wimbledon (1865)
29 Camp Road, Wimbledon Common, London, SW19 4UW
☎ **(020) 8946 2125**
🖷 (020) 8944 8652
✉ secretary@rwgc.co.uk
▥ 800
🖉 NI Smith

✓ DR Jones (020) 8946 2125
⚑ 18 L 6348 yds SSS 71
𝍣 WD–H by arrangement
££ £75 D–£100
🚗 Wimbledon Common, 2 miles S of A23 Tibbets Corner
⊕ Driving range
🏠 HS Colt
▤ www.rwgc.co.uk

Rusper (1992)
Proprietary
Rusper Road, Newdigate, RH5 5BX
☎ **(01293) 871456**
   (01293) 871871 (Bookings)
🖥 (01293) 871456
✉ jill@ruspergolfclub.co.uk
📖 350
🖉 Mrs J Thornhill
✓ Janice Arnold (01293) 871871
⚑ 18 L 6724 yds SSS 72
𝍣 U SOC
££ Fees available from Golf Shop
🚗 5 miles S of Dorking, off A24
⊕ Driving range
🏠 AW Blunden
▤ www.ruspergolfclub.co.uk

Selsdon Park Hotel (1929)
Proprietary
Addington Road, Sanderstead, South Croydon, CR2 8YA
☎ **(020) 8657 8811**
🖥 (020) 8657 3401
✉ shaun.bakker@principal-hotels.com
🖉 Mrs S Bates
✓ G Wallis (020) 8657 4129
⚑ 18 L 6473 yds SSS 71
𝍣 U SOC (min 12 golfers)
££ £28 (£36)
🚗 3 miles S of Croydon on A2022 Purley-Addington road
⊕ Driving range; putting green
🏠 JH Taylor
▤ www.principal-hotels.com

Shirley Park (1913)
194 Addiscombe Road, Croydon, CR0 7LB
☎ **(020) 8654 1143**
🖥 (020) 8654 6733
✉ secretary@shirleyparkgolfclub .co.uk
📖 600
🖉 Steve Murphy
✓ Michael Taylor (020) 8654 8767
⚑ 18 L 6170 yds Par 71 SSS 69
𝍣 WD–U WE after 3pm SOC
££ £40 (£48)
🚗 On A232, 1 mile E of East Croydon Station
⊕ Large practice area
🏠 Simpson/Fowler
▤ www.shirleyparkgolfclub.co.uk

Silvermere (1976)
Pay and play
Redhill Road, Cobham, KT11 1EF
☎ **(01932) 584300**
🖥 (01932) 584301
✉ sales@silvermere-golf.co.uk
📖 500
🖉 Mrs P Devereux

✓ D McClelland
⚑ 18 L 6027 yds SSS 71
𝍣 WD–U WE–NA before 11am SOC
££ £24 (£35)
🚗 ½ mile from M25 Junction 10 on B366 to Byfleet
⊕ Floodlit driving range
▤ www.silvermere-golf.co.uk

St George's Hill (1912)
Golf Club Road, St George's Hill, Weybridge, KT13 0NL
☎ **(01932) 847758**
🖥 (01932) 821564
✉ admin@stgeorgeshillgolfclub.co.uk
📖 600
🖉 J Robinson
✓ AC Rattue (01932) 843523
⚑ 27 L 6097-6496 yds SSS 69-71
𝍣 WD–I H WE/BH–M SOC–Wed-Fri
££ £100 – £130
🚗 2 miles N of M25/A3 Junction, on B374
🏠 HS Colt
▤ www.stgeorgeshillgolfclub.co.uk

Sunningdale (1900)
Ridgemount Road, Sunningdale, Berks, SL5 9RR
☎ **(01344) 621681**
🖥 (01344) 624154
✉ info@sunningdalegolfclub.co.uk
📖 900
🖉 S Toon
✓ K Maxwell (01344) 620128
⚑ Old 18 L 6581 yds SSS 72
   New 18 L 6617 yds SSS 73
𝍣 Mon–Thurs–I Fri/WE–M H
££ Old–£170 New–£130
🚗 Sunningdale Station ¼ mile, off A30
🏠 Willie Park/HS Colt
▤ www.sunningdale-golfclub.co.uk

Sunningdale Ladies (1902)
Cross Road, Sunningdale, SL5 9RX
☎ **(01344) 620507**
🖥 (01344) 620507
✉ slgolfclub@tiscali.co.uk
📖 400
🖉 Mr RG Mitchell
⚑ 18 L 3616 yds SSS 60
𝍣 H WD/WE–by appointment. No 3 or 4 balls before 10.30am
££ £26 (£31)
🚗 Sunningdale Station ¼ mile. M3 J3
🏠 HS Colt
▤ www.sunningdaleladies.co.uk

Surbiton (1895)
Woodstock Lane, Chessington, KT9 1UG
☎ **(020) 8398 3101**
🖥 (020) 8339 0992
✉ surbitongolfclub@btconnect.com
📖 800
🖉 CJ Cornish
✓ P Milton (020) 8398 6619
⚑ 18 L 6055 yds SSS 69
𝍣 WD–H WE/BH–M
££ £35 D–£45
🚗 2 miles E of Esher

Surrey Downs (2001)
Proprietary
Outwood Lane, Kingswood, KT20 6JS
☎ **(01737) 839090**
🖥 (01737) 839080
✉ booking@surreydownsgc.co.uk
🖉 Scott Morley
✓ S Blacklee (01737) 832726
⚑ 18 L 6356 yds Par 71 SSS 70
𝍣 U SOC
££ £25 (£37)
🚗 N of Kingswood, off A217/B2032. M25 Junction 8
⊕ Golf academy and range
🏠 Peter Alliss
▤ www.surreydownsgc.co.uk

Surrey National (1999)
Rook Lane, Chaldon, Caterham, CR3 5AA
☎ **(01883) 344555**
🖥 (01883) 344422
✉ caroline@surreynational.co.uk
📖 550
🖉 S Hodsdon (Gen Mgr)
✓ D Kent
⚑ 18 L 6858 yds Par 72 SSS 73
𝍣 WD–U WE–NA before 11.00am SOC
££ £30 (£32)
🚗 5 miles S of Croydon. M25 Jct 7
⊕ Driving range, function room, conference facilities
🏠 David Williams
▤ www.surreynational.co.uk

Sutton Green (1994)
New Lane, Sutton Green, Guildford, GU4 7QF
☎ **(01483) 747898**
🖥 (01483) 750289
✉ admin@suttongreengc.co.uk
📖 600
🖉 J Buchanan
✓ P Tedder (01483) 766849
⚑ 18 L 6300 yds Par 71 SSS 70
𝍣 WD–U WE–U after 2pm
££ £50 (£60) – reduced fees available on-line via club's website
🚗 2 miles S of Woking, just off A3, M25 J10
🏠 Walker/Davies
▤ www.suttongreengc.co.uk

The Swallow Farleigh Court (1997)
Proprietary
Old Farleigh Road, Farleigh, CR6 9PX
☎ **(01883) 627711**
🖥 (01883) 627722
✉ swallow.farleigh@swallowhotels .com
📖 550
🖉 Scott Graham (Mgr)
✓ Scott Graham (01883) 627733
⚑ 18 black tees L 7616 yds SSS 72
   18 white tees L 6409 yds SSS 70
   9 white tees L 3255 yds
𝍣 SOC WD/WE
££ 9: £9 (£12) 18 (Members): £30 (£40) 18: (Combination): £18 (£25)
🚗 5 miles SE of Croydon. M25 Junction 6

⊕ Driving range; chipping area and
putting green
🏠 John Jacobs
🖥 www.swallowhotels.com

Tandridge (1925)

Oxted, RH8 9NQ
☎ **(01883) 712273 (Clubhouse)**
🖳 (01883) 730537
📧 secretary@tandridgegolfclub.com
📖 750
🏌 Lt Cdr SE Kennard RN
(01883) 712274
✓ C Evans (01883) 713701
🏴 18 L 6277 yds SSS 70
👥 Mon/Wed/Thurs only–H
SOC–Mon/Wed/Thurs
££ On application
🚗 8 miles E of Redhill, off A25. M25
Junction 6
🏠 HS Colt
🖥 www.tandridgegolfclub.com

Thames Ditton & Esher

(1892)
Portsmouth Road, Esher, KT10 9AL
☎ **(020) 8398 1551**

Tyrrells Wood (1924)

The Drive, Tyrrells Wood, Leatherhead,
KT22 8QP
☎ **(01372) 376025 (2 lines)**
🖳 (01372) 360836
📖 744
🏌 L Edgcumbe
✓ S DeFoy (01372) 375200
🏴 18 L 6282 yds SSS 70
👥 WD–I BH/Sat+Sun NA before
noon SOC
££ £40 (£55)
🚗 2 miles SE of Leatherhead, off A24
nr Headley. M25 Junction 9, 1 mile
🏠 James Braid
🖥 www.tyrrellswoodgolfclub.com

Walton Heath (1903)

Deans Lane, Walton-on-the-Hill, Tadworth,
KT20 7TP
☎ **(01737) 812060**
🖳 (01737) 814225
📧 secretary@whgc.co.uk
📖 900
🏌 MW Bawden (01737) 812380
✓ K Macpherson (01737) 812152
🏴 Old 18 L 6836 yds SSS 73
New 18 L 6613 yds SSS 72
👥 WD/WE/BH booking necessary
SOC–WD
££ On application
🚗 18 miles S of London on
A217/B2032. 2 miles N of M25
Junction 8
🏠 WH Fowler
🖥 www.whgc.co.uk

Wentworth Club (1924)

Wentworth Drive, Virginia Water,
GU25 4LS
☎ **(01344) 842201**
🖳 (01344) 842804
🏌 Stuart Christie (Admin)

✓ Jason MacNiven (Dir of Golf)
(01344) 846306
🏴 West 18 L 7308 yds SSS 74
East 18 L 6201 yds SSS 70
Edinburgh 18 L 7004 yds SSS 74
Executive 9 L 1902 yds Par 27
👥 WD–H by prior arrangement
WE–M SOC–WD
££ On application
🚗 21 miles SW of London at
A30/A329 junction. M25 Junction
13, 3 miles
⊕ Driving range; tennis and health
club
🏠 HS Colt (East/West). Jacobs/Player
(Edinburgh)
🖥 www.wentworthclub.com

West Byfleet (1906)

Sheerwater Road, West Byfleet, KT14 6AA
☎ **(01932) 345230**
🖳 (01932) 340667
📧 admin@wbgc.co.uk
📖 550
🏌 DG Lee (Gen Mgr) (01932) 343433
✓ D Regan (01932) 346584
🏴 18 L 6211 yds SSS 70
👥 WD–U WE/BH–M SOC
££ £50 D–£75
🚗 West Byfleet ¹/₂ mile on A245. M25
Junction 10 or 11
⊕ Practice area (balls provided);
buggy hire
🏠 CS Butchart
🖥 www.wbgc.co.uk

West Hill (1909)

Bagshot Road, Brookwood, GU24 0BH
☎ **(01483) 474365**
🖳 (01483) 474252
📧 secretary@westhill-golfclub.co.uk
📖 550
🏌 I M McColl (01483) 485760
✓ G Shoesmith (01483) 473172
🏴 18 L 6350 yds Par 69 SSS 71
👥 WD–H WE–M SOC
££ £60 D–£85
🚗 5 miles S M3 J3 on A322
⊕ Winter packages available from £40
🏠 CS Butchart
🖥 www.westhill-golfclub.co.uk

West Surrey (1910)

Enton Green, Godalming, GU8 5AF
☎ **(01483) 421275**
🖳 (01483) 415419
📧 office@wsgc.co.uk
📖 620
🏌 A Gravestock
✓ A Tawse (01483) 417278
🏴 18 L 6482 yds SSS 71
👥 H SOC–Wed/Thurs/Fri
££ £40 (£50)
🚗 ¹/₂ mile SE of Milford Station
⊕ Driving range; buggy hire
🏠 Herbert Fowler
🖥 www.wsgc.co.uk

Wildwood Golf & CC

(1992)
Horsham Road, Alfold, GU6 8JE
☎ **(01403) 753255**

🖳 (01403) 752005
📧 info@wildwoodgolf.co.uk
📖 640
🏌 J Hansen
✓ Stephen Plane
🏴 27 L 6655 yds SSS 73
Par 3 course
👥 U SOC
££ £40 (£50)
🚗 10 miles S of Guildford on A281
⊕ Driving range; golf academy; junior
academy; practice room
🏠 Hawtree
🖥 www.wildwoodgolf.co.uk

Wimbledon Common

(1908)
19 Camp Road, Wimbledon Common,
London, SW19 4UW
☎ **(020) 8946 0294**
🖳 (020) 8947 8697
📧 secretary@wcgc.co.uk
📖 275
🏌 G Oakshett (020) 8946 7571
✓ JS Jukes
🏴 18 L 5438 yds SSS 66
👥 WD–U WE–M SOC
££ WD–£20 (D–£30) exc Mon–£15
(£20)
🚗 Wimbledon Common
⊕ Pillarbox red outer garment must
be worn. London Scottish play
here
🏠 Willie Dunn/Tom Dunn
🖥 www.wcgc.co.uk

Wimbledon Park (1898)

Home Park Road, London, SW19 7HR
☎ **(020) 8946 1250**
🖳 (020) 8944 8688
📧 secretary@wpgc.co.uk
📖 850
🏌 P Shanahan
✓ D Wingrove (020) 8946 4053
🏴 18 L 5483 yds SSS 66
👥 WD–H I WE/BH–after 3pm SOC
££ D–£50 (£50)
🚗 2 miles from A3 at Tibbetts
Corner
🏠 Willie Park Jnr
🖥 www.wpgc.co.uk

Windlemere (1978)

Pay and play
Windlesham Road, West End, Woking,
GU24 9QL
☎ **(01276) 858727**

Windlesham (1994)

Grove End, Bagshot, GU19 5HY
☎ **(01276) 452220**
📧 admin@windleshamgolf.com

The Wisley (1991)

Ripley, Woking, GU23 6QU
☎ **(01483) 211022**
🖳 (01483) 211662
📧 reception@thewisley.com
📖 700
🏌 T Henner (Gen Mgr)
✓ D Pugh (01483) 211213

☞ 27 holes SSS 73:
  Church 9 L 3356 yds; Garden 9 L
  3385 yds;
  Mill 9 L 3473 yds
🏠 M
🏌 1 mile S of M25 J10 (A3)
⊕ Driving range; short game practice
  area; complete learning centre
🏠 Robert Trent Jones Jr
🖥 www.thewisley.com

Woking   (1893)
Pond Road, Hook Heath, Woking,
GU22 0JZ
☎ **(01483) 760053**
🖷 (01483) 772441
📧 woking.golf@btconnect.com
📖 500
🏌 G Ritchie
✎ C Bianco (01483) 769582
☞ 18 L 6340 yds SSS 70
🏌 WD–H WE/BH–M SOC–WD
££ £45 D–£65
🏌 W of Woking in St John's / Hook
  Heath area
🏠 Tom Dunn
🖥 www.wokinggolfclub.co.uk

Woldingham   (1996)
Halliloo Valley Road, Woldingham,
CR3 7HA
☎ **(01883) 653501**
🖷 (01883) 653502
📧 enquiries@woldingham-
  golfclub.co.uk
✎ Gavin Reed
✎ James Hillen (01883) 653541
☞ 18 L 6322 yds Par 71 SSS 70
🏌 WD–U WE–NA before noon SOC
££ £26 (£30)
🏌 2½ miles N of M25 Jct 6, off A22
⊕ Practice range
🏠 Bradford Benz
🖥 www.woldingham-golfclub.co.uk

Woodcote Park   (1912)
Meadow Hill, Bridle Way, Coulsdon,
CR5 2QQ
☎ **(020) 8668 2788**
🖷 (020) 8660 0918
📧 info@woodcotepgc.com
📖 630
✎ AP Dawson
✎ W Grant (020) 8668 1843
☞ 18 L 6720 yds Par 71 SSS 72
🏌 WD WE–M
££ £50 round or all day
🏌 Purley 2 miles. M25 Junction 7
⊕ Full practice area
🏠 HS Colt
🖥 www.woodcotepgc.com

Worplesdon   (1908)
Heath House Road, Woking, GU22 0RA
☎ **(01483) 472277**

Sussex (East)

Brighton & Hove   (1887)
Devils Dyke Road, Brighton, BN1 8YJ
☎ **(01273) 556482**

🖷 (01273) 554247
📧 phil@bhgc68.fsnet.co.uk
📖 380
✎ P Bonsall (Golf Dir)
✎ P Bonsall (01273) 556686
☞ 9 L 5704 yds SSS 68
🏌 U SOC Sun–NA before noon
££ £20 (£25)
🏌 4 miles N of Brighton
🏠 James Braid
🖥 www.brightonandhovegolfclub
  .co.uk

Cooden Beach   (1912)
Cooden Sea Road, Bexhill-on-Sea,
TN39 4TR
☎ **(01424) 842040**
🖷 (01424) 842040
📧 manager@coodenbeachgc.com
📖 700
✎ KP Wiley (01424) 842040
✎ J Sim (01424) 843938
☞ 18 L 6504 yds Par 72 SSS 71
🏌 H SOC
££ £37 (£46)
🏌 W boundary of Bexhill
⊕ Full practice facility (inc driving
  range)
🏠 Herbert Fowler
🖥 www.coodenbeachgc.com

Crowborough Beacon
  (1895)
Beacon Road, Crowborough, TN6 1UJ
☎ **(01892) 661511**
🖷 (01892) 611988
📧 secretary@cbgc.co.uk
📖 700
✎ Mrs V Harwood (01892) 661511
✎ D Newnham
  (01892) 661511/653877
☞ 18 L 6273 yds SSS 70
🏌 WD–H WE/BH–H after 2.30pm
  SOC
££ 2006: £50 D–£60 (£60)
🏌 9 miles S of Tunbridge Wells on
  A26
🖥 www.crowboroughbeacongolfclub
  .co.uk

Dale Hill Hotel & GC
  (1973)
Ticehurst, Wadhurst, TN5 7DQ
☎ **(01580) 200112**
🖷 (01580) 201249
📧 golf@dalehill.co.uk
📖 1000
✎ John Tolliday (Dir of Golf)
✎ M Woods (01580) 201090
☞ 18 L 5856 yds SSS 69
  Woosnam 18 L 6512 yds SSS 72
🏌 U SOC
££ £25 (£35) Woosnam–£60 (£70)
🏌 B2087, off A21 at Flimwell from
  M25 J5
⊕ Driving range; 65 buggy fleet
🖥 www.dalehill.co.uk

Dewlands Manor   (1992)
Cottage Hill, Rotherfield, TN6 3JN
☎ **(01892) 852266**

🖷 (01892) 853015
✎ T Robins
✎ N Godin
☞ 9 L 3186 yds Par 36
🏌 U–phone first
££ 9: £16 (£18); 18: £26 (£31) 15
  minute tee times Senior (midweek
  only): 9: £14; 18: £22
🏌 ½ mile S of Rotherfield, off
  A267/B2101. 10 miles S of
  Tunbridge Wells. M25 Junction 5
🏠 Reg Godin

The Dyke   (1906)
Devil's Dyke, Devil's Dyke Road, Brighton,
BN1 8YJ
☎ **(01273) 857296**
🖷 (01273) 857078
📧 dykegolfclub@btconnect.com
📖 750
✎ SL Wise (Sec/Mgr)
✎ R Arnold (01273) 857260
☞ 18 L 6627 yds Par 72 SSS 72
🏌 WD–U WE–U after noon
  SOC–WD
££ £30 D–£43 (£40)
🏌 4 miles N of Brighton
🏠 Fred Hawtree
🖥 www.dykegolfclub.co.uk

East Brighton   (1893)
Roedean Road, Brighton, BN2 5RA
☎ **(01273) 604838**
🖷 (01273) 680277
📧 msw@ebgc.co.uk
📖 650
✎ ME Page
✎ M Stuart-William (Golf
  Mgr) (01273) 603989
☞ 18 L 6346 yds SSS 71
🏌 WD–U H after 9am WE–NA
  before 11am SOC
££ £25 (£30) 2 for 1 after 9am WD
🏌 1½ miles E of Town Centre,
  overlooking Marina
🏠 James Braid
🖥 www.ebgc.co.uk

East Sussex National Golf
  Resort and Spa   (1989)
Little Horsted, Uckfield, TN22 5ES
☎ **(01825) 880088**
🖷 (01825) 880066
📧 events@eastsussexnational.co.uk
📖 770
✎ DT Howe M.Inst, GCM (Gen Mgr)
✎ S MacLennan (01825) 880088
☞ East 18 L 7138 yds SSS 74
  West 18 L 7154 yds SSS 74
🏌 U on one course
££ Summer–£55 (£60). Winter–£35
  (£40)
🏌 2 miles S of Uckfield, on A22
⊕ Driving range; golf academy; hotel
🏠 Robert E Cupp
🖥 www.eastsussexnational.co.uk

Eastbourne Downs   (1908)
East Dean Road, Eastbourne, BN20 8ES
☎ **(01323) 720827**
🖷 (01323) 412506
📧 tony.reeves@btconnect.com

📖 550
🖎 AJ Reeves
✓ T Marshall (01323) 732264
ᗑ 18 L 6601 yds SSS 72
👫 WD–U WE–NA after 11am
££ £20 D–£25 (£28)
🔗 ¹/2 mile W of Eastbourne on A259
⌂ JH Taylor

Eastbourne Golfing Park
(1992)
Pay and play
Lottbridge Drove, Eastbourne, BN23 6QJ
☎ **(01323) 520400**
🖳 (01323) 520400
📖 250
🖎 Dawn Dunkley
✓ B Finch
ᗑ 9 L 5046 yds SSS 65
👫 U
££ £10 (£11)
🔗 ¹/2 mile S of Hampden Park
⊕ All weather floodlit driving range
⌂ David Ashton

Hastings G&CC
(1973)
Beauport Park, Battle Road, St Leonards-on-Sea, TN37 7BP
☎ **(01424) 854243**

Highwoods
(1925)
Ellerslie Lane, Bexhill-on-Sea, TN39 4LJ
☎ **(01424) 212625**
🖳 (01424) 216866
🖂 highwoods@btconnect.com
📖 800
🖎 LM Dennis-Smither
✓ MJ Andrews (01424) 212770
ᗑ 18 L 6218 yds SSS 70
👫 WD/Sat–H Sun am–M Sun pm–H
££ £30 (£35)
🔗 2 miles N of Bexhill
⌂ JH Taylor
🖥 www.highwoodsgolfclub.co.uk

Hollingbury Park
(1908)
Public
Ditchling Road, Brighton, BN1 7HS
☎ **(01273) 552010**
🖳 (01273) 552010
📖 300
🖎 Mrs M Bailey
✓ G Crompton (01273) 500086
ᗑ 18 L 6482 yds SSS 71
👫 U SOC
££ £16.50 (£22)
🔗 1 mile NE of Brighton
🖥 www.hollingburygolfclub.co.uk

Holtye
(1893)
Holtye, Cowden, Nr Edenbridge, TN8 7ED
☎ **(01342) 850635**
🖳 (01342) 850576
🖂 secretary@holtye.com
📖 350
🖎 Mrs DM Botham (01342) 850576
✓ K Hinton (01342) 850957
ᗑ 9 L 5325 yds SSS 66
👫 WD–U exc Wed/Thurs am–NA
WE–NA before 9.30 SOC–Tues &
Fri
££ D–£16 (£18)

🔗 4 miles E of E Grinstead on A264
⊕ 3-bay driving range
🖥 www.holtye.com

Horam Park
(1985)
Pay and play
Chiddingly Road, Horam, TN21 0JJ
☎ **(01435) 813477**
🖳 (01435) 813677
🖂 angie@horampark.com
📖 400
🖎 Mrs A Briggs
✓ G Velvick
ᗑ 9 L 6128 yds SSS 70
👫 U SOC
££ 9: £12 (£13) 18: £18 (£20)
🔗 ¹/2 mile S of Horam towards
Chiddingley. 12 miles N of
Eastbourne on A267
⊕ Floodlit driving range; pitch & putt
course; putting green
⌂ Glen Johnson
🖥 www.horampark.com

Lewes
(1896)
Chapel Hill, Lewes, BN7 2BB
☎ **(01273) 473245**
🖳 (01273) 483474
🖂 secretary@lewesgolfclub.co.uk
📖 500
🖎 Miss J Raffety (01273) 483474
✓ P Dobson (01273) 483823
ᗑ 18 L 6190 yds Par 71 SSS 70
👫 WD–U WE–NA before 11am SOC
££ £32 (£32)
🔗 ¹/2 mile from Lewes at E end of
Cliffe High Street
🖥 www.lewesgolfclub.co.uk

Mid Sussex
(1995)
Proprietary
Spatham Lane, Ditchling, BN6 8XJ
☎ **(01273) 846567**
🖂 admin@midsussexgolfclub.co.uk

Nevill
(1914)
Benhall Mill Road, Tunbridge Wells, TN2 5JW
☎ **(01892) 525818**
🖳 (01892) 517861
🖂 manager@nevillgolfclub.co.uk
📖 800
🖎 TJ Fensom
✓ P Huggett (01892) 532941
ᗑ 18 L 6349 yds SSS 70
👫 WD–H WE/BH–M
££ £33 D–£50
🔗 Tunbridge Wells 1 mile
🖥 www.nevillgolfclub.co.uk

Peacehaven
(1895)
Brighton Road, Newhaven, BN9 9UH
☎ **(01273) 514049**
🖳 (01273) 512571
🖂 golf@peacehavengc.freeserve.co.uk
📖 290
🖎 Mrs D Corke (01273) 512571
✓ A Tyson (01273) 512602
ᗑ 9 L 5488 yds Par 70 SSS 66
👫 WD–U WE/BH–after 11am SOC
££ £16 (£22)

🔗 8 miles E of Brighton on A259
⌂ James Braid

Piltdown
(1904)
Piltdown, Uckfield, TN22 3XB
☎ **(01825) 722033**
🖳 (01825) 724192
🖂 piltdowngolf@lineone.net
📖 400
🖎 Peter de Pinna (Hon)
✓ J Partridge (01825) 722389
ᗑ 18 L 6076 yds Par 68 SSS 69
👫 I or H exc BH/Tues am/Thurs
am/Sun am SOC
££ £34 D–£50
🔗 1 mile W of Maresfield, off A272
towards Isfield
⊕ Driving range; pitching area
🖥 www.piltdowngolfclub.co.uk

Royal Ashdown Forest
(1888)
Chapel Lane, Forest Row, East Grinstead, RH18 5LR
☎ **(01342) 822018 (Old)**
(01342) 822247 (West)
🖳 (01342) 825211
🖂 office@royalashdown.co.uk
📖 450
🖎 DED Neave
✓ MA Landsborough (01342) 822247
ᗑ Old 18 L 6502 yds SSS 71
West 18 L 5606 yds SSS 67
👫 On application–phone first
££ Old: £50 D–£70 (£70 R) West:
£27 D–£37 (£32 R)
🔗 4 miles S of E Grinstead on B2110
Hartfield road. M25 Junction 6
⌂ Rev AT Scott
🖥 www.royalashdown.co.uk

Royal Eastbourne
(1887)
Paradise Drive, Eastbourne, BN20 8BP
☎ **(01323) 729738**
🖳 (01323) 744048
🖂 sec@regc.co.uk
📖 850
🖎 David Lockyer (01323) 729278
✓ A Harrison (01323) 736986
ᗑ Devonshire 18 L 6076 yds SSS 69
Hartington 9 L 2147 yds SSS 61
👫 U H SOC–WD
££ Devonshire: £34 (£45) Hartington:
£21 (£21)
🔗 ¹/2 mile from Town Hall
🖥 www.regc.co.uk

Rye
(1894)
New Lydd Road, Camber, Rye, TN31 7QS
☎ **(01797) 225241**
🖳 (01797) 225460
🖂 links@ryegolfclub.co.uk
📖 1000 125(L) 100(J)
🖎 JAL Smith
✓ MP Lee (01797) 225218
ᗑ 18 L 6278 yds SSS 71
9 L 5848 yds SSS 68
👫 M
££ Enquiry necessary – see website
🔗 3 miles E of Rye on B2075
⌂ HS Colt
🖥 www.ryegolfclub.co.uk

For list of abbreviations and key to symbols see page 651

Seaford (1887)

Firle Road, Seaford, BN25 2JD
- ☎ **(01323) 892442**
- 🖥 (01323) 894113
- ✉ secretary@seafordgolfclub.co.uk
- ◫ 420 110(L) 37(J)
- 🏌 LM Dennis-Smither (Gen Mgr)
- ✓ (01323) 894160
- ⊩ 18 L 6546 yds SSS 71
- 👥 WD–H after 10am exc Tues
  WE–M SOC
- ££ D–£40 (£50)
- ↔ 1 mile N of Seaford (A259)
- ⊕ Driving range
- ⌂ JH Taylor
- 🖥 www.seafordgolfclub.co.uk

Seaford Head (1907)

Public
Southdown Road, Seaford, BN25 4JS
- ☎ **(01323) 890139**
- 🏌 RW Andrews (01323) 894843
- ✓ F Morley (01323) 890139
- ⊩ 18 L 5812 yds SSS 68
- 👥 U
- ££ £19 (£22)
- ↔ 8 miles W of Eastbourne. ³/₄ mile S of A259

Sedlescombe (1990)

Kent Street, Sedlescombe, TN33 0SD
- ☎ **(01424) 871700**
- ✉ golf@golfschool.co.uk

Wellshurst G&CC (1992)

North Street, Hellingly, BN27 4EE
- ☎ **(01435) 813636**
- 🖥 (01435) 812444
- ✉ info@wellshurst.com
- ◫ 400
- 🏌 M Adams (Man Dir)
- ✓ M Jarvis (01435) 813456
- ⊩ 18 L 5992 yds SSS 69
- 👥 U SOC
- ££ £20 (£24)
- ↔ 2 miles N of Hailsham on A267
- ⊕ Driving range
- 🖥 www.wellshurst.com

West Hove (1910)

Badgers Way, Hangleton, Hove, BN3 8EX
- ☎ **(01273) 413411 (Clubhouse)**
- 🖥 (01273) 439988
- ✉ info@westhovegolfclub.co.uk
- ◫ 600
- 🏌 Megan Bibby (Mgr) (01273) 419738
- ✓ D Cook (01273) 413494
- ⊩ 18 L 6226 yds SSS 70 Par 71
- 👥 U–phone first SOC
- ££ £25 (£30); after 4 pm: £16 (£21)
- ↔ N of Brighton By-pass. 2nd junction W from A23 flyover
- ⊕ Practice driving range (18 bays)
- ⌂ Hawtree
- 🖥 www.westhovegolfclub.info

Willingdon (1898)

Southdown Road, Eastbourne, BN20 9AA
- ☎ **(01323) 410981**
- 🖥 (01323) 411510
- ◫ 630

- 🏌 Mrs J Packham (01323) 410981
- ✓ T Moore (01323) 410984
- ⊩ 18 L 6049 yds SSS 69
- 👥 WD–U H WE–MH exc Sun am–NA SOC–H
- ££ D–£25 (£28)
- ↔ ¹/₂ mile N of Eastbourne, off A2200
- ⌂ JH Taylor/Dr A Mackenzie

Sussex (West)

Bognor Regis (1892)

Downview Road, Felpham, Bognor Regis, PO22 8JD
- ☎ **(01243) 865867**
- 🖥 (01243) 860719
- ✉ sec@bognorgolfclub.co.uk
- ◫ 750
- 🏌 PI Bodle (01243) 821929
- ✓ M Kirby (01243) 865209
- ⊩ 18 L 6121 yds Par 70 SSS 69
- 👥 WD–I or H after 9.30am WE/BH–M (Apr–Sept), 1 H (Oct–Mar) SOC–WD
- ££ £30 (£35)
- ↔ 2 miles E of Bognor Regis, off A259
- ⌂ James Braid
- 🖥 www.bognorgolfclub.co.uk

Burgess Hill Golf Centre (1995)

Pay and play
Cuckfield Road, Burgess Hill
- ☎ **(01444) 242993 (office)**
  (01444) 258585 (shop)
- 🖥 (01444) 247318
- ✉ enquiries@burgesshillgolfcentre .co.uk
- 🏌 CJ Collins (Mgr)
- ✓ M Groombridge
- ⊩ 9 hole Par 3 course
- 👥 U
- ££ On application
- ↔ N of Burgess Hill
- ⊕ Floodlit driving range; PGA Short Course Championship (annually)
- ⌂ Steel/Collins
- 🖥 www.burgesshillgolfcentre.co.uk

Chartham Park (1993)

Proprietary
Felcourt, East Grinstead, RH19 2JT
- ☎ **(01342) 870340**
- 🖥 (01342) 870719
- ✉ d.hobbs@clubhaus.com
- 🏌 V Machin
- ✓ D Hobbs (01342) 870008
- ⊩ 18 L 6688 yds Par 72 SSS 72
- 👥 WD–U WE–U after 2pm
- ££ £50 (£60)
- ↔ 2 miles N of East Grinstead, off A22. M25 Junction 6
- ⊕ Driving range
- ⌂ Neil Coles
- 🖥 www.clubhaus.com

Chichester (1990)

Hunston Village, Chichester, PO20 6AX
- ☎ **(01243) 533833**
- ✉ enquiries@chichestergolf.com

Copthorne (1892)

Borers Arms Road, Copthorne, RH10 3LL
- ☎ **(01342) 712508**
- 🖥 (01342) 717682
- ✉ info@copthornegolfclub.co.uk
- ◫ 565
- 🏌 JP Pyne (01342) 712033
- ✓ J Burrell (01342) 712405
- ⊩ 18 L 6435 yds SSS 71
- 👥 WD–U WE/BH–after 1pm SOC
- ££ £36 (£44)
- ↔ 1 mile E of M23 Junction 10, on A264
- ⌂ James Braid
- 🖥 www.copthornegolfclub.co.uk

Cottesmore (1975)

Proprietary
Buchan Hill, Pease Pottage, Crawley, RH11 9AT
- ☎ **(01293) 528256**
- 🖥 (01293) 522819
- ✉ cottesmore@americangolf.uk.com
- ◫ 800
- 🏌 J lavan
- ✓ C Callan (01293) 861777
- ⊩ Griffin 18 L 6248 yds Par 71 SSS 70
  Phoenix 18 L 5514 yds Par 69 SSS 66
- 👥 U SOC
- ££ Griffin–£29 (£33) Phoenix–£16 (£20)
- ↔ Pease Pottage S of Crawley, 1.5m from M23 J11
- ⌂ MD Rogerson

Cowdray Park (1920)

Petworth Road, Midhurst, GU29 0BB
- ☎ **(01730) 813599**
- 🖥 (01730) 815900
- ✉ enquiries@cowdraygolf.co.uk
- ◫ 700
- 🏌 M Upfield
- ✓ S Brown (01730) 813599
- ⊩ 18 L 6265 yds SSS 70
- 👥 H U SOC Mon–Thur
- ££ £45
- ↔ 1 mile E of Midhurst on A272
- ⊕ Driving range on site
- ⌂ T Simpson
- 🖥 www.cowdraygolf.co.uk

Effingham Park (1980)

Proprietary
West Park Road, Copthorne, RH10 3EU
- ☎ **(01342) 716528**
- ✉ mark.root@mill-cop/com

Foxbridge (1993)

Foxbridge Lane, Plaistow, RH14 0LB
- ☎ **(01403) 753303 (Bookings)**
- 🖥 (01403) 753303
- ◫ 300
- 🏌 PA Clark
- ✓ S Hall
- ⊩ 9 L 3118 yds SSS 70
- 👥 U SOC
- ££ £14 (£16) 9 hole game
- ↔ 15 miles S of Guildford, off B2133
- ⌂ Paul Clark

Golf At Goodwood   (1892)
Kennel Hill, Goodwood, Chichester,
PO18 0PN
- ☎ **(01243) 755133**
- 🖨 (01243) 755135
- ✉ golf@goodwood.co.uk
- 📖 1200
- 🏌 Mark Vickery (01243) 755130
- ⌀ Damon Allard (01243) 755133
- ⓟ 18 L 7104 yds Par 71 SSS 74
- 👥 M
- 🚗 3 miles NE of Chichester, on road to racecourse
- ⊕ Driving range and short game practice area
- 🏠 James Braid/Howard Swan
- 🖥 www.goodwood.co.uk

Ham Manor   (1936)
West Drive, Angmering, Littlehampton,
BN16 4JE
- ☎ **(01903) 783288**
- 🖨 (01903) 850886
- ✉ secretary@hammanor.co.uk
- 📖 860
- 🏌 Roy Brown
- ⌀ S Buckley (01903) 783732
- ⓟ 18 L 6301 yds SSS 70
- 👥 WD/WE–H
- ££ £35 (£50)
- 🚗 Between Worthing and Littlehampton
- 🏠 HS Colt
- 🖥 www.hammanor.co.uk

Hassocks   (1995)
Pay and play
London Road, Hassocks, BN6 9NA
- ☎ **(01273) 846990**
- 🖨 (01273) 846070
- 📖 350
- 🏌 Mrs J Brown (Gen Mgr) (01273) 846630
- ⌀ C Ledger (01273) 846990
- ⓟ 18 L 5703 yds Par 70 SSS 67
- 👥 U
- ££ £18 (£24)
- 🚗 1 mile S of Burgess Hill on A273. 7 miles N of Brighton
- ⊕ Driving range, irons only
- 🏠 Paul Wright
- 🖥 www.hassocksgolfclub.co.uk

Haywards Heath   (1922)
High Beech Lane, Haywards Heath,
RH16 1SL
- ☎ **(01444) 414457**
- 🖨 (01444) 458319
- ✉ info@haywardsheathgolfclub.co.uk
- 📖 752
- 🏌 GK Honeysett
- ⌀ M Henning (01444) 414866
- ⓟ 18 L 6216 yds SSS 70
- 👥 WD/WE–H–restricted SOC–Wed/Thurs WD/WE–M before 12 noon–H
- ££ £29 (£40)
- 🚗 1.5 miles N of Haywards Heath, off B2028
- ⊕ Driving range; short game practice area; putting green
- 🏠 James Braid
- 🖥 www.haywardsheathgolfclub.co.uk

Hill Barn   (1935)
Public
Hill Barn Lane, Worthing, BN14 9QE
- ☎ **(01903) 237301**
- ✉ info@hillbarn.com

Hilton Avisford Park   (1990)
Pay and play
Yapton Lane, Walberton, Arundel,
BN18 0LS
- ☎ **(01243) 554611**
- 🖨 (01243) 558313
- 📖 240
- 🏌 N Upjohn
- ⌀ C Rota
- ⓟ 18 L 5390 yds Par 67 SSS 66
- 👥 U SOC
- ££ £16.50 (£20) Twilight after 3pm £10
- 🚗 4 miles W of Arundel on A27
- ⊕ In grounds of Hilton Hotel

Horsham   (1993)
Pay and play
Worthing Road, Horsham, RH13 0AX
- ☎ **(01403) 271525**
- 🖨 (01403) 274528
- 📖 300
- 🏌 Elaine Purton
- ⌀ Alex Paterson
- ⓟ 9 L 2061 yds Par 33 SSS 30
- 👥 U SOC
- ££ 9: £8 (£9); 18: £11 (£13)
- 🚗 1 mile S of Horsham, off A24

Ifield   (1927)
Rusper Road, Ifield, Crawley, RH11 0LN
- ☎ **(01293) 520222**

Littlehampton   (1889)
170 Rope Walk, Littlehampton, BN17 5DL
- ☎ **(01903) 717170**
- 🖨 (01903) 726629
- ✉ lgc@talk21.com
- 📖 650
- 🏌 S Graham
- ⌀ S Fallow (ext 225)
- ⓟ 18 L 6244 yds SSS 70
- 👥 WD–U after 9am WE/BH–NA before 1pm
- ££ £30 (£40)
- 🚗 W bank of River Arun, Littlehampton
- 🏠 Hawtree
- 🖥 www.littlehamptongolf.co.uk

Mannings Heath   (1905)
Proprietary
Fullers, Hammerpond Road, Mannings Heath, Horsham, RH13 6PG
- ☎ **(01403) 210228**
- 🖨 (01403) 270974
- 📖 730
- 🏌 J Pleydell
- ⌀ C Tucker (01403) 210228
- ⓟ Waterfall 18 L 6378 yds Par 73 SSS 70 Kingfisher 18 L 6217 yds Par 70 SSS 70
- 👥 U SOC WD–U WE–U after noon
- ££ From £42
- 🚗 3 miles SE of Horsham (A281). M23 Junction 11

- ⊕ Driving range; steam room
- 🏠 Kingfisher-David Williams Waterfall-unknown
- 🖥 www.exclusivehotels.co.uk

Marriott Goodwood Park G&CC   (1989)
Goodwood, Chichester, PO18 0QB
- ☎ **(01243) 520117**
- 🖨 (01243) 520120
- ✉ adrian.wratting@marriotthotels .co.uk
- 📖 600
- 🏌 Adrian Wratting
- ⌀ Christoan Foeden
- ⓟ 18 L 6530 yds SSS 72
- 👥 SOC anytime U
- ££ £40
- 🚗 4 miles N of Chichester
- ⊕ Driving range
- 🏠 Donald Steel
- 🖥 www.marriotthotels.co.uk

Paxhill Park   (1990)
East Mascalls Lane, Lindfield, RH16 2QN
- ☎ **(01444) 484467**
- ✉ johnbowen@paxhillpark.fsnet.co.uk

Pease Pottage   (1986)
Horsham Road, Pease Pottage, Crawley,
RH11 9AP
- ☎ **(01293) 521706**

Petworth   (1989)
Pay and play
Osiers Farm, London Road, Petworth
GU28 9LX
- ☎ **(01798) 344097/ (07932) 163941 (01798) 344097 (Mgr)**
- ✉ info@petworthgolfcourse.co.uk
- 📖 150
- 🏌 John Davis (01903) 610859
- ⌀ S Hall (01798) 873487
- ⓟ 18 L 6191 yds Par 71 SSS 69
- 👥 U SOC
- ££ £15 D–£25
- 🚗 2½ miles N of Petworth on A283
- ⊕ Practice net/green
- 🏠 C & T Duncton
- 🖥 www.petworthgolfcourse.co.uk

Pyecombe   (1894)
Clayton Hill, Pyecombe, Brighton, BN45 7FF
- ☎ **(01273) 845372**
- 🖨 (01273) 843338
- ✉ info@pyecombegolfclub.com
- 📖 550
- 🏌 M Harrity
- ⌀ CR White (01273) 845398
- ⓟ 18 L 6221 yds SSS 70
- 👥 WD–U exc Tues after 9.15am WE–U after 2pm SOC–Mon/Wed/Thurs
- ££ £25 (£30)
- 🚗 6 miles N of Brighton on A273

Rustington   (1992)
Public
Golfers Lane, Angmering, BN16 4NB
- ☎ **(01903) 850790**

Selsey   (1908)
Golf Links Lane, Selsey, PO20 9DR
☎ **(01243) 605176 (Members)**
⌨ (01243) 607101
✉ secretary@selseygolfclub.co.uk
📖 400
🏌 P Carter (01243) 608936
✓ P Grindley (01243) 608936
⛳ 9 L 5834 yds SSS 68
👥 U SOC
££ 9: £11 (£12) 18: £15 (£20)
🚗 7 miles S of Chichester
🏠 JH Taylor
💻 www.selseygolfclub.co.uk

Shillinglee Park   (1980)
Pay and play
Chiddingfold, Godalming, GU8 4TA
☎ **(01428) 653237**

Singing Hills   (1992)
Proprietary
Albourne, Brighton, BN6 9EB
☎ **(01273) 835353**
⌨ (01273) 835444
✉ info@singinghills.co.uk
📖 450
🏌 Nicholas Hughes
✓ W Street
⛳ 27 holes SSS 69-72:
   River 9 L 2826 yds
   Valley 9 L 3348 yds
   Lakes 9 L 3253 yds
👥 U SOC
££ £25 (£33.50)
🚗 6 miles N of Brighton, off B2117
⊕ Driving range
🏠 MRM Sandow
💻 www.singinghills.co.uk

Slinfold Park   (1993)
*Stone Street, Slinfold, Horsham,
RH13 7RE*
☎ **(01403) 791154
   (Clubhouse)**

Tilgate Forest   (1982)
Public
*Titmus Drive, Tilgate, Crawley,
RH10 5EU*
☎ **(01293) 530103**

West Chiltington   (1988)
Proprietary
*Broadford Bridge Road, West Chiltington,
RH20 2YA*
☎ **(01798) 813574**
⌨ (01798) 812631
✉ richard@westchiltington.co.uk
📖 500
🏌 R Gough
✓ James Lockrose (01798) 812115
⛳ 18 L 5969 yds Par 70 SSS 68
   9 hole Par 3 course
👥 U SOC
££ £25 (£30)
🚗 2 miles E of Pulborough
⊕ Driving range
🏠 Faulkner/Barnes

West Sussex   (1931)
*Golf Club Lane, Wiggonholt, Pulborough,
RH20 2EN*
☎ **(01798) 872563**
⌨ (01798) 872033
✉ secretary@westsussexgolf.co.uk
📖 800
🏌 CP Simpson
✓ T Packham (01798) 872426
⛳ 18 L 6264 yds SSS 70
👥 WD–I H after 9.30am exc Fri–M
   SOC–Wed & Thurs
££ On application
🚗 1½ miles E of Pulborough on A283
⊕ Driving range
🏠 Campbell/Hutcheson/Hotchkin
💻 www.westsussexgolf.co.uk

Worthing   (1905)
Links Road, Worthing, BN14 9QZ
☎ **(01903) 260801**
⌨ (01903) 694664
✉ enquiries@worthinggolf.com
📖 1000
🏌 IJ Evans (01903) 260801
✓ S Rolley (01903) 260718
⛳ Lower 18 L 6530 yds Par 71 SSS 71
   Upper 18 L 5243 yds Par 66 SSS 65
👥 WD–U H WE–confirm in advance
   with Pro
££ On application
🚗 Central Station 1½ miles (A27), nr
   A24 Junction
🏠 HS Colt
💻 www.worthinggolf.co.uk

Tyne & Wear

Backworth   (1937)
*The Hall, Backworth, Shiremoor, Newcastle-
upon-Tyne, NE27 0AH*
☎ **(0191) 268 1048**

Birtley   (1922)
Birtley Lane, Birtley, DH3 2LR
☎ **(0191) 410 2207**
⌨ (0191) 410 2207
✉ birtleygolfclub@aol.com
📖 360
🏌 GE Barras
⛳ 9 L 5729 yds SSS 67 (men)
   9 L 5098 yds SSS 69 (ladies)
👥 WD–U before 4.30 pm WE/BH–M
   SOC
££ £15
🚗 3 miles from Birtley service area on
   A1(M)
💻 www.birtleyportobellogolfclub
   .co.uk

Boldon   (1912)
Dipe Lane, East Boldon, NE36 0PQ
☎ **(0191) 536 5360 (Clubhouse)**
⌨ (0191) 537 2270
✉ info@boldongolfclub.co.uk
📖 700
🏌 Alastair Greenfield (0191) 536
   5360
✓ Phipps Golf (0191) 536 5835
⛳ 18 L 6348 yds SSS 70

👥 WD–U WE/BH–NA before 2pm
££ £18 (£21.50)
🚗 8 miles SE of Newcastle
⊕ Driving range
🏠 H Vardon
💻 www.boldongolfclub.co.uk

City of Newcastle   (1891)
*Three Mile Bridge, Gosforth, Newcastle-
upon-Tyne, NE3 2DR*
☎ **(0191) 285 1775**
⌨ (0191) 284 0700
✉ info@cityofnewcastlegolfclub.co.uk
📖 400 110(L) 60(J)
🏌 AJ Matthew (Mgr)
✓ S McKenna (0191) 285 5481
⛳ 18 L 6523 yds SSS 71
👥 U SOC
££ £28 D–£34 (£35)
🚗 B1318, 3 miles N of Newcastle
🏠 Harry Vardon
💻 www.cityofnewcastlegolfclub.co.uk

Garesfield   (1922)
Chopwell, NE17 7AP
☎ **(01207) 561309**
⌨ (01207) 561309
✉ office@garesfieldgc.fsnet.co.uk
📖 700
🏌 Mrs J Barclay
✓ D Race (01207) 563082
⛳ 18 L 6458 yds SSS 71
👥 U (NA Sat)
££ On application
🚗 On B6315 to High Spen off A694
   from A1 at Rowlands Gill
🏠 William Woodend
💻 www.garesfieldgolf.com

Gosforth   (1906)
*Broadway East, Gosforth, Newcastle upon
Tyne, NE3 5ER*
☎ **(0191) 285 6710**
⌨ (0191) 284 6274
✉ gosforth.golf@virgin.net
📖 380 100(L) 60(J)
🏌 B Pluse (0191) 285 3495
✓ G Garland (0191) 285 0553
⛳ 18 L 6024 yds SSS 69
👥 U SOC
££ £25 (£28)
🚗 3 miles N of Newcastle, off A6125
💻 www.gosforthgolfclub.com

Hetton-le-Hill
Pay and play
*Elemore Golf Course, Elemore Lane,
DH5 0QB*
☎ **(0191) 517 3057**
⌨ (0191) 517 3054
📖 200
🏌 William Allen
⛳ 18 L 5963 yds Par 69 SSS 68
👥 U SOC
££ £12 (£15)
🚗 4 miles E of A1(M)/A690 junction

Heworth   (1912)
*Gingling Gate, Heworth, Gateshead,
NE10 8XY*
☎ **(0191) 469 9832**
⌨ (0191) 469 9898

✉ secretary@theheworthgolfclub
.co.uk
☎ 800
♨ CJ Watson
✓ A Marshall
▷ 18 L 6404 yds SSS 71
👥 WD–U WE–NA before noon
££ £22 (£25)
🚗 SE boundary of Gateshead
▤ www.theheworthgolfclub.co.uk

Houghton-le-Spring   (1908)
Copt Hill, Houghton-le-Spring, Tyne &
Wear, DH5 8LU
☎ **(0191) 584 1198 (Clubhouse)**
(0191) 584 0048 (Office)
🖵 (0191) 584 0048
✉ houghton.golf@ntlworld.com
📖 600
♨ Graeme Ferguson (Hon Sec)
(0191) 584 0048
✓ K Gow (0191) 584 7421
▷ 18 L 6381 yds Par 72 SSS 71
👥 U SOC
££ £25 D–£30 (£30 D–£35)
🚗 3 miles SW of Sunderland
▤ www.houghtongolfclub.co.uk

Newcastle United   (1892)
Ponteland Road, Cowgate, Newcastle-upon-
Tyne, NE5 3JW
☎ **(0191) 286 9998 (Clubhouse)**
🖵 (0191) 286 4323
✉ info@nugc.co.uk
📖 650
♨ S Darbyshire (Hon)
✓ (0191) 286 9998
▷ 18 L 6617 yds SSS 72
👥 WD–U WE/BH–M
££ On application
🚗 Nuns Moor, 2 miles W of city
centre
⌂ Tom Morris
▤ www.nugc.co.uk

Northumberland   (1898)
High Gosforth Park, Newcastle-upon-Tyne,
NE3 5HT
☎ **(0191) 236 2498/2009**
🖵 (0191) 236 2036
✉ sec@thengc.co.uk
📖 500
♨ Jamie Forteath
✓ None
▷ 18 L 6680 yds SSS 72
👥 WD/WE/BH–U H
££ £40 D–£50 (£50)
🚗 5 miles N of Newcastle
⌂ HS Colt/James Braid
▤ www.thengc.co.uk

Parklands   (1971)
High Gosforth Park, Newcastle-upon-Tyne,
NE3 5HQ
☎ **(0191) 236 4480**

Ravensworth   (1906)
Angel View, Long Bank, Gateshead,
NE9 7NE
☎ **(0191) 487 6014**
✉ ravensworth.golfclub@virgin.net
📖 550
♨ John Jackson

✓ S Cowell (0191) 491 3475
▷ 18 L 5872 yds SSS 69
👥 U H SOC–contact Pro
££ £20 (£25)
🚗 J65 A1(M), take A1 northbound; at
next junction take B1296
Wrekenton
▤ www.ravensworthgolfclub.co.uk

Ryton   (1891)
Doctor Stanners, Clara Vale, Ryton,
NE40 3TD
☎ **(0191) 413 3253**
🖵 (0191) 413 1642
✉ secretary@rytongolfclub.co.uk
📖 600
♨ Mrs H Oliver
▷ 18 L 5499 metres SSS 69
👥 WD–U WE–M SOC
££ £16 (£21)
🚗 7 miles W of Newcastle, off A695

South Shields   (1893)
Cleadon Hills, South Shields, NE34 8EG
☎ **(0191) 456 0475**
✉ thesecretary@south-shields-golf
.freeserve.co.uk

Tynemouth   (1913)
Spital Dene, Tynemouth, North Shields,
NE30 2ER
☎ **(0191) 257 4578**
🖵 (0191) 259 5193
✉ secretary@tynemouthgolfclub.com
📖 855
♨ TJ Scott (0191) 257 3381
✓ J McKenna (0191) 258 0728
▷ 18 L 6359 yds SSS 70
👥 WD–U (except Tue am)
9.30am–5pm –NA before 9.30am
and after 5pm WE/BH–M
££ £22.50 D–£25.50
🚗 8 miles E of Newcastle
⌂ Willie Park
▤ www.tynemouthgolfclub.com

Tyneside   (1879)
Westfield Lane, Ryton, NE40 3QE
☎ **(0191) 413 2742**
🖵 (0191) 413 0199
✉ edstephenson@tynesidegolfclub
.fsbusiness.co.uk
📖 660
♨ E Stephenson (0191) 413 2742
✓ G Dixon (0191) 413 1600
▷ 18 L 6009 yds SSS 69
👥 WD–U exc 11.30–1.30pm Sat–NA
Sun–NA before 3pm SOC
££ £30 (£30)
🚗 7 miles W of Newcastle. S of river,
off A695
⌂ HS Colt

Wallsend   (1973)
Public
Rheydt Avenue, Bigges Main, Wallsend,
NE28 8SU
☎ **(0191) 262 1973**
♨ D Souter
✓ K Phillips (0191) 262 4231
▷ 18 L 6031 yds Par 70 SSS 69
👥 U

££ £20 (£24)
🚗 Between Newcastle and Wallsend
on coast road
⊕ Driving range
⌂ G Showball

Washington   (1979)
Stone Cellar Road, High Usworth,
Washington, NE37 1PH
☎ **(0191) 417 8346**
🖵 (0191) 415 1166
✉ graeme.amanda@btopenworld.com
📖 600
♨ G Robinson
✓ G Robinson
▷ 18 L 6604 yds SSS 71
9 hole Par 3 course
👥 WD–U WE–after 10.30am SOC
££ Mon–Thur £20 (Fri–Sun £25)
🚗 Off A194 on A195
⊕ Driving range; 100 room hotel
▤ www.georgewashington.co.uk

Wearside   (1892)
Coxgreen, Sunderland, SR4 9JT
☎ **(0191) 534 2518**
🖵 (0191) 534 6186
✉ secretary@wearsidegolf.com
📖 800
♨ A Atkinson
✓ D Brolls (0191) 534 4269
▷ 18 L 6315 yds SSS 70
Par 3 course
👥 H SOC
££ £20 (£26)
🚗 2 miles W of Sunderland, off A183,
by A19
▤ www.wearsidegolf.com

Westerhope   (1941)
Whorlton Grange, Westerhope, Newcastle-
upon-Tyne, NE5 1PP
☎ **(0191) 286 9125**
🖵 (0191) 214 6287
✉ wgc@btconnect.com
📖 778
♨ B Bell (0191) 286 7636
✓ N Brown (0191) 286 0594
▷ 18 L 6407 yds SSS 71
👥 WD–U
££ £24
🚗 5 miles W of Newcastle

Whickham   (1911)
Hollinside Park, Fellside Road, Whickham,
Newcastle-upon-Tyne NE16 5BA
☎ **(0191) 488 7309 (Clubhouse)**

Whitburn   (1931)
Lizard Lane, South Shields, NE34 7AF
☎ **(0191) 529 2144**
🖵 (0191) 529 4944
✉ wgsec@ukonline.co.uk
📖 580 73(L) 85(J)
♨ Mr A Atkinson (0191) 529 4944
✓ N Whinham (0191) 529 4210
▷ 18 L 5899 yds Par 70 SSS 68
👥 U SOC–WD exc Tues
££ £22 (£27)
🚗 2 miles N of Sunderland on coast
road overlooking mouth of River
Tyne

⌂ Colt/Alison/Morrison
▤ www.golf-whitburn.co.uk

Whitley Bay (1890)
Claremont Road, Whitley Bay, NE26 3UF
☎ (0191) 252 0180
🖳 (0191) 297 0030
✉ secretary@whitleybaygolfclub.co.uk
📖 700
⛳ P Simpson (0191) 252 0180
✓ G Shipley (0191) 252 5688
🏴 18 L 6579 yds SSS 71
👥 WD–U WE–Sun only after noon
££ £30 D–£40 (£35)
⊶ 10 miles E of Newcastle
▤ www.whitleybaygolfclub.co.uk

Warwickshire

Ansty (1990)
Pay and play
Brinklow Road, Ansty, Coventry, CV7 9JL
☎ (024) 7662 1341/7660 2568
🖳 (024) 7660 2568
📖 309
⛳ K Smith
✓ M Goodwin (02476) 621341
🏴 18 L 6079 yds Par 71 SSS 69
Par 3 course
👥 U SOC WD–WE
££ £12 (£18)
⊶ Between Ansty and Brinklow
(B4029). M6 Junction 2, 1 mile.
⊕ Driving range; putting green;
practice area
⌂ D Morgan
▤ www.anstygolfcentre.co.uk

Atherstone (1894)
The Outwoods, Coleshill Road, Atherstone, CV9 2RL
☎ (01827) 713110
🖳 (01827) 715686
📖 400 40(L) 40(J)
⛳ VA Walton (01827) 892568
🏴 18 L 6012 yds Par 72 SSS 70
👥 WD–U BH/Sat–M Sun–M after
5pm SOC–WD
££ D–£25
⊶ 1/4 mile from Atherstone on
Coleshill road. M42 Jct 10
⊕ Buggies for hire - phone for details

The De Vere Belfry (1977)
Public
Wishaw, B76 9PR
☎ (01675) 470301

Boldmere (1936)
Public
Monmouth Drive, Sutton Coldfield, Birmingham, BJ3 6JR
☎ (0121) 354 3379
🖳 (0121) 353 5576
✉ boldmeregolfclub@hotmail.com
📖 300
⛳ R Leeson
✓ T Short
🏴 18 L 4463 yds SSS 62
👥 U

££ £11.50 (£13.50)
⊶ By Sutton Park, 1 mile W of Sutton
Coldfield
▤ www.boldmeregolfclub.co.uk

Bramcote Waters
Pay and play
Bazzard Road, Bramcote, Nuneaton, CV11 6QJ
☎ (01455) 220807
🖳 (02476) 388775
⛳ Sara Britain (01455) 220807
✓ N Gilks
🏴 9 L 4995 yds Par 66 SSS 64
👥 U
££ £16 (£17)
⊶ 4 miles SE of Nuneaton, off B4114
⌂ David Snell

City of Coventry (Brandon Wood) (1977)
Public
Brandon Lane, Coventry, CV8 3GQ
☎ (024) 7654 3141
🖳 (024) 7654 5108
✉ brandongolf@coventrysports.uk
📖 300
⛳ C Gledhill
✓ C Gledhill
🏴 18 L 6521 yds SSS 71
👥 U SOC
££ On application
⊶ 6 miles SE of Coventry, off A45(S)
⊕ Floodlit driving range
▤ www.brandonwood.co.uk

Copsewood Grange (1924)
Copsewood, Coventry, CV3 1HS
☎ (024) 7656 3339
📖 370
⛳ REC Jones (024) 7645 2973
🏴 9 L 6048 yds SSS 71
👥 WD–U before 2.30pm exc
Wed–NA Sat–NA Sun–NA before
noon
££ £15 (£20)
⊶ 2 1/2 miles E of Coventry on A428
⌂ TJ McAuley

Copt Heath (1907)
1220 Warwick Road, Knowle, Solihull, B93 9LN
☎ (01564) 772650
🖳 (01564) 771022
✉ golf@copt-heath.co.uk
📖 700
⛳ CV Hadley
✓ BJ Barton (01564) 776155
🏴 18 L 6522 yds SSS 71
👥 WD/WE–H BH–M SOC
££ £40 – £50
⊶ 2 miles S of Solihull on A4141. M42
J5, half a mile
▤ www.coptheathgolf.co.uk

Coventry (1887)
St Martins Road, Finham Park, Coventry, CV3 6RJ
☎ (024) 7641 4152
🖳 (024) 7669 0131
✉ coventrygolfclub@hotmail.com

📖 750
⛳ A Smith (024) 7641 4152
✓ P Weaver (024) 7641 1298
🏴 18 L 6601 yds SSS 73
👥 WD–H
££ D–£40
⊶ 2 miles S of Coventry on
A444/B4113
⌂ Vardon/Hawtree
▤ www.coventrygolfcourse.co.uk

Coventry Hearsall (1894)
Beechwood Avenue, Coventry, CV5 6DF
☎ (024) 7671 3470
🖳 (024) 7669 1534
✉ secretary
@coventryhearsallgolfclub.co.uk
📖 600
⛳ A Richards
✓ M Tarn (024) 7671 3156
🏴 18 L 6005 yds SSS 69
👥 WD–U WE–M
££ D–£35
⊶ 1 1/2 miles S of Coventry, off A45
▤ www.hearsallgolfclub.co.uk

Edgbaston (1896)
Church Road, Edgbaston, Birmingham, B15 3TB
☎ (0121) 454 1736
🖳 (0121) 454 2395
✉ secretary@edgbastongc.co.uk
📖 950
⛳ AD Grint
✓ J Cundy (0121) 454 3226
🏴 18 L 6106 yds SSS 69
👥 H SOC
££ £45 (£55)
⊶ 1 1/2 miles S of Birmingham, off A38
⌂ HS Colt
▤ www.edgbastongc.co.uk

Harborne (1893)
40 Tennal Road, Harborne, Birmingham, B32 2JE
☎ (0121) 427 1728
🖳 (0121) 427 4039
✉ harborne@hgolf.fsnet.co.uk
📖 600
⛳ GA Tozer (0121) 427 3058
✓ P Johnson (0121) 427 3512
🏴 18 L 6210 yds SSS 70
👥 WD–U WE/BH–M SOC
££ £30 D–£35
⊶ 3 miles SW of Birmingham. M5
Junction 3
⌂ HS Colt
▤ www.harbornegolfclub.com

Harborne Church Farm (1926)
Public
Vicarage Road, Harborne, Birmingham, B17 0SN
☎ (0121) 427 1204
🖳 (0121) 428 3126
📖 180
✓ P Johnson
🏴 9 L 4882 yds Par 66 SSS 64
👥 U
££ 9: £6.70 (£7.50) 18: £10.30 (£12.50)
⊶ 3 miles SW of Birmingham

⊕ Practice net
▤ www.learnaboutgolf.co.uk

Hatchford Brook (1969)
Public
Coventry Road, Sheldon, Birmingham,
B26 3PY
☎ (0121) 743 9821
🖷 (0121) 743 3420
🖂 idt@hbgc.freeserve.co.uk
▥ 400
🏌 ID Thomson (0121) 742 6643
✓ M Hampton
🏴 18 L 6137 yds Par 70 SSS 69
🏌 U SOC
££ £11.50 (£13.50) concessions
🚗 City boundary close to airport.
A45/M42 Junction
▤ www.golfpro-direct.co.uk/hbgc

Henley G&CC (1994)
Proprietary
Birmingham Road, Henley-in-Arden,
B95 5QA
☎ (01564) 793715
🖷 (01564) 795754
🖂 enquiries@henleygcc.co.uk
▥ 500
🏌 G Wright (Ch Exec)
✓ N Hyde
🏴 18 L 6933 yds SSS 73
9 hole Par 3 course
🏌 U–booking required SOC
££ £28 (£36)
🚗 Henley-in-Arden
⊕ Driving range; buggies available
🏛 N Selwyn-Smith
▤ www.henleygcc.co.uk

Hilltop (1979)
Public
Park Lane, Handsworth, Birmingham,
B21 8LJ
☎ (0121) 554 4463
🏌 K Highfield (Mgr & Sec)
✓ K Highfield
🏴 18 L 6114 yds SSS 69
🏌 U but phone to book start time
££ £11.50 (£13.50)
🚗 Sandwell Valley. M5 Jct 1 orM6
Jct 7
🏛 Hawtree

Ingon Manor (1993)
Ingon Lane, Snitterfield, Stratford-on-Avon,
CV37 0QE
☎ (01789) 731857
🖂 info@ingonmanor.co.uk
▥ 350
✓ N Evans (01789) 731938
🏴 18 L 6575 yds Par 73 SSS 71
🏌 U H SOC
££ £25 (£30)
🚗 3 miles N of Stratford-on-Avon, off
A461. M40 Junction 15
⊕ Driving range
🏛 David Hemstock
▤ www.ingonmanor.co.uk

Kenilworth (1889)
Crewe Lane, Kenilworth, CV8 2EA
☎ (01926) 854296

🖷 (01926) 864453
🖂 secretary@kenilworthgolfclub
.co.uk
▥ 750
🏌 John McTavish (01926) 858517
✓ Steve Yates (01926) 512732
🏴 18 L 6400 yds SSS 71
🏌 U H BH–M SOC–WD
££ £35 (£45) per round/day
🚗 1½ miles E of Kenilworth. 5 miles
S of Coventry
🏛 Hawtree
▤ www.kenilworthgolfclub.co.uk

Ladbrook Park (1908)
Poolhead Lane, Tanworth-in-Arden, Solihull,
B94 5ED
☎ (01564) 742264
🖷 (01564) 742909
🖂 secretary@ladbrookparkgolf.co.uk
▥ 700
🏌 MR Newman
✓ R Mountford (01564) 742581
🏴 18 L 6427 yds SSS 71
🏌 WD–U H WE/BH–M H
££ £35
🚗 12 miles S of Birmingham. M42
Junction 3
🏛 HS Colt
▤ www.ladbrookparkgolf.co.uk

Leamington & County
(1908)
Golf Lane, Whitnash, Leamington Spa,
CV31 2QA
☎ (01926) 425961
🖷 (01926) 425961
🖂 secretary@leamingtongolf.co.uk
▥ 650
🏌 David M Beck
✓ J Mellor (01926) 428014
🏴 18 L 6418 yds SSS 72
🏌 U SOC H
££ £35 (£40)
🚗 1½ miles S of Leamington Spa
🏛 HS Colt
▤ www.leamingtongolf.co.uk

Marriott Forest of Arden
Hotel (1970)
Maxstoke Lane, Meriden, Coventry,
CV7 7HR
☎ (01676) 526113
🖷 (01676) 523711
🖂 mhrs/cvtgs.golf@marriotthotels
.com
▥ 650
🏌 I Burns (Golf Dir)
✓ P Hoye
🏴 Arden 18 L 6707 yds Par 72 SSS 73
Aylesford 18 L 5801 yds Par 69
SSS 68
🏌 WD–U SOC–WE
££ Arden–£100 (£110 Fri–Sun)
Aylesford–£45 (£55 Fri–Sun)
🚗 9 miles W of Coventry, off A45.
M6 Jct 4 and M42 Jct 6
⊕ Driving range; practice area;
buggies with gps; putting green
🏛 Donald Steel
▤ www.marriott.com/cvtgs

Maxstoke Park (1898)
Castle Lane, Coleshill, Birmingham,
B46 2RD
☎ (01675) 466743
🖂 maxstokepark@btinternet.com

Menzies Welcombe Hotel
& Golf Course
Warwick Road, Stratford-on-Avon,
CV37 0NR
☎ (01789) 413800

Moor Hall (1932)
Moor Hall Drive, Four Oaks, Sutton
Coldfield, B75 6LN
☎ (0121) 308 6130
🖷 (0121) 308 9560
🖂 secretary@moorhallgolfclub.co.uk
▥ 730
🏌 DJ Etheridge
✓ Cameron Clark (0121) 308 5106
🏴 18 L 6293 yds SSS 70
🏌 WD–U H exc Thurs–U after 1pm
WE/BH–M
££ £45 D–£60
🚗 1 mile E of Sutton Coldfield
🏛 Hawtree & Taylor
▤ www.moorhallgolfclub.co.uk

Newbold Comyn (1973)
Public
Newbold Terrace East, Leamington Spa,
CV32 4EW
☎ (01926) 421157
▥ 191
🏌 CV Baker
✓ David Playdon
🏴 18 L 6315 yds SSS 70
🏌 U WE–booking 1 week in advance
SOC WD–booking 1 week in
advance
££ £10 (£14.50)
🚗 Off Willes Road (B4099)
⊕ 9-hole pitch and putt

North Warwickshire
(1894)
Hampton Lane, Meriden, Coventry,
CV7 7LL
☎ (01676) 522464 (Clubhouse)
🖷 (01676) 523004
🖂 golf@northwarwickshiregc-
fsnet.co.uk
▥ 450
🏌 Mrs A Dicks (Hon) (01676) 522915
✓ A Bownes (01676) 522259
🏴 9 L 6374 yds SSS 71
🏌 WD–U WE/BH–M SOC
££ £22 (£24)
🚗 6 miles W of Coventry, off A45

Nuneaton (1905)
Golf Drive, Whitestone, Nuneaton,
CV11 6QF
☎ (024) 7634 7810
🖷 (024) 7632 7563
🖂 nuneatongolfclub@btconnect.com
▥ 650
🏌 P Smith
✓ C Phillips (024) 7634 0201

18 L 6412 yds SSS 71
WD–U H WE–M SOC
££   £29 D–£35
⊕   2 miles S of Nuneaton, off
Lutterworth road
▤   www.nuneatongolf.com

Oakridge   (1993)
Arley Lane, Ansley Village, Nuneaton,
CV10 9PH
☎   (01676) 541389
▯   (01676) 542709
▥   500
♙   Mrs S Lovric (Admin)
▷   18 L 6242 yds Par 72 SSS 70
♟   U SOC–WD
££   £18
⊕   B4112 from Nuneaton. M6
Junction 3
⌂   Algie Jayes

Olton   (1893)
Mirfield Road, Solihull, B91 1JH
☎   (0121) 705 1083
▯   (0121) 711 2010
✉   secretary@oltongolfclub.fsnet.co.uk
▥   700
♙   R Weatherley (0121) 704 1936
✓   C Haynes (0121) 705 7296
▷   18 L 6232 yds SSS 70
♟   WD–U exc Wed am WE–M
SOC–WD
££   £40
⊕   7 m SE of Birmingham (A41); 2 m
N of M42 J5 (A41)
⊕   Driving range
▤   www.oltongolf.co.uk

Purley Chase   (1980)
Pipers Lane, Ridge Lane, Nuneaton,
CV10 0RB
☎   (024) 7639 3118
✉   enquiries@purley-chase.co.uk

Pype Hayes   (1932)
Public
Eachelhurst Road, Walmley, Sutton
Coldfield, B76 8EP
☎   (0121) 351 1014

Robin Hood   (1893)
St Bernards Road, Solihull, B92 7DJ
☎   (0121) 706 0061
▯   (0121) 700 7502
▥   650
✓   A Harvey (0121) 706 0806
▷   18 L 6635 yds SSS 72
♟   WD–U WE/BH–M SOC–WD H
££   £30 D–£35
⊕   7 miles S of Birmingham
⌂   HS Colt

Rugby   (1891)
Clifton Road, Rugby, CV21 3RD
☎   (01788) 544637 (Clubhouse)
▯   (01788) 542306
✉   golf@rugbygc.fsnet.co.uk
▥   750
♙   Brian Rose (01788) 542306
✓   D Quinn (01788) 575134
▷   18 L 5614 yds SSS 67

♟   WD–U WE–M SOC–WD
££   D–£25 £20 (£15–M)
⊕   1 mile N of Rugby on B5414. M6
J1, M1 J18 or 19
▤   www.rugbygc.co.uk

Shirley   (1956)
Stratford Road, Monkspath, Shirley, Solihull,
B90 4EW
☎   (0121) 744 6001
▯   (0121) 746 5645
✉   shirleygolfclub@btclick.com
▥   650
♙   Steve Wilkins (Gen Mgr)
✓   S Bottrill (0121) 746 5646
▷   18 L 6524 yds SSS 71
♟   WD–U M WE–M SOC (Thur)
££   £30 D–£40
⊕   8 miles S of Birmingham, nr
M42 J4
⊕   4 practice areas inc. covered range
(mid-iron play)
⌂   John Morrison
▤   www.shirleygolfclub.com

Stonebridge
Proprietary
Somers Road, Meriden, CV7 7PL
☎   (01676) 522442
▯   (01676) 522447
✉   conference.dep@stonebridge.co.uk
▥   400
♙   M Clarke
♙   Spencer Edwards
▷   18 L 6250 yds Par 70
♟   U
££   £19 (£25)
⊕   2 miles E of M42 Junction 6
⊕   Driving range; chipping green;
putting green
▤   www.stonebridgegolf.co.uk

Stoneleigh Deer Park
(1992)
The Clubhouse, Coventry Road, Stoneleigh,
CV8 3DR
☎   (024) 7663 9991
▯   (024) 7651 1533
▥   800
♙   C Reay
♙   Matt McGuire/Sarah Perkins
▷   18 L 6023 yds SSS 71
9 hole Par 3 course
♟   WD–U WE–NA before 2pm SOC
££   On application
⊕   ½ mile E of Stoneleigh
⊕   9 hole par 3 course; practice area;
putting green

Stratford Oaks   (1991)
Bearley Road, Snitterfield, Stratford-on-Avon,
CV37 0EZ
☎   (01789) 731980
▯   (01789) 731981
✉   admin@stratfordoaks.co.uk
▥   700
♙   ND Powell (Golf Dir)
✓   A Dunbar
▷   18 L 6135 yds SSS 69
♟   WD–U WE–U booking necessary
££   £25 (£30)
⊕   4 miles NE of Stratford-on-Avon

⊕   Driving range & short game
practice area; physiotherapist on
site
⌂   Howard Swann

Stratford-on-Avon   (1894)
Tiddington Road, Stratford-on-Avon,
CV37 7BA
☎   (01789) 205749
✉   sec@stratford.co.uk

Sutton Coldfield   (1889)
110 Thornhill Road, Sutton Coldfield,
B74 3ER
☎   (0121) 580 7878
▯   (0121) 353 5503
✉   admin@suttoncoldfieldgc.com
▥   600
♙   RG Mltchell, KM Tempest
(0121) 353 9633
✓   JK Hayes (0121) 580 7878
▷   18 L 6541 yds SSS 71
♟   U H SOC
££   £30 D–£40 (£40)
⊕   9 miles N of Birmingham, off B4138
⌂   Dr Mackenzie
▤   www.suttoncoldfieldgc.com

Walmley   (1902)
Brooks Road, Wylde Green, Sutton
Coldfield, B72 1HR
☎   (0121) 373 0029
▯   (0121) 377 7272
✉   walmleygolfclub@aol.com
▥   750
♙   E Barnsley
✓   CJ Wicketts (0121) 373 0029 ext 5
▷   18 L 6603yds SSS 72
♟   WD–U WE–M SOC H
££   £30 D–£35
⊕   Off A5127 (Birmingham Road), half
mile N of junction with A452. M6
Jct
⊕   Practice ground - covered bays
▤   www.walmleygolfclub.co.uk

Warwick   (1971)
Public
Warwick Racecourse, Warwick,
CV34 6HW
☎   (01926) 494316
♙   Mrs R Dunkley
✓   P Sharp (01926) 491284
▷   9 L 2682 yds SSS 66
♟   U exc while racing in progress &
Sun am
££   £13 (£14)
⊕   Centre of Warwick Racecourse
⊕   Driving range
⌂   DG Dunkley

The Warwickshire   (1993)
Proprietary
Leek Wootton, Warwick, CV35 7QT
☎   (01926) 409409

West Midlands   (2003)
Marsh House Farm Lane, Barston, Solihull
B92 0LB
☎   (01675) 444890
▯   (01675) 444891

✉ mark@wmgc.co.uk
📖 460
🏌 Ron Guthrie (01675 444894)
⌖ 18 L 6624 yds Par 72 SSS 72
👥 WD–U WE–M before 10am
££ £19.95 (£29.95am, £19.95pm)
🚗 10 min from Birmingham and Coventry, 5 min from NEC
🏠 Nigel Harrhy, Mark Harrhy, David Griffith
🖥 www.wmgc.co.uk

Whitefields (1992)
Proprietary
London Road, Thurlaston, Rugby, CV23 9LF
☎ **(01788) 815555**
🖳 (01788) 521695
✉ mail@draycote-hotel.co.uk
📖 400
🏌 B Coleman (01788) 815555
✏ David Mills (01788) 815555
⌖ 18 L 6289 yds Par 71 SSS 70
👥 U SOC WE
££ £20 (£30)
🚗 3 miles SW of Rugby at A45/M45 Junction
⊕ Driving range (floodlit); Draycote Hotel - 50 beds (adjoining); buggies
🖥 www.draycote-hotel.co.uk

Widney Manor (1993)
Pay and play
Saintbury Drive, Widney Manor, Solihull, B91 3SZ
☎ **(0121) 704 0704**

Windmill Village (1990)
Birmingham Road, Allesley, Coventry, CV5 9AL
☎ **(024) 7640 4041**
🖳 (024) 7640 4042
✉ leisure@windmillvillagehotel.co.uk
📖 450
🏌 M Hartland (Mgr)
✏ R Hunter (024) 7640 4041
⌖ 18 L 5213 yds Par 70
👥 U SOC
££ D–from £17.95
🚗 10 min from NEC and M42 link
⊕ Putting green; driving nets
🏠 Hunter/Harrhy
🖥 www.windmillvillagehotel.co.uk

Wishaw (1995)
Proprietary
Bulls Lane, Wishaw, Sutton Coldfield, B76 9QW
☎ **(0121) 313 2110**
✉ wishawgolfclub@blueyonder.co.uk
📖 340
🏌 PH Burwell
✏ A Partridge (Wishaw Academy)
⌖ 18 L 5745 yds Par 70 SSS 68
👥 U SOC
££ £15 (£22)
🚗 2 miles NW of M42 Junction 9
⊕ Chipping/putting area; practice nets
🏠 RS Wallis
🖥 www.wishaw-golfclub.co.uk

Wiltshire

Bowood G&CC (1992)
Proprietary
Derry Hill, Calne, SN11 9PQ
☎ **(01249) 822228**
✉ golfclub@bowood.org

Broome Manor (1976)
Public
Pipers Way, Swindon, SN3 1RG
☎ **(01793) 532403**
✉ bmgc.sec@eclipse.co.uk
📖 800
🏌 JE Poolman (01793) 823462
✏ B Sandry (01793) 532403
⌖ 18 L 6283 yds SSS 70
9 L 2690 yds SSS 67
👥 U
££ 18 hole: £19.10 9 hole: £11.60
🚗 Swindon 2 miles. M4 Junction 15
⊕ Floodlit driving range
🏠 F Hawtree
🖥 www.bmgc.co.uk

Chippenham (1896)
Malmesbury Road, Chippenham, SN15 5LT
☎ **(01249) 652040**
🖳 (01249) 446681
✉ chippenhamgc@onetel.com
📖 650
🏌 B Cook
✏ W Creamer (01249) 655519
⌖ 18 L 5586 yds SSS 67
👥 U WE–M SOC
££ £22 D–£30 (£27)
🚗 1 mile N of Chippenham, off A350. 2 m S of M4 Junction 17
🖥 www.chippenhamgolfclub.com

Cricklade Hotel (1992)
Common Hill, Cricklade, SN6 6HA
☎ **(01793) 750751**
🖳 (01793) 751767
📖 70
🏌 C Withers
✏ I Bolt
⌖ 9 L 1830 yds Par 62
Men: SSS 58
Women: SSS 62
👥 WD–U SOC–WD
££ £16 D–£25
🚗 ½ mile W of Cricklade on B4040. M4 Junctions 15/16
🏠 Bolt/Smith

Cumberwell Park (1994)
Bradford-on-Avon, BA15 2PQ
☎ **(01225) 863322**
🖳 (01225) 868160
✉ enquiries@cumberwellpark.com
📖 1250
✏ J Jacobs (Golf Dir)
⌖ 27 hole course
👥 U SOC
££ £27 (£33)
🚗 Between Bradford-on-Avon and Bath on A363. M4 Junction 18
⊕ Driving range
🏠 Adrian Stiff
🖥 www.cumberwellpark.com

Defence Academy (1953)
Shrivenham, Swindon, SN6 8LA
☎ **(01793) 785725**
✉ golfclub.hq@da.mod.uk
📖 500
🏌 A Willmett (Mgr)
⌖ 18 L 5671 yds SSS 68
👥 M SOC
££ £10 (£12)
🚗 Grounds of Defence Academy. Entry must be arranged with Mgr

Erlestoke (1992)
Erlestoke, Devizes, SN10 5UB
☎ **(01380) 831069**
✉ info@erlestokegolfclub.co.uk
📖 620
🏌 R Gobardansingh
✏ S Blazey (01380) 830300
⌖ 18 L 6759-6102 yds Par 72 SSS 72-69
👥 U–book with Pro SOC
££ £25 (£30)
🚗 6 miles E of Westbury on B3098
⊕ Driving range; 3 Academy holes
🏠 Adrian Stiff
🖥 www.erlestokegolfclub.co.uk

Hamptworth G&CC (1994)
Elmtree Farmhouse, Hamptworth Road, Landford, SP5 2DU
☎ **(01794) 390155**
🖳 (01794) 390022
✉ info@hamptworthgolf.co.uk
🏌 P Stevens
✏ A Beal
⌖ 18 L 6516 yds SSS 71
👥 H
££ £30 (£40)
🚗 10 miles SE of Salisbury, off A36/B3079. M27 Junction 2, 6 miles
⊕ Driving range, croquet lawns & fitness centre & tennis courts
🖥 www.hamptworthgolf.co.uk

High Post (1922)
Great Durnford, Salisbury, SP4 6AT
☎ **(01722) 782356**
🖳 (01722) 782674
✉ secretary@highpostgolfclub.co.uk
📖 625
🏌 P Hickling (01722) 782356
✏ T Isaacs
⌖ 18 L 6305 yds Par 70 SSS 70
👥 WD–U WE/BH–H SOC
££ £32 D–£42 (£42 D–£50) SOC £35 (£45)
🚗 4 miles N of Salisbury on A345
⊕ Driving range (members, fee payers & societies only)
🏠 Hawtree
🖥 www.highpostgolfclub.co.uk

Highworth (1990)
Swindon Road, Highworth, SN6 7SJ
☎ **(01793) 766014**

Kingsdown (1880)
Kingsdown, Corsham, SN13 8BS
☎ **(01225) 742530**

🖳 (01225) 743472
✉ kingsdowngolfclub@btconnect.com
🏛 640 105(L) 45(J)
🏌 N Newman (01225) 743472
✓ A Butler (01225) 742634
🏴 18 L 6445 yds SSS 71
👥 WD–H WE–M
££ £34
🔗 5 miles E of Bath
⊕ Practice area; chipping green; putting green
🖥 www.kingsdowngolfclub.co.uk

Manor House (1992)
Proprietary
Castle Combe, SN14 7JW
☎ **(01249) 782982**
🖳 (01249) 782992
✉ enquiries@manorhousegolfclub .com
🏛 400
🏌 Paul Thompson (Gen Mgr)
✓ S Slinger (Dir of Golf)
🏴 18 L 6500 yds SSS 72
👥 U H–booking necessary SOC
££ £75 Mon–Thur (£90 Fri–Sun)
🔗 N of Castle Combe, off B4039. M4 Junction 17, 4 miles
⊕ Driving range
🏠 Alliss/Clarke
🖥 www.manorhousegolfclub.com

Marlborough (1888)
The Common, Marlborough, SN8 1DU
☎ **(01672) 512147**
🖳 (01672) 513164
✉ contactus@marlboroughgolfclub .co.uk
🏛 750
🏌 JAD Sullivan
✓ S Amor (01672) 512493
🏴 18 L 6409yds SSS 71
👥 WD/WE–H SOC
££ £29 D–£40 (£38 D–£52)
🔗 ½ mile N of Marlborough (A346). 7 miles S of M4 Junction 15
🖥 www.marlboroughgolfclub.co.uk

Monkton Park Par Three
(1965)
Pay and play
Chippenham, SN15 3PP
☎ **(01249) 653928**

North Wilts (1890)
Bishops' Cannings, Devizes, SN10 2LP
☎ **(01380) 860257**
🖳 (01380) 860877
✉ secretary@northwiltsgolf.com
🏛 625 105(L) 90(J)
🏌 Mrs P Stephenson (01380) 860627
✓ GJ Laing (Golf Mgr) (01380) 860330
🏴 18 L 6414 yds SSS 71
👥 U exc Xmas Day–Jan 31–M SOC
££ D–£32 (£37/round)
🔗 1 mile from A4, E of Calne
🖥 www.northwiltsgolf.com

Oaksey Park (1991)
Pay and play
Oaksey, Malmesbury SN16 9SB
☎ **(01666) 577995**
🖳 (01666) 577174
✉ info@oakseypark.co.uk
🏌 John Cooper
✓ Andy Leith
🏴 9 L 2900 yds SSS 68
👥 U SOC
££ £10 (£15)
🔗 8 miles NE of Malmesbury, off A429
⊕ Driving range
🏠 Chapman/Warren
🖥 www.oakseyparkgolf.co.uk

Ogbourne Downs (1907)
Ogbourne St George, Marlborough, SN8 1TB
☎ **(01672) 841327**
🖳 (01672) 841101
🏛 700
🏌 Miss M Green (01672) 841327
✓ A Kirk (01672) 841287
🏴 18 L 6422 yds Par 71 SSS 71
👥 WD–H WE–M SOC–WD
££ £30 D–£40
🔗 5 miles S of M4 Junction 15, on A346
⊕ Driving range; buggy hire
🏠 JH Taylor
🖥 www.ogdgc.co.uk

Rushmore
Tollard Royal, Salisbury, SP5 5QB
☎ **(01725) 516326**
🖳 (01725) 516437
✉ andrea@rushmoregolf.co.uk
🏌 Andrea Cooper (01725) 516391
✓ P Jenkins (01725) 516326
🏴 18 L 6131 yds Par 71 SSS 70
👥 U SOC
££ £25 (£30)
🔗 8 miles SE of Shaftesbury (B3081)
⊕ Driving range
🖥 www.rushmoregolf.co.uk

Salisbury & South Wilts
(1888)
Netherhampton, Salisbury, SP2 8PR
☎ **(01722) 742645 ext.1**
🖳 (01722) 742676
✉ mail@salisburygolf.co.uk
🏛 1100
🏌 Pat Clash (Gen Mgr)
✓ Miss Gerry Teschner (01722) 742929
🏴 18 L 6485 yds SSS 71 9 hole course Par 34
👥 WD–U SOC–WD
££ £26 (£40, £30 after 2.30)
🔗 Wilton, 3 miles SW of Salisbury on A3094
🏠 Taylor/Gidman
🖥 www.salisburygolf.co.uk

Shrivenham Park (1967)
Pay and play
Pennyhooks Lane, Shrivenham, Swindon, SN6 8EX
☎ **(01793) 783853**

Tidworth Garrison
(1908)
Bulford Road, Tidworth, SP9 7AF
☎ **(01980) 842321 (Clubhouse)**
🖳 (01980) 842301
✉ tidworth@garrison-golfclub.fsnet.co.uk
🏛 750
🏌 RG Moan (01980) 842301
✓ T Gosden (01980) 842393
🏴 18 L 6320 yds Par 70 SSS 70
👥 WD–U H SOC–Tues & Thurs
££ £45
🔗 1 mile SW of Tidworth on Bulford road (A338)
🏠 Donald Steel
🖥 www.tidworthgolfclub.co.uk

Upavon (1918)
Douglas Avenue, Upavon, SN9 6BQ
☎ **(01980) 630787**
(08712) 300800 daily course info line
🖳 (01980) 635419
✉ play@upavongolfclub.co.uk
🏛 550
🏌 L Mitchell
✓ R Blake (01980) 630281
🏴 18 L 6415 yds SSS 71
👥 WD–U WE–M before noon –U after noon SOC–WD/WE after noon
££ D–£30 (£40) 2 for 1 accepted
🔗 1.5 miles SE of Upavon on A342, Andover Road
🏠 R Blake
🖥 www.upavongolfclub.co.uk

West Wilts (1891)
Elm Hill, Warminster, BA12 0AU
☎ **(01985) 213133**
🖳 (01985) 219809
✉ sec@westwiltsgolfclub.co.uk
🏛 570 70(L) 50(J)
🏌 GN Morgan
✓ R Morris (01985) 212110
🏴 18 L 5754 yds SSS 68
👥 WD–U H WE–M H NA Sat
££ £30 D–£30 (£35)
🔗 1 mile off A350, on Westbury to Warminster road
⊕ Indoor and outdoor practice facilities
🏠 JH Taylor
🖥 www.westwiltsgolfclub.co.uk

Whitley (1993)
Pay and play
Corsham Road, Whitley, Melksham, SN12 7QE
☎ **(01225) 790099**

The Wiltshire Golf & Country Club
Proprietary
Vastern, Wootton Bassett, Swindon, SN4 7PB
☎ **(01793) 849999**
🖳 (01793) 849988
✉ theclub@the-wiltshire.co.uk
🏛 600

🖉 Jennifer Shah (Gen Mgr)
🗸 Richard Lawless
🏳 18 L 6672 yds Par 72 SSS 71
   9 L 3220 yds SSS 71
👫 U SOC
££ £25 (£35)
🚗 1 mile S of Wootton Bassett on
   A3102. M4 Junction 16
⊕ Practice range
🏠 Alliss/Swan
🖥 www.the-wiltshire.co.uk

Wrag Barn G&CC (1990)

Shrivenham Road, Highworth, Swindon,
SN6 7QQ
☎ **(01793) 861327**
🖳 (01793) 861325
📖 600
🖉 T Lee
🗸 B Loughrey (01793) 766027
🏳 18 L 6633 yds SSS 72
👫 WD–U WE–NA before noon
   SOC–WD
££ £32 (£38)
🚗 6 miles NE of Swindon on B4000.
   M4 Junction 15, 8 miles
⊕ Driving range; 6-hole Academy
   course
🏠 Hawtree (Simon Gidman)
🖥 www.wragbarn.com

Worcestershire

Abbey Hotel G&CC

(1985)
Dagnell End Road, Redditch, B98 7BE
☎ **(01527) 406600**
🖂 info@theabbeyhotel.co.uk

Bank House Hotel G&CC

(1992)
Bransford, Worcester, WR6 5JD
☎ **(01886) 833545**

Blackwell (1893)

Blackwell, Bromsgrove, Worcestershire,
B60 1PY
☎ **(0121) 445 1994**
🖳 (0121) 445 4911
🖂 info@blackwellgolfclub.com
📖 269 81(L) 11(J)
🖉 JT Mead
🗸 F Clark (0121) 445 3113
🏳 18 L 6260 yds Par 70 SSS 71
👫 WD–U H WE/BH–M
££ £65 D–£75
🚗 3 miles E of Bromsgrove. M42
   Junction 1 (South)
⊕ Practice area
🏠 Herbert Fowler/Tom Simpson
🖥 www.blackwellgolfclub.com

Brandhall (1906)

Public
Heron Road, Oldbury, Warley, B68 8AQ
☎ **(0121) 552 2195**
🖳 300
🖉 J Robinson (Sandwell Leisure
   Trust)

🗸 C Yates (0121) 552 2195
🏳 18 L 5813 yds Par 71 SSS 68
👫 U exc first 1½ hrs Sat/Sun
££ £12
🚗 6 miles NW of Birmingham. M5
   Junction 2, 1½ miles
🖥 www.slt@sandwell.gov.uk

Bromsgrove Golf Centre

(1992)
Proprietary
Stratford Road, Bromsgrove, B60 1LD
☎ **(01527) 575886**
🖂 enquiries@bromsgrovegolf.f9.co.uk

Churchill & Blakedown

(1926)
Churchill Lane, Blakedown, Kidderminster,
DY10 3NB
☎ **(01562) 700018**
🖳 (08712) 422049
🖂 cbgolfclub@tiscali.co.uk
📖 380
🖉 P Bailey
🗸 G Wright (01562) 700454
🏳 9 L 6472 yds Par 72 SSS 71
👫 WD–U WE–M
££ £25
🚗 3 miles N of Kidderminster on
   A456

Cocks Moor Woods (1926)

Public
Alcester Road, South King's Heath,
Birmingham, B14 4ER
☎ **(0121) 464 3584**
📖 200
🖉 DW Wincott
🗸 S Ellis
🏳 18 L 5769 yds Par 69 SSS 68
👫 U
££ On application
🚗 6 miles S of Birmingham (A435).
   M42 3 miles south J3

Droitwich G&CC (1897)

Ford Lane, Droitwich, WR9 0BQ
☎ **(01905) 774344**
🖳 (01905) 797290
🖂 droitwich-golf-club@tiscali.co.uk
📖 782
🖉 CS Thompson
🗸 Phil Cundy (01905) 770207
🏳 18 L 6058 yds SSS 69
👫 WD–U WE/BH–M SOC–Wed &
   Fri
££ £25 – £30 £15 with member
🚗 1 mile N of Droitwich, off A38. M5
   Junction 5
⊕ Practice ground
🏠 George Cawsey, James Braid
🖥 www.droitwichgolf.co.uk

Dudley (1893)

Turners Hill, Rowley Regis, B65 9DP
☎ **(01384) 233877**
🖳 (01384) 233877
🖂 secretary@dudleygolfclub.com
📖 320
🖉 MB Pritchard
🗸 G Kilmister (01384) 254020

🏳 18 L 5730 yds Par 69 SSS 68
👫 WD–U WE–M
££ On application
🚗 2 miles S of Dudley
🖥 www.dudleygolfclub.com

Evesham (1894)

Craycombe Links, Fladbury, Pershore,
WR10 2QS
☎ **(01386) 860395**
🖂 eveshamgolf@btopenworld.com

Fulford Heath (1933)

Tanners Green Lane, Wythall, Birmingham,
B47 6BH
☎ **(01564) 822806 (Clubhouse)**
🖳 (01564) 822629
🖂 secretary@fulfordheath.co.uk
📖 660
🖉 Mrs MA Tuckett (01564) 824758
🗸 R Dunbar (01564) 822930
🏳 18 L 6179 yds SSS 70
👫 WD–H WE/BH–M SOC–Tues &
   Thurs
££ On application
🚗 8 miles S of Birmingham. M42
   Junction 3
🏠 Braid/Hawtree
🖥 www.fulfordheath.co.uk

Gay Hill (1913)

Hollywood Lane, Birmingham, B47 5PP
☎ **(0121) 430 6523/8544**
🖳 (0121) 436 7796
🖂 secretary@ghgc.org.uk
📖 700
🖉 Mrs J Morris (0121) 430 8544
🗸 C Harrison (0121) 474 6001
🏳 18 L 6406 yds SSS 72
👫 WD–U H WE–U SOC
££ £35 (18 holes), £45 (18+ holes)
🚗 7 miles S of Birmingham on A435.
   M42 Junction 3, 3 miles
🖥 www.ghgc.org.uk

Habberley (1924)

Low Habberley, Kidderminster, DY11 5RF
☎ **(01562) 745756**
📖 140
🖉 DS McDermott
🏳 9 L 5401 yds Par 69 SSS 67
👫 WD–U WE–M SOC
££ £15 (£15)
🚗 3 miles NW of Kidderminster
🖥 www.habberleygolfclub.co.uk

Hagley (1980)

Proprietary
Wassell Grove, Hagley, Stourbridge,
DY9 9JW
☎ **(01562) 883701**
🖳 (01562) 887518
🖂 manager@hagleygc.freeserve.co.uk
📖 720
🖉 GF Yardley (01562) 883701
🗸 I Clark (01562) 883852
🏳 18 L 6376 yds SSS 72
👫 WD–U WE–M after 10am
   SOC–WD
££ £30 D–£35
🚗 5 miles SW of Birmingham on
   A456. M5 Junction 3

For list of abbreviations and key to symbols see page 651

📧 www.hagleygolfandcountryclub
.co.uk

Halesowen (1906)

The Leasowes, Halesowen, B62 8QF
- ☎ (0121) 501 3606
- 📠 (0121) 501 3606
- 📧 halesowengolfclub@btconnect.com
- 📖 680
- 🏌 P Crumpton
- ⛳ J Nicholas (0121) 503 0593
- ⛳ 18 L 5754 yds SSS 69
- 🏌 WD–U WE–M SOC–WD
- ££ £28 D–£31
- 🚗 M5 Junction 3, 2 miles
- ⊕ Practice area; putting green
- 📧 www.halesowengc.co.uk

Kidderminster (1909)

Russell Road, Kidderminster, DY10 3HT
- ☎ (01562) 822303
- 📠 (01562) 827866
- 📧 info@kidderminstergolfclub.com
- 📖 900
- 🏌 David Palmer
- ⛳ P Smith (01562) 740090
- ⛳ 18 L 6422 yds Par 72 SSS 71
- 🏌 WD–H WE–M SOC–Thurs
- ££ £35 D–£35 WE with member only
- 🚗 Signposted off A449
  Wolverhampton-Worcester road;
  in Kidderminster
- 📧 www.kidderminstergolfclub.com

Kings Norton (1892)

Brockhill Lane, Weatheroak, Alvechurch,
Birmingham B48 7ED
- ☎ (01564) 826789
- 📠 (01564) 826955
- 📧 info@kingsnortongolfclub.co.uk
- 📖 1050
- 🏌 T Webb (Mgr)
- ⛳ K Hayward (01564) 822635
- ⛳ 18 L 6748 yds SSS 72
  9 L 3290 yds SSS 36
- 🏌 WD–U WE–NA SOC
- ££ £32 D–£40
- 🚗 7 miles S of Birmingham. 1 mile N
  of M42 Junction 3
- ⊕ 12 hole short course
- 🏠 Fred Hawtree
- 📧 www.kingsnortongolfclub.co.uk

Lickey Hills/Rose Hill (1927)

Public
Lickey Hills, Rednal, Birmingham,
B45 8RR
- ☎ (0121) 453 3159
- 📠 (0121) 457 8779
- 📧 mark.toombs@birmingham.gov.uk
- 📖 200
- 🏌 AG Cushing
- ⛳ Mark Toombs (Mgr)
- ⛳ 18 L 6010 yds SSS 69
- 🏌 U Pre–book tee times
- ££ £11 (£13)
- 🚗 10 miles SW of Birmingham. M5 J4.
  M42 J2

Little Lakes (1975)

Lye Head, Bewdley, Worcester,
DY12 2UZ
- ☎ (01299) 266385
- 📠 (01299) 266398
- 📖 400 50(L)
- 🏌 J Dean (01562) 741704
- ⛳ M Laing
- ⛳ 18 L 6278 yds SSS 71
- 🏌 U SOC
- ££ £19 (£24)
- 🚗 3 miles W of Bewdley, off A456

Moseley (1892)

Springfield Road, Kings Heath, Birmingham,
B14 7DX
- ☎ (0121) 444 4957
- 📠 (0121) 441 4662
- 📖 600
- 🏌 Mrs JM Hey
- ⛳ M Griffin (0121) 444 2063
- ⛳ 18 L 6315 yds SSS 71· Par 70
- 🏌 WD–H or M
- ££ £30
- 🚗 2 miles S of Birmingham off A435;
  5 miles N of M42 J3
- 🏠 HS Colt
- 📧 www.moseleygolf.co.uk

North Worcestershire (1907)

Frankley Beeches Road, Northfield,
Birmingham, B31 5LP
- ☎ (0121) 475 1047
- 📠 (0121) 476 8681
- 📖 550
- 🏌 D Wilson
- ⛳ D Cummins (0121) 475 5721
- ⛳ 18 L 5907 yds SSS 69
- 🏌 WD–U WE/BH–M
- ££ £25 D–£35
- 🚗 7 miles SW of Birmingham, off A38
- 🏠 James Braid

Ombersley (1991)

Bishopswood Road, Ombersley, Droitwich,
WR9 0LE
- ☎ (01905) 620747
- 📧 enquiries@ombersleygolfclub.co.uk

Perdiswell Park (1978)

Pay and play
Bilford Road, Worcester, WR3 8DX
- ☎ (01905) 754668
- 📠 (01905) 756608
- 📖 286
- 🏌 R Gardner (01905) 452399
- ⛳ M Woodward (01905) 754668
- ⛳ 18 L 5297 yds SSS 68
- 🏌 U
- ££ 9: £6.75 (£10.15) 18: £8.60
  (£13.85)
- 🚗 Worcester. M5 Junction 6

Pitcheroak (1973)

Public
Plymouth Road, Redditch, B97 4PB
- ☎ (01527) 541054

Ravenmeadow (1995)

Hindlip Lane, Clanes, Worcester, WR3 8SA
- ☎ (01905) 757525
- 📠 (01905) 458876
- 📖 300
- 🏌 T Senter (Mgr) (01905) 458876
- ⛳ M Slater (01905) 756665
- ⛳ 9 L 5440 yds 18 tees Par 68 SSS 68
- 🏌 U–SOC WD WE
- ££ D–£10–£14 (D–£12–£17)
- 🚗 3 miles N of Worcester, off A38.
  M5 Junction 6
- ⊕ Driving range; chipping greens;
  putting greens; 9 hole par 3 pitch &
  putt course
- 🏠 R Baldwyn

Redditch (1913)

Lower Grinsty, Green Lane, Callow Hill,
Redditch B97 5PJ
- ☎ (01527) 543079
- 📠 (01527) 547413
- 📧 redditchgolfclub@btconnect.com
- 📖 883
- 🏌 TJ Sheldon
- ⛳ D Down (01527) 546372
- ⛳ 18 L 6494 yds SSS 72
- 🏌 WD–U SOC
- ££ £35
- 🚗 3 miles SW of Redditch, off A441
- 🏠 F Pennink
- 📧 www.redditchgolfclub.com

Stourbridge (1892)

Worcester Lane, Pedmore, Stourbridge,
DY8 2RB
- ☎ (01384) 395566
- 📠 (01384) 444660
- 📧 secretary@stourbridge-golf-club
  .co.uk
- 📖 760
- 🏌 Ms M Kite
- ⛳ M Male (01384) 393129
- ⛳ 18 L 6231 yds SSS 70
- 🏌 WD–U exc Wed before 1.30pm–M
  WE/BH–M
- ££ £30
- 🚗 1 mile S of Stourbridge on
  Worcester road. M5 Junctions 3/4
- 📧 www.stourbridge-golf-club.co.uk

Tolladine (1898)

The Fairway, Tolladine Road, Worcester,
WR4 9BA
- ☎ (01905) 21074 (Clubhouse)
- 📖 270
- 🏌 P Lynas
- ⛳ M McMahon
- ⛳ 9 L 5174 yds SSS 67
- 🏌 WD–U before 4pm –M after 4pm
  WE/BH–M SOC
- ££ £12
- 🚗 M5 Junction 6, 1 mile

The Vale (1991)

Bishampton, Pershore, WR10 2LZ
- ☎ (01386) 462781
- 📠 (01386) 462597
- 📖 850
- 🏌 S lane (Gen Mgr)
- ⛳ Richard Jenkins (01386) 462520
- ⛳ 18 L 6644 yds SSS 72
  9 L 2628 yds SSS 65

🏌 WD–U WE–U after 1pm
SOC–WD
££ £25 (£35)
⛳ 6 miles NW of Evesham, off A44.
M5 Junction 6, 12 miles
⊕ Driving range
🏠 M Sandow
▤ www.crown-golf.co.uk

Warley (1921)
Public
Lightwoods Hill, Warley, B67 5EQ
☎ (0121) 429 2440
🖂 golfshop@warleywoods.org.uk
🔑 W Hardman (Course Mgr)
🏌 9 L 2673 yds SSS 66
🏌 U SOC
££ On application
⛳ 5 miles W of Birmingham, off
A456; 2 miles from M25 Jct 2

Wharton Park (1992)
Proprietary
Longbank, Bewdley, DY12 2QW
☎ (01299) 405222
(restaurant)
(01299) 405163 (pro shop)
🖳 (01299) 405121
🖂 enquiries@whartonpark.co.uk
📖 550
🔑 Elizabeth Middis
✓ A Hoare (01299) 405163
🏌 18 L 6435 yds Par 72 SSS 71
🏌 U SOC–WD
££ £30 (£35)
⛳ Bewdley Bypass on A456/ M5
Junctions 3 or 6
⊕ Practice ground; practice putting
green
🏠 Howard Swann
▤ www.whartonpark.co.uk

Worcester G&CC (1898)
Boughton Park, Worcester, WR2 4EZ
☎ (01905) 422555
🖳 (01905) 749090
🖂 worcestergcc@btconnect.com
📖 1005
🔑 PA Tredwell (01905) 422555
✓ G Farr (01905) 422044
🏌 18 L 6251 yds SSS 70
🏌 WD–H WE–M SOC
££ £30
⛳ 1 mile W of Worcester on B4485
(formerly A4103)
🏠 Dr A Mackenzie (1926)/C Colenso
(1991)
▤ www.worcestergcc.co.uk

Worcestershire (1879)
Wood Farm, Malvern Wells, WR14 4PP
☎ (01684) 575992
🖳 (01684) 893334
🖂 secretary
@theworcestershiregolfclub.co.uk
📖 770
🔑 Mrs JP Howe
(Sec/Mgr) (01684) 575992
✓ RAF Lewis (01684) 564428
🏌 18 L 6449 yds SSS 71
🏌 WD–H WE–H after 10am
££ £30 D–£36 (£34 D–£40)

⛳ 2 miles S of Gt Malvern, off
A449/B4209
▤ www.theworcestershiregolfclub
.co.uk

Wyre Forest Golf Centre
Pay and play
Zortech Avenue, Kidderminster, DY11 7EX
☎ (01299) 822682
🖂 chris@wyreforestgolf.com

Yorkshire (East)

Allerthorpe Park (1994)
Proprietary
Allerthorpe, York, YO42 4RL
☎ (01759) 306686
🖳 (01759) 304308
🖂 allerthorpepark@aol.com
📖 500
🔑 JD Atkinson (01759) 304744
✓ J Calam (01759) 306686
🏌 18 L 6430 yds Par 70 SSS 70
🏌 U SOC
££ £20 D–£30
⛳ 2 miles W of Pocklington, off
A1079
⊕ Teaching academy
🏠 JG Hatcliffe & Partners
▤ www.allerthorpeparkgolfclub.com

Beverley & East Riding
(1889)
The Westwood, Beverley, HU17 8RG
☎ (01482) 868757
🖳 (01482) 868757
🖂 golf@beverleygolfclub.karoo.co.uk
📖 550
🔑 M Drew (01482) 868757
✓ A Ashby (01482) 869519
🏌 18 L 5972 yds SSS 69
🏌 U SOC
££ £17 (£24)
⛳ Beverley-Walkington road (B1230)
▤ www.beverleyandeast-
ridinggolfclub.co.uk

Boothferry (1982)
Proprietary
Spaldington Lane, Spaldington, Nr Howden,
DN14 7NG
☎ (01430) 430364
🖳 (01430) 430567
🖂 info@boothferrygolfclub.co.uk
📖 300
🔑 Matthew Rumble
✓ Matthew Rumble (Dir of Golf)
🏌 18 L 6651 yds SSS 72 Par 73
🏌 U SOC
££ £15 (£18)
⛳ 3 miles N of Howden on B1288.
M62 Junction 37, 2 miles
⊕ Driving range; 9 hole pay & play
course; large practice ground;
short game area
🏠 Donald Steel
▤ www.boothferrygolfclub.co.uk

Bridlington (1905)
Belvedere Road, Bridlington, YO15 3NA
☎ (01262) 672092/606367
🖳 (01262) 606367
🖂 enquiries@bridlingtongolfclub.co.uk
📖 500
🔑 CB Rhodes (01262) 606367
✓ ARA Howarth (01262) 674721
🏌 18 L 6638 yds Par 72 SSS 72
🏌 U exc Sun–before 2.30pm
££ £23 D–£30 (£32 D–£40)
⛳ 1½ miles S of Bridlington, off A165
🏠 James Braid
▤ www.bridlingtongolfclub.co.uk

The Bridlington Links
(1993)
Pay and play
Flamborough Road, Marton, Bridlington,
YO15 1DW
☎ (01262) 401584

Brough (1893)
Cave Road, Brough, HU15 1HB
☎ (01482) 667374
🖳 (01482) 669873
🖂 gt@brough-golfclub.co.uk
📖 700
🔑 GW Townhill (Golf Dir)
(01482) 667291
✓ GW Townhill (01482) 667483
🏌 18 L 6075 yds SSS 69
🏌 WD–U exc Wed–NA
££ £35 (£50)
⛳ 10 miles W of Hull on A63
▤ www.brough-golfclub.co.uk

Cave Castle (1989)
South Cave, Nr Brough, HU15 2EU
☎ (01430) 421286
🖳 (01430) 421118
🖂 admin@cavecastlegc.co.uk
🔑 J Simpson (Admin) P Coyne (Golf
Coordinator)
✓ S MacKinder (01430) 421286
🏌 18 L 6524 yds SSS 71
🏌 U SOC
££ £18 (£25)
⛳ 15 miles W of Hull. Junction of
A63/M62
▤ www.cavecastlegc.co.uk

Cherry Burton (1993)
Pay and play
Leconfield Road, Cherry Burton, Beverley,
HU17 7RB
☎ (01964) 550924

Cottingham (1984)
Woodhill Way, Cottingham, Hull,
HU16 5RZ
☎ (01482) 846030
🖳 (01482) 845932
📖 600
🔑 RJ Wiles (01482) 846030
✓ CW Gray (01482) 842394
🏌 18 L 6453 yds Par 72 SSS 71
🏌 WD–U WE/BH–restricted SOC
after 2pm
££ £20 D–£30 (£30 D–£45)
⛳ 3 miles N of Hull, off A164

For list of abbreviations and key to symbols see page 651

⊕ Driving range, health club, pool
♔ Wiles/Litten
▤ www.cottinghamparks.co.uk

Driffield   (1923)
Sunderlandwick, Driffield, YO25 9AD
☎ **(01377) 240448 (Clubhouse)**
    (01377) 253116 (Office)
🖳 (01377) 240599
✉ info@driffieldgolfclub.co.uk
▥ 670
♊ JR Nicholson, M.Inst.GCM
✓ K Wright (01377) 241224
↦ 18 L 6212 yds SSS 70
♛ H1SOC
££ £26 D–£35 (£35 D–£45)
⊕ S of Driffield on A164
▤ www.driffieldgolfclub.co.uk

Flamborough Head   (1932)
*Lighthouse Road, Flamborough, Bridlington,
YO15 1AR*
☎ **(01262) 850333/850279**
🖳 (01262) 850333
✉ secretary@flamboroughheadgolfclub
    .co.uk
▥ 400
♊ GS Thornton
✓ P Harrison (01262) 850333
↦ 18 L 6185 yds Par 71 SSS 69
♛ U
££ £20 (£25) 5D–£80
⊕ 5 miles NE of Bridlington
▤ www.flamboroughheadgolfclub
    .co.uk

Ganstead Park   (1976)
Longdales Lane, Coniston, Hull, HU11 4LB
☎ **(01482) 811280 (Steward)**
🖳 (01482) 817754
✉ secretary@gansteadpark.co.uk
▥ 700
♊ M Milner (01482) 817754
✓ M Smee (01482) 811121
↦ 18 L 6801 yds SSS 73
♛ U H WE–NA before noon SOC
££ On application
⊕ 5 miles E of Hull on A165
♔ Peter Green
▤ www.gansteadpark.co.uk

Hainsworth Park   (1983)
Brandesburton, Driffield, YO25 8RT
☎ **(01964) 542362**
🖳 (01964) 542362
▥ 550
♊ R Hounsfield, BW Atkin (Prop)
✓ P Myers (01964) 542362
↦ 18 L 6362 yds SSS 71
♛ SOC
££ £20–£24 (£24–£29)
⊕ 6 miles NW of Beverley, off A165
    at Brandesburton roundabout

Hessle   (1898)
*Westfield Road, Raywell, Cottingham,
HU16 5YL*
☎ **(01482) 306840**
🖳 (01482) 652679
✉ secretary@hessle-golf-club.co.uk
▥ 680

♊ D Pettit
✓ G Fieldsend (01482) 306842
↦ 18 L 6608 yds SSS 72
♛ WD–U exc Tues 9am–1pm
    WE–NA before 12 noon
££ £26 (£34)
⊕ 3 miles SW of Cottingham
♔ Thomas/Alliss
▤ www.hessle-golf-club.co.uk

Hornsea   (1898)
Rolston Road, Hornsea, HU18 1XG
☎ **(01964) 532020**
🖳 (01964) 532080
✉ hornseagolfclub@aol.com
▥ 600
♊ Geoff Drewery (01964) 532020
✓ S Wright (01964) 534989
↦ 18 L 6661 yds SSS 72
♛ WD–U WE–restricted SOC
££ £30 D–£36
⊕ 300 yds past Hornsea Free Port
♔ Mackenzie/Braid
▤ www.hornseagolfclub.co.uk

Hull   (1904)
*The Hall, 27 Packman Lane, Kirk Ella, Hull
HU10 7TJ*
☎ **(01482) 653026/658919**
🖳 (01482) 658919
▥ 821
♊ DJ Crossley (01482) 658919
✓ D Jagger (01482) 653074/658919
↦ 18 L 6246 yds SSS 70
♛ WD–U WE–by arrangement
££ £26.50 D–£32
⊕ 5 miles W of Hull
♔ James Braid

Kilnwick Percy   (1995)
*Pocklington, York, East Yorkshire,
YO42 1UF*
☎ **(01759) 303090**
▥ 420
♊ A Pheasant
✓ A Pheasant
↦ 18 L 6218 yds Par 70 SSS 70
♛ U SOC
££ £18 (£20)
⊕ 1 mile E of Pocklington, off B1246
♔ John Day
▤ www.kilnwickpercygolfclub.co.uk

Springhead Park   (1930)
Public
Willerby Road, Hull, HU5 5JE
☎ **(01482) 656309**
♊ Mr R Taylor (01482) 654875
↦ 18 L 6402 yds SSS 71
♛ U SOC–WD
££ £12.50–£14.25
⊕ 4 miles W of Hull

Sutton Park   (1935)
Public
Salthouse Road, Hull, HU8 9HF
☎ **(01482) 374242**

Withernsea   (1909)
Chestnut Avenue, Withernsea, HU19 2PG
☎ **(01964) 612258 (Clubhouse)**

🖳 (01964) 612078
✉ golf@withernseagolfclub.fsnet
    .co.uk
▥ 329 30(L) 36(J)
♊ J Boasman (Admin) (01694) 612078
↦ 9 L 6207 yds Par 72 SSS 70
♛ WD–U WE/BH–M before 1pm
    SOC
££ £15
⊕ 17 miles E of Hull on A1033. S side
    of Withernsea

Yorkshire (North)

Aldwark Manor   (1978)
Aldwark, Alne, York, YO61 1UF
☎ **(01347) 838353**
🖳 (01347) 833991
▥ 400
♊ GF Platt (Mgr) (01347) 838353
↦ 18 L 6187 yds Par 72 SSS 70
♛ U SOC
££ £25 D–£35 (£30 D–£40)
⊕ 5 miles SE of Boroughbridge, off
    A1. 13 miles NW of York, off A19
▤ www.marstongolf.com

Ampleforth College   (1972)
Castle Drive, Gilling East, York, YO62 4HP
☎ **(01439) 788212**
🖳 (01904) 762012
✉ sec@ampleforthcollege.co.uk
▥ 280
♊ Dr M Wilson (01904) 768861
✓ Ken Howarth (01439) 788243
↦ 9 L 5600 yds Par 69 SSS 69
♛ U exc 2–4pm during term time
££ D–£15 (D–£15)
⊕ Gilling East, 18 miles N of York
    (B1363)
⊕ Short game practice area
♔ Rev Jerome Lambert OSB
▤ www.ampleforthgolf.co.uk

Bedale   (1894)
Leyburn Road, Bedale, DL8 1EZ
☎ **(01677) 422451**
🖳 (01677) 427143
✉ bedalegolfclub@aol.com
▥ 600 100(J)
♊ KJ Rhodes (01677) 422451
✓ AD Johnson (01677) 422443
↦ 18 L 6610 yds SSS 72
♛ U SOC
££ 18: £26 (£35) 27: £32 (£40)
⊕ N boundary of Bedale
⊕ Practice ground
♔ Hawtree
▤ www.bedalegolfclub.com

Bentham   (1922)
Robin Lane, Bentham, Lancaster, LA2 7AG
☎ **(015242) 62455**
🖳 (015242) 62470
✉ secretary@benthamgolfclub.co.uk
▥ 450
♊ J Mann (015242) 62455
✓ A Watson (01524) 262455
↦ 18 L 6000 yds SSS 69
♛ U SOC

££ D–£30
NE of Lancaster on B6480 towards Settle. 13 miles E of M6 Junction 34
www.benthamgolfclub.co.uk

Catterick   (1930)

Leyburn Road, Catterick Garrison, DL9 3QE
☎ **(01748) 833268**
(01748) 833268
secretary@catterickgolfclub.co.uk
525
L Layton (Hon. Sec.)
A Marshall (01748) 833671/833263
18 L 6378 yds SSS 70
U – check with Sec first
££ £25 (£35)
6 miles SW of Scotch Corner, via AI
Large practice ground
Arthur Day
www.catterickgolfclub.co.uk

Cleveland   (1887)

Majuba Road, Redcar, TS10 5BJ
☎ **(01642) 471798**
(01642) 487619
majuba@btconnect.com
800
JA Moran (01642) 471798
Craig Donaldson (01642) 483462
18 L 6696 yds SSS 70
WD–U WE/BH–by arrangement SOC
££ £28 (£35)
S bank of River Tees
www.clevelandgolfclub.co.uk

Cocksford   (1992)

Stutton, Tadcaster, LS24 9NG
☎ **(01937) 834253**

Crimple Valley   (1976)

Pay and play
Hookstone Wood Road, Harrogate, HG2 8PN
☎ **(01423) 883485**

Drax   (1989)

Drax, Selby, YO8 8PQ
☎ **(01757) 617228**
draxgolfclub@fsmail.net

Easingwold   (1930)

Stillington Road, Easingwold, York, YO61 3ET
☎ **(01347) 821486**
(01347) 822474
brian@easingwold-golf-club.fsnet.co.uk
730
DB Stockley (01347) 822474
J Hughes (01347) 821964
18 L 6717 yds Par 73 SSS 72
U SOC
££ £28 D–£35 (£35) – £12 junior
12 miles N of York on A19. S end of Easingwold
Full practice facilities
Hawtree/OCM
www.easingwold-golf-club.co.uk

Filey   (1897)

West Ave, Filey, YO14 9BQ
☎ **(01723) 513293**
(01723) 514952
secretary@fileygolfclub.com
768
Mrs DA Willis
GM Hutchinson (01723) 513134
18 L 6112 yds SSS 69
9 L 1513 yds Par 30
U H SOC
££ £30 (£35) Summer. £25 (£30) Winter
1 mile S of Filey centre
James Braid
www.fileygolfclub.com

Forest of Galtres   (1993)

Proprietary
Moorlands Road, Skelton, York, YO32 2RF
☎ **(01904) 766198**
(01904) 769400
secretary@forestofgaltres.co.uk
450
Mrs SJ Procter
P Bradley
18 L 6534 yds Par 72 SSS 71
U SOC–WD/Sun
££ £25 (£30)
Skelton, 4 miles N of York. 1½ miles off A19 Thursk Rd
Driving range
Simon Gidman
www.forestofgaltres.co.uk

Forest Park   (1991)

Stockton-on Forest, York, YO32 9UW
☎ **(01904) 400425**
admin@forestparkgolfclub.co.uk
650
N Crossley (01904) 400688
M Winterburn (01904) 400425
18 L 6673 yds Par 71 SSS 72
9 L 3186 yds Par 70 SSS 70
U SOC
££ 9: £10 (£12) 18: £23 D–£30 (£30 D–£40)
1½ miles from E end of A64 York By-pass
Driving range + undercover driving range
www.forestparkgolfclub.co.uk

Fulford   (1906)

Heslington Lane, York, YO10 5DY
☎ **(01904) 413579**
(01904) 416918
info@fulfordgolfclub.co.uk
750
Mrs L Gurnell
M Brown (01904) 412882
18 L 6775 yds SSS 72
By arrangement with Mgr
££ £45 D–£55 (£55)
2 miles S of York (A64)
Major C McKenzie
www.fulfordgolfclub.co.uk

Ganton   (1891)

Station Road, Ganton, Scarborough, YO12 4PA
☎ **(01944) 710329**

(01944) 710922
secretary@gantongolfclub.com
550
Maj RG Woolsey
G Brown (01944) 710260
18 L 6753 yds SSS 73
By prior arrangement
££ On application
11 miles SW of Scarborough on A64
Dunn/Vardon/Braid/Colt
www.gantongolfclub.com

Harrogate   (1892)

Forest Lane Head, Harrogate, HG2 7TF
☎ **(01423) 863158 (Clubhouse)**
(01423) 860073
secretary@harrogate-gc.co.uk
700
Peter Banks (01423) 862999
P Johnson (01423) 862547
18 L 6241 yds SSS 70
WD–U WE/BH–enquire first SOC–WD exc Tues
££ £35 D–£40 (£45)
2 miles E of Harrogate on Knaresborough road (A59)
Sandy Herd
www.harrogate-gc.co.uk

Heworth   (1911)

Muncaster House, Muncastergate, York, YO31 9JY
☎ **(01904) 424618**
(01904) 426156
golf@heworth-gc.fsnet.co.uk
345 80(L) 50(J)
RJ Hunt (01904) 426156
S Burdett (01904) 422389
12 L 6105 yds Par 69 SSS 69
U
££ £15 (£20)
NE boundary of York (A1036)
C Heal
www.heworthgolfclub.co.uk

Hunley Hall   (1993)

Brotton, Saltburn, TS12 2QQ
☎ **(01287) 676216**
(01287) 678250
enquiries@hunleyhall.co.uk
500
E Lillie (01287) 676216
A Brook (01287) 677444
27 holes:
5948-6918 yds Par/SSS 68-73
U SOC–exc Sun
££ £25 (£35)
15 miles SE of Middlesbrough on A174
Floodlit driving range; hotel; buggies
John Morgan
www.hunleyhall.co.uk

Kirkbymoorside   (1951)

Manor Vale, Kirkbymoorside, York, YO62 6EG
☎ **(01751) 431525**
(01751) 433190
enqs@kirkbymoorsidegolf.co.uk
600

🏌 Mrs R Rivis
✏ J Hinchliffe (01751) 430402
▷ 18 L 6207 yds SSS 69
👥 U after 9am
££ £22 (£32)
🏌 A170 between Helmsley and
Pickering
▣ www.kirkbymoorsidegolf.co.uk

Knaresborough   (1920)
*Boroughbridge Road, Knaresborough,
HG5 0QQ*
☎ **(01423) 862690**
🖥 (01423) 869345
📧 thekgc@btconnect.com
📖 795
🏌 C Hill
✏ D Tear (01423) 864865
▷ 18 L 6780 yds Par 72 SSS 72
👥 U SOC WD WE
££ £30 (£40)
🏌 1½ miles N of Knaresborough on
A6055
⊕ Practice facilities
🏠 Hawtree
▣ www.knaresboroughgolfclub.co.uk

Malton & Norton   (1910)
*Welham Park, Welham Road, Norton,
Malton YO17 9QE*
☎ **(01653) 697912**
🖥 (01653) 697912
📧 maltonandnorton@btconnect.com
📖 820
🏌 Mrs L Gurnell (01653) 697912
✏ SI Robinson (01653) 693882
▷ 27 holes:
Welham L 6456 yds SSS 71
Park L 6242 yds SSS 70
Derwent L 6286 yds SSS 70
👥 WD–U WE–restricted on match
days H SOC
££ £27 (£32)
🏌 18 miles NE of York (A64)
⊕ Driving range; short game practice
area
▣ www.maltonandnortongolfclub
.co.uk

Masham   (1895)
*Burnholme, Swinton Road, Masham, Ripon,
HG4 4HT*
☎ **(01765) 688054**
🖥 (01765) 688054
📧 info@mashamgolfclub.co.uk
📖 327
🏌 D Wall
▷ 9 L 6088 yds SSS 69
👥 WD–U before 5pm WE–M
BH–NA
££ £17 D–£20 (18 holes)
🏌 10 miles N of Ripon, off A6108
▣ www.mashamgolfclub.co.uk

Middlesbrough   (1908)
*Brass Castle Lane, Marton, Middlesbrough,
TS8 9EE*
☎ **(01642) 311515**
🖥 (01642) 319607
📧 enquiries@middlesbroughgolfclub
.net
📖 975

🏌 PM Jackson
✏ DJ Jones (01642) 311766
▷ 18 L 6278 yds SSS 70
👥 WD–U exc Tues–H Sat–NA SOC
££ D–£37 (£42)
🏌 5 miles S of Middlesbrough
🏠 James Braid
▣ www.middlesbroughgolfclub.co.uk

Middlesbrough Municipal
(1977)
Public
Ladgate Lane, Middlesbrough, TS5 7YZ
☎ **(01642) 315533**
🖥 (01642) 300726
📖 480
🏌 J Brannagan (Hon Sec)
✏ A Hope (01642) 300720
▷ 18 L 6333 yds SSS 70
👥 U
££ £12.30 (£15.50)
🏌 2 miles S of Middlesbrough on
A174
⊕ Floodlit driving range
🏠 Shuttleworth

Oakdale   (1914)
Oakdale, Harrogate, HG1 2LN
☎ **(01423) 567162**
🖥 (01423) 536030
📧 sec@oakdale-golfclub.com
📖 775
🏌 MJ Cross
✏ C Dell (01423) 560510
▷ 18 L 6456 yds SSS 71
👥 WD–U 9.30–12.30 and after 2pm
SOC–WD
££ £39 (£55)
🏌 ½ mile NE of Royal Hall,
Harrogate
🏠 Dr A Mackenzie
▣ www.oakdale-golfclub.com

The Oaks   (1996)
*Aughton Common, Aughton, York,
YO42 4PW*
☎ **(01757) 288001 (Clubhouse)**
   (01757) 288007 (Bookings)
🖥 (01757) 288232
📧 sheila@theoaksgolfclub.co.uk
📖 700
🏌 Mrs S Nutt (01757) 288577
✏ Graham Walker & Lysa Jones
(01757) 288007
▷ 18 L 6792 yds Par 72 SSS 72
👥 WD–U WE–M SOC–WD
££ D–£25
🏌 1 mile N of Bubwith on B1228. 14
miles SE of York. M62 Junction 37
⊕ Driving range; full practice facilities;
Graham Walker Golf Academy
🏠 Julian Covey
▣ www.theoaksgolfclub.co.uk

Pannal   (1906)
Follifoot Road, Pannal, Harrogate, HG3 1ES
☎ **(01423) 872628**
🖥 (01423) 870043
📧 secretary@pannalgc.co.uk
📖 780
🏌 R Braddon
✏ D Padgett

▷ 18 L 6622 yds SSS 72
👥 WD–H 9.30–12 and after 1.30pm
WE–H 11–12 and after 2.30pm
SOC
££ £45 D–£55 (£55)
🏌 2½ miles S of Harrogate, on A61
⊕ Driving range
🏠 Herd/Mackenzie
▣ www.pannalgc.co.uk

Pike Hills   (1904)
*Tadcaster Road, Askham Bryan, York,
YO23 3UW*
☎ **(01904) 700797**
🖥 (01904) 700797
📧 thesecretary@pikehills.fsnet.co.uk
📖 750
🏌 Garry Dunn
✏ I Gradwell (01904) 708756
▷ 18 L 6146 yds SSS 70
👥 WD–U H before 4.30pm –M after
4.30pm SOC–WD
££ £26 D–£32
🏌 3 miles SW of York on A64
⊕ Driving range
▣ www.pikehillsgolfclub.co.uk

Richmond   (1892)
Bend Hagg, Richmond, DL10 5EX
☎ **(01748) 825319**
🖥 (01748) 821709
📖 600
🏌 BD Aston (01748) 823231
✏ P Jackson (01748) 822457
▷ 18 L 6073 yds SSS 69
👥 U
££ £23 D–£25 (£25 D–£30)
🏌 3 miles SW of Scotch Corner
🏠 Frank Pennink
▣ www.therichmondgolfclub.co.uk

Ripon City   (1908)
Palace Road, Ripon, HG4 3HH
☎ **(01765) 603640**
🖥 (01765) 692880
📧 secretary@riponcitygolfclub.com
📖 671 86(L) 59(J)
🏌 MJ Doig MBE
✏ T Davis (01765) 600411
▷ 18 L 6084 yds SSS 69
👥 U SOC
££ £30 (£40)
🏌 1 mile N of Ripon on A6108
⊕ Driving range
🏠 ADAS
▣ www.riponcitygolfclub.com

Romanby   (1993)
Pay and play
Yafforth Road, Northallerton, DL7 0PE
☎ **(01609) 778855**

Rudding Park   (1995)
Pay and play
Rudding Park, Harrogate, HG3 1JH
☎ **(01423) 872100**
🖥 (01423) 873011
📧 sales@ruddingpark.com
📖 700
🏌 J King
✏ M Moore (01423) 873400

18 L 6883 yds SSS 73
U H SOC
££ £33, Fri/WE–£38.50
2 miles S of Harrogate (A658)
Driving range; Golf Academy; 6-hole short course opening April 2008
Hawtree
www.ruddingpark.com

Saltburn   (1894)

Hob Hill, Saltburn-by-the-Sea, TS12 1NJ
☎ (01287) 622812
(01287) 625988
info@saltburngolf.co.uk
900
M Murtha
P Bolton (01287) 624653
18 L 5897 yds Par 70 SSS 68
U H SOC
££ £26 (£31)
East on A174, right at Quarry Lane, left at lights, 1 mile on right
James Braid
www.saltburngolf.co.uk

Scarborough North Cliff
(1909)

North Cliff Avenue, Burniston Road, Scarborough, YO12 6PP
☎ (01723) 360786
(01723) 362134
info@northcliff.co.uk
860
Mrs JH Lloyd
SN Deller (01723) 365920
18 L 6425 yds Par 71 SSS 71
U H exc Sat am/Sun before 10am and comp days SOC
££ £33 D–£39 (£40 D–£45)
2 miles N of Scarborough on coast road
James Braid
www.ncgc.co.uk

Scarborough South Cliff
(1902)

Deepdale Avenue, Scarborough, YO11 2UE
☎ (01723) 374737
(01723) 374737
clubsecretary.sscgc@virgin.net
700
D Roberts
T Skingle (01723) 365150
18 L 6422 yds Par 72 SSS 71
U H SOC
££ D–£35 (£40)
1 mile S of Scarborough, off A165
Dr A Mackenzie
www.scarboroughgolfclub.co.uk

Scarthingwell   (1993)

Scarthingwell, Tadcaster, LS24 9DG
☎ (01937) 557878
(01937) 557909
400
S Footman (01937) 557864
18 L 6642 yds Par 72 SSS 72
U SOC
££ £20 (£25)
4 miles S of Tadcaster on A162
www.scarthingwellgolfcourse.co.uk

Selby   (1907)

Mill Lane, Brayton, Selby, YO8 9LD
☎ (01757) 228622
(01757) 228785
selbygolfclub@aol.com
749
JN Proctor
N Ludwell (01757) 228785
18 L 6374 yds SSS 71
WD–H WE–NA SOC–WD
££ £32 D–£37
3 miles SW of Selby, off A19 at Brayton. 5 miles N of M62 Junction 34
JH Taylor/Hawtree
www.selbygolfclub.co.uk

Settle   (1895)

Giggleswick, Settle, BD24 0DH
☎ (01729) 825288
info@settlegolfclub.co.uk
250
J Ketchell (01729) 841140
9 L 6089 yds SSS 72
U exc Sun–restricted SOC
££ D–£17
1 mile N of Settle on A65
Tom Vardon
www.settlegolfclub.co.uk

Skipton   (1893)

Short Lee Lane, Skipton, BD23 3LF
☎ (01756) 793922 (bar)
(01756) 796665
enquiries@skiptongolfclub.co.uk
720
Karen Chapman (01756) 795657
P Robinson (01756) 793257
18 L 6090 yds SSS 70
U SOC
££ £26 (£30)
1 mile N of Skipton on A59
www.skiptongolfclub.co.uk

Teesside   (1900)

Acklam Road, Thornaby, TS17 7JS
☎ (01642) 676249
(01642) 676252
teessidegolfclub@btconnect.com
730
M Fleming (01642) 616516
K Hall (01642) 673822
18 L 6535 yds Par 72 SSS 71
WD–U before 4.30pm WE–U after 11am BH–M before 11am SOC
££ D–£26 (£30)
2 miles S of Stockton on A1130. ½ mile from A19 on A1130
Makepeace/Summerville
www.teessidegolfclub.com

Thirsk & Northallerton
(1914)

Thornton-le-Street, Thirsk, YO7 4AB
☎ (01845) 522170
(01845) 525115
secretary@tngc.co.uk
550
SC Owram (01845) 525115
R Garner (01845) 526216
18 L 6495 yds SSS 71

WD/Sat–U H Sun–M SOC
££ £26 D–£32 Sat/BH–£32 D–£42
2 miles N of Thirsk, nr A19 and A168 roundabout
ADAS
www.tngc.co.uk

Whitby   (1892)

Sandsend Road, Low Straggleton, Whitby, YO21 3SR
☎ (01947) 600660
(01947) 600660
office@whitbygolfclub.co.uk
450
TJ Wilkinson (Mgr)
T Mason (01947) 602719
18 L 6003 yds SSS 69
U SOC WD WE
££ £25 (£31)
2 miles N of Whitby on A174
Simon Gidman (new holes only)
www.whitbygolfclub.co.uk

Wilton   (1952)

Wilton, Redcar, Cleveland, TS10 4QY
☎ (01642) 465265/465886
(01642) 465463
secretary@wiltongolfclub.co.uk
720
R Douglas (01642) 465265
Pat Smillie (01642) 452730
18 L 6276 yds Par 70 SSS 69
Mon–Fri after 10 am U; Sat NA; Sun after 10 am U
££ D–£26 (D–£32)
3 miles W of Redcar on A174–signs to Wilton Castle
JFS Morrison
www.wiltongolfclub.co.uk

York   (1890)

Lords Moor Lane, Strensall, York, YO32 5XF
☎ (01904) 491840
(01904) 491852
secretary@yorkgolfclub.co.uk
468(M) 160(L) 80(J)
MJ Wells
AP Hoyles (01904) 490304
18 L 6301 yds SSS 70
U–phone Sec SOC
££ £36–£50 (£45–£50)
4 miles N of York ring road (A1237)
JH Taylor
www.yorkgolfclub.co.uk

Yorkshire (South)

Abbeydale   (1895)

Twentywell Rise, Twentywell Lane, Dore, Sheffield, S17 4QA
☎ (0114) 236 0763
(0114) 236 0762
abbeygolf@compuserve.com
650
GL Lord
N Perry (0114) 236 5633
18 L 6241 yds SSS 70
U SOC–H by arrangement

££ £30 (£45)
🚗 5 miles S of Sheffield, off A621
🏛 Herbert Fowler
🖥 www.abbeydalegolf.co.uk

Barnsley (1925)
Public
*Wakefield Road, Staincross, Barnsley,
S75 6JZ*
☎ **(01226) 382856**
✉ barnsleygolfclub@hotmail.com
🏠 450
✍ B Caunt
✓ S Wyke (01226) 380358
🏳 18 L 5951 yds Par 69 SSS 69
🏌 U
££ £12.50 (£14.50)
🚗 4 miles N of Barnsley on A61

Bawtry (1974)
*Cross Lane, Austerfield, Doncaster,
DN10 6RF*
☎ **(01302) 711755**
🏠 460 34(L) 40(J)
✓ D Roberts (01302) 710841
🏳 18 L 6994 yds Par 73 SSS 73
🏌 U SOC
££ £15 (£20)
🚗 2 miles NE of Bawtry, on A614
⊕ Driving range
🏛 E & M Baker
🖥 www.bawtrygolfclub.co.uk

Beauchief (1925)
Public
Abbey Lane, Beauchief, Sheffield, S8 0DB
☎ **(0114) 236 7274**
✉ e-mail@beauchiefgolfclub.co.uk
🏠 450
✍ Mrs B Fryer
✓ Mark Tripplett
🏳 18 L 5452 yds SSS 66
🏌 U
££ £11 (£13)
🚗 A621 Sheffield. M1 jct 33
🖥 www.beauchiefgolfclub.co.uk

Birley Wood (1974)
Public
Birley Lane, Sheffield, S12 3BP
☎ **(0114) 264 7262**
✉ birleysec@hotmail.com

Concord Park (1952)
Pay and play
Shiregreen Lane, Sheffield, S5 6AE
☎ **(0114) 257 7378**
✉ concordparkgc@tiscali.co.uk

Crookhill Park (1974)
Public
Conisborough, Doncaster, DN12 2AH
☎ **(01709) 862979**

Doncaster (1894)
*Bawtry Road, Bessacarr, Doncaster,
DN4 7PD*
☎ **(01302) 865632**
🖨 (01302) 865994
✉ doncastergolf@aol.com

🏠 576
✍ GJ Needham
✓ G Bailey (01302) 868404
🏳 18 L 6220 yds SSS 70
🏌 WD–U H WE/BH–NA before
　11.30am SOC–WD
££ £32 D–£36 (£36)
🚗 4¹/₂ miles S of Doncaster on
　A638
⊕ Practice area
🏛 Mackenzie/Hawtree
🖥 www.doncastergolfclub.org.uk

Doncaster Town Moor
(1895)
*Bawtry Road, Belle Vue, Doncaster,
DN4 5HU*
☎ **(01302) 533778**
🖨 (01302) 533778
✉ dtmgc@btconnect.com
🏠 540
✍ Mrs S Foy
✓ S Shaw (01302) 535286
🏳 18 L 6141 yds SSS 69
🏌 U exc Sun–NA before 3.30pm
　SOC
££ £24 (£26)
🚗 Inside racecourse, clubhouse on
　A638
⊕ Practice facility; junior coaching; full
　catering facility
🖥 www.doncastertownmoorgolfclub
　.co.uk

Dore & Totley (1913)
*Bradway Road, Bradway, Sheffield,
S17 4QR*
☎ **(0114) 236 0492**
🖨 (0114) 235 3436
✉ dore.totley@btconnect.com
🏠 580
✍ Mrs SD Haslehurst (0114) 236
　9872
✓ G Roberts (0114) 236 6844
🏳 18 L 6763 yds Par 72 SSS 72
🏌 WD–restricted Sat–NA
　Sun–restricted before 1pm
　SOC–by arrangement
££ £30 (£34) Sun–£22 after 4pm
🚗 5 miles SW of Sheffield, off A61
🖥 www.doreandtotleygolf.co.uk

Grange Park (1972)
Pay and play
*Upper Wortley Road, Kimberworth,
Rotherham, S61 2SJ*
☎ **(01709) 558884**

Hallamshire (1897)
Sandygate, Sheffield, S10 4LA
☎ **(0114) 230 1007**
🖨 (0114) 230 5413
🏠 600
✍ R Hill (0114) 230 2153
✓ G Tickell (0114) 230 5222
🏳 18 L 6346 yds SSS 71
🏌 H SOC–WD
££ £45 (£60)
🚗 W boundary of Sheffield

Hallowes (1892)
Dronfield, Sheffield, S18 1UR
☎ **(01246) 413734**
🖨 (01246) 413753
✉ secretary@hallowesgolfclub.org
🏠 665
✍ N Ogden
✓ J Oates (01246) 411196
🏳 18 L 6342 yds SSS 71
🏌 WD–U WE–M
££ £37 D–£42 (£22)
🚗 6 miles S of Sheffield on B6057
🖥 www.hallowesgolfclub.org

Hickleton (1909)
Hickleton, Doncaster, DN5 7BE
☎ **(01709) 896081**
🖨 (01709) 896083
✉ john@hickletongolfclub.co.uk
🏠 600
✍ JM Little (Mgr)
✓ PJ Audsley (01709) 888436
🏳 18 L 6446 yds SSS 71
🏌 WD–U WE–NA before noon SOC
££ £30 (£35)
🚗 On A635 3 miles A1(M) J37
🏛 Huggett/Coles
🖥 www.hickletongolfclub.co.uk

Hillsborough (1920)
Worrall Road, Sheffield, S6 4BE
☎ **(0114) 234 9151 (Secretary)**
🖨 (0114) 229 4105
✉ admin@hillsboroughgolfclub.co.uk
🏠 534
✍ G Smalley (0114) 234 9151
✓ L Horsman (0114) 229 4100
🏳 18 L 6035 yds SSS 70
🏌 H SOC
££ £30 (£35)
🚗 Wadsley, Sheffield

Lees Hall (1907)
Hemsworth Road, Norton, Sheffield, S8 8LL
☎ **(0114) 255 4402**
✉ secretary@leeshallgolfclub.co.uk

Lindrick (1891)
*Lindrick Common, Worksop, Notts,
S81 8BH*
☎ **(01909) 485802**
🖨 (01909) 488685
✉ lgc@ansbronze.com
🏠 500
✍ J Armitage (01909) 475282
✓ JR King (01909) 475820
🏳 18 L 6486 yds Par 71 SSS 71
🏌 U H–by prior arrangement exc
　Tues SOC–WD WE (limited Sun)
££ £50 D–£65 (£65)
🚗 4 miles W of Worksop on A57. M1
　Junction 31
⊕ Practice grounds; teaching bays
🏛 Various
🖥 www.lindrickgolfclub.co.uk

Owston Hall (the Robin Hood golf course) (1996)
*Owston Hall Hotel & Golf Club, Owston,
Doncaster, DN6 9JF*
☎ **(01302) 722800**

☎ (01302) 728885
✉ proshop@owstonhall.com
📖 250
🏌 Gerry Briggs
✓ J Laszkowicz (01302) 722231
🏴 18 L 6937 yds Par 72 SSS 73
👥 U SOC
££ £20 (£28)
🏌 7 miles N of Doncaster on A19 (B1220)
🏠 Will Adamson
🖥 www.owstonhall.com

Owston Park (1988)

Public
Owston Lane, Owston, Carcroft, DN6 8EF
☎ (01302) 330821
🏌 MT Parker
✓ M Parker
🏴 9 L 6148 yds SSS 71
👥 U
££ On application
🏌 5 miles N of Doncaster on A19
🏠 Michael Parker

Phoenix (1932)

Pavilion Lane, Brinsworth, Rotherham, S60 5PA
☎ (01709) 363788
☐ (01709) 363788
✉ secretary@phoenixgolfclub.co.uk
📖 700
🏌 I Gregory (01709) 363788
✓ M Roberts (01709) 382624
🏴 18 L 6181 yds SSS 70
👥 U
££ £19 D–£25 (£25 D–£33)
🏌 2 miles S of Rotherham. M1 Junction 34
⊕ Driving range
🏠 H Cotton
🖥 www.phoenixgolfclub.co.uk

Renishaw Park (1911)

Golf House, Mill Lane, Renishaw, Sheffield S21 3UZ
☎ (01246) 432044
☐ (01246) 432116
📖 550
🏌 TJ Childs
✓ J Oates (01246) 435484
🏴 18 L 6262 yds SSS 70
👥 H SOC
££ £28 D–£37.50 (£42)
🏌 7 miles SE of Sheffield. 2 miles W of M1 Junction 30
🖥 www.renishawparkgolf.co.uk

Rother Valley Golf Centre (1997)

Mansfield Road, Wales Bar, Sheffield, S26 5PQ
☎ (0114) 247 3000
☐ (0114) 247 6000
✉ rother-jackbarker@btinternet.com
📖 300
🏌 Mrs M Goodman
✓ JK Ripley
🏴 18 L 6602 yds Par 72 SSS 72
9 hole Par 3 course
👥 U SOC

££ Mon–Thur £15, Fri £17, Sat–Sun £19.50
🏌 Rother Valley Country Park, 2 miles S of M1 Junction 31
⊕ Floodlit driving range
🏠 Shattock/Roe
🖥 www.jackbarker.com

Rotherham (1902)

Thrybergh Park, Rotherham, S65 4NU
☎ (01709) 850466
☐ (01709) 859517
✉ manager@rotherhamgolfclub.com
📖 540
🏌 Maj GJ Mason BEM (01709) 859500
✓ S Thornhill (01709) 850480
🏴 18 L 6327 yds SSS 70
👥 WD–U SOC WE (18 holes after 2pm)
££ £30 (£40)
🏌 4 miles E of Rotherham on A630
🏠 Alec (Sandy) Herd and James Braid
🖥 www.rotherhamgolfclub.com

Roundwood (1976)

Green Lane, Rawmarsh, Rotherham, S62 6LA
☎ (01709) 523471
📖 700
🏌 M Johnson (01709) 522463
🏴 18 L 5620 yds Par 67 SSS 67
👥 SOC–WD Sun from 11am U Mon–Fri, from 11am Sun
££ With member: £10 (£18) Without member: £15 (£20) Juniors £5
🏌 2 miles N of Rotherham on A633

Sandhill (1993)

Pay and play
Little Houghton, Barnsley, S72 0HW
☎ (01226) 753444
☐ (01226) 753444
📖 420
🏌 BD Murray
🏴 18 L 6250 yds SSS 70
👥 U SOC
££ £13 (£18)
🏌 6 miles E of Barnsley, off A635
⊕ Driving range
🏠 John Royston

Sheffield Transport (1923)

Meadow Head, Sheffield, S8 7RE
☎ (0114) 237 3216

Silkstone (1893)

Field Head, Elmhirst Lane, Silkstone, Barnsley, S75 4LD
☎ (01226) 790328
☐ (01226) 794902
✉ silkstonegolf@hotmail.co.uk
📖 600
🏌 Alan Butcher
✓ K Guy (01226) 790128
🏴 18 L 6069 yds SSS 70
👥 WD–U SOC–WD
££ £26 D–£34
🏌 1 mile W of M1 Junction 37 on A628
🖥 www.silkstone-golf-club.co.uk

Sitwell Park (1913)

Shrogs Wood Road, Rotherham, S60 4BY
☎ (01709) 541046
☐ (01709) 703637
✉ secretary@sitwellgolf.co.uk
📖 500
🏌 WE Hardy
✓ N Taylor (01709) 540961
🏴 18 L 6250 yds SSS 70
👥 WD–U Sat–M Sun–NA before 11.30am SOC
££ £26 (£32); D–£34 (£40)
🏌 2½ miles E of Rotherham on A631. M18 Junction 1
🏠 Dr A Mackenzie
🖥 www.sitwellgolf.co.uk

Stocksbridge & District (1924)

Royd Lane, Deepcar, Sheffield, S36 2RZ
☎ (0114) 288 7479/288 2003
☐ (0114) 283 1460
✉ secretary@stocksbridgeanddistrict golfclub.com
📖 400
🏌 D Haley (0114) 288 2003
✓ R Broad (0114) 288 2779
🏴 18 L 5200 yds Par 65 SSS 65
👥 U SOC
££ £21 (£31)
🏌 9 miles W of Sheffield (A616)
🖥 www.stocksbridgeanddistrict golfclub.com

Styrrup Hall (2000)

Main Street, Styrrup, Doncaster DN11 8NB
☎ (01302) 751112 (Golf)
(01302) 759933 (Clubhouse)
☐ (01302) 750622
✉ office@styrrupgolf.co.uk
📖 410
🏌 Dianne Stockoe (Sec/Mgr)
✓ Richard Allen
🏴 18 L 6745 yds SSS 72
👥 SOC WD–U WE–afternoons
££ £16 (£22 + Bank Hols)
🏌 2 miles from Blyth Services on A1M
⊕ Driving range; function room
🖥 www.styrrupgolf.co.uk

Tankersley Park (1907)

Park Lane, High Green, Sheffield, S35 4LG
☎ (0114) 246 8247
☐ (0114) 245 7818
✉ secretary@tpgc.freeserve.co.uk
📖 574
🏌 A Brownhill (0114) 246 8247
✓ I Kirk (0114) 245 5583
🏴 18 L 6212 yds Par 69 SSS 70
👥 WD–U WE–M SOC–WD
££ £27 D–£36 (£36)
🏌 Chapeltown, 7 miles N of Sheffield. M1 Junctions 35A/36
🏠 Hawtree
🖥 www.tankersleyparkgolfclub.org.uk

Thorne (1980)

Pay and play
Kirton Lane, Thorne, Doncaster, DN8 5RJ
☎ (01405) 815173

☎ (01405) 741899
⌨ 120
♬ R Highfield
✓ ED Highfield (01405) 812084
⏴ 18 L 5294 yds SSS 66 Par 68
⚇ U SOC WD+WE
££ £11 (£12)
⊕ 10 miles NE of Doncaster. M18 Junction 5/6
⌂ RD Highfield
⊟ www.thorneolf.co.uk

Tinsley Park   (1920)
Public
High Hazels Park, Darnall, Sheffield, S9 4PE
☎ (0114) 203 7435

Wath   (1904)
Abdy Rawmarsh, Rotherham, S62 7SJ
☎ (01709) 878609
⌨ (01709) 877097
✉ golf@wathgolfclub.co.uk
⌨ 630
♬ M Godfrey (01709) 583174
✓ C Bassett (01709) 878609
⏴ 18 L 6086 yds SSS 70
⚇ WD–U WE/BH–M SOC
££ £25 D–£30
⊕ Abdy Farm, 1½ miles S of Wath-upon-Dearne. M1 junction 36. A1M junction if appropriate
⊕ Practice area; buggie & trolly hire

Wheatley   (1913)
Armthorpe Road, Doncaster, DN2 5QB
☎ (01302) 831655
⌨ (01302) 812736
✉ secretary@wheatleygolfclub.co.uk
⌨ 430 100(L) 50(J)
♬ Trevor Roberts
✓ S Fox (01302) 834085
⏴ 18 L 6405 yds SSS 71
⚇ U SOC
££ £30 (£40)
⊕ 3 miles NE of Doncaster
⌂ George Duncan

Wombwell Hillies   (1989)
Public
Wentworth View, Wombwell, Barnsley, S73 0LA
☎ (01226) 754433

Wortley   (1894)
Hermit Hill Lane, Wortley, Sheffield, S35 7DF
☎ (0114) 288 8469
⌨ (0114) 288 8488
✉ wortley.golfclub@btconnect.com
⌨ 500
♬ Dr FA Wilson
✓ I Kirk (0114) 288 6490
⏴ 18 L 6035 yds SSS 69
⚇ WD–U WE–NA before 10.30am SOC
££ £28 (£35)
⊕ 2 miles W of M1 Junction 36, off A629
⊕ Large practice area
⊟ www.wortleygolfclub.co.uk

Yorkshire (West)

The Alwoodley   (1907)
Wigton Lane, Alwoodley, Leeds, LS17 8SA
☎ (0113) 268 1680
⌨ (0113) 293 9458
✉ via website
⌨ 450
♬ Mrs J Slater
✓ JR Green (0113) 268 9603
⏴ 18 L 6322 yds SSS 71 Yellow
⚇ U SOC–WD
££ £60 (£85) summer £55 winter WD
⊕ 5 miles N of Leeds on A61
⌂ Dr A MacKenzie
⊟ www.alwoodley.co.uk

Bagden Hall Hotel   (1993)
Wakefield Road, Scissett, HD8 9LE
☎ (01484) 865330

Baildon   (1896)
Moorgate, Baildon, Shipley, BD17 5PP
☎ (01274) 584266
✉ sec@baildongolfclub.freeserve.co.uk
⌨ 750
♬ JA Cooley (01274) 584266
✓ R Masters (01274) 595162
⏴ 18 L 6231 yds par 70 SSS 70
⚇ WD–U before 5pm (restricted Tues) WE/BH–restricted
££ £26 (£30)
⊕ 5 miles N of Bradford, off A6038
⌂ Tom Morris/James Braid
⊟ www.baildongolfclub.com

Ben Rhydding   (1947)
High Wood, Ben Rhydding, Ilkley, LS9 8SB
☎ (01943) 608759
✉ secretary@benrhyddinggc .freeserve.co.uk
⌨ 180 45(L) 40(J)
♬ JR Hartley
⏴ 9 L 4611 yds SSS 63
⚇ WD–U exc Wed pm & Thurs am WE–after 4pm
££ £15 (£20)
⊕ 2 miles SE of Ilkley

Bingley St Ives   (1931)
St Ives Estate, Bingley, BD16 1AT
☎ (01274) 562436
⌨ (01274) 511788
✉ bingleyst-ives@harden.freeserve .co.uk
♬ RA Adams
✓ R Firth (01274) 562506
⏴ 18 L 6480 yds SSS 71
⚇ WD–U before 4pm
££ £25 D–£30
⊕ 6 miles NW of Bradford, off A650
⊕ Driving range

Bracken Ghyll   (1993)
Skipton Road, Addingham, Ilkley, LS29 0SL
☎ (01943) 831207
⌨ (01943) 839453
✉ office@brackenghyll.co.uk
⌨ 400
♬ Mrs EG Vriesendorp

✓ None
⏴ 18 L 5600 yds Par 69 SSS 67
⚇ WD/BH–U WE–NA before 11am on comp days SOC
££ £20 (£24)
⊕ 3 miles W of Ilkley on old A65 to Addingham
⊕ Indoor practice area
⊟ www.brackenghyll.co.uk

Bradford   (1891)
Hawksworth Lane, Guiseley, Leeds, LS20 8NP
☎ (01943) 875570
⌨ (01943) 875570
⌨ 700
♬ T Eagle
✓ S Weldon (01943) 873719
⏴ 18 L 6259 yds SSS 71
⚇ WD–U WE–NA before noon SOC–WD
££ On application
⊕ 8 miles N of Bradford, off A6038. 10 miles N of Leeds on A650
⊕ Range available for members and green fee paying visitors
⌂ WH Fowler
⊟ www.bradfordgolfclub.co.uk

Bradford Moor   (1906)
Scarr Hall, Pollard Lane, Bradford, BD2 4RW
☎ (01274) 771716
⌨ 300
♬ GW Lee (01274) 771693
⏴ 9 L 5854 yds SSS 68
⚇ WD–U
££ £12
⊕ 2 miles N of Bradford

Bradley Park   (1978)
Public
Bradley Road, Huddersfield, HD2 1PZ
☎ (01484) 223772
⌨ (01484) 451613
⌨ 300
♬ K Blackwell
✓ PE Reilly
⏴ 18 L 6202 yds SSS 70
9 hole Par 3 course
⚇ WE–NA
££ £15.50 (£17.50)
⊕ 2 miles N of Huddersfield, off A6107, M62 Junction 25
⊕ Floodlit driving range

Branshaw   (1912)
Branshaw Moor, Oakworth, Keighley, BD22 7ES
☎ (01535) 643235
✉ branshaw@golfclub.fslife.co.uk

Calverley   (1980)
Woodhall Lane, Pudsey, LS28 5QY
☎ (0113) 256 9244
⌨ (0113) 256 4362
✉ golf@cgc1.freeserve.co.uk
⌨ 560
♬ N Wendel-Jones (Mgr)
✓ N Wendel-Jones
⏴ 18 L 5527 yds SSS 67
9 L 3100 yds Par 36
⚇ WD–U WE–pm only H SOC

££ £14 (£17)
⊕ 4 miles NE of Bradford

Castlefields (1903)

Rastrick Common, Brighouse, HD6 3HL
☎ **(01484) 713276**
🕮 180
✍ FC Tolley (Acting Sec)
🏌 6 L 2406 yds Par 54 SSS 50
🚶 M
££ £6 (£10)
⊕ 1 mile S of Brighouse

City Golf Course (1997)

Pay and play
*Red Cote Lane, Kirkstall Road, Leeds
LS4 2AW*
☎ **(0113) 263 3030**
🖳 (0113) 263 3044
✍ P Cole (Mgr)
🏌 9 hole course, pay and play
££ £5 9–18 holes
⊕ 2 miles from Leeds centre, M62–M1

City of Wakefield (1936)

Public
*Lupset Park, Horbury Road, Wakefield,
WF2 8QS*
☎ **(01924) 367442**
✍ D Bagg (01924) 360282
🏌 18 L 6319 yds SSS 70
🚶 U SOC–WD
££ £11.80
⊕ A642, 2 miles W of Wakefield. 2
miles E of M1 Junction 39/40
🏠 JSF Morrison

Clayton (1906)

*Thornton View Road, Clayton, Bradford,
BD14 6JX*
☎ **(01274) 880047**
✉ tking@otto-uk.com
🕮 168 17(L) 56(J)
✍ DA Smith (01274) 572311
🏌 9 L 6237 yds SSS 70
🚶 WD–U Sat–U Sun–after 4pm
££ D–£17 (£18)
⊕ 3 miles W of Bradford, off A647
🖥 www.claytongolfclub.co.uk

Cleckheaton & District
(1900)

*483 Bradford Road, Cleckheaton,
BD19 6BU*
☎ **(01274) 851266 (Manager)**
🖳 (01274) 871382
✉ info@cleckheatongolfclub.co.uk
🕮 594
✍ Andrew Callaway
✍ M Ingham (01274) 851267
🏌 18 L 5860 yds SSS 69
🚶 U SOC
££ £30 (£35)
⊕ Nr M62 Junction 26-A638
🏠 Alister Mackenzie
🖥 www.cleckheatongolfclub.fsnet.co.uk

Cookridge Hall (1997)

Proprietary
*Cookridge Lane, Cookridge, Leeds,
LS16 7NL*
☎ **(0113) 230 0641**

🖳 (0113) 203 0198
✉ info@cookridgehall.co.uk
🕮 570
✍ Gary Day (0113) 230 0641
✍ M Pinkett
🏌 18 L 6788 yds Par 72 SSS 72
🚶 WD–U Sat–U after 2pm Sun–U
after 12 noon SOC
££ £22 (£25)
⊕ 5 miles NW of Leeds, via A660
⊕ Floodlit driving range
🏠 Karl Litten
🖥 www.cookridgehall.co.uk

Crosland Heath (1914)

*Felks Stile Road, Crosland Heath,
Huddersfield, HD4 7AF*
☎ **(01484) 653216**
🖳 (01484) 461079
✉ golf@croslandheath.co.uk
🕮 600
✍ S Robinson (01484) 653216
✍ J Eyre (01484) 653877
🏌 18 L 6087 yds Par 71 SSS 70
🚶 U SOC H WD
££ On application
⊕ 3 miles W of Huddersfield, off A62
🏠 Dr A Mackenzie
🖥 www.croslandheath.co.uk

Crow Nest Park (1994)

*Coach Road, Hove Edge, Brighouse,
HD6 2LN*
☎ **(01484) 401121**
🖳 (01484) 720975
✉ crownest@btconnect.com
🕮 300
✍ A Naylor
✍ P Everitt (01484) 401121
🏌 9 L 6020 yds Par 70 SSS 69
🚶 WD–U WE–U before noon
££ 18 holes–£24. 9 holes–£12
⊕ 5 miles E of Halifax. M62 Jct 25
⊕ Driving range with Power Tees and
Swingcam
🏠 Will Adamson
🖥 www.crownestgolf.co.uk

Dewsbury District (1891)

*The Pinnacle, Sands Lane, Mirfield,
WF14 8HJ*
☎ **(01924) 492399**
🖳 (01924) 492399
✉ dewsbury.golf@btconnect.com
🕮 650
✍ DM Ellis
✍ N Hirst (01924) 496030
🏌 18 L 6360 yds SSS 71
🚶 WD–U WE–U after 3pm SOC
££ £20 (£17.50)
⊕ 2 miles W of Dewsbury, off A644
🏠 Tom Morris/Alliss/Thomas
🖥 www.dewsburygolf.co.uk

East Bierley (1928)

*South View Road, Bierley, Bradford,
BD4 6PP*
☎ **(01274) 681023**
✉ rjwelch@ebgc.fsnet.co.uk
🕮 156 47(L) 30(J)
✍ RJ Welch (01274) 683666
✍ J Whittam (07904) 141248
🏌 9 L 4692 yds SSS 63

🚶 U exc Mon–NA after 4pm Sun–by
prior arrangement
££ £14 (£16)
⊕ 4 miles SE of Bradford. M62-M606

Elland (1910)

*Hammerstone Leach Lane, Hullen Edge,
Elland, HX5 0TA*
☎ **(01422) 372505**
🕮 280
✍ RF Winterbottom (01422) 379174
✍ N Krzywicki (01422) 374886
🏌 9 L 5498 yds Par 66 SSS 67
🚶 U
££ £18 (£30)
⊕ Elland 1 mile. M62 Junction 24,
signpost Blackley

Fardew (1993)

Pay and play
*Nursery Farm, Carr Lane, East Morton,
Keighley, BD20 5RY*
☎ **(01274) 561438**
🖳 (01274) 561229
✉ fardew@dial.pipex.com
🕮 100
✍ SC Mann
✍ I Bottomley
🏌 9 L 3104 yds Par 72 SSS 70
🚶 U SOC
££ 9 holes–£8 (£9)
18 holes–£14 (£16)
⊕ 2 miles W of Bingley on A650
🏠 Will Adamson

Ferrybridge (2002)

*PO Box 39, Stranglands Lane, Knottingley,
WF11 8SQ*
☎ **(01977) 884165**
🖳 (01977) 884001
✉ Trevor.Ellis@Scottish-southern
🕮 305
✍ TD Ellis
✍ Alistair Cobbett (01977) 884204
🏌 9 L 6047 yds SSS 69 Par 71
🚶 U
££ D–£12 (D–£12)
⊕ ¹/₂ mile off A1, on B6136
⊕ Practice area; buggies available
🏠 G Barton

Fulneck (1892)

Fulneck, Pudsey, LS28 8NT
☎ **(0113) 256 5191**

Garforth (1913)

Long Lane, Garforth, Leeds, LS25 2DS
☎ **(0113) 286 3308**
🖳 (0113) 286 3308
✉ garforthgcltd@lineone.net
🕮 629
✍ Richard H Green
(0113) 286 3308
✍ K Findlater (0113) 286 2063
🏌 18 L 6304 yds SSS 70
🚶 WD–U H WE/BH–M SOC
££ £36 D–£42
⊕ 9 miles E of Leeds, between
Garforth and Barwick-in-Elmet
⊕ Practice grounds
🏠 Dr A Mackenzie
🖥 www.garforthgolfclub.co.uk

Gotts Park   (1933)
Public
Armley Ridge Road, Armley, Leeds,
LS12 2QX
☎ **(0113) 234 2019**

Halifax   (1895)
Union Lane, Ogden, Halifax, HX2 8XR
☎ **(01422) 244171**
🖷 (01422) 241459
✉ halifax.golfclub@virgin.net
📖 450
🏌 John Abson
⚲ M Delaney (01422) 240047
🏳 18 L 6037 yds SSS 69
👥 U WD–parties welcome SOC WE
by arrangement; special offers
Tues/Wed
££ £30 (£36)
⛳ 4 miles N of Halifax on A629
🏠 Alex Herd/James Braid
🖳 www.halifaxgolfclub.co.uk

Halifax Bradley Hall
(1907)
Holywell Green, Halifax, HX4 9AN
☎ **(01422) 374108**
📖 608
🏌 M Dredge
⚲ P Wood (01422) 370231
🏳 18 L 6138 yds SSS 70
👥 U SOC
££ £26 (£32)
⛳ S of Halifax on A6112

Halifax West End   (1906)
Paddock Lane, Highroad Well, Halifax,
HX2 0NT
☎ **(01422) 341878**
🖷 (01442) 341878
✉ westendgc@btinternet.com
📖 580 100(L) 60(J)
🏌 G Gower (01422) 341878
⚲ D Rishworth (01422) 341878
🏳 18 L 5951 yds SSS 69
👥 U SOC
££ £29 (£32) plus special offers
⛳ 2 miles NW of Halifax
🖳 www.westendgc.co.uk

Hanging Heaton   (1922)
Whitecross Road, Bennett Lane, Dewsbury,
WF12 7DT
☎ **(01924) 461606**
✉ john.whelan@hhgc.org

Headingley   (1892)
Back Church Lane, Adel, Leeds, LS16 8DW
☎ **(0113) 267 3052
(Clubhouse)**
🖷 (0113) 281 7334
📖 675
🏌 JR Burns JP (Mgr) (0113) 267 9573
⚲ NM Harvey (0113) 267 5100
🏳 18 L 6608 yds Par 71 SSS 72
👥 WD–U before 3.30pm SOC
££ £36 D–£45 (£45)
⛳ 5 miles NW of Leeds, off A660
(Church Lane lights)
🏠 Dr A MacKenzie

Headley   (1907)
Headley Lane, Thornton, Bradford,
BD13 3LX
☎ **(01274) 833481**
🖷 (01274) 833481
📖 270 35(L) 35(J)
🏌 K Allan
🏳 9 L 4914 yds SSS 65
👥 WD–U WE–M SOC
££ On application
⛳ 5 miles W of Bradford (B6145)
🖳 www.headleygolfclub.co.uk

Hebden Bridge   (1930)
Great Mount, Wadsworth, Hebden Bridge,
HX7 8PH
☎ **(01422) 842896**
📖 300
🏌 R Priestley (01422) 842896
🏳 9 L 5242 yds Par 68 SSS 67
👥 WD–U
££ £10–£12 (£15)
⛳ 1 mile N of Hebden Bridge

Horsforth   (1906)
Layton Rise, Layton Road, Horsforth, Leeds,
LS18 5EX
☎ **(0113) 258 6819**
🖷 (0113) 258 9336
✉ secretary@horsforthgolfclubltd
.co.uk
📖 365 90(L) 85(J)
🏌 Mrs LA Harrison
⚲ Simon Booth & Dean Stokes
(0113) 258 5200
🏳 18 L 6258 yds SSS 70
👥 WD–U WD–SOC WE–after 3pm
(contact Pro)
££ D–£36 (£40)
⛳ M62 - follow signs for Leeds
Bradford Airport
⊕ Practice field
🏠 Dr Alistair Mackenzie
🖳 www.horsforthgolfclubltd.co.uk

Howley Hall   (1900)
Scotchman Lane, Morley, Leeds,
LS27 0NX
☎ **(01924) 350100**
🖷 (01924) 350104
✉ office@howleyhall.co.uk
📖 492
🏌 D Jones (01924) 350100
⚲ G Watkinson (01924) 350102
🏳 18 L 6454 yds Par 71 SSS 71
👥 U SOC–WD/Sun
££ £30 D–£36 (£40)
⛳ 4 miles SW of Leeds on B6123
🖳 www.howleyhall.co.uk

Huddersfield   (1891)
Fixby Hall, Lightridge Road, Huddersfield,
HD2 2EP
☎ **(01484) 426203**
🖷 (01484) 424623
✉ secretary@huddersfield-golf.co.uk
📖 656
🏌 Mrs S Dennis (Gen Mgr)
⚲ P Carman (01484) 426463
🏳 18 L 6391 yds SSS 71
👥 U SOC–WD
££ £45 D–£55 (£55 D–£65)

⛳ 2 miles N of Huddersfield, off
A6107. M62 Junction 24
⊕ Driving range
🏠 Tom Dunn
🖳 www.huddersfield-golf.co.uk

Ilkley   (1890)
Myddleton, Ilkley, LS29 0BE
☎ **(01943) 607277**
🖷 (01943) 816130
✉ honsec@ilkleygolfclub.co.uk
📖 530
🏌 PG Richardson (01943) 600214
⚲ JL Hammond (01943) 607463
🏳 18 L 6260 yds SSS 70
👥 U–H
££ £45 (£55). Winter rate 01/11 to
31/03 £27
⛳ NW of Ilkley, off A65
⊕ Practice ground
🖳 www.ilkleygolfclub.co.uk

Keighley   (1904)
Howden Park, Utley, Keighley, BD20 6DH
☎ **(01535) 604778**
🖷 (01535) 604778
✉ manager@keighleygolfclub.com
📖 600
🏌 G Cameron Dawson
⚲ A Rhodes (01535) 665370
🏳 18 L 6141 yds SSS 70
👥 WD–NA before 9.30am &
12–1.30pm Sat–NA Sun/BH–NA
before 2pm
££ £35 D–£43 (£39 D–£47)
⛳ 1 mile W of Keighley on B6265
🖳 www.keighleygolfclub.com

Leeds   (1896)
Elmete Road, Roundhay, Leeds, LS8 2LJ
☎ **(0113) 265 8775**
🖷 (0113) 232 3369
✉ secretary@leedsgolfclub.com
📖 545
🏌 SJ Clarkson (0113) 265 9203
⚲ S Longster (0113) 265 8786
🏳 18 L 6092 yds SSS 69
👥 WD–U WE–M SOC
££ £25 D–£32
⛳ 4 miles NE of Leeds, off A58
🖳 www.leedsgolfclub.com

Leeds Golf Centre   (1994)
Pay and play
Wike Ridge Lane, Shadwell, Leeds,
LS17 9JW
☎ **(0113) 288 6000**
✉ info@leedsgolfcentre.com

Lightcliffe   (1907)
Knowle Top Road, Lightcliffe, HX3 8SW
☎ **(01422) 202459**
📖 180 95(L) 84(J)
🏌 RP Crampton (01484) 384672
⚲ R Tickle
🏳 9 L 5368 metres SSS 68
👥 U H–exc Wed Sun am–M SOC
££ £16 (£20)
⛳ 3 miles E of Halifax (A58)
⊕ Practice field adjacent

Lofthouse Hill

Leeds Road, Lofthouse Hill, Wakefield,
WF3 3LR
- ☎ **(01924) 823703**
- 🖴 (01924) 823703
- ✍ D Nicklin
- ✓ D Johnson (01924) 823703
- ▷ 18 L 5988 yds Par 70
- 👥 U
- ££ 9: £6 18: £12
- ⛳ Between Leeds and Wakefield on A61
- 🖥 www.lofthousehillgolfclub.co.uk

Longley Park   (1910)

Maple Street, Huddersfield, HD5 9AX
- ☎ **(01484) 426932**
- 🖴 (01484) 515280
- ✉ longleyparkgolfclub@12freeukisp .co.uk
- 📖 400
- ✍ D Palliser (01484) 422304
- ✓ N Leeming (01484) 422304
- ▷ 9 L 5212 yds Par 66 SSS 66
- 👥 WD–U exc Thurs WE–restricted
- ££ £16 (£20)
- ⛳ Huddersfield ½ mile

Low Laithes   (1925)

Park Mill Lane, Flushdyke, Ossett,
WF5 9AP
- ☎ **(01924) 273275**
- ✉ info@low-laithes-golf-club.co.uk

The Manor   (1993)

Proprietary
Bradford Road, Drighlington, Bradford,
BD11 1AB
- ☎ **(01132) 852644**
- 🖴 (01132) 879961
- ✉ themanorgolfclub@hotmail.co.uk
- 📖 300
- ✍ G Thompson (Sec/Mgr)
- ✓ G Thompson
- ▷ 18 L 6508 yds Par 72 SSS 71
- 👥 U SOC–exc Sat
- ££ £16 (£20; after 3.30pm £12.50)
- ⛳ 3 miles from M62 J27, off A650
- ⊕ Floodlit driving range; 6 holes pitch & putt course
- 🏠 David Hemstock

Marriott Hollins Hall Hotel
(1999)

Hollins Hill, Baildon, Shipley, BD17 7QW
- ☎ **(01274) 534212**
- 🖴 (01274) 534220
- ✉ mhrs.lbags@marriotthotels.com
- 📖 300
- ✍ Peter Rishworth (01274) 534250
- ✓ Gordon Brand Jr, Mark Wood
- ▷ 18 L 6700 yds Par 71 SSS 72
- 👥 H WD–U WE–NA before 1pm
- ££ £40 (£50)
- ⛳ 6 miles N of Bradford on A6038
- ⊕ Driving range, leisure facilities, 4-star hotel; short game practice area
- 🏠 Ross McMurray
- 🖥 www.marriotthollinshall.com

Marsden   (1921)

Hemplow, Marsden, Huddersfield,
HD7 6NN
- ☎ **(01484) 844253**
- ✉ secretary@marsdengolf.co.uk
- 📖 200 50(L) 50(J)
- ✍ SJ Boustead (01457) 874158
- ✓ D Pemberton-Nash
- ▷ 9 L 5702 yds SSS 68
- 👥 WD–U Sat–NA before 4pm Sun–M SOC
- ££ £15 (£20)
- ⛳ 8 miles W of Huddersfield, off A62
- 🏠 Dr A Mackenzie
- 🖥 www.marsdengolf.co.uk

Meltham   (1908)

Thick Hollins Hall, Meltham, Huddersfield,
HD9 4DQ
- ☎ **(01484) 850227**
- 🖴 (01484) 850227
- ✉ admin@meltham-golf.co.uk
- 📖 700
- ✍ GW Hopwood (Hon)
- ✓ PF Davies (01484) 851521
- ▷ 18 L 6407 yds SSS 70
- 👥 SOC WD–WE
- ££ £28 (£33)
- ⛳ 5 miles SW of Huddersfield (B6107)
- 🖥 www.meltham-golf.co.uk

Mid Yorkshire   (1993)

Proprietary
Havercroft Lane, Darrington, Pontefract,
WF8 3BP
- ☎ **(01977) 704522**
- 🖴 (01977) 600823
- ✉ admin@midyorkshiregolfclub.com
- 📖 600
- ✍ Tony Harris, MInstGCM
- ✓ Michael Hessay (01977) 704522
- ▷ 18 L 308 yds Par 70 SSS 70
- 👥 U SOC WD WE
- ££ £20 (£30)
- ⛳ Nr A1/M62 junction
- ⊕ Floodlit driving range
- 🏠 Steve Marnoch
- 🖥 www.midyorkshiregolfclub.com

Middleton Park   (1933)

Public
Ring Road, Beeston Park, Middleton,
LS10 3TN
- ☎ **(0113) 270 0449**
- ✉ secretary@middletonparkgolfclub .co.uk
- 📖 250
- ✓ (0113) 270 9506
- ▷ 18 L 5233 yds SSS 66
- 👥 U
- ££ On application
- ⛳ 3 miles S of Leeds
- 🖥 www.middletonparkgolfclub.co.uk

Moor Allerton   (1923)

Coal Road, Wike, Leeds, LS17 9NH
- ☎ **(0113) 266 1154**
- 🖴 (0113) 268 0559
- 📖 750
- ✍ RM Crann (Mgr)
- ✓ R Lane (0113) 266 5209

- ▷ 27 L 6470–6843 yds SSS 73–74
- ££ £55–£75 (£65–£85)
- ⛳ 5½ miles N of Leeds, off A61
- ⊕ Driving range
- 🏠 Robert Trent Jones Sr

Moortown   (1909)

Harrogate Road, Leeds, LS17 7DB
- ☎ **(0113) 268 6521**
- 🖴 (0113) 268 0986
- ✉ secretary@moortown-gc.co.uk
- 📖 600
- ✓ Martin Heggie (0113) 268 3636
- ▷ 18 L 7002 yds SSS 74
- 👥 U
- ££ £65 D–£75
- ⛳ 5½ miles N of Leeds on A61
- ⊕ Complimentary warm-up facilities for visitors
- 🏠 Dr A Mackenzie
- 🖥 www.moortown-gc.co.uk

Normanton   (1903)

Hatfeild Hall, Aberford Road, Stanley,
Wakefield, WF3 4JP
- ☎ **(01924) 377943**
- 🖴 (01924) 200777
- ✉ office@normantongolf.co.uk
- 📖 800
- ✍ D Styles
- ✓ G Pritchard (01924) 200900
- ▷ 18 L 6191 yds Par 72 SSS 69
- 👥 WD SOC
- ££ £27
- ⛳ 3 miles N of Wakefield (A642). M62 Junction 30
- 🏠 Patrick Dawson
- 🖥 www.normantongolf.co.uk

Northcliffe   (1921)

High Bank Lane, Shipley, Bradford,
BD18 4LJ
- ☎ **(01274) 584085**
- 🖴 (01274) 584148
- ✉ northcliffegc@hotmail.com
- 📖 500
- ✍ I Collins (01274) 596731
- ✓ M Hillas (01274) 587193
- ▷ 18 L 6113 yds SSS 71
- 👥 U SOC
- ££ £25 (£30)
- ⛳ 3 miles NW of Bradford, off A650 Keighley road
- 🏠 James Braid
- 🖥 www.northcliffegolfclubshipley .co.uk

Otley   (1906)

West Busk Lane, Otley, LS21 3NG
- ☎ **(01943) 465329**
- 🖴 (01943) 850387
- ✉ office@otley-golfclub.co.uk
- 📖 700
- ✍ PJ Clarke Ext 202
- ✓ S Tomkinson Ext 203
- ▷ 18 L 6211 yds SSS 70
- 👥 U exc Sat–NA SOC
- ££ £34 D–£40 (£38)
- ⛳ 1 mile W of Otley, off A6038
- ⊕ Extensive practice facilities
- 🖥 www.otley-golfclub.co.uk

Oulton Park (1990)
Public
Oulton, Rothwell, Leeds, LS26 8EX
☎ (0113) 282 3152

Outlane (1906)
Slack Lane, off New Hey Road, Outlane, Huddersfield HD3 3YL
☎ (01422) 374762
🖥 (01422) 311789
✉ secretary@outlanegolfclub.ltd.uk
📖 500
🏌 P Jackson
✓ D Chapman
ⓟ 18 L 6010 yds SSS 69
👥 U SOC
££ £22 (£32)
🚗 4 miles W of Huddersfield, off A640. M62 Junction 23
⊕ Practice ground and nets; putting green
🖳 www.outlanegolfclub.ltd.uk

Painthorpe House (1961)
Painthorpe Lane, Crigglestone, Wakefield, WF4 3HE
🏌 TJ Mead (01924) 254737
ⓟ 9 L 4506 yds SSS 62
👥 WD–U WE–U
££ £5 (£5)
🚗 1 mile SE of M1 Junction 39

Phoenix Park (1922)
Dick Lane, Thornbury, Bradford, BD3 7AT
☎ (01274) 667573

Pontefract & District (1904)
Park Lane, Pontefract, WF8 4QS
☎ (01977) 792241
🖥 (01977) 792241
✉ manager@pdgc.co.uk
📖 620
🏌 J Heald (Mgr) (01977) 792241
✓ NJ Newman (01977) 706806
ⓟ 18 L 6227 yds SSS 70
👥 WD–U 9.30–12 noon and after 2 pm WE–after 3pm SOC–WD exc Wed & WE
££ £25 (£32)
🚗 Pontefract 1 mile on B6134. M62 Junction 32
🏠 Alistair Mackenzie
🖳 www.pdgc.co.uk

Queensbury (1923)
Brighouse Road, Queensbury, Bradford, BD13 1QF
☎ (01274) 882155
🖥 (01274) 882155
✉ queensburygolf@supanet.com
📖 400 48(L) 47(J)
✓ MH Heptinstall
✓ N Stead (01274) 816864
ⓟ 9 L 5008 yds SSS 65
👥 U
££ £15 (£30)
🚗 4 miles SW of Bradford (A647)
🖳 www.queensburygc.co.uk

Rawdon (1896)
Buckstone Drive, Micklefield Lane, Rawdon, LS19 6BD
☎ (0113) 250 6040

Riddlesden (1927)
Howden Rough, Riddlesden, Keighley, BD20 5QN
☎ (01535) 602148
📖 400
🏌 Mrs R Bottomley (01535) 602148
ⓟ 18 L 4295 yds Par 63 SSS 61
👥 U exc Sun–NA before 2pm WD–U before 5pm SOC WE after 2pm
££ £15 (£20)
🚗 1 mile from Riddlesden, off Scott Lane West. 3 miles N of Keighley, off A650

Roundhay (1923)
Public
Park Lane, Leeds, LS8 2EJ
☎ (0113) 266 2695
📖 230
🏌 RH McLauchlan (0113) 266 4225
✓ JA Pape (0113) 266 1686
ⓟ 9 L 5322 yds SSS 65
👥 U
££ On application
🚗 N of Leeds, off Moortown Ring Rd

Ryburn (1910)
Norland, Sowerby Bridge, Halifax, HX6 3QP
☎ (01422) 831355
📖 300
🏌 J Hoyle (01422) 843070
ⓟ 9 L 5127 yds SSS 65
👥 U
££ £15 (£20)
🚗 3 miles S of Halifax

Sand Moor (1926)
Alwoodley Lane, Leeds, LS17 7DJ
☎ (0113) 268 5180
🖥 (0113) 266 1105
✉ info@sandmoorgolf.co.uk
📖 540
🏌 I Kerr (0113) 268 5180
✓ F Houlgate (0113) 268 3925
ⓟ 18 L 6446 yds SSS 71
👥 WD–H by arrangement SOC
££ £40 (£50)
🚗 5 miles N of Leeds, off A61
⊕ Practice ground
🏠 Dr A Mackenzie
🖳 www.sandmoorgolf.co.uk

Scarcroft (1937)
Syke Lane, Leeds, LS14 3BQ
☎ (0113) 289 2311
🖥 (0113) 289 3835
✉ secretary@scarcroftgolfclub.com
📖 660
🏌 M Gallagher (Sec/Mgr) (0113) 289 2311
✓ D Hughes (0113) 289 2780
ⓟ 18 L 6456 yds SSS 71
👥 WD–U WE/BH by arrangement SOC

££ £40 D–£50 (£50)
🚗 7 miles N of Leeds, off A58
🏠 A Mackenzie
🖳 www.scarcroftgolfclub.com

Shipley (1896)
Beckfoot Lane, Cottingley Bridge, Bingley, BD16 1LX
☎ (01274) 568652
🖥 (01274) 567739
✉ office@shipleygc.co.uk
📖 500
🏌 Mrs MJ Bryan (01274) 568652
✓ JR Parry (01274) 563674
ⓟ 18 L 6209 yds SSS 70
👥 WD–U exc Tues–NA before 2pm Sat–NA before 4pm
££ D–£35 (D–£40)
🚗 6 miles N of Bradford on A650
🏠 Colt/Alison/Mackenzie/Braid
🖳 www.shipleygc.co.uk

Silsden (1913)
Brunthwaite Lane, Brunthwaite, Silsden, BD20 0ND
☎ (01535) 652998
✉ info@silsdengolfclub.co.uk
📖 300
🏌 J Bellerby
ⓟ 18 L 5259 yds Par 67 SSS 64
👥 Sat–restricted
££ £15 (£20 Sat only)
🚗 5 miles N of Keighley, off A6034
🖳 www.silsdengolfclub.co.uk

South Bradford (1906)
Pearson Road, Odsal, Bradford, BD6 1BH
☎ (01274) 679195
📖 200
🏌 B Broadbent (01274) 690643
✓ P Cooke (01274) 673346
ⓟ 9 L 6076 yds SSS 69
👥 WD–U WE–M
££ On application
🚗 Bradford 2 miles, nr Odsal Stadium

South Leeds (1906)
Gipsy Lane, Ring Road, Beeston, Leeds LS11 5TU
☎ (0113) 277 1676
✉ sec@slgc.freeserve.co.uk
📖 450
🏌 B Clayton (0113) 277 1676
✓ L Turner (0113) 270 2598
ⓟ 18 L 5865 yds SSS 68
👥 WD–U WE–M SOC
££ £18 (£25)
🚗 4 miles S of Leeds. 2 miles from M62 and M1
🏠 Dr Alister Mackenzie
🖳 www.southleedsgolfclub.co.uk

Temple Newsam (1923)
Public
Temple Newsam Road, Halton, Leeds, LS15 0LN
☎ (0113) 264 5624
✉ secretary@tngc.co.uk
📖 500
🏌 Mrs Christine P Wood
✓ A Newboult (0113) 264 7362

▷ Lord Irwin 18 L 6448 yds SSS 71
Lady Dorothy Wood 18 L 6229
yds SSS 70
⋔ U SOC
££ £9.50 (£12.50)
⊷ 5 miles E of Leeds, off A63
⊕ Practice green; bunker area; putting
green
▤ www.tngolfclub.co.uk

Todmorden   (1894)
Rive Rocks, Cross Stone, Todmorden,
OL14 8RD
☎ **(01706) 812986**
▢ 165 43(L) 24(J)
🖎 Peter H Eastwood
▷ 9 L 5874 yds SSS 68
⋔ WD/BH–U WE–M SOC–WD
££ £15 (£20)
⊷ 1 mile N of Todmorden, off A646

Wakefield   (1891)
28 Woodthorpe Lane, Sandal, Wakefield,
WF2 6JH
☎ **(01924) 258778**
▢ (01924) 242752
▨ wakefieldgolfclub
@woodthorpelane.freeserve
.co.uk
▢ 500
🖎 Elizabeth Newton
(01924) 258778
⌁ IM Wright (01924) 258778
▷ 18 L 6653 yds SSS 72
⋔ U H SOC–Wed–Fri
££ On application
⊷ 3 miles S of Wakefield on A61. M1
Junction 39
⋔ Alex Herd

Waterton Park   (1995)
The Balk, Walton, Wakefield, WF2 6QL
☎ **(01924) 259525**
▢ (01924) 256969
▨ watertonparkgolfclub@tiscali
.co.uk
▢ 600
🖎 M Pearson (01924) 255557
⌁ M Pearson (01924) 255557
▷ 18 L 6843 yds Par 72 SSS 73
⋔ WD–H SOC

££ D–£40
⊷ 4 miles SE of Wakefield centre
⊕ Driving range
⋔ Simon Gidman

West Bradford   (1900)
Chellow Grange Road, Haworth Road,
Bradford, BD9 6NP
☎ **(01274) 542767**
▢ (01274) 482079
▨ secretary@westbradfordgolfclub
.co.uk
▢ 450
🖎 NS Bey (Hon) (01274) 542767
⌁ NM Barber (01274) 542102
▷ 18 L 5738 yds SSS 68 Par 69
⋔ WD–U WE–U after 3.00 pm
££ £32 (£32)
⊷ 3 miles NW of Bradford (B6144)
▤ www.westbradfordgolfclub.co.uk

Wetherby   (1910)
Linton Lane, Linton, Wetherby, LS22 4JF
☎ **(01937) 580089**
▢ (01937) 581915
▨ manager@wetherbygolfclub.fsnet
.co.uk
▢ 760
🖎 Matthew Streets
⌁ M Daubney
▷ 18 L 6670 yds SSS 72
⋔ WE–U after 10am SOC–WD H
££ £30 (£44)
⊷ ³/₄ mile W of Wetherby. A1
Wetherby roundabout
⊕ Driving range
▤ www.wetherbygolfclub.co.uk

Whitwood   (1987)
Public
Altofts Lane, Whitwood, Castleford,
WF10 5PZ
☎ **(01977) 512835**

Willow Valley   (1993)
Pay and play
Clifton, Brighouse, HD6 4JB
☎ **(01274) 878624**
▨ sales@wvgc.co.uk

Woodhall Hills   (1905)
Woodhall Road, Calverley, Pudsey,
LS28 5UN
☎ **(0113) 256 4771**
(Clubhouse)
▢ (0113) 295 4594
▨ whhgc@tiscali.co.uk
▢ 550
🖎 BM Court (0113) 255 4594
⌁ W Lockett (0113) 256 2857
▷ 18 L 6184 yds SSS 70
⋔ WD–U Sat–U after 4.30pm Sun–U
after 9.30am
££ £24 (£29)
⊷ 4 miles E of Bradford, off A647,
past Calverley GC

Woodsome Hall   (1922)
Woodsome Hall, Fenay Bridge,
Huddersfield, HD8 0LQ
☎ **(01484) 602971**
▢ (01484) 608260
▢ 360 130(L) 90(J)
🖎 TJ Mee (01484) 602739 RB Shaw
(Hon)
⌁ M Higginbottom (01484) 602034
▷ 18 L 6080 yds SSS 69
⋔ U H exc Tues–NA before 4pm
SOC
££ £32 D–£43 (£43 D–£53)
⊷ 6 miles SE of Huddersfield on A629
Penistone road
▤ www.woodsomehall.co.uk

Woolley Park   (1995)
Proprietary
Woolley, Wakefield, WF4 2JS
☎ **(01226) 380144 (Bookings)**
▢ (01226) 390295
▢ 500
🖎 D Rowbottom (Prop)
(01226) 382209
⌁ J Baldwin
▷ 18 L 6636 yds Par 71 SSS 72
⋔ WD–U WE–restricted SOC
££ £19 (£26)
⊷ 5 miles S of Wakefield on A61. M1
Junction 38, 2 miles
⊕ Driving range; putting green
⋔ M Shattock
▤ www.woolleyparkgolfclub.co.uk

Ireland

Co Antrim

Antrim   (1997)
Allen Park Golf Centre, 45 Castle Road, Antrim, BT41 4NA
- ☎ **(028) 9442 9001**
- ✉ allenpark@antrim.gov.uk
- 📖 500
- 🏌 Marie Agnew (Mgr)
- ∕ Neil Graham
- ⏴ 18 L 6110 m Par 72 SSS 72
- 🏌 U
- ££ £16.50 (£18.50)
- ⛳ Antrim
- ⊕ Driving range
- 🖥 www.antrim.gov.uk

Ballycastle   (1890)
Cushendall Road, Ballycastle, BT64 6QP
- ☎ **(028) 2076 2536**
- ☎ (028) 2076 9909
- ✉ info@ballycastlegolfclub.com
- 📖 820
- 🏌 BJ Dillon (Hon)
- ∕ I McLaughlin (028) 2076 2506
- ⏴ 18 L 5927 yds SSS 70
- 🏌 U H SOC
- ££ £25 (£35)
- ⛳ Between Portrush and Cushendall (A2)
- 🖥 www.ballycastlegolfclub.com

Ballyclare   (1923)
25 Springvale Road, Ballyclare, BT39 9JW
- ☎ **(028) 9334 2352 (Clubhouse)**
- ✉ ballyclaregolfclub@supanet.com

Ballymena   (1903)
128 Raceview Road, Ballymena, BT42 4HY
- ☎ **(028) 2586 1207/1487**

Bentra
Public
Slaughterford Road, Whitehead, BT38 9TG
- ☎ **(028) 9335 8000**
- ☎ (028) 9336 6676
- ✉ greenspace@carrickfergus.org
- 🏌 S Daye (028) 9335 8039
- ⏴ 9 L 3042 yds Par 36 SSS 35
- 🏌 U
- ££ 18 holes, adult: £9.50 (£13)
  18 holes, U16/OAP: £5 (£6.50)
  Membership from £95
- ⛳ 4 miles N of Carrickfergus on A2 Larne road
- 🏠 James Braid
- 🖥 www.bentragolf.co.uk

Burnfield House
10 Cullyburn Road, Newtownabbey, BT36 5BN
- ☎ **(028) 9083 8737**
- ✉ michaelhj@ntlworld.com

Bushfoot   (1890)
50 Bushfoot Road, Portballintrae, BT57 8RR
- ☎ **(028) 2073 1317**
- ☎ (028) 2073 1852
- ✉ bushfootgolfclub@btconnect.com
- 📖 684
- 🏌 J Knox Thompson (Sec/Mgr)
- ⏴ 9 L 6001 yds SSS 68
- 🏌 U Sat–NA after noon SOC
- ££ £9 (£9) – 9 hole rate
- ⛳ I mile N of Bushmills. 4 miles E of Portrush
- ⊕ Pitch & putt 9 hole course

Cairndhu   (1928)
192 Coast Road, Ballygally, Larne, BT40 2QG
- ☎ **(028) 285 83954**
- ☎ (028) 285 83324
- ✉ cairndhugc@btconnect.com
- 📖 875
- 🏌 N Moore
- ∕ S Hood (028) 285 83954
- ⏴ 18 L 6112 yds SSS 69
- 🏌 U exc Sat–NA
- ££ £20 (£25)
- ⛳ 4 miles N of Larne
- 🏠 JSF Morrison

Carrickfergus   (1926)
35 North Road, Carrickfergus, BT38 8LP
- ☎ **(028) 9336 3713**
- ☎ (028) 9336 3023
- ✉ carrickfergusgc@btconnect.com
- 📖 967
- 🏌 I McLean (Hon Sec)
- ∕ Gary Mercer
- ⏴ 18 L 5713 yds SSS 68
- 🏌 U SOC
- ££ £18 (£24)
- ⛳ 7 miles E of Belfast via M5

Cushendall   (1937)
21 Shore Road, Cushendall, BT44 0NG
- ☎ **(028) 2177 1318**
- ☎ (028) 2177 1318
- ✉ cushendallgc@btconnect.com
- 📖 834
- 🏌 S McLaughlin (028) 2175 8366
- ⏴ 9 L 4834 m SSS 63
- 🏌 WE–restricted SOC
- ££ £13 (£18)
- ⛳ Cushendall, 25 miles N of Larne
- ⊕ Practice green/area/bunker
- 🏠 Denis Delargy

Down Royal   (1990)
Dungarton Road, Maze, Lisburn, BT27 5RT
- ☎ **(028) 9262 1339**

Galgorm Castle   (1997)
200 Galgorm Road, Ballymena, BT42 1HL
- ☎ **(028) 256 46161**
- ✉ golf@galgormcastle.com

Gracehill   (1995)
Proprietary
141 Ballinlea Road, Stranocum, Ballymoney, BT53 8PX
- ☎ **(028) 2075 1209**
- ☎ (028) 2075 1074
- ✉ info@gracehillgolfclub.co.uk
- 📖 425
- 🏌 M McClure (Mgr)
- ∕ None
- ⏴ 18 L 6600 yds Par 72
- 🏌 U SOC
- ££ £25 (£30 +BH)
- ⛳ 6 miles N of Ballymoney (B66)
- ⊕ Driving range
- 🏠 Frank Ainsworth
- 🖥 www.gracehillgolfclub.co.uk

Greenacres   (1996)
153 Ballyrobert Road, Ballyclare, BT39 9RT
- ☎ **(028) 933 54111**
- ☎ (028) 933 44509
- 📖 511
- 🏌 Colin Crawford
- ⏴ 18 L 6031 yds Par 70 SSS 68
- 🏌 U
- ££ £16 (£22)
- ⛳ 3 miles from Corrs Corner on B56
- ⊕ Floodlit driving range; Par 3 course; 18-hole minigolf
- 🖥 www.greenacresgolfclub.co.uk

Greenisland   (1894)
156 Upper Road, Greenisland, Carrickfergus, BT38 8RW
- ☎ **(028) 9086 2236**
- ✉ greenisland.golf@btconnect.com
- 📖 740
- 🏌 WJ McLaughlin (Hon) (028) 9086 3232
- ⏴ 9 L 6045 metres Par 71 SSS 69
- 🏌 WD–U Sat–NA before 5pm SOC–exc Sat
- ££ £12 (£18)
- ⛳ 9 miles NE of Belfast
- 🏠 H Middleton

Hilton Templepatrick   (1999)
Proprietary
Castle Upton Estate, Paradise Walk, Templepatrick, BT39 0DD
- ☎ **(028) 9443 5542**
- ☎ (028) 9443 5511
- ✉ eamonn.logue@hilton.com
- 📖 350
- 🏌 Eamonn Logue (Golf Ops Mgr)
- ∕ E Logue and M Twitchett
- ⏴ 18 L 7077 yds Par 71 SSS 71
- 🏌 U SOC WD WE
- ££ £45 (£45)
- ⛳ 12 miles N of Belfast. M2 Junction 5. Belfast Airport 6 miles
- ⊕ Driving range
- 🏠 Jones/Feherty
- 🖥 www.hilton.com

Lambeg (1986)

Bells Lane, Lambeg, Lisburn, BT27 4QH
☎ **(028) 9266 2738**

Larne (1894)

54 Ferris Bay Road, Islandmagee, Larne, BT40 3RJ
☎ **(028) 9338 2228**
⌨ (028) 9338 2088
✉ info@larnegolfclub.co.uk
▢ 420
✍ RJ Johnston
ⴖ 9 L 6288 yds SSS 70
👥 WD–U WE–M after 5pm SOC–WD/Sun
£€ £15 (£20)
⚒ 6 miles N of Whitehead on Browns Bay road
🏠 George Baillie

Lisburn (1891)

68 Eglantine Road, Lisburn, BT27 5RQ
☎ **(028) 9267 7216**
⌨ (028) 9260 3608
✉ info@lisburngolfclub.com
▢ 1250
✍ Andrew Crawford (Hon Sec)
✍ Stephen Hamill (028) 9267 7217
ⴖ 18 L 6647 yds Par 72 SSS 72
👥 WD–U WE–M SOC–Mon & Thurs
£€ £35 (£40)
⚒ 3 miles S of Lisburn on A1
🏠 Hawtree
🖥 www.lisburngolfclub.com

Mallusk (1992)

Antrim Road, Glengormley, Newtownabbey, BT36 4RF
☎ **(028) 9084 3799**

Massereene (1895)

51 Lough Road, Antrim, BT41 4DQ
☎ **(028) 9442 9293**
⌨ (028) 9448 7661
✉ info@massereene.com
▢ 850
✍ K Stevens (028) 9442 8096
✍ J Smyth (028) 9446 4074
ⴖ 18 L 6602 yds SSS 72
👥 U SOC
£€ £25 (£30)
⚒ 1 mile S of Antrim
🏠 Fred Hawtree
🖥 www.massereene.com

Rathmore

Bushmills Road, Portrush, BT56 8JG
☎ **(028) 7082 2996**
ⴖ 18 L 6304 yds Par 69
👥 U
£€ £30 (£35)
⚒ Portrush
⊕ Tee reservations via Royal Portrush GC – 028 798 2311

Royal Portrush (1888)

Dunluce Road, Portrush, BT56 8JQ
☎ **(028) 7082 2311**
⌨ (028) 7082 3139
✉ info@royalportrushgolfclub.com
▢ 997 297(L)
✍ Miss W Erskine
✍ G McNeill (028) 7082 3335
ⴖ Dunluce 18 L 6772 yds SSS 73
Valley 18 L 6273 yds SSS 70
Skerries-9 hole course
👥 WD–I H exc Mon, Wed & Fri pm–NA Sat–NA before 3pm Sun–NA before 10.30am SOC
£€ Dunluce £110 (£125)
Valley £35 (£40)
⚒ Portrush Coastal Rd ½ mile
⊕ Driving range
🏠 HS Colt
🖥 www.royalportrushgolfclub.com

Whitehead (1904)

McCrae's Brae, Whitehead, Carrickfergus, BT38 9NZ
☎ **(028) 9337 0820**
✉ robin@whiteheadgc.fsnet.co.uk

Co Armagh

Ashfield (1990)

Freeduff, Cullyhanna, Newry, BT35 0JJ
☎ **(028) 3086 8180**

Cloverhill

Lough Road, Mullaghbawn, BT35 9XP
☎ **(028) 3088 9374**

County Armagh (1893)

Newry Road, Armagh, BT60 1EN
☎ **(028) 3752 2501**
⌨ (028) 3752 5861
✉ lynne@golfarmagh.co.uk
▢ 1350
✍ Mrs Lynne Fleming (028) 3752 5861
✍ A Rankin (028) 3752 5864
ⴖ 18 L 6184 yds SSS 69
👥 SOC
£€ £15 (£20)
⚒ 40 miles SW of Belfast by M1
🖥 www.golfarmagh.co.uk

Edenmore G&CC (1992)

Edenmore House, 70 Drumnabreeze Road, Magheralin, Craigavon BT67 0RH
☎ **(028) 9261 1310**
⌨ (028) 9261 3310
✉ info@edenmore.com
▢ 620
✍ K Logan (Sec/Mgr)
✍ Andrew Manson (028) 9261 9241
ⴖ 18 L 6278 yds Par 71 SSS 69
👥 WD–U WE–Sat after 3pm, Sun booking required
£€ £18 (£24)
⚒ Central location 4 miles E of Lurgan on A3
⊕ Five practice greens
🏠 F Ainsworth
🖥 www.edenmore.com

Loughgall Country Park & Golf Course

11-14 Main Street, Loughgall
☎ **(028) 3889 2900**
⌨ (028) 3889 2902
✉ g.ferson@btinternet.com
✍ G Ferson (Mgr)
ⴖ 18 L 6229 yds Par 72
👥 U SOC
£€ £15 (£17.50)
⚒ 8 miles W of Portadown (B77)
⊕ Practice area; putting green
🏠 Don Patterson
🖥 www.armagh.gov.uk

Lurgan (1893)

The Demesne, Lurgan, BT67 9BN
☎ **(028) 3832 2087 (Clubhouse)**
⌨ (028) 3831 6166
✉ lurgangolfclub@utvinternet.com
▢ 918
✍ Mrs M Sharpe
✍ D Paul (028) 3832 1068
ⴖ 18 L 6257 yds SSS 70
👥 U SOC–Mon/Thurs/Fri am/Sun am
£€ £17 (£21)
⚒ Nr Brownlow Castle, Lurgan
🏠 Frank Pennink
🖥 www.lurgangolfclub.co.uk

Portadown (1902)

192 Gilford Road, Portadown, BT63 5LF
☎ **(028) 383 55356**
⌨ (028) 383 91394
✉ portadown.gc@btconnect.com
▢ 731
✍ Nicola Greene (Gen Mgr)
✍ P Stevenson (028) 383 34655
ⴖ 18 L 5786 yds SSS 70
👥 WD–U exc Tues SOC WE after 3pm Sat
£€ £18 (£22)
⚒ 3 miles from centre of Portadown, towards Gilford and Banbridge
⊕ Practice area; indoor teaching area
🖥 www.portadowngolfclub.co.uk

Silverwood (1983)

Turmoyra Lane, Silverwood, Lurgan, BT66 6NG
☎ **(028) 3832 6606**

Tandragee (1922)

Markethill Road, Tandragee, BT62 2ER
☎ **(028) 3884 0727 (Clubhouse)**
⌨ (028) 3884 0664
✉ office@tandragee.co.uk
▢ 1205
✍ A Hewitt (028) 3884 1272
✍ D Keenan (028) 3884 1761
ⴖ 18 L 5754 m Par 71 SSS 70
👥 U SOC
£€ £16 (£21)
⚒ 5 miles S of Portadown on A27
🏠 F Hawtree
🖥 www.tandragee.co.uk

Belfast

Ballyearl Golf Centre
Public
*585 Doagh Road, Newtownabbey,
BT36 5RZ*
- ☎ **(028) 9084 8287**
- 📠 (028) 9084 4896
- ✉ sbartley@newtownabbey.gov.uk
- 🏌 R Johnston (028) 9084 0899
- ⛳ 9 L 2362 yds Par 3 course
- 👥 U
- ££ £6.30 (£9.50)
- ⛳ N of Mossley on B59, via A8
- ⊕ Floodlit driving range
- 🖥 wwwnewtownabbey.gov.uk

Balmoral   (1914)
518 Lisburn Road, Belfast, BT9 6GX
- ☎ **(028) 9038 1514**
- ✉ admin@balmoralgolf.com

Belvoir Park   (1927)
*73 Church Road, Newtownbreda, Belfast,
BT8 7AN*
- ☎ **(028) 9049 1693**
- 📠 (028) 9064 6113
- ✉ info@belvoirparkgolfclub.com
- 📖 1100
- 🏌 Ann Vaughan (028) 9049 1693
- 🏌 M McGivern
- ⛳ 18 L 6501 yds SSS 71
- 👥 U–booking necessary
- ££ £45 (£55)
- ⛳ 3 miles S of Belfast centre, off
  Newcastle road
- 🏠 HS Colt
- 🖥 www.belvoirparkgolfclub.com

Dunmurry   (1905)
*91 Dunmurry Lane, Dunmurry, Belfast,
BT17 9JS*
- ☎ **(028) 9061 0834**
- ✉ dunmurrygc@hotmail.com

Fortwilliam   (1891)
Downview Avenue, Belfast, B15 4EZ
- ☎ **(028) 9037 0770**
- 📠 (028) 9078 1891
- ✉ michael@fortwilliam.co.uk
- 📖 1100
- 🏌 M Purdy
- 🏌 P Hanna (028) 9077 0980
- ⛳ 18 L 6030 yds SSS 69
- 👥 U SOC
- ££ £22 (£29)
- ⛳ 2 miles N of Belfast on M2
- ⊕ Driving range; 2-seater buggies
- 🏠 Mr Butchart
- 🖥 www.fortwilliam.co.uk

Gilnahirk   (1983)
*Manns Corner, Upper Braniel Road, Belfast,
BT5 7TX*
- ☎ **(028) 9044 8477**

The Knock Club   (1895)
*Summerfield, Dundonald, Belfast,
BT16 2QX*
- ☎ **(028) 9048 2249**
- 📠 (028) 9048 7277
- ✉ knockgolfclub@btconnect.com
- 📖 900
- 🏌 Anne Armstrong (028) 9048 3251
- 🏌 G Fairweather (028) 9048 3825
- ⛳ 18 L 6407 yds SSS 71
- 👥 U SOC–Mon & Thurs
- ££ D–£25 (£40)
- ⛳ 4 miles E of Belfast on the Upper
  Newtownards Road
- 🏠 Colt/Mackenzie/Alison

Malone   (1895)
*240 Upper Malone Road, Dunmurry,
Belfast, BT17 9LB*
- ☎ **(028) 9061 2758**
- ✉ manager@malonegolfclub.co.uk

Ormeau   (1893)
50 Park Road, Belfast, BT7 2FX
- ☎ **(028) 9064 1069 (Members)**

Shandon Park   (1926)
73 Shandon Park, Belfast, BT5 6NY
- ☎ **(028) 9080 5030**
- 📠 (028) 9080 5999
- ✉ shandonpark@btconnect.com
- 📖 1100
- 🏌 GA Bailie (Gen Mgr)
- 🏌 B Wilson (028) 9080 5031
- ⛳ 18 L 6261 yds SSS 70
- 👥 WD–U Sat–NA before 5pm SOC
- ££ £25 (£27.50)
- ⛳ 3 miles E of Belfast on the Knock
  road
- 🖥 www.shandonpark.com

Co Carlow

Borris   (1907)
Deerpark, Borris
- ☎ **(059) 977 3310 (office),
  (059) 977 3143 (bar)**
- 📠 (0503) 73750
- ✉ borrisgolfclub@eircom.net
- 📖 675
- 🏌 Nollaig Lucas (Sec/Mgr)
  (0503) 73310
- ⛳ 9 L 5680 m Par 70 SSS 69
- 👥 WD–U Sun–M SOC–WD/Sat
- ££ €25 (18 holes)
- ⛳ Borris

Carlow   (1899)
Deer Park, Dublin Road, Carlow
- ☎ **(059) 913 1695**
- ✉ carlowgolfclub@eircom.net

Mount Wolseley   (1996)
Tullow
- ☎ **(059) 915 1674**
- ✉ wolseley@iol.ie

Co Cavan

Belturbet   (1950)
Erne Hill, Belturbet
- ☎ **(049) 952 2287**

Blacklion   (1962)
Toam, Blacklion, via Sligo
- ☎ **(072) 53024**

Cabra Castle   (1978)
Kingscourt
- ☎ **(042) 966 7030**
- 📠 (042) 966 7039
- 📖 160
- 🏌 Thomas O'Rourke (087) 259 7437
- ⛳ 9 L 5261 m Par 70
- 👥 U exc Sun–NA SOC
- ££ €15
- ⛳ 2 miles E of Kingscourt

County Cavan   (1894)
Arnmore House, Drumelis, Cavan
- ☎ **(049) 433 1541**
- ✉ info@cavangolf.ie

Slieve Russell G&CC
   (1994)
Ballyconnell
- ☎ **(049) 952 6458**
- ✉ slieve-russell@quinn-hotels.com

Virginia   (1945)
Park Hotel, Virginia
- ☎ **(049) 854 8066**

Co Clare

Clonlara   (1993)
Clonlara
- ☎ **(061) 354141**

Doonbeg   (2002)
Doonbeg, Co Clare
- ☎ **(065) 905 5600**
- 📠 (065) 905 5247
- ✉ doonbeggolfclub@eircom.net
- 📖 400
- 🏌 Joe Russell (Gen Mgr)
- 🏌 Brian Shaw (Head Pro)
- ⛳ 18 L 6870 yds Par 72 SSS 74
- 👥 U
- ££ On application
- ⛳ 10 miles N of Kilkee
- ⊕ Driving range
- 🏠 Greg Norman
- 🖥 www.doonbeggolfclub.com

Dromoland Castle   (1964)
Newmarket-on-Fergus
- ☎ **353 (61) 368444**
- 📠 353 (61) 368498
- ✉ golf@dromoland.ie
- 📖 400

✍ J O'Halloran
✓ D Foley
☞ 18 L 6850 yds SSS 72
👫 U H SOC
££ €110
🚗 N18 to Dromoland Interchange, 18 miles NW of Limerick. Shannon Airport
⊕ Buggies and trolley available. Caddies must be booked in advance
🏠 R Kirby and JB Carr (2004)
🖥 www.dromoland.ie

East Clare   (1992)
Bodyke
☎ (061) 921322

Ennis   (1907)
Drumbiggle, Ennis
☎ (065) 682 4074
🖥 (065) 684 1848
📧 info@ennisgolfclub.com
📖 1383
✍ Pat McCarthy
☞ 18 L 5706 m Par 70 SSS 69
👫 U SOC
££ €35
🚗 ¹/₂ mile NW of Ennis, off N18
🖥 www.ennisgolfclub.com

Kilkee   (1896)
East End, Kilkee
☎ (065) 905 6048
🖥 (065) 905 6977
📧 kilkeegolfclub@eircom.net
📖 750
✍ M Culligan (Sec/Mgr)
☞ 18 L 5555 m Par 70 SSS 69
👫 U SOC
££ €24 (€30)
🚗 End of Kilkee Promenade. 50 miles west of Shannon Airport
🏠 Eddie Hackett
🖥 www.kilkeegolfclub.ie

Kilrush   (1934)
Parknamoney, Kilrush
☎ (065) 905 1138
🖥 (065) 905 2633
📧 info@kilrushgolfclub.com
📖 700
✍ DF Nagle (Sec/Mgr) (087) 623 7557
   G Kelly (Hon Sec)
✓ J McDermott
☞ 18 L 5986 yds Par 70 SSS 69
👫 U SOC
££ €30 (€35)
🚗 25 miles SW of Ennis on Lahinch-Ballybunion road
🏠 Arthur Spring
🖥 www.kilrushgolfclub.com

Lahinch   (1892)
Lahinch
☎ (065) 708 1003
🖥 (065) 708 1592
📧 info@lahinchgolf.com
📖 1250
✍ A Reardon (Sec/Mgr)
✓ R McCavery (065) 708 1408

☞ Old 18 L 6950 yds SSS 74
   Castle 18 L 5556 yds SSS 67
👫 WD–U WE–NA 8–10.30am and 1–2pm SOC
££ Old–€145. Castle–€50 (2006 rates)
🚗 20 miles NW of Ennis on T69
⊕ Practice net and practice ground
🏠 Old – Morris/Gibson/Mackenzie/Hawtree; Castle – Harris
🖥 www.lahinchgolf.com

Shannon   (1966)
Shannon
☎ (061) 471020

Spanish Point   (1915)
Spanish Point, Miltown Malbay
☎ (065) 708 4219

Woodstock   (1993)
Shanaway Road, Ennis
☎ (065) 682 9463
📧 woodstock.ennis@eircom.net

Co Cork

Bandon   (1910)
Castlebernard, Bandon
☎ (023) 41111
🖥 (023) 44690
📧 enquiries@bandongolfclub.com
📖 1200
✍ Denise Barrett
✓ P O'Boyle (023) 42224
☞ 18 L 6334 m Par 71 SSS 72
👫 U SOC
££ On application
🚗 Bandon 1¹/₂ miles. 18 miles SW of Cork
🖥 www.bandongolfclub.com

Bantry Bay   (1975)
Donemark, Bantry, West Cork
☎ (027) 50579/53773
🖥 (027) 53790
📧 info@bantrygolf.com
📖 650
✍ J O'Sullivan (Mgr) (027) 50579
☞ 18 L 6117 m Par 71 SSS 72
👫 WE/BH–booking necessary SOC
££ €40 (€50)
🚗 1 mile N of Bantry on Glengarriff road (N71)
🏠 E Hackett/C O'Connor, Jnr
🖥 www.bantrygolf.com

Berehaven   (1902)
Millcove, Castletownbere
☎ (027) 70700
🖥 (027) 71957
📧 bearagolfglub@eircom.net
📖 208
✍ B Twomey (Hon)
☞ 9 L 5121 m SSS 68 (ladies), SSS 67 (men)
👫 U SOC
££ €20 (€25)

🚗 2 miles E of Castletownbere on Glengarriff road
⊕ Practice putting green
🏠 James Healy
🖥 www.bearagolf.com

Charleville   (1909)
Charleville
☎ (063) 81257
📧 charlevillegolf@eircom.net

Cobh   (1987)
Ballywilliam, Cobh
☎ (021) 812399

Coosheen   (1989)
Coosheen, Schull
☎ (028) 28182

Cork   (1888)
Little Island, Cork
☎ (021) 435 3451/3037
🖥 (021) 435 3410
📧 corkgolfclub@eircom.net
📖 366 176 (L)
✍ M Sands (021) 435 3451
✓ P Hickey (021) 435 3421
☞ 18 L 6065 m SSS 72
👫 WD–U H exc 12–2pm –M after 4pm Thurs–(Ladies Day)–phone in advance WE–NA before 2.30pm H
££ €85 (€95)
🚗 5 miles E of Cork, off N25
⊕ Range balls for hire; buggy hire
🏠 Dr A Mackenzie
🖥 www.corkgolfclub.ie

Doneraile   (1927)
Doneraile
☎ (022) 24137

Douglas   (1909)
Douglas, Cork
☎ (021) 489 1086
🖥 (021) 436 7200
📧 admin@douglasgolfclub.ie
📖 839
✍ Ronan Burke (Mgr)
✓ GS Nicholson (021) 436 2055
☞ 18 L 5972 m SSS 71
👫 WD–U exc Tues WE–NA before 2pm SOC–WD
££ €40 (€45)
🚗 Cork 3 miles
⊕ Driving range; practice chipping & putting greens
🏠 Jeff Howes
🖥 www.douglasgolfclub.ie

Dunmore   (1967)
Muckross, Clonakilty
☎ (023) 34644

East Cork   (1971)
Gortacrue, Midleton
☎ (021) 463 1687
🖥 (021) 461 3695
📧 eastcorkgolfclub@eircom.net
📖 900

M Moloney (Sec/Mgr)
D MacFarlane
18 L 5207 m SSS 67
WD–U WE–NA before noon
BH–U
£€ €30
2 miles N of Midleton on L35
Driving range
Eddie Hackett
www.eastcorkgolfclub.com

Fermoy   (1892)
Corrin, Fermoy
(025) 32694
(025) 33072
fermoygolfclub@eircom.net
1000
K Murphy
B Moriarty (025) 31472
18 L 5847 m SSS 70
U SOC
£€ €20 (€30)
2 miles S of Fermoy, off N8
Cdr John Harris
www.fermoygolfclub.ie

Fernhill   (1994)
Carrigaline
(021) 437 2226
fernhill@iol.ie

Fota Island   (1993)
Proprietary
Carrigtwohill, Cork
(021) 488 3710
(021) 453 2047
reservations@fotaisland.ie
650
Jonathon Woods
K Morris (021) 453 2032
18 L 6927 yds Par 71 SSS 73
new 9 opening spring 2007
U
£€ €65–€120
8 miles E of Cork on N25
Driving range & practice facilities;
golf academy with swing analysis
O'Connor Jr/McEvoy/Howes
www.fotaisland.ie

Frankfield   (1984)
Frankfield, Douglas
(0214) 363124/3611299

Glengarriff   (1935)
Glengarriff
(027) 63150

Harbour Point   (1991)
Clash, Little Island
(021) 353094

Kanturk   (1971)
Fairyhill, Kanturk
(029) 50534

Kinsale Farrangalway   (1993)
Farrangalway, Kinsale
(021) 477 4722

(021) 477 3114
office@kinsalegolf.com
830
Michael Power
G Broderick (021) 477 3258
18 L 6609 yds SSS 72
WD–U WE–NA SOC
£€ €35 (€40)
3 miles NW of Kinsale. 18 miles S
of Cork
Jack Kenneally
www.kinsalegolf.com

Kinsale Ringenane   (1912)
Ringenane, Belgooly, Kinsale
(021) 477 2197
740
Michael Power
None
9 L 5332 yds SSS 68
U SOC
£€ €25
2 miles E of Kinsale (R600). 16
miles S of Cork

Lee Valley G&CC   (1993)
Clashanure, Ovens, Cork
(021) 733 1721
(021) 733 1695
reservations@leevalleygcc.ie
450
D Keohane
J Savage (021) 733 1758
18 L 6800 yds SSS 72
U SOC WD WE
£€ €50 (€60)
8 miles W of Cork (N22)
4* accom; complimentary bus
service
C O'Connor Jr
www.leevalleygcc.ie

Macroom   (1924)
Lackaduve, Macroom
(026) 41072
(026) 41391
mcroomgc@iol.com
750
C O'Sullivan (Mgr)
None
18 L 5605 m Par 71 SSS 69
U SOC
£€ €35 (€40)
Macroom Town, through Castle
Arch. 25 miles W of Cork
Eddie Hackett
www.macroomgolfclub.ie

Mahon   (1980)
Clover Hill, Blackrock, Cork
(021) 429 2543
mahon@golfnet.ie

Mallow   (1948)
Ballyellis, Mallow
(022) 21145
(022) 42501
golfmall@gofree.indigo.ie
1500
D Curtin (Sec/Mgr)
S Conway (022) 43424

18 L 6559 yds SSS 72
WD–U before 5pm SOC
£€ €45 (€50)
1 mile SE of Mallow Bridge on
Killavullen road
Practice facility
J Harris
www.mallowgolfclub.net

Mitchelstown   (1908)
Gurrane, Mitchelstown
(025) 24072
(025) 86631
info@mitchelstown-golf.com
500
D Gorey
18 L 5773 m Par 71
U SOC
£€ €25 (€30)
30 miles NE of Cork off N8
David Jones
www.mitchelstown-golf.com

Monkstown   (1908)
Parkgarriffe, Monkstown
(021) 484 1376
(021) 484 1722
office@monkstowngolfclub.com
900
H Madden (Sec/Mgr) (021) 486
3910
B Murphy (021) 486 3912
18 L 5669 m Par 70 SSS 69
U SOC
£€ €43 (€50)
7 miles SE of Cork
Tom Carey and Peter O'Hare
www.monkstowngolfclub.com

Muskerry   (1907)
Carrigrohane, Co. Cork
(021) 438 5297
(021) 451 6860
muskgc@eircom.net
803
H Gallagher
WM Lehane (021) 438 1445
18 L 5786 m SSS 70
Restricted at certain times–phone
first SOC
£€ €35
7 miles NW of Cork. 2 miles W of
Blarney
Dr A McKenzie contribution

Old Head Golf Links
(1997)
Kinsale
(021) 477 8444
(021) 477 8022
info@oldheadgolf.ie
350
Danny Brassil (Dir of Golf)
18 L 7300 yds SSS 72
U H
£€ €250
7 miles S of Kinsale
Driving range; putting green;
chipping green
Carr/Merrigan/Kirby/Hackett
www.oldheadgolflinks.com

Raffeen Creek   (1989)
Ringaskiddy
☎ **(021) 437 8430**

Skibbereen   (1904)
Licknavar, Skibbereen
☎ **(028) 21227**
✉ info@skibbgolf.com

Youghal   (1898)
Knockaverry, Youghal
☎ **(024) 92787/92861**
✉ youghalgolfclub@eircom.net

Co Donegal

Ballybofey & Stranorlar
(1957)
The Glebe, Stranorlar
☎ **(074) 31093**

Ballyliffin   (1947)
Ballyliffin, Inishowen
☎ **(07493) 76119**
🖷 (07493) 76672
✉ info@ballyliffingolfclub.com
📖 1200
🖉 John Farren (Gen Mgr)
✓ John Dolan
⊳ Old 18 L 6611 yds Par 71 SSS 72
   Glashedy 18 L 7217 yds Par 72
   SSS 74
👥 U SOC–WD/WE
££ Old: €60/€65 Glashedy: €70/€80
🚗 8 miles N of Buncrana. 15 miles N
   of Londonderry
🏠 Glashedy-Craddock/Ruddy
📧 www.ballyliffingolfclub.com

Buncrana   (1951)
Public
Buncrana
☎ **(077) 62279/20749**
✉ buncranagc@eircom.net
📖 300
🖉 F McGrory (Hon) (07493) 20749
✓ J Doherty
⊳ 9 L 4310 m SSS 62
👥 U
££ Men: €13; Women: €8; Juv. €5
🚗 In Buncrana, nr Inishowen
   (Gateway Hotel)

Bundoran   (1894)
Bundoran
☎ **(072) 41302**
🖷 (072) 42014
✉ bundorangolfclub@eircom.net
📖 620
🖉 J McGagh (Sec/Mgr)
✓ D Robinson
⊳ 18 L 5688 m Par 70 SSS 70
👥 WD–U WE–restricted SOC
££ €40 (€50)
🚗 E boundary of Bundoran. 20 miles S
   of Donegal
🏠 H Vardon
📧 www.bundorangolfclub.com

Cruit Island   (1985)
Kincasslagh, Dunglow
☎ **(074) 954 3296**

Donegal   (1960)
Murvagh, Laghey
☎ **(074) 973 4054**

Dunfanaghy   (1906)
Kill, Dunfanaghy, Letterkenny
☎ **(074) 913 6335**
🖷 (074) 913 6684
✉ dunfanaghygolf@eircom.net
📖 390
🖉 Sandra McGinley
⊳ 18 L 5350 m Par 68 SSS 66
👥 Timesheets in operation – please
   phone
££ €30 (€40)
🚗 25 miles NW of Letterkenny on
   N56
⊕ Practice area
🏠 Harry Vardon
📧 www.dunfanaghygolfclub.com

Greencastle   (1892)
Greencastle
☎ **(074) 93 81013**
🖷 (074) 93 81015
✉ b_mc_caul@yahoo.com
📖 750
🖉 Billy McCaul
✓ None
⊳ 18 L 5334 m SSS 68
👥 WD–U WE–restricted SOC
££ €30 (€40)
🚗 21 miles NE of Londonderry, nr
   Moville
🏠 Eddie Hackett/David Jones
📧 www.greencastlegolfclub.com

Gweedore   (1926)
Pay and play
Magheragallon, Derrybeg, Letterkenny
☎ **(075) 31140**
📖 250
🖉 Eric Campbell
⊳ 9 L 6201 yds SSS 69
👥 U
££ €20 (€20)
🚗 3 miles N of Gweedore, off R257

Letterkenny   (1913)
Barnhill, Letterkenny
☎ **(+353) 7491 21150**
🖷 (+353) 7491 21175
✉ letterkennygc@eircom.net
📖 800
🖉 B O'Donnell (+353) 7491 21150
✓ S Duffy
⊳ 18 L 6353 yds SSS 72
👥 U–booking necessary SOC
££ €30 (€35)
🚗 1 mile E of Letterkenny
🏠 Declan Brannigan

Narin & Portnoo   (1930)
Narin, Portnoo
☎ **(074) 954 5107**
🖷 (074) 945 5994

✉ narinportnoo@eircom.net
📖 750
🖉 Willie Quinn (Hon)
✓ None
⊳ 18 L 5950 yds Par 69
👥 WD WE SOC–WE after 11.30am
££ €35 (€40) SOC–€25 (€30)
🚗 6 miles N of Ardara. West
   Donegal. 30 min from Donegal
   Airport
⊕ Practice net
🏠 Leo Wallace, Hughie McNeill
📧 www.narinportnoogolfclub.ie

North West   (1891)
Lisfannon, Fahan
☎ **(074) 936 0127**
🖷 (074) 936 3284
✉ secretary@northwestgolfclub.com
📖 555
🖉 D Coyle (086) 604 7299
✓ S McBriarty (074) 936 1715
⊳ 18 L 6239 yds SSS 70
👥 U
££ €30 (€35)
🚗 2 km S of Buncrana. 15 km N of
   Derry
📧 www.northwestgolfclub.com

Otway   (1893)
Saltpans, Rathmullan, Letterkenny
☎ **(074) 915 1665**
   (074) 914 8319 (Club House)
✉ tolandkevin@eircom.net
📖 97
🖉 Kevin Toland
⊳ 9 L 4234 yds SSS 60
👥 U
££ €15
🚗 15 miles NE of Letterkenny, by
   Lough Swilly

Portsalon   (1891)
Portsalon, Fanad
☎ **(074) 915 9459**
🖷 (074) 915 9919
📖 550
🖉 P Doherty
⊳ 18 L 6185m Par 72 SSS 72
👥 U–phone in advance
££ €35 (€40 +BH) €20 with member
🚗 20 miles N of Letterkenny (R246)
🏠 Pat Ruddy

Redcastle   (1983)
Redcastle, Moville
☎ **(074) 938 2073**

Rosapenna   (1894)
Downings, Rosapenna
☎ **(074) 55301**
🖷 (074) 55128
✉ rosapenna@eircom.net
📖 250
🖉 J Sweeney
✓ B Patterson
⊳ Old: 18 L 7155 yds Par 71 SSS 73
   Sandy Hill Links: 18 L 6254 yds Par
   70 SSS 71
👥 U
££ Old: €50; Sandy Hills: €75

⚑ 20 miles N of Letterkenny
⊕ Golf academy; driving range
⌂ Morris/Vardon/Braid/Ruddy; Sandy Hills designed by Pat Ruddy
▤ www.rosapenna.ie

St Patricks Courses   (1994)
Carrigart
☎ **(074) 55114**

Co Down

Ardglass   (1896)
Castle Place, Ardglass, BT30 7PP
☎ **(028) 4484 1219**

Ardminnan   (1995)
15 Ardminnan Road, Portaferry, BT22 1QJ
☎ **(028) 4277 1321**
🖳 (028) 4277 1321
🖂 lesliejardine104@yahoo.co.uk
⊞ 100
🏌 L Jardine
ℙ 9 L 2766 m Par 70
👥 U
££ £10 (£15)
⚑ 10 miles E of Downpatrick via ferry. 18 miles SE of Newtownards (A20)
⌂ Frank Ainsworth

Banbridge   (1912)
116 Huntly Road, Banbridge, BT32 3UR
☎ **(028) 4066 2342 (restaurant)**
🖳 (028) 4066 9400
⊞ 850
🏌 J McKeown (028) 4066 2211
✓ Jason Greenaway
ℙ 18 L 5590 m SSS 69
👥 U SOC
££ £17 (£22)
⚑ 1 mile W of Banbridge
⌂ F Ainsworth
▤ www.banbridge-golf@btconnect.com

Bangor   (1903)
Broadway, Bangor, BT20 4RH
☎ **(028) 9127 0922**
🖳 (028) 9145 3394
🖂 bangorgolfclubni@btconnect.com
⊞ 900
🏌 Mrs EP Roberts
✓ M Bannon
ℙ 18 L 6424 yds SSS 71
👥 WD–U exc –M 1–2pm Wed–U before 4pm Sat–NA SOC
££ £25 (£33); SOC £21 (£27)
⚑ 1 mile S of Bangor, off Donaghadee road
⌂ James Braid
▤ www.bangorgolfclubni.co.uk

Blackwood   (1995)
150 Crawfordsburn Road, Bangor, BT19 1GB
☎ **(028) 9185 2706**
🖳 (028) 9185 3785

🖂 blackwoodgc@btopenworld.com
⊞ 265
🏌 James Kennedy
✓ Debbie Hanna
ℙ 18 L 6392 yds SSS 70
👥 U
££ On application
⚑ W of Bangor
⊕ Driving range

Bright Castle   (1970)
14 Coniamstown Road, Bright, Downpatrick, BT30 8LU
☎ **(028) 4484 1319**

Carnalea   (1927)
Station Road, Bangor, BT19 1EZ
☎ **(028) 9146 5004**
🖳 (028) 9127 3989
⊞ 800
🏌 GY Steele (028) 9127 0368
✓ T Loughran (028) 9127 0122
ℙ 18 L 5647 yds SSS 67
👥 U SOC–WD
££ £17.50 (£22)
⚑ By Carnalea Station, Bangor

Clandeboye   (1933)
Conlig, Newtownards, BT23 7PN
☎ **(028) 9127 1767 (office)**
   (028) 9147 3706 (bar)
🖳 (028) 9147 3711
🖂 cgc-ni.@btconnect.com
⊞ 1456
🏌 JW Thomson (Gen Mgr) (028) 9127 1767
✓ P Gregory (028) 9127 1750
ℙ Dufferin 18 L 6559 yds SSS 71
   Ava 18 L 5755 yds SSS 68
👥 WD–U WE–M SOC
££ Dufferin–£27.50 (£33) Ava–£22
⚑ Conlig, off A21 Bangor-Newtownards road
⌂ Von Limburger/Alliss/Thomas
▤ www.cgc-ni.com

Crossgar   (1993)
231 Derryboye Road, Crossgar, BT30 9DL
☎ **(028) 4483 1523**

Donaghadee   (1899)
84 Warren Road, Donaghadee, BT21 0PQ
☎ **(028) 9188 3624**
🖂 deegolf@freenet.co.uk

Downpatrick   (1930)
Saul Road, Downpatrick, BT30 6PA
☎ **(028) 4461 5947/2152**
🖳 (028) 4461 7502
⊞ 960
🏌 Elaine Carson (028) 4461 5947
✓ Robert Hutton (028) 4461 5167
ℙ 18 L 5702 m SSS 69
👥 U SOC
££ £22
⚑ 25 miles SE of Belfast (A1). Downpatrick 1½ miles
⌂ Hawtree
▤ www.downpatrickgolfclub.co.uk

Helen's Bay   (1896)
Golf Road, Helen's Bay, Bangor, BT19 1TL
☎ **(028) 9185 2815 (office)**
🖳 (028) 9185 2660
🖂 mail@helensbaygc.com
⊞ 700
🏌 Alan Briggs
ℙ 9 L 5261 m Par 68 SSS 67
👥 WD/Sun–U Tues/Thurs/Sat–restricted SOC–WD
££ £18 (£20)
⚑ 9 miles E of Belfast, off A2
▤ www.helensbaygc.com

Holywood   (1904)
Nuns Walk, Demesne Road, Holywood, BT18 9LE
☎ **(028) 9042 2138**
🖳 (028) 9042 5040
🖂 mail@holywoodgolfclub.co.uk
⊞ 1000
🏌 KC Stevens (Gen Mgr) (028) 9042 3135
✓ P Gray (028) 9042 5503
ℙ 18 L 5885 yds SSS 68
👥 WD–U exc 1.30–2.15pm Sat–after 5pm
££ £18 (£25)
⚑ 5 miles E of Belfast on Bangor road
▤ www.holywoodgolfclub.co.uk

Kilkeel   (1948)
Mourne Park, Kilkeel, BT34 4LB
☎ **(028) 4176 2296/5095**
🖳 (028) 4176 5579
🖂 kilkeelgolfclub@gmail.com
⊞ 720
🏌 SC McBride (Hon) (028) 4176 5095
✓ None
ℙ 18 L 6579 yds SSS 72
👥 U SOC–exc Sat
££ £23 (£28)
⚑ 3 miles W of Kilkeel on Newry road
⌂ Badington/Hackett

Kirkistown Castle   (1902)
142 Main Road, Cloughey, Newtownards, BT22 1JA
☎ **(028) 4277 1233**
🖳 (028) 4277 1699
🖂 kirkistown@supanet.com
⊞ 948
🏌 R Coulter (028) 4277 1233
✓ A Ferguson (028) 4277 1004
ℙ 18 L 5616 m Par 69 SSS 70
👥 WD/Sun–U Sat–NA before 2.30pm
££ £25 (£30)
⚑ 25 miles SE of Belfast
⌂ James Braid
▤ www.linksgolfkirkistown.com

Mahee Island   (1929)
Comber, Newtownlands, BT23 6ET
☎ **(028) 9754 1234**
🖳 (028) 9754 1234
⊞ 500
🏌 M Marshall (Hon)
✓ C Macaw (shop)

9 L 5822 yds Par 71 SSS 70
- U exc Sat–NA before 5pm SOC–WD exc Mon
- ££ £12 (£17)
- Strangford Lough, 14 miles SE of Belfast
- Mr Robinson

Mount Ober G&CC
(1985)

Ballymaconaghy Road, Knockbracken, Belfast, BT8 6SB
- ☎ (028) 9079 2108 (Bookings)
- (028) 9070 5862
- mt.ober@ukonline.co.uk
- 500
- E Williams (Sec/Mgr)
- W Ramsay (028) 9070 1648
- 18 L 5281 yds SSS 66
- WD–U Sat–NA before 3pm Sun–NA before 10.30am SOC
- ££ £16.50 (£18.50)
- 2 miles SW of Belfast, nr Four Winds
- Floodlit driving range
- www.mountober.com

Mourne
(1946)

Club
36 Golf Links Road, Newcastle, BT33 0AN
- ☎ (028) 4372 3218
- (028) 4372 2575
- secretary@mourne.freeserve.co.uk
- 385
- P Keown (Hon)
- See Royal Co Down
- Play over Royal Co Down
- See Royal Co Down
- See Royal Co Down
- See Royal Co Down
- See Royal Co Down
- www.mournegc.freeserve.co.uk

Ringdufferin
(1993)

Ringdufferin Road, Toye, Downpatrick, BT30 9PH
- ☎ (028) 4482 8812

Rockmount
(1995)

28 Drumalig Road, Carryduff, Belfast, BT8 8EQ
- ☎ (028) 9081 2279
- d.patterson@btconnect.com

Royal Belfast
(1881)

Holywood, Craigavad, BT18 0BP
- ☎ (028) 9042 8165
- (028) 9042 1404
- royalbelfast@btconnect.com
- 1200
- Mrs SH Morrison
- C Spence (028) 9042 8586
- 18 L 6184 yds SSS 70
- 1 Sat–NA before 4.30pm
- ££ £46 (£56)
- E of Belfast on A2
- HC Colt
- www.royalbelfast.com

Royal County Down
(1889)

Newcastle, BT33 0AN
- ☎ (028) 4372 3314
- (028) 4372 6281
- golf@royalcountydown.org
- 450
- JH Laidler
- KJ Whitson (028) 4372 2419
- Ch'ship 18 L 7181 yds SSS 74
- Annesley 18 L 4708 yds SSS 63
- Contact Sec
- ££ Ch'ship–£125 (£140) Annesley–£30 (£35)
- 30 miles S of Belfast
- Tom Morris
- www.royalcountydown.org

Scrabo
(1907)

233 Scrabo Road, Newtownards, BT23 4SL
- ☎ (028) 9181 2355
- (028) 9182 2919
- admin.scrabogc@btconnect.com
- 600
- WJ Brown (Gen Mgr)
- P McCrystal (028) 9181 7848
- 18 L 5699 m SSS 71
- WD–U WE–11am Sun SOC
- ££ £19 (£24)
- 2 miles W of Newtownards, by Scrabo Tower
- 6-hole pitch & putt course
- www.scrabo-golf-club.org

The Spa
(1907)

Grove Road, Ballynahinch, BT24 8BR
- ☎ (028) 9756 2365
- (028) 9756 4158
- spagolfclub@btconnect.com
- 920
- TG Magee
- 18 L 6003 m SSS 72
- U exc Wed–NA after 3pm Sat–NA
- ££ £18 (£23)
- 1 mile S of Ballynahinch. 15 miles S of Belfast

Temple
(1994)

60 Church Road, Boardmills, Lisburn, BT27 6UP
- ☎ (028) 9263 9213

Warrenpoint
(1893)

Lower Dromore Rd, Warrenpoint, BT34 3LN
- ☎ (028) 4175 2219 (Clubhouse)
- (028) 4175 2918
- office@warrenpointgolf.com
- 1575
- M Trainor (028) 4175 3695
- N Shaw (028) 4175 2371
- 18 L 5628 m SSS 70
- U SOC
- ££ £28 (£34)
- 5 miles S of Newry
- Tom Craddock
- www.warrenpointgolf.com

Balbriggan
(1945)

Blackhall, Balbriggan
- ☎ (01) 841 2229
- (01) 841 3927
- 600
- Nigel Howley
- 18 L 5881 m SSS 71
- WD–U WE–M SOC
- ££ €35 (€45)
- 1 mile S of Balbriggan on N1. 18 miles N of Dublin
- Paramour/Stillwell/Ruddy
- www.balbriggangolfclub.com

Balcarrick
(1972)

Corballis, Donabate
- ☎ (01) 843 6957

Beaverstown
(1985)

Beaverstown, Donabate
- ☎ (01) 843 6439/6721
- (01) 843 5059
- manager@beaverstown.com
- 921
- Stephen Ennis (Sec Mgr)
- Marcus Casey PGA (01) 843 4655
- 18 L 5972 m Par 72 SSS 72
- WD–U WE–phone first SOC
- ££ €50 (€60)
- 4 miles N of Dublin Airport
- Chipping and putting practice area; pro shop
- Hackett/McEvoy
- www.beaverstown.com

Beech Park
(1983)

Johnstown, Rathcoole
- ☎ (01) 458 0522
- (01) 458 8365
- info@beechpark.ie
- 750
- F Kennedy (Hon), G Nolan (Mgr)
- Zak Rouiller
- 18 L 5730 m SSS 70
- WD–U exc Tues/Wed–M WE–M BH–NA
- ££ €40
- Rathcoole is on N7; club is 2 miles on Kilteel road from Rathcoole Vil
- Eddie Hackett
- www.beechpark.ie

Coldwinters
(1994)

Newtown House, St Margaret's
- ☎ (01) 864 0324

Corrstown
(1993)

Corrstown, Killsallaghan
- ☎ (01) 864 0533
- (01) 864 0537
- info@corrstowngolfclub.com
- 1050
- M Jeanes
- P Gittens (01) 864 3322
- River 18 L 6077 m Par 72 SSS 71 Orchard 9 L 2792 m Par 35 SSS 69
- Booking necessary

££   €40 (€50)
⛳   Dublin Airport 6 miles
⊕   Driving range
🏠   E Connaughton
▤   www.corrstowngolfclub.com

Donabate   (1925)

Balcarrick, Donabate
☎   (01) 843 6346
🖥   (01) 843 4488
✉   info@donabategolfclub.com
📖   913
✍   Betty O'Connor (01) 843 6346
     Brian May (01) 843 6346 (Golf
     Administrator)
⚊   H Jackson
⛳   18 L 6670 yds SSS 73
     9 L 3200 yds Par 36
👤   U (booking system)
££   €50 (€65); €30 (€40) before 10
⛳   6 miles N of Dublin Airport on N1
⊕   Practice range, putting green, buggy
     hire
▤   www.donabategolfclub.com

Dublin Mountain   (1993)

Gortlum, Brittas
☎   (01) 458 2622
🖥   (01) 458 2048
📖   430
✍   F Carolan
⛳   18 L 5433 m Par 71
👤   U
££   €15 (€20)
⛳   SW of Dublin

Dun Laoghaire   (1910)

Eglinton Park, Tivoli Road, Dun Laoghaire
☎   (01) 280 3916
🖥   (01) 280 4868
📖   880
✍   D Murphy (Gen Mgr) (01) 280
     3916
⚊   V Carey (01) 280 3916
⛳   18 L 5478 m SSS 69
👤   WD–U exc 12–1.30pm SOC WE
     (Sun only)
££   €55 Group reductions on request
⛳   7 miles S of Dublin. Ferry Port 1
     mile
⊕   Small practice area
🏠   HS Colt
▤   www.dunlaoghairegolfclub.ie

Forrest Little   (1940)

Forrest Little, Cloghran
☎   (01) 840 1763
🖥   (01) 840 1000
✉   forrestlittle@eircom.net
📖   1000
✍   Shirley Sleator
⚊   T Judd (01) 840 7670
⛳   18 L 5900 m Par 72 SSS 72
👤   WD–U WE–NA SOC
££   €50
⛳   Approx. 1/2 mile from Dublin
     Airport
⊕   Practice ground; chipping green;
     putting greens
🏠   F Hawtree/E Connaughton
▤   www.forrestlittle.com

Glencullen

Glencullen, Co Dublin
☎   (01) 295 2895

Hermitage   (1905)

Lucan
☎   (01) 626 5396
🖥   (01) 623 8881
✉   hermitagegolf@eircom.net
📖   1153
✍   Eddie Farrell
⚊   S Byrne (01) 626 8072
⛳   18 L 6032 m SSS 71
👤   U SOC–WD
££   €75 (€85)
⛳   Lucan 2 miles. 8 miles W of Dublin
🏠   James McKenna
▤   www.hermitagegolf.ie

Hibernian   (1994)

City West Hotel, Saggert
☎   (01) 851 0565

Hollywood Lakes
     (1992)

Ballyboughal, Co Dublin
☎   (01) 843 3406/7
✉   hollywoodlakesgc@eircom.net

The Island   (1890)

Corballis, Donabate, Co Dublin
☎   +353 1843 6205
✉   reservations@theislandgolfclub
     .com

Killiney   (1903)

Ballinclea Road, Killiney
☎   (01) 285 2823
🖥   (01) 285 2861
✉   killineygolfclub@eircom.net
📖   520
✍   MF Walsh
⚊   P O'Boyle (01) 285 6294
⛳   9 L 6220 yds SSS 70
👤   WD
££   €50
⛳   8 miles S of Dublin
🏠   E Connaughton

Kilternan   (1987)

Kilternan
☎   (01) 295 5559
🖥   (01) 295 5670
✉   kgc@kilternan-hotel.ie
⊕   Closed until further notice due to
     redevelopment

Lucan   (1897)

Celbridge Road, Lucan
☎   (01) 628 2106
🖥   (01) 628 2929
✉   lucangolf@eircom.net
📖   840
✍   Eddie Meehan (Sec/Mgr)
     (01) 628 2106
⛳   18 L 5958 m Par 71 SSS 70
👤   WD–U WE/BH–M SOC–WD exc
     Wed/Thurs

££   €45
⛳   14 miles W of Dublin, nr Lucan on
     N4
🏠   Eddie Hackett
▤   www.lucangolfclub.ie

Luttrellstown Castle G&CC
     (1993)

Castleknock, Dublin 15
☎   (353) 1 808 9988
✉   golf@luttrellstown.ie

Malahide   (1892)

Beechwood, The Grange, Malahide
☎   (01) 846 1611
✉   malgc@clubi.ie

Milltown   (1907)

*Lower Churchtown Road, Milltown,
Dublin 14*
☎   (01) 497 6090
🖥   (01) 497 6008
✉   reception@milltowngolfclub.ie
📖   1432
✍   E Lawless (Gen Mgr)
⚊   J Harnett (01) 497 7072
⛳   18 L 5638 m Par 71 SSS 69
👤   WD–U exc Tues & Wed pm
     Fri/WE–M BH–NA SOC–Mon &
     Thurs before 3.45pm
££   €80
⛳   4 miles S of Dublin centre
🏠   Freddie Davis

Portmarnock   (1894)

Portmarnock
☎   (01) 846 2794 (Clubhouse)

Portmarnock Hotel & Golf
     Links   (1995)
Proprietary
Strand Road, Portmarnock
☎   (01) 846 1800
🖥   (01) 846 1077
✉   golfres@portmarnock.com
✍   Moira Cassidy (Golf Dir) (01) 846
     1800
⛳   18 L 6260 m Par 71 SSS 73
👤   U H
££   €125 Residents–€85
⛳   8 miles NE of Dublin. Airport 15
     mins
🏠   Bernhard Langer
▤   www.portmarnock.com

Rush   (1943)

Rush
☎   (01) 843 8177
🖥   (01) 843 8177
✉   info@rushgolfclub.com
📖   450
✍   Noeline Quirke (Sec/Mgr)
⛳   9 L 5639 m Par 69 SSS 68
👤   WD–U WE–M
££   €32
⛳   16 miles N of Dublin, off N1
▤   www.rushgolfclub.com

Silloge Park (1994)

Ballymun Road, Swords, Co Dublin
- ☎ **(01) 862 0464**
- 📠 (01) 842 9956
- ✉ peteroconnorgolf@gmail.com
- 📖 400
- ✍ Leo Lennon Maher
- ⚲ P O'Connor
- ► 18 L 5924 m Par 71
- 👥 U
- ££ €18 (€25)
- ⛳ Swords, N of Dublin
- ⊕ Practice ground
- ⌂ Gerry Barry & Eoin Ward
- 🖥 www.christyoconnor.com

Skerries (1905)

Hacketstown, Skerries
- ☎ **(01) 849 1567 (Clubhouse)**
- 📠 (01) 849 1591
- ✉ skerriesgolfclub@eircom.net
- 📖 1060
- ✍ B Meehan (01) 849 1567
- ⚲ J Kinsella (01) 849 0925
- ► 18 L 6107 m Par 73 SSS 72
- 👥 U SOC
- ££ €50 (€60)
- ⛳ 20 miles N of Dublin
- 🖥 www.skerriesgolfclub.ie

Slade Valley (1970)

Lynch Park, Brittas
- ☎ **(01) 458 2183**
- 📠 (01) 458 2784
- ✉ sladevalleygc@eircom.net
- 📖 800
- ✍ D Clancy
- ⚲ J Dignam
- ► 18 L 5468 m SSS 68
- 👥 WD–U am WE–M
- ££ €30 (€40)
- ⛳ 8 miles W of Dublin, off N4
- ⌂ Sullivan/O'Brien
- 🖥 www.sladevalleygolfclub.ie

The South County (1998)

Lisheen Road, Brittas, Co Dublin
- ☎ **(01) 458 2965**
- 📠 (01) 458 2842
- ✉ info@southcountygolf.ie
- 📖 500
- ✍ R Yates
- ► 18 L 7013 yds Par 72
- 👥 U SOC
- ££ On application
- ⛳ SW of Dublin (N81)
- ⊕ Practice area; covered bays; pitching area; practice putting green
- ⌂ Dr N Bielenberg
- 🖥 www.southcountygolf.com

St Margaret's G&CC (1993)

St Margaret's, Dublin
- ☎ **(01) 864 0400**

Swords (1996)

Balheary Avenue, Swords
- ☎ **(01) 840 9819**

- 📠 (01) 840 9819
- ✉ info@swordsopengolfcourse.com
- 📖 505
- ✍ O McGuinness (Mgr)
- ► 18 L 5631 m Par 71 SSS 69
- 👥 U
- ££ €18 (€25)
- ⛳ 10 miles N of Dublin, nr Airport
- ⊕ Putting green
- ⌂ T Halpin
- 🖥 www.swordsopengolfcourse.com

Turvey (1994)

Turvey Avenue, Donabate
- ☎ **(01) 843 5169**
- 📠 (01) 843 5179
- ✉ turveygc@eircom.net
- 📖 335
- ✍ Sean McNolis
- ⚲ Domnic Carty
- ► 18 L 5825 m Par 71 SSS 71
- 👥 U
- ££ €35 (€40)
- ⛳ Donabate off M1 near airport
- ⊕ Practice area; putting green
- ⌂ Paddy McGuirk
- 🖥 www.turveygolfclub.com

Westmanstown (1988)

Clonsilla, Dublin 15
- ☎ **(01) 820 5817**
- 📠 (01) 820 5858
- ✉ info@westmanstowngolfclub.ie
- 📖 1000
- ✍ Stephen Crosbie (Hon)
- ► 18 L 5826 m SSS 71
- 👥 U SOC
- ££ €45 (€50)
- ⛳ 5 miles W of Dublin, nr Lucan
- ⌂ Eddie Hackett
- 🖥 www.westmanstowngolfclub.ie

Woodbrook (1926)

Dublin Road, Bray
- ☎ **(01) 282 4799**
- 📠 (01) 282 1950
- ✉ golf@woodbrook.ie
- 📖 1100
- ✍ PF Byrne (Gen Mgr) (01) 282 4799
- ► 18 L 6221 m SSS 72
- 👥 WD–U WE–phone Sec SOC
- ££ €95 (€100)
- ⛳ 11 miles SE of Dublin on N11
- ⌂ P McEvoy
- 🖥 www.woodbrook.ie

Dublin City

Carrickmines (1900)

Golf Lane, Carrickmines, Dublin 18
- ☎ **(01) 295 5972**
- 📠 (01) 214 9674
- 📖 650
- ✍ CR Bailey (Hon)
- ► 9 L 6063 yds Par 71 SSS 69
  Alternate tees make 18 holes
- 👥 U exc Wed/Sat–NA

- ££ 9: €20 Mon–Sat (€25 Sun) 18: €35 Mon–Sat (€40 Sun)
- ⛳ 6 miles S of Dublin

Castle (1913)

Woodside Drive, Rathfarnham, Dublin 14
- ☎ **(01) 490 4207**
- 📠 (01) 492 0264
- ✉ info@castlegc.ie
- 📖 1400
- ✍ John McCormack (Gen Mgr)
- ⚲ D Kinsella (01) 492 0272
- ► 18 L 6270 yds SSS 71
- 👥 Mon/Thurs/Fri–U Wed–U before 12.30pm WE/BH–M SOC
- ££ €80
- ⛳ 5 miles S of Dublin
- ⌂ Harry Colt
- 🖥 www.castlegc.ie

Clontarf (1912)

Donnycarney House, Malahide Road, Dublin 3
- ☎ **(01) 833 1892**
- 📠 (01) 833 1933
- ✉ info.cgc@indigo.ie
- 📖 1066
- ✍ A Cahill (Mgr)
- ⚲ M Callan (01) 833 1877
- ► 18 L 5317 m SSS 68
- 👥 U SOC
- ££ €50 (€60)
- ⛳ 2 miles NE of Dublin city centre
- ⌂ HS Colt
- 🖥 www.clontarfgolfclub.ie

Deer Park (1974)

Deer Park Hotel, Howth
- ☎ **(01) 832 6039**

Edmondstown (1944)

Rathfarnham, Dublin 16
- ☎ **(01) 493 2461**
- 📠 (01) 493 3152
- ✉ info@edmondstowngolfclub.ie
- 📖 700
- ✍ SS Davies (01) 493 1082
- ⚲ G McShea (01) 494 1049
- ► 18 L 6011 m Par 71 SSS 73
- 👥 WD/BH–U SOC
- ££ €55 (€65)
- ⛳ 5 miles S of Dublin. M50 Junction 12
- ⌂ McEvoy/Cooke
- 🖥 www.edmondstowngolfclub.ie

Elm Park (1927)

Nutley House, Donnybrook, Dublin 4
- ☎ **(01) 269 3438/269 3014**
- 📠 (01) 269 4505
- ✉ office@elmparkgolfclub.ie
- 📖 1750
- ✍ A McCormack (01) 269 3438
- ⚲ S Green (01) 269 2650
- ► 18 L 5374 m SSS 69
- 👥 U–phone Pro
- ££ €70 (€90)
- ⛳ 3 miles S of Dublin
- 🖥 www.elmparkgolfclub.ie

Grange (1911)

Whitechurch Road, Rathfarnham, Dublin 14
☎ **(01) 493 2889**

Hazel Grove (1988)

Mount Seskin Road, Jobstown, Dublin 24
☎ **(01) 452 0911**
🖳 400 175(L)
🖎 Paddy Massey
 (+353 86 235 9624)
✓ None
⊳ 9 L 5300 m SSS 67
👯 Mon/Wed/Fri–U Sun–NA
 Tues/Thurs/Sat–restricted
££ €15
⚬⚬ 3 miles from Tallaght, off
 Blessington road
⌂ Eddie Hackett

Howth (1916)

Carrickbrack Road, Sutton, Dublin 13
☎ **(01) 832 3055**
🖵 (01) 832 1793
🖎 manager@howthgolfclub.ie
🖳 1200
🖎 Paul Kennedy (01) 832 3055
✓ John McGuirk (01) 839 3895
⊳ 18 L 5672 m SSS 69
👯 WD–U exc Wed & Thur WE after
 4pm SOC Mon, Tue, Fri
££ €50 Reductions for groups
⚬⚬ 9 miles NE of Dublin, nr Sutton
 Cross
⌂ James Braid
🖅 www.howthgolfclub.ie

Kilmashogue (1994)

*St Columba's College, Whitechurch,
Dublin 16*
☎ **(087) 274 9844**

Newlands (1926)

Newlands Cross, Dublin 22
☎ **(01) 459 3157**
🖵 (01) 459 3498
🖎 info@newlandsgolf.com
🖳 1086
🖎 Amber Dungan (Golf
 Operations) (01) 459 3157
✓ K O'Donnell (01) 459 3538
⊳ 18 L 5947 m SSS 71
👯 WD–U am WE/BH–NA SOC
££ €75 – discounts may apply
⚬⚬ 6 miles SW of Dublin at Newlands
 Cross (N7)
⌂ James Braid
🖅 www.newlandsgolf.com

Rathfarnham (1899)

Newtown, Dublin 16
☎ **(01) 493 1201/493 1561**
🖎 rgc@oceanfree.net

Royal Dublin (1885)

*North Bull Island Nature Reserve,
Dollymount, Dublin 3*
☎ **(01) 833 6346/1262**
🖵 (01) 833 6504
🖎 info@theroyaldublingolfclub.com
🖳 1250

🖎 Raul Muldowney (01) 833 1262
✓ L Owens (01) 833 6477 (Senior
 Pro C O'Connor Sr)
⊳ 18 L 7100 yds SSS 74
👯 U H exc Wed Sat–NA before 4pm
 Sun–NA exc 10.30–12 noon
 SOC–WD
££ D–€150 (D–€170)
⚬⚬ 3 miles NE of Dublin, on coast
 road to Howth on Bull Island
⊕ Practice range; driving range
⌂ HS Colt
🖅 www.theroyaldublingolfclub.com

St Anne's (1921)

North Bull Island, Dollymount, Dublin 5
☎ **(01) 833 6471**
🖵 (01) 833 4618
🖎 info@stanneslinksgolf.com
🖳 850
🖎 Ted Power
⊳ 18 L 6443 m Par 71 SSS 72
👯 WE/BH–NA SOC WD available,
 Sat am
££ €75 (€90)
⚬⚬ Dublin 5 miles. M50, 5 miles
⌂ Eddie Hackett
🖅 www.stanneslinksgolf.com

Stackstown (1975)

Kellystown Road, Rathfarnham, Dublin 16
☎ **(01) 494 2338**
🖵 (01) 493 3934
🖎 stackstowngc@eircom.net
🖳 1300
🖎 Larry Clarke (Gen Mgr) (01) 494
 1993
✓ M Kavanagh (01) 494 4561
⊳ 18 L 6494 m SSS 70
👯 WD Mon/Thur/Fri; WE Sun
 12–2.00
££ €30 (€40)
⚬⚬ 7 miles SE of Dublin. M50 junction
 13, 2 miles
🖅 www.stackstowngolfclub.com

Sutton (1890)

Cush Point, Sutton, Dublin 13
☎ **(01) 832 3013**
🖵 (01) 832 1603
🖎 info@suttongolfclub.org
🖳 625
🖎 S Carroll (Hon)
✓ N Lynch (01) 832 1703
⊳ 9 L 5624 m Par 70 SSS 67
👯 Tues–NA Sat–NA before 5.30pm
££ €50
⚬⚬ 7 miles E of Dublin, 15 min Dublin
 Airport
🖅 www.suttongolfclub.org

Co Fermanagh

Castle Hume (1991)

Belleek Road, Enniskillen, BT93 7ED
☎ **(028) 6632 7077**
🖵 (028) 6632 7076
🖎 info@castlehumegolf.com
🖳 270
🖎 Wilma Connor (Admin)

✓ S Donnelly (028) 6632 7077
⊳ 18 L 5932 m Par 72 SSS 71
 Additional 18-hole championship
 course under construction
👯 U
££ £25 (+BH £30) Special rates for
 groups and societies
⚬⚬ A46 Belleek/Donegal road
⊕ 5-bay driving range, covered and
 floodlit
⌂ Tony Carroll
🖅 www.castlehumegolf.com

Enniskillen (1896)

Castlecoole, Enniskillen, BT74 6HZ
☎ **(028) 6632 5250**
🖎 enquiries@enniskillengolfclub.com

Co Galway

Ardacong

Milltown Road, Tuam, Co Galway
☎ **(093) 25525**

Athenry (1902)

Palmerstown, Oranmore
☎ **(091) 794466**
🖵 (091) 794971
🖎 athenrygc@eircom.net
🖳 800
🖎 P Flattery (Sec/Mgr) (086) 825
 4454
✓ R Ryan (091) 790599
⊳ 18 L 6300 yds Par 70 SSS 70
👯 WD/Sat–U Sun–NA SOC
££ D–€35 (D–€40)
⚬⚬ 10 miles E of Galway on Athenry
 road (R348), off N6
⊕ Driving range
⌂ Eddie Hackett
🖅 www.athenrygolfclub.net

Ballinasloe (1894)

Rosgloss, Ballinasloe
☎ **(0905) 42126**

Bearna (1996)

Corboley, Bearna
☎ **(091) 592677**
🖎 info@bearnagolfclub.com

Connemara (1973)

Public
Ballyconneely, Clifden
☎ **(095) 23502/23602**
🖵 (095) 23662
🖎 links@iol.ie
🖳 900
🖎 R Flaherty (Sec/Mgr)
✓ H O'Neill (095) 23502
⊳ 27 L 6560 m SSS 72
👯 U H SOC
££ €60
⚬⚬ 8 miles SW of Clifden
⌂ Eddie Hackett
🖅 www.connemaragolflinks.com

Connemara Isles

Annaghvane, Lettermore, Connemara
☎ **(091) 572498**

Curra West   (1996)

Curra, Kylebrack, Loughrea
☎ **(091) 45121**

Galway   (1895)

Blackrock, Salthill, Galway
☎ **(091) 522033**
🖥 (091) 529783
📧 galwaygolf@eircom.net
📖 1250
🏌 P Fahy
⚲ D Wallace (091) 523038
🏁 18 L 5828 m SSS 70
👯 Restricted Tues & Sun
££ €50 (€60)
⛳ 3 miles W of Galway City
🏠 Dr Alister MacKenzie
📰 www.galwaygolf.com

Galway Bay Golf Resort
(1993)

Renville, Oranmore
☎ **+353 (91) 790711/2**
🖥 +353 (91) 792510
📖 270
🏌 Ann Hanley (Golf Dir)
⚲ E O'Connor (091) 790503
🏁 18 L 6350 m SSS 73
👯 U H SOC
££ €55–€70
⛳ 10 miles E of Galway City (N18)
⊕ Driving range; Golf Academy
🏠 C O'Connor Jr
📰 www.galwaybaygolfresort.com

Glenlo Abbey

Glenlo Abbey Hotel, Bushy Park, Galway
☎ **(091) 519698**

Gort   (1924)

Castlequarter, Gort
☎ **(091) 632244**
🖥 (091) 632387
📧 info@gortgolf.com
📖 997
🏌 J Skehill (Hon) (091) 631789
⚲ None
🏁 18 L 5974 m Par 71
👯 U exc Sun am SOC
££ €25 (€30)
⛳ 20 miles S of Galway
🏠 C O'Connor Jr
📰 www.gortgolf.com

Loughrea   (1924)

Graigue, Loughrea
☎ **(091) 841049**
🖥 (091) 847472
📧 loughreagolfclub@eircom.net
📖 400
🏁 18 L 5825 m Par 71
👯 U SOC
££ D–€25
⛳ 1 mile N of Loughrea, off Dublin-Galway road. 20 miles E of Galway
🏠 Eddie Hackett

Mountbellew   (1929)

Shankill, Mountbellew, Ballinasloe
☎ **(0905) 79259**

Oughterard   (1973)

Gortreevagh, Oughterard
☎ **(091) 552131**
📧 oughterardgc@eircom.net

Portumna   (1913)

Ennis Road, Portumna
☎ **(090) 97 41059**
🖥 (090) 97 41798
📧 portumnagc@eircom.net
📖 1100
🏌 J Harte (Hon)
⚲ R Clarke
🏁 18 L 6100 m Par 72 SSS 72
👯 U WD WE except Sat/Sun pm SOC
££ €30 (€35 subject to availability)
⛳ 40 miles SE of Galway on Lough Derg
⊕ Practice area
🏠 E Connaughton
📰 www.portumnagolfclub.ie

Tuam   (1904)

Barnacurragh, Tuam
☎ **(093) 28993**
🖥 (093) 26003
📧 tuamgolfclub@eircom.net
📖 700
🏌 John Costello (Sec/Mgr)
⚲ L Smyth (093) 24091
🏁 18 L 5944 m Par 72 SSS 71
👯 Sun–NA SOC–WD
££ €30
⛳ 20 miles N of Galway
🏠 Eddie Hackett
📰 www.tuamgolfclub.com

Co Kerry

Ardfert   (1993)

Sackville, Ardfert, Tralee
☎ **(066) 713 4744**

Ballybeggan Park

Ballybeggan, Tralee, Co Kerry
☎ **(066) 712 6188**

Ballybunion   (1893)

Sandhill Road, Ballybunion
☎ **(068) 27146**
🖥 (068) 27387
📖 648
🏌 J McKenna (Sec/Mgr)
⚲ B O'Callaghan
🏁 Old 18 L 6542 yds SSS 72
   Cashen 18 L 6477 yds SSS 70
👯 U am SOC WE–NA H
££ Old: €165 Ashen: €110
   Both same day: €240
⛳ 2 miles S of Ballybunion. 50 miles W of Limerick, via Tarbert

⊕ Driving range; practice facility
🏠 Simpson

Ballyheigue Castle   (1995)

Ballyheigue, Tralee
☎ **(066) 713 3555**

Beaufort   (1994)

Churchtown, Beaufort, Killarney
☎ **(064) 44440**
🖥 (064) 44752
📧 beaufortgc@eircom.net
📖 300
🏌 C Kelly
⚲ Keith Coveney
🏁 18 L 6605 yds Par 71 SSS 72
👯 WD–H SOC WE
££ €50 (€60)
⛳ 7 miles W of Killarney, off N72
🏠 Dr Arthur Spring
📰 www.beaufortgolfclub.com

Castlegregory   (1989)

Stradbally, Castlegregory
☎ **(066) 713 9444**
🖥 (066) 713 9958
📖 400
🏌 M Lynch (Hon Sec)
🏁 9 L 5340 m SSS 68
👯 U SOC
££ €30
⛳ 18 miles W of Tralee
🏠 Arthur Spring

Ceann Sibéal   (1924)

Ballyferriter
☎ **(066) 915 6255/6408**
🖥 (066) 915 6409
📧 dinglegc@iol.ie
📖 460
🏌 S Fahy (Mgr)
🏁 18 L 6690 yds SSS 71
👯 U SOC
££ €60 – €80
⛳ Dingle Peninsula, W of Tralee
🏠 Hackett/O'Connor Jr
📰 www.dinglelinks.com

Dooks   (1889)

Glenbeigh
☎ **(066) 976 8205**
🖥 (066) 976 8476
📧 office@dooks.com
📖 900
🏌 D Mangan
🏁 18 L 6000 m Par 71 SSS 71
👯 WD–U H before 5pm
   WE/BH–phone first SOC
££ €80
⛳ 3 miles N of Glenbeigh, on Ring of Kerry (N70)
🏠 M Hawtree
📰 www.dooks.com

Kenmare   (1903)

Kenmare
☎ **(064) 41291**
🖥 (064) 42061
📧 info@kenmaregolfclub.com
📖 600

✓ None
🏳 18 L 5441 m SSS 69
👤 U SOC
££ €45
🚗 20 miles S of Killarney on Cork road
🏠 Eddie Hackett
📧 www.kenmaregolfclub.com

Kerries   (1995)
Tralee
☎ (066) 712 2112

Killarney   (1893)
Mahoney's Point, Killarney
☎ (064) 31034
📠 (064) 33065
📧 reservations@killarney-golf.com
📖 1500
✎ T Prendergast
✓ T Coveney (064) 31615
🏳 Mahoney's Point 18 L 6164 m SSS 72
Killeen 18 L 6475 m SSS 73
Lackabane 18 L 6410 m SSS 73
👤 H SOC
££ On application
🚗 3 miles W of Killarney (N72)
⊕ Driving range
🏠 Mahoney's Point – Longhurst/ Campbell; Killeen – Hackett/ O'Sullivan; Lackabane – Donald Steel
📧 www.killarney-golf.com

Killorglin   (1992)
Stealroe, Killorglin
☎ (669) 761 979
📠 (669) 761 437
📧 kilgolf@iol.ie
📖 450
✎ B Dodd
✓ None
🏳 18 L 6464 yds SSS 72
👤 U SOC
££ €30 (€35)
🚗 1 mile from Killorglin on Tralee road (N70). 12 miles W of Killarney
🏠 Eddie Hackett
📧 www.killorglingolf.ie

Listowel   (1993)
Pay and play
Feale View, Listowel
☎ (068) 21592

Parknasilla   (1974)
Parknasilla, Sneem
☎ (064) 45195
📧 parknasillagolfclub@eircom.net

Ring of Kerry G&CC
(1998)
Proprietary
Templenoe, Kenmare
☎ (064) 42000
📠 (064) 42533
📧 reservations@ringofkerrygolf.com
📖 251

✎ James Mitchell (Ops Mgr)
✓ Adrian Whitehead
🏳 18 L 6820 yds Par 72 SSS 73
👤 U H SOC
££ €70 (€80)
🚗 4 miles W of Kenmare on N70
⊕ Driving range; putting green; buggies
🏠 Eddie Hackett
📧 www.ringofkerrygolf.com

Ross   (1995)
Ross Road, Killarney
☎ (064) 31125

Tralee   (1896)
West Barrow, Ardfert
☎ (066) 713 6379
📧 info@traleegolfclub.com

Waterville   (1889)
Waterville Golf Links, Ring of Kerry, Waterville
☎ +353-66-9474102

Co Kildare

Athy   (1906)
Geraldine, Athy
☎ (059) 863 1729
📠 (059) 863 4710
📧 info@athygolfclub.com
📖 848
✎ T O'Callaghan (Hon)
✓ None
🏳 18 L 6475 yds Par 72 SSS 71
👤 W–U (Mon, Tue, Wed, Fri), Thur (Ladies Day) 11.30–1pm only) Sat–M SOC
££ €25 (€35)
🚗 1 mile N of Athy on Kildare road
📧 www.athygolfclub.com

Bodenstown   (1983)
Bodenstown, Sallins
☎ (045) 897096

Carton House   (2002)
Carton House, Maynooth, Co Kildare
☎ +353 (0)1 505 2000
📠 +353 (0)1 628 6555
📧 reservations@carton.ie
📖 700
✎ John Lawler (Ops Mgr)
✓ Francis Howley
🏳 O'Meara: 18 L 7006 yds Par 72 Montgomerie: 18 L 7300 yds par 72
👤 SOC/U
££ €75–€115 (€135)
🚗 14 miles W of Dublin (N4)
⊕ Driving range; putting green; tuition with Pro
🏠 Mark O'Meara/Colin Montgomerie
📧 www.carton.ie

Castlewarden G&CC
(1989)
Straffan
☎ (01) 458 9254
📠 (01) 458 8972
📧 info@castlewardengolfclub.com
📖 565 225(L)
✎ Emer O'Flaherty (Hon)
✓ B O'Brien
🏳 18 L 6731 yds Par 72 SSS 71
👤 WD–U WE–M SOC
££ €35–€45
🚗 13 miles W of Dublin, off N7, exit 6
🏠 Halpin/Browne
📧 www.castlewardengolfclub.com

Celbridge Elm Hall
Elmhall, Celbridge, Co Kildare
☎ (01) 628 8208

Cill Dara   (1920)
Little Curragh, Kildare Town
☎ (045) 521295

Craddockstown   (1991)
Blessington Road, Naas
☎ (045) 897610
📠 (045) 896968
📧 gaynolan@craddockstown.com
📖 580
✎ Gay Nolan
🏳 18 L 6134 m Par 71 SSS 70
👤 U
££ €38 (€45)
🚗 Naas
🏠 Arthur Spring
📧 www.craddockstown.com

The Curragh   (1883)
Curragh
☎ (045) 441238/441714
📠 (045) 442476
📧 curraghgolf@eircom.net
📖 500 176(L)
✎ D Higgins (045) 441714
✓ G Burke (045) 441896
🏳 18 L 6035 m SSS 71
👤 WD–U exc Tues–phone Sec
££ €30 (€40)
🚗 3 miles S of Newbridge via M7 from Dublin
📧 www.curraghgolf-club.com

Highfield   (1992)
Proprietary
Carbury
☎ (046) 973 1021
📠 (046) 973 1021
📧 highfieldgolf@eircom.net
📖 550
✎ Philomena Duggan (Sec/Mgr)
✓ Conor Devery
🏳 18 L 5707 m SSS 69
👤 WD–U WE–U after 12 noon
££ €30 (€40)
🚗 32 miles W of Dublin off N4
⊕ Driving range
🏠 Alan Duggan
📧 www.highfield-golf.ie

The K Club   (1991)
Straffan
☎ +353 (0)1 601 7300
⌨ +353 (0)1 601 7399
✉ golf@kclub.ie
⌗ 610
✍ P Crowe (Golf Dir)
√ P O'Hagan, J McHenry
↦ Palmer: 18 L 7377 yds SSS 74
Smurfit: 18 L 7277 yds SSS 74
♟ U H SOC–WD
£€ €350 Palmer, €245 Smurfit Peak
season prices – reduced in off
season
⊶ 18 miles SW of Dublin (N7)
⊕ Driving range; chipping green;
putting green
⌂ Arnold Palmer (Palmer & Smurfit)
▤ www.kclub.ie

Kilkea Castle   (1995)
Castledermot
☎ (059) 914 5555
✉ kilkeagolfclub@eircom.net

Killeen   (1986)
Killeenbeg, Kill
☎ (045) 866003
⌨ (045) 875881
✉ admin@killeengc.ie
⌗ 170
✍ M Kelly
√ None
↦ 18 L 6732 yds Par 72 SSS 72
♟ WD–U WE–NA before 10am
£€ €35 (€50)
⊶ 2 miles off N7 on Sallins road
⌂ Ruddy/Craddock
▤ www.killeengolf.com

Knockanally   (1985)
Donadea, North Kildare
☎ (045) 869322
⌨ (045) 869322
✉ golf@knockanally.com
⌗ 500
✍ D Monaghan
√ M Darcy
↦ 18 L 6424 yds SSS 72
♟ U
£€ €35 (€50)
⊶ 20 miles W of Dublin on Galway
road (M4), Jct 8
⌂ N Lyons
▤ www.knockanally.com

Naas   (1896)
Kerdiffstown, Naas
☎ (045) 874644
⌨ (045) 896109
✉ info@naasgolfclub.com
⌗ 1400
✍ Denis Mahon (Mgr)
↦ 18 L 6278 yds Par 71 SSS 71
♟ U SOC
£€ €40 (€45)
⊶ 2 miles N of Naas
⊕ Privately-owned driving range
beside course
⌂ Jeff Howes Design
▤ www.naasgolfclub.com

Newbridge   (1997)
Tankardsgarden, Newbridge
☎ (045) 486110

Woodlands   (1985)
Cooleragh, Coill Dubh
☎ (045) 860777

Co Kilkenny

Callan   (1929)
Geraldine, Callan
☎ (056) 7725136/7725949
⌨ (056) 7755155
✉ info@callangolfclub.com
⌗ 750
✍ M Duggan (Sec/Mgr)
(056) 7755875
√ M O'Shea (087) 6240599
↦ 18 L 6422 yds Par 71 SSS 69
♟ U SOC
£€ €25 (€30)
⊶ 1 mile SE of Callan. 10 miles SW of
Kilkenny
⌂ Bryan Moor
▤ www.callangolfclub.com

Castlecomer   (1935)
Dromgoole, Castlecomer
☎ (056) 4441139
⌨ (056) 4441139
✉ castlecomergolf@eircom.net
⌗ 700
✍ M Dooley (Hon)
↦ 18 L 6175 m Par 72 SSS 72
♟ U SOC–WD WE
£€ €35 (€40)
⊶ 11 miles N of Kilkenny on N7
⌂ Pat Ruddy
▤ www.castlecomergolfclub.com

Kilkenny   (1896)
Glendine, Kilkenny
☎ (056) 776 5400
⌨ (056) 772 3593
✉ enquiries@kilkennygolfclub.com
⌗ 950
✍ A O'Neill (056) 776 5400
√ J Bolger (056) 776 1730
↦ 18 L 6500 yds SSS 70
♟ U
£€ €35 (€45); special rates available
for groups and early birds
⊶ 1 mile N of Kilkenny, off N77
▤ www.kilkennygolfclub.com

Mount Juliet   (1991)
Thomastown
☎ (056) 777 3071
⌨ (056) 777 3078
✉ golfinfo@mountjuliet.ie
⌗ 500
✍ S O'Neill (Golf Mgr) (056) 777
3063
√ S Cotter
↦ 18 L 7264 yds SSS 74
♟ U

£€ €125–€180 May/June/July/Sept
€100–€150 Apr/Aug/Oct
€85–€105 Nov 05–Mar 06
⊶ 10 miles S of Kilkenny, off Dublin-
Waterford road (N9)
⊕ Driving range-residents and green
fees; Golf Academy
⌂ Jack Nicklaus
▤ www.mountjuliet.com

Co Laois

Abbeyleix   (1895)
Rathmoyle, Abbeyleix
☎ (0502) 31450
⌨ (0502) 130108
✉ info@abbeyleixgolfclub.ie
⌗ 601
✍ M Fogarty (Hon Sec)
↦ 18 L 6031 yds Par 72 SSS 70
♟ WD–U WE–NA SOC–WD/WE
£€ €20 (€30)
⊶ 10 miles S of Portlaoise. 60 miles
SW of Dublin on Cork road
⊕ Open singles every Fri during
summer
⌂ Mel Flanagan
▤ www.abbeyleixgolfclub.ie

The Heath   (1930)
The Heath, Portlaoise
☎ (0502) 46533
✉ info@theheathgc.ie

The Heritage G&CC
(2004)
Proprietary
The Heritage Golf & Country Club, Killenard
☎ (057) 864 2321
⌨ (057) 864 2392
✉ info@theheritagegc.com
⌗ 200
✍ Niall Carroll (Golf Co-ordinator)
√ Eddie Doyle – head pro
(0502) 45994
Eamonn O'Flanagan – teaching pro
(0502) 45300
↦ 18 L 7319 yds Par 72
♟ H SOC WD WE
£€ €115 (€130)
⊶ 2 miles off M7, 40 miles S of Dublin
⊕ Driving range; Seve Ballesteros
Natural Golf School
⌂ Seve Ballesteros/Jeff Howes
▤ www.theheritagegc.com

Mountrath   (1929)
Knockanina, Mountrath
☎ (0502) 32558/32643
⌨ (0502) 56735
✉ mountrathgc@eircom.net
⌗ 800
✍ D Kingsley (0502) 22782
↦ 18 L 5643 m Par 71 SSS 69
♟ U WD WE after 4pm SOC
£€ €20 (€30)
⊶ 10 miles W of Portlaoise.
Mountrath 2 miles; N7/M7
▤ www.mountrathgolfclub.ie

Portarlington   (1908)

Garryhinch, Portarlington
☎ **(0502) 23115**
✉ portarlingtongc@eircom.net

Rathdowney   (1930)

Coulnaboul West, Rathdowney
☎ **(0505) 46170**
🖷 (0505) 46065
✉ rathdowneygolf@eircom.net
📖 700
🏌 S Bolger (Hon) (0505) 46233
🏳 18 L 5864 m Par 71 SSS 70
🏌 U exc Sun–NA Sat–SOC
££ €25
⛳ Half mile S of Rathdowney. 20 miles SW of Portlaoise
🏠 Hackett/Suttle
🖥 www.rathdowneygolfclub.com

Co Leitrim

Ballinamore   (1941)

Creevy, Ballinamore
☎ **(078) 44346**

Carrick-on-Shannon   (1910)

Woodbrook, Carrick-on-Shannon
☎ **(079) 67015**

Co Limerick

Abbeyfeale   (1993)

Dromtrasna, Collins Abbeyfeale
☎ **(068) 32033**
🖷 (068) 51871
✉ abbeyfealegolf@eircim.net
📖 85
🏌 Conleth Dillon (Hon Sec) (087) 418 4197
🏳 9 L 4072 yds Par 62
🏌 H SOC WD–U
££ €15
⛳ 12 miles SW of Newcastle West
⊕ 20 bay floodlit driving range
🏠 Dr Arthur Spring
🖥 www.abbeyfealegolfclub.com

Adare Manor   (1900)

Adare
☎ **(061) 396204**
🖷 (061) 396800
✉ info@adaremanorgolfclub.com
📖 750
🏌 P O'Brien
🏳 18 L 5764 yds SSS 69
🏌 WD–U WE–U SOC
££ €40
⛳ 10 miles SW of Limerick (N21)
🏠 Sayers/Hackett
🖥 www.adaremanorgolfclub.com

Castletroy   (1937)

Golf Links Road, Castleroy, Co. Limerick
☎ **(061) 335753 (club)**
   (061) 330450 (shop)

🖷 (061) 335373
✉ cgc@iol.ie
📖 1033
🏌 Patrick Keane (Gen Mgr)
🏳 18: Blue L 6284 m Par 72 SSS 73; White L 6046 m Par 72 SSS 72; Red L 5453 Par 74 SSS 75
🏌 WD–U Sat am–U Sat pm/Sun–M SOC–Mon/Wed/Fri/Sat
££ €50 (€60)
⛳ Less than 3 miles from Limerick City off N7 to Dublin
🏠 Eddie Connaughton
🖥 www.castletroygolfclub.ie

Limerick   (1891)

Ballyclough, Limerick
☎ **(061) 414083**
🖷 (061) 319219
✉ lgc@eircom.net
   pat.murray@limerickgc.com
📖 1325
🏌 P Murray (Gen Mgr) (061) 415146
🏌 L Harrington (061) 412492
🏳 18 L 6479 yds SSS 71
🏌 WD–U before 5pm exc Tues WE–M SOC–WD prior booking essential
££ €50 (€70)
⛳ 3 miles S of Limerick
🖥 www.limerickgc.com

Limerick County G&CC
(1994)

Ballyneety
☎ **(061) 351881**
🖷 (061) 351384
✉ lcgolf@iol.ie
📖 800
🏌 Gerry McKeon (Mgr)
🏌 Donal McSweeney
🏳 18 L 5686 m Par 71 SSS 70
🏌 U SOC
££ €40 (€50)
⛳ 5 miles S of Limerick (R512)
⊕ Driving range
🏠 Des Smyth
🖥 www.limerickcounty.com

Newcastle West
(1938)

Rathgonan, Ardagh, Co. Limerick
☎ **(069) 76500**
🖷 (069) 76511
✉ n.c.w.golf@eircom.net
📖 950
🏌 Richard J Collins (Gen Mgr)
🏌 Conor McCormick (069) 76500 ext 21
🏳 18 L 6141 m Medal 6444 m Championship SSS 72
🏌 U exc Sun–U after 4pm SOC
££ €45 (€35)
⛳ 6 miles N of Newcastle West, off N21
⊕ Floodlit driving range; putting green; buggy hire
🏠 Arthur Spring
🖥 www.newgolf.com

Rathbane   (1998)

Public
Rathbane, Crossagalla, Limerick
☎ **(061) 313655**
🖷 (061) 313655
📖 800 approx
🏌 John O'Sullivan
🏌 Barbara Hackett (086) 811 6255
🏳 18 L 5671 m Par 70
🏌 U
££ €10–€20 (€15–€25)
⛳ Limerick
⊕ Buggies & clubs for hire

Co Londonderry

Benone Par Three

53 Benone Avenue, Benone, Limavady, BT49 0LQ
☎ **(028) 7775 0555**
🏌 Ml Clark
🏳 9 L 1427 yds Par 3 course
🏌 U
££ £5.75 (£6.40)
⛳ 12 miles N of Limavady on A2 coast road
⊕ Driving range

Brown Trout   (1984)

209 Agivey Road, Aghadowey, Coleraine, BT51 4AD
☎ **(028) 7086 8209**
🖷 (028) 7086 8878
✉ bill@browntroutinn.com
📖 150
🏌 B O'Hara (Sec/Mgr)
🏌 K Revie
🏳 9 L 2800 yds SSS 68
🏌 U SOC
££ £10 (£15)
⛳ 8 miles S of Coleraine at junction of A54/B66
🏠 W O'Hara Sr
🖥 www.browntroutinn.com

Castlerock   (1901)

65 Circular Road, Castlerock, BT51 4TJ
☎ **(028) 7084 8314**
🖷 (028) 7084 9440
✉ info@castlerockgc.co.uk
📖 1260
🏌 M Steen (Sec/Mgr)
🏌 Ian Blair (028) 7084 9424
🏳 18 L 6121 m SSS 72
   9 L 2457 m SSS 34
🏌 WD–U exc Fri SOC
££ 9 (Bann): £12 (£15) 18 (Mussenden Links): £60 (£75 inc BH)
⛳ 5 miles W of Coleraine on A2
🏠 Ben Sayers
🖥 www.castlerockgc.co.uk

City of Derry   (1912)

49 Victoria Road, Londonderry, BT47 2PU
☎ **(028) 7134 6369**
🖷 (028) 7131 0008
✉ info@cityofderrygolfclub.com
📖 775
🏌 Noreen Allen

✓ M Doherty (028) 7131 1496
P Prehen 18 L 6487 yds SSS 71
Dunhugh 9 L 4708 yds SSS 63
🏌 WD–U before 4pm –M after 4pm
WE–UH SOC
££ £20 (£25)
🚗 3 miles from E end of Craigavon
Bridge, towards Strabane
🏠 Harry S Colt
📧 www.cityofderrygolfclub.com

Foyle   (1994)
Proprietary
12 Alder Road, Londonderry, BT48 8DB
☎ **(028) 7135 2222**
🖳 (028) 7135 3967
📧 mail@foylegolf.club24.co.uk
📖 265
⛳ M Lapsley (028) 7135 2222
✓ D Morrison and S Young
P 18 L 6643 m SSS 71
9 hole course
🏌 U
££ £15 (£18)
🚗 Londonderry
⊕ Driving range; 2 putting greens
🏠 Frank Ainsworth
📧 www.foylegolfcentre.co.uk

Kilrea   (1920)
47a Lisnagrot Road, Kilrea
☎ **(028) 295 40044**

Moyola Park   (1976)
*15 Curran Road, Castledawson,
Magherafelt, BT45 8DG*
☎ **(028) 7946 8468**
🖳 (028) 7946 8626
📧 moyolapark@btconnect.com
📖 940
⛳ S McKenna (Hon)
✓ Bob Cockcroft (028) 7946 8830
P 18 L 6519 yds Par 71
🏌 U SOC exc Sat
££ £24 (£30)
🚗 40 miles NW of Belfast by M2.
35 miles S of Coleraine
🏠 Don Patterson
📧 www.moyolapark.com

Portstewart   (1894)
117 Strand Road, Portstewart, BT55 7PG
☎ **(028) 7083 2015**
🖳 (028) 7083 4097
📧 info@portstewartgc.co.uk
📖 1673
⛳ M Moss BA (028) 7083 3839
✓ A Hunter (028) 7083 2601
P Strand: 18 L 6895 yds SSS 73
Riverside: 18 L 5725 yds SSS 68
Old: 18 L 4733 yds SSS 62
🏌 SOC–by arrangement
££ Strand: £70 (£90) Riverside: £20
(£25) Old £10 (£15)
🚗 W boundary of Portstewart
🏠 Des Griffin
📧 www.portstewartgc.co.uk

Roe Park   (1993)
Roe Park Hotel, Limavady, BT49 9LB
☎ **(028) 7776 0105**

🖳 (02877) 722313
📧 sales@radissonroepark.com
📖 550
✓ D Brockerton (02877) 760105
✓ Shaun Devenney
P 18 L 6318 yds Par 70 SSS 71
🏌 U
££ £25 (£30)
🚗 Limavady
⊕ Covered driving range; golf
academy
📧 www.radissonroepark.com

Traad Ponds
Shore Road, Magherafelt, BT45 6LR
☎ **(028) 7941 8865**

Co Longford

County Longford   (1900)
Glack, Dublin Road, Longford
☎ **(043) 46310**

Co Louth

Ardee   (1911)
Townparks, Ardee
☎ **(041) 685 3227**
🖳 (041) 685 6137
📧 ardeegolfclub@eircom.net
📖 700
⛳ Seamus Rooney (Sec/Mgr)
✓ Scott Kirkpatrick
P 18 L 6490 yds Par 71 SSS 72
🏌 U SOC
££ £35 (€50)
🚗 1km N of Ardee, 7km to M1
⊕ Driving range
🏠 Eddie Hackett
📧 www.ardeegolfclub.com

Carnbeg   (1996)
Pay and play
Carnbeg, Dundalk, Co Louth
☎ **(042) 933 2518**
⛳ P Kirk
✓ J Frawley
P Championship: 18 L 5645 m
Par 72
Ladies: 18 L 4656 m Par 72
🏌 U
££ €25 (€33)
🚗 1 mile from Dundalk Road on R177
Armagh Road
⊕ Practice green and net
🏠 Eddie Hackett and Tom Croddock

County Louth   (1892)
Baltray, Drogheda
☎ **(041) 988 1530**
🖳 (041) 988 1531
📧 reservations@countylouthgolfclub
.com
📖 1400
⛳ M Delany
✓ P McGuirk (041) 988 1536

P 18 L 7035 yds SSS 73
🏌 By prior arrangement
££ €120
🚗 3 miles NE of Drogheda
🏠 Tom Simpson
📧 www.countylouthgolfclub.com

Dundalk   (1905)
Blackrock, Dundalk
☎ **(042) 932 1731**
🖳 (042) 932 2022
📧 manager@dundalkgolfclub.ie
📖 1250
⛳ T Sloane (Sec/Mgr)
✓ Leslie Walker (042) 932 2102
P 18 holes
Championship tees: L 6206 m
Par 72 SSS 72
Medal tees: L 6024 m Par 72
SSS 71
Forward tees: L 5713 Par 72
SSS 70
Ladies tees: L 5222 m Par 73
SSS 72
🏌 U SOC
££ €55 (€20 with member)
🚗 3 miles S of Dundalk
⊕ Large practice area; pitching green;
putting green
🏠 Dave Thomas, Peter Alliss
📧 www.dundalkgolfclub.ie

Greenore   (1896)
Greenore
☎ **(042) 937 3212/3678**
🖳 (042) 937 3678
📧 greenoregolfclub@eircom.net
📖 1100
⛳ Linda Clarke
✓ Robert Giles (042) 937 3951
P 18 L 6514 yds Par 71 SSS 71
🏌 WD–U before 5pm WE/BH–by
arrangement SOC
££ €35 (€50)
🚗 15 miles E of Dundalk on
Carlingford Lough. M1
Dublin/Belfast
⊕ Driving range
🏠 Eddie Hackett
📧 www.greenoregolfclub.com

Killinbeg   (1991)
Killin Park, Dundalk
☎ **(042) 933 9303**
🖳 (042) 932 0848
📖 350
⛳ Pat Reynolds (Sec/Mgr)
✓ None
P 18 L 4717 m Par 69 SSS 64
🏌 U SOC
££ €22 (€27)
🚗 2 miles NW of Dundalk on
Castletown road
🏠 Eddie Hackett

Seapoint   (1993)
Termonfeckin, Drogheda
☎ **(041) 982 2333**
🖳 (041) 982 2331
📧 golflinks@seapoint.ie
📖 530

⚐ K Carrie
✓ D Carroll (041) 988 1066
▷ 18 L 6473 m Par 72 SSS 75 –
   links course
👥 U–WE SOC
££ €60–€75
⚐ M1
⊕ Driving range; large short game
   practice academy
⌂ Des Smyth
▤ www.seapointgolfclub.com

Townley Hall   (1994)
Tullyallen, Drogheda
☎ **(041) 984 2229**
✉ townleyhall@oceanfree.net

Co Mayo

Achill   (1951)
Keel, Achill
☎ **(098) 43456**

Ashford Castle
Cong
☎ **(092) 46003**

Ballina   (1910)
Mossgrove, Shanaghy, Ballina
☎ **(096) 21050**

Ballinrobe   (1895)
Clooncastle, Ballinrobe
☎ **(04) 954 1118**
🖷 (094) 954 1889
✉ info@ballinrobegolfclub.com
📖 700
⚐ J McMahon (Sec/Mgr)
▷ 18 L 6354 m Par 73 SSS 72
U exc Sun–NA SOC
££ €28–€33
⊶ 2 miles NW of Ballinrobe on R331
⊕ Foodlit driving range
⌂ Eddie Hackett
▤ www.ballinrobegolfclub.com

Ballyhaunis   (1929)
Coolnaha, Ballyhaunis
☎ **(0907) 30014**

Belmullet   (1925)
Carne, Belmullet
☎ **(00353) 97 82292**
✉ terryswinson@esatclear.ie
📖 386
⚐ T Swinson (Hon Sec)
   (00353) 97 85786
▷ Blue: 18 L 6119 m SSS 72
   Medal: 18 L 5819 m Par 72 SSS 71
👥 U
££ D–€60 (€60)
⊶ 1 mile from Belmullet
⊕ Belmullet is the permanent resident
   club at Carne Golf Links
⌂ Eddie Hackett
▤ www.belmulletgolfclub.ie

Castlebar   (1910)
Hawthorn Avenue, Rocklands, Castlebar
☎ **(094) 21649**
🖷 (094) 26088
📖 950
⚐ Bernie Murray (087) 657 7640
✓ David McQuillan
▷ 18 L 6500 yds Par 71 SSS 72
👥 WD/Sat–U Sun–NA Pre–booking
   for time sheets advisable
££ €24 (€30)
⊶ 1 mile S of Castlebar, on Galway
   road
⌂ P McEvoy (1999)
▤ www.castlebar.ie/golf

Claremorris   (1917)
Castlemacgarrett, Claremorris
☎ **(094) 937 1527**
🖷 (094) 937 2919
✉ info@claremorrisgolfclub.com
📖 700
⚐ A Finn (Hon)
▷ 18 L 5827 yds Par 73 SSS 71
👥 WD–U before noon Sat–U before
   noon SOC
££ €30 (€33)
⊶ 2 miles S of Claremorris (N17)
⌂ Tom Craddock
▤ www.claremorrisgolfclub.com

Mulranny   (1968)
Mulranny, Westport
☎ **(098) 36262**

Swinford   (1922)
Brabazon Park, Swinford
☎ **(+353) 94 925 1378**
🖷 (+353) 94 925 1378
📖 300
⚐ T Regan (087) 291 3067
▷ 9 L 5901 yds SSS 68
👥 U SOC–exc Sun
££ €15
⊶ S of Swinford, off Kiltimagh road

Westport   (1908)
Carrowholly, Westport
☎ **(098) 28262/27070**
🖷 (098) 27217
✉ info@westportgolfclub.com
📖 850
⚐ Paul O'Neill
✓ Alex Mealia
▷ 18 L 6724 yds SSS 72
👥 U SOC
££ €42 (€55)
⊶ 2 miles W of Westport
⊕ Driving range
⌂ F Hawtree
▤ www.westportgolfclub.com

Co Meath

Ashbourne   (1991)
Archerstown, Ashbourne
☎ **(01) 835 2005**

Black Bush   (1987)
Thomastown, Dunshaughlin
☎ **(01) 825 0021**
🖷 (01) 825 0400
✉ info@blackbushgolfclub.ie
📖 1050
⚐ Kate O'Rourke (Admin)
   (01) 825 0021
✓ S O'Grady (01) 825 0793
▷ 18 L 6930 yds SSS 73
   9 L 2800 yds SSS 35
👥 WD–to 4pm WE–2 hrs Sat
   Sun–NA SOC to 4pm
££ €30 (€45)
⊶ 1 mile E of Dunshaughlin, off N3.
   20 miles NW of Dublin
⊕ Driving range for members and
   green fees
⌂ Robert J Browne
▤ www.blackbushgolfclub.ie

County Meath   (1898)
Newtownmoynagh, Trim
☎ **(046) 9431463**

Gormanston College
   (1961)
Franciscan College, Gormanston
☎ **(01) 841 2203**

Headfort   (1928)
Kells
☎ **(046) 924 0146**
🖷 (046) 924 9282
✉ hgcadmin@eircom.net
📖 1100
⚐ Nora Murphy (Admin)
   (046) 924 0146
✓ B McGovern (046) 924 0639
▷ New 18 L 6164 m SSS 74
   Old 18 L 5973 m SSS 71
👥 U before 4pm exc NA 12.30–2pm
   SOC
££ New: €60 Mon–Thur
   (€65 Fri–Sun)
   Old: €45 Mon–Thur
   (€50 Fri–Sun)
⊶ 65km NW of Dublin on N3
⌂ Christy O'Connor Jr
▤ www.headfortgolfclub.ie

Kilcock   (1985)
Gallow, Kilcock
☎ **(01) 628 7592**
🖷 (01) 628 7283
✉ kilcockgolfclub@eircom.net
📖 650
⚐ S Kelly (Sec/Mgr)
▷ 18 L 5794 m SSS 71
👥 U SOC
££ €25 Mon–Thur (Fri–Sun €30)
⊶ 20 miles W of Dublin (N4)
⌂ E Hackett
▤ www.kilcockgolfclub.com

Laytown & Bettystown
   (1909)
Bettystown, Co. Meath
☎ **(041) 982 7170**
🖷 (041) 982 8506

links@landb.ie
850
Helen Finnegan
(041) 982 7170 ext 1
RJ Browne (041) 982 8793
18 L 6454 yds SSS 72
U SOC–WD
€60 (€75) – 2005 prices
25 miles N of Dublin; junction
Layton and Drogheda South
www.landb.ie

Moor Park (1993)
Moortown, Navan
(046) 27661

Navan (1996)
Public
Proudstown, Navan, Co Meath
(046) 907 2888
(046) 907 6722
jmc@navangolfclub.ie
530
J McCann
E Riblet
18 L 6114 m Par 72
U
€20 (€29)
2 miles N of Navan
RJ Browne
www.navangolfandracecourse
.com

Royal Tara (1906)
Bellinter, Navan
(046) 902 5244/
902 5508/902 5584
info@royaltaragolfclub.com

Summerhill
Agher, Rathmoylan, Co Meath
(046) 955 7857

Co Monaghan

Castleblayney (1985)
Onomy, Castleblayney
(042) 974 9485
castleblayney@golfnet.ie
275
R Kernan (042) 974 0451
9 L 2678 yds SSS 66
U SOC
€12 (€15)
Castleblayney town centre. 18
miles SE of Monaghan
R Browne
www.castleblayneygolfclub.com

Clones (1913)
Hilton Demesne, Clones
(047) 56017/56913
(047) 56017
clonesgolfclub@eircom.net
400
M Taylor (049) 555 2354
18 L 6100 yds Par 70 SSS 69

WD–U WE–book in advance
€30
Hilton Park, 3km from Clones on
Scotshouse Road
Practice putting area; practice
ground
Dr Arthur Spring
www.clonesgolf.com

Mannan Castle (1993)
Donaghmoyne, Carrickmacross
(042) 966 3308

Nuremore Hotel & CC
(1964)
Nuremore, Carrickmacross
(042) 967 1368
(042) 966 1853
nuremore@eircom.net
300
N Power
M Cassidy
18 L 5870 m Par 71 SSS 69
U
€40 (€45)
1 mile S of Carrickmacross off M1,
take Derry exit
Eddie Hackett
www.nuremore-hotel.ie

Rossmore (1916)
Rossmore Park, Monaghan
(047) 81316
(047) 71227
rossmoregolfclub@eircom.net
750
J McKenna (Hon)
Ciaran Smyth (047) 71222
18 L 6082 yds Par 70 SSS 69
WD–U SOC WE/BH–U SOC
€25 (€35)
2 miles S of Monaghan on Cootehill
road
Des Smyth
www.rossmoregolfclub.com

Co Offaly

Birr (1893)
The Glenns, Birr
(0509) 20082
(0509) 22155
birrgolfclub@eircom.net
750
Mary O'Gorman (Hon)
Kevin McGrath (0509) 21606
18 L 6216 yds SSS 70
U SOC–exc Sun–NA (except
11–12 on certain Sundays)
€25
2 miles W of Birr
Driving range
Eddie Connaughton
www.birrgolfclub.ie

Castle Barna (1992)
Castlebarnagh, Daingean
(057) 935 3384

(057) 935 3077
info@castlebarna.ie
600
E Mangan
18 L5595 m Par 72 SSS 69
U
€25 (€35)
10 miles E of Tullamore (R402)
Alan Duggan
www.castlebarna.ie

Edenderry (1910)
Kishawanny, Edenderry
(046) 973 1072
(046) 973 3911
enquiries@edenderrygolfclub.com
1000
Noel Usher
18 L 6121 m Par 72 SSS 72
WD–U exc Thurs (Ladies Day)
WE–restricted SOC
On application
1 mile E of Edenderry town
Havers/Hackett
www.edenderrygolfclub.com

Esker Hills G&CC (1966)
Proprietary
Tullamore, Co Offaly
(057) 93 55999
(057) 93 55021
info@eskerhillsgolf.com
200
C Guinan
18 L 6669 yds Par 71
U
€35 (€45)
Tullamore
Putting green; practice area
Christy O'Connor Jr
www.eskerhillsgolf.com

Tullamore (1896)
Brookfield, Tullamore
(0506) 21439
(0506) 41806
tullamoregolfclub@eircom.net
1000
J Barber-Loughnane
(0506) 21439
D McArdle (0506) 51757
18 L 6428 yds Par 70 SSS 71
WD exc Tues–U Sat–restricted
Sun–NA SOC
€37 (€48)
2½ miles S of Tullamore, off N52
Braid/Merrigan
www.tullamoregolfclub.com

Co Roscommon

Athlone (1892)
Hodson Bay, Athlone
(090) 649 2073/649 2235
(090) 649 4080
1000
I Dockery
Kevin Grealy
18 L 5854 m SSS 71 white, 73 blue

U SOC
££ D–€30 (€35)
⚵ 3 miles N of Athlone on Roscommon road
⌂ F Hawtree

Ballaghaderreen   (1937)
Aughalustia, Ballaghaderreen
☎ (094) 986 0295
▭ 350
⚐ J Cawley (Hon)
⚑ 9 L 5663 yds Par 70 SSS 67
⚵ U SOC
££ €15
⚵ Ballaghaderreen 3 miles
⌂ P Skerritt

Boyle   (1911)
Knockadoo, Brusna, Boyle
☎ (071) 966 2594
▭ 145
⚐ J Mooney (Hon)
(087) 776 0161
⚑ 9 L 5105 m Par 68 SSS 66
⚵ U SOC
££ D–€15
⚵ 1½ miles S of Boyle
⌂ Eddie Hackett

Castlerea   (1905)
Clonallis, Castlerea
☎ (0907) 21214

Roscommon   (1904)
Moate Park, Roscommon
☎ (09066) 26382
✉ rosgolf@eircom.net

Strokestown   (1995)
Strokestown
▭ 350
⚐ L Glover (Hon)
(07196) 33528
⚑ 9 L 5230 m Par 68 SSS 67
⚵ U
££ €15
⚵ 15 miles N of Roscommon (R368). N5 to Longford/Westport

Co Sligo

Ballymote   (1943)
Ballinascarrow, Ballymote
☎ (071) 83504

County Sligo   (1894)
Rosses Point
☎ (071) 9177134/9177186
🖷 (071) 9177460
✉ teresa@countysligogolfclub.ie
▭ 1200
⚐ H O'Neill (Mgr)
(071) 9177134
⚐ J Robinson (071) 9177171
⚑ 18 L 6136 m SSS 72
9 L 2795 m SSS 35
⚵ U H–booking required SOC

££ Mon–Thur €75 Fri/WE–€90
⚵ 5 miles NW of Sligo
⌂ Colt/Allison
🖥 www.countysligogolfclub.ie

Enniscrone   (1931)
Ballina Road, Enniscrone
☎ (096) 36297

Strandhill   (1932)
Strandhill
☎ (00353) 71 91 68188
✉ strandhillgc@eircom.net

Tubbercurry   (1990)
Ballymote Road, Tubbercurry
☎ (071) 85849
✉ contact@tubbercurrygolfclub.com

Co Tipperary

Ramada Hotel & Suites, Ballykisteen   (1994)
Proprietary
Ballykisteen, Limerick Junction
☎ (062) 33333 (hotel)
(062) 31555 (golf)
✉ golf.ballykisteen@ramadaireland.com
▭ 350
⚐ James Harris, PGA
⚑ 18 L 5765 yds Par 72
⚵ U SOC WD WE
££ €40 (€50)
⚵ 3 miles NW of Tipperary town; 25 min from Limerick City
⊕ Driving range
⌂ Des Smyth
🖥 www.ballykisteenramada.com

Cahir Park   (1967)
Kilcommon, Cahir, Co Tipperary
☎ (052) 41474
🖷 (052) 42717
✉ management@cahirparkgolfclub.com
▭ 700
⚐ J Costigan (052) 41146
⚐ D Ryan (052) 43944
⚑ 18 L 6351 yds Par 71 SSS 71
⚵ U SOC–WD/Sat
££ €30 (€35)
⚵ 1 mile S of Cahir
⊕ Driving range
⌂ Eddie Hackett
🖥 www.cahirgolfclub.com

Carrick-on-Suir   (1939)
Garravoone, Carrick-on-Suir
☎ (051) 640047

Clonmel   (1911)
Lyreanearla, Mountain Road, Clonmel
☎ (052) 24050
🖷 (052) 83349
✉ cgc@indigo.ie

▭ 820
⚐ A Myles-Keating (052) 24050
⚐ R Hayes (052) 24050
⚑ 18 L 6347 yds SSS 71
⚵ WD–U WE–SOC before noon
££ €25 (€35) €20 with member WD: 3 courses for €60 (Carrick, Clonmel, Cahir Park)
⚵ 3 miles SW of Clonmel
⊕ Putting green
⌂ Eddie Hackett
🖥 www.clonmelgolfclub.com

County Tipperary   (1993)
Dundrum, Cashel
☎ (062) 71717

Nenagh   (1929)
Beechwood, Nenagh
☎ (067) 31476
🖷 (067) 34808
✉ nenaghgolfclub@eircom.net
▭ 1200
⚐ Alice Varley
⚐ R Kelly (067) 33242
⚑ 18 L 6009 m Par 72 SSS 72
⚵ U SOC
££ €30 reduced fees for groups
⚵ 3 miles NE of Nenagh on old Birr road
⌂ Patrick Merrigan
🖥 www.nenaghgolf.com

Roscrea   (1892)
Derryvale, Roscrea
☎ (0505) 21130
🖷 (0505) 23410
✉ roscreagolf@hotmail.com
▭ 500
⚐ S Crofton (Hon)
⚑ 18 L 5782 m SSS 71
⚵ U
££ €20 (€25)
⚵ 2 miles E of Roscrea on Dublin road (N7)
⌂ Arthur Spring

Slievenamon   (1999)
Proprietary
Clonacody, Lisronagh, Co Tipperary
☎ (052) 32213
🖷 (052) 30875
✉ info@slievnamongolfclub.com
▭ 700
⚐ B Kenny (052) 32213
⚐ D Kiely (087) 238 8856
⚑ 18 L 5000 m Par 67
⚵ U
££ €10 (€15)
⚵ 4 miles N of Clonmel off Fethard Rd
⊕ Practice area
🖥 www.slievnamongolfclub.com

Templemore   (1970)
Manna South, Templemore
☎ (0504) 32923/31400
✉ johnkm@tinet.ie

Thurles   (1909)
Turtulla, Thurles
☎ (0504) 21983

☎ (0504) 90806
✉ thurlesgolf@eircom.net
📖 1200
🏌 Mort Taylor
✓ S Hunt
▷ 18 L 5904 yds SSS 71
👥 U
€€ €40 (€50)
🚗 1 miles S of Thurles
⊕ Driving range
🖅 www.thurlesgolfclub.com

Tipperary   (1896)
Rathanny, Tipperary
☎ (062) 51119
✉ tipperarygolfclub@eircom.net

Co Tyrone

Auchnacloy   (1995)
99 Tullyvar Road, Auchnacloy
☎ (028) 8255 7050
✉ sidney.houston@btopenworld.com
📖 180
🏌 S Houston
▷ 9 L 5017 m Par 70 SSS 68
👥 U
€€ £12 (£15)
🚗 12 miles SW of Dungannon (B35)
⊕ Driving range

Benburb Valley
Maydown Road, Benburb, BT71 7LJ
☎ (028) 3754 9868

Dungannon   (1890)
34 Springfield Lane, Mullaghmore, Dungannon, BT70 1QX
☎ (028) 8772 2098
🖷 (028) 8772 7338
✉ info@dungannongolfclub.com
📖 840
🏌 ST Hughes
✓ Vivian Teague
▷ 18 L 6046 yds SSS 72
👥 U
€€ £20, £14 with member (£25, £16 with member)
🚗 ½ mile NW of Dungannon on Donaghmore road
🖅 www.dungannongolfclub.com

Fintona   (1904)
Eccleville Desmesne, 1 Kiln Street, Fintona, BT78 2BJ
☎ (028) 8284 1480

Killymoon   (1889)
200 Killymoon Road, Cookstown, BT80 8TW
☎ (028) 8676 3762
🖷 (028) 8676 3762
✉ killymoongolf@btconnect.com
📖 950
🏌 N Weir
✓ G Chambers
▷ 18 L 6202 yds SSS 69
👥 U H SOC
€€ £21 (£26)
🚗 1 mile S of Cookstown, off A29
🖅 www.killymoongolfclub.com

Newtownstewart   (1914)
38 Golf Course Road, Newtownstewart, BT78 4HU
☎ (028) 8166 1466
✉ newtown.stewart@lineone.net

Omagh   (1910)
83A Dublin Road, Omagh, BT78 1HQ
☎ (028) 8224 3160/1442
🖷 (028) 8224 3160
📖 817
🏌 Mrs F Caldwell
✓ None
▷ 18 L 5364 m SSS 68
👥 U SOC
€€ £15 (£20)
🚗 1 mile from Omagh on Belfast-Dublin road

Strabane   (1908)
Ballycolman, Strabane, BT82 9PH
☎ (028) 7138 2271/2007
🖷 (028) 7188 6514
✉ strabanegc@btconnect.com
📖 600
🏌 Claire Keys (028) 7138 2007
✓ None
▷ 18 L 5552 m SSS 69
👥 WD–U WE–by arrangement SOC
€€ £12 (£15)
🚗 ½ mile from Strabane, nr Fir Trees Hotel

Co Waterford

Dungarvan   (1924)
Knocknagranagh, Dungarvan
☎ (058) 43310/41605
✉ dungarvangc@eircom.net

Dunmore East   (1993)
Dunmore East
☎ (051) 383151
🖷 (051) 383151
✉ info@dunmoreeastgolfclub.ie
📖 450
🏌 Sadie Whittle
✓ Derry Kiely
▷ 18 L 6070 m Par 72 SSS 70
👥 U
€€ €30 (€35)
🚗 10 miles S of Waterford (R684)
⊕ Accom. on site
🏠 J O'Riordan
🖅 www.dunmoreeastgolfclub.ie

Faithlegg   (1993)
Faithlegg House, Faithlegg
☎ (051) 382000
🖷 (051) 382010
✉ golf@fhh.ie
📖 260
🏌 Ryan Hunt (051) 380588
✓ Derry Kiely
▷ 18 L 6690 yds SSS 72
👥 U SOC (corporate specialists) WD–U WE–Sun U after 12
€€ €50 (€65) Soc negotiated
🚗 6 miles E of Waterford City on

Dunmore East road
⊕ Short game practice area; putting green; driving nets; practice bunkers
🏠 Patrick Merrigan
🖅 www.faithlegg.com

Gold Coast   (1993)
Ballinacourty, Dungarvan
☎ (058) 42249/44055
🖷 (058) 43378
✉ info@goldcoastgolfclub.com
📖 600
🏌 T Considine (058) 44055
✓ None
▷ 18 L 6171 m Par 72 SSS 72
👥 U SOC
€€ €35 (€45)
🚗 E of Dungarvan, off R675
🏠 M Fives
🖅 www.goldcoastgolfclub.com

Lismore   (1965)
Ballyin, Lismore
☎ (058) 54026

Tramore   (1894)
Newtown Hill, Tramore
☎ (051) 386170/381247

Waterford   (1912)
Newrath, Waterford
☎ +353 (0) 51 876748
🖷 +353 (0) 51 853405
✉ info@waterfordgolfclub.com
📖 961
🏌 Damien Maquire (Sec/Mgr) (051) 876748
✓ Harry Ewing +353 (0) 51 830628
▷ 18 L 5722 m Par 71 SSS 70
👥 U
€€ €40 (€50)
🚗 1 mile N of Waterford
⊕ Practice ground; driving range; buggy hire
🏠 Willie Park/James Braid
🖅 www.waterfordgolfclub.com

Waterford Castle   (1991)
The Island, Ballinakill, Waterford
☎ (051) 871633
🖷 (051) 871634
✉ golf@waterfordcastle.com
📖 750
🏌 M Garland (Dir. of Golf)
▷ 18 L 6231 m Par 72 SSS 71
👥 U H SOC
€€ €50 (€60+BH)
🚗 2 miles E of Waterford, off R683. Island in River Suir. Access by private ferry
⊕ Driving range; putting green
🏠 Des Smyth
🖅 www.waterfordcastle.com

West Waterford G&CC   (1993)
Dungarvan
☎ (058) 43216/41475
🖷 (058) 44343

🖾 info@westwaterfordgolf.com
📖 425
🖋 T Whelan (Sec/Mgr)
⛳ 18 L 6712 yds Par 72
👤 U SOC
££ €33 (€44)
🚗 4km W of Dungarvan, off N25
⊕ Practice range
🏠 Eddie Hackett
🖳 www.westwaterfordgolf.com

Co Westmeath

Ballinlough Castle
Clonmellon, Co Westmeath
☎ (044) 64544

Delvin Castle   (1992)
Clonyn, Delvin
☎ (044) 96 64315
🖾 info@delvincastlegolf.com
📖 450
🖋 F Dillon
✓ D Keenaghan
⛳ 18 L 5818 m Par 70 SSS 68
👤 U SOC
££ €28 (€38)
🚗 15 miles NE of Mullingar (N52)
🏠 John Day
🖳 www.delvincastlegolf.com

Glasson Hotel   (1993)
Glasson, Athlone
☎ (090) 648 5120
🖾 info@glassongolf.ie

Moate   (1900)
Aghanargit, Moate
☎ (090) 648 1271
📟 (090) 648 2645
🖾 moategolfclub@eircom.net
📖 600
🖋 A O'Brien
⛳ 18 L 6294 yds SSS 70
👤 U SOC–WD Sun after 3pm
££ €30 – €10 with member (€35 – €15 with member)
🚗 Moate town centre
🏠 Bobby Browne
🖳 www.moategolfclub.ie

Mount Temple G&CC
   (1991)
Proprietary
Mount Temple, Moate
☎ (090) 648 1841

Mullingar   (1894)
Belvedere, Mullingar
☎ (0 0353 44) 9348366
📟 (0 0353 44) 9341495
🖾 mullingargolfclub@hotmail.com
📖 1,200
🖋 Ann McLoughlin (Sec/Mgr)
✓ John Burns
⛳ 18 L 6685 yds SSS 73
👤 U SOC
££ €40 (€45)
🚗 3 miles S of Mullingar on N52

🏠 James Braid/David Jones
🖳 www.mullingargolfclub.com

Co Wexford

Courtown   (1936)
Kiltennel, Gorey
☎ (055) 25166
🖾 courtown@aol.ie

Enniscorthy   (1907)
Knockmarshall, Enniscorthy
☎ (054) 921 3191
📟 (053) 923 7637
📖 1200
🖋 AP Colley
✓ M Sludds (053) 923 7600
⛳ 18 L 6115 m Par 72 SSS 72
👤 U–phone first SOC
££ Mon–Thur €30 (Fri–Sun + PH €40)
🚗 1½ miles SW of Enniscorthy on New Ross road, N30
⊕ Driving range; trollies; golf carts; on-line booking system
🏠 Eddie Hackett
🖳 www.enniscorthygc.ie

New Ross   (1905)
Tinneranny, New Ross
☎ (051) 421433
📟 (051) 420098
🖾 newrossgolf@eircom.net
📖 700
🖋 Kathleen Daly (Sec/Mgr) (051) 421433
⛳ 18 L 5751 m SSS 70
👤 U exc Sun SOC
££ €30 (€40)
🚗 1 mile W of New Ross
🖳 www.newrossgolfclub.net

Rosslare   (1905)
Rosslare Strand, Rosslare
☎ (053) 913 2113 (Clubhouse)
   (053) 913 2203 (Bookings)
📟 (053) 913 2263
🖾 office@rosslaregolf.com
📖 1000
🖋 JP Hanrick (Gen Mgr)
✓ J Young (053) 913 2032
⛳ 18 L 6782 yds Par 72 SSS 72
   12 L 3887 yds Par 46
👤 U SOC
££ 12: €20 18: €40 (€60)
🚗 10 miles S of Wexford. Rosslare Ferry 6 miles
⊕ Iron range; chipping green
🏠 Hawtree/Taylor/O'Connor Jr
🖳 www.rosslaregolf.com

St Helen's Bay   (1993)
St Helen's, Kilrane, Rosslare Harbour
☎ (053) 33234
🖾 sthelens@iol.ie

Tara Glen   (1993)
Ballymoney, Gorey, Co Wexford
☎ (053) 942 5413

📟 (053) 942 5612
🖾 taraglen@eircom.net
🖋 Marion Siggins
⛳ 9 L 5826 m Par 72 SSS 70
👤 U H SOC WD WE (not during June, July Aug)
££ €22
🚗 4 miles E of Gorey. 12 miles S of Arklow

Wexford   (1960)
Mulgannon, Wexford
☎ (053) 42238
📟 (053) 42243
🖾 info@wexfordgolfclub.ie
📖 805
🖋 Terry Ryan (Hon)
✓ Liam Bowler (053) 46300
⛳ 18 L 6338 yds Par 72 SSS 70
👤 U SOC
££ €32 (€38)
🚗 Wexford ½ mile
🏠 Jeff Howes
🖳 www.wexfordgolfclub.ie

Co Wicklow

Arklow   (1927)
Abbeylands, Arklow
☎ (0402) 32492
🖾 arklowgolflinks@eircom.net

Baltinglass   (1928)
Baltinglass
☎ (059) 648 1350
🖾 baltinglassgc@eircom.net

Blainroe   (1978)
Blainroe
☎ (0404) 68168
📟 (0404) 69369
🖾 blainroegolfclub@eircom.net
📖 1100
✓ J McDonald
⛳ 18 L 6175 m SSS 72
👤 U
££ €50 (€70)
🚗 3 miles S of Wicklow on coast
⊕ Putting green
🏠 FW Hawtree
🖳 www.blainrow.com

Boystown
Baltyboys, Blessington, Co Wicklow
☎ (045) 867146

Bray   (1897)
Greystones Road, Bray
☎ (01) 276 3200
📟 (01) 276 3262
🖾 info@braygolfclub.com
📖 808
🖋 Alan Threadgold (Gen Mgr)
✓ Ciaron Carroll
⛳ Men: Blue tees 18 L 5990 m Par 71 SSS 72
   White tees 18 L 5545 m Par 71 SSS 71

Yellow tees 18 L 5198 m Par 71
SSS 69
Ladies: Red tees 18 L 5077 m
Par 72 SSS 72
- U before 4.30pm SOC–WD
- €€ €35 (€55 Sat/Bank Hol) winter €50 (€70 Sat/Bank Hol) summer
- 12 miles S of Dublin
- Driving range; chipping green; putting green
- Des Smyth/Declan Brannigan
- www.braygolfclub.com

Charlesland G&CC   (1993)

Greystones
- ☎ **(01) 287 4350**
- 📠 (01) 287 4360
- 📧 teetimes@charlesland.com
- 📖 830
- Rosaleen Horan (Mgr) (01) 287 8200
- P Duignan
- 18 L 6739 yds Par 72 SSS 71
- U SOC
- €€ €50 (€60)
- 18 miles SE of Dublin, take Greystones exit on N11
- Full practice ground/range facilities
- Eddie Hackett
- www.charlesland.com

Delgany   (1908)

Delgany
- ☎ **(01) 287 4536**
- 📠 (01) 287 3977
- 📧 delganygolf@eircom.net
- 📖 1084
- Peter Ribeiro (Gen Mgr)
- G Kavanagh (01) 287 4697
- 18 L 5473 yds SSS 69
- U exc comp days SOC–Mon/Thurs/Fri
- €€ €45 (€55)
- 30 min from Dublin just off N11 to Wexford
- H Vardon/P Merrigan
- www.delganygolfclub.com

Djouce   (1995)

Roundwood
- ☎ **(01) 281 8585**

Druid's Glen   (1995)

Newtownmountkennedy
- ☎ **(01) 287 3600**
- 📠 (01) 287 3699
- 📧 info@druidsglen.ie
- 📖 250
- D Flinn (Gen Mgr)
- G Henry
- 18 L 7026 yds Par 71 SSS 74
- U SOC
- €€ €180
- 20 miles S of Dublin (N11)
- Golf Academy
- Craddock/Ruddy
- www.druidsglen.ie

Druid's Heath   (2003)

Newtownmountkennedy
- ☎ **(01) 287 3600**

- 📠 (01) 287 3699
- 📧 info@druidsglen.ie
- 📖 250
- D Flinn (Gen Mgr)
- G Henry
- 18 L 7434 yds Par 71 SSS 75
- U SOC
- €€ €130
- 20 miles S of Dublin (N11)
- Golf academy
- Pat Ruddy
- www.druidsglen.ie

The European Club   (1989)

Brittas Bay, Wicklow
- ☎ **(0404) 47415**
- 📠 (0404) 47449
- 📧 info@theeuropeanclub.com
- 📖 100
- P Ruddy
- None
- 18 L 7323 yds SSS 71
- H SOC
- €€ €80 – €150
- 30 miles S of Dublin, off N11
- Large practice area; pitching green; 3 putting greens
- Pat Ruddy
- www.theeuropeanclub.com

Glen of the Downs

Coolnaskeagh, Delgany, Co Wicklow
- ☎ **(01) 287 6240**
- 📠 (01) 287 0063
- 📧 info@glenofthedowns.com
- 📖 650
- James Murphy
- 18 L 5891 m Par 71
- U
- €€ Summer €65 (€80) – early bird rates also available Winter €65 (€50)
- Off N11, nr Delgany
- Peter McEvoy
- www.glenofthedowns.com

Glenmalure   (1993)

Greenane, Rathdrum
- ☎ **(0404) 46679**
- 📧 glenmal@glenmalure-golf.ie

Greystones   (1895)

Greystones
- ☎ **(01) 287 6624/4136**
- 📧 secretary@greystonesgc.com

Kilcoole   (1992)

Kilcoole
- ☎ **(01) 287 2066**
- 📧 adminkg@eircom.net

Old Conna   (1987)

Ferndale Road, Bray
- ☎ **(01) 282 6055**
- 📠 (01) 282 5611
- 📧 info@oldconna.com
- 📖 1000
- Tom Sheridan (Gen Mgr)
- M Langford (01) 272 0022

- 18 L 6551 yds SSS 72
- WD–U before 4pm WE/BH–NA SOC
- €€ €50 WD before 4pm
- 2 miles N of Bray. 12 miles S of Dublin
- Eddie Hackett
- www.oldconna.com

Powerscourt (East)   (1996)

Powerscourt Estate, Enniskerry
- ☎ **(01) 204 6033**
- 📠 (01) 276 1303
- 📖 627
- B Gibbons (Mgr)
- P Thompson
- East: 18 L 5858 m Par 72 SSS 72 West: 18 L 6345 m
- U
- €€ East: €130 West: €130
- Half hour outside Dublin city centre
- Driving range; putting green; chipping area; apartments; conference facilities
- Peter McEvoy/ David McLay Kidd
- www.powerscourt.ie

Powerscourt (West)   (2003)

Powerscourt Estate, Enniskerry
- ☎ **(01) 204 6033**
- 📠 (01) 276 1303
- B Gibbons (Mgr)
- P Thompson
- 18 L 5906 m Par 72 SSS 72
- U
- €€ €130
- Half an hour outside Dublin City Centre
- Driving range; putting green; chipping area; apartments; conference facilities
- David McLay Kidd
- www.powerscourt.ie

Rathsallagh   (1993)

Dunlavin
- ☎ **(045) 403316**
- 📠 (045) 403295
- 📧 info@rathsallagh.com golf@rathsallagh.com
- 📖 320
- J O'Flynn (045) 403316
- B McDaid (045) 403316
- 18 L 6885 yds Par 72 SSS 72
- U
- €€ Mon–Thur €60 (€75)
- 14 miles S of Naas (R412). Just off N9 and N81.
- Driving range; pitching and putting greens
- McEvoy/O'Connor Jr
- www.rathsallagh.com

Roundwood   (1995)

Ballinahinch, Newtownmountkennedy
- ☎ **(01) 281 8488**
- 📠 (01) 284 3642
- 📧 rwood@indigo.ie
- M McGuirk
- 18 L 6685 yds Par 72 SSS 72

For list of abbreviations, key to symbols and international dialling codes see page 651

U

£€ €38 (€55)

⌖ 2.5 miles from N11 at Druids Glen exit on R765

🖥 www.roundwoodgolf.com

Tulfarris (1987)

Blessington Lakes

☎ (045) 867644

🖷 (045) 867565

✉ golf@tulfarris.com

📖 300

✍ A Williams (Mgr)

⚒ Ray Williams

⛳ 18 L 7172 m SSS 74

U SOC

£€ €80 (€100)

⌖ 30 miles S of Dublin, off N81

⊕ Driving range

⌂ Patrick Merrigan

Vartry Lakes (1997)

Proprietary

Roundwood

☎ (01) 281 7006

Wicklow (1904)

Dunbur Road, Wicklow

☎ (0404) 67379

🖷 (0404) 64756

✉ info@wicklowgolfclub.ie

📖 550

✍ J Kelly

⚒ E McLoughlin (0404) 66122

⛳ 18 L 5695 m SSS 70

SOC–WD/Sat U–WD/Sat

£€ €40 (€45)

⌖ 30 miles S of Dublin, in Wicklow town off main N11 route

⌂ Craddock/Ruddy

🖥 www.wicklowgolfclub.ie

Woodenbridge (1884)

Vale of Avoca, Arklow

☎ (0402) 35202

✉ wgc@eircom.net

Scotland

Aberdeenshire

Aboyne (1883)

Formaston Park, Aboyne, AB34 5HP
- ☎ (013398) 86328
- 🖥 (013398) 87078
- ✉ aboynegolf@btconnect.com
- 📖 725 180(J)
- ✍ Mrs M Ferries (013398) 87078
- ⚐ S Moir (013398) 86328
- ▷ 18 L 5910 yds SSS 68
- ⚙ U
- ££ On application
- 🚗 E end of Aboyne. 30 miles W of Aberdeen (A93)
- 🖳 www.aboynegolfclub.co.uk

Aboyne Loch Golf Centre (2000)

Pay and play
Aboyne Loch, Aboyne, AB34 5BR
- ☎ (013398) 86444
- 🖥 (013398) 86488
- ✉ info@thelodgeontheloch.com
- 📖 50
- ✍ Derek McCulloch
- ▷ 9 L 2610 yds Par 34(68) SSS 65
- ⚙ U
- ££ £10 D–£14 (£12 D–£16)
- 🚗 1 mile east of Aboyne on A93
- 🏠 Derek McCulloch
- 🖳 www.thelodgeontheloch.com

Alford

Montgarrie Road, Alford, AB33 8AE
- ☎ (019755) 62178
- ✉ info@alford-golf-club.co.uk

Auchenblae (1894)

Pay and play
Auchenblae, Laurencekirk, AB30 1TX
- ☎ (01561) 320002 (Bookings)
- 📖 480
- ✍ J Thomson (01561) 320245
- ▷ 9 L 2217 yds Par 64 SSS 61
- ⚙ U phone for details of club activities
- ££ D–£10 (D–£12)
- 🚗 11 miles SW of Stonehaven. 3 miles W of A90

Ballater (1892)

Victoria Road, Ballater, AB35 5LX
- ☎ (013397) 55567
- ✉ sec@ballatergolfclub.co.uk
- 📖 700
- ✍ Jennifer or Irene
- ⚐ W Yule (013397) 55658
- ▷ 18 L 6094 yds SSS 69
- ⚙ U
- ££ On application
- 🚗 42 miles W of Aberdeen on A93
- 🖳 www.ballatergolfclub.co.uk

Ballindalloch Castle (2003)

Pay and play
Lagmore, Ballindalloch, Banffshire, AB37 9AA
- ☎ (01807) 500305
- 🖥 (01807) 500226
- ✉ golf@ballindallochcastle.co.uk
- ⚐ Alan Rodger
- ▷ 9 greens 18 tees L 6495 yds Par 72 SSS 71
- ⚙ WD & WE U & SOC
- ££ 9: £15 18: £20
- 🚗 Just off A95 between Grantown-on-Spey and Aberlour
- ⊕ Practice area (230 yds); putting green
- 🏠 Donald Steel and Tom Mackenzie
- 🖳 www.ballindallochcastle.co.uk

Banchory (1904)

Kinneskie Road, Banchory, AB31 5TA
- ☎ (01330) 822365
- 🖥 (01330) 822491
- ✉ info@banchorygolfclub.co.uk
- 📖 1000
- ✍ W Crighton
- ⚐ D Naylor (01330) 822447
- ▷ 18 L 5801 yds Par 69 SSS 68
- ⚙ WD–U WE–restricted
- ££ £26 (£35)
- 🚗 W of Banchory, off A93
- 🖳 www.banchorygolfclub.co.uk

Braemar (1902)

Cluniebank Road, Braemar, AB35 5XX
- ☎ (013397) 41618
- ✉ colin.mcintosh4@virgin.net
- 📖 450
- ✍ C McIntosh (01339) 741595
- ▷ 18 L 4916 yds SSS 64
- ⚙ U SOC WD WE
- ££ £20 D–£25 (£25 D–£30) W–£90
- 🚗 Braemar ½ mile. 17 miles W of Ballater
- 🏠 J Anderson
- 🖳 www.braemargolfclub.co.uk

Craibstone (1999)

Public
Craibstone Estate, Bucksburn, Aberdeen, AB29 9YA
- ☎ (01224) 716777
- ✉ craibstonegolf@sac.co.uk
- 📖 425
- ✍ Iain Buchan
- ⚐ Iain Buchan
- ▷ 18 L 5780 yds Par 69 SSS 69
- ⚙ WD–NA Weds after 4 pm WE–NA Sat before 10 am NA Sat between 12 noon and 2 pm SOC welcome 7 days a week H not required No jeans allowed
- ££ £17 D–£28 (£22 D–£35)
- 🚗 Off A96, 5 min from Dyce Airport

Cruden Bay (1899)

Cruden Bay, Peterhead, AB42 0NN
- ☎ (01779) 812285
- ✉ bookings@crudenbaygolfclub.co.uk
- 🖥 (01779) 812945
- ✉ secretary@crudenbaygolfclub.co.uk
- 📖 1070
- ✍ Mrs R Pittendrigh (Sec/Mgr)
- ⚐ RG Stewart (01779) 812414
- ▷ 18 L 6291 yds SSS 72 9 L 4926 yds SSS 64
- ⚙ WD–U WE–H exc comp days
- ££ £55 D–£80 (£70)
- 🚗 22 miles NE of Aberdeen (A90)
- ⊕ Driving range
- 🏠 Thomas Simpson
- 🖳 www.crudenbaygolfclub.co.uk

Cullen (1879)

The Links, Cullen, Buckie, AB56 4WB
- ☎ (01542) 840685
- ✉ cullengolfclub@btinternet.com
- 📖 625
- ✍ Mrs H Bavidge
- ⚐ None
- ▷ 18 L 4610 yds Par 63 SSS 62
- ⚙ U SOC
- ££ £17 D–£25 (£21 D–£28)
- 🚗 5 miles E of Buckie, off A98 between Aberdeen and Inverness
- 🏠 Tom Morris
- 🖳 www.cullengolfclub.co.uk

Duff House Royal (1910)

The Barnyards, Banff, AB45 3SX
- ☎ (01261) 812062
- 🖥 (01261) 812224
- ✉ duff-house-royal@btinternet.com
- 📖 547 167(L) 132(J)
- ✍ Mrs J Corbett
- ⚐ Gary Holland (01261) 812075
- ▷ 18 L 6161 yds SSS 70
- ⚙ WD–U H WE–H 8.30–11am and 12.30–3pm
- ££ £25–£32 (£31–£37) – 2006 rates
- 🚗 Moray Firth coast, between Buckie and Fraserburgh
- 🏠 Dr A & Maj CA Mackenzie
- 🖳 www.theduffhouseroyalgolfclub.co.uk

Fraserburgh (1777)

Philorth Links, Fraserburgh, AB43 8TL
- ☎ (01346) 516616
- 🖥 (01346) 516616
- ✉ george-young@btconnect.com
- 📖 642 56(L) 119(J)
- ✍ George M Young
- ▷ 18 L 6308 yds SSS 70 9 L 2400 yds Par 64
- ⚙ U SOC
- ££ £30 D–£35 (£35 D–£40)
- 🚗 1 mile SE of Fraserburgh
- ⊕ Practice area and practice putting green

⛳ James Braid
📧 www.fraserburghgolfclub.net

Huntly   (1892)
Cooper Park, Huntly, AB54 4SH
☎ **(01466) 792643**
📠 (01466) 792643
📧 huntlygc1@tiscali.co.uk
🛏 500
🏌 A Donald (01466) 792360
🏁 18 L 5399 yds Par 67 SSS 66
👥 U SOC
££ £16 D–£21 (£20 D–£27) W–£75
⛳ N side of Huntly. 38 miles NW of Aberdeen, off A96
📧 www.huntlygc.com

Inchmarlo   (1995)
Proprietary
Glassel Road, Banchory, AB31 4BQ
☎ **(01330) 826424**
📠 (01330) 826425
📧 info@inchmarlo.com
🏌 HG Emslie (Deputy MD) Andrew Shinie (Sec) (01330) 826422
🏌 P Lovie (01330) 826422
🏁 18 L 6218 yds Par 71 SSS 71
   9 L 4300 yds Par 64 SSS 62
👥 U SOC–WD
££ 9: £11 (£12) 18: £30 (£35)
⛳ ½ mile W of Banchory on A93
⊕ 30 bay floodlit driving range; practice putting green
⛳ Graeme Webster
📧 www.inchmarlo.com

Insch   (1906)
Golf Terrace, Insch, AB52 6JY
☎ **(01464) 820363**
📠 (01464) 820363
📧 inschgolfclub@tiscali.co.uk
🛏 400
🏌 A Hunter
🏁 18 L 5350 yds SSS 67
👥 U
££ £16 (£20) special offers on application
⛳ 28 miles NW of Aberdeen, off A96
⛳ Greens of Scotland
📧 www.insch4golf.com

Inverallochy
Public
Whitelink, Inverallochy, Fraserburgh, AB43 8XY
☎ **(01346) 582000**
🛏 400
🏌 GM Young
🏌 None
🏁 18 L 5300 yds SSS 66
👥 U
££ D–£15 (£20)
⛳ 4 miles E of Fraserburgh, off A92

Inverurie   (1923)
Davah Wood, Inverurie, AB51 5JB
☎ **(01467) 624080**
📠 (01467) 672869
📧 administrator@inveruriegc.co.uk
🛏 780

🏌 John Burns (01467) 624080
🏌 Steven McLean (01467) 672863
🏁 18 L 5711 yds SSS 68
👥 U SOC
££ £20 D–£24 (£24 D–£30)
⛳ Off the A96 at the Blackhall roundabout
📧 www.inveruriegc.co.uk

Keith   (1963)
Mar Court, Fife Keith, Keith, AB55 5GF
☎ **(01542) 882469**
📧 secretary@keithgolfclub.org.uk
🛏 250
🏌 Graeme Cruickshank
🏁 18 L 5802 yds SSS 69
👥 U
££ £15 D–£17 (£20 D–£22)
⛳ Fife Park, W side of Keith
📧 www.keithgolfclub.org.uk

Kemnay   (1908)
Monymusk Road, Kemnay, AB51 5RA
☎ **(01467) 642060 (Clubhouse)**
   (01467) 643746 (Office)
📠 (01467) 643746
📧 administrator@kemnaygolfclub.co.uk
🛏 820
🏌 Y Moir
🏌 R McDonald (01647) 642225
🏁 18 L 6362 yds Par 71 SSS 71
👥 U
££ £20 D–£26 (£24 D–£30)
⛳ 15 miles W of Aberdeen (B994, off A96)
📧 www.kemnaygolfclub.co.uk

Kintore   (1911)
Balbithan Road, Kintore, AB51 0UR
☎ **(01467) 632631**
📠 (01467) 632995
📧 kintoregolfclub@lineone.net
🛏 700
🏌 C Lindsay
🏁 18 L 6019 yds SSS 69
👥 U
££ £20 (£25)
⛳ 12 miles NW of Aberdeen on A96
📧 www.kintoregolfclub.net

Longside
West End, Longside, Peterhead, AB42 7XJ
☎ **(01779) 821558**
📠 (01779) 821564
🛏 750
🏌 K Allan (01771) 622424
🏌 None
🏁 18 L 5225 yds Par 66 SSS 66
👥 U exc Sun–NA before 10.30am SOC
££ £12 D–£16 Sun–£18 D–£22
⛳ 5 miles W of Peterhead on A590

Lumphanan   (1924)
10 Main Road, Lumphanan, Banchory, AB31 4PY
☎ **(013398) 83480**
📧 lumphanan.golf.club@lineone.net

McDonald   (1927)
Hospital Road, Ellon, AB41 9AW
☎ **(01358) 720576**
📠 (01358) 720001
📧 mcdonald.golf@virgin.net
🛏 750
🏌 G Gerrard
🏌 R Urquhart (01358) 722891
🏁 18 L 5991 yds Par 70 SSS 70
👥 U
££ On application
⛳ 15 miles N of Aberdeen, off A90
📧 www.mcdonaldellongolfclub.co.uk

Meldrum House   (1998)
Meldrum House Estate, Oldmeldrum, AB51 0AE
☎ **(01651) 873553**
📠 (01651) 873635
📧 info@meldrumhousegolfclub.co.uk
🛏 400
🏌 B Smith (Operations Mgr)
🏌 N Marr
🏁 18 L 6379 yds Par 70 SSS 72
👥 M
££ N/A
⛳ 11 miles N of Aberdeen on A947
⛳ Graeme Webster
📧 www.meldrumhousegolfclub.com

Newburgh-on-Ythan
   (1888)
Beach Road, Newburgh, Aberdeenshire, AB41 6BY
☎ **(01358) 789058**
📠 (01358) 788104
📧 secretary@newburgh-on-ythan.co.uk
🛏 400 40(L) 70(J)
🏌 H Marr (Administrator) (01358) 789084
🏌 Ian Bratton
🏁 18 L 6373 yds Par 72 SSS 71
👥 U exc Tues after 3pm & Sat before 1pm–NA
££ £25 (£30)
⛳ 12 miles N of Aberdeen (A975)
⊕ 4 hole practice course; putting green; nets
⛳ David Warrender
📧 www.newburgh-on-ythan.co.uk

Newmachar   (1989)
Swailend, Newmachar, Aberdeen, AB21 7UU
☎ **(01651) 863002**
📠 (01651) 863055
📧 info@newmachargolfclub.co.uk
🛏 1040
🏌 DS Wade
🏌 A Cooper (01651) 863222
🏁 18 L 6670 yds Par 72 SSS 74
   18 L 6388 yds Par 72 SSS 71
👥 H SOC
££ Hawkshill £35 (£50) Swailend £20 (£30)
⛳ 12 miles N of Aberdeen on A947
⊕ Driving range
⛳ Dave Thomas
📧 www.newmachargolfclub.co.uk

Oldmeldrum   (1885)

Kirk Brae, Oldmeldrum, AB51 0DJ
- ☎ **(01651) 872648/873555**
- 🖥 (01651) 873555
- 📖 800
- ✍ J Page (01651) 872315
- ✔ H Love (01651) 873555
- ⛳ 18 L 5988 yds Par 70 SSS 69
- 👥 WD–U before 5pm WE–phone first
- ££ £20 (D–£26)
- ⊶ 17 miles N of Aberdeen on A947

Peterhead   (1841)

Craigewan Links, Peterhead, AB42 1LT
- ☎ **(01779) 472149/480725**
- 🖥 (01779) 480725
- ✉ phdgc@freenetname.co.uk
- 📖 500 45(L)
- ⛳ 18 L 6173 yds SSS 71
  9 L 2237 yds SSS 62
- 👥 U exc Sat–restricted
- ££ On application
- ⊶ 1 mile N of Peterhead
- ⌂ Willie Park Jr/James Braid
- 🖳 www.peterheadgolfclub.co.uk

Rosehearty

c/o Mason's Arms Hotel, Rosehearty, Fraserburgh, AB43 7JJ
- ☎ **(01346) 571250 (Capt)**
- 🖥 (01346) 571306
- 📖 220
- ✍ S Hornal
- ✔ S Hornal (01346) 571250
- ⛳ 9 L 2197 yds SSS 62
- 👥 U
- ££ D–£10 (D–£12)
- ⊶ 4 miles W of Fraserburgh (B9031)
- ⊕ Driving range; tuition bays

Rothes   (1990)

Blackhall, Rothes, Aberlour, AB38 7AN
- ☎ **(01340) 831443**
- 🖥 (01340) 831443
- ✉ rothesgolfclub.co.uk
- 📖 340
- ✍ Kenneth MacPhee (01340) 831676
- ✔ None
- ⛳ 9 L 4972 yds Par 68 SSS 64
- 👥 U SOC
- ££ 9: £19 (£12) 18: £15 (£20)
- ⊶ ½ mile SW of Rothes. 10 miles S of Elgin on A941
- ⌂ John Souter
- 🖳 www.rothesgolfclub.co.uk

Royal Tarlair   (1926)

Buchan Street, Macduff, AB44 1TA
- ☎ **(01261) 832897**
- 🖥 (01261) 833455
- ✉ info@royaltarlair.co.uk
- 📖 520
- ✍ Mrs Muriel McMurray
- ⛳ 18 L 5866 yds SSS 68
- 👥 U
- ££ £15 D–£20 (£18–£22)
- ⊶ Macduff, 4 miles E of Banff. 45 miles E of Aberdeen
- 🖳 www.royaltarlair.co.uk

Stonehaven   (1888)

Cowie, Stonehaven, AB39 3RH
- ☎ **(01569) 762124**
- 🖥 (01569) 765973
- ✉ stonehaven.golfclub@virgin.net
- 📖 500
- ✍ WA Donald
- ✔ None
- ⛳ 18 L 5128 yds Par 66 SSS 65
- 👥 Sat–NA before 3.45pm Sun–NA before 10.45am
- ££ £18 (£20)
- ⊶ 1 mile N of Stonehaven
- ⌂ A Simpson

Strathlene   (1877)

Portessie, Buckie, AB56 2DJ
- ☎ **(01542) 831798**
- 🖥 (01542) 831798
- ✉ strathgolf@ukonline.co.uk
- 📖 375
- ✍ G Jappy
- ⛳ 18 L 5977 yds SSS 69
- 👥 U SOC
- ££ £16 D–£21 (£20 D–£27)
- ⊶ ½ mile E of Buckie
- ⊕ Driving range on site; pitch & putt and putting facilities
- ⌂ G Smith
- 🖳 www.strathlenegolfclub.co.uk

Tarland   (1908)

Aberdeen Road, Tarland, AB34 4TB
- ☎ **(013398) 81000**
- 🖥 (013398) 81000
- 📖 350
- ✍ Mrs J Joseph
- ⛳ 9 L 5875 yds SSS 68
- 👥 WD–U WE–enquiry advisable SOC–WD only
- ££ D–£18 (£24)
- ⊶ 5 miles NW of Aboyne. 30 miles W of Aberdeen
- ⌂ Tom Morris

Torphins   (1896)

Bog Road, Torphins, AB31 4JU
- ☎ **(013398) 82115**
- ✉ stuartmacgregor5@btinternet.com
- 📖 310
- ✍ S MacGregor (013398) 82402
- ⛳ 9 L 4777 yds SSS 64
- 👥 U SOC
- ££ £13 (£15); £8 for 9 holes
- ⊶ 1½ miles W of Torphins towards Lumphanan
- 🖳 www.torphinsgolfclub.com

Turriff   (1896)

Rosehall, Turriff, AB53 4HD
- ☎ **(01888) 562982**
- 🖥 (01888) 568050
- ✉ secretary@turriffgolf.sol.co.uk
- 📖 794
- ✍ GA Robertson
- ✔ C Mackie (01888) 563025
- ⛳ 18 L 6145 yds SSS 70
- 👥 WD–U before 5pm WE after 10am
- ££ £21 D–£25 (£25 D–£31)
- ⊶ 35 miles N of Aberdeen (A947)
- ⊕ Putting green; practice areas

- ⌂ GM Fraser
- 🖳 www.turriffgolfclub.com

Aberdeen Clubs

Bon Accord   (1872)

Club
19 Golf Road, Aberdeen, AB24 5QB
- ☎ **(01224) 633464**

Caledonian   (1899)

Club
20 Golf Road, Aberdeen, AB2 1QB
- ☎ **(01224) 632443**
- 📖 620
- ✍ JA Bridgeford
- ⛳ Play over King's Links

Northern   (1897)

Public
22 Golf Road, Aberdeen, AB24 5QB
- ☎ **(01224) 636440**
- 🖥 (01224) 622679
- 📖 561
- ✍ AW Garner
- ⛳ Play over King's Links Municipal
  18 L Medal 71 6270 yds, Yellow 67 5762 yds
- ££ £11.25
- ⊶ Alongside Pittodrie Stadium
- ⊕ Driving range 100 yds from tee

Aberdeen Courses

Auchmill   (1975)

Bonnyview Road, West Heatheryfold, Aberdeen, AB2 7FQ
- ☎ **(01224) 715214**
- 🖥 (01224) 715226
- ✉ auchmill.golfclub@virgin.net
- 📖 300
- ✍ G Adams (01224) 715214
- ✔ None
- ⛳ 18 L 5883 yds Par 70 SSS 68
- 👥 U
- ££ On application
- ⊶ 3 miles NW of Aberdeen city centre
- ⌂ Coles/Huggett

Balnagask   (1955)

Public
St Fitticks Road, Aberdeen
- ☎ **(01224) 871286**

Deeside   (1903)

Golf Road, Bieldside, Aberdeen, AB15 9DL
- ☎ **(01224) 869457**
- 🖥 (01224) 861800
- ✉ admin@deesidegolfclub.com
- 📖 1100
- ✍ Ms D Pern (01224) 869457
- ✔ FJ Coutts (01224) 861041
- ⛳ 18 L 6407 yds SSS 72
  9 L 5042 yds SSS 68

H
£€ £50 (£65)
🚗 3 miles SW of Aberdeen on A93
▤ www.deesidegolfclub.com

Fyvie   (2003)
Pay and play
Fyvie, Turriff, Aberdeenshire AB53 8QR
☎ (01651) 891166
🖷 (01651) 891166
✉ info@fyviegolfcourse.co.uk
📖 44
🏌 Alexander Rankin
↦ 9 L 5476 yds Par 35 SSS 67
H U SOC
£€ 9: £10 D–£20 (£12) 18: £14 D–£25
    (£17)
🚗 8 m south of Turriff off A947
🏠 Alexander Rankin & George McRae
▤ www.fyviegolfcourse.co.uk

King's Links
Public
*Golf Road, King's Links, Aberdeen,
AB24 5QB*
☎ (01224) 632269

Murcar Links   (1909)
Bridge of Don, Aberdeen, AB23 8BD
☎ (01224) 704354
🖷 (01224) 704354
✉ golf@murcarlinks.com
📖 850
🏌 Joanne Mitchell/Karen McKechnie
✎ Gary Forbes (01224) 704370
↦ 18 L 6325 yds SSS 71
    9 L 5369 yds SSS 67
H H
£€ £65 (£85) D–£90
🚗 5 miles N of Aberdeen, off A90
⊕ Driving range; practice facilities
🏠 Archie Simpson/James Braid
▤ www.murcarlinks.com

Peterculter   (1989)
*Oldtown, Burnside Road, Peterculter,
AB14 0LN*
☎ (01224) 735245
🖷 (01224) 735580
✉ info@petercultergolfclub.co.uk
📖 925
🏌 D Vannet
✎ D Vannet (01224) 734994
↦ 18 L 6219 yds SSS 70
H WD–U before 3pm WE–U SOC
£€ £22–£27 (£27–£35)
🚗 8 miles W of Aberdeen on A93
▤ www.petercultergolfclub.co.uk

Portlethen   (1983)
*Badentoy Road, Portlethen, Aberdeen,
AB12 4YA*
☎ (01224) 781090
🖷 (01224) 783383
✉ info@portlethengc.fsnet.co.uk
📖 1100
✎ Muriel Thomson (01224) 782571
↦ 18 L 6670 yds SSS 72
H WD–U exc Wed after 2pm
    Sat–NA before 4pm Sun–NA
    before 1pm

£€ £20 D–£30 (£30)
🚗 6 miles S of Aberdeen on A90
⊕ Driving range; putting green
🏠 Donald Steel
▤ www.portlethengolfclub.com

Royal Aberdeen   (1780)
*Links Road, Bridge of Don, Aberdeen, AB23
8AT*
☎ (01224) 702571
🖷 (01224) 826591
✉ admin@royalaberdeengolf.com
📖 350 100(J)
🏌 GF Webster
✎ R MacAskill (Golf Dir)
    (01224) 702221
↦ 18 L 6843 yds SSS 74
    18 L 4066 yds SSS 60
H I H SOC
£€ £80 D–£120 (£90)
🚗 2 miles N of Aberdeen on A90
⊕ Short game practice area
🏠 Simpson/Braid
▤ www.royalaberdeengolf.com

Westhill   (1977)
Westhill Heights, Westhill, AB32 6RY
☎ (01224) 742567
🖷 (01224) 749124
✉ westhillgolfclub@btinternet.com
📖 900
🏌 Amelia Burt (Admin)
✎ G Bruce (01224) 740159
↦ 18 L 5849 yds SSS 69
H WD–U before 4.30pm Sat Sun–U
£€ £14 D–£20 (£20 D–£25)
🚗 8 miles W of Aberdeen, off A944
🏠 Charles Lawrie
▤ www.westhillgolfclub.co.uk

Angus

Arbroath Artisan   (1903)
Public
Elliot, Arbroath, DD11 2PE
☎ (01241) 872069
    (01241) 875837 (Bookings)
🖷 (01241) 875837
✉ captain@arbroathartisangolfclub
    .co.uk
📖 650
🏌 RA Atkinson
✎ L Ewart (01241) 875837
↦ 18 L 6185 yds Par 70 SSS 69
H WD–U SOC WE–NA before 10am
£€ £20 D–£25 (£25 D–£35) 2006
    prices
🚗 1 mile SW of Arbroath on A92
🏠 James Braid
▤ www.arbroathartisangolfclub.co.uk

Ballumbie Castle
(2000)
3 Old Quarry Road, Dundee DD4 0SY
☎ (01382) 770028
🖷 (01382) 730008
✉ ballumbie2000@yahoo.com
📖 425
🏌 Steve Harrod

✎ Lee Sutherland
↦ 18 L 6157 yds Par 69 SSS 70
H U SOC
£€ £25 7 days a week
🚗 NE outskirts of Dundee, off A90 to
    Arbroath
⊕ 20-bay driving range with power
    tees; putting green; chipping green
▤ www.ballumbiecastlegolfclub.com

Brechin   (1893)
Trinity, Brechin, DD9 7PD
☎ (01356) 622383
🖷 (01356) 625270
✉ brechingolfclub@tiscali.co.uk
📖 750
🏌 IA Jardine
✎ S Rennie (01356) 625270
↦ 18 L 6137 yds SSS 70
H U SOC welcome 7 days
£€ £25 D–£33 (£30 D–£40)
🚗 1 mile N of Brechin on M90
⊕ Putting green/practice area
🏠 James Braid
▤ www.brechingolfclub.co.uk

Caird Park   (1926)
Public
Mains Loan, Caird Park, Dundee, DD4 9BX
☎ (01382) 453606/461460
    (01382) 438871 (Starter)
🖷 (01382) 461460
✉ cairdparkgolfclub@tiscali.co.uk
📖 280
🏌 G Martin (07800) 939876
✎ J Black (01382) 459438
↦ 18 L 6303 yds SSS 70
    Yellow 9 L 1692 yds SSS 29
    Red 9 L 1983 yds SSS 29
H U SOC
£€ Contact Starter
🚗 Off Kingsway by-pass, N of Dundee

Camperdown   (1960)
Public
Camperdown Park, Dundee, DD2 4TF
☎ (01382) 623398

Downfield   (1932)
Turnberry Ave, Dundee, DD2 3QP
☎ (01382) 825595
🖷 (01382) 813111
✉ downfieldgc@aol.com
📖 750
🏌 Mrs M Stewart
✎ KS Hutton (01382) 889246
↦ 18 L 6822 yds SSS 73
H WD–U 9.30–11.16 and
    2.18–3.42pm WE–limited access
    after 2pm (Sun only)
£€ 18 holes: £49 D–£59 36 hole
    package £69
🚗 N of Dundee, off A923
🏠 James Braid, CK Cotton
▤ www.downfieldgolf.co.uk

Edzell   (1895)
High St, Edzell, DD9 7TF
☎ (01356) 647283
🖷 (01356) 648094
✉ secretary@edzellgolfclub.net

📖 885
🏌 IG Farquhar (01356) 647283
✍ AJ Webster (01356) 648462
▷ 18 L 6367 yds SSS 71
  9 L 2057 yds Par 32
  West Water 9 hole course
  9 holes £12, 18 holes £16
👫 WD–NA 4.45–6.15pm WE–NA
  7.30–10am & 12–2pm SOC
££ £33 D–£40 (£40 D–£56)
🚗 6 miles N of Brechin on B966
⊕ Driving range
🏠 Bob Simpson
🖳 www.edzellgolfclub.net

Forfar (1871)

Cunninghill, Arbroath Road, Forfar,
DD8 2RL
☎ (01307) 463773/462120
🖥 (01307) 468495
✉ info@forfargolfclub.com
📖 885
🏌 D Wilson
✍ P McNiven (01307) 465683
▷ 18 L 6066 yds Par 69 SSS 70
👫 U (SOC: WD & Sun 10–11.30am
  and 2.30–4pm, Sat 2.30–4pm)
££ £24 D–£30 (£24 D–£30)
🚗 1½ miles E of Forfar on A932
🏠 Tom Morris/James Braid
🖳 www.forfargolfclub.com

Kirriemuir (1884)

Northmuir, Kirriemuir, DD8 4LN
☎ (01575) 573317

Letham Grange (1987)

Letham Grange, Colliston, Arbroath,
DD11 4RL
☎ (01241) 890377

Monifieth Golf Links

Medal Starter's Box, Princes Street,
Monifieth, DD5 4AW
☎ (01382) 532767 (Medal)
  (01382) 532967 (Ashludie)

Montrose (1562)

Public
Traill Drive, Montrose, DD10 8SW
☎ (01674) 672932
🖥 (01674) 671800
✉ secretary@montroselinks.co.uk
📖 1300
🏌 Mrs M Stewart
✍ J Boyd (01674) 672634
▷ Medal 18 L 6544 yds SSS 72
  Broomfield 18 L 4830 yds SSS 63
👫 Medal–WD–U Sat–NA before
  2.30pm Sun–NA before 10am
  Broomfield–U
££ Medal £42 (£46) Broomfield £20
  (£22)
🚗 1 mile from Montrose centre, off
  A92
⊕ Royal Montrose, Caledonia and
  Mercantile clubs play here
🏠 Willie Park (1903)
🖳 www.montroselinks.co.uk

Montrose Caledonia

(1896)
Club
Dorward Road, Montrose, DD10 8SW
☎ (01674) 672313
🏌 Mrs S Burness (01674 672416)
▷ Play over Montrose courses

Montrose Mercantile

Club
East Links, Montrose, DD10 8SW
☎ (01674) 672408

Panmure (1845)

Barry, Carnoustie, DD7 7RT
☎ (01241) 855120
🖥 (01241) 859737
✉ secretary@panmuregolfclub.co.uk
📖 500
🏌 Charles JR Philip (01241) 855120
✍ N Mackintosh
▷ 18 L 6330 yds Par 70 SSS 71
👫 WD/Sun–U Sat–NA before 4 pm
££ On application
🚗 2 miles W of Carnoustie, off A930
⊕ Practice range
🖳 www.panmuregolfclub.co.uk

Royal Montrose (1810)

Club
Dorward Road, Montrose, DD10 8SW
☎ (01674) 672376
🖥 (01674) 678125
✉ secretary@royalmontrosegolf.com
📖 650
🏌 Michael J Cummins (01674) 662045
✍ Jason Boyd
▷ Play over Montrose courses
££ See Montrose Golf Links
🚗 Adjacent to Montrose Medal 1st
  and 18th
🖳 www.royalmontrosegolf.com

Carnoustie Clubs

Carnoustie (1842)

Club
3 Links Parade, Carnoustie, DD7 7JE
☎ (01241) 852480
🖥 (01241) 856459
✉ admin@carnoustiegolfclub.com
📖 900
🏌 WH Law
▷ Play over Carnoustie courses
🖳 www.carnoustiegolfclub.com

Carnoustie Caledonia

(1887)
Club
Links Parade, Carnoustie, DD7 7JF
☎ (01241) 852115

Carnoustie Ladies (1873)

Club
12 Links Parade, Carnoustie, DD7 7JF
☎ (01241) 855252

Carnoustie Mercantile

(1896)
Club
Links Parade, Carnoustie, DD7 7JE
📖 40
🏌 GJA Murray (01241) 854420
▷ Play over Carnoustie courses

Dalhousie (1868)

Club
c/o Glencoe Hotel, Links Parade, Carnoustie,
DD7 7JF
☎ (01241) 853273

Carnoustie Courses

Buddon Links (1981)

Public
Links Parade, Carnoustie, DD7 7JE
☎ (01241) 853249 (Starter)
  (01241) 853789 (Bookings)
🖥 (01241) 853720
✉ golf@carnoustiegolflinks.co.uk
🏌 G Duncan
▷ 18 L 5420 yds SSS 66
👫 WD–U WE–U after 11.30am
££ £28
🚗 12 miles E of Dundee, by A92 or
  A930
⊕ Practice facilities
🏠 Peter Alliss/David Thomas
🖳 www.carnoustiegolflinks.co.uk

Burnside (1914)

Public
Links Parade, Carnoustie, DD7 7JE
☎ (01241) 855344 (Starter)
  (01241) 853789 (Bookings)
🖥 (01241) 853720
✉ golf@carnoustiegolflinks.co.uk
🏌 G Duncan
▷ 18 L 6028 yds SSS 70
👫 WD–U Sat–U after 2pm Sun–U
  after 11.30am
££ £33
🚗 12 miles E of Dundee, by A92 or
  A930
⊕ Practice facilities
🖳 www.carnoustiegolflinks.co.uk

Carnoustie Championship

(16th Century)
Public
Links Parade, Carnoustie, DD7 7JE
☎ (01241) 853249 (Starter)
  (01241) 853789 (Bookings)
🖥 (01241) 853720
✉ golf@carnoustiegolflinks.co.uk
🏌 G Duncan
▷ 18 L 6941 yds SSS 75
👫 WD–H Sat–H after 2pm Sun–H
  after 11.30am
££ £115
🚗 12 miles E of Dundee, by A92 or
  A930
⊕ Practice facilities
🖳 www.carnoustiegolflinks.co.uk

Argyll & Bute

Blairmore & Strone
(1896)
High Road, Strone, Dunoon, PA23 8JJ
- ☎ **(01369) 840676**
- ☐ 120
- ✍ JC Fleming (01369) 860307
- ⮞ 9 L 2122 yds SSS 62
- ⚲ Mon–NA after 6pm Sat–NA 12–4pm
- ££ D–£10
- ⮞⮞ Strone, 8 miles N of Dunoon
- ♔ James Braid

Bute   (1888)
32 Marine Place, Ardbeg, Rothesay, Isle of Bute PA20 0LF
- ☎ **(01700) 502158**
- ✉ info@butegolfclub.com
- ☐ 234
- ✍ F Robinson (01700) 502158
- ⮞ 9 L 2497 yds SSS 64
- ⚲ U Sat–U after 11.30am
- ££ D–£10; Juniors £5
- ⮞⮞ Stravanan Bay, 6 miles S of Rothesay, off A845
- 🖥 www.butegolfclub.com

Carradale   (1906)
Carradale, Campbeltown, PA28 6QT
- ☎ **(01583) 431321**
- ☐ 260
- ✍ Dr RJ Abernethy
- ✓ None
- ⮞ 9 L 2370 yds SSS 64
- ⚲ U
- ££ D–£15
- ⮞⮞ Carradale, 15 miles N of Campbeltown (B842)

Colonsay
Owned privately
Isle of Colonsay, PA61 7YR
- ☎ **(01951) 200290**
- ☐ (01951) 200290
- ☐ 200
- ✍ Eleanor McNeill (01951) 200210
- ⮞ 18 L 4775 yds Par 72
- ⚲ U
- ££ On application
- ⮞⮞ W coast of Colonsay, at Machrins

Cowal   (1891)
Ardenslate Road, Dunoon, PA23 8LT
- ☎ **(01369) 705673**
- ✉ secretary@cowalgolfclub.com

Craignure   (1895)
Scallastle, Craignure, Isle of Mull, PA65 6BA
- ☎ **(01688) 302517**
- ✉ pvnbook2@aol.com

Dalmally   (1986)
Old Saw Mill, Dalmally, PA33 1AS
- ☎ **(01838) 200370**
- ☐ 150
- ✍ R Johnston (01838) 200487

- ✓ None
- ⮞ 9 L 2277 yds Par 64 SSS 63
- ⚲ U SOC
- ££ D–£12
- ⮞⮞ 1 mile W of Dalmally on A85
- 🖥 www.loch-awe.com/golfclub

Dunaverty   (1889)
Southend, Campbeltown, PA28 6RW
- ☎ **(01586) 830677**
- ☐ (01586) 830677
- ✉ dunavertygc@aol.com
- ☐ 430
- ✍ James Robertson
- ⮞ 18 L 4799 yds SSS 63
- ⚲ U
- ££ £19 (£23)
- ⮞⮞ 10 miles S of Campbeltown

Gigha   (1992)
Isle of Gigha, Kintyre, PA41 7AA
- ☎ **(01583) 505242**
- ✉ golf@gigha.net
- ☐ 30
- ✍ J Bannatyne
- ⮞ 9 L 5042 yds SSS 65
- ⚲ U
- ££ D–£10
- ⮞⮞ Off W coast of Kintyre
- 🖥 www.gigha.org

Glencruitten   (1908)
Glencruitten Road, Oban, PA34 4PU
- ☎ **(01631) 562868**
- ✉ enquiries@obangolf.com
- ☐ 450
- ✍ AG Brown (01631) 564604
- ✓ Shop (01631) 564115
- ⮞ 18 L 4452 yds SSS 63
- ⚲ U
- ££ £25 D or R (£30 D or R)
- ⮞⮞ Oban 1 mile
- ⊕ Practice area; putting green
- ♔ James Braid
- 🖥 www.obangolf.com

Helensburgh   (1893)
25 East Abercromby Street, Helensburgh, G84 9HZ
- ☎ **(01436) 674173**
- ☐ (01436) 671170
- ✉ thesecretary@helensburghgolfclub.co.uk
- ☐ 863
- ✍ K Print (01436) 674173
- ✓ F Hall (01436) 675505
- ⮞ 18 L 5942 yds Par 69 SSS 69
- ⚲ WD–U WE–NA
- ££ £30 D–£40
- ⮞⮞ N of Helensburgh and A814. 8 miles W of Dumbarton
- ♔ Tom Morris
- 🖥 www.helensburghgolfclub.co.uk

Innellan   (1891)
Knockamillie Road, Innellan, Dunoon
- ☎ **(01369) 830242**
- ☐ 200
- ✍ A Wilson (01369) 702573
- ⮞ 9 L 4878 yds SSS 64

- ⚲ U SOC
- ££ 9: £10, 18: £13 (£15)
- ⮞⮞ 4 miles S of Dunoon (A815)

Inveraray   (1893)
North Cromalt, Inveraray, Argyll
- ☎ **(01499) 302079**

Islay   (1891)
25 Charlotte St, Port Ellen, Isle of Islay, PA42 7DF
- ☎ **(01496) 300094**

Isle of Seil   (1996)
Pay and play
Balvicar, Isle of Seil, PA34 4TL
- ☎ **(01852) 300348**
- ☐ (01852) 300392
- ✉ b.r.m@tesco.net
- ☐ 100
- ✍ B Mitchell
- ✓ None
- ⮞ 9 L 2141 yds Par 31
- ⚲ U
- ££ D–£10
- ⮞⮞ 13 miles S of Oban, Argyll. Take A816 to Kilniver then B844 to Balvica
- ♔ Donald Campbell

Kyles of Bute   (1906)
Tighnabruaich, PA21 2EE
- ☎ **(01700) 811603**
- ☐ 160
- ✍ Dr J Thomson
- ⮞ 9 L 2389 yds SSS 32
- ⚲ U
- ££ D–£10 (£10) Honesty box
- ⮞⮞ 26 miles W of Dunoon

Lochgilphead   (1963)
Blarbuie Road, Lochgilphead, PA31 8LE
- ☎ **(01546) 602340**
- ☐ 250
- ✍ R Foyle (01546) 510383
- ⮞ 9 L 4484 yds SSS 63
- ⚲ U SOC
- ££ D–£15 (D–£20)
- ⮞⮞ ½ mile N of Lochgilphead by Hospital
- 🖥 www.lochgilphead-golf.com

Lochgoilhead   (1994)
Drymsynie Estates, Lochgoilhead, PA24 8AD
- ☎ **(01301) 703247**

Machrihanish   (1876)
Machrihanish, Campbeltown, PA28 6PT
- ☎ **(01586) 810213**
- ☐ (01586) 810221
- ✉ secretary@machgolf.com
- ☐ 890 152(L) 150(J)
- ✍ Mrs A Anderson
- ✓ K Campbell (01586) 810277
- ⮞ 18 L 6225 yds SSS 71
  9 hole course
- ⚲ U
- ££ £40 D–£60 exc Sat £50 D–£75
- ⮞⮞ 5 miles W of Campbeltown

♞ Tom Morris
🖳 www.machgolf.com

Millport (1888)

Millport, Isle of Cumbrae, KA28 0HB
☎ (01475) 530311
🖥 (01475) 530306
📧 secretary@millportgolfclub.co.uk
📖 288 120(L) 78(J)
✍ William Reid (01475) 530306
✇ (01475) 530305
⯈ 18 L 5828 yds SSS 69
♟ U SOC
££ £22 D–£28 (£28 D–£35) W–£90
⛳ W of Millport (Largs car ferry)
♞ James Braid
🖳 www.millportgolfclub.co.uk

Port Bannatyne (1912)

Bannatyne Mains Road, Port Bannatyne, Isle of Bute, PA20 0PH
☎ (01700) 504544
📖 170
✍ J Bicker (01700) 504270
⯈ 13 L 5085 yds Par 68 SSS 65
♟ U
££ £15 (£18) – special packages available on website
⛳ 2 miles N of Rothesay
♞ Peter Morrison
🖳 www.portbannatynegolf.co.uk

Rothesay (1892)

Canada Hill, Rothesay, Isle of Bute, PA20 9HN
☎ (01700) 503554
📧 pro@rothesaygolfclub.com

Tarbert (1910)

Kilberry Road, Tarbert, PA29 6XX
☎ (01880) 820565
📖 101
✍ P Cupples (01546) 606896
⯈ 9 L 4460 yds SSS 63
♟ U SOC
££ D–£15
⛳ 1 mile W of Tarbert on B8024, off A83

Taynuilt (1987)

Taynuilt, PA35 1JE
☎ (01866) 822429
🖥 (01866) 822255 (phone first)
📧 michaelurwin152@btinternet.com
✍ MJP Urwin (Hon) (01866) 833341
⯈ 9 L 4510 yds Par 64 SSS 63
♟ U
££ £10 for 9 holes
⛳ 12 miles E of Oban on A85
🖳 www.taynuiltgolfclub.co.uk

Tobermory (1896)

Erray Road, Tobermory, Isle of Mull, PA75 6PS
☎ (01688) 302387
🖥 (01688) 302140
📧 secretary@tobermorygolfclub.com
📖 180
✍ J Weir (01688) 302338
⯈ 9 L 2492 yds SSS 64

♟ U
££ D–£16 W–£60
⛳ Tobermory, Isle of Mull
⊕ Tickets from Western Isles Hotel, Brown's shop and Ptarmigan clubhouse (Apr–Sep); practice ground and net
♞ David Adams
🖳 www.tobermorygolfclub.com

Ayrshire

Annanhill (1957)

Public
Irvine Road, Kilmarnock, KA3 2RT
☎ (01563) 521512 (Starter)
📖 350
✍ T Denham (01563) 521644/525557
⯈ 18 L 6270 yds SSS 70
♟ WD/Sat/Sun–U SOC–exc Sat
££ On application
⛳ 1 mile N of Kilmarnock
♞ J McLean

Ardeer (1880)

Greenhead Avenue, Stevenston, KA20 4LB
☎ (01294) 464542/465316
🖥 (01294) 465316
📖 700
✍ P Watson (01294) 465316
✇ P Forbes (Starter) (01294) 601327
⯈ 18 L 6409 yds SSS 71
♟ U exc Sat–NA SOC–WD
££ £25 D–£40 Sun–£35 D–£50
⛳ 1/2 mile N of Stevenston, off A78
♞ H Stutt

Auchenharvie (1981)

Public
Moor Park Road, West Brewery Park, Saltcoats, KA20 3HU
☎ (01294) 603103

Ballochmyle (1937)

Ballochmyle, Mauchline, KA5 6LE
☎ (01290) 550469
🖥 (01290) 553657
📧 secretary @ballochmylegolf.wanadoo.co.uk
📖 750
✍ RL Crawford
✇ None
⯈ 18 L 5952 yds SSS 69
♟ WD/WE–U BH–M SOC exc Sat
££ £20 D–£30 (£25 D–£35)
⛳ 1 mile S of Mauchline on B705, off A76

Beith (1896)

Threepwood Road, Beith, KA15 2JR
☎ (01505) 503166 (Clubhouse)
🖥 (01505) 506814
📧 beith_secretary@btconnect.com
📖 550
✍ M Murphy (01505) 506814 (am only)
⯈ 18 L 5625 yds SSS 68

♟ WD–U exc Tues 9–10.30am/4.30–6.30pm; Thur 9–10.30am; Sat–NA before 2pm; Sun–NA
££ £20 (£25)
⛳ Off Beith By-pass on A737
🖳 www.beithgolfclub.co.uk

Brodick (1897)

Brodick, Isle of Arran, KA27 8DL
☎ (01770) 302349
📧 secretary@brodickgolfclub.org

Brunston Castle (1992)

Golf Course Road, Dailly, Girvan, KA26 9GD
☎ (01465) 811471
🖥 (01465) 811545
📖 450
✍ F Mills
✇ S Smith
⯈ 18 L 6792 yds SSS 72
♟ U–booking necessary SOC
££ £28 D–£45
⛳ 4 miles E of Girvan
⊕ Driving range
♞ Donald Steel
🖳 www.brunstoncastle.co.uk

Caprington (1958)

Public
Ayr Road, Kilmarnock, KA1 4UW
☎ (01563) 53702 (Club)
(01563) 521915 (Starter)
📧 caprington.golf@btconnect.com
📖 400
✍ Jim Pearson (Club Sec) 07919 388517 Billy Richmond (Match Sec) 07803 592970
⯈ 18 L 5810 yds SSS 68
9 L 1731 yds SSS 30
♟ U
££ On application
⛳ 1 mile S of Kilmarnock (B7038)

Corrie (1892)

Corrie, Sannox, Isle of Arran, KA27 8JD
☎ (01770) 810223/810606
📖 270
✍ J Miles (01770) 850247
⯈ 9 L 1948 yds SSS 61
♟ U exc Thurs 12–2.30pm & Sat–NA
££ D–£15 W–£60
⛳ 6 miles N of Brodick

Dalmilling (1961)

Public
Westwood Avenue, Ayr, KA8 0QY
☎ (01292) 263893
🖥 (01292) 610543
📖 110
✍ Raymond Smith (01292) 289206
✇ P Cheyney (Golf Mgr)
⯈ 18 L 5724 yds SSS 68
♟ U – phone to book tee times
££ £14 D–£20 (£17.50 D–£27)
⛳ NE boundary of Ayr, nr Ayr racecourse

Doon Valley (1927)

I Hillside, Patna, Ayr, KA6 7JT
☎ **(01292) 531607**
🖂 (01292) 532489
📖 90
✍ H Johnstone
✓ None
🏳 9 L 5858 yds SSS 70
👤 U
££ £12
⚶ 8 miles SE of Ayr (A713)

Girvan (1860)

Public
Golf Course Road, Girvan, KA26 9HW
☎ **(01465) 714272/714346**
(Starter)
🖂 (01465) 714346
📖 170
✍ WB Tait
🏳 18 L 5095 yds SSS 64
👤 U
££ £13–£25
⚶ N side of Girvan (A77). 22 miles S of Ayr
🏠 James Braid

Glasgow GC Gailes (1892)

Gailes, Irvine, KA11 5AE
☎ **(01294) 311258**
🖂 (01294) 279366
✉ secretary@glasgow-golf.com
📖 1200
✍ DW Deas (0141) 942 2011 Fax (0141) 942 0770
✓ J Steven (01294) 311561
🏳 18 L 6535 yds Par 71 SSS 72
👤 WD WE/BH–NA before 2.30pm SOC
££ £60 D–£75 (£70)
⚶ 1 mile S of Irvine, off A78
⊕ Practice area
🏠 Willie Park Jr
🖥 www.glasgowgolfclub.com

Irvine (1887)

Bogside, Irvine, KA8 8SN
☎ **(01294) 275979**
📖 450
✍ W McMahon
✓ J McKinnon (01294) 275626
🏳 18 L 6408 yds SSS 71
👤 U SOC–WD
££ On application
⚶ 1 mile N of Irvine towards Kilwinning
🏠 James Braid

Irvine Ravenspark (1907)

Public
Kidsneuk Lane, Irvine, KA12 8SR
☎ **(01294) 271293**
✉ secretary@irgc.co.uk
📖 400
✍ M Murray (Sec) (01294) 213537
A Campbell (Steward) (01294) 271293
✓ P Bond (01294) 276467
🏳 18 L 6429 yds SSS 71
👤 U exc Sat–U after 2.30pm Apr–Sep only SOC

££ £16 D–£29
⚶ N side of Irvine, off A737. 7 miles N of Troon
🖥 www.irgc.co.uk

Kilbirnie Place (1922)

Largs Road, Kilbirnie, KA25 7AT
☎ **(01505) 683398**

Kilmarnock (Barassie) (1887)

29 Hillhouse Road, Barassie, Troon, KA10 6SY
☎ **(01292) 313920/311077**
🖂 (01292) 318300
✉ info@kbgc.co.uk
📖 600
✍ D Wilson (01292) 313920
J Howie (01292) 311322
🏳 18 L 6484 yds SSS 72
9 L 2888 yds SSS 34
👤 WD–U WE–NA before 2pm Sun only SOC–Mon/Tues & Thurs
££ D–£65 (£75)
⚶ Opp Barassie Railway Station
🏠 Theodore Moone
🖥 www.kbgc.co.uk

Lamlash (1889)

Lamlash, Isle of Arran, KA27 8JU
☎ **(01770) 600296 (Clubhouse)**
(01770) 600196 (Starter)
🖂 (01770) 600296
✉ lamlashgolfclub@connectfree.co.uk
📖 450
✍ J Henderson
✓ None
🏳 18 L 4510 yds SSS 64
👤 U SOC
££ On application
⚶ 3 miles S of Brodick on A841
🏠 Auchterlonie/Fernie
🖥 www.lamashgolfclub.co.uk

Largs (1891)

Irvine Road, Largs, KA30 8EU
☎ **(01475) 673594**
(Secretary's office)
🖂 (01475) 673594
✉ secretary@largsgolfclub.co.uk
📖 800
✍ J Callaghan (01475) 673594
✓ K Docherty (01475) 686192
🏳 18 L 6140 yds Par 70 SSS 71
👤 U SOC–WD
££ £35 D–£47 (£47)
⚶ 1 mile S of Largs on A78
🏠 JH Stutt
🖥 www.largsgolfclub.co.uk

Lochranza (1991)

Pay and play
Lochranza, Isle of Arran, KA27 8HJ
☎ **(0177083) 0273**
✉ office@lochgolf.demon.co.uk
✍ IM Robertson
🏳 18 L 5470 yds SSS 70
👤 U SOC–Apr–Oct
££ £18 (£18)
⚶ 14 miles N of Brodick

🏠 IM Robertson
🖥 www.lochranzagolf.com

Loudoun Gowf (1909)

Galston, KA4 8PA
☎ **(01563) 821993/820551**
🖂 (01563) 820011
✉ secy@loudoungowfclub.co.uk
📖 850
✍ WB Buchanan (01563) 821993
🏳 18 L 6005 yds SSS 69
👤 WE–NA WD–R 9–12 and 2–3 only
££ £25 D–£35
⚶ 5 miles E of Kilmarnock on A71
🖥 www.loudoungowfclub.co.uk

Machrie Bay (1900)

Machrie Bay, Brodick, Isle of Arran, KA27 8DZ
☎ **(01770) 850232**
🖂 (01770) 850247
📖 160
✍ PW Easley
✓ None
🏳 9 L 2200 yds Par 66 SSS 62
👤 U
££ D–£13 W–£65
⚶ 10 miles W of Brodick
⊕ Putting green; small practice area
🏠 William Fernie

Maybole (1970)

Public
Memorial Park, Maybole, KA19
☎ **(01655) 889770**

Muirkirk (1991)

Pay and play
c/o 65 Main Street, Muirkirk, KA18 3QR
☎ **(01290) 660184 (night)**
(01290) 570728 (day)
📖 100
✍ R Bradford
🏳 9 L 5366 yds SSS 66
👤 U SOC
££ £10
⚶ 12 miles W of M74 Junction 12 on A70

New Cumnock (1902)

Lochill, Cumnock Road, New Cumnock, KA18 4BQ
☎ **(01290) 338000**
📖 250
✍ J McGinn
🏳 9 L 2588 yds SSS 67
👤 U exc Sun am–NA
££ £8 D–£10
⚶ 1 mile W of New Cumnock
🏠 William Fernie

Prestwick (1851)

2 Links Road, Prestwick, KA9 1QG
☎ **(01292) 477404**
🖂 (01292) 477255
✉ bookings@prestwickgc.co.uk
📖 580
✍ IT Bunch
✓ DA Fleming (01292) 479483

☞ 18 L 6544 yds SSS 73 Medal
Course
18 L 6778 yds SSS 74
Championship Course
👥 WD/Sun–I on application only
££ £110 D–£165
🚗 Prestwick Airport I mile, nr
Railway Station
🏠 Tom Morris
📧 www.prestwickgc.co.uk

Prestwick St Cuthbert
(1899)
East Road, Prestwick, KA9 2SX
☎ **(01292) 477101**
🖥 (01292) 671730
📧 secretary@stcuthbert.co.uk
📖 865
🎣 Jim Jess
☞ 18 L 6470 yds SSS 71
👥 WD–U WE/BH–M SOC–WD
££ £30 D–£40
🚗 ¹/₂ mile E of Prestwick
📧 www.stcuthbert.co.uk

Prestwick St Nicholas
(1851)
Grangemuir Road, Prestwick, KA9 ISN
☎ **(01292) 477608**
🖥 (01292) 473900
📧 secretary@prestwickstnicholas
.com
📖 600 155(L) 68(J)
🎣 Tom Hepburn
✓ Starter (01292) 473904
☞ 18 L 5952 yds SSS 69
👥 WD–U WE–NA exc Sun pm
££ £55 D–£65 Sun pm–£60
🚗 Prestwick
🏠 C Hunter
📧 www.prestwickstnicholas.com

Routenburn
(1914)
Greenock Road, Largs, KA30 9AH
☎ **(01475) 673230 – public**
(01475) 686475 – steward
📖 350
🎣 RB Connal (Mgr)
(01475) 672757
✓ G McQueen (01475) 687240
☞ 18 L 5650 yds SSS 68
👥 U–phone Pro SOC–WD/WE
££ £16.50
🚗 N of Largs, off A78
⊕ Routenburn GC is a private club
attached to a public course
🏠 James Braid

Royal Troon
(1878)
Craigend Road, Troon, KA10 6EP
☎ **(01292) 311555**
🖥 (01292) 318204
📧 admin@royaltroon.com
📖 800
🎣 JW Chandler
✓ RB Anderson (01292) 313281
☞ Old 18 L 7150 yds SSS 74
Portland 18 L 6289 yds SSS 75
👥 Booking required – h/cap limit:
men 20, ladies 30. Mon/Tues/Thurs
only–H

££ Old + Portland D–£220 (incl
Lunch). Portland D–£125 (inc
Lunch)
🚗 SE of Troon (B749). Prestwick
Airport 3 miles
⊕ Practice range
🏠 W Fernie
📧 www.royaltroon.com

Seafield
(1930)
Public
*Belleisle Park, Doonfoot Road, Ayr,
KA7 4DU*
☎ **(01292) 441258**
🖥 (01292) 442632
📧 info@ayrseafieldgolfclub.co.uk
📖 105
🎣 Brian Milligan (01292) 445144
✓ David Gemmell (01292) 441314
☞ 18 L 5498 yds SSS 67
👥 U
££ £17.50 (£20)
🚗 S of Ayr in Belleisle Park
🏠 James Braid
📧 www.ayrseafieldgolfclub.co.uk

Shiskine
(1896)
*Shiskine, Blackwaterfoot, Isle of Arran,
KA27 8HA*
☎ **(01770) 860226**
🖥 (01770) 860205
📧 info@shiskinegolf.com
📖 550 154(L) 42(J)
🎣 Mrs F Crawford (Mgr)
(01770) 860548
☞ 12 L 2990 yds SSS 42
👥 U SOC
££ £15 D–£25 (£19 D–£30)
🚗 11 miles SW of Brodick
⊕ Putting green
🏠 Willie Fernie
📧 www.shiskinegolf.com

Skelmorlie
(1891)
Skelmorlie, PA17 5ES
☎ **(01475) 520152**
📖 429
🎣 Mrs Ellen Linton (Hon)
☞ 18 L 5030 yds SSS 65
👥 U exc Sat (Apr–Oct)
££ D–£20 Sun–£25
🚗 Wemyss Bay Station 1¹/₂ miles
🏠 James Braid
📧 www.skelmorliegolf.co.uk

Troon Municipal
Public
Harling Drive, Troon, KA10 6NF
☎ **(01292) 312464**
🖥 (01292) 312578
✓ G McKinlay
☞ Lochgreen 18 L 6785 yds SSS 73
Darley 18 L 6501 yds SSS 72
Fullarton 18 L 4822 yds SSS 63
👥 U SOC
££ Lochgreen £19–£31. Darley
£15–£29. Fullarton £13–£25
🚗 4 miles N of Prestwick at Station
Brae

Troon Portland
(1894)
Club
I Crosbie Road, Troon KA10
☎ **(01292) 313488**
📖 120
🎣 R McEwan (01292) 313602
☞ Play over Portland at Royal
Troon

Troon St Meddans
(1909)
Club
Harling Drive, Troon, KA10 6NF
📧 troonstmeddans@btinternet.com
📖 264
🎣 John Dedholm (01560) 482748
☞ Play over Troon Municipal courses
Lochgreen and Darley

Turnberry Hotel
(1906)
Turnberry, KA26 9LT
☎ **(01655) 331000**
🖥 (01655) 331069
📧 turnberry.reservations@westin
.com
📖 440
🎣 Paul Burley (Golf Dir)
(01655) 334000
✓ Paul Burley (01655) 334000
☞ Ailsa 18 L 6976 yds SSS 73
Kintyre 18 L 6861 yds SSS 72
Arran 9 L 1996 yds Par 31
👥 On application
££ On application
🚗 18 miles S of Ayr on A77
⊕ Colin Montgomerie Links Golf
Academy
🏠 Ailsa-Mackenzie Ross. Kintyre-
Donald Steel
📧 www.westin.com/turnberry

West Kilbride
(1893)
*Fullerton Drive, Seamill, West Kilbride,
KA23 9HT*
☎ **(01294) 823911**
🖥 (01294) 829573
📧 golf@westkilbridegolfclub.com
📖 900
🎣 H Armour
✓ G Ross (01294) 823042
☞ 18 L 6452 yds SSS 71
👥 WD–U WE–M BH–NA SOC
££ On application
🚗 West Kilbride
🏠 Old Tom Morris/James Braid
📧 www.westkilbridegolfclub.com

Western Gailes
(1897)
Gailes, Irvine, KA11 5AE
☎ **(01294) 311649**
🖥 (01294) 312312
📧 enquiries@westerngailes.com
📖 450
🎣 IF Sproule
☞ 18 L 6639 yds SSS 74
👥 WD–H Mon/Wed/Fri only
(booking necessary) Sun pm
££ £100 D–£150 Sun pm–£110
(2007 tba)
🚗 3 miles N of Troon (A78), Marine
Drive

For list of abbreviations and key to symbols see page 651

⊕ Practice, chipping and bunker area;
putting green
▤ www.westerngailes.com

Whiting Bay (1895)
Golf Course Road, Whiting Bay, Isle of Arran, KA27 8PR
☎ **(01770) 700487**
✉ m.auld@connectfree.co.uk
▥ 290
✍ Mrs M Auld (01770) 820208
► 18 L 4405 yds SSS 63
♔ U
££ On application
⇌ 8 miles S of Brodick

Borders

Duns (1894)
Hardens Road, Duns, TD11 3NR
☎ **(01361) 882194**
🖷 (01361) 883599
✉ secretary@dunsgolfclub.com
▥ 400
✍ A Preston (01361) 882194
✓ None
► 18 L 6298 yds Par 71 SSS 70
♔ U SOC WD WE
££ £25 D–£32 (£30 D–£38)
⇌ 1 mile W of Duns, off A6105
⊕ Driving range 2 miles S of course
🏠 EH Scott
▤ www.dunsgolfclub.com

Eyemouth (1894)
Gunsgreen House, Eyemouth, TD14 5DX
☎ **(018907) 50551**
(Clubhouse)

Galashiels (1884)
Ladhope Recreation Ground, Galashiels, TD1 2NJ
☎ **(01896) 753724**

Hawick (1877)
Vertish Hill, Hawick, TD9 0NY
☎ **(01450) 372293**
🖷 (01450) 375594
✉ thesecretary@hawickgolfclub.fsnet .co.uk
▥ 600
✍ J Reilly
► 18 L 5929 yds SSS 69
♔ U
££ £27
⇌ 46 miles from M6 at Carlisle. 50 miles S of Edinburgh

The Hirsel (1948)
Kelso Road, Coldstream, TD12 4NJ
☎ **(01890) 882678**
🖷 (01890) 882233
✉ bookings@hirselgc.co.uk
▥ 700
✍ Mrs Diane Nichol
► 18 L 6024 yds SSS 70
♔ U SOC
££ £30 (£36)

⇌ ½ mile W of Coldstream (A697)
▤ www.hirsel.co.uk

Jedburgh (1892)
Dunion Road, Jedburgh, TD8 6TA
☎ **(01835) 863587**
🖷 (01835) 862360
✉ jedburgh-golfclub@btinternet.com
▥ 300
✍ H Hogg (01835) 862851
► 9 L 5700 yds Par 68 SSS 67
♔ U
££ £22 (£25) per round or day
⇌ Jedburgh 1 mile (signs from centre)
🏠 Willie Park
▤ www.tweeddalepress.co.uk

Kelso (1887)
Golf Course Road, Kelso, TD5 7SL
☎ **(01573) 223009**
✉ golf@kelsogc.fsnet.co.uk

Langholm (1892)
Langholm, DG13 0JR
☎ **(07724) 875151**
✉ golf@langholmgolfclub.co.uk
▥ 150
✍ WT Goodfellow
► 9 L 3090 yds SSS 69
♔ U
££ £10 (£10)
⇌ 21 miles N of Carlisle on A7
▤ www.langholmgolfclub.co.uk

Lauder (1896)
Pay and play
Galashiels Road, Lauder, TD2 6RS
☎ **(01578) 722526**
🖷 (01578) 722526
✉ secretary@laudergolfclub.co.uk
▥ 250
✍ D Dickson (01578) 722526
✓ Craig Lumsden (07759) 591252
► 9 L 6050 yds Par 72 SSS 69
♔ U SOC
££ £15 (£15)
⇌ ½ mile W of Lauder
⊕ Practice fairway
🏠 W Park Jr
▤ www.laudergolfclub.co.uk

Melrose (1880)
Dingleton Road, Melrose, TD6 9HS
☎ **(01896) 822855**
🖷 (01896) 822855
✉ melrosegolfclub@tiscali.co.uk
▥ 360
✍ LM Wallace (01835) 823553
► 9 L 5562 yds Par 70 SSS 68
♔ U exc during competitions
££ £20 D–£20
⇌ S boundary of Melrose, off A68
🏠 James Braid

Minto (1928)
Denholm, Hawick, TD9 8SH
☎ **(01450) 870220**
🖷 (01450) 870126
✉ mintogolfclub@btconnect.com
▥ 500

✍ J Simpson
✓ None
► 18 L 5542 yds SSS 67
♔ H SOC WD–U WE–certain times
££ £27 (£30)
⇌ Minto near Denholm. 6 miles E of Hawick along A698
▤ www.mintogolf.co.uk

Newcastleton (1894)
Holm Hill, Newcastleton, TD9 0QD
☎ **(013873) 75608**
✍ GA Wilson
✓ None
► 9 L 5491 yds Par 69 SSS 70
♔ U SOC
££ £12 D–£12 (£12) 9 holes half price
⇌ W of Newcastleton, off B6357 (via A7). M6 Junction 44
🏠 John Shade

Peebles (1892)
Kirkland Street, Peebles, EH45 8EU
☎ **(01721) 720197**
✉ secretary@peeblesgolfclub.co.uk
▥ 650
✍ H Gilmore
✓ C Imlah
► 18 L 6160 yds SSS 70
♔ SOC WD–U WE–Sun only
££ From £25 (£30) Group discounts apply
⇌ 23 miles S of Edinburgh, via A703
⊕ Buggy hire
🏠 James Braid/HS Colt
▤ www.peeblesgolfclub.co.uk

The Roxburghe Hotel (1997)
Heiton, Kelso, TD5 8JZ
☎ **(01573) 450331**
✉ golf@roxburghe.net

Selkirk (1883)
The Hill, Selkirk, TD7 4NW
☎ **(01750) 20621**
(01750) 20857 (Bookings)
✉ secretary@selkirkgolfclub.co.uk
▥ 300
✍ JM Hay
► 9 L 5560 yds SSS 68
♔ WD–U exc Mon pm WE–phone first SOC
££ D–£20 (£20) 9 holes £10 (£10)
⇌ 1 mile S of Selkirk on A7
🏠 Willie Park

St Boswells (1899)
St Boswells, Melrose, TD6 0DE
☎ **(01835) 823527**
🖷 (01835) 823527
✉ secretary@stboswellsgolfclub.co.uk
▥ 320
✍ JG Phillips
► 9 L 5274 yds SSS 66
♔ U SOC
££ £20 D–£24 (D–£20)
⇌ Off A68 at St Boswells Green, by River Tweed
🏠 Willie Park/Shade

Torwoodlee (1895)

Edinburgh Road, Galashiels, Torwoodlee, TD1 2NE
- ☎ **(01896) 752260**
- 🖳 (01896) 752306
- ✉ thesecretary@torwoodleegolfclub.org.uk
- 📖 550
- ✍ A Owenson
- ⊢ 18 L 6021 yds Par 69 SSS 70
- 👥 WD–U from 9.30am–12.30pm and after 1.30pm exc Thurs–NA from 9.30–10.14 & 4–6pm WE–by arrangement SOC
- ££ £26 D–£36 (£32 D–£42)
- 🚗 1 mile N of Galashiels on A7
- 🏠 Willie Park
- 📧 www.torwoodleegolfclub.org.uk

Woll (1993)

Proprietary
New Woll Estate, Ashkirk, Selkirkshire, TD7 4PE
- ☎ **(01750) 32711**
- ✉ wollgolf@btinternet.com
- 📖 475
- ✍ Nicholas Brown (01750) 32711
- ⊢ 18 L 6051 yds Par 70 SSS 69
- 👥 U SOC
- ££ £26 D–£32 (£26 D–£32)
- 🚗 Ashkirk, just off A7 between Selkirk and Hawick
- ⊕ Driving range nearby; accommodation on site
- 📧 www.wollgolf.co.uk

Clackmannanshire

Alloa (1891)

Schawpark, Sauchie, Alloa, FK10 3AX
- ☎ **(01259) 722745**
- 🖳 (01259) 218796
- ✉ alloagolf2@tiscali.co.uk
- 📖 550 80(L) 130(J)
- ✍ T Crampton (Admin)
- ✓ W Bennett (01259) 724476
- ⊢ 18 L 6229 yds Par 70 SSS 71
- 👥 WD–U WE–parties restricted
- ££ £26 D–£30 (£36 D–£40)
- 🚗 Sauchie, N of Alloa on A908
- 🏠 James Braid
- 📧 www.alloagolfclub.co.uk

Alva

Beauclerc Street, Alva, FK12 5LH
- ☎ **(01259) 760431**
- 📖 320
- ⊢ 9 L 2423 yds SSS 64
- 👥 U
- ££ On application
- 🚗 Back Road, Alva, on A91 Stirling-St Andrews road. Signs to Alva Glen

Braehead (1891)

Cambus, Alloa, FK10 2NT
- ☎ **(01259) 725766**
- 🖳 (01259) 214070
- ✉ braehead.gc@btinternet.com
- 📖 800
- ✍ Ronald Murray
- ✓ Jamie Stevenson (01259) 722078
- ⊢ 18 L 6053 yds SSS 70
- 👥 U–booking necessary SOC
- ££ £24 D–£32 (£32 D–£40)
- 🚗 2 miles W of Alloa (A907)
- ⊕ Small practice area
- 🏠 Robert Tait
- 📧 www.braehead.gc.co.uk

Dollar (1890)

Brewlands House, Dollar, FK14 7EA
- ☎ **(01259) 742400**
- 🖳 (01259) 743497
- ✉ info@dollargolfclub.com
- 📖 375
- ✍ WS Morrison/J Crossan
- ⊢ 18 L 5242 yds SSS 66
- 👥 U SOC
- ££ £13.50 D–£17.50 (£22)
- 🚗 Dollar, off A91
- 🏠 Ben Sayers
- 📧 www.dollargolf.com

Tillicoultry (1899)

Alva Road, Tillicoultry, FK13 6BL
- ☎ **(01259) 750124**
- 🖳 (01259) 750124
- ✉ golf@tillygc.freeserve.co.uk
- 📖 400
- ✍ M Todd
- ⊢ 9 L 2761 yds SSS 67
- 👥 WD/WE–U SOC
- ££ £12 (£17)
- 🚗 9 miles E of Stirling on A91

Tulliallan (1902)

Kincardine, Alloa, FK10 4BB
- ☎ **(01259) 730396**
- 🖳 (01259) 733950
- ✉ tulliallangolf@btconnect.com
- 📖 600 50(L) 50(J)
- ✍ Amanda Aitken
- ✓ S Kelly (01259) 730798
- ⊢ 18 L 5982 yds SSS 69
- 👥 U exc comp days
- ££ £20 D–£35 (£25 D–£42)
- 🚗 5 miles SE of Alloa
- 📧 www.tulliallangolf.co.uk

Dumfries & Galloway

Brighouse Bay (1999)

Pay and play
Borgue, Kirkcudbright, DG6 4TS
- ☎ **(01557) 870509**
- ✉ admin@brighousebaygolfclub.co.uk

Castle Douglas (1905)

Abercromby Road, Castle Douglas, DG7 1BA
- ☎ **(01556) 502801**
- 🖳 (01556) 502509
- ✉ cdgolfclub@aol.com
- 📖 300
- ✍ J Greenfield (01556) 502509
- ⊢ 9 L 6254 yds SSS 71
- 👥 WD–U before 4pm Tue+Thur WE–U SOC
- ££ D–£15 (2006 price)
- 🚗 Off A75/A713, NE of Castle Douglas
- 📧 www.cdgolf.co.uk

Colvend (1905)

Sandyhills, Dalbeattie, DG5 4PY
- ☎ **(01556) 630398**
- 🖳 (01556) 630495
- ✉ sec.@colvendgolfclub.co.uk
- 📖 500
- ✍ JB Henderson
- ⊢ 18 L 5200 yds SSS 67
- 👥 U
- ££ D–£25
- 🚗 6 miles S of Dalbeattie on A710
- 🏠 Fernie/Soutar
- 📧 www.colvendgolfclub.co.uk

Crichton (1884)

Bankend Road, Dumfries, DG1 4TH
- ☎ **(01387) 247894**
- 🖳 (01387) 257616
- ✉ admin@crichton.co.uk
- 📖 400
- ⊢ 9 L 2903 yds SSS 69
- 👥 WD–U before 3pm SOC
- ££ £18.50 (£18.50)
- 🚗 1 mile from Dumfries, nr Hospital

Dalbeattie (1894)

19 Maxwell Park, Dalbeattie, DG5 4LR
- ☎ **(01556) 611421/610666**
- 🖳 (01556) 612247
- ✉ ocm@associates.ltd.fsnet.co.uk
- 📖 300
- ✍ BC Moor (01556) 610666
- ✓ None
- ⊢ 9 L 5710 yds SSS 68
- 👥 U SOC
- ££ 18: £16; 9: £10; D–£20
- 🚗 14 miles SW of Dumfries on A711/B794
- ⊕ Practice ground; putting green
- 🏠 OCM Golf Design
- 📧 www.dalbeattiegc.co.uk

Dumfries & County (1912)

Nunfield, Edinburgh Road, Dumfries, DG1 1JX
- ☎ **(01387) 253585**
- 🖳 (01387) 253585
- ✉ dumfriesc@aol.com
- 📖 620 120(J)
- ✍ BRM Duguid (01387) 253585
- ✓ S Syme (01387) 268918
- ⊢ 18 L 5918 yds Par 69 SSS 69
- 👥 WD–U ex 11.30–2pm–NA Sat–NA Sun–NA before 10am
- ££ £30 D–£40 (Sun £35 D–£45)
- 🚗 1 mile NE of Dumfries, on A701
- 🏠 W Fernie
- 📧 www.thecounty.org.uk

Dumfries & Galloway (1880)

2 Laurieston Avenue, Maxwelltown, Dumfries, DG2 7NY
- ☎ **(01387) 253582**

(01387) 263848
info@dandggolfclub.co.uk
750
AT Miller (01387) 263848
J Fergusson (01387) 256902
18 L 6309 yds Par 70 SSS 71
U
£27 (£33)
Dumfries
Willie Fernie
www.dandggolfclub.co.uk

Gatehouse   (1921)

Lauriston Road, Gatehouse of Fleet, Castle Douglas, DG7 2BE
☎ (01557) 814766
   (Clubhouse – unmanned)
300
(01644) 450260
9 L 2521 yds SSS 66
WD–U WE–not before noon Sun
£ D–£15 (D–£15)
¾ mile N of Gatehouse, off A75. 9 miles NW of Kirkcudbright

Hoddom Castle   (1973)

Pay and play
Hoddom Bridge, Ecclefechan, DG11 1AS
☎ (01576) 300251
(01576) 300757
hoddomcastle@aol.com
G Condron
9 L 2274 yds SSS 33
U
£8.10 (£12)
2 miles SW of Ecclefechan on B725. M74 J19
David Rothwell
www.hoddomcastle.co.uk

Kirkcudbright   (1893)

Stirling Crescent, Kirkcudbright, DG6 4EZ
☎ (01557) 330314
(01557) 330314
david@kirkcudbrightgolf.co.uk
500
DA MacKenzie
18 L 5739 yds SSS 69
U after 10 am H–phone first SOC
£22 D–£27
½ mile from Kirkcudbright town centre
www.kirkcudbrightgolf.co.uk

Lochmaben   (1926)

Castlehill Gate, Lochmaben, DG11 1NT
☎ (01387) 810552
lgc@naims.co.uk
670
JM Dickie
18 L 5933 yds SSS 70
WD–U before 5pm WE–U exc comp days SOC
£28 D–£33 (£30 D–£38)
4 miles W of Lockerbie on A709. 8 miles NE of Dumfries
James Braid
www.lochmabengolf.co.uk

Lockerbie   (1889)

Corrie Road, Lockerbie, DG11 2ND
☎ (01576) 203363
(01576) 203363
enquiries@lockerbiegolf
430
J Thomson
18 L 5418 yds SSS 67
U exc Sun–NA before 11.30am
£22 (£25)
½ mile NE of Lockerbie, on Corrie road
James Braid

Moffat   (1884)

Coatshill, Moffat, DG10 9SB
☎ (01683) 220020
bookings@moffatgolfclub.co.uk
380
J Rogers (01683) 220020
None
18 L 5259 yds Par 69 SSS 67
U exc Wed–NA after 3pm SOC
£20 D–£28 (£30 D–£36)
A74(M) Junction 15. Follow signs to Moffat
Ben Sayers
www.moffatgolfclub.co.uk

New Galloway   (1902)

New Galloway, Dumfries, DG7 3RN
☎ (01644) 450685

Newton Stewart   (1981)

Kirroughtree Avenue, Minnigaff, Newton Stewart, DG8 6PF
☎ (01671) 402172
enquiries@newtonstewartgolfclub.com
380
R McClymont
18 L 5840 yds Par 69 SSS 70
U
£25 D–£33 (£28 D–£36)
E of Newton Stewart, off A75
Nets & practice area
www.newtonstewartgolfclub.com

Pines Golf Centre   (1998)

Pay and play
Lockerbie Road, Dumfries, DG1 3PF
☎ (01387) 247444
(01387) 249600
admin@pinesgolf.com
160
Bruce Gray
B Gemmell (01387) 247444
18 L 5870 yds Par 68 SSS 68
U SOC
£20 D–£24 (£22)
Bt A75 Dumfries by-pass. M74 Junctions 15 or 17
Duncan Gray
Driving range; public putting green; short game area
www.pinesgolf.com

Portpatrick   (1903)

Golf Course Road, Portpatrick, DG9 8TB
☎ (01776) 810273

(01776) 810811
enquiries@portpatrickgolfclub.com
550
J McPhail
H Lee (01776) 810880
Dunskey 18 L 5913 yds SSS 69
Dinvin 9 L 1504 yds Par 27
U H SOC
£30 D–£40 (£35 D–£45) W–£125
Dinvin £12 D–£18
8 miles SW of Stranraer
CW Hunter
www.portpatrickgolfclub.com

Powfoot   (1903)

Cummertrees, Annan, DG12 5QE
☎ (01461) 204100
(01461) 204111
par71@powfootgolfclub.fsnet.com
920
SR Gardner (Mgr)
18 L 6266 yds SSS 71
WD 9.00–11.00, 13.00–15.30 Sat 14.30–15.30 Sun 10.30–11.15, 13.00–15.30
Winter £16 D–£21 Summer £33 D–£44
4 miles W of Annan. 15 miles SE of Dumfries, off B724
James Braid
www.powfootgolfclub.com

Sanquhar   (1894)

Blackaddie Road, Sanquhar, Dumfries, DG4 6JZ
☎ (01659) 50577
tich@rossirene.fsnet.co.uk
180
Ian Macfarlane
9 L 5630 yds SSS 68
U–parties welcome
D–£10 (D–£12); parties of 12 and over £25 per person
½ mile W of Sanquhar (A76). 30 miles N of Dumfries
W Fernie
www.scottishgolf.com

Southerness   (1947)

Southerness, Dumfries, DG2 8AZ
☎ (01387) 880677

St Medan   (1904)

Monreith, Newton Stewart, DG8 8NJ
☎ (01988) 700358
150
I Broadfoot (01988) 500539
9 L 4520 yds Par 64 SSS 64
U SOC
£15 (£15)
3 miles S of Port William, off A747
James Braid

Stranraer   (1905)

Creachmore, Leswalt, Stranraer, DG9 0LF
☎ (01776) 870245
(01776) 870445
stranraergolf@btclick.com
700
BC Kelly
18 L 6308 yds SSS 72

ᝍ WE–NA before 9.30am and
11.45am–1.45pm
£€ £28 (£33)
⊶ 2 miles NW of Stranraer on A718
⌂ James Braid
▤ www.stranraergolfclub.net

Thornhill (1893)

Blacknest, Thornhill, DG3 5DW
☎ (01848) 330546 (clubhouse)
(01848) 331779 (office)
✉ thornhillgc@fsmail.net

Wigtown & Bladnoch

(1960)
Lightlands Terrace, Wigtown, DG8 9EF
☎ (01988) 403354
▱ 170
⚹ IM Thin
▷ 9 L 2731 yds SSS 67
ᝍ U SOC
£€ £17 D–£22 (£17)
⊶ Between Wigtown and Bladnoch,
off A714
⌂ J Muir

Wigtownshire County

(1894)
Mains of Park, Glenluce, Newton Stewart,
DG8 0NN
☎ (01581) 300420
✉ enquiries
@wigtownshirecountygolfclub.com
▱ 420
⚹ R McKnight
✓ None
▷ 18 L 5907 yds SSS 69
ᝍ U exc Wed–NA after 6pm
£€ £23 D–£30 (£25 D–£32)
⊶ 8 miles E of Stranraer on A75
⌂ W Gordon Cunningham
▤ www.wigtownshirecountygolfclub
.com

Dunbartonshire

Balmore (1894)

Balmore, Torrance, G64 4AW
☎ (01360) 620284
▱ (01360) 622742
✉ secretary@balmoregolfclub.co.uk
▱ 750
⚹ Christine Campbell
(01360) 620284
✓ K Craggs (01360) 620123
▷ 18 L 5584 yds SSS 67
ᝍ WD–U SOC
£€ On application
⊶ 4 miles N of Glasgow, off A807
▤ www.balmoregolfclub.co.uk

Bearsden (1891)

Thorn Road, Bearsden, Glasgow, G61 4BP
☎ (0141) 586 5300
✉ secretary@bearsdengolfclub.com
▱ 500
⚹ Alan Harris
▷ 9 L 6014 yds SSS 69

ᝍ By arrangement
⊶ 6 miles NW of Glasgow
▤ www.bearsdengolfclub.com

Cardross (1895)

Main Road, Cardross, Dumbarton, G82 5LB
☎ (01389) 841213 (Clubhouse)
▱ (01389) 842162
✉ golf@cardross.com
▱ 810
⚹ IT Waugh (01389) 841754
✓ R Farrell (01389) 841350
▷ 18 L 6469 yds SSS 72
ᝍ WD–U WE–M
£€ £35 D–£50
⊶ 4 miles W of Dumbarton on A814
⌂ Fernie (1904)/Braid(1921)
▤ www.cardross.com

Clober (1951)

Craigton Road, Milngavie, Glasgow,
G62 7HP
☎ (0141) 956 1685
▱ (0141) 955 1416
✉ clobergolfclub@btopenworld.com
▱ 700
⚹ B Davidson
✓ J McFadyen (0141) 956 6963 (Golf
Shop)
▷ 18 L 4963 yds SSS 65
ᝍ WD–U before 4pm WE–M
BH–NA SOC–WD
£€ £22
⊶ 7 miles NW of Glasgow
▤ www.clober.com

Clydebank & District

(1905)
Hardgate, Clydebank, G81 5QY
☎ (01389) 383833
▱ (01389) 383831
▱ 780
⚹ Mrs K Stoddart (01389) 383831
✓ A Waugh (01389) 383835
▷ 18 L 5823 yds SSS 68
ᝍ WD–H
£€ On application
⊶ 2 miles N of Clydebank

Clydebank Overtoun

(1927)
Public
Overtoun Road, Dalmuir, Clydebank,
G81 3RE
☎ (0141) 952 2070 (Clubhouse)
(0141) 952 6372
(Pro Shop/Starter)
⚹ Jim Woolfries (01389) 876869
✓ S Savage (0141) 952 6372
▷ 18 L 5349 yds SSS 66
ᝍ U exc Sat–NA 11am–2.30pm
£€ On application
⊶ 8 miles W of Glasgow

Dougalston (1977)

Strathblane Road, Milngavie, Glasgow,
G62 8HJ
☎ (0141) 955 2404
▱ (0141) 955 2406
▱ 770

⚹ Mrs H Everett
✓ C Everett
▷ 18 L 6120 yds Par 70 SSS 71
ᝍ WD–U SOC WE afternoon subject
to availability
£€ £25 (£32)
⊶ 7 miles N of Glasgow on A81
⊕ Putting green & practice area
⌂ J Harris
▤ www.esporta.com

Douglas Park (1897)

Hillfoot, Bearsden, Glasgow, G61 2TJ
☎ (0141) 942 2220 (Clubhouse)
▱ (0141) 942 0985
✉ secretary@douglasparkgolfclub
.co.uk
▱ 550 210(L) 140(J)
⚹ JG Fergusson (0141) 942 0985
✓ D Scott (0141) 942 1482
▷ 18 L 5962 yds SSS 69
ᝍ M SOC
£€ WD–£25 D–£35
⊶ 6 miles NW of Glasgow, nr
Hillfoot Station
⌂ Willie Fernie
▤ www.douglasparkgolfclub.co.uk

Dullatur (1896)

1a Glendouglas Drive, Craigmarloch,
Cumbernauld, G68 0DW
☎ (01236) 723230
▱ (01236) 727271
▱ 580 64(L)
⚹ William Crombie (01236) 723230
✓ D Sinclair (01236) 794721
▷ 18 L 6312 yds SSS 70
18 L 5875 yds SSS 68
ᝍ WD–U WE SOC
£€ £20 (£30)
⊶ 3 miles N of Cumbernauld

Dumbarton (1888)

Broadmeadow, Dumbarton, G82 2BQ
☎ (01389) 765995
▱ (01389) 765995
✉ golf@dumbartongolfclub.co.uk
▱ 700
⚹ W McMonagle
✓ David Muir (01389) 600537
▷ 18 L 6018 yds SSS 69
ᝍ WD–U WE–NA
£€ £20 D–£30
⊶ 1 mile off A82
▤ www.dumbartongolfclub.co.uk

Hayston (1926)

Campsie Road, Kirkintilloch, Glasgow,
G66 1RN
☎ (0141) 775 0723
▱ (0141) 776 9030
✉ secretary@haystongolf.com
▱ 440 59(L) 80(J)
⚹ Barbara Rogerson
✓ S Barnett (0141) 775 0882
▷ 18 L 6042 yds SSS 70
ᝍ WD–I before 4.30pm –M after
4.30pm WE–M
£€ £20 D–£39
⊶ 1 mile N of Kirkintilloch
⌂ James Braid
▤ www.haystongolf.com

Hilton Park (1927)

Auldmarroch Estate, Stockiemuir Road, Milngavie, G62 7HB
- ☎ **(0141) 956 4657/5124**
- 🖷 (0141) 956 4657
- ✉ info@hiltonparkgolfclub.fsnet.co.uk
- 🖳 1200
- ♙ Mrs JA Dawson (0141) 956 4657
- ✎ W McCondichie (0141) 956 5125
- ▷ Hilton 18 L 6089 yds SSS 70
  Allander 18 L 5487 yds SSS 69
- ⚘ WD–U before 4pm
- ££ On application
- ⊕ 8 miles NW of Glasgow on A809
- ⌂ James Braid
- 🖳 www.hiltonpark.co.uk

Kirkintilloch (1895)

Todhill, Campsie Road, Kirkintilloch, G66 1RN
- ☎ **(0141) 776 1256**
- 🖷 (0141) 775 2424
- ✉ secretary@kirkintillochgolfclub
  .co.uk
- 🖳 450 100(L) 100(J)
- ♙ CA Harris (0141) 775 2387
- ✎ Jamie Good (07789) 207101
- ▷ 18 L 5860 yds SSS 69
- ⚘ M SOC
- ££ £6 D–£20 (WE on application)
- ⊕ 7 miles NE of Glasgow
- ⊕ Large practice ground; practice net
- ⌂ James Braid
- 🖳 www.kirkintillochgolfclub.co.uk

Lenzie (1889)

19 Crosshill Road, Lenzie, G66 5DA
- ☎ **(0141) 776 1535**
- 🖷 (0141) 777 7748
- 🖳 501 125(L) 125(J)
- ♙ SM Davidson (0141) 812 3018
- ✎ J McCallum (0141) 777 7748
- ▷ 18 L 5984 yds SSS 69
- ⚘ M SOC
- ££ £25 D–£30
- ⊕ 6 miles NE of Glasgow
- 🖳 www.lenziegolfclub.co.uk

Loch Lomond (1994)

Rossdhu House, Luss, G83 8NT
- ☎ **(01436) 655555**
- 🖷 (01436) 655500
- ✉ info@lochlomond.com
- ♙ K Williams
- ✎ C Campbell
- ▷ 18 L 7160 yds Par 71
- ⚘ M
- ⊕ 20 miles NW of Glasgow on A82
- ⌂ Weiskopf/Morrish
- 🖳 www.lochlomond.com

Milngavie (1895)

Laighpark, Milngavie, Glasgow, G62 8EP
- ☎ **(0141) 956 1619**
- 🖷 (0141) 956 4252
- ✉ secretary@milngaviegc.fsnet.co.uk
- 🖳 700
- ♙ S Woods
- ✎ None
- ▷ 18 L 5818 yds SSS 68
- ⚘ M SOC

- ££ £30 D–£55 (£40 D–£60)
- ⊕ 7 miles NW of Glasgow
- 🖳 www.milngaviegc.com

Palacerigg (1975)

Public
Palacerigg Country Park, Cumbernauld, G67 3HU
- ☎ **(01236) 734969**
- 🖷 (01236) 721461
- ✉ palacerigg-golfclub@lineone.net
- 🖳 300
- ♙ DSA Cooper
- ✎ J Murphy (Starter) (01236) 721461
- ▷ 18 L 6444 yds Par 72 SSS 71
- ⚘ U SOC
- ££ £8 (£10)
- ⊕ 3 miles SE of Cumbernauld, off A80. Within Palacerigg Country Park
- ⌂ Henry Cotton
- 🖳 www.palacerigggolfclub.co.uk

Ross Priory (1978)

Proprietary
Ross Loan, Gartocharn, Alexandria, G83 8NL
- ☎ **(01389) 830398**
- 🖷 (01389) 830357
- 🖳 800
- ♙ R Cook
- ✎ None
- ▷ 9 L 5758 yds Par 70 SSS 68
- ⚘ M SOC WD–U
- ££ D–£17
- ⊕ Off A881 at Gartocharn
- ⌂ George Campbell

Vale of Leven (1907)

Northfield Road, Bonhill, Alexandria, G83 9ET
- ☎ **(01389) 752351**
- 🖷 (08707) 498950
- ✉ rbarclay@volgc.org
- 🖳 750
- ♙ R Barclay
- ✎ B Campbell (08707) 498914
- ▷ 18 L 5277 yds Par 67 SSS 67
- ⚘ U H exc Sat (Apr–Sept) SOC
- ££ £20 D–£30 (£25 D–£37.50)
- ⊕ Bonhill, 3 miles N of Dumbarton, off A82
- 🖳 www.volgc.org

Westerwood Hotel G&CC (1989)

St Andrews Drive, Cumbernauld, G68 0EW
- ☎ **(01236) 725281**
- 🖷 (01236) 738478
- ✉ atait@ghotels.co.uk
- 🖳 400
- ♙ A Tait
- ✎ A Tait
- ▷ 18 L 6616 yds SSS 72
- ⚘ U SOC WD WE
- ££ £30 (£40)
- ⊕ 13 miles NE of Glasgow, off A80
- ⌂ Thomas/Ballesteros
- 🖳 www.qhotels.co.uk

Windyhill (1908)

Windyhill, Bearsden, G61 4QQ
- ☎ **(0141) 942 2349**
- 🖷 (0141) 942 5874
- ✉ secretary@windyhillgolfclub.co.uk
- 🖳 650
- ♙ JM Young
- ✎ C Duffy (0141) 942 7157
- ▷ 18 L 6254 yds SSS 70
- ⚘ WD–U Sun–M SOC–WD
- ££ £25
- ⊕ 8 miles NW of Glasgow
- ⌂ James Braid
- 🖳 www.windyhillgolfclub.co.uk

Fife

Aberdour (1896)

Seaside Place, Aberdour, KY3 0TX
- ☎ **(01383) 860080**
- 🖷 (01383) 860050
- ✉ aberdourgc@aol.com
- 🖳 670
- ♙ Sharon Hill
- ✎ D Gemmell (01383) 860256
- ▷ 18 L 5460 yds Par 67 SSS 66
- ⚘ WD–book with Pro Sat–NA SOC
- ££ £22 D–£30 (£35)
- ⊕ 8 miles SE of Dunfermline, on coast
- ⌂ Robertson/Anderson
- 🖳 www.aberdourgolfclub.co.uk

Anstruther (1890)

Marsfield Shore Road, Anstruther, KY10 3DZ
- ☎ **(01333) 310956**
- 🖷 (01333) 310956
- ✉ captain@anstruther.co.uk
- 🖳 500
- ♙ S Gardner
- ▷ 9 L 4504 yds Par 62 SSS 63
- ⚘ U SOC
- ££ £16 (£18)
- ⊕ 9 miles S of St Andrews
- 🖳 www.anstruther.co.uk

Auchterderran (1904)

Public
Woodend Road, Cardenden, KY5 0NH
- ☎ **(01592) 721579**

Balbirnie Park (1983)

Balbirnie Park, Markinch, Glenrothes, KY7 6NR
- ☎ **(01592) 612095**
- 🖷 (01592) 612383
- ✉ bp-gc@tiscali.co.uk
- 🖳 800
- ♙ S Oliver (Club Administrator)
- ✎ C Donnelly (01592) 752006
- ▷ 18 L 6275 yds SSS 71
- ⚘ WE–booking essential
- ££ £35 D–£45 (£40 D–£55)
- ⊕ 2 miles E of Glenrothes
- ⌂ Fraser Middleton
- 🖳 www.balbirniegolf.com

For list of abbreviations and key to symbols see page 651

Ballingry
Pay and play
Lochore Meadows Country Park, Crosshill, Lochgelly, KY5 8BA
☎ (01592) 860086

Burntisland (1797)
Club
51 Craigkennochie Terrace, Burntisland, KY3 9EN
☎ (01592) 872728
✉ bigmac@waitrose.com
🏛 70
♙ AD McPherson
▷ Play over Dodhead Course, Burntisland
⌂ Willie Park
▤ www.burntislandgolfclub.co.uk

Burntisland Golf House Club (1898)
Dodhead, Kirkcaldy Road, Burntisland, KY3 9LQ
☎ (01592) 874093
🖥 (01592) 874093
✉ wktbghc@aol.com
🏛 800
♙ WK Taylor (Mgr) (01592) 874093
✓ Paul Wytrazek (01592) 872116
▷ 18 L 5965 yds SSS 70
♟ U SOC WE NA Sat before 2.30pm
££ £25 D–£35 (£30 D–£42)
⚭ 1 mile E of Burntisland on B923; 9 miles E of M90 J1
⊕ Practice ground; putting green; buggies, power trollies
⌂ Willie Park Jr/James Braid
▤ www.burntislandgolfhouseclub.co.uk

Canmore (1897)
Venturefair Avenue, Dunfermline, KY12 0PE
☎ (01383) 724969
🖥 (01383) 731649
✉ canmoregolfclub@aol.com
🏛 547 70(L) 85(J)
♙ A Watson (01383) 513604
✓ D Cochrane (01383) 728416
▷ 18 L 5437 yds SSS 66
♟ WD–U WE–restricted
££ £19 D–£25 (£25 D–£32)
⚭ 1 mile N of Dunfermline on A823
⌂ Ben Sayers
▤ www.canmoregolf.co.uk

Charleton (1994)
Pay and play
Charleton, Colinsburgh, KY9 1HG
☎ (01333) 340505
✉ clubhouse@charleton.co.uk

Cowdenbeath (1991)
Public
Seco Place, Cowdenbeath, KY4 8PD
☎ (01383) 511918
🏛 200
♙ DK Mitchell
▷ 18 L 6207 yds Par 71 SSS 70
♟ U
££ On application

⚭ In Cowdenbeath, signposted from A909/A92
⊕ Practice ground & putting green; separate chipping area

Crail Golfing Society (1786)
Balcomie Clubhouse, Fifeness, Crail, KY10 3XN
☎ (01333) 450686
🖥 (01333) 450416
✉ info@crailgolfingsociety.co.uk
🏛 1600
♙ D Roy (01333) 450686
✓ G Lennie (01333) 450960/450967
▷ Balcomie 18 L 5922 yds SSS 69
  Craighead 18 L 6728 yds Par 72 SSS 74
♟ U
££ £45 (£55)
⚭ 11 miles SE of St Andrews
⊕ Driving range
⌂ Balcomie-Tom Morris. Craighead-Gil Hanse
▤ www.crailgolfingsociety.co.uk

Cupar (1855)
Hilltarvit, Cupar, KY15 5JT
☎ (01334) 653549
🖥 (01334) 653549
✉ cupargc@fsmail.net
🏛 350
♙ JM Houston (01334) 654101
▷ 2 x 9 L 5153 yds SSS 66
♟ WD–U SOC–WD/WE
££ D–£20
⚭ 10 miles W of St Andrews
⊕ Putting green
▤ www.cupargolfclub.co.uk

Drumoig (1996)
Drumoig Hotel, Drumoig, Leuchars, St Andrews, Fife KY16 0BE
☎ (01382) 541898
🖥 (01382) 541898
✉ drumoiggolf@netbreeze.co.uk
🏛 350
♙ Douglas Sievwright Gordon Taylor
▷ 18 L 6835 yds par 72
♟ U
££ £15 D–£23 (£30 D–£38) Special deals for visiting parties
⚭ 7 miles NW of St Andrews on A919; 4 miles S of Dundee
⊕ Driving range with covered bays; short game practice area and grass tees; buggies
⌂ Dave Thomas
▤ www.drumoigleisure.com

Dunfermline (1887)
Pitfirrane, Crossford, Dunfermline, KY12 8QW
☎ (01383) 723534
🖥 (01383) 723547
✉ secretary@dunfermlinegolfclub.com
🏛 720
♙ R De Rose
✓ C Nugent (01383) 729061
▷ 18 L 6121 yds SSS 70

♟ WD–U 9.30am–4pm Sat–NA SOC–WD 9.30am–3.30pm
££ £28 D–£40 (£35)
⚭ 2 miles W of Dunfermline on A994
⌂ JR Stutt
▤ www.dunfermlinegolfclub.com

Dunnikier Park (1963)
Public
Dunnikier Way, Kirkcaldy, KY1 3LP
☎ (01592) 261599
🖥 (01592) 642541
✉ dunnikierparkgolfclub@btinternet.com
🏛 600 35(L) 75(J)
♙ R Johnston
✓ G Whyte (01592) 642121
▷ 18 L 6601 yds SSS 72
♟ U SOC
££ £15 (£20)
⚭ N boundary of Kirkcaldy
⌂ R Stutt
▤ www.dunnikierparkgolfclub.com

Earlsferry Thistle (1875)
Club
Melon Park, Elie, KY9 1AS
🏛 60
♙ A Muir (01333) 330363
▷ Play over Elie Golf House Club Course
See Elie Golf House Club for other info

Elmwood Golf Course
Pay and play
Stratheden, Nr Cupar, KY15 5RS
☎ (01334) 658780
🖥 (01334) 658781
✉ clubhouse@elmwood.co.uk
♙ Sharif Sulaiman (Golf Admin) (01334) 658780
✓ Graeme McDowall (01334) 658780
▷ 18 L 5653 yds SSS 67
♟ U SOC
££ £19 (£24 +BH)
⚭ M90 J7 (southbound)/J8 (northbound). A91 to St Andrews
⊕ Practice area; indoor video analysis studio
▤ www.elmwoodgc.co.uk

Falkland (1976)
The Myre, Falkland, KY15 7AA
☎ (01337) 857404

Glenrothes (1958)
Public
Golf Course Road, Glenrothes, KY6 2LA
☎ (01592) 754561/758686
✉ secretary@glenrothesgolf.org.uk
🏛 600 35(L) 50(J)
♙ Miss C Dawson
▷ 18 L 6444 yds SSS 71
♟ U
££ £16 (£21)
⚭ Glenrothes West, off A92. M90 Junction 29
⌂ JR Stutt
▤ www.glenrothesgolf.org.uk

Golf House Club   (1875)

Elie, Leven, KY9 IAS
☎ **(01333) 330301**
🖳 (01333) 330895
📧 secretary@golfhouseclub.org
📖 500
🏌 G Scott (01333) 330301
⛳ I Muir (01333) 330955
▷ 18 L 6273 yds SSS 70
    9 L 2277 yds SSS 32
👥 July–Aug ballot. WE–no party
    bookings. WE–NA before 10am
    (May–Sept)
££ £60 D–£80 (£70 D–£90)
⊶ 12 miles S of St Andrews
⊕ Driving range; putting green
🖥 www.golfhouseclub.org

Kinghorn   (1887)

Public
McDuff Crescent, Kinghorn, KY3 9RE
☎ **(01592) 890345**
📖 10
🏌 Gordon Tulloch
    (01592) 891008
⛳ None
▷ 18 L 5629 yds Par 65 SSS 66
👥 U SOC
££ £16 (£21)
⊶ 3 miles S of Kirkcaldy (A921)
⊕ Kinghorn and Kinghorn Thistle
    Clubs play here
🏠 Tom Morris
🖥 www.kinghorngolfclub.co.uk

Kinghorn Ladies   (1894)

Club
*Golf Clubhouse, McDuff Crescent, Kinghorn,
KY3 9RE*
☎ **(01592) 890345**

Kingsbarns Golf Links

(2000)
Pay and play
Kingsbarns, Fife, KY16 8QD
☎ **(01334) 460860**
🖳 (01334) 460877
📧 info@kingsbarns.com
🏌 S McEwen (Gen Mgr)
⛳ D Scott
▷ 18 hole course
👥 U
££ £150 D–£225 June–Nov
⊶ Between St Andrews and Crail on
    coast road (A917)
⊕ Driving range
🏠 Phillips/Parsinen
🖥 www.kingsbarns.com

Kirkcaldy   (1904)

Balwearie Road, Kirkcaldy, KY2 5LT
☎ **(01592) 205240**
🖳 (01592) 205240
📧 enquiries@kirkcaldygolfclub.sol
    .co.uk
📖 600
🏌 A Wood
⛳ A Caira (01592) 203258
▷ 18 L 6086 yds SSS 69
👥 U exc Sat–NA
££ £28 D–£34 (£34 D–£42)

☒ W side of Kirkcaldy; A92 exit
    Kirkcaldy West
🏠 Old Tom Morris
🖥 www.kirkcaldygolfclub.co.uk

Ladybank   (1879)

Annsmuir, Ladybank, Fife KY15 7RA
☎ **(01337) 830814**
🖳 (01337) 831505
📧 info@ladybankgolf.co.uk
📖 1000
🏌 FH McCluskey
⛳ S Smith (01337) 830725
▷ 18 L 6601 yds SSS 72
👥 WD–U 9.30am–4pm M–after 4pm
    WE–NA Sat
££ £46 (£56)
⊶ 6 miles SW of Cupar, off A92 from
    Melville Lodges roundabout
🏠 Old Tom Morris
🖥 www.ladybankgolf.co.uk

Leslie   (1898)

Balsillie Laws, Leslie, Glenrothes, KY6 3EZ
☎ **(01592) 620040**
📧 iandonnachie@ukonline.co.uk
📖 120
🏌 IM Donnachie
▷ 9 L 4940 yds Par 62 SSS 65
👥 U
££ £10 (£12)
⊶ 3 miles W of Glenrothes. M90
    Junction 5/7, 11 miles

Leven Golfing Society

(1820)
Club
Links Road, Leven, KY8 4HS
☎ **(01333) 426096/424229**
🖳 (01333) 424229
📧 LGS@bosinternet.com
📖 500
🏌 Verne Greger
▷ Play over Leven Links:
    18 L 6506 yds Par 71 SSS 72
👥 U Fri–NA after 12
££ £40 D–£55 (£50 D–£65)
⊶ See website
🖥 www.levengolfingsociety.co.uk

Leven Links   (1846)

The Promenade, Leven, KY8 4HS
☎ **(01333) 421390 (Starter)**
🖳 (01333) 428859
📧 secretary@leven-links.com
📖 1200
🏌 (01333) 428859 (Links
    Committee)
👥 18 L 6506 yds Par 71 SSS 72
    WD–U before 5pm Sat–no parties
    Sun–NA before 10.30am SOC
££ £45 (£60)
⊶ E of Leven, on promenade. 12
    miles SW of St Andrews
🖥 www.leven-links.com

Leven Thistle   (1867)

Club
Balfour Street, Leven, KY8 4JF
☎ **(01333) 426333**
🖳 (01333) 439910

☒ secretary@leventhistlegolfclub
    .fsnet.co.uk
📖 500
🏌 J Scott (01333) 426333
▷ Play over Leven Links

Lundin   (1868)

Golf Road, Lundin links, KY8 6BA
☎ **(01333) 320202**
🖳 (01333) 329743
📧 secretary@lundingolfclub.co.uk
📖 900
🏌 AJ McDonald
⛳ DK Webster (01333) 320051
▷ 18 L 6371 yds SSS 71
👥 WD–U between 9am–3pm Sat–NA
    before 2.30pm Sun–restricted 12
    noon–3pm
££ £47 D–£65 (£50)
⊶ 3 miles E of Leven
🏠 James Braid
🖥 www.lundingolfclub.co.uk

Lundin Ladies   (1891)

Woodielea Road, Lundin Links, KY8 6AR
☎ **(01333) 320022 (Starter)**
    (01333) 320832 (Sec)
📧 secretary@lundinladies.co.uk
📖 375
▷ 9 L 2365 yds SSS 68 Par 68
👥 U Tue, Thur, Fri, Sat, Sun.
    Restricted Wed April–Sept
££ On application
⊶ 3 miles E of Leven
🏠 James Braid

Methil   (1892)

Club
Links House, Links Road, Leven, KY8 4HS
☎ **(01333) 425535**
🖳 (01333) 425187
📖 50
🏌 ATJ Traill
▷ Play over Leven Links

Pitreavie   (1922)

Queensferry Road, Dunfermline, KY11 8PR
☎ **(01383) 722591**
🖳 (01383) 722591
📖 800
🏌 E Comerford
⛳ P Brookes (01383) 723151
▷ 18 L 6031 yds SSS 69
👥 U–phone Pro SOC (Parties–max
    36–must be booked in advance)
££ £25 D–£35 (£30 D–£40)
⊶ 2 miles off M90 Junction 2,
    between Rosyth and Dunfermline
🏠 Dr A Mackenzie

Saline   (1912)

Kinneddar Hill, Saline, KY12 9LT
☎ **(01383) 852591**
🖳 (01383) 853517
📧 saline-golf-club@supanet.com
📖 300
🏌 A Lyon (01383) 852218
▷ 9 L 5384 yds SSS 66
👥 U exc medal Sat
££ £11.50 (£14) Reduction for Jun &
    OAP

⚜ 5 miles NW of Dunfermline; M90
Jct 4
▤ www.saline-golf-club.co.uk

Scoonie (1951)
Public
North Links, Leven, KY8 4SP
☎ **(01333) 307007**
▱ (01333) 307008
✉ manager@scooniegolfclub.com
▥ 160
✎ S Kuczerepa
▷ 18 L 4979 m Par 67 SSS 66
👥 U SOC
€€ On application
⚜ Adjoins Leven Links
▤ www.scooniegolfclub.com

Scotscraig (1817)
Golf Road, Tayport, DD6 9DZ
☎ **(01382) 552515**
▱ (01382) 553130
✉ scotscraig@scottishgolf.com
▥ 850
✎ BD Liddle
✓ C Mackie (0138) 552855
▷ 18 L 6550 yds SSS 72
👥 WD–U WE–by prior arrangement
SOC
€€ On application
⚜ 10 miles N of St Andrews
⊕ Practice area
⌂ James Braid
▤ www.scottscraiggolfclub.com

St Michaels (1903)
Leuchars, St Andrews, KY16 0DX
☎ **(01334) 839365 (Clubhouse)**
▱ (01334) 838789
✉ stmichaelsgc@btclick.com
▥ 400
✎ GD Dignan (01334) 838666
▷ 18 L 5802 yds SSS 68
👥 Sun am–NA (Mar–Oct) SOC
€€ D–£25 (£32)
⚜ 5 miles N of St Andrews on
Dundee road (A919)
▤ www.stmichaelsgc.co.uk

Thornton (1921)
Station Road, Thornton, KY1 4DW
☎ **(01592) 771173 (Starter)**
▱ (01592) 774955
▥ 700
✎ WD Rae (01592) 771111
▷ 18 L 6170 yds Par 70 SSS 69
👥 U
€€ £20 D–£30 (£30 D–£40)
⚜ 5 miles N of Kirkcaldy, off A92
▤ www.thorntongolfclubfife.co.uk

St Andrews Clubs

New (1902)
Club
3-5 Gibson Place, St Andrews, KY16 9JE
☎ **(01334) 473426**
▱ (01334) 477570

✉ admin@standrewsnewgolfclub
.co.uk
▥ 1750
✎ H Campbell Graham (Sec/Mgr)
▷ Play over St Andrews Links
courses
▤ www.standrewsnewgolfclub.com

The Royal and Ancient Golf Club of St Andrews
(1754)
Club
St Andrews, KY16 9JD
☎ **(01334) 460000**
▱ (01334) 460001
✉ thesecretary@randagc.org
▥ 1800
✎ P Dawson
▷ Play over St Andrews Links
▤ www.theroyalandancientgolfclub
.org

St Andrews (1843)
Club
*Links House, 13 The Links, St Andrews,
KY16 9JB*
☎ **(01334) 479799**
▱ (01334) 479577
✉ sec@thestandrewsgolfclub.co.uk
▥ 1600
✎ T Gallacher (01334) 479799
▷ Play over St Andrews Links
▤ www.thestandrewsgolfclub.co.uk

St Andrews Thistle
(1817)
Club
25 Frazer Avenue, St Andrews, KY16 8HT
☎ **(01334) 475928**
✉ kkkbbr@aol.com
▥ 180
✎ K Barber (01334) 475928
▷ Play over St Andrews Links

St Regulus Ladies'
(1913)
Club
9 Pilmour Links, St Andrews, KY16 9JG
☎ **(01334) 477797**
▱ (01334) 477887
✉ admin@st-regulus-lgc.fsnet.co.uk
▥ 273
✎ Mrs L Graham
▷ Play over St Andrews Links (six
courses)
👥 WD–U
€€ Varies depending on course

The St Rule Club
(1898)
Club
12 The Links, St Andrews, KY16 9JB
☎ **(01334) 472988**
▱ (01334) 472988
✉ struleclub@fsmail.net
▥ 289
✎ Mrs J Allan
▷ Play over St Andrews Links
⚜ St Andrews

St Andrews Courses

Balgove Course (1993)
Public
*St Andrews Links Trust, Pilmour House, St
Andrews, KY16 9SF*
☎ **(01334) 466666**
▱ (01334) 479555
✉ reservations@standrews.org.uk
✎ AJR McGregor (Gen Mgr)
▷ 9 L 1520 yds Par 30
👥 U
€€ £8–£12
⚜ St Andrews Links, on A91
⊕ Driving range: 3 day £15–£21,
weekly £30–£42; St Andrews Links
Golf Academy; St Andrews Links
Clubhouse; Eden Clubhouse
⌂ Donald Steel
▤ www.standrews.org.uk

Duke's (1995)
Craigtoun, St Andrews, KY16 8NS
☎ **(01334) 474371**
✉ reservations@oldcoursehotel
.co.uk

Eden Course (1914)
Public
*St Andrews Links Trust, Pilmour House, St
Andrews, KY16 9SF*
☎ **(01334) 466666**
▱ (01334) 479555
✉ reservations@standrews.org.uk
✎ AJR McGregor (Gen Mgr)
▷ 18 L 6195 yds Par 70 SSS 70
👥 U SOC
€€ £17–£35 3D–£66–£135
W–£132–£270 (unlimited
play–Jubilee, New, Eden &
Strathtyrum courses)
⚜ St Andrews Links, on A91
⊕ Driving range; St Andrews Links
Golf Academy; St Andrews Links
Clubhouse; Eden Clubhouse
⌂ HS Colt
▤ www.standrews.org.uk

Jubilee Course (1897)
Public
*St Andrews Links Trust, Pilmour House, St
Andrews, KY16 9SF*
☎ **(01334) 466666**
▱ (01334) 479555
✉ reservations@standrews.org.uk
✎ AJR McGregor (Gen Mgr)
▷ 18 L 6742 yds Par 72 SSS 73
👥 U SOC
€€ £32–£65 3D–£66–£135
W–£132–£270 (unlimited
play–Jubilee, New, Eden &
Strathtyrum courses)
⚜ St Andrews Links, on A91. Signs to
West Sands
⊕ Driving range; St Andrews Links
Golf Academy; St Andrews Links
Clubhouse; Eden Clubhouse
⌂ Angus/Auchterlonie/Steel
▤ www.standrews.org.uk

New Course   (1895)

Public
St Andrews Links Trust, Pilmour House, St Andrews, KY16 9SF
☎ **(01334) 466666**
📠 (01334) 479555
📧 reservations@standrews.org.uk
🏌 AJR McGregor (Gen Mgr)
▷ 18 L 6625 yds Par 71 SSS 73
👥 U SOC
££ £32–£65 3D–£66–£135
   W–£132–£270 (unlimited play–Jubilee, New, Eden & Strathtyrum courses)
⛳ St Andrews Links, on A91. Signs to West Sands
⊕ Driving range; St Andrews Links Golf Academy; St Andrews Links Clubhouse; Eden Clubhouse
🏠 Old Tom Morris
🖥 www.standrews.org.uk

Old Course (15th Century)

Public
St Andrews Links Trust, Pilmour House, St Andrews, KY16 9SF
☎ **(01334) 466666**
📠 (01334) 479555
📧 reservations@standrews.org.uk
🏌 AJR McGregor (Gen Mgr)
▷ 18 L 6721 yds Par 72 SSS 73
👥 H I No Sun play
££ £61–£125
⛳ St Andrews Links, on A91. Signs to West Sands
⊕ Driving range; St Andrews Links Golf Academy; St Andrews Links Clubhouse; Eden Clubhouse
🖥 www.standrews.org.uk

Strathtyrum Course   (1993)

Public
St Andrews Links Trust, Pilmour House, St Andrews, KY16 9SF
☎ **(01334) 466666**
📠 (01334) 479555
📧 reservations@standrews.org.uk
🏌 AJR McGregor (Gen Mgr)
▷ 18 L 5620 yds Par 69 SSS 67
👥 U SOC
££ £12–£24 3D–£65–£135
   W–£132–£270 (unlimited play–Jubilee, New, Eden & Strathtyrum courses)
⛳ St Andrews Links, on A91
⊕ Driving range; St Andrews Links Golf Academy; St Andrews Links Clubhouse; Eden Clubhouse
🏠 Donald Steel
🖥 www.standrews.org.uk

Glasgow

Alexandra Park   (1880)

Public
Alexandra Park, Dennistoun, Glasgow, G31 8SE
☎ **(0141) 556 1294**
📖 250
🏌 G Campbell

▷ 9 L 4562 yds Par 62
👥 U
££ On application
⛳ ½ mile E of Glasgow, nr M8
🏠 Graham McArthur

Bishopbriggs   (1907)

Brackenbrae Road, Bishopbriggs, Glasgow, G64 2DX
☎ **(0141) 772 1810**
📧 thesecretarybgc@yahoo.co.uk

Cathcart Castle   (1895)

Mearns Road, Clarkston, G76 7YL
☎ **(0141) 638 0082**
📠 (0141) 638 1201
📧 secretary@cathcartcastle.com
📖 950
🏌 IG Sutherland (0141) 638 9449
✓ S Duncan (0141) 638 3436
▷ 18 L 5865 yds SSS 69
👥 M SOC
££ £30 D–£45
⛳ I mile from Clarkston on B767
🖥 www.cathcartcastle.com

Cawder   (1933)

Cadder Road, Bishopbriggs, Glasgow, G64 3QD
☎ **(0141) 761 1281**
📠 (0141) 761 1285
📧 secretary@cawdergolfclub.org.uk
📖 1400
🏌 (0141) 761 1282
✓ K Stevely (0141) 772 7102
▷ Cawder 18 L 6279 yds SSS 71
   Keir 18 L 5880 yds SSS 68
👥 WD–H SOC–WD
££ £30
⛳ N of Glasgow, off A803 Kirkintilloch Road
🏠 Braid/Steel
🖥 www.cawdergolfclub.org.uk

Cowglen   (1906)

301 Barrhead Road, Glasgow, G43 1EU
☎ **(0141) 632 0556**
📠 (01505) 503000
📧 r.jamieson-accountants@fsmail.net
📖 625
🏌 RJG Jamieson (01505) 503000
✓ S Payne (0141) 649 9401
▷ 18 L 6079 yds SSS 69
👥 WD–by arrangement with Sec WE–M
££ £35 D–£45
⛳ Take Pollok junction from M77 and course is half mile towards Pollok
⊕ Driving/long iron facilities; pitching green and putting green
🏠 James Braid
🖥 www.cowglengolfclub.co.uk

Glasgow   (1787)

Killermont, Bearsden, Glasgow, G61 2TW
☎ **(0141) 942 1713**
📠 (0141) 942 0770
📧 secretary@glasgow-golf.com
📖 800
🏌 DW Deas (0141) 942 2011
✓ J Steven (0141) 942 8507

▷ 18 L 5957 yds Par 70 SSS 69
👥 M SOC WD
⛳ 4 miles NW of Glasgow
🏠 Tom Morris Sr
🖥 www.glasgowgolfclub.com

Haggs Castle   (1910)

70 Dumbreck Road, Dumbreck, Glasgow, G41 4SN
☎ **(0141) 427 0480**
📠 (0141) 427 1157
📧 secretary@haggscastlegolfclub.com
📖 900
🏌 A Williams (0141) 427 1157
✓ C Elliott (0141) 427 3355
▷ 18 L 6426 yds SSS 71
👥 WD–H SOC–Weds only
££ SOC–£40
⛳ SW Glasgow (B768). M77 Jct 1
🏠 Dave Thomas (1998)
🖥 www.haggscastlegolfclub.com

Knightswood   (1929)

Public
Knightswood Park, Lincoln Avenue, Glasgow, G13 3DN
☎ **(0141) 959 6358**

Lethamhill   (1933)

Public
Cumbernauld Road, Glasgow, G33 1AH
☎ **(0141) 770 6220**

Linn Park   (1924)

Public
Simshill Road, Glasgow, G44 5TA
☎ **(0141) 633 0377**
▷ 18 L 5295 yds SSS 65
👥 U–phone 1 day in advance
££ £10
⛳ 4 miles S of Glasgow, W of B766

Pollok   (1892)

90 Barrhead Road, Glasgow, G43 1BG
☎ **(0141) 632 1080**
📠 (0141) 649 1398
📧 secretary@pollokgolf.com
📖 650
🏌 D Morgan (0141) 632 4351
✓ None
▷ 18 L 6358 yds SSS 70
👥 WD/WE by arrangement SOC–WD
££ £50
⛳ 3 miles SW of Glasgow (B762). M77 Junction 2
🏠 James Douglas, altered by Dr Alastair Mckenzie
🖥 www.pollokgolf.com

Ralston   (1904)

Strathmore Avenue, Ralston, Paisley, PA1 3DT
☎ **(0141) 882 1349**
📠 (0141) 883 9837
📧 thesecretary@ralstongolf.co.uk
📖 440 165(L) 100(J)
🏌 J Pearson
✓ C Munro (0141) 882 1349
▷ 18 L 6100 yds SSS 69

ꙮ M SOC
££ £27 D–£42 (£27 D–£42)
⊛ 2 miles E of Paisley (A761); M8 Jct
26
ⴼ Braid
🖃 www.ralstongolfclub.co.uk

Rouken Glen (1922)
Pay and play
*Stewarton Road, Thornliebank, Glasgow,
G46 7UZ*
☎ (0141) 638 7044
📠 (0141) 638 6115
🖂 deaconsbank@ngclubs.co.uk
⚐ S Armstrong
ⴼ 18 L 4800 yds SSS 63
ꙮ U SOC
££ £10 (£13)
⊛ 5 miles S of Glasgow, W of A77
⊕ Driving range

Sandyhills (1905)
223 Sandyhills Road, Glasgow, G32 9NA
☎ (0141) 778 1179
▥ 700
⚐ CJ Wilson
ⴼ 18 L 6253 yds SSS 71
ꙮ M SOC
££ £18 WD only for v/tors
⊛ 4 miles SE of Glasgow, N of A74

Williamwood (1906)
*Clarkston Road, Netherlee, Glasgow,
G44 3YR*
☎ (0141) 637 1783
📠 (0141) 571 0166
🖂 secretary@williamwoodgc.fsnet
.co.uk
▥ 911
⚐ RJ Templeton
✓ S Marshall (0141) 637 2715
ⴼ 18 L 5878 yds SSS 69
ꙮ WD–H
££ £30 D–£40
⊛ 5 miles S of Glasgow
ⴼ James Braid

Highland

Caithness & Sutherland

Bonar Bridge/Ardgay
(1904)
Bonar-Bridge, Ardgay, IV24 3EJ
☎ (01863) 766199 (Clubhouse)
🖂 bonarardgaygolf@aol.com
▥ 250
⚐ R Thomson (01862) 892443
ⴼ 9 L 5162 yds SSS 65 Par 68
ꙮ U
££ D–£15 (£15)
⊛ ¹/₂ mile N of Bonar-Bridge on
A836. 12 miles W of Dornoch

Brora (1891)
Golf Road, Brora, KW9 6QS
☎ (01408) 621417

📠 (01408) 622157
🖂 secretary@broragolf.co.uk
⚐ AJA Gill
✓ B Anderson (01408) 621473
ⴼ 18 L 6110 yds SSS 70
ꙮ U exc comp days –H for open
comps SOC
££ £35 D–£40 (£40 D–£45)
⊛ 18 miles N of Dornoch (A9)
ⴼ James Braid
🖃 www.broragolf.co.uk

The Carnegie Club (1995)
*Skibo Castle, Dornoch, Sutherland,
IV25 3RQ*
☎ (01862) 881 260
🖂 sharon.stewart@carnegieclubs.com

Durness (1988)
Pay and play
Balnakeil, Durness, IV27 4PN
☎ (01971) 511364
📠 (01971) 511321
🖂 lucy@durnessgolfclub.org
▥ 150
⚐ Mrs L Mackay (01971) 511364
ⴼ 9 L 5555 yds SSS 67
ꙮ U
££ D–£15 W–£50
⊛ 57 miles NW of Lairg on A838
⊕ Putting green; practice net
🖃 www.durnessgolfclub.org

Golspie (1889)
Ferry Road, Golspie, KW10 6ST
☎ (01408) 633266
📠 (01408) 633393
🖂 info@golspie-golf-club.co.uk
▥ 260
✓ None
ⴼ 18 L 5990 yds SSS 68
ꙮ U after 9.30 am daily SOC
WD/WE
££ £30 D–£40
⊛ Golspie on A9, 11 miles N of
Dornoch
ⴼ James Braid
🖃 www.golspie-golf-club.co.uk

Lybster (1926)
Main Street, Lybster, KW1 6BL
▥ 100
⚐ AG Calder (01595) 721316
ⴼ 9 L 1896 yds SSS 61
ꙮ U
££ D–£10
⊛ 13 miles S of Wick on A99
🖃 www.lybstergolfclub.co.uk

Reay (1893)
Reay, Thurso, Caithness, KW14 7RE
☎ (01847) 811288
🖂 info@reaygolfclub.co.uk

Royal Dornoch (1877)
Golf Road, Dornoch, IV25 3LW
☎ (01862) 810219
📠 (01862) 810792
🖂 bookings@royaldornoch.com
▥ 1048 211(L) 62(J) 402(Struie)

⚐ JS Duncan
(Sec/Mgr) (01862) 811220 ext 22
✓ A Skinner (01862) 810902
ⴼ C'ship 18 L 6514 yds SSS 73
Struie 18 L 6276 yds SSS 70
ꙮ C'ship–H Struie–U
££ £75 (£85) Championship £35
Struie
⊛ 45 miles N of Inverness, off A9, N
of Dornoch
⊕ Helipad by clubhouse; airstrip
nearby; practice ground nearby
ⴼ Morris/Sutherland/Duncan
🖃 www.royaldornoch.com

Thurso (1893)
Pay and play
Newlands of Geise, Thurso, KW14 7XD
☎ (01847) 893807
📠 (01847) 892575
🖂 info@thursogolfclub.co.uk
▥ 300
⚐ RM Black (01847) 892575
ⴼ 18 L 5828 yds SSS 69
ꙮ U
££ £20 (£20)
⊛ 2 miles SW of Thurso
⊕ Two-bay driving range
ⴼ WS Stewart
🖃 www.thursogolfclub.co.uk

Ullapool (1998)
Pay and play
North Road, Ullapool, IV26 2TH
☎ (01854) 613323
📠 (01854) 612911
🖂 info@ullapool-golf.co.uk
▥ 220
⚐ A Paterson
✓ None
ⴼ 9 L 5281 yds Par 70 SSS 67 (18
tees)
ꙮ U
££ Mon–Sun: D–£18, Mon–Fri £55
⊛ Ullapool
🖃 www.ullapool-golf.co.uk

Wick (1870)
Reiss, Wick, KW1 5LJ
☎ (01955) 602726
🖂 wickgolfclub@hotmail.com
▥ 320
⚐ D Shearer (01955) 602935
ⴼ 18 L 6123 yds SSS 71
ꙮ U
££ £20 (£20)
⊛ 3 miles N of Wick on A99
🖃 www.wickgolfclub.com

Inverness

Abernethy (1893)
Nethy Bridge, PH25 3EB
☎ (01479) 821305
📠 (01479) 821305
🖂 info@abernethygolfclub.com
▥ 400
⚐ Mrs J McCool
ⴼ 9 L 2520 yds SSS 66

U SOC
££ £17 (£19)
🚗 5 miles S of Grantown (B970)
🖥 www.abernethygolfclub.com

Aigas

Proprietary
mains of Aigas, Beauly, Inverness, IV4 7AD
☎ (01463) 782942
✉ info@aigas-holidays.co.uk
📖 120
🏌 Graham Clark (01463) 870889
🏴 9 L 2339 yds Par 66 SSS 63
U SOC WD WE
££ £15 (£17)
🚗 6 miles west of Beauly on A831
⊕ Practice net; putting green
🖥 www.cali.co.uk/aigas/

Alness   (1904)

Ardross Rd, Alness, Ross-shire, IV17 0QA
☎ (01349) 883877
✉ info@alnessgolfclub.co.uk
📖 300
🏌 Mrs A Black
✏ Gary Lister
🏴 18 L 4976 yds Par 67 SSS 64
U SOC
££ £23 D–£28 (£25 D–£30)
🚗 ¼ mile N of Alness. 20 miles N of Inverness
🏠 I Scott Taylor
🖥 www.alness-golf.com

Boat-of-Garten   (1898)

Boat-of-Garten, PH24 3BQ
☎ (01479) 831282
🖨 (01479) 831523
✉ office@boatgolf.com
📖 650
🏌 N McConachie
🏴 18 L 5876 yds SSS 69
U–booking advisable
££ £32 D–£42 (£37 D–£47)
🚗 27 miles SE of Inverness (A95)
⊕ Driving range, net and putting green
🏠 James Braid
🖥 www.boatgolf.com

Carrbridge   (1980)

Inverness Road, Carrbridge, PH23 3AU
☎ (08444) 141415 (Clubhouse)
✉ katie@carrbridgegolf.co.uk
📖 450
🏌 Mrs Katie Fenton
🏴 9 L 2623 yds Par 71 SSS 68
U exc comp days; please phone to book and check availability
££ 9: £15 D–£21 18: £20 D–£25 (£25)
🚗 20 miles SE of Inverness, off A9
⊕ Putting green & practice area
🖥 www.carrbridgegolf.com

Fort Augustus   (1926)

Pay and play
Markethill, Fort Augustus, PH32 4AU
✉ alex.barnett@freeuk.com

Fort William   (1974)

North Road, Fort William, PH33 6SN
☎ (01397) 704464
📖 430
🏌 R Macintyre
🏴 18 L 5686 metres SSS 70
U
££ £25 (£28)
🚗 3 miles N of Fort William (A82)
🏠 JR Stutt
🖥 www.fortwilliamgolf.co.uk

Fortrose & Rosemarkie   (1888)

Ness Road East, Fortrose, IV10 8SE
☎ (01381) 620529
🖨 (01381) 621328
✉ secretary@fortrosegolfclub.co.uk
📖 750
🏌 M MacDonald
🏴 18 L 5881 yds Par 71 SSS 69
U SOC
££ £32 (£38)
🚗 Black Isle, 12 miles N of Inverness
⊕ Driving range; 2 putting greens; practice net ; golf shop
🏠 James Braid
🖥 www.fortrosegolfclub.co.uk

Grantown-on-Spey   (1890)

Golf Course Road, Grantown-on-Spey, PH26 3HY
☎ (01479) 872079
✉ secretary @grantownonspeygolfclub.co.uk

Invergordon   (1893)

King George Street, Invergordon, IV18 0BD
☎ (01349) 852715
✉ invergordongolf@tiscali.co.uk
📖 170 30(L) 50(J)
🏴 18 L 6030 yds Par 69 SSS 69
U SOC
££ £25
🚗 15 miles NE of Dingwall (A9/B817)
🏠 A Rae (1994)
🖥 www.invergordongolf.co.uk

Inverness   (1883)

Culcabock Road, Inverness, IV2 3XQ
☎ (01463) 239882
🖨 (01463) 240616
✉ igc@freeuk.com
📖 1100
🏌 JS Thomson
✏ AP Thomson (01463) 231989
🏴 18 L 6256 yds SSS 70
WE/BH–restricted SOC
££ £33 D–£42 (£33 D–£42)
🚗 1 mile S of Inverness
🏠 George Smith/JJ Fraser; alterations by James Braid
🖥 www.invernessgolfclub.co.uk

Kingussie   (1891)

Gynack Road, Kingussie, PH21 1LR
☎ (01540) 661600 (Office)
🖨 (01540) 662066
✉ sec@kingussie-golf.co.uk
📖 600

🏌 WT Baird
✏ None
🏴 18 L 5555 yds SSS 68
U
££ £23 D–£30 (£26 D–£32)
🚗 Kingussie (A9)
🏠 H Vardon
🖥 www.kingussie-golf.co.uk

Loch Ness   (1996)

Castle Heather, Inverness, IV2 6AA
☎ (01463) 713334/5
🖨 (01463) 712695
✉ info@golflochness.com
📖 550
🏌 ND Hampton (01463) 713335
✏ M Piggot (01463) 713334
🏴 18 L 5907 yds Par 70 SSS 69
U SOC
££ £25 D–£40 (£30 D–£50)
🚗 Culduthel, SW Inverness (A9)
⊕ Floodlit driving range; putting green; pitching/bunker area
🏠 Caddies Golf Course Design
🖥 www.golflochness.com

Muir of Ord   (1875)

Great North Road, Muir of Ord, IV6 7SX
☎ (01463) 870825
🖨 (01463) 871867
✉ muirgolf@supanet.com
📖 700
🏌 Mrs J Gibson
✏ Shop (01463) 871311
🏴 18 L 5557 yds SSS 68
U SOC
££ £20 D–£25 (£25 D–£30); week £50
🚗 15 miles N of Inverness (A862)
🏠 James Braid

Nairn   (1887)

Seabank Road, Nairn, IV12 4HB
☎ (01667) 453208
✉ bookings@nairngolfclub.co.uk

Nairn Dunbar   (1899)

Lochloy Road, Nairn, IV12 5AE
☎ (01667) 452741
🖨 (01667) 456897
✉ secretary@nairndunbar.com
📖 1200
🏌 JS Falconer
✏ DH Torrance (01667) 453964
🏴 18 L 6765 yds SSS 74 SR 139
U
££ £45 D–£65 (£55 D–£75)
🚗 In Nairn
⊕ Practice area
🖥 www.nairndunbar.com

Newtonmore   (1893)

Golf Course Road, Newtonmore, PH20 1AT
☎ (01540) 673878
✉ secretary@newtonmoregolf.com

Strathpeffer Spa   (1888)

Golf Course Road, Strathpeffer, IV14 9AS
☎ (01997) 421219
🖨 (01997) 421011

mail@strathpeffergolfclub.co.uk
360 50(L) 85(J)
Gayle Anderson (01997) 421011
18 L 4956 yds SSS 64
U SOC
£20 D–£25 (inc WE)
¼ mile N of Strathpeffer. 5 miles W of Dingwall
Putting green + small practice area
Willie Park/Tom Morris
www.strathpeffergolf.co.uk

Tain (1890)
Chapel Road, Tain, IV19 1JE
(01862) 892314
(01862) 892099
info@tain-golfclub.co.uk
560
Mrs J Bell
None
18 L 6404 yds SSS 71
U
£40 D–£45 (£45 D–£55)
35 miles N of Inverness (A9). 8 miles S of Dornoch
Practice area, net and putting green
Old Tom Morris
www.tain-golfclub.co.uk

Tarbat (1909)
Pay and play
Portmahomack, Tain, IV20 1YB
(01862) 871278
(01862) 871598
240
9 L 2568 yds SSS 65
U SOC
D–£17
10 miles E of Tain

Torvean (1962)
Public
Glenurquhart Road, Inverness, IV3 8JN
(01463) 711434 (Starter)
(01463) 711417
info@torveangolfclub.com
850
Susan F Menzies (Mgr) (01463) 225651
None
18 L 5799 yds SSS 68
U
£24 (£26.50)
SW of Inverness on A82 1 mile from city centre
Practice nets; putting green
www.torveangolfclub.co.uk

Orkney & Shetland

Orkney (1889)
Grainbank, Kirkwall, Orkney, KW15 1RD
(01856) 872457
(01856) 872457
330
Andrew Bonner
18 L 5411 yds SSS 67
U

££ D–£20 W–£60
1 mile W of Kirkwall
www.orkneygolfclub.co.uk

Sanday (1977)
Sanday, Orkney, KW17 2BW
(01857) 600341
(01857) 600341
20
R Thorne
9 L 2600 yds Par 35 SSS 36
U
D–£5, £10 per annum, no further green fees
2 miles N of Lady on B9069

Shetland (1891)
Dale, Gott, Shetland, ZE2 9SB
(01595) 840369
(01595) 840369
shetlandgolfclub@btopenworld.com
400
A Henderson
18 L 5562 yds SSS 68
U SOC
D–£20
4 miles N of Lerwick (A907)
Putting green; chipping green; driving nets
Fraser Middleton
www.shetlandgolfclub.co.uk

Stromness (1890)
Stromness, Orkney, KW16 3DU
(01856) 850772
250
GA Bevan (01856) 850885
18 L 4762 yds SSS 63
U
D–£20
Stromness, 16 miles W of Kirkwall on Hoy Sound
www.stromnessgc.co.uk

Whalsay (1976)
Skaw Taing, Whalsay, Shetland, ZE2 9AL
(01806) 566450/566481

West Coast

Askernish (1891)
Lochboisdale, Askernish, South Uist, HS81 5ST
(01878) 710312

Gairloch (1898)
Gairloch, IV21 2BE
(01445) 712407
(01445) 712865
secretary@gairlochgc.freeserve.co.uk
285
B Jeffrey
9 L 2267 yds SSS 63
U–phone first
D–£16 W–£60 D–£10 W–£35 (Junior)

60 miles W of Dingwall in Wester Ross
www.gairlochgolfclub.com

Isle of Harris
Scarista, Isle of Harris, HS5 3HX
(01859) 550226
harrisgolf@ic24.net
72
J MacLean
None
9 L 2442 yds Par 68 SSS 64
U
£12 (£12)
13 miles S of Tarbert on W coast
www.harrisgolf.com

Isle of Skye (1964)
Sconser, Isle of Skye, IV48 8TD
(01478) 650414
250
I Macmillan
9 L 4798 yds Par 66 SSS 64
U
£18 D–£22 (£18)
Between Broadford and Sligachan

Lochcarron (1908)
Lochcarron, Strathcarron, IV54 8YS
secretary@lochcarrongolf.co.uk
124
PC White (01520) 722206
9 L 3575 yds Par 60 SSS 60
U exc Sat 2–5pm–NA
D–£12 W–£50
½ mile E of Lochcarron in Wester Ross
www.lochcarrongolf.co.uk

Skeabost (1982)
Skeabost Bridge, Isle of Skye, IV51 9NP
(01470) 532202

Stornoway (1890)
Lady Lever Park, Stornoway, Isle of Lewis, HS2 0XP
(01851) 702240
admin@stornowaygolfclub.co.uk
400
KW Galloway (01851) 702533
18 L 5252 yds Par 68 SSS 67
U exc Sun–NA SOC
D–£20 W–£60
Off A857 in Lews Castle grounds, Isle of Lewis
J & R Stutt (most recent alterations)
www.stornowaygolfclub.co.uk

Traigh (1947)
Arisaig, Inverness-shire, PH39 4NT
(01687) 450337
160
H MacDougal (01687) 450628
None
9 L 2456 yds Par 68 SSS 65
U
D–£16
2 miles N of Arisaig off A830 Fort William-Mallaig road

⋔ John Salvesen; redesigned and enlarged 1995
▤ www.traighgolf.co.uk

Lanarkshire

Airdrie   (1877)
Rochsoles, Airdrie, ML6 0PQ
☎ (01236) 762195
🖳 (01236) 760584
✉ airdrie.golfclub@virgin.net
▦ 450
♤ W Campbell
✓ S McLean (01236) 754360
↦ 18 L 6004 yds SSS 68
⚭ U SOC WD WE H
££ £20 D–£30
⊕ Airdrie 1 mile
⊕ Putting green; practice net
⋔ James Braid

Bellshill   (1905)
Community Road, Orbiston, Bellshill, ML4 2RZ
☎ (01698) 745124
✉ info@bellshillgolfclub.com
▦ 680
♤ T McLaughlin
↦ 18 L 5900 yds Par 69 SSS 69
⚭ WD–U Sun–NA before 1.30pm SOC. No visiting parties
££ £26 D–£32 (+ BH £32 D–£42) Juniors £5 (£10)
⊕ 30 miles W (A725) M74 Junction 5

Biggar   (1895)
Public
The Park, Broughton Road, Biggar, ML12 6AH
☎ (01899) 220618 (Clubhouse)
    (01899) 220319 (Bookings)
▦ 140
♤ T Rodger (01698) 382311
✓ None
↦ 18 L 5662 yds SSS 68
⚭ U–booking recommended
££ £10 (£12)
⊕ 12 miles SE of Lanark (A702)
⋔ Willie Park

Blairbeth   (1910)
Burnside, Rutherglen, Glasgow, G73 4SF
☎ (0141) 634 3355 (Clubhouse)
✉ bgc1910@yahoo.co.uk
▦ 450
♤ John Bell (0141) 634 3325
↦ 18 L 5537 yds Par 70 SSS 68
⚭ SOC–WD WE–NA after 2pm
££ £15 D–£22 (£20)
⊕ 1 mile S of Rutherglen
▤ www.blairbeth.com

Bothwell Castle   (1922)
Uddington Road, Bothwell, Glasgow, G71 8TD
☎ (01698) 801973
🖳 (01698) 801971
✉ bcgolf@btconnect.com

▦ 1000
♤ DA McNaught (01698) 801971
✓ A McCloskey (01698) 801969
↦ 18 L 6220 yds SSS 70
⚭ WD–U 9.30–10.30am & 2.30–3.30pm
££ £24 D–£32
⊕ 2 miles N of Hamilton. M74 Junction 5
▤ www.bcgolf.co.uk

Calderbraes   (1891)
57 Roundknowe Road, Uddingston, G71 7TS
☎ (01698) 813425
▦ 300
♤ S McGuigan (0141) 573 2497
↦ 9 L 5046 yds Par 66 SSS 67
⚭ WD–U WE–M
££ D–£13
⊕ Start of M74

Cambuslang   (1892)
30 Westburn Drive, Cambuslang, G72 7NA
☎ (0141) 641 3130
🖳 (0141) 641 3130
✉ cambuslanggolfclub@tiscali.co.uk
▦ 200 100(L) 40(J)
♤ RM Dunlop
↦ 9 L 5942 yds SSS 69
⚭ M
££ On application
⊕ Cambuslang Station ³/₄ mile

Carluke   (1894)
Hallcraig, Mauldslie Road, Carluke, ML8 5HG
☎ (01555) 770574/771070
🖳 (01555) 770574
▦ 505 100(L)
♤ DT Stewart (01555) 770574
✓ C Ronald (01555) 751053
↦ 18 L 5919 yds SSS 69
⚭ WD–U before 4pm WE/BH–NA SOC
££ £25 D–£35
⊕ 20 miles SE of Glasgow

Carnwath   (1907)
1 Main Street, Carnwath, ML11 8JX
☎ (01555) 840251
🖳 (01555) 841070
✉ carnwathgc@hotmail.co.uk
▦ 582
♤ Mrs L McPate
✓ None
↦ 18 L 5955 yds SSS 69
⚭ WD–U before 4pm Sat–NA Sun–restricted
££ £20 D–£30 (Sun–£26 D–£36)
⊕ 7 miles E of Lanark
▤ www.carnwathgc.co.uk

Cathkin Braes   (1888)
Cathkin Road, Rutherglen, Glasgow, G73 4SE
☎ (0141) 634 6605
✉ golf@cathkinbraes.freeserve.co.uk
▦ 930
♤ DE Moir
✓ S Bree (0141) 634 0650

↦ 18 L 6208 yds SSS 71
⚭ WD–U
££ £33
⊕ 5 miles S of Glasgow (B759)
⋔ James Braid
▤ www.cathkinbraesgolfclub.co.uk

Coatbridge Municipal   (1971)
Public
Townhead Road, Coatbridge, ML52 2HX
☎ (01236) 28975

Colville Park   (1923)
Jerviston Estate, Motherwell, ML1 4UG
☎ (01698) 263017
🖳 (01698) 230418
▦ 900 64(L) 140(J)
♤ L Innes (01698) 262808
✓ J Stark (01698) 265779
↦ 18 L 6301 yds Par 71 SSS 70
⚭ WD–U 11am–3pm (exc Fri–NA) WE–NA SOC–WD
££ £18 D–£27
⊕ 1 mile NE of Motherwell on A723
⋔ James Braid
▤ www.colvillepark.co.uk

Crow Wood   (1925)
Cumbernauld Road, Muirhead, Glasgow, G69 9JF
☎ (0141) 799 2011
🖳 (0141) 779 4873
✉ secretary@crowwood-golfclub.co.uk
▦ 700
♤ G Blyth (0141) 779 4954
✓ B Moffat (0141) 779 1943
↦ 18 L 6168 yds Par 71 SSS 70
⚭ WD–H (prior notice required) SOC
££ £30 D–£40
⊕ 5 miles NE of Glasgow, off A80
⋔ James Braid
▤ www.crowwood-golfclub.co.uk

Dalziel Park   (1997)
100 Hagen Drive, Motherwell, ML1 5RZ
☎ (01698) 862862

Douglas Water   (1922)
Rigside, Lanark, ML11 9NB
☎ (01555) 880361

Drumpellier   (1894)
Drumpellier Ave, Coatbridge, ML5 1RX
☎ (01236) 424139
🖳 (01236) 428723
✉ administrator@drumpelliergc.freeserve.co.uk
▦ 500
♤ JM Craig
✓ JM Carver (01236) 432971
↦ 18 L 6227 yds SSS 70
⚭ I H SOC WD
££ £30 D–£40
⊕ 8 miles E of Glasgow
⋔ James Braid
▤ www.drumpellier.com

East Kilbride (1900)

Chapelside Road, Nerston, East Kilbride, G74 4PH

☎ **(01355) 220913 (Clubhouse)**

Easter Moffat (1922)

Mansion House, Plains, Airdrie, ML6 8NP

☎ **(01236) 842878**
🖥 (01236) 842904
📧 secretary@emgc.co.uk
📖 600
🏌 G Miller (01236) 620972
🏌 G King (01236) 843015
🏴 18 L 6221 yds SSS 70
🏌 WD only
££ £22 D–£33
🚗 3 miles E of Airdrie

Hamilton (1892)

Riccarton, Ferniegair, Hamilton, ML3 7UE

☎ **(01698) 282872**
🖥 (01698) 204650
📧 secretary@hamiltongolfclub.co.uk
📖 500
🏌 GM Chapman
🏌 D Wright
🏴 18 L 6463 yds SSS 71
🏌 M or by arrangement with Sec
££ On application
🚗 1¹/₂ miles S of Hamilton
🏠 James Braid
🖥 www.hamiltongolfclub.co.uk

Hollandbush (1954)

Public
Acre Tophead, Lesmahagow, Coalburn, ML11 0JS

☎ **(01555) 893484**
📧 mail@hollandbushgolfclub.co.uk
📖 420
🏌 J Hamilton
🏴 18 L 6246 yds SSS 70
🏌 U
££ £9.70 (£11.20)
🚗 10 miles SW of Lanark, off A74, between Lesmahagow and Coalburn
⊕ 3 full hole practice area
🖥 www.hollandbushgolfclub.co.uk

Kirkhill (1910)

Greenlees Road, Cambuslang, Glasgow, G72 8YN

☎ **(0141) 641 3083 (Clubhouse)**
🖥 (0141) 641 8499
📧 secretary@kirkhillgolfclub.org.uk
📖 570
🏌 C Downes (0141) 641 8499
🏌 D Williamson (0141) 641 7972
🏴 18 L 6030 yds SSS 70
🏌 WD–by prior arrangement WE/BH–NA SOC
££ On application
🚗 Cambuslang, SE Glasgow
🏠 James Braid
🖥 www.kirkhillgolfclub.org.uk

Lanark (1851)

The Moor, Lanark, ML11 7RX

☎ **(01555) 663219**

🖥 (01555) 663219
📧 lanarkgolfclub@supanet.com
📖 550 130(L) 150(J)
🏌 GH Cuthill
🏌 A White (01555) 661456
🏴 18 L 6306 yds SSS 71
9 hole course
🏌 WD–U until 4pm WE–M
££ 9: £8 adult, £4 under 18 18: £35 D–£45 (2004 prices)
🚗 30 miles S of Glasgow, off A74
🏠 Tom Morris
🖥 www.lanarkgolfclub.co.uk

Langlands (1985)

Public
Langlands Road, East Kilbride, G75 0QQ

☎ **(01355) 248173**
☎ **(01355) 224685 (Starter)**

Larkhall

Public
Burnhead Road, Larkhall, Glasgow

☎ **(01698) 881113**

Leadhills (1895)

The Lowthers, Horners Place, Leadhills, Nr Biggar ML12 6YQ

☎ **(01659) 74456**
🖥 (01654) 74356
📧 harry@glenfranka.fsnet.co.uk
📖 80
🏌 Harry Shaw
🏴 9 L 4404 yds Par 66 SSS 64
🏌 U
££ Over 18 years: £10 round or day Under 18 years: £7 round or day
🚗 6 miles S of Abington, off M74
⊕ Trolley and club hire
🖥 See Golf Central

Mount Ellen (1905)

Lochend Road, Gartcosh, Glasgow, G69 9EY

☎ **(01236) 872277**
🖥 (01236) 872249
📧 archiewylie@hotmail.com
📖 480
🏌 Archie Wylie
🏌 I Bilsborough (01236) 872632
🏴 18 L 5525 yds SSS 68
🏌 WD–U from 9am–4pm WE–NA
££ £25 D–£32 (NA)
🚗 8 miles NE of Glasgow, W of M73
🖥 www.ourgolfclub.co.uk/megc.php

Mouse Valley (1993)

East End, Cleghorn, Lanark, ML11 8NR

☎ **(01555) 870015**
🖥 (01555) 870022
📧 info@kames-golf-club.com
📖 300
🏴 18 L 6300 yds SSS 72 9 L 2200 yds SSS 65
🏌 U
££ 18 hole: £15 (£20) 9 hole: £8 (£11)
🚗 2 miles W of Carnwath on A721
🏠 Graham Taylor
🖥 www.kames-golf-club.com

Shotts (1895)

Blairhead, Benhar Road, Shotts, ML7 5BJ

☎ **(01501) 820431**
🖥 (01501) 825868
📧 info@shottsgolfclub.co.uk
📖 700
🏌 GT Stoddart (01501) 825868
🏌 J Strachan (01501) 822658
🏴 18 L 6205 yds SSS 70
🏌 WD–U Sat–NA before 4.30pm
££ £18 (£26)
🚗 18 miles E of Glasgow on B7057. M8 Junction 5, 1¹/₂ miles
🏠 James Braid
🖥 www.shottsgolfclub.co.uk

Strathaven (1908)

Glasgow Road, Strathaven, ML10 6NL

☎ **(01357) 520421**
🖥 (01357) 520539
📧 info@strathavengc.com
📖 1000
🏌 AW Wallace
🏌 S Kerr (01357) 521812
🏴 18 L 6226 yds SSS 71
🏌 WD–I before 4pm WE–NA
££ £27 D–£37
🚗 N of Strathaven, off Glasgow road (A726)

Strathclyde Park

Public
Mote Hill, Hamilton, ML3 6BY

☎ **(01698) 429350**
📖 200
🏌 K Will
🏌 W Walker (01698) 285511
🏴 9 L 6350 yds SSS 70
🏌 U exc medal days (phone booking)
££ 18: £3.60 (£4.20) – adult; 9: £1.80 (£2.10) – Jnr, unwaged & senior
🚗 Hamilton. M74 Junction 5
⊕ Driving range

Torrance House (1969)

Public
Strathaven Road, East Kilbride, Glasgow, G75 0QZ

☎ **(01355) 248638**
📖 560
🏌 Margaret D McKerlie (01355) 249720
🏌 J Dunlop (07795) 090269
🏴 18 L 6415 yds SSS 71
🏌 U
££ £9.70 (£11.20)
🚗 S of East Kilbride, off Strathaven road (A726)
⊕ Practice ground

Wishaw (1897)

55 Cleland Road, Wishaw, ML2 7PH

☎ **(01698) 372869 (Clubhouse)**
🖥 (01698) 356930
📧 jwdouglas@btconnect.com
📖 475 80(L)
🏌 JW Douglas (01698) 357480
🏌 S Adair (01698) 358247
🏴 18 L 5999 yds SSS 69
🏌 WD–U until 4pm NA–Sat Sun–U
££ £24 D–£34 Sun–£28 D–£38

↝ N of Wishaw town centre
⌂ James Braid

Lothians

East Lothian

Aberlady   (1912)
Club
Aberlady, EH32 0RB
✉ ithomps3@aol.com

Archerfield Links   (2004)
Dirleton, East Lothian, EH39 5HQ
☎ (01620) 850542
🖥 (01620) 850630
✉ mail:archerfieldgolfclub.com
♨ Golf Admin (01620) 850552
✓ Paul Lightbody
↣ 36
♟ M
⊕ Double-ended driving range, 2 short game areas; putting green
⌂ DJ Russell
🖳 www.archerfieldgolfclub.com

Bass Rock   (1873)
Club
4 Sainthill Court, North Berwick, EH39 4RL
☎ (01620) 894071
✉ bassrockgolfclub@hotmail.com
🕮 110
♨ J Bullough (01620) 893391
↣ Play over North Berwick

Castle Park   (1994)
Pay and play
Gifford, Haddington, EH41 4PL
☎ (01620) 810733
✉ castleparkgolf@hotmail.com

Dirleton Castle   (1854)
Club
15 The Pines, Gullane, EH31 2DT
☎ (01620) 843591
🕮 100
♨ J Taylor
↣ Play over Gullane courses

Dunbar   (1856)
East Links, Dunbar, EH42 1LL
☎ (01368) 862317
🖥 (01368) 865202
✉ secretary@dunbargolfclub.sol.co.uk
🕮 998
♨ Kevin Johnston
✓ J Montgomery (01368) 862086
↣ 18 L 6404 yds Par 71 SSS 71
♟ U SOC–exc Thurs
££ £50–£60 (£65–£85)
↝ ¹/₂ mile E of Dunbar. 30 miles E of Edinburgh, off A1
⌂ Tom Morris
🖳 www.dunbar-golfclub.co.uk

Gifford   (1904)
Edinburgh Road, Gifford, EH41 4JE
☎ (01620) 810591 (Starter)
🖥 (01620) 810267
✉ thesecretary@giffordgolfclub.fsnet .co.uk
🕮 570
♨ G MacColl (01620) 810267
↣ 9 L 6050 yds SSS 69
♟ U–booking required
££ 9: £12 (£14) 18: £18 D–£25 (£20 D–£30)
↝ 4 miles S of Haddington. 20 miles SE of Edinburgh (B6355)
🖳 www.giffordgolfclub.com

Glen (North Berwick)   (1906)
East Links, Tantallon Terrace, North Berwick, EH39 4LE
☎ (01620) 892726
✉ secretary@glengolfclub.co.uk

Gullane   (1882)
Gullane, EH31 2BB
☎ (01620) 842255
    (01620) 843115 (Starter)
🖥 (01620) 842327
✉ secretary@gullanegolfclub.com
🕮 1100 450(L) 100(J)
♨ NGM Watt (01620) 842255
✓ AL Good (01620) 843111
↣ No 1 18 L 6466 yds SSS 72
    No 2 18 L 6244 yds SSS 71
    No 3 18 L 5252 yds SSS 66
    6 hole children's course
♟ No 1–H Nos 2/3–U
££ No 1 £80 D–£100 (£95) No 2 £32 D–£50 (£43) No 3 £20 D–£26 (£26) Children's course free
↝ 18 miles E of Edinburgh on A198
⊕ Advance booking advisable
🖳 www.gullanegolfclub.com

Haddington   (1865)
Amisfield Park, Haddington, EH41 4PT
☎ (01620) 823627
🖥 (01620) 826580
✉ info@haddingtongolf.co.uk
🕮 850
♨ KA Nicholson (Mgr)
✓ J Sandilands (01620) 822727
↣ 18 L 6335 yds Par 71 SSS 71
♟ WD–U WE–U 10am–12 & 2–4pm SOC
££ £25 (£35)
↝ 17 miles E of Edinburgh on A1. ³/₄ mile E of Haddington
🖳 www.haddingtongolf.co.uk

The Honourable Company of Edinburgh Golfers   (1744)
Muirfield, Gullane, EH31 2EG
☎ (01620) 842123
🖥 (01620) 842977
✉ hceg@muirfield.org.uk
🕮 625
♨ ANG Brown
↣ 18 L 6673 yds SSS 73
    (Championship L 7034 yds)

♟ WD–Tues & Thurs only except public hols H
££ 1 round £145, 2 rounds £180
↝ NE outskirts of Gullane, opposite sign for Greywalls Hotel on A198
⊕ Practice range
⌂ Harry Colt
🖳 www.muirfield.org.uk

Kilspindie   (1867)
Aberlady, EH32 0QD
☎ (01875) 870358
🖥 (01875) 870358
✉ kilspindie@btconnect.com
🕮 440 160(L) 70(J)
♨ PB Casely
✓ GJ Sked (01875) 870695
↣ 18 L 5030 m SSS 66
♟ Phone Sec in advance WD–U after 9.45am WE–U after 11am SOC
££ £34 D–£52.50 (£43 D–£62.50)
↝ Aberlady, 17 miles E of Edinburgh on A198 (off A1)
⊕ Putting green; practice nets; practice green with bunker
⌂ Ross/Sayers
🖳 www.golfeastlothian.com

Longniddry   (1921)
Links Road, Longniddry, EH32 0NL
☎ (01875) 852141
🖥 (01875) 853371
✉ secretary@longniddrygolfclub .co.uk
🕮 1100
♨ RMS Gunning
✓ WJ Gray (01875) 852228
↣ 18 L 6260 yds SSS 70
♟ WD–U H SOC–WD after 9.18am
££ £42 D–£65 (£60)
↝ 13 miles E of Edinburgh, off A1
⌂ HS Colt
🖳 www.longniddrygolfclub.co.uk

Luffness New   (1894)
Aberlady, EH32 0QA
☎ (01620) 843114
🖥 (01620) 842933
✉ secretary@luffnessnew.com
🕮 700
♨ Gp Capt AG Yeates (01620) 843336
✓ None
↣ 18 L 6122 yds SSS 70
♟ H or I XL before 9.30am WE/BH–NA SOC
££ £65 D–£85
↝ 1 mile W of Gullane (A198)
⌂ Morris/Braid
🖳 www.luffnessgolf.com

Musselburgh   (1938)
Monktonhall, Musselburgh, EH21 6SA
☎ (0131) 665 2005
🖥 (0131) 665 4435
✉ secretary@themusselburghgolfclub .com
🕮 1000
♨ P Millar
✓ F Mann (0131) 665 7055
↣ 18 L 6725 yds SSS 72
♟ WD–U before 4.30pm WE–NA Sat

££ £35 (£40)
⊶ I mile S of Musselburgh on B6415
⌂ James Braid
▤ www.themusselburghgolfclub.com

Musselburgh Old Course
(1982)
Public
10 Balcarres Road, Musselburgh,
EH21 7SD
☎ **(0131) 665 6981**
  (0131) 665 5438 (Starter)
✉ mocgc@breathemail.net
▦ 270
⚲ R McGregor (0771) 461 0549
✓ None
⊳ 9 L 5748 yds SSS 69
▦ WD/BH–U WE–U after 1pm
££ 9: £9
⊶ 7 miles E of Edinburgh on A1
▤ www.musselburgholdlinks.co.uk

North Berwick (1832)
West Links, Beach Road, North Berwick,
EH39 4BB
☎ **(01620) 890312**
  (01620) 893274
✉ secretary@northberwickgolfclub
  .com
▦ 550
⚲ John Douglass (01620) 895040
✓ D Huish (01620) 893233
⊳ 18 L 6456 yds SSS 71
▦ U H
££ £62 D–£90 (£80) Winter–£35
  D–£25 (£40)
⊶ Centre of North Berwick. 24 miles
  E of Edinburgh (A198)
▤ www.northberwickgolfclub.com

Royal Musselburgh
(1774)
Prestongrange House, Prestonpans,
EH32 9RP
☎ **(01875) 810276**
  (advance bookings)
  (01875) 810276
✉ royalmusselburgh@btinternet
  .com
▦ 800
⚲ TH Hardie (Sec/Mgr) J Hanratty
  (Golf Sec) (01875) 819000
✓ J Henderson (01875) 810139
⊳ 18 L 6254 yds SSS 70
▦ U SOC
££ £30 D–£40 (£35)
⊶ 8 miles E of Edinburgh on B1361
  North Berwick road
⊕ Driving range
⌂ James Braid
▤ www.royalmusselburgh.co.uk

Tantallon (1853)
Club
32 Westgate, North Berwick, EH39 4AH
☎ **(01620) 892114**
  (01620) 894399
✉ tantallongc@talk21.com
▦ 441
⚲ DA Leckie
✓ D Huish (01620) 893233

⊳ Play over North Berwick West
  Links
▦ See North Berwick Golf Club
££ See North Berwick Golf Club
▤ www.north-berwick.co.uk/tantallon

Thorntree (1856)
Club
Prestongrange House, Prestonpans,
EH32 9RP
☎ **(01875) 810139**

Whitekirk (1995)
Whitekirk, North Berwick, EH39 5PR
☎ **(01620) 870300**
  (01620) 870330
✉ countryclub@whitekirk.com
▦ 400
⚲ D Brodie
✓ P Wardell
⊳ 18 L 6526 yds Par 72 SSS 72
▦ U SOC
££ £28 (£42)
⊶ 3 miles SE of North Berwick
  (A198)
⊕ Practice range
⌂ Cameron Sinclair
▤ www.whitekirk.com

Winterfield (1935)
Public
St Margarets, North Road, Dunbar,
EH42 1AU
☎ **(01368) 862280**
✉ kevinphillips@tiscali.co.uk
▦ 350
✓ K Phillips (01368) 863562
⊳ 18 L 5053 yds SSS 65
▦ U
££ On application–phone Pro
⊶ W side of Dunbar. 28 miles E of
  Edinburgh (A1)

Midlothian

Baberton (1893)
50 Baberton Avenue, Juniper Green,
Edinburgh, EH14 5DU
☎ **(0131) 453 4911**
  (0131) 453 4678
✉ manager@baberton.co.uk
▦ 900
⚲ BM Flockhart (0131) 453 4911
✓ K Kelly (0131) 453 3555
⊳ 18 L 6129 yds SSS 70
▦ WD–U before 5pm; Sat–after 3pm;
  Sun–after 1pm
££ £27 D–£37 (£30 D–£40)
⊶ 5 miles SW of Edinburgh (A70)
⌂ Willie Park Jr
▤ www.baberton.co.uk

Braid Hills (1893)
Public
Braid Hills Road, Edinburgh, EH10 6JY
☎ **(0131) 447 6666 (Starter)**

Braids United (1897)
Club
22 Braid Hills Approach, Edinburgh,
EH10 6JY
☎ **(0131) 452 9408**

Broomieknowe (1905)
36 Golf Course Road, Bonnyrigg,
EH19 2HZ
☎ **(0131) 663 9317**
  (0131) 663 2152
▦ 500
⚲ JD Fisher
✓ M Patchett (0131) 660 2035
⊳ 18 L 6200 yds Par 70
▦ WD–U WE/BH–NA
££ £26 D–£36 (£28)
⊶ 7 miles SE of Edinburgh
⌂ Braid/Hawtree
▤ www.broomieknowe.com

Bruntsfield Links Golfing
Society (1761)
The Clubhouse, 32 Barnton Avenue,
Edinburgh, EH4 6JH
☎ **(0131) 336 2006**
  (0131) 336 5538
✉ secretary@bruntsfield.sol.co.uk
▦ 1185
⚲ Cdr DM Sandford (0131) 336 1479
✓ B Mackenzie (0131) 336 4050
⊳ 18 L 6428 yds SSS 71
▦ WD–U WE–apply to Sec SOC–H
££ £52 D–£75 (£60 D–£80)
⊶ 3 miles NW of Edinburgh, off A90
  at Davidson Mains
⌂ Willie Park/Mackenzie/Hawtree
▤ www.sol.co.uk/bruntsfieldlinks/

Carrick Knowe (1930)
Public
Glendevon Park, Edinburgh, EH12 5VZ
☎ **(0131) 337 1096 (Starter)**

Craigmillar Park (1895)
1 Observatory Road, Edinburgh, EH9 3HG
☎ **(0131) 667 2837**
  (0131) 662 8091
✉ secretary@craigmillarpark.co.uk
▦ 440 120(L) 70(J)
⚲ B Knowles (0131) 667 0047
✓ S Gourlay (0131) 667 2850
⊳ 18 L 5859 yds SSS 69
▦ WD–I or H before 3.30pm
  WE/BH–NA
££ On application
⊶ Blackford, S of Edinburgh
⌂ James Braid
▤ www.craigmillarpark.co.uk

Duddingston (1895)
Duddingston Road West, Edinburgh,
EH15 3QD
☎ **(0131) 661 7688**
  (0131) 652 6057
✉ admin@duddingstongolf.co.uk
▦ 800
⚲ Terry Christie
✓ Alistair McLean (0131) 661 4301
  Fax (0131) 661 4301

18 L 4525 yds SSS 72
WD–U WE–phone Pro SOC–Tues & Thurs
££ £38 D–£48 SOC–£30 D–£40
SE Edinburgh
Two practice areas; putting green; buggies
Willie Park
www.duddingstongolfclub.co.uk

Glencorse (1890)

Milton Bridge, Penicuik, EH26 0RD
☎ (01968) 677177
(01968) 674399
glencorsegc@btconnect.com
700
W Oliver (01968) 677189
C Jones (01968) 676481
18 L 5217 yds Par 64 SSS 66
WD–U SOC–WD/Sun pm
££ £25 (£32)
8 miles S of Edinburgh (A701)
Willie Park
glencorsegolfclub.com

Kings Acre (1997)

Pay and play
Lasswade, EH18 1AU
☎ (0131) 663 3456
(0131) 663 7076
info@kings-acregolf.com
Alan Murdoch (Dir of Golf)
A Murdoch (0131) 663 3456
18 L 6031 yds Par 70
Junior Par 3 course
U SOC
££ £24 (£32)
3 miles S of Edinburgh, off A720
Floodlit driving range
Graeme Webster
www.kings-acregolf.com

Kingsknowe (1907)

326 Lanark Road, Edinburgh, EH14 2JD
☎ (0131) 441 1144
(0131) 441 2079
louise@kingsknowe.com
871
LI Fairlie (0131) 441 1145
C Morris (0131) 441 4030
18 L 5981 yds SSS 69
WD–U before 4pm WE–phone Pro SOC–WD before 4pm
££ £25 (£32)
SW Edinburgh
Herd/Braid
www.kingsknowe.com

Liberton (1920)

Kingston Grange, 297 Gilmerton Road, Edinburgh, EH16 5UJ
☎ (0131) 664 3009
(0131) 666 0853
info@libertongc.co.uk
797
AG McMillan
I Seath (0131) 664 1056
18 L 5344 yds SSS 66
WD–U before 5pm WE–NA before 2pm
££ £25 D–£30

3 miles S of Edinburgh
www.libertongc.co.uk

Lothianburn (1893)

106a Biggar Road, Edinburgh, EH10 7DU
☎ (0131) 445 2206
(0131) 445 5067
info@lothianburngc.co.uk
600 75(L) 100(J)
DP MacLaren (0131) 445 5067
K Mungall (0131) 445 2288
18 L 5662 yds SSS 69 Par 71
WD–U before 4.30pm –M after 4.30pm WE–NA SOC–H
££ £19 D–£25 (£25 D–£30)
S of Edinburgh, on A702. Lothianburn exit from Edinburgh Bypass
Motorised buggies for hire
James Braid (1928)
www.lothianburngc.co.uk

Marriott Dalmahoy Hotel & CC

Dalmahoy, Kirknewton, EH27 8EB
☎ (0131) 335 8010
(0131) 335 3577
Neal Graham (Golf Dir), Gordon Watt
Scott Dixon
East 18 L 7055 yds SSS 74
West 18 L 5168 yds SSS 66
WD–U H SOC–WD
££ East–£65 (£80) West–£35 (£40)
7 miles W of Edinburgh on A71
Floodlit driving range
James Braid

Melville Golf Centre (1995)

Proprietary
Lasswade, Edinburgh, EH18 1AN
☎ (0131) 663 8038
(range, shop, tuition)
(0131) 654 0224 (course)
(0131) 654 0814
golf@melvillegolf.co.uk
60
Mr & Mrs MacFarlane (Props)
G Carter (0131) 663 8038
9 L 4604 yds Par 66 SSS 62
U SOC
££ £10–£18 (£12–£22)
7 miles S of Edinburgh, signposted off city bypass on A7 (South)
Floodlit range; practice bunker; Pay & Play 9-hole course; 4-hole practice area; putting green; golf shop & tuition
G Webster
www.melvillegolf.co.uk

Merchants of Edinburgh (1907)

10 Craighill Gardens, Morningside, Edinburgh, EH10 5PY
☎ (0131) 447 1219
(0131) 446 9833
admin@merchantsgolf.com
1011
J Leslie
NEM Colquhoun (0131) 447 8709

18 L 4924 yds SSS 64
WD–U before 4pm SOC–WD
££ £20 (£27)
SW of Edinburgh, off A701
Braid/Letters
www.merchantsgolf.com

Mortonhall (1892)

231 Braid Road, Edinburgh, EH10 6PB
☎ (0131) 447 6974
(0131) 447 8712
clubhouse@mortonhallgc.co.uk
1000
Ms BM Giefer
MT Leighton (0131) 447 5185
18 L 6502 yds SSS 72
SOC WE–NA before 10.30
££ £35 (£50)
2 miles S of Edinburgh on A702
James Braid/FW Hawtree
www.mortonhallgc.co.uk

Murrayfield (1896)

43 Murrayfield Road, Edinburgh, EH12 6EU
☎ (0131) 337 1009
(0131) 313 0721
marjorie@murrayfieldgolfclub.ltd.uk
815
Mrs MK Thomson (0131) 337 3478
Kieron Stevenson (0131) 337 3479
18 L 5794 yds Par 70 SSS 69
WD–I WE–M
££ £35 (£45)
2 miles W of Edinburgh centre, 2 miles E of airport
www.murrayfieldgolfclub.co.uk

Newbattle (1896)

Abbey Road, Eskbank, Dalkeith, EH22 3AD
☎ (0131) 663 2123
(0131) 654 1810
mail@newbattlegolfclub.com
600
HG Stanners (0131) 663 1819
S McDonald (0131) 660 1631
18 L 6025 yds SSS 70
WD–U before 4pm WE–after 2pm
££ £25 D–£35
6 miles S of Edinburgh on A7/A68
HS Colt
www.newbattlegolfclub.com

Prestonfield (1920)

6 Priestfield Road North, Edinburgh, EH16 5HS
☎ (0131) 667 9665
(0131) 777 2727
generalmanager@prestonfieldgolf.com
900
JI Archibald (Gen Mgr) (0131) 667 9665
G Cook (0131) 667 8597
18 L 6207 yds SSS 70 Par 70
WD–U WE–Sat/Sun after 3.00pm SOC–WD & Sat/Sun after 3pm
££ £29 D–£39 (£35)
2 miles NE of Edinburgh City Centre, off A7 Dalkeith Road

⊕ Two practice areas with full facilities
⌂ Peter Robertson, modified by James Braid
▤ www.prestonfieldgolf.com

Ratho Park (1928)
Ratho, Edinburgh, EH28 8NX
☎ (0131) 335 0068
🖵 (0131) 333 1752
✉ secretary@rathoparkgolfclub.co.uk
📖 550 106(L) 72(J)
♠ CR Innes (0131) 335 0068
✓ A Pate (0131) 333 1406
🏴 18 L 5960 yds SSS 68
👥 U SOC – Mon–Fri
££ £27 D–£37 (£37)
🚗 8 miles W of Edinburgh centre (A71)
⌂ James Braid
▤ www.rathoparkgolfclub.co.uk

Ravelston (1912)
24 Ravelston Dykes Road, Edinburgh, EH4 3NZ
☎ (0131) 315 2486
📖 610
♠ Jim Lowrie
🏴 9 L 5170 yds SSS 66
👥 WD–H
££ WD–£18
🚗 Off Queensferry Road (A90). Turn S at Blackhall
⌂ James Braid

Royal Burgess Golfing Society of Edinburgh
(1735)
181 Whitehouse Road, Barnton, Edinburgh, EH4 6BU
☎ (0131) 339 2075
🖵 (0131) 339 3712
✉ secretary@royalburgess.co.uk
📖 635 60(J)
♠ G Seeley (0131) 339 2075
✓ S Brian (0131) 339 6474
🏴 18 L 6486 yds Par 71 SSS 71
👥 I SOC
££ £65 D–£65 (£75)
🚗 Queensferry Road (A90)
⊕ Putting green
⌂ Tom Morris
▤ www.royalburgess.co.uk

Silverknowes (1947)
Public
Silverknowes Parkway, Edinburgh, EH4 5ET
☎ (0131) 336 3843 (Starter)

Swanston (1927)
111 Swanston Road, Fairmilehead, Edinburgh, EH10 7DS
☎ (0131) 445 2239
🖵 (0131) 445 2239
📖 350
♠ RL Knowles
✓ S Pardoe (0131) 445 4002
🏴 18 L 5004 yds SSS 65
👥 U exc comp days–NA WE–NA after 1pm

££ £15 D–£20 (£20 D–£25)
🚗 S of Edinburgh, off Biggar road (A702) Edinburgh Bypass

Torphin Hill (1895)
37-39 Torphin Road, Edinburgh, EH13 0PG
☎ (0131) 441 1100
🖵 (0131) 441 7166
✉ torphinhillgc@btconnect.com
📖 450
♠ WH McCathie
✓ J Browne (0131) 441 4061)
🏴 18 L 5285 yds SSS 67
👥 WD–U WE–U exc comp days SOC
££ D–£15 (£20)
🚗 SW boundary of Edinburgh

Turnhouse (1897)
154 Turnhouse Road, Corstorphine, Edinburgh, EH12 0AD
☎ (0131) 339 1014
🖵 (0131) 339 1844
✉ secretary@turnhousegc.com
📖 640
♠ DJ Cullum
✓ J Murray (0131) 339 7701
🏴 18 L 6153 yds SSS 70
👥 WD WE SOC
££ On application
🚗 W of Edinburgh (A9080) at end of city bypass
⊕ Large practice area
⌂ James Braid
▤ www.turnhousegc.com

West Lothian

Bathgate (1892)
Edinburgh Road, Bathgate, EH48 1BA
☎ (01506) 652232
🖵 (01506) 636775
✉ bathgate.golfclub@lineone.net
📖 760
♠ WA Osborne (01506) 630505
✓ S Strachan (01506) 630553
🏴 18 L 6328 yds SSS 71
👥 U
££ £20 (£25)
🚗 15 miles W of Edinburgh. M8 Junction 4
⌂ Wm Park Sr
▤ www.bathgategolfclub.visps.com

Bridgend & District
(1994)
Willowdean, Bridgend, Linlithgow, EH49 6NW
☎ (01506) 834140

Deer Park G&CC (1978)
Golf Course Road, Knightsridge, Livingston, EH54 8AB
☎ (01506) 446699
🖵 (01506) 435608
✉ deerpark@muir-group.co.uk
📖 850
♠ Joe Gallacher (Gen Mgr)

✓ B Dunbar
🏴 18 L 6688 yds SSS 72
👥 U SOC
££ £25 (£35)
🚗 N of Livingston. M8 Junction 3
▤ www.deer-park.co.uk

Dundas Parks (1957)
South Queensferry, EH30 9SS
☎ (0131)331 4252
📖 550
♠ Mrs C Wood (0131) 319 1347
🏴 9 L 6056 yds SSS 69
👥 M I SOC
££ D–£15
🚗 Dundas Estate (Private). 1 mile S of Queensferry (A8000)
▤ www.dundasparks.co.uk

Greenburn (1953)
6 Greenburn Road, Fauldhouse, EH47 9HJ
☎ (01501) 770292
🖵 (01501) 772615
✉ administrator@greenburngolfclub .freeserve.co.uk
📖 730
♠ Adrian McGowan
✓ Scott Catlin (01501) 771187
🏴 18 L 6067 yds SSS 71
👥 U
££ On application
🚗 4 miles S of M8 Junction 4 (East)/Junction 5 (West)
▤ www.greenburngolfclub.co.uk

Harburn (1933)
West Calder, EH55 8RS
☎ (01506) 871256
🖵 (01506) 870286
✉ info@harburngolfclub.co.uk
📖 600 80(L) 120(J)
♠ J McLinden (01506) 871131
✓ S Mills (01506) 871582
🏴 18 L 6125 yds SSS 69
👥 U
££ £20 (£30)
🚗 2 miles S of W Calder on B7008, via A70 or A71
▤ www.harburngolfclub.co.uk

Linlithgow (1913)
Braehead, Linlithgow, EH49 6QF
☎ (01506) 842585
🖵 (01506) 842764
✉ linlithgowgolf@talk21.com
📖 430
♠ TI Adams
✓ S Rosie (01506) 844356
🏴 18 L 5813 yds SSS 68
👥 U exc Sat–NA SOC
££ £20 D–£25 Sun–£25 D–£30
🚗 SW of Linlithgow, off M9
⌂ Robert Simpson

Niddry Castle (1983)
Castle Road, Winchburgh, EH52 2RQ
☎ (01506) 891097
🖵 (01506) 891097
📖 500
♠ G McLeod
🏴 18 L 5914 yds SSS 69

👤 U
💷 £15 (£22)
🚗 10 miles W of Edinburgh (B9080)
🖥 www.niddrycastlegc.co.uk

Oatridge   (2000)
Pay and play
Ecclesmachen, Broxburn, West Lothian, EH52 6NH
☎ (01506) 859636
📧 oatridge@btconnect.com
🏛 250
✍ Brian Inglis
🏌 9 L 2770 yds Par 69 SSS 67 for 18 holes
👤 U
💷 9: £10 (£13); 18: £16 (£20)
🚗 1 mile W of Broxham off M8 J3
🖥 www.oatridge.ac.uk

Polkemmet   (1981)
Public
Whitburn, Bathgate, EH47 0AD
☎ (01501) 743905
📠 (01501) 744780
📧 mail@beecraigs.com
🏌 9 L 2946 metres SSS 37
👤 U
💷 £5.50 (£6.50)
🚗 Between Whitburn and Harthill on B7066. M8 Junctions 4/5
⊕ Driving range

Pumpherston   (1895)
Drumshoreland Road, Pumpherston, EH53 0LH
☎ (01506) 432869/433336
📠 (01506) 438250
📧 sheena.corner@tiscali.co.uk
🏛 537 33(L) 126(J)
✍ GC Walker (01506) 882904
✓ R Fyvie (01506) 433337
🏌 18 L 6006 yds Par 70 SSS 69
👤 WD–U SOC–WD
💷 £21 D–£28 (£27 D–£40)
🚗 14 miles W of Edinburgh. M8 Junction 3
⊕ Practice putting, bunkers & pitching area; driving range
🏠 Graeme Webster
🖥 www.pumpherstongolfclub.co.uk

Rutherford Castle
(1998)
West Linton, EH46 7AS
☎ (01968) 661233
📠 (01968) 661233
📧 info@ruth-castlegc.co.uk
🏛 150
✓ None
🏌 18 L 6558 yds Par 72 SSS 71
👤 U SOC
💷 £15 (£25)
🚗 10 miles S of Edinburgh on A702
🏠 Bryan Moor
🖥 www.ruth-castlegc.co.uk

Uphall   (1895)
Houston Mains, Uphall, EH52 6JT
☎ (01506) 856404

📠 (01506) 855358
📧 uphallgolfclub@business-unmetered.com
🏛 650
✍ JA Little
✓ G Law (01506) 855553
🏌 18 L 5588 yds Par 69 SSS 67
👤 U
💷 £15 D–£20 (£20 D–£30)
🚗 7 miles W of Edinburgh Airport (A8). M8 Junction 3

West Linton   (1890)
Medwin Road, West Linton, EH46 7HN
☎ (01968) 660970
📠 (01968) 660970
📧 secretarywlgc@btinternet.com
🏛 750 100 (J)
✍ JS Macnab (01968) 660970
✓ I Wright (01968) 660256
🏌 18 L 6132 yds SSS 70
👤 WD–U WE–phone Pro
💷 £25 D–£40 (£40)
🚗 18 miles S of Edinburgh on A702
🖥 www.wlgc.co.uk

West Lothian   (1892)
Airngath Hill, Linlithgow, EH49 7RH
☎ (01506) 826030
📠 (01506) 826462
🏛 850
✍ I Osborough
✓ I Taylor (01506) 825060
🏌 18 L 6249 yds SSS 70
👤 WD–NA after 4pm WE–by arrangement
💷 On application
🚗 1 mile N of Linlithgow, towards Bo'ness
⊕ Buggies for hire
🏠 W Park Jr/Adams/Middleton
🖥 www.thewestlothiangolfclub.co.uk

Moray

Buckpool   (1933)
Barhill Road, Buckie, AB56 1DU
☎ (01542) 832236
📠 (01542) 832236
📧 golf@buckpoolgolf.com
🏛 500
✍ Mrs M Robertson
🏌 18 L 6097 yds SSS 69
👤 U
💷 £18 D–£23 (£23 D–£28)
🚗 W end of Buckpool, ¹/₂ mile off A98
🖥 www.buckpoolgolf.com

Dufftown   (1896)
Tomintoul Road, Dufftown, AB55 4BS
☎ (01340) 820325
📠 (01340) 820325
📧 admin@dufftowngolfclub.com
🏛 310
✍ IR Montgomery
✓ None
🏌 18 L 5308 yds SSS 67
👤 U

💷 £15 D–£20
🚗 1 mile SW of Dufftown on B9009
🏠 A Simpson
🖥 www.dufftowngolfclub.com

Elgin   (1906)
Hardhillock, Birnie Road, Elgin, IV30 8SX
☎ (01343) 542338
📠 (01343) 542341
📧 secretary@elgingolfclub.com
🏛 732 150(L) 144(J)
✍ JS Macpherson
✓ K Stables (01343) 542884
🏌 18 L 6449 yds SSS 71
👤 WD–U after 9.30am WE–U after 10am SOC–WD SOC–WE by arrangement
💷 £30 D–£40
🚗 1 mile S of Elgin on A941
⊕ Driving range
🏠 John MacPherson
🖥 www.elgingolfclub.com

Forres   (1889)
Muiryshade, Forres, IV36 2RD
☎ (01309) 672949
📠 (01309) 672261
📧 forresgolfclub@tiscali.co.uk
🏛 950 150(J)
✍ David Mackintosh
✓ S Aird (01309) 672250
🏌 18 L 6141 yds SSS 70
👤 U SOC
💷 £24 (£22)
🚗 1 mile SE of Forres, off B9010
⊕ Practice range
🖥 www.forresgolf.org.uk

Garmouth & Kingston
(1932)
Spey Street, Garmouth, Fochabers, IV32 7NJ
☎ (01343) 870388
📠 (01343) 870388
📧 garmouthgolfclub@aol.com
🏛 600
✍ Mrs I Fraser
🏌 18 L 5935 yds SSS 69
👤 U SOC
💷 £20 D–£25 (£25 D–£28)
🚗 8 miles NE of Elgin

Hopeman   (1909)
Hopeman, Moray, IV30 5YA
☎ (01343) 830578
📠 (01343) 830152
📧 hopemangc@aol.com
🏛 700
✍ J Fraser (01343) 835068
🏌 18 L 5624 yds SSS 68
👤 WD–NA between 12.45–1.15 Sat–NA before 10am and 12.30–2pm Sun–NA before 9am SOC
💷 £20 (£25)
🚗 7 miles NW of Elgin on B9012
🏠 J McKenzie
🖥 www.hopemangc.co.uk

Moray (1889)
Stotfield Road, Lossiemouth, IV31 6QS
- ☎ **(01343) 812018**
- 🖳 (01343) 815102
- ✉ secretary@moraygolf.co.uk
- 📖 1500
- ✍ SM Crane
- ⌁ A Thomson (01343) 813330
- � Old 18 L 6697yds SSS 73
  New 18 L 6005 yds SSS 69
- 👥 U H SOC WD/WE after 10am
- ££ On application
- ⛳ 6 miles N of Elgin
- ⊕ Practice range; golf buggies
- ⌂ Old Tom Morris
- 📧 www.moraygolf.co.uk

Spey Bay (1904)
Spey Bay Hotel, Spey Bay, Fochabers,
IV32 7PJ
- ☎ **(01343) 820424**
- ✉ info@speybay.com

Perth & Kinross

Aberfeldy (1895)
Taybridge Road, Aberfeldy, PH15 2BH
- ☎ **(01887) 820535**
- 🖳 (01887) 820535
- ✉ abergc@tiscali.co.uk
- 📖 130
- ✍ AR Menzies (01887) 820535
- ⛛ 18 L 5600 yds Par 68 SSS 66
- 👥 U
- ££ £20 (£25)
- ⛳ 10 miles W of Ballinluig, off A9
- ⌂ Souters
- 📧 www.aberfeldygolfclub.co.uk

Alyth (1894)
Pitcrocknie, Alyth, PH11 8HF
- ☎ **(01828) 632268**
- 🖳 (01828) 633491
- ✉ enquiries@alythgolfclub.co.uk
- 📖 850
- ✍ J Docherty
- ⌁ T Melville (01828) 632411
- ⛛ 18 L 6205 yds SSS 70
- 👥 U SOC
- ££ On application
- ⛳ 16 miles NW of Dundee (A91)
- ⌂ Tom Morris/James Braid
- 📧 www.alythgolfclub.co.uk

Auchterarder (1892)
Orchil Road, Auchterarder, PH3 1LS
- ☎ **(01764) 662804**
- 🖳 (01764) 664423
- ✉ secretary@auchterardergolf.co.uk
- 📖 820
- ✍ WM Campbell
- ⌁ G Baxter (01764) 663711
- ⛛ 18 L 5757 yds SSS 68
- 👥 U SOC
- ££ £25 D–£35 (£30 D–£45)
- ⛳ 1 mile SW of Auchterarder
- 📧 www.auchterardergolf.co.uk

Bishopshire (1903)
Pay and play
Kinnesswood, Woodmarch, Kinross,
KY13 9HX
- 📖 100
- ✍ T Cascarino (01592) 783003
- ⛛ 10 L 4707 yds SSS 63
- 👥 U
- ££ £6 (£12)
- ⛳ 3 miles E of Kinross (A911). M90
  Junction 6
- ⌂ W Park

Blair Atholl (1896)
Invertilt Road, Blair Atholl, PH18 5TG
- ☎ **(01796) 481407**
- 🖳 (01796) 481751
- 📖 445
- ✍ T Boon
- ⛛ 9 L 5816 yds SSS 68
- 👥 U
- ££ £20 (£22)
- ⛳ 35 miles N of Perth, off A9

Blairgowrie (1889)
Rosemount, Blairgowrie, PH10 6LG
- ☎ **(01250) 872622**
- 🖳 (01250) 875451
- ✉ office@theblairgowriegolfclub
  .co.uk
- 📖 1700
- ✍ D Swarbrick (Managing Sec)
  (01250) 872622
- ⌁ C Dernie (01250) 873116
- ⛛ Rosemount 18 L 6588 yds SSS 72
  Landsdowne 18 L 6895 yds SSS 73
  Wee 9 L 4614 yds SSS 63
- 👥 Mon/Tues/Thurs–U H 8am–12 &
  2–3.30pm Wed/Fri/WE–restricted
- ££ On application
- ⛳ 1 mile S of Blairgowrie, off A93. 15
  miles N of Perth
- ⌂ Rosemount-Braid; Lansdowne-
  Alliss/Thomas; Wee-Old Tom
  Morris
- 📧 www.theblairgowriegolfclub.co.uk

Callander (1890)
Aveland Road, Callander, FK17 8EN
- ☎ **(01877) 330090**
- 🖳 (01877) 330062
- ✉ callandergc@nextcall.net
- 📖 500
- ✍ Mrs S Smart
- ⌁ A Martin (01877) 330975
- ⛛ 18 L 5185 yds SSS 65
- 👥 U SOC
- ££ £20 (£28)
- ⛳ Off A84, E end of Callander
- ⊕ Putting green; practice area
  (covered bay); swing analysis
  (indoor); indoor training room
- ⌂ Tom Morris
- 📧 www.callandergolfclub.co.uk

Comrie (1891)
Laggan Braes, Comrie, PH6 2LR
- ☎ **(01764) 670055**
- ✉ enquiries@comriegolf.co.uk
- 📖 400
- ⛛ 9 L 3020 yds Par 70 SSS 70

- 👥 U exc Mon 4.00 pm onwards
- ££ D–£20 (£25)
- ⛳ 7 miles W of Crieff (A85)
- 📧 www.comriegolf.co.uk

Craigie Hill (1909)
Cherrybank, Perth, PH2 0NE
- ☎ **(01738) 620829**
- 🖳 (01738) 624250
- ✉ golf@craigiehill.com
- 📖 625
- ✍ Administration (01738) 620829
- ⌁ K Esson (01738) 622644
- ⛛ 18 L 5386 yds SSS 67
- 👥 U exc Sat
- ££ £20 (£25)
- ⛳ W boundary of Perth
- ⊕ Practice area; putting green
- ⌂ Fernie/Anderson
- 📧 www.craigiehill.scottishgolf.co.uk

Crieff (1891)
Perth Road, Crieff, PH7 3LR
- ☎ **(01764) 652909**
  (Bookings)
- 🖳 (01764) 655096
- ✉ secretary@crieffgolf.co.uk
- 📖 803
- ✍ JS Miller (01764) 652397
- ⌁ DJW Murchie
- ⛛ Ferntower 18 L 6474 yds SSS 72
  Dornock 9 L 4772 yds SSS 63
- 👥 U H NA–12–2pm or after 5pm
  SOC
- ££ Ferntower £33 (£42) Dornock £16
- ⛳ 1 mile NE of Crieff (A85). 17 miles
  W of Perth
- ⌂ James Braid
- 📧 www.crieffgolf.co.uk

Dalmunzie (1948)
Glenshee, Blairgowrie, PH10 7QE
- ☎ **(01250) 885226**
- ✉ enquiries@dalmunziecottages.com
- 📖 80
- ✍ S Winton (Mgr)
- ⛛ 9 L 2099 yds SSS 61
- 👥 U
- ££ D–£14
- ⛳ 20 miles N of Blairgowrie on A93.
  (Dalmunzie Hotel sign)
- ⌂ Alistair MacKenzie
- 📧 www.dalmunziecottages.com

Dunkeld & Birnam
(1892)
Fungarth, Dunkeld, PH8 0ES
- ☎ **(01350) 727524**
- 🖳 (01350) 728660
- ✉ secretary-dunkeld@tiscali.co.uk
- 📖 590
- ✍ RW Baldie
- ⌁ None
- ⛛ 18 L 5511 yds SSS 67
- 👥 WD–U WE–phone first
- ££ On application
- ⛳ Dunkeld 1 mile, off A923. 15 miles
  N of Perth
- 📧 www.dunkeldandbirnamgolfclub
  .co.uk

Dunning   (1953)
Rollo Park, Dunning, PH2 0QX
☎ **(01764) 684747**

Foulford Inn   (1995)
Pay and play
Crieff, PH7 3LN
☎ **(01764) 652407**
📠 (01764) 652407
📧 foulford@btconnect.com
♘ M Beaumont
⤷ 9 hole Par 3 course
♙ U
££ £5 D–£7
🖳 www.foulfordinn.co.uk

The Gleneagles Hotel
Auchterarder, PH3 1NF
☎ **(01764) 662231**
    (01764) 662231 (Hotel)
📠 (01764) 662134
📧 resort.sales@gleneagles.com
♘ Patrick Elsmie (Hotel)
⤏ Russell Smith (01764) 694343
⤷ King's 18 L 6471 yds SSS 71
    Queen's 18 L 5965 yds SSS 69
    PGA Centenary 18 L 7081 SSS 74
    9 hole Par 3 course
♙ U
££ May–Sept £115
⊛ 16 miles SW of Perth on A9
⊕ Driving range; golf academy
♙ Braid/Nicklaus
🖳 www.gleneagles.com

Glenisla   (1998)
Proprietary
Pitcrocknie Farm, Alyth, PH11 8JJ
☎ **(01828) 632445**
📠 (01828) 633749
📖 300
♘ Alison Stubbington (Mgr)
⤷ 18 L 6402 yds Par 71 SSS 72
♙ U H
££ £24 (£29)
⊛ Nr Alyth (B954)
⊕ Driving range
♙ Tony Wardle
🖳 www.golf-glenisla.co.uk

Kenmore   (1992)
Pay and play
Mains of Taymouth, Kenmore, Aberfeldy, PH15 2HN
☎ **(01887) 830226**
📠 (01887) 829059
📧 info@taymouth.co.uk
📖 200
♘ R Menzies (Mgr)
⤏ None
⤷ 9 L 6052 yds SSS 69
♙ U SOC
££ 9: £15 (£17) 18: £20 (£25)
⊛ Kenmore, 6 miles W of Aberfeldy on A827
♙ D Menzies & Partners
🖳 www.taymouth.co.uk

Killin   (1911)
Killin, FK21 8TX
☎ **(01567) 820312**
📠 (01567) 820312
📧 info@killingolfclub.co.uk
📖 253
♘ Rev TR Taylor (01838) 411 083
⤏ (0771) 374 1578
⤷ 9 L 5036 yds Par 66 SSS 65
♙ U SOC–Apr–Oct
££ £18 (£18)
⊛ Killin, W end of Loch Tay
♙ John Duncan
🖳 www.killingolfclub.co.uk

King James VI   (1858)
Moncreiffe Island, Perth, PH2 8NR
☎ **(01738) 625170**
    (01738) 632460 (Starter)
📠 (01738) 445132
📧 info@kingjamesvi.co.uk
📖 675
♘ M Butler (01738) 445132
⤏ A Crerar (01738) 632460
⤷ 18 L 6038 yds SSS 69
♙ U exc Sat Sun–by reservation
££ £22 D–£30 Sun D–£32
⊛ Island in River Tay, Perth
♙ Tom Morris
🖳 www.kingjamesvi.co.uk

Kinross Golf Courses
    (1900)
c/o The Green Hotel, 2 The Muirs, Kinross, KY13 8AS
☎ **(01577) 863407**
📠 (01577) 863180
📧 bookings@golfkinross.com
📖 450
♘ Eileen Gray
⤏ Stuart Geraghty (01577) 865125
⤷ The Bruce: 18 L 6231 yds SSS 71
    The Montgomery: 18 L 6452 yds SSS 72
♙ U
££ The Bruce: £25 D–£35 (£35 D–£4
    The Montgomerey: £30 D–£45
    (£40 D–£55); 1 round on each
    course: D–£40 (D–£50)
⊛ Mile from M90 jct 6
♙ Sir David Montgomery
🖳 www.golfkinross.com

Milnathort   (1910)
South Street, Milnathort, Kinross, KY13 9XA
☎ **(01577) 864069**
📧 milnathort.gc@btconnect.com
📖 575
♘ K Dziennik (Admin. Mgr)
⤷ 9 L 5985 yds SSS 69
♙ U SOC
££ £15 D–£22 (£17 D–£25)
⊛ 1 mile N of Kinross. M90 Junction 6/7

Muckhart   (1908)
Drumburn Road, Muckhart, Dollar, FK14 7JH
☎ **(01259) 781423**
📠 (01259) 781544

📧 enquiries@muckhartgolf.com
📖 550 125(L) 100(J)
♘ A Houston (01259) 781423
⤏ K Salmoni (01259) 781493
⤷ 27 L 6174-6069 yds SSS 70-71
♙ U SOC
££ £25 D–£35 (£30 D–£40)
⊛ A91, 3 miles E of Dollar, towards Rumbling Bridge
⊕ Practice area; pro shop
🖳 www.muckhartgolf.com

Murrayshall   (1981)
Murrayshall, New Scone, Perth, PH2 7PH
☎ **(01738) 554804**
📠 (01738) 552595
📧 info@murrayshall.co.uk
📖 300
♘ M Lloyd (Mgr)
⤏ AT Reid (01738) 552784
⤷ Murrayshall 18 L 6489 yds SSS 72
    Lynedoch 18 L 5362 yds SSS 69
♙ U SOC
££ Murrayshall £35 D–£45 Lynedoch £20 D–£35
⊛ 3 miles NE of Perth, off A94
⊕ Driving range
♙ Hamilton Stutt
🖳 www.murrayshall.co.uk

Muthill   (1911)
Peat Road, Muthill, PH5 2DA
☎ **(01764) 681523**
📠 (01764) 681557
📧 muthillgolfclub@lineone.net
📖 350
♘ Alex T Fernie
⤷ 9 L 2371 yds SSS 63
    Different tees for back 9
♙ U SOC
££ £15 (£18)
⊛ 3 miles S of Crieff on A822
🖳 www.muthillgolfclub.co.uk

North Inch
Public
c/o Perth & Kinross Council, Environment Services, Pollar House, 35 Kinncoll St, Perth PH1 5GD
☎ **(01738) 636481 (Starter)**

Pitlochry   (1909)
Pitlochry Estate Office, Pitlochry, PH16 5NE
☎ **(01796) 472792 (Bookings)**
📠 (01796) 473947 (bookings)
📧 pro@pitlochrygolf.co.uk
📖 400 approx.
♘ DCM McKenzie JP (01796) 472114
⤏ M Pirie (01796) 472792 (PGA Pro)
⤷ 18 L 5670 yds SSS 69
♙ U SOC
££ On application
⊛ N side of Pitlochry (A9). 28 miles NW of Perth
⊕ Putting green; practice area with bunker and golf net
♙ Fernie/Hutchison
🖳 www.pitlochrygolf.co.uk

Royal Perth Golfing Society
(1824)

Club

1/2 Atholl Crescent, Perth, PH1 5NG

☎ **(01738) 622265**
✉ royal.perth@virgin.net
📖 200
🏌 DP McDonald (Gen Sec)
(01738) 622265, L Rutherford
(Golf Sec) (01764) 664049
🏴 Play over North Inch, Perth &
Strathmore courses
🖥 www.royal-perth-golfing-
society.org.uk

St Fillans (1903)

South Lochearn Rd, St Fillans, PH26 2NJ

☎ **(01764) 685312**
✉ stfillansgolf@aol.com

Strathmore Golf Centre
(1995)

Pay and play

Leroch, Alyth, Blairgowrie, PH11 8NZ

☎ **(01828) 633322**
✉ enquiries@strathmoregolf.com

Strathtay (1909)

Upper Derculich, Strathtay, Pitlochry,
PH9 0LR

☎ **(01887) 840373**
📠 (01887) 840777
✉ aivr@aol.com
📖 210
🏌 AIV Robinson
🏴 9 L 4082 yds Par 62 SSS 61
👥 U SOC Tee reserved Sun 12–2
££ D–£12 (£15)
⛳ 4 miles W of Ballinluig (A827),
towards Aberfeldy

Taymouth Castle (1923)

Kenmore, Aberfeldy, PH15 2NT

☎ **(01887) 830228**

Whitemoss (1994)

Whitemoss Road, Dunning, Perth,
PH2 0QX

☎ **(01738) 730300**
📠 (01738) 730490
✉ enquiries@whiterossgolfclub.com
📖 500
🏌 A Nicolson
✓ None
🏴 18 L 6200 yds Par 69 SSS 69
👥 U SOC
££ £15 (£20)
⛳ Aberuthven, 10 miles SW of Perth,
off A9
🖥 www.whiterossgolfclub.com

Renfrewshire

Barshaw (1927)

Public

Barshaw Park, Glasgow Road, Paisley, PA2

☎ **(0141) 889 2908**

Bonnyton (1957)

Eaglesham, Glasgow, G76 0QA

☎ **(01355) 302781**
📠 (01355) 303151
📖 950
🏌 A Hughes
✓ K McWade (01355) 302256
🏴 18 L 6255 yds SSS 71
👥 I SOC–WD
££ £40
⛳ 2 miles W of Eaglesham. 6 miles S
of Glasgow

Caldwell (1903)

Caldwell, Uplawmoor, G78 4AU

☎ **(01505) 850329**
📠 (01505) 850604
✉ CaldwellGolfClub@aol.com
📖 450
🏌 HIF Harper (01505) 850366
✓ S Forbes (01505) 850616
🏴 18 L 6335 yds SSS 71
👥 WD–booking before 4pm–M after
4pm WE–M
££ On application
⛳ 5 miles SW of Barrhead on A736
Glasgow-Irvine road
🖥 www.caldwellgolfclub.i8.com

Cochrane Castle (1895)

Scott Avenue, Craigston, Johnstone,
PA5 0HF

☎ **(01505) 320146**
📠 (01505) 325338
✉ secretary@cochranecastle.sol
.co.uk
📖 425
🏌 Mrs PlJ Quin
✓ A Logan (01505) 328465
🏴 18 L 6194 yds Par 71 SSS 71
👥 WD–U WE–M
££ £22 (£30)
⛳ ½ mile S of Beith Road,
Johnstone
🏛 Charles Hunter
🖥 www.cochranecastle.com

East Renfrewshire
(1922)

Pilmuir, Newton Mearns, G77 6RT

☎ **(01355) 500256**
📠 (01355) 500323
✉ secretary@eastrengolfclub.co.uk
📖 450
🏌 G J Tennant (01355) 500256
✓ S Russell (01355) 500206
🏴 18 L 6107 yds Par 70 SSS 70
👥 WD–H SOC on application
££ £40 D–£50
⛳ 2 miles SW of Newton Mearns –
M77 J5
🏛 James Braid
🖥 www.eastrengolfclub.co.uk

Eastwood (1893)

Muirshield, Loganswell, Newton Mearns,
Glasgow G77 6RX

☎ **(01355) 500261**
📠 (01355) 500333
✉ eastwoodgolfclub@btconnect.com
📖 900

🏌 I Brown (01355) 500280
✓ I Darroch (01355) 500285
🏴 18 L 6071 yds SSS 70
👥 WD SOC
££ £30 D–£40
⛳ 9 miles SW of Glasgow off M77.
Take A726/A77 turnoff then A77 S
1m
🏛 Theodore Moone/Graeme
Webster
🖥 www.eastwoodgolfclub.co.uk

Elderslie (1908)

63 Main Road, Elderslie, PA5 9AZ

☎ **(01505) 323956**
📠 (01505) 340346
📖 450
🏌 Mrs A Anderson
✓ R Bowman (01505) 320032
🏴 18 L 6165 yds SSS 70
👥 M–WE SOC–WD
££ £26 D–£36
⛳ 2 miles SW of Paisley
⊕ Practice area; putting green

Erskine (1904)

Golf Road, Bishopton, PA7 5PH

☎ **(01505) 862302**
📠 (01505) 862898
✉ manager@erskinegolfclublimited
.co.uk
📖 850
🏌 DF McKellar
✓ P Thomson (01505) 862108
🏴 18 L 6372 yds SSS 71
👥 WD SOC
££ £31 D–£42
⛳ 5 miles NW of Paisley; M8
🏛 James Braid, Willie Fernie,
Dr Alister Mackenzie
🖥 www.erskinegolfclublimited.co.uk

Fereneze (1904)

Fereneze Avenue, Barrhead, G78 1HJ

☎ **(0141) 881 1519**
📠 (0141) 881 1519
✉ ferenezegc@lineone.net
📖 700
🏌 G McCreadie (0141) 881 7149
✓ J Smallwood (0141) 880 7058
🏴 18 L 5962 yds SSS 70
👥 SOC–WD
££ £30 D–£35
⛳ 9 miles SW of Glasgow
🖥 www.ferenezegolfclub.co.uk

Gleddoch (1974)

Langbank, PA14 6YE

☎ **(01475) 540711**
📖 450
🏌 DW Tierney
✓ K Campbell (01475) 540704
🏴 18 L 6375 yds SSS 71
👥 WD–U WE–restricted SOC
££ £30 (£40)
⛳ 16 miles W of Glasgow (M8/A8)
⊕ Four-hole golf academy; driving
range
🏛 J Hamilton Stutt

Gourock   (1896)
Cowal View, Gourock, PA19 1HD
☎ **(01475) 631001**
📠 (01475) 631001
📧 secretary@gourockgolfclub.com
📖 497 79(L) 198(J)
🖈 AD Taylor
⌛ J Mooney (01475) 636834
🏳 18 L 6408 yds Par 73 SSS 72
👤 WD–I before 4.30pm SOC
££ £25 (D–£32)
🗺 3 miles SW of Greenock, off A770.
   7 miles W of Port Glasgow
🖥 www.gourockgolfclub.com

Greenock   (1890)
Forsyth Street, Greenock, PA16 8RE
☎ **(01475) 720793**

Kilmacolm   (1891)
Porterfield Road, Kilmacolm, PA13 4PD
☎ **(01505) 872139**

Lochwinnoch   (1897)
Burnfoot Road, Lochwinnoch, PA12 4AN
☎ **(01505) 842153**

Old Ranfurly – Old Course Ranfurly   (1905)
Ranfurly Place, Bridge of Weir, PA11 3DE
☎ **(01505) 613612 (Clubhouse)**
📠 (01505) 613214
📧 secretary@oldranfurly.com
📖 817
🖈 QJ McClymont (01505) 613214
⌛ Grant Miller
🏳 18 L 6089 yds SSS 70
👤 WD–I WE–M SOC
££ £25–£35 round/day. No WE visitors
🗺 7 miles W of Paisley, off A761
🏠 W Campbell
🖥 www.oldranfurly.com

Paisley   (1895)
Braehead Road, Paisley, PA2 8TZ
☎ **(0141) 884 2292 (Clubhouse)**
📠 (0141) 884 3903
📧 paisleygolfclub@btconnect.com
📖 820
🖈 J Hillis (0141) 884 3903
⌛ G Stewart (0141) 884 4114
🏳 18 L 6466 yds Par 71 SSS 72
👤 WD–H SOC
££ £30 D–£40
🗺 Glenburn, S of Paisley, M8 Jct 27
🏠 John H Stutt
🖥 www.paisleygolfclub.com

Port Glasgow   (1895)
Devol Road, Port Glasgow, PA14 5XE
☎ **(01475) 704181**
📧 secretary@portglasgowgolfclub.com
📖 265
🖈 H McGuiness
🏳 18 L 5712 yds SSS 68

👤 WD–U before 5pm –M after 5pm WE–NA SOC
££ £18 D–£24 (£24 D–£34)
🗺 1 mile S of Port Glasgow at end of M8 west
🏠 James Braid
🖥 www.portglasgowgolfclub.com

Ranfurly Castle   (1889)
Golf Road, Bridge of Weir, PA11 3HN
☎ **(01505) 612609**
📠 (01505) 610406
📧 secranfur@aol.com
📖 400 160(A) 120(J)
🖈 J King
⌛ T Eckford (01505) 614795
🏳 18 L 6284 yds SSS 71
👤 WD–H WE–NA before noon SOC–WD
££ £30 D–£40
🗺 7 miles W of Paisley (A761)
🏠 Kirkcaldy/Auchterlonie
🖥 www.ranfurlycastle.co.uk

Renfrew   (1894)
Blythswood Estate, Inchinnan Road, Renfrew, PA4 9EG
☎ **(0141) 886 6692**
📠 (0141) 886 1808
📧 secretary@renfrew.scottishgolf.com
📖 465 110(L) 80(J)
🖈 Martin Kinghorn
⌛ D Grant (0141) 885 1754
🏳 18 L 6818 yds SSS 73
👤 WD–H WE–M SOC–WD
££ £30
🗺 3 miles N of Paisley, nr Airport. M8 Junctions 26 or 27
🏠 Cdr JD Harris
🖥 www.renfrewgolfclub.co.uk

Whitecraigs   (1905)
72 Ayr Road, Giffnock, Glasgow, G46 6SW
☎ **(0141) 639 4530**
📠 (0141) 616 3648
📧 whitecraigsgc@btconnect.com
📖 1150
🖈 AG Keith CA
⌛ A Forrow (0141) 639 2140
🏳 18 L 6013 yds SSS 70
👤 WD–U before 5pm WE–M SOC–WD
££ £40 D–£50 (£40 D–£50)
🗺 6 miles S of Glasgow (A77), nr Whitecraigs Station
⊕ Practice ground
🏠 Fernie
🖥 www.whitecraigsgolfclub.co.uk

Stirlingshire

Aberfoyle   (1890)
Braeval, Aberfoyle, FK8 3UY
☎ **(01877) 382493**
📖 550
🖈 EJ Barnard (01360) 550847
🏳 18 L 5218 yds SSS 66
👤 WD–U WE–NA before 11.30am

££ £18 D–£24 (£24 D–£30)
🗺 Aberfoyle, 18 miles W of Stirling (A81)
🖥 www.aberfoylegolf.com

Balfron   (1992)
Kepculloch Road, Balfron, G63 0QP
☎ **(0781) 482 7620**
📧 brian.a.davidson@btopenworld.com
📖 600
🖈 Brian Davidson (01360) 550613
⌛ None
🏳 18 L 5903 yds Par 72 SSS 70
👤 WD–U before 4pm WE–restricted SOC
££ £15 (£15)
🗺 18 miles NW of Glasgow, off A81
🖥 www.balfrongolfsociety.org.uk

Bonnybridge   (1925)
Larbert Road, Bonnybridge, Falkirk, FK4 1NY
☎ **(01324) 812822/812323**
📠 (01324) 812323
📧 bonnybridgegolfclub@btinternet.com
📖 425
🖈 J Mullen (01324) 812323
🏳 9 L 6058 yds SSS 70
👤 WD–I SOC
££ £16 D–£20
🗺 3 miles W of Falkirk. M876 Junction 1
⊕ Practice area

Bridge of Allan   (1895)
Sunnylaw, Bridge of Allan, Stirling
☎ **(01786) 832332**
📧 secretary@bofagc.com
📖 513
🖈 AA Blackstock
🏳 9 L 4932 yds SSS 66
👤 U exc Sat SOC (by arrangement)
££ £14 (£18)
🗺 4 miles N of Stirling, off A9
🏠 Tom Morris Sr
🖥 bridgeofallangolfclub.com

Buchanan Castle   (1936)
Proprietary
Drymen, G63 0HY
☎ **(01360) 660307**
📠 (01360) 660993
📖 730
🖈 Ms JA Dawson
⌛ K Baxter (01360) 660330
🏳 18 L 6047 yds SSS 69
👤 By prior arrangement with Pro
££ £38 D–£48 (D–£48)
🗺 18 miles NW of Glasgow. 25 miles W of Stirling, off A811
🏠 James Braid
🖥 www.buchanancastlegolfclub.com

Campsie   (1897)
Crow Road, Lennoxtown, Glasgow, G66 7HX
☎ **(01360) 310244**
📧 campsiegolfclub@aol.com

650
H Weston (Mgr)
M Brennan (01360) 310920
18 L 5517 yds SSS 68
WD–U before 4.30pm SOC;
Visitors WE by arrangement
££ £15 D–£25 (£20)
N of Lennoxtown on B822 Fintry road
Auchterlonie/Stark
www.campsiegolfclub.org.uk

Dunblane New   (1923)

Perth Road, Dunblane, FK15 0LJ
☎ (01786) 821521
(01786) 821522
secretary@dngc.co.uk
700
RD Morrison
RM Jamieson
18 L 5930 yds SSS 69
WD–U WE–M SOC
££ £25 (£35)
E side of Dunblane. 6 miles N of Stirling
James Braid

Falkirk   (1922)

Stirling Road, Camelon, Falkirk, FK2 7YP
☎ (01324) 611061/612219
(01324) 639573
falkirkgolfclub@btconnect.com
700
J Elliott
Stewart Craig
18 L 6282 yds SSS 70
WD–U until 4pm Sat–NA SOC–exc Sat
££ £20 D–£30 Sun–£40
1¹/2 miles W of Falkirk on A9
James Braid
www.falkirkcarmuirsgolfclub.co.uk

Falkirk Tryst   (1885)

86 Burnhead Road, Larbert, FK5 4BD
☎ (01324) 562415
(01324) 562054
secretary@falkirktrystgolfclub.com
800
RC Chalmers (01324) 562054
S Dunsmore (01324) 562091
18 L 6053 yds SSS 69
WD–U WE–M SOC–WD
££ £24 D–£30
3 miles NW of Falkirk on A88
www.falkirktrystgolfclub.com

Glenbervie   (1932)

Stirling Road, Larbert, FK5 4SJ
☎ (01324) 562605
(01324) 551054
secretary@glenberviegolfclub.com
700
IR Webster CA
David Ross (01324) 562725
18 L 6438 yds Par 71 SSS 71
WD–U before 4pm WE–M SOC–Tues & Thurs
££ £35 D–£50
1 mile N of Larbert on A9. M876 Junction 2 (from Cumbernauld)
James Braid
www.glenberviegolfclub.com

Grangemouth   (1973)

Public
Polmonthill, Polmont, FK2 0YA
☎ (01324) 711500
700
Jim McNairney
G McFarlane (01324) 503840
18 L 6527 yds SSS 70
U–book with Pro SOC
££ £17 D–£25 (£21 D–£29)
3 miles NE of Falkirk. M9 Jct 4

Kilsyth Lennox   (1905)

Tak-Ma-Doon Road, Kilsyth, G65 0RS
☎ (01236) 824115 (Bookings)
info@klgs.co.uk

Polmont   (1901)

Manuel Rigg, Maddiston, Falkirk, FK2 0LS
☎ (01324) 711277 (Clubhouse)
(01324) 712504
polmontgolfclub@btconnect.com
300
J Ingram (01324) 711277
9 L 3044 yds SSS 70
U exc Sat–NA
££ £10, Sun–£15
4 miles SE of Falkirk on B805

Stirling   (1869)

Queen's Road, Stirling, FK8 3AA
☎ (01786) 464098
(01786) 460090
enquiries@stirlinggolfclub.tv
1000
AMS Rankin (01786) 464098
I Collins (01786) 471490
18 L 6409 yds SSS 71
WD–U SOC WE–NA
££ £30 D–£45
¹/2 mile from Stirling centre. M9 Junction 10
Braid/Cotton
www.stirlinggolfclub.com

Strathendrick   (1901)

Glasgow Road, Drymen, G63 0AA
☎ (01360) 660695

Wales

Cardiganshire

Aberystwyth (1911)
Bryn-y-Mor, Aberystwyth, SY23 2HY
☎ **(01970) 615104**
🖬 (01970) 626622
🖂 aberystwythgolf@talk21.com
📖 390
✒ (01970) 625301
🏌 18 L 6119 yds Par 70 SSS 71
👥 U SOC
££ £25 (£30)
🚗 Aberystwyth ½ mile
🏠 H Varden
🖥 www.aberystwythgolfclub.com

Borth & Ynyslas (1885)
Borth, Ceredigion, SY24 5JS
☎ **(01970) 871202**
🖬 (01970) 871202
🖂 secretary@borthgolf.co.uk
📖 550
✒ GJ Pritchard
✒ JG Lewis (01970) 871557
🏌 18 L 6100 yds SSS 70
👥 WD–U WE/BH–by prior arrangement SOC
££ £28
🚗 8 miles N of Aberystwyth (B4353), off A487
⊕ Practice ground
🖥 www.borthgolf.co.uk

Cardigan (1895)
Gwbert-on-Sea, Cardigan, SA43 1PR
☎ **(01239) 612035/621775**
🖬 (01239) 621775
🖂 golf@cardigan.fsnet.co.uk
📖 600
✒ JJ Jones (01239) 621775
✒ S Parsons (01239) 615359
🏌 18 L 6687 yds SSS 73
👥 H SOC
££ D–£27.50 (£35) W–£110
🚗 3 miles N of Cardigan
⊕ Practice area; junior golf academy
🏠 Grant/Hawtree
🖥 www.cardigangolf.co.uk

Cilgwyn (1905)
Llangybi, Lampeter, SA48 8NN
☎ **(01570) 493286**
📖 160
✒ JD Morgan
🏌 9 L 5327 yds SSS 67
👥 U SOC
££ £15 (£20)
🚗 5 miles NE of Lampeter, off A485 at Llangybi
⊕ Practice area
🖥 www.cilgwyngolf.co.uk

Penrhos G&CC (1991)
Llanrhystud, Ceredigion, SY23 5AY
☎ **(01974) 202999**
🖬 (01974) 202100
🖂 info@Penrhosgolf.co.uk
📖 300
✒ R Rees-Evans
✒ P Diamond
🏌 18 L 6660 yds SSS 73
9 hole Par 3 course/Par 4
👥 U SOC
££ £25 (£35)
🚗 9 miles S of Aberystwyth, signposted off A487
⊕ Driving range
🏠 Jim Walters
🖥 www.Penrhosgolf.co.uk

Carmarthenshire

Ashburnham (1894)
Cliffe Terrace, Burry Port, SA16 0HN
☎ **(01554) 832269**
🖬 (01554) 832269
🖂 golf@ashburnhamgolfclub.co.uk
📖 500
✒ Ian K Church
✒ RA Ryder (01554) 833846
🏌 18 L 6916 yds SSS 73
👥 WD–H WE–H after 12 noon only
££ £50 D–£60 (£65)
🚗 5 miles W of Llanelli (A484)
🏠 JH Taylor
🖥 www.ashburnhamgolfclub.co.uk

Carmarthen (1907)
Blaenycoed Road, Carmarthen, SA33 6EH
☎ **(01267) 281588**
🖬 (01267) 281493
🖂 carmarthengolfc@aol.com
📖 700
✒ Clive Edwards
✒ John Hartley (01267) 281493
🏌 18 L 6245 yds SSS 71
👥 U
££ £20 (£25)
🚗 4 miles NW of Carmarthen
⊕ Driving range
🏠 JH Taylor
🖥 www.carmarthengolfclub.com

Derllys Court (1993)
Proprietary
Derllys Court, Llysonnen Road, Carmarthen, SA33 5DT
☎ **(01267) 211575**
🖬 (01267) 211575
🖂 derllys@hotmail.com
✒ R Walters
🏌 18 L 5847 yds Par 70 SSS 68
👥 U SOC
🚗 4 miles W of Carmarthen, off A40
⊕ Practice area
🏠 P Johnson/S Finney
🖥 www.derllyscourtgolfclub.com

Garnant Park (1997)
Garnant, Ammanford, SA18 1NP
☎ **(01269) 823365**
🖬 (01269) 823365
🖂 garnantgolf@carmarthenshire.gov.uk
📖 400
✒ Kerry Jones (Mgr)
✒ Gethin Collins
🏌 18 L 6575 yds Par 72 SSS 72
👥 U SOC
££ £14.50 (£20)
🚗 On A474, between Ammanford and Pontardawe. M4 Junction 45
⊕ Driving range; starter course; practice nets
🏠 Roger Jones
🖥 www.parcgarnantholf.co.uk

Glyn Abbey (1992)
Proprietary
Trimsaran, SA17 4LB
☎ **(01554) 810278**
🖬 (01554) 810889
🖂 course-enquiries@glynabbey.co.uk
📖 450
✒ Martin Lane (Mgr) (01554) 810278
✒ Darren Griffiths (01554) 810278
🏌 18 L 6173 yds Par 70 SSS 70
👥 U SOC
££ £18 (£25)
🚗 4 miles NW of Llanelli, between Trimsaran and Carway
⊕ Driving range; gym; 9-hole course
🏠 Hawtree
🖥 www.glynabbey.co.uk

Glynhir (1909)
Glynhir Road, Llandybie, Ammanford, SA18 2TF
☎ **(01269) 850472**
🖬 (01269) 851365
🖂 glynhir.golfclub@virgin.net
📖 457
✒ D Davies, G Sadd (01269) 851365
✒ Richard Herbert (01269) 851010
🏌 18 L 6006 yds SSS 70
👥 WD/Sat–H Sun–NA SOC–WD
££ Winter £13 (£20) 5D–£45
Summer £19 (£25) 5D–£70
🚗 3½miles N of Ammanford
🏠 Hawtree
🖥 www.glynhirgolfclub.co.uk

Saron Golf Course (1990)
Pay and play
Penwern, Saron, Llandysul, SA44 4EL
☎ **(01559) 370705**
🖂 c9mbl@sarongolf.freeserve.co.uk
✒ Mr C Searle
🏌 9 L 2091 yds Par 32 (18 tees)
18 L 4412 yds par 66
👥 U
££ 9: £8 (Jnr £5) 18: £11 (Jnr £8)
🚗 On A484 Newcastle Emlyn to Carmarthen road
⊕ Putting green

Conwy

Abergele (1910)
Tan-y-Gopa Road, Abergele, LL22 8DS
☎ **(01745) 824034**
🖷 (01745) 824772
📧 secretary@abergelegolfclub.co.uk
🛏 1250
🏌 CP Langdon
⛳ I Runcie (01745) 823813
📏 18 L 6520 yds SSS 71
👥 U SOC
££ On application
🚗 Abergele Castle Grounds
🏠 David Williams
🖳 www.abergelegolfclub.co.uk

Betws-y-Coed (1977)
Clubhouse, Betws-y-Coed, LL24 0AL
☎ **(01690) 710556**
📧 info@golf-betws-y-coed.co.uk
🛏 280
🏌 Mrs P Rowley
📏 9 L 4996 yds SSS 64
9 greens 18 tees
👥 U SOC
££ £15 (£20)
🚗 ¼ mile off A5, in Betws-y-Coed
🖳 www.golf-betws-y-coed.co.uk

Conwy (Caernarvonshire)
(1890)
Beacons Way, Morfa, Conwy, LL32 8ER
☎ **(01492) 592423**
🖷 (01492) 593363
📧 secretary@conwygolfclub.co.uk
🛏 1000
🏌 DL Brown (01492) 592423
⛳ JP Lees (01492) 593225
📏 18 L 6936 yds SSS 74
👥 H WE–restricted SOC
££ £38 D–£43 (£43 D–£48)
🚗 ½ mile W of Conway, off A55 Jct 17
🖳 www.conwygolfclub.co.uk

Llandudno (Maesdu) (1915)
Hospital Road, Llandudno, LL30 1HU
☎ **(01492) 876450**
🖷 (01492) 876450
📧 secretary@maesdugolfclub.co.uk
🛏 1109
🏌 G Dean
⛳ S Boulden (01492) 875195
📏 18 L 6513 yds SSS 72
👥 U H–recognised GC members SOC
££ £25 (£35)
🚗 I mile S of Llandudno Station, nr Hospital
🖳 www.maesdugolfclub.co.uk

Llandudno (North Wales) (1894)
72 Bryniau Road, West Shore, Llandudno, LL30 2DZ
☎ **(01492) 875325**
🖷 (01492) 873355
📧 golf@nwgc.freeserve.co.uk

🛏 691
🏌 Gren Jones (01492) 875325
⛳ RA Bradbury (01492) 876878
📏 18 L 6247 yds Par 71 SSS 71
👥 U SOC–phone Sec WE–NA before 10.30 am
££ £30 D–£40 (£40 D–£50)
🚗 ¾ mile from Llandudno on West Shore. Jct 18 A55 Expressway
⊕ Practice ground; putting green; pitch and putt area
🖳 www.northwalesgolfclub.co.uk

Llanfairfechan (1971)
Llannerch Road, Llanfairfechan, LL33 0EB
☎ **(01248) 680144**
🛏 16
🏌 MJ Charlesworth (01248) 680524
📏 9 L 3119 yds SSS 57
👥 U
££ £10 (£10)
🚗 7 miles E of Bangor on A55

Old Colwyn (1907)
Woodland Avenue, Old Colwyn, LL29 9NL
☎ **(01492) 515581**

Penmaenmawr (1910)
Conway Old Road, Penmaenmawr, LL34 6RD
☎ **(01492) 623330**
🖷 (01492) 622105
📧 clubhouse@pengolfclub.co.uk
🛏 600
🏌 Mrs AH greenwood
📏 9 L 5143 yds SSS 66
👥 U SOC
££ £15 (£20)
🚗 4 miles W of Conway
🖳 www.pengolf.co.uk

Rhos-on-Sea (1899)
Penrhyn Bay, Llandudno, LL30 3PU
☎ **(01492) 549641**
🖷 (01492) 549100
📧 rhosonseagolfclub@btinternet.com
🛏 600
🏌 Gordon Downs
⛳ Jon Kelly
📏 18 L 6064 yds SSS 69
👥 U
££ £15 (£22)
🚗 On coast at Rhos-on-Sea. 4 miles E of Llandudno
⊕ 12 en-suite rooms (01492) 549641
🏠 Simpson
🖳 www.rhosgolf.co.uk

Denbighshire

Bryn Morfydd Hotel (1982)
Llanrhaeadr, Denbigh, LL16 4NP
☎ **(01745) 890280**
🖷 (01745) 890488
🛏 250
🏌 BW Astle (07752) 527257
📏 18 L 5800 yds Par 70 SSS 67
9 hole Par 3 course

👥 U SOC
££ £15 (£20)
🚗 2½ miles SE of Denbigh on A525
🏠 Duchess-Alliss/Thomas. Dukes-Muirhead/Henderson
🖳 www.bryn-morfydd.co.uk

Denbigh (1922)
Henllan Road, Denbigh, LL16 5AA
☎ **(01745) 814159**
🖷 (01745) 814888
📧 denbighgolfclub@aol.com
🛏 620
🏌 JR Williams (01745) 816669
⛳ M Jones (01745) 814159
📏 18 L 5712 yds SSS 69
👥 U SOC
££ On application
🚗 I mile NW of Denbigh (B5382)
🖳 www.denbighgolfclub.co.uk

Kinmel Park (1989)
Pay and play
Bodelwyddan, LL18 5SR
☎ **(01745) 833548**
🏌 Mrs Fetherstonhaugh
⛳ Rhodri Lloyd Jones (07916) 346602
📏 9 L 1550 yds Par 29
👥 U
££ £4 (£5)
🚗 Off A55, Jct 25
⊕ Driving range
🏠 Peter Stebbings
🖳 www.kinmelgolf.co.uk

Prestatyn (1905)
Marine Road East, Prestatyn, LL19 7HS
☎ **(01745) 854320**
🖷 (01745) 834320
📧 prestatyngcmanager@freenet.co.uk
🛏 513
🏌 SL Owen
⛳ D Ames
📏 18 L 6825 yds SSS 73
👥 H SOC WD WE
££ £25 (£30)
🚗 I mile E of Prestatyn
🏠 S Collins
🖳 www.prestatyngolfclub.co.uk

Rhuddlan (1930)
Meliden Road, Rhuddlan, LL18 6LB
☎ **(01745) 590217**
🖷 (01745) 590472
📧 secretary@rhuddlangolfclub.co.uk
🛏 560(M) 109(L) 122(J)
🏌 Mrs J Roberts
⛳ A Carr (01745) 590898
📏 18 L 6473 yds SSS 70
👥 H SOC–WD
££ £30 (£35)
🚗 2 miles N of St Asaph, J27 off A55
⊕ Pro shop
🏠 F Hawtree
🖳 www.rhuddlangolfclub.co.uk

Rhyl (1890)
Coast Road, Rhyl, LL18 3RE
☎ **(01745) 353171**
🖷 (01745) 353171

✉ rhylgolfclub@il2.com
🏠 450
🏌 Gill Davies
🏌 John Stubbs
🏌 9 L 6220 yds SSS 70
🏌 U SOC
££ £20 (£25)
🚗 On A548 between Rhyl and Prestatyn
🏠 James Braid
🖥 www.rhylgolfclub.com

Ruthin-Pwllglas (1920)

Pwllglas, Ruthin, LL15 2PE
☎ **(01824) 702296**
🏠 360
🏌 Eric Owen (01824) 702383
🏌 Michael Jones
🏌 10 L 5362 yds SSS 66
🏌 U SOC
££ £16 (£22)
🚗 2¹/₂ miles S of Ruthin in village of Pwllglas on Ruthin to Corwen road (A494)

St Melyd (1922)

The Paddock, Meliden Road, Prestatyn, LL19 8NB
☎ **(01745) 854405**
📠 (01745) 856908
✉ info@stmelydgolf.co.uk
🏠 400
🏌 Miss J McCormick
🏌 9 L 5857 yds SSS 68
🏌 U SOC
££ £18 (£22)
🚗 S of Prestatyn on A547
🖥 www.stmelydgolf.co.uk

Vale of Llangollen (1908)

Holyhead Road, Llangollen, LL20 7PR
☎ **(01978) 860906**
📠 (01978) 869165
✉ secretary@vlgc.co.uk
🏠 850
🏌 Bob Hardy
🏌 DI Vaughan (01978) 860040
🏌 18 L 6656 yds Par 72 SSS 73
🏌 U–check first SOC–WD only
££ £35 D–£55 (£40 D–£60)
🚗 1¹/₂ miles E of Llangollen on A5; 20 miles S of Chester
⊕ Practice ground; chipping area; buggies for hire
🖥 www.vlgc.co.uk

Flintshire

Caerwys (1989)

Pay and play
Caerwys, Mold, CH7 5AQ
☎ **(01352) 721222**

Hawarden (1911)

Groomsdale Lane, Hawarden, Deeside, CH5 3EH
☎ **(01244) 531447**
📠 (01244) 536901
✉ secretary@hawardengolfclub.co.uk

🏠 750
🏌 MB Coppack
🏌 A Rowland (01244) 520809
🏌 18 L 5809 yds SSS 69
🏌 H SOC–WD
££ £19 (£25)
🚗 6 miles W of Chester, off A55
🖥 www.hawardengolfclub.co.uk

Holywell (1906)

Brynford, Holywell, CH8 8LQ
☎ **(01352) 710040/713937**
📠 (01352) 713937
✉ holywell_golf_club@lineone.net
🏠 400 50(L)
🏌 RF Fiddaman (01352) 713937
🏌 M Parsley (01352) 710040
🏌 18 L 6100 yds Par 70 SSS 70
🏌 WD–U WE–SOC
££ £20 (£25)
🚗 2 miles S of Holywell, off A5026
🖥 www.holywellgolfclub.holywellgc.co.uk

Kinsale

Pay and play
Llanerchymor, Holywell, CH8 9DX
☎ **(01745) 561080**
🏠 85
🏌 K Davies
🏌 9 holes Par 71 SSS 70
🏌 U
££ 9: £8. 18: £12
🚗 4 miles N of Holywell on A548
⊕ Floodlit driving range
🏠 K Smith

Mold (1909)

Cilcain Road, Pantymwyn, Mold, CH7 5EH
☎ **(01352) 740318/741513**
📠 (01352) 741517
✉ info@moldgolfclub.co.uk
🏠 450 90(L) 95(J)
🏌 C Mills (01352) 741513
🏌 M Jordan (01352) 740318
🏌 18 L 5512 yds Par 68 SSS 67
🏌 U SOC
££ £20 (£25)
🚗 3 miles W of Mold
🏠 Hawtree
🖥 www.moldgolfclub.com

Northop Country Park (1994)

Northop, Chester, CH7 6WA
☎ **(01352) 840440**
📠 (01352) 840445
🏌 P Mesham/M Pritchard
🏌 M Pritchard
🏌 18 L 6802 yds Par 72
🏌 U–phone first SOC
££ £40
🚗 3 miles S of Flint, off A55
⊕ Driving range
🏠 John Jacobs

Old Padeswood (1978)

Station Road, Padeswood, Mold, CH7 4JL
☎ **(01244) 547701 (Clubhouse)**
🏠 500

🏌 B Slater (Hon) (01244) 816753
🏌 A Davies (01244) 547401
🏌 18 L 6728 yds SSS 72
🏌 U exc comp days SOC–WD
££ £25 (£30)
🚗 2 miles from Mold on A5118
🖥 www.oldpadeswoodgolfclub.co.uk

Padeswood & Buckley (1933)

The Caia, Station Lane, Padeswood, Mold, CH7 4JD
☎ **(01244) 550537**
📠 (01244) 541600
✉ admin@padeswoodgolf.com
🏠 592
🏌 JM Conway
🏌 D Ashton (01244) 543636
🏌 18 L 6042 yds Par 70 SSS 69
🏌 WD–U 9am–4pm –M after 4pm Sat–U Sun–NA SOC–WD Ladies Day–Wed
££ £25 (£30)
🚗 8 miles W of Chester, off A5118. 2nd golf club on right
⊕ Practice area; nets
🏠 D Williams Partnership

Pennant Park (1998)

Proprietary
Whitford, Holywell, CH8 9AE
☎ **(01745) 563000**
🏠 210
🏌 R Jones
🏌 18 L 6059 yds Par 70 whites
🏌 U SOC WD WE
££ £20 (£25)
🚗 Nr North Wales Expressway (A55); take Jct 32 to Holywell and follow signs
⊕ Practice range. Academy course
🏠 Roger Jones
🖥 www.pennant-park.co.uk

Gwynedd

Aberdovey (1892)

Aberdovey, LL35 0RT
☎ **(01654) 767210**
📠 (01654) 767027
✉ info@aberdoveygolf.co.uk
🏠 800
🏌 JM Griffiths (01654) 767493
🏌 J Davies (01654) 767602
🏌 18 L 6454 yds SSS 72
🏌 NA–8–9.30am & 1–2pm
££ On application (guide: £40 per round)
🚗 ¹/₂ mile W of Aberdovey (A493)
🏠 Braid/Fowler/Swan
🖥 www.aberdoveygolf.co.uk

Abersoch (1907)

Golf Road, Abersoch, LL53 7EY
☎ **(01758) 712636**

Bala (1973)

Penlan, Bala, LL23 7YD
- ☎ **(01678) 520359**
- 🖨 (01678) 521361
- ✉ balagolfclub@onetel.com
- 📖 340
- 🏌 G Rhys Jones
- 🏊 T Davies (visiting)
- ⛳ 10 L 4962 yds SSS 64
- 🏌 WD–U WE–NA pm SOC
- ££ £20 (£25) W–£50
- ⛳ 1/2 mile SW of Bala, off A494 to Dolgellau
- ⊕ Practice net; putting green
- 🏠 Sid Collins

Dolgellau (1910)

Proprietary
Hengwrt Estate, Pencefn Road, Dolgellau, LL40 2ES
- ☎ **(01341) 422603**
- ✉ richard@dolgellaugolfclub.com
- 📖 300
- 🏌 R Stockdale
- 🏊 R Stockdale
- ⛳ 9 L 4671 yds Par 66 SSS 63
- 🏌 U
- ££ £18 (£22.50)
- ⛳ 1/2 mile N of Dolgellau
- ⊕ Practice area; chipping green
- 🏠 J Medway
- 🖥 www.dolgellaugolfclub.com

Ffestiniog (1893)

Y Cefn, Ffestiniog
- ☎ **(01766) 762637 (Clubhouse)**
- ✉ info@ffestinioggolf.org
- 📖 138
- 🏌 A Roberts (01766) 831829
- ⛳ 9 L 4570 metres Par 68 SSS 66
- 🏌 U
- ££ £10 (£10)
- ⛳ 1 mile E of Ffestiniog on Bala road (B4391)
- 🖥 www.ffestinioggolf.org

Nefyn & District (1907)

Morfa Nefyn, Pwllheli, LL53 6DA
- ☎ **(01758) 720218 (Clubhouse)**
- 🖨 (01758) 720476
- ✉ secretary@nefyn-golf-club.com
- 📖 880
- 🏌 JB Owens (01758) 720966
- 🏊 J Froom (01758) 720102
- ⛳ 18 L 6548 yds SSS 71
    9 L 2618 yds SSS 34
- 🏌 U SOC
- ££ £31 D–£39 (£37 D–£48)
- ⛳ 11/2 miles W of Nefyn. 20 miles W of Caernarfon
- 🖥 www.nefyn-golf-club.com

Porthmadog (1905)

Morfa Bychan, Porthmadog, LL49 9UU
- ☎ **(01766) 514124**
- 🖨 (01766) 514124
- ✉ secretary@porthmadog-golf-club .co.uk
- 📖 860
- 🏌 GT Jones (Mgr)
- 🏊 P Bright (01766) 513828
- ⛳ 18 L 6322 yds Par 71 SSS 71
- 🏌 U H SOC
- ££ £30 D–£37 (£35 D–£47)
- ⛳ 2 miles S of Porthmadog, towards Black Rock Sands
- 🏠 James Braid
- 🖥 www.porthmadog-golf-club.co.uk

Pwllheli (1900)

Golf Road, Pwllheli, LL53 5PS
- ☎ **(01758) 701644**
- 🖨 (01758) 701644
- ✉ admin@pwllheligolfclub.co.uk
- 📖 920
- 🏌 Dennis Moore (Gen Mgr)
- 🏊 S Pilkington (01758) 701644
- ⛳ 18 L 6091 yds SSS 70
- 🏌 U
- ££ D–£30 (D–£35) – 2006 fees
- ⛳ 1/2 mile SW of Pwllheli
- 🏠 James Braid
- 🖥 www.pwllheligolf.co.uk

Royal St David's (1894)

Harlech, LL46 2UB
- ☎ **(01766) 780203**
- 🖨 (01766) 781110
- ✉ secretary@royalstdavids.co.uk
- 📖 880
- 🏌 DL Morkill (01766) 780361
- 🏊 J Barnett (01766) 780857
- ⛳ 18 L 6601 yds Par 69 SSS 73
- 🏌 U H–booking necessary SOC
- ££ £45 D–£55 (£55 D–£65)
- ⛳ W of Harlech on A496
- 🏠 H Finch-Hatton
- 🖥 www.royalstdavids.co.uk

Royal Town of Caernarfon (1909)

Aberforeshore, LLanfaglan, Caernarfon, LL54 5RP
- ☎ **(01286) 673783**
- 🖨 (01286) 673783
- ✉ caerngc@talk21.com
- 📖 702
- 🏌 EG Angel
- 🏊 A Owen (01286) 678359
- ⛳ 18 L 5941 yds SSS 68
- 🏌 U SOC
- ££ £25 (£30) + special offers
- ⛳ 21/2 miles SW of Caernarfon
- 🖥 www.caernarfongolfclub.co.uk

St Deiniol (1906)

Penybryn, Bangor, LL57 1PX
- ☎ **(01248) 353098**
- 🖨 (01248) 370792
- ✉ secretary@stdeiniol.fsbusiness .co.uk
- 📖 300
- 🏌 RD Thomas MBE (01248) 353098
- 🏊 No pro - golf shop proprietor
- ⛳ 18 L 5656 yds SSS 67
- 🏌 U SOC
- ££ £20 (£25)
- ⛳ Off A5/A55 Junction 11, 1 mile E of Bangor on A5122
- ⊕ Buggies available; practice nets
- 🏠 James Braid
- 🖥 www.st-deiniol.co.uk

Anglesey (1914)

Station Road, Rhosneigr, LL64 5QX
- ☎ **(01407) 810219 (Clubhouse)**
- 🖨 (01407) 811127
- ✉ info@theangleseygolfclub.com
- 📖 450
- 🏌 MI Parry (01407) 811127
- 🏊 M Parry (01407)811202
- ⛳ 18 L 6330 yds SSS 71
- 🏌 U H SOC
- ££ £22 (£25)
- ⛳ 8 miles SE of Holyhead, off A55 J5
- ⊕ Practice facilities
- 🏠 H Hilton
- 🖥 www.angleseygolfclub.co.uk

Baron Hill (1895)

Beaumaris, LL58 8YW
- ☎ **(01248) 810231**
- ✉ golf@baronhill.co.uk
- 📖 360
- 🏌 A Pleming
- ⛳ 9 L 5062 metres SSS 68
- 🏌 U exc comp days SOC–WD & Sat (apply Sec)
- ££ £15 W–£45
- ⛳ Off A545 on approach to Beaumaris
- 🏠 Evolved over 110 years, with adjustments by Frank Pennink
- 🖥 www.baronhill.co.uk

Bull Bay (1913)

Bull Bay Road, Amlwch, LL68 9RY
- ☎ **(01407) 830213**
- 🖨 (01407) 832612
- 📖 700
- 🏌 John Burns (01407) 830960
- 🏊 J Burns (01407) 831188
- ⛳ 18 L 6276 yds SSS 70
- 🏌 U SOC WD WE
- ££ £27 (£33)
- ⛳ 1/2 mile W of Amlwch on A5025
- 🏠 WH Fowler
- 🖥 www.bullbaygc.co.uk

Henllys Hall

LLanfaes, Beaumaris, LL58 8HU
- ☎ **(01248) 811717**
- 🖨 (01248) 811511
- 🏊 P Maton
- ⛳ 18 L 6062 yds Par 71
- 🏌 U SOC
- ££ £22 (£28)
- ⛳ 2 miles N of Beaumaris (B5109)
- 🏠 Roger Jones

Holyhead (1912)

Trearddur Bay, Anglesey, LL65 2YL
- ☎ **(01407) 763279/762119**
- 🖨 (01407) 763279
- ✉ mgrsec@aol.com
- 📖 790 396(L)
- 🏌 RD Barrance
- 🏊 S Elliott (01407) 762022
- ⛳ 18 L 5540 metres SSS 70
- 🏌 H SOC
- ££ £30 (£33)

🏌 2 miles S of Holyhead off A55
⌂ James Braid
▤ www.holyheadgolfclub.co.uk

Llangefni (1983)
Public
Llangefni, LL77 8YQ
☎ **(01248) 722193**

RAF Valley
Anglesey, LL65 3NY
☎ **(01407) 762241**
📠 (01407) 762241 ext 7705
✉ constables@constables.wanadoo
.com
▥ 150
🏌 MJ Constable (Mgr) ext 7716
🏴 9 L 5604 yards SSS 68
👥 U – booking necessary
££ D–£6 (£6)
🏌 RAF Valley base, off A55
⌂ Sgts Mess members
▤ www.rafvalleygolfclub.co.uk

Storws Wen (1996)
Proprietary
Brynteg, Benllech, LL78 8JY
☎ **(01248) 852673**

Mid Glamorgan

Aberdare (1921)
Abernant, Aberdare, CF44 0RY
☎ **(01685) 871188 (Clubhouse)**
📠 (01685) 872797
✉ sec-agc@tiscali.co.uk
▥ 500
🏌 T Mears (01685) 872797
✓ AW Palmer (01685) 878735
🏴 18 L 5875 yds SSS 69
👥 H SOC
££ £17 (£21)
🏌 ½ mile E of Aberdare. 12 miles
NW of Pontypridd
⊕ 3 practice nets; putting green
▤ www.aberdaregolfclub.com

Bargoed (1913)
Heolddu, Bargoed, CF81 9GF
☎ **(01443) 830143**
📠 (01443) 830608
▥ 548
🏌 G Williams (01443) 830608
✓ Craig Easton (01443) 836179
🏴 18 L 6233 yds SSS 70
👥 WD–U WE–M SOC–WD
££ £17.50
🏌 NW boundary of Bargoed. 8 miles
N of Caerphilly (A469)

Bryn Meadows Golf Hotel (1973)
Maes-y-Cwmmer, Ystrad Mynach, Nr Caerphilly, CF82 7SN
☎ **(01495) 225590/224103**

Caerphilly (1905)
Pencapel, Mountain Road, Caerphilly, CF83 1HJ
☎ **(029) 2086 3441**
📠 (029) 2086 3441
✉ secretary&caerphillygolfclub.com
▥ 650
🏌 Alun Sedgmore (029) 2086 3441
✓ J Lee (029) 2086 9104
🏴 18 L 5728 yds SSS 69 Par 71
👥 WD–U H WE–M
££ £15 with member £30 without member
🏌 7 miles N of Cardiff, off A469
▤ www.caerphillygolfclub.com

Coed-y-Mwstwr (1994)
Coychurch, Bridgend, CF35 6AF
☎ **(01656) 864934**
📠 (01656) 864934
✉ secretary@coed-y-mwstrw.co.uk
▥ 490
🏌 JR North (Sec/Mgr)
🏴 18 L 5703 yds par 69 SSS 68
👥 WE–U Sun WE–M Sat WD–U SOC–WD only
££ £20 (£25)
🏌 2 miles W of M4 Junction 35
⊕ Putting green; chipping green; bunker; nets
▤ www.coed-y-mstwr.co.uk

Creigiau (1921)
Creigiau, Cardiff, CF15 9NN
☎ **(029) 2089 0263**
📠 (029) 2089 0706
✉ manager@creigiaugolf.co.uk
▥ 810
🏌 RJ Neill
✓ I Luntz (029) 2089 0263
🏴 18 L 6063 yds SSS 70 Par 71
👥 WD–U WE/BH–M SOC–WD
££ £35 (£15)
🏌 7 miles NW of Cardiff. M4 Junction 34
▤ www.creigiaugolf.co.uk

Grove
South Cornelly, Bridgend, CF33 4RP
☎ **(01656) 788771**
📠 (01656) 788414
✉ enquiries@grovegolf.com
▥ 540
🏌 R Bourne
✓ L Warne (01656) 788300
🏴 18 L 5884 yds Par 70 SSS 69
👥 WD–U WE–NA before 3pm WD/WE–SOC contact Sec
££ £18 (£20)
🏌 1.5 miles from Porthcawl, M4 J37
▤ www.grovegolf.com

Llantrisant & Pontyclun (1927)
Ely Valley Road, Talbot Green, Llantrisant, CF72 8AL
☎ **(01443) 222148**
📠 (01443) 224601
✉ golf@lpgc.wanadoo.co.uk
▥ 600

🏌 Theresa Morgan (Admin) (01443) 224601
✓ Andrew Bowen (01443) 228169
🏴 18 L 5328 yds SSS 68
👥 WD–H WE/BH–M SOC–WD
££ On application
🏌 10 miles NW of Cardiff. 2 miles N of M4 Junction 34
▤ www.llantristantandpontyclungc.co.uk

Maesteg (1912)
Mount Pleasant, Neath Road, Maesteg, CF34 9PR
☎ **(01656) 734106**
✉ ijm@fsmail.net
info@maesteg-golf.co.uk

Merthyr Tydfil (1909)
Cilsanws Mountain, Cefn Coed, Merthyr Tydfil, CF48 2NT
☎ **(01685) 723308**
▥ 200
🏌 V Price
✓ None
🏴 18 L 5622 yds SSS 68
👥 U SOC–WD
££ £10 (£15)
🏌 2 miles N of Merthyr Tydfil, off A470 at Cefn Coed
⌂ Viv Price/Richard Mathias (new holes); original architect unknown

Mountain Ash (1907)
Cefnpennar, Mountain Ash, CF45 4DT
☎ **(01443) 472265 (Clubhouse)**
📠 (01443) 479628
✉ sec@magc.fsnet.co.uk
▥ 530
🏌 Sharon Rees (01443) 479459
✓ No Pro at present
🏴 18 L 5535 yds SSS 67
👥 WD–U H WE–M
££ £20 (£30)
🏌 9 miles NW of Pontypridd
▤ www.mountainashgc.co.uk

Mountain Lakes (1988)
Heol Penbryn, Blaengwynlais, Caerphilly, CF83 1NG
☎ **(029) 2086 1128**
📠 (029) 2086 3243
▥ 480
🏌 GM Richards (Hon)
🏴 18 L 6300 yds SSS 72
👥 U SOC
££ £18 (£18)
🏌 4 miles from M4 Junction 32
⌂ R Sandow

Pontypridd (1905)
Ty Gwyn Road, Pontypridd, CF37 4DJ
☎ **(01443) 402359**
📠 (01443) 491622
▥ 850
🏌 Vikki Hooley (01443) 409904
✓ W Walters (01443) 409904
🏴 18 L 5725 yds SSS 68
👥 WD–U H WE/BH–M H SOC–WD H

££ On application
⊶ E of Pontypridd, off A470. 12 miles NW of Cardiff

Pyle & Kenfig (1922)
Waun-y-Mer, Kenfig, Bridgend, CF33 4PU
☎ **(01656) 783093**
🖥 (01656) 772822
✉ secretary@pandkgolfclub.co.uk
📖 875
🏌 DA Fellowes (01656) 771613
⟋ R Evans (01656) 772446
⟱ 18 L 6588 yds Par 71 SSS 73
👥 WD–U WE (Sun) H SOC
££ D–£50 (£70)
⊶ 2 miles NW of Porthcawl. M4 J37
⊕ Practice facilities
⌂ HS Colt
🖳 www.pandkgolfclub.co.uk

Rhondda (1910)
Penrhys, Ferndale, Rhondda, CF43 3PW
☎ **(01443) 441384**
🖥 (01443) 441384
✉ rhonddagolf@aol.com
📖 500
🏌 Mrs P Norman (01443) 441384
⟱ 18 L 6428 yds SSS 71
👥 U H SOC
££ May–Oct: £20 (£25) Winter: £15 (£20)
⊶ 6 miles W of Pontypridd

Ridgeway (1997)
Caerphilly Mountain, Caerphilly, CF83 1LY
☎ **(029) 2088 2255**
✉ petetheplod@ntlworld.com
🏌 R Jones
⟋ Peter Johnson
⟱ 9 L 4800 yds SSS 64 (18 tees)
👥 U
££ D–£10
⊶ 3 miles from M4 J32 at top of Caerphilly Mountain on A469
⊕ 22 bay driving range

Royal Porthcawl (1891)
Rest Bay, Porthcawl, CF36 3UW
☎ **(01656) 782251**
🖥 (01656) 771687
✉ royalporthcawl@btconnect.com
📖 800
⟋ JV Dinsdale
⟋ P Evans (01656) 773702
⟱ 18 L 6829 yds Par 72 SSS 74
👥 WD–I or H WE/BH–M SOC–H
££ £120 (£150)
⊶ 22 miles W of Cardiff. M4 Junction 37
⊕ Driving range; Dormy House
⌂ Charles Gibson
🖳 www.royalporthcawl.com

Southerndown (1905)
Ogmore-by-Sea, Bridgend, CF32 0QP
☎ **(01656) 880476**
🖥 (01656) 880317
✉ southerndowngolf@btconnect.com
📖 600
🏌 AJ Hughes (01656) 881111

⟋ DG McMonagle
⟱ 18 L 6449 yds SSS 72
👥 U H
££ £45 D–£55 (£65)
⊶ 3 miles S of Bridgend, nr Ogmore Castle ruins
⌂ W Fernie
🖳 www.southerndowngolfclub.co.uk

Whitehall (1922)
The Pavilion, Nelson, Treharris, CF46 6ST
☎ **(01443) 740245**
📖 300
🏌 PM Wilde
⟱ 9 L 5666 yds SSS 68
👥 WD–U WE–M SOC
££ £10
⊶ 15 miles NW of Cardiff
🖳 www.whitehallgolfclub1922.co.uk

Monmouthshire

Alice Springs (1989)
Kemeys Commander, Usk, NP15 1JY
☎ **(01873) 880708**
✉ alice@springs18.fsnet.co.uk

Blackwood (1914)
Cwmgelli, Blackwood, NP12 1BR
☎ **(01495) 223152**
📖 300
🏌 GA Batty
⟋ None
⟱ 9 L 5304 yds SSS 66
👥 WD–I SOC WE/BH–M
££ £14
⊶ ¼ mile N of Blackwood

The Celtic Manor Resort (1995)
Coldra Woods, Newport, NP6 1JQ
☎ **(01633) 413000**
🖥 (01633) 410309
📖 450
🏌 S Wesson (01633) 413000
⟋ S Patience (01633) 413000
⟱ 18 L 7001 yds Par 70 SSS 74
18 L 4094 yds par 61 SSS 60
18 L 7403 yds par 72 SSS 77
👥 H SOC
££ On application
⊶ E of Newport on A48. M4 Jct 24
⊕ Golf academy; driving range
⌂ Robert Trent Jones Sr

Dewstow (1988)
Proprietary
Caerwent, NP26 5AH
☎ **(01291) 430444**
🖥 (01291) 425816
✉ info@dewstow.com
📖 850
🏌 D Bradbury
⟋ S Price
⟱ Valley 18 L 6091 yds Par 72 SSS 70
Park 18 L 6226 yds Par 69 SSS 69
👥 U SOC

££ £19 (£22)
⊶ Caerwent, 5 miles W of old Severn Bridge, off A48
⊕ Driving range
🖳 www.dewstow.com

Greenmeadow G&CC (1979)
Treherbert Road, Croesyceiliog, Cwmbran, NP44 2BZ
☎ **(01633) 869321**
🖥 (01633) 868430
✉ info@greenmeadowgolf.com
📖 610
🏌 PJ Richardson (01633) 869321
⟋ D Woodman (01633) 862626
⟱ 18 L 6078 yds Par 70 SSS 70
👥 WD–U WE–NA before 11am SOC
££ On application
⊶ 4 miles N of Newport on A4042. M4 Junction 26
⊕ Floodlit driving range
🖳 www.greenmeadowgolf.com

Llanwern (1928)
Tennyson Avenue, Llanwern, Newport, NP18 2DY
☎ **(01633) 412029**
🖥 (01633) 412029
✉ llanwerngolfclub@btconnect.com
📖 650
🏌 Peter Probert
⟋ S Price (01633) 413233
⟱ 18 L 6115 yds SSS 70
👥 WD–U WE–restricted I H SOC
££ £25 (£30)
⊶ 1 mile S of M4 Junction 24
⊕ 2 practice grounds; putting green
🖳 www.llanwerngolfclub.co.uk

Marriott St Pierre Hotel & CC (1962)
St Pierre Park, Chepstow, NP16 6YA
☎ **(01291) 625261**

Monmouth (1896)
Leasbrook Lane, Monmouth, NP25 3SN
☎ **(01600) 712212**
🖥 (01600) 772399
✉ sec.mongc@barbox.net
📖 500
🏌 P Tully (01600) 712212
⟋ Mike Waldron (01600) 712212
⟱ 18 L 5698 yds Par 69 SSS 68
👥 U SOC WD WE (Sun only after 11.30am)
££ £22 (£26)
⊶ Signposted ¼ mile along A40 Monmouth-Ross road
⊕ Putting green; practice area; driving net
⌂ George Walden
🖳 www.monmouthgolfclub.co.uk

Monmouthshire (1892)
Llanfoist, Abergavenny, NP7 9HE
☎ **(01873) 852606**
🖥 (01873) 850470
✉ secretary@mgcabergavenny.fsnet.co.uk

⌂ 518 99(L) 45(J)
🏌 R Bradley
✎ (01873) 852532
🏳 18 L 5978 yds SSS 70
👥 WD–H SOC
££ D–£35 (D–£40)
⚬ 2 miles SW of Abergavenny on B4269
🏠 James Braid
▤ www.themonmouthshiregolfclub.com

Newport   (1903)
Great Oak, Rogerstone, Newport, NP10 9FX
☎ **(01633) 892643/894496**
🖥 (01633) 896676
✉ newportgolfclub@btconnect.com
⌂ 800
🏌 C Duffield (01633) 892643
✎ PM Mayo (01633) 893271
🏳 18 L 6500 yds SSS 71
👥 WD–H
££ £40 (£45)
⚬ 3 miles W of Newport on B4591. M4 Junction 27, 1 mile
🏠 Ross/Fernie
▤ www.newportgolfclub.org.uk

Oakdale   (1990)
Pay and play
Llwynon Lane, Oakdale, NP2 0NF
☎ **(01495) 220044**
🏌 M Lewis (Dir)
✎ (01495) 220440
🏳 9 L 1344 yds Par 28
👥 U SOC
££ On application
⚬ 15 miles NW of Newport via A467/B4251. M4 Junction 28
⊕ Driving range
🏠 Ian Goodenough

Pontnewydd   (1875)
Maesgwyn Farm, Upper Cwmbran, Cwmbran, Torfaen, NP44 1AB
☎ **(01633) 482170**
🖥 (01633) 838598
✉ ctphillips@virgin.net
⌂ 422
🏌 CT Phillips (01633) 484447
🏳 11 L 5278 yds SSS 67
👥 WD–U WE–M SOC
££ £15 (£15)
⚬ W outskirts of Cwmbran

Pontypool   (1903)
Lasgarn Lane, Trevethin, Pontypool, NP4 8TR
☎ **(01495) 763655**
🖥 (01495) 755564
✉ pontypoolgolf@btconnect.com
⌂ 581 41(L) 80(J)
🏌 L Dodd
✎ N Matthews (01495) 755544
🏳 18 L 5712 yds SSS 69
👥 U H SOC
££ £25 (£30)
⚬ 1 mile N of Pontypool (A4042). M4 Junction 26

⊕ Practice ground; indoor teaching academy
▤ www.pontypoolgolf.co.uk

Raglan Parc   (1994)
Parc Lodge, Raglan, NP5 2ER
☎ **(01291) 690077**
🖥 (01291) 69075
✉ golf@raglanparc.co.uk
⌂ 400
🏌 S Dobney
✎ C Murphy
🏳 18 L 6604 yds Par 73
👥 U
££ £18 (£26)
⚬ Nr A40/A449 junction
▤ www.raglanparc.co.uk

The Rolls of Monmouth   (1982)
The Hendre, Monmouth, NP25 5HG
☎ **(01600) 715353**
🖥 (01600) 713115
✉ sandra@therollsgolfclub.co.uk
⌂ 200
🏌 Mrs SJ Orton
✎ None
🏳 18 L 6733 yds SSS 73
👥 U SOC
££ £38 (£42)
⚬ 3½ miles W of Monmouth on B4233
▤ www.therollsgolfclub.co.uk

Shirenewton   (1995)
Shirenewton, Chepstow, NP16 6RL
☎ **(01291) 641642**

Tredegar & Rhymney   (1921)
Tredegar, Rhymney, NP2 5HA
☎ **(01685) 840743**
✉ tandrgc@googlemail.com
⌂ 180
🏌 Will Price (07761) 005184
🏳 18 L 5316 yds SSS 67
👥 U
££ £10
⚬ 1½ miles W of Tredegar (B4256)

Tredegar Park   (1923)
Parc-y-Brain Road, Rogerstone, Newport, NP10 9TG
☎ **(01633) 895219**
🖥 (01633) 897152
✉ secretary@tredegarparkgolfclub.co.uk
⌂ 800
🏌 K Buse (01633) 894433
✎ Lee Pagett (01633) 894517
🏳 18 L 6564 yds SSS 72
👥 H SOC–WD
££ D–£20 (£25)
⚬ W of Newport, off M4 Junction 27
🏠 R Sandow
▤ www.tredegarparkgolfclub.co.uk

Wernddu Golf Centre
Old Ross Road, Abergavenny, NP7 8NG
☎ **(01873) 856223**
✉ info@wernddu-golf-club.co.uk

West Monmouthshire   (1906)
Golf Road, Pond Road, Nantyglo, Ebbw Vale, NP23 4QT
☎ **(01495) 310233**
⌂ 300
🏌 SE Williams (01495) 310233
🏳 18 L 6118 yds SSS 69
👥 WD/Sat–U Sun–M SOC–WD
££ £15
⚬ Nr Dunlop Semtex, off Brynmawr Bypass, towards Winchestown
⊕ 20-bay driving range
🏠 Ben Sayers

Woodlake Park   (1993)
Proprietary
Glascoed, Usk, NP4 0TE
☎ **(01291) 673933**
🖥 (01291) 673811
✉ golf@woodlake.co.uk
⌂ 500
🏌 MJ Wood
✎ L Lancey (01291) 671135
🏳 18 L 6300 yds Par 71 SSS 72
👥 H SOC WD WE
££ Summer–£25 (£32) Winter–£18 (£20)
⚬ 3 miles W of Usk, nr Llandegfedd reservoir
▤ www.woodlake.co.uk

Pembrokeshire

Haverfordwest   (1904)
Arnolds Down, Haverfordwest, SA61 2XQ
☎ **(01437) 763565**
🖥 (01437) 764143
✉ haverfordwestgc@btconnect.com
⌂ 740
🏌 M Foley (01437) 764523
✎ A Pile (01437) 768409
🏳 18 L 5986 yds Par 70 SSS 69
👥 U SOC
££ £30 (£33)
⚬ 1 mile E of Haverfordwest on A40
⊕ Practice area; putting green; pro shop
▤ www.haverfordwestgolfclub.co.uk

Milford Haven   (1913)
Hubberston, Milford Haven, SA72 3RX
☎ **(01646) 697762**
🖥 (01646) 697870
✉ cerlthmhgc@aol.com
⌂ 380 65(L) 90(J)
🏌 CW Pugh (01646) 697822
✎ M Stimson (01646) 697762
🏳 18 L 6071 yds SSS 71
👥 U SOC
££ £20 (£25)
⚬ W boundary of Milford Haven
▤ www.mhgc.co.uk

Newport Links (1925)

Newport, SA42 0NR
- ☎ **(01239) 820244**
- 🖶 (01239) 820085
- ✉ newportgc@lineone.net
- 📖 500
- ✍ Mrs A Payne (Mgr)
- 🏌 Mr J Noott
- ⛳ 9 L 3089 yds SSS 68
- 👥 U SOC
- £€ £22 (£25)
- 🚗 2¹/₂ miles NW of Newport, towards Newport Beach
- ⊕ Driving range; chipping green; putting green
- 🏠 James Braid
- 📧 www.newportlinks.co.uk

Priskilly Forest (1992)

Castle Morris, Haverfordwest, SA62 5EH
- ☎ **(01348) 840276**
- 🖶 (01348) 840276
- ✉ jevans@priskilly-forest.co.uk
- ✍ P Evans
- ⛳ 9 L 5874 yds Par 70 SSS 69
- 👥 U SOC
- £€ 9: £15 18: £20 D–£24 (£22 D–£27)
- 🚗 2 miles off A40 at Letterston
- ⊕ Practice area
- 🏠 J Walters
- 📧 www.priskilly-forest.co.uk

South Pembrokeshire (1970)

Military Road, Pembroke Dock, SA72 6SE
- ☎ **(01646) 621453**

St Davids City (1903)

Whitesands Bay, St Davids, SA62 6PT
- ☎ **(01437) 721751 (Clubhouse)**
- ✉ wjwilcox@hotmail.com

Tenby (1888)

The Burrows, Tenby, SA70 7NP
- ☎ **(01834) 842978**
- 🖶 (01834) 842978
- ✉ tenbygolfclub@ukk.co.uk
- 📖 700
- ✍ DJ Hancock (01834) 842978
- 🏌 M Hawkey (01834) 844447
- ⛳ 18 L 373 yds SSS 72
- 👥 H SOC
- £€ £36 D–£54 (£45 D–£67)
- 🚗 Tenby, South Beach
- 🏠 James Braid
- 📧 www.tenbygolf.co.uk

Trefloyne (1996)

Trefloyne Park, Penally, Tenby, SA70 7RG
- ☎ **(01834) 842165**

Powys

Brecon (1902)

Newton Park, Llanfaes, Brecon, LD3 8PA
- ☎ **(01874) 622004**

Builth Wells (1923)

Golf Club Road, Builth Wells, LD2 3NF
- ☎ **(01982) 553296**
- 🖶 (01982) 551064
- ✉ info@builthwellsgolf.co.uk
- 📖 400
- ✍ S Edwards (01982) 551155
- 🏌 S Edwards
- ⛳ 18 L 5424 yds SSS 66
- 👥 U H SOC
- £€ £21 D–£27 (£25 D–£30)
- 🚗 W of Builth Wells on Llandovery road (A483)
- 📧 www.builthwellsgolf.co.uk

Cradoc (1967)

Penoyre Park, Cradoc, Brecon, LD3 9LP
- ☎ **(01874) 623658**
- 🖶 (01874) 611711
- ✉ secretary@cradoc.co.uk
- 📖 750
- ✍ Bob Barnet (01874) 623658
- 🏌 R Davies (01874) 625524
- ⛳ 18 L 6188 yds Par 71 SSS 71
- 👥 U SOC
- £€ £26 (£32)
- 🚗 2 miles NW of Brecon, off B4520
- ⊕ Driving range; chipping area; practice putting green
- 🏠 CK Cotton
- 📧 www.cradoc.co.uk

Knighton (1906)

Ffrydd Wood, Knighton, LD7 1EF
- ☎ **(01547) 528646**
- 📖 150
- ✍ DB Williams (Hon) (01547) 528046
- ⛳ 9 L 5362 yds Par 68 SSS 66
- 👥 U SOC WD–U WE–NA before 5pm
- £€ £10 (£15)
- 🚗 SW of Knighton. 20 miles NE of Llandrindod Wells
- 🏠 H Vardon
- 📧 www.knightongolfclub.co.uk

Llandrindod Wells (1905)

The Clubhouse, Llandrindod Wells, LD1 5NY
- ☎ **(01597) 823873**
- 🖶 (01597) 823873
- ✉ secretary@lwgc.co.uk
- 📖 400
- ✍ R Southcott (01597) 823873
- 🏌 P Davies (01597) 822247
- ⛳ 18 L 5759 yds Par 69 SSS 69
- 👥 U SOC
- £€ £20 (£25)
- 🚗 ¹/₂ mile E of Llandrindod Wells centre
- ⊕ Driving range
- 🏠 Harry Vardon
- 📧 www.lwgc.co.uk

Machynlleth (1904)

Felingerrig, Machynlleth, SY20 8UH
- ☎ **(01654) 702000**
- ✉ machgolf2@tiscali.co.uk

- 📖 250
- ⛳ 9 L 5726 yds SSS 67
- 👥 U Sun–NA before 11.30am SOC
- £€ £18 (£18)
- 🚗 1 mile E of Machynlleth, off A489

Rhosgoch (1984)

Proprietary
Rhosgoch, Builth Wells, LD2 3JY
- ☎ **(01497) 851251**
- ✉ enquiries@rhosgoch-golf.co.uk
- 📖 80
- ✍ C Dance
- ⛳ 9 L 4955 yds SSS 66
- 👥 U SOC
- £€ £10 (£12)
- 🚗 5 miles N of Hay-on-Wye
- 📧 www.rhosgoch-golf.co.uk

St Giles Newtown (1895)

Pool Road, Newtown, SY16 3AJ
- ☎ **(01686) 625844**

St Idloes (1920)

Owned privately
Penrhallt, Llanidloes, SY18 6LG
- ☎ **(01686) 412559**
- 🖶 (01926) 889536
- 📖 320
- ✍ Martin Warr
- ⛳ 9 L 5510 yds SSS 66
- 👥 U H Sun–restricted SOC
- £€ £15 (£20)
- 🚗 ¹/₂ mile from Llanidloes on Trefeglwys road (B4569)
- ⊕ Practice putting green

Welsh Border Golf Complex (1991)

Bulthy Farm, Bulthy, Middletown, ISY21 8ER
- ☎ **(01743) 884247**
- ✉ jaykay@fsmail.net
- 📖 200
- ✍ K Farr (07966) 530042
- 🏌 M Kendal (01686) 530042
- ⛳ 9 L 3050 yds SSS 69
- 9 hole course Pay & Play Par 3
- 👥 U SOC WD/WE
- £€ £12
- 🚗 Between Shrewsbury and Welshpool on A458
- ⊕ Driving range
- 🏠 A Griffiths

Welshpool (1907)

Golfa Hill, Welshpool, SY21 9AQ
- ☎ **(01938) 850249**
- ✉ welshpool.golfclub@virgin.net
- 📖 400
- ✍ D Lewis (01938) 810757
- 🏌 None
- ⛳ 18 L 5716 yds Par 71 SSS 69
- 👥 U
- £€ £15.50 (£15.50) winter, £25.50
- 🚗 4¹/₂ miles W of Welshpool, on Dolgellau road (A458)
- 🏠 James Braid
- 📧 www.welshpoolgolfclub.co.uk

South Glamorgan

Brynhill   (1921)
Port Road, Barry, CF62 8PN
- ☎ **(01446) 720277**
- 🖷 (01446) 740422
- ✉ postbox@brynhillgolfclub.co.uk
- ⊞ 700
- ♗ R Cook/S Clarke (01446) 720277
- ⌖ D Prior (01446) 740004
- ⊳ 18 L 6516 yds SSS 72
- ♖ WD/Sat–H Sun–NA SOC–WD
- ££ £25 SOC–£20
- ⚭ A4050, 8 miles SW of Cardiff; M4 J33
- 🖳 www.brynhillgolfclub.co.uk

Cardiff   (1921)
Sherborne Avenue, Cyncoed, Cardiff, CF23 6SJ
- ☎ **(029) 2075 3067**
- 🖷 (029) 2068 0011
- ✉ cardiff.golfclub@virgin.net
- ⊞ 850
- ♗ Mrs K Newling (029) 2075 3320
- ⌖ T Hanson (029) 2075 4772
- ⊳ 18 L 6015 yds SSS 70
- ♖ WD–H WE–H SOC–Fri
- ££ £45
- ⚭ 3 miles N of Cardiff. 2 miles W of Pentwyn exit of A48(M). M4 Junction 29
- 🖳 www.cardiffgc.co.uk

Cottrell Park   (1996)
St Nicholas, Cardiff, CF5 6JY
- ☎ **(01446) 781781**
- 🖷 (01446) 781187
- ✉ admin@cottrell-park.co.uk
- ⊞ 1300
- ♗ IG Ross
- ⌖ R Donovan
- ⊳ 18 L 6606 yds Par 72 SSS 72
- 18 L 6156 yds Par 71 SSS 68
- ♖ U SOC–WD–WE
- ££ 18 hole: £25 (£35)
- ⚭ 4 miles W of Cardiff on A48. M4 Junction 33
- ⊕ Driving range
- ⌂ Bob Sandow
- 🖳 www.cottrell-park.co.uk

Dinas Powis   (1914)
Old Highwalls, Dinas Powis, CF64 4AJ
- ☎ **(029) 2051 2727**
- 🖷 (029) 2051 2727
- ⊞ 490
- ♗ Chris Miller
- ⌖ G Bennett (029) 2051 3682
- ⊳ 18 L 5532 yds SSS 67
- ♖ H SOC
- ££ D–£25 (£30)
- ⚭ 3 miles SW of Cardiff (A4055)

Glamorganshire   (1890)
Lavernock Road, Penarth, CF64 5UP
- ☎ **(029) 2070 1185**
- 🖷 (029) 2070 1185
- ✉ glamgolf@btconnect.com
- ⊞ 1100
- ♗ BM Williams (029) 2070 1185
- ⌖ A Kerr-Smith (029) 2070 7401
- ⊳ 18 L 6181 yds SSS 70
- ♖ WD/WE–H SOC
- ££ £35 (£40)
- ⚭ 5 miles SW of Cardiff, M4 J33
- 🖳 www.glamorganshiregolfclub.co.uk

Llanishen   (1905)
Heol Hir, Cardiff, CF14 9UD
- ☎ **(029) 207 55078**
- 🖷 (029) 207 65253
- ⊞ 850
- ✉ secretary.llanishen@virgin.net
- ♗ Bill Hough (029) 207 55078
- ⌖ RA Jones (029) 207 55076
- ⊳ 18 L 5301 yds SSS 67
- ♖ WD–U H WE–U H Sun pm only SOC Thur/Fri
- ££ £20 D–£32
- ⚭ 5 miles N of Cardiff

Peterstone Lakes   (1990)
Proprietary
Peterstone, Wentloog, Cardiff, CF3 2TN
- ☎ **(01633) 680009**
- 🖷 (01633) 680563
- ✉ peterstone_lakes@yahoo.com
- ⊞ 600
- ♗ P Millar
- ⌖ P Glynn (01633) 680075
- ⊳ 18 L 6555 yds Par 72 SSS 72
- ♖ U SOC
- ££ £19 (£29)
- ⚭ 3 miles S of Castleton, off A48. M4 Junction 28
- ⌂ Robert Sandow
- 🖳 www.peterstonelakes.com

Radyr   (1902)
Drysgol Road, Radyr, Cardiff, CF15 8BS
- ☎ **(029) 2084 2408**
- 🖷 (029) 2084 3914
- ✉ manager@radyrgolf.co.uk
- ⊞ 935
- ♗ Steve Dance (Mgr)
- ⌖ S Swales (029) 2084 2476
- ⊳ 18 L 6053 yds SSS 70
- ♖ H SOC–Mon/Wed/Thurs
- ££ D–£40.50
- ⚭ 5 miles NW of Cardiff, off A470. M4 Junction 32
- ⊕ Large practice area
- ⌂ Braid/Holt
- 🖳 www.radyrgolf.co.uk

RAF St Athan   (1977)
Clive Road, St Athan, CF62 4JD
- ☎ **(01446) 751043**
- 🖷 (01446) 751862
- ✉ rafstathan@golfclub.fsbusiness.co.uk
- ⊞ 450
- ♗ PF Woodhouse (01446) 797186
- ⊳ 9 L 6452 yds SSS 72
- ♖ U exc Sun am–NA
- ££ £15 (£20)
- ⚭ 2 miles E of Llantwit Major. 10 miles S of Bridgend

St Andrews Major   (1993)
Proprietary
Coldbrook Road East, Cadoxton, Barry, CF6 3BB
- ☎ **(01446) 722227**
- 🖷 (01446) 748953
- ✉ standrewsmajor@hotmail.co.uk
- ⊞ 470
- ♗ A Edmunds
- ⌖ I Taylor (07779) 712164
- ⊳ 18 L 5425 yds par 71 SSS 66
- ♖ U SOC
- ££ 18: £16 (£18)
- ⚭ Barry Docks Link road. M4 Jct 33
- ⊕ 12 bay floodlit driving range
- ⌂ MRM Leisure
- 🖳 www.standrewsmajorgolfclub.co.uk

St Mellons   (1937)
St Mellons, Cardiff, CF3 2XS
- ☎ **(01633) 680408**
- 🖷 (01633) 681219
- ✉ stmellons@golf2003.fsnet.co.uk
- ⊞ 536 89(L) 67(J)
- ♗ RH Boyce (01633) 680408
- ⌖ B Thomas (01633) 680101
- ⊳ 18 L 6225 yds SSS 70
- ♖ U exc Sat WD SOC
- ££ £32
- ⚭ 4 miles E of Cardiff on A48. M4 Junction 28
- 🖳 www.stmellonsgolfclub.co.uk

Vale Hotel Golf & Spa Resort   (1994)
Hensol Park, Hensol, CF7 8JY
- ☎ **(01443) 665899**
- 🖷 (01443) 222220
- ✉ golf@vale-hotel.com
- ⊞ 1200
- ♗ Clive Coombs
- ⌖ Clive Coombs
- ⊳ Lake 18 L 6426 yds Par 72
- National L 7413 yds Par 73
- ♖ H SOC WD WE
- ££ Lake £40, National £70 Ring for WE price
- ⚭ 1 mile from M 4 Junction 34
- ⊕ Driving range; Golf Academy; practice bunkers & putting greens; short course practice zone
- ⌂ Terry Jones
- 🖳 www.vale-hotel.com

Wenvoe Castle   (1936)
Wenvoe, Cardiff, CF5 6BE
- ☎ **(029) 205 94371**
- 🖷 (029) 205 94371
- ✉ wenvoe-castlegc@virgin.net
- ⊞ 600
- ♗ N Sims (029) 2059 4371
- ⌖ J Harris (029) 2059 3649
- ⊳ 18 L 6444 yds SSS 72
- ♖ WD–H SOC–WD WE–H
- ££ £30 (£40)
- ⚭ 4 miles W of Cardiff, off A4050

Whitchurch (Cardiff)   (1914)
Pantmawr Road, Whitchurch, Cardiff, CF14 7TD
- ☎ **(029) 2062 0985**

☎ (029) 2052 9860
✉ secretary
@whitchurchcardiffgolfclub.com
⌂ 780
♟ G Perrott
✓ R Davies (029) 2061 4660
▷ 18 L 6258 yds Par 71 SSS 71
♙ U H SOC–Thurs
££ £40 (£45)
🚗 3 miles NW of Cardiff on A470.
M4 Junction 32
⌂ F Jones

West Glamorgan

Allt-y-Graban (1993)
*Allt-y-Graban Road, Pontlliw, Swansea,
SA1 1DT*
☎ (01792) 885757

Clyne (1920)
*120 Owls Lodge Lane, Mayals, Swansea,
SA3 5DP*
☎ (01792) 401989
🖥 (01792) 401078
✉ clyngolfclub@supanet.com
⌂ 900
♟ RH Thompson FCA (Mgr)
✓ J Clewett (01792) 402094
▷ 18 L 6323 yds Par 70 SSS 72
♙ U H SOC
££ £28 (£36)
🚗 3 miles SW of Swansea
⊕ Extensive practice area; chipping
green; indoor and outdoor nets
⌂ Colt/Harris
🖥 www.clyngolfclub.com

Fairwood Park (1969)
*Blackhills Lane, Fairwood, Swansea,
SA2 7JN*
☎ (01792) 297849
🖥 (01792) 297849
✉ info@fairwoodpark.com
⌂ 600
♟ D Giltrap, E Golbas (Mgr)
✓ G Hughes (01792) 299194
▷ 18 L 6650 yds SSS 73
♙ U SOC
££ £20 (£25)
🚗 4 miles W of Swansea (A4118)
⌂ Hawtree
🖥 www.fairwoodpark.com

Glynneath (1931)
*Penygraig, Pontneathvaughan, Glynneath,
SA11 5UH*
☎ (01639) 720452
🖥 (01639) 720452
✉ enquiries@glynneathgc.co.uk
⌂ 570
♟ TA Roberts
✓ S McMenamin (01639) 720872
▷ 18 L 6090 yds Par 71 SSS 70
♙ U SOC
££ £17 (£22) Mon £10
🚗 2 miles NW of Glynneath on
Pontneathvaughan Road. 15 miles
NE of Swans

⊕ 3 hole junior academy
⌂ Cotton/Pennink/Lawrie/Williams
🖥 www.glynneathgc.co.uk

Gower
*Cefn Goleu, Three Crosses, Gowerton,
Swansea SA4 3HS*
☎ (01792) 872480
✉ adrian.richards@btconnect.com

Inco (1965)
Clydach, Swansea, SA6 5QR
☎ (01792) 841257
✉ secretaryinco.golf@amserve.com
⌂ 600
♟ DE Jones (01792) 842929
▷ 18 L 6064 yds Par 70 SSS 69
♙ U
££ £18 (£23)
🚗 N of Swansea (A4067)

Lakeside (1992)
*Water Street, Margam, Port Talbot,
SA13 2PA*
☎ (01639) 899959
⌂ 150
♟ B Channell
✓ M Wootton
▷ 18 L 4550 yds Par 63 SSS 63
♙ U SOC
££ £12–£14
🚗 Nr M4 Junction 38
⊕ Driving range
⌂ M Wootton
🖥 www.lakesidegolf.co.uk

Langland Bay (1904)
*Langland Bay Road, Langland, Swansea,
SA3 4QR*
☎ (01792) 366023
🖥 (01792) 361082
✉ info@langlandbaygolfclub.com
⌂ 800
♟ Mrs L Coleman (01792) 361721
✓ M Evans (01792) 366186
▷ 18 L 5857 yds SSS 70
♙ H SOC WD
££ £40 (£50)
🚗 6 miles S of Swansea (A4067). M4
Junction 45
🖥 www.langlandbaygolfclub.com

Morriston (1919)
*160 Clasemont Road, Morriston, Swansea,
SA6 6AJ*
☎ (01792) 771079
🖥 (01792) 796528
✉ morristongolf@btconnect.com
⌂ 600+
♟ KJ Hackford (Sec/Mgr)
(01792) 796528
✓ Mark Govier (01792) 772335
▷ 18 L 5755 yds SSS 68
♙ U H SOC–WD
££ £21 (£30)
🚗 4 miles N of Swansea on A48. M4
Junction 46, 1 mile

Neath (1934)
Cadoxton, Neath, SA10 8AH
☎ (01639) 632759

⌂ (01639) 632759
✉ neathgolf:btconnect.com
⌂ 750
♟ DR Thomas
✓ RM Bennett (01639) 633693
▷ 18 L 6490 yds Par 72 SSS 72
♙ WD–U WE–U SOC
££ Apr–Sep: £25 (£30); Oct–Mar: £17;
Nov–Dec: £15 Dec–Jan: £12;
special rates for Soc of 8 or more
🚗 2 miles NE of Neath (B4434). M4
J46 to A465
⊕ Short game practice area; 4 driving
nets; 2 practice putting greens
⌂ James Braid
🖥 www.neathgolfclub.com

Palleg (1930)
*Palleg Road, Lower Cwmtwrch, Swansea
Valley, SA9 2QQ*
☎ (01639) 842193
🖥 (01639) 845661
✉ gc.gcgs@btinternet.com
⌂ 280
♟ Graham Coombe
✓ Baden Jones (01639) 842193
▷ 18 L 5902 yds Par 72 SSS 70
♙ WD–U Sat/Sun/BH–phone first
SOC
££ £12 D–£12 £10 with member £5
junior
🚗 15 miles NE of Swansea (A4067).
M4 Junction 45
⊕ Junior Starter Centre
⌂ Cotten
🖥 www.palleg-golf.co.uk

Pennard (1896)
*2 Southgate Road, Southgate, Swansea,
SA3 2BT*
☎ (01792) 233131
🖥 (01792) 234797
✉ sec@pennardgolfclub.com
⌂ 775
♟ EM Howell (01792) 233131
✓ MV Bennett (01792) 233451
▷ 18 L 6267 yds Par 71 SSS 72
♙ U H SOC–WD WE by
arrangement
££ £40 (£50)
🚗 8 miles W of Swansea, by A4067
and B4436
⊕ Driving range
⌂ James Braid
🖥 www.pennardgolfclub.com

Pontardawe (1924)
Cefn Llan, Pontardawe, Swansea, SA8 4SH
☎ (01792) 863118
🖥 (01792) 830041
✉ pontardawe@btopenworld.com
⌂ 574
♟ N Bowden (Hon), Mrs M Griffiths
(Admin)
✓ G Hopkins (01792) 830977
▷ 18 L 6101 yds SSS 70
♙ H SOC–WD
££ £20; £54 for 4 ball Mon–Thur
🚗 5 miles N of M4 Junction 45, off
A4067
🖥 www.pontardawegc.co.uk

Swansea Bay   (1892)

Jersey Marine, Neath, SA10 6JP
- ☎ **(01792) 812198**
- 📖 400
- ✍ Mrs D Goatcher (01792) 814153
- ✓ M Day (01792) 816159
- ⊳ 18 L 6256 yds Par 72 SSS 71
  (Yellow)
- 👥 U SOC
- ££ £18 (£25)
- ⊸ 5 miles E of Swansea, off A483
  (B4290). M4 Junction 42

Wrexham

Chirk   (1990)

Proprietary
Chirk, Wrexham, LL14 5AD
- ☎ **(01691) 774407**
- 📠 (01691) 773878
- ✉ chirk-jackbarker@btinternet
  .com
- 📖 300
- ✍ Trudi Jones

- ✓ M Maddison
- ⊳ 18 L 7045 yds Par 72 SSS 73
  9 hole Par 3 course
- 👥 U after 10am SOC
- ££ £14 (£18)
- ⊸ 8 miles S of Wrexham on A483
- ⊕ Driving range
- 🖥 www.jackbarker.com

Clays Golf Centre   (1992)

Bryn Estyn Road, Wrexham, LL13 9UB
- ☎ **(01978) 661406**
- ✉ clays@wrexhamgolf.fsnet.co.uk

Moss Valley   (1990)

Moss Road, Wrexham, LL11 6HA
- ☎ **(01978) 720518**

Plassey Oaks Golf Complex
(1992)

Eyton, Wrexham, LL13 0SP
- ☎ **(01978) 780020**
- 📠 (01978) 781397
- 📖 165

- ✍ Matthew Ellis (01978) 780020
- ⊳ 9 L 4962 yds Par 66 SSS 64
- 👥 U SOC
- ££ £10 (£10)
- ⊸ 2 miles SW of Wrexham, off A483
- ⊕ 9 hole pitch & putt course
- 🏠 K Williams

Wrexham   (1906)

Holt Road, Wrexham, LL13 9SB
- ☎ **(01978) 261033**
- 📠 (01978) 362168
- ✉ info@wrexhamgolfclub.co.uk
- 📖 650
- ✍ J Johnson (01978) 364268
- ✓ P Williams (01978) 351476
- ⊳ 18 L 6233 yds Par 70 SSS 70
- 👥 H SOC–WD
- ££ £30 (£35)
- ⊸ 2 miles NE of Wrexham on A534
- 🏠 James Braid
- 🖥 www.wrexhamgolfclub.co.uk

Continent of Europe – Country and Region Index

Austria

Innsbruck & Tirol

Achensee (1934)
Golf und Landclub Achensee,
6213 Pertisau/Tirol
☎ (05243) 5377
🖷 (05243) 6202
📧 golfclub-achensee@tirol.com
🅿 18 L 6018 m Par 71
👥 U H
££ €50 (€55)
🔊 Pertisau, 50km NE of Innsbruck
🏠 Fahrenleitnner
🖥 www.golfclub-achensee.com

Innsbruck-Igls (1935)
Oberdorf 11, 6074 Rinn
☎ (05223) 78177
🖷 (05223) 78177-77
📧 office@golfclub-innsbruck-igls.at
🅿 Rinn 18 L 6055 m Par 71 CR 71.3
SR 129
Lans 9 L 4597 m Par 66 CR 64.8
👥 H–booking necessary
££ €60 (€60)
🔊 Rinn, 10km E of Innsbruck. Lans,
8km from Innsbruck
🏠 G & G Hauser. Re-design D
Fahrenleitner
🖥 www.golfclub-innsbruck-igls.at

Kaiserwinkl GC Kössen
(1988)
6345 Kössen, Mühlau 1
☎ (05375) 2122
🖷 (05375) 2122-13
📧 club@golf-koessen.at
🅿 18 L 5645 m CR 70.7 SR 127
👥 H
££ €60 (€60)
🔊 30km N of Kitzbühel, nr German
border
🏠 Donald Harradine
🖥 www.golf-koessen.at

Kitzbühel (1955)
Schloss Kaps, 6370 Kitzbühel
☎ (05356) 63007

Kitzbühel-Schwarzsee
(1988)
6370 Kitzbühel, Golfweg Schwarzsee 35
☎ (05356) 71645

Seefeld-Wildmoos (1969)
6100 Seefeld, Postfach 22
☎ (0699) 1-606606-0
🖷 (0699) 4-606606-3
📧 info@seefeldgolf.com
🅿 18 L 5894 m CR 72 SR 130
👥 H–booking necessary
££ €46–€63
🔊 7 km W of Seefeld. 24 km W of
Innsbruck

🏠 Donald Harradine
🖥 www.seefeldgolf.com

Klagenfurt & South

Bad Kleinkirchheim-Reichenau (1977)
9564 Padergassen, Plass 19
☎ (04275) 594

Kärntner GC Dellach
(1927)
Golfstrasse 3, 9082 Maria Wörth, Golfstr 3
☎ (04273) 2515
🖷 (04273) 2515-20
📧 office@kgcdellach.at
🅿 18 L 5609 m Par 71 CR 70.5 SL
134 (men, yellow)
👥 H
££ €70
🔊 Dellach, S side of Wörther See.
15km W of Klagenfurt
🖥 www.kgcdellach.at

Golfclub Klagenfurt-Seltenheim
Seltenheimerstr. 137, A-9061 Wolfnitz
☎ 0043 463 40223
🖷 0043 463 4022320
📧 office@gcseltenheim.at
🅿 18 hole Championship Course
9 hole Romantic Course
👥 H
££ €65
🔊 8km Klagenfurt
🏠 Perry O'Dye
🖥 www.gcseltenheim.at

Klopeiner See-Turnersee
(1988)
9122 St Kanzian, Grabelsdorf 94
☎ (04239) 3800-0
🖷 (04239) 3800-18
📧 office@golfklopein.at
🅿 18 L 6073 m CR 71.3 SR 122
👥 U
££ €48
🔊 25km E of Klagenfurt
🏠 Donald Harradine
🖥 www.golfklopein.at

Golfclub Millstatter See
Am Golfplatz 1, 9872 Millstatt
☎ +43 (0)4762 82542
🖷 +43 (0)4762 82548-10
📧 gcmillstatt@golf.at
🅿 18 Par 71
Men: CR 70.9 SR 126
Women: CR 72.2 SR 125
👥 H WD/WE–all day
££ €60
🔊 Seeboden near Klagenfurt
🖥 www.golf-millstatt.at

Moosburg-Pörtschach
(1986)
9062 Moosburg, Golfstr 2
☎ (04272) 83486
🖷 (04272) 834 8620
📧 moosburg@golfktn.at
🅿 18 L 6011 m SSS 72
9 L 2341 m SSS 35
👥 U
££ 9: €30; 18: €55
🔊 3km N of Wörther See/Pörtschach
🏠 G Hauser
🖥 www.golfmoosburg.at

Wörthersee-Velden (1988)
9231 Köstenberg, Golfweg 41
☎ (04274) 7045
🖷 (04274) 7087-15
📧 golf-velden@golfktn.at
🛏 330
🅿 18 L 6081 m SSS 72
👥 H
££ €66
🔊 30km W of Klagenfurt. 12km from
Velden
🏠 Erhardt/Rossknecht
🖥 www.golfvelden.at

Linz & North

Amstetten-Ferschnitz
(1972)
3325 Ferschnitz, Gut Edla 18
☎ (07473) 8293
📧 office@golfclub-amstetten.at

Böhmerwald GC Ulrichsberg (1990)
4161 Ulrichsberg, Seitelschlag 50
☎ (07288) 8200
🖷 (07288) 82004
📧 office@boehmerwaldgolf.at
🅿 18 L 6240 m SSS 73
9 hole Par 3 course
👥 U H
££ €40 (€50)
🔊 65km NW of Linz
🏠 Rossknecht/Erhardt
🖥 www.boehmerwaldgolf.at

Celtic Golf Course – Schärding (1994)
Maad 2, 4775 Taufkirchen/Pram
☎ (0043) 7719 8110
🖷 (0043) 7719 811015
📧 office@gcschaerding.at
🅿 Championship:
Men: 18 L 6392 m CR 73.2 SR 124
Women: 18 L 5582 m CR 74.2
SR 122
6 hole Josko Academy Course Par
18
👥 H
££ Championship: €45 (€55);
Academy: €16, Juniors/Students €8
🔊 8km S of Schärding on B137
🖥 www.gcschaerding.at

Golfresort Haugschlag
(1987)

3874 Haugschlag 160
- ☎ **(02865) 8441**
- 🖥 (02865) 8441-22
- ✉ info@golfresort.at
- ⛳ 18 L 6262 m CR 72.8 SL 125
  18 L 6395 m CR 72.5 SL 123
  18 hole Par 3 course
- ⛳ H
- €€ €59 (€69)
- ⊶ 25km N of Gmund. 140km NW of Vienna
- 🏠 Max Lamberg
- 🖥 www.golfresort.at

Herzog Tassilo   (1991)
Blankenbergerstr 30, 4540 Bad Hall
- ☎ **(07258) 5480**

PGC Kremstal   (1989)
Schachen 20, 4531 Kematen/Krems
- ☎ **(07228) 7644-0**

Linz-St Florian   (1960)
4490 St Florian, Tillysburg 28
- ☎ **(07223) 828730**
- 🖥 (07223) 828737
- ✉ gclinz@golf.at
- ⛳ 18 L 5864 m Par 72 SSS 72
- ⛳ H
- €€ Mon–Thur €60 (Fri–Sun €70+BH)
- ⊶ St Florian, 15km SE of Linz
- 🏠 Original Donald Harradine; redesign Hans Georg Erhardt
- 🖥 www.gclinz.at

Linzer Golf Club Luftenberg
(1990)

4222 Luftenberg, Am Luftenberg 1a
- ☎ **(07237) 3893**
- 🖥 (07237) 3893-40
- ✉ gclinz-luftenberg@golf.at
- ⛳ 18 L 6075 m CR 70.7 SR 118
- ⛳ U H
- €€ €50 (€60); early morning Mon–Thur before 10.30 €35
- ⊶ 15km NE of Linz
- 🏠 Keith Preston
- 🖥 www.gclinz-luftenberg.at

Maria Theresia   (1989)
Letten 5, 4680 Haag am Hausruck
- ☎ **(07732) 3944**

Ottenstein   (1988)
3532 Niedergrünbach 60
- ☎ **(02826) 7476**
- 🖥 (02826) 7476-4
- ✉ info@golfclub-ottenstein.at
- ⛳ 18 L 6129 m CR 71.9 SR 125
- ⛳ U
- €€ €45 (€55)
- ⊶ 90km NE of Linz. 100km NW of Vienna
- 🏠 Preston/Zinterl/Erhardt
- 🖥 www.golfclub-ottenstein.at

St Oswald-Freistadt
(1988)

Promenade 22, 4271 St Oswald
- ☎ **(07945) 7938**

St Pölten Schloss Goldegg
(1989)

3100 St Pölten Schloss Goldegg
- ☎ **(02741) 7360/7060**

Schloss Ernegg   (1973)
3261 Steinakirchen, Schloss Ernegg
- ☎ **+43 (0) 7488) 76770**
- 🖥 +43 (0) 7488) 76771/71171
- ✉ info@schlossernegg.com
- ⛳ 18 L 5803 m SSS 71
  9 L 2076 m SSS 62
- ⛳ U
- €€ €33 (€40)
- ⊶ Steinakirchen, 80km SE of Linz. 125km W of Vienna
- 🏠 Tucker/Day
- 🖥 www.ernegg.at

Traunsee Kircham
4656 Kircham, Kampesberg 38
- ☎ **(07619) 2576**

Weitra   (1989)
3970 Weitra, Hausschachen
- ☎ **(02856) 2058**
- 🖥 (02856) 2058-4
- ✉ gcweitra@golf.at
- ⛳ 18 L 5916 m Par 72
- ⛳ WD–U WE–H
- €€ €50 (€60)
- ⊶ 75km NE of Linz, nr Czech border
- 🏠 M Gansdorfer
- 🖥 www.gcweitra.at

Wels   (1981)
4616 Weisskirchen, Golfplatzstrasse 2
- ☎ **(07243) 56038**
- 🖥 (07243) 56685
- ✉ gcwels@golf.at
- ⛳ 18 L 6098 m Par 72
  Yellow: CR 71.9 SR 124
  Red: CR 74.5 SR 123
- ⛳ H
- €€ €50 (€60)
- ⊶ 5 km from Salzburg-Vienna highway. 8km SE of Wels
- 🏠 Hauser/Hunt Hastings
- 🖥 www.golfclub-wels.at

Salzburg Region

Bad Gastein   (1960)
5640 Bad Gastein, Golfstrasse 6
- ☎ **(06434) 2775**
- 🖥 (06434) 2775-4
- ✉ info@golfclub-gastein.com
- ⛳ 18 L 5639 m
  Yellow Par 71 CR 69.4 SR 125
  Red Par 71 CR 70.8 SR 122
- ⛳ H SOC WD WE
- €€ €54 (€54)
- ⊶ Bad Gastein 2 km. Salzburg 100km
- 🏠 B von Limburger and Keith Preston
- 🖥 www.golfclub-gastein.com

Goldegg
5622 Goldegg, Postfach 6
- ☎ **(06415) 8585**

Gut Altentann   (1989)
Hof 54, 5302 Henndorf am Wallersee
- ☎ **(06214) 6026-0**
- 🖥 (06214) 6105-81
- ✉ office@gutaltentann.com
- ⛳ 18 L 6103 m CR 70 SR 125
- ⛳ H (max 34) – booking necessary
- €€ €60 (€90)
- ⊶ Henndorf, 16km NE of Salzburg
- 🏠 Jack Nicklaus
- 🖥 www.gutaltentann.com

Gut Brandlhof G&CC
(1983)

5760 Saalfelden am Steinernen Meer, Hohlwegen 4
- ☎ **(06582) 7800-555**

GC Kobernausserwald
(1993)

5241 Höhnart, Strass 1
- ☎ **0043 (7743) 20066**
- 🖥 0043 (7743) 20077
- ✉ office@gckobernausserwald.at
- ✍ E Reinhard (Mgr)
- ⛳ Men: 18 L 5112 m Par 70
  Ladies: 18 L 4532 m par 70
- ⛳ H
- €€ €45 (€50)
- ⊶ 50km from Salzburg. 100km from Linz. 150km from Munich
- 🏠 Heinz Schmidbauer
- 🖥 www.gckobernausserwald.at

Lungau   (1991)
5582 St Michael, Feldnergasse 165
- ☎ **(06477) 7448**

Am Mondsee   (1986)
St Lorenz 1, 5310 Mondsee
- ☎ **(06232) 3835-0**

Radstadt Tauerngolf
(1991)

Römerstrasse 18, 5550 Radstadt
- ☎ **(06452) 5111**
- 🖥 (06452) 7336
- ✉ info@radstadtgolf.at
- ⛳ 18 L 5962 m Par 71
  Men: CR 70.5 SR 127. Women: CR 72.5 SR 127
  9 hole Par 71 course
- ⛳ U
- €€ Mon–Thur €58 (Fri–Sun €66)
- ⊶ 70km NW of Salzburg
- 🖥 www.radstadtgolf.at

For list of abbreviations, key to symbols and international dialling codes see page 651

Salzburg Fuschl (1995)

5322 Hof/Salzburg
- ☎ **(06229) 2390**
- 🖥 (06229) 2390
- ➢ 9 L 3650 m Par 62
- 9 hole Par 3 course
- ⚇ U
- ££ 9: €30 (€30); 18: €50 (€50)
- ⊶ Hof, 12km E of Salzburg
- 🖥 www.golfclub.klessheim.com

Salzburg G&CC (1955)

Schloss Klessheim, 5071 Wals
- ☎ **(0662) 850851**
- ✉ gccsalzburg@golf.at

Salzkammergut (1933)

4820 Bad Ischl
- ☎ **(06132) 26340**
- 🖥 (06132) 26708
- ✉ office@salzkammergut-golf.at
- ➢ 18 L 5673 m Par 72
- ⚇ U
- ££ April–June, Sept–Nov, Mon–Thur €50 Fri–Sun €60 July–Aug W–€60
- ⊶ 6 km W of Bad Ischl, nr Strobl. 50 km E of Salzburg
- 🖥 www.salzkammergut-golf.at

Urslautal (1991)

Schinking 81, 5760 Saalfelden
- ☎ **(06584) 2000**
- 🖥 (06584) 7475-10
- ✉ info@golf-urslautal.at
- ➢ 18 L 6030 m SSS 71
- ⚇ U H
- ££ €60 (€65)
- ⊶ 80km SW of Salzburg
- ⛫ Keith Preston
- 🖥 www.golf-urslautal.at

Zell am See-Kaprun (1983)

5700 Zell am See-Kaprun, Golfstr 25
- ☎ **(06542) 56161**
- ✉ gc.zellamsee-kaprun@telecom.at

Steiermark

Bad Gleichenberg (1984)

Am Hoffeld 3, 8344 Bad Gleichenberg
- ☎ **(03159) 3717**
- ✉ gcgleichenberg@golf.at

Dachstein Tauern (1990)

8967 Haus/Ennstal, Oberhaus 59
- ☎ **(03686) 2630**
- 🖥 (03686) 2630-15
- ➢ 18 L 5910 m SSS 71
- ⚇ U
- ££ €70 (€75 July/Aug)
- ⊶ 2km from Schladming. 100km SE of Salzburg
- ⛫ Bernhard Langer
- 🖥 www.schladming-golf.at

Ennstal-Weissenbach G&LC (1978)

8940 Liezen, Postfach 193
- ☎ **(03612) 24821**

Furstenfeld (1984)

8282 Loipersdorf, Gillersdorf 50
- ☎ **(03382) 8533**

Graz (1989)

8051 Graz-Thal, Windhof 137
- ☎ **(0316) 572867**

Gut Murstätten (1989)

8403 Lebring, Oedt 14
- ☎ **(03182) 3555**
- 🖥 (03182) 3688
- ✉ gcmurstaetten@golf.at
- ➢ 18 L 6395 m CR 73.1 SR 123
- 9 L 6006 m CR 70.4 SR 113
- ⚇ H
- ££ €55 (€65)
- ⊶ 25km S of Graz
- ⛫ J Dudok van Heel
- 🖥 www.gcmurstaetten.at

Maria Lankowitz (1992)

Puchbacher Str 109, 8591 Maria Lankowitz
- ☎ **(03144) 6970**

Murhof (1963)

8130 Frohnleiten, Adriach 53
- ☎ **(03126) 3010**

Murtal (1995)

Frauenbachstr 51, 8724 Spielberg
- ☎ **(03512) 75213**

Reiting G&CC (1990)

8772 Traboch, Schulweg 7
- ☎ **(0663) 833308/(03847) 5008**

St Lorenzen (1990)

8642 St Lorenzen, Gassing 22
- ☎ **(03864) 3961**

Schloss Frauenthal (1988)

8530 Deutschlandsberg, Ulrichsberg 7
- ☎ **(03462) 5717**
- 🖥 (03462) 5717-5
- ✉ office@gcfrauenthal.at
- ➢ 18 L 5447 m SSS 70
- ⚇ U H
- ££ Mon–Thur am €50 Fri pm–Sat–Sun €60 Seniors half price Mon/Tue
- ⊶ 30km SW of Graz
- ⛫ Stephan Breisach
- 🖥 www.gcfrauenthal.at

Schloss Pichlarn (1972)

8952 Irdning/Ennstal, Gatschen 28
- ☎ **(03682) 22841-540**

Vienna & East

Adamstal (1994)

Gaupmannsgraben 21, 3172 Ramsal
- ☎ **(02764) 3500**

Bad Tatzmannsdorf Reiters G&CC (1991)

Am Golfplatz 2, 7431 Bad Tatzmannsdorf
- ☎ **(0043) 3353 8282-0**
- 🖥 (0043) 3353 8282-1735
- ✉ golfclub@burgenlandresort.at
- ➢ 18 L 6180m Par 73 CR 72.7 SR 129
- 9 L 3660 m Par 60 CR 60.2 Slope 103
- ⚇ U H
- ££ 9: €30 (€35) 18: €45 (€55)
- ⊶ 120km SE of Vienna
- ⛫ Rossknecht/Erhardt
- 🖥 www.reitersburgenlandresort.at

Brunn G&CC (1988)

2345 Brunn/Gebirge, Rennweg 50
- ☎ **(02236) 33711**
- 🖥 (02236) 33863
- ✉ club@gccbrunn.at
- ➢ 18 L 5749 m Par 70 CR 70 SR 121
- ⚇ H – soft spikes only
- ££ €50 (€65)
- ⊶ 10km S of Vienna
- ⛫ G Hauser
- 🖥 www.gccbrunn.at

Colony Club Gutenhof (1988)

2325 Himberg, Gutenhof
- ☎ **(02235) 87055-0**
- 🖥 (02235) 87055-14
- ✉ club@colonygolf.com
- ➢ East 18 L 6404 m CR 73.9 SR 132 (Backtee)
- West 18 L 6483 m CR 74.5 SR 132 (Backtee)
- ⚇ WE only before 10am and after 2pm WD/WE–H
- ££ €50 Mon–Tue €55 Wed–Fri 12pm €80 Fri 12pm–Sun
- ⊶ 7km SE of Vienna
- ⛫ Rossknecht/Erhardt
- 🖥 www.colonygolf.com

Eldorado Bucklige Welt (1990)

Golfplatz 1, 2871 Zöbern
- ☎ **(02642) 8451**

Enzesfeld (1970)

2551 Enzesfeld
- ☎ **(02256) 81272**
- ✉ gcenzesfeld@golf.at

Föhrenwald (1968)

2700 Wiener Neustadt, Postfach 105
- ☎ **(02622) 29171**
- ✉ gcfoehrenwald@golf.at

Fontana   (1996)

Fontana Allee 1, 2522 Oberwaltersdorf
- ☎ (02253) 606401
- 📠 (02253) 606403
- ✉ gcfontana@mide.co.at
- ⛳ 18 L 6088 m Par 72
- 👤 U–booking necessary. Soft spikes only
- ££ €99 (€125)
- 🚗 20km S of Vienna
- 🏠 Carrick/Erhardt
- 🖥 www.fontana.at

Hainburg/Donau
(1977)

2410 Hainburg, Auf der Heide 762
- ☎ (02165) 62628
- 📠 (02165) 626283
- ✉ info@golfclub-hainburg.at
- ⛳ 18 L 6064 m SSS 72
- 👤 H
- ££ €40 (€60)
- 🚗 50km E of Vienna; 19km W of Bratislava
- 🏠 G Hauser
- 🖥 www.golfclub-hainburg.at

Lengenfeld   (1995)

Am Golfplatz 1, 3552 Lengenfeld
- ☎ (02719) 8710

Neusiedlersee-
Donnerskirchen   (1988)

7082 Donnerskirchen
- ☎ (02683) 8171

Schloss Ebreichsdorf   (1988)

2483 Ebreichsdorf, Schlossallee 1
- ☎ (02254)73888
- ✉ office@gcebreichsdorf.at

Schloss Schönborn   (1987)

2013 Schönborn 4
- ☎ (02267) 2863/2879
- ✉ golfclub@gcschoenborn.com

Schönfeld   (1989)

A-2291 Schönfeld, Am Golfplatz 1
- ☎ +43 (02213) 2063
- ✉ gcschoenfeld@golf.at

Semmering   (1926)

2680 Semmering
- ☎ (02664) 8154

Golfclub Spillern

Wiesenerstrasse 100, A-2104 Spillern
- ☎ +43 (0)2 668 1211
- 📠 +43 (0)22 668 121120
- ✉ gcspillern.at
- ⛳ 18 + 3 Par 72
- 👤 U (member of reg club with known course)
- ££ €43 (€58)
- 🚗 20km from downtown Vienna
- 🏠 Haluschan

Thayatal Drosendorf
(1994)

Autendorf 18, 2095 Drosendorf
- ☎ (02915) 62625

Wien   (1901)

1020 Wien, Freudenau 65a
- ☎ (01) 728 9564 (Clubhouse)
  (01) 728 9564-13 (Caddymaster)
- 📠 (01) 728 9564-20
- ✉ gcwien@golf.at
- ⛳ 18 L 5861 m SSS 71
- 👤 WE–NA
- ££ €70
- 🚗 10 mins SE of Vienna
- 🖥 www.gcwien.at

Wien-Süssenbrunn
(1995)

Weingartenallee 22, 1220 Wien
- ☎ (01) 256 8282
- 📠 (01) 246 8282 -44
- ✉ golf@sportparkwien.at
- ⛳ 18 L 6130 m SSS 72
  6 hole Par 3 course
- 👤 H
- ££ €50 (€62) 6 hole: €23 (€27)
- 🚗 15km NE of Vienna
- 🏠 Rossknecht/Erhardt
- 🖥 www.sportparkwien.at

Wienerberg   (1989)

1100 Wien, Gutheil Schoder 9
- ☎ (0222) 66123-7000

Wienerwald   (1981)

1130 Wien, Altgasse 27
- ☎ (0222) 877 3111 (Sec)

Vorarlberg

Bludenz-Braz   (1996)

Oberradin 60, 6751 Braz bei Bludenz
- ☎ (05552) 33503
- 📠 (05552) 33503-3
- ✉ gcbraz@golf.at
- ⛳ 18 L 5121 m Par 68
- 👤 M H
- ££ D–€48 (€58)
- 🚗 5km E of Bludenz
- 🏠 Kurt Rosknecht
- 🖥 www.gc-bludenz-braz.at

Bregenzerwald   (1997)

Unterlitten 3a, 6943 Riefensberg
- ☎ (05513) 8400
- ✉ office@golf-bregenzerwald.com

Montafon   (1992)

6774 Tschagguns, Zelfenstrasse 110
- ☎ (05556) 77011
- ✉ info@golfclub-montafon.at

Belgium

Antwerp Region

Bossenstein   (1989)

Moor 16, Bossenstein Kasteel, 2520 Broechem
- ☎ (03) 485 64 46
- ✉ bossenstein.shop@skynet.be

Cleydael G&CC   (1988)

Groenenhoek 7-9, 2630 Aartselaar
- ☎ (03) 870 56 80
- 📠 (03) 887 14 75
- ✉ info@cleydael.be
- ⛳ 18 L 6059 m SSS 72
- 👤 H WE–NA before 2pm
- ££ €50 (€65)
- 🚗 8km S of Antwerp. 40km N of Brussels
- 🏠 Paul Rolin
- 🖥 www.cleydael.be

Kempense   (1986)

Kiezelweg 78, 2400 Mol-Rauw
- ☎ 00 32 (0)14 81 46 41 (Clubhouse)
  00 32 (0)14 81 62 34 (start res.)
- 📠 00 32 (0)14 81 62 78
- ✉ kempense@pandora.be
- ⛳ 18 L 5904 m Par 72
- 👤 U H–36 WD WE
- ££ €45 (€55)
- 🚗 60km E of Antwerp
- 🏠 Marc de Keyser
- 🖥 www.golf.be/kempense

Lilse   (1988)

Haarlebeek 3, 2275 Lille
- ☎ (014) 55 19 30
- 📠 (014) 55 19 31
- ⛳ 9 holes Par 66
- 👤 U
- ££ €15 (€24)
- 🚗 Lille, 10km SW of Turnhout, nr E7. 25km E of Antwerp

Nuclea Mol   (1984)

Goorstraat, 2400 Mol
- ☎ (011) 39 17 80

Rinkven G&CC   (1980)

Sint Jobsteenweg 120, 2970 Schilde
- ☎ (03) 380 12 85
- 📠 (03) 384 29 33
- ✉ info@rinkven.be
- ⛳ 36 hole course
- 👤 H–phone before visit
- ££ €55 (€75)
- 🚗 17 km NE of Antwerp, off E19
- 🏠 Paul Rolin
- 🖥 www.rinkven.be

Royal Antwerp   (1888)

Georges Capiaulei 2, 2950 Kapellen
- ☎ (03) 666 84 56

Steenhoven   (1985)
Steenhoven 89, 2400 Postel-Mol
- ☎ **(014) 37 36 61**
- 🖳 (014) 37 36 62
- ✉ info@steenhoven.be
- ⮂ 18 L 5950 m SSS 71
- ⚭ H–booking necessary
- ££ €55 (€65)
- ⮂ 30 mins W of Antwerp
- ⌂ Pierre de Broqueville
- 🖥 www.steenhoven.be

Ternesse G&CC   (1976)
Uilenbaan 15, 2160 Wommelgem
- ☎ **(03) 355 14 30**

Ardennes & South

Andenne   (1988)
Ferme du Moulin 52, Stud, 5300 Andenne
- ☎ **(085) 84 34 04**

Château Royal d'Ardenne
Tour Léopold, Ardenne 6, 5560 Houyet
- ☎ **(082) 66 62 28**

Falnuée   (1987)
Rue E Pirson 55, 5032 Mazy
- ☎ **(081) 63 30 90**
- 🖳 (081) 63 21 91
- ✉ info@falnuee.be
- ⮂ 18 L 5820 m SSS 72
- ⚭ H
- ££ €38 (€55)
- ⮂ 18km NW of Namur. Mons-Liège highway Junction 13
- ⌂ J Jottrand
- 🖥 www.falnuee.be

Five Nations C C   (1990)
Ferme du Grand Scley, 5372 Méan (Havelange)
- ☎ **(086) 32 32 32**

Mont Garni   (1989)
Rue du Mont Garni 3, 7331 Saint Ghislain
- ☎ **(065) 62 27 19**
- 🖳 (065) 62 34 10
- ✉ secretariat@golfmontgarni.de
- ⮂ 18 L 6353 m Par 74
- ⚭ H
- ££ €40 (€60)
- ⮂ St Ghislain, 15km W of Mons. 65km SW of Brussels
- ⌂ T Macaulay
- 🖥 www.golfmontgarni.be

Rougemont
Chemin du Beau Vallon 45, 5170 Profondeville
- ☎ **(081) 41 14 18**

Royal GC du Hainaut   (1933)
Rue de la Verrerie 2, 7050 Erbisoeul
- ☎ **(065) 22 96 10 (Clubhouse)**
  (065) 22 02 00 (Sec)

Brussels & Brabant

Bercuit   (1965)
Les Gottes 3, 1390 Grez-Doiceau
- ☎ **(010) 84 15 01**

Brabantse   (1982)
Steenwagenstraat 11, 1820 Melsbroek
- ☎ **(02) 751 82 05**
- ✉ brabantse.golf@skynet.be

La Bruyère   (1988)
Rue Jumerée 1, 1495 Sart-Dames-Avelines
- ☎ **(071) 87 72 67**
- ✉ info@golflabruyere.be

Golf du Château de la Bawette   (1988)
Chaussée du Chateau de la Bawette 5, 1300 Wavre
- ☎ **(010) 22 33 32**
- 🖳 (010) 22 90 04
- ✉ info@labawette.com
- ⮂ Parc 18 L 6076 m SSS 72
  Champs 9 L 2146 m SSS 63
- ⚭ H–booking required
- ££ Parc €45 (€70)
- ££ Champs €40 (€50)
- ⮂ 1km N of Wavre. 15km S of Brussels. E411 Exit 5
- ⌂ Tom Macauley
- 🖥 www.labawette.com

Château de la Tournette
Chemin de Baudemont 21, 1400 Nivelles
- ☎ **(067) 89 42 66**
- 🖳 (067) 21 95 17
- ✉ info@tournette.com
- ⮂ US course: 18 L 6198 m Par 72
  UK course: 18 L 6103 m Par 71
- ⚭ H
- ££ Mon–Thur €48 (Fri–Sun €80)
- ⮂ 29km S of Brussels (E19)
- ⌂ Alliss/Clark
- 🖥 www.tournette.com

L'Empereur   (1989)
Rue Emile François No.31, 1474 Ways (Genappe)
- ☎ **(067) 77 15 71**
- 🖳 (067) 77 18 33
- ✉ info@golfempereur.com
- ⮂ Empereur: 18 L 6201 m Par 72
  La Hutte: 9 L 1650 m Par 31
- ⚭ U H
- ££ 9: €20 (€35) 18: €35 (€68)
- ⮂ 25km S of Brussels
- ⌂ Marcel Vercruyce
- 🖥 www.golfempereur.com

Hulencourt   (1989)
Bruyère d'Hulencourt 15, 1472 Vieux Genappe
- ☎ **(067) 79 40 40**

- 🖳 (067) 79 40 48
- ✉ info@golfhulencourt.be
- ⮂ 18 L 6215 m Par 72
  9 hole Par 3 course
- ⚭ H–max 36
- ££ €65 (€95)
- ⮂ 30km SE of Brussels
- ⌂ JM Rossi
- 🖥 www.golfhulencourt.be

Kampenhout   (1989)
Wildersedreef 56, 1910 Kampenhout
- ☎ **(016) 65 12 16**
- 🖳 (016) 65 16 80
- ✉ golfclubkampenhout@skynet.be
- ⮂ 18 L 6142 m SSS 72
- ⚭ H
- ££ €40 (€55) – 2005
- ⮂ 15km NE of Brussels (E19)
- ⌂ R de Vooght
- 🖥 www.golfclubkampenhout.be

Keerbergen   (1968)
Vlieghavenlaan 50, 3140 Keerbergen
- ☎ **(015) 122 68 78**
- 🖳 (015) 23 57 37
- ✉ keerbergen.golfclub@skynet.be
- ⮂ 18 L 5503 m SSS 70
- ⚭ H
- ££ €40 (€60)
- ⮂ 30km NE of Brussels
- ⌂ Frank Pennink
- 🖥 www.golf.be/keerbergen

Louvain-la-Neuve
Rue A Hardy 68, 1348 Louvain-la-Neuve
- ☎ **(010) 45 05 15**

Overijse   (1986)
Gemslaan 55, 3090 Overijse
- ☎ **(02) 687 50 30**
- 🖳 (02) 687 37 68
- ✉ ogc@golf-overijse.be
- ⮂ 9 L 5723 m Par 71
- ⚭ H
- ££ €20 (€37)
- ⮂ 10km S of Brussels
- ⌂ Rossi
- 🖥 www.golf.be/overijse

Pierpont   (1992)
1 Grand Pierpont, 6210 Frasnes-lez-Gosselies
- ☎ **(071) 8808 30**
- 🖳 (071) 85 15 43
- ✉ info@pierpont.be
- ⮂ 18 L 6232 m Par 72
  5 hole Par 3 course
- ⚭ U
- ££ €38 (€65)
- ⮂ 30km S of Brussels via N5/15km S of Waterloo
- ⌂ J Dudok van Heel
- 🖥 www.pierpont.be

Rigenée   (1981)
Rue de Châtelet 62, 1495 Villers-la-Ville
- ☎ **(071) 87 77 65**
- 🖳 (071) 87 77 83
- ✉ golf@rigenee.be
- ⮂ 18 L 6360 m Par 73 CR 74.1 SR 128

𝕎 H
££ €35 (€65)
⊗ 35km S of Brussels towards Charleroi
🏠 Rolin/Descampe
🖥 www.rigenee.be

Royal Amicale Anderlecht

(1987)

Rue Schollestraat 1, 1070 Brussels

☎ (02) 521 16 87
🖳 (02) 521 51 56
✉ info@golf-anderlecht.com
🏴 18 L 5037 m Par 70 CR 68.7 SR 123
𝕎 WD–H WE–booking required
££ €35 (€50)
⊗ Brussels Capital Region (Anderlecht)
🖥 www.golf-anderlecht.com

Royal Golf Club de Belgique

(1906)

Château de Ravenstein, 3080 Tervuren

☎ (02) 767 58 01
🖳 (02) 767 28 41
✉ ravenstein.golfclub@skynet.be
🏴 18 L 6041 m SSS 72
   9 L 1937 m Par 32
𝕎 WD–H–max 20(men) 24(ladies)–phone first. Course closed Mon
££ €100
⊗ Tervuren, 10km E of Brussels
🏠 Simpson
🖥 www.rgcb.be

Royal Waterloo

(1923)

Vieux Chemin de Wavre 50, 1380 Lasne

☎ (00) 322 633 1850
🖳 (00) 322 633 2866
✉ infos@golfwaterloo.be
🏴 La Marache: 18 L 6371 m Par 72
   Le Lion: 18 L 6215 m Par 72
   Le Bois-Heros: 9 L 2160 m Par 33
𝕎 WD–H
££ €90
⊗ 22km SE of Brussels
🏠 Hawtree
🖥 www.rwgc.be

Sept Fontaines

(1987)

1021, Chaussée d'Alsemberg, 1420 Braine L'Alleud

☎ (02) 353 02 46/353 03 46
🖳 (02) 354 68 75
✉ info@golf7fontaines.be
🏴 18 L 6000 m Par 72 SSS 72
   18 L 4874 m Par 69 SSS 67
   9 hole short course
𝕎 U H
££ €45 (€80)
⊗ Braine L'Alleud, 15km S of Brussels. E40 exit 29 direction Huizingen
🏠 Rossi
🖥 www.golf7fontaines.be

Winge G&CC

(1988)

Leuvensesteenweg 252, 3390 Sint Joris Winge

☎ (016) 63 40 53

🖳 (016) 63 21 40
✉ winge@golf.be
🏴 18 L 6049 m Par 72 CR 72.3
𝕎 H
££ €45 (€60)
⊗ 35km E of Brussels via Leuven
🏠 P Townsend
🖥 www.golf.be/winge

East

Avernas

Route de Grand Hallet 19A, 4280 Hannut

☎ (019) 51 30 66
🖳 (019) 51 53 43
✉ info@golfavernas.be
🏴 9 L 2674 m SSS 68
   Men: CR 68.6 SR 122
   Women: CR 68.3 SR 116
𝕎 H
££ €20 (€28)
⊗ 40km W of Liège. Brussels 50km
🏠 Hawtree/Cappart
🖥 www.golfavernas.be

Durbuy (1991)

Route d'Oppagne 34, 6940 Barvaux-su-Ourthe

☎ (086) 21 44 54

Flanders Nippon Hasselt

(1988)

Vissenbroekstraat 15, 3500 Hasselt

☎ (011) 26 34 82
🖳 (011) 26 34 83
✉ flanders.nippon.golf@pandora.be
🏴 18 L 5966 m SSS 72
   9 L 1883 m SSS 33
𝕎 U H (for 18 only)
££ €45 (€55)
⊗ 5km E of Hasselt. 85km E of Brussels
🏠 Rolin/Wirtz
🖥 www.golf.be/flanders.nippon

Henri-Chapelle (1988)

Rue du Vivier 3, B-4841 Henri-Chapelle

☎ (087) 88 19 91
🖳 (087) 88 36 55
✉ info@golfhenrichapelle.be
🏴 18 L 6040 m SSS 72
   9 L 2168 m SSS 34
   6 hole Par 20 course
𝕎 9 and 18 holes: (WD+WE) H; 6 holes: U
££ 6: €10 (€15); 9: €25 (€30); 2x9: €40 (€45); 18: €50 (€60)
⊗ 15km NE of Liège. Aachen 10km
🏠 Steensels/Dudok van Heel
🖥 www.golfhenrichapelle.be

International Gomze

(1986)

Sur Counachamps 8, 4140 Gomze Andoumont

☎ (04) 360 92 07
🖳 (04) 360 92 06
✉ gomzegolf@skynet.be

🏴 18 L 5918 m SSS 72
𝕎 U H
££ On application
⊗ 15km S of Liège. Spa 20km
🏠 Paul Rolin

Limburg G&CC (1966)

Golfstraat 1, 3530 Houthalen

☎ (089) 38 35 43
🖳 (089) 84 12 08
✉ limburggolf@skynet.be
🏴 18 L 6049 m SSS 72
𝕎 WD WE H
££ €60 (€75)
⊗ Houthalen, 15km N of Hasselt
🏠 Hawtree
🖥 www.golf.be

Royal GC du Sart Tilman

(1939)

Route du Condroz 541, 4031 Liège

☎ (041) 336 20 21
🖳 (041) 337 20 26
✉ secretariat@rgcst.be
🏴 18 L 6002 m SSS 72
𝕎 H–booking required
££ €50 (€65)
⊗ 10km S of Liège on Route 620 (N35), towards Marche
🏠 T Simpson
🖥 www.rgcst.be

Royal Golf des Fagnes

(1930)

1 Ave de l'Hippodrome, 4900 Spa

☎ (087) 79 30 30

Spiegelven GC Genk (1988)

Wiemesmeerstraat 109, 3600 Genk

☎ (0032) 893 59616
🖳 (0032) 893 64184
✉ info@spiegelven.be
🏴 Men: 18 L 6098 m SSS 72 SR 133
   Women: 18 L 5293 m SSS 72 SR 128
   9 hole Par 3 course
𝕎 H
££ €50 (€60)
⊗ Genk, 18km E of Hasselt. 20km N of Maastricht
🏠 Ron Kirby
🖥 www.spiegelven.be

West & Oost Vlaanderen

Damme G&CC (1987)

Doornstraat 16, 8340 Damme-Sijsele

☎ (050) 35 35 72
🖳 (050) 35 89 25
✉ damme.gcc@skynet.be
🏴 18 L 6046 m SSS 72
   9 hole short course
𝕎 H 35
££ €64 (€68)
⊗ 7km E of Bruges. Knokke 15km
🏠 J Dudok van Heel
🖥 www.golf.be/damme

Oudenaarde G&CC
(1975)
Kasteel Petegem, Kortrykstraat 52, 9790 Wortegem-Petegem
☎ **(055) 33 41 61**
▢ (055) 31 98 49
☞ 2 x 18 L 6172 m Par 72
9 L 2536 m Par 34
⚇ H
££ €55 (€70)
⚘ 4 km SW of Oudenaarde
⌂ HJ Baker
▤ www.golfoudenaarde.be

De Palingbeek   (1991)
Eekhofstraat 14, 8902 Hollebeke-Ieper
☎ **(057) 20 04 36**
▢ (057) 21 89 58
⊠ golfpalinbeek@skynet.be
⚇ 18 L 6165 m Par 72
⚇ H
££ €50 (€60)
⚘ 5km SE of Ieper, nr Hollebeke
⌂ HJ Baker
▤ www.golfpalingbeek.be

Royal Latem   (1909)
9830 St Martens-Latem
☎ **(092) 82 54 11**
▢ (092) 82 90 19
⊠ latem@golf.be
☞ 18 L 5767 m Par 72 SR 123
⚇ H
££ €60 (€70)
⚘ 10 km SW of Ghent on route N43
Ghent-Deinze
▤ www.golf.be/latem

Royal Ostend   (1903)
Koninklijke Baan 2, 8420 De Haan
☎ **(059) 23 32 83**

Royal Zoute   (1899)
Caddiespad 14, 8300 Knokke-le-Zoute
☎ **(050) 60 16 17 (Clubhouse)**
(050) 60 37 81 (Starter)
▢ (050) 62 30 29
⊠ golf@zoute.be
☞ No 1 18 L 6172 m Par 72
No 2 18 L 3607 m Par 64
⚇ H No 1 course–max 20
WE–restricted
££ €95 Par 72; €55 Par 64
⚘ Knokke-Heist
⌂ HS Colt

Waregem   (1988)
Bergstraat 41, 8790 Waregem
☎ **(056) 60 88 08**
▢ (056) 62 18 23
⊠ waregem@golf.be
☞ 18 L 6038 m SSS 72
⚇ H Sun–NA before 2 p.m.
££ €45 (€55)
⚘ 30km SW of Ghent (E17)
⌂ Paul Rolin
▤ www.golf.be/waregem

Czech Republic

Karlovy Vary   (1904)
Prazska 125, PO Box 67, 360 01 Karlovy Vary
☎ **(017) 333 1001-2**

Lísnice   (1928)
252 10 Mnísek pod Brdy
☎ **(0318) 599 151**

Mariánské Lázne
(1905)
PO Box 267, 353 01 Mariánské Lázne
☎ **(0165) 4300**

Park GC Ostrava   (1968)
Dolni 412, 747 15 Silherovice
☎ **(+420) 595 054 144**
▢ (+420) 595 054 144
⊠ office@golf-ostrava.cz
⚐ Michal Navrat (Mgr)
☞ 18 L 5593 m CR 70.3 SR 125
⚇ H
££ 600–800czk (800–1200czk)
⚘ 15km N of Ostrava
⌂ Jan Cieslar
▤ www.golf-ostrava.cz

Podebrady   (1964)
Na Zalesi 530, 29080 Podebrady
☎ **(0324) 610928**

Semily   (1970)
Bavlnarska 521, 513 01 Semily
☎ **(0431) 622443/624428**

Denmark

Bornholm Island

Bornholm   (1972)
Plantagevej 3B, 3700 Rønne
☎ **56 95 68 54**
▢ 56 95 68 53
⊠ info@bornholmsgolfklub.dk
☞ 18 L 4819 m Par 68
9 hole Par 3 course
⚇ H
££ 250kr
⚘ 4km E of Rønne, off Route 38
towards Aakirkeby
⌂ Frederik Dreyer
▤ www.bornholmsgolfklub.dk

Nexø
Dueodde Golfbane, Strandmarksvejen 14, 3730 Nexø
☎ **56 48 89 87**
▢ 56 48 89 69
☞ 18 L 5470 m CR 69.4 SR 124
⚇ H
££ 250kr (250kr)
⚘ 12km S of Nexø, nr Dueodde beach
⌂ Frederik Dreyer
▤ www.dueodde-golf.dk

Nordbornholm-Rø   (1987)
Spellingevej 3, Rø, 3760 Gudhjem
☎ **56 48 40 50**
▢ 56 48 40 52
⊠ mail@roegolfbane.dk
☞ 18 L 5369 m SSS 71 (Old Course)
18 L 6469 m SSS 72 (New Course)
⚇ WD–U WE–H
££ 325kr
⚘ Rø, 8km W of Gudhjem. 22km NE of Rønne
⌂ Anders Amilon
▤ www.roegolfbane.dk

Funen

Faaborg   (1989)
Dalkildegards Allee 1, 5600 Faaborg
☎ **62 61 77 43**

Lillebaelt   (1990)
O.Hougvej 130, 5500 Middelfart
☎ **64 41 80 11**
⊠ gkl@posf10.tele.dk

Odense   (1927)
Hestehaven 200, 5220 Odense SØ
☎ **65 95 90 00**

Odense Eventyr Golf Centre   (1993)
Falen 227, 5250 Odense SV
☎ **6565 2020**
▢ 6562 2021
⊠ oegc@golfin.dk
☞ 18 hole course Par 72
9 hole course + 9 holes Pay & Play
⚇ H
££ 320kr (360kr)
⚘ 5km SW of Odense
⌂ Michael Møller
▤ www.golfin.dk

SCT Knuds   (1954)
Slipshavnsvej 16, 5800 Nyborg
☎ **65 31 12 12**
▢ 65 30 28 04
⊠ mail@sct-knuds.dk
☞ 18 L 5792 m CR 71.1
⚇ H
££ 300kr (350kr) (2D–560kr)
⚘ 3km SE of Nyborg
⌂ Cotton/Dreyer
▤ www.sct-knuds.dk

Svendborg (1970)

Tordensgaardevej 5, Sørup,
5700 Svendborg
☎ 62 22 40 77
🖥 62 20 29 77
✉ info@svendborg-golf.dk
🏌 9 L 2034 m CR 61.9 SR 106
   18 L 5781 m CR 72.0 SR 138
👥 H–max 36 WE 42 WD
££ D–300kr
🚗 4km NW of Svendborg
🏠 Frederik Dreyer/Henrick J Jacobsen
🖳 www.svendborg-golf.dk

Vestfyns (1974)

Rønnemosegård, Krengerupvej 27,
5620 Glamsbjerg
☎ 63 72 19 20
✉ vestfyn@golfonline.dk

Greenland

Sondie Arctic Desert (1990)

Box 58, 3910 Kangerlussuaq, Greenland
☎ 29 91 14 13

Jutland

Aalborg (1908)

Jaegersprisvej 35, Restrup Enge,
9000 Aalborg
☎ 98 34 14 76
🖥 98 34 15 84
✉ mail@aalborggolfklub.dk
🏌 18 L 6087 m CR 71
👥 H (max 36)
££ D–300kr (D–400kr)
🚗 7 km SW of Aalborg
🏠 R Harris
🖳 www.aalborgolfklub.dk

Aarhus (1931)

Ny Moesgaardvej 50, 8270 Hojbjerg
☎ 86 27 63 22

Blokhus Klit (1993)

Hunetorpvej 115, Box 37, 9492 Blokhus
☎ 98 20 95 00
🖥 98 20 95 01
🏌 18 L 5584 m CR 70.5
👥 U H
££ 260kr (350kr)
🚗 35km NW of Aalborg
🏠 Frederik Dreyer

Breinholtgård (1992)

Koksspangvej 17-19, 6710 Esbjerg V
☎ 75 11 57 00

Brønderslev (1971)

PO Box 94, 9700 Brønderslev
☎ 98 82 32 81

Brundtlandbanen (2000)

Brundtland Allé 1-3, 6520 Toftlund
☎ 73 83 16 00
🖥 73 83 16 19
✉ info@brundtland.dk
📖 600
🏌 18 L 5890 m Par 73
   9 L 1255 m Par 29
👥 H (+W 9–hole course)
££ 250kr (300kr)
🚗 Toftlund, central Jutland
🏠 Henrik Jacobsen
🖳 www.brundtland.dk

Dejbjerg (1966)

Letagervej 1, Dejbjerg, 6900 Skjern
☎ 97 35 00 09
🖥 96 80 11 18
✉ kontor@dejbjerggk.dk
🏌 18 L 5794 m Par 72
   CR 71.1 SR 132 (men)
   CR 72.2 SR 125 (women)
👥 U
££ D–250kr (D–250kr)
🚗 6km N of Skjern. 25km from W
   coast on Skjern-Ringkøbing road
   (Route 28)
🏠 Schnack/Dreyer
🖳 www.dejbjerggk.dk

Ebeltoft (1966)

Galgebakken 14, 8400 Ebeltoft
☎ 87 59 6000
✉ post@ebeltoft-golfclub.dk

Esbjerg (1921)

Sønderhedevej 11, Marbaek, 6710 Esbjerg
☎ 75 26 92 19
🖥 75 26 94 19
✉ kontor@esbjerg-golfklub.dk
🏌 18 L 6347 m Par 71 CR 74.1
   9 L 5520 m Par 70 CR 69.6
👥 U H
££ 350kr/€50 (400kr/€60)
🚗 15km N of Esbjerg
🏠 Frederik Dreyer
🖳 www.esbjerg-golfklub.dk

Fanø Golf Links (1901)

Golfvejen 5, 6720 Fanø
☎ 76 66 00 77
🖥 76 66 00 44
✉ golf@fanonet.dk
🏌 18 L 5080 m CR 68.7
👥 H
££ D–220kr (D–280kr)
🚗 W side of Fanø Island. Ferry from
   Esbjerg 15 mins; 3 km
🖳 www.fanoe-golf-links.dk

Grenaa (1981)

Vestermarken 1, DK-8500 Grenaa
☎ +45 863 27929
🖥 +45 863 09654
✉ info@grenaagolfklub.dk
🏌 18 L 5782 m Par 70
👥 U
££ D–250kr (250kr)
🚗 1km W of Grenaa. 60km NE of
   Aarhus

Dreyer/Sommer
🖳 www.grenaagolfklub.dk

Gyttegård (1974)

Billundvej 43, 7250 Hejnsvig
☎ +45 75 33 63 82
🖥 +45 75 33 68 20
✉ info@gyttegaardgolfklub.dk
🏌 18 L 5548 m Par 70 CR 69.3 SR
   122
👥 H
££ 220kr (300kr)
🚗 2km NE of Hejnsvig. 5km SW of
   Billund
🏠 Amilon/Bossen
🖳 www.gyttegaardgolfklub.dk

Haderslev (1971)

Viggo Carstensvej 7, 6100 Haderslev
☎ 74 52 83 01

Han Herreds

Starkaervej 20, 9690 Fjerritslev
☎ 98 21 26 66 / 98 21 26 78

Henne (1989)

Hennebysvej 30, 6854 Henne
☎ 75 25 56 10
🖥 75 25 56 30
✉ post@hennegolfklub.dk
🏌 18 L 5998 m Par 71 CR 72.5
   9 hole Par 3 course
👥 U H
££ 230kr
🚗 19km NW of Varde. 35km N of
   Esbjerg
🏠 Frederik Dreyer
🖳 www.hennegolfklub.dk

Herning (1964)

Golfvej 2, 7400 Herning
☎ 97 21 00 33
🖥 97 21 00 34
✉ info@herninggolfklub.dk
🏌 18 L 5571 m CR 71.8
👥 H
££ 200kr (250kr)
🚗 2km E of Herning on Route 15
🏠 Dreyer/Baekgaard
🖳 www.herninggolfklub.dk

Himmerland G&CC (1979)

Centervej 1, Gatten, 9640 Farsö
☎ 96 49 61 00
✉ hgcc@himmerlandgolf.dk

Hirtshals (1990)

Kjulvej 10, PO Box 51, 9850 Hirtshals
☎ 98 94 94 08

Hjarbaek Fjord (1992)

Lynderup, 8832 Skals
☎ 86 69 62 88

Hjorring (1985)

Vinstrupvej 30, 9800 Hjorring
☎ 98 91 18 28

98 90 31 00
info@hjoerringgolf.dk
36 (4 x 9)
Booking start time
www.hjoerringgolf.dk
H
£€ 250kr (300kr)
N of Hjorring. 50km N of Aalborg
Erik Schnack and Michael Traadsdal Møller
www.hjoerringgolf.dk

Holmsland Klit
Klevevej 19, Søndervig, 6950 Ringkøbing
☎ 97 33 88 00

Holstebro   (1970)
Råsted, 7570 Vemb
☎ 97 48 51 55
97 48 51 11
post@holstebro-golfklub.dk
18 L 5921 m CR 71.9
9 L 2510 m
H
£€ 300kr (350kr)
13km W of Holstebro (Route 16)
Erik Schnack, Robert Trent Jones Jr (2004)
www.holstebro-golfklub.dk

Horsens   (1972)
Silkeborgvej 44, 8700 Horsens
☎ 75 61 51 51

Hvide Klit   (1972)
Hvideklitvej 28, 9982 Aalbaek
☎ 98 48 90 21
98 48 91 12
info@hvideklit.dk
18 L 5875 m SSS 72
H
£€ 250kr (300kr)
3km N of Aalbaek. 24km N of Frederikshavn
Anders Amilon
www.hvideklit.dk

Juelsminde   (1973)
Bobroholtvej 11a, 7130 Juelsminde
☎ 75 69 34 92
golf@juelsmindegolf.dk

Kaj Lykke   (1988)
Kirkebrovej 5, 6740 Bramming
☎ 75 10 22 46
75 10 26 68
post@kaj-lykke-golfklub.dk
18 L 5975 m CR 72.3 SR 131
Par 3 course
H U–par 3 course
£€ 300kr
18km E of Esbjerg
Bent Nielsen
www.kaj-lykke-golfklub.dk

Kalo   (1992)
Aarhusvej 32, 8410 Rønde
☎ 86 37 36 00

Kolding   (1933)
Egtved Alle 10, 6000 Kolding
☎ 75 52 37 93
75 52 42 42
kgc@koldinggolfclub.dk
18 hole course under development; front 9 ready May 2007; back 9 Aug 2007; while under development, 9 hole course used to make up 18
9 L 2065 m Par 31 SSS 62 SR 101
U H
£€ 250kr (300kr)
3km N of Kolding
Jan Sederholm
www.koldinggolfclub.dk

Lemvig   (1986)
Søgårdevejen 6, 7620 Lemvig
☎ 97 81 09 20
lemviggolfklub@lemviggolfklub.dk

Løkken   (1990)
Vrenstedvej 226, PO Box 43, 9480 Løkken
☎ 98 99 26 57
98 99 26 58
info@loekken-golfklub.dk
18 L 5902 m CR 72.3 SR 127
9 L 2964 m Par 29
U H
£€ 220kr (250kr) WD July 250kr
45km NW of Aalborg
Kaj Andersen
www.loekken-golfklub.dk

Nordvestjysk   (1971)
Nystrupvej 19, 7700 Thisted
☎ 97 97 41 41

Odder   (1990)
Akjaervej 200, Postbox 46, 8300 Odder
☎ 86 54 54 51
86 54 54 58
oddergolf@oddergolf.dk
Red: 18 L 4682 m Par 70 CR 70 SR 118
Yellow: 18 L 5473 m Par 70 CR 70 SR 123
U H 45+
£€ 250kr (300kr)
4km SW of Odder, off Route 451
Frederik Dreyer
www.oddergolf.dk

Ornehoj Golfklub
Lundegard 70, 9260 Gistrup-Aalborg, Denmark
☎ 98 31 43 44
98 32 39 45
golfklubben@mail.dk
£€ 300kr
8 km from Aalborg
Henrik Jacobsen
www.ornehojgolfklub.dk

Randers   (1958)
Himmelbovej 22, Fladbro, 8900 Randers
☎ 86 42 88 69
postmaster@randersgolf.dk

Ribe   (1979)
Rønnehave, Snepsgårdevej 14, 6760 Ribe
☎ 30 73 65 18

Rold Skov   (1991)
Golfvej 1, 9520 Skørping
☎ 96 82 8300
96 82 8309
info@roldskovgolf.dk
18 L 5789 m Par 72 CR 71.4 SR 129
U H
£€ 250kr (300kr)
30km S of Aalborg
Henrik Jacobsen
www.roldskovgolf.dk

Royal Oak   (1992)
Golfvej, Jels, 6630 Rødding
☎ 74 55 32 94
74 55 32 95
golf@royal-oak.dk
18 L 5967 m Par 72
H–booking necessary. Soft spikes only
£€ 300/400kr
25km SW of Kolding
Per Gundtodt
www.royal-oak.dk

Silkeborg   (1966)
Sensommervej 15C, 8600 Silkeborg
☎ 86 85 33 99
86 85 35 22
kontor@silkeborggolf.dk
18 L 5788 m par 71 CR 71.7 SSS 133
H
£€ 300kr (400kr)
5km E of Silkeborg
Frederik Dreyer
www.silkeborggolf.dk

Sønderjyllands   (1968)
Uge Hedegård, 6360 Tinglev
☎ 74 68 75 25
74 68 75 05
sonderjylland@mail.dk
18 L 5856 m Par 71
H
£€ 250kr (300kr)
9km NE of Tinglev. 9km S of Abenraa
Erik Schnack
www.sdj-golfklub.dk

Varde   (1991)
Gellerupvej 111b, 6800 Varde
☎ 75 22 49 44
75 22 48 35
18 L 6104 m Par 71
H
£€ 200kr (300kr)
20km N of Esbjerg
Erik Fauerholt

Vejle   (1970)
Faellessletgard, Ibaekvej, 7100 Vejle
☎ 75 85 81 85
vejle@golfonline.dk

Viborg (1973)
Spangsbjerg Alle 50, Overlund, 8800 Viborg
☎ 86 67 30 10
✉ mail@viborggolfklub.dk

Zealand

Asserbo (1946)
Bødkergaardsvej 9, 3300 Frederiksvaerk
☎ 47 72 14 90
📠 47 72 14 26
🏳 18 L 5851 m Par 72
♟ H
££ 350kr (450kr) WE + July
🚗 2km from Frederiksvaerk towards Liseleje
🏠 Ross/Samuelsen
✉ www.agc.dk

Copenhagen (1898)
Dyrehaven 2, 2800 Kgs. Lyngby
☎ 39 63 04 83
✉ info@kghgolf.dk

Dragør GolfKlub (1991)
Kalvebodvej 100, 2791 Dragør
☎ 32 53 89 75
📠 32 53 88 09
✉ post@dragor-golf.dk
🏳 18 L 5636 m SSS 71
6 hole Par 3 course
♟ WD–U WE–U H
££ 310kr (360kr) Booking from 08.00–16.52
🚗 15km SE of Copenhagen centre, nr Airport
🏠 Henning Jensen/Kierkegaard
✉ www.dragor-golf.dk

Falster (1994)
Virketvej 44, 4863 Eskilstrup, Falster Island
☎ 54 43 81 43

Frederikssund (1974)
Egelundsgården, Skovnaesvej 9, 3630 Jaegerspris
☎ 47 31 08 77
📠 47 31 21 88
✉ fgk@sport.dk
🏳 18 L 5868 m SSS 71
♟ WD–U H WE–H 30
££ 250kr (350kr)
🚗 3km S of Frederikssund towards Skibby (Route 53)
🏠 Dreyer/Samuelsen
✉ www.frederikssundgolfklub.dk

Furesø (1974)
Hestkøbgård, Hestkøb Vaenge 4, 3460 Birkerød
☎ 45 81 74 44
📠 45 82 02 24
✉ info@furesogolfklub.dk
🏳 27 holes:
5328-5641 m CR 70-71
♟ H WD–NA before 7am WE–NA before 11

££ 400kr (500kr)
🚗 25 km N of Copenhagen
🏠 Jan Sederholm
✉ www.furesoegolfklub.dk

Gilleleje (1970)
Ferlevej 52, 3250 Gilleleje
☎ 49 71 80 56
📠 49 71 80 86
🏳 18 L 6641 yds Par 72 CR 71
♟ H–max 32
££ 350kr (450kr)
🚗 62km N of Copenhagen
🏠 Jan Sederholm
✉ www.gillelejegolfklub.dk

Hedeland (1980)
Staerkendevej 232A, 2640 Hedehusene
☎ 46 13 61 88/46 13 61 69

Helsingør
GL Hellebaekvej, 3000 Helsingør
☎ 49 21 29 70

Hillerød (1966)
Nysøgårdsvej 9, Ny Hammersholt, 3400 Hillerød
☎ 48 26 50 46/48 25 40 30 (Pro)
📠 48 25 29 87
🏳 18 L 5255 m CR 70
♟ H WE–NA before noon
££ 350kr (400kr)
🚗 3 km S of Hillerød
🏠 Sederholm/Knudsen

Holbaek (1964)
Dragerupvej 50, 4300 Holbaek
☎ 59 43 45 79
📠 59 43 51 61
✉ info@holbakgolfcklub.dk
🏳 18 Par 70
Yellow: L 5315 m
Red: L 4607 m
Men: CR 68.5 SR119
Women: CR 69.8 SR 119
♟ U H(35)
££ 285Dkr (340Dkr)
🚗 Kirsebaerholmen, 2km E of Holbaek
🏠 Dreyer/Sederholm
✉ www.holbakgolfklub.dk

Køge (1970)
Gl.Hastrupvej12, 4600 Køge
☎ 56 65 10 00
✉ admin@kogegolf.dk

Kokkedal (1971)
Kokkedal Alle 9, 2970 Horsholm
☎ 45 76 99 59
📠 45 76 99 03
✉ kg@kokkedalgolf.dk
🏳 18 L 5936 m Par 72
♟ H–WE pm only
££ 350kr (450kr)
🚗 Hørsholm, 30 km N of Copenhagen

🏠 Frank Pennink
✉ www.kokkedalgolf.dk

Korsør (1996)
Ornumvej 8, Postbox 53, 4220 Korsør
☎ 58 37 18 36
📠 58 37 18 39
✉ golf@korsoergolf.dk
🏳 18 L 5752 m CR 71.1 SR 130
♟ H–NA before 9am
££ 275kr (325kr) €40 (€47)
🚗 1km E of Korsør, on Korsør Bay
🏠 Arne Jørgensen, Morten L Mortensen
✉ www.korsoergolf.dk

Mølleåens (1970)
Stenbaekgård, Rosenlundvej 3, 3540 Lynge
☎ 48 18 86 31/48 18 86 36 (Pro)

Odsherred (1967)
4573 Hojby
☎ 59 30 20 76
📠 59 30 36 76
✉ sek@odsherredgolf.dk
🏳 18 L 5536 m Par 71
Men: CR 70.3 SR 126
Women: CR 71.5 SR 123
♟ H
££ €38 (€45)
🚗 5km SW of Nykøbing
🏠 Amilon/Dreyer/Mortensen
✉ www.odsherredgolf.dk

Roskilde (1973)
Gedevad, Kongemarken 34, 4000 Roskilde
☎ 46 37 01 81

Rungsted (1937)
Vestre Stationsvej 16, 2960 Rungsted Kyst
☎ 45 86 34 44
📠 45 86 57 70
✉ info@rungstedgolfklub.dk
🏳 18 L 5681 m Par 72 CR 71.0 SR 128 (yellow tee-men)
♟ H–max 26 (WE–21) WE–NA before noon
££ 550Dkr
🚗 Rungsted, 24km N of Copenhagen
🏠 Maj CA Mackenzie
✉ www.rungstedgolfklub.dk

Simon's (1993)
Nybovej 5, 3490 Kvistgaard
☎ 49 19 14 78
📠 49 19 14 70
✉ info@simonsgolf.dk
🏳 18 L 6401 m SSS 75
♟ H–max men 25.6, women 25.1 WE–NA before 7pm
££ 450kr (600kr)
🚗 10km S of Helsingør. 35km N of Copenhagen
🏠 Martin Hawtree
✉ www.simonsgolf.dk

For list of abbreviations, key to symbols and international dialling codes see page 651

Skjoldenaesholm   (1992)
Skjoldenawsvej 101, 4174 Jystrup
☎ 57 53 87 00
🖨 57 53 87 15
✉ sgc@golfin.dk
🏳 36 L 5958 & 6604 m Par 71/72
👤 H–max 36
££ 310kr (395kr)
🚗 10km N of Ringsted. 60km SW of Copenhagen
🏠 Otto Bojesen/Robert Trent Jones II
▤ www.golfin.dk

Skovlunde Herlev   (1980)
Syvendehusvej 111, 2730 Herlev
☎ 44 68 90 09
   44 68 90 04
✉ post@shgk.dk
🏳 18 L 5125 m CR 67.8 SR 122
   9 hole Par 3 course
👤 H WE–NA before 11am
££ 300kr (350kr)
🚗 Herlev/Ballerup, 15km NW of Copenhagen
🏠 Torben Starup
▤ www.shgk.dk

Søllerød   (1972)
Brillerne 9, 2840 Holte
☎ 45 80 17 84
   45 80 18 77
🖨 45 80 70 08
✉ info@sollerodgolf.dk
🏳 18 L 5913 m SSS 72
👤 U
££ 350kr (400kr)
🚗 19km N of Copenhagen
▤ www.sollerodgolf.dk

Sorø   (1979)
Suserupvej 7a, 4180 Sorø
☎ 57 84 93 95

Sydsjaellands   (1974)
Borupgården, Mogenstrup, 4700 Naestved
☎ 55 76 15 55
🖨 55 76 15 88
✉ sydsjaelland@golfonline.dk
🏳 18 L 5663 m CR 70.5
👤 H
££ 275kr (325kr)
🚗 10km SE of Naestved towards Praestø
🏠 Dreyer/Amillon
▤ www.sydsjaellandsgolfklub.dk

Vaerlose Golfklub
(1993)
Christianshovej 22, 3500 Vaerlose
☎ (+45) 4447 2124
   (+45) 4447 2128
✉ mail@vaerloese-golfklub.dk
🏳 18 L 5800 m Par 72 CR 71.3 SR 128
👤 H WD WE
££ 350kr (450kr)
🚗 15km from Copenhagen
🏠 Sederholm
▤ www.vaerloese-golfklub.dk

Finland

Etelä-Pohjanmaan   (1986)
P O Box 136, 60101 Seinäjoki
☎ (06) 423 4545

Karelia Golf   (1987)
Vaskiportintie, 80780 Kontioniemi
☎ (013) 732411

Kokkolan   (1957)
P O Box 164, 67101 Kokkola
☎ (06) 823 8600
🖨 (06) 822 1630
✉ tolmisto@kokkolangolf.fi
🏳 18 L 5572 m SSS 71
👤 U H
££ €35
🚗 3km S of Kokkola. 500km N of Helsinki
🏠 KJ Indola
▤ www.kokkolangolf.fi

Laukaan Peurunkagolf
(1989)
Valkolantie 68, 41530 Laukaa
☎ (014) 3377 300

Tarina Golf   (1988)
Golftie 135, 71800 Siilinjärvi
☎ (017) 462 5299
🖨 (017) 462 5269
✉ toimisto@tarinagolf.fi
🏳 Old 18 L 5593 m CR 70.2 SR 130
   New 18 L 5866 m CR 71.5 SR 128
👤 U H
££ €35 (€45)
🚗 21km N of Kuopio (Route 5)
🏠 Kuronen/Sederholm
▤ www.tarinagolf.fi

Vaasan Golf   (1969)
Golfkenttätie 61, 65380 Vaasa
☎ (06) 356 9989
🖨 (06) 356 9091
✉ toimisto@vaasangolf.fi
🏳 27 holes
👤 H or Green card
££ €35
🚗 Kraklund, 6km SE of Vaasa on Route 724. 417km NW of Helsinki
🏠 Björn Eriksson
▤ www.golf.fi/vag

Aura Golf   (1958)
Ruissalon Puistotie 536, 20100 Turku
☎ (02) 258 9201/9221
🖨 (02) 258 9121
✉ office@auragolf.fi

🏳 18 L 5843 m SSS 71
👤 H–max 30 (men) 36 (women)
££ €50 (€55)
🚗 Ruissalo Island, 9km W of Turku
🏠 Pekka Sivula
▤ www.auragolf.fi

Espoo Ringside Golf   (1990)
Nurmikartanontie 5, 02920 Espoo
☎ (09) 849 4940
🖨 (09) 853 7132
✉ caddie@ringsidegolf.fi
🏳 18 L 5855 m SSS 72
👤 H
££ €40 D–€60 (€60)
🚗 20km NW of Helsinki
🏠 Kosti Kuronen
▤ www.ringsidegolf.fi

Espoon Golfseura   (1982)
Mynttiläntie 1, 02780 Espoo
☎ (09) 8190 3444
🖨 (09) 8190 3434
🏳 18 L 5920 m CR 72.3
👤 H
££ €50
🚗 Espoo, 24km W of Helsinki
🏠 Jan Sederholm
▤ www.espoongolfseura.fi

Harjattula G&CC   (1989)
Harjattulantie 84, 20960 Turku
☎ (02) 276 2180

Helsingin Golfklubi   (1932)
Talin Kartano, 00350 Helsinki
☎ +358 9 225 23710
🖨 +358 9 225 23737
✉ toimisto@helsingingolfklubi.fi
🏳 18 L 5486 m CR 70.4 SR 131
👤 H (max 24 men; max 30 women)
££ €50
🚗 7km W of Helsinki City Centre
🏠 Lauri Arkkola, Kosti Kuronen
▤ www.helsingingolfklubi.fi

Hyvinkään   (1989)
Golftie 63, 05880 Hyvinkää
☎ (019) 456 2400
🖨 (019) 456 2410
✉ caddiemaster@hyvigolf.fi
🏳 18 L 5457 m CR 72.1
👤 U H
££ €35 (€45)
🚗 3km N of Hyvinkää. 50km N of Helsinki
🏠 Kosti Kuronen
▤ www.hyvigolf.fi

Keimola Golf   (1988)
Kirkantie 32, 01750 Vantaa
☎ (09) 276 6650

Kurk Golf   (1985)
02550 Evitskog
☎ (09) 819 0480
✉ kurk@kurkgolf.fi

Master Golf (1988)
Bodomintie 4, 029400 Espoo
☎ (09) 849 2300

Meri-Teijo (1990)
Mathildedalin Kartano, 25660 Mathildedal
☎ (02) 736 3955

Messilä (1988)
Messiläntie 240, 15980 Messilä
☎ (03) 884040

Nevas Golf (1988)
01190 Box
☎ (09) 272 6313

Nordcenter G&CC (1988)
10410 Aminnefors
☎ (019) 2766850

Nurmijärven (1990)
Ratasillantie, 05100 Röykkä
☎ (09) 276 6230

Peuramaa Golf (1991)
Peuramaantie 152, 02400 Kirkkonummi
☎ (09) 295 588
🖳 (09) 295 58210
📧 office@peuramaagolf.com
🏌 36 holes
👥 H
££ €38 (€46) – 2006
🚗 27km W of Helsinki
🏠 Kuronen/Persson
🖥 www.peuramaagolf.com

Pickala Golf (1986)
Golfkuja 5, 02580 Siuntio
☎ (09) 221 9080
🖳 (09) 221 90899
📧 toimisto@pickalagolf.fi
🏌 Seaside 18 L 5745 m SSS 72
Park 18 L 5866 m SSS 72
Forest 18 L 5775 m SSS 72
👥 H
££ €55 (€65)
🚗 42km W of Helsinki, on South coast
🏠 Reijo Hillberg (Seaside and Park), Jan Sederholm (Forest)
🖥 www.pickalagolf.fi

Ruukkigolf (1986)
PL 9, 10420 Skuru
☎ (019) 245 4485
🖳 (019) 245 4285
📧 toimisto@ruukkigolf.fi
🏌 18 L 6156 m Par 72
👥 U
££ €25 (€35)
🚗 85km W of Helsinki
🏠 Lasse Heikkinen
🖥 www.ruukkigolf.fi

Sarfvik (1984)
P O Box 27, 02321 Espoo
☎ (09) 221 9000
📧 sarfvik@golfsarfvik.fi

Sea Golf Rönnäs (1989)
Rönnäs, 07750 Isnäs
☎ +358 (0) 19 634 434
📧 seagolf@co.inet.fi

St Laurence Golf (1989)
Kaivurinkatu 133, 08200 Lohja
☎ +358 (0)19 357 821
🖳 +358 (0)19 386 666
📧 caddie.master@stlaurencegolf.fi
🏌 18 L 6240 m CR 71.5 SR 128
18 L 6340 m CR 70.7 SR 120
👥 WD–H M after 3pm WE–M H
££ D–€50
🚗 50km W of Helsinki
🏠 Kosti Kuronen
🖥 www.stlaurencegolf.fi

Suur-Helsingin Golf (1965)
Rinnekodintie 29, 02980 Espoo
☎ +358 9 4399 7110
🖳 +358 9 4399 7110
📧 toimisto@shg.fi
🏌 Lakisto 18 L 5551 m
Par 72 CR 70.7 SR 129
Luukki 18 L 5085 m
Par 70 CR 69.3 SR 125
👥 H
££ €35 (€45)
🚗 25km N of Helsinki
🖥 www.shg.fi

Golf Talma (1989)
Nygårdintie 115-6, 04240 Talma
☎ (09) 274 6540
🖳 (09) 274 65432
📧 golftalma@golftalma.fi
🏌 18 L 5809 m SSS 72
18 L 5758 m SSS 72
9 hole Par 3 course
👥 WD–H WE–H
££ €50 (€60)
🚗 35km N of Helsinki
🏠 Henrik Wartiainen
🖥 www.golftalma.fi

Tuusula (1983)
Kirkkotie 51, 04301 Tuusula
☎ (042) 410241

Virvik Golf (1981)
Virvik, 06100 Porvoo
☎ (915) 579292

North

Green Zone Golf (1987)
Näräntie, 95400 Tornio
☎ (016) 431711

Katinkulta (1990)
88610 Vuokatti
☎ (08) 669 7488
📧 golf.katinkulta@holidayclub.fi
🏌 18 L 6000 m Par 72 CR 73.5 SR 129

👥 H
££ €49
🚗 36km E of Kajaani. 600km N of Helsinki
🏠 Jan Sederholm
🖥 www.holidayclub.fi

Oulu (1964)
Sankivaarab Golfkeskus, 90650 Oulu
☎ (08) 531 5222
🖳 (08) 531 5129
📧 caddiemaster@oulugolf.fi
🏌 Sanki: 18 holes
Vaara: 18 holes
👥 H
££ €45–€50
🚗 Sanginsuu, 17km E of Oulu
🏠 Ronald Fream
🖥 www.golfpiste.com/ogk

South East

Imatran Golf (1986)
Golftie 11, 55800 Imatra
☎ (05) 473 4954

Kartano Golf (1988)
P O Box 60, 79601 Joroinen
☎ (017) 572257
🖳 (017) 572263
🏌 18 L 5597 m Par 72 CR 71 SR 123
👥 U
££ €32 (€37)
🚗 20km S of Varkaus. 330km NE of Helsinki
🏠 Ake Persson

Kerigolf (1990)
Kerimaantie 65, 58200 Kerimäki
☎ (015) 252600
🖳 (015) 252606
📧 clubhouse@kerigolf.fi
🏌 18 L 6218 m Par 72 SSS 75
👥 H
££ €40
🚗 15km E of Savonlinna. 350km NE of Helsinki
🏠 Ronald Fream
🖥 www.kerigolf.fi

Koski Golf (1987)
Eerolanväylä 126, 45700 Kuusankoski
☎ +358 5 864 4600
🖳 +358 5 864 4644
📧 toimisto@koskigolf.fi
🏌 18 L 6375 m Par 73
👥 H I
££ €40 (€45)
🚗 3km E of Kuusankoski. 70km E of Lahti
🏠 Kosti Kuronen
🖥 www.koskigolf.fi

Kymen Golf (1964)
Mussalo Golfcourse, 48310 Kotka
☎ (05) 210 3700

Lahden Golf (1959)
Takkulantie, 15230 Lahti
☎ (03) 784 1311

Porrassalmi (1989)
Annila, 50100 Mikkeli
☎ (015) 335518/335446
🖥 (015) 335682
🏌 18 L 5601 m CR 70.6
👥 H
££ €36–€42
⊶ 5km S of Mikkeli

Vierumäen Golfseura
(1988)
Sport Institute of Finland, Vierumäki,
Suomen Urheiluopisto, 19120 Vierumäki
☎ +358 3 842 4501
🖥 +358 3 842 4630
✉ caddiemaster@vierumaki.fi
🏌 18 L 5580 m CR 71.1
Cooke L 4732-6048 m
Classic L 4730-5691 m
9-hole Par 3
👥 U
££ €32 (€42) (2006)
⊶ 25km NE of Lahti
🖥 www.vierumakigolf.fi

South West

Porin Golfkerho (1939)
P O Box 25, 28601 Pori
☎ (02) 630 3888
🖥 (02) 630 38813
✉ toimisto@kalafornia.com
🏌 18 L 6160 m SSS 74
👥 H
££ €40
⊶ 5km NW of Pori, at Kalafornia
🏠 Reijo Louhimo
🖥 www.kalafornia.com

River Golf (1988)
Taivalkunta, 37120 Nokia
☎ (03) 340 0234

Salo Golf (1988)
Liikuntapuisto 8, 24100 Salo
☎ (02) 731 7321

Tammer Golf (1965)
Toimelankatu 4, 33560 Tampere
☎ (03) 261 3316

Tawast Golf (1987)
Tawastintie 48, 13270 Hämeenlinna
☎ (03) 630 610
🖥 (03) 630 6120
✉ tawast@tawastgolf.fi
🏌 18 L 6063 m Par 72
👥 WD/WE–H Men 30 Women 36
££ €40
⊶ 5km E of Hämeenlinna
🏠 Reijo Hillberg
🖥 www.tawastgolf.fi

Vammala (1991)
38100 Karkku
☎ (03) 513 4070

Wiurila G&CC (1990)
Viurilantie 126, 24910 Halikko
☎ (02) 737 1400

Yyteri Golf (1988)
Karhuluodontie 85, 28840 Pori
☎ (02) 638 0380

France

Bordeaux & South West

Albret (1986)
Le Pusocq, 47230 Barbaste
☎ 05 53 65 53 69

Arcachon (1955)
Golf International d'Arcachon, 35 Bd
d'Arcachon, 33260 La Teste De Buch
☎ 05 56 54 44 00
✉ golfarcach@aol.com

Arcangues (1991)
64200 Arcangues
☎ 05 59 43 10 56

Biarritz (1888)
Ave Edith Cavell, 64200 Biarritz
☎ 05 59 03 71 80
🖥 05 59 03 26 74
✉ info@golfbiarritz.com
🏌 18 L 5376 m:
White CR 69.0 SR 121
Yellow CR 67.2 SR 118
Blue CR 69.8 SR 116
Red CR 68.8 SR 113
👥 U H36 WD WE
££ €55 (€50)
⊶ 400 m from the town
🏠 Willie Dunn
🖥 www.golf-biarritz.com

Biscarrosse (1989)
Avenue du Golf, F-40600 Biscarrosse
☎ 05 58 09 84 93
🖥 05 58 09 84 50
✉ golfdebiscarrosse@wanadoo.fr
🏌 Lake 9 L 2172 m SSS 32
Forest & Ocean 18 L 5784 m Par 72
👥 U (Lake) H (Forest & Ocean)
££ €30–€50
⊶ 80km SW of Bordeaux
🏠 Brizon/Veyssieres
🖥 www.biscarrossegolf.com

Blue Green–Artiguelouve
(1986)
Domaine St Michel, Pau-Artiguelouve,
64230 Artiguelouve
☎ 05 59 83 09 29

Blue Green-Seignosse
(1989)
Avenue du Belvédère, 40510 Seignosse
☎ 05 58 41 68 30
✉ golfseignosse@wanadoo.fr

Bordeaux-Cameyrac (1972)
33450 St Sulpice-et-Cameyrac
☎ (+33) (0)5 56 72 96 79
✉ contact@golf-bordeaux-cameyrac
.com

Bordeaux-Lac (1976)
Public
Avenue de Pernon, 33300 Bordeaux
☎ 05 56 50 92 72
🖥 05 56 29 01 84
✉ golf.bordeaux@wanadoo.fr
🏌 18 L 6156 m SSS 72
18 L 6159 m SSS 72
👥 U
££ €34 (€44)
⊶ 2km N of Bordeaux
🏠 Jean Bourret
🖥 www.golfbordeauxlac.com

Bordelais (1900)
Domaine de Kater, Allee F Arago,
33200 Bordeaux-Caudéran
☎ 05 56 28 56 04
🖥 05 56 28 59 71
✉ golfbordelais@wanadoo.fr
🏌 18 L 4727 m Par 67 SSS 67
CR men 113, women 115
👥 H–restricted Tues
££ €35 (€45)
⊶ 3km NW of Bordeaux
🏠 Colt

Casteljaloux (1989)
Route de Mont de Marsan,
47700 Casteljaloux
☎ 05 53 93 51 60
✉ golfdecasteljaloux@tiscali.fr

Chantaco (1928)
Route d'Ascain, 64500 St Jean-de-Luz
☎ 05 59 26 14 22
05 59 26 19 22
✉ pierre@golfdechantaco.com

Château des Vigiers (1992)
24240 Monestier
☎ 05 53 61 50 33
🖥 05 53 61 50 31
✉ reserve@vigiers.com
🏌 18 L 6003 m Par 72
6 hole Academy course
👥 H
££ €45–€65
⊶ 15km SW of Bergerac. 75km E of Bordeaux

🏠 Donald Steel
📧 www.vigiers.com

Chiberta (1926)
Boulevard des Plages, 64600 Anglet
☎ 05 59 63 83 20

Domaine de la Marterie (1987)
St Felix de Reillac, 24260 Le Bugue
☎ 05 53 05 61 00

Graves et Sauternais (1989)
St Pardon de Conques, 33210 Langon
☎ 05 56 62 25 43
🖥 05 56 76 83 72
📧 golf.laugon@laposte.net
🏴 18 L 5810 m SSS 71
👥 U
££ Summer: €32 (€38) Winter: €28 (€34)
🚗 5km from Langon. 45km SW of Bordeaux via A62

Gujan (1990)
Route de Souguinet, 33470 Gujan Mestras
☎ 05 57 52 73 73

Hossegor (1930)
333 Ave du Golf, 40150 Hossegor
☎ 05 58 43 56 99
🖥 05 58 43 98 52
📧 golf.hossegor@wanadoo.fr
🏴 18 L 6001 m SSS 72
👥 H–max 35
££ €45.50–€60
🚗 15km N of Bayonne, on coast
🏠 J Morrison
📧 www.golfhossegor.com

Lacanau Golf & Hotel (1980)
Domaine de l'Ardilouse, 33680 Lacanau-Océan
☎ (+33) 556 039292
🖥 (+33) 556 263057
📧 info@golf-hotel-lacanau.fr
🏴 18 L 5932 m SSS 72
👥 H
🚗 45km W of Bordeaux
🏠 John Harris
📧 www.golf-hotel-lacanau.fr

Makila
Route de Cambo, 64200 Bassussarry
☎ 05 59 58 42 42

Médoc
Chemin de Courmateau, Louens, 33290 Le Pian Médoc
☎ 05 56 70 11 90

Moliets (1989)
Public
Rue Mathieu Desbieys, 40660 Moliets
☎ 05 58 48 54 65

🖥 05 58 48 54 88
📧 resa@golfmoliets.com
🏴 18 L 6172 m SSS 73
9 hole course
👥 U H–max 30
££ €50–€63
🚗 Moliets, 40km N of Bayonne. 40km W of Dax
🏠 Robert Trent Jones Sr
📧 www.golfmoliets.com

La Nivelle (1907)
Place William Sharp, 64500 Ciboure
☎ 05 59 47 18 99
05 59 47 19 72

Pau (1856)
Rue du Golf, 64140 Billère, France
☎ +33 (05) 5913 1856
🖥 +33 (0) 5913 1857
📧 pau.golfclub@wanadoo.fr
🏴 18 L 5314 m Par 69 SSS 67.9 CR 124
👥 U
££ €45 (€50)
🚗 2km S of Pau. 150km Biarritz. 200 km Bordeau
🏠 Willie Dunn Sr
📧 www.paugolfclub.com

Périgueux (1980)
Public
Domaine de Saltgourde, 24430 Marsac
☎ 05 53 53 02 35

Pessac (1989)
Rue de la Princesse, 33600 Pessac
☎ 05 57 26 03 33

Stade Montois (1993)
Pessourdat, 40090 Saint Avit
☎ 05 58 75 63 05

Villeneuve sur Lot G&CC (1987)
'La Menuisière', 47290 Castelnaud de Gratecambe
☎ 05 53 01 60 19
🖥 05 53 01 78 99
📧 info@vsgolf.com
🏴 18 L 6107 m SSS 72
9 L 2184 m SSS 27
👥 H U
££ €59.50
🚗 10km N of Villeneuve on N21. 40km N of Agen
🏠 R Berthet
📧 www.vsgolf.com

Brittany

Ajoncs d'Or (1976)
Kergrain Lantic, 22410 Saint-Quay Portrieux
☎ 02 96 71 90 74
🖥 02 96 71 40 83

📧 golfdesajoncsdor@wanadoo.fr
🏴 18 L 6078 m SSS 72
👥 U
££ €27–€40 (€37–€40)
🚗 17km N of Saint-Brieuc. 6km W of Étables-sur-Mer
🏠 Carlian-Des Heulles

Baden
Kernic, 56870 Baden
☎ 02 97 57 18 96

Belle Ile en Mer (1987)
Les Poulins, 56360 Belle-Ile-en-Mer
☎ 02 97 31 64 65

Brest Les Abers (1990)
Kerhoaden, 29810 Plouarzel
☎ 02 98 89 68 33

Brest-Iroise (1976)
Parc de Lann-Rohou, Saint-Urbain, 29800 Landerneau
☎ 02 98 85 16 17
🖥 02 98 85 19 39
📧 golfhotel@brest-iroise.com
🏴 18 L 5672 m Par 71
9 L 3329 m Par 37
👥 U
££ €40 (€47)
🚗 25km E of Brest
🏠 M Fenn
📧 www.brest-iroise.com

Cicé-Blossac (1992)
Domaine de Cicé-Blossac, 35170 Bruz
☎ 02 99 52 79 79

Dinard (1890)
35800 St-Briac-sur-Mer
☎ 02 99 88 32 07

La Freslonnière (1989)
Le Bois Briand, 35650 Le Rheu
☎ 02 99 14 84 09
🖥 02 99 14 94 98
📧 lafreslo@wanadoo.fr
🏴 18 L 5756 m SSS 72 SR 125
👥 U
££ €37–€52
🚗 4km SW of Rennes, off N24
🏠 A du Bouexic
📧 www.lafreslonniere.com

L'Odet (1936)
Clohars-Fouesnant, 29950 Benodet
☎ 02 98 54 87 88
🖥 02 98 54 61 40
📧 golf.odet@wanadoo.fr
🏴 18 L 5843 m SSS 72
9 hole Par 3 course
👥 U H
££ €35–€49
🚗 6km S of Benodet. 15km SE of Quimper
🏠 Robert Berthet
📧 www.formule-golf.com

Les Ormes   (1988)
Château des Ormes, Epiniac, 35120 Dol-de-Bretagne
☎ 02 99 73 54 44

Pléneuf-Val André
Rue de la Plage des Vallées, 22370 Pléneuf-Val André
☎ 02 96 63 01 12

Ploemeur Océan Formule Golf   (1990)
Kerham Saint-Jude, 56270 Ploemeur
☎ 02 97 32 81 82

Quimper-Cornouaille   (1959)
Manoir du Mesmeur, 29940 La Forêt-Fouesnant
☎ 02 98 56 97 09

Rennes   (1957)
Le Temple du Cerisier, 35136 St-Jacques-de-la-Lande
☎ 02 99 30 18 18
🖳 02 99 30 10 25
✉ directeur.rennes@formulegolf.com
⌱ 18 L 6135 m Par 72
    9 L 2100 m Par 32
    9 hole short course
👫 U
££ €48 (€72)
⊕ 3km SW of Rennes
⌂ Robert Berthet

Rhuys-Kerver   (1988)
Public
Formule Golf, Domaine de Kerver, 56730 St-Gildas-de-Rhuys
☎ 02 97 45 30 09

Les Rochers   (1989)
Route d'Argentré du Plessis 3, 35500 Vitré
☎ 02 99 96 52 52

Sables-d'Or-les-Pins   (1925)
22240 Fréhel
☎ 02 96 41 42 57

St Cast Pen Guen   (1926)
22380 Saint-Cast-le-Guildo
☎ 02 96 41 91 20

St Laurent   (1975)
Ploemel, 56400 Auray
☎ 02 97 56 85 18
🖳 02 97 56 89 99
✉ golf.stlaurent@formule-golf.com
✍ 6
⌱ 18 L 6128 m SSS 72
    9 L 2705 m SSS 35
👫 U
££ 9: Low season €24, high season
    €30; 18: Low season €35, high
    season €49
⊕ Ploemel, 6km W of Auray

St Malo Hotel G&CC   (1986)
Le Tronchet, 35540 Miniac-Morvan
☎ 02 99 58 96 69
🖳 02 99 58 10 39
✉ saintmalogolf@st-malo.com
⌱ 18 L 6014 m SSS 72
    9 L 2684 m SSS 36
👫 U
££ D—€35–€50 30% reduction for
    hotel
⊕ 23km S of St Malo, off RN 137
⌂ Hubert Chesneau
✉ www.saintmalogolf.com

St Samson   (1965)
Route de Kérénoc, 22560 Pleumeur-Bodou
☎ 02 96 23 87 34

Val Queven   (1990)
Public
Kerruisseau, 56530 Queven
☎ 02 97 05 17 96

Burgundy & Auvergne

Aubazine   (1977)
Public
19190 Aubazine
☎ 03 55 27 25 66

Beaune-Levernois   (1990)
21200 Levernois
☎ 03 80 24 10 29

Chalon-sur-Saône   (1976)
Parc de Saint Nicolas, 71380 Chatenoy-en-Bresse
☎ 03 85 93 49 65
🖳 03 85 93 56 95
✉ contact@golfchalon.com
⌱ 18 L 5859 m SSS 71
👫 U
££ €30 (€30)
⊕ 3km SE of Chalon. 125km N of
    Lyon
⌂ Michel Rio
✉ www.golf_chalon_sur_saone.com

Chambon-sur-Lignon   (1986)
Riondet, La Pierre de la Lune, 43400
Le Chambon-sur-Lignon
☎ 04 71 59 28 10

Château d'Avoise   (1992)
9 Rue de Mâcon, 71210 Montchanin
☎ 03 85 78 19 19

Château de Chailly   (1990)
Chailly-sur-Armançon, 21320 Pouilly-en-Auxois
☎ 03 80 90 30 40

🖳 03 80 90 30 05
✉ reservation@chailly.com
⌱ 18 L 6146 m SSS 72
    SR 130 (White), 124 (Yellow), 126
    (Blue),
    195 (Red)
👫 U
££ €40 (€55)
⊕ A6 motorway, Pouilly-en-Auxois
    exit. 45km SW of Dijon. 40km NW
    of Beau
⌂ Sprecher/Watine
✉ www.chailly.com

Dijon-Bourgogne   (1972)
Bois des Norges, 21490 Norges-la-Ville
☎ 03 80 35 71 10
🖳 03 80 35 79 27
✉ contacts@golfdijonbourgogne.com
⌱ 18 L 6179 m SSS 72
👫 U
££ €39 (€49)
⊕ 7km N of Dijon towards Langres
⌂ Fenn/Radcliffe
✉ www.golfdijonbourgogne.com

Domaine de Roncemay   (1989)
89110 Aillant-sur-Tholon
☎ 03 86 73 50 50
🖳 03 86 73 69 46
✉ reservation@roncemay.com
⌱ 18 Par 72
    Men: white L 6270 m CR 73.9 SR
    140
    yellow L 5702 m CR 71.0 SR 128
    Women: blue L CR 73.6 SR 132
    red L 4864 m CR 73.8 SR 128
👫 U
££ High season: €48–€60 Low season:
    €40–€50
⊕ 15km W of Auxerre
⌂ Jeremy Pern & Jean Garaïlde
✉ www.roncemay.com

Limoges-St Lazare   (1976)
Public
Avenue du Golf, 87000 Limoges
☎ 05 55 28 30 02

Mâcon La Salle   (1989)
La Salle-Mâcon Nord, 71260 La Salle
☎ 03 85 36 09 71
🖳 03 85 36 06 70
✉ golf.maconlasalle@wanadoo.fr
⌱ 18 L 6024 m Par 71
👫 H or green card
££ €36 (€42)
⊕ 5km N of Mâcon (A6)
⌂ Robert Berthet
✉ www.golfmacon.com

Le Nivernais
Public
Le Bardonnay, 58470 Magny Cours
☎ 03 58 18 30

La Porcelaine

Célicroux, 87350 Panazol
☎ 05 55 31 10 69
✉ golf@golf.porcelaine.com

St Junien (1997)

Les Jouberties, 87200 Saint Junien
☎ 05 55 02 96 96
🖨 05 55 02 32 52
✉ info@golfdesaintjunien.com
➢ 18 L 5516 m Par 72 SSS 76.2
👥 U
££ €29 (€35)
🚗 30km W of Limoges (N141)
🖥 www.golfdesaintjunien.com

Sporting Club de Vichy

(1907)
Allée Baugnies, 03700 Bellerive/Allier
☎ 04 70 32 39 11

Val de Cher (1975)

03190 Nassigny
☎ 04 70 06 71 15
🖨 04 70 06 70 00
✉ golfvaldecher@free.fr
➢ 18 L 5450 m Par 70
👥 U
££ €25–€35
🚗 20km N of Montluçon on N144
🏠 Bourret/Vigand
🖥 http://golfclub.valdecher.free.fr

Les Volcans (1984)

La Bruyère des Moines, 63870 Orcines
☎ 04 73 62 15 51
🖨 04 73 62 26 52
✉ golfdesvolcans@nat.fr
➢ 18 L 6286 m SSS 73
   9 L 1377 m SSS 29
👥 U H
££ €46 (€52)
🚗 12km W of Clermont-Ferrand on RN41
🏠 Lucien Roux
🖥 www.golfdesvolcans.com

Centre

Les Aisses (1992)

RN20 Sud, 45240 La Ferté St Aubin
☎ 02 38 64 80 87
🖨 02 38 64 80 85
✉ golfdesaisses@wanadoo.fr
➢ 27 L 6200 m Par 72
👥 U
££ 9: Low season: €25 (€30) High season: €30 (€40) 18: Low: €40 D–€60 (€50 D–€70) High: €50D–€70 (€60 D–€90)
🚗 30km S of Orléans. 140km S of Paris
🏠 Olivier Brizon
🖥 www.aissesgolf.com

Ardrée (1988)

37360 St Antoine-du-Rocher
☎ 02 47 56 77 38

☎ 02 47 56 79 96
✉ tours.ardree@bluegreen.com
➢ 18 L 5745 m Par 71
👥 U H (green card)
££ 9: €27 (€32) 18: €37 (€54) Special rates Tues €32
🚗 10km N of Tours
🏠 Olivier Brizon
🖥 www.bluegreen.com/tours
   www.golf-ardree.com

Les Bordes (1987)

41220 Saint Laurent-Nouan
☎ 02 54 87 72 13
🖨 02 54 87 78 61
✉ golf.les.bordes@wanadoo.fr
➢ 18 L 6412 m Par 72
👥 U M H (max 36) SOC WD WE
££ €120 (€150)
🚗 30km SW of Orléans
🏠 Robert van Hagge
🖥 www.lesbordes.com

Château de Cheverny

(1089)
La Rousselière, 41700 Cheverny
☎ 02 54 79 24 70
🖨 02 54 79 25 52
✉ contact@golf-cheverny.com
➢ 18 L 6279 m Par 71
👥 U
££ High season D–€48; low season D–€30
🚗 15km S of Blois. 200km SW of Paris, via A10
🏠 O Van der Vynckt
🖥 www.golf-cheverny.com

Château de Maintenon

(1989)
Route de Gallardon, 28130 Maintenon
☎ 02 37 27 18 09

Château des Sept Tours

(1989)
Le Vivier des Landes, 37330 Courcelles de Touraine
☎ 02 47 24 69 75

Cognac (1987)

Saint-Brice, 16100 Cognac
☎ 05 45 32 18 17

Le Connétable (1987)

Parc Thermal, 86270 La Roche Posay
☎ 05 49 86 25 10

Domaine de Vaugouard

(1987)
Chemin des Bois, Fontenay-sur-Loing, 45210 Ferrières
☎ 02 38 89 79 00

Les Dryades (1987)

36160 Pouligny-Notre-Dame
☎ 02 54 30 28 00

Ganay (1993)

Prieuré de Ganay, 41220 St Laurent-Nouan
☎ 02 54 87 26 24
✉ golfdeganay2@wanadoo.fr
➢ Men: 18 L 6132/5646/6030/5672 m Par 72 CR 72.5/69.7/72.1/69.9 SR 126/122/120/118
   Women: 18 L 5095/4826/5225/4847 m Par 72 CR 72.3/70.5/72.2/70.7 SR 121/119/122/117
👥 U
££ 9: €17 (€23) 18: €25 (€35)
🚗 130km S of Paris. 30km (30 min) from Orleans and Blois
🏠 Jim Shirley
🖥 www.golf-ganay.com

Haut-Poitou (1987)

86130 Saint-Cyr
☎ 05 49 62 53 62
🖨 05 49 88 77 14
✉ contact@golfduhautpoitou.com
➢ 18 L 6590 m SSS 75
   9 L 1800 m Par 31
👥 U
££ 9: €14; 18: €50 every day
🚗 20km N of Poitiers. 70km S of Tours
🏠 HG Baker

Loudun-Roiffe (1985)

Domaine St Hilaire, 86120 Roiffe
☎ 05 49 98 78 06

Marcilly (1986)

Domaine de la Plaine, 45240 Marcilly-en-Villette
☎ 02 38 76 11 73
🖨 02 38 76 18 73
✉ golf@marcilly.com
➢ 18 L 6324 m SSS 73
   9 L 1301 SSS 27
👥 U
££ €32 (€38)
🚗 20km SE of Orléans
🏠 Olivier Brizon
🖥 www.marcilly.com

Niort

Chemin du Grand Ormeau, 79000 Niort Romagne
☎ 05 49 09 01 41

Orléans Donnery

Château de la Touche, 45450 Donnery
☎ 02 38 59 25 15

Golf du Perche (1987)

La Vallée des Aulnes, 28400 Souancé au Perche
☎ 02 37 29 17 33
🖨 02 37 29 12 88
✉ golfduperche@wanadoo.fr
➢ 18 L 6073 m Par 72
👥 U
££ €35 (€47)
🚗 60km SW of Chartres (D9). 130km SW of Paris

🏠 Laurent Heckly
📧 www.golfduperche.fr

Petit Chêne   (1987)
Le Petit Chêne, 79310 Mazières-en-Gâtine
☎ 05 49 63 20 95

La Picardière
Chemin de la Picardière, 18100 Vierzon
☎ 02 48 75 21 43

Poitiers
Domaine de Beauvoir, 86550
Mignaloux Beauvoir
☎ 05 49 46 70 27

Poitou   (1991)
Domaine des Forges, 79340 Menigoute
☎ 0549 69 91 77
🖥 0549 69 96 84
📧 info@golfdesforges.com
🏌 18 L 6400 m Par 74
   9 L 3200 m Par 37
👥 U SOC WD WE
££ 9: €26 (€34) 18: €37 (€42) High
   season
🚗 30km W of Poitiers
🏠 Bjorn Eriksson
📧 www.golfdesforges.com

La Prée-La Rochelle   (1988)
La Richardière, 17137 Marsilly
☎ 05 46 01 24 42
🖥 05 46 01 25 84
📧 golflarochelle@wanadoo.fr
🏌 18 L 5931 m Par 72 CR 71.8
   White SR 136, Yellow SR 134,
   Blue SR 128, Red SR 125
👥 U
££ High season: €50 (€45) Low
   season: €39 (€41) 2006 prices
🚗 6km N of La Rochelle
🏠 Olivier Brizon
📧 www.golflarochelle.com

Royan   (1977)
Maine-Gaudin, 17420 Saint-Palais
☎ 05 46 23 16 24
🖥 05 46 23 23 38
📧 golfderoyan@wanadoo.fr
🏌 18 L 5924 m SSS 71
   6 hole short course 920 m ·
👥 U
££ €3–€58
🚗 Saint-Palais, 7km W of Royan
🏠 Robert Berthet
📧 www.golfderoyan.com

Saintonge   (1953)
Fontcouverte, 17100 Saintes
☎ 05 46 74 27 61

Sancerrois   (1989)
St Thibault, 18300 Sancerre
☎ 02 48 54 11 22
🖥 02 48 54 28 03
📧 golf.sancerre@wanadoo.fr
🏌 18 L 5820 m SSS 71

👥 U
££ €25–€34 (€36–€44)
🚗 45km NE of Bourges
🏠 Didier Fruchet
📧 www.sancerre.net/golf

Touraine   (1971)
Château de la Touche, 37510 Ballan-Miré
☎ 02 47 53 20 28

Val de l'Indre   (1989)
Villedieu-sur-Indre, 36320 Tregonce
☎ 02 54 26 59 44

Channel Coast & North

Abbeville   (1989)
Route du Val, 80132 Grand-Laviers
☎ 03 22 24 98 58
🖥 03 22 24 98 58
📧 abbeville.golfclub@wanadoo.fr
🏌 18 L 5924 m Par 72
👥 H
££ €25–€30 (€35–€40)
🚗 3km NW of Abbeville
🏠 Didier Fruchet
📧 www.golf.abbeville.com

L'Ailette
02860 Cerny en Laonnois
☎ 03 23 24 83 99
📧 golfdelailette@wanadoo.fr

Amiens   (1925)
80115 Querrieu
☎ 03 22 93 04 26
🖥 03 22 93 04 61
📧 golfamiens@aol.com
🏌 18 L 6114 m SSS 72
👥 U H
££ €27–€37 (€37–€49)
🚗 7km NE of Amiens (D929)
🏠 Ross/Pennink
📧 www.golfamiens.fr

Apremont   (1992)
60300 Apremont
☎ 03 44 25 61 11

Arras   (1989)
Rue Briquet Taillandier, 62223 Anzin-St-Aubin
☎ 03 21 50 24 24

Belle Dune
Promenade de Marquenterre, 80790 Fort-Mahon-Plage
☎ 03 22 23 45 50

Bois de Ruminghem   (1991)
1613 Rue St Antoine, 62370 Ruminghem
☎ 03 21 85 30 33

Bondues   (1968)
Château de la Vigne, BP 70054, 59587
Bondues Cedex
☎ 03 20 23 20 62
🖥 03 20 23 24 11
📧 contact@golfdebondues.com
🏌 18 L 6163 m SSS 73 SR 130
   18 L 6009 m SSS 72 SR 127
👥 H–max 30. Closed Tues
££ €55 (€75 July/Aug only)
🚗 10km NE of Lille
🏠 Hawtree/Trent Jones
📧 www.golfdebondues.com

Champagne   (1986)
02130 Villers-Agron
☎ 03 23 71 62 08
🖥 03 23 71 50 40
📧 golf.de.champagne@wanadoo.fr
🏌 18 L 5760 m SSS 72 SR 132
👥 H
££ €30–€40 (€40–€50)
🚗 25km SW of Reims, via E50/A4
🏠 JC Cornillot
📧 www.golf-de-champagne.com

Chantilly   (1909)
Allée de la Ménagerie, 60500 Chantilly
☎ 03 44 57 04 43
🖥 03 44 57 26 54
📧 golfchan@club-internet.fr
🏌 Vineuil 18 L 6597 m SSS 71
   Longeres 18 L 6378 m SSS 72
👥 WE–NA
££ WD–€90
🚗 45km N of Paris
🏠 Tom Simpson
📧 www.golfdechantilly.com

Château de Raray
4 Rue Nicolas de Lancy, 60810 Raray
☎ 03 44 54 70 61

Chaumont-en-Vexin   (1968)
Château de Bertichère, 60240 Chaumont-en-Vexin
☎ 03 44 49 00 81
🖥 03 44 49 32 71
📧 golfdechaumont@golf-paris.net
🏌 18 L 6195 m SSS 72
👥 U
££ €33 (€55)
🚗 65km NW of Paris. 15km Beauvais
   airport
🏠 Donald Harradine
📧 www.golf-paris.net

Compiègne   (1896)
Ave Royale, 60200 Compiègne
☎ 03 44 38 48 00

Deauville l'Amiraute   (1992)
CD 278, Tourgéville, 14800 Deauville
☎ 02 31 14 42 00
🖥 02 31 88 32 00
🏌 18 L 6055 m Par 73

ᴪ U
££ €57 (€60)
ᐁ 4km S of Deauville
⌂ Bill Baker
▤ www.amiraute-resort.com

Domaine du Tilleul (1984)
Landouzy-la-Ville, 02140 Vervins
☎ 03 23 98 48 00

Dunkerque (1991)
Public
*Fort Vallières, Coudekerque-Village,
59380 Coudekerque*
☎ 03 28 61 07 43
✉ golf@golf-dk.com

Golf Dolce Chantilly (1991)
Route d'Apremont, 60500 Vineuil St-Firmin
☎ 03 44 58 47 74
✉ golf.dolce.chantilly@wanadoo.fr

Hardelot Dunes Course
(1991)
Ave du Golf, 62152 Hardelot
☎ 03 21 83 73 10
⌨ 03 21 83 24 33
✉ hardelot@opengolfclub.com
ᐟ 18 L 5713 m SSS 72
ᴪ U H
££ High season: €59 Mon–Thur (€69
Fri–Sun) Low season: €45
Mon–Thur (€55 Fri–Sun)
ᐁ 15km S of Boulogne
⌂ JC Cornillot
▤ www.opengolfclub.com

Hardelot Pins Course
Ave du Golf, 62152 Hardelot
☎ 03 21 83 73 10
⌨ 03 21 83 24 33
✉ hardelot@opengolfclub.com
ᐟ 18 L 5911 m SSS 73
ᴪ U
££ High season: €59 Mon–Thur (€69
Fri–Sun) Low season: €45
Mon–Thur (€55 Fri–Sun)
ᐁ 15km S of Boulogne
⌂ Tom Simpson (1931)
▤ www.opengolfclub.com

International Club du Lys
(1929)
*Rond-Point du Grand Cerf,
60260 Lamorlaye*
☎ 03 44 21 26 00

Morfontaine (1907)
60128 Mortefontaine
☎ 03 44 54 68 27
⌨ 03 44 54 60 57
ᐟ 18 L 5985 m Par 70 SSS 71.9 SR
135
9 L 2526 m Par 36
ᴪ Members' guests only
££ NA
ᐁ 10km S of Senlis. N of Paris
⌂ Tom Simpson

Mormal (1991)
Bois St Pierre, 59144 Preux-au-Sart
☎ 03 27 63 07 00
⌨ 03 27 39 93 62
✉ info@golf-mormal.com
ᐟ 18 L 6022 m Par 72
ᴪ H
££ €37 (€50)
ᐁ 15km E of Valenciennes, off RN49
⌂ JC Cornillot
▤ www.golf-mormal.com

Nampont-St-Martin (1978)
Maison Forte, 80120 Nampont-St-Martin
☎ 03 22 29 92 90
   03 22 29 89 87

Rebetz (1988)
*Route de Noailles, 60240 Chaumont-en-
Vexin*
☎ 03 44 49 15 54

Saint-Omer
*Chemin des Bois, Acquin-Westbécourt,
62380 Lumbres*
☎ 03 21 38 59 90

Le Sart (1910)
5 Rue Jean-Jaurès, 59650 Villeneuve D'Ascq
☎ 03 20 72 02 51

Thumeries (1935)
Bois Lenglart, 59239 Thumeries
☎ 03 20 86 58 98

Le Touquet 'La Forêt'
(1904)
Ave du Golf, BP 41, 62520 Le Touquet
☎ 03 21 06 28 00
⌨ 03 21 06 28 01
✉ letouquet@opengolfclub.com
ᐟ 18 L 5827 m CR 71.0 SR 128
ᴪ U H
££ €66 (€79)
ᐁ 2km S of Le Touquet. 30km S of
Boulogne
⌂ H Hutchinson
▤ www.opengolfclub.com

Le Touquet 'La Mer'
(1930)
Ave du Golf, BP 41, 62520 Le Touquet
☎ 03 21 06 28 00
⌨ 03 21 06 28 01
✉ letouquet@opengolfclub.com
ᐟ 18 L 6275 m CR 74.9 SR 131
ᴪ U H
££ €66 (€79)
ᐁ As 'La Forêt'
⌂ HS Colt
▤ www.opengolfclub.com

Le Touquet 'Le Manoir'
(1994)
Ave du Golf, BP 41, 62520 Le Touquet
☎ 03 21 06 28 00

⌨ 03 21 06 28 01
✉ letouquet@opengolfclub.com
ᐟ 9 L 2817 m Par 35 SR 118
ᴪ U
££ €35 (€45)
ᐁ As 'La Forêt'
⌂ HJ Baker
▤ www.opengolfclub.com

Val Secret (1984)
Brasles, 02400 Château Thierry
☎ 03 23 83 07 25
⌨ 03 23 83 92 73
✉ accueil@golfvalsecret.com
ᐟ 18 L 5703 m Par 72 SR 141
ᴪ U
££ €31 (€46)
ᐁ 58km W of Reims via A4. Paris
89km via A4
⌂ Paul Lennaerts
▤ www.golfvalsecret.com

Vert Parc (1991)
3 Route d'Ecuelles, 59480 Illies
☎ 03 20 29 37 87

Wimereux (1901)
Avenue F. Mitterrand, 62930 Wimereux
☎ 03 21 32 43 20
⌨ 03 21 33 62 21
✉ accueil@golf-wimereux.com
ᐟ 18 L 6150 m Par 72 SR 132 white
ᴪ U
££ €37–€61
ᐁ 6km N of Boulogne on D940.
30km S of Calais
⌂ Campbell/Hutchinson
▤ www.golf-wimereux.com

Corsica

Sperone (1990)
Domaine de Sperone, 20169 Bonifacio
☎ 04 95 73 17 13
⌨ 04 95 73 17 85
✉ golf@sperone.com
ᐟ 18 L 6106 m Par 72;
Black: SR 159, White: SR 158,
Yellow: SR 148, Blue: SR 143,
Red: SR 137
ᴪ H–max 28 or green card
££ €55–€83 (high season) or packages
of 4 or 7 green fees (low rate)
ᐁ S point of Corsica, SE of Bonifacio.
25km S of Figari Airport
⌂ Robert Trent Jones Sr
▤ www.sperone.com

Ile de France

Ableiges (1989)
95450 Ableiges
☎ 01 30 27 97 00

Bellefontaine   (1987)

95270 Bellefontaine
☎ 01 34 71 05 02

Bondoufle   (1990)

Departmentale 31, 91070 Bondoufle
☎ 01 60 86 41 71

Bussy-St-Georges   (1988)

Promenade des Golfeurs, 77600 Bussy-St-Georges
☎ 01 64 66 00 00
🖥 01 64 66 22 92
▷ 18 L 5890 m SSS 72 SR 135
👫 U
££ €36 (€60)
⊕ 20km E of Paris. Motorway A4 Junction 12
🏠 Rolin/Cornillot

Cély   (1990)

Le Château, Route de Saint-Germain, 77930 Cély-en-Bière
☎ 01 64 38 03 07

Cergy Pontoise   (1988)

2 Allee de l'Obstacle d'Eau, 95490 Vaureal
☎ 01 34 21 03 48

Chevannes-Mennecy   (1994)

91750 Chevannes
☎ 01 64 99 88 74
✉ legolfchevannes@wanadoo.fr

Clement Ader   (1990)

Domaine Château Pereire, 77220 Gretz
☎ 01 64 07 34 10
✉ golfclementader@voila.fr

Coudray   (1960)

Ave du Coudray, 91830 Le Coudray-Montceaux
☎ 01 64 93 81 76
🖥 01 64 93 99 95
✉ golf.du.coudray@wanadoo.fr
▷ 18 L 5761 m Par 71
9 L 1350 m Par 29
👫 H (men 28, women 35) WE WD–NA
££ €36 (€70)
⊕ 35km S of Paris on A6 (Junction 11)
🏠 CK Cotton
▤ www.golfcoudray.org

Courson Monteloup   (1991)

91680 Bruyères-le-Chatel
☎ 01 64 58 80 80

Crécy-la-Chapelle   (1987)

Domaine de la Brie, Route de Guérard, F 77580 Crécy-la-Chapelle
☎ 01 64 75 34 44
✉ info@domainedelabrie.com

Disneyland Golf   (1992)

1 Allee de la Mare Houleuse, 77700 Magny-le-Hongre
☎ 01 60 45 68 90
✉ dlp.nwy.golf@disney.com

Domaine de Belesbat   (1989)

Courdimanche-sur-Essonne, 91820 Boutigny-sur-Essonne
☎ 01 69 23 19 10

Domont-Montmorency

Route de Montmorency, 95330 Domont
☎ 01 39 91 07 50

Étiolles Colonial CC   (1990)

Vieux Chemin de Paris, 91450 Étiolles
☎ 01 69 89 59 59
🖥 01 69 89 59 60
✉ contact@etiollescolonial.com
▷ 18 L 6239 m Par 74
9 L 2665 m SSS 36
👫 U
££ €47.50 (€70)
⊕ 30km S of Paris
🏠 Michel Gayon
▤ www.etiollescolonial.com

Fontainebleau   (1909)

Route d'Orleans, 77300 Fontainebleau
☎ 01 64 22 22 95

Fontenailles   (1991)

Domaine de Bois Boudran, 77370 Fontenailles
☎ 01 64 60 51 00

Forges-les-Bains   (1989)

Rue du Général Leclerc, 91470 Forges-les-Bains
☎ 01 64 91 48 18
🖥 01 64 91 40 52
▷ 18 L 6167 m SSS 72
👫 H or Green card
££ €32 (€50)
⊕ 35km S of Paris, off A10
🏠 JM Rossi
▤ www.golf-forgelesbains.com

Greenparc   (1993)

Route de Villepech, 91280 St Pierre-du-Perray
☎ 01 60 75 40 60

L'Isle Adam   (1995)

1 Chemin des Vanneaux, 95290 L'Isle Adam
☎ 01 34 08 11 11

Marivaux   (1992)

Bois de Marivaux, 91640 Janvry
☎ 01 64 90 85 85
🖥 01 64 90 82 22
✉ contact@golfmarivaux.com

▷ 18 L 6116 m Par 72
👫 U
££ €39–€45 (€53–€62)
⊕ 25km SW of Paris
🏠 Macauley/Quenouille
▤ www.golfmarivaux.com

Meaux-Boutigny   (1985)

Rue de Barrois, 77470 Boutigny
☎ 01 60 25 63 98

Mont Griffon

RD 909, 95270 Luzarches
☎ 01 34 68 10 10
✉ golf.mont.griffon@wanadoo.fr

Montereau La Forteresse   (1989)

Domaine de la Forteresse, 77940 Thoury-Ferrottes
☎ (+33) 01 60 96 95 10
🖥 (+33) 01 60 96 01 41
✉ contact@golf-forteresse.com
▷ 18 L 5888 m Par 72
👫 H or Green card
££ €32 (€55)
⊕ 25km SE of Fontainebleau
🏠 Fromanger/Adam
▤ www.golf-forteresse.com

Ormesson   (1969)

Chemin du Belvedère, 94490 Ormesson-sur-Marne
☎ 01 45 76 20 71

Ozoir-la-Ferrière   (1926)

Château des Agneaux, 77330 Ozoir-la-Ferrière
☎ 01 60 02 60 79

Paris International   (1991)

18 Route du Golf, 95560 Baillet-en-France
☎ 01 34 69 90 00

St Aubin   (1976)

Public
Route du Golf, 91190 St Aubin
☎ 01 69 41 25 19

St Germain-les-Corbeil

6 Ave du Golf, 91250 St Germain-les-Corbeil
☎ 01 60 75 81 54

Seraincourt   (1964)

Gaillonnet-Seraincourt, 95450 Vigny
☎ 01 34 75 47 28

Villarceaux   (1971)

Château du Couvent, 95710 Chaussy
☎ 01 34 67 73 83
🖥 01 34 67 72 66
✉ villarceaux@wanadoo.fr
▷ 18 L 6059 m Par 72
SSS 72.4 SR 129 (men)
SSS 72.2 SR 122 (ladies)

H
££ €35 (€60)
🚗 60km NW of Paris
🏠 M Backer
▤ www.villarceaux.com

Villeray (1974)
Public
Melun-Sénart, St Pierre du Perray,
91100 Corbeil
☎ 01 60 75 17 47

Languedoc-Roussillon

Cap d'Agde (1989)
Public
4 Ave des Alizés, 34300 Cap d'Agde
☎ 04 67 26 54 40
🖥 04 67 26 97 00
✉ golf@ville-agde.fr
🏴 18 L 6286 m SSS 72
U
££ High season: €56 Low season: €46
(€56)
🚗 25km E of Béziers
🏠 Ronald Fream
▤ www.ville-agde.fr

Carcassonne (1988)
Route de Ste-Hilaire, 11000 Carcassonne
☎ 06 13 20 85 43

Coulondres (1984)
72 Rue des Erables, 34980 Saint-Gely-du-Fesc
☎ 04 67 84 13 75

Domaine de Falgos (1992)
BP 9, 66260 St Laurent-de-Cerdans
☎ 04 68 39 51 42
🖥 04 68 39 52 30
✉ contact@falgos.com
🏴 18 L 5177 m SSS 69
U
££ €29–€58
🚗 60km S of Perpignan, nr Spanish border (D115)
🏠 Alain Dehaye
▤ www.falgos.com

Fontcaude (1991)
Route de Lodève, Domaine de Fontcaude, 34990 Juvignac
☎ 04 67 45 90 10
🖥 04 67 45 90 20
✉ golf@golfhotelmontpellier.com
🏴 18 L 5992 m SSS 72
9 hole short course
U
££ €47–€55
🚗 6km W of Montpellier
🏠 C Pitman
▤ www.golfhotelmontpellier.com

La Grande-Motte (1987)
Clubhouse du Golf, 34280 La Grande-Motte
☎ 04 67 56 05 00

Montpellier Massane
(1988)
Domaine de Massane, 34670 Baillargues
☎ 04 67 87 87 87

Nîmes Campagne
(1968)
Route de Saint Gilles, 30900 Nîmes
☎ 04 66 70 17 37

Nîmes-Vacquerolles (1990)
1075 chemin du golf, 30900 Nîmes
☎ 04 66 23 33 33
🖥 04 66 23 94 94
✉ vacquerolles.opengolfclub
@wanadoo.fr
🏴 18 L 6300 m SSS 72
U
££ €53
🚗 W of Nîmes centre (D999)
🏠 W Baker
▤ www.golf-nimes.com

St Cyprien (1974)
Le Mas D'Huston, 66750 St Cyprien Plage
☎ 04 68 37 63 63
🖥 04 68 37 64 64
✉ contack@golf_st_cyprien.com
🏴 18 L 6480 m SSS 73
9 L 2724 m SSS 35
U H
££ €55
🚗 15km SE of Perpignan
🏠 Wright/Tomlinson
▤ www.golf_st_cyprien.com

St Thomas (1992)
Route de Bessan, 34500 Béziers
☎ 04 67 39 03 09
🖥 04 67 39 10 65
✉ info@golfsaintthomas.com
🏴 18 L 6130 m Par 72
U
££ On application
🚗 7km NE of Béziers (RN 113)
🏠 Patrice Lambert
▤ www.golfsaintthomas.com

Loire Valley

Anjou G&CC (1990)
Route de Cheffes, 49330 Champigné
☎ 02 41 42 01 01
🖥 02 41 42 04 37
✉ info@anjougolf.com
🏴 18 L 6227 m SSS 72
6 hole short course
U H
££ €29 (€34)
🚗 23km N of Angers
🏠 F Hawtree
▤ www.anjougolf.com

Avrillé (1988)
Château de la Perrière, 49240 Avrillé
☎ 02 41 69 22 50

🖥 02 41 34 44 60
✉ avrille@bluegreen.com
✏ J Goudard (Dir)
🏴 18 L 6116 m SSS 71
9 hole Par 3 course
U
££ €27 (€33)
🚗 5km N of Angers
🏠 Robert Berthet
▤ www.bluegreen.com

Baugé-Pontigné (1994)
Public
Route de Tours, 49150 Baugé
☎ 02 41 89 01 27
✉ golf.bauge@wanadoo.fr

La Bretesche (1967)
Domaine de la Bretesche, 44780 Missillac
☎ 02 51 76 86 86

Carquefou (1991)
Boulevard de l'Epinay, 44470 Carquefou
☎ 02 40 52 73 74

Cholet (1989)
Allée du Chêne Landry, 49300 Cholet
☎ 02 41 71 05 01

La Domangère
La Roche-sur-Yon, Route de la Rochelle, 85310 Nesmy
☎ 02 51 07 65 90

Fontenelles
Public
Saint-Gilles-Croix-de-Vie, 85220 Aiguillon-sur-Vie
☎ 02 51 54 13 94

Ile d'Or (1988)
BP 90410, 49270 La Varenne
☎ 02 40 98 58 00
🖥 02 40 98 51 62
✉ nantesiledor@wanadoo.fr
🏴 18 L 6292 m Par 72
9 L 1217 m Par 27
U H
££ €16–€38
🚗 25km NE of Nantes
🏠 Michel Gayon

International Barriere-
La Baule (1976)
44117 Saint-André-des Eaux
☎ 02 40 60 46 18
🖥 02 40 60 41 41
✉ golfinterlabaule@lucienbarriere
.com
🏴 18 L 6055 m Par 72 SSS 73
18 L 6301 m Par 72 SSS 74
9 L 2969 m Par 36
H
££ 9: €26 – €41; 18: €46 – €72
🚗 Avrillac, 3km NE of La Baule
🏠 Alliss/Thomas/Gayon
▤ www.lucienbarriere.com

Laval-Changé　(1972)
Le Jariel, 53000 Changé-les-Laval
☎ 02 43 53 16 03

Le Mansgolfier　(1990)
Rue du Golf, 72190 Sargé les Le Mans
☎ 02 43 76 25 07
🖳 02 43 76 45 25
✉ lemansgolfier@wanadoo.fr
⊢ 18 L 6054 m SSS 72
👥 U
££ €35 (€40)
🚗 6km NE of Le Mans
🏠 Antoine d'Ormesson

Le Mans Mulsanne　(1961)
Route de Tours, 72230 Mulsanne
☎ 02 43 42 00 36

Nantes　(1967)
44360 Vigneux de Bretagne
☎ 02 40 63 25 82
🖳 02 40 63 64 86
✉ golfclubnantes@aol.com
⊢ 18 L 5940 m SSS 72
👥 H
££ €40 (€52)
🚗 12km NW of Nantes
🏠 Frank Pennink
🖥 www.golfclubnantes.com

Nantes Erdre　(1990)
Chemin du Bout des Landes, 44300 Nantes
☎ 02 40 59 21 21

Les Olonnes
Gazé, 85340 Olonne-sur-Mer
☎ 02 51 33 16 16

Pornic　(1912)
49 Boulevard de l'Océan, Sainte-Marie/Mer, 44210 Pornic
☎ 02 40 82 06 69

Port Bourgenay　(1990)
Avenue de la Mine, Port Bourgenay, 85440 Talmont-St-Hilaire
☎ 02 51 23 35 45

Sablé-Solesmes
Domaine de l'Outinière, Route de Pincé, 72300 Sablé-sur-Sarthe
☎ 02 43 95 28 78

St Jean-de-Monts　(1988)
Ave des Pays de la Loire, 85160 Saint Jean-de-Monts
☎ 02 51 58 82 73

Savenay　(1990)
44260 Savenay
☎ 02 40 56 88 05

Normandy

Bellême-St-Martin
(1988)
Les Sablons, 61130 Bellême
☎ 02 33 73 00 07

Cabourg-Le Home　(1907)
38 Av Président Réné Coty, Le Home Varaville, 14390 Cabourg
☎ 02 31 91 25 56
🖳 02 31 91 18 30
✉ golf-cabourg-le-home@worldonline.fr
⊢ 18 L 5234 m SSS 68
👥 H
££ €20–€40
🚗 4km W of Cabourg
🏠 Jackson/Brizon

Caen　(1990)
Le Vallon, 14112 Bieville-Beuville
☎ 02 31 94 72 09

Champ de Bataille
Château du Champ de Bataille, 27110 Le Neubourg
☎ 02 32 35 03 72

Clécy　(1988)
Manoir de Cantelou, 14570 Clécy
☎ 02 31 69 72 72
✉ golf-de-clecy@golf-de-clecy.com

Coutainville　(1925)
Ave du Golf, 50230 Agon-Coutainville
☎ 02 33 47 03 31

Deauville St Gatien　(1987)
14130 St Gatien-des-Bois
☎ 02 31 65 19 99
🖳 02 31 65 11 24
✉ contact@golfdeauville.com
⊢ 18 L 6272 m Par 72
　 9 L 3035 m Par 36
👥 U
££ €31 (€46)
🚗 8km E of Deauville; 8km W of Honfleur
🏠 Olivier Brizon
🖥 www.golfdeauville.com

Dieppe-Pourville　(1897)
51 Route de Pourville, 76200 Dieppe
☎ 02 35 84 25 05
🖳 02 35 84 97 11
✉ golf-de-dieppe@wanadoo.fr
⊢ 18 L 5780 m Par 70
👥 U
££ €32 (€58)
🚗 2km W of Dieppe towards Pourville
🏠 Willie Park Jr
🖥 www.golf-dieppe.com

Étretat　(1908)
BP No 7, Route du Havre, 76790 Étretat
☎ 02 35 27 04 89

Forêt Verte
Bosc Guerard, 76710 Montville
☎ 02 35 33 62 94

Golf barrière de Deauville
(1929)
14 Saint Arnoult, 14800 Deauville
☎ 02 31 14 24 24
✉ golfdeauville@lucienbarriere.com

Granville　(1912)
Bréville, 50290 Bréhal
☎ 02 33 50 23 06
✉ contact@golfdegranville.com

Le Havre　(1933)
Hameau Saint-Supplix, 76930 Octeville-sur-Mer
☎ 02 35 46 36 50
✉ golf.le-havre@wanadoo.fr

Houlgate　(1981)
Route de Gonneville, 14510 Houlgate
☎ 02 31 24 80 49

Léry Poses　(1989)
BP 7, 27740 Poses
☎ 02 32 59 47 42

Omaha Beach　(1986)
Ferme St Sauveur, 14520 Port-en-Bessin
☎ 02 31 22 12 12
🖳 02 31 22 12 13
✉ omaha.beach@wanadoo.fr
⊢ 18 L 6216 m SSS 72
　 9 L 2693 m SSS 35
👥 U H
££ €30–€60
🚗 8km N of Bayeux
🏠 Yves Bureau
🖥 www.omahabeachgolfclub.com

Parc de Brotonne　(1991)
Jumièges, 76480 Duclair
☎ 02 35 05 32 97

Rouen-Mont St Aignan
(1911)
Rue Francis Poulenc, 76130 Mont St Aignan
☎ 02 35 76 38 65
🖳 02 35 75 13 86
⊢ 18 L 5522 m SSS 70
　 SR 126 (white tees)
👥 H WE–H after 4pm
££ €28–€35 (after 4pm €50)
🚗 4km N of Rouen

Golf-hotel St Saëns　(1987)
Domaine du Vaudichon, 76680 St Saëns
☎ 02 35 34 25 24
🖳 02 35 34 43 33

✉ golf-st-saens@infonie.fr
⚐ 18 L 6009 m Par 71
👤 U
££ €35 (€50)
⛳ 30km NE of Rouen
🏠 D Robinson
📧 www.golfstsaens.com

Golf barrière de St Julien
(1987)
St Julien-sur-Calonne, 14130 Pont-l'Évêque
☎ 02 31 64 30 30
✉ golfsaintjulien@lucienbarriere.com

Le Vaudreuil (1962)
27100 Le Vaudreuil
☎ 02 32 59 02 60

North East

Ammerschwihr
*BP 19, Route des Trois Épis,
68770 Ammerschwihr*
☎ 03 89 47 17 30

Bâle G&CC (1926)
Rue de Wentzwiller, 68220 Hagenthal-le-Bas
☎ +33 (0)3 89 68 50 91
🖨 +33 (0)3 89 68 55 66
✉ info@gccbasel.ch
⚐ 18 L 6255 m Par 72 SSS 73
👤 WD–H (max 36) WE–M
££ €70
⛳ 15km SW of Bâle
🏠 B von Limburger
📧 www.swissgolfnetwork.ch

Besançon (1968)
La Chevillote, 25620 Mamirolle
☎ 03 81 55 73 54

Bitche (1988)
Rue des Prés, 57230 Bitche
☎ 03 87 96 15 30

Château de Bournel (1990)
25680 Cubry
☎ 03 81 86 00 10
✉ info@bournel.com

Combles-en-Barrois (1948)
14 Rue Basse, 55000 Combles-en-Barrois
☎ 03 29 45 16 03

Épinal (1985)
Public
Rue du Merle-Blanc, 88001 Épinal
☎ 03 29 34 65 97

Golf de Faulquemont-Pontpierre (1993)
Avenue Jean Monnett, 57380 Faulquemont
☎ 03 87 81 30 52

☎ 03 87 81 30 62
✉ golf.faulquemont@wanadoo.fr
✍ Michel Goedert (Pres)
⚐ 18 L 5985 m
Men: SR 133 (white), 140 (yellow);
Ladies: SR 132 (blue), 128 (red)
👤 U
££ €32 (€44) – high season; €20 (€25)
– low season (2006 prices)
⛳ A14 towards Metz, exit Boulay
🏠 Flipo/Fourès

Forêt d'Orient
BP13 Rouilly-Sacey, 10220 Piney
☎ 03 25 46 37 78

Grande Romanie (1988)
La Grande Romanie, 51460 Courtisols
☎ 06 61 50 01 00
🖨 03 26 66 65 97
✉ at@par72.net
⚐ 18 L 6578 m SSS 76
👤 U
££ €36 (€45)
⛳ St Etienne-au-Temple, 6km from A4 Junction 28
🏠 Alain Tribout
📧 wwwpar72.net

La Grange aux Ormes
La Grange aux Ormes, 57155 Marly
☎ 03 87 63 10 62

Kempferhof (1988)
Golf-Hôtel-Academie, 67115 Plobsheim
☎ 0033 (0) 3 88 98 72 72
🖨 0033 (0) 3 88 98 74 76
✉ info@golf-kempferhof.com
⚐ 18 L 6024 m SSS 73 SR 145
👤 H
££ Low season: €65 (€75) High season: €80 (€105)
⛳ 15km S of Strasbourg
🏠 Bob von Hagge
📧 www.golf-kempferhof.com

La Largue G&CC (1988)
25 Rue du Golf, 68580 Mooslargue
☎ 03 89 07 67 67
🖨 03 89 25 62 83
✉ lalargue@golf-lalargue.com
⚐ 18 L 6142 m CR 73.1 SR 138
9 Par 30
👤 U H36
££ €60 (€70)
⛳ 25km W of Basle
🏠 Jeremy Pern
📧 www.golf-lalargue.com

Les Rousses (1986)
*1305 Route du Noirmont, 39220
Les Rousses*
☎ 03 84 60 06 25

Metz Technopole
*Rue Félix Savart, 57070 Metz
Technopole 2000*
☎ 03 87 39 95 95

Metz-Cherisey (1963)
Château de Cherisey, 57420 Cherisey
☎ 03 87 52 70 18
🖨 03 87 52 42 44
⚐ 18 L 6172 m SSS 72
👤 H
££ 9: €25 (€35); 18: €40 (€46)
⛳ 15km SE of Metz
🏠 Donald Harradine

Nancy-Aingeray (1962)
Aingeray, 54460 Liverdun
☎ 03 83 24 53 87

Nancy-Pulnoy (1993)
10 Rue du Golf, 54425 Pulnoy
☎ 03 83 18 10 18

Prunevelle (1930)
Ferme des Petits-Bans, 25420 Dampierre-sur-le-Doubs
☎ 03 81 98 11 77

Reims-Champagne (1928)
*Château des Dames de France,
51390 Gueux*
☎ 03 26 05 46 10

Rhin Mulhouse (1969)
Ile du Rhin, F-68490 Chalampe
☎ +33 3 89 83 28 32
🖨 +33 3 89 83 28 42
✉ golfdurhin@wanadoo.fr
⚐ 18 L 5977 m SSS 72
👤 WE–M
££ €55 (€65)
⛳ 20km E of Mulhouse
🏠 Donald Harradine
📧 www.golf-rhin.com

Rougemont-le-Château (1990)
Route de Masevaux, 90110 Rougemont-le-Château
☎ 03 84 23 74 74
🖨 03 84 23 03 15
✉ golf.rougemont@wanadoo.fr
⚐ 18 L 6002 m SSS 72
👤 U
££ Low season €35–€45 High season €55
⛳ 18km NE of Belfort. 25km NW of Mulhouse
🏠 Robert Berthet
📧 www.golf.rougemont.com

Strasbourg (1934)
Route du Rhin, 67400 Illkirch
☎ 03 88 66 17 22
🖨 03 88 65 05 67
✉ golf.strasbourg@wanadoo.fr
⚐ 27 holes:
6105-6138 m SSS 72-73
👤 WD–H (max 35)
££ WD only–€52
⛳ 10km S of Strasbourg
🏠 Donald Harradine
📧 www.golf-strasbourg.com

Troyes-Cordelière   (1957)
Château de la Cordelière, 10210 Chaource
☎ 03 25 40 18 76

Domaine du Val de Sorne
(1989)
Domaine de Val de Sorne,
39570 Vernantois
☎ 03 84 43 04 80
🖥 03 84 47 31 21
🖂 info@valdesorne.com
🏌 18 L 6000 m SSS 72
🏌 U
£€ High season: €43–€54 Low season:
     €31–€37
🚗 5km SE of Lons-le-Saunier,
     between Dijon, Lyon and Geneva
🏠 Hugues Lambert
🖥 www.valdesorne.com

Vittel
BP 122, 88804 Vittel-Cedex
☎ 03 29 08 18 80

La Wantzenau   (1991)
C D 302, 67610 La Wantzenau
☎ 03 88 96 37 73

Paris Region

Béthemont-Chisan CC
(1989)
12 Rue du Parc de Béthemont,
78300 Poissy
☎ 01 39 75 51 13

La Boulie
La Boulie, 78000 Versailles
☎ 01 39 50 59 41

Feucherolles   (1992)
78810 Feucherolles
☎ 01 30 54 94 94

Fourqueux   (1963)
Rue Saint Nom 36, 78112 Fourqueux
☎ 01 34 51 41 47

Golf National   (1990)
2 Avenue du Golf, 78280 Guyancourt
☎ 01 30 43 36 00
🖥 01 30 43 85 58
🖂 gn@golf-national.com
🏌 Albatros 18 L 6600 m Par 72
     Aigle 18 L 5961 m Par 71
     Oiselet 9 L 1955 m Par 32
🏌 H max 28 on Albatros, H or Green
     Card on Aigle, U on Oiselet
£€ Albatros: €75 (€100) Aigle: €60
     (€70) Oiselet: €30 (€30)
🚗 St Quentin-en-Yvelines, SW of
     Paris (D36 or A13+A12); Paris
     25km; Vers
🏠 H Chesneau
🖥 www.golf-national.com

Isabella   (1969)
RN12, Sainte-Appoline, 78370 Plaisir
☎ 01 30 54 10 62

Joyenval   (1992)
Chemin de la Tuilerie, 78240
Chambourcy
☎ 01 39 22 27 50
🖂 joyenval@wanadoo.fr

Rochefort   (1964)
78730 Rochefort-en-Yvelines
☎ 01 30 41 31 81

St Cloud   (1911)
60 Rue du 19 Janvier, Garches 92380
☎ 01 47 01 01 85

St Germain   (1922)
Route de Poissy, 78100 St Germain-en-
Laye
☎ 01 39 10 30 30
🖥 01 39 10 30 31
🖂 info@golfsaintgermain.org
🏌 18 L 6117 m SSS 72
     9 L 2030 m SSS 33
🏌 WD–H (men 24, ladies 28)
     WE–M
£€ €100 (€80 with French Federation
     licence)
🚗 20km W of Paris
🏠 HS Colt
🖥 www.golfsaintgermain.org

St Quentin-en-Yvelines
Public
RD 912, 78190 Trappes
☎ 01 30 50 86 40

St Nom-La-Bretêche
(1959)
Hameau Tuilerie-Bignon, 78860 St Nom-
La-Bretèche
☎ 01 30 80 04 40

La Vaucouleurs   (1987)
Rue de l'Eglise, 78910 Civry-la-Forêt
☎ 01 34 87 62 29
🖥 01 34 87 70 09
🖂 vaucouleurs@vaucouleurs.fr
✍ J Pelard
🏌 Rivière 18 L 6138 m CR 73.2 SR
     138
     Vallons 18 L 5553 m Par 70 CR
     68.6 SR 115
🏌 H or Green card
£€ €44 (€65)
🚗 50km W of Paris, between Mantes
     and Houdan
🏠 Michel Gayon
🖥 www.vaucouleurs.fr

Les Yvelines
Château de la Couharde, 78940 La-Queue-
les-Yvelines
☎ 01 34 86 48 89

Provence & Côte d'Azur

Aix Marseille   (1935)
13290 Les Milles
☎ 04 42 24 40 41
     04 42 24 23 01
🖂 golfaixmarseille@aol.com

Barbaroux   (1989)
Route de Cabasse, 83170 Brignoles
☎ 04 94 69 63 63

Les Baux de Provence
(1989)
Domaine de Manville, 13520 Les Baux-de-
Provence
☎ 04 90 54 40 20
🖥 04 90 54 40 93
🖂 golfbauxdeprovence@wanadoo.fr
🏌 9 L 2812 m SSS 36
🏌 U H
£€ €34 (€34) high season €28 (€34)
     low season
🚗 15km NE of Arles. 15km S of
     Avignon. 80km W of Marseilles
🏠 Martin Hawtree
🖥 www.golfbauxdeprovence.com

Beauvallon-Grimaud
Boulevard des Collines, 83120 Sainte-
Maxime
☎ 04 94 96 16 98

Biot   (1930)
La Bastide du Roy, 06410 Biot
☎ 04 93 65 08 48
🖥 04 93 65 05 63
🏌 18 L 4511 m CR 62.7 SR 94
🏌 U
£€ €40 (€45)
🚗 Antibes 5km. Nice 15km

Cannes Mandelieu   (1891)
Route de Golf, 06210 Mandelieu
☎ 04 92 97 32 00

Cannes Mandelieu Riviera
(1990)
Avenue des Amazones, 06210 Mandelieu
☎ 04 92 97 49 49

Cannes Mougins   (1923)
175 Avenue du Golf, 06250 Mougins
☎ 04 93 75 79 13
🖥 04 93 75 27 60
🖂 golf-cannes-mougins@wanadoo.fr
🏌 18 L 6263 m SSS 72
🏌 H–max 28
£€ €120
🚗 8km NE of Cannes (D35)
🏠 Alliss/Thomas (1977)
🖥 www.golf-cannes-mougins.com

Châteaublanc

Les Plans, 84310 Morières-les-Avignon
☎ 04 90 33 39 08

Digne-les-Bains (1990)

Public
57 Route du Chaffaut, 0400 Digne-les-Bains
☎ 04 92 30 58 00
🖥 04 92 30 58 13
📧 info@golfdigne.com
🏳 23 L 5556 m SSS 71
👫 U
££ €5
🏌 100km NE of Aix-en-Provence. 5km from Digne-les-Bains
🏠 Robert Berthet
🖥 www.golfdigne.com

Estérel Latitudes (1989)

Ave du Golf, 83700 St Raphaël
☎ 04 94 52 68 30

Frégate (1992)

Dolce Frégate, RD 559, 83270 St Cyr-sur-Mer
☎ 04 94 29 38 00
🖥 04 94 29 96 94
📧 golf-fregate@wanadoo.fr
🏳 Frégate 18 L 6210 m SSS 72
\ Frégalon 9 hole short course
👫 U
££ Jan 1-Apr 30 & Nov 10-Dec 31: Frégate-18: €53, 9: €40; May 1-Oct 31: Frégate-18: €68, 9: €45; Frégalon- €37
🏌 25km W of Toulon on coast
🏠 Ronald Fream
🖥 www.fregate.dolce.com

Gap-Bayard (1988)

Centre d'Oxygénation, 05000 Gap
☎ 04 92 50 16 83
🖥 04 92 50 17 05
📧 gap-bayard@wanadoo.fr
🏳 18 L 6023 m SSS 72
👫 U
££ €36 (€42)
🏌 7km N of Gap. 80km S of Grenoble
🏠 Hugues Lambert
🖥 www.ville-gap.fr

Golf Claux-Amic (1992)

1 Route des Trois Ponts, 06130 Grasse
☎ 04 93 60 55 44
📧 info@claux-amic.com

Grand Avignon (1989)

Les Chênes Verts, 84270 Vedene - Avignon
☎ 04 90 31 49 94
🖥 04 90 31 01 21
📧 info@golfgrandavignon.com
🏳 18 L 6046 m Par 72
👫 U
££ High season €60 Low season €50
🏌 Vedene, 10km NE of Avignon
🏠 Georges Roumeas
🖥 www.golfgrandavignon.com

La Grande Bastide (1990)

Chemin des Picholines, 06740 Châteauneuf de Grasse
☎ 04 93 77 70 08

Luberon (1986)

La Grande Gardette, 04860 Pierrevert
☎ 04 92 72 17 19
🖥 04 92 72 59 12
📧 info@golf-du-luberon.com
🏳 18 L 5623 m SSS 72
👫 U
££ €52
🏌 5km SW of Manosque. 45km NE of Aix-en-Provence
🏠 Artea
🖥 www.golf-du-luberon.com

Marseille La Salette (1988)

65 Impasse des Vaudrans, 13011 2a Valentine Marseille
☎ 04 91 27 12 16
🖥 04 91 27 21 33
📧 lasalette@opengolfclub.com
🏳 18 L 5214 m Par 69 SR 135
👫 H
££ €38 (€48)
🏌 Nr centre of Marseilles
🏠 Michel Gayon
🖥 www.opengolfclub.com

Miramas (1993)

Mas de Combe, 13140 Miramas
☎ 04 90 58 56 55

Monte Carlo (1910)

Route du Mont-Agel, 06320 La Turbie
☎ 04 92 41 50 70
🖥 04 93 41 09 55
📧 monte-carlo-golf-club@wanadoo.fr
🏳 18 L 5811 m SSS 71
👫 H
££ €100 (€120)
🏌 Mont Agel, La Turbie, 10km M of Monte Carlo
🏠 The committee

Opio-Valbonne (1966)

Route de Roquefort-les-Pins, 06650 Opio
☎ 04 93 12 00 08

Pont Royal (1992)

Pont Royal, 13370 Mallemort
☎ 04 90 57 40 79

Provence G&CC (1991)

Route de Fontaine de Vaucluse, L'Isle sur la Sorgue, 84800 Saumane
☎ 04 90 20 20 65

Le Roc/Golf de Roquebrune (1989)

Golf de Roquebrune, CD7, 83520 Roquebrune-sur-Argens
☎ 04 94 19 60 35
🖥 04 94 82 90 22
📧 golf@le-roc.eu
🏳 9 holes – new 18 hole championship and 9 hole academic courses will open in 2008
👫 H
££ 9 holes €24 low season, €30 high season 2 x 9 holes €40 low season, €45 high season
🏌 35km N of Saint-Tropez. 40km SW of Cannes
🏠 Udo Barth
🖥 www.le-roc.eu

Royal Mougins (1993)

424 Avenue du Roi, 06250 Mougins
☎ 04 92 92 49 69 (reception)
   04 92 92 49 79 (pro shop)
🖥 04 92 92 49 70
📧 contact@royalmougins.fr
🏳 18 L 6004 m
   Ladies CR 71.1-73.5 SR 129-137
   Men CR 70.8-72.1 SR 136-144
👫 H
££ €175 (€225) inc. buggy
🏌 5km N of Cannes
🏠 Robert von Hagge
🖥 www.royalmougins.fr

Saint Donat G&CC (1993)

270 Route de Cannes, 06130 Grasse
☎ +33 493 097660
🖥 +33 493 93097663
📧 mail@golfsaintdonat.com
🏳 18 L 6000 m Par 71 SR 129
   9 L 600 m Par 27
👫 U SOC
££ High season €75 Low season €67 week Discounts for jun/students (2005 rates)
🏌 Between Cannes and Grasse, exit 4 from m/way. 30 min Nice Airport
🏠 Robert Trent Jones jun
🖥 www.golfsaintdonat.com

Les Domaines de Saint Endréol Golf & Spa Resort (1992)

Route de Bagnols-en-Fôret, 83 920 La Motte-en-Provence
☎ 04 94 51 89 89
🖥 04 94 51 89 90
📧 accueil.golf@st-endreol.com
🏳 18 L 6219 m Par 72
   Men: white SR 142, yellow SR 134
   Ladies: blue SR 129, red SR 125
👫 U H
££ €69
🏌 Situated in La Motte in the Var countryside between Cannes and St Tropez
🏠 Michel Gayon
🖥 www.st-endreol.com

Sainte Victoire (1985)

Domaine de Château L'Arc, 13710 Fuveau
☎ 04 42 53 89 09

La Sainte-Baume
(1988)
Golf Hotel, Domaine de Châteauneuf, 83860 Nans-les-Pins
☎ 04 94 78 60 12
📠 04 94 78 63 52
✉ saintebaume@opengolfclub.com
⌀ 18 L 6062 m Par 72 SSS 72 SR 124
👥 U
££ High season: 9: €61; 18: €61 Low season: 9: €36 (€45); 18: €46 (€57)
⛳ 30km SE of Aix-en-Provence, via A8 (exit Saint-Maximin)
🏠 Robert Berthet
▤ www.opengolfclub.com

Sainte-Maxime
Route de Débarquement, 83120 Sainte-Maxime
☎ 04 94 55 02 02

Servanes
(1989)
Domaine de Servanes, 13890 Mouriès
☎ 04 90 47 59 95
📠 04 90 47 52 58
✉ servanes@opengolfclub.com
⌀ 18 L 6161m Par 72 SSS 74.3
👥 U H WD/WE
££ Low season: €48 High season: €59
⛳ 35km S of Avignon
🏠 Sprecher/Watine
▤ www.opengolfclub.com

Taulane
Domaine du Château de Taulane, RN 85, 83840 La Martre
☎ 04 93 60 31 30
📠 04 93 60 33 23
✉ resagolf@chateau-taulane.com
⌀ 18 L 6250 m Par 72
👥 H
££ April €60, May–Nov €85 (inc. meal at buffet)
⛳ 55km N of Cannes on N85 (Route Napoleon)
🏠 Gary Player
▤ www.chateau-de-taulane.com

Valcros
(1964)
Domaine de Valcros, 83250 La Londe-les-Maures
☎ 04 94 66 81 02

Valescure
(1895)
BP 451, 83704 St-Raphaël Cedex
☎ 04 94 82 40 46

Rhone-Alps

Aix-les-Bains
(1904)
Avenue du Golf, 73100 Aix-les-Bains
☎ 04 79 61 23 35
📠 04 79 34 06 01
✉ info@golf-aixlesbains.com
⌀ 18 L 5519 m Par 70 SR 124
👥 H

££ Jan–Mar, Nov–Dec €45 (€52) Apr–June, Sept–Oct €55 (€59) July–Aug €59
⛳ 3km S of Aix
▤ www.golf-aixlesbains.com

Albon
(1989)
Domaine de Senaud, Albon, 26140 St Rambert d'Albon
☎ 04 75 03 03 90
📠 04 75 03 11 01
✉ golf.albon@wanadoo.fr
⌀ 18 L 6087 m CR 72.5 SR 135
   9 L 1260 m Par 29
👥 U
££ €42–€48
⛳ 60km S of Lyon, motorway exit Chanas
🏠 Antoine d'Ormesson/Roger Guvgui
▤ www.golf-albon.com

Annecy
(1953)
Echarvines, 74290 Talloires
☎ 04 50 60 12 89
✉ golflocannecy@wanadoo.fr

Annonay-Gourdan
(1988)
Domaine de Gourdan, 07430 Saint Clair
☎ 04 75 67 03 84

Les Arcs
B P 18, 73706 Les Arcs Cedex
☎ 04 79 07 43 95

Le Beaujolais
(1991)
69480 Lucenay-Anse
☎ 04 74 67 04 44

Bossey G&CC
(1985)
Château de Crevin, 74160 Bossey
☎ 04 50 43 95 50
📠 04 50 95 32 57
✉ accueilgolf@golfbossey.com
⌀ 18 L 5954 m Par 71
👥 WD–U WE–NA
££ €75
⛳ 6km S of Geneva
🏠 Robert Trent Jones Jr
▤ www.golfbossey.com

La Bresse
Domaine de Mary, 01400 Condessiat
☎ 04 74 51 42 09

Chamonix
(1934)
35 Route du Golf, 74400 Chamonix
☎ 04 50 53 06 28
📠 04 50 53 38 69
✉ info@golfdechamonix.com
⌀ 18 L 6087 m SSS 72
👥 H
££ €34–€70 (€43–€70)
⛳ 3km N of Chamonix (RN 506). Geneva 80km
🏠 Robert Trent Jones Sr
▤ www.golfdechamonix.com

Le Clou
(1985)
01330 Villars-les-Dombes
☎ 04 74 98 19 65
✉ golfduclou.fr@freesbee.fr

La Commanderie
(1964)
L'Aumusse-Crottet, 01290 Pont-de-Veyle
☎ 04 85 30 44 12

Divonne
(1931)
Ave des Thermes, 01220 Divonne-les-Bains
☎ 04 50 40 34 11
📠 04 50 40 34 25
✉ golf@domaine-de-divonne.com
⌀ 18 L 5858 m SSS 72
👥 H–max 30
££ €50 (€80)
⛳ Divonne 1/2 km. 18km N of Geneva
🏠 Nakowski
▤ www.domaine-de-divonne.com

Esery
(1990)
Esery, 74930 Reignier
☎ 04 50 36 58 70
📠 04 50 36 57 62
✉ golf.esery@wanadoo.fr
⌀ 18 L 6350 m SSS 73
   9 L 2024 m SSS 31
👥 WD–H WE
££ €70
⛳ 10km S of Geneva
🏠 Michel Gayon
▤ www.golf-club-esery.com

Evian Masters
(1904)
Rive Sud du lac de Genève, 74500 Évian
☎ 04 50 26 85 00
📠 04 50 75 65 54
✉ golf@evianroyalresort.com
⌀ 18 L 6006 m SSS 72
👥 H
££ €36–€57 (€46–€67)
⛳ 2km W of Évian. 40km NE of Geneva Airport
🏠 Cabell Robinson
▤ www.evianroyalresort.com

Giez
(1991)
Lac d'Annecy, 74210 Giez
☎ 04 50 44 48 41
📠 04 50 32 55 93
✉ asgolfdeguer@wanadoo.fr
⌀ 18 L 5820 m Par 72
   9 L 2250 m Par 33
👥 H or Green card
££ €46–€59
⛳ 20km SE of Annecy
🏠 Didier Fruchet
▤ www.golfdegiez.fr

Le Gouverneur
Château du Breuil, 01390 Monthieux
☎ 04 72 26 40 34
✉ golfgouverneur@worldonline.fr

Grenoble-Bresson
(1990)
Route de Montavie, 38320 Eybens
☎ 04 76 73 65 00

Grenoble-Charmeil   (1988)

38210 St Quentin-sur-Isère
☎   04 76 93 67 28
🖥   04 76 93 62 04
✉   info@golfhotelgrenoble.com
🏳   18 L 5733 m Par 73
👯   U
££   €40 (€50)
⛳   15km NW of Grenoble, off A49
🏠   Perl/Garaialde
📧   www.golfhotelgrenoble.com

Grenoble-Uriage   (1921)

Les Alberges, 38410 Uriage
☎   04 76 89 03 47
🖥   04 76 73 15 80
✉   golfuriage@wanadoo.fr
🏳   9 L 2004 m Par 64 CR 61.3 SR 112
👯   U
££   €24 (€28)
⛳   15km E of Grenoble
🏠   Watine/Sprecher
📧   www.golfuriage.com

Lyon   (1921)

38280 Villette-d'Anthon
☎   04 78 31 11 33
🖥   04 72 02 48 27
✉   gcl2@wanadoo.fr
🏳   18 L 6229 m SSS 72
     18 L 6727 m SSS 74
👯   U H
££   €34 (€50)
⛳   20km E of Lyon
🏠   Fenn/Lambert
📧   www.golfclubdelyon.com

Lyon-Chassieu

Route de Lyon, 69680 Chassieu
☎   04 78 90 84 77

Lyon-Verger   (1977)

69360 Saint-Symphorien D'Ozon
☎   04 78 02 84 20

Maison Blanche G&CC

(1991)
01170 Echenevex
☎   04 50 42 44 42

Méribel   (1973)

BP 54, 73553 Méribel Cedex
☎   04 79 00 52 67

Mionnay La Dombes

(1986)
Chemin de Beau-Logis, 01390 Mionnay
☎   04 78 91 84 84

Mont-d'Arbois   (1964)

74120 Megève
☎   04 50 21 29 79

Pierre Carée   (1984)

74300 Flaine
☎   04 50 90 85 44

St Etienne   (1989)

62 Rue St Simon, 42000 St Etienne
☎   04 77 32 14 63

Salvagny

100 Rue des Granges, 69890 La Tour de Salvagny
☎   04 78 48 83 60

La Sorelle   (1991)

Domaine de Gravagnieux, 01320 Villette-sur-Ain
☎   04 74 35 47 27

Tignes   (1968)

Val Claret, 73320 Tignes
☎   04 79 06 37 42 (Summer)
🖥   04 79 06 35 64
✉   golf.tignes@compagniedesalpes.fr
🏳   18 L 5030 m SSS 68 SR 112
👯   H–max 35
££   €39
⛳   50km E of Moutiers, off D902, nr Italian border. 90km S of Chamonix
🏠   Philippe Vallant

Valdaine   (1989)

Domaine de la Valdaine, Montboucher/Jabron, 26740 Montelimar-Montboucher
☎   04 75 00 71 33

Valence St Didier   (1983)

26300 St Didier de Charpey
☎   04 75 59 67 01

Toulouse & Pyrenees

Albi Lasbordes   (1989)

Château de Lasbordes, 81000 Albi
☎   05 63 54 98 07
🖥   05 63 54 98 06
✉   contact@golfalbi.com
🏳   18 L 6200 m SSS 72
👯   U
££   €45 (€55) July/Aug D–€55
⛳   70km NE of Toulouse
🏠   Garaialde/Pern
📧   www.golfalbi.com

Ariège   (1986)

Unjat, 09240 La Bastide-de-Serou
☎   05 61 64 56 78

La Bigorre   (1992)

Pouzac, 65200 Bagnères de Bigorre
☎   05 62 91 06 20

Embats

Route de Montesquiou, 32000 Auch
☎   05 62 05 20 80
     05 62 61 10 11

Étangs de Fiac   (1987)

Brazis, 81500 Fiac
☎   05 63 70 64 70

Florentin-Gaillac   (1990)

Le Bosc, Florentin, 81150 Marssac-sur-Tarn
☎   05 63 55 20 50

Golf de tarbes   (1987)

1 Rue du Bois, 65310 Laloubère
☎   05 62 45 14 50
✉   golf.des.tumulus@wanadoo.fr

Guinlet   (1986)

32800 Eauze
☎   05 62 09 80 84

Lannemezan

La Demi-Lune, 65300 Lannemezan
☎   05 62 98 01 01

Lourdes   (1988)

Chemin du Lac, 65100 Lourdes
☎   05 62 42 02 06
🖥   05 62 42 02 06
✉   golf.lourdes@wanadoo.fr
🏳   18 L 5482 m Par 72 SSS 71.4
👯   U
££   Low season €25–€30
     High season €40–€40
⛳   4km W of Lourdes, off D940
🏠   Olivier Brizon

Mazamet-La Barouge

(1956)
81660 Pont de l'Arn
☎   05 63 61 08 00
     05 63 67 06 72

Toulouse   (1951)

31320 Vieille-Toulouse
☎   05 61 73 45 48

Toulouse-La Ramée

Ferme Cousturier, 31170 Tournefeuille
☎   05 61 07 09 09

Toulouse-Palmola

(1974)
Route d'Albi, 31660 Buzet-sur-Tarn
☎   05 61 84 20 50
✉   golf.palmola@wanadoo.fr

Toulouse-Teoula

(1991)
71 Avenue des Landes, 31830 Plaisance du Touch
☎   05 61 91 98 80
🖥   05 61 91 49 66
✉   contact@golftoulouseteoula.com
🏳   18 L 5500 m Par 69
👯   H or green card
££   €33 (€49)
⛳   15km W of Toulouse
🏠   Martin Hawtree
📧   www.golftoulouseteoula.com

For list of abbreviations, key to symbols and international dialling codes see page 651

Germany

Berlin & East

Balmer See   (1995)
Drewinscher Weg 1, 17429 Neppermin
☎ **(038379) 28199**
✉ info@golfhotel-usedom.de

Golf- und Land-Club Berlin-Wannsee e.V.
(1895)
Golfweg 22, 14109 Berlin
☎ **(030) 806 7060**
🖳 (030) 806 706-10
✉ info@glcbw.de
⚑ 18 L 6088 m SR 127
   9 L 4442 m SR 102
👥 WD–U H WE–M
££ €80, €60 with member WE with members only €70
♣ Berlin (SW)
⌂ Harris Brothers (1925)
▤ www.glcbw.de

Berliner G&CC Motzener See   (1991)
Am Golfplatz 5, 15749 Mittenwalde OT Motzen
☎ **(033769) 50130**
🖳 (033769) 50134
✉ info@golfclubmotzen.de
⚑ 18 L 5900 m Par 72
   9 L 2640 m Par 54
👥 H U
££ €35–€70
♣ 30km S of Berlin
⌂ Kurt Rossknecht
▤ www.golfclubmotzen.de

Elbflorenz GC Dresden
(1992)
Ferdinand von Schillstr 4a, 01728 Possendorf
☎ **(035206) 2430**

Potsdamer GC   (1990)
Tremmener Landstrasse, 14641 Tremmen
☎ **(033233) 80244**
✉ potsdammer.golfclub@berlin.de

Schloss Meisdorf   (1996)
Petersberger Trift 33, 06463 Meisdorf
☎ **(034743) 98450**

Golfclub Schloss Wilkendorf   (1991)
Am Weiher 1, 15345 Altlandsberg-Wilkendorf
☎ **(0049) 3341 330960**
🖳 (0049) 3341 330961
✉ service@golfpark-schloss-wilkendorf.com

⚑ Men: 18 L 6096 m
   Par 72 CR 72.7 SR 132
   Women: 18 L 5302 m
   Par 72 CR 74.0 SR 127
👥 U H with reservation (WD 45, WE 36)
££ Mon–Wed €40, Thur €45, Fri €45, Sat–Sun €60
♣ 5km to Strausberg. 40km to Berlin
⌂ Sandy Lyle
▤ www.golfpark-schloss-wilkendorf.com

Seddiner See   (1993)
Zum Weiher 44, 14552 Wildenbruch
☎ **(033205) 7320**

Golfresort Semlin am See
(1992)
Ferchesarerstrasse 8b, 14712 Semlin
☎ **(03385) 554410**
🖳 (03385) 554400
✉ golf@golfresort-semlin.de
⚑ 27 holes
   Men: CR 71.7 SR 130;
   CR 71.3 SR 127; CR 72.5 SR 127
   Women: CR 73.9 SR 127;
   CR 73.1 SR 126; CR 74.5 SR 124
   6 hole public course
👥 H
££ €35 (€60) – visitors €25 (€40) – hotel guest
♣ 75km W of Berlin (B5/B188)
⌂ Christoph Städler
▤ www.golfresort-semlin.de

Sporting Club Berlin Sport & Spa Resort   (1991)
Parkallee 1, 15526 Bad Sarrow
☎ **(033631) 63300**
🖳 (033631) 63310
✉ info@sporting-club-berlin.de
⚑ 18 L 6118 m Par 72
   18 L 6084 m Par 72
   18 L 5593 m Par 71
   9 hole course
👥 U
££ Eby: €40 guest, €60 visitor Palmer: €50 guest, €70 visitor Faldo: €70 guest, €90 visitor McEwan: €10 guest, €15 visitor
♣ 70km SE of Berlin
⌂ Palmer/Faldo/Eby/McEwan
▤ www.sporting-club-berlin.com

Bremen & North West

Bremer Schweiz   (1991)
Wölpscherstr 4, 28779 Bremen
☎ **(0421) 609 5331**
🖳 (0421) 609 5333
✉ info@golfclub-bremerschweiz.de
⚑ 18 L 5865 m Par 72
👥 H WD WE
££ Mon €20, Tue–Fri €30 (€35)
♣ N of Bremen
⌂ Wolfgang Siegmann
▤ www.golfclub-bremerschweiz.de

Herzogstadt Celle   (1985)
Beukenbusch 1, 29229 Celle
☎ **(05086) 395**

Küsten GC Hohe Klint
(1978)
Hohe Klint, 27478 Cuxhaven
☎ **(04723) 2737**

Münster-Wilkinghege
(1963)
Steinfurterstr 448, 48159 Münster
☎ **(0251) 214090**

Oldenburgischer   (1964)
Am Golfplatz 1, 26180 Rastede
☎ **(04402) 7240**
🖳 (04402) 70417
✉ oldenburgischer.golfclub@golf.de
⚑ 18 L 6109 m SSS 72 SR 132
👥 WD–U WE–U H
££ €40 (€50)
♣ 10km N of Oldenburg, nr Rastede
⌂ Von Limburger/Schnatmeyer
▤ www.oldenburgischer.golfclub.de

Ostfriesland   (1980)
Postbox 1220, 26634 Wiesmoor
☎ **(04944) 6440**
🖳 (04944) 6441
✉ golfclubostfriesland@golf.de
⚑ 18 L 6183 m CR 72.7 SR 124
👥 U
££ €30 (€40)
♣ 25km SW of Wilhelmshaven
⌂ Frank Pennink
▤ www.golfclub-ostfriesland.de

Soltau   (1982)
Hof Loh, 29614 Soltau
☎ **(05191) 967 63 33**
🖳 (05191) 967 63 34
✉ info@golf-soltau.de
⚑ 18 L 6011 m SSS 73
   9 L 2340 m SSS 54
👥 H
££ €30 (€40)
♣ Tetendorf, S of Soltau
▤ www.golf-soltau.de

Syke   (1989)
Schultenweg 1, 28857 Syke-Okel
☎ **(04242) 8230**

Tietlingen   (1979)
29683 Fallingbostel
☎ **(05162) 3889**

Verden   (1988)
Holtumer Str 24, 27283 Verden
☎ **(04230) 1470**

Worpswede   (1974)
Giehlermühlen, 27729 Vollersode
☎ **(04763) 7313**

Club Zur Vahr (1905)

Bgm-Spitta-Allee 34, 28329 Bremen

☎ **Bremen (0421) 204480**
　Garlstedt (04795) 953316
☏ (0421) 244 9248
✉ info@club-zur-vahr-bremen.de
⛳ Garlstedt 18 L 6283 m CR 72.9
　SR 134
　Bremen 9 L 5777 m CR 68.5
　SR 111
♟ WD–H WE–M
££ Garlstedt–€45 €55)
　Bremen–€30
⊶ Garlstedt-30km N of Bremen.
　Vahr-Bremen
♙ B von Limburger
🖥 www.club-zur-vahr-bremen.de

Central North

Dillenburg

Auf dem Altscheid, 35687 Dillenburg
☎ **(02771) 5001**
✉ info@gc-dillenburg.de

Hofgut Praforst (1992)

Postfach 1137, 36081 Hünfeld
☎ **(06652) 9970**

Kassel-Wilhelmshöhe
(1958)

Ehlenerstr 21, 34131 Kassel
☎ **(0561) 33509**

Kurhessischer GC Oberaula
(1987)

Am Golfplatz, 36278 Oberaula
☎ **(06628) 91540**

Licher (1992)

35423 Lich
☎ **(06404) 91071**
☏ (06404) 91072
✉ info@licher-golf-club.de
⛳ 18 L 6418 m Par 72 CR 73.9 SR
　131
♟ H SOC
££ €40 (Mon/Tue until 12 €25)
　Sat €65, Sun €70
⊶ 45km N of Frankfurt
♙ Heinz Fehring
🖥 www.licher-golf-club.de

Rhoen (1971)

Am Golfplatz, 36145 Hofbieber
☎ **(06657) 1334**
☏ (06657) 914809
✉ info@golfclub-fulda.de
⛳ 18 L 5521 m CR 68.6 SR 126
♟ H
££ €30 (€40)
⊶ Hofbieber, 11km E of Fulda
♙ Kurt Peters
🖥 www.golfclub-fulda.de

Schloss Braunfels (1970)

Homburger Hof, 35619 Braunfels
☎ **(06442) 4530**
☏ (06442) 6683
✉ info@golfclub-braunfels.de
⛳ 18 L 6085 m Par 73
　Men: CR 71.7 SR 127
　Women: CR 73.0 SR 127
♟ WD–H (max 36) WE–H NA
　10am–2pm
££ D–€35 (€50)
⊶ 70km N of Frankfurt
♙ Bernhard von Limburger
🖥 www.golfclub-braunfels.de

Schloss Sickendorf (1990)

Schloss Sickendorf, 36341 Lauterbach
☎ **(06641) 96130**
☏ (06641) 961335
✉ info@gc-lauterbach.de
⛳ 18 L 6045 m Par 72 SSS 72
♟ H
££ €30 (€40)
⊶ 30km W of Fulda. 120km E of
　Frankfurt
♙ Spangemacher
🖥 www.gc-lauterbach.de

Winnerod

Parkstr 22, 35447 Reiskirchen
☎ **(06408) 9513-0**
☏ (06408) 9513-13
✉ winnerod@golfpark.de
⛳ 18 L 6069 m Par 72
　9 hole Par 3 course
♟ U H (WD45, WE36)
££ €40 (€60)
⊶ Hessen, 30km N of Frankfurt/Main
♙ Michael Pinner
🖥 www.golfpark.de

Zierenberg Gut Escheberg
(1995)

Gut Escheberg, 34289 Zierenberg
☎ **(05606) 2608**

Central South

Bad Kissingen (1910)

Euerdorferstr 11, 97688 Bad Kissingen
☎ **(0971) 3608**
☏ (0971) 60140
⛳ 18 L 5699 m SSS 70
♟ U H
££ €55 (€60)
⊶ Bad Kissingen 2km. 65km N of
　Würzburg

Bad Vilbeler Golfclub
Lindenhof e.V. (1994)

61118 Bad Vilbel-Dortelweil
☎ **+49 (0)6101 5245200**
☏ +49 (0)6101 5245202
✉ info@bvgc.de
⛳ 18 holes
♟ H membership card required
££ €40–€65 (€50–€75)

⊶ 7km to Frankfurt Main
♙ Dr Siegmann, Hannover
🖥 www.bvgc.de

Golfclub Eschenrod e.V.
(1996)

*Postfach 1227, Lindenstr. 46,
63679 Schotten*
☎ **(06044) 8401**
☏ (06044) 951159
✉ br.golf@t-online.de
⛳ 18 Par 72 CR 69.0 SR 122
♟ H WD/WD–U
££ €22 (€33)
⊶ Hessen near Hanau & Giessen
🖥 www.eschenrod.de

Frankfurter (1913)

Golfstrasse 41, 60528 Frankfurt/Main
☎ **(069) 666 2318**

Hanau-Wilhelmsbad
(1958)

Wilhelmsbader Allee 32, 63454 Hanau
☎ **(06181) 82071**

Hof Trages

Hofgut Trages, 63579 Freigericht
☎ **(06055) 91380**

Homburger (1899)

Saalburgchaussee 2, 61350 Bad Homburg
☎ **(06172) 306808**

Idstein (2001)

Am Nassen Berg, 65510 Idstein
☎ **(06126) 9322-13**

Idstein-Wörsdorf (1989)

Gut Henriettenthal, 65510 Idstein
☎ **(06126) 9322-0**

Kitzingen (1980)

*Zufahrt über Winterleitenweg,
97318 Kitzingen*
☎ **(09321) 4956**
☏ (09321) 21936
✉ golfkitzingen@aol.com
⛳ 18 L 6093 m (men), 5373 m (ladies)
　Par 72 CR 71.4 (men), 73.1 (ladies)
♟ U H WD/WE
££ €30 (€35)
⊶ 20km E of Würzburg
♙ Greens of Scotland
🖥 www.golfclub-kitzingen.de

Kronberg G&LC (1954)

*Schloss Friedrichshof, Hainstr 25,
61476 Kronberg/Taunus*
☎ **(06173) 1426**
☏ (06173) 5953
⛳ 18 L 4941 m SSS 68
♟ WD–U H WE–M H
££ €45 (€55)
⊶ 16km NW of Frankfurt
🖥 www.gc-kronberg.de

Main-Spessart   (1990)

Postfach 1204, 97821 Marktheidenfeld-
Eichenfürst
☎ **(09391) 8435**
🖳 (09391) 8816
⮞ 18 holes Par 72
   6 hole short course
👥 H–max 36
££ €30 (€40)
⮞⮞ 80km E of Frankfurt/Main
🏠 Harradine
🖥 www.main-spessart-golf.de

Main-Taunus   (1979)

Lange Seegewann 2, 65205 Wiesbaden
☎ **(06122) 588680 (Sec)**
📧 clubinfo@golf-club-maintanus.de

Mannheim-Viernheim

(1930)
Alte Mannheimer Str 3, 68519 Viernheim
☎ **(06204) 607020**

Maria Bildhausen   (1992)

Rindhof 1, 97702 Münnerstadt
☎ **(09766) 1601**
🖳 (09766) 1602
📧 golf@maria-bildhausen.de
⮞ 18 L 6047 m Par 72
   6 hole short course
👥 U
££ €31 (€40)
⮞⮞ 80km NE of Wurzburg
🏠 Christian Habeck
🖥 www.maria-bildhausen.de

Neuhof

Hofgut Neuhof, 63303 Dreieich
☎ **(06102) 327927/327010**
🖳 (06102) 327012
📧 info@golfclubneuhof.de
⮞ 18 L 6177 m SSS 72
   3 x 9 holes
👥 WD–H WE–M
££ €70
⮞⮞ Hofgut Neuhof, S of Frankfurt, off
   A3
🏠 Christoph Städler
🖥 www.golfclubneuhof.de

Rhein Main   (1977)

Steubenstrasse 9, 65189 Wiesbaden
☎ **(0611) 373014**

Rheinblick

Weisser Weg, 65201 Wiesbaden-
Frauenstein
☎ **(0611) 420675**

Rheintal   (1971)

An der Bundesstrr 291, 68723 Oftersheim
☎ **(06202) 56390**

St Leon-Rot   (1996)

Opelstrasse 30, 68789 St Leon-Rot
☎ **(06227) 86080**

Spessart   (1972)

Golfplatz Alsberg, 63628 Bad Soden-
Salmünster
☎ **(06056) 91580**

Taunus Weilrod   (1979)

Merzhäuser Strasse, 61276 Weilrod-
Altweilnau
☎ **(06083) 95050**
📧 golfclub-taunus-weilrod.de

Wiesbadener   (1893)

Chausseehaus 17, 65199 Wiesbaden
☎ **(0611) 460238**
🖳 (0611) 463251
⮞ 9 L 5172 m
   Par 68 CR 68.6 SR 124 (men)
   Par 68 CR 70.2 SR 125 (ladies)
👥 WD–H (max 36) WE–H (max 28)
££ €35 (€45)
⮞⮞ 8km NW of Wiesbaden, towards
   Schlangenbad
🏠 Hirsch
🖥 www.wiesbadener-golfclub.de

Golf- und Landclub Wiesloch   (1983)

Hohenhardter Hof, 69168 Wiesloch-
Baiertal
☎ **(06222) 78811-0**

Hamburg & North

Altenhof   (1971)

Eckernförde, 24340 Altenhof
☎ **(04351) 41227**
   (04351) 45800 (Pro)

Berhinderten Golf Club Deutschland e.V.   (1994)

Gustav-Delle Str 18a, 22926 Ahrensburg
☎ **(04102) 41544**
🖳 (04102) 44516
📧 klausahrensbgc@aol.com
⮞ 18 hole course
👥 U SOC only
££ On application
⮞⮞ 20km NE of Hamburg
🖥 www.bgc-golf.de

Brodauer Mühle   (1986)

Baumallee 14, 23730 Gut Beusloe
☎ **(04561) 8140**
🖳 (04561) 407397
📧 gc-brodauermuehle@t-online.de
⮞ 18 L 6113 m Par 72 SSS 72
👥 U H–36
££ €35 (€45)
⮞⮞ 30km N of Lübeck
🏠 Siegmann/Osterkamp
🖥 www.gc-brodauermuehle.de

Buchholz-Nordheide

An der Rehm 25, 21244 Bucholz
☎ **(04181) 36200**

Buxtehude   (1982)

Zum Lehmfeld 1, 21614 Buxtehude
☎ **(04161) 81333**
🖳 (04161) 87268
📧 post@golfclubbuxtehude.de
⮞ 18 L 6480 m CR 73.6 SR 132
👥 WD–H WE–H before 10am
££ €35 (€45)
⮞⮞ 30km SW of Hamburg on Route 73
   from Harburg
🏠 Wolfgang Siegmann
🖥 www.golfclubbuxtehude.de

Deinster Mühle   (1994)

Im Mühlenfeld 30, 21717 Deinste
☎ **(04149) 925112**
🖳 (04149) 925111
📧 golfpark@allesistgdn.de
⮞ 18 L 5986 m CR 71.6 SR 129
👥 U H
££ €39 (€49)
⮞⮞ 50km SW of Hamburg
🏠 David Krause
🖥 www.allesistgdn.de

Föhr   (1966)

25938 Nieblum
☎ **(04681) 580455**

Gut Apeldör   (1996)

Gut Apeldör, 25779 Hennstedt
☎ **(04836) 9960-0**
🖳 (04836) 9960-33
📧 info@apeldoer.de
⮞ 18 hole Championship course Par
   72:
   Men: L 5762 m CR 72.5 SR 134
   Women: L 5347 m CR 75.5 SR 134
   9 hole Pay & Play course (Par 72):
   Men: L 5994 m CR 71.5 SR 123
   Women: L 5046 m CR 72.7 SR 128
👥 U
££ 9: €15 18: €39 (€49)
⮞⮞ 11km W of Heide. 110km N of
   Hamburg
🏠 David John Krause
🖥 www.apeldoer.de

Gut Grambek   (1981)

Schlosstr 21, 23883 Grambek
☎ **(04542) 841474**
🖳 (04542) 841476
📧 info@gcgrambek.de
⮞ 18 L 5907 m SSS 71
👥 H
££ €30 (€45)
⮞⮞ 30km S of Lübeck. 50km E of
   Hamburg
🏠 Kurt Peters
🖥 www.gcgrambek.de

Gut Kaden   (1984)

Kadenerstrasse 9, 25486 Alveslohe
☎ **(04193) 9929-0**

Gut Uhlenhorst   (1989)

24229 Uhlenhorst
☎ **(04349) 91700**
📧 E-mail:golf@gut-uhlenhorst.de

Gut Waldhof (1969)
Am Waldhof, 24629 Kisdorferwohld
☎ (04194) 99740

Gut Waldshagen (1996)
24306 Gut Waldshagen
☎ (04522) 766766
🖥 (04522) 766767
📧 info@gut-golf.de
⊳ 18 L 6369 m CR 73.7 SR 131
6 hole short course
👥 U
££ €40 (€50)
🚗 35km S of Kiel. 91km NE of Hamburg
📧 www.gut-golf.de

Hamburg (1906)
In de Bargen 59, 22587 Hamburg
☎ (040) 812177

Hamburg Ahrensburg (1964)
Am Haidschlag 39-45, 22926 Ahrensburg
☎ (04102) 51309

Hamburg Hittfeld (1957)
Am Golfplatz 24, 21218 Seevetal
☎ (04105) 2331

Hamburg Holm (1993)
Haverkamp 1, 25488 Holm
☎ (04103) 91330
🖥 (04103) 913313
📧 info@hchh.de
⊳ 27 holes CR 72.3 SR 124
👥 WD–U WE–M H
££ D–€45 (D–€50)
🚗 20km W of Hamburg
🏠 Harradine/Rossknecht
📧 www.gchh.de

Hamburg Walddörfer (1960)
Schevenbarg, 22949 Ammersbek
☎ (040) 605 1337
📧 info@gchw.de

Golfclub Hohen-Wieschendorf (1993)
Am Golfplatz 1, 23968 Hohen-Wieschendorf
☎ (0049) 384 28660
🖥 (0049) 384 286666
📧 info@howido.de
⊳ 18
👥 U H SOC
££ D–€36
🚗 13km west of Wismar. 40km east of Lübeck
🏠 Peter Tolgreve
📧 www.ostseegolfschule.de

Hoisdorf (1977)
Hof Bornbek/Hoisdorf, 22952 Lütjensee
☎ (04107) 7831

Jersbek (1986)
GolfClub Jersbek e.V., Oberteicher Weg, 22941 Jersbek
☎ (040) 20950
🖥 (040) 24779
📧 gcjersbek@t-online.de
⊳ 18 L 5921 m (men) 5220 (ladies)
SSS 71
CR 70.7 (men) 72.2 (ladies) SR 125
👥 U H36 WD WE
££ €50 (€60)
🚗 20km N of Hamburg
🏠 Von Schinkel
📧 www.golfclub-jersbek.de

Kieler GC Havighorst (1988)
Havighorster Weg 20, 24211 Havighorst
☎ (04302) 965980
🖥 (04302) 965981
📧 golfclub.havighorst@t-online.de
⊳ 18 L 6234 m Par 72 CR 73.9 SR 130
👥 WD–U H WE–H
££ €50 (€55)
🚗 7km S of Kiel. 85km N of Hamburg
🏠 Udo Barth

Lübeck-Travemünder (1921)
Kowitzberg 41, 23570 Lübeck-Travemünde
☎ (04502) 74018
🖥 (04502) 72182
📧 info@ltgk.de
⊳ 27 L 6063 - 6152 m CR 72.7 - 74.5
SR 125 - 134
👥 H
££ Mon–Thur: D–€45 Fri–Sun + Hols: D–€55
🚗 18km NE of Lübeck. 70km NE of Hamburg
📧 www.ltgk.de

Maritim Timmendorfer Strand (1973)
Am Golfplatz 3, 23669 Timmendorfer Strand
☎ (04503) 5152

Mittelholsteinischer Aukrug (1969)
Zum Glasberg 9, 24613 Aukrug-Bargfeld
☎ (04873) 595

Peiner Hof
Peiner Hag, 25497 Prisdorf
☎ (04101) 73790

An der Pinnau (1982)
Pinnebergerstr 81a, 25451 Quickborn-Rensel
☎ (04106) 81800
🖥 (04106) 82003
📧 info@pinnau.de
⊳ 18 L 6023 m Par 72 SR 127
18 L 5231 m Par 72 SR 127
👥 U H

££ €40 (€45)
🚗 25km NW of Hamburg, nr Quickborn
🏠 David Krause
📧 www.pinnau.de

Am Sachsenwald (1985)
Am Riesenbett, 21521 Dassendorf
☎ (04104) 6120

Schloss Breitenburg
25524 Breitenburg
☎ (04828) 8188
🖥 (04828) 8100
📧 golfclubschlossbreitenburg@t-online.de
⊳ 27 hole course
👥 H
££ €40 (€50)
🚗 50km N of Hamburg
🏠 Osterkamp/Krause
📧 www.golfclubschlossbreitenburg.de

Schloss Lüdersburg (1985)
Lüdersburger Strasse 21, 21379 Lüdersburg
☎ (04139) 6970-0
🖥 (04139) 6970 70
📧 info@luedersburg.de
⊳ 18 L 6568 m SSS 73
18 L 6169 m SSS 72
4 hole par 3 course
👥 U H
££ €45 (€65)
🚗 12km E of Lüneburg. 55km SE of Hamburg
🏠 Wolfgang Siegmann/Nicklaus Design
📧 www.luedersburg.de

St Dionys (1972)
Widukindweg, 21357 St Dionys
☎ (04133) 213311
🖥 (04133) 213313
📧 info@golfclub-st-dionys.de
⊳ 18 standard tees:
Red: par 72 CR 72.3 SR 125
Yellow: par 72 CR 72.1 SR 127
👥 By appointment only
££ €50 (€60)
🚗 10km N of Lüneburg
📧 www.golfclub-st-dionys.de

GC Sylt e.V. (1982)
Norderrung 5, 25996 Wenningstedt
☎ (04651) 99598-0
🖥 (04651) 99598-19
📧 golfclubsylt@t-online.de
⊳ 18 L 6200 m Par 72
👥 H–max 36
££ €55
🚗 Sylt Island, 75km W of Flensburg
🏠 D Harradine
📧 www.golfclubsylt.de

Treudelberg G&CC (1990)
Lemsahler Landstr 45, 22397 Hamburg
☎ (040) 608 22500

Auf der Wendlohe
Oldesloerstr 251, 22457 Hamburg
☎ **(040) 550 5014/5**

Wentorf-Reinbeker   (1901)
Golfstrasse 2, 21465 Wentorf
☎ **(040) 72 97 80 68**
📠 (040) 72 97 80 67
📧 sekretariat@wrgc.de
ℙ 18 L 5821 m CR 72.2 SR 127
🏌 WD–U H WE–M
£€ €45
🚗 20km SE of Hamburg
🏠 Ernst Hess
🖥 www.wrgc.de

Hanover & Weserbergland

Bad Salzuflen G&LC
(1956)
Schwaghof 4, 32108 Bad Salzuflen
☎ **(05222) 10773**

British Army Golf Club (Sennelager)   (1963)
Bad Lippspringe, BFPO 16
☎ **(05252) 53794**
📠 (05252) 53811
📧 manager@sennelagergolfclub.de
ℙ 18 L 5658 m SSS 72
   9 L 5214 m SSS 68
🏌 H
£€ (Forces) €25 (€30) (Civilians) €35 (€40)
🚗 9km E of Paderborn, off Route B1
🖥 www.sennelagergolfclub.de

Burgdorf   (1970)
Waldstr 27, 31303 Burgdorf-Ehlershausen
☎ **(05085) 7628**
📠 (05085) 6617
📧 info@burgdorfer-golfclub.de
ℙ 18 L 6426 m SSS 74
🏌 H U
£€ D–€35 (D–€45)
🚗 Burgdorf-Ehlershausen, 25km NE of Hanover
🖥 www.burgdorfer-golfclub.de

Gifhorn   (1982)
Wilscher Weg 69, 38518 Gifhorn
☎ **(05371) 16737**

Gütersloh Garrison   (1963)
Princess Royal Barracks, BFPO 47
☎ **(05241) 842606**

Hamelner Golfclub e.V.
(1985)
Schwöbber 8, 31855 Aerzen
☎ **(05154) 987 0**
📠 (05154) 987 0
📧 info@hamelner-golfclub.de

ℙ 2 x 18 holes SR 96 and SR 139
🏌 U
£€ €20–€40
🚗 10km SW of Hameln. 60km SW of Hanover
🖥 www.hamelner-golfclub.de

Hannover   (1923)
Am Blauen See, 30823 Garbsen
☎ **(05137) 73068**
📠 (05137) 75851
📧 info@golfclub-hannover.de
ℙ 18 L 5685 m Par 71 SSS 71
   Men: CR 71.7 SR 136
   Ladies: CR 74.0 SR 133
🏌 WD–U H 36 WE–M
£€ €35 (€45)
🚗 15km NW of Hanover
🖥 www.golfclub-hannover.de

Hardenberg   (1969)
Gut Levershausen, 37154 Northeim
☎ **(05551) 61915**

Isernhagen   (1983)
Auf Gut Lohne 22, 30916 Isernhagen
☎ **(05139) 893185**

Langenhagen   (1989)
Hainhaus 22, D-30855 Langenhagen
☎ **(0511) 736832**
📠 (0511) 726 1190
📧 golf-club-langenhagen@online.de
ℙ 27 L 6161 m Par 72
🏌 H
£€ €35 (€45)
🚗 25km N of Hannover
🏠 Siegmann
🖥 www.golf-club-langenhagen.de

Lippischer   (1980)
Huxoll 14, 32825 Blomberg-Cappel
☎ **(05236) 459**
📠 (05236) 8102
📧 lippischer-golfclub@t-online.de
ℙ 18 L 5990 m CR 71.5 SR 126
🏌 H WD WE
£€ €35 (€45) – 2006 prices
🚗 12km E of Detmold; 9km from Blomberg
🖥 www.lippischergolfclub.de

Marienfeld   (1986)
Remse 27, 33428 Marienfeld
☎ **(05247) 8880**

Paderborner Land   (1983)
Wilseder Weg 25, 33102 Paderborn
☎ **(05251) 4377**

Pyrmonter   (1961)
Postfach 100 828, 31758 Hameln
☎ **(05281) 8196**

Ravensberger Land
Sudstrasse 96, 32130 Enger-Pödinghausen
☎ **(09224) 79751**

Senne GC Gut Welschof
(1992)
Augustdorferstr 72, 33758 Schloss Holte-Stukenbrock
☎ **(05207) 920936**
📠 (05207) 88788
📧 info@senne-golfclub.de
ℙ 18 L 6246 m SSS 72
🏌 U H 45
£€ €36 (€48)
🚗 20km S of Bielefeld
🏠 Christoph Städler
🖥 www.senne-golfclub.de

Sieben-Berge Rheden
(1965)
Postfach 1152, 31021 Gronau
☎ **(05182) 52336**

Weserbergland   (1982)
Weissenfelder Mühle, 37647 Polle
☎ **(05535) 8842**

Westfälischer Gütersloh
Gütersloher Str 127, 33397 Rietberg
☎ **(05244) 2340/10528**
📠 (05244) 1388
📧 golf-club@golf-gt.de
ℙ 18 L 6135 m CR 71.6 SR 124
🏌 U H
£€ €40 (€50)
🚗 8km SE of Gütersloh, nr Neuenkirchen
🏠 B von Limburger
🖥 www.golf-gt.de

Widukind-Land   (1985)
Auf dem Stickdorn 63, 32584 Löhne
☎ **(05228) 7050**

Munich & South Bavaria

Allgäuer G&LC   (1984)
Hofgut Boschach, 87724 Ottobeuren
☎ **(08332) 1310**

Altötting-Burghausen
(1986)
Piesing 4, 84533 Haiming
☎ **(08678) 986903**
📠 (08678) 986905
ℙ 18 L 5948 m Par 70 CR 70.7 SR 122 (men)
   18 L 5376 m Par 72 CR 73.2 SR 123 (ladies)
   18 L 6028 m Par 72 CR 71.6 SR 124 (men)
   18 L 5319 m Par 72 CR 73.6 SR125 (ladies)
🏌 U
£€ €40 (€40)
🚗 Schloss Piesing, 4km N of Burghausen
🏠 G von Mecklenberg
🖥 www.gc-altoetting-burghausen.de

Augsburg (1959)

Engelshofer Str 2, 86399 Bobingen-
Burgwalden

☎ (08234) 5621

Bad Tölz (1973)

83646 Wackersberg
☎ (08041) 9994

Beuerberg (1982)

Gut Sterz, 82547 Beuerberg
☎ (08179) 671 or 782
⌨ (08179) 5234
✉ beurberg@golf.de
➢ 18 L 6250 m SL 132 CR 72.6
👥 WD–H WE–M H
££ €60 (€70)
⛳ Beuerberg, 45km SW of Munich
🏠 Donald Harradine
📧 www.gc-beurberg.de

Chieming (1982)

Kötzing 1, D-83339 Chieming
☎ (08669) 87330
⌨ (08669) 873333
✉ info@golfchieming.de
✍ Inger Schmid
➢ Men: white 18 L 6250 m white
CR 72.0 SR 133,
yellow 18 L 5933 m CR 70.8
SR 134;
Women: black 18 L 5508 m
CR 74.7 SR 128,
red L 5254 m CR 73.8 SR 127
9 L 1188 m Par 3
👥 H 36
££ 9: €15; 18: €45 (€60 – inc Fri after
12 noon); Students/Juniors €25
(€35)
⛳ On A8 Salzburg-Munich. 40km W
of Salzburg. Munich 100km
🏠 Thomas Himmel
📧 www.golfchieming.de

Donauwörth (1995)

Lederstatt 1, 86609 Donauwörth
☎ (0906) 4044

Ebersberg (1988)

Postfach 1351, 85554 Ebersberg
☎ (08094) 8106
⌨ (08094) 8386
✉ info@gc-ebersberg.de
➢ 18 L 5907 m Par 72
9 hole Par 3/Par 4 course
👥 U H
££ €40 (€50)
⛳ Zaissing, 35km E of Munich
🏠 Thomas Himmel
📧 www.gc-ebersberg.de

Erding-Grünbach (1973)

Am Kellerberg, 85461 Grünbach
☎ (08122) 49650

Eschenried (1983)

Kurfürstenweg 10, 85232 Eschenried
☎ (08131) 56740

⌨ (08131) 567418
✉ info@golf-eschenried.de
➢ Eschenried 18 L 5935 m Par 72 SR
129
Eschenhof 18 L 5550 m Par 70 SR
117
Gut Häusern 18 L 6710 m Par 72
SR 129
Gut Häusern 6 L 690 m Par 19
Gröbenbach 9 L 1774 m Par 32
👥 U H; Gut Häusern H
££ Eschenried €55 (€70) Eschenhof
€45 (€55) Gut Häusern €60 (€75)
Gröbenbach €28 (€35)
⛳ 8km NW of Munich
🏠 G von Mecklenburg/P Haradine
📧 www.gc-eschenried.de

Feldafing (1926)

Tutzinger Str 15, 82340 Feldafing
☎ (08157) 9334-0
✉ info@golfclub-Feldafing.de

Garmisch-Partenkirchen
(1928)

Gut Buchwies, 82496 Oberau
☎ (08824) 8344
⌨ (08824) 944198
✉ golfclubGAP@onlinehome.de
➢ 18 L 6210 m Par 72
👥 U H
££ €50 (€60)
⛳ 10km N of Garmisch-
Partenkirchen
📧 www.golfclub-garmisch-
partenkirchen.de

Gut Ludwigsberg (1989)

Augsburgerstr 51, 86842 Turkheim
☎ (08245) 3322

Gut Rieden

Gut Rieden, 82319 Starnberg
☎ (08151) 90770

Hohenpähl (1988)

82396 Pähl
☎ (08808) 9202-0
⌨ (08808) 9202-22
✉ info@gchp.de
✍ Gabriele Gestner, Susanne Ott
➢ 18 L 5971 m Par 71 CR 71.9 SR
131
👥 H36; dogs allowed
££ €50 (€70)
⛳ 40km S of Munich on B2 (km 41)
🏠 Kurt Rossknecht
📧 www.golfclub-hohenpaehl.de

Holledau

Weihern 3, 84104 Rudelzhausen
☎ (08756) 96010

Höslwang im Chiemgau
(1975)

Kronberg 3, 83129 Höslwang
☎ (08075) 714
⌨ (08075) 8134

✉ info@golfclub-hoeslwang.de
➢ 18 L 6110 m Par 72 CT 72.1 SR
126
👥 H
££ €43 (€55)
⛳ 80km S of Munich
🏠 Thomas Himmel
📧 www.golfclub-hoeslwang.de

Iffeldorf (1989)

Gut Rettenberg, 82393 Iffeldorf
☎ 0049 (8856) 92550
⌨ 0049 (8856) 925559
✉ sekretariat@golf-iffeldorf.de
➢ 18 L 5883 m Par 72 CR 1.7
SR 128
👥 H
££ D–€45 before 10am; D–€55 after
10am (€70)
⛳ 45km S of Munich
🏠 Peter Postel
📧 www.golf-iffeldorf.de

Landshut (1989)

Oberlippach 2, 84095 Furth-Landshut
☎ (08704) 8378
⌨ (08704) 8379
✉ gc.landshut@t-online.de
➢ 18 L 6130 m Par 73 CR 72.5 SR
131
👥 H
££ €45 (€60)
⛳ 65 km E of Munich
🏠 Kurt Rossknecht
📧 www.golf-landshut.de

Mangfalltal G&LC

Oed 1, 83620 Feldkirchen-Westerham
☎ (08063) 6300

Margarethenhof (1982)

Gut Steinberg,
83666 Waakirchen/Marienstein
☎ (08022) 7506-0
⌨ (08022) 74818
✉ info@margarethenhof.com
➢ 18 L 5730 m Par 71
👥 WD–H WE–before 10am
££ €60 (€80)
⛳ Tegernsee, 45km S of Munich
🏠 Frank Pennink
📧 www.margarethenhof.com

Memmingen Gut
Westerhart (1994)

Westerhart 1b, 87740 Buxheim
☎ (08331) 71016
⌨ (08331) 71018
✉ gc-memmingen@t-online.de
➢ 18 Par 72
Men (yellow): L 6077 m CR 72.3
SR 127
Women (red): L 5276 m CR 73.8
SR 126
👥 U H
££ €40 (€50)
⛳ 120km W of Munich. Memmingen
5km

Golfclub München Nord-Eichenried   (1989)

Münchnerstr 57, 85452 Eichenried
- ☎ **(08123) 93080**
- 🖳 (08123) 930893
- 🖂 info@gc-eichenried.de
- ℗ 27 L 6318 m Par 73/74
- 👥 WD–U H
- ££ €60 (€90)
- 🚗 19km NE of Munich
- 🏠 Kurt Rossknecht
- 🖳 www.gc-eichenried.de

München West-Odelzhausen   (1988)

Gut Todtenried, 85235 Odelzhausen
- ☎ **(08134) 1618**

München-Riedhof e.V.   (1991)

82544 Egling-Riedhof, Riedhof 16
- ☎ **(08171) 21950**
- 🖳 (08171) 219511
- 🖂 info@riedhof.de
- ℗ 18 L 6216 m SSS 72 SR 126 CR 71.3
- 👥 WD–U H WE–M NA
- ££ €90
- 🚗 25km S of Munich
- 🏠 Heinz Fehring
- 🖳 www.riedhof.de

Münchener   (1910)

Tölzerstrasse 95, 82064 Strasslach
- ☎ **(08170) 450**

Olching   (1980)

Feursstrasse 89, 82140 Olching
- ☎ **(08142) 48290**
- 🖳 (08142) 482914
- 🖂 sportbuero@golfclub-olching.de
- ℗ 18 L 6028 m Par 72 CR 71.6 SR 125 (men) CR 74.2 SR 127 (ladies)
- 👥 H WE–NA
- ££ €50 (€60)
- 🚗 15km W of Munich
- 🏠 Kurt Rosshnecht
- 🖳 www.golfclub-olching.de

Pfaffing Wasserburger

Golfclub Pfaffing München-Ost e.V, wsw Golf AG, Köckmühle 132, 83539 Pfaffing
- ☎ **(08076) 91650**
- 🖂 info@golfclub-pfaffing.de

Reit im Winkl-Kössen   (1986)

Postfach 1101, 83237 Reit im Winkl
- ☎ **(08640) 798250**

Rottaler G&CC   (1972)

Am Fischgartl 2, 84332 Herbertsfelden
- ☎ **(08561) 5969**

Rottbach   (1997)

Weiherhaus 5, 82216 Rottbach
- ☎ **(08135) 93290**
- 🖳 (08135) 932911
- 🖂 info@rottbach.de
- ℗ 18 L 6409 m Par 72
- 👥 U
- ££ €40 (€55)
- 🚗 20km NW of Munich
- 🏠 Thomas Himmel
- 🖳 www.golfanlage-rottbach.de

St Eurach G&LC   (1973)

Eurach 8, 82393 Iffeldorf
- ☎ **(08801) 1332**

Schloss Maxlrain

Freiung 14, 83104 Maxlrain-Tuntenhausen
- ☎ **(08061) 1403**

Sonnenalp   (1976)

Hotel Sonnenalp, 87527 Ofterschwang
- ☎ **(08321) 272181 (Sec)**

Starnberg   (1986)

Uneringerstr, 82319 Starnberg
- ☎ **(08151) 12157**

Tegernseer GC Bad Wiessee   (1958)

Rohbognerhof, 83707 Bad Wiessee
- ☎ **(08022) 8769**
- 🖳 (08022) 82747
- 🖂 info@tegernseer-golf-club.de
- ℗ 18 L 5459 m CR 68.6 SR 130
- 👥 WD–H WE–H before 9.30am
- ££ €60 (€70)
- 🚗 Tegernsee, 50km S of Munich
- 🏠 D Harradine
- 🖳 www.tegernseer-golf-club.de

Tutzing   (1983)

82327 Tutzing-Deixlfurt
- ☎ **(08158) 3600**

Waldegg-Wiggensbach   (1988)

Hof Waldegg, 87487 Wiggensbach
- ☎ **(08370) 93073**
- 🖂 info@golf-wiggensbach.com

Wittelsbacher GC Rohrenfeld-Neuburg   (1988)

Rohrenfeld, 86633 Neuburg/Donau
- ☎ **(08431) 44118**
- 🖳 (08431) 41301
- 🖂 info@wittelsbacher-golf.de
- ℗ 18 L 6350 m SSS 73
- 👥 U H
- ££ €50 (€60)
- 🚗 7km E of Neuburg. 70km NW of Munich
- 🏠 J Dudok van Heel
- 🖳 www.wittelsbacher-golf.de

Wörthsee   (1982)

Gut Schluifeld, 82237 Wörthsee
- ☎ **(08153) 93477-0**
- 🖳 (08153) 93477-40
- 🖂 info@golfclub-woerthsee.de
- ℗ 18 L 5913 m CR 70.2 SR 118
- 👥 WD–H WE–M
- ££ €60 (€75)
- 🚗 Wörthsee, 20km SW of Munich
- 🏠 Kurt Rossknecht
- 🖳 www.golfclub-woerthsee.de

Nuremberg & North Bavaria

Abenberg   (1988)

Am Golfplatz 19, 91183 Abenberg
- ☎ **(09178) 98960**

Bad Windsheim   (1992)

Am Weinturm 2, 91438 Bad Windsheim
- ☎ **(09841) 5027**
- 🖂 gcbadwindsheim@t-online.de

Bamberg   (1973)

Postfach 1525, 96006 Bamberg
- ☎ **(09547) 7109**
- 🖳 (09547) 7817
- 🖂 leimershof@golfclubbamberg.de
- ℗ 18 L 6175 m SSS 72
- 👥 H
- ££ €35 (€45)
- 🚗 Gut Leimershof, 16km N of Bamberg
- 🏠 Dieter Sziedat
- 🖳 www.golfclubbamberg.de

Donau GC Passau-Rassbach   (1986)

Rassbach 8, 94136 Thyrnau-Passau
- ☎ **(08501) 91313**
- 🖳 (08501) 91314
- 🖂 info@golf-passau.de
- ℗ 24 Par 71
- 👥 U
- ££ €40 (€48)
- 🚗 10km E of Passau
- 🏠 Götz Mecklenburg
- 🖳 www.golf-passau.de

Fränkische Schweiz   (1974)

Kanndorf 8, 91316 Ebermannstadt
- ☎ **(09194) 4827**

Golf Club Fürth e.V.   (1951)

Am Golfplatz 10, 90768 Fürth
- ☎ **(0911) 757522**
- 🖳 (0911) 973 2989
- 🖂 info@golfclub-fuerth.de
- ℗ 18 L 6478 yds SSS 71
- 👥 H tee reservations WE
- ££ €35 (D–€45) 9 holes €20 WD only
- 🚗 10km W of Nuremburg

♔ Dr Bernhard von Limburger (1971)
🖥 www.golfclub-fuerth.de

Gäuboden   (1992)
Gut Fruhstorf, 94330 Aiterhofen
☎ **(09421) 72804**

Hartl Golf Resort Bad Griesbach   (1989)
Holzhäuser 8, 94086 Bad Griesbach
☎ **(08532) 790-0**
🖶 (08532) 790-45
📠 info@hartl.de
🏌 Uttlau 18 L 6115 m SSS 72
    Lederbach 18 L 5998 m SSS 71
    Brunnwies 18 L 6029 m SSS 71
    Beckenbauer 18 L 6500 m SSS 72
    Jaguar 18 L 6037 SSS 71
👥 I H
£€ €39 (€66)
⛳ 28km SW of Passau
♔ Kurt Rossknecht
🖥 www.hartl.de

Hof   (1985)
Postfach 1324, 95012 Hof
☎ **(09281) 470155**

Lauterhofen   (1987)
Ruppertslohe 18, 92283 Lauterhofen
☎ **(09186) 1574**

Lichtenau-Weickershof   (1980)
Weickershof 1, 91586 Lichtenau
☎ **(09827) 92040**

Oberfranken Thurnau   (1965)
Postfach 1349, 95304 Kulmbach
☎ **(09228) 319**

Oberpfälzer Wald G&LC   (1977)
Ödengrub, 92431 Kemnath bei Fuhrn
☎ **(09439) 466**

Oberzwieselau   (1990)
94227 Lindberg
☎ **(01049) 9922/2367**

Regensburg   (1966)
93093 Jagdschloss Thiergarten
☎ **(09403) 505**
🖶 (09403) 4391
📠 gcregensburg@freenet.de
🏌 18 L 5734 m CR 71.5 SR 138
👥 U H
£€ €45 (€60)
⛳ 14km E of Regensburg, nr Walhalla
♔ Harradine/Himmel
🖥 www.golfclub-regensburg.de

Regensburg-Sinzing
Minoritenhof 1, 93161 Sinzing
☎ **(0941) 32504**

Am Reichswald   (1960)
Schiestlstr 100, 90427 Nürnberg
☎ **(0911) 305730**
🖶 (0911) 301200
📠 info@golfclub-nurnberg.de
🏌 18 L 6041 m CR 71.8 SR 129
👥 U H
£€ €50 (€65)
⛳ 10km N of Nuremberg
♔ Dr Bernhard von Limburger/Thomas Himmel

Sagmühle   (1984)
Golfplatz Sagmühle 1, 94086 Bad Griesbach
☎ **(08532) 2038**

Schloss Fahrenbach   (1993)
95709 Tröstau
☎ **(09232) 882-256**

Schloss Reichmannsdorf   (1991)
Schlosshof 4, 96132 Schlüsselfeld
☎ **(09546) 9215-10**
🖶 (09546) 9215-20
📠 info@golfanlage-reichmannsdorf.de
🏌 18 L 5800 m CR 70.8 SR 128
👥 H
£€ €30 (€35)
⛳ 7km from Schlüsselfeld
🖥 www.golfanlage-reichmannsdorf.de

Schlossberg   (1985)
Grünbach 8, 94419 Reisbach
☎ **(08734) 7035**

Schwanhof   (1994)
Klaus Conrad Allee 1, 92706 Luhe-Wildenau
☎ **(09607) 92020**

Die Wutzschleife   (1997)
Hillstraße 40, 92444 Rötz
☎ **(09976) 18460**
🖶 (09976) 18180
📠 info@golfanlage-wutzschleife.de
🏌 18 L 4728 m Par 65
👥 U
£€ €15.50–€31 (€18–€36)
⛳ 70km N of Regensburg. 180km NE of Munich
♔ Deutsche Golf Consult
🖥 www.golfanlage-wutzschleife.de

Rhineland North

Aachen   (1927)
Schurzelter Str 300, 52074 Aachen
☎ **(0241) 12501**
🖶 (0241) 171075

📠 info@agc-ev.de
🏌 18 L 6063 m Par 72
👥 H
£€ €50 (€60)
⛳ Seffent, 5km NW of Aachen
♔ Murray/Morrison/Pennink
🖥 www.aachener-golfclub.de

Ahaus   (1982)
Schmäinghook 36, 48683 Ahaus-Alstätte
☎ **(02567) 405**
🖶 (02567) 3524
📠 info@aglc-ahaus.de
🏌 27 hole course
    9 hole course
👥 U H
£€ €50 (€70)
⛳ 60km W of Münster
♔ Deutsche Golf Consult
🖥 www.glc-ahaus.de

Alten Fliess   (1995)
Am Alten Fliess 66, 50129 Bergheim
☎ **(02238) 94410**

Artland   (1988)
Westerholte 23, 49577 Ankum
☎ **(05466) 301**

Bergisch-Land
Siebeneickerst 386, 42111 Wuppertal
☎ **(02053) 7177**

Bochum   (1982)
Im Mailand 127, 44797 Bochum
☎ **(0234) 799832**

Castrop-Rauxel
Dortmunder Str 383, 44577 Castrop-Rauxel
☎ **(02305) 62027**

Dortmund   (1956)
Reichmarkstr 12, 44265 Dortmund
☎ **(0231) 774133/774609**

Düsseldorfer   (1961)
Rommeljansweg 12, D-40882 Ratingen
☎ **0049 (0) 2102 81092**
🖶 0049 (0) 2102 81782
📠 info@duesseldorfer-golf-club.de
🏌 18 holes: Medal tee: 5781 m
    Par 71 CR 70.8 SR 131
    ladies tee: L 5105 m Par 71
    CR 72.4 SR 126
👥 WD–U WE–M
£€ €60
⛳ 11km from Düsseldorf. Take A44 in direction of Ratingen until junction Ratingen Ost then follow signs for Ratingen
♔ FW Hawtree
🖥 www.duesseldorfer-golf-club.de

Elfrather Mühle   (1991)
An der Elfrather Mühle 145, 47802 Krefeld
☎ **(02151) 4969-0**

Erftaue (1991)

Zur Mühlenerft 1, 41517 Grevenbroich
☎ **(02181) 280637**
🖥 (02181) 280639
📧 gc.erftaue@t-online.de
🏤 18 L 6003 m Par 72 CR 71.2 SR 126
👥 WD–H WE–H after 1pm
££ €40 (€50)
🚗 25km SW of Düsseldorf
🏠 Karl Grohs
🖥 www.golf-erftaue.de

Essen Haus Oefte (1959)

Laupendahler Landstr, 45219 Essen-Kettwig
☎ **(02054) 83911**

Euregio Bad Bentheim

(1987)
Postbox 1205, Am Hauptelick 8, 48443 Bad Bentheim
☎ **(05922) 7776-0**

Golf- und Landclub Schmitzhof (1975)

Arsbeckerstr 160, 41844 Wegberg
☎ **(02436) 39090**
🖥 (02436) 390915
📧 info@golfclubschmitzhof.de
🏤 18 L 6115 m CR 71.6 SR 132
👥 H
££ €40 (€50)
🚗 Wegberg-Merbeck, 20km SW of Mönchengladbach
🏠 Don Harradine
🖥 www.golfclubschmitzhof.de

Grevenmühle Ratingen

(1988)
Grevenmühle, 40882 Ratingen-Homberg
☎ **(02102) 9595-0**

Haus Bey (1992)

An Haus bey 16, 41334 Nettetal
☎ **(02153) 9197-0**
🖥 (02153) 919750
📧 info@hausbey.de
🏤 18 L 5948 m CR 71.8 SR 122
👥 U H(30)
££ €50 (€60)
🚗 40km NW of Düsseldorf
🏠 Paul Krings
🖥 www.hausbey.de

Haus Kambach (1989)

Kambachstrasse 9-13, 52249 Eschweiler-Kinzweiler
☎ **(02403) 50890**
🖥 (02403) 21270
📧 info@golf-kambach.de
🏤 18 L 6178 m SSS 72 CR 71.4 SR 123
👥 U – please contact for tee time reservation
££ €45 (€55)
🚗 20km E of Aachen
🏠 Dieter Sziedat
🖥 www.golf-kambach.de

Hubbelrath (1961)

Bergische Landstr 700, 40629 Düsseldorf
☎ **(02104) 72178/71848**

Hummelbachaue Neuss

(1987)
Norfer Kirchstrasse, 41469 Neuss
☎ **(02137) 91910**

Issum-Niederrhein (1973)

Pauenweg 68, 47661 Issum 1
☎ **(02835) 92310**

Juliana (1979)

Frielinghausen 1, 45549 Sprockhövel
☎ **(02202) 647070/648220**

Golf- and Land-Club Köln e.V. (1906)

Golfplatz 2, 51429 Bergisch Gladbach
☎ **0049 (0) 2204-9276-0**
🖥 0049 (0) 2204-9276-15
📧 info@glckoeln.de
🖊 Andreas Döring (Gen Mgr)
🏤 18 L Men 5980 m, Ladies 5286 m
 Men: white Par 72 CR 72.2 SR 137
 yellow Par 72 CR 71.4 SR 134
 Ladies: black Par 72 CR 74.3 SR 138
 red Par 72 CR 73.4 SR 136
👥 WD–H WE–M
££ €80 (WE members' guests only)
🚗 15km East from Cologne
🏠 Bernhard von Limburger
🖥 www.glckoeln.de

Kosaido International

Am Schmidtberg 11, 40629 Düsseldorf
☎ **(02104) 77060**

Krefeld (1930)

Eltweg 2, 47809 Krefeld
☎ **(02151) 156030**
🖥 (02151) 15603 222
📧 kgc@krefeldergc.de
🏤 18 L 6082 m SSS 72
👥 WD–U H–max 28
££ €45 (€55)
🚗 7km SE of Krefeld. Düsseldorf 16km
🏠 B von Limburger
🖥 www.krefeldergc.de

Mühlenhof G&CC (1990)

Rheinstr., 47546 Kalkar
☎ **(02824) 924092**
🖥 (02824) 924093
📧 awilmsen@muehlenhof.net
🏤 18 L 6103 m Par 72 CR 72.5 SR 125 (men)
 L 5301 m Par 72 CR 74.2 SR 126 (ladies)
👥 U
££ €45 (€50)
🚗 80km N of Düsseldorf (B57)
🏠 Hans Herkberger
🖥 www.muehlenhof.net

Nordkirchen (1974)

Am Golfplatz 6, 59394 Nordkirchen
☎ **(02596) 9191**

Op de Niep (1995)

Bergschenweg 71, 47506 Neukirchen-Vluyn
☎ **(02845) 28051**

Osnabrück (1955)

Sekretariat Herr Thomas Page, Am Golfplatz 3, 49143 Bissendorf
☎ **(05402) 5636**
🖥 (05402) 5257
📧 info@ogc.de
🏤 18 L 5731 m Par 71
👥 U
££ €40 (€60)
🚗 13km SE of Osnabrück
🏠 Frank Pennink
🖥 www.ogc.de

Rheine/Mesum (1998)

Wörstr 201, 48432 Rheine
☎ **(05975) 9490**
📧 info@golfclub-rheine.de

Rittergut Birkhof (1996)

Rittergut Birkhof, 41352 Korschenbroich
☎ **(02131) 510660**

St Barbara's Royal Dortmund (1969)

Hesslingweg, 44309 Dortmund
☎ **(0231) 202551**

Schloss Georghausen

(1962)
Georghausen 8, 51789 Lindlar-Hommerich
☎ **(02207) 4938**
📧 gcschlossgeorghausengolf.de

Schloss Haag (1996)

Bartelter Weg 8, 47608 Geldern
☎ **(02831) 94777**

Schloss Myllendonk (1965)

Myllendonkerstr 113, 41352 Korschenbroich 1
☎ **(02161) 641049**
🖥 (02161) 648806
📧 info@gcsm.de
🏤 18 L 5955 m CR 72.2 SR 133
👥 H
££ €50 (€60)
🚗 1km E of Korschenbroich. 5km E of Mönchengladbach. 20km E of Düsseldorf
🏠 Donald Harradine
🖥 www.gcsm.de

Golfclub Schloss Westerholt e.V.

Schloss Strasse 1, 45701 Herten-Westerholt
☎ **(0209) 620044**
🖥 (0209) 620065

✉ info@gc-westerholt.de
🏠 18 Par 72
Men: yellow L 6052 m CR 71.5 SR 125
white L 6250 m CR 72.6 SR 126
Women: red L 5365 m CR 73.6 SR 125
black L 5534 m CR 74.7 SR 126
👥 H (36) SOC–WD WE–NA
££ €35
🚗 10km Recklinghausen. 20km Essen
🖥 www.gc-westerholt.de

Schwarze Heide
Gahlenerstrasse 44, 46244 Bottrop-Kirchellen
☎ (02045) 82488

Siegen-Olpe (1966)
Am Golfplatz, 57482 Wenden
☎ (02762) 9762-0
🖰 (02762) 9762-12
✉ gcso@ccwsieg.gov.de
🏠 18 L 5959 m CR 71.1 SR 127
👥 U H–max 36
££ €45 (€50)
🚗 20km NW of Siegen
🖥 www.gcso.de

Golfclub Siegerland e.V.
(1993)
Berghäuser Weg, 57223 Kreuztal-Mittelhees
☎ (02732) 59470
🖰 (02732) 594724
✉ info@golfclub-siegerland.de
🏠 18 Par 72
Men: L 5865 m CR 71.0 SR 129
Ladies: L 5162 m CR 72.9 SR 125
👥 H
££ €40 (€45)
🚗 15km N of Siegen
🏠 Spangemacher
🖥 www.golfclub-siegerland.de

Teutoburger Wald
Postfach 1250, 33777 Halle/Westfalen
☎ +49 5201 6279
🖰 +49 5201 6222
✉ info@gctw-halle.de
🏠 27
👥 H
££ €35 (€50)
🏠 Rosknecht
🖥 www.gctw.de

Unna-Fröndenberg
(1985)
Schwarzer Weg 1, 58730 Fröndenberg
☎ (02373) 70068
🖰 (02373) 70069
✉ golf-club-unf@t-online.de
🏠 18 L 6061 m CR 71.2 SR 123
9 hole Par 3 course
👥 M H (max 36)
££ €40 (€50)
🚗 25km W of Dortmund
🏠 Karl Grohs
🖥 www.gcuf.de

Vechta-Welpe (1989)
Welpe 2, 49377 Vechta
☎ (04441) 5539/82168
🖰 (04441) 852480
✉ info@golfclub-vechta-de
🏠 18 L 5957 m Par 72 CR 72.0 SR 133
👥 H
££ €30 (€40)
🚗 50km SW of Bremen
🏠 Rainer Preissmann
🖥 www.golfclub-vechta.de

Velbert – Gut Kuhlendahl
Kuhlendahler Str 283, 42553 Velbert
☎ (02053) 923290
🖰 (02053) 923291
✉ golfclub-velbert@t-online.de
🏠 18 L 5608 m CR 71.1 SR 136 (men)
CR 72.8 SR 129 (ladies)
👥 WD H (36), WE M H (36)
££ €40 (€60)
🚗 Between Düsseldorf and Wuppertal
🏠 Grohs/Preissmann
🖥 www.gcvelbert.de

Golfclub Velderhof
Velderhof, 50259 Pulheim
☎ (02238) 923940
🖰 (02238) 9239400
✉ info@velderhof.de
👥 WD/WE H–36
££ Mon €40, Tue–Fri €55 (€65)
🚗 Köln + Düsseldorf 20km
🏠 Dieter R Sziedal
🖥 www.velderhof.de

Vestischer GC Recklinghausen (1974)
Bockholterstr 475, 45659 Recklinghausen
☎ (02361) 93420
✉ vest.golfclub@t-online.de

Wasserburg Anholt (1972)
Schloss 3, 46419 Isselburg Anholt
☎ (02874) 915120
✉ sekretariat@golfclub-anholt.de

Golfclub Weselerwald
Steenbecksweg 12, 46514 Schermbeck
☎ (02856) 91370
🖰 (02856) 913715
✉ info@gcww.de
🏠 18 Par 72
Men: L 6047 m CR 71.8 SR 127
Women: L 5274m CR 74.1 SR 124
👥 U H WE–M
££ €40 (€55)
🚗 10km Wesel. 60km Düsseldorf
🖥 www.gcww.de

West Rhine (1956)
Javelin Barracks, BFPO 35
☎ +49 2163 974463
🖰 +49 2163 80049
✉ westrhinegolfclub@yahoo.co.uk
✏ Maj (Retd) VJ Chaszczewski

🏠 18 L 6522 yds SSS 71
👥 WD–U WE–M
££ €35 (€40)
🚗 On B230, 1km from Dutch/German border. 25km W of Mönchengladbach
🖥 www.westrhinegc.co.uk

Westerwald (1979)
Steinebacherstr, 57629 Dreifelden
☎ (02666) 8220

Rhineland South

Bad Neuenahr G&LC
(1979)
Remagener Weg, 53474 Bad Neuenahr-Ahrweiler
☎ (02641) 950950

Golf-Resort Bitburger Land
(1993)
Zur Weilersheck 1, 54636 Wissmannsdorf
☎ (06527) 9272-0
🖰 (06527) 9272-30
✉ info@bitgolf.de
🏠 18 L 6104 m Par 72 SR 133
👥 H
££ €40 (€50)
🚗 25km NE of Trier. 40km NE of Luxembourg
🏠 Karl Grohs
🖥 www.bitgolf.de

Bonn-Godesberg in Wachtberg (1960)
Landgrabenweg, 53343 Wachtberg-Niederbachen
☎ (0228) 344003

Burg Overbach (1984)
Postfach 1213, 53799 Much
☎ (02245) 5550
🖰 (02245) 8247
🏠 18 L 5913 m SSS 72
👥 H
££ €40 (€50)
🚗 Much, 45km E of Cologne, off A4
🏠 Deutsch Golf Consult
🖥 www.golfclub-burg-overbach.de

Burg Zievel (1994)
Burg Zievel, 53894 Mechernich
☎ (02256) 1651

Eifel (1977)
Kölner Str, 54576 Hillesheim
☎ (06593) 1241

Gut Heckenhof (1993)
53783 Eitorf
☎ (02243) 9232-0
🖰 (02243) 923299
✉ info@gut-heckenhof.de
🏠 27 L 6214 m SSS 72

H
€€ €45 (€55)
⚒ 40km SE of Cologne
🏠 William Amick
🖳 www.gut-heckenhof.de

Internationaler GC Bonn
(1992)
Gut Grossenbusch, 53757 St Augustin
☎ (02241) 39880
🖳 (02241) 398888
📧 info@gcbonn.de
⮞ 18 L 5927 m Par 72
⚒ U H
€€ €45 (€60)
⚒ 6km E of Bonn
🏠 Karl Grohs
🖳 www.golf-course-bonn.de

Jakobsberg   (1990)
Im Tal der Loreley, 56154 Boppard
☎ (06742) 808491
🖳 (06742) 808493
📧 golf@jakobsberg.de
⮞ 18 L 5950 m Par 72 SSS 72
⚒ U
€€ €45 (€60)
⚒ 80km N of Mainz
🏠 Wolfgang Jersombek
🖳 www.jakobsberg.de

Kyllburger Waldeifel
Lietzenhof, 54597 Burbach
☎ (06553) 961039

Mittelrheinischer Bad Ems
(1938)
Denzerheide, 56130 Bad Ems
☎ (02603) 6541

Nahetal   (1971)
Drei Buchen, 55583 Bad Münster am Stein
☎ (06708) 2145

Stromberg-Schindeldorf
(1987)
*Park Village Golfanlagen, Buchenring 6,
55442 Stromberg*
☎ (06724) 93080

Trier   (1977)
54340 Ensch-Birkenheck
☎ (06507) 993255
🖳 (06507) 993257
📧 info@golf-club-trier-de
⮞ 18 L 6069 m Par 72
⚒ H–max 36
€€ €40 (€50)
⚒ Trier 20km. Koblenz 80km.
   Highway H1, exit 'Föhren'
🖳 www.golf-club-trier.de

Waldbrunnen   (1983)
Brunnenstr 11, 53578 Windhagen
☎ (02645) 8041
🖳 (02645) 8042
📧 info@golfclub-waldbrunnen.de

⮞ 18 L 5787 m Par 71
⚒ U
€€ €30 before 10am €40 after 10am
   (€50)
⚒ 30km S of Bonn/Cologne
🏠 Donald Harradine
🖳 www.golfclub-waldebrunnen.de

Wiesensee   (1992)
*Am Wiesensee, 56459 Westerburg-
Stahlhofen*
☎ (02663) 991192
🖳 (02663) 991193
📧 golfclub.wiesensee@lindner.de
⮞ 18 L 5917 m Par 72
   White CR 72.2 SR 130
   Yellow CR 71.3 SR 127
   Black CR 75.3 SR 136
   Red CR 72.8 SR 128
   9 hole Par 3 course
⚒ H
€€ €46 (€55)
⚒ 100km NW of Frankfurt. Cologne
   80KM
🏠 E Bensing
🖳 www.golfclub-wiesensee.de

Saar-Pfalz

Pfalz Neustadt   (1971)
Im Lochbusch, 67435 Neustadt-Geinsheim
☎ (06327) 97420
🖳 (06327) 974218
📧 gc-pfalz@t-online.de
⮞ 18 L 6064 m CR 72.1 SR 130
⚒ U H WE–NA
€€ €40 (€55)
⚒ Geinsheim, 15km SE of Neustadt
   towards Speyer
🏠 B von Limburger
🖳 www.gc-pfalz.de

Saarbrücken   (1961)
*Oberlimbergerweg, 66798 Wallerfangen-
Gisingen*
☎ (06837) 91800/1584
🖳 (06837) 91801
⮞ 18 L 5971 m CR 71.9 SR 130
⚒ H
€€ €45 (€55)
⚒ B406 towards Wallerfangen. 8km
   N of Saarlouis
🏠 Donald Harradine
🖳 www.golfclub-saarbruecken.de

Websweiler Hof   (1991)
Websweiler Hof, 66424 Homburg/Saar
☎ (06841) 7777-60

Westpfalz Schwarzbachtal
(1988)
66509 Rieschweiler
☎ (06336) 6442
🖳 (06336) 6408
📧 egw@golf.de
⮞ 18 L 5599 m Par 70
⚒ H
€€ €35 (€50)

⚒ 40km E of Saarbrücken
🖳 www.gcwestpfalz.de

Woodlawn Golf Course
6792 Ramstein Flugplatz
☎ (06371) 476240

Stuttgart & South West

Bad Liebenzell
Golfplatz 1-9, 75378 Bad Liebenzell
☎ (07052) 9325-0

Bad Rappenau   (1989)
*Ehrenbergstrasse 25a, 74906
Bad Rappenau*
☎ (07264) 3666

Bad Salgau   (1995)
Koppelweg 103, 88348 Bad Salgau
☎ (07581) 527459
🖳 (07581) 527487
📧 info@gc-bs.de
⮞ 18 L 6190 m CR 71.6 SR 124
⚒ U
€€ €35 (€45)
⚒ 5km SW of Bad Salgau
🖳 www.gc-bs.de

Baden Hills GC Rastatt
(1982)
Cabot Trail G208, 77836 Rheinmünster
☎ (07229) 661501

Baden-Baden   (1901)
Fremersbergstr 127, 76530 Baden-Baden
☎ (07221) 23579

GC Bodensee Weissenberg
e.V.   (1986)
Lampertsweiler 51, D-88138 Weissensberg
☎ +41 (8389) 89190
🖳 +41 (8389) 923907
📧 info@gcbw.de
⮞ Champs: 18 L 6079 m CR 73.4 SR
   143
   Men: 18 L 5858 m CR 71.2 SR 141
   Champs L: 18 L 5373 m CR 75.4
   SR 137
   Ladies: 18 L 5185 m CR 74.3 SR
   137
⚒ WD–H 36 WE–H 35 WD+WE
   teetime reservations obligatory
€€ €56 (€69 + holidays)
⚒ 5km NE of Lindau, Lake Constance
   (Bodensee)
🏠 Robert Trent Jones Sr
🖳 www.gcbw.de

Freiburg   (1970)
Krüttweg 1, 79199 Kirchzarten
☎ (07661) 9847-0
🖳 (07661) 984747
📧 fgc@freiburger-golfclub.de
⮞ 18 L 5945 m CR 71.8 SR 127

⑳ H
££ €43 (€50)
⚬ Freiburg-Kappel/Kirchzarten
⌂ B von Limburger
▣ www.freiburger-golfclub.de

Fürstlicher Golfclub Waldsee (1998)

Hopfenweiler, 88339 Bad Waldsee
☎ (07524) 4017 200

Hechingen Hohenzollern (1955)

Postfach 1124, 72379 Hechingen
☎ (07471) 6478
▯ (07471) 14776
✉ info@golfclub-hechingen.de
▷ 18 holes SSS 72
126/124 men; 125/122 ladies
⑳ U H
££ On application
⚬ Hechingen, 50km S of Stuttgart
⌂ Bernhard von Limbürger,
Götz Mecklenbürg
▣ www.golfclub-hechingen.de

Heidelberg-Lobenfeld (1968)

Biddersbacherhof, 74931 Lobbach-Lobenfeld
☎ (06226) 952110
▯ (06226) 952111
✉ golf@gc-heidelberg-lobenfeld.de
▷ 18 L 5989 m SSS 72
⑳ WD–H WE–M H
££ €50 (€60)
⚬ 20km E of Heidelberg
⌂ Donald Harradine
▣ www.gc-heidelberg-lobenfeld.de

Heilbronn-Hohenlohe (1964)

Hofgasse, 74639 Zweiflingen-Friedrichsruhe
☎ (07941) 920810

Hetzenhof

Hetzenhof 7, 73547 Lorch, GERMANY
☎ (07172) 9180-0
▯ (07172) 9180-30
✉ info@golfclub-hetzenhof.de
▷ 27 Holes Par 72 SR 131
6 hole short course
⑳ WD–H WE–M
££ €40 (€50)
⚬ 35km E of Stuttgart Airport, via B29 and B297
⌂ Thomas Himmel
▣ www.golfclub-hetzenhof.de

Hohenstaufen (1959)

Unter den Ramsberg, 73072 Donzdorf-Reichenbach
☎ (07162) 27171
▯ (07162) 25744
✉ gc-hohenstaufen@online.de
▷ 18 L 6540 yds SSS 72
⑳ H
££ €40 (€50)

⚬ 15km E of Goppingen. 45km E of Stuttgart
▣ www.gc-hohenstaufen.de

Kaiserhöhe (1995)

Im Laber 4a, 74747 Ravenstein
☎ (06297) 399
▯ (06297) 599
✉ info@gck.geoid.de
▷ 18 L 6049 m CR 71.5 SR 124 (men)
18 L 5196 m CR 73.4 SR 123 (women)
9 hole Par 3 course
⑳ U H
££ €35 (€50)
⚬ 60km S of Würzburg
⌂ Kurt Rossknecht
▣ www.gck.geoid.de

Golf-Club Konstanz e.V. (1965)

Hofgut Kargegg 1, D-78476 Allensbach-Langenrain
☎ +49 (0) 75 33 93 03 - 0
✉ info@golfclubkonstanz.de

Lindau-Bad Schachen (1954)

Am Schönbühl 5, 88131 Lindau
☎ (08382) 96170
▯ (08382) 961750
✉ info@gc-lindau-bad-schachen.de
▷ 18 L 5776 m Par 71 SSS 71
⑳ H36
££ €55 (€65)
⚬ Nr Lindau, Bodensee
⌂ Kurt Rossknecht
▣ www.gc-lindau-bad-schachen.de

Markgräflerland Kandern (1984)

Feuerbacher Str 35, 79400 Kandern
☎ (07626) 97799-0
▯ (07626) 97799-22
✉ info@gc-mk.com
▷ 18 L 5931 m CR 71.5 SR 131
⑳ WD–H WE–M
££ €70 only by members invitation
⚬ Kandern, 10km N of Lörrach. 14km NW of Basle
⌂ Grohs/Benz
▣ www.golfclub-markgraeferland.com

Neckartal (1974)

Aldinger Str. 975, 70806 Kornwestheim
☎ (07141) 871319
▯ (07141) 81716
✉ info@gc-neckartal.de
▷ 18 L 6159 m Par 73 CR 71.6 SR 127
⑳ WD–U WE–M
££ €45 (€60)
⚬ 5km NE of Stuttgart, nr Kornwestheim
⌂ B von Limburger
▣ www.golf.de/gcneckartal

Nippenburg (1993)

Nippenburg 21, 71701 Schwieberdingen
☎ (07150) 39530

Obere Alp (1989)

Am Golfplatz 1-3, 79780 Stühlingen
☎ (07703) 9203-0

Oberschwaben-Bad Waldsee (1968)

Hopfenweiler 2d, 88339 Bad Waldsee
☎ (07524) 5900

Oeschberghof L & GC (1976)

Golfplatz 1, 78166 Donaueschingen
☎ (0771) 84525

Owingen-Überlingen (1989)

Alte Owinger Str, 88696 Owingen
☎ (07551) 83040
▯ (07551) 830422
✉ welcome@golfclub-owingen.de
▷ Men: 18 L 6179 m CR 73.0 SR 132
Ladies: 18 L 5550 m CR 75.7 SR 130
⑳ H
££ €50 (€65)
⚬ 5km N of Überlingen, nr Lake Konstanz
▣ www.golfclub-owingen.de

Pforzheim Karlshäuser Hof (1987)

Karlshäuser Weg, 75248 Ölbronn-Dürrn
☎ (07237) 9100
▯ (07237) 5161
✉ info@gc-pf.de
▷ 18 hole course SSS 72
⑳ H–max 36
££ €40 (€50)
⚬ 6km N of Pforzheim. 30km E of Karlsruhe
⌂ Reinhold Weishaupt
▣ www.gc-pf.de

Reischenhof (1987)

Industriestrasse 12, 88489 Wain
☎ (07353) 1732
▯ (07373) 3824
▷ 27 L 5998 m CR 71.9 SR 129
⑳ H
££ €45 (€60)
⚬ 30km S of Ulm
⌂ Wolfgang Jersombeck
▣ www.golf.de/gc-reischenhof

Reutlingen-Sonnenbühl (1987)

Im Zerg, 72820 Sonnenbühl
☎ (07128) 92660

Rhein Badenweiler (1971)

79401 Badenweiler
☎ (07632) 7970

Rickenbach   (1979)

Hennematt 20, 79736 Rickenbach
☎ (07765) 777

Schloss Klingenburg-
Günzburg   (1978)

Schloss Klingenburg, 89343 Jettingen-
Scheppach
☎ (08225) 3030

Schloss Langenstein   (1991)

Schloss Langenstein, 78359 Orsingen-
Nenzingen
☎ (07774) 50651
✉ golf-sekretariat@schloss-
langenstein.com

Schloss Liebenstein   (1982)

Postfach 27, 74380 Neckarwestheim
☎ (07133) 9878-0
🖥 (07133) 9878-18
✉ gcliebenstein@uumail.de
▷ 27 L 5890-6361 m SSS 71-73
⛳ U
££ €40 (€50)
⬤ 35km N of Stuttgart
🏠 Donald Harradine/Deutsche Golf
Consult
▤ www.golfclubliebenstein.de

Schloss Weitenburg   (1984)

Sommerhalde 11, 72181 Starzach-Sulzau
☎ (07472) 15050
🖥 (07472) 15051
✉ info@gcsw.de
▷ 18 L 5978 m CR 71.3 SR 123
9 hole course
⛳ 1 or U
££ 9: €15; 18: €50 (€60)
⬤ 50km SW of Stuttgart in Neckar
Valley
🏠 Heinz Fehring
▤ www.gcsw.de

Sinsheim-Buchenauerhof
(1993)

Buchenauerhof 4, 74889 Sinsheim
☎ (07265) 7258
🖥 (07265) 7379
✉ mail@golfclubsinsheim.de
▷ 18 hole course
Yellow: L 5760 m CR 71.1 SR 131
Red: L 5125 m CR 73.2 SR 130
⛳ H
££ €40 (€50)
⬤ 35km S of Heidelberg
🏠 Georg Boehm
▤ www.golfclubsinsheim.de

Steisslingen   (1991)

Brunnenstr 4b, 78256 Steisslingen-Wiechs
☎ (07738) 7196
🖥 (07738) 923297
✉ info@golfclub-steisslingen.de
▷ 18 L 6145 m Par 72
6 hole course
⛳ U
££ €48 (€68)

⬤ 30km N of Konstanz
🏠 Dave Thomas
▤ www.golfclub-steisslingen.de

Stuttgarter Golf-Club
Solitude   (1927)

Schlossfeld, 71297 Mönsheim
☎ (07044) 911 0410
🖥 (07044) 911 0420
✉ info@golfclub-stuttgart.com
▷ Men: 18 L 5949 m Par 72 CR 72 SR
128
Women: 18 L 5335 m Par 72 CR
74.4 SR 125
⛳ WD–H max 26.5 WE–M
££ €45 (€55)
⬤ 30km W of Stuttgart
🏠 B von Limburger
▤ www.golfclub-stuttgart.com

Ulm e.V.   (1963)

Wochenauer Hof 2, 89186 Illerrieden
☎ (07306) 929500
🖥 (07306) 9295025
✉ GolfClubUlm@t-online.de
▷ 18 L 6076 m SSS 72
⛳ H–max 36
££ €48 (€65)
⬤ 15km S of Ulm
🏠 Deutsche Golf Consult
▤ www.GolfClubUlm.de

Greece

Afandou   (1973)

Afandou, Rhodes
☎ (0241) 51255

Corfu   (1972)

PO Box 71, Ropa Valley, 49100 Corfu
☎ (26610) 94220
🖥 (26610) 94221
✉ cfugolf@hol.gr
▷ 18 L 6183 m SSS 72
⛳ U
££ €25–€50
⬤ Ermones Bay, 16km W of Corfu
town
🏠 Donald Harradine
▤ www.corfugolfclub.com

Glyfada   (1962)

PO Box 70116, 166-10 Glyfada, Athens
☎ (01) 894 6459

Hungary

Birdland G&CC   (1991)

Thermal krt.10, 9740 Bükfürdö
☎ (94) 358060

Budapest G&CC

Golf u.1, 2024 Kisoroszi
☎ (1) 36 26 392 465

European Lakes G&CC

Kossuth u.3, 7232 Hencse
☎ (82) 481245
🖥 (82) 481248
✉ info@europeanlakes.com
▷ 18 L 6231 m Par 72
⛳ U
££ €55 (package €80)
⬤ 20km from Kaposvar (SW
Hungary)
🏠 J Dudok van Heel
▤ www.europeanlakes.com

Old Lake

PO Box 127, 2890 Tata-Remeteségpuszta
☎ (34) 587620

Pannonia G&CC   (1996)

Alcsútdoboz, 8087 Mariavölgy
☎ 0036 (22) 594200
🖥 0036 (22) 594205
✉ info@golfclub.hu
▷ 18 L 5969 yds Par 72 CR 72.5 SR
124
Yellow Par 72 CR 71.6 SR 129
⛳ Semi–private H (Golf Assn Card)
££ €58 (€79)
⬤ Outside Budapest 30km
🏠 H Erhardt
▤ www.golfclub.hu

St Lorence G&CC

Pellérdi ut 55, 7634 Pécs
☎ (72) 252844/252142

Iceland

Akureyri   (1935)

PO Box 317, 602 Akureyri
☎ (462) 2974
🖥 (461) 1755
✉ gagolf@simnet.is
▷ 18 L 5783 m Par 71
⛳ U H
££ 3000 Ikr (3800 Ikr)
⬤ 1km from Akureyri (N coast)
🏠 Solnes/Gudmundsson
▤ www.nett.is/ga

Borgarness   (1973)

Hamar, 310 Borgarnes
☎ (345) 437 1663
✉ hamar@gbborgarnes.net

Húsavík   (1967)

PO Box 23, Kötlum, 640 Húsavík
☎ (464) 1000
✉ palmi.palmason@tmd.is

Isafjardar (1978)

PO Box 367, 400 Isafjördur
☎ (456) 5081
✉ gi@snerpa.is

Jökull (1973)

Postholf 67, 355 Olafsvik
☎ (436) 1666

Keilir (1967)

Box 148, 222 Hafnarfjördur
☎ (565) 3360
☐ (565) 2560
✉ keilir@ishoff.is
⮞ 18 L 5449 m Par 71
9 L 2748 m Par 36
👥 U H (36)
££ 9: 2000 Ikr 18: 4000 Ikr
⛳ Hafnarfjördur, 10km S of Reykjavik
🏠 Hannes Thorsteinsson
▦ www.keilir.is

Kopavogs og Gardabaejar
(1994)

Postholf 214, 212 Gardabaer
☎ (+354) 565 7373
☐ (+354) 565 9190
✉ gkg@gkg.is
⮞ 18 L 5347 m Par 70 CR 70.9 SR 133
👥 WD–H 16:00–20:00 WD–U before 14:00 WE–U after 14:00
££ 4,500 ikr (4,500 ikr)
⛳ Gardabaer, S of Reykjavik
🏠 Jan Sederholm (Sweden), Andres Godmundsson (Iceland)
▦ www.gkg.is

Leynir (1965)

PO Box 9, Akranes
☎ (00354) 431 2771
(00354) 863 4985
☐ (00354) 431 3711
✉ leynir@simnet.is
⮞ 18 L 6006 m Par 72 SR 137
👥 U
££ 3500lkr
⛳ 2km from Akranes (SW coast)
🏠 H Thorsteinsson
▦ www.golf.is/gl   www.leynir.is

Ness-Nesklúbburinn
(1964)

PO Box 66, 172 Seltjarnarnes
☎ (561) 1930
☐ (561) 1966
✉ nk@centrum.is
⮞ 9 L 5396 m Par 72 CR 71.2 SR 121
👥 U
££ 2500 lkr before 13.00; 3500 lkr after 13.00 and WE
⛳ 3km W of Reykjavik
▦ www.golf.is/nk

Oddafellowa (1990)

Urridavatnsdölum, 210 Gardabaer
☎ (565) 9094

Olafsfjardar (1968)

Skeggjabrekku, 625 Olafsfjördur
☎ (466) 2611

Reykjavíkur (1934)

Grafarholt, 112 Reykjavík
☎ +354 (585) 0200/0210
☐ +354 (585) 0201
✉ gr@grgolf.is
⮞ 18 L 6030 m Par 71
18 L 6001 m Par 71
9 L 3522 m Par 32
👥 U H
££ 4000–5500kr
⛳ 10km E of Reykjavík
🏠 Skjold/Thorsteinsson
▦ www.grgolf.is

Saudárkróks (1970)

Hlidarendi, Postholf 56, 550 Saudárkrókur
☎ (453) 5075

Sudurnesja (1964)

PO Box 112, 232 Keflavik
☎ (421) 4100

Vestmannaeyja (1938)

Postholf 168, 902 Vestmannaeyar
☎ (481) 2363

Italy

Como/Milan/Bergamo

Ambrosiano (1994)

Cascina Bertacca, 20080 Bubbiano-Milan
☎ (0290) 840820
☐ (0290) 849365
✉ info@golfclubambrosiano.com
⮞ 18 L 6047 m Par 72
👥 U
££ €37 (€60)
⛳ 25km SW of Milan
🏠 Cornish/Silva
▦ www.golfclubambrosiano.com

Barlassina CC (1956)

Via Privata Golf 42, 20030 Birago di Camnago (MI)
☎ (0362) 560621/2
☐ (0362) 560934
✉ bccgolf@libero.it
⮞ 18 L 6197 m SSS 72
👥 WD–U
££ €60 (€100)
⛳ 22km N of Milan
🏠 D Harradine

Bergamo L'Albenza (1961)

Via Longoni 12, 24030 Almenno S. Bartolomeo (BG)
☎ (035) 640028

Bogogno (1996)

Via Sant'Isidoro 1, 28010 Bogogno
☎ (0322) 863794
✉ info@circologolfbogogno.com

Brianza (1996)

Cascina Cazzu, 20040 Usmate Velate (Mi)
☎ (039) 682 9089/079
☐ (039) 682 9059
✉ brianzagolf@tin.it
⮞ 18 L 5709 m Par 72 SSS 71
👥 U
££ €42 (€58)
⛳ 24km NE of Milan. Monza 6km
🏠 Marco Croze
▦ www.brianzagolf.it

Carimate (1962)

Via Airoldi 2, 22060 Carimate (CO)
☎ (031) 790226
☐ (031) 791927
✉ golfcarimate@virgilio.it
⮞ 18 L 6021 m SSS 71 SR 1290
👥 U H
££ €45 (€65)
⛳ 15km from Como. 20km from Milan
🏠 Piero Mancinelli
▦ www.golfcarimate.it

Castelconturbia (1984)

Via Suno, 28010 Agrate Conturbia
☎ (0322) 832093
☐ (0322) 832428
✉ castelconturbia@tin.it
⮞ Red 9 L 3330 m Par 36
Yellow 9 L 3070 m Par 36
Blue 9 L 3210 m Par 36
👥 WD–H WE–M H
££ €66 (€102)
⛳ 23km N of Novara. Milan 60 km
🏠 Robert Trent Jones Sr
▦ www.golfclubcastelconturbia.it

Castello di Tolcinasco
(1993)

20090 Pieve Emanuele (MI)
☎ (02) 9042 8035
☐ (02) 9078 9051
✉ golf@golftolcinasco.it
⮞ 27 L 6253–6322 m Par 72
9 hole Par 3 course
👥 U
££ €45 (€80)
⛳ 12km S of Milan
🏠 Arnold Palmer
▦ www.golftolcinasco.it

Franciacorta (1986)

Via Provinciale 34b, 25040 Nigoline di Corte Franca, (Brescia)
☎ (030) 984167
☐ (030) 984393
✉ franciacortagolfclub@libero.it
⮞ 18 L 5924 m Par 72 SSS 72
9 hole Par 3 course
👥 WD-U WE–NA before 2pm
££ €45 (€65)

⚘ Nigoline, 25km E of Bergamo,
   Autostrada A4 exit Rovato
🏠 Dye/Croze

Menaggio & Cadenabbia
   (1907)
Via Golf 12, 22010 Grandola E Uniti
☎ **(0344) 32103**
📠 (0344) 30780
✉ segretaria@golfclubmenaggio.it
⛳ 18 L 5455 m Par 70 CR 68.8 SR
   122
👥 WD–H WE–H restricted
££ €55 (€70)
⚘ 5km W of Menaggio. 40km N of
   Como
🏠 John Harris
🖥 www.menaggio.it

Milano   (1928)
20052 Parco di Monza (MI)
☎ **(039) 303081/2/3**

Molinetto CC   (1982)
*SS Padana Superiore 11, 20063 Cernusco
S/N (MI)*
☎ **(02) 9210 5128/9210 5983**

Monticello   (1975)
Via Volta 4, 22070 Cassina Rizzardi
☎ **(031) 928055**

La Pinetina   (1971)
Via al Golf 4, 22070 Appiano Gentile (CO)
☎ **(031) 933202**
📠 (031) 890342
✉ info@golfpinetina.it
⛳ 18 L 5754 m Par 70
   Men: white CR70.8; yellow CR
   69.6
   Women: white CR 72.5; yellow CR
   70.9
👥 WD–U WE–booking necessary –
   H
££ €54 (€78)
⚘ 25m SW of Como. Milan 30m
🏠 Harris/ Albertini/Mezzacane
🖥 www.golfpinetina.it

Le Robinie   (1992)
*Via per Busto Arsizio 9, 21058 Solbiate
Olona (VA)*
☎ **(039) 331 329260**
📠 (039) 331 329266
✉ info@lerobinie.com
⛳ 18 L 6250 m Par 72 SSS 74
👥 WD–H WE–H
££ €46 (€67)
⚘ 25km NW of Milan. Malpensa
   Airport 6km
🏠 Jack Nicklaus
🖥 www.lerobinie.com

La Rossera   (1970)
Via Montebello 4, 24060 Chiuduno
☎ **(035) 838600**
📠 (035) 442 7047
✉ golfrossera@libero.it

⛳ 9 L 2510 m SSS 68
👥 U
££ €30 (€45)
⚘ 2km from Chiuduno. 18km SE of
   Bergamo

Le Rovedine   (1978)
*Via Karl Marx, 20090 Noverasco di
Opera (Mi)*
☎ **(02) 5760 6420**
✉ info@rovedine.com

Varese   (1934)
Via Vittorio Veneto 32, 21020 Luvinate (VA)
☎ **(0332) 227394/229302**

Vigevano   (1974)
Via Chitola 49, 27029 Vigevano (PV)
☎ **(0381) 346628/346077**

Villa D'Este   (1926)
Via Cantù 13, 22030 Montorfano (CO)
☎ **(031) 200200**
📠 (031) 200786
✉ golf.villadeste@tin.it
⛳ 18 L 5727 m Par 69
   White CR 71.0 SR 130
   Yellow CR 70.0 SR 129
   Black CR 72.2 SR 124
   Red CR 71.3 SR 123
👥 U H
££ €60 Italian, €70 foreign (€80
   Italian, €90 foreign)
⚘ Montorfano, 7km SE of Como
🏠 Peter Gannon
🖥 www.golfvilladeste.com

Zoate
20067 Zoate di Tribiano (MI)
☎ **(02) 9063 2183/9063 1861**

Elba

Acquabona   (1971)
57037 Portoferraio, Isola di Elba (LI)
☎ **(0565) 940066**

Emilia Romagna

Adriatic GC Cervia   (1985)
*Via Jelenia Gora No 6, 48016 Cervia-
Milano Marittima*
☎ **(0544) 992786**

Bologna   (1959)
*Via Sabattini 69, 40050 Monte San
Pietro (BO)*
☎ **(051) 969100**

Croara Country Club
   (1976)
Loc. Croara Nuova 23010 Gazzola (PC)
☎ **(0523) 977105**

📠 (0523) 977100
✉ info@croaracountryclub.com
⛳ 18 L 6065 m SSS 72
👥 H
££ €45 (€60)
⚘ 16km SW of Piacenza. 84km SE of
   Milan
🏠 Buratti/Croze
🖥 www.croaracountryclub.com

Matilde di Canossa
   (1987)
*Via Casinazzo 1, 42100 San Bartolomeo,
Reggio Emilia*
☎ **(0522) 371295**
📠 (0522) 371204
✉ golfcanossa@libero.it
⛳ 18 L 6231 m SSS 72
👥 U
££ €35 (€45)
⚘ 50km NW of Bologna
🏠 Marco Croze
🖥 www.tiscali.it/golfcanossa

Modena G&CC   (1987)
*Via Castelnuovo Rangone 4, 41050
Colombaro di Formigine (MO)*
☎ **(059) 553482**
📠 (059) 553696
✉ segretaria@modenagolf.it
⛳ 18 L 6423 m Par 72 SSS 74
   Men: CR 73.6 SR 131 (champ.)
   72.2/128 (am)
   Ladies: CR 74.9 SR 130 (champ.)
   74.9/127 (am)
   9 hole Par 3 course
👥 H
££ €45 (€60)
⚘ Formigine, 10km SW of Modena
🏠 Bernhard Langer and J Jim Engh
🖥 www.modenagolf.it

Golf Club Riolo   (1992)
Via Limisano 10, Riolo Terme (RA)
☎ **(0546) 74035**
📠 (0546) 74076
✉ riologolf@tele2.it
⛳ 18 L 6350 m Par 72
££ €35 (€45)
⚘ 50km SW of Bologna. 15km Imola.
   15km Faenza
🏠 Alberto Croze
🖥 www.riologolf.it

La Rocca   (1985)
Via Campi 8, 43038 Sala Baganza (PR)
☎ **(0521) 834037**

Gulf of Genoa

Garlenda   (1965)
Via Golf 7, 17033 Garlenda
☎ **(0182) 580012**
📠 (0182) 580561
✉ info@garlendagolf.it
⛳ 18 L 6085 m Par 72 SSS 72
👥 H

££ €58 (€78)
⌖ 7km N of Alassio. Genoa 90km
⌂ John Harris
▤ www.garlendagolf.it

Marigola (1975)
Via Biaggini 5, 19032 Lerici (SP)
☎ (0187) 970193
⌨ (0187) 970193
✉ info@golfmarigola.it
▷ 9 L 2116 m Par 49
☊ U
££ €15 (€20)
⌖ 6km SE of La Spezia
⌂ Franco Marmori
▤ www.golfmarigola.it

Pineta di Arenzano
(1959)
Piazza del Golf 3, 16011 Arenzano (GE)
☎ (010) 911 1817

Rapallo (1930)
Via Mameli 377, 16035 Rapallo (GE)
☎ (0185) 261777

Sanremo–Circolo Golf degli Ulivi (1932)
Via Campo Golf 59, 18038 Sanremo
☎ (0184) 557093
⌨ (0184) 557388
✉ info@golfsanremo.com
▷ 18 L 5203 m SSS 67
Men: CR 68.7 SR 119
Women: CR 71.0 SR 120
☊ U
££ €40 (€60)
⌖ 5km N of Sanremo
⌂ Peter Gannon
▤ www.golfsanremo.com

Versilia (1990)
Via Sipe 100, 55045 Pietrasanta (LU)
☎ (0584) 88 15 74

Lake Garda & Dolomites

Asiago (1967)
Via Meltar 2, 36012 Asiago (VI)
☎ (0424) 462721

Bogliaco (1912)
Via Golf 21, 25088 Toscolano-Maderno
☎ (0365) 643006
⌨ (0365) 643006
✉ golfbogliaco@tin.it
▷ 18 L 4600 m Par 67
CR 64.0 SR 120
☊ H
££ €45 (€52)
⌖ Lake Garda, 40km NE of Brescia
▤ www.bogliaco.com

Ca' degli Ulivi (1988)
Via Ghindare 2, 37010 Marciaga di Costermano (VR)
☎ (045) 725 6463/725 6485

Campo Carlo Magno
(1922)
Golf Hotel, 38084 Madonna di Campiglio (TN)
☎ (0465) 440622

Folgaria (1987)
Loc Costa di Folgaria, 38064 Folgaria (TN)
☎ (0464) 720480

Gardagolf CC (1985)
Via Angelo Omodeo 2, 25080 Soiano Del Lago (BS)
☎ (0365) 674707 (Sec)
⌨ (0365) 674788
✉ info@gardagolf.it
▷ 18 L 6505 m SSS 74
Men: CR 75.0 SR 139
Women: CR 77.3 SR 140
9 L 2758 m Par 36
☊ H (min 36)
££ €70 (€80)
⌖ Lake Garda, 30 km NE of Brescia.
⌂ Cotton/Pennink/Steel
▤ www.gardagolf.it

Karersee-Carezza
Loc Carezza 171, 39056 Welschofen-Nova Levante
☎ (0471) 612200

Petersberg (1987)
Unterwinkel 5, 39040 Petersberg (BZ)
☎ +39 (0)471 615122
⌨ +39 (0)471 615229
✉ info@golfclubpetersberg.it
▷ 18 L 5800 m Par 71
Men: CR 70.1 SR128
Women: CR 72.0 SR 126
☊ U
££ €59 (€66)
⌖ 35km SE of Bolzano, nr Nova Ponente
⌂ Marco Croze
▤ www.golfclubpetersberg.it

Ponte di Legno (1980)
Corso Milano 36, 25056 Ponte di Legno (BS)
☎ (0364) 900306

Verona (1963)
Ca' del Sale 15, 37066 Sommacampagna
☎ (045) 510060
⌨ (045) 510242
✉ golfverona@libero.it
▷ 18 L 6054 m CR 71.4 SR 124
☊ H
££ €60 (€70)
⌖ 7km W of Verona
⌂ John Harris
▤ www.golfclubverona.com

Naples & South

Napoli (1983)
Via Campiglione 11, 80072 Arco Felice (NA)
☎ (081) 526 4296

Riva Dei Tessali (1971)
74011 Castellaneta
☎ (099) 843 9251

San Michele
Loc Bosco 8/9, 87022 Cetraro (CS)
☎ (0982) 91012
✉ sanmichele@sanmichele.it

Rome & Centre

Castelgandolfo (1987)
Via Santo Spirito 13, 00040 Castelgandolfo
☎ (06) 931 2301/931 3084

Eucalyptus (1988)
Via Cogna 5, 04011 Aprilia (Roma)
☎ (06) 927 46252/926 8120
⌨ (06) 926 8502
✉ info@eucalyptusgolfclub.it
▷ 18 L 6310 m Par 72 SSS 73
☊ WD–U WE–U
££ €30 (€35) low season €40 (€50) high season (Easter, June–Sept)
⌖ 20km S of Rome on Aprilia-Anzio road
⌂ D'Onofrio
▤ www.eucalyptusgolfclub.it

Fioranello
CP 96, 00134 Roma (RM)
☎ (06) 713 8080 - 213
⌨ (06) 713 8212
✉ info@fioranellogolf.it
▷ 18 L 5360 m Par 70
☊ U
££ €54 (€60)
⌖ Rome
⌂ David Mezzacane
▤ www.fioranellogolf.com

Marco Simone (1989)
Via di Marco Simone, 00012 Guidonia (RM)
☎ (0774) 366469

Marediroma
Via Enna 30, 00040 Ardea (RM)
☎ (06) 913 3250
⌨ (06) 913 3592
✉ info@golfmarediroma.it
▷ 9 L 5100 m CR 66.7 SR 112
☊ H
££ €20
⌖ 30km S of Rome
⌂ Leonardo Basili/Paolo Croce
▤ www.golfmarediroma.it

For list of abbreviations, key to symbols and international dialling codes see page 651

Nettuno
Via della Campana 18, 00048
Nettuno (RM)
☎ **(06) 981 9419**

Olgiata   (1961)
Largo Olgiata 15, 00123 Roma
☎ **(06) 308 89141**
🖳 (06) 308 89968
📧 secretaria@olgiatagolfclub.it
⛳ 18 L 6347 m
    9 L 2947 m
🏌 WE–H
££ €60 (€90)
⛴ 19km NW of Rome, nr La Storta
🏠 CK Cotton
🖥 www.olgiatagolfclub.it

Parco de' Medici   (1989)
Viale Salvatore Rebecchini, 00148 Roma
☎ **(06) 655 3477**
🖳 (06) 655 3344
📧 info@sheratongolf.it
⛳ 18 L 6303 m Par 71 SSS 71
    Yellow tees CR 70.7 SR 174
    9 L 2805 m Par 35
🏌 U
££ €70 (€80) Special offers to
    Sheraton guests
⛴ 15km SW of Rome, nr Airport
🏠 Mezzacane/Rebecchini
🖥 www.sheraton.com/golfrome
    www.golfclubparcodemedici.com

Pescara   (1992)
Contrado Cerreto 58, 66010
Miglianico (CH)
☎ **(0871) 959566**

Le Querce
San Martino, 01015 Sutri (VT)
☎ **(0761) 68789**

Roma   (1903)
Via Appia Nuova 716A, 00178 Roma
☎ **(06) 780 3407**

Tarquinia
Loc Pian di Spille, Via degli Alina 271,
01016 Marina Velca/Tarquinia (VT)
☎ **(0766) 812109**

Sardinia

Is Molas   (1975)
CP 49, 09010 Pula
☎ **(070) 924 1013/4**

Pevero GC Costa Smeralda
    (1972)
07020 Porto Cervo
☎ **(0789) 96072/96210/96211**

Sicily

Il Pìcciolo   (1988)
Via Picciolo 1, 95030 Castiglione di Sicilia
☎ **(0942) 986252**
🖳 (0942) 986252
📧 segretia@ilpicciologolf.com
⛳ 18 L 5810 m Par 72 SSS 71
🏌 H SOC WD/WE
££ €55 (€65)
⛴ 18km E of Taormina
🏠 Rota Caremoli
🖥 www.ilpicciologolf.com

Turin & Piemonte

Alpino Di Stresa   (1924)
Viale Golf Panorama 489, 28839
Vezzo (VB)
☎ **(0323) 20642**
🖳 (0323) 208900
📧 info@golfalpino.it
⛳ 9 L 5397 m Par 69
    Men: CR 67.9 SR 131
    Women: CR 69.9 SR122
🏌 WE–WE H
££ 9: €22 (€32) 18: €33 (€50)
⛴ 7km W of Stresa. Milan 80km
🏠 Peter Gannon
🖥 www.golfalpino.it

Biella Le Betulle   (1958)
Valcarozza, 13887 Magnano (BI)
☎ **(015) 679151**
🖳 (015) 679276
📧 info@golfclubbiella.it
⛳ 18 L 6427 m CR 73.1 SR 141
🏌 H
££ €60 (€96)
⛴ 17km SW of Biella
🏠 John Morrison
🖥 www.golfclubbiella.it

Golf Club del Cervino
    (1955)
11021 Breuil- Cervinia (AO)
☎ **+39 0166 949131**
🖳 +39 0166 940700
📧 info@golfcervino.com
⛳ 9 L 4796 m CR 65.0 SR 112
    (18 holes from 2008)
🏌 U
££ €30–€50
⛴ Aosta Valley - 120 km N of Turin
🏠 Donald Harradine/Luigi Rota
    Caremoli
🖥 www.golfcervino.com

Cherasco CC   (1982)
Via Fraschetta 8, 12062 Cherasco (CN)
☎ **(0172) 489772/488489**
🖳 (0172) 488304
📧 info@golfcherasco.com
⛳ 18 L 6050m Par 72 CR 71.4 SR 129
🏌 U
££ €35 (€50)
⛴ Cherasco, 45km S of Turin

🏠 Gianmarco Croze
🖥 www.golfcherasco.com

Claviere   (1923)
Strada Nazionale 45, 10050 Claviere (TO)
☎ **(0122) 878917**

Courmayeur
11013 Courmayeur (AO)
☎ **(0165) 89103**

Cuneo   (1990)
Via degli Angeli 3, 12012 Mellana-
Bóves (CN)
☎ **(0171) 387041**

Le Fronde   (1973)
Via Sant-Agostino 68, 10051 Avigliana (TO)
☎ **(011) 932 8053/0540**

I Girasoli   (1991)
Via Pralormo 315, 10022 Carmagnola (TO)
☎ **(011) 979 5088**
🖳 (011) 979 5228
📧 info@girasoligolf.it
⛳ 18 L 5760 m Par 71
    Men: CR 70.7 SR 132
    Ladies: CR 73.0 SR 122
🏌 H
££ €30 (€40)
⛴ 25km S of Turin
🖥 www.girasoligolf.it

Iles Borromees   (1987)
Loc Motta Rossa, 28833 Brovello
Carpugnino (VB)
☎ **(0323) 929285**
🖳 (0323) 929190
📧 info@golfdesilesborromees.it
⛳ 18 L 6445 m SSS 72
🏌 U
££ €42 (€65)
⛴ 5km S of Stresa. 80km NW of
    Milan
🏠 Marco Croze
🖥 www.golfdesilesborromees.it

Golf dei Laghi   (1993)
Via Trevisani 6, 21028 Travedona
Monate (VA)
☎ **(0332) 978101**

Margara   (1975)
Via Tenuta Margara 5, 15043 Fubine (AL)
☎ **(0131) 778555**

La Margherita
Strada Pralormo 29, Carmagnola (TO)
☎ **(011) 979 5113**
📧 golf.lamargherita@libero.it

Piandisole   (1964)
Via Pineta 1, 28057 Premeno (NO)
☎ **(0323) 587100**

La Serra (1970)
Via Astigliano 42, 15048 Valenza (AL)
☎ **(0131) 954778**
🖳 (0131) 928294
✉ golfclublaserra@tin.it
🏴 9 L 2820 m Par 72 CR 68.6 SR 135
👥 H
££ €26 (€40)
🚗 4km W of Valenza. 7km N of Alessandria
🏠 Migliorini

Sestrieres (1932)
Piazza Agnelli 4, 10058 Sestrieres (TO)
☎ **(0122) 755170/76243**

Stupinigi (1972)
Corso Unione Sovietica 506, 10135 Torino
☎ **(011) 347 2640**

Torino (1924)
Via Agnelli 40, 10070 Fiano Torinese
☎ **(011) 923 5440/923 5670**
🖳 (011) 923 5886
✉ info@circologolftorino.it
🏴 18 L 6054 m (Blue)
18 L 6038 m SSS 72 (Yellow)
👥 U H
££ €72 (€95)
🚗 23km NW of Turin
🏠 Morrison/Croze/Cooke
🖥 www.circologolftorino.it

Vinovo (1986)
Via Stupinigi 182, 10048 Vinovo (TO)
☎ **(011) 965 3880**

Tuscany & Umbria

Casentino (1985)
6 Via Fronzola, 52014 Poppi (Arezzo)
☎ **(0575) 529810**
🖳 (0575) 520167
✉ info@golfclubcasentino.it
✍ Luca Alterini
🏴 9 L 5550 m Par 72
Men CR 70.6 SR 123
Women CR 73.0 SR 131
👥 WD–U WE–H
££ €30 (€35)
🚗 Poppi, 50km SE of Florence. 35kn N of Arezzo
🏠 Brami/Baracchi
🖥 www.golfclubcasentino.it

Castelfalfi G&CC
50050 Montaione (FI)
☎ **(0571) 698093/4**

Circolo Golf Ugolino
(1933)
Strada Chiantigiana 3, 50015 Grassina
☎ **(055) 230 1009/1085**
✉ info@golfugolino.it

Conero GC Sirolo (1987)
Via Betellico 6, 60020 Sirolo (AN)
☎ **(071) 736 0613**

Cosmopolitan G&CC
(1992)
Viale Pisorno 60, 56018 Tirrenia
☎ **(050) 33633**
🖳 (050) 384707
🏴 18 L 6291 m Par 72
Yellow (men) CR71.8 SR 129
Red (ladies) CR 73.8 SR 126
👥 U
££ €55 (€65)
🚗 15km SW of Pisa
🏠 David Mezzacane

Lamborghini-Panicale
(1992)
Loc Soderi 1, 06064 Panicale (PG)
☎ **(075) 837582**

Montecatini (1985)
Via Dei Brogi 5, Loc Pievaccia, 51015 Monsummano Terme
☎ **(0572) 62218**
(+39) 3291 790808 (mobile)

Le Pavoniere (1986)
Via Traversa Il Crocifisso, 59100 Prato
☎ **(0574) 620855**

Perugia (1959)
06074 Santa Sabina-Ellera
☎ **(075) 517 2204**
🖳 (075) 517 2370
✉ segreteria@golfclubperugia.it
🏴 18 L 5735 m Par 70 SSS 72
CR 70.3 SR 123
👥 H
££ €50 (€60)
🚗 6km NW of Perugia
🏠 David Mezzacane
🖥 www.golfclubperugia.it

Poggio dei Medici (1995)
Via San Gavino, 27 - Loc. Cignano, I-50038 Scarperia, (Florence)
☎ **(+39) 055 84350**
✉ info@poggiodeimedici.com

Punta Ala (1964)
Via del Golf 1, 58040 Punta Ala (GR)
☎ **(0564) 922121/922719**

Tirrenia (1968)
Viale San Guido, 56018 Tirrenia (PI)
☎ **(050) 37518**

Venice & North East

Albarella
Isola di Albarella, 45010 Rosolina (RO)
☎ **(0426) 330124**

Ca' della Nave (1986)
Piazza Vittoria 14, 30030 Martellago
☎ **(041) 540 1555**

Cansiglio (1956)
CP 152, 31029 Vittorio Veneto
☎ **(0438) 585398**
🖳 (0438) 585398
✉ golfcansiglio@tin.it
🏴 18 L 6007 m SSS 71 CR 69.8 SR 129
👥 WD–U WE–H
££ €42 (€52)
🚗 21km NE of Vittorio Veneto. 80km NE of Venice
🏠 Trent Jones/Croze
🖥 www.golfclubcansiglio.it

Colli Berici (1986)
Strada Monti Comunali, 36040 Brendola (VI)
☎ **(0444) 601780**

Frassanelle (1990)
35030 Frassanelle di Rovolon (PD)
☎ **(049) 991 0722**
🖳 (049) 991 0691
✉ info@golffrassanelle.it
🏴 18 L 6180 m SSS 72
👥 H
££ €60 (€75)
🚗 20km S of Padova, nr Via dei Colli
🏠 Marco Croze
🖥 www.golffrassanelle.it

Lignano
Via Bonifica 3, 33054 Lignano Sabbiadoro (UD)
☎ **(0431) 428025**

La Montecchia (1989)
Via Montecchia 12, 35030 Selvazzano (PD)
☎ **(049) 805 5550**

Padova (1964)
35050 Valsanzibio di Galzigano Terme (PD)
☎ **(049) 913 0078**
🖳 (049) 913 1193
✉ info@golfpadova.it
🏴 9 L 3001 m Par 36 (Blue)
9 L 3046 m Par 36 (Yellow)
9 L 3049 m Par 36 (Red)
👥 H WD–U WE–M
££ €50 (€58) Low season €60 (€68) High season
🚗 Valsanzibio, 20km S of Padua
🏠 John D Harris (18), Marco Crozo (9)
🖥 www.golfpadova.it

San Floriano-Gorizia (1987)
Castello di San Floriano, 34070 San Floriano del Collio (GO)
☎ **(0481) 884252/884234**

Trieste   (1954)

Via Padriciano 80, 34012 Trieste
☎ **(040) 226159/226270**

Udine   (1971)

*Via dei Faggi 1, Località Villaverde, 33034
Fagagna (UD)*
☎ **(0432) 800418**
🖬 (0432) 801312
✉ info@golfudine.com
🏴 18 L 6088 m Par 72 CR 72.1 SR
129
👥 H
££ €53 (€63)
⛳ 15km NW of Udine
🏠 Marco Croze/John D Harris
🖻 www.golfudine.com

Venezia   (1928)

Strada Vecchia 1, 30126 Alberoni (Venezia)
☎ **(041) 731333**
🖬 (041) 731339
✉ info@circologolfvenezia.it
🏴 18 L 6199 m Par 72
👥 U H
££ €65 (€75)
⛳ Venice Lido
🏠 Cruickshank/Cotton/Croze
🖻 www.circologolfvenezia.it

Villa Condulmer   (1960)

*Via della Croce 3, 31021 Zerman di
Mogliano Veneto*
☎ **(041) 457062**
🖬 (041) 457202
🏴 18 L 5995 m SSS 71
9 hole short course
👥 H
££ €50 (Sun–€60)
⛳ Mogliano Veneto, 17km N of
Venice
🏠 Harris/Croze

Luxembourg

Christnach   (1993)

Am Lahr, 7641 Christnach
☎ **87 83 83**
🖬 87 95 64
✉ gcc@gns.lu
🏴 18 L 5311 m Par 70 CR 70.2
SR 122
9 hole compact course
All training facilities are floodlit
👥 Greencard
££ 9: €30 (€40); 18: €40 (€55)
Driving range & compact course
€12 (€15)
⛳ 25 km E of Luxembourg city
🏠 Volker Päschel
🖻 www.golfclubchristnach.lu

Clervaux   (1992)

Mecherwee, 9748 Eselborn
☎ **92 93 95**

🖬 92 94 51
✉ gcclerv@pt.lu
🏴 18 L 6144 m Par 72
Men: White CR 72.0 SR 133
Yellow CR 70.3˙128
Women: Blue CR 70.9 SR 128
Red CR 70.9 SR 128
👥 H
££ €33 (€45)
⛳ 3km from Clervaux, North
Luxembourg
🏠 Green Concept
🖻 www.golfclervaux.lu

Gaichel

Rue de Eischen, 8469 Gaichel
☎ **39 71 08**

Golf de Luxembourg
(1993)

Domaine de Belenhaff, L-6141 Junglinster
☎ **(00252) 78 00 68-1**
🖬 (00352) 78 71 28
✉ info@golfdeluxembourg.lu
🏴 18 L 6094 m Par 72 CR 73.5 SR
131
👥 U–unrestricted (Green card)
££ €58 (€75)
⛳ 17km NE of Luxembourg City
🏠 Green Concept, Lyon, France
🖻 www.golfdeluxembourg.lu

Grand-Ducal de
Luxembourg   (1936)

1 Route de Trèves, 2633 Senningerberg
☎ **34 00 90-1**
🖬 34 83 91
✉ gcgd@pt.lu
🏴 18 L 5765 m SSS 71
👥 H WD only
££ €50
⛳ 7km N of Luxembourg
🏠 Maj. Simpson and Maj. Symonds
🖻 www.gcgd.lu

Kikuoka Country Club
(1991)

Scheierhaff, L-5412 Canach
☎ **+352 35 61 35**
🖬 +352 35 74 50
✉ playgolf@kikuoka.lu
🏴 18 L 6412 m SSS 73.4 SR 128
👥 H 35 WD H28 WE
££ €70 (€90)
⛳ 15 km from Luxembourg Airport
🏠 Iwao Uematsu
🖻 www.kikuoka.lu

Malta

Royal Malta   (1888)

Marsa LQA 06, Malta
☎ **(356) 21 22 70 19**
✉ info@maltagolf.org

Netherlands

Amsterdam & Noord Holland

Amsterdam Old Course
(1990)

Zwarte Laantje 4, 1099 CE Amsterdam
☎ **(020) 663 1766**
🖬 (020) 663 4621
✉ info@amsterdamoldcourse.nl
🏴 9 L 4925 m SSS 68
👥 WE–H
££ €50
⛳ 5km SE of Amsterdam
🏠 Harry Colt
🖻 www.amsterdamoldcourse.nl

Amsterdamse   (1934)

Bauduinlaan 35, 1047 HK Amsterdam
☎ **(020) 497 7866**
🖬 (020) 497 5966
✉ agc1934@wxs.nl
🏴 18 L 6124 m CR 73.1
👥 WD–H WE–M
££ €55–€65
⛳ 10km W of Amsterdam
🏠 Rolin/Jol
🖻 www.amsterdamsegolfclub.nl

BurgGolf Purmerend
(1989)

Westerweg 60, 1445 AD Purmerend
☎ **(+31) 299 689160**
✉ purmerend@burggolf.nl

Haarlemmermeersche

Spieringweg 745, 2142 ED Cruquius
☎ **(023) 558 9000**

Heemskerkse   (1998)

Communicatieweg 18, 1967 PR Heemskerk
☎ **(0251) 250088**

Kennemer G&CC   (1910)

Kennemerweg 78, 2042 XT Zandvoort
☎ **+31 (0)23 571 2836/8456**
🖬 +31 (0)23 571 9520
✉ kgcc@wxs.nl
🏴 27 holes CR 71.5-73.2
Van Hengel 9 L 2951 m
Pennink 9 L 2916 m
Colt 9 L 2942 m
👥 H WE–NA before 3pm
££ €110
⛳ Zandvoort, 6km W of Haarlem
🏠 Colt/Pennink/Van Hengel
🖻 www.kennemergolf.nl

De Noordhollandse   (1982)

Sluispolderweg 6, 1817 BM Alkmaar
☎ **(072) 515 6807**
🖬 (072) 520 9918
🏴 18 L 5865 m CR 70.6

H 36
££ €39.50–€45 (€49.50–€57.50)
⚐ 2km N of Alkmaar
🏠 Ryks/Dudok van Heel
🖥 www.dnhgc.nl

Olympus (1976)
*Abcouderstraatweg 46, 1105 AA
Amsterdam Zuid-Oost*
☎ (0294) 281241
🖳 (0294) 286347
🏌 18 L 5722 m SSS 71
9 hole par 3/4
👥 U–phone first
££ €37 (€42)
⚐ SE of Amsterdam, nr A2 and AMC
Hospital
🏠 Dudok van Heel/Gerard Jol
🖥 www.olympusgolf.nl

Spaarnwoude (1977)
Het Hoge Land 5, 1981 LT Velsen-Zuid
☎ (023) 538 2708 (club)
(023) 538 5599 (5)
(reservations)

Waterlandse (1990)
*Buikslotermeerdijk 141, 1027
AC Amsterdam*
☎ (020) 636 1040
🖳 (020) 634 3506
🖂 info@golfbaanamsterdam.nl
🏌 18 L 5156 m Par 71
👥 U
££ €30 (€40)
⚐ 5km N of Amsterdam
🖥 www.golfbaanamsterdam.nl

Zaanse (1988)
Zuiderweg 68, 1456 NH Wijdewormer
☎ (0299) 438199
🖳 (0299) 438199
🖂 zaansegolfclub@planet.nl
🏌 9 L 5282 m Par 70
👥 WD–H WE–M
££ €35
⚐ 15km NE of Amsterdam
🏠 Gerard Jol
🖥 www.zaansegolfclub.com

Breda & South West

Brugse Vaart (1993)
Brugse Vaart 10, 4501 NE Oostburg
☎ (0117) 453410
🖳 (0117) 455511
🖂 golfoostburg@hotmail.com
🏌 18 L 6409 m SSS 73
👥 H
££ €45 (€55)
⚐ 15km N of Bruges, nr Knokke,
Belgium
🏠 Bram de Vos/Ron Kirby
🖥 www.golfoostburg.com

Domburgsche (1914)
Schelpweg 26, 4357 BP Domburg
☎ (0118) 586106
🖳 (0118) 586109
🖂 golfdgc@zeelandnet.nl
🏌 9 L 5435 m CR 69 SR 127
👥 H
££ €45–€45 (€45–€50)
⚐ 15km NW of Middelburg
🏠 Alan Ryks
🖥 www.domburgschegolfclub.nl

Efteling (1994)
Veldstraat 6, 5176 NB Kaatsheuvel
☎ (0416) 288389
🖂 golfpark@mail.efteling.nl

Grevelingenhout (1988)
Oudendijk 3, 4311 NA Bruinisse
☎ (0111) 482650

Oosterhoutse (1985)
Dukaatstraat 21, 4903 RN Oosterhout
☎ (0162) 458759
🖳 (0162) 433285
🖂 info@ogcgolf.nl
🏌 18 L 6172 m CR 73.4 SR 137
👥 WD–H WE–M
££ €60
⚐ 10km NE of Breda
🏠 J Dudok van Heel
🖥 www.ogcgolf.nl

Princenbosch (1991)
Bavelseweg 153, 5126 PX Molenschot
☎ (0161) 431811
🖂 info@princenbosch.net

Reymerswael (1986)
Grensweg 21, 4411 ST Rilland Bath
☎ (0113) 551265
🖳 (0113) 551264
🖂 golf@reymerswael.nl
🏌 18 holes Par 71
L 5444 m CR 70.8 SR 123 (men)
L 4885 m CR 72.4 SR 117 (ladies)
👥 H
££ €45 (€50)
⚐ 20km W of Bergen op Zoom.
50km W of Breda, off A58
🏠 Dudok van Heel/Rijks
🖥 www.reymerswael.nl

Toxandria (1928)
Veenstraat 89, 5124 NC Molenschot
☎ (0161) 411200
🖳 (0161) 411715
🖂 bestuur:toxandria.bl
🏌 18 L 5834 m Par 72 CR 70.2 SR
131
👥 WD–I Phone first H
££ €60 (€75)
⚐ 8km E of Breda
🏠 Morrison/Dudok van Heel
🖥 www.toxandria.nl

De Woeste Kop (1986)
Justaasweg 4, 4571 NB Axel
☎ (0115) 564467
🖂 dewoestekop@planet.nl
🏌 18 L 5473 m Par 71 SSS 71
👥 U
££ €40 (€50)
⚐ 45km W of Antwerp
🏠 Paneels/Bosch
🖥 www.dewoestekop.nl

Wouwse Plantage (1981)
*Zoomvlietweg 66, 4624 RP Bergen
op Zoom*
☎ (0165) 377100
🖳 (0165) 377101
🖂 secretariaat@golfwouwseplantage
.nl
🏌 18 L 6162 m CR 72.1 SR 131
👥 H–WD WE Sat only
££ €70
⚐ 10km E of Bergen-op-Zoom, nr
Roosendaal
🏠 Pennink/Rolin
🖥 www.golfwouwseplantage.nl

East Central

Breuninkhof
Bussloselaan 6, 7383 RP Bussloo
☎ (0571) 261955
🖂 carla@unigolf.ni

Edese (1978)
Papendallaan 22, 6816 VD Arnhem
☎ (026) 482 1985
🖳 (026) 482 1348
🖂 info@edesegolf.nl
🏌 18 L 5947 m SSS 70
👥 H
££ €50 (€55)
⚐ National Sportcentrum Papendal.
NW of Arnhem, towards Ede
🏠 Pennink/Dudok van Heel
🖥 www.edesegolf.nl

De Graafschap (1987)
Sluitdijk 4, 7241 RR Lochem
☎ (0573) 254323

Hattemse G&CC (1930)
Veenwal 11, 8051 AS Hattem
☎ (038) 444 1909
🖂 secretariaat@golfclub-hattemse.nl
🏌 9 L 5808 yds SSS 68
👥 WD–H WE–M+H
££ €45
⚐ Hattem, 5km S of Zwolle
🏠 Del Court van Krimpen
🖥 www.golfclub-hattem.nl

Keppelse (1926)
*Oude Zutphenseweg 15, 6997 CH Hoog-
Keppel*
☎ (0314) 301416
🖂 dekeppelse@planet.nl
🏌 9 L 5360 m Par 70

H
££ €30 (€40)
⊶ Hoog-Keppel, 25km E of Arnhem
⌂ JP Eschauzier
🖳 www.keppelse.com

De Koepel   (1983)
Postbox 88, 7640 AB Wierden
☎ (0546) 576150/574070
✉ secretariaat@golfclubdekoepel.nl

Het Rÿk van Nunspeet
(1987)
Plesmanlaan 30, 8072 PT Nunspeet
☎ (0341) 255255
📠 (0341) 255285
✉ info@golfbaanhetrykvannunspeet.nl
🏴 27 L 6100 m Par 72
U
££ €50 (€57.50)
⊶ Nunspeet, 80km E of Amsterdam
⌂ Paul Rolin
🖳 www.golfenophetryk.nl

Rosendaelsche   (1895)
Apeldoornseweg 450, 6816 SN Arnhem
☎ (026) 442 1438
📠 (026) 351 1196
🏴 18 L 6057 m CR 72.3 SR 132
WD–H WE–NA
££ €70
⊶ 5km N of Arnhem on Route N50
⌂ Frank Pennink

Sallandsche De Hoek
(1934)
PO Box 24, 7430 AA Diepenveen
☎ (0570) 593269

Sybrook   (1992)
Veendijk 100, 7525 PZ Enschede
☎ (0541) 530331
📠 (0541) 531690
✉ info@sybrook.nl
🏴 27 L 5806 m Par 72
WD–H WE–M
££ €50
⊶ 10km N of Enschede
⌂ Rolin/Rijks
🖳 www.sybrook.nl

Twentsche   (1926)
Almelosestraat 17, 7495 TG Ambt Delden
☎ (074) 384 1167
📠 (074) 384 1067
✉ info@twentschegolfclub.nl
🏴 18 L 6178 m SSS 72
H
££ €50 (€60)
⊶ 4km N of Delden
⌂ TJ McAuley
🖳 www.twentschegolfclub.nl

Veluwse   (1957)
Nr 57, 7346 AC Hoog Soeren
☎ (055) 519 1275

Welderen   (1994)
Grote Molenstraat 173, 6661 NH Elst
☎ (0481) 376591
📠 (0481) 377055
🏴 18 L 6015 m Par 72
WD–H WE–M
££ €39.50 (WE with member only)
⊶ Elst, S of Arnhem via A325 or A15
⌂ JE Eschauzier
🖳 www.welderen.nl

Eindhoven & South East

Best G&CC   (1988)
Golflaan 1, 5683 RZ Best
☎ (0499) 391443
📠 (0499) 393221
✉ vereniging@bestgolf.nl
🏴 18 L 6079 m CR 71.7 SR 131
H
££ €45 (€55)
⊶ Best, 5km NW of Eindhoven
⌂ J Dudok van Heel
🖳 www.bestgolf.nl

BurgGolf Gendersteyn
Veldhoven   (1994)
Locht 140, 5504 RP Veldhoven
☎ (040) 253 4444
📠 (040) 254 9742
✉ gendersteyn@burggolf.nl
🏴 18 L 5739 m Par 71
7 L 2164 m Par 68
U
££ €47.50 (€57.50)
⊶ 10km SW of Eindhoven
⌂ Alan Rijks
🖳 www.burggolf.nl

Golfclub BurgGolf Wijchen
(1985)
Public
Weg Door de Berendonck 40, 6603
LP Wijchen
☎ (024) 642 0039
📠 (024) 641 1254
✉ wijchen@burggolf.nl
🏴 18 L 5671 m Par 71 SSS 70
9 hole par 3 course
WD/WE–U
££ €47.50 (€57.50)
⊶ 5km SW of Nijmegen
⌂ J Dudok van Heel
🖳 www.burggolf.nl

Crossmoor G&CC   (1986)
Laurabosweg 8, 6006 VR Weert
☎ (0495) 518438
📠 (0495) 518709
✉ crossmoor@planel.nl
🏴 18 L 6043 m Par 72
9 hole Par 3 course
H
££ €50 (€60)
⊶ Weert/Altweertheide, 30km SE of
Eindhoven

⌂ J Dudok van Heel
🖳 www.crossmoor.nl

De Dommel   (1928)
Zegenwerp 12, 5271 NC St Michielsgestel
☎ (073) 551 9168
📠 (073) 551 9441
✉ info@gcdedommel.nl
🏴 18 L 5404 m CR 67.8 SR 119
WD–H WE–NA
££ €50 (€50)
⊶ 10km S of Hertogenbosch
⌂ Colt/Steel
🖳 www.gcdedommel.nl

Eindhovensche Golf
(1930)
Eindhovenseweg 300, 5553
VB Valkenswaard
☎ (040) 201 4816
📠 (040) 207 6177
✉ eg@iae.nl
🏴 18 L 5923 CR 71.9 SR130/6223
CR 72.6 SR 135
H
££ €80 (€80)
⊶ 8km S of Eindhoven
⌂ HS Colt
🖳 www.eindhovenschegolf.nl

Geijsteren G&CC   (1974)
Het Spekt 2, 5862 AZ Geijsteren
☎ (0478) 531809/532592
📠 (0478) 532963
✉ gc.geijsteren@wxl.nl
🏴 18 L 6090 m Par 72
U but phone first (06) 537 22551
££ D–€55 (€60)
⊶ Off A73 Junction 9. N270 to
Wanssum. 25km N of Venlo
⌂ Pennink/Steel
🖳 www.golfclubgeijsteren.nl

Havelte   (1986)
Kolonieweg 2, 7970 AA Havelte
☎ (0521) 342200
📠 (0521) 343152
✉ info@golfclubhavelte.nl
🏴 18 L 5154 m CR 71.8 SR 120
18 L 6027 m CR 71.4 SR 126
H
££ €45 (€55)
⊶ 30km SW of Assen (N371)
⌂ Donald Steel
🖳 www.golfclubhavelte.nl

Haviksoord   (1976)
Maarheezerweg Nrd 11, 5595 XG
Leende (NB)
☎ (040) 206 1818
📠 (040) 206 2761
✉ info@haviksoord.nl
🏴 9 L 5948 m CR 71.1 SR 136
H
££ €37 (€43)
⊶ 10km S of Eindhoven
🖳 www.haviksoord.nl

Herkenbosch (1991)

Stationsweg 100, 6075 CD Herkenbosch
☎ **(0475) 529529**
📠 (0475) 533580
✉ herkenbosch@burggolf.nl
⤷ 18 L 5758 m Par 72
👥 U WD + WE H
££ €55 (€65)
🚗 20km S of Venlo, nr German border
🏠 van Heel
▤ www.gccherkenbosch.nl

Het Rijk van Nijmegen
(1985)

Postweg 17, 6561 KJ Groesbeek
☎ **(024) 397 6644**
📠 (024) 397 6942
✉ info@golfbaanhetrijkvannijmegen.nl
⤷ 18 L 6010 m CR 70.3
18 L 5717 m CR 69.8
👥 H
££ €50 (€57.50) – 2006
🚗 5km E of Nijmegen
🏠 Paul Rolin
▤ www.golfenophetryk.nl

De Peelse Golf (1991)

Maasduinenweg 1, 5977 NP Evertsoord-Sevenum
☎ **(077) 467 8030**
✉ info@depeelsegolf.nl

De Schoot (1973)

Schootsedijk 18, 5491 TD Sint Oedenrode
☎ **(04134) 73011**

Tongelreep G&CC (1984)

Charles Roelslaan 15, 5644 HX Eindhoven
☎ **(040) 252 0962**
✉ gcc@golfdetongelreep.nl

Welschap (1993)

Welschapsedijk 164, 5657 BB Eindhoven
☎ **(040) 251 5797**
✉ secretariaat@golfclubwelschap.nl

Limburg Province

Brunssummerheide
(1985)

Rimburgerweg 50, Brunssum
☎ **(045) 527 0968**

Hoenshuis G&CC (1987)

Hoensweg 17, 6367 GN Voerendaal
☎ **(045) 575 3300**

De Zuid Limburgse G&CC
(1956)

Dalbissenweg 22, 6281 NC Gulpen-Wittem, (GPS: Landsraderweg 2, Gulpen-Wittem)
☎ **(043) 455 1397/1254**
📠 (043) 455 1576

✉ zlgolf@zlgolf.nl
⤷ 18 L 5902 m Par 71
👥 WD–H36 WE–H28–U before 10am – after 3pm
££ €40 (€50)
🚗 Gulpen-Wittem (Mechelen), 25km SE of Maastricht
🏠 Hawtree/Snelder/Rolin
▤ www.zlgolf.nl

North

BurgGolf St Nicobasga
(1990)

Legemeersterweg 16-18, 8527 DS Legemeer
☎ **(0513) 499466**
📠 (0513) 499777
✉ st.nicobasga@burggolf.nl
⤷ 18 L 5765 m SSS 71
👥 H
££ €47.50 (€57.50)
🚗 120km NE of Amsterdam
🏠 Allen Rijks
▤ www.burggolf.nl

Gelpenberg (1970)

Gebbeveenweg 1, 7854 TD Aalden
☎ **(0591) 371929**
📠 (0591) 372422
✉ info@dgcdegelpenberg/nl
⤷ 18 L 6031 m Par 71
👥 H
££ €45 (€55)
🚗 16km W of Emmen
🏠 Pennink/Steel
▤ www.dgcdegelpenberg.nl

Holthuizen (1985)

Oosteinde 7a, 9301 ZP Roden
☎ **(050) 501 5103**
📠 (050) 501 3685
✉ golfclub.holthuizen@planet.nl
⤷ 9 L 6079 m SSS 72
👥 H
££ €20–€30 (€30–€45)
🚗 10km S of Groningen
🏠 Rijks/Eschauzier
▤ www.gc-holthuizen.nl

Lauswolt G&CC (1964)

Van Harinxmaweg 8A, PO Box 36, 9244 ZN Beetsterzwaag
☎ **(0512) 383590**
📠 (0512) 383739
✉ algemeen@golfclublauswolt.nl
⤷ 18 L 6087 m CR 71.5
👥 H
££ €55 (€75)
🚗 Beetsterzwaag, 5km S of Drachten
🏠 Pennink/Steel
▤ www.golfclublauswolt.nl

Noord-Nederlandse G&CC
(1950)

Pollselaan 5, 9756 CJ Glimmen
☎ **(050) 406 2004**

📠 (050) 406 1922
✉ secretariaat@nngcc.nl
⤷ 18 L 5660/4906 m CR 69.9/72.2
👥 H
££ €52.50 (€62.50)
🚗 12km S of Groningen, off A28
🏠 Campbell (1950), Pennick/Steel (1987)
▤ www.nngcc.nl

De Semslanden (1986)

Nieuwe Dijk 1, 9514 BX Gasselternijveen
☎ **(0599) 564661/565531**
✉ semslanden@planet.nl

Rotterdam & The Hague

Broekpolder (1981)

Watersportweg 100, 3138 HD Vlaardingen
☎ **(010) 249 5566**
(010) 249 5555/249 5577
📠 (010) 249 5579
✉ secretariaat@golfclubbroekpolder.nl
⤷ 18 L 6010 m CR 71.7 SR 125
👥 H WE–NA
££ €85 (€115)
🚗 15km W of Rotterdam, off A20
🏠 Frank Pennink/Gerard Jol
▤ www.golfclubbroekpolder.nl

Golf & Country Club Capelle a/d IJssel (1977)

Gravenweg 311, 2905 LB Capelle a/d IJssel
☎ **(010) 442 2485**
📠 (010) 284 0606
✉ info@golfclubcapelle.nl
⤷ 18 L 5220 m CR 67.4 SR 115
👥 WD–U WE–M
££ €50
🚗 5km S of Rotterdam
🏠 Donald Harradine
▤ www.golfclubcapelle.nl

Cromstrijen (1989)

Veerweg 26, 3281 LX Numansdorp
☎ **(0186) 654455**
📠 (0186) 654681
✉ info@golfclubcromstrijen.nl
⤷ 18 L 6107 m Par 72
9 L 3800 m Par 62
👥 H
££ €60 (€70)
🚗 30km S of Rotterdam (A29)
🏠 Tom McAuley
▤ www.golfclubcromstrijen.nl

De Hooge Bergsche
(1989)

Rottebandreef 40, 2661 JK Bergschenhoek
☎ **(010) 522 0052/522 0703**
📠 (08) 422 32305
✉ secretariaat@hoogebergsche.nl
⤷ 18 L 5336 m Par 71 SR 119
👥 U
££ €43.50 (€57.50)

For list of abbreviations, key to symbols and international dialling codes see page 651

&ofo Bergschenhoek, 2km NE of
Rotterdam
🏠 Gerard Jol
🖳 www.hoogebergsche.nl

Koninklijke Haagsche G&CC   (1893)
Groot Haesebroekeseweg 22, 2243 EC Wassenaar
☎ (070) 517 9607
🖳 (070) 514 0171
✉ khaagolf@bart.nl
⏩ 18 L 5674 m Par 72 SR 129
👫 WD–H (max 24) WE–M
££ €100
&ofo 6km N of The Hague
🏠 Allison/Colt
🖳 www.khgcc.nl

Kralingen
Kralingseweg 200, 3062 CG Rotterdam
☎ (010) 452 2283
✉ secretaris@gckralingen.nl
⏩ Men: 9 L 5327 yds CR 66.9 SR 114
Ladies: 9 L 4678 yds CR 67.4 SR 119
👫 H
££ €40 (€50)
&ofo 5km from centre of Rotterdam
🏠 Copijn/Cotton
🖳 www.gckralingen.nl

Leidschendamse Leeuwenbergh   (1988)
Elzenlaan 31, 2495 AZ Den Haag
☎ (070) 395 4556
🖳 (070) 399 8615
✉ secretariaas@leeuwenburgh.nl
⏩ 18 L 5461 m Par 70
👫 H
££ €57.50
&ofo E side of The Hague
🏠 Bernard Jol
🖳 www.leeuwenburgh.nl

De Merwelanden   (1985)
Public
Golfbaan Crayestein, Baanhoekweg 50, 3313 LP Dordrecht
☎ (078) 621 1221

Noordwijkse   (1915)
Randweg 25, PO Box 70, 2200 AB Noordwijk
☎ (0252) 373761
🖳 (0252) 370044
✉ info@noordwijksegolfclub.nl
⏩ 18 L 5810 m CR 71.9 SR 134 (men)
18 L4967 m CR 72.7 SR 126 (women)
👫 WD–H Reservations required
££ €110 (2006 price)
&ofo 5km N of Noordwyk. 15 km NW of Leiden
🏠 Frank Pennink
🖳 www.noordwijksegolfclub.nl

Oude Maas   (1975)
(Rhoon Golfcenter), Veerweg 2a, 3161 EX Rhoon
☎ (010) 501 5135
🖳 (010) 501 5604
✉ golfcluboudemaas@kebelfoon.nl
⏩ 18 L 5481 m Par 71
👫 H
££ €49 (€57.50)
&ofo Rhoon, 10km S of Rotterdam via A15
🏠 Pennink/Jol/Rijks
🖳 www.golfcluboudemaas.nl

Rijswijkse   (1987)
Delftweg 58, 2289 AL Rijswijk
☎ (070) 395 4864
🖳 (070) 399 5040
✉ secretariaat@rijswijksegolf.nl
⏩ 18 L 5681 m Par 71 CR 69.6
👫 H
££ €48 (€63)
&ofo 5km SE of The Hague
🏠 Steel/Rijks
🖳 www.rijswijksegolf.nl

Wassenaarse Golfclub Rozenstein   (1984)
Dr Mansveltkade 15, 2242 TZ Wassenaar
☎ (070) 511 7846
🖳 (070) 511 9302
✉ info@rozenstein.nl
⏩ 18 L 5820 m SSS 70
👫 H
££ €55 (€65)
&ofo 14km NE of The Hague
🏠 Dudok van Heel/Jol
🖳 www.rozenstein.nl

Westerpark Zoetermeer   (1985)
Heuvelweg 3, 2716 DZ Zoetermeer
☎ (079) 351 7283

Zeegersloot   (1984)
Kromme Aarweg 5, PO Box 190, 2400 AD Alphen a/d Rijn
☎ (0172) 474567
🖳 (0172) 494660
✉ secretariaat@zeegersloot.nl
⏩ 18 L 5793 m SSS 70
9 hole Par 3 course
👫 U H
££ 9: €20 (€25) 18: €42 (€60)
&ofo Alphen, 15km N of Gouda. 20km S of Amsterdam
🏠 Gerard Jol
🖳 www.zeegersloot.nl

Utrecht & Hilversum

Almeerderhout   (1986)
Watersnipweg 19-21, 1341 AA Almere
☎ (036) 521 9130

Anderstein
Woudenbergseweg 13a, 3953 ME Maarsbergen
☎ (0343) 431330

De Batouwe   (1990)
Oost Kanaalweg 1, 4011 LA Zoelen
☎ (0344) 624370

Flevoland   (1979)
Farlaan 2A, 8241 BG Lelystad
☎ (0320) 230077
🖳 (0320) 230932
✉ info@golfflevo.nl
⏩ 18 L 5836 m Par 71
👫 WD–U H WE–U+H
££ €30 (€42)
&ofo Polder of Flevoland. 1km NW of Lelystad. 45km N of Hilversum
🏠 JS Eschauzier
🖳 www.golfflevo.nl

De Haar   (1974)
PO Box 104, Parkweg 5, 3450 AC Vleuten
☎ (030) 677 2860

Hilversumsche   (1910)
Soestdijkerstraatweg 172, 1213 XJ Hilversum
☎ (035) 685 7060
🖳 (035) 685 3813
⏩ 18 L 5859 m Par 72 CR 71.2 SR 135
👫 Phone booking necessary H WE-NA
££ €100
&ofo 3km E of Hilversum, nr Baarn
🏠 Burrows/Colt

De Hoge Kleij   (1985)
Appelweg 4, 3832 RK Leusden
☎ (033) 461 6944

Nieuwegeinse   (1985)
Postbus 486, 3437 AL Nieuwegein
☎ (030) 604 2192

Utrechtse Golf Club 'De Pan'   (1894)
Amersfoortseweg 1, 3735 LJ Bosch en Duin
☎ (030) 695 6427
🖳 (030) 696 3769
✉ secretariaat@ugcdepan.nl
⏩ 18 L 5701 m Par 72 CR 70.1 SR 124
👫 WD–M WE–NA
££ €85
&ofo 10km E of Utrecht, off A28
🏠 HS Colt
🖳 www.ugcdepan.nl

Zeewolde   (1984)
Golflaan 1, 3896 LL Zeewolde
☎ (036) 522 2103
🖳 (036) 522 4100
✉ secretariaat@golfclub-zeewolde.nl

For list of abbreviations, key to symbols and international dialling codes see page 651

▷ 27 L 6259 m Par 72
9 hole course Par 58
ⁱⁱ H
£€ €55 (€65)
⇘ 20km N of Hilversum. 60km NE of Amsterdam
⌂ A Rijks
▤ www.golfclub-zeewolde.nl

Norway

Arendal og Omegn (1986)
Nes Verk, 4900 Tvedestrand
☎ 37 19 90 30
⌨ 37 16 02 11
✉ post@arendalgk.no
▷ 18 L 5528 m Par 72
9 hole P&P course
ⁱⁱ U
£€ 350kr (400kr)
⇘ Nes Verk, 20km E of Arendal (E18). 95km NE of Kristiansand
▤ www.arendalgk.no

Baerum (1972)
Hellerudveien 26, 1350 Lommedalen
☎ 67 87 67 00
⌨ 67 87 67 20
✉ bmgk@bmgk.no
▷ 18 L 5300 m Par 71
9 hole short course
ⁱⁱ U H Booking advisable
£€ 400kr (450kr)
⇘ 10km W of Oslo. 10km N of Sandvika
⌂ Jeremy Turner
▤ www.bmgk.no

Bergen (1937)
Erikveien 120, 5080 Eidsvåg
☎ 05 18 20 77

Borre (1991)
Semb Hovedgaard, 3186 Horten
☎ 416 27000
⌨ 33 07 15 16
✉ borregb@online.no
▷ 18 L 6265 m Par 72 CR 73.7
9 L 2927 m Par 36 CR 72.1
ⁱⁱ
£€ 9: D–300kr 18: 400kr (450kr)
⇘ In Horten, 50km S of Drammen. 100km SW of Oslo. 30kn N Torp Airport
⌂ T Nordström
▤ wwww.borregb.no

Borregaard (1927)
PO Box 348, 1702 Sarpsborg
☎ 69 12 15 00
✉ borregaardgk@golf.no

Drøbak (1988)
Belsjøveien 50, 1440 Drøbak
☎ 64 98 96 40

Elverum (1980)
PO Box 71, 2401 Elverum
☎ 62 41 35 88
⌨ 62 41 55 13
✉ post@elverumgolf.no
▷ 18 L 5845 m Par 72
ⁱⁱ U
£€ 250kr (350kr)
⇘ Starmoen Fritidspark, 10km E of Elverum. 35km E of Hamar. 150km N of Oslo
▤ www.elverumgolf.no

Grenland (1976)
Luksefjellvn 578, 3721 Skien
☎ 35 50 62 70
⌨ 35 59 06 10
✉ post@grenlandgolf.no
▷ 18 L 5777 m Par 72
ⁱⁱ U
£€ 325kr (375kr)
⇘ 6km from Skien
⌂ Jan Sederholm/Tor Eia
▤ www.grenlandgolf.no

Groruddalen (1988)
Postboks 37, Stovner, 0913 Oslo
☎ 22 79 05 60
⌨ 22 79 05 79
✉ post@grorudgk.no
▷ 9 L 2844 m CR 58.2 SR 101
ⁱⁱ U
£€ 200kr
⇘ 15km N of Oslo
⌂ Leif Nilsson
▤ www.grorudgk.no

Hemsedal (1994)
3560 Hemsedal
☎ 32 06 23 77

Kjekstad (1976)
PO Box 201, 3440 Royken
☎ 31 29 79 90

Kristiansand (2003)
PO Box 6090 Søm, 4691 Kristiansand
☎ 38 14 85 60
⌨ 38 04 34 15
✉ post@kristiansandgk.no
▷ 9 L 2488 m SSS 72 CR 68.6 SR 133
ⁱⁱ U
£€ D–250Nkr (D–250 Nkr)
⇘ 8 km E of Kristiansand (E18)
⌂ Nils Skøld
▤ www.kristiansandgk.no

Larvik (1989)
Fritzøe Gård, 3267 Larvik
☎ 33 14 01 45
⌨ 33 14 01 49
✉ klubben@larvikgolf.no
▷ 18 L 6147 m Par 72
ⁱⁱ U
£€ 400kr (450kr)
⇘ 3km S of Larvik on R301 to Stavern
⌂ Jan Sederholm
▤ www.larvikgolf.no

Narvik (1992)
8523 Elvegard
☎ 76 95 12 01

Nes (1988)
Rommen Golfpark, 2160 Vormsund
☎ 63 91 20 30
⌨ 63 91 20 31
✉ bente@nesgolfklubb.no
▷ 18 L 5962 m CR 71.5 SR 128
ⁱⁱ H or Green card
£€ 280kr (340kr)
⇘ 50km NE of Oslo, via E6/RV2
⌂ Hauser/own design
▤ www.nesgolfklubb.no

Onsøy (1987)
Golfveien, 1626 Manstad
☎ +47 69 33 91 50
⌨ +47 69 33 91 51
▷ 18 L 5731 m Par 72 SR 120
ⁱⁱ WD–U WE–U
£€ 400kr
⇘ 10km W of Fredrikstad. Oslo 80km
⌂ Andersen/Mejstedt

Oppdal (1987)
PO Box 19, 7340 Oppdal
☎ 72 42 25 10

Oppegård (1985)
Kongeveien 198, PO Box 50, 1416 Oppegård
☎ 66 81 59 90
⌨ 66 81 59 91
✉ leder@oppegardgk.no
▷ 18 L 5280 m Par 71
ⁱⁱ U H
£€ 250kr (350kr)
⇘ 17km S of Oslo
▤ www.oppegardgk.no

Oslo (1924)
Bogstad, 0757 Oslo
☎ 22 51 05 60

Ostmarka (1989)
Postboks 63, 1914 Ytre Enebakk
☎ 64 92 38 40

Oustoen CC (1965)
PO Box 100, 1330 Fornebu
☎ 67 83 23 80/22 56 33 54
✉ occ@occ.no

Skjeberg (1986)
PO Box 528, 1701 Sarpsborg
☎ 69 16 63 10

Sorknes (1990)
Sorknes Gaard, 2450 Rena
☎ 62 44 18 70
⌨ 62 44 00 27
✉ post@sorknes.no
▷ 18 L 6150 m SSS 72
ⁱⁱ U

££ 300–350kr (400kr)
⮔ 170km N of Oslo
🏠 Juul Soegaard
▤ www.sorknes.no

Stavanger   (1956)
Longebakke 45, 4042 Hafrsfjord
☎ 519 39100
🖥 519 39110
📧 steinar@sgk.no
▷ 18 L 5751 m Par 71
👥 H
££ 400kr
⮔ 6km SW of Stavanger
🏠 F Smith
▤ www.sgk.no

Trondheim   (1950)
PO Box 169, 7401 Trondheim
☎ 73 53 18 85

Tyrifjord   (1982)
Postboks 91, 3529 Røyse
☎ 32 16 13 30

Vestfold   (1958)
PO Box 64, 3108 Vear
☎ 33 36 25 00
🖥 33 36 25 01
📧 vgk@vestfoldgolfklubb.no
▷ 18 L 6414 / 5979 / 4877 m SSS 72
   9 hole course Par 64
👥 H
££ 400kr
⮔ Tønsberg 8km
🏠 Smith/Turner
▤ www.vgk.no

Poland

Amber Baltic   (1993)
Baltycka Street 13, 72-514 Kołczewo
☎ (091) 32 65 110/120

Portugal

Algarve

Alto Golf   (1991)
Quinta do Alto do Poço, P O Box 1, 8501
906 Alvor
☎ (00351) 282 460870
🖥 (00351) 282 460879
📧 golf@altoclub.com
▷ 18 L 5812 m Par 70 SR 121
👥 U H
££ €56–€70
⮔ 2km W of Portimão; 4km from
   A22 J4
🏠 Sir Henry Cotton
▤ www.altoclub.com

Floresta Parque   (1987)
Vale do Poço, Budens, 8650 Vila do Bispo
☎ (0282) 695333

Palmares   (1975)
Apartado 74, Meia Praia, 8601 901 Lagos
☎ +351 282 790500
🖥 +351 282 290509
📧 golf@palmaresgolf.com
▷ 18 L 5961 m Par 71 SSS 72
👥 U H
££ Low season: €59 High season: €89
⮔ Meia Praia, 5km E of Lagos
🏠 Frank Pennink
▤ www.palmaresgolf.com

Penina   (1966)
PO Box 146, Penina, 8502 Portimao
☎ (351) 282 420223
🖥 (351) 282 420252
▷ Ch'ship 18 L 6343 m SSS 73;
   Resort 9 L 3987 m SSS 71;
   Academy 9 L 1851 m Par 30
👥 H–max 28 (M) or 36 (L) – soft
   spikes only; visitors welcome
   according to availability of courses
££ Ch'ship €77 low season, €110 high
   season Resort €38, Academy €33
⮔ 5km W of Portimao. 12km E of
   Lagos
🏠 Sir Henry Cotton

Pestana   (1991)
Apartado 1011, 8400-908 Carvoeiro Lga
☎ (0282) 340900

Pine Cliffs G&CC   (1991)
Praia da Falesia, PO Box 644, 8200-
909 Albufeira
☎ (+351) 289 500100
📧 sheraton.algarve@starwoodhotels
   .com

Pinheiros Altos   (1992)
Quinta do Lago, 8135 Almancil
☎ (0289) 359910
🖥 (0289) 394392
📧 golf@pinheirosaltos.pt
▷ 18 L 6236 m Par 72
👥 H–phone first. Soft spikes only
££ €120
⮔ Quinta do Lago, 15km W of Faro;
   7km Almansil
🏠 Ronald Fream
▤ www.pinheirosaltos.pt

Quinta do Lago   (1974)
Quinta Do Lago, 8135 Almancil
☎ (0289) 390700/9
🖥 (0289) 394013
▷ Quinta do Lago 18 L 6488 m
   SSS 72
   Ria Formosa 18 L 6205 m SSS 72
👥 H–by prior arrangement
££ €65
⮔ 15km W of Faro. Airport 20km
🏠 Mitchell/Lee

Salgados
Apartado 2362, Vale do Rabelho, 8200
917 Albufeira
☎ (0289) 583030

San Lorenzo   (1988)
Quinta do Lago, 8135 Almancil
☎ (289) 396522
🖥 (289) 396908
▷ 18 L 6238 m SSS 73
👥 H–restricted
££ €150
⮔ 16km W of Faro
🏠 Joseph Lee

Vale de Milho   (1990)
Apartado 1273, Praia do Carvoeiro,
8401-911 Carvoeiro Lga
☎ (282) 358502
📧 valedemilhogolf@mail.telepac.pt

Vale do Lobo   (1968)
Vale Do Lobo, 8135-864 Vale do Lobo-
Almançil
☎ (0289) 353535

Vila Sol Spa & Golf Resort
   (1991)
Alto do Semino, Morgadinhos,
Vilamoura, 8125-307-Quarteira
☎ (+351) 289 300505
🖥 (+351) 289 316499
📧 golfreservation@vilasol.pt
▷ 27 L 6335 m Par SSS 72
👥 U H
££ Low season: €75; mid season: €100
   high season: €110
⮔ 5km E of Vilamoura. Faro Airport
   10km
🏠 Donald Steel
▤ www.vilasol.pt

Vilamoura Laguna   (1990)
8125-507 Vilamoura, Algarve
☎ (0289) 310180

Vilamoura Millennium
   (2000)
8125-507 Vilamoura, Algarve
☎ (0289) 310188

Vilamoura Old Course
   (1969)
8125-507 Vilamoura, Algarve
☎ (289) 310341

Vilamoura Pinhal   (1976)
8125-507 Vilamoura, Algarve
☎ (0289) 310390

Azores

Batalha   (1996)
Rua do Bom Jesus, Aflitos, 9545-234 Fenais
da Luz (Açores)
☎ +351 296 498 599/560

☎ +351 296 498 284
✉ verdegolf@virtualazores.com
⌖ 27 holes:
White: L 6435 m CR 73.9 SR 144
Yellow: L 6120 m CR 72.1 SR 140
Red: L 5366 m CR 74.4 SR 132
♟ H
€€ €55
⊶ São Miguel Island. Ponta Delgada
10km (45 min)
⌂ Cameron & Powell
▤ www.verdegolf.net

Furnas (1939)
Achada das Furnas, 9675 Furnas
☎ (+351) 296 498559
✉ (+351) 296 498284
✉ verdegolf@virtualazores.com
✍ Luís Inio (Dir of Golf)
⌖ 18 L 6232 m CR 71.8 SR 121
(White)
18 L 5955 m CR 70.1 SR 117
(Yellow)
18 L 5256 m CR 71.6 SR 118
(Red)
♟ H
€€ €55
⊶ São Miguel Island. Furnas Villa 5km
⌂ Mackenzie Ross/Cameron &
Powell
▤ www.verdegolf.net

Terceira Island (1954)
Caixa Postal 15, 9760 909 Praia da
Victória (Açores)
☎ (0295) 902444

Lisbon & Central Portugal

Aroeira (1972)
Herdade da Aroeira, 2820-567 Charneca
da Caparica
☎ +351 (212) 979 110/1
✉ +351 (212) 971 238
✉ golf.reservas@aroeira.com
⌖ 18 L 6044 m Par 72 SR 123
18 L 6367 m Par 72 SR 122
♟ U H
€€ €48 (€75)
⊶ 20km S of Lisbon, off Setúbal/Costa
da Caparica road
⌂ Frank Pennink/Donald Steel
▤ www.aroeira.com

Belas Clube de Campo
(1998)
Alameda do Aqueduto, Belas Clube de
Campo, 2605-199 Belas
☎ (00351) 21 962 6600
✉ golf@planbelas.pt

Estoril (1945)
Avenida da República, 2765-273 Estoril
☎ (021) 466 0367
✉ reserva@golfestoril.com

Estoril-Sol Golf Academy
(1976)
Quinta do Outeira, Linhó, 2710 Sintra
☎ (01) 923 2461

Lisbon Sports Club (1922)
Casal da Carregueira, 2605-213 Belas
☎ (21) 431 0077
✉ (21) 431 2482
✉ geral@lisbonclub.com
⌖ 18 L 5216 m Par 69 SSS 69
♟ U (WE–NA before noon)
€€ €52 (€57)
⊶ Belas, 20km NW of Lisbon
⌂ Hawtree
▤ www.lisbonclub.com

Marvão (1998)
Quinta do Prado, São Salvador da
Aramenha, 7330-328 Marvão
☎ (245) 993 755
✉ (245) 993 805
✍ R Wilson (Dir)
⌖ 18 Par 72
White: L 6036 m CR 72.4 SR 124
Yellow: L 5518 m CR 69.8 SR 119
Blue: L 5103 m CR 73.9 SR 116
Red: L 4649 m CR 71.2 SR 110
♟ U SOC some restrictions
€€ 9: €21 (€27) 18: €35 (€45)
Juniors: 9: €10.50 (€13.50)
18: €17.50 (€22.50)
⊶ 15km N of Portalegre, nr Spanish
border (N118/N246)
⌂ Jorge Santana da Silva

Golf do Montado (1992)
Urbanização do Golf Montando, Lte no.1 –
Algeruz, 2950-051 Palmela
☎ (265) 708150
✉ (265) 708159
✉ geral@golfdomontando.com.pt
⌖ 18 L 6334 m Par 72
♟ U
€€ €55 (€70)
⊶ 5km E of Setúbal. 40km S of Lisbon
⌂ Duarte Sottomayor/Jorge Santana
da Silva
▤ www.golfmontando.com.pt

Penha Longa (1992)
Estrada da Lagoa Azul, Linhó,
2714–511 Sintra
☎ (021) 924 9011
✉ (021) 924 9024
✉ reservas.golf@penhalonga.com
⌖ 18 L 6290 m CR 70.2 SR 120
9 L 2588 m Par 35
♟ U H
€€ 9: €33 (€43) 18: €90 (€120)
⊶ 8km N of Estoril. 17km W of
Lisbon
⌂ Robert Trent Jones Jr
▤ www.penhalonga.com

Quinta da Beloura (1994)
Estrada de Albarraque, 2710 692 Sintra
☎ (021) 910 6350
✉ (021) 910 6359

✉ beloura.golfe@pestana.com
⌖ 18 L 5774 m Par 73 CR 71.2 SR
128
♟ U
€€ D–€48 (D–€65)
⊶ Between Estoril and Sintra, off N9.
Lisbon 34km
⌂ Rocky Roquemore
▤ www.pestanagolf.com

Quinta da Marinha Oitavos Golfe (2001)
Quinta da Marinha, Casa da Quinta No25,
2750-715 Cascais
☎ 351 21 486 06 00
✉ 351 21 486 06 09
✉ oitavosgolfe@quinta-da-marinha.pt
⌖ 18 holes Par 71
White: L 6379 m CR73.8 SR 134
Yellow: L 5974 m CR 70.7 SR 128
Blue: L 5322 m CR 73.8 SR 126
Red: L 4573 m CR 69.2 SR 118
♟ U WE–NA after 9.30
€€ €150
⊶ 2km W of Cascais. 30km W of
Lisbon
⌂ Arthur Hills
▤ www.quintadamarinha-
oitavosgolfe.pt

Quinta do Perú
Alameda da Serra 2, 2975-666 Quinta
do Conde
☎ (021) 213 4320
✉ play@golfquintadoperu.com

Tróia Golf Championship Course (1980)
Tróia, 7570-789 Carvalhal, Portugal
☎ (+351) 265 494 112
✉ trioagolf@sonae.pt

Vimeiro
Praia do Porto Novo, Vimeiro, 2560
Torres Vedras
☎ (061) 984157

Madeira

Madeira (1991)
Sto Antonio da Serra, 9200
Machico, Madeira
☎ (091) 552345/552356

Palheiro (1993)
Rua do Balancal No.29, 9060-414
Funchal, Madeira
☎ (00351) 291 790 120
(00351) 291 790 125
(Bookings)
✉ (00351) 291 792 456
✉ reservations@palheirogolf.com
⌖ 18 L 6086 m Par 72 CR 71.6 SR
130
♟ May–Sept–U Oct–April–H
€€ €85

For list of abbreviations, key to symbols and international dialling codes see page 651

🕸 5km from Funchal, off Airport road
to Camacha
🏠 Cabell Robinson
🖥 www.palheirogolf.com

North

Amarante   (1997)
Quinta da Deveza, Fregim, 4600-
593 Amarante
☎ +351 255 44 60 60
🖳 +351 255 44 62 02
🖂 sgagolfeamarante@oninet.pl
🏌 18 L 5030 m Par 68 CR 64.2 SR
114
👬 U H
££ €37 (€49)
🕸 60km from Oporto and 45km from
Vila Real
🏠 J Santana da Silva
🖥 www.amarantegolfclube.com

Golden Eagle, Clube de
Golfe   (1994)
E.N. 1, Km 63/64, Asseiceira, 2040–481
Rio Maior
☎ +351 243 940040/
960 148425
🖳 +351 243 940049
🖂 golf@goldeneagle-golfresort.com
🏌 18 Par 72
White 6623 m, yellow 5899 m,
blue 5456 m, red 4850 m
CR (men) white 74.2, yellow 70.7;
(ladies) blue 73.9, red 70.5
SR (men) white 134, yello 127;
(ladies) blue 128, red 119
👬 H
££ €75 (€90)
🕸 55km from Lisbon – access via A1
motorway
🏠 Rocky Roquemore
🖥 www.goldeneagle-golfresort.com

Miramar   (1932)
Av Sacadura Cabral, Miramar, 4405-
013 Arcozelo
☎ (022) 762 2067
🖳 (022) 762 7859
🖂 golf.miramar@mail.telepac.pt
🏌 9 L 2655 m Par 70 SSS 69
👬 H WD WE
££ €50 (€70)
🕸 8km S of Oporto
🏠 Swan/Gordon
🖥 www.cgm.pt

Montebelo
Farminhão, 3510 Viseu
☎ (032) 856464

Oporto   (1890)
Sisto-Paramos, 4500 Espinho
☎ (022) 734 2008

Ponte de Lima
Quinta de Pias, Fornelos, 4490 Ponte
de Lima
☎ (058) 43414

Praia d'el Rey G&CC
(1997)
Vale de Janelas, Apartado 2, 2510
Obidos
☎ (+351) 262 905005
🖂 golf@praia-del-rey.com

Golfe Quinta da Barca
(1997)
Barca do Lago, 4740-476 Esposende
☎ (+351) 2539 66723
🖂 lcatarino@quintabarca.com

Vidago
Parque de Vidago, Apartado 16, 5425-
307 Vidago
☎ +351 276 990 900
🖂 vidago.palace@unicer.pt

Slovenia

Bled G&CC   (1937)
Public
Kidriceva 10 c, 4260 Bled
☎ +386 (0)4 537 77711
🖳 +386 (0)4 537 77722
🖂 info@golf.bled.si
🏌 18 L 6325 m SSS 73
9 L 3092 m SSS 72
👬 H–36 max
££ €55 (€65 inc. Red Letter Days)
Many possible discounts
🕸 3km W of Bled. 50km NW of
Ljubljana, nr Austro-Italian border
🏠 Donald Harradine
🖥 www.golf.bled.si

Castle Mokrice   (1992)
Terme Catez, Topliska Cesta 35,
8250 Brezice
☎ (00386) 7 457 4260

Lipica   (1989)
Lipica 5, 66210 Sezana
☎ +386 (0)5 734 6373
🖳 +386 (0)5 739 1725
🖂 golf@lipica.org
🏌 9 L 6318 m par 74 CR 71.9
SR 119
👬 U
££ 9: €19 (€24) 18: €27 (€35)
20% discount for hotel guests
(Maestoso Klub Hotel)
🕸 11km NE of Trieste. 85km SW of
Ljubljana
🏠 Donald Harradine
🖥 www.lipica.org

Spain

Alicante & Murcia

Alicante   (1998)
Av. Locutor Vicente Hipolito 37, Playa San
Juan, 03540 Alicante
☎ (96) 515 37 94/515 20 43

Altorreal   (1994)
Urb Altorreal, 30500 Molina de
Segura (Murcia)
☎ (968) 64 81 44

Bonalba   (1993)
Partida de Bonalba, 03110
Mutxamiel (Alicante)
☎ (96) 595 5955
🖳 (96) 595 5985
🖂 golfbonalba@golfbonalba.com
🏌 18 L 6190m Par 72 SSS 73
👬 U
££ €65
🕸 10km N of Alicante. A7 Junction
67. Road number 340
🏠 Ramón Espinosa
🖥 www.golfbonalba.com

Don Cayo   (1974)
Apartado 341, 03599 Altea La
Vieja (Alicante)
☎ (96) 584 80 46
🖳 (96) 584 65 19
🖂 doncayo@ctv.es
🏌 9 L 6156 m SSS 72
👬 U H
££ 9: €32 18: €45
🕸 4km N of Altea, nr Callosa
🏠 Barber/Sanz

Ifach   (1974)
Crta Moraira-Calpe Km 3, Apdo 28, 03720
Benisa (Alicante)
☎ (96) 649 71 14
🖳 (96) 649 9908
🖂 golfifach@wanadoo.es
🏌 9 L 3408 m SSS 60
👬 U
££ D–€28/€38
🕸 9km N of Calpe, towards Moraira
🏠 Javier Arana

Jávea   (1981)
Apartado 148, 03730 Jávea, (Alicante)
☎ (96) 579 25 84

La Manga   (1971)
Los Belones, 30385 Cartagena (Murcia)
☎ (968) 13 72 34

La Marquesa   (1989)
Ciudad Quesada II, 03170
Rojales, (Alicante)
☎ (+34) 96 671 42 58
🖳 (+34) 96 671 42 67

✉ golflamarquesa@ctv.es
⏵ 18 L 6111 Par 72 CR 72.5 SR 132
👫 U
££ D–€56
🚗 Rojales, 40km S of Alicante
🏠 Justo Quesada Samper

Las Ramblas (1991)
Crta Alicante-Cartagena Km48, 03189 Urb
Villamartin, Orihuela (Alicante)
☎ (96) 677 4728

Real Campoamor (1989)
Crta Cartagena-Alicante Km48, Apdo 17,
03189 Orihuela-Costa (Alicante)
☎ (96) 532 13 66

La Sella (1991)
Ctra La Xara-Jesús Pobre, 03749 Jesús
Pobre (Alicante)
☎ (96) 645 42 52/645 41 10

Villamartin (1972)
Crta Alicante-Cartagena Km50, 03189 Urb
Villamartin, Orihuela (Alicante)
☎ (96) 676 51 27/676 51 60
🖨 (96) 676 51 70
✉ golfvillamartin@grupoquara.com
⏵ 18 L 6132 m SSS 72
👫 U H
££ €60
🚗 8km S of Torrevieja
🏠 Paul Putman
🖥 www.grupoquara.com

Almería

Almerimar (1976)
Urb Almerimar, 04700 El Ejido (Almería)
☎ (950) 48 02 34

Cortijo Grande (1976)
Apdo 2, Cortijo Grande, 04639
Turre (Almería)
☎ (951) 47 91 76

La Envia (1993)
Apdo 51, 04720 Aguadulce (Almería)
☎ (950) 55 96 41

Playa Serena (1979)
Urb Playa Serena, 04740 Roquetas de
Mar (Almería)
☎ (950) 33 30 55

Badajoz & West

Guadiana (1992)
Crta Madrid-Lisboa Km 393, Apdo 171,
06080 Badajoz
☎ (924) 44 81 88

Norba (1988)
Apdo 880, 10080 Cáceres
☎ (927) 23 14 41

Salamanca (1988)
Monte de Zarapicos, 37170
Zarapicos (Salamanca)
☎ (923) 32 91 02

Balearic Islands

Canyamel
Urb Canyamel, Crta de Cuevas, 07580
Capdepera, (Mallorca)
☎ (971) 56 44 57

Capdepera (1989)
Apdo 6, 07580 Capdepera, Mallorca
☎ (971) 56 58 75/56 58 57

Ibiza (1990)
Apdo 1270, 07840 Santa Eulalia, (Ibiza)
☎ (971) 19 61 18

Pollensa (1986)
Ctra Palma-Pollensa Km 49, 07460
Pollensa, (Mallorca)
☎ (971) 53 32 16
🖨 (971) 53 32 65
✉ rec@golfpollensa.com
⏵ 9 L 5304 m Par 70 SSS 70
👫 U H
££ 9: €38 18: €65
🚗 Pollensa, 45km N of Palma
🏠 José Gancedo
🖥 www.golfpollensa.com

Poniente (1978)
Costa de Calvia, 07181 Calvia (Mallorca)
☎ (971) 13 01 48
🖨 (971) 13 01 76
✉ golf@ponientegolf.com
⏵ 18 L 6430 m SSS 72
👫 U H
££ €74 (€74) valid until 31/08/07
🚗 12km SW of Palma towards Cala
Figuera
🏠 John Harris
🖥 www.ponientegolf.com

Pula Golf (1995)
Ctra. Son Servera-Capdepera, E-07550
Son Servera-Mallorca
☎ (971) 81 70 34
🖨 (971) 81 70 35
✉ reservas@pulagolf.com
🖋 Rahel Wanke
⏵ 18 L 5758 m Par 72 CR 70.5 SR
132
👫 U H
££ 9: Oct–Feb/June–Sept €55,
Mar–May €65; 18:
Oct–Feb/June–Sept €100, Mar–May
€125
🚗 70km NE of Palma
🏠 JM Olazábal
🖥 www.pulagolf.com

Real Golf Bendinat (1986)
C. Campoamor, 07015 Calviá, (Mallorca)
☎ (971) 40 52 00
🖨 (971) 70 07 86
✉ golfbendinat@terra.es
⏵ 18 L 5768 m SSS 71
👫 U H
££ €70
🚗 7km W of Palma
🏠 Martin Hawtree
🖥 www.realgolfbendinat.com

Santa Ponsa (1976)
Santa Ponsa, 07180 Calvia (Mallorca)
☎ (971) 69 02 11/69 08 00
✉ golf1@habitatgolf.es

Son Antem (1993)
Ctra. Llucmajor, PN 602, Km 3,4, E-
07620 Llucmajor-Mallorca
☎ (971) 12 92 00
🖨 (971) 12 92 01
✉ mhrs.pmigs.golf.reservation
@marriott.com
🖋 Bernat Hobera (Pres)
⏵ East: 18
Men: L 6327 m CR 72.7 SR 123
Women: L 5098 m CR 72.7 SR 130
West: 18
Men: L 6293 m CR 71.9 SR 133
Women: L 5395 m CR 73.0 SR 130
👫 U H–East H–West
££ East: 9: €39 (€39) 18: €69 (€69)
West: 9: €42 (€42) 18: €74 (€74)
🚗 20km E of Palma (Route 717)
🏠 F López Segales
🖥 www.marriotthotels.com/pmigs

Golf Son Parc Menorca
(1977)
Urb. Son Parc s/n, ES Mercadal-
Menorca, Baleares
☎ +34 (971)-188875/359059
🖨 +34 (971)-359591
✉ info@golfsonparc.com
⏵ 18 Par 69
👫 U
££ €55 until 30/04/07 then check with
shop. Ask about special offers
🚗 North side of island; 8km Mercadal.
12km Alaior. 18km Mahon
🏠 Dave Thomas Ltd
🖥 www.golfsonparc.com

Son Servera (1967)
Costa de Los Pinos, 07759 Son
Servera, (Mallorca)
☎ (971) 84 00 96

Son Vida (1964)
Urb Son Vida, 07013 Palma (Mallorca)
☎ (971) 79 12 10

Vall d'Or Golf (1985)
Apdo 23, 07660 Cala D'Or, (Mallorca)
☎ (971) 83 70 68/83 70 01
🖨 (971) 83 72 99
✉ valldorgolf@valldorgolf.com

18 L 5602 m SSS 71
H
££ €75
⚲ 60km E of Palma, between Cala d'Or and Porto Colóm
⌂ Benz/Bendly
▤ www.valldorgolf.com

Barcelona & Cataluña

Aro-Mas Nou (1990)
Apdo 429, 17250 Playa de Aro
☎ (972) 82 69 00
　(972) 81 67 27 (Bookings)

Bonmont Terres Noves
(1990)
Urb Terres Noves, 43300 Montroig (Tarragona)
☎ (977) 81 81 40

Caldes Internacional (1992)
Apdo 200, 08140 Caldes de Montbui (Barcelona)
☎ (93) 865 38 28

Costa Brava (1962)
La Masia, 17246 Sta Cristina d'Aro (Gerona)
☎ (972) 83 71 50

Costa Dorada (1983)
Apartado 600, 43080 Tarragona
☎ (977) 65 33 61

Empordà (1990)
Crta Torroella de Montgri, 17257 Gualta (Gerona)
☎ (972) 76 04 50/76 01 36

Fontanals de Cerdanya
(1994)
Fontanals de Cerdanya, 17538 Soriguerola (Girona)
☎ (972) 14 43 74

Golf Girona (1992)
Urbanització Golf Girona s/n, 17481 Sant Julia de Ramis, (Girona)
☎ (972) 17 16 41
✉ golfgirona@golfgirona.com

Llavaneras (1945)
Cami del Golf 45-51, 08392 San Andreu de Llavaneras, (Barcelona)
☎ (93) 792 60 50
　(93) 792 62 27 (Bookings)
🖴 (93) 795 25 58
✉ club@golfllavaneras.com
⛳ 18 Par 70 L 5028 (Yellow)
　L 4481 m (Red)
🚶 U H
££ €60 (€155)
⚲ 34km N of Barcelona (A19), C32 Motorway Jct 105

⌂ Hawtree/Espinosa/Sardà/Viador
▤ www.golfllavaneras.com

Masia Bach (1990)
Ctra Martorell-Capellades, 08635 Sant Esteve Sesrovires
☎ (93) 772 8800

Osona Montanya (1988)
Masia L'Estanyol, 08553 El Brull (Barcelona)
☎ (93) 884 01 70

Peralada Golf (1993)
La Garriga, 17491 Peralada, Girona
☎ (972) 53 82 87
🖴 (972) 53 82 36
✉ casa/club@golfperalada.com
⛳ 18 L 5990 m SSS 71
　9 holes Par 3
🚶 H
££ €50 low season €56 mid season
　€75 high season
⚲ Costa Brava, on French border. 40km S of Perpignan Airport, nr Figueres
⌂ Jorge Soler
▤ www.golfperalada.com

Golf Platja de Pals (1966)
Pay and play
Ctra. Golf S/N, 17230 Pals - Girona
☎ (+34) 972 66 77 39
🖴 (+34) 972 63 67 99
✉ recep@golfplatjadepals.com
✍ Alexandra Reig (Mgr)
⛳ 18 Par 73 SSS 72
　White: L 6222 m CR 72.0 SR 127
　Yellow: L 5940 m CR 70.5 SR 122
　Blue: L 5360 m CR 72.9 SR 123
　Red: L 5089 m CR 71.2 SR 120
🚶 H-WD/WE
££ Low season: 9: €43, 18: €54 Mid Season: 9: €47, 18: €59 High Season & WE: 9: €56, 18: €75
⚲ 40km E of Gerona, 135km NE of Barcelona
⌂ FW Hawtree
▤ www.golfplatjadepals.com

Real Golf El Prat (1956)
⚲ The club moved to a new site near Barcelona in 2004. Please see website for details
▤ www.realclubdegolfelprat.com

Reus Aigüesverds (1989)
Crta de Cambrils, Mas Guardià, E-43206 Reus-Tarragona
☎ (977) 75 27 25
✉ golf@aiguesverds.com

Sant Jordi
Urb Sant Jordi d'Alfama, 43860 Ametlla de Mar, (Tarragona)
☎ (977) 49 34 57

Terramar (1922)
Apdo 6, 08870 Sitges
☎ (93) 894 05 80/894 20 43
🖴 (93) 894 70 51
✉ reservas@golfterramar.com
⛳ 18 L 5878 m Par 72
🚶 H
££ €75 (€115)
⚲ Sitges, 37km S of Barcelona
⌂ Hawtree/Piñero/Fazio
▤ www.golfterramar.com

Torremirona (1994)
Ctra N-260 Km 46, 17744 Navata (Girona)
☎ (+34) 972 55 37 37
✉ golf@torremirona.com

Vallromanes (1972)
C/Afveras, 08188 Vallromanes, (Barcelona)
☎ (93) 572 90 64

Burgos & North

Castillo de Gorraiz (1993)
Urb Castillo de Gorraiz, 31620 Valle de Egues (Navarra)
☎ (948) 33 70 73
✉ administracion@golfgorraiz.com

La Cuesta
Apdo 40, 33500 Llanes
☎ (98) 541 7084

Izki Golf (1992)
C/Arriba, S/N, 01119 Urturi (Alava)
☎ (945) 378262
✉ izkigolf@izkigolf.com

Larrabea (1989)
Crta de Landa, 01170 Legutiano, (Alava)
☎ (945) 46 58 44/46 58 41

Lerma (1991)
Ctra Madrid-Burgos Km195, 09340 Lerma (Burgos)
☎ (947) 17 12 14/17 12 16
✉ golflerma@csa.es

La Llorea (1994)
Crta Nacional 632, Km 62, 33394 Lloreda (Gijón)
☎ (985) 18 10 30

Real Golf Castiello (1958)
Apdo Correos 161, 33200 Gijón
☎ (985) 36 63 13
✉ administracion@castiello.com

Real Golf Pedreña (1928)
Apartado 233, Santander
☎ (942) 50 00 01/50 02 66

For list of abbreviations, key to symbols and international dialling codes see page 651

Real San Sebastián (1910)
PO Box 6, Fuenterrabia, (Guipúzcoa)
☎ (943) 61 68 45/61 68 46

Real Zarauz (1916)
Apartado 82, Zarauz, (Guipúzcoa)
☎ (943) 83 01 45

Ulzama (1965)
31779 Guerendiain (Navarra)
☎ (948) 30 51 62

Canary Islands

Amarilla (1988)
Urb Amarilla Golf, San Miguel de Abona,
38630 Santa Cruz de Tenerife
☎ (922) 73 03 19

Costa Teguise (1978)
Apdo 170, 35080 Arrecife de Lanzarote
☎ (928) 59 05 12

Maspalomas (1968)
Av de Neckerman, Maspalomas, 35100
Gran Canaria
☎ (928) 76 25 81/76 73 43

**Real Club de Golf de
Tenerife** (1932)
Campo de Golf No.1 38350,
Tacoronte, Tenerife
☎ (922) 63 66 07
✉ director.golf@interbook.net

**Real Club de Golf de Las
Palmas** (1891)
PO Box 93, 35380 Santa Brigida,
Gran Canaria
☎ (928) 35 10 50/35 01 04
🖳 (928) 35 01 10
✉ rcglp@realclubdegolfdelaspalmas.com
👫 18 L 5919 m SSS 71
👥 WD 8am to 12.45pm WE–M
££ €48–€73
🚗 Bandama, Las Palmas 14km
🏠 Mackenzie Ross
📧 www.realclubdegolfdelaspalmas.com

Golf del Sur (1987)
San Miguel de Abona, 38620
Tenerife (Canarias)
☎ (922) 73 81 70

Córdoba

Club de Campo de Córdoba
(1976)
Apartado 436, 14080 Córdoba
☎ (957) 35 02 08
✉ administracion@golfcordoba.com
👫 18 L 5964 m Par 72 SSS 73
👥 U H36

££ €45 (€65)
🚗 9km N of Córdoba
📧 www.golfcordoba.com

Pozoblanco (1984)
Apdo 118, 14400 Pozoblanco, (Córdoba)
☎ (957) 33 91 71

Galicia

Aero Club de Santiago
(1976)
General Pardiñas 34, Santiago de
Compostela (La Coruña)
☎ (981) 59 24 00
🖳 (981) 50 95 03
✉ reception@aerosantiago.es
👫 9 L 5816 m SSS 70
18 holes Par 72
👥 U
££ €40 (€60)
🚗 Santiago Airport
🏠 José Luis Tarriq
📧 www.aerosantiago.es

Aero Club de Vigo (1951)
Reconquista 7, 36201 Vigo
☎ (986) 48 66 45/48 75 09

La Toja (1970)
Isla de La Toja, El Grove, Pontevedra
☎ (986) 73 01 58/73 08 18

Ria de Vigo (1993)
San Lorenzo-Domaio, 36957
Moaña (Pontevedra)
☎ (986) 32 70 51
🖳 (986) 32 70 53
✉ info@riadevigogolf.com
✍ Cholmin Kwon (Gen Mgr)
👫 18 L 6110 m
Men: CR 71.1 SR 136
Women: CR 72.2 SR 123
👥 H (26.4)
££ €50
🚗 Vigo 12km. Ponevedra 21km.
Santiago 78km
🏠 Ramón Espinosa
📧 www.riadevigogolf.com

Granada

Granada
Avda de los Corsarios, 18110 Las
Gabias (Granada)
☎ (958) 58 44 36

Madrid Region

Barberán (1967)
Apartado 150.239, Cuatro Vientos,
28080 Madrid
☎ (91) 509 00 59/509 11 40

La Dehesa (1991)
Avda. de la Universidad, 10, 28691
Villanueva La Cañada
☎ (91) 815 70 22
🖳 (91) 815 54 68
✉ dehesa-direccion@infonegocio.com
👫 18 L 6444 m SSS 72
👥 WD–U WE–NA H
££ WD D–€75
🚗 35km NW of Madrid
🏠 Manuel Piñero

Herreria (1966)
PO Box 28200, San Lorenzo del
Escorial, (Madrid)
☎ (91) 890 51 11
🖳 (91) 890 26 13
✉ lsveiro@golflaherreria.com
👫 18 L 6050 m SSS 72
££ €60 (€104)
🚗 Escorial, 50km W of Madrid
🏠 Antonio Lucena/José Cancedo
📧 www.golflaherreria.com

Jarama R.A.C.E. (1967)
Urb Ciudalcampo, 28707 San Sebastian de
los Reyes, (Madrid)
☎ (91) 657 00 11
🖳 (91) 657 04 62
✉ golf@race.es
👫 18 L 6505 m Par 72
9 hole Par 3 course
👥 M H
££ €67.30 (€113.90)
🚗 28km N of Madrid on Burgos road
🏠 Javier Arana
📧 www.race.es

Lomas-Bosque (1973)
Urb El Bosque, 28670 Villaviciosa de
Odón, (Madrid)
☎ (91) 616 75 00

La Moraleja (1976)
La Moraleja, Alcobendas (Madrid)
☎ (91) 650 07 00
🖳 (91) 650 43 31
✉ info@golflamoraleja.com
👫 18 L 6451 m SSS 72
18 L 5958 SSS 72
👥 M H
££ €80 (€160)
🚗 9km N of Madrid on Burgos road
🏠 Jack Nicklaus
📧 www.golflamoraleja.com

Olivar de la Hinojosa
(1995)
Avda de Dublin, Campo de las Naciones,
28042 Madrid
☎ (91) 721 18 89

Puerta de Hierro (1896)
Avda de Miraflores, Ciudad Puerta de
Hierro, 28035 Madrid
☎ (91) 316 1745
✉ deportes1@realclubpuertadehierro
.es

For list of abbreviations, key to symbols and international dialling codes see page 651

Los Retamares   (1991)
Crta Algete-Alalpardo Km 2300, 28130
Valdeolmos (Madrid)
☎ (91) 620 25 40

Somosaguas   (1971)
Avda de la Cabaña, 28223 Pozuelo de
Alarcón, (Madrid)
☎ (91) 352 16 47

Valdeláguila   (1975)
Apdo 9, Alcalá de Henares, (Madrid)
☎ (91) 885 96 59

Villa de Madrid CC   (1932)
Crta Castilla, 28040 Madrid
☎ (91) 550 2010
🖳 (91) 550 2031
⊳ 27 L 5900-6321 m SSS 73-74
⋔ U H
££ €46.50 (€87.50)
⊶ 4km NW of Madrid, in the Casa
del Campo
⌂ Javier Arana
▤ www.clubvillademadrid.com

Malaga Region

Alhaurín   (1994)
Crta 426 Km15, Alhaurín el Grande
☎ (952) 59 59 70
🖳 (952) 59 45 86
✉ reservasgolf@alhauringolf.com
⊳ 18 L 6221 m Par 72
18 hole Par 3 course
9 hole Par 3 course
⋔ U
££ €33 low season €57 high season,
any day
⊶ 6km from Mijas; 3km from
Alhaurín el Grande
⌂ Severiano Ballesteros
▤ www.alhauringolf.com

Añoreta   (1989)
Avenida del Golf, 29730 Rincón de la
Victoria, (Málaga)
☎ (952) 40 40 00

La Cala Resort   (1991)
La Cala de Mijas, 29649 Mijas-
Costa (Málaga)
☎ (952) 66 90 00
(952) 66 90 33
🖳 (952) 66 90 34
✉ golf@lacala.com
⊳ America 18 L 6187 m Par 73
Asia 18 L 5925 m Par 72
Europa 18 L 6014 m Par 71
6 hole Par 3 course
⋔ U H
££ €70 (summer €45)
⊶ 6km from Cala de Mijas, between
Fuengirola and Marbella
⌂ Cabell B Robinson
▤ www.lacala.com

El Chaparral
Urb El Chaparral, Mijas-Costa
☎ (952) 49 38 00

Guadalhorce   (1988)
Crtra de Cártama Km7, Apartado 48,
29590 Campanillas (Málaga)
☎ (952) 17 93 78

Lauro   (1992)
Los Caracolillos, 29130 Alhaurín de la
Torre, (Málaga)
☎ (95) 241 2767/296 3091
🖳 (95) 241 4757
✉ info@laurogolf.com
⊳ 27 L 6067 m Slope 135
⋔ U
££ €50 (€30 in summer)
⊶ Drive west from Málaga airport.
Take exit 'Coín' onto A-366
towards 'Alhaurin el Grande, Coín'.
Lauro Golf is 77km
⌂ Folco Nardi, Mariano Benítet
▤ www.laurogolf.com

Málaga Club de Campo
(1925)
Parador de Golf, Apdo 324, 29080 Málaga
☎ (952) 38 12 55

Mijas Golf International
(1976)
Apartado 145, Fuengirola, Málaga
☎ (952) 47 68 43
🖳 (952) 46 79 43
✉ info@ mijasgolf.org
⊳ Los Lagos: 18 Par 71
white L 6367 m, yellow L 6007 m,
red L 5148 m
Los Olivos: 18 Par 70
white L 5840 m, yellow L 5601 m,
red L 4877 m
⋔ H–booking required Oct–Apr
££ €44–€70
⊶ 4km NW of Fuengirola (Mijas
Valley)
⌂ Robert Trent Jones
▤ www.mijasgolf.org

Miraflores   (1989)
Urb Riviera del Sol, 29647 Mijas-Costa
☎ +34 (952) 93 19 60

Los Moriscos   (1974)
Costa Granada, Motril (Granada)
☎ (958) 82 55 27

Torrequebrada   (1976)
Public
Apdo 120, Crta de Cadiz Km 220,
29630 Benalmadena
☎ (95) 244 27 42
✉ torrequebrada@grn.es

Marbella & Estepona

Alcaidesa Links   (1992)
CN-340 Km124.6, 11315 La Linea (Cádiz)
☎ (956) 79 10 40

Aloha   (1975)
Nueva Andalucía, 29660 Marbella
☎ (952) 81 37 50/90 70 85/86
(952) 81 23 88
(Caddymaster)
🖳 (952) 81 23 89
✉ office@clubdegolfaloha.com
⊳ 18 L 6261 m SSS 72
9 hole short course
⋔ H–booking necessary
££ €120
⊶ 8km W of Marbella, nr Puerto
Banus
⌂ Javier Arana
▤ www.clubdegolfaloha.com

Los Arqueros   (1991)
Crta de Ronda Km44.5, 29679
Benahavis (Málaga)
☎ (952) 78 46 00
🖳 (952) 78 67 07
✉ caddiemaster@es.taylorwoodrow
.com
⊳ 18 L 5729 m Par 71 SSS 72
⋔ H U
££ 9: May/Oct €30, Feb/May €40 18:
May/Oct €30, Feb/May €60
⊶ 5km N of San Pedro de Alcántara
⌂ Severiano Ballesteros

Atalaya G&CC   (1968)
Crta Benahavis 7, 29688 Málaga
☎ (952) 88 28 12

Las Brisas   (1968)
Apdo 147, 29660 Nueva
Andalucía, (Málaga)
☎ (952) 81 08 75/81 30 21
🖳 (952) 81 55 18
✉ info@lasbrisasgolf.com
⊳ 18 L 6094 m SSS 72
⋔ H–restricted
££ €150
⊶ 8km S of Marbella, nr Puerto Banus
⌂ Robert Trent Jones
▤ www.lasbrisasgolf.com

La Cañada   (1982)
Ctra Guadiaro Km 1, 11311
Guadiaro (Cádiz)
☎ (956) 79 41 00

Estepona   (1989)
Arroyo Vaquero, Apartado 532, 29680
Estepona (Málaga)
☎ (+34) 95 293 7605
🖳 (+34) 95 293 7600
✉ information@esteponagolf.com
⊳ 18 L 5893 m Par 72 SSS 71
⋔ U
££ Feb–May €57.50 June–Oct €39.00
⊶ 5km W of Estepona (CN340)

⌂ Luis López
▤ www.esteponagolf.com

Guadalmina (1959)
Guadalmina Alta, San Pedro de Alcántara,
29678 Marbella (Málaga)
☎ (952) 88 65 22

Marbella (1994)
CN 340 Km 188, 29600
Marbella (Málaga)
☎ (952) 83 05 00

Monte Mayor (1989)
PO Box 962, 29679 Benahavis (Málaga)
☎ (+34) 95 293 7111
🖳 (+34) 95 293 7112
📧 reservations@montemayorgolf
   .com
🏳 18 L 5652 m Par 71 SSS 71
👥 H
££ €90 high season (inc. buggy)
   €60 low season (inc. buggy)
🏌 Exit on N340 at km 165.5
   Cancelada
⌂ Jose Gancedo
▤ www.montemayorgolf.com

Los Naranjos (1977)
Apdo 64, 29660 Nueva
Andalucía, Marbella
☎ (952) 81 52 06/81 24 28

El Paraiso (1973)
Ctra Cádiz-Màlaga Km 167, 29680
Estepona (Málaga)
☎ (95) 288 38 35
🖳 (95) 288 58 27
📧 info@elparaisogolfclub.com
🏳 18 L 6116 m SSS 72
👥 U H
££ €75 (summer and winter offers
   available)
🏌 14km S of Marbella
⌂ Player/Kirby
▤ www.elparaisogolfclub.com

La Quinta G&CC (1989)
Urb. La Quinta, Nueva Andalucía
29660, (Marbella-Málaga)
☎ +34 (952) 76 23 90
🖳 +34 (952) 76 23 99
📧 reservas@laquintagolf.com
🏳 27 L 602, 5749, 5915 m
   SSS 70, 71, 71
   SR 125, 123, 125
👥 U H
££ Oct–Nov & Feb–May: 9: €53; 18:
   €82 Dec–Feb & May–Sept: 9: €43;
   18: €66
🏌 3km N of San Pedro de Alcántara
⌂ Piñero/García-Garrido
▤ www.laquintagolf.com

Rio Real (1965)
Urb Rio Real, PO Box 82, 29600
Marbella (Málaga)
☎ (95) 277 95 09

San Roque (1990)
CN 340 Km 126, San Roque, 11360
Cádiz
☎ (956) 61 30 30/60/90

Santa María G&CC
Urb. Elviria, Crta N340 Km 192, 29600
Marbella (Málaga)
☎ (952) 83 10 36
🖳 (952) 83 47 97
📧 info@santamariagolfclub.com
🏳 18 L 5586 m Par 70
👥 U
££ €75
🏌 10km E of Marbella, opp Hotel
   Don Carlos
⌂ A García Garrido (1st 9 holes),
   Santa Maria's Technical Team (2nd
   9 holes)
▤ www.santamariagolfclub.com

Sotogrande (1964)
Paseo del Parque, s/n, 11310
Sotogrande, Cádiz
☎ +34 956 785014
🖳 +34 956 795029
📧 info@golfsotogrande.com
🏳 18 L 6394 m Par 72
   white CR 73.1 SR 125
   yellow CR 70.9 SR 131
   blue CR 73.9 SR 129
   red CR 72.1 SR 125
   9 L 1299 m Par 29
👥 U WD–4 starting times only
££ €160 (€135 tour operators)
🏌 30km N of Gibraltar, nr Guadiaro
⌂ Robert Trent Jones
▤ www.golfsotogrande.com

Valderrama (1985)
Avenida de los Cortjos S/N, 11310
Sotogrande (Cádiz)
☎ (956) 79 12 00

La Zagaleta (1994)
Crta San Pedro-Ronda Km 9,
29679 Benahavis
☎ (95) 285 54 53

Seville & Gulf of Cádiz

Costa Ballena (1997)
Crta Sta Maria-Chipiona, 11520 Rota
☎ (956) 84 70 70

Isla Canela (1993)
Crta de la Playa, 21400 Ayamonte (Huelva)
☎ (959) 47 72 63
📧 golf@islacanela.es

Islantilla (1993)
Urb Islantilla, Apdo 52, 21410 Isla
Cristina (Huelva)
☎ (959) 48 60 39/48 60 49

Montecastillo (1992)
Carretera de Arcos, 11406 Jérez
☎ (956) 15 12 00
🖳 (956) 15 12 09
📧 commercial@montecastillo.com
🏳 18 L 6494 m SSS 72
👥 H
££ €90
🏌 10km NE of Jérez. 75km S of
   Seville
⌂ Jack Nicklaus
▤ www.montecastillo.com

Montenmedio G&CC
(1996)
A-48 Km 42.5, 11150 Vejer-
Barbate (Cádiz)
☎ (956) 45 12 16
🖳 (956) 45 12 95
📧 commercial@monteenmedio.com
🏳 18 L 5897 m Par 72 SSS 72
👥 U
££ €78
🏌 Cádiz-Algeciras road (CN 340),
   42.5km; Vejer 5km
⌂ A Maldonado
▤ www.monteenmedio.com

Novo Sancti Petri
(1990)
Urb Novo Sancti Petri, Playa de la Barrosa,
11139 Chiclana de la Frontera
☎ (956) 49 22 33
🖳 (956) 49 43 50
📧 sales@golf-novosancti.es
🏳 18 L 6071 m Par 72
   18 L 6476 m Par 72
👥 U H
££ €60–€75
🏌 La Barrosa, 24km SE of Cádiz. Jérez
   Airport 50km
⌂ Severiano Ballesteros
▤ www.golf-novosancti.es

Pineda De Sevilla (1939)
Apartado 1049, 41080 Sevilla
☎ (954) 61 14 00

Real Sevilla (1992)
Autovía Sevilla-Utrera, 41089
Montequinto (Sevilla)
☎ (954) 12 43 01

Vista Hermosa (1975)
Apartado 77, Urb Vista Hermosa, 11500
Puerto de Santa María, Cádiz
☎ (956) 87 56 05

Zaudin
Crta Tomares-Mairena, 41940
Tomares (Sevilla)
☎ (954) 15 41 59
   (954) 15 25 52
   (reservations)

For list of abbreviations, key to symbols and international dialling codes see page 651

Valencia & Castellón

El Bosque   (1989)
Crta Godelleta, 46370 Chiva-Valencia
☎ (96) 180 41 42

Costa de Azahar   (1960)
Ctra Grao-Benicasim, Castellón de la Plana
☎ (964) 22 70 64

Escorpión   (1975)
Apartado Correos 1, Betera (Valencia)
☎ (96) 160 12 11

Manises   (1964)
Apartado 22.029, Manises (Valencia)
☎ (96) 152 18 71

Mediterraneo CC   (1978)
Urb La Coma, 12190 Borriol, (Castellón)
☎ (964) 32 1653 (bookings)
🖳 (964) 65 77 34
📧 club@ccmediterraneo.com
🏌 18 L 6227 m Par 72
♟ H WD before 1pm WE–after 12
££ €50 (€60)
🚗 Borriol, 4km NW of Castellón
🏠 Ramón Espinosa
🖥 www.ccmediterraneo.com

Oliva Nova   (1995)
46780 Oliva (Valencia)
☎ (096) 285 76 66
🖳 (096) 285 76 67
📧 golf@chg.es
🏌 18 L 6270m Par 72
    5 hole Par 3 course
♟ H
££ €69
🚗 15km N of Denia on N332. A7
    Junction 61
🏠 Severiano Ballesteros
🖥 www.olivanovagolf.com

Panorámica   (1995)
Urb Panorámica, 12320 San
Jorge (Castellón)
☎ (964) 49 30 72

El Saler   (1968)
Avd. de los pinares 151, 46012 El
Saler (Valencia)
☎ (96) 161 0384
📧 saler.golf@parador.es

Valladolid

Entrepinos   (1990)
Avda del Golf 2, Urb Entrepinos, 47130
Simancas (Valladolid)
☎ (983) 59 05 11/59 05 61
🖳 (983) 59 07 65
📧 golfentrepinos@golfentrepinos
    .com

🏌 18 L 5349 m Par 69 CR 68.6 SR
    123
♟ U H
££ €36 (€60)
🚗 15km SW of Valladolid. N-620 exit
    135 towards Simancas
🏠 Manuel Piñero
🖥 www.golfentrepinos.com

Zaragoza

La Penaza   (1973)
Apartado 3039, Zaragoza
☎ (976) 34 28 00/34 22 48

Sweden

East Central

Ängsö   (1979)
Box 1007, 72126 Västerås
☎ (0171) 441012

Arboga
PO Box 263, 732 25 Arboga
☎ (0589) 70100
🖳 (0589) 701 90
📧 arbogagk@arbogagk.nu
🐾 Gun Peterson
🏌 18 L 5890 m Par 72
♟ U
££ 250kr (300kr)
🚗 5km S of Arboga
🏠 Sune Linde
🖥 www.arbogagk.nu

Ärila   (1951)
Nicolai, 611 92 Nyköping
☎ (0155) 216617

Askersund   (1980)
Box 3002, 696 03 Ammeberg
☎ (0583) 34943

Burvik   (1990)
Burvik, 740 12 Knutby
☎ (0174) 43060
🖳 (0174) 43062
📧 info:burvik.se
🏌 18 L 5785 m SSS 72
♟ U
££ On application
🚗 45km E of Uppsala. 70km N of
    Stockholm
🏠 Bengt Lorichs
🖥 www.burvik.se

Edenhof   (1991)
740 22 Bälinge
☎ (018) 334185
📧 info@edenhof.se

Enköping   (1970)
Box 2006, 745 02 Enköping
☎ (0171) 20830

Eskilstuna   (1951)
Strängnäsvägen, 633 49 Eskilstuna
☎ (016) 142629
🖳 (016) 148729
📧 info@eskilstunagk.se
🏌 18 L 5610 m SSS 70
♟ H
££ 220kr (320kr)
🚗 2km E of Eskilstuna. 20km E of
    Örebro
🏠 Douglas Brasier
🖥 www.eskilstunagk.se

Fagersta   (1970)
Box 2051, 737 02 Fagersta
☎ (0223) 54060

Frösåker   (1989)
Frösåker Gård, Box 17015, 720
17 Västerås
☎ (021) 25401
🖳 (021) 25485
📧 fgcc@telia.com
🏌 18 L 5820 m Par 72
♟ U H
££ 350kr (450kr)
🚗 15km SE of Västerås
🏠 Sune Linde
🖥 www.fgcc.se

Fullerö   (1988)
Jotsberga, 725 91 Västerås
☎ (021) 50132
🖳 (021) 50431
🏌 18 L 5633 m SSS 71
♟ H
££ 240kr (320kr)
🚗 6km SW of Västerås
🏠 Hultström/Sjöberg
🖥 www.fullerogk.se

Gripsholm   (1991)
Box 133, 647 23 Mariefred
☎ (0159) 350050
🖳 (0159) 350059
🏌 18 L 6203 m Par 73 SR 128
♟ H
££ 350kr (450kr)
🚗 Mariefred, 70km SW of Stockholm
🏠 Bengt Lorichs
🖥 www.golf.se/gripsholmsgk

Grönlund   (1989)
PO Box 38, 740 10 Almunge
☎ (0174) 20670

Gustavsvik   (1988)
Box 22033, 702 02 Örebro
☎ (019) 244486
🖳 (019) 246490
📧 info@gvgk.se
🏌 18 holes SSS 72
♟ H
££ 280kr (340kr)

恢 4km S of Örebro
🏠 Turner/Wirhed
📱 www.gvgk.se

Katrineholm (1959)
Jättorp, 641 93 Katrineholm
☎ **(0150) 39270**
💻 (0150) 39011
├ 18 L 5850 m SSS 72
9 L 2850 m
🚹 U
££ 300kr (350kr)
恢 7km E of Katrineholm
🏠 Skjöld/Lorichs

Köping (1963)
Box 278, 731 26 Köping
☎ **(0221) 81090**

Kumla (1987)
Box 46, 692 21 Kumla
☎ **(019) 577370**

Linde (1984)
Dalkarlshyttan, 711 31 Lindesberg
☎ **(0581) 13960**

Mosjö (1989)
Mosjö Gård, 705 94 Örebrö
☎ **(019) 225780**

Nora (1988)
Box 108, 713 23 Nora
☎ **(0587) 311660**

Örebro (1939)
Lanna, 719 93 Vintrosa
☎ **(019) 164070**

Roslagen
Box 110, 761 22 Norrtälje
☎ **(0176) 237194**

Sala (1970)
Norby Fallet 100, 733 92 Sala
☎ **(0224) 53077/53055/53064**
✉ kansli@salagk.nu

Sigtunabygden (1961)
Box 89, 193 22 Sigtuna
☎ **(08) 592 54012**

Skepptuna
Skepptuna, 195 93 Märsta
☎ **(08) 512 93069**

Södertälje (1952)
Box 9074, 151 09 Södertälje
☎ **(08) 550 91995**

Strängnäs (1968)
Kilenlundavägen, 645 91 Strängnäs
☎ **(0152) 14731**

Torshälla (1960)
Box 128, 64422 Torshälla
☎ **(016) 358722**
💻 (016) 357491
✉ kansli@telia.com
├ 18 L 5934 m Par 72
🚹 H
££ 220kr (300kr)
恢 5km N of Eskilstuna
🏠 Brasier/Linde
📱 www.torshallagk.com

Tortuna
Nicktuna, Tortuna, 725 96 Västerås
☎ **(021) 65300**
✉ kansli@tortunagk.com

Trosa (1972)
Box 80, 619 22 Trosa
☎ **(0156) 22458**

Upsala (1937)
Håmö Gård, Läby, 755 92 Uppsala
☎ **(018) 460120**
💻 (018) 461205
✉ info@upsalagk.golf.se
├ 18 L 5818 m SSS 72 CR 72.0 SR
128
9 L 2674 m SSS 70 CR 68.1 SR 112
9 L 1673 m SSS 58 CR 58.7 SR 96
🚹 H
££ 300kr (350kr)
恢 10km W of Uppsala
🏠 Greger Paulsson/Peter
Nordwall/Nils Nyberg/Einar
Jansson
📱 www.upsalagk.com

Vassunda (1989)
Smedby Gård, 741 91 Knivsta
☎ **+46 (0) 185 72040**
💻 (018) 381416
✉ info@vassundagk.se
├ 18 L 6141 m Par 72
🚹 H
££ 280kr (360kr)
恢 45km N of Stockholm
🏠 Sune Linde
📱 www.vassundagk.se

Västerås (1931)
Bjärby, 724 81 Västerås
☎ **(021) 357543**
💻 (021) 357573
✉ info@vasterasgk.se
├ 18 L 5575 m Par 70 SSS 75
🚹 U
££ 250kr (300kr)
恢 2km N of Västerås
🏠 Nils Sköld
📱 www.vasterasgk.se

Far North

Boden (1946)
Tallkronsvägen 2, 961 51 Boden
☎ **(0921) 72051**

Funäsdalsfjällen (1972)
Golfbanevägen 8, 840 96 Ljusnedal
☎ **(0684) 668241**
💻 (0684) 21142
✉ kansli@ffjgk.nu
├ 18 L 5300 m SSS 72
🚹 U
££ 275kr (290kr)
恢 Funäsdalen, nr Norwegian border
🏠 Sköld/Linde
📱 www.ffjgk.nu

Gällivare-Malmberget (1973)
Box 35, 983 21 Malmberget
☎ **(0970) 20770**
💻 (0970) 20776
✉ gmgk@telia.com
├ 18 L 5528 m Par 71
🚹 H
££ 250kr
恢 4km NW of Gällivare, towards
Malmberget
🏠 Jan Sederholm
📱 www.gmgk.se

Haparanda (1989)
Mattila 140, 953 35 Haparanda
☎ **(0922) 10660**

Härnösand (1957)
Box 52, 871 22 Härnösand
☎ **(0611) 67000**

Kalix (1990)
Box 32, 952 21 Kalix
☎ **(0923) 15945/15935**

Luleå (1955)
Golfbaneväg 80, 975 96 Luleå
☎ **(0920) 256300**
💻 (0920) 256362
├ 27 L 8930 m Par 72
🚹 H
££ 300kr
恢 Rutvik, 12km E of Luleå
🏠 Skjöld/Tideman/Eriksson

Norrmjöle (1992)
905 82 Umeå
☎ **(090) 81581**
💻 (090) 81565
✉ kanslie@norrmjole-golf.se
├ 18 L 5619 m Par 72
🚹 U
££ 250kr (350kr); 300kr (400kr) in
July
恢 19km S of Umeå
🏠 Acke Lundgren
📱 www.norrmjole-golf.se

Örnsköldsviks GK Puttom (1967)
Ovansjö 232, 891 95 Arnäsvall
☎ **(0660) 254001**
💻 (0660) 254040
✉ kansli@puttom.se

For list of abbreviations, key to symbols and international dialling codes see page 651

18 L 5795 m SSS 72
H
£€ 250kr (300kr)
⊷ 15km N of Örnsköldsvik on E4
⌂ Nils Sköld
🖳 www.puttom.se

Östersund-Frösö (1947)
Kungsgården 205, 832 96 Frösön
☎ (063) 576030

Piteå (1960)
Nötöv 119, 941 41 Piteå
☎ (0911) 14990

Skellefteå (1967)
Rönnbäcken, 931 92 Skellefteå
☎ (0910) 779333
✉ info@skelleftegolf.nu

Sollefteå (1970)
Box 213, 881 25 Sollefteå
☎ (0620) 21477/12670

Sundsvall (1952)
Golfvägen 5, 86234 Kvissleby
☎ +46 60 515175
🖳 +46 60 515170
✉ info@sundsvallgk.golf.se
ℙ 18 L 5885 m SSS 72
WD–H WE–H after 10am
£€ 250kr (300r)
⊷ Skottsund, 15km S of Sundsvall
⌂ Rafael Lindholm, Nils Sköld
🖳 www.sundsvallgk.com

Timrå
Golfbanevägen 2, 860 32 Fagervik
☎ (060) 570153
🖳 (060) 578136
✉ info@timragk.golf.se
ℙ 18 L 5715 m Par 72
H
£€ D–300kr
⊷ 1km S of Sundsvall airport
⌂ Sune Linde
🖳 www.timragk.se

Umeå (1954)
Lövön, 913 35 Holmsund
☎ (090) 41071/41066

Gothenburg

Albatross (1973)
Lillhagsvägen, 422 50 Hisings-Backa
☎ (031) 551901/550500

Chalmers
Härrydavägen 50, 438 91 Landvetter
☎ +46 (0) 31 91 84 30
✉ info@chgk.se

Delsjö (1962)
Kallebäck, 412 76 Göteborg
☎ (031) 406959

Forsgårdens (1982)
Gamla Forsv 1, 434 47 Kungsbacka
☎ (0300) 566350

Göteborg (1902)
Box 2056, 436 02 Hovås
☎ (031) 282444

Gullbringa G&CC (1968)
Kulperödsvägen 6, 442 95 Håtta
☎ (0303) 227161
🖳 (0303) 227778
✉ kansli@gullbringa.o.se
ℙ 27 (3 x 9):
Blue Par 71, Red Par 70, Yellow
Par 69
U
£€ D–350kr/€38
⊷ 14km W of Kungälv, towards
Marstrand; 25km from Gothenburg
⌂ Douglas Brasier
🖳 www.gullbringa.o.se

Kungälv-Kode
Ö Knaverstad 140, 442 97 Kode
☎ (0303) 51300

Kungsbacka (1971)
Hamravägen 15, 429 44 Särö
☎ (031) 938180

Lysegården (1966)
Box 532, 442 15 Kungälv
☎ (0303) 223426
🖳 (0303) 223075
✉ info@lysegarden.sgk.golf.se
ℙ 18 L 5670 m SSS 71
9 L 5444 m SSS 70
H
£€ 300kr
⊷ 10km N of Kungälv
⌂ Röhss/Engström
🖳 www.lysegarden.sgk.se

Mölndals (1979)
Box 77, 437 21 Lindome
☎ (031) 993030
🖳 (031) 994901
✉ molndalsgk@telia.com
ℙ 18 L 5625 m SSS 73
£€ 300kr (350kr)
⊷ Lindome, 20km S of Gothenburg
⌂ Ronald Fream
🖳 www.molndalsgk.se

Öijared (1958)
Pl 1082, 448 92 Floda
☎ (0302) 30604

Partille (1986)
Box 234, 433 24 Partille
☎ (031) 987043

Sjögärde
430 30 Frillesås
☎ (0340) 657860

Stenungsund (1993)
Lundby Pl 7480, 444 93 Spekeröd
☎ (0303) 778470

Stora Lundby (1983)
Valters Väg 2, 443 71 Grabo
☎ (0302) 44200

Malmö & South Coast

Abbekas (1989)
Kroppsmarksvagen, 274 56 Abbekas
☎ (0411) 533233
🖳 (0411) 533419
✉ info@abbekasgk.golf.se
ℙ 18 L 5817 m Par 72
U H
£€ 300kr (350kr)
⊷ 20km W of Ystad
⌂ Tommy Nordström
🖳 www.abbekas.nu

Barsebäck G&CC (1969)
246 55 Löddeköpinge
☎ (046) 776230

Bokskogen (1963)
Torupsvägen 408-140, 230 40 Bara
☎ (040) 406900

Falsterbo (1909)
Fyrvägen 34, 239 40 Falsterbo
☎ +46 (0)40 470078/475078
🖳 +46 (0)40 472722
✉ info@falsterbogk..se
ℙ 18 L 6577 yds Par 71 CR 73.2 SR
129
H
£€ €50.65 (€60.65)
⊷ 30km SW of Malmö
⌂ Gunnar Bauer; Peter Champerlain/
Peter Nordwall
🖳 www.falsterbogk.com

Flommens (1935)
239 40 Falsterbo
☎ (040) 475016
🖳 (040) 473157
✉ info@flommensgk.se
ℙ 18 L 5735 m SSS 72
U H
£€ 400kr
⊷ 35km SW of Malmö
⌂ Bergendorff/Kristersson
🖳 www.flommensgk.se

Kävlinge (1989)
Box 138, 244 22 Kävlinge
☎ (046) 736270
🖳 (046) 728486
✉ info@kavlingegk.golf.se

18 L 5800 m SSS 72
H
££ 280kr (350kr)
♣ 12km N of Lund
⌂ Rolf Collijn
▤ www.kavlingegk.com

Ljunghusen (1932)
Kinellsvag, Ljunghusen, 236 42 Höllviken
☎ (040) 458000
▭ (040) 454265
✉ info@ljgk.se
↦ 27 holes:
L 5455-5895 m SSS 70-73
WD–U H WE–M before noon
££ 400kr (500kr)
♣ Falsterbo Peninsula. 30km SW of
Malmö
⌂ Douglas Brasier
▤ www.ljgk.se

Lunds Akademiska (1936)
Kungsmarken, 225 92 Lund
☎ (046) 99005
▭ (046) 99146
✉ info@lagk.se
↦ 18 L 5780 m
H
££ 350kr (450kr)
♣ 5km E of Lund
⌂ Boström/Morrison/Fjallman
▤ www.lagk.se

Malmö Burlöv (1981)
Segesvängen, 212 27 Malmö
☎ (040) 292535/292536
▭ (040) 292228
✉ malmogolfklubb@teua.com
↦ 18 L 5750 m SSS 71
H
££ 320kr
♣ NE of Malmö
⌂ Jan Sederholm and Tommy
Nordstrom
▤ www.malmogolfklubb.com

Örestad (1986)
Golfvägen, Habo Ljung, 234 22 Lomma
☎ (040) 410580
▭ (040) 416320
✉ info@orestadsgk.com
↦ 18 L 6046 m Par 71
9 L 3116 m Par 36
18 hole Par 3 course
H
££ 280kr (340kr)
♣ 15km N of Malmö
⌂ Åke Persson
▤ www.orestadsgk.com

Österlen (1945)
Lilla Vik, 272 95 Simrishamn
☎ (0414) 412550
▭ (0414) 412551
✉ osterlengolfklubb@telia.com
↦ 18 L 5835 m CR 69.8
18 L 5741 m CR 71.3
H
££ 300kr (400kr)
♣ Vik, 8km N of Simrishamn

⌂ Tommy Nordström
▤ www.osterlensgk.com

Romeleåsen (1969)
Kvarnbrodda, 240 14 Veberöd
☎ (046) 82012
▭ (046) 82113
✉ info@ragk.se
↦ 18 L 5783 m Par 72
H
££ 30kr (350kr)
♣ 6km S of Veberöd. 25km E of
Malmö
⌂ Douglas Brasier
▤ www.ragk.se

Söderslätts (1993)
Ellaboda Grevier 260, 235 94 Vellinge
☎ (040) 429680
▭ (040) 429684
✉ info@soderslattsgK.golf.se
↦ 18 L 5800 m SSS 72
9 hole Par 3 course
WD–H WE–M H before noon
££ Jan–May and Sept–Dec 300kr;
June–Aug 350kr
♣ 15km SE of Malmö
⌂ Sune Linde
▤ www.golf/se/soderslattsgk

Tegelberga (1988)
Alstad Pl 140, 231 96 Trelleborg
☎ (040) 485690
▭ (040) 485691
↦ 27 L 6011 m CR 73.5
U H
££ 300kr (360kr)
♣ 11km N of Trelleborg. 25km E of
Malmö
⌂ Peter Chamberlain
▤ www.golf.se/tegelbergagk

Tomelilla (1987)
Ullstorp, 273 94 Tomelilla
☎ (0417) 19430
▭ (0417) 13657
✉ info@tomelillagolfklub.com
↦ 18 L 6455 m Par 73 SSS 75
H
££ 370kr
♣ 15km N of Ystad. 60km E of
Malmö
⌂ Tommy Nordström
▤ www.tomelillagolfklubb.com

Trelleborg (1963)
Maglarp, Pl 431, 231 93 Trelleborg
☎ (0410) 330460
▭ (0410) 330281
✉ info@trelleborgsgk.golf.se
↦ 18 L 5299 m Par 70
U H
££ 350kr
♣ 5km W of Trelleborg
⌂ Brasier/Chamberlain
▤ www.trelleborgsgk.com

Vellinge (1991)
Toftadals Gård, 235 41 Vellinge
☎ (040) 443255

Ystad (1930)
Långrevsvägen, 270 22 Köpingebro
☎ (0411) 550350
▭ (0411) 550392
✉ info@ystadgk.com
↦ 18 L 5800 m Par 72
U
££ 250–350kr
♣ 7km E of Ystad, towards
Simrishamn
⌂ Thure Bruce
▤ www.ystadgk.se

North

Alvkarleby
Västanåvägen 5, 814 94 Alvkarleby
☎ (026) 72757
✉ info@alvkarlebygk.se

Avesta (1963)
Friluftsvägen 10, 774 61 Avesta
☎ (0226) 55913/10866/12766
▭ (0226) 12578
↦ 18 L 5560 m SSS 71
H
££ 250kr (300kr)
♣ 3km NE of Avesta
⌂ Sune Linde
▤ www.golf.se/golfklubbar/avestagk

Bollnäs (1963)
Norrfly 1634, 823 91 Kilafors
☎ (0278) 650540
▭ (0278) 651220
✉ info@bollnasgk.com
↦ 18 L 5870 m Par 72
H
££ 250kr (300kr)
♣ 15km S of Bollnäs (Route 83)
⌂ Sune Lindhe
▤ www.bollnasgk.com

Dalsjö (1989)
Dalsjö 3, 781 94 Borlänge
☎ (0243) 220080
▭ (0243) 220140
✉ info@dalsjogolf.se
↦ 18 L 5715 m Par 72
H
££ 290kr
♣ 5km NE of Borlänge
⌂ Jeremy Turner/Peter Nordvall
▤ www.dalsjogolf.se

Falun-Borlänge (1956)
Storgarden 10, 791 93 Falun
☎ (023) 31015

Gävle (1949)
Bönavägen 23, 805 95 Gävle
☎ (026) 120333/120338

Hagge   (1963)
Hagge, 771 90 Ludvika
☎ **(0240) 28087/28513**

Hofors   (1965)
Box 117, 813 22 Hofors
☎ **(0290) 85125**

Högbo   (1962)
Daniel Tilas Väg 4, 811 92 Sandviken
☎ **(026) 215015**

Hudiksvall   (1964)
Tjuvskär, 824 01 Hudiksvall
☎ **+46 (0) 650 542080**

Leksand   (1977)
Box 25, 793 21 Leksand
☎ **(0247) 14640**

Ljusdal   (1973)
Svinhammarsv.2, 827 23 Ljusdal
☎ **(0651) 16883**
   (0651) 12566 (shop)

Mora   (1980)
Box 264, 792 24 Mora
☎ **(0250) 592990**
🖳 (0250) 592995
✉ info@moragk.se
▥ 1100
▷ 18 L 5600 m Par 72
££ 260kr
🚗 1km N of Mora. 40km NW of
   Rättvik
🏠 Sune Linde
▤ www.moragk.se

Rättvik   (1954)
Box 29, 795 21 Rättvik
☎ **(0248) 51030**

Sälenfjallens   (1991)
Box 20, 780 67 Sälen
☎ **(0280) 20670**
🖳 (0280) 20671
✉ info@salenfjallensgk.se
▷ 18 L 5702 m Par 72
👤 U H
££ 250kr
🚗 230km NW of Borlänge. 400km
   NW of Stockholm
🏠 Sune Linde
▤ www.salenfjallensgk.se

Säter   (1984)
Box 89, 783 22 Säter
☎ **(0225) 50030**

Snöå   (1990)
Snöå Bruk, 780 51 Dala-Järna
☎ **(0281) 24072**

Söderhamn   (1961)
Box 117, 826 23 Söderhamn
☎ **(0270) 281300**

Sollerö   (1991)
Levsnäs, 79290 Sollerön
☎ **(0250) 22236**

Skane & South

Allerum   (1992)
Pl 7592, 260 35 Ödåkra
☎ **(042) 93051**

Ängelholm   (1973)
Box 1117, 262 22 Ängelholm
☎ **(0431) 430260/431460**

Araslöv
Starvägen 1, 291 75 Färlöv
☎ **(044) 71600**

Båstad   (1929)
Box 1037, 269 21 Båstad
☎ **(0431) 78370**

Bedinge   (1931)
Golfbanevägen, 231 76 Beddingestrand
☎ **(0410) 25514**

Bjäre
Salomonhög 3086, 269 93 Båstad
☎ **(0431) 361053**

Bosjökloster   (1974)
243 95 Höör
☎ **(0413) 25858**

Carlskrona   (1949)
PO Almö, 370 24 Nättraby
☎ **(0457) 35123**

Degeberga-Widtsköfle
Segholmsu.126, Box 71, 297 21 Degeberga
☎ **(044) 355035**
🖳 (044) 355075
✉ dwgk@telia.com
▷ 18 L 6129 m SSS 72
   9 hole Par 3 course
👤 U
££ 250kr–300kr
🚗 20km S of Kristianstad
▤ www.dwgolfklubb.com

Eslöv   (1966)
Box 150, 241 22 Eslöv
☎ **(0413) 18610**
🖳 (0413) 18613
✉ info@eslovsgk.golf.se
▷ 18 L 5610 m CR 70.7 SR 133
   Par 70
👤 H
££ 300kr (340kr)
🚗 4km S of Eslöv (Route 113)

🏠 Thure Bruce
▤ www.golf.se/golfklubbar/eslovsgk

Hässleholm   (1978)
Skyrup, 282 95 Tyringe
☎ **(0451) 53111**

Helsingborg   (1924)
260 40 Viken
☎ **(042) 236147**
✉ office@helsingborgsgk.com
▷ 9 L 4578 m Par 68
👤 U
££ 200kr (220kr)
🚗 15km NW of Helsingborg
🏠 W Hester
▤ www.helsingborgsgk.com

Karlshamn   (1962)
Box 188, 374 23 Karlshamn
☎ **(0454) 50085**

Kristianstad   (1924)
Box 41, 296 21 Åhus
☎ **(044) 247656**
🖳 (044) 247635
✉ info@kristianstadsgk.com
▷ 18 L 5810 m SSS 72
   9 L 2945 m SSS 36
👤 H
££ 350kr
🚗 18km SE of Kristianstad. Airport
   20km
🏠 Brasier/Nordström
▤ www.kristianstadsgk.com

Landskrona   (1960)
Erikstorp, 261 61 Landskrona
☎ **(0418) 446260**

Mölle   (1943)
260 42 Mölle
☎ **(042) 347520**
🖳 (042) 347523
✉ info@mollgk.se
▷ 18 L 5292 m Par 70
👤 H–max 36
££ 350kr
🚗 Mölle, 35km NW of Helsingborg
🏠 Thure Bruce
▤ www.mollegk.se

Örkelljunga   (1989)
Rya 472, 286 91 Örkelljunga
☎ **(0435) 53690/53640**
🖳 (0435) 53670
✉ info@orkelljungagk.com
▷ 18 L 5700 m SSS 72
👤 H
££ 250kr (350kr)
🚗 8km S of Örkelljunga. 40km NE of
   Helsingborg (E4)
🏠 Hans Fock
▤ www.orkelljungagk.com

Östra Göinge   (1981)
Riksvägen 12, 289 21 Knislinge
☎ **(044) 60060**

(044) 67862
info@ostragoinge.golf.se
18 L 5906 m Par 72
H
220kr (280kr)
20km N of Kristianstad
T Nordström
www.golf.se/ostragoingegk

Perstorp (1964)
Gustavsborg 501, 284 91 Perstorp
(0435) 35411

Ronneby (1963)
Box 26, 372 21 Ronneby
(0457) 10315

Rya (1934)
PL 5500, 255 92 Helsingborg
(042) 220182
(042) 220394
kansli@ryagolf.se
18 L 5558 m Par 72
H
450kr
10km S of Helsingborg
Petterson/Sundblom
www.ryagolf.se

St Arild (1987)
Golfvagen 48, 260 41 Nyhamnsläge
(042) 346860
(042) 346042
kansliet@starild.se
18 L 5805 m Par 72
H
350kr (350kr) = £25
50km N of Helsingborg
Jan Sederholm
www.starild.se

Skepparslov (1984)
Sätesvägen 14, 291 92 Kristianstad
(044) 229508
(044) 229503
kansli@skepparslovgk.se
18 L 5996 m SSS 73
U
220kr (300kr)
7km W of Kristianstad
Rolf Collijn
www.skepparslovsgk.se

Söderåsen (1966)
Box 41, 260 50 Billesholm
(042) 73337
(042) 73963
info@soderasensgk.golf.se
18 L 5633 m Par 71 CR 70.8 SR 134
U H
320kr (380kr)
20km E of Helsingborg
Thure Bruce
www.golf.se

Sölvesborg
Box 204, 294 25 Sölvesborg
(0456) 70650

(0456) 70650
info@solvesborggk.se
18 L 5900 m Par 72
U
300kr
30km E of Kristianstad
Sune Linde
www.solvesborggk.se

Svalöv (1989)
Månstorp Pl 1365, 268 90 Svalöv
(0418) 662462

Torekov (1924)
Råledsv 31, 260 93 Torekov
(0431) 449840
(0431) 364916
info@togk.se
18 L 5525 m Par 71
H WE–M before noon
400kr (450kr)
3km N of Torekov
Nils Sköld
www.togk.se

Trummenas
373 02 Ramdala
(0455) 60505

Vasatorp (1973)
Box 13035, 250 13 Helsingborg
(042) 235058

Wittsjö (1962)
Ubbaltsgården, 280 22 Vittsjö
(0451) 22635

South East

A 6 Golfklubb (1985)
Centralvägen, 553 05 Jönköping
(036) 308130
(036) 308140
a6gk@a6gk.se
27 hole course:
9 L 3185 m Par 38
9 L 3115 m Par 37
9 L 2935 m Par 36
U H
300kr–350kr
2km SE of Jönköping
Peter Nordwall
www.a6gk.se

Älmhult (1975)
Pl 1215, 343 90 Älmhult
(0476) 14135

Åtvidaberg (1954)
Västantorp, 597 41 Åtvidaberg
(0120) 35425

Ekerum
387 92 Borgholm, Öland
(0485) 80000

(0485) 80010
18 L 5975 m Par 73
18 L 5862 m Par 72
U H
250kr–400kr
12km S of Borgholm. 25km N of Öland bridge
Peter Nordwall
www.ekerum.com
www.ekerum.se

Eksjö (1938)
Skedhult, 575 96 Eksjö
(0381) 13525
(0381) 12405
info@eksjogk.nu
18 L 5930 m SSS 72
WD–U WE–H
300kr
6km W of Eksjö on Nässjö road
Anders Amilon
www.eksjogk.nu

Emmaboda (1976)
Kyrkogatan, 360 60 Vissefjärda
(0471) 20505/20540
info@emmabodagk.golf.se

Finspångs (1965)
Viberga Gård, 612 92 Finspång
(0122) 13940
(0122) 18888
info@finspangsgk.golf.se
27 L 5800 m CR 71.1 SR 124
H
250kr (300kr)
2km E of Finspång, Route 51. Norrköping 25km.
Sköld/Linde/Chamberlain
www.finspang.se/golf

Gotska (1986)
Box 1119, 621 22 Visby, Gotland
(0498) 215545
(0498) 256332
info@gotskagk.golf.se
18 L 5202 m Par 69
9 L 5414 m Par 72
U H
9: D–100kr 18: D–280kr
N outskirts of Visby
Jack Wenman
www.gotskagk.se

Grönhögen (1996)
PL 1270, 380 65 Öland
(0485) 665995

Gumbalde
Box 35, 620 13 Ståga, Gotland
(0498) 482880

Hooks
560 13 Hok
(0393) 21420

Isaberg (1968)
Nissafors Bruk, 330 27 Hestra
☎ (0370) 336330

Jönköping (1936)
Kettilstorp, 556 27 Jönköping
☎ (036) 76567

Kalmar (1947)
Box 278, 391 23 Kalmar
☎ (0480) 472111
🖳 (0480) 472314
📧 reception.kalmar.gk@telia.com
🏴 Blue 18 L 5700 m SSS 72
  Red 18 L 5634 m SSS 72
👥 H
££ 350kr (400kr)
🚗 9km N of Kalmar via E22
🏠 Brasier/Sköld/Linde
📋 www.kalmargk.se

Lagan (1966)
Box 63, 340 14 Lagan
☎ (0372) 30450/35460

Landeryd (1987)
Bogestad Gård, 585 93 Linköping
☎ (013) 362200
🖳 (013) 362208
🏴 North 18 L 5675 m SSS 72
  South 18 L 5085 m SSS 68
  9 hole short course
👥 U
££ 300–350kr (400–450kr)
🚗 7km SE of Linköping
🏠 Nordström/Persson

Lidhems (1988)
360 14 Väckelsång
☎ (0470) 33660

Linköping (1945)
Box 15054, 580 15 Linköping
☎ (013) 262990
🖳 (013) 140769
📧 lggolf@telia.com
🏴 18 L 5659 m SSS 71
👥 H
££ 300kr (400kr)
🚗 3km SW of Linköping
🏠 Sundblom/Brasier
📋 www.linkopingsgK.se

Mjölby (1986)
Blixberg, Miskarp, 595 92 Mjölby
☎ (0142) 12570
🖳 (0142) 16553
📧 kansli@mjolbygk.com
🏴 18 L 5485 m SSS 71
👥 H
££ 260kr (320kr)
🚗 35km WSW of Linköping (E4), exit
  108
🏠 Åke Persson
📋 www.mjolbygk.com

Motala (1956)
PO Box 264, 591 23 Motala
☎ (0141) 50840
🖳 (0141) 208990
📧 info@motalagk.golf.se
🏴 18 L 5563 m Par 71
👥 U
££ 260kr (320kr)
🚗 3km S of Motala via Route 50
🏠 Sköld/Sederholm
📋 www.motalagk.se

Nässjö (1988)
Box 5, 571 21 Nässjö
☎ (0380) 10022

Norrköping (1928)
Borg, 605 97 Norrköping
☎ (011) 158240
🖳 (011) 158249
📧 info@ngk.nu
🏴 18 L 5860 m SSS 73
👥 U H
££ 300kr (350kr)
🚗 Klinga, 9km S of Norrköping on E4
🏠 Nils Sköld
📋 www.ngk.nu

Oskarshamn (1972)
Box 148, 572 23 Oskarshamn
☎ (0491) 94033

Skinnarebo
Skinnarebo, 555 93 Jönköping
☎ (036) 69075

Söderköping (1983)
Hylinge, 605 96 Norrköping
☎ (011) 70579

Tobo (1971)
Fredensborg 133, 598 91 Vimmerby
☎ (0492) 30346

Tranås (1952)
Box 430, 573 25 Tranås
☎ (0140) 311661

Vadstena (1957)
Hagalund, Box 122, 592 23 Vadstena
☎ (0143) 12440
🖳 (0143) 12709
📧 kansli@vadstenagk.nu
🏴 18 L 5850 m (men) 4992 m
  (Ladies)
  Par 72
👥 U
££ 280kr (350kr)
🚗 3km S of Vadstena, towards
  Vaderstad
📋 www.vadstenagk.nu

Värnamo (1962)
Box 146, 331 21 Värnamo
☎ (0370) 23991
🖳 (0370) 23992
📧 info@varnamogk.se

🏴 27 L 6253 m SSS 72
👥 U
££ 300kr (350kr)
🚗 8km E of Värnamo on Route 127
🏠 Nils Sköld, Björn Magnusson
📋 www.varnamogk.com

Västervik (1959)
Box 62, Ekhagen, 593 22 Västervik
☎ (0490) 32420

Växjö (1959)
Box 227, 351 05 Växjö
☎ (0470) 21515

Vetlanda (1983)
Box 249, 574 23 Vetlanda
☎ (0383) 18310

Visby
Västergarn Kronholmen 415, 622 30
Gotlands Tofta
☎ +46 498 200930
🖳 +46 498 200932
🏴 18 L 5875 m Par 72
  9 L 9277 m Par 36
👥 Jun–Aug–H
££ 300–450kr
🚗 Kronholmen, 25km S of Visby,
  Gotland island
🏠 Nordwall/Sköld
📋 www.visbygk.com

Vreta Kloster
Box 144, 590 70 Ljungsbro
☎ (013) 169700
📧 info@vkgk.se

South West

Alingsås (1985)
Hjälmared 4050, 441 95 Alingsås
☎ (0322) 52421

Bäckavattnet (1977)
Marbäck, 305 94 Halmstad
☎ (035) 162040

Billingens GK (1949)
St Kulhult, 540 17 Lerdala
☎ +46 511 80291
🖳 +46 511 80244
📧 info@billingensgk.se
🏴 18 L 5470 m Par 71
👥 U
££ 200kr (270kr)
🚗 20km NW of Skövde
🏠 Douglas Brasier
📋 www.billingensgk.se

Borås (1933)
Östra Vik, Kråkered, 504 95 Borås
☎ (033) 250250

Ekarnas (1970)

Balders Väg 12, 467 31 Grästorp
- ☎ (0514) 12061
- 🖨 (0514) 12062
- ✉ info@ekarnasgk.golf.se
- ⴑ 18 L 5501 m SSS 71
- ⴱ H
- £€ 250kr (300kr)
- ⛽ 25km E of Trollhätten; 35km SW of Lidköping
- ⌂ Jan Andersson
- 🖥 www.golf.se//ekarnasgk

Falkenberg (1949)

Golfvägen, 311 72 Falkenberg
- ☎ (0346) 50287
- 🖨 (0346) 50997
- ✉ info@falkenberggk.golf.se
- ⴑ 27 L 5575-5680 m SSS 72
- ⴱ H
- £€ 360kr
- ⛽ 5km S of Falkenberg
- ⌂ Sköld-Sundblom-Sederholf-Nordström
- 🖥 www.falkenberggolfklubb.com

Falköping (1965)

Box 99, 521 02 Falköping
- ☎ (0515) 31270

Halmstad (1930)

302 73 Halmstad
- ☎ (035) 176800/176801
- 🖨 (035) 176820
- ✉ info@halmstad.golf.se
- ⴑ North: 18 L 5955 m CR 72.4 South: 18 L 5542 m CR 69.9
- ⴱ H
- £€ North: 600kr South: 500kr
- ⛽ Tylosand, 9km W of Halmstad
- ⌂ Sundblom/Sköld/Pennink
- 🖥 www.hgk.se

Haverdals (1988)

Slingervägen 35, 31042 Haverdal
- ☎ (035) 144990
- 🖨 (035) 53890
- ✉ info@haverdalsgk-golf.se
- ⴑ 18 L 5840 m Par 72
- ⴱ H
- £€ 360Skr
- ⛽ 11km NW of Halmstad
- ⌂ Anders Amilon/Bjorn Magnusson
- 🖥 www.haverdalsgk.com

Hökensås (1962)

PO Box 116, 544 22 Hjo
- ☎ (0503) 16059

Holms (1990)

Nannarp, 305 92 Halmstad
- ☎ (035) 38189
- ✉ info@holmsgk.golf.se

Hulta (1972)

Box 54, 517 22 Bollebygd
- ☎ (033) 204340

Knistad G&CC

541 92 Skövde
- ☎ (0500) 463170

Laholm (1964)

Box 101, 312 22 Laholm
- ☎ (0430) 30601
- 🖨 (0430) 30891
- ✉ info@laholmgk.com
- ⴑ 18 L 5430 m Par 70 CR 69.5 SR 128
  9 L 2660 m Par 72 CR 71.0 SR 135
- ⴱ U H
- £€ 300kr (320kr)
- ⛽ 5 miles E of Laholm on Route 24
- ⌂ Jan Sederholm
- 🖥 www.laholmgk.com

Lidköping (1967)

Box 2029, 531 02 Lidköping
- ☎ (0510) 546144

Mariestads Golf Course (1975)

Gummerstadsvägen 45, 542 94 Mariestad
- ☎ (0501) 47147
- 🖨 (0501) 78117
- ✉ info@mariestadsgk.se
- ⴑ 18 L 5970 m SSS 73
- ⴱ H
- £€ 250kr
- ⛽ 4km W of Mariestad, at Lake Vänern
- 🖥 www.mariestadsgk.com

Marks (1962)

Brättingstorpsvägen 28, 511 58 Kinna
- ☎ (0320) 14220
- 🖨 (0320) 12516
- ✉ info@marksgk.se
- ⴑ 18 L 5530 m Par 70 CR 70.7 (men); 73.1 (ladies)
  9 L 2675 m Par 35
- ⴱ H
- £€ 300kr
- ⛽ Kinna, 30km S of Borås
- ⌂ Sköld/Sederholm
- 🖥 www.marksgk.se

Onsjö (1974)

Box 6331 A, 462 42 Vänersborg
- ☎ (0521) 68870
- 🖨 (0521) 17106
- ⴑ 18 L 5730 m SSS 72
- ⴱ U
- £€ 250kr (300kr)
- ⛽ 3km S of Vänersborg. 80km N of Gothenburg
- ⌂ Sköld/Linde
- 🖥 www.onsjogk.com

Ringenäs (1987)

Strandlida, 305 91 Halmstad
- ☎ (035) 161590
- 🖨 (035) 161599
- ✉ ringenas.golf@telia.com
- ⴑ 27 L 5395-5615 m Par 71-72
- ⴱ H

Ringenäs (continued)

- £€ 280kr-370kr (380kr)
- ⛽ 10km NW of Halmstad
- ⌂ Sune Linde
- 🖥 www.ringenasgolfbana.com

Skogaby (1988)

312 93 Laholm
- ☎ (0430) 60190
- ✉ skogaby.gk@telia.com

Sotenas Golfklubb (1988)

Pl Onna, 450 46 Hunnebostrand
- ☎ (0523) 52302

Töreboda (1965)

Box 18, 545 21 Töreboda
- ☎ (0506) 12305

Trollhättan (1963)

Stora Ekeskogen, 466 91 Sollebrunn
- ☎ (0520) 441000

Ulricehamn (1947)

523 33 Ulricehamn
- ☎ (0321) 27950
- 🖨 (0321) 27959
- ✉ info@ulricehamngk.golf.se
- ⴑ 18 L 5509 m Par 71
- ⴱ WD-H
- £€ 230kr (260kr)
- ⛽ Lassalyckan, 2km E of Ulricehamn
- ⌂ Anders Amilion, Rafael Sundborn
- 🖥 www.golf.se/ulricehamngk

Vara-Bjertorp

Bjertorp, 535 91 Kvänum
- ☎ (0512) 20261

Varberg (1950)

430 10 Tvååker
- ☎ +46 340 480380
- 🖨 +46 340 480388
- ✉ info@varbergsgk.se
- ⴑ East 18 L 5440 m Par 71 CR 71 West 18 L 6435 m Par 72 CR 76
- ⴱ H
- £€ 320kr-380kr (£25-£28)
- ⛽ East: 15km E of Varberg. West: 8km S of Varberg, nr E6
- ⌂ Sköld/Nordström
- 🖥 www.varbergsgk.se

Vinberg (1992)

Sannagård, 311 95 Falkenberg
- ☎ (0346) 19020

Stockholm

Ågesta (1958)

123 52 Farsta
- ☎ (08) 447 3330

Botkyrka

Malmbro Gård, 147 91 Grödinge
- ☎ (08) 530 29650

For list of abbreviations, key to symbols and international dialling codes see page 651

☎ (08) 530 29409
✉ info@botkyrkagk.golf.se
☞ 18 holes Par 73
9 hole Par 3 course
👥 WD–U H WE–H after 1pm
££ 350kr (400kr)
🚗 30km S of Stockholm
▤ www.golf.se/botkyrkagk

Bro-Bålsta   (1978)
Ginnlögs Väg, 197 91 Bro
☎ (08) 582 41310

Djursholm   (1931)
Hagbardsvägen 1, 182 63 Djursholm
☎ (08) 5449 6451
☎ (08) 5449 6456
✉ robert@dgk.nu
☞ 18 L 5569 m SSS 71
9 L 2135 m SSS 34
👥 WD–U H before 5pm M after 5pm
WE–M before noon U H after
noon
££ 500kr (500kr)
🚗 12km N of Stockholm
▤ www.dgk.nu (Swedish only)

Fågelbro G&CC   (1991)
Fågelbro Säteri, 139 60 Värmdö
☎ +46 (08) 571 41800
☎ +46 (08) 571 40671
✉ info.fagelbro@telia.com
☞ 18 L 5522 m Par 71
👥 WD–H WE
££ 500kr (600kr)
🚗 35km E of Stockholm
🏠 Eriksson/Oredsson
▤ www.fagelbrogolf.se

Haninge   (1983)
Årsta Slott, 136 91 Haninge
☎ (08) 500 32850
☎ (08) 500 32851
✉ info@haninggk.golf.se
☞ 27 L 5930 m Par 73
👥 WD–U before 1pm –M after 1pm
WE–M before 1pm –U after 1pm
££ 400kr (450kr)
🚗 30km S of Stockholm towards
Nynäshamn
🏠 Jan Sederholm
▤ www.haningegk.se

Huvudstadens
Lindö Park, 186 92 Vallentuna
☎ (08) 511 70055 (Bookings)
☎ (08) 511 70613
☞ 18 L 5800 m SSS 72
18 L 5795 m SSS 72
👥 U H–book 3 days before play
££ 150kr–395kr (395kr–595kr)
🚗 30km N of Stockholm
🏠 Persson/Bruce/Eriksson
▤ www.huvudstadensgolf.se

Ingarö   (1962)
Fogelvik, 134 64 Ingarö
☎ (08) 570 28870

Kungsängen   (1992)
Box 133, 196 21 Kungsängen
☎ (08) 584 50730
☎ (08) 581 71002
✉ info@kungsangengc.se
☞ Kings 18 L 6100 m Par 71
Queens 18 L 5300 m Par 69
👥 U H
££ Kings–600kr. Queens–400kr
🚗 25km W of Stockholm via E18 to
Brunna
🏠 Anders Forsbrand
▤ www.kungsangengc.se

Lidingö   (1933)
Box 1035, 181 21 Lidingö
☎ (08) 731 7900
☎ (08) 731 7900
✉ kansli@lidingogk.se
☞ 18 L 5647 m SSS 72
👥 WD–U H before 3pm –NA after
3pm Sat–NA Sun–NA before
1pm
££ 450kr
🚗 6km NE of Stockholm
🏠 MacDonald/Sundblom
▤ www.lidingogk.se

Lindö   (1978)
186 92 Vallentuna
☎ (08) 514 30990

Nya Johannesberg G&CC
(1990)
762 95 Rimbo
☎ (08) 514 50000

Nynäshamn   (1977)
Korunda 40, 148 91 Ösmo
☎ (08) 524 30590/524 30599
☎ (08) 524 30598
✉ kanslp@nynashamnsgk.a.se
☞ 27 L 5690 m SSS 72
9 hole par 29 course rated
👥 H–phone first
££ 340kr (390kr)
🚗 Ösmo, 40km S of Stockholm
🏠 Sune Linde, Åbe Persson, Rolf
Colijn
▤ www.nynashamnsgk.a.se

Österakers
Hagby 1, 184 92 Akersberga
☎ (08) 540 85165
☎ (08) 540 66832
✉ kansli@ostgk.se
☞ 18 L 5792 m Par 72
18 L 5780 m Par 72
9 L 2740 m Par 35
👥 U on the 9 hole course (Pay &
Play); H on the 18 hole course
££ 9: 180kr (200kr) 18: 350kr–400kr
(400kr–450kr)
🚗 30km NE of Stockholm
🏠 Sederholm/Tumba
▤ www.ostgk.se
www.hagbygolf.se

Österhaninge   (1992)
Husby, 136 91 Haninge
☎ (08) 500 32285
☎ (08) 500 32293
✉ info@osterhaningegk.golf.se
☞ 18 L 5600 m Par 70
👥 H
££ 300sek (350sek)
🚗 20km S of Stockholm
🏠 Bengt Lorichs and Jeremy Turner
▤ www.osterhaningegk.se

Royal Drottningholm
(1958)
PO Box 183, 178 93 Drottningholm
☎ (08) 759 0085
☎ (08) 759 0851
☞ 18 L 5745 m SSS 71
👥 WD–U H before 3pm –M after
3pm WE–M before 3pm –U H
after 3pm
££ 450kr
🚗 16km W of Stockholm
🏠 Sundblom/Sköld
▤ www.kdrgk.se

Saltsjöbaden   (1929)
Box 51, 133 21 Saltsjöbaden
☎ +46 (0)8 717 0125
☎ +46 (0)8 717 9713
✉ klubb@saltsjobadengk.se
☞ 18 L 5436 m SSS 71
9 L 3756 m SSS 64
👥 WD–U WE–M H before 2pm
££ 9: 200kr (250kr) 18: 380kr (450kr)
🚗 15km E of Stockholm city, via
Route 228
▤ www.saltsjobadengk.se

Sollentuna   (1967)
Skillingegården, 192 77 Sollentuna
☎ (08) 594 70995

Stockholm   (1904)
Kevingestrand 20, 182 57 Danderyd
☎ (08) 544 90710

Täby   (1968)
Skålhamra Gård, 187 70 Täby
☎ (08) 510 23261

Ullna   (1981)
Rosenkälla, 184 94 Åkersberga
☎ (08) 514 41230

Ulriksdal
Box 8088, 170 08 Solna
☎ (08) 855393
☞ 18 L 3900 m SSS 63
👥 H
££ 200kr (250kr)
🚗 8km N of Stockholm
🏠 Alec Backhurst

Vallentuna   (1989)
Box 266, 186 24 Vallentuna
☎ (08) 514 30560/1

Viksjö (1969)
Fjällens Gård, 175 45 Järfälla
☎ **(08) 580 31300/31310**

Wäsby
Box 2017, 194 02 Upplands Väsby
☎ **(08) 514 103 50**

Wermdö G&CC (1966)
Torpa, 139 40 Värmdö
☎ **(08) 574 60700**

West Central

Arvika (1974)
Box 197, 671 25 Arvika
☎ **(0570) 54133**

Billerud (1961)
Valnäs, 660 40 Segmon
☎ **(0555) 91313**
📞 (0555) 91306
📧 kansli@billerudsgk.se
⯈ 18 L 5465 m SSS 71
  Men: CR 69.6 SR 129
  Ladies: CR 71.9 SR 127
👥 H
££ D–260(300kr 15/6–31/8) (300kr)
🚗 Valnäs, 15km N of Säffle
🏠 Brasier/Sköld
🖥 www.billerudsgk.se

Eda (1992)
Noresund, 670 40 Åmotfors
☎ **(0571) 34101**

Färgelanda
Box 23, 458 21 Färgelanda
☎ **(0528) 20385**

Fjällbacka (1965)
450 71 Fjällbacka
☎ **(0525) 31150**

Forsbacka (1969)
Box 137, 662 23 Åmål
☎ **(0532) 61690**
📞 (0532) 61699
📧 info@forsbackagk.golf.se
⯈ 18 L 5860 m SSS 72
👥 H
££ D–250kr (300kr)
🚗 6km W of Åmål (Route 164)
🏠 Nils Sköld
🖥 www.golf.se/golfklubbar
  /forsbackagk/

Hammarö (1991)
Sätter Tallbacken, 663 91 Hammarö
☎ **(054) 522650**
📞 (054) 521863
📧 info@hammarogk.se
⯈ 18 L 6075 m Par 71
👥 H
££ 260kr (320kr)

🚗 11km S of Karlstad
🏠 Sune Linde
🖥 www.hammarogk.se

Karlskoga (1975)
Bricketorp 647, 691 94 Karlskoga
☎ **(0586) 728190**

Karlstad (1957)
Höja 510, 655 92 Karlstad
☎ **(054) 866353**
📞 (054) 866478
📧 info@karlstadgk.se
⯈ 18 L 5970 m Par 72
  9 L 2875 m Par 36
👥 H
££ 280 kr (320kr)
🚗 8km N of Karlstad (Route 63)
🏠 Sköld/Linde
🖥 www.karlstadgk.com

Kristinehamn (1974)
Box 337, 681 26 Kristinehamn
☎ **(0550) 82310**
📞 (0550) 19535
📧 kristinehamnsgk@telia.com
⯈ 18 L 5800 m SSS 72
👥 H
££ 250kr–300kr
🚗 3km N of Kristinehamn
🏠 Sune Linde
🖥 www.golf.se/golfklubbar
  /kristinehamnsgk

Lyckorna (1967)
Box 66, 459 22 Ljungskile
☎ **(0522) 20176**

Orust (1981)
Morlanda 135, 474 93 Ellös
☎ **(0304) 53170**
📞 (0304) 53174
📧 orustgk@telia.com
⯈ 18 L 5770 m SSS 72
👥 H
££ 250kr–360kr
🚗 Ellös, 10km from Henån. 80km N
  of Gothenburg
🏠 Lars Andreasson
🖥 www.orustgk.org

Saxå (1964)
Saxån, 682 92 Filipstad
☎ **(0590) 24070**

Skaftö (1963)
Stockeviksvägen 2, 450 34 Fiskebäckskil
☎ **+0046 (523) 23211**
📞 +0046 (0523) 23215
📧 kansliet@skaftogk.se
⯈ 18 L 4831 m SSS 69
👥 WD–H
££ 150kr–300kr
🚗 40km W of Uddevalla, through
  Fiskebäckskil
🏠 Sköld/Sederholm
🖥 www.skaftogk.se

Strömstad (1967)
Golfbanevägen, 452 90 Strömstad 1
☎ **(0526) 61788**

Sunne (1970)
Box 108, 686 23 Sunne
☎ **(0565) 14100/14210**

Torreby (1961)
Torreby Slott, 455 93 Munkedal
☎ **(0524) 21365/21109**

Uddeholm (1965)
Risäter 20, 683 93 Råda
☎ **(0563) 60564**

Switzerland

Bern

G&CC Blumisberg
(1959)
3184 Wünnewil
☎ **(026) 496 34 38**
📞 (026) 496 35 23
📧 secretariat@blumisberg.ch
⯈ 18 L 6048 m Par 72
👥 WD–U H WE–M
££ 100fr (100fr)
🚗 Wünnewil, 16km SW of Bern
🏠 B von Limburger

Les Bois (1988)
Case Postale 26, 2336 Les Bois
☎ **(032) 961 10 03**

Neuchâtel (1925)
Hameau de Voëns, 2072 Saint-Blaise
☎ **(032) 753 55 50**
📞 (032) 753 29 40
📧 secretariat@golfdeneuchatel.ch
⯈ 18 L 5917 m SSS 71
👥 H
££ 90fr (110fr)
🚗 Voëns/Saint-Blaise, 5km E of
  Neuchâtel. 30km W of Bern
🏠 Von Limberger/Peter Herrodine
🖥 www.golfdeneuchatel.ch

Payerne (1996)
Public
Domaine des Invuardes, 1530 Payerne
☎ **(026) 662 4220**
📞 (026) 662 4221
📧 golf.payerne@vtx.ch
⯈ 18 L 5450 m Par 70
👥 U H
££ 80fr (100fr)
🚗 50km W of Bern. 50km NE of
  Lausanne
🏠 Yves Bureau
🖥 www.golfpayerne.ch

Wallenried   (1994)

1784 Wallenried
☎ **(026) 684 84 80**
📠 (026) 684 84 90
📧 info@golf-wallenried.ch
🏷 18 L 6042 m Par 72
👥 WD–U H WE–U H
££ 80fr (100fr)
🚗 6km W of Fribourg
🏠 Ruzzo Reuss
📧 www.swissgolfnetwork.ch

Wylihof   (1994)

4542 Luterbach
☎ **(032) 682 28 28**
📠 (032 682 65 17
📧 wylihof-sekr@bluewin.ch
🏷 18 L 6580 yds Par 73
👥 WD–U H–max 36 WE–M H
££ 120fr
🚗 40km N of Bern. 90km W of Zürich
🏠 Ruzzo Reuss von Plauen
📧 www.golfclub.ch

Bernese Oberland

Interlaken-Unterseen
(1964)

Postfach 110, 3800 Interlaken
☎ **(033) 823 60 16**
📠 (033) 823 42 03
📧 interlakengolf@bluewin.ch
🏷 18 L 6143 m Par 72 CR 73.0 SR 129
👥 H max 36
££ 90fr (105fr)
🚗 Interlaken 3km
🏠 Donald Harradine; remodelled by John Chilver-Stainer
📧 www.interlakengolf.ch

Riederalp   (1986)

3987 Riederalp
☎ **(027) 927 29 32**
📠 (027) 927 29 23
📧 info@golfclub-riederalp.ch
🏷 9 L 3066 m Par 60 CR 57/8 SR 100
👥 U
££ 9: 45fr 18: 60fr
🚗 10km NE of Brig
🏠 Donald Harradine, John Shilver-Steiner
📧 www.golfclub-riederalp.ch

Lake Geneva & South West

Bonmont   (1983)

Château de Bonmont, 1275 Chéserex
☎ **(022) 369 99 00**
📠 (022) 369 99 09
📧 golfhotel@bonmont.com
🏷 18 L 6080m CR 71.6 SR 126 (white repairs)

👥 WD–restricted WE–M
££ WD–150chf
🚗 3km from Nyon. 30km NE of Geneva
🏠 Donald Harradine (1983), renewed by Peter Harradine (2003)
📧 www.bonmont.com

Les Coullaux   (1989)

1846 Chessel
☎ **(024) 481 22 46**
📠 (024) 481 66 46
🏷 9 L 2940 m Par 58
👥 U
££ 9 holes: 30fr (45fr) 2x9 holes: 35fr (55fr)
🚗 Chessel, between Evian and Montreux
🏠 Donald Harradine

Crans-sur-Sierre   (1906)

C P 112, 3963 Crans-sur-Sierre
☎ **(027) 485 97 97**
📠 (027) 485 9798
📧 info@golfcrans.ch
🏷 18 L 6341 m SSS 72
   9 L 2729 m SSS 35
👥 H
££ On application
🚗 20km E of Sion. Geneva 2 hrs
🏠 Severiano Ballesteros
📧 www.golfcrans.ch

Domaine Impérial   (1987)

Villa Prangins, 1196 Gland
☎ **(022) 999 06 00**
📧 info@golfdomaineimperial.com

Geneva   (1923)

70 Route de la Capite, 1223 Cologny
☎ **(+41) 22 707 48 00**
📠 (+41) 22 707 48 20
📧 secretariat@golfgeneve.ch
🏷 18 L 6150 m Par 72
👥 WD–am only Tues–Fri WE–M
££ 150fr
🚗 4km from centre of Geneva
🏠 Robert Trent Jones Sr

Lausanne   (1921)

Route du Golf 3, 1000 Lausanne 25
☎ **(021) 784 84 84**
📠 (021) 784 84 80
📧 info@golflausanne.ch
🏷 18 L 6295 m Par 72 CR 72.1 SR 135
👥 H
££ 100fr (130fr)
🚗 7km N of Lausanne towards Le Mont
🏠 Narbel/Harradine/Pern
📧 www.golflausanne.ch

Montreux   (1900)

54 Route d'Evian, 1860 Aigle
☎ **(024) 466 46 16**
📠 (024) 466 60 47
📧 gcmtx@swissonline.ch

🏷 18 L 6207 m Par 72
👥 H
££ Visitors 130fr ASG members 110fr
🚗 Aigle, 15km S of Montreux
🏠 Ronald Fream & Dale
📧 www.swissgolfnetwork.ch

Sion   (2002)

CP 639, Rte Vissigen 150, 1950 Sion
☎ **(+41) (0) 027 203 79 00**
📠 (+41) (0) 027 203 79 01
📧 info@golfclubsion.ch
✍ Guy Reynard
🏷 18 L 5543 m Par 70 SR 120 (mens champion)
   18 L 5095 m Par 70 SR 118 (men)
   18 L 4859 m Par 70 SR 123 (ladies champion)
   18 L 4423 m Par 70 SR 119 (ladies)
👥 H–booking necessary
££ 90 fr (100 fr)
🚗 Sion, 80km SE of Montreux
🏠 Harradine
📧 www.golfclubsion.ch

Verbier   (1970)

1936 Verbier
☎ **(027) 771 53 14**
📠 (027) 771 60 93
📧 golf.club@verbier.ch
🏷 18 L 4880 m Par 69
👥 U
££ 50fr–70fr (80fr)
🚗 Centre of Verbier
🏠 Donald Harradine
📧 www.verbiergolf.com

Villars   (1922)

CP 118, 1884 Villars
☎ **(024) 495 42 14**
📠 (024) 495 42 18
📧 info@golf-villars.ch
✍ Eric Krol (Mgr)
🏷 18 L 5288 m SSS 70
👥 U
££ 70fr (90fr)
🚗 5km E of Villars towards Les Diablerets; 20km Montreux
🏠 Thierry Sprecher
📧 www.golf-villars.ch

Lugano & Ticino

Lugano   (1923)

6983 Magliaso
☎ **(091) 606 15 57**
📠 (091) 606 65 58
📧 info@golflugano.ch
🏷 18 L 5575 m Par 70
👥 H–max 36
££ 90fr (110fr)
🚗 8km W of Lugano towards Ponte Tresa
🏠 Harradine/Robinson
📧 www.golflugano.ch

Patriziale Ascona   (1928)
Via al Lido 81, 6612 Ascona
☎ **(091) 791 21 32**
📠 (091) 791 07 06
📧 info@golf.ascona.ch
⏸ 18 L 5933 m Par 71
👭 H–max 30
££ 100fr (110fr)
⛳ 5km W of Locarno
🏠 CK Cotton
🖥 www.golf.ascona.ch

St Moritz & Engadine

Arosa   (1944)
Postfach 95, 7050 Arosa
☎ **(081) 377 42 42**
📠 (081) 377 46 77
📧 golf@arosa.ch
⏸ 18 L 4340 m Par 65 CR 63.6 SR 116
👭 U
££ 75fr (85fr)
⛳ 30km S of Chur
🏠 D Harradine/P Harradine
🖥 www.arosa.ch/golf

Bad Ragaz   (1957)
Hans Albrecht Strasse, 7310 Bad Ragaz
☎ **(081) 303 37 17**
📧 golfclub@resortragaz.ch

Davos   (1929)
Postfach, 7260 Davos Dorf
☎ **(081) 46 56 34**

Engadin   (1893)
7503 Samedan
☎ **(081) 851 04 66**

Lenzerheide Valbella   (1950)
7078 Lenzerheide
☎ **(081) 385 13 13**
📠 (081) 385 13 19
📧 info@golf-lenzerheide.ch
⏸ 18 L 5253 m CR 66.9 SR 124
👭 H 30 high season
££ 60fr–90fr
⛳ 20km S of Chur towards St Moritz
🏠 Donald Harradine/Kurt Rossknecht
🖥 www.golf-lenzerheide.ch

Vulpera   (1923)
7552 Vulpera Spa
☎ **(081) 864 96 88**

Zürich & North

Breitenloo   (1964)
8309 Oberwil b. Bassersdorf
☎ **(01) 836 40 80**

Bürgenstock   (1928)
6363 Bürgenstock
☎ **(041) 610 2434**
📠 (041) 610 3761
📧 club@buergenstock-hotels.ch
⏸ 9 L 2200 m Par 33
👭 H
££ 70fr (90fr) Season May–October
⛳ 15km S of Lucerne
🏠 Fritz Frey
🖥 www.buergenstock-hotels.com

Dolder   (1907)
Kurhausstrasse 66, 8032 Zürich
☎ **(01) 261 50 45**

Entfelden   (1988)
Muhenstrasse 52, 5036 Oberentfelden
☎ **(062) 723 89 84**
📠 (062) 723 84 36
⏸ 18 L 4194 m Par 66, CR 63.2 SR 107
👭 H
££ 70fr (90fr)
⛳ 50km W of Zürich
🏠 Donald Harradine (9 hole)
   Christian Affolter (18 and 9 holes)

Erlen   (1994)
Schlossgut Eppishausen, Schlossstr 7, 8586 Erlen
☎ **(071) 648 29 30**
📠 (071) 648 29 40
📧 info@erlengolf.ch
⏸ 18 L 5694 m SSS 71
👭 H–WD
££ 80fr
⛳ 30km NW of St Gallen. 60km W of Zürich
🏠 Gross J Preismann
🖥 www.erlengolf.ch

Hittnau-Zürich G&CC   (1964)
8335 Hittnau
☎ **(01) 950 24 42**

Küssnacht   (1994)
Sekretariat/Grossarni, 6403 Küssnacht am Rigi
☎ **(041) 850 70 60**

Golf Kyburg   (2004)
CH-8310 Kempthal, Zürich
☎ **(052) 355 06 06**
📠 (052) 355 06 16
📧 info@golf-kyburg.ch
⏸ 18 L 6015 m Par 71 CR 72.4 SR 132
👭 WD–U H WE–M H
££ 100 fr
⛳ 20 km NW of Zürich
🏠 Kurt Rossknecht
🖥 www.golf-kyburg.ch

Lucerne   (1903)
Dietschiberg, 6006 Luzern
☎ **(041) 420 97 87**

📠 (041) 420 82 48
📧 info@golfclubluzern.ch
⏸ 18 L 6067 m Par 73 SSS 71-73
👭 H max 30
££ 110fr (130fr)
⛳ Lucerne 2km
🏠 Krebs & Reuss
🖥 www.golfclublucerne.ch

Ostschweizerischer   (1948)
Club
9246 Niederbüren
☎ **(071) 422 18 56**
📠 (071) 422 18 25
📧 osgc@bluewin.ch
⏸ 18 L 5920 m SSS 71
👭 WD–H
££ D–90fr
⛳ Niederbüren, 25km NW of St Gallen
🏠 Donald Harradine
🖥 www.osgc.ch

Schinznach-Bad   (1929)
5116 Schinznach-Bad
☎ **(056) 443 12 26**
📠 (056) 443 34 83
📧 golfclub.schinznach@bluewin.ch
⏸ 9 L 5670 m Par 71
👭 WD–U
££ 100fr
⛳ 6km S of Brugg. 35km W of Zürich

Schönenberg G&CC   (1967)
8824 Schönenberg
☎ **(01) 788 90 40**
📠 (01) 788 90 45
📧 gccs@swissonline.ch
⏸ 18 L 6205 m CR 73.4 SR 137
👭 WD–H–by appointment WE–M H
££ 120fr
⛳ 20km S of Zürich
🏠 Donald Harradine
🖥 www.swissgolfnetwork.ch

Golf Sempachersee   (1996)
CH-6024 Hildisrieden, Lucerne
☎ **(041) 462 71 71**
📠 (041) 462 71 72
📧 info@golf-sempachersee.ch
⏸ 2 x 18 L 6600/5900 m Par 72/70
👭 WD–U H WE–M H
££ Par 72: 110 fr Par 70: 100 fr
⛳ 13km NW of Lucerne
🏠 Kurt Rossknecht
🖥 www.golf-sempachersee.ch

Zürich-Zumikon   (1929)
Weid 9, 8126 Zumikon
☎ **(6041) 43 288 1078**
📠 (6041) 43 288 1077
📧 gccz.zumikon@ggaweb.ch
⏸ 18 L 6389 m Par 72 CR 73.6 SR 134
👭 WD–H by appointment WE–M
££ WD–150fr
⛳ 10km SE of Zürich
🏠 Donald Harradine
🖥 www.swissgolfnetwork.ch

Turkey

Gloria Golf
Acisu Mevkii PK27 Belek, Serik, Antalya
☎ **(242) 715 15 20**

Kemer G&CC
Goturk Koyu Mevkii Kemerburgaz,
Eyup, Istanbul
☎ **(212) 239 70 10**

Klassis G&CC
Silivri, Istanbul
☎ **(212) 748 46 00**

National Golf Club, Antalya
(1994)
Belek Turizm Merkezi, 07500 Serik,
Antalya
☎ **(242) 725 46 20**
📠 (242) 725 46 23
▷ 18 L 6279 m Par 72 SSS 72
   White CR 73.9 SR 138
   Yellow CR 69.8 SR 129
   Red CR 72.0 SR 131
   9 L 1547 m Par 29
⚐ H
£€ £50
⊶ Belek, 30km from Antalya
🏠 Feherty/Jones
▤ www.nationalturkey.com

Robinson Golf Club Nobilis
(1998)
Acisu Mevkii, Belek, 07500
Serik/Antalya, Antalya
☎ **(+90) 242 715 1491**
✉ golf.nobilis@robinson.de

Tat Golf International
Belek International Golf, Kum Tepesi Belek,
07500 Serik, Antalya
☎ **(242) 725 53 03**

Immelman and Romero are top US Tour rookies

South African Trevor Immelman, who won the Cialis Western Open and collected more than $3.8 million in earnings finishing seventh on the money list, is the 2006 US PGA Tour Rookie of the Year. Earlier, Eduardo Romero of Argentina was named Champions Tour Rookie of the Year.

Steve Stricker, who began the year with only partially exempt status, was named the PGA Tour Comeback Player of the Year. In 17 starts, Stricker posted seven top ten finishes, including a tie for second at the Booz Allen Classic and finished 34th on the money list with more than $1.8 million. Tim Simpson collected the Champions Tour Comeback Player of the Year award.

Index

Guatemala Open, 213
Guildford, 745
Guinlet, 869
Gujan, 857
Gullane, 822
Gullbringa G & CC, 904
Gumbalde, 907
Gustavsvik, 902
Gut Altentann, 845
Gut Apeldör, 872
Gut Brandlhof G & CC, 845
Gut Grambek, 872
Gut Heckenhof, 879
Gut Kaden, 872
Gut Ludwigsberg, 875
Gut Murstätten, 846
Gut Rieden, 875
Gut Uhlenhorst, 872
Gut Waldhof, 873
Gut Waldshagen, 873
Gütersloh Garrison, 874
Gweedore, 781
Gwent, 318
Gyttegård, 851

De Haar, 892
Haarlemmermeersche, 888
Habberley, 761
Hadden Hill, 730
Haddington, 822
Haderslev, 851
Hadley Wood, 694
Hagge, 906
Haggs Castle, 816
Hagley, 761
Haigh Hall, 706
Hainburg/Donau, 847
Hainsworth Park, 764
Hale, 664
Halesowen, 762
Halesworth, 741
Halford-Hewitt Cup, 309
Halifax, 772
Halifax Bradley Hall, 772
Halifax West End, 772
Hallamshire, 768
Hallowes, 768
Halmstad, 909
Halstock, 677
Haltwhistle, 670
Ham Manor, 753
Hamburg, 873
Hamburg Ahrensburg, 873
Hamburg Hittfeld, 873
Hamburg Holm, 873
Hamburg Walddörfer, 873
Hamelner Golfclub e.V., 874
Hamilton, 821
Hammarö, 911
The Hampshire, 689
Hampshire Hog, 302

Hampshire, Isle of Wight and
    Channel Islands Open, 208
Hampshire Ladies', 364
Hampshire Match Play, 208
Hampshire PGA, 208
Hampshire Rose, 360
Hampshire Salver, 291
Hampshire, Isle of Wight and
    Channel Islands, 315
Hampstead, 720
Hampton Court Palace, 745
Hamptworth G & CC, 759
Han Herreds, 851
Hanau-Wilhelmsbad, 871
Hanbury Manor G & CC, 694
Handigolf, 400
Handsworth, 737
Hanging Heaton, 772
Haninge, 910
Hankley Common, 745
Hannover, 874
Hanover G & CC, 683
Haparanda, 903
Harborne, 756
Harborne Church Farm, 756
Harbour Point, 780
Harburn, 825
Hardelot Dunes Course, 861
Hardelot Pins Course, 861
Hardenberg, 874
Harewood Downs, 657
Harjattula G & CC, 854
Harleyford, 657
Härnösand, 903
Harpenden, 694
Harpenden Common, 694
Harrogate, 765
Harrow Hill Golf Course, 720
Harrow School, 720
Harry Vardon Award, 430
Hart Common, 706
Hartl Golf Resort Bad Griesbach,
    877
Hartland Forest, 674
Hartlepool, 679
Hartley Wintney, 689
Hartsbourne G & CC, 694
Hartswood, 683
Harwich & Dovercourt, 683
Harwood, 706
Hassan II Trophy, 185
Hässleholm, 906
Hassocks, 753
Haste Hill, 720
Hastings G & CC, 751
Hatchford Brook, 757
Hatfield London CC, 694
Hattemse G & CC, 889
Golfresort Haugschlag, 845
Haus Bey, 878
Haus Kambach, 878

Haut-Poitou, 859
Havelte, 890
Haverdals, 909
Haverfordwest, 838
Haverhill, 741
Haviksoord, 890
Le Havre, 864
Hawarden, 834
Hawick, 808
Hawkhurst, 700
Hawkstone Park, 733
Haydock Park, 717
Hayling, 689
Hayston, 811
Haywards Heath, 753
Hazel Grove, 664, 786
Hazelwood Golf Centre, 745
Hazlemere, 658
Headfort, 792
Headingley, 772
Headley, 772
The Heath, 789
Heath Park, 720
Heaton Moor, 664
Heaton Park Golf Centre, 715
Hebden Bridge, 772
Hechingen Hohenzollern, 881
Hedeland, 853
Hedsor, 658
Heemskerkse, 888
Heidelberg-Lobenfeld, 881
Heilbronn-Hohenlohe, 881
Hele Park Golf Centre, 674
Helen's Bay, 782
Helensburgh, 804
Hellidon Lakes Hotel G & CC,
    724
Helsby, 664
Helsingborg, 906
Helsingin Golfklubi, 854
Helsingør, 853
Hemingford Abbots, 660
Hemsedal, 893
Hemsted Forest, 700
Henbury, 686
Hendon, 720
Henley, 731
Henley G & CC, 757
Henllys Hall, 835
Henlow, 653
Henne, 851
Hennerton, 655
Henri-Chapelle, 849
Hereford Municipal, 692
Herefordshire, 692
The Heritage G & CC, 789
Herkenbosch, 891
Hermitage, 784
Herne Bay, 700
Herning, 851
De Vere Herons Reach, 706

Compiling the *Golfer's Handbook* is a team effort. Thanks
are due to Mike Aitken, David Davies, Andy Farrell, Mark
Garrod, John Hopkins, Keith Mackie, Lewine Mair and Jock
McVicar for their literary contributions, to Shirley and
Michael Card for their enthusiasm and sterling work at "the
coal face", St Andrew's-based Heather and Alan Elliott who
helped in so many other ways and to the Phil Sheldon Photo
Library and Getty Images.

Renton Laidlaw